KT-560-989

THE GREAT WAR

VOLUME 9

This Volume Combines Volume 9 & Volume 10
of an Original 13 Volume Set.

Reprinted 1999 from the 1917 & 1918 editions
TRIDENT PRESS INTERNATIONAL
Copyright 1999

ISBN 1-582790-29-9 Standard Edition

Printed in Croatia

Subject Index to THE GREAT WAR Volumes I. to IX.

Enabling the reader to refer back to any chapter in the first nine volumes by consulting the section in which it may be expected to appear. Black Roman numerals indicate the number of the volume, ordinary figures the first page of each chapter.

List of Maps in Volumes I.-IX. of "The Great War"

Arranged According to Battle Areas

Frontispiece Vol. IX "THE GREAT WAR".

Specially painted by CHAS. SHELDON

The Music of Triumph: Victorious Australians Entering Bapaume. March 17th, 1917.

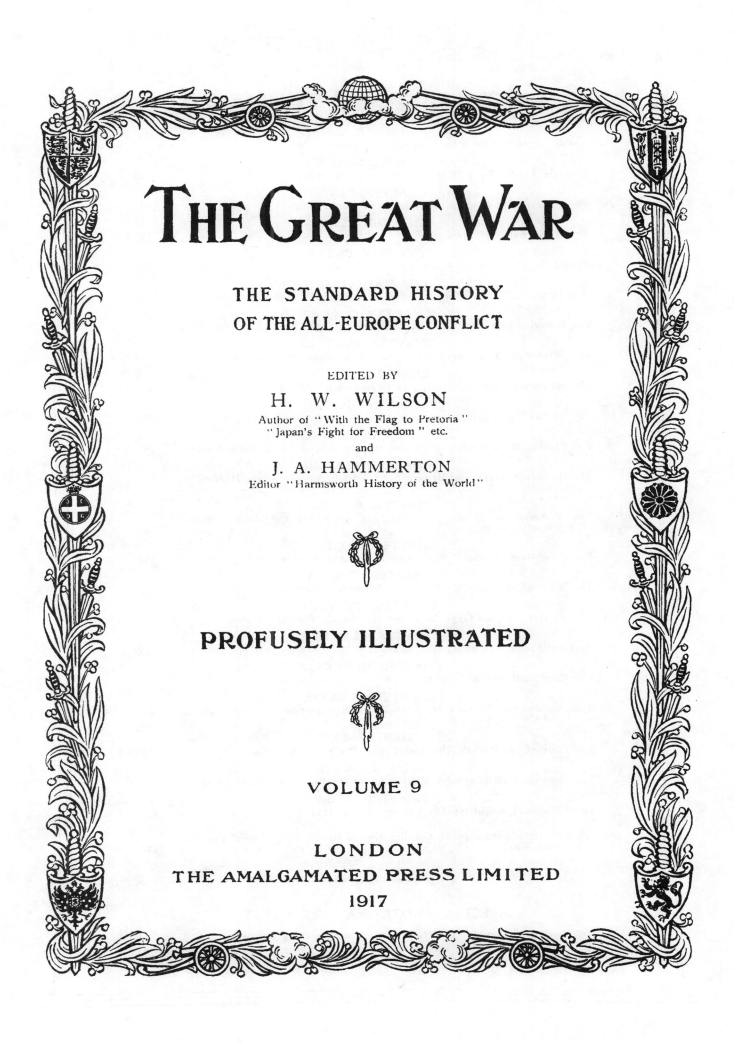

THE GREAT WAR

THE STANDARD HISTORY
OF THE ALL-EUROPE CONFLICT

EDITED BY

H. W. WILSON

Author of "With the Flag to Pretoria"
"Japan's Fight for Freedom" etc.

and

J. A. HAMMERTON

Editor "Harmsworth History of the World"

PROFUSELY ILLUSTRATED

VOLUME 9

LONDON
THE AMALGAMATED PRESS LIMITED
1917

CONTENTS OF VOLUME 9

SPECIAL PHOTOGRAVURE PLATE

THE GREAT WAR

THE STANDARD HISTORY OF THE ALL-EUROPE CONFLICT

VOLUME 9

CHAPTER CLXXI.

THE STRUGGLE OF LAND-POWER AGAINST SEA-POWER.

By H. W. Wilson.

Importance of Decisive Victory at Sea—Changed Conditions—Peril of Zeebrugge—Airships and Mine-fields—Meaning of the Submarine War—The New German Submarines—Consequences of Submarine War—Rail Power—The Blockade Does Not Starve Germany—Her Financial Strength—Zeebrugge Skirmishes—High Sea Fleet Out—Its Escape—Germans Preparing for Submarine Campaign—Voyage of the Deutschland—Neutrals and Submarines—U53 Blockades New York—Fierce Attacks on Neutrals—British "Wait and See"—The Channel Raid—Admiralty Reorganised—Submarines at Madeira—German Raider at Sea—Arming of Merchantmen—Measures Taken against Submarines—Admiral Jellicoe's Appeal—Destroyer Fight in the North Sea—German Threat to Hospital Ships—Eve of the New German Blockade—Its Announcement—Germans Believe Victory Certain—Insolent Contempt for the United States—Terror of Smaller Neutrals—President Wilson Breaks Off Relations with Germany—"The Supreme and Terrible Climax of the War"—Number of German Submarines—First Results—The Laconia Sunk—The U.S. Orders to its Merchantmen.

THE great naval Battle of Jutland had been fought, and its result could be summed up by reversing Nelson's phrase; it was not annihilation, but victory. The German Fleet had not been destroyed; it was battered, shaken, severely handled in those brief minutes of firing in the mist, before it vanished altogether. Beaten it was, and forced to retire. It was able to escape, as has been shown already, because of the British want of aircraft, because of the mist, and because the British destroyer flotillas were not sufficiently numerous to encircle it and definitely ascertain the direction of its retreat. But it had survived a day of immense peril; and in ships actually sunk it had inflicted as heavy loss as it sustained itself. How catastrophic to Germany, how precious to the Allies would have been such a victory as that of Trafalgar or the Nile or Tsushima, gained by close action and the determination to force decisive results,

can be best understood from the chapter of history which followed, and from studying the probable consequences of a decisive German defeat.

If the German Fleet had been destroyed—if, that is to say, the enemy's battle-cruisers and Dreadnoughts had been taken or sent to the bottom—then the route into the Baltic could have been cleared, and communications opened up with Russia, who could have been aided in equipping her new armies and repairing her worn-out railways. The British flotillas could have pressed close up to the German coast, and by watching the stretch of water between Schleswig and Emden—the Bight of Heligoland—t h e y could have made the blockade far stricter and greatly hampered the passage in and out of the German submarines. The whole aspect of the war at sea would have changed; the war on land would have been profoundly modified to Germany's disadvantage. Such difficulties would have been placed in the way of the German

[British official photograph.

BRITISH NAVAL 15 IN. GUNS.
Tested at the Dardanelles in the Queen Elizabeth, the first super-Dreadnought to be armed with these monster pieces of ordnance, the 15 in. gun has been declared to be "the best gun we ever had," accurate at all ranges and "exceptionally long lived."

[*British official photograph.*

DIVERS AT WORK ON A DAMAGED VESSEL AT SALONIKA.

At work with a floating workshop in Salonika Harbour. The large vessel had been extensively damaged as the result of a collision. Despite, however, the great gash in her side, she was successfully kept afloat. The divers seen in the photograph were engaged in surveying the nature of the underwater damage.

had packed the waters round their coast with mine-fields, and when German submarines cruised by the dozen in the North Sea. The object of sea-power in the old days was to blockade, to cut the enemy off entirely from the sea, and either to prevent his warships from leaving harbour or to make certain that, if they did, they would be brought to battle and swiftly defeated. There were then no mines and no submarines. It was impossible for two fleets to occupy the same waters—one on and the other below the surface. The ship of the line had nothing to fear from any vessels smaller than herself. In the Great War the battleship could be sunk by the enemy's submarines and destroyers, provided these could get to close quarters.

The torpedo was a weapon which had transformed naval war by giving small vessels this capacity of dealing a death-blow to the armoured monsters. The mine, scattered by submarine mine-layers and by German surface craft — often under a neutral flag — was nearly as dangerous and was full of strategic menace. Lines of mines could be used to close large areas of water, and so almost to turn the sea into dry land, but with this proviso—that the fleet which sowed the mines had secret passages available through its mine-fields. It was suggested that the Germans might thus carry protected lanes or covered ways between rows of mines, and down them move transports across the North Sea for the invasion of Great Britain.

The Germans had an excellent base for torpedo warfare close to the Strait of Dover and the eastern entrance to the Channel in Zeebrugge, which had fallen into their hands in the disastrous weeks of 1914 when Belgium was overrun. It was of the most vital importance for the British to hold this place, but at that date there were not the men, guns and ammunition required. It supplied the enemy with a respectable harbour for small craft. Destroyers of the most powerful type were gradually brought down to **Vital Importance of Zeebrugge** it from the north, the British forces in the North Sea being unable to prevent their transit along the Dutch coast. Smaller vessels were built at Antwerp and forwarded to Zeebrugge by the excellent canal system. The place itself was fortified by the enemy with extraordinary care. A large number of 15 in. and 11 in. guns and howitzers were mounted in the dunes so as to be invisible from the sea. The whole coastline bristled with smaller guns, and the waters near the coast were sown with mines so as to render approach extremely difficult. No serious naval attack on it was attempted in 1916, because long experience in naval war indicated that for ships—unless these were specially designed and armed ships—to assail fortifications

submarine campaign that little could have been hoped of it. For ten years before the war, however, a doctrine had been allowed to gain ground in the British Navy that fleets existed for other purposes than destroying the enemy's organised forces in battle. They were to protect the country against invasion, to blockade, to safeguard commerce, to cover the movements of transports. Ministers seemed to forget that the destruction of the enemy's fighting fleet was the quickest and surest method of attaining all these ends. It was now shown that so long as the enemy's fighting fleet remained virtually intact, the other objects could not be fully achieved. In the old days the war waged against commerce by destroying British merchantmen was deadliest when it was supported by a powerful fleet. It languished after Trafalgar. So with the submarine. It was most threatening with a great force of battleships behind it.

All things had changed at sea except the fundamental law—" Destroy the enemy's fleet, and everything else shall be added to you." The British Admiralty was faced with baffling conditions. The old close blockade of the weak fleet by the strong was no longer possible when the Germans

ashore was useless. Nelson never engaged the batteries at Toulon. The bombardments at the Dardanelles had proved that forts could resist the fire of Dreadnoughts, even when these were armed with 15 in. guns.

Zeebrugge was not only a nest of destroyers, submarines, and mine-layers; it was also a point from which Germany could deliver air attacks on the British coast. Aircraft operating from it could and did watch all Dutch shipping moving in and out of the Scheldt, and could also observe British shipping approaching the Thames. A circle with a radius of 100 miles from it—an hour's run in a modern fast seaplane—included Dover and Harwich, while Lowestoft and Yarmouth were only just outside. A circle with a radius of 150 miles included London. Because of this Zeebrugge hornets' nest, which the British **Disadvantages** strategists left intact, an elaborate system **of the British Fleet** of British air patrols had to be maintained on the East Coast, and then was not always effective. Constant seaplane raids were made by the Germans on the East and South-East Coasts during 1915 and 1916, though with only the most trivial result. But the real object of these visits of German aircraft was probably rather reconnaissance than destruction—to ascertain exactly what was being done and what were the positions of the British troops and the anti-aircraft defences.

In North Sea war the British Fleet suffered from another signal disadvantage. It was without powerful rigid airships of the Zeppelin type. The small airships, of which it possessed a good number, were not capable of long-distance work at sea, and could not patrol far from the coast. The German Zeppelins could do so in any but the worst weather.

If they cruised at a height of 4,000 feet—and on occasions they were seen at 10,000 feet—they could sweep with their telescopes a circle of which the radius was 67 miles, and in clear weather ascertain what the British Fleet was doing, and whether there was much shipping about. They could then direct their destroyers and submarines how to act. At every turn, owing to the fatal neglect of airships in the past before the war, and the astonishing failure to build them after the war had begun, British naval officers were like men who, with bandages over their eyes, fenced against opponents with perfect vision. The work of patrolling the North Sea could have been easily and cheaply carried out with airships. As it was, it had to be expensively performed by an enormous number of trawlers and small armed vessels which burned much coal, required many men, were good targets for the enemy's attacks, and were vulnerable to mine or torpedo.

PASSING THROUGH SEAS RENDERED PERILOUS BY SUBMARINES.
Orient Line steamer outward-bound for Australia with mails and passengers. Germany's " unrestricted submarine warfare," or the running amok of U boats among the world's shipping, did not scare the mercantile marine off the seas, as its blockaded perpetrators hoped, though it necessitated a constant watch being kept on board ship. Above: Officers on an Orient liner on the look-out for enemy submarines.

Looking aft, it is seen that the "living space" is yet more restricted. The crew had to accustom themselves to very limited quarters. The man to the right was engaged in observing through a periscope.

"Living space" on board a submarine, looking forward. At some of their work while tending the machinery the men had to sit cross-legged in the time-honoured fashion associated with tailors.

(British official photographs.)

Main engines of a submarine. The machinery was of a kind which required that, those who worked and tended it, whose very lives depended on it, should have highly specialised training.

Foremost torpedoes on board a submarine, showing the situation from which they would be fired when discharged through the torpedo-tubes on their destructive journey.

SEEMING MEDLEY OF MACHINERY BY WHICH THE SUBMARINES ACHIEVED THEIR WONDERFUL WORK.

Early in the war a British mine-field had been laid at the northern entrance to the Channel and publicly notified, but though this should have hampered the movements of the enemy in Zeebrugge, it did not appear to trouble the Germans much, nor did it entirely prevent attacks on traffic in the Channel, as will appear later. Another British mine-field, laid early in the war, after Lord Fisher's accession to the Admiralty, closed the North Channel leading into the Irish Sea, between Scotland and Ireland, except for a narrow passage near the Irish coast.

Because of the imperfect British control of the North Sea and the British inability to blockade closely, or seal with mines, the German harbours and Zeebrugge, the Germans were able to employ the submarine with great effect. In their hands it became a pirate craft, possessing the terrible power of suddenly becoming invisible, like Mr. Wells' ghastly "Invisible Man." The German submarine officers behaved with the inhumanity of pirates. They murdered women and children with less compunction than a Captain Kidd or Captain Teach. They were ready to sink neutral ships without warning, so long as these neutral vessels did not belong to a formidable Power, and sometimes even then. Their chief aim was to destroy shipping. The German Staff argued that with each ton of shipping sunk the scarcity of ships was augmented, the price of freight rose, and the dearness of food increased. It did not greatly matter whether the ships sunk were neutral or British, provided that the neutrals were too weak or too timid to cause Germany alarm.

The struggle, as has been well said, was one between force and invisibility. The invisible German pirates stole out of the German harbours and Zeebrugge, and voyaged under water through the zone where the British cruisers and patrols were most active. Even there they often contrived to sink ships. All through 1916 the

Force versus invisibility Germans were building submarines of much larger type and much greater sea-keeping capacity than the earlier boats with which they had carried out their blockade in 1915. Then they had perhaps fifty boats. Now they aspired to place hundreds at sea. The older boats were capable of 16 to 17 knots on the surface, and 10 knots under water. They had a radius of perhaps 3,000 miles. They could remain ten days or a fortnight on their cruising ground. The new boats could move at 18 to 21, or even 25 knots on the surface. They had a radius of 10,000 miles, and could remain at sea six weeks or two months, and much longer if they were supplied with torpedoes, oil, and food by submarine cargo carriers or neutrals.

According to certain Austrian newspapers, which cannot, however, be implicitly trusted, a radical change was made in the new German submarines. The older boats employed oil-engines on the surface and electric-motors under water. In the new boats, it was stated, oil-motors were used below water as well as on the surface. A boat dependent on electric-motors and accumulators below could only move very slowly beneath the surface, and must re-emerge at short intervals if she kept her motors going, to recharge the accumulators from the main oil-engines. The boat with oil-engines could move as fast below the surface as on it, and need only emerge at long intervals. It was alleged that the German scientists had discovered a method of dealing with the exhaust of their oil-engines, without discharging it from the boat, which would have left a trail of bubbles and instantly have revealed her presence below to the British patrols. Whether this report was as apocryphal as that which asserted that non-inflammable gas was employed in the German super-Zeppelins of 1916, remained to be proved.

In the armament of the new boats there was an equal advance. The older submarines were sharply specialised for torpedo work or mine-laying. The new submarines were fitted in many cases to lay mines as well as fire torpedoes, of which the larger vessels are said to have carried 20. The older submarines carried a 12-pounder gun with a small 1-pounder for anti-aircraft work. The new boats mounted 4.1 in. guns of the semi-automatic type, firing a 35 lb. shell with great rapidity to a range of 6,000 yards.

A few of the largest were said to have attained the proportions of veritable cruisers, and to carry 6 in. guns firing 100 lb. shells. They were vessels that could be used for bombardments, and that could not easily be beaten in an artillery fight by anything smaller than one of the latest and largest destroyers.

The older patrol boats and armed yachts employed by the Allies, and equipped only with one or two small guns, were not of much service against them. They were also much more difficult to sink. The conning-towers and upper works were armoured lightly, and the conning-tower was completely separated from the

[British official photograph.

BRITAIN'S PART IN THE SUBMARINE WAR.
Scanning the surface through the periscope of a British submarine. Although German submarines chiefly held the world's attention owing to their nefarious activities, the British submarines did invaluable work.

interior of the boat, so that it could be riddled without the loss of the boat. It was fitted with automatic valves, allowing the air to be drawn in while the boat was on the surface, but closing when she submerged. There were undoubtedly cases—as was disclosed by neutral witnesses who were taken against their will on board these craft—when the conning-towers were hit by the British guns without sinking the boat. The hull was double, and to the outer space in it the sea was admitted, so that to ram one of these submarines was not to sink her.

The periscopes carried were two in number, of extraordinary clarity and power. One led down to the main compartment in the conning-tower where the boat was manoeuvred; it was raised and lowered by electricity.

MAP SHOWING THE PRINCIPAL BRITISH AND GERMAN MINE-FIELDS IN THE NORTH SEA.

In 1914 British mine-fields were laid to protect the northern entrance to the English Channel and the North Channel leading into the Irish Sea. In January, 1917, a new mine-field was notified in the North Sea, from Flamborough Head 320 miles north-eastwards to Denmark and southeastwards to the Dutch Frisian Islands. This blocked the approach to the North Sea coast of Germany, except through neutral territorial waters.

A second periscope went down to the engine-room, and was worked by hand-power. There were two masts of steel, lying flush with the deck in pockets when folded down, and telescopic. They were raised and lowered by electric-motors, and were fitted with wireless. They could be so disguised with sails and spars as to give the boat the appearance of an innocent sailing ship at some distance.

These vessels could proceed to favourable points on the great routes and attack commerce with the utmost effect. It was as though not one Emden, but a hundred Emdens, each able to submerge at will, had been turned loose. Their power of submerging enabled them to escape from warships sent on patrol duty or in search of them, and even to attack them if any carelessness was shown by the surface craft.

They could commit any outrage with impunity. One submarine is exactly like another submarine. If the German boats carried numbers on a thin steel plate, this plate could be removed or hidden, and nearly always was removed. There was no check whatever upon their conduct, such as exists in ordinary surface vessels of war. If only for that reason, they were a deadly menace to neutrals as well as to the Allies. Nothing whatever like them existed in the warfare of the past. Then commerce was attacked by vessels moving on the surface, which with more or less difficulty could always be hunted down. The first result of the submarine war was that the sea Power controlling the surface lost many of the advantages of its position. The ocean routes behind its blockading fleets were no longer safe. Its communications were liable to constant interruption. On the other hand, land-power had gained prodigiously, owing to the general introduction of railways, since the Napoleonic Wars. Germany, with her central position stretching across Europe and Western Asia, enjoyed perfectly secure communications. No raider could attack her trunk railways except through the air, and here Germany in 1917 was able to hold her own, or something more. The great artery which ran from Zeebrugge and Hamburg by Berlin and Vienna, through Sofia and Constantinople towards Bagdad and the Egyptian frontier, gave her safe lines of attack and operations against Great Britain in three different directions—at Salonika, in Mesopotamia, and in Egypt.

More than this, in the old days the sea Power could threaten the land Power with attack on every part of the land Power's coastline, while itself enjoying safety from menace. In the Great War, however, the gigantic scale of operations and the prodigious force needed to produce any

Land and sea mobility contrasted effect, rendered the rapid movement of armies by sea out of the question. The Dardanelles Expedition was an example of the immense difficulties incurred and the perils that waited upon failure. The land Power, however, with its railways could transfer enormous forces with extraordinary speed. In a week a German army corps was transferred from Verdun to the Russian front, which meant that some 40,000 men with 160 guns were moved 1,000 miles. In two days 160,000 men were moved 200 miles from one part of the east front to another. British troops sent by sea from London to Salonika had to cover 3,510 miles of water, and the transports conveying them had to be escorted every mile of the distance. German troops en route from Zeebrugge or the western front to Salonika had a distance of only 1,730 miles to cover, and could make the journey in complete security. With railway communications a commander was always certain of receiving what supplies and munitions he needed, while the commander who depended on transport by sea might discover that some particular munitions of which he stood in great need had been loaded in a ship that had been torpedoed and sunk. Transport by sea was also much slower than

movement by railway. Troop trains could usually be trusted to do 20 miles an hour, and on well-constructed and organised lines 30 miles. Ships could not average more than 10 or 15 land miles an hour. In the Napoleonic Wars it was calculated that armies could be moved nearly twice as fast by sea as by land; that on land the average marching distance was 12 miles a day. In the Great War it was possible to move troops 500 miles in a day. Here again the tables had been turned upon sea-power. The sea was betraying those who trusted in it.

FRENCH SUBMARINE-CARRIER KANGUROO TORPEDOED IN FUNCHAL HARBOUR, MADEIRA.
On December 3rd, 1916, a large German submarine appeared at Funchal, in the island of Madeira, and torpedoed the French gunboat Surprise and submarine-carrier Kanguroo, and the British cable-ship Dacia, which were lying in the harbour, and afterwards bombarded the town. The fore part of the Kanguroo was detachable, giving access to a sort of dock into which the submarine entered. Above : Submarine in position in the mother-ship.

HIT FULL AMIDSHIPS.
Alleged to be carrying contraband, this vessel, nationality not specified, was sunk by gun fire from a German submarine.

The distance to be covered by the German railways from Zeebrugge (which is chosen as the extreme point in the west occupied by the German armies) to the railhead on the Egyptian frontier was little over 3,000 miles, while the distance by sea from London to Port Said was 3,730 land (not nautical) miles. The most southward point attained by the vast German railway network, in early 1917, was Medina, in Arabia, 3,750 miles from Zeebrugge, but an extension was under construction to Mecca prior to the revolt of the Arabs. The equipment of the Hedjaz Railway, as this line into Arabia was called, was bad, but it was slowly improved, and with the enormous efforts made by Germany in 1916-17, material for it was available from the German works and factories. To a corresponding point in the Red Sea the distance by sea from London was 4,250 miles, so that the sea route was much longer and subject to all the dangers and uncertainties of submarine interruption. The last of the great tunnels in Asia Minor had

The Berlin-Bagdad Line been pierced in the autumn of 1916, and it was reported that the Bagdad line might be open for through traffic in the summer of 1917 as far as Nisibin, in the direction of Bagdad, or possibly to the neighbourhood of Bagdad itself, a distance of 3,290 miles from Zeebrugge, and greater than that from New York to San Francisco, measuring in a straight line. To reach Mesopotamia, British shipping had to cover a distance of 7,680 miles to Basra from London, or more than twice as far, passing through much more inclement regions. The Germans had thus everywhere distance on their side, and with distance, time.

It might have seemed obvious strategy to cut this great trunk system of railways which exercised such a profound and ever-growing influence on the war. The risk of attack

from the sea, however, had been foreseen by the Germans, and provision had been made against it. The Bagdad line was everywhere carried at a safe distance from the sea, and where it approached closest, at the point where Asia Minor meets Syria, it was ten miles from the Mediterranean, and protected by formidable fortifications. It was a German rule to leave nothing to chance, as it was the British policy in time of peace to leave everything to it and to shut the eyes to all unpleasant possibilities.

In the Napoleonic Wars each country was, as a rule, able to produce the food which it needed, and the British blockade did not bring starvation into view. It cut off all or most trade by sea,

THE END OF HER DAY: GOING DOWN WITH THE SUN.
Torpedoed vessel sinking off the North Cape. Impressed by the beauty of the spectacle, an exponent of "Kultur" aboard the submarine produced his camera and secured this photograph of his victim's end, subsequently publishing it in a German newspaper, from which it is reproduced here.

and it deprived the peoples under Napoleon's rule of such luxuries as tobacco, sugar, coffee, and tea, to which they were then beginning to get accustomed. In the Great War, Germany, with her dependents and the conquered areas, controlled 1,400,000 square miles of continuous territory, populated by 170,000,000 of people, of whom nearly 30,000,000 were in the position of slaves, and were compelled to labour on State farms or in the German munition factories. The food raised in this enormous area was almost, but not quite, sufficient to feed the population; the Germans, as has already been shown, were generally hungry, though not actually starving; while the conquered population was often in the most miserable plight conceivable, and cruelly stinted of food. Had the British Navy blockaded vigorously and closely at the outset, Germany might have swiftly succumbed, but because the blockade was not pressed with energy, the German organisation was given the opportunity of laying up stupendous reserves, adapting itself to the new conditions, and making immense preparations. By the opening of 1917 Germany had organised herself perfectly, while

Great Britain had done little or nothing to increase food production. Thenceforward the real danger which Germany had to fear was the failure of cotton, leather, rubber, wool, vegetable oils, alcohol (for explosives), fats, and nitrates, rather than an insurmountable shortage of food.

In the matter of food production, as in other directions, the Germans had made far-seeing preparations, recognising that wars are won in advance by taking care and thought, and always intending to attack their neighbours. In spite of the rapid increase of urban population and manufactures in the twenty years before the war, they had enormously increased the annual production of corn and potatoes from

A LOST HARVEST.
This fishing steamer, sent to the bottom by German pirates, was said to have a cargo of herrings aboard worth about £50,000.

HER LAST—AND VAIN—APPEAL FOR HELP FROM SHORE.
Torpedoed within sight of shore, a sinking steamer shrilly blew her siren in appeal for succour for the crew, but in vain. Aboard the waiting submarine her callous destroyers remained listening to her swan-song until she went down, meanwhile taking this photograph during her last moments.

15,000,000 tons of corn to 27,000,000, and they had at the same time raised the number of live stock from 50,000,000 to 56,000,000. They grew at home in 1913 all the rye they required, 67·7 per cent. of the wheat consumed, 97 per cent. of the oats, and 98·6 per cent. of the potatoes. They exported sugar largely. They had a sufficient supply of potatoes not only to feed human beings and animals, but also to provide raw material for starch and spirit manufacture. While good land in improvident Great Britain was lying derelict, waste land in Germany was being eagerly reclaimed. A sturdy population was maintained, at the cost of great sacrifice, on the soil to form the backbone of the German armies; whereas in Great Britain, at every turn, the interests of agriculture were neglected. The immense agricultural strength of Germany was one of the factors which enabled her to withstand the pressure of the blockade.

The blockade did not exhaust Germany's food supply with the rapidity that many expected. It also did not affect her finances so seriously as might have been anticipated. She had seized the richest mineral areas in Belgium

and France, and had obtained in them assets of incalculable value which she utilised with an entire disregard for the rights of property. The rich Belgian and French coal and iron fields were exploited, so as to give the largest possible yield, with forced labour, and with no care for the future of the mines. The heart was picked out of them, and the coal and iron ore thus secured were worked up in French or Belgian or German factories and foundries, again with forced labour, into products of which neighbouring neutrals stood most sorely in need. Switzerland, Holland, and Sweden were supplied with a certain quantity of coal, iron, and steel, on condition that they paid for it in gold or food, and complied with Germany's diplomatic demands. Thus these products not only strengthened German finances and enabled Germany to carry on a very valuable trade, but they also served as counters in the diplomatic game. The Allies were bled while Germany drank up their blood. Without the iron ore of the Briey district of France, east of Verdun, the German output of munitions could not have been maintained. The ore fields there were of extraordinary richness, and their loss was an immense catastrophe for the Allies and a prodigious success for Germany.

German industrial organisation

In time of peace and several years before the war the German industrial organisation had been equipped on a scale equal to the supply of all Europe, especially in such machine-tools as the big lathes used for big-gun production. Warning had been given of this in 1908 to the British Government, which treated it with ridicule. Hence Germany had no need to transform herself, at incalculable expense, for the manufacture of munitions when she began the war. Everything was ready to hand, and she had not to make the machinery to make rifles and guns, or to

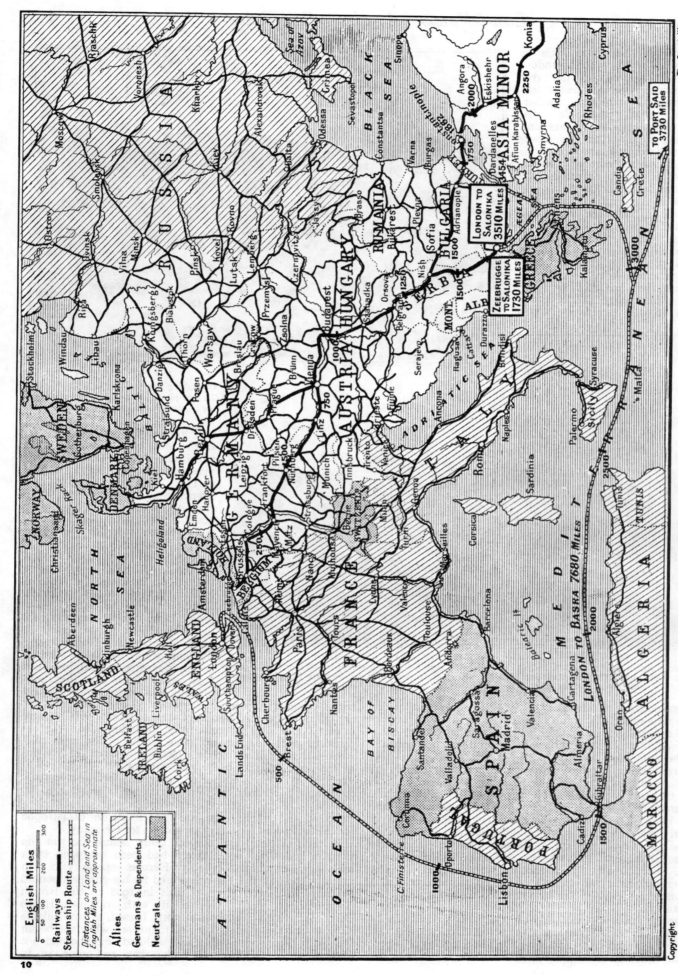

Copyright

The Great War

MAP TO ILLUSTRATE THE SUPERIOR TRANSPORT FACILITIES OF THE GERMANS AS COMPARED WITH THOSE OF THE ALLIES.

Germany, with her central position and network of railways, enjoyed prodigious advantages over Great Britain with her long lines of communication by sea. From Zeebrugge to Constantinople the railway distance is 1,862 miles : from London to the Dardanelles, by sea, it is 3,454 miles, and the men and munitions conveyed by sea were threatened by submarines throughout the entire route. Submarines and railways had completely altered the relative position of sea and land Powers since the Napoleonic era, for troop trains could cover a given distance in a third to a half of the time taken by sea transport.

import it oversea. With the system which she introduced, the discipline she maintained, the millions of slave-workers whom she commanded among the conquered allied populations, she could manufacture munitions cheaply. There were no strikes (despite legends to that effect circulated by German agents in Holland, probably to stimulate unrest in Great Britain). There were no " war-bonuses " for the women and the Belgian slaves, who were tortured and starved if they refused to work. There was no " ca' canny," or deliberately reducing the output, for selfish and unpatriotic reasons. The whole vast machinery of the Fatherland roared in continual full blast.

As the war progressed the Germans obtained additional and very valuable resources by the capture of iron and coal fields in Poland, of rich copper mines in Serbia, of the great oil-field in Rumania (though the wells had been temporarily put out of action), and of the magnificent wheatlands of the Danube plain. The cash value of their conquests cannot be stated at less than £1,000,000 000. and may very greatly have exceeded that sum. As they methodically stripped the territory which fell into their hands of raw materials, manufactured goods, machinery, and furniture, the total of such re-

Germany's colossal " booty " movable plunder cannot be placed at less than £500,000,000. The property seized in Northern France alone was estimated by Dr. Gustav Streseman, a member of the Reichstag, so early as January, 1915, at several hundred millions. The agricultural and industrial produce carried off from Belgium was estimated at £200,000,000 at the close of 1916. From Poland timber, pianos, furniture, and even the miserable rags of the people were taken, as was disclosed in the Hungarian Chamber in February, 1917. Railways were removed wholesale from occupied districts when the Germans did not need them, and transferred to totally different areas. If the German claim is correct, 10,000 miles of new line were laid during the war, largely on the Russian front, and some considerable part of the material for them was taken from the conquered territory.

It was estimated by the " Frankfurter Zeitung " in February, 1917, that the Allies were then spending and had continuously spent £2 for each £1 that the Germans spent. There were no large assets in the hands of the Allies to offset the colossal German " booty." The value of the German Colonies, which had all been conquered except East Africa, was not great, and the Allies showed extreme reluctance to seize German property in their territory, Thus Germany was given great advantages in a war of exhaustion. Each allied ship that she sunk, each allied life or dwelling that she destroyed in her attacks with submarine or aircraft, weakened the allied resources. Germany suffered no corresponding injury, as there was no German shipping at sea, and the allied Governments carefully abstained from bombardments for the sake of mere destruction.

For some weeks after the Battle of Jutland the German Fleet was undergoing repairs, but continual skirmishing proceeded between the British and German light craft in the North Sea. The German destroyers at Zeebrugge made frequent sorties, and eluded destruction at the hands of the British with extreme good fortune, or possibly through the scouting of the Zeppelins. On June 8th, 1916, a few shots were fired, and the British flotillas drove the Germans back into port.

On June 23rd the Germans came out again and seized the British passenger steamer Brussels, Captain Charles Fryatt. She was taken into Zeebrugge, as there was no British warship to protect her — the line of traffic to Holland was left open to interruption by the enemy all through 1916 — and Captain Fryatt was separated from those on board her, tried by court-martial on July 27th, and sentenced to death. He was shot by special instructions of the German Emperor, after a council at the German Headquarters had determined on his fate, on the

BRITISH NAVAL OFFICERS LOOK FOR THE ENEMY.
Officers on board a British cruiser scanning the horizon for a sight of the enemy. They were well-equipped with life-saving appliances against any eventuality from a suddenly appearing submarine or mine danger.

charge that he had been guilty of acting as a " franc-tireur," or guerilla, because on March 28th, 1915, he had tried to ram a German submarine which was attacking him. The German naval prize regulations, issued on the eve of war, recognised the perfect legality of his conduct, for from time immemorial it had been the universally admitted right of a merchantman to be armed and to defend herself.

On July 11th a German submarine shelled the small defenceless town of Seaham, on the Durham coast, killing a woman and hitting a colliery and a house.

On July 23rd there was a double skirmish with German small craft from Zeebrugge. According to the British report, three German destroyers were encountered by British light craft off the North Hinder (a shallow in the North Sea north-west of Zeebrugge), and retired at once. The Germans professed **Destroyer skirmishes** that they had reconnoitred to the Thames **in North Sea** mouth, and that on their return they had met a number of British light cruisers and destroyers, on which they made some hits. The second affair was off the Schouwen Bank, which lies almost due north of Zeebrugge in the North Sea. Six German destroyers were encountered there, and after being repeatedly hit by the British fire went off at great speed. According to Dutch reports, when the German destroyers returned two of them were seen to have a heavy list. No damage was done to the British vessels, and the enemy's escape appears to have been due to the very high speed of his newer destroyers. For some years before the war the Germans had built faster destroyers—as they built faster cruisers and battle-cruisers—than the British ; and as the result of this far-seeing policy they were often able to get away when in dangerous positions.

On August 13th the British destroyer Lassoo was torpedoed and sunk. A few days later the German Fleet put to sea in strength for the first time since the Battle of Jutland. The weather was dull, cold, and misty, and the Germans may have hoped to steal across the North Sea bombard some British town, and perhaps destroy some weak British detachment. A great array of German Dreadnoughts, twenty-one in number, was seen by Dutch fishermen moving west early in the morning of August 19th, preceded by three Zeppelins and a number of submarines which were obviously scouting for it The general direction of the course was towards Hull. At noon the German Fleet had reached the Dogger Bank. By that time one of its Dreadnoughts had been put out of action. The British submarine E23, Lieut.-Commander Turner, managed to get near the German battle squadrons, and fired a torpedo at the battleship Westfalen, which was seen to be hit. Re-emerging cautiously a little later, Lieut.-Commander Turner saw that the Westfalen had separated from the Fleet and was returning to a German base, escorted by five destroyers. With great daring he contrived to run in

GUNS SALVED FROM THE SEA TO DO SERVICE ON LAND.
Two naval guns that did useful work in the rounding up of the Germans in East Africa, the last of their Colonies. The guns had been salved from H.M.S. Pegasus, which had been sunk by the German ship Königsberg while in Zanzibar Harbour on September 20th, 1914.

once more within range and to fire another torpedo at her, which hit. None the less, she was able to regain harbour, according to the German reports. Possibly her elaborate system of sub-division saved her in the same way that the British Dreadnought Marlborough was saved in the Battle of Jutland.

The Germans, according to the Dutch trawlers' statements, had now concentrated between fifty and sixty ships in the centre of the North Sea. They were steaming very slowly east at noon, possibly waiting for the reports of their scouts and Zeppelins. Speedily there were signs that the British were approaching from two or three different directions. The Dutch saw a squadron of British light cruisers come up swiftly from the south ; about that time the German Fleet increased speed and retired, steaming fast towards its ports. It was not out to fight, and that was the last seen of it. In his speech on January 11th, 1917, Sir John Jellicoe gave this account of the affair : " Our enemies have only on one occasion ventured sufficiently far with their main fleet to give us an opportunity to engage them." [He meant on May 31st, at the Battle of Jutland.] " No vessels, neutral or British, have sighted the High Sea Fleet far from its ports on any other occasion. It is true that on August 19th the enemy fleet came within measurable distance of the English coast, being sighted by

German Fleet · in the North Sea

some of our patrols, but turned back, presumably because the presence of our fleet was reported by their aircraft." This was a plain hint that if the British Fleet had been equipped with airships as fast and powerful as the German ones, Von Scheer's fleet might have been brought to action and the decisive battle fought. Thus another great opportunity was lost through the want of foresight which had neglected aircraft.

The Germans reported seeing five British light cruisers, with two destroyer flotillas and six great battle-cruisers behind them, steaming swiftly down from the north-west — presumably Admiral Beatty's " Cat Squadron," hurrying down full of fight and fire to draw the enemy once more into battle. At five p.m. a German submarine torpedoed one of the British light cruisers, apparently the Nottingham, hitting her twice. She did not sink at once, but was being escorted back by British destroyers when the submarine, according to the German report, slipped in again and discharged a third torpedo, which sank her. About the same time another German submarine torpedoed and sank the light cruiser Falmouth. Both these vessels were excellent, if somewhat slow, ships of about 5,500 tons, with crews of 380 men ; the loss of life was fortunately small, only 39 being killed. The British Fleet claimed to have destroyed one German submarine and rammed another ; the loss of neither was admitted by Berlin.

Two British cruisers lost

Two other sorties of minor importance were made by the German Fleet during the last three months of the year. On October 21st a British submarine got close up to a squadron of German light cruisers and fired a torpedo which hit the München. She was seen steaming off with difficulty, but there is no reason to think that she sank. On November 5th a number of large German ships were sighted by British submarines, one of which, under Commander Laurence, with great skill and boldness approached the German line sufficiently close to attack it. Two German Dreadnoughts were hit. One was of the Kaiser class, and was severely damaged in her stern, but was believed to have reached harbour. Of the injuries to the other there were no particulars, and the Germans professed that the second torpedo missed. Probably Commander Laurence found things too warm to permit of his making further observations.

Throughout this stage of the war the Baltic was a sealed lake so far as the British were concerned. Their submarines were no longer able to pass freely in and out. The Germans had placed an elaborate series of mine-fields at the entrance to the Sound, and had brought pressure to bear on Sweden to induce her, in defiance of an ancient treaty with Great Britain, to forbid the passage of all but Swedish vessels through her territorial waters, which could not be mined by Germany without an open breach of Swedish neutrality. Swedish warships were also instructed to destroy all submarines which were not commercial submarines. As Germany alone employed—or pretended to employ—commercial submarines, the effect of this regulation was that allied submarines were sunk without warning if they entered Swedish waters, even inadvertently, whereas German submarines were merely warned to withdraw. In another way Swedish regulations assisted Germany. They allowed German shipping to proceed through Swedish waters from Kalmar to Lulea, the route

Submarine hunting: Small naval dirigible, introduced by the British Navy, for scouting.

Rescue in sight: Soldiers aboard one of the Ivernia's rafts watching an approaching patrol boat.

Coolness and courage: Troops on the Ivernia facing the camera before taking to the boats.

Swamped by breakers: One of the boats from the transport Ivernia, torpedoed January 1st, 1917.

15

Coming down for news: Air=scout hailing a vessel from an altitude of 230 feet.

Flying over the fleet: Naval scouting dirigible passing over allied warships.

which was followed by vessels carrying the rich Swedish iron ore, needed for the best qualities of steel, from the mines to the Krupp works. In Swedish waters they could not be attacked by the British and Russian submarines. Meanwhile, the Germans with destroyers, Zeppelins, and armed trawlers diligently watched the Sound and the Cattegat.

All through these weeks the German preparations for the great submarine campaign, which they believed would close the war, were going forward silently. Types were being tested and arrangements made, though for the time being it suited the German Government to profess that it would faithfully observe the rules laid down by President Wilson. The torpedoing of the Channel steamer Sussex, on March 24th, 1916, when eighty innocent civilians were killed or wounded, had brought on a fresh crisis between Germany and the United States. The German Government at first declared that the ship had struck a British mine, and then that it had been torpedoed with a British torpedo. It pretended that a report from the only German submarine near the scene showed that her captain had torpedoed a vessel " near the Sussex," but that this vessel did not resemble the Sussex, as a drawing of it—which was enclosed in the report—showed. The actual fact was that the guilty submarine had been destroyed, and that her captain, who was either dead or in the hands of the Allies, never made any report at all. Moreover, portions of the torpedo remained in the vessel's hull, and were examined by United States officers, who at once identified them as German. This impudent trickery would have exasperated a less pacific and long-suffering politician than President Wilson. He replied to it with a Note requiring the German Government " now, without delay, to proclaim and make effective renunciation of its present methods of submarine warfare against passenger and cargo ships," or the United States would break off diplomatic relations. On May 4th Germany simulated obedience, and informed the United States that an order had been issued to the effect that merchantmen " both within and without the area declared a naval war zone, shall not be sunk without warning, and without the saving of human lives, unless the ships attempt to escape or offer resistance." The German Government at the same time called on the United States to force the British Government to abandon the blockade, as otherwise Germany must reserve herself " complete liberty of action."

This outward surrender raised a furious storm in Germany, where it was not understood that the German submarines had not, in actual fact, in any degree altered their methods. If they were less successful than previously, it was because of the precautions taken by the British Navy. They still sank ships without warning ; indeed, on May 8th, when the German Government's order forbidding this ought to have been in the hands of the submarine commanders—supposing it to have been genuine —the unarmed British liner Cymric was sunk without warning. There were so many subsequent instances of Germany's disregard of her pledges as to show the utter worthlessness of any undertaking given by the German

Torpedoing of the Sussex

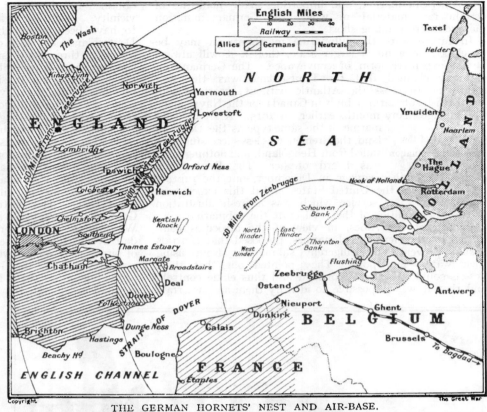

THE GERMAN HORNETS' NEST AND AIR-BASE.
Zeebrugge, a most important coastal point, was secured by the enemy in his early onslaught into Belgium. Strongly fortified, it became a formidable base for his destroyers, submarines, and aircraft. The fifty-mile sections on plan show Zeebrugge's relationship to London and South-East Coast.

Government. A few typical examples may be mentioned. On June 9th the Norwegian steamer Orkedal, on a voyage from the Argentine with a cargo of maize for Denmark, was sunk without warning off the Dutch coast. She was proceeding from one neutral port to another neutral port, and her cargo would ultimately have reached Germany in the shape of Danish butter and bacon. Her destruction was thus an insane outrage. Again, the Kelvinia, with twenty-seven American horse-tenders on board, was sunk without warning on September 2nd. The German submarines did, however, show a certain caution when they suspected that there were American citizens on board ships attacked. But as Herr Bethmann-Hollweg told the Reichstag on January 31st, 1917, he never opposed the ruthless use of submarines from principle, but only because " according to the unanimous judgment of the political and military authorities, the question was not ripe for decision." It was not that the German Government cared for humanity or American scruples. It had not enough submarines ready to make it worth while for Germany to defy the United States.

On July 9th a German submarine, the Deutschland, claiming to be a merchantman, arrived at Baltimore from Bremen, having left Germany on June 14th—according to her captain's statements—with a cargo and mails on board. The figures in her bill of health indicated a tonnage of 791 and a carrying capacity of 441 tons, though her captain stated her tonnage at 1,000. She had 290 tons of dye-stuffs on board. The American authorities permitted her to embark a cargo of nickel and rubber, of both of which Germany was in extreme need. The event was one of great importance. This was the first occasion on which a submarine was used for cargo-carrying work, and the success of the voyage for the time being gave Germany a means of communicating secretly with her diplomatic agents in the United States, obtaining information from her army of spies there, despatching securities for sale in

Exploit of the Deutschland

the American market, and importing small quantities of certain raw material of which the German munition factories were running short.

In future wars the submarine merchantman may be developed on a much larger scale, though it will always be an expensive form of conveyance. The Germans incorrectly claimed that the Deutschland was the first submarine to cross the Atlantic without escort or aid. Ten British submarines, built in Canada for the Navy, made the passage many months earlier, in 1915. A second submarine of the same type as the Deutschland, the Bremen, was less successful. She sailed from Heligoland, and nothing more was heard of her. The Deutschland completed another voyage in December, but the rupture of relations by the United States ended this experiment of an underwater service which was a fresh illustration of the potentialities of that evil craft the submarine.

Gravity of the submarine situation

In August the Allies, in view of the atrocities committed by the German submarines, proposed that neutrals should prevent all belligerent submarines from using their waters and ports. They pointed out that these vessels could navigate submerged and thus elude control ; and that it was impossible to identify them and ascertain

obtained full details of allied and neutral shipping in the vicinity. From such facts as were disclosed she seems to have been larger than the British E boats and the Deutschland, a vessel of about 1,000 tons. She put to sea after three hours' stay, without taking on board any supplies, and in the absence of the British patrols, the presence of which President Wilson had denounced in a previous Note as "vexatious and uncourteous," she could do what she liked. She cruised off the American coast without asking whether such conduct was "vexatious and uncourteous," and torpedoed in quick succession the British ships Westpoint, Strathdene, Stephano, and Kingston ; the Dutch steamer Blommersdijk, and the Norwegian vessel Christian Knudsen. The Blommersdijk was on a voyage from one neutral port to another, and was not inside what the German called their "war zone." Her destruction was not permitted by the German proclamations, and was an act of senseless piracy. While these things were being done, the United States destroyer Benham cruised close at hand, watching the acts of piracy. It was, however, false that her commander—as was pretended by the Germans—was ordered to move out of the line of fire at the Blommersdijk and submitted to the German order. In the Stephano were a large number of American passengers, who were treated with easy insolence and discourtesy.

A tiger is not soothed by smiling at him ; and immediately after this sinister visit, Mr. Gerard, the United States Ambassador in Berlin, and Mr. Swope, one of the coolest and best-known American editors, who had spent two months in Berlin, reached the United States. They carried news of the gravest character. Both agreed that Germany was determined on an unrestricted submarine campaign to be waged with the most savage brutality, and that she would not be deterred by any fear of war with the United States. At her own chosen moment, when she had enough submarines ready, she would fall to work. It was further known, subsequently, that Mr. Gerard gave information as to stupendous preparations by Germany to fill the sea surrounding the British Isles with submarines.

SUBMARINE WAR ON PEACEFUL PASSENGERS.
Cross-channel passenger steamer Sussex, which was torpedoed on her way to Dieppe on March 24th, 1916, when about fifty persons lost their lives. The passengers included a number of Americans, and the outrage led to an emphatic exchange of views between the United States and Germany.

whether they were combatant or non-combatant, and in the latter case to remove " the capacity for harm inherent in the nature of such vessels." These invisible pirates had, in fact, confronted the world with a new and terrible problem. The neutral response to these proposals was most unsatisfactory. The United States flatly refused to exclude combatant or non-combatant submarines from its ports or waters, and almost pushed its Note to a point of unreasonableness by calling on the Allies to " distinguish between submarines of neutral and belligerent nationality," ignoring the fact that a surface ship could not possibly tell from the appearance of a periscope whether it belonged to a German or a neutral submarine ; and that, if she waited to investigate and did not fire, she would almost certainly be sunk.

The question was one of extreme gravity, as was seen on October 7th, when submarine U53, for which the way had been left clear by the withdrawal of the British patrols, arrived at Newport. She was a war submarine fully armed ; her captain is said to have been personally guilty of dastardly outrages on Americans, neutrals, and non-combatant subjects of the Allies. She was allowed to communicate with the shore, where she

In the early days of the war Great Britain had been defined as " a piece of land entirely surrounded by the British Navy." The new version was to run " a piece of land entirely surrounded by German submarines."

The attack on neutral shipping was prosecuted by the Germans with fury. The destruction of neutral craft was a relatively safe business, as they were never armed and did not venture to defend themselves. A particular set was made against Norway, whose Government had had the temerity to propose the introduction of the Swedish rule, forbidding the presence of any belligerent submarines in her territorial waters. These waters were constantly used by the German underwater boats attacking the munition ships en route to the Russian bases in the White Sea. Germans argued that Sweden was right to apply the principle because in her case it helped them, but they contended that Norway was wrong to apply it because in her case it hurt them. When the Norwegian Government hesitated to accept this remarkable logic they sank Norwegian ships. By the close of the year they had destroyed 400,000 tons ; though somewhat to their disgust, as fast as they sank Norwegian vessels the shipowners,

Attacks on neutral shipping

out of their fabulous profits, bought or built new tonnage. Spanish shipping was just as roughly used, though the German submarines stealthily created bases and supply-depots on the Spanish coast. Early in October it was announced that one-twelfth of the Spanish tonnage had been destroyed by the pirates.

Depredations on such a scale ought to have roused the British Government to intense energy. Mr. Runciman announced on October 17th that Great Britain had lost 2,000,000 tons of shipping during the war, intimated that there would be difficulties of food supply, and, incidentally, gave the Germans the valuable information that the British Government had purchased 500,000 tons of wheat in Australia. This was immediately followed by a development of German submarine war on the Australian routes, through the Mediterranean and Atlantic. The most important measure requisite was to reassure farmers and organise agriculture for the largest possible production of food. This was not taken. The Cabinet had been advised by an authoritative committee, so far back as 1915, to guarantee a minimum price for wheat and other food products, so as to give the farmers confidence—for the seizure of their crops for military purposes at a price well below market rates had left them in great uncertainty. Unfortunately it could not make up its mind to abandon old doctrines in that hour of destiny. It disputed and debated while the weeks wore on ; and its half measures and irresolution were among the chief causes of the political revolution in December. The inaction of the Food Production Department was paralleled by the inadequate and

Australian food route attacked

unimaginative measures of the Admiralty, face to face with the deadliest peril that had ever threatened the British Empire, and by the spiritual bankruptcy revealed in the leadership which failed to tell the nation plainly that it must gird itself with all its heroism, patience, and endurance. None that knows British history can believe that the British people would not have responded gloriously to such an appeal.

Anxiety as to the management of the Admiralty was deepened by the incident of the Channel raid on the night of October 26th, which was in itself a trifling affair, though it showed very plainly the danger of Zeebrugge and the difficulty of guarding the Channel against alert German torpedo officers. It was a moonless night with a high tide, when the mines in the British mine-field at the entrance to the Channel would be well submerged. It was therefore a night when an attack might have been expected and watched for. Ten large German destroyers put out of Zeebrugge, steamed into the Channel, and reached a point not far from Folkestone. They sank eleven small drifters or trawlers and captured some few of their crews. They came upon the British Channel steamer Queen, which fortunately had no troops or passengers on board her, and placed bombs in her after her crew had made their escape. Encountering a detachment of British destroyers they sank the Flirt, an old boat of 380 tons, with most of her crew. They torpedoed the larger and modern destroyer Nubian, which vessel had to be beached owing to the storm that was raging, and eventually became a total loss. They then disappeared. The first British official report claimed

German destroyers in the Channel

AMERICAN COAST CUTTER SALVING A DERELICT DANGER TO NAVIGATION.

Derelict Brazilian ship Nephthis being salved by a United States coast cutter. Vessels which have had to be abandoned by their crews, and drift water-logged at the mercy of the tides and currents, are a constant danger to navigation at all times. When the running amok of German submarines threatened to diminish seriously the world's tonnage every effort was made to bring such derelicts into port rather than sink them.

that two German destroyers had been sunk, but the German Admiralty at once repudiated this assertion. That was not in itself conclusive, but it subsequently appeared that the British officer in command only thought that the destroyers had been sunk because he had heard the noise of two violent explosions, and did not claim to have seen them go down. It is therefore probable that the German official report was on this occasion approximately correct.

The German destroyers engaged in this raid appear to have been very large, fast, and heavily-armed vessels, carrying 4·1 in. semi-automatic guns or even 6 in. weapons. They had this great advantage that, as there were no other German ships at sea, they were able to fire at everything they met without challenging. The British, before they opened fire, had to ascertain whether the vessels which they suspected were British or neutral, and it was quite easy for the Germans to discharge their torpedoes at the challenge, thus dealing a deadly blow at once. None the less, the fact that the German destroyers were able to get

back to port came as a disagreeable surprise to the House of Commons and the British public.

Another attempt to enter the Channel was made on November 23rd by six of the Zeebrugge destroyers. The night was dark; the tide was high; but on this occasion they did not come farther than the neighbourhood of Ramsgate, off which port they encountered a number of small British patrol craft and retired after firing a few shots which did no damage. They falsely claimed to have bombarded the "fortified port" of Ramsgate. Again they regained Zeebrugge without being intercepted and brought to action. A third sally was made on November 25th, when a British armed trawler on duty off the East Coast was sunk and her crew captured. The Germans claim to have searched a number of neutral steamers for contraband, but to have released them as they carried nothing objectionable. For the third time they returned safely. Throughout the summer and autumn the German molestation of shipping on the route between England and Holland continued, and between the date of the capture of the Brussels and the end of November no fewer than twelve vessels were seized and taken into Zeebrugge for examination, some of them being condemned.

Changes at the Admiralty

The effect of these minor German successes was to strengthen the desire for a stronger policy at the Admiralty, conducted by men with actual experience at sea in the Great War. Most of the Board had seen no service in the new conditions, and as a whole the Board could show no real success at sea, for the Battle of Jutland was not the great blow which the Navy had wished to inflict on the enemy. On November 29th Sir Henry Jackson, the First Sea Lord, was replaced by Sir John Jellicoe, who again was replaced in command of the Grand Fleet by Sir David Beatty. The command of the Battle-Cruiser Fleet was taken over by Sir William Pakenham. Sir Cecil Burney became Second Sea Lord. On December 10th, with the formation of Mr. Lloyd George's National Government, Mr. Balfour, the First Lord and political head of the Admiralty, was succeeded by Sir Edward Carson, a man of action of remarkable determination and driving power, who, the nation hoped, would insist on the blockade being made effective and on all the channels by which supplies leaked into Germany being stopped.

A few days before the new First Lord entered office the German submarines gave a fresh proof of their audacity. A large German submarine appeared at Funchal, in the island of Madeira, on December 3rd, torpedoed the French gunboat Surprise, which was lying there, a small vessel of 620 tons built for river work; destroyed the British cable-ship

SIGNALLING TO THE GREAT: "GO SLOWLY FOR SAKE OF THE SMALL."
British submarine, alongside her "mother-ship" for small repairs, signalling "M F" to an American vessel. This in the new international code indicated "Reduce speed," and was adopted owing to the damage often caused to vessels alongside piers or other vessels by the wash from ships passing at a high rate of speed.

Dacia and the French transport Kanguroo, which were in the harbour; and then wantonly bombarded the town for two hours, causing great alarm among the Portuguese but without doing any serious damage. In all, thirty-four men were killed or drowned in the ships sunk. Six hundred miles from Lisbon, Madeira is on the routes to South Africa and South America by which the Germans expected the wheat purchased by Mr. Runciman in Australia to be conveyed to Great Britain. A few days later several German submarines were reported off the Canaries, 300 miles south-east of Madeira, in the Central Atlantic, and their appearance in this quarter caused acute distress, as they practically blockaded these Spanish islands.

A fresh embarrassment was provided by the appearance of a German surface commerce-destroyer in the Atlantic on December 4th. This successor of the Möwe—or as some of those captured by her declared, the Möwe herself — carried supplies and provisions sufficient to enable her to remain at sea till April, 1917. She was equipped for mine-laying and carried a very powerful battery, apparently four 6 in. guns, besides a number of smaller weapons. Her speed was estimated at 18 to 19 knots. As usually seen she had a most innocent appearance, resembling a tramp, with one funnel and two masts. It was alleged, however, that she had contrivances by which additional funnels could be shown and the rig and disposition of her masts completely altered. She had four torpedo-tubes, which would enable her to sink any warship that unwarily approached her. She passed the British patrols disguised as a neutral, with a deck-load of hay, flying a neutral flag in bad weather when there was difficulty in boarding suspected vessels. A favourite device of hers was to make the distress signal and then disloyally to destroy ships which came to render aid. She achieved considerable success. The names of eleven ships sunk by her were published in January, 1917, with a total displacement exceeding 70,000 tons.

Methods of the Möwe As for the method employed, the case of the Dramatist may be taken as typical. On December 18th she sighted a vessel approaching on the same course but closing in on her. Suddenly the stranger increased speed, and came up fast alongside. The bulwarks were dropped, revealing a couple of small guns, and the Dramatist had no course but to surrender. She was boarded, a detachment of Germans was placed in her, and most of her crew were transferred to the raider, where they were kept below in the stifling heat when any vessel was sighted. The Dramatist was sunk with bombs the night of her capture.

Two ships, the Yarrowdale and St. Theodore, each of about 4,500 tons, were kept afloat by the Germans after capture and used as tenders. A third, the Japanese vessel Hudson Maru, was spared, and directed to proceed to

WAVES THAT GERMANY CLAIMED TO RULE FROM UNDERNEATH.
The waters "barred" by Germans to all shipping after February 1st, 1917, included the whole of the Mediterranean (except a "lane" twenty miles wide leading to the Greek coast), the whole of the North Sea, and an area extending from the Faroe Islands to 260 miles west of Ireland and twenty miles north of Cape Finisterre to the French frontier.

the Brazilian port of Pernambuco with 237 prisoners. Of the remaining prisoners 441 were placed on board the Yarrowdale, which, with a prize crew, contrived to reach the German port of Swinemunde, first proceeding to the north of Iceland and then through Norwegian territorial waters. The St. Theodore was reported to have been armed and commissioned as another commerce-destroyer, after her decks had been strengthened at sea to take guns; but, according to other reports, she was sunk at sea in January. The island of Fernando de Noronha, in the Central Atlantic, which belongs to Brazil, was for several days the raider's headquarters. Then she vanished, possibly to the base which the Germans were said to have secretly prepared and provisioned at the mouth of the Amazon, possibly to the Indian Ocean, where mines were presently laid in the Gulf of Aden and off Ceylon. Off the Cape of Good Hope other mines were laid. On March 22nd the German Admiralty reported that she had returned to Germany with 593 prisoners, and that in all she had taken twenty-two steamers and five sailing vessels of 123,100 tons gross register. Another German vessel with a large quantity of arms and supplies on board stole out of a Chilian port on the eve of the Möwe's departure, and may have joined the raider. There was reason to believe that a number of neutral steamers laden with coal and supplies—and, it was alleged, with mines—had also been instructed to meet the German at some secret rendezvous. That the raider was not able to do more damage was due to the generally effective patrol of the ocean routes by the Navy. She was a far less formidable antagonist than the German submarines, but her promiscuous scattering of mines made even distant waters dangerous.

Her operations and the work of the German submarines would have been greatly hampered by the effective arming of British merchantmen. The need of this had been often pointed out before the Great War, and, very tardily in 1913, the Admiralty began to supply guns to certain vessels on the South American routes. Forty had received two guns apiece, both mounted in the stern, by the spring of 1914. This restriction was imposed by the British Foreign Office, which throughout the years before the war had been willing to hamper the Royal Navy by every kind of concession to German diplomacy. Germany viewed the arming of British ships with great alarm, and stirred up the pacifists in the British House of Commons and the Press to protest vehemently against it and oppose it at every turn. When the war came the United States

THE INNOCENT-LOOKING GERMAN PIRATE MÖWE.
On December 4th, 1916, a German raider carrying a formidable armament appeared in the Atlantic and had considerable success. Her identity with the Möwe seems to have been established by one of her captives, the skipper of the Nantes, who from German photographs identified Count von Dohna-Schlodien and other officers of the Möwe.

let it be known that it would regard the equipment of merchant vessels with guns forward—so as to enable them to resist attack from ahead—as transforming them into warships, and the British Foreign Office accepted this view, though the custom of the past in the United States merchant service, as in the British, during war was always to sail armed and to carry guns wherever they could be most effectively mounted.

The new Admiralty showed far more vigour in arming the merchantmen and in giving them guns forward as well as aft. Finally, but not till March, **Arming the** 1917, the United States Government **mercantile marine** acquiesced in the allied view, which was undoubtedly the sound one, that guns could be carried anywhere. For some weeks and months, however, allied ships carrying guns forward for their safety had to land those guns at the Canadian port of Halifax and reship them on their return voyage from the United States. The value of an effective armament can be understood from these facts. While only 25 per cent. of unarmed merchantmen escaped when attacked up to February, 75 per cent. of armed merchantmen escaped.

Not content with arming merchantmen on a larger scale and in a more effective manner than its predecessors, the

new Admiralty Board appointed a special committee of young officers with experience at sea in the Great War to deal with the submarine campaign. It developed all the measures which had been employed by Lord Fisher in his successful period of office. An excellent account of the special means employed during 1916, so far as they may be disclosed, was given by the French expert, M. Blanchon, in "La Guerre Nouvelle." The chief characteristics of the earlier German submarine war were the practice of resting on the bottom of the sea, employed by the submarine **Meeting the sub-** captains, and the organisation of a supply **marine menace** system from neutral vessels and accomplices on neutral coasts. Resting at the bottom of the sea, so as to allow the crews to sleep, was easy only in shallow water such as that of the North Sea, but it was possible in deeper seas and oceans to arrange floating anchors. As for the supply system, secret bases were discovered at different times on the Greek and Spanish coast.

The vessels engaged in patrolling for and attacking submarines, stated M. Blanchon, had various methods of making them very uncomfortable. The surface of the sea in calm weather would be watched, and a slight disturbance moving along it would be noted. That indicated a submarine. Fast vessels then hastened to the point and towed mines so as to hit the submarine, when they were exploded against her. Or they tried to envelop her in nets and loose hawsers which would foul her screws. They fished for her as men fish for whales. In straits and harbour entrances nets were fixed with explosive charges and cables were arranged to catch the screws. The newer German submarines, however, were fitted with apparatus for cutting or lifting the nets. A touch none the less gave the alarm on the surface and showed, like the bobbing of a fishing float, that there was something below, and this something could be attacked.

Microphonic appliances enabled the beat of the submarines' screws to be heard to a great distance. Aircraft were utilised, both in the shape of small airships and of seaplanes. An observer in the air looks downward through the water, and, if the sea is clear and the weather fair, can often detect a submarine which would not be visible from a ship. If the submarine was right under him he could usually see it without being seen, for the periscope of 1916 was so constructed as to sweep the horizon but not the zenith. The aircraft could then signal the position to surface craft, or could drop heavy charges on the submarine. In one or two cases British airmen claimed to have destroyed German submarines, and, though the claims were always disputed by the German Admiralty, they were probably correct. The closing of the submarine routes with mines was another method of dealing with the German boats, but these mines could with time be removed by sweeping. Early in 1917, however, neutrals were warned that an enormous area in the centre of the North Sea was, thenceforth, to be regarded as a danger zone. This covered the entire coast of Germany on the North Sea, and only left two channels, one along the Danish and the other along the Dutch coast, open to her submarines. These channels could be watched.

Another measure was the building of standardised merchantmen on the largest possible scale to replace the

About 10.30 a.m. on December 20th, 1916, the raider Möwe held up the French sailing-ship Nantes between Cape Verde and the West Indies.

The Nantes was boarded by two officers, who confiscated her papers and some stores and sent her crew aboard the raider.

At 1.30 a first bomb, fixed aft by the pirates, exploded, and at once the ship took a heavy list to port.

Shortly afterwards a second bomb, fixed forward near the main hatch, exploded, and the ship at once began to go down.

In ten minutes the Nantes went down by the head, watched by her skipper from the bridge of the pirate ship whereon he and his crew were prisoners. These photographs were taken by an American sailor from the St. Theodore, a ship captured by the pirates and used as an auxiliary raider.

PIRACY ON THE HIGH SEAS: SINKING OF THE NANTES BY THE MÖWE.

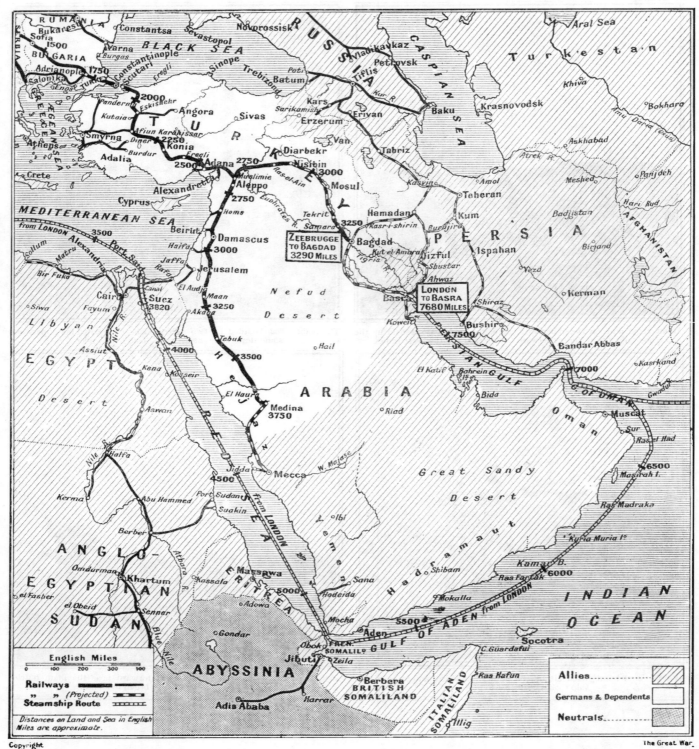

COMMUNICATIONS IN MODERN WARFARE: ADVANTAGE OF LAND-POWER OVER SEA-POWER.

This map illustrates the advantage possessed by the Central Powers over the Allies in respect of communications with the forces fighting in Meso- potamia. From Zeebrugge to Nisibin, above Bagdad, Germany had 3,000 miles of railway secure from all save air attack. From London to Basra the steamship route is 7,680 miles, all exposed to submarine dangers. Moreover, troops could be moved far more rapidly by rail than by sea.

British losses. This, unfortunately, absorbed much labour and raw material which would more profitably have been employed in building warships or making shells for the defeat of the enemy. It was at best a remedy and not a cure. "Lanes," or routes in the oceans guarded by patrol vessels, were established. Yet another step taken by the Government was to restrict the importation of all non- essentials, thereby liberating shipping for vital articles of food and raw materials, and, though only very tardily and after much hesitation and many mistakes, to grant special advantages to the farmers for the production of food. That the situation in January, 1917, was an exceed- ingly serious one was pointed out by the First Sea Lord, Sir

John Jellicoe, in a notable speech on January 11th. "The submarine menace to the merchant service," he said, "is far greater now than at any period of the war, and it requires all our energy to combat it. It must and will be dealt with, of that I am confident." Even then, in the third year of the war, he had to make an appeal to the shipyards, begging the men there—who do not seem to have fully realised the tremendous danger—not to strike or keep bad time or idle.

The situation in January, 1917

The fate of the nation, indeed, was going to depend on whether the workers could or would redouble their energy, increase their output, and so meet the enormous mechanical resources of Germany. The British blockade of Germany had so far failed to stop many necessaries: There would be no make-believe about the German blockade of Great Britain. Unless the British people broke the submarine menace the British Empire must fall, the allied munition factories, deprived of iron ore, petrol, oil, nitrates, glycerine, cotton, and all the ingredients of explosives that could not be obtained in the British Isles, must be gradually brought to a standstill, the British people be slowly starved, and the British Empire cut up into a number of disconnected fragments. Moreover, the Empire could never reunite unless the submarine challenge could be defeated. The British Islands would lie at the mercy of the vast German organisation that stretched across Central Europe and Western Asia.

CAPTAIN JAMES BLAIKIE.
Taken prisoner after his ship, the s.s. Caledonia, was sunk by submarine on December 4th, 1916.

The opening of what the Germans called their unrestricted submarine blockade was fixed for February 1st, and was preceded by a fresh series of minor German successes or British misadventures. On December 21st, in stormy weather, two British destroyers collided in the North Sea, and both went down with a loss of 6 officers and 49 men. On January 1st the troopship Ivernia was sunk in the Mediterranean with the loss of 153 men on board. A peculiar atrocity was committed by a German submarine, apparently in the Atlantic. She torpedoed and sank the British steamer Westminster, and, after the ship had sunk, opened fire on the Westminster's boats, killing the captain and chief engineer deliberately and wantonly. Another German submarine captured Captain Blaikie, of the steamer Caledonia, which was sunk after firing on the submarine. The German semi-official Press announced that he would be executed as Captain Fryatt had been. Luckily, the German Government changed its mind, perhaps recognising that Mr. Lloyd George's Ministry would not shrink from reprisals. On January 9th the old British battleship Cornwallis was sunk by a submarine in the Mediterranean, but all her crew escaped except 13 men, who were killed by the explosion.

On January 23rd two sharp actions were fought between a number of destroyers from Zeebrugge and British craft in the North Sea. The first of these encounters took place off the Schouwen Bank, which lay off the Dutch coast, thirty miles north of Zeebrugge. The night was dark but very cold, with a stiff easterly wind and occasional showers of sleet. Both the British and German destroyers were whirling along at high speed, with all lights out, through the gloom when suddenly came the flash of guns, the detonation of quick-firers, and the rush of torpedoes through the water. The two forces had met. Unfortunately a German torpedo struck a British destroyer, damaging her and killing 47 officers and men. As she remained afloat, but could not be towed back to port in the heavy sea running, she had to be sunk by the other vessels in the British detachment. Otherwise the British vessels were untouched, and owing to the pitchy blackness nothing could be learned of injury to the Germans.

Two destroyer actions

The second was a fiercer and closer fight. A number of new and powerful German destroyers, whose leading boat was V69, laid down in late 1914 and mounting several 4·1 in. semi-automatic guns on a displacement of 1,200 tons, met a flotilla of British destroyers in the darkness and instantly received a violent fire. V69 was hit on the bridge by a shell which shattered the wheel, killed the officer in charge of the flotilla, Commander Schultz, two other officers, and two or three of the crew. The British salvos damaged one of her funnels and dislodged two of her torpedo-tubes from their pivot. Another shell

FINE DISCIPLINE ON THE TORPEDOED LINER ARABIA.
Saving women and children from the P. and O. liner Arabia, torpedoed without warning in the Mediterranean on November 6th, 1916. The 437 passengers included 169 women and children. Thanks to coolness and discipline all on board were saved, except two engineers probably killed by the explosion.

put the relief steering-gear out of action, and the vessel had to be manœuvred with her screws. She made repeated attempts to escape northwards towards the German coast, but on each occasion she was headed off. About four she was rammed by a British destroyer, which ran at her fiercely and struck her with such violence as to bring the damaged funnel down and to cause a serious leak. Meanwhile, the other German destroyers were in full flight, making no attempt to support their leader. About 7 a.m., after five hours of intermittent firing, the **V69 at Ymuiden** combat ended indecisively. V69 was able to struggle into Dutch waters at Ymuiden, and, as the morning advanced, was brought into harbour, with a man's arm blown off and frozen into her rigging and eight corpses frozen firmly to her deck. It was reported that 80 of her crew of 116 had been killed or wounded, but this appears an excessive figure. The British report claimed that one German destroyer had been sunk (though this may possibly have been the V69), and that others had suffered " considerable punishment." Another damaged destroyer was seen off the north coast of Holland, but it presumably made its escape.

The Germans admitted that they were on an " enterprise," which probably meant that they were preparing an attack on some point of the British coast. The British patrols, however, on this occasion were on the spot, and were able to prevent them from accomplishing anything. V69 was not interned, by some surprising Dutch jugglery with international law, but was repaired and released, and though ample warning had been given of the fact that she was preparing for sea, she was able unmolested

to steam the hundred miles between Ymuiden and Zeebrugge on the night of February 10th. In the second engagement the British suffered no loss, and no damage worth reporting. In return for the exceptional favour which the Dutch showed the German Navy, their ships were relentlessly torpedoed.

In the night of January 25th, about eleven o'clock, a German vessel approached a place on the Suffolk coast which the German official report described as " the fortified town of Southwold," and fired two star-shells which lighted up the coast as though it had been day. Immediately afterwards the vessel opened fire. She discharged in all thirty or forty shells, most of which fell in fields, and then she disappeared. No lives were lost, and only the most trivial damage was inflicted. The vessel appears to have been a submarine.

The various peace intrigues of Germany and the efforts of President Wilson do not fall within the province of this chapter. The German proposals were never sincere, and were intended **" Ruthless " employ-** only to lead up to and prepare the way **ment of submarines** for the introduction of yet more savage methods of war and the perpetration of yet more appalling atrocities the moment a considerable number of large submarines were complete. The usual agitation in Germany preceded the German Admiralty's action. The Hamburg Chamber of Commerce, in January, 1917, entreated the Emperor to permit " the ruthless employment of our submarines for an effective blockade " of Great Britain. His Majesty replied that the " sharp weapons " of the German people would not be allowed to rest till victory had been won.

GUARDING A CHANNEL STEAMER FROM POSSIBLE ATTACK BY SUBMARINE.
British destroyer convoying a cross-Channel steamer. When German submarines made war on passenger steamers, neutral vessels, hospital ships—any peaceful floating target by preference—the English Channel was, apart from occasional espisodes, kept wonderfully free of them. The system of convoy—suggestive of the wars of an earlier age—was resorted to, and warships accompanied defenceless vessels on their journeys.

Early in 1917 preparations were made by all German ships lying in neutral ports to put to sea. Apparently orders had been secretly sent to them to break out if they were not closely guarded. The next step of the German Government was to announce that it had " conclusive proof that in several instances enemy hospital ships have been misused for the transport of munitions and troops. It has at the same time declared that the traffic of hospital ships within a line drawn between Flamborough Head and Terschelling on the one hand, and from Ushant to Land's End on the other, will no longer be tolerated." The British

issues at stake, concerted plans for a counter-campaign. In January a Naval Conference met in London, mainly to discuss policy in the Mediterranean, where the submarines were becoming peculiarly active and dangerous. The proceedings were opened by Mr. Lloyd George. The British, French, and Italian Navies were represented, among the officers present being Rear-Admiral Lacaze, the French Minister of Marine, and Vice-Admiral Corsi, the Italian Minister of Marine, and various Staff officers and experts. Important decisions were reached affecting naval operations, the use of shipping, and the control of the trade routes.

Shipping casualty lists

On the eve of the German proclamation of unrestricted submarine war on shipping the situation was this : The Germans were destroying shipping, according to the lists of vessels which were then published day by day in the Press, at the rate of at least 150 a month. The ships which appeared by name in these mortality lists between December 1st and 31st numbered 147 ; and between January 1st and 31st, 148. The lists were not quite complete, as a certain number of allied and neutral vessels were sunk without figuring in the British reports, A valuable analysis of the losses for various periods of fifteen days

DAMAGED GERMAN DESTROYER V69 AT YMUIDEN.
German destroyer that sought harbourage in Holland after being battered in a "scrap" with a British patrolling force in the North Sea on January 23rd, 1917. Above and right: Other views of the same vessel.

Government made the only reply possible to this infamous declaration. It stated that "if the threat is carried out, reprisals will immediately be taken." As a matter of fact, the Germans long before this impudent Note had attacked hospital ships. On November 21st a submarine sank the 48,000-ton Britannic in Greek waters, with a loss of 60 lives. A day or two later the hospital ship Braemar Castle was sunk in the Ægean, but with the loss of only one life.

Those last days of January were marked by the tremors which in political as well as in terrestrial catastrophes precede the greatest shocks. Norway, despite all the German bullying, decided to prohibit belligerent submarines from entering her waters. A Royal proclamation informed the combatants that any submarines entering Norwegian waters would be attacked without warning. Damaged boats or boats driven into harbour by stress of weather would only be allowed in territorial waters provided they navigated on the surface and showed their colours. The Germans at once savagely redoubled their attacks on Norwegian shipping.

The Allies, aware of what was coming and the immense

Norway and the submarines

was published in the " Daily Chronicle," and showed the following results :

	TOTAL SUNK	OF WHICH BRITISH
October 26th—November 9th	82	28
November 10th—November 24th.. ..	62	29
November 25th—December 9th	105	42
December 10th—December 24th	70	27
December 25th—January 8th	63	21
January 9th—January 23rd	88	40
TOTAL	470	187

This rate of loss was three times heavier than in the earlier submarine blockade which began in February, 1915. It was not so heavy as the loss of British shipping in certain periods of past wars. The loss of British merchantmen in the most unfortunate year of the Revolutionary War with France, 1797, for example, was 949 vessels taken by the enemy, an average of nearly 80 a month, though naturally they were ships of very much smaller size. In those old days, however, Great Britain grew her own food. Nine-tenths of all that she required was produced at home, and even for munitions of war she had not seriously to rely on importation for anything except hemp, tallow and spars.

The German decision to disregard the Notes of President Wilson and openly repudiate all respect for humanity, was notified to the Reichstag by Herr Bethmann Hollweg on January 31st. He told that assembly that "the moment has now arrived. Last autumn the time was not ripe." There had been, he declared, several changes in the position. "The number of our submarines has been very greatly increased as compared with last spring, and thereby a firm basis has been created for success." The harvest had failed in Great Britain and the allied States. The coal question was becoming critical for France and Italy, which depended on sea-borne British fuel. In Great Britain there was a shortage of ore for munition manufacture and of timber for pit-props, without which coal could not be raised.

There was a great scarcity of allied cargo ships owing to the earlier operations of the German submarines, which had thus prepared the way for a decisive blow. Austria was acting in conjunction with Germany, and while Germany drew a blockade round Great Britain, she would encircle Italy with her submarines. He concluded by discussing the risks of war with the United States, which event had been carefully studied for months before by the German Staff.

The effect of the submarine campaign was necessarily cumulative. It aggravated other troubles. It was true that 2,000,000 tons of new shipping had been built to replace that lost by Great Britain in the first two years of the war. But one of the difficulties of the Allies was that each ship in the war did only about two-thirds the amount of work that she had done before the war. This was due to delays caused by waiting for instructions, by the congestion of certain ports, and by the lack of labour to unload and load. Each reduction of tonnage or **German bid** of carrying power was felt, as each suc-**for victory** cessive reduction of a man's food would be, more and more severely. So the Germans hoped that each successive destruction of shipping would tighten the garotte round the neck of the Allies.

It would be a mistake to accept the view, which was current in some quarters, that Germany adopted this plan of merciless submarine war as "a last throw" of the gambler's dice, or with some desperate desire to drag the United States into the war, and then make a hurried peace. Germany, as we have seen, had long been preparing the campaign; she opened it not with any intention of "riding for a fall," a practice unknown to the German Staff, but

because her experts were firmly convinced that it meant victory—and speedy victory. They declared on every hand that while they had greatly underrated the capacity of the British Army, they had overrated the energy and leadership of the British Navy. In a curious, confidential circular, which was issued to the German Press, and a copy of which came into the possession of the British Government in February, 1917, the German newspapers were told that there must be no doubts or discussions as to the usefulness of unrestricted submarine war.   **Position of the United States**

The determined approval of the entire people must ring out from the Press. It is a question, not of a movement of desperation—all the factors have been carefully weighed after conscientious technical naval preparation—but of the best and only means to a speedy, victorious ending of the war. . . . Material, personnel, and appliances are being increased and improved continually; trained reserves are ready. Britain's references to the perfection of her means of defence, which are intended to reassure the British people, are refuted by the good results of the last months. Each result is now much more important, because the enemy's mercantile marine is already weakened, the material used up in much coloured personnel. The psychological influence should not be underestimated. Fear among the enemy and neutrals adds to difficulties with the crews and may induce neutrals to keep ships in harbour.

ABOVE THE CLOUDS IN A SEAPLANE.
Naval aerial scout, above Salonika, passing through heavy clouds into the clear air above. Looking on this remarkable photograph almost imparts the sensation of being actually in the machine from which the picture was taken.

As for the United States, the German view was that President Wilson would take several weeks or months to make up his mind, and even then would probably not act with any energy. The German Press was directed to "use the outward forms of friendliness." An immense contempt for democracy and a total disbelief in its capacity to wage war with success overwhelmed the German leaders. They hated the United States because, in perfect conformity with international law, it had supplied the Allies with large quantities of munitions. They hoped much from the intrigues and plots of their agents, from the votes of the German-American population, from the connivance of certain powerful German-American politicians. They had also mobilised the extreme Irish element. At the worst they knew that the United States Navy was weak in men, and that the United States Army hardly existed at all. They saw that it had taken Great Britain two years to organise herself for war. No serious attack from the United States was therefore to be feared before a decision had been reached. Arrangements were made to paralyse the American Government by fomenting trouble in Mexico and in Cuba, with a complete and saturnine disregard of the cherished Monroe Doctrine.

The German plan was a clever one, if the Germans had not fatally misunderstood the American character. It was to begin by making outrageous demands on the United States, which perhaps were not intended to be carried out in their entirety. On January 31st an arrogant German Note was despatched to President Wilson. It stated that German submarines would thereafter observe no restraints. It forbade neutral shipping to enter the waters round Great Britain, France and Italy, or to voyage in the Eastern Mediterranean. Concessions were offered of a nature that was merely derisive.

This extraordinary document concluded with an ironical announcement that the German Government was actuated by "the highest sense to serve humanity," and expressed the hope that the people and Government of the United States would "appreciate the new state of affairs from the right standpoint of impartiality." Every other neutral Power received a similar communication from the Foreign Office in Berlin. To the Dutch, who were powerless to object or resist, in view of a great concentration of German troops on their frontier and of threatening hints in the German Press, the German Government offered as a special privilege the right to send one paddle-steamer a week to and from Southwold, subject to the restriction that it must be painted zebra-wise and must carry no contraband. This service was obviously allowed to remain because it was most useful to German spies and secret agents.

To the smaller and weaker neutrals these haughty Notes brought utter consternation. They were now shown what was the German idea of the "freedom of the seas," which the German Government had professed itself so supremely anxious to secure. The "freedom of the seas" meant, in effect, the freedom of the German submarines from all regard for honour and law of humanity, and the utter destruction of all ocean traffic. It meant **Germany and** sowing not merely the North Sea and the **neutral shipping** Mediterranean with mines; it meant sowing every sea and ocean with them. It meant that the German submarines would treacherously torpedo any vessel which they encountered anywhere. The example of U53 off New York had illustrated the German naval officers' regard for such flimsy restrictions as their own Government pretended to impose on them. Never before had the whole civilised world been menaced with such horrors, with indiscriminate massacre at sea on so colossal a scale. The weaker neutrals flinched. In

Holland, Sweden, and Denmark it was decided that ships should, as far as possible, remain in port until it was seen what the Germans could do. By such acquiescence, passive it may be, but yet in effect involving tame obedience to the German will, these smaller neutrals complied with Germany's demands and served her aims. So long as neutral shipping vanished from the sea, she was satisfied. That was what she required to destroy Great Britain and the Allies.

Norway showed greater courage and independence. Though her losses by February 11th had reached 338 vessels of 464,900 tons, her merchant navy con tinued its voyages and her seamen faced **Norway's courageous** the risks from the German murder vessels **independence** unperturbed. The Norwegian Government protested against the German blockade, in common with the other Scandinavian Power, but appears to have permitted Sweden to weaken the force of its remonstrance. If it did not go to war, it was because it had seen the fate of Rumania, which was hardly such as to encourage the smaller neutrals to resolute action. The Spanish Government despatched a very forcible Note to Germany, but as yet made no other move, though many Spanish ships had been wantonly sunk by the German submarines. "The decision," stated this protest, "completely to close certain sea routes by substituting for the indisputable right of capture in certain cases the alleged right of destruction in every case, exceeds the legal principles of international life . . . and is contrary to the principle observed by all nations even in moments of the most extreme violence."

The United States did not show the feebleness and hesitation that Germany had expected. The country which had tolerated the Lusitania outrage, the incessant floutings of its Government by German diplomacy, and the frequent and callous murders of United States citizens on

SECTIONAL VIEW OF A GERMAN SUBMARINE MINE-LAYER.

A.—Engine-room with electric motors and oil engines. B.—Trimming-tank with oil for engine. C.—Screw-shaft attached to propeller. D.—Rudder for steering controlled from deck or conning-tower. E.—Bunks for the crew. F.—Mine-tubes from which the sinking mines have been released G.—Mines in tubes. H.—Mushroom-shaped anchor. J.—External steering wheel. K.—Conning-tower.

CAPTAIN-LIEUT. PETZ,
Commandant of a U boat, who claimed to have sunk 51,000 tons, February 6th-7th, 1917.

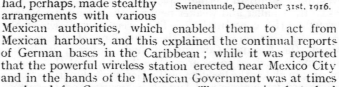

DEPUTY-LIEUT. BADEWITZ.
Took the Yarrowdale and four hundred and sixty-nine prisoners into Swinemunde, December 31st. 1916.

the high seas by German officers, received the new orders of Germany with a stupefaction which immediately developed into fierce indignation. It was as though the veil of the temple had been rent. The real meaning of German policy became clear. On February 3rd President Wilson announced to Congress " that diplomatic relations between the United States and the German Empire are severed," that the American Ambassador in Berlin would be forthwith withdrawn, that the German Ambassador in Washington had received his passports, and that a sum of £50,000,000 was required to complete warships. The House of Representatives was crowded as never before. Its galleries were packed to listen to an announcement which must make history, and which marked one of the most solemn moments in the war. As each firm sentence came from President Wilson it was answered with bursts of applause from the members and by the waving of handkerchiefs from the gallery. When at last the President concluded with the epoch-making declaration — that " if American ships and American lives should in fact be sacrificed by their (the German) naval commanders, in heedless contravention of the just and reasonable understandings of international law and the obvious dictates of humanity, I shall take the liberty of again coming before Congress to ask that authority be given me to use any means that may be necessary for the protection of our seamen and our people "— then all, able no longer to observe the convention which forbade cheering by strangers, broke forth into eager applause.

At first sight the action of the United States looked like a half measure. Its effects were not the less far-reaching. The hands of the Allies were no longer tied in their blockade of Germany. But important above all was the decisive act of President Wilson in stamping with eternal infamy the conduct of Germany. Bismarck, who was not a scrupulous man, once, in a moment of insight into the forces which ultimately sway the destinies of mankind, warned his countrymen against setting against themselves " the imponderabilia of Europe," by which he meant the moral feeling of mankind. Now the world was to be shown, amidst this final clash of all nations, whether Bismarck was right or William II.

A point of further importance was that the Germans could no longer use bases, which they had perhaps secretly prepared, on United States territory, nor employ secret wireless installations in the United States, which they had as certainly arranged, nor charter United States steamers for the conveyance of oil, food, and munitions to their submarines in the Western Atlantic. They had, perhaps, made stealthy arrangements with various Mexican authorities, which enabled them to act from Mexican harbours, and this explained the continual reports of German bases in the Caribbean ; while it was reported that the powerful wireless station erected near Mexico City and in the hands of the Mexican Government was at times employed for German purposes. The war, in fact, had crossed the Atlantic before President Wilson spoke his fateful words. The Monroe Doctrine had been insolently defied.

With the exception of Brazil and Chile, who took up a firm attitude, much resembling that of the United States, the other Republics of Central and South America made no decided move. German influence was so strong with them, and dislike of the powerful United States so general, that they did not respond to President Wilson's new policy, but rather threw cold water on it and on the diplomacy of Brazil, who suggested a combination against Germany ; and this though the prosperity of the Argentine entirely depended on free traffic by sea between her magnificent pampas and estancias and the markets of Europe and the United States. In Asia the great State of China followed the lead of the United States. On March 14th the Chinese Government broke off relations with Germany and seized German shipping in its ports.

And so the " unrestricted " submarine war began. In the hour of its inception the German Staff published certain figures on which all its forecasts were based. These are of such importance that they must be reproduced from the Berlin " Lokalanzeiger." The total British tonnage the German Staff estimated at 20,000,000 tons, of which 8,600,000 had been requisitioned for military and naval purposes ; 500,000 was employed in coastal trade ; 1,000,000 was under repair ; 2,000,000 was employed in the service of the Allies ; and only 8,000,000 tons, at most, was available for the supply of Great Britain. It was

PIRATE'S QUICK-FIRER.
Quick-firing gun on a U boat. Improved U boats mounted 4'1 in. guns of semi-automatic type, firing a 35 lb. shell with great rapidity.

FULL SPEED ON THE SURFACE.
The newer German submarines in commission in 1917 could travel at eighteen to twenty-one, and even twenty-five, knots on the surface. With their low freeboard they were naturally awash when moving at that speed.

calculated that no more than 6,750,000 tons of British shipping had been serving Great Britain from July to September, 1916, eked out by 900,000 tons of allied shipping, and 3,000,000 tons of neutral vessels. This was barely sufficient, while a stoppage of neutral shipping between Denmark and Holland and Great Britain would at once produce a fat famine in the last country, as the British depended on Holland for margarine and on Denmark for butter. "Scarcity and high prices," already prevailed in Great Britain, stated the German Staff. The conditions were therefore "the most favourable conceivable" for the German campaign. At the same time it was announced that after the exhaustion caused by submarine attacks had been allowed to develop, the German High Sea Fleet might also come into action. These estimates were generally correct, and in accord with those of British unofficial authorities.

The British counterprecautions were indicated in Parliament, but the full gravity of the position was disclosed by Lord Lytton, speaking for the Admiralty on February 13th. He warned the public that, even if there were no submarines, there would be need for drastic restriction of imports, owing to the absorption of tonnage for military and naval purposes and the service of the Allies. "We are now approaching the supreme and terrible climax of the war," Lord Curzon stated. He added that further counter-measures had been taken. Scientific inventions were being employed and developed for the discovery and detection of submarines, and "lanes" of safety were being

THE SOWER OF DEATH.
German mine-laying steamer busy— near the German coasts.

FISHING FOR MINES: A CATCH.
Crew of a German mine-sweeper watching a mine rising to the surface. Trawling for mines was most dangerous work, requiring great vigilance and courage. Mines brought up by the cables were exploded by rifle fire.

organised over the oceans, which were guarded for neutral and British shipping.

The number of submarines which Germany had available was estimated very variously. A German deserter put it at 1,000, but this fantastic figure certainly included vessels on the stocks, and was grossly exaggerated. A Swiss calculation gave the number as 300. The Americans, with Mr. Gerard, who had just left Germany, gave it as between 200 and 300 large boats, to which a considerable number of small boats had to be added. Whatever the number, it could be very rapidly increased, as arrangements had been made in Germany to build these craft, which were all standardised on two or three designs, with extreme speed. The various parts were made in works inland, and were put together on the sea-coast. Skilled workers were even brought back from the German Army in France. Three hundred large oil-engines were ordered in Switzerland, which would probably provide the motive power for one hundred large submarines. The real difficulty in augmenting the number of submarines necessarily lay in the provision of trained officers and men, but for them demands were made on the German Army, thus supplementing the personnel of the German Navy.

The zone which was barred to all shipping was enclosed by an imaginary line running 20 miles west of the Dutch coast, and then north and west to a point 3 miles south of the Faroe Islands, whence it turned south-westward, and then again south, 260 miles west of the Irish coast. It finally turned in and approached the Spanish coast near Cape Finisterre, running 20 miles north of that coast to the French

HOW THE ENEMY DEPICTED AN ALLEGED GERMAN SUCCESS.
German cruiser out on patrol destroying an English mine-layer. This illustration, like others on pages 30, 31, 32, is reproduced from a German newspaper, and may be founded on fact. No enemy surface mine-layers ventured near the English coast, but British mine-layers had to operate near German waters.

frontier. In the Mediterranean the barred zone included all the waters westward from a line drawn from the Gulf of Lyons, east of the Balearics, to the Algerian coast, but a narrow "corridor," 20 miles wide, was to be left open leading south of Sicily and Crete to the Greek coast. As the Germans scattered drifting mines everywhere, it was certain that even waters which were not professedly barred would gradually become dangerous to the most innocent neutrals. German piracy was, in fact, steadily becoming intolerable to the rest of the civilised world which had not been bred up in the peculiar Teuton code of brutality.

One of the first and most barbarous acts of German submarine officers was the destruction of the Belgian relief-ship Lars Kruse, voyaging with a safe-conduct, which was torpedoed and sunk. This cruel act did not injure Great Britain, but it increased the anguish of the miserable victims of Germany in Belgium. A Peruvian vessel, the Lorton, was sunk by a German submarine inside Spanish territorial waters on February 5th. The British liner Port Adelaide, with passengers on board, was sunk without warning about the same time. Other vessels with wheat and flour on their way to Greece, whose Government gave every sign of acting in concert with the Germans, were destroyed. Yet, though the losses were very heavy in the first week of the blockade, they were very far from answering the sanguine German hopes, which looked for at least 250,000 tons of shipping sunk a week. The following side by side are the records of ships, the destruction of which was published in the British Press in the first week of February (" unrestricted ' blockade) and January (" restricted ") :

DATE	FEBRUARY	JANUARY
1st	4	11
2nd	7	8
3rd	10	1
4th	11	7
5th	4	6
6th	16	3
7th	12	7
	64	43

The rate of destruction was increased 50 per cent. But if it was far below what Germany hoped, it was yet grave enough. It was not the case that the losses in February were light, but rather that those in January, before the "unrestricted" war, were very heavy. In the first fourteen days of February no fewer than 7,981 British ships entered or cleared at British ports, besides 452 allied and 858 neutral vessels. The British loss reported in the Press in the first fourteen days—some of it representing vessels destroyed before February 1st—was

The crew of a U boat on deck doing various small repairs necessitated by mishaps during a spell of dirty weather.

Pirates on the look-out in the North Sea. Outlaws, as they must have known themselves to be, the crews of German submarines had need of vigilance not to be caught unawares.

LIFE UNDER THE " JOLLY ROGER."

34 ships, in addition to 25 fishing vessels and small craft.

Among the German victims were the large White Star steamer Afric, sunk about February 12th. On the previous day the Norwegian steamer Dalmata was sunk in the Atlantic, and the captain, with his wife and the crew, were bundled into small open boats in a heavy sea and bitter weather and left to die. One of the crew perished of cold, and three others were frost-bitten before a small Danish vessel chanced upon them. Even Swedish ships were not spared. The largest Swedish sailing vessel, the Hugo Hamilton, and the Swedish steamer Vaering, though en route from one neutral port to another, were both sent to the bottom, despite the fact that they had nothing which even lunatics could have called contraband on board.

The humbler and feebler the Dutch became the more the Germans, like all bullies, delighted to injure and annoy the people that had once boasted a Van Tromp and a De Ruyter. On February 22nd seven Dutch steamers which left Falmouth were attacked at 5 p.m. in daylight by a single submarine, U3. This vessel went to work in the most leisurely fashion. She must have been, on the most moderate computation, thirty or forty minutes at her business. Three of the Dutch ships were torpedoed, and all these went down. In the other four, bombs were placed, a process requiring time. One of these four remained afloat, and was towed into port by a British trawler, which at last appeared on the scene. Nothing was ever published as to the fate of the other three. The Dutch had declined to accept British warnings or escort. They neither asked nor received instructions as to their route from the Admiralty, being, like very simple people, content with the promises made them from Berlin. They carried the usual navigation lights, though it was day when they were sunk. Two of them were laden with wheat and flour for Holland, a very considerable part of which might ultimately have reached Germany. It subsequently appeared that the Dutch Government had been informed by the Germans that its ships could leave with "relative security" on February 22nd, or with "absolute security" on March 17th, as it would be impossible to inform the German submarine officers at sea by February 22nd. Remembering that the German Admiralty had at its disposal high-power wireless installations which could communicate with every German submarine within 500 miles of Europe, without delay, the innocent Dutch sent orders to these vessels to sail. Another eleven vessels were ordered to leave at the same time. The German submarines had therefore plenty of notice, and could post themselves in readiness. When the ships were thus attacked and the German pledge was violated, the Dutch Press did not venture to utter more than a few timorous complaints. Indeed, certain of its organs attacked the British Government for detaining these ships, needless to say without rhyme or reason.

On February 25th the Germans attempted to repeat their Lusitania coup by sinking the Cunard liner Laconia, a vessel of 18,099 tons. The attack was delivered without the slightest warning, off the Irish coast, the happy hunting-ground of the German submarines. The crime was committed in the darkness. Suddenly a great crash was heard as though many tons of steel-plate had fallen from an immense height on to hollow steel. There was no panic. The vessel had been hit aft, and all the lights were turned on while the signal of distress was made by wireless. Meanwhile, the boats were lowered. After the ship had floated for a quarter of an hour the submarine drew up a second time and fired a torpedo into the Laconia's engine-room, whereupon instantly the lights went out and she sank very rapidly. In the vessel, among other women passengers, were two United States citizens, Mrs. Hoy and her daughter.

Sinking of the Laconia

The night was an intensely cold one, and, after suffering tortures, they died of exhaustion in one of the boats which had been smashed in lowering. The son and brother of the dead women telegraphed to President Wilson these words : " My beloved mother and sister, passengers in the Laconia, have been foully murdered on the high seas. As an American citizen outraged, and as such fully within my rights, as an American son and brother bereaved, I call upon my Government to preserve its citizens' self-respect, and to save others of my countrymen from such deep grief as I now feel. If my country can use me against these brutal assassins, I am at its call. If it stultifies my manhood and my nation's by remaining passive under outrage, I shall seek a man's chance under another flag." The crowning touch was given to the whole episode by a remark which the commander of the submarine made when he came close up to a boat, demanding the Laconia's captain, whom he did not ultimately find. He was told that he had sunk a vessel carrying women and children. " They are all right " was the cynically indifferent answer of the murderer.

American's passionate protest

Three days later President Wilson asked for power to arm American merchantmen. The Rubicon had been crossed and a new force was about to enter the field.

Figures for the week ending February 25th showed that 4,541 vessels of all nationalities over 100 tons had arrived in British ports. Of these 15 British ships over and 5 under 1,600 tons had been sunk, besides 4 British fishing vessels. Twelve British ships had been unsuccessfully attacked by submarines.

ABOARD A TROOPSHIP : INSPECTION TO THE MUSIC OF THE BAND.

Upon the British Navy rested the greatest part of the burden of the oversea transport for all the Allies. By a mobilisation of her mercantile marine Great Britain compassed the stupendous task satisfactorily, and by February, 1917, she had conveyed no fewer than eight million men by sea to the various fronts on which her armies were operating.

promoted from the field-artillery, where they handled little guns. The technique of the new big howitzers, with the new system of aerial control from kite-balloons and aeroplanes, was a perplexing matter even for a field-artillery officer of experience. It was as if the British Army, mainly accustomed to 3·3 in. guns, were suddenly to be provided with as large ordnance as the British Navy, and set to fire against British gun-layers and British gunnery lieutenants who had been practising for ten years with their gigantic pieces.

Germany's new magazine-rifle

The training of the new British infantry was good. Indeed, it was miraculously good, and in one branch of attack—bomb-throwing—its skill seems to have been at least equal to all that which the troops of Germany had acquired in a year of trench warfare. The musketry of the infantry, though far from equalling that of the incomparable riflemen at Mons and Ypres, appears to have been almost as effective as that which the French conscripts attained with their inferior Lebel rifle. The Germans had a new magazine rifle, holding twenty rounds, but did not use it as well as the new British soldier used his Lee-Enfield. And even in bayonet work the new British soldier was not at much disadvantage when charging an average German force. The British machine-gunner was also good, having been promoted by reason of his special marksmanship from the multitude of the new infantry.

The new British field-artillery seems to have been of fair quality. Before the war the French used to say it took ten years to make a first-class man for their 3 in. gun. Naturally, British civilians who entered the Army in 1914 and 1915 were not transformed by the summer of 1916 into the peers of the field-gunners of France. But their native alertness of mind and the fine system of accelerated training designed for them, together with the opportunities for battle practice they received on first going to the front, transformed them into men of a useful sort. They needed an abundance of shell, though with this abundance they did not always breach the hostile zones of wire entanglement ; still less could they sweep with unexpected gusts difficult bits of land as French gunners could. But having regard to the extraordinary circumstances, their work was most praiseworthy. All this the German Staff allowed in its study of the situation on the western front. Having achieved most of its great successes east and west by means of siege-guns, worked by the most highly trained body of expert gunners outside the British Navy, the German High Command concluded that the British attack would be wrecked through inefficient handling of the British heavy artillery.

What the enemy expected

The enemy expected that there would be no close and precise co-operation between the advancing waves of British infantry and the battering-ram of British heavy shell fire. Sir Douglas Haig divined what the enemy thought in the matter, and frankly recognised the factors of weakness in his own vast but improvised forces. In the first grand clash of Briton and Teuton he took all possible steps to remedy the inexperience of his troops.

[*British official photograph.*

THE STRUGGLE FOR THE SPUR : SHELLS BURSTING NEAR THIEPVAL.

Thiepval was won by the British, September 27th, 1916, after terrific fighting, and with its capture—and that of Combles by the French and British in co-operation—the whole Bapaume Valley was dominated.

RUSSIAN INFANTRY | CHAPTER CLXXII. | ON THE MARCH.

RUSSIA'S TRAGIC STRUGGLE TO THE EVE OF THE REVOLUTION.

By Edward Wright.

Half a Million Germans Rescue Austria-Hungary—Railway Weakness of Southern Russia—Brussiloff has Only One Line to His Southern Base and no Proper Connections with Rumania—How Bismarck Triumphed over Alexeieff—Opening of New Offensive in Galicia —Desperate Battles around Halicz—Finns and Russians Break Across the River but Lose Ground in Counter-attack—Germany's Stronger Artillery with Ampler Munitions Dominates the Battlefield—Terrific Struggle on the Lysonia and Lechitsky's Drive Across the Carpathians—Failure of Rumanian Invasion Checks the Russian Offensive—Corrupt Russian Bureaucracy Tries to Make Separate Peace—Stürmer Overthrown by the Progressives in the Duma—Russian Nobility and Russian Princes of the Blood Royal Rally to the People—Sinister Power of Rasputin over Tsar and Tsaritza—Ministers of War and Marine Fight against Stürmer and Rasputin—Trepoff and Protopopoff Struggle for Autocracy and Democracy—Execution of Rasputin by a Grand Duke and Rise of Protopopoff as the New "Dark Force" in Russia—Radko Dimitrieff Cheers the Despairing Russian People by a Surprising Victory—Reopening of the Duma and Preparations for the Revolution.

THE position of Russia at the end of August, 1916, seemed to be of astonishing resurgent strength, as was shown in Chapter CXXXVII. (Vol. VII., page 319) She had again overthrown the main armies of Austria-Hungary, captured 360,000 foes, over 400 guns, and put out of action a million men. So great was the force of the Russian blow that the Germans had entirely to reorganise the eastern front. They were no longer able to hold the line by merely stiffening the broken forces of their allies with occasional German units. Hindenburg took over the command, and though, after a quarrel with Austro-Hungarian Headquarters, he allowed the Austrians to save their face by retaining some nominal positions, all the real work of army control and army administration was carried out by German generals. A strong Turkish force that had been trained and armed in Germany was diverted to the defence of the Lemberg line. Many of the new divisions that General von Falkenhayn had been creating for a final offensive against Russia were sent to the help of the stricken Austrians and Magyars.

General Friedrich von Bernhardi, the famous cavalry leader and preacher of Prussian militarism, was amongst the new army commanders selected to defend the Lemberg line. He fought on the Stokhod River, with a Hungarian general, Fath, nominally above him, but actually serving only as a political ornament. South of Bernhardi were Marwitz and Litzmann and Schmidt von Knobelsdorff— all three of them Germans exercising actual command, with another political ornament, Tersztyansky, nominally representing the Austro-Hungarians. Directly covering Lemberg were three more German generals, Eben, Melchior, and Wilhelmi, carrying out the work of defence which the Austrian Arab, Ermolli, pretended he was still conducting. Next came the army of the highly-capable Bavarian, Count Bothmer, who by a three months' struggle had saved the position in Galicia. Between the Dniester River and the Carpathian Mountains, where the army of the Austrian, Pflanzer-Baltin, had been annihilated, Prussians, Bavarians, and Hessians were mingled with Austrian and Magyar troops under the nominal command of two Austrians.

In all about half a million German soldiers came to the rescue. The general result was that the Prussians annexed Austria-Hungary and its remaining military resources. A separate peace on the part of the subject Empire became impossible, and when Francis Joseph died, towards the end of the year, and was succeeded by

RUSSIAN SCOUTS HOT ON THE TRAIL.
In the broken country near the Dniester River the Germans had deeply excavated machine-gun positions which the Russians could only discover by scouting or by launching costly infantry attacks to draw their fire.

the Emperor Charles, this young man was actually in a more subordinate position to the Hohenzollerns than were the Kings of Bavaria, Saxony, and Würtemberg. Hindenburg, who was somewhat of a figurehead himself, with his Chief of Staff, Ludendorff, who was the new directing mind of Germany, exercised despotic control; and any point in Austro-Hungarian affairs with which they did not deal was settled by the former German Commander-in-Chief, Falkenhayn, who **Alexeieff checks** co-operated in the defence of Hungarian **Falkenhayn's plan** territory with the most brilliant of German commanders, Mackensen.

The original German plan, as devised by Falkenhayn when he was Commander-in-Chief, was to make a grand drive towards the Black Sea port of Odessa. It was with this design that many fresh German divisions had been created, and the entire organisation of the German armies remodelled. The army corps had been abolished, and a small unit, formed out of three regiments of three thousand men each, constituted the new style of division. This was somewhat of a return to the old British practice of divisional commands, but the Prussians made their new divisions weak in infantry yet enormously strong in artillery. The underlying idea was to improve upon Falkenhayn's and Mackensen's artillery tactics of 1915, and blast a path to the Black Sea through millions of Russian soldiers, while using only hundreds of thousands of Teutonic troops. It was to nullify this scheme by forestalling it that the Russian Commander-in-Chief, General Alexeieff, concentrated in the south, and there gave General Brussiloff the main striking force of the resurgent Empire.

It may be doubted whether the Russian commander expected to win a great decision on the Galician battlefield. He may have contemplated the recapture of Lemberg; but that must have been almost the limit of his possible substantial gains. And though he did not reach Lemberg, he succeeded in one of his principal strategic aims. For by the middle of August the Russian offensive had so crippled Austria-Hungary as to relieve the pressure on the Italians on the Trentino front and enable them successfully to resume their attack upon Gorizia. It also reduced, but in a much slighter manner, the pressure against the French armies, as German divisions were brought both from Verdun and from the Somme in order to strengthen the defensive line near Lemberg. Then, as had been arranged at the Conference of the Allied Staffs, the Franco-British offensive, which opened on July 1st, 1916, and continued until November, 1916, helped the Russian armies in turn, by using up many of the German divisions that had been prepared for the drive towards the Black Sea.

But though Russia seemed, in the summer of 1916, to have recovered her strength, there was a most serious element of weakness in her **Russian deficiency** general situation. As will be seen from **of railways** the map (pages 48 and 49), a single railway line between Odessa and Tarnopol fed and munitioned General Brussiloff's southern armies. The Russians had no good railway system extending from the Black Sea to the Rumanian frontier and Bukovina. The frontier province of Bessarabia was only scantily provided with poor branch tracks from the Odessa-Tarnopol line. Imagine Sir Douglas Haig conducting a battle all along the British front with only one bad railway line linking his forces to his sea-base.

WATERING HORSES AT A RUSSIAN FARMSTEAD.
Owing to the inadequacy of railway communications and the lack of good roads in Southern Russia, horses played a more important part with the Russian than with any other of the belligerent armies. Horse-power was the only means by which guns and munitions could be brought up to the front, and General Alexeieff employed countless trains of horse-drawn carts to cope, however slowly, with this vital need of his army.

RUSSIAN CAVALRY SCOUTS IN THE CARPATHIANS.
Party of scouts on the snow-clad slopes of the wooded Carpathians. The Russians gained some notable successes in the mountains, and while fighting in the most adverse conditions, again and again pressed back not only the Austrians. but also the German troops which had been sent to "stiffen" them.

that made it look as if Russia was blockaded, the trains, diverted almost entirely to military uses, did not suffice for the Army.

At the beginning of his offensive General Brussiloff had evaded some of his insuperable railway difficulties by accumulating large stores of shell and slowly marching his men up in masses, while supplying them by means of tens of thousands of pony-carts. So long as he continued to move directly forward towards Galicia his slow and primitive cart system and tramping bodies of reinforcements enabled him to maintain the force of his thrust. The Germans used the superior Galician and Hungarian railway systems to their utmost capacity, transporting new armies by the half-million, new guns by hundreds, and shells by tens of millions ; yet they continued to give ground on the Zlota Lipa and in the Carpathians. In the end, however, the railway completely triumphed over the pony-cart and the marching power of the Russian soldier.

Such was actually the position of the Russian armies in Bukovina and Eastern Galicia in the summer of 1916. Only across the old frontier in the northern Kovel sector was there good railway communication with Kiev and Moscow. The principal Russian armies in the south had only one good line running to their bases of supply.

The enemy, on the other hand, had a network of lines behind his front. All the resources of Western Galicia and Poland, Hungary, Austria, Eastern Germany, and Serbia could, if occasion required, be rapidly concentrated against the southern Russian armies. A vast gridiron of railways existed. Tracks ran over the Carpathians at five points ; main lines came down Silesia towards Lemberg ; and new lines, both light and heavy, had been constructed since 1915 to feed the battle-front with munitions and men.

The Russian railway system had been inadequate to the needs of Southern Russia before the war. It was overstrained and greatly damaged by the unforeseen amount of traffic required in two years of terrific warfare. In the greatest agricultural Empire in the world the urban population almost starved because trains were lacking to carry the crops from the country-side to the towns. In some places mining and iron-making stopped owing to men being called up for the Army, when the Army needed material far more urgently than men. The Russian bureaucracy was slow in adapting itself to the extraordinary needs of an extraordinary war, and what remained of the comparatively small industrial and transport powers of the Empire was tragically insufficient to supply the wants of the fighting forces alone. Though the civil population suffered in the cities in a way

When the plans of the Rumanian Staff failed and the Rumanian forces withdrew from Transylvania, disaster followed, because there was no Russian railway running lengthwise through Bessarabia. The Russians were stuck. They formed a huge, primitive battering-ram, set in one direction, that could not be moved quickly enough towards a different target. They could not transfer their guns from the Galician front into Western Rumania. They could not throw a force of any great striking power across the Danube towards the Bulgarian frontier. There was no railway by which ordnance and shells, troops and supplies, could be moved. It may be doubted whether, even had the tracks existed, Russia could have found locomotives

Bessarabia an impassable barrier

IN TOUCH WITH THE ENEMY ON THE RUSSIAN FRONT.
Hillside Russian trench with the enemy within range. The officer with field-glasses was evidently directing the fire of the small group of riflemen. To the left a man had been hit, and to the right a stretcher was being taken down for removing him to a dressing-station.

E

WINTER IN THE RUSSIAN TRENCHES.
Russian troops endured the rigours of the winter campaigns well. The Austro-Hungarians, badly hammered during 1916, had to be carefully nursed by the German Command to face another winter of hardship.

Between the Dniester River and the Pruth River there were only two roundabout branch railways, both depending on the utterly overworked Odessa line. In the days before the war Rumania had lived in fear of Russia, and had indeed relied upon Germany and Austria-Hungary to save her from attack. With this view she had constructed five direct lines, running through the mountain valleys into Hungarian territory, and there linking up with two main networks of their new railways. But on her Russian frontier she had connection, near Jassy and Reni, merely with two poor Russian subsidiary lines, which became one track on the Dniester and thence ran as a single-line branch to the Odessa and Galician

and rolling-stock by which to transport a modern army, with its great train of siege-guns, rapidly to the assistance of Rumania.

Undoubtedly Russia would have done better had she refused to co-operate with the former Rumanian Commander-in-Chief when he arranged to leave his Bulgarian frontier weak and invade Transylvania. But General Alexeieff, who had shown such remarkable skill during the great Russian retreat in 1915, appears to have miscalculated the situation in Germany. In the middle of August, for instance, the chief organ of the Russian Staff published the extraordinary statement that the lack of free reserves in the Central Empires would quickly lead to enormous changes on the eastern front. Yet at this time Germany, as we all now know, possessed quite a large number of free reserves. She had a new army, perfectly prepared for action, provided by General von Falkenhayn, and waiting only the turn of events in order to make a new drive against the Russian lines, or against Rumania,

Hindenburg's hidden reserve forces or to change the situation on the Somme. Therefore, when Hindenburg succeeded Falkenhayn, he inherited a reserved and hidden power of initiative which seems to have been much greater than any of the Allied Staffs calculated.

Hindenburg would have thrown this new army with its new guns into the furnace of the Somme had he reckoned that his line there was in serious danger of breaking. As a matter of fact, there was more danger of a break, especially on the Bazentin Ridge, than he could at the time foresee. Nevertheless, he accepted this risk, and more by his good luck in weather than by good generalship, succeeded in holding Bapaume, when his free reserves were at last deployed on a new battle-line, under the direction of Falkenhayn, around the passes of the Transylvanian Alps.

After Hindenburg, who was largely influenced in the matter by Falkenhayn, had surmounted the perils of the Somme, the unexpected new army which he railed to the eastern front upset all the calculations of the Russian Commander-in-Chief and his Staff. Had General Alexeieff possessed the means of rapidly manœuvring large forces, he would have probably outplayed Hindenburg and held up first Mackensen and then Falkenhayn. But there was no main Russian railway line near the new critical theatre of war.

INSTRUCTIONS BY TELEPHONE.
Telephone operators attached to a Russian field battery engaged in the Eastern Carpathians taking instructions from the officers who were checking the results attained from the observation-post.

railway. This lack of Russian railways in Bessarabia used to please the Rumanians in the days of peace. They regarded it as their technical security against attack by their old allies. Under King Carol, Rumania had been organised to fight against Russia and receive abundant supplies through Hungary. When, therefore, she returned, under the stress of circumstances, to the natural alliance she had formed in the days of Plevna, her railways were as inadequate to the new conditions as was the Southern Russian railway system.

Had Russia been a great industrial State she might still have saved the situation by the same means as the French saved Verdun. She could have brought up thousands of motor-lorries and used them incessantly while constructing new light railways. In Bessarabia, however, there were few of the fine strong roads that the French had to build and fewer great river bridges. The Danube was so wide that even a light temporary bridge of pontoons taxed the resources of military engineers. In the southern part of Bessarabia there was a strange outlying German settlement wedged between the Slavs and Latins of this frontier province. Naturally, all these Germans were not loyal subjects of the Tsar, and their ca' canny methods added to the difficulties of moving a Russian army to the help of Rumania.

In the absence of a huge fleet of motor-lorries, the genius of dead Bismarck vanquished the living minds of General Brussiloff and General Alexcieff. As a direct result of Bismarck's skill in diplomacy, the outlets of Rumania were turned in the wrong direction and she had no strategic links with her proper allies. Under these conditions—as everyone can now see, wise after the event—Rumania might have been of most service to the Entente if she had continued her cautious and subtle policy of benevolent neutrality. The utmost she could have done in military action would have been to entrench on the Transylvanian Alps, and stand there strongly on the defensive, with a fair railway system feeding her troops, while using what striking power she possessed in attacking the Bulgarians across the Danube. This scheme of action would have

Probably the Germans had both a larger reserve than the Russian Staff calculated and stronger artillery than the Rumanian Staff was prepared to meet.

On the Russian front the number of hostile troops was suddenly increased in a remarkable manner. Count Bothmer's army, for example, had consisted in June, 1916, of six Austrian divisions and one German division. When the Austrian forces were half shattered and withdrawn, they were replaced by seven fresh German divisions, a Turkish army corps, and two fresh Austrian army corps. This army thus became, after a great defeat, stronger than it had been when it was attacked. A similar strengthening process went on all along the front General Brussiloff was assailing. The organising skill of the Germans transformed the scattered remnants of the Austro-Hungarian Army into good fighting material. The men were for the first time fed in a regular and sufficient manner. They were treated as a good farmer treats his cattle, and properly prepared as valuable material for slaughtering. No longer were they marched thirty miles **Germany reorganises Austrian army** a day along the lines where trains were passing with empty cars. As an Austrian private put it: "The Germans looked after us better than our own officers!"

The consequence was that the spirit of the troops steadily rose with the improvement of their commissariat, transport, and general management. There was good fighting material in the Hapsburg Empire, and the great defeats had been largely due to the lack of business capacity in the matter of food and arrangement of work on the part of the self-conceited and lazily-brutal Austrian upper class. The Germans were quite as brutal as the Austrians, but they did not waste the strength of the manhood of the country like the domineering spendthrifts of the Austrian nobility. When, however, the Germans had rested, fed, and re-equipped the Austrian, Magyar, and Slav races, and brought them under an iron but efficient discipline, they employed them in the most cynical manner. "When an attack begins," said an Austrian, "we are placed in front.

RUSSIAN OBSERVATION-POST.
Careful ingenuity was exercised in hiding these points, vitally necessary to accurate gun fire, from enemy scouting aeroplanes.

enabled the slowly-moving Russians gradually to reinforce the main Rumanian front, while imposing on the new army of the Central Empires the difficult task of attacking upon tremendous and entrenched mountain slopes.

General Alexcieff, however, appears to have shared to some extent in the over-confidence of the Rumanian Staff. He calculated that Rumania would scarcely need any assistance, and that the entire reserves of Germany would be soon exhausted in the Transylvanian battles. It was not clear whether the famous Russian Secret Service was at fault in the matter, or whether the element of surprise resided mainly in the unexpected quantity of heavy artillery with which the new German divisions were supplied.

PUTTING THE FINISHING TOUCHES TO A SHELL.
A Russian heavy battery at work in a well-concealed thicket. Before loading the shell in the gun the kneeling artilleryman set the movable time-fuse to agree with the number of seconds it would take to reach the point where it was intended that the shell was to burst.

AREA OF FOURTH GREAT GALICIAN BATTLE.
Map to illustrate the operations in Galicia, August-September, 1916, when General Shcherbacheff broke across the Zlota Lipa and the Dniester.

Then, when we have been killed, our bodies make cover for a German advance."

But even the Austrians could not deny that their Machiavellian allies were justified by the results obtained. Victories were won, and though the Austrians in the first line paid the larger price in blood, and the Germans in the second line won most of the laurels, the successes were practically decisive. For the Austrian breakdown in 1916 was remedied in a more brilliant manner than the similar breakdown in 1914. The able Germans used Austria as a grinding-wheel against Russia. They **Austria subjected** exhausted the strength of their ally even **to Prussia** more thoroughly than they weakened the thrusting force of Russia, and thus furthered the political design, underlying their military plan, of making the Hapsburg Empire permanently subject to Prussian control.

After the retreat of Bothmer's army from the Strypa River line in the middle of August, the Russian armies under General Shcherbacheff and General Lechitsky advanced in an enveloping movement south-east of Lemberg. Bothmer took up a new position on the Zlota Lipa River line, with his right wing slanting backward to the town of Halicz on the Dniester. While falling back, Bothmer received as a reinforcement the new Turco-German army

already mentioned, the aim of the General Staff being apparently to make the new Bothmer army one of the principal thrusting forces of an intending drive towards Odessa if Rumania remained neutral. Bothmer's forces occupied a front of fifty miles, from Halicz on the Dniester to the village of Pluhov on the Lemberg and Tarnopol branch railway line.

A range of hills stretches from Pluhov to the sources of the Zlota Lipa River, and extends farther southward in a tract of high broken country to the Dniester River. While Bothmer had been making his long stand farther eastward, multitudes of men, under the direction of German engineers, had been fortifying the high wooded hills and the steep grassy valley slopes. In some places extensive wire entanglements were erected, and on the edges of all the high oak forests were screened and deeply-excavated machine-gun positions, which the Russians could only discover by launching infantry against them. By his great stand in Eastern Galicia, Bothmer had gained three months' grace for the engineering work in his rear. Consequently, when he retired he possessed, in addition to a new army, one of the strongest fortified lines on any front.

The Russian generals then needed parks of gigantic ordnance such as Sir Douglas Haig and General Foch were using on the Somme. Yet such guns, which might have been obtained from Japanese, British, and American armament firms, were useless **The Fourth** in themselves. Both for mobility in hand- **Galician Battle** ling and for rapidity of shell supply, monster guns of the new type needed light railways in a network behind the fighting-line, with several main lines of track running towards the Russian bases of supply. But, as we have seen, the Russians had neither the building material nor the rolling-stock to create a vast modern system of railways as an answer to the new fortifications the Germans had constructed. They had to continue to use only such guns of medium calibre as could be slowly hauled about by horse-power and supplied with shells by cartage. It was, therefore, by the concentration of field-artillery very close to the fire-trench that the Russian commanders strove to break the Zlota Lipa line.

They opened the fourth great Galician battle on August 29th, 1916, by an attack on a height covering the town of Zawalow, on the lower course of the Zlota Lipa. At this point Bothmer's wing began to bend back towards Halicz, forming a salient exposed to assault on two sides. But the position had been selected with good judgment. A great height, now famous as Hill 413, covers the river town, and by means of its artillery swept part of the river valley. Yet, climbing up the slopes, with their artillery behind them making lanes through the Teutonic entanglements, the Russian infantry won by hand-power the great hill, which had seemed invincible to any force but the fire of heavy modern guns. Then, with this important key position in their hands, the soldiers of General Shcherbacheff delivered a general assault on the whole length of Bothmer's southern flank, from Zawalow to Mariampol on the Dniester. They broke across the Zlota Lipa some ten miles north of Zawalow, and also penetrated across the Dniester between Mariampol and Halicz.

Day and night the struggle raged from August 30th to September 3rd. When both rivers were forced, the advance lay through successive lines of hills and deep woods, where the German troops fought with splendid courage. In the forests between Zawalow and Halicz the Russians were three times repulsed by the Brandenburgers and Pomeranians. But in the afternoon of September 3rd the right flank of the Germans was turned, after most bitter hand-to-hand fighting, and, after covering four square miles of woodland with their own bodies and hostile corpses, the Russian infantry pierced the German flank and let their cavalry through the gap. Germans, Turks, and Austrians were overwhelmed, four thousand prisoners were

The Grand Duke Michael, to whom Tsar Nicholas II. abdicated his crown, March, 1917.

Keeping the Feast of Pentecost in a Russian Camp, Valley of Tchorok, Caucasus.

General Baratoff (wearing a white fez) leading Russian troops into a Persian town.

Scene on the route of the Russian advance through Persia towards Bagdad.

The Shah of Persia with his chief officers of State advancing to meet General Baratoff

When winter held the western front in thrall: Icebound advanced post of the Russian contingent in France.

taken, and Lemberg again seemed about to fall to General Brussiloff by the same manœuvre as that which he had employed in 1914.

Halicz, which he had captured in September, 1914, was once more enveloped on three sides. The Turks had been broken in the central portions of the Zlota Lipa, south of the town of Brzezany, and the victors stormed westward and arrived within gunshot of the railway feeding Halicz. Thereupon, the line of battle moved from the Zlota Lipa River line to the Gnila Lipa River line. At the same time as the army of General Shcherbacheff pressed back the enemy's south-eastern flank and assailed his front, the army of General Lechitsky, operating on the Dniester line, gained a series of remarkable successes. Lechitsky's men stormed the railway-station of Halicz, and then swerving to the north-west, crossed the Dniester and cleared the corner between the main river and its tributary, the Gnila Lipa. Pursuing their stricken enemy, they also crossed the Gnila Lipa in the night of September 4th, the heralds apparently of one of the grandest victories in Russian history.

Some twenty miles of fortified hills and forests had been stormed in a battle lasting one hundred and fifty hours. The broken enemy wing had withdrawn in remnants northward and westward along the railways connecting with Lemberg. Of the three hostile bastion railway towns on the fifty-mile front, Halicz in the south seemed about to fall, Brzezany in the centre appeared to be tottering, and Pluhov in the north was menaced by the wings of two Russian armies. The forces holding the bending line were, as General Brussiloff stated at the time, "the last living rampart of the Austro-Hungarian monarchy."

It is composed (he continued) of the very last soldiers that Austria-Hungary can still put into the line. Some have been hurriedly withdrawn from the Italian front; then a number of Germans have been brought rom our northern front and from the French front; and, finally, there are some Turks. The hostile army I had in front of me in June is almost destroyed or captured. The more numerous and conglomerate new army is resisting desperately on strong mountain positions, which have to be carried by storm one after the other. Step by step we are advancing—only step by step. Yet we do advance, and the spirit of my men remains very bright and very high. Soon the co-operation of the brave Rumanian Army will make it easier for us to win a decisive result.

Value of Brussiloff's success negatived

It is clear from this statement that the commander of the southern armies of Russia had largely based his new campaign upon the pressure which the Rumanian forces in Transylvania were expected to bring upon the last free reserves of the Central Empires. But owing to General von Falkenhayn's creation of some twenty-three new divisions, equipped with powerful artillery, the enemy's free reserves were capable of throwing back and breaking the forces of Rumania while resisting the weight of the Russian attacks.

General Brussiloff, it is patent, was relying upon information collected by the Staff of his Commander-in-Chief, General Alexeieff, and reckoning confidently that either the Germans would break in front of him, if they went to the assistance of the Austrians in Transylvania, or that the Austrians, left unassisted, would break in front of the Rumanians. But the arrival of General von Falkenhayn, with a new German army on the Transylvanian front, and the appearance of General Mackensen with an unexpected force of artillery on the Danube front, entirely altered the complexion of affairs, and deprived the successes of the Russian armies of much of their value.

Meanwhile, General Brussiloff's campaign, which had opened victoriously, went on for a while in a promising manner. The second great Battle of Halicz began on September 5th, 1916. The Russians strengthened themselves on the Gnila Lipa, in their position behind the town, and the Germans retired from the southern bank of the Dniester River and entrenched on the higher ground across the river. They blew up the forts and the bridge, and removed their stores, while all the civilian population fled excepting the little sect of curious Jews of Tartar strain, the Karites. The Karites refused to leave their street, and going down into the cellars stayed there throughout the battle. The Germans were picked troops, including some of the 3rd Division of the Guard, with the Fusiliers of the Guard and the Pomeranian Grenadiers. They held the river-line of the Narayowka tributary, between the Zlota Lipa and the Gnila Lipa, and along their river-line ran the branch railway linking Halicz with Lemberg. In a fierce first drive the Russians stormed across the river, some twenty-two miles north of Halicz, and constructed an entrenchment on the western bank. They fortified a forest and two mountains on a semicircular front three miles long and two miles deep.

Then with one Finnish and one Russian division operating

THE GRAND DUKE NICHOLAS.

As supreme Commander of all the Russian Armies and later as Commander-in-Chief in the Caucasus, the Grand Duke Nicholas proved himself a great general, but the Provisional Government deemed it wise to supersede him.

in the salient across the river, General Shcherbacheff tried to break the last living rampart of the Hapsburg Empire and obtain a decisive victory.

The Germans had artillery of larger calibre and longer range, and drenched with barrier fire the portion of their river-line taken by the Russians. The Russians had but 6 in. and 7·2 in. guns, for their new 11·2 in. howitzer, firing a new Japanese high explosive, did not come into action for another month, owing to railway difficulties. But despite the enemy's superiority in material, and his concentration of the finest German troops, he was at last thrown back after terrible slaughter and the capture by the Russians of three thousand prisoners. This happened on September 17th, when the struggle in the salient had lasted for ten days.

The German commander, General von Gerok, at once brought up reinforcements and, counter-attacking on both sides of the river, recovered some of the lost ground, and took in turn more than three thousand prisoners. The wood by the village of Svistelniky was the main pivot of

[British official photograph.

SAPPERS OF A TURKESTAN BATTALION BEING DECORATED FOR DISTINGUISHED SERVICES.

General Prschevalski decorating sappers of the 2nd Turkestan Battalion for their distinguished services on the Russian front. The man-power that formed the great Russian armies was drawn from all parts of the vast dominions that stretch from the Baltic to the Pacific, and these sturdy fighters had travelled from the distant province of Turkestan to take their part and win distinction in the European fighting-line.

this almost decisive clash of Slav and Teuton. The wood changed hands six times a day on some occasions. The German Guardsmen and the Finns and Russians swayed continually to and fro in bayonet and hand-bomb combats between the blasted trees and over the shell-ploughed ground. The Russian armoured cars fought like old-fashioned cavalry in advance of the infantry, steering under shell fire through the German wire entanglements and keeping down the German machine-gunners until their own bayonets arrived. In the end, however, the longer-ranged German guns dominated the battlefield, and though the struggle went on until the first week in October, the opposing forces then remained in much the same positions as those which had been held in the first week of September.

The Second Battle of Halicz

General von Gerok, by his great counter-attack of September 19th, had saved Halicz from falling, and while General Brussiloff was preparing in turn to send out new divisions for a final blow from the river salient, the unfortunate turn of events on both frontiers of Rumania compelled him to cease his own thrusting operations.

About twenty miles north-east of the Svistelniky salient there was another prolonged and intense struggle around the northern course of the Zlota Lipa and the railway junction near Brzezany. There, in a diversified region of river marshes, upland forests, and high, bare rock, the left wing of General Shcherbacheff's army tried to crown the operations by breaking the German centre and striking through directly to Lemberg. South-east of the town rises a hill, Lysonia, which overlooks the valleys of the Zlota Lipa and its tributaries and dominates the railway lines and the river fords. On September 2nd the Russian guns began to bombard the Lysonia mass of chalk and rock, and the high explosive broke the stones into murderous splinters that hurtled among the defending troops. Nearly all the German artillery on the height was silenced, when the Russian infantry clambered up from the valley and, in a hand-to-hand combat that went on all day and through the night, carried the Lysonia and the other hills south-east of the town. In the end the bodies were heaped like ramparts ; but they were mostly Austrian and Polish corpses. The German commander in this sector, General von Eben, merely used the troops of his ally to wear out the Russians, and kept his own Bavarian regiments in reserve.

When the Russians had carried all the heights and taken 2,700 prisoners, they were counter-attacked before dawn the next day (September 3rd) and driven from the Lysonia height by the fresh Bavarian reserves. Fatigued though the Russians were, they managed to hold one of the main hills in the angle between the rivers, and after another month of terrific fighting, similar to that of the Somme, they captured the important village of Potutory, at the point where two railways crossed below the bastion town. But Brzezany remained—like Halicz near by and like Bapaume far distant—an unbroken tide-mark of the Allies' slow progress in the summer offensive of 1916.

Farther northward, in the neighbourhood of Vladimir Volinsk, in a land of low hills watered by tributaries of the Bug River, there was also heavy fighting. The army of General Kaledin, which had captured Lutsk (Luck) and advanced across the Stokhod towards Kovel, opened another offensive around the village of Shelvov, amid the marshes and forests of the Luga River. This operation was subsidiary to the main southern actions around Lemberg, and was designed to prevent the Germans from reinforcing the critical front. The battle ceased for a while when the principal Russian thrust in the south failed of effect. It was resumed in the latter part of September, and continued until the middle of October. But all the October actions by General Brussiloff's armies were of a defensive nature. They were partly intended to relieve the pressure on the Rumanian Army, and also to veil the withdrawal of the central Russian army under General Sakharoff, as it moved southward to save the upper corner of Rumania from the invaders.

Second Battle of the Carpathians

On the northern Rumanian frontier another fine fighting force of Russians, under General Lechitsky, had originally prepared to break across the Carpathians into the Hungarian Plain. By the middle of August the Tartar Pass, leading to Maramaros Sziget, was stormed and held, and by the end of the same month the Pantyr Pass, farther north, was also occupied. General Lechitsky's southern forces then began a great mountain battle on a front of ninety miles, from the Rumanian frontier to the central Hungarian border. Amid peaks rising to 7,000 feet, the Carpathian Battle, that had been broken off in 1915, was resumed with greater fury. Each side had guns of heavier calibre, such as the 6 in. which was hauled behind the light artillery to points of vantage on the great Carpathian slopes. Primeval forests, through which only a few paths were kept, were the scene of machine-gun ambushes and arduous enveloping movements. Around every great mountain the fighting increased in intensity during the first part of September, when the Rumanian advance into Transylvania seemed to promise a great combined Russo-Rumanian success. General Lechitsky's forces were divided into small groups by the peaks and ridges of naked rock. No manœuvring by rapid concentration was possible.

End of Second Carpathian Battle Only from the distant Army Headquarters could any large surprise effect be engineered by the slow process of sending up reinforcements, with a new supply train, wearily to tramp to the scene of action.

The enemy incessantly poured his men and supplies forward, and continually recovered from the defeats inflicted upon him. Nevertheless, the three Russian army corps detached for the mountain operations gradually worked forward. By the middle of September five of the great heights between Mount Pantyr and Dorna Vatra had been captured, each with a considerable remnant of its garrison. Then towards the end of the month, when nearly all the main crests

had been occupied and the Russians were fighting their way down some of the eastern ravines towards the Hungarian villages, the general scheme of the offensive was completely checked by the failure of the Rumanian wing to maintain the ground it had won. After the retreat of the old allies of Russia the Second Battle of the Carpathians came to an end, with the Russians still holding on to the ninety miles of crest and forest they had vainly won.

Generally speaking, the great Russian offensive of the summer of 1916 achieved a measure of partial success, similar to that attained in the Franco-British offensive on the Somme. No decision was effected, but debilitating losses were inflicted on the forces of the Central Empires. By far the greater portion of these losses fell upon Austria-Hungary, who was most seriously crippled in man-power thereby. But the Austro-Hungarian munition works

British official photograph.

TURKS AND TEUTONS TAKEN PRISONER ON THE RUSSIAN FRONTS.
Group of Turkish prisoners with a German officer, to the left, at Erzingan in Armenia. The rough-looking crowd was part of the forces which had been captured by the army of the Grand Duke Nicholas on its triumphant way to the taking of that town. Above: Batch of German prisoners who had been taken by the Russians during the advance of General Kaledin's army on the Lutsk-Kovel road.

remained in full productiveness, and, under German supervision, were again speeded-up to replace by machinery the million of men that had been lost. The Russian capacity for the production of shells, explosives, and guns fell behind that of Austria-Hungary, owing to the fact that the rich industrial and mining districts of Russian Poland were occupied by the enemy. Russia had lost an army of trained mechanics as well as mines and factories and plant of many kinds. Under the new conditions of warfare she was still able to defeat Austria-Hungary and a part of the forces of Germany, but she could not make her superior man-power tell in a **Despotism *versus*** decisive manner because of her much **Mandarin system** inferior industrial power and political organisation.

Germany remained enormously strong, by reason both of her supremacy in steel-making and of her extraordinarily efficient bureaucratic and military systems. The German Empire was a true despotism, possessing in almost practical perfection the military virtues of a despotism. There was no serious element of weakness in the German organisation. The official class was hard-working and, on the whole, remarkably honest, and the military class was of similar character. Very powerful caste interests, such as those of the large landed estates, were no doubt able to bring

influence to bear upon the Government which did not always make for general national strength. Yet even in the case of the agrarian interest there was some attempt to reconcile the needs of the urban populace with the requirements of the producers of food. The farmers were favoured for much the same reason as the troops were fostered. They were recognised, long before the outbreak of hostilities, as a grand, essential element in the strength of the nation for war.

Russia, on the other hand, was not a despotism, though several Tsars had occasionally endeavoured to follow the German example. The Russian system of Government was more of an Oriental than a European type. In its virtues and defects it somewhat resembled the mandarin system of China. The official class was underpaid and yet well-to-do, because it obtained money from persons who had occasion to use the machinery of the State for their private advantage. The corruption, however, was itself of a slack, easy-going nature, the money obtained being regarded rather as the perquisite of office than as blackmail or bribery. Routine was esteemed the master principle in the Russian Civil Service. Any sign of initiative was considered either an unfair attempt to attract attention and secure rapid promotion or an unscrupulous trick to obtain a larger field for money-making.

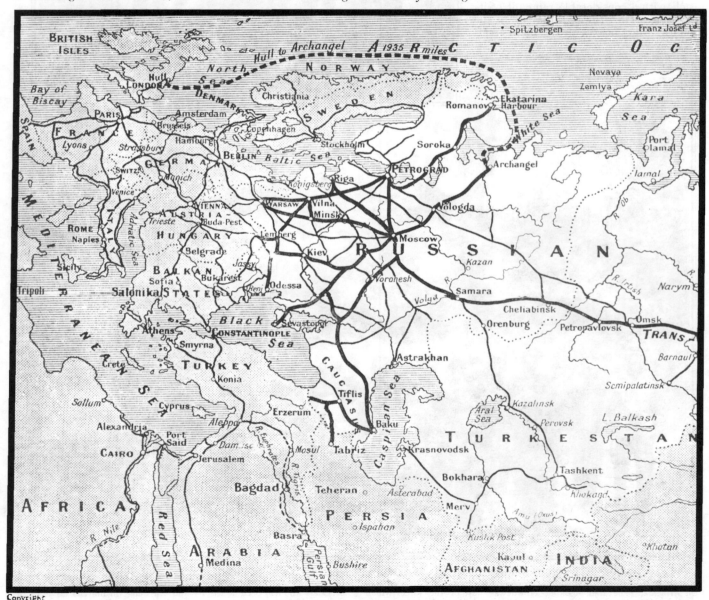

Copyright

MAP SHOWING THE SEA AND RAILWAY COMMUNICATIONS BY WHICH
The position of the Russian armies in Bukovina and Eastern Galicia in the summer of 1916 may be likened to that of the British armies in France, had Kovel sector was there good railway communication with Kiev and Moscow. Our map also

Under peace conditions this system, which was historically connected with the system established in Russia by Mongol conquerors, more or less met the needs of the Empire, which was still young and rapidly developing. The breeding and colonising power of the race, with its traditions of local co-operation, made strongly for ultimate stability and progress. Russia was growing enormously strong by practically the same means as the races of China were spreading, without a struggle, over the earth. The inefficiency of the Russian bureaucracy was almost a praiseworthy quality, as, unlike the Prussian system of machine-like despotism, it allowed scope for the evolution of a healthy Government.

Under war conditions the loose, careless, and corrupt system of Russian officialism proved disastrously inadequate. The situation in the European War was far more complicated than it had been in the Manchurian campaign. In the war with Japan the strong and efficient German elements in Russia, drawn from the Baltic provinces and from the German settlements in Russian Poland, Volhynia, and the Chersonese, were loyal to the land of their birth and vehement against the Japanese. Indeed, it was the large and powerful German element in Russia that agitated against any peace with Japan, and tried to force a fight to the utter finish. At one time it is reported that nearly

eighty out of a hundred officers in the Russian Army were men of Teutonic stock.

In the war with Germany and Austria-Hungary a considerable proportion of the German-Russians remained loyal to the land of their birth. Among the barons of the Baltic provinces, for example, were several leading men who were firmly attached to the cause of the Allies. But, as was to be expected, after years of world-wide intrigue of an intensive nature on the part of the Germans, some of the Teutonic settlers scattered about Russia entered on a campaign of treachery. In military matters operations skilfully planned by the General Staff, which should have issued in victory, ended strangely in defeat, owing to the conduct of some German-Russians occupying positions of authority. After this direct kind of treason on the battlefield had been generally checked, by the removal of suspected commanders and Staff officers and certain persons at Headquarters, the disloyal element in the Russian national life began to work less directly but more perniciously upon the political administration of the Empire. **Treachery of German-Russians**

In the Russian Civil Service the methodical, businesslike, and hard-working German-Russian was generally the master of the ordinary, easy-going Russian official. He

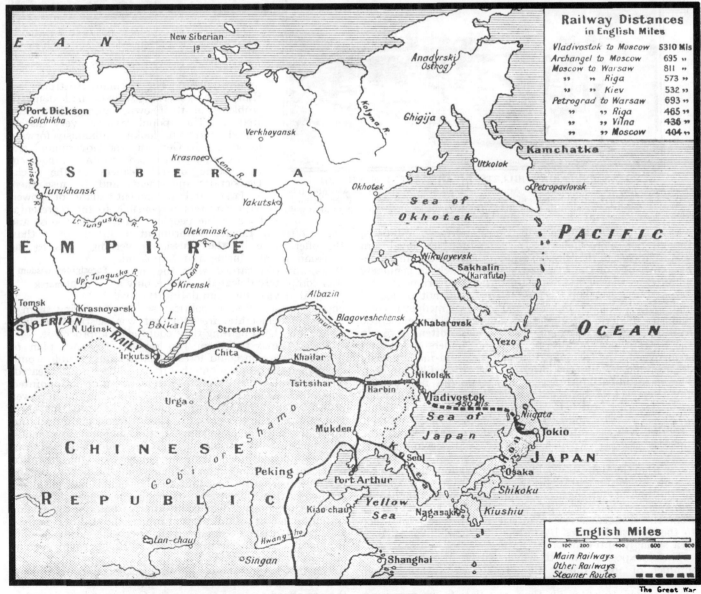

RUSSIA RECEIVED SUPPLIES FROM HER BRITISH AND JAPANESE ALLIES.
the latter been compelled to fight with only one poor railway line linking them with their sea-base. Only across the old frontier in the northern shows in English miles the distances supplies had to be brought from Great Britain and Japan.

[British official photograph.

RUSSIAN TRANSPORT IN ASIA MINOR.
The camel was largely utilised for carrying the necessaries for an army pushing far from its bases of supply, in the difficult mountainous country of the Caucasus.

RUSSIANS PREPARING BILLETS IN AN ARMENIAN VILLAGE.
Mud-plastering the flat roof of an Armenian dwelling to be utilised as a winter billet by Russian soldiers. The houses in many Armenian villages were of a very primitive character, consisting of but little more than irregularly-shaped stones roughly piled as walls.

was more practical, more industrious, and more ambitious, though not more honest. In peace-time his loyal aim was to impart to the Russian system the stern and machine-like efficiency of the Prussian system, which he genuinely admired as the highest standard of good government. He despised the Russians because they would not be logical and strict and hard, but wavered between mediæval communism, modern bureaucratism, and essays in democratic institutions. The German of this class often gave up the Russian idea, because he could not understand it, and went over to the clean-cut Prussian idea of a modern caste organisation, because the latter at least satisfied his intellect. The most important men of this type did not commit any overt act of treason towards Russia. They did not wish to see her beaten to the ground and reft of her Baltic and Black Sea provinces. In spite of their **Prussian ideals and** intellectual prejudices, they loved the **Russian character** Russian character, and the most they wanted was to see Russia receive such a lesson from Germany as would force her to adopt the Prussian system of social and political organisation, and acquire all the military strength appertaining to a thoroughgoing autocracy. Their principal aim was to detach Russia from the democracies of Western Europe, and bind her to the Central Empires by means of a new Holy Alliance of a strongly anti-democratic nature.

The unexpected strength which Russia displayed in the summer of 1916, during the operations in Galicia and Volhynia, enabled the Russian-Germans of the bureaucratic school to enter on their negotiations in promising

circumstances. The German, Austrian, and Hungarian governing classes had domestic problems of their own, causing them deep anxiety. Their populaces were very discontented, and were looking anxiously forward to peace. In Germany the Government had been compelled to come to an arrangement with some of the leaders of the Social Democratic movement, and promise them a large and permanent share of power, with Ministers responsible to the representatives of the people. In itself this loose and vague offer of Liberal Government meant no more than the offer made by the Prussian governing class to the Prussian people during the Napoleonic Wars, and disregarded when the enemy **Foresighted wisdom** was completely defeated. It was only a **of Bismarck** political device for stimulating the last energies of a nation of political serfs by showing them a mirage of democratic freedom that was destined to fade away, if by hard fighting they could ever approach it.

Nevertheless, the men who revived this old plan of popular deception could foresee that serious trouble would arise when the people found that they had been again cheated. In nineteenth-century Germany the ferment of disappointed hopes had lasted for two generations, until the rise to power of Bismarck; and Bismarck had largely saved his class and stopped the movement towards democracy by relying upon Russia as the main support of reactionary movements. The successors of Bismarck, who had once despised him and abandoned his system of policy through ignorance of its subtle bearing upon German domestic policy, began, in September, 1916, to admit that Bismarck had all along been wiser than they knew. Germany, it appeared, needed a strong reactionary Russia in order to balance the democratic influences of Western Europe, the United States, and the British Commonwealths oversea. Austria and Hungary were too weak to support the German system of caste organisation.

The Austrian and Magyar governing classes were more likely to need German troops to shoot down their revolutionary mobs than to afford any assistance to the German ruling classes.

Great Britain was apparently regarded with indifference. Her unique amalgamation of democratic forms, plutocratic powers, and aristocratic leadership was too singular a thing to exercise any profound influence upon the Continental populaces. France was the State which was feared, because of her plain and logical middle-class polity and the incessant fertility of political ideas in her working class. French ideas were as contagious as the plague, and often as mortal to the interests with which they conflicted.

Why Germany feared France

Some time before the war the French working men had abandoned the idea of State Socialism because they saw how easily any governing class could use it to their own ends, and had begun to spread throughout Europe new doctrines of guild communism and syndicalism. These new ideas alarmed the industrial magnates of Germany, and largely influenced them to combine with their military class in a plan for the conquest of France. The fact that France was still unconquered, and practically certain, with the help of the British Empire, to remain unconquered, made it more necessary for the German Government to come to some arrangement with Russia.

At the head of the Russian Ministry was M. Boris Stürmer, who had succeeded M. Goremykin in February, 1916. M. Stürmer, a man of Austrian stock, a Court favourite, and a bureaucrat of the reactionary school, was suspected of engineering a movement for peace with the enemy. In his Ministry were men attached to the Black Hundred organisations, who maintained subsidised newspapers which openly attacked Great Britain and France and worked for a friendly settlement with Germany. In any other country than Russia such patent signs of intrigue on the part of one principal section of the administration would have been good evidence of the underlying intention of the Government. But in easy-going Russia, in a condition of disorganisation, the wheels of the official machine often revolved in opposite directions, and merely checked each other without driving the country along any clear path.

Since the great munition crisis of 1915, which made bankrupt the reputation of the bureaucracy, the majority of the nobility had begun a movement with some remote resemblance to the action of the English barons at Runnymede. Without definitely infringing the privileges of the Tsar they took steps to diminish the inefficient power of the bureaucracy by transforming many of the Zemstvos and municipal assemblies into practical instruments of local organisation and government. Alongside the patriotic country gentry, who were thoroughly aroused by the need of national defence, there worked most of the best business men of the towns.

The Duma of Moscow, in particular, became once more the grand focus of the fighting spirit of the Russian race, and showed at times a hostile attitude to M. Stürmer because he was suspected of using the machinery of his administration in the interests of a settlement with Germany and Austria-Hungary on an anti-democratic basis.

Certainly there were "dark forces" then in Russia, working in all kinds of underhand ways, sometimes against the fluctuating mind of the Tsar, and continually against the will of his nobles and his people. Great Britain was bitterly attacked by this sinister conspiracy. As the British Ambassador at Petrograd complained in a speech at Moscow, his country was at first assailed for doing too little in the war and then maligned for doing too much. One of the principal pro-German statesmen, Count de Witte, invented an epigram that ran like fire through all levels of Russian society. "Britain will fight Germany to the last drop of Russian blood" was the first and most telling of the slanders of the great bureaucrat. But in the autumn of 1916, when the military power of Great Britain had at

Movement of the "dark forces"

MISHAP TO SLEDGE TRANSPORT ON THE RUSSIAN FRONT.

Temporary hindrance to transport: A Russian Army sledge which had slipped from the road and overturned on reaching the end of a simple but strong and shapely bridge. The men were compelled to wade into the stream and remove much of the load before they were able to right the sledge and continue their interrupted journey. The sledge is sometimes employed in Russia for ordinary road purposes as well as over snow.

last been fully displayed on the Somme, the leaders of the "dark forces" entirely changed their ground of attack, and alleged that Great Britain had become so great a military Power as well as so mighty a sea Power that Russia would be helpless in the future unless she made a fighting alliance with Germany.

After the check to General Brussiloff's armies in Galicia and Volhynia, and the defeat of Rumania on both frontiers, the pro-German conspiracy in the bureaucracy and in the entourage of the Court began to increase in scope and power in a formidable manner. Even some Ministers, who were loyal to their race and confident in its great destiny, seemed to lose hope for a while, and think that

DINNER ON THE FIELD OF BATTLE.
This cheery company of Russian soldiers laughed and chatted over their dinner which was served on tables, though on the field where military operations were proceeding, as is shown by the sentry posted beyond them.

Russia would do well to make the best peace she could obtain. The disorganisation of the country was deplorable, and it appeared to them that it would be wisest again to rely upon the Russian outbreeding the Teuton, and wait another generation in order to win Constantinople and collect the Poles into a firm bulwark State against the Germans. Many of the large Russian towns were running short of food, and the native production of munitions of war was still quite inadequate to the needs of the Army, in spite of the help given by Japan, Great Britain, and the United States.

When honest and patriotic Russians began sombrely to incline to this view, it can easily be imagined what were the opinions spread in thousands of channels **Failure of the ad-** by the "dark forces" of disloyal and **ministrative machine** corrupt pro-Germans. The leading men in the Imperial Duma, the town Dumas, and the County Councils did not, however, lose heart. The Tsar seemed determined to pursue the war, and the Grand Duke Nicholas and other Princes of the Blood Royal were far more resolute than the head of their house. It was the administrative machine, as reconstructed by Peter the Great on the German model, which chiefly failed the Empire in military virtue as well as in civil efficiency. As was afterwards seen in the Congress of the Nobility, practically all the descendants of the ancient fighting boyars, who under their Tsars had broken the rule of the Mongols and checked the aggressions of Poles, Swedes, Turks, and Frenchmen, were eager to continue the war, and also resolved to find in the development of representative forms of government an improvement upon the bankrupt system of bureaucracy.

The result was that Russia for the time blended the main

elements of her domestic crisis with the main elements in her military problems and conflicting foreign policies. In almost every representative group in the Imperial Duma, the municipal assemblies, and the rural councils the controlling majorities were averse to a German peace and desirous of extending the system of representative government, as both a means of victory and an instrument of Russia's soundness and greatness in the period of reconstruction following the war. The leading statesmen of the bureaucratic school, on the other hand, were more alarmed by the signs of growth of free institutions in their country than by the disasters in Rumania and the unexpected strength shown by the enemy in Galicia. Like Chinese mandarins under Manchu rule, some of the Russian reactionists had made money by devious ways during the war and wanted to save their face and their fortune by making a fairly favourable peace with the enemy. Then, if possible, they designed to employ their own Army, after the Red Sunday fashion, in repressing the new spirit of liberty and abolishing the Duma and the smaller local forms of representative government.

It was not known who was the governing mind of the "dark

JUST TIME FOR A MOUTHFUL.
Russian telephone operators glad of a free minute in which they could lay aside their apparatus and enjoy an alfresco meal and a cigarette outside the wattled shelter in which their work was done.

forces" in Russia. Possibly there was no governing mind planning and directing all the details of conspiracy. There may have been only separate agents, more or less in touch with Teutonic influences and acting mainly on the immediate circles around them. But one sinister figure, of a weird, mediæval type, swiftly emerged into the daylight of history. He was Rasputin—a kind of fakir or wizard, such as flourished in all lands of twilight culture before the daybreak of modern science. Such men were known in pagan Rome and in the heathen Orient. In Christendom they continued to appear until the seventeenth century. Indeed Cagliostro was something of a Rasputin, and in Great Britain and the United States there were hundreds of male and female Rasputins of an inferior and less powerful kind.

Gregory Rasputin was one of the older representatives of that school of magic to which many modern spiritualists, Christian scientists, and practitioners of the " Higher Thought " belong. Starting as a Siberian peasant with some religious instruction but no position as a monastic priest, he developed into a sort of " holy man," wandering about the country-side and professing to cure diseases by hypnotic suggestion of a religious colouring. For some time his position was similar to that of hundreds of other Russian fakirs, but at last he won the favour of a lady at the Russian Court who suffered from the modern disease of nervous debility, and was by her introduced to the Imperial household.

The Tsarevitch was unwell, and Rasputin undertook to endow the heir to the throne with a strong constitution. What sinister means he used are unknown,

The diabolical but as the prince usually became unwell **Gregory Rasputin** when Rasputin was sent away and recovered if the quack was allowed to return, it was thought that Rasputin had means of slightly poisoning the Royal child when removed from him. The Tsaritza was naturally influenced by the fact that these extraordinary changes in the health of her son seemed to depend entirely upon the presence or absence of Rasputin. The man, therefore, came to enjoy a larger measure of influence, and while conducting himself with all seemliness in the Imperial palace, flaunted outside in the manner of an almighty favourite. Either by some hypnotic power or by downright unscrupulous force he ruined many women of position, overthrew Princes of the Blood Royal, and became a diabolical influence behind the Russian throne. Whether he was actually in the service of Germany was a matter not clearly determined ; but he was a creature who would do anything for money, and a poisoner as well as an extraordinary libertine.

He undermined the Russian Church to a very considerable extent by getting men of his own stamp into such important positions as the metropolitanate of Petrograd. To him directly was due the dismissal of the Grand Duke Nicholas from the post of Commander-in-Chief, and the appointment of Boris Stürmer to the position of Prime Minister and of Protopopoff to the position of Minister of the Interior. The fall of M. Sazonoff, the dismissal of General Alexcieff from the supreme command of the armies, and of General Polivanoff from the Ministry of War were also the work of the Court fakir. To a considerable extent Rasputin had the Tsar as well as the Tsaritza under his strange and evil influence. He did more than any man to pervert the liberal ideas of the Russian Emperor and make him as personally autocratic as the Kaiser. It is, however, possible that Rasputin's power for evil would not have effected anything of large importance had it not been that some of the principal bureaucrats began continually to work, directly or indirectly, in the German interests.

In these circumstances, the first great open clash between the bureaucracy and the constitutional party occurred. A rumour went through the country that the Premier, M. Stürmer, who was also acting as Minister for Foreign Affairs, intended to negotiate a separate peace. Thereupon, more than three-fourths of the members of the Imperial Duma gathered together in a solid, patriotic *bloc*, with the declared intention of carrying on the war to a decisive victory. M. Stürmer made an ineffectual effort to alter the date fixed by Imperial order for the meeting of the Duma. But his intrigues were defeated, and on November 14th, 1916, the assembly met. Professor Miliukoff, the leader of the Progressive Party, then made an historic speech charging M. Stürmer with treacherous conduct. The Ministers of State withdrew from the Duma in a pointed manner, and the debate continued in a hush of expectation. Two days after the Premier had been denounced by Miliukoff an even more telling attack was made by M. Shulgin from the Conservative side of the House.

The situation somewhat resembled that in England in the seventeenth century, when the Ministers of the Crown were in conflict with Parliament. There can be little doubt that M. Stürmer meant to close the Duma by military power. But, to the deep relief of all the Russian people, the Minister of War and the Minister of Marine broke away from him and from the reactionary group of irresponsible bureaucrats and openly sided with the progressive *bloc*. In ordinary circumstances, General Shuvaeff and Admiral Grigorevich would have been the two Ministers most independent of Duma influences. Their estimates and demands could not be contested, and only by express permission from the Tsar were they able to attend the National Assembly. The design was that these two Ministers of Imperial Defence should not be in any way restrained by the popular representatives. But, by the irony of history, it was these **Indictment of** two Ministers who, for the sake of the **M. Stürmer** Army and the Navy, abandoned the bureaucratic system and supported the Duma. Their official act was insignificant in itself. They merely attended the Assembly, when all other Ministers of State had deserted it, and spoke about the increase in the production of munitions, and declared that the war would be carried on to a finish.

But, after their speeches, the two departmental chiefs descended into the body of the House, and General Shuvaeff walked towards M. Miliukoff and stretching out his hand said : " I thank you." Great was the significance of the three commonplace words spoken by the Minister for War. They constituted the briefest and most important speech in the annals of Russia, and directly led to the downfall of M. Stürmer. The Russian Zemstvo Union, the Duma of Moscow, and many other public bodies telegraphed to the Ministers of War and Marine, thanking them for their action in the National Assembly, and the Tsar, shaken for the moment by the defection of his military Minister, also telegraphed to the Council of State reaffirming his decision to continue the war until Russia was victorious.

On November 24th one of the most enterprising of Russian Ministers, M. Trepoff, was appointed Premier.

RUSSIAN MOUNTED TROOPS AND ARTILLERY ON THE WAY TO THE FRONT.
Mounted troops on the march in Russia. Cavalry had for long more opportunity of service on parts of the eastern front than anywhere else on the battlefields of Europe, and the Cavalry, which had always been a famous branch of the Russian Army, distinguished itself anew in many actions, even as it had done in the successes which the Russians had achieved in Galicia in the earlier stages of the war.

WINTER FIGHTING ON THE MOUNTAIN RANGE OF THE DORNA VATRA.
Russian soldiers storming one of the heights in the mountains of the Dorna Vatra, where Rumania,
Bukovina, and Hungary join. In the fight which was put up on this mountainous front to lessen Falkenhayn's
attack farther south, great heights were captured by the Russians in the face of fearful difficulties.

a speech of a promising constitutional character. He declared that it was the desire of his Government to work energetically with the legislative institutions, and he praised the patriotic activities of the town Dumas and provincial councils. Then he revealed that an agreement had been made in 1915 with Great Britain, France, and Italy, establishing the right of Russia to Constantinople and the waterway between the Black Sea and the Mediterranean. " It is time," he said, " that the Russian people should know for what they are shedding their blood, and, with the consent of our Allies, I to-day make from this tribune the announcement of the agreement." Wide and deep was the impression made by M. Trepoff's speech. His revelation in regard to Constantinople and the Straits strengthened the bond between Russia and her Allies, and undid, among the Russian people, all the underground intrigues of the German reactionary party.

The Duma, however, was not satisfied with all the members of the new Ministry, and, in particular, one of the most prominent members of the Conservative group attacked the Minister of the Interior, M. Protopopoff. M. Protopopoff had been Vice-President of the Duma, and he was at first looked upon as the agent of the people's representatives in the bureaucratic Ministry. He began, in the first week of November, by trying to establish a new electoral system of an oligarchical kind, by which only persons paying rates to the amount of £100 were to be allowed to vote. Then he tried to requisition all the corn in the country from both peasants and landowners, through the Zemstvos. This seemed to be, from the point of view of the Duma, an unpractical and disorganising measure, subtly calculated to disgust the peasantry with the local representative bodies that had done good work in the war and had supported the principal organ of Russian freedom.

M. Protopopoff soon became the **Protopopoff as** man of mystery in Russia. On the **man of mystery** one hand the majority in the Duma alleged he was working towards the same end as M. Stürmer, but employing more subtlety and power of mind. On the other hand the friends of the Minister of the Interior acclaimed him a dictator of genius, who intended to save the country in his own way, and for the time merely wanted to work on bureaucratic lines because all the representative bodies, local and Imperial, were lacking in experience of departmental work. M. Protopopoff controlled all the domestic government, including the censorship, the police, the political Secret Service, and the governorships. His power was enormous, and his Ministry, having been the centre of reactionary repression, contained many adepts in

As former Controller of Ways and Communications, M. Trepoff was well aware of the internal difficulties of the Empire and of the good work done by all the representative bodies, and he therefore arranged to work with the Duma. But the intrigues of the German party were not completely defeated. Some of the reactionaries tried to throw the Empire into the wildest possible disorder with a view to helping the Teutons. Certain sections of the Russian Secret Service, under the control of persons in the Ministry, were set to work upon men in munition factories and lead them to strike or attempt a Revolution. In Petrograd it was rumoured that Moscow was a scene of riot and slaughter. In Moscow it was whispered that the streets of Petrograd were barricaded and that fierce fighting was going on. Happily, the leaders of the working classes intervened ; they posted notices in the war factories revealing the plot, and advising the men to work on steadily and trust in the Duma.

On December 2nd M. Trepoff, the new Premier, made

the science of misgovernment. Thus a large part of the machine, which the former champion of liberty handled, was of a corrupt and sinister character, bearing the mould of men who had been notorious reactionaries of the Prussian school. The old Ministry of the Interior had engineered practically every m o v e m e n t against representative institutions, Polish and Catholic organisations, and Jewish and Socialistic groups. It had been concerned of old in the Black Hundred pogroms and the Red Sunday massacre. It had worked for the bureaucratic interests, without labouring to carry on its proper task of domestic organisation. Owing to the corruption of its officials, the people had to rely upon their municipalities and Zemstvos to organise their social activities on a war basis.

The suspicions against M. Protopopoff increased; but he countered the movement against himself by augmenting his ministerial power. He practically silenced the Duma by censoring the speeches that indicted the reactionary school, and incited and aggravated the misery of the people by causing greater disorder in the transport of food and other necessities of life. But by the middle of December, 1916, the Russian nobility broke away from the bureaucracy, and displayed in their old and new assemblies a marked tendency towards Liberal representative Government. In the Council of Empire—the Upper House of the Imperial legislative chambers —a direct movement was made against the maleficent influence of Rasputin. Then, at the annual Congress of the United Nobility of Russia, the oldest institution in the Empire, a resolution was passed against Rasputin and the German party.

WOUNDED RUSSIAN SOLDIERS REWOUNDED FROM THE AIR.
Russian soldiers who had been wounded during the advance by General Lesh to the River Stokhod, in July, 1916, were being taken in pony-cart transport to the rear when they were attacked by German aeroplanes, and a number of them and their Red Cross attendants were hit.

The resolution of the United Nobility, which was passed on December 15th, ran:

Doom of Gregory Rasputin

Into the heart of the administration of the Russian State there have penetrated obscure forces, irresponsible and outside the power of the law. These forces are subjecting to their influence the supreme power, and are even making attempts upon the government of the Church.

Meanwhile, in the opinion of many of the best men in the Duma and the United Nobility, the Empire was moving, under the control of the reactionary Ministers, towards a hunger-born Revolution that would leave Germany and Austria-Hungary victorious in the eastern theatre of war. Some of the Liberal politicians reckoned that nearly ninetenths of the inhabitants of Petrograd were slowly famishing, and only living on because of their grim determination that the war must be seen through. M. Protopopoff continued his sinister course as leader of the reactionaries. He prohibited, towards the end of December, the congress of the union of country and town representative bodies, thus openly acting against the declared policy of the new Premier, M. Trepoff.

It appeared that in the bureaucratic Cabinet the Minister of the Interior had become supreme and the Prime Minister a mere figurehead. Thereupon, some leading members of the Royal House saw no other way to save their country but to dispose of the most sinister and notorious figure in Russian history. On Friday night, December 29th, 1916, two young officers drove up in a motor-car to the house in Petrograd occupied by Gregory Rasputin. They carried him off, and after they had called on him to shoot himself as penalty for the crimes with which they reproached him, an affray took place. In this the notorious monk was shot. They thrust the body into a motor-car, made a hole in the ice in the Neva, and pushed the corpse down into the water. Two Grand Dukes took an active part in the drama, which was as significant in Russian history as the affair of the

Diamond Necklace had been in French history. The execution of Rasputin indicated that most of the Royal forces of the House of Romanoff were on the side of the Russian people, in addition to the United Nobility and the majority of the Council of Empire.

The immediate result of the disappearance of Rasputin was not promising. The Duma was postponed, nominally on account of the Christmas holidays, and, after much intrigue, its reassembly was delayed until the end of February, 1917. In the meantime the reactionary forces were greatly strengthened. The Moderate Premier, M. Trepoff, was overthrown, and succeeded by a man of the extreme school, Prince Galitsin. The Ministers of War and Marine who had supported the Duma in the movement against M. Stürmer were removed, and M. Protopopoff, who was largely responsible for bringing about all these

struck a great blow and broke through the German front between Tirul Marsh and the River Aa.

A blizzard of snow was raging at the time, and, screened by the storm, the attacking troops, composed of local levies of Letts and a Siberian corps, carried position after position at the point of the bayonet. **Eve of the** The Germans were blinded by the snow **Revolution** and weakened by the heavy frost. Tier after tier of their fortified lines, rising above the flat country, was stormed by the Courlanders and the Siberians. Twenty-one heavy guns and eleven field-guns were captured, and the main German northern base at Mitau was threatened.

It was one of the greatest surprise attacks in the war. The Russian troops made no artillery preparation and fired no shot, but went forward, as in a scouting adventure, under cover of night and the snowstorm, and pierced the German line, pursuing the enemy to Mitau. Had Mitau fallen, the larger part of Courland would have been at once recovered. The enemy, however, managed to bring up reserves in time to save his base. Yet the happy blow had a most important result, in that it cheered the spirit of the Russian people when they were in a more profound abyss of despair than they had been since the Tartar period.

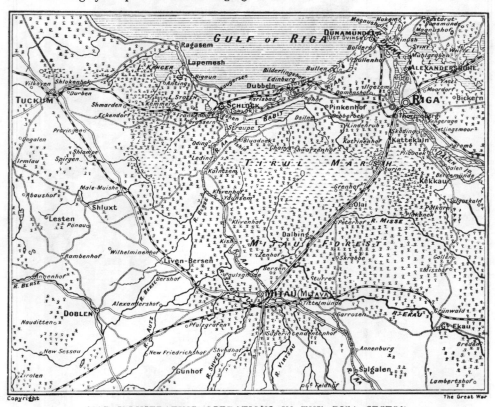

MAP ILLUSTRATING OPERATIONS IN THE RIGA SECTOR.
In January, 1917, General Dimitrieff, commanding the right wing of the Russian northern army, delivered one of the greatest surprise attacks in the war, breaking through the German front between Tirul Marsh and the River Aa, and threatening the enemy base at Mitau.

They had borne the news of the great retreat of 1915 with the same patient confidence as their forefathers had endured the miseries of the Napoleonic invasion. Yet, though their armies had not only held the line reached in 1915, but had made another partial forward movement towards Lemberg, the people had begun to lose confidence because they felt there were traitors in high positions. It was openly alleged that the official mismanagement of the food supplies of large cities was part of a far-reaching German plot to bring about a Revolution in the interests of Germany and Austria-Hungary.

changes, seemed to become for the time controller of the destinies of Russia.

Secret agents again attempted to incite the working people against the Duma, and arranged for strikes and street demonstrations against the Imperial legislative chamber. But the leaders of the working classes once more stopped the extraordinary plot, and when the deputies met at Petrograd in the last week of **Dimitrieff's blow** February there was no demonstration of **for the Duma** importance. Meanwhile the right wing of the northern army, under the Bulgarian general, Radko Dimitrieff, made an unexpected forward movement in the Riga sector. Little had been heard of General Dimitrieff since his retreat from the Dunajec line in Western Galicia. His failure there was not entirely his fault, and General Russky had given him one of the most important commands in the northern army. He fought the Germans to a standstill round Riga in 1915 and 1916. Then in the first days of January, 1917, he began some outpost fighting across the ice-bound Tirul Marsh. This great barrier to all operations on either side had become passable, and on January 8th General Dimitrieff abruptly

In these circumstances, the unexpected advance of General Dimitrieff's army in the depth of the terrible Russian winter had a strangely inspiriting effect upon the nation. A few days after the victory the new feeling of confidence was again disturbed by the publication of a rescript from the Tsar to Prince Galitsin, the new Prime Minister, in which the local organizations such as the County Councils, which had been threatened with extinction by the repressive measures of M. Protopopoff, were singled out for praise for the invaluable work they had done in both peace and war. But, while praising the County Councils, Nicholas abruptly deprived them of power and placed them under the rule of Protopopoff.

When in February, 1917, Lord Milner went to Russia with a view to strengthening the general cause of the Allies and assisting the British Ambassador, Sir George Buchanan, in his important and delicate work, it was apparent to all the world that Russia was about to transform herself. Neither friend nor foe, however, could then discern whether either of the extremists would prevail and establish a despotism or an anarchy, or whether a well-based, constitutional form of Government would be constructed amid both Revolutionary conflicts and battles with external enemies.

PRESIDENT WILSON **CHAPTER CLXXIII.** ADDRESSING CONGRESS.

THE INTERVENTION OF THE UNITED STATES OF AMERICA.
By Edward Wright.

Woodrow Wilson's Struggle with Tirpitz—Destruction of the Sussex and Anti-American Plot in Mexico—Wilson Helps Hollweg against Tirpitz—Note to Germany Threatening an Immediate Rupture—Germans Yield to American Demands and Temporarily Restrict Submarine Warfare—Wilson Attempts to Bring About Peace—American People Shrink from War—Clamour and Confusion of Presidential Campaign—Surprising Defeat of Mr. Hughes—The Girl of the Golden West Responds to the Peace Cry—German Plot to Make American Election a Weapon against Allies—Wilson Threatened with Unrestricted Submarine Piracy Appeals for Peace without Victory—Historic Reply by Mr. Arthur Balfour—Discovery of German Plot in Mexico—President Severs Relations with the Enemy—Mr. Gerard Held as Hostage—Filibustering Senators and Measure of Armed Neutrality—Inaugural Address by American President to Congress—Banks Allowed to Finance Allies—Discovery of Submarine Plot in Cuba—Russian Revolution Affects German-American Jewish Finance—American People Fired by Success of Russian Democracy—President Appeals to Congress—Historic Speech against German Government—Hindenburg Jeers while America Arms for the Struggle—Reconciliation of the Two Great English-speaking Nations.

I N Chapter CIII. (Vol. VI., page 85) the history of the difficulties in the relations between the United States of America and the Central Empires was brought down to February 1916. President Woodrow Wilson was then seen to be standing in direct opposition to Grand-Admiral von Tirpitz with regard to the policy of submarine piracy pursued by the Teutonic Powers. Tirpitz was in a desperate mood. His plans and preparations for war had proved inadequate to their special purpose, and his countrymen rightly accused him of having failed to foresee in the submarine the only weapon by which British sea-power could be strongly attacked. The Grand-Admiral was really a defeated and discredited man, striving to palliate the bankruptcy of his naval policy by recklessly involving his country in a struggle with another powerful enemy. According to a German allegation, he was as reckless at home as he was abroad, and doctored the reports of his first submarine campaign in order to induce the Kaiser to permit him to enlarge his scheme of operations against neutral as well as enemy merchant ships.

As a matter of fact, he had no instrument immediately available for a general campaign of piracy. His submarines were of the old type, and needed secret depots or secret

SIR CECIL SPRING-RICE, K.C.M.G., G.C.V.O.
Appointed British Ambassador to the United States in 1912, after long diplomatic experience in Sweden, Persia, Petrograd, Constantinople, Tokyo, and Brussels.

store-ships to enable them to operate in the Mediterranean. The new ocean-going submarine had been designed and tested, and was in progress of being manufactured in standardised parts, but more than six months were required to produce and man any considerable flotillas of improved U boats. In the meantime the British Fleet, with its large force of submarine-hunting vessels, was inflicting heavy losses upon Tirpitz's underwater craft and gradually reducing the first German campaign of piracy to a condition of comparative unimportance. Tirpitz became more ruthless as he grew more feeble. He made false claims of success, deceiving the German Emperor and the Council at Headquarters, and in March, 1916, proclaimed to the world that an intensified submarine campaign would be conducted against all shipping trading with the British Isles.

This was a direct movement against the legitimate commerce of the United States, and a defiance of the international laws that President Wilson was resolved to maintain. An attempt was made by the party of compromise in Germany, led by Herr Bethmann-Hollweg and Dr. Helfferich, to appease the American people by accusing Great Britain of illegally cutting off neutral trade with Germany. A Note of this nature was presented by Count Bernstorff, the German Ambassador at Washington.

to Mr. Lansing, the American Secretary of State. Count Bernstorff also set energetically in motion all the Press and political machinery he controlled in the United States with a view to making the people think that German and British methods were each as bad as the other. At the same time the attacks upon both neutral and allied shipping were resumed with spasmodic violence, as related in Chapter CLXXI.

In January and February, 1916, numerous Germans, acting with the revolutionary forces in Mexico, planned a raid into American territory, and induced one of the strongest of the Mexican rebels, Pancho Villa, to attack an American border town. Thereupon, from the German party in the Senate and in the House of Representatives, there was a renewed agitation for a Mexican campaign on a grand scale, which, it was hoped, would gradually absorb a large part of the munitions being manufactured for the Allies.

The pro-Germans were represented in Mr. Wilson's Cabinet, as in all other seats of authority. The result was that, pressed by the Germanic party and the Republican party in the critical year of the Presidential election, Mr. Wilson decided to send an expedition into Mexico to capture Villa. The task of the American Commander - in - Chief, G e n e r a l Funston, was an impossible one. He had fifteen hundred miles of marches to guard by means of feeble patrols, and only a small active force under General Pershing for operations over the frontier. At the end of the first month's operations a detachment of his troops was badly trapped in circumstances which showed that the nominally friendly Mexican leader, General Carranza, with whom the American force was supposed to be co-operating, was as hostile as Pancho Villa.

CAPTAIN VON PAPEN.
Formerly German Military Attaché in the U.S.A. Captain von Papen was recalled by request in December, 1915, as a result of his incrimination in the plot to destroy the Welland Canal.

The attitude of the American people in regard to the Mexican expedition was strange and disturbing. The border States of Texas, New Mexico, and Arizona were most concerned in the frontier raids, and apparently most clamant for punitive measures. But when General Funston, after the Parral episode, ordered the militia of these three States to turn out on active service along the border, weeks passed before a single militiaman, out of twelve thousand available, answered the call.

This made it plain that the popular agitation for intervention in Mexico was factitious, even in the border States. The expedition had mainly been engineered, by the bribery of Villa and the working of Teutonic plotters of all kinds in the United States, in preparation for Grand-Admiral von Tirpitz's new submarine campaign. The Germans in both Europe and America reckoned, at the end of March, 1916, that they had securely entangled President Wilson in an exhausting and prolonged action in Mexico. But to make sure that he would have no means of intervening in European affairs, the plotters also stirred up movements in Cuba and disturbances in Haiti and San Domingo, and elsewhere, which were calculated to engross the activities of the small remaining forces of Marines and regular troops that were not required on the Mexican frontier.

Such was the situation created by Count Bernstorff in Washington and Herr von Eckhardt in Mexico City, on the instructions of Tirpitz and the German Naval Staff. Captain von Papen's secretary, Wolfe von Igels, remained in America after his master had been practically deported, and continued to plot outrages while serving Count Bernstorff. The Fenian and Sinn Fein organisations in the United States, vigorously represented in the Senate and the Lower

Dr. Helfferich, German Vice-Chancellor and Minister of Finance, actively associated himself with the policy of unrestricted submarine warfare against all shipping.

Count Bernstorff, German Ambassador to the United States, and master of intrigue, received his passports from President Wilson in February, 1917.

Herr Wolff, head of Wolff Agency, a main instrument for the dissemination of German propaganda in America and of lying accounts. of the progress of the war.

PROMINENT GERMANS WHOSE SINISTER ACTIVITIES CONTRIBUTED TO THE GERMAN-AMERICAN RUPTURE.

LIBERTY IN PARIS.
Replica of Bartholdi's famous statue, presented to France in 1889 by the United States and sited on an island in the Seine. Appropriately one of the American ambulances is seen standing by it.

House, were connected with the Teutonic plotters of murder, revolutions, and frontier wars. President Woodrow Wilson, however, was not turned from his purpose by the far-stretched web of intrigues radiating from the German Embassy at Washington. The American Secret Service men were confident that they held in their hands the larger part of the web, and could break it in a few hours. As afterwards appeared by the confession of the German Foreign Minister in Berlin, his secret means of communication with Count Bernstorff was known to the American Secret Service men, and they had the key to the special cipher in which messages of decisive importance were sent to the German Ambassadors in Washington and Mexico City.

The German Emperor appears at first to have been averse to any compromise with pro-Americans in Germany. He was always a man who lived in the moment. Immediate military considerations outweighed with him all possible plans for the future commercial strength of his Empire. So long as he believed in the power of Tirpitz to starve out Great Britain by means of an unrestrained submarine piracy, he cared nothing about the present and future attitude of the United States. The complexion of affairs, however, abruptly changed when Tirpitz was convicted of having concealed his losses in submarines. In the middle of March the Grand-Admiral, with two of his principal lieutenants, was dismissed from the Marine Office, at a time when his intrigues in Mexico appeared to him to reach a point of success that freed him from all danger of active American intervention. Count Bernstorff, quickly tacking

in a new direction on the skirt of the gale that had sunk Tirpitz, turned to his own advantage the overthrow of the man he had been serving, and publicly claimed that he had been mainly responsible for defeating the inventor of submarine atrocities.

After the fall of Tirpitz, President Wilson began to explain his position to the American people. On April 13th, 1916, he spoke at a Democratic banquet at Washington, and asked his audience, in the veiled yet transparent manner peculiar to him, if they were ready to abandon the Mexican expedition and take action in a larger affair where the interests of America were coincident with the interests of humanity. His audience gave him the answer he required. So he set out, in an address to Congress, the substance of the Note to Germany, in which he threatened a rupture over the submarine campaign.

Sinking of the Sussex

He pointed out that the Government of the United States had from the beginning protested that the German submarine policy could not be pursued without gross and palpable violation of the law of nations. In spite of the assurances given by the German Government, there had been no check at all upon the destruction of ships of all kinds. In a speech that afterwards became of world-wide importance President Wilson continued:

Again and again Germany has given this Government solemn assurances that at least passenger ships will not be thus dealt with, yet she has again and again permitted her under-sea commanders to disregard those assurances with entire impunity.

Great liners like the Lusitania and the Arabic, and mere ferry-boats like the Sussex, have been attacked without a moment's warning—sometimes before they were even aware that they were in the presence of an armed vessel of the enemy; and the lives of non-combatants, both passengers and crew, have been sacrificed wholesale in a manner which the Government of the United States cannot but regard as wanton and without the slightest colour of justification. No limit of any kind has, in fact, been set to the indiscriminate pursuit and destruction of merchantmen of all kinds and all nationalities within waters constantly extending in the area where operations are carried on, and the roll of Americans who have lost their lives on ships thus attacked and destroyed has grown month by month until it is ominous—until it has mounted into hundreds.

One of the latest and most shocking instances of this method of warfare was that of the destruction of the French cross-Channel steamer Sussex. It must stand forth, as the sinking of the Lusitania did, so singularly tragical and unjustifiable as to constitute a truly terrible example of the inhumanity of submarine warfare as the commanders of German vessels for the past twelve months have been conducting it. If this instance stood alone, some explanation, some disavowal by the German Government, some evidence of a criminal mistake or of wilful disobedience on the part of the commander of the vessel that fired the torpedo might be sought or entertained; but, unhappily, it does not stand alone. Recent events make the conclusion inevitable that it is only one instance, even though one of the most extreme and most distressing instances, of the spirit and method of warfare which Germany has mistakenly adopted, and which from the first has exposed that Government to the reproach of thrusting all neutral rights aside in the pursuit of its immediate object.

The Government of the United States has been very patient. At every stage of this distressing experience of tragedy after tragedy, in which its own citizens have been involved, it has sought to be restrained from any extreme course of action or protest by thoughtful consideration of the extraordinary circumstances of this unprecedented war, and has been actuated in all it said and did by the sentiments of genuine friendship which the people of the United States have always entertained, and continue to entertain, towards the German nation.

LIBERTY ILLUMINATES THE WESTERN WORLD.
Bartholdi's Statue of Liberty in New York Harbour with the great torch illuminated. This colossal statue was presented to America by France in 1886 in commemoration of the centenary of its independence.

NOTIFYING NEUTRALITY.
Liner St. Louis as labelled during the period when the United States sought to maintain neutrality despite German provocation.

It has, of course, accepted the successive explanations and assurances of Germany, as given in entire sincerity and good faith, and has hoped even against hope that it would prove possible for Germany so to order and control the acts of her naval commanders as to square her policy with the principles of humanity as embodied in the law of nations. It has been willing to wait until the significance of the facts became absolutely unmistakable and susceptible of but one interpretation.

That point has now unhappily been reached. The facts are susceptible of but one interpretation. The Imperial German Government has been unable to put any limits or restraint upon its warfare against either freight or passenger ships. Therefore it has become painfully evident that the position which this Government took at the very outset is inevitable—namely, that the use of the submarine for the destruction of the enemy's commerce of necessity, because of the very character of the vessels employed and of the very methods of attack which their employment involves, is incompatible with the principles of humanity, the long-established and incontrovertible rights of neutrals, and the sacred immunities of non-combatants.

President Wilson's threat to Germany

I have deemed it my duty, therefore, to say to the Imperial German Government that if it is still its purpose to prosecute relentless indiscriminate warfare against vessels of commerce by the use of submarines, notwithstanding the now demonstrated impossibility of conducting that warfare in accordance with what the Government of the United States must consider the sacred and indisputable rules of international law and the universally recognised dictates of humanity, the Government of the United States is at last forced to the conclusion that there is but one course it can pursue, and unless the Imperial German Government now immediately declare and effect the abandonment of its present methods of warfare against passenger and freight-carrying vessels, this Government will have no choice but to sever diplomatic relations with the Government of the German Empire altogether.

The German Government seemed at first inclined to defy the United States Government. This was probably only a domestic political manœuvre, made with a view to preparing the German people for a partial restriction of the policy of Tirpitz. Discussions went on for some time at Imperial Headquarters, to which Mr. Gerard was invited, with Herr Bethmann-Hollweg and Dr. Helfferich. According to a German report, Dr. Helfferich, as Minister of Finance, took a most important part in bearing down all naval and military opposition to a compromise with the United States. In his view the financial and commercial situation was such that peace without victory, but with the friendship of the

American people, was necessary to enable the new Middle Europe system to survive and develop in full strength and security.

The lack of sufficient submarines and trained submarine crews finally decided the matter—for the time. On May 4th a Note was handed to Mr. Gerard in Berlin, replying to the American Note of April 20th, and practically yielding to the principal demand made by President Wilson.

There can be little doubt that Germans hoped, as the result of the discussions at German Imperial Headquarters in May, 1916, that the President of the United States would endeavour to promote peace among the belligerent Powers if the submarine attacks on neutral shipping ceased. On May 21st President Wilson made his first speech in North Carolina in favour of negotiated settlement of the affairs of Europe. An apostolic delegate arrived at the White House with a sealed message from Pope Benedict, in which the President was said to have been urged to mediate between the contending nations. In Germany public opinion was at once skilfully prepared for a negotiated peace through the mediation of President Wilson.

KEEPING WATCH ON INTERNED GERMAN LINERS.
New York police guarding piers at which interned German liners were moored. Over a score of such liners were interned at New York, and a close guard was necessary to ensure that none of them put to sea or was damaged as American and German relations neared breaking-point.

In the United States the same public expectation was created by all the means of publicity at the disposal of the Government. Then, on May 27th, at a meeting of the League to Enforce Peace, President Wilson made his first strong and direct attempt to bring about a settlement by compromise.

The idea of a League to Enforce Peace had first been developed by a former President of the United States, Mr. Taft, and had been supported by several eminent leaders of American opinion. It had attracted attention in both Great Britain and Germany, and Lord Grey of Fallodon and other powerful Liberal Ministers were in favour of it. In the land of its origin, however, the scheme remained an academic proposal, in which neither the people nor the main body of politicians took any practical interest.

GERMAN STEAMER HAMBURG IN CHARGE OF N.Y. POLICE.
Police guard mounted over the interned German s.s. Hamburg at New York. Despite the guards that were maintained, and daily inspections on board, the crews of the interned vessels wrought much damage to the machinery in many of the ships when war became inevitable.

In his speech President Wilson neatly reduced the ideas of the new league into a paragraph. It ran as follows:

We believe in these fundamental things: Firstly, that every people has a right to choose the sovereignty under which it shall live; secondly, that the small States of the world have the right to enjoy the same respect for their sovereignty and their territory and integrity that the great and powerful nations expect and insist upon; and thirdly, that the world has the right to be freed from every disturbance of its peace that has its origin in aggression and disregard of the rights of peoples and nations. So sincerely do we believe these things that I am sure that I speak the mind and wish of the people of America when I say that the United States is willing to become a partner in any feasible association of nations formed in order to realise these objects and make them secure against violation.

He argued that if such an association of nations had existed before the outbreak of the war the struggle would have been averted. He went on to suggest that the belligerents should negotiate among themselves a settlement on lines approved by the United States, and then form a universal association of nations to secure a highway of the seas for the common and unhindered use of all peoples, and to prevent any war being begun either contrary to treaty covenants or without warning and full submission of the causes to the opinion of the world.

The speech failed to effect the desired peace. The American people were, on the whole, indifferent. Of most of them it could truly have been said that with the causes and objects of the war they were not concerned. From the Alleghany Mountains to the Pacific Ocean there was as yet no weight of public opinion behind President Wilson, even in his struggle to save American merchant ships and passenger liners from being torpedoed by German submarines. Only in the Eastern States did intense indignation against the piratical methods of the Central Empires prevail.

The President was well aware that the apathetic majority in the States was inclined to remain prosperously at peace during the struggle, and rely upon increased wealth and

U.S. MARINE RECRUITS.
Enrolling men in New York for the Marine Service, an instant increase of 4,000 recruits for which was called for.

NEW YORK HOME DEFENCE LEAGUE.
Men of the Home Defence League of special policemen setting off for duty on Staten Island. As soon as war became inevitable the New York Police Commissioner appointed these special constables to act as guards over public property.

industrial power in dealing with the international problems of the future. The campaign for preparedness and an increase in armament had so far not touched the general mind.

The United States remained pacific at heart. The Navy was not prepared to deal with submarine attack upon American shipping. National pride was flattered by large projects in battleship construction. Capital ships, with 16 in. guns and 35 knot speed, were designed, amid the acclamations of the Press. Small, fast vessels and quick-firing guns in large numbers, however, were most urgently required, in order to protect American commerce against the new German ocean-going submarines.

Senator Root's leading question

The American people visibly shrank from war. Since the days of the Civil War they had been transformed apparently from the most blustering of modern democracies into the most pacific. For nearly two years they had hourly been reading of scenes of extreme carnage and misery in Belgium, Northern France, Poland, Galicia, and Serbia. Everything of this nature that they read made most of them more than naturally anxious to avoid being drawn into the dreadful conflict.

In the Middle and Western States the mere spectacular interest in the clash of the armed nations of the Old World ceased to engage the general attention. Conversation usually turned upon some little local affair. It appeared at times as though the Westerners especially wanted to forget that half the earth was at war. Yet they did not forget. Towards the close of the year they carried Mr. Woodrow Wilson back to White House in expressed gratitude for the success with which he had kept them out of the struggle.

A considerable number of Americans thought that the later medley of races peopling their continent had a weaker fibre of character than the almost purely Northern European strains that had carried on the Civil War. "Have selfish living, factional quarrelling, and easy prosperity obscured the spiritual vision of our country?" asked Senator Root.

SPECIAL GUARD FOR NEW YORK'S WATER SUPPLY.
Patrolman instructing a squad of recruits for the special police raised to guard the great New York aqueduct. The men, clothed in khaki and armed with shot-guns, revolvers, and clubs, relieved the members of the National Guard who had done the work previously.

" Has the patriotism of a generation, never summoned to sacrifice, become lifeless ? Is our nation one, or a discordant multitude ? " Professor J. M. Baldwin, after his voyage in the Sussex, answered : " The name of our country to-day is a synonym for cowardice, commercialism, and hypocrisy." This was really not so. Only the Germans in Germany regarded the people of the United States as timorous and intimidated.

The Americans were still very confident of their strength, and only sobered in the expression of their growing power and quietly thoughtful over the part they might play in shaping civilisation. Their increasing wealth, that changed them suddenly from a debtor nation into a creditor nation, did not lead them into the error of thinking that gold had at last become the master of iron. It was on their enlarged power as munition providers to the Allies, in which they clean outraced the Japanese, their competitors for the

TYPICAL GUN-TURRET OF AN AMERICAN BATTLESHIP.
American initial naval plans provided for the protection and patrolling of home waters, policing the high seas against commerce-destroyers, and helping the fleets of the Allies in European waters.

dominion of the Pacific Ocean, that their confidence chiefly rested.

Their Army was very small, their Navy was inadequate to the defence of their coasts, but their war plant had grown, without any expense to themselves, to enormous capacity. It was indeed their lively sense of their potential strength that made them largely averse to organising a Continental army before it was immediately required for action. Herein they somewhat resembled the British people of the ante-bellum era. In their own view they stood to the militarised and commercially advancing Japanese in much the same relation as the British had stood to the Germans. They continued to watch Japan and her policy in regard to China more intently than they followed the struggle in Europe. The comparative failure of the Panama Canal, through incessant landslides, with **the** consequent check **to** the American plans of naval con-**centration,** had more to do with the grand new scheme of

battleship construction than had the events and incidents of naval operations in Europe. The United States was really looking very far ahead. In the meantime many Americans wanted to keep out of the war in order to conserve their strength.

One of their parties was moved to urge participation in the European conflict, for the reason that that would organise the country as thoroughly as Japan was organised. The majority of the American people, however, was averse to this policy. They could not be induced to see that their interests were in any way directly engaged in helping the British Empire and defeating the German Empire. They misconceived the British aim and over-estimated the British strength. There was a large element of national egotism in their attitude. They regarded the British Fleet as the shield of their Atlantic shores and the eastern defence of their Monroe Doctrine. They felt entirely safe from Teutonic aggression while the British Fleet held the seas, and too lightly they reckoned that British sea-power was so enormously prepotent that it was being exerted without serious strain.

    U.S. attitude to the belligerents

Great Britain was commonly regarded as the most successful of the combatants—pursuing business while making war, and with easy effort gathering new colonies and piling up investments among her Allies. France was the only Great Power that excited American sympathy in a struggle which was considered mainly as a duel between British sea-power and German land-power. A few Americans would have liked the war to end by the mutual exhaustion of Great Britain and Germany, leaving the United States the potential leader of civilisation.

Not until the new German campaign of submarine piracy was seen patently to threaten the British Isles with famine and general enfeeblement did American people begin to recognise the fact that Britons were sacrificing themselves equally with the French and Belgians.

The cold, proud, reserved, and academic attempts to explain the British cause to the populace of the United States were largely responsible for the American lack of sympathy. Under the administration of Mr. Asquith, no British statesman of authority acted as Abraham Lincoln had acted in the Civil War and appealed directly to democratic feeling across the Atlantic. The British Government of the old school, though perplexed and distressed by its difficulties, maintained a curious kind of aristocratic reserve with both Allies and friendly neutrals. Certainly, there was something not ignoble in this attitude. Yet, as a matter of practical politics, it was a costly affair. For two years and a half it cost the British nation the sympathy of the generous but unawakened American democracy.

In the meantime President Woodrow Wilson failed to get any response to his peace movement. Becoming at last aware that a great Franco-British offensive was preparing, he prudently postponed his direct attempt at mediation until the result of the new struggle in the west was clear. Diplomatic remonstrances with the British and French Governments in regard to the seizure of mails served to maintain an active neutrality between the belligerent groups. The dispute about the seizure of mails, like the similar dispute over the blacklisting of pro-German firms known to have helped the enemy, was not a very serious matter. At worst it would have led to claims for damages after the war, somewhat after the Alabama precedent. As a matter of fact, the British and French Governments had a good case underlying all these developments of the modern blockade system, and kept up a spirited correspondence with the American Secretary of State.

    British Government's reserve

His design was apparently to maintain strict impartiality after the apparent defeat of the Tirpitz party in Germany. The Americans themselves admitted, however, that they were

United States Fleet arriving off New York. The ships were passing the colossal Statue of Liberty Enlightening the World, which so finely symbolises all those things that had been placed in jeopardy by the action of the Central Powers of Europe, which the President of the United States pledged his country to uphold. The United States had at the outbreak of the Great War the third largest Navy in the world.

Fighting-tops of the Kentucky, one of the battleships of the United States Navy. The lattice-work system on which these fighting-tops were devised was designed with a view to minimising the extent of the damage likely to result from a hit. The Kentucky, a vessel of 11,520 tons, was laid down in 1896, launched in 1898, and completed in 1900, with an armament of four 13-inch guns besides lesser weapons, and a complement of 726 men.

SHIPS OF THE UNITED STATES NAVY, ONE OF THE GREATEST IN THE WORLD.

IN NEW YORK ARMOURY.
Cleaning and polishing rifles and bayonets in the New York Armoury, for America's fighting forces.

Many of the Republican leaders, and, in particular, Senator Root and Senator Lodge, agreed with the fighting policy of Mr. Roosevelt. Their known enthusiasm for the cause of the Allies was not to be destroyed by the bribe of the German vote. The German Government, however, miscalculated the spirit of the American people and the strength of judgment of character of the American leaders. They considered that the pacifism of the Middle West and Western States was based on timidity, and that this timidity could be worked upon with a view to increasing the effect of the German vote. Therefore, on July 9th, 1916, when the political campaign was proceeding and

prevented, by their own Civil War practices, from seriously interfering with the main lines of the British blockade. Even in regard to the British censorship of mails and despatches, on August 10th, 1916, a remarkable incident was reported from Berlin. Several German-American war correspondents in Germany complained that the British Censor was unreasonably interfering with their work. They approached the American Ambassador in Berlin, and asked him to forward a petition to the American Government. Mr. Gerard forwarded the petition, but with a disconcerting note of his own, stating that he could not endorse the protest against the British Censorship until the German Censorship permitted proper reports to be transmitted from American newspaper correspondents in Berlin.

ENROLLING SPECIAL POLICEMEN IN NEW YORK.
American citizens enrolling as special policemen in the Armoury of the 69th New York Regiment. Following on the declaration of war against Germany, on April 6th, 1917, a force of special police was formed to relieve the soldiers of the National Guard stationed on the Catskill Aqueduct.

By this time, however, the clamour and confusion of the Presidential election campaign silenced and overwhelmed everything else in the national life of America. The influence of the war in Europe told upon the political crisis in various indirect ways; but it had no immediate bearing upon the struggle between the Democrats and Republicans. Mr. Woodrow Wilson was opposed by the German-American associations and certain Irish-American associations.

The Presidential election campaign

It was reported that the Republican candidate, Mr. Hughes, would receive the entire German vote, not because he favoured Germany, but because the Central Empires wished to make Mr. Wilson a permanent example of the power they exercised in American politics. Throughout the election campaign Mr. Hughes continued to preserve a diplomatic reticence, but his campaigning lieutenant, Mr. Roosevelt, attacked the Germans in a most vigorous and emphatic manner, and practically made it clear that the Republican Party would, if it carried its candidate to power, be rather less pacific than the Democratic Party had been.

skirmishes were taking place on the Mexican frontier, the German ocean-going submarine Deutschland arrived at Norfolk, on the Virginian coast, with a cargo of costly merchandise, as already chronicled in Chapter CLXXI. (Vol. IX., page 17). The threat was very gently and subtly made. The Deutschland was unarmed, being a new type of underwater craft intended to be used as a depot of supplies in the forthcoming intensification of piracy. She was sent to the United States in order to indicate to the American people that the arm of German piracy now extended to their shores. Then in October 1916, when the struggle between Mr. Wilson and Mr. Hughes was at its height, the hint given by the Deutschland was abruptly and most unexpectedly driven home by the depredations of the ocean-going submarine U53, off the New England coast, on October 7th, as described in Chapter CLXXI.

No doubt the German Government reckoned that President Wilson would be unable to make any serious attempt to break off relations with the Central Empires. In the second week of October it seemed very uncertain whether Mr. Wilson would continue in power. The Republican candidate, Mr. Hughes, appeared then to be increasing his hold upon the country. When, however, the election results were gradually disclosed, there was a succession of surprises for everybody. Most of the Eastern States, with a large industrial population to which Mr. Wilson had appealed by establishing an eight-hour working day law for railways, with a promised extension to other fields, turned against the new Liberalism of the Democratic Party and voted for Mr. Hughes. Practically all the old President-making States swung over to Mr. Hughes, until in both America and Europe the election of a Republican President was regarded as a definite fact. The Germans began to claim the defeat of Mr. Wilson as a magnificent and decisive illustration of their Transatlantic power. But while European countries were disputing whether

YOUNG AMERICA IN TRAINING.
Definitely committed to entrance into the arena of war Young America began to train for the struggle.

the women had not won the suffrage, they yet managed practically to exercise it by their influence on the vote of their husbands.

In those States where the women had voting power the hand that rocked the cradle swung the election. As the Americans themselves put it: "The girl of the Golden West carried the day for Wilson!" Of the twelve suffrage States ten voted for the man who had kept them out of the war; and, in the final close and critical count, the women voters of California changed the verdict of the Eastern States and thus upset all the

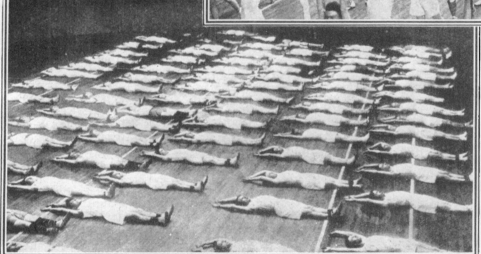

FOUNDATION WORK IN THE MAKING OF A SOLDIER.
At the Stevens Institute of Hoboken, New Jersey, courses of physical training were provided on a system which the Canadian authorities had found highly successful for developing the muscles and hardening the physique of recruits.

the apparent Republican victory indicated a more warlike temper in the people or a success for Teutonic intrigues, the women voters of the Western States entirely changed the issue of the election, and carried Mr. Wilson back to White House.

There was then no doubt of the double significance of the President's victory. On the one hand, he completely defeated the organisers of the German vote and maintained the integrity of American nationality. Many German-Americans refused to follow their leaders, and voted for either candidate according to their old party predilections, or for other reasons, just as other men did. Where they answered to disloyal leadership, they happily did it so ostentatiously as to arouse the passion of ordinary Americans, who thereupon swamped the German vote and swung the State round to Wilson. The Irish-Americans appeared, in some important places, to have been a more effective Germanic force than were the Germans, Austrians, and Hungarians. Yet, though they turned the vote against Mr. Wilson in New York and New Jersey, the entire German-American plot failed, by reason of a strange and surprising movement in the Middle West and the West.

The cry: "He kept us out of the war!" rang from Kansas to California, and, taken up by the women, it ensured the continuance of power of the President. Where

traditions of American politics. Nevertheless, the woman vote was divided like the German vote, though perhaps not in the same measure. From Montana there came, in the handsome person of Miss Jeannette Rankin, the first Congresswoman in history. She sat as a Republican for her State in the House of Representatives. Important Republican masses went over to the Democratic Party and won all the frontier States menaced by Villa and Carranza for the President who had prudently refrained from launching a great punitive expedition in Mexico.

Count Bernstorff was not discon- **Bernstorff's fresh** certed by the failure of his political plot **intrigue** against the President. On the contrary, he skilfully seized upon the successful pacifist movement, to which Mr. Wilson's re-election was largely due, and made it the groundwork of a new and more promising intrigue. He convinced the German Emperor, Herr Bethmann-Hollweg, and Dr. Helfferich that the American peace movement could be transformed into an instrument against the Entente Powers. It was known, from the declaration of Mr. Lloyd George, that Great Britain intended a fight to the finish. France, especially after her victory at Douaumont, was also strongly averse to a negotiated peace. Russia, too, had rejected a private offer to negotiate; while Italy, having enormously increased her output of

ARTILLERY MANŒUVRES AT FOX BLISS, TEXAS.
The possibility of war between Mexico and the United States, insidiously engineered by German agents, required the presence of considerable American forces on the Mexican border.

NATIONAL GUARD AT MANŒUVRES.
Rushing up ammunition. On June 30th, 1915, the United States National Guard, or organised Militia, comprised 8,705 officers and 120,693 men of whom three-fourths could actually be put in the field.

munitions and arrayed large reserves of men, was resolute to increase the advantage she had won at Gorizia and slowly grind forward to Trieste and all her unredeemed territory.

In these circumstances it seemed to Count Bernstorff that there was a great opportunity for entering into sincere friendly relations with the United States President. The design was to employ him, with the pacifist vote behind him, to bring the Allies to negotiate for a settlement. The Central Powers were in a difficult position. They had a shortage in food. Their railway material was wearing badly from over use, and their army on the western front was, for the time, dispirited by a year of terrific punishment at Verdun and on the Somme. Hindenburg could not promise a grand decision by military means, and, like former captains of Continental warfare perplexed by the amphibious power of Great Britain, he inclined at last to look for some naval means of obtaining a short cut to a victorious peace. In the new ocean-going submarines that Tirpitz had ordered in large numbers before his fall he had an instrument. In order to use these new submarines with complete effect, the promise given to the United States must be repudiated, and an utterly unrestricted campaign of ruthless piracy started against all neutral as well as belligerent vessels trading to the British Isles, France, Northern Russia, Italy, Egypt, and Northern Africa.

Perhaps, if the American people had elected a President in a warlike temper after the act of piracy committed by the German submarine near the Nantucket Lighthouse, Hindenburg would at once have proceeded to involve the whole world in war in the hope of starving out the people of the British Isles. This measure was avoided, for the time at least, by the talent for diplomacy displayed by Count Bernstorff. At his suggestion Mr. Gerard, the American Ambassador in Berlin, was approached by the Imperial authorities and informed that the mediation of the United States could alone save the world from complete and general disaster. No direct threat appeared to be employed. That would have been too clumsy a **German submarine threats** method in such delicate circumstances. The Teutons displayed an unusual degree of adroitness. Under Government impetus a violent and widespread political campaign was opened for the restoration to power of Grand-Admiral Tirpitz, who was loudly commended for the position of Imperial Chancellor, in place of Herr Bethmann-Hollweg.

It is just possible that Herr Bethmann-Hollweg secretly helped in this campaign against himself. He was accused of being too weak, too considerate, and too humane, when, as a matter of fact, he really combined an extreme of pitiless ferocity with as much cunning as a Prussian could develop. During this attack upon himself the Imperial Chancellor, with Dr. Helfferich and other nominal pro-Americans, pretended to seek for help from Mr. Gerard and President Wilson. They implored the United States authorities to assist them in the peace movement and prevent Tirpitz and the apostles of ruthlessness from winning complete power and outraging humanity. It it is not probable that the directors of the policy of the United States were deceived by Herr Bethmann Hollweg and by the German Emperor, who was acting through his Chancellor. In any case, it is clear that the threat of intensified submarine piracy was aimed at President Wilson, in the design to spur him to offer to mediate between the contending Powers. Either he did not act quickly enough, or the German Emperor thought he would win advantage by making a peace proposal first in his peculiar and histrionic manner. So the President of the United States was anticipated by the impossible peace speech delivered by Herr Bethmann-Hollweg under theatrical circumstances in Berlin on December 12th, 1916. The rise of Mr. Lloyd George to a position of dominant authority in the War Council of Great Britain, perhaps, induced the Germans to propose negotiations for peace before Mr. Wilson took any definite action in the matter.

This created considerable embarrassment for the American President. Nevertheless, he found himself drawn so near the verge of war that he opened his movement for peace on December 20th, 1916, a week after the report of the speech of the German Chancellor had been received and the German offer to negotiate had been transmitted to the Grand Alliance. In a Note to all **President Wilson's** the belligerents Mr. Wilson asked each **proposal** nation at war to state the terms upon which it would make peace, and indicate what arrangements it would consider satisfactory in providing against any similar conflict in the future. Two paragraphs in the American peace Note that attracted special attention ran as follows :

The President takes the liberty of calling attention to the fact that the objects which the statesmen of the belligerents on both sides have in mind in this war are virtually the same, as stated in general terms to their own people and to the world. Each side desires to make the rights and privileges of weak peoples and small States as secure against aggression or denial in the future as the rights and privileges of the great and powerful States now at war. Each wishes itself to be made secure in the future, along with all other nations and peoples, against the recurrence of wars like this, and against aggression or selfish interference of any kind. Each would be jealous of the formation of any more rival leagues to preserve an uncertain balance of power amidst multiplying suspicions; but each is ready to consider the formation of a league of nations to ensure peace and justice throughout the world. Before that final

step can be taken, however, each deems it necessary first to settle the issues of the present war upon terms which will certainly safeguard the independence, the territorial integrity, and the political and commercial freedom of the nations involved.

In the measures to be taken to secure the future peace of the world, the people and the Government of the United States are as vitally and as directly interested as the Governments now at war. Their interest, moreover, in the means to be adopted to relieve the smaller and weaker peoples of the world of the peril of wrong and violence is as quick and ardent as that of any other people or Government. They stand ready, and even eager, to co-operate in the accomplishment of these ends when the war is over with every influence and resource at their command. But the war must first be concluded. The terms upon which it is to be concluded they are not at liberty to suggest ; but the President does feel that it is his right and his duty to point out their intimate interest in its conclusion, lest it should presently be too late to accomplish the greater things which lie beyond its conclusion, lest the situation of neutral nations, now exceedingly hard to endure, be rendered altogether intolerable, and lest, more than all, an injury be done civilisation itself which can never be atoned or repaired.

The first paragraph was resented by some of the Allies, as they mistakenly thought it implied that their aims in the war were virtually the same as those of Germany, Austria-Hungary, Turkey, and Bulgaria. All that the President said, however, was that each belligerent Government

ARTILLERY PRACTICE OF THE NEW YORK NATIONAL GUARD AT MANŒUVRES.
Battery practice of the New York National Guard. The artillery observation officer, it will be noticed, was perched on a high pole so that he could look from above the denser part of the smoke emitted from the guns. Above : Unloading a projectile from the magazine to the truck for conveyance to the gun during the testing of the American coast defences at Fort Totten, protecting New York Harbour.

AT A LOOK-OUT POINT OVER NEW YORK HARBOUR.
In the observation-tower at Fort Totten. After the fateful decision of April 6th, 1917, a close watch had to be kept for German submarines near N.Y. Harbour, one approach to which is protected by Fort Totten.

had, in general terms, professed somewhat similar objects. President Wilson did not really believe in all these professions. It was for this reason he asked for more particular statements of terms. Moreover, the alarm he expressed in the second paragraph was genuine, and his Secretary of War caused a panic in the American markets by frankly explaining that the underlying situation was bringing the United States very close to an outbreak of hostilities. One of the aims of the Note was to test the sincerity of all the combatants, and especially to discover, if possible, whether Germany would make any large concessions and avoid breaking her pledge in regard to U boat warfare.

Allies indicate their terms

The effect of the American Note upon the German Government was such as to gratify the Allied Powers. Under direct invitation to make good his rhetoric about peace, and to substantiate the offer to negotiate made under his direction, the German Emperor became confused and disconcerted.

Through his Ministers he rejected the request to state his terms, and vainly tried to shuffle away from the issue by proposing a conference at which his unexplained demands could be examined by the Allies. The Allies, on the other hand, consulted together in accordance with the desire of President Wilson, and boldly outlined their terms of peace, in a Note presented on January 10th, 1917, by the Premier of France to the American Ambassador in Paris.

It was impossible, stated the Allied Governments, to obtain at the moment such a peace as would not only secure to them reparation, restitution, and guarantees, but enable the European nations of the future to be established on a sure foundation. The Allies challenged the analogy drawn between the two groups of belligerents in the American Note, and suggested that President Woodrow Wilson could not himself have thought that the aims of the Central Powers were virtually the same as those of the Allied Powers. They alluded to the horrors of the invasions of Belgium and Serbia, to the massacres in Armenia and Syria, the barbarities of airship raids on open towns, submarine piracy, and the deportation and enslavement of civil populations. Then, without formulating in detail their terms of peace, the Allied Governments gave the following indications of their demands and intentions :

The evacuation of the invaded territories in France, Russia, and Rumania, with fitting reparation ;

The reorganisation of Europe, guaranteed by a stable settlement, based alike upon the principle of nationalities, on the right which all peoples, whether small or great, have to the enjoyment of full security and free economic development, and also upon territorial agreements and international arrangements so framed as to guarantee land and sea frontiers against unjust attacks ;

Mr. Balfour's great letter

The restitution of provinces or territories formerly torn from the Allies by force or contrary to the wishes of their inhabitants ;

The liberation of Italians, Slavs, Rumanians, Czechs, and Slovaks from foreign domination ;

The liberation of the peoples who now lie beneath the murderous tyranny of the Turks ; and the expulsion from Europe of the Ottoman Empire, which has proved itself so radically alien to Western civilisation.

The allied Note was sent to the British Ambassador in Washington with a covering despatch from the new Secretary of State for Foreign Affairs, Mr. Arthur J. Balfour.

As a document of diplomacy the letter of Mr. Balfour was a masterpiece. The impression it made upon American opinion constituted a moral victory for the allied cause. For more than two years the people of the United States had been waiting for an appeal to their instincts of liberty and justice, similar to the appeal that Abraham Lincoln made to the British people at a time when the issues of the Civil War were obscured in the European Press. Mr. Balfour had for years seemed to be almost an extinct force in British politics. As he had not distinguished himself as First Lord of the Admiralty in the last Asquith administration his appointment to the position vacated by Viscount Grey was thought at the time to be a mistake. In his address to the American people, however, the old brilliant Foreign Minister, who in his younger days attended the Berlin Congress, recovered the genius of his prime, and stated the case for the Allies in passages of lucid and telling power. What the British official propaganda had been unable to accomplish in thirty months Mr. Balfour achieved in one day. Owing to its historic importance, and its value for future reference, we print in full this famous despatch :

Sir,--In sending you a translation of the allied Note, I desire to make the following observations, which you should bring to the notice of the United States Government.

I gather from the general tenor of the President's Note that while he is animated by an intense desire that peace should come soon, and that when it comes it should be lasting, he does not, for the moment at least, concern himself with the terms on which it should be arranged.

His Majesty's Government entirely share the President's ideals ; but they feel strongly that the durability of the peace must largely depend on its character, and that no stable system of international relations can be built on foundations which are essentially and hopelessly defective.

This becomes clearly apparent if we consider the main conditions which rendered possible the calamities from which the world is now suffering. These were the existence of a Great Power consumed with the lust of domination, in the midst of a community of nations ill-prepared for defence, plentifully supplied indeed with international laws, but with no machinery for enforcing them, and weakened by the fact that neither the boundaries of the various States nor their internal constitution harmonised with the aspirations of their constituent races, or secured to them just and equal treatment.

President Woodrow Wilson, who led the United States into the fight for civilisation.

HON. ROBERT LANSING.
SECRETARY OF STATE.

HON. NEWTON D. BAKER.
SECRETARY OF WAR.

GENERAL LEONARD WOOD.
COMMANDER-IN-CHIEF OF THE ARMY.

MR. JAMES W. GERARD.
EX-AMBASSADOR TO GERMANY.

Leaders of American opinion: Ministerial Secretaries, Ambassadors, and Army

HON. JOSEPHUS DANIELS,
SECRETARY OF THE NAVY.

COL. THEODORE ROOSEVELT,
PRESIDENT OF THE U.S.A. 1901-8.

DR. WALTER H. PAGE,
AMBASSADOR TO GREAT BRITAIN.

ADMIRAL HENRY T. MAYO,
COMMANDING THE ATLANTIC FLEET.

Navy Chiefs when the United States declared war on Germany, April 6th, 1917.

America's coastal defences: Powerful mortar in action.

That this last evil would be greatly mitigated if the Allies secured the changes in the map of Europe outlined in their joint Note is manifest, and I need not labour the point.

It has been argued, indeed, that the expulsion of the Turks from Europe forms no proper or logical part of this general scheme. The maintenance of the Turkish Empire was during many generations regarded by statesmen of world-wide authority as essential to the maintenance of European peace. Why, it is asked, should the cause of peace be now associated with a complete reversal of this traditional policy?

The answer is that circumstances have completely changed. It is unnecessary to consider now whether the creation of a reformed Turkey mediating between hostile races in the Near East was a scheme which, had the Sultan been sincere and the Powers united, could ever have been realised. It certainly cannot be realised now. The Turkey of "Union and Progress" is at least as barbarous and is far more aggressive than the Turkey of Sultan Abdul Hamid. In the hands of Germany it has ceased even in appearance to be a bulwark of peace, and is openly used as an instrument of conquest.

Changed conditions in Europe

Under German officers, Turkish soldiers are now fighting in lands from which they had long been expelled, and a Turkish Government, controlled, subsidised, and supported by Germany, has been guilty of massacres in Armenia and Syria more horrible than any recorded in the history even of those unhappy countries. Evidently the interests of peace and the claims of nationality alike require that Turkish rule over alien races shall, if possible, be brought to an end; and we may hope that the expulsion of Turkey from Europe will contribute as much to the cause of peace as the restoration of Alsace-Lorraine to France, of Italia Irredenta to Italy, or any of the other territorial changes indicated in the allied Note.

Evidently, however, such territorial rearrangements, though they may diminish the occasions of war, provide no sufficient security against its recurrence. If Germany, or rather those in Germany who mould its opinions and control its destinies, again set out to dominate the world, they may find that by the new order of things the adventure is made more difficult, but hardly that it is made impossible. They may still have ready to their hand a political system organised through and through on a military basis; they may still accumulate vast stores of military equipment; they may still perfect their methods of attack, so that their more pacific neighbours will be struck down before they can prepare themselves for defence. If so, Europe, when the war is over, will be far poorer in men, in money, and in mutual goodwill than it was when the war began, but it will not be safer; and the hopes for the future of the world entertained by the President will be as far as ever from fulfilment.

There are those who think that, for this disease, international treaties and international laws may provide a sufficient cure. But such persons have ill-learned the lessons so clearly taught by recent history.

While other nations, notably the United States of America and Britain, were striving by treaties of arbitration to make sure that no chance quarrel should mar the peace they desired to make perpetual, Germany stood aloof. Her historians and philosophers preached the splendours of war; power was proclaimed as the true end of the State; the General Staff forged with untiring industry the weapons by which, at the appointed moment, power might be achieved. These facts proved clearly enough that treaty arrangements for maintaining peace were not likely to find much favour at Berlin; they did not prove that such treaties, once made, would be utterly ineffectual. This became evident only when war had broken out; though the demonstration, when it came, was overwhelming. So long as Germany remains the Germany which, without a shadow of justification, overran and barbarously ill-treated a country it was pledged to defend, *no State can regard its rights as secure if they have no better protection than a solemn treaty.*

The case is made worse by the reflection that these methods of calculated brutality were designed by the Central Powers not merely to crush to the dust those with whom they were at war, but to intimidate those with whom they were still at peace. Belgium was not only a victim, it was an example. Neutrals were intended to note the outrages which accompanied its conquest, the reign of terror which followed on its occupation, the deportation of a portion of its population, the cruel oppression of the remainder. And lest nations happily protected, either by British fleets or their own, from German armies, should suppose themselves safe from German methods, the submarine has (within its limits) assiduously imitated the barbaric practices of the sister service. The War Staffs of the Central Powers are well content to horrify the world if at the same time they can terrorise it.

If, then, the Central Powers succeed, it will be to methods like these that they will owe their success. How can any form of international relations be based on a peace thus obtained? Such a peace would represent the triumph of all the forces which make war certain and make it brutal. It would advertise the futility of all the methods on which civilisation relies to eliminate the occasions of international dispute and to mitigate their ferocity. Germany and Austria made the present war inevitable by attacking the rights of one small State, and they gained their initial triumphs by violating the treaty-guarded territories of another.

Are small States going to find in them their future protectors, or in treaties made by them a bulwark against aggression? Terrorism by land and sea will have proved itself the instrument of victory. Are the victors likely to abandon it on the appeal of the neutrals? If existing treaties are no more than scraps of paper, can fresh treaties help us? If the violation of the most fundamental canons of international law be crowned with success, will it not be in vain that the assembled nations labour to improve their code? None will profit by their rules but the criminals who break them. It is those who keep them that will suffer.

Though, therefore, the people of this country share to the full the desire of the President for peace, they do not believe that peace can be durable if it be not based on the success of the allied cause. For a durable peace can hardly be expected unless three conditions are fulfilled:

DEFENCES OF NEW YORK HARBOUR.
View of Fort Totten, which is situated at Willett's Point, opposite Fort Schuyler at the entrance to Long Island Sound. The gun crews are seen at battle practice, the photograph having been taken at the moment when one of the huge mortars was about to be fired.

The first is that the existing causes of international unrest should be as far as possible removed or weakened.

The second is that the aggressive aims and the unscrupulous methods of the Central Powers should fall into disrepute among their own peoples.

The third is that behind international law, and behind all treaty arrangements for preventing or limiting hostilities, some form of international sanction should be devised which would give pause to the hardiest aggressor.

These conditions may be difficult of fulfilment. But we believe them to be in general harmony with the President's ideals, and we are confident that none of them can be satisfied, even imperfectly, unless peace be secured on the general lines indicated (so far as Europe is concerned) in the joint Note. **Conditions of durable peace** Therefore, it is that this country has made, is making, and is prepared to make, sacrifices of blood and treasure unparalleled in its history.

It bears these heavy burdens not merely that it may thus fulfil its treaty obligations, nor yet that it may secure a barren triumph of one group of nations over another. It bears them because it firmly believes that on the success of the Allies depend the prospects of peaceful civilisation, and of those international reforms which the best thinkers of the New World, as of the Old, dare to hope may follow on the cessation of our present calamities.

I am, with great truth and respect, Sir, your Excellency's most obedient, humble servant, ARTHUR JAMES BALFOUR.

Many Americans admitted that the ideas expressed

by Mr. Balfour were in the tradition that the American people had inherited from Abraham Lincoln. The only dissonant note of importance came from Mr. Bertrand Russell, who smuggled through a letter to President Wilson demanding peace without victory. The President was informed that:

However the war may be prolonged, negotiations will ultimately have to take place on the basis of what will be substantially the present balance of gains and losses, and will result in terms not very different from those which might be obtained now. The Allied Governments have not had the courage to acknowledge publicly what they cannot deny in private, that the hope of a sweeping victory is one which cannot now be obtained. Such acquiescence as there is in continued hostilities is due entirely to fear. The harm done by a peace, done by what we do not desire, is as nothing in comparison to the harm done by the continuance of the fighting.

This false and unpatriotic letter, published by the notorious anti-British newspaper owner, Mr. W. R. Hearst, in the "American" of New York, might quickly have been forgotten, as being merely a singular expression of opinion by one of those friends of every country except his own, who have been clamant in England in all great crises of modern times.

On January 22nd, 1917, however, President Wilson made a speech to the Senate in which there were curiously disturbing indications of the influence of Mr. Bertrand Russell. He said: "There must be a peace without victory. A peace forced upon the loser would leave a bitter memory — leave only a quicksand for the security of the world to rest on." Among the terms of peace that President Wilson advocated was a direct outlet to the great highways of the sea for every great people. By this he apparently meant the neutralisation of territory in a part of Turkey for the benefit of the Black Sea commerce of Russia, a similar neutralisation of Trieste for the benefit of Austro-Hungarian commerce, and possibly some direct access to the sea for an independent and autonomous Poland.

In order to induce the Allied Powers to accept peace without victory, President Wilson again brought forward the American idea of a League to Enforce Peace, with limitation of armaments and co-operation of navies. With wonderful daring he held out the expectation that the people and Government of the United States would join the other civilised nations of the world in guaranteeing the permanency of peace and applying the Monroe Doctrine to all Continents. The Americans themselves, however, immediately replied that their chief magistrate was exceeding his powers in holding out the expectation that the United States would enter the proposed league. The necessary treaties would need the sanction of Congress, and it was at the time most unlikely that the nation and its legislators would mortgage the destinies of the country in the manner suggested by the President.

The offer made by Mr. Wilson was not designed as a snare. Still, the fact remained that, in order to tempt the Allies to consent to a peace without victory, the President offered

DR. CHARLES W. ELIOT.
Ex-President of Harvard University. One of the chief leaders of the U.S. pro-Ally movement.

DR. CHARLES PARSONS.
Distinguished American chemist. Appointed on the outbreak of war chief chemist to the War Department.

MR. CHARLES M. SCHWAB.
Successively President of the Carnegie Steel Company and of the United States Steel Corporation.

HERR ZIMMERMANN.
German Foreign Secretary, November, 1916. Plotted to make Mexico attack the U.S.

them a guarantee against future wars, which guarantee he was absolutely incapable of fulfilling. He might vainly have spent the rest of his life in a political campaign to engage the forces and diplomacy of the United States in establishing the Monroe Doctrine for all the world. His offer may have had an educating influence upon American opinion, causing millions of men immersed in local affairs to ponder what great international policy their country might have to adopt in the changed and changing conditions of the modern era of instant transoceanic speech and accelerated transport of great masses of men, material, and armament. As, however, the American people had recently re-elected Mr. Wilson on the ground that he had kept them out of war, there seemed to be, to the majority of their observers, little reason for expecting they would follow their President in his strangely new and revolutionary policy in foreign affairs.

Mr. Bonar Law made an immediate reply to the proposal:

What President Wilson is longing for (he said) we are fighting for, our sons and brothers are dying for, and we mean to secure it. The hearts of the people of this country are longing for peace—a peace which will bring back in safety those who are dear to us, but a peace which will mean that those who will never come back shall not have laid down their lives in vain.

Meanwhile, there was no response in the United States to the proposal laid before the Senate. The idea of a League to Enforce Peace was generally condemned as a thing that might lead to disastrous intrigues and unnecessary wars.

The United States, when this proposal was made, was, as Mr. Lansing had said, on the verge of war. Germany was entering upon her intensified submarine campaign against both neutral and allied shipping, and the pledge given to President Wilson in May, 1916, was openly and most cynically about to be broken.

Three days before the President went to the Senate his Secret Service had accomplished one of the most dramatic coups in the history of diplomacy. Herr Zimmermann, the German Foreign Secretary, forwarded to the German Ambassador in Mexico, Herr von Eckhardt, instructions to plot against the United States. The instructions were sent in a special secret code by a devious secret channel.

Yet the brilliant American Secret Service men were able to lay before their President the following authentic instructions from Herr Zimmermann to Herr Eckhardt:

January 19th, 1917.

On February 1st we intend to begin unrestricted warfare. In spite of this it is our endeavour to keep the United States neutral. If this attempt is not successful we propose an alliance with Mexico on the following basis:

That we shall make war together, and together make peace. We shall give general financial support, and it is understood that

GUNNERS OF THE U.S. FIELD ARTILLERY.

E Battery, 5th U.S. Field Artillery, with one of its 4·7 in. guns. It formed part of the forces sent to the Mexican border in 1916 when German intrigue was fomenting trouble between Mexico and the U.S.

Mexico is to reconquer her lost territory in New Mexico, Texas, and Arizona.

Details are left to you for settlement.

You are instructed to inform the President of Mexico, or myself, in greatest confidence, as soon as it is certain there will be an outbreak of war with the United States, and suggest that the President of Mexico, on his own initiative, should communicate with Japan, suggesting adherence at once to this plan, and, at the same time, offer to mediate between Germany and Japan.

Please call the attention of the President of Mexico to the fact that the employment of ruthless submarine warfare now promises to compel Great Britain to make peace in a few months.—(Signed) ZIMMERMANN.

About the same time the American Secret Service also tapped a secret code message to Count Bernstorff, directing him to damage the engines and machinery of all German and Austrian vessels in American ports, **Germany withdraws** and thereby prevent them being used on **pledge to U.S.** the outbreak of war. It is thus clear that President Wilson's suggestion to arrange a League to Enforce Peace was little more than an impossible attempt to keep the United States out of the war.

Though in making the offer the President exceeded his constitutional powers, he at least served his people to the extreme limit of diplomatic action. The Germans, however, acted like men bent on self-destruction. As an American put it : " Again let us thank God for that when He made the Prussian He made a fool." On January 31st, 1917, the German authorities formally withdrew their pledge to President Wilson and proclaimed a new campaign of unlimited submarine piracy. But, as though intentionally to add insult to injury, Herr Zimmermann informed the American Secretary of State that one American passenger steamer would be allowed to enter Falmouth once a week, on the farcical condition that the vessel was painted with vertical stripes, three yards wide, alternating white and red, with a red-and-white checkered flag showing on each mast.

On the same day as Herr Zimmermann's Note was dispatched, Herr Bethmann-Hollweg made in the Reichstag a speech containing a blunder as disastrous to his country as the " scrap of paper " conversation by which he sought to keep Great Britain from helping Belgium. His aim in this new case was to prevent the United States from fighting for her old, sound, international sea rights. But far from attempting to placate the Americans, he went out of his way, with cynical stupidity, to inform them that he had been deceiving them.

NAVAL GUNNERS OF A U.S. BATTLESHIP.

The scheme of naval construction authorised in August, 1916, aimed at making the United States Navy the second largest in the world in every unit essential to a powerful fighting force.

President Wilson then had a difficult domestic problem. He could have brought his nation at once into the war by going to Congress and revealing Zimmermann's despatch about Mexico, and instantly deepening the impression upon the American mind made by Herr Bethmann-Hollweg's speech. Such a storm of indignation would have swept the States that war would have been declared almost within a day. For various reasons, political as well as military, the President, however, decided to act in a gradual manner. Proceeding nominally only upon the open declarations of the German authorities, he severed relations with Germany by sending away Count Bernstorff and recalling Mr. Gerard. The Senate ratified his action by seventy-eight votes against five. But there was no agitation for immediate **U.S. breaks relations** hostilities, and the possibility of war was **with Germany** generally regarded with a kind of regretful patience. The President stated that, if American ships were destroyed, he would again come before Congress—meaning, of course, that he would then ask for military powers.

Meanwhile, he clearly succeeded in carrying the country with him as far as he cared to go. This he did without revealing the German threat against the Southern and Western States. It must be remembered that only the Eastern States had ever displayed a resolute temper. These States were of Republican colour, and unrepresented in all the intimate councils of the President's own party. His power and his political organisation were founded upon the Southern, Middle, and Western States, and the

DETAILED TO JOIN THE ATLANTIC FLEET.
L2 and L9, two of the United States submarines completed in 1915, lying in dock at Norfolk, Virginia. Submarines of this and the later classes carried 3 in. guns and had large cruising range.

pacific feeling in these States was alone fully and continually expressed in all Democratic Party meetings. Naturally, therefore, the mind of the President was influenced by the views of the Senators, representatives, governors, and numerous officers of the States on which both his personal and his party power were based. When at last he was himself convinced that the employment of armed force was necessary for the honour and safety of the nation, he had still to educate the larger part of the electorate into a lively appreciation of the dangerous situation.

The United States had been called the melting-pot of the world. But in the hour of crisis its chief magistrate did not seem assured that all the main elements of the coming American race had thoroughly amalgamated into one solid new human alloy. His governing design was to prepare the future solidity of the medley of old and new settlers by gradually inducing all the sound, strong, and larger Germanic element to see the absolute need for armed and bitter conflict with the land from which they or their fathers had sprung. He knew that he could have swept most of the German-Americans abruptly into the war by revealing Herr Zimmerman's despatch to Herr Eckhardt. He did not, however, **Berlin's** want a straw fire of indignation under **calculations upset** the melting-pot, but a slow, steady, enduring flame of patriotism, coming from the inmost conscience and heart of the Germanic and all other elements.

The German authorities in Berlin appear to have been staggered by the abruptness with which President Wilson severed relations. They fell into the same error with regard to the United States in 1917 as they did in regard to Great Britain in 1914. The American department of the Foreign Office in Berlin had laboriously and learnedly studied the American temperament. Going by the Presidential election and by the successes won by Mr. Wilson by his policy of keeping the country out of the war, the German specialists in Wilhelmstrasse worked out a theory that the United States would never intervene. This extraordinary theory became one of the bases of their new submarine policy. They expected President Wilson would resume Note writing, but his instant recourse to action entirely upset the German plan. Herr Bethmann-Hollweg and Herr Zimmermann are reported to have prearranged to submit to making certain concessions to the United States, and to have employed abrupt and rough measures at the outset merely in order to intimidate the American people as much as possible, and make the later and inadequate concessions

UNITS OF A RAPIDLY-GROWING SUBMARINE FLEET.
The submarine Octopus, partly submerged, and (above) a flotilla of submarines of the United States Navy. In October, 1916, the United States had fifty submarines completed and a further twenty-four in the course of construction, while the revised programme provided for an addition of sixty-eight, of which fifty-eight were to be coast submarines, nine Fleet submarines, and one on the Neff system.

ARMED SUBMARINE CHASER.
New type of motor-boat, sixty feet long and with a speed of forty knots, privately built and offered to the United States Government as a "submarine chaser" in the spring of 1917.

appear more valuable by relieving the tension deliberately created. But in Berlin they were not aware that the details of their plot with Mexico were fully known to President Wilson, and that he was also well acquainted with every secret message of importance sent to Count Bernstorff. To use a cant phrase, Mr. Wilson had "called the bluff" of the German Foreign Office. He was in the happy position of knowing all the cards in his opponents' hands, and of possessing in Herr Zimmermann's despatch the "straight flush."

Being ignorant of this, Count Montegelas, the chief of the American department in Wilhelmstrasse, crowned all the indignities and injuries inflicted upon the United States by an amazing treatment of the American Ambassador, Mr. Gerard. There was an ancient treaty between Prussia and the United States, in which each country agreed, in case of war, to allow the merchants and other nationals of the opposing nation to trade and reside for some nine months in its territory, and freely to depart without hindrance. This treaty had not been renewed on the foundation of the German Empire. So, at the last moment, the German Government endeavoured by violence to compel Mr. Gerard to sign a new agreement, securing large commercial advantages to the Germans in the United States, protecting German boats from seizure, and all German patents, contracts, and businesses from forfeiture Mr. Gerard was held as hostage, and refused means of communicating with his Government. Count Montegelas further threatened to imprison all Americans in Germany if Mr. Gerard would not sign the treaty. "I can't be

U BOAT CHASER LYNX.
Another form of "submarine chaser" named the Lynx. This was also the outcome of private American enterprise under the impetus provided by Prussian piracy.

sand-bagged in this way," said Mr. Gerard. After a detention lasting several days he was allowed to leave Germany, and many Americans went with him.

Even this barbaric treatment of their Ambassador did not rouse the American people to action. In the middle of February, 1917, the administration leaders, in both the Senate and the House of Representatives, warned the President that if he went to Congress to obtain a declaration of war against Germany the declaration probably would not be given. Even if a resolution were carried, the discussion, it was calculated, would reveal so strong an opposition as would have encouraged the enemy, and perhaps provoked outbursts of Teutonic rebellion. Large forces of pacifists, under Mr. W. J. Bryan, were acting more or less loosely with the German organisations, and spending money abundantly in the leading newspapers and other directions. Amid the somewhat sinister resurgence and extension of all the forces of pacifism that occurred at the time when German reservists in the United States were crowding into Mexico, Germany tried to reopen negotiations for means of assuring the safety of American shipping To the proposal, which was made through the Swiss Minister, President Wilson replied that he could not resume negotiations unless the German Government restored the pledge they had given in May, 1916.

U.S. public opinion apathetic

About this time two American ships, the Housatonic and the Lyman M. Law, were sunk by Teutonic submarines. Then, on February 25th, 1917, the Cunard liner Laconia was sunk off the Irish coast with the loss of the lives of two American citizens. These were clearly overt acts of hostility, and on February 26th President Wilson returned to Congress and asked for powers to protect the shipping of the country. He met with strong

DESIGNED TO MEET THE UNDERSEA PIRATES.
Side view of the Lynx. This little vessel, of which it was estimated large numbers of sister-vessels could be turned out very rapidly by American shipyards, had a length of about thirty-nine feet.

opposition. Strongly then he countered both the pacifists and the disloyalists by publishing the despatch sent on January 19th by the German Foreign Minister to the German Ambassador in Mexico City. The effect of the disclosures was to unite the Eastern, Middle, Southern, and Western States in earnest preparation for war. Had Herr Zimmermann been a traitor to his own country, he could not have done more to injure Germany and to benefit the United States than he accomplished by his idle and senseless attempt at a Mexican-Japanese plot. Had he kept to the bare possibility of the situation and arranged to subsidise an insignificant Mexican invasion of American territory, he would not greatly have disturbed the popular mind. But all along the Pacific coast there had for years been a certain fear of Japanese action. It was because Japan was leagued with the Allied Powers that a majority of the people of the Pacific States looked coldly upon the cause of the Allies and partly inclined to hope for something like a German victory. In wildly and foolishly proposing that Japan should be detached from the Grand Alliance by Mexico, the German Foreign Minister made himself ridiculous, and yet alarmed the

MONSTER SEARCHLIGHT OF THE AMERICAN ARMY.
Huge travelling searchlight which could be moved about on rails. America was able to boast the possession of the largest searchlight in the world. The lens shown above was between five and six feet in diameter.

Western States and turned there the current of unenlightened popular opinion violently against Germany.

The result was that when a remnant of pro-German and pacifist Senators defeated President Wilson's measure of armed neutrality in the Senate, by the sorry device of talking out the Bill, the educative process in the nation was completed. "A little group of wilful men, representing no opinion but their own," said President Wilson in an unwonted mood of anger, "have made the great Government of the United States helpless and contemptible." More than five hundred out of the five hundred and thirty-one members of the two Houses were ready and anxious to take action against the Central Empires. Means, therefore, were quickly devised to restore to the overwhelming majority of legislators their usurped rights. The Senate passed, by seventy-six votes to three, a new closure rule which completely crippled the power of the small band of malignants. American vessels were armed with guns, provided with picket-boats for launching against submarines when approaching the danger zone, and sent out to encounter German and Austrian submarines.

With intense yet quiet energy the most powerful industrial and financial State in the world, with a population of a hundred million, organised itself for war against the piratical Central Empires. No declaration of war was at first made, but the work of practical co-operation with the Allied Powers was rapidly carried on. The Allies were in no immediate need of military help, and the American people was not in a position to afford such help. Great Britain, France, and Italy were sufficiently strong on land and on the surface of the seas. What they needed was food, metal, and general supplies of military material. To some extent they also needed financial aid, and this the United States could lavishly provide. It seemed as though the American nation had only to maintain a large and regular Transatlantic traffic, in despite of the enemy's submarine operations, in order powerfully to assist in the ultimate defeat of the anarchists of Central Europe and Asia Minor. The intervention of the United States appeared to mark a turning-point in the history of civilisation. It was pregnant with noble possibilities of development in the international problems of the future, and it promised to prove finally decisive of the issue of the war, provided in the meantime that the British Navy and the British people succeeded in defeating the methods of submarine piracy by which the enemy sought to starve the Allies into submission.

United States prepares for war

The inaugural address of President Wilson on March 5th, 1917, had that quality of strange quietness and soberness with which the race, usually the loudest in the world, turns to some heavy and grim task. "We are provincials no longer," said the President. "The tragical events of thirty months of vital turmoil through which we have just passed have made us citizens of the world." In this reticent way the chief magistrate of the United States burst through the political traditions held from the age of Washington and prepared to make common cause with the Entente Powers.

The Federal Reserve Board which, as late as November, 1916, had prohibited American banks from investing in foreign loans, withdrew the restriction, and thus enabled the Allies to obtain vast financial aid. Then, largely under American influence, the Chinese Government severed diplomatic relations with Germany and began to seize German ships. The Cuban Government likewise proceeded towards a working alliance against the Teutons. For it was revealed about the middle of March that the Cuban rising under the former President, Gomez, had been engineered by Germany, partly in the general design to embarrass the American Government, and with the more particular aim of establishing submarine bases near the American coast. One point, a hundred and fifty miles from Florida, had especially been chosen by the Teuton plotters as a centre of operations against American commerce. Just as this revelation added the last flames of anger to the fire of indignation caused by the exposure of the Mexican plot, and quickened the war feeling in the Southern States, whose sea-borne traffic would have been seriously menaced by secret German submarine bases in Cuba, news of the Russian Revolution removed all cause of hesitation from the mind of the American democracy.

From the outbreak of war the powerful and tentacular influence of German-American Jewish finance had told heavily against the Allies. Many Russian Jewish settlers in America, who sympathised more or less with the aims of the Entente, were bent into a show of pro-Germanism by pressure from their stronger brethren in the synagogues, who were working with the masterful Hebrews of Germany. Memories of Russian pogroms and Russian oppressions weighed indeed upon all Hebrews. Even in Great Britain some of the most brilliant of Jews continued to protest against such enlightened and tolerant people as the British and French leaguing themselves with the "dark forces"

Attitude of the Jews

President Wilson reviewing some of the State troops of New Jersey during the United States Army manœuvres. When a state of war with Germany was declared the President was emphatic in calling for a conscript army.

Machine-gun detachment of the United States Army at practice. Boxes, it will be seen, were carried which served the purpose of gun-rests when firing from a prone position in open country.

Cadets undergoing a course of training to take their places as officers of the United States Army. They were receiving instruction in the use of the 10 in. disappearing gun which was employed by the artillery entrusted with the coast defences of America. In circle: Men of the United States infantry at drill beside one of the powerful anti-aircraft guns with which the American Army was provided.

MEN OF THE UNITED STATES ARMY IN PREPARATION FOR ACTIVE SERVICE.

U.S. COUNCIL OF NATIONAL DEFENCE AND ADVISORY COMMITTEE.
Seated (from left): David F. Houston, Secretary of Agriculture; Josephus Daniels, Secretary of the Navy; Newton D. Baker, Secretary of War; Franklin K. Lane, Secretary of the Interior; William B. Wilson, Secretary of Labour. Standing (from left): Grosvenor B. Clarke, Secretary of the Council; Julius Rosenwald, Chairman of Committee on Supplies; Bernard M. Baruch, Raw Materials; Daniel Willard, Transportation; Dr. F. H. Matlin, Medicine and Sanitation; Dr. Hollis Godfrey, Science and Research; Howard Coffin, Munitions; and W. S. Gifford, Director of the Council.

of his Hebrew subjects beyond the high social pale and refusing them the privileges of gentlemen.

The contrast between the instant magnanimity of free Russia and the subtle exclusiveness of autocratic Germany produced a profound change of opinion among the leaders of the American Jews. Powerful financial houses, such as Kühn, Loeb & Company, at once proclaimed themselves allies of the European democracies. In the previous month there had been some dangerous food riots in New York, where there was a large Jewish population, and it was known that the most active rioters and some of the principal food speculators had worked under Germanic influence. The design was to induce Congress to place an embargo on the exportation of foodstuffs, and thereby aid the murderous campaign of German submarines and increase the difficulty of rationing Great Britain, France, and Italy. Even in the second week of March there had been thousands of clamorous Germanic agents in

of Russia. The sudden liberation of the Russian people, with the complete enfranchisement of the Russian Hebrews, fired the imagination of the American Jews. They began to direct their contempt and anger towards the military caste of Germany, which still kept all save the most highly-placed Hebrews in a social ghetto, while professing that only the Russian bureaucracy was so sunk in mediæval barbarism as to refuse full rights of civilisation to men of all religions. The German governing class had merely been more skilful and more tactful than the reactionaries of Russia. While refraining from massacre, and using German-Jewish finance as a weapon of national aggression, they had retained the Jew under a system of ostracism. The treacherous Kaiser had patronised a few very successful German Jews, such as Ballin, Rathenau, Dernburg, and Bleichröder, because he recognised they were among the main instruments of Teutonic power. Nevertheless, he maintained the general system of keeping the majority

New York who openly continued the plot against President Wilson, and accused him of starving his own people in order to feed the armies of the Allies. There was some natural stringency in breadstuffs and vegetables, owing to bad weather and bad harvests; but the partial failure of crops had been transformed into an artificial instrument of economic attack against Great Britain, France, and Italy. When the success of the Russian Revolution was announced the food riots almost ceased. A still more formidable general railway strike, which would have stopped the export of munitions and other supplies, was also prevented. The American people were excited to an ecstasy of political fervour by the abrupt and inspiring birth of an immense new democracy. They dreamt noble dreams and saw glorious visions of a universal confraternity of democracies being wrought into practical and lasting shape in their own lifetime.

Failure of the plotters

SENATOR ROOT.
Who declared that no nation had a greater stake in the success of the Allies than had the United States.

SENATOR LODGE.
Well-known Republican leader, who warmly advocated the fighting policy of the United States.

MR. W. H. TAFT.
Who immediately preceded President Wilson as President of the United States, occupying the position 1909-1913.

EMINENT REPUBLICAN LEADERS WHO SUPPORTED PRESIDENT WILSON'S WAR POLICY.

President Wilson was deeply stirred by the unexpected Russian miracle. He at once shortened, by two weeks, the date for the convening of Congress and the declaration of war against Germany. On April 2nd he asked Congress to declare that a state of war existed between the United States and Germany. In an address that ranked with the most famous declarations of Lincoln he carried the country with him in a crusade against all the forces of Prussianism that had perverted the soul of the Germanic race. Abandoning the policy of armed neutrality which he had advocated on February 26th, 1917, he preached full and strenuous war against the enemies of mankind. He said:

There is one choice we cannot make and are incapable of making. We will not choose the path of submission and suffer the most sacred rights of our nation and our people to be ignored and violated. The wrongs against which we now array ourselves are not common wrongs; they cut to the very root of human life.

With a profound sense of the solemn event and the tragical character of the step I am taking, and of the grave responsibilities which it involves, but in unhesitating obedience to what I deem my constitutional duty, I advise that Congress declare that the recent course of the Imperial German Government to be in fact nothing less than war against the Government and people of the United States, that it formally accepts the status of a belligerent which is thus thrust upon it, and that it take immediate steps, not only to put the country in a more thorough state of defence, but also to exert all its power and to employ its resources to bring the Government of the German Empire to terms and end the war.

President Wilson's historic address

We are at the beginning of an age in which it will be insisted that the same standards of conduct and responsibility for wrong done shall be observed among nations and their Governments that are observed among individual citizens of civilised States. We have not quarrelled with the German people. We have no feeling towards them but one of sympathy and friendship. It was not upon their impulse that their Government acted in entering this war. It was not with their previous knowledge or approval.

It was a war determined upon as wars used to be determined upon in the old unhappy days when people were nowhere consulted by their rulers, and wars were provoked and waged in the interest

PRESIDENT WOODROW WILSON AND HIS CABINET.
Back row (left to right): President Wilson; William G. McAdoo, Secretary of the Treasury; Thomas W. Gregory, Attorney-General; Josephus Daniels, Secretary of the Navy; David F. Houston, Secretary of Agriculture; William B. Wilson, Secretary of Labour. Front row (left to right): Robert Lansing, Secretary of State; Newton D. Baker, Secretary of War; Albert S. Burleson, Postmaster-General; Franklin K. Lane, Secretary of the Interior; William C. Redfield, Secretary of Commerce.

of dynasties, or little groups of ambitious men, who were accustomed to use their fellow-men as pawns and tools. Self-governed nations do not fill their neighbour States with spies, or set in course an intrigue to bring about some critical posture of affairs which would give them an opportunity to strike and make a conquest. Such designs can be successfully worked only under cover, where no one has a right to ask questions. Cunningly contrived plans of deception or impression, carried, it may be, from generation to generation, can be worked out and kept from light only within the privacy of Courts or behind the carefully-guarded confidences of a narrow, privileged class. They are happily impossible where public opinion commands and insists upon full information concerning all the nation's affairs.

A steadfast concert for peace can never be maintained except by the partnership of democratic nations. No autocratic Government could be trusted to keep faith within it or observe its covenants. There must be a league of honour and partnership of opinion. Intrigue would eat its vitals away. Plottings by inner circles, who would plan what they would and render an account to no one, would be corruption seated at its very heart. Only free peoples can hold their purpose and their honour steady to the common end, and prefer the interests of mankind to the narrow interests of their own.

Does not every American feel that assurance has been added to

MR. JOSEPH H. CHOATE.
U.S. Ambassador to Great Britain, 1899-1905. He represented the United States at the Second Hague Conference.

COLONEL HOUSE.
An intimate friend of President Wilson, who sent him as a private emissary to Germany and Great Britain in 1916.

WILLIAM G. McADOO.
Secretary of the United States Treasury in President Wilson's Cabinet, who introduced the first War Budget in 1917.

THREE REPRESENTATIVE AMERICAN CITIZENS WHO STOOD HIGH IN BRITISH ESTIMATION.

MR. G. W. GOETHALS.
Appointed to direct the construction of 1,000 wooden merchantmen for the United States.

ADMIRAL SIMS.
Special Envoy from the United States to confer with the British Naval Board on naval co-operation.

known any other fealty or allegiance. They will be prompt to stand with us in rebuking and restraining the few who may be of different mind and purpose. If there should be disloyalty it will be dealt with with the firm hand of stern repression, but, if it lifts its head at all, it will lift it only here and there, and without countenance, except from the lawless and malignant few.

It is a distressing and oppressive duty, gentlemen of Congress, which I have performed in thus addressing you. There are, it may be, many months of fiery trial and sacrifice ahead of us. It is a fearful thing to lead this great and peaceful people into war, into the most terrible and disastrous of all wars. Civilisation itself seems to be in the balance, but right is more precious than peace, and we shall fight for the things which we have always carried nearest our hearts, for democracy, for the right of those who submit to authority to have a voice in their own government, for the rights and liberties of small nations, for the universal domination of right by such a concert of free peoples as will bring peace and safety to all nations, and make the world itself at last free.

To such a task we can dedicate our lives, our fortunes, everything we are, everything we have, with the pride of those who know the day has come when America is privileged to spend her blood and might for the principles that gave her birth and the happiness and peace which she has treasured. God helping her, she can do no other.

The distinction which President Wilson made in his address between the autocratic German Government and the unfree German people was a stroke of policy of the

our hope for the future peace of the world by the wonderful heartening things that have been happening within the last few weeks in Russia? Russia was known by those who knew her best to have been always in fact democratic at heart in all her vital habits, in her thought, and in all intimate relations of her people that spoke of their natural instinct and their habitual attitude towards life. The autocracy that crowned the summit of her political structure, long as it had stood and terrible as it was in the reality of its power, was not in fact Russian in origin, character, or purpose, and now it has been shaken, and the great, generous Russian people have been added in all their native majesty and might to the forces that are fighting for freedom in the world, for justice, and for peace. Here is a fit partner for a league of honour.

It will be easier for us to conduct ourselves as belligerents in a high spirit of right and fairness because we act without animus, not in enmity towards a people, or with a desire to bring any injury or disadvantage upon them, but only in **Friends of the German people** armed opposition to an irresponsible Government, which has thrown aside all considerations of humanity and right, and is running amok.

We are, let me say again, sincere friends of the German people, and shall desire nothing so much as an early re-establishment of intimate relations to our mutual advantage.

However hard it may be for them for the time being to believe this, it is spoken from our hearts. We have borne with their present Government through all these bitter months, because of that friendship, exercising patience and forbearance which otherwise would have been impossible. We shall happily still have an opportunity to prove that friendship in our daily attitude and actions towards millions of men and women of German birth and native sympathy who live amongst us and share our life, and we shall be proud to prove it towards all who in fact are loyal to their neighbours and to the Government in the hour of test. They are most of them as true and loyal Americans as if they had never

REAR-ADMIRAL GRANT.
Commanding the Submarine Division of the United States Navy.

ADMIRAL GLEAVES.
Commanding the Destroyer Division of the United States Navy.

highest skill. It was directly intended for the large, hesitant, and powerful body of German-Americans who were either descended from immigrants rebellious to Prussian rule or were themselves men and women who had left the Central Empires in search of more freedom.

BRIG.-GENERAL CLARENCE EDWARDS.
Commanding the North-Eastern Department of the New England States.

ADMIRAL BENSON.
Chief of Staff of the United States Navy.

ADMIRAL FLETCHER.
Commander of the Second Atlantic Squadron of the United States Navy.

SOME PROMINENT FIGURES IN THE UNITED STATES SERVICES AT THE OUTBREAK OF WAR.

Scene on a United States battleship, showing types of the sailors, Marines, and chief petty-officers. The United States Navy is manned by voluntary enlistment, and the total number of enlisted men in the Navy and Marines at the end of 1916 was 67,644. On the right : Looking down on the after-deck and fighting-tops of the Nevada, a Dreadnought completed in January, 1915.

The Dreadnought Utah going at full speed with oil fuel. The designed horse-power of the Utah, launched in 1911, was 28,000, equivalent to a speed of 20·75 knots. Left : The Brooklyn, a first-class armoured cruiser launched in 1895.

United States battleships in line formation. In October, 1916, America's strength in battleships was thirty-seven, with five building and four included in the new programme. The projected battleships were to have a displacement of 32,600 tons, a speed of 21 knots, an armament of eight 16 in. guns, eighteen 5 in. guns, and four 3 in. anti-aircraft guns, and an exceptionally large cruising range.

SOME DREADNOUGHTS AND BATTLE-CRUISERS OF THE UNITED STATES NAVY.

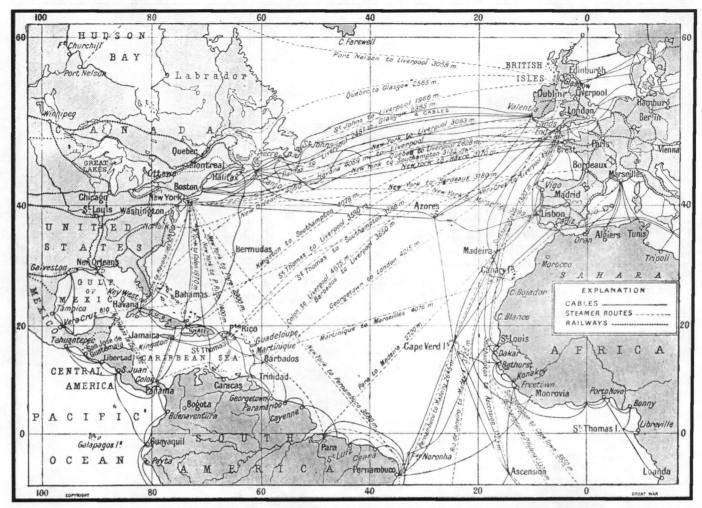

MAP SHOWING THE COMMUNICATIONS BETWEEN AMERICA AND EUROPE.

On this map may be seen the principal steamer routes and distances from Europe to the United States and South American ports, and also the cable lines.

Upon both of these classes President Wilson's policy told with considerable effect, as they were well aware of the fact that the spirit of the German military caste, displayed at Zabern before the war, remained throughout the struggle the ruling factor in the Fatherland.

In addition to the direct intention of the President's policy, there was an indirect appeal to the German people to bring the war to an end by following the example of the Russians and establishing a democracy. The bitter violence with which the Government-controlled German Press vituperated the President of the United States seemed to show that the shaft he aimed had gone home. Though the Germans remained far more docile than the Russians, the moral effect of the great address was felt throughout the world. To the Allies it was a refreshment and a renewed inspiration, confirming them in the high ideas with which they had entered the war. At last all the great democracies of the earth stood solid and four-square against the restrictive and degrading principles of government of the Central Empires, the Ottoman Empire, and Bulgaria. The pro-German governing class of Sweden was shaken with a double wind of liberty blowing from Russia and the United States. Most of the strong commonwealths of South America, which had been continually recalcitrant to the leadership of the United States, began to feel the influence of President Wilson's fine mind, and Brazil, on April 9th, being strongly attached to the Republic of Portugal, broke off diplomatic relations with the outlaws of civilisation.

In the meantime, Congress, by overwhelming majorities in both Houses, voted for military operations. National guards were called out to defend Government and munition works, railways and military depots ; plans were pushed forward for an immense loan and the financing of the Allies ; the output of merchant ships was speeded up, and flotillas of submarine chasers were devised to assist the British and French Navies. A large army on the Continental scale was planned, and the great munition works of the United States were further extended. Everything that could possibly be done to quicken the organisation of the striking power of the country was done by the enemy. The German Press, German agents, and Hindenburg himself jeered at the American effort, and foretold it would come too late to determine the issue of the war. The destruction of American steamers increased, and the first blow against an American liner occurred in the first week of April, 1917. In these circumstances the great federal State accelerated her preparations for war, throwing her entire strength into the contest and breaking with Austria-Hungary while arming for battle with Germany.

The German jeers at the intervention of the United States were really an expression of profound nervousness. Like Figaro in Beaumarchais' play, the enemy laughed to prevent himself from weeping. He knew that his grand stake in the world was lost, and that an overwhelming tide of all the democratic forces of mankind was sweeping against him. The instant effect of the decision of the American Government was to clarify the atmosphere of battle and make it clear to every nation that the struggle was a final, era-marking conflict between autocracy and democracy. The peoples of France, Belgium, Great Britain, and Italy had long known the true character of the contest ; yet they had sometimes been hard put to it to make plain the absolute purity of their motives.

Their alliance with the Russian autocracy, notorious for political and religious persecution, had tended to obscure the democratic nature of the struggle, so that Socialist organisations in the principal neutral States and in some of the Entente countries had been able, subtly and somewhat treacherously, to confuse the large and righteous issue of the war.

The Revolution in Russia and the conversion of the American people made everything plain. From Brazil and Bolivia, and from other South American States, as well as from the populace of parts of neutral Europe, there came, in deep waves of fighting democratic sentiment, an increasing strengthening of the cause of the Allies. The Allies themselves were then much in need of help of both spiritual and material kind. The armies of free Russia were enfeebled by the disorganisation of anarchistic and traitorous agitators. There was danger that the massed might of the Central Empires would be almost entirely directed against Italy, France, and Great Britain. The peoples of these countries were beginning to suffer from shortage of food, and though their moral power remained high and firm, the strain was growing very severe. France had no great store of men in reserve ; Italy expected a terrific attack by Germans as well as Austrians ; Great Britain was seriously menaced by submarine operations, and in extreme need of more shipping.

In these circumstances the action of President Wilson, and the magnificent support he received from both Congress and country, proved a blessing and a confirmation to the struggling democracies of Europe. It nerved them for the grand battles of the third year of war, and while producing at the time little direct change in the military

Moral effect of U.S. action

TESTING A "CATERPILLAR." Armoured "caterpillar" car, made by a private American firm, undergoing practical tests before its adoption for military purposes.

situation, afforded immediate relief in other directions. In the first place, the problem of financing the war to a victorious conclusion was definitely solved. The British people were lightened of their heaviest burden, just at the time when the strain of their money and money-making resources was becoming grave. The national income of the United States had reached the enormous figure of ten thousand million pounds a year, which was five times the annual income of Germany. The annual balance of trade was more than six hundred million pounds. Such was the glut of gold that the banks were in a position to make a loan of fourteen hundred million pounds sterling, on the basis of their gold reserves, by putting out notes without any further authorisation or legislation. The American Government, therefore, was at once enabled to make arrangements for a loan of this enormous size, and provide the Allies with a separate sum of six hundred million pounds at the remarkably low interest of 3½ per cent.

Consequently, all the available material resources of the mighty Commonwealth were unlocked, at reduced prices, for Britain, France, Italy, and Russia. Not only was the export of gold made unnecessary, but more labour in many exporting industries in the Entente countries was set free for recruiting and other military purposes. There was

Immediate material gains

no longer any immediate vital need for Great Britain to check the progress of her armies through lack of reinforcements, as occurred in the Somme campaign, in order to maintain an unparalleled outflow of manufactures wherewith to purchase American materials of war for herself and for her Allies. When Sir William Robertson called for another

TAKING A STIFF BANK. On its demonstration trials the "caterpillar" had to prove its fitness for going over rough ground and diverse obstacles.

EXPERIMENTAL TRIALS OF AN AMERICAN "TANK" RECRUIT. This "caterpillar" tractor—suggested by such tractors as had been employed in logging camps—was armoured and adapted for military purposes by a private American firm. Inventors and capitalists were given full scope in adapting such ideas to war-time needs.

h

half a million men to sustain and increase the force with which Sir Douglas Haig was battering the Hindenburg line, it was at last possible to diminish the manufacturing output of his country and organise its man-power, in the French fashion, entirely for direct war needs. The United States became the new Atlas of finance, that sustained on broad, strong shoulders the Allies' power of universal import.

In the second place, the United States, while ensuring the ultimate economic defeat of the Teutons, was able to give equally important help in overcoming the effects of the enemy's campaign of submarine piracy. As Mr. Lloyd George stated in the fine speech in which he welcomed the new ally, shipping had become the chief instrument of victory. Great Britain then knew she had made tragic mistakes in wasting her merchant ships in aimless adventures, while reducing her construction of tonnage from 1,200,000 net tons in 1913 to 410,000 tons in 1915. Upon the sum of this series of perilous errors the enemy had built his hopes of starving out the Western Allies and impoverishing their fighting forces. The entrance of America into the war promised to relieve the tension in shipping, and eventually to retrieve the errors of the old British War Cabinet.

In the ports of the United States were interned about

RECONCILIATION !

On April 19th, 1917, on the occasion of the Anglo-American service at St. Paul's Cathedral, the Union Jack and the Stars and Stripes flew together over the Houses of Parliament at Westminster. Speaking in 1887, John Bright declared that an alliance between America and Great Britain would be one of the greatest factors for peace the world had ever known.

HOSTS AND GUESTS AT AN ANGLO-AMERICAN GATHERING.

On April 12th, 1917, the Americans in London gave a luncheon to the Prime Minister, Mr. Lloyd George, at the Savoy Hotel. From left : The Italian Ambassador (Marquis Imperiali di Francavilla), Mr. Lloyd George, the United States Ambassador (Dr. Walter H. Page), Colonel H. W. Thornton, of the Engineer and Railway Staff Corps, and Director of Inland Waterways, who came from America in 1914 to be manager of the Great Eastern Railway.

one hundred and five German and Austrian vessels, totalling 622,513 tons. Then in the ports of Brazil, which was following the northern Republic into the war, were another forty-nine enemy vessels, aggregating 250,000 tons. Few of these ships were ready for service. Some of them had been damaged by the crews ; others had been crippled by the removal of vital parts of the machinery ; the rest were temporarily injured by long detention in harbour and lack of care. Among them, however, were some of the largest liners of the Norddeutscher-Lloyd and the Hamburg-Amerikan Line, forming magnificent transports or hospital ships, and capable of being fitted for sea in a few months by American repairing yards.

In addition to their vast haul of hostile shipping the American people possessed 3,300,000 tons of Atlantic and Pacific shipping. Furthermore, they had very large fleets of steamers on the Great Lakes, including many vessels serviceable in good weather for Transatlantic traffic. The resources of American shipyards and engine-rooms had been greatly developed during the war, and were again speeded-up for the production of steel-built freighters. No doubt all this had been foreseen by Hindenburg and Ludendorff and their Staff when they decided that the cost of provoking American hostility would be well repaid by the immediate chances of starving out Great Britain, France, and Italy. The German commanders, however, did not allow for the inventiveness of the American mind. As soon as the Americans saw that they were about to be drawn into the struggle, they attacked, in a surprising manner, the fundamental shipping problem which underlay all the troubles of the Western Allies. The problem was to get the surplus harvest of Northern America to Great Britain, France, and Italy early in the autumn of 1917, when all Europe would be hungering for corn. The enemy reckoned that his submarine operations would so seriously reduce all shipping as to hold up the bulk of American foodstuffs. The Federal Shipping Board, however, accepted a striking proposal made by a New York mining engineer, and engaged Colonel Goethals, the builder of the Panama Canal, to organise the new scheme for countering the results of Teutonic piracy. The scheme consisted in reviving the American industry of timber-built ships, and making use of all the apparently antiquated clipper-building yards, in order to obtain, from September, 1917, a monthly output of 200,000 tons of wooden ships. These ships were to be engined with oil-driven motors and armed for defence. Unlike iron or steel cargo-ships, which were big tin cans that sank when holed, the wooden freighters were designed to float, by the natural buoyancy of their timber-work, even when they had sustained considerable damage. Thus they promised to prove difficult opponents for any enemy submarines that attacked by means of gun fire, as their primitive material made the sinking of them an expensive task. One thousand ships of this kind were planned, under technical conditions enabling rapid

Inventiveness of American genius

Fight on a hillside. "Blue" infantry making for the cover of a wall, the "Red" enemy holding a commanding position on the edge of a thicket. Right: Officers engaged in placing skirmishers.

Advancing in rushes towards an enemy position in heavily-timbered ground—a thrilling moment even in peace manœuvres. The conditions under which troops performed this perilous operation in the Great War, heavily cumbered and through devastating artillery fire, rendered the progress slow.

MILITARY MANŒUVRES IN THE UNITED STATES: BATTLE BETWEEN THE "REDS" AND "BLUES."

WATCH AND WARD OVER THE HOOSAC TUNNEL.
U.S. soldiers searched all trains before allowing them to enter the Hoosac tunnel on the Boston and Maine Railway, in case any German agents should attempt the destruction of that great engineering work. The tunnel, which has a length of four miles and three-quarters, is the largest in New England

Navy barely had sufficient of these light craft of the newest type to cover their capital ships in any general action near a hostile base. Happily, the American shore was far removed from all German war ports, so that the harm enemy submarines could do in American waters seemed to be limited. U boats could not remain more than a few days on the other side of the Atlantic, unless they possessed secret local bases or secret relief-ships. Off the ports of the United States they could be fought by nets, mines, and patrols and a few quick-firing guns.

It was, expected that some ocean-going German submarines would be used to alarm the American population, and induce them to press for naval material to be wasted on purely defensive schemes. The U.S.A. admirals, however, were stern and scientific fighters. Though their politicians had not fully provided them with the light craft especially needed in the latest kind of warfare, they began to invent and improvise naval surprises for the enemy of mankind. Co-operation with the Allies was seen to be essential to success, and Admiral Sims, a brilliant American

use to be made of both the United States and Canadian forests

This surprising modernisation of the wooden ship had the additional merit of conserving the enormous steel production of the United States for other useful purposes. Among these was the creation of an improved type of submarine chaser, of which scores were ordered. As we have already seen, the intervention of the U.S.A. Navy did not immediately add any decisive factor to the critical anti-submarine campaign of the Allies. The American Fleet had developed battleship strength somewhat out of proportion to fast light-cruiser and destroyer strength. In the new anti-submarine warfare warships of a light and quick class were the principal weapons of the offensive-defensive necessary to save the mercantile marine of the world. The U.S.A.

Fighting quality of the U.S. Navy

OFF INLAND OUT OF HARM'S WAY.
Crews of German raiders were at first interned at League Island, Navy Yard, Philadelphia; but, warned by plots menacing the naval station, the U.S.A. authorities removed them to Fort McPherson, Atlanta, Georgia.

strategist, visited London early in April to consult with Sir John Jellicoe. Arrangements were made for the United States Navy to patrol the waters from Nova Scotia to the Caribbean Sea, to act with allied vessels in policing the Atlantic against commerce-destroyers, and to assist the allied fleets in European waters. In any naval engagement between the forces of barbarism and civilisation the addition of the United States Navy made assured success surer.

In fighting strength the American Fleet was the third in the world. It ranked somewhat below that of the German Fleet in material, and had the further disadvantage of lacking the battle experience of Admiral von Scheer's personnel; but the men were inspired by the true sea spirit, and their officers, inheriting the glorious tradition of Farragut, were keen and resourceful. When the American Fleet was proposed for employment as one of the main branches of the naval forces of the democracies of Europe

GERMAN RAIDERS ARRIVING AT FORT McPHERSON.
Captain Thierfelder, of the Kronprinz Wilhelm (with hand in pocket) and his aide, with Major Wise, who conducted the Germans to Fort McPherson —the first internment camp in the United States.

the general strength of strangling sea-power arrayed against the Central Empires became for the time immense beyond public calculation. For, as the forces of the Grand Fleet of Great Britain were unknown in a general way, no estimate could be given of the comparative value of the additional capital ships, cruisers, and destroyers which the great Republic added to the common strength available for fleet action.

With regard to the fourth chief means by which the United States could assist the Allies, her available resources were insignificant and yet tremendous. As a military State the Republic was actually weak and potentially strong. She possessed only another "contemptible little army," which, however, could gradually be developed into a host of five million and more fighting men. She had at first to act as Great Britain had acted between the retreat from Mons and the advance on the Somme, and afford her Allies great help in finance, shipping, munitions, and naval affairs while building up a national army. This army, when it was absolutely non-existent, still helped to govern the general military situation. For in the spring of 1917 it formed one of the main allied reserves for 1918. At first sight the condition of the American Army seemed deplorable. Including the militia, which was unfit for service, it numbered less than a quarter of a million men. The regular force was so small that many authorities doubted whether it would be safe to send a single army corps quickly to France.

For three years Major-General Leonard Wood had endeavoured to rouse the country to the need of national defence by a campaign of enlightenment similar to that which Lord Roberts had vainly carried out in Great Britain. As former Chief of Staff, General Wood could speak with patriotic authority to his fellow-citizens, but he evoked as little general response as did Lord Roberts. Only in the universities did General Wood produce any effect of importance. University training corps were formed, in which fine material for the cadres of a national army was collected ; but the number of trained officers with active service experience was very small. The regular troops were too few even for an expedition across the southern frontier, and the second line was weak and lacking in training. It was foreseen that, in order to create a national army capable of being used within a year against the **Profiting by British** veteran German troops, most of the **experience** regular force would have to be retained in the country to train and stiffen the large body of recruits. The U.S.A. Government intended to profit by British experience, and raise its forces in masses of half millions until victory was achieved. In its population of a hundred million souls man-power was abundant. Weapons were also plentiful, as American munition factories had expanded in a gigantic way under the stimulus of orders from the Allies.

At this time the direct military effort of the United States was a matter of secondary importance. Even had a large, perfectly-trained army been available, its transport across the Atlantic would have been an affair of great difficulty. The danger of the passage of American troops to Europe, by reason of the intensification of the enemy's submarine operations, would not have checked the movement. But the troops, with their armament and supplies, would have required so many ships that the aim of the enemy would almost have been achieved, and the populations of Great Britain, France, and Italy would have starved for want of shipping. It was sufficient for the immediate occasion that the United States stood behind the Allies as an immense reservoir of fighting men, while her Fleet, her mercantile marine, and her shipyards actively contended against the underwater assassins.

Transcending all the actual and potential reinforcements brought by the American democracies to the fighting democracies of Europe were the political possibilities of the new international situation. The design upon which

the leaders of the great Republic entered the war extended far beyond the immediate military issue of the struggle. In one way it might have been said, as an English poet put it, that the sons were coming home. The people of Brazil turned to Portugal, the people of the United States turned to Great Britain, and the Spanish populations of the larger part of Central and Southern America began to look eagerly for their mother country—Spain—to join them in the crusade for civilisation.

Over the reconciliation of the two great English-speaking federations the spirits of Chatham and Burke brooded prophetically. The common rich heritage, from the ages of Drake and Shakespeare, Cromwell and Milton, had been at last developed by diverse ways towards a community of larger and higher sentiments, principles, and ends. Though a union of the two **A democratic League** systems would have practically formed a **of Honour** controlling power on earth, neither side regarded such a design as entirely admirable. Something larger, nobler, and more universal, including all the Allies and all stable free nations, appeared to be adumbrated. The first American scheme of a League to Enforce Peace was modified into a League of Honour between all democracies. As the lines of the plan became curiously vaguer the feeling that inspired the plan grew stronger and more definite. Above the fiery thunderclouds of battle there seemed to break faintly the light of a larger day than the contending races of men had yet known. Visionary it still seemed as the guns rang over the Hindenburg line ; yet was it an inspiration to every free man struggling against the last autocracies of Europe.

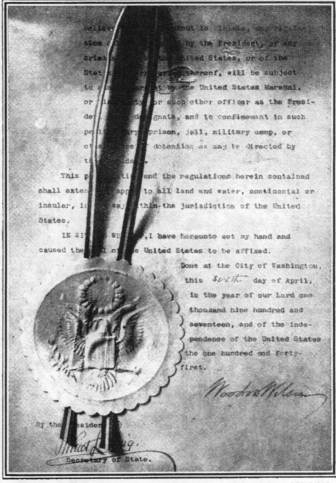

THE MOST MOMENTOUS DEED IN AMERICAN HISTORY.
President Woodrow Wilson's signature to the Declaration of War, sealed with the seal of the United States and attested by Robert Lansing, Secretary of State.

THE LAST SALUTE: TOUCHING TRIBUTE OF ITALIAN TROOPS TO A COMRADE WHO GAVE HIS LIFE FOR HIS COUNTRY.

A deep religious sense of duty inspires the Italian soldier, who feels that the most fitting commemoration of his dead will be to carry on the battle of the comrades whose bodies lie in the wake of the advance. "Remember your dead!" was a cry that often rose above the roar of the battles on the Italian mountain fronts and on the Carso. The Italian artist Signor Amato here portrays a touching scene peculiar to Italian warfare. A soldier had fallen wounded outside a trench, in so exposed a position that it was impossible to bring him in. When he finally expired his comrades lined up and presented arms in honour of his heroism.

CHAPTER CLXXIV.

THE GREAT BATTLE OF THE CARSO.

By Dr. James Murphy.

Preparation for the Second Phase of the Austro-Italian Campaign—Trieste the Objective—Italian Series of Offensives Forming the Battle of the Carso, September-November, 1916—Three Zones of Action from San Grado on the Left Wing to Hill 144 on the Right—Hand-to-Hand Struggle Followed by Flight and Surrender of Many Austrians—Triple Attack on Hill 144—Italians Suffer Heavily but Hold Firm—Skill and Gallantry of the Austrian Defence—Renewal of the Attack, Culminating in Victory of the Italians and Taking of nearly 1,000 Prisoners—Results of the Three Days' Struggle—Description of the Terrain—Trieste the Heart of Austria and the Carso its Pericardium—Abandonment of the Austrian First Line—Italian Infantry Assault of October 10th—Deadly Attack on San Marco : Two Austrian Regiments Exterminated—Stubborn Austrian Defence of the Veliki Hriback—Gigantic Contest near the Castagnevizza Road—Austrian Reserves Hurried from Other Fronts—Italian Attack of November 1st—Great Fight at a Fortified Cavern which was Finally Cleared of the Austrians—Struggle for the Veliki Summit—Gabriele d'Annunzio's Silken Banner—"Victors of Gorizia, Remember Your Dead !"—Brilliant Italian Success with Capture of an Austrian Brigade Commander and his Staff—An Austrian Strategic Centre Reached—Extent of the Austrian Losses—Effect of the Battle of the Carso on the General Position of the Allied Armies.

I N Chapter CXXXV. (Vol. VII., page 281) the narrative of the Austro-Italian Campaign was brought forward as far as the fall of Gorizia, August 9th, 1916. With the series of battles which culminated in that victory the first phase of the great Italian offensive came to a close. Before the opening of the second phase, which happened a month later, the work of preparatory organisation engaged all the energies of the Army. Staff officers were busy re-forming the regiments and drafting in new forces where gaps had been made. The Air Service explored the new battlefield, photographing the Austrian positions, and accurately mapping them for the guidance of infantry and artillery commanders. The Engineering Corps employed its huge mass of military labourers to consolidate the positions won and fit them as jumping-off ground for a new attack.

The amount of labour expended in fortifying trenches and dug-outs and artillery emplacements can be realised only by remembering how the line of battle lay along a stony waste of mountain, where the surface is at best only a thin skin of withered moss and heather. To use spade and shovel for the digging of trenches in such a terrain was out of the question. For the housing of munitions and general stores

ITALIAN AND RUSSIAN ALLIES.
The Duke of Aosta (right), whose troops won Gorizia on August 9th, 1916, and the officer at the head of the Russian Military Mission with the Italian Army.

caverns had to be blasted in the hard rock. In excavating gun emplacements electric and steam drills had to be employed. The material for the building of parapets was brought from the plain beneath. Quarries were opened for the supply of stone, and millions of sand-bags were dragged up the hill-sides. To supply and organise the driving force for this immense industry, electric-power plants were installed, roadways were laid along the hill-crests, bridges built across the ravines, telegraph stations, kitchens, store-houses, and dwelling-quarters constructed.

Trieste had become the direct though not the immediate objective of the Italian forces. In conquering Gorizia and the western Heights of the Carso they had broken down the principal outer defences of Trieste. Between this first-line barrier and the Hermada group of hills, which formed the immediate defence of the Triestine Plain, lay a block of rugged territory known as the Eastern Carso. It is a weird, wild terrain, partly wooded, but almost entirely bare of other vegetation and fertile soil, furrowed by a confused maze of valleys and gorges, pockmarked by innumerable *doline* (funnel-shaped hollows in limestone rock), and gored by subterranean river-beds. There are no springs, for all water percolates through the porous limestone and

AERIAL TRANSPORT BASE.
The Italians freely used aerial transport in difficult country for the conveyance of wounded and supplies.

runs to the sea in underground channels.

Standing at Gorizia and looking towards the southeast, the horizon is everywhere broken by a bewildering mass of hills, varying in altitude from a few hundred to about two thousand feet, irregular in outline, with rugged slopes fitfully wooded and barren brows where every vestige of plant life is destroyed by the merciless *bora*, or north wind. To conquer this territory was the objective of the three great offensives launched by the Italian Army during September, October, and November. The whole movement is generally called the Battle of the Carso, and the Carso, it must be remembered, is a generic term, like that of the Alps; it does not apply to a single mountain, but to that vast hilly region which lies on the north-eastern shore of the Adriatic.

The Battle of the Carso was begun in the middle of September. In order to understand the reasons for the plan of attack formulated by the Italian commander, two outstanding features of the strategic **Strategic situation** situation after the conquest of Gorizia **after Gorizia** must be recalled. Though the capture of the Isonzo citadel was a great feat of arms both in the tactical and strategic sense, from the strategic point of view it was not a complete success. The Austrians had held their ground on Monte Santo and San Gabriele, directly north of the city, and on the fortified heights of Duino, the extreme left of their lateral defence. This condition of affairs seriously influenced the subsequent phases of the Italian programme. The original Italian plan, if it were to reap the full harvest of success, was to open the attack on Gorizia by a heavy thrust against the Austrian left, thus attracting the enemy's centre of gravity southwards towards Monfalcone; then to get round

behind him through the Vipacco Valley, thus cutting the communications with Lubiana (Laibach) and inflicting a complete defeat. But Monte Santo controlled the mouth of the Vipacco from the north and hindered the Italian advance through the valley. This hitch might have been countered if the Duino position could have been taken, for then the obvious rôle of the Italian Army would have been a direct thrust southwards along the shore route to Trieste, turning the Austrian left and rolling it back towards Lubiana; but the Duino position held out as firmly as that on Monte Santo. The result was **Scope of the** that the Italians broke through the **September attack** centre, while the wings remained firm.

The defeat of the Austrians on the Isonzo was therefore incomplete, and its incompleteness changed the character of the Italian advance. It became necessary to adopt a defensive rôle on the northern and southern wings, while thrusting forward with the centre, in the hope of breaking through the second and third lines and curling them round the Hermada group, which is the great mountain bulwark directly north of Trieste. This movement would have completely isolated the Austrian left; but before it could be undertaken it was necessary for the Italians to better their positions on the extremities of both wings, so that the flanks might have room to manœuvre in the defensive struggle while the centre was pushed forward.

This offensive-defensive stroke on the flanks was the scope of the September attack. On the morning of September 14th the action opened. The solemn roar of the big guns was the prelude of the symphony. About ten o'clock a great crescendo was reached. An hour later the medium and

LIGHT LINE OF COMMUNICATION ON THE ITALIAN FRONT.
Terminus of an overhead transport line in the mountains, and (in circle) passengers en route. In the "cradle" men, or supplies, were rapidly conveyed over ground only otherwise crossed slowly and with difficulty.

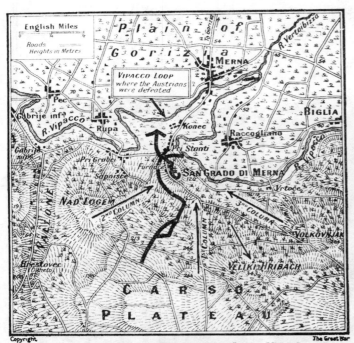

PLAN OF THE ATTACK ON SAN GRADO.
On the left wing of the Italian attack of September 14th, 1916, San Grado
was captured on the following day.

smaller calibres joined in. The whole Carso, from Gorizia to the sea, was fire and flame. In the interludes of silence the gun - waggons could be heard rattling along the roads at the rear of the Austrian lines. Reinforcements were swiftly rolling up. Towards midday the Austrian artillery answered with a tremendous antiphony.

Owing to the controlling positions which they held on the surrounding hills they were enabled to search out the Italian trenches and inflict some damage. The sun was still on the Austrian side, throwing its rays directly against the Italian positions and dazzling the outlook of the gunners. The soldiers were gathered for the attack, bayonets fixed, bombs in hand, each unit instructed in the special work allotted to it. The officers scanned their watches, the priests uttered a prayer, in which the soldiers joined *sotto voce*. At two o'clock the sun was on the Italian side. Half-past two was the moment chosen for the charge.

The sphere of action divided itself into three well-defined zones. The conquest of San Grado was the task allotted to the left wing. Hill 144 was the main **Strategic importance** objective of the right. The rôle assigned **of San Grado** to the centre was to support the attack on the wings and move accordingly. The Austrians had guessed where the main effort would be launched, but they did not know its purport. They were puzzled to find out whether the Italians intended clearing the way for the main advance through Duino or through the Vipacco. In other words, they could not guess whether the Italian purpose was to encircle the Hermada or take it by direct assault. The action in each zone may be followed separately.

San Grado di Merna is a circular mound, some three hundred and seventy feet in height, situated on the southern bank of the Vipacco, about three miles southeast of Gorizia. On their retirement from Monte San Michele, on August 8th, the Austrians chose this as the pivot of their defence east of Gorizia. It served as a sort of universal joint, keeping their line on the Carso firmly articulated with that on Monte Santo. A reference to the map will at once make clear the strategic importance of the position. Not only does it control the Vipacco road on the north, but also from the western side it overlooks the important route which runs from the Plain of Gorizia

through the Vallone to the Adriatic. It was, therefore, a central pillar supporting the twin gates of the Vipacco and Vallone. As long as it remained in Austrian hands the Italians could make no headway.

San Grado is reminiscent of an ancient Celtic dun (hillfort); and there is a possibility that at one time it served such a purpose, for the Celts were here in the days of the world's youth, and have left their traces not only in the nomenclature of mountains and rivers, but also in the fairy legends which abound among the people of the Carso. In any case, it will help the reader to visualise the course of the battle if he pictures San Grado as a circular Celtic dun, with a Christian sanctuary on the summit. Its northern slope is barren, the southern side is slightly wooded, and on the western side there is a large oblong crater somewhat like the *doline*, which are such familiar phenomena in the geography of the Carso.

The Italian plan was to attack the stronghold from the west and south simultaneously. At four o'clock in the afternoon the assault was launched by the infantry of the Eleventh Army Corps. The Austrian artillery enveloped the western and **Italians assault** southern approaches in a dense curtain **the position** of fire, so as to hold back the Italian advance, while the Italians pounded the reverse slope and the summit of the hill, with the result that only a fraction of the Austrian reinforcements could reach their objective. Bursting through the enemy's barrage in a brilliant dash, the first waves of the attacking infantry were soon pouring into the front trenches. These were found to have been partially demolished by the preparatory bombardment. A sprinkling of dead bodies lay strewn along the irregular furrow at the foot of the hill, but the bulk of the defending troops had taken shelter in the crater on the escarpment and in the covered communication-trenches. To clear the crater was the heavy task then ahead of the Italians.

The terrain of the struggle resembled a mammoth witch's cave, furnished in every nook and cranny with the engines of destruction. From inner recesses, where the satanic cauldrons of German chemists were a-boil, issued heavy clouds of poisonous vapour. A thick covering of ragged shrubbery clothed the inner walls of the crater, hiding the openings of large caves which had been excavated in the limestone rock by the long action of rains filtering through.

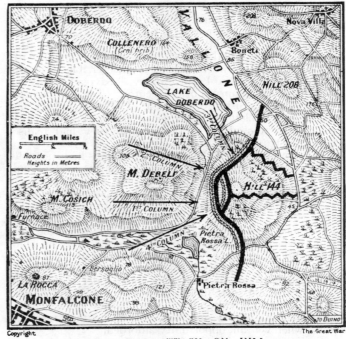

PLAN OF THE ATTACK ON HILL 144.
In the opening of the battle on September 14th, 1916, Hill 144 was the main objective of the Italian right wing

L

ON THE EASTERN CARSO: AUSTRIAN TRENCHES IN ITALIAN HANDS.

Italian infantry repairing trenches taken from the Austrians in the Carso di San Martino : part of a typical " d line," showing an entrance to caves. The " d line " are funnel-shaped hollows in the limestone rock, countless numbers of which pockmark the whole of the rugged territory which lies between the western heights of the Carso, near Gorizia, and the Hermada group of hills which form the immediate defence of the Triestine Plain.

From the observatories on Nad Logem the troops could be seen passing over the embankment and descending into the unknown. They ceased to be visible, save where the polished discs, which were carried as signals for the artillery, glittered like fire-flies above the torn mass of shrub and foliage. Then, after an hour or so, a stream of prisoners and wounded began to trickle towards the Italian rear.

They told stirring tales of the fight. It was a hand-to-hand struggle, bayonet against bayonet, bomb against bomb, rifle-stock against rifle-stock, rocks hurled from one side and the other as in a primeval barbaric contest. The Austrians fought desperately, always hoping that reinforcements would arrive ; but nothing could withstand the fury of the Italians. In the terrible melée the sonorous notes of the Latin war-cry, " Savoia ! " rang out above the hoarse hurrah of the Teuton. Towards nightfall the Austrian resistance wavered. Only one officer and ten men were left in a corner of the cavern, but they steadfastly refused to surrender until they had realised that the struggle was hopeless.

When morning broke, the flanking columns had succeeded in overcoming the resistance on the southern slope, and before midday they were nearing the **Capture of** summit. There the Austrians were firmly **San Grado** entrenched in the pilgrim-church and in the cellars of the surrounding houses. A well-aimed shell from the Italian artillery struck the campanile, which had served as an observatory, utterly smashing it and breaking in the roof of the church. Sheltered by the débris, the defenders still held out. With a wild rush, the Italian troops, led by their commander, entered the churchyard and surrounded the houses. " Fuori ! Fuori, tutti ! " (" Out ! Out, all of you ! ") they cried, hurling bombs through every opening and playing their machine-guns wherever an opportunity afforded.

Casting away rifles and accoutrements, six hundred Austrians fled down the northern slope towards the Vipacco, hoping to regain their lines at Raccogliano. But they could not cross the river. Sullenly they threw up their hands and rushed towards the Italian lines. From their dominating positions behind the line the Austrian guns were now turned on the fleeing mass. Escaping from the destructive fury of their own companions, the conquered heroes of Francis Joseph's Army called out for Italian protection, raising their hands in supplication, trembling and dazed.

The majority of these prisoners were Hungarians belonging to the 39th Regiment. Lamenting the fate which had compelled them to fight on Austrian soil while their own country was in the throes **Strategic value** of the Rumanian invasion, they explained **of Hill 144** that they would have surrendered more readily but that Austrian officers stood behind them with pistols in hand, ready to shoot the first man who should cry " Kamerad ! " Interspersed with the Hungarians were Slavonians and Croats from the Austro-Italian provinces. One man said that his home was in Cormons—one of the towns conquered by the Italians during the first days of the war—and asked leave to visit his family. This was readily granted. On reaching his home he found a happy community living peacefully and contentedly under the benign rule of their deliverers. Good bread and cheese and wine and fresh water formed luxuries which he had almost forgotten. For him the agony of Galician, Carpathian, and Carso battlefields was at an end.

On the extreme right the struggle was of a similar character. Here the Austrians had held a position which might be called the twin hinge of San Grado. This position is always called " Hill 144 " (its height in metres) in the military notices. Standing beyond the eastern slope of Monte Debeli it served the purpose of a watch-tower at the southern exit of the Vallone, controlling the road which runs from Gorizia to Trieste through the Vallone and

Duino. In Austrian hands Hill 144 had a further defensive value, for it stands in front of the junction where an important highway branches from the Vallone and runs directly eastwards at the northern foot of the Hermada. In conjunction with the Vallone road this forms an outer loop which receives several tributary roads from the important strategic centres on the Carso Plateau. Therefore, the fall of Hill 144 would unshield the arterial supply system of the Austrian defence.

On the western glacis of the stronghold the Austrians had constructed a deep zigzag trench, so well covered and protected that it looked like the casemate of some mammoth fortress. The protecting wall was a cyclopean structure of rocks and sand-bags, with thousands of embrasures for the play of machine-guns. Along the escarpment two strong fences of barbed-wire defended the approaches. Lower down, at different points of vantage on the slope, batteries of machine-guns were installed, connected with the main trench by protected channels. Close to the summit, about sixty yards above the main trench, ran another deep furrow, completely encircling the brow of the hill. A series of covered channels **Strength of** connected both trenches and led into **Austrian defences** spacious caves where munitions and men could be held in reserve.

The Italian plan was to attack the position from three different points. On the southern shore of the Doberdo Lake one column awaited the order to advance southwards against the northern glacis of the Austrian stronghold. From Pietra Rossa, on the south, another column was to advance northwards. On Monte Debeli, on the west, two columns were ready to launch the frontal attack. During the first stages of the struggle these two central columns would have to bear the brunt of the enemy's resistance.

Between them and the foot of Hill 144 lay a strip of ground about a thousand yards in depth ; but that stretch was under the open fire of the enemy's guns, not only from the stronghold itself, but also from the higher mountains to the rear and south.

About three o'clock in the afternoon of September 14th the flanking columns launched their attack. Within half an hour the troops from the north had gained the foot of the hill and begun to fight their way upwards with bomb and bayonet. Simultaneously the southern column advanced, driving the Austrians **Spirited attack** from the roadway at the point of the **on the Hill** bayonet and entering the wood on the southern slope. The central columns then began to move. Before them lay the descending slope on the eastern side of Monte Debeli, the valley beneath, the roadway, and the western glacis of the stronghold. They set forward at full sprint, covering a distance of nearly a thousand yards within ten minutes. Then the gruelling work commenced. The lateral columns began to suffer heavily, under the raking fire from Medeazza on the south and Hill 238 on the north. The centre toiled forward through the tree-trunks and caverns and rock-built barricades. The machine-guns of the enemy opened great gaps in the advancing files. Volleys of hand-grenades burst against the stony crust of the hill, scattering showers of splintered rock, denser and deadlier than shrapnel. But the Italian line held firm. Leading their companies, pistol in hand, the officers shouted rallying cries to their men.

It was a strange scene, bringing together in one great mêlée the characteristic elements of primeval and mediæval and modern warfare. While the heavy guns lifted their shells over the hill, across a distance of five and six miles, the machine-guns and rifles rang out at short range,

FORTIFIED POSITION IN THE EASTERN CARSO.

In the weird, wild terrain of the Eastern Carso, furrowed by a maze of valleys and gorges the Italians adapted the "doline," or hollow parts of the surface, for defensive purposes. Blasting out these hollows where they were not deep enough for the purpose in hand, they succeeded in converting some of them into veritable sunken forts, building up "dug-outs" with pieces of rock and sand-bags.

AWAITING THE WORD TO GO FORWARD.
Italian reserves in waiting during an action. The men had been assembled within easy distance of the fighting, and were awaiting the signal that should send them to the support of their comrades in the front lines.

aeroplanes fought one another in the skies, men fought hand to hand with bayonet and rifle-stock, and when the rifles were broken they hurled rocks at one another. Some of the Austrians carried heavy shields, which looked like specimens from some museum of classic antiquities. An Austrian officer challenged an Italian to a separate duel. They fought with pistols, as in olden days, and both fell. As the attendants stood over the dead bodies of their masters the first impulse was to rush at one another with bare bayonets, but the more human sentiment of loyalty conquered. Each lifted the corpse of his master and bore it back to the rear of the fighting. Rain fell heavily. The smoke of exploding shells and the steam

Tribalism in modern warfare

rising from mountain torrents, mingled with the waves of earth and splintered rock cast up by the high explosives, concealed the outlines of the struggle. Twilight began to descend. Men called out to one another—the Austrians in a strange babel of tongues—Slav, German, and Magyar ; the Italians in the different Latin dialects which are to be heard from the Alps to Sicily and Sardinia.

Foreign writers have often criticised regionalism in Italy, and counted it as a disintegrating force in national life ; but here it proved a rich source of appeal for the outpouring of blood in the national cause. The officers appealed to the tribal instincts of their followers. Many forgotten war-cries, appealing to the honour of home and kindred were heard. " La Brigata Sassari non si arrende mai e non indietreggia ! " " I laceri, ma indomiti della

Brigata Perugia sanno qual 'è il loro dovere ! " " Bersaglieri di Lamarmora, sempre avanti ! " " Garibaldini del San Michele, ricordatevi dei vostri morti ! " " Brigata Ferrara, o Brigata Brescia, fate onore alla fiera Calabria, alle generose Puglie ! " (" The Sassari Brigade never yields nor turns back ! " " The wounded but unconquered men of the Perugia Brigade know their duty ! " " Onward, ever onward, Bersaglieri of Lamarmora ! " " Garibaldians of San Michele, remember your dead ! " " Brigade of Ferrara, Brigade of Brescia, onward for the glory of dauntless Calabria and bountiful Apulia ! ")

But the fiery courage called forth by memories of home and fallen comrades could not break through the Austrian barrier of fire. Men had fallen in sheaves, and wounded comrades were crying out in agony. Yet the line did not waver or break. Clinging for bare life to every yard they had won, the heroic aggressors sought such cover as scattered rocks and shell-riven trunks of trees could afford. The barrage of the Austrians held back the Italian reinforcements. Fearing lest this might develop into a decisive thrust along the shore route to Trieste, the Austrians defended their ground with extraordinary skill and gallantry.

Night came on—a night of terrific wind and rain. Under cover of the darkness and blinding storm the Italians were enabled to move up reinforcements. Barricades were hurriedly built and wire entanglements erected. Morning found the troops holding a stronger footing on the ground they had won the day before. The Austrians now launched several counter-strokes. Six times they came on in dense waves ; six times they were hurled back,

Desperate Austrian counter-attacks

always with heavy slaughter. Throughout the day the Italians were strengthening their hold and repairing the damage which the units had suffered ; when night came on the whole series of positions had been consolidated and the ranks made ready for a new start.

The morning of the 16th dawned clear and calm. About eight o'clock the infantry columns were in motion. Led by a young Calabrian, Roberto Taverniti, who had been a journalist in civil life, the right central column went bounding up the slope and along the gorges. Within a few minutes the Calabrians had lost their leader. The Southern blood was now up and the terrible vendetta was sworn. The Bersaglieri had also lost their favourite colonel and several officers. All the more reason why the combat must go on with increasing vigour ; for when a comrade falls beside an Italian soldier the soul of the dying man seems for the moment to take up its abode in the living companion, giving him a double strength.

At ten o'clock the Bersaglieri were over the parapet, and about three hundred Austrian survivors were captured. But the conquest of the hill was not yet completed, for the defenders still held to the topmost part and the concealed communication-trenches. After two hours' further fighting, man to man and hand to hand, the aggressors succeeded in routing the enemy from the summit. He was now driven down the reverse slope, where he entrenched and held fast. Here he was no longer a menace on the Italian flank, nor could he hinder the manœuvring of the troops on the immediate sectors of the centre. When the fresh relief columns came up they found the trenches and caves and open escarpment of Hill 144 littered with dead. About one thousand prisoners had fallen into the hands of the victors.

Though the advance on the wings, for the purpose of gaining freedom of movement for the main offensive against the Carso, was the primary object of the September attack, the centre also bettered its position. Here, however, the advantages could not be fully maintained, for several battalions which had gained a footing east of Loquizza and Oppacchiasella had to be withdrawn in order to save them from the enemy's artillery on the flanks. Still, the gains were important. West of Loquizza,

Battle of the Carso: Victorious colours of the Lombardian Brigade.

Sand-bag trench above Redipuglia on the Carso, terrain where it was impossible to dig.

Type of fortress trench built by the Austrians in many of their strategic centres.

Improvised trench built of stones placed within wicker baskets on Lago Mucile, Carso di Monfalcone.

Telephone post in the Italian lines on Podgora, the famous "Hill of Death," near Gorizia.

Laborious progress over obstacles imposed by inexorable Nature: Italian troops advancing on skis along the Alpine front.

amongst the outlying houses of the village fortress, a number of trenches were taken and successfully held. East of Oppacchiasella the line moved forward on the fortified Castagnevizza road. Farther south, between Nova Villa and the Lake of Doberdo, one of the twin " 202 " hills had been conquered and the second partially outflanked. During the operations in this sector upwards of a thousand prisoners were taken.

Violent storms and the necessity of consolidating the new positions brought about a pause in the action. During the three days' struggle, from September 14th to 17th, the Italians had taken 4,104 prisoners,

Geographical aspects of the Carso including 111 officers, together with a considerable quantity of arms and ammunition and various military stores.

Before passing on to the second phase of the Battle of the Carso it is necessary to examine more closely the geographical aspects of the territory that lay ahead of the advancing troops. Once again it was not merely a question of one army against another, but that of an army unaided by any natural advantages of position against an army whose power of resistance was primarily due to the strength of the great fortresses which Nature had placed at its disposal. It is not easy for one who has not tramped it in times of peace to call up a vision of the geographical difficulties which beset a military traveller on the road which winds round the Eastern Carso towards Trieste.

Leaving Gorizia, and bending his steps to the south-east, the traveller follows the Vipacco road onwards and upwards towards the source of the river amid the hills. On his right rises the tier-like ridge of mountains — Veliki Hriback (1,190 feet), Faiti Hrib (1,247 feet), and Golnek (1,470 feet) — which stand as sentinels along the ascent. On reaching the village of Ranziano, he leaves the Vipacco road and turns directly southwards, on the winding ascent which brings him to the shoulder of Monte Golnek. Faiti Hrib is now on his right, the brow of Golnek on his left. At his feet the rugged upland of the Eastern Carso extends. The landscape framed before his eyes is the scene of the great Austrian defence. The distant horizon, beyond which lies the Plain of Trieste, is broken by the blunt peaks of the Hermada group. The foreground is a weird upland scene which looks like the handiwork of some delirious cubist artist who has allowed his gargantuan brush to splash mountains and roads and villages on the canvas in defiance of all proportion of symmetry.

In the general ensemble there is a point of central interest around which it is possible to group the jumble of objects which fall within the field of vision. It is the town of Castagnevizza, almost in the centre of the foreground. On their retirement in August the Austrians chose this as the centre of their defensive system. It was made the focus towards which a number of newly-made railways converged. Tapping the main line between Trieste and Lubiana, these arteries poured men and supplies into Castagnevizza, to be transferred from there by a system of radiating mountain roads to all parts of the Carso. The town and outlying district became the site of an entrenched camp, holding much the same relation to the new line as Gorizia had held to the old.

Barracks and arsenals were erected, and the heavy guns taken from Gorizia were installed in a position which gave them a pivotal control of the plateau. The masses of manœuvre were held in leash within the town and its outskirts. As a revolving searchlight sweeps the horizon, concentrating its rays wherever danger may be suspected to lurk, the military strength held in reserve at Castagnevizza could be sent forth at a moment's notice along any given radius, and concentrated wherever the Italian line looked threatening.

It would be impossible to give a definite numerical estimate of the forces employed for the defence of this area, but we may be quite certain that since the fall of Gorizia their ranks had been greatly strengthened. In the general outburst of vituperation which followed the fall of the great Isonzo citadel, the divisional commanders were made the scapegoats of the popular outcry. General Zeidler, who had commanded at Gorizia, was promptly dismissed. General Würm, who had had control of the Sixteenth Army Corps on the Western Carso, was relegated to an inferior position in some unknown section of the Imperial battle-line. It was decided to reorganise the Staff thoroughly and reconstruct the general system of

PLACING A CHEVAL-DE-FRISE ALONG A MOUNTAIN FRONT.
Digging trenches to consolidate positions won in the mountainous area where the Italians fought was generally impossible. The most the Italians could do was hurriedly to build barricades of fragments of rock and erect wire entanglements along the ice-bound zone before them.

defence. General Boroevic still remained commander of the Isonzo Army, and he was now supported by a Staff of the ablest generals at the disposal of the Imperial Army. Among these were Generals Lukacich, Scheider, Scharizen, and Schench.. The Archduke Charles, who succeeded his uncle, the Emperor Francis Joseph, as the Emperor Charles, on November 21st, 1916, took personal control of the Seventh Army Corps.

We know that at least three army **Numerical strength** corps were employed—namely, the **of the Austrians** Eighth, Ninth, and Seventeenth—but it would be impossible to say whether they were present in full strength. From the examination of prisoners, and other information gathered from captured documents, it was fairly well established that at least eight divisions were employed between the Vipacco and Duino, a front of about eight miles. As to the general fighting quality of the troops, we know, on Boroevic's own showing, that they were the best Austria-Hungary could afford. The majority of the regiments were exclusively Hungarian.

BROAD BARBED-WIRE ENTANGLEMENTS THAT PROTECTED THE ITALIAN FRONT.

Snowy slopes on the Italian front, with belts of barbed-wire protecting the sinuous trenches. In advancing on the Austrian positions among the mountains the Italians found that the enemy had made particularly extensive use of wire. In some places deep layers of entanglements were concealed in a way which made it impossible to sight them from any distance, so that the Italian artillery could not always be trained on them.

Next in strength of numbers came the Croatian and Bosnian regiments. These were all first-class troops, the only troops of second-rate quality present being a few Austrian Landwehr and Landsturm regiments. What was the strength of the masses of manœuvre held in reserve it would be impossible to say, especially in view of the fact that it was constantly on the increase; for trainloads of troops from the eastern front arrived every day. The artillery and engineering equipment had been strongly reinforced from Germany, as the defence of Trieste had become a problem of vital interest for the Central Empires. "Trieste," said a captured officer, "is the heart of Austria and the Carso is its pericardium."

On October 9th the Italians began the second stage of the offensive. From the Vipacco to the sea the whole line was subjected to a violent bombardment, so violent indeed that on the Carso the waves of earth and stone and smoke constantly cast up by the exploding shells entirely obscured the outline of the terrain. Those who witnessed a bombardment on the Carso could realise to the full the power of modern artillery. The high-explosive shells dug slight openings in the stony crust of the mountain. The rocks split and heaved. Volumes of broken stone and earth leapt upwards, like eruptions from a volcano, and then descended in heavy showers on the trenches. The high explosives performed the double duty of wrecking the trenches and killing the inhabitants. There was no shrapnel in France and Flanders to compare with this deadly rain of splintered stone. The enemy deserted his trenches for the time being and hid in the rock-hewn caverns. When the range began to lengthen, so as to allow the attacking infantry to advance, he came forth and worked furiously at reorganising his defences. Hence it was always necessary that the rush of the attacking troops should follow immediately on the heels of the lengthening curtain, and that the attack should be sharp and decisive. Yet that was not so easy as where the trenches ran through a stretch of level ground, for these mountain positions were often at a considerable distance across ravines and valleys from the trenches of the attacking foe.

Second stage of the offensive

On the morning of October 10th the prisoners began to filter through the dense screen of fire and smoke. With hands raised, trembling and semi-delirious, they cried out for deliverance from the terrible inferno in which they were suffering. Among these first prisoners some were Ruthenians and Dalmatians. How had they escaped the vigilance of the Austrian officers, who stood behind their men and shot them down mercilessly the moment the least tendency to surrender was manifested?

"Our officers have deserted us," the prisoners proclaimed. "Our trenches are full of dead and wounded. You have destroyed our parapets and entanglements." Among them was a Hungarian sergeant-major, who had come as an emissary from his men. Abandoned by the commissioned officers, on whose shoulders rested the responsibility of defending the position, and seeing no hopes of holding out against the expected infantry attack, the sergeant chose discretion as the better part of valour. He would surrender. But how? He would come alone, and convince the Italians of his sincerity. Having listened to his story, they agreed to grant a safe-conduct for the men. The artillery ceased fire for a moment, signals were made, and the whole company made good its escape.

Surrender of Hungarian company

What had happened in the Austrian lines? Owing to the destructive violence of the bombardment it had already been decided to abandon the front line of trenches and concentrate the defence on strong strategic points, such as Veliki Hriback and Nova Villa. Furthermore, it had been decided to establish a new series of trenches as a subsidiary front line. Without parapets or entanglements, these were simply narrow channels delved in the soil among the rocks, connected with underground caverns by an elaborate system of concealed corridors. This arrangement enabled the defenders to fill the main channel at a moment's notice. An enormous number of machine-guns had been hastily brought up and posted in hiding-places throughout the rugged uplands. It was clear that the Austrians had abandoned the idea of holding a definite linear frontage against the brunt of the attack. They would force the Italians to accept a system of fighting which was a scientific development of guerilla warfare. The character of the terrain was well suited to such a method of defence.

At half-past three in the afternoon of October 10th the infantry assault was launched. The battlefield was divided into three separate zones—namely (1) the territory immediately north of the Vipacco, on the lower spurs of the Julian Hills; (2) the ascending ridge on the southern bank of the Vipacco; and (3) the Carso Plateau east of the Vallone. We shall follow the course of the action in these zones separately.

On the heights east of Gorizia and north of the Vipacco some units of the Second Army co-operated with the Treviso and Cuneo Brigades of the Third Army. The object of this movement was to enlarge the manœuvring-ground for the troops which operated on the Vipacco. It would also compel the enemy to keep a mass of reserves

here and thus weaken his resistance on the Carso. Besides, every new position gained on the Sober Ridge would drive home a little further the right arm of the forceps, by means of which the Italians were striving to tear the Monte Santo molar from the Austrian jaw.

In Chapter CXXXV. the importance of Monte Santo and San Gabriele was explained. After the fall of Gorizia the Austrian guns on Monte Santo still dominated the city and the opening of the Vipacco road. They might reduce Gorizia to ruins, as they had reduced Gradisca and Monfalcone, but they fondly hoped that one day they would retake the city. Should an Austro-German drive on the grand scale again become a practical part of the Teutonic military programme, not only would the position on Monte Santo be a serious hindrance on the flanks of the Italian defence, but it would be a magnificent support for the flank of the Austrian **Attempt to encircle** attack. Having failed to conquer it by a **Monte Santo** direct assault from the west, the Italians attempted to encircle it by operating from the northern bank of the Vipacco along the bed of the Vertoibizza.

Leaving the summit of Monte Santo and descending the southern slope of the hill, the traveller comes to a broad furrow which extends to his left and carries the road from Gorizia to Tivoli and Aisovizza. Between this furrow and the foot of the mountain there is a triangular block of hills, known as the Rosenthal group. These form the residential suburb of Gorizia. It is a beautifully-wooded hillside facing the southern sun, rich in flower-gardens and olive groves, vineyards and orchards. Numerous parks nestle in its folds, and there are clusters of beautiful villas where wealthy Austrian pensioners were wont to spend the declining years of lives that had been given to the service of the House of Hapsburg.

The outstanding feature of the landscape is the Hill of San Marco (750 feet), the southern slope of which

FRENCH COMMANDER-IN-CHIEF AT ITALIAN HEADQUARTERS.

General Nivelle, visiting the Italian Headquarters to concert plans with General Cadorna, took advantage of the opportunity personally to decorate an Italian officer with the Croix de la Guerre. Behind the French Commander-in-Chief stood the Italian Commander-in-Chief (wearing a fur coat thrown open) and General Porro, the Italian Chief of Staff. In circle : General Cadorna (left) and General Nivelle.

ITALIAN "DUG-OUTS" ARRANGED ON THE SLOPE OF A CARSO "DOLINA."

In the "doline," or hollows, of the limestone rock of the bare and broken Carso the Italians contrived the to the whole of the vast hilly region which lies on the north-eastern shore of the Adriatic. It is a bewildering nearest approach to dug-outs which the nature of the ground permitted. The Carso is a general term applying mass of hills, irregular in height and rugged in form, sparsely grown with trees, and bare of all other vegetation.

runs down to the railroad and the northern bank of the river. For practical strategic purposes it is a low spur of Monte Santo and San Gabriele, a sort of bridge-head position shielding the approaches to the main block of hills. In like manner San Marco has several lower spurs, which may also be regarded as bridge-head positions in relation to the summit of the hill. The obvious Italian plan, subsequent to the capture of Gorizia, was to lay siege to San Marco, as a first step towards the encirclement of Monte Santo. This was to be the task of the extreme left during the attacks on the Carso.

Owing to the advantageous positions which the Italians occupied to the south of Gorizia, it was possible to open a devastating fire against San Marco and its surroundings. So violent and precise was the bombardment that, even before the infantry advanced, the defenders had already lost sixty per cent. of their effectives. At half-past three in the afternoon of the 10th the infantry attack was launched. As the Italians entered the wooded terrain on the southern slope of the hill, the Austrians took shelter in the parks behind the ruins of the once princely villas. Through the night of the 11th and the morning of the 12th the struggle continued. The Italian artillery had succeeded in gaining control of the Austrian approaches, so that no further reinforcements could be sent. Again and again the defending commander signalled for help, but received none. Still he defended every yard of his ground. Prisoners yielded only in twos and threes. They came from places of ambush in the hedges and arbours and amid the broken statues of the once beautiful parks.

It was a weird, semi-ludicrous, semi-tragic spectacle. Above the débris of broken walls and statues and garden-seats glittered the familiar Teuton formula " Verboten "— " Forbidden to walk on the grass or injure the shrubs." About midday the main redoubts had fallen and two Austrian regiments had been practically exterminated. A rich booty in machine-guns and bomb-throwers fell into Italian hands. Towards evening the remaining subsidiary spurs of San Marco had been taken, but the Austrians still held the summit. Several times they counter-attacked, but failed on each occasion. Though **Italians isolate San Marco** unable to press the attack as far as the summit of the hill, the victors held all the ground that had been gained, and were firmly consolidated when the fury of the battle began to wane. The winning of these spurs was a very important success, for it robbed the enemy of valuable tactical supports and rendered his position on the summit extremely difficult. From that day onward San Marco remained isolated on two sides and a part of the third, with the result that the bringing up of supplies became difficult and dangerous.

While these successes were being gained by the left wing, the centre was pushing forward against the Carso Pentagon. At three o'clock in the afternoon of the 10th the assault was launched against the powerful line which ran from the northern ridge of the Carso to the Oppacchiasella-Castagnevizza road, a distance of about three miles. On this front the Austrians had built their trenches on the classic style, protecting them by walls of rocks and sand-bags covered with metal shields. Deep layers of entanglements lay in

DRIVING A MACHINE ROCK-DRILL ON THE CARSO FRONT.
In the fighting on the Carso gun-emplacements and caverns for housing munitions and general stores had to be blasted out of the solid rock, and for this purpose numbers of electric and steam driven machine rock-drills were used. The Italian Engineering Corps comprised a huge mass of military labourers.

front of each line, so cleverly concealed in parts as to make it impossible for the Italian gunners to sight them.

In occupying the front line little difficulty was experienced, for the preparatory artillery fire had demolished the parapets and strewn the ditches with dead and wounded. The thin group of survivors frantically cried for mercy, shouting out " Nichts dum-dum ! "—for General Cadorna had issued an order, copies of which Italian airmen had dropped into the enemy's lines, proclaiming that any soldier found possessing explosive bullets would be shot forthwith. Within a few hours the northern section of the line had fallen ; but to the south, around Point 201, the resistance was more stubborn, for this blocked the road to Castagnevizza. Here the Austrians **Successes of the** had constructed a series of trenches in **Italian centre** quadrangular formation, protected by dense rows of barbed-wire and connected with one another by a labyrinth of underground channels. A new brigade, which was to experience its first battle, attacked the position. After several hours of desperate fighting with bomb and bayonet the defenders surrendered. " Genug, Genug ! " they cried. " We cannot stand it any longer ! " When night came the village of Loquizza had been reached, and farther north the attacking troops were laying siege to the western slope of Veliki Hriback.

Next morning the attack was renewed. The Italians commenced to ascend the mammoth staircase. On Veliki Hriback the Austrians contended every yard of ground. This terrain was more difficult than that over which the battle of the previous day had been fought. Advancing upwards, the leading columns found in their path a thickly-wooded crater which had not been mapped by the aeroplane observers. Here the Austrians had employed every means at their disposal to make the ground impassable. Densely woven nets of barbed-wire lay concealed in the undergrowth. Stout fences of the same material ran from tree to tree in the wood. Alcoves for the harbouring of machine-guns had been constructed amid the rocks ; like traps set by hunters for the capture of game, clusters of percussion bombs lay ingeniously concealed beside the pathways. Any attempt to encircle the hollow would have exposed the troops to the enemy's artillery on the flanks. The only hope was to advance cautiously and clear the ground yard by yard. After two days' terrific struggle a firm footing had been gained in the centre and on the rim of the crater. But it was impossible to proceed farther until the ground had been subjected to an artillery bombardment.

South of the Castagnevizza road the contest assumed gigantic proportions. In this sector the main storm-centre was the fortified ruins of Nova Villa, which stood south of Oppacchiasella, at a distance of about a thousand yards. In times of peace Nova Villa sheltered about two hundred and fifty souls, but the experience of war had now reduced its houses to a mass of débris. Through the western outskirts the Austrians had built a deep trench, and another through the heart of the village. The strong point of the latter was the piazza and campanile of the church, which had offered a good opportunity for the emplacement of artillery. Both these trenches ran to the foot of the neighbouring Hill 208, outside the south-western corner of the village, whence they branched into a deep causeway that encircled the hill-top. The position was of vital importance, for it was an effective obstacle in the flank of any attempt to advance towards Castagnevizza.

The "Iron Brigade" of Calabria (59th and 60th Regiments), consisting chiefly of the Calabrians, Sicilians, and Apulians, led by two Sardinian generals, **Capture of Hill 208** had been entrusted with the task of conquering Hill 208. The first onslaught brought them astride the front line of trenches between the village and the hill, but the Austrians now pivoted their immediate defence of the hill on a system of irregularly grouped redoubts which were very difficult to reduce. During the first day's fighting a thousand prisoners fell into the hands of the Italians. On the

third day of the struggle the village fell and the hill was carried by the force of a terrific simultaneous attack on left, right, and centre. By the evening of the 14th the position was solidly held, and the advancing troops had entrenched amid the outlying houses of the village of Hudilog.

For the moment the offensive was over. It had succeeded in pressing forward the line over a distance of five hundred yards at some points and nearly two miles at others, and, more important **Austrian reserves** than mere territorial advance, it had also **brought up** taken from the enemy several strongly fortified positions of great strategic value. During the whole of the action the Italians had taken 8,219 prisoners, including 254 officers, 31 trench-mortars, 82 cases of cartridges, and a rich booty in general war material. The declarations of prisoners bore unanimous testimony to the heavy losses sustained by enemy regiments, several of which had been practically wiped out.

On several occasions towards the end of October attempts were made to prepare the ground for a new offensive, but the heavy rains and fogs prevented their continuance. Thus, warned of the forthcoming onslaught, the Austrians spared no pains in strengthening themselves against it. During the latter half of October, Italian airmen reported an incessant stream of daily and nightly traffic through the railway-stations of Opicina, Nabresina, and Duttole Duttagliano. This meant that the Austrians were bringing up their reserves from the home bases and effectives from the eastern front in order to make the road to Trieste impassable.

From the declarations of prisoners subsequently taken

AT THE END OF THE MULE-PATH: UNLOADING SUPPLIES AT THE MOST ADVANCED DEPOT.
Ten men were required, on the average, to supply one man fighting on the Alps. This picture shows the end of the mule-trail but not the end of the route. Here were the kitchens where the food was cooked. The provisions were carried the rest of the journey by expert climbers who set out for the front line three times daily. Their journey usually took them six or seven hours, but they arrived with marvellous punctuality.

ALPINE SPORT ADAPTED TO WARFARE.
Italian soldiers ski-ing along pine-grown slopes on their mountainous front. They carried their rifles slung across their backs to leave their hands free for using the steadying sticks.

SKI-ING SCOUTS AMID ROCKY SUMMITS
Alpine soldiers of the Italian Army scouting among the grand summits of the mountains on their Carso front. It was only by means of the ski that the deep snow could be traversed.

the extent and character of these movements became known. Besides several Landwehr and Landsturm battalions, Ruthenian, Rumanian, and Bosnian troops of the line had been brought from the interior of the country. These were reinforced by heavy drafts of Hungarians hastily brought from Transylvania. So expeditious was the transport that some regiments made the journey from the Carpathians within two days and some from Volhynia within three. When the whole reorganisation was complete the army which now faced the Italians was almost entirely new to this front. Not more than a fourth of the original Carso Army had remained, and a large part of this had been relegated to the reserve.

On October 31st the weather improved and the demolition fire of the artillery began. It was sustained throughout the night and intensified on the following morning. Scouting parties having ascertained that great gaps had been opened in the enemy's line, the order to advance was given. The immediate objective of the attack was the second line on the Carso Plateau from the Vipacco to the Hermada Mountains. This line passed along the western slope of Veliki Hriback, at a distance of about a thousand yards from the summit, and descended in a southerly direction as far as Lukatic. Here it joined the sector of the first line, which had remained firm during the October advance. But in the most important area, the northern Carso Ridge, the Austrians had built a subsidiary line at a distance of about eight hundred yards from the first. The strong points of this were the summits of Veliki Hriback and Monte Pecinka.

At half-past ten on the morning of November 1st the curtain fire lifted and the batteries lengthened the range so as to lash the storm of projectiles on the Austrian approaches. At eleven o'clock the infantry leaped from their trenches. Against all the strongholds along the front—Veliki Hriback, Pecinka, the village of Loquizza, and the southern flank of the Castagnevizza road—a simultaneous onslaught was launched. At 11.30 four dense columns on the extreme right of the attack had already driven the enemy from his main **Austrian second** positions to the south of the road. In one **line rushed** wild rush the Spezia Brigade, with the Cremona Brigade on the left, carried every obstacle in its path. So sudden was the avalanche and so fierce the driving force, carving its way principally by the aid of bomb and bayonet, that it dazed and bewildered the enemy. Time was not given even for signals of surrender. Within half an hour the Italians were in the Austrian second line of defence, without having halted to clear the battlefield or send back prisoners. Stricken friend and foe, dead and dying and wounded, now littered the wake of the advancing troops. It was one of the strangest spectacles of the war. Within a radius of about two miles over half a dozen races had met in battle shock. In over half a dozen different tongues—Italian, German, Magyar, Rumanian, Croatian, Polish, Bohemian—the wounded cried out for help, the conquered for mercy. Lukatic was swiftly encircled and before midday the victors were entrenching amid its ruins.

Then the famous *dolina* (the *dolina* of the brigands) beyond the village became the scene of a desperate conflict. This cavern was about one hundred and fifty yards in length and an average of forty yards in depth. Fortified

REGIMENT OF ITALIAN INFANTRY WHICH WON NEW LAURELS IN THE CARSO.

The men are clad in winter uniform and wearing steel helmets in readiness for their service at the the barrage fire of their own artillery. Their officers led them on with half-forgotten war-cries, front. The infantry of King Victor Emmanuel's gallant Army behaved magnificently in the Carso fighting. appealing to the honour of home and of kindred; and even when they were met by machine-gun Sometimes the men went forward with an impetuosity which almost carried them into danger from fire and grenades that made great gaps in their advancing files, "the Italian line held firm."

in every nook and cranny, floored with dense entanglements and explosive mines, with thousands of openings like rabbit-burrows, behind which machine-guns lurked in well-constructed caves, it formed one of the strongest positions along the whole line. The shock of the conflict was terrible. On the Italian side six battalions took part in it. The cries of the Austrians reached beyond the village as they were poniarded in their lairs. The struggle grew fiercer with the despair of the defenders, who now contested the positions foot by foot. Several separate duels were fought. During the opening stages an Austrian captain stood alone and pointed his pistol at an Italian lieutenant. The challenge was readily taken up and both combatants fell. Later in the day orders were given that the two brave enemies should be buried side by side in the same grave.

At one o'clock in the afternoon the defenders were already giving way, and an hour later the cavern had been fully cleared. The Latin troops were now beyond Segeti. So swift had **The Brigands'** been their onrush that they were already **Cavern cleared** on the fringe of their own curtain fire, and only with difficulty could the officers restrain them until the gunners had been signalled to lengthen the range.

On the immediate left of this thrust another force, composed of the 6th and 12th Bersaglieri, pushed forward on the southern slope of Monte Pecinka. There the rush was also like that of a pent-up torrent suddenly let loose. Before the gunners on the summit of the hill could realise the precise direction of the attack the Italians had pounced upon them. The surprise was largely due to the fact that the Austrian gunners had expected the full blow to come on the ridge between Veliki Hriback and Pecinka. Now they were suddenly seized from the south, while the north remained quiet. But as they were reorganising their plans of defence a swift blow was struck in the north. Both attacks had been carried out by young Bersaglieri regiments, which have the speed of mountain deer. Finding themselves so suddenly encircled, the Austrians surrendered the two batteries, containing six 4.13 in. cannon, which had defended the position, together with large supplies of ammunition and food stores.

The Italian Command had planned this thrust with the object of clearing the ground for an attack on Veliki Hriback. Thus supported from the south, the blow against the summit of Veliki was now guaranteed its full striking force. The deep cavern and heavily-fortified wood which had so stubbornly held back the advance in October were carried in the first rush. But the struggle for the summit turned out to be an arduous task. Here the terrain was a barren patch of rocky hill, cleft in twain by a deep seimcircular fosse.

The attack was one of the most dramatic spectacles witnessed on the Carso. The principal actors in the great scene were the troops of the Tuscan Brigade (77th and 78th Regiments) and **Attack on** the Lombardian Brigade (73rd and 74th **Veliki Hriback** Regiments) which had conquered the heights of Sabotino during the epic struggle for Gorizia. From every observatory in the immediate rear of the advancing lines binoculars were levelled on the bare brow of the hill. A warm sun drew clouds of vapour from the rain-sodden valley of the Vipacco. Standing out, gaunt and defiant, above this mass of cloud and shell smoke, Veliki Hriback—the second San Michele—seemed destined to resist all attack. Will it hold out, or will it fall? the officers asked one another. If Veliki should hold out, the conquest of Monte Pecinka would have been in vain. Since the famous day in August when the Latin troops were struggling up the side of San Michele no moment so pregnant with destiny had dawned on the standards of Rome.

At half-past eleven the bright discs which signalled the position of the front line began to glitter like fire-flies wherever the sunlight broke through the mist. They were working ahead and upwards. That at least was a comfort. But the pace was slow, for it was in the teeth of a raking fire from the summit. The great trench was like the balcony of a castle, commanding a steep lawn in front. Would steady-plodding progress bring the besiegers to their goal? The onlooking officers shook their heads doubtfully, for experience had taught them that the only hope of success in such a manœuvre lies in a great lightning thrust, where the speed and agility of the troops make it difficult for the defenders to get the best out of their machine-gun batteries. The quivering line of discs seemed almost stationary.

Suddenly a wave of excitement passed along the groups of onlookers who crouched in the Italian observatories. "Ecco! Ecco! Savoia! Avanti, Savoia!" they shouted frantically. Triumphantly a row of hands was pointed towards the southern slopes of Veliki, where nobody — except those in the official secret — had expected an attack. Out from the heavy wreaths of fog and smoke, like boys leaping through bracken after a pack of hounds, wave after wave of Bersaglieri sprang upwards. They were bounding up the hill-side. The Austrians had not expected nor prepared for this charge. Within half an hour the foremost Bersaglieri were already on the summit. The Austrian gunners were attacked at close quarters before they had time to organise a defence. The observatories telephoned to the batteries on the surrounding hills, but it was too late. The Bersaglieri waved a tricolour in the sun. The Tuscans, who had been toiling up the western slope, now came forward with a bound. At midday the position was won, and remained firmly in Italian hands.

A specially dramatic incident in the attack deserves mention; it is the story of the banner that was waved on Veliki Hriback. On the eve of the attack Gabriele d'Annunzio, the national poet, who had served in the Flying Corps until he met with a serious accident to his sight, and was subsequently gazetted as a captain in one of the infantry regiments of the Tuscan Brigade, provided himself with a silken banner which he folded and concealed in his knapsack. At the head of his battalion he fought his way upwards, bounding over the heather as lithely as the youngest peasant in the regiment. Having reached the summit he unfolded the banner, which was the signal for a mighty cheer from the Tuscan ranks. But a brother officer, fearing lest the signal might attract the Austrian fire, cried out: "Hold! Hold! Give me the banner! Let us bear it farther onward still!" D'Annunzio relinquished his treasure. Jumping forward along the reverse slope of Veliki, the streaming banner laid the trail for

Gabriele d'Annunzio's silken banner

WITH THE ITALIAN GUNNERS: AN AWKWARD TURNING.
Bringing a gun round a precipitous curve on a mountain road built by Italian military engineers. The soldier on the left had descended to make sure that the passing of the weighty weapon had not displaced any of the supporting balks of timber.

the Italian huntsmen who were after the Austrian game. That evening they had reached the foot of another towering hill beyond.

Another incident of a picturesque character is worthy of record. As the Bersaglieri rushed forward on the ridge which runs from Veliki Hriback southwards to Pecinka they encountered a train of Austrian mules laden with provisions and ammunition for the front line. One of the drivers, a native of Trieste, spoke for his companions and surrendered. "Signor Tenente," he said, addressing the Italian lieutenant, "I know the road to Italy." "Good! Good!" answered the Italian. "Go to Italy and take your company with you!" The mule-driver, so unexpectedly gazetted to the rank of captain, jauntily led his column along the road to the Vallone, explaining to the wondering Italians as he arrived that he had been suddenly promoted for discretion shown on the field of battle. His ammunition he could recommend. It would serve for use in the captured guns. But as for the quality of his bread and coffee and meat—well, if the signori did not mind, he would prefer to sample their *minestrone* and *pane commune*.

Throughout that night, the night of November 1st, tremendous difficulty was experienced in holding the positions which had been won. The Italians were clinging to the lower flight of steps on the mountain staircase, while the Austrians held the main landing, from which their guns mercilessly swept the positions beneath. For the aggressors the attack could have no halt until the enemy had been driven from his post of vantage. The principal position which he held was the towering hill beyond Veliki Hriback overlooking the Carso Plateau to the south and the Vipacco to the north. Beyond Veliki, at a distance of about one and a half miles, the summit of Faiti Hrib (1,247 feet) was now the immediate and indispensable objective of the attack. The conquest of Faiti occupied four hours. The struggle proved to be one of the most interesting in the annals of the campaign ; not merely because of its epic heroism, but largely because it offered a telling example of the triumph of Latin intelligence over the mechanical military mind of the Teuton.

Conquest of Faiti Hrib

It was November 2nd, the Feast of All Souls, a day on which a deep religious sense of duty inspires the Italian soldier, for he feels that the most fitting commemoration of his dead will be to carry on the battle of his fallen comrades whose bodies lie in the wake of the advance. On that day the shout was often re-echoed on the hill-side : " Vincitori di Gorizia, ricordatevi dei vostri morti ! " (" Victors of Gorizia, remember your dead ! ")

As on the previous day, the troops advanced in three separate columns, a heavy central column making the frontal attack and a column on each wing moving somewhat ahead, with the idea of encircling the Austrian position. As the central column advanced it soon found itself exchanging shots with the advance guards of an Austrian column, counter-attacking along the ridge which runs directly westwards from Faiti Hrib. Realising the meaning of the situation, the Italian commander made a bold decision on the spur of the moment. Wheeling suddenly to the right, he detached the main body of his forces from the

impact of the counter-attack and threw them into the line of advance along the right wing. This lightning stroke immensely strengthened the impetus of the advance. The Austrians on the summit were taken unawares, but they made a desperate resistance. Machine-guns opened gaps in the advancing troops ; the hail of bombs was terrific. For the Italians the main hope was in the force of numbers and the lightning speed at which their troops could work. It was a bomb and bayonet fight, with more of bayonet than of bomb, for in a mountain advance it proved difficult to keep the bombers supplied.

The Austrians were magnificently fortified behind stout rows of rocks and sand-bags which had been protected by iron shields. The communication-trenches led into roomy caverns where whole companies could shelter at a time. From these communication-trenches and caverns they had to be driven at the point of the bayonet. The defenders, who were mostly composed of Hungarians and Croats, fought like wild animals cornered by hunters. For three hours they fought the Italian hand to hand, but his hand was more dexterous than theirs. And he won. The communication-trenches were choked with dead and wounded, friend and foe lying side by side. At six o'clock in the evening the position was safely in Italian hands. Waves of reinforcements and military

HIT BY AN AUSTRIAN SHELL.
Private house which was wrecked as a result of the first Austrian projectile that was fired on an Italian village.

labourers, for the work of consolidation, were already surging upwards along the western and southern slopes of the hill.

During the struggle a brigade commander and his Staff were taken prisoners. Having occupied the summit, the Italians set out to explore the surrounding ridges and spurs. They came upon a group of huts screened from the view of the airmen by layers of thick foliage. From the roof of one hut a number of telephone wires radiated. Here was big game. It was evidently the headquarters of the general commanding the sector. If it could be taken by a surprise dash valuable documents and maps would fall into the hands of the victors.

ITALIAN OUTLOOK ON A ROCKY SUMMIT.
Observation-post on the Italian front. Many of these vertical heights, as one visitor put it, could only be scaled by placing ladders one above the other. As each of these ladders was secured in position it was mounted to find a place for the next.

AUSTRIAN PRISONERS TAKEN ON THE CARSO BEING ESCORTED TO THE REAR.

In the first three days of the Battle of the Carso, September 14th to 17th, 1916, the Italians took 4,104 prisoners, including 111 officers; in the second phase of the battle, beginning October 9th, they took 8,219 more, including 254 officers; between November 1st and 3rd they took 8,982 more, including 259 officers. In addition to this grand total of 21,305 prisoners, they captured also guns and a rich booty in general war material.

Getting down on all fours, the Italians began to creep stealthily towards the sheds. They saw an officer come out and put up his binoculars for a scrutiny of the surroundings. Soon the group of buildings was surrounded. The Austrians rushed out. "Siamo Italiani! Arrendetevi! ("We are Italians! Surrender!") A few pistol shots rang out as the entrapped Austrians tried to open a gap in the ring that surrounded them. But it was a hopeless attempt. The commander and officers laid down their arms and surrendered all their material—maps, documents, etc.—to the conquerors. Then the Italians discovered that the establishment had been the headquarters of General Stankl, who had been in command of the 55th Brigade. The general, however, was not there in person. Having been seriously wounded a few days previously, he had surrendered the command to Colonel Skofo, who now found himself in Italian hands. Skofo, who was a native of Budapest and evidently a rather good type of Hungarian, did not unreasonably quarrel with his fate. When the first moments of surprise were over he and his Staff readily fraternised with their Italian hosts.

So ended All Souls' Day, with a list of deeds that might be accounted a worthy commemoration of the heroic dead whose graves are on the Carso. The memory of the fallen brave had given rise to a touching episode which proves that beneath the roaring seas of war, which separate the men of one nation from those of another, lies the deep bedrock of human nature where all men are united. In a little graveyard behind the Austrian lines some Hungarian soldiers had written the following inscription on a prominent slab as a touching reminder and request to the conqueror:

An historic All Souls' Day

Italians! If your advance should reach thus far, let not your engines of war profane the soil on which you tread. Respect this cemetery and preserve it; for we have tears in store within our eyes wherewith we shall bathe this soil above our buried kindred when the scourge of war shall have passed and all shall be friends once again.

Before the morning of November 3rd all the outlying positions between Faiti and the Vipacco had been taken, and on the Carso Plateau the troops had brought forward their line to a depth of about a mile, between Faiti Hrib and the Castagnevizza road. During November 3rd a vigorous push south of the road sent the line forward in that section another four hundred yards, so that the Italian entrenchments now ran through the western outskirts of Castagnevizza. The Austrian strategic centre on the Eastern Carso had been reached. The enemy had been forced to evacuate a position which he had deemed impregnable. He was now faced with the possibility of an encirclement of the Hermada mountains, and the immediate defence of Trieste became his main concern.

Thus ended the second phase of the Battle of the Carso. Realising that winter was coming on and that no other great advance could take place during the close of the year, the Italians settled down to the winter war work of organising the positions and strengthening their ranks so as to be ready, when the weather conditions would be suitable once more, for the great thrust which should bring them to the gates of Trieste.

End of the second phase

In the general reckoning of the losses that had been inflicted on the enemy it was found that during the action which opened on November 1st and closed with the fall of Volkovniak on November 3rd, the victors had taken 8,982 prisoners, including 259 officers, 24 guns (of which 13 were of medium calibre) 9 bomb-throwers, 62 machine-guns, some thousands of rifles, a large quantity of ammunition and vast military stores of various kinds. According to a semi-official account published by themselves, the Austrians had lost 33,000 men during the three days' battle from November 1st to November 3rd.

The record of these splendid deeds would lack completeness if the main points of comment suggested by the narrative were not placed before the reader's mind. Let us, therefore, discuss briefly the position which the Battle of the Carso occupies in the history of the war during 1916. What was its effect on the general position of the allied armies? How far did it bring the Italians towards the realisation of their immediate national objectives?

In answering these questions, it is necessary to distinguish between material and moral values, though it must be remembered that in the objective order of things there is an interplay of forces between both spheres.

MAP OF THE CARSO BATTLEFIELD, SEPTEMBER-NOVEMBER, 1916.

In this map of the whole of the Carso region, extending from Gorizia in the north to Trieste in the south, may be readily identified the centres of the fighting during the autumn of 1916. The battlegrounds—San

Grado, Veliki Hriback, Hill 144, etc.—may be seen immediately to the right of an imaginary line drawn from Gorizia to Montalcone, near the head of the Gulf of Panzano.

From the material point of view the loss inflicted on the Austro-German forces was serious in the extreme.

In order to realise this to the full extent we must look upon the Battle of the Carso as a subsequent phase of the conquest of Gorizia, and we must view the conquest of Gorizia as part of the counter-offensive in Trentino. These three movements were closely linked together, in fact, and they must be linked together in any study of general value. Now, during the period of Italian onslaught against Austria, from Gorizia to Castagnevizza, 42,000 prisoners were taken, together with 60 guns, 200 machine-guns, and a vast booty in general war material. Judging by statistics compiled from the information given by prisoners, and verified by careful comparison with data otherwise obtained, the proportion between the number of prisoners taken and the actual casualties suffered in the enemy's ranks was far higher than the normal proportion in other parts of the allied battle-front. T h i s phenomenon was due to conditions which are peculiar to the Italian front. In the first place comes the demolition of stone trenches effected by the artillery. On the Carso there was little necessity for the use of shrapnel; for the high-explosive shells did double work. By destroying the parapets and blasting the rocks beneath the enemy's feet, a deadly hail of splintered stone was showered on his troops. On many parts of the Carso it was discovered that even before the advance of the infantry the enemy had lost sixty per cent. of his effectives in the front line. We may, therefore, suppose that three times the number of prisoners taken would be a very conservative estimate of the total casualties. Adding the number thus obtained to the amount of casualties which are known to have been suffered in the Trentino—namely 140,000—we

arrive at a number approaching 300,000 as the sum total of the Austrian casualties on the Italian front during the summer and autumn campaigns. But the real number is probably much higher. Relating this figure to that which measures the results of the Battle of the Somme, where the combined Franco-British forces captured 51,000 Germans, we find that in the magnitude of the losses inflicted on the common enemy the Italian victory achieved results which stood well beside those of the classic Franco-British offensive.

It is a fine record, but the importance of it is intensified when we come to consider the peculiar conditions of the Austro-Italian conflict. The military value of the positions held by Austria on the Carso and Isonzo was the main source of her strength. Several of those positions, such as San Michele, Sabotino, and Veliki Hriback, were such that to maintain them against an attacking force the defenders needed only a small percentage of the forces necessary for a successful assault. Indeed, it is doubtful if Gorizia would have been taken had it not been for the able strategy employed by General Cadorna. And once it had fallen, Austria could not hope to retake it, if she were not prepared to employ forces at least four or five times greater than those with which she had originally held it. In driving them farther backwards towards a territory which is far more difficult to defend, the Battle of the Carso forced the Austrian armies not only to make up for their losses but to increase enormously the number of effectives. Reacting on the whole Austro-German line in the east and in the west, this state of affairs seriously weakened the resistance of the common enemy.

But there is another aspect of the matter which reveals in a stronger light the value of Italy's stroke. The most

ANTI-AIRCRAFT GUN ON MONTE NERO.
When M. Chavez first flew over the Alps in 1910 the world marvelled at the achievement. In the Great War, however, scouting airmen soared frequently above the Julian Alps and anti-aircraft guns studded many of the mountain peaks.

RETURN OF A SEAPLANE TO ITS BASE ON ITALIAN SHORES.
Italy is poorly provided with harbours on her Adriatic littoral, whereas Austria at the beginning of the war had many fine bases between Trieste and the southern extremity of Dalmatia, whence she might have despatched strong forces against her enemy. Italian seaplanes did important service watching for any such attempt until the Italian Navy had "bottled up" the Austrian Navy in its bases and secured full control of the Adriatic.

N

vital portion of the whole Austro-German battle-front was that block of territory lying between the Isonzo, the Vipacco, and the Plain of Trieste. It defended not only the Adriatic seaport, but also the road to Lubiana (Laibach), which is the principal junction of the main railroads between Austria and her Adriatic provinces. The Battle of the Carso brought the Italian Army into contact with the main outer defences of Trieste and practically within striking distance of the commercial arteries which supply the city.

Only one line of positions now remained along the mountain defences; to construct a second and a third it was necessary to entrench on the plain. A large force of German engineers was employed in the construction of these defences, for the Central Empires **In touch with** had fully realised the peril which threat- **Trieste's defences** ened them. They were fully cognisant of the fact that, should Trieste fall, the Istrian Peninsula would probably follow suit, Pola would have to be evacuated by the Fleet, and the position of the Austrian naval forces in the Adriatic seriously jeopardised. If the Battle of the Carso had done no more than to compel the military leaders of the Central Empires to concentrate large bodies of their forces on the defence of the Adriatic it had rendered a service of immense value to the allied cause.

Coming to the more restricted question of the strategic position which the Italian Army occupied in relation to its particular objective, we can easily discover the point of convergence towards which the Carso movements were directed. And when viewed in that light the offensives of September, October, and November assume an aspect which has a dramatic interest; for each of them was an act in a great military drama, carrying on and developing the

A NEST OF WAR EAGLES IN THE ALPS.
Headquarters of an outpost constructed by Italian engineers in a mountain cleft on the Alpine front. Here at intervals the men were able to enjoy some rude comforts in comparative security.

central theme towards a majestic climax. After the conquest of Gorizia the Austrian official bulletins assured the Teutonic populace that the fall of the city was not a matter of deep concern in the general military situation, for the positions on the Carso Plateau were stronger than the original primary line on the Isonzo. The German correspondents at the Austrian front were at pains to popularise the same theory among their readers, adding that the Isonzo citadel could be easily recaptured.

It would be a mistake to suppose that these statements were entirely without foundation. Having held firm at Monte Santo and Duino the Austrians judged, with a good show of reason, that **Austria's mis-** it would be impossible for the Italians to **leading calculations** manœuvre against their flanks. They, therefore, concluded that the pentagon of the Eastern Carso would withstand the heaviest attacks. The pentagon was formed of five great strongholds, linked to one another by an elaborate series of defences and supported by a number of subsidiary positions both within and without. All these points have been already mentioned. During the offensives of September, October, and November they all went down before the Italian blows.

The new line reached in November brought the aggressors into close contact with the last defences on the Carso. In August Trieste was thirty-two kilometres away; in November that distance had been reduced to twenty-two kilometres; but of these remaining twenty-two about eighteen lay on the lowland surrounding the city. Therefore

HOW THE ROCKY AERIE WAS REACHED.
Rope ladder by which the hut shown above was attained. The ladder was some hundreds of feet in length, and to ascend it called for the steady nerve of the experienced mountain climber.

IN MONFALCONE SHIPYARD.
Interior of the works of the Austrian shipyard at Monfalcone which was captured by the Italians.

who had shown a lack of ability had been replaced by men of approved worth. General Boroevic was supplied with troops and artillery and ammunition to the full extent of his request. And the quality of the troops put at his disposal could be objected to by no commander in Europe. He had several divisions of Hungarian soldiers, hardy Croat and Bosnian mountaineers, and only very few regiments of Austrian Landwehr or Landsturm. On October 23rd Archduke Frederick, then Commander-in-Chief of the Imperial Army, visited the Carso front and inspected all its defences. In company with General Boroevic he examined the immediate defences of Trieste. Then he visited the Archduke Charles Joseph—who in the following month became Emperor of Austria—on the Carso. He spoke with the Staffs of the different sections, and was assured of the Austrian power to resist at every point. Concluding his tour at Villach, after an inspection of the forces fighting in Carinthia, he returned to Supreme Headquarters on October 25th, well pleased (according to one of the Vienna journals) with all that he had seen. **General Boroevic's elaborate plans** To make assurance doubly sure, he ordered further reinforcements to the Carso. During the following week the bases at Komen and Temnizza were busy receiving and distributing additional supplies of men and artillery, machine-guns, bomb-throwers, and ammunition.

But within the three first days of November this elaborate system of defence had fallen. The Austrians did not attribute the disaster to fate or accident, but to the military superiority of their rival. For a people who place so high a military value on the will to conquer and the consciousness of superiority in the rank and file of the Army, this enforced change of appreciation was a more crushing blow than the material loss of men and guns. The old idea of Teutonic superiority and Latin inferiority was gone. The " Deutschland über Alles " spirit, which the military caste had made

the Italians had succeeded in breaking down more than three-fourths of the mountain defences which had formed the great bulwark of the Adriatic seaport.

In the moral sphere the value of the conquest was marked by an entire volte-face on the part of the Teuton military authorities. Articles in praise of the Italian Army were now allowed to appear in the Press, and nothing more was heard of the old superstition about the " mandolin players." On November 9th the " Neue Freie Presse," of Vienna, uttered a jeremiad which probably reflected the general state of mind in the Dual Monarchy.

Teutonic respect for Italy " Quiet reigns on the Carso," said the Vienna journal. " Is the battle over, or will it break out anew ? Probably the Italian Supreme Command wishes to consolidate the gains of November 1st and 2nd and to rest the troops. Then there will be a new assault, for the conquest of further ground to a depth of four or five kilometres. Another period of rest will follow, and so on."

It was no longer argued, as it had been argued in the case of Gorizia, that the Austrian commanders were taken unawares, for on the Carso they well knew what was coming and had prepared for it accordingly. Commanders

CORNER OF AUSTRIA'S LOST SHIPYARD.
Part of the Monfalcone shipyard which the Italians succeeded in taking from the Austrians in 1915. It long continued to be dominated by the artillery of the ejected enemy, who subjected it to frequent bombardment from the heights which they held to the east.

the dominant characteristic of the Teuton populace, was waning fast.

Among the Staff officers captured on Faiti Hrib was one who declared openly his impression of the Italian Army, vouching for the fact that he gave expression to the general state of mind among his confrères. Speaking with the correspondent of the Rome " Tribuna," he said :

" I have never seen General Cadorna personally, but I once saw a portrait of him and I read an article about him, published originally in an Italian paper and subsequently copied in the Austrian Press. My impression of your Generalissimo is that he is unerschütterlich."

" What do you mean by that ? " asked the correspondent.

" I will tell you," replied the Austrian. " Cadorna

AUSTRIAN DEFENSIVE LINES ON THE CARSO.
Diagram of the Austrian trench system east of the Vallone. At the end of the Italian offensive in the autumn of 1916 the Austrians held only the third main line terminating at the Hermada Mountains, the last position covering the Triestine Plain.

strikes me as a piece of massive sculpture, roughly shaped, as if from one of those rocks on the Carso. I do not say that through want of respect; but that convex forehead, that head which looks almost like a piece of primitive carving, reveals to us, your enemies, a danger in itself. He is like a tower, a fortress which you have raised to encompass our downfall. In our journals the caricaturists have outlined him as a man of stone, and stone is hard. That is why our Austrian soldiers hate Cadorna, but they are forced to look upon him as a dreadful enemy."

"Have you nothing more to say?"

"Oh, yes!" said the Teuton officer. "Cadorna has deceived us many times. In one week last spring he gathered together a new army, rushed it to the Trentino, and blew our offensive to pieces. He then showed a quickness of insight which is a mark of genius. On the Isonzo

he has upset our plans several times, and he has done it by that cursed habit of silence."

On December 26th the Italian Supreme Command published a general summary of the year's work and commented on the position then held by the Army. The concluding paragraphs, full of justified pride and hope, form a fitting close to the story of the Battle of the Carso:

Looking back on the year which is drawing to its close, the Italian Army has reason for legitimate satisfaction and pride in all the efforts made, the difficulties overcome, and the victories achieved.

The development of its military power was effected in the winter of 1915-16, thanks to the wonderful work of reorganisation and production, in which the whole nation participated. In the spring we sustained in the Trentino the powerful, long-prepared Austrian offensive, which the enemy, with insolent effrontery, styled a punitive expedition against our country. But after the first successes, which were due to the preponderance of material means collected, above all in artillery, the proposed invasion was quickly stopped, and the enemy was counter-attacked and forced to retire in haste into the mountains, leaving on the Alpine slopes the flower of his Army, and paying bitterly the price for his fallacious enterprise, not only here, but also on the plains of Galicia.

Our Army did not rest after its wonderful effort. While maintaining a vigorous pressure on the Trentino front, in order to gain better positions and to deceive the enemy as to our intentions, a rapid retransfer of strong forces to the Julian front was made. In the first days of August began that irresistible offensive which, in two days only, caused the fall of the very strong fortress of Gorizia and of the formidable system of defences on the Carso, to the west of the Vallone. Doberdo, San Michele, Sabotino —names recalling sanguinary struggles and slaughter—ceased to be for the Austro-Hungarian Army the symbols of a resistance vaunted insuperable, and became the emblems of brilliant Italian victories. The enemy's boastful assertions of having inexorably arrested our invasion on the front selected and desired by himself were refuted at one stroke.

The year's work summarised

From that day our advance on the Carso was developed constantly and irresistibly. It was interrupted by pauses, indispensable for the preparation of the mechanical means of destruction without which the bravest attacks would lead only to the vain sacrifice of precious human lives.

Our constant and full success on the Julian front is witnessed by 42,000 prisoners, 60 guns, 200 machine-guns, and the rich booty taken between the beginning of August and December.

Also on the rest of the front our indefatigable troops roused the admiration of all who saw them for their extraordinary efforts to overcome not only the forces of the enemy, but also the difficulties of Nature.

The coming year is looked forward to by our Army with serenity and confidence. Our soldiers are supported by the unanimous approval of the nation, and by faith in themselves and in the justice of their cause. They face willingly their hard and perilous life, under the guidance of their beloved Sovereign, who, from the first day of war, with a rare constancy has shared their fortunes. Our Army is waiting in perfect readiness to renew the effort which will carry it to the fulfilment of the unfailing destiny of our people.

COMMANDO SUPREMO, *December 26th, 1916.*

WHERE NATURE FROWNED UPON THE WORK OF WAR.
Sheds and refuges on Monte Nero, suggesting to the imagination something of the natural difficulties which the Italians had to overcome in their theatre of the war merely in respect of keeping their men supplied with the bare necessaries of existence.

CHAPTER CLXXV.

RUSSIA IN THE THROES OF REVOLUTION.

Imminence of Civil War—Grand Duke Denounces the German Empress of Russia—Tsarevitch Poisoned by the "Dark Forces"— How Protopopoff Succeeded to Rasputin—Preparations for Another Red Sunday—Plot to Starve the People of Petrograd into Rebellion—Protopopoff's Agents Begin the Riot—Petrograd Revolutionary Groups Turn the Pseudo-Revolution into a Real Revolution—Half-Starved Soldiers Shoot their Officers and Side with the People—Tsar Refuses to Meet the Popular Demands—White Sunday and the Birth of Free Russia—General Russky Compels the Tsar to Abdicate—All Army Leaders Go Over to the Provisional Government—Communists of Petrograd Endeavour to Promote Peace with Germany and Civil War at Home—German and Austrian Socialists' Scheme to Drown Russian People in their Own Blood—Wild Machinations of the Communists—Disorganisation of Russian Armies—Communists Try to Arrest Members of Provisional Government and Duma—Russian Armies Threaten to March Against the Petrograd Commune—Agitators Work Upon the Peasantry to Bring About Confiscation of all Property—Attacks on Landowners and Huge Waste of Agricultural Effort—Sobering Effect of Reverse on the Stokhod—Cossack League and First Army Declare Against the Commune—Lenin's Plot Against the Allies—Victory of Communists Over Miliukoff—Prince Lvoff Transforms a Difficulty into an Opportunity—Russian Revolutionists Challenge Teutonic Revolutionists to Overthrow all Autocracies.

ON February 27th, 1917, the Conference of the Allies at Petrograd, referred to at the close of Chapter CLXXII. (Vol. IX., p. 35), came to an end, and the chief British representative, Lord Milner, left for England in a troubled frame of mind. In the afternoon of the same day the Duma reopened, with the British Ambassador, Sir George Buchanan, sitting in the centre of the diplomatic box, grimly watching the final efforts of the "dark forces" of Russia which he had boldly denounced.

Everybody knew that civil warfare was imminent; nobody knew what the result would be. The Allied Conference, at which the new Russian Minister of War, General Bieliaeff, and all the other reactionary intriguers had spoken fair words and given fair promises, had proved only an historic farce. The Russian Ministry had already arranged terms of peace with Germany, Austria-Hungary, Bulgaria, and Turkey, and was secretly prepared, if France stood out for the return of all Alsace and Lorraine, to make a separate peace with the Teutons, Bulgars, and Turks.

The action of Sir George Buchanan in denouncing at Moscow the sinister favourite of the Tsar and the Tsaritza seems to have provoked in the Russian Court a

SIR GEORGE BUCHANAN, BRITISH AMBASSADOR IN RUSSIA.
At the reception of the allied Ambassadors at the Marinsky Palace, Petrograd, in March, 1917, Sir George Buchanan, the British Ambassador, addressing the Council of Ministers, conveyed to them "the most heartfelt greetings of a friendly and allied nation," and looked forward to "a new era of prosperity, progress, and glory" opening before Russia.

violent feeling of enmity against Great Britain. Stimulated by the speech of the British Ambassador, one of the leading men of the House of Romanoff, the Grand Duke Dmitri Pavlovitch, had killed Gregory Rasputin in a bold and open manner, and had practically dared the weak chief of his family to avenge the murder of his favourite.

Nearly all the men and women of the House of Romanoff drew away from their crowned kinsman, and in one of their palaces in Petrograd held conferences throughout January and February, 1917, with the leading men of the Duma and the Council of Empire. Another Prince of Royal Blood, the Grand Duke Nicholas Michailovitch, had in December, 1916, called upon the Tsar and denounced the Tsaritza as a treacherous and hostile German woman.

"I have said my say," said the Grand Duke, "and now you can have me shot and bury me in your palace garden."

Nicholas looked at him with glassy eyes, but went on offering him lighted matches for his cigarettes, and shook hands with him when he left. The Grand Duke thereupon wrote the Tsar a letter, in which he again accused the Tsaritza of being a false adviser and a traitress to Russia. Save that the Grand Duke was banished to his country estate, nothing was done to him.

MADAME VYRUBOVA.
Original centre of the Russian "dark forces," she introduced Rasputin to the Court circle.

One more effort was made by the Imperial Family to prevent civil war or a German peace. The Tsaritza Alexandra, who was a granddaughter of Queen Victoria and a daughter of Princess Alice and the Grand Duke of Hesse, was visited by the divorced wife of her own brother, the reigning Grand Duke of Hesse. Having remarried a prince of the House of Romanoff, the lady had the interests of Russia at heart, and in the frankest of conversations she informed the German Tsaritza of the danger she was running.

Nothing, however, could move the strange, wild woman from her evil course. She exclaimed that the Romanoff princess knew nothing about anything except bridge-playing, and that she had sat on the throne for twenty-two years and thoroughly understood the Russian people. In her view the Russians would fight for autocracy, and the only persons in favour of a Liberal Government were a small pack of traitors who could easily be dealt with.

In regard to the policy of maintaining autocratic rule, the Tsar was as resolute as his German wife. The difference between husband and wife was that Nicholas was also determined to continue the war and overthrow William of Hohenzollern, whom he personally disliked and patriotically regarded as a bitter enemy of all the Slav races. At Field Headquarters, amid his leading generals, the Tsar did all he could to pursue the war with vigour. But, in his capital, the well-meaning, feeble, and yet honest autocrat allowed himself to be misled on political grounds by his intriguing wife and her creatures in the bureaucratic Ministry. He became afraid of allowing the local assemblies or national representatives in his Empire to exercise any power.

Crisis after crisis occurred in the supply of food and production of munitions, owing to the way in which the corrupt and traitorous bureaucracy interfered with the organisation created by the representative bodies. On practically every occasion of domestic conflict the Tsar, while still hoping to win the war, put down the men who were loyal to him and to the Army and the nation, and increased the powers of his treacherous and irresponsible Ministers. He removed loyal Russian ecclesiastics from the metropolitan sees of Petrograd and Moscow, and to these positions, which were superior to those of archbishoprics, he appointed, at the suggestion of his wife and favourite, two notorious agents of Germany. The Russian Church became corrupt in its centres of power and administration, resembling in this respect the Russian Civil Service.

A German potentate, the Duke of Mecklenburg-Strelitz, obtained an important position in the

GREGORY RASPUTIN.
Monk, who for years exercised a sinister influence in the Russian Court. "Removed," December, 1916.

M. BORIS STÜRMER.
The pro-German Prime Minister of Russia who had sought to make separate peace. Notoriously a creature of the Tsaritza.

Palace of the Tsar, there acting as counsellor to the Tsaritza while she worked to delude her husband and defeat his armies. Outside the palace the principal agent of the Empress was the new Minister of the Interior, Protopopoff, who became, on the death of Rasputin, the most active plotter in the German cause.

The Austrian, Boris Stürmer, who, as former Prime Minister, had tried to make a separate peace with Germany and had been overthrown by Professor Paul Miliukoff, in the Duma, remained in the palace with the Empress, and assisted Protopopoff in the schemes.

Kurloff, another treacherous bureaucrat, sat in the Ministry of the Interior at Petrograd, and there collected the gangs of the Black Hundred, and clothed these hired assassins

DUKE CHARLES MICHAEL.
Heir to Grand Duchy of Mecklenburg-Strelitz, but naturalised, July, 1914. Arrested by the Duma.

GRAND DUKE NICHOLAS.
In December, 1916, the Grand Duke Nicholas Michailovitch had warned the Tsar with outspoken courage.

M. PROTOPOPOFF.
Russian Minister of the Interior; after the death of Rasputin the most powerful of pro-German plotters.

GRAND DUKE DMITRI.
The Grand Duke Dmitri Pavlovitch was responsible for the bold and open "removal" of Rasputin.

in police uniforms and trained them in machine-gun practice.

The new Minister of War, who was carefully chosen so that he would not act like his predecessor and support the Duma, brought thirty thousand troops to the capital, under officers of the reactionary school, and placed them under the command of another reactionary commander, General Khabaloff.

Protopopoff, however, remained the dominant figure in all the intrigues and preparations. Without him the Tsaritza and the Tsar would have been almost impotent. Unlike all the creatures of routine with whom he worked, the new Minister was possessed of original power. His associates had edged themselves into their positions by toadying to Court favourites, and by accumulating the proceeds of blackmail and bribery until they were able to purchase high positions in which they could rapidly make a fortune at the expense of the nation.

Protopopoff's subtle intrigues From Stürmer down to Stürmer's secretary they lacked creative force of intellect. Protopopoff, on the other hand, was a wealthy landowner and a capable man of business, who had first distinguished himself as a champion of freedom in the Duma. There he became Vice-President, in which capacity he visited Great Britain in the early part of the war, and again made himself remarkable by his advocacy of the common cause of the Allies. He saw the new British munition factories and the expanding British Fleet some months before the Battle of Jutland Bank, and was able to foresee the sudden rise of Great Britain into a great military as well as a great naval Power.

Extraordinary as it now seems, the sights that he saw in Great Britain helped to alter the frame of mind of the Vice-President of the Duma. Apparently, fear and jealousy of the British power were stirred within him. On his return to Russia he opened negotiations with a representative of the German Government in Sweden, and then seemingly made up his mind that a separate peace with Germany and the repression of the democratic movement in Russia were required in the interests of his country. He entered into an alliance with Stürmer, and, while pretending to be still a Liberal, strengthened the bureaucracy as Minister of the Interior, **Madame Vyrubova and Rasputin** and through Rasputin and the creatures of Rasputin acquired the confidence of the Tsaritza and the Tsar. Upon the death of Rasputin he became the power behind the throne. By working directly upon the Tsar and indirectly assisting the Tsaritza and the Germans he became the virtual controller of the destinies of Eastern Europe.

Behind him was the repulsive figure of Madame Vyrubova. This woman may fairly be regarded as the original centre of all the "dark forces" of Russia. She was, as leading lady-in-waiting, the chamber confidante of both Tsar and Tsaritza, and took a leading part in the spiritualistic vagaries in which the Frenchman Philippe and the Russian monk Helidor played upon the minds of the rulers. When Helidor fell out of favour, Madame Vyrubova introduced Rasputin, and became, with this infernal witch-doctor, the leading conspirator against the Russian throne and the Russian people.

The Emperor's heir, Alexis, had inherited through his

A MILITARY CEREMONIAL ABOLISHED BY THE REVOLUTION.

Changing guard at the Winter Palace in Petrograd. As a result of the most rapid and least bloody Revolution in history this ceremony was swept away within a week of the outbreak. The Imperial Guard promptly took the oath of allegiance to the new Provisional Government, the Imperial ensign and symbols were at once removed from the Palace, and the building itself was henceforth appropriated to national uses.

mother a tendency to bleed to a dangerous extent from the slightest wound or from sudden internal injury. Rasputin knew two Chinese drugs that stimulated the action of the heart and produced bleeding. He gave these drugs to Madame Vyrubova when he was dismissed from the palace, and she poisoned the young prince and made him bleed, and only stopped poisoning him when her fellow-conspirator was recalled to favour. By this means the two murderous charlatans obtained an amazing power over both the Emperor and the Empress.

The execution of Rasputin by the Grand Duke Dmitri Pavlovitch in no way cleansed the Russian Court. Madame Vyrubova remained in constant intercourse with the perturbed and angry Emperor and Empress, and urged them to maintain the autocracy for the sake of their son, whom she had really arranged to poison in response to the dying order of Rasputin. Rasputin had always prophesied that the young prince would die forty days after his own death, and the preparations he had made for this diabolical vengeance can easily be imagined. The woman, however,

first sought for another man to help her, and selected Protopopoff as her new partner in crime.

At the suggestion of Madame Vyrubova the renegade Vice-President of the Duma practised some of the arts of spiritualism, and gave a séance at the palace. In the presence of the Emperor and Empress he pretended to summon the spirit of Rasputin. This trick of his had an astonishing success upon the superstitious Emperor. For years Nicholas had followed the advice of Rasputin, and he now obeyed any order that Protopopoff delivered while pretending to act as a spiritualistic medium.

Thus, with Madame Vyrubova controlling the affairs of the Palace and watching every current of thought in Emperor and Empress and communicating all information to Protopopoff, the new successor to Rasputin was able, with his great business ability and his connection with all the other pro-German leading bureaucrats, to become the master of the Russian Empire.

The self-styled Russian Richelieu

In his own opinion Protopopoff was the Richelieu and Bismarck of the new age. His former friends and admirers in the Duma refused to have anything to do with him. They would not even allow him to address them in the House, as other bureaucratic Ministers did. In various ways and on different occasions the National Assembly warned the Tsar that the removal of Protopopoff from the Ministry was the chief preliminary to any reconciliation or compromise with the autocratic system. The constitutional movement against the renegade only increased his sinister and widespread power.

Before the Duma reopened Protopopoff concocted a very subtle plot against the representatives of the people. As Minister of the Interior he knew the names and places of residence of thousands of Russian Revolutionists of the extreme school. He could have placed them in prison or had them tried by court-martial and shot in the course of a few days. Far, however, from repressing them, he sent his agents among them with funds, and arranged for a considerable number of German Social Democrats to enter Petrograd and work alongside the Russian Anarchists, Tolstoyans, Pacifists, Communists, and Red Socialists. In the munition factories, especially, Protopopoff's men were the wildest and fiercest of agitators. They continually urged the working men to strike and riot, and begin the movement that was to make Europe a federation of Socialistic republics. Men were disguised and dressed so as to resemble Professor Miliukoff and other popular leaders of the Duma, and sent into the munition factories to induce the working men to erect barricades in the streets. To an extent arms and ammunition

FIERCE STREET FIGHTING BETWEEN COSSACKS AND POLICE.
From the first the Cossacks were sympathetic with the people, and on March 11th and 12th, 1917, the really decisive days of the Revolution, when the police, secreted in garrets and on roofs, began firing wildly on the populace, they engaged them fiercely and drove them out of their strongholds.

were provided; but this was only done in a small way, as Protopopoff designed to produce his own "revolution" within such limits that he hoped easily to control it.

When the Duma opened the grand plotter employed two methods of causing the insurrection he had so carefully prepared. His early system of engineering strikes had been defeated by the organising talent of a former President of the Duma, M. Gutchkoff, who had become one of the leading men in the Upper House, the Council of Empire. M. Gutchkoff was a man of large experience, who had fought for the Boers in the South African War, worked in the Manchurian campaign, and done much to assist the Grand Duke Nicholas and General Alexeieff in the munition crisis of 1915. He was Director of the Committee of War Industries, and into this committee he introduced some highly capable Labour delegates, who moved among the munition workers and prevented them from striking when Protopopoff tried to make them do so.

So Protopopoff's first step was to arrest the leading Labour members of M. Gutchkoff's committee. This not only angered the National Assembly but removed from the working class of Petrograd their principal protectors against the false "revolutionary" movement. The Duma, however, remained grimly patient under this foul stroke, and though Professor Miliukoff made a speech proclaiming that the struggle for liberty was about to open, no signal for it was given by the representatives of the people.

The tension increased in a desperate manner during the first week of March, 1917. Protopopoff then used his second method. He brought terrific pressure to bear upon the populace by withholding food supplies from them. While one of his creatures, the Minister of Agriculture, blandly explained to the Duma that the lack of food was caused by snowstorms—as though snowstorms were unexpected things in a Russian winter—the governors of the provinces, who were directly controlled by Protopopoff, artfully induced the peasants to hold back their crops for higher prices.

Engineering an artificial famine

In the early part of the war, urban difficulties in regard to food supply in the greatest agricultural State in the world had arisen through pure incompetence on the part of the bureaucracy. The bureaucrats had foreseen nothing and arranged nothing; but the municipalities and the local councils had prevented famine. These local bodies, indeed, could have soon arranged for all the people to be fed, had it not been for the Tsar's personal fear that the local councils would so grow in power as to make autocratic government impossible. Until Protopopoff became

REVOLUTIONISTS WRECKING THE HOTEL ASTORIA.
As some sailors were marching past the Hotel Astoria, Petrograd, a machine-gun secreted on the top floor opened fire, whereupon the mob stormed and wrecked the hotel and killed the gunners.

dictator the people continued to go short of food, merely in order that the bureaucratic system should remain in full and futile force.

With diabolical ingenuity the renegade turned the defects of the bureaucratic system into an instrument of popular oppression and political intrigue. After deliberately aggravating all the difficulties of food supply, he pretended to ask the advice of the Duma as to the best means of obtaining grain. In the National Assembly, as he knew, there were two parties which disagreed over the method of fighting the artificial famine. One party, desiring to get food at any cost, was ready to offer the peasants the highest possible price; while the other party thought that a lower price, combined with a system of requisition, would meet the situation. The food debate, therefore, caused considerable differences of opinion. In the first week of March Protopopoff informed the Tsar that he had broken the power of the Duma and avoided all real danger to the dynasty.

The Tsar went to the front, confident and pleased, while Protopopoff arranged his little pseudo-revolution, which

o

was intended to be the decisive weapon against the popular Assembly. The rations in Petrograd were suddenly reduced to a starvation level. But an historic blunder was committed by the agent of the subtle and tricky dictator. He thoughtlessly held up all food supplies, some of which were scarcely more than a day's journey from the capital. There were 35,000 troops in the city, and by way of keeping them faithful to the Crown and ready to shoot the hungry populace, their daily allowance of rye-bread was reduced from 3 lb. to 1¾ lb.

This diminution of the ration of the Petrograd garrison changed the fate of Russia and of mankind. Most of the soldiers were reservists, with families, **Reactionary agent's** recently called to the Colours, and in sym- **historic blunder** pathy with the people from whom they were drawn. The Revolutionary ferment was working in them, owing to the fact that the students, who were the principal intellectual force in the movement towards free government, were mingling with the troops and preaching every variety of doctrine of revolt. Protopopoff had not foreseen any possibility of serious disaffection among the soldiers. He had confined himself to organising the police and the secret police, and bringing up to the capital from all parts of the country gangs of Government bravoes such as had formerly been used in massacres of the Jews.

In regard to the military forces Protopopoff relied upon the new reactionary Minister of War and the reactionary commander of the Petrograd garrison. These two men, happily for the popular cause, were blind both to the changes that had taken place in the Army and to the propaganda which was spreading among the troops who were half-starving on

UNDER THE NEW FLAG.
Russian sailor, with the red flag of Revolution, leading a company of soldiers on a police hunt in Petrograd.

insufficient rations. On Wednesday, March 7th, 1917, Protopopoff opened his own little false "revolution." Some of his bands, led by his secret police, held demonstrations in the streets and raised the cry of "Give us bread!" Numerous attempts were made to induce the working men to join in the demonstrations when they left the factories in the evening. The people, however, remained under the control of their own organisers, and a happy phrase went round in which the true state of the situation was expressed in a sort of a pun. The phrase ran, "This is not a strike, but a false strike." But the word used for "false strike" was "protopofka," which had the merit of approaching the sound of the name of the man who was trying to murder Russian freedom.

A few Cossack patrols moved about the streets, but did not interfere with the people or with the pseudo-revolutionaries whom Protopopoff was employing. On Thursday, March 8th, the agitation continued and increased. A new force appeared on the **Socialist leaders** scene in the Russian Social Democrats, **force the pace** directed by M. Kerensky, a brilliant and perfervid young lawyer, who was a deputy in the Duma, and by M. Cheidze, another impassioned Revolutionary orator of the same stamp. Being far less cautious than the constitutional members of the National Assembly, these two Socialist leaders at once forced the pace of the popular movement, and began to fight Protopopoff with his own weapons of street rioting. Genuine working men in large numbers joined the false demonstrators and started wrecking the bakers' shops. Thereupon the Cossack patrols opened fire, and the armed police tried to form a cordon through the city and confine the rioters to the working-class quarters.

So far all had gone excellently from the point of view of Protopopoff. He had provoked the kind of riot which he needed as an excuse for closing the Duma, for silencing the Press, and for establishing absolute autocratic

SEARCHING FOR WEAPONS.
After the Arsenal at Petrograd had been rushed the crowd helped themselves to arms and ammunition, and civilians were searched for these when the troops began to restore order. In circle: Searching for police spies.

house-tops, and roofs of Government buildings and churches, where they had placed machine-guns, rifles, and stores of ammunition in preparation for an insurrection. Since the opening of the Duma they had been eagerly waiting the order to fire, and at last they opened the battle between the Crown and the people without any provocation.

Protopopoff, no doubt, gave the signal. For his own purposes he wanted a great riot at all costs, and he proceeded to provoke it. He was a man of nervous temperament, playing in blood for a mighty stake. Against him were three Russian gentlemen—Prince Lvoff (the President of the Union of County Councils), M. Rodzianko (the President of the Duma), and Professor Miliukoff (the leader of the Constitutional Democratic Party). The longer the outbreak was delayed the greater grew their influence over the national forces. Their agents were busy throughout the country, where their power became so great that even a temporary defeat in Petrograd would not have permanently overthrown them.

Playing for a mighty stake

They, therefore, remained quietly expectant. The Social Democrats, with yet wilder schools of Revolutionaries, arrayed themselves for battle, and with Protopopoff's agents urging them on, swept over all the bounds that the reactionary Minister had attempted to impose. They set up clubs in both munition factories and barracks, and with thousands of delegates from the working-class and military groups, they improvised a cumbrous yet far-ranging system of control that much exceeded in power the Jacobin organisation in the French Revolution. When the infantry were brought out in the afternoon of Saturday,

RED FLAG IN PETROGRAD.
Soldiers on a motor-car bearing the red flag on their bayonets through the snowy streets of the Russian capital.

government. In the Lower House there was an open conflict between the Constitutional group and the Socialist group in regard to the conquest of Constantinople and the Dardanelles. Moreover, as we have already seen, the Constitutionalists themselves were divided over the problem of obtaining food supplies.

Protopopoff tried to increase the division among the deputies over the urgent question of food, and a conference was arranged between some of the reactionary Ministers and the leading members of the National Assembly. In this fateful conference, held while the hungry crowds were demonstrating in the streets of the capital, the representatives of the nation completely disconcerted both the Tsar and his bureaucrats by showing a solid front. They required that the local councils, which had proved their organising powers in the munition crisis, should be made the principal collectors of grain, and that the distribution of supplies should be managed by the municipal authorities. Protopopoff did not appear at the conference. Acting through the undistinguished Ministers who were his creatures, the sinister dictator rejected the help of the local councils and arranged to end both the Duma and the Council of Empire, deal with the recalcitrant members as the Kaiser had dealt with some of his political opponents, send them into the Army, and bring the "revolution" to a bloody finish.

Protopopoff's police open battle

On March 9th, when the failure of the conference was known, the bulk of the working men of Petrograd joined in the demonstration, and surged along the Nevsky and other main streets in a mood of apparent good-humour, singing songs and offering some of the soldiers cigarettes. The people did not expect a struggle would take place, and many of them were curious sightseers rather than potential rebels. It was Protopopoff's armed police who deliberately excited the fighting passions of the mob. For more than a fortnight these men had been occupying attics,

SOLDIERS WHO JOINED THE REVOLUTIONISTS.
Civilian cutting a piece off a soldier's red ribbon, in order that he might show that he, too, was of the Duma Party and on the side of the revolution. In circle: Soldier wearing the ribbon round his arm.

March 10th, and ordered to shoot down the people, only a few troops fired a few rounds. Others mutinied and killed their officers. Protopopoff's police became more violent, but as they lacked military support they were in places killed by the mob.

By this time the real Revolution was in train, and General Khabaloff, backed by General Bieliaeff, the new Minister for War, resolved to hold the capital down by armed force until the Tsar could arrange to rail an army back from the front under General Ivanoff, who was apparently the only first-rate Army leader who remained loyal to the weak and decadent autocrat.

On Sunday, March 11th, the commander of the Petrograd army issued a proclamation warning the people that the soldiers would use force to preserve order. The newspapers were not printed, the tramways ceased running, and the capital became the supreme battlefield of the Empire. The Guards were called out to shoot down the

THE ABDICATION SCENE AT PSKOFF.
On March 15th, 1917, MM. Gutchkoff and Schulgin, representing the Duma, arrived at Pskoff, where Nicholas II. received them in the Imperial train and signed the manifesto announcing his abdication.

people, but the character of these household troops had completely changed. Hindenburg had destroyed most of the old Guards regiments in the early battle amid the Masurian Lakes. Both officers and men of the old school had vanished, and their places had been supplied by new recruits who were in sympathy with the people from whom they were drawn.

Every heavy blow delivered by Hindenburg and Mackensen had indirectly served the purpose of purging the Russian Army of officers and non-commissioned officers ready to support autocracy, and had introduced fresher and more liberal forces into all the regiments. From the beginning of the struggle the Duma and the National Assembly knew that the character of the Army was changed, and that with the return of General Alexeieff, a champion

of Constitutionalism, to the High Command the Army would not remain at the service of the reactionists.

On White Sunday things fell out very differently from the events of Red Sunday twelve years previously. The famishing Petrograd garrison was almost as discontented as the populace, and was organising for revolt. A non-commissioned officer of the Volynski Guards, by name Kirpitchnikoff, went round the barracks and won over all the other non-commissioned officers and all the men. They discussed the case of their officers, and decided they were all likely to be loyal to the Duma with the exception of one company commander. Him they tried and shot, and then went out into the streets and persuaded the Sappers of the Guard and the Preobrajenski Regiment to join them.

These combined forces of Guardsmen were the mainspring of the Revolution, for they gradually won over the rest of the garrison and defeated Protopopoff's armed police. One company of the Pavlovski Guards, after first **Mainspring of the Revolution** firing on the mob on the Nevsky and killing and wounding a hundred people, mutinied and shot their own officers. Then the Cossacks came over in considerable numbers with large bodies of infantry of the line.

Many of the soldiers of liberty marched to the Taurida Palace, where the Duma sat, and asked the deputies for orders. This was a moment when the National Assembly lost a splendid opportunity of controlling the situation. The deputies should have kept the troops, who came over to them, wholly under their command, and should have vigorously directed their negotiations with the rest of the garrison and their conflicts with the reactionary police. It almost seems, however, as though the leaders of the Duma were oppressed by their memories of Red Sunday and feared that the popular effort would be again defeated. It was left to the Anarchist council of workmen's delegates to form an alliance with the victorious troops by co-opting representatives of the soldiers into the council.

Protopopoff was seriously alarmed, and, pretending to be ill, withdrew to the background, and induced the Tsar to issue ukases suspending the session of the National Assembly. This suspension had been his aim throughout, but his long-prepared stroke fell too late. By the time the ukases were published the Taurida Palace was defended by revolted Guardsmen. The deputies continued their sitting all through the night, while in other rooms of the palace a multitude of delegates from groups of soldiers and workmen continued to direct the fighting in the capital.

When the members of the Duma tried to govern, they found themselves outside the centre of affairs. The men who had raised the whirlwind continued to direct the storm. They were non-commissioned officers and enterprising privates with a gift of eloquence, with the orators of the working-men's sections and numerous agents of the secret police. **Position of the secret agents** If the people were victorious, the false agitators were in a position to prove that they had been actively loyal throughout the Revolution, and had merely pretended to serve Protopopoff in order to strike him down.

If the people were defeated, the agents were able to say they had fully carried out the bureaucrats' orders and induced the working men to come out and be shot. Meanwhile, most of these men were the loudest and most violent of all the mob leaders and the most hostile to any measures of control by the laggard Duma. Joining with the honest and rabid working-class Revolutionists, they preached to the soldiers every variety of Socialism, Communism, and Anarchism, in order to seduce the troops from their free allegiance to the National Assembly.

The leaders of the Duma were almost as much dismayed by the character of their new friends as by the menace by their old foes. On Monday, March 12th, the President of the Duma telegraphed to the Tsar, making a last appeal to him to meet the people's demands. The struggle for

Street fighting in Petrograd: Students and soldiers firing at police across the Moika Canal.

Empty frame in the Duma whence the Tsar's portrait was removed ; and covered insignia on the Palace gates.

Eagles and heraldic pomps that adorned the Imperial Palace were torn down and burnt in the courtyard.

Shadows of glory in Petrograd where Democracy broke the i

Barricades at the corner of the Liteini Prospect and the Sergievskaya, showing a munition factory.

Barricades across a main street in Petrograd defended by guns decorated with the red flag.

of Autocracy and brought sceptre and crown tumbling down.

On March 12th, 1917, the Tsar prorogued the Duma. On March 15th the Duma forced the Tsar to abdicate.

Last session of the Duma under the Empire: Ignoring the ukase proroguing it, the Duma, instead, abolished Tsardom.

liberty was then practically decided, as nearly all the Petrograd garrison had sided with the revolted Guardsmen. Yet Protopopoff, General Khabaloff, and the reactionary Minister of War would not save further bloodshed by admitting they were beaten. So the battle went on.

The Guards stormed the Arsenal and Artillery Department and closed round all buildings where the police and troops under reactionary officers were holding out. As a considerable number of able officers remained with the revolted troops, many of the actions were conducted in a skilful manner and with comparatively small loss of life to the attackers. In the case of regiments that had shot most of their officers, there were, however, privates who rose by self-assertion and Revolutionary eloquence to commanding positions. In one instance it was reported that a private became a general in a single day, although he could not capably handle a platoon in battle.

TOWN MILITIA SEARCHING A MOTOR-CAR IN PETROGRAD.
After the first few days of Revolutionary excitement the Russian Provisional Government took control of all motor-lorries and private motor-cars, and ordered the Town Militia to search all motor-vehicles for arms and to ascertain on what business they were being employed at the moment.

Generalship was scarcely needed in the closing phase of the street fighting. In addition to nearly three divisions of revolted troops there were some forty thousand civilians who had obtained arms and fought against the police. They captured and set on fire the reactionists' central position, broke into the gaols in order to liberate all political prisoners, and in the confusion allowed many ordinary criminals to escape. In spite, however, of the presence of some desperadoes amid the fighting mobs, the overthrow of Tsardom was conducted with extraordinary order and coolness. Only the reactionary police, who had secret stores of drink, showed signs of drunken frenzy.

Provisional Government formed

The Russian people have always been distinguished by a genuine feeling of brotherly charity. This feeling prevailed during the four days' battle in Petrograd. As Protopopoff's forces weakened, the curious spectacle of policemen being arrested and taken to prison by the public was seen in many streets. The resistance of the last remnants of autocratic power was overcome on Tuesday and on Wednesday, March 14th, 1917, the bureaucratic Ministry resigned and a Provisional Government was formed by members of the National Assembly and the Union of Local Councils.

Two days before this the Tsaritza, who was in residence at Tsarskoye Selo, summoned a new large force to guard her palace. But the entire garrison rose and marched through the grounds; the pickets of her household guard went over to them, and the officers entered the Imperial apartments and met the authoress of all the misfortunes of the Romanoff dynasty. "Please do not shoot," she said. "I am now only a Sister of Mercy, tending my children!" In the hour of her overthrow her condition was piteous. Her children were suffering from an infectious disease, and her only son Alexis, for whom she had always striven to preserve all the privileges of autocracy, was in danger of death.

The Tsar was at Field Headquarters at Mohileff when the news of the success of the Revolution reached him. At first he did not understand what forces were arrayed against him, and sent General Ivanoff with a battalion of the Knights of St. George to retake Petrograd. General Ivanoff had proved himself a commander of genius during the great retreat from Galicia, and it was somewhat tragic that he should be the only Russian captain of fame who was ready to fight against free Russia. His trainload of troops, however, was utterly inadequate for the task assigned it. His train was forcibly turned back near Tsarskoye Selo, and it then wandered to and fro along the line until it was stopped by General Russky, the Army commander on the north-west front.

It was afterwards alleged that General Ivanoff's final advice to the Tsar was to open the Dwina line and let the Germans in upon the Petrograd mob. General Russky however, upheld the popular cause. The Tsar went in person to General Russky's headquarters at the town of Pskoff. Pskoff was the nearest active Army centre to the capital, and the Emperor no doubt hoped to obtain from General Russky an army strong enough to break the Revolution. Russky was of the same mind as Alexeieff, Evert, Brussiloff, and the Grand Duke Nicholas. That is to say, he was angry with the bureaucratic Ministry, by reason both of their inefficiency and their treacherous pro-Germanism. He had little interest in politics, but he judged the local and national representative bodies by the good work they had done in the war, and preferred that they should have free scope to organise victory rather than that Protopopoff should have renewed power to organise defeat. When the Tsar found that Russky would not move, he offered, after a midnight discussion on March 14th, to grant responsible government to the people.

Abdication of the Tsar

Russky, however, knew that abdication had become necessary now the Tsar was two days late in answering the last telegraphed appeal from the Duma. He communicated with President Rodzianko by telephone, and also sent an outline of the case to the Grand Duke Nicholas in the Caucasus, to Alexeieff at General Headquarters, and to Brussiloff and Evert. They all agreed upon abdication, and in the morning of March 15th Russky informed the Tsar of the general decision. Thereupon, the Tsar wrote out an abdication in favour of his son. Before this was despatched, two representatives of the Provisional Government arrived and had an interview with the beaten and hopeless man. When he learnt that his bodyguard had gone over to the people he changed his mind in regard to his heir, and, stating that he would not be separated from the ailing boy, signed a form of abdication in favour of his brother the Grand Duke Michael. He then tried to go to the Crimea, but was stopped by General Alexcieff.

Thus, by the evening of March 15th, 1917, the movement directed by the National Assembly and Zemstvos was apparently accomplished. Russia was **Cost of the four days' fighting** transformed with amazing swiftness from the greatest autocracy in the world into a progressive and Constitutional monarchy somewhat resembling the British monarchy. Having regard to the immensity and complexity of the Russian Empire, its inadequate communications, diversity of races, and the dominating and penetrating power of the bureaucracy, the Revolution was carried out at comparatively little cost of life.

The people of Petrograd suffered most, but their casualties of 2,500 killed, and severely and slightly wounded, were small for four days of street fighting. In Moscow there were only six people killed and eight wounded, and, save at Kronstadt and in some parts of Finland, where one of the most brutal of reactionary commanders held sway, the provinces carried out the great change in government as easily as did the ancient capital. Both the Baltic Fleet and the Black Sea Fleet came over to the popular side without any serious disturbance or loss of material and men. It was only in the remote east, in the Amur region, that any commander of a considerable force of troops made any show of resistance to the Provisional Government.

GENERAL BIELIAEFF.
Russian Minister of War at the time of the Revolution.

One foolish Grand Duchess did great harm to the Romanoff family by sending a letter to the Grand Duke Nicholas, commanding the Army of the Caucasus, advising him to start a counter-revolution. The only result of this act of folly was that the Grand Duke Nicholas, who had been loyal to the Constitutional movement, was relieved of his command and prevented from aiding General Alexcieff in the struggle with Germany and Austria-Hungary. Seeing that the gallant Grand Duke had originally been removed from the post of Commander-in-Chief by Rasputin and the Tsaritza, who disliked him because he was a fierce anti-German and feared him because she thought he coveted the throne, the suggestion that he was the man to organise a counter-revolution and restore the power of the bureaucracy seems to have been as idle as it was mischievous.

While the country was swaying between the propaganda of the Petrograd Commune and the organising efforts of the local councils, the Provisional Government constituted itself in day and night sittings at the Taurida Palace. Prince George Lvoff, the President of the Union of County Councils, was made Prime Minister and Minister of the Interior. Professor Paul Miliukoff, the leader of the Constitutional Democratic Party, became Foreign Minister. M. A. I. Gutchkoff, the chairman of the War Industries

Committee, which had accelerated the supply of munitions, was appointed Minister of War and Marine. M. Kerensky, the young lawyer leader of the Social Democrats, was made Minister of Justice, and M. Shingareff and other brilliant men of the Constitutional Party filled various important posts. M. Rodzianko, the President of the Duma and chief director of the Revolution, did not take office ; neither did M. Cheidze, the Socialist Revolutionist, who had played the main part in provoking the battle to which Protopopoff had challenged the Duma. **Dreams of a Socialistic Utopia**

As a result of the activity and clamour of the Social Democratic organisation in Petrograd the popular victory in the capital was entirely claimed by the Labour delegates. These men, mainly of the fire-brand type, were so numerous that they reduced Petrograd to the condition described by W. S. Gilbert, in one of his comic operas, of a land where dukes could be bought at three a penny, while field-marshals crowded all the pavements and every street resounded with the political debates of two or three party leaders.

In Petrograd, in the middle of March, 1917, there were 1,300 party leaders. By the middle of the next month they numbered 4,000. Each was a delegate of either the working men or the soldiers. There were occasions when the greater part of a battalion of newly-trained peasants transformed itself into a parliament. One of the Guards regiments, for instance, killed its officers, fought one of its companies that began to fire on the people, and then came leaderless to the Taurida Palace for the purpose of placing itself under the orders of the Duma. Instead, however, of doing any more fighting or engaging in public work, the battalion divided itself into committees, to consider and solve all the problems of Russia and mankind in general, and spent weeks wrangling over the details of the glorious Utopia pictured by the Communists. Not one man said anything about the war. The battalion considered that the war was over, because the Social Democrats of Germany were rumoured to have made common cause with the Russian people. They thought the only remaining business was to settle all details for the new Socialistic Utopia before going back to their homes, there to enjoy the earthly paradise which they imagined they had created. In many of the officerless regiments quite a considerable portion of the men deserted and returned home, or wandered about the capital talkatively idle. Some of the munition factories, on which General Russky's army vitally depended,

TAURIDA PALACE : THE CENTRE OF THE REVOLUTION.
When the Duma, or Russian National Parliament, was created by Tsar Nicholas II., in 1905, he gave as its meeting-place the Taurida Palace in Petrograd, near the banks of the Neva. The Duma became the directing power of the forces of Revolution.

also stopped work, while the men demanded to be paid higher wages for discussing all the problems of the universe.

Had Hindenburg been ready to strike with his men and artillery he would have again broken Radko Dimitrieff on the Riga front, and swept up towards General Russky's headquarters at Pskoff, and immediately menaced the debating Revolutionary mobs of Petrograd. Happily for Russia, Hindenburg was not ready. His reserves were in the middle of Germany, poised between the imperilled

M. GUTCHKOFF.
Minister of War and Marine in the
first Russian National Cabinet.

M. KERENSKY.
Leader of the Labour Party, who
became Minister of Justice

M. KONOVALOFF.
Minister of Commerce and Industry
in the first Russian National Cabinet

M. MILIUKOFF.
Deputy for Petrograd in the Duma
and Minister for Foreign Affairs.

western front and the weak but distant eastern front. His Chief of Staff was fully engaged in the delicate operation of withdrawing to the new line in Northern France, having based his plan of action upon the early arrangement for a negotiated peace with the Ministry that Protopopoff had controlled. The sudden success of the Russian Revolution surprised Germany and Austria as completely as it surprised the Russian bureaucracy. Berlin had expected only some feeble street rioting in Petrograd, followed by the suspension of the Duma and the rise to practically absolute power of Protopopoff, with the German Empress of Russia behind him, eager to make peace with the Central Empires in order to safeguard the principle of autocracy.

Germany was thus caught unawares by the movement in Russia. Its immediate effect was to stagger and dismay the Kaiser and his Ministers. Bethmann - Hollweg tried to anticipate the impression that the Russian Revolution would make upon the German people by unexpectedly proposing another vague and unsubstantial offer of political reform. This offer, abruptly made when the events in Russia were still hidden from the German people, was afterwards withdrawn by the Imperial Chancellor, under energetic pressure from the Prussian governing class and their political allies, the German industrial magnates. But the promise of political

M. RODZIANKO.
President of the Duma, who might have become Prime Minister if he had not preferred to retain the position to which he had given such weight and distinction.

reform, made to quieten the German populace on March 14th, 1917, showed that the German military authorities were not in a position to take immediate advantage of the state of utter disorganisation in Petrograd. They were, indeed, more fearful of contagious outbreaks among their own large urban populations than ready to profit by the temporary weakness of the Slav race.

Meanwhile, the unpractical and misled agitators in Petrograd proceeded in their attempt to reduce an empire to anarchy. There were powerful forces of treason and perfidy acting alongside the honest but wild popular forces of revolution. Germanic agents dominated some of the gatherings of workmen and soldiers, and worked upon them to enfeeble the Army and make it an easy prey for hostile despotism. Munition makers and the troops were falsely told that the German and Austrian Social Democrats were prepared at once to follow their example and rise in mutiny along the battle-front, as well as in the cities. In some cases the Russian soldiers were advised that they should kill their officers and advance unarmed from the fire-trench, when they would be received as brothers by equally mutinous Teuton soldiers. Demonstrations were engineered by duped and excited crowds carrying banners with such legends as, "Down with the war with Germany!" "Hurrah for the struggle between the masses and the classes!"

PRINCE GEORGE LVOFF.
First Premier under the new régime, had been President of the National
Union of Zemstvos.

PROFESSOR IMANUILOFF.
Of Moscow University, who became
Minister of Public Instruction.

M. SHINGAREFF.
Deputy for Petrograd, who was
appointed Minister of Agriculture.

M. CHEIDZE.
One of the Social Democrat leaders
in the Duma.

M. LVOFF.
Member of the Duma, who became
Procurator of the Holy Synod.

EMINENT AND PATRIOTIC RUSSIANS WHO GUIDED THE FORCES OF REVOLUTION.

At home the German Social Democracy was the tamest of all slave organisations in history. It lovingly ate out of the hands of the Hohenzollern, and exerted all the cunning of the slave mind to excuse and palliate the ghastly inhumanities practised by the despotism to which it was attached. But, through its international connection with the Russian Social Democracy, it cynically worked for the overthrow of the newly-born Russian Provisional Government, and strove to drown the Russian people in their own blood, in order to procure an easy and complete victory for the Hohenzollern dynasty.

Surrender of Protopopoff This subtle intrigue against free Russia was assisted by the agents of the fallen Russian bureaucracy. Protopopoff came of his own will to the Duma, and, in a condition of nervous collapse, surrendered to the Provisional Government. Most of his associates had been captured and imprisoned, and his armed police were arrested or killed. But the secret agents he had introduced into the factories and into the Revolutionary clubs were still at large. Some of them, as we have seen, had been frightened into a show of patriotism by the course of events, and had compounded for their crimes against the people by becoming the wildest of the Revolutionists. Others, in vain wisdom, still anticipated a successful counter-revolution, and continued to carry out the orders of the old Ministry of the Interior, by allying themselves with the German Social Democratic Party and urging the workmen, soldiers, and peasants on courses calculated to weaken and disperse the national forces.

There was a remarkable strain of fervent humanitarianism in the populace of Petrograd, and a noble idealism in the minds of the loyal leaders of many sections. But even the loyal Russian Communists were unwittingly made to play into the hands of the enemy. They belonged to a European race that was, in general, illiterate and entirely lacking in large political experience. The peasantry was living in the atmosphere of the Middle Ages, governed by, tradition and swayed by superstitions that had faded from the intellect of Europe and America.

The principal leaders of the Petrograd Commune were entirely out of touch with the majority of the Russian race. Indeed, they were not Russians themselves. M. Cheidze, the principal Communist, was a Georgian ; his most active lieutenant was a Hebrew ; the large majority of lesser Communists were infidels, agnostics, and disciples of every fashionable form of every decadent Western European school of scepticism and neo-paganism. Their book knowledge of the latest theories in French and German forms of political thought was often brilliant and comprehensive. They knew everything, but were practised in nothing. Their lack of the ballast of experience made them the most blindly audacious pilots with which any civilised race in the day of danger was cursed.

The wildest follies of the ancient French Jacobins were prudent social experiments compared with the schemes worked out by the orators of the Petrograd Commune. They would have required all the forces employed against Germany, Austria-Hungary, and Turkey to enforce their plans of action upon the enormous mass of Orthodox, uneducated, and backward peasantry.

The most progressive of democratic communities, such as New Zealand and Australia, would have been staggered by **Intoxication of success** the proposals of the utterly inexperienced Petrograd agitators.

Yet to the strange successors of those old Paris Communists, who nearly wrecked the French Republic, everything seemed possible on the day when they were intoxicated by success, blinded by their own vanity, and misled by numerous traitors. They opened their extraordinary campaign on March 15th, by sending to the armies delegates who ordered the men not to obey their officers, but to elect new commanders. Had this unparalleled act of folly been consummated, the disorganised

RUSSIA REBORN AMID FLAMES AND FUSILLADES.

Much of the bloodshed which stained the streets of Petrograd when Russian liberty was born was due to the action of the police, who had promoted disturbances among the disaffected expressly in order to suppress them by force. When the soldiers threw in their lot with the populace the police were in a hopeless position, and those who were not shot were imprisoned. In the street fighting in Petrograd about 2,500 people were killed and wounded.

THE END OF POLICE TERRORISM IN RUSSIA: REVOLUTIONISTS STARTING ON A POLICE HUNT.
Animosity against the police, creatures of the old bureaucracy, suppressed through long years of terrorism, burst into full flame when the day of the Revolution dawned. Armed civilians, and soldiers with them, crowded into motor-lorries and raced from point to point, driving the police by a hail of bullets from coigns of vantage on roofs and in garrets whence they had been firing their last shots in defence of doomed tyranny.

Russian troops would have been at the mercy of their enemies, and German and Austrian forces would have been able to close upon Petrograd, Moscow, and Odessa. Then, after battering and starving out the Russian people, they would have taken the wheatlands and ports of Little Russia, drained the Muscovites completely of strength and treasure, and either left them in utter anarchy or have imposed autocratic rule again upon them. There can be little doubt that treacherous Germanic influences,

Difficulties of the new situation

as well as bureaucratic forces plotting a counter-revolution, were active in the Petrograd Commune during this phase of the Revolution.

The honest fanatics of pacifism were misled by the more practical agents of the enemy. A ghastly intestinal conflict seemed imminent, for the Russian people had more powerful representatives than the Petrograd Communists possessed. The Provisional Government, with the old National Assembly and the Army commanders behind it, rightly refused to surrender the conduct of the State to the mob of the capital, and prepared to retire to Moscow and bring an army against the rebels. The situation somewhat resembled that which obtained in France in 1871, when the Communists of Paris were in conflict with the forces of the new National Assembly. In France, however, the representatives of the nation sat outside the capital and directed the army that quelled the city. In Russia the deputies and councillors of the country sat in the rebellious capital, with a small bodyguard of soldiers, whom the agitators continually tried to seduce. The larger part of the former Petrograd garrison was controlled by the delegates of the Commune, and was carried away by lies, treacheries, empty idealisms, and vain dreams.

There were four institutions exercising power—the Provisional Government, the Executive Committee of the Duma, the Military Commission of the Duma, and the Council of Workmen's and Soldiers' Delegates. The first three bodies worked in cordial support of the new order of things, but the delegates of the Petrograd mobs showed many signs of disloyalty to the nation. In the last week of March, 1917, they sent mandatories to the Taurida Palace, with orders to arrest the members of the Provisional Government and of the Executive Committee of the Duma. Some misguided soldiers, with fixed bayonets, accompanied the delegates with the intention of effecting the arrests by force.

The palace, however, was defended by a strong force of Guardsmen, who asked the traitors what their business was. "What!" the Guardsmen exclaimed. "You want to imprison the members of the Duma? Go away!" The delegates went away, and in an endeavour to recover their prestige sent a hundred and fifty armed soldiers to Tsarskoye Selo with a written order to arrest the Emperor and imprison him in the Fortress of Peter and Paul. Again the forces controlled by the Provisional Government daunted the unrepresentative leaders of the city mobs. The small Communist force withdrew without a struggle, after being allowed to peep at "Colonel Romanoff" walking in the guarded grounds.

Communists and the Army

After the failure of the attempt to arrest the members of the Provisional Government, the directors of the Petrograd Commune tried to capture the armies. They despatched thousands of missionaries and delegates to the forces at the front. No Army commander or general, however, was ready to have all his officers selected for him by the privates. General Brussiloff, commanding in the south, would not allow his forces to be interfered with. General Evert, commanding in the centre, so fiercely resisted the

MINISTER OF JUSTICE IN THE PROVISIONAL GOVERNMENT.
M. Kerensky, Minister of Justice, the Commandant of the Palace of
Tsarskoye Selo, and the two adjutants who placed the ex-Tsar Nicholas
and his family under arrest at the Palace.

unauthorised power of the Communists
that they afterwards intrigued against
him with remarkable persistence.

Only in the north-western army,
under General Russky, were there any
serious disorders, when the Communists tried to overcome the officers
and make the troops a helpless,
leaderless mob. As this army was
nearest the capital, it was more subject than the others to Anarchist
influences. General Russky and his
subordinate commanders were not,
however, men to be daunted or

ON GUARD AT THE PRISON-PALACE OF THE EX-TSAR.
Sentry on duty at Tsarskoye Selo. He was being visited by Prince
Gagarine, who always accompanied the ex-Tsar Nicholas when he went
for a walk. The Emperor was kept closely guarded.

duped by a medley of dreamers and traitors. Discipline
was restored after a fortnight of confusion and enfeeblement,
and before the Germans could strike at any leaderless
and loquacious division, the north-western army again
stood firm from Riga to the lakelands of the Dwina.

By this time it was fairly clear that the armies in the
fighting-line would detach troops to march against Petrograd
and overthrow the Commune, if the Provisional Government and the members of the Duma were arrested. Thereupon, the allies of the Hohenzollern and Hapsburg changed
their tactics. They endeavoured to procure the defeat
of the armed forces of the Russian
Commonwealth by creating disorders in   **Reactionary forces**
the great garrison towns in the rear   **at work**
of the battle-line. The reserve troops
were told that they need not obey their officers, and that
the great estates near their villages were being divided
among the people.

By suggestion rather than by definite statement the men
were induced to desert and return to their families, so as
to secure a large share in the new land. In the agricultural
districts of South Russia, especially, certain organisations
connected with both the Black Hundred and with the
Petrograd Commune actively stirred the peasantry to
invade private estates and divide them up. In some
places massacres also occurred, and as these were said
to have been committed against unoffending Jews, it
seemed as though some of the old secret forces of the most
criminal department of the fallen bureaucracy were craftily

CONSULTATION AT TSARSKOYE SELO.
Officers and privates of the Guard in consultation. After the Provisional
Government decided to arrest the ex-Tsar and his family they were kept
under guard at Tsarskoye Selo, fifteen miles south of Petrograd.

working with the Communists in preparation for some
counter-revolutionary movement.

General Brussiloff succeeded in maintaining command
of his reserves at Kieff, but lost for a time control of
Odessa and other bases. Moscow remained firm behind
the central army, yet the general condition in the urban
centres was for some weeks one of profound disorganisation.

The Commune of Petrograd exhibited remarkable activity
in producing smaller Communes in many
other centres of industry where the work-   **Helpful work of**
ing class was more or less prepared for   **the Zemstvos**
Social Democratic movements. All the
disturbances and changes in urban centres were not mischievous. It had been found during the disorders in the Army
that where the men cast their officers out these officers were
usually unfitted to command, being incompetent, cowards,
or bullies. In the same way, where municipal authorities
were overthrown by movements of working men, it was
often discovered that the popular decision was well founded,
and that the old town council was corrupt and inefficient.
The Zemstvos, or local councils, controlled by the new
Prime Minister, Prince George Lvoff, best weathered the

storm of civil and military commotion. They were, indeed, the soundest and strongest organ of national strength, connecting the Army, the peasantry, the gentry, and the middle classes with the large body of trained mechanics and other skilled men. Zemstvos had saved Russia in 1915, and they worked intensely yet quietly to save her again in 1917.

From the middle of March to the middle of April the divided and confused Russian people wavered between the Communists and the Constitutionalists. Happily, some of the leaders of the Commune came to terms with the Provisional Government. M. Kerensky accepted the position of Minister of Justice in the new Government, and proved himself a reconciling and moderating force.

Communists versus Constitutionalists

At gathering after gathering he faced the wilder agitators, and seemed gradually to educate his audiences into an appreciation of the realities of the general position. M. Cheidze and his lieutenants became more reasonable and anxious to avoid civil war. While insisting on important concessions from the Provisional Government, the leaders of the Commune agreed to submit some of the matters in dispute to a Constituent Assembly, which was to be elected upon democratic lines.

Before the country was ready for a General Election, however, the leaders of the Petrograd delegates forced some profound modifications in policy upon Prince Lvoff.

In the first place, the idea of making Grand Duke Michael a Constitutional monarch was annulled. Russia was to decide by the vote whether it would be a monarchy or a

REPUBLICAN GUARDS IN IMPERIAL GROUNDS.
General Korniloff, Military Governor of Petrograd, inspecting the Republican Guards after the burial of the men who fell during the Revolution at Tsarskoye Selo. Thousands of people marched past their graves.

WINDOWS OF THE PALACE-PRISON.
The suite of apartments in the Palace of Tsarskoye Selo assigned to the ex-Tsar and his family, who were placed under the strictest surveillance and completely isolated from the world outside.

the Church still exercised enormous influence over the people, who were not prepared for such practical measures of religious reform.

The confiscation of all property was the idea at the back of the agrarian reform. The land greed of the peasantry was merely excited by the agitators as an instrument for ultimately establishing a complete system of National Communism. The immediate result was an outburst of peasant risings that continued through

republic. It was at first thought that the majority of peasants would hold to their ancient traditions and require a Tsar. But the Communists quickly showed they were able to shake the peasant out of his conservative attitude. Upon the country and upon the Army they poured a stream of lurid stories concerning Rasputin and other evil figures in the Russian Court. From newspapers and public speeches the tales travelled with the strange speed of oral communication to camp and village.

Peasantry and Republicanism

So general an emotion of disgust was excited that the spirit of Republicanism began to penetrate the peasantry. Some members of the Provisional Government responded to the new feeling of the nation and planned a republic on the modern French model. But a middle-class polity of this kind did not suit the aspirations of the Communists. They endeavoured to win over the peasantry in a furious and extensive campaign for agrarian reform. All the estates of the Crown and the Church and the monasteries were to be confiscated and divided among the villagers. This was a possible though rather dangerous scheme, as

STRANGE MANTLING FOR HERALDIC CIPHERS.
Red flags hung over panels of the Palace gates concealed the Imperial cipher of Nicholas II., as a smiling sentry showed by raising one with the point of his bayonet.

April. In the Saratov Province, for example, where a remote German settlement had spread along the Volga, there were serious attacks on landowners, led by soldiers who had deserted from the garrison towns. Yet, after the peasants had forcibly occupied the lands, they found they could not sow them, owing to lack of seed and badness of weather. Consequently, the outrages only tended to reduce the harvests for 1917. It is scarcely too much to say that all the blunders and deliberate errors for which the old bureaucracy was responsible were exceeded by the wild visionaries and the treacherous elements of the Petrograd Commune. The fanatics were ready to wreck their country in the hope of getting an opportunity to build the paradise of their dreams out of the ruins.

The patience of the members of the Provisional Government was marvellous. The men of the Duma, the Council

divisions of General Brussiloff's southern army were holding debates on political matters and leaving their lines in a criminal state of weakness.

The Germans were well aware of what was going on. With a favouring wind they rolled cloud after cloud of poison gas over the Russian fire-trench, flung out a heavy curtain fire over the political meeting, and stormed down to the river. The larger part of a Russian army corps was killed or captured, losing guns and a large amount of ammunition. Treachery, incompetence, and faction among the beaten troops were the causes of this serious reverse. Yet it was, in a paradoxical way, a moral victory for the Provisional Government. It brought home to every Russian soldier and citizen the danger of indiscipline and disorganisation. All the other troops in the firing-line became alarmed and turned more willingly to their

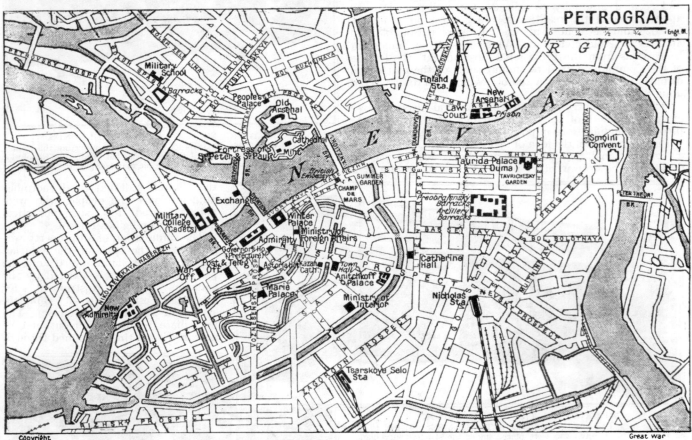

CAPITAL OF THE NEW DEMOCRATIC GOVERNMENT OF EASTERN EUROPE.
Plan of Petrograd, showing streets and buildings which were the scenes of notable events during the Revolution of March, 1917: The Taurida Palace, home of the Duma, where the Provisional Government was set up; the Fortress of St. Peter and St. Paul, the British Embassy, the Winter Palace, afterwards appropriated to national uses; the Arsenal, Barracks, and thoroughfares at the corners of which barricades were built during the street fighting.

of Empire, and the Zemstvos had been trained in endurance by their long struggle with their old enemy the corrupt bureaucracy, and they met their new internal foes with the same patient confidence in the ultimate soundness of the nation. There were occasions when they were tempted to abandon Petrograd for the ancient capital of Moscow and try to reduce the Commune to reason before Hindenburg could strike. It is doubtful whether any French or British Committee of Safety would have delayed to take forcible measures when the armies were behind them.

The Russian Provisional Government, however, recognised that a large part of the disorder was due to the uneducated minds of honest men intoxicated by one of the most successful Revolutions in history. So they waited, anxiously but not without hope, for the people to come to their senses. Happily, one of the German commanders on the Russian front intervened, on April 3rd, 1917, in a manner that greatly helped to sober the popular mind. In the salient of a bridge-head on the Stokhod River some

officers for direction. They also became angry with the idle garrisons in Petrograd and in other bases, and volunteered to conduct military police operations in the cities, and compel the Revolutionary soldiers to take a turn in the trenches.

Two days after the Stokhod reverse the Cossack League met in the capital. The soldier delegates from the front and the representatives of all Cossack armies swore to support the Provisional Government and to continue the war to a victorious peace. The Cossacks held brilliant parades in the streets and marched to the British Embassy, and there declared that Russia would be faithful to her Allies. The next day delegates from the First Russian Army also came to Petrograd. They protested against the anarchical propaganda which the Communists were conducting without the consent of the Provisional Government, and affirmed that the Government was the sole organ of national direction until the new Constituent Committee was elected. This, however, was not the case.

Troops in the Liteini Prospect halting on their way to the Duma.   Right : Arrival of prisoners of the Duma.   By order of the Provisional Government many adherents of the old régime were arrested, and some of them were brought before the former at the Taurida Palace.

The Taurida Palace, the home of the Duma, was naturally the focus of general attention.   Large crowds gathered round the building to witness the many spectacles of historic interest provided by the coming and going of Ministers, the passing of troops, and other events incidental to the establishment of the Democratic Government.   There, too, the crowds were addressed from time to time by members of the Provisional Government

STIRRING SCENES IN PETROGRAD DURING THE REVOLUTION.

HOMAGE TO THE DEAD. At the public funeral of those who fell in Petrograd. Second from left: M. Rodzianko (President of the Duma).

The Provisional Government was still compelled to divide all exercise of power with the Petrograd Commune. The Communists pretended they were only acting as a sort of legal opposition, but as their method of opposing every measure they disliked or commending any action they required was to prepare for civil war, they remained in many ways the forcible controllers of the national policy.

Each side was organising for armed conflict. The Communists were trying to steal men away from the armies and hinder the output of munitions that might be used against them. The Constitutionalists were approaching the men through their officers and their factory managers. The confusion of voices was worse than that of a genuine General Election. Rare were the cases in the rear where munition makers stood steadily to their task, as they did in the famous Ochta Works on the Neva. Rare also were the instances in which divisions in the rear of the armies were not troubled by some preacher of German Socialism.

Lenin's return through Germany On April 9th the wilder spirits of the Commune were excited to further excesses by the arrival of a political exile, Lenin, who had long exercised marked influence over the Revolutionary forces. Lenin had come to Russia with thirty companions by a sinister route, travelling from Switzerland through Germany with the gracious help of the Prussian autocracy. His manner of arrival in Russia was somewhat similar to the manner of Casement's arrival in Ireland. He at once showed himself worthy of all the attentions paid him by the Prussians. He denounced Great Britain, France, and Italy, and urged that instant peace should be made separately with Teuton and Turk.

Behind Lenin quickly massed all the treacherous forces of the system of Social Democracy founded in Germany and spread through Europe. Swiss, Dutch, Danish, and Norwegian Socialists conferred with German and Austrian Socialists, and, with certain Russian Socialists, drew up proposals for peace. It was arranged that Alsace and Lorraine were to be left to the mercy of the Kaiser, together with the Posen province of Poland, and that the Russian Baltic provinces, peopled by Slav races, were to be surrendered to Prussian masters. Constantinople and the Straits were to become a Turkish protectorate with **Treacherous proposals for peace** Germany as the practical protector, while Serbia was to be merged in the Austrian dominions. Finally, as a concession to British sea-power, Belgium was to be evacuated, on condition that the Belgian people did not maintain an army.

These proposals of the Social Democratic International groups were the meanest and blackest concatenation of treacheries ever attempted in the annals of mankind. Upon every Socialist of neutral and Russian nationality engaged in the proceedings they stamped such infamy as was likely permanently to alter the International Labour system. Some of those concerned may have been sincere fanatics, and others blind dreamers; but the nature of the proposals proved that the men who tried to carry them through were servile agents of the Hohenzollern and the Hapsburg There were, however, some Continental Socialists unwilling to act as betrayers of liberty and humanity. In Sweden, for example, though the Government was pro-German, the working classes were faithful to the cause of democracy, and their Socialist leader, M. Branting, stood out strongly against Russia concluding a separate peace.

CROWD AT THE GREAT GRAVESIDE IN PETROGRAD. Those who had fallen in Petrograd in establishing the Revolution were buried near the suggested site of the new Houses of Parliament. Members of the Government, M. Miliukoff (marked with an x), released victims of the old régime, soldiers, and populace mingled at the graveside.

Meanwhile, Petrograd was shaken by another popular agitation. Great Britain was assailed by the wildest slanders and the basest lies. All the machinery of disloyalty formerly employed by Rasputin and the reactionists was revived and expanded by many of the delegates of the Workmen's and Soldiers' groups. The British, French, and Italian democracies were violently condemned as the worst enemies of the human race because they were bent on fighting for a victorious peace. Then the German view was adopted that Great Britain was the only Power eager to continue the war for the profits she could make out of it.

The leading members of the Provisional Government had to interrupt their work of reorganising the country in order to conduct a campaign of oratory on behalf of Great Britain. This led to another approach to civil war. After some of the Ministers had explained that the British Fleet saved Petrograd in August, 1914, and that the British Army relieved the pressure upon Russia in 1915 and 1916, reference was made to the apparently gratifying fact that with British help the grand ambition of the Russian race would be achieved and the holy city of Constantinople become again the centre of the Orthodox religion.

On April 7th, 1917, Professor Paul Miliukoff, speaking as Foreign Minister, stated that the occupation of

Constantinople and the Dardanelles was essential to his country. He pointed out that the neutralisation of the Straits would leave Russia weaker than she was before, and compel her to think perpetually about the fortification of the Black Sea coast and maintain a more powerful fleet in the Black Sea.

His views were correct, and supported by the existing military situation. Turkey was seriously weakened and Austria-Hungary half broken, so that the eventual conquest of Constantinople was practically certain if only Russia could recover her fighting strength. But,

"Free Russia" and Constantinople to the amazement of Professor Miliukoff and his fellow-Ministers, the reference to Constantinople almost produced a Socialist insurrection at a time when the menace of internal strife seemed to have abated. The four thousand agitators in the capital worked up a great show of popular excitement, and the leaders addressed a practical ultimatum to Prince Lvoff, the Prime Minister. So extreme was the pressure of the Communists that the published statement of the Foreign Minister had to be contradicted by a proclamation that Russia no longer aimed at extending her territory or strengthening her power at the expense of other nations.

The way in which the proclamation was composed clearly indicated that it had been written under outside pressure against the will of the writer. "Free Russia," it was said, "does not aim at dominating other nations or depriving them of their national patrimony or occupying foreign territories by force; her object is to found a lasting peace upon the basis of the right of nations to decide their own destiny." The last phrase, as will be observed, was turned in such a way as to prevent the Armenians in the conquered eastern province of Turkey from falling by treaty under their enfeebled oppressors. Then the second and more curious phrase appeared to leave it undecided whether the conquests made by the Ottomans in Europe were part of their national patrimony.

On the whole, Prince Lvoff transformed an acute domestic crisis into a masterly snare for the enemy, who had done so much to produce the crisis. All the honest men among the Petrograd agitators had joined in making the practical suggestion that the declaration of Russia's intention of making no territorial gains would increase the war-weariness of the Germanic working classes and middle classes. At this time the Russian Communists still believed that the Social Democracy of Germany was only waiting the signal to overthrow the Prussian autocracy. The Kaisers of the Central Empires were using Scheidemann, Adler, and other Social Democratic decoys to induce the Russians to make a weak separate peace, on the pretence that the German, Austrian, and Hungarian peoples would break out in violent and general revolt as soon as the Russian Socialist Republic was successfully established on the ruins of the Provisional Government.

Prince Lvoff steered the leaders of the Commune away from this booby-trap by proposing a sound and practical form of co-operation with the Teutonic Social Democracy. The free Russian people were to assist their brothers in Germany, Austria-Hungary, and Bulgaria in overthrowing the remaining autocracies in Europe. Democratic Russia had clearly shown that she was fighting only to defend herself. She had restored the liberties of Finland, arranged for the practical independence of Poland, and established political equality of all races and creeds in her dominions.

Therefore, it was soon argued by many Russian Communists as well as by all the Constitutionalists, the next step in the permanent pacification of Europe was for the German, Austrian, and Bulgarian peoples to strike for free Government and enter on peace negotiations as democrats among democrats. As a matter of fact, there was then no evidence whatever that the Teutonic Socialists could or would carry out this great task. From the international standpoint the proposal was vain. Yet it was valuable in that it served to steady the Russian mind and give the excited imagination of the Russian people a new object on which to dwell. In effect the challenge to Scheidemann and Adler to follow Cheidze and Kerensky and attack autocracy in its last centres seriously disconcerted all the Social Democratic intriguers and confused the forces of treachery in Petrograd. The first peace negotiations failed.

In the second week in April a congress of Workmen's and Soldiers' Delegates from all parts of Russia was held in the capital, and by 325 votes to 57 the continuance of the war was advocated. But the next day the congress unanimously passed a resolution affirming the necessity for the Commune to maintain control over the Provisional Government. The Russian people were asked to rally round the Workmen's and Soldiers' Delegates, as these were the only power capable of counteracting any reactionary movement! The Provisional Government was to be supported only so long as it carried out the policy of the four thousand Petrograd delegates and the

Prince Lvoff's statesmanship

AT THE GRAVES OF THOSE WHO FELL IN THE REVOLUTION IN PETROGRAD.
Taking a record of the names of the dead. View of one of the four graves, showing the arrangement of the coffins. Above: French officers at the graveside. Among the people who paid homage to those who had died in the cause of freedom were many representatives of Russia's Allies.

DOOM OF THE IMPERIAL EAGLE.

The potency of symbols on the imagination was proved anew by the fact that one of the first things the Russian Revolutionists did was to hack down and destroy the double-headed Imperial eagles and other emblems of Tsardom that had hitherto decorated the Government buildings.

The German Fleet was reported to be moving in force into the Baltic, preparatory to a great amphibious operation in the rear of the Russian north-western army. Many soldiers, wasting their time in garrison towns, began to feel the call of patriotism and inclined to resume their duties. By a gigantic effort Great Britain and France had held the principal German armies down to the Hindenburg line in the west, and, assisted by the prolonged winter, had given free Russia time to recover from the disorder of a mighty internal explosion.

Yet the time thus strenuously won by her Allies had been extremely short for all the strengthening work Russia had to do. The Provisional Government, while carrying on an incessant and intense struggle with the Communists, had to improvise a new Civil Service in place of the vicious, ineffectual, and often treacherous bureaucratic system. When the representative organisations of the county councils and urban councils were rapidly extended and linked with village systems and co-operative systems, there remained a vast administrative machine to clean, repair, and restaff. In many positions, that were notoriously corrupt, it was not sufficient to remove the old chiefs and appoint able and patriotic men. The subordinates were often worse than their old superiors, whom they had assisted in ill-doing.

Many of these subordinates had to remain in the Civil Service and the State Railways and industries because they were too numerous to replace and they knew their work better than new men. In this connection there was a special source of trouble in the lowest branches of the bureaucracy. Many of the honest and embittered men working at the base of the old Government machine, like Omar Khayyám, wanted "to grasp this sorry scheme of things entire" and shatter it to bits, and then "remould it nearer to the heart's desire." That is to say, they preferred the impossible to the possible. They became some of the wildest agitators in the Commune.

In the last week of April, 1917, the general situation still was doubtful. The Communists and the Constitutionalists were still arrayed against each other, and working vehemently for a victorious majority in the future Constituent Assembly. The Germans and the Austrians were gathering against the new-born democracy for a terrible trial **Foes within and without** of strength, and only the Army and Navy leaders were in a position to estimate if free Russia would prove more powerful than enslaved Russia. In many ways the position was similar to that obtaining in Republican France immediately before the Battle of Valmy. Owing to the Commune, the Russian democracy had not had time or proper opportunity to organise itself for defence. It had foes within as well as foes without, and its internal enemies were its gravest danger.

thousands of new delegates elected by other small and irresponsible groups of idle workmen and deserting troops in other towns. Meanwhile, according to the modest programme of the delegates, the election of the Constituent Assembly was to be hastened and all the voting was to be controlled by the multitudinous members of the Commune.

"If we can overcome you by the ballot, we shall not use the bullet. But——" Such seemed to be the implied menace of the fiercer section of delegates against the members of the Provisional Government. The delegates were then apparently confident that they could obtain a majority in the civilian population, and were doubtful only about the men of the active armies. These, they thought, ought to be ordered to vote separately, so as to avoid the danger of their turning the balance against the peacemongers and the Anarchists in constituencies where there might be close contests. In the middle of March the Army, in the opinion of the Communists, had been the complete incarnation of the national will. But by the middle of April it had ceased to be so.

Even the Guards Regiments in Petrograd were then tiring of political debates and organising battalions for the front.

A GURKHA DRAFT

CHAPTER CLXXVI.

IN MESOPOTAMIA.

MESOPOTAMIA : THE VICTORIOUS ADVANCE TO BAGDAD.

By Edward Wright.

Serious Consequences of Kut Disaster—Emperor of Abyssinia Goes Over to the Enemy—Ottoman Advance into Persia—How Sir Percy Sykes Saved Southern Persia—Princes of Arabia Rise against Turks—Reorganisation of India Command and Mesopotamian Forces—Battling with the River Floods and Building the Railway of Victory—Germans Weaken the Turks, thinking that Indo-British Army is Stalemated—Sir Stanley Maude's Unexpected Drive on Turkish Flank—Preparations for an Ottoman Sedan on the Tigris—Brilliant Turkish Tactics in Hassan Bend—Recovery of Liquorice Factory and Advance against Shumran Position—Fierce Demonstrations at Sanna-i-Yat—Turkish Commander Completely Misled—Forcing of the Tigris and Envelopment of Main Turkish Forces—Terrific Pursuit of the Broken Enemy—Glorious Night Watch by the Arch of Ctesiphon—Cavalry Overtake and Pierce the Enemy at Laj—Magnificent Courage of Lancashire Men in the Diala River Action—Heroic Stand in an Improvised Fort—Smashing In of Turkish Front and Turning Movement Across the Desert—Occupation of Bagdad and Pursuit of the Divided Turkish Forces—Turks Prepare a Trap between Diala and Adhaim Rivers—Trappers are Trapped, and British and Russian Armies Unite—Continuing Battles Along the Upper Tigris and Capture of Holy Places of Samarra and Kerbela—All the Bagdad Railway Line Taken from the Turks—Ancient Babylonia Becomes a British Possession—End of Teutonic Dream of a Bagdad-Berlin Empire—Profound Depression in Germany and Recovery of British Prestige Throughout the Islamic World.

THE surrender of the Indo-British garrison of Kut-el-Amara on April 29th, 1916, with an account of which Chapter CXXXIII. closed, had serious consequences. In both Asia and Africa the prestige of British power declined. In Egypt the success with which Senussi and Ottoman attacks were repelled helped to mitigate the effects of the double disasters in the Dardanelles and Mesopotamian campaigns. Yet the victories achieved against the armies of the British Empire by the strongest of Mohammedan Powers had political results surpassing their direct military value.

Some of the men round the young Emperor of the barbaric Christian State of Abyssinia were so extravagantly impressed by the Turkish successes that they tried to enter into league with the Ottomans and Teutons, with the aim of making a flank attack upon the Sudan. In Persia there was a force of rebels and native and European mercenaries who became more active and mischievous, thinking that the power of the British had been irremediably broken, and

that the Germans, with a large Turkish army, would sweep through Persia, crush the Russian and British troops there, and invade India. There were signs of unrest in various directions, and the faith of many native leaders in the permanent might of the British Empire was severely tested by all manner of political and religious intrigues.

Happily, the main structure of British influence in Asia and North - Eastern Africa resisted temporary defeat and incessant plotting. The British race profited by the traditions of tenacity it had established in the Sudan, in South Africa, and in Flanders. In Abyssinia, in Persia, in Afghanistan, and in Arabia loyal rulers and. princes felt that the nation which had avenged Gordon would avenge General Townshend.

The Turks themselves, though inflated by victory, did not turn upon the outworn and suffering British and Indian troops that had failed to relieve the Kut-el-Amara garrison. The 7th Division and the 13th Division were held up by the Sanna-i-Yat position. Repeatedly the same troops had assaulted the enemy's lines and done all that men could do to overcome a

FIELD-AMBULANCE IN MESOPOTAMIA.
Many ingenious methods were devised for transporting casualties in outlying theatres of the war. In Egypt and Mesopotamia bucket-seat saddles borne by camels were adopted for slightly-wounded men.

OLD-TIME TRANSPORT ADAPTED TO MODERN NEEDS.
Camels on war service, with their Arab drivers, somewhere on the shores of the Tigris. On every hand in Mesopotamia old and new jostled one another, and of the former the "ships of the desert" were once again requisitioned for transport purposes.

MODERN HOSPITAL SHIPS: THE MADRAS.
On the Tigris modern hospital ships, with the Red Cross and green band on their white hulls, became familiar objects to the natives. This photograph shows the Madras arriving at Basra.

SIEGE-TRAIN BULLOCKS UNDER THE PALMS.
Mild-eyed bullocks, picturesquely suggestive of peaceful Eastern indolence, drew Western 5 in. guns, and at the end of the march were tethered beneath the palms to chew the cud in philosophic patience. Meanwhile, the next task for which they were fitted was being prepared for them.

determined foe and the exceptional climatic and physical obstacles. Shortage of river transport, for which the Indian Government was responsible, had made it impossible to augment the insufficient rations on which the troops fought, and as the result of battle losses, sickness, and exhaustion, the limit of human endurance had been reached.

There was then a grand opportunity for the Ottomans and their Teutonic directors to complete their success in Mesopotamia by breaking and routing the forces under Sir Percy Lake. Apparently the Turks had no faith in their own power of making an offensive movement. Instead of advancing against the baffled Indo-British army of relief, they abandoned part of the ground they had held and resumed a purely defensive attitude. On May 19th, 1916, the Turks retired from their advanced positions by Es Sinn, on the right bank of the Tigris. This withdrawal was followed up, and by the evening of the next day most of the right bank of the Tigris was clear of the enemy as far as the Hai River, which connects the Tigris and the Euphrates between Kut-el-Amara and Nasiriyeh. Turkish rearguards only remained to cover the bridges over the Hai River, which was in flood and unfordable.

The immediate effect of this unusual retreat, which followed upon a brilliant success, was to throw upon the British forces the burden of the offensive. Naturally, no offensive was attempted. The troops were too exhausted, too poorly supplied, and the flooded marshland in the angle of the Tigris and Hai was so dangerous as to render it difficult or impossible to hold any ground gained. The large angle of water and marsh was a trap. Any British force that entered it without firmly securing its position and communication was liable to be cut off by two sudden Turkish thrusts from the Tigris and the Hai.

It was stalemate in Mesopotamia. Neither side was in a position to make any further movement; the Turks because they dared not, and the British because they could not. The enemy, however, was far from idle. The stalemate he had established on the Tigris was only part of a grandiose scheme of action which he at once attempted to carry out. As soon as all British action was checked in the direction of Bagdad, and when the Turkish defences had been greatly improved from Sanna-i-Yat to Kut-el-Amara, a considerable number of Ottoman troops marched against the Russian army under General Baratoff, which had driven down to Karind.

Karind was only one hundred and fifty miles from Bagdad, lying in the heart of the tangle of mountains, through which ran

Stalemate on the Tigris

the immemorial route of trade and conquest from Bagdad to Teheran. In the early plan of the Allies it had been arranged that General Baratoff should move towards Bagdad from the north, while General Townshend advanced from the east. With the failure of the British movement the Russian column at Karind became too weak to withstand the increasing forces brought against it. The Russians fell back from Karind to Kirmanshah. There they were again assailed by part of the army from Kut-el-Amara, with reinforcements from other corps. They were compelled to abandon Kirmanshah, and in a prolonged retreat, that ended two hundred and fifty miles beyond the Persian frontier, they at last checked the great Ottoman advance and saved Northern Persia from being entirely overrun by the enemy.

Meanwhile, Southern Persia was also saved from ruin and anarchy and utter spoliation by an unexpected British movement. This developed into one of the most romantic episodes in the general history of the war. Sir Percy Sykes landed at Bandar Abbas, at the entrance of the Persian Gulf, some months before the fall of Kut. As originally designed, his work was only to have extended the British successes in Mesopotamia by restoring order in the disturbed regions in Southern Persia. When, however, the British successes in Mesopotamia ended in utter failure, and Turks, Teutons, Persian rebels, and neutral mercenaries endeavoured to transform Persia into a base of operations against India, the task of Sir Percy Sykes became one of great importance.

Sir Percy Sykes' great march

The man was equal to his work. Sir Percy had begun life as a subaltern of cavalry, and had found more scope as an explorer. After serving five years in the Army he settled in an obscure but congenial post in the Persian city of Kerman, near the desert route to Afghanistan. After exploring the surrounding waste and highlands he obtained a position as Consul-General in the still wilder and more remote Persian town of Meshed, in the mountainous angle where the deserts of Persia, Russia, and Afghanistan meet. For more than twenty years Sir Percy Sykes travelled and explored, becoming the supreme British authority on all Persian problems and the leading historian of the country.

Early in 1916 he returned to Persia at the head of a small British column, but armed with such knowledge and such power of personality as made him worth an army corps in himself. His design was to enlist, train, and arm the tribes of Persia, and transform Persia herself into a wall of defence against Turks, Teutons, brigands, and the treacherous Swedish officers of the old military police. By a

WATERING HORSES IN THE TIGRIS AT THE END OF THE DAY.
Warring horsemen have spurred over the plains of the Euphrates and Tigris for at least five thousand years, but not even the Arabs, famous as lovers of horses, gave more attention to their steeds than did the British soldiers in the twentieth century.

TERRITORIALS FOR THE TIGRIS.
Men of a battalion of the Hampshires parading on board the transport that took them out to share in the capture of Bagdad, one of the most signal victories of the Great War.

STRETCHER-BEARERS BRINGING A CASUALTY INTO HOSPITAL.
The occupation of Bagdad on March 11th, 1917, gave opportunity to the General Staff to express its satisfaction with all concerned in providing for the needs of Sir Stanley Maude's forces. Special word of praise was given to the attention that had been available for the sick and wounded.

marvellous march of more than a thousand miles through hostile regions where the tribes had been armed by the Germans, Sir Percy Sykes saved the situation that had been imperilled by the surrender at Kut and the failure at the Dardanelles.

The gallant explorer first moved up to his old post at Kerman and connected the trade of this highland town with the sea-borne traffic at Bandar Abbas. Then, in a great **British influence** march between the central mountains, he **in Persia** pushed on to Yezd and reached Ispahan. Thence he turned south to Shiraz and Bushire. Tribe after tribe was adroitly and tactfully drawn to the British side, until some eleven thousand young and warlike Persians were enlisted in his military police. A vast tract of fresh country was added to the British sphere of influence and connected with the valuable British petroleum fields north-east of Basra.

When the great march of Sir Percy Sykes was completed, the direct influence of the British Empire extended from the Baluchistan frontier of India, entirely across Southern Persia, to a point near Kut-el-Amara on the Tigris. At the outbreak of war British influence in Persia had reached only to Bandar Abbas at the entrance to the Persian Gulf. Only a small corner of Persian territory was still occupied by the Turks, and from this corner they were soon expelled under the combined pressure of Russian and British forces.

Thus from defeat the British peoples, by their great virtue of tenacity, rose to larger victory. Another corner in the map of the world was painted red.

Great Britain entertained no designs on the independence of Persia. That country had indeed been left as a sort of buffer State between Russian and British fields of influence. Only the over-reaching intrigues of Teuton and Turk had transformed the Shiraz regions into a scene of conflict, and the Turkish success at Kut had finally made the occupation of the whole of Southern Persia obligatory upon the menaced British forces. If the Germans had not first armed the tribesmen and the Turks had not first tried to incite them to help in operations against India, this great new protectorate would not have been added to the British Empire.

In Abyssinia there was less trouble in putting down the movement against British dominion. The men around the young Emperor were so madly excited by the news of the Turkish victory on the Tigris that they went too far for their own people. They proposed suddenly and violently to turn Abyssinia from a Christian State into a Mohammedan State. This extraordinary design was suggested to them by agents of that German Empire which, before the war, had intrigued against its own Mohammedans in East Africa, and sought to use pig-breeding as a weapon of conversion, as the pig is regarded as an unclean animal by Moslems. Now, Germans of the same intriguing school endeavoured, by the gospel of Ottoman victories and British defeats, to transform the Abyssinians into a Moslem race, and league them with the Mullah of Somaliland, the Sultan of Darfur, and some discontented remnants of the old Mahdi's levies in the Sudan, for a combined attack upon the British forces holding the Nile.

The plot, however, was almost as fantastic as Herr Zimmermann's later attempt to unite the bandit chiefs of Mexico with the great and splendid armies of Japan against the United States.

In Abyssinia the most powerful chiefs of the Christian clans turned upon the miscreant Court party, defeated the forces of the Emperor, drove him from the throne, and placed a Christian upon it. In Afghanistan the Amir loyally continued his policy of amity with both Russia and Great Britain. Neither the retirement from the Dardanelles nor the fall of Kut inclined him to become the tool of the Ottoman intriguers who plied him and his feudal chiefs with mischievous advice.

With Afghanistan standing firm, and with Persia in course of conversion from a condition of hostility and anarchy to one of friendship and order, while the **Friendship succeeds,** Sherif of Mecca, the Prince of Nedj, **to hostility** and other Arabian rulers were showing antagonism to Ottoman power, the situation of the Indo-British forces in Mesopotamia improved. The immense resources in man-power in India, though still greatly restricted in operation by the poverty of cadres, were gradually employed in the neighbouring field of war. The military classes and races of India were especially suited to the climatic conditions of warfare on the Tigris and

SIR VICTOR HORSLEY,
C.B., F.R.S. This distinguished surgeon died of heat-stroke on July 16th, 1916, while acting as temporary Colonel A.M.S. in Mesopotamia. He volunteered for service in the previous March.

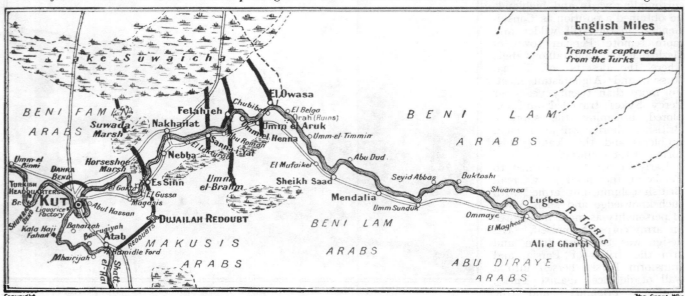

MAP SHOWING THE TURKISH DEFENCES BEFORE KUT.
During the months of preparation for Sir Stanley Maude's advance on Kut-el-Amara the Turks occupied some thirty miles of lines along the Tigris. At Sanna-i-Yat their trench system formed a narrow front between the flooded Suwaicha Marsh, or Lake, and the swollen Tigris.

On the Bagdad Railway in the Amanus Mountains, north-west of Aleppo, and part of the Taurus range. One of the difficult tunnelling sections.

Journey of inspection via the military railway in the Amanus range, where the engineers met with most formidable natural obstacles.

Turkish transport passing over a military road in the mountains. Some of these roads were very fine pieces of work.

Turkish military caravan crossing a bridge at the head station of a military road in the south of Turkey in Asia.

A Turkish military camp on the Bagdad Railway. The Bagdad Railway Concession was one of the early achievements of German *Welt-politik*.

Building station of the great Amanus Tunnel. This tunnel, three miles long, was one of the greatest engineering feats of the undertaking.

Great bridge over the Euphrates near Jerablus, north-east of Aleppo. There is a steamer service from Jerablus to Bagdad.

Kurd navvies between Adana and Aleppo. Between Konia and Bagdad, 1,117 miles of the total 1,509 were working at the end of 1915.

SCENES ON THE AMANUS (OR ELMA DAGH) SECTION OF THE BAGDAD RAILWAY.

BOUND FOR BASRA.
Wounded soldiers being removed from an ambulance by Indian Red Cross orderlies for the passage by steamer to Basra.

Euphrates. Less resistant to the heat of the desert than the native Arabs, they were at least as well able to bear the tropical temperature, the sandstorms and plague of insects as the Ottomans of the Anatolian Highlands.

At first some of the younger Indian troops scarcely showed the same qualities as their veteran countrymen, many of whom had fought in France and Egypt and on the Gallipoli Peninsula. Their training had been short, and their military experience had to be gradually won. Opposing them was a picked force of the finest fighting race on the Asiatic mainland.

Mesopotamia thus became the great testing place for the soul of the young new India that had grown up under the fostering rule of the British race. Brilliant British generals, who had watched the work of the old Indian Army in the days of tragic stress around Ypres, came to the Orient to train and lead the new generation to battle.

RED CROSS SLEDGE.
With linen covers for protection from sand, sun, and the flies, these sledges provided fairly comfortable means of conveyance for the wounded over the Mesopotamian sands.

EARTHWORKS ON THE TIGRIS.
Dug-outs with sand-bagged parapets afforded a striking contrast to the palms and ruins along the shores of the Tigris.

succeeded Sir Percy Lake and Sir John Nixon as commander of the army of Mesopotamia, had been a colonel at the outbreak of hostilities. Then as brigadier he had distinguished himself, and been promoted major-general in 1915. After being wounded on the western front and mentioned five times in despatches he went to Mesopotamia with the 13th Division.

It was he who had broken the Turks in the Henna position on April 5th, 1916, and endeavoured to save General Townshend at the last moment by storming the Felahieh lines, through which his men victoriously passed. Again, he had launched the Lancashires and North Lancashires, Welsh Fusiliers and Wiltshires into the enemy's front at Sanna-i-Yat, but failed to get completely through, owing to some troops losing their direction. Of all the generals in the baffled army of relief, Sir Stanley Maude had shown most skill, and came, in circumstances of hopeless difficulty, nearest to decisive success.

Such was the commander chosen to avenge General Townshend and restore throughout Asia and Northern Africa the prestige of the British Empire. He enjoyed many material advantages over his predecessors. Under the severe pressure of British opinion, inflamed by disclosure of scandalous neglect and lack of foresight on the part of the Indo-British bureaucracy, the measures that should have been taken in 1914 and 1915 were at last energetically carried out in 1916.

A considerable fleet of river steamers was collected. Munitions were provided of the quality and quantity required. Hospital accommodation was enlarged from

Sir Stanley Maude in command Sir Charles Monro, the former Army commander at Ypres and director of the withdrawal from the Gallipoli Peninsula, was appointed Commander-in-Chief. He succeeded Sir Beauchamp Duff, and from India organised victory on the Tigris. His work was closely linked with the activities of all the British armies and allied forces. It was controlled from London by the Imperial Chief of Staff, Sir William Robertson.

The result of this rearrangement was that the practical conduct of affairs was removed from the lax and fumbling hands of Indo-British administration and entrusted to men whose high ability had been proved in continual warfare of the most violent kind. Sir Stanley Maude, who

4,700 beds in January, 1916, to 18,000 beds in August, 1916, Medical men, practised in preventive treatment and bacteriological measures, were encouraged and greatly increased in numbers. Drugs and vaccines were obtained and an outbreak of cholera checked.

The antiquated aeroplanes, outpaced and outclimbed by the German machines employed by the Turks, were replaced by more modern and powerful fighting, bombing, and scouting machines. The large guns brought by the Turks from Adrianople were outranged by new British heavy artillery, and the wonderful Stokes gun travelled to the Tigris front with fleets of motor-lorries and other aids to rapid transport. Ice plants were erected, green food was grown in abundance, and insect pests were combated; the able war correspondent, Mr. Edmund Candler, strangely distinguishing himself as a strategic genius in the battle against Beelzebub, the god of flies.

Finally, and crowning all the works of re-organisation, the railway, long refused by the Indo-British administration, was begun. The line and the improved river transport system enabled concentrations of men and material to be made against the

of which the ancient tradition comes down to us in the early chapters of the Bible. At Basra, by which a constant stream of troops and stores poured, ground space was won for camps, huts, magazines, and hospitals. A great embankment was raised from Magil to Shaiba. From the main embankment another rampart against the waters branched off to Basra. This was followed by further works on a total front of twenty miles.

Wharves were constructed by which ocean-going steamers could stop and unload. Large waterworks were made **Transformation of Basra** at the port and the towns on the upper reaches. Direct wireless communication was established with London, and Basra was transformed into one of the great seaports of the world, exceeding in importance, if not in romantic picturesqueness, the glories it had enjoyed in the days of Sindbad the Sailor. Then it had been the great Moslem gate to the Orient, trafficking in spices, silk, and pearls, and jealously guarding its secrets of commerce from the barbaric European world. In those days Mesopotamia was so fertile and so well peopled that the farm-houses almost touched from Basra to Bagdad.

For thousands of years before the reign of Haroun-al-Raschid the great desert between the rivers had blossomed like the rose. Vague swells of buried mud-bricks, veiled in blown sand, dimly remained to show where lived the first dynasties of the world, men who were masters of both the Mediterranean Sea and Indian Ocean. Some of their ancient seaports had been removed hundreds of miles from the sea, owing to the enormous masses of earth brought down by the rivers since the dawn of

RAILWAY-YARD IN THE DESERT.
Only a year before this photograph was taken the spot was bare desert. In oval: Making a pontoon bridge over the Tigris.

enemy, with a rapidity to which he could not reply by means of the incomplete Bagdad Railway line. As Lord Kitchener had avenged Gordon by driving a railway towards Khartoum, so the engineers of Sir Stanley Maude avenged Townshend by driving a railway towards Bagdad. The speed with which the river line was constructed was unparalleled in overseas warfare. Able and determined men organised the railway of victory along the Tigris.

Before, however, the railway was built, it was necessary to roll back the great river floods,

WHERE THE RAILWAY RAN OVER ANCIENT CARAVAN ROUTES.
One of the locomotives of the Mesopotamian railway. The operations that resulted in Sir Stanley Maude's recapture of Kut, and his triumphs at Bagdad and beyond, were immeasurably facilitated by the rapid establishment of railways and other means of supplementing the slower river transport.

CAPTURED TURKS IN THEIR FLOATING PRISON.

Turkish prisoners taking exercise on board a steamer in which they were interned at Basra. Many of the thousands of Turks taken by Sir Stanley Maude during his advance were sent down the Tigris to this port.

through Nejd to Mecca. No doubt the news was also carried northward to Bagdad, Mosul. Aleppo, and thence to Constantinople. The Turk and the Teuton, however, appear to have been somewhat incredulous of the reports conveyed to them by numberless spies. They did not believe that the great works were being achieved in time to have any decisive effect upon the course of the war.

The Turkish military authorities, inflated with conceit in their victorious power, neglected to strengthen their Tigris front, and spent men by tens of thousands in helping the Austrians in Galicia. They made also another vain adventure in the direction of the Suez Canal, and assisted the Bulgarians around Salonika, while maintaining a strong line of battle against the Russians in Armenia, and pursuing their wild plan of invading India through Persia. According to a German allegation, made in a belated manner after the disaster, the Turkish Staff conducted the later Mesopotamian campaign according to its own views, and did not submit its problems in strategy to the successor of Von der Goltz. Seeing, however, that both Falkenhayn and Hindenburg greedily and selfishly took large Turkish forces away from Turkey, and exhausted them against the south-eastern Russian army under General Brussiloff, it would appear that the Germans misled the Turks.

Germans mislead the Turks

civilisation. Eden after Eden had flourished and faded, conqueror after conqueror had triumphed and vanished. The tall cane-brake grew where illimitable levels of wheat had shone. The lion prowled where sheep once had grazed. Palaces and temples, hanging-gardens and millions of happy homes had fallen into the dust. The last inheritor of the ancient paradise of the earth—the Arab—had seen the land laid waste by tribe after tribe of Mongols, and had been thrown back to primitive savagery by his fellow-Mohammedan—the Turk.

The Arab had finally watched the Turk defeat the Briton. For a generation he had been inclined to trust in British power, and half to believe the extraordinary promise of a renaissance of Mesopotamia through British agency. But when General Townshend's column turned back from the great arch at Ctesiphon, many Arab tribesmen lost their faith in a British regeneration of their country, and, going over to the apparent victor, helped the Turk to pursue and surround the Indo-British force. The gigantic transformation of Basra, carried out with a speed like that of the miracles performed by a magician of "The Arabian Nights," served once more to impress the imagination of the tribesmen.

As the great effort of organisation proceeded with equal intensity of achievement at Amara and other distant river towns, the tale of wonders spread across Arabia

It was the General Staff of Germany that misappreciated the situation on the Tigris. The enemy's military authorities either overlooked the older lessons in British tenacity, or concluded that time would not allow the disaster at Kut to be retrieved. A very strong Ottoman force was left on the banks of the Tigris; but considerable as was its power, its strength was not properly adjusted to meet the very violent and prolonged effort which the British might have been expected to make. Falkenhayn, Hindenburg, and Ludendorff did not understand the British mind and

TEUTONIC LEADERS OF THE TURKISH RED CRESCENT.

Contingent of Turkish Red Crescent ambulance men marching in the desert with German officers and doctors at the head of the detachment. Above: Building a desert portion of Germany's dream railway from Berlin to Bagdad. The dream of this railway as an important factor in Germany's progress to world-power was shattered by Sir Stanley Maude's victories at Bagdad and beyond.

character. They did the ordinary things, while Sir William Robertson, Sir Charles Monro, and Sir Stanley Maude were strenuously preparing extraordinary feats.

Seven months and a half were silently spent by the Mesopotamian army in organising the territory it occupied, speeding-up methods of transport, collecting reinforcements, and devising improved means of warfare. The ground abandoned by the enemy between the Tigris and the Hai was gradually consolidated and strongly occupied, in a manner permitting swift concentration against the long stretch of Turkish fortifications.

The Turks then occupied some thirty miles of lines along the loops and bends of the Tigris. At Sanna-i-Yat their deep and intricate trench system formed a narrow, profound front between the flooded Suwaicha Marsh and the swollen Tigris. On the opposite bank was a large patch of water-logged ground extending close to a second zone of strong defences at Es Sinn. At Es Sinn was another swamp, the Suwada Marsh, on which the second zone of Turkish fortifications rested. The low land was badly water-logged by winter floods, hindering operations in the cool season when battles could best be fought.

Feint attack on the Hai   Sir Stanley Maude, however, crept upon the enemy in the night of December 13th, 1916. From Imam Ali Mansur, a force of cavalry and infantry marched in the darkness across the seven miles of desert to the fords of the River Hai, an almost stagnant hidden river edged with scrub. The infantry rushed the Turkish outposts and threw a pontoon bridge across the stream near Atab. Then the cavalry also crossed the Hai as dawn was breaking, and swept along the western bank of the river to a point two miles from Kut. Thereupon the infantry in turn again advanced and entrenched in a large bridge-head on the

CAVALRY HORSES THAT HAD PLENTY TO DO.
Horses of British hussars embarked on a barge for conveyance up-stream. In the final advance upon Bagdad the British cavalry did much successful work, extending their raiding operations on wide flanks and sometimes far inside enemy territory.

ground they had won, while the cavalry made a sudden raid towards the Shumran bridge on the Upper Tigris, nine miles beyond Kut. All these surprise operations were carried out with slight casualties, and perturbed and confused the enemy.

It was against the distant Shumran bridge, well behind Kut and far in the rear of the principal zones of the Turkish defences, that Sir Stanley Maude intended to make his main attack. Apparently, he considered that the Turkish commander would regard the operations across the Hai as a feint, designed to distract him and induce him to weaken his forces at Sanna-i-Yat. This was exactly how the Turkish general looked at the matter. On the night of December 14th his pontoons at Kut were bombed by the British Flying Corps, and so wrecked and scattered that the Turks had to ferry their troops across the river.

When the enemy was thus temporarily lamed, the Indo-British forces on the Hai pressed onward, and won all the ground within a quarter of a mile of Kut. From their new camp the attacking troops were able to see the townspeople gazing from their roofs. The line of white houses, thrown out against the dark palm-groves, could have been reduced in a day to a heap of mud-bricks had the British gunners been ordered to bombard. But though their guns were within three miles' range of Kut, the town was not attacked. All the head of shell was poured upon the eastern Turkish front of Sanna-i-Yat, where the bombardment began on

SOLDIERS OF THE SULTAN WHO FELL PRISONER TO THE BRITISH.
Turkish prisoners lined up to have new clothes distributed to them. In the series of operations which began on December 13th, 1916, and ended with the capture of Bagdad on March 11th, 1917, a large number of Turks were taken prisoner; 7,000 were reported up to February 28th. Above: An Arab village on the Tigris. Much of the Mesopotamian lowland is water-logged, and habitations are few between Basra and Bagdad.

December 14th. This was done in order to lead the enemy to think that the movement across the Hai was only a preliminary diversion.

The cavalry that had crossed the Hai extended its raiding operations twenty miles inside the enemy's territory, breaking bands of hostile Arabs and capturing the important position of Gassab Fort, where cattle and grain had been stored. The enemy's river communications were also raided ten miles behind Kut, and some of his bridges destroyed. The Flying Corps co-operated admirably with the horsemen and, using a ton of bombs on a single journey, sank enemy steamers and exploded ammunition dumps.

By Christmas the army of Mesopotamia was in high spirits, confident in its increased strength and in the skill of its commander. The Turks, however, were also in good fighting form, and as full of dogged courage as in the days of Plevna. On January 9th, 1917, an Indian division made a sudden superb attack on the Turkish lines in the bend of the Tigris north of Kut. Here, in a position known as Mohamed Abul Hassan, both ends of the loop were stormed by Indian troops. They advanced through the morning mist, and, with very few casualties, occupied the

Turk doesn't know he is beaten until he is dead." For nine days the force defending Mohamed Abul Hassan held out in the river loop. Then the Turks buried their dead in their trenches, filling up all the earthworks, and when their surrender was expected, slipped away in the darkness in boats and coracles to their main position on the left bank of the Tigris. The British divisional commander thought the Turks had been digging themselves in deeper against his artillery fire. When day broke, the enemy had vanished, leaving no works to serve as cover for the Indian troops when they advanced toward the river-bank. By general consent the action at Mohamed Abul Hassan was regarded as a Turkish rearguard victory. Seldom had the Ottoman fought with more skill and determination.

Garrison vanishes in the night

On the other hand, the attacking troops were handled in scientific fashion. Economy in life was the rule on the British side. The attacking trenches were gradually thrown forward, while the enemy was driven back by hurricane gusts of high explosives from trench-mortars and field and heavy artillery. More than a thousand dead Turks were found in the bend.

While the Turkish commander was massing east of Kut against the river loop he had lost, the Indo-British forces resumed their operations west of Kut, across the Hai. After working some days in getting their guns and munitions forward, they opened an intense bombardment against the enemy's position south-west of Kut. Screened by the barrage, the attacking infantry stormed a position known as the lunette in the Dahra bend. The lunette extended from the end of the Hai River to the right bank of the Tigris, between Kut and the Shumran bridge. The enemy withdrew from his firing-trenches when the bombardment began, and lost a large stretch of his first line and a considerable portion of his second line. As soon, however, as the Indo-British force began to occupy the lost ground, the Turkish commander began launching counter-attacks. For two days and three nights the contending troops swayed to and fro. Twice the Turks recovered the ground from

VIEW OF THE MAIN STREET IN MODERN BAGDAD.
All the streets are narrow and filthy in Bagdad, an architecturally ugly town described as being " a little like Cairo, a little like Lourdes, a little like Monte Carlo, and a little like Clapham Junction."

eastern mounds of Kut and the river-bank, at a point nearly a day's march behind the Sanna-i-Yat lines.

The position of the Turkish garrison seemed hopeless. It had the swollen Tigris at its back, with no bridge and only some primitive basket boats as communications. The British guns hammered the enemy into a narrow area; but instead of breaking or surrendering, the hard-pressed Turks made an unexpected counter-attack along some of the river nullahs and recovered part of the lost ground. The Indian division attacked again in the evening, and again won all the ground. The battle continued all the night and the next day. Though the Turks fought on splendidly, they once more were penned by the evening into a narrow triangle on the river-bank. But the following afternoon, when the attacking division was closing for the final assault, the Turks made a most gallant sally.

Turks' dogged courage

They broke into both flanks of the Indian line, in the face of a terrific tempest of artillery, machine-gun, and rifle fire. Though thrown out with heavy losses, they continued to make sorties and counter-attacks. " It seems to me," said a British private taking part in the action. " the old

which they had been dislodged, only to be again blasted and bayoneted out of their lines. In one place the Turks erected a barricade of their dead as a protection from Indian and British bombers.

With the same economy of life as was observed in the conquest of the eastern river loop at Kut, the thrust into the western Dahra bend was maintained. All the lunette was occupied on a front of two miles and a half by January 28th. By February 3rd the mouth of the Hai River was controlled by the attacking force. The Turks then retired to the liquorice factory, famous for the gallant exploits of two battalions of General Townshend's forces during the great siege. The group of buildings was surrounded by a moat, and formed a large and magnificent machine-gun position. Using the factory as a flanking fort, the retreating Turks occupied a line of works extending westward for four miles, and rejoining the Tigris at the Shumran bridge of boats. The boat bridge was soon wrecked by British guns, the enemy's shipping shattered, and a considerable amount of his grain captured by a cavalry raid. Then the liquorice factory, that had been held by General Townshend throughout the siege of Kut, was stormed in a single

The conqueror of Bagdad: Lieut.-Gen. Sir Frederick Stanley Maude, K.C.B., C.M.G., D.S.O.

Troops crossing a pontoon bridge over a marshy section of the Tigris Valley.

Station on the Tigris bank used by the river transports carrying small detachments.

British airman flying over Sheikh Saad on the way to Kut=el=Amara.

Camel supply=train passing through abandoned trenches on the way to Kut.

The Bridge of Boats across the Tigris at Bagdad, looking westwards to the warehouse quarter.

Palm-grove encampment of the cavalry attached to General Lake's Kut relief force.

General view over Bagdad, "Queen of Cities" of the East, captured March 11th, 1917.

Arabs unloading the sailing boats which ply the Tigris with cargoes of grain and fodder.

Picturesque scenes in the victorious advance to the old capital of the Caliphate.

operation on February 10th, the enemy being pushed back half a mile closer to the river in the critical Dahra bend.

The distance between the Turkish front at Sanna-i-Yat and the Turkish rear at Shumran in the Dahra bend was thirty miles. It was more than two days' march for an army of the modern type, dragging a large amount of heavy artillery and constricted in its march to the river road between the Tigris and the northern swamps. The Ottoman commander was risking something like a Sedan; for it was clear that, if his lines were pierced in his rear at Shumran, his main body of troops would be enveloped.

Occupation of Shumran bend The British pressure on the Dahra bend was resumed on February 15th, in circumstances resembling the earlier attack on the Mohamed Abul Hassan river loop. On this occasion, however, the defeated Turkish garrison was not allowed to escape by a clever ruse. First the enemy's right flank was driven in, then his right centre, and while he was making weak counter-attacks, his left centre was broken and two thousand prisoners were taken. The pontoons by which the Turks endeavoured to escape across the river were smashed by shell fire, and the bend was occupied as far as Shumran.

The enemy commander still persisted in regarding this instant and formidable threat to his rear as a feint intended to weaken him at Sanna-i-Yat. His German airmen may have informed him, as the result of their reconnaissances, that the long British line beyond the Hai River showed no menacing concentration of men, guns, and material. The transport arrangements of Sir Stanley Maude's army were, in fact, concealed from hostile eyes. The enemy checked all river traffic from Sanna-i-Yat, and his own movements by water were hindered from Shumran onward. Both sides had to rely on road transport, and the Turks occupied the better road. For a week all the British preparations for a swift movement were quietly yet vehemently made. In the meantime the main Turkish forces were fiercely held in the trap they had made for themselves between the flooded Tigris and the Suwaicha and Suwada Marshes.

On the afternoon of February 17th the long-impending operations against the Sanna-i-Yat position were begun. A strong frontal attack was delivered, and the enemy's two first lines were carried. The Turks immediately counter-attacked, according to their custom. Their first rush was completely shattered, but their second wave broke into the right flank of the assailants. Thereupon, the left flank also withdrew in the evening, leaving the enemy in possession of all his lines. Yet the effect of this preliminary demonstration in force was not at all vain.

After the interval of reorganisation the Sanna-i-Yat position was more methodically reduced on February 22nd. Two lines of trenches by the Tigris were suddenly carried. This local success provoked the enemy to counter-attack. He had been carefully trained in this method of trench-holding by the German officers sent to instruct him in the latest advances in warfare. The Germans had learned the methods from the French, who held their front lines feebly, and relied largely on the speed of fire and semi-automatic action of their light artillery to beat an attacking force into bayonet-fodder for their counter-attack.

The Ottoman officers did not always appreciate the rationale of the modern counter-attack. They regarded it superstitiously as a certain recipe for victory, whereas it had become rather an outworn artillery trick, easily countered by a force with superior heavy guns and flying trench-photographers.

Sir Stanley Maude's brigadiers photographed and measured the Turkish lines and instructed their gunners in the exact ranges. A few registering shots were tried. The infantry, under cover of a strong but limited curtain of shell fire, occupied the first Turkish line. The Turks brought all their guns to bear on their lost works, and, while a fierce artillery duel opened, counter-attacked. Six times they counter-attacked, losing thousands of men. The heavy, long-ranged British artillery, joining with the lighter guns, mowed down the brave but ineffectual enemy. Once, through sheer power of manhood and mass of sacrifice, the Turk almost touched success. In the end, however, he was beaten. His counter-attack method had been turned against him and used to exhaust him. Two of his Sanna-i-Yat lines were consolidated by the victors.

This was the subtly decisive and indirect winning stroke in the conquest of Mesopotamia. The Ottoman commander was entirely deceived. He reinforced his front at Sanna-i-Yat when, thirty miles distant against his rear, the main

THE CITADEL, BAGDAD, WHERE GENERAL MAUDE HOISTED THE UNION JACK.
The military quarter of Bagdad is situated on the left (the eastern) bank of the Tigris, at the end of the town farthest up-stream, between the Government offices and the cemetery. It comprises the lofty Citadel, a military hospital, and cavalry barracks to the rear inland.

struggle gently opened in the Shumran bend. Just before daybreak on February 23rd covering parties were ferried across the Tigris. Britons and Gurkhas they were. The Britons got within a few yards of the river-bank held by the Turks before a single outpost spied the leading boat. Machine-gun fire and musketry fire then broke out against the boat, but the British guns across the river helped to stamp down all opposition, and the enemy pickets were captured.

The Gurkhas crossed farther down-stream, and, meeting with stronger resistance, conducted a fierce little action before they gained the other bank. After getting through a strong machine-gun fusillade the Gurkha boats were attacked with grenades as the men were landing. **Gurkhas cross the Shumran bend**

There was a bombing match between boat and river-bank, in which the hardy mountaineers of Nepal bore down the Turks. Then, hanging on under an intense artillery fire, they joined up with the British regiment that had extended from its crossing point up-stream. Britons and Gurkhas advanced through the Shumran peninsula, sweeping the Turks before them, and covering the engineering work on the Tigris.

The great river was a thousand feet broad, with a flood

SYMBOL OF BRITISH SUPREMACY.
When the Turks intervened in the war they commandeered this British vessel, then trading on the Tigris, and used her as a transport. She was recaptured by the British during their pursuit of the Turks to Bagdad, and the Union Jack was hoisted above the Turkish Crescent.

current running at five knots. The sappers drove in their first shore anchorage at half-past eight. By half-past four the Tigris was bridged and an army was crossing it. Turkish guns swept the point of crossing, but with little effect. One pontoon only was hit, and that was not sunk. The tremendous speed with which the bridge was thrown across the river was the grand surprise. The enemy thought the slow work of ferrying small parties over would go on all night and the next day. Consequently, where he had expected to meet with patrols he encountered an army.

In preparation for the sweep for the Shumran peninsula

GUNS THAT WERE TWICE TAKEN FROM THE TURKS.
In the first Battle of Kut, in September, 1915, General Townshend captured these guns from the Turks. Then when the heroic defenders of Kut had to surrender in April, 1916, the Turks again got possession of their lost guns, though it was only for a time. In February, 1917, Sir Stanley Maude recaptured them when he took the town.

the British guns on the southern bank had been massed in a large arc. The Turkish guns were soon beaten down, and the British and Indian infantry stormed forward in the night of February 23rd, and, when day broke, the ridge across the neck of the peninsula was conquered and occupied. Well within gunshot of the ridge was the immemorial river road running from Bagdad to Kut. Two days' march beyond was the front of the Ottoman army, still blindly fighting in the Sanna-i-Yat position, where the third and fourth lines had been stormed by an Indo-British division.

The breaking blow had not yet been struck, yet one of the great decisive battles of history was

QUAINT TURKISH ORDNANCE.
The Turks lost two-thirds of their artillery, captured by the British or thrown into the Tigris by themselves. This quaint gun was among the British spoil.

already won. In the year 1638 the Ottoman conqueror, Murad IV., had driven in triumph through Bagdad, passing under an ancient tower built by the old Caliphs of Mesopotamia. The vaulted gateway running through the tower had been walled up immediately after the barbaric conqueror passed through. The rough wall, strangely contrasting with the finished and lovely Arab work it stultified, still stood as a symbol of the imprisonment of the Arab spirit, but the guns that roared over the Shumran bend, ninety miles distant, were opening all the gateways of Mesopotamian civilisation. Between daybreak and nightfall, on February 24th, 1917, the enveloped Ottoman army of Irak was destroyed.

At eight o'clock in the morning a strong force of Indo-British cavalry manœuvred against the flank of the Turkish line of retreat. At the same time the Indo-British infantry drove from the Shumran bridge upon the fugitive enemy, and, taking him unawares, inflicted upon him crippling losses. Then while cavalry, infantry, and gunners were already chasing the Turk north-westward towards Bagdela, on the way to Bagdad, Sir Stanley Maude's eastern forces broke fiercely upon what had been the Turks' front and was now their scattered rear.

Like a gigantic pair of pincers, of which the handle rested on the Hai River, the points of the widely-

THREE CHAPTERS IN A GUNBOAT'S STORY. I.—IN PEACE.
Turkish gunboat lying at anchor in the Tigris before the Ottoman Empire was beguiled by Germany into alliance with the Central Powers—a picture of halcyon days of peace upon the river.

II.—AT WAR.
Fired by shells from a British warship, the gunboat burned fiercely, the dense smoke being visible miles away.

little river town, though in itself a romance, was almost lost to sight in the tremendous drama that was now being enacted. The victors had no time to pause when the jaws of their vice came together near Kut, leaving but remnants of the Turks reduced from an army into a mob. Upon the rapid organisation of the pursuit depended the immediate fate of Bagdad. Men, horses, and engines were worked to the utmost energy in order to reap the full harvest of victory.

The line of the Turkish flight was intersected by numerous stream beds and irrigation ditches, and dotted with peasants' huts. Under all this cover the Turks fought a series of rearguard actions. In the night of February 24th a strong Turkish force, with artillery, was discovered in

separated Indo-British army closed upon the breaking enemy. He fled into the desert, into the swamps and the cane-brakes. His magazines went up in flames, his guns were flung into the river, and, as he ran from position after position, British gunboats steamed up the Tigris with decks cleared for action, and acted as pursuing cavalry. Group after group of the fugitives leading the rout was overtaken by British machine-gunners in flying machines.

The recovery of Kut became an unimportant episode in the triumphant march of victory. Like the recapture of the British gunboat, the Firefly, which had been lost on the retreat from Ctesiphon, the occupation of the famous

III.—SALVED, BUT A PRIZE IN BRITISH HANDS.
Some time after the action, the British naval contingent with the Mesopotamian Expeditionary Force salved and captured the vessel and put her under repair. A shell had penetrated to her oil-tank, causing the conflagration shown in the centre picture.

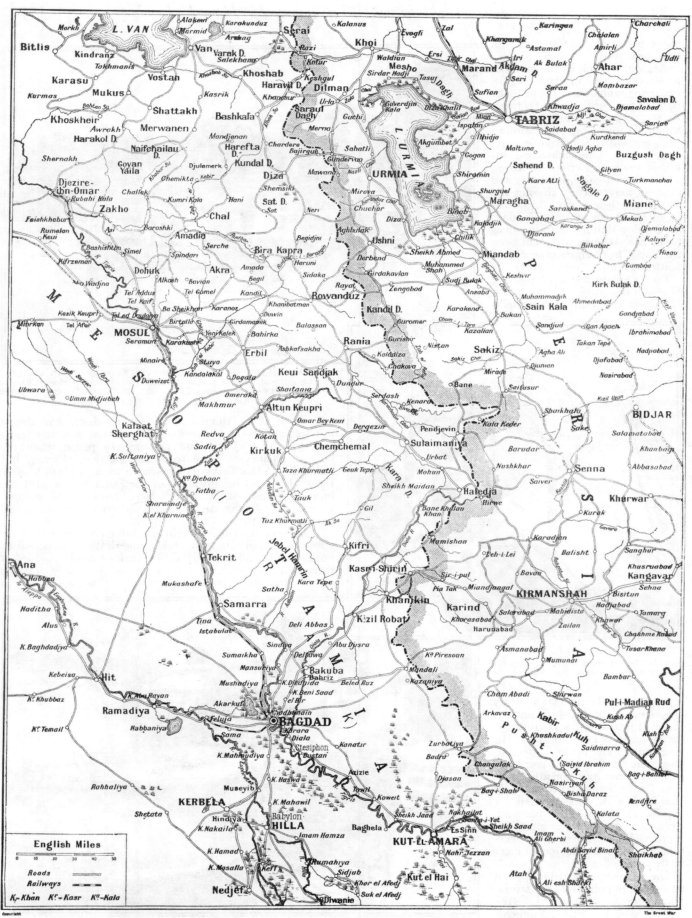

MAP ILLUSTRATING THE OPERATIONS ROUND BAGDAD.

By the end of April, 1917, the Indo-British forces under Sir Stanley Maude operating in the ancient country of Mesopotamia had reached to Feluja, on the Euphrates, about forty miles west of Bagdad, to Samarra, about a hundred and fifty miles north of that city on the Tigris, and had linked up with the Russian forces at Kizil Robat, not far from the Persian frontier to the north-east.

a series of entrenched positions fifteen miles west of Kut. It was clear that this rearguard was covering the withdrawal of guns and stores from Baghela, farther up the stream. But early in the morning of February 25th the British gunboats and Indo-British cavalry and infantry swept in and around the last strong hostile rearguard.

The cavalry enveloped, by a ride round the river marshes, the northern flank of the Turks. The gunboats steaming up the river, in an artillery duel with the hostile guns, obtained a field of fire on the enemy's rear, where British airmen were watching him. As the rearguard shook under the menace of complete envelopment, the infantry charged and broke down all resistance. Thereupon, the general flight of the enemy went on in increasing confusion and disorder. Although only 4,300 prisoners were taken between February 24th and February 27th, the blow to the enemy's strength was tremendous.

The beaten troops had been the pick of their race—veterans from the Gallipoli and Ctesiphon fields of victory. Many of them had fought to the death, their total losses probably reaching 30,000. Those who had died fighting were the cement of the Army. When they vanished nothing was left but a panic-stricken mob. This mob, by the evening of February 27th, passed through Azizie, on the north bank of the Tigris, fifty-five miles from Kut and forty-five miles from Bagdad.

The trail showed the changes in the Turkish mind. At first a continuous battlefield stretched from Sanna-i-Yat to Imam Mehdi. The ground was pitted with shell-holes and strewn with dead troops and shell-cases. Farther westward there were few dead Turks, but many dead mules and horses and dying animals exhausted in the flight. Along the roadside lay live shells flung from the limbers to lighten the burden. Rarer became the intervals where the guns of the gunboats and horse-artillery had shelled a Turkish rearguard and made another scene of battle.

Across the undulating desert, broken by mounds and ruined canal-banks, the pursuit continued by the tree-fringed river from Azizie to Laj, twenty miles nearer Bagdad. A force of Turkish infantry, on March 5th, endeavoured to check the pursuit at Laj. Covered by the thick haze of a sandstorm, the leading body of British cavalry rode through the nullah in which the Turks had entrenched and compelled them to **At Ctesiphon** abandon the position. On March 6th **once more** the farthest point attained by General Townshend in his advance was reached. For one tropical, starry night the grievous burdens of the day—scorching heat, lashing sandstorm, desert thirst, and intolerable fatigue—were lightened by visions of ancient grandeur mingled with prospects of a great modern achievement.

By the edge of a reed-grown marsh rose the huge vault and gigantic eastern wing of the Palace of Chosroes, the fire-worshipping Emperor of the Mediterranean and Indian Ocean. Where the Great King had sat in glory, heir of the dominions of Alexander and his Macedonian captains, there the small heroic expedition of Townshend had won victory and then retreated, as fresh Turkish reserves from the Russian front reinforced the half-shattered Ottoman army that had vainly defended the approaches to Bagdad.

Once more British and Indian troops, excited by victory, lighted their camp-fires round the mighty arch built by the race of fire-worshippers, of which the last remnant had become the Parsees of the new Indo-British Empire. No doubt there were some Parsees in Sir Stanley Maude's host of Christian, Moslem, Hindu, and Arab troops. Far back in time their thoughts must have ranged as they gazed upon the most imposing ruin in all the world, built by their forefathers in the days when Persia had vanquished the power of Rome.

The thoughts of the British troops **Russians capture** must, too, have been bitter-sweet. Their **Kirmanshah** fellow-countrymen were captives of the barbarous Turk ; them they could not yet rescue. Nevertheless, they could soothe their sufferings and exalt their pride of race by a march of conquest which made a new chapter in modern history.

The situation was in some ways similar to that which obtained when General Townshend camped by the Palace of Chosroes. For the second time the Ottoman army in Irak had been hammered up the Tigris, from the Suwaicha Marsh to the Diala River. It had retreated with the utmost rapidity, with the same design as before, which was to get in touch with large reinforcements hastening

KUT: WHERE AN EARLIER DEFEAT WAS SPLENDIDLY AVENGED.
British troops in Kut-el-Amara, on the Tigris. Captured by General Townshend on September 29th, 1915, Kut was then besieged by the Turks, and after an heroic defence surrendered on April 29th, 1916. Nearly a year later, on February 24th, 1917, it was brilliantly recaptured by Sir Stanley Maude.

from the Turkish forces in Persia and the Turkish reserves near Mosul. Immediately on the fall of Kut the Turks in the heart of Persia began quickly to retire. General Baratoff, acting in concert with General Maude, pressed the retiring enemy, and in the first week of March recovered the important provincial capital of Kirmanshah, commanding the main caravan route between Bagdad and Teheran. The Russians were then one hundred and sixty-seven miles from Bagdad, and the British merely fourteen miles.

Consequently, the Turkish army in Persia was in danger of having its chief lines of communication cut above Bagdad if it stayed to offer any opposition to General Baratoff's advance. The fugitives from Kut were dragging with them another mass of fugitives from Persia. Neither of the retreating forces could help the other. The only hope of both was that the general Turkish reserves from Mosul would again arrive in time to strengthen the broken forces near Bagdad and check the British advance.

Sir Stanley Maude, however, was overwhelmingly strong and surpassingly swift. His means of river transport were incomparably superior to those possessed by General

LANDING OF BRITISH SAILORS ON THE TIGRIS.

In Sir Stanley Maude's advance up the Tigris to Kut, and the subsequent rapid pursuit of the Turks to Bagdad and beyond, gunboats of the British Navy rendered valuable assistance to the land forces not only from the river, but also by means of landing-parties.

Townshend. His railway on the lower course of the Tigris set free a large fleet of vessels for immediate battle service up-stream. While the infantry was camped at Ctesiphon the cavalry bivouacked near the Diala River, within gunshot of the suburbs of Bagdad. The retiring Turkish rearguard, which had been pierced by the cavalry, fell back across the Diala, and destroyed the bridge at the point where the tributary stream joins the Tigris.

On the morning of March 7th the manœuvring of forces for the Battle of Bagdad opened. The Indo-British cavalry, with two columns of infantry, began to work round the right bank of the Tigris River, so as to make an enveloping movement on Bagdad from the south-west. At the same time a direct frontal attack was organised against the Diala stream line, which was held by the main Turkish forces and strengthened by fresh troops brought by railway to Bagdad

The operation was a double movement like that conducted east and west of Kut. The enemy was assailed front and rear, so that if he resisted too strongly the attack on the Diala line, a rapid concentration on his flank would lead to envelopment. A frontal attack alone would not have succeeded. The ground was too favourable to the enemy's defensive. The Diala stream was three hundred and sixty feet wide, and screened by houses, trees, and walled gardens. The cover enjoyed by the enemy's observers, machine-gunners, and sharpshooters made it impossible to repeat the Shumran tactics and bridge the river secretly and swiftly.

At any unusual point of embarkation a road and ramps would have been required for bringing up the pontoons, and the enemy would have ascertained from these preparations where the passage would be attempted. The bridge, therefore, had to be constructed openly, and completed by sheer hard fighting. The old bridge-head site was chosen by reason of its convenience. and on the

night of March 7th the first pontoon was lowered over the ramp in bright moonlight. The watchful Turks, massed in the houses on the opposite bank, turned their machine-guns and rifles on the launching-party and shot them all down. The second pontoon was caught in the middle of the stream and the crew killed. The third nearly reached the opposite bank, the men rowing with calm, fierce courage, but it was sunk by a bomb. The fourth crossing-party was annihilated in the same manner. Still there was no holding back. Band after band of volunteers came out into the moonlight from the brigade, and the struggle went on across the stream until the loss of available pontoons prevented all further attempts.

The gunners had not been able to help. The pursuit had been conducted with such speed that they had no time to register on their targets. The work of getting the exact ranges was carried out on March 8th. Then, again, in the clear moonlight night the river battle for the bridge-head was resumed. The new curtain fire of shell made for success. The explosions, though apparently injuring few of the concealed enemy machine-gunners and sharpshooters, had an important indirect effect. The dust raised by the shells formed so thick a fog that ten boats were able to cross and secure a footing. Only when the dust died down were succeeding crossing-parties slaughtered with the same deadly precision as on the previous night.

Lancashires' splendid exploit

In all some sixty Lancashire men crossed the Diala and, joining up, began bombing along the bank. The Turks, finding how small was the landing-party, pressed it in on either flank between two woods. In ordinary circumstances the little detachment, surrounded on three sides by thousands of foes, and cut off at the back by the moonlit, bullet-swept river, would have been exterminated. Happily, the river embankment had been broken by a

GALLANT GURKHAS ON THE SHUMRAN BEND.

One of the most brilliant episodes preceding the capture of Kut in February, 1917, was the bridging of the Shumran bend, seven miles beyond that town. Two Gurkha regiments effected a crossing in the face of strong opposition by means of an heroic bombing attack on the bank.

former flood, and, instead of repairing the mud wall, the Arabs had constructed a new interior embankment, of crescent shape, behind the breached rampart.

Their recent work was a perfect lunette from the military point of view. The Lancashire men at once manned the chance fort, and held it against strong and repeated attacks all the night, all the next day, and the following night. At midnight on March 9th the Turks, by mass attack, reached the top of the embankment, and with one more determined rush would have carried the fort. The Lancashire men were reduced in number to forty, and their ammunition was running out. Yet with steady courage they economised their bombs and cartridges, killing or wounding men at every stroke. They threw the Turks off the parapet, and when the main force at last crossed the river to their

DIFFICULTIES BY THE WAY: MESOPOTAMIAN PALM-GROWN SWAMP.
Contrasting desert and swamp were among the obstacles to the Mesopotamian advance. In some parts of the water-logged country along the Tigris the troops pursuing the Turks had at times to wade almost waist-deep through morass-like stretches of country.

help, the lunette was still held, with a stock of ammunition consisting of one hand-bomb and one clip of cartridges. The Lancashires on the Diala achieved one of the finest feats in the entire range of the war.

Meanwhile, on the last night of the ordeal, the Turks at length showed signs of anxiety at the progress of the cavalry and the infantry columns working south-west of Bagdad. They began to withdraw their machine-guns from the Diala. Fresh Indo-British parties crossed the stream, and by slipping through the Turkish rearguard, gained dead ground, outflanked the Turks on both sides, and captured a company of them. One crossing up-stream was so unexpected that a Turk was bayoneted as he lay stretched at full length, covering the opposite bank with his rifle.

Union Jack over Bagdad

By the morning of March 10th the brigade was across the Diala, and pursuing the Turks into the palm-groves of Saida. The guns quickly followed, and raked the palm-groves with shells before the infantry went in with the bayonet. The Turks then retired northwards to an

entrenched line four miles from the Tigris. This line was attacked on the flank and also assailed in front, and to avoid envelopment the enemy again fled, leaving the victors to enter Bagdad from the east. Thus the frontal attack on the capital of Mesopotamia succeeded, despite the fact that the Ottoman commander had received reinforcements enabling him to offer a stubborn resistance.

The flank attack was equally successful. On the night of March 7th, when the first terrible crossing of the Diala was checked, the Indo-British cavalry, with its two infantry columns, threw a bridge across the Tigris and swept up the right bank of the river towards the road from Aleppo to Bagdad. In great heat and blinding dust-storms the troops marched eighteen miles through the desert, and found the enemy strongly posted south-west of Bagdad. Immediately attacking, they forced the Turks back two miles. Then on March 10th, in a stinging, choking, blinding gale of sand, they pressed their advantage and again turned the defending forces out of a new position only three miles from Bagdad. Broken on the Diala and driven in by the Tigris, the Ottoman army abandoned Bagdad and, in two confused lines of flight along the railway and along the Diala, separated into divergent, hurrying crowds, one seeking help from the north, the other hoping for aid from the west. On March 11th, 1917, the Union Jack flew from the citadel of the city of "The Arabian Nights."

As the vanguard entered, crowds of Arabs, Jews, Persians, Armenians, and Chaldeans came out to meet the dust-covered, red-eyed, weary victors. Children danced before the troops; women put on their festival dresses and clapped from roofs and balconies; the streets were lined with cheering crowds. Some Kurds, however, were looting the bazaars at the farther end of the town, and battalions had at once to be detailed for police work against the last of the marauders of the Ottoman Empire.

TURKISH PRISONERS TAKEN IN THE ADVANCE ALONG THE TIGRIS.
Gurkha guards making sure of Turkish prisoners before sending them back through the British lines. These prisoners were blindfolded by having their caps reversed and the back flap pulled down over their faces. Their wrists were then securely bound behind them.

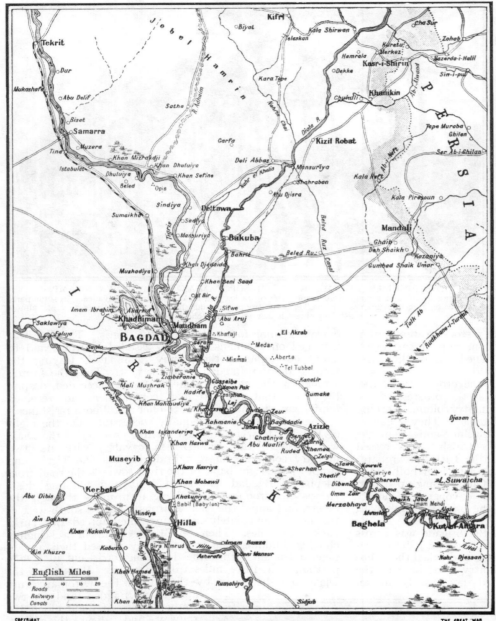

MAP OF THE TIGRIS FROM KUT-EL-AMARA TO BAGDAD.
It was on February 24th, 1917, that Sir Stanley Maude recaptured Kut and started in pursuit of the retreating Turks. A fortnight later the victorious Indo-British army under this brilliant leader entered Bagdad.

pressed onward along the left bank of the Tigris, and, by another extraordinary effort, reached in less than twenty-four hours a point thirty miles upstream from Bagdad. Sweeping along the railway line, the cavalry, with considerable assistance from the British gunboats, got another good day's march behind the rear of the Turkish forces, which were retiring on the right bank of the river. These forces consisted of the remnants of three Turkish divisions. They were overtaken by infantry on March 14th, and again broken at the railway-station of Mushadiya and driven in full flight towards Samarra.

While these operations were proceeding up the Tigris, another strong Indo-British force pursued the second Turkish army that was retreating up the Diala River, in order to unite with the enemy forces retiring from the Russians in Persia. The fighting along the northern tributary was difficult, as the country was intersected with numerous canals and rivers, most of which had to be bridged. The region through which the Russians were operating was also against rapid movement, as the old caravan route ran through narrow mountain passes and great stretches of snow. The town of Kizil Robat, on the upper reach of the Diala tributary, was fixed as the junction-point of the Russian and Indo-British forces.

At first it looked as though the Allies would effect their junction without any great difficulty, and combine to crush the defeated and scattered Ottoman divisions. Someone on the Turkish Staff, however, kept a clear and active head. Probably he was a German commander sent in haste to the scene of disaster. For the plan he made was somewhat similar to that devised by Frederick the Great in an extreme difficulty. He tried to trap that portion of the Indo-British army which had been detached, after the conquest of Bagdad, to move northward up the Diala towards the Persian frontier and link up with General Baratoff's vanguard.

Collecting the three divisions that were retiring along the Tigris on Samarra, he stiffened them with reinforcements. **Clever Turkish attempt defeated** Then he brought them back along the road to Bagdad towards the Adhaim River, which ran at an interval of thirty miles, roughly parallel with the Diala stream. The Turkish force retreating before the Russians was ordered to entrench, and while conducting a containing movement northward to send all the troops it could spare southward to co-operate with the Turkish force on the Upper Diala.

The scheme was that this combined force should close down from the north against the British and Indian troops on the Diala, while the re-formed Turkish divisions on the Adhaim River advanced westward and likewise attacked the Indo-British. Cleverly as the converging attack was planned it did not succeed. The British commander also followed the methods of Frederick the Great. He detached

The joy of the townspeople was most genuine. The oppression they had endured was as savage as that of the Mongol era. It had become brigandage on a vast scale, though townsmen and soldiers were nominally fellow-countrymen and largely fellow-Moslems. The despoiled and downtrodden people of Bagdad hailed with delight the prospect of coming under the orderly and progressive administration of the race that had built up Egypt and made India strong and prosperous.

On the day of victory, however, little time could be given to the affairs of the city. Only a few battalions could be spared to deal with the looting Kurds and guard the streets. As at Kut, the immediate pursuit of the enemy was the task of supreme importance. General Maude had in fifteen days advanced a hundred and ten miles, fighting rearguard after rearguard, crossing the Tigris three times, and engaging in two great pitched battles. The country through which he worked was destitute of supplies, but such was his organisation that he not only fed his army on the march, but arrived in Bagdad with ample resources for rapid, continuous action.

When Bagdad was occupied, the Indo-British cavalry

NO BARS, BUT STILL A CAGE.
Sir Charles Townshend's house on Prinkipo Island. It stood on the cliffs with a view over the sea, and had a garden a quarter of a mile long and very beautiful.

SIR CHARLES TOWNSHEND, THE HERO OF KUT, IN CAPTIVITY.
Full of admiration of Sir Charles Townshend's heroic defence of Kut-el-Amara, the Turks treated him with honour and assigned him quarters on Prinkipo Island, near Constantinople, where he was allowed full freedom. Left to right: Corporal Boggis (orderly), Tewfik Bey, General Townshend, Captain Morland, Private Hoskyns. Above: Sir Charles Townshend driving with the Commandant of Constantinople.

a small force that countered the northern body of newly-combined Turks near Deli Abbas. With his main strength he met the forces coming from the Adhaim River line and broke them, so that they fled back over the river on March 29th. This cleared the way for the junction of the Allies. On April 2nd the Indian Lancers and the Cossacks met at Kazil Robat, and the victories of Kut and Bagdad were consummated by a union of the two allied armies, who then formed an uninterrupted line of front protecting Persia from invasion.

Much still remained to be done before the concentrated Ottoman forces were decisively broken. These forces were strengthened with fresh troops and placed under a new commander with talent and character. There was, indeed, a report that Mackensen, the ablest of all German generals, was coming to Mesopotamia to retrieve the fortunes of the Turks. He probably sent a very able man from his Staff, and promised to come himself as soon as affairs on the Danube allowed. Certainly the enemy needed assistance, both moral and material. The spirit of the Turkish infantry was, for the time at least, remarkably low. This was proved in the series of actions between the Diala and the Adhaim, which occurred after the junction of the Russian and British armies.

On April 10th Sir Stanley Maude, by drawing in his detachments on the right bank of the Diala River, lured the Turks to return to the rich region of Deltawah, only thirty miles north of Bagdad. The following night the British commander made a night march from the Tigris, struck the surprised Turks on their flank, and drove them back for many miles with heavy losses. But for a mirage that screened the battlefield in a critical moment the enemy would have been trapped and annihilated. Again, on April 18th, the Turkish divisions operating from the Adhaim River were attacked on two sides, one thrust being delivered by the Tigris and another across the northern tributary. The Turks were routed, and only saved their guns because the horses of the British cavalry were completely exhausted by the heat. Fifteen hundred prisoners were taken, and the enemy's losses in dead and wounded were in proportion. Yet the total casualties of the attackers numbered only seventy-three. Clearly the Turks in Mesopotamia knew that they were beaten. Scarcely any fight was left in them, and only the tropical weather and the waterless condition of the desert prevented another long and victorious march by the army of Mesopotamia.

By the end of April, 1917, Sir Stanley Maude was master of the Euphrates as far as Feluja, where one of his columns had pushed across the rivers intersecting the desert. All the Bagdad Railway, stretching seventy miles to the terminus at Samarra, was also conquered. The broken Turkish forces were pushed nearly a hundred miles away from Bagdad, in spite of the terrible heat in which the pursuit was continued. Ancient Babylonia was a British possession, and the famous Moslem shrines of Kerbela and Samarra were recovered from the Turanians.

To the green-robed Persians Kerbela was as sacred a spot as Mecca. For there Hussein had perished in circumstances that led to the great schism in the Mohammedan world. Then at Samarra, under a dome of gold, slept the Imam of Allah—the mysterious prophet, who was expected by the Persians to rise again, when the time was ripe, and establish righteousness throughout the earth. Under British protection, these homes of the Shiah faith, which had been looted of their treasures by the enemy, served strongly to attach the Persian people to the Allies and complete the work carried out by Sir Percy Sykes and General Baratoff.

Revival of the Arabs

The succession of diverse defeats incurred by the Ottomans took from them all their practical means of religious control. The Orthodox Moslems recovered the shrine of the Prophet, while the Shiahs were rejoicing in liberty at the shrine of Hussein. In the heart of Arabia the direct descendant of Mohammed, the Sherif of Mecca, had proclaimed the independence of his people and become King Hussan of the Hedjaz. He formed a league with other independent princes of Arabia whose territories were nearly as large as India. By common action against the Turk the Arab race organised itself. Clear signs could be seen of one of those great movements of the Arab spirit which in the past had been turning-points in the annals of both Asia and Europe.

In many ways the decision achieved at Kut and confirmed at Bagdad was of far-reaching consequence. Not only did it restore the prestige of British arms in Asia and Northern Africa, but it weakened the reputation of the Germans even more profoundly than it depressed the spirit of the Turks. Some years before the date when the Teuton definitely determined to break the peace of the world, the British Government tried to placate them by allowing them a large sphere of influence in the Near East. The Germans then devised their Berlin-Bagdad route, and continually put pressure upon the British Government to gain the control of the Persian Gulf. For some years their apparent design was merely one of commercial expansion towards their chosen "place in the sun" at Bagdad. Beneath their engineering and commercial designs, however, was a military plan for an overland route of advance to India, with the practical absorption and reorganisation of the great potential fighting power of the races of the Ottoman Empire.

British prestige restored

The British Government was at first inclined to think that the movement was intended against Russia. But the attack was really directed against the tropical possessions of the British Empire. Austria-Hungary entered into league with Germany, and, acting as the spear-head of that Central Europe that aimed to dominate the earth, began to thrust through Serbian territory in the design to prepare the way for the Berlin-Bagdad movement. From 1909 to 1913 Europe shook with preparations for war and threats for war, because the eyes of the Teutons were fixed on the strange, distant, and romantic goal of the city of " The Arabian Nights." In the end it was the Austrian pressure on Serbia, made with the view to annexing the railway corridor to the Orient, that directly brought about the awful conflict of all the Great Powers of the world.

The Germans then had, of course, more practical and immediate schemes of conquest than they had previously entertained in regard to Mesopotamia. They had estimated that a generation of quiet, gradual work would have been required to consolidate themselves on the Tigris and the Euphrates.

When, however, their great armies in Europe were checked, and a peace by negotiation seemed to them the best way out of their difficulties, Bagdad again became one of the great bases of their hopes of permanent expansion.

Germany and Austria-Hungary were to unite in forming a Central Europe State, to reach through the railway corridor of Serbia, Bulgaria, European Turkey, Asia Minor, Arabia, and the Persian Gulf. These countries were to form an economic and military confederation. Mesopotamia was to be developed by German engineers and agricultural experts, and made the granary of the Teuton-Ottoman Bund and the future base for operations against the communications of India and Egypt.

All this was little more than a dream, yet it was ever present to the German mind. After every severe check in the principal theatre of war the Germans resumed their boastings of the Berlin-Bagdad line.

The world continually rang with German voices spreading the fame of Bagdad. Immense, therefore, was the moral effect when the city of ancient enchantments was taken by Sir Stanley Maude.

CHAPTER CLXXVII.

THE INTRIGUES AND TRIALS OF NEUTRAL EUROPE.

German Intimidation of the Smaller Neutral States—Anti-German Feeling Among the People of Holland Coincident with Pro-German Sympathy among the Jonkheers and Leading Merchants—Dutch Army Mobilised to Meet a British Invasion of Holland Artfully Suggested by the German General Staff—Holland Perturbed by American Proposal to Stop Superfluous Exports—Political Isolation of Sweden Before the War—Reactionary Coup d'Etat by the Swedish Aristocracy—King Gustav's Proposal for an Anti-British Scandinavian Union Declined by the Kings of Norway and Denmark—The Transito Established in Sweden by Great Britain—Trouble Over the Parcels Mails—The Closing of the Sound—Effect of the Russian Revolution Upon the Swedish Reactionaries—Norwegian Democracy Benevolently Neutral Towards the Allies—Friction Over the Blockade Problem of the Export of Norwegian Copper to Germany—Passive Responsiveness of Denmark to Pressure—Purchase of the Danish West Indies by the United States—Sincerity of All Neutral Socialists Tested by the Russian Revolution—German Intrigues in Switzerland—Cleavage between the French-Swiss and German-Swiss—The Stegemann Case—Economic Pressure by Germany upon Switzerland—Overtures for a Commercial Rapprochement between Great Britain and Spain—Reactionary Noble and Clerical Forces in Spain Reinforced by the Organised German Population in that Country—Subtle and Persistent German Intrigues in Spain.

FROM the spring of 1915, when the course of Germanic intrigues in the neutral world was described in Chapter LI. (Vol. III.), to the spring of 1917 no decisive change of conditions occurred in the Scandinavian countries, Switzerland, Holland, and Spain. At intervals the Germans made threats of invasion against Norway, Switzerland, and Holland. These threats, however, were designed only to terrorise the small neighbouring neutral States, make them submit to the effects of submarine piracy, and compel them to yield further under the economic pressure of the Teutons. So long as the countries bordering on Germany continued to feed the German armies their existence was tolerated by the enemy. Their absorption into the Middle Europe system was temporarily postponed, owing to circumstances over which the German General Staff and Marine Office had no proper control.

In Holland, in Sweden, and in German-speaking Switzerland there was some partial inclination to unite

THE KING OF SPAIN.
Alfonso XIII. became protector, in Germany and Austria-Hungary, of the interests and subjects of several belligerent countries.

THE QUEEN OF SPAIN.
Victoria Eugenie Julia Ena Maria Christina, daughter of Prince and Princess Henry of Battenberg. Born October 24th, 1887.

with the Central Empires. In Holland popular feeling ran against the Germans. Only the landed gentry and the large business interests linked with the German export trade saw any solid and permanent advantages in the proposed scheme of military, political, and economic serfdom. The ancient nobility of Holland —headed by the Bentinck family—had sent sons as volunteer officers into the German Army, and some of their older men, occupying important positions in the Dutch Army, made no secret of the fact that they desired to see a general triumph of German arms. A Dutch general was on Mackensen's Staff.

The Dutch Jonkheers sympathised with the Prussian Junkers for selfish class interests. There was no national base for their policy. Quite the contrary. They were disturbed by the growth of democratic and socialistic activities among their own populace, and hoped eventually to obtain the help of a victorious and reactionary Prussia in repressing and chaining down the Dutch working classes.

A considerable number of Dutchmen of the upper middle class took the same view. Not only did they want as docile and serf-like a proletariat as Prussia possessed, but they required a mighty and prosperous German Empire, to which they could continue profitably to act as export agents. Their principal port, Rotterdam, was the grand outlet of the immense industries of the Rhine basin. Anything that damaged the Germans damaged also the Dutch. On the other hand, anything that injured Antwerp profited Rotterdam ; and, among other things, the German occupation of Zeebrugge, the great new base for Belgian ocean traffic, gave considerable relief to some menaced Dutch mercantile interests.

Pro-German party in Holland Members of leading Dutch business houses would have lost nothing if the Germans had succeeded in dominating the world. They would have amalgamated on fair terms with German business houses, and become prosperous partners in the supreme Teutonic system, bringing in their rich East Indian plantations as a great asset of the new partnership.

On the whole, therefore, the *haute bourgeoisie* of Holland inclined to the same policy as the Jonkheeren. The farming class did not worry about any policy, being content to enjoy its advantages of making enormous profits out of the ineffectual British blockade. Agricultural Holland, built up by exports to Great Britain under the British Free Trade system, was transformed into a huge factory for transforming American cattle-cake and fodder into highly-priced provisions for German soldiers and munition makers. All that the ruling and influential classes of Holland feared was that Great Britain would intervene and forcibly stop the huge leak in the blockade of the Central Empires.

[British official photograph.
INSPECTING THE RUINS.
Spanish officers visiting a wrecked village retaken by the British on the western front.

The attempt to control the commerce between the Netherlands and Germany by means of an oversea trading trust, directed by a British commercial attaché at The Hague, was farcically inept. Dutch newspapers openly proclaimed that the means of control had failed. The strong pro-German party of Jonkheers, merchants, and farmers at last became alarmed by their own success in helping the enemy.

By March, 1916, Sir Edward Grey was commonly regarded in the Netherlands as the most Machiavellian statesman that ever existed. It was supposed he had let the Dutch treat him as a blind weakling, until he had accumulated against them an overwhelming case for warlike action. The loss of the rich plantations of Java and Sumatra and the capture or internment of Dutch shipping were, so rumour ran, only part of the price that Holland would have to pay. The great new national **A farce with** armies of the British Empire were **a moral** ready for action, and Lord Kitchener, so the Dutch Staff apparently believed, intended to kill two birds with one stone—invade Holland and turn the flank of the German forces.

The Dutch Army actually mobilised to meet the attack. On March 31st, 1916, the General Staff requisitioned the railways and strengthened the personnel at strategic stations. All leave for military and naval officers and men was stopped. Guns were expedited to the coast and the defences of the estuaries of the Scheldt and Rhine were reinforced. On the Stock Exchange there was a general slump in prices, steamship shares falling in an especially heavy manner. Some liners postponed their

British official photograph.
AT A TRENCH ENTRANCE.
British Staff officer explaining the construction of modern trenches to the Spanish visitors.

[British official photograph.
SPANISH OFFICERS VISITING THE WESTERN FRONT.
Members of the Spanish Mission in a mine-crater ; an aeroplane was passing overhead. A number of Spanish officers were taken round part of the British front in France to study the actual conditions of modern warfare.

sailings, and there was a furious run on the banks. A secret session of Parliament was held, and the general perturbation continued for more than a week. Very gradually, as the anxiety of the people calmed, the reason for all the military, naval, and political activity was revealed. The German General Staff had warned the Dutch General Staff of a British attack near the mouth of the Scheldt, and had suggested that if Holland did not feel strong enough to oppose the disembarkation of the British Army, the German forces in Belgium would undertake the task.

The affair was an historic farce with a moral. It indicated the weight of German influence upon the uneasy mind of the Dutch governing class. The larger part of the Dutch Press was then rabidly hostile to Great Britain, who was accused of tyrannic

ANOTHER UNIT OF SPAIN'S SUBMARINE ARMADA.
The submarines which American shipyards built to Spanish orders were of the 800-ton type, 200 feet in length, with a cruising radius of 5,500 miles. They attained the latest and highest standard of submarine construction at the time of being laid down.

SPANISH SUBMARINE IN AMERICAN WATERS.
Preparing for eventualities, Spain, while preserving neutrality, ordered new submarines from American yards. One is shown here passing through the Cape Cod Canal, Massachusetts.

endeavours to reduce the Netherland nation to a condition of vassalage. When, for example, the Tubantia was torpedoed by a German submarine, the "Niewe Rotterdamsche Courant" insinuated that the liner had been sunk by a British submarine. Then, after the Berkelstroom was openly torpedoed by the U18, in inhuman circumstances, the same organ of the Dutch merchant classes mildly remarked that the incident would tend to tell against the general sympathy felt throughout Holland for the German people.

At the opening of the campaign of Germanic piracy, in 1917, seven Dutch steamers were torpedoed on leaving Falmouth, after an assurance had been given by enemy authorities that the vessels would not be attacked. Some were outward-bound in ballast to neutral ports, one was returning to Holland with wheat for the Dutch Government. All were destroyed. Yet the majority of the directing and influential classes did not lose faith in their neighbours. Only the Dutch Radical groups, with the circles represented by the "Telegraaf" and "Handelsblad" newspapers, remained concerned for the honour of their country and the free development of civilisation.

In so far as the Dutch working classes were organised for political action in the interests of labour their influence was employed to promote the intrigues of the Prussian masters of Middle Europe. Mynheer Troelstra, the leader of the Social Democrat movement in the Netherlands, cooperated with Herren Scheidemann and Ebert and other Socialist jackals of the Kaiser. In July, 1916, he welcomed them in a German speech to a conference at which an attempt was made to revive the international organisation as an instrument for obtaining a German peace. He also took an important part in arranging, in 1917, a Socialist conference at Stockholm, in which the Russian Revolutionists were to be tempted to break with the democracies of France, the United States, Italy, and the British Empire and make a separate peace with the autocracies of Germany and Austria.

In addition to Dutch Socialism, Dutch religion was transformed into a political weapon against the Entente Powers. A leading politician, Dr. Kuyper, was the head of a Calvinist league directed against "atheistic and revolutionary France." The leader of the league applauded the destruction of the Lusitania, and said the victims had been punished for trying to act as a shield to the cargoes despatched by American armament firms. Alongside the Protestant pro-German force was an **Religious political intrigues** equally powerful Roman Catholic group, directed by Cardinal van Rossum and the Archbishop of Utrecht. Dutch priests and ministers at times proclaimed from the pulpit the righteousness and glory of Germany's war.

Only a powerless minority of Dutchmen retained the independent spirit of their forefathers, and their chief spokesman, the editor of the "Telegraaf," was at last imprisoned by the Netherlands Government for the crime of publishing his opinion of the scoundrels of Germany. Virulent attacks upon Great Britain and France by men of the school of Dr. Kuyper were not checked by similar police proceedings. It seems to have been thought, after the panic of March, 1916, that Great Britain could not afford to take any action which would throw Holland into the arms of Germany and make the North Sea coast, from Groningen to the Scheldt, a new base for submarine operations against all ships trading to the British Isles. The calculating Dutchmen reckoned that the German submarine menace was their protection, and the means by which they retained their East Indian colonies and oversea imports. The ships they lost by German attacks represented the cost of insurance against British action. Most of the lost ships did not belong to members of the Teutonising party. The menace of German absorption did not trouble the majority of the directing and commercial Dutchmen. As one of them put it, in a veiled sneer over the misfortunes of the heroic Belgians : " After all, it would be better to be annexed and alive than independent and dead."

Not until the United States entered the war did the governing and trading classes in Holland become perturbed. What perturbed them was the American proposal to stop all superfluous provisioning of countries bordering on Germany, by reducing the supply of American grain and cattle food to the proportion required for home consumption. America had been providing Dutchmen with food, while the Dutch sold their own produce at famine prices to the Germans. The peril of a stoppage of superfluous American imports upset the Dutch people far more than anything they had suffered in the German submarine campaigns. The Dutch heart was hard and so was the Dutch head, but the Dutch purse was extremely sensitive to the shocks of war. Enormously fat it had grown, and as it covered the remnants of the Dutch conscience as well as riches accumulated by years of national smuggling, the intervention of the United States and some of the principal countries of South America seemed to many Dutchmen a far greater calamity than any German atrocities in Belgium.

Effect of American action

Sweden was also sobered in the spring of 1917, by the American scheme of restricting exports to neutral States that neighboured Germany. For thirty-four months of the war Sweden had been a potential ally of the Central Empires. On several occasions there was danger of a Swedish advance through Finland towards Petrograd. If Great Britain had not entered the struggle, and if Russia, France, Belgium, and Serbia had fought unaided, the action of Sweden would probably have been belligerent in August, 1914.

SENOR MAURA ADDRESSING A VAST MEETING AT MADRID FOR MAINTAINING NEUTRALITY.

In the Plaza de Toros, Madrid, Señor Maura, ex-Premier, under the motto of " No human power shall make us deviate from neutrality," addressed a crowd of twenty thousand people on April 29th, 1917. He declared that Spain must continue to maintain absolute neutrality, but that her international policy after the war should favour a rapprochement with the Western Powers. Above : Señor Maura speaking.

FIRST MEETING OF THE SPANISH CABINET, FORMED APRIL 19TH, 1917

From left to right: Señor Juan Alvarado, Minister for Foreign Affairs; Señor Garcia Prieto, Premier; Señor Ruis Valarino, Minister of Justice; Señor Julio Burell, Minister of the Interior; Señor José Franco Rodriguez, Minister of Public Instruction; the Duke of Almodovar del Valle, Minister of Public Works; General Aguilera, Minister of War; Admiral Miranda, Minister of Marine; Señor Santiago Alba, Minister of Finance.

It is now possible to trace, in the domestic history of Sweden, one of the great preparatory steps to the outbreak of the universal conflict. In the year 1913 Sweden was outside the field of influence of both the Central Europe Alliance and the Triple Entente. She was governed by a Liberal Ministry, which was absorbed in internal problems and poised between a sweeping Labour movement and a violent Conservative reaction.

The King was married to a German princess, and admired the Prussian system of repressive government. He forgot that he was the great-great-grandson of a common soldier in the army of the French Revolution, and being alarmed by the prospect of a Swedish Labour Ministry, he favoured the plan for a *coup d'état*, which was carried out in March, 1914, by the Swedish aristocracy and their supporters.

A great mob of peasant farmers was organised by the large landowners to demonstrate against the Government. Thereupon, the Liberal Ministry was dismissed, and a reactionary group established by means that were not above criticism. Looking at the affair in the light of the war, there can scarcely be any doubt that the Swedish aristocracy knew something about the plans of the German General Staff, and seized upon the powers of government in the design to resume the struggle with Russia that had ended at Poltava. The Swedish nobility had formerly grown rich and powerful from the spoils of war. It was largely formed of German adventurers from the Baltic provinces afterwards conquered by Russia. It had fought under Gustavus the Great and Charles XII., and had exhausted Sweden for centuries by rapid and inordinate conquests which could not be held.

Memories of the days when Sweden lived on the spoil

SEÑOR GARCIA PRIETO.
Chief of the Spanish Democratic Party and President of the Senate, Señor Prieto became Premier, April 19th, 1917.

of Germany, Poland, and Russia stirred in the minds of the descendants of the old adventurers. It was their ancestors who had first taught the Prussians that war could be made a profitable business affair. They themselves, however, were a chafing military caste, with aims larger than their resources. They needed to conquer new lands for recruitment. The population of their country had been reduced to five and a half millions, possessing an Army of some two hundred thousand men, to which another three hundred thousand could only be added in special circumstances.

These special circumstances were principally of a moral nature. The recalcitrant working classes, with socialistic views, and the angry middle classes, with democratic opinions, had first to be converted to a common faith in aggression, similar to that with which the German people went to war. This could have been done had action been taken solely against Russia, on the plea of liberating Finland from government by the knout.

The affair, however, became difficult to conduct, when it was clearly evident that Germany was massing only against the democracy of republican France. M. Branting, the leader of the Swedish Socialists and chief of the largest political group, was a champion of France, and an upholder of the French rights over Alsace and Lorraine. His influence over the working classes was too great to be contemned, especially when it was also seen that Sweden might be suffocated by an Atlantic blockade if she actively moved against the Grand Alliance.

For some months the Swedish camarilla was foiled by the force of circumstances. Their Government, under Herr Hammarskjöld, whose sympathies were openly German, had to let "I dare not" wait upon "I would." With a remarkable amount of assistance from Swedish publicists belonging to the Swedish Court party the Swedes were inundated with

German news and views and verbosities. Well-known British men of letters were not allowed to give addresses explaining the cause of the western democracies. The machinery of administration, education, and social influence was directed entirely to the effort of convincing the Swedish people that the *coup d'état* had been carried out in their own interests, and that it was their duty to advance the cause of liberty on the Prussian system. They were told that the age of democracy had passed and the age of organisation had arrived. This meant that they had to work as long as their masters thought fit, that they would be shot down if they **Swedish animosity** tried to strike, and **against Britain** also march against Russia in order to ensure the destruction of the French democracy.

The stubborn Swedish working men could not be convinced. They made neither threat nor movement. Yet their attitude was such that the reactionary Government was still afraid to strike at Russia in the critical weeks in the summer of 1915 when all the Russian armies were in retreat

When, however, the Swedish Government saw that, as a matter of fact, the recovery of the Russian power of offensive largely depended upon the transit of munitions through Swedish territory there opened a long, intense, and yet quiet struggle between Great Britain and Sweden.

The Swedish reactionaries acted as though they desired to bring about armed conflict, but so that it would seem to have been forced upon them by the "maritime tyranny" of Great Britain. The interruption of the huge Swedish traffic in contraband in the Baltic, by the British submarine operations of 1915, was one of the motives for the Swedish action.

The King of Sweden invited the Kings of Denmark and Norway to a conference, and endeavoured to induce them to combine in forming a Scandinavian union to battle against British sea-power.

The constitutional monarchs of Denmark and Norway refused to take common action with the Swedish reactionaries. In the first place, they could not bind their democratic peoples. In the second place, they were less afraid of Great Britain than of Germany. In the third place, their western coasts would have been exposed to British attack, while the coasts of Sweden would have continued to remain fairly well protected so long as the German Fleet was in being.

After the Queen of Sweden returned from Germany, where she publicly prophesied the triumph of German arms, her husband and his Ministers openly began to play their part in the Teutonic plan of action for 1916. The British Government arranged, with considerable difficulty, a Swedish

MARQUIS CORTINA.
In April, 1917, the marquis negotiated a commercial agreement between Great Britain and Spain for the exchange of certain commodities.

system of controlling imports, similar to the systems established in Switzerland, Holland, Denmark, and Norway. The control was loose and leaky, and allowed enormous profits to be made by devious methods of contraband traffic.

Yet the Swedish Ministers fought furiously against the Transito, as the control system was named. When borne down by the pressure of public and political opinion, they nevertheless introduced in the act of legislation a clause that undid everything the ruling opinion of the country desired to establish. It was, for example, made illegal for a Swedish importer of British goods to inform the British manufacturer of the names of the person or persons to whom the goods would ultimately go. Not improbably, therefore, the goods would have gone to Germany.

In the debates on the affair it was clearly revealed that the intention of the Swedish Ministry was to encourage the entrepôt traffic in contraband between America and Germany.

Failing to obtain complete success in regard to the Transito, the men who were intriguing for war selected another point **Contraband in** of dispute with Great **Swedish mailbags** Britain, and narrowly missed the declaration of hostilities which they desired.

In December, 1915, a Danish steamer, Hellig Olaf, was brought to Kirkwall for examination of the Swedish parcels mail she was carrying from the United States. One third of the parcels addressed through Sweden were found to contain contraband of war destined for Germany. The parcels of contraband were put in the Prize Court, and the remainder of the mail was forwarded to Sweden.

The action of the British naval authorities was undoubtedly sound in international law, but the Swedish war party thought it gave a fit opportunity to make the case the ground for their long-contemplated struggle with Great Britain.

By way of reprisal, the British parcels mail for Russia was detained while passing through Sweden. The mail was detained until August, 1916.

Then, when releasing most of the parcels, the Swedish Government refused to allow the further transit of the mail.

The transparent intention was to stop all transport of munitions to Russia over the land route through Sweden to Finland. There was a rough, slow traffic route through Northern

OLD FRIENDS AND COLLEAGUES IN SPANISH AFFAIRS.
Count Romanones (on the right) who, failing to persuade his Cabinet to join the Allies, resigned the Premiership. On the left: His old friend and colleague Señor Juan Alvarado, Minister for Foreign Affairs in Señor Prieto's Government.

Norway to Finland—but without a railway, and employing reindeer sledges, available only for small parcels—in the critical winter months when Archangel was ice-bound. The new Russian ice-free port near Kola was not ready, and the Murman railway was still in course of construction.

Regiment of the Spanish Queen's Lancers engaged in tactical exercises in the presence of King Alfonso in the Cerro de los Retamares. In Spain, by the Army Law of 1911, personal military service was obligatory on all, with but few special exceptions; three years being spent with the Colours, five in the Second Portion of the Army, six in the Reserve, and four in the Territorial Reserve. The war strength of the Army was 400,000 men.

Review of Marines at Santander, on the Bay of Biscay, by the King of Spain. The Spanish Navy, which had been destroyed during the Cuban War of 1898, was being rebuilt and reorganised in 1917, at the commence-ment of which year it consisted of three modern battleships of 15,700 tons and one old one, three modern cruisers and four old ones, eight torpedo-boat destroyers, twenty-four torpedo-boats, and ten gunboats.

KING ALFONSO OF SPAIN WITH SOME OF HIS SEA AND LAND FIGHTING FORCES.

THE QUEEN OF HOLLAND.
Under Queen Wilhelmina's guidance, Holland showed impartial kindness to interned soldiers of all nations.

In August, 1916, when the quarrel over the parcels mails became most acute, the Swedish Government adopted another method capable of provoking war. The Sound was strongly closed to British warships, by laying a minefield in the Kogrund Channel and setting Swedish naval forces to watch over the passage.

The pretence was that all belligerent vessels, and especially all belligerent submarines, were to be prevented from entering or leaving the Baltic through Swedish waters. A farcical report was spread that a German warship was sunk in August, 1916, when

trying to make the forbidden passage. It was against the victors of the Battle of Jutland that the mine-layers and warships of Sweden acted.

The Swedes helped to hold the Baltic until the German Navy had recovered its strength. Not until May, 1917, was there any movement by Sweden to open the Kogrund Channel. Foreign merchant ships and steamers trading between foreign ports were shut out from traffic through the inner Falsterbo route on another amazing pretence that German contraband traffic would thereby be prevented.

Fine iron ore from the State mines of Sweden poured into Germany. The German Baltic ports could not make use of all the ore, owing to the lack of coal in North Germany. Therefore, a considerable portion of the ore was carried to the foundries on the Rhine coal basis by a voyage through the territorial waters of Sweden and Denmark, and behind the mine-fields of the German North Sea

Closing of the Kogrund Channel coast, and thence along the territorial waters of Holland to the Rhine. Yet, according to an official Swedish shipping organ, the Falsterbo passage was shut to prevent the contraband traffic of the Germans! The Germans themselves publicly praised one of the later Swedish Ministers of the reactionary school for the good work he had done in preventing a British syndicate from obtaining control of a new Swedish iron mine, by purchasing a large number of shares for the Government. Apparently, the German idea was that everything controlled by the Swedish Government was available for German use.

Such appeared to be the position of affairs in the critical summer of 1916, when the Russian drive into Galicia was

checked and the Franco-British offensive on the Somme still left Germany sufficiently strong to overthrow the army of Rumania. Had the elections to the Swedish Landthing produced in that year the results expected by the reactionaries, there might have occurred another intervention on the side of the Central Empires.

The Swedish war party conducted a campaign of a virulent character against the pacific Socialist Party. The Socialists, however, though divided into two schools, showed great political power, and by balancing the reactionary group, left the Liberals as the deciding factor in the assembly. By combining on any vitally important matter the Socialists and Liberals could clean out-vote the promoters of the former *coup d'état*.

Swedish Socialists' political power

The reactionaries, therefore, were compelled to be careful and subtle in their intrigues against the Allies. They succeeded, however, in exhausting the patience of Viscount Grey, and practically every man in Great Britain acquainted with the trouble with Sweden expected a declaration of war by the autumn of 1916. The Russian bureaucracy, however, became alarmed. They protested that the stoppage of the transport of munitions through Sweden was in itself sufficient to destroy the striking power of the Russian armies.

The ways of Russian authorities in the days of Rasputin, Stürmer, and Protopopoff were dark and tortuous. It is possible that Protopopoff had then arranged for peace and alliance between the autocracies of Russia, Prussia, and Austria. Belated hostilities against King Gustav of Sweden, who was a promising embryo of an autocrat, were likely to be upsetting, especially if Great Britain, a Liberal

A ROYAL INSPECTION IN HOLLAND.
Queen Wilhelmina reviewing some of her troops. The war strength of the Dutch Army in 1917 was about 200,000 men—a small defensive force against possible aggression by the neighbouring might of Germany.

between foreign ports were shut out from traffic through the inner Falsterbo route on another amazing pretence that German contraband traffic would thereby be prevented.

Power, opened the action. A long-distance British blockade from the gateways of the Atlantic might have quickly produced such discomfort among the Swedish population as would lead the angry Socialists to rise in insurrection. Then an insurrection in Stockholm might have had a contagious effect upon the Revolutionary forces in Petrograd. The oppressed Finns were already in a fiercely Revolutionary frame of mind and assisting the enemy in many ways. They could have spread the insurrection from Stockholm to Petrograd.

However this may be, the British Coalition Cabinet, under Mr. Asquith's

THE DUTCH PRINCE CONSORT.
Though German by birth and sympathy Prince Henry of the Netherlands preserved a correct demeanour in a very difficult position.

QUEEN WILHELMINA WITH HER SOLDIERS AT LEYDEN.
The Queen of the Netherlands with some of her chief military leaders at a sham fight at Leyden. Her Majesty is seen in the centre of the photograph. They are in the outer defences of a large block-house.

GUARDING NEUTRALITY ON THE DUTCH FRONTIER.
Representative men of the Dutch Frontier Guards, equipped in the new steel helmets, which were called into being among neutrals as well as among belligerents by the conditions of the Great War.

and Lord Grey's guidance, had to use more patience and quietly exact more pressure in regard to Sweden. British exports to Sweden and Swedish exports to Great Britain were prevented by Government action on both sides. Traffic between the two countries in cotton and woollen goods, timber and iron ore, and other merchandise diminished. A great stoppage of coal imports occurred in Sweden, which the distant German mines, of inferior quality, were unable, in spite of great effort, to remedy. Avaricious Swedish exporters had denuded their land of stock, crops, and farm horses for the benefit of Germany. The universal failure of harvests in the autumn of 1916 aggravated the results of the impoverishment of Swedish farms. The wealth of the farmers could not be transformed again into live stock and grain. Denmark, Norway, and Holland were in a similar condition of vital penury. All had oversold into the German markets, and possessed no rapid means of recovery. The unusually prolonged and severe winter of 1916-17 told on the small remaining stocks of sheep, hurt the more delicate breeds of cattle, and diminished the store of fodder. Great Britain added to the natural and economic difficulties of Sweden by holding up some grain-ships.

THE BINNENHOF—HOUSE OF PARLIAMENT—THE HAGUE.
The Dutch Parliament (the States-General) is composed of two Chambers. The Upper, or First, Chamber contains fifty members, elected by the Provincial States from among the most highly assessed inhabitants of the eleven provinces, and from high functionaries mentioned by law. The Second Chamber numbers one hundred deputies, who are elected directly.

The Swedish people had to be placed on rations. The rations were afterwards reduced, and food riots began to occur. The leaders of the reactionary party then openly prepared for war on the ancient plan of preventing intestinal struggles by action against any foreign nation within reach. They asked the Landthing for a large sum of money to enable stronger measures to be taken for the preservation of neutrality. The Liberals and Socialists did not consider that more armament was necessary for purely pacific purposes. They did not, in fact, think that anything of a pacific nature was intended. So they combined and voted down the proposals of Hammarskjöld's Ministry.

King Gustav intervened and tried to effect a compromise between the warlike anti-British camarilla and the peaceful anti-German majority. Herr Hammarskjöld, however, was, after long negotiations, compelled to resign. Another Ministry was formed, under Royal influence, again from the reactionary group. Most of the new Ministers, however, had no record of hostile actions against the Western Allies. Ill-service was done to them by the German Press Bureau, which indicated every incident in their education in German universities or in their past political career that made them likely to prove agents of Germany.

Undoubtedly the Swedish King, backed by the Swedish nobility, exercised power in establishing the new Ministry. By the middle of March, 1917, the reactionary party of Sweden and the Scandinavian counterpart of Constantine of Greece had other things to think of besides their struggle against British "navalism." The spirit of Revolution was again loosened in Europe and clothed in such might as had not been seen since the fall of the Bastille. The disturbances of 1830 and 1848 were but ripples around the seats of despotism compared with the flood of popular passion in which the remote descendant of the Viking Rurik had been submerged.

Relaxation of the tension

The Royal descendant of the French lawyer's son, Bernadotte, had in strange vanity modelled himself upon the Hohenzollerns. He possessed a military caste, largely of Prussian origin and exuberant with the Prussian spirit. He lacked, however, a Liberal Party similar to the National Liberals of Germany, and his Socialists were not of the same plastic quality of character as the majority of German Socialists.

Rumour ran, in April, 1917, that some Swedish naval men and soldiers were inclined to side with the people

GUN PRACTICE ABOARD A DUTCH BATTLESHIP.
On July 1st, 1916, the Dutch Royal Navy possessed seven ironclad battleships, four protected cruisers, eight torpedo-boat destroyers, thirty-eight torpedo-boats and seven submarines, besides a considerable number of coast and harbour defence vessels, river gunboats, and special service vessels.

in a hunger born revolution. A month afterwards there were discussions in the Congress of the United States on the policy of imparting new and deadly rigour to the British blockade of Germany by depriving Scandinavia and Holland of all imports not actually needed to feed those neutral States.

In these circumstances the new Swedish Ministry, in May, 1917, reopened negotiations with the new British Ministry. The long period of tension was over, for the time at least, and the rations of the Swedish nation were increased. Stockholm became for a while the most agitated centre of pacifism in the world.

All the Social Democrats of the Germanic school made arrangements to meet there that they might devise means of saving the Prussian system of kindly internal government and the humane, enlightened rule of the Turkish Party of Union and Progress! At the same time the Cabinets of Scandinavia held another conference at Stockholm, at which the problem of destroying the maritime supremacy of Great Britain was not the principal topic of discussion.

The previous meetings of Scandinavian Kings and Ministers had been more menacing to the common interests of the Allies than appeared on the surface of Press comment in the western democracies. German agents had attempted to make Norway believe she was in danger of Russian attack since 1909. The Norwegians were passionately implored by

the Swedish war party to co-operate with Germany in putting an end to the Russian menace.

When the war broke out the Norwegian people remained profoundly distrustful of the Russian Government, yet confident in the protecting influences of Great Britain and France. Great Britain, in particular, had been the stay of the Norwegian democracy in 1905, during the definite break with the oligarchy of Sweden. A British princess had become Queen of an independent Norway, and Norway was, moreover, related closely by language and historic tradition with the Denmark that had been maimed by Bismarck in order to consolidate German sea-power by means of the Kiel Canal.

From Denmark the enfranchised Norse people had chosen their King. Denmark retained their romantic Viking colony of Iceland and their old Faroe settlement; yet they had no grudge against the Danes, but rather affection for their kinsmen. The general result was that the majority of Norsemen refused to be frightened by the Russian bogy and sympathised with the Allies.

They were not averse to profiting by the first sham blockade which Sir Edward Grey maintained from 1914 to 1916. As readers of Ibsen will remember, the Norwegians have an average amount of original sin, and some of their pillars of society greatly increased their banking accounts by trafficking in war material with the Germans. Until the British Government entirely repudiated the Declaration of London and partly resumed the old sea rights of the days of Nelson, there was no objection to Norwegian mineral workers, manufacturers, and merchants making fortunes out of the difficulties of the enemy. The proportion of profiteers in Norway was possibly not larger than that of the profiteers in Great Britain.

On the whole, the Norwegian democracy was as benevolently neutral towards the Entente as the Swedish oligarchy was determinedly hostile. Most of the Norse shipowners and seamen became actively friendly to the Allies during the campaign of German submarine piracy. Norway possessed the largest mercantile marine in the world in proportion to population. Her modern power in shipping was indeed practical evidence of the fact that the spirit of the Vikings fully survived, amid all change of circumstances, in their descendants.

The modern Norsemen were born seamen, with their natural hardihood set off by great practical skill. There was no political reason why they should have coolly undertaken continually to run through the zones of enemy submarine activity. It would have been fairly easy for them to have restricted their traffic to American

Benevolent neutrality of Norway

and other neutral ports, and remained spectators of the violent struggle between Briton and Teuton. American coal and American manufactures would have been high in price in Norway, yet Norway might have tranquilly existed throughout the war, at some economic sacrifice, had she tacitly agreed to observe the outrageous conditions of marine traffic which the Germans endeavoured to enforce.

The Norsemen, however, were not made that way. Partly out of downright pride in their manhood, partly out of a Viking zest for the profits of adventure, and largely out of indignation over the Lusitania affair and a general sympathy with the cause of the Allies, the sailors of Norway carried on. By the spring of 1917 their losses

JOHN TRAVERS CORNWELL, V.C.
By Frank O. Salisbury.
First-Class Boy Hero of H.M.S. Chester.

LIEUT.-GENERAL SIR JOHN COWANS, K.C.B.
By William Orpen, A.R.A.
Sir John Cowans won high distinction as Q.M.G. of the Forces.

COLONEL ELKINGTON, D.S.O.
By William Orpen, A.R.A.
Colonel Elkington was reinstated and awarded the D.S.O. in 1916.

MAJOR WM. LA TOUCHE CONGREVE, V.C.
By J. St. Helier Lander.
Also awarded D.S.O., M.C., & Legion of Honour.

The Cornwell portrait by permission of the John Cornwell Memorial Committee, on whose behalf the Fine Arts Publishing Co., Ltd., London, issue prints.
Copyrights of all other pictures in these four pages strictly reserved for the artists by Walter Judd, Ltd., Publishers of "The Royal Academy Illustrated."

AN ARMED MERCHANTMAN: A FALMOUTH PACKET, ABOUT 1790, BEATING OFF AN ENEMY NEAR THE MANACLES.
By C. Napier Hemy, R.A.

THE WRECKED ZEPPELIN: A GERMAN AIRSHIP BROUGHT DOWN IN THE CHANNEL.
By Bernard F. Gribble.

NOTABLE PICTURES OF BATTLE ON SEA AND LAND

BATTLE OF THE SOMME: THE ATTACK BY THE ULSTER DIVISION ON THE 1st OF JULY, 1916.
By J. Prinsep Beadle.

THE LONDON TERRITORIALS AT POZIÈRES. BATTLE OF THE SOMME.
By W. B. Wollen.

FRATERNITÉ.

[By courtesy of Frost & Reed, Ltd., Bristol.

By J. C. Dollman.

A STRAY SHOT.

By Gemmell Hutchison.

GLIMPSES OF THE PITY OF WAR SHOWN IN THE ROYAL ACADEMY 1917.

in ships were tremendous, and their losses in lives were considerable. During March and April, 1917, for example, they lost one hundred and thirty-six ships—an average of seventeen a week when the British losses were twenty-four a week. Having regard to the smaller tonnage of Norway, her losses were far heavier than those of the grand belligerent, Great Britain.

Still the Norsemen carried on. As already stated, Hindenburg, when in control of both the German Army and Navy, let it be known that he contemplated employing part of his general reserve in an attack upon Norway. It appeared an idle threat. That it should have influenced the Norwegians shows how the passive policy of the British in naval affairs had affected Europe. It scarcely made for the ultimate advantage of Germany that she should go out of her way to find a new enemy, in attacking whom she would expose herself to British sea-power. The distance between the Orkney Islands and the Western Norwegian coast was not very great—in fact, it was much less than the distance between Wilhelmshaven and Christiania.

Had two German army corps been thrown into Norway there would have been two army corps less in the reserve available for strengthening the front between Lens and A u b e r i v e. The scabbard that Hindenburg rattled at Norway was really empty. On his submarines only did the German dictator depend for stopping the commerce between the Norse and the British kingdoms. German submarines ranged to the northernmost part of the Norwegian coast, in the operations directed against the commerce of the Kola and White Sea ports of Russia. There was reason to suppose that the territorial waters of Norway were often employed as cover by the German submarines. The Norwegian Government, therefore, at last followed, on January 30th, 1917, a policy similar to that of the Swedish Government, and forbade all belligerent submarines to use their territorial waters. All submarines in the forbidden area were liable to attack by armed Norwegian forces.

The Germans had not shown any indignation over the action of the Swedish Government, yet the much slighter precautions taken by the Norwegian Government provoked a tempest of angry passion in Germany. The difference between the two Scandinavian States was that the Swedes helped the Germans by taking vigorous measures against British warships, while the Norsemen only indirectly helped the Allies by policing their own waters with a view to protecting their own mercantile marine.

The interests of the Allies were likewise promoted, in an indirect and unintended manner, by a new pacific movement of Socialism among the Norwegian people. As in nearly all countries in Western Europe, there was in Norway a group of young, ambitious men who desired to succeed to the power exercised by the older leaders of the orthodox Socialist groups. The phenomena were almost universal in Europe, being, under diverse forms, an ebullition of ambition in the younger generation, who for personal motives sought for instruments to overthrow the older men who stood in their way.

Socialist movement in Norway

The same thing was going on in the South Wales coalfields and the shops on the Clyde. Happily, the younger school of Norse Socialists developed a special kind of actively passive resistance to the war. Their battle-cry

was: "It is better to fall fighting in the street than to perish in the trenches!" The movement was of little importance in Norway, as no responsible man there intended to bring the nation into the European struggle.

The Norwegian movement, however, spread to Sweden, and developed in a remarkable manner. The battle-cry then had an immediate political interest. It told heavily against the secret design of the Swedish oligarchy, and largely helped to sap all the pernicious aggressiveness out of their military camarilla. The Swedish Socialist leader, M. Branting, suffered from the eruption of the ambitious spirits of the younger generation, who preached the new Norwegian doctrine. Nevertheless, the general Socialist movement for absolute neutrality throughout Scandinavia was considerably strengthened. Thus there was in warring Europe one class of conscientious objectors who directly and actively fought against Prussian militarism. The new Norse movement also had the advantage, from the Allies' point of view, that it undermined the authority of many older Scandinavian Social Democrat leaders, who were consciously or unconsciously moved by a sort of

Norwegian Socialism infects Sweden

BRITISH SAILORS INTERNED IN HOLLAND.

On the way to the camp kitchen. After the withdrawal from Antwerp, in October, 1914, one of the British naval brigades that had taken part in the defence of the city got cut off, and crossed into Holland, where the men were interned.

religious bias towards the race that had produced Karl Marx and Scheidemann, Lassalle and Sudeküm.

In spite, however, of the general friendly feeling obtaining between Great Britain and Norway, a quarrel arose in the summer of 1916 over the blockade problem of the export of copper and pyrites from Norwegian mines to German munition works. In August, 1916, Lord Robert Cecil, as Minister of Blockade, arranged that no British coal should be supplied to Norwegian ships maintaining trade with Germany. The Norwegian skippers, however, managed to continue working across to Germany, by means of German coal and secret supplies of British coal.

A large haul of fish was despatched to Germany in the autumn of 1916 against British interests. The export of copper and pyrites, however, remained the chief matter of contention, and from the Norse mines there continued to flow, in diverse channels, a stream of copper for the manufacture of German shells. In both Sweden and Norway the copper was often made into sham manufactured articles, such as tanks that would not hold water, and forwarded to Germany as raw metal of high price.

When Mr. Lloyd George became Prime Minister means were at last adopted to bring the Norwegians clearly to appreciate the British view. No hostile measures of any kind were taken, but during one of the longest and severest winters on record the entire export of British coal to Norway was stopped. Owing to the season of the year, the water power of every Norwegian river and stream, harnessed to a turbine or dynamo, was reduced practically to nothing. The country people had an abundance of log-wood for domestic fires, and some of the southern towns managed to obtain a little dear and costly German coal.

But the general economic pressure of the stoppage of British coal supply was irresistible. Early in the spring of 1917 the Norwegian Government agreed to prohibit the export of copper and pyrites to Germany, and the Norwegian fish harvest was largely sold in Great Britain. The historic salt herring, which might have **British coal and** fed millions of Teutons, **Norwegian herrings** became an object of affection to the new British Food Controller. He expended a considerable amount of valuable wood-pulp in expounding the virtues of the Norse fish to unenlightened English housewives. Scotswomen needed no instruction in the matter, but the British victory over the salt herring caused much trouble in English kitchens. If the Norwegians suffered for months from lack of British coal, they had their full revenge when English folk endeavoured to obey the orders of the Food Controller and consume the enormous cargoes of salt herring which many of them could not learn properly to prepare and cook.

The position of Denmark was one of passive responsiveness to pressure. The Danes had no wealth of iron and copper ore to provoke alternating pressure from the British and German Governments. The Danish dairy farmers were a source of vital strength to the enemy, yet they maintained a fair show of distributing their produce westward and southward, taking smaller prices from Great Britain than they obtained from Germany.

Denmark was a little nation fallen from greatness, resigned to her fate, and cynical of any profession of idealism by the belligerent countries. Her grudge against Prussia for robbing her of a part of her territory was scarcely deeper than her resentment against Great Britain for promising help in the Schleswig-Holstein War, and leaving her entirely helpless when the attack was made.

The Danes made no allowance for the fact that Lord Palmerston would have fought the Prussians, but was held back by German influence. Rather did they regard the rise of German sea-power, by means of the

DR. JOHN LOUDON,
Dutch Minister for Foreign Affairs.

CHIEFS OF THE DUTCH MILITARY FORCES.
Left : General Smyders, Commander-in-Chief of the Dutch Army and Navy. Right : Major-General Bosboom, Dutch Minister for War.

ANXIOUS DAYS FOR THE NETHERLANDS.
Mr. Cort van der Linden, Prime Minister and Minister of the Interior (on the left) with Dr. John Loudon, Minister for Foreign Affairs, returning from a special sitting of the Cabinet.

canal through their lost provinces, as a tardy punishment upon the British nation. They were very sorry for the Belgians in a dulled way. It seemed to them that all small things were doomed—small businesses by Trust systems and small nations by Imperial systems. They hoped for eventual salvation in a Scandinavian union, but were unable to reconcile their very democratic tendencies with the oligarchical fabric of Sweden. In the meantime, they were not only between the hammer and anvil of Great Britain and Germany in the matter of the blockade, but torn between the United States and Germany in a perplexing Colonial problem.

The Danish West Indian islands, on a great traffic route to the Panama Canal, had become valueless to the Danes. The German **America buys Danish** Government saw in them **West Indies** a means of dominating the United States, and after the Hamburg-Amerika line established a coaling-station there, it tried to purchase the islands.

The United States seemed asleep, yet was really in a state of quiet, intense watchfulness. In the European difficulties of the Great War came America's opportunity, and in the summer of 1916 President Wilson, apparently calmly unconscious of the German intrigues in the Caribbean Sea, offered to purchase the Danish West Indies. The Danish Cabinet wished to remain on friendly terms with everybody. The islands were worth nothing to Denmark ; were, indeed, an economic burden ; and the sum of about £5,000,000, which the United States was willing to pay, could be employed in some important social reforms by the dominant Labour Party of Denmark. It was clear that Great Britain would never permit Germany to obtain an important naval harbour and submarine base off Central America. As the United States was, at the time, a neutral country, it appeared to the Danish Government that the proposed sale was a happy solution of a grave international difficulty. The Danish Ministers underestimated the tenacity of the Germans. The matter of the sale of the islands suddenly became a tempestuous problem of domestic politics. The extraordinary amount of opposition created was a measure of the extraordinary influence the Germans exercised among the people they had defeated and oppressed. The sufferings of the Danes in the conquered frontier province had endured for two generations, and made the Danish gentry and Danish middle classes more subservient to the Hohenzollern.

The affair might have become

very serious, had the opposition lasted until the United States entered the war against Germany. The Germans then would have been able openly and forcibly to protest against one of their valuable private coaling-stations being sold to an enemy. Happily, the danger was avoided by means of a referendum, before hostilities opened between the Americans and Germans. The United States acquired the Virgin Islands at considerable cost, and safeguarded the eastern approach to the Panama Canal from domination by the Teutons.

DUTCH VICTIM OF GERMAN PIRACY.
On the night of March 15th, 1916, the Dutch liner Tubantia, outward-bound from Ymuiden to Buenos Aires, was torpedoed off the North Hinder Lightship by a German submarine.

BUSY CENTRE OF HOLLAND'S COLONIAL TRADE.
Commercial activity on the Java Quay at Amsterdam, to which ships bring the rich merchandise from the Sunda Islands and Moluccas, and the other large possessions of the Netherlands in the East Indies.

It must be confessed that the curious quarrel among the Danes themselves over the sale of their West Indian colonies had a disturbing effect upon British and French opinion. It revealed the extent and depth of Germanic control in Denmark, which had greatly increased during the commerce in imported war material. New vested interests of subtle and far-reaching power had been estab-
Germanic control in Denmark lished by the first futile attempts at a British blockade, and the corrosive action of gold upon the character of an influential body of Danes became clearly evident.

The Danish Jews, who, by the brilliance of their talent, exercised an intellectual and political sway out of proportion to their numbers, were mainly German agents. Georg Brandes, the greatest of European men of letters, inclined to the enemy, and was denounced by Clemenceau and other leading Frenchmen as a renegade. Brandes'

brother was Minister of Finance, and Brandes himself the director of the young Danish democratic mind.

Probably the German Jews, who were distinguished by brilliance of talent, managed to impress Brandes by frightening him with the nightmare of a triumphant Russian despotism permanently over shadowing the whole of Western Europe. It must be remembered **The Labour Party in Denmark** that Lassalle and Marx, the inspirer and the organiser of the Social Democracy movement, were Hebrews, with a kind of secular Messianic appeal that touched the temperament of many men of their race. Brandes was touched by it, and though a rationalist, he regarded Germany, where Social Democracy had risen and spread, with a sentiment of piety.

Behind Brandes, in Denmark, was a ruling Labour Party, largely of Socialistic tendency, that shared in a

THE DUTCH NAVY AND MERCANTILE MARINE.
Arrival of a Dutch armoured ship, the Utrecht, welcomed by large crowds. Above: View of the Docks, Amsterdam, showing in the foreground the buildings of the Dutch Steamship Company.

feeling of reverence for the fatherland of internationalism. And as for the time German-Jewish capitalism was co-operating with German-Jewish and German anti-capitalism, the union of forces was of remarkable strength and scope. Some leading Danish Socialists were men of the stamp of Scheidemann; like him, they were, for all immediate practical purposes, base and cunning lackeys of the German despot. If Scheidemann was an honest but deluded man, they were honest but deluded men. If he was a traitor to the cause he pretended to captain, so were they.

THE QUEEN OF NORWAY.
Daughter of King Edward VII. and sister of King George V., Queen Maud's sympathies were naturally with the Allies.

The Russian Revolution was the test of the sincerity of Danish - Jewish a n d Danish and other neutral Socialists. They could no longer maintain the pretence that Tsarism was a greater danger to t h e world than Prussianism. Months before war broke out, the leading Socialists of Europe knew that an armed movement of liberty was preparing in Russia. When the war broke out they also knew that the German Staff based its plan of campaign on the expectation of a Russian Revolution, which was to leave Russia in anarchy while France was being d e s t r o y e d. Therefore, t h e Social Democracy pretence of combating Tsarism was an hypocrisy from the outset.

The long - delayed but effective Russian Revolution left the traitorous party of Labour leaders in neutral Europe without any further means of concealing their attachment to the enemy. In Denmark the Socialist, M. Borgbjerg, came forward as the open agent of the German Government, and, travelling to Petrograd in May, 1917, presented the Communists with the offer of an Imperial German peace. Even men of the extremist school of Russian Revolutionists were thereupon moved to denounce Borgbjerg as an agent of Teutonic autocracy.

The intrigues of the Danish Labour Party in regard to the proposed Stockholm Peace Conference, and the manœuvres among the Danish gentry and middle classes in connection with the opposition to the sale of the West Indian colonies to America, combined to show that, for all practical international purposes, Denmark had become, in varying degrees, one of the neutral allies of the Central Empires. In Holland, Denmark, and Sweden strong outposts of the Prussian scheme of a Middle Europe Bund were patently established before January, 1917.

Switzerland also was, to a considerable extent, quietly won over by the enemy. The French-Swiss were outnumbered by three to one by the German-Swiss, and their forces were controlled by a German-Swiss commander, General Wille, and a German-Swiss Staff that did not trouble to conceal its sympathies with the Prussian military monarchy. The merchant patricians of Berne, Zurich, and Basle were intimately connected with the German industrial magnates, represented by the National Liberal Party, which was even more greedily aggressive than the Junker Party. The Swiss Socialist Party was similarly linked with the German Social Democrat Majority Party, and continually acted as the go-betweens of the Kaiser in intrigues with Italian and French deputies and delegates.

German influence in Switzerland

All the noble and impartial work of humanity conducted in Switzerland was created and organised by the French-Swiss. The Red Cross of Geneva was a French-Swiss invention, in the reflected glory of which the ruling German-Swiss pursued their special interests and the general interests of the Germanic races. From Germany was derived the coal, iron, and steel upon which most of the fine Swiss engineering work was based. The Swiss were the discoverers of the dynamo and several other important mechanical principles, and their turbine and oil and petrol engine manufactures were of high class. Their watchmaking industry was also of great military value, as it could be transformed into a fuse-making industry for high-explosive shells.

The German design was to make the main industries of Switzerland auxiliary to their own enormous production of general war material. They increased their financial interests and commercial interests in the country, and, with the tacit consent of the Swiss Government, maintained a strong and intensive system of propaganda in the German cantons. In many notorious instances lectures and books, newspaper articles and pamphlets, vehemently ventilating the wrongs of the Belgians and Frenchmen, were forbidden by the German-Swiss censorship, while the false and abusive German attacks upon the Allies were at times positively favoured.

Propaganda by military criticism

For example, a German journalist, Herr Stegemann, made himself notorious as a supposed neutral military critic on the pro-German Bernese journal, " Der Bund." He exercised the art of concealing the defeats and exaggerating the victories of Germany, and executed many variations upon the theme that the French armies were exhausted and the British forces ineffectual. Like other journalists of the same school, his " Kaiserlich " task was to make the Swiss people still more amenable to Prussian influences by convincing them that the success of the Allies was hopeless, and that it was most profitable to make early arrangements with the assured victors.

Stegemann did his work so well that Ludendorff proceeded to make him the grand organ of pure, neutral, disinterested military criticism in Europe. The Philosophical Faculty of Berne University was a representative German-Swiss

THREE MEMBERS OF THE BROTHERHOOD OF KINGS.
From left to right: Haakon VII. of Norway, Gustav V. of Sweden, Christian X. of Denmark, blood brother of the King of Norway. The King of Sweden sought to form a Scandinavian union against Britain.

institution, for it consisted of nineteen professors, of whom eight were Imperial Germans. At a meeting at which only three Swiss but all eight German members were present, it was resolved by a majority rule that Herr Stegemann should be proposed to the Canton Council as University Lecturer on Military Science. The Swiss Commander - in - Chief, General Wille, appears to have recommended the appointment, as also did the Swiss Staff authority, Colonel Sprecher. But so widespread was the opposition to the sorry intrigue, especially in French-Switzerland, that the Berne Council refused to sanction the appointment. From the pro-German point of view the affair became dangerous when it began to excite attention in France and Great Britain and Italy.

The Stegemann case, which ended in April, 1917, was only a straw in the current of German-Swiss opinion. Floating on that current, however, were other straws, far too numerous even to catalogue, and they all showed the same trend. Brilliant exceptions, of course, occurred, among whom was the fine poet, Carl Spitteler. Seeing that in Germany itself there was a small anti-Prussian minority, it was only to be expected that a similar minority should flourish more freely in German-Switzerland.

There was, however, a military caste in Switzerland that had never been described by Freeman and other British historians of the Germanic school. The Swiss military caste was similar in character to the Prussian, only more flexible and civilised, with glorious traditions behind it. From its Hapsburg family it had given an Emperor to Austria, and provided in the course of ages princes to many small States.

The Republican system of Switzerland was the work of this fighting gentry of the Alps. They wanted no emperor or king to limit their personal independence, and they so skilfully trained and led their peasantry as to make the ancient Swiss mercenary armies the stay of any monarch or Pope that purchased their services. For centuries war was the only industry of the Swiss. The Swiss Guard at the Vatican is the historic vestige of ancient Swiss militarism, which was finally broken by Napoleon when in a state of utter decay.

With the renaissance of the German genius, under the Hohenzollern Empire, the old military class of German-Switzerland acquired fresh interest in its profession. Studying in the school of Moltke, and developing the sport of marksmanship among the Swiss people, it managed, in spite of the militia system, to make an Army of which it was properly proud. When the Kaiser, in 1913, attended the Swiss manœuvres, meeting there General Beyers, with

KING HAAKON OF NORWAY.
Haakon VII. (second from the right) riding with some of his cavalry officers When Norway and Sweden separated, Prince Charles of Denmark was offered the crown of Norway, and assumed the name of Haakon on becoming King, November 18th, 1905.

GENERAL T. O. KLINGENBERG.
General Klingenberg, chief officer in command of the artillery branch of the Norwegian Army.

from other stocks it had ages princes to many small

results afterwards seen in South Africa, he also seems to have talked over some matters with certain leading German-Swiss.

The event of the Battle of the Marne, combined with the more distant menace of the pressure of British sea-power, made the German-Swiss camarilla cautious and politic. Only when the Imperial armies had definitely broken the back of France could any action be safely undertaken; for the German-Swiss caste had exceptional difficulties of a domestic kind. Not only were its working classes largely infected with French doctrines, but one-third of its forces were of French stock, and likely to rebel or secede if Switzerland attempted to march with the Central Empires.

The mobilised French-Swiss force was kept from its own frontier, and dragooned in Prussian style, to make it obedient to any commands of the German-Swiss. The French-Swiss territory was **Switzerland menaced** held by troops of Germanic stock. **with invasion** Nothing occurred, except that at intervals the Imperial forces were rumoured to be massing for a drive through Switzerland. In 1916 Falkenhayn was said to be preparing to thrust through the Alps into Italy. In the early spring of 1917 Hindenburg was reported to have gathered a large army in the Black Forest, in the design to break across the Jura Mountains and enter France below Belfort.

Naturally, the German-Swiss leaders adopted an independent attitude on these occasions. Happily, Hindenburg's reserves were soon required to fill the gaps in the Lens-Auberive line, and Switzerland was saved from the dreadful ordeal of battle. There had been some scandals in regard to the authorities on the Swiss Staff communicating to German Headquarters information of the movements of French troops. Yet the national honour of Switzerland was not touched.

In addition to the show of military pressure by Germany, the Swiss were subjected to some economic pressure. It was in Switzerland that the enemy secretly set up a system of controlling neutral commerce, which was gradually and inefficiently imitated by the Allies. The Germans stipulated that the raw materials they supplied should not be used directly or indirectly for the eventual benefit of France or Great Britain. Quite early in the war they blacklisted Swiss firms that continued to trade with the Allies, and established a thorough system of espionage to strengthen their control.

When the Allies countered, by organising a Swiss society for handling French and British imports, the Germans made some savage attempts to break the new system. On June 8th, 1916, the Swiss Government was staggered by a Note from the German Government threatening that

STEEL-HELMETED SOLDIERS OF THE SWISS CONFEDERATION.
Her mountainous terrain was Switzerland's best safeguard against violation of her studied neutrality by Germany, who would have liked to outflank the extreme right of the French defensive line by pouring troops through Swiss territory. Nevertheless, her Army was an important factor in her safety.

the supply of coal would be stopped unless stocks of cotton and fats were given in exchange.

The enemy hoped to obtain the contraband war material secretly, through the Swiss authorities fraudulently breaking their agreement with the Allies. The news of the Note transpired, however. The Allies stood firm, and the German coal supply was not stopped.

Again in January, 1917, economic pressure was brutally applied to Switzerland. Swiss imports were interdicted by Germany, and practically stopped by Austria-Hungary. This was in preparation for the revival of the submarine campaign against neutral and belligerent shipping.

Economic pressure upon Switzerland

On February 1st, 1917, the Swiss people were allowed one line of sea-borne import through Cette. This port was utterly insufficient for the commerce of Switzerland, and the French railways behind the French port were largely required for French purposes. The situation of Switzerland was further aggravated by the entrance of the United States into the war, with the plan, already mentioned, for placing an embargo upon superfluous food supplies to neutral States adjoining enemy countries.

For Germany insisted upon the Swiss having a superfluity of imported goods from the Allies and forwarding the stores across the Rhine. She again stopped the export of coal to Basle, and most seriously diminished the goods-train service.

At this time the Swiss themselves were beginning to suffer from a shortage of food. They had sold too much to Germany. So many tens of thousands of cattle had gone every season to feed the enemy armies that Switzerland, the land of milk, was short of milk for her own towns. Another sixty thousand head of cattle had to be apportioned to the Germans, in May, 1917, in order to obtain coal from Westphalia. This demand the Swiss resisted. Apparently the Teutons had no further prospect of winning the military aid of the German-Swiss, and were bent merely upon draining Switzerland to the uttermost, while famishing her partly by general submarine piracy effects.

Submarine piracy and the neutrals

In regard to this matter we may remark, by way of summarising the story of all the neutral States adjoining Germany, that they enjoyed incomparable prosperity during the first two years of the British blockade, but felt the pinch of misery immediately the Germans opened their submarine piratic operations in ferocious earnestness. It was not merely the murderous character of the enemy's campaign against shipping that made the difference, but the military efficiency of his system.

By the middle of May, 1917, the industries of Denmark were stagnant for lack of coal. Gas works and electric works reported they would have to close if commerce with Great Britain were not resumed quickly. The stock of petrol was exhausted, and only a small store of candles remained for lighting purposes. In Sweden political discontent increased with the increase of the general rigour of living. In Norway the Government had to adopt extraordinary measures to calm popular indignation over the condition of affairs.

In Holland there were symptoms of a similar ferment, but the defenders of Germany there tried to turn against the Allies the anger born of apprehension of the results of the U boat campaign and discomfort at the stoppage of trade. In Switzerland the disillusion of the majority of German-Swiss was profound. So profound was it that at times they were almost inclined to believe the statements in the French and British communiqués. This was remarkable. For a considerable part of German-Switzerland was not yet able to accept the Allies' version of the Battle of the Marne.

In some cases hunger has an educative effect. Germany was educating her neutrals.

Spain had the peculiar distinction, among European neutral States, of standing outside the immediate commercial radius of the Central Empires. She could not send iron ore or other contraband material to Germany without her ships running the Franco-British blockade. Some Spanish iron ore reached the Rhine foundries by way of the river passage of Holland, but this was eccentric to the main line of Spain's commerce during the war. Great Britain, France, and Italy took all that Spain could get ships to carry, and were in a position to maintain

General Wille, in command of the Swiss Army, addressing a number of his officers on the subject of the military manoeuvres in which they had been engaged. General Wille belonged to the German-Swiss part of the Republic.

Swiss howitzer battery marching through a village. The Swiss Army is a militia, the men of the artillery doing a recruit course of seventy-seven days during their first year of service.

Making trenches on the Swiss frontier. The position of Switzerland was a difficult one, and its Government, while maintaining strict neutrality, made full preparation for resisting any violation of that neutrality.

An anti-aircraft gun mounted on a turn-table. The Swiss erected these weapons near their frontier, in accordance with the President's emphatic decision to preserve the freedom of the country at any cost.

MEN AND MATERIALS READY TO DEFEND THE FREEDOM OF SWITZERLAND.

THE QUEEN OF DENMARK.
Queen Alexandrine, a princess of Mecklenburg-Schwerin, married in 1898 Prince Christian of Denmark, who succeeded to the throne in 1912.

discoursed on the solidarity of Latin civilisation. British scholars and their patrons established Chairs of Spanish Literature and exploited the common centenary of Cervantes and Shakespeare for all it was politically worth. British business men, in rather small number, drove in practical fashion at the realities of an alliance. Spain and Great Britain, it was pointed out, completed each other. Spain had iron; Great Britain had coal. Spain had large undeveloped resources; Great Britain had remarkable financial power and first-rate engineering experience. A short sea passage separated the countries, with the advantage that sea carriage was cheaper than railway carriage. "Señorita, let us have a *mariage de convenance;* it will end in love!" said John Bull.

Spain's desire to be peacemaker

Spain smiled a Monna Lisa smile. She was extremely complex. Indeed, she could not understand herself. She was wildly, fondly romantic. She wanted Gibraltar and a larger share of Morocco as a wedding portion, with the benediction of her old kinsman, Austria, and the services of her new friend, Germany, as trustee for the marriage settlement. In vain did the suitor and his circle point out they were at war with Austria and Germany. The dearest desire of Spain was to act as peacemaker and show herself the Power that shaped the destinies of Europe and mankind.

permanently important commercial relations with the Spaniards.

It is true that France had recently discovered in Algeria an enormous wealth of iron ore, reputed to be of as high a quality as Bilbao ore. Bilbao, nevertheless, was closer than Bizerta and Bône to the British and Northern French coalfields, so that there was a solid economic basis for a Franco-British rapprochement with Spain.

Yet Spain remained remarkably aloof. French and Italian publicists frequently and eloquently

She was the motherland of the rich Spanish-American States. Her prestige over their social leaders was still considerable, although politically they were quite independent of her. The warring races—Teuton and Briton, Frenchman, Italian, and, later, Northern American—were anxious to obtain commercial advantages in Spanish-America. Each reckoned that friendship with Spain would be a help in the contest for Spanish-American trade.

It was for this reason that Spain set a high price on herself. From Germany she then received large but vague promises, all conditional upon a decisive German victory. From Great Britain came a more definite offer of a smaller kind, implying effort and sacrifice on the part of the receiver.

The Spaniards were violently divided among themselves. The Spanish aristocracy wanted an alliance with a victorious Teutonic nobility for frankly selfish reasons. Their estates and their privileges were menaced by the Socialist Revolutionary party. Therefore, they revered the Kaiser and his Junkers as the champions of their class interests, and

AT THE ENTRANCE TO THE BALTIC.
On the Narrows between Denmark and Sweden. The Castle on the left is that of Kronborg, in Denmark. From Kronborg to Helsingborg, in Sweden, is but a twenty minutes' journey in the ferry steamer.

passionately desired to see such a complete defeat of the western democracies as would establish their own authority in Spain for generations. No disinterested arguments touched the Spaniards of this order. They were realistic politicians, with their special aim clear in view.

The Spanish ecclesiastics were closely allied with them in principle and in action. The Spanish Church was

CONFERENCE OF DANISH AND SWEDISH MINISTERS AT COPENHAGEN.
King Christian of Denmark in the pilot's seat of a military aeroplane. His Majesty was being shown the way in which his airmen controlled their machines. Right: A conference of Swedish and Danish Ministers at Copenhagen on March 9th, 1916. The Ministers are (from right to left) M. Scavenius, Danish Foreign Affairs; M. Wallenberg, Swedish Foreign Affairs; M. Zahle, Danish Premier; M. Hammarskjöld, Swedish Premier.

KING GUSTAV OF SWEDEN.
Gustav V., " King of Sweden of the Goths and Vandals," was born in 1858 and succeeded to the throne in 1907.

QUEEN VICTORIA OF SWEDEN.
Daughter of the Grand Duke of Baden. Photographed as colonel of a German cavalry regiment.

CROWN PRINCE OF SWEDEN.
Gustav Adolf, Duke of Skone, Heir Apparent to the Swedish Crown, was born in 1882 and in 1905 married Princess Margaret of Connaught.

troubled by an anti-clerical movement, conducted by men of Republican temper and French inspiration. To the Spanish Clerical Party the overthrow of France was necessary for the salvation of Christendom. Strange are the political colourings of creeds. The Roman Catholic Irish priesthood, long and intimately connected with Spanish ecclesiastic institutions, was by historic accident Democratic and at last even Revolutionary in temper. It largely ran the Sinn Fein.

The Spanish priesthood was violently reactionary. To it France was Antichrist, despite the fact that, with the exception of Anatole France, most of the leading French writers, such as Faguet, Barrès, Bourget, were returning

SWEDISH GUARDS NEAR THE RUSSIAN FRONTIER.
Frontier station and guards at the Swedish seaport of Haparanda, with a distant view across the water to the Russian town of Tornea, passengers from which had just landed from a steamer.

to the faith of their fathers, and generally trying to evoke a national reversion to Catholicism. The clergy of Spain never thought of assisting the French clergy. They were absorbed in the problem of preventing the Gambettas and Combes in the Peninsula from extending their influence from Portugal and Catalonia into the Castilles and Andalusia. They badly needed a smashing defeat of France to achieve their short-sighted aim. Vehement political passion led them into the camp of the **Aid to the** Germans. They took a large propor- **reactionary forces** tion of the Spanish middle-class and peasantry with them.

There can be no doubt that the reactionary noble and clerical forces in Spain would have failed to check the tendency towards a fighting alliance with the Entente Powers had they received no powerful help. Spain would gradually have followed the same course as Italy. There were, however, the extraordinary number of eighty thousand Germans in the country. Some of them were refugees from France, some were crews of interned ships, a large number were German soldiers from Cameroon, who had

crossed to Spanish territory in Africa and been conveyed to the healthier climate of Spain.

They formed two army corps of able, active men, skilfully disciplined. They were sorted out according to their social attainments. Some went to the industrial centres of Northern Spain to preach Revolution, organise strikes and hold up exports to France and Great Britain. Others settled in Spanish ports, and did all they could to bedevil things there. Lonely points on the Spanish coast were occupied by the Teutons, with conse- quences seen when their countrymen were **German activities** operating off the shore in submarines. **in Spain**

German financial houses in the chief Spanish cities augmented their funds and established new branches. Periodicals and daily newspapers were acquired, not only in Madrid and the other large cities, but in hundreds of small places. The Teuton combined wisdom with economy, and, appreciating the cheapness and intensive authority of small country-side papers, he obtained the control of them, and worked them with his usual energy. The local clergy and sometimes the grandees readily assisted him. In turn he organised the peasants as a modern political force.

SOLDIERS OF THE SWEDISH ARMY.
Men of the Crown Prince's Infantry Regiment taking part in field exercises. With universal and compulsory military service, Sweden had, in 1916, an Army which at war strength numbered nearly 200,000.

The first two and a half years of the war were a busy and troubled period in Spain. The amount of unrest was amazing. Strikes occurred on little or no provocation, and there were threats of revolution, needing the temporary application of martial law. All this was extremely mysterious, because the Labour organisations sympathised with the embattled French Democracy, and produced war material for the Allies. Mephistopheles from Germany was behind all the disorders.

Spanish Cabinet changes

He was suspicious of King Alfonso. It was rather a wonder that the young patriot King was not assassinated. Perhaps the agents of the Hohenzollern considered that would have been too dangerous an example to set in the circumstances. During the period of German intrigue there was a change in the Ministry, Señor Dato being succeeded as Premier by Count Romanones, who also conducted Foreign Affairs. Two pro-German politicians were included in the Ministry, apparently by way of notification of neutrality. Their presence, however, did not lead to any lessening of the artificial Labour unrest. There were eighty thousand Germans in the country, and they had to continue doing something to earn their keep and lift *Deutschland über alles*.

Much that was prevented from happening in Spain had a bearing on the course of the war; but little that actually occurred had any immediate relation of importance to the events of the battlefields until the historic date, February 1st, 1917. The futile anxiety of some Spaniards that their King should be the peacemaker of the world, their anger when President Wilson was still essaying to win the position, the fine work done personally by King Alfonso to mitigate the miseries of war, and the noble protest made by a large body of leading Spaniards against the action of the Germans in Belgium, these were among the incidents of Spanish history in the middle of the struggle.

With the opening of the Teutonic submarine attack on both neutral and belligerent shipping the position of Spain became endangered. One of her merchant ships, the Ferrucio, was torpedoed by the Germans on February 6th, 1917. It was soon afterwards discovered that the German Consul at Cartagena was providing with stores a German submarine operating off the port between Cape Palos and Tarragona. German action was also traced in the origin of a serious explosion in a Bilbao shipyard, and in the placing of an infernal machine in a load of coal about to be delivered to a British steamer. Spanish oranges for export to the Allies were poisoned while being packed.

All the murderous devices that Captain von Papen and Count Bernstorff had employed in the United States were used in Spain. The day after the Ferrucio was torpedoed a band of workmen and students demonstrated in Madrid in favour of maintaining neutrality. It was a suggestive coincidence that the demonstration should have taken place on the day when Count Romanones sent a strong Note against the German submarine policy. The Teutons were undoubtedly splendid stage-managers.

Fall of Count Romanones

Also, they were not always inexpert in constructing a plot. The diplomatic Note by Count Romanones had as little effect as the diplomatic Notes of President Wilson. The Spanish Premier prepared for warlike action. But he was suddenly overthrown on April 19th, 1917, by the pro-German Ministers, who sought to maintain Spain in a state of passive neutrality while her commerce was being ruined by the German submarine operations.

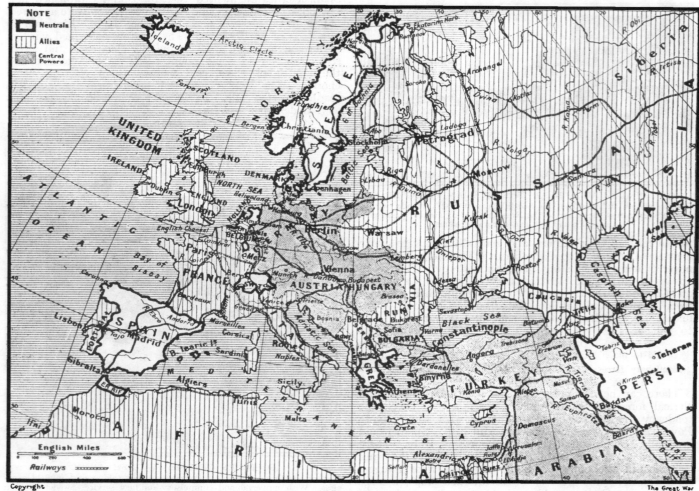

MAP OF EUROPE SHOWING THE RELATIVE POSITIONS OF BELLIGERENTS AND NEUTRALS IN 1917.
In this map the neutral countries dealt with in the preceding chapter are indicated by a thick line enclosing their frontiers.

CHAPTER CLXXVIII.

THE WINTER RAIDS BETWEEN THE BATTLES OF THE SOMME AND ARRAS.

By F. A. McKenzie.

Somme Advance Checked by Break-up of the Weather—Winter Activity of the British General Staff—Canadian Plan of Night Raids Standardised—Terror Inspired in the Enemy by British Raids—Transfer of the Canadians to Vimy—Daylight Raids by Canadian Mounted Rifles Outside Roclincourt—Epic Raid of December 20th, 1916—Nova Scotians Celebrate Christmas Day by a Surprise Raid—Comparison of the British Military Machine in 1917 with that of 1915—Bombs and Unlimited Shells Instead of " Tickler's Artillery " and Gun Rations—Telescopic Sights and Disguises for Snipers—Steel Helmets and Gas Masks —Multiplication of Machine-Guns : Vickers-Maxim, Lewis, and Stokes—Military Observation by Balloon and Aeroplane—. Minor Raids by Men of Montreal and New Brunswick Battalions—Big Raid by Ontario Battalions, January 31st, 1917—Splendidly Successful Raid by London Territorials on Hill 60, Ypres—New South Wales Battalion's Raid at Gueudecourt : Captain Bean's Account—Canadian Raid in Ladies' Night-Dresses—Some Dramatic Incidents—How the Germans Met the British Activities— Best German Fighting Material Conserved for Later Use—German Raids on the British Lines—Failure of a Raid by the Canadians in February : Lieut.-Colonels Kemball and Beckett Killed.

AFTER the great Somme offensive, dealt with in Chapters CXLIX.-CLV. (Vol. VIII.), the break-up of the weather in the autumn of 1916 made a further immediate sustained advance impossible. The whole of the front was one great quagmire of sticky, gluey mud, interspersed with numerous specially deep mud-holes caused by shell fire. The ground had been so torn and blown up by the action of high explosives that it was sifted with almost incredible fineness for many feet down. This loose, pulverised earth quickly turned into deep mire. It was impossible to move guns through it, and scarcely possible to bring up supplies. Horses were suffocated in mud as they tried to advance, and often men would have been lost had not their comrades dug them out. British and Germans faced one another in their hastily-dug trenches on the Somme, and settled down for a test of endurance under winter conditions.

While, h o w e v e r, great movements were, for the time, made impossible by the weather, there was no

[*British official photograph.*]

STUDYING THE LIE OF THE NEWLY-TAKEN GROUND.
Consulting the map. British officers in command of working-parties seeking to ascertain the significance of recently-captured ground on the western front which they had been sent forward to consolidate.

intention on the part of the British General Staff to allow the Germans to remain quiet and to renew their strength. The activities of the winter, while less dramatic than the incidents of the great summer campaign, were of vital importance. Our lines were readjusted. Fresh methods of battalion organisation, making each platoon still more independent, were perfected. The vast reserves of ammunition behind t h e British lines were enormously augmented. Large numbers of fresh guns, trench - mortars, howitzers, and long-range guns were brought into position. The British line was extended southwards in order further to relieve the French. At the same time, winter raids were begun on the new plan —raids which caused much loss to the enemy and had a damaging effect on his moral.

In the summer of 1915 t w o Canadian o f f i c e r s, Colonel (afterwards Brigadier-General) Odlum, a n d Colonel (afterwards Brigadier-General) Tuxford, introduced a new system of night raids which for a time was very successful indeed. These raids, based upon a careful training of a number of men for one specific task, provided various precautions to ensure secrecy, rapidity, and the terrorising of the enemy. For a time they carried all before them.

The Canadian plan was standardised for all the British and French forces; but gradually the Germans came to appreciate their opponents' methods of night raiding, and to take fresh precautions against them. Their wire entanglements were strengthened to resist wire-cutters, some of the strands of wire being as thick as two fingers of a man's hand. They arranged double rows of wire with spaces between, along which patrols moved all night long. Despite this, the British troops made their way through on many occasions.

Prisoners who were brought in often described the terrorising effects of our raids. Their accounts were strikingly confirmed by Mr. J. P. Whitaker, of Bradford, an Englishman who, after living for two years inside the German lines, returned to England. Writing in the "Times," Mr. Whitaker said:

This is how a German soldier gave me his impressions of the British raids: "They are the worst horror we have to contend with. The English seem to do it for sport, not for war. You do not know when or where a raid is coming. These Englishmen daub their faces with clay, come along the ground on all fours, smother our advance posts, and are in our trenches before we know where we are. They come not with rifles and revolvers, but with knives and sledge-hammers and bombs. We cannot use our rifles against them. They are too near, and perhaps we have not fixed our bayonets. We must either run or be killed. The English will clear a trench on a stretch of a hundred and fifty yards and get away again without losing a man." It would be difficult to exaggerate the genuine terror with which the raids have filled German soldiers of all ranks and regiments.

It soon became evident that the hour had come for fresh developments. The Canadians now led the way in the new system of raiding as they had done before. Four Canadian divisions, after their brilliant victories around Courcelette, were moved from the Somme to the lines facing Vimy Ridge, running roughly from north of Arras to the north of Bully-Grenay. Their casualties on the Somme had been heavy. Some battalions that had **Canadians moved** marched a few weeks earlier under **to Vimy Ridge** the hanging golden Virgin of Albert twelve hundred strong, marched back on their way northwards counting their effectives by the score. Their new position, facing the great Vimy Ridge, had been reckoned a little time previously one of the quietest parts of the line. Earlier in the war some of the most tragic and costly fighting had taken place there, and the French and German dead buried in the Souchez Valley were numbered by many scores of thousands. Towns and villages such as Souchez, originally as prosperous and delightful as any in France, were nothing but masses of ruins, presenting pictures of desolation as dreadful as

could be seen in any part of the field of war. In villages a little farther behind, a few bold peasants and farmers still lived, maintaining their footing and carrying on their work under frequent shell fire. Their homes were cellars, their children had been sent away, each man had his gas-mask to protect himself, and all were ready for anything that might come.

The Canadians were sent to Vimy to rest and recruit their strength. They did not rest for long. They immediately began to make things so lively that, ten days after their arrival, the Germans on one section of the line opposite them put out a notice:

CUT OUT YOUR DAMNED ARTILLERY.
WE, TOO, ARE FROM THE SOMME.

Evidently some German-American had written the notice.

It was resolved now to have raids on entirely new lines. Hitherto our raids had been at night time, and the Germans thought themselves comparatively safe during the day. Now the British raids took place in full daylight. The section chosen was on the front outside Roclincourt, when the Canadian Mounted Rifles were in the line. The trenches and No Man's Land here were very muddy. There were sectors in the advanced trenches where men at times got stuck and had to be dug out by their comrades; sectors as nearly impassable as anything could be. Out in No Man's Land some of the saps contained two feet of icy, muddy water.

For men to move in these positions without betraying themselves to the enemy was exceedingly difficult; but they promptly began raiding the German lines One of the most formidable of these early raids took place on December 2nd, 1916. Previous attempts made to penetrate one part of the German lines had failed. Then a battalion volunteered to make another attempt. The raiders were divided into three parties. Those to the right and the left succeeded in reaching the German trenches after heavy fighting. The centre party, however, was held up by very strong wire entanglements. which could not be broken through.

The Canadians held both sides of **Deadly raid at** the trench. There was no communi- **Roclincourt** cating-trench through which the enemy might retire. Packed in, they could not retreat. The officer of the middle section of the Canadians gave the command. His men stretched out quickly in front of the wire through which they could not pass, and threw their bombs right over it along the line of cooped-up Germans. Then the men to the right and left closed in. There was little more fighting to be done, for they found the trench heaped up with dead. One hundred Germans had been blown to bits. A young Michigan boy, Lieutenant MacCormack, who acted as reconnoitring officer, was

GENERAL SIR HENRY SINCLAIR HORNE, K.C.B.
Sir Henry Horne was in command of the First Army on the western front, and, with General Allenby, was in charge of the great Arras offensive, which began on April 9th, 1917. The above is a reproduction from a portrait by Mr. Francis Dodd, one of the official artists at the front.

Most of the troops of the front trenches were down in their dug-outs taking shelter from our fire. The Canadians knew the position of nearly every dug-out. A sergeant or officer went to the head of each and called to the men inside to come out. Those who came out and surrendered were taken prisoners. Those who did not were blown up together with the dug-outs. Mobile charges, brought for the purpose, were thrown in—mobile charges sufficiently strong to send the deepest dug-out into irretrievable ruin. At one point the Canadians came on a dug-out full of supplies. It was treated in the same fashion.

The German machine-gunners on the other side of the smoke barrier were now firing wildly. Supplementary parties of Canadians pushed down the communicating-trenches to the second lines. The raiding-party remained in the German trenches for ninety minutes. During that time they blew up every dug-out and destroyed every store. Then **Counter-attack on** they quietly returned over No Man's **empty trenches** Land, bringing fifty-eight prisoners, including one officer, with them. They had killed at least twice as many in the trenches. The Canadian losses could be counted on the fingers of both hands.

While the Canadians were resting after the battle, the Germans, who had not yet discovered that they had gone, flung up reserve forces to attack them. The Canadians had the satisfaction of listening to the Germans recovering their own lines. They first of all opened concentrated artillery fire upon them, then they advanced, section by section, bombing each point before rushing it, only to find each section deserted. Suspecting a trap, they continued in the same slow way. A few days later the German official account of the action was published. It stated that the British had penetrated the German lines but had been

LIEUT.-GENERAL HON. SIR JULIAN H. G. BYNG, K.C.B.
Sir Julian Byng, who was General Officer Commanding in Egypt from 1912 to 1914, and had already distinguished himself both in France and in the Dardanelles, succeeded General Alderson in the command of the Canadian Army Corps early in the summer of 1916.

decorated with the Military Cross for his work that day. He was one of many thousands of Americans then in the Canadian Army fighting with enthusiasm for the Allies.

In mid-December the British began to concentrate fire upon one picked section of the German position. A stretch of line four hundred yards long was marked off. On the morning of December 20th it was suddenly boxed in by gun fire. A line of smoke-bombs was sent behind the first set of trenches so as to make a screen between it and the German machine-gun positions. On both sides a machine-gun barrage was opened. This machine-gun barrage, a comparatively new thing in war, was of the most terrifying and formidable kind, the machine-guns **Impassable machine-** creating for the time a sheet of living **gun barrage** steel through which none could pass and live. Men familiar with older forms of barrages declared that that of the machine-gun was the most awe-inspiring of all.

The Canadian Mounted Rifles, who were largely a Western corps, had in the meantime taken up their positions at jumping-off places in No Man's Land, where they crouched low to avoid observation. At a given moment the divisional artillery behind opened a heavy fire upon the rear of the German lines and a barrage on the German trenches. Under the shelter of this barrage the Canadians moved forward. The enemy was taken by surprise. Our artillery had already inflicted great destruction. Most of his machine-guns were unable to take aim because of the line of smoke from the Stokes bombs which acted as a barrier. Here and there, individuals tried to put up a fight. Two or three men around a front-line machine-gun attempted to turn it on the Canadians, but before they could do so they were bayoneted.

GENERAL SIR EDMUND H. H. ALLENBY, K.C.B.
Sir Edmund Allenby, in command of the Third Army on the western front, had gained a brilliant reputation as cavalry leader in South Africa, and won new laurels in the retreat from Mons. Both drawings on this page are reproduced from portraits by Mr. Francis Dodd.

PERILS OF WIRING WORK: "FROZEN" BY THE COLD GLARE OF A STAR-SHELL.

Erecting barbed-wire entanglements was work that could only be done at night. Even then the wiring-parties were liable to discovery by enemy star-shells soaring up and revealing them to enemy machine-gunners waiting to fire at any suspicious objects. When a flare burst every man "froze" hard in the position in which he was surprised, absolute immobility being the only chance of escaping observation.

driven out with heavy losses by a German counter-attack. Actually, the counter-attack had been against empty trenches, for it had never been our intention to hold the place.

The victory of December 20th was so brilliantly successful at so small a cost that it was quickly copied, and was the beginning of a new series of similar raids along the British front. This did not mean, however, that the old plan of raiding at night was wholly given up. A Nova Scotian battalion gave a good example of the old-time raids on Christmas morning. The commander of this battalion argued rightly that the Germans would not be expecting an attack on Christmas Day. Therefore, he would give them a little surprise. No special preliminary artillery work was done, our guns only keeping up their usual occasional fire. It was starlight and quite cold. The Nova Scotians had taken very exact observation of the German front ahead, particularly noting the position of machine-guns, sniping-posts, observation-posts, and listening-posts.

The raiding-party consisted of five officers and one hundred men, divided into four groups, each under an officer. At a fixed moment the German **Nova Scotians'** wire entanglements were blown up. The **Christmas raid** sound of the explosions had barely died away before the Nova Scotians ran forward. Forcing their way into the trenches, they swept the surprised Germans clean before them. One sergeant went to a dug-out. Three Germans were there. He shot two of them and took the third prisoner. A big Nova Scotian corporal lunged at a man showing fight and bayoneted him. The Germans behind hastily sent up red flares, bursting into great golden showers—"SOS" signs calling for artillery aid and for reinforcements. All the dug-outs were searched and every man within a considerable area killed or taken prisoner. Just as German reinforcements were coming up in great strength, the Nova Scotians slipped back, taking their prisoners with them. The Canadian casualties were one killed and three slightly wounded. At least fifty-five Germans were killed and wounded that night and a considerable number made prisoners.

The German commanders were evidently greatly mortified by this surprise raid. They promptly hit back with a barrage of rifle-grenades, and for hours afterwards sought to wreck the Canadian lines at this point with shell fire. It is one of the laws of trench war that if you hit, the other side hits back; so the Canadians were not surprised. A few days later, however, the Germans attempted a still more formidable punishment for this raid. At ten o'clock in the evening they started a phosgene gas shell attack on the ruined coal-mining towns of Bully and Grenay. The bombardment was maintained until four o'clock in the morning. Sometimes it reached an intensity of ten shells a minute. In all about three thousand shells were thrown. The attack had been very carefully elaborated, with the intention of wiping out every living person in the country-side around. Phosgene is one of the most deadly of all gases. The Germans had, however, overlooked one thing, and consequently their bombardment was a failure. The total losses from this heavy bombardment were seven French civilians, six of whom died during the night and one who died in the following afternoon.

In studying the raids of 1917 it must be remembered that the British Army was equipped as never before, and was able to undertake tasks previously impossible. This can be well seen by comparing the conditions in 1915 and 1917.

In two years the British Army had been transformed, save in spirit and courage, for everyone gladly recognised that the pluck and endurance of the First Expeditionary Force could never be surpassed. Means of communication, weapons, and methods of war had been revolutionised. In the grim winter of 1914-15 the contest was between ill-equipped courage on the side of the British and an almost perfect military machine on the German side. In the winter

[*British official photograph.*

BRITISH ARTILLERY OBSERVATION-POST.

Artillery observation-posts—O.P.'s or "O-Pips"—were built up in trees, and connected with the batteries by telephone. These positions were exceptionally perilous, for discovery immediately made them the target for every enemy gun within range.

of 1916-17 the British had an almost perfect machine, while on the enemy's side there were armies seeking by retirement to escape from the tremendous punishment that was being inflicted on them.

In 1915 the British pinned their faith to the motor-car. Railways were few and inadequate. Heavy military automobiles tore the roads of Northern France and Belgium to pieces, day and night, bringing up supplies. The system was costly, wasteful, and inadequate. An army of men was kept busy doing nothing but repairing the thoroughfares. The cost was ten times what railway transit would have been, and the result was insufficient. Had the British then broken through the German lines, they would not have been able to advance far, for their lines of communication would have inevitably been blocked up, being inadequate for the necessary traffic. This was now no longer true. For considerably over a **British railway** year the British had been building rail- **organisation perfected** ways as fast as they could. Sir Eric Geddes, who was in command of this work, was a live railway organiser. Much of the new railway construction was being done by men from overseas.

Readers of trench literature of early 1915 will remember the frequent references to "Tickler's Artillery." Tickler was the famous maker of plum-and-apple jam, then so liberally served out to the Army. The jam was sent out in tins. Our boys in the trenches made the empty tins into bombs to fling at the Germans—Tickler's Artillery! In other words, there were no proper bombs for them. They had to make their own to answer the German hand-grenades. In 1917 the bomb was the most familiar weapon of the infantryman. In every attack it was the bomb, and not the rifle, that did the work, and when a man was too near to use the bomb, the trench-dagger completed the business. There was now no need for the men in the trenches to make Tickler's Artillery. The bombs served out to them were the finest in the world, and the supply of them was equal to all requirements.

In the spring of 1915 the British guns were on rations. Even in a heavy attack, when the Germans were attacking with concentrated fire, the artillery opposed to them at times had to cease fire by ten o'clock in the morning. Three shells a day was the usual allowance. Theoretically, the British field-guns were supposed to carry or have in reserve 1,000 rounds, and the howitzers and heavy guns from 500 to 800 rounds. Every soldier knew that the shells needed in serious fighting must be counted by the thousand, for in the previous great war—the Russo-Japanese—both the Russians and the Japanese batteries frequently fired 500 rounds a day. But the British had not the shells.

Shell supply in 1915 and 1917

In 1917 there was no "rationing." On most parts of the British line a minimum of four shells was normally returned for every one the Germans sent over. If a battalion commander telephoned to the artillery behind to retaliate on a particular position, the enemy quickly got it, full measure, pressed down and running over. If, in the afternoon, more was wanted, he got some more. There was no limit. The British had all the shells they needed, and more artillery in proportion to infantry than any army since war began.

There was never anything to complain about the small arms, and the British infantry fire from the first was unequalled for rapidity and accuracy. But when it came to sniping there was a different story to tell. The Boer War showed the advantage of telescopic sights for rifles. When the Germans retreated from the Marne their snipers inflicted great damage. They left men behind in villages or woods, expert foresters, with rifles fitted with telescopic sights. They had supplies of provisions and clothes skilfully coloured to resemble their surroundings. They picked off officer after officer at leisure.

There quickly came a demand for telescopic sights that could not be provided. The old optical industry of Birmingham had been killed, and the sights were made in Austria or Germany. A new industry had to be created. By 1917, however, British-made telescopic sights were as good as the German, and the art of disguising men for sniping work had been brought to a point equal at least to the best that the enemy had done.

When, early in the war, a British officer made a scene in the House of Commons, declaring that British soldiers were being murdered by the absence of steel helmets, the average stay-at-home was inclined to ridicule him. Those who had ever had to stand along the line when the "Minnies" were bursting near by, and the ugly black fragments were hissing as they dropped, were not altogether so indifferent.

Even early in 1916 it was customary, when a battalion was setting out for the front lines, for the officers to toss up for their supply of steel helmets, to decide who should have them and who should not. The man who went out without one knew that his chances of death under trench-mortar fire were increased by about fifty per cent. Every battalion in 1917 could show steel helmets torn with fragments of high explosive, the men who wore them having escaped either wholly unhurt or with mere surface wounds. But for their helmets they would have been killed.

Steel helmets and gas-masks

By 1917 there were helmets for everyone—the best helmets in the world. They were, maybe, not so pretty and not so comfortable as the French, but they gave a maximum of protection. The newest helmets even had steel chain-armour for the front, protecting the eyes. Gas-masks had kept pace with steel helmets. By 1917 the

[*British official photograph.*]

NATURE'S AID ENLISTED IN THE ART AND CRAFT OF ENTRENCHMENT.

A well-concealed trench adapted by the British from a gully between a double line of trees upon the western front. As the advance grew more rapid the labour of consolidating positions won and entrenching new ones grew more severe, and ingenuity availed itself of every scrap of advantage offered by the natural conformation of the terrain when time did not permit of trenches being burrowed deep and concreted.

British had not only the best gas-masks, but the man who was without one had no one but himself to blame.

At the beginning of the war two machine-guns to a battalion was the ideal. By 1917 machine-guns had been multiplied many times. The Vickers-Maxim was, in the opinion of military observers, the best in the world. The Lewis seemed the last word in portable machine-guns. Here was a little weapon which one man could easily carry about with him, with which a whole line of advance could be swept in a few seconds with a merciless hail of fire. One man, with steady finger on his trigger, could sweep down a charging battalion. Naturally, a small weapon was more likely to get out of order than a heavier one.

The British Army had brought machine-gun fire to the ultimate

[*British official photograph.*
THE HIGHWAY TO VICTORY.
Typical mud on the Somme battlefield, and the typical smile with which it was encountered by the British soldiers.

[*British official photograph.*
GROUP OF ANZACS WHO TOOK PART IN THE WINTER RAIDS.
Sent first to Egypt and Gallipoli, it was the supreme desire of the Australian and New Zealand Contingents to be transferred to the western front to meet the arch-enemy. When their wish was gratified they had abundant opportunities of fighting, and won imperishable renown against the flower of the German Army.

The art of military observation had been revolutionised. The gas-balloons spread along over the British front lines kept the enemy position in constant surveillance. It was scarcely possible for the enemy to put up a fresh fence of light wire for some distance behind his lines but it was at once noted and recorded. Aerial photography gave permanent records. The Army airmen — the *corps d'élite*—had come into their own.

A whole series of raids, both day and night, followed the preliminary successes. Sometimes they were small, undertaken by seven or eight men; sometimes they were on a considerable scale, the raiders being counted by the thousand. As an example of the minor raids, reference may be made to an expedition by two officers and five men of a Montreal battalion who left the Canadian lines on New Year's Eve after dark,

point of perfection. The machine-gun barrage, which acted so effectively at the Somme and elsewhere, was like nothing so much as a continuous sheet of steel sweeping overhead. The Stokes gun was a gem. For months everyone familiar with trench life had recognised the Stokes as the ideal trench-gun. For simplicity, rapidity of fire, and portability there was nothing like it. In the view of many soldiers, under almost any conditions a German advance could have been made impossible by Stokes gun fire alone. Further, by use of smoke-shells, it was possible quickly to build up a barrier behind which men could move out of sight and take cover from the fire of the enemy gunners.

and fifteen minutes later had crossed the enemy's wires and entered his front trench without being detected. No German was to be seen, so they moved down the **A New Year's Eve adventure** trench, full of mud and water, to a point where they believed a sentry-post was located. Here they waited twenty minutes until the sentry approached. He was seized and overpowered. A second German, coming out of the dug-out, was also seized; and, with these two prisoners, the raiders returned safely home. In one way this enterprise was little more than an adventurous jaunt, but the army that is in the humour for games such as these, where the stake is the life of the players, is the army that is likely to win.

The most considerable and successful of the Canadian raids was made on January 31st, 1917. On the previous day a New Brunswick battalion rushed into the German trenches after the explosion of a mine and penetrated to the support line, meeting with no resistance. Thirty Germans were met in a communication-trench, and hastily retiring, took refuge in their dug-outs. Called upon to emerge and surrender, they refused to stir, whereupon mobile charges were flung down the dug-outs, destroying them. Four Germans were taken prisoners, but while they were being escorted along No Man's Land a shell fell and killed all of them.

The bigger raid began at 7.45 in the morning of the last day of January. Two Ontario battalions set out under exceedingly unfavourable conditions. There was snow on the ground, making the uniforms of the men conspicuous. The wind prevented the formation of a smoke barrage, and the enemy's wire entanglements were known to be strong. The men had hardly left the trenches before the machine-guns opened out on them from the German lines. Now, however, the great excellence of the supporting artillery became apparent. The enemy machine-guns were almost instantly silenced. When the troops got to the German wire the gun fire had already cleared the position for them.

The German trenches were smashed by heavy shells. When the Ontario troops vaulted into the German lines they found a scene of desolation and ruin. Every deep dug-out and machine-gun emplacement was quickly destroyed. An hour after their start the Canadians were back in their own trenches, bringing one hundred prisoners, two machine-guns, and a mechanical bomb-thrower with them.

This list of captures was up to now the greatest in any

[British official photograph.

CHEERFULNESS IN A CHILLY CORNER.
Winter on the western front. The British soldier, warmly clad, was able to keep himself cheerful even when sudden frost following on heavy rain had turned his shelter into a cave of stalactitic icicles.

of these winter raids, but it was surpassed shortly afterwards by some Imperial Territorial troops on the Ypres salient. On February 21st a London Territorial battalion attacked an inconvenient German salient, five hundred feet wide, between Hill 60 and the Bluff. This point was long considered one of the best prepared along the whole German front, for around Hill 60 British and Germans had for about two years exchanged almost daily battle. It was here that the Londoners—shopmen, warehousemen, and clerks, many of them, in the old days— elected to drive home their attack. The principle that audacity always pays was rarely better illustrated. The audacity was all the greater when it is realised that the majority of the lads who took part in the attack had never up till then been "over the top."

The attack was preceded by a heavy bombardment which smashed up the German wires. Then, in the evening, the bombardment suddenly concentrated on the German side of Hill 60. Believing that the raid was coming at this point, the Germans quickly concentrated their defence here; but while they were doing so, and while the hurricane of Stokes bombs shut out their view, the Londoners quietly advanced closely behind their own curtain of Stokes bombs a little to the side of where the Germans expected them.

The lie of the German position had been closely studied, and every man had been very carefully drilled in advance as to his particular part in the work. When they reached the German front trench a certain number of men were nerve-broken and ready to surrender. These prisoners were secured by some, while others of the raiders, provided with the right quantity of aminol, tackled the dug-outs. Still others went to the communication-

[British official photograph.

WOUNDED MAN ON THE WESTERN FRONT GETS BACK TO SAFETY FROM NO MAN'S LAND.
British soldier who, having been wounded during the course of a wintry trench raid and got lost, yet managed to crawl back, and was nearing the security of his own trenches. There were many such wonderful escapes of men who succeeded in getting back, despite the target which, except at night-time, they afforded to the watchful enemy snipers, and that, short of recognition, they were in danger from their own side, too.

EXTRAORDINARY EXPLOSION OF A HAND-GRENADE.
In this remarkable photograph of bomb practice a grenade, thrown just as the men went "over the top," is seen as it exploded well ahead of them. It suggests the destructive character of these small bombs in trench warfare.

[British official photographs.

LOOKING AFTER THE WOUNDED ALONG THE WESTERN FRONT.
With the motor-ambulance brought as near as the condition of the ground would permit, the ready men of the R.A.M.C. and other comrades helped the disabled over difficult "bits" to the vehicle that would convey them to surgical attention. Above: Carrying a wounded man from a dressing-station.

IN A WRECKED VILLAGE ON THE WESTERN FRONT.
[British official photograph.
Arrival of a British Staff car at a gas-alarm point. The man being assisted into the car was evidently a wounded despatch-rider. His motor-cycle is by the dug-out entrance beneath one of the ruined houses.

trenches, carefully hemming in men from the German front who had begun to retreat. The Londoners entered into the spirit of the game as though it were a hunt, calling "Tally-ho!" as they ran. They moved round in such fashion that the Germans left in the position were surrounded on all sides. The German commanders behind knew that serious work was afoot, but could not locate where the British raiders were. The raiders had seen to it with the utmost expedition that the telephonic communications were cut off. Consequently, the German heavy artillery concentrated on other points, giving the Londoners time to go through the position at leisure. The Germans were given every chance to surrender, and many of them elected to do so, but others fought to the end.

When at last, having completed their work, the London troops retired, they took with them one German officer, one hundred and nineteen rank and file, seven **London Territorials'** machine-guns, and much else. They had **raid near Ypres** destroyed every dug-out and every store in the position; they had blown up a fine mine-shaft. A concrete section of the German trench with stores of hand-grenades had been destroyed; and it was not until the raiders had been back in their own lines with their prisoners that the German heavy artillery turned on the position they had raided and smashed it still further, greatly to the delight of the Londoners, who watched it from the safety of their own lines with unconcealed glee.

This raid was the most successful of any undertaken until the spring advance began. There were reports that, in their turn, the Canadians were determined to beat the British records. The Canadians rejoiced in the Londoners' success as though it had been their own, and smiled grimly. "Anyone would think," muttered one captain from Saskatoon, "that it was a baseball game to hear people talk in that way, in place of a mighty serious business."

One of the most considerable of the raids undertaken by the Australians was at Gueudecourt, on the night of February 4th, when the New South Wales Battalion attacked and took six hundred yards of trenches. Here,

after the usual artillery bombardment, the Australians advanced. The account that follows is based largely on the description by Captain C. E. W. Bean, the Australian official Press representative. The Australian line got into the German trench, following its own barrage very closely, so closely that, to use a German phrase, "it was not behind the bombardment but with it." The Germans on the greater part of the position surrendered like lambs; but a flanking company of New South Wales men, that had to swerve to avoid some unbroken wire, met with very severe opposition. It leaped into the German trench just as the Germans were tumbling out of the mouth of their dug-outs. A hand-to-hand fight followed, the Australians fighting up the trench. Some of them jumped up on the parapets and hurried across No Man's Land to get quickly on to the enemy. Quick as they were, the Germans had time to make a stand and to defend their position. A German counter-attack was crushed by the whole section being wiped out. The flanking company of the Australians closed its end of the trench, but already Germans in the support trenches were preparing a big counter-attack.

Australian raid at Gueudecourt

"It fell immediately," wrote Captain Bean.

There was a sudden burst of something like twenty high-explosive bombs in a single shower over the barricade which the flank company had built. An incessant stream of bombs followed. The company bombers suffered, and the men behind them fell back a little. But the company officer was on the spot in a flash. A private—the last of the regular bombers except one who remained unwounded—shouted to five other privates—simple riflemen—to follow him and take up the bomb fight. The Lewis machine-gunner fought his gun until the German bombs began to fall around that also, when he immediately got it on to them again from a better vantage point. And then, before the Germans had time to take advantage of their success, the Australians were into it again. The company officer shot three Germans himself; the amateur bombers were sweating with the effort of throwing; and the artillery, which had stood by our men so well in the attack, crashed down on the lines which were supporting the German attack.

The support withered in an instant under that hail. But the German bombers in front fought on for nearly thirty wild minutes. Five separate times they appeared to come on. They were in No Man's Land on both sides of the Australians and in the trench, and they hung on and threw stubbornly. Then, without warning, a portion of the flank company, with bombs and bayonets, swarmed out of the trench, and the Germans, good fighters though they were, could not face them. Some were bayoneted, more were bombed, and the rest fled.

After that the Germans turned their artillery on to this trench and the trenches around it. In these little sectional attacks it is, of course, possible for the Germans to concentrate all the guns they have to spare for miles around on to a little portion of trench;

[British official photograph.
OFFICERS IN THE MAKING ENGAGED IN BAYONET EXERCISE.
Learning command of the bayonet as weapon of offence and defence. These men, who had been recommended for commissions, were at a school of instruction for officers in France, where the experience gained at the fighting-front was supplemented by further training to fit them for leadership.

Bitter work: Fusing shells in a winter action.

Pack=mules bringing up shells by night.

Getting to grips with cold steel: British infantry rushing a German trench on the Somme.

[British official photograph.

British troops crossing a temporary bridge replacing that destroyed by the retreating enemy.

British official photograph

" We carried out a raid this morning": An officer leading under heavy shell fire.

A trench bridge over an empty gully, once a strongly held German position.

[British official photograph.

[Canadian War Records

"Time's up. Over you go!" A Canadian battalion going "over the top" to new triumphs.

Behind the lines in France: An evening concert in the officers' mess of the Artists Rifles.

and the hail of shell fire was very heavy indeed. The company which had done most of the fighting so far was not the one on which the brunt of this fell, but rather the small carrying-parties, which accounted for a good part of the success of this intricately organised and well carried out attack. The attacking troops had so far been doing all their own carrying. When this heavy German barrage came down, some Victorian troops, who had watched the New South Wales battalion go forward magnificently under the bombardment, voluntarily undertook the carrying ; and from that time on throughout the night the Victorians, through heavy shell fire, carried this duty on.

The Germans made another attack in the early hours of the morning, but in vain. The following evening a Western Australian battalion was asked to provide a company to take the place of the flanking company of New South Wales men, who were almost done in. Every man of the Western Australians volunteered. The flanking company had lost nearly three-quarters of its men, but, in the language of the Australian historian, " It beat the Germans and held on, and came out fighting still."

The raids were naturally full of incident. **Humorous incidents of the raids** On one occasion a company of Canadians, led by a young officer noted in amateur theatricals, bought a consignment of ladies' " nighties " from a village shop, and put them over their uniforms in order to make themselves less visible in the snow. The scene, as the grim and muddied Westerners covered their uniforms with the dainty, blue-ribboned white garments, stirred everyone to laughter. This *ruse de guerre* was, of course, a very old one. The Germans, two years before, had bought large quantities of cotton goods in order to make similar disguises for their troops on the Russian front.

On another occasion a Canadian raider, going to the mouth of a dug-out, called to the Germans to come up and surrender. There was only one German there, and he hurried up the steps with hands raised. The Canadian greeted him with a yell. " Where is your helmet ? " he asked, pointing to the man's head. The German, who knew a little English, shook his head and pointed below.

" You hustle down like a streak of greased lightning and get it, if you don't want to be blown up," shouted the Canadian. " Do you think I came all this way over No

[*British official photograph.*
BRITISH SENTRY AT THE CHURCHYARD GATE.
This God's Acre had been shattered by German "frightfulness," but the whole line of the western front became holy ground, consecrated by the blood of self-sacrificing soldiers.

Man's Land to go back without a souvenir ? I want that helmet quick ! "

A Canadian officer, with a handful of bombs, stood at the mouth of a deep dug-out and shouted, " *Rous !* Come out ! " A voice replied, in excellent English, " Yes, we are coming ! " The officer called again, and told them to hurry. " Yes, yes ; one minute, please ! " came the reply. A third time the officer shouted. Time was precious, and he must go. " Come out of that ! " he yelled. " I won't call again. I'll throw a bomb next time ! " Even then there was a pause before the Germans poured out. Their officer came last of all. " I had to burn my papers," he said apologetically. The Canadian glared at him, and then his face relaxed, as he saw the humour of the thing. " All right," said he, " we'll call it square, but two seconds more and you would have been in Kingdom Come."

All this time raids were going on all along our front. Scarcely a night passed in which two or three or more parties —Imperial, Canadian, Australian, Newfoundland—did not start out to harry the enemy lines. It was the boast along a section of the British lines that No Man's Land really belonged to us, and no Germans dared show their faces in it. The Germans met the British activities in two ways. The first sets of trenches, with their triple lines, while very important, were not the sole barriers of the German defence. Behind them lay set after set of other trenches. The German front might be broken at fifty points, and yet the main German scheme of defence not be vitally affected. Accordingly, the enemy held large sections of these front lines very lightly, and often with second-class troops — reserve battalions of a poor type, mere cannon-fodder.

There was one section of the German line where a division of what were probably the poorest troops in the German Army was placed. On one occasion they were raided, and a number of them killed. Three prisoners were

[*British official photograph.*
GERMAN AMMUNITION-WAGGONS DESTROYED BY BRITISH ARTILLERY.
Accuracy as well as intensity of fire gave the British supremacy over the German artillery when the early deficiency of munitions had been supplied. Directed by their airmen, they frequently destroyed ammunition-dumps behind the enemy lines and ammunition-waggons rushing shells up to the front.

WINTER WARFARE ON THE WESTERN FRONT: A SUCCESSFUL SURPRISE ATTACK ON FROST-BOUND TRENCHES.

Early one winter morning, after a terrific crash of guns, some British troops rushed across a hundred yards ot No Man's Land, pockmarked with shell-holes and frozen hard as iron, and utterly surprised the Würtembergers in the trenches. Although these sent up distress signals and evoked furious fire from the German gunners, they went back prisoners to the British lines, while their captors took their dug-outs.

brought back. The prisoners averaged 5 ft. 3 in. in height. One was blind in one eye, one was an idiot, and the third an enfeebled youth. But, while a division like this might occupy one point, a section a little distance away would possibly be held by picked men. The best of the German troops, however, the men who were being reserved for the spring offensive, were mostly kept back, saved for special operations. The whole German policy was to conserve the best fighting troops until they were actually wanted, and not to fritter away their energies in winter trench work.

An army cannot, however, always live on the defensive without losing moral. In February the Germans began to follow the example of the British raiders. Early one morning, late in February, a heavy bombardment opened on parts of the British lines, and shortly afterwards from thirty to fifty Germans were seen massing in the front lines, waist high above the parapet. Our **Terrific** sentries at once opened rapid fire on them, **hand-to-hand battle** and the British artillery concentrated its retaliation on that point, smashing up the Germans before they got out of their trenches. Next morning the British troops counter - attacked. The Germans offered desperate resistance at one point, but while they were holding their own there, a second party of raiders moved in on their flank and swept through them, killing or capturing every man in the entire position. Three large mine-shafts were completely wrecked, every dug-out was destroyed, and forty-seven prisoners, including one officer, taken back. The excitement of this big attack had scarcely subsided when, four hours later, in broad daylight, a second raid was made from the British lines. Ten large dug-outs, apparently full of men, were destroyed, sixteen Germans killed in the trenches, and two prisoners captured. On one occasion a German raiding-party succeeded in entering our trenches and getting a man or two.

Almost universally the score was heavily on the side of the British. There was one occasion, however, on which the enemy succeded in inflicting somewhat severe punishment. Late in February two of the most famous Canadian brigades prepared for a raid in great force on the German lines. The position was difficult, the enemy occupying rising ground. Gas was to be used. The whole movement was rehearsed with the greatest care, and the ground was prepared by a very heavy artillery bombardment.

The raid was timed for the early hours of a Tuesday morning ; but, owing to the uncertainty of the wind, it had to be abandoned at the last moment. Some hours previously two Germans had escaped from a French prison compound. Whether they had anything to do with conveying warning to the Germans, or whether the enemy learned of the intended raid by observation, cannot be said.

INDIAN CAVALRY TAKE THE OPEN FIELD.
[British official photograph.
When the winter of 1916-17 ended, the Arras Battle brought a resumption of open warfare in place of raids and trench-fighting.

" LIAISON " OFFICER CONTROLLING THE BARRAGE FIRE
When the infantry advanced, liaison officers followed with a telephone-box, and accompanied by signallers paying out wire, to which the instrument was attached, when the officer stopped to report to the battery behind.

Obviously, the delay gave the Germans a much greater opportunity of learning the details of the British operations.

The wind continued unfavourable until early on Thursday morning. The troops, occupying the trenches night after night in the mud and bitter cold, found their powers of endurance taxed to the full, but all were keen. Early in the morning, following a terrific bombardment, a first gas wave was sent over, apparently successfully. About six o'clock a second wave followed, and the Canadians went after it. The Germans, from their positions, opened a terrific fire with machine-guns. The Canadians who were left jumped for temporary shelter into the shell-holes and replied vigorously. But every effort on their part was in vain ; they were overwhelmed. Party after party of them was wiped out, and the remainder were forced sullenly back into their trenches.

Defeat, however, was not to be accepted. The British artillery redoubled its fire on the German front. Another wave of gas was sent over, and the Canadians again followed it. The wind, however, had now veered, and blew the gas back on the Canadians. The Germans had been greatly strengthened, and poured over their trenches. A terrific hand-to-hand battle ensued. Some of the Canadians got into the enemy lines, doing great damage, but the fortune of war was against them. Two well-known colonels—Lieut.-Colonel H. G. Kemball (of British Columbia) and Lieut.-Colonel Samuel G. Beckett (of Toronto) were killed. It would be foolish to minimise the reality of the disaster on this occasion, but it was the only serious repulse in a long list of brilliant winter engagements—engagements which showed in the best possible way not only how well equipped the new British troops were, but how these young men, many of them fighting for the first time, drawn from every part of the Empire, were prepared worthily to maintain the traditions of our armies in the Great War in any month that followed. When winter raids were merged into the great spring offensive this promise was made good.

Troops of the 2nd South African Infantry Brigade marching into Mbuyuni Camp from Martau. Mbuyuni was captured by the 2nd Division, under Brigadier-General Malleson, on January 22nd, 1916. With the occupation of the adjacent Serengeti Camp the enemy evacuated Kasigan. On taking over the command in February, General Smuts, in planning his campaign, retained this brigade as a reserve force.

Ox convoy crossing improvised bridge across the River Himo, on the Taveta-Moshi Road. General Van Deventer, commanding the 1st South African Mounted Brigade, after occupying Chala, pushed on to Taveta, where the enemy were encountered in considerable force, and defeated on March 9th, 1916; but succeeded in withdrawing his main force, the exact line of his retirement being difficult to establish.

SUNSET STUDIES OF TROOPS AND TRANSPORT ADVANCING INTO GERMAN EAST AFRICA.

CHAPTER CLXXIX.

GENERAL SMUTS' GREAT CAMPAIGN IN GERMAN EAST AFRICA.

II.—The Central Railway Conquered.

By Robert Machray.

The Central Railway—Dominant Feature of German East Africa—General Smuts' Fine Strategy—Successes of Van Deventer and Hoskins—Co-operation of the Belgians with Crewe—Difficulties Overcome—Tombeur's Victorious Movements—Brilliant Capture of Mwanza by the British—Five Lines of Attack on the Railway from the North—The Sixth Line from the South-West—Operations of the Portuguese—Van Deventer Captures Dodoma—The Belgians at Ujiji-Kigoma on Same Day—Splendid March of the South Africans to Kilosa—General Smuts' Rapid Advance from Mziha—His Hard Task—Cutting a Way through Roadless Mountains—Encircling Plan Fails, but Enemy Defeated and Driven South—Mrogoro on the Railway Occupied—Escape of the Germans—Heavy Work in the Uluguru Range—Enemy Retreating to Mahenge—Fall of Dar-es-Salaam—Whole Coast Seized —Belgians Take Tabora after Bitter Struggle—Crewe also Reaches the Railway—Allies in Possession of All the Railway in September, 1916—Northey's Force at Iringa—Germans Hemmed In on Every Side.

THE history of the progressive conquest of the last and most important of the colonies of Germany, up to and including the capture of the Usambara Railway, was told in Chapter CXXIX. (Vol. VII.). The whole of the Usambara line was in the effective occupation of the British on July 21st, 1916, a result that was attained only by the most splendid persistence and devoted effort on the part of all ranks in the face of a brave and skilful enemy, who knew the country and took every advantage of its naturally strong defensive opportunities. Chapter CXXIX. further briefly touched on the two significant developments of General Smuts' Usambara operations; first, the advance of General van Deventer from Arusha to Kondoa Irangi and thence to Dodoma, on the Central Railway; secondly, the advance of General Hoskins from Mombo to Handeni and the Luki- gura River, with the Central Railway also as its objective.

There were just these two railways in the colony. Having taken the one in the north- east area, General Smuts next set about the

capture of the other, which ran from the Indian Ocean to Lake Tanganyika, its total length from Dar-es-Salaam on the east to Ujiji-Kigoma on the west being about seven hundred and eighty miles, or nearly four times that of the Usambara Railway. The longer line had been completed only in 1914, two or three months before the outbreak of the war, and in itself constituted the best and the greatest work that Germany had then accomplished in all her Colonial Empire. No branch connected the two railways, and the shortest distance between them was over a hundred miles. They approached each other most nearly on the coast at Tanga and Dar-es-Salaam, and in the west by the light railway from Mombo, at Handeni and Kilosa or Mrogoro. The only good road which linked them together lay along the seashore, by way of Pangani, Saadani, and Bagamoyo. After leaving Mombo the Usambara Railway struck up north into the Moshi-Kiliman- jaro district at an ever- widening distance from the Central Railway till it joined the new line which the British had built from Moshi east- ward to Voi, on the Uganda Railway, ninety miles from Mombasa.

STRANGE RAILWAY ACCIDENT IN EAST AFRICA.
Train conveying British pioneers and native troops derailed and overturned in British East Africa. It was fortunate that the accident did not happen a few seconds later, for at the moment it did occur the train was within thirty feet of the bridge, part of which is seen in the foreground of the photograph.

TANGANYIKA FORT CAPTURED BY GENERAL NORTHEY.
Fort Namema, near the southern end of Lake Tanganyika, which was captured by the Rhodesian force under Brigadier-General Northey on June 2nd, 1916, a few days after that force had crossed the frontier.

General Smuts planned to conquer the entire colony, and the occupation of the Usambara Railway with the surrounding country, though valuable in itself, and helpful as a base for further operations, was but a small part of the vast undertaking. The total area of German East Africa was about 385,000 square miles, and so far only a few thousand square miles had been wrested from the enemy. Of the immense region that had yet to be subjugated the dominant feature was the

Strategical importance Central Railway, and it was natural that
of the railway the Commander-in-Chief should fix his closest attention and co-ordinate all the movements of his forces with the object of gaining possession of this line. From the great length of the railway, as well as the nature of the country across which it had to be reached, this could be no easy business, but even its successful accomplishment was not the end of his task, unless in the process he was fortunate enough to destroy or capture the Germans and their troops, for south of the line lay rather more than half of the colony.

In a lengthy but most interesting and illuminating despatch, dated October 27th, 1916, from General Headquarters, East Africa, and published by the War Office

NATIVE SENTRY ON GUARD AT A CAPTURED FORT.
One of the entrances to Fort Namema at which one of the native soldiers of General Northey's force had been posted. After being captured, Namema was organised as a strong post before General Northey continued his brilliant campaign in the direction of Iringa.

on January 17th, 1917, General Smuts made known the considerations which determined the strategy that he pursued in the campaign after the conquest of the Kilimanjaro-Arusha districts in March, 1916. All the information that came to hand at that time was to the effect that the Germans intended to make an obstinate defence along the Usambara Railway, and thereafter to retire to Tabora, on the Central Railway, for a last stand. Ruling out, as undesirable at the moment, an advance from the coast or from Victoria Nyanza with Belgian support from Lake Kivu, and taking advantage of the fact that practically the entire fighting force of the enemy was aligned on the Usambara Railway, General Smuts decided on an advance from Arusha into the interior, towards the Central Railway, during April and May. These were the months in which the rains were most violent in the Usambara quarter—a period when operations were

SIMPLE BUT SIGNIFICANT CEREMONY AT NAMEMA.
Hoisting the Union Jack over captured Fort Namema. The place had been invested by the Rhodesians shortly after the crossing of the frontier, and, though the garrison broke out on June 2nd, it suffered heavily. The German commandant was made prisoner and the place captured.

impossible there until well into May. But farther west and south the rains usually were not so heavy as seriously to interfere with, far less to prevent, military movements. Accordingly, General van Deventer, with the 2nd Division, pushed on south from Arusha, as was narrated in Chapter CXXIX., and after a swift march of one hundred and twenty-five miles, captured Kondoa Irangi, which was only a hundred miles from the Central Railway, with fairly good roads in between. This thrust, which the Germans had not expected, had the result, as General Smuts anticipated, of causing them to withdraw a considerable number of their troops from the Usambara Railway in an endeavour to stem the tide of invasion into the interior, and thus his capture of that line was facilitated.

Meanwhile, Deventer concentrated his men at Kondoa Irangi. He had gained the high, healthy, and fertile plateau connecting Arusha with the Central Railway, and had occupied the chief strategic points for any further advance; but by the middle of April his position was jeopardised by bad weather. Rains of extraordinary heaviness flooded the region, and cut off all supplies from the main depots in the north, so that he was dependent on what could be collected locally, or brought by porters from Kissale, one hundred and twenty miles away. The deluge thus forbade his advance southward, defeated his intention of reaching the Central Railway rapidly and of striking a formidable blow at the rear of the principal German forces, and had the unwelcome effect of giving time for the hurried transfer of German troops from the Usambara to the Central Railway sooner than General Smuts had bargained for.

KING'S AFRICAN RIFLES ON THE MARCH.
Men of the 3rd King's African Rifles marching through the wooded hills of East Africa. This battalion, said General Smuts, was hotly engaged in the capture of Kilimanjaro, when it had the misfortune to lose its gallant commander, Lieut.-Colonel B. R. Graham.

In this isolated position of Kondoa Irangi, with their communications "in the air," Deventer and the 2nd Division subsisted on short rations for several weeks, and when in the second week of May the enemy attacked in strength, privation and disease had so told on its defenders that they were unable to oppose to him more than three thousand rifles. Von Lettow, the German Commander-in-Chief, learning how matters stood, had brought up from Dodoma, where he had concentrated the troops withdrawn from the Usambara Railway, upwards of four thousand fighting men, with considerable artillery, to overwhelm Deventer. But after he had made four desperate assaults, the brunt of which fell on the 11th South African Infantry, supported by the 12th South African Infantry, and in the

SUN-SIGNALLERS AT WORK IN EAST AFRICA.
Party of the King's African Rifles at a helio station during the operations in German East Africa. These native troops, under British officers, played a notable part in the arduous but brilliant campaign.

course of which the Germans repeatedly charged right up to the trenches, Von Lettow was decisively repulsed with heavy losses, including one battalion commander killed and another wounded. The fighting throughout was of a most determined character, and if there were moments when the issue appeared to be in doubt, the heroism and steadiness of the South African soldiers won in the end a glorious victory, and compelled the Germans to retreat south into the thick bush. "With this defeat," General Smuts reported in his despatch, "the enemy's last hope of success- **German defeat at** ful resistance to any large portion **Kondoa Irangi** of our forces was extinguished."

Though splendidly successful in beating back the attempt of the Germans to take Kondoa, Deventer was in too weak strength to follow up the advantage he had gained; on the other hand, he had mauled Von Lettow's contingents in such a manner that they ventured on no further offensive movement, but perforce had to content themselves with patrol work and occasional long-range bombardments. Things remained in this state throughout the rest of May and the greater part of June. Early in the latter month General Smuts paid a flying visit to Deventer, to arrange personally the plans for the future co-operation of their two widely-separated forces, and in a day or two

HALTING ON THE WAY.
King's African Rifles taking a rest on the march. These troops had a goodly share in the conquest of the Kilimanjaro district, which General Smuts described, in one of his very notable despatches, as probably the richest and most desirable part of German East Africa.

was back again on the other front, which was then on the Pangani River. In the meantime Deventer's main body at Kondoa was strengthened by the arrival of three South African regiments and additional artillery and machine-guns. Thus reinforced, and with the weather vastly improved and supplies of all kinds coming forward sufficiently, Deventer recommenced operations.

His first business was to clear his front, and on June 24th he drove the Germans from all their positions in the neighbourhood of Kondoa, and occupied them at a comparatively small cost. Thereafter he proceeded to get everything in readiness for his march to the Central Railway. "My orders to him," said General Smuts in his despatch of October 27th, 1916, "were to clear his right flank towards Singida, to move a small column along the Saranda road towards Kilimatinde, and farther east on the road to Mpapwa. My object was not only the occupation of the Central Railway, but more especially the movement of Van Deventer's force to the east, so as to get into closer co-operation with the force at the Nguru Mountains in

General Smuts' orders to Deventer

TROOPERS OF BELFIELD'S SCOUTS EXAMINING THEIR HORSES FOR SORES AND STINGS.
Belfield's Scouts served with the 1st East African Brigade, under General Tighe, in the notable fighting at Latema Nek in March, 1916, and took part in the successful operations on the Pangani River in May of the same year, assisting in the capture of the rich Usambara Highlands.

dealing with the main enemy forces as they fell back to the Central Railway."

In the last paragraph but one of the chapter which narrated the capture of the Usambara Railway, it was shown briefly how an advance towards the Central Railway was begun by General Hoskins' march from Mombo, on the former line, to Handeni, and followed a few miles farther on by the heavy defeat of the enemy on the Lukigura River on June 24th, the very day when Deventer struck his blow at the Germans near Kondoa and commenced his final preparations for his offensive southward. Hoskins had then reached the eastern slopes of the Nguru Mountains, and immediately in front of him towered the lofty mountain known as Kanga. For various reasons, but chiefly because his plans required that Deventer should be more advanced before the combined movement against the main strength of the Germans should start, General Smuts formed a large standing camp on the Msiha River, about eight miles beyond the Lukigura, and rested and refitted his troops, who remained there until the end of the first week in August. Here was assembled the larger part of the army of invasion, which was more directly under the command of General Smuts.

This army consisted of three divisions, together with the troops on the lines of communications, under Brigadier-General W. F. S. Edwards, D.S.O. Of these divisions the 1st and 3rd were at Msiha. The former, under Major-General Hoskins, comprised the 1st East African Brigade, under Brigadier-General Sheppard, and the 2nd East African Brigade, under Brigadier-General Hannyngton, as previously stated. But to this division was now joined the 3rd Division, under Major-General Coen Brits, which was made up of the 2nd South African Mounted Brigade, under Brigadier-General B. Enslin, and the 2nd South African Infantry Brigade, under Brigadier-General P. S. Beves. General Enslin's brigade had arrived in East Africa in May, and was ready to take the field in the latter half of June. The 2nd Division, which was with Deventer, consisted of the 1st South African Mounted Brigade, under Brigadier-General Manie Botha, and the 3rd South African Infantry Brigade, under Brigadier-General C. A. L. Berrange. Among the reinforcements sent to Deventer in May were two South African Infantry regiments that had been taken from the 3rd Division.

In addition to these forces, which were the mainstay of the general campaign of the Allies in German East Africa, there were, both in the west and in the south-west, other forces of considerable importance that at this time were converging, or about to converge, on the Central Railway. The first of these was what was designated the "Lake Detachment," and it consisted of the 98th Infantry, the 4th Battalion of the famous King's African Rifles, the Baganda Rifles, the Nandi Scouts, and some small irregular units. The initial task of this detachment had been the defence of the frontier on both sides of Victoria Nyanza —a stretch in all of about three hundred miles ; and this it continued to perform with marked success for many long months. During April, May, and June, 1916, the troops of the Lake Detachment on the west side of Victoria Nyanza became more aggressive, and gradually forced the Germans from their advanced posts on the Kagera River, south of the Uganda Protectorate. On June 9th, Ukerewe, the largest island in the lake, and only a few hours' distance from Mwanza, the fortified German port on the southern shore, was occupied, the capture being most skilfully effected by surprise by Lieut.-Colonel D. R. Adye, then commanding the detachment, and the naval flotilla under Commander Thornley, R.N. Some seventy prisoners were taken, as well as two small Krupp field-guns, but the chief value of this operation was that it provided a favourable base for an assault on Mwanza.

In the middle of June, Brigadier-General Sir Charles Crewe, K.C.M.G., who was a member of General Smuts' Staff, was appointed to the Lake Command, to which a particular significance was then coming to be attached. Sir Charles was member for East London in the Union Parliament, and had seen much active service in South Africa. Prior to taking over his new command he had been for some time in the Victoria Nyanza region, acting as chief representative of General Smuts in the making of various arrangements for facilitating the movements of the Belgians in the north-west corner of the colony. As the Lake Detachment formed the first of the forces, apart from the

Work of the Lake Detachment

German soldiers and sailors in an East African gun-pit aiming their machine-gun at an approaching British aeroplane.

Observation-post of men from the cruiser Königsberg, discovered up the Rufiji and destroyed by the British, July 11th, 1915.

Well-masked German naval gun in East Africa. Besides the natural shelter afforded by the palms, the gun-crew had made elaborate brushwood cover.

"German band," making use of a strange medley of instruments, giving an alfresco concert outside their huts in East Africa.

Machine-gun corner, with a German sailor training his weapon (firing Maxim ammunition) on an attacking British force.

Aiming a German machine-gun at a British aeroplane. The gunner lay down flat on his back to take his sight.

German machine-gun shelter. These photographs of Germans in action in East Africa were found on a prisoner captured by the British.

Firing a German gun in East Africa from within a very substantial and evidently well-masked and protected gun emplacement.

ENEMY PHOTOGRAPHS FROM SCENES OF THE OPERATIONS IN EAST AFRICA.

MARCHING THROUGH BUSH IN NORTHERN RHODESIA.
Rhodesian troops did fine work in German East Africa. Much of their campaigning was in country where dangerous carnivora abounded and in bush so dense that they could only advance in single file.

heavy casualties that they cleared off overnight. In the latter region there was a protracted struggle of intense bitterness around Ngoma and Kissengi, fortified posts on the boundary, the one Belgian, the other German, but after various mutations of fortune Kissengi passed finally into the hands of the Belgians in May, 1915, thanks to a successful surprise organised by Lieutenant Puck-Chaudoir, the commandant at Ngoma, an officer who had served in the opening weeks of the war at Liège and elsewhere, and had won both the Order of Leopold and the Legion of Honour decorations. In 1916 the Belgians were planted firmly on German soil in the two areas, and ready and eager to continue the struggle.

All difficulties having been met and overcome by General Tombeur and General Crewe in combination, one Belgian column, under the leadership of Colonel Molitor, was sent forward by Tombeur, and about the end of April it arrived at Kamwezi, ten miles south-east of Lutobo. Rapid progress and sharp fighting gave Kigali to the Belgians on May 6th, the effect of which gain was to render untenable the position of the Germans farther west on the border, and consequently **Capture of Bukoba** to enable Tombeur to advance his troops **and Mwanza** from the north and the south of Kivu. Molitor's column reached the Kagera River on June 24th, and, as that month closed, his advanced guards occupied Namirembe, in the south-west corner of Victoria Nyanza, while his main body was hotly engaged with the retreating Germans on his right.

Meanwhile, the men of the scattered posts in the Lake Command had been formed into a mobile fighting force by Sir Charles Crewe, who proceeded to get possession of Bukoba, which had previously been held by the British for a short time. It was the chief German port on the west side of the lake, and after he had taken it he occupied the district of Karagwe, between the lake and the Kagera River. He thereupon went south to arrange a combined forward movement with Tombeur's forces. On July 3rd the strong German force which Crewe had dislodged found its retreat barred at Busirayambo by a much weaker body of Belgian troops, who, however, completely routed it after a stiff fight, the bulk of the German Europeans being killed or captured, while the remnant of the enemy fled, closely pursued, towards Maria-hilf, in the direction of Tabora. Among the prisoners was Herr Godovius, the German commander.

General Crewe's next achievement was the taking of Mwanza. He had come to the sound conclusion, as General Smuts approvingly noted, that the course which promised the best results was a movement of his force against this important fortified place, the occupation of which would furnish an excellent base at the south of Victoria Nyanza for the advance of the combined British and Belgian columns to the Central Railway at Tabora. "Accordingly," added General Smuts, in his description of the event, "on July 9th, 10th, and 11th he embarked his force, consisting of about 1,800 rifles, at Namirembe and Ukerewe Island, and on the night of the 11th landed a column, under Lieut.-Colonel C. R. Burgess, at Kongoro Point, east of Mwanza, and the following day another column, under Lieut.-Colonel H. B. Towse, farther north at Senga Point. By his skilful disposition and movement of both columns—the one from the east, the other from the north-east—on Mwanza, he made it impossible for the enemy to withstand his advance; and the threat to the enemy's retreat from Burgess's column made the enemy evacuate the town on July 14th."

The Germans were ousted from one of their principal strongholds in East Africa with quite insignificant loss to their assailants, but most of the enemy whites, after destroying the powerful wireless station, made good their escape in the steamers Mwanza, Heinrich Otto, and Schwaben, while some five hundred Askaris got away down the main road to Tabora.

three divisions in the east, which, with the others, were to converge on the Central Railway, so these Belgians were the second. The Belgian troops had as their Commander-in-Chief a distinguished Colonial soldier in Major-General Tombeur, with headquarters at Kibati, north of Lake Kivu. An advance from Kibati direct on the German positions in that quarter being impracticable on account of the barren, volcanic country which lay between, it had earlier been agreed that Tombeur's force was to move north-east to Lutobo, from which it was to descend in a southerly direction on Kigali, the chief town of the rich and prosperous German province of Ruanda, and that a base for it should be established at Bukakata, on Victoria Nyanza, one hundred and fifty miles **Belgian co-operation** farther east, the British making them- **with British** selves responsible for the transport and supply arrangements there. The carrying out, however, of those arrangements proved a difficult matter, and it was to overcome it that Crewe was sent by General Smuts.

Along the Congo frontier there had been lively fighting between the Belgians and the Germans ever since the outbreak of the war, both in the plain north of Lake Tanganyika and on the northern slope of Lake Kivu. In the former region the Germans made a strong attack on the Belgian post of Luvugu on September 29th, 1915; but, after what seemed an inconclusive battle, suffered such

Subsequently General Crewe advanced to Misungi, opposite the southern end of Stuhlmann's Sound, and found that the steamers had been abandoned, as well as a Colt gun, much baggage, stores, ammunition, and a considerable sum of money in specie. The Mwanza was afterwards salved and employed on the lake.

Meanwhile, General Tombeur's second force, which marched from the south of Lake Kivu under the command of Colonel Olsen, had defeated the Germans at Kitwitawe on June 6th, and again on the road to Kitega. Making good progress in the direction of Lake Tanganyika and east of that lake, it swiftly advanced during June and July towards the western end of the Central Railway at Ujiji and Kigoma, while a Belgian flotilla co-operated on Tanganyika itself. As the general result of all these highly-successful operations of Crewe and Tombeur, the Germans were swept out of their fine provinces of Ruanda and Urundi, and the menace to the great railway had become very pronounced both at Tabora and at Ujiji and Kigoma. Seeing the rapidity with which the enemy had quitted his valuable Lake Provinces and Mwanza, General Smuts now arrived at the conclusion that the German retreat finally would not be towards Tabora, as he had at first supposed, but farther east towards Dar-es-Salaam, or south to Mahenge, the plateau lying about half-way between the Central Railway and the Portuguese frontier. The latter idea involved the conclusion that the Germans would make their last stand not on the railway, but in the vast and almost roadless region south of it. In any case, however, the capture of the railway was of predominant importance.

Strategical lines of attack

To sum up. In the beginning of July, 1916, there were four distinct but closely related lines of assault developing against the Central Railway from its northern side. The first, from the Mziha Camp, under the personal leadership of General Smuts, on the east side of the colony, had Kilosa and Mrogoro as objectives. The second, from Kondoa Irangi, under Deventer, some distance east of the middle of the railway, aimed at Dodoma. The third, from Mwanza and the south of the Victoria Nyanza, under Crewe, with Belgian support, west of the middle of the railway, was directed against Tabora. The fourth, from Lake Tanganyika, and entirely Belgian, struck at the western terminus. To these must be added a fifth line of assault—that of a small but competent force working along the sea-coast, in conjunction with the Navy, the objective being Dar-es-Salaam, the eastern terminus.

Victory that saved Nyasaland

Not only were these offensive movements in course of maturing on the north side of the railway, there also was from the south-west area of the colony the beginning of an offensive on its south side, striking up towards it north-eastward. British forces, which had been concentrated at various points along the northern borders of Rhodesia and Nyasaland, with Brigadier-General E. Northey in chief command, advanced into German territory on May 25th to a distance of twenty miles on the whole front between Lake Nyasa and Lake Tanganyika. Prior to this date a good deal of fighting had occurred in this frontier district, the chief physical feature of which was the British road—known as the Stevenson Road after the name of its builder—passing from Karonga, on Nyasa, through Fife and Abercorn to Kituta, on Tanganyika. The principal event in the southern district was the total defeat of a surprise German assault on Karonga, in 1914, by a small body composed of part of a battalion of the King's African Rifles, with some reservists of that corps and a little company of local volunteers, commanded by Captain Barton, D.S.O., of the Northamptonshire Regiment. This victory saved Nyasaland from invasion. In January, 1915, an internal disturbance that might have had dangerous consequences was frustrated. The natives of the Shiré Highlands revolted against the British through the incitement of a negro preacher, who had been educated in America, and

TRENCH FIGHTING UNDER DIFFICULTIES IN GERMAN EAST AFRICA.
British soldiers in well-protected but badly-flooded trenches in German East Africa. The conditions of fighting in the course of the campaign in Germany's last colony were very varied, according to the district and season. The country operated in ranged from bare, open plains to dense and almost impenetrable forests, and from lofty heights to low-lying lands, which the torrential, seasonal rains converted into morasses.

GERMAN OFFICERS IN EAST AFRICA.
Colonel von Lettow-Vorbeck (second from right), German Commander-in-Chief in German East Africa, with Dr. Schnee, the Governor, and Commander Müller, of the Königsberg.

district, while in the Tanganyika district he occupied Bismarckburg on June 8th. From New Langenburg and Bismarckburg respectively roads ran north-westerly to Kilimatinde and Kilosa, on the Central Railway, the more important being that from New Langenburg to Kilosa through Iringa, and it was by this route that the main body of the Germans in the south-west retreated, with Northey in hot pursuit. On June 30th he drove the enemy out of Ubena, and in July was advancing towards Iringa.

To complete the picture presented in the preceding narrative of the situation in German East Africa, as it stood at the end of June and in the first weeks of July, 1916, it must be noted that

was an inflammatory exponent of "Ethiopianism" (Africa for the Africans—*i.e.*, the negroes), but the rising was quickly suppressed, its leader being killed in action. During the rest of the year nothing of importance occurred, though patrol skirmishes were frequent on the border.

Higher up in this area, towards Tanganyika, the outstanding incidents took place in 1915, and there the British were assisted in repelling the Germans by native Belgian troops, the combined allied strength being only about three thousand men to a frontier of some one hundred and fifty miles in length. General Edwards was in chief command. In March the enemy attacked Abercorn, but was driven off. In July he assaulted Saisi with as scant success, though on that occasion he had two thousand men, several 12-pounders, and a number of machine-guns. In this latter affair the British and Belgians, who were not half as numerous as their assailants, were most ably handled by Major J. J. O'Sullevan, of the Northern Rhodesian Police, and his splendid defence of the position was rewarded with the D.S.O. A German force which later in the same year was concentrated near Saisi was tackled courageously and dispersed by the Belgians.

Towards the close of 1915 the British were reinforced along the whole of this border region, and the Belgians, **General Northey's vigorous offensive** whose help had proved most material, then proceeded north along Tanganyika to join their comrades of the Olsen Brigade under General Tombeur, participating afterwards in the advance on Ujiji and Kigoma, on the Central Railway. The Nyasaland and Northern Rhodesian Commands were merged into one under General Northey, and vigorous offensive action was begun in the following May, the movement corresponding in time with the invasion of German East Africa by the Belgians from Lake Kivu, in the north-west of the colony. In addition to the local Rhodesian and Nyasaland forces, consisting chiefly of trained police and volunteers, with some detachments of the King's African Rifles, Northey had at his disposal the Imperial Service Contingent, which had been raised in 1915 in the Union of South Africa. Before the month closed he took New Langenburg, his casualties being slight, and within a little more than a fortnight also captured Old Langenburg, beating off a heavy counter-attack there on the night of June 14th, in the Nyasa

COLONEL VON LETTOW-VORBECK.
Commander-in-Chief of the German forces in East Africa. This photograph and the one above were found on a German prisoner captured during General Smuts' brilliant campaign.

in March of that year Portugal, the ancient ally of England, threw in her lot with the Entente Powers, and that Portuguese troops were fighting the Germans on the southern frontier of the colony. On April 23rd an enemy force was defeated on the Rovuma River, with the loss of a gun and several prisoners, and in the course of May and June relatively heavy attacks on the Portuguese posts at Nikha, Namaka, and Undi on that boundary river were dealt with successfully. Further, the entry of Portugal into the war signified that the last stage in the military encirclement of the sole remaining oversea possession of Germany had been reached. As the "Cologne Gazette" sorrowfully confessed, the position in East Africa was hopeless, and all that was left was to make as good an effort as was possible till the inevitable end. To do the Germans justice, they fought bravely and well in the colony, protracting the unequal struggle for a longer period than had generally been expected.

Of the various offensive movements that were directed on the Central Railway, two attained their objectives, but at wide distances apart, on the same day, July 29th.

On that date one of Deventer's columns occupied Dodoma, and the Belgians were in Ujiji and Kigoma.

After extensive preparation, Deventer resumed his advance south of Kondoa Irangi in the middle of July. Throwing off a column, under Lieut.-Colonel A. J. Taylor, to take Singida, eighty miles west of Kondoa, he despatched on July 14th another column, under Lieut.-Colonel H. J. Kirkpatrick, towards Saranda, on the railway. Singida was captured on August 2nd. Kirkpatrick encountered little opposition on his line of march until he arrived before Mpondi, some twenty-four miles north of the station. There the country was covered with thick bush, which made scouting almost impossible. He suddenly found himself confronted by a strong hostile position, and was assailed by heavy machine-gun fire. Going straight for the Germans in a frontal attack, he utterly routed them, and took Mpondi within a few hours. Continuing his progress, he was in Saranda on July 31st, and also on the same day occupied Kilimatinde, seven miles farther south, and one of the chief points on the railway.

PEACEFUL SCENE IN THE MIDST OF WAR.
Church parade with the German forces in East Africa. The men on the right were German sailors, and facing them was a company of the sturdy Askaris, or native troops. With the officers about the improvised pulpit may be observed a lady member of the German Red Cross.

Nyangalo, with orders to its commander, General Manie Botha, to advance towards Kikombo Station. The other, under General Berrange, and comprising two infantry battalions, a motor-cycle corps, and mounted scouts, he ordered to move along the road through Tschenene and Meia Meia towards the station at Dodoma. Berrange was the first to gain his objective. On July 25th he took Tschenene. In spite of its being well fortified, its losses were small, owing to the first-class work of the Armoured Motor Battery, which engaged the enemy at close range. Two days afterwards he was in occupation of Meia Meia, capturing part of a mounted detachment, and on July 29th he took possession of Dodoma.

General Manie Botha's column, which was marching on the line by the road farther west, had to face a more determined opposition. On July 22nd General Manie Botha took Tisu Kwa Meda, but not till after a sharp engagement. From this place he returned to South Africa, being compelled by urgent private business to relinquish his brigade, at the head of which he had rendered great

GERMANS ON TREK WITH AN ANTI-AIRCRAFT GUN.
Anti-aircraft gun-crew of Germans in East Africa. The men were evidently sailors, natives being pressed into the service as a team for dragging the weapon. Above: German East African field-hospital. The figure on the left is a woman.

In the meantime, however, Deventer's main force had already got astride of the Central Railway. Marching south from Kondoa along the Dodoma road, Deventer entered Champalla (otherwise Jambalo) on July 18th, and Aneti on the following day, without fighting. Hearing that the route farther south was destitute of water, and that the Germans were entrenched at the waterholes at Tisu Kwa Meda and Tschenene, he divided his men into two forces. One, consisting of the 1st Mounted Brigade, he placed on the road which went through Tisu Kwa Meda and Kwa

COMPANY OF ASKARIS IN THE GERMAN SERVICE.
Askaris—native troops trained by European officers—were largely employed by both British and Germans during the campaign. Those employed by the British were commended by General Smuts for their loyal devotion to duty. The photographs on this page were found on a German prisoner taken in East Africa.

service in the campaign, as General Smuts put on record. He was replaced by Brigadier-General A. H. M. Nussey, D.S.O., who had been Chief Staff officer to Deventer. Nussey now pushed on to Nayu and Membe, and on July 28th came upon the enemy in a strong position at Nyangalo. After spirited fighting he defeated and drove on the Germans, who suffered considerable casualties, besides losing fifteen hundred head of cattle. On July 30th he reached Kikombo Station, a few miles east of Dodoma, where Berrange had already established himself. As Saranda and Kilima-

Deventer's difficult advance westward tinde were next day in the hands of Kirkpatrick, something like a hundred continuous miles of the Central Railway passed under Deventer's control by the end of July, a notable achievement, and one that was significant of the speedy fate of the whole line.

An integral part of the masterly plan of General Smuts was that Deventer, after occupying the railway at Dodoma, should advance with his troops westward along the track so as to take in flank and rear the main forces of the Germans in their retreat from the Nguru Mountains. To effect this object, Van Deventer spent the first week of August in

GERMANS ENTRAINING NATIVE TROOPS IN EAST AFRICA.
Mrogoro Station, in German East Africa, whence Askaris were about to be taken to one of the fronts threatened by General Smuts. Mrogoro, which is on the Central Railway, over a hundred miles west of Dar-es-Salaam, was captured by the British on August 26th, 1916.

concentrating his forces, then scattered along the railway from Saranda to Kikombo, at Nyangalo, on the main road to Mpapwa, a town a short distance north of the track. He was ready to move in a wonderfully short time, everything considered. His chief difficulty was concerned with questions of transport and supply, which had been serious enough at Kondoa Irangi, when he was two hundred miles from Moshi, but now were made even graver by his being a hundred miles farther away from that base on the Usambara Railway. And with every mile that he advanced to the west on the Central Railway that difficulty could only be increased.

It was not that the actual road-bed of the railway had been destroyed by the Germans, for Deventer's movements had been too rapid for that, though they had managed to blow up practically every bridge and culvert. It was the fact that all his supplies had to be obtained from the north. But in one way or another the problems that were involved were faced and overcome. For his advance to Kilosa, one hundred and twenty miles westward, and his next objective, the railway was rendered available by a

simple but ingenious device of the South African Pioneers. As it was impossible, without months of strenuous labour, to restore the demolished bridges, some of which were of considerable length, so as to bear heavy locomotives, the pioneers patched them up with such material as they discovered locally, so as to carry a weight of about six tons, and at the same time they narrowed the gauge of the large motor-lorries in such a manner that these could run on railway trolly wheels over the line when repaired in this way. Thus Deventer was able to supply his division till it reached Kilosa, and but for this solution of his transport trouble his march south from that station to the Great Ruaha River, the next stage in this part of the campaign, would, according to General Smuts' testimony, have been a physical impossibility.

Having completed his concentration, Deventer commenced his advance westward from Nyangalo on August 9th. His immediate objective was Tschunjo, in the pass of the same name, and the road to it lay across a waterless district. The enemy, who was about twelve companies strong (1,800 men) with artillery, was known to hold the pass well entrenched, his left being at Gulwe and his right at Kongoa. Having disposed his troops so as to assault the Germans on the centre and to envelop them on the flanks, Deventer came into contact with the enemy at the pass, after a most trying march, on the afternoon of the 11th. Without taking a rest he attacked at once, and brisk fighting continued during the remainder of the day and nearly all the following night. Owing to the difficulty of the country the flanking movements he had ordered were delayed, but his frontal operations were successful. On the morning of the 12th it was found that the Germans, who had been punished severely, had evacuated their positions and withdrawn towards Mpapwa. Proceeding forthwith in pursuit, he came up with them on the same day at that place, promptly engaged and, before the night fell, defeated them, though he had been marching and fighting without a halt for forty-two hours. It was a fine effort, made very gamely by all ranks.

Having occupied Mpapwa, Deventer next moved on Kidete, a station on the railway where the Germans held a strong position and were supported by heavy guns, field-artillery, and machine-guns. Fighting began on August 15th, and went on without intermission until late next day, but finally a flanking movement by his mounted troops, who fell on the rear of the enemy, gave the place into his hands. During the ensuing week Deventer gradually drove the Germans from Kidete along the railway to Kilosa and Kimamba, both of which he occupied **Deventer's report to** on August 22nd. In reporting these **General Smuts** operations, which were of an extremely arduous nature, to General Smuts, Deventer wrote:

The railway from Kidete to Kilosa, for a distance of twenty-five miles, follows a narrow defile through the Usagara Mountains by the Mukondokwa River; every yard of advance was stubbornly resisted by the enemy. Of the more important engagements, those on the 19th at Mzagara and on the 21st before Kilosa should be mentioned. In all the actions on this advance the fighting consisted of the enemy receiving our advanced guard with one or several ambushes, then falling back on a well-prepared position and retiring from that on to further well-selected ambush places and positions. All the time our less advanced troops were subjected

In a German mess tent.   Right : German naval band.   Men from the cruiser Königsberg—which had been destroyed by the British when it was hidden up the Rufiji River in July, 1915—giving a performance to their comrades beneath East African palms.

Trenches, masked by palms and backed by scrub, which were made by the Germans among the tropical growth of East Africa.   Right : Another view of well-planned trenches, the course of which it would be difficult to determine from aerial or distant observation.

Well-hidden German gun.   The abundant vegetation afforded unlimited material for effective masking of gun-positions. Right : Trench with loopholed parapet, fronted by a screen of scrub through which the men could fire.

LIFE WITH THE GERMANS IN EAST AFRICA AS REVEALED BY AN ENEMY CAMERA.

to vigorous shelling by means of long-range naval guns. Since leaving Kondoa Irangi the troops who have reached Kilosa by the shortest route have done at least two hundred and twenty miles. Those troops who have gone via Kilimatinde and other places have done many more miles. Owing to bad roads, shortage of transport, and the rapidity of advance, the adequate rationing of the troops was not possible. The underfeeding and overworking are sadly reflected in their state of health. Regarding the animals of my division, the advance from Mpapwa to Kilosa was through one continual fly belt, where practically all the animals were infected.

Gallant endurance of South Africans — With the occupation of Kilosa, Deventer now held upwards of two hundred miles of the Central Railway, or a good deal more than a quarter of its entire extent. His gallant South Africans, strained by incessant marching and fighting under such hard conditions, imperatively needed rest, but the necessities of the situation at the moment even more imperatively forbade it. The 1st and 3rd Divisions had moved south from the Mziha Camp, and were pressing the Germans down from the Nguru Mountains. Deventer's mounted brigade, less one regiment, was sent on August 25th to Mlali, farther east, to co-operate. But there was no rest for the balance of his sorely-tried men. On August 26th he received a message from General Smuts ordering him to advance from Kilosa to Ulaia, twenty miles south, on the main road to Iringa, and despite the exhausted state of his force the command was obeyed, the place being taken before the day was over. The Germans had held it in strength, and were being reinforced by detachments who had been opposing General Northey's march towards Iringa from the direction of New Langenburg. Thereafter, Deventer's line of route led him on to the Great Ruaha River, one of the principal affluents of the Rufiji River, and over which went the Iringa road.

It had been with a view to assisting their main body then retreating from the Nguru Mountains to the Central Railway that the Germans had been concentrating a force at Ulaia, and Deventer now drove it southwards towards Kidode, along the road to Iringa. The operation involved an extraordinary amount of mountain climbing and constant fighting. The country was ridged with high mountains running across the road for several miles, and every ridge had been fortified previously by the enemy, who, after losing one, would fall back on the next, a mile or two in the rear. In fact, Deventer's advance encountered difficulties at every point from the character of the terrain, dongas and all sorts of natural traps strewing his path. Yet his casualties were surprisingly light, this being mainly due to his avoiding, as far as might be, all frontal attacks. His strategy was to carry out flanking movements, while holding the Germans to the position occupied by them, but once the pressure he thus exerted became marked they usually broke off the engagement under cover of the night and stole away in the darkness.

OVERLAND TREK OF BRITISH NAVAL DIVISION.
The overland transport of two armoured motor-boats to Lake Tanganyika was a remarkable feat in the East African Campaign. In the course of the long trek seventeen bridges more than eighty feet long had to be built.

Forcing them on in this fashion, he took Kidode on September 10th, having reached his objective for the time being. Deventer was emphatic in his appreciation of the conduct and the spirit of his troops, declaring that their determination and zeal, their endurance of hardships during long marches through dry and waterless stretches on scanty rations formed an achievement worthy of South African soldiers.

Meanwhile, the great move of the 1st and 3rd Divisions from the Mziha Camp south to the Central Railway on the east was well under way. But, before this most vital operation started, General Smuts saw to the clearing of his flank to the Indian Ocean by the occupation of the coastal area from Tanga, the terminus of the Usambara Railway, to Saadani Bay, which was taken by the Navy on August 1st, Pangani having been captured by it a week previously. A detachment of the West India Regiment was landed at Saadani, and in union with a contingent of the 40th Pathans drove the enemy from the Lower Wami River. The combined force marched south-east to Bagamoyo, which was captured in brilliant style by the Navy on August 15th, a 4.1 in. naval gun with ammunition being included in the spoil. Dar-es-Salaam lay a short distance south, and it was evident that no long time could elapse before the British would close in and seize the capital of the colony. The military operations on the coast and parallel to it were under the command of Colonel C. U. Price, C.M.G., subject to the orders of Brigadier-General Edwards, the Inspector-General of Communications. With the area on his extreme left thus in his possession, General Smuts began the advance from Mziha through the Nguru Mountains to the railway, his hope then being that if he failed to corner the Germans in those mountains, he, in conjunction with Deventer from Dodoma, would bring them to bay somewhere about Kilosa Station.

General Smuts' task was exceedingly formidable by reason of the difficult character of the terrain, of which naturally the Germans took care to make the most. The main road to the Central Railway, for about forty-five miles, passed close under the Nguru Mountains and Mount Kanga. In the mountains and across this road the enemy had disposed about three thousand rifles, with much heavy and light artillery, trenches having been dug athwart the foot-hills in the best positions, and every conceivable measure adopted that would add to the strength of the **Germans favoured by the terrain** defence. If General Smuts forced his way by frontal attacks along the road, or moved by his left through the scrub and high elephant-grass, there was something more than a chance that the Germans on his right would get behind him, and at the very least put his communications in serious danger of being cut. In these circumstances he considered it of paramount importance to advance through the mountains themselves, and to clear them of the enemy as he

LIEUT.-GEN. HOSKINS, C.M.G.
General Hoskins succeeded General
Smuts in command in East Africa.

BRIG.-GEN. P. S. BEVES.
Commanded 2nd S.A. Infantry
Brigade. Mentioned in despatches.

BRIG.-GEN. SHEPPARD, D.S.O.
In command of 1st E.A. Brigade.
Mentioned by General Smuts.

BRIG.-GEN. BERRANGE, C.M.G.
At the head of the 3rd S.A. Infantry
Brigade, in the 2nd Division.

R.-ADMIRAL CHARLTON, C.B.
In command off East Africa. Mentioned in despatches by Gen. Smuts.

BRIG.-GEN. COLLYER, C.M.G.
Chief of the Staff to General Smuts.
Mentioned in despatches.

BRIG.-GEN. HANNYNGTON.
Commanded 2nd E.A. Brigade.
Mentioned for ability as commander.

CAPT. HON. F. E. GUEST, M.P.
Mentioned in despatches by General
Smuts for meritorious services.

marched to the south. He decided that the most effective strategy for carrying out this aim was to institute a series of turning movements, which would result in threatening the retreat of the Germans, or of cutting off that retirement if it was delayed too long.

A mass of the Nguru Mountains lay on the west, while the lower hills and spurs of the range, with lofty Mount Kanga, stretched to the east, the division between them being the rugged valley of the Mjonga River, which flowed from Mahazi on the north almost due south towards Turiani, where the road round Kanga crossed it. Above Turiani two streams ran from the north-west through gaps in the Ngurus into the Mjonga; one entered the valley near Matamondo, under the shadow of Kanga, and the other, some miles south, came along into it past Mhonda Mission, not far from Turiani itself. All the way from Mahazi to Turiani the enemy was strongly posted along the banks of the Mjonga, and a turning movement had to be made farther west, so as to strike in at either Matamondo or Mhonda. General Smuts' design was threefold. First, General Sheppard's brigade was to make a feint from Mziha directly against the German position at **General Smuts'** Ruhungu, on the main road to the rail- **threefold design** way, while in reality he was moving the bulk of his men by the left so as to gain the Russongo River, six miles in rear of Ruhungu. Secondly, General Hannyngton was previously to have marched to Mahazi, and from there, accompanied by General Hoskins, was to drive the Germans along the valley of the Mjonga. Thirdly, the 3rd Division under General Brits was simultaneously to make a detour northward to the Lukigura, and then westerly through Kimbe to enter the Ngurus farther west of Mahazi, emerging from them through the Mhonda gap in the rear of the forces of the enemy on the slopes of Kanga and the Mjonga valley.

On August 5th General Enslin, with the 2nd South African Mounted Brigade, 3rd Division, marched from the Lukigura via Kimbe, and struck the Nguru Mountains eight miles west of Mahazi on the following day. Making rapid progress, he arrived at the Mhonda gap, and occupied Mhonda on August 8th. But as he sent back word that the route through the mountains was entirely impracticable for wheeled traffic, his transport had to return to the Lukigura. On August 6th the 2nd South African Brigade, with General Beves in command, set out by the same way, while General Hannyngton, with the 2nd East African Brigade, advanced by the mountain footpaths direct from the Lukigura to Mahazi, and working steadily down the valley of the Mjonga encountered no keen opposition until he reached Matamondo on the 9th. Two days previously General Sheppard and the 1st **Enemy abandons** East African Brigade left the Mziha Camp, **his defence** and progressing slowly through the dense bush which enveloped the enemy's positions on the sides of Mount Kanga gained the Russongo on August 11th. But by this time it was clear that the clever scheme of General Smuts for the encirclement of the Germans was not destined to be a success.

According to his plan the whole of the 3rd Division was to have proceeded to Mhonda, but the difficulty of the country, with its absence of anything like a road, defeated it. Had it not been for the impossibility of transport, the idea would not have proved unprofitable; but, on the contrary, would in all probability have resulted in the complete cutting off of the retreat of the Germans from these mountains and their capture or destruction. As things were, General Smuts, baffled by the terrain so far as wheeled transport was concerned, was compelled to tell General Brits to divert the 2nd South African Infantry Brigade, under Beves, down the footpath to Matamondo, where Hannyngton was having heavy fighting. One of Enslin's mounted regiments, as it happened, had lost its way in these trackless hills, but finally emerged also at this place. Yet a vigorous attempt to carry out the original plan, so

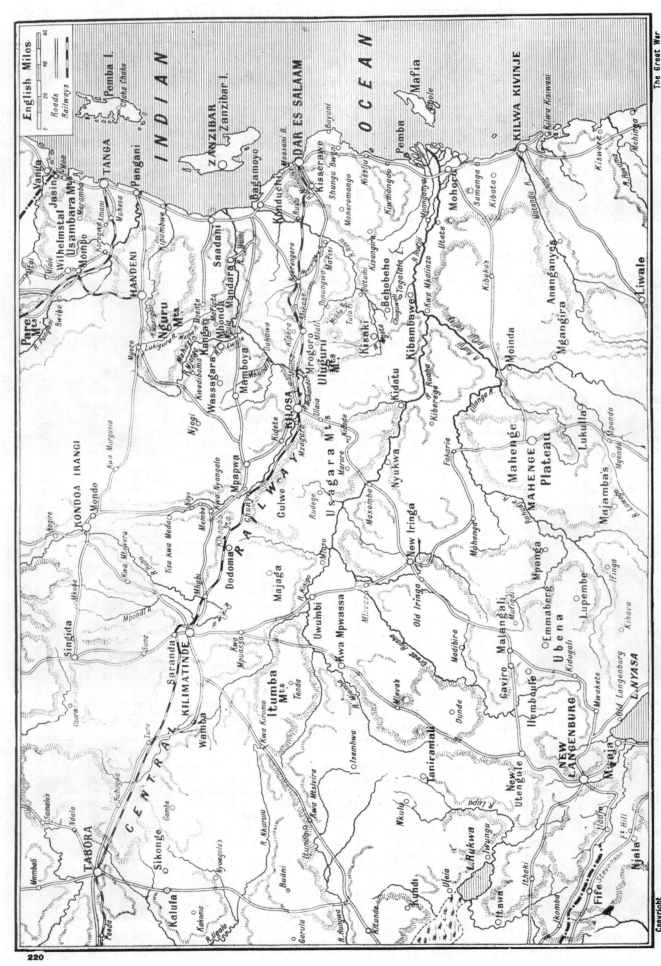

Copyright

The Great War

MAP SHOWING THE AREA OF GENERAL SMUTS' OPERATIONS IN EAST AFRICA FOR THE CONQUEST OF THE CENTRAL RAILWAY.

far as circumstances permitted, was made by Enslin with the rest of his command. Passing through the Mhonda gap, he endeavoured most gallantly to cut off the enemy by seizing a series of positions by which the retreating Germans must go. But in the upshot he found that he was not able to retain these dominating positions in the rear because of the smallness of his force, the safety of which was gravely compromised on the flanks by the far more numerous men opposed to it. Still, he was able to maintain himself at the Mhonda Mission, whence his continued threat was so strong that the enemy had to abandon his whole defence in the mountains and retire as fast as he could.

BROUGHT-TO WITH ITS DECKS AWASH.
German blockade-runner after it had been brought-to by British fire. The natives pressed into the service of the Teutons do not appear to have found their lot a particularly happy one.

GERMAN EAST AFRICAN BLOCKADE-RUNNER.
Result of trying to run the blockade on the coast of German East Africa. The vessel was sunk in shallow water by British naval gunners, and the marks of many hits are observable in the above photograph.

After sharp engagements lasting over two days Hannyngton drove the enemy south from Matamondo on August 11th with great loss, his own casualties being about sixty killed and wounded. On the 12th and 13th Hannyngton's brigade and the brigades of Brits reached Turiani, at the end of the Mjonga valley through the mountains, the Germans having withdrawn some miles farther south. It was, however, becoming clear to General Smuts that he now was dealing with part only of the enemy's force, and that the balance was streaming southward towards the Central Railway, making for Mrogoro or Kilosa. He moved on at once, though he was much hampered by the numerous rivers flowing across his path from the Nguru and Kanga Mountains. The bridges, including some of very considerable span, had been demolished, and had to be rebuilt. In spite of these and other difficulties, he decided to give the enemy no time. On August 13th Enslin's mounted brigade proceeded round the left flank along the Lwale River to Ngula, where he was joined by the 130th Baluchis from Kipera, at which place Sheppard's brigade had arrived by way

of Mafleta, after driving off a small German body. Hannyngton worked his way south along the main road. On the 15th Enslin and Hannyngton were at Kwediboma and Mwomoro, where the roads to Mrogoro and Kilosa respectively left the Ngurus. Both of the former points were occupied with little fighting. The larger number of the Germans retired along the road to Mrogoro, their immediate objective being Dakawa, on the Wami, while the smaller part, consisting of a few companies, made off along the road to Kilosa. General Smuts pressed on in pursuit.

General Hannyngton marched from Mwomoro hot-foot along the Kilosa road to the Mkundi River, while General Enslin moved in the direction of Dakawa. General Sheppard had been ordered to cross the Wami River from Kipera, and to advance along the right or southern bank of that stream to Dakawa Crossing. This meant that the British would be on both sides of the river at Dakawa. Sheppard and Enslin arrived on opposite banks at the enemy position on August 16th, but the Germans were in sufficient strength to **Severe fighting** hold the former at bay two miles on the **at Dakawa** north and, at the same time, to prevent the latter from attempting to get across the stream, which there was both wide and deep. Enslin succeeded next day in crossing the Wami higher up, and the enemy retreated hurriedly when he discovered that this movement had outflanked him and threatened his line of escape. Dakawa Crossing was occupied on the 18th. In the fighting, which was severe in these operations, the British lost about one hundred and twenty men, but the Germans were very badly mauled. A halt was made at Dakawa in order to bridge the Wami, and this involved a delay of several days. Meanwhile, Hannyngton was recalled to Dakawa from pursuing the party which was fleeing to Kilosa, and the Cape Corps was sent to perform the task instead.

General Smuts had been under the impression that the Germans would retreat to Kilosa, and then, having lost the railway there, that they would withdraw to the Mahenge plateau. Kilosa was the most convenient point of departure for this proceeding, and the impression had a good reason behind it; but he now was aware that only a small body of the enemy was on the road to Kilosa, and that the main enemy force was retiring to Mrogoro, a considerable distance farther east. The reason for this choice of the alternative routes was most probably the rapid advance towards Kilosa of Deventer, who, as was previously shown, was progressing eastward along the railway from Kidete, and on August 18th, the date on which Dakawa Crossing was occupied, was only four days away from his then objective. The next effort of General Smuts was to try to bring the Germans to a stand, if it were possible, at Mrogoro. For this purpose he despatched Enslin with the mounted troops to the Central Railway on August 21st, and Mkata Station was occupied two days later. Enslin, without halting, pushed on to Mlali, which lay about fifteen miles south-west of Mrogoro, on the road to Kisaki, round the west of the Uluguru Mountains, and the place was in his hands on August 24th.

Enemy escapes by unknown track

It was then that Deventer sent the 1st South African Mounted Brigade, under Nussey, to reinforce Enslin, the strength of their combined forces being such as to render extremely unlikely any attempt of the enemy to break through to the south in that direction.

ARMOURED STEAMER ON VICTORIA NYANZA.
Under Commander Thornley, R.N., the naval flotilla on Victoria Nyanza did important work, preliminary to the advance on the Central Railway, in the capture of islands and in helping General Crewe to force the Germans from Mwanza, their fortified post at the southern end of the lake.

Simultaneously the Commander-in-Chief arranged that his other troops from Dakawa should advance so as to block also the road to Mrogoro through Kiroka, round the eastern slopes of the Uluguru range. These moves looked as if the "bottling up" of the chief German forces in and around Mrogoro was a certainty. Unfortunately there was a fatal flaw in this promising scheme. "I was not then aware that a track went due south from Mrogoro through the mountains to Kisaki," General Smuts recorded in his despatch, "and that the capture of the flanks of the mountains would not achieve the end in view." On the morning of August 23rd the rest of the British forces crossed the Wami River at Dakawa by the new bridge which had been completed, but instead of marching on Mrogoro direct by the road, which ran nearly due south, General Smuts moved backward down the right bank of the river for some nine miles, and from the point thus reached struck east to the Ngerengere River, in the vicinity of Msungulu, north-east of Mrogoro. He had to traverse a desert belt about twenty-five miles wide, and owing to the denseness of the scrub, the heat, and the lack of water, this movement, which was spread over two days, proved one of the most trying of the whole campaign. However, on the night of the 24th General Smuts encamped on the Ngerengere, eighteen miles from his objective. Earlier on that day a mounted contingent under Colonel Brink, chief Staff officer to General Coen Brits, had gone on in front and seized Mkogwa Hill, three miles farther south-east, and on the south side of the river.

Owing to the exhaustion of man and beast, General Smuts had to halt for a day, but he employed the time in reconnoitring the country. His forces were again in motion on August 26th. Hannyngton with his brigade advanced towards Mikese, on the Central Railway, twenty miles east of Mrogoro, and on the same day occupied that station. Meanwhile Sheppard and Beves, with their respective troops, marched up the Ngerengere on Mrogoro, which was taken also on August 26th. Then it was discovered that the Germans had succeeded in escaping the enveloping net. One lot had got away by the eastern route through Kiroka, another was struggling with Enslin at Mlali; but Col. Lettow-Vorbeck, with Dr. Schnee, the Governor of German East Africa, and the bulk of their men, had made off by the track—of whose existence General Smuts had been ignorant—that passed from Mrogoro south into the mountains. At Mrogoro General Smuts found so many proofs of the precipitate flight of the enemy and of his demoralised condition that he resolved to continue the pursuit, notwithstanding the fact that his troops and animals were worn out with the exertions of the past three weeks, and that his transport had reached its extreme radius of action. Nearly half of the Central Railway was in his possession by this time, but the principal forces of the Germans were still in being, and had to be crushed. There seemed to be a fair chance that they might be rounded up in the Uluguru Mountains, and he devoted himself to the effort. In any case, he had to secure his hold on the railway by driving the enemy well to the south of it.

The 1st Division operated on the eastern slopes of the Ulugurus. Sheppard occupied Kiroka, east of Mrogoro, on August 26th, and Hannyngton advanced southward. By the end of the month, after continuous fighting from the 27th, the enemy was pressed to the other side of the Ruvu River. Then several days had to be spent in throwing a bridge across that stream. The terrain to be negotiated was extremely difficult, the road passing through numerous broken foot-hills, covered with bush or grass from six to twelve feet high, so that progress was slow, painful, and dangerous. The country there, as in so many other parts of the colony, was particularly well suited to defensive tactics, and the Germans held up the British at every convenient place, retiring after as long a delaying action as was possible in the circumstances. From the Ruvu the road for some distance went along the face of precipitous rocks, round which the enemy had constructed a gallery on piles as a track for his transport; but as this structure was not sufficiently strong to carry the mechanical transport of the 1st Division, a path was made by blasting away the mountain-side. Near the river a 4·1 in. German naval gun was found destroyed.

Sheppard occupies Kiroka

When the new path was ready, and the forward movement was resumed, the 1st Division marched towards the

Lieut.=General J. L. Van Deventer, C.B., and some members of his Staff.

British foodships successfully convoyed by seaplanes in clear weather when U boats were easier to detec

A friend in need: Destroyer towing home a "Blimp" dirigible whose engine has failed.

A timely shot: Passengers on a liner cheering a destroyer's direct hit on a German submarine.

225

A heliograph signalling post in General Van Deventer's East African operations.

Postal carriers with General Northey's column toiling through the East African scrub.

Mvuha River by three routes. The first led by the main road to Tulo, the second, by a track west of the first, to Kassanga, and the third, by a track on the east side, to the Tunungo Mission. Brisk fighting took place every day, and road-making with bridge-building employed not only the pioneers but also a large portion of the troops. Swampy tracts as well as rocky stretches abounded between the Ruvu and the Mvuha. A way had to be cut down the precipitous face of a spur of the Ulugurus, and this took the technical corps and most of Sheppard's brigade several weeks, but the result was a notable and enduring feat of engineering. The advance could not be rapid in such conditions, but Tulo was occupied on September 10th and Dutumi taken three days later. It was only after very hard efforts that the Germans were finally beaten south to the Mgeta River.

While these operations were proceeding on the eastern side of the Uluguru range, the South African brigades, under General Brits, and Enslin's brigade were busy in the interior and on the western side of it. Enslin's men had reached Mlali on August 24th, and early in the morning his advanced scouts rushed Kisagale, a **Germans driven to Kisaki** small isolated hill on the road to the south, capturing an ammunition depôt in which were stored about a thousand shells for naval and other guns. At the same time one of his regiments galloped up the valley to the north of this eminence, and took up positions among the foot-hills in the vicinity, at the very moment when an enemy force retreating from Mrogoro was coming down the road. A severe engagement ensued, and the South African soldiers, finding that they were being gradually outflanked with a heavy fire converging on them, withdrew a short distance, but retained effective possession of the road on the south during that day and the next. When the Germans saw that they could not dislodge these determined combatants, they drew off into the mountains towards Mgeta Mission, ten miles away, after destroying two naval guns, one a 3·4 in. and the other a 4·1 in. Leaving their horses behind, Enslin and his troopers footed their way into the hills after the foe, but farther to the south, with the intention of cutting him off. In the meantime, General Nussey's brigade had come up, and on August 27th it occupied Mgeta Mission; thereafter it followed the enemy through the mountains along the course of the Mgeta River.

Enslin then marched back to the trail which went round the west of the Ulugurus by the Msongosi River and Mahalaka and came out at Kisaki, on the southern edge of the range. In this advance to Kisaki two infantry regiments of Beves' command supported Enslin.

BELGIAN ASKARIS MARCHING THROUGH A NATIVE VILLAGE.
Belgian troops co-operated with the forces under General Crewe directed against Tabora, and another exclusively Belgian force operated from Lake Tanganyika against the western terminus of the Central Railway.

SOME BELGIAN ASKARIS. Belgian native troops were recruited from the various Congo tribes and proved excellent fighting material.

the Mgeta with porter transport only, and Brits, in command of Enslin's and Beves' brigades, moved to the Msongosi River, but found it impracticable to take his guns or waggons beyond it, and had to send them back to Mrogoro. From Mahalaka Brits advanced, however, in light order by the elephant track along which Burton and Speke had travelled into the interior in 1857, and on September 5th he reached the neighbourhood of Kisaki after slight opposition. Nussey, however, had not yet come up; and, owing to an accident to his wireless, was not able to get into communication with Brits, but the latter decided to attack the enemy on the 7th. Kisaki was found strongly held by a large enemy force, the bulk being on the right bank of the Mgeta in front of Enslin, while dense bush prevented Beves on the other side of the stream from giving effective assistance to him. In danger of envelopment on his left and then on his right, Enslin decided to

From all points in the Uluguru Mountains the Germans were retreating on Kisaki, very much against their will. General Smuts had been too quick for them. As was apparent from the vast quantities of heavy-gun ammunition captured from them at various points, they had planned a protracted and elaborate defence of these mountains. It was the unexpected arrival of Enslin at Mlali, and the audacious and successful pursuit which thereafter took place, combined with the operations of the 1st Division on the east, that compelled them to abandon their scheme and retire to Kisaki.

Converging on Kisaki, Nussey marched south along

SWAMPS OF LAKE BANGWELO.
Small canoes used by the natives who were attached to the British Naval Expedition which was sent to Lake Tanganyika.

SKINNING A LEOPARD "ON BOARD SHIP."
The British Naval Expedition that took out two armed motor-boats from England to Lake Tanganyika in 1915, and cleared the Germans off the lake, had an adventurous trip overland and by rivers and lakes. In Northern Rhodesia unlimited sport was forthcoming.

retire at night. Beves also withdrew, and their joint forces entrenched six miles north of Kisaki, awaiting the arrival of Nussey. That general, not knowing what had occurred or where Brits was, reached Kisaki early next day, and, gallantly going into action at once, held his ground against much superior numbers till the evening, when messengers from Brits came to him with an order to proceed to Little Whigu, the place to which Enslin, and Beves had gone.

This unfortunate affair would hardly have happened if Brits had been in touch with Nussey. It was not till a week later that Kisaki was captured as the result of flanking movements round the north-east; but the Germans made good their retreat. They left behind them a hospital full of sick and some seventy Europeans, but all supplies had been removed or destroyed.

General Smuts' tribute to his troops Driven everywhere from the Uluguru Mountains, the enemy took up a line of defence along the Mgeta, south of Dutumi. and farther to the west, across the road, from Kisaki to the Rufiji River. As his men were thoroughly spent after their hard march through this most difficult region, generally on half rations or less, and needed a complete rest on medical as well as military grounds, General Smuts did not press an attack at that time against the Germans in their new positions, and for a short period something approaching trench warfare supervened. Writing of his men, General Smuts delivered this eulogy:

The plain tale of their achievements bears the most convincing testimony to the spirit, determination, and prodigious efforts of all. Their work has been done under tropical conditions, which not only produce bodily weariness and unfitness, but which create mental languour and depression and finally appal the stoutest hearts. To march day by day and week by week through the African jungle or high grass, in which vision is limited to a few

yards, in which danger always lurks near but seldom becomes visible even when experienced, supplies a test to human nature often in the long run beyond the limits of human endurance. And what is true of the fighting troops applies in one degree or another to all the subsidiary and administrative services. The efforts of all have been beyond praise; the strain on all has been overwhelming.

So far as the Central Railway had been affected by the operations of General Smuts' three divisions, the whole of it, from Saranda on the west to Miroka on the east, was in the occupation of the British on August 26th, and was made available for motor traction, by the methods already

GERMAN FORT CAPTURED BY SOUTH AFRICANS.
South African troops constituted the 2nd Division, commanded by General Van Deventer, of the military forces at General Smuts' disposal. They also formed the bulk of the 3rd Division under General Brits.

explained, with all expedition. As regards the line itself, and simultaneously with the movements of these divisions in the interior, the forces at work near and on the coast, in union with the Navy, made rapid progress towards Dar-es-Salaam, the western terminus. After the capture of Bagamoyo, General Edwards concentrated there about eighteen hundred rifles, under Colonel Price, for the march against Dar-es-Salaam. Dividing this force into two bodies, Price, with the larger of the two, moved down the coast on the capital, while the smaller struck off towards the railway at the Ruvu bridge, with the object of seizing that structure before the Germans had destroyed it, and thereafter of swinging in on the city.

By this time the enemy had come to understand that there was no hope of his being able to hold Dar-es-Salaam, and, anxious to avoid an assault, or perhaps a siege of a town containing a large German non-combatant population, had resolved to make no attempt to defend it. Consequently, the advancing columns met with little serious opposition. The larger occupied Konduchi and Msasani Bay, and then bivouacked on the Msimbuzi River, which flowed round the city on the west and north. The smaller

ON THE MOUNTAIN BORDER OF EAST AFRICA.
Native soldier on the look-out in the mountainous Kilimanjaro district. Much fighting took place there during the earlier part of General Smuts' campaign for the capture of the Usambara Railway.

and fine permanent Government and other buildings, to say nothing of the Transcolonial Railway, as one of their greatest achievements—as it was.

Though the capital, as a whole, passed into the hands of the conquerors practically undamaged, the railway-station and the harbour works had been demolished, and the harbour itself rendered as of little service to the victors as was possible. The Germans did their utmost to hamper the British by running their locomotives and rolling-stock into the harbour, thus annulling transport facilities and preventing the unloading of ships. Dar-es-Salaam had been an important German naval base; the **Capture of Dar-es-Salaam** floating-dock and the enemy vessels were found sunk in the harbour. The Tabora, König, and Möwe had been wrecked too thoroughly to admit any prospect of their being salved, but the Feldmärschall and the floating-dock were recovered. With Dar-es-Salaam the whole of the Central Railway west to Saranda fell into the hands of General Smuts. The business of clearing the harbour, and also of restoring the line westward, was taken in hand promptly and successfully. By October 6th the track was open for motor traffic all the way to Dodoma, a distance of nearly three hundred miles, and beyond it towards Tabora, while

ADAPTABLE MOTOR IN E. AFRICA.
Taking a boat by railway to Lake Nyasa on a train which was drawn by a Napier motor adapted for the purpose.

marched to the Ruvu bridge, but found that it had been wrecked. After dispersing to the south a small hostile body at Ruvu, this force turned east and moved on Dar-es-Salaam. While these two columns were thus converging on the place, the British ships appeared on the scene, and the capital surrendered on September 3rd, all the German troops having retired to the south a few days earlier, with their artillery, except one 6 in. gun which they had blown up. On the morning of the 4th the British flag waved over the chief centre of German East Africa—to the bitter regret of the Colonial party in Germany, who had always regarded Dar-es-Salaam, with its excellent harbour

RED CROSS TRAIN ON THE CAPTURED CENTRAL RAILWAY.
Motor-drawn hospital train, conveying sick and wounded, at Mikese, which was captured by the British under General Hannyngton on August 26th, 1916. The train was drawn by a Napier business motor fitted with flanged wheels for rail traction.

the British forces in the western midland area were being supplied from Dar-es-Salaam as sea base.

Having gained Dar-es-Salaam, General Smuts considered that the time had arrived for the effective occupation of the whole coast of the colony. Accordingly, he arranged with Rear-Admiral E. F. B. Charlton, C.B., who was in command of the fleet operating in these waters, for the convoying of forces south, and for co-operation in the seizure of all the chief points on the seaboard to the Portuguese frontier. Kilwa Kivinje (commonly known as Kilwa) and Kilwa Kisiwani, some miles farther down, were taken on September 7th, while Mikindani, Sudi Bay, Lindi, and Kiswere were all occupied before the close of the month. The penning in of the Germans in the interior was thus accomplished, nor did it seem at all likely that any assistance could reach them from oversea. A strong column was landed at Kilwa, which General Smuts made into a base of operations in the south-east, his intention being to assemble the 1st Division there later, with a view to its taking part in a great encircling movement south of the Rufiji.

Brilliant work of the Belgians

West of Saranda the whole of the Central Railway to Lake Tanganyika was taken from the Germans by the joint work of the British and the Belgians before the close of September, 1916. As far back as July 29th the Belgian 110th Regiment and a Belgian flotilla, forming part of the force under Colonel Olsen, one of General Tombeur's two chief subordinate officers, had captured Ujiji and Kigoma, and on the following day another part of the same force occupied Ruchugi, nearly seventy miles farther east on the railway. During these operations the Belgians killed over a hundred of the enemy and took some European prisoners. Among the spoil were two of the Königsberg's guns. In the first weeks of August Olsen's column was moving steadily eastward on Tabora, one of the main points on the line, and a strong enemy centre, towards

THE UNION JACK FOR IRINGA.
General Northey, marching from the south-west of the colony towards the Central Railway, occupied Iringa, August 29th, 1916. Lieut-Colonel Murray is seen advancing to take the surrender of the town.

which also the Lake Force, under Sir Charles Crewe, and Colonel Molitor's Belgians were marching from the north-west, the one from Misungi, south of Mwanza, and the other from Biaramulo and Niemirambe, in the southern Victoria Nyanza region.

General Crewe had arranged with General Tombeur that their forces should advance simultaneously from Victoria Nyanza along the two roads that converged on Tabora, the British taking the eastern route through Ivingo and the Belgians the western through St. Michael. But transport difficulties, the bane of the Allies in German East Africa, caused delay, and Crewe did not reach Ivingo till August 7th, while Molitor, though he captured St. Michael on August 12th, and got into touch with Crewe, was not able to concentrate there before the 22nd. The Germans had taken up strong positions in the Kahama Mountains, south of St. Michael, and for a while stoutly opposed the Belgians, but were cleverly driven out by turning movements, and compelled to withdraw towards Tabora by the end of

RELIEVED OF HIS POST.
The German commandant of Bukoota, who was taken prisoner when the British captured the German fort.

August. The British arrived at Shinyanga on the 30th. In the meantime, Olsen's column from Ujiji, having gained Ugaga on the railway on August 14th, was approaching Tabora. The Belgians had transported railway material across Tanganyika from Lukugu to the Central Railway, and on the 25th ran their first train along the track to supply their troops, then in contact with the enemy on the east. Brisk actions took place on September 1st and 2nd, some twenty miles west and south-west of Tabora. Tombeur, thereupon, pushed forward Molitor's force from the north with all speed, so as to co-operate with Olsen, and after stubborn and almost continuous fighting the town fell to the Belgians on September 19th.

Over a hundred British prisoners of war, most of whom had been interned for two years, were found in Tabora, among them being several women. The conditions of the camp were frightful. When, towards the end of 1916, a number of the released arrived in London, they **German cruelty to British prisoners** told a story as revolting as anything appearing in all the horrible records of German Kultur.

East of Tabora General Crewe's advanced guards occupied the railway at Igalulu, about a week after the fall of Tabora, and gradually the British linked up all along the line eastward. A portion of the enemy force which had been driven out of Tabora retired southward into the Itumba Mountains, while the remainder also withdrew to the south by way of Sikonge. From their headquarters at Tabora the Belgians harried the retreat of both German columns, who were making off in the direction of the Great Ruaha River in order eventually to form a junction with the main German forces on the Mahenge plateau. With their disappearance the Central Railway from end to end was in the possession of the Allies in less than three months from the capture of the Usambara Railway.

In July, as was noted, General Northey was marching from the south-west of the colony towards the Central Railway via Iringa. After winning some small engagements

A company of the 1st King's African Rifles on parade in an open space somewhere in the region of Lake Nyasa, East Africa.

Learning the art of modern warfare. Stalwart men of an ancient race at the musketry butts. Right: Units of the King's African Rifles drilling in Central Africa. This notable regiment took part in the conquest of Kilimanjaro under General Sheppard.

Native troops erecting palisade fortifications somewhere in East Africa. There was no dearth of timber available for such defence works. Right: Tree-trunks sawn into logs about ten feet in length formed effective barricades against raiders. Native troops at work under British officers.

COLOURED SOLDIERS UPHOLDING THE GREAT WHITE CAUSE: KING'S AFRICAN RIFLES IN THE SERVICE OF THE EMPIRE.

Copyright.

MAP SHOWING THE LINES OF ASSAULT DEVELOPED AGAINST THE CENTRAL RAILWAY.

General Smuts' strategy devised distinct but related lines of attack upon the Central Railway. In the east, General Hoskins moved towards Mrogoro; in the centre, General Van Deventer worked from Kondoa Irangi towards Dodoma; in the north-west, General Crewe moved from Mwanza towards Tabora, which also was the objective of Colonel Molitor's Belgian troops. Colonel Olsen's Belgian force operated from the north and south of Lake Tanganyika, and General Northey worked north-eastwards from the top of Lake Nyasa.

Northey fought a considerable action on the 24th of that month at Malangali, and completely routed the enemy, who hastily retreated to Madibira and to Iringa   In the following month Northey occupied Lupembe on the 19th and Iringa ten days afterwards, but the latter town might have been taken much earlier had it not been that General Smuts advised him to slow down while the line of retreat of the Germans from the railway was still uncertain. It was towards Malangali and Iringa that the enemy retired after being forced out of Tabora, and had definitely lost the railway. The part of Northey's command which had taken Lupembe moved on to the Ruhudje River south-west of Mahenge, and that which had captured Iringa remained there and near the Ulanga River, north-west of Mahenge. In that area Northey, in conjunction with Deventer from the Great Ruaha River, was assigned the difficult task of preventing the Germans from Tabora from breaking through to the east to join up with their main body under Col. Lettow-Vorbeck on the plateau.

On October 27th, 1916, General Smuts said that the net results on that date of all the various co-ordinated operations of the Allies were that the Germans had been driven south over the Central Railway, and, with the solitary exception of the Mahenge plateau, out of every healthy or valuable part of what had once been their premier colony, while on the east they were cut off from the sea, and on the south a Portuguese army had advanced north of the Rovuma River. The enemy was hemmed in on all sides, but the end was not yet.

TORPEDO PRACTICE FROM

A TORPEDO-BOAT DESTROYER.

WAR BY SEA: THE GREAT DEVELOPMENT OF GERMAN U-BOAT PIRACY IN 1917.

By H. W. Wilson, Author of "Ironclads in Action."

Great Britain's Utter Dependence on the Sea Her One Source of Weakness—Wheat Failure and Inclement Weather Favour German Designs—Leakage in the British Blockade through Neutral Countries—Gravity of the Food and Economic Situation in Germany—German Determination Fortified by Hopes of the Submarine Campaign—Destroyer Raids from Zeebrugge—Aeroplane Raids on England—Zeppelin Raid on Kent: L39 Destroyed at Compiègne—"Tip-and-Run" Raids—British Naval and Air Attack on Zeebrugge: German Destroyer G88 Sunk—The Great Fight of H.M.S. Swift and Broke with Six Large Destroyers—The Gena Torpedoed by a German Seaplane—Fine Reconnaissance Work of the R.N.A.S.—First Aeroplane Night Raid on London—British Naval Forces Destroy Zeppelin L22 in the North Sea—The Vital Menace of the Submarine—Admiralty Shipping Returns and German Claims—The Story of the Alnwick Castle—German Attacks on Hospital Ships: The Asturias, Gloucester Castle, and Salta—Reprisal Raid on Freiburg—Cowardice of the Prussian Guard Prisoners on the Torpedoed Lanfranc—Detention of the Wounded in France—British Transports Sunk—Naval Resources of the United States at the Time of Their Intervention in the War—Practical Co-operation of the Atlantic Fleet—Changes at the British Admiralty.

THROUGH the spring and early summer of 1917, while the army fought army, blockade was matched against blockade, the Allies pressing Germany with surface ships and Germany pressing the Allies with submarines.

In the submarine blockade, the cumulative effect of which to February, 1917, was dealt with in Chapter CLXXI. (Vol. IX.) the Germans placed all their hopes upon the fact that Great Britain depended on the sea for her supplies of food and raw materials, for munitions and for manufacture. They aimed not so much at completely cutting off all sea-borne products from her as at rendering them so scarce and expensive as to destroy her industries and strain her population beyond endurance. The problem presented by the British food supply and the measures taken to deal with it will be dealt with in a subsequent chapter. Here it will be enough to say that since the days of the Napoleonic Wars, when Great Britain fed herself, she had come to rely on imported food to an enormous extent. In 1916, on the eve of the intensified submarine blockade, the British imports of food

SIR ERIC GEDDES.
On the reorganisation of the Admiralty Staff in May, 1917, Sir Eric Geddes was appointed Controller of the Navy with the temporary rank of Vice-Admiral.

totalled £419,000,000 in value, and included four-fifths of the wheat consumed in the country. In addition, large quantities of food were imported by the British Government for the use of the Army, and did not appear in the returns. In this utter dependence on the sea were Great Britain's feet of clay.

Two natural causes assisted the Germans in their blockade. Throughout the world there had been a failure in 1916-17 in the wheat harvest, which totalled only 94,750,000 tons, against 110,800,000 tons in 1915-16. There was thus an initial shortage of about 15 per cent. in the available supply. This was the more serious matter because in war more food is eaten. The shortage would have sent up the price of bread had there been no blockade. A second complication which favoured Germany was the extraordinarily inclement weather of 1916-17. The late autumn was wet and cold; the winter was one of intense severity accompanied by frequent snowfalls. The spring was unusually late. The bad weather caused the failure of the potato crop generally in Western Europe. The British crop in 1915-16 had been 7,540,000 tons, which met all the needs of the population.

CLEARED FOR ACTION AND FULL SPEED AHEAD IN THE NORTH SEA.

British cruiser showing almost the whole depth of her keel as she rushes full speed ahead through the choppy seas. From the stern of the vessel, from which this fine photograph was taken, it will be seen that the vessels were "cleared for action." The cruisers that kept watch and ward in the North Sea only had occasional "scraps" with units of the German Fleet, while they were waiting for a general and decisive engagement.

In 1916-17 it sank to 5,473,000 tons, a reduction of nearly 30 per cent. Through the want of home-grown potatoes there was a heavier run on imported foods, and an increased strain on the British merchant service.

The weather filled Germany with ecstasy; indeed, they saw in it positive proof that their "old God" was working in their interests, though in actual fact the failure of the crop extended to Germany and affected her even more severely. Their calculations were thus set forth by the "Frankfurter Zeitung" early in May.

Optimistic German calculations

It is beyond doubt that the anxieties of our enemies are already very great, and it is certain that these anxieties must increase greatly, even if they surmount the present crisis. They will be faced by another bad harvest in North America, which is still their chief source of supply of corn. They will still be faced by the steadily increasing want of ships. We, on the contrary, can obtain what is urgently necessary from our own resources, and we have also at our disposal fruitful acres and rich herds in Northern France, Courland, and Lithuania. Above all, we have the soil of Rumania, which we can retain until the peace, and which our armies can sow. We shall have relative want, but our enemies are moving towards absolute want. They desired a war of attrition. They will regret it because, if only we do not now give way, the exhaustion of the world's supplies of food will bring peace in other fashion than they had calculated, and that perhaps more quickly than at present appears.

The Germans controlled a continuous area of territory with every variety of climate, and, when once they had organised agriculture on a large scale in the conquered territories, believed that they could easily produce enough food to feed themselves. In the spring of 1917 they had not by any means reached that position. But the blockade which the surface fleets of the Allies inflicted on them had up to that date been very far from complete. Germany had been able to import enormous quantities of food from neutral States on her frontier. The "Washington Times" spoke bitterly of the "hocus-pocus" by which people in

Holland and Denmark "put imported food on their table," and "slipped their own dinners out to Germany by the back door." It was a process that had continued on a gigantic scale for two and a half years under the very nose of the British Foreign Office, which strictly limited the activity of the British cruisers. Statistics officially published in France asserted that while from Denmark there went to Germany in 1913 only 1,448 tons of pork, 3,341 of lard, 106 tons of fat, and 113 of preserved meat, in 1916 14,280 tons of pork, 96,720 of lard, 72,000 of fat, and 100,800 tons of preserved meat were sent to Germany. From Holland the export of foodstuffs to Germany in 1916 was placed at 1,200,000 tons, including immense quantities of fish, meat, butter, eggs, and cheese. The figures were similar in the case of Switzerland, where the export of cereals to Germany rose from 228,000 tons in the first nine months of 1913 to 1,155,000 tons in the same period of 1916. The German Navy could smile at these results. It showed no mercy to neutrals, and sank their ships remorselessly, but it reaped extraordinary profit from British tenderness to them.

It is true that in 1916 little food was imported by these neutral States. They imported, however, great quantities of raw material for food in the form of fertilisers and feeding stuffs for cattle. Thus Denmark imported 150,000 tons of soya beans, most of which probably went later to Germany in the shape of lard or bacon. The entry of the United States into the war at last destroyed this trade;

Incompleteness of British blockade

but, unfortunately, Germany had been given time to make her arrangements. It has repeatedly been pointed out and, indeed, is hardly denied by the officials of the British Foreign Office and Admiralty—that a severe blockade from the opening of war would have brought Germany's collapse. If Mr. Asquith's Government neglected the most powerful weapon that it possessed, surely it must have been because Ministers were obsessed by mistaken theories of war and were not well advised by their Naval Staff. The people who had agreed to the Declaration of London showed by that act a strange misconception of the value of a navy and the power of a blockade.

The policy which could have been followed was to put to the neutral States adjacent to Germany these alternatives: " Either cease altogether exporting foodstuffs to Germany, or cease importing." Holland and Denmark were capable of maintaining themselves on the products of their own soil. But not until the late spring of 1917 was this course taken—years too late—and then it was necessitated by the loss of shipping destroyed by the enemy in the submarine campaign. A last chance of bringing Germany down by a close blockade in the winter of 1916-17 was probably lost by this delay. The fact was disclosed by Herr Batocki, the German Food Dictator, that the German potato crop had been a complete failure. In 1915-16 it was 50,000,000 tons. In 1916-17 it sank to 20,000,000 tons. In 1915-16, after allowing potatoes for distilling alcohol (required for munition factories) and for feeding cattle, a surplus of 40,000,000 tons had remained

German potato crop failure for human consumption. In 1916-17 the quantity available was only 16,000,000 tons, a reduction of 60 per cent., though it was still about three times the quantity available in Great Britain. Had the blockade been impervious, it is doubtful if Germany could have survived.

Even with the defective blockade the strain on Germany was intense, though Austria, Bulgaria, and Turkey were, so far as these weak vassal States would permit, stripped of their food in the German interest. The early months of 1917 were marked by many official admissions of the gravity of the food situation in Germany. In March, for example, Herr Michaelis, the Prussian Food Commissioner, stated that there was a great shortage of provisions, and that the outlook was dark. He predicted that the result of a food census (which had just been taken) would show that there were even lower stocks of food than had been believed, and that yet more drastic restrictions on consumption would be necessary. Herr Schorlemer, the Prussian Minister of Agriculture, warned the Prussian Parliament not to **Food restrictions** expect any improvement in 1917, as **in Germany** there would be a smaller area of potatoes and beet under cultivation, and the output of milk and butter, which had already fallen, would yet further decline.

The conditions were worst in the large towns; best in the country districts, where the pressure of hunger was scarcely felt at all. In Hamburg, in the severest weeks of the winter, a price of £3 had to be paid for 100 eggs of a very doubtful kind, and in Stettin it was officially admitted that the output of the working class had fallen 25 per cent. owing to underfeeding. Food was deficient in quality as well as quantity. Ptomaine poisoning, caused by eating unsound meat, was unusually rife. Owing to want of green food, scurvy broke out in some districts. Some of the substitute foods which had been introduced (there was a substitute coffee, and a substitute marmalade) proved to be not only nauseous but also injurious to life.

Demands were pressed by the trade unions for larger rations, on the plea that the output of factories was falling through underfeeding, and the German Chancellor agreed to continue during severe weather an additional meat ration of rather less than a quarter of a pound per week. German bread then consisted of 55 per cent. of rye,

GERMAN NAVAL BATTERY IN POSITION ON THE COAST OF FLANDERS.
Sea-pointing German gun near Westende, not far from the end of the enemy line in Flanders. The British maintained from the air so constant a photographic reconnaissance of the coast that it was said not a spadeful of earth could be turned over, not a trowel of cement added to a bastion, but a note appeared a day or two later in the long chart which was brought daily up to date at headquarters.

35 per cent. of wheat, and 10 per cent. of other materials (by which any edible root was meant), but was on the whole better than it had been. Bread, which could only be bought with bread tickets, was, for the cheapest quality, 8d. a loaf of slightly over 4 lb., so that it was distinctly cheaper than wheaten bread in London. Owing to the wholesale forgeries of bread tickets, which could be bought by those who knew where to go, the well-to-do could get as much bread as they wanted, if they were ready to traffic with the criminals. The bread

German Government and labour ration was reduced on April 15th, amid outcries from "Vorwärts," which declared that " the British blockade makes the import of provisions from foreign markets impossible and imposes on us heavy privations." The German public, however, was bidden to remember that the reduction would only last a few weeks, till the new harvest. The reduction was felt the more because the ration of potatoes had been cut down to ¾ lb. a day per head on account of the bad crop, and in some localities to less than ½ lb. a day. No general increase in the allowance of meat was possible. In Saxony, indeed, the weekly ration, including sausage and fat, was reduced from 9 oz. a week per head to 7 oz., though for men in laborious trades 13 oz. was allowed. The price for a goose in Berlin was between £4 and £5. Even herrings had become almost unprocurable, costing 9d. to 1s. each, but this was probably due to the severe weather in the early spring, to the bad catches of the Swedish, Danish, and Dutch fishermen, and to the purchase of their fish by Great Britain.

The Germans, however, were buoyed up in their hardships by the firm belief that Great Britain was on the brink of starvation and the submarine campaign a most dazzling success, and, after the Russian Revolution, by the expectation of a speedy peace on the eastern front. The temper of the people was indicated by the letter of an officer, who said that the Germans would hold out for another year

Now, however, there were indications of considerable unrest in the munition factories. On April 16th over 300 munition works were idle in Berlin and the district, and 210,000 men were on strike, according to the statements of " Vorwärts "—the State-controlled Socialist newspaper. The trouble was ascribed to the difficulty of obtaining food. Neutrals arriving from Germany asserted that 35,000 men were on strike in Hamburg. In the coal-mining districts it was alleged that many thousands of men had ceased work. Swift and summary measures were taken. Instructions were given that if the strikers did not return to work by April 21st they were to consider themselves ordinary soldiers and would be treated as such. The

[Crown copyright reserved.

THE ADMIRAL COMES ABOARD.
Boatswains piping the arrival of Admiral Madden aboard H.M.S. Royal Oak, one of the ships of his squadron.

munition works in the Berlin district were placed under military law. The obedient and patriotic German at once submitted. The men were reported back at work on the 22nd. Some disturbances occurred in the German shipyards, as was admitted by Admiral von Capelle in the Reichstag early in May, but he added that work was speedily resumed.

At the end of May the German ration of food in most towns stood at 8 oz. of meat a week, 3 lb. of flour or 3½ lb. of bread, 3 to 4 lb. of potatoes supplemented by swedes or turnips, slightly over 2 oz. of butter, 1 oz. of margarine, 3¾ oz. of rice, and 3¾ oz. of barley;

[Crown copyright reserved.

PUBLIC RECOGNITION OF A BRAVE MAN'S GALLANT DEED.
One dark night in midwinter Boy Batty fell overboard, whereupon Leading-Stoker Shaw jumped after him and rescued him. The Royal Humane Society awarded its medal for life-saving to Shaw, to whom it was presented by Admiral Madden, in presence of the entire ship's company.

even if they had to eat wood. Many reports reached Holland and Great Britain of strikes and riots, some of which were said to have been of a serious nature. Down to this date the German working man had shown extreme docility, and done whatever the military party told him to do without question or remonstrance, and there had been nothing more dangerous than raids by hungry women upon food-shops in such cities as Hamburg. These had been repressed with the customary German severity.

while during the early spring only one egg per fortnight was allowed. These rations were not always procurable in the quantities specified. They and very many other articles could only be obtained by card. In the case of working people, and especially of munition workers, larger rations were allowed, and there was an extra allowance for the young. A promise had been made of an increase in the ratio of meat to 1 lb. a week, but there seems to have been difficulty in carrying it out.

German organisation was so thorough, and such careful steps were taken to assist extreme poverty that the labouring class did not suffer so much as might have been expected. On no point was unbiased evidence so difficult to obtain. One United States official, who left Germany late in the spring, said that while the Germans were usually hungry they had actually improved in health, because they were no longer able habitually to over-eat themselves. This seems to have been too optimistic a view. Dr. Keuchenius, a Dutch specialist in nerve disease, who left Berlin in May, said that the workers were suffering less than the lower middle class owing to the high wages paid in the munition factories. He thought there had been a deterioration in physique, but he declared that the determination of the German nation was unfaltering as ever. Germans still believed that they had been treacherously attacked by Russia.

One certainty emerged from the conflicting accounts of German conditions—that the chief source and stay of Germany's determination was the hope entertained of the submarine campaign. Had this been ably met and promptly crushed in the early spring of 1917 the Germans might have given way. Unfortunately, for many weeks the German submarines were unexpectedly successful.

The submarine campaign was energetically supported by the action of German surface ships, which nowhere were more constantly on the offensive than at Zeebrugge.

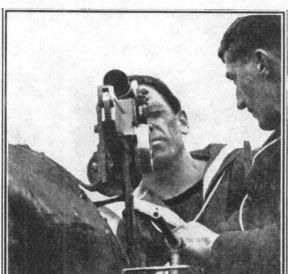

MEN BEHIND THE GUN.
Spotter and gunlayer on a British battleship—two of the most important units of the gunnery staff passed out of gunnery establishments for distribution through the Grand Fleet.

The powerful German destroyer flotilla which was stationed there was commanded by officers who incessantly attacked, and it was not completely paralysed—as might have been hoped—by the British Navy. The approaches to the port were heavily mined by the Germans, and the mine-fields were commanded by their powerful shore batteries, to the shelter of which they could always retire when the North Sea became too hot for them.

On Sunday, February 25th, the Zeebrugge destroyers came out, under Commanders Tillesen and Albrecht, and steamed unopposed to the British coast. According to the official British report, they were off the coast of Kent about 11.15 p.m. and fired at long range on Broadstairs and Margate. They opened their proceedings by discharging star-shells, which lighted up the country as though it had been under the beams of a searchlight. At Broadstairs the bombardment lasted ten minutes. A cottage near that town was hit and a woman in it was killed, while her baby was mortally wounded and three other children were injured. At Margate the attack lasted six minutes, and did remarkably little damage. Most of the shells fell in fields, and while three or four buildings were hit, in no case were they much harmed. The Germans claimed to have pushed into the Channel beyond the Dover-Calais line and to have reconnoitred the Downs. They alleged that they had encountered and driven off a force of British destroyers in the Channel, inflicting on them several direct hits, and that they had

POWERLESS FOR FURTHER EVIL: A PIRATE'S END.
On November 5th, 1916, the German submarine, U20, of 750 tons, ran ashore in a gale near Harboöre, on the west coast of Jutland, and began to break up. Seeing that it would be impossible to get her off, her crew subsequently blew her up.

FF

HONOURABLE SCARS OF THE VICTOR IN A DEEP-SEA DUEL.
British destroyer in dry-dock for repairs after having successfully rammed a German submarine. The force of the impact is strikingly indicated by the damage which had been done to the destroyer's bows.

engaged in these attacks were probably watching shipping in the Channel; but they wantonly attacked undefended seaside towns, and no attempt was yet made by the British authorities to retaliate or deter the German airmen from these assaults upon women and children by reprisals on German towns. On March 16th there was another aeroplane raid on the Kent coast, this time near Margate, where a few bombs were dropped without doing any damage.

It was possibly in connection with the German operations against shipping that the first Zeppelin raid of the spring took place. On the night of March 16th three Zeppelins crossed the Kent coast-line and dropped a number of bombs on British soil, but without causing any injury

returned without sustaining loss or damage. Sir Edward Carson, in the House of Commons, gave a different account of the affair. He said that one British destroyer had encountered a force of several German destroyers, and that, although she came under a "very heavy fire," she was not damaged. "The enemy vessels," he said, "were pursued, but were lost in the darkness." While this skirmish was in progress a separate German force had attacked Margate and Broadstairs, but on British vessels steaming to the scene of firing the Germans were found to have already withdrawn.

This British official account showed, at least, that the British, at an important point, were inferior in force to the Germans, and that, though these sorties from Zeebrugge were becoming a matter of regular routine, a method of making them exceedingly dangerous to the Germans had not yet been devised. In all the raids up to that point the Germans had escaped with comparatively little damage; but they had contrived to inflict considerable injury on the British flotillas.

Destroyer sorties from Zeebrugge

In part, no doubt, this was due to the strictly defensive policy which had been adopted by the British in the Channel.

The Germans were able to deal their blows and to get away after delivering them. They contrived to bombard towns and villages on the Kent coast, while the British strategists were seemingly unable to give the people of those towns and villages security. The plan of watching the wasps' nest of Zeebrugge itself does not seem to have been adopted, no doubt for good and sufficient reasons, but with painful results for the people of Kent.

The destroyer attacks were accompanied by aeroplane raids, which were attempted at intervals when the weather was specially favourable. On March 1st, early in the morning, a German aeroplane dropped several bombs at Broadstairs, most of which fell into the sea. One dropped in a garden and another outside an infants' school, fortunately without serious injury to anyone, though one person was slightly wounded in the head. The aircraft

[*Canadian War Records.*

BATTLESHIP TAKING IN STORES.
Busy scene on board a British super-Dreadnought. The maintenance of supplies to the Fleet which watchfully awaited the opportunity of meeting the enemy was carried on with unfailing regularity.

to property or loss of life. The hostile airships wandered about apparently uncertain of their position, and made grotesque reports to Berlin of their achievements.

They did not all escape. One of the three, L.39, a super-Zeppelin of the same type as those destroyed with such precision by the British airmen in 1916, appears to have been hit by anti-aircraft fire, or to have had an engine failure.

A strong northerly wind sprang up during the night of the 16th-17th, and this swept her south into France. She was seen at Beauvais, at 4.30 a.m. in the morning of the 17th, at a distance of about forty-five miles north of Paris, when she was flying slowly towards the German lines. She was near Compiègne at 5.30, and the French airmen and artillery were ready for her. At that time she was moving very slowly indeed at a height of 10,000 feet. A French aeroplane was up chasing her, but it drew off to allow the guns to attack her. Fire was opened on her with incendiary projectiles, which burst all round her. At 5.40 a "75" shell struck her framework near the stern. A line of blue flame ran along the top of the gasbags and spread rapidly. In the light of early day she could be seen blazing aloft,

[*Canadian War Records.*
GUNNERY PRACTICE ON A CRUISER.
Firing practice aboard one of the light cruisers of the Arethusa class which had been added to the British Navy in the year of the outbreak of the war.

[*Canadian War Records.*
GREAT BRITAIN'S FIRST LINE OF DEFENCE.
Guns of a British battleship as seen from the fighting-top—formidable weapons which the German High Sea Fleet evinced an intelligible reluctance to meet.

like a gigantic torch, and then, as the gas was consumed and its lifting power was dissipated, the whole structure buckled and fell, still burning. A large part of it, probably the forward gondola, detached itself and struck the ground first. Three or four of the crew leaped from it as it came down. They were instantly killed. The

rest of the airship and the twenty men in her fell with a great crash in a piece of waste ground, where the wreckage lay blazing, with the body of the captain on the top of the débris. The L39 had previously dropped her bombs, but the machine-gun ammunition on board her continued to explode for some time. It was noted that she carried inflammable bullets, although the Germans—who first introduced them in 1914—had had the impudence to complain of their employment by allied airmen. This was the first Zeppelin victim of the Allies in 1917, but the Germans had by March learnt that their airships were of trifling value for offensive work by land, and were beginning to keep them out of the reach of the allied airmen and gunners.

Early in the morning of March 18th a number of German destroyers from Zeebrugge approached the Kentish coast and shelled one of the towns there, firing nine projectiles in three minutes at Margate. Two empty houses were wrecked by one shell. Another **British destroyer** house was hit and badly damaged; but **torpedoed** the wife of a soldier who lived there had left it with her baby on the previous evening, feeling, strangely enough, a presentiment that some disaster was about to happen. The Germans succeeded in inflicting another loss on the British Navy. About the time when the bombardment began a number of German destroyers discovered and attacked a British destroyer east of the Strait of Dover and fired a torpedo at her, sinking her. She also fired a torpedo, but without effect. She went down with all her officers and all her crew but eight men. While another British destroyer was endeavouring to rescue men from the water, she, too, was torpedoed, but was stated not to have been "seriously damaged." The Germans also claimed to have sunk a steamer of 1,500 tons in the north part of the Downs. Once more they escaped intact, and reported, probably with truth, that they had returned "free from damage and casualties."

A few days later, on the 26th, they made yet another raid, this time steaming to Dunkirk and viciously shelling that port, which is only forty miles distant from Zeebrugge.

first occasion on which an aeroplane had been employed in attacking British towns during the hours of darkness.

A novel attack was delivered on certain German destroyers which were lying outside Zeebrugge on April 7th. The British Admiralty announced that two German destroyers had been torpedoed, and that one of the two was undoubtedly sunk. The fate of the other was not definitely ascertained, but she was severely damaged, if she was not sunk. The destroyer sunk was G88, one of the new and powerful torpedo craft completed for the German Navy since the outbreak of war, and brought openly down the North Sea in spite of the British Fleet. She was of much the same type as the destroyer driven into Ymuiden, but was of even later build, and was reported to steam about thirty-five knots and to carry four semi-automatic 4·1 in. guns. The Germans stated that she was sunk by a British submarine, and that many of her crew were saved. This naval attack was accompanied by an air

BRITISH T.B.D. TORPEDO PRACTICE.
Crew, wearing life-belts in case of accident, getting into the whaler to go and recover a torpedo which had just been fired.

They arrived about two a.m. and fired about sixty shells, which did some damage but only caused slight loss of life. Two persons were killed. The firing only lasted three minutes, and when the Dunkirk flotilla put to sea the German torpedo craft are said to have steamed off at thirty-five knots. Their superiority in speed and the absence of any strict blockade of Zeebrugge enabled them to engage in these "tip-and-run" raids, the object of which was undoubtedly to weaken the prestige of the British Navy exhibit it to neutrals as unable to protect its own coast, and attract the attention of the largest possible number of destroyers and British small craft, thus assisting the German submarines indirectly.

On March 28th the German destroyers were out again. On this occasion they claimed to have cruised close to the British coast, and their claim was indirectly confirmed by the British official statement that "some firing was observed some miles off shore from Lowestoft. Our patrols were sent to the scene at utmost speed, but nothing was seen of the enemy, who had made off." The Germans stated that they sank the British armed steamer Mascot (apparently the armed trawler of that name) and took seven of her crew prisoners. They added that they saw no British naval forces and no merchant vessels. This was an unfortunate month for the British Navy, as the loss of two destroyers was announced late in March. One had struck a mine in the Channel (probably laid by a German submarine) and gone down with all the crew except four officers and seventeen men. The other had been sunk in collision with the sacrifice of one life. A few days later the destruction of a mine-sweeper "of an old type," with twenty-four of her crew, was announced.

German destroyers torpedoed

An air raid of a new kind took place on the night of April 5th, at 10.45 p.m. It was a beautiful, clear moonlight night, and the opportunity was seized by a German aeroplane to visit the Kent coast. Eight bombs in all were dropped, but in every case harmlessly, doing no more damage than breaking some glass. Night aeroplane attacks had become common enough on the front, but this was the

SWINGING A TORPEDO ON BOARD A T.B.D. AFTER ITS RECOVERY.
Incident in torpedo practice on board a British destroyer. After it had been fired at its "target," a boat's crew was sent off to secure the dummy torpedo. By constant practice the men of the British Navy attained a degree of deadly accuracy with the real destructive weapon.

attack carried out by the Royal Naval Air Service. Many bombs were dropped on the Zeebrugge Mole and on ammunition-dumps near, at Ghent and Bruges, in co-operation with the Royal Flying Corps. The damage done to Zeebrugge, however, was not such as to destroy, or even seriously to affect, its value as a naval base. A fortnight later the German flotilla which had its headquarters there was again active. The hope that a vigorous, sustained offensive against Zeebrugge would follow was not fulfilled.

On the night of April 20th the German destroyer flotillas came out of Zeebrugge in great force and proceeded into the Channel. One section of them opened a heavy fire on Calais, throwing about five hundred shells into that port, killing two women, injuring about a dozen people, and doing considerable damage. Six of the German destroyers steamed towards Dover and opened fire on the town, but only hit a ploughed field. So far the British Navy had not appeared on the scene. The Germans, after these bombardments, claim to have sunk a British "outpost" vessel, by which they probably meant a trawler or small armed drifter. Many of these were employed in the Strait of Dover, and they depended for their safety upon the activity and energetic support of the Royal Navy. As the German destroyers were still unchallenged, they "cruised towards the outlet of the Channel." Then at last they met the British, but the British Navy was in greatly inferior force.

Against six large German destroyers, all seemingly of

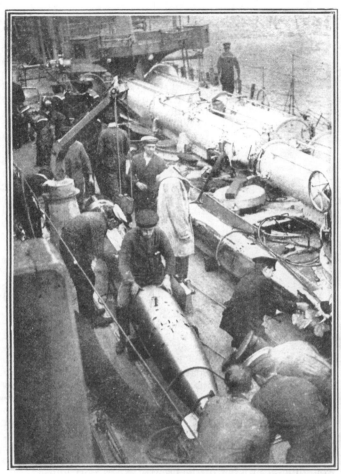

Cleaning and readjusting torpedoes on board a destroyer after they had been employed in practice-firing.

Torpedo retrieved after firing. The smoke was caused by the action of water on a charge of calcium carbide in its head.

Sailors on board a torpedo-boat destroyer hauling at the davit-falls to bring aboard a recovered torpedo.

Explosion of a mine which, having been located by the crew of a mine-sweeper, was destroyed by a rifle-shot.

TORPEDO AND MINE PRACTICE IN THE BRITISH FLEET.

KEEPING THEIR HANDS IN FOR THE JOURNEY'S END.
British soldiers on board a troopship bound for a distant front—note the sun helmets and the "shorts" which some of the men were wearing. The squad lying prone was engaged in practising the proper positions for carrying on rapid firing.

the latest type, there were but two British vessels. These two were the Swift and Broke. The Swift was the first of a class of large and very swift flotilla-leaders (or vessels built to act as the flagships of destroyer flotillas), but had never quite come up to the expectations entertained of her. Her nominal speed was 35 knots, and she mounted four 4 in. guns on a displacement of 2,170 tons. She carried a crew of 150 officers and men, and was thus about twice the size of an old-fashioned destroyer, though probably not much larger than the German vessels against which she was to be matched. The Broke was a large flotilla-leader of about 1,800 tons, which before the war had been laid down for the Chilian Navy, and after the war had been taken over by the British Government. She mounted six 4 in. guns, had a nominal speed of 31 knots, and carried a crew of 160 officers and men. She was equipped with six 21 in. torpedo-tubes, against the Swift's torpedo armament of four 18 in. tubes. Commander A. M. Peck commanded the Swift ; Commander E. R. G. R. Evans, famous as an Antarctic explorer, the Broke.

It was 12.40 a.m. when the Swift sighted the Germans on her port bow, proceeding east at great speed, only six hundred yards away. The night was very dark, and as the Germans were made out they, too, saw the British, and the sound of their gongs calling the crews to general quarters (the battle stations) rang down the line and came over the water. They opened fire. The Swift, which was steaming ahead of the Broke, replied at once, and Commander Peck determined to close and ram the leading German vessel. The wheel was wrenched round, and the Swift, running at high speed, dashed at the foremost German destroyer, which was steaming between 20 and 30 knots. The operation, as was pointed out in the official account issued of the engagement, was an exceedingly delicate one. " An initial miscalculation of a few degrees of helm, a few revolutions of the propellers more or less, spell failure. Failure may, and probably does, mean being rammed by the next boat in the enemy line." The Swift missed her quarry. The German boat manœuvred well. The British vessel was not, however, caught by the second destroyer in the German line but passed unscathed through the narrow gap between in the line and, turning, fired a torpedo which hit a German

Gallantry of H.M.S. Swift

destroyer. She then made a fresh attempt to ram the leading German destroyer. A second time she missed. The German boat made off into the darkness, the Swift in eager pursuit.

While this fierce encounter was in progress the Broke was furiously engaged. As the Swift turned, the Broke discharged a torpedo, which ran straight at the second German destroyer and hit her, exploding well. Then the Broke opened fire from every gun that would bear and —after waiting a minute or so to gather speed, as the German boats were stoking vehemently and a dull glare was showing from their funnels—swung round to ram the third German destroyer. The Broke struck her with a great crash full on the side, abreast the after-funnel, which in the largest German destroyers is about the centre of the vessel, but did not cut her in two or sink her then and there. The two boats were locked together, every man in each firing at the other at point-blank range, while the undamaged German destroyers also fired their hardest into the Broke. It was a fight sterner than most of the sea-encounters of the Napoleonic Wars. A shell hit the Broke's bridge at the very opening of the struggle, killing and wounding several men on it, and also wounding a number of the crew of No. 2 port gun.

Midshipman Gyles, who was stationed forward, was struck by a fragment of shrapnel in his right eye and was wounded in his right leg and arm. Stunned by the force of the blows, he was thrown down on the deck. An instant later, recovering himself, he found the blood pouring from his eye and face. He wiped it away, and most gallantly scrambled on to the forecastle, where of eighteen men who composed the two forward gun-crews only five were left alive. They were aided by Able-Seaman Ingleson, whose gun was out of action ; and the six men and Midshipman Gyles between them loaded and fired both forward guns. While they were thus engaged a number of Germans boarded from the rammed destroyer. They scrambled up, yelling and frantically shouting something the Broke's men could not understand. Midshipman Gyles met the rush, levelling his automatic pistol at them, and ordered them forward, apparently intending to take their surrender. Suddenly a huge German lunged at him, seized his arm, and tried to wrench the pistol from him. There was a hand-to-hand scuffle. Fortunately the gun-crews had cutlasses and rifles with fixed bayonets ready. Petty-Officer Woodfield struck at the German, who eluded the blow. Then Ingleson drove his cutlass through the German seaman's body and ended the fight. The man's body was hurled overboard, and the rest of the Germans were flung into the water or secured and made prisoners. Two were found skulking forward feigning death.

The steersman of the Broke, Able-Seaman Rawles, behaved as magnificently. A projectile burst near the wheel (probably the same shell that wounded Midshipman Gyles), and four fragments hit him in the back and on each leg, but though dazed, bleeding from all these wounds and severely shaken, he remained gallantly at his post, taking orders from Commander Evans through the speaking-tube. With the words, " I'm going off now, sir," he revealed to the captain his wounds and his critical condition. He fainted as the engagement closed, about five minutes after the Broke had fired her first shot

Great fight of H.M.S. Broke

Three German destroyers still remained in line when the Broke swung clear of the sinking German destroyer which she had rammed, and, turning, endeavoured to ram the last German boat in line. She missed, unfortunately, but struck another German destroyer on the very bow with a torpedo, apparently only inflicting slight damage. As all the German flotilla had now taken to flight, she followed them towards Zeebrugge. At this juncture she was hit in the engine-room by a shell, which disabled her main turbines. She drifted down towards the destroyer which she had previously rammed. The German vessel was badly on fire and the crew were screaming for mercy. The Broke could only move with difficulty and approached it slowly, notwithstanding the risk that its magazines might explode, in order to take off its crew. The Germans were shouting "Save! Save!" in a frenzied manner, but they behaved with their usual treachery. As the Broke drew close they opened fire. The British vessel was no longer under control, but she was able to deal a death-blow to the German. She fired four shots, and then discharged a torpedo which hit the German vessel amidships and sent it to the bottom.

Triumph of Swift and Broke The destroyer which the Broke had torpedoed early in the fight was sinking at some distance from the Broke when the Swift returned from her chase of the other German destroyers. The injuries she had received in the initial stage of the action had reduced her speed and rendered it impossible for her to overtake her enemies. Her crew in the darkness sighted a stationary vessel and heard from it the confused sound of many voices shouting together in time. Knowing the methods of the German Navy and its disregard of honour, the Swift approached, keeping her guns trained on the damaged destroyer. The Germans were yelling in unison, "We surrender! We surrender!" The Swift avoided closing and waited. The German destroyer heeled over and sank stern first, and then the Swift turned on her searchlights, after the enemy had vanished, and proceeded to rescue the men swimming in the water. While this work was in progress the Broke, whose electric circuits were out of action, flashed the news of her share in the engagement by an electric torch to the Swift, and the crews of the two destroyer leaders cheered one another.

Their conduct had been worthy of the greatest traditions

BURIAL OF SAILORS WHO FELL IN A CHANNEL FIGHT.
Impressive scene at the graveside where sailors, soldiers, and civilians gathered to pay tribute to the men of H.M.S. Swift and Broke who had fallen in their great fight on April 20th, 1917.

RESCUED ENEMY SAILORS.
German sailors saved from the sea by men of the Broke and Swift after their striking victory in the Channel.

of the British Navy. In all the war there was no finer example of judgment on the part of the commanders and courage and steadfastness on the part of the men. There was none of the defensive spirit about Commanders Peck and Evans. Yet they did not rashly take extravagant risks. They attacked the Germans with such skill as to do their work with the minimum of loss, and though both the Swift and Broke necessarily suffered in the engagement, important results were secured. The Germans admitted the loss of destroyers G85 and G42. Both of these were new vessels, built in 1914

ON BOARD H.M.S. DESTROYER LEADER BROKE.
Bridge and deck of H.M.S. Broke, showing two of the 4 in. forward guns. In the early hours of April 20th, 1917, the Broke (Commander Edward R. G. R. Evans, C.B.) and the Swift (Commander A. M. Peck) had a victorious fight in the Channel against six German destroyers.

or subsequently, displacing something over 1,000 tons (according to some accounts 1,500 tons), and mounting in all probability four 4·1 in. semi-automatic guns. Their speed was alleged to be 35 knots, and it was certainly sufficient to enable them to escape from the older British destroyers, which had speeds of 29 or 30 knots. The German Navy thus suffered a sharp blow, though the British public was hoping for news that the whole Zeebrugge squadron had been destroyed.

The loss inflicted by the Swift and Broke showed what might have been expected had the British been in equal or superior force to the Germans. In that case all the six German destroyers should have been cap-

Honours for officers and men tured or sunk. In all, ten German officers and one hundred and eight men were picked up from the two vessels which were sunk, but of these apparently thirty died after being got on board the British ships. They were buried on April 24th, when some comment was provoked by the Vice-Admiral commanding at Dover sending a wreath to the "brave and gallant" enemy, epithets which, after the bombardments of defenceless towns, the treachery shown to the Broke, and the abominable crimes of the German submarines, were universally regarded as misplaced.

The Germans claimed to have sunk the leading British ship, hitting her with a torpedo under the bridge, and to have torpedoed another British destroyer with three funnels. They asserted that they only retired when "other enemy ships appeared," and professed that they were much inferior in force to the British. Special honours were bestowed on the officers and men of the two British vessels.

Commanders Peck and Evans were promoted to captain's rank and received the D.S.O. Midshipman Gyles, Lieutenants Hickman, King-Harman, Despard, and Simpson, Probationary-Surgeons Helsham and Westwater,

BRITISH HANDY-MEN COUNTERACT GERMAN HANDIWORK.
It would seem an almost hopeless task to reproduce order from this chaotic scrap-heap. British handy-men, however, regard no ship as lost until it has been sunk, and can repair and restore to active use the most battered hulk that ever kept afloat. Above: British sailors engaged in salvage operations on a damaged vessel in the North Sea, the first job being to pump the water out of the flooded holds and prevent the inrush of more.

and Gunners Turner and Grinney received the Distinguished Service Cross ; Able-Seaman Rawles was given the Conspicuous Gallantry Medal. In granting these distinctions—which were accompanied by special promotion for both the engineer officers, Lieut.-Commanders Hughes and Coomber—the King added : " I have much pleasure in approving these awards in recognition of the splendid action of the Swift and Broke. . . Officers and men did more than uphold the grand traditions of the British Navy."

The Zeebrugge hornets were only scotched and not killed. On April 21st, the morning after this brilliant action, a small British airship was destroyed in the Strait of Dover. The vessel in question was apparently one of the so-called "blimps" (an aeroplane fuselage attached to a gasbag, carrying two or three officers and men, and used for reconnaissance and observation on the British coast).

Aeroplane destroys a British "blimp" According to the official account, an aeroplane was observed near her, and soon afterwards she was " seen to descend in flames." As she was at a considerable distance from her proper position, it was surmised that her engine had broken down, and that she had drifted a long distance before the wind, which on that day was blowing from the north-west with considerable strength. Search was made at the place where she had disappeared, but no more trace of her or of the men in her could be found. It was obvious that they perished when she fell. She was of a type which was not meant for offensive work, and was not designed to resist aeroplane attack, so that, if employed within the zone of hostile aircraft action, she needed an escort.

On the afternoon of April 23rd the German destroyers at Zeebrugge once more put to sea ; but their movements were at once observed by British reconnoitring aircraft, whereupon three British naval machines, carrying bombs, were despatched to attack them. Five German destroyers were overtaken on a north-easterly course, between Blankenberghe and Zeebrugge, five miles from the coast, at 4.10. The leading British machine at once attacked, dropping sixteen bombs, one of which was seen to hit a German destroyer. The other four destroyers **British aircraft rout destroyers** scattered to avoid the attack, but thirty-two bombs were dropped on them by the other two aeroplanes, apparently without obtaining any hits. After all the bombs had been dropped and the airmen had done their work, one of the German destroyers was seen to have a list to port and to have stopped. The other four closed round her. Meanwhile, a German seaplane came out to attack the British aircraft, but was easily beaten off. Reconnoitring aeroplanes saw four destroyers enter Zeebrugge at 6.10. What had become of the fifth is not known. The Germans did not admit her loss, but she had vanished, and it is therefore not improbable that she sank ; though, if so, this was the first occasion on which a surface vessel was sunk by a bomb from aircraft.

On the night of April 24th the German destroyers were again at sea. According to the German report, under the

CHEERFUL CONFIDENCE AND EFFICIENCY IN A SOMEWHAT CRITICAL CASE.
Ships have their human personality, and this damaged vessel resting quietly alongside the unit of the British Navy that has come to her aid suggests the acquiescence and confidence in the event with which the human victim of an accident awaits the curative treatment of a trusted surgeon—the smiling naval officers and unhurried sailormen representing the cheerful efficiency of a trained hospital staff.

GG

CREW OF A BRITISH MINE-SWEEPER.
Men of the mine-sweeping service with their small craft carried on their work of incalculable value with the greatest heroism. They faced constant peril while seeking for and destroying floating mines, and did so without any of the glamorous excitement attendant upon actual fighting.

A new weapon, which had for nearly two years been in the possession of the British Navy without, so far, being employed in large-scale operations, was now turned against Great Britain by the Germans. It was announced on May 3rd that on the previous day "the British steamer Gena was sunk by a torpedo discharged from a German seaplane off Aldeburgh. Another seaplane concerned in this attack was brought down by gun fire from the Gena, and the crew were made prisoners." The Germans stated that "a number of our seaplanes attacked enemy merchant ships off the Thames, and sank a large steamer of about 3,000 tons." The Gena was, in fact, a vessel of 2,784 tons, and she was attacked by two seaplanes, one on each side. She fired at and disabled one, but the other, which had alighted on the water, discharged its torpedo and sank her.

An aeroplane armed with a torpedo-tube had been designed and patented in England shortly before the war. Unfortunately, the Admiralty Staff of that period had not appreciated the value of aircraft, and its conservatism prevented the construction on a large scale of an appliance that might have been used very effectively in the earlier months of the war. Much comment was aroused by this incident, and the Admiralty announced that seaplanes armed with torpedoes had been actually used by the British forces in the Dardanelles campaign, and had sunk Turkish vessels. The Germans had in this way obtained information of the existence of this new weapon—which they were not clever or **Aeroplanes armed** inventive enough to devise themselves— **with torpedoes** and, with their usual patient imitativeness, they immediately adopted it and employed it. Their air services were not handicapped by conservative views or the belief that aircraft were little more than elegant toys.

The method of attack with a seaplane was thus described in the "Daily Mail": "The torpedo could be fired either from a tube, which is a form of gun, or from a special launching apparatus. The seaplane, when firing it, might be in the air, though then the chance of a hit would not be great; or it might fire after alighting on the water at a safe distance from the ship, but within torpedo range of her. A torpedo of 5,000 or 6,000 yards' range could be carried in view of the size and power of modern seaplanes. The accuracy of the torpedo, fitted with the gyroscope (or contrivance for automatically keeping the torpedo to the line of direction) was great. When the torpedo had been fired the seaplane could rise from the water and be gone like a flash."

The day on which this historic event took place a British destroyer struck a mine in the Channel, and was lost with one officer and sixty-nine men. Aircraft, at least, were free from the mine peril, and in daylight had extraordinary range of vision from the height at which they could cruise. Their weakness in gun fire was accompanied by elements of strength in other directions. While the war showed sea-power to be losing much of its value, it incessantly emphasised the importance of air-power and the necessity

orders of Captain Assmann, they attacked the port and town of Dunkirk. Star-shells were fired first of all to light up the place, and then some three hundred and fifty shells were discharged into the town—not, as the Germans pretended, at the batteries and forts. After this bombardment, during which "two destroyers, apparently French," arrived, they attacked these two vessels and sank one with gun fire. They also claimed to have destroyed a patrol vessel, but added that they could not rescue any of the crew of either vessel, owing to the heavy fire from Dunkirk. The German flotilla admitted neither damage nor loss. According to the French report, it withdrew at great speed towards Ostend when French and British patrol vessels arrived.

Two nights later the Germans steamed towards the Kentish coast and heavily bombarded Ramsgate. Over one hundred shells were fired, and though many of the projectiles fell in the country, twenty-one houses were damaged and two persons were killed, while two **Zeebrugge flotilla's** were wounded. This was the third raid **busy week** carried out by the Zeebrugge flotilla in a week. On the 20th it had bombarded Calais and had lost two destroyers, but had escaped annihilation; on the 24th it had bombarded Dunkirk and sunk a French destroyer and a patrol trawler; on the 26th it had shelled Ramsgate and got away without a scratch. The evidence given at the inquests on the victims showed that the shelling of Ramsgate continued for ten minutes, and that the alarm was given after the attack was over. That same night twenty-eight shells fell in Margate, severely damaging one house, but causing no injury to any human being. Other projectiles fell in St. Peter's. The jury invited the coroner to forward to the Admiralty an appeal for greater protection to be given to the district in view of the recurrence of the bombardments.

ENG. LT.-COM. J. HUGHES. R.N.,
MENTIONED IN DESPATCHES.

LT. R. KING-HARMAN.
D.S.C., R.N., H.M.S. SWIFT.

LT. G. V. HICKMAN, D.S.C., R.N.,
H.M.S. BROKE.

CAPT. EDWARD R. G. R. EVANS,
C.B., D.S.O., R.N., H.M.S. BROKE.

CAPT. AMBROSE M. PECK. D.S.O.,
R.N., H.M.S SWIFT.

ABLE-SEAMAN E. INGLESON,
D.S.M., H.M.S. BROKE.

ABLE-SEAMAN W. G. RAWLES,
C.G.M., H.M.S. BROKE.

MID. DONALD GYLES, D.S.C.,
H.M.S. BROKE.

Officers and men "who did more than uphold the grand traditions of the British Navy."
—H.M. King George.

HH   247

Mammoth "tips" emptying 20=ton railway trucks of coal at one time into colliers.

Triumphs of marine engineering: A 200=ton crane lowering a boiler into a liner.

Hun tricks at sea: Raider's double decoy of S O S signals and sham fire aboard.

U.S. destroyers beating off German submarines while escorting the Adriatic to Queenstown.

Replenishing the bunkers: Coal being taken aboard from lighters at sea.

Battleship undergoing repairs in the floating dry=dock of a great English shipbuilding yard.

of developing in the most strenuous manner and with the utmost boldness the construction and design of aircraft. With a proper supply of aircraft there was no reason why Zeebrugge, instead of being bombed once a month, should not have been kept under a continual bombardment ; and why its destroyers, instead of being left free to harry the British coast, should not have been constantly attacked from the air in their own lair. What some observers in touch with airmanship had foreseen before the war had come true. "The seaplane was Britain's best weapon"—at sea. Unfortunately, they had not been able to convince the British Governments of 1913, 1914, and 1915.

But though the flying navy had hardly put off its swaddling-clothes, and though the officer representing it on the Admiralty Board was the Fifth Sea Lord (and not the Second), though its work had as yet not been co-ordinated with that of the surface and submarine navies, so that it did not bring the immense results that might have been looked for, it still did something to annoy the Germans.

Reconnaissance work of the R.N.A.S. A constant photographic reconnaissance of the Belgian (though not of the German) coast was carried out. "The work in progress at Ostend and Zeebrugge," stated an account of its operations, "the activities of submarines and destroyers inside the basins, locks, quays, and gun emplacements, and the results of bombs dropped thereon the night before, were all faithfully recorded by aerial cameras. The negatives were developed and printed, the resultant bird-pictures enlarged, studied through stereoscopic lenses, and finally given to the monitors for information and guidance. Not a spadeful of earth can be turned over nor a trowel of cement added to a bastion along the coast but a note appears a day or two later in the long chart." Great heroism and magnificent airmanship were displayed by the officers of the Royal Naval Air Service who carried out these reconnaissances. The best of material was available, and only waiting to be used. And many were the fights with German machines, whirling along at a speed which was rarely less than 100 miles an hour, and might be much more, and many the victims on both sides.

On the night of May 7th the first German night air raid was made with aeroplane on London. A solitary aeroplane appeared soon after midnight and dropped four bombs in a residential district. Some slight damage was done ; one man was killed and a woman was injured. Few people in the capital would have known anything of the affair but for the newspaper notices and the official report. The aeroplane escaped, though the night was very fine and bright. It had committed an act of mere murder. No military purpose whatever was to be served by wantonly dropping a few bombs from an immense height on a part of London where there were no munition works of any kind. No attempt at reprisal was yet made by the British Government or military authorities, but the fact remained that the certainty of swift and effective reprisals was the only protection against such attacks.

On May 10th, under Commodore Tyrwhitt, one of the most enterprising and energetic squadron leaders in the British Navy, a force proceeded towards Zeebrugge, acting in combination with British aircraft, which very early that morning bombed the port. Loud explosions were heard in Holland. The object of the attack was apparently to drive the German destroyers out to sea, and thus to give Commodore Tyrwhitt a chance of dealing with them. The Germans came out in due course. Eleven destroyers were discovered by the British light craft proceeding southward between the Dutch and British coasts in the North Sea. Chase was at once given to them, but the German boats were of the very fast type, built with the foresight which the German Naval Staff displayed, and went off at great speed under cover of a dense smoke-screen. For eighty minutes the pursuit continued, and the Germans were engaged at long range, but they could not be overtaken.

[Canadian War Records.

WITH THE GRAND FLEET IN THE NORTH SEA.
H.M.S. Lion with another battle-cruiser astern. The Lion, as the flagship of Vice-Admiral Sir David Beatty, played a great part in the Jutland Battle, when, said Sir John Jellicoe in his despatch on that battle, " Sir David Beatty once again showed his fine qualities of gallant leadership, firm determination, and correct strategic insight."

The British did not draw off till four of their destroyers had come within range of the Zeebrugge coast-batteries. The British loss was only one man wounded. The German destroyers were seen to be hit. The Germans professed that the British force was much superior—which it seems to have been—including light cruisers as well as destroyers, and alleged that when it retired they gave chase. In the bombing of Zeebrugge they stated that the British dropped sixty bombs, did no military damage whatever, and had two aeroplanes shot down.

On May 12th the "Vice-Admiral, Dover" carried out what was officially described as a "very heavy bombardment of an important area at Zeebrugge." A number of monitors were employed, with the special maps that had been prepared by the previous air survey, and a strong force of aeroplanes accompanied the warships and observed for their artillery. The fire, according to the Germans, was directed from "a great distance," and the weather was foggy, so that it is doubtful whether any very great result was obtained. The sound **Monitors bombard Zeebrugge** could be plainly heard on the British coast from 3 to 8 a.m., and it was also noted in Holland. No fewer than fifteen aerial engagements took place between British and German machines, in which four German aeroplanes, according to the British official account, were destroyed and five others driven down out of control. It was at first supposed that the attack marked the opening of continued operations against Zeebrugge, but this proved not to be the case. The French Press commented with a great deal of force on the policy followed :

Foresight (said the " Figaro ") would have dictated an unceasing renewal of the attacks. The enemy should have been harassed and allowed no rest. The attacks should have been persisted in until the new naval stronghold had been destroyed. But a contrary view has prevailed. Operations have only been carried out at periodic intervals. The fear of losses paralyses any energetic and continuous action. In war no success is obtained without losses. All that is necessary to know is whether the losses to be expected are worth the result achieved. Who could doubt the capital advantage that would have accrued to the Allies with Zeebrugge annihilated and made unfit to serve as a base for the German fleets? There should be no more of these periodic attacks.

These words expressed the opinion of almost the entire British public, who watched, without being able to understand, the desultory attacks on the German naval base. At the same time, naval force pure and simple has always been unable to attack fortifications with effect. It appears to be one of the few "iron laws" of war that for ordinary ships to contend with forts involves hopelessly disproportionate risks to the ships. Monitors were repeatedly tried against forts in the American Civil War, and invariably failed.

The practical comment on the sanguine accounts of the damage inflicted at Zeebrugge which were published in England was the speedy reappearance of the German destroyers at sea a week later. They were sighted off Dunkirk by a patrol of four French destroyers early on

the Schleswig airship sheds of March 25th, 1916, when three British seaplanes and a good British destroyer were lost, with trifling damage to the Germans—had the German aircraft been attacked so near their own coast. The airship in question was L22, and though there is some uncertainty as to her exact pattern, she appears to have been a vessel of the large type, but not of the largest, such as the super-Zeppelins of the L30-39 build. She was probably equipped with five propellers (against the six of the L30) and engines of **Zeppelin destroyed** about 1,000 horse-power (against the **in North Sea** 1,440 horse-power of the latest airships)

She was seen from the Dutch coast majestically sailing through the air early in the morning of the 14th at a height of about 4,000 feet, north-east of the island of Terschelling, some forty to forty-five miles from the German island of Borkum. A little later she was seen north-north-west of Terschelling. After that the noise of firing was heard, and observers noted that the airship had suddenly been shrouded by heavy clouds of smoke, from which flashed flame, and over the sea came the sound of a tremendous detonation. A haze near the sea prevented the spectators from learning what became of her, but presently the cloud had gone, and with it the airship. That same day the British Admiralty made the curt announcement: "Our naval forces destroyed Zeppelin L22 in the North Sea this morning." This was the end of the German Zeppelin command of the air over the North Sea, and an event of historic importance. The German Fleet could no longer cruise in safety covered by the reconnaissance of its Zeppelins. That the German Admiralty, however, would make the most determined effort to recover control of the air was to be foreseen, and was a risk against which the British Admiralty was bound to guard with energy, insight, and vigilance.

GERMAN DISREGARD OF THE RED CROSS.
On the night of March 30th, 1917, the British hospital ship Gloucester Castle was torpedoed without warning by the Germans in mid-Channel. Fortunately, the weather was good, and succouring craft protected the crippled ship from further injury, while the four hundred and fifty wounded aboard and the staff were rescued.

The exact method in which L22 was destroyed was not officially disclosed. But the Paris "Matin" stated a few days after this event that she had been cut off by a squadron of British seaplanes and set on fire after an engagement of a few minutes. Two of the crew fell into the sea, it added, but the rest were burnt in her.

The power of the Zeppelin had gone. It is true that a few days later, in the night of May 23rd-24th, five Zeppelins, in cloudy weather, stole over to the British coast, where they dropped several bombs on the Norfolk seaboard. But they were careful not to venture inland, and they only killed one man. The cloudy weather prevented effective attack on them by the British aircraft.

Through all these weeks the German submarine war on Great Britain and on neutrals continued with varying result. Now at last Great Britain fought for her very life. Yet the fact was still obscured from the knowledge of her people by contradictory statements on the part of Ministers and by the misleading manner in which the statistics of losses were issued. A nation which knows that it is fighting for life will put forth unexpected strength, but it cannot be said that Great Britain really knew. And thus, amidst the sinking of ships and the agony of British seamen, the strikes and squabbles which rendered the industrial history of the war so melancholy and dispiriting

May 20th, while it was still dark, and were engaged, but they made off at full speed without loss or damage after injuring a French destroyer.

The Germans, throughout the naval war, owed very much to the work of their aircraft scouting over the North Sea. The unfortunate lack of foresight on the part of the British Admiralty had, as has been previously stated, left the British admirals in the position of blind men fencing with an antagonist who had full possession **Zeppelin air** of his sight. The supremacy of the **supremacy ended** Zeppelins as scouting craft over the North Sea area had been favoured by the policy which failed to attack them resolutely so soon as they put to sea. This state of affairs was, however, beginning to alter, though very slowly, by the late spring of 1917. The Germans had already discovered that airship raids over British soil meant funeral parties for the Zeppelin crews. They were now to find that other perils awaited them in the North Sea. On May 14th a brilliant piece of work was accomplished in destroying a Zeppelin close to her lair. Never before—except in the futile raid against

continued with unabated violence. Significant of forces more injurious to the nation's honour than even the successes of the German submarines was a prosecution, on March 6th, of a Birmingham munition worker, named William Slim, for "writing a note to a fellow-workman urging him to take his time, and make the job on which he was engaged last the week."

At the end of February the publication of the returns of ships lost, and the number of ships arriving and sailing weekly, was begun by the Admiralty. The figures were correct, but unsatisfactory because of two faults. They did not disclose the tonnage of shipping sunk, and tonnage was one of the most important factors. The loss of fifteen ships, averaging 3,000 tons and totalling 45,000 tons, mattered less than the loss of ten ships averaging 8,000 tons and totalling 80,000 tons. The second defect was that the sailings and arrivals necessarily exaggerated the number of ships moving, and made the percentage of loss seem smaller than it really was. The same ship might figure more than once if she went from port to port. People were improperly reassured when they saw that in the first week of March 2,528 vessels of all nationalities over 100 tons

Admiralty returns of shipping in displacement had arrived at British ports, and 2,477 had sailed from them, while only 14 British vessels of and over 1,600 tons and 9 under 1,600 had been sunk. It looked as though the week's losses only represented $\frac{1}{2}$ per cent. of ships sailing from and arriving at British ports. Men did not reflect that $\frac{1}{2}$ per cent. a week is 25 per cent. in a year (or one-fourth), or that neutrals and Allies were included in the ships arriving and departing, but not in the losses, though the losses, of course, included vessels sunk in the Mediterranean and Central Atlantic. While it was of extreme importance not to disclose to the Germans the precise name and description of the ships sunk, they knew approximately the tonnage destroyed, and thus the publication of the figures would have told them nothing.

After these limits and qualifications have been pointed

Return of the Möwe. The commander, Count Dohna-Schlodien, addressing his crew.

Crew of a British ship being taken as prisoners aboard the German Möwe after their own vessel had been sent to the bottom by the commerce-raider that so long eluded capture.

Prisoners, of whom on her return to Germany there were five hundred and ninety-three, on board the Möwe. They had been taken from the various peaceful vessels which the raider had sunk or captured

on her mission of destruction. Right: The crew of the raider, with some of the pets which they had taken from the ships they had destroyed. The photographs on this page are from an enemy source.

SCENES ABOARD GERMANY'S MOST SUCCESSFUL COMMERCE-RAIDER: THE MÖWE.

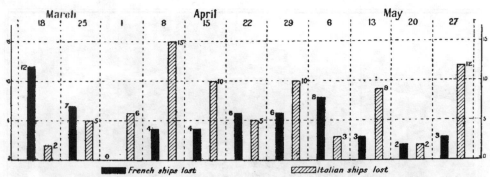

FRENCH AND ITALIAN LOSSES BY ENEMY SUBMARINES, 1917.
Diagram showing the destruction of French and Italian shipping through a period of the eleven most critical weeks. The fluctuations were more marked than in the British losses. Many of the Italian vessels sunk were very small craft.

out, the figures for the first three months of the blockade must be given, because of their historic importance, and because they afford, as it were, a bird's-eye picture of the campaign. They were:

1917.	All Ships at British Ports.		British Ships Sunk. 1,600 Tons and Over.	Under 1,600 Tons.	British Ships Unsuccessfully Attacked.
	Arrivals.	Sailings.			
Feb. 25	1,985	1,959	15	6	12
March 4	2,528	2,477	14	9	12
,, 11	1,985	1,959	13	4	16
,, 18	2,528	2,554	16	8	19
,, 25	2,314	2,433	18	7	13
April 1	2,281	2,399	18	13	17
,, 8	2,406	2,367	17	2	14
,, 15	2,379	2,331	19	9	15
,, 22	2,585	2,621	40	15	27
,, 29	2,716	2,690	38	13	24
May 6	2,374	2,499	24	22	34
,, 13	2,568	2,552	18	5	19
,, 20	2,664	2,759	18	9	9
,, 27	2,719	2,768	18	1	17

The campaign, then, fluctuated greatly from week to week. This was to be expected, because certain of the German submarine commanders were more skilful than others, and as every submarine had from time to time to go back to port to refit and rest her crew, there were periods during which the best commanders were absent. Moreover, the disclosures of the German Press showed that officers of exceptional skill or brutality in the art of submarine murder had disappeared, never to be seen again. Such a one was Lieutenant-Commander Petz, who sank 50,000 tons in a single day in February, and vanished in March. Their removal by the agency of the allied fleets and flotillas was an unpleasant interference with what Germans had come to regard as an agreeable and comparatively safe pastime. Weather certainly influenced the losses. Very cold and stormy conditions seemed to hamper the submarines, as also did very fine weather.

As to the German losses, Admiral von Capelle claimed in the Reichstag that in the first two months of the campaign, apparently February and March, only six submarines had failed to report, and stated that many

more than that number had been completed in the same period. His assertions could not be accepted as true, but it is not probable that in the early weeks of the campaign the British Navy was very successful. It had allowed itself to be surprised. For reasons which have been given, no one could be certain when a German submarine was sunk. If prisoners were captured —as they were still in some instances, notwithstanding the appalling barbarities of the submarine crews—that was proof. But there were necessarily many cases in which boats were sunk without any person escaping, and in these instances the British had no means of verifying or checking the loss of the boat. Oil on the surface was not a certain indication of a boat's destruction, as the oil-tanks in the German submarines were disposed in the outer hull, and could be damaged without the inner hull being breached. The real test of the Navy and of the Admiralty which controlled it was to be found in the losses. An efficient Admiralty would prevent all but a mini- **Uncertainty as to** mum of loss by harrying the submarines **results** and giving them no leisure to attack merchant shipping. It would show results from the first, because it would be ready to meet new German moves.

Undisturbed by peril, faithful to the great call of duty, receiving scanty honour and little attention from those who ruled the country, the officers and men of the British merchant service " carried on." Theirs was a page of unmatched glory in the troubled history of the war. They had not signed on to confront one of the deadliest perils

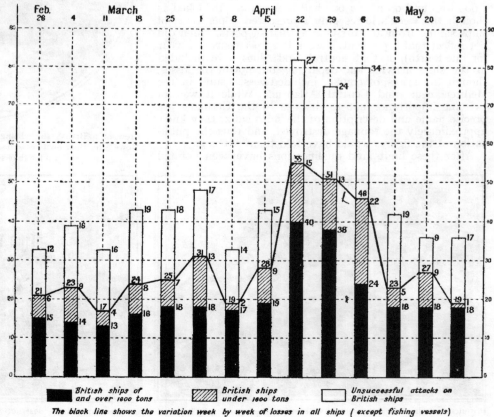

The black line shows the variation week by week of losses in all ships (except fishing vessels)

CHART OF THE INTENSITY OF THE SUBMARINE WAR, 1917.
This diagram shows the weekly losses of British shipping in the spring of 1917. The important figures are those of the losses, but the unsuccessful attacks also indicate the activity of the submarines.

known to mankind. They wore no military uniform and could look forward to no medals. For this reason their vocation was on occasions mistaken, and they were presented with white feathers and other tributes which, not unrightly, the women of England and Scotland showered on those whom they suspected to be shirkers. The speeches of politicians and even of naval officials could be searched, and would yield scarcely an inkling of the fact that during the most critical period of the war, when the Navy failed to give the protection expected of it, the merchant service rose to the emergency. Where so many faltered or fell below the occasion, its men were true, and this though their ranks had been depleted by the withdrawal of thousands of good officers and seamen for purely naval service, where they did magnificent work. They might have been a race of Drakes and Blakes and Nelsons, all of whom had served in the merchant service and ever admired it.

The sufferings which they often had to endure were shown in the case of the Alnwick Castle, whose commander, Captain Chave, wrote a report of his experiences which has already become a classic, worthy of the pages of **Story of the** Hakluyt. His ship was torpedoed with-**Alnwick Castle** out notice in the Atlantic on March 19th, three hundred and twenty miles from the Scilly Islands. Extreme precautions had been taken and a thorough look-out had been kept, there being at the moment of attack two look-outs on the foremast, a steward on the forebridge, two cadets on the lower bridge, and the chief officer himself and fourth officer on the bridge. The six boats were lowered immediately after the explosion as the ship sank rapidly. The submarine emerged, showing a conning-tower and gun, trained on the sinking vessel, but then went off in pursuit of another ship, which she destroyed. In one boat was a woman with her baby, left callously by the submarine criminals on the open sea. After dark the wind freshened and the twenty-nine souls in the boat suffered piteously. All the 20th they spent " fighting the sea, struggling with oars to assist the sea anchor to head the boat up to the waves, constantly soaked with cold spray and pierced with the bitter wind, which was now from the north." Their torments increased. Some of the men became delirious from cold and thirst and want of food. Once the boat was swamped by a breaking sea in the dark, and it seemed that the agony was over. " A moan of despair rose in the darkness," wrote Captain Chave, " but I shouted to them, ' Bale, bale, bale ! ' and assured them that the boat could not sink." They got the water under, and at last, on the 23rd, after five men had perished in the boat, the surviving twenty-four were picked up in the last stage of misery and exhaustion by a French steamer, which treated them with noble tenderness.

The case of the Alnwick Castle was typical of hundreds ; with the sudden explosion, the disappearance of the great ship, the miserable struggle for life in open boats on a stormy sea by men who had no comforts and no warmth, and who were exposed to the waves and the bitter cold, with every prospect of perishing of starvation and thirst. Many boats were never heard of again ; many ships vanished leaving no trace. What aggravated the infamy and inhumanity of the " brave and gallant " enemy was the German abuse of all laws regarded as sacred by seamen. The submarines persistently used the call of distress to attract other ships to them, when they callously destroyed these vessels. They tried even baser and more horrible stratagems. They set boats adrift, which looked as though they had human beings in them, poor derelicts of this war of murder, to which explosives and mines were attached. They disguised their submarines as fishing boats and ships' lifeboats, and hoisted in them the distress signal.

Attacks on hospital ships had been deliberately ordered by the German Admiralty, and were carried out with apparent enjoyment by the German submarine crews. The Note in which the German Government had publicly

KULTUR AT SEA : LURE OF THE GERMAN CORSAIRS.
A mean device of the pirates was to launch boats with dummy figures flying a distress signal. The pirate then submerged and torpedoed the first ship that came to rescue the apparently shipwrecked mariners.

intimated this barbarous intention on January 29th, 1917, has been mentioned already, and will remain as one of the most damning articles in the indictment against the Kaiser and Admiral Capelle. On the night of March 20th the British hospital ship Asturias, at which the Germans had fired a torpedo without making a hit in 1915, was torpedoed without warning and sank. She was steaming with navigation lights burning and with the Red Cross sign brilliantly illuminated, which, it need scarcely be said, made the work of the German miscreants much easier. She had nine hundred cases on board and a large number of R.A.M.C., nurses, and attendants. Forty-three persons, including two women, were killed and thirty-nine injured. The outrage had some importance from the light which it shed on British war organisation. The Government had announced in January that, if the Germans sank hospital ships, reprisals **German war on** would be taken. The hospital ship had **hospital ships** been sunk, yet the crime seemed to find the Admiralty without any definite plan of reprisal or redress. Further crimes followed, and illustrated the need of a stronger forethought department at Whitehall.

On the night of March 30th-31st the hospital ship Gloucester Castle was torpedoed in mid-Channel, and the fact was announced by the German Admiralty in the wireless report which it issued. On this occasion all the wounded were removed, including a number of German prisoners, and there was no loss of life. On April 10th the hospital ship Salta was sunk during very bad weather by a mine which German submarines had laid. There were no wounded on board, but nine nursing Sisters and thirty-eight of the R.A.M.C. were drowned. And still the reprisals did not come. The delay, combined with the losses to British shipping, strengthened the general conviction that changes were urgently required at the Admiralty.

At last, on the night of April 14th, the reprisals took place. They assumed the form of an aeroplane bombardment of Freiburg, in Baden, an important military centre and headquarters of the 29th German Artillery Brigade, where were large munition works, so that, quite apart from the crime committed by the German submarines, an attack on the place would have been amply justified. It was, in fact, much as though the British batteries at Arras had fired a few extra rounds at the German trenches. Three British machines were lost in the bombardment, which took place at five in the afternoon by German time, and, according to the German reports, resulted in the death of seven women and four men or soldiers, and in injuries to

twenty-seven men, women, and children. The German Government, which had killed and wounded some 1,200 women and children in the wanton bombardments of the North-East and South-East Coasts by Admiral Hipper's cruisers, in the Zeebrugge destroyer attacks, and in the cowardly Zeppelin raids, had the effrontery to complain that the British had attacked "an open town out of revenge." Its own "War Book," however, declared that military policy should be guided not by "sentimentality and flabby emotion," but only by "the fear of reprisals."

On April 17th a submarine attacked and sank the hospital ship Lanfranc, on board which were a number of British wounded and also of Prussian Guards **Sinking of the Lanfranc** taken prisoners by the merciful British Army in the Battle of Arras. The moment they heard the explosion all the Prussian Guards who could stand rushed for the lifeboats, to the general contempt of the nurses and British wounded. Howling and panic-stricken, they demanded first place, and tried to fight their way into the boats till they were beaten back. They managed to secure one, but they so overcrowded it in their miserable cowardice that it capsized when it reached the water and they were thrown out. They struggled with one another and tried to fight their way into another already overladen boat crowded with badly-wounded British. The British wounded showed their usual calmness and forbearance. That same night another hospital ship, the Donegal, was sunk with wounded on board.

HEROISM OF AUSTRALIANS ON BOARD A TORPEDOED TROOPSHIP.

It was on April 25th, 1917, that the homeward-bound troopship Ballarat, carrying a large number of the Australian Imperial Forces, was torpedoed by an enemy submarine when about thirty-five miles from land. Thanks to the magnificent steadiness and discipline displayed, which, as the official notification put it, "were in keeping with the finest traditions of the British Army," everybody on board was safely transferred to patrol craft.

Not the least sad feature of the story was that, when the Lanfranc's wounded were taken ashore and placed in a Y.M.C.A. hut used by British dockers, these dock labourers, who earned high wages in perfect security, grumbled and complained and were rough to the wounded who were in their way. For war brings out the best and the worst in men; and the best suffer for the worst, which is the law of human life. In the Lanfranc perished thirty-four souls, among them fifteen Germans; in the Donegal forty-one. Both ships were convoyed by destroyers.

The authorities now decided on a change of policy regarding the treatment of the wounded. The Navy, for the first time in the war, had met with failure in its efforts to protect the transport of men in the narrow waters of the Channel. New methods were necessary in view of this. Hospital ships were no **New methods** longer sent out ablaze with lights to **made necessary** enable the German destroyers to find and sink them readily. German prisoners were usually carried in them when they went to sea, as there was scarcely a day on which a number of men were not captured by the British forces. The British wounded were, as far as possible, treated in hospital in France and not sent home.

This course involved some hardships for the men, but it had the very important military result of keeping the railways clear behind Sir Douglas Haig for the movement of troops and munitions. With the large British armies at that date in France it was becoming increasingly difficult to move the Red Cross trains across the rear if any manœuvring was required.

Two more hospital ships were torpedoed in early May without further reprisals.

LINED UP FOR LEAVING THE TORPEDOED SHIP.
Within four minutes of the bugle sounding when the Ballarat was torpedoed every man was in his place and everything ready for abandoning ship. The men remained imperturbably cheerful in the hour of their peril.

The Navy in the early part of the war had generally been able to protect transports, but when the intensified submarine campaign became acute these also suffered. One of the most notable incidents of the war was the conduct of a battalion of the Middlesex Regiment in the Tyndareus, which struck a mine on February 9th off the coast of South Africa. The ship at once began to settle. The "Assembly" was sounded and the men put on their life-belts, paraded in excellent order, and at the command "Stand easy!" with death staring them in the face, they began to sing. They sang "The Long, Long Trail," and then "Tipperary." Lower and lower sank the ship, but the men maintained their calmness and their choruses, at intervals cheering the **The Birkenhead** captain, who upheld the noble traditions **tradition** of the merchant service by his firmness and skill. Help came in time, and they were rescued; the ship was eventually got into port not very greatly damaged.

Three British transports were torpedoed in the Mediterranean in April—the Cameronian on April 15th, with the loss of one hundred and forty lives; and the Arcadian, the same day, with a loss of nineteen officers and two hundred and sixty men. On April 25th the Ballarat was sunk with Australian troops on board, but in her case there was no loss of life. In the case of the Cameronian the heavy loss was in large part due to the violence of the explosion, which undoubtedly killed many of the troops and crew. The Cameronian's chief officer, Robert McBurnie, after exhausting his energy in getting out the lifeboats, had boarded a destroyer, when, seeing a man struggling in the water, he dived to the rescue and gave his heroic life to save another. In the Arcadian the wireless operator went

AWAITING THEIR TURN IN THE BALLARAT'S BOATS.
Australia's brave sons—worthy of the Empire's Birkenhead tradition—stood singing or engaged in chaff while waiting orders to take to the boats, responding to their colonel's "Be steady!" with "We're all right!"

AFTER THE EXPLOSION.
On February 9th, 1917, the Tyndareus, Captain G. Flynn, struck a mine off Cape Agulhas, 105 miles south-east of Cape Town.

down in the ship with the receiver on his head, sending and receiving messages, faithful unto death. Always the troops behaved with a courage and composure that covered them with glory. Not in one but in every instance was the heroism of the soldiers who met death in the Birkenhead repeated.

The sinking of neutral ships proceeded monotonously. On April 2nd, almost the eve of the United States declaration of war, the first American armed ship to sail for Europe was torpedoed. She was the Aztec, carrying two 5 in. guns, manned by gunners of the United States Navy, but as the attack was made on a stormy night they never saw the submarine, and were unable to fire. The Aztec went to the bottom very quickly, taking with her twenty-eight officers and men.

Some days later the first German submarine was fired at by an American armed ship. This was the Mongolia, which, while on a voyage to a British port, sighted a German submarine, when the American naval gunners on board opened and obtained a clear hit on the submarine. Much oil was seen after a violent explosion.

The United States declared war on April 6th. The incalculable historic importance of this event is dealt with elsewhere. Here its naval consequences have to be set forth. It placed on the side of the Allies a Navy of great strength with magnificent traditions, though unfortunately that Navy was weak in men. There were at the date of war no fewer than fourteen American battleships of the Dreadnought

type completed for sea, and most of these were vessels of extraordinary gun-power. In weight of metal the American Dreadnoughts were equal to the German Dreadnought battleships. Thus the force of heavy ships which the Allies now had available was so crushingly superior as to enable the High Commands to take risks which had previously been impossible or inexpedient to face, and to remove any excuse for want of enterprise. The British Battle Fleet in itself might be calculated to have had a superiority of over 60 per cent. in weight of metal, and now this further reinforcement was thrown into the scale and ready to aid it. In small craft the American Navy was relatively weak. The German 1916 "Naval Pocket Book" showed forty-seven large modern destroyers complete and sixteen older destroyers ready for sea, in addition to eleven large boats which were building. Another weakness was in the fast light cruisers, which had proved their value so remarkably in the war. Of these the United States Navy had only three. It was peculiarly well equipped in the matter of naval bases on the western side of the Atlantic, while the denial of the American ports to the German submarines was a very serious further blow to the pirate Navy. Probably that had been anticipated from the first by the German Staff, but it is also probable that they counted on obtaining secret aid from sympathisers in the United States. This now carried with it the grave penalties of treason.

The shipbuilding resources of the United States were great,

SAVED BY SEAMANSHIP: THE TYNDAREUS NEARING PORT.
The Tyndareus was carrying a battalion of the Middlesex Regiment, commanded by Lieut.-Colonel J. Ward, M.P. (above). All ranks displayed conduct which "upheld the splendid tradition of the Birkenhead," and by "devotion and perseverance" Captain Flynn brought his ship to port without loss of life.

FIRING THE 15 IN. GUNS OF A BRITISH BATTLESHIP.

[Canadian War Records.]

The Queen Elizabeth, completed in 1914, was the first British Dreadnought to be armed with 15 in. guns, of which she carried eight, representing 15,600 lb. weight of projectiles discharged by a single broadside. In theory a direct hit from a 15 in. gun will pierce nine inches of the best type of armour from a distance of eight miles. Practically, the biggest gun is the most accurate gun for long-range firing.

only surpassed by those of Great Britain and Germany, and they were not, like the British and German yards, affected by the withdrawal of hundreds of thousands of able-bodied workers for service in the fighting ranks. The output of merchant tonnage a year was estimated at over 1,200,000 tons, while warship tonnage could also be produced with reasonable speed. Though many of the great American engineering and munition works had, prior to the declaration of war, been engaged in work for the Allies, the Government arsenals and dockyards, which had not hitherto been employed to anything like their full power, were now available. In addition to this, one hundred and nineteen German and Austrian ships of 719,000 tons were in American ports, and were promptly seized, repaired, and put into use.

Naval results of U.S. intervention

The total strength of the American naval personnel before the war was about 66,000 officers and men, which was the strength of the German Navy in 1912.

The first attack upon an American warship was made on April 17th, when a submarine fired at the destroyer Smith a hundred miles south of New York. The torpedo missed the Smith by thirty yards, and the submarine, which was running submerged, disappeared. The German Admiralty subsequently declared that no German submarine was on the western side of the Atlantic, but to such a statement no value could be attached, in view of the German record for mendacity. Early in May a powerful contingent of American destroyers, which had

been detached from the American Atlantic Fleet and despatched to Europe, arrived in a British port, and was welcomed with the greatest enthusiasm by the British Navy. Sir David Beatty, commanding the Grand Fleet, telegraphed this message in honour of the event, and of the glorious comradeship of the two great Navies:

> The Grand Fleet rejoices that the Atlantic Fleet will now share the task of preserving the liberties of the world and maintaining the chivalry of the sea.

To which Admiral Henry T. Mayo, commanding the Atlantic Fleet, replied:

> The United States Atlantic Fleet appreciates the message from the British Fleet, and welcomes the opportunities for work with the British Fleet for the freedom of the seas.

The Atlantic Fleet further undertook the patrol of the Western and Southern Atlantic, thus freeing large British forces for work in the North Sea.

This help came most opportunely at one of the critical moments of the war, when to all appearances the German submarines were fulfilling the hopes that the German Staff had entertained of them. They were being turned out, according to an able American official who left Germany late in March, at a maximum rate of ten a month. There were then, according to his information, three hundred submarines in existence ranging from 300 tons to 1,500 tons. The smallest type of submarine mine-layer does not seem to have been included in this estimate; it operated mainly from Zeebrugge and infested the Channel

Atlantic fleet gets to work

259

and southern parts of the North Sea. The submarines, this authority stated, were constructed in sections at Barmen, Elberfeld, Düsseldorf, and other manufacturing centres, and were then sent to Hamburg or Stettin to be assembled. There were usually sixty submarines at sea at any given time, and as these returned or were captured or sunk others took their place.

No respect was shown by the German commanders for humanity or international law. On April 4th the Brazilian steamer Paraná was torpedoed and sunk with heavy loss of life ; and, failing to obtain any satisfaction, Brazil seized all the German shipping in her ports, a total of 240,000 tons, and opened her ports to allied warships. On April 10th, the Argentine Government in a Note recorded its con-demnation of German submarine prac-tices ; but, despite this protest, placed an embargo on the export of grain, thus hampering the Allies. The turn of Spain came next. On April 10th the Spanish steamer San Fulgencio, with a German safe-conduct, was sunk without warning, and the Spanish Government, which had hitherto maintained a masterly inactivity, protested vehemently. Nor was the slightest regard shown for the limits of the " danger zone." Several steamers flying the Norwegian flag were sunk in early April off Bergen, which was well outside. No State suffered more cruelly than Norway. In the single month of April she lost seventy-two ships destroyed by the pirates, some of them in Norwegian territorial waters, and many of them outside the " danger zone." In all, since the outbreak of war, she had lost four hundred and seventy-six vessels of 675,000 tons by the end of May, 1917. Sweden, despite the strong anti-Ally sympathies of her upper classes, did not escape. Three Swedish steamers carrying food to Sweden were wantonly sunk, with the loss of ten lives, in May.

Utter disregard of Neutral rights

Through all this, while State after State broke off relations, the Germans continued their insolent boasting over their crimes. Never did a people so preen itself on its infamy. At the close of April, Admiral Capelle declared that all expectations had, been confirmed, that the reduction of allied tonnage was proceeding with mathematical regularity, that the U boat war had " hit the vital nerve of England." Dr. Helfferich, the German Minister of the Interior, announced that 1,600,000 tons of shipping had been sunk in February and March, of which 1,000,000 were British, and that the British Government dared not disclose the facts. Admiral Capelle, on May 9th, stated that not less than a million tons had been sunk in April, and said that while the Staff had calculated upon a total destruction of 1,800,000 tons in the first three months, the tonnage actually sunk had been 2,800,000, and the number of ships 1,325. Moreover, the German submarines were constantly growing in skill and experience ; their weapons were being improved ; new boats and new torpedoes were constantly being completed ; officers and men crowded forward for submarine service ; the losses were small beyond expectation, and the British reports of large numbers of U boats destroyed were false. In the better weather of the summer even higher figures of destruction were to be expected. The tone was confident, even jubilant.

A state of affairs in which the Germans sank fifty British ships a week and 1,000,000 tons of shipping a month made the British command of the surface of the sea a mockery, and must have been speedily fatal to an island State. Anxiety as to British naval policy deepened. It was pointed out in the Press that the Admiralty, as it existed at the opening of the war, as it still remained in that fateful April when the destinies of nations trembled on the knees of the gods, was not a good instrument for the conduct of operations. Critics alleged that no member of it had studied deeply the scientific side of war. Yet science was everywhere conquering. The British Admiralty doubtless included many able officers, but they were, said the reformers,

specialists—gunnery men, torpedo men—rather than strategists. The War Staff was alleged to be comparatively uninfluential, the humble subordinate of the Board, which was at once unwieldy and oddly composed for the control of so highly technical a business as naval war.

Five Sea Lords, all of them naval officers, figured on the Board ; but, instead of being free to consider strategy, they were said to be for the most part overwhelmed in administrative detail. The First Sea Lord had in practice to look after most things, for all the business was centralised to a remarkable degree. The Second Sea Lord was in charge of personnel ; the Third Sea Lord attended to material ; the Fourth Sea Lord controlled supplies ; the Fifth Sea Lord directed the Naval Air Service. In addition to these there were five civilians on the Board, the First Lord, Civil Lord, Additional Civil Lord, Parliamentary Secretary, and Permanent Secretary, the last one of the most powerful figures in the organisation. This was not an Admiralty of the kind which had fought and won the great wars of the remoter past, but a body which had been designed for peace conditions and their own convenience by politicians. Naval strategy was left very largely to chance and hurried decisions. The Chief of the Staff, Sir Henry Oliver, had held his office since the autumn of 1914, through a period when there had been frequent warnings that a great submarine campaign was imminent. Yet the success of the German U boats seems to have come on the Admiralty as a great surprise.

The nation and its Allies naturally asked for results in the shape of submarines sunk and British ships protected from attack. Victory or defeat hung in the balance. Whether it was to be victory or defeat for the Allies depended ultimately on the British Admiralty and, at the British Admiralty, on the ability of the War Staff to foresee German moves, to parry them when made, to co-ordinate the naval action of the Allies, to meet the submarines with such energy, skill, and resource as to overcome them. The chief charge brought against the Admiralty in the Press was that it had played for safety rather than victory, and that, as the result of playing for safety, as many ships and lives had been lost as would have given victory. Now there was overwhelming force available owing to the addition of the United States Fleet to the allied forces, so that on no theory was ultra-caution necessary. The question put was whether the Admiralty could change its whole habit of mind and cast of thought—could turn instantly from the passive defensive to an active and resolute offensive.

The first requisite of such a change was a good Staff, to plan operations systematically and scientifically. A department similar to the Ministry of Munitions in the War Office was created under a new official—though his title was old—the Controller. To this post a civilian, Sir Eric Geddes, was appointed with rank of a vice-admiral. Vice-Admiral Oliver became an additional member of the Admiralty Board with Rear-Admiral A. L. Duff, who had previously been in charge of the anti-submarine operations, under the respective titles of Deputy-Chief and Assistant-Chief of the Staff. Sir John Jellicoe, the First Sea Lord, took the additional title of Chief of the Naval Staff. It now remained to be seen whether this advance in the dignity of the War Staff and the renaming of officials would bring the desired result. The submarine campaign had brought the bankruptcy of the old system, the failure of which every thinker had predicted for twenty years. Now this recon-struction of it was to be tried in the fiercest of furnaces.

Changes at the Admiralty

At the end of May there was some improvement in the British position. Though the British shipping losses continued to be heavy, Mr. Lloyd George was able to tell the House of Commons on May 25th : " We are making substantial progress. During the last three weeks or a month we have dealt more effective blows at the submarines than during any corresponding period of the war."

THE CLOSING BATTLES OF THE ANCRE AND THE OPENING OF THE GERMAN RETREAT.

By Edward Wright, Author of "The Great British Battles of the Somme."

Ludendorff Uses Hindenburg as a Screen—Plans for the Great Retirement to the Arras-Laon Line—Manœuvring Masses Used to Threaten Italy and Southern France—Sir Hubert Gough Opens the Great Advance—Scotsmen and Irishmen in the Le Transloy Salient—Breaking of German Line at River Trench and Capture of Grandcourt—Why the Hamburgers Surrendered at Baillescourt Farm—Capture of the Supreme Key Position on the Ancre Front—Nemesis Overtakes the Militarised German Tribes—Signal of British Victory from German Trenches—Main Enemy Line by Bapaume Breaks and Retreats—Prussian Guard at Gommecourt Abandons Position against Orders—British Advance Hindered by Lack of Ample Superior Flying Machines—Sir Douglas Haig Dominates the European Theatre of War—Marshal Joffre's Opinion on the Situation—Allies' Plan of Action Disarranged by Weakness of Russian Democracy—New British Railway System Counters New U-Boat Campaign—Balance of Opposing Forces on Western Front—Why the Army Council Called For another Half a Million Men—Grand Importance of the Huge American Reserves.

AT the end of November, 1916, the British armies on the Somme and Ancre, as described in Chapters CLIV. and CLV. (Vol. VIII.), had a strong sense of victory. The German armies on the two rivers had a deep sense of defeat. The natural consequence was for the enemy to profit by the winter standstill and gradually withdraw to a new line. The British, however, hoped that considerations of both civilian and military moral in Germany would induce the enemy to continue to fight desperately on the weakened river lines.

Ludendorff, the new dictator of the Central Empires, thought of a way out of the difficulty. It was Ludendorff who had picked out Hindenburg from a Hanover café, won the victory of Tannenberg for him, and turned all the limelight of the German Press Bureau upon the picturesque figurehead he used. Ludendorff had stilled all the jealousies in the German General Staff against himself by making Hindenburg the popular idol. Then, under cover of Hindenburg's artificial popularity, Ludendorff had stalked and brought down

Falkenhayn and became the secret master of Middle Europe. He conquered Bethmann-Hollweg, and as Hollweg was little more than the gramophone of the Kaiser, Ludendorff actually brought the German Kaiser under his control.

At the same time he became the practical master of the young Austrian Kaiser. He had all the principal Austrian and Hungarian forces sandwiched between German troops, directed by German Staffs, and controlled by German commanders. Some important Turkish and Bulgarian divisions were also directly under his orders. Bismarck never enjoyed, never dreamt of enjoying, such power as Ludendorff exercised. The position of this bull-necked, energetic, cruelly jovial master of the Central Empires resembled that of a mayor of the palace under the decadent Merovingian Frankish kings.

He possessed the unusual virtue of preferring real power to outward fame. Herein he resembled Bismarck, and, like Bismarck, he was a man of veritable genius, loyal to his caste and esteeming his Emperor and all the rest of Germany and Austria as a means to the triumph of Prussian Junkerdom. The lack of personal ambition in

GOOD HEART MAKES LABOUR LIGHT.
[Canadian War Records.
Working a heavy howitzer on the Canadian section of the Somme battle-front; labour in which there was practically no intermission after the great British offensive began in July, 1916.

Ludendorff was one of the main elements of his strength. Not only was he neither a Cromwell nor a Napoleon, he was not even a Hindenburg. He did not merely allow the old Field-Marshal all the popular applause; he went out of his way to help in the campaign of advertisement of his nominally commanding officer.

There seems to have been no friction between him and Hindenburg. He was absolutely necessary to the man whose reputation he had created, and he was also the ablest politician on the reorganised General Staff. He appointed one of the German generals who had been defeated on the Somme—General Stein—to be Minister of War in Berlin. Stein became his faithful and obedient ally occupying the place from which Falkenhayn had worked against Moltke. Mackensen, one **The man behind** of the ablest of German commanders in **Hindenburg** the field, owed his position largely to Ludendorff, and though he had been put forward by Falkenhayn in 1915 as a rival to the Hindenburg-Ludendorff partnership, Mackensen was ready to act with the new dictator.

Falkenhayn had not done so well as he should have done in Rumania. Moreover, he had exposed Mackensen, who was a vehement gambler in war, to serious risks in the Argesh River action. Ludendorff, who waged war in much the same way as Steinitz in his prime played chess, was a sound, careful, and very patient strategist of the unadventurous, scientific school.

In the winter of 1916 he fully possessed the confidence of all the other leading German commanders, most of whom were, like himself, unknown to fame, and acting behind the Crown Princes of Prussia and Bavaria and behind

GENERAL SIR HUBERT GOUGH, K.C.B.
Commanding the 3rd Cavalry Brigade in the early stages of the war, Sir Hubert was afterwards given command of the Fifth Army, and did splendid work in the Battles of the Somme and Arras.

Duke Albrecht of Würtemberg and Prince Leopold of Bavaria.

Ludendorff, being as resolute as Bismarck, resolved to sacrifice the Press-made fame of Hindenburg to the task of evading the British trap on the Somme. He ordered a retirement to be at once organised, instructing the official Press controllers to work the Hindenburg legend for all that it was worth, and thus steady public opinion against the effects of the extraordinary retreat.

The proposed withdrawal was more significant than the retirement from the Marne. The Battle of the Marne was an open-field struggle, from which the worsted enemy had drawn back to a strong natural fortress line, with caves and quarries, on which he made a victorious stand. On the Somme, however, he was arranging to give up the most powerful fortified line in the world, and flee beyond the range of the medium **Marne and Somme** heavy British artillery, simply because he **contrasted** had been hammered out of the positions he had spent two years in fortifying. The line to which he was fleeing was weaker than the lines from which he was being driven. Therefore, he could not use any excuses similar to those with which the younger Moltke had fairly successfully covered the failure on the Marne.

It was a testimony to the inventive mind of Ludendorff that he lighted upon the figure of his nominal chief as a screen against the general depression that would have invaded the Teutonic soul had the movement of confessed defeat been conducted without any plausible explanation.

Hindenburg, who had recoiled for a victorious spring in both East Prussia and Russian Poland, was supposed to be entirely responsible for the proposed withdrawal from the Somme and Ancre. The argument, as prepared by

[*British official photograph.*]
THREE DISTINGUISHED BRITISH GENERALS.
Sir Herbert Plumer, K.C.B., commanding the Second Army, to whose care and thoroughness the success at Messines was chiefly due in June, 1917, and Generals Sir E. H. H. Allenby and Sir H. S. Horne, who commanded the Third and First Armies on the western front.

Ludendorff, ran at first that no admission of the pressure on the part of the allied armies was implied by the retreat. When this excuse had worn too thin to quieten the German mind, Ludendorff assuaged the growing unrest by mysteriously hinting at the preparation of a grand and masterly plan of an offensive to which the partial withdrawal was a key.

All the winter work energetically proceeded upon the new line, running from Arras to Laon, and commonly known as the Hindenburg line. General Stein and his subordinates in Berlin rigorously "combed" the Central Empires of their last recruits of good quality. The new system of industrial compulsion was vigorously applied in order to dilute skilled labour in munition works, railway transport, and other industries of vital importance. Young men and men in the prime of life were obtained in great numbers, with the remarkable result that Ludendorff was able at the beginning of 1917 to reckon on a new general reserve amounting to about one million men.

He placed the enormous number of four hundred thousand troops in and about the Black Forest. They were echeloned from Basle to Constance, and from Mulhouse to Strassburg. **Germany's new general reserve** Thus they threatened the French Vosges line on the one side and the Swiss Jura line on the other side, and were popularly supposed to be aimed at turning the French flank below Belfort by a drive through Switzerland.

Another group of four hundred thousand troops of the new reserve was more loosely collected in Southern Germany, menacing Italy by means of an enormous reinforcement of the Austro-Hungarian troops in the Trentino. There was, however, no sure ground for supposing that either of these preliminary great concentrations was definitely intended for use against South-Eastern France or Lombardy. Indeed, Ludendorff is said to have decided against the Austrian scheme for a renewal of the Trentino offensive.

Ludendorff and his Staff well knew that the concentrations would be soon known to the Allies. The two new masses were in the nature of demonstrations, intended to facilitate operations in the spring, and meanwhile confuse and mislead the Allies. Ludendorff was still relying upon the German railway system for a rapid rehandling of **Ludendorff's plans delayed** his striking forces. There were indications that a sudden thrust at the Russian front at Riga was among the strokes contemplated, and that very strong forces of men and artillery were being directed towards the Champagne front in France and the Yser and Ypres line in Flanders.

Undoubtedly, Ludendorff intended to strike with his grand reserve, but he met with a series of difficulties during his winter preparations. The German railway system was wearing out, owing to the pressure put upon it by the British Fleet. Lack of sufficient lubricating oil, combined with incessant traffic, seems to have produced serious damage to the rolling-stock. Troop and munition trains in motion could be heard at a distance of ten miles, through the wheels shrieking upon the axles. When the stock was sadly in need of a period of relief for repairs, an extraordinary spell of long and severe frost froze the German canals and navigable rivers, caused great disorder in the transport of war stores and general goods, and increased the burden upon the overloaded railways. Such a winter had not been known for the best part of a century. By stopping all the canal traffic it upset the plans of the German Staff and disastrously delayed the rearrangement and munitioning of their armies.

GERMANY'S WAR-LORD ON THE SOMME.

The Kaiser with his Staff watching the operations at one point of the Battle of the Somme, 1916. He is the third figure from the right of the photograph, apparently looking at a map. Ironical fate decreed that the presence of the German War-Lord at a battle should have almost invariably presaged victory for the other side, and this occasion was no exception to what had come to be looked upon as the rule.

[British official photograph.

THE VICTORY LINE.
British soldiers laying a railroad on ground
they had newly captured in the course
of their victorious eastward advance.

disconcerting retreats rested with the side that possessed the best and most numerous means of movement and supply.

It was the merit of Sir Douglas Haig and his Staff that they clearly perceived these primal conditions of modern warfare in its latest developments, and energetically worked all through the winter of 1916 to improve their means of communication. Two hundred miles of main railway track were added behind the British front, together with new lines of light railways and new motor roads.

By February, 1917, Sir Douglas Haig began to reckon that the tonnage his improved railways were capable of carrying was fairly commensurate with the tonnage

Sir Douglas Haig was in the same difficulty as Ludendorff. He had not sufficient railway power. The British commander may not have known what the enemy intended to do. Indeed, he may not have much cared; for his design was once more to compel the Germans to meet him in a grand battle on the ground he again chose. In order, however, to select his own ground, Sir Douglas Haig needed more railways, and needed them at once The chief reason why he had been unable, in the summer and autumn of 1916, to open and maintain a double offensive at widely separated points was that he lacked the lines, locomotives, and trucks necessary for feeding two mighty and separated battle forces.

In the winter of 1916 Sir Douglas Haig appealed to the British railway companies to help him. Magnificent was the effort they made. First, with the consent of the British Government, the passenger traffic in Great Britain was restricted and the carriage of many kinds of material was diminished. This enabled rolling-stock to be moved to France and Flanders, and at the same time entire tracks were transported by patriotic railway companies. Even the ballast was con-

Triumphs of British engineering veyed to France. Tens of thousands of tons of macadam for new road-making were given to the sappers of the British armies, who, under officers of genius, developed quite an incomparable speed in road-making and track construction.

All this railway work and engineering work was the fundamental factor of future successes. The war had become an engineering affair. Even superior troops with superior guns could not achieve victory by their own exertions. Success in both victorious advances and

[British official photograph.

PLEASURABLE PROSPECT OF A MEAL IN SECURITY.
German prisoners drawing rations, watched with interest by their comrades behind the wires. Many of the
Germans captured were half-famished, the intense and incessant British artillery fire having effectually
served to prevent rations being brought up to them in their trenches.

landed at his sea bases. All that he then wanted was more heavy artillery and a larger reserve of men. Some of his heavy guns had to be lent to Italy, and strikes in the British engineering trades hindered vital output. Yet the British commander was able to obtain sufficient shell to enable him at last to throw at the enemy forty thousand tons a week. This, however, did not content him. He wanted still more heavy guns and more heavy shells, as it was his design to blast the Germans out of their lines by an unending hurricane of high explosives of unparalleled intensity, and thereby save his infantry the immense sacrifices they had made on the Somme.

The campaign that had been checked in November, 1916, by the swimming clay in the Ancre Valley, was, notwithstanding the check, carried on in the latter part of the same month, through December, and through January. The British infantry did not make any important move but, as described in Chapter CLXXVIII., continually raided the hostile lines in an intensification of the ferocious winter sport of the previous year. The campaign was mainly continued by the artillery. In the Somme area the Germans were under observation from the great ridge they had lost, and from the sky immediately above them, where their fighting pilots had temporarily lost the lead in aerial warfare. The plight of the beaten German forces was hopeless, and the British guns never ceased, either by day or night, to hammer the shallow hostile line.

At first the men in the firing-trenches on both sides were in a deplorable condition. On the ground where the action had been broken off there was little more than rough connections between shell-holes, undrained and without protection of either parapets or dug-outs. In some places, such as our position near Grandcourt, no connected lines existed, but merely a series of rough outpost positions with the approaches covered by British and German batteries.

The predominance of the British artillery told upon the physical condition of the front-line German troops.

into the neutral zone and there erected new barbed-wire entanglements sometimes seven feet high and fifty feet broad. Thereupon, the British troops also came out in the night mist to the neutral zone and bombed and dispersed the night workers. In the day-time, when the mist lifted, the Stokes mortars and field-artillery shattered the enemy's labour of the night, and if his guns tried to engage in a duel the heavy ordnance of Sir Henry Rawlinson's and Sir Hubert Gough's armies beat down all opposition.

German retreat preparations

The German commanders prepared for the great retreat by leaving only outposts in the broken, shallow fire-trench and small reinforcements in the support line. Both these German positions on the Somme front were open to shrapnel fire and entirely without shelter from high explosives. Only in the third reserve line were there tunnel dug-outs in which the main bodies of defending troops could sit with some security. The Germans had no leather, fur, or sheepskin coats, and took no change of clothes into the trenches. They suffered badly from stomach and chest complaints, and when sick were often harshly treated as malingerers. Many of their rest billets were within the range of the British railway guns, so that when they escaped from the misery of the wet trenches they had to crowd together in damp cellars.

Towards Christmas the activity of the British raiding-parties increased all along the hundred-mile front. They made daylight swoops behind gas-clouds and smoke-screens, explored the German lines at night, often without meeting a German soldier, and generally did all they could to keep the enemy nervous and subdued. During this display of force the British troops began their new southward extension towards Roye, and took over from the French a sector of the Somme.

Sir Hubert Gough, the conqueror of Beaumont-Hamel, and

[*British official photograph.*
AN IMPROVISED "BILLET."
British soldiers had here arranged a "billet" with corrugated iron and tarpaulin against the remnants of a French farmhouse.

They were unable to get up provisions in a regular manner, or obtain boarding for revetting their trenches and lifting them out of the mud.

On the other hand, British soldiers in a similar position were well served and regularly rationed, and by the first week in December some means of comfort were installed in most of the transformed shell-hole lines.

When the wet weather was succeeded by sharp frosts the Germans were helped by the light white mist rising at night. Covered by the haze, they came out

[*British official photograph.*
AT AN UNDERGROUND CANTEEN ON THE WESTERN FRONT.
Men of the British force making purchases at a trench canteen. During the long trench warfare on the western front in some places dug-outs were conveniently converted into canteens, where the soldiers could get such "extras" as imparted greater variety to their daily fare.

[British official photograph.

FETCHING RATIONS FROM THE RAILHEAD "DUMP."
Rations were sent up daily to divisional rail-heads, where waggons attended to take them on to battalion quartermasters at some convenient point nearer the front for further subdivision among companies.

the brilliant partner of Sir Henry Rawlinson in the Somme campaign, remained in control of affairs along the Ancre and the Serre plateau, ready for the drive through Bapaume and the struggle along the middle of the Hindenburg line. General Allenby, with his army reinforced for a new offensive around Arras, maintained his old position on the left of the forces of Sir Hubert Gough, with the upper part of the Hindenburg line as his objective. Sir Henry Horne, one of the master British gunners, moved from the Somme towards Arras to assist in the next grand offensive.

The Canadians, under Sir Julian Byng, were transferred from the scene of their victory south of the Ancre to the

Canadians moved to Vimy lower slopes of the Vimy Ridge, south of Lens. This was the critical point in the new line the enemy was arranging, and the position of attack given to the conquerors of Courcelette was a telling tribute to their fighting fame. Their offensive was planned long in advance, in February, 1917, thus anticipating Ludendorff's scheme for retiring his centre and striking with his wings. The Australians were also given an important line of assault that afterwards led them into the Hindenburg system at Bullecourt; while the South Africans, covered in tragic glory by their stand in Delville Wood, were so placed as to enter the still greater battle in a scene of even more terrible trial.

Sir Hubert Gough opened the infantry advance towards the new German line. On the night of January 2nd, 1917, the Germans provoked the new Ancre campaign by

jumping one of the British advanced posts in front of Serre. A Staff officer, inquiring into the affair, found a dead British sentry amid a quagmire of ponds and mud-swamps, through which it was impossible to build a strong line.

The only way in which to strengthen the front was to capture the nearest German positions and link them together into a protective barrier. In the night of January 5th two small parties crawled through the mud towards the German posts. The first party of twenty men

[British official photograph.

FRIENDLY NEUTRALS SAMPLE BRITISH RATIONS.
General Primo de Rivera, one of the Spanish officers who visited the allied armies in the field in France, inspecting the bread turned out from one of the Army bakeries.

rushed their objective and made forty-four German prisoners, at no cost to themselves in fatal casualties. The second party, that attacked a strong point on the right, also trapped the defending troops, but were counter-attacked by a detachment of Bavarian bombers. After a sharp fight the enemy's supporting force was shattered and the conquered position consolidated.

The points thus won commanded an important system of enemy trenches. The German commander, therefore, would not give up the struggle. On January 7th he turned his guns on to his lost positions and, after a heavy bombardment, made another vain counter-attack. The consequence was that the British artillery also opened heavily and on a wider front of two miles, and on January 10th English patrols climbed up the battered slopes behind their deadly barrage, and took one hundred and twenty prisoners from an upper line of dug-outs. As in the previous case, the prisoners were more numerous than the attackers and the cost of the little local victory was slight.

These things showed that the enemy was enfeebled and disheartened. Sir Hubert Gough, therefore, resolved to press onward and upward, in spite of the severe weather conditions. So on January 11th, when a thick morning mist, followed by a snowstorm, veiled all the Serre plateau, a strong attack was delivered by English county regiments on the high ground above the Ancre.

Very slowly the English troops moved. They were ankle-deep in mud on the firm ground and up to their thighs in slime in other places. Sometimes, when an officer was sucked in the mud he had first to pull his feet out of his long boots and go on in his stockings until his boots were dug out. Notwithstanding all the difficulties of the ground the German line

[British official photograph.

DRAWING RATIONS FROM THE BATTALION QUARTERMASTER.
Company quartermasters served out the meat to their cooks and divided the rations into portions for platoons, labelling them and sending them on to the company ration-parties still farther forward, by whom they were distributed to the men in the front line.

was reached, under cover of mist and snow, before the hostile machine-gunners could get to work. Some of the German officers fought to the death, but their men surrendered by the hundred without a struggle.

When the German artillery tried to put a shell curtain over the edge of the plateau, something went wrong with their fire-control system. Their observation-officers had been killed or captured, and the falling snow prevented the others from seeing what had happened. The wild shooting did scarcely any damage, and, when the weather cleared, the forward observation-officers of General Gough's army were securely fixed upon the high ground of the Serre plateau, and thence directed their massed guns upon the enemy's lines.

Holding attack at Le Transloy

Then came the great frost that whitened the battlefield for weeks. The mud hardened, the shell-pools froze, the brown, rusty barriers of barbed-wire put on beauty, and became looped and graceful tangles of ice crystals and clinging snow. But winter could not silence and frost could not subdue the tireless British guns. The general bombardment of the enemy's reserve line and communications increased rather than diminished, and the continual thick fogs were employed as screens in great raids all along the front.

On January 27th the raids were varied by a holding attack against one of the positions on the Bapaume sector. The enemy occupied a sunken road at Le Transloy, on a

slope going down to the ruined village. It was a bitter morning, with a sharp wind blowing over the snow. Three German battalions were making coffee in their dug-outs, leaving only a few numbed sentries watching the breadth of a hundred yards between the lines.

Suddenly, at half-past five o'clock, there was a clash of artillery and, as the guns spoke, a force of Scotsmen and Irishmen charged across the snow. Before the Germans could man their trenches or use a single machine-gun they were trapped and bundled into old London omnibuses which used to run to the Bank. Only from two isolated trenches on the right was there any rifle fire, and the victorious troops at first drove a third of a mile beyond their objective. But finding the ground there was too hard to

[British official photographs.

BUSY HOUR AT THE PORTABLE FIELD-KITCHENS ON THE ANCRE.

British soldiers drawing their dinner rations from the field-kitchens near the fighting-front on the Ancre. The feeding of the vast numbers of troops was a triumph of organisation. The method by which the supplies were taken up and distributed to the various units is graphically described in an earlier volume of this work (Vol. VIII., p. 447). Above: Huge stacks of supplies accumulated for British troops on the western front.

NATURE'S PROTECTIVE COLOURING ADOPTED BY HIGHLANDERS ON A SNOWY BATTLEFIELD.

Men of a Highland regiment, clad in white, making a night raid over snow on German trenches on the western front. With their steel helmets painted white, with white smocks reaching below their kilts, with rifles ready loaded and bayonets fixed to avoid making any noise, the Highlanders crept silently over the snowy space of No Man's Land to the hidden dug-outs of a German company. When they reached their objective they called to the men to surrender, and a few did so, after which bombs were thrown in and the nest of dug-outs effectually destroyed before the White Company returned with their prisoners.

dig, they drew back to the sheltered dug-outs in the sunken road.

The German gunners then endeavoured to bombard the Scotsmen and Irishmen out of the Le Transloy salient. This only led to further trouble for the enemy. All his movements and attempts to organise counter-attacks were defeated by the power of absolute observation which the British had won by their former victories on the great ridge by the Somme. The Germans soon tired of provoking an artillery duel, and began to remove their guns towards St. Quentin. The continual mist in the Somme Valley favoured the enemy's retirement of his heavy pieces. Nothing, however, could screen the increasing weakness of his lines, as these were being incessantly tested by vigorous raids. The German commanders had to sacrifice thousands of men in demonstrative counter-attacks, in a vain endeavour to maintain an appearance of strength.

Yet the first and preliminary British thrust between the Ancre and the Serre plateau steadily and methodically continued. On February 3rd Sir Hubert Gough made a moonlight attack from Holland Wood over a valley to a crest dominating the village of Miraumont. The ground was white with snow and the moon shining in a clear sky, but happily a low-lying mist veiled the movement of the khaki figures, crawling forward and dragging their rifles and trench spades.

Just before midnight the British guns crashed with the same surprise effect as before. The defending troops fled to their dug-outs, as sudden bombardments of this kind with no infantry action following had become common. On this occasion the infantry were scarcely more than twenty-five yards behind the volcanic line of shell fire. They overran the enemy's fire-trench, and then followed their own pillars of fire and smoke and stormed a strong position known as the River Trench in which there were three strong redoubts. Two hundred prisoners were made, all of them men from Schleswig-Holstein. They were Danes, especially selected for the work of holding the worst position on the German front so that their Prussian masters would profit almost as much by their death as by any victorious stand made by them. They had been sent out to die in order that, when peace came, there should be fewer recalcitrant Norsemen in the country near the Kiel Canal.

The next morning the hostile commander furiously and continually launched real German troops in counter-attack after counter-attack upon his lost line of redoubts. Wave after wave of grey figures went down under rifle fire, machine-gun fire and great explosions from the new Stokes gun. Each assembling force was also caught flank and front by the British artillery. At a disastrous cost in life the Germans recovered one of the redoubts on the southern part of the River Trench, but lost the position again as the British troops returned to the conflict with hand-grenades and trench-mortars. One German machine-gun party in a shell-crater made a long and heroic fight, but was at last enveloped.

About this time the enemy tried, on the southern part

Fight on the River Trench

of the Ypres salient, a trick he had used on the Russian front. A German force was dressed in white sheets, with the men's heads concealed in white hoods, and their faces whitened with chalk, and was sent over the snow in the moonlight to make a surprise attack. After the elaborate preparation in make-up all surprise effect was exploded by a preliminary bombardment. The two ghostly attacking parties were broken by machine-gun fire and rifle fire, in spite of the fact that most of the British troops in the section were new recruits undergoing their baptism of battle.

German retreat definitely begun

Meanwhile, on the Ancre front the German High Command and General von Below, the commander of the

[*Canadian War Records.*
LIEUT.-GENERAL SIR JULIAN BYNG,
K.C.B., K.C.M.G.
After magnificent service at Ypres and the Dardanelles, Sir Julian Byng was appointed in 1916 to the command of the Canadian Expeditionary Force, and won the victories at Courcelette and Vimy Ridge.

First German Army, gave up the struggle. On February 7th, 1917, the retreat towards the Hindenburg line definitely began by the evacuation of the riverside village of Grandcourt. British patrols cautiously advanced into the trenches west of the village and, after exploring the snow-mantled walls and cellars, established a new line on the road to Miraumont. The German position had become a neck of shell-craters, broken walls, and dug-outs, overlooked by the new British positions on the Serre plateau.

Combles was the first place from which the Germans crept without a fight. Grandcourt was the second place. In both cases the enemy was caught in the pincer-like movement of two enveloping forces, so that he was compelled to retreat in order to avoid heavy and utterly useless losses. It was at Grandcourt that the German artillery had massed during the Somme battles at Contalmaison and the Pozières ridge. A small German rearguard came out with their hands up, being so terrified by the creeping barrage of British shells that they refused to carry out their orders and make a last, desperate, delaying resistance.

Sir Hubert Gough pressed the advantage he had won by attacking in the night the fortress manor-house of Baillescourt, whose gabled roofs and massive walls rose, like an observation-tower, above the furrowed landscape between Grandcourt and Miraumont. German engineers had done all they could to make Baillescourt a position of strength by means of loopholed galleries, machine-gun emplacements, and bomb-proof caverns. A hundred Hamburgers—sturdy dockers and factory hands—garrisoned the ancient buildings and the dug-outs round about. But, like the other rearguard, they surrendered practically without a struggle. Helped by the clear moonlight, the British gunners swept the farm with a whirlwind of heavy shell, causing the Hamburgers to retire to their underground shelters. Before they could regain their fire-trenches the bombers of General Gough's army were outside the dug-outs demanding surrender. The unusual rapidity of interaction between the lines of attacking artillery and infantry surprised the German force, and they gave in without any attempt at resistance.

An incident to which reference has been made already occurred at about this time. Some of the Canadians, hearing of the German white-sheet attack at Ypres, bought a hundred women's night-dresses and, crawling in them

A LINK IN THE AMMUNITION SUPPLY.

[British official photograph.

Section of a British supply column waiting to fetch ammunition for the guns. Throughout the pauses caused by weather and other conditions in the offensive campaign that began in July, 1916, the British artillery continued its incessant hammering of the hostile lines, whose supply service was almost broken up.

across the snow, made a very successful raid. The Gordon Highlanders likewise dressed themselves in white smocks, and went over the German line in two waves, trapped and killed an entire company in a large cavern, and blew up a bomb-store.

By reason of the strategic conquest of the Grandcourt line and the high ground north of the Ancre the German positions on the dominating Serre plateau were endangered. Almost daily small bits of ground were seized by the British troops, enabling them to reach out farther round the last remaining buttresses of the Germans' original first line of defence.

On the night of February 10th a force of North-countrymen stormed into the south-eastern approaches to Serre. They had to cover eight hundred yards of difficult ground that dipped and rose and then dipped again, and ended beneath the main plateau from which the enemy stared down. Moreover, there was a deep gully cutting across the line of attack, and in this gully was a German outpost force with machine-guns and the usual underground retreats.

The movement had to be conducted by stealth, with no sight or sound to give the enemy warning. The guns bombarded the hostile position without creating any alarm, as bursts of artillery fire had been the regular characteristic of the British winter campaign. Nearly **Important gain** half an hour after the barrage opened, the **near Serre** crawling North-countrymen covered the half a mile of No Man's Land and, after a fierce fight in the ravine, stormed the higher German position, breaking up a Prussian regiment and taking more prisoners than their own casualties.

The importance of the gain was shown next morning by the heavy counter-attack which the German commander vainly delivered with a view to getting back the edge of the plateau. Only a few of his men arrived within bombing distance of his lost line. The British artillery, firing from both the southern and the western sides of the downland,

completely shattered the counter-attacking masses. On February 17th the men of London and Southern England and the Midland Counties drove in a wedge south of the Ancre. The advance was made on a front of two miles, and stretched across the river to Baillescourt.

The ground was thawing and greasy and shrouded in a thick mist. The fog prevented observation and hindered artillery action. Nevertheless, all the decisive objectives on the northern bank of the Ancre were won with little difficulty, and the line of posts forming the enemy's centre was also secured. But on the south there was a fierce struggle over a steep and isolated hill that commanded Miraumont, Petit Miraumont, and Pys.

The English troops secured their first goal, consisting of a few trenches at the base of the hill, and then, by a bitter fight lasting two hours, they climbed up the height and pushed the Germans well over the crest. A fresh, strong German force, however, came unperceived through the mist and attacked the English right flank, compelling a withdrawal to the foot of the high position. In spite of this check, the advance was a general success. The British line was advanced five hundred yards on a front of two miles, six hundred Prussians were captured, and Miraumont was completely dominated from the new high ground captured north of Baillescourt Farm.

The hill above the farm was the supreme key-position to the German front on the Ancre. It overlooked the enemy's intricate rear **Key-position** positions on the Serre plateau, and **at Baillescourt** enabled tornadoes of fire to be directed on three sides of the peninsula of downland to which the Germans were clinging. It also overlooked the upper valley of the Ancre, running north of Pys, and thus prevented the enemy from concealing his forces on the open, rolling ground by the Ancre.

In addition to these two advantages of this position, the Baillescourt Hill rose well above the northern valley of Puisieux brook, and afforded direct observation across a large space of ground to the enemy's railway junction at Achiet-le-Grand. The German main gun-positions came under observation. In many cases the flames from the hostile guns could be seen by British forward observing-officers, and these officers could also steadily and minutely measure the answering effect of the fire of their own howitzers.

The consequence was the Germans had either to submit to the rapid destruction of both their artillery and their infantry or retire under cover of the mist, tacitly acknowledging complete defeat in the Battle of the Ancre. The German commander made one last desperate attempt on Saturday, February 24th, 1917, to recover the hill that dominated his line. In the darkness of early morning his troops came on in fierce waves of assault, only to be swept by shrapnel and raked by machine-guns. Large fresh reinforcements were employed in this forlorn hope, and their determined gallantry showed that the German Army still had plenty of fight left in it.

On the other hand, the extraordinary persistence with

End of the vigil in a German observation post.

Tolling the gas alarm on a sanctuary bell

Surprising an enemy patrol in No Man's Land.

"Come on, you fellows, there is no one here."

[British official photograph.

Placidity in midst of peril: Cycle orderlies at work under heavy shell fire.

[British official photograph.

A corner of the battlefield near Arras, with "tank" in the background on the left.

[British official photograph.

irresistible determination on the move : British infantry moving up in " artillery formation " to the attack

[Canadian War Records.

Canadians establishing a signalling headquarters and communication post for British aeroplanes.

[Canadian War Records.

Heavy ordnance behind the Canadians: Making ready to fire a large naval gun.

[Canadian War Records

Crushing the foe by sheer weight of metal: Heavy guns at the moment of discharge.

which the attack was maintained indicated a mere brutal stupidity of mind on the part of the hostile commander and his Staff. When the first grey wave was obliterated, long before it reached the British defences, it must have been patent to the enemy that all succeeding attacks would be only vain and appalling sacrifices of life. There was no military justification for the ghastly slaughter of some ten thousand men of some famous Prussian regiments. They perished by the useless and irresponsible act of a defeated German general, who wasted brigade after brigade in the sorry personal design of preventing himself being relieved of his command.

In this way Nemesis overtook the militarised federation of German tribes. For more than a generation the Teutons had devoted themselves, in both body and mind, to the organisation of a system of universal preying, submitting to the loss of all real independence in the prospect of becoming the master race of the earth. In almost every defeat, however, their own system was turned against them, and their national strength was viciously and foolishly wasted by men of the Zabern school, who were only anxious for their own damaged personal reputation. The Germans were at first sacrificed by the hundred thousand to save the individual position of some army commander. Then they were destroyed, actually by the million, to salve the dynastic interests of the Hohenzollern family and the connecting interests of the German nobility.

Sacrifices to militarism

After the great counter-attacks on Baillescourt Hill were shattered, and the remnants of the Prussian regiments were pursued beyond the railway junction of Achiet-le-Grand, the First German Army retired from the Ancre in worse condition than it had retired from the Marne. It was a pretty piece of historic irony that the former command of General von Kluck, whose first orders were to destroy "the contemptible little British Army," should have been the first German host fully to feel the weight of power wielded by the most able of British generals at Mons. Sir Douglas Haig had not reaped in the autumn of 1916 the full harvest of his victory on the Somme. Lack of reinforcements and imperfect railway communications had compelled him to wait, and give the enemy the winter months in which to recuperate and reorganise. Yet, such was the strength of the new British war-machine, that an interval of hard frost and clearer air in February, 1917, was sufficient to enable it victoriously to end the first great battles on the north-eastern rivers of France.

Ludendorff could neither stand nor counter in strength, on the original great German fortressed line of downland running down from Gommecourt. His front-line troops could not be properly fed or reinforced, as their communications were dominated by the deep crescent of British artillery. The German railway line was destroyed, only a ditch of shell-craters indicating where the track had been laid. For some time signs of a general retirement from the great Gommecourt salient had been visible, and British preparations were speeded up for a modern kind of pursuit.

Had the frost held and the air remained fairly clear the German commander would have had great difficulty in effecting a withdrawal. His forces would have been deluged with long-range heavy shell fire, controlled from

WHERE THREE LINES MET ON THE WESTERN FRONT.
Examination of a British despatch-rider's papers. The rider had reached a point on his journey where British, French, and Belgian lines ran together, and was held up by the sentries representing the three Allies of the western front that his bona fides might be established.

high observing positions. The darkness of night would not have saved the enemy, as the breadth of eight thousand yards between the Bapaume ridge and the hills of the Ancre would have been illuminated by the incessant play of searchlights. Unhappily, the fog that came with the great thaw in the latter part of February saved the enemy from the gravest disaster. The persistent thickness of the air enabled him to get most of his guns away, though he paid a heavy toll while traversing the great zones of curtain fire maintained on three sides of the salient by the British artillery.

The German gunners began their operations by working their ordnance in a remarkable manner. They seemed to have received a sudden abundance of shell, enabling them to cope with the increasing power of the British artillery. This, however, was only a sign of weakness. The Germans were merely firing off their shell-dumps because they had no time to remove them. In the evening of February 23rd, 1917, just after the breaking of the German counter-attack against the Baillescourt Hill, the German Army ceased the struggle and, for the first time since the Battle of the Marne in September, 1914, drew back without a battle on the western front, in patent confession of a great defeat.

The signal of the British victory was a line of fire from the German trenches. The enemy was burning his timber-lined dug-outs with a view to making them useless to the conquerors. Through the blurring fog and over a sea of thawing mud British patrols went forward and cautiously felt their way among wire entanglements and ruined and steaming earthworks. Obstructing parties of German troops were scattered in shell-holes and supported by machine-gun posts all along the enemy's rear.

Fire signal of victory

At every likely place traps were laid for the advancing forces of Sir Hubert Gough.

Trip-mines and other devices, such as the Australasian and British forces had employed in the Dardanelles retirement, were largely used. Objects likely to be picked up as souvenirs were filled with high explosives. Charges were laid in the streets and in the underground galleries between the concrete forts from which machine-gun batteries had played. In some cases the larger mines were exploded just as the last Germans tramped away. This was done so that no cover should remain against the

FORCED TO DESCEND BEHIND THE LINES ON THE WESTERN FRONT.

[British official photograph.

Dismantling a damaged British aeroplane that had been compelled to descend. The personal skill, individual courage, and heroic sacrifice of British airmen prevented any important check to the advance on the Ancre, despite the temporary superiority snatched by German aviators.

barrage of heavy shelling intended to hinder the progress of the main British forces.

These forces, however, did not move forward into the traps set for them. They merely sent out increasing numbers of patrols to secure the ground and discover where the First German Army proposed to make its next stand. Petit Miraumont was first occupied in the night of February 23rd. About the same time a forward movement was made north of the Ancre down the road to Miraumont village. By the morning of February 25th all the German line from Serre and Pys to the Butte de Warlencourt was being occupied by the British patrols. In some places the German retirement reached in the evening a depth of two miles.

This historic advance was strangely devoid of any large dramatic interest. As one officer said, when returning from the reclaimed village of Pys, the affair was as exciting as searching a muddy field for a lost trinket. Only occasionally did a knot of Germans open a fierce little rearguard action and need handling by a slowly exploring, enveloping movement by the patrols.

Some of the hostile snipers showed high spirit, and fully carried out their orders to display as much activity as possible and make the utmost noise. Their object was to induce the reconnoitring parties of British troops to expect a strong resistance and call **Delaying rearguard** for reinforcements before advancing. **work** Then, before the advance was made, the bravest Germans stealthily retired, feeling they had successfully gained time for the rearrangement of their main forces.

Although, however, the enemy command selected special men for this delaying rearguard work and promised them special privileges, they were not always equal to the task assigned to them. For example, a Guards battalion was ordered to hold the fortress of Gommecourt to the very last moment. Gommecourt was the pivot on which the German line was swinging back. But when a British patrol entered Gommecourt in the evening of February 27th no resistance whatever was made. The famous

works on the high westernmost point of the German lines was tenanted only by a blind man. He was a Guardsman who had lost his sight, and his battalion fled so hastily that he still thought the stronghold was well held. The Guardsmen seem to have perceived some British patrols pushing northward from Serre, and became fearful that they were about to be cut off. Instead of attempting to make a stand they bolted at once to Bicquoy, and their dug-outs were still burning when the British detachment arrived.

The morning after the memorable capture of Gommecourt the British line was pushed forward a thousand yards north-east of the **Eleven villages** fortressed down, and the defences imme- **recovered** diately in front of the city of Bapaume were driven in by the capture of the villages of Le Barque and Ligny. At the same time the western and northern trench systems around Puisieux were occupied. During the month of February eleven villages were either captured by the British or surrendered to them by the Germans. Some twenty-one hundred German troops were captured, including thirty-six officers. The villages recovered were Grandcourt, Petit Miraumont, Miraumont, Serre, Warlencourt, Pys, Le Barque, Ligny, Gommecourt, Thilloy, and Puisieux.

Sir Hubert Gough's army would probably have worked forward more quickly and with less loss had the pilots of the Royal Flying Corps been provided with all the machines of superior type of which they could make use. It will be remembered that, at the close of the Battle of the Somme, Sir Douglas Haig especially demanded in his famous despatch that aeroplanes of the most modern and progressive type should be abundantly provided.

Owing, however, to the imperfect conditions of construction established during previous years, the output of British-designed and British-made aero-motors had been much inferior to the output of German engines. For this practical lesson in the application of British State Socialism in a progressive industry the British forces in the field had to pay. There had been amply sufficient engineering talent in England and Scotland to counter the engineering talent in Germany. British officialism had, however, proved less enlightened for a time than German officialism. Private British motor designers, such as the very able men working for the Sunbeam Company and the Rolls-Royce Company, were not encouraged, either before the war or during the first phase of the war, as the German Government had encouraged their leading private engine designers.

The later public agitation in Great Britain in regard to the fighting inferiority of Royal Aircraft Factory machines seems to have produced no immediate effect. A scheme of reorganisation was gradually established, but this scheme came into operation just at the time when the British Navy wanted powerful aero-motors for anti-submarine purposes, while the British Army also required similar motors to cope with the enemy's military aeroplanes.

The Admiralty authorities appear to have been at least more foresightful than the War Office authorities. They were able to make some claim to some of the most promising British engines. The result was that when **Insufficiency of fighting aircraft** the Germans covered their retreat by sending up scores of fighting machines of first-rate quality in the early spring of 1917, the lieutenants of Sir Douglas Haig had only a comparatively small number of the latest and most powerful British machines with which to contend for the practical mastery of the air.

At the beginning of the German retreat the enemy employed two large forces of machines of the newest type, under Captain Baron von Richtofen and Captain von Bülow. In superior masses these two formations swooped upon the smaller squadrons of new fighting machines sent up by the British commanders. The personal skill, individual courage, and large sacrifices of life of British pilots happily prevented any **Air-mastery temporarily lost** important check to the advance of the attacking army.

Apparently, there had been no time between the receipt of Sir Douglas Haig's despatch and the opening of the German movement of withdrawal to effect in aerial material a revolution similar to that which Mr. Lloyd George had previously effected in the production of heavy artillery material. The new German machines were not superior to the newest British machines; but, unfortunately, they were at first more numerous. Consequently, the British Army was not able to maintain during the closing operations on the Ancre front that practical mastery of the air which it had managed to assert during some of the most critical days of the battles on the Somme front.

The continual misty weather aggravated the difficulties of the advancing British Army and lightened the task of the retreating German Army. On the whole, the enemy escaped from an impossible position almost as lightly as the British and French Mediterranean armies escaped from their lines on the Gallipoli Peninsula. The Germans got practically all their guns away, left nothing behind

[British official photograph.

FIELD-ARTILLERY GETTING A GUN INTO POSITION IN THE ADVANCE.

Hindenburg's retreat, which was described as being "according to plan," in the spring of 1917, was conducted with a celerity that imposed most strenuous work upon the British artillery following hot upon his heels.

Batteries limbered up and galloped over ground gaping with pits, intentionally exploded by the Germans in the vain hope of retarding pursuit, and took up new positions whence to speed the parting foe.

[*Canadian War Records.*

LOADING LARGE NAVAL GUN ON THE CANADIANS' FRONT.
Artillerymen at work on part of the western front, held by the Canadians. Sir Douglas Haig, in the Ancre advance, was enabled to throw at the enemy forty thousand tons of shells a week.

in munition work compensated for the tragic weakness of Russia.

As against her chief original opponents—Russia and France—Germany had won some striking advantages. Either by means of a separate peace with Russian autocracy, or by a cunning armistice with the Russian peoples, she might have been able to negotiate a European settlement that would have left France very weak and still overshadowed by the prestige of Prussian militarism. France might have obtained Metz by negotiation. She certainly would not have recovered the most valuable part of Lorraine and the potash mines of Alsace. She would have remained in economic servitude to the German Empire, and been crippled during the reconstruction period by the impossibility of working her ruined northern coal-fields.

of material importance, and ferociously wasted and bedevilled the territory from which they withdrew.

The remarkable power of the machine-gun, with curtain fire from long-range artillery, was the instrument of the successful retreat. As Sir Charles Monro had shown on the Gallipoli Peninsula, after his masterly experience in holding the Ypres salient, modern artillery had a tremendous defensive value. The Germans faithfully copied all the British tactics of the Dardanelles withdrawal, and, wherever time permitted, they constructed numerous traps for the advancing victors.

In their Ancre retirement, however, they were considerably hurried. They left behind them new artesian wells, with other recent important works, showing that it had been their original intention in January, 1917, to stand on the Ancre front for at least several months longer.

British Empire dominates the world Their new lines, on both the Bapaume ridge and on the Hindenburg system, were far from being properly completed.

Ludendorff had proposed but Sir Hubert Gough had disposed. By his sudden break into and over the Baillescourt Hill the famous kinsman of the conqueror of the Sikhs upset all the plans of the German dictator, and compelled him abruptly to alter his arrangements for the spring campaign. The German drive at the Russian front had to be countermanded, and the still more important threat against the eastern French flank had also to be allowed to fade into a vain shadow of action.

The intention of Sir Douglas Haig dominated the entire theatre of war in Europe. The German Empire, which had entered the struggle for world-dominion in the expectation of meeting only some sixty thousand British troops, was in February, 1917, opposed by a British Army stronger than the enormous active German Army that had joyously taken the field in August, 1914. Russia was weakened, and France, though magnificent in spirit and strong in machinery, was lacking in a decisively large reserve power. The British Empire, however, supplied the lack of great French reserves, and by a gigantic and unparalleled effort

[*Canadian War Records.*

OPENING THE BREECH AFTER FIRING.
Large naval gun on the Canadians' front, which had just been fired, showing the volume of smoke and fumes released on the opening of the breech preparatory to the reloading.

No Frenchman had anticipated at the outbreak of war the enormous development of the military strength of the British Commonwealth, which was clearly evident on March 1st, 1917. The British, Canadian, Australasian, and South African forces, extending from the north of Ypres towards Roye, had grown into the grand, human battering-ram of the Alliance. The forces of the Oversea Dominions approached three-quarters of a million men under arms.

In the opinion of an officer on the Staff of Marshal Joffre, it was then certain that the Germans could be pushed out of Belgium and France at the cost of one million lives among the attacking forces. According to the same authority, this expense of a rapid movement to the German frontier was considered to be too high from a political point of view. It was thought that a slow, steady pressure would eventually so tell upon the moral of the German

[British official photograph.

In November, 1916, bad weather set in, turning the Valley of the Ancre into a vast morass of swimming clay, which entirely precluded any important move by the infantry, and thereby interrupted the offensive campaign so vigorously waged by the British since the previous July.

[British official photograph.

Throughout this interval the artillerymen were busy, laboriously bringing up heavy guns and shells to satisfy their infinite requirements by sheer man-power, through the seas of mud, to new more advanced positions in anticipation of the resumption of the offensive in the spring.

WINTER WORK IN PREPARATION FOR THE CLOSING BATTLES OF THE ANCRE.

[*British official photographs.*

WARRIORS OF THE EAST AT WORK IN THE WEST.
Indian Hotchkiss gun-crew at their sand-bagged gun emplacement on the western front, and (above) Indian cavalry engaged in studying the lie of the land, preparatory to taking a share in the advance.

[*British official photograph.*

CONSOLIDATING A NEWLY-WON POSITION.
Working-parties in a great mine-crater on the British front in France. Putting aside for awhile the rifle and bayonet, the soldiers shouldered picks and shovels and set to work making good the ways of the devastated country over which the advance had passed.

nation as to achieve victory at less cost in life to the British, French, and Belgian races.

By an arrangement made between the French and British authorities the mighty New Army of Sir Douglas Haig remained under the direction of the French High Command. It was most important that the Western Allies should act as an organised whole. Had they not so acted, the enemy would have enjoyed an important advantage by reason of his centralised power over all the forces of Middle Europe. He would have been in a position similar to that occupied by Napoleon when fighting against loosely connected and self-centred nations.

Happily, the feeling of loyalty and absolute comradeship between the French, Belgian, and British High Commands was strong, enlightened, and permanent. France had borne heroically and skilfully the main burden of the long western campaign, and it seemed both fair and sound that her Commander-in-Chief should continue to exercise the supreme direction in the conduct of the war of liberation. Thus the relation between Sir Douglas Haig and General Nivelle and General Pétain was different from the relation between the Duke of Wellington and Blücher and Gneisenau. Owing to the reserves behind it the British Army had become more powerful than the French Army. It was indeed almost strong enough to engage the entire remaining forces of Germany in an open-field conflict with a probability of final though costly victory.

Loyalty among the Allies

On the other hand, the struggle was not taking place in the open field. The enemy was still ably placed in lines of fortified earthworks. In front of him extended long, gradual downward slopes, which the British infantry had to climb against machine-gun fire and under curtains of artillery fire. It was not, therefore, practically certain that the existing force of British soldiers could either break through or press back the German line when Ludendorff brought up the larger part of his huge reserve.

Like General Grant before the long, fortified line of General Lee, Sir Douglas Haig needed, for assured success, a large superiority in men and guns over his opponent. When the attacking force was only about equal in number to the total available defending force there was no sure prospect of a grand decision. In combination the British, French and Belgian Armies were more powerful than the western German armies, even when full allowance was made for the strength of the enemy's fortifications. In the first week of March, however, it was becoming clear that the reactionary Ministers of Russia were intriguing for a separate peace which would have enabled the Germans to concentrate entirely against the western democracies.

A general allied plan had already been worked out in detail for a series of combined movements in great strength by the Allies. Great Britain, who had been the last to move in 1916, was to be the first to resume the offensive in 1917. France was to follow, with a great and persistent attack, as soon as it was seen that the British were attracting the enemy's reserve from Alsace. Then, when the reserve forces in Southern Germany clearly separated from the Austrian forces and moved into France, the main Italian Army was to renew its assault upon the mountainous approaches to Trieste. Afterwards the allied army around Salonika was to engage and hold the principal Bulgarian force. Finally, the Russian Army and the reorganised Rumanian Army were to assail the weakened German, Austro-Hungarian, and Bulgarian Armies on the eastern front, and help to maintain an enveloping and increasing pressure all through the summer and autumn on the Central Empires.

This general allied plan had soon to be altered. By the second week in March the Western Allies **British Empire's** began to see that they could not count **heavy burden** upon Russia again putting forth her full power for at least a considerable time. The British Commonwealth had to shoulder the main burden of the land war as well as the naval struggle, while suffering under the grievous disadvantage that all the main sea paths of communication were partly invaded by hostile submarines.

The German dictator was inclined publicly to admit the superior strength of the British armies opposed to him, and to confess that he was employing a system of submarine piracy in the final hope of evading defeat on land by successful operations under the sea. His desperate submarine campaign served at least one of his purposes in that it kept the spirit of the German people from breaking during the spring of 1917.

Strange and distracting at first was the apparent revolution in the positions of the British Commonwealth and the German Empire. The mistress of the seas promised to become a dominant Power on land, while the greatest military State on earth was trying to save itself by asserting a practical control of the seas.

Happily, in regard to the enemy's interference with communications of Great Britain and France, the power exercised by hundreds of new U boats was not so disturbing as Ludendorff and his advisers had calculated. From a purely military point of view the

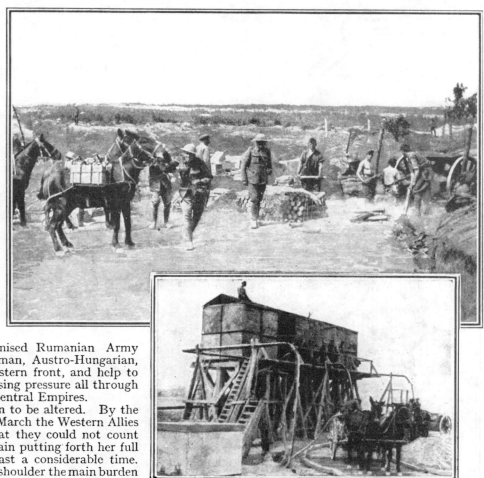

[British official photograph.

WATER SUPPLY TANK IN THE SOMME AREA.

A big water depot on the western front—a form of tank with which the whole zone of military operations was studded. Above: Mules bringing up water for the toiling gun-crews.

[British official photograph.

AFTER THE "ASSEMBLY" HAD SOUNDED.

British infantry, under the doubtful cover of a battered chateau, awaiting the order to move forward. Although one or two of the men appear to have been interested in the dilapidated state of the house, the attention of most was focused on the official camera.

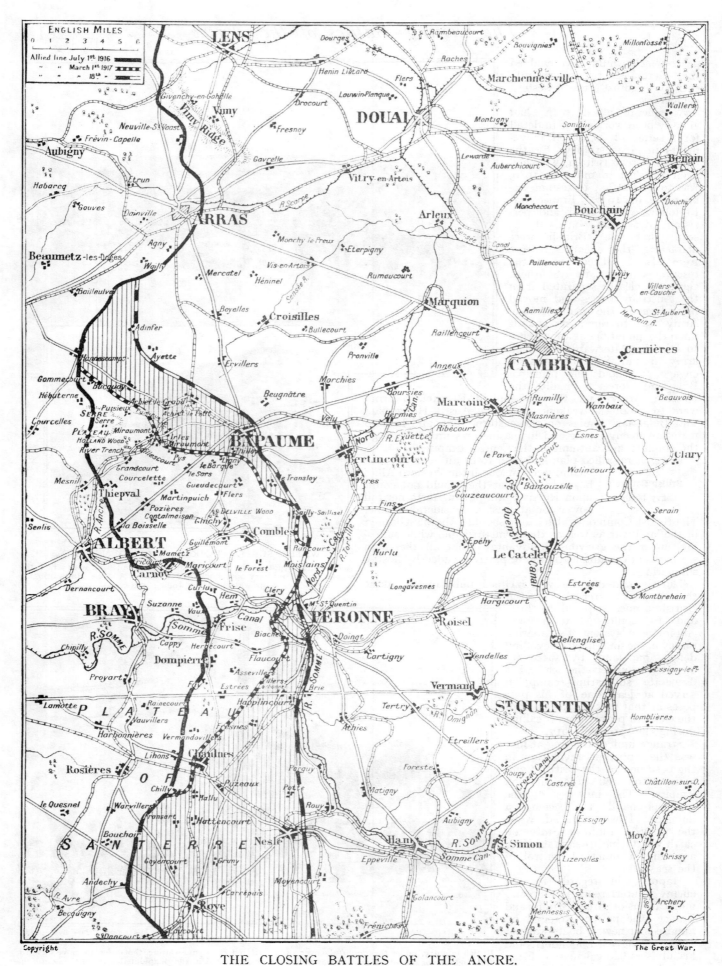

THE CLOSING BATTLES OF THE ANCRE.
Map showing the area of the British advances on the Somme and Ancre between July 1st, 1916, and March 18th, 1917.

new railways Sir Douglas Haig had constructed and the large additional number of locomotives and trucks he had obtained more than compensated for the direct and indirect damage done to the British sources of manufacture, food supply, and means of sea transport.

He suffered at times some serious losses in transit, both to the war factories behind him and to his sea bases on the Continent. Yet the speed with which he was able to move all the material brought to him balanced the delays and losses inflicted by the enemy at sea. His general power was greater in the spring of 1917 than it had been in the summer of 1916.

According to an estimate from

[*British official photograph.*
WAITING TO GO FORWARD.
British troops ready for the signal to go up and over during the advance on the Ancre.

million seven hundred thousand Germans, Great Britain, France, and Belgium had deployed some three million fighting troops in the line and in reserve.

A Washington report, claiming to derive information from the American War Commissions that visited the western front, stated that there were six million men —Britons, Overseas Britons, Frenchmen, and Belgians—under arms from the North Sea to Switzerland. About half of

[*British official photograph.*
VISUAL SIGNALLING DURING THE ADVANCE.
Heliographing by British soldiers in France. As the advance became more pronounced it became possible to use this method on the western front. The man at the telescope was reading the answering flashes. With a large mirror this sun-signalling can be used over a range of many miles.

French Headquarters, the total strength of the German forces was two hundred and nineteen divisions, consisting of about two million six hundred and fifty thousand fighting men. It was reckoned that some seventy-six of these divisions were in the eastern and south-western theatres of war. The western front was held by one million two hundred German combatant troops, at the back of whom was a strategic reserve of another five hundred thousand men. Against this total force of one

[*British official photograph.*
THE POINTING FINGER IN THE ADVANCE ON THE ANCRE.
Sign which there was no mistaking. This eloquent notice-board was put up behind the lines on the western front, and the British soldiers followed its simple direction when the opportunity offered, and, having secured Pozières, passed on and captured Bapaume.

these men, however, were auxiliary to the actual fighting forces. The Kaiser, in a message which he sent to the Sultan of Turkey, referred to the superiority of his opponents on the western front in regard to numbers and material.

In mere numbers the Germans were scarcely so inferior as they tried to make out. In addition to their first strategic reserve of five hundred thousand troops, mentioned in the report from French Headquarters, **Germany's strategic reserves** the enemy appears to have possessed a second strategic reserve of similar proportion, with which he at first contemplated striking at Russia. When through force of circumstances General von Ludendorff was compelled to divert this second reserve to the western front, and was further allowed by the action of the wilder among the Russian Revolutionists also to shift from east to west a considerable number of competent divisions, the balance of opposing forces in France and Flanders became practically equal for the time.

The British Army Council then called forth another half a million men. There was, unfortunately, some delay in raising in England, Scotland, and Wales the new army that would be badly needed by the autumn. British local tribunals did not seem to be alert to the vital need for more men wherewith to achieve a decision in 1917, and thus save the enormous cost in life and treasure of a more prolonged and dragging war.

Happily, at the time when the enemy began to retire towards the Hindenburg line, an important new factor was introduced into the military situation by the entrance of the United States into the struggle. A vast new source of reserve power came suddenly into existence and influenced the plans of the commanders of the western democratic armies.

Although they could not expect any immediate military aid of decisive importance from the great American nation, they could yet confidently look forward to receiving help from a new army of at least half a million men at the end of a year.

This prospect of the future accession to the fighting forces on the western front of so considerable a factor enabled the British, French, Belgian, and Italian High Commands to recover from the disappointment in connection with the Russian part of the grand operations. They then felt strong enough to continue to fight forward in a thrusting and very violent manner, instead of adopting a cautious and **Influence of the** waiting attitude, which would have **American factor** permitted the enemy to exercise the power of initiative. The great American reserves, that were expected to come into action in 1918, were a dominating influence upon the awful battlefield of Europe in the early part of 1917, when Sir Douglas Haig moved against the Hindenburg line, and there began to grind down the last huge accumulation of troops of good quality with which Ludendorff was prepared to make a desperate stand.

WAYSIDE REST OF BRITISH CAVALRY ON THE WESTERN FRONT.

Off-saddle halt for lunch of British horsemen behind the lines in France. During the retreat of the Germans on the western front in the spring of 1917, a retreat which was rapidly accelerated though the German command claimed it was "according to plan," the cavalry got into action on several occasions, their patrols getting well forward into the country from which the enemy had been pressed back on to his Hindenburg line.

OFF TO ATTACK

CHAPTER CLXXXII.

AT EARLY DAWN.

[*British official photograph.*]

THE GERMAN RETREAT FROM BAPAUME AND BRITISH ADVANCE TO THE HINDENBURG LINE.

By Edward Wright.

Ludendorff Achieves Nothing by Retreating from the Ancre—Remarkable Failure of Prussian Guard—Whirlwind Attack on Irles—Great Key Position Won in German Panic—Ludendorff Has to Change His Plans Through Defeat—Grand Retirement from Arras to Soissons Hurriedly Prepared—Why the Germans Thought the British Could Not Follow Them—The Siegfried Line, the Siegfried Troops, and the Siegfried Myth—Victory of Loupart and Capture of Bapaume Ridge—Australians and Prussian Guardsmen—Battle for Bapaume—Victorious St. Patrick's Day—The Mark of the Beast as He Fled from the Guns—Dreadful Condition of Bapaume and Péronne—Poisoning of Wells and Destruction of Historic Edifices—The Australians in the Apple Orchards—Liberation of Forty-five Thousand French People—Skirmishes between British and German Cavalry with Airmen Intervening—Magnificent Charges at Twenty-three Miles an Hour Through Village after Village—Fine Work by the British Patrols in the Hindenburg Line—Australians Give Battle in Beaumetz and Advance on Lagnicourt—Alarm of Ludendorff at the Speed of the British Pursuit—Swift Thrusting Actions all Along the Hindenburg Line—Battles at Doignies and Croisilles—Great British Successes Around St. Quentin—Ronssoy Garrison Forced Against Its Own Wire Entanglements—Results of the Superb Strategy of Sir Douglas Haig—German Reserves Concentrated in the Wrong Positions—Grand British Offensive Opens.

AT the beginning of March, 1917, General von Ludendorff, who was personally directing the operations on the western front, had retired the First German Army to the Monchy-Bapaume Ridge. This ridge runs from Monchy, south-east of Arras, to Bapaume, south-west of Cambrai. The new German position formed a large salient, projecting between Arras and Bapaume. The salient was about fourteen miles broad along the Arras-Bapaume highway, and about eight miles deep at its extreme point on the Hill of Monchy.

The heavy British artillery dominated the whole of this salient. Extending for four miles in front of the Monchy point was a great plateau of land, more than three hundred and twenty-five feet above sea-level, running from Berles to Gommecourt, and occupied by British infantry and artillery and observation-officers. The enemy held only a small patch of land of similar altitude at Monchy, with still smaller patches

near Essarts and near Bucquoy. Between the isolated high downs retained by the enemy were valley gaps in his line, through which British gunnery officers could both fire and observe. The railway system that served the forces in the Monchy salient naturally worked at grave disadvantage, as the British heavy ordnance had a plunging fire across the northern, western, and southern sides of the large German wedge. Even the rearmost German line of communication was at the mercy of the 15 in. howitzers employed by the British gunners.

The Monchy - Bapaume Ridge is one of the most important geographical features of France. It forms the dividing watershed between the North Sea and the English Channel, separating the drainage of the Scheldt from the basin of the Somme River. The hills of which the ridge is composed are not formidable in themselves, because all the rolling, broken country is about four hundred and sixty feet above sea-level. The topmost heights are barely more

[*British official photograph.*]

STUDYING THE NEXT STAGE FORWARD.
British officers in Péronne studying maps in preparation for their continued advance eastward—a stimulating change from their long concentration on maps of the trenches behind the Bapaume Ridge.

REINFORCEMENTS ON THEIR WAY TO THE FIGHTING.
British troops passing through a battered town on the way to reinforce their advancing comrades.
Shattered walls and gaping roofs were familiar objects of the advance, for what artillery had spared had
been wantonly and even viciously destroyed by the retreating Germans.

than sixty-five feet above the valleys. In most places the enemy had only winding vales, about sixty feet deep, in which to shelter his howitzers and his brigade reserves. Into these shallow vales the British guns threw a plunging fire from the higher ground which they occupied.

It was thus clear that General von Ludendorff had achieved nothing by his retreat from the hills above the Ancre. He had merely narrowed the Monchy salient by some three miles. Over these three miles, between Gommecourt and Loupart Wood, the British commander speedily pushed all his artillery. The consequence was that his guns came three miles closer to the heart of the German salient, and thereby obtained a more deadly power of fire against the enemy garrisons.

On the other hand, the German commander acquired considerable advantages of position against infantry attack. In order to reach his new lines the British troops had to cross, by the Upper Ancre, a wide, shallow valley raked by high-placed machine-guns and artillery of every kind.

It was the intention of the German High Command to make a long stand on the Monchy-Bapaume Ridge, and use it as the main pivot for a great retreat southward at Noyon. The enemy had spent months in erecting a formidable new double barrier behind Gommecourt and Irles, and was still engaged making many new trenches. In advance of his

two new lines of defence he retained a connected string of outpost positions, of which the more important were Nightingale Wood, on a spur between Gommecourt and Puisieux, and the village of Irles and Loupart Wood.

The weather in the first week of March was foggy and favoured the enemy by hindering observation for the British artillery. Some ten days were spent by Sir Hubert Gough in bringing his guns forward, constructing new roads and lengthening railways. His infantry profited by the haze and advanced to a depth of a quarter of a mile near Gommecourt on March 3rd, and the following day broke into the German front by the wood of St. Pierre Vaast, taking a considerable number of prisoners.

In the movement from Gommecourt more progress was made for another half a mile, and the Prussian Guardsmen were driven from the forested spur of Nightingale Wood and from their more northern positions in Biez Wood. The Guardsmen fled in the night from the high wooded ground which dominated the way of advance between Gommecourt and Bucquoy.

After the surrender of the woods, which surrender did not speak well for the courage of the most famous of Prussian corps, another intricate system of defences was abandoned without a struggle. This was the farmstead of Rettemoy, which was so fortified and so connected

WATCHING THE TIDE GO FORWARD ON THE WEST.
Members of the British R.A.M.C. and some of their combatant comrades watching the advance from
the remnant walls of a ruined building. From some of the higher parts of the long front over which the
Germans retreated extensive views of the operations of their pursuers were obtainable.

with switch-lines that it exceeded in strength and strategic value the famous farm of Mouquet. It had a labyrinth of underground communications and machine-gun positions, against which brigade after brigade of British troops might have broken. Yet the position was conquered without any important loss by a small British patrolling force, that worked from one end of all the linked positions to the other end, meeting only with some weak parties of bombers, who came from Essarts, and retired more quickly than they came.

On March 6th there were snowstorms along the western front, but around the Somme the air cleared and the Royal Flying Corps became very active, photographing the enemy's new positions, bombing his depots, and controlling a series of fierce outbursts of artillery fire. With drying winds and clearing air the enemy would have been placed in grave difficulties. General Gough had a magnificent force of road-builders and railway constructors, including some fine Canadian hustlers, and they all drove forward the British communications with a surprising speed.

[*British official photograph*

IN A RUINED VILLAGE OF THE ARRAS DISTRICT.
British troops marching past Athies Church, which had been destroyed by the Germans in their enforced retirement from its neighbourhood. The village of Athies is on the left bank of the Scarpe, about three miles east of Arras and about half that distance from the southern end of Vimy Ridge.

Entire parks of field-howitzers pursued the enemy over the broken downland country and kept remarkably close behind the advancing infantry.

The weather dominated everything, and the British Army found that its special weather-lore Staff was of supreme importance in arranging operations. Unhappily, mist and mud continued to serve the enemy. His vast preparations for retreat were veiled in haze or completely blanketed by fog. General Gough could do little more than prepare for pursuit, as General Rawlinson was also doing, and make use of the mist for local operations of high tactical value.

On March 10th the fortified village of Irles, lying in front of Pys and defending the height known as Hill 129, was carried by an enveloping movement. The position was held by a battalion of the Prussian Guard, who was acting merely as a rearguard, and intended to retire to Hill 129 when the new defences were completed. Only two hours before the German plan of retirement was executed the British field-howitzers opened one of their whirlwind bombardments, in which Sir Hubert Gough had specialised. Under cover of the massed fire one British force of infantry worked up from the south, while another swung round northward towards the shoulder of the down. At the same time a detachment of Fusiliers swept up a sunken road which was held by hostile machine-gun crews, and broke the farther flank of the Irles garrison.

The Germans were mastered by very little fighting. They were completely overcome by panic when they perceived the British troops streaming behind them. Surrendering in hundreds, they

[*British official photograph.*

BRITISH ARTILLERYMEN FIRING CAPTURED ENEMY GUNS.
Artillery in one of the devastated villages on the western front from which the Germans had been driven. In his hurried retreat the enemy was compelled to abandon some of his guns, which were effectively turned on him to accelerate further his movement.

BRITISH HEAVY ARTILLERY TAKING UP A NEW POSITION DURING THE ADVANCE.

It was largely the surprising rapidity with which the British Army organised its advanced field-howitzer positions and brought forward its 8 in. and still heavier siege ordnance, rushing up ammunition to the guns and timber for the works in great motor-lorries, that frightened the German Command, and made it seek security and freedom of action by withdrawing prematurely to the new lines it had been preparing.

enabled the conquerors, whose casualties were remarkably small, to snatch the fortified system on the hill slopes and get within a few hundred yards of the wire entanglement at Loupart Wood.

Slight in extent as the British advance was, and small as were the forces engaged, the action was of tremendous importance. Sir Hubert Gough had not merely repeated the success he had won at Baillescourt Hill, by abruptly breaking into the heart of the enemy's defence system, but he had entirely disarranged the plan of General von Ludendorff in regard to the western front.

Irles Hill was a little lower than Loupart Wood. Nevertheless, it was the key-position to practically the whole of the Bapaume Ridge; for its possession enabled the British forces to turn the western side of the main down. The enemy commander had placed the Prussian Guard at Irles, because of the supreme importance of the hill behind it. When the best soldiers in Germany became so panic-stricken that they could not fight their way back to the hill of which they were the advanced guard, and allowed the British troops to occupy the slope, the scheme upon which Ludendorff had worked since October, 1916, had hastily to be altered.

Vital importance of Irles The day after the capture of Irles Hill open preparations were made for a gigantic retirement over a winding front of about one hundred miles. From a point near Arras to a point near Soissons the German forces prepared in anxious haste to withdraw towards Cambrai, St. Quentin, and Laon.

Nothing, of course, will be certainly known about the intentions of the enemy, unless the German General Staff publishes an honest history of the war. Seeing that this Staff grossly falsified its story of the Franco-Prussian War, and made the luckiest chance strokes of the older Moltke appear to be the result of wonderful calculation, it is not likely that the truth about the great German retirement from Bapaume to Noyon will ever be related frankly by German Staff historians.

In these circumstances, one can only consider the matter thoroughly from the British side. From this point of view,

it is almost certain that General von Ludendorff intended to make a long and fierce stand upon the Bapaume Ridge. As was afterwards discovered by British patrols, an enormous amount of new fortification work was being carried on when Irles Hill was lost. Vast triple-thick barbed-wire entanglements had been recently erected. Intricate new trench systems were being excavated, and the ground was marked for further long extensions at Achiet-le-Grand and elsewhere. Thousands of German troops and allied prisoners were being employed in transforming the great lumpy ridge of chalk into a mighty modern fortress system. Clearly it was intended to use the ridge as an **Ludendorff's aim in retreating** obstacle that would delay the army of Sir Hubert Gough for several months.

Immediately after the fall of Irles Hill, however, the French people in towns and villages and hamlets in German possession, from the vicinity of Arras to the neighbourhood of Soissons, became aware that a great general enemy retirement was being hurriedly prepared.

The panic of the Prussian Guard produced something like a panic in the mind of Ludendorff and his lieutenants. As German Staff publicists afterwards admitted, their ablest commander became afraid of the power and speed of movement of the British artillery and the British road-makers. It was largely the surprising rapidity with which the attacking army organised its advanced field-howitzer positions, and brought forward its 8 in. and still heavier siege ordnance, that frightened Ludendorff and made him seek security and freedom of action by withdrawing prematurely to the new line he had been preparing since the autumn of the previous year.

Ludendorff had a double aim. He wished to escape from the overwhelming British gun fire around the Ancre and the Somme, and to avoid being compelled to waste his reserves there in another gigantic pitched battle. He calculated that Sir Douglas Haig would require months of new preparation to organise the country which was to be abandoned to him, or to move his main armies for a prolonged offensive in another direction.

Technical considerations formed the base of the German dictator's plan. Close behind the British armies, north and south of the Somme, were reservoirs of drinking water of a size suitable for London. There was also a system of main and light railways, motor roads, store and provisioning depots, which had taken nearly a year to construct. The system of works was so vast that if, for instance, it were transferred to Canada, it would have provided for years for the needs of all new immigrants. The task of moving this system forward or northward or southward seemed almost as stupendous as would be the removal of London to the sea-coast.

The Germans, on the other hand, had already spent six months' labour of their own troops, and of enslaved civil and military prisoners, in constructing huge water supplies, new railways, stations, store places, gun-pits, and trench systems at a distance of about a day's march behind their front. Their commander, therefore, reckoned that he could stand in full strength on his new front between Arras and St. Quentin, and send out rearguards in superior numbers and with superior equipment, while the British commander would be able only to send out small advance guards.

German plans to hinder pursuit The essence of the German plan was to make the vast new zone of evacuation an utter desert. Large British or French forces were to be prevented from quickly traversing the zone of retreat by blasting up the roads, poisoning the wells, destroying all towns and villages that afforded cover, and arranging numberless machine-gun ambushes along all the ways of advance.

This, at least, was what Ludendorff proposed to do and ordered to be done. Members of his Staff, who frequently and regularly instructed the military writers on the German Press, informed them of the great new plan for open-field warfare conducted over open country from a strongly

fortified line. Thereupon, all German newspapers began first to hint of the invention of a promising new way of warfare, and then openly to expatiate upon the glorious and scientific advantages of Hindenburg's scheme for bringing the half-trained British troops out into the open field, where their inexpertness in rapid manœuvre would lead to their defeat.

Hindenburg, it will be observed, was still credited with the supreme invention of the man who was using him as an advertisement marionette. The old wooden idol of Berlin still served as cover to Ludendorff, who at first named his new system the **Working the** Hindenburg line, and only later divided it **Siegfried tradition** into the local distinction of Siegfried and Wotan lines. From the beginning of the operations, however, the more westerly line was known to the German Army by its Wagnerian title, and special bodies of troops, picked for bodily strength and firmness of character, were formed into Siegfried forces, for the dangerous work of open warfare in front of the new line.

It is hard to believe that Ludendorff himself had such a strain of romance in his temperament as to turn to the greatest of German dramatic musicians as a source of inspiring courage for his rank and file. Ludendorff had as much feeling for poetry as Hindenburg. Yet he had sufficient versatility to discern the moral value of the Wagnerian tradition, with its glorification of the ancient German legends of the heroic age.

He adopted the Siegfried idea and worked it with characteristic energy in his Press Bureau. He also supplied a sound, prosaic foundation for the poetic superstructure of Siegfried warfare by arranging that every Siegfried soldier should be allowed especially luxurious rations during the period of food shortage, when ordinary German troops were kept on limited diet in the manner in which farmers were keeping their store animals during the hard, long winter.

REINFORCING THE BRITISH BARRAGE DURING THE ADVANCE ON THE WESTERN FRONT.
Royal Horse Artillery batteries that had just been galloped into a fresh position to reinforce the barrage behind which the British infantry was pressing forward. The rapid movement of the artillery of different calibres formed a great feature of the advance, and entire parks of field-howitzers pursued the enemy over the broken downland country and kept so close behind the infantry as to disarrange the German plans.

[Canadian War Records

BRINGING IN THE WOUNDED BY LIGHT RAILWAY.
Again and again during the German retreat parties of their delaying forces surrendered to the rapidly following British forces, and were marched back with the wounded, sometimes acting as stretcher-bearers.

Ludendorff was undoubtedly a master of men. Yet he could not master the Briton or the Frenchman. In the Ancre section his half-broken and critical positions were subjected to continuous bombardment immediately after the capture of Irles Hill. Especially upon the thick, black, high belt of trees, rising against the sky on Loupart Down, were convergent streams of smashing shell fire directed. The Germans were caught just as they were removing their field-artillery, and could only reply with their distant heavy guns.

Rain came down in a dense drizzle and blotted out Loupart Wood. The German gunners ceased to shoot except in a mechanical way. Yet, despite the weather, all the roads along which they were dragging their heavy pieces were continually kept under fire. The British army quickly brought forward a large number of 8 in. howitzers and, placing them close behind the field-artillery, maintained a tornado of light and heavy shell from Monchy to the southern bastion of Bapaume at Le Transloy. The

British capture Bapaume Ridge

pieces were aimed through the curtain of rain by means of photographs of the enemy's lines taken by the Royal Flying Corps.

Screened by the rain and heralded by a line of havocking shells, strong British patrols started to work round the great down of Loupart and the smaller hill in front of Grévillers. When the weather cleared on March 12th, enabling the British gunners to see their immediate targets, the decisive struggle for the Bapaume Ridge was concluded in a remarkable manner. The German troops fled. They could not stand against the gigantic British war-machine that slew them at long range with merciless thoroughness. The reconnoitring-parties of British infantry met with only slight resistance from a few machine-guns and snipers. In a morning of mist, on March 13th, they stormed right through Loupart Wood, topped the dominant height, and, going down the farther slope, completed the work done at Irles.

Before them stretched the low plain of French Flanders, where the lazy Scheldt rose and slowly wound northward towards Antwerp. From the last ridge of downland there could be seen no high position from which enemy gunnery officers could direct their artillery against the advancing

British army. German rearguard batteries still fired over the ridge, working by the maps they had made and ranges they had measured before the retreat began.

Yet, save for the information wirelessed to them by a few daring aerial observers, they could only guess by what paths the British troops were working forward, and sprinkle high explosive and shrapnel in a blind and wasteful manner. By the evening of March 13th Grévillers Hill and Grévillers village were occupied by British troops, who began to work westward around Bapaume.

As night fell, the enemy was still holding on to the north-western end of the ridge from

[Canadian War Records.

GERMAN PRISONERS SERVING AS STRETCHER-BEARERS.
Canadian soldier bringing in a wounded comrade and three prisoners—one of them of the German Red Cross—who were apparently glad to be on their way to the safety of internment.

Monchy to the Achiets. But close to Bapaume itself he had only a line of rearguards at Logeast Wood and the low hills around. For all practical purposes the enemy's salient between Arras and Péronne, which since 1914 had formed his most westerly line of advance in France, was pierced and overwhelmed. At the northern end British reconnoitring-parties were progressing from Gommecourt. At its southern end a strong force of patrols was penetrating, by the help of a whirlwind bombardment, into the famous fortified wood of St. Pierre Vaast, against which the French offensive had stopped in the autumn of 1916.

In the clear sunshine of March 15th it seemed unlikely that the enemy would escape from the great salient without severe damage. There were, indeed, great hopes that he would be unable to avoid grave disaster if only the weather remained clear for combined aerial observation and exact and heavy gun fire. Unhappily, rain again beat on the battlefield and veiled the enemy's withdrawing movements. By means of maps the British gunners maintained a fierce and far-ranging fire. They hammered the last

German rearguard out of the great jungle of St. Pierre Vaast, and enabled their infantry to sweep so quickly through the wood as to trap and annihilate a German company and make a breach of two miles and a half in the hostile line between Bapaume and Péronne.

The tempest of rain in the middle of March was, however, the last aid that Thor gave to the errant branch of his former worshippers. The weather became fine and dry, hardening the ground, making rapid movement possible, and facilitating the frenzied labours of the British track builders. British flying squadrons obtained a clear view over the enemy's line of activities, and all the British forces around the Somme soon knew that a great event was impending.

In vain did the German commander pretend he was still standing in strength on his old line. On March 15th he sacrificed a large body of men in making a sally from the Achiets, which was beaten off. On March 16th he launched on the British line above Gommecourt another fierce assault which was also easily broken. He made the mistake of demonstrating in the wrong places.

[*Canadian War Records.*
WOUNDED AWAITING REMOVAL.
Stretcher cases ready for transference to a light railway for conveyance from the battlefield to the base.

The British commander only pressed forward more strongly in the face of the enemy's show of resistance. Instead of striking back at the points from which an attempt had been made to strike him, he suddenly and violently thrust clean through the German front at Bapaume. Between Arras and Noyon were two German salients, with a wider British salient extending between them. Sir Douglas Haig left the German forces in their own two wedges, and struck directly eastward from each side of the Albert-Cambrai high road, along which he had been fighting since July 1st, 1916.

The German commander feared that a violent attempt to break

his line would be delivered from the extreme point of the British salient. He placed a fresh force of Prussian Guards around Bapaume and excavated a new and strong system of earthworks on either side of the Albert road. Three great belts of new and unbroken wire covered the new system of defences, on which the Foot Guards were still working when the final storm of shell broke upon them in the grey dawn of St. Patrick's Day. From the west and south-west approaches to the city strong Australian and British patrols came forward with ladders, bombs, and machine-guns. They climbed over the unbroken wire and, in a fierce, short action, scattered the Prussian Guards. As one company fled it was trapped in a machine-gun barrage and destroyed. The Australians then entered the town in pursuit of the enemy, who detonated charge after charge of high explosive to cover his retreat.

Soon after Bapaume fell, Le Transloy, forming the southernmost defence of Bapaume, was surrendered by the enemy without a shot, the garrison retiring eastward to the village of Rocquigny. They were pursued by British patrols and thrown out of Rocquigny by nightfall. Then, on the other side of Bapaume, a more daring and rapid method of advance **Victorious** was made. A force of British cavalry **St. Patrick's Day** worked past the high wood of Logeast, and, penetrating eastward of the great, new, vain system of defences at Achiet-le-Grand, turned the whole German line and reached to open country towards Béhagnies. Achiet-le-Petit and Biefvillers were taken, and British airmen, cavalry, and infantry scouts were, by the evening, moving beyond the old shell-ploughed battlefields into the Siegfried zone of warfare.

The darkened theatre of the new campaign was horribly picturesque. A great belt of burning villages and smoking towns marked the ebb of strength of the most powerful army of invaders in history. The nocturnal sky was illumined with infernal splendour by their star-shells, by green clouds of fire from their shrapnel shells, and by volcanic bursts of high-explosive projectiles from their rearguarding batteries. The ancient, charming city of Bapaume was an indescribable ruin. Scarcely one house remained intact. Inside and out were the marks of the beast.

Every dwelling was looted, and where there had been

[*British official photograph.*
INTERROGATING GERMAN PRISONERS JUST BROUGHT IN.
British officers questioning a batch of prisoners immediately on their arrival at a base. The Germans, whose supplies had been held up sometimes for days by the deadly fire of the British guns, frequently arrived in a half-famished condition and were immediately given food.

BRITISH FIELD-BATTERIES RUSHING FORWARD TO PRECIPITATE THE GERMAN RETREAT FROM BAPAUME.

The Germans expected that the British Army would be tied to its positions by the mass of material accumulated during the winter, and were disconcerted by the marvellous rapidity with which the artillery pursued them. Mud was thick over all the terrain, but eight horses were furnished to each gun instead of the usual six, and extra ammunition was sent up on pack-horses, each carrying six to eight rounds in panniers.

no time to cart the furniture away it had been broken up. Family portraits were rent, and in some cases smeared with human ordure. The only unbroken thing left in the town seems to have been a trunk, that was found in the open street. A charge of explosive was placed in it, so arranged as to shatter any British soldier who tried to open it. Small war souvenirs were also scattered about to tempt the inexperienced Australian and Briton.

The Australians, however, had played similar tricks upon the Turks when evacuating the Anzac position on the Gallipoli Peninsula. The Briton, also, was well instructed in the art of avoiding booby-traps and trip-mines. The Germans were like savages with inferior cunning. They wasted their labour and their material on insignificant devices, and neglected tasks of great importance. The time they spent in setting fire to Bapaume, in breaking up the furniture of the townspeople, spoiling the houses and destroying the ornamental trees must have amounted to a week.

They were so thoroughly occupied with a great variety of dirty monkey tricks, directed against the feelings of the civil population of France, that they were finally in too great a hurry to complete the destructive work of real military importance. Bapaume was **Insane destruction** a city of deep cellars, which the invaders **in Bapaume** had connected and extended into an immense system of bomb-proof shelters. Had all these old and new dug-outs been thoroughly blown in when the Australians entered the city under a heavy bombardment from the distant German batteries, the victors' casualties from gun fire might have been very heavy.

The foolishly savage Germans, however, had blown up only a part of the great underground retreats. They had been too busy destroying the homes of the civil population of Bapaume, and hacking pictures and furniture, and putting paraffin and petrol in private houses. As a military position Bapaume, though but a smoking ruin

above ground, was still an admirable concentration base for operations eastward.

Even the highway from Albert remained available for traffic. There were about three mine-craters in it, but British army vehicles were able to swing round them and quickly bring up the food material required by the advancing army. The damage to the road was speedily made good, and the British railway lines prolonged across the old battlefield.

In the night of March 17th, while the conquerors of Bapaume were extending their gains northward and east-ward, other British forces were working into and around Péronne. Patrols had **British occupation** begun to feel their way, in the afternoon **of Peronne** of St. Patrick's Day, towards the dominant mass of Mont St. Quentin. It was against the hill of St. Quentin that the armies of General Fayolle had been stayed both north and south of the Somme. The French Ordnance Department had even had a special gun at last made for action against Mont St. Quentin without, however, succeeding in mastering the hostile batteries concealed in and about the historic down.

With the breaking of the enemy's line at Irles Hill, which directly opened Bapaume, Mont St. Quentin was in great danger of being stormed by a sudden flank attack. The Germans hastily removed their powerful batteries. On March 17th there were only a few machine-gun teams and snipers clinging to the crest and watching the British movements at Biaches and in the Tortille ravine.

By midnight strong scouting-parties were gathering at the foot of the height and clearing Moislains and the hamlets by the bend of the Somme. In the morning of March 18th a party of field-grey figures was seen escaping from Mont St. Quentin to avoid envelopment, and soon afterward both the height and Péronne town were occupied by the British army.

Some of the men crossing the river from Biaches had an unexpected bath. The retreating Germans had broken the wooden bridges over the Somme, and then artfully covered the gaps with straw screens to prevent British aerial observers from noticing the evidence of withdrawal by the breaking of communications. This was an ingenious trick that met with the success it deserved. Not only was the destruction of the bridges unperceived, but some British soldiers thought the straw was solid and fell through into the water. The cost in life of taking Péronne, however, was nil.

The enemy prepared explosive devices in habitual ape-like imitation of the Dardanelles evacuation traps. But there was not, so report ran at the time, a single British casualty. A cavalry patrol first entered, followed by Midland and London infantry. The condition of the renowned old lovely town that used to adorn the curve of the Somme was heart-breaking. The heart that bled for Louvain must have run white for Péronne.

For example, after blowing out the front of the beautiful fifteenth-century town hall of Péronne, the wreckers placed **Wreck of Péronne's ancient town-hall** high upon the ruins a large placard with the cynical message: "Nicht ärgern, nur wundern!"—"Don't get angry, simply wonder!"

The ruins of this ancient jewel of the country-side of Picardy were a monument to the character of the modern descendants of the race that had produced Bach, Goethe, Schiller, Wagner, and Hauptmann. The destructiveness of scientific barbarians was combined with the filthiness of sewer rats. High-explosives, solidified paraffin, and the contents of latrines were employed by the new Siegfrieds to shatter, fire, and sully the houses they had completely looted.

In the village of Barleux, close to Péronne, the discovery was made of the poisoning of wells by the Germans. They began in scientific fashion by using arsenic, and ended in bestial manner by throwing in ordure. This was done to hinder the advance of the British armies by infecting the natural water supplies and compelling the troops to wait for pure water to be brought forward.

The chief design of the gigantic system of destruction, extending from the Arras suburbs to the villages near Soissons, was not, however, of a direct military nature. The intention was to appal the imagination of the civilian population of France. Apparently Ludendorff fancied that the intrigues for a negotiated peace, which he was about to conduct through **Object of the** Scheidemann, Troelstra, Lenin, Stauning, **wholesale destruction** and the Socialist minorities of Great Britain, France, and Italy, would be facilitated by the methods he employed in surrendering French territory.

The Australian forces, advancing from Bapaume, were the first troops of the British Commonwealth to respond to these methods. They did so in a manner peculiarly British. Nothing they heard or saw seemed to touch them keenly until they came to an orchard in which all the fruit-trees had been felled. The enemy had destroyed towns and burnt hundreds of villages and thousands of farms. He had left behind starving crowds of pitiful children, parchment-faced women, and enfeebled old men. The girls with any beauty surviving his manner of rule had been taken away, nominally as officers' servants, but really for purposes of a most dreadful kind.

Yet it was the sight of some felled or ringed fruit-trees that loosed a passion of anger in the Australians. From the Australians the fierce emotion spread to the home divisions. A stranger might have thought that it was a foolish sentiment.

It was merely a symbol. The men had grown full of

A "MOPPING-UP" PARTY BOMBING A CAPTURED TRENCH WHENCE SHOTS HAD BEEN FIRED.
In the Battles of the Somme and Ancre the Germans, when driven out of positions, left men in dug-outs to come up later and attack the conquerors from behind. Having been taught by experience, however, the British troops organised "mopping-up" parties to follow close on the heels of the attack and bomb all lurking Germans out of their captured trenches while the attack was being pressed on.

explosive rage, while continually suppressing it and endeavouring to keep cool and calm. Mastered at last by their feelings, they saw some broken fruit-trees, and, with disconcerting abruptness, took the ruined orchard as a small but significant token. During the Indian Mutiny British troops in the relieving army took with them fragments of the clothing of the murdered women of their race to inspire them in avenging victory. The Australians and their comrades took with them only the memory of some gashed

Symbol of the orchards

and broken apple-trees. But, when they afterwards went into action at Bulle-court, the armed forces of Germany fully paid for all the vile, mean things they had done around Bapaume, Péronne, Nesle, and Roye.

At Rouy, by the Somme, the Germans placed some hundreds of women, children, and old men in the ruined village, fired all the hamlets from which the people had been collected, and then trained their guns upon the place. When the British patrols entered Rouy a storm of shell was directed upon the famished, starving people before they could be rescued and removed.

GENERAL VIEW OF BAPAUME AFTER ITS RECAPTURE.
Bapaume, an ancient, charming town, was deliberately wrecked by the Germans before they surrendered it. Every house was looted, soaked with paraffin, and fired. Yet, though but a smoking ruin, Bapaume remained a military position of great importance for the British operations eastward.

The British Army liberated nearly ten thousand of the French population, and the French Army set free more than thirty-five thousand of its compatriots. In all cases only the " useless mouths " in the evacuated territory were left behind by the retreating invaders. Any adult or young person whose slave labour was likely to pay the cost of inadequate feeding was carried off behind the Hindenburg line.

By the evening of March 18th the British armies had advanced on a front of forty-five miles to a depth of ten miles in some places. In addition to the four towns of Bapaume, Péronne, Nesle, and Chaulnes, some fifty-five villages were recovered from the enemy, and two hundred square miles of land. The French armies from Roye to Soissons swept over a still larger tract of country, recovering Roye, Lassigny, and Noyon, and reaching towards Ham and liberating nearly a hundred villages.

The scattered fighting between British reconnoitring-

parties and German rearguards was continuous. The enemy employed Uhlans and mounted Jägers to cover his retirement, and against these enemy mounted forces British cavalry patrols worked forward in difficult circumstances. Machine-gun ambushes, with hidden barbed-wire defences and other devices, were naturally employed by the enemy. Rare were any of the old-fashioned straight-forward charges of sabre against sabre. If a party of German cavalry was sighted and seen galloping away, it was rather unwise to pursue them at the charge. For near the tail of an apparent flight a hostile ambuscade was to be suspected.

At first the cavalryman seemed to have become only a reconnoitring infantryman who sometimes used a horse, though this state of things changed in splendid fashion A large part of the advanced-guard work, formerly carried out by cavalry, was performed by squadrons of aeroplanes. At the beginning of the great retreat a British airman reconnoitring over the Somme spied a hostile cavalry screen near the hamlet of Ennemain, and chased it with machine-gun fire, bringing down one man and stampeding all the others. In another action a British cavalry patrol was surprised by a party of German snipers concealed in a stranded omnibus. Just as the Germans opened fire a British pilot swooped upon them, falcon-like, and smote them with a drum of his Lewis gun.

Airmen, Regular cavalry, Yeomen, and picturesque turbanned Indian horsemen, cyclists and motor-cyclists, with horse-artillery behind them all, probed into the vague and yielding long German line. British and Australian infantry, with their light artillery, Stokes guns, and supply trains, worked close behind the forward reconnoitring-parties to afford rapid support.

The dangerous art of drawing the enemy's fire was pursued with zest by the advanced guards of the victorious armies. Only a remnant of the little original Expeditionary Force had any happy memories of chasing the beaten armies of the German Empire. To the new national forces, trench-trained for nine months in the science of slowly pushing back the stubborn enemy, the feel of sudden and complete weakness in the foe was a great exhilaration. Men wounded in the skirmishes came back congratulating themselves on having been in " a jolly little scrap."

The eagerness of the British cavalry again to get in contact with the long-ranged German snipers was amusing to the plodding infantry. Most gladly did they search for trouble, while **British cavalry** skilfully trying to avoid all possible **capture Equancourt** ambushes. In the end, however, the British infantrymen had an exceeding admiration for the lance as a storming weapon.

At Equancourt, a little place on the Tortille River near the junction with the North Canal, the enemy was expected to make a very strong stand. The Germans held a wood in front of the village and also another hamlet, Sorel, on the right, commanding the field of fire before Equancourt. Both German forces were on high ground, and the only means of approaching them were two gullies, down which

(Australian official photograph.

Australians crossing a sleeper=log road over a crater blown to delay their advance near Bapaume.

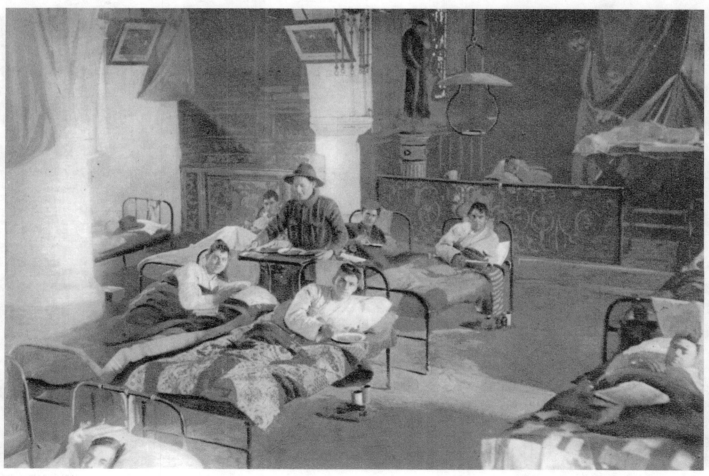

(Australian official photograph.

Mid=day dinner in a hospital established in the chapel at Millencourt, west of Albert.

[British official photograph

Ruined but rescued: Havoc in the outskirts of Péronne, recovered from the enemy March 18th, 1917

[Australian official photograph

Vanguard of the liberators: Australians passing through the wrecked Rue de Péronne, Bapaume.

[British official photograph.

First across the Somme near Péronne: Over the wooden bridges broken by the retreating foe.

[British official photograph.

British advance guard entering Péronne: Once a fair jewel of the country-side of Picardy.

[British official photograph.

Street in Bapaume burned by German incendiaries.

[British official photograph.

In the heart of ancient Bapaume during the conflagration.

[British official photograph.

A violated sanctuary as left by the Huns in Bapaume.

Main street in Bapaume immediately after the town had fallen.

their machine-guns played. Some British infantry came to the scene of action, six hours before they were due, in order to watch how the cavalry did it.

The cavalry commander divided his men into three parties. One was posted on rising ground on the left, to bring machine-gun fire to bear on the wood. Another small detachment dismounted on the right and engaged the garrison of Sorel with machine-gun fire. Then down the outer gully the attacking force of cavalry was launched at the pace of twenty-three miles an hour. The Germans opened with a few bursts of machine-gun fire, and then fled in a panic behind a railway embankment at the rear of the village, from which they scattered in wild flight. Owing to the speed of the charge only a few of the mounted men were hit.

The little action was a revelation of the insignificance of machine-gun fire against a cavalry target. By the time the gunners fired their first shots the horsemen swept on, and the defending teams then had the alternative of missing their mark or losing their nerve. Owing to the lightning pace with which the lances came to them, they usually lost their nerve. "Look at the beggars!" shouted one of the British infantrymen as the cavalry swept past. "That's the style to take a village. No blighted bombs for them, but hell-for-leather all the way!"

Equancourt fell on March 26th, and the same day the British cavalry also took the large village of Longavesnes, on the way to Épéhy. The country round about was wooded, which is what all cavalrymen like. Under cover of the trees several troops converged upon the village, and, charging through musketry and machine-gun fire, drove the enemy back towards the Hindenburg line.

Advancing from the new lines they had won, the cavalry forces on March 28th broke a series of German rearguards at Villers-Faucon and Saulcourt and other villages, five and a half miles from St. Quentin.

Sometimes they rode the enemy down at the point of the lance by a surprise charge on his flank, capturing his machine-guns and making prisoners. More often the Germans bolted like rabbits, leaving their guns, flinging away their arms, and speeding off on the cycles they kept by the nearest road in the rear.

For more than a week the weather was, on the whole, brilliant for both cavalry work and aerial scouting. There was a keen wind, tempered by sunshine, with an unusually clear air, giving unusual facilities for observation. There was less rain than sunshine, and most of the roads were in good order.

Superiority of British cavalry The German cavalry were found poor in quality. They avoided encounter, and appeared only on the sky-line, riding away at the first sight of British troops. Many of them seemed to have no confidence or skill in the use of the lance. They held it awkwardly, showing that they were not the same class of men that rode to the shock in the early actions between the Lys and the English Channel. It was on the pistol that they seemed to rely, and in the lightning clash of conflicting cavalry the British and Indian lances were much the surer weapons. After one skirmish

twenty German lances were picked up by British troopers.

Night after night the British cavalry went out in patrols. The leader was ahead and alone; two men followed him, while behind a small body kept in touch. Silently they rode, like moving shadows, with no clatter of stirrup or clank of bit. Their task was to find gaps in the enemy's wire, creep close to his outposts, ride softly into the black ruins, and come back with news of the enemy's positions.

They captured at least eight villages at the gallop, by sweeping round on both sides in wide order, with lowered lances. One daring cavalry patrol penetrated the Hindenburg line on March 26th. It stole into the Forest of Holnon, north of St. Quentin, picked up information by listening to the talk of the Germans, and stole out undiscovered. Holnon soon afterwards was captured, largely through this fine piece of scouting. **Villages captured at the gallop**

After a heavy snowstorm on March 22nd the German commander threw out stronger forces from the Siegfried

[*British official photograph.*]

NEATLY BRIDGING A DESTROYED LIGHT RAILWAY.

British working-party making good the ways behind the advance with the materials that the enemy had left behind. The men erected this neat and serviceable structure across a sunken road, the light-rail track along which had been destroyed by the rapidly retreating Germans.

line, and increased his resistance between Arras and St. Quentin. Ruined villages, which were thought to be occupied by British cavalry, were shelled, and the important railway junction of Roisel, seven miles beyond Péronne, was the scene of several fierce little actions. It changed hands three times in two days, but was finally abandoned by Uhlans and cycling riflemen without a shot.

These reactions by the enemy were principally due to a lack of courage by his Siegfried forces. They abandoned several important positions in which they had been ordered to make a desperate stand. The village of Beaumetz, standing on high ground between Cambrai and Bapaume, was a striking example of the fluctuating quality of the picked German storming troops. First, an Australian patrol drew heavy fire from Beaumetz and the neighbouring hamlet of Morchies. It drew back for reinforcements with field-artillery, and then skirmished forward. Morchies was occupied without a struggle, and Beaumetz

[*British official photographs*.

HERO-WORSHIP WELL EARNED.

French villagers' interest in a machine-gun and gunner that had helped in their deliverance.

[*British official photographs*.

LEARNING ALL THE GLAD TRUTH AT LAST.

Smiling hospitality was offered by the French people to their British rescuers. Not least of the pleasure these brought were the French newspapers, of which the people had been deprived throughout the German occupation. Above: Curiosity in a newly-recovered village over the arrival of a British motor-car.

was outflanked, bombarded, and occupied, the enemy bolting before he could be seriously engaged.

The German Staff, on hearing the news, required the village to be reconquered at any cost. The light surrender was a grave error, and interfered with Ludendorff's plan and endangered the Hindenburg line, which ran near by. After a lull of two days a special German force, with guns, made a surprise attack upon a small Victorian sniping-party holding, with one machine-gun, the day post in front of the village. The little band of Australians charged to the death, but though most of them fell, the survivors brought back their gun into safety.

At other points the Germans worked through the Australians' outpost line, but were broken in a wild street-fight and driven back down the Bapaume road. The next day the Germans attacked in stronger force. Their colonel had called for volunteers, and, when no man came forward, he ordered two infantry companies to go with a company of special storming troops.

The attack was made from two sides. On one side the ordinary German infantry advanced in column of fours, only to be caught at close range by a machine-gun. Fifteen men dropped, and the rest of the gallant five hundred rushed back to any cover they could find and disappeared from the battle. The storming troops were of tougher fibre. Working forward silently on leather

Long struggle for Beaumetz

knee-pads and leather elbow-pads, armed with short rifles and little dagger-like bayonets, they made a rush attack upon the village, entered the main street, met the tree-lovers from Australia, and went down before them.

The remnant was driven back into two ruined houses at the end of Beaumetz. On one house a British field-gun was trained at a range of 500 yards, and under one shell the shelter of the storming troops collapsed. The other house was left until dusk, when a young Victorian officer, who had led the charge the previous day, stalked the building, shot one of the snipers, and, seizing the sniper's rifle, as his own was empty, killed another fleeing German. Upon the last German was found an interesting diary, one passage of which ran: "Attacked Beaumetz last night, but found the place too strongly held. Shall probably attack again to-night, *as the position was surrendered sooner than was intended.*"

On March 26th, while the struggle for Beaumetz was violently raging, the main Australian force attempted a diversion. Instead, however, of effecting a diversion, General Birdwood and his able lieutenants victoriously opened the great battle on the Hindenburg system. The point selected for attack was the village of Lagnicourt. It was a dominant position, close to the most critical position in the enemy's new defences. In the neighbouring village of Quéant the long Wotan switch-line running down from Drocourt made a junction with the outer Siegfried line. As British aerial observers had found, Lagnicourt village was the most delicate spot over the heart of the new front that Ludendorff had constructed. Fighting was going on at Croisilles northward, as well as at Beaumetz southward, when the Australian patrols, extending from Morchies, surprised the German garrison of Lagnicourt and captured the key-position with few casualties.

After a sharp fight in the streets and around the sawmill and windmill in the morning with a fresh German force in new uniforms, the Australians outflanked the enemy, under cover of Chaufour Wood, ate the breakfast of brown bread, brawn, and ale of the vanquished troops, and prepared for stormy weather. The following day the official enemy communiqué stated that the victors had purchased their success at the cost of a thousand men killed. The local German commander apparently reported that his Staff had counted this number of slain Australians,

Capture of Lagnicourt so that it might be estimated that, with the wounded, the total casualties on the British side exceeded four thousand. As a matter of fact, the Australians lost at the outside only fifty men killed in the advance from Morchies and the capture of Lagnicourt.

The ease and the speed with which the outer defence of the main junction of the great Hindenburg line had been stormed alarmed the German commander. He ceased the struggle to recover Beaumetz and massed at Quéant the best troops he had available for the recovery of Lagnicourt. He counter-attacked in strength from the direction of the Wotan line, employing selected troops from a Prussian Guard division. They were shot down. Again he launched the Guardsmen later in the day, but by this time British field-guns had been moved up to answer the artillery the enemy was using. As the Germans came out in the open, preparatory for a rush attack, they were swept by shell fire and dispersed.

It was reckoned that the enemy had some fifteen batteries of machine-guns grouped in one small depression between Lagnicourt and the neighbouring village. He raked the ridge with them, while his heavy guns, in permanent new emplacements behind the Hindenburg system, bombarded the lost ground in terrific fashion. Nevertheless, the Australians repulsed every counter-attack,

[*British official photograph.*
A REAL JOY-RIDE.
French children, mounted on British soldiers' bicycles, piloting their liberators to their billets.

[*British official photographs.*
HARBINGERS OF HAPPINESS AFTER LONG DISTRESS.
British soldiers won the confidence of the French children at once, and many scenes of unintentional pathos were witnessed as the children gathered round the improvised stoves for the warmth and food and kindness to which they had been strangers so long. Above: A British general greeting a little French maiden.

[British official photograph.
DAMAGED PERONNE
FORT.
Before evacuating Péronne the
Germans damaged much of
the old town, including its
quaint mediæval fort.

with very heavy losses
to the Germans, and
in the night began to
advance along the road
to L o u v e r v a l and
Doignies.

Then there followed
a series of British
thrusts all along the
line between Arras and
St. Quentin. On March
28th the enemy positions
at Croisilles were tested,
and found to be strongly
held, yet ground was
won against fierce resistance. The next day
the south-western ap-
proaches to Cambrai were attacked, the village of Neuville-
Bourjonval being stormed and held against a fierce counter-
stroke. On March 30th Ruyaulcourt, a little farther north,
was taken, opening the way to Havrincourt Wood, destined
to become famous as one of the grand fortresses of the
Hindenburg entrenched line. Immediately afterwards
another line of convergence was cleared towards Cambrai,
still in a south-westerly direction, by a succession of
brilliant little British victories around the Péronne and
Cambrai high-road at Fins, Sorel, and Heudicourt.

North-west of Cambrai, and above Bullecourt, there was
a very weak point in the terrain that Ludendorff had
carefully selected for a decisive battle. The little
Cojeul stream, tributary to the Scarpe River, flowed
from Hénin, over low ground. This tract of low ground
was liable to be narrowed on either side and transformed
into a death-trap salient. The British
Preparing the Commander - in - Chief arranged for
Battle of Arras General Gough and General Allenby
and General Horne to co-operate in this
scheme of action. Thus the Battle of Arras was prepared.
As a preliminary measure some of the enemy's posts at
Hénin were rushed at the end of March, while he was being
severely pressed by British and French forces far southward
at St. Quentin. Then, on April 2nd, when the St. Quentin
Battle was growing more violent, General Gough's forces
of Australian and British troops fought forward towards

the Cambrai sector of the Hindenburg system and penetrated the outworks on a front of ten miles. Hénin was
entirely taken, together with Croisilles, Ecoust-St. Mein,
Noreuil, Longatte, Louverval, and Doignies.

It was the opening of the terrible and incessant pitched
battle of 1917. Ludendorff's calculations of the time it
would take the British Army commanders to bring their
artillery across the deep zone of wasted and befouled
country were wide of the mark. A few days before his
outpost barrier line was broken by surprise assault he had
gone out of his way openly to jeer at the apparent slowness
with which the British forces were advancing, comparing
it with the speed of the French movement, and drawing
very foolish conclusions as to the lack of manœuvring
power and skill of the trench-trained new British soldier.

The Teutonic dictator and his Staff and his dependent
military publicists were duped in manifold ways by self-
conceit and ignorance. In the first place, they seem
seriously to have underestimated the decisive impetuosity
of British cavalry and
infantry a t t a c k s in
open - field operations.
They lost many impor-
tant positions through
under-garrisoning them.
In the second place,
they failed to foresee
the speed with which
the vast construction of
n e w communications
and new p o s i t i o n s
would be carried out by
the s a p p e r s, road-
makers, and railway-
builders of the advancing
British armies. In the
third place, they would
not, in their plans and
forecasts, allow for the
fact that the nation that
took six months to con-
struct the Hindenburg
line was likely to be
excelled in rapid and
gigantic reorganisation
by the B r i t i s h, in
their aroused and in-

[British official photograph.
BRITISH WORKING-PARTY IN A GREAT MINE-CRATER.
Working-party who had " camped " with tent and dug-out in an extensive mine-
crater, from which they could set out to carry on their important work of maintaining
the lines of communication.

calculable mood of fiercely strenuous effort.

Ludendorff's army commanders, from the beginning of
the sudden period of disillusion, wasted men in army corps
in attempts to retrieve the original
errors in the plans of their chief. On　**Costly German**
April 2nd large numbers of men, drawn　**counter-attacks**
from one division of the Prussian Guard
and two divisions of ordinary infantry, were exhausted in
repeated counter-attacks between Hénin and Doignies. The
British first won the village by a trick. The troops streamed out
at dawn, unheralded by the customary artillery barrages,
and got in among the nests of snipers, machine-gunners,
and bombers before the Germans could rally. Doignies was
carried from Beaumetz in almost a minute, the garrison bolting to Demicourt and firing mines behind them as they fled.

Almost as suddenly, Louverval, with its glorious château
by the Cambrai road, was stormed ; while Croisilles and
the other northern villages were more gradually reduced
by house-to-house fighting. Then it was that the German
Staff reacted with wild violence. Their heavy howitzers,
emplaced in the Hindenburg system, shattered the lost
villages and entirely destroyed Louverval Château. Under
the hurricane of big shell the counter-attacks went on in
furious extravagance. Seven were broken in the course
of the day at Doignies, while at Croisilles, which the enemy
was grimly resolved to retake at any sacrifice, the struggle
was continuous.

British soldiers making friends in one of the French villages which they had forced the ruthless invader to evacuate. The children thus restored to France eagerly welcomed their deliverers, who found joy for themselves in giving joy to the youngsters. After the bullying Germans, the children found that the cheery and friendly new-comers imparted something of a holiday atmosphere to their shattered homes.

Welcoming the British troops into a French town which they had delivered from the tyranny of German occupation. By the spring of 1917 the British Army had liberated nearly ten thousand of the French population, and the French Army more than thirty-five thousand of its compatriots. The Germans only left the old people and young children, "useless mouths," in the territory from which they were forced.

IN THE HOUR OF DELIVERANCE FROM THE HORROR OF THE HUN.

AUSTRALIAN BAND PLAYING THE OCCUPYING FORCES INTO BAPAUME.

[British official photograph.

Strong and fresh forces of the Prussian Guard were still fortifying Bapaume with a new system of defences when the final storm of shell broke upon them in the grey dawn of St. Patrick's Day. From west and south-west Australian and British patrols advanced and scattered the Prussian Guard, and then the Australians entered and took possession of the town, an important base for operations eastward.

Several times the grey hostile waves broke into the villages and ebbed into the ruined cottages. By means of bombs, bayonets, and rifle fire each remnant was destroyed or compelled to scatter back. At last only broken and dispirited bodies of German troops remained in the cover of neighbouring farmsteads and woods, and were withdrawn towards Fontaine.

On the same day the new German line was bent back badly round St. Quentin by the southernmost British army. Savy village and Savy Wood, west of the city, had already been carried by Midland troops' hard fighting. Developing this advantage, the British commander, on April 2nd, hunted the Germans round both sides of Holnon Wood, captured Bihécourt, and Villécholles, Francilly, Selency, and St. Quentin Wood, thus enveloping the town, west and north at a distance of two miles. Near Savy Wood a battery of six German field-guns was taken by the Midlanders, but could not be at once removed.

The German commander, in the night of April 3rd, made a violent effort to recover his guns, the capture of which had been mentioned in Sir Douglas **British advance on** Haig's report. A strong force of storm- **St. Quentin** ing troops worked forward for a rush in the darkness, but were completely broken in a hand-to-hand tussle. The guns were then brought into the British lines.

Meeting with more resistance, as Ludendorff threw in part of his enormous reserves, the southernmost British forces continued slowly and stubbornly to thrust farther into the St. Quentin sector of the Hindenburg system. Maissemy was taken, on the Omignon brook, and Pontru and Le Verguier were occupied, near the St. Quentin-Cambrai highway, by April 8th.

In the next enemy sector northward, in front of Le Catelet, there was a similar series of vehement British thrusts. After the cavalry rode down the Siegfried troops in Liéramont, Epéhy and Peizière were captured, though held by strong hostile detachments. On April 5th the British patrols, having surprised and scattered the Bavarians at St. Emilie and Templeux, stormed into Ronssoy.

At Ronssoy, the garrison had erected a mesh of heavy wire, and placed machine-guns in copses commanding the routes of advance on the village. An abrupt and utterly unexpected rush at dawn, however, undid all the preparations of the Germans. Their **Important victory** machine-gunners were dislodged before **at Ronssoy** they could bring their batteries properly into action, and though their wire entanglements were rather troublesome, they did not delay the little but important victory. Quite the contrary. By an extraordinary reversal of positions the Germans were driven against their own wire, and there either killed or captured. Next day the neighbouring hamlet of Lempire was taken, bringing the attacking forces well within battle range of the main defences of the enemy.

To the north-west of Epéhy, another line of approach to the Hindenburg system was rapidly won by a driving sweep through Metz-en-Couture on April 3rd. Two days later the outskirts of Gouzeaucourt and the southern edge of Havrincourt were reached. As Havrincourt Wood was likewise occupied along its northern edge, it seemed likely at the time quickly to fall.

The great jutting wood was surrounded on three sides, and some British forces had entered it. Yet it did not fall. For months it remained a breakwater against all the British waves of attack that beat on its front and flanks. Like Greenland Hill, Riencourt Hill, and the suburbs of

Lens, Havrincourt Wood was one of the grand bastions of the enemy's line.

Still, there is no doubt that the German High Command was seriously disconcerted by the speed with which British advance-guards, with mobile artillery, moved across the evacuated territory. At Emilie, Ronnsoy, Savy, and other barrier positions the Siegfried garrisons were dazed and staggered by the rapidity of the assault. Their machine-guns were taken by the hundred, and they themselves were buried by the thousand. One of their greatest common defects was their lack of alertness. This seems largely to have been due to the fact that their Army Staffs, influenced by the calculations of their General Staff, did not for the time expect any strong and sustained British movements against the Siegfried line.

General von Ludendorff manœuvred with pen as well as with spade and reserves. For some reason he continually set his publicity agents to boast about his coming achievements.

Ludendorff's various excuses At first he was reported to be preparing to engage in terrific open-field warfare between the Cambrai-Laon line and the Arras-Soissons line. Next, in contradiction to this statement, the new commander was said by his henchmen to be conducting a subtle scheme for dodging out of range of the British war-machine on the Somme, and thereby winning ample time to employ his grand reserve in recovering a decisive striking power in a new direction. Lastly, it was admitted that Ludendorff hoped for no great triumph on the western front, and retired simply to escape

heavy losses on land, while his submarines achieved a practical decision against the mercantile marine of the Allies.

The German people regarded the last statement as being nearest the truth. They knew what the stand on the Somme had cost, and applauded the plan for avoiding the terrible grip of the strengthened British armies, and for starving out the island population. There was undoubtedly some possibility, in April, 1917, of British shipping being **German hopes from the submarine** disastrously crippled by the German submarine campaign. The menace at sea inspired Sir Douglas Haig and all his officers and men in their enormous effort to close with the enemy.

Fierce as was the leap they made from Bapaume and Chaulnes towards Cambrai and St. Quentin, this was not in itself a matter of the highest importance. The extraordinary rush against the lower Hindenburg system was at first a great feint. It was intended to surprise and alarm the enemy, and induce him to increase his forces in positions of comparative unimportance. The French Commander-in-Chief did not design to make St. Quentin the objective of another mighty Franco-British offensive. The old French battlefield by Rheims, where the principal Gallic war-machine had been long in position, and was being improved by General Pétain, was the scene of the French preparations, as German aerial observers knew.

These observers also knew that similar preparations for offensive movements on a large scale were proceeding

WELCOMING THE PRESIDENT OF THE FRENCH REPUBLIC IN PERONNE.

[*British official photograph.*

Péronne was occupied by the British Army in the morning of March 18th, 1917. A cavalry patrol entered first, followed by Midland and London infantry. President Poincaré took the earliest possible opportunity to visit the recovered town—lovely no longer, but more glorious in history. He was received with full military honours in the main street of the town, where a band and Guard of Honour were stationed.

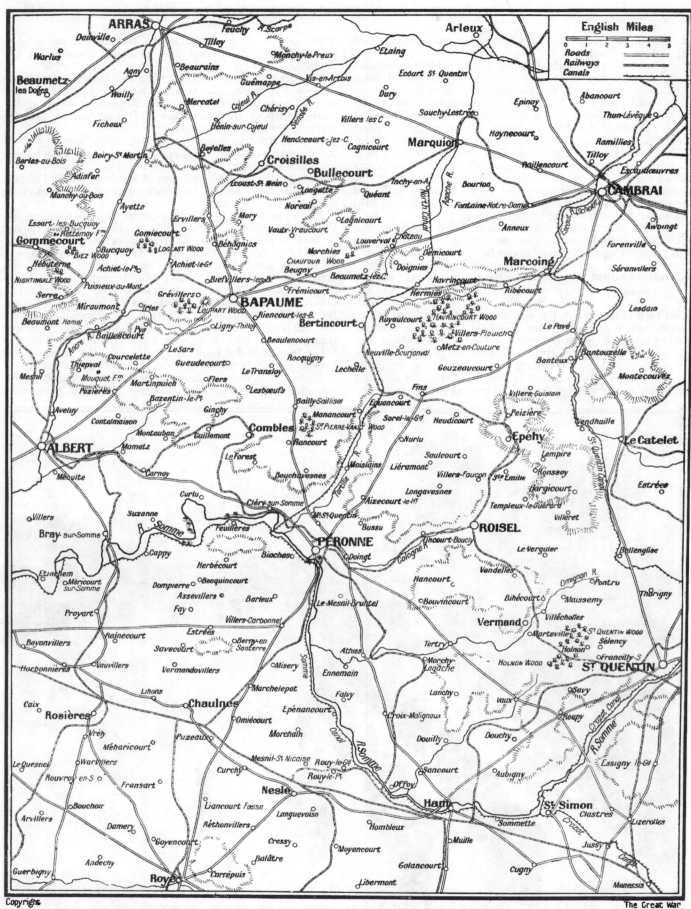

LINE OF THE GERMAN RETREAT FROM BAPAUME AND PÉRONNE TO CAMBRAI.

In this map are shown all the places involved in the fighting which followed the first menace to the German positions on the Bapaume Ridge caused by the British capture of the village of Irles, with the almost immediately consequent fall of Bapaume and Péronne and the premature German retreat to the Hindenburg positions in preparation on the Cambrai-St. Quentin line.

round Ypres and Arras. For nearly eleven months the northern and central British armies had visibly been organising their striking power. It could be seen that very remarkable extensions of their railway systems were energetically carried out. Ludendorff, therefore, had good grounds for anticipating a gigantic renewal of attack on his old lines in the northern sectors. Yet in all probability he much underestimated the speed with which Sir Douglas Haig's engineers could answer the German withdrawal by a grand move at Arras or Ypres.

Accumulation of local surprises

It appears to have been one of the main purposes of Sir Hubert Gough and Sir Henry Rawlinson, in crashing quickly and violently into the Hindenburg system at Bullecourt, Havrincourt, and Savy, to mislead the German High Command in regard to the direction of the main British attack. Pace combined with strength was the essence of the great demonstrating advance, the details of which have just been related.

The accumulation of local surprises against the Siegfried troops and the storming troops weighed upon Ludendorff and his Staff. This was clearly evident in the series of gross, clumsy lies with which Ludendorff personally endeavoured, in his daily communiqués, to palliate his small but worrying defeats. With a view to eventually making good his perversion of facts, the German commander had to check all further progress of the British armies between St. Quentin and the Scarpe River. For example, having slain, by the pen, some thousand Australians, he had to prevent their very

[*British official photograph.*
PÉRONNE RAILWAY STATION.
One of the few pieces of German destruction to be recognised as legitimate in war.

[*British official photograph.*
SPOOR OF THE BAFFLED AND RETREATING HUN.
A main street in Péronne, where the Germans "combined the destructiveness of scientific barbarians with the filthiness of sewer rats." They employed high-explosives, solidified paraffin, and the contents of latrines to shatter fire, and sully the once lovely town, from sheer rage at being unable to hold what they had taken.

[*British official photograph.*
LEGACY OF "KULTUR."
The condition of Péronne as left by the Germans was heart-breaking —even worse than that of Louvain.

vigorous ghosts from storming through Bullecourt to the heart of the Hindenburg line at Riencourt. He had heavily engaged both his own and Hindenburg's credit by his forged drafts upon the remnant of credulity of the Teutonic populace. Military considerations, therefore, had to rank for the occasion subsidiary to considerations of a social-politic kind.

The immediate consequence was that an important part of the immense new German reserve had to be railed round from Alsace to the Cambrai-St. Quentin sectors of the Hindenburg line. In vain did Ludendorff repent of attaching to his new defensive works the name of the old Field-Marshal. Having rashly attached the legend of impregnability to lines which were inferior to those from which he had retired, he tried to undo the effects of his early Press campaign. The Central Empires and the world at large were informed that there was no Hindenburg line, but only two ordinary systems, named the Siegfried and Wotan trenches.

Retracting the Hindenburg myth

The retraction came too late. As well-trained and well-controlled moulders of general opinion, German journalists had decisively executed the original orders given to them by the Staff officers of the High Command. Popular faith in the Hindenburg line, in conjunction with universal belief in a victorious peace by U-boat piracy, was the chief remaining barrier against national demoralisation. Ludendorff had at all costs to hold the Hindenburg line, not only as a rampart against the British armies, but as a dam against the rising passions of the half-disillusioned German populace. There was a wind blowing from Russia—blowing strange thoughts into the minds of the German people.

In the camps where British prisoners were being slowly killed by methodical ill-treatment the ordinary German guards began to appear a little more humane. Their conversion was not due to official orders. Their Emperor was still preaching to the troops in a mood of extreme ferocity and inciting them to a war of extermination against the "odious Englishmen." Yet German privates guarding British prisoners began to explain to them that the war was a "capitalists' war," and that peace must be made so that the real wrongdoers could be punished.

The German people did not seem to be in a revolutionary frame of mind; but their nerves were raw from want of good food and their minds were troubled by the apprehension of possible defeat, followed by a world-wide boycott. A serious disaster on the Hindenburg line, at a time when the impressions and suggestions of the transformation of Russia were fresh and vivid, might have had a still more serious domestic repercussion.

Apprehension of possible defeat

Certainly the German Emperor thought so. So did Bethmann-Hollweg. Ludendorff inclined to the same view. It was barely a fortnight since the tale of events in Russia was fully known, and the influence upon German opinion of the sudden warlike action of the United States had likewise to be taken into account.

In these circumstances the enemy High Command played for safety. The result was one of the most brilliant, strategic, and easy victories won in the Great War. Largely by superb advance-guard actions, the Fourth and Fifth British Armies succeeded in compelling Ludendorff to misplace his reserves on the Cambrai-St. Quentin front, and expose his more critical position on the distant Vimy Ridge to extreme danger from the British First and Third Armies. Finding himself clean outplayed, the new dictator of the Teutons whimpered like a spoilt, peevish child. Piteously he complained to all the world that the British nation had brutally accumulated an overwhelming mass of war material instead of keeping to 3 in. field-guns and shrapnel shell and allowing the real lords of the earth a monopoly in monster guns and high-explosive projectiles. Apparently he regarded it as a crime against the superior German genius in organisation and technical science for the effete Briton to excel in the rapid production of military weapons.

Of course he was only trying to cover up his failure in strategy by making a frenzied appeal to his munition-makers to speed up their output. In the meantime, he began to waste his general reserve by using them as cannon-fodder to retrieve the errors he had made between Bapaume and Cambrai, Péronne and St. Quentin. He employed a large amount of naval material, especially guns running right up the scale of heavy calibres, to strengthen his artillery power. He postponed both the plan of a spring offensive against Russia and the scheme for a combined Austro-German attack on Italy. The great duel between the British Commonwealth and the German Empire was opening. The front from Lens to Arras was ablaze, and Sir Henry Horne and Sir Edmund Allenby, with the First and Third British Armies, were opening the campaign of Vimy Ridge and the Scarpe.

Ludendorff's strategic failure

[*British official photograph.*

CLEARING OBSTRUCTIONS TO THE BRITISH ADVANCE AT PÉRONNE.

Roadside trees felled at Péronne by the Germans to delay the advance of the British troops. So hastily had the enemy left the town that some of the trees were but partly cut through, while a hurriedly dropped axe was left beside one of them. When the first British troops entered Péronne, working parties were at once told off to remove the obstructions on the roads leading into the town caused by the felled timber.

CHAPTER CLXXXIII.

THE VICTORIES OF VIMY AND ARRAS, AND THE RUPTURE OF THE HINDENBURG LINE.

By Edward Wright.

New Engines of War for the First and Third British Armies—Development of the Raid into the Rush—General Horne's Tremendous Barrage—How the Canadians Stormed Up the Vimy Ridge—Arnuld and Völker Tunnels and the German Stratagem that Failed—Capture of Hill 140 and Thelus—German Stand upon Crowning Hummock of Vimy Cliffs—Nocturnal Success of Red-Indian Methods of Warfare—Prussian Guards Gather for a Counter-Attack—Heroic Achievement of Irish, English, and Canadian Troops at Bois-en-Hache and The Pimple—Charging in a Snowstorm Through Waist-deep Mud—Terrific Bayonet Battle with the Prussian Guard—Ludendorff Staggered by Loss of Vimy Rampart—Scots and South Africans at Point du Jour and Hyderabad Position—German Guns Turned Upon German Fugitives—Difficulties of Attack by British Third Army—Hand-to-hand Underground Struggle at Blangy—Why the Barrage Missed the Railway Triangle—British Advance Checked—Battles of Feuchy and Advance on Monchy—Tale of the Tank and the Harp—Storming of Tilloy and the Capture of Church and Chapel Redoubts—Critical Success at Fampoux—Race for Monchy and Amazing Charge of British Cavalry—Wancourt and Heninel Tanks, their Great Adventures—Splendid Determination of English Divisions—Bavarians and Prussians Broken in Front of Monchy.

AS soon as the Germans retired from Bapaume, Péronne, and Chaulnes, the British High Command speeded up its preparations for an attack upon the more northerly and unyielding enemy front, from Vimy Ridge to the suburbs of Arras. The plan of the new offensive was elaborated in detail in February, 1917 —a month before Ludendorff ordered his armies to withdraw from the Somme and Ancre sectors.

Large forces had been moved already from the Somme to the north, while General Rawlinson's old army was strengthened, so that it could extend southward towards the Avre River near Roye. The great Scots master-gunner, Sir Henry Sinclair Horne, who had assisted General Nivelle at Verdun, and developed his special invention of the new technique of the creeping barrage, was promoted to the command of the First Army in recognition of the great successes he had won in the Somme actions beginning at Fricourt. General Horne's army was deployed below Vimy cliffs, alongside the Third Army, which was commanded by Sir Edmund Allenby and arrayed about Arras.

It was these two powerful forces that prepared to engage the enemy along the old and tremendous fortressed front of some fourteen miles from the Souchez River to Cojeul River. New engines of war were placed at the service of General Allenby and General Horne. They were given an improved kind of caterpillar-wheeled mobile fortress, which was not only heavier and more strongly gunned than the original "tank," but considerably more numerous. The supply of Stokes guns was increased, as this powerful new invention in artillery had rapidly developed into a master weapon in the hands of attacking infantry.

The Stokes gun was employed to form blinding smoke-screens against hostile machine-gun lines, as well as to overwhelm machine-gun positions by an extraordinary, rapid fire of aerial torpedoes. The First and Third Armies were, moreover, at last provided with a complete answer to the horrible flame-projectors, which the enemy had used in various ways from the beginning of the war. Means were discovered by British inventors for firing large drums of flaming petrol over hostile positions and discharging bursts of molten metal upon the enemy. Methods of gas attack, originated by the Germans in contravention of their engagements at The Hague Conference, were likewise improved by British men of science. The Germans

[British official photograph.

ARTILLERY OFFICER'S LONELY QUEST.
British officer riding forward to find new positions for his guns. With shell-shattered tree stumps still marking the straightness of its course, this road remained in an unusually good condition for transport purposes.

[Canadian War Records.

H.M. PIGEON POSTAL
SERVICE.
Releasing a pigeon from the front
trenches with a message to headquarters behind the line.

had begun with chlorine
and ended with the terrible
poison of phosgene gas.

Their phosgene gas had
wrought considerable harm
upon the British armies on
the Somme, but full
reprisals were exacted from
the scientific barbarians by
the new school of British
chemical artillerists. The
Germans had spent years
in elaborating their methods
of frightfulness, only to be
excelled, on the infernal
ground they had selected,
by the brilliant and rapid
inventiveness of their most
hated opponents. There
was good reason for the
German Emperor's procla-
mation that he regarded the Britons as the "most odious"
of his foes.

In the production of artillery and shell the new
munition factories of Great Britain overwhelmed the
enemy. The Germans possessed more coal-mines and
larger iron-fields. Yet, as General von Ludendorff admitted at the time, they could not equal, on the critical
fields of conflict, the British power of bombardment.

The guns between Lens and Arras opened fire at the
beginning of April, 1917. At the same time the First and
Third Armies made fierce raiding expedi-
Development of tions on a broad front, in order to dis-
the raid cover the German positions and exercise
themselves in the arrangements for the
great attack. Since the winter of 1915 the raid had
developed in an extraordinary way. Employed first to
shake the nerve of the enemy and worry him, it had become
the finishing instrument of infantry education in the grand
offensive. Battalions went "over the top" in the order
fixed for the battle, entered the terrain which was to be
part of their objective, and came back with increased

confidence and a valuable haul of prisoners. From the
prisoners there could be discovered exactly the names
of the German forces holding the positions, the generals
in command, and the average quality of the troops.

It was, however, the scheme of exercising the attacking
forces directly on the ground that they were about to be
set to conquer which was the most important characteristic of the new raiding method. Man becomes accustomed to anything. The Germans be-
came accustomed to lulls in the British **Battle of Arras**
bombardment, followed by raids. When **opens**
they were thus habituated to tip-and-run
tactics on the part of the British and Canadian infantry,
they were at last surprised by a gigantic raid, which
transformed itself into one of the most powerful offensive
movements in the history of war.

On April 9th, 1917, after an intense artillery duel, the
Battle of Arras opened. It had been heralded by a great
aerial struggle, in which British pilots, supplied at length
with a large number of machines of first-rate quality,
began to recover the practical mastery of the air.
According to General Smuts, who watched the battle, the
enemy's lines were domi-
nated for a depth of nearly
twenty miles by the Royal
Flying Corps, assisted by
the Royal Naval Air Wing.

[Canadian War Records.

ATTACHING THE MESSAGE TO THE BIRD.
The use of pigeons to carry despatches from points whence other means
of communication were not available or were especially dangerous was
a device adopted quite early in the prolonged trench warfare.

When the vast battle
opened, in the dim dawn
at half-past five in the
morning, the weather, as
usual, changed for the worse.
The wind shifted into the
west, bringing a curtaining
drizzle of rain with it. It
did not, however, hinder the
enormous action of parks
of British artillery, which
were firing some five million
shells well on to their
targets.

Two previous days of fine
Easter weather made the
artillerymen almost
independent of chance
conditions of visibility.
Everything in the German
lines had been photographed
from the air, marked for
the precise range, and
registered by a gun or so
from each battery. Models
of the enemy front, to the
depth fixed for the offensive, were prepared from the
aerial photographs and closely studied by all arms. All
the preliminary bombardments were carried out with but
a small part of the immense artillery concentration. Not
until the dawn of Easter Monday, April 9th, did the
entire masses of guns reveal their full strength by the
roar and flame of an attack of surprising magnitude.

All along the circuit of the horizon rockets rose from
the stricken German trenches, calling for help by means
of red, white, green, and golden fountains of fire. Then,
brighter than all the firework display of the doomed
German troops, shone the awful cascades of liquid metal
and bursting drums of petrol launched by the new British
engines of war. Amid this new and ghastly picturesque
splendour played the flame-shot volcanic bursts of high-
explosive shell and aerial torpedoes. The scene was soon
veiled in places by the smoke-screens created by the
Stokes gun in preparation for some difficult infantry
advances.

In retrospect it seems utterly amazing that General von
Ludendorff should have spent so much time in loudly

boasting that, by his flight from the Somme and Ancre, he had delayed the British offensive movement for several months. He had definitely retired his troops in the night of March 16th, and at dawn on April 9th his principal armies on his most important sectors were gripped and shattered. In spite of the labour of arranging the concentration of British guns and British infantry, with the gigantic supplies and great communications needed for two powerful armies, less than four weeks elapsed between the enemy's movement of evasion and the terrific answer to it.

It must also be remembered that the heavy engineering labour of pursuing two of the retreating German armies was also being speedily carried out by Sir Hubert Gough and Sir Henry Rawlinson. So successful were their efforts that preparations for another great British offensive were completed a few days after the opening of the Battle of Arras and Vimy.

At the same time the Second British Army, operating around Ypres under Sir Herbert Plumer, was also completing a marvellous amount of prepara-

Marvels of British engineering tions for another offensive on the grand scale. The engineering power and transport organisation behind Sir Douglas Haig's armies were of a quality and scope that the German Secret Service could not fully have measured. Otherwise, Ludendorff would have been less inclined to boasting before the event.

On the north of the great line of attack the Canadian divisions, under Sir Julian Byng, achieved the greatest success in western trench warfare since the recapture of Douaumont and Louvemont. They equalled the best achievement of their French comrades, and maybe, in some respects, almost sur-

Canadians attack Vimy Ridge passed it. They were set the task of storming up and over the famous Vimy Ridge, which covered the top of the Hindenburg line—those great coal-fields so valuable to France. In May and September, 1915, a magnificent French army, controlled by General Foch and commanded by General d'Urbal, had been twice checked by the Gibraltar-like defences of the Vimy Ridge. General Pétain, who then commanded only a small force, had skilfully fought over the advanced hill positions and, by an effort that made him famous, came close to a decisive victory.

Yet the great main plateau remained unconquered when the British Army extended southward past it. A British assault had been broken in the summer of 1916, and the ridge still loomed above the Canadian divisions, as the German Gibraltar of the western front, in the grey, rainy Easter dawn of battle on April 9th.

Flurries of snow came with the rain as the Canadians left their assembling trenches. The dawn-light remained sufficient for the manœuvring of the forces of attack, yet obscured the vision of the defending machine-gunners

[*British official photograph.*

WAR'S LITTLE IRONIES: A BRITISH SENTRY-BOX FASHIONED FROM GERMAN AMMUNITION CARRIERS AT FEUCHY.
Feuchy, a little to the east of Arras, was one of a group of fortified villages which, with other powerful trench systems, composed the enemy's rearward defences on the Arras front, extending about twelve miles from Hénin-sur-Cojeul to the southern outskirts of Givenchy-en-Gohelle. These were all captured by the British troops on April 9th, 1917, the enemy garrison being practically wiped out.

and riflemen. In three waves of assault the victors of Courcelette set out to add to the tale of victories they had won since they saved the situation in the Second Battle of Ypres. At first the Canadians advanced without serious opposition on their centre and their right. Preceded by a great stamping barrage of shell fire, they passed the great tunnels in the enemy's line and, under bursts of German shrapnel and close-range machine-gun fire, climbed half-way up the ridge.

The left wing of the Canadians was, however, checked around the low northern height known as the "Pimple."

Check on the "Pimple" The attacking troops in this sector had a most arduous struggle lasting from 5.30 a.m. to 10 p.m. By downright valour and skill in manœuvre they gradually captured a considerable part of the hostile trenches; but when another heavy snowstorm intervened at night their commander wisely arranged first to repulse the inevitable German counter-attack, and postponed operations against Pimple Hill.

In the meantime the main Canadian forces conducted a terrific battle between the first and second German lines. In their rear a considerable force of Germans emerged from the tunnels, and, reoccupying their old front with unusual determination, opened fire upon the backs of the advanced Canadians. For a time the situation somewhat resembled that obtaining on Thiepval Down on July 1st, 1916. The underground force of enemies, supplied with a large number of machine-guns, emerged between the first waves of Canadians and their reserves.

Fortunately, both the British and the overseas British armies had learnt a great deal since the opening of the Somme offensive. In a series of fierce advances, the foremost Dominion troops bombed the enemy out of his second line on the great ridge. Then, instead of making a wild sweep over the crest, they strengthened their newly-won positions on the second line, and turned back and dealt with the subterranean force that was shooting them in the back.

There were two immense galleries running through the ridge, known as the Prinz Arnuld and Völker tunnels. In spite of the extraordinary destructive power of the British artillery, both of these series of corridored caverns remained intact at the moment when the Canadians went over their parapets and began to climb the cliffs. Filled with confidence at the slight harm done to them by the millions of shells pitched upon the slopes, the emerging Germans at first showed quite a remarkable quality of dauntlessness.

When, however, they were attacked from behind by the Canadian regiments that had first passed over them, and also assailed in front from the lower slope by Sir Julian Byng's supporting troops, and likewise surrounded on both flanks, the courage of the Teutons evaporated. They surrendered in hundreds, and at last in thousands. The prisoners from the Völker tunnel left the place mined and ready to be blown up. Happily, the victors detected the trap and, cutting the leads, saved themselves from destruction, and secured an enormous shelter and place of concentration for further operations. **Völker tunnel trap detected**

During a pause on the conquered German second line fresh Canadian troops came up and deployed into position, while a tremendous British curtain of shell held the enemy off and hammered him into a condition of despair. Then, two divisions strong, the Canadians climbed up the slippery hillside and captured the German third line, pausing once more for a final drive through the enemy's centre. Again they advanced in a magnificent sweep of two-thirds of a mile.

ATTACKING GERMAN TRENCHES BEHIND AN ARTILLERY BARRAGE.
British infantry with a "tank" going forward during the Battle of Arras. The first line of enemy trenches had been taken already, and some of the men and the "tank" had reached the second line, beyond which was the "barrage" smashing any attempt at sending up German reinforcements. In the left foreground is a group of German prisoners, of whom 18,000 were captured during the first eighteen days of the battle.

"TANKS" IN ACTION AT THE CAPTURE OF VIMY RIDGE.

At one point on Vimy Ridge the British infantry attack was held up by wire that had escaped destruction, and the machine-guns it protected. "Two 'tanks' came to the rescue, and did most daring things." One of them is seen crushing in the machine-gun position on the German crews, while its companion (seen in the distance to the right) was smashing down wire obstructions and clearing a way for the infantry.

Before them went the rampart of smoke and fire of their barrage, and as it stamped the Germans into their dug-outs the Canadian infantry dashed forward, capturing Hill 140 and a variety of fortified woods and several villages. At each stage of progress of the two divisions the enemy's resistance grew feebler. Hundreds of pairs of hands were lifted beyond the belts of wire before signs of surrender were expected.

At ten o'clock in the morning, as the Canadians climbed to the top of the hill rampart and commanded a view of the enemy line eastward, a heavy snowstorm again blotted out the landscape. Once more the Canadians turned to the work of consolidation and, converting to their own advantage the covering curtain of snow, worked along the third line, which they had penetrated, and gradually cleared it. At half-past ten o'clock the snowfall ceased, the great black clouds silvered and thinned away, and a fitful sun brightened the blasted and thundering ridge of battle. The Canadian centre became more active, and in another two and a half hours of magnificent fighting cleared every part of the enemy's third line, secured all their objectives, captured three German commandants, and more than two thousand rank and file.

Enemy's third line cleared

The British divisions on the right of the Canadians fought forward with equal success. They topped the southern slopes of the Vimy system by twelve o'clock, and their leading battalion met and broke three strong counter-attacks. Soon afterwards the troops overlooking the enemy's low positions eastward reported that a great mass of Germans was concentrating, near Vimy village, for a grand attempt to recover the ridge. Forward observing-officers measured the distance, and directed a preliminary shell or two on the road by which the enemy was advancing. Quickly the exact range was discovered, and the heavy British howitzers fired over the ridge with such effect that the counter-attacking force was smashed and dispersed.

The right wing of Canadian and British troops then pressed home their swinging advance. Passing through the wide gaps, torn by their heavy artillery at fixed intervals in the last wire entanglements fringing the tableland, they went down the eastern slopes of Vimy Ridge. Below them were the villages of Farbus, Vimy, and Little Vimy, all shattered by the fire of the British railway guns. Beyond, on the level plain of Douai, were the hamlets of Arleux, Willerval, Bailleux, with Fresnoy, Oppy, and Gavrelle, which were soon the scene of another great battle. Just a couple of miles beyond was the once unimportant village of Drocourt, which had become doubly famous as the northern base of the Wotan, or switch-line, in the Ludendorff-Hindenburg system of defence.

The conquerors of the historic line of heights descended into Farbus Wood and Goulot Wood, taking on their way batteries of German guns and large dumps of German ammunition. In the early part of the afternoon of Easter Monday the front of the victorious thrust reached the limits of advance covered by its own heavy guns. When night fell the Germans held only a few trenches on Hill 145. All the rest of the great ridge was not only conquered, but refortified eastward, by the Canadian divisions and the Scottish division operating on their right.

Round Hill 145, north-west of La Folie Wood, a small detachment of Germans on the crowning hummock of the ridge maintained a most gallant resistance all through Easter Monday. With their massed machine-guns they shattered every daylight attempt to rush or encircle them. No doubt the nature of the ground favoured them, as they had a long, clear field of fire. Nevertheless, their tenacity of resistance at a time when other Germans were surrendering in thousands was rather striking.

German resistance on Hill 145

They were left alone on Easter Monday afternoon, because it was seen that they were not worth the cost in life they would exact. During the night a Canadian patrol reverted to that Red Indian form of warfare from which their countrymen had originated the famous trench-raiding system. In the windy darkness the patrol got into the dominating machine-gun fortress, and, as soon as day broke and gave them clear vision, they rapidly cleared it, and completed, at little sacrifice of life, the

[Canadian War Records.

Laying a road over No Man's Land to the British front line troops at Vimy Ridge. Unprecedented demands were made upon the engineers in coping with the question of transport in the battle area, and their rapid solution of these problems largely contributed to the success of the operations.

[Canadian War Records.

"In spite of the enormous difficulties which the condition of the ground and the ingenuity of the enemy had placed in the way, the work of repairing and constructing bridges, roads, and railways was carried forward with most commendable rapidity." (Sir Douglas Haig's despatch, May, 1917.)

[Canadian War Records.

Pushing a railway through captured territory on Vimy Ridge. The problem of railway transport could not have been solved without the patriotic co-operation of the railway companies, who readily tore up tracks in order to provide the Army with the necessary rails.

DRIVING NEW ROADS AND RAILWAYS THROUGH TERRITORY RECOVERED FROM THE ENEMY.

entire conquest of the most important natural rampart in the western German line.

The village of Thelus, which had been the base from which the enemy held up the French offensive by weeks of resistance in the historic Labyrinth, was completely shattered beforehand by the new railway guns of the British armies. In the obliterated ruins, through which ran the German's second-line system, some enemy bombers and machine-gunners bravely

[*Canadian War Records.*]

OPENING THE NEW VIMY RIDGE LINE.
The first train over the new railroad on Vimy Ridge. Material, rails, and rolling stock followed the advancing troops, who spun new lines behind them as a spider spins its web.

[*Canadian War Records.*]

TENTACLES OF VICTORY.
Canadians laying a light railway close on the heels of their victorious comrades who had captured the ground. The engineering power and transport organisation of the British Army were astounding.

endeavoured for a time to stem the advance. The works on either side of them were rapidly broken under the thrust of the Canadian battalions, and the forlorn hope of Thelus was caught on both flanks and killed or captured, the stand made being too long to allow many of the fugitives to escape.

Squalls of snow veiled all the Douai Plain in the morning of Tuesday, April 10th, when the Canadian divisions worked, with patrols, towards the railway line running from Lens towards the eastern suburbs of Arras. Their advanced guards met with little opposition from the fragments of German forces, and fought through the hamlet of Little Vimy and Ville Wood towards the village of Vimy on the foot-hills, almost directly south of Lens.

Fight for Vimy foot-hills By the morning of Thursday, April 12th, the new British line ran from a point just below Givenchy-en-Gohelle to the south of Vimy village and the south of Bailleul.

At its widest the depth of the Canadian advance was about five thousand yards, covering hundreds of miles of trenches, protected by barbed-wire and machine-guns, with numerous redoubts, fortressed woods, and fortified swells of ground.

In a frantic endeavour to hold on to the extreme northern spur of the Vimy Ridge the German commander sent out a regiment of the Prussian Grenadier Guards to strengthen the battered Bavarian troops massed in and

about the ruined woodland of Bois-de-Hirondelle. Near this wood was a rise of ground commanding the little valley of Souchez River. This ground was known as Bois-en-Hache, and it was connected with the foot-hill of the Vimy Ridge, scornfully known as the "Pimple." The "Pimple" and Bois-en-Hache were of much higher military importance than their small altitude suggested. They were the only enemy positions that gave observation over part of the lost ridge. This was why the enemy had poured out troops from the Lens area on Easter Monday to retain the lower heights north of the lost rampart.

It was the intention of the German commander to make a heavy counter-attack by way of Bois-en-Hache and Pimple Hill against the northern edge of the Vimy Ridge. But on April 12th, as his forces massed in a snow blizzard, his operation was anticipated by a sudden movement by General Horne's forces.

The snow veiled the waves of Canadian, Irish, and English infantry, yet it did not protect the enemy. Through the snowstorm a squadron of British pilots swooped low down above **Airmen bomb the** the wood, where the Prussian Guard had **Prussian Guard** concentrated, and discharged upon them bombs of a new kind that wrought terrible havoc. Never before had this aerial manœuvre against infantry been employed with such deadly success.

As the British hawks rose above the smoking wood a whirlwind of shell smote the wooded rise and Pimple Hill. Neither the gunners nor their observation-officers could see the targets, by reason of the thickly-falling snow. But the ranges had been finely measured in intervals of clear air on previous days. General Horne's barrage went forward with time-tabled exactitude, and close behind it came the charging Canadian, Irish, and English troops, happy in the fact that the snow was blowing on their backs and driving into the faces of their enemies.

The ground was a bog of shell-craters and mud, making the attacking movement slow and difficult. German machine-gunners on the knoll and the wooded hump maintained a barrage of machine-gun fire against the men who were slipping and stumbling forward, falling into shell-holes and trying to keep their bombs and rifles dry.

The Prussian Guardsmen fought with heroic determination. Far from giving any ground under either the aerial attack or the whirlwind bombardment, they waited for a personal trial of strength, and, after sweeping the attackers with the machine-gun fire, came out of their trenches and opened a terrific hand-to-hand combat with bomb and bayonet.

The only result of their desperate stand was to increase their losses. For neither the Northern nor Southern

German of the best class was a match for the Canadian, Gael, or Briton. Furious was the charge of the Irishmen on the Prussian Guard in Bois-en-Hache. Thigh-deep in mud at times, the assailants gripped their enemies and fought to the death. The conquerors made but a hundred prisoners. Thousands of dead and wounded foes marked their trail of victory over Pimple Hill and Bois-en-Hache and along the Souchez stream. The Irish and English troops extended their line towards the village of Givenchy-en-Gohelle, while the Canadians also advanced towards the village on its southerly side.

During the struggle in the snowstorm the main mass of General Horne's artillery held the enemy down in Vimy village and the country beyond with such intensity of fire that no German gunner cared to leave the shelter of his dug-out. Captured German guns were employed with their own ammunition against their former owners. By the village of Bailleul were a number of German batteries abandoned between the contending armies and desperately eyed by the beaten foe. Again and again he tried to recover the guns and haul them away. But from the ridge the batteries were so continually smothered by British shrapnel fire that the Germans lost men and horses until they were tired of the vain sacrifice.

Enemy batteries lost at Bailleul

With the successes at Pimple Hill and Bois-en-Hache the commander of the First British Army obtained full and absolute observation over the Vimy Ridge. Only the continual snowstorms that veiled the enemy's movements in the Douai Plain prevented Sir Henry Horne from overwhelming the shattered German forces before they could be pieced together again and strongly reinforced from the grand reserve.

Though the enemy clung to Vimy village, on the other side of the slopes, and to the railway on the farther side of Farbus, he merely increased his losses. The positions, to which he held with blind courage, were ranged and registered by the heavy British artillery, as well as by the field-guns and howitzers that had, somehow, climbed the smashed and pulpy ridge.

Life was made hideous for all German soldiers holding on to the nearest villages on the plain for a distance of four miles from the light British howitzers. The local German commander would have done better had he used the extraordinary April snowstorms as cover for a withdrawal from the Vimy village line.

[*Canadian War Records.*

Some of the German trench mortars captured by the Canadians, and (right) a direct hit scored by them on a German gun emplacement on Vimy Ridge. Above (in centre) some of the machine-guns and other booty taken by the Canadians at Vimy Ridge, with French village children playing alongside them; and (top) examining a German naval 8 in. gun which the Canadians secured on the railway at Farbus.

GUNS AND TRENCH ARTILLERY TROPHIES CAPTURED BY THE CANADIANS.

The German High Command, however, seemed ready to spend another hundred thousand men in the defence of a mile or two of low-lying country eastward of the Vimy heights. The reason was that the coal-fields of Lens would have been quickly wrested from the invader if he had acted solely from a military point of view, and withdrawn to save further and much larger wastage of men and material.

Lens itself was an enormous fortress of an intricately laborious kind. When the ridge was lost, and the main Hindenburg front turned in the north and pierced in other places, the enemy was left only with the smaller and weaker second Hindenburg system running from Drocourt to Quéant, on which he could make a stand with his reserves. Lens and its easterly mining suburbs covered Drocourt. Had Lens been allowed to fall, the capture of the entire Drocourt line would quickly have followed.

Ludendorff had not completed the construction of the Drocourt line. He had spent six months on it, and yet had to sacrifice men by the hundred thousand in order to win time for making big-gun emplacements and other heavy works. Thus, had he been rapidly

Ludendorff has to change his plans pushed back from the Lens area, and violently struck in an unprepared state at Drocourt, he would have been unable to resite his heavier ordnance. Everything that impeded the advance of the British armies would have more seriously retarded the definite German retirement. The snow, mud, and rain would have exhausted the energy of the German gunners, compelled the German infantry to enormous sacrifices to save the guns, and yet allowed the mounted British forces and light British infantry forces to achieve the great decision, after the period of admirable training in their first successful advances against the first Hindenburg line.

Ludendorff had, therefore, to cling in sheer desperation, and at any cost to the strength of his nation, to the ground between the Vimy Ridge and Lens. It was soon known to the British High Command that the German dictator was staggered and dumbfounded over the sudden loss of the high Vimy positions. He had to change all his plans, and devote to a purely defensive scheme not only his available portion of the grand reserve, but many men and guns liberated on the Russian front by the armistice established by Germanic agents in the Russian Revolutionary parties.

[Canadian War Records.

Canadians firing upon the enemy one of their own guns, a 4·2 in. howitzer that had been taken at Vimy Ridge, and (right) a German 5·9 in. gun which had been effectually put out of action by a direct hit from the

Canadian artillery. In circle : Some varied types (observe the miniature one on the left) of the German trench mortars that were taken in the fighting near Arras, and (top) taking back to the base a captured German gun.

FURTHER GERMAN GUNS AND MORTARS TAKEN BY THE VICTORS OF VIMY.

R.B

A considerable part of the German reserves of one million men, together with part of the men and material withdrawn from Russia, were deployed against the French armies on the Aisne and on the Champagne line. The rest were moved as rapidly as possible against the British armies, in the design to balance at a tremendous cost in German life the magnificent victory won at Vimy by the Canadian and Scottish divisions.

The ·Scotsmen, who advanced on the right of the Canadian divisions at dawn on April 9th, were as successful as their comrades of the Dominion. Their line stretched from the southern edge of the ridge towards the suburbs of Arras. The German forces opposed to them were based upon a series of fortified lines and labyrinthine underground fortresses. The works at Le Point du Jour were among the principal enemy systems assailed by the Scottish regiments. But even stronger than Le Point du Jour was another network of positions known as the Hyderabad Redoubt.

The guns of Great Britain were as mighty in destructive

[*Canadian War Records.*]
TANGLED WILDERNESS OF WIRE IN WAR-SCARRED ARRAS.
For three months after the Germans were driven from the positions in Arras to which they had clung since 1914, they continued to bombard the old-time city, playing havoc with the picturesque residences in front of which the tangled wire of German and British positions still remained.

power on this sector of the front as they were on the Vimy cliffs. Tons of high explosive, used in both mines and in shell fire, destroyed most of the enemy's works of warlike industry between Thelus and Arras.· Then the new British engines of war launched upon the hungry and thirsty Germans missiles more terrifying than the spouts of burning petrol on the use of which Ludendorff was relying to a considerable extent.

German flame-projectors outdone In the Battles of the Somme the German corps commander, General von Armin, had especially recommended to the consideration of his new High Command the extended use of flame-projectors. Though Armin lost the battles in which he was engaged, the criticisms he made upon the deficiencies in German material and German personnel enabled him to win the confidence of Ludendorff. During the rearrangement of forces Armin was given the important army command in the Messines sector at Ypres.

His suggestions for a larger use of modern Greek fire in

trench warfare seems to have been adopted by his new Commander-in-Chief. Unfortunately, however, from the Teutonic point of view, the British Command was also alert to the great tactical value of the horrifying weapon of dropping fire.

Pursuing a policy of more vigorous invention than the plodding and routine Prussians could adopt, the Britons elaborated methods of launching the most panic-creating forms of fire at entrenched hostile troops. Over distances which no improved flame-projector could carry, cascades of fiery liquid metal and geysers of flaming oil hurtled and rained upon Bavarians, Prussians, Saxons, and Würtembergers. **New British engines of war**

It was a form of reprisals such as the Hun could appreciate. For years he had gloried in his own infernal weapon, and regarded it as triumphant evidence of his superior talent in science. He would not have been alarmed if his flame-projector had been copied by Britons and employed against him. While fleeing from the flame he would have, at least, been able to assert that the diabolical instrument was invented by his own race and employed in hundreds of little successes before it was imitated by the foe.

When, however, Sir Henry Horne and Sir Edmund Allenby brought into action new engines of utter terror, that reduced the flame-projector to insignificance, the German was demoralised. His pride of intellect was seared within his frightened body. He was outmatched in big guns, in trench-mortars, in methods of gas attack, and in machine-gun fire. His hand-bombs were scarcely as variably useful as the British grenade.

His flame-projector, which he had first used in August, 1914, in burning down Belgian and French villages, appeared to him to be the only superior instrument he retained. While he was in this frame of mind, and rocking under a whirlwind storm of shell, what first seemed like a strange and gigantic display of fireworks played above his trenches. The wet ground then steamed about him, and in splashes and torrents the lava and oil hissed and burnt, surprised and terrified.

There was hardly any resistance in the first German system when the Scotsmen went over the ground. Afterwards, the enemy machine-gunners brought a severe fire to bear upon the attacking forces. Nevertheless, the Highlanders and Lowlanders steadily and skilfully worked forward. They fought their way over Point du Jour, and in the stronger system of Hyderabad Work their closing success was so rapid that a German general of brigade and his Staff were captured. The German commander, it was reported, wept at the way in which thousands of his unwounded men surrendered. Besides taking more than 3,600 prisoners, the Scotsmen seized a considerable number of enemy guns, including some very useful 5·9 in. howitzers. A great amount of German ammunition lay in dumps in the conquered ground, and the victors turned the pieces about and shelled the broken foe.

The South Africans combined with some of the Scottish battalions in the historic battle. They were said to have

[Canadian War Records.

Canadian road=makers at work on a cordwood track for supply traffic, on the Western front.

[British official photograph.

British cavalry scouts on the move over newly=won ground in France.

[British official photograph.

All that was left of the Hotel de Ville, Arras, when the Huns were driven from the suburbs.

[British official photograph.

Winter of discontent for man and beast: Mules quartered in a shattered French village.

[British official photograph.

General view of Feuchy, east of Arras, as it was when retaken by the British, April 9th, 1917.

[British official photograph.

German shell bursting in a wire=tangled street in Arras during the great April battle.

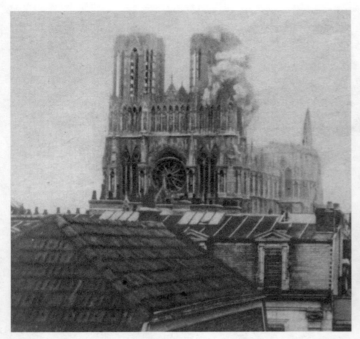

Shell bursting on south tower of the Cathedral.   *Simultaneous shells on south transept and apse.*

The systematic bombardment of Rheims Cathedral: A heavy shell bursting on the transepts.

taken the first hostile line without a single casualty. Then, going onward against a violent fire, they swept all before them, gathering hundreds of prisoners, and contributing largely to the bag of guns made by the united division. Altogether, the division captured 2,200 Germans, with 52 officers, including the Hyderabad brigadier and his Staff, 37 machine-guns, 17 5·9 in. guns, and two 8 in. howitzers.

The South Africans had bitter memories of German gun fire in Delville, where they made a despairing yet effective **South Africans** stand alongside their old comrades the **at Arras** Scots. In the great Arras victory they were among those who smote the enemy at last with his own weapons, and thus triumphantly paid off some of the " Devil's Wood " score.

From Vimy Ridge to Point du Jour and the fields north of Arras the artillery of Sir Henry Horne dominated the zone of battle from dawn to nightfall on Easter Monday. In the Arras sector, where Sir Edmund Allenby commanded, it was in places impossible, however, for the gunners behind the attacking English and Scottish troops to lay flat all the enemy's front line. There was no front line.

Britons and Teutons were, for example, less than five yards from each other in Blangy suburb. Only the foundation walls of one ruined house after another separated them. Mining from cellar to cellar had for years been the sole way of progress attempted by the opposing forces. Overground rushes were dangerous. For if a fragment of the burrows were occupied in this fashion, the apparent loser was likely to retaliate by firing a hidden mine under the apparent conquerors, and thereby suddenly reversing the positions.

The French forces under General Pétain had wrestled underground with the Germans in the eastern suburbs of Arras. When British troops took over the Arras sector, they could, for more than a year, do little more than continue the methods of their allies. It remained unsafe to show oneself above ground in daylight on the northern, eastern, and southern outskirts of the battered old city. Enemy machine-gunners and snipers commanded St. Sauveur, Baudmont, Ronville, and other thresholds of Arras.

The glorious edifices of the old-time city of Spanish Flanders were vanishing like the monuments of priceless beauty in Ypres. The Gothic buildings in the Grande Place and the belfried Town Hall, showing the final manner of the architecture of the master weavers of old Europe, were in the same state as Rheims Cathedral. Only by happy chance was Arras saved from complete destruction with the remnant of her civil population.

Ludendorff seems to have decided, towards the end of March, 1917, to wheel away from the Arras suburbs. His object was to repeat the manœuvre of the Somme withdrawal, and evade for a while the great British offensive, preparations for which had been reported by his aerial scouts. It was said by German prisoners that the Arras retreat was originally fixed for the first week in April. However this may be, it was finally arranged for April 15th.

In the meantime, instead of decreasing the forces in and around the suburbs of Blangy and St. Laurent, the German commander strengthened them. He intended to deliver a devilish stroke against the shattered city before he withdrew, and to continue his policy of appalling the French mind by the total destruction of all territory from which he was compelled to retreat. He reckoned this was the way to bring about negotiations for peace.

Dumps of huge shells, filled with prussic acid and other poison gases, were formed near Fampoux village, in advance of the Drocourt line. By the dumps ordinary heavy artillery was sited, and two 16·8 in. Krupp howitzers were specially ordered forward to Fampoux, for the diabolical work of flooding with poison gas the cellars of the ruined city, in which the townspeople were sheltering.

Happily, Sir Douglas Haig struck before Ludendorff. In the grand heralding bombardment, long-range British guns, mounted on railway carriages and designed to wreck the enemy's rearward depôts and communications, assailed Fampoux and other neighbouring villages. The German gunners were overborne and generally confined to their caverned refuges. The monster Krupp guns

[*British official photograph.*

FORMIDABLE BARRICADE FORMED BY THE RETREATING GERMANS.
Clearing away the débris of a church which the Germans had blown up across a road to hinder the British advance. How considerable were some of the tasks in opening up the way for that advance is well shown in this mighty mass of bricks and masonry.

were not risked, so that when Fampoux was captured only some of the unused 16·8 in. gas shells, left behind in the hurry of flight, told the tale of Ludendorff's baffled devilry.

As already remarked, both the long, preparatory British gun fire and the moving line of bursting shells at dawn on Easter Monday had little effect upon the hostile underground line in Blangy. English and Scottish infantrymen at this tangled point had to attack a practically unbroken front of subter- **Desperate fighting** ranean forts. Most gallantly did the **at Blangy** bombing-parties advance and try to find a way through the dreadful machine-gun fire barrages. A complete and sustained machine-gun barrage was the latest and absolutely the most deadly of wholesale forms of slaughter. A shell barrage was a mechanical and purblind thing, arranged in advance by gunners four miles and more away. The machine-gun barrage had eyes and brains immediately behind it—skilled shooters, studying every detail

contentedly carry bricks all their life for the erection of copies. Taking up some foreign idea of proved fertility, the German man of science will joyfully devote his existence to applying it in every way he can discern.

In the case under consideration the Teuton's unwearied power in repetition work was annulled by the Briton's faculty for inventing new means to an end. The city of forts was first badly shattered by a long, fierce bombardment, pierced by an heroic hand-to-hand bomb fight, and then overwhelmed by smashing barrages of exact howitzer fire. The Scottish and English bombing-parties were so close behind the shell that many of the hostile garrisons of the forts were unable to make a strong stand.

In the Railway Triangle, however, a German force

of the situation. When the guns were close enough together, and fed with unending ammunition just as fast as they could use it, the sleet of lead was of dreadful efficacy.

Fortunately there was space between the British and German lines above and below Blangy, enabling the attacking artillery to pour hurricanes of shell upon the opposing defences. A Hamburg division withdrew from its ruined first system, leaving a small rearguard which surrendered rather than fight. Wedges were driven around Blangy Park, and at last, after heavy sacrifice, a famous British battalion, in an hour of deft bombing rushes amid the Blangy posts, carried the suburb.

Another memorable scene of conflict was the triangle of railway lines east of Blangy. All the German works on three sides of Arras were of immeasurable strength. The British Staff could not find room in its largest map of this enemy sector to mark all the enemy positions. There were some four square miles of forts of all patterns and sizes—forts sunk in craters, with only a foot or so of loopholed machine-gun emplacement visible at close range; forts rising daringly above belts of wire, as though challenging observation; forts stuck in marshes; forts hidden in the pious façades of church and chapel. It was a large city of forts, indicative of enormous and uninventive labour.

Check at the Railway Triangle

The Prussian, and to a less extent, all Northern Germans, are the natural hodmen of Europe. Rare among them is the faculty of invention ; they try to supply by patience their want of originating power. If they can steal or honestly acquire a useful original design, they will patiently and

[*Canadian War Records.*

THUNDER AND FLAME AND FLYING DEATH.
Two exceptionally fine photographs of a big German shell bursting on Vimy Ridge, at the northern end of which the enemy had retained a footing at the close of the first day's fighting. He was ejected during the night, and his fierce counter-attacks failed to materialise.

threatened to disarrange the plans of the advance. The Triangle was formed by the junction of the lines from Lens and Douai, and a branch track connecting the two lines before they merged. On the farther railway embankment, some thirty to forty feet high, the enemy had constructed a deep trench and lined it with dug-outs and machine-guns. The guns were placed in redoubts, consisting of two feet of armoured concrete and additional steel girders, all banked with earth within a foot of the domed top. They formed targets only a square yard in size, and by their narrowness escaped the bombardment and barrage. The blind barrage went onward according to time-table, leaving the English and Scottish infantry, coming through Blangy Park, faced with an impossible task. For three hours the attackers were checked, and all their fine, forlorn attempts to get within bomb-casting distance of the extraordinary rampart failed.

In the campaigns of 1914, 1915, and part of 1916, the check at the Triangle would probably have developed into a local defensive victory for the enemy. But Sir Henry Horne had won the command of the First British Army by, among other great achievements, the invention of a device for plucking victory out of a defeat of this kind. He had become the master-gunner of Sir Douglas Haig, and Sir Edmund Allenby's artillerists around Arras had constantly practised the various uses of Horne's creeping barrage.

After crawling too far in front of the helpless infantry the line of roaring fire and pillared smoke halted for a moment, **Triumph of the creeping barrage** and came threshing back like an infernal flail. Again it halted. Then it stamped about and upon the high, fort-lined embankment, and the waiting Scots and Englishmen were occasionally splashed with bits of concrete as they watched gun-mountings and girders spin through the air. "Our barrage," said an admiring spectator, "just sat upon the forts, and all the works disappeared. It was as if it had been pulled back by a leash."

A cleaning-up party of infantry entered the wreck of the best designed of German forts, while the Scots and Englishmen followed their barrage, on a rearranged time-table, towards the second Hindenburg line. Meanwhile, a series of similar fortifications, such as Haugest Work and Holte Work, Horn and Hamel Works, were exploded into the tragic rubble of the battlefield of Arras, after checking other English regiments.

The victors of Blangy fought onward **Enemy obliterated at Feuchy** to the Feuchy Redoubt. Here their dreadful creeping barrage more than compensated for its preliminary failure at the Triangle. The entire enemy garrison at Feuchy Work had been so buried by the moving tempest of British shell that none escaped alive. At Feuchy Weir some prisoners were taken—an unarmed party of electrical engineers, under a captain.

Passing through Feuchy village, some time before the German gunners began to shell it, the men from the Triangle dug themselves in for the night close by a deep pit, where four 8 in. howitzers had been captured by a fine brigade of British cavalry. Being within striking distance of the important hostile hill position at Monchy, and at very short range from the heavy ordnance defending the Drocourt line, the conquering Britons were subjected

[Canadian War Records.

GERMAN PRISONERS RUNNING THE GAUNTLET OF THEIR OWN BARRAGE INTO CAPTIVITY.

Vimy Ridge was carried by Canadians troops early in the morning of April 9th, 1917, and in the course of that one day more than nine thousand of the enemy were taken prisoners. The King telegraphed the Empire's congratulations to all who took part in the day's successful operations and in the splendid achievement of taking that "coveted" Ridge which had so long dominated the Allies' line north of Arras.

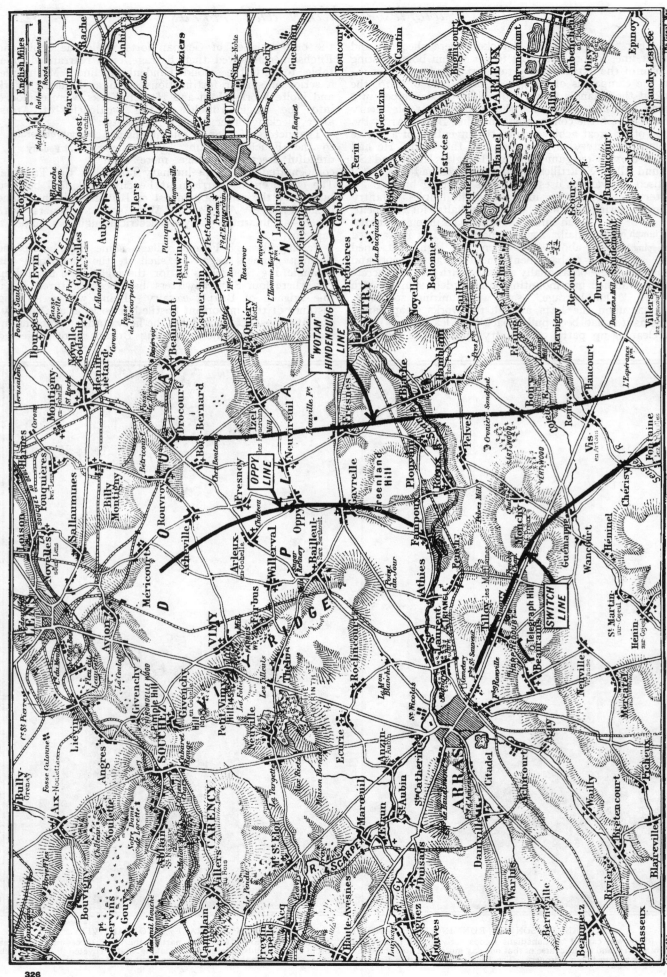

AREA OF THE FIGHTING ON THE OLD GERMAN FORTRESS FRONT, BETWEEN LENS AND ARRAS, APRIL 9TH TO 14TH, 1917.

ON THE LINE OF RETREAT.
Teuton soldiers on a light railway behind the boasted Hindenburg line. (From a German photograph.)

to terrific shell fire. They clung to their line all Easter Tuesday, while more English troops lined up with the Scots on the right and the cavalry assembled on their left, for a combined surprise stroke that was to shake Ludendorff almost as much as did the loss of the Vimy cliffs.

In the meantime another mass of British troops worked towards the Monchy line from a series of positions south of Blangy and the Douai railway. Near Beaurains, south-east of Arras, was a great German system known as the Harp. It was built on a hill, in a large irregular oval of earthworks and armoured forts, commanding a hollow over which the British troops had to advance. Telegraph Hill, a higher height, was close by.

Neither bombardment nor barrage seriously injured the strength of the Harp. When the attacking lines of troops reached the hollow, a murderous fire from the fortified rise stopped all progress. Attempts were made to get machine-guns to sweep the enemy trenches, and so keep down the Germans while bombing-parties worked forward. The plan, however, did not work quickly enough. The strong place was so intricately designed, with tier after tier of plunging fire positions, that the assault was held up by seven o'clock on Easter Monday.

Then from their lair behind a screen of trees some "tanks"

slithered to the holed and muddy top of Telegraph Hill. Squatting in this dominating position, above the Harp, they exercised a very perturbing influence upon the German force. The Harp was bombarded until it gave forth the music of a British victory, with a "Kamerad" chorus provided by a thousand prisoners.

In the neighbouring village of Tilloy, on the highway to Cambrai, with the Harp south-west and Feuchy north-east of it, a "tank" again broke into a fortified swell of ground and enabled the infantry to enter the village. There the German works had been terribly wrecked by the distant British guns. The land was smashed into shell-holes, the fields of barbed wire were torn into scattered strands, and the trenches turned into shapeless ditches. Devil's Wood, Tilloy Quarry, and other strong points around the Cambrai road were all occupied by eight o'clock in the morning. The survivors of the garrison surrendered quickly, and the British troops continued their progress along the highway to the Hindenburg switch-line. They were impeded, however, by some works erected at Feuchy chapel, on commanding ground at the junction of the lane from Feuchy village and the Cambrai high-road. The enemy had constructed two strong positions, known as Church Redoubt and Chapel Redoubt, and though the

[British and Canadian official photographs.

ON A RIVER OF MANY BATTLE MEMORIES.
British soldiers crossing the Scarpe by means of a light, partially destroyed footbridge and a pontoon. At the villages—Athies, Feuchy, Fampoux, Rœux—along this small river much severe fighting took place in the Arras battle. Above: British car passing over the old German front line on Vimy Ridge.

garrisons were weakened by the British gun fire, they survived in sufficient strength to make a brave and most desperate stand.

The Church Work was gradually reduced by bombing operations on April 9th, but at the Chapel, which was anything but a chapel of ease, according to an officer who led one of the assaults, a handful of gallant enemies held out until the following morning. Once more the ubiquitous "tank" lumbered up and settled the affair at the Chapel of Feuchy, thus clearing the last obstacle to the movement against Monchy plateau.

All the succession of victories around Arras by the Third Army, under Sir Edmund Allenby, opened a wide line of attack upon Monchy. The hill at Monchy was the last patch of high ground, held by the enemy for a breadth of thirty miles, between Orange Hill, conquered by the British, and the city of Valenciennes. The little plateau of Monchy, on the edge of which the village rose, was only about ninety feet above the great plain of French Flanders.

Importance of Monchy plateau Yet it was twenty-five higher than Orange Hill, intervening westward between it and Arras city; while eastward, looking over the territory held by the enemy, it gave as spacious and deadly a field of artillery observation as did the higher Vimy Ridge.

It was the grand prize of war in the Battle of Arras. So long as Ludendorff held it he still overlooked his lost line and safeguarded his new Drocourt front. In the ordinary way the German commander would have launched fierce, heavy, and persistent counter-attacks

from Monchy during the decisive time when the Third British Army was organising the ground it had won and bringing up its guns.

It had been Ludendorff's braggart design to employ his Drocourt line, with a mass of heavy artillery placed behind it, for the purpose of making irresistible Parthian-like rushes backward in great force against the tired advancing British troops, who possessed for immediate action only some field-guns.

Village of Fampoux stormed At Monchy, however, the shattered Germans were too hard put to it to maintain a good rearguard defence. Even with reinforcements they could not counter-attack rapidly in strength. Ludendorff found his line extended almost to breaking point.

His principal available reserves had to be sent towards the Lens sector, and other reserves had to be railed towards the Quéant region; for Sir Douglas Haig was stretching his original twelve-mile front of advance on either side of Arras to a fifty-mile battle-line, running from Loos to St. Quentin.

On the morning of Tuesday, April 10th, the British troops working between Vimy Ridge and the northern Scarpe River, made a magnificent bound forward and stormed into the village of Fampoux. Fampoux was about two miles beyond Monchy plateau, lying in the marsh of the Scarpe Valley, between the river and the enemy's railway communications with Douai. The conquerors of Fampoux achieved one of the pivoting successes of the campaign. They made a large dent, more

[Canadian War Records.

LOOKING DOWN ON THE VALLEY FROM VIMY'S CONQUERED RIDGE.
No ground on the western front had been more fiercely fought for than Vimy Ridge, and its capture on April 9th, 1917, was a great triumph for the Canadian and other British troops engaged. The Germans, who had regarded it as impregnable, yielded most of the ridge on the first day of the battle. Rising gradually on the western side, Vimy Ridge is more abrupt where it overlooks the coalfield plain on the east.

than five thousand yards deep, into the German line. They outflanked the hill fortress of Monchy in the south, and they also outflanked in the north the enemy positions at Bailleul and other places below the end of the Vimy Ridge.

The attack on Fampoux was made in worse conditions than the advance on Easter Monday. The snow fell more thickly, the soaked, broken ground was a deeper sea of mud, and the gale blew furiously. Maybe this bitter winter storm told on the weary, defeated Germans, and led them to think that the pursuing force would be as exhausted as they were. Victory, however, is a wonderful tonic. To the attacking Scotsmen the blinding snow seemed providential. It was better than any smoke-screen, being a natural battle blanket that did not herald any operation. The Germans were surprised and shattered ; their artillery was blinded and Fampoux secured.

This was the reason why the Scotsmen, Midlanders, and other Englishmen who had won towards Monchy Hill in the first day of battle were allowed to rest on Tuesday. Alongside them was the marvellous cavalry brigade, that had also won up the Scarpe valley, taking big guns on the way, and adventuring well beyond the foremost infantry. The victory at **Allenby's brilliant encircling manœuvre** Fampoux eased the situation of the Third Army in a remarkable way, and gave Sir Edmund Allenby the opportunity for one of the most brilliant encircling manœuvres in modern trench warfare.

Elbow-room had been won between the first and second Hindenburg systems for something like open-field action. Vexed and dulled by the great snowstorm, the German Staff officers at Monchy completely lost their grip of the situation. Either their means of communication were disorganised, or they did not understand what the news from Fampoux meant to them. They went to sleep in Monchy manor-house and in the village houses which had hastily been prepared for a state of siege.

[British official photographs.

British cavalry advancing through newly-captured territory, and, above, an impression of the broken ground over which they had to operate.

[Canadian War Records.

Canadian Light Horse going into action on Vimy Ridge. British cavalry got their chance in the Battle of Arras, and used it to the full, particularly at Monchy, south-east of Arras, where a clever encircling movement ended in a triumphant charge.
BRITISH CAVALRY IN THE BATTLE OF ARRAS.

The general of a defeated Prussian division, which had been pursued by British cavalry into the fringe of open country, retired from his old headquarters at Monchy Château. He left only a brigadier, with one battered brigade, to hold the all-important height. The worn and reduced force of Prussians was, of course, ordered to maintain the ground at any sacrifice. Fresh regiments, they were informed, were hurrying to their aid from rest billets in Douai and Cambrai. It was merely a matter of hours when they would be relieved.

This was so. Monchy had become the prize in a race against time by the opposing armies. The Britons won the race, because they did not wait for reinforcements, but struck with all their remaining strength. Sorely had they been tried by three nights and days of terrific fighting, marching in snow, rain and tempest, with little food and less sleep, harassed continually by hidden, hostile machine-guns and shelled by undiscoverable batteries.

Yet when the Prussian divisions, which had broken, had to be taken out of the battle, the British troops merely

cavalry and infantry encircled Monchy in a series of lightning manœuvres. The movements at times did not seem rapid. The infantry stumbled up snow slopes, slipping under the double blast of a gale and a rain of bullets. Heads down, they went upward, many falling, yet always with others to take their place.

The Prussians fired from the whitened roofs of the village, and poured machine-gun showers from windows and ditches. Their airmen also used machine-gun fire. "It was a rain of bullets," said a Londoner, who survived. "They couldn't miss us, but they couldn't stop us." Before the snipers could get off the gabled roofs of the cottages the attacking force reached the southern part of the village, and began to chase the fugitives up the narrow streets and across the square. Thereupon, as a long, bitter house-to-house conflict seemed to open, and give the enemy time to fight till reinforcements arrived, the combined British movements locked together.

Monchy height captured

The cavalry had formed up in a slight hollow north of the village, under a severe fire. The horses wheeled into position, and with amazing suddenness the wild, mud-plastered, unrecognisable figures of Dragoons, Lancers, and Hussars, their faces lost in metal bonnets and three days' growth of hair and grime, emerged on the plateau. They were greeted with cheers by thousands of other British troops scattered about the country-side.

They had slept for nights in shell holes, in a bath of rain, snow, and mud, with soaking greatcoats around them, chilled to the marrow, hungry and utterly worn out. Yet they charged with superb and victorious fury and perfect, deadly skill. When at last they halted, at the end of a good half mile, not a single Prussian was in view. Machine-guns, that had vainly been used against the too rapid target, were abandoned to them. They linked up with their infantry, who began to search the village, manor-house, and park for concealed prisoners, guns, ammunition, and food. The cavalry brought up their Hotchkiss and Lewis guns, and

[Canadian War Records.
WHERE A GREAT HIGHWAY CROSSED VIMY RIDGE.
Ruined roadway, from Arras to Lens and Lille, where it crossed Vimy Ridge. The way in which the ground had been torn up by the shattering bombardment that preceded the successful attack on the ridge is well shown by the state of the surface on which the British soldiers were standing. Near the centre of the photograph is a destroyed German machine-gun emplacement.

got their second wind, and went forward for another intense and prolonged effort. That is the reason why they won the critical race for time, and altered, greatly for the better, the conditions under which Ludendorff's grand reserve was ground to death between the Hindenburg lines.

In the lulls between the obscuring snow-squalls the German machine-gunners were able to observe every movement of their opponents in the little hollows beneath the dominating height. The stoic Britons calmly dug themselves in, in the finest tradition of the first Ypres battle. Their losses were considerable, but they stuck close to the hill, instead of withdrawing to a safer, less exposed holding position. The cavalry worked forward on both sides of the Cambrai road, beyond the famous Feuchy Chapel Work.

Cavalry on the Cambrai road

Then early in the morning of Wednesday April 11th, the long-enduring Scots, English, and mounted troops claimed their reward. Assisted by a gallant "tank," and yet counter-attacked by swooping German aeroplanes, the

turned to ride down the fugitives in the trenches east of the village.

Between Monchy and Sart Wood they found, in a hollow, a badly-sited entrenched line of German machine-guns. Dismounting, they brought the old Hotchkiss and the new Lewis guns into position above the German line, and, overcoming the enemy, threw him into Sart Wood. British horse-artillery, bumping and lurching, came over holes and dikes and through mud and snow slush, as a preliminary measure for transforming the little Monchy height into the master artillery position against the Drocourt line. It was still a race for time.

The German guns beyond Sart Wood began to shell the lost plateau about two hours after the British forces completely occupied it. When night fell, the village and château were smashed into the usual heap of ruins. Long before this the Prussians re-formed and strengthened under cover of Sart Wood, and came out in storming parties to recover the great key-position. Less than a hundred yards from the wood the counter-attack was so

[*Canadian War Records.*

German shells bursting behind the dug-in Canadian troops on Vimy Ridge, which " loomed above the Canadian divisions as a German Gibraltar on the western front in the grey, rainy dawn of battle " on April 9th, 1917, but before the close of that day had, all but a small northern portion, been captured by the assaulting troops. Thousands of the enemy were taken prisoner and many guns captured on the Ridge.

[*Canadian War Records.*

Collecting the wounded on the battlefield of Vimy Ridge, for conveyance by light railway to the base. The railway was rapidly laid behind the advancing troops, fresh sections of rails being taken up on the open trucks which returned with the wounded. Three German prisoners were assisting their captors in placing a stretcher case on the second truck. Ahead men were carrying the railway line further forward.

ON THE BATTLEFIELD OF VIMY RIDGE, WHERE THE CANADIANS WON UNFADING LAURELS.

smitten by the plunging fire from the hill that it faded into nothingness.

The British front was driven forward half a mile east of Monchy during the enemy's evidence of weakness. This won more flexibility for the British defence when the alarmed German High Command drew on its grand reserve for a pitched battle on a great scale for the only hill of supreme importance for thirty miles. Soon German howitzers began to increase the weight of their bombardment, and towards the evening another series of assaulting waves issued from Sart Wood.

When the height of Monchy was securely conquered, and posts thrown out into La Bergère and the country near Guémappe, another important operation was directed by Sir Edmund Allenby against the Hindenburg line at the point where it had been broken and turned by the thrust from the south-east of Arras. In the offensive of Easter Monday the hostile line had been assailed as far south as the Cojeul stream, near Henin-sur-Cojeul, while the armies of Sir Hubert Gough and Sir Henry Rawlinson violently held and occupied the enemy by thrusting actions around Quéant and St. Quentin.

Along the main line of battle, south of Telegraph Hill, near Arras, the village of Neuville Vitasse was carried through a network of trenches on April 9th. The enemy's defences on the western bank of the Cojeul stream were also broken. This advance, in combination with the later conquest of Fampoux and Monchy, left the village of Wancourt jutting, like a German bridge-head, into the field of victories of the Third Army.

Wancourt and its neighbouring cluster of cottages and farms, Heninel, across the Cojeul River, formed positions of difficulty to attack. They were on the slope of the river valley, and the approaches to them were fiercely swept by fire from other German works, especially at Guémappe northward and Cherisy south-eastward. Great zones of uncut wire entanglements stretched between the villages and the waiting London and English county men, lying out in deep snow and icy gales, with shrapnel and high-explosive shell bursting above them.

On Thursday, April 12th, as the struggle around Monchy slackened for a very brief period, Sir Edmund Allenby widened his great Arras salient of new ground by striking southward at Wancourt and Heninel. At first some things did not go very well. The English troops were checked by the thickets of uncut wire and by various strong places, from which enemy gunners poured out enfilading streams of bullets. One heroic division helped the force on its left by attacking without artillery support, before the arranged hour, penetrating the uncut wire and raiding a trench. When the time for the battle came they withdrew from the demonstrating and distracting affair, and opened their part of the general team-work, in which they again bore themselves with gallant distinction.

Wancourt and Heninel At the two villages the infantry were checked by machine-gun fire and unbroken wire. Happily, two "tanks" came forward in their laborious gait and, guided by young officers and crews of a daring spirit and fine skill, drove at the hedges of wire. Shooting from machine-guns at the Germans entrenched behind the entanglement, one "tank" flattened out two belts of entanglements, thus opening the gate for the infantry. Then it climbed the northern slope and fought down the German gunners there, and advanced, dauntless and terrifying, into Wancourt village.

It crawled in and out of Wancourt, panic-striking the garrison as well as shooting them. The cheering English infantry followed it into the village. This incident was merely the beginning of a record voyage by H.M. Landship. For two days and a night—some forty hours in all—the "tank" continued to cruise about the country, nosing out machine-gun posts and squirting death into enemy hiding-places. Bumped and battered, and as worn as ship-wrecked sailors, with almost all ammunition spent, the officer and crew turned the snout of their slithering vessel homeward.

In Heninel the second "tank" zigzagged amid the buildings and swept down the German troops so ferociously that they fled from the thing in terror, like the panic in the Somme action that marked the first appearance of the new machine of war. Then, with its sister of Wancourt, the Heninel "tank" fiercely explored the land about the Cojeul River, clearing the way for the splendid infantry.

In spite of the decisive help given by the "tanks," the attacking Englishmen had no easy triumph. In places the Germans continued stubbornly to hold to their pits and trenches, and the fire from the high, raking positions north and south continued to be severe. At length, on Friday, April 13th, as one bombing force worked down the trenches towards Wancourt, another strong force worked upward from the south, and met each other behind the Hindenburg line and cheered their common victory.

On a front of seven miles the new Siegfried system of the Hindenburg line was definitely pierced, turned, and occupied. The **German Lens-Arras** Wotan switch system was partially pene- **front shattered** trated and generally menaced. The old German fortress front between Lens and Arras was completely shattered, and the gigantic pivot city of forts around Blangy, designed as the hinge of Ludendorff's plan for fighting withdrawal battles, was entirely destroyed. Some twelve Teutonic divisions, with Silesian and Alsatian elements, had held the main systems or come out in support. They lost, by April 14th, 14,000 men as prisoners, with one hundred and ninety-four guns, that were soon increased to the number of two hundred and twenty-eight. A remarkable feature of the German losses was the proportion of Bavarians taken, killed, and wounded. The population of Bavaria was seven millions, the population of Prussia twenty millions, and the entire population of Germany was nearly seventy millions. In the most violent battles, if all Teuton tribes had been represented in proportion, the losses of the Bavarians should have been one-tenth of the whole. They were, however, more than one-third. Bavaria, the only possible rival to Prussia, was treated like a nation of Uriahs by the Prussian High Command.

Little Bavaria was set against the stronger British forces, so that she should be drained of strength and placed at the mercy of cunning Prussia. Some Bavarian writers had recommended that the Wittelbach dynasty should replace the Hohenzollern line as German Emperors, in order to restore the confidence of Europe in the future good intentions of the Teutonic race. The tremendous losses of the Bavarian troops in the Battles of Vimy Ridge and Arras formed the subtle Prussian reply to this suggestion.

On Friday, April 13th, when the Wancourt-Heninel action was proceeding, the 3rd Bavarian Division, which had fought bravely at Loos and on the Somme ridge, was railed to Douai, and made the spear-head force of a counter-attack on Monchy Hill, with the defeated and re-formed Prussian division in support. Under cover of as sustained and intense a bombardment as the German commander could organise, the attempt to recover the dominating height was developed with crippling losses.

Some of the advanced posts of defence were taken by the enemy by sheer weight and pressure of numbers, recovered by the British forces, taken again by the enemy, and once more regained. The Bavarians were at last cut to pieces and the Prussians so weakened they could not carry out the design of a final successful rush, enabling them to claim they had accomplished that which their screen of Bavarians had failed to achieve. The British positions, at the close of the struggle, were firmly held, and, with this victorious defence of the Monchy key-position, the Battle of Arras ended and the new Battle of the Scarpe began, while Lens rocked and flamed northward and Bullecourt in the south became a tangle of slaughter.

THE FIRST GREAT SOLDIERS' BATTLES ALONG THE ARTOIS RIVERS.

By Edward Wright.

General Haig in the Position of General Grant—Germany Fighting With Only One Arm—British Conscripted Population only Three-Fourths of German Population—British Commonwealth's Superiority in Man-Power Still Badly Undeveloped—Haig Skilfully Works German Reserves Round to His Wings, and Strikes from His Centre—Great Wing Attack on Lens—Storming of Angres and Liévin—Desperate Fighting in the Cités of Lens—Midlanders in the Crook and Crazy Line—Germans Prepare to Retire from Lens, but Return in Greater Force—Ludendorff Lacks Infantry to Counter-Attack—Opening of Terrific Battle of St. George's Day—The M.E.B.U.'s and the Part They Played in the Great German Manœuvre—Striking Preliminary British Successes All Along the Line—Enemy's Main Forces Overthrow the British Advance Guards—Victorious Heroism of Newfoundland Men—Magnificent Stand Made by the Middlesex and Argyll and Sutherlands—Victory of Worcester Battalion When Encircled for Nine Days—British Main Masses Attack German Main Masses—Unparalleled Scene of Open-Field Warfare—Horne Recovers Gavrelle—Allenby Regains Guémappe—Great Swaying Battles of Fontaine and Chérisy—German Armies Become too Exhausted to Continue Their Massed Counter-Attacks—Import of the British Victory.

THE situation on the western British front in the middle of April, 1917, was of complex interest. The Fifth British Army, under Sir Hubert Gough, and the Fourth Army, under Sir Henry Rawlinson, had overtaken the defenders of the Hindenburg line and driven wedges into the enemy's new system. The Third British Army, under Sir Edmund Allenby, had broken and turned the top of the main Hindenburg system and advanced along the Scarpe River, threatening the secondary and half-constructed Hindenburg system. The First British Army, under Sir Henry Horne, had stormed the hill rampart near the top of the enemy's Drocourt or Wotan line, and prolonged the attack directly against Lens and its coal-fields and Drocourt and its unfinished fortifications.

There was no complexity in the view of Sir Douglas Haig and his able Army Commanders. Their task was direct and grandly simple. All they had to do was to continue battering against the enemy and

AMONG THE RUINS OF TILLOY.
Interesting legacy from the enemy evicted from Tilloy—a German machine-gun emplacement on wheels. Tilloy was captured in the first attack on April 9th, 1917, but was practically demolished by shell fire.

[British official photographs.

incessantly weakening him, to the best of their ability, until he broke, retreated, or sued for peace. They needed more railways, more heavy artillery and larger reserves, with more aeroplanes, and more shells of large calibre.

General strength, as overwhelming as the resources of the British Commonwealth would allow, was their plain and only need. Their essential policy was the same as that of General Grant in the mighty intestinal struggle with General Lee. They intended to wear the enemy down until he was utterly enfeebled. They had won a series of very advantageous positions, and from these positions they had only to continue to attack, in order to bring to battle a larger part of the reserves which the enemy possessed.

It was open to Sir Douglas Haig to intensify the process of attrition, by bringing into action his Second Army, under Sir Herbert Plumer, in the Ypres section. He decided, however, to keep this army in reserve, as it had been arranged with the French Commander-in-Chief that the main French Army should first increase the

WHERE MERCY BRAVED THE FLYING MENACE OF THE GUNS.

[British official photograph.]

Heavy shell bursting almost upon an advanced dressing-station on the western front. The Red Cross flag was flown over all medical stations, from regimental aid-posts back to base hospitals; but many of these unavoidably came into the line of shell fire, and when bombardment was heavy the wounded were carried to underground cellars or dug-outs till the bombardment ceased and they could be moved farther back.

terrific pressure upon the forces and resources of Germany by a general offensive, opening on April 16th, 1917, along the Aisne and the hills of Champagne.

Ludendorff was troubled and perplexed in his view of the situation by the complexity of the problem he had to face. He seems to have been unable to fight without a flow of braggart loquacity. He was a **Ludendorff loquacious in perplexity** buck nigger with a white skin. He jeered and sneered at his opponent while delivering his strokes. Partly he thought that a stream of abuse was of fighting value, in that it was calculated to distract his foe and make him blindly angry. Mainly, it was merely the expression of the nature of the man. It was his own way of keeping up his own courage. When Jack Johnson, the negro prize-fighter, felt the superior power of Willard, the white champion, he became quiet and touched with commonsense and common decency. When Ludendorff, however, felt the full weight of the power wielded by Sir Douglas Haig, he merely became wilder and more extravagant in his language. For he was trying to keep up the courage of his people, in addition to making a noise to stir up his own energies.

The greater his perplexity became, the louder and wilder became his speech. All his personal ambitions were suddenly defeated in the Battles of Vimy Ridge and Arras. He could not initiate any new operation of importance during the spring of 1917. The most he could do was to stand on the defensive, and struggle to save his guns and his fortified lines, by means of an enormous sacrifice of human material.

By reason of his grand reserve of a million men, he retained a considerable measure of tactical control. He had merely to counter-attack in heavy and persistent force, against some points seized by the armies of Sir Douglas Haig, in order to provoke a great battle in the place he selected. Naturally, the British commander could not allow his opponent to win back any height or other position of military importance or political prestige. Therefore, masses of British troops had to be concentrated behind every sector of the Hindenburg line from which the enemy strongly and persistently counter-attacked.

With this exception, Sir Douglas Haig imposed upon General von Ludendorff the time and direction of the stupendous conflict of the armies of the two nations. Ludendorff had to provide against the coming French offensive, and, for a week or two, he had also to consider seriously the possibility of a movement on the Russian front by General Brussiloff. He could not immediately withdraw a large proportion of German troops and German guns from the **Germany menaced on two fronts** eastern theatre of war without running a gambling risk.

He was not by nature a gambler, but rather a backer of what seemed to be military certainties. He usually introduced elements of surprise in an obvious situation by organising a greater and more rapid striking power than his opponent expected to meet. Between Lens and St. Quentin he had been mastered by his own method. Four British armies had been driven at him on an expected course, but with unexpected speed and power. By sheer drive and pressure, Sir Douglas Haig practically compelled him to submit to a downright naked trial of strength.

334

It must be remembered that the German Empire was fighting against the British Empire with only one arm, while the British Empire was fighting against the German Empire with two arms, and indeed two feet. The British Commonwealth was somewhat distracted by operations against the Turks in Mesopotamia and Palestine, and against the Bulgars and Turks in Macedonia. By way of balance, however, Germany had to provide Austria-Hungary with both commanding officers and troops, and a considerable number of her best class of professional officers were engaged in Turkey and Bulgaria.

France still attracted a huge force of the enemy troops, guns, munitions, and general war material. To a much less extent Russia, even in a pacific mood, succeeded in retaining against her passive battle-line about half **Handicap on** a million German sentinel troops of **German Empire** second-rate quality, together with a considerable amount of artillery.

Thus, it can scarcely be said that Germany had her right hand entirely free during the conflict with two-handed Britain. In the matter of population, the white races of the British Empire were not much inferior in strength to the people of the German Empire. Had the system of universal service obtained in Ireland and the overseas British Dominions, the actual British forces in the field would have outnumbered the forces available in Germany after thirty-four months of most costly warfare. Also, if the leading statesmen of the Union of South Africa had not been averse to the enlistment of warlike Bantu tribesmen, the British commander would have had, in British black Africa, an enor- **Enormous ultimate** mous field of enlistment for infantry of **British resources** good quality in bayonet attacks. The military castes and races of India were largely absorbed in the Mesopotamian campaign, though they gave some fine cavalry to the French front.

In summer campaigning in France, the warlike section of the great Indian population might profitably have been employed, if circumstances had permitted, withdrawing from the winter campaigning when weather conditions favoured only men hardened to the climate of the temperate zone.

Had the Bantus been employed, they would have done best, in the European theatre of war, when employed in the French fashion of storming attacks, covered by a bombardment that temporally overwhelmed the foes and enabled white support troops to hold the ground won by the black troops.

Thus the ultimate resources of the British Commonwealth

[*Canadian War Records.*

SYMBOLS OF THE PASSING OF GERMANY'S MILITARY SUPREMACY.

British soldiers outside a former German headquarters in one of the re-captured towns. The French tricolour replaced the German flag over the doorway immediately after the re-occupation, but the liberators had not troubled to paint out the black, white, and red stripes upon the sentry-box, the national colours of the hated invader. It was enough that the late occupant had been evicted and that a British sentry occupied it.

were enormous. Nevertheless, mere population did not count in this case, as the adult males among the seventy millions of Germans were of higher personal fighting strength than many of the non-military nations of all classes in large parts of British territory. The intricate and terrifying machinery of modern warfare tended to give the men of European stock, who manufactured it, a certain superiority in temperament and intelligence over less experienced, more emotional, and uneducated warriors of semi-tropical origin.

As things stood at the time, England, Scotland, and Wales, with some help from northern and southern Ireland, and generous voluntary aid from Canada, Australia, New Zealand, and South Africa, maintained the largest burden in the struggle against the Germans. In the area to which conscription had been applied, the total population was only about four-sevenths of the German population. Germany also started with a larger absolute proportion of males, which originally served greatly to increase her military strength. Her acknowledged heavy losses did but give her a surplus female population similar to that of her principal foe.

The general result was that the British Commonwealth, in the third year of war, still had only the potentiality of a marked superiority in man-power over the German Empire. Actually, in the spring of 1917, Sir Douglas Haig could not safely proceed to obtain a decision by a sustained gigantic thrusting movement, requiring entire armies to be propelled forward until the strength of Germany was worn out. He had still to nibble, in the manner of Marshal Joffre. Yet his nibbles became large bites, and he greatly accelerated the process of

reducing Germany to the condition in which the Confederate States of America were left after four years of grinding warfare.

It will be remembered that in the Somme Battle, a fortnight elapsed between the first successes of General Horne and General Congreve and the resumption of their advance in full force. A similar period of preparation occurred on the Hindenburg line of battle. After his victories of April 9th, 1917, Sir Edmund Allenby required a fortnight in order to bring forward his guns, railways, and roads for a terrific battle against the **Sir Douglas Haig's** enemy's Drocourt front. Even then the **design** Third Army was not completely ready, as the great extent of conquered ground needed months to organise fully.

In the meantime, Sir Henry Horne, with his brilliant lieutenants, including the Canadian Corps Commander, Sir Julian Byng, occupied the enemy in a fierce struggle around Lens, while Sir Hubert Gough assailed the southern end of the Drocourt line near Quéant, and Sir Henry Rawlinson went on with his series of actions north of St. Quentin.

Sir Douglas Haig's design was to attract Ludendorff's reserves of men and guns towards the wings of the half-broken Hindenburg line, during the period in which he was assisting Sir Edmund Allenby in preparations for another fierce and sustained stroke against the centre of the Hindenburg system. The Canadian victory on the Vimy Ridge had opened a promising line of approach against the southern outskirts of the mining city of Lens.

Sir Henry Horne silently and rapidly organised an attack, employing the English, Irish, and Canadian troops who had fought up and over Bois-en-Hache and Pimple Hill on April 12th. Fresh British troops were brought into action against the northern and western sides of the Lens salient, and the operation immediately began on Friday, April 13th.

General Horne began by throwing his main forces of Canadians and Scotsmen down the eastern slopes of the Vimy heights. Employing captured German guns and thousands of rounds of German shells, the attacking forces bombarded the Douai plains, and in a series of brilliant actions seized the villages of Vimy, Petit Vimy, Willerval, and Bailleul, taking more guns and ammunition and more prisoners.

At the same time, the battle for Lens opened. The troops who conquered Vimy village were able to outflank all the important German positions westward of Lens. The village of Angres and the town of Liévin, with many of the pit-head hamlets of the

[*British official photographs.*]

RESTFUL MOMENTS IN THE FORWARD FIGHTING.
Crossing a flooded road near Tincourt, about five miles east of Péronne; in the distance a number of British cavalry horses brought down for watering. In circle: A group of British soldiers resting in the corner of a battered building after a period of strenuous fighting.

great French coal-field district, were then well behind the Canadian front. Also, the village of Givenchy-en-Gohelle and Riaumont Wood, with a considerable stretch of Souchez River, were subjected to terrific flanking fire from the Vimy positions and the old Loos positions on the northern side.

The British army around Loos, on the other side of the river, was almost directly in line with the Canadian forces at Vimy. The Germans in Angres, Liévin, Givenchy, and the various groups of miners' cottages round about, were caught in the artillery pincers of the Loos and Vimy armies. Time was not allowed the enemy to retire without a struggle. He had been utterly surprised by the loss of the Vimy positions, and possessed an abundance of war material in the Lens salient, for which he was ready to sacrifice his infantry. Instead of withdrawing guns and men, he lost time in sending the Prussian Guard forward to Bois-en-Hache in a vain attempt to recover the lost heights. By the time the Prussian Guard was broken there was no opportunity left for a pacific retirement. The English and Irish conquerors of Bois-en-Hache at once drove into the town of Liévin, on April 13th, on the heels of the retreating enemy.

Again the Anglo-Celts had in some places to fight forward up to their waists in mud. Before them was the large fortified line of Riaumont Wood, dotted with machine-gun forts, and another couple of elaborate redoubts, known as Crook and Crazy Redoubts, with a series of strong positions extending a thousand yards east of Liévin.

From Bois-en-Hache the clay-caked waders worked forward to the outskirts of Lens, swept by machine-gun fire from the sunken redoubts and fortified cottages. In a grim spirit, their bombers rushed many of the armoured concrete forts, and came to a smooth rise and the wire entanglements of Riaumont Wood. The position was practically impregnable, so the German garrison waited for the easy work of repelling an impossible advance. They waited in vain.

Capture of Riaumont Wood

All day and all night enormous explosions rose in flame and smoke and thunder from Lens and Liévin. The enemy was blowing up mine-shafts, flooding mines, and destroying all buildings of either military or civilian service. Meanwhile, his westernmost rearguards in the village of Angres were overcome by a fierce hand-to-hand combat in which there were some touches of humour. One Irishman, for example, came upon a German at the entrance to a dug-out, fought him down, and then agreed

[*British official photograph.*

AT A MINED CROSS ROAD.
Boiry-Becquerelle, south-east of Arras, showing the German guide-marks (left to Mercatel and right to Henin) and the mine they exploded on being forced to retire.

[*British official photograph.*

OUTSIDE AN ADVANCED DRESSING-STATION.
Cases waiting for attention at an advanced dressing-station, with German prisoners assisting in carrying stretchers. Casualties whose condition permitted their removal were carried hence by motor-ambulance farther down the line.

to accept breakfast before taking his prisoner. He took a good share of German sausage, cheese, black bread, and wine, and came back arm-in-arm with his prisoner. Eating German breakfasts was the great game in Angres, as the enemy troops there were uncommonly well supplied with food.

Since the Battle of Loos their position had been the most dangerous on either the western or the eastern front. It was overlapped on each side by the allied positions at Loos and Souchez, yet had to be held at heavy cost to the enemy, being a valuable advanced position along the British rear. Since the winter of 1914 it had been repeatedly attacked by French and British forces, yet had never been seriously endangered. Communicating with it ran a large series of miners' cottages, usually arranged each in a quadrangle and known as Cités. There was nothing of a city appearance about Cité St. Pierre, Cité Jeanne d'Arc, Cité St. Theodore, west and north-westward; Cité St. Dourard, Cité St. Laurent, Cité Ste. Auguste, Cité St. Edouard, and Cité Ste. Elizabeth, northward; with Cité de Riaumont, Cité du Moulin and Cité du Bois de Liévin southward. They were nearly all square blocks of French colliers' cottages, formerly housing a population of twelve thousand people in addition to the twenty-eight thousand inhabitants of Lens.

The squares made admirable machine-gun positions. Each had its sand-bag barricades, its distinct systems of wire entanglements, and its nests of machine-guns. Rearguard forces were set to serve the guns, and ordered to save the retreating army by holding out to the last desperate moment. Therefore, on all sides, the British advanced troops were at first checked by a scything fire of bullets from the Cités. Any attempt to storm forward in force would have entailed great losses. So the British infantry took cover in the nearest shell-holes, while their artillery added to the smoking ruin of the mining centre by a prolonged and devastating bombardment.

Then, in the sunlit morning of April 14th, the fortressed hillside of Riaumont Wood was captured in brilliant fashion. Small parties of English troops came out in two thin waves, and, after taking cover and concentrating under an embankment, went at the double towards the bare, sudden slope of the wooded rise where the German gunners were still waiting for them. Instead, however, of pressing up to the crest in a frontal attack, they swerved and disappeared down a tree-fringed street.

As soon as they vanished the enemy flung out a barrage that caught the embankment where the English troops had assembled. Tragic would have been the fate of the attacking force had they waited a little longer. The Englishmen, however, worked around the left of the wooded hill and emerged, amid a tangle of protecting cottages, on high ground on the north-western side. Thence, with their own machine-guns, they barraged the flank of the enemy's position, and, taking him unawares, fought through the undefended side of Riaumont Wood and captured it, together with a mining village in the rear. All the wood was won by noon. An hour afterwards the Crook Redoubt was entirely taken and Crazy Redoubt was entered and rapidly cleared.

The top of the Crook and Crazy line was driven in by an officer of a Midland battalion with half a dozen of his men. He worked along the attics of a row of **Crook and Crazy** houses, and found a window from which **line breached** he could snipe the gunners in the topmost machine-gun post. By good shooting, at the range of four hundred yards, the seven Midlanders sniped all the German gunners and made a breach in the Crook and Crazy line through which the entire position could be turned. By the time the German garrisons grasped the situation, an English machine-gun was already trained on their rear, and as they bolted across the open they were unexpectedly swept by a deadly fire.

The action raged northwards as well as westward and southward. The British forces in Loos fought onward to their old line, coming again in view of the fortified mound of Hill 70 which had been temporarily occupied by Scottish Territorials and Guards in the battle of 1915. The historic embankment of coal-mine refuse, known as the Double Crassier, which had been stormed by British Territorials in the earlier struggle and lost by the French, was again occupied. The town of Liévin was taken, with a great store of trucks, artillery dumps, engineering tools, and undamaged railway lines. The Germans were compelled to retire in such a hurry that they could not fire their stores or remove their guns.

At first it seemed as though Lens was also about to fall. Night and day, in sunshine, and mist, and drizzling darkness, it was enveloped in whirlpools of smoke. The enemy sappers were using **Weakening German** up thousands of tons of high-explosives, **resistance at Lens** partly to prevent the material from falling into British hands and partly to prevent the mines being useful to the French people in the coming winter. The resistance of the rearguards suddenly grew weaker all along the line, indicating that they intended soon to retire.

Then, in the afternoon of Sunday, April 15th, the entire situation changed. It seemed as if the local army commander had first decided to retire from the half-encircled mining city and base his defence upon Hill 70 and Cité Ste. Auguste and the eastern colliers' blocks and rises of ground running southward to Méricourt. He was outflanked in the south, near the village of Avion, by the artillery of the Canadian corps advancing down from the ridge. The course he was taking seemed to be wise, as his position was becoming a very expensive one, being under close and direct observation from the ridge and the other lost heights near Souchez River. The wide panorama of battle could be studied in detail in clear weather from the commanding positions conquered by Sir Henry Horne's forces.

In the sunshine of Saturday British observers looked down into the streets of Lens, and if a single German came out of one of the red houses his movements were followed. The slag hills stood out in clear outline upon the plain near the tall chimneys of the power-stations and the gantries of the pit-heads. Close at hand were the electric works, soon to become memorable, and the dome of the great waterworks, with Lens Church in the distance, rising behind the hill across a stretch of red streets. The red dust of the cottages coloured the volcanic

[*Canadian War Records.*

TAKING COVER FROM A HIGH-EXPLOSIVE SHELL BURSTING ON A BARREN PLATEAU.

In the absence of an immediately adjacent shell-hole, the only course for men not actually in a trench to pursue was to drop flat to the ground, and hope that the shell splinters flung upwards by the explosion would be thrown sufficiently far to fall clear of them. The men learned to judge approximately where a high-explosive shell, which could be seen, as well as heard, approaching, was likely to burst.

[Canadian War Records.
AN OBSTACLE THAT FAILED TO BAR THE WAY.
British soldiers examining a German machine-gun emplacement at Thelus, near the famous Labyrinth, destroyed by the terrific bombardment that preceded the recapture of the village on the glorious Ninth of April.

[British official photograph.
COUNTING THE BAG AFTER A GOOD DAY.
British conquerors of Tilloy looking at their trophies. In the first five days of the Arras Battle one hundred and sixty-three machine-guns were captured, and more than a hundred guns, many of them of large calibre.

smoke of the enemy's devastating explosions, while the fume of fires drifted in grey clouds over the mine-fields. Prisoners stated that hundreds of thousands of hand-grenades were being used in the destruction of the town because there was no time to carry them away.

Everything pointed to an evacuation similar to that of Bapaume and Péronne. But Ludendorff either intervened or changed his mind. Fresh German troops were poured into the smouldering ruins, and the withdrawing German guns were turned about and worked at express speed; 8-inch howitzers, in large numbers, curtained all the British line of approach, and late on Sunday night the first counter-attack came. New German batteries were brought up and massed around Loos and Lens, to deluge with heavy projectiles the wreckage of Angres, Liévin, Riaumont, and the lost suburbs of Lens.

A change in the weather made the shooting on both sides somewhat feeble in effect, in spite of its strength. The rain curtained the grim theatre of war, black clouds scudded across the sky in a fierce gale, most of the observation-balloons had to be hauled down, and the long-ranged guns were trained in haphazard fashion by the map.

The storm scarcely interfered with the British operations. The infantry had pressed forward with little artillery support, and had carried out a good deal of their work on the northern and western outskirts of the town by means of patrols. It was nearly a six-mile tramp, on the larger part of the original British front, to the new line running through the Lens suburbs. The heavy British artillery had been left too far behind, and could not give sufficient support to the infantry as an attacking force.

Guns, with shells weighing more than half a ton, could not gallop after an enemy along a damaged highway. They could not even crawl over a shell-ploughed field, streaming with melted snow and falling rain. Gunners and drivers worked in super-human fashion, and, in spite of everything, brought their pieces and limbers forward in a manner very remarkable in the circumstances. But, in addition to guns and shells, pits, emplacements, bomb-proof shelters, firm roads, light railways, and munition depots, food stores and water were required.

Germans reinforced in Lens

A considerable period of organisation had to elapse between the first rapid advance and the second attack. It would have been bad generalship to allow the infantry to press into Lens when Ludendorff had brought up hundreds more guns of long range. He had been able to increase the range of his field artillery by means

[*British official photograph*
WHEN THE ADVANCE BEGAN.
On Easter Sunday, 1917, the entire British Army quickened into activity. Soon baggage trains were passing infantry still in trenches, and the ground was heaped with material for wiring positions to be won farther forward.

of a new device that increased the velocity of the shell. It was reported that his field pieces could cover the remarkable distance of nine thousand yards. This was an increase of two thousand yards beyond the previous range of German field artillery.

The German 9·6 in. gun had a range of twenty-eight thousand yards, and, being employed in larger number than the British 9·4 in. gun, it was able to do a disturbing amount of damage to British communications. Especially was this the case when the heavy British artillery was something like ten miles away from the new line won from the enemy.

German engineers built a dam across the Souchez River and the Lens Canal, with which the stream merged, and caused the flood of melting snow and rain to inundate parts of the town and some of its suburbs as well as

Skirmishing in the suburbs

to make the mines unworkable. The enemy was apprehensive of British attacks being delivered through the mine galleries, from the pit-heads won around Liévin. At least, he pretended to be apprehensive in the matter, and his fear served as an excuse for his usual plan of destroying everything of possible use to the civil population of France.

In spite of floods, German reinforcements, and increased power in the German artillery, British patrols worked within four hundred yards of the streets leading to the centre of the town. At the beginning of the third week in April lively skirmishing went on in the western suburbs

of Lens, and the British cordon, forming nearly a semi-circle around the town, was drawn still tighter by fierce little bursts of outpost fighting among the coal dumps, slag heaps, and battered cottages.

The lull that followed on Ludendorff's decision to make a stand around Lens merely covered an immense amount of frenzied preparation on both sides. The German worked day and night to strengthen his Wotan line, running from the south-east of Lens to Drocourt, and his Alberich line, extending to Laon. These elements of the Hindenburg system, though strong in parts, were often patchy and weak, consisting of shallow, unfinished trenches, without dug-outs or gun emplacements. The time-table of Ludendorff and his Staff had completely failed to adjust itself to the speed and

ONLY WAITING THE WORD.　　　　　　　　[*British official photograph.*
British cavalrymen resting in a shell hole awaiting the order to advance. Although nothing like a general cavalry operation took place in the Battle of Arras, some corps cavalry did notably useful work.

reach of the British advance. On the other hand, the successful British forces found it very difficult to build forward at the pace with which they fought. Having left their own heavy guns far behind, and approached closer to the enemy's large pieces, the infantry had themselves greatly to endure, and they had to throw much of the burden of victory upon the heroic Pioneers, who slaved in the open, under violent shell fire, while making roads and emplacements for the advance of the British guns.

In the Somme Battles the big guns did not need to move for some weeks. The depth of ground gained was so much smaller that the heavy artillery had been able to cover the successive stages of attack from their old sites. In the Arras, Vimy, and Lens actions a great breadth of country was abruptly wrested from the enemy. But for his strength in heavy ordnance his front would have been pierced. As it was, he was not only enabled to reorganise, under shelter of his siege guns, but to win by means of them a temporary tactical advantage.

Between April 15th and April 23rd it was open to Ludendorff to make tremendous counterattacks with a considerable superiority in heavy gun power. He did not do so, simply because he could not. In the first place, the new French offensive occupied him and attracted his free reserves. In the second place, he had massed too many of his former reserves around Quéant and St. Quentin, where they were fully occupied by the strong demonstrating forces of Sir Hubert Gough and Sir Henry Rawlinson. Not having anticipated the loss of the Vimy Ridge and Liévin, the German commander had no large, fresh forces ready in this section to make a grand attempt to recover the

[*British official photograph.*

BRITISH CAVALRY ON THE MOVE.
The cavalry seized their longed-for chance at Arras. One body captured a pair of heavy howitzers mounted on the bank of the Scarpe, charging and cutting down the gunners in the fine old style.

BRITISH INFANTRY ADVANCING TO ATTACK. [*British official photograph.*
The wonderful scenes on the Somme in July, 1916, were eclipsed by the amazing activity developed on the Scarpe in April, 1917. Troops of all arms combined in one simultaneous, irresistible offensive.

heights. Moreover, in the terrific artillery duels, with which the Battle of Arras opened, Ludendorff's lieutenants had lost more than one thousand two hundred guns through direct hits from the magnificent British gunners. At least two hundred important German ammunition dumps had also been destroyed in the artillery duel and others were captured, together with more than two hundred guns. It was, therefore, as much as Ludendorff could do, by working all his men and means of communication to the uttermost, to replace his losses in war machinery.

He retained the advantage of some heavy guns placed near the new battlefields, and the superiority of having practically unbroken communications behind him. His front, however, was so much bent back at the top of the Siegfried line, and near the top of the Wotan line, that he had to prepare against new violent thrusts from two directions.

He did not know in advance whether the heaviest

weight of attack would be behind the Third British Army along the Scarpe River, or behind the First British Army along the Souchez River. He had also to take into reckoning the possibility of a fierce assault by the Australian and other spear-head forces of Sir Hubert Gough's army.

In these circumstances the German dictator appears to have brought forward his grand reserve, and echelonned it behind Lens and above the Scarpe, Sensée, and Scheldt Rivers to balance all possible British attacks. At the same time, he placed great reserve forces close to the Aisne and Champagne front, where a great French enveloping movement was opening.

Although the lull on the British front lasted a full week the Germans enjoyed no rest. Immediately the advance on Lens came to a standstill the armies of France opened a grand offensive on a wide front from Soissons to Auberive. The Franco-British commands were employing their old method **French grand** of alternate heavy shocks against the **offensive opens** enemy's wings, according to the first plan originated by Marshal Joffre. The second plan, worked out by Marshal Joffre, General Foch, and Sir Douglas Haig, could not be followed. It consisted in massing the main British and French armies side by side, as in the Somme operations, and thus getting the utmost concentration of effort. This second and better plan, however, had been invalidated by the enemy's retreat from the Somme. Yet the return to the first plan was not without compensation. The weight of the British and French strokes had enormously

[*British official photograph.*

HAIG'S MEN IN POSSESSION OF A BASTION OF HINDENBURG'S LINE.

On April 10th, 1917, Hindenburg declared that the western front was so strong that it could withstand every attack. That very same day the British troops in effect really broke through the extreme end of the famous Hindenburg line, just to the south-east of Arras.

increased since 1915, partly owing to the great increase in munition production, and partly owing to the still more remarkable increase in numbers and technical skill of the British forces.

France no longer had to send two or three of her best armies north-westward to bring the British striking power to the level of the need of the strategic situation. The armies of the British Commonwealth had grown so amazingly large and strong that all the main forces of the French Republic could be concentrated against the right wing of the enemy's principal positions.

On St. George's Day, April 23rd, as soon as the powerful French stroke had drawn off part of the reserves Ludendorff was pouring into France, the British Commander-in-Chief made another attack in force. Sir Douglas Haig's immediate aim was to bring relief to the French armies, who had met with more resistance than General Nivelle had anticipated. The British forces had to strike again before they were ready, for the loyal purpose of enabling the French High Command to resume its effort in better circumstances. On the other hand, Sir Douglas Haig's larger design was to continue to grind down the strength of the enemy at the moment when General Pétain was holding down vast German forces.

The scene of the new battle was a continuation of the terrain of the struggle around Arras. Sir Edmund Allenby's Third Army swung out against Roeux and Pelves, Sart Wood, and Vert Wood, Guémappe, Chérisy, and Fontaine, and the country north of Croisilles, and Sir Henry Horne sent one of his corps against Gavrelle.

Battle of St. George's Day

The front of attack was about twelve miles. As there was no continuous and definite system of fortification facing the British troops, the operation was a kind of open-field warfare interrupted by scattered redoubts. On the slopes about the Scarpe River, and the little swells of ground between the Cojeul and Sensée streams, the German engineers had constructed a multitude of remarkable detached forts.

These forts often consisted of three separate armoured concrete cellars, in each of which was a machine-gun, covered by a dome about the size of a coal-cellar plate. The top was only an inch or two above ground, with a sideway slit in it, through which the machine-gun played. Farther underground was a connecting gallery, by which the gun teams could communicate with each other. Trenches were scattered among the forts, in important tactical positions. There was not, however, any general system of communication trenches, as the enemy had not had time to dig them. Scattered garrisons usually had to wait until the cover of night for supplies or reliefs to reach them across the open rolling country. The entire arrangement of forts, pieces of trench, and local stretches of wire entanglement fulfilled the purpose of barbed wire. It was an obstacle to the British attacking forces, intended to delay and confuse and weaken it before the main battle was joined.

Ludendorff certainly displayed high ability in the mechanics of war when he devised this system of interrupting obstacles. He placed only an advance guard in the immediate battle-line, and kept back his large striking forces for a countering blow. His tactics were in turn answered by Sir Edmund Allenby. The British general seems at first to have sent forward patrols against the scattered forts and entrenched positions, and kept a large reserve in hand for the terrific conflict of mass against mass.

The general result was one of the most sanguinary and close-fought battles in history. Three days of fine weather preceded the action, and enabled the Royal Flying Corps and the Royal Naval Air Wing to show what they could do when they had a good number **British dominion of the air** of machines equal in quality to the best German machines. Seldom did any enemy aerial observers cross the British lines. On Sunday, April 22nd, twenty-one German machines and seven German kite balloons were destroyed. On the Monday, thirty-nine German machines were crashed, leaving the enemy's territory open to a larger number of bombing raids on railways, dumps, and aerodromes than had occurred in any previous action.

For a brief but critical period the British fighting pilots recovered the mastery of the air. As the weather was remarkably clear, the dominion of the sky was an advantage of high importance. By a violent bombardment, continued throughout Sunday night, the British artillery challenged the German gunners, and inflicted considerable preliminary losses upon his infantry. The weight of British pieces, hastily brought up over bad roads and long distances, was indeed very remarkable. It was one of the finest triumphs of British organisation.

The nearest villages to the German lines were wiped out, and the nearest trenches with their garrisons were battered out of existence or reduced to ruins. Only a few men were left with any fight in them. The German artillery, however, escaped the crippling damage inflicted upon it in the Vimy and Arras battles. Many German gunners held their fire during the British bombardment, so as to escape counter-battery attack. Ludendorff's aim was

Every building bristled with machine-guns. Final mêlée at Monchy, captured April 11th, 1917

Rushing the last barricade of the retreating German rearguard at Heudicourt, March 31st, 1917.

Mowing=time at Tilloy: Concentrated machine=guns cut the massed Germans down in swathes.

Evening on the Somme: British patrol stalking a German machine=gun post outside a village

Wild fight for guns near St. Quentin : Repulse of the last German attempt to save a battery.

Lair of the "Potsdam giants": Thrusting the Prussian Guard out of Bullecourt, May, 1917.

Pressing the German retreat : British cavalry patrol dispersing rearguard detachment of Uhlans.

The dreadful hollows that led to Oppy Wood : British bombers working along the German trenches.

THE GUARDS' CLUB—NOT IN PALL MALL. [*British official photograph*.]
Canteens where wounded soldiers could obtain tea, coffee, and other light refreshments without payment, and where other soldiers could get them at purely nominal charges, studded the western front. This one was run by the Guards Division in the field in connection with a Divisonal Club.

to sacrifice his advanced infantry forces, in order to save his guns for the main battle.

When, therefore, the British patrols advanced, they were swept by a barrage of unusual intensity, resembling that of the early Gommecourt and Ancre valley actions. Nevertheless, they won through the great shell curtain, and began to penetrate the enemy's line. In the first phase of the action, a series of magnificent British successes was won, although many of the men

Fontaine, Guémappe, and Chérisy were drawn from Sir Douglas Haig's new reserves, and were receiving their baptism of fire.

Southward, progress was made, by furious fighting, to the outskirts of Fontaine. Here there was an extremely strong series of positions at the point where the Hindenburg line crossed the Sensée River.

Many German machine-gunners were specially ordered to adopt the tactics of the Gommecourt battle. They allowed the British troops to advance and pass their hidden forts, and then suddenly fired on their backs from a rear loop-hole. Bayonet and bullet were seldom of much use in attacking the forts; light hand-bombs could not break through the dome. Only a Stokes' gun crew, or the cannon carried by the new and larger tanks could easily master the garrison of a sunken fort that had escaped the British barrage and allowed the first lines of infantry to pass.

In spite of the enemy's machinery of resistance Fontaine was almost conquered in the first gallant attack in the morning. Between Fontaine and Guémappe, in open undulating country, was a commanding height crowned by an old tower which had served as a valuable observation post for the enemy. Nearly all the ground was carried against the German 35th Reserve Divison, which had jeered at the men of the 18th Division, who had been broken previously. Under British gun-fire and bayonet and bomb attacks, the Pomeranians of the new Division surrendered in masses, in the early morning, even more readily than the men they had scoffed at. So severely did they suffer under the British bombardment, that they

retired to their dug-outs in the support line, and when their empty fire trench was taken by the attacking troops and a tank appeared on the Hindenburg line on their left, they surrendered in a block of five hundred without attempting to fight.

The neighbouring village of Guémappe, on the low ground of the Cojeul River, was another storm centre. It was taken in the morning by Scottish troops, after a hard fight that broke the enemy. The Germans evacuated the ruins, leaving not a single corpse or a wounded man. They held on, however, to the machine-gun forts in the neighbourhood, and did not retire until they were hammered out.

Between Guémappe and Fontaine, other British forces advanced southward towards the cross-ways hamlet of Chérisy, which formed an important German knot of highway communications. Over the rolling fields, rising to two hundred and eighty feet above sea level, the attacking troops fought onward with extraordinary fury. For the enemy was employing the dirtiest of tricks. In places near his concealed machine-gun forts, men often came forward with uplifted hands and cries of " Kamerad!" in order to lure the English and Scottish troops into the field of fire of the hidden machine-guns.

Such a Berserker mood invaded many of the new British battalions that, in the battle of the rivers, they thrust onward like madmen. The Arras and Vimy actions had been generals' battles. They had been planned on large plaster models and executed with clock-work precision. The Scarpe, Cojeul, and Sensée actions were soldiers' battles.

In the open field warfare, in undulating new country, dotted with masked underground forts, that no aerial photographer could discover beforehand and no barrage could destroy, the attacking battalions had to work forward largely by the chances of fighting. Sometimes a brigade would divide in separate courses, one part being checked by slopes commanded by hostile guns, while another part found an opening and furiously developed their lucky advantage.

The enemy's heavy curtain fire impeded, at times, both brigade and divisional communication. Even battalions often lost touch with some of their companies. In the forefront of the khaki waves of attack, subalterns, sergeants, and even privates had to conduct the advance. It was on the high average of personal initiative and force of character of ordinary men from England, Scotland, Wales, **British initiative v.** and Newfoundland that the issue **German drill** of the wild struggle largely depended.

It was the day of the ordinary soldier. In many cases, utterly inexperienced men belonging to the fresh forces poured up to strengthen Sir Edmund Allenby's army, were set to out-manœuvre and out-fight the best veteran divisions of the German Empire. What they were set to do they did.

Above Guémappe, in the morning of St. George's Day, there was a more definite field of conflict than that which obtained southward along the Sensée River. Ludendorff had been much concerned about the loss of Monchy,

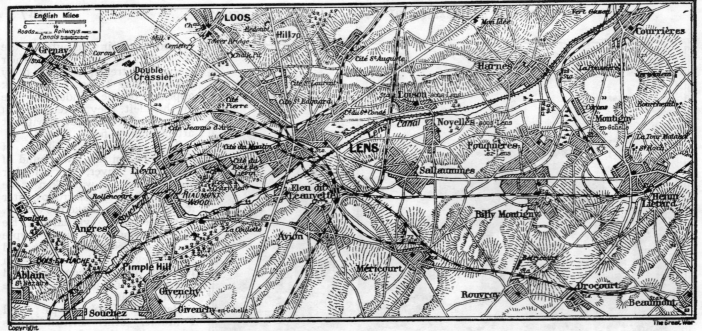

LENS AND ITS ENVIRONS TO DROCOURT ON THE "WOTAN" LINE.

Haig's renewed attack on Lens began April 13th, 1917. The cités, quadrangles of miners' cottages, were strong machine-gun positions, and the fighting there was severe. Savage encounters also took place at Riaumont Wood, the Crook and Crazy Redoubts, and La Coulotte.

as the plateau dominated all his line. Between April 10th and April 23rd he massed a very large number of heavy guns in Sart Wood, Vert Wood, and the country around Pelves and Boiry villages.

In the first British advance at dawn, the small German force facing Monchy fled or surrendered as the forward wave of advance reached them. Most of the garrison ran up their own slope to the cover of Sart Wood. This early flight, however, may have been cleverly based upon tactical considerations. Between Guémappe and Monchy, along the road running to Cambrai, the Germans had built a series of redoubts, from which they could bring enfilading fire upon the slopes between Monchy and the opposing woods.

Roeux and Gavrelle stormed

Northward around Roeux and Pelves were other systems of hostile positions from which the British attacking forces could be swept. Therefore, the Englishmen coming down the Monchy Hill were smitten in the face and on both sides, when they endeavoured to storm in and through Sart and Vert Woods, and advance on their left towards Pelves.

Not until Guémappe was consolidated for a further advance along the Cambrai road, and not until Roeux was entirely won and held along the Scarpe, could a rapid British movement be developed from the Monchy plateau in the centre of the battle line. A superb force of Scottish battalions made a gallant attack upon Roeux village, by way of Gavrelle Road, towards a fortified farm and fortressed chemical works. They were swept by a furnace blast of machine-guns and trench mortar fire, from the ruins about Roeux and from redoubts on the slopes of the famous Greenland Hill.

Yet by noon the farm redoubt and the chemical works on the Gavrelle road, north of Roeux village, were captured, and the Scotsmen were progressing eastward against desperate resistance.

Southward across the River Scarpe an English assailing force was held up by intense gun-fire, and had to wait for the help of a tank, which crawled up through a long copse. Then a position known as Shrapnel and Bayonet Trench was carried, and the troops slowly pressed forward, under a heavy curtain of shell and a rain of bullets. Their advance along the south bank of the Scarpe was extremely difficult. They were faced by a crescent of fortified slopes, running from Roeux and Greenland Hill to Plouvain.

The English action in this centre remained, therefore, somewhat in the nature of a demonstration along the Scarpe lowland, being designed to assist the more important thrusts against the northern heights.

Above Roeux and somewhat flanking it was the village of Gavrelle, forming a main point in the second improvised Hindenburg system, known as the Drocourt line. The enemy had two main roads running south of Gavrelle towards Roeux, with another main road running southeast to Plouvain. Gavrelle was also connected, by a fine French national road, with Douai, and by a northward branch road with Oppy. It was thus a most important knot of communications, and as it was a hundred and sixty feet high, it formed the enemy's chief observation-point in the battleground below the southernmost slopes of the Vimy Ridge.

On the other hand, it had the disadvantage of being overlooked by the Vimy foothills, and was dominated by the artillery of the great master gunner, Sir Henry Horne. The Scottish troops who stormed into Gavrelle, under cover of a magnificent barrage, were opposed by Hamburgers and Rhinelanders. With comparative ease they captured many of these sturdy Germans in their dug-outs, and began to turn the conquered line about, so as to resist the coming counter-attack.

Then, all along the twelve miles of broken enemy positions, the German commander launched his main forces. The weight and persistence of this German counter movement were tremendous. Ludendorff had often used the method of mass attack on the Russian front, and backed his infantry with a gigantic accumulation of artillery; but never before had he been master of such multitudes of **Tremendous German** men and such parks of heavy ordnance **counter-movement** as he employed on the Drocourt line.

He had held silent a large number of his biggest guns during the first British advance, so as to prevent them being injured by counter-battery work before the critical moment. Only when he thought that the force of the British attack had been weakened did he fully disclose the striking power he had been preparing. His plan was entirely based on the fact that he possessed practically uninjured communications between Douai and Cambrai, while the British forces had immediately behind them roads and lines and tracks wrecked by their own artillery in the previous battles.

At first the German commander won a remarkable series of victories, from end to end of the open battle-front. By hurricanes of shell fire, the British forces in Gavrelle were compelled to retire. The Scotsmen in Roeux were driven beyond the ruins of the village and the fortified cemetery. The English troops on the southern side of the Scarpe were forced back. The victors of Guémappe village were smashed out of their defences, which had already been ruined by British gun fire, and then compelled to retreat, against fresh German troops pouring across the fields from Vitry-en-Artois.

Newfoundlanders at Monchy-le-Preux

Between the Cojeul and the Sensée Rivers the breaking of the English offensive seemed complete. The British troops were forced away from the positions around Chérisy and from Fontaine. The Pomeranians they had captured were recovered, and the battery of field guns they had taken was likely to be turned against them. In many places the German waves came over the low ridges and over their own dead, in solid lines of mechanical rigidity. The hill village of Monchy, which had been taken by the British in a fairly intact state, was reduced to a heap of powdered bricks. Cottage after cottage vanished in great pink clouds of smoke and brick-dust, until not a single wall remained with any semblance of the outline of a building. So it was all along the line. Ludendorff's concealed reserve of artillery power was as formidable as his hidden reserves of infantry.

Though overwhelmed by the tremendous weight and driving power of the enemy's counter movement, the advanced British forces rose to the highest military traditions of their race, and made a series of heroic, and often scattered, stands. The New-foundland troops, who had proved their desperate valour on the Somme, had pushed to the farthest point of the preliminary advance in a most difficult part of the battle front. They were assailed by two fresh German columns, possessing a great superiority in numbers. Yet only some Newfoundland outposts were cut off. The main body of Newfoundlanders fell back in orderly fashion, keeping off the German masses by means of skilful and dauntless rearguards of machine-gunners and riflemen.

Reaching the trenches beyond the main British positions the enemy was caught by the British guns. In search of cover, he dropped into the advanced position that had been held by the Newfoundlanders. Without waiting for supports, the troops from the great island in the Atlantic surged forward again like men lashed to madness. For thirty minutes there raged, in and around their lost position, such a hand-to-hand fight as had rarely been seen in the whole course of the war. Good judges doubt whether such a fury of slaughter occurred more than once before along the British front. It was believed that not a single German got back to his own lines. In the trenches in which the Newfoundlanders again settled, and over the ground which they had counter-attacked, there were fifteen hundred German corpses, and many others wounded.

The Lincolns, helped by some North-Country troops, performed a similar achievement. They met a body of Bavarians who much outnumbered them. Nevertheless, attacking on both sides, first with the rifle, then with the bayonet and the butt, and at last with fists, they annihilated the enemy. For the Bavarians refused to surrender, and all went down to death. The Northumberland Fusiliers were another noble spear-head of the British Army. In a magnificent struggle they took and held one of the most important German strategic positions. The Shropshires, Londoners, Black Watch, and numerous other troops nobly distinguished themselves.

Some of the Middlesex and Argyll and Sutherlands touched the record of the Royal West Kents in the Somme Battle. In the great German counter-attack the two English and Highland battalions were driven right back to their original line. Only one company of the Middlesex and one company of the Argyll and Sutherlands remained, like khaki islands, in the grey inundation. Fighting on both flanks and on their rear, and breaking the German waves by machine-gun and musketry fire on their front, the five hundred enveloped men clung to two German officers and fourteen men they had taken prisoners, and

[Canadian War Records.

THE WINNING SPIRIT ON A RE-WON ROAD.

Exceedingly bad weather—gales and snow and howling storms—occurred during the second week of Sir Douglas Haig's thrust in April, 1917, covering the ground with mud ankle-deep. The victorious British troops, however, found any road from which they had driven the enemy a good enough road.

swept with fire each German wave that broke against them and passed, under raking range, by their flanks. Theirs was a glorious example, under modern conditions of warfare, of the strength of the old British square formation by which Waterloo was won.

The square, however, had become obsolete, except for the purpose of hand-to-hand fighting. Against a ploughing, thundering modern barrage it was the easiest of targets. At first the men thought that they would be slain by their own guns. The British artillery put a terrific shell curtain upon the large German forces. Steadily, yet with apparently blind mechanicalness, the dreadful line of thunder, flame, and steel worked over the ground, blasting it into dust and preparing the way for the resurgent English and Scottish battalions.

Gallant Middlesex and Highlanders

Happily, some acute-eyed British forward observation officer glimpsed the island of khaki in the ocean of grey. The British barrage swept up to the rear of the two companies, jumped over their heads, in a strange, tense lull.

and again descended, just beyond the front of the little encircled force. There it remained, protecting the two gallant companies from further attack from the east.

Instead of profiting by this unexpected help by making a desperate dash backward through the advanced enemy lines, the English and Scottish captains wisely decided to hold on until the British movement in force developed. In the triumphant moment, when the Germans broke and retreated, the fugitives were taken in the rear. The band of Highlanders, Londoners, and Middlesex county-lads avenged themselves upon the flying enemy, made a gap in the retreating German line, and then ranged in line with the main British force and continued the advance.

A Worcester regiment, in another part of the field, made a similar stand on a larger scale and for a much longer period. Two great German charges **Magnificent stand** swept back their comrades on both their **of the Worcesters** flanks. Being well entrenched, the Worcesters were able to maintain a more deadly defence. They broke one wave of three thousand Germans, and, when the enemy commander launched another four thousand men, the Worcesters again withstood the solid waves and swept the divided force as it swirled along their flanks.

Soon afterwards all the German and British guns pounded the battlefield in dreadful and repeated hurricanes of shell. The Worcesters ran out of water, and became agonised by thirst, and the dust and smoke of the artillery action increased their sufferings and the strain on their bodies and minds.

Still they gave no ground. They were able to signal to their main forces, and they were confident that the tide of British victory would flow back to them. Husbanding their munitions, they fought the enemy off for thirty-six waterless, arduous hours, and were at last joined by the main British forces. The wood held by the Worcesters had been reached by them on April 14th. Thus, in addition to the magnificent stand they made in the acute phase of the battle of April 23rd, they fought for a previous eight days with their communications cut.

In the closing scene of this series of heroic stands the whole battlefield was veiled in the smoke of thousands

CAMERA IMPRESSION OF PART OF THE STORIED VIMY FIELD.
Canadian machine-gunners dug-in in shell-holes during the Vimy advance. Above : Thirsty soldiers flocking to a water-cart for water. The reservoirs of drinking water behind the British armies on the Somme were of a size suitable for London, and the difficulty which he anticipated the British would have in moving this vast system of works influenced Ludendorff in deciding on retreat. (*British official photograph.*)

HUN HANDIWORK IN MISERY—A TOWN WITH A SADLY APPROPRIATE NAME.

[Canadian War Records.

Misery was once a large village about six miles south-west of Péronne, on the line to Chaulnes. The photo shows it completely demolished by the Germans before evacuation, without any military justification, but in accordance with their idea of appalling the imagination of the civil population of France, and thereby facilitating the intrigues for a negotiated peace which were being conducted through the medium of German socialists.

of bursting shells. Above the smoke the sky was full of fighting aeroplanes. In the rents of the smoke the grey German infantry could be seen forming in the open and marching resolutely through the British barrage. British pilots sailed through the clouds of shrapnel, and, darting down on the German formations, swept them at the range of a few score yards. Above the batteries on both sides more pilots hovered, watching the tongues of flame, signalling the positions to their own guns, and telling, as the shells thundered beneath them, whether the target was reached or the distance of the miss.

While everything still apparently indicated a decisive British check, the British forces regathered, with their main supports, for the grand clash of the Battle of St. George's Day. Between Gavrelle and the Douai railway and Scarpe River parks of British guns opened upon the solid lines of Germans advancing from Fresnes. Gavrelle and Guémappe were again ground to powder, while Chérisy, Vis, Fontaine, and other villages on which the victorious Germans had based themselves were caught in tempestuous blasts of high-explosives and incendiary shells.

Grand clash of the battle Then, amid and around the dreadful shell curtains, maintained by the artillery on either side, the Scottish, English, Welsh, and Newfoundland troops closed upon Ludendorff's main armies. Gavrelle was recovered by bitter fighting by Sir Henry Horne's corps, and then held against incessant assaults by enemy storming troops. Again and again the Germans gathered, in a wood by the Douai Road, only to be more than decimated by the British barrage, and finally dispersed by the machine-guns of the British garrison in Gavrelle. The struggle went on for thirty-six hours. The survivors of each broken German force were sorted out, reduced from battalions to companies, and held in reserve for another attack. Meanwhile, fresh regiments, after toiling from Douai under long-ranged British gunfire and aeroplane attacks, were deployed near Fresnes, and sent into the defender's barrage and against the machine-guns behind the flaming, smoking, thundering line of shell. It was all in vain.

Nothing could shake the garrison at Gavrelle. They were a small number of men in comparison with the German divisions repeatedly thrown against them, and the victory they won was vividly illustrative of the superiority of the British tactics. In an attempt to break an already-shattered British position, which had not been organised for defence on its eastward side, the German commander lost men by the ten thousand, although the troops he continually tried to hammer out of the village numbered only some hundreds. He extended his attacks by column to the long road between Gavrelle and Roeux, trying to pierce section after section. But all the British line held firm.

British triumph at Gavrelle

The battle continued all night, and ended about mid-day on April 24th by the complete exhaustion of the German forces. The British garrison could then see on the fields in front of them an immense grey covering of German bodies. The action at Gavrelle was accounted the most successful along the front.

The Scotsmen, immediately southward along the Gavrelle road and in the outskirts of Roeux, also held most of their ground against incessant and very heavy storming attacks. They had captured, in their first advance, the chemical works on the Gavrelle road, which contained a useful amount of material, including some mine-throwers. The Germans held on to the village, or rather the site of the village, and retained the edges of the Scarpe River abreast of the ruins. They also won back the crest

351

[British official photograph.

Animated scene of cavalry assembled on an open plateau for an operation on a large scale. Cavalry of Monchy-le-Preux itself. Here, after the infantry had got in on the southern side, the cavalry, by a rendered useful service in the Pelves-Monchy area of fighting on April 11th, 1917, especially at the village gallant charge, occupied and held the western and northern parts, and beat off counter-attacks.

[British official photograph.

Typical scene outside an advanced dressing-station when an engagement was proceeding in the near on stretchers to await their turn for attention. When they had received this they were conveyed the next neighbourhood. Casualties were brought in from the regimental aid-posts by R.A.M.C. men, and laid down stage of their journey hospital-wards in the ambulances here shown waiting for full complements.

BEFORE AND AFTER BATTLE: ASSEMBLING CAVALRY AND CLEARING CASUALTIES DURING THE BRITISH ADVANCE FROM ARRAS, APRIL, 1917.

of Greenland Hill, and from all their vantage points they made continual rushes against the Scotsmen.

Neither the British nor German artillery could directly intervene in the swaying body-to-body infantry struggle. They could only curtain off supplies and reinforcements and take terrible toll of all supporting troops and marching reserves. Largely by reason of the nature of the ground, and especially by reason of the strength of the dominating Greenland Hill position, Ludendorff won an important defensive victory at Roeux.

He completely checked an extremely dangerous British thrust north of the Scarpe, which would have turned his position south of the river and pierced the Drocourt-Quéant line in the neighbourhood of Douai. For months after the battle of St. George's Day, Greenland Hill remained an impregnable German salient, rising between the British positions at Monchy and Gavrelle. It became the principal point of conflict between the British forces based on Arras and the German forces based on Douai.

Germans hold Greenland Hill

Immense was the sacrifice of life by which Ludendorff retained his hold on Greenland Hill. It is possible that his stern judgment in the affair was sound ; for, as we have seen, his defences existed only in outline, being largely mere scratches in the earth, with no bomb-proof shelters for a large defending force. In some places there were dug-outs, while in some places there were practically none.

In fact, the Wotan line of the Hindenburg system seems originally to have run through Greenland Hill. The small concealed German forts of the new type, called by the British soldier a " Maybush," and known to the Germans by the more technical term of a M.E.B.U., were devised as part of the second Hindenburg line. It was only because the intended Wotan line, with its legendary vast caverns and its fabulous chain of impregnable fortresses, did not exist, in the fourth week of April, 1917, that Ludendorff fought an open-field battle.

His M.E.B.U. defences, or *Maschinen Eisen Betun Unterstand*—armoured concrete machine-gun positions— were first sited in the autumn of 1916, as outposts of a long, deep underground fortress, expected to excel, in the power of resisting heavy shell, Beaumont Hamel, Thiepval Ridge, and other lost works by the Somme and Ancre. The immensity of the design defeated its designer. He could not procure the needed labour, either from Germany or from occupied territories and prisoners' camps, within the short space allowed him by the advancing British armies. The long, hard, freezing winter had made digging slow and difficult, and both Sir Henry Horne and Sir Edmund Allenby drove into parts of the Wotan line before it really existed.

From the military point of view Ludendorff might have done well in continuing his retreat. He seems to have wavered when the Vimy Ridge was lost, and hesitated for some days to reinforce his troops at Lens. Having checked, by April 17th, the great French offensive along the tableland of the Aisne and the hills of Champagne, he might have pivoted on Lille and wheeled away from Douai, Cambrai, and St. Quentin, and created another deep zone of evacuation in front of the main British forces.

Reasons governing Ludendorff's action

Probably he would have lost some guns and some valuable railway communications, and provoked new British offensives against Messines Hill and the Ridges of Lille. On the other hand, he would have conserved nearly all his enormous forces of six million men, instead of losing some eight hundred thousand first-line troops. By transferring a large part of his reserves to the Ypres and Lille areas, he could have fought with the old advantage of standing upon a system of completely fortified lines.

There were, however, other points of view besides the military one. There was the naval view. The submarine campaign against shipping depended to a considerable

extent upon the retention of the Flemish coast and the port of Zeebrugge. It seemed better to engage the extraordinary power of the British armies on the Douai-Cambrai-St. Quentin front, than to withdraw from there and allowing Sir Douglas Haig to bring most of his striking power to bear against the Flemish sector, close to the Flemish coast.

Finally, from the political point of view, the rapid surrender of the Hindenburg system, which the German population had been taught to regard as absolutely impregnable, might have produced a lowering of the German moral such as would have been most perilous between the general winter shortage of food and the harvesting of the potato and grain crops.

This seems to be the reason why Ludendorff judged it wise to hold on to Roeux and Greenland Hill, at the cost of enormous wastage in men. He was master of an army larger than existed in 1914, 1915, and 1916. By an effort of organisation, comparable with the British effort, he had given his nation, in the third year of a war of terrific attrition, four and a half million active troops, half a

[*British official photograph.*

HOUSEBREAKERS' "LAWFUL OCCASIONS."
The Labour Battalions won immense credit for their unceasing work, which seldom brought them a share in the glory of war. In the Arras fighting, however, one party found, attacked, and captured eighteen Germans in a dug-out by the side of a road where they were working.

million line of communication troops, and one million reserve troops. He was thus very strong in regard to man-power ; but in gun-power he was somewhat weak. He considered at the time he could sacrifice men, in order to grind down the British man-power before American man-power began to tell heavily upon the issue of the struggle.

He made the mistake of being too bull-necked. His method of attacking in solid lines may have produced good results when employed against the poorly-armed and badly-gunned Russian armies of the old régime ; it did not make for eventual success against the superior machinery of war controlled by Sir Douglas Haig and his able lieutenants. Moltke and Falkenhayn had learnt by experience the worth of the British military organisation, even in the days when it was weak in machinery. Ludendorff, in turn, had to learn what it was worth in the period when its railways and roads, guns and shell supplies, surpassed those of any German army group.

At Guémappe the British troops repeated their success of Gavrelle. After losing the village in the morning, by

GERMANY'S CROWNING DISGRACE: LEADING THE WOMEN AND CHILDREN INTO SLAVERY.

This poignant painting by Signor Matania illustrates the German iniquity which, more than any other, aroused the passionate protest of the entire civilised world—the deportation into captivity in Germany of women and children from the occupied districts of Belgium and France. Lille was particularly victimised in this barbaric fashion. Twenty-five thousand persons were deported in Holy Week, 1916, to slavery or worse.

being hammered out with heavy shell and swept in the flank by machine-gun fire, the British force went forward again in the evening against the famous 3rd Bavarian Division. They bombed and bayoneted the Southern Germans out of the ruins, and swept them back for half a mile or more. Towards nightfall, the German commander threw in fresh troops, but they were smashed up in the open near some farm buildings by artillery fire.

Around Fontaine, by the Sensée River, the remnant of the Pomeranian regiment, captured by the British infantry and released by the German counter-attacking forces, did not long remain free. They were caught, before they could recover their arms, in the grand return attack, and sent into the British cages. With them went prisoners from sixteen battalions, shattered in the raging, fluctuant series of actions around the bridge-head of Fontaine.

This village was as important to the enemy's system of defence as was Greenland Hill. It was not merely a bridge-head over the obstacle of the Sensée River. Scarcely two miles down the road was Hendecourt, with Riencourt about another mile away on the same road. South-west of Hendecourt and Riencourt was Bullecourt, where the Australians and the Londoners were fiercely thrusting at the Quéant end of the Hindenburg switch-line. Fontaine was the gateway leading behind both the Hindenburg systems. So Fontaine had to be held by the enemy at any sacrifice of life.

Importance of Fontaine

Seven or more divisions were brought up and poured through Chérisy to defend the flank of the Fontaine positions. Around Fontaine itself more German forces were sent forward, to get through the British barrage and strengthen the front running along the river towards Croisilles.

In this action the British artillery had a great superiority of position. From Ecoust St. Mein to Croisilles, some of the guns of the Fifth Army took in flank the large German forces on the Sensée River line. These same German forces were smitten on the river front by the guns of the Third Army. The Germans were in a large salient, subjected to cross fires by two masses of heavy British artillery. Sir Edmund Allenby's men held the great observation point on Tower Hill, which had been taken in the first British attack, and the forward observation officers were soon able to train their guns upon the enemy formations as these came into view over the lower undulations of ground. In the end, though neither Fontaine nor Chérisy was occupied, the enemy's losses were immense, and one of the two main objects of the battle was attained.

Sir Douglas Haig's object

Sir Douglas Haig's object was principally to wage a war of attrition on a grand scale, in order to relieve the French armies, whose Champagne offensive had been checked, and to recover the entire initiative in the European struggle. This initiative had been lost in a general way by the Entente Powers through the extraordinary disorganisation of the Russian forces.

German agents, in Petrograd and behind the Russian front, accomplished that which the German soldiers could not have effected. They had prevented the Allies from obtaining a series of decisive victories in the summer of 1917. Moreover, they made it possible for the German High Command to look forward to recovering some measure of initiative. Thereupon, Sir Douglas Haig decided at all cost to wear down Ludendorff's reserves.

Had both elements of the Franco-British plan developed prosperously, the French offensive of April 16th would have completely carried on the work begun by the British troops at Arras and Vimy. Sir Henry Horne and Sir Edmund Allenby would have had another fortnight for railway building, road-making, constructing heavy gun-emplacements, and accumulating shell. As it was, the British advance on April 23rd against the Gavrelle and Sensée River line had to be hastily prepared to give breathing time to General Pétain's army group, whose progress had been seriously arrested.

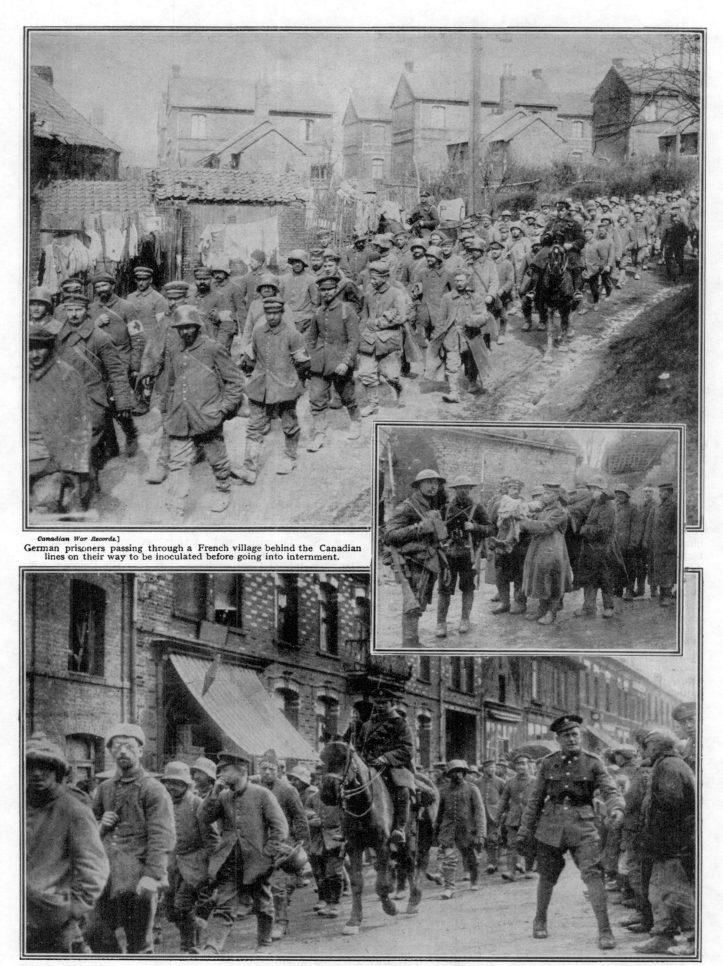

Canadian War Records.]

German prisoners passing through a French village behind the Canadian
lines on their way to be inoculated before going into internment.

[*Canadian War Records.*

Germans captured by the Canadians at Vimy Ridge being shepherded   them carrying a severely-wounded comrade (British official photograph).
through a French town.   Above : A group of enemy prisoners, four of   During this day, April 9th, more than nine thousand prisoners were taken.

GERMANY'S WANING MAN-POWER: THE EVER-GROWING LIST OF PRISONERS.

BREAKING A FORLORN HOPE OF BAVARIAN STORM-TROOPS AT GAVRELLE MILL.

Gavrelle Mill, an important position on the north side of the Scarpe, near Roueux and Oppy, changed hands eight times before it was finally secured by the British. The last German attack, made by a forlorn hope of picked Bavarian storm-troops, who had been specially incited to do their utmost, was repulsed after a desperate bomb and bayonet struggle, and most of the few survivors were taken prisoners.

Therefore the British victory of St. George's Day was not to be measured merely by the gain of ground and the capture of Gavrelle and Guémappe. Sir Douglas Haig aimed only indirectly at any further recovery of French territory. His target was Ludendorff's grand reserve. This target he struck and badly holed, and he continued to strike and damage it through the spring and summer of 1917, waiting somewhat anxiously all the time for news of the definite recovery of fighting power by the armies of revolutionary Russia.

Meanwhile, the magnificent forces of republican France made another great rush against the plateau above the Aisne, and stormed over Craonne, and exerted more pressure upon the German reserve. Some French military writers then suggested that the British Commonwealth forces should take over another large part of the French front, in view of the great strain upon the man-

power of their country. Happily, the High Command of France appeared well content with the fact that the British forces were closely échelonned between Ypres and St. Quentin, and acting as an incessant and stupendous battering-ram against the most sensitive long stretch of German lines. It was the Belgian army that was relieved, near the coast, by the expanding, victorious forces of the British Commonwealth. A well-trained body of Portuguese troops joined the British armies, and only the urgent immediate want of another half a million new recruits prevented Sir Douglas Haig from rapidly developing the great advantages he had won. For at the end of April, 1917, he had to ensure himself against the situation on the Russian front, and prepare to meet, alongside the French and Belgian armies, the entire weight of practically five and a half million German troops.

BRITISH HEAVY GUN IN ACTION. [British official photograph.
One of the finest triumphs of British organisation was the persistence with which, despite the many difficulties of the terrain, the heavy artillery was brought up behind the rapidly-advancing infantry.

CHAPTER CLXXXV.

THE WORK OF THE NAVY ENGINEERS : A SPLENDID RECORD.

By Percival A. Hislam.

EDITORIAL NOTE.—In earlier chapters of THE GREAT WAR the Navy has been treated chiefly in its aspect as a fighting force. The efficiency of each ship as a fighting unit depends, however, upon the men who control and feed the engines, and although the splendid service of the lower deck throughout the war has been fully recognised, the nature of their work and the manner of their life are not generally known to the public. The Editors, therefore, asked Mr. Hislam to write the accompanying chapter to describe the work of the Navy Engineers. and of the many interesting points he takes, the following may be mentioned by way of summary :
Traditions of the Sailing Era Inherited by the Engineers—Initial Prejudice against Machinery, and Anomalous Position of Naval Engineers at the Outbreak of War—Demands which Could not be Met from Depleted Ranks of Officers Satisfied by the Lower Deck and the Mercantile Marine—Engine-room Artificers and the Submarine Service—Engine Power and the Stoker Branch—Advantages of Oil Fuel and its Influence on the War—Work of the Engine-room Departments in Action –Targets for Attack by Torpedoes and Mines—Tributes of Sir John Jellicoe, Sir David Beatty, and Others—Principal Engineer Officers at the Admiralty and Afloat—Growth of the Branch in the War.

N the great wars of the past, upon which the enduring tradition of British naval supremacy was erected, mechanics, in the modern sense of the word, played but a little part. At the same time, from the earliest records of maritime affairs, the company of a ship of war has always been divided into two separate and quite distinct groups, the one responsible for the driving and the manœuvring of the ship, and the other for dealing with the enemy when the vessel had been brought by the seamen into the necessary position.

In the days of Alfred and the Vikings the galley-men, labouring at their great oars, carried the "keel" to where her presence was demanded by strategy or tactics. From before the time of Elizabeth—when the crews of English warships were made up of "mariners," "gunners," and "soldiers"—to past the middle of the nineteenth century, the seamen of the Navy, working amid a maze of rope and a cloud of canvas, built up a tradition of smart and fearless seamanship that no other fleet has ever been able to approach ; and it was indubitable superiority in this

CAPTAIN W. R. HALL, C.B.
Appointed Director of the Intelligence Service of the War Staff at the Admiralty, October, 1914. He commanded the Queen Mary in the action of Heligoland Bight, August 28th, 1914.

direction as much as anything else that was responsible for the opposition of the naval authorities to the introduction of steam in the first half of last century.

Many of the soundest of foreign critics also held the sincere belief that the substitution of steam for sails would make for the depreciation of British sea-power by wiping out its traditions and rendering useless, or at any rate reducing to the Continental level, the vast resources of Great Britain's seafaring population ; and, as these views were widely shared in this country as well, it is no wonder that for generations both the marine steam-engine and those who managed it were looked upon with anything but favour.

It was not until the year of Queen Victoria's accession that naval engineers were permitted to reach the rank of warrant officer, nor were the commissioned ranks opened to them until ten years later — 1847. Five years after this, the first line-of-battle ship to be designed for screw propulsion, the Agamemnon, was launched at Woolwich, but for many years subsequently, and even when ironclads were protected with several inches of side armour, the first-rate warships continued

TAKING COAL ABOARD IN ARCTIC COLD.
Naval men had to be prepared for all variations of climate. Even in summer, those stationed or calling in the far north were compelled to keep their hands and ears well protected though engaged in the strenuous and warming work of coaling their vessel.

to carry a spread of canvas as big as, and often bigger than, that of any vessel afloat in the days of Nelson.

The sailing tradition died hard. Engines were distrusted, and engineers suspected of a jeopardising inability to live up to the high professional standards of their lineal predecessors, the mast-and-sail men. Even as late as 1902 the latter phase of this distrust existed in the most malignant and uninstructed form, and it was then decided that the engineer officers of the Navy should no longer be recruited from the ranks of trained engineers, and devote the whole of their service to their intricate and highly-specialised profession, but that the machinery departments of the Fleet should be officered by men who, entered in the ordinary way as naval cadets, should combine and alternate the supervision of masses of highly-complicated machinery with the ordinary duties of a naval officer.

In order to appreciate fully the incomparable work of the Navy's engineers during the war, it is necessary that their position at the outbreak of hostilities should be understood. In pursuance of the policy adopted in 1902, the entry of professional engineer officers was gradually slackened off, and came to an end with the commissioning of a small batch of sub-lieutenants in 1910. The original idea was that from this time onwards the natural wastage among the existing officers, together with the expanding needs of the Fleet, would be met by the voluntary specialisation of a sufficient number of officers entered in the ordinary way at the Naval College at Osborne; but, in point of fact, not a single officer had so specialised down to the actual start of the war, and this in spite of the heavy demands thrown upon the engineering personnel by the commissioning of great battle-cruisers like the Lion and Princess Royal, with their 70,000 h.p. turbines, and the multiplication of small craft of the light cruiser and destroyer types.

Failure of voluntary specialisation

During the four years preceding the war the only source from which the Navy drew its engineer officers was the ranks of the chief artificer engineers—chief warrant officers who, entering the Service as competent fitters, turners, boilermakers, and so forth, had, after many years of service, been promoted to the small number of lieutenancies held available for rankers. In 1914 a new scheme was instituted whereby the best of the younger artificers could be passed through the rank of "Mate (E)" and become engineer lieutenants in two or three years. The first lieutenants under this arrangement were commissioned in November, 1916.

It will be seen from this brief survey that, so far as the engineering branch of the Fleet is concerned, the war came upon Britain at an inopportune moment. The old supply of engineers had been allowed to dry up, and the new had not begun to be productive. Indeed, when the war had been in progress nearly three years, the number of officers who had temporarily specialised in engineering under the "new scheme" of 1902 was fewer than forty. The naval authorities were thus faced with a shortage of trained personnel that might easily have been attended with disastrous consequences.

When ships were taken over from the mercantile marine for service as armed cruisers or fleet auxiliaries, the whole of their original engine-room staffs as a rule went into the naval Service with them, so that no additional strain was thus involved. On the other hand, not only was it necessary to increase the staffs of ships already in full commission in order to cope with war conditions, but every warship capable of doing anything at all was hurried out of the reserve into active service, while the immediate ordering of scores of warships of all types necessitated the despatch, to supervise their construction, of engineer officers thoroughly conversant with the special and peculiar needs of the naval Service. The needs of these new craft when in commission had also to be provided for.

In such circumstances it was indeed fortunate that the Admiralty was able to fall back upon the artificers and those who had risen from them to warrant and chief warrant rank. In fact, it is no exaggeration to say that the engineering department of the Fleet was saved from chaos and breakdown only by these men, who had **Warrant officers promoted** not been affected by the scheme of 1902, and whose numbers had therefore continued to advance with the growth of the Navy. Within a few weeks of the outbreak of war the Admiralty began to remove commissioned engineer officers from the older destroyers and similar small craft, and to replace them by warrant officers, while the warrant officers were relieved in turn by engine-room artificers (chief petty-officers), or by men joining up in the Royal Naval Reserve from the merchant service. In numbers of big ships throughout the Fleet the process was repeated, a warrant officer or petty-officer taking the place of a junior commissioned officer, and the change so justified itself that in the course of a few months more than fifty per cent. of the destroyer flotillas had been taken over, so far as their engine-rooms were concerned, by men who had risen from the ranks.

In a perfectly governed world we should probably have seen the substitutes given the same rank—or at any rate something like the same pay—as the officers whose places they so efficiently filled; but nothing of the sort was actually done, with the result that some very striking comparisons became apparent. To take but one instance. For three years before the outbreak of war the engineer officer of the Firedrake, one of the fastest of our existing destroyers in 1914, with turbines of 20,000 h.p., was a lieutenant-commander whose service pay was 17s. a day; but the war had not been in progress very long when his place was taken by an artificer engineer—a warrant officer—whose pay was only 8s. 6d. a day, or exactly one half of what was paid to the former holder of the appointment for having charge of the same vessel's machinery in time of peace.

It says much for the loyalty of the artificers and artificer engineers of the Navy, who are as keen trade unionists as can be found anywhere, that they accepted such conditions as these without a trace of complaint, rejoicing in the confidence thus reposed in their professional capabilities.

As for the rest of our mosquito craft—the older torpedo-boats, the coast-service monitors of the " M " class, some of the special patrol boats known as the " P's," and the small monitors (officially known as " China gunboats ") specially designed for work in Mesopotamia—practically the whole of these were put in charge of engine-room artificers, who are chief petty-officers. To these men also

Artificer engineers for submarines fell almost the entire responsibility for running and maintaining the submarine service, a work demanding the highest degree of professional knowledge, an intimate acquaintance not only with steam engineering, but with oil-engines, electrical propulsion, and all the paraphernalia of machinery that make up the bulk of a submarine's interior ; and, on top of all this, as senior mechanical rating in the boat the artificer was responsible for keeping her structure in a proper state of sea-worthiness and for dealing with all repairs that might be necessitated either by engagements with the enemy or by those accidents of navigation to which the submarine is always liable, such as striking the bottom when hurriedly diving to get out of the way of a hostile vessel on murder bent.

Mr. Rudyard Kipling, in his " Tales of ' The Trade, " told of one engine-room artificer whose record is typical of this branch of the Navy. Mr. Kipling was writing of the official reports of submarine E14, for whose work

in the Sea of Marmora her commanding officer, Commander E. Courtney Boyle, was awarded the V.C. ; and this is what he said after recounting some of her adventures : " But that, again, was only in the day's work. The point she insisted upon was that she had been for seventy days in the Sea of Marmora with no securer base for refit than the centre of the same, and during all that while she had not had ' any engine-room defect which has not been put right by the engine-room staff of the boat.' The commander and the third officer went sick for a while ; the first-lieutenant got gastro-enteritis and was in

ON THE STOCKS IN ONE OF BRITANNIA'S WORKSHOPS.   [*British official photographs.*
A large destroyer in the course of construction in a British naval shipbuilding yard. In circle : A ferry boat for the Bosphorus, which was being built in a British yard for the Turkish Government. When the war broke out all further work on it was suspended.

HANDLING A FIFTEEN-INCH SHELL.
The weight of a 15 in. projectile was not much short of a ton, and the normal possible rate of fire was about 1·2 per minute. The 100 lb. projectile of the 6 in. gun is the largest that in practice can be efficiently man-handled for any length of time.

bed (if you could see that bed !) 'for the remainder of our stay in the Sea of Marmora,' but 'this boat has never been out of running order.' The credit is ascribed to 'the excellence of my chief engine-room artificer, James Hollier Hague, O.N. 227715,' whose name is duly submitted to the authorities 'for your consideration for advancement to the rank of warrant officer.'

"Seventy days of every conceivable sort of risk, within and without, in a boat which is all engine-room except where she is sick-bay; twelve thousand miles covered since last overhaul and 'never out of running order '—thanks to Mr. Hague. Such artists as he are the kind of engine-room artificers that commanders intrigue to get hold of—each for his own boat—and when the tales are told in the Trade their names, like Abou Ben Adhem's, lead all the rest." Hague was awarded the Distinguished Service Medal, and the Admiralty were not long in carrying out his commanding officer's recommendation, for in August, 1915, he was promoted to the warrant-officer rank of artificer engineer. What Mr. Hague, engine-room artificer, did for the E14, engine-room artificers were doing for every other submarine in the Service, some under better conditions, and some, at times, under worse, and it would be impossible to exaggerate the debt of gratitude the country owed to these men or to speak too highly in

Expansion of the stoker branch praise of their professional attainments, involving a wider knowledge of the various branches of engineering—mechanical, motor, electrical, hydraulic, and constructional—than is required in any other department of the naval Service.

So far we have glanced in a general way only at the higher grades of the naval engineering profession, but there remain to be mentioned those whose laborious and prosaic task it is to produce in the stokeholds the energy that is so marvellously harnessed and manipulated by the officers and artificers in the engine-rooms. For many years before the outbreak of hostilities the proportionate strength of the stoker branch had been steadily increasing until, in the year of the war's commencement, the number of stoker petty-officers and men authorised for the active list of the Fleet was very little short of the corresponding number of seamen, the actual figure being 39,274 and 44,947 respectively. The relative expansion of the stoker branch was, of course, directly due to the high speed of all recent warships, calling in the larger vessels for phenomenal engine-power and a correspondingly extensive

steam-raising plant. In the Crimean War no British ship had machinery of more than 700 h.p., while in the victorious Japanese Fleet that beat the Russians in 1904-5 there was no more powerfully-engined vessel than the armoured cruiser Tokiwa, of 18,000 h.p.; but all the modern light cruisers in the British Navy in 1914 equalled or exceeded the latter figure, the slower battleships ranged up to 27,000 h.p., and the battle-cruisers, beginning with 41,000 h.p. in the original trio of the Invincible class, ran up to 70,000 in the Lion and Princess Royal and 75,000 in the Queen Mary.

Fortunately, the expansion in the stoker branch which these facts involved was begun to be offset not long before the outbreak of war by the wider application of oil fuel for steam-raising purposes. The naval authorities had begun to experiment with oil-burning furnaces many years before, and such success had been attained that from 1905 onwards all British destroyers, with the exception of those built under the 1908 programme, were entirely independent of coal and used only oil in their furnaces. The advantages of oil over coal for this purpose **Advantages of oil fuel** are enormous. For a given space occupied, the distance that can be covered on a single supply is increased about fifty per cent.; higher speeds can be reached, and can be maintained much longer, because the burning oil causes neither sooty deposits to form in the flues and between the boiler-tubes nor slag in the furnaces; the number of men required to attend to the latter is reduced about sixty per cent., because, instead of coal having to be brought from the bunkers to the stokehold and there fed into the fires, oil is mechanically pumped from the tanks and double bottoms right up to boilers, where it exhausts itself in a series of blazing sprays, each requiring only the careful attention of two or three well-trained men.

Quite as important as anything else, however, is the wiping out of that exhausting and nightmarish evolution known as "coaling ship." A vessel like the Iron Duke, carrying about 1,000 tons of oil as an auxiliary, has

HOLYSTONING THE DECK.
"Ship-shape," as a synonym for cleanliness and order, is the world's tribute to the British Navy's methods. The "holystone" is said to have got its name from being used to clean up before Sunday Church Service aboard ship.

accommodation also for a storage of 2,700 tons of coal, and with the entire crew working at top speed—as crews always do when "coal ship" is the order—it would be impossible to get such an amount on board in less than from twelve to fifteen hours. After that the ship has to be thoroughly cleaned down, and by the time everything is ship-shape again and the men have had a little rest, anything from one to two days may have elapsed, during which period the ship is for all practical purposes demobilised. How different it is for everyone and everything concerned when the ship is an oiler! Then, when she wants a fresh supply of fuel, she simply makes herself fast alongside a wharf, various hoses leading into various tanks are connected up with the main pipe-line leading down from the storage depot somewhere in the background, and the whole business is completed quickly and cleanly, without more than ten per cent. or so of the ship's company having anything at all to do with it.

It was in 1912, with the battleships of the Queen Elizabeth class, and the light **Problem of the** cruisers of the Arethusa group, **oil supply** that the Admiralty took the bold and inevitable step of applying the "all oil" principle to every type of naval unit. From the details already given it will be seen how thoroughly justified the decision was, but there was still one very serious objection remaining to be overcome. England has a monopoly in the production of the best coal in the world for steam-raising purposes, while her domestic supply of oil, confined to certain districts of Scotland, would be altogether inadequate for the requirements of an "all oil" fleet. The change meant, in short, that the Navy would have to depend for its mobility upon imported supplies— that, while fighting for the command of the sea, it would depend upon that command for its ability to fight at all.

To meet this difficulty the Admiralty at once took in hand the enlargement of old and the construction of new reservoirs for the storage of reserve stocks of fuel at various points round the coast and overseas. It is still too early to write of what was done in this direction after the outbreak

[*British official photograph.*

PIPE-LINES ON A BRITISH WARSHIP.
With the adoption of oil as generator of power in the Navy, the operation of taking fuel on board became greatly simplified. The gain in time was very considerable, and the dust and dirt inevitably associated with "coaling" were unknown in "oiling."

of war, but an examination of the Navy Estimates for 1914-15 shows that there were oil-fuel depots then in hand at Dover, Port Victoria (on the Medway), Immingham (on the Humber), Rosyth, Invergordon (on Cromarty Firth), Portland, Portsmouth, Gibraltar, Malta, and Hong-Kong, the total estimated cost of these works, in hand at that moment, being over one and a quarter millions sterling. The Admiralty also acquired interests in various oil-producing areas, and laid down "tankers," or "oilers," for bringing the liquid home.

If Britain's command of the sea had ever been in serious jeopardy all these arrangements might not have helped her much, for any reserve is likely to be exhausted before very long when it takes something like 4,000 tons of fuel— in other figures, the phenomenal total of 1,196,800 gallons —to provide such a vessel as the Queen Elizabeth with as much as she is able to stow. However, the official theory probably was that if the British nation was ever reduced to such a state that it could not get the oil needed, it would have reached such a hopeless position at sea that neither oil nor anything else could save it.

When the war began, the "oiling" of the Fleet had not proceeded to such an extent as to diminish the value of the old-time stoker. How valuable a man he really is is but dimly realised **The all-important** even to-day. Strategy and tactics alike **stoker** depend essentially upon a ship being in a certain spot at a certain moment—indeed, that is the essence of both departments of naval warfare. The commanding officer is entirely dependent upon the "chief" of the engineering department for the speed and mobility of the ship, but the engineer, no matter how experienced and adept he may be, can do nothing by coaxing and manipulating his machinery unless he has the necessary steam pressure to work upon, and it is the stokers, and they alone, who can give him what he wants in that direction.

The stoker is to the modern fleet what Boreas was to the fleets of Nelson—a Queen Elizabeth without steam is as helpless as a Victory without wind—and it is all the more right and proper that the part he played in the war should be recognised by the country that owes him so much, because the conditions under which he works are well calculated to keep him out of the limelight. It is greatly to the credit of the Admiralty that in the years immediately leading up to the war, as well as in the course of that conflict, they did much to encourage the stoker and to recognise his merit. The man in the street probably

MEN WHO SEARCHED THE SEAS FOR HIDDEN MINES.
Repairing a "sweep" cable. With these cables attached from one trawler to another, the brave men of the Mine-sweeping Service went to and fro over the waters for the locating of mines, which were fired as soon as found.

[*British official photograph.*

IN THE BOILER-ROOM.
One of the " vitals " of a battleship, the boiler-room, may be described as the heart which makes a living creature of what would otherwise be a mass of inert metal.

on a more or less parallel course with the Cleopatra, and the people in the cruiser, putting two and two together, decided that she was an enemy up to mischief. Wherefore the British ship suddenly swung round her bows, and, heading straight for the source from which the tell-tale sparks were issuing, cut so cleanly through the mysterious craft that in the darkness of the night the two halves of her could be seen drifting by, one on either side. It turned out afterwards that the Cleopatra had sent to the bottom the German destroyer G194—a vessel which might have been afloat to this day, and which might have succeeded in torpedoing one of our ships that night into the bargain, had her presence not been betrayed by the unscientific handling of the stokers' shovels and rakes.

The feeding of fires, however, is the lowest and most elementary form of a stoker's work. If he wants to get on at all in his profession he must prove himself capable of looking after the various types of auxiliary machinery that are to be found in every nook and corner of a modern ship of war; he must also attend a mechanical training course and pass a satisfactory examination at the end of it; and he must prove himself to be fairly capable in some such trade as fitter and turner, boilermaker and smith, coppersmith, or moulder.

Career open to stokers

In short, the Navy takes its stokers as absolutely untrained youths and turns them in a very few years into skilled mechanics. So successful has this policy been that in 1904 a new rating, that of mechanician (chief petty-officer) was instituted for stokers up to twenty-eight of proved efficiency and intelligence, and so well have the " shovellers " responded to the opportunity that it is now possible for a man who joins as a stoker (the sole requirements being a very good character and physical fitness) to become in time a com-

thinks of him as a mere shoveller of coal—but even the firing and trimming of a boiler furnace calls for a degree of skill, to say nothing of physical stamina, that comes only with long experience. Faulty stoking, by betraying the position of a ship and her consorts, may easily lead to the miscarriage of some plan, and even to disaster.

In the rather ludicrous air raid that was made by some British seaplanes on the German Zeppelin sheds at Tondern, behind the island of Sylt, in March, 1916, the seaplane carriers were convoyed by a force of light cruisers and destroyers all of which were exclusively oil-burners. While running for home on the 25th, in a dark night and a heavy snow-storm, the look-out in the light cruiser Cleopatra sighted not far away a stream of sparks driving with the wind. It was obvious that it was not a British vessel, for oil-burners do not throw sparks out of the funnel. It was equally obvious that the ship concerned was steaming for all she was worth, and the high speed her commander was trying to get out of her was leading to frantic and faulty stoking down below.

Finally, the sparks showed that she was steaming

[*British official photograph.*

IN THE ENGINE-ROOM OF A BRITISH BATTLESHIP.
Another of the battleship's " vitals "—all of which are grouped below the waterline and protected above by a curved armoured deck of thick steel. The engineers, knowing nothing of what was going on overhead in a battle, thus carried on in a " steel box, suspended, as it were, under the fighting body of the ship."

missioned officer with the rank of engineer-lieutenant. This is, indeed, a remarkable testimony to the efficiency of these men and the efficiency of the Navy system of training, and should abolish for ever the idea that all the Service wants in its stokers is brawn and the ability to work four hours at a stretch in the melting inferno of a warship's boiler-room. The opening of the ward-room (commissioned rank) to stokers was a direct outcome of the Jutland Battle. Mr. Clayton Hartnup, who was one of the first stokers to reach warrant rank (warrant mechanician) and chief warrant rank (commissioned mechanician), was serving at that time in the armoured cruiser Shannon, and was very highly commended for his services by his commanding officer, Captain J. S. Dumaresq.

The commendation was repeated by the Commander-in-Chief in his despatch, with the note that he recommended the officer for "early promotion." The Admiralty in turn included Mr. Hartnup among the "officers noted for early promotion," although at that time it was quite impossible for him to be advanced above the rank he then held. However, as the authorities—quite possibly in a moment of forgetfulness—had promised to accelerate his advancement, they were morally bound to open up some rank to which he could be advanced ; and, therefore, in the course of a few months came the announcement that warrant and commissioned mechanicians (who enter as stokers, second class, at one-and-eightpence a day) should be eligible for promotion to engineer-lieutenant for long and zealous service. It was one of the most democratic little innovations that the Navy has ever witnessed.

It would be difficult to exaggerate the drab monotony of the life of the officers and men of the engineering branch of the Fleet in war. Cruising, or on patrol, engines and boilers must be kept continuously at work, and when the ship returns to harbour for her periodical rest there are coal-bunkers or oil-tanks to be replenished, boiler-tubes to be examined and perhaps replaced, and a hundred and one little defects to attend to that could not be remedied while the ship was at sea. The general method of working the engineers' department at sea was "four hours on, eight hours off," but naturally this was an elastic sort of rule entirely dependent upon circumstances. As soon as the "Action" call sounded every man had to make at once for his allotted station. During the war the "normal" complements of our ships were increased twenty-five or thirty per cent., so that the strain of constant working and constant watching might

The call for speed

be the better distributed ; but in action there was never a surplus man in a ship's company. Only a certain number of men could be employed in working the guns and torpedo-tubes, in passing up ammunition from the magazines and shell-rooms, and in keeping the boilers charged with a full head of steam, but there was never any difficulty in finding ample employment for the increased complement of stokers.

In nearly every action fought the call from the first sign or news of the enemy until the last shot was fired was for speed, more speed, and still more speed, and as a boiler-room, even in a big ship, is hardly remarkable for its roominess, the demand had to be met not by increasing the number of stokers at work, but by getting those already there to work twice as hard. This, again, meant more frequent reliefs, and in some ships—as, for instance, the Glasgow and the Kent in the fight off the Falklands in December, 1914—the cry for speed was so urgent and insistent that numbers of seamen and Marines took a hand down below in order to give the stokers a brief respite. The innumerable pieces of auxiliary machinery all over the ship would each demand its special party of attendants, usually consisting of a few stokers in charge of a petty-officer, while others of the engineer's men would be attached to the various "fire-parties" detailed to quench any outbreak that might be caused by the enemy's bursting shells.

The position of those actually in the engine and boiler-

NOT AFRAID OF THE GERMAN UNDERWATER PIRATES.

A British trawler, equipped with two guns, was attacked by a submarine more heavily armed. With a couple of shots she forced the pirate to submerge, and, though badly damaged herself, survived to fight four others before her plucky career ended.

rooms during an action is one of the few things in modern naval warfare for which no parallel can be found in the fleets of the past. There are certain parts of a modern battleship known collectively as her "vitals," and consisting of the engine and boiler-rooms, the shell-rooms, and the magazines. It is necessary above everything else that these "vitals" should be protected from the enemy's fire.

A single shell bursting among the machinery or boilers might convert a great, fast-steaming steel fortress into a mass of inert metal, while an explosion in the magazines would send the ship instantly to the bottom and everyone on board to eternity. Therefore the "vitals" are all placed below the water-line, while over the top of them, forming a roof that runs from end to end of the ship, is a curved, protective deck of steel two or three inches thick designed as a defence against shell splinters and dropping fire.

In this steel box, suspended, as it were, under the fighting body of the ship, the engineers and the stokers work. For them the battle has few excitements. The chief engineer has a loud-speaking tele- **Engineers and stokers** phone at his ear, leading down from the **in action** commanding officer in the conning tower ; before his eyes is the engine-room telegraph, registering on a dial the orders transmitted from above, while around him on all sides are other dials each automatically recording in its own way what every boiler and every bit of machinery is doing. A single word comes down from the conning-tower, and in a twinkling the engineer has translated it into action, controlling with a wheel here, a lever there, and a few bawled orders to his subordinates, a moving,

setting up friction and tending to hold her back. So it is with the stoker. He knows nothing of either speed or revolutions. His business is simply to keep up the pressure of steam, so that when the captain rings down for more speed the engineer passes on the word to the stokers for a few more "pounds per square inch," for without the steam pressure he cannot get his "revolutions."

For those who can look about them a naval action is full of incident, excitement, and achievement, while down below there is nothing but the roar of furnaces and machinery, a concentration of mental and physical energy on what lies immediately to hand, and utter ignorance of the progress of the fight until it is over, or until a blow from the enemy lays them under tribute. It is impossible to imagine, and the men themselves found it almost equally difficult to explain, what their feelings are during a fight. In the battle off the Falklands it fell to the lot of the Kent to attend to the German cruiser Nürnberg, which was nominally her superior in speed by half a knot. The German was well out of range when the chase began, and both ships were short of fuel—though, of course, neither ship knew the state of the other. The problem on board the Kent was to overtake a nominally faster ship and bring her within decisive range before the bunkers were swept clean, and there is perhaps no more brilliant incident in the war record of the naval engineering department than the fact that the Kent's "black squad" acquitted themselves "as requisite," and had quite a good supply of fuel left in their bunkers when the Nürnberg went to the bottom.

Stokers of H.M.S. Kent

One of the Kent's chief stokers, speaking of this action to the writer, said: "We had treble odds against us— the Nürnberg's ten-mile start, her extra half-knot in speed, and our own bunker shortage. While we had to go top speed to catch her we had to be on the look-out against running dry ourselves. Every shovel of coal had to be handled like gold-dust, and if we hadn't had good, experienced men we should have burned ourselves out and lost the Nürnberg into the bargain." In order to encourage the stokers, word was frequently passed down as to the progress made in the chase, but "when we heard our 6 in. bow-chasers let fly, and knew we had got them in range at last, the men gave a tremendous yell and seemed to redouble their efforts— though Heaven knows they had been going 'all out' before."

The great development of underwater attack during the war added very considerably to the immediate risks of those serving in the engine- and boiler-rooms. Anchored mines and torpedoes are alike designed to strike their victims several feet below the water-line, and although it would at first appear that in the case of mines, at all events, the chances were heavy that the extreme bows would, in the majority of cases, bear the full force of the explosion, this was not in actual fact the case. Unless a ship bore down on a mine in an absolutely straight line, what usually happened was that the cushion of water carried along ahead of the ship and around the bows pushed the mine slightly out of the way, and it would remain a small distance from the side of the ship until about half the latter's length had passed,

AWAITING HAMMOCK INSPECTION.
Hammocks and bedding laid out for inspection by the divisional officer, with the owners standing by awaiting his arrival.

living mass of machinery which, in such a ship as the Queen Elizabeth, cost more than it did to build and complete outright any ten of such three-deckers as Nelson commanded at Trafalgar.

In the stokeholds the dripping firemen, stripped to the waist, frequently with no more covering than a loin-cloth, give their unremitting attention to the furnaces. In an oiler they were lucky, but it can well be imagined what it must sometimes have been like in such a vessel as the Lion, which, when running at full speed, could eat up coal at the rate of forty tons an hour —2,240 lb. every ninety seconds. Speed was no concern of the stoker—nor, indeed, of the "chief." Once a ship settled down after her commissioning trials the engineer ceased to think in terms of speed and concerned himself only with the "revolutions per minute" of the screw propellers. The reason for this will be readily understood. The engineer can see just what his machinery is doing, and knows what, in theory, should be the speed of the ship for any given number of revolutions; but he can know nothing of the currents through which the vessel may be steaming at the moment, of the wind which may be helping or retarding her progress, or of the marine growths on the ship's bottom

LASHING UP AFTER INSPECTION.
Blankets and bedding are folded longitudinally in the hammock and rolled up in it, the whole being then lashed up with rope. This photograph shows clearly the several stages of the process.

when the mine would sweep inwards and strike the vessel's side.

In November, 1916, the destroyer Zulu was badly mined in this way. As a result of the explosion the bottom of the after-part of the engine-room was blown out and the whole compartment reduced to a mass of débris and broken steam and water pipes. Immediately after the explosion Engine-Room Artificer Michael Joyce and Stoker Petty-Officer Walter Kimber made their way to the engine-room, the latter not leaving the boilers of which he was in charge

" Well done, stokers ! " until he had shut off the oil supply and sent his men on deck. From the inside of the engine-room came the sound of groans, and both men tried to enter it by way of the foremost hatch and ladder. The heat, however, was intense, and volumes of scalding steam were pouring out of the hatchway, so they went farther aft, wrenched off one of the ventilating hatches over the engine-room casing, and lowered themselves into the rapidly-filling compartment over the steam-pipes, which were extremely hot.

Scrambling over the débris, they discovered well over on the starboard side a stoker petty officer named Smith, who had been badly injured and was nearly unconscious, and quite unable to keep himself clear of the rising water, which was already up to his neck. He was, indeed, held fast by the twisted pipes and other wreckage flung about the engine-room by the explosion, but a rope was lowered from above, and with great difficulty Joyce and Kimber succeeded in extricating him, and he was hoisted safely to the deck. Another stoker petty-officer was hauled out in the same way, but he was, unfortunately, dead ; and by this time the water had risen so high in the engine-room as to make it impossible for the two rescuers to work there any longer, and their search for the body of another man who was known to be there had to be abandoned. Joyce and Kimber both received the Albert Medal (second class), while the Zulu was ultimately got into port.

Torpedoes, being set as a rule to run about nine or ten feet below the surface in order to strike a battleship under the lower edge of its main armour belt, will, if they hit at all, probably strike a ship either in the machinery or boiler compartments, or abreast of the magazines lying under the main turrets fore and aft. In either case it is those down below who have to bear the brunt of the explosion, and one may well imagine the ghastly and terrible result of the detonation of 420 lb. of trinitrotoluol among high-pressure boilers or a mass of machinery. There is no possible escape for officers or men. Those who are not killed by the force of the explosion or the flying fragments of metal as the interior of the ship is blown to pieces are bound to be caught in the floods of steam, boiling water, and, possibly, blazing oil. For those who are above the protecting deck, whether on duty or off, there may be some hope of escape, but there is precious little chance for those below.

Every one for himself is the only possible order after

[Swaine.

WING-COM. E. F. BRIGGS, D.S.O.
One of the R.N.A.S. men who bombed Friedrichshafen in October, 1914, when he was taken prisoner. Nearly two and a half years later he escaped from Germany.

everything possible has been done to secure the safety of the ship, but even then the chances are that the shock of the explosion will have dislocated the hatchways and sliding doors, cutting off all hope of escape, and confining the men to their terrible prison until death ends all. It is some slight consolation to reflect that in such cases as these death must nearly always be instantaneous. Happily, too, there have been many cases in which the main shock of the torpedo attack has been absorbed by the coal-bunkers, which, when possible, are always so arranged as to flank the "vitals," and in such instances the casualties were small and the vessel was able to make her way into port.

In practically every naval action of importance the work of the engine-room staffs of British warships was singled out for special praise. In the Dogger Bank fight of January 24th, 1915, which from start to finish was a speed contest between Sir David Beatty's and the enemy's battle-cruisers, resulting in the sinking of the Blücher, the British vice-admiral reported that "the behaviour of officers and men was only what was expected, and great credit is due to the engine-room staffs for the fine steaming of the squadron." The Indomitable especially distinguished herself on that occasion by well exceeding her designed speed, and those responsible were more than rewarded when Sir David Beatty, at the close of the action, made the special signal, "Well done, Indomitable stokers ! "

Vice-Admiral Sir Frederick Sturdee, the victor of the Falklands fight, recorded in his despatch : " I have pleasure in reporting that the officers and men under my orders carried out their duties with admirable efficiency and coolness, and great credit is due to the engineer officers of all the

[Heath.

ENG.-CAPT. C. G. TAYLOR,
Who became soon after the outbreak of the war principal engineer staff officer to Sir David Beatty. Killed in the Dogger Bank fight of January 24th, 1915.

ships, many of which exceeded their normal full speed." Captain J. C. T. Glossop, of the Australian cruiser Sydney, wrote of his successful action with the Emden (November 9th, 1914) : " I have great pleasure in stating that the behaviour of the ship's company was excellent in every way, and with such a large proportion of young hands and people under training it is all the more gratifying. The engines worked magnificently, and higher results than trials were obtained."

Most emphatic of all, however, were the remarks of the principal flag officers engaged in the Jutland Battle of May 31st-June 1st, 1916. Admiral Sir John Jellicoe, Commander-in-Chief, **Engineers in the** wrote : " I cannot adequately express the **Jutland Battle** pride with which the spirit of the Fleet filled me. . . . It must never be forgotten, however, that the prelude to action is the work of the engine-room department, and that during action the officers and men of that department perform their most important duties without the incentive which a knowledge of the course of the action gives to those on deck. The qualities of discipline and endurance are taxed to the utmost under these conditions, and they were, as always, most fully maintained throughout the operations under review. Several ships attained speeds that had never before been reached, thus showing very clearly their high state of steaming efficiency. Failures

zz

in material were conspicuous by their absence, and several instances are reported of magnificent work on the part of the engine-room departments of injured ships."

Vice-Admiral Sir David Beatty was briefer, but no less eulogistic. "As usual," he wrote, "the engine-room departments of all ships displayed the highest qualities of technical skill, discipline, and endurance. High speed is a primary factor in the tactics of the squadrons under my command"—there were then under his orders the Battle Cruiser Fleet, and its attendant squadrons of light cruisers

Engineers of "emergency" ships and flotillas of destroyers—"and the engine-room departments never fail." Higher praise than that there could not be.

It would be altogether improper here not to make some further mention of those skilled engineers who came into the Navy from the mercantile marine at the outbreak of war, and put their services at the disposal of the country, very often at considerable financial sacrifice. In nearly all the "emergency" ships—armed liners, mercantile fleet auxiliaries, and such small craft as trawlers and drifters— the original staffs remained—a double advantage to the Service, inasmuch as it left officers and men in the ships.

[*Canadian War Records.*

JEALOUS FOR THEIR GUN'S APPEARANCE.
Gun crew cleaning their 6 in. gun after firing practice aboard one of the light cruisers of the Arethusa class with the Grand Fleet. This gun can fire about ten rounds per minute, the projectile weighing about 100 lb.

and with the engines and boilers to which they were accustomed, and relieved the already short-handed Navy from the impossible task of providing for these vessels' requirements. The extraordinary value of the assistance rendered from this quarter is to be seen in the fact that although, in the spring of 1917, there were in service just about three hundred armed merchantmen and mercantile fleet auxiliaries, absorbing almost exactly nine hundred engineer officers, there was in the whole of them but one officer of the engineering branch of the Royal Navy, and he was serving on the Staff of Vice-Admiral R. G. O. Tupper, commanding the 10th (Blockade) Cruiser Squadron. The whole of the others had taken commissions in the Naval Reserve, and for the most part were serving in the same ships as they had done before the war. There were, of course, large numbers of other Royal Naval Reserve engineer officers scattered throughout the Fleet as watch-keepers in battleships, cruisers, and so forth, while the machinery of the trawlers and drifters was exclusively in the hands of their own "enginemen" of pre-war days.

For nearly the first three years of the war the superintendence of British naval engineering was in the hands of Engineer Vice-Admiral Sir Henry J. Oram, who had been appointed Engineer-in-Chief of the Fleet in 1907. Admiral Oram entered the Service in 1879—the year after Sir John Jellicoe received his first commission as a sub-lieutenant— and his administrative talents and the broadness of his grasp of naval engineering problems so quickly asserted themselves that after serving a commission in the Crocodile, an Indian troopship, he was appointed to the Naval Engineering Department at the Admiralty in May, 1884, and never left it until his retirement on June 8th, 1917. There is possibly something in this record that is reminiscent of Gilbert's famous gibe at Mr. W. H. Smith, who, though he had "never been to sea," yet became First Lord of the Admiralty. The requirements of a navy are, however, far too varied for any man to become familiar with them by first-hand acquaintance, and it is only in the Admiralty, where the experience of every ship of every type is concentrated in analytical reports, and where engineering progress the world over can be closely followed in its entirety, that a comprehensive view of the needs of the Fleet can be obtained. Throughout the nineteen years when the late Sir A. J. Durston was Engineer-in-Chief, Admiral Oram was closely associated with him, and it was towards the end of that period—in the opening years of the twentieth century—that some of the most vital revolutions in warship machinery had been effected. The water-tube boiler was introduced and established; the turbine, experimentally installed in the ill-fated destroyers Cobra and Viper, was first applied to a cruiser (Amethyst) in 1903, and to a battleship (Dreadnought) in 1906; while experiments with oil fuel, begun in the 'nineties, had so far prospered that by the time Sir Albert Durston handed over his office to Admiral Oram we had in commission thirty-six torpedo-boats using turbines for propulsion and oil exclusively for steam-raising. In ten thousand minor ways the mechanical equipment of the Fleet was improved, and Admiral Oram, being at the hub of things, necessarily had a full and complete knowledge of everything that was going forward not only in our own Fleet, but elsewhere. He went to the Admiralty, as has been said, in 1884, and he left it after a most successful career in 1917. In that period the speed and power of battleships was raised from 16·75 knots and 11,500 h.p. to 25 knots and 58,000 h.p.; of cruisers from 22 knots and 20,000 h.p. to well over 30 knots and 100,000 h.p.; while destroyers, submarines, and aircraft were all introduced and most successfully established. The years during which Sir Henry Oram was Engineer-in-Chief were not marked by any large innovations, but by the most profound developments in speed, power, and equipment; and the almost monotonous tribute paid by commanders afloat to the excellence of the engine departments, as regards both their materiel and their personnel, is the greatest testimony that could be desired to the soundness of his work. In June, 1917, he was succeeded by Engineer Vice-Admiral George Goodwin, **Engineers'** who for the previous ten years had served **headquarters work** at the Admiralty as Deputy Engineer-in-Chief. By his appointment there was secured a continuity of tradition, as well as the certainty that the new chief would be no less familiar than his predecessor with the position and requirements of naval engineering in all its branches.

In the Admiralty itself the principal work of engineer officers lay in designing machinery for such ships as were deemed by the Board to be necessary for the prosecution of the war, so that the Engineering Branch came for the most part under the Department of the Director of Naval Construction. The Board of Admiralty, for instance, would say that they wanted a ship to carry so many guns of such and such a calibre, to make a certain speed, be able to steam so many miles, carry so much defensive armour,

Training torpedo deck tubes on the target before dropping the torpedoes into the water.

[British official photograph.

[British official photographs.

Torpedo taking the water. Right : Coming to the surface at the end of the run.

Keeping in form for the next sea affair : Torpedo practice in the British Navy.

Hit in the stokehold! The appalling risk engineers and stokers faced unflinchingly.

British submarine officer examining the periscope in the hope of finding an enemy target.

[British official photograph.

Destroyers starting to make a smoke-screen to reduce or veil the visibility of their fleet.

[British official photograph.

Weaving the web of the veil : Destroyers altering their course and digging into the sea.

[British official photograph.

An effective smoke-screen drawn before the fleet in long and heavy sable convolutions.

A lesson man learned from the cuttlefish, which hides itself in its own inky fluid.

and, in some cases, to draw no more than a certain amount of water; and it is obvious that the Department of the Director of Naval Construction could make no progress with the plans until the machinery details had been drawn out; because, for one thing, the engines, boilers, and fuel spaces often account for a third or more of the entire structure of a ship. But the "headquarter" work of the engineers extended far beyond this. Engineer officers figured in the Intelligence and the Trade Divisions of the War Staff, and in the Departments of the Directors of Naval Ordnance and Naval Equipment. In the Air Department of the Admiralty and the R.N. Air Service engineers figured prominently. Engineer Lieutenant-Commander E. F. Briggs was one of the trio who raided the Zeppelin factory at Friedrichshafen in October, 1914. His machine was brought down and he was taken prisoner, but nearly two and a half years afterwards he made his escape, and returned to England for further service.

In the Grand Fleet the individual "chief" in each ship was naturally responsible for the efficiency of his own engines, but the most responsible work fell upon those officers who were borne on the Staffs of the principal flag officers. During the time that Sir John Jellicoe commanded the Grand Fleet the principal engineer officer on his Staff was Engineer Captain Howard Bone, who was appointed to that post in November, 1914, after having been for two and a half years Chief Engineer at Haulbowline Dockyard. Captain Bone entered the Navy as an assistant engineer in July, 1889, and, unlike most officers of his branch, divided his time fairly evenly between sea and shore service. In 1906 he was appointed assistant to the Chief Engineer at Chatham Dockyard, quitting that post three years later to go afloat in the armoured cruiser Natal (since lost), which was at that time commanded by Captain W. R. Hall, who became Director of the Intelligence Division of the War Staff a few months after the outbreak of war. When Sir John Jellicoe left the Grand Fleet for the Admiralty, Captain Bone went from the Grand Fleet flagship to the Lion, in which vessel he joined the Staff of Rear-Admiral Sir W. C. Pakenham, who succeeded Sir David Beatty in command of the battle-cruiser force. Captain Bone was made a C.B. in the Birthday Honours of 1917.

Engineer Captain Fred Hore was senior engineer officer on the staff of the second-in-command of the Grand Fleet from February, 1915, until June, 1917, when he was appointed to the position of Chief Engineer at Haulbowline. He entered the Navy in January, 1885, and served in the Royal yacht Osborne in 1893-97, and in the battleship Albemarle in 1908-9, during which period that vessel carried the flag of Admiral Jellicoe in the Atlantic Fleet. From 1909 to 1913 he was associated in various ways with the torpedo branch of the Service, but just a year before the war began he went on the Staff of the admiral commanding the 2nd Cruiser Squadron, where he remained until his transference to the Marlborough, flagship of Admiral Sir Cecil Burney (second in command of the Grand Fleet) in February, 1915.

In the Battle-Cruiser Fleet there were fewer ships than in the battle squadrons forming the backbone of the Grand Fleet, but each vessel was much faster than any battleship, and, what was **Battle-cruisers'** equally or more important, speed counted **greater speed** for much more in the general "make-up" of the force. Soon after the outbreak of war Sir David Beatty took as his principal engineer staff officer Engineer Captain C. G. Taylor, but that officer, accommodated at the time in the battle-cruiser Tiger, was unfortunately killed in the Dogger Bank fight of January 24th, 1915. He was succeeded by Engineer Captain D. P. Green, who had actually been in charge of the machinery of the Lion (Admiral

Beatty's flagship) since she was first passed into service. Joining the Navy in 1887, Captain Green had spent many years in instructional work, and the fact that he was selected in 1910 to take charge of the Lion, whose engines were almost twice as powerful as any ever built into a ship of war, is sufficient testimony to the confidence placed in him by the authorities. He was made a C.B. in the Birthday Honours of 1916, and—perhaps more significant from a professional **Increased numbers** point of view—was taken by Sir David **of the engineers** Beatty to be his principal engineer adviser when that officer assumed chief command of the Grand Fleet in December, 1916. From one point of view it is perhaps unfortunate that it is impossible to give a more picturesque atmosphere to the work of the most important of the Navy's engineers; but there is little that is picturesque about their work. They are to the Fleet what the officer in command of communications is to the Army. They have to guarantee the ability of the Fleet to move at any moment, at any time, at any speed, and to any distance that may be required by the circumstances of the moment. To bring it to that state of efficiency calls for a measure of professional

[*Canadian War Records.*

TAKING SHELLS ABOARD A BRITISH BATTLESHIP.
Vitally important work was the maintaining of ample supplies of munitions to all units of the Navy. In the receiving of these on board a big warship, and the moving of them on their way to the ship's magazines, the Marines lent a helping hand.

capability which, though invariably forthcoming, is never likely to be given its due place among the factors that go to the achievement of victory.

The expansion of the engineering branch of the Fleet between the outbreak of war and the spring of 1917 is broadly shown in the following comparison:

	August, 1914.	April, 1917.
Commissioned Engineer Officers, R.N.	833	819
Ditto, for temporary service	—	219
Lieutenants (E.)	—	37
Mates (E.)	—	73
Chief Warrant and Warrant Officers, R.N.	752	852
Ditto, for temporary service	—	20
Commissioned Engineer Officers, R.N.R.	142	1,772
Chief Warrant and Warrant Officers, R.N.R.	176	243
	1,903	4,035

The war decorations won by officers and men of the branch down to April, 1917, included, for those who then survived, eight C.B.'s, seventeen D.S.O.'s, ten D.S.C.'s, twelve Conspicuous Gallantry Medals, and three hundred and nine Distinguished Service Medals. In addition, numerous special promotions had been made.

[British official photograph.

The transport train of the Newfoundland Regiment and (right) the regiment marching back elated and triumphant from Monchy-le-Preux, where it added glory to the renown it had gained at Gommecourt on July 1st, 1916.

[British official photograph.

Newfoundland officers resting in billets after their return from Monchy. Monchy-le-Preux was a dominating position in the Switch line, south-east of Arras. The Newfoundlanders held out there for three days against savage German counter-attacks, winning special praise from General Allenby.

HEROES OF GOMMECOURT WHO GATHERED NEW GLORY AT MONCHY-LE-PREUX.

FOOTPRINT OF THE HUN:

CHAPTER CLXXXVI.

CROSS-ROADS MINE CRATER.

THE VICTORIES ON THE OPPY LINE AND THE SENSÉE FORTRESS SYSTEM.

By Edward Wright.

Haig Comes to the Rescue of Nivelle—Sacrifice of a Fortnight's British Preparations to Help French at Craonne—Magnificent Feat by Canadians at Arleux—Sand-Spouts Dancing Upon Volcanoes—Secret of Oppy Wood—Terrific Swaying Battles Round and In Village—Attacking Prussians Surprised and Enveloped in Fresnoy—Three German Divisions Counter-Attack English Garrison—Excessive Price Paid by Enemy—Field of Slaughter Around Gavrelle—Strange Adventures of London Company—How the Men of Kent Returned Home—Annihilating Struggles at Roeux—A Comedy of the War—Enemy Defeated by His Own Engineers—Fierce Actions at Monchy—Breakfast-Snatching at Infantry Hill—Why Ludendorff Poured Reinforcements Towards Guemappe—Triangle Wood and the Advance Towards Chérisy—Enemy Recovers Cavalry Farm—Resurgence of British Attacking Force—Discovery of Ludendorff's Vast Tunnel—Battles Around Fontaine—German Shock Troops and their Tragic Cost to Germany—Enemy's Rabbit-Hole Tactics Restore Confidence to his Troops—Allenby Teaches German Private that the Great Hindenburg Rabbit-Hole is Imperfect—Extraordinary Duel Between Tunnel and Gun—Triumph of British Gunners and Munition-Makers—Germany Can Only Fight With Her Left Hand—British Victory Between Bullecourt and Fontaine.

AFTER the Third British Army, under Sir Edmund Allenby, fought forward on April 23rd and April 24th, 1917, from Roeux to the ground near Fontaine-les-Croisilles, the First British Army, under Sir Henry Horne, resumed its action in strength. As before explained, the immediate aim of the British High Command was to compel Ludendorff to swing over a large part of his reserves, from the Laon front to the Douai and Cambrai front, and thereby facilitate the second great French offensive arranged for May 4th.

In this view, it was absolutely necessary for Sir Douglas Haig to put aside his own scientific plan for a battle of artillery, based upon his Vimy Ridge and Arras victory, and rush his infantry onward against the Wotan and Siegfried lines. As soon as any considerable part of the British artillery could be brought forward, the struggle was continued, up and down the Hindenburg

system, in order to attract, hold, and waste the German reserves.

Immediately the battle of the rivers ended in a final repulse of a large body of German troops near Gavrelle, on April 25th, Sir Henry Horne turned the main mass of advanced guns against the top of the Wotan line. The villages of Acheville, Arleux, and Oppy had been transformed into fortresses, to protect the top of the Hindenburg switch system at Drocourt and all the southern side of the Lens salient from Avion and Méricourt to Rouvroy.

These last three villages were built on or among a series of foot hills, some three hundred feet lower than the topmost points of the Vimy Ridge. The lighter British artillery, which was hauled up to the great crest, had Avion at about a three miles range, Méricourt at about four miles range, and Acheville at a little more than a five miles range. In all three places a plunging fire effect could be obtained by the guns

[British official photograph.]

BRITISH GUNNERS IN THE OPEN.
During the first phase of the advance on Oppy, Sir Henry Horne, commanding the First Army, worked forward mainly with his field-guns, sending out only comparatively light infantrymen behind his barrage.

[British official photograph.

ALL GOES WELL.
Sir Edmund Allenby showing the King of the Belgians over ground which had been newly recovered from the common enemy.

British forces in Gavrelle swept forward more than half a mile south of the village, and reached the western slope of that low ridge of blood and mud known as Greenland Hill.

The capture of Arleux was a gallant feat. It was carried out by a Canadian force that fought on April 9th from Neuville St. Vaast over the Vimy Ridge, and continued its great drive for a depth of six miles into the German front. When the attacking troops leaped over their parapets before dawn on April 28th, the German wire entanglements remained uncut over several long stretches, and

on the Vimy cliffs, giving the cannon almost as much power of pitching its shells behind the German foot-hills as the howitzer possessed.

The ordinary British howitzer, with good aerial and hill fire controlling observation, could smash up any hostile concrete fort by its creeping barrage. If General Horne had had another fortnight to site his heavier artillery, accumulate shell, and photograph and register upon all German works within a range of six miles, he could have paralleled his Vimy success. Having to act quickly in order to assist the French armies, the brilliant Scots gunner-general attacked the new enemy line in piecemeal fashion. He was opposed by a reorganised and greatly strengthened German army, under General von Reiser, which he had driven from the Ridge to its fourth line, which originally ran from Fampoux and Gavrelle to Arleux and Méricourt. The enemy retained only the upper part of this last system of his original front.

[British official photograph.

LAND LEFT UNCOVERED BY THE RECEDING TIDE.
The King of the Belgians seldom left the narrow strip that remained to him of his own kingdom except to pay a few brief visits to the fighting line in France. Here he is seen standing with General Sir Hubert Gough at the entrance to a captured German dug-out.

The part which he held divided at Oppy into two branches, making a loop at Arleux. General Horne worked forward mainly with his field guns, sending out only comparatively light infantry forces behind his barrage.

Large scale skirmishing

He was well aware, from his experiences at Gavrelle, that the German commander would hold his main infantry divisions in reserve, until the force of the British attack seemed to be spent, and then thrust back furiously with overwhelming masses.

The first phase of the battle was therefore in the nature of a skirmish on a large scale. Storming parties of Canadian, English, and Scottish troops fought into Oppy, and broke into and beyond the junction point of the German system at Arleux. At the same time, the

behind the wire was a Prussian Division, the 111th, who also held the crest of a slight slope running towards Oppy.

Arleux was a straggling street, flanked by groups of cottages, small gardens, and orchards. All these were fortified by the enemy, together with some sunken roads at the northern end of the village. At first, the Canadian battalions, who advanced against the uncut wire entanglements, were compelled to lie down under a rain of machine-gun bullets. On their wings, however, other Canadian battalions found paths for them, through the wire broken for them by the guns. Bombing and bayoneting along the flanks, the Canadian wings shook the nerves of the enemy machine-gunners, and enabled the held up Canadians in the unbroken sections to tear over the finger-thick wire, and arrive, with their clothes ripped to rags, against the enemy's centre.

The Prussians endeavoured to hold out until reinforcements arrived from the neighbouring village of Fresnoy; but the Canadians pressed their attack with such fury that Arleux fell in two hours of very fierce hand-to-hand fighting. The isolated cottages, gardens, and orchards were bombed until the dogged Prussians were forced out into the open. Some of the enemy then surrendered, and others did not cease fighting until they were bayoneted.

At the end of the two hours' action, only one enemy detachment held out in the village. The Canadians drew well away from the position, and it was levelled to the ground by some fine shooting from the batteries on Vimy Ridge. In the sunken roads a line of German machine-guns continued to worry the conquerors until night-fall. Then they were rushed by the same tactics as had won the crowning hummock of the Vimy cliffs. The crest between Arleux and Oppy was stormed in a very few minutes after the opening of the attack, and the Prussians were driven along the two roads to the village and there slowly broken in the hand-to-hand action already described.

As soon as news of the defeat reached the German gunners, they made Arleux look like a sandspout dancing upon a volcano. When the clouds of red **Canadians in** and yellow dust cleared, the buildings **Arleux and Fresnoy** of Arleux were scattered around the fields. Yet the Canadians held on to the spot where the village had been. Fierce counter-attacks were launched by the German commander. He barraged the village with gun fire, and swept it with an arc of machine-guns before sending his infantry into the open. It was all in vain. Every time his troops came out, they were seen from the Vimy Ridge, and shelled into scattered impotence. Not only did the Canadians hold on, but a few days afterwards they magnificently celebrated their month of continual fighting by breaking into the German position at Fresnoy.

Captured German officers were incredulous when told that Arleux and Fresnoy had been taken by the same troops that had stormed over the Vimy Ridge. They thought that all the original British attacking forces of the Easter Monday battle had been so wasted by four weeks of fighting as to **Fortified wood** need withdrawing and reorganisation. **at Oppy** As a matter of fact, the Canadians had suffered rather heavily, and had found the action at Arleux more arduous than that at the Vimy Heights. Yet, by some wonderful power of recoil, it was the battalions that lost most men which were the most high-spirited and grimly enduring. The pipers of the Canadian Scots played their men into the battle and out again; the bandsmen of other Canadian regiments made music under shell-fire, and then brought up supplies through the enemy's barrage around Arleux.

With the storming of the crest between Arleux and Oppy another important success seemed to be assured. Oppy, however, was a more difficult position to assail. It was farther removed from direct observation from the Ridge and from the British batteries around the conquered heights. The key to Oppy was a wood beside the village, and this wood the enemy had fortified in an amazing manner. It was a grand rookery of machine-guns. The guns were mostly placed in the budding boughs twenty to thirty feet above ground, and the gunners took shelter during a bombardment on ladders running down the eastern side of the trunks. On the ground, the deep dugouts placed behind barricades were concealed and strengthened by felled trees.

In the first advance, the British troops penetrated the

[British official photograph.

DEVASTATION WROUGHT IN ONE OF THE RECAPTURED VILLAGES.

British waggons passing through a ruined village on the western front. Partly by the artillery fire of modern war conditions, and partly by the Germans who indulged in frenzies of wanton destruction, many places when retaken by Sir Douglas Haig's armies were found thus reduced to heaps of rubble. In this instance the crossed timber that remained upright seemed symbolical of the regeneration which was being won.

ONE OF H.M. "LANDCRUISERS" FIGHTING ITS WAY INTO WANCOURT.
On April 12th, 1917, " tanks " played a great part in the forward movement of Sir Douglas Haig's armies, especially in the capture of the villages of Wancourt and Heninel on the Cojeul River, where two of these landcruisers carried on what was described as a forty hours' duel with the foe.

village and reached the wood and then swayed backwards and forwards for hours in attack and counter-attack against tremendous odds. German reinforcements came up in columns of motor omnibuses as well as by rail, and from Neuvireuil filtered into the wood and the groups of houses near the white manor-house to reinforce the garrison.

In almost regular periods, the fresh enemy forces surged up in three, four, or five successive waves. The struggle grew so close that the gunners on either side had to stop shooting at the village, and barrage the hostile communications. For example, three Englishmen, carrying up ammunition for a Stokes' gun, captured, amid the storm of German shrapnel, an enemy detachment who were crouching in a shell hole against their own gun fire. In the end, the German reinforcements worked back through the wood, and round the Church and recovered the village.

It was a costly recovery. The atmosphere was bright and very clear. From the eastern slopes of the Vimy heights, the field of war was spread out to view in minute distinctness. German observation officers enjoyed a clear view of the Vimy slope, but they could not see down into the hollows between the slope and the Oppy line, and they could not overlook the preparations in the British rear. British observation officers, on the other hand, were able to study all the enemy's movements as far as Douai.

Only in some crinkles of ground, close to the fire trenches, were German troops able to gather without being seen from the Vimy Ridge. Even there they were exposed to the view of the pilots and observers of the Royal Flying Corps, who often bombed them or raked them with Lewis gun fire. For the rest, the individual horses, waggons, omnibuses, trains, and marching columns of men on the German front were visible at a distance of several miles

from their fighting-line. They had to move through a storm of shrapnel and high explosive, so that some German battalions were reduced from a thousand to four hundred men before they got into action.

Oppy was bound to fall, as the capture of Arleux and Gavrelle, on either side of it, left it projecting into the new British line. Sir Henry Horne brought forward his heavy guns, and lashed the village with big shell and hammered at all its communications.

Yet for days the big white manor-house survived, with its broken roofs and empty windows clearly visible through a thin fringe of dead trees. The German commander seemed to be defying all military doctrine by clinging to the remnant of the Oppy line, and wasting battalions day after day on bits of low ground, almost surrounded by British infantry and entirely dominated by British guns. Through gaps in the shattered wood, observers on the Ridge could at last espy the Oppy trenches, filled with dead Prussians and wrecked machine-guns.

Nevertheless, the German commander would not give ground. He retired the broken garrison and sent forward the Second Guard's Reserve to man the village, wood, church, and manor-house. When the British troops again attacked Oppy, in darkness before dawn on May 3rd, they came at once under a hail of machine-gun bullets, and afterwards under a hurricane of shell fire. Again they penetrated into Oppy Wood, only to be thrown out by the massed counter-attacking forces of the Prussian Guards, and forced back, for the second time, to the outskirts of the village.

Obstinate German resistance

While the British barrage went ahead to the eastern end of the village, with the assaulting troops following close behind it, the Guard's reserve drove in sideways in a

TRIUMPHANT ENTRY OF A "TANK" INTO THE VILLAGE OF HENINEL.
Extraordinary work was achieved by the " tanks " which cleared the way for the British infantry into the twin villages of Heninel and Wancourt. That which reached Heninel swept down numbers of the enemy, many of whom fled from the monster against which rifles and bombs were of no avail.

southernly direction, through the wood and across the village. This compelled the British flank to fall back over the Gavrelle Road. Oppy again was won and lost.

Northward, however, the second British offensive on the Oppy front was more successful. Long stretches of trenches were stormed between Oppy and Arleux, enabling the line to be linked up with the Canadians in Arleux.

The superb Canadians were by this time known to the enemy command, and regarded by them as their prey. Sir Julian Byng, so the Germans thought, had kept the division so long in action that its strength was gone. The 15th Reserve Division of Prussians was informed that it had weak troops in front of it, and was deployed in and around Fresnoy, with orders to attack in the morning of May 3rd.

The result was that before morning dawned, the f r e s h Prussian division was surrounded in Fresnoy village. By six o'clock in the morning the Canadian encircling movement was completed. The enemy's front was strongly defended with machine-guns and wire entanglements, and as at Arleux, part of the Canadian force was held up in the centre. But again on the wings, the Canadians broke through, linked together along the enemy's rear,

Canadians beat the Prussian Guards
and, after a short, fierce bomb and bayonet attack, captured the remnants of the Prussian division. Only two hundred men and eight officers were taken, as the nine Prussian battalions had been under British gun fire all the way from Douai.

Fresnoy, however, then became a British salient between the enemy positions at Acheville and Oppy. A counter-attack by the First Reserve Division of the Prussian Guards was shattered by high explosive shell and shrapnel from British guns on the Vimy positions. This repulse enabled the Canadians to improve their lines beyond Fresnoy by the capture of another German trench. The

ARMOURED MONSTER THAT THERE WAS NO WITHSTANDING.
During the fighting to the south-east of Arras the "tanks" were taken by their crews wherever their irresistible force could be best employed. Many thousands of yards of wire were flattened out, dug-outs broken in, and machine-gun corners destroyed by them in the fighting along this front.

Canadians, however, remained with two flanks to defend, and when they were relieved by English troops the enemy continued to thrust in on either flank to prevent the new garrison from working forward throughout the line.

Then at dawn on May 9th the German artillery around Lens, together with every available gun north of the Scarpe, drenched the five hundred yards of front at Fresnoy with shells of all calibres. The enemy's new high velocity guns, throwing 5 in. shell a distance of ten miles and 13·5 shell a distance of twenty miles, were employed in large numbers for making gas bombardments of British artillery positions, amid hurricanes of black smoke projectiles. Dense white smoke screens were skilfully used by the enemy to hide his firing artillery as well as to cover his infantry advance.

The men of the 15th Reserve Division advanced at dawn in dense columns, and were repulsed as they reached the fire trench. At nine o'clock in the morning the First Reserve Division of Prussian Guards, which had been detached from the Oppy sector, also attacked in column formation, and, after tremendous losses, gained a foothold on the outskirts of the village. For several hours the struggle continued, but though hard pressed, the English troops gradually won the mastery, and took prisoners from both Prussian forces which surrounded them on three sides.

Just as a defensive victory against great odds was shaping, the German commander brought up a third division, the 5th Bavarian. Through the lines of the weakened 15th Division the Bavarian troops p a s s e d in columns with a battering ram effect against the lads from the English Southern Counties. In spite of the intense bombardments and extraordinary pressure of the enemy, the Englishmen served their machine-guns to the last moment, and when the village, or rather the cellars of the village, was choked with gas and blown in by high explosive, they fell

PRISONERS CARRYING THEIR GUN FOR THEIR CAPTORS.
Many of the underground fortresses which the Germans had constructed to withstand any advance from Arras proved of little avail against the terrific British artillery fire, and the advancing infantry were frequently able to compel dazed prisoners to bring up their own guns with them.

ENEMY CAVALRY IN THE FIELD.
German photograph showing cavalry ready for action. When in the spring of 1917 the cavalry came into contact during the fighting to the east of Arras the enemy horsemen were found of poor quality compared with those who had fought in the earlier actions of the war.

While fighting was going on at Greenland Hill on April 28th, some of the forces on the left, including a London battalion, dug themselves in and stayed there, and stubbornly broke a number of German counter-attacks. It was, however, very disappointing to them to have to stop owing to a check at Roeux of which they knew nothing at the time.

They had completely shattered all the enemy forces in front of them, and could have won, at scarcely any cost, for the time being another two miles of territory. They might have suffered badly from flanking counter-attacks from Fresnes, Plouvain, and the miners' cottages between the two villages, after the Germans had again strengthened themselves at Roeux. It was absolutely sound tactics to dig in between Gavrelle and Greenland Hill.

Yet the remarkable adventures of some two hundred London men showed what possibilities lay in the situation, had Roeux only been captured. On the left of the attack a company of London troops had all their officers either killed or wounded, and were left to do what they liked. A German company under the same conditions would have withdrawn; but, as always happened among British troops in such cases, the officerless Londoners worked forward in a spirit of savage adventure.

They scouted ahead to discover something worth attacking, and, about a thousand yards from Greenland Hill, they saw a small patch of woodland known as Square Wood. Here, they said to themselves, was a visible objective in the feature- **Square Wood and** less countryside. So they gathered **Railway Copse** and headed for the woodland. Greatly were they cheered on finding that the first German trench, on the skirts of the wood from which the enemy had been firing at them, was obliterated by their own barrage.

In spite of the fact that the British artillery was still bombarding the patch of trees, the Londoners ran through their own shell curtain rather than be baulked of the kind of fighting they wanted. Square Wood was a strong fortress, originally intended to strengthen the German defences south of Gavrelle. After Gavrelle was captured it was used as a concentration place for some of the unceasing enemy counter-attacks.

Arriving unexpectedly in front of their barrage, the band of Londoners took the garrison by surprise, bayoneted them, and occupied the wood. It was a lonely place to hold, and the conquerors were hungry for more hand-to-hand fighting. They did not care to go back to their main body, as this seemed a tame ending to an extraordinary outing. A thousand yards in front of them was another and larger wood, known as Railway Copse, from which enemy gunners began to fire at them.

In wide order they charged for the best part of a mile against the hostile batteries, leaving behind only a handful of men to hold Square Wood. When they closed upon the German guns, the gunners fled, thinking that the entire British Army had broken through the line, and was storming upon them. The London men fired upon the fugitives, and some German infantry at a distance also brought machine-guns and rifles to bear upon their own frightened gunners.

Since April 9th there had been a very fierce bitterness

back to Fresnoy Wood. Thence they recovered part of the lost ground by a counter-attack, and from the north-west corner of the wood defied the Prussian and Bavarian masses to shift them. Canadian officers, fighting alongside the South-country Englishmen, were full of praise for the manner in which their comrades fought.

The enemy High Command paid an excessive price for the recovery of Fresnoy. Any commander could have broken into a salient, only five hundred yards in breadth, by concentrating the guns of two armies upon the small patch of ground and its neighbouring batteries, and deploying three divisions of the first class to wear down the physical power of the small garrison. It was mere bludgeon work, this counter-attack by 27,000 men in dense column formation, and as the field of war was dominated by the Vimy Ridge, the destruction of German men, guns, and material was enormous. The same conditions obtained at Oppy and along **Gavrelle and** the next village southward at Gavrelle. **Greenland Hill** While the forces of the First, Third, and Fifth British armies swayed to and fro on the wings of the battlefield, their centre stood almost motionless during weeks of incessant slaughter.

The garrison of Gavrelle had heaps of dead grey figures before it in the action of April 23rd. In the next action, on April 28th, the British forces that attacked from the south of Gavrelle village achieved a remarkable success. They swept over a wide tract of vague country, which had no special landmarks, and reached the western slopes of Greenland Hill. At that time Greenland Hill could have been transformed into another dominating British position, and saved from becoming one of the most terrible of enemy obstacles. The movement, however, was checked by flanking fire from the next German position southward around Roeux. Until Roeux fell Greenland Hill could not be entirely conquered.

among the German infantry over the lack of support they received from their artillery. In the prison cages the gunners had at times to implore the help of the British guards to prevent them from being done to death by their angry countrymen. It was a fact that many German artillerymen had been so panic-stricken by the British bombardment that they kept in their dugouts instead of courageously trying to cover their infantry. This was the reason why the men serving German batteries in Railway Copse were shot down by German troops as they fled.

End of a gay adventure Decisive was the assistance the Londoners received from their enemies. They could have taken the guns back to their own line, had they been a little stronger and possessed the necessary horses. As it was, the Germans closed on their rear, and swept them with fire from all directions. The Londoners dug themselves in and arranged outposts all around and beat the enemy off.

They got in touch with the few men they had left in Square Wood, and in the evening the tiny Square Wood garrison communicated with the main body, near Greenland Hill. Thereupon, some officers went out and brought most of the adventurers back. Their losses were remarkably slight in proportion to their achievements. The entire battalion to which they belonged had less than sixty casualties throughout the day's fighting, so that the small advanced party, which engaged in one of the most audacious escapades of the war, got off practically scot free.

Their feat indicated how near the German line was to breaking. When, however, the London men withdrew, Ludendorff reoccupied Railway Copse and Square Wood with division after division, and, after another fortnight of intense fighting, the main British forces only won one quarter of the ground through which the two hundred Londoners had penetrated. Greenland · Hill, which they could have swept on the rear with the German guns they might have captured, remained for months the base of the German defences on the Douai road. It was not until the first week in June, after a month of terrific battering, that the British hold on the western slopes of Greenland Hill was for the time assured. The eastern slopes were still occupied by the enemy.

In another part of the field, during the struggle along the three rivers of Artois, forty Kentish men had an experience somewhat similar to that of the Londoners. They went out to attack in one of those remarkable nocturnal offensives which have great advantages and great disadvantages. British commanders often used the night attack on the grand scale, because it forced the enemy artillery to reveal itself against the dark sky, and come under the superior and heavier

counter-battery fire of the British artillery. The cover of darkness also impeded the work of German machine-gunners, as they usually retired to their covering when the bombardment opened, expecting only a raid. If they emerged before the attacking infantry reached them, they had to wait for star shells and other illuminating devices, in order to mark their targets. On the other hand, it was difficult for the assailants to maintain communications during a night action, and the fighting tended at times to grow confused and full of incredible incidents.

The forty men from Kent were among those who lost direction in the darkness. They went far beyond the rest of their line, and settled in a small copse, considerably more than half a mile beyond their comrades. Being well out in the middle of the enemy territory, and having a machine-gun with them and Germans all round them, they settled down to do all the damage they could.

No German discovered from what direction the deadly, unexpected fire came, as the spurts of flame from the Kentish rifles, with the longer flame from their machine-gun, looked like the work of a German supporting force, covering a counter-attack. Shrapnel was

[*Canadian War Records.*
CANADIAN GUNNERS DRAWING AMMUNITION.
Ammunition dumps presented an incessant sequence of scenes like this, waggons running in an endless chain to the batteries in front. When the great advance of April, 1917, began specially arduous work devolved upon the field artillery until ways had been made on which heavy ordnance could move forward.

falling everywhere, and the comrades of the men that fell put the casualties down to gun fire.

Throughout the night and all through the next day the men from Kent held on to the copse. When evening came their ammunition was running low, and they resolved to cut a way back. Between them and their friends were scattered posts and two well made trenches full of Germans. They evaded the posts, and, screened by the dusk, reached the first German trench without being detected. But in the trench a German officer, with drawn sword, and the two orderlies beside him, saw enough of the Kents' uniform to detect them. There was a call to surrender.

In reply, one of the little Kentish force shot the officer, and the two orderlies were killed at the same moment. As the whole trench sprang to life, the men from Kent charged. A wild, sharp bout of fighting followed. The Englishmen disengaged themselves, and, amid a hail of bullets and bombs, sprinted to the second trench. By good luck this trench was deep and narrow, and the Kents' leaped it, over the Germans, who took pot shots as the unexpected figures made flying jumps above their heads. The remnant of the little party still had the zone of fire to cross. In the first rush two officers and thirteen men came in unwounded, and a few wounded stragglers

[*Canadian War Records.*

MEN OF THE MAPLE LEAF BOUND FOR THE TRENCHES.
Canadian troops going forward. Several of the men had fixed to the muzzles of their rifles special wire-cutting machines, designed to help them in getting through any wire that had remained standing after the preliminary bombardment that preceded their attack on enemy trenches.

kept turning up at night. In all, twenty men out of the original forty got home.

In another strange episode of the nocturnal battles, some British troops north of the Scarpe, near Roeux, rushed a position from which, for the first time, they could look down and take in enfilade a hostile position on the south side of the river. Dimly they saw that the enemy trench was full of Germans, and, therefore, they furiously raked it with machine-guns. Their smashing fire, however, did not seem to worry the garrison. Only when day broke was it discovered that the men who filled the trench had been killed by gun fire before the British infantry arrived on the scene.

On April 30th the Germans round Gavrelle re-organised the ground they had temporarily lost to the London group, and, on a day of brilliant weather, stormed back towards the village. The great counter-attack was ineffectual, and resulted only in fresh and larger grey swathes being piled upon the barren fields of dead bodies. On May 3rd the British troops in turn resumed the battle in the Gavrelle sector.

They were met by masses of Germans in a violent hand-to-hand combat round a windmill north of the Douai road. Eight times the windmill changed hands while the gunners on both sides looked on helpless. Few were the rockets that could be carried to the opposing fighting-lines, and artillery observers were often afraid to act on the signals they perceived, because of the sandwich medley of the action.

Sometimes British rockets went up on the rear of strong parties of Germans, with the result that the enemy was shelled by his own guns. The German gunners acted too readily on the informa- **Another Prussian** tion conveyed by the British rockets, and **Guard defeat** thinking that the entire ground was lost, deluged it with shell, effecting more demoralisation among the Germans than slaughter among the British.

Another division of the Prussian Guard was engaged in the struggle around Gavrelle on May 3rd. It was supported by the Reserve Guards Division, which was detached for the first counter-attack at Fresnoy. In these circumstances the nine battalions of Guardsmen completely lost the day, and, leaving the windmill in the hands of the British troops, after seven vain counter-attacks, retired, after piling the field of death with thousands more of their newly dead.

In all cases, the number of British troops engaged against the Hindenburg system at the end of April to the beginning of May was small in comparison with the number of German troops. Ludendorff went out of his way to state in his official reports that the British attack on April 28th was of terrific weight, while the attack delivered on May 3rd was feeble.

On both occasions the British Army commanders used almost a similar weight in the offensive, and obtained almost similar results. The Germans employed more troops and lost more from shell fire during the preliminary operations. Moreover, by reason of their system of mass attack, either in solid lines or in solid columns, they lost far more from machine-gun and musketry fire.

The German anticipation of the tactics of the Hindenburg system was reversed. Ludendorff had arranged that Sir Douglas Haig's lieutenants should launch dense, large forces against the invincible machine-gunners and long range artillery of Germany. This arrangement did not prove practical. Such was the danger to the Hindenburg lines that the German command had to employ men by the mass in its defence, while the British command generally used troops in open order to induce the foe to gather in large targets for the British artillery.

Around Roeux the fighting on April 28th and May 3rd was as terrible as at Gavrelle. The English troops who relieved the gallant Scotsmen had a most bitter time in and about the chemical **Fierce fighting** works and on Greenland Hill. Having **around Roeux** recovered the factory, the enemy made it a machine-gun and trench-mortar position, from which a blast of fire swept the attacking troops. Many leading English officers fell, but subalterns and sergeants succeeded them, and with brilliant initiative held on to important points of ground, and made fierce attacks against the increasing pressure of the enemy.

In the afternoon of April 28th the German commander collected a great force of men and launched them in wave after wave. Happily, the preparations for the grand counter-stroke were observed by British pilots. Their signalling helped the British gunners to get quickly upon the moving target.

Three counter-attacks were completely broken, between Plouvain and Roeux and Greenland Hill, by intense artillery fire. The English battalions, though enfiladed northward from the high ground of the Douai road, and caught on the flank by a line of German machine-guns on a slope between the Scarpe River and Monchy Hill, retook the chemical works as the Scotsmen had done, but had to fall back.

Violent enemy counter-attacks The enemy had a labyrinth of defences knitted together from the ruins of the railway station, manor-house, chemical works, cemetery, churchyard, and cottages. They also held two dominating positions north and south of the village. Bombarded out of the chemical works on April 28th, the English troops resumed their attack, and again entered the factory and captured a hundred German Poles in and around the works. Again, however, they were driven back, the ground being untenable because of its exposure to the German positions beyond.

Owing to the formation of the terrain, the enemy was able to bring up continuous reinforcements along the north bank of the River Scarpe, where there was a winding, sheltering hollow that could only be reached by indirect fire from the British artillery. When a British pilot was circling above the hollow lane, amid innumerable bursts of shrapnel from hostile anti-aircraft guns, a considerable amount of damage could be inflicted upon the fresh hostile forces before they reached the caverns below the complicated nest of machine-gun defences.

British airmen, however, could not bide all day over Roeux on observation work at a low level. Not only were the enemy's anti-aircraft guns numerous and manned by very skilful men, but there were other important sectors of the great battlefield where aerial observation work was so vital as to tax the material resources of the Royal Flying Corps.

However, in the action of May 3rd the British troops, south of Roeux and the Scarpe River, succeeded in taking and holding two new German trench lines, thereby much improving the conditions for a further advance. Continuous fighting went on around Roeux for the first two weeks of May. Finally, in the evening of Friday, May 11th, the English troops, with Irishmen and Scotsmen helping them, completely broke **British win the** the enemy's grip upon this group of **chemical works** fortified buildings which had been one of the most intense centres of conflict since the second phase of the Arras Battle opened. In the great night attack the sand-bagged cellars of the chemical works, which had changed hands almost as frequently as the Gavrelle windmill two miles northward, were cleared and reorganised. The quarry by the chemical factory yielded two hundred and fifty prisoners, and some four hundred

[*Canadian War Records.*

HAULING A GUN INTO POSITION ON THE CANADIAN FRONT.
Great work was done by the Canadians during the fighting to the east of that Vimy Ridge with which their fame will be ever gloriously associated. On April 28th, 1917, they captured most of Arleux, but one enemy position still held out; the Canadians then drew well away while their guns were turned on to this position and levelled it with the ground, after which they successfully completed a dashing performance.

BBB

and fifty more were taken in the works and the churchyard, in the tunnels and open fields.

The Bavarian and Würtemberg battalions had come straight from Douai to garrison Roeux. So frequent had been the British attacks that the enemy commander did not expect another assault until the morning. He reckoned that fresh British troops would have to be brought forward in the night. As night was falling a terrific bombardment of shrapnel rained upon the network of defences and drove the garrison underground. The attacking troops followed so close behind their barrage that they carried many of the enemy machine-gun posts before the gunners came out to fire.

The larger part of the German garrison fled across the open fields of Plouvain, only to find this way of escape closed by another British barrage. Some of them went through the curtain of death, and paid heavily for their gallantry; other groups, caught between two fires, and hammered also by English, Scottish, and Irish infantry, surrendered, bringing the tale of prisoners to seven hundred.

[*Canadian War Records.*

FARBUS STATION AS RECOVERED BY THE CANADIANS.
Farbus village, with a station on the Arras-Lens railway, was in the heart of the Vimy Ridge fighting area, and was demolished. Both the village and Farbus Wood, west of it, were cleared in the morning of April 10th, 1917, after heavy fighting in generally unfavourable weather conditions.

The total British casualties were below this figure, while the losses of the two German regiments amounted to two thousand men, in addition to the unknown number of fugitives caught in the enveloping curtain of shell near Plouvain. The English troops cleaned out the nests of machine-guns behind the broken gravestones in the churchyard, and were helped in their work by the Scotsmen. From the cemetery there extended a large tunnel, entered through an old well among the tombstones and running westward, with openings at intervals for machine-guns. The machine-gunners, however, were held down by the hurricane of shrapnel, and, after some savage fighting underground, in which all the defenders were either killed or captured, the tunnel was taken.

Savage fighting underground

Meanwhile, the Irish troops worked among the wrecked houses between the churchyard and the village, cleaned out more German machine-gunners from the cellars, and broke up all counter-attacks on this flank. The English

troops stormed the Manor House in a remarkable manner. The German sappers had fortified it in front and on both flanks, and placed in it an extraordinary machine-gun redoubt that could fire in three directions. But the English troops attacked the building from the rear, where there were no machine-guns sweeping all the approaches. Though in the confusion of the fighting some of the attacking troops lost their way, and, as usual, went ahead two hundred yards beyond their objective, the advanced line on which they dug themselves in proved a better position than that which their Staff had fixed on. Its value was decisive.

English enterprise rewarded

One incident in the fighting formed a notable comedy of the dreadful war. A German doctor was found in a dug-out, and instead of taking the trouble of explaining the position to him and making him a prisoner, he was given the work of attending to wounded British soldiers. He worked well and quickly, and dressed more than a hundred injured men. Each one he labelled for Berlin, and sadly was he surprised when he learnt that his patients were not prisoners of the Germans but that he was a captive attending to his conquerors.

The victorious troops spent the night and the following day in turning the labyrinth of tunnels, dug-outs, and machine-gun emplacements to their own use. Only when their explorations and repairs were thoroughly carried out were they able to appreciate their own valiant tenacity. Not since the Ulstermen charged up the Ancre valley on July 1st, 1916, had anything been seen like the first Scottish and English attacks against Roeux.

The tunnelled and caverned position, lying in an arc of German dominating heights, seemed impregnable. In the Manor House the roof above a central machine-gun position consisted of seven feet of concrete. Roeux had originally been a warren of ancient tunnels and large cellars, to which the villagers fled for refuge from Germanic invading forces in the sixteenth and seventeenth centuries. Modern German engineers had extended and linked the old underground ways; and then, with tons of concrete and an infinite number of sand-bags, they had made the village safe from high-explosive shell.

As we have seen, it was captured merely by shrapnel that held the enemy down until all his rabbit holes were guarded by British bombers. After spending a day in the work of consolidation the conquering force again advanced in the evening, and steadily worked through the village, which was entirely conquered against incessant German counter-attacks by May 16th. The last German assaults were made under deadly disadvantages.

Fresh battalions were sent out from the fringed woodland along the Scarpe Marshes, and over the broken ground by the Douai railway line. They had to sit in makeshift shallow trenches along the river-bank, entirely exposed to the fire of the British artillery. The new defenders of Roeux held the tunnels and concrete pits, while the ruins above them rocked and smoked under an equally terrific German shell fire.

In the supreme counter-attack the enemy reached the famous chemical works and the railway-station after plunging through the British barrage. There was a desperate struggle with bomb and bayonet in and around the cellars, but finally the Germans were forced back in headlong flight into the British shell curtain.

Another wave of Germans—Bavarians as usual — broke against the great tunnel, Manor House, and churchyard. Parties of enemy gunners tried to work forward among the shell craters, while machine-gun teams nosed warily along the ground. At times the pressure of the assault was very strong. In one place a single British soldier surviving from a machine-gun team retrieved the critical situation. Single-handed he swept the Bavarians back until they gathered in such force as to break the line. He then helped to rally the broken, scattered defenders against the enemy's shock troops who had converged for a final winning thrust.

In one way the enemy owed his defeat to his own engineers. The German-built defences, with concrete, loopholed bastions, with lines of machine-gun posts and with tunnel connections, were too well designed and constructed for the enemy's new purpose. Their makers had regarded them as impregnable, and so they were against German troops.

Boomerang recoil of thoroughness

After May 16th the German Army Headquarters at Douai resigned themselves to the loss of Roeux, and, with Roeux, to the loss also of the command of the Scarpe valley and the flanking position in which the western slope of Greenland Hill could be swept with fire. Some two miles south of Roeux was the famous dominating British position, the hill of Monchy, which looked across the valley to Infantry Hill and the slope on which Sart Wood and Vert Wood rose.

In spite of the fact that the British artillery on and behind the Monchy plateau could fire, with continual and exact information, upon the enemy's trenches and gun-pits on the rolling eastern plain, it was very difficult for the British infantry at Monchy to storm down and up to the wooded slope. North and south of the valley, around Pelves, and on the Arras highroad near Guémappe, the Germans had some skilfully-sited M.E.B.U. sunken machine-gun forts, that were very difficult to knock out with gun fire. Every night German Pioneer companies excavated new dug-outs, trenches, and redoubts, so that the positions constantly increased in strength, after the first battle of the rivers on April 23rd. By machine gun and rifle fire the

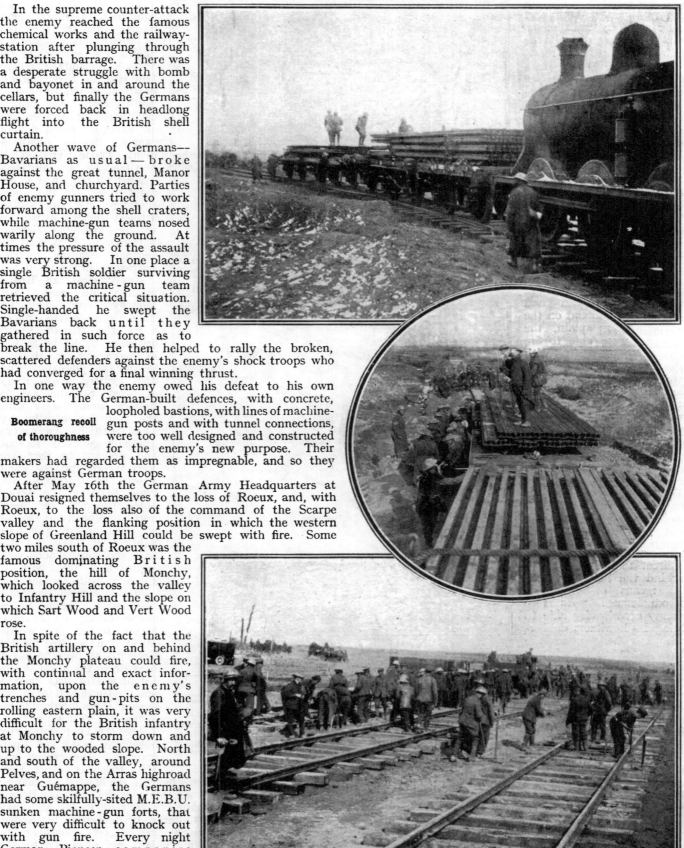

VITAL CO-OPERATION BETWEEN THE PIONEERS AND ARTILLERY.
Laying a triple railroad over recaptured ground. In circle: Unloading rails for a permanent way under construction. Above: Bringing up rails along the lengthening line. The work of the pioneers and other construction forces in organising new lines of communication from Arras to Fampoux, Monchy, Guémappe, and Wancourt for the artillery was amazing in scope and rapidity.

[*British official photographs.*

enemy garrison swept Guémappe in enfilade, as well as raking directly the hillside and hollow at Monchy.

In every action the German artillery was massed in remarkable force upon Monchy. The aim apparently was to kill the British observation officers peering from the hillside and telephoning to their guns, and to smash up the British troops gathered upon and around the plateau. As has been seen in the Verdun and Somme Battles, great hill positions, with long slopes, had their weak side.

With a very powerful artillery, concealed in creases of ground and patches of woodland on the rolling eastern plain, the Germans were able to fire tornadoes of shell, with direct observation, upon the eastern slopes of Monchy. They checked many of the British advances against Sart and Vert Woods, but in turn lost still more heavily when they endeavoured to send their infantry forward under direct observation of British fire control officers. The Third Army possessed a magnificent cover along the western side of the plateau, but had to use a large number of howitzers for indirect and sheltered fire behind the height. Only by means of aeroplane reconnaissance was the enemy occasionally able to bring his howitzers deliberately to bear upon the hidden British howitzer batteries.

A grand increase of heavy British artillery, sited behind the Monchy Plateau, was a fundamental condition of a successful British advance on Monchy. The artillery problem could only be solved by a vast amount of organising work on the new lines of communication from Arras to Fampoux, Monchy, Guémappe, and Wancourt. Magnificent in scope, intensity, and rapidity were the labours of the British pioneers and other construction forces. Yet they needed time to carry out their mighty work, by reason not only of its magnitude, but of the continual harassing effects of the enemy's long-ranged gun fire. His new field guns reached Arras; his new, big, naval guns, with flat trajectory, could have havocked Dover from Calais. Both of these pieces were used largely in imitation of the British naval ordnance employed in the Somme Battles to disorganise the German rear.

BATTLE FRONT FROM LENS TO THE SENSÉE RIVER.
On this map may be followed the course of the fighting during the spring of 1917 from Acheville, Arleux, and Oppy—which had been transformed into fortresses to protect the top of the Hindenburg switch system at Drocourt—to the Fontaine salient, where on May 20th the British consolidated their victory on the Hindenburg line.

Yet the Germans were subjected to much more damage than they were able to inflict. Their loss of the dominating positions of the Vimy Ridge and the Monchy Hill laid all their communications generally open to well-directed gun fire in clear daylight, and enabled an exactly registered long-ranged British bombardment from invisible howitzers to be maintained against all their rear in the night-time. On the whole, therefore, the incessant artillery duel was as wearing to the low-lying German batteries as it was to the German infantry forces burrowing in the plain.

Nevertheless, all British infantry advances from Monchy were conducted under local disadvantages, until the British siege ordnance could be massed in overwhelming strength behind the plateau. From the valley positions, captured by the cavalry brigade immediately after the storming of Monchy, the British infantry gradually worked forward and upward to Sart and Vert Woods and the knoll, known as Infantry Hill, lying between the woods. Some progress was made north of Monchy at the end of April, and in the hard fighting of May 3rd the Sart and Vert Woods were approached and part of Infantry Hill occupied. A continual British bombardment on the enemy forces, concentrating for counter-attacks in the large woods, made it impossible for the Germans at once to sweep back down the lower slopes. Infantry Hill was carried, and the German lines driven in some three hundred yards in front of Vert Wood.

The British success, however, was not permanent. The enemy was able to filter large reinforcements into the caverns beneath the blasted woodlands. Though the woods were smitten constantly by the British artillery with an increasing weight of metal and high explosive, the enemy countered by deepening his underground works and pouring thicker concrete upon his roofs. The result was that Infantry Hill was recovered by the Germans, and carried again by the English and Scottish troops, who were in turn thrown back.

On June 14th, 1917, the knoll was again stormed on a front of three-quarters of a mile, and the survivors of the garrison were captured. Scarcely more than two minutes elapsed between the beginning of the assault and the victorious end of it. It was a brilliant feat of surprise, as the Scotsmen and East Anglians went forward without artillery support, snatched the hill from the Germans, and ate their breakfasts. Once more the Germans counter-attacked in great force, and drove the British troops from the crest. Yet again the Englishmen and Scotsmen returned the attack, and recovered their advanced posts on Infantry Hill after shattering a violent thrust by the enemy.

About a mile and a half below Monchy was the village of Guémappe, consisting merely of a chaos of shell holes near the Arras-Cambrai highroad. After the victory of St. George's Day Ludendorff's lieutenant sent the famous Third Bavarian Division forward, and when this in turn was broken he brought up an increasing number of larger forces.

His aim was to retain a series of machine-gun positions on the Cambrai Road, from which the flank of the British from Monchy could be swept. He rightly regarded attack as the best form of defence in the circumstances. Dragging up many new batteries of heavy guns, that began firing night and day at long range, he **British thrust** became especially powerful in 5.9 in. **from Guémappe** pieces, which were the favourite German weapon for general bombardment and counter-battery work.

In spite of the renewed strength of the enemy in both guns and men, the British troops at Guémappe heroically fought forward, on May 3rd, towards St. Rohart factory, near the enemy village of Vis-en-Artois, at the junction of the Sensée stream and the Cambrai highroad. This advance was of enormous importance. Had it been allowed fully to develop it would have cut through and behind the supreme German fortress system around the Sensée River and around Bullecourt, Quéant, Riencourt, Chérisy, and Cagnicourt.

The entire Hindenburg system, with its illimitable tunnels, its thousands of M.E.B.U. forts, redoubts, and earthworks, would have been decisively pierced. Months of incessant and most murderous work would have been spared the English, Australian, and Scots forces on the Sensée River and Bullecourt sectors, and the enemy would have been compelled to make a longer retirement to a weaker line.

As will be seen from the map, the **Hindenburg system** junction, at Quéant, of the remnant of **threatened** the Siegfried line and the Wotan line had been reduced to a salient by the magnificent series of victories won by the Third Army under Sir Edmund Allenby. Basing his observation posts on the dominant position on the hill at Monchy, Sir Edmund Allenby, the moment he launched from Guémappe on May 3rd, threatened to cut through the base of the great German salient.

Naturally, the German High Command could not permit the Guémappe operation to proceed so long as any strength remained in their Empire. They massed more guns and more of the forces of their grand reserve in the Cambrai area. When at last even their great reserve was in danger of exhaustion they brought guns and men from the Russian front.

As the Russian Commander-in-Chief, General Alexeieff, explained to his officers, scarcely any German artillery of importance was left to hold back the disorganised Russian armies. All the German active and reserve troops were moved westward. Their place in the eastern theatre of war was supplied by Landwehr and Landsturm troops, with shattered active divisions, that were merely sent into Russia to recuperate and train their new young drafts.

[French official photograph.

GERMAN PRISONERS IN A CROWDED "CAGE" ON THE WESTERN FRONT.

Sir Douglas Haig's statement of captures by the British during the month of April, 1917, reported 19,343 German prisoners, of whom 393 were officers. Between April 16th, when their offensive began, and April 30th, the French took over 22,000 prisoners, bringing the German losses through capture alone to more than 41,000 men. Letters found on them testified to general depreciation of moral in the troops in the German front line.

BATTLE OF THE SAPPERS.
Where the ground won by the British neared the new German line, working parties sometimes came into contact, when picks and shovels were promptly exchanged for bombs and rifles.

In this way, the German High Command brought absolutely the whole of the sound fighting forces, in its army of six million men, against the British front of battle and the French front of battle. The British troops at Guémappe, notwithstanding, succeeded in pressing back the most intense concentration of enemy forces. South of the Cambrai road, at a distance of about a mile from the Sensée River, the Germans were imbedded in three quarries and a triangular wood, all connected with each other by means of tunnels, and likewise provided with underground galleries running to the Sensée brook.

The fighting in Triangle Wood was extremely arduous. The German garrison resisted hard and steadily, and was driven out slowly. But the troops in the three quarries were of poorer quality. After a mere show of battle, consisting of a few spurts of machine-gun fire and some disconnected bombing, they endeavoured to withdraw to Vis, and came under a formidable British barrage. Most of them, it was reckoned, were killed.

The victorious British troops then crossed the Sensée River, south of Vis, and, swinging their right wing along the Guémappe-Chérisy road, stormed into Chérisy village. So easy were the first stages of this advance that one English battalion had no casualties. The success was, how-

Chérisy won and lost

ever, only a prelude to main battles, for the German position at this point was extremely strong. The trenches were heavily held, as also were two difficult sunken roads which had been converted into lines of machine-gun forts. In addition, the narrow valley of the Sensée brook, that ran across the new British front immediately behind the village, formed a very formidable obstacle.

On May 3rd the British advanced troops broke clean through the village, fought across the river, and began to progress towards the rear communications of the Fontaine-Bullecourt-Riencourt-Quéant salient. Thereupon, the

German Commander brought up an overwhelming counter-attacking force, and from woods, hollows, and tunnels sent them, in convergent mass, storming against the new temporary British line.

Though the fresh German reserves greatly outnumbered the advanced British forces, they could not easily recover Chérisy. They did not have everything their own way. S.O.S. signals went up from the British outposts, and, in answer to these signals, a blasting British barrage fell upon the German multitudes. Yet in some places the enemy came through the fire in sufficient force to press back the British troops.

STERN STRUGGLE IN THE FORTIFIED OPPY WOOD.
Never before had the machine-gun been employed in trees on any such scale as by the Germans in defending Oppy Wood. The British troops, however, fought their way despite the tangled wire stretched from bole to bole, and of the firing from above in the trees and from the veritable warren of machine-gun pits which had been established in the ground below.

Chérisy was lost, and soon afterwards the Germans recovered the strong point of Cavalry Farm, lying east of Guémappe, and almost as tragically famous, for the times it changed hands, as was the mill by Gavrelle.

Except for the enemy's tunnels, the ground that was given up by the English forces was of no value. It was wholly exposed to gun fire and unprotected by trenches, save for fragments of shallow ditches that had been wrecked by the opposing artilleries. Sir Edmund Allenby relied, in this kind of open field warfare, more upon his guns than upon his men. His method was to use fewer

Allenby's open field tactics

troops than did the enemy, while bringing a heavier gun fire to bear upon the great counter-attacking masses he provoked into action.

The additional guns employed by the enemy at the beginning of May did not increase his fire power proportionately to their number. Many of the new pieces were needed to replace the batteries which the British gunners had rooted out with remarkable accuracy. In one part of the field, where three German batteries were grouped, two of them were completely destroyed by British counter-battery fire, and the third was badly damaged. Therefore, when the German infantry came back to the exposed ground between Chérisy and Cavalry Farm, they had again to suffer terribly, until they could construct fresh earthworks and excavate new dug-outs.

Night and day they were bombarded, as they laboured in the open fields; then, by a nocturnal attack delivered by the British troops along the Arras-Cambrai road, on May 12th, 1917, Cavalry Farm was again recovered, together with twelve hundred yards of German trenches. West and north-west of Chérisy village the British regiments slowly gained more **Amazing German** ground by slight pushes, but no further **tunnel system** general assault was delivered for many weeks.

One of the reasons for this was that the extraordinary strength of the southern end of the Hindenburg systems had been revealed in the intense fighting around the Sensée brook salient. The German stand was based upon two continuous tunnels, placed about a hundred yards apart, and apparently extending for many miles like the underground electric railways of London. There were innumerable exits to each tunnel, and an unparalleled number of sunken concrete machine-gun redoubts. A rush across one of the tunnels was usually ineffective. German reinforcements were sent, in continual streams along the subterranean galleries, against both sides of the attacking force. At the same time the main masses of German reserves came out into the open, and stormed against the British front.

For the purpose of grinding down the enemy's strength Sir Douglas Haig decided it was wisest merely to nibble at the strong, completed path of the Hindenburg tunnel system, and induce the enemy to counter-attack in the open. At Fontaine-lez-Croisilles the tunnel system was as perfect as it was at Bullecourt. In the battle of May 3rd the English regiments, on the Fontaine section of the Sensée line, stormed forward at dawn, and captured all the enemy's first zone of defences, including the important observation position known as the Hump.

Then they carried six hundred yards along the first Hindenburg line and took Fontaine Wood, north of the village. The Germans, however, remained in the south and south-east trenches and occupied the sunken roads west of Fontaine.

Also, near the wood on its southern side there was a very strong system of hostile defences, and all the ground which the Germans lost was pounded in fearful fashion by a barrage of heavy shell-fire. The British detachments in the wood obtained contact with the forces in Chérisy, but the enemy remained pocketed along the western side of the Sensée brook and immediately below it, and made the most of the cover afforded by the sunken roads.

When the British advanced forces were weakened by the tremendous barrage, the new German shock troops crept forward in the converging movements of which they were excessively proud. These "stosstruppen" were regarded by themselves as being a great improvement upon the older storming troops. In the original German plan there were one or two battalions of shock troops to an entire German army. Afterwards numerous new battalions of these troops were formed out of able-bodied unmarried men, youngish married men without children, bad characters of the regiments, and even convicts, with unusual strength of body. First, each German Army Corps was given a battalion of shock troops. Then one battalion was allotted to each division, and at very critical points **German shock** brigades of shock troops seem at **troops method** times to have been employed.

The method was bad, and was not adopted by the British and French armies. All the attacking infantry of the Western Allies were shock troops. The effect of this element of Ludendorff's reorganisation in the western theatre of war was to empty the main body of eight thousand men in every division of its most powerful fighting men. The general quality was much reduced, while the men who were regarded as the cement of each battalion were

BRITISH INFANTRY CAPTURE A GERMAN BATTERY AT THE POINT OF THE BAYONET.
Early in the April offensive some British troops rushed a battery which the enemy, not expecting so determined an assault just then, had left posted in the open. As the attackers got up to the battery with the bayonet the gunners threw up their hands. Only the captain refused to surrender, and fought to the last. The victorious British captured six field-guns on this occasion—the first taken in open warfare since 1914.

DESOLATION WROUGHT THROUGH RUTHLESS INVASION.

[British official photographs.

View of Puisieux as it appeared when re-won for France; (in oval) the road into Puisieux and (top) wrecked houses of the town. The photographs indicate in graphic fashion the ruin which desolated the French countryside from which the invading Germans had been driven.

removed, and exposed to greater wastage than the less valuable main force.

The shock troops were an expedient of desperation. From Fresnoy to Bullecourt parcels of the enlarged Prussian Guard were sandwiched between ordinary divisions, with a view to supplying the strength that had been sapped by the formation of shock troops. Other German divisions, who had proved themselves finer men than the best of the Guards, were also sandwiched between the ordinary masses of German soldiers. Yet, as nearly all the best divisions had their shock battalions, which were terribly shattered by the incessant counter-attacks they conducted, there ensued a natural and widespread decline in the fighting quality of the picked divisions as well as of the ordinary divisions.

Never in all their history had the German tribes been so winnowed of their strength as they were in the prolonged operations along the rivers of Artois. At Fontaine the German shock troops succeeded at heavy cost in holding the village and pressing the British battalions back. Nevertheless, the British retained the supreme advantage of the possession of the high observation point known as the Hump.

Immediately after the battle **Intense bombardment** of May 3rd, Sir Edmund Allenby **of Fontaine** massed an enormous weight of artillery south-east of Arras. Employing the dominating height as a permanent fire-control position, and sending up squadrons of machines to assist in discovering hostile battery sites and movements in the enemy's rear, the British Army commander broke up the Hindenburg system round Fontaine by a fortnight of intense bombardment. The artillery of Sir Hubert Gough's Fifth Army strongly assisted in the work of shattering the German front between Fontaine and Bullecourt.

The enemy's main communication tunnel was the supreme masterpiece in modern military engineering. It was lined as comfortably as the hall of a new dwelling-house, with countless alcoves, containing sleeping bunks, shelves for rifles, small arms ammunition, and bomb supplies. Electric light was employed in lavish fashion, and many dynamos were fitted to supply fresh air even in the event of the machine-gun shafts being blown in by British shells. Great underground caverns were connected with the main tunnel, into which were also built concreted shafts, running outward to enable machine-guns to be thrust up into the shell holes of No Man's Land on one side, and shell holes in the rear of the tunnel on the other side. In some cases the protective wire was of the marvellous depth of six hundred yards. It was arranged in a zigzag pattern, so that any attacking force, seeking the line of least resistance, would become enmeshed in an angle lined with the machine-gun positions extending in the tunnel. Mole warfare was developed by the Germans to its extreme possibilities.

It was only when the British troops reached the main Hindenburg tunnel, largely constructed by British, French, and Russian prisoners of war and **Weakness of** Belgian and French deportees, that they **strength exposed** could appreciate the basis of the early boasts of invincibility made by Hindenburg and Ludendorff. During the battles of April and May the German High Command sacrificed men by the hundred thousand in order to win time to complete the construction of the great tunnel and the various subsidiary underground galleries connected with the gigantic rabbit run.

Like the formation of hundreds of battalions of storm troops, the scheme of the great tunnel and its subsidiary works was a confession of general weakness. The German troops as a whole would not face the British gun fire. Their own commanders thought that they would break unless they were comforted by some new protective invention that promised to save them from the suffering they had endured on the Somme.

The great tunnel seems to have been at first a successful means of reviving the confidence of the German soldier. Many of the numerous prisoners captured by the British Army became, after they recovered from fear of instant reprisals for the way in which British prisoners were treated by the enemy, as full of proud confidence in the resisting power of the Hindenburg tunnel as their comrades used to be of the attacking power of their national armies.

It was, therefore, one of the main objects of Sir Douglas Haig and his commanders of the Third and Fifth Armies to prove to the German ordinary soldier that the Hindenburg tunnel was merely a trap for rabbit-hearted men.

Between Fontaine and Bullecourt the heaviest British artillery poured hundreds of thousands of the new British high-explosive shell upon the tunnelled line. The effect was terrifying.

Deep as the German garrisons had burrowed, they could not stay far below ground for a fortnight. In shifts they had to man their trenches and serve in their machine-gun forts. Many of them were blasted out of existence. Very many more were reduced by varying degrees of shell-shock into hopeless, human wrecks or enfeebled, nervous hospital cases.

For ten days and nights the overwhelming parks of British artillery played incessantly upon the surface and surroundings of the tunnel. Concreted and heavily-banked pits, enormous zones of thick wire, deep and well-timbered dug-outs, and reveted fort lines vanished in the smoke of hurricanes of shell. Where aerial photographs first revealed the most intricate system of defences that military engineers could construct, there remained at last only a tortured stretch of brown, beaten, and featureless earth.

Great were the British gunners, and the men who trained them, and the men and women who worked for them. Besides the grind of incessant labour, at sustained topmost speed, with the air continually in concussion, and the fumes of the charges blowing into mouth and eyes, the gunners had to share most **Incomparable** of the battle with the infantrymen. They **British gunners** escaped usually the agony of thirst and the weakness of hunger, with machine-gun fire and hand-bomb explosions. Yet their foes tried to smother them with gas shells containing the newest poisons, to put them out of action with shrapnel, and destroy them and their guns with concentrated bursts of high explosive.

As the Germans possessed high-velocity guns that could have bombarded Dover from Calais, any former British recruit that enlisted in the Royal Garrison or Field Artillery, to escape the ordeal of the Infantry, must have been sadly disappointed. All held to their wearing,

BRITISH RAID ON GERMAN TRENCHES.

Night raiding of the enemy trenches was a constant feature of the fighting on the western front between the operations on a more extended scale. In this picture a raiding party is shown after it has reached its objective. Some of the soldiers are bombing the German trenches on the left, while in the foreground a couple of their comrades are seen to be shepherding three prisoners towards the British line.

perilous labour. The German foot soldier wished to shoot or strangle his gunners. The British soldier wanted to worship his protectors, but contented himself with joking at them as he passed, and offering them a cigarette if, by a miracle of forgetfulness or economy, he had one left as he came back from the trenches.

Experienced as the British infantryman was in the effect of high explosive, he was amazed when he saw what his guns had done between Fontaine and Bullecourt. At times the German expenditure of munitions was only one-tenth of that of the British. Apparently, they did not lack shell, but had to be frugal in the matter of guns. When taking over supreme control of all German forces, during the battles of the Somme, Ludendorff and Hindenburg had promised to double their artillery by the spring of 1917.

Superior British gun power

They had not done so. Ludendorff was considerably inferior in gun power to Sir Douglas Haig, though he showed some progress since the days of Falkenhayn. Either he was still bent upon an offensive in another direction, upon saving his material and guns as much as

[Canadian War Records.
SETTING A TRENCH-MORTAR IN POSITION FOR FIRING.
Directly our infantry had rushed a position previously hammered by their guns, they reorganised and consolidated it, converting parados into parapet, and arming it with machine-guns and trench-mortars.

possible and storing shell, or his final combing out of German productive labour had prevented his munition factories from carrying out his artillery programme. The latter appeared the more probable.

All the German dictator had to fear was that important American forces would arrive before Sir Douglas Haig was constrained, by exhaustion, to a standstill. In these circumstances the German High Command must have employed all its available artillery power on the western front in order to support all its available infantry power. Consequently, it may be concluded that the munition workers of Great Britain had surpassed all the productive energies which German workers could devote to supply their men along the British front of battle.

This did not mean that the munition factories of Great Britain had excelled in output the German factories. Germany still remained the master industrial country of Europe. Against her were the refined and most expert mechanics, male and female turners, chemists, and engineers of France, with the larger part of the engineering plant and personnel of the industrial regions of the United States, and all the male and female munition workers of England, Scotland, Wales, and the Belfast nook of Ulster. This fact

deserves to be kept in perpetual remembrance. Great Britain was only one of three great Powers who, in combination, defeated the possessors of the Lorraine iron mines, the Lorraine coal-field, the vast Westphalian coal-field, the smaller Saxony coal-fields, and the large coal-fields in German, Russian, and Austrian Silesia.

British sea power it was that originally tapped the industrial resources of the United States, the iron mountains of Spain, and the British and French colonial ores. Notwithstanding this means of increasing the native resources of Great Britain, France, and Italy, the fact remained that Germany alone was stronger in warlike productive power than Great Britain was.

On the other hand, Ludendorff had to recognise that practically the entire world was against him. The only foreign help he received, in direct military material, was derived from the iron mountains of Sweden and to a less extent the iron fields of Norway. He was compelled to economise in gun power, and chiefly for this reason he extended the tunnel tactics in defence which Falkenhayn had really originally invented.

The battle in the Fontaine salient became a decisive duel between the gun and the tunnel. The gun won. In the early morning of May 20th, 1917, the British infantry advanced between Fontaine and Bullecourt, and carried the first Hindenburg line. When night fell the attacking forces were firmly in the support line above the tunnel.

English and Scottish battalions went into the wreckage. They met with no opposition from the fire trench, because no fire trench remained. A scattering machine-gun fire from the tunnel outlets delayed, for a time, the British troops, yet before noon they had driven right across the flanking systems, between the enemy's first and second lines, and reached the alley ways in the support line.

Thereupon the German commander launched his reserves in open warfare according to the ordinary Ludendorff plan. The fresh German troops fought well, and held the Englishmen and Scotsmen back until the afternoon, while the German artillery no longer practised economy, but ravaged the lost territory and the British rear with whirlwinds of shell.

In the meantime the British gunners had obtained information of the positions of their advanced artillery. In the evening the undulating land for miles along the British front again flamed and thundered, and, assisted by their overpowering barrage, the British troops obtained a firm footing in the last German trenches and consolidated their victory on the Hindenburg line.

The 49th German Reserve Division, composed mainly of Poles who garrisoned the Fontaine salient, was in such a condition that officers and men did not care whether they lived or died. The division had come to France from Rumania in February, and after being in the trenches for twenty-one days the troops were so dazed by the shock of the continuous bombardment that those who escaped and were captured staggered along the road like drunken men, and were so spent that they did not want food when placed in the wired cage.

The next day, when they were able to talk, they explained that they had never slept at night. The garrison remained in their tunnel, with a few sentries posted at intervals on the open ground. The sentries, however, became nervous, and frequently in the afternoon brought the troops up the steep stairways from the caverns on a false alarm. After the battle of May 20th only two thousand yards of the Hindenburg tunnel remained in the possession of the Germans between Fontaine and Bullecourt. What was of more importance, the new undergrounds of confidence supplied by Ludendorff to his troops had been shattered by British gun fire. Closely connected with this result was the magnificent work of the Australians, Englishmen, and Scotsmen in Bullecourt, which deserves a special chapter.

Hindenburg tunnel failure

Back at Victoria for his first furlough.

Flowers for the brave at Charing Cross.

Soldiers bound for the front leaving Euston in volunteer motor transports for the boat trains.

Scenes of poignant joy and pathos enacted at the great railway=stations of London.

Cornish prize-winner for harrowing, driving, and costume.

Carriage-washers on the Great Eastern Railway.

[British official photograph

Handling long steel bars in a shipyard.

Wheeling coke to tracks at Coventry gasworks.

Cleaning brewery vats at Burton-on-Trent.

Helpmates at home for heroes abroad: Some of the many diversities of national service wherei

Carrying sacks of coke in a London gasworks.

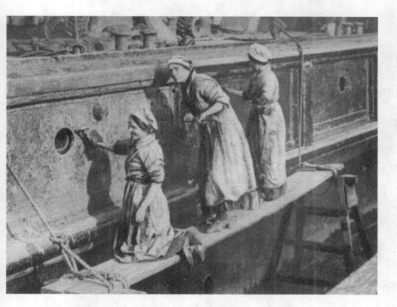

Cleaning and painting a trawler salvaged at Rainham.

Lumber-women sawing pit-props near Ludlow.

Coal-women on a daily round in Glasgow.

Bricklayer's labourer in an English village.

women quickly proved their adaptability and endurance, and released men for military service.

[Drawing.]

Welcome guests in a stately home of England: Wounded soldiers at Longleat Hall, the seat of the Marquis of Bath.

CHAPTER CLXXXVII.

NATIONAL PSYCHOLOGY AND SOCIAL CHANGES.

By Harold Owen.

A New Experience for Mankind—All " Precedents " Valueless—New and Magnified Factors—Our Unpreparedness—The End of an Era
—The Unknown—The Red Dawn—An Awed Nation—The Crowd before the Palace—Hasty Provisioning—Five-Pound Notes
and Gold Shortage—Holiday-makers Stampede—The Veil of Secrecy and the Growth of Rumour—" Business as Usual " Folly—
Lord Rosebery's Plea for War Derbys—The New-comers in the City Trains—The " Nut " : What he Was and What he Became—
Changed Outlook of Society—National Slackness—A Nation without Leaders—Our Immunity from the Realities of War—
The First Wounded—A Quick Acceptance of the Horrors of War—The Reaction to a False Gaiety—The First Zepps—" Full
Moon " in London—Changes in the Small Things of Life—" Do you Take Sugar ? "—Closer Mingling of the Classes—A Blow
to Snobbery—Decrease of Drunkenness—Disappearance of the Tramp and Gutter Merchant—Trains that Did Not Run—Travel
Stopped—The Vain Lure of Holiday Posters—Passports—The Cocaine Habit—Fortune-telling Epidemic—The New Class—
" Equality of Sacrifice "—The War as a Boon—The Things that Could Not be Done—The Things that Had to be Done Without—
A Nation of Gardeners—Spade Work in the Suburbs—The War and the Homes—The Mansions of the Rich—Migrations to London
—" To Let "—Broken Hearts and Broken Lives—War Weddings—New Buildings Everywhere, but No New Homes—Canteens
for Women and Crèches for Babes—Less Cooking at Home—Domestic Shopping—Children Left to Themselves—Increase of
Juvenile Crime, but Decrease of all Serious Crime—No Murder " Sensations "—Decrease in Litigation—Changes to Come.

LOOKING back on those fateful days of August, 1914, the imagination and memory must be struck by one outstanding feature : the disparity between the great event then looming upon us and the outward signs of it. One chapter in the history of mankind had been closed, and the book of Fate lay open before our eyes, but with the record still to be written upon it. What would that record be ? To a few, a very few, the record was to be brief. There were prophets who said that it would "all be over in six months," and their confidence was even unchecked by the recollection that the same prophecies of time, money, and men required to bring another war to its conclusion had been made and falsified. But these baleful optimists, soon to realise how greatly they were to be confounded, were few and for the most part unheeded. No man, however ignorant of the rudiments of military knowledge, or of those larger considerations which might determine the course of Armageddon, could fail to reflect that there was about to burst upon the world something so

ST. GEORGE FOR ENGLAND.

St. George's Day, 1917, was celebrated throughout England by much charitable work. At Windsor Queen Mary drove through the town and bought flowers wholesale for hospitals, accepting a bouquet from the Festival Committee on her way.

different from everything that had ever preceded it as to amount to almost a new experience for mankind, in which all " precedents " would be valueless and even positively misleading. The mere extent of the theatre of war—even as the scene was then set upon the stage of Europe—rebuked all *a priori* reasoning and theory, for though the tide of battle had flooded the same countries in other wars, the world of Napoleon was not that of to-day. Then the resources of mankind for its own destruction were small indeed. The armies were but a fragment of the peoples engaged in war, great battles that settled the fate of Europe (as our forefathers thought, just as we, perhaps as mistakenly, hope that this most dire tragedy will settle the fate of mankind, in the end beneficently, for countless generations to come) were decided on a few acres of ground between sunrise and sunset. Then the resources of money and material were as limited as the armies engaged, and then the powers of offence and of destruction were on the same small scale, so that the Marquess of Anglesey could almost see trundling across the ground the solid shot which a moment afterwards made him exclaim : " By God, duke, I've lost my leg!" and brought from the Iron Duke, sitting his horse but hardly turning his head away from the battle that was to settle Europe, the laconic reply: "By God, have you?" But looming over us now was something not to be measured by the mind of man, with every factor that was a delusive "precedent" magnified enormously—the first war of *nations* since civilised man had deputed the defence of his countries to standing armies.

The first war of nations

The territory to be fought over, limited as it then was compared to its future extension, had been fought over before, in little patches that the mapmakers had shown on the map with signs of crossed swords—here a battle-ground and there a battle-ground, in clusters here (as in Flanders, that predestined cockpit) and there in simple isolation. But, though the veil had not then lifted to disclose to us how this dire event would shape (in battle-lines that extended from sea to sea across all Europe, so that the mapmaker's crossed swords would look like so

SORTING THE SOLDIERS' POST IN THE GENERAL POST OFFICE.
Men of the Royal Engineers instructing women at the G.P.O. in the sorting of letters addressed to men on military service. In June, 1917, the Postmaster-General stated that his department dealt every week with nearly twenty million letters and parcels to and from members of the British fighting forces.

many thousand miles of barbed-wire or chevaux de frise), we knew that the territory involved was the least instructive factor, except in technical military considerations, in the whole sum. For it was not the miles that stretched from the Ural Mountains to the Belgian coast, from the Baltic to the South Coast of France, or the vast oceans that we should have to guard to preserve the highways of our Empire—it was not these geographical factors that would decide the magnitude and the intensity of the coming struggle. What counted most were the armies to be engaged—the millions who would shake the earth with their marching, the amazing intricacies of modern life and economic interests, and, above all, the actual powers of destruction that had been perfected and increased since the last great scourge of war in Europe. Even since the Boer War—that trivial incident, though rich in consequences, that was then called "a dress rehearsal for Armageddon"—two military factors had arisen that were, in practice, totally new to mankind: the submarine,

which had only emerged from the experimental stage since the Treaty of Vereeniging, and the aeroplane. That is to say, to the old elements of sea and land were now to be added two imponderable factors—the element of the air, and the new element (in a military sense) of under the sea.

But, above all these material magnifications and complications of all precedents and experience, there was the moral and political factor of our unreadiness for the bursting storm. War is not *our* national industry—it has never been, except during the progress of a war, our national or political preoccupation, and Armageddon burst upon us as an incredible thing. When the history of these years comes finally to be written, and the judgment of the historian is mellowed by time so that he can see the essentials clearly, perhaps that which will most astonish the generations that will read of these days is the contrast furnished by our general, national, and political preoccupation with everything but Armageddon and the imminence of that calamity. Not until it was, so to speak, thrust under the noses of the statesmen did they give any indication to the nation whose destinies they largely controlled that even its possibility was present in their minds. As to the nation itself, it could not learn what it had not been taught, and obviously a country which was so habituated in Parliament to all deprecation of "provocative armaments," and which never heard any warning uttered half so loudly as the voices of protest that drowned the warning—a nation accustomed for more than a decade to seeing military problems debated in a thin House of Commons by experts who were thought to be cranks and were stigmatised as Jingoes—such a nation, lulled into a false sense of security by its public instructors, accustomed to hear every problem debated to rags except the problem of national defence, and somnolent with prosperity, peace, and plenty, and politically active only in internal dissensions—such a nation was manifestly unprepared for the red dawn of Armageddon.

Yet, the moment it became probable, all saw that it had been inevitable. To the shocked mind leaped all sorts of recollections of symptoms, warnings, and ominous truths. In a flash those who had been derided became suddenly right, those who had scoffed became silent. Perhaps our political history does not afford a more bitter irony than was furnished by this swift and terrible disillusionment of those idealists who had so largely affected our policy during the critical years when our unreadiness for Armageddon was being so sedulously prepared. Perhaps never has there been such a contrast as that provided by the intensity of our party political "warfare" and our obliviousness to the shadows cast before by the coming war of the world.

Suddenness of the storm

The suddenness of it all—the first mutterings of the coming storm passing so quickly into the onset of the storm itself—awed the nation. It all seemed incredible, yet it was all true. It had been talked of as something remote in time and even in probability—yet here it was. It "could never be," it "must not be," "it would be a crime if ever such a thing came to pass "—so the politicians' clichés had run, to take our minds off its probability—and now, under lowering August skies that seemed heavy with Fate, we had, almost in the twinkling of an eye, to realise that it had come, and that the last days of one great era of mankind were yesterday and the day before, and the first days of a new era of mankind, be it what it might be, were to-morrow and the day after. To some there was an overpowering awe even in the reflection that it had come in our time—that we, even we, were to live in the most majestically critical days and years of the history of man—that it had come to us and to our generation to stand out in the pages of history

SOCKS FOR THE TROOPS.
Lady Byron (left) enlisted the aid of many helpers in providing socks for sailors and soldiers.

QUEEN MARY'S BIRTHDAY GIFT FOR SAILORS AND SOLDIERS.
In celebration of Queen Mary's birthday, May 28th, 1917, the many branches of her Needlework Guild in the United Kingdom and Canada sent a " shower of gifts " to her Majesty for the sailors and soldiers. Over one hundred thousand gifts of all kinds—games, pipes, walking-sticks, writing materials, blankets, etc.—were received by Queen Mary at St. James's Palace on behalf of the fighting forces.

pride by victories, preparing in peace only for the last great effort that was to establish for her the hegemony of the world. And the sudden and supreme infamy of the invasion of Belgium, with Visé burning as soon as the grey hordes had crossed the frontier and violated the territory of a little nation trusting in Germany's word and relying on even her protection, luridly showed from the first moments of the war what we were now confronted with—a Power mighty in its preparations, united as one man in its policy of conquest (the success of which was then doubted by no individual German, however much individual Germans may have come to " repudiate " aims of conquest when those aims had been finally frustrated)—and a Power

as the generation that bore upon its shoulders the burdens of the greatest tragedy ever brought upon mankind by man.

To all, even the least reflective and imaginative, there came a sense of dismay before the vast uncertainties that stretched onward. For it was now seen how true it was that Germany had been working to this end. We had been warned not to heed the warnings—we had been told that Germany's aim was merely an economic expansion, that she had no rivalry with us except in the markets of the world, that our Free Trade policy was in itself a bulwark of peace, that we must distrust even the evidence of our eyes and of our ears in order not wickedly to contemplate as a possibility that which had now become a reality.

But once the great shadow fell across the world men realised, in a flash, in what a cave of delusion we had been living. The course of the diplomatic events of those last few days of peace showed us a Germany true to the revelation of Germans themselves—a hectoring, bullying race, aggrandised by conquest and swollen in

that had cast behind it all considerations of humanity to alleviate the horrors of war, but was prepared from the very first day to march through terror and "frightfulness": to triumph—the triumph of barbarism over justice and right.

It was clear that this was to be a war *à outrance*— a war, if necessary, to exhaustion—a war that must extend as the weeks and months went on until it embraced practically the whole world, for **Elemental principles** there could only be two sides in such a **at stake** struggle for elemental things : the side of right and the side of wrong. So, in those heavy August days —the culminating days of a feverish era of unbridled luxury and of great industrial prosperity, and yet of acute and constant social unrest, of violent theories and fantastic ideals, of fads and follies in every department of life, of weak statesmanship and of political turbulence about every issue except that great issue which was now to dwarf all others—in those sinister August days men peered into the future as into the unknown, into a future without

MR. LLOYD GEORGE AT A "POTATO SPRAYING."
The Prime Minister (left) and Sir George Riddell (third) witnessing Mr. Waldron Rose (right), of the Food Production Department, demonstrating the spraying of potato crops with sulphate of copper.

horizons. There we were, in a few fateful days set "in the foremost files of time," and the future stretched onward veiled in the dark uncertainty that was lit only by the red gleams of war. All our little puny dissensions became suddenly irrelevant, all our fixed ideas came loose from their moorings, all our plans became suddenly suspended, nothing seemed normal, and men knew, though they could not say how, that nothing in the world as they knew it would be quite the same again. We held our breath—waiting. We held our breath so that we did not even cheer in the streets.

It has been necessary to recall some of those wider impressions and memories of those days in order to see the small things in their true perspective. How did we then greet the red dawn? In silence and in awe. There were no boisterous crowds in the streets, no war fever, no Jingo demonstrations, no paradings of high-spirited crowds bawling defiance of the enemy. Round Buckingham Palace, on the eve of war, a respectful crowd had assembled—a quiet, orderly, much-moved crowd, that had gathered there, as at the very heart and hearth of our kingdom and Empire, to give their token of loyalty and duty, and to strike as soon as possible the note of national unity. They sang "Rule, Britannia" lustily but not boastfully, they cheered the King, they sang his anthem, and quietly dispersed.

Note of national unity

Whitehall became suddenly busy, and lights shone in the Admiralty until the dawn came to extinguish them, and the new War Office, now dealing with its first war, looked big and apt for its task. But the outward signs of war were not greatly to be seen—only because the signs were hidden. One vituperative writer has spoken of "the blue funk" of the nation during those first few days. He libelled the race to which he does not belong. There was no "blue funk," and no sign of it, even to the man looking for it. For the hasty buying of provisions, which went on quite on a small scale, was due not to panic, but to the simple fact that men and women were suddenly confronted with something utterly outside either their experience or their belief, and they did not know what might happen. Gold had become suddenly scarce, and amongst the minor comedies of those days was the difficulty of changing a five-pound note. One member

of Parliament, wishing to get home to the North in his Rolls-Royce car, suddenly found that he had no petrol and no money to buy it, with the banks closed over the Bank Holiday, and he then could not change the five-pound notes he had borrowed from a friend for his railway journey. Many little devices were invented for circumventing the new state of affairs, so that men would go to a post-office and buy five postal-orders of a pound each, and then change them—one by one. For there was a pitfall even in that trick, as one man discovered who, having been told of the innocent dodge, promptly handed in his five postal-orders all at once, only to receive his original five-pound note back

THE PRIME MINISTER TRIES HIS HAND.
Mr. Lloyd George directing the nozzle of the potato sprayer which Mr. Waldron Rose carried. During the 1917 campaign for increasing the home-grown food in Britain these potato sprayers were widely employed.

again. Such incidents as these gave people a distorted idea of what might happen. Thus they hurried away from the seaside — especially the South-East Coast—and countermanded their lodgings, so that the first economic effect of the war was felt by the hotel-keepers and the lodging-house keepers of Margate, Ramsgate, and Broadstairs—which soon were to be full of refugees flying in fishing-smacks from Ostend, until Ramsgate had its little harbour full of boats marked "O" on their brown sails, with a yacht or two of prosperous Belgians among the craft.

Arrival of first refugees

In the upheaval and uncertainty of those early days there was a little hasty buying of foodstuffs—and many sides of bacon purchased on or about August 6th were unfit for human consumption before the hot days had passed. But this was not panic buying; there was no lack of faith then in the power of the Navy to maintain our food supplies; but Armageddon had come, and no man knew what was going to happen next, and rumours of collapse in the City and the sudden shortage of gold had made people here and there determined to be "prepared for the worst."

The veil of secrecy that had fallen upon all movements of Army and Navy helped to bring forth a crop of rumours. On the second day of the war "a decisive battle" had been fought in the North Sea. Some said the German Navy was at the bottom, others said that all our Dreadnoughts had been either sunk or damaged, and there was no ground whatever for the rumour except that of the uninstructed expectation that, naturally, as soon as war began, the two Fleets would come into action, for there was then no public knowledge of the mine-fields the Germans were laying to keep our Navy at arm's length. Then came stories—told under the strictest pledge of secrecy—that troop trains were rushing through the night to take out the Expeditionary Force, and by the time the official announcement was made that our gallant little Army, hastily and secretly shipped across the Channel, had entered upon its high ordeal at Mons, the

Rumour running mad Russian rumour had acquired a vitality that no denial seemed able to affect and which positively throve on incredulity. Yet there was no Russian army rushing through the night in crowded trains from the north of England to be taken hastily over to France to aid our little army there. The Battle of Tannenberg had not then been fought, and we did not then know that Russia needed all the men she could mobilise and arm for the urgent defence of her own soil.

But soon enough the nation settled down to the great fact of war, and began to take in the truth that we had started on an enterprise that would need all our fortitude and patience. Hence, perhaps, arose the mistaken cry of "Business as usual." People argued, no doubt, that it would be fine evidence of our national self-confidence if we were to go on as though nothing in particular was happening, and allow our national life to be as little disturbed as possible.

This mood was perhaps one of the most dangerous and undesirable reactions from the early days of sobriety and bewilderment. For it afterwards became clear enough that our politicians had missed the moment when they could have welded the nation right away into one single aim : the war. Hence the " Business as usual " mood, following upon a reluctant acceptance of Lord Kitchener's prediction of a three years' war (which for long was wrongly interpreted as meaning that we could

WOUNDED SOLDIERS AT A LONGLEAT BEAUTY SPOT.
Among the many owners of " the stately homes of England " who placed their mansions at the service of the wounded were the Marquis and Marchioness of Bath, who established a Relief Hospital at Longleat.

go about our business quite leisurely, as " time was on our side "), succeeded to a mood in which anything could have been done by the Government with the people. Thus, the question of compulsory service came to be agitated in an atmosphere unfavourable to its immediate adoption, and the opposition to it had had time to consolidate long before it was a concrete proposal ; whereas, the bold policy of National Service, if propounded or even authoritatively foreshadowed from the first day of war, would have materially and favourably affected the psychology of the nation.

As things were, it took the nation a long time to disabuse itself of the leisurely policy indicated by the cry of " Everything as usual," so that, even in the spring of 1915, a man of such general discernment as Lord Rosebery could be found protesting against the abandonment of the Derby on the ground that horse-races were run in the year of Waterloo !

Yet the golf-links, which later on were to grow potatoes, were already deserted, and the City trains began to tell their tale as the months went on. They were still as crowded as ever. But young men became scarcer, and young women and girls more numerous, so that some- **Last of the dandies** times a carriage on the Underground was to be seen with almost every seat occupied by typists and girl clerks who were returning home from the City, and every strap taken up by men.

From the streets and the haunts of fashion soon disappeared the " nut." The " nut " was the finest flower of youthful male fashion. He was an elegant idler, strenuous only in getting " the last ounce " out of his motor-car. He smoked incessant cigarettes. He cultivated a manner almost effeminate. He made harmonies of neckties and symphonies of socks. Golf was too strenuous for him, and most things " too much fag." His chief attitude to life was to be " fed-up " with everything that imposed any

BY FOUR-IN-HAND ON THE ROAD TO HEALTH.
This party of wounded soldiers, crossing Hammersmith Bridge, was one of many taken by coach from London hospitals to be entertained at Laleham. Such healthful trips relieved the tedium of convalescence.

AGRICULTURAL TRAINING FOR DISCHARGED SOLDIERS.
Lifting and carting potatoes on the land of the Cheshire County College of Agriculture, where a course of general training in agriculture was provided for soldiers who had been released from military service.

response to the "Business as usual" cry, or else by turning their efforts into one of the many and ever increasing channels of supplementary work for the war. Furthermore the response made to voluntary recruiting was large enough to rebuke any generalisation concerning the apathy of the working classes. Clerks and workers rolled up to the flag in far larger numbers than could have been justly expected of a race bred for generations away from the ideal and duty of national defence.

Yet there was amongst all classes a failure to reach the high standard of devotion and concentration to the one supreme task which should have followed from the first outbreak of war—

strain, physical, moral, or mental. To social observers he was quite a perplexing portent, for his advent and presence, an apparently decadent type of masculinism, synchronised with the advent of a strenuous feminism, so that the easiest explanation of both seemed to be that each phenomenon explained the other. He furnished a text for many homilies, and when the "flapper" emerged into the public limelight to keep him company, there did in truth seem every justification for pessimism concerning the future of the race if "nut" and "flapper" were to be the parents of the next generation. Yet, apparently, the "nut" was merely suffering from the general malaise induced by the social and spiritual conditions of the time—conditions which had many manifestations, though a general defiance of "authority" and rebellion against fixed laws and canons in politics, art, religion and morals were the most outstanding features of them all. But the "nut" was not vicious. He was merely "bored" and "fed-up" and "at a loose end" generally, and there was no authority to set his feet on the right path, for **Coming of the young Briton** parental authority, like that of the State, was being flouted and derided at every turn.

And then with the war the "nut" vanished and the Young Briton leapt to life. The call of his race was answered in his blood, and his fripperies dropped from him. He now lies under many a white cross in the fair land of France—shot as he rode his despatch-rider's motor-cycle in those early days of still moving armies, or brought to earth from Icarian flights high in the blue above the smoke and din of the battle-front—so that the despair of many a father's heart became one of the glories of his race.

His case deserves this special and particular mention, for it was possible to generalise more about him than perhaps about any other class. On the whole, Society—the sober leaders of social life—met the change with a corresponding change in its daily routine and outlook. It gave liberally of its wealth to the many funds that sprang into being, it cut down its entertainments, and began to engage in the many subsidiary activities of the war. On the whole, too, the middle classes rose to the emergency —the sons enlisted, the daughters took up V.A.D. work, and the fathers went about their business—either in

LEARNING TO MAKE CHESHIRE CHEESE.
Cheesemaking and general dairy work naturally formed an important part of the curriculum in the Cheshire County College of Agriculture. Preparing and vatting the curd before pressing.

a devotion to the task commensurate with both its magnitude and the supreme issue for mankind that depended upon it. The truth is that the nation was without leaders. It was the day of great events and small men. Events were bigger than the men who had to meet them. There was a lamentable lack of decision in the high places of government, and this irresolution, combined with a wide tolerance for opinions in conflict with the national **Compulsory** purpose and a reluctance to assert the **military service** principle that citizenship could not have its rights without its duties, infected the general body of the nation. The tardy recognition, by the pressure of events, of the need for compulsory military service was practically the first impulse the nation received from its leaders to brace itself for the huge and unaccomplished task, but once that principle was affirmed the nation, as might have been expected from any elementary psychologist, began to adjust its outlook more resolutely to the national peril. Thereafter, the war left its mark more deeply upon contemporary life, and then began to be seen those social changes which were largely due to the increasing stringency of the war.

For it must be remembered, in mitigation of that national slackness, which was so little discouraged by the responsible leaders of the nation, that up to almost the end of the second year of war the nation had had little first-hand acquaintance with the hardships of war. Perhaps the first shock to the laggard imagination was that banner which was hung across the Strand in the first autumn, with a strange device, bidding "Quiet for the wounded"—the first wounded who lay in Charing Cross Hospital, men from Mons and the Marne and the Aisne, the early forerunners of those stricken men who afterwards were to become so familiar in the streets of every town and city in the land. But it is permissible for a contemporary observer to record how strangely and quickly the nation settled down to the war and its horrors. Future generations will undoubtedly wonder what manner of heroic folk they were who lived through those awful days, when each succeeding day brought its own full tale of horror and inhumanity.

The fact is that there was a speedy accommodation of the emotional and moral sense to the horrors of war. Things daily happened that no lurid writer of fiction had ever conceived, or would have had the courage to set down if he had conceived them; yet the theatres were still packed, the restaurants still gay and busy, the trains **Saturation point of** still full of people who talked about the **emotion** commonplaces of life, night clubs increased until the scandal was checked, and things went on pretty much the same while our men were being infected and neglected at Wittenburg and the frequent casualty lists were still being published in full in the newspapers not yet suffering from paper shortage. And perhaps it is a psychological truth that the human heart, saturated with horror and grief, can at length take up no more impressions of pity, but turns to a false gaiety as a deliberate relief from horror.

It must be remembered, however, that for two years the biggest war in history had been waged with little breach of our territorial immunity from it. Scarborough and Hartlepool had been raided before 1914 was out, but though that fact brought the war home to Scarborough and Hartlepool it had no marked effect upon the rest of the nation, though it sent up local recruiting. Zeppelins had appeared north and east, but London was not touched until that May evening in 1915 when three Zeppelins sailed over the North Foreland, in the hardihood of twilight, killed a few women and children in the East of London, and leisurely went home again unscathed. That brought the war home to London, but it still missed the effect of intimidating the nation, which, as the enemy was slow to learn, is so little **London discovers** inclined to panic that its fault is **the moon** rather an excessive belief in its security.

Then came those "Zeppelin nights"—nights of almost Cimmerian gloom, when familiar streets became strange and pedestrians went about with electric torches so discreet and fitful in their gleams as to make them look like glow-worms, and London became as dark as it was in the days of footpads. Among one of the minor curiosities of the time was a notice to a meeting announcing that that night there was "full moon," for the "Zepps" taught the Londoner to esteem the moon and to follow her phases as though he were a dweller in the country-side where streets and illuminants are alike absent.

After the end of the second year of the war it began to tell its tale in the minute things of life. Matches became scarce, so that it almost became "bad form" for one smoker in a train to ask another for a light. The newspapers began to shrink, and then the posters disappeared, and chalked improvisations of the newsvendors became a poor substitute for the aggressive contents bill. Trains were "knocked off" and stations closed, for miles and miles of railway metals were torn up to be sent over to France for the supply lines behind the Western front. Sugar became scarce, and by and by in the teashops the waitresses would offer sugar with every discouragement to take it, and would deposit an inadequate lump if the answer to the question was "Yes"; and "Do you take sugar?"—so

VOLUNTEERS ASSEMBLED ON THE HORSE GUARDS' PARADE FOR INSPECTION BY LORD FRENCH.
In March, 1916, the Volunteer Act of 1863 was revived, and the Volunteer Forces were constituted and recognised for purposes of Home Defence, being placed, in the following December, under the administration of the Territorial Force Associations. Viscount French, in command of the Home Forces, warmly supported the Volunteer movement and held an inspection of eleven thousand of London's Volunteers in Hyde Park.

far from being an aimless if polite question at a five o'clock tea-table—became a very pertinent inquiry indeed.

Private entertaining disappeared altogether, except in a furtive and ashamed fashion, and though the dressmakers were busy, the hoardings told us to wear our old clothes and to economise at Christmas—that third Christmas of the war that all hoped would be the last. Snobbery received a wound that might not prove mortal, but must at least check its vitality. For the even dis-

Disappearing class distinctions tribution of sorrow and sacrifice had very naturally engendered a common human sympathy, and people saw how little some of those social distinctions and observances upon which they had set such store really mattered. And with the " Society " volunteer rubbing shoulders with the working woman in the munition factories, and wealthy people deliberately forgoing the exclusiveness of first-class travel, it was inevitable that there should be a closer mingling of classes, most marked at the beginning of the war, then

WOMEN COOKS WITH THE BRITISH ARMY.
Mess orderlies receiving dinner rations from women cooks. Early in 1917 it was decided to employ women for work where they could release soldiers, and many women cooks were enlisted for service in France.

lapsing back again after the war had become a daily feature, but reappearing again in increasing measure as the war went on and sacrifices mounted high. The trades-men assisted the recoil from snobbery, for they reinforced their appeal that customers should carry their own parcels when practicable by refusing to give any date for delivery when the purchaser would not take his or her own parcel away.

Thus up many a suburban street struggled the professional man who formerly would as soon have thought of carrying home in broad daylight half a ham as going to church in a check suit. Tradesmen became, in fact, very " independent," and take-it-or-leave-it became the order of the day. Errand boys graduated into munition workers, and errand girls straddled on their " bikes," and waitresses appeared in clubs that had never seen a petticoat within their portals, and domestic servants made themselves scarce in more than the colloquial sense. So that Mrs. Brown, emulating her husband with the ham—and even with the loaf from the local baker's—cleaned her front door-

step courageously, and polished up the little brass plate on her front gate which announced " The Geraniums " or " Ivydene," hoping that her neighbours were not looking.

In the theatres evening dress became bad form, just as theatre suppers became simply impossible, owing to the increasing stringency of licensing hours, which also told their tale in the streets, where a drunken man became rarer than unnaturalised Germans still walking freely about. Motors were laid up, or sold to those optimists who still thought motoring would go on for ever. Whisky became more aqueous, and yet with each dilution more expensive, every other month, while club life became almost limited to the luncheon hour and a brief after-dinner gossip.

Letters became rarer, and the post less secure, and the few postmen left were oldish men who cleared the boxes and did the heavier parcel work ; for the postwoman came on the scene, and the telegraph girl kept her company, for telegraph messengers had joined the ranks of industry, receiving a man's wages, and looking forward to the time when their eighteenth birthday would begin for them that process which would make men and soldiers of them.

The tramp disappeared from the country-side, and the casual ward, like the casual labourer, went out of date, never, it is to be hoped, to have resurrection ; so that one might truly say, even after the first six months of war, that there were no poor in England except those who had hardly known want until the war began—the professional men, writers, architects, musicians, and those who flourish only in times of peace as the fine fruits of civilisation, but who are supernumeraries in the days of horrid war and elemental strife.

Railway travel became uncomfortable and expensive, and long-distance trains were deprived of their restaurant-cars, so that travellers provisioned themselves for the journey with packets of home-cut sandwiches and vacuum flasks. Theatrical touring companies endured added dis-comfort to the normal discomforts of their calling, and waited long hours at junctions for slow trains to take them to the " next town," and missed their reserved carriages, and suffered pangs of suspense concerning the safe delivery of their scenery and " effects." On the walls of the railway-stations still lingered the travel bills and pictures, but " Lovely Lucerne " was inaccessible. " Gay Boulogne," alas ! was sad with military hospitals and busy with troops, and did not merely not welcome the traveller, but refused him. Norwegian fiords and Swiss Alps still beckoned from the walls the traveller who could not go near them, and as for the Rhine——! For foreign travel became reserved only for those who had urgent business to cross the seas, and if the submarine menace was not enough in the early days to deter wealthy and middle-aged people from adventuring forth, the increasing stringency of passports and travel permits acted more effectively.

Never since Britain was had so many **Restrictions on** passports been sought as those issued **foreign travel** during the war ; never has the implied protection of *Civis Britannicus Sum* been more valued and coveted, so much so that half the work of the Passport Departments and officials was to prevent a British passport being granted to a Swiss or an " American " who had anglicised a Teuton name.

Travel became increasingly difficult even in the streets of London, for the rationing of petrol to the omnibuses drove many of those vehicles off their routes, establishing queues of waiting passengers along the pavements ; and the same scarcity of petrol limited the number of taxi-cabs, and so brought the hansom cab back on the streets of London. Only three or four years before the war a hansom cab had been solemnly acquired by the London Museum as an exhibit of antiquarian interest, and at auction sales that most typical of London vehicles had often fetched no more than the value of the rubber tyres with which they began to be " shod " during the nineties. Time and the war, however, fetched them out of their hiding-places, and the jingle of the hansom was heard on London streets again, bringing back to many memories of those pleasant days when life went very well in London town, and the trot and jingle of its hansoms on a summer night in the bright West End were the most characteristic sounds of London life.

Holidays there were none, for though the festivals came round with time, they were not marked off in Labour's calendar, and not until the Whitsuntide of the third year of war—a glorious burst of summer after a winter that had protracted itself into the season that should have been spring— was the holiday spirit really manifested or felt. And probably it was this deprivation of the excitements and relief of holiday and travel that accounted for two undesirable developments— that of the cocaine habit and of fortune-telling. The strain of war and the need of some relief and reaction from its burdens and anxieties drove many men and women to those desperate alleviations for mind, body, and soul—drugs and "psychic consolation." The drug habit increased to such an extent that the mere possession of cocaine became an offence, punishable, oddly enough, by the precise penalty attaching to the new "crime" of "treating"—

VOLUNTEERS AT WORK.
Members of London's Corps of Citizens helping to pull a heavy watercart up a hill to their camp.

one hundred pounds' fine and six months' imprisonment. Fortune-tellers were raided and prosecuted by the dozen, but their prosperity still continued unabated, for the worn and anxious heart turned to them for the solace that faith could not give but credulity grasped. And the plentifulness of money still kept the shopping streets thronged.

There were no matchsellers or boot-lace vendors in the gutter, for the war had gathered up even the fringes of humanity and ravelled them into its wonderful garment, and there were no hawkers going from door to door, and no mendicants singing in the suburban streets, and no outcasts sleeping on the Embankment or in "the Arches"—though soldiers on leave who had missed their last train to camp or depot, and who had spent all their money, sometimes wandered up and down rather than present themselves at one of the many hostels for their shelter or Y.M.C.A. recreation huts that sprang up all over the place. Yes, the streets were gay on summer days in war time, with the awnings from the drapers' shops making cool shade for those who shopped to satisfy not their need but their vanities while men were falling every hour for liberty. In

SOLDIERS ON "AGRICULTURAL FURLOUGH."
The soldiers helping the veteran labourers in spreading manure for the crops. In circle: Some of King George's ploughmen at work on the Royal farms at Windsor, during leave granted that they might help in getting as much land as possible under cultivation for the harvest of 1917.

June of 1917 it was possible for an obscure little news paragraph to chronicle the humiliating fact that women had begun to line-up for the summer bargain sales at three o'clock in the morning, and that the crowd that surged round the doors when they were opened at nine smashed the plate-glass windows in their frantic eagerness for " bargains."

A new class had, to some extent, sprung up—a class of Government officials and service contractors—those who dipped their hands into the five, six, and seven millions a day that the war progressively cost. To many the night of August 4th had been the night of doom. At a breath commercial and financial stability or professional position had been blown away, and age became suddenly confronted with penury, with the bitter loss yet to be faced of those young lives which would have stood as a bulwark between it and the worst blows of adversity. Much was said of " equality of sacrifice " as an ideal to be striven for so far as legal obligations could impose it. But what equality of sacrifice could there be between, say, the architect of sixty years of age, whose profession became suddenly a national superfluity, and who, too old to turn to anything else, was yet not too old to have three sons destined to lie under white crosses in France, Mesopotamia, and Salonika ; and the Midland bootmaker on a small scale who soon, perhaps, was taking a Government contract for a million boots, and successfully pleaded before the tribunals that his sons were essential to the conduct of the business ?

The new bureaucratic class

Thus it was that a new class of *nouveaux riches* sprang up, to whom the war was not primarily even a national calamity, still less a personal one, and they spent their money lavishly, just as the munition workers spent their wages in higher living than they had been accustomed to, and to whom the war was—while it lasted—the sun of industrial prosperity. Indeed, so far had economic values altered that it was possible to read without surprise in May, 1917, of the excuse made by a boy of sixteen to the magistrate for stealing, that his wages of a pound a week " were not sufficient for him to keep up his appearances on." There were thousands of people to whom one could put the question, " How has the war affected you ? " and receive the answer, if it were true and honest, " Oh, I am doing very well indeed, thank you ! "

Yet there was every discouragement to individual self-gratification in the public appeals for thrift and economy, in the official deprecation of luxury, and, above all, in the newspapers, which told day after day and year after year the same story, in an apparently unending narrative, of slaughter, suffering, barbarity, heroism on all the seas and in nearly all the lands of our tortured world. Never since England had a Parliament, never since the first dawn of representative government in Saxon witenagemot, had there been so many laws interfering with the daily life of the people and governing actions, normal and ordinary in other times, with so many " don'ts ! " The Defence of the Realm Act (which is dealt with in greater detail in a later chapter), frequently enlarged and amended, and supplemented by Orders-in-Council, practically abolished civil liberty—or, much more truly, suspended it—a distinction not easily grasped by those eager searchers for " reactionary tendencies " to whom the war was not a grave peril so much as an opportunity for detecting infringements of " principle " and " liberty." Amongst the many things " you must not do," under that very elastic Act, were these :

Talk about naval or military affairs in any restaurant, railway carriage, or any public place.

Repeat any unofficial account of military operations or any projects and plans.

Say anything to give the impression of being employed in any Government department when not so employed.

Say or do anything which might cast aspersions upon the armies or other forces of the allied Powers, or prejudice the relation of the country with the neutral Powers.

Repeat any unfounded report of a Zeppelin scare, or of any reverse or disaster to British arms.

Ask any sailor to what ship he belonged, or any soldier concerning the disposition of his unit.

Ask any officer to tell anything " which the public did not know."

Write to anyone living in a military area asking for information about what was being done in that area.

Use any cipher code in correspondence with any neutral country.

Send any letter abroad written wholly or in part in invisible ink

Receive letters or telegrams for any fee, unless the police were notified.

Trespass on railways, or loiter anywhere near railway arches, bridges, or tunnels.

Send any newspaper to a neutral country except through an authorised agent.

Enter any Government factory without specific permission, or walk over any trenches constructed by the military.

Trespass on or damage any allotment-plots.

Show any films or pictures of any kind discrediting the Army, or produce any plays on the stage that were prejudicial to military discipline.

Wear any uniform of the forces, unless a member of them, even as an actor on the stage. (In the case of one play produced during the war, before this regulation was added, the naval and military uniforms were taken to the authorities to be elaborately altered and made " incorrect " though the whole object of the manager, of course, had been to boast of them as elaborately " correct.")

Make, buy, or send any picture postcard giving a picture of any ship in the Navy.

Buy any binocular glasses of the prismatic type without an official authorisation.

Fly any kite that could be used for signalling.

Send up a fire balloon or give a display of fireworks, or light a bonfire, even of garden refuse, to be still alight after 5 p.m., or the " lights down " time fixed according to the period of the year.

Buy any whisky, or other spirits, on a Saturday or Sunday, or on any other day except between noon and half-past two in the afternoon.

Buy a flask of whisky, brandy, or any spirits in a railway refreshment-room or similar place.

Pay for any intoxicating liquor for another person, except as the host of that person, at lunch, dinner, or supper.

Give or offer any intoxicating liquor to a soldier at or going to any port of embarkation, or to any soldier or sailor in hospital garb.

Melt down gold, silver, or bronze.

Buy any lead or other metal above prescribed weights.

Have in possession any document the publication of which would be forbidden.

Attempt to leave the country as the member of the crew of a neutral ship.

Give bread to any dog, poultry, horse, or other animal.

Fail or neglect to report any bomb dropped from enemy aircraft, or any part of the aircraft or its machinery, or to deliver up these things to the authorities when asked to do so.

If there were many things that could not be done, there were also many things that had to be done without. A contemporary writer was able to say, on the completion of the second year of war : " If any Englishman had been told two years ago that a day was coming soon when he could not travel to Paris or Brussels, or even north to Inverness "—for the *Ultima Thule* of Britain was south of that town for all but established residents, and the few spies who may have had the luck and hardihood to get past a barrier behind which lay many secrets—" that there would be no Boat Race, Derby, Ascot, or Goodwood, no Henley or Cowes, no cricket match or football ' final ' ; that there would be no dining-cars on his trains, no lights in his towns, hardly a murder and yet unparalleled bloodshed, no conductors on his trams, women porters on the Underground, no waiters in his clubs ;

Suspension of civil liberty

that the law would make it a penal offence for him to buy a glass of wine for his wife or treat a long-absent brother to ' a drink ' . . . that Englishman would have looked very hard indeed at the prophet."

The war turned the nation into a nation of gardeners ; even " the backyards of England " became green with growing vegetables, for no change was more general than that induced, especially in the spring of 1917, by the official exhortations that every householder having a patch of garden should make it yield its full capacity of food.

One of the pleasantest sights in a journey through the suburbs of London was to see how general was the response to this behest, which had all the validity of an order in the public mind. All the vacant building sites were taken over by the local allotment and garden-produce societies and let out to applicants, and the gardening amateur became a person of note and consequence to his neighbours, for he could give advice on soils, seasons, seeds, and "best croppers" to those who remained unenlightened. In the spring days of 1917 men, "unfit" or "over age," renewed their youth with spade-work. They hurried home to change their City clothing, to emerge in the suburban streets looking as much like agricultural labourers as old clothes and stout boots could make them, carried their tools to the allotment area, and began to turn the most unpromising plots, with a sparse "top-spit" and a subsoil of London clay, into potato-patches. Lawns were dug up, and the flower-beds were put to utilitarian ends; and an amateur gardener, summoned for some mild offence, was let off on his declaration that he had torn up a hundred pounds' worth of choice "blooms" in order to grow twenty pounds' worth of potatoes. Gardening tools became so scarce that neighbourly borrowings and lendings went on. Railway sidings and waste spaces were tilled industriously, and England never looked so green as it did in the third June of the Great War.

And how did the Great War affect the homes of Great Britain? Many homes were broken up that would never be the same again, for their mainstay had gone never to return, and widow and children became absorbed in other families. But even in those homes where that dark shadow had not fallen, the sense of "home" departed when "the man" went forth to the unknown chance of war, and furniture was stored, so that the wife could be free to go to her parents', waiting for the first leave, yet

GIRL GUIDES: A GENERAL INSPECTION.
Lady Baden-Powell, wife of Sir Robert Baden-Powell, who founded the world-wide Boy Scout movement, inspecting the South-Western Division of the Girl Guides at Balham.

dreading a more poignant message. After the Military Service Bill had come into operation provision was made by the authorities for the storing of furniture, so that disused chapels and warehouses, made idle by the war, were filled with household effects of many homes that would never be homes again. The mansions of the rich in town, and those stately homes of England in whose parks fallow deer ran—until they were slaughtered for food economy— were given up to soldiers as hospitals for the wounded and homes of rest for the convalescent, and for those suffering, rather than recovering, from "shell shock." And to the credit of those who had "many mansions" it may be said that they did their part, on the whole, very creditably, either limiting themselves to two or three rooms in town or country house, or abandoning their homes entirely to their new function and living in London hotels. There were great transferences of population—town-dwellers went back to the country for agricultural work when the labour shortage and the food shortage made agriculture "a work of national importance," and country people flocked to the towns and smaller urban districts to find the work and wages that were so plentiful in munition factories, clothing factories, aeroplane works, and all the other accessory industries of war. There was a constant migration to London from all parts of the kingdom, supplemented by the comings and goings of the wives of Colonial soldiers, who had come from far oversea to be (vain hope!) near their men-folk, and by the return home from every part of our wide Empire of the women and children of men who had thrown up their berths in Hong Kong, the Cape, the Malay Peninsula, or elsewhere, to come home to fight. And so there was quite a big demand for furnished flats and houses, and the estate agents, who had resigned themselves when the war broke out to facing lean and hungry years, found that the demand created by those wishing to find temporary homes was to be

WOMEN'S ARMY CORPS: THE RAW MATERIAL AND THE FINISHED ARTICLE.
In the early summer of 1917 a Women's Army Corps was raised officially to serve with the field army in various capacities, chiefly in connection with clerical and telegraphic work, but also for other branches such as carpentering and motor-driving. These photographs show some of the recruits fallen in for drill and (right) a trained company ready for France. Over a hundred trained women were passed out to the front every week.

GERMAN PRISONERS EMPLOYED ON LAND WORK.
Pausing during hot weather work for a welcome drink. In different parts of the country prisoners of war were employed in various agricultural operations. These men worked on farms in Hainault Forest, Essex.

supplied by those who temporarily had to give up keeping house. Hence they were kept busy, even though "long lets" were few, and though in many a suburban street the "To Let" boards, facing each other from front gardens, made a gloomy avenue. Those empty houses of Suburbia, each with its own separate story to tell of why it was empty and whither the inmates had gone, with their individual fates all merged into the great tragedy that engulfed the world! Broken homes, broken lives, broken hearts, far from the actual devastation of war.

The marriage rate increased, but few new homes were "set up." For the marriages were "war weddings," with honeymoons just snatched from a few days' leave, and with bridegrooms that were to pass from new-wed happiness to the trenches, and with wives who might be widows ere they knew whether a young life would blossom from the brief union. So that few new homes were set up, though many were broken and scattered, and no new homes were built, for all building except that of national purpose and importance was stopped throughout the war. Yet even the building necessary for national work was restricted by the compulsory renting of hotels and clubs for war staffs, though many square miles of Britain were covered by munition buildings

that sprang up in all sorts of strange and hitherto inaccessible places, with special railways laid down to a spot that was but a stretch of moorland ere the war came, but afterwards became a sudden little town humming with machinery.

In London mushroom buildings went up on roofs of Government offices, in the Embankment Gardens, and in the parks ; and one of the oddest surprises of the town was to come suddenly upon a pile of "temporary" Government offices built upon ground once covered by a beautiful stretch of ornamental water in a public park. But of homes there was no increase, and villadom did not add a cubit to its range.

Within the homes much was altered, for mothers went out to work, with many effects on domestic economy. One outstanding effect was that, with the mothers' absence, something had to be done with **Changes in** the babes, and so crèches sprang up in the **the home** industrial quarters of the town—neat and pleasant places, with tiled walls and blue cots in which the babes lay, tended by volunteer nurses, and watched by lady doctors, with wide verandas where the infants could spend sunny days in the fresh air, and sand-pits for the "toddlers" near by.

Co-operative kitchens sprang up, but were only a partial solution of the housewife's problem, for the housewife had become the worker, and realised by experience that she could not be both. So domestic cookery became, if not a lost art, a neglected one. The Government stepped in here to supplement the enforced deficiencies of the women workers. In the canteens of the "controlled" factories up and down the land over a million meals were daily provided for the women workers ; and outside working hours the tendency was to improvise meals and to

PRISONERS OF WAR USING THE PITCHFORKS OF PEACE.
German prisoners engaged in hoeing the crops on a farm in Hainault Forest, and (above) helping in the work of gathering in the hay in the same district, the men bringing heavy pitchfork loads to the waiting cart.

These prisoners were sent in batches to various farms in the neighbourhood, each party being under an armed guard during the time that they were away from their internment camp.

purchase them ready-made; for after an ordinary day's work a munition worker had no heart or strength to go home to a domestic task, and so the ham-and-beef shop did an enormous trade in spite of the increased prices; and the fried-fish shops did a brisker trade than ever, despite the shortage in the accompanying "chips." The economy of the better-class homes was also affected. With coals so scarce in the third winter that ladies wrapped in furs chartered taxi-cabs to bring home from the coal-yard half a hundredweight of coals, and with cooks and "generals" hard to get and harder to keep, and with prices soaring until household shopping (as distinct from that pastime pursued in Oxford Street) became an interesting perplexity and annoyance, many households came to rely in greater measure upon the prepared and cooked foods which the large stores began to stock, or went out to dine at the restaurants, until it was found that the rise in the price of food had produced this paradoxical effect — that the portions were halved as a matter of patriotism, and the prices were doubled as a matter of further profit.

In one other respect the war had a marked effect, for children, liberated from stricter surveillance both at school and home, and growing up in such an atmosphere of war that some of them could at length hardly recall the time when war was not with us, became precocious, adventurous, and free. Errand-boys, who before the war used to whistle up the street and occasionally interrupt themselves by delivering a parcel, found themselves, though only a year or two older, suddenly matured and promoted to adult tasks and almost adult wages. So the cinema-houses, despite the new amusements tax, never throve better; and the stimulus received by the youthful imagination, fostered in an atmosphere of war, and then stimulated by cinematic dramas, overflowed into action, with a consequent increase of juvenile crime in all the big cities. Still, petty larcenies largely accounted for the fifty per cent. increase of "cases," and it is to be noted, as one

Diminution of serious crime of the minor compensations of the war, that serious crime diminished throughout the whole community. Newspapers, indeed, had no "sensations" to record except the daily sensation of an unparalleled war, so far as the Censorship permitted—for though much may have been recorded that did not happen, much more that happened had to go unrecorded—and in the third year of the war the newspapers were unable to flick up public interest in the mystery of the apparent murder of a girl in a wood. But more spies were shot within the Tower than there were murderers hanged in Britain during the war. Litigation, too, largely diminished, and it seemed as though private feuds (except

STAGE PERFORMANCE FOR SOLDIERS BLINDED IN THE WAR.
Among the many entertainments which were devised for the blind at St. Dunstan's Hostel in Regent's Park, London, was a performance of "Daddy Long-Legs," given in March, 1917, without scenery and in everyday costume, by the company then performing in that piece at the Duke of York's Theatre.

in politics) had been obliterated by the great feud between peoples and principles.

Yet in one class of litigation—that of the Divorce Division—the increase was very marked. For the Trinity Sittings of 1917 the divorce cases set down for hearing were the highest number on record. Of the 394 cases, no fewer than 330 were marked undefended, and an indication of the direct connection between this phenomenon and the war was clearly given in the statement that " a considerable number of them have been instituted by soldiers under the ' Poor Persons' scheme for judicial relief and assistance."

Great and numerous, however, as were the changes in the normal life of all during the war, they were probably, for the most part, transient, and the greater changes to be made by the Great War, not only in the settlement of the war itself and its direct consequences, but in those entailed by the redistribution of wealth and in all the allied phenomena of a great social and economic upheaval, could for long remain matter only for speculation and intelligent anticipation, not for history.

[British official photograph.

Working-party on the western front, engaged in consolidating ground already re-won, pause to observe the explosion of enemy shells between them and their comrades in the trenches. Whenever the line was pushed forward the men behind immediately set about making good the ways for bringing up those guns and reinforcements which were essential to the preparation for pushing yet farther forward.

In the support lines of the advancing Australians on the western front. As part of the left wing of the Fifth Army under Sir Hubert Gough, which was co-operating with the Third Army under Sir Edmund Allenby, the Australians, at the end of the first week of April, 1917, fought forward and approached one of the supreme battlefields of the Great War—Bullecourt —where, by their combined dash and tenacity, they won great glory.

IN THE LINES BEHIND AS THE FRONT LINE WAS MOVING FORWARD.

[British official photograph.

THE EPIC BATTLES OF BULLECOURT.

By Edward Wright.

Australians' Road of Glory—Asked to Demonstrate, Make Terrific Thrust into [Riencourt—Climbing through Unbroken Wire—Victorious Defeat of Australian Division—German Counter-move at Lagnicourt—Rally of Queenslanders and New South Wales Men—Recovery of Guns and Slaughter of Fugitive Enemy—Londoners and Australians Advance on Bullecourt—A Check and a Victory—Australians Left in the Air—Swaying, Furious Conflict on Hindenburg Line—Penned-in Troops Ordered to Retire—Plucking Victory out of Defeat—British Renew Attack on Bullecourt Village—Enemy's Dense Columns Destroyed by Gun fire—Englishmen and Scotsmen Envelop Village—Australians Ambush Fugitives—Terrific British Barrages Ensure Victory—Incomparable Shooting by Gunners and Infantry—Revival of Mad Minute Method—Lowering the Pride of " Stosstruppen "—Bullecourt a Charnel-house, with Corpses Piled like Human Sandbags—Final Desperate Attempt at Recovery by Germans—Indomitable Tenacity of Imperial British Forces—Extraordinary Power of Sir Hubert Gough's Men—Extension of Gains on Bullecourt and Fontaine Sectors.

HERE is a road in France of sacred interest to the people of the Australian Commonwealth. It runs by Albert, through Bapaume, to Cambrai. Between Albert and Bapaume are Pozières and Mouquet Farm, and between Bapaume and Cambrai is a scatter of villages, lying mainly north of the great national road—Boursies, Beaumetz, Morchies, Lagnicourt, Bullecourt, and others.

Heroic as was the fighting power of the Australians on the Gallipoli Peninsula when battling against the Turk, the mettle of the men of the island continent was far more severely tested during nearly a year of fighting against the Germans on and around the Albert-Cambrai highway. The Germans themselves went out of their way publicly to confess that, in striking and resisting power, the Australian, with the Canadian, New Zealand, and South African forces, were equal to their own best troops.

No doubt the underlying intention of the enemy was to exalt the soldiers of the overseas democracies at the expense of the British home divisions. Making all allowance for this, the guarded confession of equality extorted from the enemy after his defeats at Vimy Ridge and Bullecourt practically amounted to an admission of German inferiority. The overweening and vain Prussian would never have admitted a mere equality in valour. He would have deceived himself in this case rather than go out of his way to admit the truth.

Only when broken by men of a higher personal courage did he try to soothe his wounded pride by accepting his victors as his peers in battle.

Some of the exploits of the Australian force during the advance from Bapaume to the double Hindenburg line covering Cambrai have already been related in Chapter CLXXXII. Sir William Birdwood, after exhausting the enemy forces on the Beaumetz line, stormed into Lagnicourt on March 26th, 1917, thereby reaching, within two miles, the Quéant junction of the Siegfried and Wotan lines of the Hindenburg system.

Probably the Australians did not know the

[Australian official photograph.
CONSOLIDATING THE ADVANCE.
Australians filling sand-bags for the new trenches dug and the old German trenches converted to British use, in the course of the slow but steady eastward move that began with the opening of the Battle of the Somme in July, 1916.

extraordinary value of their achievement at Lagnicourt. By their audacious stroke in the critical direction of Quéant, they imperilled the entire plan of General von Ludendorff, and opened the vast battle along the Hindenburg line fourteen days before the First and Third British Armies drove in enormous strength through the enemy's front.

After swinging forward his left wing, the commander of the Australian troops, on April 2nd, thrust forward with his right wing, and carried all the enemy's advanced line at Louverval and Doignies. At the same time he also lengthened his hold around the Quéant pivot by moving forward on the left to Noreuil and Longatte. At the end of the first week in April the Australians fought forward from Noreuil, and approached one of the supreme battle-fields of the great war—Bullecourt.

They were a part of the left wing of the Fifth Army, under Sir Hubert Gough, which was co-operating with the Third Army under Sir Edmund Allenby. There was, however, a great difference between the offensive power of the Fifth and Third Armies. For example, the Australian and British troops of the Fifth Army had so rapidly advanced from Bapaume that they had left most of their heavy artillery behind them. They set out from the neighbourhood of Bapaume on March 17th, and in nine days of marching, attacking, and resisting counter-attacks they arrived at the Hindenburg line, with only light artillery to support them.

Rapidity of preparation

In an ordinary way, months of constructive and engineering work were needed to build new roads, new railways, gun pits, and traffic stations, and to make huge dumps of munitions and supplies, in order to concentrate in force against the positions the enemy had been preparing for at least six months.

By an intense speeding up of all the vast work, the period of British preparation was considerably shortened. In the meantime, the Third Army that faced the enemy in positions established in October, 1914, had been preparing since the spring of 1916 for the blow it delivered on April 9th, 1917. The Third Army attacked the Germans with an equality in the matter of preparations.

When, however, Sir Edmund Allenby's forces victoriously advanced beyond the range of their large number of medium-calibre guns, their situation became, for a time, rather awkward. While they were dragging up, through snow and slush, their 6 in. guns, they required some remarkable movement by the Fifth Army in order to occupy the enemy and force him to weaken the front which they intended to attack. In these circumstances the

Australian division, which had approached the Bullecourt section of the Hindenburg line, was ordered to make a strong demonstration.

The Australians did not demonstrate. They made an attack in force which, in personal valour and downright vehemence, surpassed all their own previous achievements, and excelled the charge of the Light Brigade and practically all the most famous exploits in British military history. Even the charge of the dismounted Australian Horse, in the last great battle for the Peak in the Gallipoli Peninsula, was not of such heroic scope as the wonderful drive of an entire infantry division across the Hindenburg system on April 11th, 1917.

The Australian infantry advanced over the snow, at

[*British official photograph.*
AN INTERESTING OPERATION.
Serving out dinner to men of the Newfoundland Regiment. Their honest interest in the cook's equity in the matter of "helpings" was patent proof that good digestion waited on their appetite, and health on both.

five o'clock in the morning, while the guns of the Third Army were flashing like summer lightning over the north-western horizon. There was no time for the British artillery to attempt to break the wire of the Hindenburg system by means of a whirlwind bombardment. Not enough guns had yet been brought forward to carry out this preliminary work. It was left to some "tanks" to crawl over the snowfields in the darkness before dawn and attempt, under fire of the new German anti-"tank"

[*Canadian War Records.*
FIRST-AID FOR AN INJURED AIRMAN.
Men of an R.A.M.C. aid post attending to an aviator brought down behind the lines on the western front. After receiving first-aid the wounded man was sent to the base for necessary surgical treatment.

[*British official photograph.*
SLIGHT ACCIDENT ON A LIGHT RAILWAY.
Stretcher-bearing truck that had left the track. The patient, removed to safety by the wayside, was evidently interested in the efforts of his comrades to get the truck wheels back on to the rails

guns, to flatten out some of the zones of entanglements that protected the great tunnel.

In and around the tunnel there were two enemy battalions in the front line, and the rest of a division in support and reserve. M.E.B.U. machine-gun forts of the latest model were skilfully placed along the hostile front, and behind the Australians there was not sufficient heavy artillery and accumulations of shell to stamp out these forts and the trenches they defended, with the main lines of earthworks and caverns built above the great tunnel.

An hour before dawn a few big British guns began to shell Bullecourt and Riencourt. Half an hour afterwards the slight preliminary bombardment of hostile trenches quickened. Still the great shell bursts only occurred

AN ALFRESCO MEAL.
[British official photograph.

Newfoundlanders at dinner behind the British lines on the western front where, while waiting to take their turn in the trenches, they were billeted about the buildings of an old French farmstead.

slowly in couples against the darkness of the fading night. They were merely intended to distract the enemy while the British "tanks" snailed over the snow to the enormous band of German barbed wire.

At ten minutes to five the guns ceased fire. At five o'clock, just before the grey light of dawn appeared and showed the khaki figures outlined against the white ground, the Australian infantry climbed from their newly-made trenches on the right of Bullecourt, and stormed across

the great tunnel towards the main German artillery position at Riencourt. Twenty-five minutes afterwards it was light enough to see the Australian support troops going over the snow in extended order, with cavalry behind them, hoping for the chance of a charge upon the enemy batteries. The Germans were able to observe all the movements. A great line of red flares went up from their trenches, and their massed artillery poured curtains of shrapnel shell upon the figures standing out against the snow, and moving calmly to the dark belt of barbed wire running across the sides of the hills.

After clearing the wire, by dropping overcoats on it and climbing over, or finding paths left for German snipers, many of the Australians changed from a walking pace into a run. Horsemen went with them through the wire, and a "tank" joined the infantry. This was probably one of the "tanks" that were afterwards shattered by the enemy, but she did fine work in the great rush into Riencourt. Her gun fired continually at top speed, while her machine-guns produced an unending spout of flame. Now and then a party of Australian foot soldiers came and talked to her crew, indicating some machine-gun fort which was checking the rush attack.

The "tank," meanwhile, had become the target of both German field-guns and anti-"tank" guns. But, escaping **Tank's fine work at Riencourt** for a time the high-explosive shells which were aimed at her, she crawled into a dimple of ground, and lashed with her single gun the fort that was holding up the advance. Her shells exploded on the mark. The Australians were able to cross the hollow and mount the crest of the hill. With them went the "tank," looking like an enormous black slug, and continually spouting flame as she slid along over the snow and topped and descended the crest.

Towards seven o'clock the Australian forces on the left closed towards Bullecourt, while the Australian right went over the hill that protected Riencourt, and reached the village. The first "tank" came back wounded, and another "tank" worked forward to assist the infantry that were working around Bullecourt. The second "tank," however, did not get very far. She was bracketed by a great black German shell thirty yards behind her, with another shell about the same distance in front of her. She zigzagged in an endeavour to avoid being hit, but the German gunners overwhelmed her by concentrated battery work. In about a minute she was pierced on her front, and her crew escaped. A third of them were, however, struck as they emerged by a shower of shells pouring upon their stricken landship.

TRAFFIC WAS THEN RESUMED.
[British official photograph.

The mishap to the trolley, shown on the opposite page, having been put right, the placid patient proceeded on his journey, returning reassuring replies to the enquiries of the Padre who now accompanied him.

TAKING UP FRESH PASSENGERS.
[Australian official photograph.

Placing wounded men on an ambulance trolley. These light railways, spun like a spider's filaments by the advancing army, provided an expeditious means of conveying casualties off the battlefield.

[British official photograph.

NEW RAILROAD IN THE MAKING.
Bird's-eye view of British soldiers engaged in making a light railway to facilitate the advance on the western front.

which their comrades were desperately fighting against superior numbers of German bomb-throwers. Strong German forces advanced, in artillery order, over the hill behind Riencourt, and steadily marched against the Australian flank at Bullecourt. Had it been a veritable pitched battle, with the full strength of British artillery ranging over the fighting line, the clearly visible groups of German reinforcements would have been cut off by a barrage and scattered, and the German batteries, that maintained the enormous shrapnel curtain, would have been silenced by fierce and rapid counter-battery work.

But no British barrage in full strength could yet be produced. Without strong artillery protection, the Australian forces had broken clean through the Hindenburg system, but they could not get up the necessary stream of supplies. About noon the enemy began to work forward by incessant bomb attacks, conducted with overwhelming weight of material. The Australians gradually made their last few throws, and moved back across the open fields when their bombs were finished.

Intricacies of the Great Tunnel

Enemy forces came up in unexpected ways through the great tunnel, the intricate extent of which was not known at the time to the attacking troops. The Australians were swept in rear and flank as well as bombed in front. Their new line was broken in several places, and they were forced back out of the Hindenburg line to their original positions. A thousand of their advanced troops who had pushed into Hendecourt village and taken Riencourt, both far behind Bullecourt, fell into the hands of the enemy, and were most barbarously ill-treated.

Yet, grievous as were the losses of the gallant division, it accomplished the main task set it. The troops who

In spite of this little set-back, all the section of the Hindenburg line was stormed by the Australians. They entered Riencourt, but could not take the German guns. They almost enveloped Bullecourt, and attained every point they were ordered to reach. For the most part they got through the wire around the Hindenburg system without help from their own guns or from their "tanks." Only at one point had one or two "tanks" given any help. Most of them had been foiled by the fall of snow, which was quite an unexpected event in the middle of April.

[British official photograph.

PEACEFUL CAMP ON WAR-SCARRED GROUND.
Tents pitched in a mine-crater on the British front in France. The men who had here their temporary home had formed a series of steps leading down into their little valley, and made roughly-fenced pathways leading to the tents, which were well hidden from observation by the sides of the crater.

Three and a half hours after the first advance the Australians still held the main tactical positions near the junction point of the Hindenburg system. All they required, in order to hold all that they had marvellously won, was a good supply of bombs, cartridges, mortars, and big mortar bombs. Here it was, however, that the enemy's overpowering strength in artillery decisively told upon the event of the battle.

As the snow melted under the springtide sun, and the white slopes began to turn as brown as the rusty wire that laced them, the hillsides and hollows were swept by a continual hailstorm of round shrapnel bullets. Ammunition carriers could not reach the distant positions in

reached Hendecourt were a good five miles in the rear of the enemy's Cojeul River line, running by Wancourt. The troops who thrust into Riencourt were more than six miles behind the German Cojeul River system, and nearly three miles north-west of Quéant. They were also well behind the enemy's main tunnel line at Fontaine and Chérisy.

The result was that the enemy had to draw off forces from the Cojeul River and Sensée River works, in order to deal with the daring Australians. By the time he had dealt with them, the right wing of the British Third Army, under Sir Edmund Allenby, drove in victorious force against Wancourt and Héninel, crossed the Cojeul stream,

HURRYING FORWARD WITH THE AUSTRALIAN ARTILLERY.

[Australian official photograph.

Men of the Australian forces "rushing" a gun along a light railway in support of their advancing troops. The heroism and dash of the Australians at Riencourt and Hendecourt, on April 11th, 1917, glorified one of the outstanding episodes of the struggle between Arras and Cambrai, though the retention of those two villages beyond Bullecourt was then impossible owing to enemy superiority in artillery.

and obtained elbow room in the new British salient at Arras for siting more guns against the Hindenburg system.

The Australians were defeated, but theirs was a victorious defeat. The German commander on the Bullecourt front, however, thought he had so shaken the Australian Expeditionary Force that he could press it back towards Bapaume, and thus compel an interruption of the Arras battle. He immediately brought down to Quéant the 3rd Division of the Prussian Guard, together with troops from two other Guards divisions, and squeezed these powerful reinforcements alongside the German division holding the Quéant front.

The shock troops of the Guards came out at dawn on April 15th, and cut off two Australian advanced posts, allowing the main forces to debouch into Lagnicourt village and advance towards Noreuil. Along most of the line, however, the advanced guards of Australians and British troops shattered the attacks with machine-gun fire. Only by Lagnicourt were a couple of outposts rushed, while those on either side were bent back, though still holding out. Through the gap the Guardsmen, Bavarians, and other German troops of the line poured in overwhelming mass.

Brief loss of British guns They broke through Lagnicourt, and took about twenty-two field-guns and held them for half an hour. Happily, they were unable to use them against the rallying Australian line, as the surprised and almost naked Australian gunners had dismantled their pieces by taking away the breech-blocks.

As the Guardsmen were placing charges in the guns to smash the barrels, a magnificent counter-attack by Queenslanders and New South Wales men caught and broke the Lehr regiment (formed from the Lehr-Bataillon, or Instructional battalion, which was one of the smartest German units), and the Fusilier regiment of the Guards and other crack forces. As the fugitives raced back to their own lines, where they had not cut their wire, many of them were caught in the Hindenburg entanglements and slain by the artillery of the Australian force.

Each opening in the wire was ranged almost to an inch. As the successive parties of Guardsmen, Bavarians, and other German troops were ordered through by their officers, they disappeared in bursts of black smoke shells from the British heavy artillery.

Thousands of Germans, who could not find any gap in the wire, ran wildly up and down seeking a way through. The Australian riflemen flung themselves on the grass, and maintained such an intensity of rifle-fire as had not been seen since the first battle of Ypres. Many of the men got off more than a hundred rounds rapid in the old "mad minute" manner. The despairing remnant of Germans, trapped at last, with arms raised and quivering mouths shrieking for mercy, ran to the Australians, **Fine counter-attack** and, to the number of four hundred, were **at Lagnicourt** taken prisoners. The enemy lost in total casualties at least two-thirds of a division—fifteen hundred German corpses being found in and around Lagnicourt alone when the positions were recovered.

The counter-attack of the Australians was a pretty piece of work. The battalions advanced by alternate companies, one halting and firing while the men in the other fought onward, partly covered by their comrades' flanking fusillade. These tactics were executed along the entire front. In spectacular effect it was reminiscent of a field-day in manœuvres. As practical open field warfare it was so brilliantly successful that the final scene of slaughter was terrifying. Some of the Australians fought in their shirts, stretched on the damp ground, shooting the Germans down for an hour. An officer asked one of them whether he wasn't very cold. "For another chance like this," was the answer, "I would go without trousers all my life." In fact, he took to shorts when summer came on, to maintain the Gallipoli tradition.

Only 190 men from the Australian outposts were missing, though the German staff claimed to have taken 475 prisoners and destroyed twenty-two guns. Seventeen of the guns that had been destroyed were in action against the Germans three hours after the Prussian Guardsmen began their attack. The Australian gunners who had fled in their shirts carrying their breech-blocks with them, returned in time to put a shrapnel curtain over the flying enemy before he could get through the few paths in his wire.

After this great and heartening success the Australians and their British comrades worked with furious energy to increase their artillery power. A larger number of heavy guns were brought from the Bapaume area and sited around the Quéant salient. The Pioneers drove their tracks and roads across the muddy Bapaume chaos, and the Sappers prolonged the huge system of communications close to the Hindenburg line. In six weeks after the great devastating German retreat the northern army corps of Sir Hubert Gough's Fifth Army were in a position to renew their offensive on the scale of the Ancre and Somme actions.

On May 3rd, as the Third British Army was fighting on the Sensée River flank of the Quéant salient, the British and Australian forces of the Fifth Army again broke into the Bullecourt and Riencourt sector of the Hindenburg system. Upon this occasion the attacking infantry was fairly well provided with heavy artillery support, and the field batteries roared and blazed for mile upon mile behind them. The enemy called it drum-fire, but the guns roared faster than the rolling of a kettle-drum.

[*British official photograph.*

A RELIC OF THE INVASION.
A dug-out in the garden of a French villa which had been occupied as a German headquarters: fraught with painful memories to the old, but an object of endless interest to the younger generation.

The wire was excellently cut, and the line of the British barrage was as easy to follow as a line of human guides would have been. The attacking forces walked forward, with their shrapnel bursting nearly over their heads. In a quarter of an hour they were in the front line of the Hindenburg system. In another fifteen minutes they followed their barrage into the enemy's second line.

Then, from the second line, the Australians worked over a slope into a tramway cutting running towards Riencourt. Only on their right were the men of the Commonwealth checked. As happened at the Triangle in the Arras battle, the barrage went over the enemy's line of sunken forts without putting them out of action. The German machine-gunners had time to man their hidden concreted works, and after some of the attackers had rushed across the hostile trenches, this part of the British commanders' plan of action went to pieces.

Serious check at Riencourt

There followed a long, fierce, and confused struggle between scattered Australian troops and the German supports

creeping up from the tunnel. Gradually the fragments of the Australian battalions worked round the machine-gun positions, and, by intense persistence and splendid bombing work, the force recovered from its early check, and by the end of the day won, by hand-to-hand fighting, all its objectives.

Meanwhile, the London troops, who directly attacked Bullecourt village, failed completely, through no fault of their own, in working through the ruined houses and linking with the left of the Australian attackers. Early in the day they took the village, and one of their detachments, consisting of about forty men, drove clean through and got in touch with the Australians, according to the general programme of the action. But over the great tunnel it was easier to carry the surface trenches and redoubts than to hold them. Where there were ruined houses, with many cellars connecting with the enemy's underground caverns and galleries, the ordeal of holding what had been won was superhuman. The Londoners, nevertheless, would have taken and held the village had not the troops on their left been unable to get forward and shield their exposed left flank.

The German artillery put a great barrage upon the British trenches and over the neutral zone and their own lost line. Having thus interfered with the forwarding of supplies to the attacking troops, the German Commander brought his men up from the great tunnel, where large stores of supplies of ammunition and bombs were ready to hand, and filtered them into the stairways leading back to the brick ruins. The London troops were thus scattered into broken parties, and kept in incessant action until, like the Australians on April 11th, their bombs were finished, and they had to retire.

Londoners isolated at Bullecourt

This withdrawal left the Australian attack clean in the air. By midday Bullecourt village projected like a flat promontory on their left, where isolated London troops were still holding out against the reconquering Germans. In front was the ridge on which Riencourt stands, pitted with battery sites that drenched the Australians with shrapnel and high explosive. On the right was another promontory at Quéant, where the hostile heavy batteries were fighting under the protection of the Riencourt Ridge. Between the two promontories, in a small section of double trench varying with the sway of battle from five hundred to twelve hundred yards, were the encircled yet indomitable Australians. At times the German machine-gunners, operating from the great tunnel, fired from the right rear of the Australians and from their left rear, while other enemy gunners swept all the front.

The position was an impossible one, but the overseas Britons would not admit the word impossible into their vocabulary. They did not know clearly that they were fighting over a vast underground system, through which counter-attacking forces could climb among them and behind them. What held them up was the fact that already an Australian division, without preliminary bombardment, had gone much farther ahead than they had done. They did not, perhaps, fully appreciate the fact that, by going so far ahead in April, the first attacking force had exposed itself to entire destruction from enemy reserves hidden in the underground tunnel in its rear. All they considered was that what men had done, men could do. So they held their ground to the death, with intense and ever resurgent energy.

In the night, on the extreme left of the Australian position, where a small force had been attacked by machine-gun fire and isolated, some New South Wales troops bombed along this part of the Hindenburg line and reached the extreme point fixed to be taken in the original battle plan. The enemy counter-attacked heavily both night and day. His first counter-attack was memorable by reason of its comic yet deadly character. At noon on the first day of the action some three hundred shock troops advanced from the sunken roads on the right, and dived from shell-hole to shell-hole like a school of seals.

The new method of attack was well executed, but almost amusing to watch. The Australians stood breast high over

(Canadian War Records

Lieut.-General Sir A. W. Currie, K.C.B., commanding Canadian Forces in France, June, 1917

Conveying wounded by sledge=transport.   *Gunners taking cover under a hot bombardment*

Village under heavy shell=fire: Sketched by Mr. F. Matania.

Retribution : Surprise attack by British patrol on enemy cyclists looting a French village.

French peasants awaiting motor-transport to take them back to their ruined but redeemed villages.

Burning refuse in the incinerators of the Army Sanitary Service.

Cheshires charging unbroken wire before a trench at Messines.

First-aid and shelter for the wounded at Messines.

Australians crossing the Douve, Messines, under machine-gun fire.

their parapet, with cigarettes in their mouths, and practised human seal shooting with decisive effect. Only a handful of resolute Germans arrived within a dozen yards of the trench, and there died. At the same time, a bombing attack was made against the left flank of the new Australian position, to divert attention from the frontal assault. A shower of Stokes aerial torpedoes blew the bombing detachment into eternity. One German was hurled thirty feet into the air, turning over and over as he spun. So the flank diversion ended.

The enemy, however, also possessed a large number of trench mortars. By means of a powerful bombardment on the Australian right, they forced this flank back completely to the left flank, seriously reducing the length of the thrust across the Hindenburg line. Thereupon, a Western Australian battalion resumed the struggle and bombed back to the limit of the trench and recovered the whole of the objective. Yet they in turn were smashed back by the concentrated fire of German trench mortars.

Failure of a German trick Then the enemy infantry drove furiously down the trench into the bare five hundred yards of German territory in which the Australians were penned.

The position became tragically critical, as other German forces in the tunnel brought their machine-guns to bear from both the left rear and the right rear. When, from the Australian point of view, everything seemed past praying for, the enemy played his last trick. From one of the outlets of the tunnel system, a man appeared, speaking excellent English and wearing the uniform of an Australian officer. He gave the order to retire, and his order passed along the hard-pressed and almost breaking line.

It was a brilliant ruse which would have succeeded in ordinary circumstances. The circumstances, however, were extraordinary. By a miraculous reversion of effect, the false order given by the disguised German produced a German defeat. As the order passed along, the Australians said: " What officer of ours gave that order ? " They knew none of their officers would have said such a thing. For all officers and men had determined beforehand that they never would retire, even if they were entirely encircled. They had arranged to stay until they were wholly enveloped, and then cut their way back through the enemy. Recognising at once the German trick, they were so stiffened in spirit that they fought the enemy down at all points. Although the German commander used the best forces of his Empire, including the Third Guard Division, the Second Guard Reserve, and a very large body of storm troops, most of these battalions had already been smashed by the Australians in the Lagnicourt battle. Though filled out with fresh drafts, they could not, in the five hundred yard fragment of the Hindenburg line, hold with the men who had already inflicted such heavy slaughter upon them.

The following afternoon, the gallant troops of New South Wales, who had restored the extreme position on the left attack, came forward and again bombed their way for more than six hundred yards over other ground that had been temporarily lost. Then once more the Prussian Guard and the shock troops counter-attacked in the night of May 5th. Three times the shock troops and the Guard supports tried to break through. They only penetrated one trench, and were soon thrown back from it.

Continually pressed on three sides and threatened in the rear, the superb Australians not only held to what they had won, but, in sudden fierce leaps, made after the German counter-attacks were broken, they slowly enlarged the narrow gap into which they had thrust.

There was no definite line of conflict. The opposing forces were wedged into each other, in a tangle of deep ditch fighting. The enemy tried to tire out the Australians by continually feeding up attacking forces from Quéant,

TYPICAL GERMAN DUG-OUT ON THE HINDENBURG LINE. Where the famous Hindenburg line was dented numerous ingeniously built and luxuriously fitted dug-outs were found, some of them picturesquely situated, as the one shown in the above enemy photograph.

from Riencourt, from Bullecourt, and from the east of Bullecourt. As each counter-attacking force relaxed in vigour, it was relieved by new forces. No sacrifice of life was spared in order to recover the Hindenburg line.

The German sappers had not completed their work on April 11th. The spades of the working parties were observed when the Australians went forward without artillery preparation. On May 3rd, the defences were still unfinished. The works were excavated on a massive pattern, with wide **Use of enemy** traverses capable of preventing the **defence works** biggest British shell from enfilading the bays. The magnificent design was very helpful to the penned-in attacking force, when pounded by the heavy German artillery.

The German sappers, however, had not had time to revet the enormous ditches by means of hurdles or galvanised iron. The dug-outs also had not been cemented, though the wood-lined staircases were good, and the caverns were upheld with stout logs. Moreover, many of the neighbouring machine-gun positions still lacked connecting galleries. Yet all the works were so well on the way to completion that the German commander could quickly have made the line practically impregnable

ACTIVITY AT AN AID-POST NEAR THE BULLECOURT BATTLEFIELD.

Stretcher-bearers bringing in wounded, while a despatch-rider goes off with the latest information. In the tense struggle around Bullecourt which preceded its capture on May 17th, 1917, all branches of the Army shared the honours with the infantry and gunners. The stretcher-bearers were acclaimed the greatest of all heroes by hundreds of thousands of men who had proved themselves to be of the finest heroic type.

had he been able to keep the Australians out of it for a few days.

This was why he sternly exhausted army corps after army corps of his finest troops in attempts to recover the little patch of ground. From his point of view there was no reason why the Australians should be allowed to continue to occupy an impossible position. "You are merely madmen from the Antipodes," said a captured Prussian soldier of the professional school. He pointed out that his opponents were defying all the principles of warfare, in clinging to a position in mid-air from which they were certain to be driven.

"Madmen from the Antipodes"

The Australians were like their British ancestors, who fought against Soult in Spain, and after being defeated by all canons of strategy, remained victorious on the hard-won battle ground. By sheer primitive hand-to-hand struggles, with the heavy artillery on both sides smashing up communications and playing upon all visible reinforcements, the struggle went on by the Riencourt road and around Bullecourt village.

On the morning of May 7th some of the English troops, who had fought around Bullecourt village, came forward, with a fine Scottish force, to co-operate again with the bull-dog fighters of the Island Continent. In close bomb-fighting the Scots blasted the enemy down the trenches, and fought into the village, dragging a bunch of prisoners out of it. They sliced off the south-east corner of Bullecourt, linked it with the part of the Hindenburg line held by the Australians, and rescued ten London men who had been taken prisoners in the battle of May 3rd.

On the same day some British artillery observers spied a German division trying to dig a trench behind Bullecourt, set their guns on to the large force, and killed many of the diggers just behind the village. As the struggle on the Bullecourt line became more clearly defined, the most

horrible weapons were employed on both sides. The Germans used their flame projectors and their poison gas shells, only to be answered by liquid metal shells, far-flung barrels of flaming petrol and a new British gas shell of dreadful quality. According to prisoners, their masks gave no protection from the new British gas. One shell, exploding in a crowded dug-out, killed all the occupants, in spite of their gas helmets. In another battalion at Bullecourt, so men taken from the battalion said, there were two hundred and thirty casualties from gas shell bombardment.

By this time part of the great Hindenburg tunnel was solidly occupied by the Australian forces, and found to be sufficiently high and wide to allow the enemy quickly to move troops from point to point. It was also known that at Riencourt there was a series of mediæval catacombs, capable of sheltering six thousand German troops. All these advantages which the enemy possessed, together with the chain of great caverns he was constructing, were fairly balanced by the continually increasing power of the heavy British artillery.

The big guns maintained such a plastering barrage over the hostile rear that the Germans could not move across open country into their subterranean fortresses without very grave losses. They had also to stop working on a new switch line, which was intended to give them communication with Quéant when they were driven out of the Bullecourt salient. Indescribable—within, at least, the limits of this voluminous history—were the stupendous labours of the organisation forces behind the Imperial British attack.

Superb British organisation

The vast and rapid concentration of British heavy guns across the wide zone of territory evacuated by Ludendorff was answered by the enemy with a strenuous effort. Never had he massed more guns on a small area than on the Bullecourt sector in the first weeks of May. He tried to spare his Hindenburg line, shooting merely behind it and on the saps in front of it, as he did not want to foul his own nest, which he hoped to retake.

When, however, he began to see that the heroic defence of the Australians was unlikely to be broken, he endeavoured to smash up the great system he had lost. Tens of thousands of heavy shells, fired from three sides, fell upon the Australian, Scottish, and English troops, who gradually broadened the front of the wedge of territory they had conquered by means of perpetual bombing attacks, entailing the carrying forward of tons of munitions through the hostile shell curtain.

After the action in Bullecourt village on May 7th the enemy took a full day to recover. He launched his customary counter-attack on May 9th, and was caught by machine-gun fire while trying to cross the open. Severe and continuous fighting raged all around Bullecourt, and in spite of the vehement repeated counter-assaults by the enemy, progress was made by the Imperial Forces.

The Germans began with a terrific bombardment, followed by storming operations all along the line. They were repulsed everywhere, with very **Unavailing German** great losses, and the victorious Austra-**counter-attacks** lians, Scotsmen, and Englishmen came out against their broken foes and bombed them out of some of the most important positions. Again, on Friday evening, May 11th, the Germans were observed to be massing for another great storming operation in the neighbourhood of Bullecourt. A tempest of shrapnel unexpectedly fell upon them, and the survivors scattered into shelter.

The British Commander was quick to seize the advantage his guns had won for him. Just as twilight was deepening into night he launched his English and Scottish troops into the historic village, through which the men of London had battled with desperate valour on May 3rd, when their supporting wing was checked. The linked cellars beneath the ruined cottages, with the armoured machine-gun forts and the caverns of the great tunnel, once more enabled a considerable part of the garrison to maintain a fierce defence, and escape, when beaten, by unseen subterranean ways.

Violent hand-to-hand bomb-fighting **Enemy surrounded** went on all night, and continued **in Bullecourt** in the morning of Sunday, May 13th.

The British troops attacked both sides of the village. The Scotsmen, in the south-eastern corner, sent out parties of bombers, who worked up the trenches on the right and reached the road running across the village of Bullecourt from east to west. Other English bombers blasted their way through the eastern end of the village towards the same road, with the effect that the Germans discovered they were being entirely surrounded.

In an endeavour to escape the flanking operations, they bolted along the trenches eastward, only to find the Australians waiting for them there. After a brief fight, some two hundred prisoners were taken by the forces of the Commonwealth. Nevertheless, after the encircling movement, remnants of the German garrison continued to hold out in the underground works in the middle of the village. There they waited, in darkness and silence, for the great German counter-attack that was to bring them again into their own lines.

The first attempt at rescue and recovery was extraordinarily disastrous to the enemy. Early in the morning the German gunners tried, by means of a heavy barrage, to break a path for their battalions massing behind the

TRYING THEIR HANDS AT A NEW WEAPON DEVISED IN THE GREAT WAR.
New Zealand troops engaged in practising a smoke attack, using portable smoke generators. For use in trenches a much larger apparatus was invented. It was a curious development that was manifested when belligerents, who for long had been perfecting a smokeless powder for rifles and artillery, had to turn their attention to devising fresh means of producing smoke-clouds that should serve to mask an advance or hinder an attack.

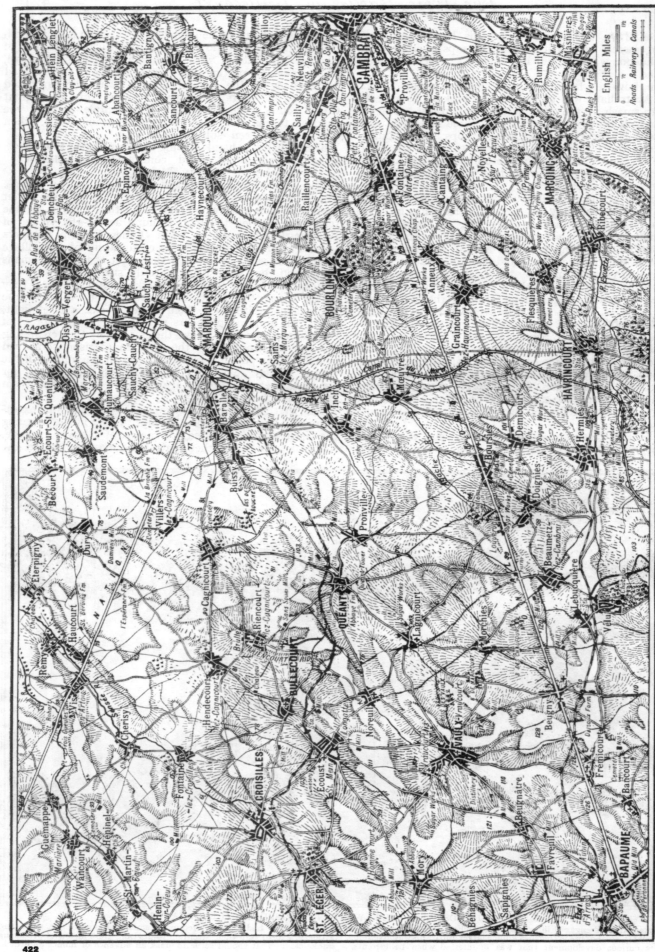

422

Copyright

AREA OF THE FIGHTING FOR POSSESSION OF BULLECOURT AND THE NATIONAL ROAD NORTH OF IT FROM ARRAS TO CAMBRAI.

village. The infantry was sent forward, shoulder to shoulder, in columns of fours, to win back Bullecourt by sheer weight of numbers. The moment their barrage lifted the British curtain fire fell on the road they had to travel. With a degree of courage that must be recognised, one well-disciplined German column went steadily forward into the hurricane of artillery fire and was torn to fragments. Only twelve Germans got within bombing distance. Three were mortally wounded, and nine were killed.

One hour afterwards the heavy German artillery again hammered at the British line in the village, and provoked another British shell curtain, through which the German columns again went forward. On this occasion twenty of the counter-attackers arrived near an English trench. Of them, nineteen were killed, and one was captured.

Success of British artillery

The dreadful success of these two British barrages decided the battle for Bullecourt. Final victory was the result of one of those highly technical dispositions which the enemy thought was impossible to such an upstart, newly-created national army as the British Empire put into the field. The liaison between artillery and infantry was practically perfect.

Though the gunners worked under most frightful diffi-

a gift of steady vision and rapid calculation inherited from the bowmen of Crecy and Agincourt, and from the gunners of Drake, Blake, and Nelson. Yet, if this were so, the larger part of the success remained traceable to the science and intensive instruction communicated by a small band of professional British gunners to the multitudes of new officers and men whom they had trained at unparalleled speed.

Ludendorff reckoned upon a raggedness in the British co-operation of guns and bayonets. Especially did he anticipate encountering only a weak British artillery at the pivot point of his Hindenburg system. Here the British heavy artillery had to advance more than twelve miles, and construct new emplacements, dug-outs, underground store chambers, light railways, and other vast works.

Yet by May 12th Ludendorff knew that he had been entirely mistaken in all his anticipations. Around Bullecourt he was opposed by ordinary British Imperial troops of the line, whose fighting qualities exceeded those of his best shock troops, crack Guardsmen, and Bavarians. All his artillery, which he had been emplacing and strengthening for at least nine months,. was over-borne by British artillery, which had taken less than two months to haul forward, emplace, and provide with abundant shell.

Bullecourt was a great testing-place of the strategy of

[*British official photograph.*

CANAL BRIDGE THAT STOOD, THOUGH THE WATERWAY WAS FILLED WITH THE DEBRIS OF BOMBARDMENT.
Despite the terrific bombardment to which every square inch of the ground between the opposed guns was subjected, some few objects, even of military importance, escaped destruction. Among them was this bridge over the canal between Péronne and Bapaume, which was left standing, although the canal itself was filled with broken rubbish and that which had been a peaceful waterway was converted into a dried-up sunken road.

culties, with, day and night, storms of explosives searching for their batteries, they and their forward observation officers and aerial observers ranged with marvellous quickness on all living German targets during the repeated counter-attacks. Again and again, in the first fortnight of May, the enemy's dense masses were shattered before they could close upon the Australian, Scottish, and South of England troops.

This thing it was that staggered Ludendorff and his lieutenants. Some of the shooting of the British artillery in the opening of the Somme battles had undoubtedly been poor. Many were the British artillerymen who fired their first gun between Gommecourt and Montauban. They had a certain knowledge of the theory of gunnery; they had practised their work without using shell; but, being very new recruits, from a country whose gun production first lagged behind its potential man-power, many of the men opened their real apprenticeship on the battle-field. Only as they acquired a mastery of their mighty and complicated weapons were their armies able to work forward at lighter loss than the enemy suffered.

On the other hand, it had taken much less than a year to transform these apprenticed artillerists into the master gunners of the world. Perhaps it was a quality of race—

General von Ludendorff and the strategy of Sir Douglas Haig. At Bullecourt the German dictator at first accomplished all he had designed to achieve. He withdrew his First Army safely from Bapaume. Near his new line he lost some important villages which he had intended to hold as outpost fortresses. Still, he succeeded in firmly establishing himself in the immense new earthworks above his gigantic tunnel and below his new high artillery positions. Behind the ordinary " cannon fodder " manning his first line was concentrated the finest flower of his forces, and, though his fortifications were not entirely completed, the excavation of the main huge trench system and the secret tunnel ways had been carried out. Finally, in spite of the fact that he had been taken by surprise by the Australian division, in the second week of April, he was able to use his superior artillery power and tunnel devices in a successful manner, and recover and strengthen the Hindenburg line.

British versus German strategy

He therefore felt confident that the scheme of defence which he had carried out, by enormous industry, would win him sufficient time to employ his submarines in starving out the British races. When, however, the awful British barrages absolutely destroyed his massed counter-attacking forces around Bullecourt, the principal element in his original plan was seen to be ineffectual.

At Arras and Vimy the British and Canadian forces had, from the German point of view, merely repeated, with accelerating skill, the form of the British successes on the Somme and Ancre. The troops of the British Empire there fought a pitched battle on old ground which they and the French armies had been organising since October, 1914. For more than a year, the British gunners had been able to register on all enemy positions on the fixed line extending from Lens to Arras.

On the Bullecourt front the British and Australian gunners had slowly to discover their targets, in an unknown tract of country containing tunnels, **Germans' tactical advantages** galleries, catacombs, and thousands of other underground shelters of which they were ignorant. Not until an enemy gun fired could they learn its position. Their artillery had to provoke the enemy gunners into counter-battery work before anything of importance could be carried out. Every possible tactical advantage was enjoyed by the enemy in and around Bullecourt.

Nevertheless, he was thoroughly beaten. In other words, the technique of the British Empire forces, composed mainly of troops who did not know anything of war before August, 1914, proved superior to the technique of the German armies, which had been training in military technique, with the utmost scope and energy, since Roon and Moltke prepared in the middle of the nineteenth century for the series of victorious campaigns against Denmark, Austria, Hanover, other German States, France and Russia. It was as though the first Surrey cricket

[*Australian official photograph.*

TENANTS ON A REPAIRING LEASE.
Australians at work on a captured German trench to render it available for their own occupation : Converting parados into parapet, and pulling bundles of broken barbed-wire out of the clearway.

eleven was beaten again and again by some boys from an unknown Cornish village.

At the suggestion of Ludendorff, the German Press began to expatiate upon the large war experience won by the small British regular army in continual little conflicts with the tribes of north-western India and the Somali clans of north-eastern Africa. This explanation did not explain. The larger part of the original British Army was out of action. The most effectual weapons, used in the enormous parallel battle, were of a kind with which only the Teutonic armies had practised before the war. The German 16.8 in. guns, the Austrian 12 in. guns, the German 11 in. pieces of siege ordnance were unknown even to the regular British Army. The British Garrison Artillery **Superiority of** originally possessed only a few 9.2 in. **British technique** guns in coast defence batteries.

The technique of connecting the heaviest siege ordnance with aeroplane direction, was practically entirely of Germanic use. Aeroplane direction had never been practised in British colonial wars. The extraordinary advances made by the British, in the intricate technique of attack upon subterranean fortifications of incomparable strength, were a result of rapid improvisation and invention. The enemy possessed all possible original advantages because of his intensive and enormous preparations for war. He gradually failed to maintain his advantages, because he was at last outclassed in both foresight and inventive power.

With the help of Royal Marine and Naval gunners the British Master-General of Ordnance transformed raw recruits into good artillerists at a speed which was marvellous. In regard to musketry instruction, the method of rapid fire, developed by the regular army

[*British official photograph.*

MACHINE-GUN STAND OF FLESH AND BLOOD.
Canadian machine-gunners driving away an enemy aeroplane. One powerful fellow shouldered the weapon, instinctively shutting his eyes in anticipation of the sudden shock of the explosion.

between the South African Campaign and the battles of Mons and Ypres, was so superbly perfected that the new armies could cause as much execution in thirty seconds as the troops at Ypres inflicted in a minute.

In this respect, however, some ground was lost during the middle period of trench warfare. For a time the bomb and the bayonet seemed to be more important than intensely rapid, well-aimed, rifle fire. Most of the small local and temporary reverses incurred along the Hindenburg line, after the victories of Vimy Ridge and Arras, were largely attributable to a certain slackness in maintaining all the British infantry in the perfected art of incomparably deadly, rapid musketry fire. This British lapse may have been partly due to the erroneous influence of some brilliant French Army Commanders, who openly professed that the rifle was scarcely of any importance in comparison with bomb, bayonet, and machine-gun. After the first great battles along the Hindenburg line, however, every British commanding officer, from lieutenant-generals commanding armies to lieutenant-colonels commanding battalions, returned to his original faith in the fire-power of the Lee-Enfield.

Importance of rifle fire

The marksmen of Australia achieved wonderful things by means of their undiminished skill in intense and aimed rifle fire. When the Germans were bunched together in thousands, the Australians did not fire "into the brown" as was the general manner of all Continental infantry. Every man got between his sights one grey figure, fired at it, covered another grey figure and fired, and so on, with remarkable speed, until his supply of a hundred rounds of cartridges in clips was quite or nearly exhausted.

Many British battalions, directly inheriting the musketry tradition of the original seven divisions, proved themselves as deadly masters of all their approaches as the men at Le Cateau had been. Yet among other new British divisions there seemed to remain ample room for improvement and return to the great tradition. Perhaps, in the well-known perfecting school of infantry training in France, commonly known as "the Bull-Ring," the hand-bomb had been too much exalted over the magazine and barrel of the rifle. This error, at the base behind the fighting-line, seems to have spread to the home training centres.

Germany's "stosstruppen"

With this exception, the military technique of the forces of two million front-line men of all the British Commonwealth armies was magnificently effective, excelling the technique of the common forces of the German armies, and at least equalling in expertness that of the special German shock troops. It is, in fact, scarcely extravagant to say that the average British infantryman proved as fine a fighting man as a member of the comparatively small German forces of picked and specially trained "stosstruppen."

These stosstruppen were killed in thousands in the actions in and around Bullecourt. For the most part they only came into action in the dark hours when their common infantry had been thoroughly defeated. They were filled with pride when they first came forward to attempt the counter-attacks intended to retrieve the entire situation. When, however, they were entirely defeated by the ordinary Australian, English, and Scottish soldier the moral result was far-reaching. Not only was the personal pride of the shock troops lowered and broken,

[*Canadian War Records.*

SOLDIERS GREETING THE RETURN OF A LANDSHIP FROM A VICTORIOUS CRUISE.

"Tanks" made their first appearance at Thiepval on September 16th, 1916, and were greeted with hilarious delight by the British troops and with terrified denunciation by the enemy. Thereafter they continued to render valuable assistance on all fronts, especially to attacking infantry. Though they soon lost their novelty, they never ceased to cause amusement by their ungainly movements when performing seemingly impossible feats.

SCOTTISH TROOPS GOING "OVER THE TOP" TO TAKE PART IN A NIGHT RAID ON THE WESTERN FRONT.

In this very impressive picture, the artist, Mr. D. Macpherson, presents from an eye-witness's account something of the solemnity and grim splendour of one of those night raids on the enemy trenches behind barrage fire which formed an important and more or less constant feature of the fighting along all parts of the British front in France. The heavy barrage from the British artillery held the enemy from sending relief up to their front lines, while behind that barrage the raiding parties reached the German trenches, bombed their dug-outs, and generally returned with a number of prisoners.

but the men of the numerous divisions, whom they had gone forward to help, became despondent. Each ordinary German private thought to himself, in various ways: "If our picked shock troops cannot throw back the terrible 'Englishmen,' how ever can a common soldier like me hope to achieve anything?"

After the great Bullecourt battle, at the end of the second week in May, there remained on May 14th only two posts of the original German garrison holding out in the village. Groups of fugitive bombers were unearthed slowly from unlikely corners in an oppressive heat like that of August. Through nights that brought them no fresh air to cool them at their task, the British bombing parties fed as they went on with their deadly work, and snatched brief periods of rest in horribly strange places.

Clearing out Bullecourt

In the great charnel-house of ruins the dead stared at the groups of living, sleeping victors from winding alleyways and the rubble of unroofed and broken walled cottages. All the time the heavy German guns hammered at the wreckage and flogged the corpses that were at last piled like human sand-bags around the living.

The remnants of the German infantry, sheltering in their last dug-outs, were often afraid of being annihilated by their own artillery before the British bombers discovered their hiding places. On the other hand, nothing of the exhilaration of battle sustained the attacking troops, engaged in sifting out Germans from the village cellars, and fighting for a strip of trench a few yards long. It was like digging out rats. In places, an entire morning was spent in the wearying work of excavating a single ruined covered corner, on the chance of finding a handful of Prussians cowering beneath broken roof beams and mounds of lath and plaster.

Cleaning up parties worked gradually, yet energetically, along the village uncovering and exploring a cottage at a time, under a continuous fire of enemy shrapnel, varied by shell bursts sufficiently powerful to penetrate dugouts. Dead Prussian Guardsmen carpeted the earth round Bullecourt, and choked the new ditches linking the village with the rest of the Hindenburg system.

Heavy German losses

Each of the enemy's vain counter-attacks could be traced by successive trails of corpses. First, on the open cratered fields were masses of bodies shattered by the British barrages. Closer at hand were thinner layers of the brief survivors of the shell curtain, who were brought down by British machine-gunners. Lastly, inside the ruins were the final remnants of the counter-attacks, consisting of little groups of grey motionless figures, killed, almost at arm's length, by British bombers and riflemen.

There was a dramatic episode when the English troops were fighting through the village and an Australian bombing party was blasting forward to meet them. Only a small number of Germans at last separated the two spear heads. Some of the Englishmen happily observed the distinctive features of their oversea comrades, and at once shortened the throw of their bombs for fear of accidents. The Australians were fighting forward in such wild fury that they did not notice that their bombs would soon explode beyond the small stretch of trench held by the Germans.

They felt, however, that the enemy's resistance was weakening, and came upon some bodies which they knew they could not have killed. They interrupted their action to puzzle over the problem of the dead Germans. This saved the English troops. During the pause, an English soldier jumped on the parapet and shouted.

Bombing parties' dramatic meeting The Australians answered with a ringing cheer, and both parties ran forward and shook hands over the German dead.

The Third Prussian Guards Division, with a regiment of Grenadiers and a division brought down from Ypres, were shattered in the final battle of Bullecourt. Still the enemy Army Commander was not content to stand upon his new line and regard the village as permanently lost. As soon as he was certain that all his garrison had been killed, captured, or driven out from the upper part of the village by May 14th, leaving only a few pockets of men southward, more or less connected with the great tunnel, he resolved to make a final attempt to turn defeat into victory.

Early in the morning of Tuesday, May 15th, Bullecourt was again ploughed up by a smoking, flaming tempest of German projectiles, and drenched for hours with gas shells. The intense and heavy fire stamped up and down the section of the Hindenburg line won by the Australians, as well as thundering in flame and poison upon the village.

Then, at dawn, when the British batteries were fiercely shooting at the German gunners, the first German masses advanced in the open upon the right flank of the lost German line. The position was held by New South Wales troops. After passing through the British barrages of guns and machine-guns, at four o'clock in the morning, the German infantry survived in sufficient strength to penetrate the Australian centre for thirty yards. They were, however, immediately counter-attacked with bombs, bayonets, and trench mortars, and by the rallying men from New South Wales. By eleven o'clock no living German remained in the trench, but more than two hundred dead Germans were found in it. Moreover, as the enemy was held in the rear by a shell curtain, through which he had to flee, his total losses were very much greater.

Another counter-attack directed on the left flank of the British position, about the same time, did not reach the defending outposts. The British artillery entirely smashed up the German columns as they were advancing, with trench mortars firing behind them and big guns clearing a path in front of them. From the British point of view, it was one of those overwhelming artillery successes that made the infantryman adore his gunners.

Later in the morning a third attack was delivered upon the north-east corner of Bullecourt. This also was successfully repulsed, with staggering loss to the enemy, by shrapnel curtains, machine-gun barrage, and gusts of rifle fire. In the afternoon, however, the German commander won a local, but apparently definite success. He launched his fourth and strongest counter-attack upon the south and south-west of Bullecourt village, and sent his troops up in such continuous dense formations that the British gunners could not kill them quickly enough. The

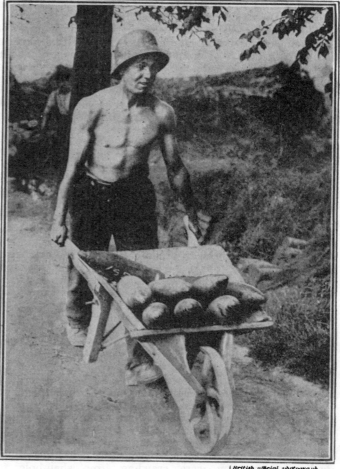

[British official photograph.

LIGHTLY CLAD FOR WEIGHTY WORK.
British soldier—who it will be observed was wearing an enemy helmet which he had secured as a trench souvenir—wheeling up shells in a barrow for keeping the guns supplied on the western front.

Germans drove back some posts near the lower end of the village in hard fighting above ground, while the remnant of the old garrison in the ruins was reinforced from the main tunnel.

The subterranean force began to emerge on the rear of the Scottish and English troops, and swept them with unexpected bursts of fire and volleys of bombs as the British companies were struggling against the overland shock troops. At this time, all that could be seen of Bullecourt was about half a dozen stumps of trees, rising above flattened heaps of broken brick and narrow ditches, blown in by blasts of high explosives. A few sticks of timber were regarded as a refreshing cover, while a cellar only half full of wreckage seemed like a little paradise in hell.

Wild groups of dust-covered, tired, bristly-faced fighting-men talked to each other about hurrying to the church, where the line was sagging, or supporting the **Fighting in a smoking desert** men at the cross-roads, and bombing back down the main street. But there were not any church, high street, cross-roads, churchyards, or other features in the blind and desolate place. The men merely named the various vanished features from memory of what they had been.

The last-made shell-hole was regarded as the best cover, because it seemed unlikely that another shell would fall immediately in the same crater. Nevertheless, the lunar wilderness incessantly fluctuated, the craters flowing over each other and hollowing out in new ways, like a waste of deep water labouring under a heavy gale. Stronger than any tempest were the concussions of air from the high explosive shells. Amid these violent and stunning ripples of the atmosphere, there drifted, more slowly, the choking fumes of exploding chemicals and wafts of poison gas from the quieter kind of projectiles.

The masked, grimed, powdered, fantastic figures of Englishmen and Scotsmen travelled through this modern inferno to reinforce their comrades holding out around the section of ruins, where the Germans were increasing in numbers and drawing fresh supplies from the Hindenburg tunnel.

Fighting went on all night and continued throughout Wednesday, May 16th. The British troops gradually, but continually, gained ground by their amazing tenacity and personal prowess. Sometimes, where the enemy's position was clearly defined, British fighting-men would suddenly draw back a little, to allow their artillery observation officers exactly to place a tremendous mass of shell capable of shattering dug-outs around the German galleries connecting with the tunnel.

After the high explosive projectiles there often followed a hurricane of the new British gas-shell, if the wind happened to set in a quarter that would not **Prolonged and** bring the gas back upon the attacking **unremitting ordeal** troops. Finally, after high explosive and gas, shrapnel would be flung steadily upon the positions which the Germans had regained, in order to force all their infantry to withdraw underground. Then, with the backing of trench-mortars, the British bombers would again work forward, win a scrap of ground, and dig themselves in like madmen. The quicker they dug, the better was their chance of surviving.

They, however, had also to submit to the same ordeal, prolonged and unremitting, which slowly broke the spirit and strength of their foes. The German gunners battered in their cover with shell, ranging from 5.9 in. to the largest calibres. Horrible gases burst about them in clouds, and intense shrapnel fire tested their steel hats when they were able to stand in the trench, and penetrated their bodies when they were crawling from shell-hole to shell-hole.

Happily, there was a considerable difference between the rate of fire of the opposing batteries. The British gunners had more guns, more shell, and a much wider arc of siting positions. As has already been explained, the enemy around Riencourt occupied a narrowing salient. It was overreached by the howitzers of the British Third Army on the Sensée stream line on the German right, and hammered in front by the guns which the Fifth British Army had arranged to the depth of some miles. Wholesale was the destruction wrought by the counter-battery work of these two great cross-firing combinations of British artillery, daringly and skilfully assisted by aeroplane observation and hill fire-controlling positions.

The German artillery appeared to have been ordered to be as economical as possible in its bombardment and counter-battery work. Either the tubes of the guns were wearing badly or the British naval and railway guns were interfering with the enemy's transport of shell. The hostile gun-fire only on rare occasions equalled the intensity of the British gun-fire. The German gunners generally used whirlwind bombardments for important purposes, but did not maintain the incessant storm of shell with which the British artillerymen opened the way into the great tunnel, both in Bullecourt and in the large space between Bullecourt and Fontaine.

The consequence was that a task which would have been impossible for the men of the Fifth Army in ordinary circumstances became practicable owing to the extraordinary rate at which great masses of artillery had been brought from the Bapaume front. On Thursday, May 17th, after continual fighting for nearly three hundred and fifty hours, the village of Bullecourt was entirely conquered, with all its difficult underground tunnel connections.

When everything is considered, the achievement of the Australian, English, and Scottish troops of Sir Hubert Gough's army appears to be the most striking success of the Imperial British forces in the spring campaign of 1917. The storming of Vimy Ridge and the advance from Arras to Monchy Hill and the upper part of the Hindenburg Line had larger strategic importance than the break made between Riencourt and beyond Bullecourt.

Yet, regarded as an affair of sheer human effort in fighting, engineering, heavy gun transport and improvised organisation, the advance of the left wing of the Fifth Army over the broad wasted zone between Bapaume and Bullecourt, followed by an amazingly rapid and victorious thrust across the works of the great Hindenburg tunnel, lifted the victors in the Ancre and Somme Battles to a glorious pinnacle of military power.

Every man in the army of Sir Hubert Gough shared the honours with the infantry and the gunners. The pioneers were indeed beyond praise; the cavalry, who took machine-gun villages at the charge and on some occasions rode over the Hindenburg Line, may be esteemed the finest horsemen that ever lowered a lance; the stretcher-bearers were acclaimed the greatest of all heroes by hundreds of thousands of men who were themselves of the finest heroic mould. Even the men of the Army Service Corps did so splendidly that the fighting-men scarcely grudged the fact that the more sheltered, non-combatant corps was better paid than the men who won the battles.

On Sunday, May 20th, when the conquered position at Bullecourt was fairly consolidated, the considerable break in the Hindenburg Line was extended by an English advance north of the village. By an assault at dawn, more than a mile of tunnelled front was carried and held by very violent fighting against the enemy's counter-attacking forces. The struggle continued until the evening, by which time the Germans showed clear signs of exhaustion.

The hostile force consisted of two first-class divisions with a large number of shock troops. Yet at the end of the day they were so thoroughly beaten that the English troops again stormed forward, behind their smashing barrage, and captured the hostile support system. All through the night the contending armies clashed amid the volcanic thunder of the guns.

The enemy forces engaged on the surface of the ground were thrown back with terrible losses. Only in a small sector of the great tunnel above Bulle- **Holding the main** court was the underground German **enemy masses** garrison able to hold out, by means of a subterranean feed of reinforcements.

With this exception, the Germans were thoroughly beaten and driven out of their fortress tunnel between Bullecourt and Arras. The nature of the ground made it too costly an affair for the British troops to continue merely a local action on the two thousand yards of tunnel west above Bullecourt. Another great offensive by the Third and Fifth Armies would have been necessary in order to capture the fragment of the Hindenburg Line and extend the British gains around Riencourt, Fontaine, and Chérisy.

Sir Douglas Haig ordered a strong British artillery demonstration, apparently indicative of another combined operation by the forces of Sir Edmund Allenby and Sir Hubert Gough. But no large infantry action followed. The British Commander-in-Chief was merely holding the main enemy masses on the old battlefield, in the design to facilitate the new campaign by the Second British Army on the distant Messines Ridge. In the first week of June the new battle opened under the direction of Sir Herbert Plumer, and the Bullecourt front relapsed into a condition of comparative calm.

BRITISH TROOPS ADVANCING

[British official photograph.
ALONG A SALONIKA RAILWAY.

RUMANIA AND THE BALKANS FROM THE FALL OF BUKAREST TO THE DETHRONEMENT OF CONSTANTINE.

By Robert Machray.

In Face of Disaster Rumania Carries On—Bravery of Peasant Army Recognised—Changes in the Commands—How the Front was Held
—Germans Baulked of the Oil—Rumanian and Russian Fighting Retreat Continues—Fierce Struggles in the Wallachian Plain
and in the Moldavian Mountains—Allies Lose Ramnicu Sarat—Enemy's Slow Progress South-East of Bukarest—Sakharoff's
Strategic Retirement in the Dobruja—Converging Attacks on Braila—Evacuation of the Grain Town—Its Grain Saved—Strong
German Push Against the Sereth Line—Its Comparative Failure—Severe Cold Grips All Rumania—Offensive Stopped at the
Sereth—Germans Held Up in Moldavia—Lull Sets In—Enemy Brutality in Rumania—Questionings in Great Britain Regarding
the Salonika Expedition—Government Reply—Pause in Macedonia—Allied Front Extended from the Adriatic to the Ægean—
Independence of Albania Proclaimed—Rising in Serbia Crushed by the Bulgaro-Germans—Renewal of Brisk Warfare by Sarrail
—British and Other Allied Successes—German Effort Splendidly Countered—Bulgarians Defeated near Doiran—Constantine
and the Entente—The Greek King Still Playing his Old Game—Intrigue and Treachery—Allies' Long Patience Exhausted at Last
—High Commissioner Appointed—Entrusted with Full Powers—Radical Change in the Situation—Constantine Compelled to
Abdicate and Leave Greece—Thessaly Occupied—Venizelos Returns from Salonika—Balkans in a New Phase.

R UMANIA'S most gallant struggle against
very heavy odds, with its varying phases
of success and failure deepening into
tragedy, was nar-
rated in Chapter
CLIX. (Vol. 8, p.
247) up to and including the
occupation of Bukarest by Field-
Marshal Mackensen on December
6th, 1916. By that date the
greater part of Wallachia had
passed into the ruthless hands of
Germany, and while the Rumanians, with the preponderant forces
of Russia, were successfully holding
the enemy on the western frontier
of Moldavia, the more important
portion of the Dobruja had also
been lost. Since the Second Battle
of Targu Jiu and the fall of
Craiova in November the whole
situation had developed unfortunately for Rumania and the
Entente, and the outlook was
distinctly dark and depressing,
though **not** entirely destitute of
the hope **that** something might
be saved from the spreading ruin.

Germany had taken a considerable area of the country, with the
best of its rich corn lands, but she
had failed to achieve what had
been her greatest aim—namely,
the capture or destruction of the
Rumanian Army. That Army had

[Elliott & Fry.
COLONEL J. NORTON GRIFFITHS, M.P.
Colonel Norton Griffiths, M.P. for Wednesbury, was
sent out from England to see that the petroleum wells
in Rumania with their plans and buildings were rendered
useless for the German invaders.

been seriously depleted by more than three months of
bitter and incessant fighting against superior numbers,
artillery, and science, but even the disastrous issue of
the terrible Battle of the Argesul,
which sealed the fate of the capital,
did not result in such an impair-
ment of its cohesion or of its
spirit as would have been fatal.
All along the line from the
Carpathians to the Danube, north
and south of Bukarest, it retreated
eastward in fairly good order, the
Russians helping effectively in
covering and securing its withdrawal intact. It suffered losses,
some of them severe enough, but
in the main it made good its
retirement to the line of the
Sereth, behind which it was
reorganised, refitted, and put in
even better fighting trim than
before.

Yet neither the Army nor the
people of Rumania lost heart on
account of the blackness of the
position at the time, or ceased to
be confident as regarded the
future. Among the many fairy
tales spread broadcast over the
world by the Germans none was
more specious than that which
represented Bukarest as receiving
Mackensen and his soldiers with
enthusiasm, none more false than
that which described the

HHH **429**

IN THE TRAIL OF THE SAPPERS.
Trestle bridge built across a river in East Macedonia by the British troops, who were placed on the right wing of the Allied Army of the Orient.

retained his place as Prime Minister and Minister for Foreign Affairs, and directed the Administration.

Two outstanding features of the struggle so far had been the heroism of Rumania's peasant soldiers and the incompetence, if nothing worse, of a large proportion of their commanding officers. In recognition of the bravery and constancy of the one, and as a stimulus to further effort, agrarian reforms of a thoroughgoing description were promised in Parliament, while, as a remedy for the other, sweeping and salutary changes were effected in the commands.

Rumanians as welcoming the invaders. The truth was that during the long reign of King Carol, who was far more of a German than a Rumanian, the country had become infested with Germans and Austrians, the majority of whom remained after war had been declared—to the serious prejudice, no doubt whatever, of the success of the Rumanian arms. As the red tide advanced and overflowed the land, these enemies, who had kept quiet at first, showed their real nature, and they were the people who showered congratulations on the victors. This was particularly the case in Bukarest, where, according to a candid correspondent of the "Arbeiter-Zeitung" of Vienna, the "Germans, Austrians, and Hungarians resident in the town, who had hitherto preserved silence, rediscovered their German hearts"—and acted as might be expected in the circumstances.

Genuine Rumanians had no bouquets, no garlands of flowers for the brutal conquerors of their native soil. The

"German hearts" in Bukarest

deep and abiding feeling of the little country, which had already endured so much, and was to be called on to bear still more, was manifested when, summoned by its King, its Parliament met in Jassy, the temporary capital, in the fourth week of that same dark month of December. By that time nearly the whole of Wallachia and practically all the Dobruja had been subjugated by the Germans. In his speech from the throne, which was frequently and fervently applauded, King Ferdinand said that up till then the war had imposed great hardships and sacrifices on the country, which, however, was bearing them with courage and resolution. He stated emphatically that the Rumanians, in spite of their difficulties and sufferings, were determined to continue the contest with all their energies by the side of the Allies. In the debates which followed, the members of the Legislature unanimously declared against any idea of a separate peace, and strongly advocated a still more strenuous prosecution of the conflict. To increase the solidarity of the Government with the nation, the Cabinet was reconstituted by the inclusion of several former political opponents of M. Bratiano, the most distinguished of them being M. Take Jonescu. As the chief Rumanian statesman, Bratiano

NO PASSAGE WITHOUT PERMISSION.
Military police-station of the Allies at the frontier of the Neutral Zone delimited across Greece between the Greek Royalist and Venizelist troops from the Gulf of Salonika to Albania.

MACEDONIA—BUT FOR EVER FRANCE.
French cemetery by the little Greek church of Brod, on the Cherna River. There was heavy fighting in all this district in 1916 between the Bulgarians and the Serbo-French troops pressing on Monastir.

Apart from the industrial and commercial class, the population of Rumania was sharply divided into two classes—the aristocracy, composed of the landowners or boyars, who were comparatively few in number; and the tillers of the soil, who formed the bulk of the people, and whose condition was not much better than that of serfs. As a consequence of what had taken place in the field, it was seen that the status of the peasants had to be raised, and that too much had been left to officers drawn from the aristocracy. Large political concessions to the peasantry were, in fact, long overdue.

SCENE OF A SERBIAN TRIUMPH.
The village of Brod on the Cherna, taken by the Serbians October 17th, 1916, when with a sudden thrust they crossed the river and chased the Bulgarians across the hills in the direction of Monastir.

PRUSSIAN METHODS IN THE AUSTRIAN ARMY.
Recaptured deserters from the Austrian troops fighting in the Balkans being led back to certain execution. German military tyranny caused much disaffection among the soldiery of Germany's allies.

BRITISH CAMP IN MACEDONIA.
At the opening of the allied offensive the British held the line of the Struma northward to Lake Butkova, and thence westward, south of Lake Doiran, to the Vardar River near Smol.

With respect to the commands, most of the generals were removed and replaced by men who had proved their ability in the campaign. Many of the superseded officers were of high social position, but that did not save them.

If the result of the Battle of the Argesul could not have been a victory for the Rumanians, it would have been much less of a defeat, and probably indecisive with respect to Bukarest, but for the culpable indolence and sluggishness of movement of certain of the subordinate commanders, and the criminal negligence, amounting to treachery, of one of them, a naturalised German, whose original name of Sosek had been altered into Sosescu. This general was the son of a Saxon, who had established himself in the capital about fifty years before the war, and his loyalty had been questioned on several occasions, but he had contrived to retain his rank. For his conduct —or rather misconduct—in the Argesul operations he was tried by court-martial, cashiered, and given five years' penal servitude. Of the Rumanian high commanders, only two really had distinguished themselves —always excepting General Dragalina, **Naturalised general** whose strategy and gallantry won the **cashiered** First Battle of Targu Jiu, in which he fell gloriously. These two generals were Avarescu, the Commander-in-Chief, and Presan, who was in command of the troops that fought, not altogether without success, that part of the great Battle of the Argesul which took place south-west of Bukarest, and was specifically known as the Battle of the Neajlov. General Presan afterwards became Chief of the General Staff, and General Avarescu, who was beloved by his soldiers, was confirmed in his post as head, under the King, of the Rumanian Army.

From the outset of the campaign Russia had assisted Rumania in both Moldavia and the Dobruja. By the beginning of December very large Russian forces were actively co-operating with the Rumanians along the whole battle-line. They had taken over nearly the entire Moldavian frontier, with its extremely difficult mountain warfare. They were strung along the Wallachian front, being particularly strong in the southern area, north of the Danube. Under Sakharoff they were fighting in the Dobruja. In that darkening stage of the struggle which followed Rumania's early successes in Transylvania, and

RUMANIAN ARTILLERY RETREATING UNDER HEAVY FIRE.
German representation of a Rumanian battery caught by enemy artillery while retreating at the end of the Battle of the Argesul. This stubbornly contested fight lasted for three days, December 1st to 3rd, 1916, and ended in the complete victory of Mackensen's army and his occupation of Bukarest which he entered in state on December 6th.

roads to Buzau and Braila respectively, that the Russians, with some Rumanian troops, were holding up the invaders in Moldavia along the line of the mountains, and that while there was a lull in the Dobruja, circumstances indicated a retirement to the north by the Russo-Rumanian forces in that region. Heavy fighting had been going on for more than a week in the Carpathians, and still continued. In Wallachia the Rumanians, with whom were mingling more and more Russians, were endeavouring to check the advance of the enemy by incessant rearguard actions, some of which had a temporary success, but it was already clear that no prolonged stand could be made until the line of the Sereth, which was fortified, was attained, and that whether the Germans would be brought definitely to a standstill there was a question that could be answered in the affirmative only if they also failed to penetrate into Moldavia from the north-western passes. An uncompromised defence of the mountains was therefore a matter of cardinal importance, though the rival forces operating in that rugged area were much smaller numerically than those fighting in the Wallachian plain, which at the moment attracted the larger share of public attention and interest, as was natural enough, inasmuch as the bulk of the Rumanian Army was still in that quarter.

In Wallachia the following was the manner in which the opposing armies were distributed. On the north the Second Rumanian Army, then commanded in person when it was becoming evident that the Germans were winning, there had been some voices raised suggesting that Russia was lukewarm in support of her little neighbour, but M. Take Jonescu and others, who were well informed, denied that this was the case, and maintained that Russia had done all and more than all she had covenanted to perform. What seemed to be authoritative statements to the same effect were published in the British Press. However, after the Russian Revolution of March, 1917, when, figuratively speaking, "many graves were opened," the "Matin" of Paris printed an interview with General Iliescu, formerly Chief of the Rumanian General Staff, in which he made a grave accusation against the old Russian régime. He asserted that the initial cause of the overthrow of Rumania was the "disloyal plan of the Germanophil (Stürmer) Government of Petrograd, who played with the fate of Rumania to facilitate a premeditated act of treachery." This plan was to allow the Germans to invade Rumania as far as the Sereth, and then to make a separate peace, which was to be represented as the inevitable consequence of a Rumanian—and not of a Russian—defeat.

On December 6th, the day on which Mackensen entered Bukarest, the general situation was that the main Rumanian armies were retreating in Wallachia by the by General Avarescu, had its right in the mountains east of the Predeal Pass, from which it had effected its retirement, though mendacious German reports stated that it had been captured or destroyed; but it had been compelled to sacrifice its rearguards, who fought bravely to the last, and had been forced to blow up many of its guns. It had thereafter got into touch with the First Rumanian Army, which had been concentrated around Ploesti, and retreated from that capital of the oil-fields on December 6th in the direction of Buzau. These two armies, thus combined, were moving backward in the district north-west of Bukarest. **Rumanian retreat** South-west of the capital were the **from Ploesti** Third and Fourth Rumanian Armies under General Presan. Over against the first group was the Ninth German Army, under Falkenhayn, and against the second was what was styled the "Danube Army," under General von Kosch. Of the enemy forces, Falkenhayn's was predominantly German, while Kosch's was made up of Germans, Austro-Hungarians, Bulgarians, and Turks, the nationals of the two last named constituting its principal strength.

The retreat of the First and Second Rumanian Armies from Ploesti and the line north and south of it took place under a thick pall of smoke, which made the sky for many leagues as black as if it had been night. This Egyptian darkness was occasioned by the destruction of the oil industry. To prevent the Germans from getting the valuable, and to them essential, supplies of the petroleum of Rumania, the wells had been blocked, the oil set on fire and burned, and all the plant and buildings systematically wrecked. Prominent in the work of devastation—which was a serious loss to Rumania as it involved the loss of many million pounds sterling, but which was necessary in her own interests as well as in those of her allies—was Colonel J. Norton Griffiths, M.P. for Wednesbury, whose energetic methods surprised not only the Rumanians but also Americans who happened to be there. Of him a correspondent wrote: "To see him swinging a big hammer round his head and smashing up machinery with it, just to show how the thing should be done, made one poetical mine-manager describe him as being in love with ruin. Neither weariness nor danger could daunt him. When the petrol in basins would not light quickly, he took bundles of straw, thrust them into

Destruction of the oil-wells it, and set them alight, escaping just in time." Colonel Griffiths had been sent out from England to see that this wholesale and thorough business of destruction should be carried out, in case the advance of the Germans demanded this heavy sacrifice, and he did it well, to the intense, raging disappointment of the baffled enemy, who had counted on obtaining immediately the oil in sufficiently large quantities to be of vital service to him.

By the railway which branched eastward from Ploesti, and along the high-road in the same direction, the main body of the Rumanians in the north-west retreated to the Cricovu River, where it took up a position, and succeeded in checking the Germans for a while, but the pressure was too severe to permit of a long stand, and it fell back on the town of Mizil, through which from Cislau passed the road from the Buzau Pass to Bukarest by way of Urziceni, and to the Danube via Slobozia, whence one arm went northward to Braila, the second eastward to Harsova, and the third southward to Silistria. Higher up on the same front Avarescu fought a successful delaying action in the valley of the Buzau River, near Cislau. Lower down, the Jalomita, a stream of some size after its junction with the Prahova and the Cricovu, and then swollen by heavy rains, presented a natural obstacle of importance to the onward march of the enemy, and on its banks, in front of Urziceni and elsewhere,

Fall of Mizil and Urziceni

there were several sharp encounters. But the Germans, who had brought up fresh troops, were forcing the pace, and determined to move forward with their occupation of the country, though by this time they must have lost all hope of cornering any large amount of the Rumanian Army. By this time, also, considerable bodies of Russian cavalry had made their appearance in this area, and were reinforcing the tired and overworked Rumanians, who were now being withdrawn gradually to the rear.

It was not till December 12th, and only after bitter struggles, that the Germans took Mizil and Urziceni. The Rumanians resisted the enemy gamely at Cislau, but were compelled to retreat eastward from it about the same date. From Mizil the Germans pressed on towards the town of Buzau, their chief objective in this district, but suffered a distinct reverse on the 13th. South of the high-road between these places the Rumanians turned and, boldly taking the offensive, drove their foes out of a whole row of villages which had previously been lost. More than that, the Germans farther south were thrown

AUSTRO-HUNGARIAN GUNS IN POSITION COMMANDING A RUMANIAN PASS.

Another German artist's impression of the Central Powers' operations in Rumania—an Austro-Hungarian battery of mountain howitzers sited in a pass. Hindenburg's plan was that Falkenhayn should maintain heavy pressure on all the passes leading into Wallachia while holding a large force in reserve at the Vulkan Pass, which Mackensen should join after crossing the Danube, and then drive in force upon the Rumanians.

THE COURAGE OF THE SERBIANS.
Wounded Serbians on their way from the front. British doctors and nurses were full of admiration for the courage with which the Serbian soldier endured all suffering.

back across the Jalomita, thanks to the support given to the attack by impetuous rushes of the Cossack horsemen, backed up by some companies of Russian infantry. These successes, however, had only a temporary effect, and the enemy was in sufficient strength to resume his advance on Buzau, which fell into his hands on the 14th, marking a further stage in his invasion of Wallachia.

Buzau, as the centre on the east side of the great oil tract, had a high value from the commercial point of view, but there, as elsewhere, wells, machinery, and the petroleum itself had been destroyed, and the Germans again were baulked of this particular prey, which they so much desired. Yet they found recompense in the strategical significance of the place, as it was the meeting of several roads, one of them being the most important in that part of the land, and a railway junction, a line running from it to Braila, fifty-six miles away, and another, the continuation of the Bukarest-Ploesti line eastward, going up northerly through Ramnicu Sarat and Focsani to the Bukovina and Russia.

The capture of Buzau

Simultaneously with the advance of the Ninth German Army north-west of Bukarest, that of the Danube Army was making progress south-west of the capital. In the latter area the Third and Fourth Rumanian Armies were supported by the 40th Russian Division. Following on the retreat, after the Battle of the Argesul, of these forces, which were commanded by General Presan with great ability, the enemy swarmed across the Danube south-east of Bukarest, the Bulgarians occupying the left bank between Silistria and Cerna Voda, and taking the town of Oltenitsa, with little or no opposition. Oltenitsa had been evacuated by the Rumanians so thoroughly that the Sofia communiqué described it as having been " looted" before the Bulgarians got into possession of it. Another communiqué spoke of the capture of Calarasi and of the bridge-head on the left side of the Danube opposite Cerna Voda, but these were easy captures, the truth being that Presan was withdrawing north and east to the Lower Jalomita, and was avoiding engagements till he reached the line of that river, where he purposed making a stand if the circumstances were favourable. By December 14th all Great Wallachia, according to a Berlin message of that

date, was in the hands of the Danube Army south of the railway from Bukarest to Cerna Voda. On the evening of that day Kosch forced a passage of the Jalomita, and the Bulgarians were in Fetesti. As the Russo-Rumanian troops were retiring from Buzau on the north-west, Presan withdrew his whole forces from the positions he had taken up on the Jalomita—otherwise he might have been cut off from the north—and rapidly made for Filipesti and Braila.

Thus, north-west and south-west of Bukarest, the Rumanians made good their retreat. Since the Battle of the Argesul their losses had not been serious, and they had succeeded in inflicting considerable damage on the enemy, besides slowing down his advance. Meanwhile, the Russians and the Rumanians held him

" HITS WERE MADE AND GOOD RESULTS OBSERVED."
Fire caused by bombs dropped from enemy aircraft on material belonging to the Allies operating in Serbia. All the belligerents in Macedonia displayed great aerial activity, but only aeroplanes were used after the enemy lost a Zeppelin in the Vardar Marshes early in the campaign.

up on the Moldavian frontier—a factor in the struggle of the utmost importance. As far back as November 28th the Russians had started a great relief offensive, but it came too late to save Bukarest and Wallachia. It did very materially contribute, however, to the salvation of the Rumanian Army and of Moldavia, by depriving the Germans of the initiative on that front and bringing to naught their plans. From the Bukovina and all down the Carpathians the armies of General Lechitsky and General Kaledin—names for ever memorable in connection with Brussiloff's splendid campaign in the summer of the same year—covered the mountain approaches into Moldavia, and in the beginning of December joined up with the Rumanians about the Trotus Valley south of the Gyimes Pass. Opposed to them in the north was the army of General von Kövess, who had co-operated with Mackensen in the subjugation of Serbia, and it was composed mainly of Austrians and Hungarians ; while in the south they were faced by the First Austro-Hungarian Army under the leadership of General von Arz.

Russia's effective assistance

Day after day fighting of the most bitter and determined character continued, almost without intermission, in this most difficult region. Amidst deep snow and piercing blasts various mountains and heights were taken by storm, lost, recaptured, and lost again ; but nowhere did the enemy get a real chance of breaking through, which was his aim, though he made out that his effort was to hold off the Russians and Rumanians. A Vienna official telegram of December 11th showed this pretended attitude, but also showed how magnificent were the efforts of the Russians. It said : " In the Carpathians the Russians, in spite of heavy losses, which during the last few weeks at a low estimate amount to 30,000 men, continue to assail our positions without success." These figures doubtless were excessive—like so many other calculations of the enemy—but they bore eloquent testimony to what must have been his corresponding losses in that sector alone. The communiqué next week went into details : " The army of General von Kövess on both sides of the road from Vale Putna to Jacobeny (in the extreme southern corner of the Bukovina), where the enemy since the beginning of his relief offensive has, with particular stubbornness, been assaulting the troops of General von Habermann, and in the region north of the Jablonica Pass, there was fierce fighting. All the sacrifices of the Russians were unavailing." With respect to the part of this front that lay farther south, it observed : " The army of General von Arz, in the frontier sector west and north-west of Ocna (in the Trotus Valley below the Gyimes Pass), beat off again several attacks." Typical of the struggle was the fight for a height north of Sulta, in the Trotus district —one day the Austrians had it, the next saw it taken from them, and on the third day it was once more reft from the Allies, after the most sanguinary conflict in each case. On December 15th there was very little change in the Moldavian line generally, but fighting went on and on.

Operations in the Dobruja

In the Dobruja the Russians, under General Sakharoff, with Rumanians and Serbians, in late November and in the first days of December, had sought to help their forces on the other side of the Danube by a series of vigorous attacks on the Bulgarians ; but these had had no appreciable influence on the issue of the great battle which gave Bukarest to the Germans. After the fall of the capital there ensued a lull on this front, the Russians remaining stationary on the line they had taken up some miles south of Harsova, and about an equal distance north of the Cerna Voda bridge. They were waiting on developments

CROSSING THE LINE.
Military train passing from Greek on to Serbian territory, watched by a British soldier from one of the stones marking the frontier.

north of the Danube, as their own movements had to conform with them. By December 15th the situation in Wallachia was, unfortunately, only too plainly inimical to Rumania, and compelled a retirement in the Dobruja. On the 16th Berlin announced that the Russians had evacuated their positions, and that Bulgarian, Turkish, and German troops, moving up after them, had crossed the Harsova-Cartal-Cogealac line. The allied force retreated steadily, fighting occasional rearguard actions, to the wooded district of the Northern Dobruja. A striking episode in the Dobruja operations was the bombardment of Baltchik, in the extreme south, by the Russian Black Sea Fleet on December 13th, with a view

to the destruction of the mills there which supplied the Bulgarian Army with flour. The Russian ships were shelled by the shore batteries, and attacked by seaplanes and a submarine, but, after executing their task, got away with very slight damage.

In Wallachia the main body of the Ninth German Army was, on December 15th, marching along the high-road from Buzau towards Ramnicu Sarat (otherwise Rimnic), while another portion of it, moving some miles to the east of Buzau, in the neighbourhood of the river of the same name, was attempting to cross the Calmatuiul lowlands. On the 16th the Russians inflicted a severe check on the enemy in the former district, the Cossacks driving him back for some distance, and in the latter sector repelled all assaults near Batogu, thirty miles south-west of Braila, and smothered by their fire attacks south of Filipesti—so that the Germans gained even no local advantage, and were unable to advance for several days. Along the whole front raged a stubborn battle, in which the Russians more than held their own, and for a while stemmed the tide of invasion. For the best part of a week the enemy had to admit that the situation exhibited no improvement for him, but meanwhile he was bringing up his heavy guns wherewith to batter down the not too strong entrenchments that had been hurriedly improvised by the Russians during the retreat ; and, at the same time, in order to divert the flow of Russian reinforcements to Rumania, he initiated an offensive in Volhynia and Galicia.

Russians more than hold their own

Not till December 25th were the Germans really making any progress worthy of the name, but their powerful artillery was then beginning to tell. In the morning of that day they commenced a violent bombardment of the Russian positions on both sides of the Buzau-Ramnicu Sarat road, and in the region of Socariciul-Balaceanul, about nine miles south of Ramnicu. Under cover of the fire of immense quantities of both light and heavy guns they launched a fierce assault on the north of the high-road, and after ineffectual attempts captured a height lying south of Racovitseni, eight miles west of Ramnicu. By a brilliantly-executed counter-attack the Russians retook the height, but had to abandon it, as the enemy swept it with his shells. Next day the unrelaxing pressure of the German

FIRE CAUSED BY ENEMY AIRCRAFT.
Dense columns of smoke rising from an object fired by incendiary bombs dropped by enemy aviators, watched from the Serbian heights with unconcern by men of the allied armies.

GREECE IN RELATION TO THE SALONIKA EXPEDITION.

This map shows the geographical importance of Greece as a factor in the problem confronting the Allied Army of the Orient, which lay in an arc from the Gulf of Rendina to Lake Prespa, with a possibly hostile Greek army in its rear. The Neutral Zone cut across the north of Thessaly was the frontier which both forces were pledged not to pass.

front of Ramnicu Sarat, gained a complete victory over the Russians "sent forward for the defence of Rumania."

This communiqué further stated : "The enemy, who was defeated on December 26th, attempted to recapture the lost territory by means of counter-attacks delivered by strong masses of troops which failed. Prussian and Bavarian Infantry detachments, pursuing the retreating Russians, swarmed into his new positions constructed during the night and penetrated beyond Ramnicu Sarat." Berlin reported that over ten thousand Russians were captured in the course of the fighting for the place. But south-east of Ramnicu Sarat, on a line from the Ramnicu River through Boldu, Filipesti, and Viziru to the Danube, south of Braila, the Germans were held at this time.

There their objective was Braila, and the Russians sought with tremendous effort to save it, or at least to give such pause to the German advance that it could be evacuated with little loss. Though on December 25th the "well-seasoned German divisions, supported by Hungarian battalions," as Berlin put it, "stormed the stubbornly defended village of Filipesti, and the strongly entrenched adjoining Russian positions on both sides of the village," the Russians retired only a short distance, and there "stubbornly defended" themselves with more success for several days. Filipesti was destroyed by the fire of the enemy's heavy guns, which had been moved up the railway from Buzau. Wherever there were no railway facilities for the heavy artillery the Germans advanced either very slowly or not at all in this part of the field.

Farther east on this front the Danube Army of Von Kosch took up the German line from Filipesti to the Danube. On December 20th it had progressed as far as Pirlita, south of Viziru, or about twenty-five miles south of Braila, but had been repulsed by the Russians, who, however, were pressed slightly back on the south-east near Stancuta. Five days later Petrograd announced that all attacks in this region had been baffled by the Russian fire. Yet on the 27th Kosch's persistent assaults prevailed. Capturing several fortified villages, he forced his way, after repeated attacks, **Danube Army** counter-attacks, and desperate hand-to- **reaches Pirlita** hand encounters, into the front of the Russians, who were compelled to return to positions northward which they had previously prepared. The Germans confessed that the fighting here was bitter, which meant that their own losses were heavy, and said that their success was due to "the energy of the command and the complete devotion of the troops." But the Russians did not retire very far, and almost immediately were standing their ground with the greatest bravery and resolution. West of Viziru the

guns was too strong for the Allies, who were forced to yield ground and withdraw towards the town. In the fighting on this and the preceding day the Germans claimed to have made prisoners upwards of 5,000 men. West of Ramnicu they were not at first successful, but on the contrary were beaten back. On the 27th the battle reached a pitch of great intensity, the Germans thrusting forward with all their might and the Russians resisting with the most tenacious valour. Here and there the latter maintained themselves splendidly, but south-west of the town, on a front of about eleven miles, their trenches were demolished and rushed. Before the close of the day Ramnicu Sarat was in the hands of the enemy, and the Russians were withdrawing to the fortified line of the Sereth at Focsani, on the railway, and Maicanesti, about half-way between Focsani and Braila.

According to the official German account, published on December 28th, it was not till that day that the Ninth Army under Falkenhayn, in this very considerable battle in

Germans were thrown back with many casualties. In this last engagement British armoured motor-cars played a prominent rôle. They had last been heard of as fighting in the Dobruja, and months before that they had won renown in Armenia in the operations against the Turks. Of them a Russian communiqué of December 28th reported: "The famous British armoured cars took part in beating off the attacks of the Germans. The gallant

Success of British armoured cars commander of the car detachment was wounded during the battle of December 26th when repulsing the enemy. Never-

theless, on the 27th he again directed the operations of his force, and put the enemy to flight." It was a fine tribute to the admirable work of this small but efficient British contingent, and of the courage and energy of its head.

South of Janca, a station on the railway from Buzau to Braila, east of Filipesti, the Germans also were repelled, the Cossack horsemen thrusting boldly into them, and casting their ranks into confusion. In spite of this and similar checks the Danube Army advanced generally, if slowly, on this front, and by the last day of the year was attacking the bridge-head of Braila, some ten or twelve miles from the port itself. The Germans now were both south and west of the town. On the other side of the Danube, in the Dobruja, the Bulgarians, with German and Turkish supports, were by the same date approaching

at the beginning of the third week in December, the Russo-Rumanians, under the leadership of General Sakharoff, withdrew in good order, and by the 18th were forty miles north of the line they had held when the Battle of the Argesul was fought. As they retired they fired the villages, evacuated the population, and when the enemy entered Babadag, the only place of any importance in the district, it was to find a mass of smoking ruins. On the 20th a Bulgarian communiqué stated that Sakharoff was preparing a stand in the broken, hilly region south of the Danube. Heavy fighting continued throughout the next two days for the possession of several heights, which changed hands more than once. By a brilliant attack a Russian regiment threw back a portion of the Bulgarians, who had advanced east of Lake Babadag from Enisala, most of its units being drowned in the lake or neighbouring marshes, and the remainder, over a hundred in number, taken prisoner. But **Turks and Bulgars take Rachel** the enemy on this front was in much superior strength, and on the 25th the Russo-Rumanian left wing abandoned both Isaccea and Tultcha, respectively twenty-five and forty miles east of Braila. The right wing, however, offered strong artillery opposition near the village of Greci, some fourteen miles south-east of the grain town, in an attempt to cover the bridge-head at Macin, six miles away. On the 28th combined assaults of Bulgarian and Turkish troops succeeded in driving

[*French official photograph.*

A LONELY VIGIL.
Sentry on duty at a vantage point on the Macedonian front, where he could maintain observation over wide distances.

the Russians from the fortified hills immediately east of Macin, and then took Rachel, about seventeen miles from Braila. At Macin the Russians resisted with admirable tenacity, but in spite of their efforts the bridge-head was slowly narrowed by the fierce and persistent attacks of the enemy, and by New Year's Day had been considerably reduced in extent.

Braila was now closely invested on all sides except on the north, where it lay in front of the Sereth line. Without natural defences, the town stood on a bluff on the edge of a wide plain, a melancholy fenland, tenanted solely by herds of swine and innumerable wild birds. Situated on

very close to the great Rumanian grain centre on the east. In conformity with the gradual, orderly, fighting retirement of the Russian forces across the Eastern Wallachian plain to the line of the Sereth, the Russo-Rumanian troops had withdrawn northward in the Dobruja, but as in Wallachia, so in the Dobruja, the enemy was made to pay a considerable price for all the territory he gained. No longer did he progress by leaps and bounds, as had been the case after the fateful Second Battle of Targu Jiu.

Having given up most of their southerly positions in the Dobruja

[*British official photograph.*
MINERS CONSTRUCTING DUG-OUTS UNDER A MOUNTAIN-SIDE.
This fine photograph gives an illuminating insight into the development of trench architecture under pressure of modern artillery, which rendered useless the strongest and most elaborate fortifications of steel and concrete built upon the surface of the earth. As the war progressed it became always more apparent that only subterranean fortresses were of any use.

the left bank of the Danube, where the river, after dividing into several arms near Harsova, resumed its normal appearance and was wide and deep, Braila was at the head of navigation for sea-going ships by the Sulina Channel into the Black Sea. A flourishing commercial entrepôt, its prosperity dated from about half a century before, when its waterway was vastly improved by the work of the European Commission set up on that behalf by the Treaty of Paris. Vessels of 4,000 tons were able to go up to it, and before the war British shipping was more in evidence at the wharves than any other, the English tongue being almost the second language of the place.

After the Russo-Turkish War Braila **The enemy enters** became, with its near neighbour, Galatz, **Braila** the centre of the Rumanian grain trade, the granaries of the two towns ranking with the largest in the world, each holding about a quarter of a million quarters of wheat, or nearly two million bushels. Its population was not far from seventy thousand; but, apart from its commercial side, it had few claims to notice. In 1854 the Russians crossed the Danube from it into the Dobruja, but in 1878 they crossed from Galatz. Its wheat gave it its vital importance, and made it of enormous prospective value to the Germans. Here, again, they were destined to be balked.

Of the three converging attacks on the town, the one which got home first was that from the east. At Macin and Jijila, a short distance to the north, the Russians continued to offer a most stubborn resistance, but on January 3rd they were overborne, and had to abandon both of these places. Next day Berlin announced that "German and Bulgarian regiments, fighting shoulder to shoulder, had taken by storm" these "obstinately-defended villages," capturing a thousand prisoners and ten machine-guns. It was added that by this action the Dobruja had been cleared, with the exception of a narrow strip of land running in the direction of Galatz, where the Russians still held their ground. On the 5th Petrograd admitted that a retirement was being made to the other bank of the Danube, after an all-day battle. With the loss of Macin, Braila was open from the east, and as it was impossible to defend it any longer, the Russians evacuated the grain town on January 4th-5th; but before leaving it they destroyed the granaries and factories. From Macin the Bulgarians marched into the empty and desolated streets, while German and Bulgarian cavalry entered from the west. At the end of a long message, dated January 6th, Berlin pompously maintained that in the Dobruja the Third Bulgarian Army, including German, Bulgarian, and Turkish troops, under the command of General Neresoff, had swiftly and definitely completed its task. "There are no more Russian or Rumanian soldiers in the country," it declared; and concluded by stating that Galatz was under fire. But it had nothing to say regarding the fact that no booty was obtained in Braila.

From the point of view of supply—the point of view that bulked so largely with the Germans and their allies— Braila proved a keen disappointment. **Balked of the** Deep as had been the rage and vexation **hoped-for grain** of the enemy over the thorough destruction of the great Rumanian oil-fields, it might be doubted whether, having in mind the grave food problems which confronted the peoples of the Central Empires, the loss of by far the larger part of the grain of Rumania, if not of nearly the whole of it, was not even a more bitter blow. The protracted delaying retirement of the Russians had afforded plenty of time for getting the wheat away from Braila, or for rendering it unfit for use. Nor did the Germans get much grain in any other part of the country. As was seen in a previous chapter, one of the cogent reasons that impelled them to invade and seize the land was to gain possession of the grain of Rumania, which, with her petroleum, was her great economic asset. A Hungarian

correspondent put it on record that the total quantity of wheat, barley, maize, and other foodstuffs—wrung from the peasants and shopkeepers by the usual German methods of persuasion—which was obtained in Rumania by the enemy did not exceed one-fifth of the quantity exported from Rumania to the Central Empires during each of the years 1915 and 1916. Herr von Batocki, Germany's Food Dictator, to assuage the bitterness of the defeat of the tremendous expectations that had been raised, significantly warned his countrymen that the extent of the plunder must not be overestimated. Under Government direction the newspapers of Germany published cautions to their hungry readers not to pitch their hopes too high. Besides, the Bulgarians and the Turks desperately wanted a share. The truth was that neither Germany nor Austria-Hungary got anything like what they had anticipated. On the other side of the account, however, there was the potential value of the occupied corn and oil lands; but that needed time for its realisation, and, in the case of the petroleum, the expenditure of a good deal of money.

While the various operations which resulted in the fall of Braila were going forward, strenuous fighting was taking place along the railway and the high-road between Ramnicu Sarat and Focsani; and, at the same time, heavy enemy pressure was incessantly exerted in the mountains and in the valleys leading from them on the north into Moldavia and North-Eastern Wallachia. On January 1st the Russians were withdrawing nearer Focsani, on the fortified line of the Sereth, and stood about half-way between Ramnicu Sarat and Focsani itself. Next day there was a sharp fight, but it was only with Russian rear-guards, as the main force went on with its retirement. That day's German communiqué stated that the German and Austro-Hungarian troops of the Ninth Army were approaching the Focsani and Fundeni bridge-heads—the latter on the Sereth **Intense struggle** midway between the former and Galatz. **for Focsani** It claimed the taking of many prisoners.

Bitter and violent conflicts developed in this sector on January 3rd. South-west of Focsani the Germans, under cover of a drum-fire bombardment with asphyxiating shells, attacked a Russian regiment along the railway, but the Russian artillery was well handled and made great rents in their close formation. South-east of the Ramnicu River a Russian rifle detachment took by assault the village of Guleanca, capturing over two hundred men, five guns, and eight machine-guns. Nevertheless, the enemy was successful on the Milcovu River, gaining both Pantecesti and Meru; and on the 4th had advanced above Odobesti, eight miles north-west of Focsani.

The Milcovu, an affluent of the Sereth, was the stream which separated the old principalities of Wallachia and Moldavia, and what was designated the Milcovu sector formed a prolongation of the permanent system of fortifications called the Sereth line. Its conquest by the enemy gave him an important advantage, as it covered the farther advance of Falkenhayn's centre on Focsani. South-east of that town Slobozia and Rotesti were stormed by the 152nd West Prussian Regiment, these villages lying a few miles south of the junction of the Ramnicu River and the Sereth. On January 5th and 6th the struggle for Focsani became greatly intensified, the Germans bringing up their heaviest guns and attacking fiercely in massed formation. On the 6th a concentrated fire of extreme violence was directed on Ramniceni, and under its cover the enemy advanced nearly three miles easterly. According to the official German account, General Knobelsdorf and General Oettinger's divisions, under the command of General Kuhne, stormed and captured the strongly-consolidated Russian position on the road from Tatarani to Ramniceni, in spite of its having been strengthened by wire entanglements and flanking devices, and thereafter they advanced across the marshes towards the Sereth.

Greece makes amends for an unfortunate incident.

In addition to formal apologies by the Greek Government for the attack on allied troops in Athens on December 1st, 1916, the French British, Italian, and Russian flags were formally saluted by Greek troops in front of the Zappeion on January 30th, 1917.

[British official photograph.

Supplies moving up to a division by light railway to avoid the Macedonian mud.

Prince Alexander of Serbia visiting a Serbian encampment while on a tour of inspection.

[British official photograph.

Men of the Oxford and Bucks Light Infantry advancing over ground captured near Salonika.

[French official photograph.

French sentry on guard in an Athens suburb on the day of King Constantine's abdication.

Serbian cavalry, wearing steel helmets similar to those of the French Army, taking up positions during the recapture of Monastir.

Farther to the south-east a reinforced cavalry division under Count Schmettow took Olaneasca, Guleanca, and Maxineni. Next morning the Russians launched a great relief offensive between Focsani and Fundeni on a front of nearly sixteen miles, but they only gained ground near Obilesti, and Focsani shortly afterwards fell into German hands. North-west of the town, while the enemy was breaking into it on the south and from the east, Russian and Rumanian troops, after a desperate and most tenacious defence, were driven out of the mountain pass near Odobesti towards the Putna. Early in the morning of the 8th the Russians withdrew from Focsani, with a loss in prisoners of close upon 4,000 men, in addition to some guns and machine-guns.

Hailed throughout Germany as a great victory, the capture of Focsani, the western bastion of the fortified Sereth line, did not bring the enemy all the success he anticipated with regard to the swift rolling up of that line. The first step in the process had been taken, but practically it remained the only step. The Russians retired from Focsani to the Sereth itself and to its western tributary, the Putna, forming there a strong new line which linked up with the old Sereth line eastward. The Germans progressed to the Putna to find a difficult position, on which they had not reckoned, right in front of them. On both sides of Fundeni, between Focsani and Galatz, the Russian retreat continued to the Crangeni-Nanesti line, two or three miles south of the Sereth, and the village of Garleasca was lost in the same district. On the 10th the enemy succeeded in getting a footing on the farther bank of the Putna under cover of a fog, but he did not hold it long, for by an impetuous counter-attack, in which Russian bayonets made quick play, he was driven across the river again with considerable loss. A few days later an Austrian attack in the Putna valley was repulsed. For a week little of interest occurred on this part of the **Bulgarians' costly** front, but eastward the Turks stormed **adventure** Mihalea, north-west of Braila and west of Vadeni, and also took the last-named village, on January 13th. Vadeni, which lay two miles south of the Sereth, was recaptured by the Russians on the 17th by a well-prepared effort, and was held despite a determined Turkish onslaught.

By this time the weather in all Rumania had become most severe, an Arctic cold, with frost and snow, making extensive military movements well-nigh impossible. Mackensen did not attempt any operations of conspicuous importance. Galatz was within range of his guns, but though it was bombarded in a desultory fashion by the Turks of the Danube Army, an attack was not pressed. From the junction of the Sereth with the Danube, except about Vadeni, the enemy now occupied the right bank of the stream for a distance of nearly fifty miles westward. Higher up at Radulesti he was checked and thrown back, as also at Ciuslea, eight miles north-east of Focsani. On the 16th the Germans were actually standing on the defensive near Fundeni, but on the 20th they stormed Nanesti, after strong artillery preparation and hard fighting, with hand-to-hand struggles in the streets and houses, and then carried the bridge-head of Fundeni itself south of the river. The Russians made good their retreat to the opposite bank and destroyed the bridges. Thereafter nothing of importance happened on this front east as far as the Black Sea. But there was one curious episode—for a moment it appeared as if it might be something much more than an episode. Screened by a thick mist, Bulgarians from Tultcha crossed the St. George's Channel of the Danube, the southern arm of the estuary, the others being the Sulina Channel in the middle, and the Kilia Channel on the north. It looked as if an invasion of Russian Bessarabia was intended, but evidently this was a mistaken impression. The Russians counterattacked by night, and, according to their own communiqué, without a single shot being fired, annihilated the force

which had crossed the channel, except about three hundred and fifty men whom they made prisoners, while their loss was only one man killed and some forty men wounded. The Bulgarians did not try to cross over again, and the affair lost all significance.

Within a short space of time it was obvious that the great combined advance of the enemy was stayed, whatever were the reasons, on a line just south of the Danube, the Sereth, and the Putna, with a net result to him, since the invasion, of the subjugation of Wallachia and the Dobruja, or about three-fourths of Rumania, by the third week of January, 1917. Though it had to be admitted by the Allies that the enemy's gain in territory was considerable, they had the **Sanguinary fighting** satisfaction of knowing he had expected **in Moldavia** nothing less than the complete conquest of the country, and had failed to accomplish it owing to his being held up on the Moldavian front. His protracted and determined effort to break through or outflank the Russo-Rumanians from the Carpathians had met with absolute failure, notwithstanding some successes which seemed to promise well for his scheme, and many desperate, indecisive actions in the early part of that terrible winter. This front made a sharp angle from the mountains southward; at this bend the Russians and the Rumanians joined up, and though he attacked along the whole line, it was at this elbow that he made his pressure most felt in co-operation with his advance to the Sereth lower down.

Generally referred to as the "Front of the Archduke Joseph" in German despatches, the Moldavian mountain sectors saw the fiercest combats in the region that extended on both sides of the valley of the Oitoz, from the Trotus in the north to the Savala in the south. During the last week of December, 1916, and the first two weeks of January, 1917, fighting of the most sanguinary kind hardly ever intermitted. In this area the leader of the enemy's troops was General von Gerok, who had been transferred from Galicia towards the end of the year. On December 28th he took the offensive with considerable forces around Sosmezo, a Transylvanian frontier village in the Oitoz Pass, and pressing back the Russians captured some heights, but south of the place he was checked by the Russian artillery. Next day he made a slight farther advance in this difficult highland district, storming slowly his way eastward from hill to hill. Simultaneously he attacked the Rumanians in the valley of the Casin, a few miles to the south, and pushed them on for about a mile. On New Year's Eve he drove with all his might against both Russians and Rumanians from Sulta, in the Trotus sector, to the head-waters of the Putna, making gains at some points, but elsewhere being checked, and even defeated, as on the upper stream of the Susita. On January 1st the conflict continued with varying fortune; but in the Savala valley the Austrians, under General von Ruiz, captured the villages of Herestrau and Ungureni, both about ten miles within the frontier of Southern Moldavia, and also moved some distance down the valleys of the Putna and the Naruja. The following day saw the intense struggle maintained, the enemy making little out of it, as the Allies **Gerok reports** fought him foot by foot and, as a rule, **some progress** held on to their positions. His one distinct success was the storming of Soveia, in the Susita valley, and nine miles inside the frontier.

On January 3rd Gerok was able to report some progress between the Susita and the Putna. Beating down violent counter-attacks by Russian and Rumanian contingents, he occupied, after a stiff engagement, both Barsesti and Topesti, two villages about twenty-six miles north-west of Focsani, and midway between the frontier and the plain. To the north of the Oitoz road, and on both sides of Soveia, Gerok stormed several hills, and though the Allies strongly counter-attacked he was able to retain the positions he had captured. But in the Trotus district, where he delivered

ALLIED BATTLESHIPS IN GREEK WATERS.
Admiral du Fournet, commanding an Allied Fleet of British, French, and Italian warships, took practical control of Greek waters in September, 1916, and by threats of a blockade became master of the situation.

therefore that he would need all the men he could get together. He had vastly shortened his line in Rumania—no inconsiderable advantage. Various German divisions were withdrawn from the Sereth and sent to their home depôts, their places being taken by Austrian and Turkish troops.

Nothing of special importance took place on the Rumanian front during the months of February, March, April, May, and June. General Gourko had taken over the chief command of the Russo - Rumanian forces, with General Avarescu as his colleague; but after the Russian Revolution Gourko was superseded. Behind the front all that part of the Rumanian Army which was not in the trenches was thoroughly fitted for its duties in every way.

six separate assaults, he was repulsed with heavy loss. His progress continued, however, down the valleys of the Putna, the Naruja, and the Savala, and on the 5th the Rumanians on the Susita were forced to retire towards Racosa. Then came blinding snowstorms, with the thermometer well below zero, and the advance of the enemy, which had been far from rapid, almost ceased. In the upper valleys the Russians more than held their own.

Why the invasion stopped

Near Racosa the Rumanians yielded some ground on January 9th, and two days later the Russians lost some heights in the Gitoz district. On the 12th the Rumanians turned on their foe, and forced him back over a mile in the Casin valley; continuing their offensive they retrieved further lost ground in the same district during the next two or three days.

The progress of Gerok's flanking force met everywhere with stubborn and sometimes successful opposition. Apart from isolated operations, the fighting gradually died down along this whole front, practically coming to a close in the fourth week of January. A lull, in fact, had set in over the entire Rumanian theatre.

Resting on a line from the Bukovina nearly due south to the valley of the Oitoz, and thence south-eastward across the mountains to the Putna-Sereth-Danube front, the German invasion definitely stopped. Among the reasons given for the closing of the German operations against Rumania were the steadily increasing Russian opposition, with the great strength of the allied positions and the reorganised Rumanian Army in the background, and the inclemency of the weather, which was far beyond general experience. These reasons must have had due effect, but there was another which must greatly have contributed to bring about the decision. This was that Hindenburg, in carrying out his plan for the conquest of Rumania, had been able to attain the large measure of success achieved only by the employment of his strategic reserves, and that he was now under the necessity during that winter of building them up again, if he desired—as he did desire—to have them available for service in the larger and more important theatres of the war as required. He knew, for instance, that he would have to meet a great offensive of the British and French in the spring, and

GENERAL VIEW OF THE PIRÆUS.
The historic harbour of Athens, at which the British, French, and Italian contingents landed in December, 1916, to compel King Constantine's compliance with the requirements of the Allied Governments.

On the front itself there were few incidents, other than small raids and patrol encounters, during February and March, when the great cold still gripped the country; but the British armoured-car detachment in February added to its fame by attacking Bulgarian detachments south of the Sereth and inflicting relatively heavy loss upon them. After one engagement two hundred and sixty dead Bulgarians remained in front of the cars. Two Bulgarian outposts were completely demolished. Russia was too closely united to Rumania for the Russian Revolution not to have a marked effect on the Rumanian front, and on April 21st M. Gutchkoff, then Minister of War in the Russian Provisional Government, arrived in Jassy. A council of commanders was held immediately. Gutchkoff presided, and the situation was discussed. Later, he received a deputation of Russian officers and men, who assured him that they **German military** were determined to fight the invaders. **governors appointed** But throughout April, May, and June only small encounters were recorded, and these occurred chiefly in the mountain area.

With her usual unscrupulous thoroughness Germany took good care to establish herself in the subjugated portion of Rumania. On December 4th, 1916, General Tulff von Tschep und Weidenbach was appointed military Governor-General, with Austrian and Bulgarian vice-governors under him. At the outbreak of war he had been commander of the Eighth Rhenish Army Corps, with head-quarters at Coblenz. His instructions from the German High Command were that Rumania was to be treated exactly as Belgium and Poland had been ; and, as he had taken part in the invasion of Belgium, he knew precisely what these instructions meant. His business was to get out of the occupied territory all that could be got by any methods whatsoever. Over Bukarest a military governor was appointed of the same kidney—General von Heinrich, who had been Governor of Lille. As a matter of course, heavy money contributions were levied. An edict was published forbidding the circulation of paper money, unless marked good by the Germans—for which surcharge thirty per cent. of the value was demanded. A similar contribution of fifteen per cent., amounting to two millions sterling, was exacted from Craiova. The lives of the Rumanians were made as bitter as those of the Belgians, and great gangs of people were deported from the country to work in Germany at the most menial toil. Rumanian ladies were insulted and persecuted. So Germany wrote another dark page in her own history.

As was stated in Chapter CLXV. (Vol. 8, p. 399), which dealt with the Balkan "Allied Offensive of 1916, the Capture of Monastir, and the Greek Imbroglio," General Sarrail's efforts, though they had some distinctly excellent results, had had no appreciable effect on the fate of Rumania. The taking of Monastir was important from both the military and the political points of view, and it was altogether a good thing that the Serbians should have **Greece and** regained a portion, even if a compara-**Macedonia** tively small one, of their own country. These were positive advantages for the Entente, but with these progress in this area of the world-war seemed to end—did practically end for several months. Monastir was in the hands of the Allies in November, 1916, and more than half a year later it still marked the height of Sarrail's advance. The winter of 1916-1917 saw some heavy fighting, mainly in the shape of trench warfare ; but the Army of the Orient, as the composite force of the Entente was compendiously named by the French, made no sharp push forward that inflicted grave injury on the enemy or led to the reconquest of territory. The natural difficulty of the terrain and the severity of the winter had

much to do with the arrest of the offensive, which, more-over, appeared to be inadequately furnished with men and material in face of a brave and tenacious foe, who had been strongly reinforced, and in any case held dominating positions. Added to these factors was the uncertainty that existed till June with respect to the action of the Greek King.

In Great Britain, during the winter of 1916-1917, the question of the utility of the Salonika Expedition was much discussed. The original purpose had been to save Serbia, and Serbia had not been saved ; the expedition was sent too late, nor was it large enough to have achieved its aim. Then the Entente **Record of the** decided that Salonika, having been occu- **Salonika Expedition** pied, should be retained and made into a great military and naval base. Very considerable forces were landed at the port, and these, gradually moving upward, had taken possession of a fairly extensive block of Macedonia. Enraged by the tame surrender of the east side of Greek Macedonia to the Bulgarians, and encouraged by the presence of the Allies in strength, the Venizelists, who were dead against Germany and Austria, had broken away from King Constantine and the Royalists, formed a National Government with Salonika as its seat, and received recognition and support from the Entente. The next development of the war which materially affected this area had been the appearance in the field of Rumania in opposition to the Germanic League ; and, to help her in the struggle, Sarrail had taken the offensive, but without success in that particular direction. On the whole, the record of the Salonika Expedition had been one, broadly speaking, of failure, inasmuch as the objects chiefly desired had not been attained.

From the very start there had been a sharp division of opinion among the Allies regarding the expedition. One school of thought, which included some eminent men, took the view that in the Balkans lay the key to the whole war, and declared that an energetic and powerful offensive in that region would have decisive results. The other school, which embraced most military authorities, held an expedition in that quarter to be ill-advised, as involving the Allies in a serious diversion of their effective strength from other fronts of vastly greater importance, notably

WHERE ANCIENT ATTICA OVERCAME THE PERSIAN INVADERS.
British, French, and Italian battleships lying off Salamis, to the west of the Piræus. Salamis has been the scene of many great events in its long history of 2,500 years, including the victory of the Greeks over the Persians in 480 B.C. ; but it has witnessed none more vital to civilisation than the struggle in the twentieth century between the barbarism of Teutonic ideals and the principle of the liberty of nations for which the Allies contended.

the Franco-British front, on which was concentrated the mass of the troops of Germany. Maintaining that it was only on these fronts, and more especially the Franco-British front, that the enemy could be decisively beaten, they asserted that in despatching the expedition political considerations were allowed to override those of sound strategy. The latter school by this time could point to the incommensurate results obtained by the expedition, which now was known to be an extremely expensive affair in several ways.

Opinion in the Commons

In summer the climate of Macedonia was unhealthy, and told heavily on the allied forces. All supplies had to be brought oversea, and consequently a severe strain was imposed on the navies and merchant service of the Entente—a strain which could not but increase with the development of the submarine campaign against shipping. The district itself had poor railways and was nearly destitute of roads. The terrain to be negotiated in an advance was mountainous and capable of almost insuperable defence. In a word, the difficulties that inhered in the expedition were of the most formidable description, entailing a lavish expenditure in life and treasure, which could only be justified by proportionate gains—and these had not been procured. To this the other school retorted that the expedition had not been on a sufficiently large scale.

On March 6th the subject was debated at some length in the House of Commons, several prominent members taking part in the discussion, and exhibiting in their speeches that diversity of opinion which had obtained from the beginning with respect to the expedition. Summing up, Mr. Bonar Law, Chancellor of the Exchequer and Leader of the House, said it was impossible for the Government to give any indication of their intentions with regard to the Salonika Army. Continuing, he observed :

[*British official photograph.*]
THE ALLIES' HIGH COMMISSIONER IN GREECE.
M. Charles Jonnart, High Commissioner of the Protecting Powers of Greece, who on June 11th, 1917, demanded the abdication of King Constantine, guarantees for the safety of the Army of the Orient, and restoration of the Greek Constitution.

I have heard the question asked : Is the force at Salonika intended to be offensive or defensive ? I am sure the Germans would like very much if we would give an answer. It is precisely to that kind of question that it is impossible to give any answer. There is one set of members who have definitely taken the view that we ought not to have a Salonika Expedition. There is another section who think it is one of the vital operations of the war. I am not going into the merits of the expedition at all. But I do wish to point out that we are engaged in a war with many Allies. The policy as a whole cannot by any possibility be the policy of this Government alone. Therefore, if we took the view of those who think the expedition is a mistake, it does not follow that it would be possible for us to act in any other way. But I am very far from admitting that that view is correct. . . . We must not merely act in concert with our Allies. What has happened has laid obligations on us which it is necessary for us to fulfil, if we can. Let me point out the obvious fact.

If by any chance this expedition were taken away, the first thing that would happen would be that Greece would be overrun, that the whole Balkan Peninsula, without exception, would be in the hands of our enemies, and that—what from the point of view of the British House of Commons is not less important—those who have helped us from the beginning would be at the mercy of our enemies, and we know precisely how they would be treated. . . . Nothing has exercised the Government more than the whole subject of Salonika. It has been difficult because the Allies who are interested in Greece and the Balkan Peninsula have not always taken the same view as to the right policy to adopt. . . . I think we are now carrying out a common policy, and the main object of that policy is to make sure that if our German enemies choose to advance against us there, we shall not run the risk that we would have run a few months ago of being attacked from behind.

This statement of the attitude of the British Government to the Salonika Expedition referred in the concluding sentence to the belief that the Allies' measures for preventing the Greek King from falling on the Army of the Orient from the rear were adequate. But besides that, there was another element in Greece that required protection from Constantine and his malevolent activities. Venizelos and his party had stood squarely by the Entente. Many Venizelists had already suffered death, imprisonment, or serious loss of property for their devotion to the common cause, particularly during the dark days in Athens at the commencement of December, 1916, when the Allies had been in force insufficient to defend them against the rage of the King and the fury of the Royalists. Mr. Law brought forward an argument against a withdrawal from Salonika which it was impossible to rebut— the certain and terrible fate that would be the lot of the Venizelists in such an eventuality. Thousands of Venizelists had joined the Salonika Army ; they had been eager to take their share in manning the trenches on the front, and they had displayed great courage in action. In May, M. Gennadius, who had been Greek Minister in London before the establishment of the Government of Venizelos, and who after renouncing his allegiance to Constantine had become Venizelist Minister to Great Britain, publicly stated that at that time 45,000 Venizelist soldiers were fighting alongside the Allies. In May three Venizelist companies captured a hill from the Bulgarians, and held it through seven hours' heavy bombardment, at the end of which only seventeen men were not killed or seriously wounded. Such brave fighters deserved well of the Entente. Then there were the Serbians, whose claims to generous consideration were at least equally strong.

After the fall of Monastir and the immediate subsequent fighting, the struggle on the Macedonian front died away, partly, at any rate, owing to bad weather, into a patchwork affair of patrol encounters, air and other raids, artillery duels and naval bombardments, none of which was of high military importance ; and this continued into the second week of February, 1917. On the 12th of that month, the weather having somewhat improved, operations became more active. The British raided Palmis and some points in the Doiran sector, capturing several prisoners and doing much damage. On that day the Germans, after heavy preparatory shelling, delivered an attack in considerable force on the Italian positions on Hill 1,050, a height east of Paralovo, six miles east of Monastir, and succeeded in gaining a foothold at various places in the first-line trenches, in spite of the valiant resistance of the Italians. During the ensuing night the Italians replied with a desperate counter-attack, which resulted in their retaking the greater part of the trenches they had previously occupied. Next day the counter-attack was maintained with ardour, and on the 15th the enemy was completely ousted, with heavy losses. In this fighting the Germans used flame-machines for the first time in the Balkans.

Franco-Italian achievement

Meanwhile, the Italians had done very good work farther west. Italian and French cavalry patrols had been in contact all the way from the Adriatic to Monastir for some time before, but the route had not been cleared of the enemy. It was announced from Salonika that on February 18th complete union was established between the French and the Italian troops, and that the road from Liaskovici to Korcha (Koritza) had been thoroughly freed from Austrians and hostile Albanians in Austrian pay. This achievement was of distinct importance, as it cut off communication between Athens and the Central Powers, except by wireless or aeroplanes. Korcha and Liaskovici lay south-west of Monastir, along the south-eastern frontier of Albania. The French had occupied Korcha some time previously, and the statement indicated that the Italians from Valona (Avlona) on the Adriatic had linked up solidly with them. With this the front of the Allies now stretched in an unbroken line from the Adriatic to the Ægean.

As far back as January the Italians had organised Southern Albania and Northern Epirus into separate provinces, called Valona and Argyrokastro respectively, with administrations of their own. According to a communiqué which

FATHER AND SON.

Ex-King Constantine, who abdicated, and King Alexander, who took the oath to the Constitution, June 12th, 1917.

ROYAL EXILES' ARRIVAL AT MESSINA.

Accompanied by ex-Queen Sophia, the ex-Crown Prince, and his younger children, ex-King Constantine left Greece in the Royal yacht, June 14th, 1917, and landed at Messina, whence the party proceeded to Switzerland.

was quoted in the Salonika papers, the Italians hoisted the flag of Albania on March 1st over the chief places in Northern Epirus— a proceeding which the Venizelists, who regarded that district as Greek, did not like. In the meantime Austria, still in occupation of the greater part of Albania, announced that she had granted "autonomy" to Albania under the protection of the Dual Monarchy; but influential Albanian chiefs protested that Albania was independent, and through Essad Pasha, its greatest chief, had already declared war on the enemies of the Entente. What Austria really was aiming at was to give a show of justification for making a levy of Albanians for her Army. The French at Korcha proclaimed the independence of Albania, and hundreds of Albanians were brigaded with French troops on this front.

From time to time during the winter vague reports found their way into the Press of a rising of the Serbians in Serbia against their oppressors, who treated the poor people of the conquered land with a perfectly fiendish cruelty, many important citizens who had remained in the country being executed on the slightest pretexts, and the whole population reduced to the most abject slavery. From the fastnesses of the mountains small bands of Serbians had maintained a guerilla warfare after the occupation, and these united in a formidable movement under the leadership of Kosta Pestanatch in the district of Prokuplie, the rugged, hilly country west of Nish. Kurshumlia was captured from the Bulgarians, who were driven as far as Vranja, and the Bulgarian line of communications between Nish and Uskub was threatened. Greatly alarmed by the growing success of the rising, which was participated in by fifteen thousand Serbians, and fearing that it was connected with an allied offensive from Monastir, Bulgaria speedily concentrated large bodies of troops, among whom were German contingents, and defeated the Serbians, whose plans had been betrayed by a Bulgarian agent, who had posed as a pro-Russian and a hater of Tsar Ferdinand. By the end of February the insurrection was stamped out. Of six thousand Serbians who were taken prisoners, two thousand were summarily done to death by Germans with **Wholesale murder of Serbians** machine-guns. Long, deep trenches were dug, in front of which the victims were bound to stakes and shot in groups, their bodies being flung into the trenches immediately and buried. Many Serbians, however, escaped to the mountains, and continued to carry on a desperate guerilla campaign.

March set in with bitter cold and heavy snowstorms on the whole Macedonian front, but in spite of the weather the Italians on the 3rd made a successful assault on the enemy's trenches in the vicinity of Hill 1,050, wrecked them, and repulsed a determined attack of the Prussian Guard, who attempted to regain the lost positions. In the second week of the month violent actions took place on several sectors. During the night of the 12th the British line south-west of Doiran was advanced a thousand

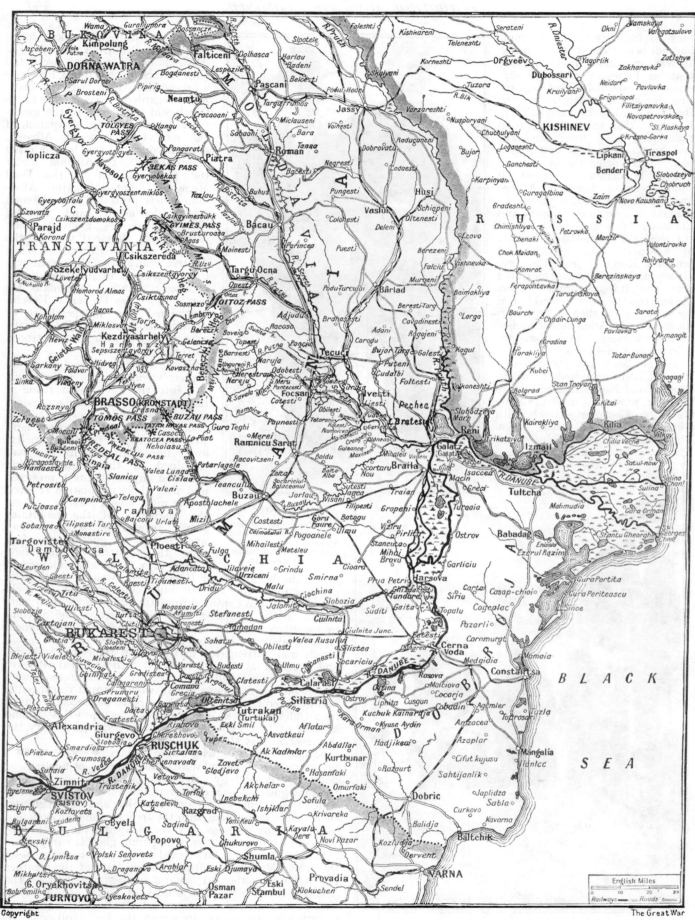

Copyright

The Great War

GENERAL MAP OF THE AREA OF COMBINED RUSSO-RUMANIAN MILITARY OPERATIONS AGAINST
THE CENTRAL POWERS.

yards on a front of 3,500 yards without opposition, the Bulgarians being caught napping; but next day there was lively fighting, as the result of which the British retained their new line and consolidated it. In co-operation with this movement the French and other Allies attacked near Monastir, and after a continuous contest extending over a week in severe weather captured Hill 1,248, an important height due north of the city. All the way from the famous Cherna Bend fierce struggles occurred for many miles westward, the French, Russians, Italians and Serbians fighting gallantly in the most difficult conditions. A furious battle raged in the region between Lake Prespa and Lake Ochrida, and east of the former the Bulgaro-Germans were driven from the Chervena Stena ridge that ran down from the mountain at Pisoderi to within two or three miles of Monastir. It was from positions in this neighbourhood that the Bulgarians had bombarded the town, causing considerable loss of life and much damage to buildings.

On March 7th the Bulgarian gunners had a distinguished victim in Mrs. Harley, a sister of Lord French. In charge of a motor-ambulance unit with the Serbian Army, she was wounded in the head by a shell that burst near an ambulance in which she was sitting, and died shortly afterwards in hospital. Early in the war Mrs. Harley had worked in France with the Scottish Women's Hospitals organisation at Royaume, and afterwards with the Girton and Newnham Unit at Troyes. Later, this unit accompanied the French Expeditionary Force to Salonika, and she went with it. In 1916 Mrs. Harley took charge of a flying column of Serbian motor-ambulances, but in December she left the Scottish Women's Hospitals and transferred her very efficient energies to an independent motor-ambulance for the Serbian civilian population at Monastir. Her self-sacrificing services had been greatly appreciated, and her death was much deplored. The Serbian Crown Prince sent an affecting message of **Lord French's sister killed** condolence to Lord French, in which he spoke in the highest terms of her as the " worthy sister of a great soldier."

To regain the slopes of the Chervena Stena the enemy put forth a mighty effort in April. Here he was in strength, having a German division, a Turkish force, and at least two Bulgarian divisions, with proportionate artillery. His assault began on the 18th, and was vigorously pressed for two days, but after some initial successes it failed. The French counter-attacked magnificently, and on the 20th drove him back completely with heavy casualties, among them being many Germans. In the Doiran sector the British, after three days' artillery preparation, began after dark on the 24th an attack on the Bulgarian positions along a three-mile front on the western side of the lake. By half-past five in the morning of the 25th more than fifteen hundred yards of the enemy's first system of trenches was carried by the British infantry, who had to advance through a barrage of mortars and 8 in. howitzers, which the steep contours of the terrain made particularly deadly. Though not equally successful at all points, the attack gained a good deal of ground, nor were the Bulgarians able to reconquer it, though they strove hard to do so by formidable assaults repeated several times during the next three nights. Then there was another lull, which extended over all Macedonia.

In the second week of May brisk fighting broke out once more in this area. On the night of May 9th the Bulgarians delivered a powerful assault on the new positions of the British in the Doiran sector, south-west of Krastali, three miles south-west of Doiran town. The enemy at first obtained a footing on Goldies Hill, which was held as an advanced post in the middle of the British line, but he was almost at once driven out by a splendid infantry counter-attack. Next day the Bulgarians were again heavily repulsed. About this time an offensive was begun by the other allied armies along the whole

Balkan front as far as Monastir. French and Venizelist troops stormed forward on the west bank of the Vardar, Serbians and Russians attacked in the Moglena Mountains and on the east bank of the Cherna, while French, Russian, and Italian forces advanced from the Cherna Bend to the hills west of Monastir. In the region of Dobropolie, in the precipitous Moglena range, the Serbians, fighting with their usual ardour, made good progress, and took Hill 1,824. The French, on May 10th, captured the Skra di Legen, west of Liumnitza, and Venizelists distinguished themselves by taking a strong work near Liumnitza itself. On the Struma the British defeated two heavy Bulgarian assaults against Kiupri on the 15th, taking a hundred prisoners, and on the following day the French captured a series of works west of the Cherna on a front of eight hundred yards. The enemy now brought up reinforce-

ALLIED TROOPS IN OCCUPATION OF ATHENS.
French troops landed at the Piræus, June 12th, 1917, the day King Constantine abdicated, and were joined by British and Russian forces, their mission being to re-establish liberty under the Constitutional Monarchy.

ments, the weather turned unfavourable, and for the rest of the month there was little except cannonading on both sides.

In the beginning of June, Italy took a further step with respect to Albania. On the 3rd, General Ferrero, the commander of the Italian Army of Occupation, issued, " by order of the Government of King Victor Emmanuel III.," a proclamation guaranteeing the " unity and independence of all Albania under the ægis and protection of the Kingdom of Italy." He promised to the Albanians free institutions, and troops, law courts, and schools of their own, with security for their property and the reaping of the fruits of their labours. Reminding them of the old memories and traditions that had allied them in the past with Rome and Venice, and of the community of interests existing between them and Italy in the Adriatic, he invited them to take the oath of allegiance to the new

A PATRIOT WHO VINDICATED THE HONOUR OF GREECE.

[British official photograph.]

General Christodoulos interrogating Bulgarians taken prisoner by the Greeks fighting under his command. It was this patriotic soldier who, resenting the surrender of the Greek forts at Seres to the Bulgarians early in the war, repudiated his allegiance to King Constantine, who had betrayed Greek honour, and threw in his lot with the Venizelists.

imprisoned Venizelists had been released, that the Leagues of Reservists had been dissolved, and that the military withdrawals from the north (Thessaly) and the surrender of arms, which had been specified as essential, had been carried out to a large extent, and were in course of being completed. The Anglo-Hellenic League, a Venizelist organisation which kept close watch over the deeds of the King, intimated that it was not the case that all the Venizelists had been set free. The indemnification question had not been settled, but had only been referred to a commission, which was in no hurry over the business. From the same source came news that the Minister of War had granted leave to an extraordinary number of officers and soldiers, thus enabling them to remain in the area from which they should have been withdrawn. Though the Government protested that the Reservists had been disarmed, the Military Control which the Allies had instituted was aware that these extremely troublesome irregulars still had artillery and rifles in their possession. The Greek populace complained of the want of food, but it was known that the King had immense quantities of provisions stored in Thessaly and sufficient to supply for three months an army of 100,000 men. In these circumstances there could be no relaxation of the blockade in any marked degree, and in the third week of February the Allied Ministers issued a statement to that effect, dwelling particularly on the great quantity of arms there still was in Thessaly and on the continued hostility to the Entente of the Athens Press.

Allies maintain the blockade

To influence the Allied Ministers' decision the Greek Government, on February 23rd, stated officially that 16,000 soldiers, 313 guns, 155 machine-guns, 140,000 rifles, and about 2,000,000 shells of different sizes and cartridges had been removed from the north to the Peloponnesus. The blockade, however, was not raised, but as an act of grace the Allies permitted some cargoes of grain to enter the Greek ports. The Ministers made further representations with respect to the disarming of Thessaly, as they were not satisfied that it was thorough, and on March 16th the Greek authorities announced that by that date nearly 300,000 rifles had been transferred to the Peloponnesus. Meanwhile, an order had been published in Athens forbidding the local papers to attack foreign States. In spite of some unpleasant incidents, which indicated antagonism to the Entente, the Allied Ministers once again took up their residence in Athens about March 19th, showing their confidence apparently that the situation warranted this proceeding. A sign seemingly in the same direction was the reappearance of two Venizelist journals in the capital—even in Athens Venizelism was far from being dead. But there was no real change in the mind of the King, as was soon manifest again. He was still surrounded by the same pro-German camarilla, which was secretly, and openly so far as it dared, as active in intrigue as ever before.

Venizelism continued a growing power. April showed a remarkable development of it in the Greek islands, and, at the same time, indicated a change of profound significance in the attitude of the Entente Powers towards King Constantine. In that month the rule of the King

régime. According to Italian accounts, his action was received with enthusiasm. Before the war Austria and Italy had been co-protectors of Albania, and that arrangement was now terminated. In reply to a question in the British Parliament, it was officially stated that the proclamation did not apply to Greek Epirus. On June 8th the Italians occupied Janina in that district, the reasons for this move being the strengthening of the Italian occupation of Southern Albania and the creation there of a safe base for a line of communication across the Adriatic with the allied army in Macedonia, in place of the roundabout Ægean route.

Chapter CLXV. told the story of the Greek Imbroglio down to the end of January, 1917. Under the pressure of the blockade King Constantine had apparently yielded completely to the demands of the Entente Powers, and in token of apology representative groups of his Army had saluted the flags of the Allies in Athens. But normal relations were not re-established, as some time had to elapse before it could be seen whether he would fulfil the conditions which had been imposed, and which had been accepted by him. After what had happened in the past, he had to prove his sincerity, and this could only be tested by his acts, not by his professions, of which he had been profuse when they served his purpose. The chief preoccupations of the Allies with respect to Greece were the protection of the rear of the Salonika Army from attack by Greek Royalist troops or irregulars, and the release from prison and the indemnification of the Venizelists for the misery and loss to which they had been subjected, as the result of the outrageous events of December 1st and the following days in the Greek capital and other towns in Old Greece.

King Constantine's insincerity

From the date when M. Venizelos had been dismissed from office the various Prime Ministers who had succeeded him had been, with their Governments, the puppets of the King, who had made himself autocrat in defiance of the Constitution. In the beginning of February the nominal Government, in reality Constantine, addressed a Note to the Entente Powers asking for a relaxation of the blockade on the ground that the demands of the Allies had been complied with. It stated that the

was repudiated in Zante and Cephalonia, and his representatives were expelled from Corfu. The Ionian Islands became definitely Venizelist. Cythera, which had previously been evacuated by the Venizelist forces in compliance with a request, or rather order, of the Allies, was reoccupied by the Venizelists, who also took possession of the Sporades. The notable thing was that these transferences from the Royal Government to the National Government of Venizelos were effected in each case by the naval troops of the Entente in the first instance, and signalised a complete alteration in the point of view of the Allies with regard to Constantine, who had been given a promise, conditioned by certain stipulations, that Venizelism should not be allowed to be spread in those parts of his kingdom over which he still ruled. He could hardly have been aware of it, else he would have bent once more that supple back of his, but he had been given his last chance—and the sands were already fast running out.

IN A GARDEN AT LUGANO.

Ex-King Constantine of Greece with his eldest son, the ex-Crown Prince George, and his daughters the Princesses Helene (left) and Irene, at Lugano, whither the Allies permitted the Royal family to retire after their compulsory departure from Greece, June 14th, 1917.

As the weeks had gone past it had become more and more evident to the Entente Ministers that the stipulations which they had made, and to which the King had agreed, were not being observed and carried out in the spirit, or even in the letter, where evasion and delay were possible. It was in reality the old story with little variation. Soldiers and arms still remained in far from negligible quantity in Thessaly, nor had the King removed from the Army those of its officers who had been convicted of being concerned in the organisation of the bands of Reservists and Comitadjis who attacked the French in the Neutral Zone and, on one occasion, immediately after a visit to the district of Saghias, President of the Reservists' League, murdered a French patrol of Senegalese. German officers, such as

ENJOYING HIS BRIEF AUTHORITY.

General Totscheff, the Bulgarian "Governor-General of Macedonia," with his Staff in Uskub. Both this and the photograph above are reproduced from a German newspaper.

Von Falkenhausen, once military attaché at Athens, found their way mysteriously, either across the wild parts of the Neutral Zone, or from the coast, to the capital, where the King received them regularly at his palace. These Germans brought money from enemy sources for the purpose of maintaining the Reservists' League, as much as £10,000, it became known from disputes over the division of the cash, being handed over to Saghias in April. The Entente authorities in control of the Neutral Zone had definite proofs that the Reservists and Comitadjis who made trouble there were armed and organised from Athens under the personal direction of Constantine.

King Constantine's duplicity exposed

It was not till the second week of May, however, that the general public were put in possession of certain damning evidence of the complicity of the King's son and brother, of whose acts the King himself must have been quite well aware, in the plotting against the Allies. A letter, the genuineness and authenticity of which were beyond doubt, was published in the "Times" and the "Daily Mail" on May 9th, implicating in the most direct manner the Greek Crown Prince and Prince Andrew, his uncle. This letter had been written by Colonel John Metaxas, of the Greek General Staff, one of the most prominent of the personages who formed the pro-German camarilla, and it was addressed to a man called Esslin, a "Greek" of recent Bavarian origin, who had been left by Baron von Schenck to carry on the work of espionage in the German interest after his deportation (Chapter CXLV., Vol. 7, p. 484). From this letter it appeared that Metaxas gave German funds to Gounaris, the strongly anti-Ententist ex-Prime Minister, and that these funds were earmarked for "use in Thessaly." The document next referred to the Crown Prince as having requested that Metaxas' office (the Greek War Office) should "stop if possible for some time the affair of Thessaly," lest something should be discovered by the Allies, who already were suspicious because of the action of Saghias. Metaxas also alluded to General Dousmanis—another leading member of the camarilla—and said he had heard that the general was "very busy with the affair of the Neutral Zone." Then followed a bracketing of Prince Andrew and Dousmanis. Here was confirmation, past all effective denial, of the true attitude of the King.

A week or so before this letter saw the light M. Zaimis had once more become Prime Minister of Greece. The political situation had grown steadily worse. Constantine had a very special end in view—nothing less than the securing for himself, for his partisans, and for his plans of the crops in Thessaly then ripening fast. The time had arrived for the Entente to intervene—and to intervene so that there should be little possibility left of any mistake about the matter.

On June 6th there arrived a French warship at Salamis. On board her was a diplomat, who, in a **M. Charles Jonnart** very short time, effected a radical change **intervenes** in the whole situation. He stopped at first but a few hours, and then sailed to Salonika, where he conferred with General Sarrail and with M. Venizelos on the position of affairs. In a day or two he was back in Old Greece, and events began to march with startling rapidity. He was none other than the High Commissioner of the Protecting Powers of Greece, by whom he had been given full powers—the powers of a dictator. This was M. Charles Jonnart, who had been Minister of Public Works in the Casimir-Périer Government of France in 1893, but who was chiefly known for his tenure of the Governor-Generalship of Algeria. A man of excellent judgment, he was also a man of prompt decision.

On the morning of June 11th M. Charles Jonnart had an interview with M. Zaimis, and demanded the abdication of King Constantine and the designation of his successor, to the exclusion of the Crown Prince. In the course of conversation M. Jonnart told the Greek Prime Minister that the Allies intended to purchase the crops of Thessaly, and superintend their equitable distribution throughout the whole country. He said, further, that what had taken place in Greece since 1915 obliged the Protecting Powers—France, Great Britain, and Russia—to seek more complete guarantees for the safety of the Army of the Orient, to provide for the restoration of the unity of the kingdom, and to see to the working of the Constitution in its true spirit, and he appealed to the patriotism of M. Zaimis to help in carrying out the national reconciliation pacifically. That there could be no uncertainty, however, as to the position, he added that the Allies would take measures for the control of the Isthmus of Corinth, that military forces were in readiness to assure the maintenance of order in Athens, and that, in fact, everything was well in hand. Zaimis acknowledged the disinterestedness of the Protecting Powers, and recognised that their object was the re-establishment of the unity of Greece under the Constitution, but he said that the decision must be left to the King after a meeting of the Crown Council.

Dethronement of Constantine's game was up, and he **King Constantine** had at least the sense to know that the end had come. Next morning Zaimis communicated to M. Jonnart the answer of the King to the Note in which the High Commissioner had embodied his demands. This somewhat singular reply was in the form of a letter signed by Zaimis himself, and it stated that Constantine, "always solicitous solely for the interest of Greece," had decided to leave the country with the Crown Prince, and had designated Prince Alexander as his successor. The wording of this communication seemed to suggest that the King's choice of Prince Alexander, his second son, was on his own initiative, but Mr. Bonar Law, in the House of Commons, made it clear that this was not the fact. On June 12th King Alexander took the oath to the Constitution. On the same day he issued a proclamation to the Greek people in which he spoke of his grief at being separated from his "well-beloved

father," his "single consolation" being to carry out Constantine's "sacred mandate." And this he said he would endeavour to realise on the lines of his father's "brilliant reign." Such language did not appeal to the Allies, who were thoroughly weary of Constantine, but it afterwards came out that it was Zaimis who had written the proclamation in these terms in the hope of conciliating Royalist sentiment. In a letter to Zaimis, which was published shortly afterwards, the new King stated categorically that he would be faithful to the Constitution, and that, convinced of the good intentions of the Protecting Powers, he would work sincerely with these Powers for the reconciliation of the different elements of the nation.

Athens remained tranquil, and only a small affair in Thessaly broke the general acceptance of M. Jonnart's coup d'état. The ex-King was shown a consideration by the Allies which he had hardly deserved. Accompanied by Queen Sophia, the Crown Prince, Prince Paul, the princesses, and his secretary, the pro-German Streit, he was allowed to leave Greece on the Royal yacht Sphacteria, which sailed from Oropos, a small port in the Gulf of Eubœa, on the morning of June 14th, and landed him at Messina, whence he was freely permitted to journey into Switzerland. Next the High Commissioner proceeded to expel from Greece Gounaris, Metaxas, Dousmanis, and the other members of the camarilla which had shown such determined hostility to the Entente. Venizelos arrived at the Piræus from Salonika on June 21st, and shortly afterwards became Prime Minister of reunited Greece.

In the meantime, General Sarrail, in accordance with the instructions of M. Jonnart, had taken possession of Thessaly. In the evening of June 10th a Franco-British column crossed the boundary of the Neutral Zone, and entered Thessaly from the north. Two days later French cavalry occupied Larissa, the most important town in the district. General Baivas, the Greek commandant, had promised there would be no opposition, but in spite of this statement **A reassuring** some Greek soldiers under a Colonel **proclamation** Orivas treacherously opened fire. A fight ensued in which the French had six killed, the Greeks losing sixty. Baivas was arrested. This affair was practically the sole incident that marred the peaceful occupation of the region by the Allies. By the 15th all Thessaly, the Corinth district, and part of Phocea were in their hands. French troops had disembarked at the Piræus, the port of Athens, on the 12th, and were subsequently joined by British and Russian contingents.

With the situation, whether military or political, completely under control, the High Commissioner published a proclamation to the Greek nation in which he said that France, Great Britain, and Russia desired the independence, greatness, and prosperity of Greece, and were determined to put an end to the violations of the country's Constitution and of treaties, and to the intrigues which resulted in the massacre of soldiers of friendly Powers. He continued:

Until yesterday Berlin governed at Athens, and was gradually bringing the Greek people under the Bulgaro-German yoke. We have decided to re-establish constitutional liberty and the unity of Greece, and therefore the Guaranteeing Powers demanded the abdication of King Constantine. They will not, however, interfere with the Constitutional Monarchy, and they have no other ambition in Greece than to ensure the regular working of the Constitution, to which King George, of glorious memory, was ever scrupulously faithful, but which King Constantine had ceased to respect. The hour of reconciliation has arrived. The destinies of Greece are closely interwoven with those of the Guaranteeing Powers. We have the same ideals and the same aspirations. We appeal to your wisdom and patriotism.

He then informed the Greeks that the blockade was raised, but that all reprisals by or against any party among them would be pitilessly repressed. He concluded by giving an assurance that the Powers had no intention of forcing Greece to mobilise. The proclamation made an excellent impression. It was very evident besides that not only Greece but all the Balkans were entering on a fresh phase.

CHAPTER CXC.

THE STORY OF THE BRITISH WAR HORSE FROM PRAIRIE TO BATTLEFIELD.

By Basil Clarke.

Cossack's Affection for his Horse—Shared by British Soldiers—Statistics of Horses Needed for War—Where the First British Horses Were Found—Buying in the Highways and Byways—Government Buyers' Powers—" Never at Home " Horses—Civil Collecting Stations—Overseas Buying—Remount Commission at Work in Canada—Removal to America—Co-operation with American Firms—Stockyards Placed at Disposal of Commission—Selection of Animals—Testing—The " Broad Arrow " Brand—Commissioners' Names—Purchases Passed On to the Special British Depot—Description of Depot—How Horses were Fed—Darkies and " Chigoe Boys "—Rounding Up—Train Journey to Coast—The Wharf and Wharf Stables—" Shipping Day "—Animals' Last Examination at the " Cut Out "—Mechanical Counting—On Board Ship—The " Conductor " and his Crew of " Horse Boys "—'Tween Decks—Horses' Quarters—Feeding Time—German Submarines and Horse Transports—Nearing Land—Effect on Horses—The Landing in Britain—Sea Voyage Casualties—Horses Led to Remount Depots—Military Take Control of Civilian Depots—The Women's Depot—New Arrivals Put in Isolation Camps—Fear of Disease—Horses' Joy at Freedom—Recuperative Treatment—Drafted Off for War Training—France at Last—Up to the Front—The Veterinary Officer—Field Hospitals—The Painless Death—" Good-bye, Old Pal "—Care of German Horses—The Mobile Veterinary Section—Wounded Horses' Train—Base Hospitals for Horses—Special Wards for Special Wounds—The Work of the R.S.P.C.A.—The Blue Cross Fund—Unjust Attacks on the Government and the Answer—Moral Value of Care and Kindness.

ROM time to time in the course of this history it has been necessary to glance for a moment at the services and sacrifice of man's faithful friend, the horse. Although motor traction has so largely usurped the ancient functions of the horse, it requires no more than a glance at the camera records of the war to realise that machinery has by no means eliminated the animal from the scene. Mechanical traction has greatly increased military mobility, but it has still left many uses for the horse and mule, and some consideration of how the supply of animals was maintained during the war, their manifold usefulness, and the organisation for their care is required in these pages.

" His horse, his arms, his son, his wife." Such is the order of precedence of the Cossack soldier's main affections; and when they talk of revenge upon the Germans the reason of their resentment is expressed not in terms of human lives lost or of country devastated or of towns razed flat, but in terms of horses. " We will make them pay dearly," they say, " for all the horses we have lost."

This simple affection of the Cossack soldier for his horse, as noticed and expressed by a writer who had spent some time among

British official photograph.

NEW ARRIVAL ON THE WESTERN FRONT.
Mare and foal in a veterinary hospital in France. The general veterinary hospitals received all kinds of cases—surgical, medical or, as here, maternity —each type being segregated with its own class.

them, would find nowhere a more ready sympathy than among the soldiers fighting for Great Britain. This was perhaps natural: British soldiers were no more than maintaining a national tradition. To the British race the horse had long been more than a mere animal. For centuries he had had a place in their sports and pastimes and pleasures as well as in their work; and by sheer merit of his own he had won a place in the British mind not only as a faithful servant, but also as a friend and companion. At the outbreak of the war British law and usage alike reflected the esteem in which the horse was held. There was no country in the world where abuse of him was more roundly punished, no country where so many voluntary agencies and agents existed to safeguard his interests and to see that he was not ill-treated. When war began, therefore, it was only natural and fitting that this British regard for the horse in peace should be reflected in the means and measures taken for his welfare in war; and it may be said truly that not one of the fighting nations took greater care of their war-horses than did the British. How their colossal army of war-horses was raised and maintained, and the

STURDY BEASTS THAT MOVED THE GUNS ALONG THE WESTERN FRONT.
British official photograph.

How stiff a task was that which fell to the lot of the artillery horses may be seen by this equine group photographed during a moment of rest by the wayside. Mud-caked all up their legs, and even to the saddle, they suggest the condition of the roads over which they were employed.

great pains taken to look after the welfare of those horses, forms a striking item among the many great war achievements of the nation.

First, it will help towards a realisation of the enormous numbers of horses needed for warfare on the scale of the Great War if a few figures are given. The civil mind may find it hard to conceive that even an infantry brigade of four battalions (about four thousand men) could not get along in the field with less than some two hundred and fifty horses and mules. Cavalry, artillery, and supply services needed horses, of course, in far greater proportion than infantry, and a division of 18,000 men of all arms, infantry, artillery, transport, etc. (the unit used for purposes of supply and action in the field) needed, according to the official military standards in vogue in the year 1916, about 5,600 horses, distributed as follows :

	Men.		Horses.			
	Officers.	Other Ranks.	Riding.	Draught.	Heavy Draught.	Pack.
Headquarters	15	67	49	2	2	1
Three Infantry Brigades	372	11,793	195	336	102	108
Headquarters Divisional Artillery	4	18	20	—	—	—
Three Field Artillery Brigades	69	2,316	594	1,644	6	—
Field Artillery Howitzer Brigade	22	733	195	500	2	—
Heavy Battalion and Ammunition Column ..	6	192	29	6	109	—
Divisional Ammunition Column	15	553	56	625	28	—
Headquarters Divisional Engineers	3	10	5	1	2	—
Two Field Companies Engineers	12	422	34	106	4	8
Signal Company	5	157	33	37	2	8
Cavalry Squadron ..	6	153	153	10	2	2
Divisional Train	26	402	66	38	274	—
Three Field Ambulances	30	672	42	45	111	—
Totals ..	585	17,488	1,471	3,350	644	127

No great mental calculation is needed to conceive the immense number of horses needed for Great Britain's Army of "more than five million men," of which several million were on active service in the field.

How was this tremendous supply raised and maintained ? The outbreak of war gave to the Remount Department of the British Army, ably controlled by General Sir W. H. Birkbeck, the task of raising the supply of Army horses from 20,000 to 140,000 **The home** before the First Expeditionary Force was **contribution** equipped sufficiently to move out of the country. Most of these horses were raised in the highways and byways of Great Britain itself. They were bought either with the owner's consent or without it ; in other words, they were commandeered, for no private interests could be let stand in the way, and a man who grudged the sale of his horse found it taken by force and a fair price put in his hands. In justice to the nation, it must be recorded that the number of unwilling sellers was rare in the extreme. Many people were naturally reluctant to part with old favourite animals, but they saw the nation's greater need and yielded them up.

For some time after the outbreak of war the stables and country roads of Great Britain were one great mart for the buying of Army horses. The Government had appointed as their buyers men of repute and integrity and knowledge of horses, who acted in an honorary capacity. They comprised well-known breeders and trainers of horses, well-known judges at horse shows, landed gentry, masters of foxhounds, and others who were in a position to know a good horse when they saw one and the price of it. Provided with a little black tin box containing a Government cheque-book, instructions as to what kind of horses to buy, and a written authority empowering them to commandeer any horse they thought fit, these men began a round of the stables of Great Britain with a keen eye (and a good price) for any horse that might serve their purpose.

Each buyer was made responsible for a district— generally speaking, his own locality—where he knew, roughly, what horses existed and where they were to be found. To help him he was equipped with a copy of the latest horse census for that district. This document, which had been compiled in spare time by Territorial adjutants, police, and others, showed the number and the owners of all horses that had existed in the district when the census was taken. It was far from accurate, of course, when used at this later date, but it was of great value, nevertheless, in showing the Government buyer who were the usual keepers of horses in the district, and where the horses were usually stabled. These addresses were at once visited, and a valuable first collection of horses was made from them.

It was noticed, however, that—perhaps owing to coincidence, and perhaps to human nature being what it is—many much-needed horses were never " at home " when the Government buyer called to see them, and before many days were passed the buyers found that they must amplify their visits to the stables by a keen look-out on the roads and fields. Many a farmer's dogcart and country woman's gig was stopped on the high-road and its horse bought, as it were, right out of the very shafts.

Roadside horse-dealing

The writer spent a day during the first week of the war with a Government horse-buyer in the roads of Essex, and saw several tragi-comedies of this kind ; for at this time people had not awakened to the seriousness of war, and could not understand why national necessities should be allowed to ride so roughshod over personal predilections. There might be many protests, but the horse was bought in the shafts as it stood. If the owner promised to forward the animal immediately upon his return home, he was allowed to have the use of it to complete his drive. If not, the animal was taken forthwith and handed to soldiers who accompanied the Government buyer to take charge of his purchases. The trap—now horseless—was left at the nearest inn.

As horses were bought in this manner, or in stables, they were forwarded each day to a horse-collecting station. Each area of the many areas into which the country had been divided for mobilisation purposes had one or more of these collecting stations. Like the organisation for buying horses, they were run on civil lines—manned and equipped by civilian labour, and in some cases provided free of charge to the nation by public-spirited citizens and local authorities. Thus a collecting station might be the yard of some big farm or the stables of some big house, or it might be a market-place or other public space lent by a public authority. As examples of collecting stations, one may mention Colonel Hall Walker's training stables at Russley Park, Marlborough, Mr. Bibby's private stables at Hardwick, and the market-place of Market Harborough, lent by the public authorities of that town.

Collecting stations for horses

By strenuous efforts in the different districts of England, horses sufficient for the mobilisation were got together in twelve days' time. In addition, the first 150,000 horses sent out of the country were replaced as they went, and supplies sufficient for three months' war needs were obtained by impressment before the Government ventured

WATERING TIME FOR ARTILLERY HORSES ON THE FRONT IN FRANCE.
[*British official photograph.*]
Picturesque view of an important part of the gunners' arduous work — battery horses being led through an apple orchard to the watering-place. Not one of the fighting nations took greater care of their war-horses than did the British, and more than once many men were saved in critical emergency by the wonderful state of efficiency in which the horses had been kept, enabling guns to be rushed up to the point of danger

REMOUNT COMMISSIONERS
IN AMERICA.
The Director of Remounts (centre,
in profile) and members of his staff
who supervised the shipment of
horses.

to rely upon purchases in
the open market for all the
horses of which they had
need.

But it was seen from the
outset that, numerous as
were the horses in the
British Isles—and their total
even in 1917 was over two
million—they could not be
drawn upon to the extent
that was likely to prove
necessary without denuding
the country of its home
transport and power wherewith to keep going all the
home activities necessary
for a successful carrying on
of the war. In the same
month, therefore, that
horse - buying in Britain

A PROMISING RECRUIT.
At a mule-buying centre. These sturdy and serviceable if normally
intractable animals came principally from the Southern States of America.

began, special commissioners were chosen to go overseas
to organise the purchase of the many additional horses
that would be needed for an Army greatly increased in
size, and to make good the high rate of casualties among
horses which is inevitable in war.

The late Major-General Sir Frederick Benson, K.C.B.,
was at the head of these commissioners. He went out to
America, and died there after organising a splendid
system of horse-buying and seeing it well at work.

He began first in Canada, making his
Co-operation of the headquarters in Drummond Buildings, St.
stockyards Catherine Street, West Montreal, a little
centre of activity that soon became
known even in hustling Montreal as a place where
business moved swiftly. Early and late, Sir Frederick
and his helpers were interviewing the stockmen of
Montreal, Toronto, and elsewhere, visiting their stockyards
and picking out the best horses for the equipment of
Britain's Army in the field. So well did they work that
before the end of September shiploads of horses, carefully
picked and graded and tested for disease, were being
shipped from the Canadian ports to England.

When winter came the Commission moved southward
to a warmer climate, and took up quarters at Newport
News, in Virginia, later establishing a base also at New

Orleans. A horse-buying
connection which had proved
very successful at the time of the
Boer War was renewed, and by
means of it horse-buying for the
British Army was soon a stirring
business throughout all the
neighbouring States of America.

It was realised by the
Commission that they could not
hope for the success and quickness
and economy of buying at which
they aimed if they worked in
opposition to the huge stockyards
of these parts of America, who
after years of organisation had
spread a network system of
horse - buying right over the
Southern States of America. As
an indication of the immensity of
some of these concerns and their
extraordinary facilities for buying,
it may be mentioned that
one firm alone, even in
pre-war times, bought and
sold about 130,000 horses
and mules a year, the
purchases of more than five
hundred buyers distributed
all over the country.

To have set up in business
opposition to such concerns
as these would have been
merely to invite competition
and overbidding. It would
have necessitated the
appointment of local buyers
in great numbers. The
British authorities had,
moreover, the precedent of
the South African War, and
knew that they could
depend upon the best stock-
buying firms of this part
of America for loyal service
and a "straight deal."
Instead, therefore, of establishing a rival organisation
to buy horses they linked
up with some of the leading stockyards and worked
in co-operation with them. The stockyard firms, for their
part, entered into the bargain not only with loyalty, but

TRUTH FROM ITS OWN MOUTH.
Mr. John Brown, M.R.C.V.S. (right), examining the teeth of a horse
offered for sale to Major F. H. Wise, of the British Remount Commission.

with American business enthusiasm. They placed their big organisations and their immense stockyards and pastures at the disposal of the Commission. They railed off separate pastures and erected new barns and stables, light railways, and all other things necessary for equipping collecting depots specially for British Army horses.

Some system of isolation of this sort was considered necessary owing to the special liability of American horses to a kind of influenza fever which is of a very infectious nature. Horses were placed in these special camps for several weeks and observed closely for any outbreak of this fever before they were allowed to be shipped overseas, with the risk of bringing the infection with them.

To show in closer detail the work of the British Horse Buying Commission, it may be helpful to describe and give some account of one of these big American stockyards and the function that the commissioners exercised in it. The stockyards of the Guyton and Harrington Mule Co. will serve admirably for this purpose. With sales depots and feed stables in more than a dozen cities and hundreds of horse-buyers constantly out in the field, covering every State of the Union, this company could feed and stable on their own premises alone more than 100,000 horses and mules at any one time. This firm sold Great Britain some 113,000 horses and mules during the South African War.

Employing the same methods as at that time, they scoured the States of America for horses for the use of

BIG "SHIPPING OUT" ACHIEVEMENT.
Pen showing 1,550 horses in a stockyard awaiting despatch to France. They were entrained in seventy minutes.

Great Britain in the Great War. Their buyers, each in his allotted district, went direct to the producer or breeder for his purchases and not to sales or markets. This method not only insured every animal being fresh, but also eliminated middlemen's profits.

When a car load or train load had been bought in any one locality the animals were despatched to the nearest depot of the firm. Here they were carefully examined both by the veterinary surgeons of the firm and also by the United States Government "vets." Newly-arrived stock was isolated in separate stables, in order to rest and get in good condition, and to undergo rigid daily tests and inspection for sickness. Not until it was fit and guaranteed free from disease was a horse put forward for sale to the British Commissioners.

For the ordinary buyers auction sales were held weekly. These were open to farmers and any other horse-buyers, American or foreign, who cared to bid. The animals went into the auction-room one by one, and were knocked down to the highest bidder. The members of the British Government Remount Commission, however, were given special advantages. Certain **Procedure at the auctions** stables were set apart that they might inspect all animals that were on offer and make a " first pick."

First of all members of the firm made a selection of such animals as they considered came up to the necessary standard in height, condition, and soundness set by the Remount Commissioners. No other animals than these were led before the commissioners, who then made an examination of their own, aided by the expert advice of British veterinary surgeons, one of whom was attached to each commissioner and buyer.

First the commissioner had each horse mounted and run to shown that it was properly broken in, had good

INOCULATION AGAINST FEVER AND GLANDERS.
U.S. veterinary surgeon inoculating horses on arrival at one of the stockyards in co-operation with which the British Remount Commission worked.

SELECTED REMOUNTS UNDER SUPERVISION.
At the sales each horse was mounted and run to show that it was properly broken in and otherwise fit.

East Alton Horse Depot. Horses bought by the great American firms were brought to the company's depots and carefully examined by the veterinary surgeons of the firm and also by the U.S. Government "vets." Animals that came up to the necessary standard of height, condition, and soundness were then submitted to the British Government Remount Commissioners, who were given the first pick, and their purchases were then passed on to the nearest British Government Depot. Auction sales of the rest were held weekly, open to any buyers, American or foreign, who cared to bid.

Five hundred horses, forming portion of one shipment purchased from W. T. Hales at Oklahoma City, Oklahoma, U.S.A., for the British Remount Commission by Major F. H. Wise and Mr. E. C. Winter, F.R.C.V.S., in June, 1915. Years of organisation had spread a network system of horse-buying over the Southern States of America, and the huge stockyards were immense concerns with marvellous facilities for buyers. The average annual sale of one firm alone in pre-war times was 130,000 horses and mules, this huge figure representing the purchases of more than five hundred buyers distributed all over the country.

TWO OF THE AMERICAN DEPOTS WHERE THE VAST WORK OF PROVIDING HORSES FOR THE BRITISH ARMY WAS UNDERTAKEN.

action and wind and strength. Next the veterinary surgeon went over it, giving it certain tests. When both commissioner and veterinary surgeon were satisfied that the animal was sound it was led away to a special stable where the British brand marks were burnt on its hindquarters. The brand contained not only the broad arrow (common to all British Government property from field-guns to pillow-slips), but also the initial of the buyer, so that responsibility for the wisdom of the purchase rested ever upon the buyer who had made it.

Some of the buyers Next the horse went to the "roaching," or "hogging," room, where manes were trimmed and tails "squared." The United States surgeons then submitted each animal to a strict test for ophthalmia before it was taken away to the British Army feeding-grounds to await shipment. The names of a few of the men who served as buyers of horses for the British Government will give some index to the suitability of the experts chosen for this work. Besides military officers of the Remount Commission, all expert judges of horses, there were Mr. Alexander Parker, of the Hunters' Improvement Association, Sir Merrick Burrell, Mr. F. L. Fenwick, Mr. James Maher, Mr. Blennerhassett, Mr. Gordon Cunard, and Mr. Charles McNeill—names that were known wherever good horseflesh was known. The buyers, and the British veterinary surgeons attached to them, were provided with quarters at the depots and stockyards, so as to be on the spot to inspect every horse that came in.

The purchases, now branded as British and with the buyer's initial, passed on to the British depot some forty miles away, where they were kept and carefully fed and watched for a period of several weeks before shipment.

This place, which had been especially made by Major-General Moore for the British Army at the time of the Boer War and taken over by a private firm at the end of the war, was retaken for use in the European War and put in the control of Colonel E. de Gray Hassell, who organised the system by which horses and mules were shipped over to Great Britain. It comprised nearly thirty-six square miles of pasture lands, yielding the finest "blue grass." Between its many low hills lay tiny springs of blue crystal-like water, pouring off into small streams and creeks. About the estate were stables, barns, grain elevators, and hospitals for every kind of sickness a horse is liable to. Railways ran into the estate at various points, so that none of its many feeding-stations was more than three miles away from the central entraining point.

Probably at no other place in the world were there so many conveniences for the care of horses in large numbers. The natural springs and streams had in many places been dammed up by concrete to form artificial reservoirs. That no horse should have far to go for water, the streams and creeks had been supplemented by the provision of more than twelve hundred drinking-troughs, supplied by some twenty miles of two-inch piping. For feeding the horses, immense hay storage sheds with iron roofs had been put up, capable of storing 5,000 tons of hay. There were also grain elevators, feed mills, and granaries, and, in the feeding-fields, haystacks, and feeding-troughs enough for 25,000 horses and mules.

"Feeding-time" at this depot was a thing that many visitors came to see. More than a hundred waggons, many of them pulled by four horses, scampered about the plains, and more than two hundred men were at work filling the troughs and hay-racks. The hospital accommodation included fine stables, special cookers, hot-water baths for horses, and everything that veterinary skill could suggest.

The staffs at these depots comprised darkies of the Southern States of America and "round-up men," or "chigoe boys," mounted on saddle horses. These men, the darkies especially, were keen supporters of the Allies' cause. They felt that they were an integral part of the British Army, and went about their work with keenest zest, with much merriment and shouting.

The "chigoe boys" in their caps and soft felt hats were especially picturesque. Mounted on beautiful horses, they were men of greatest skill both in riding and

PEASANT WITH HIS HORSE AT A MILITARY DEPOT, SALONIKA.
As was done in England at the beginning of the war, the Greek War Office commandeered all the horses it required for military purposes. Owners had to bring them in to depots, where they received payment for them on a generous scale from the Government buyers.

in handling horses. Many were expert in the use of the lasso, and a frisky young horse who refused to be "rounded up" soon found his "capers" brought to a sudden finish by a noose cunningly thrown.

They also showed the liveliest enthusiasm in the work of policing and patrolling the feeding grounds, and any suspicious-looking person found about the stables and pastures met with the fiercest reception and handling. This work was really most important, for German agents tried every conceivable means to destroy British war-horses before they were shipped. In several cases disease germs were poured into depot **Outrages of** water supplies; in another case small steel **German agents** spikes, each of them barbed at the sides like the end of a fish hook, were mixed with oats intended for horse food. These, if swallowed by a horse, were calculated to perforate the stomach and bowels—a most barbarous thing to do to any horse. No outrage that was calculated to kill a horse or to give him disease that would spread to other horses—in fact, no outrage of any kind—was too bad for these German agents to attempt, and the watch maintained to prevent this sort of thing had to be most strict. The difficulty of proof of intent was, of course, considerable, and after one or two failures to bring home charges of outrages against persons strongly suspected the "chigoe boys" took justice into their own hands and

HORSES AS AMMUNITION CARRIERS.
Where the use of waggons was impracticable owing to the nature of the terrain, shells were brought up to the guns in special wicker panniers hung on each side of horses.

any unauthorised person found near the horses or their pasture was well-nigh lynched. This was rough justice, but it served very well.

When the time for sending a batch of horses down to the coast was nearly due the " chigoe boys " began a round up of the pastures and shepherded the horses needed for shipment into a central station. These contained pens leading out on to a railway siding. Each pen had three exits or " chutes," and every " chute " faced a waggon of the train. A train of thirty long cars, each car holding twenty-five horses, could be loaded in thirty minutes.

Working on very similar lines to this were other British depots in different parts of the country, all under the personal supervision of members of the British Remount Commission, officer or civilian. Each depot, after conditioning its horses, sent them along to
At the port of the coast. The train journey was made
embarkation easier for the animals by stops at regular intervals for feeding, watering and rest ; for it was found that the long railway journeys of America, when taken without halt, made a horse in but poor condition for the trying sea voyage to Europe.

The chief port of embarkation used by the British was designed with the same efficiency and thoroughness as the collecting and conditioning depots. The wharves, half a mile in length, were covered with fine stables built of brick. Behind, were some square miles of pasture land and feeding-grounds. So ample was the accommodation that 12,000 horses could be handled in one day without difficulty.

The buildings were originally designed as fireproof cotton warehouses, but were converted into horse and mule stables purely for the purpose of shipping horses away to England. They were used for this purpose in the Boer War. On arrival by train from the British depots,

away inland, the animals were driven down plank roads to enclosures behind the wharf. British veterinary surgeons examined each of them as it passed, and should any of them prove to have been injured on the train journey it was picked out and placed in a " hospital pen " for surgical treatment. The sound horses were passed on into isolated pens and stables, where they were allowed to rest quietly for a day or two before being sent to the main feeding-grounds and stables.

So warm was the climate here that open-air feeding all the year round was possible, and animals bought from the colder Northern States soon showed a great improvement in condition. Still some sickness was inevitable, and plenty of work was forthcoming for the British veterinary surgeons who ran the horse hospitals here under the charge of Mr. A. Hunt, M.R.C.V.S.

" Shipping day " provided one of the busiest scenes. As the steamer drew alongside the wharf the whole organisation of the depot was busily astir.
Members of the Commission were in the   **Busy scenes**
feeding-grounds behind, picking out **on " shipping day "**
horses suitable for shipment. Noisy
" chigoe boys " were catching them or roping them and leading them into special pens. At the wharves, meanwhile, a crowd of niggers and others were erecting timber chutes, long and sloping, leading from the wharf to the steamer's deck.

When all was ready, one or more members of the British Commission took their places in the " cut out " station of each pen behind the wharf, and as the animals passed before them, pointed out any which, on this closer examination, seemed not quite in condition for shipment. Any such animal was headed off into the " cut out," while the fit and well passed on. Thence they passed over a wooden viaduct to the wharf half a mile away. At the entrance to the wharf was a gate, at which stood a commissioner, who, with the aid of mechanical counters, assured himself that the number of horses and mules thus delivered for shipment was correct.

On the wharf itself the horses passed through special driveways into narrow " halter-pens," where each was seized and fitted with a halter to take him on shipboard. With one man holding each horse's halter they were led up the sloping " chutes " to the steamer's main deck, from which they were distributed about the ship and made secure.

In a British Government horse ship, which the writer of this chapter was given an opportunity of visiting, the animals were loaded on two decks, each deck being under cover. There were some seven hundred animals on board, and the mules, as being the " tougher " creatures, were given the lower deck, while the horses, more delicate and liable to lose condition at sea, were given the upper deck. The air there was considerably better than down below.

The horses were packed in pens, five or six in a pen, with their heads facing an alleyway that ran round the ship. This alleyway was narrow, and to walk along it one had to push aside the heads of horses from both right and left of one's path. A vicious horse could have bitten one quite easily, for he had at his mercy anyone scrambling along the narrow passage. Yet not one of them seemed maliciously inclined. All good-temperedly moved their heads aside for one to pass.

On the voyage the animals were under the charge of a " conductor," who, if not actually a veterinary surgeon by academic qualification, had nevertheless a complete knowledge of horses and their ways and ailments. Under him were some forty horsemen—a crew of tough Americans, some black, some white, who made the round trip out and home with the boat. They were split up into gangs and squads under foremen, and each gang was responsible to the " conductor " for watering, feeding, and otherwise caring for the horses in certain stalls every day. The conductor, in turn, was responsible to the shipping company and the Government, and his earnings depended on his success in bringing over horses without sickness or injury. Every horse lost meant a loss to him. He saw to it that horses were well fed and watered, and were given as good a voyage as might be.

At feeding-time the "horse boys" filled portable iron troughs with "feed" and squeezed their way along the alley-ways, fixing a trough on the wooden bar under each horse's head. Water had next to be carried round, and each horse watered individually. To water a horse in a rolling ship, standing in a narrow alley, with horses' heads all around one, each trying to force its mouth into your bucket, was no easy task.

Life on the ocean wave Sometimes a horse might strain a limb on the voyage, in which event a sling was run to a roof bolt over his head, and he was given support to keep his weight off his legs. But no very complex surgical treatment was possible on shipboard, and little more could be done than to make the horse as easy as possible pending his arrival on land.

It might be thought that to horses standing athwart ship in this way, the rolling of the ship would cause great hardship. When the rolling was severe this was the case, but a slight roll was regarded as more beneficial than harmful, in that it kept the horses mildly exercised, seeing that their leg muscles had to be constantly in use to enable them to maintain their balance.

Sometimes German submarines made a bid to sink British horse transports, and after a time it was found necessary to arm these ships with a gun or more and gun crews for purely defensive purposes. More than one good Army horse had his first taste of war and gun fire as he was crossing the sea from his native land. Some of them showed nervousness, others were calm and placid, and it was noticed that the calm ones

seemed to reassure the nervous ones. Is it not so with human beings, too?

After days at sea, with all the adventures and anxieties that sea travelling during the Great War had for sailors, a curious restiveness would become manifest among the horses below decks. It might be night-time. First would begin a restless tugging at head-ropes; then perhaps a beating of hoofs, which gradually increased, like the approaching of drums. The "horse boys" and officers took no notice. They knew the signs only too well. The restlessness would increase till at last the emotions of some horse found vent in a long-drawn whinny or neigh.

Land! He had smelt the land. It might be a hundred miles away, but he had smelt it, and he gave vent to his joy in the only way he knew. **Welcome scent of the land** He even tried to cut a little caper in his narrow stall.

Soon the cry would be taken up by horses on both decks all round the ship, and from the lower deck the queer, unmusical, almost pathetic trumpeting of the mules would join in the horse chorus of the upper deck. In every alleyway horses' heads would be tossing high, right to the beams overhead, and nostrils, widely dilated, taking in long sniffs of that new and welcome scent—the land. Even sick horses seemed to brighten up after that great shout from their comrades. From that moment onwards the horses would be all impatience till land was reached.

In the case of the horse transport visited by the writer, the ship glided smoothly to the dock-side, and was met by nearly two hundred soldiers working under the direction of a Staff transport officer and officers of the Remount Department. Gangways for horses, or "horse brows," as they are called, were run up from dock-side to deck. The "horse boys" of the ship, quaintly dressed in sacks, and with cloths tied round their boots to prevent slipping, led

THE LONSDALE HORSE AMBULANCE ADOPTED BY THE BLUE CROSS SOCIETY.
This ingenious ambulance was invented by a private in the Army. It is fitted with a reversible body working on a pivot, so that the horse can enter and leave it by walking forward on to a platform lowered for the purpose. These photographs show: On the left, a horse just led into the ambulance; in circle, swinging the body of the ambulance round to unload; on the right, leading the horse out.

out the animals one by one from the alleyways with halters. They coaxed them up a sloping brow to the upper deck, and there handed them to soldiers, who piloted each horse down the " brow " to the dock-side. In many cases it was the horse rather than the soldier who did the piloting, for they were so glad to get to land once more that they scampered down the brows, pulling the soldier with them. Others, nervous creatures, had to be persuaded and helped along, and one saw at intervals half a dozen " horse boys "—white men and darkies—literally pushing a horse up the brows and shouting like savages.

The whole disembarkation was done without mishap. A veterinary officer examined each horse immediately on landing, and but for one or two animals that had developed disease on the voyage, there were no casualties.

Before leaving the subject of horse transport at sea, it may be mentioned that the rate of sea-voyage casualties was very slight indeed, averaging barely

Low casualty rate at sea one per cent. Among the first 540,000 horses and mules landed from America the losses were no more than 6,000. Compared with the horse transport of some other nations, whose losses varied between seven and fifteen per voyage, and even more, this was a fine achievement indeed, and spoke well for the care expended on the work.

On arrival in England from the ships, the horses were taken to remount depots. Every port of disembarkation had its depots within easy reach. Some of these were old military remount depots, much enlarged to meet the increased demands upon them ; others were quite new, specially established for the war. Among the latter may be mentioned the civilian depots which by a stroke of the pen became military depots. Mention was made early in this chapter of civilian collecting-stations established at the beginning of the war for the collection of horses bought and commandeered in England. When the commandeering of horses in Britain ceased some of these places were closed, but the best of them were retained and used for a time as civilian remount depots, working in touch with and exactly on the same lines as the military depots. But for purposes of uniformity and control it was thought better that these depots should be made military if possible.

The idea was put to the men who manned them, and, with one accord, they voluntarily agreed to enlist right away. The masters of hounds, horse-breeders, and others in control of these depots were given commissions ; the grooms, saddlers, farriers, and others who had manned them, were made privates and non-commissioned officers. Thus, apart from a change on the part of the staffs from stable-clothes to khaki, the work of the depots went on virtually as before. Only slight changes were needed. The depots were standardised on Army lines. A hundred horses now formed a " troop," and its

Military control of all depots staff of twenty-five grooms and one foreman became twenty-five privates and one N.C.O. Five troops made a " squadron," each squad with its three officers, 165 grooms and riders, shoeing-smiths, " vets.," and N.C.O.'s. But, apart from such changes in nomenclature, the taking over of the civilian depots brought about no great change.

It is worthy of record that one of the best civilian depots was run exclusively by women. After the taking over of the other depots it continued its work with the same staff, and worked on lines quite parallel to those of the depots that had now become military. Its staff had a khaki uniform of their own, and were, to all intents and purposes, a women's military unit. Many forage depots were also run by women.

The moment horses landed in England the care for them, begun in British hands over the water, was continued, and even increased. The veterinary officer, standing at the brow on the dock-side, had a quick eye for any horses that did not look up to the mark. They were promptly separated from their fellows, and sent straight to the depot infirmary. A " float " was at hand to carry off horses not able to walk. The strong horses were marched off to the depot by road. Their unshod hoofs on the hard English roads made an unusual patter. Arrived at the depot, they did not mix with other horses, but were tethered to horse-lines in an isolation camp of their own. Here they stood for two days under the closest observation for any symptoms of disease. Their temperature was taken, and the " mallein " test for glanders—a sort of inoculation either in the neck or in the eyelid—was made. At any sign of a " temperature " or other symptom of sickness, a horse was drafted off at once to the sick lines.

After two days' examination, horses apparently fit were turned loose. Their joy on feeling themselves free at last was stirring to watch. Following the example of some leader, they careered about the fields like mad things, kicking up their heels, shaking their manes, and neighing with all the spirit of youth on holiday. This, in fact, was their holiday, their last holiday before beginning the serious work of war.

As they came back to condition and robust health they were drafted to the stables in batches. The dirt and mud of the voyage were still upon them. First they were scrubbed—literally given a bath with soap-and-water ; their hoofs cleaned, their manes cut off (unless they were meant for cavalry use), their tails " pulled," and their forefeet shod. Then followed a further period of feeding-up and conditioning, with nicely-graded exercises every day. For this purpose the horses were turned into a circular track enclosed by a double line of railings, in which two mounted soldiers, one riding in front, the other behind, were able to exercise forty horses at once.

It was to be noticed that in each group of forty horses the same horse invariably took the lead every day, and followed in the wake of the leading mounted soldier. What determined **Training for active service** leadership among the horses was never discovered. It was not sex, for sometimes the leader was male, and sometimes female. Some close observers held that it was a question of " spirit " or " devil."

It was not until the horses had been in England for four or five weeks, and had reached a thoroughly good condition—so good that some of them were more than eighty pounds heavier than when they left America—that they were considered as fit for issue to the fighting units. Carefully graded, according to strength, size, and condition, they were drafted off to reserve units—cavalry or artillery, or transport—to begin the learning of their war duties.

Here at least another six weeks was spent, and more in the case of cavalry horses, for there are many tricks in the war-horses' trade. Much patience and care must be expended on the teaching. Oddly enough, it was found that the best teachers were other horses ; the skilled horse trained the novice.

Then came at last the great day when the horse was ready for the war zone itself. Three or more months had elapsed since its landing in Great Britain, and in many cases a horse, on leaving for the front, would hardly have been recognised as the same animal, so much altered for the better was it in both appearance and real condition.

It was taken to a British port of embarkation, of which several were used, and rested there for three or four days before undergoing even the shortest journey overseas, as, for instance, to France, whither the great bulk of them went.

On landing, a horse received a similar rest at the depot of the port at which it arrived. Every British Army base had its remount depots, one or more ; also a vast horse hospital for the reception of casualties in the field due to either wounds or sickness. Of these, more later.

Horses from the base depots overseas were issued to the fighting troops as and when required to replace losses in

After the charge: A wounded chum.

Under shell fire: A trying time for horse and man

Sikh cavalry in pursuit of a German rearguard.

With the Red Cross in France: An advanced dressing=station.

The Blue Cross: Care of wounded horses on the battlefield.

The Lancers at Monchy.   *A successful skirmish.*

'Halt!" Advancing artillery checked by explosion of an enemy shell.

the field. Every British unit, whether infantry, artillery, or transport, had one or more executive veterinary officers attached to it. In the case of infantry of the line the veterinary officer attached to each battalion was to be found ever in the neighbourhood of the nearest point to which horses were allowed to approach the lines. Stationed at the "horse-lines"—or at Échelon B—he kept an eye not only upon all transport and baggage trains moving backwards to rail-head or rendezvous for supplies, but also on the pack mules going forward with daily rations to points nearer the trenches. He had men of his own to correspond roughly with the stretcher-bearers attached to each regimental medical officer and his men, and he performed much the same services for the horses of the unit as the medical officer and his men performed for the men. It was not to be expected, of course, that these veterinary workers could exercise quite the same degree of supervision and surgical attention as was given to human beings, but a very efficient care of the physical welfare of all war-horses was maintained, nevertheless.

These regimental veterinary officers nearest the front of the battle and their men were equipped with field-dressings, splints, and the like for giving efficient first-aid to horses. They might run, moreover, rough little field hospitals of their own for the treatment of minor wounds and sicknesses not entailing a long curative course. They carried drugs and remedies for all the minor ailments that horseflesh is heir to, and, as a last resource, they carried one humane little weapon for putting a painless end to any poor animal so stricken with wounds as to be beyond hope of cure. This instrument was a Greener's Cattle Killer. Loaded with a powerful explosive charge, it was capable of penetrating a horse's skull instantly. Held against the horse's forehead, one tap on the cap was enough—the suffering animal lay still, his sufferings over.

Euthanasia for the suffering — Many a merciful end to a wounded horse was given by British veterinary officers in this way. According to regulations, it was for a veterinary officer alone to decide whether a horse should be killed straightaway or whether it should be kept alive for hospital treatment. But such was the concern of British soldiers for their horses that in many cases, where a horse was obviously wounded beyond repair, and the veterinary officer was not close at hand, a soldier himself performed this merciful office with his rifle. It was done *sub rosa*, of course, and men did not hesitate to assert that it was a shrapnel bullet or an enemy rifle-bullet that had struck their horse so neatly and exactly between the temples after he had been wounded in some other place. The veterinary officers knew better, of course; but they were, after all, as human as the soldiers and kept their own counsel.

Many touching scenes occurred on the battlefields, not only in France but elsewhere, where British soldiers lost horses in this way. Men who in times of shortage or danger had shared rations with their horses, or even risked their lives to save them from danger—as had many British soldiers—could not come to this tragic parting without real sorrow. One of the most human pictures of the war represented a British soldier on the battlefield holding up the head of his wounded horse and saying "Good-bye, old pal!" It was no mere flight of imagination on the part of the artist, for that scene occurred over and over again in actual fact.

While dealing with events here near the forefront of the battle, it may be fitting to mention the good feeling and care which British troops showed towards the German horses which fell into their hands in the course of battle. Not only were they kindly treated or humanely killed if they had been left suffering by the Germans (as was often the case), but they were given surgical treatment if it was practicable; and many a horse that had fought for the Germans came to be the pet of some British soldier, who regarded him as no less a "pal" because of his enemy origin.

It often seemed as though the Germans had neither the time nor the means nor yet the wish to look well after their horses. The diet they gave them was evidently not suitable, as was shown by the number of horses found dead with widely distended bellies. It used to be said out at the front, in fact, that a dead German horse could always be told from an English horse by his distended belly. British horses were fed largely on corn. The Germans gave their horses too much green food.

In close touch with every veterinary officer posted to a fighting unit was the Mobile Veterinary Section, who performed for the care of horses much the same duties as the field-ambulance units of the R.A.M.C. performed for men. They had vehicles and men and officers for the collection of horses wounded in the field, and for transporting them either to field hospitals for the treatment of minor wounds and sickness, or to base hospitals for the treatment of serious cases. **Mobile Veterinary Section's work** These hospitals in the field were adjuncts to collecting-stations from which wounded horses could be sent by train down to a base hospital.

They had all sorts of up-to-date means and tackle for lifting horses and supporting them, besides surgical means for making every animal as secure and comfortable as possible for his journey down to the coast. Any cases capable of treatment at the collecting-stations were, of course, kept there and treated by the Mobile Veterinary Section themselves. Other cases were packed off in long trains to the base hospitals.

One sad memory picture which the writer brought away from the British front in France was of a long line of horse-boxes lying in a siding, each horse-box containing eight cases of horse casualties in the field. The animals were bandaged and splintered just like human beings. Some were supported by a broad band and were standing on three legs, the other being hung up in a sling. Some looked out with one eye through a casing of head bandages, but the big majority had their wounds naked, covered only with the stain of some antiseptic dressing; for it was found that horse wounds, in ordinarily clean surroundings, do better when left exposed to the open air.

The base hospitals for horses were either general hospitals or special, just as in the case of the men. There were special hospitals, for instance, for the treatment of mange and skin troubles. The general hospitals took all sorts of cases, surgical or medical, but each type of case was segregated with its own class. A big hospital visited by the writer followed strictly a group system by which all cases of a similar nature were placed in the same stables or horse-lines, and put in charge of particular officers who had special knowledge and skill in the treatment of that class of case. **Base hospitals for horses** Officers of the Veterinary Corps did not specialise in quite the same way as the officers of the R.A.M.C., one taking surgery, one public health, one skin troubles, and so on. Members of the Veterinary Corps were supposed to have an equal skill all round, but in actual practice it was found that men showed a preference for one or other class of work, and had special skill in that class. Commanding officers tried as far as possible to find an officer's strong point, and to use it.

The hospitals were divided into wards quite on the lines of a human hospital, though very different, of course, in detail. The reception ward of this hospital was no more than a series of posts and ropes in a big enclosed field. The cases on arrival were taken to these reception lines, pending their distribution into separate wards suited to their case. For the little ticket appended to each horse, showing his complaint—in some cases it was no more than a chalk mark across his back—a disc was substituted. Upon it was written the date of admission to hospital, and then it was tied to the patient's tail.

[Canadian War Records.

HOW HORSES HELPED AT VIMY.
Canadian Horse Artillery bringing up their guns and getting into position for the action which resulted in their capture of Vimy Ridge, April 9th, 1917.

From the reception lines the horses were taken, according to their complaint, to a surgical ward, or a medical ward, or an isolation ward. These wards, each of which was a great quadrangle surrounded with stables, was again subdivided. A surgical ward, which was really an amalgamation of several wards, was subdivided into the wounds, bullet wounds, foot wounds, and lameness, etc. The medical ward was subdivided again into groups or lines for catarrh, strangles, pneumonia, exhaustion, general debility, etc. In the isolation ward were segregated mange and other skin cases.

As far as possible, heavy draught horses, light horses, riding horses, ponies, and mules were placed together in their respective groups, one explanation of this being the very human one that when a big horse is put next to a little one he is apt to reach over and steal his neighbour's food. This is less liable to happen when the other horse is capable of " reprisals."

To enumerate the many methods and appliances used in the treatment of wounds and diseases in British horse hospitals in France would hardly be within the scope of any work save a veterinary history of the war. One or two points that struck the writer as being of more general and human interest may, however, be recorded. Every horse undergoing painful operation at the hands of veterinary surgeons was given an anæsthetic. The writer saw, for instance, a big brown mare lying on her side on a mattress undergoing an operation for some injury to the head. A solid leather muzzle containing a wad of cotton soaked in chloroform enclosed her mouth and nostrils, and although two white-coated surgeons were busy with instruments inside the skull itself, the good creature lay quiet, snoring peacefully. The four grooms who sat by her extended limbs had no work to do. In the isolation ward, which was entered by a narrow gap through which a man but not a horse could pass, stood a row of patients suffering from skin trouble. They were all a greeny-blue in colour, like that of German uniforms, owing to liberal baths and sprays with copper sulphate. Here were special tanks for horses to bathe in, and water-sprays, hot and cold. Farther along, the catarrh cases were having their noses and mouths swabbed out with soothing lotions. In a neighbouring ward men were hurrying along with little bags of steaming linseed for application as poultices to the " strangles " cases. In the surgical wards were poor old fellows standing patiently on three feet, holding up a painful fourth limb. Beyond were horses with great open wounds in various stages of cure. Such is the healthiness of the horse that a wound will begin to

Anæsthetics for operations

468

[British official photograph

BRITISH WIRING-PARTY NEAR PILKEM.
Loading a pack-horse for a wiring-party near Pilkem, which was stormed by the British on July 31st, 1917, during the Third Battle of Ypres.

granulate and heal very rapidly after it is caused. The surgeons left them, where possible, without any covering. This could not have been done save in clean and healthy surroundings ; but in the matter of cleanliness the care exercised in British horse hospitals at the war was well-nigh as great as in the hospitals for men. Not a speck of dirt was to be seen ; the horses themselves were scrubbed spotless before admission to the ward.

A disinfecting plant, generating a heat of 220 deg. centigrade dry-heat, was available for the disinfection of all halters and horsecloths that might be likely to lead to infection. There were even arrangements for the care of horses' teeth, and the writer saw one poor creature who had been " off its food " for months, and was now restored to good appetite and a quickly-increasing fatness simply by repaired teeth. Its teeth, it seemed, had been turning inwards and hurting it every time it ate. Therefore it would not eat. After a dental operation, it picked up amazingly, and its appetite, said its attendant, was now more like a mule's. The appetite of mules, and their catholicity in the choice of food, was proverbial among our soldiers at the front. But, after recovering from an illness, a mule's appetite became a fearful and wonderful thing. A hospital groom, pointing out such an animal to the writer, said, " He eats and he eats, he eats the wood of his stable, and he eats even the rope he is tethered by. He likes poultices, and he seems to regard newspaper and print as a special luxury. He has his ' Daily Mail ' regular every morning, and eats it with his breakfast ! "

Supplementing the British Army's measures in the field for the welfare of horses were those of different voluntary organisations in Great Britain, and no record of this subject would be complete without mention of the war-work of the Royal Society for the Prevention of Cruelty to Animals and of the Blue Cross Fund. The " R.S.P.C.A.," as it was familiarly called, greatly assisted the British

Appetite of convalescent mules

Army Veterinary Corps by erecting and equipping horse hospitals in the field. Financed by voluntary contributions of private subscribers, they were able to supply hospital equipment and means on far more generous lines than would have been possible to the Veterinary Corps themselves, working with strict regard to the exacting requirements of Government regulations and Government auditors.

To the normal comforts allowed by the Army Regulations these societies added others, with the result that British field hospitals and base hospitals were more complete and comfortable for their dumb patients than those of any other army in the field.

Then the Blue Cross Fund, founded under the ægis of Our Dumb Friends' League, of which the president was the Earl of Lonsdale, one of the best friends that the British horse ever had, supplemented the good work of the R.S.P.C.A. for British horses by supplying many special drugs, veterinary requisites, and horse comforts to the various British regiments.

They made a point of supplying a number of things that were not always included in the Army scheme of pro-

[*British official photograph.*

"SLIGHTLY WOUNDED."
Men of a Mobile Veterinary Section dressing the wounds of a mule outside a veterinary field hospital.

[*British official photograph.*
PERFORMING A MAJOR OPERATION.
Anæsthetics were given to horses undergoing painful operations in the horse hospitals, a solid leather muzzle containing a wad of cotton soaked in chloroform being placed over their mouths and nostrils.

vision for horses—little extras which made all the difference between "treatment" and "kind treatment."

More than a thousand units had to thank the Blue Cross Fund for their extra supplies of veterinary requisites —for the horserugs, chaff - cutters, portable forges, humane killers, and such things. They received sometimes letters from officers in the field, and even from privates, saying what a difference these extras made to the comfort of horses; and it was characteristic of the British regard for horses that the writers wrote as warmly and as enthusiastically as though the gift had been a personal one to themselves.

The Blue Cross had no regard for the nationality of a horse. They erected, equipped, and worked a series of hospitals for the French Army, whose arrangements for the care of horses were hardly so complete as those of the British Army. Their hospitals at Moret, St. Mames, Provines, La Grande Romaine, Favière, comprised in all some thirty huge wards, and were models of their kind; in fact, the French themselves used to say that the British Blue Cross hospitals had set a new standard to the French

FIRST-AID ON THE BATTLEFIELD. [*British official photograph.*
Wounded horses received rough first-aid on the field from their immediate masters, and then were seen by the executive veterinary officer attached to the unit, who either committed them to the care of the Mobile Veterinary Section in the locality or packed them off to a base hospital.

Army in the humane treatment of horses. The society was the means of establishing similar treatment for horses of the Italian Army, and gave grants to supplement the funds raised for this work in Italy. The Belgian Army horses also benefited by the gifts of money and stores from the fund.

One of the Blue Cross measures in other fields of the war is deserving of special mention. Its provision of fly-nets for horses wounded in the Near East brought an incalculable relief to stricken animals. Thousands of flies

Fly-nets for the Near East swarmed in the open wounds of horses injured in battle, causing an agony of restlessness which often resulted in the horse's death from sheer exhaustion.

The careful treatment meted out to British war-horses, not only in the field, but even from the first moment of their selection and enlistment for the purposes of war, had a commercial as well as a moral value. British horses, thanks to the time and trouble taken upon their care, conditioning, and training, arrived in the field in better condition than the horses of any other army, and were, in fact, looked upon with wondering admiration not by our Allies alone, but even by the enemy. As good results of this care, the horses, in the long run, cost less, owing to fewer losses from disease, debility, and exhaustion in the field ; and, secondly, they yielded a more efficient service.

[Canadian War Records.

BORN ON THE BATTLEFIELD.

The mother and baby. The foal was born on Vimy Ridge and was called Vimy in commemoration of its personal association with one of the most glorious events in Canadian history.

More than once, in emergencies, the British were saved by the wonderful efficiency of their horses. Mr. Beach Thomas, in one of his war despatches in the " Daily Mail," described how plans for a German attack in a new place were suddenly discovered. He went on to explain how urgent and vital it was that the British artillery should be shifted to more advantageous positions if they were to repel the attack. The ground was a quagmire, with guns up to their axles in mud. Time was pressing. They must be moved somehow. He continued :

Our Horse Artillery bumped and lurched and tore their way forward over holes and dykes and deep mud and slush. Picked teams of splendid horses, excited as a hunter on a hunting morning, dragged their hearts out in this noble venture, and an hour before the Germans' charge was ready the guns were unlimbered and in position. . . . Who said that horses were no use in war ? We have lost many noble animals, but they have done their part indeed.

Losses, of course, were very heavy. Of more than a million war-horses bought by the British Government previous to May, 1917, one in every four gave its life either through wounds or disease. One hundred and forty-three thousand died in France alone, 12,000 in Egypt,

15,000 at Salonika, and 42,000 at home. This was a very heavy toll, and various attacks were made against the Government in both the Press and the House of Commons on the score of these figures. It was probably true that at the beginning of the war a number of horses were bought that were not as good as they might have been. But in the rush to make good the Army's vital need for horses this was well-nigh inevitable. The first commissioners and buyers who went to America were faced with a similar need for urgency. They had to buy not only the best of horses, but also the horses they could get quickly. The Germans would not await battle while their enemy was picking and choosing horses. But after the first and most urgent demand for war-horses had been met— and it was met with amazing promptitude considering the circumstances—the buying became much more methodical and critical. The methods of transport were also systematised, so that losses were reduced to a minimum.

The high rate of casualties in the field was also made the ground for criticism, and the fact that more horses died from disease and exposure than died from wounds received in battle was hurled at the Government as conclusive proof of waste and lack of care. This was quite an ill-considered argument. To anyone who saw at close quarters the conditions in which war was carried on it became ground for wonder that more horses did not perish. Not only horses but men were standing, in France, for instance, up to their waists in mud for days on end in the most bitter of weather. To argue that the horses should have had protection and cover is to argue that the horses should have had better treatment than was possible even for the men.

The horse, though so strong of bone and muscle, is an animal of delicate constitution. He is as liable to coughs and colds and lung troubles as any human being, and probably more so. That far more horses did not die in Flanders and in the mud of the Somme was testimony to their original fitness.

A most conclusive and detailed answer to those who criticised the Government for their treatment of horses was given by the Under-Secretary for War, Mr. Macpherson. Replying to Colonel Sanders in the House of Commons on August 1st, 1917, he said it was true that more than a quarter of a million horses and mules had been destroyed or cast or sold in the various theatres of war in the previous three years. This wastage worked out at less than one and a half per cent. per month on the monthly strength of horses since the outbreak of the war. Commercial firms using many horses estimated that every year they had to replace twenty out of every hundred horses used. The wastage in the stables of two of the largest railway companies during 1916 was nineteen and a half per cent. and seventeen and a half per cent. respectively. The figures of wastage in the British Army were, therefore, extraordinarily small. They have never been approached in any campaign in history. The loss of horses bought in America had been five per cent., and at sea one per cent.

A large number, however, developed influenza or pneumonia in spite of vet-**Relatively small horse mortality** erinary care. Considering the variety of adverse circumstances, including infections and attempted poisonings by enemy agents, one could only marvel that the loss had been so small. It was due chiefly to the system of keeping our horses till they were " salted " or clear from infection that we had attained the remarkably small figure of one per cent. loss on shipboard, which was a quarter of the loss at sea during the South African War. British figures were believed to compare more than favourably with the losses that had occurred, both on land and sea, among the animals bought by our Allies in the same market.

Such facts as these were conclusive, and before them all attacks upon the Government's methods petered out.

MR. ASQUITH INSPECTING

CHAPTER CXCI.

GERMAN AMMUNITION.

THE GROWTH OF OFFICIALDOM: BRITAIN UNDER THE BURDEN OF BUREAUCRACY.

By Jesse Quail.

The Nation Unorganised for War—Organisation Rapidly Carried Out on Bureaucratic Lines Similar to those of Germany—Costliness of the System—Previous Tendency of Legislative and Administrative Activity in this Direction—Consequent Growth of Expenditure—Report of Committee on Extravagance in the Civil Service—National Outlay for War Purposes on Yet More Lavish Scale—Public Services Taken Over by Government—Industries Controlled—Irksome Restrictions and Regulations Imposed—Demand for "Business Heads" of Government Departments—Official Ignorance and Mistakes—Advisory Committees Appointed—A "Business Ministry"—Ministers Without Salaries—Great Increase of Number of Paid Officials—Government by Commissions—Business Advisers of Departments Ignored by Permanent Officials—Large Hotels and Club Houses Commandeered for Departmental Staffs, and New Offices Built in the Parks—Unnecessarily Large Establishments—"Anomalies, Blunders, and Possible Absurdities" Ministerially Admitted—Obstructive Departments—Overlapping and Lack of Official Co-operation—Costly Publicity Scheme of National Service Department—Triple Registrations—Muddling in Shipping and Shipbuilding Management—Delay in Carrying Out Labour Agreement—Congestion of Goods at Ports and on Rail—Export Trade "Throttled"—Contradictory and Irritating Food Control Orders—View of Labour M.P. Thereon—30,000 Officials Wanted to Distribute Bread Tickets—Unknown Cost of Officialism—Absence of Parliamentary Control of Expenditure—Nation Submits to Inconvenience and Sacrifice of Liberty in Order to Win the War.

AMONG the remarkable changes which came over the political and social life of the people of Great Britain during the war, perhaps the most striking was a rapid development of bureaucratic government and methods, accompanied by a large increase in the official class and a correspondingly enormous growth of public expenditure.

The nation had given expression in many ways to its dislike of anything savouring of German — or, rather, Prussian— bureaucracy, for the system held the German people in a condition of servility abhorrent to British love of freedom. Yet the exigencies of the war compelled the country to organise most of its public and supply services on bureaucratic lines not very dissimiliar from those of Germany. Mr. Lloyd George, in one of his speeches in June, 1915, affirmed that Great

Britain was at the outset the "worst organised nation in the world" for carrying on this war. Probably it never was at any time the best organised of the belligerent States, but vast changes directed towards complete utilisation of the national activities were carried out with more or less success. The object in view was to "put the nation on its full strength," and this was done, on the whole, with less friction and inconvenience than might have been anticipated, though the changes developed, perhaps inevitably, along bureaucratic lines little less mechanical and arbitrary than those of Germany.

There was a rapid multiplication of Government departments and sub-departments, with local branches throughout the Kingdom. These had under their control eventually almost the entire industrial, commercial, and civic life of the people, entailing a vast increase in the army of Government officials, many

[British official photographs.
WHERE THE ROSE OF YORK BLOOMS.
Mr. Lloyd George and Lord Reading with French soldiers on King George's Hill, an eminence overlooking the Somme Valley, so named after its recapture by the British in the July offensive, 1916.

471

irksome restrictions on individual freedom, and an excessive growth of public expenditure. A very large, but not definitely ascertainable, part of the colossal sum of close upon eight millions per day, which the war ultimately cost, must be debited to this expansion of Officialdom.

In reviewing some of the methods adopted to organise the forces of the nation, it would be a mistake to attribute the bureaucratic trend and its resulting lavish expenditure entirely to the exigencies of the war. A decided impetus or bias in this direction had previously been given to public policy. For some years before the great European convulsion occurred there had been a steady and, at times, heavy increase in national outlay on Government departments, mainly due to the extension of State interference and control to many matters which had formerly been left to voluntary individual or associated initiative and effort. Social legislation had imposed new tasks upon **Increase in national** Government which could only be dis-
expenditure charged at great cost, involving increased taxation. In the twenty years previous to 1914 the national expenditure had more than doubled, rising from £92,000,000 to £200,000,000 per annum. Of this vast increase the larger part was due to new essays in State Socialism, which necessitated continual additions to the numbers of the official class. The outlay on Government services mounted up at almost double the rate of increase of the population. It was only £2 4s. 3d. per head in 1890, and had risen to £4 6s. per head in the year of the war. It was, therefore, only to be expected that, when the Great War came and imposed many fresh and unwonted duties on the Government, the official element would be rapidly swollen out of all proportion even to its previous development, and expenditure thereon would go up by even greater leaps and bounds.

In a report, issued in February, 1916, of a Government Committee on Public Expenditure, some particulars were given of lack of economy and instances of extravagance in various branches of the Civil Service. These were not necessarily due to the war, though, continuing at a time when the war services required such a vast diversion of public wealth, they were regarded by the committee as adding unnecessarily to the burden on taxpayers. Among the instances given were the continued erection of new public buildings on too costly a scale of magnificence ; the receipt by certain members of the Legislature of double salaries—one as a member of Parliament, and a second as holder of an official position ; and an unnecessary plethora of lunacy and other commissioners whose work had diminished in recent years. Thus, there were ten Lunacy Commissioners holding salaries rising to £1,500 a year each, whereas a board of five commissioners, assisted by several lower salaried officials, was held sufficient to discharge the duties.
Extravagance in Again, the Light Railways Commissioners
Civil Service had dealt with only nine applications in twelve months, and the work did not justify the expenditure of nearly £4,000, which it cost during the year. At the Board of Agriculture there were five assistant secretaries with salaries of £1,000 to £1,200 a year, a chief agricultural adviser at £1,200, and a chief veterinary officer at £1,000 to £1,200 a year. Both salaries and number of these officials, the committee reported, might be reduced without sacrificing efficiency. Then there were twenty-one National Insurance Commissioners with salaries aggregating £24,000 a year. The working of the Act, the report stated, could be simplified and economies introduced.

Instead of savings of the kind recommended having been carried out, the expenditure on various departments of the Civil Service criticised in this report was largely increased, for the official elements of almost all departments expanded during the war at a more rapid rate than before. The fashion of expenditure had been set on the ascending curve by bureaucratic advances following upon the social and political legislation of the previous decade. As a special instance outside those mentioned in the Civil Service reports, reference may be made to the new valuation machinery instituted for land-tax purposes, which employed about 2,000 officials at an annual cost of some £600,000, though the tax collected was but a tithe of this.

The way having been so well prepared for bureaucratic expansion and encroachments, war exigencies afforded an easy pretext for the taking over by Government, and running by means of its officials, of a large number of the services which private enterprise had carried on with success. In the early days of the war, in August, 1914, the new movement began by the acquisition of the railways ; most of the lines of the kingdom, save a few unimportant local branches, were officially taken over, and afterwards run mainly for the conveyance of troops and munitions. The facilities for travelling afforded the general public were gradually curtailed, and in 1917, in addition to many trains being taken off, fares were raised 50 per cent. This was very largely prohibitive of travel, and besides inflicting hardship by preventing people of small means from visiting their friends at a distance, it imposed a heavy embargo on many industries, for the success of which cheap transport is an essential.

Following the railways, Government next acquired practically the whole shipping industry of the country, including the shipbuilding yards. Then, the manufacture of munitions of war was organised on Government lines, and all works which could in any way be utilised for the purpose were taken under control throughout the country. A Minister of Munitions—Mr. Lloyd George being the first to hold the position — was appointed, with a new and numerous staff of officials. By degrees, between 4,000 and 5,000 works or factories were taken over and controlled **State control of** by the new Ministry, and some two **industry** millions of workers became in a very real sense State employees. Among other trades, the coal, iron, sugar, wool, then food generally, and finally agriculture, were practically " commandeered " and controlled by State officials. Each fresh acquisition brought with it new restrictive regulations or " orders," many of them of a vexatious character, and an increase in the number of officials appointed to carry these out. That not a few such regulations were unnecessary was made apparent by the fact that they were soon countermanded and new ones substituted ; in some cases contradictory orders were issued by overlapping and conflicting authorities—as in the case of the licences which had to be obtained by shippers of staple goods. Yet firms and individuals were heavily fined for non-compliance with regulations difficult to understand, some of which were speedily withdrawn, and others of which had not been made sufficiently known to the trades concerned.

There were very few trades or industries in the country which did not feel the arbitrary pressure of these official restraints, and certain trades, which it was desirable in the interests of the nation to maintain in a condition of efficiency, were virtually paralysed by them. The legend of " business as usual during the war," which was adopted in the early days of the struggle, soon had to be dropped, and the complaint was heard, in some branches of the iron trade, for instance, that its export trade was being " strangled with red tape."

The unreasonable character of some of the restrictive orders and the numerous mistakes that were made were at first attributed to the absence of " business heads " of the Government departments which issued them. This, too, was especially urged as the cause of much of the vast waste observable in military camps, hospitals, and other Government establishments, and also in connection with chartering, transport, and other arrangements. Lord

Sydenham was responsible for the statement that " in the chartering of ships, in hut building, billeting, and other matters tens of millions had been squandered "; and in one of the many discussions which took place in Parliament on this subject, a member asserted that not less than £250,000 per day might be saved the taxpayers by the appointment of a business head at the War Office. The " biggest business undertaking ever known in the world's history," it was said, " was being run by soldiers, lawyers, civil servants, and politicians who knew nothing of business."

The absence of business acumen in administrative work became marked very early in the war, and it did not escape public notice that many Government officials were dealing with matters of which they had no practical experience or actual cognisance. In such circumstances blunders and muddling, sometimes of a costly character, were inevitable. The same thing had been **New War Ministry** noticeable, though on a smaller scale, **appointed** during the Crimean Campaign and again in the Boer War, but apparently the nation had to repeat its experience on the grander scale imposed by a conflict of vastly greater magnitude.

With a view to remedying the chaotic conditions brought about by official lack of knowledge, a large number of advisory committees, partly composed of business men, were appointed. But as popular dissatisfaction with the conduct of affairs still continued, in December, 1916, Mr. Asquith and his Coalition Ministry resigned, and a new War Ministry under Mr. Lloyd George, who had organised the manufacture of munitions with much success, took its place. Business heads were appointed as directors or controllers of a number of new State departments which were created; Dr. Addison, a physician and surgeon of eminence, succeeded Mr. Lloyd George as Minister of Munitions; Sir Joseph Maclay was appointed Shipping Controller; Sir Albert Stanley, President of the Board of Trade; Lord Rhondda, President of the Local Government Board; Lord Devonport, Food Controller (until June, 1917, when he was succeeded in that office by Lord Rhondda); Sir George Cave, Home Secretary; Mr. R. E. Prothero, Minister of Agriculture; Sir Alfred Mond, First Commissioner of Works; Lord Cowdray, Chairman of the Air Board (controlling the manufacture of aircraft), and Mr. John Hodge, Minister of Labour. These were either men of reputation and experience in various branches of trade and commerce, or had special technical experience fitting them for the posts to which they were assigned. A number of Parliamentary secretaries were also appointed from among the business men in the House of Commons. Various changes were subsequently made in the above list, and Sir Eric Geddes, a successful railway manager, was appointed First Lord of the Admiralty.

Multiplication of official salaries It should be explained that not all of the new Ministerial appointments involved new Ministerial salaries. On February 13th, 1917, Mr. Bonar Law stated in the House of Commons that the following Ministers were not drawing their salaries : Earl Crawford (Lord Privy Seal), Sir S. H. Lever (Financial Secretary of the Treasury), Viscount Cowdray (President of the Air Board), Sir Joseph Maclay (Controller of Shipping), Lord Devonport (then Food Controller), and Captain Bathurst (Parliamentary Secretary of the Food Control Department).

On the other hand, it is not clear to what figure the cost to the nation of the continued additions to the official staffs of the new departments and the increases of the old staffs really amounted, for information respecting salaries, etc., was only given piecemeal, while Parliamentary Votes in Supply were for gross or " lump " sums. Thus, on April 2nd, 1917, it was stated that in connection with the National Service Bureau, which had its headquarters at St. Ermin's Hotel, Westminster, there had been

appointed twelve commissioners at £500 per annum ; two deputy commissioners at £300 per annum ; thirty-eight sub-commissioners at £250 per annum, two at £200, and one at £150 per annum. The Ministry of Munitions, however, had a much more numerous and costly staff than this, for in the previous year (1916) its officials numbered between 3,000 and 4,000, and new posts had been created involving an expenditure of £100,000 a year in salaries. The increase did not stop there, and the multiplication of official salaries went on apace in this and other departments.

Then, as regards the numerous committees and commissions instituted as advisory bodies in connection with various departments, although membership of these was for the most part honorary and voluntary, they required paid clerical staffs. The number of such bodies appointed, by 1917, was not far short of two hundred. In that year also eight further special commissions of employers

VOLUNTEERS FOR NATIONAL SERVICE.
When Mr. Neville Chamberlain outlined his plan to enrol volunteers between the ages of 18 and 61 for National Service the post-offices were besieged by applicants for the official " forms of offer."

and employed were appointed to deal with and settle disputes that had arisen in various groups of controlled trades, in which trade union regulations had been set aside and the " dilution " of skilled with unskilled labour introduced. Other commissions were formed in connection with the Liquor Control Board, to negotiate terms between Government and various branches of the liquor trade with a view, should Parliament give its sanction, to the purchase of the trade by the State. Besides the above, many local committees were instituted in connection with central boards. All these entailed increases in official staffs and gave new power and influence to the fast-growing Officialdom. It was, indeed, contended by some that the entire Government of the country had for the time passed from Parliament to officially-appointed commissions and committees.

It did not appear that the substitution of " business heads " for politicians in Government departments made

CAPTAINS IN COUNCIL.
General Sir William Robertson, Chief of the Imperial General Staff, with General Cadorna, Italian Commander-in-Chief (right), and General Gilinski, of the Russian Army, leaving a conference in Paris.

and several piles of offices recently erected were thus acquired, or clerical staffs were temporarily lodged in them. Even the Somerset House staff overflowed its spacious historic pile, and new offices were taken in Kingsway for several of its departments. The large buildings so acquired by Government did not suffice, and extensive temporary structures were erected in several of the London parks and public gardens; even the ornamental water in one of them was drained, and the greater part of its area covered over with wood or iron buildings for temporarily housing official staffs. When a question was asked in the House of Commons, in July, 1917, as to the number of officials employed in these various buildings, the reply given on behalf of the Office of Works was: "It is not possible, at short notice, to give even an approximate return of the particulars asked for, and the preparation of such a return would entail undue pressure on a staff already overworked"—a reply received by the House with an outburst of incredulous laughter.

It is worthy of note that even the "Times," though it consistently supported the "Business Government" of Mr. Lloyd George, strongly protested against this growth of Officialdom. It pointed **Public protests** out that the new Ministry was going the **against Officialdom** way of its predecessors in encouraging "a gigantic and apparently unchecked growth of Ministerial establishments. Every fresh department or sub-department required new and costly staffs, and these great establishments," the leading journal averred, "were in many cases not only unnecessary, but a definite cause of friction and delay." They were due to the "time-honoured belief that the importance of a Government department varies with the number of clerks employed, and to sheer ignorance of the machinery which was already available."

Replying early in 1917, in the House of Lords, to criticisms evoked by the blunders of some of the new departments and boards, Lord Curzon, on behalf of the Government, confessed that their creation entailed "anomalies, blunders, and possible absurdities," but these were excused on the ground that the system "had been hastily improvised under pressure." Although that excuse did not hold good in all cases, it made a large admission as to the cause of many of the failures in efficiency.

any great improvement, either in the smooth and efficient working of the official machinery or in point of economy, and complaints continued rife of friction, waste, and needless restrictions of the liberties of the subject. In many cases the permanent officials proved stronger than the new men; the business members of advisory committees found their recommendations overruled or ignored by permanent officials at Whitehall or other central offices, unacquainted with the actual conditions. A number of these committees disappeared without results, others were superseded by the Ministerial controller or director, but some of them continued to carry on their work more or less successfully in the face of many drawbacks.

To accommodate the "monstrous regiments" of clerks appointed, the Government took over one by one some dozen or more of the principal hotels and club-houses of London, and also a number of the palatial private residences in the West End. The National Liberal Club, the Constitutional Club, the Victoria Hotel, De Keyser's Royal Hotel, the Hotel Cecil, St. Ermin's Hotel,

COUNCILLORS OF THE KING IN CONFERENCE.
Mr. Lloyd George and Mr. Arthur Balfour leaving a conference in Paris. Frequent conferences were held in Paris and elsewhere to arrange for the closest co-operation between all the Allies in political and financial as well as in military affairs.

A few instances of the somewhat chaotic working of the official bodies, and of how, incidentally, departments overburdened with officials obstructed one another and displayed official jealousy, may be given. In the early days of the war the Local Government Board was asked by the War Office to ascertain what skilled mechanics employed by local authorities could be spared for munition making. The Local Government Board sent inspectors round the country and obtained the names of several thousands of men who, they reported to the War Office, were available at once. For a considerable time no notice was taken of this return, and it was not acted upon. The local authorities began to complain of the delay in learning whether the officials they had offered to give up would be required for the national service. A correspondence ensued, and the War Office was pressed to make known its wishes in the matter. It subsequently transpired that the Local Government Board had been in communication with the Board of Trade, which ran the Labour Exchanges, and that this department was the obstacle to a settlement of the business.

Ineffectual National Service Scheme It insisted that if the skilled municipal workers whose names and qualifications had been registered by the Local Government Board wanted employment, they must apply through the Labour Exchanges. Thus, the registration at the public cost was rendered futile, and a second registration through the Labour Exchanges (also at public cost) was required. This is a luminous instance of the " red tape " methods which prevented co-operation between Government departments even under the pressure of a great war ; and there were many such.

The National Service Scheme, instituted in March, 1917, under the Act of Parliament creating a Ministry of National Service, to the head of which Mr. Neville Chamberlain was appointed, proved a practical failure, probably due to the methods employed. The department, with a great staff of clerks, was installed at St. Ermin's Hotel, Westminster, and an extensive publicity scheme appealing for volunteer workers was instituted. According to a statement made in Parliament on April 14th, 1917, the cost of this scheme was £62,000. At least 500,000 registrations were asked for, but only 163,161 individuals had been registered. Of these 93,622

REPRESENTATIVES OF TWO GREAT REPUBLICS.
Admiral Sims, commanding the U.S. Atlantic Squadron (left), shaking hands with General Nivelle—a photograph which strikingly symbolises the friendship of France for the Western Republic whom she helped in the early days of its history.

were men already at work in " trades of primary importance," or otherwise not available for various reasons ; 26,873 only of the balance were suitable for work in trades in which there was a considerable demand for male labour ; 16,000 of these had been offered to employers, of whom 2,804 had started work, and 11,826 were awaiting replies from employers. In addition, 5,765 were awaiting decision by the National Service Sub-Commissioners on protests made against their transfer from their old occupations. At the end of May, Mr. Walsh, speaking for the Government, admitted that only 13,000 National Service Volunteers had been placed under the scheme, at a cost of £123,540, or over £9 10s. per head. National Service Committees were subsequently set up, consisting of representatives of employers and workmen, in each borough in the county, with a view to enrol men for necessary trades, and later the department was amalgamated with the Labour Exchanges.

The registration under the National Service Scheme was practically the third to which a

THE BRITISH GENERALISSIMO IN PARIS.
Field-Marshal Sir Douglas Haig, with two of his Staff, in Paris. The great soldier was always in closest communication with the French War Office, and he was an object of particular attention and admiration when on his visits to the French capital.

great part of the industrial classes had been subjected during the war. Each time the names, addresses, and other particulars of those registered were card-indexed, involving an immense amount of clerical labour, a great part of which proved futile, and could have been employed to better purpose for the interests of the nation.

The famine in mercantile tonnage, from which the country suffered during a great part of the time it had been at war, was not due wholly to the losses inflicted by the German submarine campaign. Much of it was caused by official mismanagement of the shipping and ship-building which had been taken under Government control. At the outset, steamers were chartered far in excess of the amount of tonnage which Government required. A great part of the mercantile tonnage of the nation was thus held up, and freights rose to excessive figures in consequence. In the meantime, many of the steamers which the Government had comman- **Deficiency of** deered were lying idle in ports and rivers, **mercantile tonnage** waiting orders for their employment, while piles of goods lay spoiling on the quays, waiting for tonnage. In the latter part of 1916 the Government had to alter its plans, in order to liberate for commercial purposes much of the shipping for which they had no immediate use. Sir Joseph Maclay, an experienced shipowner, was appointed controller of the department. He dispensed with the advisory committee which had up to then been in evidence, and adopted new plans for the distribution of tonnage between Government and the mercantile service, which eased the situation somewhat.

The Government embargo on shipbuilding similarly prevented tonnage being built for necessary oversea traffic, although in some of the large shipyards there were shipways unoccupied, and even gangs of workmen doing nothing but receiving wages. The serious delays in providing the tonnage which the nation required for its necessary supplies, and to keep open essential channels of foreign trade, were often ascribed to the action of labour unions, although, under the Defence of the Realm Acts, Government had powers of "dilution" and transfer which, if exercised, would have removed these difficulties.

Similiar complaints were made of the congestion of goods lying at ports awaiting shipment, and of delays in transit on the railways, owing to the Government holding up freight waggons. It took, for instance, six weeks for goods put on rail at Rochdale and other Lancashire towns to reach the Liverpool and Birkenhead docks, where steamers were waiting for them. South Wales collieries were, at times, laid idle, and the colliers had to "play," because the coal already raised could not be got away from the pit-head for lack of trucks, which meddling Government officials had "side-tracked" somewhere on the line or at the ports of shipment. **Food Controller's** Useless restrictions, unreasonable delays, **regulations** and obstructive regulations in regard to the licences required for shipment were said to have "throttled" important branches of our export trade, the vigorous prosecution of which would have assisted the nation during the war, and which were sure to be urgently needed after it was over.

Perhaps the regulations which evoked the sharpest criticism were those issued from the Department of the Food Controller. All classes felt the pressure of these, which were not only arbitrary, but in some cases due to official ignorance of prevailing conditions, and had soon to be modified or withdrawn. Placing of the supplies of food under control of Government had been advocated by the Labour Party, and it may, therefore, not be out of place to record the views of Mr. W. C. Anderson, M.P., on the way in which this control sometimes worked. Writing in May, 1917, he said:

What has been set up is something in the nature of a bureaucracy many times removed from the life and toil of the working people.

The country, in point of fact, is threatened with an increasing supply of food controllers and a decreasing supply of food. Orders apparently sent out from the department one day had been countermanded the next. Systems of distribution, abandoned after a time, have been persisted in for months, though failure was written legibly all over them. Commissioners have been appointed, committees have afterwards had to be set up to investigate the work and methods of the commissions. Committees have sprung up in bewildering welter. It is the view of officialism that if we leave one extreme we must go to another. If we quit the present chaos we must swing to another chaos equally vast and complicated.

The alternative referred to here was that with which the nation was threatened during 1917, when arrangements for compulsory rationing of the people and the issue of bread tickets were made. To give effect to this scheme, it was then announced, an entirely new army corps of 30,000 officials would be required; but the success which attended the voluntary bread-saving arrangements which were adopted caused its postponement. When Lord Rhondda succeeded Lord Devonport as Food Controller, in June, 1917, he instituted a new "Costings Department," consisting of highly-skilled accountants, and had local committees formed under municipal authorities throughout the kingdom for rationing the people, with a view to a stricter control of food prices.

As to the actual cost of the system of Officialdom which grew to such alarming proportions, only scraps of information on the subject were given to Parliament, and on certain phases of it the facts were altogether withheld. Thus, after the railways were taken over by the Government in 1914, only "skeleton" accounts of the meagrest character were issued in place of the very full and detailed half-yearly or yearly statements previously published. As the Government guaranteed a continuation of the shareholders' dividends at the rate of the last year of the companies' control, and as their public services and traffic were very materially **Costliness of** curtailed, there was reason to apprehend **bureaucracy** that the nation may have been carrying on the lines at a loss. Only the country's total expenditure in connection with the war—which rose in 1917 to £7,752,000 per day—can be spoken of with any certainty. Even the German military bureaucracy was not so costly as the British, for it cost Great Britain as much to mobilise one million men as it cost the Germans to mobilise four millions.

In the spring of 1917 a large number of members of Parliament petitioned the Government to exercise more rigid control over expenditure in the direction of economy, and a resolution affirming the desirability of steps in this direction was agreed to by the House of Commons. A Select Committee was subsequently appointed to examine current expenditure, and make recommendations with a view to its more effective control by the House. But that branch of the Legislature had in great measure abdicated its function of checking expenditure, and retained little or no control over Government extravagance. The duties of the Controller and Auditor-General, who is an officer of Parliament appointed to make an independent audit or check of expenditure and point out unnecessary outlay in any department, could not well be exercised under the prevailing conditions, and became nominal and perfunctory; while Parliament itself passed great Votes of Credit of hundreds of millions and Supply Votes *en bloc*, without detailed estimates. The more or less effective supervision previously exercised by Parliament was thus, like other guarantees of public rights and liberties, practically suspended in war-time. The Treasury itself had no effective means of controlling the spending departments, but had simply to find the money they required. The nation submitted to its increased burdens with the best grace it could, in the hope that its liberties, so curtailed during the war, would be restored to it when the looked-for victory over its enemies had been won.

CANADIAN GUN

IN ACTION.

[Canadian War Records.

THREE YEARS OF ANGUISH : THE LESSONS OF 1914-1917.

By H. W. Wilson, Author of " Ironclads in Action," etc.

In the following survey of the first three years of the world-war Mr. Wilson has endeavoured to mark a great opportunity with a chapter of history that might be thought worthy of its engrossing theme. Explaining first the fourfold surprise which enabled Germany to take possession of vast areas of her enemies' territory, he proceeds to indicate eight main periods into which the war had fallen up to August, 1917. Drawing attention to the fact that this was the first occasion when man had fought man on more than one plane or level, he dwells upon the effect which the introduction of aircraft and submarines had upon military operations, and notices the new weapons which had been invented to meet new conditions. He comments on the stupendous financial outlay involved in modern war, and the social upheaval caused by the necessary regimentation of the civilian populations. Having indicated the broad strategical plan of Germany at the end of the third year of conflict, he dwells upon the noble inspiration of the British race since it was confronted with the ultimate realities of life and death ; and after painting, in a few unstrained touches, the awe-inspiring scene amid which so many heroes went to their glorious death, he concludes with an expression of confidence in the triumph of their righteous cause and of the faith in which they died.

THAT the close of the third year of the war found Germany still in possession of 170,000 square miles of conquered Ally territory, with a population of nearly 30,000,000 Ally subjects or slaves, must be ascribed to the enormous advantage that she gained at the outset by surprising the Allies. A criminal who stealthily arms to the teeth and falls unexpectedly on a victim, may usually count on success. "Surprise," wrote Clausewitz, the greatest of all German theorists on war, " lies at the foundation of all military enterprises." It is the chief secret of victory; it gives the most prodigious triumphs.

If in this war Germany accomplished the most stupendous surprise in history, her misjudgments were also stupendous. Her Staff was composed of soldiers, devoid alike of pity and respect for law, recognising no obligations of humanity and religion, trained by

[Belgian official photograph.

RESTORING WYTSCHAETE'S BELL TO KING ALBERT.
General Plumer presenting a recovered piece of Belgian property to King Albert (with whom he is shaking hands). When the British recaptured Wytschaete during the Battle of Messines, this bell of the church was found intact among the ruins.

years of education to the highest pitch of proficiency in their specialist work, and doing it so well that in some respects they seemed to have attained a superhuman efficiency. They were, however, wrong in all their fundamental judgments. " In a fortnight—yes, in a fortnight my Army will be in Paris ! " the German Emperor told a British visitor shortly before the war. He said this because he was so advised by his experts. The German Foreign Office, in August, 1914, informed the American Government that its troops were shortly about to enter Paris, and asked the American authorities to take certain steps for the security of American citizens. "Belgium will never resist ! " was another doctrine that had been accepted by the Staff, which had drawn up its time-table for reaching Paris accordingly. "Great Britain will betray her engagements, steal her Allies' trade (a course which was recommended in effect by certain British newspapers, including the

HANDING OUT RATIONS TO HUNGRY PRISONERS.
Scene in a barbed-wire encampment or "cage" for German prisoners taken during the Messines fighting during the summer of 1917. From the platforms of their elevated sentry-boxes the armed guards were able to keep watch over the whole enclosed space in which the prisoners were confined.

system of organised ferocity. The British Government was goaded out of its habitual lethargy by the wanton bomb-throwing of the Zeppelins and aeroplanes and the bombardments of the open coast-towns by the German battle-cruisers, and adopted compulsory service the sooner. The American nation was roused to action by the slaughter of its citizens on the high seas, by the vision of daily atrocity, by the cruelties to Belgium, by the shameless shelling of noble cathedrals, by the systematic destruction of everything precious and lovely in Northern France. Nor were these crimes essential to the successful conduct of war. The Japanese in 1904-5, during their struggle with Russia, found that strict compliance with the letter and spirit of The Hague Conventions did not prevent their victory.

'Daily News' and enter the war too late," was the belief of the Staff, which had therefore not made arrangements for attacking her commerce at the very outset. "The United States will never fight, and President Wilson's Notes may be contemptuously tossed into the waste-paper basket!" had been so confidently repeated by the Staff that all Germans had come to believe it. "The submarine campaign will bring England down in six months with certainty!" the German Admiralty declared to all in January, 1917. Six months later the British Empire still stood, though the submarine campaign had not been met with any notable degree of energy or organisation.

At every turn in the first three years of the war Germany came within a hairsbreadth of complete success, yet at every turn success slipped from her. Whenever she had to deal with the sense of honour and duty in nations she was wrong, perhaps because she was led by men who openly proclaimed their disbelief in the claims of honour and duty. Their doctrine was that stated by Herr Bethmann-Hollweg—"Necessity knows no law"—which meant that Germany could commit any crime that suited her purpose of the moment. Yet, as the war progressed, other States showed that they recognised the existence of law and justice, and these States attracted to themselves the steadily-growing support of such neutrals as could not be terrorised or bribed.

The German Staff calculated that the Allies could be cowed by cruelty. The massacres in Belgium and Serbia, the murders of wounded, the frightful outrages on women and children, the devilish submarine atrocities, the devastation of Northern France, were all moves in a game made by men whose morals were of the Stone Age. These moves caused the Allies enormous suffering and loss, enormous economic injury, but they failed in their main object. The Belgians and French were exasperated by this vast

The surprise which the Germans sprang upon Europe in July, 1914, was so stupendous that it all but brought civilisation down in ruins. It was a fourfold surprise. Germany mobilised and was ready to strike before the Allies knew that she was mobilising. She was able to do this because early in 1914 her autocrat and Staff had decided to attack in the summer of 1914, and had fixed the very moment of action—for which they had been systematically preparing during forty years. So far back as May, 1914, before **Germany's fourfold** the murder of the Archduke Francis **surprise** Ferdinand, they began to call up reservists, buy food, and lay up immense reserves of supplies and munitions. In June they placed contracts in the United States for the coaling at sea of cruisers that were to prey on French trade. During July they stealthily raised the German troops with the colours to a strength of two and a half million men. Germany's confederate and ally, Austria, simultaneously carried out similar measures, and also immensely extended her munition works. The position at the end of July, 1914, was that the Allies were still

INTERROGATING GERMAN PRISONERS NEAR MESSINES.
British officers visiting a "cage" and examining German prisoners who had been taken in the Battle of Messines on June 7th, 1917. Over five thousand prisoners were taken by the British during the course of the fighting which resulted in the capture of Messines Ridge and its defence system.

thinking of peace and arbitration, and (except Russia) had scarcely begun to mobilise, while Germany was fully mobilised and Austria had completed all her most important preparations.

A second surprise which affected France was that Germany decided to march on Paris by the shortest routes, through Belgium, violating Belgian neutrality. In this way the extensive and costly defences which the French had constructed on the frontier of Alsace-Lorraine were rendered valueless. French strategists had constantly discussed the possibility of attack by Germany through Belgium in the days before the war.

Belgium's sacrifice saves France When it came, France, for some unknown reason, was quite unprepared to meet it. Her Army had deployed on the frontier of Alsace-Lorraine, leaving the north bare. As soon as it was certain that the Germans were moving in a wide sweep through Western Belgium, the whole disposition of the French forces had to be rearranged at the last moment, and almost under the enemy's fire. Swift and terrible disaster must have followed but for the heroic resistance of Belgium, who gained by her immense sacrifice the respite needed to save France and the world.

A third surprise was that the Germans placed their reserve troops in the fighting-line, whereas the French Staff had calculated that the attack would be made with

[British official photograph.
BRITISH HONOURS FOR HEROES FROM FRENCH TRENCHES.
Group of sturdy French soldiers who had come straight from the trenches to receive British decorations at the hands of Prince Arthur of Connaught, who distributed them on behalf of King George.

VERDUN'S JUSTIFIED MOTTO: "THOU SHALT NOT PASS."
Medal struck to commemorate the French victory of Verdun in the early part of 1916, when Germany's repeated desperate attempts on the great fortress system were successively and successfully thrown back.

the active army corps only. The French had expected to meet in the initial shock 1,200,000 Germans with 1,000,000 Frenchmen—odds by no means hopeless even if the Belgians failed and the British were slow in arriving. They calculated on 800,000 Germans being detached to meet the Russians. Actually, the German Staff flung over 2,000,000 men upon France, and had at least another million at the front against Russia, with a further million in reserve. The French generals found their men outnumbered on the battlefield by two to one, odds which would have rendered victory impossible even if their equipment had been equally good.

Another surprise was the superiority of the German equipment and armament at the outset. The French had the best field-gun, but in every other respect they were poorly found. Their uniform was a bad one, revealing the position of their

troops, while the German field-grey was perfection. They lacked rifles and boots and heavy artillery, while the Germans had large numbers of 6 in. and 8 in. howitzers, and a certain number of huge 11 in., 12 in., and 17 in. weapons. This was no secret, but none of the Allied Governments had grasped its importance, though the Austrian 12 in. howitzer had been shown in manœuvres shortly before the war, and the 11 in. howitzer had been described in German technical periodicals. The German superiority in these monster high-angle fire weapons was the more serious because, as events speedily showed—as had been foreshadowed at Port Arthur in 1904— **German superiority** they rendered old-type fortresses useless. **in armament** Again, the French were badly supplied with machine-guns, of which the Germans had eight to twelve per battalion. Though France had led the world in developing the aeroplane, the French Army was short of serviceable machines. Germany had a very large number trained to act in concert with her heavy guns, and with their aid was able in the initial battles to paralyse the French artillery.

All the elements of an immense catastrophe for France were here, and yet, through the sublime qualities of the French people, that catastrophe was averted, though

SURRENDER OF GERMANS IN THEIR FIRST LINE.
French soldiers, who had successfully attacked an enemy first-line trench, taking German prisoners. When the photograph was taken one of the Poilus was engaged in searching his captive.

France was torn as a body on the rack. Spellbound, the world watched during those first weeks of August, 1914, the most terrible that have been known on our earth since man maintained records, the swift and irresistible progress of the Germans, not aware that it was as though two men with rifles chased one with a smooth-bore shotgun. Then gradually the supreme violence of the offensive declined. The French, after a series of initial defeats the history of which had not been disclosed at the end of the third year of war, fell back and allowed the enemy to expend the full fury of his onset in the air. Men cannot march far and fast, and fight hard day after day. At the close of the first month the Germans were within sight of Paris, and everything tottered. But they exhausted themselves; while they had inflicted frightful suffering on the invaded districts, the defence began to hold them, and afterwards very slowly to push them back. The tide ebbed. Month by month the equipment of the British and French Armies improved, and their numerical strength grew with the enrolment of large forces in Great Britain. The peculiar advantage which Germany enjoyed passed very slowly away. Prussia, who, as Mirabeau said, made war her national industry, had failed to annihilate her peace-loving neighbours in the first shock. There was no Sedan in 1914. But a great extent of allied territory was surrendered to the enemy, and its recovery was to prove a task of unimagined difficulty.

That France did not support Belgium at the outset was due to the fact that no measures had been concerted beforehand and to the concentration of the French Army in the wrong direction. France could not justly be blamed for it. It lay deep in the nature of things and in the guilelessness of the Belgian Government, which had actually prepared the ruin of its own country by allowing the construction shortly before the war of the railways that the Germans needed for their treacherous rush on Liège. Great Britain could not give aid with sufficient speed because the movement of even so small a force as the 80,000 men of the Expeditionary Force involved careful preliminary arrangements. The British military attachés in Brussels in 1906 and 1912 had discussed with the Belgian Command the possibility of British action in case Germany violated Belgian neutrality, but on each occasion the Belgian Government had declined even to consider the possibility, and the British Government, believing pathetically in peace, did not press the point.

Only in one direction was Germany incompletely prepared. At sea she had a perfectly trained and organised Fleet, but it was not large enough to meet the full force of the British Navy. Her admirals displayed an unexpected timidity, and attempted no violent and dashing offensive before the British had concentrated. On the other side, the British Fleet made no resolute initial attack on the German naval forces, nor were the submarines which the British and French possessed thrown remorselessly on the German battleships. Each side at the outset

[*French official photograph.*

SORROW TEMPERS JOY AT COMING HOME.
Serbian women returning to their houses in Monastir after its liberation were filled with sorrow and indignation at the pillage to which their homes had been subjected at the hands of the Bulgarian invaders.

[*French official photograph.*

LEADERS OF THE LIBERATING ARMIES.
Vice-Admiral Troubridge, accompanied by one of the Serbian princes, walking through the streets of Monastir after its reoccupation by the allied troops, November 19th, 1916.

[*British official photograph.*

SPOKESMAN OF A GRATEFUL NATION.
General Vassitch, commander of a Serbian army corps, thanking the British troops for their fine work in feeding destitute Serbians during the Austrian invasion. The general spoke in English.

[*Belgian official photograph.*
GENERAL RUCQUOY.
Appointed Commander-in-Chief
of the Belgian Army in 1917.

seemed content at sea to watch the other. Nor was the German attack on British commerce of that energy which had been predicted by German strategists. Timidly conceived, it was half-heartedly delivered by a bare score of ships. Every opportunity for it had been given by the withdrawal of the fast and powerful British cruisers from the trade routes, and by Germany's creation of numerous well-fortified coaling stations, which in 1914 were still in her hands. The Berlin Staff blundered badly. This was another of those fundamental errors that marked its prosecution of the war.

Germany enjoyed an advantage in her central position which told greatly as the war advanced. She could transfer men from one front to another as occasion arose. Divisions would appear on the French front before it was even known that they had left Poland. Thus throughout the war the Allies were exposed to a peculiarly damaging kind of surprise, as it was always possible for the Germans to hold one or more fronts thinly with a screen of troops and machine-guns, and to mass the forces thus liberated at some selected point. Eighteen through railways ran from the eastern to the western fronts in Germany, prepared long beforehand for this war, and the services which they rendered were priceless. North and south the lines leading to the Italian frontier were constantly improved. The Allies had always to be ready to meet a treacherous stroke through Switzerland at Milan.

Again, the Germans secured complete unity in the command of their confederate States. Hindenburg possessed a power which no leader among the Allies enjoyed. The men on the German Staff did not shrink from assassination when any of the German vassals became dangerous. The Turkish heir-apparent, Yussuf-ed-Din, was suspected of goodwill to the Allies, and he immediately disappeared, committing suicide (as was pretended). The Allies were separate States whose interests of necessity often conflicted. Yet their co-operation was one of the wonders of the war. The British Army loyally and zealously carried out the plans which the French Staff framed, though technically it was not under the French command. An allied council prepared schemes for common action by which all the armies timed their attacks.

Another German advantage lay in the German form of government. Autocracy has many grave defects, but it favours military efficiency, because it acts secretly and swiftly. German administration was organised on well-thought-out lines to combine knowledge, power, and responsibility in the same hands. It avoided the numberless committees which in democracies waste so much time and too often provide excuses for inaction. The watchword of Germany was "Thorough." Germany's opponents, with the single exception of Russia, which at the outbreak of war was a feeble autocracy of the Asiatic type, were democracies. The watchword of democracy is "Compromise," which means half-measures, drift, talk, and sluggish action. "Half-hearted measures never attain success in war," the British "Field Regulations" state. Napoleon summed up the secret of victory in three words—"Activity, activity, speed." Mr. Lloyd George, in the critical months of 1915, crystallised the history of Great Britain during the first year of war in the phrase, "We have been always six months too late!"

Military autocracy versus democracy

The war was a test of the two systems—inhuman autocracy against comfort-loving democracy. History suggested that democracy, to survive war, needed temporarily to

[*Belgian official photograph*
STANDING, EASY.
Belgian infantry halted in a village for a brief rest during their march to the front.

adopt the concentration of effort, vigour, and central control which distinguish autocracy. This was accomplished in the United States by Lincoln in the Civil War. It was to a great extent accomplished by France in this war. Failure to recognise the need for strong central control brought disaster upon Russia after the Revolution. The failure to adapt itself to the changed conditions of war was the defect which led to the defeat of the Athenians, who were the noblest and the greatest people that the ancient world knew.

Germany possessed advantages far greater than Napoleon in his bid for world-empire. His treasury was empty; his country was exhausted by revolution and misgovernment when he began his

TYPES OF BELGIAN MILITARY HEADGEAR.
Three types of head-dress were issued to the reconstituted Belgian Army: A khaki cap of British pattern, a steel helmet, and a small circular cap.

marvellous career. Germany was rich, with finances in perfect order, abundantly supplied with everything, magnificently equipped. France under Napoleon was always a house divided against itself through Royalist and Republican plots. In Germany there were no divisions and no parties, but a machine-made unity. The people who imagined that Germany would collapse through internal feuds or Socialist upheavals were cruelly undeceived. Not Germany, but her antagonists, suffered from these disorders. Lastly, while Napoleon was situated at one extremity of Europe, so that it was difficult for him to reach opponents at the other extremity, Germany lay in the centre, only a short distance from any capital in Europe.

The efficiency of autocratic government told in another and most important respect. While German expenditure was economical and careful, the Allies, and in particular Great Britain, spent money profusely and **Financial extrava-** sometimes recklessly. In part this was **gance of the Allies** due to their neglect of preparation during peace ; in part it was the result of administration by hosts of irresponsible committees (a Parliamentary return late in 1916 showed over one hundred at work in Great Britain) : in part it was the vice of an officialism which was either reckless or routine-ridden, and sometimes both. In London almost every large hotel was taken over by Government departments, and filled with thousands of unproductive officials and clerks. Yet waste proceeded on a colossal scale. Aeroplanes of defective design were built by the hundred and immediately scrapped. Bacon was imported by the hundred tons and allowed to rot. While widows were fined for wasting a crust of bread, ships with thousands of tons of wheat or sugar on board were torpedoed, and, so far as has been disclosed, no inquiry and no punishment of those responsible followed. The Mesopotamian Report was followed by Parliamentary debates, in which Ministers screened the officials whose carelessness that Report had

condemned. Contracts early in the war were awarded on a defective system. Munition works were taken over by the Government, and so managed that the owners had a positive pecuniary interest in increasing the cost of production. Wages were enormously increased without any corresponding increase in efficiency and output. In the first year of the war Mr. Bonar Law stated in Parliament that munitions were costing three or four times their pre-war figure. Thus it came to pass that by the summer of 1917 the **Eight periods of** British daily outlay on the war had risen **the war** to the stupendous figure of £7,884,000.

The first three years of the war fell into eight fairly well-defined periods. The first witnessed the triumphant advance of the German armies through Belgium and Northern France, and marked an epoch in the history of military science and of man. The collapse of Liège and Namur before the monster German guns preceded a whole catalogue of German victories. The French advance in Alsace-Lorraine was stopped by defeat at Sarrebourg. The French northern armies which, after a hurried journey from the east, were beginning to advance against the Germans in Belgium, were outflanked by a vast turning movement through Brussels, and were defeated in a series of gigantic battles. The real causes of these defeats, in which the small British Expeditionary Force was involved, were insufficient use of entrenchments and want of numbers and long-range artillery. The French Staff, commenting on them, said : " There were individual and collective failures, imprudences committed under the fire of the enemy, divisions badly engaged, rash deployments and precipitate retreats, a premature waste of men, and, finally, defects in certain of our troops and of their leaders." Similar success marked the German campaign in the east. The Russians, who alone of the Allies were tolerably prepared for war, advanced swiftly and with great energy against the Austrians, whom they defeated with surprising ease. At the hands of the Germans they suffered a terrible reverse at Tannenberg. There, at the end of August, 1914, an entire Russian army under General Samsonoff was annihilated, and this brought the invasion of East Prussia to an end. The disaster was due to treachery, to the East Prussian railway system, which enabled the Germans to concentrate a large force and fling it on the Russians, and to the German heavy artillery.

The second period of the war opened with the Battle of the Marne, a series of stubborn engagements along the whole western front that checked the German advance. The French were warned by General Joffre that " the hour has come to advance at all costs and to die where you stand rather than give

ITALIAN INFANTRY ADVANCING FOR AN ATTACK.
" First wave " of an Italian infantry attack getting over a substantially built breastwork. In circle : General Cadorna (right) and General Porro (left) on a tour of inspection at Grado, on the Adriatic, after the Italians had captured that place from the Austrians.

Italian official photograph.

way." The hardest and fiercest fighting took place at the eastern end of the line, at the Grand Couronné of Nancy, where the famous French "Iron Corps" gave abundant proof of valour and devotion. Massed assaults by the German troops under the eye of the Kaiser, though supported by a terrifying artillery, were shattered with enormous loss. At Verdun the French were equally steadfast. In the centre and west they and the British rapidly gained ground, and there was a moment when the Germans were on the edge of a great disaster. General Kluck's quickness parried the thrust, and the Marne was not a Jena. Before neutrals had grasped its true meaning, Germany had forced Turkey into war—one of the consequences that followed from the Allies' passivity at sea, as the German Admiral Souchon,

How Turkey became involved with the battle-cruiser Goeben and light cruiser Breslau, reached Constantinople, was allowed to remain there, and at once used all his arts to involve the Sultan.

The hope that the Germans might be quickly driven out of Belgium and Northern France was not destined to be fulfilled. The third period of the war was marked by trench warfare. The American Civil War had given clear indications half a century before that in large-scale war one side or the other would sooner or later entrench itself and force its opponent to undertake siege operations. In the American Civil War Grant was able to outflank Lee. Here no outflanking was possible. The German lines ran continuously from the sea to neutral frontiers. The war became one of attrition, a term dangerously resembling "wait and see," and very slowly Great Britain began to arm in earnest.

Lord Kitchener made many mistakes, but he saw one thing clearly—that the war must be long. He did not apply his knowledge unhesitatingly; but when he perished by so tragic a fate, bewailed by the country which he had striven to serve, he had at least begun the work of organising a vast army. It was an army of volunteers, raised by the crudest experiments, but the thought of it may well fill Great Britain with pride. Never in British memory had such men gone to war as marched in its ranks. The flower of the nation was there. The old regulars of the Expeditionary Force who perished in circumstances of such glory at Ypres, though surpassingly good, came of a limited circle. They were soldiers in many cases by profession, descent, and caste, and the ranks were of a

[British official photograph.
PORTUGUESE OFFICERS ON THE WESTERN FRONT.
Major-General Barnardiston (left) seated beside General Tamagnini, commander of the Portuguese Expeditionary Corps in France. Next to the chauffeur is Lieut.-Colonel Roberto Baptiste, chief of the Portuguese General Staff.

different class from the officers. But in the New Army all stations of life were found in every degree. Side by side with the millionaire (Sir H. Raphael served in the ranks) might be seen the artist, the actor, the poet, the chemist, all wearing the private's uniform. Among the officers figured many men promoted from the ranks who had earned advancement by their valour and skill on the battlefield. As in Napoleon's army, so in this, a career was open to talent. The presence in the High Command of the old British Army of Sir William Robertson, a soldier who had climbed every rung in the ladder by sheer capacity, proved it. The British Army had at last become the British nation.

The fourth period of the war was noteworthy for the diversion of large British forces from the main objective in France. The disastrous Dardanelles Expedition was undertaken to aid Russia. It failed completely, involving the loss of some 200,000 British troops in killed, wounded, and sick. Begun without plans or forethought, in defiance of all the principles of war, it never had any real prospect of success, and it led to the resignation of Lord Fisher, who during his brief tenure of the office of First Sea Lord had infused notable energy into British operations at sea. This period was marked by a deadlock in the west and a violent and successful German offensive in the east. The Germans first reorganised the Austrian Army. In April, 1915, they effected a great concentration of artillery and broke through the Russian front near its centre. Then, rapidly advancing, they conquered all Poland and much territory in Western Russia. This series of disasters was due to Russia's want of railways and shortage of ammunition, which could not be manufactured in the country and could not reach her in sufficient quantities by the routes which **Serbia overrun and crushed** remained open. The consequences to the Allies were cruel. Austrian forces were freed for an attack on Serbia. Though Italy had now entered the war on the Allies' side, she was as yet insufficiently prepared for a great offensive. In the autumn of 1915 Bulgaria joined Germany against her sister Slav State. Serbia was crushed, and direct and easy communication between Berlin and Asia Minor opened. The Allies despatched a small army to Salonika too late, and at the end of the year evacuated the Gallipoli Peninsula. Half the force wasted there might have saved Serbia and the Balkans had it been intelligently employed.

The effect of the Serbian catastrophe was at once felt in Mesopotamia, where a small, miserably-equipped British force which had been ordered to advance against a large,

[British official photograph.
MACHINE-GUN MEN OF THE PORTUGUESE CORPS.
Squad of Lewis-gun men belonging to the Portuguese Expeditionary Corps on the western front in France. When the Portuguese came into action in June, 1917, they "proved themselves in the trenches," to the admiration of their allies.

well-equipped Turkish army was captured at Kut. But the fifth period of the war was one generally of allied half-victories. It opened with the terrific Battle of Verdun, which combined an attempt to capture that fortress and to bleed France white. Germany came within very little of success. The safety of Verdun hung for some hours on a hair. But the French held with the cry, "Let the dead arise and fight with us!" though 4,000 German guns of heavy calibre rained death and mutilation on the points selected for assault. In the **Battles of Verdun** spring was fought the Battle of Jutland, **and Jutland** which was an indecisive victory, in that the German Fleet was allowed to escape after it had been brought to action by greatly superior forces. In June the allied guns opened on the Somme the fiercest bombardment that had up to that date been known, and the new British armies began the attack which they maintained throughout the rest of the year. While in these sanguinary engagements the Germans were not annihilated or decisively defeated, their reputation suffered and their losses were severe.

In the sixth period of the war, in the autumn of 1916, Rumania joined the Allies. Her intervention might have been decisive had it been combined with vigorous action from Salonika. This would have involved the removal of the German puppet-king in Greece, who intrigued against the Allies and was unaccountably spared and shielded by them. He paralysed the Salonika army at this fresh crisis, and caused the ruin of Rumania as he had previously caused the ruin of Serbia. Russia was slow in giving aid owing to the disorganisation of her railways, and also, perhaps, to treachery. The Germans were able to overwhelm Rumania. They conquered Wallachia and inflicted a fresh and quite unnecessary disaster on the Allies. This was the more tragic because General Brussiloff had just conducted a brilliant offensive on the eastern front in which he captured over 300,000 prisoners. The sixth period of the war closed in gloom.

The seventh period was marked by the Russian Revolution, which was almost as much a movement against the war as against the Tsar, and was in large measure promoted by German agents. It, for the time being, disorganised the Russian armies, shattered discipline, destroyed the Russian system of government, threatened to break Russia up into a number of weak, chaotic republics, and set free very large German and Austrian forces for work on other fronts. It was an almost unmixed misfortune to Europe and marked the collapse of the old European system. Large portions of what had been Russia declared their independence. Poland, Lithuania, and most of Courland were before the Revolution in German hands. After it Finland and the Ukraine proclaimed themselves separate States. Many towns of Russia constituted themselves independent communes, among them Sebastopol and Kronstadt, which defied the weak authorities in Petrograd. But for this collapse of Russia and the flight of the Russian armies from their positions in July, 1917, the great offensives

which began very early in 1917 in the west would probably have ended the war.

The British Army was now thoroughly trained and worked with the precision of a machine, under generals expert in handling masses. No such formidable engine had ever been in British hands, and its spirit and tenacity were such that no check daunted it. At sea the British Navy had not yet been rejuvenated in the same way, but its fleets were now commanded by men of action, and there was hope that a more aggressive strategy would be adopted.

This period saw the opening of the renewed submarine campaign, the clear meaning of which was that until the submarine had been overcome the British Empire could have no stability, and no peace could be more than a precarious truce, liable to be interrupted at any moment by a sudden attack from the German submarines. The day had passed—perhaps for ever—when Great Britain could trust for her food to supplies imported from oversea. Her whole position was transformed, an economic change in its way as tremendous as the Russian Revolution, and one the consequences of which were not at once understood.

This period was also marked by an event of immense importance—the entry of the United States into the war, which was the sole benefit brought by the change of régime in Russia. It placed vast financial resources at the disposal of the Allies and added immeasurably to their manpower. Within a few weeks American destroyers were cruising in the Channel, the advanced guard of an American army was landing in France, and a programme of 20,000 aeroplanes was under construction. Russia having temporarily fallen out of the war and admitted defeat, the United States filled her place.

Have the earlier races altered?
Do they droop and end their lesson, wearied over there beyond the seas?
We take up the task eternal, and the burden and the lesson,
Pioneers! O Pioneers!

[*French official photograph.*]

ARRIVAL OF GENERAL PERSHING IN FRANCE.
General Pershing (right) saluting at the playing of the national anthems of the Allies on his arrival at Boulogne to take up his duties as Commander of the American Troops in France.

So the great American poet had sung two generations before, and now as "the earlier races," worn and dusty and bleeding in the desperate struggle for liberty, expended their last manhood and gave their last sacrifices on those gigantic battlefields, yet another people in all its vigour and freshness of youth prepared to enter the fight.

The tide of war had now overflowed Europe, Asia, and Africa. The struggle spread to every continent and every sea. The Germans were no longer the enemies of the Allies; they were the **War in every** enemies of mankind. China and Brazil **continent** followed the lead of President Wilson, on whom the mantle of Lincoln seemed to have fallen, with such energy and insight did he guide his people when he once decided that the hour to strike had come. In the great struggles of the past, America and Asia had been involved, but the rôle of the United States in the Great War was something for which there was no precedent.

The spring and summer of 1917 formed the eighth period of the war, which was marked by a French offensive, delivered without great success owing to the fact that the Germans had been able to withdraw large forces from the east and mass them in Champagne ; by a brilliant Italian campaign on the Carso, characterised by even fighting, and by the tremendous blows which the British inflicted in the capture of the Vimy Ridge and Messines Ridge and the Ypres offensive. While these great battles were in progress on land, the Allies were making preparations to cope with the submarine campaign at sea. The weeks of March and April were critical. Then came a slight improvement, though the attack continued to be most formidable in May, June, and July, and the losses incessant.

The Great War was the first in which men fought on more than one plane or level. The change was so far-reaching that its consequences were only **War in air and** very slowly perceived by the orthodox **under water** Admiralties and War Offices, which disliked aircraft and submarines as new-fangled devices, and refused to treat them seriously. For the first time in human history aircraft were employed which made the air a common highway above both land and sea. Beneath the sea it was now possible for submarines to navigate, so that surface ships might command the surface and yet submarines could elude them, pass under their cordon, and attack commerce in their rear. The existence of devices by which man could pass over or under the defending force—for the Allies throughout, so far as concerned these new forms of war, adopted defence as their policy—exposed non-combatants and civilians to new and terrible dangers at the hand of a cruel and lawless adversary. All the security of life vanished for ever, and thus came the greatest catastrophe that has occurred in the history of man, as it is upon his security that his progress has been founded.

The importance of air warfare increased with each month of the war, though it was left to the German Air Command to show how an enemy could be remorselessly and constantly attacked, and the British air service was generally condemned by the politicians to parry the German blows when it was not employed in purely tactical work. In the earliest days of the war aeroplanes were used largely by the Germans, and to some extent by the British and French, to reconnoitre and control heavy artillery fire. They were not then employed on any considerable scale for bombing, machine-gun work, and the offensive generally, though one of the first incidents of the war was the dastardly bombing of Lunéville (August 3rd, 1914), before the Germans had declared war, and though British airmen from the first sought out German aeroplanes and resolutely attacked them. The information

obtained by the Allies early in the war was unsatisfactory because the Germans were moving in thickly-wooded country. But British aeroplanes noted General Kluck's wheel on the eve of the Battle of the Marne, and thus gave General Joffre his opportunity of outflanking the invaders.

The advance under the stimulus of war was miraculous on both sides. The Germans at the outset had the better machines ; they were quicker in introducing improvements. They were not hampered by military conservatism or by the routine methods and red tape of such institutions as the Royal Aircraft Factory. They tried every make, and their engines were better. By sheer skill and audacity the British airmen at times gained the upper hand on the British section of the front early in the war, and they never permitted the Germans to have their own way there. The Battle of the Somme was remarkable for their exploits. They appeared in hundreds and co-operated with the infantry in the attack on the German positions. Late in 1916 the Germans again made a strong bid for air power and concentrated a large number of new machines and pre-eminent airmen on the British front—in particular the famous " circuses " as they were called, under Richthofen and Bülow. But by the spring of 1917 the British had recovered their position. They paid the price in fearful sacrifices, and Captain Ball, the greatest airman that the war revealed, died the hero's death in the fighting. But at the Battle of Messines they achieved their greatest triumph. The British official report stated that " the enemy's aircraft were prevented from taking part in the battle."

This was the aim of the Air Command on the front—to put out the enemy's eyes, blind his gunners, and render his communications intolerably perilous.

As yet air offensives pure and simple **Increasing importance** were not attempted, because no one had **of aircraft** had sufficient imagination to prepare thousands of machines. The Germans lacked the material, the Allies the energy and offensive spirit. But the importance of aircraft on the battlefield was shown by the work of a British squadron at Messines, which enabled the British gunners to silence seventy-two German batteries. In the old wars nothing cheered the infantry more than the roar of their own guns bombarding the enemy. In the Great War there was one sound which the British infantryman loved above even the thunder of his incomparable artillery—it was the buzz of the indomitable British airmen over his head, like protecting gods guiding his movements and raining down death on his enemy.

Nothing more trying to the physique or nerve can be

[French official photograph.
FIRST UNITED STATES CONTINGENT FOR THE FRONT.
Part of the American troops which landed in France with General Pershing on June 12th, 1917, on the quay at Boulogne. They were pioneers of the millions the United States was then preparing to send.

AMERICA'S COMMANDER-IN-CHIEF IN FRANCE.
General Pershing, in command of the United States Expeditionary Force, visiting the French front with members of his Staff. The American leader is to the right of the picture, pointing out something to his companion.
PPP

conceived than the work of an airman in the third year of the war. In the early days Lieutenant Frankau sang in spirited verse of " the Eyes in the Air " :

Our guns are a league behind us, our targets a mile below,
And there's never a cloud to blind us from the haunts of our
    lurking foe—
Sunk pit whence his shrapnel tore us, support-trench crest-concealed,
As clear as the charts before us, his ramparts lie revealed.
His panicked watchers spy us, a droning threat in the void,
Their whistling shells outfly us—puff upon puff, deployed
Across the green beneath us, across the flanking grey.
In fume and fire to sheathe us and balk us of our prey.

But the " hawks that guide the guns " could no longer fly over the enemy's line at so low a height as a mile in 1917. The anti-aircraft fire of the Germans had become so good and their guns so powerful, including 6 in. and even 8 in. weapons, that machines rose to 7,000 or 9,000 feet, and then made the run across, **Amazing intrepidity** carrying with them the observers and **of the airmen** their paraphernalia. Thanks to them, barrages of 6 in., 8 in. or even 12 in. shells could be turned on with mathematical precision at great distances, or fire concentrated on any refractory point. Direct hits were made at Arras on machine-gun turrets, which offered only a few square feet of target.

The fighters, as distinct from the observers and bombers, climbed to ever greater and greater heights, and moved at ever increasing speed. Height was to the aeroplane what the windward gauge was to the old sailing ship. The German fighting craft early in 1915 cruised at 5,000 feet ; early in 1917 at levels of 17,000, 18,000 or even 20,000 feet. British airmen adopted the same tactics when they had good machines. The speed was terrific. The Sopwith of 1917 was capable of 152 miles an hour ; the ordinary bombing machines flew 90 miles an hour. The airmen were masters of their art. All the old tricks were utilised in battle. Captain Ball, a Titan among them all, would go up whirling round like a tumbler pigeon, almost from the ground. They could nose-dive, tail-dive, side-slip either way or make a spinning nose-dive and bring their machines up. " Looping the loop " was a very common evolution in action.

At sea aircraft grew more and more deadly. At the outset the Germans enjoyed a great advantage in their Zeppelins and big rigid airships, the value of which for naval scouting had been repeatedly indicated. They used their airships to direct their fire in the bombardment of Lowestoft, and according to some, but untrustworthy, reports in the Battle of Jutland, while, unfortunately, the British Admiralty, handicapped by the mistaken parsimony of the Governments before the war, failed to build similar airships, and for some reason did not utilise aeroplanes and seaplanes. For months the system of defence adopted permitted the Zeppelins to range the North Sea and attack British towns and villages with impunity. **Elimination of** That more active methods were adopted **Zeppelin menace** was due to public pressure. When at last Zeppelins were resolutely attacked by aeroplanes on land, and by seaplanes at sea with incendiary bullets, they ceased to cause grave danger except to their crews.

Flying torpedo craft were a new development of the war. Patents for their construction had been taken out in 1914, and they had been built for the British Navy in early 1915, but it did not turn them to any serious use. The mists and fogs of the Battle of Jutland which gave such opportunities of employing them were not utilised. The British tried them with great success against Turkish vessels and transport during the unhappy Dardanelles Expedition. As the bombs carried by aircraft grew in size so their power of attacking warships increased. There was no indication in any British report that the German heavy ships were attacked in this way, though the Germans constantly, and falsely, claimed to have made attacks on British cruisers and even battleships.

The effect of aircraft on land war was curious. By preventing surprise and revealing the enemy's intentions and concentrations of force they prevented decisive blows from being struck. The British Expeditionary Force would probably have been enveloped and destroyed by the enormously superior German force flung upon it in August, 1914, but for its eyes in the air. In the same way information obtained by their airmen enabled the Germans to meet the very formidable flank attack which General Joffre made upon them at the Marne. Decisive results might have been obtained with aircraft had they been employed in strategical work in large forces, like Murat's or Sheridan's raiding expeditions with cavalry. The demands were so heavy for aircraft for purely tactical and auxiliary work with other arms on land and sea that sufficient machines were not available for such large offensives. Ten thousand aeroplanes employed in constant large-scale attacks on the zone behind an enemy's lines would have destroyed his railways, communications, magazines, depots, and munition works, and would have rendered life and movement behind his front intolerable. The German armies might have been cut off from their bases by such an attack with allied machines, precisely as the Germans attempted to cut off the British armies and Great Britain herself from oversea supply by submarine attack.

Aircraft proved their power to inflict great loss of life and destruction when they were skilfully used. In the raid on Folkestone a contemptibly small force of German aeroplanes accounted for two hundred and fifty casualties, and escaped almost untouched. The economic effect of such an attack on a town was very serious, though it never seems to have attracted the attention of Parliament or Government. At the sacrifice of one German machine grievous pecuniary loss was inflicted on one small place. In the first important raid on London the German aeroplanes **The coming of** escaped without a scratch and caused six **the " tank "** hundred casualties. For some obscure reason, possibly because the British Government allowed its military policy to be controlled by sentimentalists, or because of the addiction to passive defence which marked the politicians' methods throughout—an addiction due to the fact that less energy and initiative are demanded in parrying than in inflicting blows—the German aeroplanes were not kept busy at home by allied attacks on German towns and fortresses.

An entirely new weapon which was employed in this war and which was of the greatest importance was the " tank," a large, heavily armoured motor-car of very special design, capable of traversing every kind of ground and of crawling over almost any obstacles. It carried either a light gun or machine-guns, and was proof against rifle fire. It was driven by powerful petrol-engines. The earlier " tanks " had one defect, that they were exceedingly slow. But though they were employed in the Battle of the Somme before the experiments to improve them were complete and before their number was large, they proved their great value. Those who saw them at their work and realised their potentialities regarded them as marking a new era in the history of war on land. They were a purely British invention, but were at once enthusiastically adopted by the French. Even when put out of action they afforded invaluable cover to the infantry. The Germans replied to them with special guns, firing a shell capable of penetrating their armour with great rapidity, but the " tanks " grew more and more dangerous to them.

Other new British weapons were the Stokes gun, the details of which were secret, but which rendered magnificent service, and the Lewis gun, a light automatic weapon which was more and more generally used as the conflict advanced. It could be carried with ease by a single man, and was thus much handier than the older types of machine-gun. Poisonous gas and liquid fire squirted from

Major=General H. M. Trenchard, C.B., D.S.O., in command of the Flying Corps in the field.
From the painting by William Orpen, A.R.A., one of the official artists on the western front.

British repelling a smoke=screened liquid=fire attack launched by Germans clad in armour

Italians on the Isonzo front dispersing Austrian asphyxiating gas by chemical fumes from braziers

French artillery of assault: "Tanks" invading German trenches on the Aisne, 1917.

Day of deliverance after the long night of terror: French troops entering a recovered town.

Soldiers and sailors leaving the great French liner Sontay before her final dive

Rescued men climbing aboard the French gunboat that raced up to the rescue.

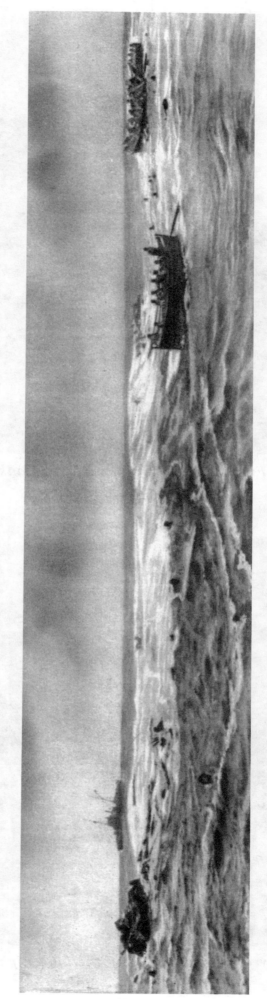

French gunboat picking up the survivors from the French transport Sontay, torpedoed without warning in the Mediterranean a hundred miles from land. *Vive la France! The cry with which Lieut. Mages, commanding the Sontay, went down with his ship, April 16th, 1917.*

tanks under pressure were two devilish devices introduced by the Germans in defiance of The Hague Conventions and reluctantly adopted by the Allies. The gas chiefly used by the Germans was chlorine, for the manufacture of which they had immense plant in their aniline and dye works, but they also from time to time employed bromine and, later in the war, phosgene, a peculiarly noxious and deadly gas. The British when they adopted gas employed it chiefly in shells, which were of such a nature as to startle even the Germans. At the outset they were hampered in its manufacture by the absence of the necessary plant, owing to the loss of the chemical trade before the war to Germany. Gas discharged from tubes proved to be a very doubtful and uncertain weapon. A shift of the wind might turn it against the army employing it with unfortunate results.

To meet gas the armies used masks which were specially designed to keep men alive in the deadly atmosphere that had so often to be breathed at the front. The efficiency of these masks rapidly improved, and there was not much to choose between either side at the close of the third year of the war. The German liquid-fire device was serviceable only at close range and was, like gas, an uncertain weapon. The British introduced a great improvement on it, which was first mentioned at the Battle of Messines, in the shape of a fearful shell which burst and poured molten metal and boiling oil on the enemy, and is said to have produced panic among the German troops against whom it was first tried.

Another new feature of war was the introduction of the " barrage " (or barrier) or curtain of shells. It was as it were a pillar of fire and cloud combined. An immense number of guns directed projectiles on one particular line of front so that one continuous sheet of shells and splinters and shrapnel bullets rained down there.

Barrages and shell consumption An improvement on the " barrage " was the " creeping barrage " which advanced at a prearranged rate in front of the assaulting infantry. In the third year of the war an effort was always made to crush the enemy's trenches and machine-gun positions before assaulting, in accordance with General Pétain's principle, " the gun conquers, the infantry occupies the position." The consumption of ammunition rose to fabulous figures. The " barrage " involved a lavish expenditure of shells, and was only possible when they were available by the million and when the concentrations of artillery were enormous. The first great concentration of artillery, that of the Germans on the Dunajec in April, 1915, was marked by the massing of 1,000 heavy guns at one point, and at that point in the crisis 700,000 rounds are said to have been fired. This was soon outdone. At Verdun 4,000 guns are said to have been in action simultaneously, and a million shells were fired by the Germans in twelve hours. One area, 500 yards by 220, was struck by 80,000 large projectiles. The German batteries at Spincourt fired so furiously that the French airmen's photographs of them showed a continual blaze of flame. At the Somme the French fired half a million rounds in one " barrage " on one single day from their field-guns alone. At Messines a single British division fired 170,000 rounds and its heavy guns 80,000 on one small sector, and according to German reports ten divisions fought in the battle. At Vimy Ridge the British artillery fired 5,000,000 rounds.

Machine-gun " barrages " were used on occasions at short range to stop movement over a particular route or past a particular point. They were controlled in the same way as gun curtains, the dust of the falling bullets showing where they were striking.

The German monster howitzers proved their utility at the outbreak of war for attacking fortresses. Their huge projectiles had also a demoralising effect on troops exposed to them, and on occasions prevented the allied artillery from acting effectively. The Allies replied as soon as they could by constructing similar howitzers and immense guns, which were mounted on carriages so as to be capable of firing from railways. By the close of the third year the Allies had more formidable weapons than the 17 in. Krupp howitzers. The cinematographs of the French front showed long naval French 16 in. guns in the act of bombarding, and it may be taken as certain that the British were in no respect behind the French. But the heaviest work fell on the 6 in., 8 in. and 9·4 in. guns and howitzers, and also on the admirable British 60-pounders. The monsters were too costly for ordinary work, though their moral influence was great, and the aid which they gave by compelling the heavy German artillery to remain at a great distance from the front was precious.

In the trench systems, which grew more and more elaborate, earthworks were replaced by elaborate steel and concrete defences that could defy anything but a direct hit from a powerful **Underground fortress** gun. The huge German fortresses, of **systems** which many were taken during the continuous battles of 1916 and 1917, had vast systems of communications and tunnels at a level of thirty or forty feet below the surface, large excavated chambers, some of them big enough to accommodate a battalion, and shafts and special lifts for machine-guns. They were equipped with periscopes, so that the defending force could watch, hidden safe below, what was passing above. Such, however, was the skill and violence of the Allies' attack that these underground labyrinths were stormed, and often turned into death-traps for all within them. Now and again monster shells from the Allies' guns would penetrate the earth above them, burying perhaps hundreds of men alive.

Trench-mortars firing a short-range projectile containing a large charge of high explosive, and aerial torpedoes similar to these projectiles, were other new weapons, or revivals and improvements of older weapons. The British trench-mortars of 1917 were of appalling efficiency, nor were the British air torpedoes inferior. Bombs had reappeared on the German side in the early battles. The Allies quickly adopted them, and by 1917 this terrible weapon was universally employed in close fighting, and again the British pattern left nothing to be desired, except perhaps that it was unnecessarily large and powerful.

Barbed-wire of extraordinary thickness was extensively used by the Germans from the first, and also by their disciples the Turks. Indeed, one of the most painful features of the Dardanelles despatches was their note of pained astonishment that the Turks should have been so well provided with the barbed-wire and machine-guns which the Allies lacked. Used in combination with machine-guns, barbed-wire gave extraordinary delaying power to the defence. At the Marne the attempt to pursue the German armies on their retreat was checked by the plentiful **Value of barbed-** employment of barbed-wire. If the **wire in defence** Russians had possessed it in the required quantity, their great retreat of 1915, which involved such disastrous loss, might never have taken place at all, or might have been conducted so slowly as to save all their material and men.

One of the curious developments of the war was the reintroduction of armour for the head and body. The French, late in 1914, adopted a strong steel helmet which gave perfect protection against spent bullets and splinters, though it was incapable of resisting direct hits at short range. The British followed, after noticeable delay, with a headpiece shaped like a pudding-basin ; this, though ugly, saved tens of thousands of men from death. The Germans, last of all, introduced a very serviceable and strong helmet, and provided their sharpshooters with a special pattern in which the front was strengthened till it would resist a direct hit at short range. Similar helmets were used in most of the armies for the men stationed at

crew. In the war she proved comparatively safe. The German losses do not appear to have been heavy, and the British losses certainly were not.

The effect of the submarine on naval operations was to produce a great uncertainty, and to render sea communications extraordinarily precarious. Large ships were chary of showing themselves at sea without escorts of destroyers—which were not always successful in protecting them—and had to proceed at high speed. The German operations were simplified by the Allies' plan of campaign, which gave them free access to the sea and did not close the holes from which they issued. On two occasions fear of submarines seems to have prevented a decisive blow from being struck. The first was at the Dogger Bank, where the pursuit of the German ships was broken off when two of them were badly on fire, one in her magazines. The second was in the Battle of Jutland, after the British Battle Fleet had appeared on the scene.

The mine was another comparatively new weapon,

[*French official photograph.*]
RUSSIAN SOLDIERS ON THE WESTERN FRONT.
Men of the Russian Contingent standing-to in the French trenches. The fine body of troops which Russia sent to fight in France acquitted itself splendidly.

observation-posts where they had to expose themselves.

Body armour was not so generally employed, because it was not in most cases provided by the military authorities and issued to all. British and French officers for the most part refused to avail themselves of a means of protection which was not supplied to their men. Heavy shields with a loophole in them were often used by the German "thrusting" troops. They were hung round the neck, and protected the heart, stomach, and groin, but they were so awkward and cumbrous that they were not in great favour. The French, so early as September, 1914, tried shields for their infantry in the Argonne, and a large number were ordered for the Russian Government.

Some few officers tried coats of light chain-mail, which gave effective protection against slight wounds and against the risk of tetanus. The cost of these appliances, so long as they were only made in small number, was so heavy that they could only be used here **Armour for men and machines** and there. Steel cylinders rolled towards the enemy represented another device which was tried in the earlier period of the war without proving a great success. Heavy shields on wheels were more satisfactory, but were afterwards more efficiently replaced by the " tank " and by armoured motor-cars. Armour appeared also in the aeroplane. There it was placed beneath the pilot. Sometimes in the earlier days it took the form of a sand-bag. Later in the war large armoured aeroplanes appeared.

At sea the new weapons made their influence felt. The submarine rapidly improved, and developed on lines generally similar to the aeroplane. The largest submarine actually in service when the war began was a vessel of about 800 tons submerged, but many Powers had larger craft under construction. The most powerful, according to the published German accounts, which may have been exaggerated or untrue, were vessels of 1,500 tons. Moderate sized submarines seem to have proved most satisfactory for the German campaign of piracy. But one or two large German submarines appear to have been constructed. Neutral newspapers printed accounts of a German submarine cruiser of 3,000 or 4,000 tons, which was said to have been seen in the Baltic. The submarine before the war had been regarded as a very dangerous craft for her

ENTERING THE BREACHED WALLS OF AN ENEMY POST.
Russian soldiers coming up from a covered trench to a commanding enemy position at Courcy, north of Rheims. The artillery had been trained previously on the post and battered the walls, through which an entrance had been broken.

though it had been employed on a considerable scale in the Russo-Japanese War, when it destroyed a large number of vessels, including two of the best Japanese battleships in a single day. It had no such success in the early part of the Great War, though it inflicted heavy and increasing destruction on merchant ships. The power of the charges in both mines and torpedoes was greatly increased. At the outbreak of war 60 lb. of high explosive was regarded as a respectable charge for an allied mine. At the end of the third year charges of 500 lb. or even **Development of mines and torpedoes** more were employed. In the case of torpedoes, charges of 400 and 500 lb. weight took the place of those in fashion at the opening of war, which rarely exceeded 150 or 200 lb.

Everything had to be systematised and organised, and so the old plan of voluntary enlistment, which had survived in Great Britain alone of European Powers, broke down. With the quickness of vision which marked President Wilson, compulsory service was adopted at once in 1917 by the United States. Great Britain clung to voluntary service for many months, until early 1916. The result was mischief and confusion. It skimmed off the bravest men at the outset instead of using them to leaven the mass. It often took the wrong men. Thus the ship-building artisans, the trained engineers, and the skilled workers in iron and steel volunteered in large numbers for the front, though they were more urgently needed at home for the manufacture of munitions. On the other hand, it permitted hundreds of thousands of unskilled young men to skulk. Even when compulsory service was introduced in Great Britain (though not in Ireland) in 1916, it was introduced in so half-hearted a way and surrounded by so many qualifications that immense injustice was done. Enormous numbers of young men escaped, and the coward had always a loophole in the clause excusing "conscientious objectors" from service.

Introduction of compulsory service

These persons were treated with special affection and tenderness by the Government, were given excellent berths, and were allowed to do much as they liked. On the other hand, men of forty, with large families and businesses dependent on them were taken for the front. Quakers were allowed to make money by the war, but were not required to fight for their country, though to their honour some of their younger men did so. But the general behaviour of the Society of Friends was as arrogant as it was unpatriotic.

The war was marked by an intensity and fury that had been apparent in no previous conflict. The scale of everything was so vast that it resembled a convulsion of Nature. A week of such fighting as began it was equivalent to any year or more of the older wars. For the first time whole nations were placed in the field. In the Franco-Prussian War Germany was credited with a stupendous feat when she assembled a million men under arms. In late 1914 she had at least four millions in the field, and in 1917, after all her losses, she had still five millions. It has been calculated that thirty-four million men in all fought during the first three years, and the casualties and prisoners were reckoned by millions. An estimate of the British War Cabinet, in May, 1917, placed the loss of lives at seven million, including in this women and children who had been starved or murdered in Belgium, Serbia, and Armenia. The German losses, as disclosed down to the end of May, 1917, were 4,356,760, of whom 1,067,000 were killed or died of sickness, 254,000 were missing, and 303,000 were prisoners. As against these appalling casualties, the Germans and their allies claimed to hold 2,080,000 Russian prisoners, 368,000 French, 154,000 Serbians, 98,000 Italians, 79,000 Rumanians, 45,000 British, and 42,000 Belgians, though included in these figures were doubtless large numbers of civilians of military age. In the Franco-Prussian War of 1870-71 the total German loss was only 46,600 killed and died of sickness, and 127,000 wounded; the French loss was 138,900 killed or died of sickness, and 131,000 wounded. In the Russo-Japanese War of 1904-5 the Japanese lost 80,000 men killed or died of sickness, and 137,000 wounded, against Russian losses estimated at 320,000 killed and wounded, and 67,700 prisoners with, in addition, a heavy loss from disease. In the American Civil War the dead in the United States armies were 360,000; in the Southern armies, from 250,000 to 300,000.

Slowly, and after generations of effort, mankind had tempered the cruelty of the laws of war. The Assyrian despots usually tortured and killed prisoners and enslaved peoples; often they massacred the whole population of conquered States. In the twilight of history the ancient Egyptians alone showed mercy, and can still be seen on

KING VAJIRAVUDH OF SIAM.
His Majesty, who was born on January 1st, 1880, and ascended the throne on October 23rd, 1910, is wearing the uniform of Commander of the Royal Guards. The Siamese Government declared war against the Central Empires on July 22nd, 1917.

their monuments rescuing their enemies from the water. Progress towards the nobler rule was slow and precarious. In the Napoleonic Wars prisoners were usually generously treated, and subject populations spared. Napoleon issued stringent orders against the ill-treatment of captives, and though he was guilty of occasional acts of severity, he could never be reproached with ferocity or wanton slaughter. As a Republican general in the fiendish Terrorist excesses he spared his own disloyal countrymen. After his day international effort built up a code to eliminate needless suffering. Until the Great War it was unhesitatingly obeyed by all but the Balkan States. In a few hours the Germans swept it all away and carried the world back to the ferocious cruelties of the Assyrian age. The savageries of inhuman Asiatics were emulated by the Kaiser's troops and the Kaiser's Navy. The assassination of Captain Fryatt, though carried out with an order and method which made it the more diabolical, stamped every German officer, from the Kaiser downward, implicated in it with ineffable shame. When in a hasty moment Napoleon directed the summary trial and execution of a German soldier, Count Bentinck, the French officers refused to obey. Their master, a nobler and juster being than the German despot, showed them no ill-will for this act of independence. With such deeds did Germany, in Professor Eucken's words, "busily and cheerfully work for the elevation of the German race."

Not only was the whole able-bodied manhood placed under arms or required to execute urgent war work in all the belligerent States except Great Britain, but also the civilian population, women and older men, was enrolled and regimented for work in munition factories, on the land, and in other directions. Nothing like this had been seen in earlier wars. In France and Germany women and children tilled the land. In Great Britain—though Ireland, all but six counties, enjoyed a dishonourable security and ease—young men gradually disappeared, except in the towns, where they were seen in numbers. The fields and farms and inns emptied. A quiet, as of a house in which the dead lie unburied, brooded over the land, the lists of those who had paid the last sacrifice grew incessantly, and in almost every window was the name of one who was fighting for freedom or whose fight had ended for ever. Silence fell upon the colleges of Oxford and Cambridge, except where the cadets messed and forgathered. The great universities were in arms, serving the nation with a heroism and devotion which the gratitude of a great race can never forget. And so it was throughout Europe. Great Britain in the far-off Napoleonic Wars had placed 500,000 men under arms. Now her Ministers claimed that she had 5,000,000 in service.

The battles of the war were interminable, obscure, gigantic struggles marked by anonymity; for at the outset **Obscurity of the great battles** each side hid from the other the names of units and generals engaged, and wrapped everything in uncertainty and mystery. Many priceless traditions were lost in this twilight. Bravery is personal, and deeds of heroism do not move mankind when sundered from the character that has produced them. Even Homer's poems without Achilles and Hector and Helen would lose their eternal beauty. So strict was the censorship that it was difficult to discover whether a battle had issued in victory or defeat.

The casualties were not divulged, and each side usually claimed that it had suffered moderate loss and inflicted on the other fearful losses. The notion that the Germans were mown down in masses sustained the constancy of the Allies in the dreadful initial period of the German advance. The gain of ground by one side or the other was the only tangible fact. Thus engagements greater by far than Austerlitz or Sadowa or Mukden produced comparatively little effect. The resisting power shown by nations in arms was astonishing. Moltke, however, had in 1880 predicted that the next great war would be long.

Vast area of battlefields No one knew when many of the great battles began or when they ceased. It was, for example, exceedingly difficult to determine at what precise moment the Battle of the Marne or the First Battle of Ypres opened and closed. Generally the great battles died down slowly, like an expiring conflagration. There were exceptions, as in the Battle of Messines. The extent of ground covered by the great battles was often enormous. The Marne was fought along a distance of two hundred miles, but there was not one continuous line of attack or resistance over this vast front. At Waterloo the space covered by the British Army and its allies was slightly over two miles

THE FLOOD AND THE EBB.
Map showing the line held in France and Flanders by the German armies of invasion at the end of the first, second, and third years of the war.

at the opening of the battle. Waterloo lasted ten hours; the Marne six days. The forces engaged in it probably exceeded two and a half million men, of whom one and a half million were Germans, and the casualties certainly reached and probably exceeded 350,000, as compared with 201,000 at Mukden in 1905. The First Battle of Arras began on May 9th, 1915, and continued for several weeks. The fighting resulted in 113,000 French casualties, and probably in a German loss of 150,000. It was composed of obscure attacks and counter-attacks, surging round a sugar refinery and a vast trench labyrinth.

The outlay on the war was stupendous. The total cost of the Franco-Prussian War to both combatants was £695,000,000, and of the Russo-Japanese war over £373,000,000. The American Civil War involved a direct outlay to the combatants of £950,000,000, apart from losses of property, which certainly reached another £100,000,000. The Napoleonic Wars cost Great Britain £800,000,000, but this expenditure was spread over

twenty-two years. The cost of the Boer War, which was little more than a series of skirmishes, was £223,000,000. Speaking for Germany in the Great War, the German Finance Minister said, in the summer of 1915, that " the expenditure in a single month is a third greater than the entire sum disbursed during the war of 1870." A calculation of the British War Cabinet, in May, 1917, placed the total war expenditure of all the Powers at nine thousand millions at that date. Great Britain had then borrowed £3,195,000,000 for the war. The figures became so immense that they failed to make any impression. The cost rose each month with the increasing fury of the fighting and the ever-advancing consumption of ammunition and multiplication of guns. The latter were used up at a great rate in the protracted bombardments which opened all the great battles.

No one had supposed that such outlay could be borne without repudiation ; few had imagined that such amounts could be raised by any device. The patriotism of the British citizen placed vast resources at the disposal of his Government, which, unfortunately, muddled a considerable part of them away. British investments abroad, particularly in the United State—the accumulation of more than a century's profit in trade and manufacture—vanished in a few months. They were sold, and their proceeds were handed to the British Treasury. Conscription of American securities was introduced for the purpose of financing the war, and though it brought heavy loss, it was cheerfully and loyally borne. The British income tax was raised to a level of 5s. in the pound on large incomes, with other taxes which in some cases brought the total up to 11s. or even 12s. in the pound, but there was no murmuring, and such burdensome imposts were never so willingly paid. Nor was this all. Taxed as he was, the British investor in the great loan of 1917 provided over a thousand millions of capital for his Government. A real peril was that throughout the first part of the war money was so easily obtained that it was carelessly spent. Whence all these funds came was a mystery which even the ablest financiers found it difficult to explain. The one certain fact was that the strain would be most felt after peace, as was the case in the Napoleonic Wars, when buildings partially completed had to be abandoned for want of money, unemployment was rife, and wages suddenly collapsed. In Germany money was raised with much greater effort, but still it was raised, and the expenditure being far more carefully controlled the German Government was able to meet all needs.

The very size of armies and the holding power of machine-guns clogged and delayed movements on land. For example, before the Somme offensive the Allies had to construct an immense system of water mains, as otherwise in that upland country an army of many hundred thousand men would have died of thirst. Roads and causeways had to be built, and railways and tramways to be laid. At Messines the mining operations occupied **Colossal work of preparation** weeks and months. It is probable that one of the causes of the German defeat on the Marne was that sufficient preparation had not been made for the advance of so enormous a force, despite the care and system shown by the German Staff in its organisation. The German troops, in fact, ran out of munitions and food. So, to inflict decisive defeats was extraordinarily difficult. A general might break the enemy's line. There were certainly moments at the Somme and at Arras where the German line was broken. For a small force to advance through the gap in such cases meant probable disaster, while had a large force attempted to pass through it could not have been supplied with food and ammunition over ground which had been rendered impassable by a week of furious bombardment. In Napoleon's day, when armies were small, it was possible to inflict such catastrophic defeats as Austerlitz and Jena. When the scale of the fighting grew, as in the Saxon campaign of 1813, even the greatest soldier of all time found that his methods broke down. The Rumanians, though weak in numbers and poorly equipped, were not completely overwhelmed when the two ablest German generals were sent against them with overpowering numbers.

The German plan on land at the close of the third year was to leave the Russians to decay by revolution and internal chaos, while the other Allies were worn down by holding a very strongly fortified trench line in Allies' territory with the minimum of troops, and all the time vigorously to attack the allied cities with aircraft and the allied commerce with submarines. This was a strategy which gave Germany marked advantages. It enabled her to save men and munitions and money, and to destroy her opponents' resources, while she employed every form of political intrigue to paralyse the energy of the Governments opposed to her. In the United States, where President Wilson knew his own mind, and was

not afraid to show a determination worthy of Lincoln, her propaganda encountered unexpected difficulties. Though opponents of compulsory service in Great Britain were allowed surprising licence, in New York one was sentenced to three years' imprisonment and payment of a fine of £2,000. German policy aimed at promoting war-weariness, and spreading the belief that the German armies could not be dislodged. But war-weariness steadily grew in Germany, and the fear of the arrival of a large United States' army became increasingly acute.

The last enemy that shall be overcome is death, and in this war it was overcome with a courage so sublime as to lift man to new heights. The war showed, as Maeterlinck justly said, " that civilisation, contrary to what was feared, so far from enervating, depraving, weakening, lowering, and dwarfing man, elevates him, purifies him, strengthens him, ennobles him, makes him capable of acts of sacrifice, generosity, and courage which he did not know before." Men marched by the hundred thousand

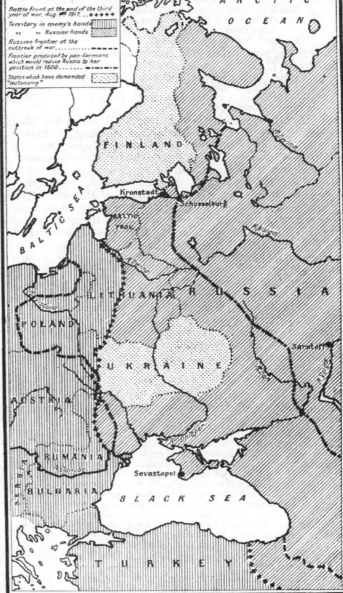

Copyright   The Great War   Copyright   The Great War

RUSSIA AS IT WAS IN 1600, AND AT THE END OF THE THIRD YEAR OF THE GREAT WAR.

The map on the left shows Russia as it was, cut off from the sea, before the days of the Tsars. That on the right indicates, beside the matters mentioned in the key, the towns, such as Cronstadt and Sebastopol, which on the outbreak of the Russian Revolution proclaimed themselves separate republics, and the frontiers of Lithuania and the Baltic Provinces, which the Germans proposed to form into protected States, with Poland.

to the bloody trial of the battlefield, and died with a smile. The airman tranquilly flew off at dawn to encounter danger alone, and too often never returned. It is not to be pretended that there were no failures. There were nations, there were troops which yielded on the battlefield. There were men whose hearts, like Peter of old when he denied his Lord, failed them before the great sacrifice. But these were few, and many even of them overcame themselves, and went back to death.

Under the stimulus of this new strange life, in which man was suddenly confronted with the ultimate realities, a nobler inspiration seemed to fire the heart of the British race. Never had it shown so many young **The voice of the** poets, nor had their poetry reached such **young poets** a plane of beauty. Many of them died, leaving imperishable work, and the example of such lives has put meaner men to shame. No generation of the race will probably forget Rifleman S. Donald Cox's half-dozen lines, " To My Mother " :

> If I should fall, grieve not that one so weak
> And poor as I
> Should die,
> Nay, though thy heart should break
> Think only this : that when at dusk they speak
> Of sons and brothers of another one,
> Then thou canst say : " I, too, had a son ;
> He died for England's sake ! "

Nor is there, perhaps, in literature a more touching epitaph than Pte. F. G. Scott's lines on a soldier's grave in Flanders :

> He found the songs for which he yearned,
> Hopes that had mocked desire ;
> His heart is resting now which burned
> With such consuming fire.

In all their verse—and the output of it was great from the multitude of writers—there was nothing of hatred for the enemy. Contempt sometimes, disgust for the cruelty and meanness which the Germans so often showed, but beyond that the great charity which was the characteristic of the British soldier. Yet it is to the poets that men must go to learn the real meaning of the war. The English prose-writers and letter-writers at the front commonly glossed over its grim facts, and there was some truth in a reminder which came from one who watched the fighting, that " humility, consideration for others, good-humoured belittlement of suffering or horror are admirable in their way, but war must not be allowed to masquerade as tolerable, enjoyable, and glorious." The men concealed " the discomfort of their lives, the unspeakable sights around them, and the risks they ran." One of the reasons why Great Britain was so slow to wake and act was, undoubtedly, the belief thus spread that war was a glorified picnic or sport and not " a savage encounter with desperate enemies who dealt death and grievous wounds with impartial hands."

The French soldier spoke out more plainly. The truest picture of life in the trenches, as it appeared to a great artist and writer who suffered and fell in battle, is painted in *Lettres d'un Soldat* :

> Our existence as infantrymen is rather like that of rabbits which are being shot. We feel pain in shaking off our habits, but perhaps we had all accustomed ourselves too completely to a degree of comfort which could not last. What passes our understanding —and yet after all it is natural enough—is that civilians are able to continue their normal existence while we are in torment. It is perhaps a destiny and privilege of which our generation should be proud to witness these horrors, but what a fearful ransom it has to pay. If there is one thing absolute in the realm of human sensation it is suffering. The true death would be to live in a conquered country. Rain in war ; it is a punishment of which you can form no idea. To sleep in a trench full of water has no equivalent in Dante's hell. But what of the awakening, when you have to count the moments before killing or being killed ?

And so to his last message, written just before the attack in the spring of 1915, in which he was lost :

> In the full possession of all my faculties, let us hope to the last, but above all have steadfastness and love. We are now at the last point of waiting. I send you my love. Whatever happens life will have been beautiful.

Thus they went to death.

The last scene in man's life in this struggle was ordered with terrors which no previous generation had known. Maeterlinck has pointed out that Homer's heroes had to face no such ordeal as met the soldier of the Great War. The ground was shaken with the concussion of interminable bombardments. The approach to the battle up the communication-trenches was like the entrance to the Valley of the Shadow of Death. The men marched into a terrain covered with smoke, into an atmosphere vitiated by the dense clouds of poisonous gas or constant explosion of the shells. Each side used smoke-clouds now that guns had become smokeless. The noise was so terrific that it drowned speech and sometimes even paralysed thought. Through the gas fumes could be perceived the heavy, sweet, evil scent of death. High above droned monstrous terrible insects, the aeroplanes of the two sides. In the advanced trenches the men waited patiently the order to go over the top, which, a French soldier has said, was as the order to mount the scaffold. As the moment approached the bombardment quickened, till sometimes its distant throbbing was heard or felt on British soil, and the mines went up in purple sheets of flame. Then through the darkness and first grey light of dawn the lines advanced, not at a run, for they were too grievously weighted, but generally at a gentle amble or walk, while the roar of the enemy's firing rose and the drumming of the machine-guns increased in violence. Now and again sheets of hissing fire from the flame-projectors would shoot through the air. Last of all, when the surge of battle had passed and peace returned before the counter-attack, a faint, whimpering noise as from a catch of fishes at sea would go up from the mortally stricken, and the salt smell of blood strike the nostril.

Conspicuous among the many brave and doomed to early death, most gallant and most beloved, moved the airmen. Something has already been said of the difficulty of their work, which was enhanced by their spiritual solitude when the moment of their great trial came. The finest at their art fought alone. They were a race apart, though the infantry officers who gave so lavishly of their lives deserved to share their immense glory. " Their flying life is reckoned," wrote a witness at the front, " not in years, or even in months, but in hours ; so that a man who has flown fifty hours is experienced, and one who has flown two hundred and fifty—ten days of time— is a veteran. These hours are numbered by fate and by the average of casualties. Fifty hours without a crash would be luck—five hundred would be practically impossible. Within such spans is the fighting pilot's life compassed." The epitaph of these valiant souls is written in the poem that commemorated Sub-Lieutenant Warneford's end :

> Whom the gods loved they gave in youth's first flower
> One infinite hour of glory. That same hour
> Before a leaf droops from the laurel, come
> Winged Death and Sleep to bear Sarpedon home.

Of the future, of the hopes that lay beyond the war, only the poets could tell. There was a revival of religious feeling, very marked in France and Belgium in the earlier period of the war and notice- **For Honour and** able also in Great Britain. Again, as at **the Cross** Marathon in the crisis of civilisation 2,400 years before, helpers from above were seen by mortal man incarnate and fighting in battle at his side. As the old world of comfort and *laissez-faire* and selfishness came down in such utter ruin, as mankind passed into a new " twilight of the gods," the end of which none could foresee, this at least could be said, that for the first time in the history of the race millions of men had been filled with the spirit which the poet put into these words :

> See young " Adventure " there
> (" Make-money-quick " that was)
> Hurls down his gods that were
> For Honour and the Cross !

Synchronised Chronology of Leading Events in the First Three Years of the War.

EVENTS PRECEDING BRITAIN'S DECLARATION OF WAR.

1914.
June 28.—Assassination of Archduke Franz Ferdinand and his wife at Sarajevo.
July 23.—Austria issues ultimatum to Serbia.
,,   25.—Russia's request for extension of time limit for Serbia refused by Austria.
,,   26.—Serbia's reply regarded as evasive by Austria. Serbian mobilisation.
,,   27.—Sir Edward Grey proposes mediation by France, Germany, Italy, and Great Britain.
             Serbian troops fire first shots in the war on the Danube.
,,   28.—Austria declares war on Serbia. Russia starts mobilising.
,,   29.—Austrians bombard Belgrade.
,,   30.—Sir Edward Grey announces Britain's refusal of neutrality at expense of France.

1914.
July 31.—Germany sends ultimatum to France and Russia.
Aug. 1.—Germany declares war on Russia.
,,   2 —Sir Edward Grey gives conditional assurances to France of British help.
             German ultimatum to Belgium.
,,   3.—Sir Edward Grey in Parliament states Britain's obligations to France.
             Germany declares war on France.
,,   4.—Germany declares war on Belgium.
             Great Britain declares war on Germany.

1914	The Western Front.	The Eastern Front.	Other European Areas.	War Outside Europe.	War by Sea and Air.	Events at Home.	1914
Aug						**Moratorium Bill passed.**	**Aug**
3	Germans invade Belgium.					Government controls railways.	3
4	Von Emmich attacks Liège.					Lord Kitchener War Minister.	4
5	Fierce fighting at Liège.				Königin Luise sunk off Harwich.	Vote of Credit for £100,000,000.	5
6		Austria declares war on Russia		Lome (German Togoland) taken	H.M.S. Amphion sunk by mine.	[£1,000,000.	6
8	French occupy Mulhouse.	[Poland.		Germans occupy Taveta.		Prince of Wales' Fund reaches	8
15	Fall of Liège.	Tsar promises Home Rule to	Serbs defeat Austrians at				15
16	British Force lands in France.		[Shabatz.				16
18	British advance in Alsace-Lorraine.	Ger. defeat near Eydtkuhnen.					18
19	Germans occupy Louvain.	Ger. defeat at Gumbinnen.		[Africa.			19
20	Germans occupy Brussels.			Germans invade British S.			20
21	Battle of Charleroi begins.			Japan declares war on Germany.			21
23	British Engaged at Mons.				Zeppelin bombs Antwerp.		23
24	Retreat from Mons. Fall of Namur.				[sunk.		24
25	Louvain destroyed.	Aust. declares war on Japan.		Germans surrender Togoland.	Kaiser Wilhelm der Grosse		25
26	British hold line Cambrai—Le Cateau.				Battle of Heligoland Bight.		26
27	Allies retired towards Somme.	Aust. declares war on Belg.		[Zealand force.			27
28	Germans bombard Malines.			Surrender of Apia to New			28
30							30
Sept					Bombs dropped on Paris.		**Sept**
1	British engaged near Compiègne.	Austrians defeated at Lemberg.			H.M.S. Speedy mined.		1
3	French Govt. moves to Bordeaux.				Two Ger. airmen capt. N. Sea.		3
5	Retreat from Mons to Marne ends.	Battle of Tannenberg.			Formation of Naval Brigades.		5
6	Battle of Marne begins.		Serbian victory near Racha.		H.M.S. Pathfinder sunk.	Lloyd George's "Silver Bullets"	6
8	Germans sack Termonde.			[to Australians.		King's Message to Overseas	8
9	British reported across the Marne.		Serbians capture Semlin.	German New Guinea surrenders.		[Dominions.	9
11	Allied advance reported.				Carmania sinks Cap Trafalgar.		11
14					[bar Harbour.		14
15	Battle of the Aisne begins.				H.M.S. Pegasus disabled Zanzi-		15
20	Germans shell Rheims Cathedral.	Russians take Jaroslav.	Serbs attack Sarajevo.		[pedoed.		20
21				[Chief	Aboukir, Hogue, Cressy tor-		21
22				Botha takes field as Com.-in-	British bomb Zepp. sheds at		22
23				[announced.	[Düsseldorf.		23
25		Battle of Augustovo begins.		Occu. Kaiser Wilhelm's Land			25
26	Indians land at Marseilles.		Serbians recapture Semlin.	German raid on Walfish Bay.			26
29	Germans bombard Antwerp.						29
Oct							**Oct**
7	Belgian Govt. removed to Ostend.			Mutiny of Maritz in S. Africa.	Brit. destroy Zepp. at Düssel-		7
8					[dorf.		8
9	Fall of Antwerp.				German air raid on Paris.		9
11	First Battle of Ypres opens.						11
13	Germans occupy Lille.						13
14	Allies occupy Ypres.	Fighting along Vistula and San			Undaunted sinks 4 destroyers.	Canadian troops arrive.	14
16					Bombardment of Tsing-tau.	Anti-German riots at Deptford.	16
17					Monitors bombard Belgian coast.		17
19	Fighting bet. Nieuport and Dixmude.			Botha routs Beyer's commando.			19
27	Ger. driven from French Lorraine.	Russ. declares war on Turkey.			Lord Fisher First Sea Lord.		27
30	Germans re-cross the Yser.				H.M.S. Hermes torpedoed.		30
					Rohilla wrecked off Whitby.		
Nov			Turkey joins Germany.		Naval action off Coronel.		**Nov**
1			Britain at war with Turkey.				1
5				Fall of Tsing-tau.	[E. Afr.		5
7					Königsberg bottled up German		7
10	Germans take Dixmude.				Emden destroyed at Keeling		10
11	Prussian Guard repulsed at Ypres.			Botha defeats De Wet.	Niger torpedoed off Deal.		11
14	Lord Roberts dies in France.				[Harbour		14
26	Germans bombard Arras.				Bulwark blown up Sheerness		26
29	King George in France.						29
Dec				Surrender of De Wet.			**Dec**
1	Allied advance bet. Bethune and Lens.						1
2			Austrians occupy Belgrade.	Collapse of S. Afr. Rebellion.			2
7							7
8	Germans shell Furnes.	Russians admit loss of Lodz.	Serbians retake Valievo.		Naval victory off Falklands.		8
15			Serbians re-enter Belgrade.				15
16					Scarborough and Whitby shelled.		16
17				Egypt a British Protectorate.			17
24					Air raid on Dover.		24
25					Brit. air raid on Cuxhaven.		25
1915							**1915**
Jan				[ported			**Jan**
1		Russian victory on Bzwra.		Success at Dar-es-Salaam re-	H.M.S. Formidable torpedoed.	King's message to Fr. President	1
2	French retake Steinbach.	German advance on Warsaw.		Swakopmund occupied.		Stock Exchange re-opened.	2
4				Turks occupy Tabriz.			4
14	French reverse north-east of Soissons.				[Lynn		14
19					Zepp. raid Yarmouth, King's		19
22				Turks engaged at El Kantara.	Air raid on Zeebrugge.		22
24				Turks advance on Egypt.	[ger Bank.		24
					Adm. Beatty's victory off Dog-		
26				Nyasaland rising ended.			26
Feb			[Sokachev.	Turkish defeat, Suez Canal.			**Feb**
1	German defeat north of La Bassée.	Hindenburg defeated near			[Zeebrugge.		1
2	Fighting near Cuinchy.				Com. Samson's squadron raids		2
12	French carry Hill 937 in Vosges.				[men.		12
16	Fren. gain bet. Perthes & Beauséjour.	[Augustovo.			Naval losses: 348 officers, 5,812		16
18		German enveloping movement			Blockade of Gt. Britain begins.		18
19	The 200th Day of the War.			Garub occupied by S. Africans.	[forts.	Notes to U.S.A. published.	19
22	French gain in Champagne.	Ger. offensive Pranysch region.			Bombardment of Dardanelles		22
					Zeppelin raid on Calais.		
23	British capture trench at Givenchy.	Russians retake Prasnysch.		Indian troops riot, Singapore.			23
27		Russ. advance Prasnysch region.			French seize the Dacia.		27
Mar							**Mar**
1	French gain about Perthes.				Brit. blockade of Ger. begins.		1
7	Heights captured near Münster.			Brit. check on Tigris reported.	British air raid on Ostend.		7
10	Battle of Neuve Chapelle.				H.M.S. Ariel sinks U12.		10
14					Glasgow and Kent sink Dresden.		14
18		Russians occupy Memel.			Irresistible, Ocean, Bouvet lost		18
					[Dardanelles.		
21	Loss of Great & Little Reichackerkopf.	Fall of Przemysl to Russia.			Zeppelin raid on Paris.		21
22		Russ. withdraw from Memel.					22
23		Russ. capt. Lupkow Pass (Carp.).		Turks routed on Suez Canal.			23
26							26
28					Falaba torpedoed.		28
Apr							**Apr**
3				Union forces seize Warmbad.			3
5	French gain south-east of St. Mihiel.	Austrian defeat at Bartfeld.			Russians engage Goeben and		5
7	French progress near St. Mihiel.	Aust. retreat across Carpathians			[Breslau		7
13		Russ. victory near Uzsok Pass.		Brit. rout Turks on Euphrates.	Zeppelins raid Tyneside.	Munitions Committee appointed.	13
14	British capture Hill 60.						14
17							17
22	Second Battle of Ypres opens.				[forts		22
24	Canadians recapture 4 guns Ypres.				Russians bombard Bosphorus		24
25			Allied forces land in Gallipoli.		Léon Gambetta sunk.		25
27	French recapt. Hartmannsweilerkopf.		Land fighting in Gallipoli.		Zepps. raid Bury S. Edmunds		27
30					[and Ipswich.		30
May							**May**
3	German gas attack Hill 60.	Germans break through in W.				Second War Budget introduced.	3
4	British line Flanders readjusted.	[Galicia.			Lusitania torpedoed.		4
7		Germans capture Libau.					7
8					Zeppelin raid on Southend.		8
9	French advance Carency—Souchez.						9
	British adv. Bois Grenier—Festubert.						
12				Union forces occupy Windhoek.	Goliath torp. Dardanelles.		12
13	French carry Carency village.			Conquest of Ger. S.W. Africa.		[Windsor.	13
14	French success south-west of Souchez.	Russ. admit retreat to the San.	Italian Cabinet resigns.			Kaiser's Garter removed from	14
23			Italy declares war on Austria.				23
24			Gen. Cadorna leaves for front.				24
26			Ital. attack on Trentino front.		Zeppelin raid on Southend.	New Cabinet announced.	26
27	French carry Ablain Cemetery.				French raid on Ludwigshafen.	Princess Irene blown up.	27
					E11 enters Sea of Marmora.		
28			Italians occupy Gradisca.				28
31	French organise "Labyrinth" gains.			Brit. occupy Amara.	Zepp. raid Outer London.	Sir Hy. Jackson First Sea Lord.	31

1915/1916	The Western Front.	The Eastern Front.	Other European Areas.	War Outside Europe.	War by Sea and Air.	Events at Home.	1915/1916
June							**June**
1		Austro-Ger. attack Przemysl.	Italians occupy Mount Zugna.				1
3	British gain at Givenchy.	Austro-Ger. retake Przemysl.				New Ministry meets Parl.	3
7			Italians capture Monfalcone.				7
9					Warneford, V.C., destroys Zepp.		9
16	British gain north of Hooge.			De Wet sentenced and fined.		[Munitions. Mr. Lloyd George Minister of	16
21	French take Metzeral.					Second War Loan announced.	21
22		Austrians retake Lemberg.					22
July							**July**
14		Germans move on Warsaw.					14
16		Russ. admit loss of Prasnysch.	Ital. success Cadore frontier.				16
18		Russ. forced back to Narew.	Italian success Isonzo anncd.				18
19		Russ. stand N.and S. of Warsaw.	Ital. victory on Lower Isonzo.				19
20		Russ. yield Bzura-Rawka front.					20
25				British take Nasiriyeh.			25
29		Russ. line Lublin-Cholm forced.					29
30	German liquid fire attack at Hooge.						30
31		Russians evacuate Lublin.					31
Aug							**Aug**
4		Fall of Warsaw.				Intercession Service St. Paul's.	4
5		Fall of Ivangorod.					5
6							6
9	British recapt. trenches near Hooge.		New landing Anzac Cove, Gallip.		French raid on Saarbrück.		9
12			Gain at Chunuk Bair reported.		Zepp. raid East Coast.		12
14			Austrians bombard Belgrade.		Royal Edward transport sunk.		14
15			Advance at Suvla.			National Register Day.	15
16		Fall of Kovno.			U boat shells Whitehaven.		16
17					Zepp. raid Eastern Counties.		17
19		Fall of Novo Georgievsk.	New landing Suvla Bay reptd.		Liner Arabic torpedoed.		19
20			Italy declares war on Turkey.				20
25		Fall of Brest Litovsk.					25
Sept							**Sept**
2		Fall of Grodno.					2
5		Grand Duke Nicholas appointed [to com. Caucasus			Zeppelin raid on London.		5
8							8
18		Fall of Vilna.					18
19							19
21	Allied adv. at Loos and in Champagne.		Bulgaria mobilises. M. Venizelos invites Allies to [Salonika.		French air raid on Metz.	War Budget introduced Parl.	21
25				Turks defeated at Kut-el-Amara			25
28							28
30		Russians abandon Lutsk.					30
Oct							**Oct**
4			Russ. ultimatum to Bulgaria	Turks defeated near Van.			4
5			Allies land at Salonika.			Lord Derby Dir. of Recruiting.	5
6	French carry village of Tahure.		M. Venizelos resigns.				6
9	British advance Hill 70—Hulluch.		Austro-Ger. occupy Belgrade.				9
11			Bulgarians invade Serbia.				11
12		Russians cross the Strypa.	Miss Edith Cavell shot.				12
13					Zeppelin raid on London.		13
15			Britain at war with Bulgaria				15
17	French regain Hartmannsweilerkopf.		Italians occupy Pregasina.				17
22			Bulgarians occupy Uskub.		Allies bombard Dedeagatch.		22
23					Prince Adalbert torpedoed.		23
27		Austrians across the Drina.	Serbs retake Uskub.	British occupy Banjo.	H.M.S. Hythe collides and sinks	General Joffre in London.	27
29			Bulgarians retake Veles.				29
Nov							**Nov**
5			Bulgarians enter Nish. [Valley French advancing up Vardar		H.M. steamer Tara sunk.		5
14	Ger. penetrate trench. in "Labyrinth."		Serbs holding Kathanik Pass.		Austrian raid on Verona.		14
15	Fighting in "Labyrinth."		Bulg. repulse Babuna Front.				15
17			Serbs lose Novi Bazar.		Anglia, hospital ship, founders.		17
20			Bulgarians occupy Prilep.				20
23			Serb. capital at Prizrend.	British victory at Ctesiphon.			23
24			Serbian retreat to Albania.	British evacuate Ctesiphon.			24
29							29
Dec							**Dec**
2			Fall of Monastir.	[Amara.			2
3	Joffre Com.-in-Chief French Armies.			Townshend reaches Kut-el-			3
4	Franco-British War Conference, Calais.		More British at Salonika.				4
6	Allies' Council of War, Paris.		French retire Demir Kapu Pass.	Russian victory in Persia.	E boat's exploit S. of Marmora.		6
9			Allied retreat in Macedonia.	Attacks on Kut-el-Amara [repulsed			9
12						Derby Recruiting Camp. ends.	12
13			Allies across Greek frontier.	Arab defeat west of Matruh.			13
15	Viscount French retires com. in France.		Italian landing Avlona ann.			[Home Forces.	15
17	Sir Douglas Haig in command, France.			Russians occupy Hamadan.	E boat sinks Bremen.	Viscount French Commander	17
19	French success Hartmannsweilerkopf.	General Russky retires.	Withdrawal from Anzac and [Suvla Bay.				19
21		Russians cross the Styr.		Russians take Kum.		Sir W. Robertson Chief of	21
31						Imperial Staff.]	31
1916 Jan							**1916 Jan**
1				Yaunde (Ger. Cam.) occupied.			1
4					Geelong sunk, Mediterranean.	Ld. Derby's Report published.	4
5			Complete evacu. of Gallipoli.			Military Service Bill introd.	5
8			Austrians attack M. Lovtchen.	Turks retr. from Sheikh Saad.	H.M.S. King Edward sinks.		8
9			Austrians take M. Lovtchen.				9
10			Fall of Cettinje.				10
13				Turkish defeat at Wadi.		Allied War Council in London.	13
19		Russ. offens. N.E. Czernovitz.			Air raid on Kent.		19
23	German attack E. of Neuville.		Austrians occupy Skutari.	Senussi defeat at Mersa Matru	Seaplane driven from Dover.	Military Service Bill passed.	23
24				Serengetti (E. Africa) occupied.			24
28	German success at Frise.		Allies occupy Kara Burun.		Zeppelin raid on Paris.		28
29					Zepp. raid Mid. and N.E. Cou.		29
31							31
Feb							**Feb**
1					Captured Appam arriv. Amer.		1
9		Russians capture Uscieczko.			Seaplanes over Margate.		9
10				Smuts in command E. Africa.			10
12				S. Afrs. engaged Ger. E. Afr.			12
14	Ger. take "International Trench."		French cross the Vardar.		Arethusa mined.		14
16				Fall of Erzerum.			16
17				Conquest Cameroon announced.			17
21	Great Verdun Battle opens.				Zepp. shot down in Lorraine.		21
26	Germans take Fort Douaumont.				Provence II. sunk.		26
Mar							**Mar**
2	Desperate Verdun fighting.			Russians take Bitlis.	Maloja mined in Channel.		2
5				Gen. Aylmer reaches Es-Sinn.	Zepp. raid 8 East. Counties.		5
6	Germans enter Forges.						6
10	Germans retake Crow's Wood.			Moshi reported taken.			10
15							15
16	Gen. Roques French War Minister.		Portugal joins the Allies.		Von Tirpitz's resignation rptd.		16
22				Russians occupy Ispahan.		General Cadorna in London.	22
23	Brit. line extended to Somme anncd.				Minneapolis mined Mediter.		23
25					British raid Schleswig.		25
27	Allied Conference in Paris.						27
31					Zeppelin L15 disabled.		31
Apr							**Apr**
1	German gain in Vaux village.				Zeppelin raid N.E. Coast.		1
2					Zeppelin raid Eng. and Scot.		2
3	British crater success at St. Eloi.			[E. Africa.			3
6				Victory Arusha district Ger.			6
14				Falahijah position carried.	British raid Constantinople.	Sir J. Nixon's desp. published. [of City of London.	14
18				Fall of Trebizond announced.		Mr.W.M.Hughes rec. Freedom	18
20	Russians at Marseilles announced.			Occupation Umbugwe anncd.		Attempt to land arms, Ireland: [Sir R. Casement a prisoner.	20
22	Struggle for Dead Man Hill.				Zepp. raid Norfolk and Suffolk [coast.	22
24				Kondoa Irangi occupied.		Irish Rebellion breaks out.	24
25					Bombardment of Lowestoft [and Yarmouth.	"Anzac Day" in London.	25
27				Fall of Kut.	H.M.S. Russell mined.	Gen. Maxwell sent to Ireland.	27
29							29
30						Irish Rebellion broken	30
May							**May**
2					Zepp. raid Eng. and Scot.		2
8	Anzacs announced in France.				Liner Cymric torpedoed.		8
14			Austrian offensive Trentino.				14
18					British raid El Arish.	Royal Com. Irish rising.	18
19			Ital. retreat in Trentino.	Gorringe takes Dujailar Re- [doubt.	Air raid Kent coast.		19
20				Russ. cavalry joins Gorringe.			20
23				Sultan of Darfur defeated.			23
25					British raid El Hanna.	Military Service Act law.	25
26	Death of General Galliéni.		Bulgar. occupy Rupel Fort.				26
27							27
30	100th Day of Verdun Battle.					Haig's first Despatch published.	30
31					Battle of Jutland.		31
June							**June**
4		Russ. offen. Pripet to Rumania.					4
5					Lord Kitchener drowned.		5
6	Fall of Vaux Fort.	Russians take Lutsk.					6
8					Allies blockade Greece.		8
9	German gain near Verdun.	Continued Russian offensive.				Allied War Council.	9
10		Russians capture Dubno.					10
12	German attack at Thiaumont repulsed	Russians regain Kolki.	Italian offensive continued.	British enter Kerman.		Lord Kitchener Mem. Service.	12
13	Canadian gain near Zillebeke.		Ital. advance Lagarina Valley.				13
14	Allied Economic Conference, Paris.			Smuts reaches Makuyni. Wilhemstal occupied.	Russian victory in Baltic.		14

1916	The Western Front.	The Eastern Front.	Other European Areas.	War Outside Europe.	War by Sea and Air.	Events at Home.	1916
June							**June**
16					H.M.T.D. Eden sunk.		16
17	French gain north of Hill 321.	Fall of Czernovitz to Russians.					17
21				Smuts reports Handeni occu.		Text of Paris Economic Conf.	21
23	Germans capture Fleury.						23
24							24
30		Russians capture Kolomea.			Blockade of Greece raised.		30
July							**July**
1	Franco-British offensive Somme.						1
2	Fricourt, Frise captured.						2
3	Fr. take Herbecourt, Chapitre Wood.	Russ. offensive Riga front.					3
4	British take La Boiselle.	Russ. gain north of Pripet.					4
5	French take Hem, Estrées.						5
6	British advance near Thiepval.						6
7	British take Leipzic Redoubt.			Tanga Ger. E. Afr. occupied		Mr. Lloyd George War Minister.	7
8	French capture Hardecourt.						8
9	French capture Biaches.						9
11				Russians occupy Mamahatun.	Aeroplane raid S.E. England.		11
14	German second line breached.			Smuts captures Muanza.	U boat shells Seaham.		14
15	British Dragoons in action.			Russians capture Baiburt.			15
16	Oviliers completely taken. [line	Russian success in Volhynia.					16
20	Brit. gain N. of Bazentin—Longueval	Russ. victory N.E. Galicia.		Russians occupy Erzindjan.			20
25							25
26	British take Pozières.	Russians capture Brody.					26
27	Captain Fryatt shot in Bruges.				Zeppelins raid East Coast.		27
29	[to Somme.	Russians force the Stokhod.					29
30	New Allied attack from Delville Wood			Smuts reports Dodoma occu.	Zepp. raid E. and S.E. Count.		30
31							31
Aug							**Aug**
3	French retake Fleury.						3
4	British gain W. of Pozières.			Belgians occupy Ujiji.		Casement hanged.	4
6	Brit. prog. towards Martinpuich.		Italian victories on Isonzo.	Turk defeat near Romani.			6
7	Brit. attack outskirts of Guillemont.	Russians capture Tlumacz.	Ital. take bridgehead Gorizia.	Turk attack Sinai repulsed.	Zepp. raid East Coast.		7
9	French advance N. of Hem Wood.	Russians capture Chryphlin.	Fall of Gorizia.				9
10	British advance N.W. of Pozières.	Russians capture Stanislau.		Deventer occupies Mpapua.	Brit. raid Brussels and Namur		10
11	French gain S. of Maurepas.		Italian troops at Salonika.		Seaplane raid on Dover.		11
12		Russians west of Zlota Lipa.	Ital. occupy Oppacchiasella.				12
15		Russians reach Solotwina.		Bagamoyo occupied.			15
17	British gain N.W. of Bazentin.		Bulg. adv. towards Kavala.				17
18	British gain Thiepval Ridge.			Smuts crosses Wami River.			18
19		Russ. advance on the Stokhod.	Serbs fight Bulgars at Florina.		German fleet out, but retires. Nottingham and Falmouth sunk		19
20	British carry Pozières Ridge.						20
22	French success N. of Maurepas.		Italian gain in Dolomites.	Deventer takes Kilossa.	Zepp. raid on East Coast.		22
23	British gain S. of Thiepval.			Russian victory at Rayat.	Zepp. raid E. and S.E. Coasts		23
24	French take Maurepas.				Zepp. raid E. and S.E. Coasts		24
25			Bulgarians enter Kavala.				25
27	British progress N.W. of Ginchy.	Russ. advance towards Halicz.	Rumania joins Allies.				27
29	Falkenhayn dismissed.	Russians take Mount Pantyr.					29
30			Enemy evac. Hermannstadt and [Brasso		Zepp. raid Bukarest.		30
Sept							**Sept**
1			Rumanian victory at Orsova.		Allied fleet outside Athens.		1
3	British capture Guillemont.				Zepp. destroyed Cuffley.		3
4	French advance on Somme.				British raid Mazar.		4
6		Russ. capt. Halicz bridgehead	Fall of Tutrakan to Bulgaria.	Surrender of Dar-es-Salaam.			6
9	British occupy Ginchy.		Enemy repulsed in Dobruja.				9
12	French capture Bouchavesnes.	Russ. carry Kapul Mountain.			Austrian raid on Venice.		12
14			Italians capture San Grado.				14
15	British take Flers, Martinpuich.		Ital. victory east of Vallone.				15
16	British advance N. of High Wood.	Russ. victory N. of Halicz	Allied advance in Macedonia.				16
17	British prog. nr. Mouquet Farm.		Franco-Russ. capt. Florina.	Brit. victory at Bir-el-Mazar.			17
20			Rum. 50 miles N.E. Brasso.		Allied blockade Greek coast.		20
22	British line on Somme advanced.		Italians carry the Gardinal.		Seaplane attack on Dover.		22
23	Brit. advance E. of Courcelette.		British cross the Struma.		Two Zepps. brought down Essex		23
24			M. Venizelos leaves Athens.		French raid on Essen.		24
25	British take Morval and Lesbœufs.				Zepp. raid N.E. Counties.		25
26	Capture of Thiepval, Combles.						26
28	British gains N. and N.E. Courcelette.		[claimed				28
29			M. Venizelos' Prov. Min. pro-				29
Oct			[Turm Pass.				**Oct**
1	British take Eaucourt l'Abbaye.		Rumanians retire through Roter		Zepp. destroyed at Potter's Bar		1
4					Troopship Gallia torpedoed.		4
7	British take Le Sars.		Enemy retake Brasso.				7
8	100th Day Battle of Somme.		Rumanians retreat to Passes.				8
10	French take Bovent.		Allied ultimatum to Greece.		Greek Fleet surrend. Allies.		10
11			Itals. carry Tooth of Pasubio		Allied landing at Athens.		11
17			Serbians take Brod.				17
18	Allied Advance N. of the Somme.		Serbians occupy Veliselo.				18
19	British prog. Butte de Warlencourt.		Rumanians evacuate Tuzla.				19
21	Brit. capt. Stuff and Regina Redoubts.		Fall of Constantsa.		Aeroplane raid Sheerness.		21
22	French carry Ridge 128.		Enemy take Predeal.		Aeroplane raid Margate.		22
23	Brit. advance E. of Gueudecourt.						23
24	French capt. Douaumont, Thiaumont.						24
25			Enemy occupy Cerna Voda.		Ger. raid Channel transports.		25
26							26
Nov							**Nov**
1	Germans evacuate Fort Vaux.		Italians advance on the Carso.		Italian naval raid on Pola.		1
2	French gain W. of Lancourt.		Italians take Faiti Hrib.		Russians bombard Constansa.		2
5	French take Vaux Village.		Fierce fight Roter Turm Pass.		Arabia torpedoed.		5
6	French adv. St. Pierre Vaast Wood.		Allied advance in Dobruja.				6
7	French take Ablaincourt, Pressoir.		Serbians take Chuke heights.		Germans shell Baltic Port.		7
10	British storm Regina Trench.		Serbians capture Iven.				10
12	French recapture Saillisel, Divion.						12
13	Brit. take Beaumont-Hamel, St. Pierre		Serbians capture Tchegel.				13
14	British take Beaucourt-sur-Ancre.						14
17	British advance on the Ancre.		Fall of Monastir.				17
18	British outside Grandcourt.		Fall of Craiova.		Hospital ship Britannic sunk.		18
21		Emperor of Austria dies.	Orsova and Turnu Severin taken		Raid by six Ger. destroyers.		21
23			Allied ultimatum to Greece.		Hosp. ship Braemar Castle sunk		23
24			Mackensen occupies Alexandria		Naval raid on Lowestoft.		24
26			Serbs capture Hill 1,050.				26
27			Enemy takes Giurgevo.		Two Zepps. down East Coast.		27
28		Russian success Carpathians.			Naval raid on Zeebrugge.		28
29			Enemy captures Pitesti.		Daylight raid on London.		29
Dec							**Dec**
1			Allied troops land Athens.		Admiral Beatty to com. Fleet	Cabinet crisis.	1
5		Russ. carry Jablonica Pass.				Mr. Asquith and Mr. Lloyd [George resign.	5
6			Fall of Bukarest.			Mr. Ll. George to form Minist.	6
7		Russ. offensive in Carpathians	Rumanian defeat Predeal Pass			Mr. Lloyd George Premier.	7
8					Allied blockade of Greece.		8
11			Enemy takes Urziceni. Allied Note to Greece. Contd. retreat of Rum. armies		Air raid on Zeebrugge.	New Ministry complete.	11
12	Gen. Nivelle French Com.-in-Chief.			Advance on Kut.			12
13		Fighting near Jablonica Pass					13
14			Rumanians evacuate Buzeu.	Further advance on Kut.	Brit. raid Kuleli-Burgas bridge		14
15	Great French victory at Verdun.		Greeks comply Allies' demands.		British raid on Razlovci.		15
16	French take Bézonvaux.		Enemy pursuit in Wallachia.				16
18	French retake Chambrettes Farm.		Enemy checked at Botogu.				18
20				Adv. to right bank of Tigris		Pres. Wilson's Peace Note.	20
21			New Note to Greece.	Capture of El Arish.	Air raid on Bargela.		21
23				Capture of Magdhaba.		Swiss Peace Note.	23
24							24
25	British line extended.		Germans take Tultcha.				25
26			Germans take Filipesti.				26
27			Rimnic-Sarat taken.		Allied raid on Dillingen, etc.		27
30			Russ. retreat Moldavian front.		Brit. airmen destroy Chikaldir [Bridge		30
1917 Jan							**1917 Jan**
1	Sir Douglas Haig Field-Marshal.			Mgeta Valley lines stormed.	Ivernia sunk Mediterranean.		1
3			Enemy capt. Macin bridgehead.		Lord Cowdray Air Minister.		3
4		Russ. gain near Mt. Botosul.	Germans capture Braila.		Brit. raid Kuleli-Burgas bridge		4
5			Allied Conference in Rome.				5
7	British raid S. of Armentières.	Russian gain on Riga front.					7
8			Germans capture Focsani.				8
9			New Allied Note to Greece.	Sinai cleared of the Turk.	Cornwallis torpedoed.		9
11	British gain N.E. Beaumont-Hamel.	Russ. gain island in Dwina.	Greeks comply Allies' demands.		Seaplane carrier Ben-my-Chree [sunk	Allies reply Wilson Note.	11
12						New War Loan issued.	12
15			Allied successes in Macedonia.				15
17	Canadian raid N.E. Cité Callonne.						17
22	Ger. attack at Verdun repulsed.	Russians retreat W. of Riga.	Bulgarians cross Danube.		Dest. actions- North Sea and [Schouwen Bank		22
23	British raid at Neuville.	German progress S.W. of Riga.	Bulg. driven across Danube.				23
24	French raids Somme & Woevre fronts.			Ger. surrender S. part G. E. [Africa.			24
25	German attack Verdun repulsed.			British gain S.W. of Kut.	Suffolk coast shelled.		25
27	British gain near Le Transloy.				Laurentic sunk.		27
29	British raids Butte de Warlencourt. [Souchez	Allied Conference at Petrograd.					29
Feb							**Feb**
1		Russ. suc. Riga and Bukovina.			Intensified U-boat war starts.		1
3	British advance E. of Beaucourt.			Rupt. bet. U.S.A. and Germany.			3
4	British gain N.E. of Gueudecourt.			Senussi defeated near Suva.	Presid. Wilson's Note Neutrals.		4
7	British capture Grandcourt.						7
9					Transport Tyndareus mined off [Cape Agulhas.		9

1917	The Western Front.	The Eastern Front.	Other European Areas.	War Outside Europe.	War by Sea and Air.	Events at Home.
Feb 10	Brit. raids nr. Vermelles & Ypres.	German repulse S. of Halicz.		Liquorice factory, Kut, capt. Turks hemmed in W. of Kut.		
11	Brit. adv. towards Puisieux-au-Mont.	Russ. re-estab. line at Zloczow.		Dahra bend of Tigris cleared.		
15	German success in Champagne.			British check at Sanna-i-Yat.		
16		Russ. gain S.W. of Ocna.			Zeppelin raid on Boulogne.	War Loan, £1,000,000,000.
17	British advance in Ancre Valley.			British success at Sanna-i-Yat		
20	British thrust N.E. of Gueudecourt.			British cross Tigris Shumran [Bend.	Dutch ships torpd. Falmouth.	
22				Fall of Kut to British.		Ll. George's speech on imports.
23	British gain near Gueudecourt.					
24	British enter Petit Miraumont.				German destroyers raid Broad-[stairs and Margate.	
25	German retreat on the Ancre.					
26	British occupy Le Barque.					
27	British take Ligny.					
28	British take Gommecourt.					
Mar 1	German retreat N. of Miraumont.			Russians retake Hamadan. Turks abandon Shalal, Sinai.	Aeroplane raid on Broadstairs.	
2	British advance beyond Warlencourt.			Brit. cross Tigris S. of Diala.		Dardanelles Com. Report pub.
5	British progress S. of Bucquoy.			British force passage of Diala.		
8	Brit. line adv. either side of Ancre.	Food riots in Petrograd.		British approaching Bagdad.		U.S.A. to arm merchantmen.
9	French success near Caurières Wood.			Fall of Bagdad.		
10	British take Irles.					
11		Riots Petrograd, many killed. Revolution in Russia.	British advance Doiran front.			
12	British adv. on Bouchavesnes Ridge.			Russians occupy Kermanshah.		
13	Germans abandon Bapaume Ridge.			China breaks with Germany.		
15	British occupy St. Pierre Vaast Wood.	Tsar abdicates.		Russians occupy Kerind.	Destroyer mined in Channel.	
16	British take Bapaume.			Russians take Harunabad.	Air raid on Kent.	
17	Fall of Péronne, Noyon, Neale, and [Chaulnes.				French destroy Zepp. L39.	
18					Ramsgate shelled.	
19	Ger. retreat; Fr. take Chauny & Ham. M. Ribot forms new Fr. Government.				Warship Danton torpedoed.	
21	French carry Jussy.				Hospital ship Asturias torp.	Imperial War Conference meets
24	British occupy Roisel.	Russian reverse Baranovitchi.	French gain W. of Monastir.	British victory near Gaza.		
26	Further Allied advance.					
27	Progress between La Fère and Laon.				Two British destroyers lost.	
29	British take Neuville-Bourjonval.			Gen. Maude at Deli Abbas. [Pass.	Hosp. ship Gloucester Castle [torpedoed.	
30	British take Fins, Heudicourt.			Gen. Baratoff through Paitak [on Diala		
31	British take Herbecourt, Vendelles.			British and Russians in contact		
Apr 1	British take Savy, Epéhy.			Russians occupy Khanikin.		
2	British take Selency, Croisilles.	Russ. reverse on the Stokhod.		U. S. at war with Germany.		
3	French take Giffecourt, Cerizy.			Cuba declares war on Germany.	Air raid on Kent.	
4	French progress towards St. Quentin.			Gen. Maude occupies Harbe.	2 Ger. dest. torp. Zeebrugge.	
5	Great air battles.			Brazil breaks with Germany.		
7	British two miles from St. Quentin.			Brit. def. Turks near Deltawa.		
9	Vimy Ridge carried.				Hospital ship Salta mined.	
10	British take Louverval.					
11	British take Monchy-le-Preux.					
12	British storm Wancourt and Heninel. British take Gouzeaucourt.					
13	British take Bailleul, Vimy, Fayet, [Givenchy-en-Gohelle.				Allied reprisals raid Freiburg. Arcadian and Cameronia torp.	
14	British take Liévin and Gricourt.					
15					Hosp. ships Donegal, Lanfranc [torpedoed.	
16	Great French attack on the Aisne.			Turk defeat Wadi-Ghuzzeh.		
17	French take Auberive.				Dests. Swift and Broke defeat [6 Ger. dests.	
18	French progress on Aisne.			Samarra Station occupied.	Germans bombard Dunkirk.	
20	British take Gonnelieu.		British advance Doiran front		Germans bombard Ramsgate.	
23	British take Gavrelle, Guémappe.					
28	Canadians take Arleux.					
May 3	Canadians take Fresnoy.					
4	French take Craonne. [des Dames.					Jellicoe Chief of Adm. War Staff
5	Fr. win Craonne Ridge, with Chemin [Cemetery.					
8	Germans recapture Fresnoy.					
10	French progress at Chevreux.				11 Ger. destroyers chased into [Zeebrugge by Com. Tyrwhitt. Zeebrugge bombarded by sea [and air.	
12	British take Cavalry Farm, Roeux.		British progress Doiran front. Italian victories Plava area.		Zepp. L22 destroyed N. Sea. Austrian defeat in Adriatic.	
14	British take Roeux.			Van Deventer C.-in-Ch. E. Afr.		Sir E. Geddes Con. Admiralty.
15	General Pétain French Com.-in-Chief.	Coalition Govt. in Russia.			U.S. destroyers in Brit. waters.	
16			Italians capture Hill 652. Ital. adv. Kostanjevica to sea. [to sea.		Zepp. raid in East Anglia.	
17	British capture Bullecourt.		Italian gains Lisert marshes Ital. progress Southern Carso. Italians approach Medeazza. Italians win San Giovanni. Italian gain near Medeazza.			
23				Brazil annuls neutrality decree.	Brit. monitors shell Aust. lines. Aerop. raid on Folkestone. Hosp. ship Dover Castle torp.	
28						Allied War Conference.
June 2						Investiture in Hyde Park.
5					Cameronian torpedoed. Aerop. raid Medway and Essex. Destroyer fight in Channel.	
6	British gain on Greenland Hill.		M. Jonnart High Commissioner [in Greece. Italians occupy Yanina.	Lord Northcliffe on Mission to [U.S.A.		
7	British capture Messines Ridge.		Italian victory in Trentino. French troops land Corinth. King Constantine abdicates. Allied troops land Piræus.			Gen. Pershing arrives in London.
8	Messines gains held.					
12	British occupy Gapaard.				Saliff captured by naval men.	
13					Aeroplane raid on London.	
14	British storm Infantry Hill.				Zepp. L43 destroyed North Sea	
15			Ital. capt. Cormo Cavento. Brit. evac. left bank Struma.		Liner Addah torpedoed.	Lord Rhondda Food Controller.
16	British progress N.W. of Bullecourt.					
17					Zepp. raid E. Anglia and Kent. Mongolia mined off Bombay.	
23	Fighting N. of the Aisne.		M. Venizelos returns Athens.			
24	French gain E. of Vauxaillon.		M. Venizelos forms a Cabinet.		British air raid on Tekrit. Allies bombard Ostend.	
25	American troops in France.					
26	British occupy La Coulotte.				French cruiser Kléber mined.	
29			Ital. evacuate Agnella Pass.	Gen. Allenby in com. Palestine. Germans driven back Nyasa-[land Border.		
30	British advance S.W. and W. of Lens.					
July 1	Ger. attack French E. of Cerny.	Russ. offensive in East Galicia. Russ. prog. around Brzezany.			Brit. air raid Bruges Docks.	
2	Ger. defeats Cerny and Verdun.	Further Russian attack on [Brzezany.			Air raid on Harwich.	
3	Ger. offens. Jouy to Craonne defeated.					
4	Slight Brit. adv. near Hollebeke.	Fighting on Brzezany front.				
5	Slight Brit. adv. S.W. of Hollebeke.	Russian attack spreading to [Stanislau.				
6	French gain Moronvillers Ridge.	Enemy line W. of Stanislau [broken.				
7	British adv. E of Wytschaete.	Russians take Wiktorow.			Great aeropl. raid on London.	
8	German attacks Aisne repulsed.	Russians take Halicz.				
9	British adv. E. of Oosttaverne.	Russians take Kalusz.				
10	German success Yser River.	Russians cross the Lomnica.				
11		Russ. progress Kalusz.		British success on Euphrates.		
12						Mesopotamia Debate Parliament.
13				Brit. raid Turk. lines, Gaza.		
14	Bethmann-Hollweg resigns. Ger. attack on Chemin des Dames.					
15	German attack Mont Haut defeated.	Political crisis, Russia. Russian retreat from Lomnica.	Italian raid near Versic.		Brit. capture 6 Ger. steamers.	Royal House takes name of [Windsor.
16		Disorders in Petrograd. Petrograd revolt crushed.		British gain Narongombe, Ger. [East Africa.		
17	French win back position Hill 304.	Russ. troops defection, Galicia.				
18	Ger. att. Verdun, St. Quentin, def.	M. Kerensky Premier.		British raid S.W. Gaza.		
19	Ger. attack S. of Lombartzyde.	Russ. retreat on the Sereth.				
20		Russian retreat extending.				
21	Ger. attack Chemin des Dames Ridge.	Fall of Halicz to enemy.				
22		Fall of Stanislau and Tarnopol [to enemy.			Otway torpedoed and sunk. Air raid Harwich and Felix-[stowe.	Lloyd George replies to Herr [Michaelis.
24	French gain around Craonne.		Russo-Ruman. success Moldavia.			
25	Artilly. Battle in Flanders increasing.	Russians evacuate Buczacz.			British capture Batavier II.	
26	Allied Conference Paris closes.	Fall of Kolomea to enemy.				
27	Germans recapture La Basse Ville.					
28		Enemy reach Russ. frontier.				
29	Fury of Artill. batt. Flanders growing.	Ger. across River Zbrucz.	Rumanian Advance. Continued Rumanian success.			
30		Russian retreat in Bukovina. [sarabia.			Ariadne torpedoed and sunk.	
31	Great Allied Offens. around Ypres.					
Aug 1	Brit. withdraw from St. Julien.	Enemy gains footing in Bes-General Brussiloff resigns.				
2	Ger. attacks N.E. Ypres repulsed.	Fall of Czernovitz to Austria.		Battle at Lindi, Ger. E. Africa.		
3	British recapture St. Julien.					

End of Volume 9.

THE GREAT WAR

VOLUME 10

Subject Index to THE GREAT WAR. Vols. I. to X.

Black Roman numerals indicate the number of the volume, ordinary figures the first page of each chapter.

Redrawn from Photographs by J. F. CAMPBELL.

Back from Hill 70: Canadian Highlanders, headed by their Pipers,

returning, after the Victory of August 15th 1917.

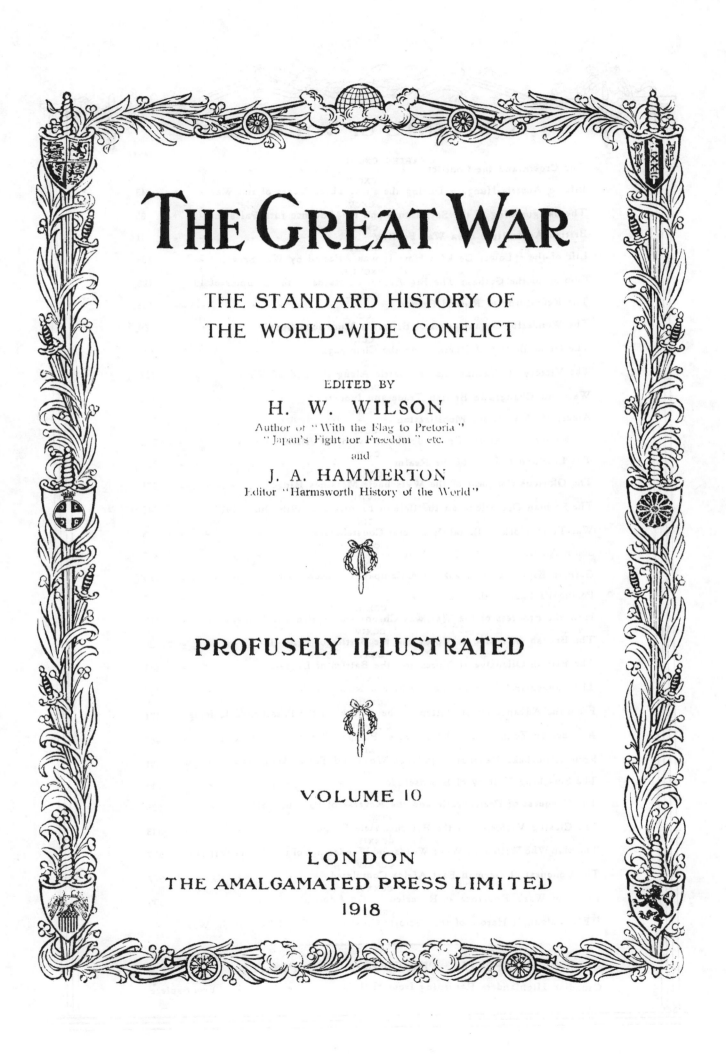

THE GREAT WAR

THE STANDARD HISTORY OF
THE WORLD-WIDE CONFLICT

EDITED BY

H. W. WILSON

Author of "With the Flag to Pretoria"
"Japan's Fight for Freedom" etc.

and

J. A. HAMMERTON

Editor "Harmsworth History of the World"

PROFUSELY ILLUSTRATED

VOLUME 10

LONDON
THE AMALGAMATED PRESS LIMITED
1918

CONTENTS OF VOLUME 10

SPECIAL PHOTOGRAVURE PLATE

THE GREAT WAR

THE STANDARD HISTORY OF THE WORLD-WIDE CONFLICT

VOLUME 10

CHAPTER CXCIII.

THE CROWN AND THE CONFLICT.

By F. A. McKenzie.

Ties of Royal Kinship—A New Departure in Modern History—The Spithead Review—King George's Message to the Tsar—King Albert's Appeal—Contrasting Demonstrations in Potsdam and London—King George and Britain's "Sure Shield"—A Triumph of Personality—Royal Inspection of the British Expeditionary Force—The Prince of Wales's Fund—At Westminster Abbey—The Queen's Work for Women Fund—"The Hardest Worked Man in the Land"—The Prince of Wales at the Front—The King's Visits to France, to the Fleet, and to the Munition Workers—Royal Lead to the Wealthy: Personal Gift of £100,000—Change in the Royal Title—Work for Soldiers and Sailors—The King's Active Interest in India and the Overseas Dominions—Food Economy Proclamation: Royal Example—The Queen and Baby Week—The Head of the Nation.

T HE outbreak of war was at once the testing time and the hour of opportunity for British Royalty. By law and by tradition the King stood forth to an even greater degree than usual as the pre-eminent figure in the nation immediately war began. The day had long passed since the monarch led his armies in person in hand-to-hand battle. King George never aimed to fill the meteoric and disturbing place assumed by Kaiser Wilhelm among his people—the instructor of generals in land war, of admirals in sea fighting, of statesmen in politics, of painters in art, and of preachers in religion. His whole temperament would have made such a course impossible, and none of his people desired it.

The British Crown had become the rallying war-point for the Empire. The King was supreme Commander-in-Chief of the Army and Admiral of the Fleet. These titles were something more than mere honorary distinctions. War was declared in the King's name. The Army was the King's, and the annual passing of a fresh Army Act— only holding good for a year—permitting the existence of a standing Army, was a remembrance of the olden days when the King's Army was thought to be a possible menace to Parliament. Each soldier was sworn to render obedience to the King and to serve him loyally. Each officer held as his most treasured document his commission signed by the King. The King was the fount of military honour. Soldiers of all ranks, whenever possible, received high honours direct from him in person. The King was no vague entity to the Navy and Army, but the living and active head of their organisation.

King George was a sailor. He had commanded his ship at sea in the days when there was little thought of his succession to the throne. As King, he kept in close and intimate touch with the Navy and Army from the commencement of his reign. To him the coming of war meant trials and anxieties that were all his own. It meant, in the first place, the tearing asunder of many ties of blood. The Royal and Imperial families of Britain and the Royal and Imperial families of Germany were closely knit. The Kaiser was son of the King's father's sister.

THE ROYAL HOUSE OF WINDSOR.
King George V. and Queen Mary, with the Prince of Wales. This photograph was taken on the British western front in July, 1917.
[British official photograph.]

King George visiting Salisbury Plain. Arrival of his Majesty on the ground for the inspection of troops from New Zealand, with the Royal Standard borne behind him.

At least one branch of the Royal Family was so placed that the mother lived in England, and worked for the British side, while the son fought for Germany. The Duke of Connaught, whose simple, strong, soldierlike qualities had won him the love and respect of every soldier, had refused the succession to a German princedom. Grandchildren of Queen Victoria, and cousins of the King, were arrayed against Britain.

The Queen's brother, son of the British Princess Mary Adelaide of Cambridge, who married a German Duke, was known by the German territorial title of the Duke of Teck (a title altered by Royal decree, in June, 1917, to Marquis of Cambridge). His brother, another British Prince, was Prince Alexander of Teck (Earl of Athlone). Prince-Leopold and Prince Alexander of Battenberg (respectively H.H. Lord Leopold of Mountbatten and the Marquis of Carisbrooke) were the sons of Queen Victoria's daughter Princess Beatrice and her German husband Prince Henry of Battenberg. Prince Louis of Battenberg, married to the granddaughter of Queen Victoria, and in the early days of the war First Sea Lord of the British Admiralty, was born in **German titles** Austria, the son of a German Prince. **abandoned** His title was altered to that of Marquis of Milford Haven. Five of the children of Queen Victoria married German Royalties, and one other became himself a German Prince.

Time after time, in the years before the war, the Kaiser had been among us, the guest of his Royal relations. The King could scarcely forget, any more than could many of his subjects, that fourteen years before, at the death of Queen Victoria, the German Emperor had cut short the bicentenary celebrations of his monarchy and had hurried to Osborne that he might pay his last respects to the Queen's memory. And it was only four years previous to 1914 that he had ridden on the right hand of King George, in the uniform of a British Field-Marshal, following the remains of King Edward to their final rest. Ties of blood are not easily sundered. Yet there was no suspicion of hesitation when the great hour came, for ties of Royal kinship counted for little indeed in face of the great issues before King George and his people.

In July, 1914, when the world at large had not fully realised the imminence of the war, King George made a bold new departure. The United Kingdom was passing

The King passing down the lines during an inspection of the Australian Imperial Forces in England. The Australian Commonwealth sent a magnificent body of troops for the defence of all that the British Empire represented, and magnificently they acquitted themselves, as the epic stories of the Gallipoli landings and the fighting at Lone Pin Hill quickly testified. In circle: King George shaking hands with a New Zealand officer.

KING GEORGE REVIEWING TROOPS FROM HIS DISTANT DOMINIONS.

through a tremendous political crisis. The Home Rule Bill was about to be carried into law, in spite of the opposition of the House of Lords. Ulster was arming, and there was real danger of civil war.

The King had been announced to visit the Fleet at Spithead. There came sudden notification that the visit had been delayed. This was followed by a statement in the "Times" that the King had called a conference of leaders from each of the four groups—Government, Unionists, Nationalists, and Ulstermen—at Buckingham Palace. The news, confirmed a few hours later by the Prime Minister, created a profound sensation. Here was a new departure in modern history. It was the tradition of our country that the King stood outside and above politics; but now, defying precedent, he was acting directly and personally in a matter of furious controversy.

The King welcomed the delegates, and made a speech to them at the opening of the conference, in which he earnestly pleaded for peace through compromise. It would be idle to deny that his action provoked a certain amount of criticism; but even those who criticised had to admit that, if ever there was a moment when the King might depart from ancient usage, this was it. Men asked one another if we were once more to see the Crown actively participating in current affairs as in the days of the Stuarts.

The great Spithead pageant In the third week in July the King reviewed his warships and seaplanes at Spithead. Each day the war-clouds in Europe were gathering more darkly. There were signs in Germany, not to be overlooked, that preparations for mobilisation were being pressed on with feverish rapidity. The negotiations between Austria and Serbia, following the murder of the Austrian heir-apparent, had almost reached breaking-point.

The procession which was inspected by the King at Spithead filled the heart of every man who saw it with pride. Here was the largest and most powerful Fleet which had ever been concentrated in British waters. Four battle-cruisers ploughed the way in single line, the Lion leading them. Then came Sir George Callaghan's flagship, followed by four First Fleet battle-squadrons, Dreadnoughts and super-Dreadnoughts, destroyers by the score, armoured cruisers, protected cruisers, and battle-ships of the most diverse types—twenty-two miles of war vessels in motion. The very air seemed alive. A Maurice Farman biplane signalled the departure of the last ship from Spithead. **Twenty-two miles** A flock of seaplanes was soon overhead. **of war vessels** Men could count sixteen of them, Shorts and Henry Farmans, Maurice Farmans and Sopwiths. Still others came after, Bristols and Avros. And the crowning moment in the air was when Commander Samson performed wonderful manœuvres high up above the Royal yacht.

The vessels ranged in size from the Queen Mary of 27,000 tons to underwater craft. Fourteen of the ships mounted the new 13'5 in. gun, the greatest weapon of death ever known at sea. Youth, energy, power seemed around. Men noticed curiously sixteen craft that passed the King. These were submarines. A week or two before, a great sailor, Sir Percy Scott, had warned the nation that submarines would render the mighty battleship obsolete. The brilliant entourage of the King may have looked smilingly at the tiny vessels as they passed by their Majesties, seemingly so trivial by the side of the titanic monsters of the Fleet.

As the King went back through the cheers of the spectators and of the crews of the great grey giants that held the sea, there must have been both pride and anxiety in his heart—pride in that he, a sailor King, was King of this mighty Fleet, the mightiest Fleet that ever sailed the seas; anxiety, because he was one of the few who knew the seriousness of the position.

Events followed rapidly. At other times of crisis British rulers had been able through their personal relations with

BIRD'S-EYE VIEW OF A ROYAL INVESTITURE AT ALDERSHOT.

On July 25th, 1917, King George, accompanied by Queen Mary, Princess Mary, and the Duke of Connaught, held an investiture on the Queen's Parade at Aldershot, when 259 decorations and medals were distributed.

One of the first public duties of the King after the declaration of war was to visit Aldershot and there bid God-speed to the original Expeditionary Force before it left for France.

the different monarchs to bring mollifying influences to bear on the disputes of statesmen. King George tried to do the same again.

It was obviously necessary that such influences should be exercised with care. The foreign policy of the nation is decided by the Government—not the King—and the Government is directly responsible for it. But in the days before the war it was inevitable that the rulers themselves should play sometimes an indirect and sometimes a deciding part in world affairs. It was to avoid any danger of conflicting activities between Government and Ministers that a practice was established in Queen Victoria's reign, and subsequently maintained, by which private letters addressed by the Sovereign to foreign princes or received from them, if they touched upon politics, were shown to the Prime Minister, to the Foreign Secretary, or to both.

Late in July, Prince Henry of Prussia, the sailor prince of Germany—who later was credited, rightly or wrongly, with supreme control of the organisation of much of the espionage in Great Britain—arrived in London and had an interview with King George. The details of that interview were not published, but they could easily be gathered from published correspondence. Prince Henry declared that the Kaiser was sincerely desirous of peace, and that he was being forced into war by the military activities of France and Russia. Both of these countries were threatening to come to the aid of Serbia when she was attacked by Austria-Hungary. Prince Henry begged the King to use his utmost influence with France and Russia to remain neutral, and to allow Austria to carry out her punitive expedition against the little Balkan State unhindered.

He further pleaded that Britain and Germany should work together to this end, and give each other mutual support. The Kaiser himself, writing a few days afterwards to the President of the United States, claimed that King George had promised British neutrality. This statement was manifestly false. The King had no power to promise British neutrality, and immediately the Kaiser's claim was made known it was specifically and authoritatively denied.

The Kaiser's statement was written in his own hand on August

LIEUTENANT PRINCE ALBERT AFLOAT.
Prince Albert (left), the second son of King George V., on board a vessel of the Grand Fleet with Lord Cromer.

PRINCE HENRY AND THE ETON O.T.C.
Prince Henry (right), the King's third son, taking part in manœuvres of the Eton College Officers Training Corps in Windsor Park.

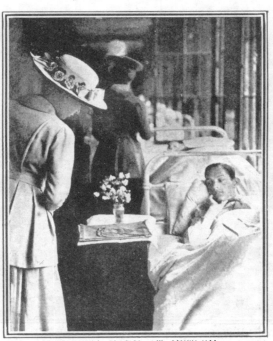

PRINCESS MARY AT NETLEY.
Princess Mary, only daughter of the King, at Netley Hospital. She was much interested in a patient's needlework.

roth, and handed by him to Mr. Gerard, the American Ambassador in Berlin, for the President of the United States personally:

H.R.H. Prince Henry was received by his Majesty King George V. in London, who empowered him to transmit to me verbally that England would remain neutral if war broke out on the Continent involving Germany and France, Austria and Russia. The message was telegraphed to me by my brother from London after his conversation with H.M. the King, and was repeated verbally on July 29th.

Prince Henry returned to Berlin, and immediately after the interview messages were exchanged between him and the King. In his first telegram, dated July 30th, 1914, he described how he had arrived at the German capital, and had told the Kaiser about the interview:

I arrived here yesterday, and have communicated what you were so good as to say to me at Buckingham Palace last Sunday to William, who was very thankful to receive your message.

William, who is very anxious, is doing his utmost to comply with the request of Nicholas to work for the maintenance of peace. He is in continual telegraphic communication with Nicholas, who has to-day confirmed the news that he has ordered military measures which amount to mobilisation, and that these measures were taken five days ago.

We have also received information that France is making military preparations, while we have not taken measures of any kind, but may be obliged to do so at any moment if our neighbours continue their preparations. This would then mean a European war.

If you seriously and earnestly desire to prevent this terrible misfortune, may I propose to you to use your influence on France, and also on Russia, that they should remain neutral. In my view this would be of the greatest use. I consider that this is a certain, and perhaps the only possible, way of maintaining the peace of Europe. I might add that Germany and England should now, more than ever, give each other mutual support in order to prevent a terrible disaster, which otherwise appears inevitable.

Believe me that William is inspired by the greatest sincerity in his efforts for the maintenance of peace. But the military preparations of his two neighbours may end in compelling him to follow their example for the safety of his own country, which otherwise would remain defenceless. I have informed William of my telegram to you, and I hope that you will receive my communication in the same friendly spirit which has inspired it.

(Signed) HENRY.

King George replied on the same date, thanking Prince Henry for his telegram, and saying that his Government was doing the utmost possible to induce Russia and France to postpone further military preparations if Austria

 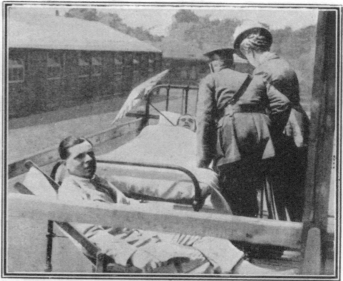

Queen Mary receiving a bouquet from a French girl at a British supply depot near the western front, and (right) her Majesty visiting the wounded at a hospital in France. The Queen showed a keen sympathy with all the beneficent activities, British, French, and Belgian.

The Queen talking with a French officer, and (right) inspecting a sturdy company of convalescent British soldiers, with a pleasant word for each of the men. Her Majesty devoted much of her time during the Royal tour to visiting centres where the sick and wounded were cared for.

[British official photographs.

A striking camera record of her Majesty's visit to a Belgian hospital, and (on the right) a photograph taken on the occasion of the Queen's inspection of a French establishment where work for the British Army was in progress. Her Majesty is seen chatting with one of the forewomen.

QUEEN MARY'S VISIT TO THE WESTERN FRONT IN JULY, 1917.

AT A COMMUNAL KITCHEN.
Queen Mary, when visiting a communal kitchen at Stepney, took part in serving some of the customers.

would be satisfied with the occupation of Belgrade and the neighbouring Serbian territory as a pledge for a satisfactory settlement of her demands.

I rely (he continued) on William applying his great influence in order to induce Austria to accept this proposal. In this way he will prove that Germany and England are working together to prevent what would be an international catastrophe. Please assure William that I am doing all I can, and will continue to do all that lies in my power to maintain the peace of Europe."

On the same day the Kaiser intimated to the King: "Your proposals coincide with my ideas." Then he went on to say that intelligence had just reached him that Nicholas had ordered the mobilisation of his entire Army and Fleet. "He has not even awaited the result of the mediation in which I am engaged, and he has left me completely without information." The King sent back saying that he had despatched an urgent telegram to Nicholas.

In a message sent, early in the morning of August 1st, to the Tsar of Russia, after repeating a statement received from the German Government that **King George's** unless Russia was prepared to suspend **efforts for peace** within twelve hours her "warlike measures against Germany and Austria" war would follow, the King added:

I cannot help thinking that some misunderstanding has produced this deadlock. I am most anxious not to miss any possibility of avoiding the terrible calamity which at present threatens the whole world. I therefore make a personal appeal to you to remove the misapprehension which I feel must have occurred, and to leave still open grounds for negotiation and possible peace. If you think I can in any way contribute to that all-important purpose, I will do everything in my power to assist in reopening the interrupted conversations between the Powers concerned. I feel confident that you are as anxious as I am that all that is possible should be done to secure the peace of the world.

QUEEN MARY AND THE BABY.
Greeting one of her little protégées. Her Majesty paying an informal visit to the Woolwich British Hospital for mothers and babies, which was under her patronage.

A reply came directly back from the Tsar. The Kaiser had already declared war. The Tsar told how he had been obliged to mobilise because of the open and secret preparations of Austria-Hungary. "In this solemn hour," wrote the Tsar, "I wish to assure you once more that I have done all in my power to avert war. Now that it has been forced on me, I trust your country will not fail to support France and Russia. God bless and protect you."

The whole conduct of the King during this period was the best proof of his sincere desire for peace. The German Government, as was shown later, had resolved to support Austria-Hungary in **The Kaiser's** its declaration of war against Serbia, even **two voices** though it knew that such a declaration would involve war with Russia. All the talk by the Kaiser of the great sincerity of his efforts to maintain peace was vain. He was willing to maintain peace provided the German allies were allowed to carry out unchecked their first forward move in their already settled plans for the domination of Europe and of the world. He was no doubt sincere in desiring that Britain should stay out of the war, for Britain would prove the fatal barrier to his ambitions. King George sought a compromise that, had Germany been sincere, would have satisfied her. He strove to avert the threatening cataclysm. But the train was already laid, and war could be avoided no longer.

Immediately after the invasion of Belgium, King Albert sent a personal telegram to King George asking his aid. "Remembering the numerous proofs of your Majesty's friendship and that of your predecessor, and the friendly attitude of England in 1870, and the proof of friendship you have just given us again, I make a supreme appeal for the diplomatic intervention of your Majesty's Government to safeguard the integrity of Belgium."

News came to England of passionate demonstrations being made in Berlin around the Kaiser. He received tremendous ovations on his way to his palace at Unter den Linden, great crowds gathering around it, cheering until they could cheer no more. It was noted in those days that the Kaiser was grave and stern, and the Crown Prince animated and smiling, saluting and nodding repeatedly. At first there were no such demonstrations in London. On the same evening that 50,000 cheering Germans stood outside the Kaiser's palace in Berlin, scarce a person, save a sentry or a policeman, was seen to be waiting outside Buckingham Palace. This was because the people of London had not yet realised what was happening. By the first Sunday in August, London really woke up to what these rapidly following events meant. In that hour enthusiasm leapt forth. On the night following, tens of thousands stood around the King's palace cheering, singing loyal songs, and waiting for their Majesties to come out and return their greetings. Time after time on the Monday and the Tuesday the King and Queen, accompanied by the Prince of Wales, appeared on the balcony above the entrance to the north side of the palace, and bowed. On Tuesday night the crowds were greater than ever. People knew well that that evening the question of peace or war was to be decided. The British Government had issued an ultimatum. All the great thoroughfares near Buckingham Palace, around by the Houses of Parliament and on to the Strand, were crowded with cheering throngs. There were signs of military preparations on all sides. Every now and then troops and munition waggons and guns would hurry by.

Outside the gates of Buckingham Palace the entire area around the Victoria Memorial was black with people. Song followed song—patriotic songs most of them. At seven o'clock, in answer to the calls of the crowd, the King stepped out, accompanied by the Queen, the Prince of Wales, and the Princess Mary. As he showed himself on the balcony the crowd began the National Anthem, followed by " He's a jolly good fellow ! " The King appeared again at half-past nine, and the scene was repeated. Shortly after eleven o'clock the King and Queen and the Prince of Wales appeared once more.

The crowds were cheering. It was not with eagerness for war, for there was a note of solemnity pervading all. In the very singing of the people it was marked that the patriotic airs were followed by hymns—hymns started by solitary individuals in the crowds and taken up by all. Then, as the fatal moment drew near, the great throng sang in time and tune, " O God, our Help in Ages Past." For King in palace and people in street knew that, in the great issue now before the nation, vain would be the strength of man, vain the might of fleets and armies, if God were not on its side. To hear these verses sung by many thousands of Englishmen and Englishwomen enabled

THE BRITISH HEIR-APPARENT.
Studio portrait of the Prince of Wales, taken in 1917. He was then a captain on the Headquarters Staff at the front.

onlookers from other lands to realise, as never before, what Britain was. Not boastingly, not lightly, not shrinkingly, had her people taken their stand. Britain was going into this war as into a holy war of liberty. Soon after the hymn was sung, the King and Queen and Prince of Wales once more stepped on to the balcony—the Prince who was shortly to go forth in his regimentals and take his part in Army duties for Britain. The cheers seemed as if they would reach the sky. The whole front of the palace was one waving mass of hats, sticks, and flags as the crowd cried out " God Save the King ! "

The King sent a personal message to the Fleet, a message communicated to the senior naval officers on all stations outside of home waters :

At this grave moment in our national history I send to you, and through you to the officers and men of the Fleets of which you have assumed command, the assurance of my confidence that under your direction they will revive and renew the old glories of the Royal Navy, and prove once again the sure shield of Britain and of her Empire in the hour of trial. GEORGE R.I.

In the anxious days that immediately followed, the personality of the King played a big part. It was around him that the Dominions, and even more particularly India, rallied. The Indian Princes used the name of the King everywhere among their people as a symbol of loyalty and devotion. Messages poured on the King from every part of the Empire, promising help—messages that came as a great comfort to him. He told the Overseas Dominions with what appreciation and pride he had received them. " I shall be strengthened in the discharge of the great responsibilities which rest upon me by the confident belief that in this time of trial my Empire will stand

THE PRINCE OF WALES IN FRANCE.
The Prince being shown the way by a British cavalry soldier in a French town, and (centre) his Royal Highness with an officer friend amid the snow on the western front. Right : The Prince, visiting one of the British base hospitals in France, has a chat with one of the nurses.

[*British official photograph.*

A TALK WITH KING ALBERT.
King George describing to King Albert an amusing incident which he had experienced in captured German trenches in 1916.

united, calm, resolute, trusting in God."

One of the first public duties of the King after the declaration of war was to visit Aldershot to inspect the Expeditionary Force before it left for France. Accompanied by the Queen, and attended by Major Clive Wigram, he drove to the camp, where he was met by Sir Douglas Haig. Here he walked around all the units, shaking hands with and congratulating each commanding officer on the appearance of his troops. He naturally received an enthusiastic demonstration. He paid special attention to the aircraft, and to the personnel of the naval and military wings of the Flying Corps. He had barely returned to London before the men started out quietly for **Farewell to the** the coast on their way to France, **B.E.F.** where, between two to three weeks later, they were to earn immortality by the most glorious defeat turned into victory ever known in the history of the world.

The Royal Family immediately took a prominent part in the work of charity. The King gave numerous personal gifts, such as an ambulance and a pair of his own horses to the Westminster Division of the Red Cross, and a gift of £200 to the Belgian Relief Fund. Queen Mary launched a scheme for a Needlework Guild, which bore her name, to organise the collection of garments for those who would suffer on account of the war. The King and the Royal Family, like the rest of the nation, were seriously concerned about the acute distress that was expected in Britain itself because of the war. Business had been seriously upset. Finances had been temporarily paralysed by the great disturbance of the stock markets. Very few, if any, people at that time realised that fresh

industries for the creation of war material would make the demand for labour so acute that the working classes would enter, within a few weeks, into an era of unexampled prosperity.

A committee was constituted by the Government to consider what should be done to meet the expected distress, and the Prince of Wales was made treasurer of a National Fund initiated by it. The Prince of Wales's Fund became one of **Prince of Wales's** the features of national life in Britain **Fund founded** during the weeks that followed. Two very energetic organisers, Mr. (afterwards Sir Arthur) Pearson and Mr. (afterwards Sir Hedley) Le Bas, undertook the details of the organisation. "All must realise," said the Prince in a public statement asking for aid, "that the present time of deep anxiety will be followed by one of considerable distress amongst the people in this country least able to bear it. We must earnestly pray that their sufferings may be neither long nor bitter, but we cannot wait until the need presses heavily upon us." He appealed for very generous aid. His appeal was supported by a letter from the Queen to the women of Britain. The response was immediate and generous. Within twenty-four hours a quarter of a million pounds had been raised. Very soon the subscriptions reached a million pounds; within two months the National Relief Fund had totalled three million pounds, and was still mounting up. The Royal Family themselves generously subscribed to the Fund. The King gave £5,000, the Queen £1,050, Queen Alexandra £500, and the Prince of Wales £3,000.

The Prince of Wales having launched the scheme, passed on to other work. He was appointed a second-

[*British official photograph.*

KING GEORGE VISITS CAPTURED ENEMY TRENCHES.
His Majesty outside a German dug-out during his visit to the western front in the summer of 1916, and (in circle) passing between two great mine-craters near Mametz.

lieutenant in the Grenadier Guards, attached to the 1st Battalion. He left Buckingham Palace at five o'clock on the Monday morning following the declaration of war to join his regiment at barracks, travelling in his own motor-car, which he drove himself. At eight o'clock that morning he appeared on parade with the regiment, which shortly afterwards set out on a route march, headed by the Prince and another junior officer.

A solemn hour came on Friday, August 21st, when the King and Queen, accompanied by Princess Mary, took part among the congregation at Westminster Abbey in a Service of Intercession. The Archbishops, Cardinal Bourne, and the Free Church leaders had united to set apart that day as one on which special services should be held in all churches—services of prayer on behalf of our soldiers and sailors. There was a large congregation at the Abbey. The two hymns that were sung had been selected by the King himself, "Holy Father, in Thy Mercy," and "God Moves in a Mysterious Way."

The Queen's next step in charity was to inaugurate a Work for Women Fund, with the object of providing employment for as many as possible of the women of the country thrown out of work by the war. This committee was a collecting and not an administrative body, and it financed schemes devised by the Central Committee on Women's Employment. Large numbers of workshops and sewing-rooms were opened for women. Schemes were initiated to find suitable employment for higher-grade workers. Here again the course of events happily made the need much less than anticipated. The centres of work begun within a few weeks included two workrooms in Bethnal Green and Stepney, each em-**The Queen's Work for Women Fund** ploying ninety-six women in making cradles out of banana crates; four workrooms in East London for making baby clothes to give away with the cradles to poor mothers; two kitchens where women were trained to cook; premises where unemployed dressmakers were being trained to teach others how to cut down and mend second-hand garments; and factories for fruit preserving, to give a new employment for women in fruit pulping, preserving vegetables, and bottling unsweetened fruits.

The work of the King during the weeks that followed may have seemed to outsiders comparatively small. The Kaiser was making the world ring with his dramatic exits and entrances. A persistent claque filled two hemispheres with tales of what he was doing and what he was about to do. Even the date of his promised entry into Paris as victor was told, and his menu at the triumphal dinner detailed. His speeches, his threats, his promises, his unending journeys, and his intrigues filled many columns. King George chose a quieter part, but a part more in keeping with the rôle of **King and Kaiser : a contrast** monarch under the British Constitution. It may, however, be questioned if the advisers of the King would not have acted more wisely had they planned more display for him. This was an hour when the very pomp of kingship could be wisely employed.

While remaining largely in the background, the King's activities were endless. Some time later Mr. Lloyd George, himself one of the hardest of workers, described the King as the hardest-worked man in the land. "There is one man who is working as hard as the hardest-worked man in this country, and he is the Sovereign of the Realm," said the Premier amid great applause. He had endless conferences with Ministers. The burden of decisions which none but he could make fell on him. There are certain crowning responsibilities which, even under a Constitutional monarchy, must be taken by the King. He eagerly assumed them all. He kept in full touch with every development in every part of the field. Each day reports from the front, both land and sea, were carefully perused by him. There were naval and military leaders to interview, foreign diplomats and attachés to receive, high administrative officers to confer with. No man left England on an important task during the war without first being received by the King, who talked with him, discussed his plans, and showed a real grasp of his work. Even when the King went abroad or in the country there was no rest for him. Couriers followed him everywhere, with endless papers of State. The mere task of signing all the documents presented to him was no light one, and the King had the habit of requiring to be satisfied about all documents apart from those of purely a formal nature.

British official photograph.

PASSING THROUGH PEACEFUL PINE-WOODS BEHIND THE BATTLE FRONT.

The Royal car during the visit of the King to the western front. On July 3rd, 1917, King George and Queen Mary arrived in France, and spent twelve days among the British fighting forces. The Queen chiefly visited hospitals and centres where women worked; while the King went to many spots made historic by his armies, and visited Vimy Ridge and other parts of the battlefield near to which shells were still bursting.

B

"IT WAS ROSES, ROSES ALL THE WAY."

Queen Alexandra and her second daughter, Princess Victoria, about to set out on a drive through London on "Alexandra Day," June 20th, 1917, when over twelve thousand ladies were engaged in selling floral emblems for the benefit of the hospitals.

A correspondent of the "Daily Mail" gathered some interesting details of the life of the King:

The King takes no holidays. He is at work from early morning until late at night.

Being the head of the biggest concern in the world, his work has to be organised on scientific lines, or it would never get done. He gets up early in the morning and goes carefully through the newspapers. By 8.30 he is ready for his secretaries, and the morning mail takes until about 10.30, though work is at high pressure. From 10.30 until luncheon there are engagements at the palace, and these are so nicely ordered that every quarter of an hour is occupied.

Between 3 and 5 p.m. the King visits institutions such as munition factories, flying grounds, military establishments, war hospitals, and the like. Between 5.30 and 8 he is again at work, for scores of papers have to be considered and scores of documents signed. To take one instance, every list of promotions has to be signed with the King's own hand. During dinner other papers have a habit of coming in, and those are dealt with before going to bed.

The King's motto is "Do it now." He is what the Americans call a "clean-desk man"; he allows no unfinished work to accumulate. Wherever he goes—to the fighting-front, to the Grand Fleet, or elsewhere—messengers follow daily with despatches to be read and papers to be signed, and they bring the completed documents back to London; no time wasted.

The King and Queen Mary were ceaseless in their visits to the sick and wounded and in their unostentatious personal service to the suffering of all ranks and classes. Innumerable movements radiated from Buckingham Palace, which became under the direction of the Queen a hive of charity. Queen Mary had never been ambitious to act as a leader of the "Smart Set." Smartness and ultra-modernism in morals and manners found in her no friend. It was the sneer of the "smart" that she indulged in "middle-class virtues," and that she stood up for the sanctity of the home, the closeness of the marriage tie, and the supremacy of the family. They dubbed her "Puritanical." She clung to old-fashioned

Personal service to the suffering

ideas in morals, but they proved very good wearing ideas in time of war. She showed the greatest tact and skill in bringing together women of all classes and in stimulating them to serve Britain better.

Many interesting tales were told of the King and Queen at this time, particularly concerning their dealings with wounded officers and men. On one occasion the same hospital was visited within twenty-four hours by the King and Queen and by a famous military leader. The military chief—it would scarcely be kind to give his name—came in great state. Everyone felt uncomfortable and on his best behaviour while he was present, and relieved when he had gone. One bold young subaltern had a bet with his ward that when the military chief came he would put one question to him. The subaltern was so awed when the great man was in the room that he never dared to open his mouth. Now for the contrast. A telephone message was received at noon that the King and Queen had an hour to spare and would like to come along and look over the hospital. As it happened, a number of fresh cases were just about to arrive from Victoria, cases straight from the front. The matron, knowing this, urged on the King's secretary that they would be very much upset during the next hour. If the King would only come an hour later, all would be ready for him.

Typical visit to a hospital

"That is exactly how the King wants to see you, when you are busy," came the reply over the telephone. "He does not want you to make specially ready for him." And so a few minutes later, just as the ambulances were beginning to discharge their loads, a quiet carriage drew up and their Majesties stepped out. They stood around, watched the men being carried in, talked with some of them, and then questioned the attendants. There were no trappings or trimmings of state about them. They were simply an Englishman and Englishwoman, anxious to do a kindly act to some of their fellow-countrymen who had suffered for England. They went in, and moved from room to room, chatting unconcernedly with everyone. The young wounded officers forgot to be awed. The King left smiles in every ward. The Queen, as a practical housewife, took a glance around the store-rooms and examined in a few minutes the organisation of the place, declaring her appreciation of all she saw.

This was typical of many of the King's calls. There were thousands of soldiers and sailors recovered from their wounds who loved to tell long afterwards how the King had stood by their beds and asked their experiences; how he had used their slang to them, and how his quiet remarks showed that he knew some of the tricks and ways of the British sailor and soldier just as well as they did.

In one hospital a boy, clearly not over sixteen, although he had declared his age on attesting at the necessary military figure of nineteen, was lying wounded in bed. He was the pet of the ward. The King, entering it, was struck by his boyish face.

"Well, my lad," he said, "how old are you?"

"Nineteen, your Majesty," replied the lad.

"Yes, I know that is your military age," said the King, "but what is your real age?" For the King was old Service man enough to know that the age on the attestation paper was not always the age on the birth certificate.

On another occasion the King was visiting a hospital when he noticed among the men sitting around on their beds a white-haired veteran. There could be no mistake that his white locks were bleached by age. The King promptly went up to him. "You are a reservist, are you not?" he asked. "No, sir," the soldier replied. "I enlisted again for the war; I wanted to have a whack at these Germans." The King glanced at his bandaged arm. "It seems to me," he said, "that these Germans have had a whack at you. How old are you?" The man glanced quickly at the card above his bed. "I'm forty-five, your Majesty." A little twinkle of amusement came

King George V. in Flanders: His Majesty on Wytschaete Ridge, July, 1917.

Viewing some of the results of the Huns' destructive fury on their enforced retirement.

[British official photographs.

His Majesty with members of his suite walking through one of the devastated streets of the town.

King George V. on his visit to the ruins of historic Péronne.

The King passing a rescued relic of Cuinchy Church, west of La Bassée.   The Prince of Wales stands by the bell.

[British official photographs.

His Majesty in Péronne, ruined but regained by his gallant troops for France on March 18th, 1917.

The Royal visit to the rewon towns of suffering France in July, 1917.

[Canadian War Records.

At an observation-post on Vimy's famous ridge.

[British official photograph.

His Majesty picks up a battered Hun helmet.

[Canadian War Records.

On the Butte de Warlencourt, taken in the Bapaume advance.

[British official photograph.

Looking at German cartridges picked up on the field.

[British official photograph.

An officer has put on German armour for the King's inspection.

[Canadian War Records.

Interested in ammunition found in an old German trench.

Incidents during King George's third visit to the western front.

into the King's eyes. "And how old are you, really?" he asked. "I'm sixty-two, sir," was the prompt reply.

On September 19th Parliament was prorogued. The King did not attend in person, but his Speech struck a note which vibrated throughout the country. "I address you," he said, "in circumstances that call for action rather than speech . . . We are fighting for a worthy purpose, and we shall not lay down our arms until that purpose has been fully achieved." The scene in both Houses was unprecedented. In the Lords, "strangers," members of the House of Commons, and others broke the rules and burst into loud cheering on the Royal assent being given to the Home Rule and the Welsh Church Bills. In the Commons, after the King's Speech was read, Mr. Will Crooks, the popular Labour member, formerly a noted pacifist but who now boldly came out for his country in the hour of crisis in his country's history, asked Mr. Whitley, who was in the chair, if the House would be in order in singing "God Save the King"? Without waiting for a reply, he struck up the first notes of the National Anthem.

There was barely a momentary hesitation before the entire body of the Commons, Ministers on the Treasury Bench, Opposition Leaders, and Nationalists rose to their feet and joined in the singing. "It was an impressive scene," wrote the Parliamentary correspondent of the "Times," "and its effectiveness was increased by its unaffected fervour and obvious spontaneity. And when the patriotic demonstration was over and members were streaming out of the Chamber, some Liberals cried, 'God save Ireland!' Back came the hearty and ready reply from the Nationalists, 'God save England!' A picturesque and moving end to the most amazing Session in our modern Parliamentary history."

In November it was announced that the Prince of Wales, who had been serving with the Grenadier Guards, had been appointed aide-de-camp to Sir John French, and had hastened to take up the duties of his new post. His appointment was dated Saturday, and on Monday he was at Headquarters in the field. It was an open secret that for some weeks the Prince had been exceedingly desirous of getting to the front. Shortly after joining the Grenadier Guards at the outbreak of the war he endeavoured to persuade Lord Kitchener, the Secretary of State for War, that he should go to France with his regiment. Lord Kitchener, however, felt obliged to advise the King that his training was insufficient to qualify him for active service. The **The Heir-Apparent** Prince thereupon set to work harder, **at the Front** trained more fully, and at last attained his desire.

The president of Magdalen College used this occasion to describe in the columns of the "Times" the Prince of Wales as he was at Oxford. The war had cut short the Prince of Wales's Oxford career. He had arrived when he was a little over eighteen, well forward in the studies and training of the Navy—moral, physical, and intellectual—but naturally somewhat newer to and less directly prepared for university life and studies than the public school boy. He soon, however, began to find his feet, and developed rapidly. He had only a short time for set studies. It was not clear at the first that he would have

a second year. French, German, and English, especially the command of literary expression in his own language, were necessary for him. History, political economy, political science, and constitutional law were desirable. He took as habitual and as consistent trouble to avoid deference or preference as others took to cultivate it. He played football, lawn-tennis, golf, tennis, and squash rackets; he motored, he ran with his college boats, he ran a great deal with the beagles, he shot at various country-houses round Oxford, he rode for exercise **Impressions of his Oxford life** and to hounds. In this last accomplishment he started at a disadvantage, but by real perseverance and pluck soon made up for it and became quite proficient, though among one of the genuine losses involved by the loss of another winter at Oxford was the missing of yet further days with the Oxford hunts. He was withal a punctual and diligent member in the ranks of the O.T.C. He drilled, he marched, he went into camp like any other private.

"Bookish," said the president, "he will never be;

OVER ONE HUNDRED THOUSAND BIRTHDAY GIFTS.
Queen Mary, with Princess Mary (right) and Princess Beatrice (left), among the books which formed part of the 102,000 birthday gifts sent from all over the world by members of her Needlework Guild in June, 1917. Her Majesty distributed the gifts among hospitals and war organisations generally.

not a 'Beauclerk,' still less a 'British Solomon.' Kings, perhaps fortunately, seldom are this last. That is not to be desired, but the Prince of Wales will not want for ready and forcible presentation, either in speech or writing. And all the time he was learning more and more every day of men, gauging character, watching its play, getting to know what Englishmen are like, both individually and still more in the mass."

Let it be said at once that the Prince, at the front, more than lived up to the good impressions he had made on dons and undergraduates alike at Oxford. There is always a danger in speaking well of kings and princes, that those who praise them should be thought to be uttering mere courtly flattery. But in the case of the Prince of Wales flattery was to a very special degree unnecessary. Every man who came in contact with him had the same to say about him. He was a simple, sincere, straightforward lad, keen on his work, active in physical exercises, a young soldier showing deference to his seniors, always ready for his duties. He lived with the same simplicity as the soldiers surrounding him, and nothing was more remarkable than the way in which this quiet boy made himself loved and admired by the men in the

MUNITION WORKERS' CHEERS FOR THE KING AND QUEEN.
During June, 1917, King George and Queen Mary made a five days' tour of the North, visiting shipyards and munition works of various kinds. They met with a fervent welcome from the armies of workers in the factories who were making possible the work of the armies in the field.

ranks of the Army. Before many months there were a hundred anecdotes about him in the trenches, and every one of the hundred was to his credit.

A few days after the Prince of Wales reached General Headquarters the King travelled over to France to pay his first visit to the Expeditionary Force. The occasion was a great one. No British sovereign had taken his place among the soldiers in the field since George II. fought at Dettingen. The " New York Times " expressed the feeling of many when it said: "The first journey of an English King to the seat of war for one hundred and seventy-one years is an incident of note. That his presence will cheer the soldiers who see him is not to be doubted. King George has sterling qualities which must commend him to all men brought to the stern realisation of the seriousness of life as soldiers are. They know him as an honest, faithful, and valiant man, who would willingly join them in the firing-line and share their luck."

The King landed in France at a critical and memorable moment in the history of our Army. General French's army had barely concluded a long spell of severe and continuous fighting. Sixteen German army corps had flung themselves against an attenuated British line to hack their way through to Calais. The Germans made no secret of their programme ; first Ypres, then Calais, then London. And there came hours in the furious fighting on the western front when it seemed that the British line could hold out no longer.

Every man who could move had been flung into the trenches. Terrific losses had been inflicted on the enemy, but at a heavy cost, for up to the end of October alone, leaving out the November

fighting, the British casualties had numbered 57,000 of all ranks. The British, however, had held firm and had won ; and now the King was going amongst his own men who had attained victory against almost impossible handicaps.

The King first went to Boulogne, in the days before the war a gay watering-place, now the town of the wounded. The Casino, big public buildings, and great hotels had been taken over wholesale, and fitted hastily with beds. Armies of doctors and nurses from England were doing their best for the thousands of men pouring in by train, by car, and by every route possible. The King, accompanied by the Prince of Wales, who had come down from St. Omer to meet him, went round the hospitals and showed by his speech and by his evident solicitude his concern at the number of the wounded. He spoke in German to a wounded German officer, and expressed a desire that the German wounded should be well supplied with literature, because their lot was doubly hard in that they could not talk with other wounded men. Going to an officers' ward of a hospital, he spoke to every officer in turn, asked their personal experiences, and heard their anecdotes.

" One officer had a story to tell which greatly interested his Majesty," wrote a correspondent. " He said that while **His Majesty at Boulogne** he was reading a newspaper in the trenches a bullet went through the page. When he examined the paper he found that the bullet had traversed the name of a great friend of his, a member of his Majesty's suite. ' Is my friend with you to-day, your Majesty ? ' he inquired. The friend was present, and was summoned to the bedside.

LINKS IN THE GREAT CHAIN OF EFFICIENCY.
King George inspecting a great chain-making works during the Royal tour in the North in the summer of 1917. It was estimated that during the tour over two million people hailed their Majesties in the seven great industrial centres that were visited.

The wounded officer explained that, directly after the paper was hit, he sat down to write a letter to his friend, relating the incident, and he cut out the burst piece of the paper to send on to him. It was while he was thus occupied that he was himself hit by a bullet."

The King also visited the Indian Hospital, where he spent forty minutes talking with the wounded Sikhs, Jats, and others. There was an officer there of the 218th Gurkhas, a regiment which had lost very heavily in the fighting in November, and the King showed a special interest in his story. At one convalescent camp, as the King was passing, a sepoy rose from his bed and shouted, "God Save the King!" He knew no other English words than these.

From Boulogne King George went up by road to St. Omer, the French country town which had been chosen for the Headquarters of the British Army. A quiet place was St. Omer, yet not without its own special interests.

THEIR MAJESTIES INSPECT A TORPEDOED SHIP.
While on a visit to one of the great shipyards at Newcastle-on-Tyne the King and Queen were shown a vessel that had been torpedoed, but had been safely brought in and was dry-docked for the necessary repairs. The King's close interest in the work that was proceeding is manifest.

It still had some great buildings, a wonderful military hospital erected on the site of a college founded by the English Jesuits centuries before, a beautiful college, a church with a tower one hundred and sixty-five feet high, and the still more majestic ruins of the Church of St. Martin, with a huge tower of one hundred and ninety feet high, dominating the country round. The life of St. Omer had completely changed. In one quiet house, somewhere around the town, Sir John French had his headquarters. Little old buildings, the ruins of the splendour of the historic mediæval north, now housed princes and generals and great military leaders. The quaint old streets that had rung to the rival cries of Catholic and Huguenot, the

From Boulogne to St. Omer

grim by-ways where mediæval bravoes had waited for their prey, the shady squares where the daughters of the Revolution had sat and knitted and had discussed the work of the guillotine in Paris, and the ruin being wrought yet nearer to hand, all these streets and squares now saw the hastening of men in khaki, the wonderful co-operation of English and French, ancient foes, present and enduring friends. St. Omer was approached along the old military roads of France, the roads where Napoleon's armies had marched, the roads where a few years earlier Dumouriez's Revolutionary battalions had poured forth to face a world in arms against France, the roads along which, generations before, Marlborough and his veterans had fought the armies of Louis.

King George must have found much food for thought as his car swept through these historic ways. For centuries the generals of his ancestors had fought France on ground in and near here. Now he was coming as friend and ally. He had barely arrived before the President of the French Republic, accompanied by the Premier and General Joffre, visited the British Headquarters. King and President had long and cordial conversations, and then they motored out together to the British front in an open car. There was a memorable dinner that night, when, at the King's invitation, the French President remained with him. Around the table were the Prince of Wales, Sir John French, the French Premier, and several French military leaders.

When dinner was over, the King set out from his billet and went forth unheralded among his troops, visiting them in their bivouacs, studying their surroundings, and seeing how they were placed. His walk was lit

ROYAL VISITORS AT A SUNDERLAND SHIPYARD.
King George and Queen Mary walking through Messrs. Pickersgill's shipyard. Their Majesties. who had a great reception at Sunderland and Stockton during the first day of their tour in June, 1917, walked at least ten miles through the yards and works they visited on that day.

THE KING AND QUEEN AMONG THE MUNITION MAKERS.
Their Majesties, while inspecting a large munition works at Stockton-on-Tees, paused to talk with some of the girl workers, who were greatly delighted at the Royal visit, and especially gratified by the sympathy manifested in their arduous work.

up by the flash of the German guns and by the distant reflection of the flare of the German lights thrown up in the sky. His soldiers had earned well of him. So far as it can be said of any men, it can be said of French's army that by stemming the German flood they had saved Great Britain itself and its monarch from destruction. To the people of France the journey of the King was one of special gratification, even though his visit on this occasion was made not to France so much as to the British Army in France. The "Temps" put the national feeling into words : "France addresses to the King an expression of her high esteem for his person and profound gratitude towards his country."

The King's first Christmas of the war was spent at York Cottage, Sandringham. Two days before Christmas the King and Queen gave a farewell family luncheon party. Queen Alexandra was there, with Princess

Victoria and the Princess Royal. Some of the King's sons had come home for their Christmas holidays — Prince Henry from Eton, Prince George from Broadstairs, and Prince Albert. The princes drove to St. Pancras, and soon afterwards were followed by the King and Queen to the Royal special, which was waiting to convey the Court to Norfolk. Some Canadian ladies who had not hitherto seen their Majesties nor the Royal children were specially permitted to have places on the platform close to the King's saloon. Just before the train left, the King turned and raised his hat to them and to the big crowd who had assembled to bid him farewell.

Christmas was no holiday for the King. There was much to be done. It was necessary to keep all the time in the closest touch with the developments of the war and the changes in the international situation. The Royal Family observed its Christmas as tens of thousands of other families did. There were Christmas cards specially designed and illustrated for them and distributed in their own circle. There were presents. The Royal party attended church in the morning, when the hymns were selected by the King and sung by a choir of village boys and girls, who also **A War Christmas** rendered a special Christmas anthem. **at Sandringham** The Royal Family had dinner early on Christmas Day, so that the children might be present at the meal. They dined on the traditional Christmas fare. The King had seen to it that every tenant and every workman on his Norfolk estate was ensured a good Christmas dinner also. On Christmas Eve six bullocks had been killed and cut up into joints—two pounds for each adult and one pound for each child. Where the father was away at the

THEIR MAJESTIES TALK WITH WORKERS, OLD AND YOUNG.
The King chatting with one of the men engaged at a brass foundry at Sunderland, and (in centre) Queen Mary receiving a bouquet from a young girl munition worker during one of the Royal tours in the North.
On their tours they always evinced a lively interest in the workers. Right : Their Majesties have introduced to them one of the oldest workmen at Messrs. Cammell Laird's shipbuilding yard at Birkenhead.

front special provision was made. There were presents of warm clothing for the old folk and dainties were cooked in the Royal kitchen for the invalids and aged in the villages around.

The opening days of 1915 were a time of great anxiety for the King himself and for all associated with him. Back in London, he resumed even more fully than was possible in the country his close and intimate touch with the most minute affairs. Every despatch of any moment came before him. Every bit of news was carefully examined by him. He naturally saw hour by hour, in the closest details, the real situation. There was at once cause for gratification and for misgiving. In Britain, Kitchener's armies had been raised by the many hundred thousand. The men from the Dominions had flocked to defend the Crown. There were Canadians by the ten thousand on Salisbury Plain and at Winchester. The Australians had not reached England, but were fighting for the Empire on the Suez Canal. Almost every village in Britain was a recruiting ground, and there was scarcely a district that was not an armed camp. The armies at the front were clamouring for more men. But a large proportion of the new soldiers were unarmed ; there were no rifles for them and no munitions. They had to practise with dummy guns. Recruits had to be hurried out to the front almost before they had mastered the elements of drill. Battalions were housed amid the mud of a record rainy winter, in leaky tents and in old houses, under conditions which tried the physique of the men to the full. In France itself soldiers were holding up the pick of the German

A time of great anxiety

THE DUKE OF CONNAUGHT AT A MUNITION WORKS.
During a tour of some of the munition-making centres the Duke of Connaught, uncle of King George, spent some time in watching the women workers who were skilfully handling the heavy shells as they were received in the stencilling sheds.

Army in trenches that were mud-holes, ill-drained and ill-built. Their very clothing was unsuitable for the conditions of modern warfare. They were being stricken wholesale by trench-foot and other ills. They were almost without hand-grenades and with insufficient shells for the big guns. Ill-equipped, they were fighting with heroism the most splendidly equipped and armed Army the world had ever seen. And it was King George's lot to maintain the enthusiasm of his soldiers at white heat by visiting them in their camps, and by sending stimulating messages to the armies at the front, while also helping to promote activity at home for the production of the needed material of war.

Thus we find him now at Salisbury Plain, being cheered to the echo by the Canadian boys who were soon to prove their heroism on the blood-soaked and gas-swept field of

ROYAL INTEREST IN THE ARMY BEHIND THE ARMY.
King George and Queen Mary talking with one of the employees who were introduced to them at a Birkenhead shipbuilding yard, and (in centre) presenting medals won in the war during their visit to Manchester.　The Queen is seen conversing with a mother who had received the medal gained by her son, a private in the Manchester Regiment, killed in action. Right : The King in a Lancashire shell factory.

AT A NORTHERN GUN FACTORY.
The King and Queen see one of the guns that were used for the defence of merchant ships against enemy submarines.

Ypres; now seeing some British division before it went off. It became a tradition with the British Army that "First you're trained; then you're polished up; then the King comes; and then you're off!"

The King paid a visit to his fighting Fleet. "I have been on board representative ships of all classes," he said, "and am much impressed by the state of their efficiency and the splendid spirit which animates both officers and men. I have not the slightest doubt that my Navy will uphold its great traditions."

The year 1915 was King George's jubilee year. On June 3rd he was fifty. The occasion was celebrated by the publication of an unusual list of honours, but there was little outward festivity. The "great push," from which so much was expected, had failed to materialise.

Day of intercession at St. Paul's

There could hardly be. The British, instead of pushing the enemy back, had been pushed back. The shortage of shells had become a matter of common knowledge. It was now more and more clear that the length of the war would be counted by years and not by months. At other times there would have been great rejoicings; now it was a day of solemn remembrance.

"On no man in all his wide Empire has the strain of war come more heavily," said one contemporary writer. "None has laboured more incessantly to play his part, to set a right example in all things, to prove himself a king indeed at a time which is full of special opportunities of leadership." Greetings came to the King not only

from his own people, but from his Allies. The French Minister of War sent on behalf of the French Army an exceedingly cordial message, to which the King as cordially replied.

The first anniversary of the outbreak of the war was celebrated by the King and nation as a day of intercession and of prayer. The King and Queen, with Queen Alexandra and the leaders of the nation, attended a great service at St. Paul's Cathedral at noon. The scene was grave and impressive. The vast area of the cathedral was filled with a packed throng representing not Britain alone but the Empire — distinguished soldiers from the Dominions, Indians, many men in khaki, statesmen, wounded men with the bandages still on them, wounded men who limped pain-

IN A SUNDERLAND SHIPBUILDING YARD.
During their visit to one of the extensive shipbuilding yards on the North-East Coast their Majesties paused to watch the operations of a huge drilling machine which, under the control of skilled workers, cut with nice exactness large discs out of thick metal plates.

fully to their seats. There were many in mourning, many whose eyes were haunted with looks of grief. Close in front of the King's chair was the Artillery band which led the singing. But the singing on this day had little of the note of triumph in it. The hymns were hymns of petition, such as "Rock of Ages" and "Through the Night of Doubt and Sorrow." The whole note of the assembly was subdued, but not despondent. Those who did not know England might have been deceived, and might have thought that the air was one of war-weariness. In truth it was rather the air of those who were only now recognising the magnitude of the task ahead, and who, having recognised it, were preparing themselves for the great fight. The service ended in a crash of music, with "God Save the King," and as the King and Queen moved outside, thousands of people, assembled for even a sight of them, rent the air with their cheers.

One of the important duties now undertaken by the King was to visit the great industrial centres of the land. He went to numerous munition works. A visit to Leeds in September, 1915, may be taken as typical of many others. Arriving at the city, he first visited a number of munition works, where he talked with the men, picking out the veterans and asking them how long they had served. Specially prominent working men were brought up to him; for example, one who was a former sergeant in the Sherwood Foresters, and who had been recalled for munition work. He tried to impress on the men individually the importance of their task. He told them one after another unless there was an adequate supply of shells the war could not be won. "He shook hands right heartily," said one man. "My black, oily fist

IN A RIVETING SHOP.
Their Majesties watching the operation of riveting a ship's plates at a Stockton shipyard during a tour in the North.

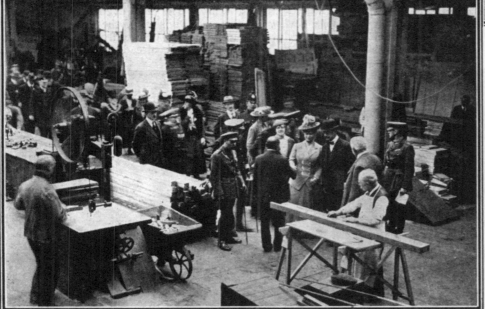

VISIT TO WOOD-WORKING SHEDS AT BIRKENHEAD.
During one of their tours of the Northern manufacturing centres the King and Queen inspected the shipbuilding yards of Messrs. Cammell, Laird & Co. at Birkenhead. They are here seen passing through the sheds devoted to shaping that wood which forms no unimportant part even of iron ships.

left a lovely mark right across his glove, but he didn't care."

Then the King went on to the hospitals, where he talked to the patients and conferred some decorations for war services. Before he left he spoke to them all gathered together. "I am very glad to be with you here to-day," he said, "and I wish to say how proud I am of the way in which you have done your duty both in France and in the Dardanelles. I trust that you will soon be restored to health and back again to your friends and your homes."

Next day he returned to the military hospital. Again he talked to the men, decorated some who had earned medals, and made another speech to them. "I have been very much pleased with everything I have seen," he said to the Lord Mayor before he left.

Then he travelled to Sheffield, where he inspected the principal munition works, and saw the students in training at the university for munition work. He lunched at the leading works in the city, where the table decorations consisted of models of British and Japanese war vessels. After lunch when he went among the workmen there was a pleasant episode, for the King recognised one of them as a man who had formerly served with him when he was a midshipman in H.M.S. Bacchante. Another man who had served for fifty years with the firm told his Majesty that he remembered King Edward coming round the works when he was the Prince of Wales. The King and the workmen got on well together.

The month of October, 1915, was marked by another visit of the King to the allied troops, and by a direct personal appeal to the nation. The King's appeal was couched in terms worthy of the ruler of the greatest Empire in history. The outlook for Great Britain was dark. The enemy was pressing her **Royal appeal to** hard, and while newer preparations for **the nation** the production of munitions and the equipment of fresh troops were progressing splendidly, she was yet suffering from great handicaps. The King spoke in terms of encouragement and of warning :

BUCKINGHAM PALACE.
TO MY PEOPLE.
At this grave moment in the struggle between my people and a highly organised enemy who has transgressed the Laws of Nations and changed the ordinance that binds civilised Europe together, I appeal to you.
I rejoice in my Empire's effort, and I feel pride in the voluntary response from my Subjects all over the world who have sacrificed

home, fortune, and life itself in order that another may not inherit the free Empire which their ancestors and mine have built.

I ask you to make good these sacrifices.

The end is not in sight. More men and yet more are wanted to keep my Armies in the Field, and through them to secure Victory and enduring Peace.

In ancient days the darkest moment has ever produced in men of our race the sternest resolve.

I ask you, men of all classes, to come forward voluntarily and take your share in the fight.

In freely responding to my appeal, you will be giving your support to our brothers who, for long months, have nobly upheld Britain's past traditions and the glory of her Arms.

GEORGE R.I.

This message came simultaneously with a gigantic recruiting canvass which raised vast numbers of men voluntarily for the Army.

The King's second visit to France   The King visited Havre, which had become an important British base, and went by motor-car to the English hospital and various English institutions. Proceeding to the front, he was met by the President of the French Republic and M. Millerand, the French Minister of War. The Royal and Presidential party was now in the actual zone of war. King and President went over some very well-known lines of defences and inspected detachments of numerous British corps. President Poincaré made the occasion one of some ceremony. The French Staff surrounding him was brilliant, and the British Staff, with the King, included leading British and Dominion generals. The President bestowed the Croix de Guerre, the most honoured and coveted of French decorations, upon the Prince of Wales, and other French decorations upon our generals. Next day, October 26th, King and President

again met, and, accompanied by General Joffre, were present at a review of the French Second Colonial Corps—some of the picked troops of the French Army, whose discipline, splendid formation, and magnificent appearance were the admiration of every British officer who saw them. The King requested the permission of the President of the French Republic to send his congratulations to the French Army. His message, which was one of great political significance, was as follows :

SOLDIERS OF FRANCE.

I am very happy to have been able to realise a desire which I have had at heart for a long time, and to express to you my profound admiration for your heroic exploits, for your dash as well as your tenacity, and those magnificent military virtues which are the proud heritage of the French Army.

Under the brilliant leadership of your eminent General-in-Chief and his distinguished collaborators you, officers, non-commissioned officers, and soldiers, have deserved well of your dear country, which will for ever be grateful to you for your brave efforts in safeguarding and defending it.   **Greetings to the French army**

My armies are very proud to fight by your side and to have you as comrades. May the bonds which unite us hold firm and the two countries remain thus intimately united for ever.

Soldiers,—Accept my most cordial and sincere greetings. I have no doubt that you will bring this gigantic struggle to a victorious conclusion, and, in the name of my soldiers and my country, I beg to address to you my warmest congratulations and best wishes.

The King went on to his own men. He spent the day with the Second Army. The chief event of that day was the review of the 2nd Division of the Canadians, which had arrived about a month before from England. The Canadian 1st Division had already made a record for

[*British official photograph.*

THE KING AND CANADA'S JUBILEE, 1917.

On the occasion of the fiftieth anniversary of the Confederation of Canada the King and Queen attended a solemn service at Westminster Abbey in memory of fallen Canadians. His Majesty inspecting the Guard of Honour.

THE DUKE OF CONNAUGHT IN ITALY.

After his return to England, on relinquishing the post of Governor-General of Canada, the Duke of Connaught visited the Italian front. The photograph shows his Royal Highness with the King of Italy standing on his left.

THE DUKE OF CONNAUGHT AT A TRAINING CENTRE.
With memories still fresh of his tenure of the Governor-Generalship of Canada, the Duke of Connaught devoted special attention to the Dominion forces in training in England. The men shown in the above photograph belonged to the Duchess of Connaught's Own Irish Rangers.

Canada in this war, at Ypres, at Givenchy, and at Festubert. The 2nd Division was keen to emulate it. The King had known the men of this division while training in England, where he had inspected them. Their leader, Major-General (afterwards Lieut.-General Sir) R. E. W. Turner, V.C., was a tried soldier, who had won the highest honour a soldier can win in the South African War.

The second main incident that day was the inspection of a mixed brigade, composed of other divisions of the First Army. The review closed fittingly. After the men had marched past the King they moved across the parade ground at the double, and they lined the roads through which he had to return. The King chatted for a time with a group of his own generals and foreign commanders who were around him. Then he entered his motor-car to drive away. The car moved through an avenue of shouting, smiling soldiers, yelling themselves hoarse in their cheers for the King. "It was the moment," said one spectator, "when the troops could really express their feeling of pride and pleasure in the

Rumour and the King's accident King's presence, and the surging sea of uplifted caps and the ripple of hurrahs that rolled up the roadway as the car passed by showed the King, as nothing else could show him, with what genuine appreciation his visit is everywhere being hailed."

A day or two later great concern was aroused in Britain by a report which rapidly spread over the country that the King had received serious injuries at the front. An official bulletin was quickly published. It told how, while he was inspecting his army in the field, his horse, excited by the cheers of the troops, rose up and fell. "The King was severely bruised, and will be confined to bed for the present." The public estimated the seriousness of the accident by the list of five doctors who signed the bulletin. Sir Arthur Sloggett was Director-General of the Army Medical Service in France, Sir Anthony Bowlby was a distinguished surgeon, Sir Bertrand Dawson had been Physician-Extraordinary to the King since 1907, Sir William Herringham was Consulting Physician to St. Bartholomew's Hospital, and Mr. Cuthbert Wallace was a surgeon attached to St. Thomas's Hospital.

The wildest reports spread rapidly. The King was already dead, said some. The accident was caused, not by a horse falling, said others, but by a German attack—a German shell had very severely wounded him. It was

INSPECTING A CANADIAN O.T.C.
The Duke of Connaught on a visit of inspection to a Canadian officers' training camp in England. In centre: His Royal Highness presenting decorations won by Canadian soldiers during the progress of the war.

23

recalled that not until almost the last moment had the physicians around the late King Edward taken the nation into their confidence about the real gravity of his illness. The worst conclusions were drawn.

The prophets of evil were wrong. The accident had occurred exactly as stated. The injury that the King had suffered was in the highest degree painful. He had just finished the second of two reviews of the troops of the First Army when his horse reared and fell on him. The animal, a mare, reared up twice, when the soldiers started cheering a few feet away from where the King was. The first time she came down again on her forefeet, the second time she fell over, severely crushing and bruising him. How it was that a horse was provided for the King which had not been properly broken in was one of those mysterious oversights which probably will never be explained.

It was evident that the King was in great pain. Messengers were sent instantly for doctors, who could not readily be found. He was raised and put in a car. Only a comparatively small number of the troops had seen the accident, and as his car moved back, the waiting regiments cheered, despite all efforts to silence them. It was some little time before they could be got to understand that this was no moment for cheering. The day was wretched —cold, gusty, and misty. Eventually the Royal patient was got on a hospital-train for England.

One of the most moving episodes of the time was when the King, while lying ill in his hospital-train in France, decorated Lance-Sergeant Oliver Brooks, of the 3rd Coldstream Guards, with a V.C. Lance-Sergeant Brooks had led a bombing-party shortly before and recaptured a trench held by the Germans, and the King, hearing of it, expressed his wish to decorate the man in person. Brooks was led to the bedside of the King in the hospital-train. He knelt on the floor and bent over the bed. The King tried to fasten the cross on his coat, but it was soon evident that he had overrated his strength, and someone had to come to his assistance to

Investiture in a hospital-train

push the pin through the stiff khaki of the soldier's uniform. He tried pluckily, but the effort was too great.

Before leaving for England, the injured King issued an impressive message to his Army:

Officers, Non-Commissioned Officers, and Men,—

I am happy to have found myself once more with my Armies. It is especially gratifying to me to have been able to see some of those that have been newly created. For I have watched with interest the growth of these Troops from the first days of Recruit Drill and through the different stages of training until their final inspection on the eve of departure for the Front as organised Divisions. Already they have justified the general conviction then formed of their splendid fighting worth.

Impressive farewell message

Since I was last among you, you have fought many strenuous battles. In all you have reaped renown and proved yourselves at least equal to the highest traditions of the British Army.

In company with our noble Allies you have baffled the infamous conspiracy against the laws and liberty of Europe, so long and insidiously prepared.

These achievements have involved vast sacrifices. But your countrymen who watch your campaign with sympathetic admiration will, I am well assured, spare no effort to fill your ranks and afford you all supplies.

I have decorated many of you. But had I decorated all who deserve recognition for conspicuous valour, there would have been no limit, for the whole Army is illustrious.

It is a matter of sincere regret to me that my accident should have prevented my seeing all the Troops I had intended, but during my stay amongst you I have seen enough to fill my heart with admiration of your patient, cheerful endurance of life in the trenches: a life either of weary monotony or of terrible tumult. It is the dogged determination evinced by all ranks which will at last bring you to victory. Keep the goal in sight and remember it is the final lap that wins.

GEORGE R.I.

The King had a rough crossing in the hospital-ship Anglia, and after reaching home he enjoyed the best night's rest experienced since his accident. He was conveyed from Victoria to Buckingham Palace on a stretcher placed in an ambulance. The bearer-party from the train to the vehicle, and from the ambulance to the palace, was composed of a specially selected party of men belonging to the British Red Cross Society, No. 1 London Detachment—the Polytechnic boys of Regent Street.

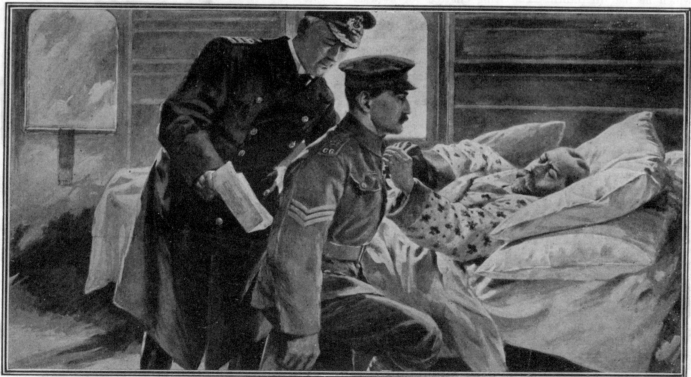

MOVING EPISODE AFTER THE KING'S ACCIDENT IN FRANCE.

On October 26th, 1915, when visiting his troops in France, the King had a severe accident, his horse rearing and falling with him. While lying ill in the hospital-train his Majesty expressed a wish personally to present the Victoria Cross won by Lance-Sergeant Oliver Brooks, of the Coldstream Guards. Brooks was taken to the bedside, and the King tried to pin on the cross, but had overrated his strength and had to be assisted.

So painful were his Majesty's injuries that the car started off only at the rate of eight miles an hour, and was promptly dropped to dead slow. Even at the pace of only three miles an hour the patient was considerably shaken up.

The King, for a time unable to visit his soldiers himself, sent messages through members of his family, telling them how grateful he was for their services, and how proud of their gallant conduct. Early in December Queen Mary took the place of the King on various occasions. More than once she visited divisions before their departure for the front, bringing with her messages from his Majesty regretting that, as a result of his accident, he could not attend.

On December 13th a bulletin was issued by Sir Frederick Treves and Sir Bertrand Dawson :

Buckingham Palace,
Dec. 13, 1915.
We are happy to report that the King has so far recovered from the grave accident of Oct. 28 as to be able to resume work with certain limitations.

The King has lost seriously in weight, and until a normal state of health is attained it is essential that his Majesty should avoid any cause of fatigue.

It has been necessary on medical grounds that the King should take a little stimulant daily during his convalescence.

As soon as the King's health is quite restored, his Majesty will resume that total abstinence which he has imposed upon himself for public reasons.

Frederick Treves.
Bertrand Dawson.

The King's second war Christmas was a very quiet one. He sent a message to the Army and to the Navy, which was published on Christmas morning in orders throughout the Empire.

Despite the trials of 1915, the year 1916 opened for King and people with a feeling of confidence and greater cheerfulness. The King's message to the President of the French Republic struck the note of the feeling in both countries—the deep admiration for the splendid qualities of the land and sea forces whose services had been of such inestimable value, and offered a sure guarantee of ultimate victory.

The King moved down to Sandringham. From Sandringham he returned to Buckingham Palace, where his life soon assumed its regular routine. For a time he walked with a stick, and showed evident signs of how great his suffering had been.

His interest in others who had been injured in the war was now greater than ever, if that were possible. One of the things planned by him early in 1916 was an entertainment to several thousand wounded men

[British official photograph.
GENERAL PÉTAIN, G.C.B.
A notable incident of King George's visit to the western front in July, 1917, was the investiture by his Majesty of General Pétain, the Commander of the French Armies, with the insignia of a G.C.B.

at Buckingham Palace. This was, in the best sense of the word, a family affair of the King and Queen. They and their entourage arranged the details, waited on the men, had them into their own home, went among them and mixed as friends with friends. The great riding-school at Buckingham Palace was turned into a monster theatre. The Queen herself selected the attendants who were to be honoured with an invitation to wait on the wounded men, and they included some of the greatest ladies in the land—the Duchess of Devonshire, the Duchess of Sutherland, the Duchess of Buccleuch, Lady Farquhar, Lady FitzWilliam, Lady Lansdowne, Lady Keppel, and others.

The men were brought into the courtyard of Buckingham Palace in motor-omnibuses from their different hospitals. Here they were greeted by the Guards' Band, playing lively tunes. Many of them were hopeless invalids and had to be carried out from the omnibuses by parties of Red Cross men who were in waiting. Quite a number were blind and had to be led along by companions who could see. Here were one-legged men and one-armed men, and men with no legs and others with no arms at all. Here were some who hopped along on crutches, some who limped, some still half-covered with bandages, some whose eyes would never see the light of day again. The onlooker was hardened indeed who could watch them without emotion as they were helped out of the motor-omnibuses.

They were quickly in their seats in the long rooms of the Palace, and here Royal fare was waiting them. Some people of lesser degree seemed to think that when they entertained wounded men, anything was good enough. The King and Queen had no such idea. The best was the only thing good enough for the soldier. All hired attendants had departed. The work of waiting, of pouring tea, and helping the men was done by the first gentlewomen of the kingdom.

Suddenly, unannounced, without any display, the men noticed the King and Queen, Queen Alexandra, and the princesses quietly walking from table to table, the King in admiral's uniform. They had a word for every man they came in contact with.

The King knew about their battles; he knew where they had fought, and he seemed to know even the individual stories of many of the men. There were Canadians and Australians here. He picked out a non-

[British official photograph.
CEREMONY OF INVESTITURE NEAR THE BATTLE-FRONT.
In addition to General Pétain, a number of other officers were decorated by the King during his stay with the armies in France and Flanders in the summer of 1917. A Guard of Honour of dismounted British Lancers formed a striking background to the ceremony on one of those occasions.

D

[*British official photograph.*
OUT OF ACTION.
The King on a light-railway journey pauses to view a broken enemy 5·9 in. gun.

[*British official photograph.*
A PAUSE AMID THE RUINS OF PÉRONNE.
King George, during his visit to the western front in July, 1917, journeyed to Péronne and other towns from which the Germans had been driven. He is here seen, with walking-stick, leaning over the bridge which his troops had built to replace that destroyed by the enemy.

commissioned officer at each table for a special word. The King was at one table, the Queen at another, while Queen Alexandra was at a third.

One young Canadian —trust a Canadian not to lose anything by failing to ask for it— pulled out his fountain-pen, presented his programme of the day, a greatly prized souvenir, to Queen Alexandra, and asked her to autograph it. The Queen-Mother smilingly assented. Encouraged by the example of the one, others pressed around. She sat down on a seat and set to work putting her name on every card that was offered, smiling, talking, to the men and evidently enjoying herself, as they were enjoying every moment of the time, too. " Gee ! " said one lad of the Fighting Tenth from Calgary. " They would not believe out West that the King asked me to tea if I had not something to show for it. I wouldn't trade Queen Alexandra's signature for a hundred dollars ! " And every man went out from the tea-room feeling that the King and Royal Family were really his friends and had a thought for him—that they were not dim and distant figures under the panoply of State, but human folk.

Entertaining the wounded

The day was by no means yet over. All went along to the great riding-school, which was beflagged and beflowered for the occasion. There was a fine stage at one end. There was a comfortable seat for everybody, and an entertainment had been prepared that far surpassed anything shown in the chief variety halls in London, for the pick of all the artistes had come. Here were Harry Lauder and Miss Ethel Levey, George Grossmith, Arthur Playfair, and Nelson Keys, Miss Gladys Cooper, Gerald du Maurier, Jack Norworth, and many others. Neil Kenyon showed himself as the golf caddie, Cornalia and Eddy played their eccentric acrobat tricks, and the corps de ballet of the Palace Theatre girls acted as chorus. There was plenty of music, and before the King and Queen came the house echoed with patriotic song after patriotic song. One man standing in front of the stage—I was there but did not catch his name—set the whole house a-singing. He had jest and quip for all the boys. There were the national songs to be sung —" Australia Will be There," " Oh, Canada ! " " Land of Hope and Glory," and, crowning all, " God Save the King." And when the King and Queen came in, and walked down the great hall to their seats in front, it seemed as though the roof would come off with the cheers and cries of the men. It was a great day. Those who watched the King, who still used a stick in getting about, could see his face lighten with joy and pride, for he was among his own men again.

Throughout the war the King tried, time after time, to give a direct lead to his people by personal example and by personal sacrifice. His personal war charities were, from the first, on the most generous scale. In the spring of 1915 the most thoughtful men in the country were profoundly concerned over the question of the consumption of alcoholic drinks. There was a keen demand that the Government should enforce Prohibition. This was generally thought to be impracticable. The King led the way in another direction. He commanded that the consumption of wines, spirits, and beer should cease in the Royal residences, and he himself became a teetotaller for the duration of the war. The only occasion on which this rule was relaxed was during his illness after his accident in the field, when the doctors ordered him to take some stimulant temporarily, as stated in the bulletin printed on the previous page.

The King's gift of £100,000

The King's decision created a profound impression throughout the country. He gave a lead to the wealthy people of the land in April, 1916, when he placed a sum of £100,000 at the disposal of the Treasury. " It is the King's wish," said Sir Frederick Ponsonby, the Keeper of the Privy Purse, announcing the gift to the Prime Minister, " that this sum which he gives in consequence of the war should be applied in whatever manner is deemed best in the opinion of his Majesty's Government."

The summer of 1916 was very fully occupied with a

hundred and one affairs of State. The King paid a visit to Lowestoft to see the Royal Naval Reserve there. The King and Queen attended the Abbey service on Anzac Day, when the Australasian forces made a great display to meet them. One very interesting occasion was on St. Patrick's Day, when he inspected the Irish Guards at Warley Barracks and decorated one officer and four men with the Distinguished Service Order and the Distinguished Conduct Medal for gallant conduct in the field.

To go from great things to small, the King and Queen showed the greatest personal interest in the proposal to cultivate medicinal home-grown herbs to replace supplies formerly received from Germany and Austria. At their Majesties' request there was a consultation with the head gardener as to what could be done in the way of growing herbs in the Royal gardens.

When the question of recruiting became acute the King gave orders that every unmarried man of military age in his Majesty's household, especially at Buckingham Palace, Windsor Castle, Balmoral, and Sandringham, no matter what the **Royal message on compulsory service** nature of his employment, was to report himself to the military authorities for service with the Colours.

When the Compulsion Bill received the Royal assent the King sent a direct message to the nation which was published throughout the country:

BUCKINGHAM PALACE, May 25, 1916.
To enable our Country to organise more effectively its military

ROYAL GROUP IN FLANDERS.

The King and Queen with the King and Queen of the Belgians, whom they visited during their stay on the western front in July, 1917. King George had bestowed the Order of the Royal Red Cross on the Queen of the Belgians for her splendid services among the wounded.

resources in the present great struggle for the cause of civilisation, I have, acting on the advice of My Ministers, deemed it necessary to enrol every able-bodied man between the ages of 18 and 41.

I desire to take this opportunity of expressing to My people My recognition and appreciation of the splendid patriotism and self-sacrifice which they have displayed in raising by voluntary enlistment since the commencement of the war no less than 5,041,000 men, an effort far surpassing that of any other nation in similar circumstances recorded in history, and one which will be a lasting source of pride to future generations.

I am confident that the magnificent spirit which has hitherto sustained My people through the trials of this terrible war will inspire them to endure the additional sacrifice now imposed upon them, and that it will, with God's help, lead us and our Allies to a victory which shall achieve the liberation of Europe.

GEORGE R.I.

In August, 1916, the King paid another visit to the front. The occasion was very different from before. His previous journeys had been, to a certain extent, visits of encouragement to armies that were resisting enemy attacks under very arduous conditions. Now he was going to an Army that had driven the Germans back. He was to stand on soil which, until a few weeks before, had been held by the Germans, and was to go over line **Third visit to the front** after line of captured German trenches. The projected visit was kept a secret save from the leaders of the Army. The King landed at Boulogne on August 8th, and had seven days in which to see as much of the front as possible. After being received by the military governor of the town, and the representative of the President of the French Republic, he went on to General Headquarters, where he met Sir Douglas Haig and studied with him the whole British position. From there he travelled on, accompanied by the Prince of Wales, Lord Stamfordham, and a number of officers, past St. Pol away to the region of Souchez, where he looked across the valley to the German positions at Lens and upwards to the Vimy Ridge, still held by the German forces.

He was now in one of the most memorable and fiercely-contested fields of the war. Many scores of thousands of French and German dead lay roughly buried in the fields of the valley around him. Souchez itself was one of the most dreadful of ruins. Behind it were whole lines of broken

LEADERS OF THE WESTERN ALLIES.

King George and Queen Mary (right) in France in the summer of 1917, with M. Poincaré, President of the French Republic, and Madame Poincaré to the left. At the back, from left to right, are the Prince of Wales, Lord Bertie (British Ambassador to France), and Sir Douglas Haig.

villages, but little earlier the homes of some of the most prosperous peoples in France, apparently absolutely and irretrievably wrecked—the houses smashed to atoms—every door burnt and broken, every bush seared, the fields a waste, and the hillsides, with all the life on them, destroyed. Thence, looking up to Vimy Ridge, he could see how the Germans had occupied one of the strongest points of the whole front, the great ridge which dominated the country for a score of miles and from which they could take heavy toll of lives from our men below them. He may have discussed even then the plans by which our men some months later were to drive the enemy back.

On the battlefield of the Somme

From here the King visited a trench-mortar school, where he saw the work of high-explosive shells and rapid firing with the most modern guns.

On August 10th he visited the battlefield of the Somme. His car travelled past Amiens towards Albert. On the sides of the road he could see the camps of the German prisoners who had been taken by our men. Farther on still he passed through Albert itself and drove under

BROUGHT DOWN BEHIND THE LINES. [*British official photograph.*
An incident of the tour of the western front in July, 1917. His Majesty was greatly interested in watching the operations of men of the Royal Flying Corps who were engaged at work on a wrecked aeroplane.

the hanging golden Virgin, the monster figure half dropping from the tower of the great church and looking as though it must come falling at any second on the passers-by below. From there he arrived, at midday amid the thunder of heavy artillery firing on the Germans, at a spot that had been specially chosen for him to get the best view of the entire fight. From that day it was named King George's Hill.

Those who imagine that kings are never allowed to go in the danger zones of war would certainly have returned wiser had they been with the King that day. The spot where the King went was, in the language of the Army, "a very warm place indeed." That very morning the enemy had been searching the ridge with heavy shells, as was his custom day after day.

As the King moved up to the front he passed over old trenches, then beside monster craters, made by the mine explosions with which the British had opened the attack. The whole country-side was one mass of shell-holes, sand-bags, craters, wire entanglements, and miscellaneous litter of war. The British labour battalions had worked magnificently clearing up and building fresh roads behind our

lines, but even they could not clear everything. There were parapets for the King to climb, trenches to be jumped, deep pits to be negotiated, and wire entanglements to be crossed.

Once he reached the hill the King was able to see as wonderful a picture of war as man has ever gazed upon. The valleys behind him spat fire and thunder as the monster 15 in. guns concealed in them shrieked their messages of death. Almost under the King's feet was Mametz, taken by our infantry a short time before at the point of the bayonet, with every house in it recording the fierce struggle that had taken place there. In the woods to the left, where the Germans suspected the presence of our troops, there would be frequent bursts of flame and clouds of smoke as German shells exploded. On the horizon shells were bursting almost everywhere, and the roar of the artillery was awesome.

Here was Delville Wood—"Devil's Wood" as the soldiers called it—where British troops were at that moment engaged in a desperate fight.

King George stood in the midst of the old German trenches. He examined with great interest the relics of war around. He noted a simple cross of the kind that is seen all over the front, with the inscription, "Here lies the body of an unknown British soldier." The King reverently saluted the grave. He went down into some of the old German dug-outs two stories deep, which had been captured. He examined the signs of luxury there—the fine wooden staircases, the well-arranged suites of rooms, the elaborate ventilating apparatus. "They know how to take care of themselves," said the King. "They evidently thought they were going to make a long stay." There was much for him to see had he set out to see it all.

The Army received him with the greatest enthusiasm. The men cheered him and showed their great delight in his presence, and also their delight in the presence of the Prince of Wales with him. One correspondent, who accompanied the King, reported an interesting incident. A big group of soldiers had met spontaneously to cheer the King as he left. In the midst of them was a battalion of the Northamptons, with their little mascot, Joseph Lefevre, a twelve-year-old Belgian boy, the son of a soldier, whom the regiment had adopted and placed on its enrolled strength. His father was wounded and a prisoner; his mother had been murdered by the German troops:

Originally he was found by some men of the Black Watch wandering round Ypres, and for a good many months now he has been with his present friends, who have put him in khaki and conferred upon him the rank of a lance-corporal. The King approached the Northamptons, who pushed the little boy in front of them. "I believe," said his Majesty, "I have found at last my youngest soldier. How old are you, my boy?" "Please, your Majesty," said a burly private of the regiment, who seemed to constitute himself the personal guard of the mascot, "he doesn't understand much English, though we're teaching him, but he speaks French." His Majesty accordingly interrogated him in the French language. "Do you like being a soldier?" the King asked. "Oui, Monsieur le Roi," replied the boy. "And do you think you will still like to be a soldier when you are grown up?" "Ah, but yes, Sir," was the answer in French, "I want to fight the Boches." "You are getting on," said the King, "I see they have made you a lance-corporal already. You will soon be a

A chat with a Belgian boy

King George on the summit of the Butte de Warlencourt, by the memorial to the gallant Durhams, who fell in November, 1916, in an attack on that hill to the south-west of Bapaume ; and (right) in a Canadian cemetery on Vimy Ridge.

His Majesty, with General Sir Arthur Currie, commanding the Canadian Forces (centre), and General Sir Henry Horne, traversing the famous Vimy Ridge. Right : The King inspecting representatives of the South African native labourers enlisted for work in France.

[British and Canadian official photographs.

A Royal greeting for the matron in charge of a military hospital on the western front ; and (right) his Majesty pauses for a chat with a heavily-equipped infantryman during his tour.

KING GEORGE'S VISIT TO HIS TROOPS IN FRANCE AND THE SCENES OF THEIR HEROISM, JULY, 1917.

general." The King expressed the hope that the men did not lead the boy into dangerous areas. "He's quite willing to go anywhere, your Majesty," said one of the men, "but we don't let him. When we are in the trenches we leave him with the transport."

The visit of the King was made the occasion for the bestowal of numerous decorations on French officers, and his Majesty also decorated a Territorial soldier, Private A. H. Proctor, of the Liverpool Regiment, with the Victoria Cross.

The King, on his way back after his memorable visit to the Somme, met the Australians, reviewed **Honour for Queen** them, and made **of the Belgians** a stay at the Anzac Headquarters. On the Friday he visited another district, inspecting, among others, a Scottish division of the South Africans. Travelling along, he passed a French village, whose broken and ancient houses were full of British troops. He went among them without any previous announcement, walked to and fro about the rooms crowded with resting men, and soldiers started up from their sleep to find their King looking at them.

He went through Arras, at that time a very dangerous city, where German shells were constantly falling and increasing the area of ruin. Going onwards he got to a casualty clearing-station and passed a regiment of Manchester men marching along the hot summer road. The King's car, with the Royal Standard at its head, attracted their attention. "The King!" the word went round. "Blest if it isn't the King!"

On the Saturday the King was largely engaged with departmental chiefs in examination of the routine organisation of the Army. Then, accompanied by Sir Douglas Haig, he made a visit to the French Mission, where he met President Poincaré and General Joffre with their suites, and the whole party lunched together in intimate domestic fashion. On the Sunday the King, after attending church and reviewing a division of Welsh troops, met the King and Queen of the Belgians, and decorated a number of Belgian soldiers. One honour which he bestowed that day is worthy of special note. It was the Order of the Royal Red Cross for the Queen of the Belgians, whose splendid service in trench, in camp, among the wounded, and among the needy of her people had given her higher rank than her title of Queen, for it had placed her among the eminent women of the world of all ages. That Sunday the King inspected a large section of the Belgian Army on the sea-beach near La Panne.

On the Monday he went south again, down to the Ypres salient. It was not thought wise that he should go into Ypres itself, for the town was at that time being

LIEUT.-COL. THE MARQUIS OF CAMBRIDGE.
Brother of Queen Mary, who before June, 1917, was known by the German territorial title of Duke of Teck.

PRINCE MAURICE OF BATTENBERG.
Cousin of King George. Died of wounds received in action in October, 1914.

LORD LEOPOLD OF MOUNTBATTEN.
Cousin of King George, known before June, 1917, as Prince Leopold of Battenberg.

THE MARQUIS OF MILFORD HAVEN.
Until June, 1917, known as Prince Louis of Battenberg. First Sea Lord of the Admiralty when the war broke out.

constantly heavily bombarded. He went among the artillery while it was "strafing" the German lines. From there he returned home, after as close and thorough an inspection of the actual fighting work of the Army as could be imagined. Before his return he sent to Sir Douglas Haig a General Order to the Army, which ran as follows:

OFFICERS, N.C.O.'S, AND MEN.

It has been a great pleasure and satisfaction to me to be with my Armies during the past week. I have been able to judge for myself of their splendid condition for war and of the spirit of cheerful confidence which animates all ranks, united in loyal co-operation to their Chiefs and to one another.

Since my last visit to the front there has been almost uninterrupted fighting on parts of our line. The offensive recently begun has since been resolutely maintained by day and by night. I have had opportunities of visiting some of the scenes of the later desperate struggles, and of appreciating to a slight extent the demands made upon your courage and physical endurance in order to assail and capture positions prepared during the past two years and stoutly defended to the last.

I have realised not only the splendid work which has been done in immediate touch with the enemy—in the air, under ground, as well as on the ground—but also the vast organisations behind the fighting-line, honourable alike to the genius of the initiators and to the heart and hand of the workers. Everywhere there is proof that all, men and women, are playing their part, and I rejoice to think their noble efforts are being heartily seconded by all classes at home.

The happy relations maintained by my Armies and those of our French Allies were equally noticeable between my troops and the inhabitants of the districts in which they are quartered, and from whom they have received a cordial welcome ever since their first arrival in France.

Do not think that I and your fellow-countrymen forget the heavy sacrifices which the Armies have made and the bravery and endurance they have displayed during the past two years of bitter conflict. These sacrifices have not been in vain; the arms of the Allies will never be laid down until our cause has triumphed.

I return home more than ever proud of you. May God guide you to Victory.

GEORGE R.I.

Back in England the regular routine of work was renewed. There came long spells when, day after day, the King and Queen, or Queen Alexandra, or all of them, were kept busy with inspections and reviews of one kind and another. Now the Queen was appealing for continued support for her Needlework Guild, which up to this time had been the means of **Queen Mary and** distributing 3,990,784 **Queen Alexandra** garments. Soon afterwards Queen Alexandra was the central figure in an interesting and picturesque little ceremony at the India Office, when a silk Union Jack and silver shield, subscribed for by the women and children of the British Isles, were handed over by her Majesty to the India Office. Queen Alexandra also associated her name with the movement for the relief of the wives, children, and dependents of soldiers and sailors. She issued another appeal for " the

ROYAL SPECTATORS AT MILITARY SPORTS.
During a visit to an Aldershot military fete, King George and Princess Mary were greatly diverted at witnessing a blindfold drill competition. Immediately behind his Majesty is Lord Derby.

and for helping to create an improved Britain. It was undesirable for the King to intervene openly in discussions over the new Constitution of the Empire which men saw looming ahead, but it was not impossible for him to show in many ways his profound concern and interest in the development. Thus we find him visiting different sections of Imperial troops and showing great honour to the Imperial and Indian delegates who came to the Imperial War Conference. This Imperial War Conference, a new thing in the history of the Empire, concluded its sittings by a gathering at Windsor Castle. The conference decided on great things. It had virtually pledged the Empire to Imperial preference. It had voiced the decision to maintain a self-supplying Empire. It had—perhaps most important of all— **The Imperial War** decided to admit India and the Indians **Conference** into partnership in the Imperial Commonwealth, not as a subject race, but with equal rights with white men. In the Green Drawing-room at Windsor the King, surrounded by the Queen and members of his family, received the members of the conference in state. Sir Robert Borden, the Premier of the Dominion of Canada, whose prudence and statesmanlike conduct and speech had played so large a part in helping to mould the work of the conference, read an address to his Majesty emphasising that the fruits of victory must not be lost by unpreparedness in peace, and that an unscrupulous enemy must not be allowed to repeat his outrages upon civilisation.

Then the King replied. He expressed his utmost satisfaction that the Indian representatives had sat with the others with equal rights. His Majesty said :

Your present gathering is a giant stride on the road of progress and Imperial development.

KING GEORGE AT ALDERSHOT.
His Majesty chatting with Lord Derby at Aldershot. From the time of his inspection of the original British Expeditionary Force, in 1914, the King paid many visits to his troops in training on the famous ground.

brave sailors and soldiers who have fallen into the hands of the enemy and are now prisoners of war in foreign lands. Our thoughts are with them at all times. . . . It is our bounden duty to do everything that is possible to alleviate their sufferings."

The King and Queen helped personally in many schemes for our soldiers. Thus, one part of Buckingham Palace was used to house soldiers and sailors who arrived at Victoria Station from the front and had nowhere to go. In mid-December the King and Queen visited a metropolitan military post-office to see for themselves how the Christmas parcels and letters were sent to the troops abroad. There were so many affairs of State to keep him busy that the King, for the first time since the outbreak of the war, found it impossible to leave **Christmas Day in** London for Christmas. Accordingly, **a hospital** Christmas Day, 1916, was spent at Buckingham Palace. In the afternoon their Majesties, accompanied by Princess Mary, Prince Henry, and Prince George, visited the King George Military Hospital in Stamford Street, vast premises originally built for the new Stationery Office, but transformed into an enormous war hospital. It would have been too much for the whole party to visit every ward, so the King and Queen and their children visited different wards. Every patient was presented with a copy of a charitable gift-book that had been named after Queen Mary, " Queen Mary's Gift Book." Some men who were occupying beds which had been given by the King and Queen were presented with photographs of their Majesties.

Among the events in which the King and Queen took a leading part in the early days of 1917 were the activities for the shaping of the new Imperial policy of the Empire,

The magnificent contributions in men, munitions, and money made by all parts of my Empire have been a source of the greatest pride and satisfaction to me. Vast armies raised in the Dominions have taken, or are taking, the field side by side with those of the United Kingdom to fight the common foe in the cause of justice and of those free institutions which are the very keystone of my Empire. It is fitting also that I should specially refer to the munificent gifts of money made towards the expenses of the war by the Government, Princes, and peoples of India.

The Queen and I recall with the liveliest and happiest recollections the visits which we have been privileged to pay to the different parts of my Dominions. I look forward to the day when some of our children will in their turn have an opportunity of acquiring similar priceless experience by such visits. I rejoice in the prospect of better means of communication which will more effectively link up the various portions of my Empire. For do not sympathy and common brotherhood help to form the surest foundations on which a State can rest?

The Maharaja of Bikanir and the other Indian delegates let their loyalty be known in no uncertain way. Their sentiments were widely appreciated, for the overwhelming sentiment among the people was one of trust and confidence in the King. This was specially marked in the days immediately following the Russian Revolution, when the Tsar of Russia lost his throne. Many people anticipated that there would be a wave of republicanism over Europe which would submerge all thrones. One English publicist, Mr. H. G. Wells, wrote a letter, which created very considerable controversy, advocating the formation of a republican society. Mr. Wells's action aroused the most vigorous protest, so much so that he was eager to explain that he was not thinking of a republic in place of our present monarchy. The hour of stress and strain following the Russian revolt made it clear how firmly the monarchy was planted in the affections of the people of the Empire of all races and colours.

There was one point, however, upon which public opinion was making itself felt. The resentment which had grown up against the German nation because of its atrocities during the war led to a keen desire that our princes should not retain German titles of honour, and that the ancient, **German titles** close association between the German **abandoned** and the British Royal Houses should not be renewed. Something had been done early in the war by the removal of the German Emperor's name from the Order of the Garter. The King, recognising the public feeling, formally ordered the discontinuance by different members of the Royal Family of their German titles, gave them instead marquisates and earldoms in the United Kingdom, and further, limited the title of prince and princess to the second generation from the Throne.

A correspondent of the "Times," who declared himself a firm believer in the principles of monarchy, especially of the British Empire, uttered a warning which was very seriously regarded concerning the future of the Prince of Wales, whose marriage had already been a subject of frequent discussion. He said that the history of the war in Greece, in Bulgaria, and in Russia—to name the instances details of which were only common knowledge—showed the danger to national policy and national liberty of kings who, in one way or another, were related to the German Royal circle.

A feeling seems growing in prevalence and in strength that the risk to their people's welfare of monarchs whose spiritual home is Berlin is too great to be borne, and the principle of monarchy **Future of the Prince of Wales** itself has now come to be criticised on that ground. It seems to me that the best way to meet and turn this drift of opinion is to show that the whole trouble arises from the comparatively modern and characteristically German idea of a separate Royal caste. Not many centuries ago kings often chose mates for themselves or for their sons from among the daughters of their own nobility. Thus the Royal House became truly a part of the nation. Let the Ministers in every Constitutional country advise their Sovereign to revert to this healthy custom when the time comes to find a wife for the Heir to the Throne. The real danger which is now in men's minds will then disappear. The inconveniences of the arrangement are, of course, obvious; but they are of little account compared with the peril of foreign influence in high places. By the action I suggest the interests of a truly national dynasty can be safeguarded, and the criticism to which I have referred will be fairly met.

The King shared to the full the anxiety of his subjects over the growing scarcity of food in the spring and early summer of 1917. The Royal House asked for no special treatment from the rest of the country. The King had, from the beginning of the war, made a definite end of the elaboration of luxury and state which naturally tends to grow up around a monarch. The stately Royal footmen had gone, most of them into the ranks of the Army, and several had distinguished themselves there by gallantry in the field. The Royal table would have been scorned by some of the King's middle-class subjects; not only were there no wines and spirits, but the daily food was simple and plain. Now the King went beyond even this. He and his household went on rations, the same amount of bread, the same amount of meat as allowed to their humblest subjects—4 lb. of bread and 2½ lb. of meat per person per week.

On May 10th the King issued a proclamation exhorting the nation to practise the greatest economy and frugality in the use of every species of grain, to reduce the consumption of bread, and to abstain from the use of flour in pastry. The text of the proclamation, so far as it was concerned with this subject of economising in the use of grain stuffs, was as follows:

ROYAL INVESTITURE ON BOARD SHIP.
King George investing Admiral Pakenham with the K.C.B. on board a battle-cruiser. During his visit to the Fleets in June, 1917, the King held investitures on board—a ceremony which the Navy had not seen since George III. conferred an earldom on Lord Howe, at Spithead, after "the Glorious First of June."

By the King.

A Proclamation.

GEORGE R.I.

WE, being persuaded that the abstention from all unnecessary consumption of grain will furnish the surest and most effectual means of defeating the devices of Our enemies, and thereby of BRINGING THE WAR TO A SPEEDY AND SUCCESSFUL TERMINATION, and out of Our resolve to leave nothing undone which can contribute to these ends or to the WELFARE OF OUR PEOPLE IN THESE TIMES OF GRAVE STRESS AND ANXIETY, have thought fit, by and with the advice of Our Privy Council, to issue this OUR ROYAL PROCLAMATION, most earnestly exhorting and charging all those of Our loving subjects the men and women of Our realm who have the means of procuring articles of food other than wheaten corn, as they tender their own immediate interests, and feel for the wants of others, especially TO PRACTISE THE GREATEST ECONOMY AND FRUGALITY IN THE USE OF EVERY SPECIES OF GRAIN, and We do for this purpose more particularly exhort and charge all heads of households

Royal Proclamation on food economy

TO REDUCE THE CONSUMPTION OF BREAD IN THEIR RESPECTIVE FAMILIES BY AT LEAST ONE-FOURTH OF THE QUANTITY CONSUMED IN ORDINARY TIMES.

TO ABSTAIN FROM THE USE OF FLOUR IN PASTRY and moreover carefully TO RESTRICT OR WHEREVER POSSIBLE TO ABANDON THE USE THEREOF IN ALL OTHER ARTICLES THAN BREAD * * *

GIVEN AT OUR COURT AT BUCKINGHAM PALACE THIS SECOND DAY OF MAY IN THE YEAR OF OUR LORD ONE THOUSAND NINE HUNDRED AND SEVENTEEN AND IN THE SEVENTH YEAR OF OUR REIGN.

GOD SAVE THE KING.

The King now had an allotment of his own at Windsor. His subjects were being urged to increase cultivation of food; he would take his own part in the work. And so it became an understood rule of the Royal Household that King and Queen and any Royal guests would definitely work at some form of food production or food distribution. It was a regular thing for guests to divide themselves after their midday meal into two groups, one group going off to help to serve munition workers with food, and the other group going off to dig at the allotment. Both the King and the Queen dug as heartily and as thoroughly as anyone.

When communal kitchens were opened in London and elsewhere Queen Mary took the most active share in planning them. She was assisted in this by Princess Mary,

THE KING ON BOARD A MINE-SWEEPING TRAWLER.

On June 24th, 1917, after the investiture on the flagship of the Grand Fleet, his Majesty went on board two of the trawlers engaged in mine-sweeping in the North Sea, and expressed warm appreciation of the work that had been done by this new branch of the naval Service. Above, with Admiral Beatty, he is seen about to go aboard one of these vessels, and, in the smaller photograph, on the mine-sweeper's deck. E

THE KING AND THE ADMIRAL OF HIS GRAND FLEET.
King George on his visit to the Grand Fleet in June, 1917, with Admiral
Sir David Beatty, who had been appointed to the chief command of
that Fleet in succession to Sir John Jellicoe, in November, 1916, when
Sir John Jellicoe became First Sea Lord of the Admiralty.

now rapidly emerging from girlhood to womanhood. Princess Mary was as keen to help as her mother. She gave in herself a lesson of simplicity of dress to the girls among whom she worked. The princess's plain-cut coat and skirt and black curly-brimmed sailor-hat became very familiar in many industrial quarters.

The Queen and Princess Mary went to the public kitchens. First they visited the store-rooms and larders. The Queen addressed herself to these not so much as a Queen as a good housewife. Then she would stand at the distributing counters talking with the women and children, finding out the actualities of their life, seeing poverty at first-hand, not dressed and decked for the occasion, but as it really was. And as the children came

Queen Mary visits public kitchens up to the princess asking for their "Penn'orth of pudding, miss," or as the overworked mothers talked informally with the Queen about their home needs, of their husband who had died at the war, of the child ill with-fever, of the difficulties of making both ends meet with food at its high prices, the Crown and its humblest subjects came perhaps closer together than they had been for generations.

In some of the poorer districts visited by the Queen the matrons and hospital workers thought to interest her by bringing into prominence the prettiest and most attractive of their young patients. Thus at one hospital, where there were a number of children, the matron and her staff picked out the nicest-looking children, dressed them in the best they could find, and put them forward for the Queen to notice. As the Queen walked round the ward

she apparently did not see these nicely-dressed children at all; probably she saw through the little plan at once. She went straight beside the cots of some of the worst cases, inquired closely about them, and, turning to the King, quoted something that had happened at one time in the Royal nurseries as illustrating what was the matter with the children. She picked out every bad case in the hospital for her personal attention, and her homely, sound common-sense concerning them left matron and staff amazed.

The Queen was also a very active worker in the Baby Week Campaign in July, 1917, an attempt at the improvement of conditions of child-life throughout the country. She opened the exhibition connected with this at the Central Hall, Westminster, on July 2nd, and talked informally for some time with the mothers of the poor who had brought their children, and with the workers. There were large numbers of mothers there, and scarcely one of them failed to attract the Queen's attention to her children and to get a few cheery and practical words from her. The mothers of the poor streets of Westminster and South London soon found that the Queen was not alone Queen but a mother like themselves, and a mother with plenty of knowledge of childish ways and childish ills, ready to impart her knowledge to her poorest sisters.

In the middle of May, 1917, considerable anxiety was felt over a certain amount of unrest evident in munition centres. The working classes of Great Britain had, on the whole, done magnificently in the war. There, had been, it is true, a few organised labour troubles on the Clyde, in South Wales, and elsewhere, but these were the rare exceptions. Trade unions had temporarily surrendered, for the purpose of the better conduct of the war, many hardly-earned privileges. They had agreed to the dilution of labour; they had allowed women and unskilled workers to come in on what **King George in touch** were hitherto the skilled men's jobs; **with Labour** they had in most cases surrendered the right to strike; and they had consented to speeding up output in a way contrary to all their traditions. What is more, there was not a labour centre that had not sent its multitudes of men as soldiers to the war, men who volunteered long before conscription came into force. Now, however, there were signs that labour was becoming restive. This restiveness was mainly due to two or three causes. The first was a suspicion that the employers intended to use war conditions to establish regulations permanently unfavourable to Labour; another was a feeling that the employers were making undue profits; but perhaps the greatest cause of all was the conviction, widely spread among the workers, that a number of speculators were forcing the prices of necessary supplies up, and were making fortunes out of the hard-earned money of the working classes. Mr. Lloyd George, the Prime Minister, was quick to recognise this, and set about reorganising the machinery of Government to get control of the profiteers. The King himself had many means of learning facts.

He was in touch with Labour. He repeatedly received Labour leaders and others at Buckingham Palace, and encouraged them to talk quite freely and openly to him. It may well be imagined that the Queen, too, in her visits down poor streets learnt much of what the poor were feeling. And so, while the Government was attempting to remove the causes of trouble, the King and Queen made a tour among the workers of the North to encourage them to keep on at their work of munition production.

The King's visit to the North was considered by many who thought themselves best acquainted with the feelings there as a somewhat bold measure. Timid employers and directors whispered to themselves that there might be hostile demonstrations; in this they little knew the real feelings of the people. The head of one great firm telegraphed to London that his men were coming out

In June, 1917, the King spent five days in the lonely and stormy Northern waters, where the Grand Fleet, with its multitudinous auxiliaries, lay waiting for the call to action. Above: His Majesty aboard one of the larger vessels.

Officers being presented to the King. For the first time since 1794 there was an investiture at sea, Sir David Beatty receiving the G.C.B., Admirals Evan-Thomas and Pakenham the K.C.B., and Admirals Madden and Sturdee the K.C.M.G.

Camera souvenirs of the King's visit to the Grand Fleet in June, 1917.

A picturesque ceremony on each ship inspected by the King during his visit to the Grand Fleet was the march-past. As the men went by to the musi of the ship's band they saluted and gave " Eyes left ! "

His Majesty walking between lines of bluejackets and lascars on board the Plassy, the P. and O. liner which had been converted into a hospital-ship. The coolies gave the King a typically Oriental welcome on his arrival.

East and West join in a cordial salute to the Sailor King.

Going below. The King made a thorough examination of what was then one of the latest of the British submarines, a vessel which was an object of very special interest to the whole Fleet. Its novel features included a bath-room for the officers.

Returning to the flagship from the submarine. Admiral Sir David Beatty, Prince Albert, the King's sailor son, and officers of the Staff are standing at the foot of the ladder by which the King is making the ascent.

His Majesty inspects a 1917 type of British submarine.

The King chats with a cabin-boy of the Plassy.

His Majesty and some " old shipmates."

A handshake with a Japanese naval attaché.

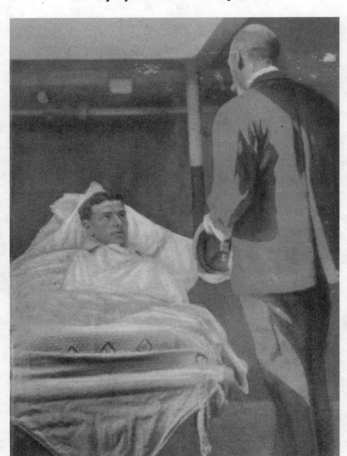

In the sick-bay of the hospital-ship Plassy.

A chat with a cabin-boy and a greeting for " old shipmates."

on strike, and he very earnestly advised that the King's visit to his works should be postponed. There came an answer promptly back that the King was going to visit the place, strike or no strike; and he did. The workmen, when they heard that the King was really coming, agreed among themselves to keep the dispute with their employers over until the King had come and gone, and they gave his Majesty the greatest of receptions.

The King and Queen began their week's tour at Chester on Monday, May 14th, by an early-morning visit to some munition works. They were welcomed by 3,000 munition girls, and spent two hours going over a monster factory which had been built up since the war. The King gave up his cigarette-case and matches, and took off his spurs as he entered the factory. From here they went on to Chester Castle, and then to some other works. Decorations were bestowed, prominent trade unionist representatives were received, and a busy day concluded with an inspection of the Transport Workers Battalion at Birkenhead, a steamer trip down and across the Mersey, and an examination of a Dockers Battalion at work. Tuesday was devoted to Liverpool and Manchester. The King went over several works, and the Queen over others.

When the King was at the docks he went on board several vessels, including two American armed liners, and the crews heartily responded to their commanders' call, " Three cheers for the King of England!" Among other things that the Queen saw was a monster canteen, where 8,000 girls were seated. They were waiting for their meal when the Queen came, and as she entered they rose and sang the National Anthem. A choir of Lancashire lasses then sang a verse from " Land of Hope and Glory," the whole of the vast body of girls joining in. At Manchester there were still more works to be seen, **Royal visits to** and on the Wednesday the King **the North** devoted considerable time to the monster factory of the British Westinghouse Company at Trafford Park. Here, as at other places, the King went freely among the workers. He asked them about their difficulties and about their troubles. " I hope you will remain at your work," he told them frankly, "for the nation needs all the service that every one of us can give."

The reception of the King and Queen seemed to grow more and more enthusiastic day by day, if that were possible. After leaving Manchester on Wednesday the King telegraphed to the Lord Mayor that the reception of the Queen and himself in that city would ever be a memorable occasion to them. At Lancaster cheering crowds filled the streets. On Thursday the King and Queen were at the great shipyards of Messrs. Vickers at Barrow, shipyards covering two hundred and seventy acres, and employing 35,000 people. Here a big strike had been threatened, and only on the previous evening had the engineers decided by ballot against coming out. Those who knew said that it was the King's visit which had been the main factor in preventing the strike. The King looked out for the shop stewards, the real organisers of the strike troubles, and urged on them, as man speaking to man, the importance of everyone keeping at his work. Friday found the party in Sunderland, Stockton-on-Tees, and the great shipbuilding districts.

This tour in May was followed by another in June to the Tyne, Tees, Wear, and Humber.

The main features of every visit were much the same. The King and Queen got among the workers; they used the opportunity to decorate in person people in localities who had done good war service. Wounded and broken soldiers were visited by them. The Queen examined the schemes of charitable relief in the districts, particularly schemes connected with the benefit of child-life. The King went among the men. Never in the records of the British monarchy had King and Queen striven so systematically and so thoroughly to bring themselves into

KING GEORGE GREETS THE HERO OF THE FALKLANDS.
His Majesty talking to Admiral Sir Doveton Sturdee during his visit to the Grand Fleet. Admiral Sturdee received the K.C.M.G. at the first of the investitures which the King held while with the Fleets in 1917.

direct touch with the people of the land, not by taking part in spectacular displays or presiding over big functions, but by going down among them and mixing freely together.

One welcome relief from the somewhat drab and wearisome monotony of the visits to factories, workshops, shipyards, and hospitals was the open-air investiture held by his Majesty on Saturday, June 2nd, in Hyde Park. It was the first thing of the kind that had been held for many years. Three hundred sailors and soldiers and the relatives of fifty more men who had distinguished themselves by special heroism were to have decorations bestowed upon them by the King in person.

Everything had been done that was possible to add to the dignity and splendour of the occasion. Nature was at its best ; it was an ideal summer day, and Hyde Park had never looked **Investiture in** finer. The flowering trees were a blaze **Hyde Park** of colour, and the massed beds of flowers glowed in the sunlight. High overhead was a group of aeroplanes guarding the park against sudden attack from enemy machines. Tens of thousands of people crowded the public spaces, and everything was done that could be done to help them to see. In the reserved enclosure there was much that was of interest. Here was a group of American nurses, advance guard of the new America that was coming into the war ; here were children from an orphanage ; here a group of distinguished soldiers. The Guards' Bands swung into place, playing British and American airs, and when the King arrived the National Anthem crashed forth and the Royal Standard broke from the flag-post. There was one great burst of enthusiastic cheering from all the onlookers. Then followed a scene of simple, restrained pathos that touched every heart. The soldiers—officers and men—who had won their decorations were brought up before the King—some stricken men, some maimed, some lacking a limb, one sightless, who had to be led up to the presence.

Not that the scene was all sad. Far from it. Most of the heroes stepped to the fore straight and whole, glowing with natural pride. There were Britons, Canadians, and Australians, men of the sea and men of the land. First to come up was Major Henry Murray, of the Australian Infantry, whose valour had won him not only the D.S.O., but a bar to the Order and the Victoria Cross. Next came Major Forbes Robertson, of the Border Regiment, given the D.S.O. and the Military Cross. Men wanted fresh voices to cheer when the next two came, for they were the captains of the Swift and the Broke, who, unsupported, had attacked a fleet of six German destroyers in the Channel, sunk two of them, and put the other four to precipitate flight. Do you wonder that the people shouted as though they would rend the skies? And so they went on—V.C.'s, D.S.O.'s, Military Crosses, and Military Medals. One who came forward was a Scottish mother, Mrs. Elizabeth Erskine, who took the V.C. that had been earned by her son when he shielded the body of his officer with his own and brought him into safety. Then came a widow, whose husband, Thomas Mottershed, of the Royal Flying Corps, died of burns after bringing back his blazing aeroplane and saving the life of his observer. But perhaps the most thrilling moment of all was when an old, grey-haired man stepped up briskly to receive the V.C. won by his son, Private James Fynn, of the South Wales Borderers, at Sanna-i-Yat, in Mesopotamia. There were nurses and doctors decorated for their brave deeds. Then, when the three hundred and fifty had passed before him, when the King had had a handshake and conversation with nearly all of them, the decorated heroes gave a cheer for the King before he went back to his palace. London for once had been able to see something of the greatness of the Empire's heroes in this war.

On July 17th the King in Council, with representatives of the Dominions present, took a formal step which still further accentuated the determination of the British House to clear itself from all association with German Royalty. The title of the Royal Family was formally changed to "The House and Family of Windsor." All German titles and dignities were relinquished, and all members of the Royal Family were directed to discontinue the use of their German honours.

The name of Windsor was chosen because it is one that has been associated with the British Royal House for generations. Windsor Castle is the best known seat of the Sovereign. Since the days of William the Conqueror, British Kings have made it their home. The history of British Royalty is written in stone on its walls, and is revealed in its monuments, its tombs, and its statues. Kings had been born there, and kings have died there. It is the burial-ground of Tudors and Stuarts, of Queen Victoria and King Edward VII. "Cynics may regard the change as a matter of no importance," said the "Times," "but they are mistaken. His Majesty has been better advised. It is not wisdom, but folly, to ignore the influence of sentiment in the populace. More than anything else it binds the Empire together, and the war has demonstrated the strength of the bonds by proofs which no man can gainsay or belittle. The King has known well how to gratify the patriotic sentiment of all the British peoples which centres in the Crown, in this as in other things."

The King's proclamation is one of great historic interest:

A PROCLAMATION

Declaring that the Name of Windsor is to be Borne by His Royal House and Family and Relinquishing the Use of All German Titles and Dignities. GEORGE R.I.

Whereas We, having taken into consideration the Name and Title of Our Royal House and Family, have determined that henceforth Our House and Family shall be styled and known as the House and Family of Windsor:

And whereas We have further determined for Ourselves and for and on behalf of Our descendants and all other the descendants of Our Grandmother Queen Victoria of blessed and glorious memory to relinquish and discontinue the use of all German Titles and Dignities:

And whereas We have declared these our determinations in Our Privy Council:

Now, therefore, We, out of Our Royal Will and Authority, do hereby declare and announce that as from the date of this Our Royal Proclamation Our House and Family shall be styled and known as the House and Family of Windsor, and that all the descendants in the male line of Our said Grandmother Queen Victoria who are subjects of these Realms, other than female descendants who may marry or may have married, shall bear the said name of Windsor:

And do hereby further declare and announce that We for Ourselves and for and on behalf of Our descendants and all other the descendants of Our said Grandmother Queen Victoria who are subjects of these Realms, relinquish and enjoin the discontinuance of the use of the Degrees, Styles, Dignities, Titles, and Honours of Dukes and Duchesses of Saxony and Princes and Princesses of Saxe-Coburg and Gotha, and all other German Degrees, Styles, Dignities, Titles, Honours and Appellations to Us or to them heretofore belonging or appertaining.

Given at Our Court at Buckingham Palace, this Seventeenth day of July, in the year of our Lord One thousand nine hundred and seventeen, and in the Eighth year of Our Reign.

GOD SAVE THE KING.

The end of June witnessed a visit of the King to his Grand Fleet in the North. In the days immediately before the war, as told in the opening of this chapter, he inspected the Grand Fleet at Spithead. To those who were present nearly three years before, the contrast between the two occasions was very striking. In July, 1914, the attention of all had been concentrated on the great grey monsters, Dreadnoughts and super-Dreadnoughts, the mightiest vessels the world had ever known. In June, 1917, even the super-Dreadnoughts of 1914 had been outdone. Among the ships that the King saw before him on this occasion were ships of a new type, with the speed of a battle-cruiser and the arms and armament of a super-Dreadnought.

In 1914 the submarine had been a minor factor. In 1917 the King saw in the submarine, which had grown in size and equipment out of all knowledge, a predominant weapon in naval warfare. The great ships that had expected to engage in hard fighting when war broke out had many of them been in no fighting at all, but had been obliged to wait for close on three years for their enemy to come out. There were some ships proudly concealing their battle scars. Some that had sailed majestically past the King at Spithead were now lying low in the depths of the North Sea. But the King found his Navy —under conditions far different from and far more difficult than those most had expected—the same faithful and watchful guardian of the seas that it had ever been.

Early in July, 1917, the King paid another visit to France, this time accompanied by the Queen. A very elaborate programme had been arranged for both of them. They arrived together at a French port on July 3rd. After lunch the King proceeded to the front, the Prince of Wales accompanying him, while the Queen undertook a series of visits behind the lines. Even among all the varied experiences of his momentous reign the days that followed must have been as crowded with interest as any the King had known. Almost every hour was full. There were large sections of our own advanced lines to be traversed. First the King visited Messines, where a month before General Plumer's army had won its brilliant victory. Later on he went to Vimy Ridge where, accompanied by General Currie, the commander of the Canadian Army Corps, he visited the memorable heights of the great ridge won back by the Canadians on April 9th.

From this ridge, amid the shell-craters, he could see far below, stretched out like a great panorama, a wonderful vision of war. From the red-brick houses of Lens to the left, Avion, and then a succession of mining villages, ruined factories, and country-houses, the rival lines stretched out away in a great arc towards Arras. In the distance could be seen on fine days the towers of the churches of Douai. All along the front fighting was in active progress. The guns were at work, the batteries far behind were keeping up their steady fire, the aircraft were sailing amid bursts of exploding shrapnel, and the infantry were waiting in their trenches.

The King visited some of the towns behind the lines. Everywhere he was among his own men. In the course of those few days he saw and talked to soldiers from every part of the Empire—British regiments that had borne the heat and burden of the day all along the line; Australians and New Zealanders who had done so splendidly at Messines; Canadians who had won **King and Queen in France** Vimy, and who were now going through some of the hardest experiences of war in the valley on the further side of the ridge; South Africans, Newfoundlanders, and labour battalions of Zulus, Basutos, and Chinamen from our Far Eastern settlements. The King was constantly and of necessity within the zone of fire. No one could visit districts like Vimy and Messines without going within the range of the enemy guns, and it must have been with

considerable relief that his Ministers heard of his safe return.

The new methods of war shown to the King would have made many soldiers of even three years before open their eyes with astonishment. He spent one morning studying the new arts of disguise. At the beginning of the war the British Army knew little of "camouflage," as it is called. The Germans hid their snipers in the woods, so carefully dressed that it was almost impossible to distinguish them. **The art of "camouflage"** Our men went out as a rule in their regular uniforms—and went out to death. But we had learned since then. Our Army authorities had called in artists and sculptors and masters of colour. They had planned dresses which allowed the sniper to go right up to the enemy lines and scarcely be seen. When lying still he seemed to be part of the country around him. Dummy figures were moulded so like life that men could be deceived by them even a few yards away. The artists elaborated colour schemes by which the roofs of houses could be so speckled and splashed that spying aircraft overhead could not tell them from the country-side itself.

The King studied some of the methods of underground war, carefully guarded secrets from the enemy. He was given an exhibition of the employment of poison gas and of the use of the latest form of flame-thrower, built on the most approved German model. He saw the use of smoke barriers. Above all, he obtained opportunities

IMPRESSIVE FAREWELL SCENE ON A BATTLE-CRUISER.

His Majesty, in the foreground at the salute, acknowledging the hearty cheers of the massed crew of one of the battle-cruisers on the conclusion of his visit in June, 1917, to that section of the Fleet. The visit was a memorable one, and in a message of congratulation to Sir David Beatty, his Majesty said, " Never has the British Navy stood higher in the estimation of friend and foe. You can assure all ranks and ratings under your command that their brothers throughout the Empire rely upon them with pride and confidence to defend our shores and commerce."

of seeing our airmen at work. He spent some hours with them, and they were around him most of the time, whole squadrons of them in the air, performing the most amazing evolutions, as he went to and fro. Then came great parades and sham fights, when armies by land and the armies in the air combined in their work. At Messines he was given an admirable example of the wonderful work of the railway construction men, for right up in the spot that had been German trenches a month before a light railway was now laid, and a miniature train was waiting to carry him along the line.

Another remarkable display was made by the newest form of "tanks," which lurched and bucked in front of him, and moved through the woods and other rough country, sweeping obstacles aside and **King's speech to** going through trenches and across **S.A. labour corps** trenches such as vehicles surely never faced before. One notable occasion was when the King inspected a number of men of the African Labour Contingent. These men, including members of the families of some of the leading chiefs, made a fine appearance, dressed in blue cavalry coats and wide-brimmed hats. The King, accompanied by Sir Douglas Haig, passed slowly down their lines, asking various questions. Then he spoke to them :

I have much pleasure in seeing you who have travelled so far over the sea to help in this great war. I take this opportunity of thanking you and your comrades for the work done in France by the South African Labour Corps. Reports have been given me of the valuable services rendered by the natives of South Africa to my Armies in German South-West Africa and German East Africa. The loyalty of my native subjects in South Africa is fully shown by the helpful part you are taking in this world-wide war. Rest assured that all you have done is of great assistance to my Armies at the front. This work of yours is second only in importance to that of my sailors and soldiers, who are bearing the brunt of the battle.

But you also are part of my great Armies which are fighting for the liberty and freedom of my subjects of all races and creeds throughout the Empire. Without munitions of war my Armies cannot fight. Without food they cannot live. You are helping to send these things to them each day, and in doing so you are hurling your assagais at the enemy and hastening the destruction which awaits him. A large corps such as yours requires drafts and reinforcements, and I am sure your chiefs will take upon themselves this duty of supporting your battalions with ever-increasing numbers. I wish them and all their peoples to share with all my loyal subjects that great and final victory which will bring peace throughout the world. I desire you to make these words of mine known to your people here, and to convey them to your chiefs in South Africa.

Immediately following this inspection the President of the French Republic with Madame Poincaré arrived. The King and Queen and the President and his wife had an informal luncheon together. Later on in the visit the King met General Pétain, the Commander of the French Army, when he was farther south revisiting the Somme battleground. The King and general had luncheon together in the heart of a town that had felt the full fury of German hate. Afterwards, in the **Royal investiture** great square surrounded by the wrecked **at the front** buildings, an investiture was held. Our troops were paraded on three sides of the square. On the fourth side were marquees with open sides. In the centre of these was the King ; on one side of him were those who were to receive honours, and on the other the Royal party. The first honour to be bestowed was a G.C.B. on General Pétain. Decorations for other French generals followed, and then others for British officers. Among those knighted here was General Currie, recently appointed to the command of the Canadian Army Corps.

The King went through many ruined towns and villages. He saw whole stretches of country-side recovered from the enemy, but reduced by them before their departure to absolute wreck. He saw districts with every tree cut down and every house smashed up. He saw ancient cities that had been deliberately burned by the enemy,

street by street, house by house, before their departure. He saw the worst that Germany could do, and he saw, too, that despite that worst, the Allies were moving on. Even in some of the places that they had left in complete ruin he already saw signs of newly-stirring life, of the revival of industry, of the recultivation of the ground, and of the beginnings of the uprising of a new France, phœnix-like, from the ashes of the invaded country.

During the first four days the King was alone, for the Queen was busy elsewhere. Afterwards she joined him. The Queen spent much of her time while alone visiting hospitals. She also witnessed a display of flame-projectors and an exhibition of flying. Accompanied by the Prince of Wales, she visited the old battlefield of Crécy, and the Prince stood on the exact spot where the Black Prince, close on six hundred years before, assumed the feathered crest hitherto worn by King John of Bohemia.

Before his departure the King issued the following message to the Army :

On the conclusion of my fourth visit to the British Armies in the Field, I leave you with feelings of admiration and gratitude for past achievements, and of confidence in future efforts.

On all sides I have witnessed the scenes of your triumphs.

The battlefields of the Somme, the Ancre, Arras, Vimy, and Messines have shown me what great results can be attained by the courage and devotion of all arms and services under efficient commanders and Staffs.

Nor do I forget the valuable work done by the various departments behind the fighting-line, including those who direct and man the highly-developed system of railways and other means of communication.

Your comrades, too—the men and women of the industrial army at home—have claims on your remembrance for their untiring service in helping you to meet the enemy on terms which are not merely equal, but daily improving.

It was a great pleasure to the Queen to accompany me, and to become personally acquainted with the excellent arrangements for the care of the sick and **King George's** wounded, whose welfare is ever close to her **message to the Army** heart.

For the past three years the Armies of the Empire and workers in the homelands behind them have risen superior to every difficulty and every trial.

The splendid successes already gained, in concert with our gallant Allies, have advanced us well on the way towards the completion of the task we undertook.

There are doubtless fierce struggles still to come and heavy strains on our endurance to be borne.

But be the road before us long or short, the spirit and pluck which have brought you so far will never fail, and, under God's guidance, the final and complete victory of our just cause is assured.

Their Majesties returned to Buckingham Palace on the evening of July 14th.

There was, in the early months of the war, an inclination on the part of some of his subjects to desire that the King should set out to rival the Kaiser as a spectacular figurehead of his people. As the months went on it became more and more clear, however, that his line of quiet service was one more in keeping with the national feeling and the national temperament. There was a time during the war when the King's advisers had kept him too much in the background, when they were over-nervous of publicity, when they failed to use as they might have used the facts about his work in such a way as to be most serviceable. There is always a natural tendency among the great to avoid new departures. This tendency was to some extent counteracted by the good sense and wide knowledge of the King himself. Quietly, steadily, unswervingly he stood at the head of the nation, showing by his every action even more than by his speeches that his deliberate and unflinching purpose to live through the hour of Britain's greatest trial as Britain's monarch should do. His one purpose was to lead a Britain true to herself and true to her greatest traditions to crowning victory. And even in the smoke, the din, the obscurity of war men could see outstanding the figure of their great monarch, who had avoided war so long as war could be avoided, but who, once he had taken the sword, held it with a strong hand to the end.

THE EMPEROR CHARLES

CHAPTER CXCIV.

INSPECTING GERMAN TROOPS.

LIFE IN AUSTRIA-HUNGARY DURING THE FIRST THREE YEARS OF THE WAR.

By Charles Lowe, M.A., formerly Berlin Correspondent of the "Times," author of "Prince Bismarck," "The German Emperor William II.," "Alexander III. of Russia," etc.

Antipathetic Races and Contending Religions of the Dual Monarchy—Dominant Influences—Dualism, Trialism, and Quadruplism—Leading Features of Government—The Austrian Reichsrath and Hungarian Parliament—Francis Joseph and Queen Victoria—Effect of the War on Popular Feeling in Vienna and Budapest—The Hearts of the Czechs—The Assassination of Stürgkh—Death of Francis Joseph—Character of the Emperor Charles—Changes in the Ministry—A Mediæval Coronation Ceremony—The Long Suspension of the Austrian Reichsrath—Crisis Follows Crisis—The New Emperor's Speech from the Throne—Count Clam-Martinitz—An Imperial Amnesty—Its Reception by Germans and Slavs—The German Kaiser and Kaiserin at the Laxenburg Palace—Czech Sympathy with Russia—The Surrender of Przemysl—German Domination—Effect of the War on Everyday Life.

BEFORE essaying the difficult, because necessarily indirect, task of constructing some sort of a picture of the internal life and condition of an enemy country like Austria-Hungary during the war, it may be as well to say something about the racial composition of this conglomerate Empire and the way in which it is ruled—an Empire (including Bosnia and Herzegovina) with an area of about 261,000 square miles and a population of over 51,000,000, as compared with the 66—or perhaps even 68—millions of Germany and the 45 millions souls of the United Kingdom.

But it is the variety and contrariety of the races forming the population of the Hapsburg Empire which have always made its government so extremely difficult. The map of Austria-Hungary is a piece of ethnographical patchwork. It is as if all the nations of Europe had flung their political parings into a common cauldron, whereunto Asia contributed some potent drug to make the mass ferment. The Magyars, for example, or dominant race in Hungary, are not of Indo-European, but Turanian origin, akin to the Turks, and perhaps also to the Finns. They were a nation of horsemen, of martial instincts, and it was from them that all other European nations derived the idea of their hussars.

In no other European country do we find such a variety of antipathetic races and contending religions:

Germans, Magyars, Rumanians, Czechs, Croats, Poles, Slovaks, Slovenes, Serbs, Ruthenes, Italians, Orthodox and Roman Catholics, Protestants, Jews, and Gipsies, with sub-divisions innumerable and shades of difference to infinity. The coat of many colours of Joseph the son of Jacob must have been drab in comparison with the parti-coloured Imperial mantle of Francis Joseph of Austria and his successor Charles.

Perhaps the nearest parallel to such a heterogeneous realm is our own conglomerate Empire of India, which has an area of over a million and three-quarter square miles—into which you could easily put fifteen times the British Isles—and a population of 315 millions as against 400 millions in Europe. "If the population," wrote General Sir O'Moore Creagh, V.C., Lord Kitchener's successor in India as Commander-in-Chief, "were uniform in character the task of government would be a comparatively easy one, but the absolute reverse is the case.

"There are complete variations in race, language, religion, and the degree of civilisation attained. India's teeming millions speak some 145 distinct tongues, and when we hear references to such a thing as Indian opinion we would do well to remember the multiplicity of languages and cautiously refrain from hasty acceptance of statements sheltered under that generalisation.

"There are in India many nations who are almost entirely unknown to one another, which is not surprising

THE EMPEROR CHARLES VIII. OF AUSTRIA.
Charles VIII., Emperor of Austria, succeeded to the throne of the Dual Monarchy on the death of the Emperor Francis Joseph on November 21st, 1916. He is here seen leaving Budapest after his coronation as King of Hungary, on December 30th, 1916.

AUSTRIAN LANDSTURM.
Men of the Landsturm leaving Vienna for the front. The Landsturm Reserve was formed of men from the ages of thirty-seven to forty-two, who had previously served with the Colours.

and then the Magyars, with over 10,000,000; so that these two races thus together form a considerable minority of the whole. Yet the Slavs of various kinds, who form throughout the Empire the bulk of the majority, are practically held in subjection by this Teuton-Magyar minority, by whom, in Lowland Scots phrase, they are " sair hauden doon." It is just as if the Irish race were somehow to impose its will on the inhabitants of Great Britain.

This most unnatural anomaly was at the bottom of all the political strife and party wrangling which distracted, embittered, and endangered the Dual Monarchy even in time of war—to an extent, indeed, as we shall afterwards see, which most seriously impaired its military power.

seeing that in length India, from Cape Comorin in the south to Chitral in the north, is over 2,000 miles. It is obvious, then, that no man can possibly know India."

Yet in spite of all the inherent difficulties of the British Raj, India has been more successfully ruled than Austria, which one may take to be testimony of the highest kind to the administrative genius of the Anglo-Saxon race. Consider the 145 distinct tongues and tribes of India as compared with the races of the Hapsburg monarchy, which may roughly be generalised as five—namely, Teutons, Magyars, Slavs of all kinds, Italians, and Rumanians. But now let us reduce them to their several component elements in tabular form, thus :

CAPTURE OF A DESERTER.
Austrian soldiers taking a comrade charged with desertion through a village. The various nationalities, willingly and unwillingly brought together under the power of the Dual Monarchy, rendered desertions or attempts at desertion a serious problem to the Army leaders on the different fronts.

	AUSTRIA.	HUNGARY.	BOSNIA.
Germans	9,950,266	2,037,435	22,968
Magyars (including 900,000 Jews)	10,974	10,050,575	6,443
Slavs ⎰ Czechs	6,435,983	⎱ —	7,045
Slovaks	—	⎰ 1,967,970	482
Poles	4,967,984	—	10,975
Ruthenes ..	3,518,854	472,587	7,431
Croats	783,334	⎰ 1,833,162	1,822,564
Serbs		⎱ 1,106,471	
Slovenes ..	1,252,940	—	3,108
Latins ⎰ Italians	768,422	27,307	2,462
⎱ Rumanians ..	275,115	2,949,032	608
Others	608,062	441,848	14,440
Total	28,571,934	20,886,387	1,898,526

51,356,847

Now, the outstanding feature of all this ethnical distribution is the fact that the dominating races—not in point of numbers, but of power and influence—are the German-speakers, with some 12,000,000 to their credit,

There is a little river, Leitha—not to be confounded, yet in some respects identical in soporific or hypnotic effect, with the Lethe of the nether world—which flows for some distance between Austria proper and Hungary, and so the German portion of the Dual Monarchy is known as Cis-Leithania, and the Hungarian or Magyar moiety as Trans-Leithania (on the analogy of Cæsar's Cis-Alpine and Trans-Alpine Gaul), the point of view being Rome in one case and Vienna in the other. This for readers who like to have obscure things simply explained to them. And now for the Dual Monarchy in the same way.

Dual it is in the sense that the Hapsburg Empire consists of two main administrative portions—Cis-Leithania, with its German-Slav elements, and Trans-Leithania, in which the dominating—which is not the same thing as numerically predominant—ingredient is Magyar, each being linked to the other by the golden nexus of the Crown, but otherwise enjoying Home Rule—nominal at least—to an extent that might even have satisfied the Irish

Nationalists. Thus the Empire is said to be based on a system of dualism.

But there are some who want trialism, not to speak of others who aim at something like quadruplism—if that is the correct word—and of these the former are the Czechs of Bohemia, Moravia, Silesia, and the Slovak districts in Hungary under the heel of the Magyars. These Czechs, forming, as they do, the largest and most cultured branch of the Slav race, clamour for the reconstitution of their ancient kingdom, from which the Princes of Wales derive their " Ich Dien " motto, which was that of the blind King John of Bohemia, who fell on the field of Crécy when opposed (on the French side) to Edward III. and his warrior son the Black Prince.

TRAVELLING HOSPITAL.
This ingenious Red Cross car of the Austrian Medical Staff was, in effect, a hospital in little, carrying six persons and all the boxes of medical stores seen in the foreground.

COLLECTING LOVE-GIFTS FOR THE AUSTRIAN TROOPS.
Waggons of the house-collecting service instituted by the Archduchess Zita, who became Empress on her husband's accession in November, 1916, for gathering " love-gifts " for the soldiers in the field and the wounded in Austrian hospitals. In 1915 gifts to the value of 4,500,000 crowns (about £180,000) were collected.

It was at Eger in Bohemia that Wallenstein, one of the foremost figures of the Thirty Years War, was assassinated by his Irish and Scottish officers. It was to Karlsbad and Marienbad in Bohemia that multitudes of valetudinarians annually flocked to woo the goddess at once of holiday, fashion, and health; it was in Bohemia, at Kolin and Königgrätz, where the Prussians of Frederick suffered their greatest defeat and those of William gained their greatest victory; it was from Bohemia that fine pottery and glassware were imported.

The Czechs desired the reconstitution of this Bohemia as a separate kingdom or commonwealth, with Prague for its capital, on a footing at least of independence as complete as that of the Hungarians.

There was even another analogous movement of the autonomous kind in the direction of a four-State system, or quadruplism, which should combine all the Jugo-Slavs (or Southern Slavs) into a homogeneous whole, corresponding to the ideal Bohemia of the Czechs. Opinions

varied as to the relation which this Jugo-Slav State should bear to the Hapsburg Empire, but the extremists advocated the formation of a " free and independent kingdom under the Karageorgevitch dynasty of Serbia, which should gather into one racial fold all the inhabitants of Serbia, Bosnia and Herzegovina, Montenegro, Croatia, and Slavonia, and to be called the ' Kingdom of the Serbs, Croats, and Slovenes,' of some 12,000,000 inhabitants, which would be a powerful bulwark against German aggression and an inseparable ally of all civilised States and peoples."

Delegates from all the Jugo-Slav provinces of Austria-Hungary, towards the end of the third year of the war, sat for six weeks in solemn conclave with the Serbian Premier at Corfu on the subject of this political creation, after which they visited the headquarters of the Serbian front in Macedonia, and were feasted by Prince Alexander.

The Archduke Franz Ferdinand, heir to the dual Crown, who fell a victim to the Southern Slavs at Serajevo, together with his morganatic wife, Countess Chotek, a Bohemian lady, was supposed **Government of the** to be favourable to the idea of trialism, **Dual Monarchy** and perhaps even to the wider " ism," such as was conceived before the war by the Jugo-Slavs; though all these schemes and outlooks were very much altered by the course of the war itself.

But now let us briefly explain how all these conflicting races and nationalities had been ruled before the war. The principle of Home Rule, as Mr. Gladstone once remarked, nowhere found more practical application than in Austria-Hungary, where each half of the Dual Monarchy had its own separate Parliament and Cabinet, nominally responsible to it for the management of its own affairs—that is to say, all affairs which did not fall within the fields of

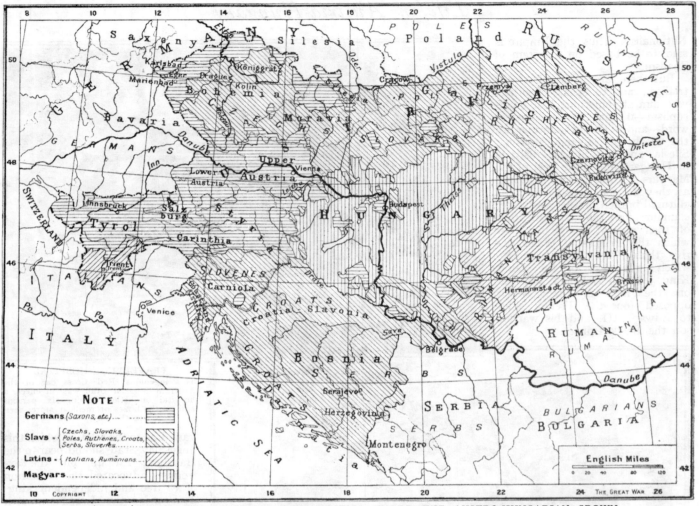

MAP INDICATING THE VARIOUS NATIONALITIES UNDER THE AUSTRO-HUNGARIAN CROWN.

foreign policy, defence, or finance, for which there were special Imperial Ministers common to both countries.

The provision of money for common objects was practically assigned to two special bodies called the "Delegations," each of sixty members, chosen by the two Chambers of each Parliament, and they met alternately at Vienna and Budapest. They were, in fact, Budget Committees of the two Legislatures, and, among other things, they saw to the payment of the Emperor-King's salary, or Civil List of £1,000,000, which was drawn in equal moities from the revenues of Austria and Hungary.

The Austrian Parliament, or Reichsrath (*i.e.* "Council of the Realm," while the German "Reichstag" means "Diet of the Realm," though their constitution and function were the same), consisted of two Houses, of which the Lower was elected for six years by universal, equal, and direct suffrage, as in Germany. The number of deputies was five hundred and sixteen, contributed in certain pro-

Constitution of the Reichsrath

portions by the seventeen provinces, each of which, for the rest, was endowed with a separate local Diet, or Assembly, which dealt with all matters not expressly reserved for the Reichsrath—local government, in fact, on a pretty extensive scale.

On the other hand, the Hungarian Parliament—of which the building fronting the Danube is perhaps the finest of its kind in Europe—was not quite so democratic in its composition and spirit as the sister assembly at Vienna. It consisted of a House of Magnates and one of popular representatives—four hundred and fifty-three—each of whom received about £270 a year, though the franchise was not of so large and free a kind as in Austria, and it was elected for five years. The official language was Magyar, though the deputies from Croatia and Slavonia might speak their own tongue, and these two provinces enjoyed a very considerable measure of Home Rule under the paramount power at Budapest.

The Parliament at Budapest, resting upon a corrupt franchise, was entirely oligarchic in its composition. In Hungary the working classes, the Magyar peasantry, and the ten millions of non-Magyars were almost entirely unrepresented; and thus the House could be relied upon to voice the wishes of those responsible for the war.

Such, then, in general outline, was the Constitution of what Mr. Lloyd George once contemptuously and truly characterised as "a ramshackle Empire."

Perhaps that was one of the bitterest taunts directed from Great Britain at Austria during the war; but, after all, there was no Austrian poet to emulate and surpass the German Lissauer's "Hymn of Hate," with its foaming-at-the-mouth venom against England and all her ways. Neither, on the other hand, did the British Press indulge in daily denunciation of the Austrian name— **British attitude towards Austria-Hungary** and for the simple reason that it never had any occasion to do so. In comparison with their Hun allies, the Austrians behaved like civilised beings and gentlemen.

For the rest, Austria was so much more remote from observation than Germany, and also much more closely sealed against inspection. It was much more difficult for "intelligent neutrals" to supply information as to the internal state of the Hapsburg than of the Hohenzollern Empire. Besides, the British had a much greater interest in knowing what was going on at Berlin than in what was happening at Vienna. Germany was their chief enemy, and to some extent Austria was regarded as a negligible quantity.

Up to well towards the end of the third year of the war she had only some dozen and a half British prisoners, including five officers, in her keeping, and in comparison with the treatment which those captives—probably from the Salonika front—would have received at the hands of the savage Huns, they were accorded something like

Arab hospitality from the humaner and more Christianlike Austro-Hungarians, who would not allow the asperities of war to efface the recollection of the long-standing friendship between the two countries.

Their conduct was even described as "magnanimous" by Captain A. Stanley Wilson, M.P., who, as a despatch-carrying passenger in a. P. and O. steamer which was torpedoed and sunk in the Mediterranean, had been taken prisoner and sent to Salzburg, and who, after twenty months' confinement was set at liberty without conditions of any kind and allowed to return to England. "I am not a bearer of peace," he said, "but I should like to see some *rapprochement* between the Entente and Austria-Hungary."

At the same time it was contended by Czech writers that the acts of cruelty committed by the Austro-Hungarians on the Slav populations of Bosnia, Serbia, and Galicia were no less appalling than those perpetrated by the Germans in Belgium and Poland. In Galicia alone, said those writers, the estimated number of persons hanged without trial was declared by Deputy Daszynski to be over 30,000.

Ever since the British alliance with Austria against Napoleon, British relations with the Hapsburg monarchy had always been cordial; nor had this amity been seriously impaired by the revolution of 1848, when British sympathies went out to the Hungarians in their efforts to achieve independence. The hero of that revolution was Louis Kossuth, who, like the Garibaldi of a later time, sought and found an asylum in Great Britain, and entranced his audiences by his remarkable mastery of Elizabethan English, which he had acquired when reading Shakespeare during his two years' incarceration in the Castle of Buda,

AUSTRIAN WOMEN ACT AS "FIREMEN."
Fire-brigade of a town in the Austrian Tyrol which, owing to the continuous drawing away of men for the armies, was mainly composed of women. In Austria, as elsewhere, women proved their readiness and capacity to take on unaccustomed work.

"keeping company with the rats." At the London Tavern, with the Lord Mayor in the chair; at Manchester, at Bradford, at Glasgow, and other large towns he thundered to cheering audiences against the despotism of Austria, whose Emperor—young Francis Joseph—he denounced as the "murderer of my nation."

As Kossuth had figured to the British people as the hero of the Hungarian rebellion, so General Haynau was its equally abhorred villain; so that when, a couple of years later, he came to London, and, among other sights, paid a visit to the brewery of Barclay & Perkins—on the site almost of Shakespeare's "Globe" Theatre, where the spirit of the English people may be said to have been enshrined—he was set upon and severely handled by the brewers and draymen, by whom he received a severe "dusting down" for his flogging of Hungarian women and other barbarities, which had caused him to be dubbed General "Hyena." The incident—which is repeatedly referred to in Queen Victoria's letters—caused a decided tension between the two **Francis Joseph and** countries, so that, two years later, Austria **Queen Victoria** was the only military State unrepresented at the funeral of the Duke of Wellington, for which, wrote the Queen, "there is but one feeling of indignation and surprise."

In the year 1880, Mr. Gladstone, as the self-constituted mouthpiece of his countrymen, in one of his famous Midlothian speeches, fiercely denounced Austria as "the unflinching foe of freedom in every country of Europe. Austria trampled underfoot, Austria resisted, the unity of Germany . . . Austria has never been the friend even of Slavonic freedom. Austria did all she could to prevent the creation of Belgium; Austria never lifted a finger for the regeneration and constitution of Greece. There is not an instance—there is not a spot upon the whole map where you can lay your finger and say: 'There Austria did good.'" On returning to power, as the result of the election which he had thus inflamed, Mr. Gladstone tendered an apology to the Austrian Ambassador, Count Karolyi, which Lord George Hamilton described as "shameful and shameless," though it did not altogether satisfy Francis Joseph.

On the other hand, that monarch was always most sincerely devoted to Queen Victoria, for whose character

NURSES OF THE AUSTRIAN ARMY.
Red Cross nurses who were attached to the Austrian Army in Vienna. They wore field-grey uniforms, with the Red Cross on collars and caps.

and sovereign wisdom he had the highest esteem, not to say admiration. He was always most friendly, not only in his private sentiments, but also in his public acts towards Great Britain, and it was only the increasing burden of age, added to his dislike of the sea, which prevented him from coming to England to thank King Edward in person for making him a British Field-Marshal and chief of the 1st Dragoon Guards.

In the year 1902 a former British Ambassador at Vienna, Sir Horace Rumbold, caused a great sensation by revealing, in a magazine article, a striking incident indicative of the friendly feeling pervading the Austrian Court during the Boer War.

"Coming up to me," wrote Sir Horace, "in the official circle preceding a great ball given at Court in January, 1900—I had not had the honour of seeing him for some time—his Majesty at once addressed me, where I stood between the Russian and French Ambassadors, with the words, 'Dans cette guerre je suis tout a fait de côté d'Angleterre '—' In this war I am altogether on the side of England.' "

But the war, of course, was bound to bring about a great change in the feelings of the Austrian people towards Great Britain. In his interesting account of "My Secret Service" (for the "Daily Mail "), "The Man who Dined with the Kaiser " (at Nish)—a daring Anglo-Dutch journalist, Mr. Loopuit— detailed a visit which he paid to Vienna on his way to the Near East in December, 1915 :

I determined (he said) to look about the city to discover what changes had taken place during the eight months that had elapsed since my previous visit. The first thing I noticed was the increased hostility on the part of the Viennese towards the English. For this there were two very obvious reasons : First, the pinch of hunger, " stomach pressure " as it has been called, the work of the British Navy ; second, the intervention of Italy, the work of British diplomatists. The Austrian is not so dramatic in his hatreds as the German ; but there is a bitter and burning feeling in his heart against a nation that has robbed him of most of the luxuries and many of the necessaries of life, and, in addition, has precipitated him into another war at a time when his hands were already over full.

But in spite of—if not, perhaps, in consequence of—this growing hatred of the British name, Mr. Loopuit found to his astonishment that the most popular play in Vienna should be the English success, " Mr. Wu." It was advertised all over the city, beneath the title in smaller letters appearing the words " Der Mandarin."

"I was at a loss to account for this anomaly. I remembered having seen the play several times in London, yet this did not supply any information as to its popularity in an enemy city." He soon discovered the reason.

Austrian treatment of British prisoners　" An English business man is shown to great disadvantage beside a Chinaman, and this seemed vastly to please the audience. At the end of every act the curtain was raised time after time and the performers loudly applauded."

Yet with regard to the British subjects—civilians— interned in Austria, the same authority wrote : " To me the real tragedy of Vienna is that Englishmen of military age cannot leave the city. They are well treated, and are allowed their liberty so long as they do not leave the city, which shows how much milder is the Austrian as compared with the German rule. They are, however, expected to be within doors by 8 p.m. Notices have appeared in the papers to the effect that subjects of

belligerent countries are to be freely allowed to use their own language in public places as long as they do not in a way that is offensive."

At Budapest the popular feeling towards England was on the whole milder than at Vienna, though, as we shall presently see, there were some Press outbursts which might have been envied at Berlin. The Hungarians had always been flattered by being called " the English of the East," partly because they were natural horsemen and sportsmen, and lovers of country life, and partly because they were united by a common love of popular liberty. Nowhere was the rebellion of 1848 against the despotism of the Hapsburgs followed with greater sympathy than in England, **Contrasting opinions** where many of the foremost victims **in Hungary** of the revolution found an asylum.

On the other hand, nowhere on the Continent was an English traveller better assured of a hospitable welcome than in Budapest, which boasted of its " Queen of England Hotel," its " English Club," its " English Garden," or promenade, and above all its beautiful English suspension bridge spanning the Danube where it is over 1,400 feet wide—the work of Tierney Clark, the engineer of Hammersmith Bridge, and the finest thing of its kind on the Continent of Europe.

COUNT CARL STÜRGKH.
Austrian Prime Minister, who was assassinated by Dr. Friedrich Adler on October 21st, 1916.

The great canal connecting the River Theiss with the Danube was the result of English enterprise, and on the outbreak of the war its manager, Mr. Yoxall, was not only allowed but positively entreated to continue his services on behalf of the Hungarian State—an act of generous confidence beyond the comprehension of the cruel gaolers of Ruhleben.

Anglomania had its votaries in most European capitals, but nowhere more numerous or more sincere than at Budapest. In the summer of 1917, when the Hungarian Premier, Count Tisza, was succeeded by Count Eszterhazy—who, like others of his countrymen, had been educated at Oxford (Queen's), and even been a member of the " Bullingdon "—an Austrian writer drew attention to the fact that his sympathies were pro-British.

" In all matters relating to the turf, the last word in tailoring, and the running of a country-house and its game preserves, not merely Count Eszterhazy, but practically the entire Hungarian aristocracy is generally pro-British " in personal sympathy, that is, if not in policy.

So also thought Mr. Gerard, late American Ambassador at Berlin, whose sister-in-law was a Hungarian lady. In his " My Four Years in Germany " he wrote :

The Hungarians, as a people, are quite like Americans. They have agreeable manners and are able to laugh in a natural way, something which seems to be a lost art in Prussia. Nearly all the members of the Hungarian noble families speak English perfectly, and model their clothes, sports, and country life as far as possible after the English.

Yet at the same time it must be owned that some mannerless Magyars of the baser sort — " slaves who took their masters' humour for a warrant "—wrote in the Press in a vein of villainy which had been borrowed from Berlin. Thus, for example, wrote " Az Ujsag," said to be—but surely not—the organ of the Premier, Count Tisza :

The plan of the war was conceived in the head of Sir E. Grey, whose mouth vomits fiery lies ; Grey is the incarnation of Britain's perfidy. Though a gentleman in his outward appearance, Grey is the greatest hangman of mankind, who only deserves to be put in the darkest prison.

DR. K. P. KRAMARZ.
Leader of the Young Czechs in the Lower Chamber of the Austrian Reichsrath.

The same journal wrote:

The first telegram announcing the Kitchener catastrophe was posted up in large characters in the windows of our office reading-room at 10.30. A large crowd collected, and when the second telegram arrived announcing that Kitchener was drowned, with his Staff, the public were moved to such an extent by this blow of Nemesis, that they could not hide their feelings. At the Gaiety Theatre, during the third act, one of the actors included the news in his rôle, and the audience rose and cried out " Eljen ! " (Hurrah !) with great enthusiasm. The orchestra played the National Anthem.

" Pesti Hirlap," June 7th :

Kitchener has been lost to his country in such an ignominious way, the like of which has never overtaken any other leading Englishman before. . . . This blow has hit England immediately after the Battle of Jutland, and when the English were declaring themselves to be still masters of the seas. This blow is particularly favourable to the Central Powers at a time when the Allies were organising a big general offensive. Lord Kitchener now lies at the bottom of the sea, with his Staff and his mission, and with him lie many, many hopes of the Allies of the Entente.

At about ten o'clock in the evening the telephone-bells of our editorial rooms began to ring. Everybody was asking whether the news was true. People coming from the theatres formed themselves into groups, and people who were strangers were asking one another whether the news was exact. Nobody evinced the slightest compassion for Kitchener and his Staff.

It was inevitable, of course, that political feeling against England should have been intensified as the war went on by the avowed sympathies of the Allies with the Irredentist hopes not only of the Italians, but also of the Serbs and Rumanians in Hungary itself.

The work of the German-Magyars

But what, then, had been the original attitude of the Hungarian people towards the war into which they had been pushed by their fellow-countryman, Count Berchtold, Austro-Hungarian Minister for Foreign Affairs, successor in the office to Count von Aehrenthal, the annexer of Bosnia-Herzegovina ; while Berchtold, in turn, at the instigation of Germany, was to let loose the dogs of the world-war on account of Serbia ?

We have it on the authority of Professor Masaryk, the Czech champion, that it was the war of the Germans and Magyars. The Austrian Parliament itself had not been convoked since March, 1914, so that war was declared without its assent ; and it was only the Chauvinistic and oligarchical Hungarian Parliament that accepted the Emperor's autocratic declaration of war. The majority of the Austro-Hungarian races and peoples were against the war ; while the German - Magyar minority forced the whole Empire to serve as the obedient slave of Pan-Germanism.

How was it, then, that the Hungarian Parliament should have given its assent to and then ratified the Emperor's declaration of war ? For the simple reason that the House of Representatives at Budapest was very much in the nature of a packed assembly. It may be said without exaggeration that this House was the most unrepresentative of its kind in all Europe. Nowhere else had the people so little to say as in Hungary, where the Socialists had not a single seat in Parliament. " Politics " in Hungary was the privilege of a few aristocrats. Hungary was a typical oligarchic and theocratic State, the very opposite of a democracy. Half the population of Hungary proper (apart from Croatia) was non-Magyar, yet they held only eight out of four hundred and thirteen seats in the Hungarian Parliament. In 1910 there were 2,202,165 Slovaks (Czechs) in Hungary, according to the official census. These two million Slovaks had only two deputies, while the 8,651,520 Magyars had four hundred and five seats ; so that every Slovak deputy represented one million voters, but every Magyar deputy 21,000.

Cases of persecution for political offences were innumerable. Slovak candidates were debarred from election by simply being imprisoned. Corruption and violence were the two main characteristics of all elections in " democratic " Hungary. No Magyar politician ever abandoned the programme of the territorial integrity of Hungary, their aim being expressed in the words of Kálmán Tisza : " For the sake of the future of the Magyar State it is necessary for Hungary to become a State where only Magyar is spoken. To gain the Slovaks, or to come to a compromise with them, is out of the question. There is only one means which is effective : Extirpation ! "

Kálmán Tisza and the Slovaks

Meanwhile, let us leave Hungary and return to the other, or Cis-Leithanian, moiety of the monarchy, which was rent by party strife and political passion throughout the war to an extent that grievously impaired its military efficiency. And perhaps the best and briefest way of giving some account of all this internal chaos and confusion will be to concentrate our narrative on the persons of two conspicuous actors in the political drama, and martyrs to their convictions, in the persons of Dr. Kramarz and Dr. Friedrich Adler—one a pure Bohemian Czech, the other a German-Austrian-Jew Socialist.

Dr. Kramarz was the leader of the Young Czechs in the Lower Chamber of the Austrian Parliament, or Reichsrath. They wanted an independent Bohemian-Slovak State whose relationship to the Hapsburg Empire would have to be specially adjusted.

" I should like to point out to you," said a prominent Czech publicist to the present writer, " that in the first instance we want to be liberated from the yoke of the Hapsburgs, Germans, and Magyars—*i.e.*, absolute political independence from Berlin, Vienna, and Budapest. The question whether Bohemia is to be a republic or a constitutional monarchy is, of course, of secondary importance, and will have to be decided later on."

Holding those views, the

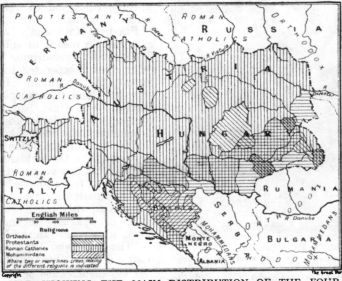

MAP SHOWING THE MAIN DISTRIBUTION OF THE FOUR CHIEF RELIGIONS PROFESSED BY THE HETEROGENEOUS POPULATION OF AUSTRIA-HUNGARY.

DR. FRIEDRICH ADLER.
Editor of the Socialist organ " Das Volk," and assassinator of Count Stürgkh.

G

hearts of the Czechs were never in a war which, they averred, was as much directed against them and the other Slav elements in Austria as against the Entente Allies. They had never been consulted on the subject; war was declared without the assent of the Austrian people as a whole, and thus they had been called upon to fight for a cause which in their heart of heart they despised and condemned.

The war (said one of their writers) is a war not only against England, Russia, and against France, but it is also a struggle against the Slavic majority living in Austria. The Bohemians, having reached the highest state of culture and development among the Austrian Slavs, are an obstacle which the Germans and Magyars seek to crush.

Now, the champion of all those Separatist, or Home Rule, ideas— a man who may be described as the Redmond of his race—was the before-mentioned Dr. Kramarz, regarded by his compatriots as

LYING-IN-STATE OF THE EMPEROR FRANCIS JOSEPH.
Francis Joseph, Emperor of Austria and King of Hungary, died at Schönnbrunn on November 21st, 1916, after a reign of sixty-eight years. He had attained his eighty-seventh year, having been born on August 18th, 1830. The assassination of his heir in 1914 was the pretext for the ultimatum to Serbia, which precipitated the world-wide war.

FUNERAL PROCESSION IN VIENNA.
Procession of Imperial and Royal mourners at the funeral of the Emperor Francis Joseph in Vienna on November 30th, 1916. At the head of the procession is his successor, the Emperor Charles VIII., and the Empress Zita, with their son the Crown Prince Francis Joseph Otto. They are immediately followed by the King of Saxony and King Ferdinand of Bulgaria.

a sort of John Huss, a prominent Bohemian who suffered at the stake for uttering such sentiments as this :

I have affirmed and yet affirm that the Bohemians should by right have the chief place in the offices in the Kingdom of Bohemia, even as they which are French-born in the Kingdom of France, and the Germans in their own countries, whereby the Bohemian might have the faculty to rule his people, and the German bear rule over Germans.

Asked by Andreas Broda, Canon of Prague, whether the enslaved country was ever likely to have a Liberator, Huss replied : "Spero quod habebimus Liberatorem"— "I hope that we shall get a Liberator." He appeared, though he was long in coming, in the person of Dr. Kramarz, who was flung into prison and sentenced to death in June, 1916, though he was afterwards set free (on certain conditions) under an Imperial amnesty.

One of the counts of the indictment against this modern Huss was that he had denounced the Triple Alliance as an "antiquarian relic," comparable to an "old clavichord," a thing belonging to "diplomatic archæology," and had warned his countrymen against the idea of Friedrich Naumann's "Mittel-Europa" **Dr. Kramarz and** as a certain means of subordinating the **the Triple Alliance** Slavs to the slave-driving Teutons. But what most exasperated the Central Government at Vienna against the Bohemian "Liberator" was its conviction, a stronger thing than suspicion, that this Dr. Kramarz, this modern John Huss, had been at the bottom of the pro-Russian sympathies of the Czechs, which had found active expression in the wholesale surrender of Bohemian regiments during the first Serbian campaign and the subsequent fighting in the Carpathians. It was calculated that, before the war was two years old, over 300,000 Czech soldiers had surrendered to, or allowed themselves to be taken prisoners by, the Russians.

Perhaps the most startling case was that of the 28th, or Prague, Regiment, whose colours, draped in black, were placed in the National Museum at Vienna.

"The Man who Dined with the Kaiser" got the story from a Polish officer there :

It was the intention of the whole of the regiment to desert to the Russians, officers as well as rank-and-file. One day, seeing before them what they took to be Russian regiments, the soldiers threw down their arms and held up their hands in token of surrender.

But the "Russians" were Prussians! The Bohemians were unaware that the round cap of Russia is practically the same as that worn in the Prussian armies. The Prussian officers immediately grasped the situation and turned machine-guns on the defenceless men, massacring them in hundreds. The remainder were taken prisoners, and eventually one out of every five was shot, and of the officers one in every three executed.

In an address delivered at Chicago in May, 1916, Dr. Pergler, a prominent Czech Separatist, said:

Revolt of the Bohemian regiments

There is reliable information that the Bohemian regiments in the Austrian Army, as soon as opportunity offered, surrendered to the "enemy." The 28th Regiment surrendered, in fact, on two occasions, once in Serbia and once in the Carpathians; the 88th in Serbia, the 11th in the Carpathians, the 8th, the 91st, as well as the 102nd in Serbia. Although subsequently again re-established after April 3rd, 1915, the 28th Regiment was dissolved by a special Army Order, signed by the Emperor himself, and its re-establishment was resorted to merely for the purpose of deceiving the outside world.

Reliable information has it that the 36th Bohemian Regiment and a Bohemian regiment from the south of Moravia revolted, and it is a fact that, after the surrender of the 28th Regiment at Bardejov, of those who did not succeed in reaching the Russian lines every fifth man was executed.

The fact remains that the number of Czechs who deserted would make six army corps. That explains many of the Austrian defeats in Serbia and Galicia.

But in order to prove that all this wholesale surrender of his Czech countrymen to the enemy was not due to fear of the Russians but to hatred of their real foes, the Germans, Dr. Pergler proceeded to show that whenever they could get an opportunity of fighting against their natural persecutors they eagerly embraced it—in France, where they distinguished themselves in Champagne; in Serbia, and

CHARLES VIII. AS KING OF HUNGARY.
Charles VIII. on the day of his coronation as King of Hungary at Budapest.

THE AUSTRIAN IMPERIAL FAMILY.
The Emperor Charles VIII. and the Empress Zita, with their son the Crown Prince. Their Majesties are wearing their coronation robes, the Emperor having on his head the ancient crown of St. Stephen, the founder of the Hungarian monarchy in the tenth century.

in Russia. Of 1,500 Bohemians (deserters) serving in a Russian regiment, "five hundred of these," boasted Dr. Pergler, "now wear the Cross of St. George, awarded only for conspicuous deeds of bravery." That was certainly an unparalleled performance—one in every three out of a regiment of 1,500 to be awarded a Russian decoration equivalent to the Victoria Cross. There was never anything like this in British regiments. As Dr. Pergler said:

It is no exaggeration to speak of the heroism of these Bohemians fighting voluntarily in the allied armies; they volunteered because they felt that no Bohemian can stand indifferent and impassive in the struggle against the German desires for world-dominion.

No wonder all these Bohemians ground their teeth and went over to the "enemy" —not the real, but the conventional one —when they thought of the Austrian terrorism that was being exercised in their beloved Bohemia to break their refractory spirit; of the prisons full of political offenders, the countless executions of patriots, wholesale hangings and shootings. "By May, 1916," says the writer of "Austrian Terrorism in Bohemia," "the death sentences on civilians pronounced in Austria since the beginning of the war already exceeded the terrific number of 4,000, nine hundred and sixty-five of the victims being Czechs. A large proportion of the condemned were women. The total of soldiers executed already amounts to several thousands."

Such was the record up to June, 1916, till when Dr. Kramarz had figured in the Dual Empire as the chief protagonist of popular freedom. But a few months later his reputation was to be paralleled by the appearance of another dramatic figure on

CORONATION OF THE EMPEROR CHARLES VIII.
On December 30th, 1916, the Austrian Emperor Charles VIII. was crowned King of Hungary. Having been robed in the mantle, girt with the sword of St. Stephen and crowned with St. Stephen's crown in the cathedral of old Buda, he proceeded to the Coronation Mound in Pest, on the other side of the Danube, where the ancient ceremony was completed.

CHAMBER OF DEPUTIES, BUDAPEST.
Interior of the Chamber of Deputies in the Hungarian Parliament buildings. It has seats for four hundred and thirty-eight members, and the walls are lined with gilt carvings.

the national stage. This man, Dr. Friedrich Adler (Eagle), a Jew journalist of Vienna, was editor of the leading Socialist organ " Das Volk " (" The People "), and son of Victor Adler, a noted Socialist. One night (October 21st, 1916) the son went to dine at an hotel, where he knew that Count Stürgkh, the Austrian Premier, was accustomed to take his evening meal. Rising from his chair and approaching the table at which the Count and several friends were seated, Adler drew a revolver and fired several shots at the Count with fatal effect.

But it was not till the following May—that is to say, after an interval of just seven months—that the assassin was brought to trial and condemned to death, though the sentence was afterwards commuted under the new Emperor Charles.

Adler's able speech in his own defence threw a lurid light on the internal state of Austria—hence its historical value for the present purpose. He opened his defence by refuting the suggestion that his act was that of a madman.

The internal state of Austria

It is my duty (he said) to contend for my convictions, which are far more sacred to me than the question whether one more human being is hanged in Austria during the war. . . . I acted, not with clouded reason, but after full deliberation, after thinking out for over eighteen months all possible consequences. . . .

I agree with the public prosecutor, that in a well-ordered State murder must not be a political weapon. . . . I will not examine our rulers as moral beings, but will ask whether we live in a well-ordered State. For me the answer to this question is the moral justification of murder as a political weapon. . . .

It was the condition of justice in Austria which I felt most keenly since the war began, and which always kindled in me the feeling of

shame that I was an Austrian. As early as July 25th, 1914, the Stürgkh-Hochenburger Cabinet issued an Imperial decree on juries—on the very day when diplomatic relations with Serbia were broken off—a decree which in itself was a real coup d'état. No one ever wrecked Parliament so deliberately as Count Stürgkh, who saw coming what actually has come. . . .

Even before the declaration of war on Serbia it had been decided to declare war upon the peoples of Austria, to treat the Constitution as a scrap of paper, and shamelessly to tread under foot all law and right in Austria ! . . . All political offences—high treason, lese-majesty, disturbance of the public peace—for which juries were really instituted, were transferred by the decrees of July 25th to the jurisdiction of the Courts-Martial. . . . We are a State which has not its equal in the whole world. In Austria justice has been degraded to a mere internal machine of war.

Adler then emphasised the double motive of his action—shame at the attitude of his party and shame at the situation to which Stürgkh had reduced Austria:

GRAND STAIRCASE, HOUSES OF PARLIAMENT, BUDAPEST.
This richly-decorated staircase leads from the main entrance of the superb edifice on the left bank of the Danube into the Domed Hall on the first floor. A feature of its rich embellishment is a fine ceiling-painting by Lotz representing Legislation.

My feeling was this : Are we dogs to be whipped ? Have we no sense of honour that we should submit to all this ? . . . For two and a half years no one in Austria knew who was governing. Russia, China, had their Parliaments, Austria had none ; we were the only really degraded ones. Stürgkh played the chief part in this. An eager opponent of universal suffrage even before the war, opposition to electoral reform had centred round him. Afterwards he became Premier, watched the powerlessness of Parliament with an air of malicious joy (*Schadenfreude*), and deliberately brought about its prorogation. He obviously wanted to rule without it. When war came Parliament was not summoned. It was an open coup d'état.

The clamour for Parliament grew steadily stronger in the summer of 1916 ; even the Feudalists in the Upper House took an interest in the Constitution. But Stürgkh systematically did everything to prevent its convocation. The Club of Socialist Deputies in September, 1916, passed a resolution demanding the summons of

Parliament as indispensable. Stürgkh gave instructions to suppress not only this pronouncement, but even the fact that the meeting had taken place. Stürgkh drew a cordon round the Emperor to prevent him from knowing anything of the whole affair. He refused Sylvester, President of the Reichsrath, access to the Emperor, and suppressed all public reference to discussion on the position of Parliament, even forbidding the Faculty of Law in the University of Vienna to hold their proposed conference on the Constitutional position of the Reichsrath.

Such was the intolerable situation in October.

Therefore (said Dr. Adler) I decided to call Stürgkh to account and fight him with the weapons which he himself had chosen. There was no other way, for if the law is violated, it is not only the right, but the duty, of every citizen to procure justice for himself.

The death of Francis Joseph

Just a month after the assassination of the Austrian Premier the Dual Monarchy was again, but still more, stirred to its depths by the death of the aged Emperor Francis Joseph, in his eighty-seventh year; and it is probable that his end had been accelerated by the worries arising from the domestic state of his distracted dominions, as much as by his anxieties resulting from the war. His whole long reign of sixty-eight years, beginning (1848) in his eighteenth year, was one continuous record of public and domestic calamity such as perhaps never fell to the lot of any other ruler. According to a writer in the "Times," the closing months of his life were marked by the establishment of a military reign of terror throughout his dominions, by the persecution of millions of his subjects taught to revere his name, and by thousands of executions for "high treason." . . . The world will reflect that an era which might have been a great era in Hapsburg history has closed amid ruin, bankruptcy, blood, and tears; but in these reflections there will be place for human compassion with the lot of a man who came as a stripling to the throne, who saw brother, wife, son, and nephew perish by violence, who lost the fairest provinces of his Empire, and who must have ended a long and chequered reign with forebodings of disaster to his House and his dominions graver than any which even he had known. . . . The direct responsibility of Francis Joseph for this criminal policy (of the war) cannot be ascertained. Age probably rendered him incapable of resisting pressure which in earlier years he might have had the strength to withstand. Rather than upon him,

responsibility falls upon the German Emperor, the German military party, and their accomplices in Austria, and particularly in Hungary, where Count Tisza worked in close agreement with German schemes.

Francis Joseph was succeeded by his grand-nephew, Archduke Charles Francis Joseph, who chose to be styled Emperor Charles (Carl), the eighth of that name to rule over Austria proper, and the first over Hungary. Born on August 17th, 1887, and thus missing the birthday of his predecessor by only a day, the new ruler was in his thirtieth year, with the training more of a soldier than a statesman. His parents were the Archduke Otto, second son of the Emperor Francis Joseph's brother Louis, and the Archduchess Maria Josepha, sister of the King of Saxony. Handsome in appearance and sporting in his tastes, Otto became popular with the Army and the people to an extent never attained by his elder brother Francis Ferdinand, the victim of Sarajevo, though he was of dissipated tastes, like most members of his family—the most degenerate and decadent of any dynasty in Europe.

Among his other escapades Archduke Otto, when riding in the country one day with several officers, met a funeral procession of a poor peasant whose relatives and friends were following the body to the grave. Otto compelled

THE ROYAL PALACE, BUDAPEST.
Grandly situated on the high right bank of the Danube, erected 1748-71 by Maria Theresa, it was rebuilt and enlarged, 1894, by Nicholas Ybl and Aloysius Hauszmann. "No princely palace in Europe can compare with it."

the bearers to put down the coffin in the road in order that he might enjoy the pleasure of jumping over it, which he did several times — backwards and forwards — while the mourners looked on indignant and helpless; after which the Archducal party continued their ride. There can be the less doubt as to the truth of this otherwise incredible story since it was detailed at the time in the Austrian Chamber by a Socialist Deputy, Pernerstorfer, who denounced the Archduke Otto as a blackguard—an act of

VIEW OF BUDAPEST FROM THE FRANCIS JOSEPH BRIDGE.
On the left is seen the slope of Mount Gellert; in the centre the Elizabeth Bridge; on the right (in the background) Castle Hill, with the Royal Palace. The capital of Hungary is one of the most finely-situated towns in the world, owing its beauty and the importance of its trade chiefly to the Danube.

VIEW OF THE CATHEDRAL AND ROYAL PALACE OF PRAGUE.
Prague, the ancient capital of the Kingdom of Bohemia, a beautiful city on both sides of the River Moldau. The Cathedral of St. Vitus and the fourteenth-century Palace form the dominating features on the left bank. To the left of the picture is the fine old many-statued Charles Bridge.

courage for which the said Pernerstorfer very nearly suffered the fate that was subsequently to befall the priest Father Rasputin at Petrograd.

Next day Pernerstorfer was found in his rooms battered nearly to the point of death, and it was subsequently discovered that the Archduke Otto and his brother Francis Ferdinand had been at the bottom of the outrage. It was one of the curious ironies of fate that some nine months after the accession to the throne of Otto's son Charles in November, 1916—the latter should have summoned Pernerstorfer to a private audience to consult with him as to the best means of safeguarding his throne.

As far as his Saxon mother was concerned, Archduke Charles—son of Otto, the coffin-jumper—enjoyed a very careful upbringing; but the vigour of a plant depends on the nature of its soil, and Hapsburg soil was notoriously poor, not to say worked out. Thus, when Charles succeeded to the sceptre of his House, it was said of him by one well qualified to judge that " much surprise would be felt by those who had known him for the last five years if he were to show in any respect the qualities of a great ruler." His wife, Princess Zita of Bourbon-Parma, was described as a " simple, unaffected woman of great charm and attractive appearance "; but more than that is wanted in a wife to make up for the character-defects and debilities of a husband.

As far as regards mere personality, the new Emperor made a favourable impression on all observers, and particularly on Mr. Ward Price, who had hurried to Vienna as a special correspondent on the eve of the war, and who gave us this pen-and-ink sketch of the new heir to the Austrian throne :

Character of the Emperor Charles

At the back of the car, sitting very upright on the edge of the seat and saluting in a way that adds even to so simple a movement the suggestion of physical vigour, is the next Austrian Emperor, in a black tunic that fits in the glove-like way that is the secret of Austrian military tailors, with a red collar and a high képi. His face is plump, with a dimple in the chin. It is very brown and sunburnt, and has the short-cropped moustache that Austrian officers have copied from their English brothers-in-arms.

An active, healthy, sensible, jolly young officer—that is the impression you would have of the Archduke Charles if you met him walking through the Graben of an afternoon. And your observation would not have deceived you, since that is exactly what he is, or has been hitherto—for what effect the anxieties of the Austrian crown may have upon his character remains to be seen. He is a soldier and a sportsman. He used to have fame as a dancer until a skating accident handicapped his waltzing. He speaks English well, French fairly, and commands an extensive collection of the difficult and sometimes non-European tongues that are spoken among the seventeen races of the Austrian Empire—Czech, Magyar, Croatian, and the rest.

Such was the simple, unaffected prince on whose brow there was soon to descend a crown of thorns such as, perhaps, no temporal sovereign in all the world had ever worn. What would he say ? What would he do ? All the world looked to him for a sign; and when at last this was forthcoming, in the shape of several edicts, addresses, and proclamations, it was seen that the voice was Jacob's, but that the hands that penned those State documents were the hands of Esau; that, in fact, the new Emperor was more of a medium than a man, more of a puppet than a personality—like the manikins which ventriloquists make use of at popular entertainments.

The new Emperor's address to his Army—which might well have been penned for him by the War Lord of Potsdam—made allusion to the fact that " up to the present I have endured with you the hard but glorious days of this gigantic struggle," though his personal participation in the war was not particularly fruitful of results—for the Austrian cause. But the course of the war itself, which had been proving favourable to the Central Powers in Rumania at least, was not so much a source of direct solicitude to the new Emperor Charles—son of Otto, the coffin-jumper—as the distracted state of his dominions, rent and imperilled as they were by racial conflict and political strife.

At his accession his Imperial and Apostolic Majesty had found the post of Austrian Premier occupied by Dr. von Körber, successor to the assassinated Count Stürgkh; but in about three weeks' time he had to be superseded by Dr. von Spitzmüller and a new Cabinet. The meaning of this change in general terms was that **Changes in the Cabinet** the young and pliable puppet-Emperor had been taught to see the wisdom of having an Austrian Premier more agreeable to the Hungarians than the " stalwart " Dr. von Körber, an Austrian through and through—the more so since, in view of the forthcoming coronation of his Apostolic Majesty as King of Hungary, it was found expedient to make certain concessions to the Magyars, who, after all, were in a racial minority in Trans-Leithania.

This change of Austrian Premier was soon followed by the substitution of the German Bohemian Count Czernin, for the Hungarian Baron Burian as Imperial (or Austro-Hungarian) Minister for Foreign Affairs; though it passed the wit of man, especially of the alien observer kind, to estimate the true meaning of all this constant shuffling of the Ministerial cards.

But for the moment public interest in all these political puzzles was merged in a picturesque ceremony—that of the coronation of the Emperor Charles and his consort as King and Queen of Hungary—on the last day but one of the year 1916. The customary ceremonial had to be somewhat curtailed owing to the war, while it also suffered from the absence of the foreign representatives, who add so much to the lustre of such occasions. Yet even so, the Royalist ritual at Budapest was, perhaps, more picturesque and interesting than any other of its kind in Europe.

After Edinburgh, with its parallel old and new towns, perhaps no city in Europe presents such an architectural contrast between past and present as the capital of Hungary, with mediæval Buda and its " castled-crag " on one bank of the broad, majestic Danube, and modern Pest on the other.

Reuter gave a very good account of the ceremony :

The two Houses of Parliament assembled together as early as six o'clock in the morning, adopting in common a resolution to attend the coronation in accordance with Constitutional law.

Escorted by the Hungarian bodyguard, the Royal couple left the Castle at 9.30 a.m. for the Cathedral, where they were received by the Cardinal Primate and the clergy, and conducted to the Loretto Chapel, where the King was robed in the mantle and girded with the sword of St. Stephen. From the Chapel the Royal couple proceeded to the high altar, where they sat on the throne surrounded by Barons of the Empire.

The mediæval character of the ceremony was emphasised **The Hungarian** by the use of its monkish Latin. High **coronation ceremony** Mass having begun, with the King—son of Otto, the coffin-jumper—kneeling at the steps of the altar, the Archbishop of Kalocsa, addressing the Primate, said:

Most reverend father, Holy Mother Catholic Church asks you to raise the most serene Charles—here present—to the rank of King of Hungary.

To which the Primate replied :

Do you know him to be fit and worthy for such a dignity ?

Whereto the Archbishop rejoined :

We know and believe him fit and worthy a member of God's Church for the governance of this realm.

Whereupon the Palatine, Count Tisza, placed the crown on the head of the King with the words, "Accipe coronam." The crown was held over the shoulder of the Queen, who then rose with her suite and left for the Castle.

The King, while on the throne, knighted several officers who had specially distinguished themselves at the front. While the guns were firing the salute and the church bells were ringing, those present at the coronation assembled on the great square in front of the Cathedral, where the King in full robes stepped on the dais before the assembled people, carrying the cross in his left hand, with his right hand raised to take the Constitutional oath.

The coronation procession was then formed in order to accompany the King to Coronation Mound, which had been formed of earth obtained from all the counties of the kingdom. The King ascended the mound and waved the sword of St. Stephen towards the four corners of the earth, in order to symbolise that he, as supreme guardian of the Empire, would protect it against all its foes.

After this ceremony the King returned to the Castle, accompanied by his suite, on horseback. The coronation banquet concluded with festivities at which all the members of Parliament and those Barons present at the coronation attended.

But all this ceremonial music was not worth its rasping jars and discords. By order of the police every fifth flag on the Royal route had to be Croatian and every tenth Dalmatian, so as thus to demonstrate the unity of the kingdom. But though Croatian flags were thus displayed, the Croats themselves held sullenly aloof. Their Diet had been invited to send a representative

DR. CHARLES GROSH,
Mayor of Prague at the time of the outbreak of the war.

number of its members to the coronation, but the Leader of the Opposition, M. Pavelic, speaking for the three Jugo-Slav parties comprising the Opposition, said :

We reject the invitation. Hungary oppresses her Slav subjects. Hungary is the cruellest oppressor of small nationalities ; the Hungarian Government is corrupt and brutal. The coronation of the King of Hungary thus represents for us the enthronement of tyranny.

The whole of the Opposition then demonstratively rose and left the building.

Otherwise the coronation was marked by striking contrasts. On one hand there were the Hungarian magnates in their gorgeous suits—from which was evolved the idea of the British hussar uniforms—and their ladies in dresses that cost thousands of pounds, with jewellery worth fortunes, passing along the streets and over Tierney Clark's beautiful suspension bridge in luxurious carriages and motor-cars, while not far off, in the market-place, rioting was going on for the purchase of provisions.

While the young Queen's coronation dress was said to have cost £5,000, a chicken or duck fetched as much as thirty shillings, and even at that price it could scarcely be got without a fight. While some gave as much as £150 for a window at Buda to view the coronation show, others had to pay—or would have been willing to pay—six shillings for a pound of butter and ten shillings for a pound of sugar if they could only have come across someone prepared to sell at those prices. The Royal Household, said the official report, needed 6,000 eggs a day, and it got them, too—but only at the expense of those who could not afford excessive prices.

At the same time, the main question then pending between the two halves of the Dual Monarchy was whether Hungary should feed Austria, as she was expected to do, or whether she could not. The relations between the two Siamese-twin-like countries were always calling for an "Ausgleich," or compromise, like that of 1867. The centrifugal forces were ever active, more particularly in Hungary, for, to tell the truth, the two moieties of the Empire were like ill-mated dogs running in the same leash.

The two countries never failed to present striking contrasts to one another, and more especially in the character of their **The closed doors of** respective Parliaments. Ever since the **the Reichsrath** outbreak of the war the Legislature at Budapest had been free to deliberate as usual, while the sister Assembly at Vienna was as a closed book.

Prorogued in March, 1914, the Austrian Reichsrath had not been allowed to meet during the critical days which decided the question of peace or war, and for nearly the next three years its doors remained closed.

GENERAL VIEW OF PRAGUE FROM THE MOLDAU, LOOKING DOWN STREAM.
The Czechs are fond of describing their capital as "The golden city of Prague." The old town, on the right bank of the Moldau, forms a comparatively small part of the modern city. Besides its fine mediæval buildings Prague has many very handsome modern ones.

The result was that Austria proper lived in a constant state of Ministerial change. Every month, every week almost, brought with it a fresh turn of the kaleidoscope. Not only was the country in a state of war, it was also in a perpetual state of political crisis. In all these crises the most hotly-contested topic was the convocation of the Reichsrath, so stoutly opposed by Count Stürgkh, who, in consequence, as we have seen, fell to the revolver bullets of Dr. Adler.

The "Mittel-Europa" project　　Count Stürgkh's successor, Dr. von Körber, was favourable to the idea, but his successor, Dr. von Spitzmüller, who failed to form a Cabinet, thought it impracticable; while the next Premier, Count Clam-Martinitz, a Bohemian noble — like the new Foreign Minister, Count Czernin — was believed to desire it, but on terms objected to by the German parties whose aim it was, by hook or by crook, to establish a German majority in the Parliament of Vienna, as well as a Magyar majority at Budapest, in conformity with the scheme of a "Mittel-Europa" (or Central Europe), under Teuton domination.

THE EMPEROR CHARLES VIII. AND HIS TROOPS.
Charles VIII. greeting a company of his soldiers on their return from the trenches on the Italian front. The difficulties of the ruler of the "ramshackle Empire" became especially complicated during the war. Many of his subjects were bitterly opposed to the Germans, and many thousands of his anti-German soldiers not only deserted to the "enemy" but readily enlisted in those enemy ranks.

Now what was the nature and object of the "Mittel-Europa," as first sketched out by Dr. Friedrich Naumann, and then elaborated by others? We cannot do better than ask an expository writer on the "Times" to step into the witness-box:

Competent observers have long understood that one of the reasons why Germany made war was to secure her road to the East, or, in other words, to extend her effective sway from the North Sea to the Persian Gulf. The realisation of this plan would involve, as a secondary result, the practical annexation of Austria by Germany, and the conversion of Trieste into a German port and of the Adriatic into a German sea. . . . From admissions in the Austrian Press, it appears that the German design—which includes the formidable economic scheme known as "Mittel-Europa," or "Central Europe"—is so to reconstruct Austria proper as to turn it into a German land; or, in other words, to make the 9,000,000 Austrian Germans absolute masters of their 22,000,000 Slav fellow-subjects. It is proposed to eliminate the Polish-Ruthene province of Galicia by giving it a "special status"; to reorganise the administrative districts of Bohemia, so as to enable the comparatively small German minority to overpower the large Czech majority; to proclaim German as the language of State in Austria in place of the eight Austrian languages hitherto recognised;

to modify Parliamentary standing orders so as to muzzle those Slav representatives whom it may be impossible entirely to suppress; and to make over to an "autonomous Southern Slav State" under Magyar-German control the kingdom of Dalmatia, which is represented by eleven Serbo-Croatian Deputies in the Reichsrath. This "State" is, apparently, to include also Croatia-Slavonia, Bosnia-Herzegovina, Montenegro, and such parts of Serbia as Germany may think it safe to release from her direct control.

While the whole Dual Monarchy, no less than Germany, was ringing with Press discussions about this "Mittel-Europa" scheme, in Austria proper crisis followed crisis in most confusing manner, till at last, towards the end of April, 1917, the new Emperor signed a decree convoking the Reichsrath for May 30th. In so acting he and his advisers undoubtedly had been influenced to some extent by the recent Revolution in Russia and the influence of the democratic spirit which had contagiously spread to the Central Powers.

At the opening sitting of the Lower House the galleries were crowded, and many deputies appeared in uniform. Wreaths were laid on the seats of four who had been killed during the war. Reference was made to "the heroic fighters who are now in the field for Austria's existence, honour, and glory, especially those now on the Carso and the Isonzo." In face of the ominous abstention of nearly two hundred of its members, the House elected as its President (or Speaker) Dr. Gross, leader of the German National League—a signal triumph for the "Mittel-Europa" dreamers and their scheme of "Deutschland über Alles."

The Emperor's Speech from the Throne was intolerably long and tedious, though evidently the handiwork of a much more capable man than himself. Perhaps its key-note was the frank confession that he meant for the time being to act as an autocratic ruler after the model set by his fellow-despot at Berlin.

Mindful (he said) of my obligation to take the oath to the Constitution, and adhering to my intention expressed immediately after my accession to fulfil this obligation truly, I must at the same time keep in mind the provision of the fundamental law which places in my hands alone the decisions to be taken at the great moment of the conclusion of peace. . . . . From these considerations I have decided to postpone the taking of the Constitutional oath until the time, which I hope is not far distant, when the foundations of a new strong and happy Austria will again for generations to come be firmly consolidated internally and externally. Already to-day, however, I declare that I shall always be a just, affectionate, and conscientious ruler of my dear peoples in the sense of the Constitutional idea which we have taken over as a heritage from our forefathers, and in the spirit of that true democracy which during the storms of the world-war has wonderfully stood the ordeal of fire in the achievements of the entire people at home and at the front.

Flouting of the Constitution, sops flung to Slav aspirations, and suggestions of a separate peace with Russia—such were the chief ingredients of the Emperor's Speech from the Throne. No wonder that, in an article on "The Vienna Sham," the "Times" wrote:

The Emperor Charles is too young for the difficult part which he had to play at the opening of the Austrian Reichsrath. Training, as well as natural aptitude, is required to sustain the character of a political Joseph Surface with any credit. His Apostolic Majesty's ally in Berlin has often won applause in it, but his own performance wholly lacked spirit. He spoke the words set down for him, but he must have been overwhelmed by consciousness that the world-wide audience for whom he was acting are cold and critical. What he will do when the screen scene is reached, we cannot imagine. There is something much worse than " a little milliner " behind it, and the time is coming when somebody will throw it down. It will be an embarrassing moment.

It was some little time before the screen with the " little milliner " behind it could be thrown down; but, meanwhile, Babel was quick to break loose in the Reichsrath itself, and nothing could better illustrate the chaos prevailing throughout the polyglot Empire than the debate which followed the speech of the Premier, Clam-Martinitz, a Bohemian noble who had given great offence to his own particular countrymen the Czechs. These deputies, disappointed and angry at Count Clam-Martinitz's virtual refusal of their nationalist demands, interrupted his speech with turbulent shouts and cries of disapproval. The speeches of the Czech deputies later further disturbed the proceedings. The Southern Slav deputy Korosec declared that not only the Slavs, but the whole **" Bohemian Club "** population, were joining more and more **in the Reichsrath** in the cries, " Away with German bureaucracy! " " Away with German officers! " In demanding their rights the South Slavs intended that all Slovenes, Croats, and Serbs living in the Monarchy should be united under the Hapsburg sceptre within a State of their own. A Czech deputy, Stranski, protested against the sentence passed on Dr. Kramarz, and said the time was coming when the Austrian Peter and Paul Fortress would be opened and political prisoners released.

Another Czech deputy, Herr Praschek (a former Cabinet Minister), excited the wrath of the German parties by declaring that, whoever was responsible for beginning the war, it was certainly not the Czechs nor the Slavs. The Czechs could only support a Government whose programme included the abolition of the dual system and the organisation of independent States in both halves of the Monarchy.

No less alarmed and indignant than the Germans were their friends and coadjutors, the Magyars, on hearing the declaration of the " Bohemian Club " in the Reichsrath to the effect that " the Czechs would insist upon the

AUSTRIA'S EMPEROR IN TRANSYLVANIA.
The Emperor Charles VIII. (left) driving through a town in Transylvania with General von Kövess. The new Emperor was known more as a soldier than as a statesman, though he had won no special distinction in the Great War, which had been in progress for over two years when the death of his grand-uncle the Emperor Francis Joseph called him to the throne.

union of all branches of the Czecho-Slovak nation in a democratic Bohemian State."

On this the Magyars accused them of high treason, asserting that it was directed against the integrity of Hungary, and, therefore, anti-monarchic and anti-dynastic. It was said of these Magyars that when they pleaded for " peace without annexations " and for the integrity of Hungary, what they wanted was to be allowed to continue oppressing and systematically Magyarising the Slavs and Rumanians of Hungary.

A few days later an immense flutter was caused at Vienna by the issue of an Imperial amnesty in favour of all civilians undergoing sentence for high treason, lese-majesty, offences against the public peace, rioting, etc., and, in fact, of all political offenders except those who had fled abroad—such as Professor Masaryk, who had found an asylum in England. Neither, of course, did it apply to the case of Dr. **Effect of the** Adler, the slayer of Count Stürgkh, who **Imperial amnesty** had first been condemned to death and then to fifteen years' hard labour. Moreover, as the Czech deputies, though released, would not be allowed to re-enter Parliament, the whole thing was regarded as an empty farce, intended to hoodwink public opinion at home and abroad.

This amnesty—couched in language of maudlin sentiment—came as a complete surprise to all, and fell like a thunderbolt on the German parties in the Reichsrath, the first intimation of it reaching there when the Premier, Dr. Seidler—who had meanwhile succeeded Clam-Martinitz, then acting as Governor of subjugated Montenegro—read the Imperial rescript in the Lower House. It was greeted with thunders of applause from the Slav deputies, while the Germans were equally loud in shouting out their protests against this sop to the Slavs. " This pardon for high treason," they exclaimed, " is a slap in the face of loyalty! " " It is only to the Czechs," said a leading Berlin organ, " that nation of colossally organised high treason, that this decree brings anything. Germans need no amnesty. There are no traitors in their ranks. Their leaders have not had to be put into gaol for the safety of the State."

THE EMPEROR CHARLES WITH HIS OFFICERS.
Charles VIII. (in the centre) chatting with some of his Army officers. Described as " a simple and unaffected prince," he was not regarded on his accession as being likely to prove a strong ruler but rather the tool of his Ministers; " in fact, the new Emperor was more of a medium than a man, more of a puppet than a personality."

" The tone of the Emperor's letter to the Premier," wrote another Junker journal, " is more fitting for melo-drama than for the serious situation which exists at the end of three years of war. Germans will not be misled by false emotions about ' the hand of a child leading back the wanderers to their father's house.' We are living," it continued, " in Central Europe, and the last act of the world-war is not in the least an act of Surrey-side melo-drama, so that few outside the Vienna boulevards will find this admixture of styles and tones suitable."

It was about this time that the German Kaiser and Kaiserin paid a return visit to their Imperial Majesties of Austria at the Laxenburg Palace, near Vienna, and there was reason for believing that the Potsdam War Lord had a considerable length of finger in the amnesty pie which had so startled and revolted the German elements in both Empires. The German General Staff **Racial differences** had been rendered very uneasy by the **in the Army** growth of the revolutionary feeling in Bohemia and the passing of so many Czech soldiers over to the Russians, and suggested the adoption of remedial measures. One of these was this amnesty which resulted in the release of some 60,000 political prisoners, though there were some who estimated their number at a far higher figure. Other measures aimed at alleviating the situation brought about by food scarcity and internal troubles throughout the Empire, which were even affecting the Army.

This Army may be said to have well reflected the patch-work character of the Dual Monarchy—the " ramshackle Empire "—from the military point of view, while its racial varieties, far from producing a spirit of noble rivalry, only proved a source of weakness and strife. A Hungarian writer, M. Szebenyei, wrote in the " Fortnightly Review ":

In Germany the soldiers are all practically of one race and speak one tongue. Accordingly, the German Army is united, patriotic, and enthusiastic. But the Army of the Dual Monarchy is a heterogeneous mass of irreconcilable elements, held together for the time by sheer force of the iron band of discipline, yet mutually repellent and constantly threatening disruption. Austrians and Hungarians have always hated each other, while the various Slav races in the Monarchy hated them both, and the war has not radically changed these sentiments. The Austrian officers have fanned the flame of ill-will by their stupid and brutal conduct. The Hungarian Parliament has often been roused to white-hot anger by tales of the treatment accorded to Hungarian soldiers by their Austrian officers, and of insults offered to the Hungarian flag.

Only a short time ago M. Urmánczy, a member of the Independence Party, declared that the Austrian General Staff had ordered all Hungarian flags to be taken down, even from the fortress of Belgrade, which the Hungarian troops had occupied, and that no Hungarian flags were to be carried into battle. He also gave instance after instance of brutal treatment. One Hungarian officer, a brave man who had been through seventy battles, had been driven to commit suicide by the long-continued persecution on the part of his Austrian colleagues. The House was intensely excited, and all kinds of furious denunciations of the Austrian officers guilty of such crimes, and demands for their punishment, were made. Officers of different nationality in the same regiment hate each other and have no social intercourse with each other, but form little hostile coteries animated by intense mutual distrust and suspicion.

Again, another source of weakness was the Austrian policy of separating officers from men of their own nationality, except in the case of **Hostility of officers** Austrians proper. The reason for this **and men** was the fear that, if officers and men of the same race were left together, they might, in the event of a revolution, prove a well-organised army difficult to overcome, whereas the men of any one nationality, if officered by Austrians, would lack cohesion. The result was that officers and men spoke entirely different languages. The bulk of the Army was Hungarian or Slav, and those troops had mainly Austrian officers.

As the words of command were in German throughout the whole Army, the men knew just enough German to understand all the orders their officers gave them. But, apart from purely military matters, men and officers had no community of interest. No good fellowship was possible, even if racial antipathies allowed it. The officers hated and persecuted their men, while the men took every opportunity of getting their revenge. Often, when the officers rushed forward during a battle, obnoxious ones were shot by their own men, and some regiments lost several commanders in succession in this way.

Allusion has been made already to the enormous deser-tions of some Austrian races and their surrender to the enemy. The truth was, as we have just seen, that there was no uniform spirit animating the entire mass of the Austro-Hungarian Army. That was perhaps the chief reason why it began by making such a poor show against the Serbians, and reached the culminating point of its disasters by the surrender of Przemysl to the Russians.

How it was that such a first-class fortress as Przemysl, with its immense military booty, came to be handed over to the armies of the Grand Duke Nicholas will surprise no one who reads the vivid account of its surrender by an eye-witness, Mr. Stanley Washburn, special correspondent of the " Times " with the Russians, an account that is quoted as supplementing the briefer narrative in Chapter LXIV. (Vol. 3, page 430) of THE GREAT WAR :

Przemysl (he wrote) is the story of an impregnable fortress two to three times over-garrisoned, with patient, haggard soldiers starving in the trenches, and sleek, faultlessly-dressed officers living on the fat of the land in fashionable hotels and restaurants. The Russians were utterly amazed at the casual reception which they received. The Austrian officers showed not the slightest sign of being disconcerted or humiliated at the collapse of their fortress. It is impossible to conceive a greater contrast than that between the businesslike Russian officers and the easy-going, dapper Austrians. The bulk of the Russian officers are barely distinguish-able from their own soldiers, and all look what they are—serious, hard-fighting men. On the other hand, the greatest stretch of imagination cannot picture the Austrian officers one sees in the streets fighting at all. Sleek cavalry officers, in smart uniforms, with trailing sabres and ringing spurs, saunter about, laughing and joking, and apparently oblivious of the fact that their equine commands have long **Object-lesson of** since been eaten up and that their troopers **Przemysl** are already on the way to Lemberg. Again one sees wasp-waisted, blue-coated infantry officers casually watching their haggard men, whose faces are pinched and wan with hunger and exposure, as they are being marched out of the town on their way to internment in Russia.

While the garrison became thin and half-starved, the mode of life of the officers in the town remained unchanged. The Café Sieber was constantly well filled with dilettante officers, who gossiped and played cards and billiards, and led the life to which they were accustomed in Vienna. Apparently very few shared any of the hardships of their men, or made any effort to relieve their condition. In the Hotel Royal, until the last, officers had their three meals a day, with fresh meat, cigars, cigarettes, wines, and every luxury, while, as a witness has informed me, their own orderlies and servants begged for a slice of bread.

There can be no question that the ultimate surrender was due to the fact that the garrison was on the verge of starvation, while the officers' diet was merely threatened with curtailment. Witnesses state that private soldiers were seen actually to fall in the streets from lack of nourishment. The officers are reported to have retained their private thoroughbred riding-horses until the day before the surrender, when 2,000 of them were killed to prevent them from falling into the hands of the Russians.

A Russian officer of high rank informed me that, when he entered the town, hundreds of these bodies of beautiful thoroughbred horses were to be seen, with half-crazed Austrian and Hungarian soldiers tearing into their bodies, their faces and hands smeared red with blood as they devoured the raw flesh. This officer stated that even his Cossack orderly, who, as he put it, was by no means of a delicate disposition, wept when he beheld the horrid spectacle of half-famished men gorging themselves on raw horse-flesh.

I believe that the Austrians, especially the Hungarians, are first-class raw material, but that now they are utterly broken and hopeless. This I consider to be due to their wretched officers, who, if those I have seen in Przemysl are at all typical, have every appearance of being the most irresponsible and incompetent in Europe. I have never witnessed a more unpleasant sight than that of the dapper, overdressed, and immaculate Austrian officers laughing and chatting gaily as they are driven in carriages to the railway-station for departure, passing through columns of their own men, pale and haggard from hardships which apparently have not been shared in any particular by their officers.

The officers, who numerically seem to be about one in thirty, strike one as having been parasites, contributing nothing whatever to the defence of the town.

[Elliott & Fry.

MAJOR-GENERAL W. A. WATSON, C.B., C.I.E.
APPOINTED COMMANDER OF THE EXPEDITIONARY FORCE OPERATING IN WESTERN EGYPT. OCTOBER, 1916.

[Swaine.

MAJOR-GENERAL SIR HENRY G. CHAUVEL, K.C.M.G., C.B.
COMMANDER OF THE AUSTRALIAN CONTINGENT WITH THE EGYPTIAN EXPEDITIONARY FORCE.

[Bassano.

LIEUT.-GENERAL SIR PHILIP CHETWODE, C.B., D.S.O.
CAPTURED RAFA FROM THE TURKS. JANUARY 9TH. 1917.

[Elliott & Fry.

MAJOR W. J. OTTLEY, SIKH PIONEERS.
LED A BRILLIANTLY SUCCESSFUL EXPEDITION INTO SINAI.

Officers who rendered conspicuous service in the defence of Egypt and the advance into Palestine.

Speeding messages across the desert.   Flag-signallers at work on the summit of a sand-hill

At the gate of Palestine.   A halt in the valley five miles south of Gaza.

Crusaders of the twentieth century on their pilgrimage into the Holy Land.

Advance of the Red Cross: An ambulance train on the march over the desert.

Engineers making a practicable crossing over a dried-up watercourse in Palestine.

Scenes with the British Expeditionary Force that marched from Egypt into Palestine.

Telephone exchange in the heart of the desert, sand-bagged against assault by aircraft

Boring apparatus for supplying the needs of the troops where the wells were few.

Miracles of modern engineering amid scenes of immemorial antiquity.

For such disasters as the fall of Przemysl, wrote M. Szebenyei :

the Austrian officers were entirely responsible; they were not only incapable, but also were jealous of each other and more intent on winning laurels for themselves than on subordinating their own petty personal interests to the success of the whole campaign. So clearly has this fact been discerned that of all the Austrian generals in command at the commencement of the war there are only four who are still (November, 1916) at their posts. The others have all been got rid of on one ground or another. General Auffenberg, the ex-Minister for War, was imprisoned, some were cashiered, and others had to retire on a pension, while of the generals who remain, not one has any power to initiate any movements, so entirely has confidence in their fitness been destroyed.

In fact, had not the Germans, in their masterful way, practically taken over the command of the Austrian Army it would speedily have ceased to exist. Soon after the fall of Przemysl disunion entirely disappeared from the Higher Command of the Austro-Hungarian Army because it became entirely German. There was no scope whatever for intrigue or wire-pulling, rivalry or favouritism. No Austrian general could now form any plans of his own, since he had but to carry out the plans supplied to him by the German General Staff. In fact, by this imposition of the military will of William II.—first on Francis Joseph and then upon his feeble successor—the first stage of converting Austria into the mere vassal and tool of Germany had been reached, and the Teutonic advocates of a " Mittel-Europa " shouted and jumped for joy.

But this German domination did not come soon enough to save the Austro-Hungarian Army from suffering vast and irreparable losses. Competent authorities (says M. Szebenyei) tell us that the retreat from Serbia was the most terrible disaster, in the magnitude **The Army's** of the losses and suffering involved, that **irreparable losses** any of the belligerent armies had to endure. Whereas the German losses were the heaviest during the opening stages of the war, and afterwards those of the Russians, the greatest losses of all were endured by the Austro-Hungarian Army.

From no point of view was the Austro-Hungarian Army ever a very happy one, and its misery was aggravated by the state of its stomach. Rarely revelling in the joy of victory, it was almost equally unfamiliar with the *joie de vivre*. The British soldiers lived like lords (and fought like lions) in comparison with the ill-fed and ill-paid soldiers of the " ramshackle Empire."

And not only (says M. Szebenyei) do the men at the front suffer discomfort through their own lack of sufficient nourishment; they suffer perhaps still more acutely from the news which keeps coming to them from home, telling them of the privations of their wives and families. For upon these the scarcity and dearness of provisions press very hardly. In Budapest and in the other large towns one sees outside the shops the same long rows of people that are to be met with in the streets of Berlin, but the food is still dearer and more scarce than it is in Germany. And the separation allowance made to the wives of soldiers is quite inadequate to their needs.

In Budapest the wife gets sevenpence a day, while in the provinces the allowance is from fivepence to sixpence, and for each child about half this amount. Out of this small sum the wife has to pay rent, fuel—which is now very dear—and other household expenses. The money which remains is barely sufficient to buy bread and potatoes, for bread is sevenpence per kilo in Budapest, and elsewhere dearer still.

A woman with four children receives about one shilling and sixpence per day. Of this, rent and fuel take at least one shilling, thus leaving sixpence a day on which to provide food for five persons.

Nevertheless, it must be admitted that the war proved the Central Empires to be much more self-sufficing than had been generally supposed, and they had the advantage of occupying territory—Rumania and the Russian provinces, for example—that were rich in natural resources. This enormously increased their powers of resistance against any attempts at economic strangulation.

Yet, in spite of all that, the pinch of hunger was felt very keenly throughout the Dual Monarchy. A well-informed correspondent, writing to the " Times " from Lausanne, in December, 1916, gave some illuminating figures :

A modest meal which formerly cost from 1s. 8d. to 2s. 1d., according to the class of establishment, costs to-day from 6s. to 7s. 6d., and even then, either from the point of view of the quality or the quantity of the food provided, there is no comparison with pre-war conditions.

Prices generally have greatly increased. For instance, 2 lb. of poor quality coffee costs from 10s. 10d. to 12s. 6d. ; 2 lb. of beef are worth at Prague 11s. 3d. ; pork costs 9s. 2d. per 2 lb. ; rice, which before the war was obtainable at about 6d., now costs 2s. 6d., and one cannot always get it even at that price. Household soap has advanced from 6½d. to 3s. 4d. ; that, at least, is the official price. In reality it is impossible to obtain it at less than from 8s. 4d. to 10s. per 2 lb. **Famine prices in** As for fancy toilet soap, all business in **the Dual Monarchy** this article was discontinued a long time ago. The rare examples that one does occasionally light upon in the chemists' and druggists' shops sell at anything from 21s. to 25s.

Boots and shoes have risen considerably in price. Ladies' low shoes are worth at the lowest 33s. 4d., and men's shoes are quite unobtainable at less than £2 1s. 8d. Military boots sell at anything up to £8 a pair.

Tobacco becomes scarcer and scarcer, and its sale is now prohibited in the cafés and restaurants. Cigarettes are no longer sold in boxes, and customers can only obtain them singly or at most two at a time in the tobacco shops.

Paper is also very dear, and books have naturally risen in price. For the better class of printed book the increase is as high as 200 per cent.

But perhaps the most interesting, because the most authentic, authority on the subject was the American Ambassador to Austria-Hungary, Mr. F. C. Penfield, who, on returning to Washington, said to an interviewer in August, 1917 :

The number of war orphans in Hungary alone exceeds 400,000, and misery is everywhere growing, while the demand for peace rings louder every day.

Austria's food supply is being so rigidly conserved that the people have now three meatless days in each week, with other days when fats of every sort and butter are forbidden. At best, the remaining days are but half-ration days. Because the Army has commandeered two-thirds of the cows there is a milk and butter famine.

The average person in Austria has not tasted butter in a year. The pinch last winter was most severe, and summer finds the people reduced to straits of genuine desperation. Starvation cannot well come to a monarchy possessing the grain-fields of Hungary and Moravia, but hunger is already there, and there are degrees of hunger.

Last winter Vienna was almost coalless, because there were no cars to haul the fuel from the mines. The authorities decreed that families could heat but a single room in their abodes, but even for this the dealers could seldom supply the necessary fuel.

There have not been sufficient cars to bring salt in needed quantity from the Salzkammergut, and housewives have had to learn to do without a necessary article of which the Dual Monarchy has a natural store sufficient to last for centuries.

One of the costliest commodities is soap of the commonest variety used by the housewife, for fats have become extremely scarce.

These conditions may be met by persons of means, but the masses are in no position to purchase food having inflated values. Great self-denial has to be practised on all sides by the millions, and the wonder is that poor people can find ways of existing.

Horse-flesh is to-day the food of millions. Poor people in Austria-Hungary have always consumed much horse-flesh, but not half the quantity as at present. The price is half that of beef or mutton, and the article is claimed not to be unwholesome.

A later recorder than Mr. Penfield was another informant of the " Times," who, **War-time contrasts** writing from Berne, on May 21st, 1917, **in Vienna** said he had received on excellent authority the following account of conditions in Austria as they existed at that time :

A person visiting Vienna to-day neither sees nor hears anything of the war. He finds the city full of people who seem to think of nothing but enjoyment; the cafés—where conversation about the war is taboo—are full of people from morning till night; the restaurants, where everything except bread and potatoes can be obtained, if one's purse is long enough, are crowded : the opera and the theatres have nearly every seat booked in advance, and the cinemas are filled at every performance.

In the fashionable streets of the city one cannot help remarking the extraordinary number of officers of all ranks and of both services, who appear to have no other duties than to make themselves agreeable to ladies. Both morning and afternoon the pavements are so crowded that progress is a matter of the utmost difficulty. On all sides are fine shops full of the latest fashions which find purchasers even at the prevailing exorbitant prices. Everything is up to date and of the best, but only within reach of the rich.

If one makes inquiries below the surface, however, one finds that housekeeping, even on the most modest scale, is almost an impossibility, owing to the difficulty of obtaining supplies. The rich solve this difficulty by giving up all idea of catering for themselves and going to a good restaurant for most of their meals, but to those of moderate or small income the food problem is an ever-increasing anxiety. The question is no longer " What shall I buy ? " but " What can I buy ? " for it is impossible to procure many articles which were formerly regarded as necessaries.

And then as to the attitude of the Austrian people towards the war :

It may be described as one of total indifference—except in regard to its duration. The only desire of the people is for peace, " no matter who wins." For some little time there have been persistent rumours that Austria was about to make a separate peace. . . . If Austria could shake off German influence and get good terms, she would make peace to-morrow ; but as she knows that she would be obliged to give up so much of her territory she is obliged to continue the fight, in the hope that something may turn up. As an Austrian soldier friend of my informant expressed it : " We are beginning to realise that all along we have been the tool of Germany, and whether we win or lose we shall have to pay, and pay dearly."

A lady who returned from Prague to England towards the end of August, 1917, described the economic situation as desperate. The crops, she said, had been most unsatisfactory. Moreover, all the fruit, cattle, potatoes, and other victuals were exported to Germany, and the native population was starving. In consequence of the scarcity of food, prices had risen enormously. A pound of rice cost 15s. or £1 ; butter (almost unobtainable), 16s. ; bacon (fat), 12s. ; chocolate, 16s. ; coffee or tea, £1 per pound. Bread was usually made of maize, but it was better when the Rumanian grain became available. Cloth cost about £2 per yard, and boots £4 per pair, generally with wooden heels.

The popular feeling in Bohemia was anti-German and anti-Austrian. Obviously the Czechs were determined to attain national independence. Food riots were frequent.

[*Elliott & Fry.*
SIR MAURICE DE BUNSEN.
British Ambassador to Austria-Hungary.

MR. F. C. PENFIELD.
United States Ambassador to Austria-Hungary.

The troops garrisoned in Prague were mostly Magyar, hostile and cruel towards the population.

The suffering was terrible, especially among the poorer classes. The mortality among the children, old people, and invalids was very high, largely owing to the lack of milk and proper nourishment. A so-called " hunger-typhoid " had broken out in some of the working-class suburbs of Prague.

So much, then, for the state of the Dual Monarchy at the end of the third year of the war, from the point of view of national food ; and now let us conclude by supplementing this with some official figures as to national finance.

Austro-Hungarian war expenditure At the beginning of June, 1917, the National Debt Committee of the Reichsrath estimated the war expenditure of Austria-Hungary to the end of 1916 at 44,000,000,000 kronen (£1,833,000,000 at the normal pre-war rate of exchange), of which Austria's share was 28,000,000,000 kronen (£1,166,000,000) and Hungary's 16,000,000,000 kronen (£666,000,000).

It was further estimated that the total Austro-Hungarian war expenditure to the end of June would reach the sum of 55,000,000,000 kronen (£2,291,000,000), and that the daily war expenditure of Austria in 1916 was 41,600,000 kronen (£1,750,000), while that of Hungary was 25,000,000

kronen (£1,040,000)—the " kronen " being reckoned at about tenpence, or a very little more than the French franc.

A little later the speech on the Austrian Budget by the new Minister of Finance, Dr. Spitzmüller (formerly Prime Minister), which was delivered in the Reichsrath, contained little more detailed information than the Budget itself, which was entirely without figures.

By way of explaining this extraordinary omission, the Minister said, in effect, that the presentation of an ordinary complete Budget would have shown an enormous deficit likely to be misinterpreted abroad, and would have placed Austria in a most painful situation before the whole world. The only actual figures contained in the exposé appeared far from satisfactory. The Minister stated that the expenditure in support of soldiers' families to the end of April, 1917, amounted to 3,500,000,000 kronen (about £146,000,000), a sum exceeding the whole Budget of the last year of peace—namely, 1913. This expenditure was increasing rapidly, and it was estimated that the total for 1917 would reach 2,100,000,000 kronen (about £87,000,000), or more than double the aggregate of all the direct and indirect taxes for the year.

An extraordinary Budget speech

Besides this, 600,000,000 kronen (£25,000,000) had been spent in relief of fugitives from Galicia, the Bukovina, and the Southern Crown lands, and 300,000,000 kronen (£12,500,000) to furnish cheap food for the poorer classes.

Several hundred millions would also be required for the restoration of damaged property in Galicia after the Russian invasion.

Regarding future plans, the Minister intimated that there would be heavy taxes on property and concentrations of capital, and confiscation of the share profits of trusts.

No wonder that the Austrian Press received the speech coldly, and expressed surprise and disappointment at the Minister's reticence. This disappointment could hardly have been lessened by the statement authorised by the Austrian Government on August 25th, 1917, that the Austrian State Budget for the year ending June 30th, 1917, showed a deficit of about £140,000,000.

In view of all those unfortunate and fatal figures, it was seen that a new meaning would have to be read into the old Hapsburg family maxim subserving the ends of State policy : " Bella gerant alii : tu, felix Austria, nube ! " (" Let others get on by waging war, but thou, more astute Austria, shalt seek to prosper in the world by means of politic marriages ") — marriages which would now have to be superseded, if possible, by money loans.

Five vowels were inscribed on all the Hapsburg palaces by Frederick III., " A.E.I.O.U.," admitting of three interpretations : " Austria erit in orbe ultima " (" Austria will be the last survival among States ") ; " Austria est imperare orbi universo " (" Austria's business is to rule the world ") ; or " Alle Erde ist Oesterreich unterthan " (" All lands are subject to Austria ").

Compare those haughty inscriptions on the walls of all the Hapsburg palaces with the real " handwriting on the wall " as engraved thereon by the events of the world war which Austria provoked !

SIGNALLERS HELIOGRAPHING

FROM AN EGYPTIAN TOMB.

THE SAFEGUARDING OF THE SUEZ CANAL AND THE ADVANCE INTO PALESTINE.

By Robert Machray.

Problem of the Defence of Egypt and Suez Canal—Conditions in the Summer of 1916—General Murray Plans an Advance across Sinai —His Military Engineers Build a Railway Eastward—How the Arabs Co-operated with the British—Daring Cavalry and Air Raids from the Canal—The Turco-German "Second Invasion of Egypt" Starts—Its Total Failure—Magnificent Victory at Romani—Enemy's Serious Losses—Pause while Railway is Pushed On—Great Air Raid on Beersheba—The Advance Begun— Swift, Sudden March on El Arish—Turks Hastily Abandon that Base—Their Flight to Magdhaba, where They are Enveloped and Completely Defeated—The Advance Continued—Battle of Rafa Splendidly Won after Hard Fighting—Palestine in Sight— The Zionist Movement—State of the Holy Land—Prevalence of German Intrigue—Cruel Turkish Oppression of both Christians and Jews—British Cross the Frontier—First Battle of Gaza—Fog Deprives British of Full Victory—Second Battle of Gaza Indecisive—Results in Stalemate—Trench Warfare—General Allenby Replaces General Murray—Operations on the West— The Grand Senussi Driven Out of the Oases—A Broken Fugitive—End of the Rebel Sultan of Darfur—Vast Improvement of the whole British Position in Egypt.

SUBSEQUENT to the complete repulse of the Turco-Germans from the Suez Canal in February, 1915, the various operations which were undertaken by the British for the further defence of Egypt were recorded in Chapter CXVIII. (Vol. 6, page 453) up to about the end of May, 1916. The narrative described the thrust forward to the east, and concluded, so far as that front was concerned, with the recapture, on April 26th, 1916, of Katia, the oasis on the great caravan road from El Kantara to Rafa and Gaza. It also chronicled the defeat in the west of the mysterious and formidable Senussi, which was nearly consummated by May, 1916, and it told of the over-throw in the south-west of Ali Dinar, the rebel Sultan of Darfur, whose capital, El Fasher, was taken on May 23rd of that year.

Apart from some successes, none of which was of lasting importance, the enemy, in what-ever guise he presented himself, had everywhere failed, while, on the other hand, the British had substantially improved their position on all sides. They now had no grounds for apprehension with respect to the west of the

ABOVE THE TAPERING MINARET.
British aeroplane flying over El Arish, about thirty miles west of Rafa, on the Mediterranean shore of Sinai—one of the important positions taken by the British during their rapid advance on Gaza.

country, and with regard to the eastern front they were preparing to take advantage of the territory which they had occupied east of the canal, and make a forward movement across Northern Sinai towards Palestine, thus providing for the safeguarding of the Suez Canal in a far more adequate manner than had been possible before.

Among the problems which the Allies had to face after the entry of Turkey into the war none was more pressing than that of the defence of Egypt— which meant chiefly of the Suez Canal, the principal artery of communication between Europe and the East, and one of perfectly enormous significance, especially to the British Empire. The difficulty of this particular problem arose from the fact that, for one reason or another, the most prominent being the Gallipoli adventure, the British were short of men on the spot. The forces in Egypt, which was turned into a sort of intermediate clearing-base, were constantly being drawn upon ; no sooner was there a strong concentration of troops than imperious demands from the field elsewhere compelled a heavy depletion. For a con-siderable period nothing beyond a stationary defensive of the

SLEDGING IN THE DESERT.
Sledges were used in great numbers by the Egyptian Expeditionary Force for transport of supplies over the sand.

HYBRID VEHICLES EVOLVED IN WAR-TIME.
Necessity, prolific mother of inventions, stimulated the native resourcefulness of the British soldier, who discovered that motor-bicycles, deprived of wheels, provided effective power for light-railway trollies.

of Egypt would be a much easier business altogether. Then perhaps more than that might come of it —Palestine lay just beyond. The Holy Land, the birthplace of the Christian faith, might be redeemed from the Turk; Jerusalem, Bethlehem, and other sacred shrines with their eternal memories, be rescued from infidel hands and cleansed of their polluting touch. Such ideas as these could not but fire the imagination and thrill the hearts of men to most of whom the Bible story was part and parcel of themselves. But these ideas, like the beginning itself of the advance into Palestine, came later. The first—prosaic, but necessary—effort of the British was the defence of Egypt and of the all-important Suez Canal.

Establishing his headquarters at Ismailia, General Sir Archibald Murray took over the defence of Eastern Egypt from General Sir John Maxwell in January, 1916. These two high officers shared the Command in Egypt for a little while, but on March 19th, 1916, the dual control ceased, and Maxwell returned to Europe. Murray, meanwhile, had gone on vigorously with the completion of the stationary defences of the canal —the great work which had been initiated by General Sir Alexander Wilson. Owing to difficulties connected with the water supply on the east bank, and vexatious delays caused by labour troubles, it was not until the last week of May, however, that the desired end was attained. By the close of the month one hundred and fourteen miles of roads had been built, one hundred and fifty-four miles of pipe-lines laid, and two hundred and fifty-two miles of railways constructed. The railways were of narrow gauge, running alongside the canal and to adjacent permanent points. But to this statement there was one extremely significant exception to be made. A broad-gauge line was started from El Kantara in an easterly direction, the general purpose of which was clearly indicated by the middle of April, when the railway, which had reached Romani, was being prolonged towards Katia.

canal could be attempted in such circumstances. It said a good deal that this defensive was sufficiently powerful to prevail over the Turkish assault of 1915, the assault which Germany had widely advertised as the "Invasion of Egypt," loudly predicting from it all manner of evil for the hated British.

During the twelve months that followed on that defeat of the ambitious plans of the enemy the flux of the war told first against and then in favour of the British in Egypt. For, if the termination of the Gallipoli Expedition resulted in setting free large numbers of Turkish soldiers for service in Syria and Sinai, the victorious campaign of General Yudenitch in Armenia, which saw the fall of Erzerum, necessitated in its turn the withdrawal of most of these regiments to the threatened area in Asia Minor. This balancing of accounts left Egypt and the canal comparatively safe from attack. To a certain extent this was satisfactory as the situation then was, but it could scarcely be considered that the line of defence, which was no other than the canal itself, was the best obtainable. It was obvious that the farther away from the canal the enemy was pressed the less would be his opportunity of doing mischief and the greater its security.

At the beginning of 1916 the Turks were in occupation of the whole of the Sinaitic Peninsula, with the exception of some stations on the Gulf of Suez. Yet the Peninsula, though it was in Asia, belonged to Egypt, and that Egypt should hold it was most desirable, if not absolutely essential, for the thorough protection of the canal. Indeed, a sound strategy required that the Peninsula should be reoccupied with all possible speed, as thereafter the defence

Egypt and the Sinaitic Peninsula

Sir Archibald Murray had made up his mind that the line of defence for the canal had to be shifted well to the eastward of its banks. In a memorandum, dated February 15th, and addressed to the Chief of the Imperial General Staff in London, he stated his opinion that the first step for securing the true base for the defence of Egypt was an advance to a suitable position east of Katia and the construction of a railway to that place. The War Office concurred, and the British Government gave its sanction to the outlined scheme. As the march of events disclosed, the new railway was designed to extend many miles east of Katia, and it was destined to have a marked effect

Sir A. Murray's railway plan

on the "offensive-defensive" campaign which Sir Archibald had in view. The line, after leaving Romani, eventually passed through Katia and followed thereafter the ancient camel road across the Wilderness of Sin, a short distance south of the Mediterranean, reaching the coast at El Arish. A great part of the region traversed consisted of drift sand, loose, soft, and infinitely fatiguing for the wayfarer, but here and there along the route were

Results of the Arab rising — oases with wells of brackish water; at El Arish itself the wells were good and fairly numerous. By nature it was a poor country for troops in any number, yet in past times great armies had marched across its wide-stretching wastes, though with difficulty and much loss. The military engineer, with his railway and its accompanying pipe-lines, was to make all the difference.

Early in May, 1916, the Turks increased their strength in Sinai by bringing up considerable reinforcements, and from a few miles east of Katia were keeping close watch on the movements of the British, who were in some force at Romani. El Arish was the Turkish base on the caravan road, and an army, composed of about 20,000 men in July, was gradually concentrated there, under the command of Colonel Kress von Kressenstein, the Bavarian officer who had been Chief of Staff to Djemal Pasha in the abortive attack on the canal in 1915. The enemy had by no means abandoned the idea of another direct assault on the canal, and in all probability had intended to assemble a much larger striking force, but the flux of the war again told against him. In this instance the effect was produced by the Arab revolt in the Hedjaz, which was headed by the Grand Sherif of Mecca, who declared his independence of Turkey—as was briefly noted in Chapter CXXVIII. (Vol. 7, p. 161). By the middle of the summer nearly all Arabia, much of which had regarded but lightly the suzerainty of the Constantinople Caliphate, was in active rebellion, and the Turks had been expelled from the most important area of the country. From Yambo on the north to Kunfidah on the south, on the eastern side of the Red Sea, with the Holy Places of Islam behind the coast, the Turks were driven out by the Grand Sherif and other princes of Western Arabia.

Two important results of the Arab rising made themselves felt at once with respect to Egypt. One was military, the other religious and political, and its influence extended over the entire Mohammedan world, but both combined to aid General Murray's plans. The Young Turk Committee at Constantinople, with the Sultan and the religious authorities in its power, had posed as the trustee of Islam. It had acclaimed the German Kaiser as Hadji Mohammed Guilliamo, and had discovered that the Hohenzollerns were descendants of the Prophet. It declared that Germany was the true friend, the benevolent protector, of Mohammedanism. A much more accurate view was presented at the beginning of the war by the Aga Khan, who, in a statement addressed to the Mohammedans of India, pointed out to his co-religionists that the Kaiser's Resident in Constantinople would be the real ruler of Turkey, and would control Mecca and Medina, the Holy Cities. The Grand Sherif had come to see that the Aga Khan was right, and in August he issued a proclamation to Moslems throughout the world, in explanation of his course of action, which had already justified itself by its rapid and remarkable success. Having in mind the fact that Turkey, egged on by Germany, had endeavoured to incite Mohammedans everywhere to engage in a Jehad, or Holy War, against the Entente Powers, the **Proclamation of the Grand Sherif** proclamation of the Grand Sherif was one of the most striking documents that saw the light in the war. He began it by saying that he and his House had acknowledged the overlordship of Turkey in order to strengthen Islam, and then went on to state that the case was altered when the Government of Turkey was usurped by the Committee of Union and Progress with Enver Pasha, Talaat Bey, and Djemal Pasha as its directors. These men were the real rulers of Turkey, and it was plain that they did whatever was good in their own eyes without reference to the precepts and claims of the Mohammedan religion or the rights of those who believed in it. They had despised God's house, and had denied the honour due to it. " Our aim," said the Grand Sherif, " is the preservation of Islam and the uplifting of its standard in the world. We fortify ourselves on our noble religion which is our

HOW THE WOUNDED WERE MOVED ACROSS THE DESERT.
One of the light mule-drawn carts, fitted with very thick tyres to avoid sticking in the sand, used by the R.A.M.C. with the Egyptian Expeditionary Force. Above: A camel carrying two casualties in a regulation double ambulance stretcher.

BRITISH DESERT COLUMN ON THE MARCH.
Much of the advance from the Suez Canal to the border of Palestine was through bare sandy wastes, very monotonous and trying to the troops, who, notwithstanding, achieved some surprising marches.

only guide." Ready himself to accept all things in harmony with the faith, he urged his fellow-believers everywhere to make a stand against Turkey, so that the " brotherhood of Islam " might be confirmed.

It was not to be expected that the committee would sit down calmly under such a challenge, preceded as it had been by such determined hostile action. Accordingly troops were despatched south in a great hurry, and part of the forces which had been assigned for a second invasion of Egypt was diverted to the Hedjaz. Thus Kressenstein's army was not nearly so strong as it might and probably would have been, and, **Daring cavalry** meanwhile, the phantasm of a Pan-**and air raids** Islamism arrayed against the Entente, which Germany had sought to endow with actuality and employ for her own purposes, had been shown to be the unreal thing it was in the circumstances of the time.

Kressenstein's attack did not develop till the beginning of August. In the meantime General Murray went on with his preparations. Permanent lines of defence were constructed from Romani to Mahemdia, on the coast along the Bay of Tineh, where the co-operation of the Navy could come into play. In these waters the British naval forces were commanded by Vice-Admiral Sir Rosslyn Wemyss, who could be depended on not to lose any opportunity that presented itself.

From various points of the front General Lawrence, who, under Sir Archibald Murray, was in command of the land operations, sent forward reconnoitring parties, and constantly harassed the Turks by raids, in which the Anzac Mounted Division made several records. On one

occasion the Canterbury Mounted Rifles, who were included in the division, rode forty miles, in heat most intense, in thirty hours, and on another the 2nd Light Horse Brigade covered sixty miles in the same number of hours and in the same tropical, sweltering conditions, destroying a Turkish camp and capturing many camels. On May 31st a most successful raid was made on the enemy's post at Bir Salmana, some twenty miles east of Katia, by the New Zealand Mounted Rifles, a regiment of Australian Light Horse, and an Ayrshire Horse Artillery battery. The post was rushed, with heavy loss to the Turks, the British casualties being only two men slightly wounded. Aeroplanes bombed the flying Turks and completed their discomfiture. In this affair the British force covered sixty **Combined attack** miles in thirty-six hours—including the **on El Arish** engagement. The Royal Flying Corps also gave a good account of itself during May, bombing all enemy camps from Bir el Mazar to Rod Salem, a distance of over forty miles.

In May the most important operation undertaken against the Turks took place on the 18th, and consisted of a combined sea and air attack on the Turkish base at El Arish. With their fire directed by seaplanes, two monitors and a sloop bombarded for two hours the fortifications, aerodrome, and camp of the enemy. Shells from the heavy guns of the monitors hit the aerodrome, a fort was destroyed, and the camp was set in flames in many parts. So overcome were the Turks that they attempted no reply, and many of them sought shelter among the palms near the shore, whereupon the sloop, under cover of the monitors, stood in close to the coast

TURKISH TROOPS FOR THE EGYPTIAN FRONT.
Body of Turkish troops marching to the sound of their brass band to reinforce their fellows on the Egyptian front, where, instead of winning forward to the canal, they were steadily pressed back into Palestine by the British forces.

and searched the trees very thoroughly with medium-sized shells. To complete the demoralisation of the enemy, six machines of the Royal Flying Corps now joined in, and dropped a large number of bombs, three of which were described as exploding in the midst of a body of a thousand troops, " evidently Germans." One of the valuable results of this assault on El Arish was that the place was well reconnoitred, several excellent photographs being taken by the flying men. Later Kressenstein provided the camp with anti-aircraft guns, and retaliated by making raids in the following month on El Kantara, Romani, Serapeum, and the canal itself with aeroplanes. On the British side June was signalised by another air attack on El Arish.

Enemy aerodrome bombed On June 13th Bir el Mazar and El Arish were visited by a squadron of British machines, the particular effort being to place definitely the whereabouts of an aerodrome known to exist in the neighbourhood of the latter town. On this occasion the Turks sent up a Fokker to try conclusions with the British flyers, but it was easily driven down, and the aerodrome that was being looked for was located to the south of the place. Having obtained the requisite information, the airmen returned and reported —with the result that on the 18th eleven aeroplanes were despatched to El Arish for the purpose of destroying the aerodrome, and very successful was the venture, which involved in all a voyage of two hundred miles. The British airmen carried out their orders most brilliantly. The first who arrived on the scene descended to a hundred feet, and blew to pieces an enemy aeroplane and its personnel. A second machine was also put out of action by bombs. The Turks now opened heavy fire from rifles and machine-guns on the attackers who, however, stuck

DEBUT OF THE " TANK " IN THE HOLY LAND.
British " tank " going into action in the fighting before Gaza, one of the ancient battlefields of the Holy Land. The figures on the sky-line are British officers observing the Turkish trenches.

intrepidly to their task. General Murray reported that altogether six out of ten of the hangars of the aerodrome were hit, and two, if not three, were burned to the ground. A party of soldiers on the aerodrome was also successfully bombed, and at the close one of the observing machines attacked the hangars with its machine-gun from a height of 1,200 feet. The British lost three machines in the action. The pilot of one set his aeroplane on fire to prevent the Turks from capturing it. A second machine fell into the sea, its pilot being rescued by a motor-boat. The third was compelled to land some miles east of El Arish, and while its pilot was trying to repair it he was seen by one of the escorting aircraft, which at once landed at considerable risk, picked him up, and flew back to El Kantara, a distance of ninety miles, carrying two passengers in addition to **The " Second** the pilot—an extremely gallant feat. **Invasion of Egypt "**

General Murray was quite ready to meet the " Second Invasion of Egypt," as it was grandiloquently called by the Germans. He was, in fact, better prepared to repel it than Kressenstein was to make it, though the latter had received large quantities of material, including tanks and pontoons, from Germany. The force of the enemy consisted of the 3rd Turkish Division, with eight machine-gun companies under German officers and partly manned by Germans, mountain artillery, and batteries of 4 in. and 6 in. howitzers and anti-aircraft guns with Austrian artillerymen. Germany had specially organised for service with the Turks the machine-gun units, heavy artillery, wireless sections, and field-hospital and supply sections, as Murray noted in his despatch of October 1st, 1916. In addition to the Turkish infantry, there was in support

TURKISH REGULARS AT A SYRIAN OUTPOST.
Turkish soldiers on outpost duty at the foot of a crumbling wall. At the moment of facing the camera the men were evidently anxious that all their arms should be in the picture.

an array of Arab camelry. Considering the nature of its task, the enemy force, though admirably equipped, was inadequate ; and when this was demonstrated by its complete defeat, surprise was expressed in many quarters that it had attempted such an effort. Kressenstein may have supposed that the British front was weakly held, as he was aware that several divisions had been sent from Egypt to France ; if this was his conception of the situation, he soon found out his mistake. Perhaps **German pressure** he thought to gain something from **on Kressenstein** launching his assault at the hottest time of the year, when it would be least expected. Probably he had penetrated Murray's plans for the building of the railway and the advance eastward across the desert, and was determined to thwart them, or at least materially delay their accomplishment. Then there was Germany urging him on, for at this juncture what was taking place on the Somme caused her to be sincerely anxious that as many British troops as possible should remain elsewhere.

Indications of the coming offensive were observed by General Murray as early as July 17th in the appearance

MAKING AN END OF DANGEROUS JETSAM.
Large numbers of floating mines were sown by the Germans in Mediterranean waters along the coasts of Sinai and Palestine. Many of them were washed up on shore, and these were collected and exploded harmlessly by the Royal Engineers with the Egyptian Expeditionary Force in the manner here shown.

of numerous Turkish aeroplanes over the Romani-Duweidar district. Two days later British scouting airmen reported that the Turks were on the move westward, and had reached Bir el Abd in considerable strength, with their line extended south-west through Bir Jamiel to Bir el Bayud. Murray's advanced troops fell back towards the Romani-Mahemdia fortifications, and reinforcements were sent forward to Romani. The Commander-in-Chief gave orders to General Lawrence, who was leading the British on the spot, not to hinder the march of the enemy by a premature counter-attack, but to allow Kressenstein to develop his movement and disclose its aim. Meanwhile cavalry kept in touch with the Turks, whose every act was closely followed by aircraft and reported to head-quarters. On the 20th Kressenstein swung forward his left from Bir el Bayud to the Magheibra Oasis and his centre from Abd to Oghratina, where in the preceding April the two squadrons of the Worcester Yeomanry had been so severely handled.

For the next succeeding days there was little change, but Kressenstein was busy entrenching and strengthening his

positions. At Magheibra, on his left, he constructed a series of redoubts, and garrisoned them with 3,000 men. Around Oghratina, his centre, he had lines dug among the groves of date-palms, and held them with a force of certainly not less than 5,000 effectives. On his right, towards the Serbonian Lake, he established rows of entrenchments, and manned them with hundreds of soldiers. He had brought with him a numerous body of labourers from Palestine for making trenches, and he worked them for all they were worth. A tract of desert about fifteen miles wide lay between his and the British lines. On the night of July 27th he made a general advance, which was most marked from Magheibra, his troops swinging up to the north-west. On his right he was checked by the Canterbury Mounted Rifles, who, in a brisk, sanguinary passage, killed fifty of his men, themselves losing only two or three. Then Kressenstein paused again. He threw up fresh entrenchments and brought forward the rest of his army till, by the end of the month, he had 18,000 men at his disposal.

Before this Sir Archibald Murray, after an exhaustive survey of the situation, had resolved that the enemy should be attacked. The difficulty with which the Commander-in-Chief was confronted lay in the fact that the huge camel transport necessary for the crossing of the strip of desert that stretched between him and Kressenstein was not immediately available, and for the moment he was unable to move in force. Orders, however, were given for getting ready with all speed a striking force on a pack basis with camel transport; but it was not till August 3rd that all formations were in a position to take the field. His intention was, unless his hand was forced, to deliver an assault on the Turks about ten days later, when it would be full moon. While these preparations for an offensive were going on, General Lawrence kept the enemy anxious and distracted by various minor operations. A mobile camel column, under Lieut.-Colonel C. V. Smith, V.C., from July 28th harried the Turkish left and rear around Magheibra and Bayud. The Royal Flying Corps ceased to perform merely scouting work, and from July 29th incessantly bombed the enemy's lines and camps, giving him no peace. On July 30th two monitors, commanded respectively by Commander Robinson, who had won the V.C. for distinguished gallantry at Gallipoli, and by Lieut.-Commander A. O. St. John, began shelling the Turkish right flank from the Bay of Tineh.

On August 2nd Kressenstein made a strong reconnaissance in the direction of Katia and Hamisah, the latter lying a little south of the former and a few miles north-west of Magheibra. And this was the position he took up next day for the main attack. The reconnaissance made a slight gain on the north, **Turkish attack** but, after sharp fighting with the Anzac **in force** Mounted Division, was held up everywhere else. For some hours General Murray was in doubt whether he or Kressenstein would attack first, but on the following day any uncertainty there was came to an end, when, about midnight of August 3rd, the Turks assaulted in force, and drove furiously at the Romani-Mahemdia fortifications. These lines were defended by the 52nd Division of Territorials from the Lowlands of Scotland. They faced east to a point east of an enormous sand-dune,

Camel train of wounded on their way to hospital in "cacolets"—military litters specially designed for transport by mules or camels.

Loading up kit and camp equipment on a camel in preparation for a move to new quarters.

Transport Corps natives shearing a camel. Left: Representative units of the Sudanese Camel Patrol—soldierly men and splendid animals.

Camels attached to the transport service of the E.E.F. at one of the huge supply dumps. Although railway lines of various gauges and motor-lorries were employed in conveying supplies to the troops, the camels were not dispossessed of their historic paramountcy as a means of desert transport.

CAMELS STILL AN INDISPENSABLE PART OF MILITARY MACHINERY IN THE DESERT.

three hundred feet high, known as Katib Gannit, and thence the British position looked south-westward, its natural features being a hill named Hod el Enna on the south, and two great sand-dunes called Mount Meredith and Mount Royston to the north, with a stretch on the east of high-lying, bright yellow sand termed Wellington Ridge. These distinctively English appellations were derived respectively from the names of Colonel Meredith, commanding the 1st Australian Light Horse ; General Royston, in command of the 2nd Australian Light Horse ; and from that of the Wellington Mounted Rifles, who hailed from New Zealand. Behind Mount Royston was Pelusium, a station on the new railway from Kantara.

Kressenstein planned to press back the British on the south, cut the railway, and then attack from the rear. Having driven in the outposts on Hod el Enna, Mount Meredith and the Wellington Ridge, he forced the British to the north of Mount Royston by mid-day on August 4th, and the situation had an alarming look, but the enemy's success was only temporary. The British troops here consisted of the 1st Australian Light Horse Brigade, between Katib Gannit and Mount Meredith, and the New Zealand mounted force, around Mount Royston. In the darkness of midnight 3,000 Turks had attacked the Australians, who kept them off with machine-gun fire. The enemy then delivered a bayonet assault on Mount Meredith, but it was repulsed ; a second attack, for which reinforcements had been brought up, met with more success, and by half-past four o'clock in the morning the Australians had lost the hill. Kressenstein next tried to outflank them on the left, and the troopers fell back slowly towards the railway. Meanwhile he had been shelling with his heavy howitzers and field-guns the whole of the fortifications stretching between Mahemdia and Romani, but was unable to effect any serious impression. Nor were the repeated assaults of his infantry able to make any change to his advantage. The Territorials stood their ground like veterans, and repelled him at every point. As evening came on the enemy fire grew less and less until it died away in this part of the field, where Kressenstein had failed altogether.

On the southern front the day had finally gone against the Turks. After fighting their way to within a mile and a half of the railway—the farthest point of their advance northward—they were counter-attacked about 12.30 by the British, who had received belated **Recapture of** reinforcements in the shape of two **Mount Royston** mounted brigades originally intended to operate on the enemy's rear. Three hours later two brigades of the East Lancashire Territorials appeared on the scene, but by this time the Anzac and other cavalry had begun to throw the Turks back, and at four o'clock the infantry was ordered to drive them out of Mount Royston and Wellington Ridge. The Yeomen dismounted and advanced side by side with the East Lancashires, all fighting with the utmost gallantry. The Turks put up a game and determined defensive for a couple of hours, but Mount Royston was recaptured from them about half-past

six o'clock, with the loss besides of five hundred men taken prisoners, a mountain battery, and several machine-guns. As daylight broke on August 5th, Wellington Ridge was stormed by Scottish Territorials, under General W. E. B. Smith, helped by some of the Anzacs, the loss of the Turks being very heavy. It included 1,500 men taken prisoners, among them being a number of Germans.

Kressenstein's attempt was, it was now clear, a complete failure; the " Second Invasion of Egypt " was destined to share the fate of **Turco-Germans again** the first invasion. On the 5th the British **in full retreat** advanced all along the line, and Scottish troops carried the enemy's strong position at Abu Hamra. The cavalry, comprising the Mounted Anzacs and the Gloucester and Warwick Yeomanry, pressed on in hot pursuit, under the leadership of General Sir H. G. Chauvel, K.C.M.G., C.B., the officer commanding the Australian force, who also was splendidly supported by batteries of Territorial horse artillery. A strong Turkish rearguard made a short stand at Katia and then at Oghratina to cover Kressenstein's retreat, but the British advance was hardly delayed. On the 8th he retired to Bir el Abd, where Chauvel nearly succeeded in enveloping him. Three days later the Turks were again in full retreat, nor did their main body halt until it had reached El Arish, only a rearguard being left at Bir el Mazar. In his despatch of October 1st, 1916, Sir Archibald Murray wrote :

The complete result of the operations in the Katia district was the decisive defeat of an enemy force amounting in all to some 18,000 men, including 15,000 rifles. Some 4,000 prisoners, including fifty officers, were captured ; and, from the number of enemy dead actually buried, it is estimated that the total number of the enemy casualties amounted to about 9,000. In addition, there were captured one Krupp 3 in. mountain battery of four guns complete with all the accessories and four hundred rounds of ammunition, nine G e r m a n machine-guns (dated 1915) and mountings, with specially constructed pack-saddles for camel transport, 2,300 rifles, one million rounds small-arms ammunition, a hundred horses and mules, five hundred camels, and a large amount of miscellaneous stores and equipment. Two field hospitals, with most of their equipment, were also abandoned by the enemy in his retreat, and large quantities of stores were burned by him at Bir el Abd to prevent their capture.

LINES OF COMMUNICATION IN THE DESERT.
An outpost British soldier on the Egyptian front telephoning to his base warning of the approach of enemy aircraft. Though the message could be sent by an up-to-date method, the messenger rode the camel, the ancient " ship of the desert," to reach his post.

Thus did the second great effort of the Turco-Germans for the possession of the Suez Canal go down in sheer disaster in this Battle of Romani, as it came to be called. The glorious victory won by the British would have been even more sweeping than it was but for difficulties in supplying the pursuing troops with water. Much had been done in overcoming these difficulties. As soon as the forward movement began, many thousands of transport camels with water, food, ammunition, and material for entrenching stretched over the desert " like veins in all directions "—to quote the description of Mr. Massey, the Press correspondent with the British Army in Egypt, who added that for three days and nights, as far as the eye could reach, there was a never-ending procession of this multitudinous array of heavily-laden camels, the only animals that could negotiate with loads the wastes of Sinai, with its drift sand and fierce summer heat.

But even camel transport had its limits, and General Murray did not push his advance beyond Bir el Abd for several weeks; and Kressenstein took enough heart of grace to reinforce his outpost at Bir el Mazar, where he entrenched on a front of three or four miles, and accumulated howitzers and field-artillery. On September 16th and 17th, however, Murray set to work to disturb him. Starting from Abd, Sir H. G. Chauvel reconnoitred Mazar with a force composed of Australian Light Horse, the Imperial Camel Corps, a mountain battery, and some batteries of the Royal Horse Artillery. Simultaneously British air-machines appeared over Mazar and seaplanes bombed the enemy's headquarters at El Arish. There was some fighting at Mazar, not of a very intense description, but it was enough for the Turks, who evacuated the position without any real attempt to check the British. Masaid was the next halting-place of the fleeing foe, some five miles from El Arish.

Three months passed before the British moved eastward in force again, but in the meantime they had been very busy getting ready, in accordance with General Murray's plans, for the expulsion of Kressenstein and the Turks from the north of the Sinaitic Peninsula. The main thing on which he relied for success in this effort was the railway, and he pushed the line on with a speed that was wonderful in the circumstances, its rate of construction being two-thirds of a mile on an average each day.

Railway and pipe-line progress From Romani it passed through Katia, and then swung across the desert through Oghratina to Bir el Abd and Bir Salmana, whence the vagaries of the drift sand raised problems almost every minute for his engineers. And with the laying of the rails went the laying, though more slowly, of the pipe-lines with the blessed water, without which no army, however fine, could march. In order to be in touch with the civil authority, the Commander-in-Chief transferred his headquarters from Ismailia to Cairo on October 23rd, the local command, with headquarters at Ismailia, devolving on Lieut.-General Sir Charles Dobell, K.C.B., C.M.G., D.S.O.

Of course, Murray saw to the assembling of the force for striking hard at El Arish when the time came, and till that arrived his aeroplanes were incessantly active in scouting, in taking photographs of the route until it was all clearly mapped out, and in bombing operations at Masaid, El Arish, and elsewhere. In the middle of November a long-distance raid was made on Beersheba, the great Turkish base on the strategic railway through Syria and Palestine, large quantities of bombs being dropped on the railway-station, sidings, and rolling-stock. Also in November, El Auja and El Kossaima, on the road from Beersheba to Nakhl, and both important points on the Turkish lines of communication westward across the central plateau of Sinai, were heavily bombed. The Turks retaliated by an air raid on Cairo, which effected nothing of military consequence, its sole result being the killing and wounding of several civilians.

Although operations now centred in the north of the Peninsula, they did not cease in other parts of it. In the **Futile air raid on Cairo** invasion of 1915 the Turco-Germans had advanced on the canal by three roads that crossed Sinai: on the north by the Serbonian Road, as it was anciently named, which was now being turned into a railroad by Murray's engineers; in the centre, from El Auja towards Serapeum, Tussum, and Ismailia; and on the south, by the Darb el Haj, or Pilgrims' Road, through Nakhl towards the town of Suez. With regard to the second of these roads, which was the route of the main Turkish advance under Djemal Pasha, the British had destroyed the wells at Jifjaffa and at Hassana by air raids in the first half of 1916. In October a mounted force, after two night marches in drift sand, reconnoitred Magara, a strong mountain position on the southern side of the desert of El Jiffar, between sixty and seventy miles east of Ismailia. In a brisk fight lasting two hours, the outposts of the Turks were driven in, with a loss of twenty-eight men, the British having only three casualties. Having ascertained the exact position of the enemy's main concentration, the mounted men returned westward; but in the middle of November the Royal Flying Corps paid the place a visit and dropped four hundred pounds of explosives on the camp and its stores with excellent results. Southward, on the third road, General Mudge raided Bir el Tawal, some thirty miles east of Kubri, in September, and taking the Turks completely by surprise, put them to flight after a brief

PIONEERS OF THE BRITISH ADVANCE OVER THE DESERT.
Engineers smoothing a crossing over a dried-up water-course on the Egyptian front. The work of the Pioneers with the Egyptian Expeditionary Force was very arduous, for the old caravan route along the north of the Desert of Sin was totally inadequate for the movement of a modern army and had to be made good along its whole length, besides being supplemented by many miles of railway.

K

SAND-BAGGED DESERT RAILWAY-STATION.
El Alamein Station on the Western Egypt coast railway. After being occupied by the Senussiyeh it was retaken by the British and fortified against further attack by sand-bag breastworks.

By the third week in December the main British force was again in motion along the northern road, in the direction of El Arish. The railway was well forward, and General Murray's plans had matured for the advance eastward. His army was small as armies went in the war, but it was composed of the same redoubtable troops who had won the Battle of Romani five months before — the Anzac Horse, Yeomanry, Territorials, and Camel Corps, a sort of epitome of the Empire. On the morning of December 20th the British marched out of Bir el Abd, accompanied by squadrons of aeroplanes, who kept the

struggle, and captured all their supplies. Thereafter he destroyed the wells and withdrew to the zone of the canal.

From the southern end of the great waterway, where the British had strongly fortified the Well of Moses, otherwise Ain Musa, for the protection of the town of Suez, frequent raids into the interior were made, which easily fulfilled the limited ends in view. Considerable activity also was shown farther south, on the Sinai shore of the Gulf of Suez, Abu Zeneima and Tor, both small ports—but the latter, at least, of some importance—being occupied by Sikh and Bikanir Camel Corps troops. From these places Major W. J. Ottley, who had previously distinguished himself at Aden, conducted a raiding expedition inland, in the course of which **British occupy El Arish** he dispersed several bodies of the enemy, took a number of prisoners, among whom was an Arab chief, rounded up a large quantity of live-stock, and traversed sixty miles of difficult hilly country all without a single casualty—a remarkable performance. On the eastern side of Sinai the port of Akaba with its forts was repeatedly shelled by British warships. About half-way between Akaba and Suez, on the Pilgrims' Road, lay Nakhl, from which also ran a road north-easterly to El Auja and Beersheba. Of strategic significance, it was one of the chief remaining Turkish centres. In December a British mobile column advanced from Suez towards it for a considerable distance, destroyed two camps en route, and was a distinct menace to the Turks in that quarter.

THE IRON ROAD ACROSS THE SANDY WASTES.
Driving in the spikes. British soldiers engaged in laying a new railway across the desert during the Egyptian campaign. The laying of railways considerably facilitated the operations in driving back the threatened Turco-German attacks on the Suez Canal and pressing the enemy back into Palestine.

command well supplied with information, besides tackling the enemy's machines. The columns swept on without opposition across the broad desert track towards Masaid, which the Turks had strongly fortified, and where they were expected to make a stand. But no stand was made. Murray had been too quick for Kressenstein, who, unable to bring up reinforcements in time to parry this sudden stroke, decided on instant retreat—not only from Masaid, but also from El Arish itself. As soon as General Murray knew that Kressenstein's men were evacuating El Arish he ordered the Anzac Mounted Division and the Camel Corps to press on and occupy the town. They had been on the move all the livelong day and were nearing Masaid. With hardly a pause they marched on through the night, found the Turkish lines at Masaid deserted, and as the day broke entered El Arish—to discover it practically abandoned, too. They made a few prisoners, but Kressenstein, with nearly his whole force, had got away, some retreating along the road to Rafa on the border, while others, the larger number, with whom was Kressenstein, fled southward along the bed, then dry, of the Wady el Arish, the ancient "River of Egypt," to Bir el Magdhaba.

El Arish fell into the hands of the British on December 21st in the course of this wonderful march of

OLD AND NEW IN STRIKING CONTRAST.
This large locomotive had been transferred from one of the great British railway lines to new service in Egypt. The camel standing by the engine affords a striking contrast of the age-long means of Eastern desert travel with the modern "iron horse" imported from the West.

twenty-four hours, an achievement in its way as memorable as any in the war. During the night of December 22nd, after a day in bivouac, Chauvel of the Australians, who was in local command, had his men once more on the road; but this time the route was south to Magdhaba, by way of the dry Wady el Arish. The enemy had thought he was safe at Magdhaba, but his calculations were to be thoroughly upset. He had no notion of the powers of endurance these Anzacs and others possessed. General Chauvel knew the kind of troops he had under him, and, acting under Murray's orders, he determined to

BRITISH CAVALRY GOING FORWARD.
British cavalry advancing across a wady—or dried-up water-course. In the foreground men of the Royal Engineers were breaking down the banks to improve the crossing.

MAKING A ROAD OVER THE DESERT.
British infantrymen of the Egyptian Expeditionary Force engaged in "digging the sand" to some purpose. They were making a road over which the necessary transport vehicles could pass. Only by such constant and indefatigable spade-work was the advance made possible.

strike at the Turks without delay. Starting off soon after midnight at a sharp trot, Chauvel and his force covered a distance of twenty miles up the oftentimes rough bed of the wady in four hours, and after reconnoitring the enemy position, began the attack at eight o'clock on the morning of the 23rd. The camelry, with a mountain battery, supported by Territorial guns, whose fire was extraordinarily accurate, began the frontal attack, while the Anzacs, who were led by Brigadier-General E. W. C. Chayton, C.B., moved north of the Turkish position, under cover of the sand-dunes, to the east and south-east of Magdhaba, to cut off the retreat of the enemy. The Turks were well entrenched, with five redoubts very cunningly placed and armed with Krupp and mountain guns.

The battle lasted eight hours, and was of a desperate character, as the Turks offered the most strenuous resistance, mainly in these redoubts. Soon after the attack commenced, aeroplanes brought word that some of the enemy's troops were already retiring, and the Anzacs on the east pushed on quickly to complete the envelopment of the Turkish force, while a reserve brigade went forward at the trot to co-operate in this movement. It was soon discovered that only small bodies of the enemy were withdrawing, and that the main position was held in very considerable

strength. The retreat was, in fact, in the nature of a ruse. The reserve brigade came under heavy machine-gun fire, and the other Anzac brigades were systematically shelled by Krupp mountain guns. The Camel Corps also suffered from the Turkish fire while moving forward across the plain, on which there was not a vestige of cover, but it continued to advance with magnificent steadiness.

To assist the frontal assault, the reserve brigade swung to the right and at the same time extended its line to the west to complete the encircling of the foe. The British gained ground, but suffered from the lack of cover. One of the redoubts which could be seen from the artillery observation-post —it was the only one that could be so seen— was blown to bits, and its survivors showed the white flag; but the other re-doubts continued firing, and the battle progressed with violence. **Rout of the enemy at Magdhaba** About noon the British advance was stopped, except at one point, and as the enemy appeared determined to resist, supporting troops were brought into action. During the next two or three hours the fighting reached the greatest intensity. Aircraft attacked the redoubts, registering many hits; the guns increased their fire, and the troopers, dismounting, swarmed forward in repeated assaults. It was not until four o'clock in the afternoon, however, that the Turkish defence, which had been most resolute, gave way.

A small number of the enemy succeeded in escaping to El Auja, but otherwise the whole force of Kressenstein was captured or fell on the field. Out of an enemy force of

BRINGING IN ROAD-MAKING MATERIALS.
Infantrymen of the E.E.F. bringing in by armfuls the desert scrub which they had been collecting for road-making. It was such material as this that helped to bind the sand and made the roads laid by the Royal Engineers suitable for heavy traffic.

over 1,600 men, the British took 1,282 prisoners, including forty-five officers, among them being Khabir Bey, the commandant. Kressenstein himself escaped capture; it was reported that he had left Magdhaba for Beersheba in his motor-car early in the morning of the battle. Most of the prisoners were Syrians, big, well-built men. Among the spoils were four mountain and three Krupp guns, a large number of rifles, a hundred thousand rounds of small-arms ammunition, some artillery ammunition, telephone and other equipment, camels, and horses.

It was a very complete affair, and relatively a heavy blow to the Turco-Germans. In this brilliant **Work of the Anzacs** exploit the Anzacs and the camelry covered **and camelry** themselves with glory. During the latter half of the battle most of the men suffered agonies from thirst, but their fighting spirit remained undiminished. Some water rations came up in the course of the afternoon, and other supplies reached the force as it was returning to El Arish, where it arrived on the 24th, and was presently joined by the Territorials, who had to slog their way through the soft sand at such speed as was possible, and thus were prevented, much to their disgust, from taking a share in the defeat of the Turks.

For a little more than a fortnight the British forces

UNDER THE CLOUD OF SUSPICION.
Bedouins suspected of communicating with the enemy being taken to Headquarters for examination. Surprise was an essential element of the British operations at several points, notably at the River of Gaza, and it was of paramount importance to prevent news of impending movements leaking out to the enemy.

halted at El Arish, the roadstead of which had been cleared of mines and made practicable for the landing of supplies, and then there was another swift night march eastward, which also produced magnificent results, the Turks being again surprised and, though they fought desperately, utterly defeated. At sunset on January 8th, 1917, the Mounted Anzacs, Yeomanry, Camel Corps, Territorial horse-batteries, and a mountain battery under the command of Lieut.-General Sir Philip Chetwode, C.B., D.S.O., set out from El Arish along the road to Rafa, the town on the coast thirty miles distant, and just on the Egyptian frontier. The guns and the wheeled transport passed over a part of the route which the Turks had made fairly firm with brushwood. Striking south of it, the mounted troops rode through the night by cross-country paths—in deep sand for ten miles, and thereafter on harder ground, the going being so good that they were able to rest for a couple of hours. At four o'clock in the morning of the 9th the cavalry and camelry reached Karm Abu Musleh, a point five miles south of Rafa. After disarming a large number of Arabs, whose attitude might have been hostile, the New Zealanders, an hour later, moved rapidly over a grassy ridge direct on Rafa, which was found to be lightly held, and was immediately occupied.

The real struggle took place at El Magruntein, a strong natural position two miles south-west of the town. After their overthrow at Magdhaba the Turks had greatly increased the military strength of this place by digging several lines of trenches and constructing six redoubts, besides building many well-concealed rifle-pits. But the capture of Rafa itself began the day splendidly, for the New Zealanders were able from it to get behind the enemy's rear and harass him considerably. One of the New Zealand regiments was sent to the east to watch the movements of the Turks in that quarter, and subsequent happenings showed the wisdom of this step.

With the dawn the attack was general. The Territorial guns were pushed forward most gallantly, in spite of their being exposed to the heavy shelling of the enemy's mountain batteries. The troopers dismounted, and though raked by incessant fire, advanced across the open with the utmost courage and coolness to the assault. As the Turks were shifting from the west to the south, they were engaged by the Yeomanry, and large bodies of Light Horse galloped into action. The Camel Corps moved steadily to extreme rifle-range, dismounted, and made a model infantry attack. Yet the progress of the British was slow. They had little or no cover, and the fire of hostile machine-guns, which were operated by Germans, and of hidden marksmen told against them. The enemy made the most of his strong position. But in the afternoon the tide turned. At three o'clock the Anzac artillery and the battery supporting the Yeomanry opened an intense bombardment, which immediately silenced two of the opposing guns and wrecked some of the Turkish trenches. In a succession of rushes the dismounted men, who had been reinforced, pressed forward towards the position. It was at this moment, when victory was still uncertain, that the wisdom of placing that New Zealand regiment well to the east was justified. From that regiment came the news that two Turkish relief forces, from three to four thousand strong, were marching from the east towards Rafa, one of them being not more than three miles away.

In the circumstances the presence of these relief forces on the battlefield would have meant a very substantial addition to the Turks at El Magruntein, and it was therefore necessary for the British to make a supreme effort for victory there, while the New Zealanders held these forces up. Splendidly did Murray's men respond to the call. In an irresistible rush two of the Anzac brigades carried the south-eastern works, and as a New Zealand regiment dashed into the enemy's strongest position from the rear, the camelry made a sustained and effective assault on the south-west, and **British victory at** the yeomen attacked stoutly and success- **Rafa** fully all along the west. The fight was won—in the nick of time. The whole of the Turks in the place surrendered. Their loss had been very great, the accuracy of the British fire having filled their trenches with dead. In the meantime the New Zealanders on the east, though in much inferior numbers, had kept the relief forces back until the struggle was over, and then they attacked and forced those to retreat. Among the spoils of the Battle of Rafa were over 1,600 unwounded prisoners, including thirty-five officers and a number of German gunners, and a quantity of mountain and machine-guns, besides rifles, ammunition, and equipment. On the other hand, the casualties of the British—which were under five hundred—were comparatively light, considering the nature of the attack. One striking result of the battle was to clear the Turks entirely out of Northern Sinai for the first time for more than two years.

At Rafa the British gazed across the frontier upon the billowy downs of Southern Palestine, the fertile region which in Biblical days was known as the Land of the Philistines. From Kantara, the fortified bridge-head on the Suez Canal, they had advanced a distance of one hundred and twenty-five miles, more than a hundred of which were sheer desert; but some nine or ten miles west by south of Rafa the nature of the country had changed, the tract of endlessly monotonous and fatiguing soft sand was passed, the troops marched on firm ground, and the animals enjoyed the luxury of fresh green food. In ancient times the cultivated area had stretched even farther westward, the Wady el Arish, the River of Egypt, having marked the limits on the east of the desert in Northern Sinai. Arabs and Turks, with their blighting slackness of method, were responsible for the encroachment later of the drift sand. From Rafa north-eastward the sand had piled itself in a succession of high dunes, swept by the winds sometimes into strange, fantastic shapes; but this was the case

A scene of enchantment

only along the fringe of the coast, behind it lying a beautiful country-side, whose waving meadows and numerous fields of grain in the season spoke of an abundance of water. In the spring the undulating expanse of this goodly land repeated to English eyes the charm of the Berkshire Downs.

Writing in the third week of March, 1917, when General Murray's army had advanced some miles across the border, Mr. Massey, the accredited correspondent, gave this graphic picture of the scene:

Before and around us everything is green and fresh. Big patches of barley, for which the plain south of Gaza is famous, shine like emeralds, and the immense tracts of pasture are to-day as bright and beautiful as the rolling downs at home. We do not see the buttercup and cowslip to remind us of the time when, the war being over, we shall return to Britain, but in their place there is an abundance of the most gorgeous flowers lighting up the vivid greenness of the plain as if in welcome to an army which is to relieve the country from the oppressors' hand. There are crimson anemones, bright as any rubies, crocuses and narcissi, irises (short in the stem but brilliant in hue), a tiny sweet-pea, clover, and many common flowers in dazzling profusion; while a few specimens of an almost black arum lily have been collected. Can you not imagine the effect this enchanting scene has had upon the condition of troops who have become desert veterans? And what of the horses, those noble beasts, whose courage and staying power helped to make possible the victories of Magdhaba and Rafa? One of the prettiest pictures I have seen for many a long day was an Australian Light Horse regiment out grazing. Each

PRISONERS FROM MAGDHABA AT EL ARISH.
Turkish prisoners of war. Above: Sorting out at El Arish the Turks captured at Magdhaba, December 23rd, 1916, when the British took 1,282 prisoners out of a force of 1,600 men.

TURKISH SOLDIERS WHO YIELDED TO BRITISH PROWESS IN EGYPT.
Group of Turkish prisoners of war. More than 4,000 unwounded prisoners were taken in the Sinai operations, nearly 1,300 at Magdhaba, 1,600 at Rafa, and 950 in the first attack on Gaza, in addition to many captured in lesser engagements fought during the advance into Palestine.

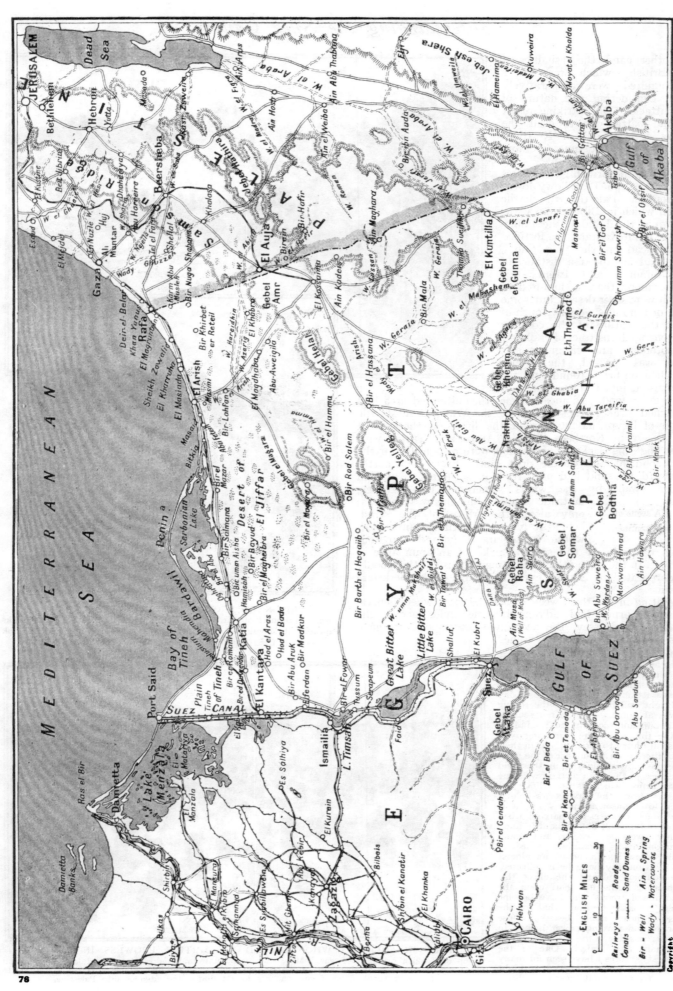

MAP OF THE NORTHERN PORTION OF THE SINAI PENINSULA, ILLUSTRATING THE BRITISH ADVANCE FROM EL KANTARA TO GAZA.

The Great War.

Copyright

ENGLISH MILES

Railways
Canals
Roads
Sand Dunes

Bir = Well   Ain = Spring
Wady = Watercourse

man was tending two horses. He was enjoying the luxury of a rest on the grass, but his pleasure was derived not so much from lying full-length on the turf as in seeing the animals revel in abundant green food. To beast as well as man it is the Promised Land.

With the British at Rafa, and in occupation of Northern Sinai, the question of Palestine and its future assumed a new and tremendous importance. Before the war the Hebrew impulse towards the resettlement of the land, which was known as the Zionist Movement, had made a good deal of progress. Many little Jewish colonies, centring in whitewashed villages of stone-built houses, had been founded, and had become flourishing agricultural communities, over which brooded a peace and a harmony that were in striking contrast with what prevailed throughout the greater part of the rest of the country. The Zionists had powerful protectors in Europe—in Germany as well as in Great Britain—and the Turk knew better than to meddle to any marked extent with their settlements. But from the outbreak of the war there was a terrible change.

Under the Constitution brought into existence by the Young Turks in 1909, Christians and Jews throughout the Turkish Empire were liable to military service, and soon after the beginning of hostilities by

German intrigue in Palestine

Germany, Turkey commenced her mobilisation, calling up all the men of military age in Palestine and Syria as elsewhere. The Zionists responded among others in these countries. According to the testimony of one of them, Alexander Aaronsohn, given in a notable book called " With the Jews in Palestine," which was published in 1917, the young Zionists were not unwilling to sustain the Turkish Government, because while the Constitution imposed the burden of militarism it also carried with it freedom of religion and equal rights ; nor could they forget that "for six hundred years Turkey had held her gates wide open to the Jews who fled from the Spanish Inquisition and similar ministrations of other civilised countries." The order for mobilisation, therefore, was well received by the Zionist colonies, but they had no suspicion that Turkey would not remain neutral. Yet they had seen much in Palestine that ought to have made them more alert and filled them with misgivings. There were plenty of signs all about them which should have indicated how things were going.

Permeated as the whole world was with German intrigue and the other workings of German policy and craft, nowhere on the globe perhaps were these more apparent than in Palestine. The German Government had done everything in its power to encourage German settlement in the country, scattered over which were German mills, though half of the time these had nothing to grind, and German hotels, often in places not usually touched by travellers. German engineers had traversed the whole land, making careful surveys, and noting its possibilities. An energetic and unscrupulous propaganda, the head of which was Lentweld von Hardegg, the German Consul at Haifa, sought to imbue the minds of the population with the idea of the greatness of Germany and of the evil disposition of Great Britain, France, Russia, and the like. Hardegg went about making speeches and distributing pamphlets in Arabic, the gist of which was that the Germans were not Christians like the British and the French, but were descendants of the Prophet, passages from the Koran being actually quoted as prophesying the coming of the Kaiser as the Saviour of Islam. The German colonists held meetings in which they descanted to the ignorant natives on the manifold excellences of Germany and the demerits of her competitors. In a word, Palestine was carefully sown with the seed of Germanism. Soon after Turkey entered the war on the side of Germany the result of this sedulous cultivation was manifest in the wholesale Germanisation of the country—in all the mosques Friday prayers sought the blessing of Allah on " Haji Guilliamo," and German officers appeared everywhere.

AT THE ENTRANCE INTO PALESTINE.
British working-party marching along a wady, under excellent cover from the Turkish guns. Nearing Gaza the troops rejoiced at exchanging the sands of Sinai for the firm earth and green pastures of Palestine.

Germany's successes in the early part of the war were exploited in Palestine to influence the people in her favour. Many of the Arab population, which even then was none too friendly to the Turks, were carried away on the tide. The Jews and Christians, who had been mobilised and had undergone military training for some months, were disarmed, turned into corps of navvies, and set to work on the roads. Turks and Arabs united in a systematic persecution of the non-Mohammedan races in the land, under the thin disguise of " requisitions." Among the rest, the Zionist colonies were overrun, robbed and devastated. The pride and arrogance of the Turk, which had been curbed in bygone days by the " capitulations," became overweening, but they were as nothing compared with those of the German, who lorded it over everybody. There was a strong reaction, however, in Palestine after the **Zionist colonies devastated** defeat of Djemal Pasha's expedition against the canal in 1915. The Germans and Turks spread about lying accounts of their dismal failure—they, of course, did not call it that. Their explanation to the people was : " A terrible sandstorm having arisen, the glorious army takes it as the wish of Allah not to continue the attack, and has therefore withdrawn in triumph." But the truth soon came out. The Arabs began to turn against the Turco-Germans. There were rumours that Djemal Pasha had been bought by the British. Some German officers were shot, and there were even fears on the part of the Germans of a general massacre of their nationals. Djemal Pasha contrived, largely by the help of his bodyguard of fanatical Anatolians, to maintain order through stern measures of repression, and the danger to the Germans passed.

FOR DESERT MARCHING.
Special sand shoes, which were devised for men marching over loose sand.

The situation in Palestine darkened for the natives during 1916. Not only were Christians and Jews subjected to harsh persecution, but the Arabs also came under the ban of the Turco-Germans. The revolt of the Grand Sherif of Mecca, who later took to himself the title of King of the Hedjaz, found a large number of sympathisers among the Arabs—especially among those of noble birth—all the way from Damascus to the frontier of Egypt. They, too, saw the true character of Enver Pasha and his associates, and would have nothing more to do with them. This, in its turn, led to severe reprisals by the Young Turk Committee which were countenanced by Germany, and many of the leading members of the highest Arab houses were executed, their families being turned adrift or deported and their property confiscated. At the end of January, 1917, authoritative information reached London that the Turks were carrying out a deliberate policy of destroying the Arabs, a policy similar to that which they had applied with such horrible success to the unfortunate Armenians. On the pretext of obtaining fuel, they had cut down the olive-trees and ruined the orange gardens in Syria and Palestine. A still more deadly blow was the prohibition of the Arabic language in the services in the mosques, as well as in the ordinary intercourse of life. But if under these heavy strokes the Arab cause languished in these lands, it went on gaining strength in Arabia. In this connection a visit paid in the winter by the King of the Hedjaz to the allied fleet at Jeddah, in the Red Sea, and reported in detail by his official newspaper, was of particular interest.

On New Year's Day, 1917, Turkey made a bid for full sovereignty within her Empire by denouncing the Treaty of Paris, 1856, and the Treaty of Berlin, 1878, in a formal Note which she addressed to the German and Austro-Hungarian Governments. The text of this Note was made public at Washington, U.S.A., and it stated that the Ottoman Empire definitely "abandoned its somewhat subordinate position under the collective guardianship of the Great Powers."

Turkey's bid for full sovereignty

At the same time Turkey abolished the autonomous organisation of the Province of the Lebanon, and established the same administrative mechanism that existed in other parts of the Empire. As a matter of fact, Turkey had disregarded the autonomy of the Lebanon soon after her entry into the war, though she was pledged to observe it, as were Germany and Austria equally bound to see that the pledge was kept. The Lebanon was a good deal more than the mountain familiar to readers of the Bible; in reality it was a beautiful region of about four thousand square miles' area. Its population, 600,000 in number, consisted of the Maronites, who were Christians, and of the Druses, who were Mohammedans, but with esoteric rites and beliefs of their own. In 1860 the Druses, joined by Turkish troops, massacred thousands of the Maronites, the Great Powers intervened, and ten thousand French troops were landed at Beyrout to restore order. Turkey was compelled to grant autonomy to the Lebanon, and the German and Austrian Governments, as well as those of France, Great Britain, and Russia, signed the guarantee of autonomy. To Germany this guarantee was only another "scrap of paper" to be torn up at pleasure. The Maronites naturally favoured the French,

but the Druses were in a measure under British influence. With the declaration of war on Turkey, both tribes were regarded with suspicion and hostility by the Turks. The province was invaded and despoiled by Turkish soldiers, some of its chiefs were hanged, and its young men were taken to serve in the Army.

Addressing the House of Commons, in May, 1917, Lord Robert Cecil, the Foreign Under-Secretary, spoke of the state of Syria and Palestine as being like that of Armenia, the greatest martyr to Turkish cruelty and fanaticism, and in answer to the "No annexations, no indemnities" theory of the Russian Socialists, argued from it that these countries could not be permitted to remain under Turkish rule after the war. Even the German newspapers, though at first they denied that the Jews in Palestine were being most harshly treated by the Turks, had to admit that from eight to nine thousand Jews had been "evacuated" from Jaffa in circumstances of revolting cruelty. The "Berliner Tageblatt," a journal run by German Jews, made an urgent appeal to Germany for better treatment of the Palestine Jews. It said that under the compulsion of the war thousands of Jews had to quit the homes they had made in Palestine by decades of hard work, and described these victims of the Turks as "at home, but homeless, surrendered to the miseries of flight and to devastating sicknesses." The German Government, unable to deny altogether the inhumanity shown to the Jews in Palestine, and not unmindful of the fact that the rich and powerful Jews of Germany were behind the Zionists, offered to agree to the appointment of a Commission of Inquiry, composed of neutral Consuls, but this proposal was justly scouted as nothing more than an astute move to obscure the situation.

Revolting cruelty to the Jews

Such, then, was the state of affairs in Palestine and Syria in 1915, 1916, and the first months of 1917. Some Palestine refugees, who had arrived on American vessels, were in Egypt, and from them, as from other sources, news had come of what was taking place in the lands north of the frontier. The British, looking out from Rafa on the Holy Land, and knowing how it was desolated and oppressed, regarded themselves as fighters in a new crusade for its rescue, and for its restoration to peace and prosperity. After the victory of Rafa, General Murray

ON THE EDGE OF THE DESERT.
Field workshop of the Army Service Corps at the limit of cultivation on the Egyptian front. The work of the A.S.C. and its handy-men was an important factor on all the fronts.

DUMMY BOMB-THROWING FROM A TRENCH.
Men of the E.E.F. receiving instruction at the Imperial School of Instruction at Zeitoun in the art of bomb-throwing from a deep trench. From the trench immediately in front of the standing men, arms may be seen raised in the act of throwing the dummy bombs.

in the victories, and declaring that it was only meet for Bagdad "to thank Almighty God for its liberation from the criminal hand of the Turanians." Enver Pasha, who had been paying a visit to Kressenstein at the Palestine front, returned in a prodigious hurry to Constantinople to see what could be done to retrieve the situation.

Kressenstein, meanwhile, was concentrating at Shellal, about ten miles from Gaza. In the first week of March, General Murray reported that in the face of his advanced troops the Turks had abandoned a very strong position at Khan Yunus, in the neighbourhood of Sheikh Nurm, west of Shellal, which lay midway between Gaza and their base at Beersheba, though they had spent

paused for a time in his advance, consolidated the position, and prepared for the next big forward movement. The railway was pushed on from El Arish eastward as rapidly as circumstances permitted, rails, sleepers, and other material being brought all the way from India, as was also the case at Salonika for the lines there. January passed without any outstanding incident. February was, however, marked by two successful operations in the south. Information had been received that the Turks were re-establishing posts at Bir el Hassana and at Nakhl, and steps were promptly taken to defeat these efforts of the enemy to regain his footing in those districts. Columns were despatched simultaneously from the Suez base. One effected a complete surprise at Hassana, the whole garrison of three officers and twenty-one men being captured; and the other drove the Turks, in number about a hundred horse, out of Nakhl on to a waterless road, with a loss to the enemy of a field-gun, guns, rifles, ammunition, explosives, and stores. The British, on **Effect of the** the other hand, suffered no casualties— **capture of Bagdad** another record in that desert warfare that bespoke both dash and skill.

A few days after the publication of the report of these brilliant if minor affairs, the British War Office made an announcement of such vast importance as to affect profoundly the whole Eastern world. This was the news of the first great result achieved by the reconstituted army in Mesopotamia, under the leadership of Sir Stanley Maude, after a long series of well-planned and methodically executed operations. As was narrated in Chapter CLXXVI. (Vol. 9, page 141), the Turks were decisively defeated on the Tigris, and Kut was recaptured on February 24th, with great loss to the enemy. Pressing on in hot pursuit, General Maude drove the shattered forces of the Turks up the river, and Bagdad was in his hands on March 11th. The taking of the ancient capital of the Caliphate was an event that reverberated throughout all lands, but the shock of it was felt most powerfully in Turkey, and scarcely less so in Arabia, Syria, and Palestine, as well as in Persia. The view which was expressed by Mohammedans, other than Turks, of the sweeping successes of the British in Mesopotamia was voiced in a telegram to the High Commissioner in Egypt from the King of the Hedjaz, rejoicing

PRACTICE WITH LIVE BOMBS IN THE DESERT.
Throwing live bombs from one somewhat shallow trench to another, in practice-preparation for the advance. In the Egyptian desert there were ample opportunities for practising the various methods of modern trench warfare of which bomb-throwing proved one of the most important.

two months in the construction there of a formidable system of defences. On the same day British airmen dropped half a ton of high explosives on the Turkish troops, railway trains, rolling-stock, and camps, doing much damage. The frontier now was crossed by the troops, the first town in Palestine to be occupied (February 28th) being Khan Yunus, which was described by Mr. Massey as "a not unlovely collection of houses amid wonderfully fertile gardens hedged around by impenetrable walls of huge cactus." In the place were the ruins of a palace, the building of which local tradition ascribed to the great Saladin. In the third week of March reconnoitring-parties came within sight of the minaret of Gaza, standing high above the trees encircling that city of the Philistines of old, with its deathless story of the romance and tragedy of Samson and Delilah, and its wealth of striking historical associations.

During the month of February the Turks were again expelled from Hassana and Nakhl, where they had

L

re-established themselves with the object of regaining their prestige among the Bedouins. General Murray ordered a combined operation against these two places by three mobile columns of cavalry and camelry, one from El Arish against Hassana, and the other two against Nakhl from Serapeum and Suez respectively. Hassana was surrounded at daybreak on the 18th, and its garrison surrendered without resistance. The other columns encountered some opposition, but Nakhl was entered on the evening of the 17th by a squad of Australian Light Horse, who found that the Turks had fled, leaving behind them one field-gun and a quantity of stores and ammunition. The operations against Nakhl were organised by Brigadier-General P. C. Palin, C.B., who was complimented by the Commander-in-Chief for the excellence of the arrangements he had made. These minor operations were

Capture of Hassana and Nakhl perfectly successful as regarded their immediate object, and, further, were of importance in view of the general campaign which was developing in Palestine. The fight for the Holy Land had begun.

Under cover of the night of March 25th-26th the British advanced in force from Rafa to the Wady Ghuzzeh, or River of Gaza, five miles south of the town, the name of which had been modernised into Guzzeh. The march, which covered a distance of fifteen miles, was one of those swift movements of which General Murray's troops had already given examples, and its immediate object was to protect the railway, which was still being pushed eastward, and was then near Rafa. In the darkness the wady was occupied without opposition by the Mounted Anzacs and Yeomanry, accompanied by horse-artillery batteries. To get the guns across, the banks of the wady, which were in places forty feet high and almost perpendicular, had to be cut down, and ramps had to be built, while the soft, sandy bed of the watercourse also had to be negotiated. When these things were accomplished the advanced troops moved on towards Gaza, but by that time a heavy fog had rolled up from the sea, and the marching had to be done by compass, so dense was the pall that lay over the land.

In itself a considerable natural obstacle, the Wady Ghuzzeh had not been made use of by the Turks to withstand or, at any rate, delay the British advance. Either they had no intention of holding it, or if they had, the rapid surprise movement of the British had anticipated them. But their real defensive position was on the other side of the wady, nearer Gaza, and it had been made exceedingly formidable. Separated from the sea by two miles of sand-dunes, which had been entrenched, it consisted of two main hills, one lying north of the other, and a smaller hill in between. The southern hill was a perfect labyrinth of deeply-cut trenches and redoubts, sited with great skill, and no lines of wire indicated how strong the place might be. The terrain was difficult,

Two days' battle at Gaza as it was intersected by ravines and nullahs, some of them being deep cracks in the ground with precipitous sides. General Sir Charles Dobell was in local command, and he had determined to force the enemy to stand and fight, his idea being to capture Gaza by a coup de main. The attack was to have been begun early in the morning of the 26th, but the fog did not lift till ten o'clock, and the delay this occasioned caused his plans to go awry, as it gave time for the Turks to bring up strong reinforcements, which put a different complexion on the battle.

As the sky cleared to a perfect arch of blue the guns belched forth, and the British troops, who all had been in position some time, moved forward to the assault. The Welsh Territorials engaged the enemy in hand-to-hand grips in a bewildering maze of zigzags, and the other infantry, taking advantage of every bit of available dead ground, rushed across the open plain amid bursts of hostile machine-gun fire. The gallant Welshmen and their supports encountered a furious resistance on the

north-west and west, and to assist them a portion of the Anzacs and the Yeomanry were ordered to close in from the north-east about one o'clock, but it was not till four o'clock that the attackers made marked progress, the enemy's first-line trenches being taken soon after that hour, with over seven hundred of his men captured. All the British fought magnificently, especially troops of the Welsh, Kent, Surrey, Sussex, Hereford, and Middlesex Regiments, as well as the Anzacs and the Yeomanry. A particularly fine instance of dashing and at the same time determined bravery was recorded of the New Zealanders. Of this Mr. Massey wrote:

> The brigade (of mounted New Zealanders) got to the sea, north of the position, and were ordered to assist the infantry attack. At half-past four, with the Yeomanry, they took an important ridge, and proceeded to cross the flats strongly opposed by the enemy in pits behind cactus hedges—very deadly obstacles—but they quickly carried them. The New Zealanders went on, got into the position, rushed the enemy battery, and captured two hundred men and howitzers, which the enemy made frequent and desperate attempts to regain. Finally, enemy gunners and some infantry got into a country-house a hundred yards off and endeavoured to prevent the removal of the guns. The New Zealanders refused to leave the guns. They loaded them and used them against the house until they had demolished it and killed the occupants. Then the Turkish infantry tried to rush the guns, but they were driven off with the bayonet. Darkness now set in. The New Zealanders were ordered to retire, but would not come away without the guns. They brought them back to our lines this morning (27th). The New Zealanders' casualties during the day were two killed and twenty-nine wounded. They took two hundred and twenty-five prisoners, and probably killed and wounded as many more.

As the battle proceeded on the afternoon of the 26th, the Turks, who fought with spirit and resolution, received strong reinforcements. Three columns came to their relief. The first marched along the coast road from the north, the second from the Huj district to the north-east, and the third from Nejeila, Sharia, and Harreira to the east. Turkish cavalry **Armoured cars** poured out from Beersheba. General **in action** Murray reported that these columns were admirably delayed by the mounted troops and the armoured cars, heavy losses being inflicted, at slight cost to the British, on the Turks, who had the commander and Staff of their 53rd Division taken prisoners during this phase of the fighting. The armoured cars had been sent out in the afternoon to assist in keeping off the reinforcements from the Huj district, who numbered five thousand men, and so well did they perform their work that they held up the whole of the enemy at a critical juncture. When it became dark the cars retired, and early next morning successfully ran the gauntlet of thousands of Turks, with artillery, getting through with one killed and four wounded, themselves inflicting, at a conservative estimate, three hundred and fifty casualties. When they were back in the British lines, the numerous bullet marks on their turrets showed how accurate had been the Turkish fire and how closely they had been assailed.

After nightfall on the 26th the British took up a defensive position from a point just south of Gaza, towards the Wady Ghuzzeh. Not only had the delay caused by the sea fog in the morning militated against the success of the coup de main by shortening the amount of daylight necessary for the enterprise, but it also had the ill-effect of giving time to the Turks for the bringing up of their reinforcements. Besides, according to General Murray's despatch of April 1st, the time during which the operation could be carried out was limited by the supply of water available for the troops, the infantry being dependent on what they took along with them. Owing to the delay occasioned by the fog the supply of water with the troops proved to be insufficient. The fog, in fact, saved the Turks. "Another two hours of daylight," wrote Mr. Massey, "and the whole town of Gaza would have been ours." Next day the Turks, with their reinforcements in line, attacked the position which the British had taken up, but they were everywhere repulsed,

REAR-ADMIRAL SIR CECIL BURNEY, K.C.B., G.C.M.G.
APPOINTED SECOND SEA LORD, DECEMBER 1916.

REAR-ADMIRAL SIR WILLIAM C. PAKENHAM, K.C.B.
COMMANDED THE SECOND BATTLE-CRUISER SQUADRON, JUTLAND.

CAPTAIN SIR REGINALD Y. TYRWHITT, K.C.B., D.S.O.
(COMMODORE 1ST CLASS.) COMMANDED DESTROYER FLOTILLAS.

REAR-ADMIRAL W. E. GOODENOUGH, C.B., D.S.O.
COMMODORE SECOND CRUISER SQUADRON.

The portraits on this and the three succeeding pages are from a large series made by Mr. Francis Dodd, who was appointed official artist, and in this capacity drew nearly all the admirals and generals on active service and some famous officers of lesser rank. Mr. Dodd received his art education in Glasgow.

LIEUT.-GEN. SIR THOMAS D'OYLY SNOW. K.C.B., K.C.M.G.
COMMANDED THE SEVENTH ARMY CORPS ON THE SOMME.

LIEUT.-GENERAL SIR CLAUD JACOB. K.C.B.
COMMANDED THE SECOND ARMY CORPS ON THE SOMME.

LIEUT.-GENERAL SIR IVOR MAXSE. K.C.B.
COMMANDED THE 18TH DIVISION ON THE WESTERN FRONT.

84

LIEUT.-GENERAL SIR WILLIAM PULTENEY. K.C.B., D.S.O.
COMMANDED THE THIRD ARMY CORPS ON THE SOMME.

LIEUT.-GENERAL SIR THOMAS L. N. MORLAND, K.C.B.
COMMANDER OF THE TENTH ARMY CORPS ON THE WESTERN FRONT.

GENERAL SIR HERBERT C. O. PLUMER, G.C.M.G., K.C.B.
COMMANDER OF THE SECOND BRITISH ARMY, WESTERN FRONT.

LIEUT.-GENERAL SIR EDWARD A. FANSHAWE, K.C.B.
KNIGHTED FOR VALUABLE SERVICES IN THE FIELD, JANUARY, 1917.

LIEUT.-GENERAL J. A. L. HALDANE, C.B., D.S.O.
COMMANDED A DIVISION ON THE WESTERN FRONT.

85

REAR-ADMIRAL HEATHCOTE S. GRANT, C.B.
COMMENDED FOR SERVICE DURING OPERATIONS IN GALLIPOLI.

REAR-ADMIRAL T. D. W. NAPIER, C.B.
COMMANDED THE THIRD LIGHT CRUISER SQUADRON. JUTLAND

CAPTAIN J. R. P. HAWKSLEY, C.B., M.V.O.
COMMANDED THE ELEVENTH FLOTILLA. JUTLAND.

REAR-ADMIRAL FREDERICK C. T. TUDOR, C.B.
APPOINTED COMMANDER-IN-CHIEF, CHINA STATION. MAY. 1917.

the guns of the British ranging perfectly and smashing up the assailing force. The Camel Corps completely defeated the Turkish Cavalry Division. On the 28th the British infantry were withdrawn to the Wady Ghuzzeh, the cavalry remaining in contact with the enemy's main position, from which the Turks showed no desire to resume the offensive.

In this battle the British took nine hundred and fifty prisoners, including some Germans and Austrians, and two howitzers, while their own loss in killed was less than four hundred. General Murray estimated the total casualties of the Turks at eight thousand. On their part, the Turks, in their official report of the two days' battle, claimed that the fighting had terminated in a brilliant victory for them, stated that they had taken two hundred prisoners, and declared that over three thousand British dead were found on the field. It was true that about two hundred men, who had penetrated into Gaza itself, were cut off and captured, but the number given of dead found on the battlefield was the wildest exaggeration, as Mr. Bonar Law, on behalf of the Government, announced in the House of Commons, after reading the despatch from General Murray referred to above. Murray's own view of the battle, as expressed in this telegram, was : " The operation was most successful, and owing to the fog and the waterless nature of the country round Gaza, just fell short of a complete disaster to the enemy." King George sent a message of congratulation to him. From France, General Nivelle wired to the British War Office, voicing the satisfaction of his country with the " favourable start for the army's campaign in Palestine and Syria." Later, a much less optimistic opinion of the result of the battle came to be held, but the fact remained that the British had advanced fifteen miles beyond the frontier.

Sir Archibald Murray and his army remained in occupation of the Wady Ghuzzeh after the battle, and no further move of importance against it took place till April 17th. In the meantime, preparations for a renewal of the advance had gone on, and the railway was well forward. On the other side of the account, the Turkish strength had been increased by bringing masses of troops to this front from the Caucasus and elsewhere, the disorganisation of the Russian Army because of the Revolution having rendered possible these withdrawals to Palestine. Kressenstein now had five divisions under him, with a considerable force of cavalry in addition. He had also heavily fortified and deeply entrenched the naturally strong defensive position at Gaza, and had made it much more formidable than before. From the sand-dunes on the coast a ridge, rising here and there into heights, extended to the Shefela range at the end of the Judean hills, its principal feature being the natural fortress of Ali Muntar, or the Watch Tower, south-east of Gaza, which from time immemorial had checked the march of hostile armies. An extraordinary variety of rifle-pits, redoubts, and trenches, most of which had been built by the poor natives under the Turco-German lash, was disposed on lines of several miles length up to the broken and waterless country on the east, where such protection was unnecessary. Over against these lines lay the British, on a front of nearly sixteen miles.

Soon after break of day the British assault opened by land and sea on the 17th. Supported by the fire of warships, some of which were French, and of the coast batteries, the infantry and cavalry moved forward, occupied the positions among the sand-dunes which had been designated as their primary objectives as well as those on their more immediate front, and stormed the Sheikh Abbas Ridge, four miles south-east of Ali Muntar. Their casualties were slight, but this was merely a preliminary affair. The marching of the mounted troops over the dry plain on the British right had filled the air with dense clouds of dust, under cover of which next day

Varying views of the Gaza battle

supplies were pushed across the wady, and all was got ready for the main attack set for dawn on the following morning.

As the sun rose on the 19th a perfect hurricane of shells from the allied ships and from the land guns, including some of 11 in. calibre, broke over the Turkish lines, tore gaps in their defences, and caused Ali Muntar to shake. After this intense bombardment the infantry came into play about half-past eight o'clock. On their left they gained the Samson Ridge, and found the trenches there filled with Turkish dead. In the centre and on the right progress was more difficult owing to the heavy fire from Ali Muntar and the neighbouring heights, but the Scots, who were fighting there, advanced steadily though slowly for nearly a mile and a half, and took an outpost hill, where they dug themselves in and consolidated the position. Throughout the day, and especially in the afternoon, the Anzacs and the Yeomanry were heavily engaged. The Turks made no fewer than five desperate counter-attacks on these mounted troops and the Camel Corps, but all of them were repulsed magnificently. At the close of the day the Turkish advanced positions had been captured on a front of six and a half miles. There was fighting all along the line on the 20th, but without any particular result. The British forces stood on the ground they had carried and consolidated it, and thenceforward for some time only trench warfare ensued.

Statements in Parliament

The British at home were warned not to expect an early decision at Gaza. In reply to questions it was officially stated in Parliament, on May 24th, that by that date the positions gained had been organised, as also had been some further ground that had been wrested from the Turks, but that progress had necessarily been slow. The British were in close touch with the enemy's main positions defending the town between the sea and Sheikh Abbas, a front of 14,000 yards. But the Turkish forces, which had again been reinforced, had made good use of the natural obstacles of the terrain, and had turned Ali Muntar, in particular, into a stronghold of the first rank. In such circumstances, it was explained, it was impossible for any advance to be rapid.

Two days before this somewhat depressing announcement was made, the British in Palestine had effected a dashing raid which was crowned with success. The Turkish railway south-west of Beersheba was attacked, and twenty miles of it were utterly destroyed. A camel corps and a column of Anzacs, with field engineers, started out on May 22nd, and returned two days later, having in the interval completely wrecked the Turks' strategic line from El Auja to within a few miles of Beersheba. While the engineers were blowing up the track and the bridges the cavalry made a strong demonstration against the latter town. They got within five miles of that important base, heavily shelled and destroyed the railway bridge to the north, and drove off two Turkish cavalry brigades which appeared to the south of Beersheba during the afternoon. Perhaps as a reprisal for the heavy blow inflicted by these daring raiders, an enemy aeroplane, on May 24th, descended at Salmena, a short distance from Bir el Abd, and attempted to cut the railway and the pipe-line. While the Turkish airmen were placing the dynamite on the rails they were fired on by a patrol, and immediately made off, incontinently leaving behind them their machine, stock of explosives, and implements.

Turks strategic railway wrecked

No change occurred in the general situation in Palestine during June. Frequent patrol encounters took place in which the British were invariably successful, as they also were in their air raids. On the 23rd of the month many hundreds of pounds of explosives were dropped on the aerodrome at Ramleh, on the railway from Joppa to Jerusalem, and on the supply depot at Tul Keram, on the road from Joppa to the north. Three days later a

AT THE JOURNEY'S END.
Desert motor-cars reach the end of their patrol at the foot of the sandhills at the base of a curiously striated cliff.

British air squadron bombed the headquarters of the Fourth Turkish Army, the Augusta Victoria Hospice, lying about a mile from the walls of Jerusalem. The Turks asserted that the British dropped their missiles within the Holy City itself, but this was a lie. The close of the month was signalised by one notable event. On the 30th the War Office announced through the Press that General Murray had been replaced by General Sir Edmund H. H. Allenby, K.C.B., who had been in command of the Third Army in France, and that Allenby had arrived in Egypt. General Allenby was fifty-six years of age, and had a long and distinguished record of service before the war, especially in connection with South Africa. Thrice mentioned in despatches during the war with the Boers, his work had been acknowledged with the brevet of colonel and a C.B. Subsequently he was Inspector of Cavalry. When in command of the Third Army in France he had a brilliant share in the great victory of Arras, April, 1917.

On his arrival at the front in Palestine, General Allenby found operations being conducted, as had been his experience in France, by the opposed forces in deep entrenchments within a short distance of each other. It was plain that any big offensive movement on his part could take place only under conditions similar to those which obtained on the French front, and must be made with large bodies of effectives, backed by the most powerful artillery. For such an offensive, if it was contemplated, a period of intense preparation was required. Meanwhile, the enemy could be worn down. The enemy's lines were incessantly bombarded, and constant air raids played havoc with his communications. On the night of July 20th the British successfully raided his trenches south-west of Gaza, killing over a hundred Turks and taking seventeen prisoners. This was the most considerable affair since the heavy fighting in April. Other raids took place during July and August which harassed the enemy, but the general situation remained unchanged.

General Allenby in command

IN PURSUIT OF THE SENUSSIYEH.
" Rough going " in the Libyan Desert for one of the transport cars that took part in the driving and defeat of the Senussiyeh in Western Egypt.

In the meantime, the Arabs had scored substantially in their own country. News came in July that the King of the Hedjaz had gained a decided victory over the Turks who, besides having seven hundred men killed, lost six hundred in prisoners and considerable territory. As the result of this important success, the Arabs advanced to the ancient land of Moab and occupied all the Turkish positions between Akaba and Maan on the Hedjaz railway, some sixty-five miles south of the Dead Sea. At Akaba, at the head of the eastern gulf of the Red Sea, they were in touch with the British in Southern Sinai, and at Maan, farther to the north-east, they were close to the south-eastern confines of Palestine. The Turks in the Yemen, with whom the British at Aden were in contact, were thus still more isolated. A few weeks previously the British, on the eastern shore of the Red Sea, had captured the port of Salif. British warships attacked the fort on June 12th, and stormed it after three hours' resistance, taking about a hundred prisoners, two mountain guns, and other booty. The place was valuable, both as a military station and as the centre of a salt industry capable of enormous expansion.

As was recorded in Chapter CXVIII., in its narration of the campaign in Western Egypt up to May, 1916, the attempt of the Grand Senussi, Seyyid Ahmed, against the British was completely defeated, the chief, with the broken remnants of his forces, fleeing to the region of Jupiter Ammon (or Siwa) Oasis.

On October 4th, 1916, Major-General W. A. Watson, C.B., C.I.E., took over the command of the Western Force, which in a little over a fortnight from that date captured both the Beharia and the Dakhla Oases, nearly five hundred men, and a number of camels. General Watson visited the Beharia Oasis on November 16th, and, under the Union Jack, which had been hoisted by the troops, held a durbar attended by the principal inhabitants. Similarly, he held a durbar at Dakhla on the 19th. In both districts the civil administration was reinstituted, to the gratification of the natives, who were glad to be freed from the burden of the Senussiyeh. Meanwhile, Seyyid Ahmed had reached the Siwa Oasis, and Sir Archibald Murray, having heard in January, 1917, that he was making preparations to leave it and to retire to Jaghbub, gave orders on the 21st of that month that operations were to be undertaken against the Siwa and Girba Oases by a force of camelry and armoured cars, but finally decided to send a column entirely composed of armoured motor-cars, and supplied by motor transport from Mersa Matruh. This place was two hundred miles from Siwa, and the road, such as it was, lay across a waterless desert. Brigadier-General H. W. Hodgson, C.V.O., C.B., was placed in command. He planned to attack the Senussi camp at Girba, which was west of Siwa, with the larger part of his force, and to detach two

Operations in Western Egypt

Motor-cars speeding over the desert sands of the Sinaitic Peninsula. The armoured cars performed invaluable work in General Murray's advance, not only as patrols, but also—as in the attack on Gaza, of March 26th, 1917—in holding off enemy reinforcements.

Difficulties of desert motoring. This car was being pushed up a soft sand slope, while its companion car, which had attained the summit, towed it also. Right : Another car, near the Beharia Oasis, in the Desert of Libya, which called for strenuous pushing up a steep, soft ascent.

Pontoon bridge built by Cheshire Engineers for the armoured cars with the E.E.F. These cars did splendid service, at one point running the gauntlet of thousands of Turks, and after inflicting 350 casualties on the enemy, got through with but one man killed and four injured.

BRITISH MOTOR-CARS' MAGNIFICENT WORK ON THE EGYPTIAN FRONT.

motor-batteries to block the solitary pass at Garet el Manâsib that was practicable for camels between Siwa and Jaghbub—so that if the Grand Senussi got away, heavy casualties might be inflicted on his reurguards and his march be deflected into the waterless sand-dunes.

On the evening of January 29th the fighting force, consisting of three light-armoured batteries and three light-car patrols, was concentrated at Mersa Matruh, but progress was delayed by a severe sandstorm, which prevented some of the lorries of the heavy supply column that was coming from Dabaa from arriving till the 31st. But on February 1st all was ready for the swift rush across the waste, and next day all units reached the point of concentration, one hundred and eighty-five miles south of Matruh. Early on the 3rd the force successfully descended the pass north-east of Girba, and moved on to the attack. The enemy was completely taken by surprise on seeing the motor column, and at once withdrew from his camps to the cliffs and hills in rear—where he showed that he did not intend to retreat farther without a fight.

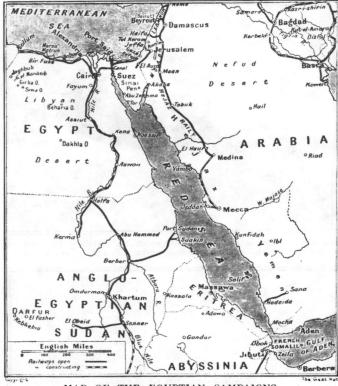

MAP OF THE EGYPTIAN CAMPAIGNS.
Showing the relative fronts—that through the Sinai Peninsula to the Palestine border at Rafa and El Auja ; Western Egypt, where the Senussiyeh were defeated ; and Darfur to the south.

At Girba the Senussiyeh were about eight hundred and fifty strong, with both guns and machine-guns, and they were led by Mohammed Saleh, the general of the Grand Senussi, who himself was at Siwa with four or five hundred men, and was already making ready to fly. Owing to the rough nature of the country, the cars could get no nearer to the Girba position than eight hundred yards, but after an action lasting all day and on into the night they compelled the Senussiyeh to withdraw. On the 4th Girba was in their possession, as was Siwa next day. The Senussi's base of Jupiter Ammon thus fell into the hands of the British with astonishing rapidity—thanks to the motor-cars, an ideal arm for the western desert. A parade, at which the local sheikhs were present, was held before the court-house at Siwa, and the inhabitants of the oasis gave the troops a friendly reception.

Meanwhile, the detachment of armoured cars and a light-car patrol which had been despatched in the direction of the pass at Manâsib, with the object of intercepting

Seyyid Ahmed—or, at least, of cutting off a considerable number of his followers as they retreated from Girba and Siwa—had reached a position some eighteen miles north of the pass, but there most of this column was forced to remain, as it was found impossible to get the armoured cars down the steep escarpment. The light-car patrol and one car, however, managed to get down to Manâsib, and take up a position, from which this force was able to cut up some of the leading parties coming from Girba. But the enemy established a post in the sand-dunes beyond the reach of the cars, and diverted to it his retreating men. There thus being no chance of further success, the detachment was ordered to withdraw. The whole column returned to Matruh on February 8th, having sustained no loss except three officers slightly wounded, and one set of broken springs. On the other hand, the Senussiyeh lost forty killed and two hundred wounded, including five Turkish officers, besides rifles and ammunition. Seyyid Ahmed and his chief **Heavy blow to the** fighting man, Mohammed Saleh, made **Senussiyeh** good their escape. Yet this expedition into the southern desert dealt, in the words of Sir Archibald Murray in his despatch of March 1st, 1917 (published July 6th), " a rude blow to the moral of the Senussiyeh, left the Grand Senussi himself painfully making his way to Jaghbub through the rugged and waterless dunes, and freed the western front from the menace of his forces."

Far to the south of the oases of the Senussiyeh, the final operations against the Sultan of Darfur (Chapter CXVIII., page 485) had earlier been brought to a termination. As was previously narrated, a mixed Egyptian force, commanded by Lieut.-Colonel P. V. Kelly, of the Egyptian Cavalry, had occupied El Fasher, the capital of Ali Dinar, the Sultan, who fled westward with a small following. On May 29th, 1916, three envoys appeared in El Fasher with an offer of surrender by the Sultan, and with some reservations the offer was accepted, but as the negotiations proceeded it became evident that Ali Dinar was acting in bad faith. A second offer of surrender, which came after the occupation of Kebkebia in September, and the surprise and flight of a force under Zacharia, the Sultan's eldest son, in October, led to nothing. The wily African prince was merely playing for time, and in the beginning of November an expedition was sent out against him. The force consisted of Sudanese troops and camelry, and was led by Major H. J. Huddleston, D.S.O., M.C., of the Dorsetshire Regiment. Disease and hunger had told on Ali Dinar's men, and there was little fight left in them. On the 3rd, Huddleston marched into Kulme, almost without opposition, and received a large number of surrenders, including two sisters of the Sultan. At dawn on the 6th, Ali Dinar was surprised at Giuba, thirty miles from Kulme, and was shot through the head as he fled. Shortly afterwards, his chiefs and headmen surrendered, all resist- **Turks driven out** ance disappeared, and the State was **of Sinai** incorporated as a province of the Sudan.

To sum up. Both east and west the British, by the summer of 1917, had added enormously to the security of the great canal, the whole area of Egypt being practically freed of enemies of every sort. Whatever disappointment there was respecting the situation at Gaza, with its protracted trench warfare, there could be nothing but satisfaction regarding the indisputable fact that the safety of the splendid waterway of Suez, so vital to the British Empire, had at last been placed almost beyond peradventure. Towards this end the Sultan of Egypt, as well as the civil authorities, whether British or Egyptian, had materially assisted by co-operating most cordially in the furtherance of the plans of the leaders of the Expeditionary Force and of the work of the soldiers. It was with immense relief and gratitude that the natives of the land saw the Turks driven out of Sinai—one of the real achievements on the side of the Allies in 1916-17.

BRITISH AGRICULTURE ON A WAR FOOTING.

By Basil Clarke.

Increased British Agriculture the Only Answer to German U Boats—Low Condition of Agriculture—Fall in Acreage Cultivated Owing to Drafting of Workmen and Horses to the Army—1915 Harvest Smallest on Record—Lord Selborne's Protests—Drain on Agriculture Continued—New Agricultural Policy of Mr. Lloyd George's Government—Foundation of the Food Production Department (" Growmore " Department)—Revolutionary Powers—British Farms Virtually Nationalised—Commandeering of Land and Supplies—Opposition of Landlords and Farmers Ruthlessly Overridden where Necessary—Farm Workers Brought Back from Army—Woman Labour—Prejudices Against It—Efforts to Stimulate It—" Rush " Order to America for Machinery—Motor Tractors and Steam Ploughs Bought and Commandeered—Fixing of Prices—National Distribution of Supplies—Farmers Helped Financially—State Guarantees for Farmers' Loans—Compulsory Cultivation—Work of Small Holders—District Food Production Committees with Powers Similar to County Committees—Help for Small Holders—Extent of Small Holding Movement about the Country—Work of Private Gardeners, Tennis Club Members, and the Royal Family—Greatest Popular Movement of the Year—1917 Harvest Saved—Plans for Increasing the 1918 Harvest to Enable Britain to be Self-Supporting—Extra Men, Horses, Machinery, Organisation—Motor Tractor Batteries for the Land—Stimulating Output of Fertilisers—Ensuring Seed Supplies—Keenness of British Farmer to Help—Prospects of Success of the Scheme for a Record British Harvest.

GERMANY'S unrestricted use of submarines, as described in Chapters CLXXI. and CLXXX. (Vol. 9, pp. 1 and 233), brought Great Britain face to face with the problem of feeding herself. For, imperfect as was the blockade which those submarines maintained, it was sufficient, nevertheless, to make appreciable inroads in the supply of ships available for carrying the food and merchandise of the country. The number of these ships was smaller by nearly one half than in normal times, owing to the great demands the war had made upon merchant shipping for vessels to carry men, munitions, and war supplies. In the fleet of vessels that remained available the shipping casualties caused by German submarines told with effect that was not made fully apparent by simply deducting these shipping losses from the total tonnage of Great Britain's ships. Their true proportionate value was more than this. It was high enough to be most disquieting, if not actually dangerous. Any increase in the number of sinkings, or even the maintenance of shipping losses at the maximum amount they attained, would have left the country to face famine unless other food sources than sources overseas had been made available. Of such other sources there remained, of course, only one possible—the farms and vacant lands of Great Britain itself. As the most elementary common-sense precaution against any

[Swaine.
MR. R. E. PROTHERO, M.V.O., M.P.
Appointed President of the Board of Agriculture in Mr. Lloyd George's National Ministry, December, 1916.

increase, or even maintenance of our shipping losses, that land, it was clear, had to be cultivated and made to yield enough food to feed the people of the country.

Until this moment it had seemed to have escaped the memory of the British Government and people that Great Britain was well able to do this and more if need be. Not fifty years had elapsed since Great Britain did actually feed herself. In the 'seventies of last century agriculturists ploughed and grew crops upon no less than 14,000,000 acres of the 37,324,000 acres of land in England and Wales available for cultivation, and the country was independent of any other country for the means of subsistence. But from that period onwards the importation of foreign food increased steadily year by year, while the cultivation of land at home steadily decreased. One after another fields that had been ploughed became grass and remained as grass. Families who for centuries had worked on the land, father and son after him, migrated to the towns. Cottages which for centuries had housed farm workers who had given birth to more farm workers, fell into disrepair and ruin, and were neither repaired nor replaced. The year 1914 found England and Wales with only 10,998,000 acres of plough land in cultivation.

But the lowest point had not been reached. Upon the already shrunken frame of British agriculture the war made a great drain. The youngest and most vigorous farm workers were recruited for the Army. Horses, too, were taken. The land was stripped of both, until farmers saw clearly that their area of cultivation must fall still lower. That year saw another 35,000 acres fall out of cultivation, and the 1915 harvest of England and Wales was from only 10,965,000 acres—the lowest on record.

The danger of allowing our agriculture to lapse in this manner was apparent, and many warnings were given by writers, politicians, and agriculturists alike. The Government of the day exhorted the farmers not to allow their acreage of cultivation to fall. This they did through Lord Selborne, President of the Board of Agriculture, who from the outset of his work in that department had always opposed vigorously any weakening of the agricultural

SPADES INSTEAD OF RIFLES.
Volunteers setting out to dig the grounds of a hospital at Englefield Green, in Surrey, with the object of making its own vegetable supply sufficient for the institution's needs.

forces of the country to strengthen its other war services. He made tremendous efforts by such means as were available to him, and notwithstanding the fact that the land had yielded a great proportion of its men and horses, he and his department, aided of course by the farmers of the country, succeeded in getting 11,051,000 acres ploughed and sown for the harvest of 1916. It was an achievement worthy of all praise.

But even yet the drain on British agriculture had not ceased. In spite of protests from the Board of Agriculture and the farmers of the country, more men were taken from the land. Tribunals, working upon instructions from the Government, "combed out" the farm workers even more rigorously. Men who had been given temporary exemptions from military service were refused renewals. By the new Compulsory Service regulations older workers who had not previously been liable were called up and enlisted. The land was skinned to the bare bone for labour.

By this time women substitutes were being hurriedly enrolled and offered to the farmers, but their lesser skill, coupled with the difficulties of housing and controlling them, made them a substitute which the farmers of the country, notoriously conservative in thought and method, were loth to accept.

Added to the labour difficulty came the difficulty of getting supplies. Through the shipping shortage, fertilisers and all farming accessories imported from overseas became most difficult to obtain, even at greatly

increased cost. Through transport difficulties at home, supplies of seed, fuel, manure, and such things became also a problem. The winter of 1916-17 found the British farmers so perplexed by all these problems and difficulties that any attempt to plan for 1917 a harvest as big as that of 1916 seemed impossible, a courting of disaster. It is a fact that the farming programme of Great Britain for the 1917 harvest, as framed by farmers at the beginning of the ploughing season, was smaller by many thousands of acres than anything known in the history of British agriculture.

Such was the dangerous state of things when the Asquith Government went out of office and was succeeded by the Lloyd George Government, a change that was to be followed before many weeks were passed by Germany's declaration of an unrestricted submarine policy and the sinking of all ships, British and other. **Food Production Department founded** It was a grave situation, one that called for immediate and masculine handling.

With the new Government, fortunately, came a new and vigorous agricultural policy. Agriculture was to be no longer the Cinderella of Government services, sacrificing men and means alike to strengthen other war services. A definite policy of increased food production was framed, and immediate steps taken to establish the means and organisation for carrying this policy into effect.

The month of January, 1917, saw the founding of the Food Production Department

VOLUNTEERS ENGAGED IN PEACEABLE TRENCHING.
Men of a Voluntary Training Corps battalion preparing the grounds of the Englefield Green Hospital for vegetable growing. Some of the wounded soldiers staying at the hospital were watching the work of their comrades of the V.T.C. with evident interest.

as a separate branch of the Board of Agriculture, to deal solely with the problem of increasing the nation's food-growing. Its function was tersely and admirably expressed in the word which constituted its telegraphic address—"Growmore." Its controller, Sir Arthur Lee, was not appointed till the middle of the following month, February. His instructions were to increase the food-growing of Great Britain at the maximum rate to its maximum capacity, or till the country was self-supporting, and independent, if need be, of overseas food. In other words, the harvest of 3,000,000 extra acres was to be added in the shortest possible time to Great Britain's home-grown food supply.

This was a tremendous task, and with the men and

means still to be found, and the ploughing season already half gone, the possibilities before the new Food Growing Department for the 1917 harvest were limited in the extreme. Even their own organisation had yet to be thought out; their powers of controlling agriculture to be defined, scheduled, and obtained from the Government before they could go out on to the broad acres of Britain telling the farmers what to do and helping them with the labour and other necessary means to do it.

Yet before the ploughing and sowing season was at an end the new Food Production Department had not only succeeded in saving the utter collapse that had threatened British agriculture two months earlier, but also in adding

Ideal of a self-supporting Britain

no less an area than 300,000 acres to the previous year's total of land ploughed and sown with foodstuffs for the nation. The area to yield food crops for the harvest of 1917 was forced up to 11,351,000 acres, or 353,000 acres more than in the year in which the war began. In addition, plans were laid, the country mapped out, and the means devised for attaining in the following year to the achievement of their final aim — that, namely, of a self-supporting Britain.

This rapid and intensive stimulation of British food-growing was not brought about without measures and steps which at any other time would have been regarded—and possibly resented—as absolutely revolutionary. Foreseeing the difficulties that might confront them from landlords and farmers, who,

PREPARING THE GROUND FOR ANOTHER YEAR.
A lady student in the Truro district harrowing a ploughed field. Besides receiving theoretical teaching at the agricultural training centres, the students acquired practical experience by working on the neighbouring farms, attending to stock and doing all the ordinary duties of farm-labourers.

through apathy or prejudice or inefficient farming methods, stood in the way of an increased cultivation of the land, the Board of Agriculture set out to obtain definite legal powers to enable them to meet all eventualities. These they obtained by an Order-in-Council passed in January, 1917, under the Defence of the Realm Act. Then the department set out to devise machinery for applying these powers to the farming of the country so as to be in touch with, and to control the work of, all farms, no matter how remote.

War Agricultural Committees had previously been established in each of the counties of England and Wales. Each of these committees was instructed to appoint an Executive Committee of not less than four nor more than seven members, and to these County Executive

Committees were delegated virtually all the powers vested in the Board of Agriculture by the Order-in-Council of January, 1917, to control and direct the farming of the country. These powers, as subsequently amended, and their transference to the County Executive Committees were detailed and confirmed by the " Cultivation of Lands Order, dated March 15th, 1917." They were numerous and drastic. The Order made it legal for the Board or for any of the County Executive Committees acting on the Board's behalf :

(a) To enter and take possession of any land which in their opinion was not being so cultivated as to increase as far as practicable the food supply of the country, and to do all things necessary to cultivate it or to adapt it for cultivation. To achieve this purpose any buildings on the land or convenient to it might be entered and seized.

HARVESTING IN THE DELECTABLE DUCHY.
Getting in the harvest at a Cornish training centre. A French-Canadian drove the binder while National Service Volunteer girls set up the shocks of corn.

(b) To take possession of any machinery, implements, or plant, or any farm produce, stock, or animals required for the cultivation of land.
(c) To seize any land or unoccupied premises to provide housing accommodation for workers.
(d) To use any water or motive power.
(e) To order any landholder to cultivate his land in such manner as the Board might think fit.
(f) To terminate forthwith the tenancy of any holder of land which in the opinion of the Board was not being cultivated so as to increase, as far as possible, the food supply of the country. (This power was vested only in the Board of Agriculture itself, but was exercised by them on the recommendation of any County Executive Committee.)
(g) After seizure of any land to arrange for its cultivation by any other person.
(h) To nullify clauses in any lease or agreement between tenant and landlord that placed restrictions on additional cultivation.
(i) To recover from any person who resumed possession of land occupied and cultivated by another at the Board's direction, the cost of such cultivation.
(j) To inspect any land, building, or farm, and their methods and means and adaptability for increasing the food supplies of the country.

The effect of these powers was to place the agricultural industry of Great Britain as directly under the control of the State as the shipping industry or the engineering industry, which earlier in the war had been virtually " commandeered " by the Government to ensure an efficient transport service and munitions supply. Armed with these powers the Board of Agriculture and its Food Production Department and their County Committees could, and actually did, control the nation's farming down to the smallest detail. They determined what additional

ORGANISED YOUTHFUL LABOUR.
Boy Scouts and Girl Guides digging up
waste land at Leigh-on-Sea in readiness
for planting potatoes.

land should be ploughed and by
what means it should be ploughed;
they determined what crops
should be grown, and discouraged
and even forbade the growing of
crops which either did not contribute to the nation's food supply
or were not — considering the
nation's agriculture as a whole—
the most suitable food contribution that could be made in the
circumstances. In other cases
they gave definite orders as to
how crops should be grown, what
manure should be used, what
additional fertilisers applied.

They met with opposition,
though far less than might have
been expected from classes so
independent and used to "doing
things their own way without
interference from anybody" as
the British landowners and
agriculturists. But all opposition
was overcome. Tactful persuasion was first employed, and
usually this persuasion, coupled
with knowledge of the powers
the authorities were able to bring
to bear for enforcing their will,
was enough to induce in the
farmer or landlord a reasonable
frame of mind. If this were not
enough, the authorities did not
hesitate to use with full rigour
the powers put into their hands.
The nation needed food, and
could not wait; the whims or
prejudices of individuals were not
allowed to stand in the way. In
the spring of 1917 the authorities
took steps to terminate the
tenancies of some fifty farmers
who either by their obstinacy or

their lack of skill stood in the
way of a full cultivation of the
lands they held. Others were
prosecuted and fined.

The number of landlords
against whom forceful measures
were applied in this period was
rather greater than this, for the
idea that a man could do what
he liked with his own land had
held place in the British mind
too long to be effectually eradi-
cated by merely one Act of
legislature.

Other farmers resisted measures
of cultivation perhaps through
differences of opinion with their
County Agricultural Committees
on points of farming method.
Not a few of them, for instance,
were opposed to manuring their
land on the lines laid down by
the authorities, and refused to
do this manuring. In these cases
they were not a little surprised
to discover men armed with the
full powers of the law at work
on their land carrying out the
orders of the County Committee,
and manuring the land in the
manner they had prescribed for
it. These farmers were more
surprised when the bill for this
work was presented to them for
payment. Until that moment they
had perhaps not regarded the new
farming committees and their
legal powers very seriously.
Special circulars issued by the
Food Production Department
were shown to them, proving
that it was each County Committee's prerogative and even

COUNCIL SCHOOLBOYS CULTIVATING THE LEICESTER PARKS.
At Leicester large portions of the public parks were put under cultivation and planted with potatoes. The
Council schools provided the labour, and prizes were offered in connection with the scheme. These photo-
graphs show the schoolboys trenching the ground, and (in circle) knocking off work for the day.

BRITISH WOMANHOOD'S REPLY TO THE GERMAN THREAT OF STARVATION BY SUBMARINE.
Women engaged in ploughing at Shackleford, near Godalming, Surrey, where a demonstration was held, of the efficient way in which women could perform all kinds of agricultural tasks. By September, 1917, it was said that 200,000 women were employed on the land, and their co-operation in this national service resulted in the acreage brought under cultivation for the harvest of 1918 exceeding all previous records.

duty to enter farms and do any "special act of cultivation" that they thought necessary for increasing the food supply, and to recover the cost from the farmer.

It may be of value, historically, to reproduce here an example of these circulars, to illustrate the vigour of the Food Production Department's methods, and the steps it took to get its orders carried out quickly.

MEMORANDUM TO WAR AGRICULTURAL EXECUTIVE COMMITTEES.

TEMPORARY ENTRY ON LAND FOR SPECIFIC ACTS OF CULTIVATION.

It has been brought to the notice of the Department that some Executive Committees do not fully realise that the Cultivation of Lands Order, 1917 (No. 3), authorises them to enter *temporarily* on any land for the purpose of doing specific acts of cultivation or adaptation for cultivation, and to recover from the occupier such amount as represents the value to him of the work done.

In the Board's circular letter of the 23rd January last (A290, C,) reference was made to this power in paragraphs 14 and 15, and the Director-General thinks it desirable to call the attention of Committees to the matter again.

If Committees are of opinion, for instance, that certain fields should be ploughed by motor-tractors or other means, and the occupiers fail to enter into contracts with the Committee for the work to be done, the Committee may enter temporarily and do the work themselves. If the occupier refuses to pay the cost the Committee should take proceedings for recovery of the amount due in accordance with paragraph 4 of Regulation 2M.

Legal powers of the committees

Similarly, the power of temporary entry may be used for the purpose of applying fertilisers to any land or doing any other acts of cultivation or adaptation for cultivation.

Action on these lines may be taken by Committees without the necessity of obtaining the previous sanction of the Board in each case. In order to avoid any unnecessary delay it might be well for Committees in connection with their ploughing programme to pass a general resolution authorising entry under Regulation 2M on all the lands included in the programme, so that in case any of the farmers fail to sign contracts, entry may be made and the ploughing done forthwith, without having to wait for the next meeting of the Committee. At the same time every endeavour should be made to conclude contracts with the farmers, so as to avoid the exercise of the powers of the Regulation, except where absolutely necessary.

FOOD PRODUCTION DEPARTMENT,
72, Victoria Street, London, S.W. 1.
16th April, 1917.

Sometimes, of course, farmers actively resisted cultivation, in which cases the County Committees had no alternative but to find new tenants. This they did as a rule by arrangement with the landlords, but if a landlord was unwilling the tenancy was terminated over his head.

In actual practice it was found that the landlords or farmers who resisted measures of cultivation for their land were very few in number and **Willing co-operation** of no great account. A South-country **with the Government** farm of some three hundred acres was the largest to change hands in this unpleasant way. To the credit of British farmers and landowners in general, it must be recorded that the great majority entered not only with good will but with a real enthusiasm into the Government scheme for increased cultivation of the land. They drew up programmes of what crops they could produce with their existing means, and how these programmes could be extended if additional means were supplied to them. These additional means the Food Production Department made it its business to supply.

Of all the things that were missing for an increased cultivation of land in Great Britain, the outstanding item was that of labour. If was clear that if a full use were to be made of the few months of the ploughing and sowing season of 1917 that remained, there must be a great influx to the land of fully skilled labour, and the only place in which skilled land labour was to be found was in the ranks of the Army itself.

The drafting back of men from the Army to do farmwork, a rock upon which previously all negotiations of the sort between the Board of Agriculture and the War Office had split, was arranged on a basis of compromise. The War Office agreed to muster such skilled agriculturists as were to be found in the ranks of the Home Defence forces, and to lend them to the Board of Agriculture for a limited and definite period—namely, the spring cultivation season. Further, they agreed to form agricultural companies from able-bodied soldiers belonging to Infantry Works Battalions, and to add to these companies enlisted men of lower medical categories who were not reserved for Home Defence. The War Office **Soldiers for** also made arrangements to send home **agricultural work** from France and other theatres of the war men skilled in ploughing, especially in the use of mechanical ploughs driven by steam or petrol.

The Home Defence men thus lent to agriculture were some 12,500 in number. The demand for men in each locality was ascertained by the War Agricultural Committee of each county and made known to the Board, who communicated these details to the War Office. Certain military depots were selected by the War Office and used as distributing centres, whence men were sent to the farming areas in the proportions required. They were subject to recall on April 15th.

The number of able-bodied soldiers belonging to Infantry Works Battalions who were transferred to agricultural companies was 4,000. They were lent to the Board of Agriculture in lieu of 4,000 combatant German prisoners of war who had been put upon farm work in the previous January. The use of these men for the purposes of agriculture had not proved a success. Many British farmers were nervous of using them, and other farmers who made the experiment were disappointed with the results. The difficulties of guarding German soldiers during work on the land, where small and detached parties might be working in many places at once, was considerable. Numerous guards had to be employed, and even then the employment of these men was attended with risks of escape.

To the 4,000 able-bodied soldiers, transferred to agricultural companies and lent in their place, were added men of lower medical categories to the number of quite 6,000, making the strength of the agricultural companies 10,000. These were lent to agriculture, subject to withdrawal should unforeseen military circumstances arise, for the period of the war. For this labour the farmer paid the current wages rate of the district, but he paid it not to the soldier himself, but to the officer commanding his agricultural company. The farmer might dismiss men at a day's notice, in which case the man returned at once to his unit. Farmers were specially urged to make the men as comfortable as possible.

Another source of farm labour, though not very extensive, was found in non-combatant prisoners of war. These men, civilians, most of whom had lived in England before the war, proved less truculent than German soldier prisoners. Moreover, they were volunteers for agricultural work, and therefore keener to give satisfaction. In batches of seventy-five and more, under military guard, they were housed on the land and used with some success.

Another most valuable contribution to the labour of British farms was made by the women of Britain. Soon after the outbreak of the war the Board encouraged women to volunteer for work on the land by offering free training at agricultural colleges and on private farms. They also stimulated **Women's work** the employment on the land of country- **on the land** women able to give part of their time to farm work. With splendid energy and devotion in all ranks of life, titled women, professional women and others, threw themselves into this movement, and the second year of the war found British agriculture using the services of ploughwomen, women cattle keepers, women grooms, milkers, harvesters, and the rest.

THE RETURN TO THE LAND FOR INCREASING THE COUNTRY'S FOOD SUPPLY.
Naval officers at their self-imposed labour of war-time economy gardening on the coast. A number of these officers took over plots of land, which they worked for the production of vegetables for supplying their hospital-ships, seen in the distance.

But the number so used was not as great as it might have been. The supply of women volunteers for the land greatly exceeded the demand. This was due chiefly to two reasons. The first was the prejudice of British farmers against women workers. They believed them incapable of efficient farm service. To combat this prejudice, farming demonstrations by women were organised by many of the County Agricultural Committees. The writer attended one of these held in Lincolnshire, and saw women doing all the tasks that fall to a man worker on a farm—ploughing, harrowing, manure spreading, threshing with machinery, gathering root crops, etc., and doing it wonderfully well. Farmers who had come to laugh were amazed at what they saw, and converted.

Efficiency of women farmworkers One girl of seventeen ploughed quarter-mile furrows as straight and true as any man could have done. Six other girls, ploughing in neighbouring fields, were almost as good. In another field a threshing-machine, driven by belting from a steam-engine, was being worked by seven girls who till a few weeks before had never done any work on a farm. One of them managed the engine, stoking it, seeing to the steam pump-water feed, and oiling it. The other girls were at work on the threshing-machine, two of them feeding it with corn from a tall stack, others carrying away the grain, tying up the straw, and so on. The only change they made in men's way of doing these things was that they carried away the grain in half sacks instead of full sacks to the grain bins, being unable to carry the weight of the full sack.

In another field two girls with a horse and cart were spreading manure, one of them leading the horse, the other inside the cart forking out the manure as the cart moved slowly along. Not far away a score of girls, with admirable skill and quickness, were gathering and "topping and tailing" turnips. In a field down the lane a man was giving demonstrations with a motor-plough driven by petrol. One of the girl "ploughmen" asked to be allowed to try it. She could ride a motor-bicycle, she said. The man gave up his seat, and after two minutes' experiment the girl and the machine were moving steadily across the field, cutting a perfect furrow alongside the last one the man had made.

Red-faced Lincolnshire farmers and their wives, who had driven in their dog-carts from places miles away "to see the fun," as more than one of them expressed it, were marvelling at what they saw. They had never believed "girls could do it." The only criticism the writer overheard came from farmers' wives who asked, "What would we do with 'educated ladies' like them about the house?"

These demonstrations of women's capabilities on the land were excellent, so far as they went, but they were too few in number to reach the bulk of British farmers, who still retained their prejudice against woman labour. One heard of farmers saying that they would give up farming rather than employ women. This, of course, was prejudice carried to absurdity. In other cases there were real difficulties in the employment of women, the greatest of which was that of housing. Farming cottages were too few to be able to house more than a small proportion of women willing to work on the land. Nor was it possible to allow women to be housed on the " bothy " system in farm buildings in the way that many men farm-hands had lived before the war.

The most successful way in which the housing difficulty was met was by the establishment of hostels, in which a number of women workers lived together under a matron or housekeeper. In some cases, rich country people lent their houses for this purpose, and they became the homes of happy gangs of girl farmworkers who had given up town life and work to take up the more active life of farmworker and make themselves "nationally useful." But, again, there were not enough of these hostels.

In 1917 the Food Production Department of the Board of Agriculture, seeing where the women's land labour movement threatened to fail, busied itself in a special effort to overcome the difficulties in the way of success, and through the Director of National Service it issued a new appeal for women workers. The official terms of employment may be quoted. They included :

Free outfit, consisting of breeches, overalls, high-boots, and hat.

Maintenance allowance (15s. a week) during three weeks' training.

Travelling expenses.

Wages after first month's training of 18s. a week, or the district rate, whichever was the higher.

Four weeks' maintenance during unemployment.

Housing and quarters, inspected and approved by the Women's War Agricultural Committee of the County.

Work on specially selected farms.

Promotion and higher pay for good work.

Special facilities for settlement at home or overseas after the war.

One other source of labour of which the Food Production Department made good use was that of workers willing to serve on the land during their holidays, especially in the summer, during harvest. Among them were many schoolboys. Some of the big public schools of England organised "holiday teams" of boy farmworkers, who worked under the direction of their own masters. So that these workers should not oust ordinary land workers, it was insisted that they must receive wages, and threepence an hour was the usual price for boy labour.

Notwithstanding these many means for making good the deficiency of labour on the land, there still remained a **Call for more machinery** shortage in spite of all the Government could do ; for it was computed that the Army, the munitions industry, and other war services had taken from the land no fewer than 250,000 people, to say nothing of all the horses, fodder, and supplies that had been taken for Army purposes. It was only by a greatly extended use of machinery in substitution of man-power and horse-power that the Food Production Department could hope to increase or even to maintain the 1917 harvest. Motor-tractors and steam-tractors offered the best means for doing the amount of ploughing and harrowing that remained to be done if

CHIEF OF BRITAIN'S ORGANISED WOMANHOOD.
Queen Mary visiting the National Welfare and Economy Exhibition, opened at the County Hall, London, June 25th, 1917, to advocate economy in the purchase and use of the necessaries of life. Prices and food values of all articles were shown and practical demonstration given of ways to prepare them.

HOEING UNDER THE JUDGE'S EYE.
An agricultural competition for girls of "All England" was held at Bishop's Stortford in 1917, when their capability was tested in a variety of farming employments. A competitor in the hoeing competition.

prospect of being used as they had been in previous years.

The Food Production Department tracked down and examined every machine, and of the five hundred that existed no fewer than four hundred and fifty-two were manned, repaired when necessary, supplied with fuel and tackle, and set working almost night and day, going from farm to farm, till square miles of country-side that had been grass became soft brown soil ready for seed. Of the remaining forty-eight sets, thirty-four were beyond repair, so that all but fourteen of the ploughing sets of the country were reclaimed and set to fullest use.

The resolute handling of the machinery difficulty contributed

the harvest were not to fall short of that of the preceding year. Yet motor-tractors and steam-ploughing "sets" were not to be had in the country in anything like the required number. Before the war the number of motor-tractors on the land was barely two hundred. Some had been imported in the earlier years of the war, but they were, of course, in the hands of private owners.

The Food Production Department sent a "rush" order to the United States, and by unprecedented hustling contrived to import no fewer than five hundred motor-tractors, and to get them into use before the spring cultivation season was through. In addition, it commandeered almost all the privately owned motor-tractors of the country, and employed them on co-operative lines to their fullest working capacity.

The machines were manned, equipped, and controlled by the Government, who, of course, also kept the new machines in its own hands. The commandeered machines were taken and paid for on a hire basis of so much an acre for work done, the owner being given priority in the use of his machine for the culti-

Government control of motor-tractors vation of his own land. After that the machine passed into the hands of the department, who controlled its programme of work, manned it, and saw to its upkeep.

Before the cultivation season was passed, the Government was controlling a force of motor-tractors for the land, six or seven hundred strong. In February it had only ten.

Another potential source of machine power for the land, that had presented itself when the Government took control in February, were the steam-ploughing sets, of which some five hundred were known to exist in the country. Hurried inquiry was made after them, and it was found that a great proportion of them was lying idle. The difficulties of getting labour, coal (which at that time it was almost impossible to obtain in some of the country districts), oil, and tackle, coupled with the fact that many machines were slightly defective and spare parts could not be obtained nor repairs be done, had decided the owners in very many cases not to attempt to use their machines that year. Hundreds of these steam-ploughing sets—worth nearly £4,000 a set—were lying rusting in farm buildings and agricultural engineers' yards, with no

MAKING UP A DIFFICULT HEDGE.
Hertfordshire girls taking part in the agricultural competition at Bishop's Stortford. The hedgers and ditchers displaying their skill on a particularly tangled stretch of hedge drew close attention from the judges.

enormously to the value of the 1917 harvest. In spite of bad weather, which included, among other evils, five weeks of hard frost, the threatened deficiency of ploughed land, as compared with the previous year's acreage, was obviated. More than this, 300,000 acres were added. It was a fine achievement, one that was not carried through without a great expenditure of energy and resourcefulness, coupled in one or two cases with the necessity of a tactful display of force and "the mailed fist."

Perhaps the next greatest difficulty in the way of increasing cultivation was that of getting supplies—fertilisers, feeding-stuffs, seeds, and the rest. The Food Production Department handled this problem also with a directness almost Napoleonic. It took control of the whole organisation of distribution and supply. In many cases it actually seized supplies of which there threatened to be some shortage, and shared them fairly among the many people who were in need of these commodities. It bought, for instance, the whole of the Scottish potato crop for use as seed; it bought seed potatoes right and left in Ireland and England, and also super-intended their distribution to farmers and smallholders. Fifteen thousand tons of seed potatoes were actually handled by the department, and the threatened shortage of seed potatoes—due largely to the poorness of the 1916 potato crop, in Scotland especially—was obviated.

The department fixed prices for all supplies used in agriculture, thereby preventing any undue profiteering which might have taken place as a result of shortage of certain commodities. It organised the supply and distribution of fertilisers to such good effect that the distribution was even better than in years before the war. The use of sulphate of ammonia, for instance, in the months of March and April in England and Wales exceeded the consumption of any whole year before the war. Basic slag and sulphate of copper (for potato-spraying) were also secured in large quantities and distributed. This was done by co-operation with the Ministry of Munitions, who made arrangements for giving every help to works making these things.

Financial loans to farmers Arrangements were also made for safe-guarding the supplies of raw phosphates, for which Britain was almost wholly dependent upon foreign countries. Importation of these commodities had, of course, been interrupted. The normal annual need of phosphates was half a million tons. The department saw that the best possible use was made of the 110,000 tons remaining in the country, and made arrangements for the supply of future years. As to potash, a most necessary ingredient, of which we used about 20,000 tons per annum, there was a great shortage ; but a valuable new source of supply was found in the flue dust from blast furnaces. Production of lime was also stimulated.

In the foregoing ways the Government handled the problems of labour, machinery, and supplies that confronted the British farmer in the spring of 1917. All these steps would, however, have been useless in many cases unless one other difficulty had been solved, too—namely, that of finance. Eager as most of the British farmers were to increase their area of cultivation, it was impossible for many of them without financial assistance. The fact that a farmer had no means was not allowed to stand in his way. Arrangements were made by the Government with the principal joint-stock banks of the country for loans to farmers to enable them to buy supplies (which in view of the high prices of all commodities entailed a much greater outlay than usual), to pay wages, and to subsist pending the sale of the increased crops which they were asked to grow. Security for these loans was naturally asked for by the banks, and in cases where the farmer could give no security, the Government gave its own guarantee for the repayment of the loan and interest. In this way many a willing farmer, who even in years before the war had been held back and cramped by lack of means, was enabled to launch out and to put his farm in the way of yielding its maxi-mum output.

So far this chapter has dealt only with the side of the Government's work which concerned the professional farmers of the country working on a large scale. The

FROM "KULTUR" TO INTENSIVE CULTURE.
Two of the company of German prisoners who had been chosen for their knowledge of agriculture to work on the land at Evesham. They were engaged in the intensive culture of vegetables.

PRISONERS OF WAR IN AGRICULTURAL OCCUPATIONS.
German prisoners at Evesham—where a party of eighty were employed in various agricultural operations —leaving their quarters under an armed guard to start work. Above Two of the prisoners engaged in planting young trees. Blue circular patches were sewn on their tunics for identification purposes.

HARVESTING POTATOES.
Cadets from an O.T.C. camp gathering potatoes in Cornwall for despatch to the Navy and the Army.

other side of the Board of Agriculture's work concerned the small food-growers, allotment-holders, gardeners, and amateurs. Its measures to help these men and to enrol others in the great movement of food production were well-nigh as great and far-reaching in extent, if not in their effect upon the food yield of the country, as the measures on behalf of the bigger food producers. As a parallel to the War Agricultural Committees set up in each county area, the Board of Agriculture established similar committees in each of the boroughs of the country. Their duty was to do for the urban areas and small urban gardeners what the County Committees did in the country-side for the farmers. They called themselves in some cases Food Production Committees, in other cases War Agricultural Committees, for they chose their own titles. They were formed by and under the authority of the borough councils and urban district councils, but responded willingly to the guidance of the central Food Production Department of the Board of Agriculture, who conferred upon them powers very similar to those conferred upon the County Committees for the acquisition of land.

Thus they were empowered to seize land, either within their own urban area or outside it, provided that such land could be conveniently cultivated by persons residing within the urban area. Common lands might be used, subject to the consent of the Board ; but consent was not given to any scheme which damaged unduly the natural beauty or amenities of a common, or which seriously prejudiced the interests of the public. A council did not have to pay for any un-occupied or common land they cultivated, and the rent to be paid for occupied land that was taken was definitely limited to provide against extortion.

Councils were further authorised to do all things necessary to adapt land for cultivation, including fencing, and to provide, at cost price to cultivators, such things as seed, manure, and tools. Councils were also urged to arrange for expert help and advice to cultivators in the preparation and sowing of their plots. The Royal Horticultural Society, with members scattered all over the country, did invaluable work in providing this expert advice. The Board aided its work by issuing leaflets telling how various crops should be grown. Some millions of these were printed and distributed, and proved of great use to the many recruits to the new army of land cultivators.

So that no expense should fall on the local rates as a result of steps taken to help smallholders, the Board of Agriculture agreed to make good any loss incurred by a council

CADET CAMP FOR FOOD-SUPPLY WORK IN CORNWALL.
Weighing the potatoes which had just been collected, and (in circle) clearing off the haulm preparatory to lifting the tubers. Scenes near one of the many camps which were formed by cadets of public school O.T.C.'s for helping in harvest work in various parts of the country.

not exceeding a total sum of £2 for each acre of ground taken by the council.

The Borough Food Production Committees, backed by these powers and guarantees, did a tremendous work for British food production in 1917. By the beginning of May nine hundred and twenty-four boroughs or urban districts had received 168,000 applications for plots, which in almost every case they were able to provide, the total acreage covered exceeding 11,000. About 14,000 applications had to be refused—in some cases owing to shortness of time available during the sowing season for obtaining the necessary land, and in other cases owing to actual absence of cultivatable land within the area or near it. Had steps been taken a little earlier there would have been no failures to supply plots.

In addition to the small-holdings provided by borough councils, many horticultural societies, that in previous years had taken land and let it out to members in allotments, greatly increased the scope of their work. The Vacant Land Cultivation Society, for instance, increased its total of allotments from a few hundreds to more than 7,000 before the spring was passed. Smaller societies whose allotments in previous years had numbered only a few score, increased that

AT THE FURROW'S END.
Lifting the blades of a motor-plough out of the furrow in order to turn at the end of the field.

number a hundredfold, and there were many of them who eventually had several thousand allotments apiece. A considerable number of new societies was also formed.

Among other helpers of the allotment movement were the railway companies and the colliery companies of the Midlands and North. The former gave free grants of vacant land on the fringe of their railways to employees and others to be worked in spare time. The colliery companies parcelled out vacant land lying over their pit-workings both to their employees and to their friends. The total acreage thus brought under cultivation, much of it for the first time, cannot be accurately estimated, but Mr. Prothero himself, President of the Board of Agriculture, in a speech made in May, 1917, assessed the number of these allotments and vegetable gardens at 500,000.

Yet one other great source of food supply for the 1917 harvest has to be mentioned—namely, the private gardens of Great Britain. By the time summer arrived there was hardly a garden in the whole country that was not making some contribution to the year's food supply. Beds which in previous years had been devoted exclusively to flowers were showing potatoes, parsnips, beans, and greenstuff well advanced in growth. Even lawns were sacrificed and dug up to grow vegetables.

RUSSIAN MOTOR-PLOUGH IN AN ESSEX FIELD.
The Russian Government lent several "caterpillar" motor-ploughs to the British Government, and the huge machines lent to farmers, together with implements and crews, became familiar objects in many parts of rural England. One is shown here at work near Braintree, with an old-fashioned harrow working beside it. In circle: The "caterpillar" crawling off to a fresh field.

THE KINDLY FRUITS OF THE EARTH.
Land Service girls harvesting in Cornwall. Bad weather in 1917 laid some of the corn, with the result that women had to acquire skill with the scythe.

Some of the tennis clubs, with commendable self-sacrifice, converted playing courts into vegetable plots, and in the spring and early summer members were to be seen busy with spade and hoe and watering-can where previously they had handled nothing heavier than a tennis racket.

Schools took up the movement, and vegetable plots and work on them became an integral part of the equipment and curriculum of almost every elementary school. Some of the City schools were hard put to it to find land for the purpose, but they found it. On the Vauxhall Bridge Road, for instance, right in the heart of London, and bounded on three sides by tall buildings, were to be seen the garden plots of an infant school of the neighbourhood, each plot, trim and carefully numbered, yielding its quota of radishes, lettuces, and such things to the food supply of the district. Many of the schools, even big public schools among them, substituted agricultural work for some of their games, and did this work either on the schools' gardens or on the farms of the district.

Food-growing the popular interest   Food-growing was undoubtedly the greatest popular movement in Great Britain in the third year of the war. Every class participated in it. Even members of the Royal Family worked industriously on their vegetable plots, Princess Mary being reported as a special enthusiast. Prince Henry at Eton and his friends often took a hand at farm work and the loading of farm trucks on the railway.

In fact, every class alike was equally interested. From spring onwards the country-side presented one great tide of agricultural activity, which crept right to the outskirts of every town, penetrating wherever a green field or bit of vacant land presented itself. And just as the tide foams whitest round some island rock that resists it, so around the large towns of England—vast islands of bricks and mortar—this agricultural tide seemed fiercest. The outskirts of London afforded wonderful sights. On a fine evening or Saturday afternoon or Sunday, food-growers were busy in their thousands —men, women, and children. One small suburb alone, that of Dulwich, had more than 3,000 allotments, upon any one of which might be seen sometimes a whole family at work. This was no more than typical of the suburbs

of London and virtually all great towns. "Tea on the allotment" became with some families a regular Sunday event. Church services for smallholders were held on the allotments, and men and women would leave their work for half an hour to gather in some corner of the field round a clergyman in white surplice from some neighbouring church, who read Divine service.

Allotment patrols were organised to guard the produce from depredations, and holders undertook this work voluntarily, taking each his turn of regular duty to guard his own and his neighbours' plots at night. The Government helped to discourage

BLACKBERRY PICKERS AT TOLLESBURY, ESSEX.
Holidays were granted to school-children throughout the country to enable them to gather blackberries to be made into jam for the troops. The children were paid for their work by weight.

thefts from plots by inflicting severe penalties. A fine of a hundred pounds might be imposed on an allotment robber, with an alternative of six months' imprisonment. Severe penalties were the more necessary because many of the plots lay in positions quite exposed, on public commons and roadsides easily accessible to anyone evilly disposed.

At first sight it might not seem that the multiplication of these small food producers and small gardens offered any very considerable contribution to the food supply. As compared with the 11,000,000 acres cultivated by the big farmers, they might seem little indeed. But these small gardens were far more valuable than their mere acreage would suggest. For these reasons : First, they were a source of extra food supply, cultivated by men and women who previously had had no touch with agriculture ; they meant extra work, done in addition to an ordinary day's work. Second, these little gardens represented no ordinary land culture, but **Great value of the** intensive culture ; each square foot was **small gardens** used to its full growing capacity. Third, the products of these gardens were food that needed no re-handling—no transport, no marketing, no middlemen. They were grown at the consumers' own door, thus effecting a most valuable saving at a critical time of the national energy. Lastly, these gardens on a small scale were making converts to agriculture. Each garden, besides being a little source of supply, much needed and in the right place, was also a little school, where a man not only learnt the detail of land work, but acquired also enthusiasm for it. All of these things stood to help enormously towards the attainment later on of the agricultural ideal which Great Britain had adopted and set before herself, which was to become self-supporting and independent of food supplies from overseas.

That was the end at which the Government aimed. "Britain must be put in the way to feed herself." Such was the instruction given by the Prime Minister to Sir Arthur Lee when he became chief of the Food Production Department in February, and it was in **Britain to be** February that details of the scheme **self-supporting** for a self-supporting Britain were begun. They would have been carried through that same year had there only remained available a greater part of the spring cultivation season ; but to increase British agriculture to this extent in the space of a few spring months was humanly impossible, and the Food Production Department divided the problem into two parts. That spring it would attempt no more than to make good the collapse which threatened agriculture, and to devise plans for carrying out the fuller scheme later on. These plans were formulated, and the means and preparations for carrying them out in the year 1918 were actively begun.

To make Britain self-supporting meant a return to the agriculture of fifty years earlier. Since that time more than

three million acres had dropped out of cultivation, though only a mere fragment of that land had been covered by bricks and mortar. Of the 37,324,000 acres available for cultivation in England and Wales in the 'seventies of the previous century, 37,137,00 acres still remained available, so that a return to the agriculture of that date was by no means impossible, so far as the availability of land was concerned.

After "stopping the rot" in time for the 1917 harvest and increasing the previous year's total of ploughed land to 11,351,000 acres, the department began work upon plans for adding no fewer than two and a half million acres to the following year's harvest for England

and Wales alone, making that total 14,000,000, the same acreage as in the 'seventies. The scheme demanded an additional 100,000 men for the land. These the Government virtually promised should be forthcoming. The whole country and its production and potential production was mapped out, and a table drawn up allotting to each area a percentage of increased cultivation necessary to attain the "objective" of 14,000,000 acres.

It was realised, of course, that to make a demand of the farmers without being able to ensure them the means for carrying out that **National programme** demand was useless, and steps were begun **for 1918** to ensure that every commodity and means of power of which a farmer might stand in need should be available.

The Government's scheme, upon which it began work about May, 1917, provided, *inter alia*, for :

1. An additional 100,000 men for agriculture.
2. An additional supply of horses on a large scale, to be purchased or obtained by Government agents.
3. Great extension of the service of motor-tractors available for the use of farmers.
4. State control and provision of supplies, with regulation of prices.
5. Establishment, by reserving and, if necessary, by importation, of a seed supply equal to 25 per cent. of the 1917 harvest.
6. Organisation of market facilities and transport facilities where needed.
7. Extension of movement for women labour on the land and arrangements for women workers' welfare.

Some of the details of this national programme followed quite new and original lines, lines suggestive of war organisation. The motor-tractors, for instance, were to be grouped in "batteries," each battery comprising ten motor-tractors and one "spare" for use in case of breakdown. All implements for use on the tractors — ploughs, harrows, and the like—were to be interchangeable. Each battery was to be a self-contained unit, having its own especial crew, its own headquarters, and its own base depot or "dump," from which to draw supplies of oil, fuel, and spare parts. Repair depots and, if necessary, travelling repair units, were also provided for.

Each battery was designed to be allocated to one

"CONSCIENTIOUS OBJECTORS" AT DARTMOOR.
Men who obtained exemption from military service on the ground of "conscientious objection" clearing ground, and (in oval) trenching on Dartmoor. They were quartered in the great convict prison at Princetown, and were allowed a latitude in the employment of their time which provoked considerable hostile criticism, the Devonshire people in particular holding public meetings of protest at Plymouth.

THIRSTY WORK ON A HOT DAY.
Party of Land Service girls hoeing weeds on a' farm in Hertfordshire, where the size of the field and the absence of all shade made the work exceedingly arduous.

or other of the County Committees, who would control its programme of work from day to day and collect the fees to be paid by farmers for the use of the battery on their lands. But the tractors themselves and their crews were to remain always in Government service as national property and servants, the County Committees acting, as it were, only in the capacity of controlling officers for the time being. A battery lent to one county one month might be allocated to another county the next, and its crew would go along with it.

Among other interesting preparations made in 1917 for bringing the 1918 crop to record size were those for the distribution of fertilisers. Arrangements were made for distributing sulphate of ammonia, for instance, at a uniform price, and a fund of £100,000 was set aside from which to make contributions towards delivery charges. To maintain supplies, export of this chemical was suspended.

In consultation with the Ministry of Munitions, steps were taken to increase the output of basic slag by 50 per cent. The reserves of lower-grade slag, which so far had not been used, were earmarked for use. To ensure supply of feeding-stuffs, the department took steps with a view to checking undue profits of middlemen. This they did partly by direct means and partly by indicating to farmers the cheapest source of supply.

A special scheme for the selection and distribution of the more prolific cereal seed, such as the Cambridge wheats and Svalov oats, was put in hand. With the first gathering of the 1917 vegetable crops the Government were in the market as big buyers of seed.

By June, 1917, all these arrangements were so well in hand and promised so well that Mr. Prothero, President of the Board of Agriculture, felt justified in making the following pronouncement: "Strict

economy is necessary, and if the worst comes to the worst we may not be able to allow any barley for brewing. But on these lines, with these allowances, I think that Germany may just as well abandon the idea of starving this country into surrender. If our agricultural programme is carried out, and if no grain of corn is brought into the country for a whole year, we shall be able to supply the normal rate of consumption of nine million loaves a day, and we shall have a margin over which will enable us to set aside liberal supplies for the live-stock of the country.

"That is the object we are aiming at. It is the most complete and effective answer to the submarine menace, and if Germany is buoying herself up with the hope that she may, if she prolongs the war to 1918, starve us out, it is worth making every effort that this nation can to make that answer. Germany knows perfectly well that time and money and men (since America joined in the war) are all on our side. It is only the food question that trembles in the balance. Once decide that question in our favour, and peace will be nearer our doors. We have silver bullets, we have lead bullets, it is up to the farmer to find us bread bullets."

A farmer of his audience shouted, "Give us the labour and we'll do it!" That admirably represented the frame of mind of the average British agriculturist at this critical moment of British history. At the end of June, Lord Milner, a member of the Cabinet, speaking in the House of Lords, expressed the opinion that the extra men needed for agriculture would be found. The Government had made arrangements for a contribution of skilled men from the Army and for additional employment, under new arrangements, of prisoners of war, both combatant and non-combatant. Though these additions to the labour problem, amounting to 80,000 men, did not entirely solve the problem, they represented a great advance and put an entirely new aspect upon the whole matter.

The Duke of Marlborough mentioned that six hundred and twenty-six motor-tractors had been obtained and eight hundred and thirty motor-ploughs.

Thus, even by the summer of 1917, the arrangements for carrying out the 1918 programme were so well in hand as to give sound promise of success.

PRACTICAL INTERESTS OF A PREMIER: MR. LLOYD GEORGE IN HIS POTATO-PATCH.
Mr. Lloyd George watching the weighing of a very satisfactory crop of King Edward potatoes grown in his garden at Walton Heath under the supervision of his housekeeper. He had previously superintended the spraying of this crop with the Government-recommended apparatus and antidote against the disease that attacked potatoes throughout England in 1917.

HOISTING A SHELL

ABOARD A BATTLESHIP.

LIFE OF THE "LOWER DECK": HOW IT WAS AFFECTED BY WAR SERVICE.

By Percival A. Hislam.

The Peace Training of the Navy—Its Man-Power at the Outbreak of War—The Mobilised Strength of the Reserves—Complex Organisation of the Personnel—Complaints Regarding Inadequate Pay and Detained Pensions—Promotion Reduced to a Minimum by the Direct Entry of Outsiders into the Commissioned Ranks—Naval Victualling in War Time—An Organised Appeal to the Press—Prize Money and Prize Bounty—How the Awards were Divided—Small Fortunes for Submarine Crews—The Bad Luck of Commander Noel Laurence—Rewards for Sinking Submarines—Prize Money in the German Fleet—The Splendid Health of the British Navy in War—Breaking the Monotony of the long North Sea Vigil—How the Medical Department Coped with its Task Afloat and Ashore—The Great Change in Naval Casualties since Nelson's Day—The British Seaman in Battle.

T is usually accepted as an axiomatic truth that during long periods of peace the efficiency of a fighting force is gradually sapped away. In the great threshing-machine of war all that is useless, is—or should be—ruthlessly swept away until, whether in men, methods, or material, there remains only that which is actively contributory to the victorious end in view. With the return of peace, however, the lessons of battle are too often forgotten. New standards are set up, moulded not upon the teachings of past wars, but upon the false supposition that the principles of war have been changed by some striking new theory or mechanical device. Combatant merit becomes less and less the avenue by which a man rises to prominence and command. This, indeed, is to a certain extent inevitable, seeing that there is no system yet devised by which combatant merit may be unfailingly detected in peace; and the general preparation of an armed force for war is very apt to be diverted into channels whose fallaciousness is the more dangerous because it cannot be effectively exposed save by war itself.

The British Navy was not subjected to any severe test between the end of the struggle with Napoleon, in 1815, and the outbreak of the Great War, in 1914, and in that century of peace many false standards were set up which tended to cripple the higher administration of the Fleet and to impose upon those who were

MEN OF "THE TRADE."
Sailors belonging to the British submarine service, or "The Trade." Boats of the "E" class had complements of from twenty-eight to thirty-three officers and men.

ambitious for advancement a wholly spurious idea of their ultimate functions. This is not the place to plunge into the intricate questions concerned with the study of the higher problems of war; but we may very plainly see one of the gravest effects of a long peace in the fact that the proper training of the Navy in the science of gunnery did not begin, in the modern era, until the twentieth century, and even then it took some years finally to eradicate the idea that officers ought to be promoted according to the smartness of their ship's appearance. The Navy will long remember the case of a distinguished admiral on the China Station who, having completed his annual inspection of a vessel that had just put up a remarkable record in shooting, found nothing more impressive on which to compliment the ship's company than the cleanliness of their bedding.

It was fortunate for Great Britain that her Navy awoke in time to the folly of this, and that the men of the Fleet turned with a will to the intensive training that was their lot for ten years before the opening of the Great War. In the annual firing under the Gunlayers' Tests, carried out in 1899, the ships that took part missed the target 3,418 more times than they hit it; but in 1907, so extraordinary had been the progress made under the new conditions, that hits exceeded the misses by 5,556, with the result that the Admiralty had to reduce the size of the target, increase the range, and in various other ways add to the difficulty of the test.

As regards battle practice, carried out at much greater distances and under much severer conditions, the comparative increase in efficiency was no less remarkable than in the case of the Gunlayers' Tests. Comparatively little was known of German gunnery in 1914, beyond the fact that on one occasion some extraordinarily good shooting had been made by the Scharnhorst, flagship in the Far East. That was in 1911, when, steaming from 14 to 17 knots and firing at a target 18 feet long, at a distance of 4,500 to 7,000 yards, she made eighteen hits in twenty-two rounds with her 8·2 in. guns, and twenty-six hits in thirty rounds with her 5·9 in. guns. In spite of, or perhaps because of, this lack of knowledge, something of a halo had been built around the German seaman, who was often held up in this country as a model to be emulated; but although he proved himself strong in that mechanical discipline and efficiency which is the especial product of the Prussian system,

Personnel of the British Fleet and never showed himself lacking in courage, the British seaman scored heavily every time by reason of his longer training, the habits of self-reliance inculcated by it, and the splendid traditions that were at the back of him.

When the war began the strength of the personnel of the British Fleet had reached a higher figure than at any previous time in its history. In 1792, immediately before the opening of the French Revolutionary Wars, the manpower of the Navy had been reduced to 16,000 officers and men, but under the influence of war it rapidly expanded, and in the year of Trafalgar the number voted by Parliament was 120,000, the average borne throughout the year (1805) on the books of the Fleet being 114,012. The actual maximum of those days was reached in 1813, when the average number borne was 147,047, though the Parliamentary vote was for only 140,000, or 5,000 fewer than in the preceding three years. During the eighty years of comparative peace at sea that followed the downfall of Napoleon, the strength of the personnel fluctuated a good deal. It rose again to 80,000 for the first time in 1894, and to 100,000 in 1898; and in the Navy Estimates for 1914-15 the House of Commons sanctioned a strength of 151,000 officers and men for the active list of the Fleet. This figure was made up of 129,425 of the Royal Navy, 3,130 of the Coastguard, and 18,445 of the Royal Marines.

In addition to the above there were various classes of reservists liable for service, and promptly called out for hostilities under proclamations of August 3rd, 1914. The most important of these at that time was the Royal Fleet Reserve, established in 1900, and consisting entirely of seamen and stoker ratings and Royal Marines, together with a few ships' police, who had completed their term of enlistment in the Navy. At the outbreak of war the R.F.R. was numerically, as well as from

The R.F.R., R.N.R., and the R.N.V.R. the point of view of efficiency, the most important of the Navy's reserves, its authorised strength being 31,137 petty-officers and men, but it was rapidly outstripped in numbers by the Royal Naval Reserve. The latter force was recruited entirely from the merchant service and the fishing fleets, officers and men being required to put in a certain amount of periodical training with the Fleet in return for a retainer, and, of course, to place their services at the disposal of the naval authorities in the event of war. The main body of the Royal Naval Reserve consisted of 1,790 officers and 17,299 men, while there were sections in Newfoundland and Malta comprising 600 and 400 men respectively. In 1911 a new branch had been created for the specific purpose of mine-sweeping in war, and in 1914 the authorised strength of this, the Trawler Section, was 142 skippers (warrant officers) and 1,136 men.

The third and youngest of the Navy's reserve forces was the Royal Naval Volunteer Reserve, established in 1903, and consisting for the most part of shore-keeping men with the necessary enthusiasm and spare time to equip themselves to stand their footing with the regular "matlo" in the event of war. Its various divisions were known as London, Clyde, Bristol, Mersey, Sussex, Tyneside, and South African, and its strength at the outbreak of war was 4,700 officers and men—a small force, but one whose efficiency was quickly established and acknowledged, and part of which formed the nucleus of the Royal Naval Division, whose splendid but ineffectual services at Antwerp in October, 1914, and later on in Gallipoli and on the western front, won such a prominent place in the records of naval fighting ashore. Finally, the Admiralty had at their immediate disposal a few hundred men in the Royal Naval Auxiliary Sick Berth Reserve, and had the right, which was naturally exercised wherever it was desirable, to call upon all pensioners up to the age of fifty.

The following is a summary of the naval man-power nominally available at the outbreak of war, apart from retired officers and pensioners and R.N.A. Sick Berth Reserve:

ACTIVE LIST.		RESERVE.	
Royal Navy ..	.. 129,425	Royal Fleet Reserve ..	31,137
Coastguard ..	.. 3,130	Royal Naval Reserve ..	20,089
Royal Marines ..	.. 18,445	R.N.R., Trawler Section	1,278
		R.N. Volunteer Reserve	4,700
Total	.. 151,000	Total ..	57,204

Two days after the declaration of war a Supplementary Naval Estimate was passed authorising the addition of 67,000 to the strength of the Fleet; 32,000 were added in February, 1915, and further additions were made at intervals until, in the spring of 1917, the total stood at 400,000 officers and men, of whom about 76,000 belonged to the Naval Reserve and 33,000 to the Volunteer Reserve. The actual number engaged upon naval operations, however, was not divulged, and many thousands would have to be deducted from the aggregate on account of the Royal Naval Division—a purely land force made up of R.N. Volunteers and a **Branches of the** Royal Marine Brigade—and the R.N. **"lower deck"** Air Service, of which a certain proportion was employed with the land forces. After making full allowance for these, however, it will still be seen that the continued existence of the German Navy was making a very heavy drain upon British resources in men, and providing a very effective answer to those who argued that it did not matter whether the enemy's Fleet were destroyed or not so long as it was content to let the command of the sea—or the sea's surface—remain with Great Britain by default.

In this chapter we are concerned only with the "lower deck"—a term which came into general use to express for the Navy what "rank and file" does for the Army. The complexities of its organisation were such that it would be quite hopeless—even if it were necessary, which it is not—to set them out here; but some idea of its intricacies may be gathered from the fact that in the armoured cruiser Good Hope, which was sunk off Coronel on November 1st, 1914, with a loss of 52 officers and 864 men, more than a hundred different ratings were represented among the crew, and even then the entire list was by no means exhausted. Broadly speaking, however, the lower deck—among whom we are including warrant officers and chief warrant officers—fell into eight branches. There was the "military" branch, comprising seamen, signalmen, telegraphists, and, curiously enough, sailmakers; the engineer branch, with its stokers, mechanicians, and engine-room artificers; the highly-diversified artisan branch, embracing carpenters, joiners, shipwrights, blacksmiths, plumbers, painters, coopers, armourers, wiremen, and electrical artificers; the medical branch of sick-berth attendants and stewards; the accountant branch, with its writers, ship's stewards, and—another curiosity—cooks; the police, with the ratings of ship's corporals and masters-at-arms; and, finally, the Royal Marine Artillery and the Royal Marine Light Infantry.

Boxing competition aboard a warship, with the crew of a second ship as additional spectators.

How the men of the Grand Fleet kept fit while waiting for "The Day."

British submarine berthed on a " hard " for painting.

American submarine at the " Laurenti " dock for pressure tests.

The neutral : Doom of a merchantman that ventured into waters proscribed by the German submarine pirates.

Incidents in the story of the underwater craft of three nations.

Suspense on a liner entering the danger zone.

End of a mine-sweeper that struck a mine.

Passing a hawser : Tugs attempting the salvage of a merchantman torpedoed by a German submarine.

Hidden perils of the deep in the heyday of German piracy.

Using the holystone to keep perfection perfect.

Inspection of bedding on the quarter-deck.

[British official photographs.

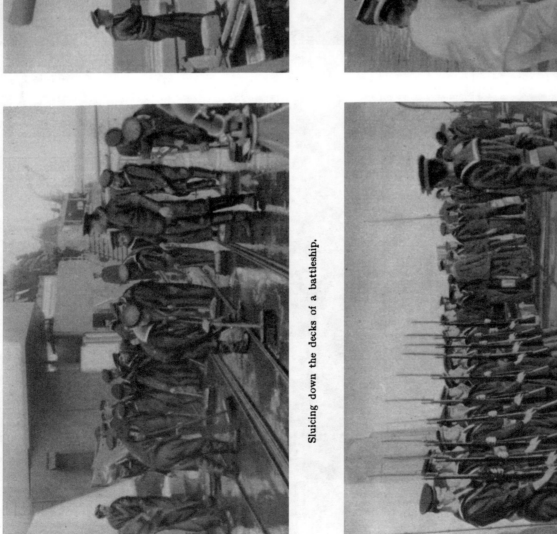

Sluicing down the decks of a battleship.

Musketry drill aboard a man-of-war.

With the British Navy in war time: *Daily routine aboard a battleship.*

110

Beyond all these—in each of which there were various "ratings" according to capacity and length of service—there were such "miscellaneous ratings" as bandsmen, officers' stewards, and cooks, schoolmasters, tailors, and shoemakers.

Long service was the keynote of enlistment in the Navy, and, without doubt, the real foundation of its superiority. Every rating, on joining, had to agree to serve for twelve years, the only exception to this being officers' stewards and cooks, and a small proportion of seamen and stokers who were enlisted as "special service" entries for five years. In order to earn a pension twenty-two years' service was required, and this brings us to the first of a number of cases in which the men, with a considerable basis of reason, thought themselves badly treated by the authorities. The Admiralty stated quite unequivocally in their recruiting pamphlets that "after twenty-two years' qualifying service pensions are awarded for life"; but on August 3rd, 1914, an Order-in-Council was issued bringing into force the Naval Enlistment Act of 1853, according to the provisions of which not only were the services of time-expired men retained, but their pensions were withheld also, 2d. a day "detained pay" being given in its place. There were several facts to justify the irritation the men felt at this treatment. The first was that they should have been deprived of their pensions in defiance of the definite statements of the recruiting circulars, and under cover of an Act of Parliament of which they were entirely ignorant. Secondly, there were the statements of two First Lords (Mr. McKenna and Mr. Churchill) made before the war to the effect that when a pension had been earned it was distinctly and definitely the property of the one who had earned it. Thirdly, there was the fact that if a man who had completed his time for pension after the outbreak of war should be killed, neither he nor his dependents would ever have touched a penny of the pension for which he had given twenty-two years of service. Most aggravating of all was Dr. Macnamara's attempt in Parliament to show that the detained pensioner receiving a meagre 2d. a day extra was better off than the man who had taken his pension before the war and was called up for service. The statement was not challenged in the House of Commons; but as the pensioner called up drew the full pay of his rating *plus* his pension, its absurdity is apparent on the surface. Another anomaly of the naval pension system was that although boys were entered from the age of fifteen, they were not allowed to start counting time for pension purposes until they were eighteen, or rated ordinary seamen. As their pay during the interval was only 6d. or 7d. a day—the latter sum being temporarily increased to 9d. in May, 1917—the cutting out of these two or three years, making them serve twenty-four or twenty-five years for a pension nominally awarded for twenty-two (and which stood at the same figure when the service required was only twenty), was not unnaturally felt to be a hardship, more especially as in the first three years of war the Navy's boys won a V.C. and more than a dozen Distinguished Service Medals, while three hundred of them laid down their lives in the Battle of Jutland alone.

Generally speaking, the policy of the Admiralty was to draft the reservists in considerable numbers to warships of the less modern and important types. Thus we find that in the sinking of the armoured cruiser Cressy, on September 22nd, 1914, out of a total of 536 men lost, there were 252 men of the Royal Fleet Reserve and 47 of the Royal Naval Reserve, in addition to a few coastguardsmen and pensioners; while of 864 in the Good Hope (November 1st, 1914), 411 belonged to the Royal Fleet Reserve. In these cases, therefore, the reservists accounted for about 50 per cent. of the entire complement. But the other aspect of the matter is to be seen in the casualties for the month of May, 1916, which were accounted for as regards at least

95 per cent., and probably more, by the Battle of Jutland. In that month the number of men killed was 5,348; but these included only 121 men of the R.F.R., 351 of the R.N.R., and 210 of the R.N. Volunteers, the majority of the last falling while on service with the Royal Naval Division in France. It is obvious, therefore, that the authorities arranged for the crews of the Grand Fleet ships to consist almost entirely of Royal Navy ratings; but it is impossible to ascertain what proportion had been entered "for hostilities only" and were still more or less under training. The fact that 5.6 per cent. of the month's killed were boys under eighteen suggests that the proportion was rather high.

The efficiency of any fighting force necessarily depends to a large extent upon the discipline and contentment of the elements of which it is composed. With regard to the former, it was customary in peace time for the Admiralty to issue an annual return of the number of courts-martial held and summary punishments awarded. In 1902 there were 373 courts-martial punishments on men for a personnel of 104,724; while in 1912 the sentences fell to 111 for a personnel of 119,903. There is no statistical information available on this head for the period of the war, during which one would naturally expect the ratio to be increased, owing to the greater severity of the conditions and the relaxation of the standards usually required of recruits in peace. In later years, however, there had been a remarkable growth in the spirit of comradeship between officers and men, while the long-service personnel itself had been recruited from a much better educated class than was formerly the case; and there is no reason to doubt the truth of the several semi-official assurances that were given from time to time, that the general level of discipline in the Fleet stood higher during the war than at any former period of its history. This must be attributed very largely to the tact of the officers, for it is impossible to doubt that serious trouble might have arisen if, for instance, the men who entered the R.N. Reserve from the merchant service so patriotically, and in such large numbers, had been suddenly called upon to conform to all the intricate and, to an outsider, often inexplicable, rules and customs that make up routine in a British man-of-war.

In the matter of pay the petty-officers and men of the Navy were, on the whole, treated considerably better than the rank and file of the Army, and the bulk of them, and their families, benefited considerably from the separation allowances that were granted close upon the outbreak of war. The principal complaint of the men—and it was one for which there was very substantial foundation—was the lack of opportunity for accelerated promotion. In the old fighting days one of the most popular toasts among the officers was "Here's to bloody wars and sickly seasons," the implied hope being that these twin calamities would kill off the seniors and give the juniors a chance to rise. Nothing like that sentiment existed among the petty-officers and men of the Navy in the Great War; but, on the other hand, when it became obvious that the Fleet would have to be enormously expanded as regards ships, officers, and men, there was a keen and bitter feeling of disappointment that the best of the warrant officers and petty-officers of the Service itself were not selected to fill at least a proportion of the higher posts that thus became available.

When the United States declared war upon Germany one of the first acts of the Navy Department was to order the selection of five hundred warrant officers for promotion to commissioned rank—the principal need there, as in the British case, being for junior officers to take command of small craft and act as watch-keepers and specialist officers in larger ships. In the British Navy there was not, and had not been in three years of war, a single promotion to fill vacancies of this sort. On the contrary,

Anomalies of the pension system

Discipline of the Grand Fleet

Naval grievances about promotion

SAILORS AT PHYSICAL DRILL.
Men of a troopship's crew engaged in barefoot "doubling" and jumping—part of the system of regular exercises which served to keep them thoroughly fit.

warrant officers who had been in command of torpedo-craft were replaced by mercantile officers from the reserve, while in large ships taken over from the merchant service a Naval Reserve lieutenant was often appointed gunnery officer of the ship on the strength of a single short course taken perhaps a dozen years before, while his subordinate—and, of course, the man really responsible for the efficiency of the armament—was a warrant officer who had very likely been a gunner for fifteen years or more.

When the Admiralty began to receive the motor-launches for patrol service, ordered in such large numbers from America, it was felt in the Navy that they would surely give the warrant officers and petty-officers of the Fleet a chance to show whether they were competent to take command of these small craft ; but nothing of the sort was done. Every officer required for these five hundred and fifty boats was recruited from outside the Navy, only the absolute minimum of sea knowledge being required of them. Needless to say, the Navy itself had no feeling of animus against the men who were given these appointments, but it would indeed have been remarkable if the disappointment felt by the men at the start had not developed as time went on into something very like resentment at the **Legitimate lower** manner in which their capabilities and **deck grievances** their legitimate claims to advancement were ignored.

The general question was raised at various times in both Houses of Parliament, and the Admiralty reply was generally to the effect that it was not good policy to promote men to commissioned rank merely for gallantry. This is perfectly sound—something more than gallantry is required in a naval officer—but it altogether begs the question. Outsiders were not given their commissions for gallantry, or even for competence, while the Navy's point of view, with which there can be no possible quarrel, was that the competent men in its own ranks should have been given the chance of promotion to commissioned rank before any other was entered from the shore into that rank. The official veto against promotion for

gallantry, too, could not be held to apply to the warrant officers of the Fleet, who had already proved by their service and advancement that they were fitted for further preferment. After the Battle of Jutland only two chief warrant officers—that is, men who had been warrant officers for more than fifteen years—were promoted to commissioned rank, which would have come automatically to both of them in a relatively short time.

The award of honours for this great battle, as for the war generally, also created more than a little heart-burning. Twenty-nine warrant officers of the military branch were mentioned in despatches for their Jutland services, but not so much as a Distinguished Service Cross was awarded among them—a very striking and significant omission, seeing that there were more than thirty appointments to the Order of the Bath alone among commanding and other officers.

Among the whole of the warrant officers, petty-officers, and men of the lower deck there were only fifty-three promotions, some of which were no more

MARINES AT EXERCISE ON A TROOPSHIP.
Physical drill of Marines on board ship. It was by regular and varied exercises of every kind possible in the space available that the " Jollies," as well as their sailor shipmates, maintained that well-being which kept them ready for the call to action.

than from able seaman to leading seaman, while forty officers were promoted to commander or captain.

These facts—which are but a few among many that might be quoted if this were a catalogue of legitimate lower-deck grievances—will serve to show how well-grounded was the feeling among the men of the Navy that they were subjected to treatment which was not only unjust but directly subversive of efficiency. At the same time, it would be distinctly unfair to omit all mention of the further opportunities for lower-deck progress that were opened in the course of the war. Between July, 1914, and July, 1917, it was made possible for men of the following branches to reach the rank of commissioned warrant officer : Telegraphists, masters-at-arms (police), mechanicians, armourers, electricians, wardmasters (sick-berth), writers, and stewards ; while for the last two branches, as well as for mechanicians and schoolmasters, further advancement to the rank of commissioned officer was made possible. The mate scheme, likewise, was considerably extended, whereby the pick of the younger petty-officers could take a short cut to the wardroom and reach the rank of lieutenant, or engineer-lieutenant, in the early thirties. This, however, still left untouched the long-service men who had had to fight their way up long before the mate scheme was thought of, and it was among them that the feeling of resentment rankled most. Even at the end of the third year of the war the warrant officers who had won their way to the top of the tree were being consistently passed over, while outsiders were entered with commissions over their heads.

In such a chapter as this it will be appropriate to say something about the victualling of the Navy. In Nelson's time there was a daily issue of a pound of biscuits and a gallon of beer (the latter partly because the water was usually undrinkable) to every one of the ship's company, while beef (2 lb. a head) or pork (1 lb.) was served out four days a week, pease, oatmeal, sugar, butter, and cheese figuring on the menu about every other day. The apparent generosity of the allowance was to some extent depreciated by the fact that messes were generally victualled on the principle of " six upon four "—that is to say, six men shared the rations of four. At the outbreak of the Great War the " standard daily ration" in the Navy was as follows: 1 lb. bread (or ¾ lb. bread and ¼ lb. flour), ½ lb. fresh meat, 1 lb. vegetables, ⅛ pint of spirit (rum), 4 oz. sugar, ½ oz. tea (or 2 oz. coffee), ½ oz. chocolate (or 1 oz. coffee), ¾ oz. condensed milk, 1 oz. jam, marmalade, or pickles, 4 oz. preserved meat on one day of the week in harbour, or on two days at sea, in lieu of fresh meat; mustard, vinegar, and salt as required. On " salt-pork day " the ordinary meat and vegetable ration was replaced by half a pound of meat, with 4 oz. of split

[*British official photograph.*
AT A BREEZY HEIGHT.
Party of stokers of a British battleship engaged in cleaning the top of a funnel — a great contrast to their work in the stokehold.

pease and 8 oz. of potatoes per man; and on "preserved-meat day " by 6 oz. of meat, 8 oz. of flour, ¾ oz. of suet, 2 oz. of raisins or jam, and 8 oz. of potatoes. In addition to the issue in kind, each mess was credited with 4d. a day per head for the purchase of further provisions from the paymaster's stores or from the canteen, a settlement being made at the end of the month. During the first three years of the war the messing allowance was increased from 4d. to 5½d., but there was a reduction in the sugar ration from 4 oz. to 2 oz., and of bread from 16 oz. to 10 oz. On a personnel of 400,000 (voted in 1917), these reductions would represent a weekly saving of no less than 1,050,000 lb. of bread and 350,000 lb. of sugar.

Generally speaking, there was no fault found with the victualling arrangements, the food being of good quality, and the cooking—especially in the later, larger, and best-fitted ships — often excellent. On the other hand, the harder work and strain, both physical and mental, imposed by war conditions naturally led to the production of heavier and more expensive appetites, with the result that instead of the messing allowance being found more or less adequate to meet the monthly bills, it became quite a general thing for men to have to find as much as 20s. a month out of their own pockets, and one case was mentioned to the writer in which it mounted to as high as £2 5s. In this way the inadequacy of pay was greatly emphasised, and a further heavy drain arose from the fact that clothing—in which seamen have to maintain themselves after receiving a free first kit—increased considerably in price, and wore out much more quickly under the severity of war conditions.

In July, 1917, the men of the Navy took the strong course of issuing a statement of their grievances to the

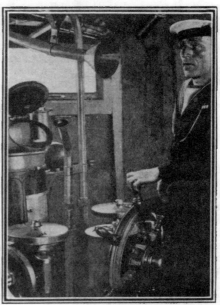

[*British official photograph.*
LOWER-DECK HEROES OF H.M. DESTROYER-LEADER BROKE.
A trophy of victory. Bell of H.M.S. Broke, inscribed " Made from the lid of torpedo-tube of C.42, rammed and sunk by H.M.S. Broke, April 21st, 1917 "; and (centre) Leading-Seaman Ingleson, C.G.M., on the forecastle of the Broke, where he bayoneted the Germans who boarded her in that fight. Right: Leading-Seaman Rawles, C.G.M., at the wheel of the Broke. Although wounded, he stuck to the wheel throughout the action.

AN INCIDENT OF THE DOCTOR'S ROUND.
The naval doctor for the day going on his visit among the ship's company satisfies himself that a sailor is not losing weight. The health of the Navy was maintained at a high level during the war.

Press—a procedure directly contrary to the Regulations, and inevitably reminiscent of the events that led up to the mutiny of 1797. It goes without saying, however, that the men submitted their case in a perfectly loyal spirit, the appeal to the public not being made until three years had passed without any concession being made as the result of " Service " representation of grievances. The principal requests were for an increase of pay ranging from 3s. 6d. to 7s. a week, for the promotion of warrant officers and petty-officers to commissioned rank in place of the entry of untrained outsiders, and for pensions to be paid to those who had earned them by twenty-two years' service. The authorities took no official cognisance of the appeal, but its subject matter was raised in both Houses of Parliament. The Admiralty did not betray any great sympathy with the demands put forward, especially in regard to promotion to commissioned rank ; but a small concession was made to men who were not receiving their pensions, their " detained pay " being raised from 2d. to 4d., 6d., and 8d. a day in the second, third, and fourth years of their detention, while it was announced that the general question of pay would be submitted to a special committee. With this the men had perforce to be content, though the refusal of what was asked for in the matter of promotion was felt very keenly indeed. ·

A protest and its effect

One of the most interesting of the side issues of the war affecting the men of the Fleet was the revival of the ancient practice of giving financial rewards to those immediately responsible for the destruction of hostile warships. In previous wars it had been customary to make periodical distributions both of prize-money—the proceeds of the capture of enemy property—and of prize bounty, which was a bonus provided by the Government for the capture or destruction of the armed ships of the enemy. In the old days huge fortunes were sometimes amassed by officers favourably situated for capturing enemy shipping. In 1762, for instance, the British ships Active and Favourite captured the Spanish ship Hermione off Cadiz, and, the prize being loaded mainly with coin and precious metals, the total net produce of her cargo amounted to £519,705, of which the commanders of the British ships took about £65,000 apiece. The unfairness of the old system, however, lay in the fact that the ships which did the most work and the hardest fighting had practically no chance whatever of taking a prize, while for those on the productive stations the principal risk—and that not a great one—lay in falling in with a straggling enemy frigate. Shortly after the outbreak of the Great War, therefore, an Order-in-Council was issued suspending the old system of distribution, and registering the intention to substitute for it " under regulations and conditions to be hereafter announced, a system of Prize Bounties or Gratuities for more general distribution to the Officers and Men " of the Navy. Down to the end of the third year of war the further announcement had not been made, and nothing was known as to the course the Government would adopt beyond the fact that no distribution would be made until after the war. Presumably the representatives of officers and men who died or were killed on service would be included, and some distinction would have to be drawn between a man who had served throughout the war and one who joined up within a few months of its conclusion. By the summer of 1917 the Prize Fund stood somewhere in the neighbourhood of £7,000,000, but owing to the great stiffening of the blockade and the fact that very few countries had any desire to see their goods shipped to Germany (since very few then remained neutral), the fund had virtually ceased to grow.

Distribution of prize bounties

With regard to Prize Bounty, however, the Government faithfully followed the established custom of the Service, and in the first claim that came before the Court—that of the armed liner Carmania for sinking the German armed liner Cap Trafalgar on September 14th, 1914, the case being heard on March 27th, 1916—Commander Maxwell Anderson, who appeared for the claimants, gave the following outline of the history of the bounty, or, as it is sometimes called, " head money." It was a grant from the Crown, provided out of money voted by Parliament as a personal reward for the sinking or capture of an armed vessel belonging to the enemy forces. In earlier days, when there was no great difference in construction or design between vessels of the Royal Navy and vessels of the mercantile marine, it was more or less customary to give the prize to the captors. In the time of the Commonwealth, however, it was felt that some special reward should be given to those who, by their personal exertions, destroyed a recognised ship of war of the enemy ; and so, in 1649, it was enacted that for all enemy ships of war burnt, sunk, or destroyed there should be paid for an admiral's ship £20 per gun, for a vice-admiral's ship £16 per gun, and for other ships £10 per gun. At the same time the captors were also allowed a certain amount of pillage or plunder out of all prizes. Everything above the gun-deck was the property of the captors ; everything else had to be brought into the Prize Court. That practice led to lawlessness, and by an act of William and Mary the captors, in lieu of plunder, were given a definite share in the proceeds of the prize, and, in addition, in the case of a warship taken or destroyed, a bounty of £10 for every gun mounted in such vessel. About that period very frequent complaints were made of the low rates of pay and lack of encouragement given to naval officers, and pamphlets were circulated showing the superior advantages offered by the French Navy. As a result of that agitation, what was commonly known as the first Prize Act was passed in 1708, by Section 8 of which it was declared that "if in any action any ship of war or privateer shall be taken from the enemy, five pounds shall be granted to the captors for every man which was living on board such ship or ships so taken at the beginning of the engagement between them." The wording of that section required the enemy ship to be "taken," and it was felt that such requirement was too restrictive. Therefore, in 1805, it was **Naval Prize Acts,** enacted that the bounty might be paid for **1708-1915** the " taking, sinking, burning, or otherwise destroying " of an armed ship of the enemy. These grants had been renewed in almost every war, and by virtue of Section 42 of the Naval Prize Act of 1864 the King declared by Order-in-Council on March 2nd, 1915, his intention to grant bounty to the officers and crews of such ships of war as were actually present at the taking or destroying of any armed ship of any of his Majesty's enemies, who should be entitled to have distributed among them as prize bounty a sum calculated at the rate of £5 for each person on board the enemy's ship at the beginning of the engagement. Comparatively speaking, the maintenance of the bounty at the old level of £5 a head meant a considerable reduction in the relative value of the reward. In the old days a first-rate ship of 100 or 120 guns carried a crew of from 750 to 900 officers and men, and yet cost only between £75,000 and £120,000, so that the bounty for the destruction or capture of such a ship amounted to something like one-third of her actual value. A super-Dreadnought battleship, however, rarely carried a crew of more than 1,000 or 1,200 ; and as the bounty in such a case would amount

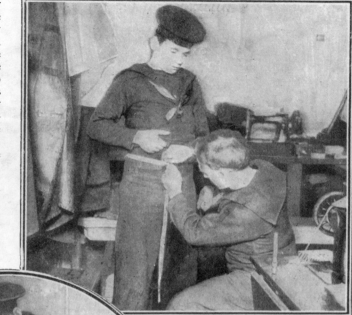

[*British official photograph.*
IN THE TAILOR'S "SHOP."
A ship's tailor measuring one of his shipmates for a new suit.

to only five or six thousand pounds, this would represent less than a quarter of 1 per cent. of the ship's value, which may be put down at about two and a half millions sterling. Some time before the war it had been unofficially suggested that the bounty should be revised and placed on a tonnage basis, but the proposal was not adopted.

A few words must be said regarding the distribution of the bounty among those sharing it. The system was rather complicated, especially as regards the higher ranks, but, generally speaking, it amounted to this : One-thirtieth part of the whole went to the flag officers, if there were any present. If there were but one, he took the whole of this, but if more than one, the senior took a half (that is, one-sixtieth part of the total), and the other half was divided equally among the remainder. One-tenth part of the remainder was then divided among officers in command of ships and commanders second-in-command under a captain, so that each captain ranked for six shares, each commander for three, and every other commanding officer for **Distribution of the** two. After these deductions had been **prize bounty** made, the residue was divided up among the officers and crews of the participating ships according to a graduated scale. Commanding officers, having already taken their share of the tenth part, came in again for a heavy share of the general distribution—a captain in command, for instance, taking eighty shares, a commander forty, a lieutenant-commander thirty, and so on. Coming down to the lower deck, we find a chief warrant officer standing in for only fifteen shares, and a warrant officer for twelve, while among the rank and file of the Fleet the shares were as follows : Chief petty-officer (and equivalent ratings, such as engine-room artificer,

[*British official photograph.*
VARIED WORK ABOARD SHIP.
Sailors and a Marine engaged in the tailor work of cutting-out and machining serge suits aboard one of the ships of the British Navy. In circle : Sailor at work making a rope mat.

BRIEF REST FOR SAILORS DURING STRENUOUS LABOUR.

A "stand easy" during the operation of provisioning a warship, after which the men would have to distribute and stow away the medley of stores in their proper places. Provisioning was an important work on the

vessels whether in home waters or abroad, a vast quantity of food and miscellaneous material being an essential part of their equipment, and the stowage of that material calling for careful organisation.

mechanician, chief stoker, ship's steward), ten ; petty-officer and equivalent ratings, eight ; leading seaman, etc., six ; able seaman, etc., five ; ordinary seaman, etc., three ; boy, one.

How the distribution of prize bounty worked out in practice may be shown from the award made in the case of the German armoured cruiser Blücher, which was sunk in the action on the Dogger Bank, on January 24th, 1915, by a British force under Vice-Admiral Sir David Beatty. The Prize Court found that the enemy ship had on board a crew of 1,050 officers and men, the bounty therefore amounting to £5,250 ; but as there were no fewer than forty-seven British vessels engaged in the running fight with the German cruiser fleet (five battle cruisers, seven light cruisers, and thirty-five destroyers), the number sharing in the award ran into several thousands. This accounts for the smallness of the individual sums apportioned, though their relative values

Bounty award for the Blücher

were, of course, unaffected. Sir David Beatty, as Vice-Admiral commanding, received £79 4s. 4d.—that is, one-half of the one-thirtieth part after deducting prize agents' fees and so forth ; and a similar sum was divided among the three other flag officers, Rear-Admiral Sir Archibald Moore, Commodore W. E. Goodenough, and Commodore Tyrwhitt, who thus received £26 8s. 1d. apiece. Among commanding officers of ships, captains received £15 13s. 3d., commanders, £7 16s. 7d., and lieutenant-commanders £5 4s. 5d. Coming down to the lower deck, we find a warrant officer receiving 14s. 5d., a petty-officer 9s. 8d., and an able seaman 6s. 1d. (or about one-fiftieth of a captain's share) ; while in the lowest class of all, boys

received the insignificant sum of 1s. 2d., which, nevertheless, represented two days' pay.

By far the most satisfactory feature about the prize bounty system was that it enabled the nation to reward financially, and more or less adequately, the splendid work of our submarines. In big fleet actions, as we have already seen from the relatively small affair of the Dogger Bank, the numbers engaged were so large that the division of the bounty brought very little to the individual, but with submarines the case was very different. Not only did they nearly always work singly and independently, but their crews were **Financial reward to** small, and they always endeavoured for **submarine crews** military reasons to select the biggest possible ship for their attacks. As a result, some very striking awards were made to these craft in the Prize Court, as will be seen from the following list of bounty awards made to British submarines in the first three years of war:

B11 (Lieut. Norman Holbrook, V.C.).—For sinking the Turkish battleship Messudiyeh on December 13th, 1914, £3,500.

E9 (Lieut.-Commander Max K. Horton, D.S.O.).—For sinking the German light cruiser Hela on September 13th, 1914, £1,050 ; the German destroyer S116 on October 6th, 1914, £350 ; and two German destroyers, on January 28th, 1915, and June 4th, 1915, respectively (both in the Baltic), £930. Total, £2,330.

E11 (Lieut.-Commander, later Captain, Martin E. Nasmith, V.C.).—For sinking the Turkish gunboat Pelenk-i-Deria on May 23rd, 1915, £655 ; the Turkish battleship Kheyr-ed-Din Barbarosse on August 8th, 1915, £3,250 ; and the Turkish destroyer Yar Hissar on December 3rd, 1915, £425. Total, £4,330.

E14 (Lieut.-Commander, later Commander, E. Courtney Boyle, V.C.).—For sinking an unnamed Turkish gunboat on May 1st, 1915, £375.

E16 (Commander C. P. Talbot, D.S.O.).—For sinking the German destroyer V188 on July 26th, 1915, £465.

E4 (Commander E. W. Leir, D.S.O.).—For sinking the German patrol vessel Senator van Berenberg Gossley on July 28th, 1916, £135.

E2 (Commander O. De B. Stocks, D.S.O.).—For sinking a Turkish mine-layer on August 14th, 1915, £400; a larger armed vessel on August 20th, £600; and an armed steamer on August 22nd, £250. Total, £1,250.

E5 (Commander C. S. Benning, D.S.O.).—For sinking a German auxiliary (name unknown) on September 25th, 1915, £1,000.

E8 (Commander F. H. H. Goodhart, D.S.O., since killed).—For sinking the German armoured cruiser Prinz Adalbert in the Baltic on October 23rd, 1915, £3,000.

E19 (Commander F. N. A. Cromie, D.S.O.).—For sinking the German light cruiser Undine in the Baltic on November 7th, 1915, £1,410.

E16 (Lieut.-Commander K. J. Duff-Dunbar, D.S.O., since killed).—For sinking a German auxiliary (name unknown) on December 22nd, 1915, £625.

As our submarines of the E class had a complement ranging only from twenty-eight to thirty-two or thirty-three officers and men, the majority of the above cases represented a very comfortable little addition to Service pay; but, although she comes second in point of amount, it was the little B11 that returned, so to speak, the highest rate of interest on the skill and courage expended by her officers and men. When she crept under five rows of Turkish mines in the Dardanelles and torpedoed the Messudiyeh, which the Germans had made their naval headquarters, her crew consisted only of two officers and fourteen men. Her commanding officer received the V.C., and the second-in-command, Lieutenant Sydney T. Winn, the D.S.O., and all the crew were awarded the Distinguished Service Medal. In addition to these well-merited decorations, prize bounty was subsequently distributed as follows:

Good fortune of Submarine B11

Lieut. N. D. Holbrook, £601 10s. 2d.; Lieut. S. T. Winn, £481 4s. 2d.; Chief Engine-Room Artificer J. Harding and Engine-Room Artificer A. Douglas (chief petty-officers), £240 12s. 1d. each; Petty-Officers W. Milsom and T. Davey, and Stoker Petty-Officer P. McKenna, £192 9s. 8d. each; Leading-Seamen A. Perry and W. Mortimer, and Acting-Leading-Stoker J. Sowden, £144 7s. 3d. each; Able-Seamen N. Rae, G. Read, E. Buckle, and T. Blake, Signalman F. Foote, and Stoker First Class S. Lovelady, £120 6s. 1d. each.

The balance of the total award was made up of the prize agent's and other charges. The comparative value of the distribution to the recipients is seen in the fact that the respective amounts mentioned represented about two years' pay to the engine-room artificers, three years' pay to the petty-officers and all the stokers, and four years' pay to the able seamen.

Comparative value of the distribution

In some cases the regulations governing the award of prize bounty seemed to work a little unreasonably, though it was, of course, necessary that there should be a hard-and-fast line about the fate of the enemy ship. In the summer of 1915, when the Germans were making their first big effort to gain control of the Gulf of Riga, submarine E1, under the command of Commander Noel Laurence, D.S.O., torpedoed the German battle-cruiser Moltke, and it was at first stated officially in Russia that the vessel had sunk. In November, 1916, the same officer, while "submarining" off the coast of Jutland, succeeded in torpedoing two enemy super-Dreadnoughts of the Kaiser class, displacing 24,700 tons each. Unfortunately, however, none of these splendid exploits seems to have ended in the actual sinking of the torpedoed ship, and therefore, in spite of the risks run, the magnificent handling of the boat which could alone have made the

OPEN-AIR CONCERT ABOARD A HOSPITAL-SHIP.

Cot patients and others on the deck of a hospital-ship enjoying an open-air concert provided by members of the ship's company. When the war broke out there was not a single hospital-ship at the disposal of the Admiralty, but by the summer of 1917 there were thirteen hospital-ships in commission.

attacks possible, and the fact that all three attacks were entirely successful so far as the placing of the torpedoes was concerned, no prize bounty could be claimed. As each of the enemy ships probably carried a crew of 1,200, this would have amounted to £18,000 in all.

An even harder case to all appearances was that of the E14, Commander E. C. Boyle, V.C., whose officers and crew presented in the Prize Court a claim for £31,000, for having on May 10th, 1915, sunk the Turkish transport Gul Djeml. This vessel was shown to be a permanent unit of the enemy forces, and it was said that such units were usually armed with about four 6-pounder guns;

The case of the Gul Djeml while the Gul Djeml was at the time of her destruction actually carrying some 6,000 troops in addition to her crew of two hundred, as well as six field-guns and several thousand rifles. The sinking of such a vessel (the loss of life was said to have been considerable) was a most desirable and highly useful operation; but in his judgment, the President of the Prize Court, Sir Samuel Evans, refused the claim, mainly on the ground that the mounting of four light guns did not make the Gul Djeml an armed ship, and that an "armed ship" within the meaning of the Prize Act was "a fighting unit of the fleet, a ship commissioned and armed for offensive action in a naval engagement." The decision was accepted without demur, though there are in all navies many ships carrying a less formidable armament, and others, such as mine-layers and commerce-destroyers, which are not armed or commissioned for the purpose of taking "offensive action in a naval engagement." As one of the Service newspapers expressed it: "If the Turk had carried a bare crew of, say, two hundred and fifty, and half a dozen 4 in. guns, the E14 would have received £1,250. As she only carried 6,000 troops, with field-guns, rifles, and ammunition, the whole cargo being believed lost, she gets nothing."

The Government made no announcement of any special bounty arrangements in respect of the destruction of hostile submarines—vessels which were certainly worth more from this point of view than the £150 or thereabouts which they would represent under the ordinary scale. It may be mentioned, however, that early in the war official notices were issued offering to "fishermen and others" a sum not exceeding £1,000 "for information which directly leads to the actual capture or destruction of an enemy vessel, down to and including a mine-layer or submarine," and up to £200 for information leading to such a vessel being sighted and chased, even though she were not destroyed. Early in 1917 a new scheme applicable to merchant vessels was drawn up, a maximum sum of £1,000 being offered for the capture or destruction of an enemy submarine or other ship of war, it being added that "a vessel contributing to, or giving information which directly leads to, the capture of an enemy submarine is eligible for some part of the reward; but a mere call for assistance when attacked does not give a claim under this

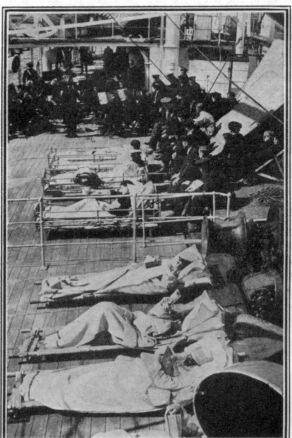

"MUSIC CAN SOFTEN PAIN TO EASE."
Cot cases on a hospital-ship laid out on deck to absorb the healing air and sunshine and forget their pain while listening to the music of the band.

head." As in a large proportion of cases where submarines are concerned, conclusive evidence of destruction would be impossible to obtain, a maximum of £300 was to be paid "in cases where the Admiralty consider the enemy submarine or other ship of war has been damaged, though not destroyed." There was no other navy in which the officers and men had the benefit of a bounty system, but prize money was fairly general, and in France the proceeds of this were applied to the relief of those disabled in the war and of the dependents of the killed.

Before leaving this subject, it will not be out of place to set out the system of prize money as applied to German submarines. Officers and men in these craft received the ordinary pay of their rank or rating, with an addition of 10 per cent. In the case of merchant vessels captured, the commander and the chief engineer each took 5 per cent. of the Prize Court value of the prize; the remaining officers shared 15 per cent. of the total (seeming thus to indicate that U boats carried at least six officers, since otherwise the juniors would receive as much as or more than the seniors); while the crew shared 25 per cent. of the total. One-half of the value of these prizes thus went to the crew of the capturing boat. In the case of merchantmen sunk the basis of the award was the insured value of the vessel, and of this the commander and the chief engineer each received 1 per cent., 4 per cent. being shared among the remaining officers and 10 per cent. among the crew. Higher rates were given to a submarine during the first six months of her commission, and there were special rewards for those destroying the greatest aggregate tonnage on a voyage, and also for particularly noteworthy feats.

One of the most important, and at the same time one of the most difficult, problems with which the naval authorities had to contend was the maintenance of the mental and physical health of officers and men. Especially so far as the mental factor was concerned the war was absolutely unique. Never before had our principal Fleets been based so far to the North, where the long nights of the winter months inevitably tended to propagate a feeling of depression. Never before had it been necessary to maintain a great Fleet in a **Mental strain on** state of instant readiness to put to sea **the personnel** and go into action, following perhaps months of monotonous routine and the strain of anxious waiting. Never in any previous war were war ships' faced with the ever-present menace of the unseen mine or submarine striking at them from below in their most vulnerable parts. Never before had the smaller units of the Fleet been called upon to maintain a ceaseless and unbroken patrol of waters strewn with mines and infested with submarines, and lying within easy striking distance of any force the enemy might choose to send out to intercept them. Never before had either the action or the relative inaction of naval warfare been carried on under such conditions of mental strain, tending inevitably to weaken the system and render the body more vulnerable to physical ills. Having these conditions in mind, it must surely be regarded as one of the most amazing facts of the war that, after two and a half years of hostilities it was possible truthfully to assert that "the general health of the Grand Fleet has been extremely good, indeed, probably better than in times of peace."

That was the statement made by Temporary Surgeon-General H. D. Rolleston, R.N., Consultant Physician to the Royal Navy and Senior Physician of St. George's Hospital, London, in an address before **Percentage of sick** the London Medical Society on February **in the Fleet** 12th, 1917, and he supplied proof of his statement in the following words:

The average daily percentage of sick in the whole Fleet in 1913 was 2·37, and in 1914 a little lower, 2·03. Since the outbreak of war cases of sickness have naturally been sent off to hospital more rapidly than in peace time, and thus the daily sickness in the Fleet is diminished. But even allowing for this, the average daily sickness in the Grand Fleet has been extremely low, almost always under 1 per cent., and, indeed, has fallen since the outbreak of war. This percentage incidence would have been less had it not been for the higher rate of sickness among the Reservists and pensioners. Most of the sickness was of a minor character, such as seasonal influenza and boils.

Surgeon-General Rolleston thus accounted for this highly satisfactory state of affairs:

1. The comparative isolation of the Fleets, and especially of the Grand Fleet, thus necessitating absence of venereal disease and of opportunities for alcoholic excess incident to the temptations of seaports. In the Fleet the men's daily allowance of stimulant is half a gill of rum, and special precautions are taken to prevent the absorption of unused allowances by other men. 2. The quarantine precautions in drafting men from the shore establishments to the Fleet, instituted by the (then) Medical Director-General, Sir Arthur May. 3. The lectures given by the medical officers to the ships' crews on personal hygiene, dealing

especially with the dangers of venereal disease and alcoholic excess These lectures appealed to the common-sense of the men, and as an illustration of their good effect it may be mentioned that on return from leave of the men (about 1,100) of one great battleship there were only three cases of gonorrhœa and one of syphilis. 4. Measures to obviate the effects of monotony entailed by awaiting events which have been long anticipated: Thus, when possible, regattas, boxing competitions, and other entertainments are got up, and both by their preparation and performance brighten up the men. In the Grand Fleet the short days of winter are the most trying, and then, in addition to entertainments, lectures, for example, by those who have made visits to the front in France, and cinema shows serve a useful purpose. Each big ship has its cinema, and there is a scheme of **Measures employed** circulating films between the various ships. **to maintain health** Periodical leave is also provided. 5. Improvement in the ventilation of the ships, due to the adoption in 1914 of the recommendations of a committee, of which Fleet-Surgeon R. C. Munday was the secretary, appointed in October, 1912, to consider the best methods of ventilating modern warships.

There is little need to expand this brief summary of the means by which the precious health of the Fleet was so splendidly maintained. Men were landed as often as possible for route marches, and physical exercises under qualified instructors were part of the regular routine on board. Twice every day — after morning and evening quarters—the entire ship's company, with the exception of such men over thirty-five years of age as liked to stay out, would for a quarter of an hour "double" round the decks to the music of the ship's band, low obstacles being placed in the way as jumps. About once a week the order was given, "Man all boats and pull round the Fleet"—a form of exercise that was further encouraged by the offering of prizes in rowing and sailing regattas. Boxing was similarly encouraged, "professors" of the art being appointed to each group of ships for the instruction of the men, and

HOW THE WOUNDED WERE MOVED AT SEA: TYPES OF STRETCHERS IN USE ON BOARD SHIP.
Lowering a wounded sailor into the sick-bay in a Faulkner swing. Right: Removing a cot case from a battleship. (British official photograph). Above: Slinging a wounded soldier aboard the S.Y. Liberty in a "Neil Robertson stretcher." The Liberty was owned by Lord Tredegar, and fitted by him to receive 897 cases, was accepted as a hospital-ship by the Admiralty in August, 1914. She did good service in many waters.

prizes being offered for competitions between ship and ship, division and division, and the Fleet championship. So great was the interest taken in this sport that no fewer than 14,000 men landed to witness the final for the Fleet championship—a fact which shows that its beneficent influence extended far beyond the relatively small numbers who were able actively to participate in it. At all the Fleet bases as many football grounds as possible were prepared (not too close to the landing-place), and as each big ship ran its own " league," with perhaps nine or a dozen teams, there was always great competition to get ashore either to play or to look on, the result being a combination of physical exercise with mental diversion. Many ships, indeed most of the larger ones, ran their own theatrical and entertainment parties, which went from one vessel to another, or to a central vessel (not a warship) for the general recreation. Ships' companies took up parcels of land ashore and proceeded to cultivate vegetables, of which there was never a super-abundance available for distribution in the ordinary way ; and all the time, of course, the Fleet was constantly exercised in the ordinary routine evolutions, and at sea in gunnery, steaming, and tactics, either as a whole under the Commander-in-Chief, or by divisions and squadrons under their respective rear-admirals and vice-admirals. In these various ways the dreadful monotony of the long wait for the enemy was effectually broken, and although there are no details available to illustrate the mental side of the Navy's bill of health, there are the best of reasons for believing that it was no less satisfactory than the physical side.

Effect of moral upon health Dealing with this aspect of the subject in the address already referred to, Surgeon-General Rolleston said :

The prolonged and monotonous strain necessitated by life in the Fleet favours mental deterioration, psychasthenia, and neurasthenia, especially in those with a neurotic taint and in those who have not been through a long training. Further, the short interludes of acute stress and excitement which punctuate the periods of monotonous alertness may so disturb the already-vibrating balance as to precipitate an acute breakdown with violent though transient symptoms and delusions. The burden of responsibility and, in a small ship, the comparative isolation of the senior officer, favour mental instability, and may lead to a want of self-confidence bred of brain-fag. In an interesting psychological study of the influence of periods of (1) monotonous watchfulness, (2) acute stress, and (3) comparative calm on a ship's company during the first six months of the war, Beaton (Temporary-Surgeon Thomas Beaton, M.D., R.N.) found that mental troubles of a really serious nature occurred in less than 1 per cent. and mild neurasthenic conditions in less than 4 per cent. With the prolongation of the war the results of the continued and monotonous strain would naturally be expected to become more noticeable, but, as far as my impression goes, not to anything like the extent that would have been expected. This happy result is, no doubt, due to several factors—the fine spirit of confident superiority in the men, and the hygienic measures already mentioned. The effect of good moral in preventing mental disturbance was seen by the freedom of the men from these manifestations after the Jutland Battle.

At the outbreak of war the medical department of the Navy comprised 521 officers, together with a Sick Berth Staff of about 1,500 warrant officers, petty-officers, and men. With the coming of hostilities numbers were rapidly increased by calling up retired officers and mobilising the surgeons of the R.N. Volunteer Reserve, while a very liberal response was made to the

Admiralty appeal for doctors to join for the period of the war, so that by the middle of 1917 no fewer than 680 temporary surgeons had been entered. Further, the rank of surgeon probationer—resembling the surgeon's mate of olden days—was created in the Volunteer Reserve, and to this there were appointed numbers of unqualified medical students who had passed their examinations in anatomy and physiology.

After a course at one of the principal naval hospitals, these officers were usually drafted singly to destroyers, large mine-sweepers, and similar minor craft which ordinarily do not carry medical officers, and many of these subsequently obtained leave to prepare for and pass their final examinations, returning then to the Service as temporary surgeons. A Medical Consultative Board was appointed early in the war to advise on large matters of policy affecting the health of the Fleet, and the fine standard maintained was undoubtedly due in large measure to its work. In July, 1917, this Board consisted of the following : **Medical Department of the Navy** The Medical Director-General of the Navy, W. H. Norman, president ; Sir W. Watson Cheyne, Bart, C.B., LL.D., M.B., D.Sc., F.R.C.S., F.R.S. ; Sir Dyce Duckworth, Bart, LL.D., M.D., F.R.C.P. ; Professor W. J. R. Simpson, C.M.G., M.D., F.R.C.P. ; Sir John Tweedy, F.R.C.S. ; Surgeon-General George Welch, C.B. ; and Fleet-Surgeon J. F. Hall, secretary.

The petty-officers and men of the Sick Berth Staff were analogous to R.A.M.C. ashore, a really high standard of competency in first-aid, nursing, and other qualifications being required of them. Their numbers were augmented by the mobilisation of the Auxiliary Sick Berth Reserve, and by the continual inflow of recruits during hostilities, and it was a cause of some discontent that these "hostility entries " not only received higher pay than the regular Service man, but were also paid a special " risk allowance " of a shilling a day when serving afloat in armed ships—such service being, of course, the everyday routine of the great majority of the long-service ratings, to whom no " risk allowance " was paid.

At the outbreak of war there was not a single hospital-ship at the disposal of the Admiralty. The only one which the Navy had possessed, the Maine, had been wrecked in

ONE OF A FAMOUS CREW.
Ship's cobbler of H.M.S. Spitfire mending the crew's boots. The T.B.D. Spitfire did conspicuously gallant work with the Fourth Flotilla in the Battle of Jutland, one of her torpedoes being seen to " take effect."

June, 1914, and there had been no opportunity to replace it. Energetic measures were taken to remedy the deficiency, and within a few weeks of the outbreak no fewer than ten were in service, including the beautiful yacht Sheelah, generously placed at the disposal of the authorities by Lady Beatty. By the middle of 1917 the following hospital-ships were in commission with the Fleet : Agadir, Berbice, China, Garth Castle, Karapara, Liberty, Magic II., Plassy, Queen Alexandra, Rewa, St. Margaret of Scotland, Sheelah, and Soudan. These ships retained their peace-time crews, and were staffed by naval medical officers, with a Fleet surgeon in charge, and by four or more Sisters of Queen Alexandra's Royal Naval Nursing Service. Owing to their lack of speed, and to the diabolical German policy, openly adopted early in 1917, of destroying hospital-ships at sight, these vessels did not accompany the Fleets to sea. They usually remained at the Fleet bases until full, when they proceeded south to discharge their patients for distribution to the various naval hospitals.

The latter operation was carried out by the Land Medical Transport branch of the Naval Medical Service, the efficiency of whose work was on more than one occasion the subject of the highest praise. A system of comfortable transportable cots was devised which enabled a patient to be received at, say, Plymouth in the same cot as that in which he was first put in the sick-bay of his own fighting ship up in the Orkneys. The hospital-trains used for transportation normally left Edinburgh once a week, travelling down the East Coast and picking up cases from sick quarters *en route*, and then proceeding across country to Plymouth, where cases belonging to that port were transferred to hospital. Thence the train went to Haslar, and finally to Chatham, the entire journey occupying thirty-four hours. The hospital-trains, fitted for one hundred and thirty-six cots and a number of sitting cases, were furnished with everything for the comfort and care of those on board, including even padded rooms for the more violent mental cases, while the staff consisted of two medical officers and thirty-six men, who lived in the train and worked in watches as if on shipboard.

Navy doctors' magnificent work

The work of the medical staff on board ships in action was often carried out under conditions of the greatest difficulty. Each large vessel was fitted with a sick-bay in a high and well-ventilated part of the ship for use as a hospital in normal times; but this would obviously be too exposed for use during battle, and large modern units were, therefore, fitted with two " distributing stations " well down below the water-line, to which the wounded were taken as soon as possible after being injured. To give some idea of the magnificent work done by the doctors and their assistants in action, one cannot do better than extract the following from an article which appeared in the " Times," written by its medical correspondent, on July 24th, 1916:

During the Battle of Jutland Bank the naval surgeons performed a terrible task. At first when the enemy was sighted there devolved upon them the work of transferring stores and equipment from the sick-bays above the armour to the fore and aft distributing stations below it. The emergency was a sudden one, and the time at disposal short. With the closing of the armoured doors the time for action was come. Soon, in their station, they heard the booming of the guns, and soon there crept down to them the fumes of the exploding charges. From that time the stations became the scene of fierce and terrible activity. In one great ship bellying smoke filled the doctors' rooms at the very moment when the stream of wounded began to flow down to them, adding suffocation to the thousand other perils of the work. The ship reeled under pounding blows; she staggered in a difficult sea; the concussion of her guns was so great as to preclude the possibility of adequate surgical assistance. Wearing gas-masks, the doctors did what they could, bending their energies selflessly to the great task, as is the tradition of their calling.

In another ship an enemy shell destroyed the after-station utterly, so that the whole work of relief fell on the remaining forward one. Hour after hour, without reck of time or exhaustion, the staff laboured to overtake its great task. Another ship was holed and had her electric light cut off. The medical station was in darkness; it was foul with the gas-fumes from the enemy's shells; water poured in by the holes in the vessel's sides. Here, single-handed, a young naval surgeon toiled by the light of an electric torch until at length he was ordered to get his wounded away because the ship was sinking. And this task he achieved so well that not a life was lost. The doctors witnessed strange scenes during these hours, and perhaps the strangest of all was that which followed the announcement that a German ship had gone down, for then all the wounded, including the man on the operating-table, began to cheer.

[*Russell.*
SURGEON THOMAS BEATON, M.D., R.N. Prosecuted useful inquiries into the effect of active service conditions on the mental health of the Navy.

One of the most striking and unexpected features of the medical side of the war was the great disproportion between the numbers of killed and of wounded in action. In the great fights of the sailing days the latter usually outnumbered the former more or less in the ratio of three to one. For instance, at the Glorious First of June, 1794, the casualties of the British Fleet were 290 killed and 858 wounded; at St. Vincent, 73 killed and 227 wounded; at the Nile, 218 killed and 678 wounded; and at Trafalgar, 449 killed and 1,242 wounded. By the time of the Russo-Japanese War, however, conditions had already changed very considerably, and in the fighting at sea that took place during that conflict the number of killed actually exceeded the wounded, the figures being 1,883 and 1,809 respectively. The reason for the change was, of course, the radical alterations that had come about in the construction of ships and in the means for destroying them. A three-decker of the old days could stand a tremendous amount of knocking about without being in any serious danger of foundering, while actions were fought at such close quarters that surrender could always be intimated by ceasing fire, lowering the colours, or even by word of mouth. Modern warships, however, are built of material that is essentially non-

Ratio of killed to wounded

Sir John Tweedy, F.R.C.S.

Sir W. Watson Cheyne, Bart., C.B.

[*Photos by Elliott & Fry.*
Sir Dyce Duckworth, Bart.

DISTINGUISHED MEMBERS OF THE NAVAL MEDICAL CONSULTATIVE BOARD.

R

included the fights of Heligoland
Bight and Coronel, the torpedoing
of the Aboukir, Hogue, and
Cressy, and the destruction of
more than a dozen enemy warships—the total of our casualties
in sea fighting was—Officers :
Killed, 208 ; wounded, 29. Men :
Killed, 4,072 ; wounded, 243.
It will be remembered that no
single soul was saved from the
Good Hope and Monmouth when
they were sunk by the Germans
on November 1st, 1914, no fewer
than 1,654 officers and men being
accounted for in these ships alone ;
while 1,459 were lost in the
Aboukir, Hogue, and Cressy. A
large number were fortunately
saved from these three ships, but
they did not include any of the

DINING-ROOM IN H.M.H.S. LIBERTY.
The beautifully appointed dining-room of Lord Tredegar's yacht never
received more appreciative guests than the sailors who stayed in her in
her time of service as a hospital-ship.

floating ; they are liable to be burst open by a torpedo
below the water-line, or a single shell, bursting and
thrusting tongues of flame down into the vitals, may
detonate a magazine stored with tons of cordite and high
explosives—which is what happened to the Indefatigable
and Queen Mary at Jutland—reducing a great ship to
débris in a moment.

In these circumstances there is little cause for wonder
that, taken in the aggregate, those killed in sea fighting
outnumbered the wounded many times over. The
Admiralty did not see fit to issue any detailed statistics
on this head after the end of the third month of the war ;
but down to November 11th, 1914—a period which

wounded. Those who were most
badly hurt in the explosion of
the torpedoes could hardly be
saved from going down with the
ship, and those who had been
injured at all would be the least
likely to survive the sudden and
long-continued immersion in the
cold water. According to Surgeon-
General Rolleston, " it is not
considered advisable in the public
interest to give the figures for
the Battle of Jutland " ; but in
this action the battle-cruisers
Queen Mary, Indefatigable, and
Invincible, and the armoured
cruisers Black Prince and Defence,
were sunk with almost everyone
on board ; and, taking the action
as a whole, the killed on the
British side probably outnumbered the wounded by more
than ten to one.

Of the manner in which the
men of the Fleet acquitted

DRAWING-ROOM AND (IN CIRCLE) OPERATING-THEATRE.
Lord Tredegar, a notable member of the Royal Yacht Squadron, placed his palatial steam-yacht Liberty
at the service of the Admiralty as a hospital-ship directly war broke out. He bore the entire cost of
refitting her for her new purposes, in the manner shown on this and the opposite page.

themselves in battle there is no need to speak in detail, for their coolness, courage, and inflexibility are recorded in every action that was fought. Nevertheless, two considered opinions expressed by Admiral Sir John Jellicoe, first Commander - in - Chief of the Grand Fleet, may fitly be quoted, the one written early in the war and the other shortly after the Battle of Jutland. The first was addressed to Lady Jellicoe, and read by her at a meeting of women in the London Guildhall on November 19th, 1914. It ran:

I know you will be meeting the wives and families of the men, and I hope you will tell them of the magnificent spirit which prevails. Our troops have covered themselves with glory during this war. The Navy has not

ONE OF THE WARDS IN H.M.H.S. LIBERTY.
As is suggested by the glass-fronted cases that line the walls, this apartment was formerly the library of the Liberty when she fulfilled her peaceful purpose as a pleasure yacht.

so that they may be worthy of their menkind, of whom it is impossible to say too much.

See now the impression left on the mind of the Commander-in-Chief after the great battle of May 31st-June 1st, 1916:

The conduct of officers and men throughout the day and night actions was entirely beyond praise. No words of mine could do them justice. On all sides it is reported to me that the glorious traditions of the past were most worthily upheld—whether in heavy ships, cruisers, light cruisers, or destroyers—the same admirable spirit prevailed. Officers and men were cool and determined, with a cheeriness that would have carried them through everything. The heroism of the wounded was the admiration of all.

I cannot adequately express the pride with which the spirit of the Fleet filled me.

yet as a whole had an opportunity of showing that the old spirit which carried us to victory in the past is with us now, but where our men have had the opportunity of fighting the foe above the water they have shown that they possess the same pluck and endurance as our comrades ashore.

Nothing can ever have been finer than the coolness and courage shown in every case where ships have been sunk by mines or torpedoes; discipline has been perfect, and men have gone to their death not only most gallantly, but most unselfishly. One hears on all sides of numerous instances of men giving up on these occasions the plank which has supported them to some more feeble comrade, and I feel prouder every day that passes that I command such men. During the period of waiting and watching they are cheerful and contented in spite of the grey dullness of their lives. I am sure you will tell the wives and children and sisters of our men of the spirit that prevails, and I know that it will make them all desire to show in their own lives that they are dominated by the same spirit to do the best they can for their country,

THE SMOKING-ROOM AND (IN CIRCLE) DISPENSARY.
As a hospital-ship the Liberty retained her peace-time crew, and was staffed by naval medical officers and Sisters of Queen Alexandra's Royal Naval Nursing Service. She served in the Mediterranean, in home waters, and off the coasts of France and Belgium.

Sir David Beatty, whose fast squadrons of battle-cruisers, light cruisers, and destroyers bore the brunt of the fighting, was no less emphatic. " A review of all the reports I have received," he wrote,

leads me to conclude that the enemy's losses were considerably greater than those which we 'had sustained—in spite of their superiority—and included battleships, battle-cruisers, light cruisers, and destroyers. This is eloquent testimony to the very high standard of gunnery and torpedo efficiency of his Majesty's ships. The control and drill remained undisturbed throughout, in many cases despite heavy damage to material and personnel. Our superiority over the enemy in this respect was very marked, their efficiency becoming rapidly reduced under punishment, while ours was maintained throughout.

As was to be expected, the behaviour of the ships' companies under the terrible conditions of a modern sea battle was magnificent without exception. The strain on their moral was a severe test of discipline and training. Officers and men were imbued with one thought—the desire to defeat the enemy. The fortitude of the wounded was admirable.

With these testimonies to the worthiness of the British seamen of the twentieth century to rank with their fore-

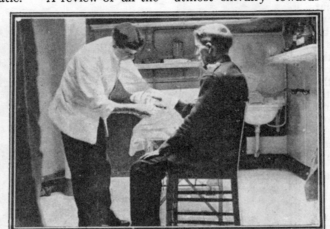

[*British official photograph.*

ATTENDING TO A PATIENT ON BOARD SHIP.
Bandaging the hand of a Marine in the operating-room on board a British battleship.

fathers this chapter may fittingly be brought to a close. It only remains to add that they invariably displayed the utmost chivalry towards the enemy, sometimes in the most dangerous and exasperating circumstances—as, for example, in the action in the Bight of Heligoland on August 28th, 1914, when the Germans turned their fire on the boats of the Defender, lowered to pick up the crew of the enemy destroyer V187, which had been sunk. There were even times when the Briton at home displayed a marked impatience with the unfailing efforts of the officers and men of the Fleet to save a beaten enemy from death, often at the risk of their own lives. A Navy that organised the murder of women and children at sea, and that used its guns for the shelling of open boats crowded with the remnants of a sunken ship's company, could not be expected to inconvenience itself to save the life of a combatant ; but the British Navy has handed down untarnished to its successors the splendid traditions of honour and clean fighting which it inherited from its forefathers.

THE FIRST PRIZE COURT HELD DURING THE GREAT WAR.

The first Prize Bounty case to come before the Prize Court, presided over at the Law Courts by Sir Samuel Evans, was heard on March 27th, 1916, the case being that of the armed liner Carmania for sinking the German armed liner Cap Trafalgar on September 14th, 1914. No cases had been heard before the Prize Court between those arising out of the Crimean War and those arising out of the Great War of sixty years later.

CHAPTER CXCVIII.

COMING OF THE GOTHAS : THE BIG AEROPLANE RAIDS OF THE SUMMER OF 1917.

By H. W. Wilson.

Revolution in Warfare Presaged by Blériot's First Crossing of the Channel—Lord Northcliffe's Propaganda to Spur the British Empire to Great Efforts—Lack of Vision on the Part of the British Authorities—Systematic and Scientific Organisation of the German Air Service—Establishment and Reorganisation of the British Air Board—German Plans for 1918—The Gotha Aeroplane—Methods of Protecting Great Britain, Offensive and Defensive—Great Aeroplane Raid on Folkestone, May 25th, 1917—Its Objects and Results—Raid on Essex and Sheerness, June 5th—First Aeroplane Raid on London, June 13th—Parliamentary and Public Criticism of the Government—Raid on Harwich, July 4th—Second Raid on London, July 7th—Optical Illusions of the Spectators—Peculiarities of the Air-Fighting Attending the Raid—Failure of the Defence to Punish the Raiders—Public Indignation and Renewed Demand for Reprisals—French Reprisals for German Raids, and Their Lessons—German Raid on Harwich and Felixstowe, July 22nd—Rocket Signal System of Warning London Tested—Raid on Southend, August 21st—Raid on Thanet, August 22nd—Probable Intention of the German High Command to Open a Campaign of Large-Scale Air Raids on Great Britain—Analysis of the Raids Between May 25th and September 24th.—Zeppelin Activities During the Summer ; The Rigid Airship Discredited as a Military Machine—Nelson's Last Order : " Engage the Enemy More Closely."

FOR three centuries British statesmanship has recognised that the presence of a Great Power on the coast of Holland and Belgium—opposite London and the mouth of the Thames—would mean mortal peril to the people of Great Britain. Because Napoleon in 1803 would not relax his grip on Holland and the Scheldt, a British Government which believed in peace at almost any price went to war with him. In 1870 even Mr. Gladstone was quick to take alarm when for a moment it seemed that the independence of Belgium might be endangered in the struggle between France and Germany. At every turn in the Great War the gravity of this menace was emphasised and illustrated. It was demonstrated that so long as the Belgian coast was in German hands there was no security for South-Eastern England. The British seaboard was harried by German destroyer raids from the Belgian bases. The Channel was beset with submarines, which put out from Zeebrugge and Ostend. But, above all, from the Belgian coast-line, left by British strategy in German hands, moved the warcraft of the new arm which was blotting out geography, and promised to decide the conflict.

As naval power had lost, so air power had gained. As the surface warship had to move ever more and more warily over a sea in the depths of which the treacherous

[Lafayette.
LIEUT. MAX A. E. CREMETTI, D.C.M., R.F.C.
During the raid of July 7th, 1917, Lieut. Cremetti charged through the enemy formation more than once, and brought down one machine at the mouth of the Thames. He was killed while flying, August 14th.

submarine might always be lurking, so aircraft developed in range and capacity of destruction. Even before the war some few thinkers had discerned the meaning of the revolution that began in 1909 with the crossing of the Channel by M. Blériot in a little 22 horse-power monoplane. They saw that for military purposes seas were disappearing, that Great Britain, now a road to her was open through the air, had ceased to be an island, and had retained only the disadvantages of insularity, that she was beset by new and unknown dangers, and that the one safe course was for her to develop aircraft and air power with might and main. In M. Blériot's flight they recognised something like the unnerving signal of the underground booming which in Mr. Wells's romance of the journey to the moon ushered in such strange and fearful events. Lord Northcliffe, with the large prizes given in the " Daily Mail," and with unceasing propaganda in every direction, did his utmost to spur the British Government and people on to the efforts which security demanded. The nation very slowly awoke, but the lethargy and scepticism of the Government were difficult to move. Ministers were always talking of "hard thinking," and of "using science," but they troubled themselves little about aircraft. Even so late as the opening of 1916, long after the Germans had begun to build on a large scale, they regarded aeroplanes as interesting and useful accessories to armies and

[*French official photograph.*

TESTING THE PROPELLER.
Mounting the propeller of a French flying machine on the trying bench.
All parts of an aeroplane have to be subjected to careful testing before
being assembled for making the complete machine.

perhaps to fleets. Of the possibility that the new arm
might eventually swallow up both the other forces and
dominate them by its importance there was never a
glimpse on the Ministerial horizon.

Even in 1914, while the war was in its earliest stages,
Professor Lanchester, an authority of European reputation
on the technical and scientific side of airmanship, had urged
that decisive results could be obtained were aircraft used
strategically as a kind of super-cavalry, to raid and sweep
the country behind the enemy's lines continuously. Under
" a continuous and unrelenting attack," he said,

depots of every kind in the rear of the enemy's lines would cease
to exist ; rolling-stock and mechanical transport would be destroyed ;
no bridge would be allowed to stand for twenty-four hours ; railway
junctions would be subject to continuous bombardments, and the
lines of railway and roads themselves broken up daily by giant
bombs to such an extent as to baffle all attempts
to maintain or restore communication. In this
manner a virtually impassable zone would be
created in the rear of the enemy's defences—a
zone varying perhaps from one hundred to two
hundred miles in width. Once this condition has been brought about,
the position of the defending force must be considered as precarious ;
not only will the defence be slowly strangled from the uncertainty and
lack of supplies of all kinds, but ultimate retreat will become impossible.

Professor Lanchester's early forecast

Professor Lanchester added that very large air forces
would be needed to accomplish such a result. He warned
the British Government of the risk of great and carefully
organised attacks upon London, and asked that Government to study protective measures as a matter of " ordinary
military precaution."

" Where there is no vision, the people perish." Before the
war the chief air-adviser of the British Army had ridiculed
and dismissed as preposterous the suggestion that German
aircraft would bomb London. When war came, aircraft

were built in 1914-16 in a hand-to-mouth fashion. Large
plans, such as Lord Northcliffe, Professor Lanchester, and
a few others had proposed, were conspicuously absent.
Indeed, the suggestion that aircraft could be employed as a
separate arm for strategic work was received in official
quarters with coldness or positive hostility. The un-
reformed War Office of 1915 imagined that it would lose
control of aeroplane construction for its special purposes.
The Admiralty of that date was not favourable to bold
ideas or vigorous execution, and was jealous of airmanship.
The difficulties in the way of a great air programme were
very great, and the intensest energy and earnestness would
have been required to overcome them. The unimaginative,
sceptical temper which could not think of shells by the
million, could not conceive the possibility of turning out
aeroplanes by the thousand—a much
more difficult business. The danger was **Government apathy**
that the German Staff would attempt to **and German energy**
carry out such plans if they were regarded
as impracticable in Great Britain, and would devise the
organisation for doing this. Before the beginning of the
war the German Staff had grasped the meaning of air war,
and had made extraordinary efforts to create large air
forces. It had been hampered by the undeveloped state
of air science and construction, by lack of material, and by
the Zeppelin obsession, though the Zeppelin had its value
in hamstringing the British Navy during a most critical
period, in paralysing large British forces, and in tying
them down to passive defence at home. By 1917 the
German Staff, as the result of practical air tests, had the
instrument necessary. As the Zeppelin degenerated in
military value—which it did so soon as the British
authorities could be induced to attack it with aircraft—
the far more formidable aeroplane took its place.

WHERE THE PILOT SAT.
The position occupied by the pilot of a German aeroplane of the Rumpier
type. From a photograph taken in a French école d'aviation.

In the winter of 1916 Hindenburg had reorganised the German air service in the most systematic and scientific manner. The disputes between the Navy and Army, which in the autumn of that year caused so much delay in Great Britain, did not trouble Germany, where Hindenburg was complete master of both services. His rule meant that the brains of the German General Staff were supreme. Elaborate plans of operation were worked out, and proper proportions of machines were ordered, and tactics devised for them, acting in bodies. Instead of trusting to chance and improvisation, Germany used experience and knowledge. It was indeed fortunate for Great Britain that the Germans had difficulty in obtaining material, and that the British airmen were generally superior in dash, initiative, courage, and individual skill, as all the odds which the most scientific direction could accumulate against the British were on the German side. The German airmen were

German appropriation of British ideas supported by a highly-efficient construction department. This scrutinised and copied the admirable new machines which private firms in Great Britain designed, and which from time to time fell into German hands, often before the British services were ready with them in any number. Thus, when one of the German Gothas—machines of the type largely employed in long-distance raids on London and other English towns—was examined, it was found to embody a number of features borrowed from a British Handley-Page of giant size, which fell into German hands in 1916.

The closest touch was kept in Germany between the airmen in the field and the constructors at home, and every effort was made to introduce new and improved designs quickly, and to standardise them. Aeroplane-making is not like shell-making, where material of the same pattern can

TRIBUTE TO AN ENEMY AIRMAN.
Wreath dropped behind the German lines by men of the R.F.C. as a tribute to Lieut. Immelmann, one of the crack German flyers, who was brought down on the western front in July, 1916.

GERMAN FLYING MEN.
General Hoepner, commanding the German air service, talking to a flying man who had just returned from a reconnaissance on the western front.
(From a German photograph.)

be turned out month after month. In aircraft there is perpetual progress ; the machine of one year is out of date the next. In Germany some months elapsed before large numbers of new machines were delivered. But the delay in England was far greater, as shown by such an example as the Sopwith two-seater. This was a very fast and extremely valuable aeroplane. According to the editor of the " Aeroplane," it made its appearance in July, 1915. It was then criticised and not accepted by British authorities. The French Government ordered a number of these machines in December, 1915 ; the British service did not give large orders for them until May, 1916, when the type was already a year old. As there were delays in delivery, they did not appear in the field in numbers before August or September, 1916 ; and contracts for their construction were still running in 1917, when the type was more than eighteen months old. If Germany was better supplied with up-to-date aeroplanes, though her patterns were inferior to the best British machines, she owed it to the absence of friction between her services, to the businesslike system of inspection, and to the importance which her authorities attached to the opinion of the German airmen. " We are always," said the " Aeroplane," " six months ahead of the enemy in design and twelve-months behind him in delivery."

Production lags behind invention

In Great Britain a new authority had to be created in 1917 to deal with the rivalry between the Royal Naval Air Service (R.N.A.S.) and Royal Flying Corps (R.F.C.), and to decide which service should have the prior right to machines. The Air Board, established in 1916, was reorganised in 1917, and placed under Lord Cowdray, with greater powers than in the past, when it had been little more than the ghost of a name. It was, however, primarily a

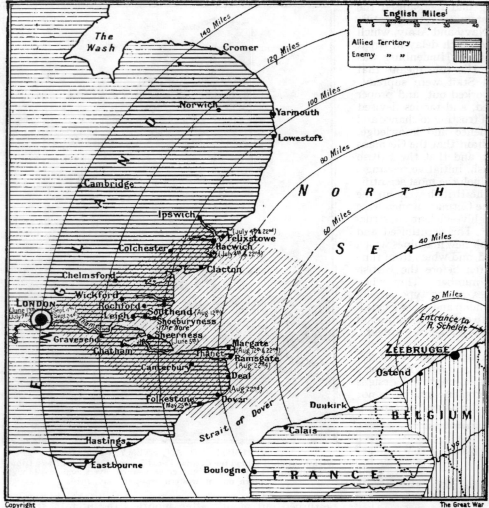

THE GERMAN AIR-RAID ZONE IN THE SUMMER OF 1917.
During the summer of 1917 the bomb-dropping German Gotha aeroplanes, fully equipped, developed a range of one hundred and forty miles. In the above map, in which the mileage from Zeebrugge is shown by semicircular lines with twenty-mile distances between them, the area of England attacked in June-September, 1917, is indicated by diagonal shading, the dates of the raids being added under the names of the towns on which bombs were dropped.

types lasted only a little over three months. If it were assumed that the Germans intended to maintain a force of 1,500 fighting and 2,000 bombing and observing machines, they would need to turn out each month 750 new fighting machines and 600 bombing machines merely to keep their force at the strength originally fixed. They would require a steady output of 1,350 machines a month, or 16,200 a year. Provision was probably made in these calculations for machines lost in the field. The severity of the air fighting constantly increased. In the first six months of the year 1917 the Allies on the western front claimed to have " brought down " or " destroyed " 1,401 German machines and 52 German kite-balloons, while the Germans claimed to have " destroyed " 955 allied machines and 45 kite-balloons. In the execution of its vast plans the German Staff was seconded by the perfect discipline and patriotism of the German workers. In Great Britain, on the other hand, in the first five months of 1916, 1,559,000 working days were lost through strikes in munition works. In the corresponding period of 1917, 540,000 days were lost. What proportion of this time was lost in aeroplane manufacture is not known, but Mr. Lloyd George asserted in the House of Commons that as the result of one strike in April, 1917, between 150 and 200 fewer aeroplanes were delivered. British airmen were killed in old-fashioned and obsolescent machines because British workers quarrelled with the Munitions Department. British women and children were bombed because the machines to meet the German aeroplanes were incomplete as the result of these pitiful squabbles.

Of the machines which the Germans constructed a number were of specially large size, and expressly designed for long-distance bombing raids. The most famous of these was the Gotha, which has already been mentioned, and which derived its name from the place where it was built. It made its appearance in numbers in 1917. Its details were ascertained, as a machine of this type was shot down by the famous airman Captain Guynemer in February, 1917, and fell in the French lines. It was a giant biplane, though smaller than the monster British Handley-Page. The span was 77 feet and the length 40 feet; **Details of the Gotha aeroplane** the height was 12 feet. By way of comparison, a standard British aeroplane before the war measured 36 feet in span and 29 feet in length, with a single engine of 80 horse-power. The Gotha had two engines, each of the famous Mercédès type, with six cylinders developing 260 horse-power, of the type used in super-Zeppelins. They were placed on either side of the body and drove " pusher " propellers (behind and not in front of the aeroplane). There were two pairs of wheels, as could be plainly observed in the case of the machines used to bomb London, placed abreast of one another, one under each engine. The aeroplane normally seated three men—an observer or gunner in front

supply department to provide aeroplanes, not to study air strategy and tactics, and it did not include any section for air operations. Even in the supply of machines it was hampered by many obstacles. For its materials and labour it had to go to Priority Boards, which decided whether at that particular moment shells, or standarised steamships, or destroyers, or mines, or aircraft were the more essential. It did not make its own engines. For these it depended on the Ministry of Munitions. The multitude of departments involved was unfavourable to the rapid execution of large programmes. Where Army, Navy, Ministry of Munitions, Controller, and Air Board all might be involved, with the best will in the world, progress was slower than in Germany, where both the air services were practically one, and where one department as far as possible dealt with the air arm and its material. Still, the Air Board as constituted by Mr. Lloyd George marked an advance from the previous chaos, if only because for the first time the air directions of both Army and Navy were housed under the same roof with the Air Board.

Early in 1917 it was known that the Germans were planning a programme which they hoped would go far to give them air supremacy in 1918. According to official information published in France, they intended to maintain a total of 3,500 machines at their front in the spring of 1918. This figure involved a very large output. The French experts calculated that the fastest machines used for fighting at the front lasted only two months, while other

in the centre line, with a clear field of view or fire ; behind, or abaft, him was the pilot, seated somewhat to the left, leaving a passage from the front to the rear of the body ; and behind him was yet another gunner. Three machine-guns were commonly mounted. One in front was placed on a turntable, and could fire forward, above, below, and on either side of the machine. A second, at the very rear, could fire on either side, and almost vertically upward and downward. A third, mounted close to the floor of the body, near the stern, could fire downwards or obliquely, and directly astern through a curious tunnel which was one of the new features of the machine. The best method of attack upon aeroplanes had previously been to approach them from below and behind, when the rudder and tail planes prevented fire from machine-guns mounted in the usual fashion. The Gotha was protected against this danger.

In the body there was accommodation for fourteen bombs which, if of 60 lb. weight, would mean a load of 840 lb. The speed would probably be 80 miles an hour with full load at a great height, and at least 90 or 100 miles an hour without a load of bombs. There was no sign of armour in the machine captured, but it is possible that some of the fighting machines were fitted **Size, speed, and** with it. Nor was there anything special **fine workmanship** except fine workmanship about the engines, though the ease with which they maintained a high speed at great altitudes where the air pressure was much reduced was certainly surprising. The machines commonly flew at 12,000 to 15,000 feet, where only the most powerful anti-aircraft guns could reach them. Their great size led spectators to imagine that they were flying very low.

These large, fast, heavily-armed machines were further drilled to act together. They moved in regular formation in all their raids, manœuvring exactly as would a squadron of battleships or a flotilla of destroyers. The arrangement was generally, but not always, triangular, with the leader at the apex of the triangle, high up, and the machines at the base flying at a greater altitude than those in front. In this order the German airmen could support one another, best beat off attacks, bring the largest volume of fire to bear, and crush isolated antagonists. The Gotha machines were said to be relegated to short-distance work after a few long-distance raids, as the strain on their structure was too great to be often repeated.

The most effective method of protecting Great Britain against these attacks lay in taking the offensive—in driving

HYDROPLANE VERSUS SUBMARINE.
French hydroplane dropping bombs—the jet of water thrown up by an exploding bomb is plainly shown. Experienced airmen, observing from a height, were able to locate underwater craft, and there were many instances of hydroplanes successfully attacking U boats.

the Germans from the Belgian coast and depriving them of their bases, or in carrying the air war resolutely into Germany and bombing the German towns and munition centres and factories. The destruction of munition works and munition-makers' dwellings in Germany would have produced important military results in many directions. It would have interfered with the German supply of ammunition and aircraft at its source. It would have affected the nerve of the German people as no raids on German depots and dumps in Northern France or Belgium could do. It would have been much less dangerous work for the British airmen, as towns are easier targets to hit than railway-stations or heaps of ammunition, and can be assailed from a much greater height—which meant less peril for the airman—and, away from the immediate front, were less vigilantly guarded. This plan would speedily have compelled the German Command to detach air squadrons from the front and to use them for passive defence in Germany. It thus would have protected the women and children of South-Eastern England, and would at the same time have lessened the pressure on the

BROUGHT DOWN AND DESTROYED.
German aeroplane brought down by Captain Guynemer, the famous French airman, on the western front. After bringing down his thirtieth machine he was promoted captain and awarded the Russian Cross of St. George. He had accounted for fifty-three enemy machines by September, 1917.

British fighting squadrons at the front. True, there were difficulties in executing it, as a barrier of allied territory in the hands of the Germans was interposed between the allied front and Germany proper. But even so, a large area of industrial Germany was within reach.

A less satisfactory plan was to adopt a pure defensive against the raiders. The difficulty of organising an effective system of passive defence was great, owing to the peculiar conditions of air war. Anti-aircraft artillery—unless the guns were of great size and power, and the gunners were constantly practising on actual aeroplanes—was not at all certain of hitting machines which flew high and fast.

Difficulties of passive defence

Attacks delivered when there was cloud or haze might be driven home without the machines ever being clearly seen by the gunners. If the artillery was of great power, firing large shells, it became very dangerous to the people of the town it was intended to defend, who would, in fact, be bombarded by their own guns. If the defenders relied upon aeroplanes, a large number of machines must always be ready to go up. A German aeroplane could travel from Zeebrugge to London in less than two hours; in little more than an hour after leaving the Belgian coast it could reach Harwich or the coast of Kent. Unless the sea were carefully and vigilantly patrolled by allied war-

A TROPHY BEHIND THE CANADIAN LINES.
[Canadian War Records.
Type of German aeroplane brought down behind the Canadian lines on the western front. Captured as it was in an almost complete condition, this example of German aircraft manufacture aroused the keenest interest on the part of its captors.

ships and allied aircraft, the movement of raiders might not be observed until they reached the British coast, and warning might be given only a few minutes before they arrived, or, indeed, might not be given at all. When it was known that the raiding force was moving, and when the general direction of its movement was ascertained, the Germans might always turn back or alter course. The defending machines could not, like a fleet, cruise aloft, waiting for the enemy. Aeroplanes only carried a limited supply of petrol, and could remain only a limited time in the air. The strain of war work on both engines and pilots could scarcely be exaggerated. If the defending machines went up too soon, their pilots might be tired out and unavailable when the real attack came. If they waited for certain news, they might not be able to climb to the height requisite for effective fighting or to take up formation. To reach a level of 15,000 or 16,000 feet at least, fifteen to twenty minutes' notice was necessary.

For all these reasons the defensive involved the use of large numbers of machines and the display of great organising skill in the employment of them. The best form of defensive lay in destroying the lairs from which the Germans

issued by bombing their aerodromes unceasingly and preventing concentrations of aeroplanes. "If you do nothing but defend yourself," said Napoleon, "you incur risk without any compensating gain." The difficulties being so great, there was a natural tendency to argue that as many machines as possible should be sent to the front, where they could always be usefully employed in the hope of attracting thither the German aeroplanes. But though it was sometimes suggested that London ought to be allowed to take its chance, rather than the front should be stinted of machines, the opinion of the greatest master of war on that head was uncompromising. "To leave so important a point as the capital undefended," Napoleon said, "reveals the most surprising inconsequence and bad reasoning." London had to be defended, as the Germans had been permitted to retain bases within aircraft range of it, and as they were not kept busy defending their own homes. The real question was how efficiently to protect it. To expose it to systematic and continued attack on a large scale by aeroplanes was out of the question, and would have involved stupendous pecuniary loss and immense injury to the British reputation for energy and common-sense. Moreover, those who talked of "the front," as opposed to London, confused the issue. With the developments of air war London had become part of the front.

Two authorities were concerned in the defence of London against air attack. The first and most seriously responsible was the Admiralty. To that body the nation had trusted for its defence against Zeppelins early in the war, but the duty was so unsatisfactorily executed that the work of meeting airship attack had to be taken from it by the Government in 1916, and given to the reformed and improved War Office, which carried it out with marked success. The Admiralty, represented by "Vice-Admiral, Dover," controlled the naval aircraft at Dunkirk, which of all the British defensive forces were closest to the German bases, and it also controlled the British warships and R.N.A.S. stations in the southern North Sea and the Channel. The Dunkirk aircraft, however, despite the extraordinary gallantry of the individual airmen, proved powerless to prevent the German raids, and did not punish the raiders severely on their return. The British warships appear to have played no part at all.

In the same way, in the earlier period of the war, the Navy had not reported or stopped the movements of Zeppelins in the North Sea. As the Navy could not defend the capital, and as its strategy was accepted as satisfactory by the Government, the task of meeting the Germans fell on the Army and the Royal Flying Corps. The task increased in difficulty with each mile that the Germans flew. Off Dunkirk they were most vulnerable because they had their full load of bombs and petrol on board, which handicapped them considerably. The Gothas used 130 lb. of petrol and oil for each hour of flight, and thus gained rapidly in manœuvring and climbing power. When their bombs had been dropped they were so much lightened that the chance of attacking them with success was not great.

Responsibility of the Admiralty

A further embarrassment of the defence, according to Lord Montagu of Beaulieu, who had made a special study of the air problem, was that the British forces were unaccountably short of effective and up-to-date machines, despite much talk and many official assurances. The

England's defences against attack from the air: Anti=aircraft gun at a coast town.

Giant British biplanes in flight: The Handley=Page bomb carrier, prototype of the German Gotha.

Raiders' fate in Thanet, August 22nd, 1917: One was brought down in a cornfield, one in the sea.

Off on patrol: R.N.A.S. men about to let go the hawsers and release a naval airship.

shortage was increased by the collapse of Russia, which set a large number of German machines free, and by the German system of air tactics adopted early in 1917 at the cost of the unfortunate German infantry, who bitterly complained. The Germans in the first half of the year generally declined to attack over the British lines, where they were likely to lose heavily. They preferred to engage the British pilots and observers over their own lines or well behind them, where a British machine that fell was lost with its pilot for good to the British cause. In the raids on England the German machines took very moderate risks. The German Staff was certainly prepared for a reasonable proportion of casualties now that aircraft were becoming regular fighting craft. In such enterprises as raids on London it was probably quite ready to sacrifice ten, fifteen, or even twenty-five per cent. of the machines engaged, so long as blows were struck which appealed to the imagination and satisfied German opinion. The delusion in Great Britain that the Germans were a kindly, affectionate, good-humoured people who had been hood-winked into war by cruel autocrats, should have been dispelled by the savage demand which went up in the Fatherland for bloodthirsty attacks on the British capital.

The first serious German aeroplane raid took place on Friday, May 25th, 1917, at Folkestone. Soon after 6 p.m.,

Serious raid on Folkestone when the streets were full after a delicious spring day, the buzz of aeroplanes was heard coming, apparently from London. No warning had been given. The people generally supposed that the machines were British, and noticed with peculiar pride the splendid order in which they were exercising. As the raiders were seen at Folkestone they numbered from eleven to sixteen machines. A single aeroplane very high up led them; then followed four or five machines in line abreast; a little behind them were another four or five in line, and a small group brought up the rear. Approaching the town, the first group swung north, the second south, and the third held straight on. The manœuvre was watched with admiration and with no suspicion of danger by the crowds below. The machines had now deployed into a single line which was either straight or slightly crescent-shaped, with the leader still in advance. They seemed very low because of their great size, but were actually, according to expert reports, at 14,000 feet. As they drew nearer they dived to 12,000 or 13,000. Then from them glistening objects dropped and, with a roar of violent explosions and the crash of shattered glass and collapsing masonry, dense clouds of smoke and sheets of flame rose from the surprised town, over which spread a black, evil-smelling pall of fumes.

There had been no firing and no attack so far by the British forces, whether of artillery or aircraft. Nor had there been the slightest premonition of danger. The bombs took cruel effect, and the streets a couple of minutes later were spattered with blood and strewn with prostrate forms and human fragments. Several of the bombs fell among a crowd of women and children who were watching, and claimed many victims. A greengrocer's shop, full of customers, was struck; it collapsed, and all in it were killed. A church-clock was hit by one fragment and stopped at 6.27.

The Germans added greatly to the effectiveness of their attack—if their object was mere slaughter—by approaching from the landward side. They crossed the coast in Essex, at a point about one hundred miles from Zeebrugge, at least forty-five minutes before they reached Folkestone, and then headed for Kent, dropping a few bombs at various places as they passed. By taking this circuitous route and feinting at London they obviously intended to hamper the defence and put their proposed victims off their guard.

The attack was very quickly over; it lasted from eight to ten minutes. Then the Germans passed out to sea under the fire of the British anti-aircraft artillery, still maintaining excellent formation, and disappeared. There

THE FORTUNE OF WAR.
German aeroplane brought down behind the French lines on the western front after being crippled by anti-aircraft gun fire. French soldiers are seen removing the severely injured enemy airman from the wreckage of his machine.

was no official claim that the Germans were attacked by British aircraft before reaching Folkestone or while they were engaged in the work of bombing. The War Office report stated that " aeroplanes of the R.F.C. went up in pursuit, and the raiding aircraft were engaged by fighting squadrons of the R.N.A.S. from Dunkirk on their return journey." The Admiralty report did not mention any attempt to attack the Germans on their way to British territory, but said:

In the evening several enemy aircraft returning from a raid on England were engaged oversea. . . . An encounter took place between one British and three hostile aeroplanes in mid-Channel, and one of the latter was destroyed. Several encounters also took place off the Belgian coast, in which two large twin-engined hostile machines were shot down. All our machines returned safely.

In the action between one British and three German machines, Flight-Commander R. F. S. Leslie was the British pilot, and most deservedly won the Distin-guished Service Cross for his splendid gallantry in following the raiders out to sea in a land machine. A German aero-plane which he attacked and repeatedly hit was seen by him to be descending in a nose-dive, emitting smoke and steam, when his attention was taken off it. Two other German machines attacked him from behind and for some moments he lost control. When he had recovered it, the two German machines which had attacked him were proceeding east at a great height above him, and the other German machine had disappeared. A French naval pilot, with an aeroplane stationed at Dunkirk, claimed to have destroyed another of the raiders—perhaps one of the two machines engaged by Commander Leslie.

In its first report the German Staff merely stated that " during a successful raid one of our squadrons dropped bombs on Dover and Folkestone. Long-distance inland flights also gave good results." A few days later a second

LONDON CHILDREN KILLED WHILE AT SCHOOL.
Funeral of some of the one hundred and twenty school-children, victims of the midday raid on London of June 13th, 1917. The pathetic procession was here turning into the street wherein stood the devastated school in which the children had been killed while at their lessons.

Government constantly indulged. The usual assurance was given to the British public that no military damage had been done, but the destruction of life and property and the shock to confidence were not to be lightly dismissed.

The total casualties officially reported were 76 killed and 174 injured, of whom 70 were women and 42 were children. In all 43 bombs were dropped. They were of four kinds— shrapnel, arranged to burst just overhead and kill human beings (as the Germans well knew that in the evening the streets would be full of women and children); 60 lb. shells of a type similar to the smaller bombs dropped by Zeppelins, with delay-action fuses, designed to penetrate buildings and explode after reaching the ground, completely wrecking the structure; incendiary bombs; and another type with highly sensitive fuse, designed to explode on merely touching the roof. Possibly this curious variety of bombs was employed to gain information through spies and German agents for the attack on London which the German Staff was then planning.

report was issued asserting that "the naval fortresses" of Dover and Folkestone were attacked:

In both these places there are miles of works and warehouses, filled with troops awaiting transport to France, and with stores, munitions, and other supplies. Among these packed masses our airmen found suitable targets. Seven enormous fires were seen from the sea by airmen who arrived after the attack had been made with success. The English profess that three German aeroplanes were lost. Only one of our machines failed to return.

This raid was probably carried out as a test of the Gotha machines' endurance and trustworthiness, and also to feel the strength of the British defences. It should be observed that for once the two sets of official reports were in general accord. The British only claimed one machine as actually destroyed, "shot down" often meaning that the enemy was forced by some injury to return to earth or thought it better to run away from the battle. The pretence that the German bombs dropped from such an immense height had hit only British troops was one of those grotesque exhibitions of hypocrisy in which the German

Variety of German bombs

The public had scarcely recovered from the surprise caused by the raid and by the escape of almost all the machines concerned in it when the Germans delivered another audacious attack. On the afternoon of June 5th a large force of German aeroplanes, from sixteen to eighteen in number, left the Belgian coast. Four machines of the R.N.A.S., which were patrolling off Dunkirk, observed them well out to sea travelling north-westwards towards England. The British machines attacked, but were too weak in numbers to stop the raiders and destroy them or drive them back. The British pilots followed for some distance towards the English coast. The Germans pursued their usual route imperturbably and steered for Southern Essex. They crossed the British coast at 6.15, when their force was counted, and observed to consist of sixteen machines flying in the regular formation, with the leader high up in advance and three lines following him at various heights. The general level was estimated

German priest as air-raider

NAVAL VICTIMS OF A GERMAN AIR RAID.
Head of the funeral procession nearing a cemetery on September 6th, 1917, when ninety-eight of the men killed by a bomb dropped on naval barracks in the Sheerness-Chatham area three days earlier were buried.

TEUTONIC "FRIGHTFULNESS" AT FOLKESTONE.
Funeral of a mother and her two children, killed in a German air raid on Folkestone. The monument on the right is to one hundred and fifty sailors of a German frigate, which foundered off Folkestone in 1878.

DARING EXPLOIT OF A BRITISH AIRMAN ON THE WESTERN FRONT.
During the Ypres fighting on July 31st, 1917, one British flying man performed a series of very daring exploits. On one occasion, descending to within twenty feet of the ground, he attacked a company of two hundred enemy infantry and scattered them with his machine-gun fire.

at 14,000 to 15,000 feet, and the great size of the machines was again noted by skilled observers.

Eleven bombs were dropped in Essex, killing a man and injuring another, but the main attack was directed against the British naval base at Sheerness and the mouth of the Medway. At 6.30 the anti-aircraft guns in the British defences came into action. The Germans, still flying at a great height in the air, were met by a number of British machines which had gone up to attack them, and a brisk encounter took place: They were not prevented from reaching Sheerness, where they dropped some forty bombs. According to the British official report, "a certain amount of damage was done to house property, but the damage done to naval and military establishments was practically negligible." The Germans followed their usual tactics. Of their three lines one steered for the town, and the second made a great sweep to attack the dockyard. They dropped their bombs with the greatest possible speed from an extreme height, and then swiftly made off.

They did not escape scathless. At the very opening of the action a German machine was hit, and fell into the water in sight of all, not far from the coast. Boats hurried to it and picked up the pilot, who had been mortally wounded by the British shells. He stated that he had been a Lutheran priest before entering the air service. His observer, a boy of eighteen, had his left arm blown off. A third man was also rescued. The

British War Office report announced that two German machines were destroyed in the Medway. According to the British Admiralty report, the Germans on their return were attacked by a naval machine from a Kent station, which drove down two German aeroplanes and afterwards landed at Dunkirk, and later by ten naval pilots from Dunkirk, when a series of air encounters took place. The

PRUSSIAN AVIATOR PRINCE'S LAST FLIGHT.
Prince Frederick Charles of Prussia setting out on his last flight in a machine constructed after his own design. He died of wounds on April 11th, 1917, after being made prisoner on the western front by the British. (This picture is reproduced from a German source.)

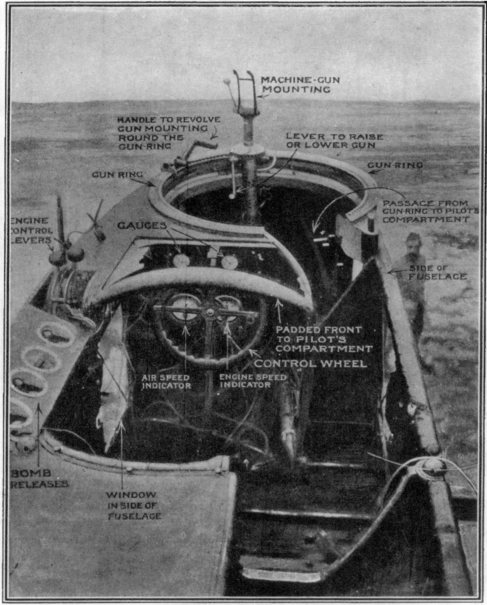

NAVIGATING AND FORWARD FIGHTING QUARTERS OF A GOTHA.

This Gotha fighting aeroplane was brought down by Captain Guynemer. The two passengers sat in the centre of the axis, while the pilot's seat was placed to the left, allowing room for a gangway, along which the occupants could pass from end to end.

but shot to pieces with explosive bullets, so that its vital structure only hung together by a miracle." What Captain Ball did often, less skilful airmen could do on occasions, and it is quite certain that machines which each side counted as "destroyed" or "driven down," often managed to struggle home safely.

The Germans in their official report alleged that over five tons of bombs had been dropped on "the military establishments of Sheerness," and that "good hits" were observed. They only admitted the loss of two machines. Had they really lost ten out of sixteen, which was the extreme British claim, it is not probable that they would have repeated their raids. As with Zeppelins so with aeroplanes, a sure method of discouraging their attacks on towns remote from the actual front was to destroy the hostile aircraft, instead of merely ex-postulating with the German Staff on its wickedness.

The next attack was a yet more serious one, and was apparently carried out by the same group of aeroplanes. The daring of the German Air Command grew with continued success. On the morning of June 13th fifteen or sixteen German machines were sighted off the North Foreland, having apparently passed the R.N.A.S. patrol off Dunkirk without being attacked or interfered with. They dropped a few bombs in Thanet, and then steered up the Thames, reaching the Essex coast some time later, and passing the Nore, about thirty-eight miles from London, at 11 a.m. Their destination was London. That city had been repeatedly attacked by Zeppelins, and on two occasions had been reached by aeroplanes. On November 28th, 1916, a German machine had dropped a few bombs on it in broad daylight, but had been captured on the return journey through the airman miscalculating his route and running out of petrol, so that he came down in France. On May 7th, 1917, another machine, attacking by night, had dropped four bombs in a northern suburb, killing or injuring three people. These raids were probably tests; in the **Home Office and raid warnings** first a seaplane seems to have been employed, and in the second one of the new Gotha machines. From the earliest days of the war the German air commanders had been eager to reach and bomb London, and in 1916-17 they were preparing a surer weapon than the Zeppelin to carry out their designs.

In spite of these indications of German intentions, no instructions were issued to the people of London, and no attempt was made to organise a system of warnings. No one studied the precautions necessary to protect life in the event of aeroplane raids. People in Paris, Milan, Venice, and the German cities were warned as a matter of course when raids were imminent, and were provided with careful advice. But it was assumed by the responsible Minister,

Admiralty claimed that two German machines were destroyed and four driven down " out of control, of which two are considered to have been destroyed," adding that all the British machines returned safely.

The British casualties were twelve killed and thirty-six wounded, as against which a doubtful number of German machines—from two to six—were destroyed. Uncertainty about the exact number was inevitable in view of the peculiar character and extraordinary swiftness of air fighting. The most careful and truthful pilot or observer might make mistakes. In naval engagements it was invariably found that far more enemy ships than had actually been sunk were reported to have been destroyed by good and competent eye-witnesses, and for much the same reason. In the air it was specially difficult to know whether a machine which went spinning down with steam pouring from it was actually "destroyed" or was only driven out of the battle. "Time after time," said an expert of Captain Ball, one of the greatest of British airmen, "he made home safely with his controls shot away and his machine, not 'riddled with bullets,' in the hallowed phrase,

Sir George Cave, the British Home Secretary, that Londoners, if told an attack was apprehended, would rush out into the streets and offer themselves as targets for falling bombs, or else would give way to wild panic. Therefore, it was argued, they ought not to be warned. It never even occurred to the Home Office or the other authorities concerned to issue plain instructions telling people what to do when they heard the ominous buzz of machines and bursting of the German bombs. In foreign cities the public did what the military authorities advised, and the citizens of London might at least have been informed where to take shelter, and what shelter to seek. Ministers had been repeatedly warned of the peril, and the "Daily Mail," in prescient articles from January, 1916, onwards, had specially called attention to the risk of daylight aeroplane raids.

About half-way to London the raiders, who appear to have been moving at eighty miles an hour, divided into two or three parties, each of five or more machines. The exact course of these parties was difficult to determine for various reasons. The day was a brilliant one, with a strong sun, but there was much light cloud at a level of 8,000 or 10,000 feet, and the raiders cleverly screened themselves behind it and travelled at an immense height, possibly 15,000 feet. At many points nothing could be seen of them, according to statements in the Press, and only the buzzing of large machines—some of which may have been British—could be plainly heard. In Northern London, which the raiders approached at about 11.30, they could not be distinctly seen, though they were heard. Loud and repeated detonations —whether from anti-aircraft guns or bombs, or from both combined, no one who was not in the actual area attacked could say—gave the first definite indication that the Germans had reached the capital. They bombed the City and the poor districts of the East End with great fury from an extreme height, and showed once more that their aim was rather to kill and destroy than to secure any so-called military results.

A railway-station was one of the objects specially attacked, and was hit by one detachment of raiders who crossed it from west to east. Four bombs were dropped, all of which passed through the glass roof. Two burst with great effect. One struck a carriage and tore it to splinters. Another fell on the permanent way, and the full violence of its explosion caught a second carriage, wrecked it, set it on fire, and fearfully injured the people in it and on the platform, who ran to and fro with clothes ablaze. Soldiers in the station displayed great coolness and gave valuable help. Here, as elsewhere, it was noticed that the people suffered most who were out of doors without cover—a fact which reflected strongly on those who were responsible for withholding warning of raids. In a few buildings, however, there were heavy casualties. The elementary schools suffered badly, as they were systematically bombed by the Germans. In one school a bomb passed through the roof, two floors, and three class-rooms, each full of children. It reached the ground-floor, and there exploded among sixty-four infants. In the words of an eye-witness, "the room was choked with struggling and screaming victims, many of them crying distractedly for their mothers. Little limbs were blown from bodies, and unrecognised remains were littered among the debris of broken desks and forms."

In some of the schools, in accordance with a drill which had been previously carried out, the children were ordered to take shelter under the desks, where they remained till the raid was over, singing songs or listening to tales read by their teachers. In the City several offices were destroyed, and many people had narrow escapes. One large building was completely wrecked in its upper stories, and there several people were killed by a single bomb, among them a woman who was terribly mutilated. Two girls who rushed out of a neighbouring building when they heard the explosion were severely injured by falling wreckage. When the bombing was at its height the streets were obscured with a thick, evil-smelling black smoke and with clouds of dust, and after the explosion they were left deep in powdered glass. The interests of national defence prevented the disclosure of the exact points where bombs fell. Generally perfect coolness was displayed, despite the universal indignation at the failure to give warning. At the Law Courts, where the noise of the bombs was plainly

Bombs dropped in City of London

Elementary schools suffer badly

SECTIONAL DIAGRAM OF A GOTHA FIGHTING AEROPLANE.

This particular Gotha carried two 260 h.p. Mercédès engines with propellers moving behind the wings, thus being really "propulsive," not "tractor." In a turret forward a gun fired forwards and, at certain angles, above and below the wings. Two others, in grooves on transverse tubes behind the rear passenger, fired, one above the body, the other in a gun-tunnel level with the floor, in the manner shown in the diagram.

heard, the judges proceeded with their work as though there had been no raid.

At Buckingham Palace an investiture had been appointed to take place at noon, and it was duly held. Immediately after it the King paid a visit to the hospitals and the bombed districts.

The Germans, when their bombs were exhausted, withdrew, still maintaining formation. According to the British official account, a large number of British aeroplanes went up in pursuit, but the raiders were not brought to action and destroyed. There was no indication that they were attacked on their return journey by the R.N.A.S. at Dunkirk, as the Admiralty maintained an entire silence as to the operations of that force.

[*French official photograph.*]

MACHINE-GUNS ON A FRENCH AEROPLANE.
" Tuning-up " the machine mounted on a French aeroplane preparatory to a flight. Two of these guns were carried, one controlled by the pilot and the other by his observer.

[*French official photograph.*]

GUNS ON A FRENCH ONE-MAN MACHINE.
French aeroplane, showing the position of the fighting pilot in relation to the two guns which his machine carried—one for firing ahead, and the other at an enemy at a higher altitude.

The casualties were returned as follows :

	Killed.	Injured.
Men	91	222
Women	24	110
Children	42	100
Total	157	432

It was observed that some ingredient in the German bombs was intensely poisonous, so that persons who handled fragments suffered from a painful skin eruption some days afterwards.

The German report was couched in the usual impudently hypocritical style :

A fleet of our large aeroplanes reached London and dropped bombs over the fort, and during clear weather observed the effect of good hits. In spite of a strong defensive fire and numerous aerial engagements, during which an English airman fell down over the Thames, all our aeroplanes returned safely.

A more flowery account was provided by the " Frank-

fürter Zeitung," as it professed, from the pen of an airman who took part in the raid :

At last (he wrote), surprisingly clear and distinct so that everything could be recognised, London was beneath us. Our first greetings dropped in rapid succession ; we gave them more and still more. Then we proceeded coolly and calmly over the suburbs, as we wanted to hit the centre. There were the Tower, Liverpool Street Station, the Bank of England, the Admiralty, and the ships on the Thames. I pressed the bomb-release and followed intently the greetings of the German people to the English. We gave them plenty—blow after blow from bursting bombs in the very heart of England. The sight over Central London was wonderfully impressive. High up, between us, were bursting shells. The squadron turned. We took a last glance at the City—" good-bye till next time." We had attained the object which not long ago was the unfulfilled dream of German airmen.

Such were this gentleman's dithyrambs, and it must be confessed that the safe passage of this large force to and from London afforded some justification for them.

The ease with which the Germans reached London, the ineffective character of the measures taken to protect the city, the entire absence of warning, and the failure to intercept the raiders on their retreat were the subject of the severest criticism in Parliament. The War Office, Admiralty, and Home Office were all in equal degree involved, and the excuses offered by Lord Derby, that " not a single soldier was killed," and that the victims were of " no military value," was not likely to deter the Germans from future raids or to reassure the people of London. Every issue raised was confused. If members called for defence by vigorous attacks on German towns—thus protecting British women and children—the question was shifted to the moral problem, whether reprisals were justifiable, an issue which did not really arise, and which, if it did, ought to have been decided on military grounds. When it was suggested that the authorities, who had left tens of thousands of people exposed in the streets to German bombs and British anti-aircraft shells and splinters, had been guilty of negligence, members were assured that workers in munition factories would go home and waste the whole day, or that idle fools would take cabs and crowd the streets to stare at the spectacle. Subsequent experience proved that these statements were most unjust to the people of London. It remained true that the only means of effectively defending London was to attack German towns, or to stop the raiders off Dunkirk. Members in the House of Commons, in reply to the Ministerial plea that British air forces were constantly bombing German shell-dumps and aerodromes, pointed out that this bombing was done in Belgium and Northern France, countries inhabited by a pro-Ally population. The German aircraft factories and munition works were left untouched, and the people of Germany were permitted—so far as the British air forces were concerned—to enjoy entire freedom from menace.

Apologists for British inaction All this storm of criticism produced no positive effect. The House of Commons no longer controlled events; it was so occupied with the discussion of secondary political questions that it could scarcely find time to deal with the war. A previous Government had pleaded for "darkness and composure" as a defence against Zeppelins, but had fortunately been overruled by the good sense of the British people. The watchword was now amended by apologists for inaction, and took the form of "dignity and composure," which, the country was assured, was the proper prescription for meeting German aeroplane raids. The value of this policy was strikingly illustrated in the weeks that followed by yet more humiliating raids on British territory.

On July 4th the same detachment of German aeroplanes, again altogether unchallenged, proceeded early in the morning from Ostend to Harwich. The distance to be covered was a little more than ninety miles over open sea, and the German airmen were never seen till they reached the British coast. Neither scouts from Dunkirk nor from any British station reported their movement. Suddenly twelve to fourteen large German machines came swiftly through the haze and cloud over the British East Coast naval base about 7.10 a.m., flying in formation. The Germans were high; they attacked as they had done previously, and disappeared after a few minutes of furious

bombing, leaving relics of their visit in eleven persons killed and thirty-six injured. Two bombs fell in Harwich, one of them at the door of the parish church, without doing any damage. The brunt of the attack fell on places near. The material damage was generally small.

The Germans suffered no visible injury from the British fire, and there was no information as to any attack on them in the air when they were over the British naval base. On their return they had to run the gauntlet of attack by the Dunkirk air forces. According to "Vice-Admiral, Dover," they were assailed by the R.N.A.S. machines, and he claimed that "two of the hostile machines were brought down in flames, and a third was seen to be damaged. All our machines returned undamaged." The German report was in flat contradiction to this. It asserted that "several tons of bombs were dropped on the objectives with good effect. All our aeroplanes returned undamaged." Whether the British were mistaken or whether the Germans lied, as they so often did, could only be decided after the war. But the loss of two machines was not sufficiently heavy to act as a deterrent upon them.

In six weeks the Germans had attacked in succession two British naval bases, a Channel port, and the capital of the Empire, all places in close proximity to numerous British defensive air stations, **Enemy airmen's** and in no case, except the doubtful one of **six weeks' record** the raid on Sheerness, had they been hit hard. They had killed and wounded nearly a thousand people, and done considerable damage to property. On July 7th they accomplished an air raid of an even more imposing character in yet more humiliating conditions. A second time in the space of a month the capital was attacked in broad daylight by a force of aircraft, which moved as if on parade, and brushed off all the defenders' attempts to interfere with it. If the loss of life was far less than in the previous attack, this was in no sense due to the authorities. The public, left entirely without guidance and warning—though every Government department received

A "SEA-BIRD" COMING ASHORE.

This striking photograph, taken from an aeroplane, shows a hydroplane returning to its hangar after a flight of reconnaissance. Despite the severely practical lines of the flying station, arranged with geometrical precision on the treeless shore, the picture is charged with poetry by the man-made bird splashing with outspread wings over the wrinkled surface of the sea, like a seamew returning to its haunts at the close of day.

timely notice and placed its employees in shelter—showed how curiously at fault was Sir George Cave's information. When the news that the Germans were approaching leaked out, very many people got under cover and remained there, without panic but with sound common-sense.

It was subsequently stated by Mr. Lloyd George that a force of British aircraft intended for the protection of London had been recalled to France on the eve of the raid at the request of Sir Douglas Haig. The Germans must have been informed of this through their spies and agents in Great Britain, and though, according to the "Aeroplane," a well-known technical journal, the aeroplanes in question were not of a pattern adapted for meeting the Gothas, their withdrawal left the road to London unguarded. At 9.30 a.m. the Germans crossed the English coast. They appear to have moved in two distinct bodies. One made for London by the old route of the Essex coast, which was fast becoming a regular German air-highway, and the other by Thanet and Kent. The two detachments proceeded by the north and south banks of the Thames at a great height. They numbered "about twenty" machines, according to the War Office report; according to unofficial estimates they may have been twenty-two or even twenty-five strong. A few bombs were dropped on the way up to London. Some few miles short of London the two bodies of raiders combined and took up formation in one large force, with the leader well in advance, and behind him the other machines in a triangular order which was **The second attack** rigidly maintained. When they neared **on London** London they moved along the northern outskirts to the north-west, and then suddenly the leader made a great sweep and was followed by the others, all altering course to steer south-east.

The exact number of machines and the exact number of lines and of machines in each line were difficult to determine because of the haze and glare and light clouds, and because when the Germans neared London numerous British machines were up in the air attacking them. The loud buzzing noise made by so large a force of powerful aeroplanes attracted instant attention, and the progress of the Germans was watched by tens of thousands who had not learnt that an attack was imminent. The aircraft were at first supposed to be British, as the public imagined—on the strength of official assurances—that effective steps had been taken for the defence of London. Moreover, the raiders flew in such perfect order that it seemed incredible they should be enemies. But as they emerged from the haze and drew nearer steadily the anti-aircraft guns opened a rapid fire. Even then few could believe their eyes or imagine that German aircraft in such force and order would be allowed to reach the capital. Many cheered them, mistaking the firing for some manœuvre, until it was seen that puffs of smoke from bursting shells followed the raiders across the sky, and until the din of bursting bombs, the crash of collapsing masonry, and the smashing of glass, with the clouds of smoke and dust, proved that a second attack on London was actually in progress.

In the area which the raiders first bombed, a building that had been a popular resort of Germans in London before the war was struck, and two old men and a lad were killed or injured. Two bombs fell in another building where a large number of women were employed, and the value of warnings was there clearly demonstrated. The women had been withdrawn from the upper stories, with the result that the casualties

CLOSE FIGHTING IN THE AIR.
German artist's view of an air fight, with one of the Black Cross machines closely pressed by an Allies' biplane. The superiority of the allied airmen was a marked feature of the fighting on the western front during the summer of 1917.

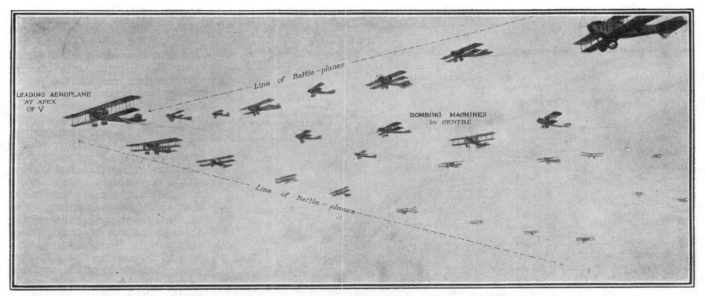

HOW THE RAIDING SQUADRON APPROACHED LONDON ON JULY 7TH, 1917.

Plan showing the "duck" formation in which the Gotha planes and their guard of battle-planes flew to London on the midday raid of July 7th, 1917. The outer, or V-shaped, line was that of the attendant battle-planes, the Gotha bombing machines flying in the centre. It was called "duck" formation from the habit that wild ducks have of flying in the form of a **V**., with a leader at the apex of the angle.

were insignificant and the damage not great. Part of the coping of the structure was thrown down and fell in the street, causing one death and injuring another man. In a third building which was struck and considerably damaged, eight people employed there had wisely retired to the basement. The whole edifice rocked under the shock, and plaster fell on them, but they escaped without a scratch. The streets had emptied as soon as the firing began, so that there was no such slaughter as in the previous raid. A large party of school-children, four hundred in number, were sent in the very nick of time to the shelter of an Underground station. Much glass was broken in the City and the top floors of a few buildings were blown away. The poor districts suffered more severely. Buildings there were of a flimsier **Curious popular** type, and against them the Germans seem **illusions** to have used their special shrapnel bomb, designed to kill rather than to wreck structures. One of their most powerful bombs, however, fell in a poor street in the midst of a granite-paved roadway, and its blast shattered the fronts of half a dozen houses, flung people inside them down, and killed or wounded some victims. Yet even there the loss was smaller than might have been expected.

There were two curious illusions among those who watched the raid, which proceeded in the midst of a continuous air battle, as the British aeroplanes were in action throughout and, though outgeneralled, held most gallantly and devotedly to their work. The first was that the Germans were flying very low. Many even averred that they could see the pilots; few estimates placed them at over 7,000 feet, yet they were really at nearly twice that height, the immense size of the machines disguising the distance. The second was that they were almost stationary or proceeding very slowly, another result of the great height at which they were flying and the absence of objects by which to measure their progress. Just as in the air the machine when high up seems to the airman to be standing still and throbbing, while an air-blast of extraordinary violence plays on him, so from the ground the far-off German machines appeared motionless, and for the same reason that all our standards of movement depend on the relation to some object.

The heaviest loss occurred under an exposed archway, where ten people who had taken shelter were killed or wounded by a bomb which fell near them. Numerous fires were caused, but in no case were they serious. The railways and tramways maintained their services throughout the brief duration of the raid. About 10.40, or a little earlier, the raiders retired, still maintaining their excellent order, unshaken by either gun fire or the defending aeroplanes,

which they beat off as an elephant brushes off flies. The total casualties, including three killed and two injured in the Isle of Thanet, were:

					Killed.	Injured.
Men	..	..	..	..	42	98
Women	..	..	..	..	9	45
Children	..	..	..	..	8	50
			Total	..	59	193

The air fighting which accompanied this raid was of a peculiar character. There was no attack by the British in formation and in a large mass of machines. Individual airmen went up and showed marvellous courage and devotion, but without combination it was in vain. One heroic airman, Lieutenant M. A. E. Cremetti, was seen to charge right through the German formation, and then to turn and repeat his charge. Another officer who distinguished himself was Second-Lieutenant J. E. R. Young; he died gallantly in action for the women and children of London. In the words of his commanding officer:

Almost single-handed he flew straight into the middle of the twenty-two machines, and both himself and his observer at once opened fire. All the enemy machines opened fire also, so he was horribly outnumbered. . . . He never hesitated in the slightest. He flew straight on till . . . he must have been riddled with bullets. The machine then put its nose right up in the air and fell over and went spinning down into the sea from 14,000 feet.

His observer, who behaved with as magnificent gallantry, was also killed. In Kent, Second-Lieutenant W. G. Salmon attacked the Germans, but after firing forty-four rounds in a most intrepid onslaught, he was shot down and killed. His machine had the petrol-tank punctured and a control-wire hit, but it might have landed safely had not the pilot been wounded and rendered unconscious. In addition to these casualties, **Heroism of British** one British pilot was wounded. Besides **airmen** the two British machines shot down by the Germans, two fell and were damaged from other causes. At the mouth of the Thames one German machine was seen to drop. It had been engaged by Lieutenant Cremetti, and now it fluttered down and disappeared in the water, and the three men in it perished.

There was still the hope that the raiders would be caught at sea on their retreat by the naval machines from Dunkirk and other stations. An Admiralty report stated that the Germans were "chased by R.N.A.S. machines from this country, and engaged forty miles out to sea off the East Coast. Two enemy machines were observed to crash into the sea; a third enemy machine was seen to fall in flames off the mouth of the Scheldt. All our machines returned

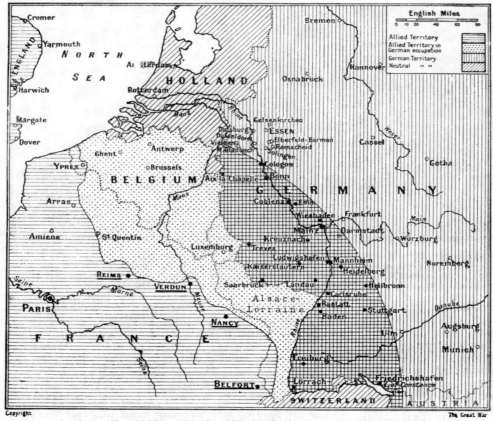

RANGE OF ALLIED AEROPLANE OFFENSIVE AGAINST GERMANY.
Map showing the German munition centres and fortresses which, in 1917, were within a radius of the allied line equal to that of the distance traversed by the Gotha aeroplanes to carry out their attacks upon London. The whole of that part of German territory marked in small squares was within this radius.

safely." The Dunkirk force was eluded by the Germans. The message received from "Vice-Admiral, Dover," dated Dunkirk, was an undoubted surprise and disappointment to the public :

On information being received that enemy aircraft were attacking England, five flights were sent up to intercept them as they returned. The raiding aircraft were not seen, but three enemy aeroplanes were encountered and destroyed, and one enemy aeroplane was driven down in the sea, and another enemy aeroplane driven down. The machines returned to replenish petrol and left again immediately. In the course of this patrol one enemy aeroplane was brought down in flames and another forced to land on the beach damaged near Ostend. During the course of their operations none of the enemy aeroplanes was encountered, and it is highly probable that they returned near the Scheldt and over Dutch territory.

The one fact which stood out from this report was that the British aircraft at Dunkirk had not been able to administer a severe lesson to the raiders. That the Germans constantly violated Dutch territory by passing above it was well known, but steps were not taken to close this line of retreat.

Disappointing report from Dover   The German report was again in entire variance with the British claims. Dropping the hypocritical pretence that only "the fort of London" was assailed, the German Staff said :

In the morning of July 7th one of our air squadrons attacked London. At about 11 a.m. bombs were freely dropped on the docks, harbour works, and warehouses on the Thames. Fires and explosions were observed. One of the English aeroplanes which went up in defence was shot down over London. Also at Margate, on the East Coast of England, bombs were dropped. Our aeroplanes all returned except one, which was compelled to make a descent in the sea, and could not be saved by our naval forces.

Thus, as against the British claim of at least four German machines disposed of, the German Staff only admitted the loss of one. It was perhaps just possible that both the British Admiralty and the German Staff were right, and that the machines which "crashed" into the sea and

the aeroplane which fell in flames over the Scheldt were able to effect repairs, but all the probabilities were against this.

The raid and the escape of most of the raiders caused great and intelligible public indignation. One sign of the feeling was a series of attacks on naturalised Germans in East London. There was a renewal of the demand for a really vigorous offensive in the air against Germany. The reasons given for not attempting this were that it involved serious risks for the British airmen, who had to fly overland where their movements could be followed and reported, whereas the Germans could make much of their journey over the sea ; that the British Army had not got sufficient machines ; and that it was "un-British" to drive home the war by bombing German towns. These excuses or arguments did not allay the strong feeling against a passive system of defence, and public impatience was increased by the discovery that the French Government could plan and could carry out with success measures which some British experts pronounced impracticable.

On the night of July 6th, not many hours before the German machines left for London, eighty-four French aeroplanes started to attack various German towns as reprisals for raids by German machines on French towns away from the front. The French authorities never permitted these to be bombed without retaliating in kind, and as the result French towns enjoyed a very large measure of security. French airmen dropped two and a half tons of bombs on the great military centre of Treves, where there were two enormous Zeppelin sheds, erected on the very eve of the war. Several fires were seen there, one in the Central Station. The important Rhine harbour of Ludwigs-hafen was bombed by another detach- **French airmen retaliate in kind** ment, and the huge factory of the Badische Aniline Company, where poison-gas was manufactured, was wrecked. Coblenz was also visited, with Phalsbourg and Thionville. One machine, piloted by Sergeant-Major Gallois, reached Essen and bombed it. The pilot described how the Rhineland and Westphalia were ablaze with the lights of towns and factories—evidence of the security Germany enjoyed as the result of her policy of attack and of always taking the offensive. From a height of 7,000 feet the airman dropped his bombs at the spot where the blaze of light from the Essen works was brightest. According to the Germans, only the most trifling damage was done and no injury of military importance was inflicted. That optimistic version was not confirmed by neutral evidence, and did not appear to be true. In this series of night raids the French lost only two machines—a practical comment on the British argument that such raids were either impracticable or too dangerous. The escape of the French was used by Mr. Lloyd George to excuse the British failure in punishing the German machines which raided England, but the Prime Minister overlooked the most important fact—that the German raids were made in daylight.

Between July 7th and 22nd there were no raids, possibly because the weather conditions were unfavourable.

On the 22nd, however, a force, variously reported as consisting of from fifteen to twenty-one aeroplanes, attacked the naval base of Harwich and the neighbouring watering-place of Felixstowe at 8.5 a.m. The weather was cloudy and hazy, and the Germans were only made out with difficulty when they were attacked by anti-aircraft fire. Many bombs fell on Harwich, yet nobody was hurt; at Felixstowe the results were more serious, and among the visitors and inhabitants several were killed or wounded. The attack took place on a Sunday, at the hour when early service was in progress in the churches. The raiders divided into two bodies, one of which speedily returned, probably because it had exhausted its bombs. The other passed down the Essex coast, dropping a few bombs. The total casualties were thirteen killed and twenty-six injured. On their retreat the raiders were pursued by British machines to sea, and a patrol of the R.F.C. encountered a party of them, engaged them, and stated that one of them was brought down and fell into the sea not far from the coast. There was no reference in the British reports to any attack by the Dunkirk aeroplanes on the Germans either going or returning. The German report declared that no machine had been lost. It asserted that "one of our air squadrons dropped bombs on Harwich with visibly good effect; the aeroplanes returned complete in number." It is therefore possible that the machine which was shot down managed after all to reach the Belgian coast.

Raid on Harwich and Felixstowe

This raid was noteworthy because it gave the occasion for the first trial of a system of warning London by rocket signals. Two hundred and thirty-seven rockets were discharged from the various fire-stations soon after the Germans passed the coast, and before it was certain or even probable that they were heading for London. The result of giving two hundred and thirty-seven warnings, spread over ten minutes of time, in place of no warning at all, was that many people in the capital supposed a raid was actually in progress, as the noise was nearly as great as that of actual gun fire. Unnecessary uneasiness was caused by this want of care, but the value of a warning far outweighed any inconvenience caused by such mistakes.

An interval of three weeks followed, during which the weather was uninterruptedly bad, and no aeroplane raids were attempted. But on the afternoon of August 12th the Germans delivered a daring attack. They selected for their raid a Sunday on which a high wind was blowing. The conditions, indeed, were stormy, and thick black clouds raced at intervals across a deep-blue sky, driven by a gusty, south-south-west wind. No attempt at a surprise was made; the raiders' intention was apparently to see what the British air forces could do when they were given ample warning. At about 5.15 that afternoon German machines were sighted almost simultaneously at two distinct points—approaching Felixstowe and off Margate. Off Margate three German machines were seen. Off Felixstowe the force of raiders numbered twenty. They were flying against the gale at a level of 12,000 to 14,000 feet in their customary formation, and, notwithstanding the strength of the wind, were maintaining admirable order. They were fired at by the local anti-aircraft guns without any visible effect, but they did no damage, and turned south along the coast to Clacton, some thirteen miles distant. There they split up into two bodies. One of about four aeroplanes steered south; the other of sixteen in formation moved towards London, and some minutes before six o'clock was above the little Essex town of Wickford. Here it turned, possibly because it had located British air forces barring its way to London, and steered east before the wind to Rochford, where a few bombs were dropped, and then to Southend.

Serious attack upon Southend

The experience of Southend was almost identical with that of Folkestone eleven weeks before. The police and

R.F.C. DESTROYERS OF L48.

Second-Lieut. F. D. Holder, M.C. (right) and his gunner, Sergt. S. Ashby, M.M., who were decorated for the part they took in the destruction of L48, one of Germany's super-Zeppelins, on June 17th, 1917.

THREE HEROES OF THE BRITISH AIR-DEFENCE.

Lieut. J. E. R. Young, R.F.C., who was killed while pursuing the Gotha machines that raided London on July 7th, 1917; and (centre) Captain R. H. M. S. Saundby, Royal Warwicks and R.F.C., awarded the Military Cross for his share in destroying the enemy airship L48 on June 17th, 1917. Right: Sec.-Lieut. W. G. Salmon, who, in an intrepid onslaught on the raiders of July 7th, 1917, was shot down and killed.

the fire-brigade had received warning that an attack was possible at 5.22, quite half an hour before the Germans arrived. No attempt was made to inform the people. The streets were crowded with a holiday throng. Very many women and children were on their way to the station.

There was no sign of danger. The evening was delightful. Then suddenly the heavy droning note of a mass of machines flying in formation was heard. The raiders were seen very high up in perfect order, and from the ease and precision with which they manœuvred were taken to be British. The people did not mark other isolated machines hanging on to the German formation and by spasmodic movements trying to break into it. These were the British aeroplanes, of which afterwards a large number was counted. But as they were not attacking in concentrated force their assaults were brushed aside, despite the magnificent courage of individual airmen. On the crowd suddenly rained bombs

AFTER AN AIR RAID.
Members of the National Motor Volunteers, with the permission of the police, arranged an effective method of making air-raid announcements. Their cars went out in all directions, bearing large notices of warning or reassurance. Rear view of a car with the "All Clear" signal.

from the German machines. The Kaiser told Mr. Gerard after the sinking of the Lusitania that no gentleman could kill so many women and children. The German airmen had even less trace of humanity and honour than his Majesty. No military purpose was to be served by this attack. There were no military works at Southend, as the German Command well knew. It was sheer slaughter. Here and there women and children were warned at the last moment to get under cover, but few received such warnings. The most of them were left exposed. In an instant the streets were full of smoke; shop-windows were blown in and the goods tossed into the streets and mingled with lamentably torn and wounded human beings. Five or six people, standing in one doorway, were killed on the spot. A little girl was torn to pieces. A mother with two babies left them outside a shop while she went in to make a purchase. At that precise moment a bomb fell, and when the smoke vanished the babies were mangled fragments of flesh. A well-known Great Eastern railway-guard, who had just come off duty, was killed.

Most of this loss could have been avoided if warning had been given and the people had been told what to do and where to go. These commonplace precautions were

AN EFFECTIVE WARNING.
Front view of a car of the National Motor Volunteers, showing the "Take Cover" warning. To draw attention to its message a couple of loud-sounding bells were attached to the front springs of the car.

neglected. Indoors the losses were small, though two persons were killed in a house which was demolished by a bomb that struck a chimney and buried several other persons. The survivors were rescued a little later. In Leigh seventeen houses were destroyed, there was much damage to property, and a very great quantity of glass was broken. The raiders drew off to sea, still in order, having suffered no loss and beaten off the attacks made on them.

In all about forty bombs were dropped on Southend. At Sheerness, which the raiders approached about 6.30, they were received with a heavy fire and withdrew without inflicting any damage, possibly because they had already dropped their bombs. In their attacks on Margate they did little damage. Four bombs were dropped, one of which hit an empty house and destroyed it. The total loss was 32 killed (of whom 22 were women and children), and 43 (of whom 30 were women and children) injured.

Gallantry of a R.N.A.S. pilot

It was apparently at this point that the Germans were attacked by a single British R.N.A.S. machine (not, as the British people had hoped to learn, by an overwhelming force of British machines). This pilot had already chased a German machine from the North Foreland to the neighbourhood of Zeebrugge, and was flying back when he observed firing at Southend, and proceeded thither, climbing. He must have covered nearly one hundred and fifty miles of sea. As he neared Southend he saw eight big German Gotha machines pursued by four British, steering north-east and flying high, 2,000 feet above him. He rose to 18,000 feet, and attacked without result, when he sighted one of the German machines 4,000 feet below the main German formation, but flying with it. He most gallantly attacked it from in front with such success that he drove it down into the water, where it capsized. One of the German airmen could be made out hanging to the tail. With singular humanity to the enemy, who had just perpetrated the butchery at Southend, he flung down a lifebelt to the German and made two or three circuits round him before returning. He also attempted to inform the British destroyers of the German's position and predicament. The loss of this machine was acknowledged by the Germans. Thus nineteen out of twenty machines escaped unhurt from this leisurely raid.

The Dunkirk air forces made no report, and seemingly saw nothing of the raiders either coming or going, or, if they sighted the Germans, failed to engage them with any result. One seaplane was brought down on this date on the coast of Flanders, but apparently it had nothing whatever to do with the force of raiding Gothas, which were aeroplanes not seaplanes.

On the morning of August 22nd, a fine day with a high southerly wind, a force of Gothas left the German bases in Belgium and, unmolested by the Dunkirk aircraft, proceeded to the British coast. Its strength was uncertain; the British War Office report placed it at ten machines when it reached Thanet; the report of "Vice-Admiral, Dover" stated it at twelve Gothas on its return, after three machines had been shot down. If his figure was correct, the German force was fifteen machines at the outset. It approached Thanet soon after ten o'clock and was at once attacked

 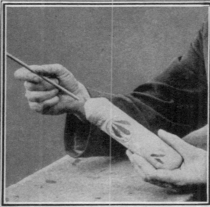

"SOUND-BOMB" WARNINGS IN LONDON AIR RAIDS.
Case of rockets, the firing of which was adopted in the summer of 1917 for warning London of imminent air raids by day; to the left of the photograph is the mortar from which they were fired. Right : Placing the time-fuse in a rocket.

by British aeroplanes and by anti-aircraft guns. The Germans were flying in formation at a height of 12,000 to 15,000 feet. Possibly their intention was to attack London. A fierce action was fought high in the air. Almost at once one of the German machines burst into flame and showed a streak of smoke from the petrol tank; it headed for the ground, but collapsed and fell just before the landing was made near Margate. Yet of the three men in it one was still alive. A second German machine nose-dived and fell into the sea, taking with it two of the men in it ; the pilot was rescued, slightly injured.

The remaining eight machines divided into two detachments. One steered for Margate; the other went south along the coast, by Deal to Dover. Four bombs were dropped at Margate, but little damage was done and no casualties were inflicted. Probably this detachment was the force which about 10.30 appeared over Ramsgate and dropped several bombs there with some effect. One large

Attacks on Ramsgate and Dover bomb fell near the harbour at a point where there were several shipwrights' stores excavated in the solid chalk under a road; it blew in the door of a store, hurling in stones and fragments of masonry, killing four men on the spot and terribly injuring another. A large area of glass in a nursery garden near the town was shattered, and some houses were damaged.

The detachment which bombed Dover was hotly engaged and did little mischief. Only four or five bombs were dropped before the Gothas retired, pursued by British machines of the R.N.A.S., which shot down one of the Germans near the coast. The raiders had again concentrated, and at this point numbered seven machines, which were now steering direct for the Belgian coast. A British R.N.A.S. pilot who chased them for some distance reported that he fired three hundred rounds into one of their machines, and that both gunners appeared to have been killed, as there was no reply even at twenty yards—a

distance which illustrated the closeness of the fighting.

The Dunkirk air forces did not intercept the Germans on their return. A weak detachment of three British machines "met twelve Gothas, thirty-five miles north of Nieuport and engaged them, chasing them to Zeebrugge, but with no decisive result," in the words of the official report. Another British patrol of ten machines from Dunkirk met and engaged twenty-five German escorting scouts which were waiting off the coast to support the returning Gothas. There was an indecisive action, in which the British claimed that five of the German scouts were "driven down completely out of control, and probably some more." This was a new development in the air war—the concentration of strong and efficient German forces to meet and support the Gothas when they came back, and when they might have been expected to be violently attacked by the British air forces at Dunkirk.

No British air losses were reported in the British official bulletin, and the number of casualties was stated at eleven killed and thirteen injured. The Germans only admitted the loss of two machines.

The rapid development of night flying by the German air forces in France was one of the characteristics of the summer campaign. The Germans from the very opening of the war had studied night work, and had arranged an excellent system of

FIRING THE WARNING SIGNAL.
The operator fired the rocket by pulling a lanyard attached to the time-fuse. In circle : Placing a rocket in the mortar ready for discharging.

CLEANING OUT THE MORTAR.
After the rocket was fired, the mortar had to be cleaned out ready for its further use. The rockets, or sound-bombs, were designed to throw out clouds of smoke, as visible signals, on exploding high in the air.

lighting for their landing-grounds. They constantly carried out experiments, and gave every scope to young officers with initiative and ideas. It thus became certain that London and the towns in the air danger zone of South-Eastern England would sooner or later have to meet night attacks. One special reason why the Germans practised them was that they deprived their foes of sleep, and thus lowered vitality and gradually affected

A TRUE BIRD'S-EYE VIEW.
Ruins of the Temple of Miletus, photographed from an aeroplane. Miletus was the southernmost of the Ionian cities built along the coast of Asia Minor.

there. Without any warning a number of bombs were dropped on the sleeping town and naval base. The British were taken completely by surprise, partly because it had been announced that anti-aircraft practice was to be carried out that night. The Germans made a complete circuit of the place and dropped seventeen bombs. One of these fell on one of the dormitories of the Royal Naval Barracks. The men had not been warned to take cover, and they were berthed in a shed, about as dangerous a place as could be found. This single bomb killed or wounded nearly two hundred men. "For s h e e r slaughter, in a small area," said a survivor who had served in the Grand Fleet, "it was worse than at the Battle of Jutland." Other bombs were dropped in Thanet without doing much damage or

nerves. The aim, as Professor Eltzbacher, a type of the German intellectual, wrote in "Das Grössere Deutschland," was "not only to interfere with the enemy's economic life but also to fill the hostile population with terror and dislike of the war." The German Command always kept psychology in view, which was a matter too little considered by the Allies.

Excellent opportunities for such air attacks were given by the fine moonlight nights of the late summer and early autumn, when flying conditions were at their very best. The first such raid, made at the end of the summer, was obviously intended as a test. About midnight on September 2nd a single German aeroplane crossed the coast and attacked Dover. The moon was full, the night was beautifully fine, and there was little wind. The airmen hurriedly

STRIKING CONTRAST OF FAR-SUNDERED AGES.
View taken from an aeroplane of the Greek theatre of Patinotiko, south of Miletus, the city where St. Paul preached to the Milesians. The portion seen of the plane of the flying machine of modern times forms a remarkable contrast with the crumbled masonry of the ancient city.

dropped six bombs and disappeared, having caused trifling damage, and killed one person and injured six. So far as could be learnt, no one saw the machine. One of the difficulties of defeating night raids was that aeroplanes were almost invisible or quite invisible when moving high and fast across the moonlit sky.

Heavy mortality in naval barracks

On the following night, September 3rd, there was a much more serious raid. Six aeroplanes crossed the coast at various points. Three steered for Chatham. The night was still and bright, with a magnificent moon, when a heavy droning, as from monstrous insects, was heard overhead. To the naked eye nothing was visible, but the sound of engines left no doubt that raiders were

causing loss of life. The disquieting fact was that the Germans had developed a new means of attacking, while remaining invisible and almost invulnerable themselves, and that as yet no remedy for it had been provided by the British, nor had precautions been taken to guard against it.

On the night of September 4th London saw its first large-scale night aeroplane raid. The weather was generally fine, and there was a bright moon, but there was much haze, and many banks of light cloud high in the sky sheltered the attacking aircraft. The Germans crossed the coast with about twenty machines, at 10.30, and travelled towards London in groups of two and three. Shortly before midnight in the capital

AIMING AT A DUMMY DREADNOUGHT.
German airmen practising bomb-dropping on a model of a British Dreadnought, which, according to the German description, was painted the exact colour of a British warship and at night-time carried the correct lights.

MACHINE-GUN ON GERMAN WARPLANE.
Striking photograph of the body of an enemy high-speed, high-power aeroplane, showing the position of the gunner and his revolving machine-gun, close to and at the rear of the pilot's seat. (From a German source.)

distant firing was heard at intervals, and then sounded the deep, disquieting buzz of the German machines. It was plainly audible over the greater part of London ; at times it was so loud that the invaders seemed to be very low. Yet nothing could be seen of them without instruments.

The sky was empty. The searchlights flashed their streaks of white light, but in their beams the Gothas—if they were Gothas and not smaller aeroplanes—could not be detected. Then sharp firing began. Undisturbed, the Germans dropped bombs in various districts which for reasons of national policy cannot be disclosed, and after the crashing of the bombs had ceased the droning died away.

Triple night attack on London It was only for a time, however. After the first attack came a second and a third, during which there was very little firing. The noise of the bombs could be heard above the occasional crack of the guns. The third attack took place about 2 a.m. Thus for rather more than two hours London was kept on tenter-hooks. The damage inflicted was small. The loss was eleven killed and sixty-two injured. Several lives would have been saved had people kept carefully indoors and shown less curiosity ; of those killed many were victims of the open door. They looked out to see what was happening, when a bomb fell in the street and a splinter struck them.

Numerous British machines were in the air during this series of attacks, but as they were usually not able to find the Germans, they could not shoot them down. One British airman, however, encountered a German machine at the closest quarters and emptied into it many rounds from his machine-gun, bringing it down. The loss was admitted by the Germans, but it was the only machine destroyed that night. After this attack the British were given a respite by a period of stormy and cloudy weather which intervened. It was remarked everywhere that, though the Germans had proved the safety with which night raids could be carried out, no effort was made by the British Government to counter these night raids by attacking German towns from the air.

Certain measures of passive defence were, however, taken to meet night attacks, and the methods which the Germans themselves applied on their front were studied. The night of September 24th ushered in the " harvest moon." The weather was again fine and favourable, and there was a tolerably brilliant moon. Early in the evening, just after dusk, seventeen German machines crossed the coast and steered for London. Shortly before eight the sound of guns at a distance could be heard, showing that the raiders were approaching. No formal warning had been given to the public, except in some districts of Central London, but almost everywhere it wisely got under cover on hearing the guns. A little after eight the distant firing increased in violence and the explosion of bombs could be very faintly heard. This was a first effort by the German machines to penetrate the London defences, and it apparently failed. About 8.30 came a second attempt. Suddenly the anti-aircraft artillery opened a fire of such violence as London had never dreamed of before. It was as though the devil was beating a terrific tattoo with giant hammers on vast plates of steel. Thirty or forty shrapnel or shells were in the air at the same moment. The din was deafening. Against the invisible enemy—who from time to time was

REMARKABLE PHOTOGRAPH OF AN ENEMY AEROPLANE.
View of a German biplane taken by an aerial observer as it passed beneath him. Wonderful work was achieved by the flying men in securing photographic data concerning enemy positions and movements, and also in obtaining definite knowledge of the damage effected by raiding-parties.

THE KING AND CAPTAIN HUCKS.
King George, visiting an aircraft factory in the London area, talked to many of the workpeople and chatted for some time with the well-known airman Captain B. C. Hucks, R.F.C., who gave an exhibition flight.

very faintly and indistinctly made out from buildings in the City, apparently flying in formation with dim, coloured lights on his machines—an invisible barrier of steel was set up by the British guns. It was awe-inspiring to watch the spectacle, and remember that on the issue of the struggle rested the lives of thousands of women and children.

The drum-fire rolled fiercely over London ; the German machines tried again and again to drive through it, but it was believed that only one, or at the most two, machines got past. The others recoiled from this curtain of moving steel and splinters, and retired, being attacked in their retreat whenever they could be made out by the numerous British machines. The few bombs which **Defence by shell curtain** were dropped by aeroplanes that worked past the curtain killed fifteen persons and injured seventy. Once again, nearly all the dead were the victims of the open door ; most of them fell just in or outside an hotel, opposite which a bomb dropped about 9 p.m., as the raid was nearly over. Some of the casualties may have been caused by the British fire.

After this vigorous engagement, by far the hottest so far of the whole air war over Great Britain, two questions remained to be answered. Was the curtain of shells an effective reply to the German attack ? Were the German attacks that night serious or only reconnaissances ? The answers could only be supplied by subsequent events, by the history of the raids that were still to come. But one fact remained evident. Nearly a month had passed since the night air raids on England began, and still Britain had not attempted to hit back. There was impatience and astonishment among the British Allies, and above all in the United States, where British prestige was adversely affected by this strange passivity. That machines were available for this purpose was plainly stated by General Smuts, on October 4th, 1917, when he said:

" It is wrong to think that we have hitherto had no means at all of carrying our aerial warfare into the enemy country."

This series of raids pointed strongly to the intention of the German Air Command to open a campaign of large-scale air raids on Great Britain, so soon as the necessary number of machines should be available. These attacks had, therefore, to be viewed as preliminary tests of the strength of the British defences ; they were greatly encouraged by repeated declarations, made by ecclesiastics, members of Parliament, peers, and pacifists, that in no circumstances would Great Britain attempt reprisals. The results were unsatisfactory enough when analysed :

Place.	Date.	Number of German Machines. Estimate. Highest. Lowest.		Machines claimed by British. "Destroyed" or "Shot down."	"Driven down."	Loss admitted by Germans.	British Casualties. Killed.	Wounded.
Folkestone	May 25	16	11	3	0	1	76	174
Sheerness	June 5	16	16	4	4	2	12	36
London	June 13	16	15	0	0	0	157	432
Harwich	July 4	14	12	0	2	0	11	36
London	July 7	22	20	4	0	1	59	193
Harwich	July 22	21	15	0	1	0	13	26
Southend	Aug. 12	23	20	1	0	1	32	43
Margate	Aug. 22	15	10	3	0	2	11	13
Chatham	Sept. 3*	6	6	0	0	0	108	92
London	Sept. 4*	20	20	0	1	1	11	62
London	Sept.24*	17	17	1	0	1	15	70
		186	162	16	8	9	505	1,177

* Night raids.

On September 2nd a single German machine attacked Dover at night, killing 1 person and injuring 6.

Of the total of between 162 and 186 machines which crossed the coast only 16 were definitely claimed by the British as destroyed (a proportion of slightly under 10 per cent.), and the loss of only nine was admitted by the Germans. The earlier attacks were made in broad daylight, in a zone where they were to be expected, where defending machines should have been numerous, and where, when the Germans were crossing the sea, there were many

GOOD COVER AT RAMSGATE.
Several hundred women and children sheltered at night-time from the German raiders in the chalk-pits at Ramsgate, where, twenty feet below the surface of the ground, they slept in absolute safety from bombs.

BUCKLING ON HIS HARNESS.

Men of the German Flying Corps helping a raider to dress for a bombing expedition to England. Thickly-padded body garments, special boots, and a shrapnel helmet were features of his kit. (From a German source.)

British vessels to observe and report them, or even to fire at them. Yet, at the most trifling cost to themselves, the Germans inflicted 1,600 casualties, heavy pecuniary loss, and distinct injury to British prestige. In the two most daring raids of all, and the most painful to British pride, only four of their machines were definitely claimed as destroyed by British airmen.

Little was heard of the Zeppelin during the summer, except for a report that the German airship factories had ceased turning out large rigid airships, which seems to have been true. Many Zeppelins, however, remained, and were gradually worn out in service or destroyed when they came into contact with the British forces. On June 14th Zeppelin L43, a very large and fast airship, was brought down by the British Navy at sea and its crew killed, though the exact conditions in which it was destroyed were not divulged.

On June 16th-17th a small number of Zeppelins crossed the coast of Kent and East Anglia. In Kent the raiders caused some damage, dropping six bombs, and killing three persons and injuring twenty. One airship was seen; it stopped its engines and remained for two minutes or so directly over a Kent coast town. It escaped, apparently uninjured, leaving behind it in the town the glow of a great fire.

Raids by Zeppelins

In East Anglia the raiders did not appear till it was almost dawn, when the noise of a Zeppelin was heard. Whether the airship was hit by the British anti-aircraft fire was not certain. The Zeppelin apparently stopped its engines or had them temporarily put out of action, and drifted for some minutes at a height of 11,000 feet. It was attacked by British aircraft. A thrilling encounter took place which could be watched far and wide; the flash of the German guns was answered by the flash of the weapons in two British aeroplanes, and then a red spark appeared in the cover of the Zeppelin. The airship dropped swiftly to the ground, stern foremost, while the flames spread.

With a crash it fell to earth in one mass of flame, but just before it fell three men contrived to leap out and to fling themselves clear of the blazing wreckage, and, though seriously hurt and shaken. survived the disaster.

The airship destroyed was L48, one of the latest super-Zeppelins, and was commanded by Captain Eschler. He perished in the wreckage, and was a distinct loss to the German air service, as he had taken part in numerous raids and was an expert in the art of air murder. The second-in-command, Lieutenant Mieth, escaped with his life and was able to walk away; he was, indeed, trying to make off when he was taken prisoner. Of the remaining two survivors, one had both legs broken, and the other one leg broken.

Four members of the Royal Flying Corps appear to have taken part in the most gallant and successful attack on L48, and received decorations for it: their names were Captain R. H. M. S. Saundby, Second-Lieutenants L. P. Watkins and F. D. Holder, and Sergeant Sydney Ashby. The name of a non-commissioned officer appeared for the first time in the roll of honour of the Zeppelin-destroyers. The Germans dejectedly remarked in their newpapers, after the loss of L48, that the plan of using Zeppelins for land raids was becoming questionable. For military work, in fact, the rigid airship was dead.

Nevertheless, when late in August a period of fine weather came, Zeppelins were again seen at sea. On the morning of August 21st one was caught by British naval forces off the coast of Jutland, and was at once engaged and destroyed with all on board. It was the third which during the summer had been brought down at sea by the British Navy. **Object of the raids** In the late evening of the same day three or four Zeppelins, acting apparently quite independently of the airship which had just been destroyed, appeared off the Yorkshire coast. One attacked at the mouth of the Humber but, being warmly received by anti-aircraft guns, retired to sea. One or two crossed the coast and dropped twenty-five bombs at three small villages near the coast, as the result of which one man was injured and several houses were damaged. On the night of September 24th two or three Zeppelins visited the Yorkshire and Lincolnshire coast and dropped bombs there, causing some slight damage and injuring three persons. They escaped uninjured.

The object of these raids was obviously to test the strength of the British defences and to divert as much force as possible from France. Thus Zeppelins were used to menace the zone which could not be reached by the Gothas. The secret of defence against both Gothas and Zeppelins was to be found in a vigorous policy at sea and in the air—by carrying out Nelson's famous last order: "Engage the enemy more closely."

PLUNGING TO HIS DOOM.

Striking photograph of the fate that befell a German air raider. His machine, shot down, plunged nose first into the North Sea, caught fire, and was consumed.

ROAD-PLANNING IN A DESTROYED FRENCH VILLAGE.

British soldiers "taping out" a road to be remade through a one-time prosperous village in France. The houses and villages close to the firing-line were reduced to mere mounds of builders' rubble, and the roadways were frequently no longer recognisable. Directly a village was reoccupied the work of road-making was begun —for on the roads depended the supply of munitions and food to the men who had pushed through and beyond.

THE REBUILDING OF RUINED FRANCE.

By F. A. McKenzie.

The Problem Awaiting France—Absolute Ruin—Arras and Dunkirk—First German Advance into France—Stories of Outrages—How the Emigrés were Received—Anticipating an Early Return Home—The Deepening Shadow of the "White Plague"—Statistics of Destruction—Under the German Heel—How the Retreat on the Somme was Planned—Systematic Destructiveness—Nothing Left Behind—Carl Rosner's Description—Protest by the French Government—What the Writer Saw—Destruction of Velu—The Plea of Military Necessity—Germany's Pledges in The Hague Convention—A German Time-Table—Resolution by the French Senate—Indemnification of the Proprietors—Immediate Relief of the People—Plans for a Better France—How Reconstruction was Financed—British Farmers Come to the Rescue—Reports by British Commissioners—Help from Canada—How Miss Daisy Polk Rebuilt Vitrimont—National Credit—M. Dariac's Report—Splendid Work of the French Army—Bringing the Land Under Cultivation Again—American Activities—The "Adoption" of French Towns—How French People Helped Themselves—The Society of Friends at Work—Evacuating Hospitals—Maternity Hospital at Chalons—Difficulties of the Sinistrés—Greater Tasks Yet Ahead—Could France Stand the Strain?—How France Would Triumph and Why.

IMMEDIATELY after the retreat of the German armies, following the Battle of the Marne, it became evident that France must enter on the work of the reconstruction of her regained territories. The Germans as they retired left many parts of the country in complete ruin. Here and there, notably at Amiens, no appreciable damage was done; the lives and private property of the citizens were respected and the public institutions left alone. Generally, however, villages were destroyed, farms burnt, cattle slaughtered, crops laid waste, bridges blown up, and often enough the leading inhabitants shot as hostages.

The work of building fresh homes and of restocking the land was undertaken at once by the French Government and by various philanthropic agencies, the British farmers, the Society of Friends, and Americans. As the war lengthened it became evident that the task of reconstruction would be more formidable than was first imagined. The long lines of the trench war, stretching from the Belgian frontier at Armentières to Alsace, became one broad swathe of ruin. The rival artillery of the opposing armies laid every town, every village, even every

IN THE RUINED CATHEDRAL OF ARRAS.
Interior of Arras Cathedral. View taken from the eastern altar, and showing something of the damage wrought in that edifice so long a centre of the severe struggle on the western front.
British official photograph.

hamlet, for a long zone about twenty miles wide, in ruin. This ruin was of the most absolute character that it is possible to imagine. The houses were wrecked and burned, mere fragments remaining. Hundreds of churches were reduced to the stage where nothing but four corner points marked the boundaries of the building. Many others were so levelled that the site of the churches could not be distinguished from the ruins of the houses. Special signposts had to be put up to mark them out so that their boundaries might not be forgotten. The fields were churned up by shell fire; the ground was so broken and the various layers of soil were so mixed and poisoned as apparently to make agriculture impossible. The forests were ruined, the old trees being chipped and torn by shrapnel and machine-gun bullets in such a way that they would eventually die. The zone of ruined farm land was not so wide as the zone of ruined houses, but it presented a graver problem, many of the fields seeming at first irretrievably destroyed.

The Germans, by the development in 1917 of special long-range artillery, carried ruin still further on the French side. Some cities, notably Rheims and Arras, had been within the range of their guns from the first, and these they had devastated. Rheims, one of the great historic cities of France, had before the war a population of 110,000. Its cathedral was among the foremost artistic treasures of the world, a building full of sacred memories for every Frenchman. Here it was that the French kings had been crowned for many generations. The cathedral formed the centre of a busy and prosperous population. Rheims was also the centre of the champagne trade of the world, the heart of the vine-growing country of France, and the home of a great woollen manufacturing industry. The German guns pounded Rheims day after day, week after week, month after month, till a city of flourishing industry became one great wreck.

Arras, the old Gallic capital and the home of mediæval chivalry, rich in traditions and in historic buildings, was treated in the same fashion. Albert, a flourishing little town on the Ancre, was another target for the German guns, the great golden Virgin which **Deliberate destruction** towered aloft on the church spire **by German guns** attracting their aim until they had forced it down from a perpendicular to a horizontal position. The hanging Virgin at Albert was an unforgettable sight to the hundreds of thousands of British soldiers who marched under it in the days of the fighting around that region.

Far behind the lines, French towns like Dunkirk became the victims of the long-range guns of the foe. First Zeppelins and aeroplanes flew over the town, dropping bombs, and then followed messengers of death from the big German guns twenty to twenty-four miles behind. Some of these guns, such as " Fat Bertha," had been cast in German foundries in the days before the war in order that they might be mounted on the heights between Calais and Boulogne to bombard Dover, Folkestone, and the country around. The Germans, foiled in this objective, took their revenge by concealing their titanic weapons somewhere in the dunes of Belgium and sending the shells occasionally into Dunkirk and into intermediate villages. At first, in the autumn of 1914, the people of Dunkirk looked upon their one or two ruined buildings as something of a curiosity ; but soon the shelling became a constant menace. Sometimes as many as four dozen monster shells would fall in and around the old French city in one day. Wherever a shell fell on a house that house disappeared. The inhabitants built themselves dug-outs and places of refuge in the main streets, to which they went at the first signal of bombardment ; but Dunkirk was being slowly and steadily destroyed.

The towns immediately behind the allied lines became overcrowded by vast numbers of refugees immediately after the first German advance into France. All who could do so fled before the German soldiery. The tales of outrage, of murder, of pillage which had preceded them sent terror into the hearts of the French **Pitiful plight of** civilian population. Old men, tottering **the refugees** grandames, and little children rushed off, abandoning homes and property and carrying their little all with them that they might escape with their lives. One of the most piteous spectacles in the winter of 1914 was the arrival in some of the towns occupied by the allied troops of these armies of refugees, footsore, hungry, broken, dressed in sombre garments, sometimes almost sinking beneath the load of their most prized household treasures. They were scrambling on through mud, mist, and rain to safety. Here was the great-grandfather of ninety helped on by his daughter, a grandmother of seventy. There was a woman with one babe in her arms, with two other children clinging to her skirts, stumbling, scarcely able to get along, crushed with weariness, and overpressed with grief. Her husband had been shot and her daughter worse than murdered in the village left behind.

What tales they had to tell—tales that they gasped out in the refuge that had been quickly arranged by pitiful souls still in safety ! Here was a workman, sixty-six years old, coming from Douy-la-Ramée. The Germans had set fire to a mill, and one rough soldier had seized him to throw him in the flames. He had struggled violently and had clutched on to a wall, until the soldier was weary of him. Then the soldier, becoming merciful, left him alone and did not shoot him. Here some people were bringing in a gentlewoman from the village of May-en-Multien. Some of the German cavalrymen had fired at her house. One of them had called for some wine. Her husband had hurried to get it ; but the soldier, impatient at the delay, had shot at the wife and wounded her badly. Her arm had been amputated. It was clear that she must soon die. Here were some other people from Courtacon, sodden with horror because of their experiences. One young man in their village had been arrested. The soldier had said he was a soldier, and if he was not, he ought to be. He belonged to the 1914 class. The mayor, examined by the troops, said that the lad had passed the medical examination, and that his class had not been called up. The Germans made the lad strip, saw that he was in good physical condition, told him to put his clothes on again, took him out, and shot him within a stone's throw of the other villagers. Here were women, the wives and daughters of decent citizens, broken by the worst of outrages. The refugees came back with hate and terror graven deeply in their hearts.

Sometimes these armies of refugees arrived at towns and villages occupied by their own kin. Then they were happy. For example, the people who escaped from the mining towns around Lens got back to Bruay—another mining town. Here their fellow-miners welcomed them with open arms. It was true that every house in Bruay was soon overcrowded, and that the normal population of 17,000 rose in a few weeks to 55,000, but everyone made the best of the new conditions. The refugees, however, were not always so fortunate. People from the Alsatian border flocked back **Problems of homes** to parts well out of their own country **and work** where they were among strange people —French folk like themselves, it is true, but people absorbed in the problems of their own affairs. These refugees, after the wave of emotion and tenderness had passed, found life by no means easy. Their new hosts expected them to pay, and to pay well, for their keep in meal or malt.

The position of these tens of thousands of refugees was one of very great difficulty. Many of them had a certain amount of money, for the French peasant is usually thrifty ; but money could buy them comparatively little comfort. Rooms were scarce and poor ; food was scarce and poor, too. The people of the districts that were flooded by these emigrés at first looked after them well, but goodwill for the stranger has its limits ; the French family in particular dislikes having strangers boarded on it. Rooms were let out at high prices. In some towns schemes were arranged for dealing with the emigrés by the thousand.

In the beginning many of these people were unwilling to take up fresh work. " What is the need ? " they asked. " Our armies will soon drive the invaders out again. We will soon be able to return home. Why make fresh plans and break up everything for no purpose at all ? " When the refugees were called on to fill up gaps caused by mobilisation there was some difficulty in persuading them to take work even in agricultural districts.

Here the Agricultural Syndicates, which play so large a part in the life of rural France, did good work. The Central Union of Agricultural Syndicates, working in connection with the Société des Agriculteurs, the organisation of great French landlords, planned on a wholesale scale to help the farmers to provide seed for spring sowing at the lowest prices, to bring in machinery where necessary, and to persuade the people from the ruined districts to settle to work on other land.

What one French soldier found on coming " home " : Wife and children alive, but all else gone.

General Pétain's Staff Headquarters during the final stages of the Battle of Verdun.

Rest and refreshment in the Forest of St. Germain for wounded soldiers from Paris hospitals.

French Chasseurs d'Afrique escorting German prisoners through the streets of a Flemish town.

British soldiers receiving hospitable welcome in billets in the war zone of France.

157

Spirited Frenchwomen tilling the soil for which all French manhood was fighting.

Peasant women reaped the harvest, staying work only to hush a drowsy child to sleep.

As months went on, this crowding of population, the difficulties in the food supply, the exposure to weather, the lack of proper accommodation, and the hardships the men were experiencing at the front led in turn to another problem which loomed greater and greater in the eyes of those responsible for New France. Tuberculosis, the "white plague," began to raise its head. In large sections of France, impoverished by the war, consumption increased with amazing rapidity. It seized the children, whose life of ample food and abundant laughter had been rudely interrupted. It grasped the young women, the mothers, the wives weeping for husbands gone, husbands who might never return, the children mourning for the absent father. It became more and more evident that no plans for the rebuilding of France after the war could leave out of sight the dire harm that this plague of armies and of nations could do.

Early in 1916 a French official commission was formed to ascertain the actual amount of the damage caused by the Germans, the number of houses existing before the war, how many of them had been destroyed, what public property had been injured, what factories and other industrial establishments ruined, and the like. This commission found that 3,554 communes in ten departments had suffered. Of these communes, 2,554 were still in German hands, and it was impossible to obtain any exact details of what had happened in them. The greater number of these were in the Departments of Nord (545), Aisne (569), and Ardennes (503). The whole of the Ardennes was occupied by the enemy.

A second division of 247 communes had been abandoned by the civil population because they were under enemy shell fire. There were 21 in the Pas-de-Calais, 27 in the Somme, 25 in the Aisne, 34 in the Marne, 88 in the Meuse, 39 in Meurthe-et-Moselle, 2 in the Nord, 10 in the Oise, and 1 in the Vosges. There remained 753 **Classification of** communes in which destruction had **communes damaged** taken place, but in which civil administration had been restored. These were divided thus: Nord, 23; Pas-de-Calais, 71; Somme, 34; Oise, 59; Seine-et-Marne, 35; Aisne, 51; Marne, 258; Aube, 2; Meuse, 59; Meurthe-et-Moselle, 109; Vosges, 53.

Thus, out of a total of 36,247 communes in France, 3,554 had been wholly ruined or partially damaged. It was only possible to obtain accurate details about the 754 communes that had been reoccupied. In 299 of these over half of the buildings had been destroyed. The total number of buildings injured was 46,263, of which 16,669 were completely destroyed, and 29,594 partly destroyed. The following table shows the destruction by departments:

DEPARTMENTS.				Completely.	Partly.	Total.
Nord	..	..	..	889 ..	2,838 ..	3,727
Pas-de-Calais	..	..	..	6,660 ..	6,792 ..	13,452
Somme	..	..	..	425 ..	1,527 ..	1,952
Oise	..	..	..	263 ..	324 ..	587
Seine-et-Marne	..	..	..	101 ..	185 ..	286
Aisne	..	..	..	93 ..	456 ..	549
Marne	..	..	..	3,499 ..	11,607 ..	15,106
Aube	..	..	..	30 ..	8 ..	38
Meuse	..	..	..	1,768 ..	679 ..	2,447
Meurthe-et-Moselle	..	..	1,685 ..	3,245 ..	4,930
Vosges	..	..	..	1,256 ..	1,933 ..	3,189
Total	..		..	16,669 ..	29,594 ..	46,263

Public buildings and monuments destroyed in the 754 communes included 221 town-halls, 379 schools, 331 churches, 306 other public buildings, and 60 works of art; 340 factories and industrial establishments had been dsetroyed which had formerly employed among them 57,633 people. Only 74 of these, however, were totally wrecked.

These figures, incomplete as they were, brought home to the world some realisation of the magnitude of the problem. The total value of the properties thus ruined was many scores of millions of pounds. But great as the destruction was in the reoccupied provinces, it was vastly greater in those communes that had been evacuated by the civil population because of proximity to the zone of fire. Of these 247 communes, the greater number were completely wiped out, and in many of them scarce one stone stood upon another, save a few crumbling and threatening walls waiting for their final shocks from artillery fire.

A further inquiry on the same lines as that of 1916 was made in the summer of 1917. A report issued late in July brought the figures of destruction up to date. It was then possible to obtain accurate details of the conditions in 1,223 communes. The actual total of communes from which the enemy had been cleared since the previous year was 499, thus reducing the total in German occupation from 2,554 at the end of May, 1916, to 2,055 at the end of May, 1917. The districts from which the Germans had been cleared were: On the Somme (182), the Aisne (152), the **Details of destruction** Oise (66), and the Nord (5). The Oise **in July, 1917** and the Somme had been entirely cleared of the enemy. The total of destruction in that time had enormously increased, as is best shown by the following figures:

			NUMBER OF HOUSES DESTROYED.	
			1916.	1917.
Completely	..	..	16,669	50,756
Partly	..	..	29,594	52,043
	Total	..	46,263	102,799

The figures of houses completely destroyed showed thus an increase of 204 per cent., and that of houses partly destroyed 75 per cent. The number of houses completely destroyed had been trebled. The increased destruction was chiefly found on the Somme and on the Aisne. The number of public buildings destroyed had risen in very similar proportion to 435 town-halls, 598 schools, 472 churches, and 377 other public buildings. Many of these places were reparable, but 136 town-halls, 170 schools, 118 churches, and 49 other buildings had been destroyed beyond all hope of repair. The total number of factories and industrial establishments destroyed had increased to 414.

What of the country still occupied by the Germans? This included some of the richest industrial areas of France. There was the big manufacturing region to the north around Lille, itself one of the greatest and richest cities of France. There was a whole succession of prosperous towns such as Valenciennes, Tourcoing, and Roubaix, in the Department du Nord. There was the rich agricultural Department of the Ardennes, with Charleville as its capital. There were the coal-mines around Lens, where a few hundred pounds of explosives might do harm that it would take years to repair. There were thousands of **Apprehension for still** factories. There were the rich districts of **occupied areas** the Meuse and of the Meurthe-et-Moselle.

When Germany was driven out of these, how would she leave them? Would she behave in accordance with the recognised traditions of war, leave civilian property unhurt, and confine herself to military action? Or would she continue to interpret war as she had already done in other parts, and destroy wherever she had power?

The answer to these questions was given when the Germans retreated in the spring of 1917 from their front on the Somme away beyond Bapaume and Velu. This retirement was carefully planned. The German position had become practically untenable after the vigorous offensive of the British armies, and the General Staff decided to fall back before a British advance, which was already well under way, might cut off the line of retreat. Before going, the Germans turned the entire countryside into a wilderness. The town of Bapaume, the centre of their position, at ordinary times a thriving country place, was wiped out. They removed all the metal work from the houses ; they burned, broke, and destroyed all that they could. They blew up prominent buildings, they wrecked streets, they went through house after house in an orgy of destructiveness. In every village, however small, they did the same, save where their retirement was hurried by the active advance of the British armies. Naturally they destroyed the railways, blowing up the lines, firing explosives under bridges, making the whole track as complete a wreck as possible. It is not surprising, either, that they did their best to destroy the magnificent new canal, whose splendid construction was at once a triumph of modern engineering and a glory of Northern France.

What, however, was utterly indefensible was the way in which the German troops before their departure wrecked and smashed everything that could give shelter or provide food for man. They levelled the villages where their own troops had found shelter for two years

Systematic destruction or more. They blew great chasms in the **by order** roads, and then they set about destroying houses. Sometimes the houses were too strong or too well built of stone to give way easily. Then in many cases they got hoists and pulleys, chained ropes around some of the joists and pillars of the buildings, and pulled with engine or horse teams until the whole collapsed. This destruction was systematic. It was done as part of the avowed German system to leave nothing behind that could be used by the advancing enemy.

The Germans made no secret of what they had done. The military correspondent of the Berlin " Lokalanzeiger " described the work in the issue of that paper of March 18th, 1917 :

> A great stretch of French territory has been turned by us into a dead country. It varies in width from 10 to 12 or 15 kilometres (6¼ to 7½ or 9 miles), and extends along the whole of our new position, presenting a terrible barrier of desolation to any enemy hardy enough to advance against our new lines. No village or farm was left standing on this glacis, no road was left passable, no railway track or embankment was left in being. Where once were woods there are gaunt rows of stumps ; the wells have been blown up, wires, cables, and pipe-lines destroyed. In front of our new positions runs, like a gigantic ribbon, an Empire of Death.

Carl Rosner, a German writer, in another issue of the same paper, gave a graphic description of what had happened. " We came," he wrote, " upon the Empire

[British official photograph.
MATERIAL FOR ROAD REPAIR IN FLANDERS.
Accumulating road metal ready for road repairs during the advance east of Ypres in 1917. The making up of the roads in reoccupied territory, necessary for lines of communication, was a valuable step towards the regeneration of the devastated country.

[British official photograph.
MAKING GOOD THE HIGHWAYS OF FRANCE.
British soldiers at work repairing the road through a reoccupied village on the western front. The ruined buildings shown in this photograph convey some idea of the devastating power of the guns.

of Death . . . that broad zone of devastation which stretches from the Scarpe to the Aisne :

> A year back and earlier I was so often in this country—and I do not know it again. The war has set its mark upon it. Old giant trees once stood here on either side of the road—they are no more. There were houses by the road and farms. There is nothing left of all that, and nothing of the bloom and prosperity of the countryside. As far as the eye can see the land is bare and desert, a uniform, forbidding, open field of fire, through which the ribbon of road we are following runs as a last remnant of extinct civilisation. And even the road will only give passage for a few days longer across the desert. At the crossways it is mined. . . .
>
> Troops meet us on the march and waggons piled high with the men's kit and properties. They have packed up at the front and have left those who will succeed them in the abandoned places nothing, nothing whatever, not a tub, not a bench. And what they could not take with them they have burnt or smashed. They have blown up behind them the shelter in which they had lodged ; they have filled up or made undrinkable the wells that gave them water ; they have destroyed the lighting and set the barracks on fire. . . .
>
> Any piece of wall that still stands after the burning, is blown up or battered down by engineers. The enemy, when they come, shall not find here so much as a miserable half-burnt wall to shelter them from the wind. Even the cellars have been blown up. But all this is not the work of **In the " Empire** a few days ; it was carried out systematically **of Death "** for weeks and months on end—it had to take months, if it was to pass unnoticed by the enemy. A zone of burning villages would have shown the enemy airmen in a flash what was afoot. No, one village was burnt somewhere one day, and the next day, if the weather was hazy and there was low visibility, two more somewhere else went up in smoke and flames. For the final days nothing was left but what was needed up to the last moment for the accommodation of the troops. And now the sorry remnant goes to ruin, that this stern work of destruction may be complete. . . .

In a formal protest to neutral Powers the French Government described the situation :

> Whole towns and villages have been pillaged, burnt, and destroyed. . . . Private houses have been stripped of all their furniture, which the enemy has carried off ; fruit trees have been torn up or rendered useless for all future production ; springs and wells have been poisoned. The comparatively few inhabitants who were not deported to the rear were left with the smallest possible ration of food, while the enemy took possession of the stocks provided by the Neutral Relief Committee and intended for the civil population.

It was the business of the writer of this chapter to travel over a large section of the recovered country a few weeks after the German retreat. It was still a land of the dead, mile after mile without any sign of life. The very trees were burned and broken, limbless, leafless, and black. In most of them, although it was high summer time, there was not a bird, for there was nowhere for birds to nest and nothing for them to feed on.

After travelling about five miles along the abandoned fronts one came on a wild cat tearing through some wires. Two miles farther on a raven fluttered overhead. Innumerable trenches, British and German, ran across the old roads. They had been hastily filled in, but the boggy earth made hard going. Big piles of German ammunition were still grouped on the roadsides. There were miles with vast masses of wire entanglements still untouched, and everywhere there were crosses marking graves, the graves of the German dead.

After a time the villages were reached, most of them still wholly deserted. Here were ruins, fantastic, gruesome, wholesale. Everywhere could be seen fine agricultural machinery smashed beyond repair, and piles of broken stones that once were homes. The **Scenes of gruesome,** villages were much worse than merely **wholesale ruin** swept away. They were left in a state of destruction which would mean immense work to clear. The countryside was full of unexploded shells and bombs, many to burst when the ploughshare of the farm-hand first struck them.

One typical village, Velu, some way beyond Bapaume, stood as a specimen of many. It was surrounded by woods recalling Fontainebleau. There was a great château here which had the reputation before the war of being the second most beautiful country-house in France. A long avenue led to it, and beyond it was a great straight road through the forest as at Versailles. The house itself was quite modern. The original building, erected by the Marquis de Couronnel in 1719, had been restored by the Baron Goer de Hervé **Typical example** in 1883. It was built in one long front, **at Velu** with the house on one end, the stables, the motor-houses, the domestic quarters, and the extensive gardens on the other.

When they swept over this country early in the war the Germans used the château as a hospital. They made the sloping lawn to the side of the house a cemetery for their dead. When they had to retire before the advancing British forces they blew up the entire building. They went through the gardens, destroying everything in sight. The main garden had been devoted to a very fine selection of fruit trees. Its central avenue had an archway of espaliers. The old red walls were covered with branches of fruit trees. In an outer garden was an orchard of standard trees. The trunk of every bush, without exception, had been cut or broken across. Sometimes a clean cut through was made by a fine saw. Sometimes the trunk was hacked in half. Sometimes it looked as though a special kind of giant nippers had been employed. Apples, peaches, pears, a monster grape-vine, nectarines, apricots, and plums all shared in the common fate. Men had gone to work deliberately, systematically, thoroughly

IN A ONE-TIME BEAUTIFUL TOWN OF CHAMPAGNE.

Ruins of Souain, on an ancient Roman road about twenty-four miles to the east of Rheims. This once beautiful town of the famous Champagne district, which had been the scene of much severe fighting, was reduced to mere remnants of walls and battered heaps of rubble. A few miles to the south-east of Souain was Valmy, where the French Revolutionists inflicted a severe defeat on the Prussians in 1792.

to leave no tree alive.   What happened at Velu happened also in scores of villages around.

The Germans attempted to justify this destruction on the plea of military necessity.   The best answer to this plea was found in The Hague Convention of 1907, to which Germany herself had given her solemn adhesion.   In it rules were laid down for the guidance of military authorities occupying the territory of an invaded State. Here are some of them :

The false plea of military necessity

Art. 46.—Family honour and right, the lives of individuals and private property, as well as religious convictions and the observances of public worship, are to be respected.   Private property cannot be confiscated.

Art. 47.—Pillage is explicitly forbidden.

Art. 55.—The occupying Power must consider itself only as the administrator and temporary recipient of the income arising from the public buildings, house property, forests, and agriculture of the enemy State within the occupied territory ; it must safeguard

[French official photograph.

COUP D'ŒIL OF RUINED COMBLES.

Outlook over Combles, about eight miles east of Albert, from a hole in the wall of its destroyed church.   The village was captured after very severe fighting on September 26th, 1916.

the funds of these properties, and administer them in accordance with the rules of usufruct.

Art. 56.—The property of Communes and of religious establishments dedicated to worship, charity, education, and the arts and sciences, will be treated as private property even when these institutions belong to the State.   All seizure, destruction, or wilful dilapidation of such establishments, of historic buildings, of works of art or of science is forbidden, and should be punished.

To this may be added these words from the preamble of the Convention :

In cases which do not come under the regulations adopted by the Powers, populations are under the safeguard and governance of the principles of international law as manifested in the customs established between civilised nations, the laws of humanity, and the demands of public conscience.

A German table of work, discovered at Bancourt, a village east of Bapaume, gave instructions to the troops how they were to carry out their work :

In the village of Bancourt, it is more important to set fire to the houses than to blow them up.

March 5th.—Straw will be heaped and tarred.

March 10th.—Explosives are to be ready for the cellars and walls in Bancourt.

March 11th.—All unused wells and watering ponds must be plentifully polluted with dung and creosote soda.   Sufficient dung and creosote soda must be placed in readiness beside the wells which are still in use.

March 12th.—Bancourt must be ready to be set on fire.

March 13th.—Parade in fighting kit, issue of iron rations, cleaning of arms, instructions regarding safe roads to be used and instructions for the demolition party.

March 14th.—Explosives to be issued for destroying the cellars and wells in Bancourt.   Bancourt church tower will be blown up.

March 16th.—All wells in Bancourt, with the exception of one, will be blown up by 5.30 p.m.

March 17th.—The road mines will be fired at 3 a.m.   The remaining cellars in Bancourt will be blown up at 3.15 a.m., and Bancourt will be set on fire at 4 a.m.

Formally on various occasions the French Government expressed its condemnation of the criminal acts of Germany on French territory.   On March 31st, 1917, a resolution was proposed to the Senate :

Denouncing to the civilised world the criminal acts committed by the Germans in the regions of France occupied by them, crimes against private property, against public buildings, against the honour, the liberty, and the life of individuals ;

Recognising that these acts of unparalleled violence have been perpetrated without the excuse of military necessity of any kind, and in systematic contempt of the International Convention of October 18th, 1907, ratified by the representatives of the German Empire ;

Holding up to universal execration the authors of these crimes, the stern repression of which is demanded by justice ;

Offering respectful sympathy to the victims, to whom the nation gives a solemn pledge, for which it will itself be guarantee, that they shall obtain full reparation from the enemy ;

Affirming more resolutely than ever the determination of France, supported by her admirable soldiers, and in concert with the Allied Nations, to carry on the struggle that has been imposed upon her, until such time as German Imperialism and Militarism, which are responsible for all the misery, ruin, and mourning heaped upon the world, have been finally crushed.

In the debate on this resolution, which was carried unanimously, numerous details were given of the destruction that had been wrought in France.   Senators who had gone over the country examining it declared that the truth of what they had seen was in itself so horrible that nothing could be gained by exaggerating it. " Everywhere we have been witnesses of the same appalling sights : the results of pillage, systematic destruction, and acts of barbarity committed without the slightest excuse on the grounds of military necessity. . . . What we have recorded are the acts of violence perpetrated in cold blood among an unarmed population for the sake of **Things seen by French senators** evil, pillage, destruction of private property, of public buildings, outrages on the lives, liberty, and honour of individuals, all things which ought to be denounced before the whole world if only to stigmatise the dishonour for all time of the accursed race and régime which claim to dominate other nations and impose on them their culture."

The Chamber of Deputies voted in favour of a resolution affirming the principle that all losses suffered by the people of France through the invasion of the country by the enemy must be fully indemnified ; but full indemnification affirmed in principle was one thing, to reinstate the people was another.   While the Senate and the Chamber of Deputies were busy recording the facts, State and private enterprise were at work tackling the problem of reconstruction.

This problem had two aspects.   First, immediate needs had to be met—fresh stock on the land, new buildings, temporary or permanent, in which the people could live, and restoration in the shortest possible time of the activity of all industry.   The numbers of people in various cities who were now crowded together as refugees among strangers had to be started afresh at work with the least possible delay.   Then came a second aspect—of reconstruction, which France and her friends could not afford to overlook.   Hundreds of the villages and farmsteads which had been destroyed were survivals of mediæval times.

A rural suburb of Arras while a heavy bombardment was in progress. Arras, once a quaintly picturesque French town, was almost wiped out of existence by gun fire during the battles to which the place gave a name in the spring of 1917.

The ruined church of Tracy-le-Val as it was in August, 1917. This old and once beautiful building stood four or five miles from Ribécourt, quite close to the German positions on the line from Albert to Ribécourt, held by them up to the Allies' advance in July, 1916.

RUIN IN PICARDY WHEN DELIVERED AT LAST FROM THE INVADER.

They had been planned and built in days when sanitation was unknown. There was usually a great midden in the centre of each farm, a vast dung-heap with buildings surrounding it on the four sides, save for one entry way. The very drinking-water supply for men and beasts was often poisoned by the overflow of the cesspools. The narrow village streets were full of festering pools. The houses were ill-drained or not drained at all. The water supply was as bad as it could be. The fact that so many survived under such insanitary conditions was best proof of the stubborn vitality of the French people. Here was an opportunity, which French sanitarians—among the foremost in the world—

Opportunity for permanent improvement immediately recognised, to make a better France. What applied to the country villages applied with tenfold force to the older sections of the great towns. Reconstruction here meant not the reproduction of the old conditions, but the building up of a new section of France where all the latest developments of knowledge in building construction, of comfort, and of health should be utilised to the full. This meant that in most of the places at least the immediate reconstruction must be temporary, awaiting the full development of carefully devised national plans.

The French Government itself determined to take the ultimate responsibility for the cost of constructing the buildings. Long-term bonds were to be issued, not only in France but in allied and neutral countries, to pay the cost of rebuilding—a cost which, it was hoped, would eventually be reimbursed by a heavy war indemnity from Germany. Almost as soon as the armies advanced in their reconquest of French land from the Germans the tide of peaceful life advanced also. Districts that had been abandoned were reoccupied. The Army cleared up the main litter of war, the barbed-wire, the heaps of shells, the broken debris, and in a few months land which at first appeared irreclaimable began to blossom again.

The French Department of Agriculture enlisted the services of farmers throughout the uninvaded territories of France to help to restock the wasted land wrecked by the Germans. Fresh cattle, poultry, and pigs were quickly brought in, horticultural experts were set to work on the broken trees seeking to save them, and agricultural implements were obtained wherever possible. New trees were planted in place of those that had been cut down, and numbers of emigrés and sinistrés were put again to work.*

The French Minister of Agriculture received valuable immediate aid from the farmers of the United Kingdom. In the war of 1870-71 the Royal Agricultural Society organised a relief fund for the war-ravaged districts of France. Soon after the outbreak of the Great War similar work was begun again under the Agricultural Relief of Allies Committee. This body, initiated by the Royal Agricultural Society of England, announced its purpose of assisting in the restoration of agriculture that had been ruined by the war in the countries of our Allies.

A representative committee was formed in almost every county, consisting of numbers of agricultural societies, farmers' clubs, farmers' unions, chambers of agriculture, breeds societies, and other bodies con-

Agricultural help from Britain nected with the land. The King was patron, the Duke of Portland president, and some very active county gentlemen took the direction of affairs, notably Mr. James McRow, hon. secretary; Mr. Charles Adeane, hon. treasurer; and Mr. Frank F. Euren, well known as organiser of the Horse Shows at Olympia, hon. assistant secretary. The committee did not confine its work to France, but covered all the allied countries in distress, so far as circumstances permitted. It organised "jumble" or gift sales throughout Great Britain. Farmers and others gave stock and gifts in kind which were

---

* By emigrés was understood people who had been driven from home by the German invaders. Sinistrés were those who, although they had suffered from the German invasion, had yet managed to remain in their own districts.

put up to auction. It sent deputations to France to inspect the recovered country to see what could best be done.

One of the first of these deputations consisted of Lord Northbrook, Mr. Anderson Graham, and Mr. Adeane. They visited some of the more devastated districts in the Departments of the Marne and the Meuse in the summer of 1915. The committee found that the worst they had heard did not exaggerate the grievous condition of affairs. They were emphatic in their praise of a people who, in spite of danger and ruin, had courageously cultivated their lands. "They are reticent, uncomplaining, and dignified," wrote Mr. Adeane. "Not once were we asked for anything by the peasant proprietors of La Champagne, but assistance they must have."

Time after time after this fresh deputations were sent to France. They all came back with the same account of the courage of the people and of the hardness of their lot. The prospect that caused the most uneasiness was the condition of the land after the sustained artillery firing along the front. Sir Herbert Matthews dealt with this in a statement in " Land and Water " after one visit:

The remark has often been made that an enemy army may burn every house and building, burn all crops and implements, drive away all the live-stock, and massacre many of the inhabitants, but they cannot permanently damage the soil. The part of the battle area of the Somme that we saw is a contradiction of that statement. The surface soil has largely disappeared. Originally it consisted of a thin chalky-clay over pure chalk, intermixed with beds of loam over gravel. Now the general displacement by trenching, shell-pits, and mine-craters has so churned up soil and subsoil that levelling will leave a surface mainly of chalk. How long Nature will take to cover this with enough to sustain vegetation, even if aided by the usual operations of husbandry, it is difficult to say, but it does not appear commercially feasible to redeem this area. If the primary work of levelling be carried out by troops, or by prisoners, the cost reckoned as military outlay, and not as a charge on the land, it might possibly be planted with beech or other forest **Alteration of** seedlings, and developed as a Government **soil formation** undertaking; but the fates forbid that any individuals should be compelled to try to wring a living from such ground. How far this soil formation extends could not be ascertained, as we were not allowed to go farther.

The deputations, having seen the need, set to work to stir the sympathies of the British farmers. They did not confine their appeal to Great Britain. The Dominions, notably Canada, co-operated with them; and Dr. J. W. Robertson, formerly Commissioner of Agriculture for the Dominion of Canada, and perhaps the most distinguished of all Canadian agricultural authorities, organised that Dominion on their behalf. South Africa, Australia, and New Zealand rivalled Canada. The slogan throughout the British Dominions was:

THE FARMERS OF OUR ALLIES
HELPED TO SAVE *YOU.*
WILL YOU HELP TO SAVE *THEM?*

The British farmers particularly devoted themselves to the provision of stock and machinery for the French farmers, leaving the question of rebuilding to others. They determined to provide the best possible stock. Thus the thousands of heads of poultry that were sent out were each of them in breeding pens of four pullets and a cockerel of good strain that should be a foundation of a new and excellent stock of poultry. It was the same with the cattle, with the pigs, and with the seed. What was worth doing at all was worth doing well, and the British farmers tried to do well. Many men gave the pick of their stock; others bred specially for France.

The list of stock and goods sent by British farmers up to the summer of 1917 is a very plain record of what really was a very romantic and splendid endeavour. The relief was distributed by the French Government itself through permanent official agricultural inspectors. The quantities sent to the Marne and the Meuse included 61 rams, 11 boars, 2 goats, 20 binders, 6 threshing-machines, 40 harrows, 50 ploughs, 20 cultivators, 15 drills, 5 tons of binder twine, 2,500 head of poultry, 800 sacks of seed wheat, 2,000 sacks of seed oats, and 900 sacks of seed potatoes. One useful gift was an enormous number of Scottish pine-trees to replant the ruined forests.

An enterprise of a different kind, touching a smaller area but admirable in its way, was undertaken by a Californian Society under the direction of Miss Daisy Polk, of San Francisco. Miss Polk went to the ruins of the village of Vitrimont, near Nancy. In August, 1914, the Germans secured possession of this place for forty-eight hours. They had bombarded it previously, blowing half of the sixty or seventy farmhouses or cottages to pieces. Before they were driven out they set every house on fire, leaving the whole village in complete ruin. When the villagers returned after the Germans had gone out they found nothing but crumbling walls, charred woodwork, and desolation. The outlook appeared hopeless. Then came the American women. They had money, but money alone could not solve their difficulties. It was very difficult to obtain labour, and there was a lack of material. They naturally desired, while observing the wishes of the owners, to make a better Vitrimont than ever before. They set out over this small area to wipe out the traces of the war.

The architect, herself a woman, prepared plans for farms and cottages to be rebuilt almost on the old foundations and in the old style. The middens were to be removed and placed in yards at the rear of the houses. **American women's work at Vitrimont** Alterations were to be made in the way of giving more air, in making the place healthier, and improving the drainage and slightly rearranging the public buildings, such as the schools, so as to make them more convenient. All these things had to be done tactfully, for the French peasants are conservative and resent change. The work was a great success. Before many months the whole aspect of the neighbourhood was transformed. Little houses, temporary structures, gave way to more permanent buildings of grey stone, roofed with red tiles in the old fashion. The work of these American women, while limited in extent, was very thorough over the district it embraced.

The Government announced its intention of allowing the people in the ruined villages 40 per cent. of the cost of reconstructing their houses and in lending them the balance of the money at an easy rate of interest.

The Department of Agriculture in France did magnificent work. A credit of twelve millions sterling was used for advancing loans to farmers who had returned to their liberated communes ; but this was not enough, and the Government demanded greater supplies. A Budget Committee considered this demand, and a report was drawn up by M. Dariac, Deputy of the Orne. " The time has now come for greater efforts," declared M. Dariac.

The agricultural region which has to be restocked and refitted was one of the most prosperous in the country. There will be need immediately after peace is signed for seeds, manure, cattle, a need varying **Agricultural** according to the season of the year when **Department's Report** hostilities cease, by the manner of the enemy's evacuation of the territory, and by the state in which the fields and crops are left. Certain wants will need to be met at once, such as cereals for human food, draught animals, seeds, and manure. Other provisions can be spread over a period of several months or even years. For example, it is evident the building up of the live-stock will move along with the building of the barns and stables and the tillage of the land, and will depend upon the cattle available from the breeding centres.

M. Dariac estimated that to begin the restocking of the farms a minimum of at least 120,000 horses, 300,000 head of cattle, 100,000 sheep, and 100,000 pigs would be needed.

" The most important work," continued the report, is to clear the surface of the soil of unexploded shells, of stakes, wire, and other material, and to fill the trenches and pits. This is in the hands of the engineer and artillery services, and a beginning has already been made at certain points (Tracy-le-Val). Subsequently a special service will be created for the purpose of getting the soil ready for cultivation. Engineer and artillery officers, State functionaries, representatives of the Ministries of Public Works and Agriculture, will collaborate to this end. In order to avoid accidents arising from the explosion of shells and other missiles hidden under the surface, and susceptible of being turned up by the ploughshare, it will be necessary to carry out a series of investigations. A sub-section of the Inter-Ministerial Committee has already considered the merits of certain machines for discovering buried explosives.

FROM ONE FIELD OF SERVICE TO ANOTHER.
Ploughing on a French farm in war time. The ex-soldier who was leading the patient bullocks that dragged the share through the yielding earth had been crippled when fighting the invader at the front, and had returned to the work of cultivating the soil. This work was as essential to the final victory as that of the trenches, and as the tide of war receded efforts were begun to win back the land to cultivation.

In the area regained by the French Army in the spring of 1917 the Germans had felled over 32,000 valuable fruit trees. In the 243 evacuated communes the French found a population of over 35,000 old men, women—mostly women with families of children to look after—and children under fifteen. Two-thirds of these people remained in their villages and endeavoured to restore them. The remainder had to be removed to the interior of France. Then the soldiers and the civilians set to work. One hundred of the communes were nothing but heaps of stone and bricks, without a habitable room or cellar among them; of the remainder, one-third were largely demolished and the rest only slightly. The military authorities promptly organised the country and its people.

In this work they were assisted by a number of British and American volunteers. First food was brought in through the military commissariat. Then the question of cultivating the 250,000 acres of agricultural land was tackled. It was late in the season. Save for one small section, this land, once among the richest in France, had been neither ploughed nor sown. It was the end of March before a beginning could be made. There were no draught animals. The Germans had taken them all. But horses were lent by the Army.

Officers of high rank were placed in charge. The recovered country was divided into seven sections. These sections were again sub-divided. The Army mechanics repaired the broken ploughs, and tractors and seeds were imported. Everyone who witnessed the work declared that the French officers showed the most amazing ingenuity and resource in utilising the machinery still left. At one place thirty American tractors were found lying idle in a depot not far from the stricken district, and were at once pressed into service.

The officers in command of the districts had each of them an agricultural expert, an architect, and about forty military engineers at their service. In addition, they were able to call upon the troops to help them. The local officials, the mayors **Resource of** of the communes — where they were **French officers** left—worked hand in hand with the Army. Soon ploughing was begun. It was thought that there would be many accidents, because of the presence of unexploded shells in the ground.

But, happily, only one actual explosion took place. By the latter part of May close on 4,000 acres had been ploughed and sown, and another 2,500 acres ploughed and cleared. Every family had been provided with seeds and roots to form a kitchen garden. All the litter of war was cleared up as quickly as possible.

The problem of shelter for the people was promptly tackled. In the 243 villages which had been completely destroyed wooden huts were erected, and the military engineers set to work to rebuild more permanent structures from the wrecks of the old houses. Schools were opened, Army doctors looked after the sick, and everything possible was done to restore normal life.

The American people as a whole revealed the keenest desire to help France. The bonds of sympathy between the two nations had always been strong since the days of the Revolutionary War. Thoughtful Americans realised how much they owed to the land of Lafayette and Rochambeau. Even while America was yet neutral, American airmen volunteered their services as fighting flyers for France. The American ambulances did splendid work with the Army, and the Rockefeller Commission investigated in the most thorough manner the problem of tuberculosis among the French people. The American Red Cross, reorganised to meet the new conditions imposed on America when she entered the war, promptly sent a commission to France to consider how best America as a whole could help. This Commission for a start arranged for the unification of all the different American charities in France in order to prevent overlapping. It

IN A CAVE CANTONMENT NEAR VERDUN.
French soldiers and their horses in one of the grottoes of La Falouse, near Verdun. Among the hills around that famous fortress were many such picturesque places, utilised by the heroic defenders who added new glory to the fame of Verdun and of France.

devoted the summer of 1917 to an inquiry into the best means of turning American sympathy into such channels as would serve France most effectively. Among the many American activities, different cities each pledged themselves to take care of one French city that had been ruined, to rebuild it as soon as war conditions permitted, and to give its people a fresh start. Thus the city of Philadelphia pledged itself to "adopt" Arras; the city of Washington "adopted" Noyon; and Detroit declared that it would make itself responsible for Soissons.

Every bit of practical assistance given by outside peoples was rendered doubly beneficial by the helpfulness and practical common-sense of the French people themselves. Even those who had had their own properties largely destroyed still found the will and the heart and the means to help those poorer than themselves. A correspondent of the "Times" described one case: "There is a completely ruined little village which has found a fairy god-mother in a kind-hearted French-woman, Mme. de Chabannes, who was made prisoner by the enemy in Maubeuge, where she was acting as a nurse at the beginning of the war, and has since been decorated with the Croix de Guerre. Her plan has been to replace the vanished cottages with portable buildings easily and q u i c k l y erected, and, given all the circumstances, that is probably as good a method of encouraging and facilitating the present repopulation of these wasted districts as can be devised."

The Society of Friends undertook work on a very wide scale for both the relief of suffering and the rebuilding of ruined districts. They opened up a great Maternity Home. They provided medical aid, and sent

THE COMING OF THE DELIVERERS.
Old people and children, all that were left of the inhabitants of a French village long at the mercy of the merciless invader, went forth to welcome those who had brought about their deliverance. Many such scenes of pathetic joy were witnessed during 1916 and 1917 as towns and villages were relieved of the nightmare horror under which they had long suffered, and, though ruined, were restored to France.

clothing of all kinds. A number of the Friends volunteered their personal services, and their work was done with a prudence, kindliness, and generosity worthy of the best traditions of the community. Some of the calls on them were tragically odd. For example, they found it necessary to provide numbers of pairs of spectacles. Many of these spectacles were to replace the glasses of people whose glasses had been broken in the great retreat; others were to aid the eyes of men and women whose sight had been weakened through excessive weeping.

Districts given over to the Friends

Certain districts in the Marne and the Meuse were given over to the Friends. Here they built 430 houses, of which 62 were of brick, housing some 1,530 persons. In some cases groups of cottages were built to house families of the labouring classes who were only tenants before the war. In another district they helped to convert a farmhouse into an orphanage for about twenty orphans.

At Dôle, in the Jura, a construction camp was begun for making portable houses in sections. These were intended for erection in destroyed villages immediately they were opened up.

One part of the work was to assist in the evacuation of people from threatened districts. Hospitals, sometimes maternity hospitals, had to be cleared suddenly. The cars had to go into towns under shell fire to carry away the wounded. Here is a notable description of one such incident:

The helpers were called on to help to evacuate civilians from Rheims. They got off with some loads, including wounded and infirm. When they left they saw flames springing up in two places and shells bursting steadily over the town. Next day they returned to get away the few remaining patients in the hospital. On Saturday we obtained permission to use a school-room at C., a village some five miles from R., as a temporary evacuation centre, the idea being to evacuate there all the morning, if necessary, while it was quiet, and to take two journeys thence to Chalons in the afternoon. When we arrived at R. we found the situation very much more serious. Thousands of shells were said to have been poured into the place the previous day, and the civil population were streaming out. There had been many deaths, and there was an indescribable atmosphere of apprehension and dismay. Avenues of trees had been mown down as with a sickle; whole streets were destroyed; and people were running about aimlessly, trying to pick out their few remaining possessions from the ruins. By this time there were fifteen seriously wounded cases in the hospital, but it was not at first proposed to remove them; and the morning was spent in searching out helpless people in the town, which took a long time, as many streets were impassable by the motors owing to the debris.

When we arrived back at the hospital we learnt that it had been decided to evacuate all the wounded, however bad. As there were fourteen stretcher cases we loaded up two cars for Chalons, to return to C. for their future loads. The ambulance car was to evacuate from R. to C. during the afternoon. The ambulance car made six trips to and fro, but much time was lost in waiting for temporary lulls in the hail of shells which were falling all round the neighbourhood of the hospital.

The Maternity Hospital for Refugees at Châlons was one of their most admirable enterprises. It included, in addition to the actual maternity work, **Help for babies at Chalons** the care of numbers of sick and refugee babies. It was found here that the war conditions, the strain and trials of living under fire, the hardship and exposure which the mothers had to contend with, told very severely on the vitality and the nerves of the young children. Now and then the workers would be aroused by the sudden arrival of fresh groups of child refugees. "We *thought* we were busy," said one of the workers, "but when two of us came in from gathering nettles we found two cars at the door and the floor of one ward literally paved with babies under eighteen months—twelve of them for us to keep and the others to be fed and to go on. They were as hungry as little wolves. I fed three who sat in a row. The one to whose mouth I held the basin gulped the food down in great snorts, and the one on each side tried to grab the basin away in little pink paws."

The experience of the Friends led them to have great sympathy for the refugees away from their homes. They found that their lot became far worse than with people beginning life again in however poor a way in their own villages. For the refugees the problems of finding work and lodging were both extremely hard of solution. A certain amount of employment could be had. An able-bodied man could always get something to do, and women could be employed on the farms for part of the year. "But a great deal of this work is intermittent and precarious," the Friends declared. "Most of it is impossible for ailing or elderly women, or mothers of small children, who cannot be out all day. The task of making ends meet, with constantly rising prices, on the Government allowance is an almost hopeless one; and there is no doubt that the families who cannot supplement their allowance by earnings suffer seriously from insufficient nourishment. The danger is aggravated by their lamentable condition as to housing. The restriction imposed upon enforcing the payment of rent during the war makes some landlords very chary of letting rooms; others charge exorbitant prices for miserable lodgings, and the **Overcrowding and tuberculosis** refugees are crowded into tumble-down hovels or slum tenements in a way which is causing very serious injury to their health, and threatens grave trouble in the years to come."

The realisation of the hardships of these people led the Friends to extend the work among the refugee population of some of the most crowded towns, concentrating upon schemes for furnishing employment, providing housing for them, enabling them to get out of expensively furnished rooms, and often enough letting them have furniture at very moderate hire or hire-purchase rates. "Of all the needs of the war victims in France there is none to compare in urgency with that of coping with the rapidly increasing ill-health, and particularly tuberculosis, among them."

Even at the end of the third year of the war it was evident that the work of reconstruction in France, considerable as were the proportions it had attained, had as yet barely begun. Men wondered doubtingly what would be the fate of great cities such as Lille. Direful rumours had come through about the misery of the population and of their impoverishment. It was told that all their manufacturing machinery was being gradually taken away to Germany, and that the enemy had resolved, when they quitted Lille, if quit it they must, to leave nothing but the empty shell and, maybe, the barren ruins.

One question that arose immediately the Allies began to recover the invaded territory was when, and under what conditions, the inhabitants who had gone away should be allowed to return. Numbers of these people were naturally anxious to get back at once. They wanted to see what was left of their farms and homes, what damage their property had suffered, and how they could best start life again. The military authorities, on the other hand, wished in most cases to keep the civilian population as far behind as possible. It was essential for military purposes that the Army should have a clear zone along the front, and should have the roads free and the houses at their disposal for their own traffic. The military authorities knew, too, that in some cases spies were bound to come in among the returning inhabitants. Regulations for the return of the people were agreed upon jointly by the Ministry of the Interior and the Ministry of War in April, 1917. It was then arranged that the recovered territory, and the parts occupied by the military, should be divided into a reserved and a non-reserved zone. In the latter an ordinary authorisation by the civilian authorities sufficed, save for people specially excluded by order of the Ministry of the Interior. In the reserved zone people could only go back after their demand had been sent by the prefect of their department to the military officer commanding, and had been signed by him.

Greater even than the problem of houses and cities was the problem of the people themselves. France had been "bled white" by war. Her population had been practically stationary in the **Vision of the New France** years before the conflict opened. Now it had been drained of the very cream of its manhood. Among those who were left grief and want were helping the growth of disease. Let peace, even victorious peace, come immediately, and France would have to settle down to years of steady national reconstruction. The whole principles on which her home life had been built would have to be reconsidered. Small families would have to give place to large. Childless couples would need to be looked upon almost as the enemies of the State. There must be a time of further national trial. France had endured her ordeal when faced by the enemy at her gates in a way that aroused the admiration even of her foes. Would she be able, when peace came, to settle patiently down to the work of internal reconstruction, or would forces of social discontent make themselves felt?

Those who knew France best were least afraid. Great Frenchmen, with the stern logic of the race, had thought out the issues ahead. France, even in the hours when conflict was fiercest, was laying the foundations of a new era, an era to be built up afresh on the foundations of the heroic yesterday, and built with a splendour and assurance such as the world had never dreamed before. For if the blood of the martyrs is the seed of the Church, then the blood of the martyrs who had died by the hundred thousand in France for Liberty might well be the seed of a new nation which, with the splendid vision, the steady heroism, the unexampled endurance and the high endeavour that for centuries had marked France out among the nations of the world, should forge ahead steadily in the ways of peaceful prosperity. The seers of France at war dreamed of a New France, with her own lawful territory regained, with the fear of war which for three generations had threatened the Old France removed, and with nothing to prevent the natural expansion of a great and heroic people.

CHAPTER CC.

THE WONDERFUL ORGANISATION OF BRITAIN'S MUNITIONS SUPPLY.

By Basil Clarke.

The " Times " Disclosure of the Shell Shortage—Public Demand High Explosive—Government Yields and Appoints Lloyd George Minister of Munitions—Organising the Nation for Shells—Lord Chetwynd's Splendid Offer—His Stop-gap Factory and the Deadly Risks He Ran—The New Function of Artillery Creates Demand for Even More Shells—A War of Munitions Begun—Trench Warfare—Problem after Problem for the Munitions Ministry—The Biggest Concern in the World—Controlled Establishments—What " Control " Meant for the Masters and for the Workers—New Factory Rules—A Controlled Establishment at Work—Better Conditions, Pay, and Feeding for Workers—National Factories—Why They Were Necessary—Women's Welfare Work—A Typical Factory—The First State Town—Its Houses and Public Services—The " Town Manager "—The Shops—The Women Police and the Soldier Guard—Making Explosives—" Nitro-Glycerine Hill"—Shell-Filling—Comparative Statistics of Shell Output—Improvement in Quality—" Prematures," " Duds," and " Flying Bands"—Defects Overcome by the Inspection Staff—30,000 Women Inspectors—Big Guns in the Making—Enormous Output Attained—Aeroplanes the " Eyes " of the Guns—How the Output was Speeded—Other Numerous and Widespread Activities of the Ministry.

" The want of an unlimited supply of high explosive was a fatal bar to our success."

PROBABLY no sentence written or uttered during the Great War had a greater or more far-reaching effect on the war and on Great Britain's share in it than this one. It appeared in the "Times" of May 14th, 1915, and was written by Colonel Repington, the famous Military Correspondent of that journal. It revealed to a nation, which it staggered, one of the inner secrets of British failure in the field in the early stages of the war. It all but upset a Government. It was responsible for a complete change both in war policy and in the public estimate of the war ; and, lastly, it brought about a movement and enterprise destined to become the greatest thing in British industry — namely, the national manufacture of munitions, the greatest industry Great Britain had ever known.

So momentous a disclosure is worthy of closer examination. It appeared in a long article

VISCOUNT CHETWYND.   [*Lafayette.*

Lord Chetwynd, when the need for shells was most urgent, made an offer to the Government to build, equip, and have in full working order within six weeks a shell-filling factory. The offer was accepted, and fulfilled to the letter, and Lord Chetwynd himself was an untiring worker in it.

dealing with the results of a British offensive that had cost many, many lives without meeting with any success. The rigorous censorship of the day limited the writer ; he could not say at what cost our men had attacked and failed ; but reading between the lines, and with the knowledge of later disclosures, it became easy to gather the full purport of his words. Here are a few quotations from the article, an article fated to become historic :

It is important for an understanding of the British share in the operations this week to realise that we are suffering from certain disadvantages which make striking successes difficult to achieve.

The result of our attacks on Sunday last in the districts of Fromelles and Richebourg were disappointing. We found the enemy much more strongly posted than we expected. The French fired 276 rounds of high explosives per gun in one day, and levelled the enemy's defences with the ground. We had not sufficient high explosive to level his parapets to the ground after the French practice, and when our infantry gallantly stormed the trenches, as they did in both attacks, they found a garrison undismayed, many entanglements still intact, and Maxims on all sides ready to pour in a stream of bullets.

The attacks were well planned and

[British official photograph,
"CAMOUFLAGED" HOWITZERS.
British howitzers on the western front masked with branches and twigs. In oval: Getting a gun into position near Ypres.

valiantly conducted, but the conditions were too hard. THE WANT OF AN UNLIMITED SUPPLY OF HIGH EXPLOSIVE WAS A FATAL BAR TO OUR SUCCESS.

The value of German troops in the attacks has greatly deteriorated, and we can deal easily with them in the open, but until we are thoroughly equipped for this trench warfare we attack under grave disadvantages.

If we can break through this hard outer crust of the German defences we believe that we can scatter the German armies . . . but to break this hard crust *we need more high explosives, more heavy howitzers, and more men.*

How did it come about that the public duty of making these serious disclosures fell to a newspaper ? That, again, is another queer story of the war. A difference of opinion between military guides was at the back of it. Leaders working with Sir John French, who saved Great Britain in the field in those disastrous early days, had seen for some time that high explosive was the only serviceable type of shell to drive an enemy out of trenches. Shrapnel, with which the Army was supplied, was serviceable against troops in the open or against troops under only light cover—and the area of the fall of shrapnel is much larger than that of high-explosive shell, which is much more concentrated in its effect ; but against **High explosive** solid trench parapets, several feet thick, **versus shrapnel** and troops sheltering, behind them, shrapnel was virtually of no use. The parapets had first to be smashed before the defenders could be hit, and to smash them nothing but high explosive was of use.

Urgent requests for high-explosive shell were forwarded home. No high explosive was sent to the Army. The urgent requests were repeated. Still none was forthcoming. No adequate arrangements for producing it had been made.

Leaders at home had made no arrangements because they had been led to put too much faith in shrapnel and had neglected high explosive. They thought shrapnel should be used. It had proved effectual in

South Africa against moving troops ; it had proved effectual against tribesmen in the Egyptian Sudan. It must be good also against Germans. This view of its chief military advisers at home the Government had blindly accepted ; the view of leaders in touch with German forces was disregarded in face of that of more forceful people nearer home, and no arrangements for the forwarding of high explosive were made.

It soon became evident that nothing but an appeal to the nation at large would bring about the reform which experience in the field showed to be vital. How was that appeal to be made ? With all the powers of the censorship to defend its attitude and to keep the country in the dark the Government seemed to hold a whip-hand ; but the "Times," at the instigation of its proprietor and chief director, Lord Northcliffe, undertook the task of disclosure and dared to tell the nation the truth. The shell muddle was disclosed. It was one of the greatest things in British journalism.

The country was aghast. Realisation that brave British soldiers had been struggling so long and so valiantly against such odds, all for want of conception on the part of leaders at home of the real needs of the case, brought about a public anger against the authorities which up to that time had never been equalled or even approached in the Government's career. It may be said, in fact, that the downfall of the Asquith Government began with the shell shortage disclosures. Public confidence in its leadership was never to be the same again. The blow did not actually upset the Government, but it shattered its foundations, and subsequent war failings led to its downfall.

The public demanded that Field-Marshal French must have high-explosive shells. The demand was unanimous and whole-hearted. The Government, badly shaken, acquiesced, and with such alacrity that it deputed its most forceful and most go-ahead member to see that high-explosive shell was forthcoming in the biggest quantities in the shortest possible time.

That man was Mr. Lloyd George, then Chancellor of the Exchequer, whose courage and skill and resource as Minister of Munitions were to prove the chief stepping-stones by which he came to win the utmost confidence of the nation, and with it, later, the Premiership.

He was created head of a new Government Department, the Ministry of Munitions. He chose as his Parliamentary Secretary Dr. Christopher Addison, M.P., who had given him invaluable help earlier in his National Health Insurance schemes. The Secretary of the new department was an experienced public servant, Sir H.

[*Canadian and British official photographs.*

IN A SHELL-DESTROYED VILLAGE.
Canadian soldier carrying shells through a recaptured village in France. In oval: Loading up limbers with ammunition on the British western front.

Llewellyn Smith, K.C.B., who had helped Mr. Lloyd George on many occasions, especially in matters connected with strikes and labour troubles, when he was at the Board of Trade. As Assistant Secretary was chosen Mr. W. H. Beveridge, head of the Labour Exchanges. Major-General Ivor Phillips, M.P., was another member of the new department.

Mr. Lloyd George went to work with all the energy and enthusiasm that made him so outstanding a man at this time and later in British affairs. The Ministry of Munitions probably established a record in the quick building of a Government Department. It was sometimes said of Mr. Lloyd George that he was no organiser. If organisation means the mere setting up and devising of a machine in microscopic detail this was perhaps true to some extent, and the nation may be thankful for it, for later days in the war were to bring forth not a few instances of new Government Departments in which so-called organisers of ability mistook details and means for ends, and lost themselves in a huge mesh of detail of their own devising, which hindered them from performing the function allotted to them. Mr. Lloyd George proved to be no organiser of this sort. "The end in view is munitions," he seems to have said to himself, "munitions in the shortest time, delivered in the greatest numbers. That

is an engineering problem and an organisation problem; two classes of men alone can solve that problem; I myself am neither an engineer nor an organiser. It follows that my first duty is to get the very best engineers and the very best organisers that are to be had, and hear what they have to say."

First of all he called a little meeting of his colleagues in the new Ministry, and won their warmest co-operation in the great task he had in hand. In a short speech he inspired them with some of his own wonderful keen-ness—and in his gift of personal magnetism Mr. Lloyd George was without equal among British statesmen. He told them of the urgency of the task, the extent of it, and the difficulties that would have to be overcome before it was achieved. From that point he went on to invite their counsel, mentioning that to him the first step necessary seemed to be to get the cream of the nation's organisers and engineers to devise details, ways, and means.

Some little light on this most historical of meetings in Britain's war history was shed later by one of the men who attended it. Dr. Addison, who had succeeded Mr. Lloyd George in the Ministry, speaking in the House of Commons at the end of June, 1917, said:

"Man-grabbing" for munitions

It is a little over two years since a small party of us gathered with my right honourable friend the Prime Minister one Wednesday afternoon in No. 6, Whitehall Gardens. We were about to open a munition shop. There was to be one aim and one aim only—to obtain the goods and make delivery of them to the Army. No other interests, no considerations of leisure, were to be entertained. At the same time a process of man-grabbing was also resolved upon. We were to seek out capable and trustworthy men, and to secure their help in this big task on the same terms.

Thus Mr. Lloyd George's plan of getting the best possible men was agreed to, and the work of "man-grabbing," as Dr. Addison picturesquely termed it, was

DRAWING SUPPLIES FROM A BOMB-STORE.
Bombing-party drawing bombs from a bomb-store during the Third Battle of Ypres. The store was in a dug-out in the support trenches, and thence the men carried the bombs up to the firing-line.

Chairman of the Advisory Committee, and holder of other important offices under the Ministry. Another man of the team was Lord Moulton, one of his Majesty's judges, who in time became Director-General of Explosives Supply. Sir Frederick Black, who was borrowed from the Admiralty, became Director-General of Munitions Supply. Of skilled engineers there were such men as Mr. (later Sir Ernest) Moir, of the great contracting firm of Weetman Pearson; and Mr. (later Sir Glynn) West, one of the brightest minds in the big engineering firm of Armstrong, Whitworth. The former eventually became Director-General of the American and the Transport Departments; the latter became Controller of Shell Manufacture. Munition work in Scotland was organised by Mr. (later Sir William) Weir, of the great firm of ships' pump-makers, a man who for energy and ability was one of the greatest discoveries of the war. Later he became Controller of Aeronautical Supplies.

Of such men as these—and there were a number of others—was Mr. Lloyd George's first "team" made up. They were a remarkable team, and they achieved wonders of work. With the old-fashioned house, No. 6, Whitehall Gardens, as their headquarters, this small staff of experts began a course of labours which for high pressure, enthusiasm, and lack of "red tape" were probably without precedent in the history of British Government Departments. It was a hive of wonderful industry. An eighteen-hour day for six days a week, with a twelve-hour day for Sundays, seemed about the standard "working week" for all heads of departments. Night and day, Sunday and week-day alike, the place was never at rest. It was quite unique among Governmental Departments for the way that all "red tape" was rigorously excluded. You could walk into the place—provided, of course, you had any reasonable business—and get a straight answer to a straight question as soon as it was asked. The Minister himself was always accessible. His two private secretaries—Mr. J. T. Davies, a Welshman, and Mr. W. D. Sutherland, a Scot, both of them drawn from the Civil Service—were just as businesslike and as free from official remoteness as their chief, and through them an **A Ministry without** answer to any important question was **"red tape"** to be had with a minimum of delay.

Other heads of sectional departments, taking the line of the Minister, were just as informal and businesslike. To each of them had been accorded a full measure of responsibility and trust in his own section, leaving him free to decide questions concerning that section on his own initiative. After the roundabout procedure and delay that had been characteristic of Government Departments up to this time, it was novel and refreshing to have

begun post-haste. The way it was done was very characteristic of Mr. Lloyd George's methods—it was thoroughly original, thoroughly unconventional. He began a little inquest of his own among all the biggest and most up-to-date concerns in the country. The question he asked of each was, in effect, this: Irrespective of all considerations of age, social position, and the like, who is the very best man you have in the place for handling big, broad-gauge propositions? To this question, which in most cases was asked by Mr. Lloyd George in person of the leading men of these big undertakings, truthful answers were forthcoming, and from the men recommended a small and select team was picked.

This team comprised types of men quite different in their knowledge and attainments, but alike in one respect— namely, their courage, go-aheadness, long-sightedness, and capacity for "hustle." All of them were proved organisers, though not necessarily of engineering experience. For instance, there was Mr. James Stevenson, who was taken from one of the largest whisky firms. Later he became Sir James Stevenson, and showed such skill and capacity that he became Director of Area Organisation, Vice-

dealings with the Ministry of Munitions. The writer can testify from personal experience as a journalist to the extraordinary saving in time, trouble, and temper to all who had anything to do with this new branch of national government.

Whether the Ministry of Munitions retained its freedom from "red tape" right through its career is a debated point. When the place grew to be the biggest of all Government Departments, and its working was reduced to fixed routine, there were people who said it was as "red-tapey" as the rest. Whatever **Germany's advantage** the truth of this later, it certainly was **over the Allies** not the case in the early days of the Ministry.

Before showing in detail how the work of feeding the guns was tackled, it will be helpful to realise how very much behind their enemy in the matter of munition production Great Britain and her Allies were at this time. By the end of 1914, Germany held 90 per cent. of the French iron-ore mines, 86 per cent. of the cast-iron foundries, and 70 per cent. of the French steelworks. Belgium, with its admirable facilities for the production of steel products, had fallen almost entirely into German hands. The great burden of munition-making thus had to fall on Great Britain. How was she equipped for it ? The position, until the spring of 1915 and even later, was this : Whereas Germany had retained all her skilled metal workers at their own work, instead of drafting them into the Army, Great Britain had allowed many metal workers to enlist under the disastrous voluntary system of recruiting. Germany had developed her own munition works to their fullest possible extent ; the captured munition works of the Allies had been manned by skilled labour drafted from Germany itself, and with unskilled labour recruited by force, if need be, from the surrounding civil population. Britain's smaller resources were far below their full strength.

Thus, at the very moment when it was evident that the war was to be, before all else, a war of munitions and a race between the munition factories and plants of the rival nations, Germany was making a million tons of steel a month when Great Britain was not turning out more than half that quantity ; Germany, with the help of the Austrian iron-works, was turning out a quarter of a million shells a day, when Great Britain was not making more than 10,000. That was how it came about that the German generals could hurl a rain of shells upon our men and positions without much risk to their infantry, whereas the Allies' artillery reply was limited to a few score rounds of shells, and their infantry had to bear the brunt of vast attacks. In one such attack the German Field-Marshal Mackensen, for example, expended 700,000 rounds of shell in four hours. There had

been nothing like it in warfare. As an additional superiority, the enemy exceeded the Allies not only in the number but also in the weight of guns. Compared with the monster howitzers which smashed up the strongest Belgian fortresses like so many walnut shells, the Allies had no adequate guns for use on land. They were forced to expend human life and limb to attack and defend positions which might have been attacked or defended by munitions and mechanical means had these means been forthcoming. The Allies paid in blood and life for the munitions they lacked.

Later on the Ministry of Munitions took under its control the whole subject of munitions of war, including even shipbuilding, farming implements, and the rest, but at the outset almost the only function of the Ministry was to provide shells. In this connection work was done that was well worthy of the adjective heroic, and it was done not only by established manufacturers, but by volunteer organisers who showed a most exhilarating enterprise, not to say audacity, in making good the Army's deficiencies.

The problem was to focus the whole of the available

FIRST STAGES IN THE MAKING OF A SHELL.
This sketch by Mr. W. Hatherell, R.I., shows a white-hot ingot, just taken from the mould, being held by one man with a huge pair of pincers, while others scrape off the scale with which it is encrusted.

[*British official photograph.*]

RUSHING SHELLS TO THE FLANDERS FRONT.
Every possible means of transport was used to get shells to the guns.
Here, ordinary ammunition waggons moved alongside a light railway, on
which a flange-wheeled motor-car drew trollies packed with shells.

shell-making. Women, especially, volunteered in great numbers. Munition-making came as almost the first outlet that had offered itself for all the pent-up energies and war enthusiasm of British women, and they greeted it eagerly. There was not a rank of society that did not yield its volunteers. For example, at the same bench in a works which the writer visited were the daughter of a carpenter, the daughter of an earl, the wife of an earl's son, the sister of a well-known M.P., the daughter of a greengrocer, and the widow of a postman. This one illustration will serve better than a column of generalisation to show how universal among all classes of women was the wish to

engineering resources quickly on shell production. There were no machines, no plant, no workshops, no workers, and no supplies—save the beggarly few which yielded the all too inadequate supplies of shell then being sent to our armies in the field. The first step taken was to commandeer all the things that were necessary. Through local munitions committees, established under the direction of Sir James Stevenson, in every area where steel and metal manufacture was carried on, a general hunt was organised for lathes and material. Every available machine was put on to the turning of shells. If its owner was willing to use his lathe for that purpose, he might keep it in his own workshop and employ his own workers. If not, his lathe was commandeered, and taken off for use in some other workshop. The local committees, consisting usually of the leading engineers and managers of their districts, made inventories of the resources of their areas, and mapped out programmes of the maximum possible output of each workshop, factory,

Work of local committees

and shed where shell-making could possibly be carried on. Working with wonderful zeal and patriotism, these local committees co-ordinated the work and output of their districts; they established clearing-houses for the supply of tools, materials, etc.; they devised local schemes for accelerating production and maintaining the right proportion of production. The Ministry of Munitions co-ordinated their efforts, and sent officials to each area to help and encourage in every possible way and to stimulate the slothful.

Soon all the country was making shells. Scores of works that had never yielded shell-cases in all their history began suddenly to produce them—works which till then had confined their energies to such prosaic and peaceful articles as cutlery, sewing-machines, bicycles, grass-mowers, and the like. Each works undertook to make either whole shells or such parts of shells as their machinery could produce. Many firms, for instance, had no machinery suitable for turning shell-cases, but they could make shell-noses (or fuses) perhaps. Each works loyally undertook such work as it could do.

In addition, new workers flowed in from all ranks of life to take a hand in this new British war industry of

[*New Zealand official photograph.*]

THE LAST STAGE BUT ONE.
Handing in shells at a New Zealand howitzer battery, carefully screened in a sunk emplacement. In this penultimate stage of their journey the shells were carried by hand along a duck-board gangway.

do something to provide Great Britain with the shells she needed.

A great engineering book will be written some day to show the resource and skill and clever makeshifts by which the shell problem was faced by the engineers and manufacturers of Great Britain. Enough here to say that this problem was tackled with a resolution hardly less than that of the British forces in the field, and notwithstanding all difficulties and all makeshift, shell parts began to appear in steadily increasing numbers. These parts—cases, fuses, detonators, and the rest—emerging piecemeal from scores of factories, were passed on to other factories to be " assembled " or to have incomplete processes completed, each works doing such part of the total work as its machinery and resources were fitted to undertake.

To co-ordinate these various stages of manufacture, done in so many different workshops, was a work of immense intricacy. Often shells were held up merely for want of one process or part. For instance, the application of their copper bands, called driving bands, was a great difficulty. They had to be squeezed on to the case of the shell by hydraulic presses of great power, and but few of these presses were to be had. Gauges were another difficulty. Only a few of them existed, and only few mechanics could make them. Existing gauges had to be passed from place to place, like books from a circulating library, for use first here, then there.

Still, even these difficulties were overcome—and to such good purpose that shell parts began to accumulate at so great a rate that the capacity of the shell-filling establishments became overtaxed; the inrush of shells was more than they could possibly cope with.

Great Britain's shell-filling factories at this time were no more than a handful. Woolwich and similar Government works had contrived in the past to fill all the shells that were made. They were greatly extended, but it was soon seen that they were still too small, and as their capacity for further extension was at an end, other filling factories had to be found. Great piles of shells were waiting in works' yards needing only to be filled with explosives to be ready for use. National shell-filling factories were then decided upon, and they were to be erected on a mammoth scale.

One may step aside for a moment at this point to give an illustration of how the urgent need **Need of** for shell-filling facilities to keep pace **shell-filling factories** with the increased output of shells was met pending the erection of the big national factories. Hearing of the difficulty in which the Ministry of Munitions was placed, a man of great public merit and not a little daring went to the Ministry and made a most generous and sporting offer. "You are behindhand with your shell-filling," he said in effect. "If you will allow

me, I will build and equip at my own expense a shell-filling factory in six weeks, and have it in full working order."

This volunteer was Lord Chetwynd. His generous offer was accepted, and he fulfilled his promise to the letter. To him and his wonderful energy and enthusiasm was due the welcome fact that British soldiers at the front were in possession **Lord Chetwynd's** of an extra shell supply long before the **splendid service** date they would otherwise have been.

Lord Chetwynd's work was that of a hero. At a time when very few people knew anything about the filling of high-explosive shells he took from flour-mills the ordinary machinery with which flour is ground, and with it treated dangerous explosives as if they had been innocent of all power to harm. "Man alive," said his friends, when they heard of it, "you will surely blow yourself and your workpeople sky-high one of these days. You've doomed yourself to death." Upon this Lord Chetwynd, loath to allow his workpeople (who had all volunteered for the work) to take greater risks than he himself took, actually went to live in the filling factory he had erected so hurriedly, sleeping and working and taking his meals within range of deadly explosives that were being treated by methods unprecedented. Working in his little office till late in the night, he not only saw to the filling of shells, but also invented a process which became a most valuable means of providing the Army with the vast supplies of high-explosive shell it needed. His new method was copied far and wide.

The decision as to the erection of national shell factories marked a turning-point in the general policy of the Ministry of Munitions and in the conduct of the war. It was the

[British official photograph.

RAMMING HOME THE SHELL IN A BIG GUN AT NIGHT.

British artillerymen loading a big gun on the Flanders front—two of them are engaged in ramming home the shell ready for the moment of firing, while two officers are examining other shells for subsequent use. Even when, in the language of the official despatches, there was "nothing to report" from the front, the artillery was maintaining a constant shell-fire against the enemy positions.

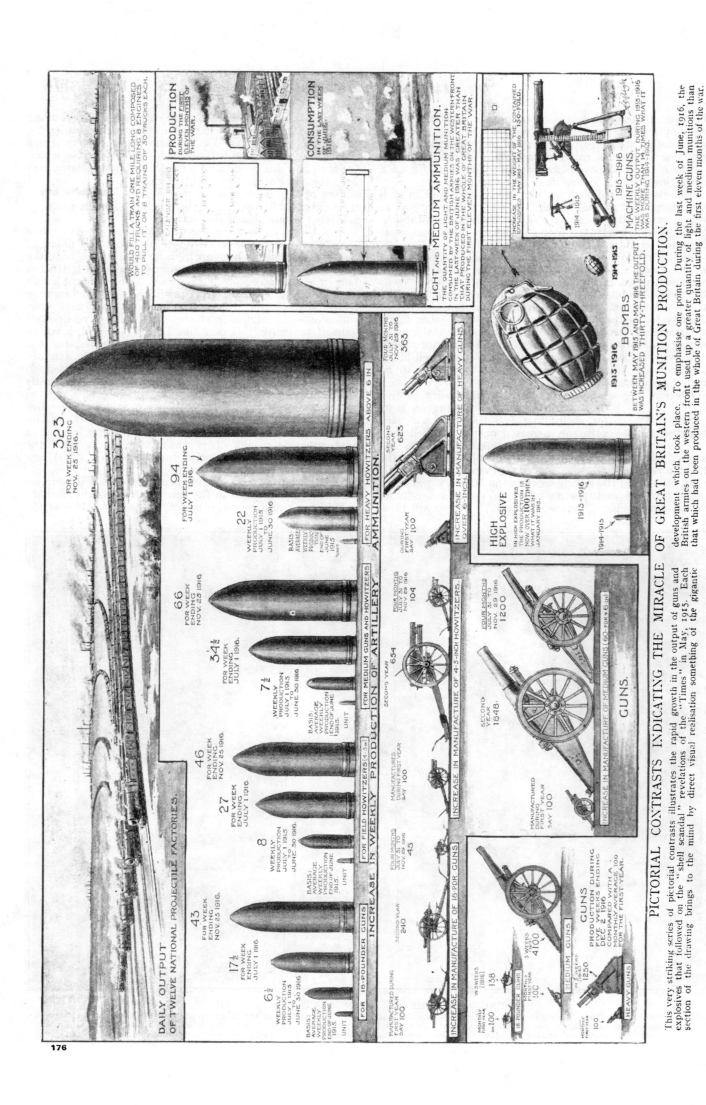

PICTORIAL CONTRASTS INDICATING THE MIRACLE OF GREAT BRITAIN'S MUNITION PRODUCTION.

This very striking series of pictorial contrasts illustrates the rapid growth in the output of guns and explosives that followed on the "shell scandal" revelations of the "Times," in May, 1915. Each section of the drawing brings to the mind by direct visual realisation something of the gigantic development which took place. To emphasise one point. During the last week of June, 1916, the British armies on the western front used up a greater quantity of light and medium munitions than that which had been produced in the whole of Great Britain during the first eleven months of the war.

DAILY OUTPUT
OF TWELVE NATIONAL PROJECTILE FACTORIES.

WOULD FILL A TRAIN ONE MILE LONG COMPOSED OF 400 TRUCKS AND REQUIRING 8 ENGINES TO PULL IT, OR 8 TRAINS OF 50 TRUCKS EACH.

PRODUCTION
DURING THE FIRST ELEVEN MONTHS OF THE WAR.

CONSUMPTION
IN THE LAST WEEK OF JUNE, 1916.

LIGHT AND **MEDIUM AMMUNITION.**
THE QUANTITY OF LIGHT AND MEDIUM MUNITION CONSUMED BY THE BRITISH ARMIES ON THE WESTERN FRONT IN THE LAST WEEK OF JUNE 1916 WAS GREATER THAN THAT PRODUCED IN THE WHOLE OF GREAT BRITAIN DURING THE FIRST ELEVEN MONTHS OF THE WAR.

323
FOR WEEK ENDING NOV. 25 1916.

94
FOR WEEK ENDING JULY 1 1916.

66
FOR WEEK ENDING NOV. 23 1916.

46
FOR WEEK ENDING NOV. 25 1916.

43
FOR WEEK ENDING NOV. 25 1916.

34½
FOR WEEK ENDING JULY 1 1916.

27
FOR WEEK ENDING JULY 1 1916.

22
WEEKLY PRODUCTION JULY 1 1915 TO JUNE 30 1916

17½
FOR WEEK ENDING JULY 1 1916.

8
WEEKLY PRODUCTION JULY 1915 JUNE 30 1916.

7½
WEEKLY PRODUCTION JULY 1 1915 JUNE 30 1916.

6½
WEEKLY PRODUCTION JULY 1 1915 JUNE 30 1916

BASIS: AVERAGE WEEKLY PRODUCTION END OF JUNE 1915.

BASIS: AVERAGE WEEKLY PRODUCTION END OF JUNE 1915.

BASIS: AVERAGE WEEKLY PRODUCTION END OF JUNE 1915.

UNIT

UNIT

UNIT

FOR 18-POUNDER GUNS

FOR FIELD HOWITZERS (4.5 IN.)

FOR MEDIUM GUNS AND HOWITZERS

FOR HEAVY HOWITZERS ABOVE 6 IN

INCREASE IN WEEKLY PRODUCTION OF ARTILLERY AMMUNITION.

INCREASE IN MANUFACTURE OF 18-PDR GUNS
MANUFACTURED DURING FIRST YEAR SAY 100
SECOND YEAR 240
FOUR MONTHS JULY 31 TO NOV 29 1916 45

INCREASE IN MANUFACTURE OF 4·5-INCH HOWITZERS
MANUFACTURED DURING FIRST YEAR SAY 100
SECOND YEAR 654
FOUR MONTHS JULY 31 TO NOV 29 1916 104

INCREASE IN MANUFACTURE OF HEAVY GUNS.
OVER 6-INCH.
DURING FIRST YEAR SAY 100
SECOND YEAR 623
FOUR MONTHS JULY 31 TO NOV 29 1916 363

INCREASE IN MANUFACTURE OF MEDIUM GUNS (60-PDR + 6 IN)
MANUFACTURED DURING FIRST YEAR SAY 100
SECOND YEAR 1848.
FOUR MONTHS JULY 31 TO NOV 29 1916 1200

GUNS.

GUNS
PRODUCTION DURING FIVE WEEKS ENDING DEC 2 1916 COMPARED WITH A MONTHLY AVERAGE 100 FOR THE FIRST YEAR.

HEAVY GUNS
MONTHLY FIRST YEAR 100
IN 5 WEEKS (1916) 1250

MEDIUM GUNS
MONTHLY FIRST YEAR 100
IN 5 WEEKS (1916) 4100

18-POUNDER GUNS
MONTHLY FIRST YEAR 100
IN 5 WEEKS (1916) 138

HIGH EXPLOSIVE
IN HIGH EXPLOSIVES THE PRODUCTION IS NOW OVER 100 TIMES WHAT IT WAS IN JANUARY 1915.
1914-1915
1915-1916

BOMBS
BETWEEN MAY 1915 AND MAY 1916 THE OUTPUT WAS INCREASED THIRTY-THREEFOLD.
1914-1915
1915-1916

MACHINE GUNS.
THE WEEKLY OUTPUT DURING 1915-1916 WAS 14½ TIMES WHAT IT WAS DURING 1914-1915.
1914-1915
1915-1916

INCREASE IN THE WEIGHT OF THE CONTAINED EXPLOSIVE MAY 1915 - MAY 1916 150-FOLD.

outward expression of a realisation on the part of the nation's military leaders that the Great War was to be, above all else, a war of munitions. It marked, moreover, an acceptance of the new military fact that artillery fire no longer had for its sole function the mere demolition of specific objects. War had shown by this time that artillery must be ready to destroy not only objects but whole areas. And even more than this—it must be ready also to keep up a compact and constant shower of shell upon whole areas, so that no military movement above ground could occur in those areas. For such work as this shells would be needed in millions where in earlier warfare they had been needed only in thousands ; guns would be needed in thousands where previously only in tens.

With this realisation of the new functions of artillery, the duty of the Ministry of Munitions increased in one bound a thousand-

KEEPING THE GUNS SUPPLIED IN BAD WEATHER.
British soldiers carrying shells to a gun on the western front over ground rendered impassable to ordinary traffic by the mud. Each man carried two or three of the heavy missiles across the sticky mud, so that the gun should not run short of ammunition.

fold. The department which had begun with the simple object of rushing out more shells to a few hundred British guns was suddenly confronted with the problem of providing millions of shells and thousands of guns — shells and guns not for Britain alone, but for those of her Allies, who were as behindhand as herself with means for artillery warfare on this scale, and who lacked the means that Great Britain still had for making up the deficiency.

Almost at the same time a full conception was reached of the new trend of trench warfare and of Britain's serious defects and deficiencies, as compared with the enemy, for carrying on this means of warfare. In fact, about this time discovery followed discovery. Problem after problem, defect after defect, want after want, in quick succession were hurled at the Ministry of Munitions to solve and make good. There was hardly a single one of our many war deficiencies that did not concern them, more or less ; and in the vast majority of cases the deficiencies discovered were ones which the Ministry of Munitions alone could attempt to make good.

Discovery follows discovery

The place and its duties grew like a mushroom. Hardly a day passed but it became evident that some new department would have to be established. One of the pleasantries exchanged between members of the Ministry about this time was, " We open a new department every day." This was almost actually true, for not only had the manufacture of a thousand and one different kinds of new things to be organised—and in many cases these things had to be designed by the Ministry—but the supply of thousands of different ingredients and materials had to be ensured. This meant activities not only at home, but in almost every part of the world.

To attempt to trace and record in the scope of this chapter the many changes and developments that occurred in the Ministry at this time would be to create a bald inventory, uninteresting in itself and unsatisfactory as a means of showing the tremendous scope and far-reaching activity that the department eventually assumed. Better to skip the period of greatest evolution in the Ministry's history and pick up the story again at a later date, when the changes were completed and in working order.

By the middle of the year 1917 a little department, that previously comprised two rooms, with a staff of less than a score of people, had become a department employing an administrative staff at its London headquarters alone

of no fewer than 12,000 people—the biggest staff of any one Ministry or concern in the whole world. The London offices alone covered acres in extent. Hotels, offices, clubs, mansions—all had been commandeered for the use of the Ministry, and even these were not enough. Wooden huts—" bungalows " as they were called—became a feature of London's open spaces.

The Ministry at this time controlled the work and destinies of no fewer than 3,000,000 workpeople engaged in the making of munitions, and this number did not include thousands of other workers employed under sub-contractors.

The Ministry controlled no fewer than one hundred national munition factories of its own building and 4,900 engineering establishments, many of which were themselves square miles in extent.

It had in its hands the manufacture of all sorts of munitions in all phases, right from the getting of supplies in the raw state to the output of the finished article. What this means may be grasped from the schedule of the Ministry's work as it was officially defined in the Acts of Parliament :

(a) Munitions work for the purposes of the Act means the manufacture or repair of arms, ammunition, ships, vessels, vehicles, and aircraft, and any other articles intended or adapted for use in war ; and of any metals, machines, or tools required for such manufacture and of the materials of any class required for such manufacture.

(b) The construction, alteration, or repair of buildings for naval or military purposes or for munitions work, and the erection of machinery and plant therein and of houses for the accommodation for persons engaged therein.

(c) The construction and alteration of docks and harbours.

(d) The supply of light, heat, water, or power, or of tramway facilities.

(e) The maintenance of fire-brigades.

The scope of these terms placed the Ministry virtually without limit as to the work it might do. The industry of munitions became by far the greatest of all British national industries. To survey this industry in **Britain's greatest national industry** detail in all its many aspects one would need to peer into almost every corner of British and foreign industrial life. It is a subject for the largest of books rather than a chapter, and here one can attempt no more than to look into some of its more striking features.

First as to the " controlled establishments," of which there were nearly five thousand dotted about the British

AA

Isles. By a simple Order, made under Section 4 of the Munitions of War Act, 1915, the Minister of Munitions could declare any establishment in which munition work was carried on a " controlled estab-

Meaning of controlled establishments

lishment." The effects of this Order concerned both the owner of the establishment and the persons employed therein. For the owner " control " meant :

(*a*) Limitation of profits by providing that the profits made on war work should not exceed the average profits of two complete years before the war, unless increased output, justifying greater profits, was achieved, or unless increased capital or some other cause justified the owner in claiming a larger profit than the average of two previous years.

(*b*) Preclusion from making any changes in the rate of wages

[*Canadian War Records.*

OUTGUNNED AND OUTMANNED IN FLANDERS.
Germans taken prisoner by the Canadians coming into the British lines carrying their own machine-guns with them. In September, 1917, three hundred and seventy-seven machine-guns were taken during the fighting on the western front alone.

paid to workpeople or managers or directors, without first submitting the proposed changes to the Ministry of Munitions.

(*c*) Obligation to run works on a set of rules drawn up by the Ministry for the use of all controlled establishments throughout the kingdom.

(*d*) Obligation to comply with all reasonable requirements of the Ministry for information as to methods, stocks, costs, and profits of the establishment.

The Order meant virtually full financial control. For the workmen " control " meant :

(*a*) A removal of all rules, practices, and customs which tended to restrict production or employment.

(*b*) Obligation to comply with certain working rules as to order, timekeeping, discipline, and efficiency laid down by the Ministry and posted in each controlled establishment.

This forced removal of the restrictions on output touched a vital spot in Trade Union practices and customs, and it was only with the greatest difficulty that the Ministry contrived to carry this important point in the face of Labour opposition and other opposition in Parliament.

The point might never have been carried but for two important concessions —the first being a promise that the enforcement of this rule was only temporary, and that immediately after the war there should be a return to the old state of things if the Trade Unions then demanded it ; the second being the limitation of profits of the employers. The men, made rather bitter by unfortunate experiences in the past whenever they had succeeded in increasing output, would consent to no speeding-up of production that was merely to put extra money into the employers' pockets. If they were to forgo all their old-established safeguards against being sweated, they argued, then the employers must be precluded from making extra profits out of their increased work.

Controlled establishments, like many other establishments, also came within the scope of the Munitions Acts of 1915-16, which made strikes and lock-outs illegal, and which made a " leaving certificate " indispensable for any workman who wished to give up his employment. The factories were also under strict regulations with regard to the issue of badges to workers ; the terms and conditions of employment and the rate of wages paid to men and women, to skilled and unskilled workers ; also as to secrecy concerning the work on which they were engaged, and as to the employment of foreigners, more particularly as regards the recruiting of foreigners by means of paid recruiting agents sent to foreign countries. This practice, it may be mentioned, which had been largely resorted to owing to the shortage of skilled mechanics, had led to the introduction into the country of aliens, some of whom were far from desirable. There is not much doubt, in fact, that Germany sent not a few spies into this country in the guise of mechanics, who joined parties of neutral mechanics recruited in Holland, Denmark, and other countries by British firms or their foreign agents.

If control, however, meant many limitations and curtailment of individual freedom for the worker, it also had its advantages ; for to enable a worker to conform to very strict rules as to attendance, timekeeping, and output, it was necessary that he or she should be supplied with all the best means for attaining these ends —that he must be well looked after, well fed, and the rest. With " control " there came along new working conditions that were incomparably better than the old conditions. As works grew and grew, the management saw to it that each extension was better than the old buildings, and that the maximum of comfort for the worker was attained.   **New conditions of labour**

The writer, at the invitation of the Government, made a round of the munition works of the country with a small party of journalists representing many nations, and the following is an extract from the notes he then made of a " controlled " factory. It gives a glimpse of some of the new conditions :

I have seen to-day all the wonders of shell-making, and I believe I could now go fairly closely into the question of shell manufacture in all its six hundred different processes.

But wonderful as these things are, their wonder pales before that contained in a chance remark made by one of the shop managers who was showing us round one of the new munition works. He had led us over acres of new workshops. We seemed to have walked miles—miles past whirring lathes and squeezing presses and guttering furnaces, miles past workers, men and women, busy in all the conceivable minutiæ of mechanical activity. And then, as we paused for a minute, overlooking a great sea of work and workers, he said : " Yes, all this place was green fields not many weeks ago."

What a picture that was ! The department I have in mind was eight acres in extent, without a single dividing wall, and it was merely one section of a " controlled " works of sixty-five acres. From a raised gallery alongside this section you looked down on what at first seemed only a medley of colour—red, white, blue, and yellow. And then you made out that it was no garden or flower market, but that the colours were flags, that each flag reared its head from some machine, and that by each machine, packed tight, row upon row, line upon line, amid thousands of lights, were men and women, girls and lads, with heads bent and fingers working, ever working, on the great war industry—munitions.

Over two thousand women and girls worked in that one shed

Loading pontoon boats with ammunition for guns at the "bridgehead" across stream.

Heavy ordnance moving forward under fire in the line of British advance on the western front.

Girl workers filing into the canteen for dinner.

Day nursery for the babies of munition workers.

As a necessary antecedent to efficient national service women in munition factories were relieved from all domestic cares.

Rest, recreation, and solicitous care of mind and body that resulted in efficiency.

Sidelights on the everyday life of the women workers in a typical national munitions factory in England.

British official photograph.

British manhood hurling the shells that British womanhood had made in loyal co-partnership.

alone, a wonderfully light, clean, and airy shed, very unlike the old-fashioned type of engineering works. Each girl had her khaki overall and her pretty khaki cap, lined with green, and each had a little flag—Belgian, or French, or British—pinned on her machine before her (as a sailor has his flag before him) to hearten her, perhaps, when fingers tired and eyes ached and temples throbbed with the beating and the whir and the clatter and glare that compassed her about.

We stepped down from the gallery, and walked in this coloured sea of industry. For some time I was unable to watch the detailed processes of munition-making with any great attention, because of interest in a greater and a newer phenomenon—the woman munition worker. Where were these girls before the war? No works manager can tell you. They have just sprung into being—a new genus. Watch them as they feed piece after piece of metal into a machine with one hand, pull a lever with another, and push a pedal with a foot, all at a rate that makes one giddy to watch. As one of our guides told us, girls soon acquire a quickness and deftness and aptitude for this kind of work that few men can attain. And one great qualification they have that few men ever learn—namely, patience. They can work for hours on one process.

We saw women with long iron tongs placing little chunks of brass into a white-hot blast furnace; others taking them out and putting them under great steam-hammer presses that came down " thump " three times and squashed the brass into little rimmed cups—the tops of gun-shells. Other women watched turret lathes with six-tooled turrets, each one of which put in some new series of cuts on the shell piece that was being made. These lathes girls worked among soapy, oily fluid that played unceasingly on the cutting edges of the tools. Yet the girls kept spotless.

One looked for signs of tiredness and paleness. Whether there is something specially healthful in the manufacture of munitions I cannot say, but certainly one would go far to find so many pink complexions and clear eyes under one working roof as were to be seen in this great hive of industry.

We happened to arrive at one of the works kitchens just about one o'clock, and even the most up-to-date hospitals could not show better cooking appliances. The roasting joints, the big baked puddings, batter puddings, milk puddings, and fruit puddings that we saw being got ready for the one o'clock inrush of hungry girls made one quite hungry, too. They dine off tables clean as white deal can be, and the prices paid are " bare cost," with all the Government-buying privileges thrown in. One girl told me she could get a dinner cheaper at the works than she could at home. The men had separate dining-rooms just as good.

This little picture of a " controlled establishment " was no more than typical of many of the five thousand similar establishments which the Munitions Ministry controlled. These establishments differed in size and in other details, of course, but the general character was very much the same everywhere. Existing engineering works had extended their buildings, running up new sheds on every acre of available space, and these extensions, equipped with new machines, staffed with new workers, men and women, many of whom were as new to engineering work as the machines they controlled, were in no way comparable with the old engineering shops that existed before the war. The buildings were better, working conditions were better, wages were better, health was better, and even spirits were better. In that it led to a more enlightened and more systematised
Development of the method of production and treatment of
" control " system labour, the call upon Great Britain for war munitions was no bad thing.

The national factories, of which by 1917 no fewer than a hundred existed in different parts of Great Britain and Ireland, were a natural development of the controlled establishment system. Every engineering concern of repute and every explosives factory had developed its resources to the utmost, and yet there remained need for still greater resources. The Ministry decided to supply these resources itself rather than to thrust more work upon private concerns already fully occupied, and the national factories were the result. One other factor that made it desirable to build new factories rather than to extend still further the existing factories was this: Experience had proved that the processes of explosives manufacture and shell-filling ought only to be carried on in isolated areas. Existing factories were nearly all in congested areas—with the dwellings of the workers clustering round about them. It was decided to go into open country.

Among many national factories visited by the writer, two may be described as examples. The first had been built on a moor some twenty miles from a Northern city, and was used for the filling of shells made in the many vast engineering shops of that city. It was merely a vast agglomeration of wooden huts dotted at equal intervals over three hundred acres of moorland. The area was surrounded by barbed-wire, around which, at all hours of night and day, elderly soldiers in khaki maintained a patrol.

Along one side of the works ran a rail-way with many sidings, and with branch **A moorland** lines running into the factory area. A **munitions area** passenger station, brand new and built entirely of wood, had been erected in the middle of this side of the factory, and from it pathways made of logs, laid transversely across the grass and heather, led to different parts of the factory. Within the outer fence were a few huts used as sleeping-places and kitchens by the military guard, but no other living places of any kind existed within the factory area. Nor were there any for miles around. The factory was on open moorland, with not even a farm in

DINNER-TIME IN A MUNITION FACTORY.
Women workers purchasing tickets, which they could exchange at the canteen for such refreshments as they required. The ticket system was found more convenient than taking the money over the counter.

sight. One wondered what became of its thousands of workers when their day's task was done. To see what became of them one had only to wait until the shift then on duty were set free. They swarmed to the railway-station. Special trains of their own were waiting to take them off to the city, whence they had come that morning. A similar train on another platform had just landed the incoming shift, and as work-girls boarded the one train, others, newly arrived, left the station and took their places in the filling-sheds. The factory worked three shifts a day and was never idle. A day's output of filled shells, when loaded on to railway trucks, made quite a large-sized goods train.

One noticeable feature about this factory was the large number of farmers' milk-carts which delivered daily at its gates. The total supply must have been several hundred gallons. It had been found that milk was in some way an antidote to the poisonous fumes of the high explosives and deadly chemicals which the girl workers were called upon to handle, and they were provided with milk several times a day free of charge by the authorities.

[*British official photograph.*
"PATIENTS" IN A "HOWITZER WARD."
Howitzers in a gun hospital during the Flanders battles of the autumn
of 1917. To this place guns that required repairs were removed, that the
results of wear and tear might be made good by the artillery artificers.

It may be mentioned that in this factory, as in most other
munition factories where a large number of women were
employed, special women officials had been appointed for
no other purpose than to see after the girl workers' welfare
and comfort.

This subject occupied a good deal of the attention of
the Munitions Ministry, and a special section, called the
Womens' Welfare Section, devoted itself entirely to
furthering the comfort, health, and general welfare of
women munition workers. In munitions areas local
committees of women saw that girls found suitable lodgings
and were well fed both at home and at their work. The
Young Women's Christian Association helped very
materially in these matters. They established and ran
many canteens and rest-rooms for girl workers ; they
also organised concerts, games, and amusements for them
in their spare time.

Another type of national factory set up by the Ministry
of Munitions presented even a greater departure from
normal commercial enterprise, for with the national factory
they established also a national "town"

The first State town for its workers to dwell in. An admirable example of this type of factory
and town may be cited. It covered
probably ten or more square miles, a long strip of land bent
at the middle. Each end was a national factory comprising
innumerable huts dotted about open land, and following
very closely on the lines of the shell-filling factory
already described ; but the thousands of workers had
no great town near at hand to house them when off
duty. The only alternative, therefore, was to build suitable
accommodation for workers at some point convenient to
these two factories.

The land in between them was chosen as the site, and
on it was built practically a little town. It differed from
the ordinary town, however, in two most striking features.
It was a town built almost entirely of wood, and it was
a State town—State owned, State built, and State controlled, the first town of its sort in British history.

Armed with a Government permit to view this new
township, the writer was met at the railway-station by one
of the factory motor-cars, driven across green, open
country and set down some half-hour later within the
township. Great Britain's first national cinema theatre

stood on the left hand ; beyond it
the first national grocery shop.
A stone's throw away was the first
national laundry, close to it the
fire-station. A woman stepped
from the back door of a State
cottage (addressed K3 West), and,
after a calculating look at the sky,
pegged out some washing on a
national clothes-line.

The main street of the town
ran almost due north. Beginning
at the bottom, near the electric
lighting station, houses stretched
away in streets to right hand
and left of the main street—that
is, east and west of it. The first
street was A Street, east or west
as the case might be, and this
letter, with the number of the
house and the word east or west,
was sufficient postal address for
any house in that street. Walking

[*British official photograph.*
BIG GUN IN "HOSPITAL."
In a British ordnance workshop, or "hospital," behind the lines during
the Flanders battles. A heavy gun which had been brought in for some
necessary repairs was receiving the requisite attention that would fit it for
renewed service.

along the main street one passed the ends of all these side
streets, also the town club and the school, the town
institute, and the cinema, before coming at length to the
town square. Here were to be found the town shops and
the chief public buildings — some of them built of
brick instead of wood — also the town bank and the
post-office.

The shops were run on co-operative principles under
the ægis of a Co-operative Society by a committee
elected by the local workers. Not far away were
the hospital and the house where the town doctors lived.
Branch surgeries were to be found also at each end of
the factory area.

In the background from here was the town laundry ;
also a beer canteen and a public-house. On one prominent
corner was the fire-station, behind it the telephone
exchange, which, it may be mentioned, was equipped
with a censor. All calls from outside the area had to be
retransmitted, and they were duly censored in the process.
Discreetly hidden in the background not far from here
was the town lock-up.

There were three types of houses in the township, all of
them made of wood, and they are deserving of description
as showing the kinds of people who worked in the munition
area. The first was a little family house comprising a
big living-room, with stove, three bed-rooms, a larder, a

scullery and wash-room, a bath-room and a lavatory. The rent for this, inclusive of rates and electric light, was five shillings a week. Next came houses of the "boarding-house" type, capable of housing eight men or eight women apiece, with separate quarters for the house-keeper and her family. These housekeepers acted as, and were officially styled, "mothers"—providing meals and attendance for their boarders. The rent of these houses was nine shillings a week. Beds and bedclothes were hired from the Government for threepence a week per bed. "Mothers" did no munition work, of course, but devoted all their energies to looking after their "families."

The third type of house held seventy men or seventy women workers apiece, with a staff to look after them. They were called "barracks," and were big places with four wings each and central dining-rooms and kitchens. All had baths and clothes-drying rooms. These "barracks," of which there were a good number, lay behind two sides of the town square, the women's houses on the east side, the men's on the west. Several thousands of workers lived here.

Near them were central bakeries which supplied 5,000 loaves at a baking; central kitchens could supply 8,000 rations three times a day.

The administration of this munitions township was on novel lines. There was no mayor, no town clerk; no watch committee or highways com- **Town manager's** mittee; no multifarious committees with **sole control** sub-committees and clerks for this and that. Nobody had time for these pleasing municipal hobbies, and the "powers" of the town were vested in one man, a Government officer, his title being "Town Manager." The official acting as town manager when the writer visited the town was a Local Government Board officer of wide experience, with an able assistant.

This vesting of all authority in one official certainly simplified domestic life. If your chimney smoked or the down spouting of your house leaked you protested not to the landlord but to the town manager. If the

electric light was dim, or the water supply muddy, you wrote not to the county water board or an electric lighting company but to the town manager. One could even foresee his receiving complaints if some citizen's Sunday beef was tough; for even though he, as town manager, did not perhaps buy the beast that was tough, he gave his ægis to the local co-operative butcher who did. Truly his post was no sinecure.

Of course citizens' committees expressed their opinions and made petitions to the town manager on different points concerning the commonweal, and every effort was made to fall in with the wishes of the majority in any point not conflicting with the town's first function—that of producing munitions. Churches and missions of different denominations were **Pure democracy** established as and when required. The **under autocracy** school was staffed and extended to growing needs. The shops committee had a good "say" as to the goods provided in the local co-operative shops. A permanent professional fire-brigade was established. Visiting nurses and an ambulance corps helped the town-ship's Government doctors.

The police were supplied by the neighbouring county police authorities, but were paid by the Government. There were also factory police—men and women. A thousand soldiers patrolled the barbed-wire fences sur-rounding the munition works. New railway-stations had

[*Canadian War Records.*

GUNNERS AND GUNS THAT CLEARED THE GERMANS FROM VIMY RIDGE.
Canadian Horse Artillery bringing up their guns into position for the operations that resulted in their capture of Vimy Ridge, April 9th, 1917. Above: A section of Canadian artillery lined up for inspection at a training camp, showing the type of gun they used so effectively on the western front.

PART OF THE PANORAMA OF FANTASTIC CONTRASTS IN THE BATTLE OF ARRAS.

Hurrying forward with guns and munitions during the great Battle of Arras, in April, 1917. Where the guns were pounding the enemy as he was being determinedly pressed back, the scenes were described by an eye-witness as forming a panorama "fantastic as a nightmare of war." "No sane man would believe it unless he saw it with his own eyes and heard it with his own ears." Guns and ammunition limbers were moving forward, a light railway was being laid, loaded transport waggons being brought up, mules kicked and rolled—and over all was the incessant thunder of the guns and bursting shells.

been erected at different points on the railways passing near the township. A set of motor-cars plied from end to end of the area at intervals.

The munition centre has been described as two national factories with a national town in the middle. Officially it was considered as one factory, but the two ends were quite different in their functions. The one end was devoted to the making of raw material. It had huge plants for the making of nitric acid and sulphuric acid of the strong, fuming variety ; plants also for the refining of crude glycerine and for the distillation of ether and alcohol. Near by were buildings where raw cotton was stored. From these places these ingredients were carried by little trucks to a hill called Nitro-Glycerine Hill. There nitro-glycerine and gun-cotton were kneaded together into a grey, viscous porridge by girls dressed in khaki, who swirled the stuff around with their hands as though it had been the most innocent of mixtures for making cakes instead of a deadly compound which, with any fault or carelessness, might blow them sky-high without a moment's warning.

Later the explosive was pressed and kneaded and squeezed through holes until it took the shape and appearance of macaroni. This was dried and cut up into lengths of exact size suitable for fitting into the shell-cases for which it was intended. Supervision was strict to make sure that the girl workers, through a misdirected patriotism, did not put into shells too strong a charge of explosive in the fond belief that it would help their soldier friends in overcoming the enemy. The filled shells, neatly packed into wooden cases, were loaded into grey-coloured railway trucks and despatched—to the war.

Such was the wonderful factory in question, one of many national factories set up to feed Britain's guns. Before leaving the subject of these national factories some tribute is due to the masters of craft whose skill and enthusiasm and wonderful energy led to their being built so well and with such amazing rapidity. **Rate of increase** Among the builders chiefly responsible **in shell production** was an American citizen, Mr. Quinan. This remarkable man, who was chemist, scientist, man of business, soldier, and architect all in one, threw up everything at the beginning of the war to give to Britain his valuable services.

Another man who did heroic labours in equipping the new factories was Sir Eric Geddes. Taken originally from the management of the North-Eastern Railway, this wonderful organiser did great war work for munitions before going over to another sphere of activity of greatest importance—at the Admiralty—where the whole question of supply organisation was put into his capable hands.

Though definite figures of the increase in shell production, due to these stupendous efforts, were not available for the purposes of this chapter—such figures would have been useful to the enemy—the writer, nevertheless, was able to obtain official figures showing the ratio of increase. Compared with the output in May, 1915, the ratio of increase attained by the middle of 1917 was as follows :

18 lb. shell production had increased 18 times.
4·5 in. howitzer shell production had increased 52 times.
Medium gun and howitzer shells increased 71 times.
Heavy howitzer shells (above 6 in.) increased 423 times.

Shown in another way : By the middle of 1917 the rate of shell production was such that the whole year's supply of 1915 could be produced in the following times :

18 lb. shells in 13 days.
4·5 in. howitzer shells in 7 days.
Medium gun and howitzer shells in 5 days.
Heavy gun shells (above 6 in.) in less than one day.

The following figures give an indication of the tremendous increase in the output of explosives used for the making of shells and other ammunition.

For every single ton of explosive used in September,

1914, the corresponding amounts used later were as follows :

In July, 1915, 350 tons.
In July, 1916, 1,100 to 1,200 tons.
In July, 1917, 2,200 to 2,400 tons.

In 1914 the Germans were able to fire ten shots to one from us. By the middle of 1917 the proportion was exactly reversed. Great Britain could fire ten shells to every German shell.

Not only was the supply of shells increased in these vast proportions but the quality was considerably improved. Two common defects in gun shells in the earlier years of the war were premature explosion, called "prematures," and "flying bands." Both were very serious defects, tending to make a shell more disastrous to the people who fired it than to the enemy at whom it was fired. Premature explosion of a shell might occur even in the barrel of the gun from which it was fired. That is to say, the shell, instead of carrying its charge of violent explosive safely through the air to explode in the enemy's position, "went off" in the gun-barrel simultaneously or almost simultaneously with the explosion of the propelling charge contained in the cartridge or packed in a silken bag behind the shell itself. Such was the strain on the gun-barrel when this double explosion occurred that the gun, even though it did not burst, swelled like a blown bubble and was rendered defective for further use. It may be interesting to mention here that the German guns, through not being wound with wire in the careful way that British guns were made, very frequently burst as a result of premature explosion of shell, killing their crews.

Improvement in quality of shells

Premature explosion might also occur during the flight of the shell, in which case it was very likely to injure men of the army that fired it, for the guns were almost always well back from the front lines, and the shells they fired passed over the heads of infantry and other troops stationed between the guns and the enemy's positions.

"Flying band," the other defect referred to, was due to defective make or fixing on of a shell's driving band, a broad and solid band of copper projecting from the steel case of the shell to come in contact with the rifling of the gun, and to bear the greater burden of the immense friction between shell and gun barrel. Copper, a softer metal than steel, did less damage to the gun and its rifling than a steel-to-steel contact would have done. These bands, as previously explained, were fixed on by hydraulic pressure. If faulty in any way, or badly fixed, they were apt to fly off during the flight of the shell and to hit men, horses, or other objects belonging to "their own side."

The writer stood once under a shell from which the band flew off. It whizzed through the air like a gleaming boomerang, struck the earth, throwing up a shower of soil, and then bounded along the surface of the ground, cutting ground, shrubs, and wire as it went. It was a most deadly missile and would have killed anyone who happened to be in its line of flight. The flight of a shell was invariably made inaccurate through the flying-off of the band. What happened to the shell in this particular

case could not be seen. Possibly no harm was done, but there were many cases of accident through shells falling short owing to faulty driving bands.

A third type of defective shell was the "dud," which, owing to faulty fuse or faulty contact detonator, failed to explode at all. Artillery officers posted in convenient "O.P.'s" (observation-posts) in advance of the guns were given great difficulties by these shells. A battery would telephone through to the O.P. that they were firing; the observers would strain their eyes for the landing of the shell—and see nothing. When the ground upon which the shells had been dropped was captured these "dud" shells could be found lying intact and unexploded, having fallen almost harmlessly on the enemy's positions.

The problem of the shell-makers was to hit the happy mean between the shell that exploded too easily, and therefore prematurely, and the shell that did not explode at all. Such was the improvement of the shells made after the Somme Battles that the Commander-in-Chief himself congratulated the Ministry of Munitions on the improvement in its work. The proportion of "prematures"

GETTING A FIELD-GUN OUT OF FLANDERS MUD. *British official photograph.*
British soldiers engaged in the strenuous task of "jacking" up a field-gun, one of the wheels of which had become embedded in a specially soft bit of ground during its removal to a fresh position.

had been reduced till it was fifteen times less than during the Somme Battles.

Much of this improvement was due to more efficient inspection. In July, 1915, the Inspection Department staff of the Ministry consisted of 8,761 persons. In July, 1917, it consisted of 48,000, of whom 8,000 were posted in the United States examining raw material. Thirty thousand of these inspectors were women, and it was found that in the more tedious and monotonous gauging processes women were more consistent and patient than men. The monotony of the work may be judged from the fact that every field-gun shell (the ordinary 18-pounder) had to go through one hundred and eighty-three different gauging operations before it could be regarded as exact.

Enormous output of guns

Of all the sound thinking done by the Ministry of Munitions in its earlier days nothing was more valuable than its foresight in the matter of guns, and especially of heavy guns. Even before the nation had realised to what extent shells would be needed in the new kind of warfare the Ministry had realised the importance of guns and had stimulated their output from existing plant

[Canadian War Records.

THROUGH FLOOD AND MUD.
Canadian soldiers moving an anti-aircraft gun on the western front along a badly flooded road. The men near the transport-waggon were ankle-deep in the mud.

[British official photograph.

PERTINACITY VERSUS TENACITY ON THE FLANDERS FRONT.
In difficulties with a field-gun during its removal to a fresh position. It had stuck firmly in the tenacious Flanders mud, and the pertinacious efforts of a number of British soldiers were necessary to drag and "jack" it out.

to the highest pitch as well as arranging for big extensions of plant. A big gun was not a thing that could be made anywhere. Very few works in the kingdom had the necessary apparatus, for the making of a big gun is a titanic labour. A quotation from the writer's diary after seeing these guns in the making will give some indication of that labour :

To-day we have been looking down the sixty-foot barrels of 15 in. guns, guns into which you can put your head and down which a man at the other end, holding an electric light seemed distant and tiny. "Gee," said an American of our party, after looking down such a barrel, "but you half expect to see the next train for Hammersmith dash out of yon tube." It had reminded him of a London underground railway.

Down this gun, with a light shining at the far end, you saw its beautiful rifling taper slowly along the barrel. Every ridge and groove shone bright as silver, till all seemed merged together in the perspective in a glittering pin-wheel of light. Here, in such a gun as this, finely exact to the finest dimensions, both outside and in, lay the final results of titanic labours. We had seen those labours from almost the start. First the smelting furnace outpouring its liquid fire, which splashed and hissed like water, though it was finest steel. Then the moulded ingot of steel which, gripped by giant claws, was carried away and passed through heatings and reheatings in order to undergo many maulings and thumpings and squeezings from hammers and from presses that squeezed it with a 10,000-ton squeeze. To see a great, red-hot trunk of steel, big as the biggest oak-tree, being punched and kneaded, cut and shaped and hollowed, as though it were so much potter's clay is one of the sights of even this wonder age. And suddenly the whole thing, red hot, scores of tons, was whisked right into the air from out of its vertical furnace (sixty feet or more high) and lowered right into an underground oil-bath, reaching

seventy feet below the earth's surface. The subterranean rumbling and gurglings and the sparks and the smoke ! You get a pocket Vesuvius in eruption with the oil-bath tempering of a 15 in. gun.

Some of the bigger guns are wrapped about their breeches with as much as two hundred miles of steel tape.

None of the many striking features of a long tour of the munition works of the country impressed the writer more than the enormous output of guns. The authorities were anxious that no indication of the extent of the output should be made known, but in general terms that output could be described as colossal. One saw acres of land covered with field-gun barrels stacked one upon another like logs around a Canadian homestead. There must have been thousands upon thousands. In other yards the big, fat barrels of howitzers were similarly piled up, all ready for mounting. It was interesting to note that some of these guns were inscribed with Russian characters. They were destined for the use of our eastern Allies, and not only the Russians, but most of Britain's Allies, had cause during the war to be thankful for the wonderful productivity of British gun-shops.

Great as was that productivity, it was not too great. In the Flanders battles of 1917, for instance, one saw a line of guns reaching from the sea to Messines Ridge, with one gun alongside another at an interval of only a few yards—actually miles of guns. There was need also for anti-aircraft guns and for guns for arming merchant ships. Remembering all these needs, and the comparatively short life of a gun-barrel, one realises the strain thrown upon the gun productivity of Great Britain. This productivity was not attained without going to the root of the whole matter, which lay in the capacity of the country to make steel ; and a programme of steel production calculated to give an increase from 7,000,000 tons a year to 12,000,000 tons had to be undertaken before Great Britain was in a position to make all the contribution she wished to make to the war resources of the allied nations. Even this was not enough, and private users of steel had to be "rationed." It was worthy of remark that at this time, notwithstanding the increased cost of material and

Regulation of steel production

labour, Great Britain was able to make steel plates at home at less than half their cost in the United States, and shell-steel at a saving of thirty per cent.

No record of the great work of feeding the guns would be complete without some reference to the work of supplying aeroplanes, which became almost as essential to the guns as their sights, for they were no less than the " eyes " of the guns. They found the positions of the enemy strong points, and recorded the effect of the allied gun fire upon those positions so far as the artillery observation officers were unable to record it. In January, 1917, it was realised that, if the Allies were to hold their own, the supply of aeroplanes would have to be increased in almost as great proportion as the supply of shells had to be increased in earlier years of the war. Till that time the supply of aeroplanes had been controlled by the flying services of the Army and the Navy respectively, with no very happy results, for the one service had been virtually competing with the other. It was with something akin to a "scare" that the position to which this state of things had led became realised. There was much severe criticism, and the whole question of the construction of aeroplanes was

Speeding up aero-plane construction handed over to the Ministry of Munitions, with instructions to reform the whole process and to speed-up production and output to an enormous extent. The Ministry put the matter in the hands of one of their expert organisers, Sir William Weir, of whom mention has already been made, and in his able hands output quickly increased. To such good purpose did he work that eight months later Dr. Addison—before leaving the Ministry of Munitions to take up the important duties of Minister of Reconstruction after the War—was able to make the following statement :

The single fact that no fewer than a thousand factories are engaged on some process or other connected with the construction and equipment of the flying machine proves the magnitude of the work we have in hand. As for output, it is increasing by leaps and bounds. If, for the purposes of comparison you put the

number of aeroplanes produced in May, 1916, at one hundred, then in May of this year the number rose to rather more than three hundred. Even this rate of increase is being accelerated. The output in December will be twice what it was in April, and the December total will be far surpassed in succeeding months. The number of aeroplane engines turned out monthly has been more than doubled this year already, and this total will be doubled again before the close of the year. What these figures involve in organisation will perhaps be appreciated when it is stated that a single cylinder of the rotary engine involves forty-eight different operations in its manufacture. As for spare parts, an enormous number has to be manufactured, as owing to the fragility of the machine its parts require frequent renewal, and "spares" must be ready to hand whenever and wherever wanted.

A growing number of workers are employed **Training-schools for** in the aeroplane factories, the increase in the **aircraft builders** last five months being twenty-five per cent. on the previous total. Along with this the replacement of skilled workers by women has gone on, the dilution percentage having risen from nineteen per cent. to thirty-seven per cent. To meet the demand for labour, special schools have been started all over the country, where a training of about two months qualifies a pupil to carry out some simple process in aeroplane manufacture. About a hundred qualified workers are supplied each week under this system. Yet the demand is not satisfied. More and more women are wanted, both in London and in the provinces, and women of good education and good physique can render the nation no better service at the present time than by undergoing the training which is offered in the schools.

The Minister of Munitions has had special difficulties to overcome to reach the present degree of output and efficiency. The technical development of the aeroplane has presented peculiar problems. New types are continually being evolved. It has never been possible to say, "This is the final form the aeroplane will assume," and lay constructional plans accordingly. Those responsible for the manufacture of our flying machines have always had to allow for a new invention coming along and revolutionising all their projects. Speed, climbing power, and armament have continually increased and improved since the outbreak of the war. An engine that can develop up to 350 horse-power, for example, and a single-seater scout able to travel at 150 miles per hour, are built on very different lines from their prototypes of August, 1914. Where there is no finality there is a limit to standardisation, except in small details, and the problem of supervising the manufacture of our aeroplanes is correspondingly complicated.

The variety of materials used in aeroplane construction, again, has been a great source of anxiety to the Ministry. Linen, timber, chemicals for tightening the fabric of wings, alloy steel, light alloys,

INTERIOR VIEW OF A MUNITION WORKS WHERE THOUSANDS OF HANDS WERE EMPLOYED.
Remarkable photograph of the interior of one of the vast factories that sprang into being when the manufacture of munitions was organised as a national industry by the Ministry of Munitions after its creation in May, 1915. By the beginning of 1917 the Ministry was in control of more than five thousand establishments, employing three million workpeople, exclusive of thousands of other workers employed under sub-contractors.

[Canadian War Records.

HEAVY HOWITZER IN ACTION ON THE WESTERN FRONT.

Canadian gun-team in charge of a heavy howitzer on the western front, having just fired their mighty weapon—the smoky fumes may be observed about the opened breech—are preparing to reload with another powerful shell. The stupendous increase in munitions after the summer of 1915 enabled the Allies to overcome and reverse the superiority in artillery which the enemy had possessed in the earlier stages of the war.

and thin tubes are among the essential requirements of the industry. Even if these were wanted in normal quantities there would be difficulty in getting enough in view of other necessities. But the needs of the aeroplane programme are enormous, almost passing belief. For our present programme of construction more spruce is wanted than the present annual output of the United States, more mahogany than Honduras can supply, and Honduras is accustomed to supply the requirements of the world. Besides this, all the linen of the type required, made in Ireland, the home of the linen industry, and the whole of the alloy steel that England can produce can be used. As for flax to meet the needs of the air service, the Government has actually to provide the seed from which to grow the plant essential for its purpose.

Programme of maximum production

Still, despite the magnitude of the demands, all the needs of aeroplane manufacture will be met, and the programme before the Ministry of Munitions is that of a maximum production.

This statement, with its full and intimate details as to the many different things and different kinds of labour and organisation of supplies needed for the making of aeroplanes, has been given in full because it is so thoroughly characteristic of other munition problems which the Ministry had had to face and overcome. For, as with aeroplanes and aeroplane parts, spruce, mahogany and the rest, so with a thousand other things needed for the making of munitions, the increased output had entailed similar activities reaching all over the world.

Great Britain's vast production in many cases had overtaken world supplies of raw material, and the Ministry had actually to send its delegates abroad in order to stimulate this world production of different commodities before Great Britain could be guaranteed supplies that should be sufficiently large to enable her to make all the munitions she wanted.

As in metals wrought from the earth in mines in remote parts of the world, so with other ingredients made at home. Special recruiting campaigns had to be undertaken in Cornwall and in the china-clay districts to obtain workers to assist in increasing the output of iron ore; a special "commando" of metal experts had to be turned aside to increase the production of tungsten for the making of high-tension steel; another "commando" was specially detailed to go into the refining and working up of copper; another to take up the production of spelter (commercial zinc); another the production of nitrates at home.

These and a thousand such problems had to be tackled as elemental problems, failing the solution of which essential programmes of munitions production could never have been successfully fulfilled.

So far this chapter has kept pretty closely to the main stream of the work of the Ministry of Munitions—namely, that of the feeding of the guns. This stream had tributaries innumerable, each of which represented a special department of the Ministry, with a special function and history of its own. The Labour Dispute Section, with its forty-five local Advisory Boards, dealt with an average of a hundred strikes a month, a thousand fair-wages-clause awards a month, and other disputes at the rate of four a day. The Labour Department of the Ministry adjusted the flow of labour to different industries and activities as and when required, fixed time rates and piece rates of pay. The Billeting Board provided housing and lodgings. The Stores Department made 60,000 individual consignments each week, and handled each

The Ministry and Labour disputes

week in its different departments no fewer than 50,000,000 articles.

Other departments of the Ministry were numerous, and they were no less complex in their make-up. Among these were the Trench Warfare Section, under the control of Sir A. F. P. Roger, responsible for the enormous variety of new sorts of trench weapons and supplies for which modern warfare had created a demand. Fireworks, hand-grenades, bombs, helmets, shields, gas-throwers, trench-mortars and their ammunition, gas-**Allied Departments** masks, steel helmets — these and a **and their chiefs** thousand other things, enough to make an immense munition section of their own, were needed in ever-increasing numbers. Whereas 7,648 tons of trench-warfare material served the needs of the armies in the month of December, 1916, the amount only six months later had risen to nearly 18,000 tons per month.

The Railway Supply Department, under Sir Ernest Moir, was another section that achieved wonders of work. The problem suddenly arose of supplying an enormous number of trucks, locomotives, and even new railways to help our Allies in France, and to keep British field forces well supplied. A collection was made from the railways of the British Empire. In reply to a telegraphed

FINISHING TOUCHES TO THE SHELLS.
Women workers in a vast British shell factory. One of them is seen engaged in stencilling the mighty missiles, each of which was placed on a separate small truck that ran on rails.

inquiry, the Government of Canada offered to pull up and send along as it stood 800 miles of track, with waggons and locomotives complete. Without calling on Canada to make this noble self-sacrifice, Sir Ernest Moir's department, between November, 1916, and June, 1917, supplied more than 2,000 miles of railway track and nearly a thousand locomotives over and above those lent by the British home railways.

The Mechanical Warfare Section, under the control of Colonel Stern,

saw to the designing and completion of new types of "tanks"; Colonel Holden and his Motor Transport Department (transferred from the War Office during 1916) saw to the needs of the immense service of motor transports needed in the field by the British Army; Mr. S. F. Edge controlled the immense output of agricultural implements needed for the Board of Agriculture's war programme; Mr. Martin, of the Birmingham Small Arms Company and the Daimler Motor Company, garnered into one department the whole supply for all departments of internal combustion engines; Mr. Herbert and his department became in a similar way a servant for all departments in the making and supply of machine-tools.

So one could go on right through the many varied phases of this vast agglomeration of the war energies of the nation centred in the Ministry of Munitions. As Dr. Addison aptly said in the House of Commons, on June 27th, 1917:

"The Ministry represents perhaps the most remarkable aggregation of men and women of diverse qualifications and attainments that has ever been got together in this country or in the world. Men from every branch of commerce and industry are serving with us, often as volunteers — scientists, lawyers, literary men, commercial men, travellers, soldiers and sailors, and I know not what besides, are working in our ranks, and faithfully have they served the State."

A word remains to be said of the millions of workers—men and women — who had sacrificed in many cases lucrative posts, careers, comfort, leisure, and contact with friends to go and help the nation during this period of danger and stress; also of the thousands of industrial workers of the country who worked unremittingly for hours and hours on **The nation's debt** end till, in some cases, their bodies **to the workers** gave out under the strain; also of the women and girls who sacrificed one of the possessions a woman holds dearest—namely, her physical beauty—to dabble in dangerous, noxious commodities which stained skin and hair and undermined health at the same time. All these workers who worked thus loyally were national heroes no less than those who fought in the field of battle. To these people who laboured, no less than to the people who organised their labour, were the thanks and praise of the nation due. British posterity for all time will owe them this debt.

THE KING AND QUEEN AMONG THE MUNITION WORKERS.
King George and Queen Mary, during their visit to centres of war activity on the North-East Coast, inspecting the girl munition workers at Sir James Laing & Sons' Deptford Yard, Sunderland.

INTERIOR OF A "TANK" BELONGING TO THE FRENCH ARTILLERY OF ASSAULT.

Gunners of a French "tank" in action. In the centre a gunner is seen reloading the forward gun, while to the right two machine-gunners are at work, one firing forward and the other laterally. One of the Press correspondents on the western front, Mr. H. Perry Robinson, in describing a trip in a British "tank," said: "It has immensely increased my admiration for them, and for the men who go down in them to battle. For a summer outing a man might reasonably prefer a caravan, for they are not luxuriously appointed. But the manageability of the great beasts is wonderful."

THE GREAT BATTLES OF RHEIMS AND THE CHAMPAGNE.

By Edward Wright.

Seven Hours' Gas Attack—Pétain Recovers Maisons de Champagne—Western French Army Breaks into Roye—Grand Pursuit Between Soissons and Roye—Monuments of Hunnishness—Germans Leave Horrible Traps for French Children—Progress Through the Land of Death—Fresh Evidence of Corpse Utilisation Processes—French Advance Stopped by Great German Inundation—Envelopment Demonstration at St. Quentin—How the Chasseurs Escaped from Ambush at Missy—Destruction of Coucy Castle—French Victory in the Lower Forest—The Pen Becomes Mightier than the Sword—Grandiose Plan of General Nivelle—Extraordinary Bad Weather Hinders French Operations—Magnificent Heroism of French Forces above Vailly—Double Wedge Attack on Braye—Victorious Enveloping Movement Round Condé—Germans Shepherded into an Artillery Massacre—Temporary Failure at Craonne—French Public Mistake Victory for Defeat—Comparison with First British Successes on the Somme—Capture of Ville-aux-Bois Position and Cavaliers de Courcy—Division of "Aces" and Russian Contingent Strive to Free Rheims—Retirement of General Nivelle—Promotion of General Foch and General Pétain—The "Bonnet Rouge" and Enemy Influences that Made a Great Victory Look Like a Defeat.

FTER General Nivelle's remarkable successes north of Verdun on December 15th, 1916 (as described in Chapter CLXII.), there was a long period of routine trench warfare by the army groups commanded by General Castelnau, General Franchet d'Espérey, and General Pétain. The new Commander-in-Chief arranged for the first blow in the new campaign to be struck by Sir Douglas Haig. In the meantime the French armies prepared to co-operate between Roye and Noyon in a resumption of the Somme Battle, and to undertake another wing offensive in the Champagne area.

The German Staff foresaw that the effect of the great retreat it was arranging would provoke a most violent reaction at the southern pivot of its proposed new line. This pivot was at Soissons, close to where the Germans possessed a bridge-head over the Aisne River. On February 14th, 1917, the armies under the Crown Prince of Prussia began to test the line held

TWO DISTINGUISHED FRENCH GENERALS.
General Guillemot (left) and General Humbert (right) at Vezaponin, on the Aisne. In March, 1917, General Guillemot was successful in breaking a fierce German attack on the French line around Caurières Wood.

by General Pétain. There was a slight French salient in the downland between Rheims and the Argonne Forest. It occurred at the spot where General Pétain, in September, 1915, won the rank of army commander by the way he led his division over the Hand of Massiges. The spot was known as the Maisons de Champagne. German engineers arranged a great line of cylinders along the whole front of attack, and for seven hours poured out asphyxiating gas in a continuous stream. Special troops, with oxygen helmets, visited the cylinders frequently to see that the gas was flowing out properly.

The design was to saturate the masks of the French defending troops and compel them to die or flee. But the danger had been foreseen by the French general, and he had furnished his men with a change of masks. The effect was that this part of the German plan was nullified.

Nevertheless, the attack succeeded. Seven hours after the gas cylinders were opened a special concentration of hostile artillery poured such a fire upon the little curve that the French outposts were cut off. Then a number of mines were exploded under the advanced French positions, and the German storming troops came forward and carried the few hundred yards of trenches. They could not, however, reach the sunken road which had formed the base of the small French salient.

Batteries of quick-firers on the Massiges heights swept the flank of the German troops, inflicting upon them losses heavier than those incurred by the light advanced force which had occupied the salient between Mesnil Down and the ruined buildings of the Maisons de Champagne.

At the beginning of March another strong enemy demonstration was directed against the French outpost position near Douaumont. In a fierce nocturnal struggle the German troops tried to penetrate two miles of French line around
Caurières Wood. When day came the **Germans broken at** enemy was completely broken on both **Caurières Wood** flanks, and holding, in his centre, feebly to a line of posts in the wood. A sharp counter-attack dislodged the Germans from the northern part of the wood, and at comparatively little cost restored practically all the lost French positions.

Following on this success of General Guillemot, General Pétain, after lengthy preparations, launched his counterstroke on the Maisons de Champagne. As was generally known after the Battle of the Marne, Pétain was a man with a motto. His motto was: "Artillery conquers; infantry merely occupies." He was an extraordinary economist in regard to the lives of his men. Having brought up an overwhelming number of guns, he smashed the German lines around the Maisons Farm on March 8th, and sent out infantry patrols to see if the ground could be easily occupied.

Only part of the shattered portions was easy to capture and reorganise. There remained a height called Down 185,

AT A DANGEROUS OBSERVATION-POST.
Moroccan marksman in the French Army who had erected a mass of leaves and twigs as a mask through which he could make observations of the enemy positions with the minimum of exposure.

which was an important observation-station overlooking the enemy's river front at Ripont. This dominating point remained well defended. General Pétain withdrew his troops for a short distance, and for another four days lashed with heavy shell the great lump of chalk and its connecting defences. Again he sent his patrols forward, and not only recovered the whole of the lost salient, but penetrated into the fortress in the original German lines. This local victory on a single mile of front had considerable political importance. On February 16th the German Emperor had vaunted his son's success, and with characteristic folly published a telegram of exaggerated felicitation. The subsequent loss of the ground by the Crown Prince and the penetration of his own line helped to maintain the tradition of the personal impotence in battle of the Hohenzollern.

It is hard to decide, however, whether this little bout was worth undertaking. Its immediate result was that an enormous amount of new work was at once put in hand along all the front **Preparations for a** nominally commanded by the Crown **German offensive** Prince. From the great ridge north of the Aisne, through the crescent of hills enveloping Rheims, and the broken downland beyond stretching to the Argonne Forest, German sappers and German troops, with tens of thousands of prisoners of war and deported French and Belgian non-combatants, were set to labour in snow and mud.

Dug-outs and caverns were enlarged and increased in number, new communicating tunnels were excavated or partly constructed, more heavy guns were brought up, and additional armoured concrete forts were sunk in the ground whenever the frost-bound surface allowed of digging. A considerable amount of expert opinion in France reckoned that Ludendorff intended to use a large part of his reserves in a great offensive movement from Champagne as soon as the land became sufficiently dry.

A PATHWAY TO SAFETY.
Two French soldiers carrying to the nearest aid-post a comrade who had been severely wounded in the firing-line. They were passing through a very deep communication-trench.

French aerial observers began to perceive that extraordinary masses of hostile forces were collecting, one behind the other, between Verdun, Rheims, and Soissons. Somewhat more than a month afterwards, captured German troops stated that it was known throughout the Crown Prince's army that an offensive, far surpassing that of Verdun, was to be launched against the French in Champagne, while the British armies were checked by Ludendorff's scheme for retiring his centre.

Ludendorff surprised and outplayed This movement against the main French forces may have been intended in the middle of March, 1917, before Sir Hubert Gough broke through the Bapaume Ridge, months in advance of the time-table fixed by the hostile High Command. When, however, Ludendorff was surprised and outplayed by the British commander, he was compelled to postpone his attempt to better the achievement of Falkenhayn, to stand on the defensive, and play as long as possible for safety.

Warned by Sir Douglas Haig that the German front was breaking under the attacks by the Fifth British Army, General Nivelle arranged with vehement speed to pursue the Germans with all his available light forces. His western army, under General Castelnau, broke into Roye before dawn on Saturday, March 17th, giving the Germans no time to set fire to the town. The barbarians had laid numerous mines under the streets and the principal buildings, and fired some of them at four o'clock in the morning, as the French forces were driving over the original front. Craters, forty feet wide and thirty feet deep, were blown into the centre of the principal thoroughfares, and many fine historic buildings were undermined and toppled into the great holes. The magnificent Town Hall was completely wrecked when the French patrols reached it, but they managed to cut the leads of some of the German mines and save the buildings of entire streets.

As at Péronne and Bapaume, the Germans had wasted time in smashing pianos, chairs, beds, looking-glasses, dishes, and other private furniture, and had not completed their real military work of destruction, though the town looked as if it had been destroyed by an earthquake. The French engineers rapidly reconstructed the roads for their pursuing forces.

Cavalry, infantry, artillery, supply convoys, and sappers poured through Roye, Lassigny, Thiescourt, and Chiry, and by the woods and farms between Ribécourt and Soissons. Before them, clouds **Outrages by the** of smoke by day and pillars of fire by **retreating foe** night, rising from burning towns, villages, hamlets, and homesteads, urged them forward to vengeance and recovery. Very quiet were the Frenchmen as they swept onward against the rearguards of the enemy. When they entered Noyon and found that fifty girls between fifteen and twenty years of age had been taken away by German officers they became still quieter.

KEEPING THE FRONT LINES WELL SUPPLIED. [*French official photograph.*]

British and French convoys passing each other behind the lines on the western front, near the junction of their armies. The British convoy, miles in length, was going up with munitions and other supplies along the roadway, while French waggons (on the left), lightened by the due delivery of their loads, were returning to their base along the rougher ground of the field edge, so that the road might be clear for their British comrades.

IN A RUINED BUT REDEEMED FRENCH VILLAGE.

[French official photograph.

French troops marching forward through Flaucourt, on the Somme, towards Péronne, in that victorious push of the summer of 1916 which began the winning back for France of a large tract of her territory that the Germans had occupied for two years. The officers were pausing to look at some of the ruins. One striking example of the fantastic effects left by shell fire or other explosion is shown in the background.

Instead of setting Noyon on fire, the unspeakable Teutons packed the streets with twelve thousand old men, women, and children, and then dammed the canals and flooded the lower parts of the town. The inundation rose very high and caused great suffering. The appearance of the starving people was terrible. They had scarcely tasted meat or good bread for eighteen months, as the food provided by the American Relief Organisation was usually seized by the invaders.

The population of Noyon was used by the enemy as a screen. He placarded the road of approach with notices, asking the French not to shell his rearguards, as the town was crowded with refugees from the surrounding villages. As soon as the rearguards safely retired, German aeroplanes dropped bombs

Thefts by Prince Eitel Frederick upon the town, killing and wounding the people there collected in a way which showed that the placarded appeals for mercy to the townspeople were only a cynically cruel manœuvre.

There were several historic manor-houses around Noyon. Most of them were, like Avricourt, exquisite examples of French architecture of the Renaissance, filled with lovely works of art and rare and valuable books. Prince Eitel Frederick, son of the German Emperor, settled in Avricourt Château and transported all its finest treasures into Germany, in the ordinary manner of the avaricious robber race descended from a usurer of Nuremberg.

When this Imperial brigand left for another plundering operation on Fretoy Château, the lovely building of Avricourt remained for a time intact. In the night of March 13th, however, his men exploded a vast mine under this jewel of French architecture, and when the French troops arrived not a fragment of wall remained above the mounds of broken brick. As Avricourt Château was in a low position that protected it from bombardment, it was utterly useless to either side as an observation-point. More- **Destruction of Avricourt Chateau** over, the Count of Avricourt was a diplomatist of the little neutral State of Monaco, and on terms of personal acquaintance with the German Emperor, his sons, and many of his Ministers. No fighting occurred in or near this lovely classic in stone. No doubt, the barbarians thought that the Minister of such a microscopic neutral country as Monaco was a person of less than no account. Yet the amazingly wanton destruction of the beautiful turreted building served vividly to illumine the permanent qualities of character of the modern Teuton.

From Noyon to Chauny the roadside orchards were destroyed in the same manner as in the British zone of advance. All agricultural machinery was either carried away or smashed up. Canals were mined to make them useless for traffic and to flood the countryside. Wells were horribly poisoned, and the most extraordinary traps were laid. To tempt the French troops, there were exploding trunks and boxes and other objects of furniture which it

196

was death to open. Then, with more subtlety, special fountain-pens were left behind apparently in the hurry of retreat, but filled with very delicate chemicals calculated to shatter the arm and blind the eyes of the man who handled them.

The horrifying brutes, however, were not content to devise booby-traps for the fighting men of France. In order to reduce to a condition of mad despair the villagers who returned to the evacuated territory, a curious variety of childish toys was placed among the litter in some of the ruined dwelling-places. There were little whistles that exploded when they were blown, spinning-tops with ammonal inside them, devised for blowing a group of playing boys into the hospital or the grave. Dolls, probably made in Nuremberg, were stuffed with something more deadly than sawdust. At Canizy a French child lost four fingers through picking up one of these toys. At Voyennes a grandfather lost his hand in an attempt to please his grandchild by bringing him something to play with. Similar incidents occurred at Languevoisin and other villages.

The Germans out-Heroded Herod by the scientific ingenuity with which they devised means of torturing and slaying, in a series of after-blows, the French children they left behind them. Their action in the matter of explosive toys can scarcely be called satanic. Lucifer himself would

WINE FOR THE FIRING-LINE.
Bringing up supplies of wine "in the wood" for the first-line fighting men on the French front.

have had more virility than to act like a human degenerate of the weakest of all Neronian types. Had the Germans pursued, like the ancient Huns, a downright policy of entire extermination, and driven their bayonets through the French children, as they did in some cases during their advance into Belgium and France, their inhuman fury would have excited less disgust than their device of leaving behind them exploding toys. Civilised beings can hardly understand the mental condition of the men who filled the toys with the horrible chemicals and carefully placed them in tempting positions, amid wreckage of humble dwelling-places of starved, ruined peasant folk. It would be a libel upon the lowest savages of the most primitive age to call this sort of thing savagery.

There were many other atrocities of a more ordinary kind. At Guiscard, for example, an aged woman endeavoured to succour her grandchild, a girl of eighteen, whom a German officer was leading away for immoral use. With a stroke of his sword the officer cut off the arm of the grandmother. Another old woman, attempting a similar rescue, had her thigh broken by a German officer. In a village near Guiscard the women and children, after being separated from their husbands, older sons, and brothers, were ordered to go along the road westward and wait for the French troops. The main body of Germans then left, but the German rearguard brought

CAVALRY DESPATCH-RIDERS ON LIAISON DUTY.
Behind the lines on the French front, where cavalrymen were stationed to form a link as despatch-riders between two parts of the French forces, so that they could be kept in touch and their movements properly correlated. Above: Trained canine messenger on "liaison" work.

```
Oberkommando 6.Armee.                          A. H. Qu.,den 21. 12. 1916.


                    Armee - Tages - Befehl vom 21. 12. 1916.


      1.      Personalien.
     IVb.     Das Kommando des Zahnarztes Oppenheim und Zahntechnikers Glander
             der Kr.Laz.Abt.1/IV zur Zahnstation der 6.B.Res.Div.wird bis 1.4.
             1917 verlängert.

      2.      Chef des Gen.Stabes d.Feldh.II № 41863 op.
     Pi. a)Hptm.Kniep besucht im Auftrage d.Chefs d.Gen.Stabes d.Feldh.die
             Armee um sich über Zufuhr und Verbrauch von Nahkampfmitteln und
             Baustoffen,für den Stellungsbau zu unterrichten.
             Die Dienststellen und Truppen werden ersucht,ihm zu diesem Zwecke
             jede Unterstützung zu gewähren und Zutritt zu allen Stellungen und
             Parks sowie vollen Einblick in die betreffenden Verhältnisse zu
             gewähren.

          b)7.Offizier-Aspiranten-Lehrkurs für Pioniere.
             Die General-Jnspektion des Jng.-u.Pion.Korps u.der Festungen teilt
             mit:
                 Nach den unter G.J.№ 6400.16.III vom 23.Februar 1916 gegebe-
             nen "Bestimmungen für die 4.Ausbildungskurse für Offizieraspiran-
             ten des Beurlaubtenstandes der Pioniere"beginnen am 5.Januar 1917
                         siebente Lehrkurse.
             Sie dauern bis zum 29.März 1917.

          c)Die Arm.Sold.Haarmann und Boller der 2./Arm.Bat.53 werden mit
             Wirksamkeit vom 21.12.16 zur Armee-Starkstromabt.6 versetzt,die
             dafur der 2./Arm.Bat.53  2 Mann als Ersatz überweist.

      3.      Organisationsänderung bei den Telegrafen-Truppen.
     Tel.    Gem.K.M.E.№ 192/12.16.A 7 V vom 14.12.16 wurde der Stabsoffizier
             der Telegrafen-Truppen beim A.O.K. in "Kommandeur der Fernsprech-
             truppen (Kofe)",
             der Kommandeur des Funker-Kommandos 6 in
             "Kommandeur der Funkertruppen (Kofu)"beim A.O.K.umgewandelt.

      4.     Gemäß Pr.K.M.E. 2675/11.16.A.2 v.12.12.16.Ziffer 1 Abs.4 ist in
     M.G.    den monatlich einzureichenden Nachweisen über M.G.von jetzt ab
             der Stand vom 1.jeden Monats zu Grunde zu legen;auf der Rückseite
             ist Art u.Anzahl der noch fehlenden Fahrzeuge - auch bei bay.,
             sächs.u.württ.Formationen - zu melden.
             Termin beim A.O.K.6 am 6.jeden Monats.

      5.      Anforderung von Geschirrleder,Filz und Rehfellen.
     IVa.a)Nach Mitteilung der Traindepotinspektion Berlin wird neues Leder
             (Blankleder,Kalbleder u.s.w.)als Flickmaterial zur Ausbesserung
             von Geschirren nicht mehr geliefert.Die Truppen haben zu diesem
             Zweck das Leder von unbrauchbaren Geschirren,für die neue angefor-
             dert wurden,zu benutzen.
             Desgleichen sind die Bedarfsanzeigen auf Filz und Rehfelle ungleich
             mehr als bisher einzuschränken.Die Verwendung von Filz als Sattel-
             unterlage ist verboten.Als Unterlagstücke bei Druckschäden oder
             Durchziehen der Pferde sind,soweit irgend möglich,Unterkummte bezw.
             Schwellkissen anzufordern.

          b)Einlieferung in die Kadaververwertungsanstalten:
             Es besteht Veranlassung,wiederholt darauf aufmerksam zu machen,
             daß bei Einlieferung von Kadavern in die Kadaververwertungsanstal-
             ten in allen Fällen Ausweise mitzugeben sind,aus denen Truppenteil,
             Todestag,Krankheit und Angaben über etwaige Seuchen zu ersehen sind

          c)Einschränkung des Karbidverbrauchs.(Telegramm des Gen.Jntdt.I
                                   № 2200/12.16 v.19.12.16)
             K.M.drahtet:Mit Rücksicht auf hohen Karbidverbrauch in Schweißin-
             dustrie und Landwirtschaft,Karbidbestände sehr knapp und größte
             Einschränkung geboten,soweit mit Kriegsinteressen vereinbar,wird
             daher ersucht,Anordnung zu treffen,daß über bisherigen Umfang
             Karbidbeleuchtung keinesfalls hinausgegangen und Beschaffung Kar-
             bidlampen in jeder Beziehung eingeschränkt wird.

          d)Neues Versandziel für Säcke und Sacklumpen. (Gen.Jntdt.W.№ 1245
                                                                    12.16)
             Neues Versandziel für Säcke und Sacklumpen;aus dem Westen:
             Firma Gebr.Blumenstein,Mannheim-Jndustriehafen,
             für Sendungen aus dem Osten: Hermann Förster,Magdeburg-Sudenburg.


                             V. S. d. O. K.

                                 J. A.

                             B r a u n
```

GERMAN "CORPSE UTILISATION" ORDER.
Photographic reproduction from the "Times" (June 5th, 1917) of the notorious Daily Army Order of the Sixth German Army. Paragraph 5b says: "It has become necessary once more to lay stress on the fact that when corpses are sent to the Corpse Utilisation Establishments returns as to the unit, date of death, illness, and information as to (contagious) diseases, if any, are to be furnished at the same time."

a machine-gun to bear upon the unhappy refugees as these were confidently awaiting the arrival of their saviours. It was mainly the children who were killed or wounded.

Everything in the zone of evacuation made the country look like a land of death. Between the ruined towns and villages were fire-blackened walls of farm-steads, ravaged orchards, flooded fields, and broken canals. More-over, the French graveyards were odiously profaned and devastated; all the tombs that promised to hold spoil were opened, and the coffins were broken. Only one kind of monument remained in-tact and insolently dominant. Standing like a permanent insult in the recovered territories were the stone monuments consecrated by the Germans to the memory of their " Helden krieger "—their " Warrior heroes." French graves were broken open and sullied with human filth. The German funereal monuments, distinguished mainly by pretentious ugliness, were clean and well tended. Im-pudently, the barbarians had endeavoured to protect their dead by burying some French soldiers between the German corpses that had escaped from the Teutonic Corpse Utilisation Society.

It had been long known that the German Staff had developed some of its new scientific knackers' businesses into factories for the extraction of fat from human bodies and turning the rest of its dead cannon-fodder into pigs' food. The " Times " first openly debated this matter, and was fiercely assailed, as an organ of inhuman slander, by certain British and French journals as well as by all the reptile Teutonic Press. It soon became evident, however, that the " Times " was right in the matter. For during the retreat of the German centre an Army Order was found, which dealt, among other things, with the collection and transport of dead German soldiers to one of the factories where their fat could be turned into lubricating oil and their flesh, sinews, and bones into meatmeal for pigs. The discovery was made during these operations.

Amid all the scenes in this province of death, which, though only a little corner of France, was sufficient to plunge a great realm into mourning, the French troops became more sternly quiet and more swift in their movements of advance. Since the age of Julius Cæsar the Gaul had been renowned for his power of speech; yet the modern Frenchman spoke but little. Bomb and sabre, bayonet and gun, were the instruments with which he expressed his feelings. He clean outraced the more cautious British soldier. By means of savage cavalry charges he rolled back rearguard after rearguard, and kept in close touch with the retiring enemy.

He swept through Ham, where the mediæval fortress had been blown, in vast rocks of masonry, into the canal. He occupied the important railway junction of Tergnier on March 20th, and arrived within four miles of St. Quentin. The next day the mounted French patrols carried Jussy against a strong defence, and touched the lower course of the Ailette stream, that ran from the old and new battlefields of tangled hills near Craonne and the Chemin des Dames, north of the Aisne River. General Castelnau kept his men tensely struggling forward in difficult weather of mud and rain and snowstorms. Frequently, a gun would get bogged on a good road, or what once had been a good road, and hold up miles of traffic. The continual search for land-mines delayed the heavy **Rapid advance of** vehicles of supply, and though the **infuriated French** cavalry, light infantry, machine-gunners, and horse artillery were often able to work over the unbroken fields, which were harder than the worn-out roads, the distressing condition of the ground told on the legs of horses and men.

Nevertheless, the fierce and inflamed French toiled forward at a remarkable pace, and rapidly consolidated their new positions. As already stated, Ludendorff

contrasted, with cynical intention, the quickness of the French advance and the slow cautiousness with which Sir Henry Rawlinson's and Sir Hubert Gough's troops went forward. In the end, however, the different methods of the allied armies achieved the same result. As the French arrived first at the Hindenburg system, they were merely the first to be strongly checked. Indeed, they were abruptly brought far more completely to a standstill than were the British.

Germans loose an inundation

Very ingenious was the means devised by the enemy to contain, with little effort, the progress of the French forces between St. Quentin and Laon. The German sappers dammed the upper course of the Oise and its tributaries, kept back also the water of the Somme, collected the winter rains and the wash of melted snow, and unexpectedly loosed a great flood upon the hostile French advanced guards between Tergnier and La Fère.

The town of La Fère rose, like a lake island, from the waste of water. The French could not attack, and the Germans did not dream of counter-attacking across the inundations. The trick the Belgians had played upon the enemy along the Yser in the autumn of 1914 was effectively imitated by him in the spring of 1917. All the left wing and left centre of General Castelnau's army was prevented from turning St. Quentin from the south and getting in the rear of the German hill positions north of the Aisne. In ordinary circumstances the French would have broken through the Alberich line of the lower

PUSHING FORWARD WITH THE ARTILLERY THROUGH A CAPTURED POSITION.

French artillery passing along a road that had been improvised by Army engineers round a great mine-crater in the highway which the Germans had sought to render impassable before their retirement from the village to which it gave approach. The French engineers proved themselves wonderfully quick and resourceful in minimising the delays to their advance which were caused by such obstacles.

Hindenburg system by the surprising vehemence of their advance in force.

Before them, protecting St. Quentin southward, was a large crescent of hills which would have been costly to assail. This great obstacle would certainly have been avoided by sweeping still more to the south, seizing La Fère and its lowlands, and dividing, by this famous gateway of battle, into two streams of flanking attack flowing against and around St. Quentin and **Relief of St. Quentin** Laon. As Sir Henry Rawlinson's army **frustrated** was then approaching well within rifle-shot of St. Quentin, and beginning to turn the historic city from the north, the expectations of the French people rose very high.

Vainly, however, they waited for news of the fall of St. Quentin. The flood between the French commander and his real goal continued to deepen and widen, as snow-falls alternated with rain downpours, while the severest of winters within memory effaced the springtide and ended only when the sudden heat of summer came. The French commander discovered the situation very quickly by means of aeroplane reconnaissance. Changing the direction of his main force, he struck towards the great hill Forest of St. Gobain, that towered like an inland Gibraltar between the floods at La Fère and the fortified plateau north of the Aisne. All the German positions for twenty-five miles north of Soissons were rapidly taken as far as Vregny—an historic point in the Franco-British campaign of September, 1914, against which General Smith-Dorrien's division and General Maunoury's forces had then vainly tried to advance.

The French armies worked down from the Oise River, along its tributary the Ailette, and worked up from the forest and fortified promontories and ridge of the Soissons Plateau. By March 22nd the advanced attacking forces were on the high ridge, in a dominating position on the Maubeuge road.

The deadly rage of the French peasants made them at times so impetuous that they fell into hostile ambuscades. Along the Aisne at Missy, of tragic memory to the 2nd British Division of the original Expeditionary Force, two companies of a crack light infantry battalion of Chasseurs were entirely enveloped by superior numbers of Germans. For some days they had been pressing hard on the heels of the retreating enemy, and their energy had been doubled by the destruction of the Soissons orchards. The Chasseurs justly complained that their barbaric foes had spared the great forest, which had a real military value, while endeavouring to ruin the peasantry by destroying fruit trees that would take twenty years to grow again.

The five hundred Chasseurs swept down on Missy with less caution than was necessary, and as the Germans had also flooded the Aisne Valley as well as the Upper Oise, the men were pressed by superior numbers to the river brink and taken between fire and water. At some distance behind them was a veteran regiment of the line, who saw the peril of the light infantry. No orders were needed. By a kind of sudden inspiration the entire regiment swept

FROM THE VIEW-POINT OF A "TANK."
View of one French "tank" as seen from another. This photograph gives an idea of the gunners' range of vision when they went into action with their "artillery of assault."

down on the Germans, and at the same time the Chasseurs rose from such cover as they had found and charged to meet their comrades. The right German flank was entirely broken by the double attack. The Germans who tried to stand their ground were cut to pieces; the others were scattered.

From the Aisne to La Fère the Germans were overwhelmed in their outpost positions by the furious rapidity of the French advance. The measure of the degree in which they had been disconcerted was indicated by the wild and repeated counter-attacks they made in the hope of recovering their important lost positions. There was bitter fighting on and around the Vregny mass of rock and along the deep ravines and high spurs running from it. The villages of Crouy and Missy, on its southern base, and Margival, at its northern angle, were also theatres of fierce conflict. Against the bridged road running towards Laon and Maubeuge, which was captured on March 22nd, the Germans stormed back three times on March 23rd and 24th. The French forces maintained their ground, and after each enemy counter-attacking force was broken, again fought forward steadily and violently. The result was that they opened the grand battle of the Hindenburg line a fortnight before the main British offensive movement began.

The southern part of the Hindenburg system ran from the old Condé Fort, by Vailly village on the inundated Aisne, through the high broken table-land where General Smith-Dorrien and General Haig had fought. It continued along the Ailette stream, through the great St. Gobain forested upland, and by the flooded marshes near La Fère to the southern crescent of heights at St. Quentin.

The principal base of the new German stand was the natural fortress of St. Gobain. It consisted of a thickly-wooded mass of rock, covering fifteen square miles and rising seven hundred feet. It was bounded by the Oise on the west, the Ailette on the south, and the Plain of Laon on the north. By March 25th the western French armies half surrounded St. Gobain. They occupied also some of the outer forts of the islanded hill of La Fère, and held the southern hill village of Margival, where the old blood-stained battle road, the Chemin des Dames, ended. They also occupied the midway position of Coucy, in the neighbourhood of which was one of the most perfect and famous examples in Europe of the castle architecture of the Middle Ages.

What Windsor Castle is to England, Coucy Castle was to France. Venerable, majestic, consecrated by history and romance, the mighty **Wanton destruction** walls and towers, set against the wild **of Coucy Castle** beauty of the forest, was, like Rheims Cathedral, one of the supreme monuments of the French people. Modern military value it had none in the circumstances. It might have served as a machine-gun position had the struggle raged around it, but owing to its position on the lower slope of the plateau it gave no observation over the tree-screened higher ground to which the Germans retired.

Ludendorff, however, ordered that many tons of high explosive should be wasted in blowing up the grand old castle. The vandal act was part of his policy of exasperating the French nation into a condition in which they would accept a servile peace. At the same time as Coucy Castle was reduced to shapeless ruin, Rheims Cathedral was pounded with extraordinary storms of heavy shell.

As was afterwards seen, Ludendorff's lieutenants could not obtain sufficient shell during the terrific fighting from Vimy to Bullecourt, and had to remain for weeks in a condition of inferior artillery power. **Blood tribute for German vandalism** Yet enough high explosive was spent on Coucy Castle as would have been sufficient to undermine all the roads in the evacuated zone, and the number of big shells pitched on Rheims Cathedral and the neighbouring buildings sometimes exceeded seven thousand, and was never less than two thousand, a day. All the main bodies of German infantry were bitterly angry in regard to the scandalously small support they received from their high-explosive weapons. It thus seemed that they paid in blood for the insane injury done to the Castles of Coucy and Ham and to the Cathedrals of Soissons and Rheims.

The German infantry also paid in another way for all the vile, obscene, dirtily-cunning, and most barbarous work of destruction they accomplished. The French soldier of Napoleon's day never fought with such sustained violence, such passion-quickened skill, and spiritual glory of sacrifice as his descendant did along the Aisne and the Hindenburg line in the spring of 1917.

Often had the Frenchman been lashed to madness. The first atrocities of the invaders lifted him above himself on the Marne. The following year he was again spurred to the fiercest fury by fresh revelations of Teutonic devilry. Again, in 1916, the deportations of his countrymen in the country occupied by the enemy, and the systematic manner in which French women and girls were horribly wronged,

worked upon the French soldier in a way that did not make for the ends the German Staff had in view.

After this long series of maddening exaltations of the French spirit, Ludendorff may have thought that the impressionable Frenchman would at last be dulled to any further intense reaction against systematic atrocities. It was not so. In spite of such incidents as that which occurred at Missy, the veteran troops of France were not generally carried away by the vehemence of their feelings. They worked quicker in the heavy, monotonous labour of organising their new communications and lines; they grumbled less when difficulties in food supply occurred owing to the speed of their advance; and they watched every possible advantage in attack while manœuvring to close upon the enemy. It was when they closed in attack and could employ bomb and bayonet that they let themselves go.

Hundreds of German patrols were wiped out neatly and completely. French field-gunners, using the new system of ranging invented by the brilliant professor of mathematics, M. Painlevé, who had become Minister of War, caught large bodies of German troops, some on the march and some ready for attack. It was on Sunday, March 25th, that the French troops first brought the enemy into action in a large way. Between the Somme and the Oise they broke the Germans south **Battle of the Coucy Forest** of St. Quentin, and began to work round the semicircle of hills. South of the Oise they entered the lower part of the forest, and drove violently forward against Folembray village and La Feuillée. The great forest battle continued day and night until Tuesday, March 27th. All the German forces were then shattered in the Lower Forest, and at various points some of the French advanced patrols penetrated, with slight losses, into the outskirts of the Upper Forest.

Servais, the village south of La Fère, with the forest hamlet of Barisis, Coucy Castle, and Coucy la Ville, were

FRENCH "TANKS" ADVANCING INTO ACTION UNDER COVER OF A WOOD.

The "artillery of assault" made its first appearance with the French armies in the spring of 1917. On April 16th it played a determining part in the capture of Juvincourt, east of Craonne, and on April 20th General Nivelle, in an Order of the Day, particularly congratulated the "tanks" on this performance, saying that the crews had won a place of honour in the army by their courage and zeal.

D D

GERMAN CURTAIN FIRE BARRING THE CHEMIN DES DAMES.
"The Ladies' Walk," north of the Aisne, was the scene of terrific fighting at several periods of the Great War. Part of it was held by the British in 1914, until they moved to Ypres to save Calais, and in April, 1917, it became the objective of General Nivelle's offensive.

among the important positions captured. Then, south of the great forest, the army of the Aisne drove through the advanced works of the Hindenburg line, between the Ailette River and the Aisne, as far as Leuilly and the Chemin des Dames. They also penetrated beyond Margival and the wooded spurs of the river plateau at Chivres—another spot well known to the little British Army in September, 1914.

With the capture of the Lower Forest, the western end of the Chemin des Dames, and the approaches to Condé Fort the operations of pursuit by the French armies, working directly with the British armies, came to an end. In order to drive with any prospect of success through the main Hindenburg system between St. Quentin and Vailly, time was needed for the difficult work of hauling big guns towards the slopes of the Gobain and Craonne Plateaux and towards the various hills and flooded waterways on the northern sectors of the new French line.

At the end of the last week in March it would have been possible for General Castelnau and Sir Henry Rawlinson strongly to combine in an enveloping attack upon the town of St. Quentin. The Fourth British Army enjoyed a better terrain, and was able to press more closely around St. Quentin than the connecting French Army. Yet, in spite of the fact that the French were held back by the arc of fortified hills, their **General position of** general position was not unfavourable. **the French Army** General Nivelle and Sir Douglas Haig, however, decided that it would be best to use St. Quentin merely as a sector of demonstrations.

The French Army was about twenty-five miles from its old line at Ribécourt when it reached the flooded marshes of the Upper Oise. In modern siege-gun warfare, requiring shells by the million for important attacks, there was bound to be a very considerable pause in the construction of new communications and new positions, at a distance of twenty-five miles from railway systems, networks of motor roads, reservoirs, underground magazines, and other vast works of excavation and general engineering.

The Fifth British Army, under Sir Hubert Gough, had less space to traverse and organise than had the armies of Sir Henry Rawlinson and General Castelnau. Only by a miracle of labour did the pioneers and sappers under Sir Hubert Gough complete their work in time to enable their

artillery and infantry to take an important part in the first terrible battles over the tunnelled Hindenburg system. The French and British forces north, west, and south of St. Quentin could not do more than better-placed armies at the top of their power could do. It was a plain matter of arithmetic that the forces which had penetrated most deeply into the old front of the invader would need the longest time to get their heavy guns forward, accumulate shell, and make preparations for a new offensive in great force.

Therefore, some of the heaviest guns, which they could not use for some months, were sent northward and southward to other allied forces, still standing in the order of parallel battle, and ready to break into the wings of the Hindenburg line. It is probable that the excitement skilfully created by the French Press in the last week of March, in regard to the promising situation round St. Quentin, was merely a brilliant ruse.

It is still at times possible for the pen to be mightier than the sword, as the German General Staff rather too vividly appreciated. It continually employed its own Press and certain organs of opinion in neighbouring neutral States to indicate coming offensive movements that never came. The General Staffs of France and Great Britain were so amused by the vain industry of the hostile Press Bureau that they scarcely troubled to use their own Press as a weapon of military demonstration.

In the affair at St. Quentin, however. the British and French Staffs resorted to journalism, and created a general impression that a **Demonstrations** premature Franco-British thrust against **against St. Quentin** St. Quentin was about to take place. Sir Douglas Haig never contemplated so eccentric a movement at his weakest point, and as the French Army was checked by the German inundations, it was unlikely that General Nivelle intended to attack at a disadvantage.

The demonstration against St. Quentin was continued by the Allies in the first week of April. While the forces of Sir Henry Rawlinson were capturing German guns north of the town, the army of General Castelnau, on April 3rd, made an attack in grand style on the southern and south-western defences. The assault was delivered on a front of eight miles from Dallon Hill to the Oise River. In spite of the strong resistance of the Germans, the French troops attained their objectives and, after capturing a series of fortified points, drove into one of the suburbs of St. Quentin. The battle continued amid heavy snowstorms on April 4th. The enemy was driven back on the whole front from the Somme to the Oise, and the important hill positions near the villages of Urvillers, Grugies, and Moy were brilliantly carried by the French Army.

The forces of France then waited for the result of the British offensive in the Vimy and Arras sections. General Nivelle had removed from active command the brilliant army leader General Foch, who had co-operated with Sir John French and Sir Douglas Haig since October, 1914. The new French Commander-in-Chief was not altogether happy in his high position. He had been appointed to the supreme command by M. Aristide Briand, owing to his remarkable successes at Verdun.

Meanwhile, M. Briand had fallen from power, being succeeded by the veteran politician M. Ribot, with the

Re-entry of the French into Noyon, March, 1917: Artillery passing through the town.

French engineers repairing the havoc caused by retreating Germans in the Rue de Paris, Noyon.

Roadside halt of a "fleet" of motor-omnibuses used for conveyance of troops to the French front.

[French official photograph]

French gunners screening their heavy ordnance with foliage on arrival at an advanced position.

[French official photograph.

Where war had passed by: Havoc on a main road through once lovely Picardy.

[French official photograph.

War architecture: A terraced town of dug=outs in an exposed sector of the western front.

Hospitality and chivalry: A French farmer welcomes a troop of horse to his old=world farm.

Pomp and circumstance of war: French infantry on the march to a general review.

famous mathematician M. Pain-levé as civilian Minister of War. There was no Chief of Staff in Paris, undertaking duties similar to those carried on in London by Sir William Robertson.

A considerable number of the French people, with their political representatives, appear to have been somewhat too optimistic in regard to the result of the method of warfare which General Nivelle had developed upon the artillery tactics invented by General Pétain and Sir Henry Horne. Indeed, General Nivelle himself was rather inclined to overestimate the general value of the new barrages which he had success-fully employed only on a small scale.

There was some raggedness, therefore, in the execution of part of the plan for a great offensive which the new French Com-mander-in-Chief launched on the Aisne on Monday, April 16th, 1917. The French artillery pre-paration was of remarkable duration. For ten days the German positions were shelled on a front of twenty-five miles. The German trenches and redoubts were ploughed up, the slopes of the plateau between Soissons and Rheims were made almost uninhabitable, and many of the enemy's hill positions between Rheims and the Argonne Forest were also badly battered in two hundred and forty hours of uninterrupted fire.

In these circumstances the new Chief of Staff of the Crown Prince of Germany was directed, by Ludendorff in person, to adopt the same tactics as were being followed against the British on the Hindenburg

Ludendorff's tactical reply to Nivelle

line. Large numbers of fresh German troops were massed behind the Aisne heights and the downland of Champagne, leaving a very strong advanced German force in the shattered fortified line.

Ludendorff had not been able to conduct an open-field battle against Sir Henry Horne and Sir Edmund Allenby on April 9th. He was then too much disconcerted by the loss of Vimy Ridge to carry out his considered plan of operations. Not until April 23rd was he able to fight on the British front in the manner he intended. Nevertheless, in the interval between the two British operations, the German War Lord managed to employ against the French armies on the Aisne the method he had been working out for some months.

In the first place he gave General Nivelle scarcely any chance of repeating on the Craonne Plateau the Canadian-Scottish success of the Vimy Ridge. Having been forewarned by the British, he was forearmed against the French. He gathered a grand reserve along the upper course of the Ailette brook, that ran in the northern hollow above the famous Ladies' Walk, or Chemin des Dames, which Sir Douglas Haig's division had reached in September, 1914.

In the second place the weather favoured the defence and impeded the attack. Rain, sleet, and snow made aerial observation almost impossible, and turned the exploded slopes of chalk into sticky slides that terribly hampered the climbing infantry. The French guns had to work blindly by the map and strictly according to time-table. When a barrage missed a hostile stronghold it

[French official photograph.

CONVEYING HEAVY SHELLS TO THE GUN-BREECH.
Heavy artillery preparation of remarkable duration and intensity preceded the French offensive in April, 1917, the German positions being shelled on a front of twenty-five miles for ten days, and the slopes of the plateau between Soissons and Rheims rendered almost uninhabitable.

could not be drawn back, and while it went vainly thunder-ing ahead the soldiers had to struggle unsupported against plunging machine-gun fire.

In the third place the German guns, from the beginning of the artillery operation, displayed great strength. Curtains of 5·9 in. and 8·2 in. shells swept the waiting French infantry, and made them at times uncertain of the success of their attack. They were told that the German batteries were all marked down, and were merely left until the morning of battle so that they should not move to new sites in the meantime.

No doubt it would have been better if General Nivelle had given orders that intense counter-battery work should be carried out during the period of preparation when the weather allowed. The enemy would have lost more guns, and would have been strained severely in the effort to replace his injured pieces. Nevertheless, in spite of the veils of snow and rain that assisted the enemy on the day of attack, many of his pieces were smothered by French gunners, who could neither see at what they were aiming nor obtain aerial information concerning the hidden targets.

Under General Gouraud, one of the heroes of the Dardanelles Campaign, under General Mangin, the conqueror of the northern heights of Verdun, and under other famous commanders the infantry operations began on the pre-arranged day. It was very difficult for the French com-mander to alter his plan owing to the change in the weather. He had carefully to measure his stock of shell and estimate the wear of his heavy guns. He could not postpone the infantry action and continue to keep the enemy under intense bombardment until the extraordinary long rains of April and the strange April snowstorms were ended.

Operations tied to time

Great as his accumulation of material had been, it was not inexhaustible. He needed to launch his action at a time when he had still ample munitions in hand to cover his struggling infantry and beat down the new batteries which the enemy was hiding for the main contest.

The French commander also had to strike along the Aisne while the enemy was kept at the highest tension by the victorious First, Third, and Fifth British Armies along the northern Hindenburg line. All the operations of the Western Allies were closely linked together, and when one started the other was almost bound to follow.

General Nivelle appears to have hoped to repeat on a grander scale the achievement of Sir Henry Horne on the Vimy Ridge. His design was to reach the herring-bone of small, connected tablelands running three hundred feet above the Aisne from Laffaux to Craonne.

The Chemin des Dames, or Ladies' Walk, constructed in the eighteenth century for the daughters of Louis XV., was the French objective. When the Ladies' Walk was reached the ground sloped down to the Ailette brook, at which some of Sir Douglas Haig's men had drunk in September, 1914. From the brook and its sources the ground again rose northwards to another range of hills known as the Mountains of St. Croix. Between gaps in the Croix

Terrain round the Ladies' Walk Hills there could be seen from the higher parts of the Aisne Plateau the Cathedral of Laon. Laon was about nine miles distant from that part of the Ladies' Walk which the French had taken over from Sir Douglas Haig's division when the British troops went west to stand at Ypres and save Calais.

The French lines had scarcely changed between Craonne and Venizel since September, 1914. The enemy held the Fort of Condé, where the position was worse than it had been when General Smith-Dorrien's division crossed the Aisne and entrenched below the hostile slopes, ravines, and promontories. After the British Expeditionary Force moved nearer the sea the Germans profited by a flood in the river, swept down to the bank, and established a bridge-head on the other side, which they still held on April 16th, 1917.

In the meantime, however, General Nivelle had advanced his forces from Soissons and closed down upon the five-mile flank of the German forces in the Condé position. The enemy was half encircled from Laffaux, where the Ladies' Walk ended, to the Condé bridge-head. Instead of opening his offensive by bearing upon this German flank, General Nivelle left the Condé position untouched, but threw his forces upward in a wedge from Vailly. His design was to enclose the Condé peninsula on the eastern side as well as on the western side, and then envelop the enemy's forces by a pincer-like movement, working round the German rear by the hamlet of Sancy.

A similar method of double enclosing thrusts was employed between the other fortified promontories, branching from the main plateau like the spine of a herring. The trouble was that many of the German positions on the flanks of the subsidiary promontories running down to the Aisne were built on dead ground. Scarcely a howitzer could drop its shell plumb enough into the works that lined the great wooded buttresses of the main plateau.

A considerable number of the attacking French infantry had come from the Somme, where, under General Foch, the work of the French gunners had been perfect. In the bend of the Somme, however, the ground had been fairly level. Though there had been some swells, behind which the enemy could take cover, it had been possible to flatten out the German lines and pierce some of his most important underground shelters.

Along the Aisne was an unbroken rampart of high, projecting cliffs of limestone. In places only a shell of limestone remained, as small underground streams had eaten the soft rock away and left huge caverns and innumerable small caves. For two and a half years the Germans had worked upon and in the limestone caverns and quarries,

AIDING A WOUNDED PRISONER.
Russian soldiers on the French front assisting towards the field-ambulance a wounded German whom they had captured.

draining them, lighting them with electricity, connecting them with tunnels, and making them magazines of munitions and perfect defences against shell fire.

Only by means of terrific curtains of shells, controlled by aerial observers, rocket-signalling companies, and heliograph operators, could the enemy garrisons in the great promontories have been kept out of action. In the snow, rain, and sleet these means of fire-control were useless. Moreover, owing to the unwonted violence and scope of the enemy's barrages, field-telephone wires were broken as soon as they were laid, and most of the messengers sent

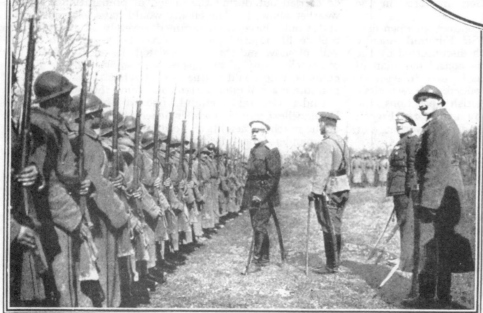

RUSSIAN VICTORS OF COURCY.
General Palitzin, one of the commanders of the Russian troops on the French front, reviewing his victorious troops who stormed Courcy, north of Rheims, in April, 1917, and held it against the most obstinate German counter-attacks.

and Foch in giving more latitude to his able lieutenants.

As it was, the French armies moved forward like a huge machine, through the blinding weather, and achieved a fine measure of preliminary success. But this success, though greater than many victories for which Berlin had been beflagged, threw Paris into a mood of despondency. Nineteen thousand German prisoners and a hundred guns were taken, yet France and her capital were deeply disappointed. The general expectation was pitched too high, and because General Nivelle could not, in his first great offensive, produce on a grand scale the marvellous results he had achieved on a small scale, he was dismissed from the supreme command as abruptly as he had been appointed to it.

Yet the Battle of Rheims was a French victory. It was indeed, at least as great a victory as Sir Douglas Haig won on the Somme in the first weeks of July, 1916. Had the French nation been less troubled by treacherous elements and less worn by the dreadful mistakes of the past, it might have supported General Nivelle with the same patience as the British nation supported Sir Douglas Haig. Though the struggle around Rheims was a soldiers' battle rather than a generals' battle, and cost more lives in proportion to results than Nivelle had lost in freeing Verdun, it was a glorious triumph of the French race.

as a last resource could not get through the enemy's zone of fire.

In these circumstances General Nivelle would have done better had he adopted the British method of attack and reached at first for the nearest subsidiary promontory by means of short-ranged, intense gun fire, such as General Horne adopted around Fricourt on the model of General Nivelle's own operations at Verdun. No doubt this is what General Nivelle would have done had he foreseen what was to happen. But he appears to have been so bent upon carrying the entire plateau by one long, forceful sweep, and all the details of his programme were so fixed, that his army commanders and army corps commanders could not alter their local operations to suit the change of weather.

The new Commander-in-Chief seems to have been somewhat too masterful and precise. Having been extremely successful himself in battles of smaller range, he applied his system of personal control of a small army to the far more intricate work of ordering the action of the great French host composed of several army groups. Everything was planned out in such exact detail that insufficient scope for initiative and improvisation appears to have been allowed to the subordinate generals. Over-anxiety in regard to the success of his first grand operation made the new Commander-in-Chief too rigorous in his personal method of control. Had he been more experienced in handling hundreds of thousands of men, he would have followed the example of Joffre, Castelnau.

HEAVY FRENCH ARTILLERY IN ACTION.

A gun of a heavy battery on the French front at the moment of discharge—the heavy smoke cloud still floating above the muzzle. Inset is a gun just ready for firing, while (above) a battery is shown having just been placed in position.

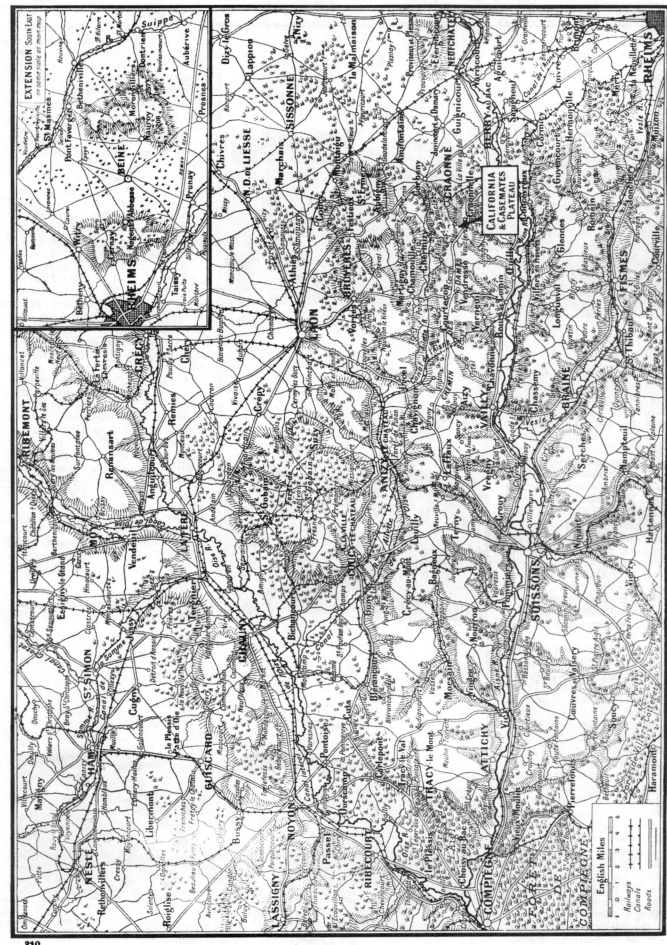

Copyright

The Great War

MAP OF THE RHEIMS AND CHAMPAGNE BATTLEFIELDS, 1917, SHOWING THE LINE OF THE CHEMIN DES DAMES AND THE MORONVILLIERS SYSTEM.

At Vailly, the westernmost base of a line of advance extending for twenty-five miles, the first wave of assault was remarkably successful. The men advanced, rifle in one hand, spade in the other, and a bag full of bombs hanging from their shoulders. The slopes in front of them seemed inaccessible, yet they climbed upward stoically, under the rattle of German machine-guns, and reached the line of shell-holes they had been ordered to take.

All the night, in a tempest of wind, rain, sleet, and shells, the attacking troops worked at connecting the holes and deepening them. At last many of the men fell asleep through absolute fatigue. Some had been ten days in the trenches before the offensive opened, and were tired before they started.

When at dawn the next morning they had again to climb upward, digging cover as they went, men who were afterwards decorated for supreme acts of cour-
Heroic endurance age confessed that they felt like cowards.
of the French On their right the Senegalese of the
African Division were gallantly working upward, in spite of the violent resistance of the Germans.

All day the Frenchmen held on to the positions they had won, and the effect of hunger began to deepen the effects of fatigue. They expected to be relieved at nightfall, but instead of returning to billets they received the order to buckle on their haversacks and renew the struggle. Going forward they took a ravine, passed through a network of German trenches, and reached some quarries on the high slopes alongside the Senegalese. After sleeping beside their African comrades, the French troops again awoke, in a dim, rainy dawn, and for the third time went upward in strength. They bombed the Germans out of their last line and, in a weak, famished condition, opened field warfare beyond the crest of the great plateau. According to an eye-witness, some of these wonderful French troops stopped and gathered

[*French official photograph.*
ENTRANCE TO A MORONVILLIERS FORT.
Substantial entrance into one of the forts in the Moronvilliers system, which were captured by the French during their successful offensive east of Rheims in the spring of 1917. The Moronvilliers heights were of exceptional value, as they formed dominating observation-posts over the whole of the Champagne district.

violets by the brookside before eating the last biscuit of their " iron " rations. In the evening of their victory in the quarries they flung out sharpshooters, occupied the fortified copses in front of them, slept in shifts, and were saved from hopeless misery by discovering food in the underground places abandoned by the Germans.

The next morning, while waiting for orders, the men organised their new line and sent down revictualling-parties to Vailly. The German war-bread they had captured did not suit their weary stomachs, but in the course of the day they obtained good white French bread. Their supports came up, and they were able to have a good sleep and a wash. " I could have slept for a week on end," said one of the victors.

East of Vailly a high buttress spur stretched down to the village of Soupir. As this spur was six hundred feet high, it was almost level with **Underground for-** the topmost ridge. Its steep slopes were **tresses at Soupir** covered by a dense wood, above which was a clearing marked by a mass of grey ruins of the farm Cour Soupir. It was against this farm that the British pursuit had been checked after the Battle of the Marne. Between the autumn of 1914 and the spring of 1917 the Germans had turned the cliffs into an amazing network of underground defences. They had, moreover, pushed the French out of some of the positions which General Haig and General Smith-Dorrien had won, and in particular had seized on the riverside at Chavonne and recrossed the Aisne.

A frontal attack upon the Soupir spur was ineffectual. The battalion that began to attack on April 16th, 1917, found that the enemy's system of trenches in the southern

AWAITING THE SIGNAL.
Heavy gun on the French front in well-chosen position behind a long ridge of rising ground. Above in the sky may be seen two observation balloons, the men in which would duly signal instructions to the gunners how best to direct their fire at the distant enemy.

ROYE STATION, MARCH 17TH, 1917.
The Germans had mined Roye, intending to raze it to the ground, but the French rushed the town so quickly that they frustrated this design and saved entire streets from wanton destruction.

wood was undestroyed. A flanking operation was at once prepared, and a famous army corps from the eastern frontier advanced in a sideways movement against the village of Braye, far behind Soupir and near the point where the canal connecting the Aisne and Oise Rivers runs in a tunnel under the Ladies' Walk.

The French artillery made a whirlwind bombardment on the German machine-gun forts around Braye, and the advanced forces of the attacking army corps pushed forward to the canal tunnel. At the same time another French force entered the southern edge of the woods, and in a fierce bomb and bayonet attack seized the higher part of it. The Germans were caught in a net. Hurriedly and desperately they made a fighting attempt to widen the narrowing path of retreat behind them ; but the Chasseurs and infantry of the line were not to be denied of their great enveloping victory. They put the larger part of the garrison out of action as it tried to flee, and at the end of three days' fighting captured two thousand prisoners, fifty guns, a large

number of machine-guns, and huge stores. All the caves had been mined, but the Germans had no time to fire the charges, and the positions remained intact when the French occupied them.

A similar enveloping operation was conducted against the strong German position around Fort Condé, from which the enemy had been bombarding Soissons. The French attacked from two sides, from Laffaux .and Margival north-westward and from Vailly south-westward. The two attacking forces had only four miles to cross in order to enclose the enemy's rear.

Enveloping attack on Fort Condé

Fort Condé was six hundred feet above the sea, being, like the Soupir defences, on the level of the main ridge on which the Ladies' Walk ran. A frontal attack against plunging machine-gun fire was again impossible, and the brilliant French general worked forward, after a check on April 16th, by means of a pincer-like movement through the ravine near Vailly, and over the Plateau of Vregny. He struck the Germans in their rear at the hill village of Aizy, near the head of the valley running from the Ladies'

Walk. The capture of Aizy, on the western side of the valley, enabled the main attack to develop across the wide hollow eastward against the hamlet of Jouy, which was directly on the path of retreat of the hostile forces around Condé. Simultaneously, the French forces on the other side of the wide spur stormed into the village of Nanteuil. Between Jouy and Nanteuil there remained only a restricted bottle-neck for the Germans in the road running through Sancy. Naturally, the enemy withdrew in extreme haste, for farther on his rear another French force was battling forward at the end of the Ladies' Walk at Laffaux.

Ludendorff reported that the large garrison of the Condé spur withdrew unmolested on April 19th to the new Siegfried line, running along the Ladies' Walk.

STATIONS WHENCE THE FRENCH EJECTED THE GERMANS IN THE SPRING.
Headquarters of the Hun commandant in Roye. In circle : The shattered railway-station at Vailly, the point on the Aisne east of Soissons whence General Nivelle made his upward thrust in April, 1917, to enclose the enemy in the Condé position already half encircled from Laffaux.

As a matter of fact, the withdrawal was a massacre. The French field-gunners at Jouy and Nanteuil, assisted by their comrades handling the heavy artillery south of the Aisne and north-east of Soissons, maintained a terrific shell curtain over Sancy. Together they blasted and shrapnelled to destruction the larger part of the enveloped German force.

In a modern battle between nations possessing on the battlefield an extraordinary number of guns, an enveloping movement need not be conducted entirely by a ring of infantrymen. Indeed, the infantry only shepherd the enemy to the place of slaughter, and leave a gap on which their guns play upon the panic-stricken enemy, as he crowds in confused masses along what seems to him to be an open path of retreat. The light and flexible French 3 in. quick-firer, throwing twenty shells a minute, practically destroyed the retreating German forces. The Chief of Staff of the Crown Prince of Prussia had to throw **Fate of the Condé** forward his reserve upon the Siegfried **garrison** line in order to make it appear that, as the village of Sancy was still held, the evacuation of the Condé position had been carried out in an orderly manner.

The result of all the operations on the western part of the great northern Plateau of the Aisne was a French victory of high importance. By April 19th the Germans were thoroughly defeated on the slopes and heights between Margival, Braye, Cerny, and Vauclerc. In similar circumstances, the British public would probably have rejoiced, and the German public would most certainly have decorated their capital and their principal towns with flags. The French public, however, were overwhelmed with melancholy, and, according to a statement made by M. Clemenceau, some of the wounded troops returning to Paris cried for peace.

This extraordinary recession of popular opinion was due to two causes. As already remarked, the great local successes along the Aisne were much less than the French people had expected General Nivelle to obtain. They

had, somewhat wildly, expected him to excel the achievement of Napoleon against Blücher, and sweep the Germans from the great plateau by one rapid attack. They had also expected that the casualties of their troops would be remarkably small in comparison with the result obtained, by reason of the economy in life with which General Nivelle had beaten the enemy back at Verdun.

Owing, however, to the great reserve that Ludendorff had massed all along his Hindenburg line from Lens to Craonne, it was impossible for either the French or the British Commanders-in-Chief to win any cheap victory. The German dictator was employing one hundred and fifty-six divisions on the western front, and of these he was keeping only forty-four divisions back from the fighting-line for general purposes in all theatres of war. He put a hundred and twelve divisions in action against the armies of Sir Douglas Haig and General Nivelle, and though he lost in the battles of March, April, and May, 1917, three

[*French official photographs.*]

FEEDING THE GUNS ON THE FRENCH FRONT.
Railway siding behind the French front, whence shells of every calibre were being constantly loaded on trucks that they might be sent forward to maintain that incessant artillery fire which grew to a mighty crescendo at every advance. Inset : Truckloads of heavy shells on a light railway being taken forward from the artillery supply base to where the guns were smashing back the invader.

hundred and fifty thousand men and hundreds of guns, his strength of resistance yet remained exceedingly formidable.

Moreover, by reason of the skilful scheme for combining open-field warfare with a fortified base line, Ludendorff was able to bring on a most costly kind of conflict in mass, at any point at which his first line was driven in and his second line attacked. The only manner in which the new German plan of defence could be economically defeated was by a slow campaign of limited objectives, each fully within the range of the attacking artillery.

Haig's methods justified again This slow and limited method was, from the beginning of the new offensive, the essential method of Sir Douglas Haig. It was also the method favoured by General Pétain and General Foch. Both French and British commanders had perfected this method in the Somme operations. There were, however, several French generals, writing in " Le Temps " and other important newspapers, who criticised Haig's tactics, and required, in the supposed interests of their country, a more rapid attempt at breaking

ENTRY OF THE FRENCH INTO LIBERATED NOYON.
[*French official photograph.*]
French patrols entered Noyon at ten o'clock in the morning of March 18th, 1917. In the afternoon a regiment of infantry, headed by drums and bugles, marched into the old grey market-place, where General Nivelle was received with passionate enthusiasm by the rescued population.

the German line and liberating the lost departments of France and Belgium.

Although General Nivelle had successfully practised, under the control of General Pétain, the limited method of attack at Verdun, he was inclined, in his preparations for the Battle of Rheims, to return to the earlier French method for winning large and rapid results. He planned to turn the Aisne Plateau from the east by a movement across the flat country north of Berry-au-Bac. While shaking the enemy on the flank in this way, he intended to pierce his centre in the middle of the Ladies' Walk, and storm over the Ailette Valley towards the hills in front of Laon. Before the battle General Nivelle felt so confident of success that he dangerously prophesied that he would pierce the enemy's Aisne line—a thing Napoleon had failed to do.

This was only a part of his scheme. One of his subsidiary aims was to liberate the city of Rheims, from which

the German lines were only a mile and a half distant. The Germans held, at Brimont and Nogent, two important heights around Rheims, from which they bombarded and wrecked the lovely old cathedral city. Their position on these neighbouring commanding heights was based upon their hold on the Champagne downland at Moronvilliers, between Rheims and Auberive.

The new French Commander-in-Chief designed to throw the Germans from the northern Aisne Plateau on April 16th, and conquer Brimont and Nogent heights, and then fend off a grand German counter-attack from the lowland road of advance from Rheims by storming the most important western downs in the Moronvilliers system.

The plan was of too grandiose a scope. It failed because the thick weather prevented the French heavy artillery on the southern heights of the Aisne and on the upland west of Rheims from continually and closely supporting the assailing French forces. It also failed because General Nivelle had insufficient reserve forces to drive home a final attack. It is, further, just possible that the special dispositions which Ludendorff had invented along his Hindenburg line also decisively checked the complete development of the grand offensive of General Nivelle. The Germans, of course, proclaimed that their defensive victory was due entirely to Ludendorff's plan of fighting from a new fortified line with a surprising mass of fresh reserves, but we may more fairly attribute to the extraordinary April snowy weather the principal part in the restriction of the largest offensive movement launched during the period of trench warfare.

On April 16th the French forces on the eastern part of the Aisne front occupied the high position near Troyon, which had been won by General Haig's division in September, 1914. They were just touching the Ladies' Walk at a point below the dominating village of Cerny, where General von Zwehl brought siege-guns down from Maubeuge to stop the early British advance.

From Troyon the French line bent a little backwards and extended eastward to Craonnelle, well below the supreme point of the great plateau at Craonne. Then below Craonne the French line made a long, backward curve for more than twenty miles southward past Rheims. When Blücher stood on the northern Aisne Plateau in 1814 he was able to force Napoleon to use up his strength in carrying the Craonne positions, so that after another battle at Laon the great captain was compelled to abdicate.

For more than a hundred years Craonne had been a glorious memory to the Prussians, although they had suffered temporary defeat there and a monument to Napoleon rose by the high **Historic battlefield** Vauclerc level. The Germans of the **of Craonne** later generation regarded their position as absolutely impregnable. They had wide zones of plunging fire from slope above slope, with trap-like hollows, fenced in with triple-wired trenches, and underground works, including such vast natural grottos in the limestone rock as the famous Dragon's Cave.

Many of the sunken German works were in dead ground beyond the pitch of the French howitzers, and as the

French guns and transport waggons passing through Noyon in pursuit of the retreating Germans on March 18th, 1917.   Right : The crowd assembled in the Place of the Hotel de Ville, Noyon, to welcome those who had delivered them from the horrors of invasion.

M. Poincaré, President of the French Republic, who paid an early visit to recaptured Noyon, saluting the French troops in that town.   Right : The President greets the Mayor of Noyon and congratulates him on its restoration to France.

Victorious French troops passing through Noyon on their return from the pursuit of the enemy beyond Chauny.   Right : French troops drawn up before the beautiful old Hotel de Ville of Noyon, awaiting inspection by General Nivelle, then Commander-in-Chief.

NOYON RESCUED FROM THE DESTROYING TEUTON.

French infantry climbed up the wet inclines, amid the winter tempest, they suffered very badly around the hostile hidden strong places. Many German batteries, that had remained silent during the bombardment, curtained off the French advance by mechanical means perfected by years of registering over known ground. The rain, sleet, and snow did not disturb the gunners handling the new parks of hostile artillery.

They merely maintained a deep unbroken zone of shell fire over their wrecked first line and over the French line and rear. The thick weather veiled the flame of their guns from French observing officers, and prevented any serious counter-battery work by the attacking armies.

Everything was against the French infantry. Yet by personal dauntlessness and magnificent endurance, combined with brilliant regimental leadership, the troops reached the top of the ridge and stormed with diminishing hand-bomb supplies into Craonne village. They conquered the high levels of the plateau between Hurtebise and Craonne, and occupied the famous plateaux known as Casemates and California in French reports and as the Winterberg in German reports.

They reached the Ailette brook, as a few of Sir Douglas Haig's men had done in September, 1914, and, more successful than General Franchet d'Espérey's troops had been in the earlier attack on the Craonne Ridge, they

IN VERDUN, THE SALLY-PORT OF FRANCE. [*French official photograph.*
French soldiers going back to billets after taking part in one of the offensives which throughout 1917 continued to drive the enemy a little farther from Verdun, the sally-port of France, which the German High Command squandered blood in vain attempts to capture.

overran the ground as far as the western ruins of the village. There was, however, one long slope which also had to be climbed in order to carry the whole ridge end by an enveloping movement. This sodden, slippery slope could not be surmounted.

It was crowned by a German machine-gun position, from which the enemy maintained a short-range, incessant barrage of bullets. The slope was some hundreds of yards high, and the time necessary to climb it gave the German gunners a deadly advantage.

All French storming-parties were swept down, all detachments that tried to crawl up were even more easily caught and entirely shattered. Widely scattered bombers, who attempted by individual heroism to get within throwing distance, were either sniped or caught in one of the wild blasts of leaden death.

In clear weather the check might have been of small importance in the general result. Field-guns, trench-mortars, and the new French armoured cars of the "tank" type would have been brought rapidly forward, and scores of the new French siege-guns would have opened a whirlwind bombardment upon the German forts.

German gunners' deadly advantage

In the blinding weather, however, no mechanical means of conversation obtained between the checked infantry and their guns. The messages that reached Headquarters came slowly, by scribbled notes carried by men who often failed to get through the enemy's barrage. As in the first Australian attack on the Hindenburg line, the new mobile forts, which the French had been constructing since the Battle of the Somme, were impeded by the mud and snow. The light artillery was delayed by the condition of the ground and its steepness. Thousands of the horses were killed or maimed in the passage through the terrific German shell barrage.

It was a dreadful battle for the attacking gunners as well as for the attacking infantrymen. Though many of the French quick-firers were at last, by superhuman efforts, hauled up to help the foot soldiers, few of them could be hauled close enough to the high plateau to command the Valley of the Ailette and the woods leading up to the Mountains of St. Croix. The clerk of the weather behaved in an unconscionable pro-German manner.

WEST FRONT OF LAON CATHEDRAL.
Laon, north of the lowland that ran like a corridor through Berry-au-Bac and Craonne, was an ultimate objective of General Nivelle's great offensive in 1917, the complete development of which was checked.

He blanketed from the French artillery observing officers the brown woods where the main German battle forces collected, and when these forces came across the Ailette Valley to attack they escaped the overwhelming howitzer barrage which General Nivelle and his lieutenants had designed as the crown of their victory.

The tired, wasted French advanced divisions on the Casemates and California Plateaux were subjected to a fearful bombardment. The German gunners needed no repeated telephone messages to tell them to continue their fire upon their targets. All they needed to know was that their high ridge line had been lost. They had every range to a yard, and stamped with their heavy shells upon the trenches and communicating ways, ravines and dug-outs, from which their men had retired. At the same time their reserve forces slowly came forward behind their picked shock troops, and by weight of numbers pressed back the battered French battalions to what cover remained in the first German line.

German success around Craonne In many respects the situation resembled that obtaining in the night of July 1st, 1916, among the British forces from Gommecourt to Montauban. The left French wing had won a splendid victory, which enabled it to top the ridge, and hold it in places and envelop various German fortified heights after the manner in which Sir Henry Horne enveloped Fricourt. The right wing of the French armies on the Aisne, however, had suffered a partial defeat, which, though not as decisive as had been the British disasters in the Ancre Valley and on the Serre Plateau, yet upset the main plan of their Commander-in-Chief. It took the French Command only a fortnight to reorganise forces that turned the check at Craonne into a brilliant victory, so that the local set-back on the Aisne did not prove to be as serious as the Gommecourt disaster.

Nevertheless, the character of the Battle of Rheims was completely changed by the temporary success of the Germans around Craonne. The great outflanking movement, eastward through the low country by Berry-au-Bac, had to be stopped at the moment when it promised the largest result obtained by the Western Allies since the Battle of the Marne. **French victory at Ville-aux-Bois** The French troops that advanced towards Laon by the high-road from Rheims were magnificently victorious. The gap in the heights between the Aisne Plateau and the Champagne Downs enabled the French heavy gunners on the hills south-east of Berry-au-Bac to work with infernal destructive power upon the enemy defences in the lowland. The French infantry, working eastward on the level with Craonne, carried the first German line with ease, and then stormed into the second German line south of Juvincourt. There they held out against the enemy's counter-attacks in mass and formed a menacing French wedge, from which Craonne could be enfiladed from their left and the German positions on the Upper Aisne taken in the rear.

Farther south of Juvincourt the Germans suffered an important local disaster in the large fortified wood by the village of Ville-aux-Bois. But there was a severe check to the French operations around Berry-au-Bac, on the

SHELL DEPOSITS LEFT BY THE FLOOD OF WAR.
Some idea of the enormous consumption of ammunition in the battles of the Great War may be formed from this photograph of the empty cases of shells fired by a single battery of "75's" during the Battle of Courcy in April, 1917.

Aisne, where the enemy had a large field of plunging machine-gun fire from the eastern and south-eastern slopes of the Craonne Plateau. Another check to the French forces was incurred south of the Aisne, around the defences of Brimont Fort, from which the Germans conducted the bombardment of Rheims. But a series of magnificent achievements by certain divisions and brigades redeemed the failure to liberate Rheims. As the network of German trenches and armoured concrete positions extended within a mile and a half of the city, the attack on the outworks of the fortified Mill of Brimont was extremely difficult.

Among the troops of the assault were the Bretons and Parisians of the 410th Regiment and the famous division of " Aces " commanded by General Philipot. The division consisted of the 42nd Regiment, which had pierced the German centre in the Battle of the Marne, with the 35th, 44th, and 60th Regiments, all of whom had been specially decorated with the *fourragere*, the rarest and most coveted distinction in the French Army. The artillery regiment of the division also won the colours of the *fourragere*. Each

brigade employed an ace as its design, and the artillery brigade used the joker, as the four aces in an ordinary pack of cards had been taken.

Between the brilliant French troops were the Russian soldiers sent to France by the ex-Tsar in token of the comradeship of the Allies. Commissaries of the Revolution had reached them, and they had rallied to the new Government, but, unlike many Russian troops, their fine native moral had not been injured by the intrigues of Lenin and the treacherous elements in the Maximalist party.

The task of the Bretons was to capture a formidable German position known as the " Cavaliers " of Courcy. A *cavalier* is a French engineering term for a spoil-bank. It was employed to denote two high embankments between which the Aisne and Marne Canal ran at Courcy. The works formed an artificial ravine, on the **" Cavaliers " of Courcy stormed** sides of which the Germans had constructed dug-outs, concrete forts, and nests of machine-guns. From the neighbouring fortress of Brimont the hostile gunners were able to enfilade the ravine and all its approaches and rear.

The men from Brittany and Paris stormed forward through the tempestuous weather of April 16th, and in a single sweep carried three German lines, conquering nearly three square miles of ground, half of which was beyond their objective.

Setting out from the north of Rheims, the three battalions reached the great artificial ramparts with extreme rapidity in an uninterrupted movement. Admirably led, they bombed, in a simultaneous action, into the right and left Cavaliers and along the sides of the canal. They smashed in the machine-gun forts, hurled their bombs

[*French official photographs*

REAPING A DOUBLE HARVEST IN THE CORNFIELDS OF FRANCE.
A French heavy gun throwing shells on enemy positions from a railway running through cornfields where the harvest was being gathered in.
Above : Getting a big gun into position on a road so worn that the carriage sank to the axle-trees in mud.

INGENIOUS LABOUR-SAVING DEVICE EMPLOYED ON THE WESTERN FRONT.
[*French official photograph.*

Careful consideration was given to every invention designed to release men for the fighting-line. This photograph shows a device adopted by French labour battalions engaged in digging operations—a series of moving belts on which the diggers deposited the soil which they had excavated to be thereby transferred to trucks that moved automatically along light railways and tipped out the contents at the required positions.

into the dug-outs, chased the Germans up the trenches, and swiftly occupied all the positions.

Their work was then finished, as it enabled the Philipot division and the Russian force to escape being enfiladed by machine-gun fire from the canal embankment. The victors, however, were still full of fight. They saw that the forces on either side of them were in difficulty, and, deploying both right and left, they went to the help of their comrades around Brimont Fort. The Russians had a hard fight in the ruins of Courcy village, but they prevailed over all the German garrison, and advanced farther towards the south-western slope of Brimont.

There were other fine French successes at Loivre and around Berméricourt, north of Brimont, and the famous division of the "Aces" swept up the lower slopes of the fortified hill, and, under a deluge of rain, sleet, snow, bullets, and shell, clung to the hillside. Once more, had the weather been clear and enabled the French gunners to mark their targets, a great and definite success might have been won, and the batteries that bombarded Rheims at short range would have been captured. All that General Philipot's men could do they did ; but the enemy's awful machine-gun barrage prevented them from topping the hill and freeing Rheims from the deadliest of her destroyers.

Heroism of the "Aces"

The fall of Brimont would have had larger consequences than the salvation of the ruins of the coronation city of old France. It would have broken the German defensive scheme, which was based on cross-firing artillery from Brimont and Nogent l'Abbesse Hills. It would likewise have exposed the Germans' more distant artillery heights at Berru to direct attack and cleared the path for a grand French movement northward through the corridor of lowland running through Berry-au-Bac and past Craonne towards Laon.

General Nivelle's first attack on the long front of twenty-five miles, from the neighbourhood of Soissons to the neighbourhood of Rheims, was delivered against sixteen German divisions in the first line and six other divisions in immediate support. A total of about a quarter of a million German soldiers were defeated at many important points. Ten thousand officers and men and about a hundred guns were captured, while in the preliminary bombardment, that lasted ten days, and in the fierce, close fighting in the infantry actions the proportion of Germans permanently put out of action was much larger than any estimate based upon the number of prisoners taken.

Change in French High Command

For it had been the policy of the German High Command to hold its first line, consisting of a fivefold system of trenches, in extraordinary strength. A Divisional Order, signed by General von Schussler, commanding on the Aisne, rebuked the officers of one of his brigades for their weakness in trying lightly to hold the first position. "Our principal line of battle is our first line," wrote the general, underlining this sentence as he wrote it.

All orders prescribed that the first line should be defended at all costs, and that if it were lost, the struggle had to

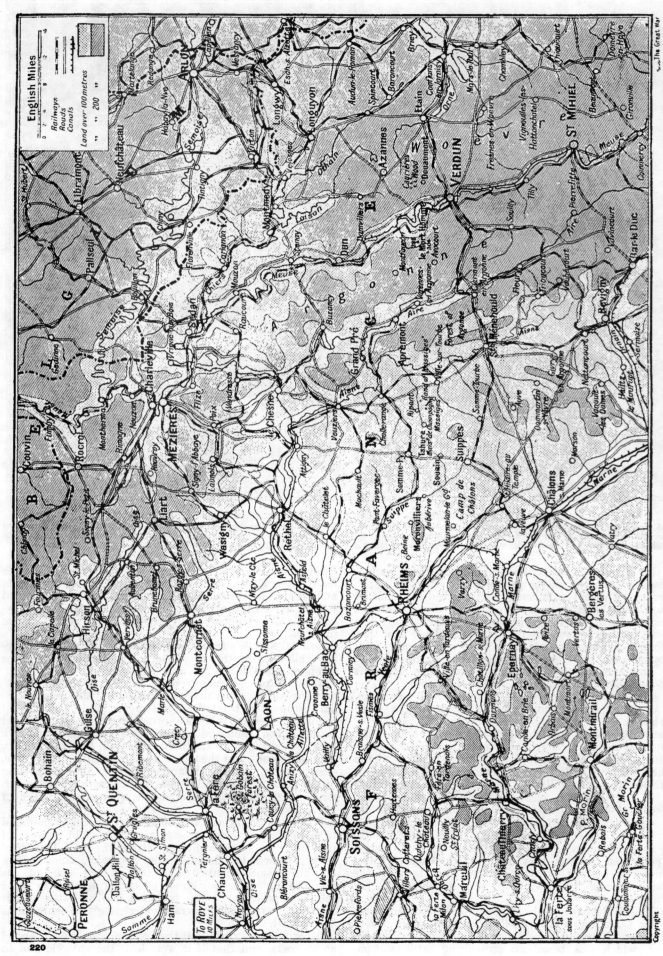

CONTOUR MAP OF THE GENERAL AREA OF FRENCH OFFENSIVE OPERATIONS BETWEEN PERONNE AND VERDUN IN 1917

be maintained until it was re-conquered. These were special German tactics designed in view of the special nature of the ground along the northern heights of the Aisne and the hilly country around Rheims. The enemy High Command could not afford lightly to lose the advantages of observation, plunging fire, and the momentum of counter-attack afforded by the steep slopes. Therefore, the German commanding officer placed a great army in his first line, and a somewhat small supporting force near his second line, in the hope that the grand Ludendorff reserve of available manœuvring masses echeloned in the rear, behind the new Siegfried line, would be

RECOVERING FRANCE, LINE BY LINE.
Two photographs of French infantrymen going into action from their second line, which was previously the German first line. The new French first line can be seen in the middle distance of the upper picture; the comparative lack of substantiality in the wire entanglements shown in the oval indicates French confidence that their advance would not be driven back again.

was not until a courageous fighting deputy came from the most critical part of the battle-line, roused the Chamber, and bore down the unnerved advocates of a lame peace, that the larger number of French politicians began to recognise that they had mistaken a French victory for a French defeat.

Meanwhile, it took some time for the public mind of France gradually to recover the feeling of confidence which it never should have lost. M. Joseph Caillaux, the leader of the powerful group of Radicals with a Socialistic colour, seemed inclined towards a German peace. His party was not at first averse to the same policy. There were some sinister organs of opinion in the country, which powerfully increased the temporary and unjustifiable epidemic of depression. Considerable sums of money were sent from Germany, through Switzerland and America, to the traitor Press, which had, among other instruments of influence, special journals for troops holding the trenches. The French successes of April, 1917, were for the time disastrously obscured by a variety of enemy influences working directly in France among all classes of the population.

Victory mistaken for defeat

Only the victorious troops, who had topped the great ridge above the Aisne and scaled some of the most important heights around Rheims, were in a triumphing mood. They could feel the enemy weakening under the combined shocks of the British offensive around Arras and their own offensive around Rheims. They gripped the steeps close to Craonne, and knew that they could surge again upward as soon as their commander sent them reinforcements. The interval between their great victories was brief, and, to the distraction of the enemy, it was filled by another great French attack on the Champagne front by part of the group of armies commanded by General Pétain.

preserved from the wastage of battle. The French losses were undoubtedly heavy. They were, in fact, heavier than the people of Paris regarded as reasonable. What was worse, a general rumour, spread by enemy agencies, put the losses at double what they actually were. A strong agitation was started in political circles against General Nivelle, who, only five months before, had been acclaimed the supreme master of war. General Foch, who had been retired from active service, was recalled to a political military consultation, and another profound change in the High Command was made towards the end of April. General Pétain was appointed Commander-in-Chief, and for General Foch there was made a new and somewhat higher position, similar to that created in London for Sir William Robertson after the Dardanelles disaster.

Public advertisement of the alterations was delayed for a time, in order to prevent the enemy Press from breaking out into jubilations in the middle of the great battle and increasing the feeling of depression among the French people. Secret sessions were held, and some of the extravagant language used there was faintly echoed outside. It

BRETON INFANTRY STORMING THE "CAVALIERS" OF COURCY, APRIL 16TH, 1917.

The "Cavaliers" were two high embankments between which the Aisne and Marne Canal ran at Courcy. held, and further protected by enfilading guns from Brimont. The Breton troops detailed for the purpose This artificial ravine had been converted by the Germans into a most formidable position very strongly bombed and smashed their way along the ramparts, and with irresistible rapidity captured all the positions.

THE VICTORY OF CRAONNE AND THE BATTLE ALONG THE LADIES' WALK.

By Edward Wright.

General Gouraud and His Attack on the Moronvilliers Downs—A Blind French Army Drags Itself Through the Slime—Importance of the Victory in Champagne—Magnificent Feat of Foreign Legion—The Grand Gunner of France Arrives—Advance of French Wing and Volcanic Struggles for Helmet and Breast Downs—Mastery Won by the Gunners of France—German Army Blinded by Loss of Observation Positions—Squid Tactics in Modern Warfare—Pétain Continues the Plan of Attack of Nivelle—Millions of Men Battling on a Front of One Hundred and Fifty Miles—How the Alpine Infantry Clambered into Craonne and on the High Plateaux—The "Blue Devils of France" Meet the Prussian Guard—Ludendorff and His Fountain-Pen Victory—General Bohm Fails to Make Good—The French Anvil that Broke the German Hammer—Terrific Wastage of Enemy Reserves—Ludendorff Tries to Turn the Ladies' Walk into a New Verdun—Monkey Hill an Example of Stonewalling Tactics—Story of the Dragon's Cave—The Finest Regiment in France and Its Battle Motto—Pétain as a Military Statesman—The French Mind and Its Incomparable Creativeness—France the Light and Glory of the World—Ludendorff Requires a Political Victory—The Hillsmen of the Vosges Remember Zabern—How the Decisive Return Match was Fought out Between the Aisne and the Ailette.

DURING the important but partial success of the French operations along the Aisne, General Nivelle extended his front of attack between Rheims and Auberive. His design, apparently, was to redeem the check around Berry-au-Bac by breaking into the enemy's strongest point of resistance on the Champagne front.

In the operations of September, 1915, in which General Pétain had distinguished himself by the capture of the heights of Massiges, the French attack had been limited by the German hill positions around the village of Moronvilliers, east of Rheims and west of Auberive.

The Moronvilliers Hills were larger, higher, and more densely wooded than the Massiges heights, and the heavy artillery sited on this buttress of the invading force was able to bring a terrific enfilading fire against the troops engaged in the earlier French attacks. Mont Haut was the highest of the Moronvilliers Downs, and being some eight hundred and forty-three feet above sea-level, it gave observation over the French positions southward as far as a telescope could reach.

Besides being the grand buttress of the German line between the Champagne front and the Argonne Forest, the Moronvilliers Downs were the mainstay of all the enemy's

FRENCH HEAVY GUN IN ACTION.
Hundreds of these monster pieces of ordnance, of 12·8 in. calibre and upwards, moved along hundreds of miles of railway laid for their passage, hurling destruction at the invading Germans.

operations around Rheims. The German guns on the great hills protected the enemy's works on Nogent Hill from direct assault, while Nogent Hill in turn protected the Brimont fortress that swept the ford of Berry-au-Bac and the levels leading round the Craonne height.

General Nivelle seems to have aimed at compelling the enemy to concentrate his main reserves on April 16th, 1917, along the northern Plateau of the Aisne, and thus weaken the resistance among the Moronvilliers heights which were assailed on April 17th.

The condition of the ground, however, was horrible. In many places the trenches had been so silted up and blown in that they had become merely shallow ditches. In these ditches the slime was so thick that the soldiers were buried up to their thighs. The attacking troops, moving upward in rain and snow, neither climbed nor crawled. They dragged themselves forward, and on reaching their objective sank into it. Their task would have been impossible but for the great superiority of their artillery.

The German guns were kept down by counter-battery work, and though they sprayed the ground with long-range shrapnel, they did not interfere in any serious way with the operations. The German machine-guns, firing from redoubts upon the slopes, were the most formidable

223

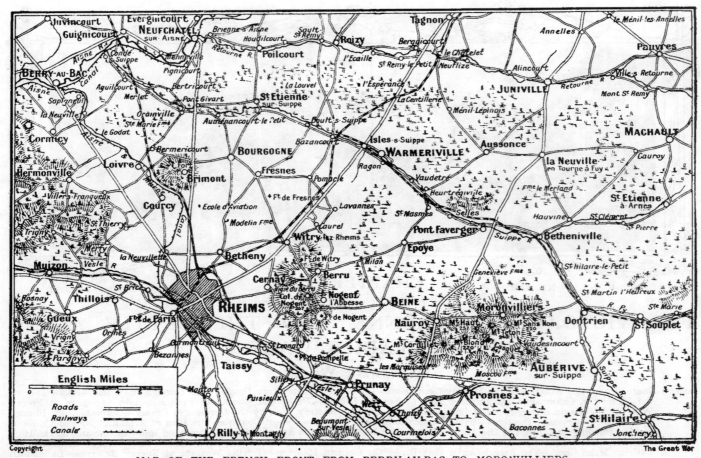

MAP OF THE FRENCH FRONT FROM BERRY-AU-BAC TO MORONVILLIERS.
The Moronvilliers system was the grand buttress of the German line and the mainstay of the enemy's operations around Rheims. The heights, whose altitude in metres is shown, were the objective of furious attacks by General Gouraud, and were finally won in July, 1917.

instruments of the defence. Yet the thick weather was not wholly an advantage to the enemy. It served to screen the French forces, though impeding their progress. Often the Germans did not perceive they were in danger until their position was partly enveloped. Then they raked the slopes furiously and incessantly from the slits in their concrete forts. The French troops fell flat and crawled into shell-holes at the point where they were in danger of being swept away, while their comrades on their flanks continued the encircling tactics.

Practically both armies were blinded by the weather. The French artillery could only continue to register upon known or suspected hostile gun sites, while the German artillery could merely proceed, with decreasing vigour, to maintain a shrapnel curtain over all ways of approach and over any German positions that were definitely known to have been lost.

A high wind made air scouting almost impossible, and the extraordinary late April snowfall completed the difficulties. Nevertheless, the French troops, that went up and over the white slime of Champagne between Prunay and the ground east of Auberive, on a front of about nine and a half miles, took all the first line of **General Gouraud's attack** downs. Mont Cornillet, eight hundred and fifty feet high, was carried, and all enemy counter-attacks were shattered.

Rapidly developing their advantage, the forces of the left French wing of attack conquered in two days a block of hills and valleys some three miles square between the village of Moronvilliers and the hamlet of Nauroy. Besides Mont Cornillet, the Nameless Mount and Mont Blond were occupied, and important ground was won around the dominating central height of Mont Haut.

General Gouraud, who conducted the action, deployed only four regiments in attacking the great clump of Champagne Downs. Among the troops were the famous thrusting forces of Africa, composed of French planters, Arabs, and Sudanese. Alongside the African battalions was the Foreign Legion. The Legion was composed of six thousand Swiss, South Americans, and other men of neutral States, who were set the tremendous task of breaking into the right of the enemy's position around Auberive.

Since the first French offensive in Champagne, Auberive had become one of the most extraordinary fortresses. It was belted with a two-mile line of redoubts, and also caverned, tunnelled, and overlaid with thick concrete. The defences, however, proved but death-traps. The tremendous weight of the French artillery was irresistible, and the Auberive salient was overrun on the first day of the offensive.

Foreign Legion at Auberive

The ground to the west of Auberive, through which the Legionaries worked, was far more difficult. It consisted of wired shell-holes, concealed machine-gun posts, and vague lines on the slopes, which were often lightly held at first and then strongly reinforced through sheltered ways. From the northern hills, as far as Berru, heavy German howitzers swept the ground of approach with a continual hurricane of shell. Three thousand shells are said to have fallen on and around a single company of the Legion, that worked through Auberive, in a single hour. As the strength of the company was then considerably reduced, more than twenty heavy shells were thrown at each surviving man. But for the thickness of the weather the Legion would have been annihilated.

Happily, the men worked forward in very wide order, gathering only when their patrols discovered some undamaged strong point to attack. One Swiss lieutenant, a corporal, and twelve men fought their way to Auberive through a mile of underground labyrinth. Then the immortal fourteen waited for a fresh supply of hand-bombs, obtained them, and continued fighting for another five days! Such was the mettle of the men of the Foreign Legion.

Copyright

In all, six days passed before the Legion won its final objective. The larger number of men were French Swiss, and the quality of endurance they showed was a glorious set-off to the pro-German intrigues of notorious members of the Swiss Staff, and Hoffman and Grimm. Their achievement was also a striking answer to the early Teutonic movement in the German cantons that had sent thousands of misled volunteers into the armies of the Nero of the Hohenzollern dynasty.

The enemy garrison in this sector was mainly Saxon. They originally outnumbered the forces of attack, and when driven backwards they were re-formed, under the orders of the angry Prussian Staff, and sent forward in continual counter-attacks. Sleepless, hungry, and terribly thirsty, the Legionaries held on for six days and nights, and, slowly extending their gains, compelled the remnant of the Saxons to retreat. The Nameless Mount fell to them, and with their two assistant regiments they

Heroic but costly victory

captured eleven hundred prisoners and twenty guns, and defeated the Germans, who were at least twice their number.

Their own losses were heavy, and included Colonel Duriez, who was acting as brigadier. As in the conquest of the Horse-shoe position in the early Champagne Battle, the Legion almost perished in its victory ; but its chain of great achievements and the spirit that inspired it made the famous corps immortal. For the third time thousands of lovers of France came, from some fifty races, to fill the large gaps in the battle formation and bring the Legion again up to the strength necessary for the accomplishment of further deeds of grandeur.

After the Legion and the African Division were relieved, the German counter-attacks went on amid an awful artillery action. Ludendorff's lieutenant made every possible effort to recover the buttress that supported both his Champagne front and his Rheims front. After the loss of Mont Haut the German commander still possessed at Berru, north-east of Rheims, one higher observation peak.

Awful artillery action

But the Berru position · was rather the safeguard against a French thrust north of Rheims than a part of the Moronvilliers hill system.

For nearly all practical purposes the forces of the Crown Prince of Prussia had to stay the advance of General Gouraud's army by means of howitzer fire directed from the Moronvilliers valleys against the summits of the lost downs. As had been seen in the Somme Battles, the tactics of hill actions were almost reversed. A well-mounted attacking force could, with comparative ease, carry the slopes directly in front of it by means of a terrific, continual bombardment of the exposed ground. The field-artillery in particular was able to overwhelm by direct short-range fire every work visible on the slopes in front of it.

When, however, the assailing force reached the summit it became in turn exposed to a devastating fire. Its assistant quick-firing cannon lost much of their value ; for, although the French field-gun had a small degree of

[French official photograph.

RESTORING ORDER IN SOISSONS AFTER THE GERMAN MENACE WAS REMOVED.
French Territorial troops relaying streets in Soissons that had been trenched and fortified against attack until the successes of General Nivelle's armies, operating in the twenty-five-mile front between Soissons and Rheims, relieved the former town from constant enemy bombardment.

indirect fire, it was only the light and heavy howitzers that decisively counted in any advance down the opposite slopes of the hills.

At an enormous cost in ammunition each side so swept the summits of the Moronvilliers system as to curtain off permanently the hostile advanced forces which went forward from the tops of the hills. Still more perilous were the work of observing officers and the task of carrying supplies up the reverse slopes and over the summit and down to the advanced and exposed forces.

General Gouraud belonged to the school of General Pétain and Sir Douglas Haig. He first rose into fame as the " Lion of the Argonne Forest," after his superb stand in the wooded, rocky region west of Verdun. Afterwards, he fought with Sir Ian Hamilton in the hill-battles at the tip of the Peninsula of Gallipoli. A severe wound compelled him to retire from service for a considerable time, but he returned to take command of General Pétain's

Pétain follows Nivelle's plan

army in the critical month of April, when the French losses in the Aisne Battles were producing consternation in Paris.

General Gouraud then could not afford to attempt to carry the entire Moronvilliers system. And when, towards the end of the month of April, General Pétain was practically made Chief of Staff, the work of the fighting wing of the Champagne army became subsidiary to a larger design for a renewal of the Aisne offensive.

General Pétain continued to work out the plan upon which General Nivelle had acted. He did not like the plan, and he was reported to have remarked that nobody could hope to succeed in a campaign in which Napoleon himself had failed. He seems to have thought that General Nivelle had been too ambitious in employing the best French troops in an attempt to break over the double ridge in front of the hill city of Laon. Had Pétain been Commander-in-Chief in the early part of 1917, he would probably have co-operated in the great British offensive by movements from the sally-port of Verdun, or from the old Champagne front.

As, however, his plan of battle had been set by the brilliant general who had been his former subordinate, General Pétain could not do anything but continue the attempt to execute the main part of the original scheme and carry the eastern and highest portion of the northern Aisne Plateau above Craonne. Happily, the enemy regarded the Battle of the Aisne as a complete German victory. General Ludendorff looked upon the loss of part of the great Hog's Back of the Ladies' Walk as a comparatively insignificant episode in a very successful scheme of defence. The violent pressure which Sir Edmund Allenby, Sir Henry Horne, and Sir Hubert Gough were exercising upon him in the closing weeks of April, 1917,

General Ludendorff's self-confidence

between Lens and Bullecourt, appeared to the German dictator to be only a loyal and gallant British effort to win breathing time for beaten France.

In these circumstances General Pétain, with whom General Foch was soon associated, prepared to profit by the self-conceit of the German dictator. Heavy as the French losses had been in the offensive movement of April 16th, they had been more than balanced by the very large casualties inflicted upon the German armies. Only the unforeseen and almost complete weakening of the Russian forces, amounting to more than ten million men under arms, told in any serious way upon the plans of the commanders of France, Great Britain, and Italy.

Towards the end of April, 1917, it was well known in headquarters in France and Italy that the magnificent strength of the re-equipped multitudes of Russian peasants had been disastrously sapped by the wilder, sinister forces in the Russian Revolutionary parties. The intervention of the United States did not immediately compensate for the effects of fraternisation on the eastern front. For the available military resources of the great new ally were feeble, and time was needed to train the men, fashion the weapons, and build the troopships and supply-ships needed to make the American Army a decisive force of action between the North Sea and Switzerland.

In the meantime France, Great Britain, and Italy had to continue to assert their power of initiative over the Central Empires. Therefore General Pétain, in agreement with the French Government, proceeded to assist the great efforts of Sir Douglas Haig and ease the offensive movement that General Cadorna was preparing.

At the end of April the new French Commander-in-Chief approved a resumption of attack by General Gouraud on the Moronvilliers system. The action began on Monday, April 30th, 1917. After an intense artillery preparation the French infantry stormed forward in clear daylight from Mont Cornillet towards Nauroy village. The main advance was supported by demonstrating attacks on either side, and but for the thick woods, in and behind which the Germans were entrenched, the assaulting force would have had a comparatively easy task.

The pine woods, however, were almost impregnable. The perennial sombre foliage, lifted high above the intricate hostile works, formed a perfect screen. Little had the French forestry authorities reckoned, in the days of Napoleon the Third, what cover they were building for future generations of invading Teutons when they planted the sterile northern region of dusty Champagne with great masses of pine. Had the downland remained bare, the marked superiority of the French artillery and its aerial observers would probably have resulted in a definite local victory.

The pine woods saved the weakened enemy. He burrowed deeply below the roots of the tall, red trunks ; he bound his finger-thick wire from bole to bole ; he kept his machine-guns underground during the bombardment,

Foe saved by Champagne pines

and survived sufficiently, in spite of the gun fire, to come up to the surface in very considerable strength when the French gunners ranged upon his rear and allowed the French infantry to advance.

When the battle was joined all the landscape was blotted out. The batteries on either side concealed themselves from counter-firing by clouds of special screening smoke. They also poured clouds of poison gas upon the hostile infantry. The German underground works in the pine woods were swamped with gas from tens of thousands of shells, but the charging French infantry had likewise to go across a gas-shell barrage, through which hundreds of thousands of shrapnel bullets also rained.

The attackers and the attacked wore gas-masks, which had become the commonplace feature of a modern battle. They had eye protectors against blinding gases and breath protectors against poison fumes. The time was soon to arrive when their uniforms also had to be altered in order to protect them from the new cloth-impregnating gas with which the subtle enemy tried to poison their skins. In appearance civilised man seemed like a monster of the pre-human age of the earth, and as he went forward in his anti-chemical attire the woods flamed and smoked around him and the tops of the downs looked like volcanoes.

Just before the assault the German commander had reinforced with a new division his troops in the line. Therefore, when hand-to-hand fighting opened in the hollows between the opposing masses of guns, the struggle was of a supremely severe character. The Germans fought desperately for every trench and redoubt, and when their efforts proved unavailing against the vehemence of the French troops, reserves were brought forward for counter-attack after counter-attack against the captured positions.

Nevertheless, the left French wing, which had the most difficult piece of work, fought forward with remarkable rapidity. Its flank was exposed to German guns in the Beine Woods and on the Berru slopes. In front of it

[French official photograph.

French troops that had relieved the town marching past Prince Arthur of Connaught at Noyon.

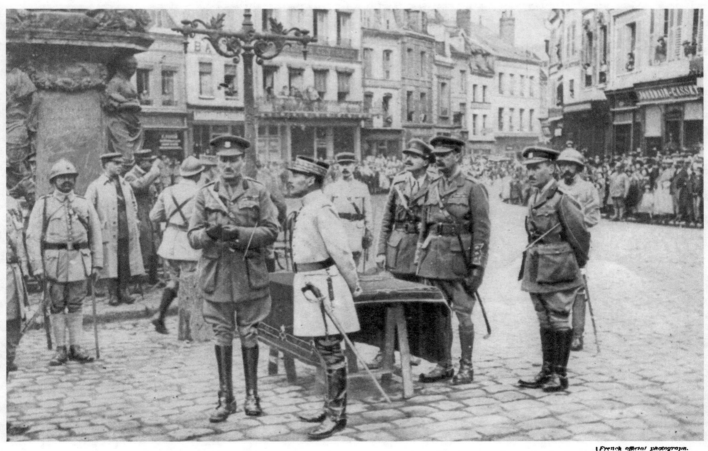

[French official photograph.

Prince Arthur of Connaught, representing King George, decorating French heroes at Noyon.

French curé preaching in his ruined church to a company of French officers.

How Nature healed the scars of France and children played where heroes fought and died.

Drums and bugles of the 8th Algerian Tirailleurs at a general review on the Oise.

French troops escorting German prisoners along roads tunnelled through valleys by German labour.

Wanton ruin wrought at Vauxaillon=en=Laonnois by the Germans before evacuating the village.

Cautious advance of French patrols to a house in Vauxaillon suspected of containing explosives.

were strong redoubts, such as the fieldwork north of Grille Wood. In spite of the obstacles and the terrible flanking fire, the French forces on and around Mont Cornillet won their objectives within an hour. They carried the enemy's fortified lines to the south of Beine village, and thus lightened the task of the French centre.

In the centre the assault was delivered from Mont Haut, down the northern slopes of the valley through which ran the road from Moronvilliers to Nauroy. The bottom of the valley was reached, but the enemy managed to maintain his position on the two downs south of Moronvilliers village. These two downs, known as the Casque and the Téton, flanked the valley road westward, and gave observation over part of the eastern side of Mont Haut. They also commanded the roads running southward and south-eastward to the French lines. Moreover, the Germans also held a series of lower but very useful heights beyond the Casque and the Téton.

As the weather was misty and the scene of battle was smoking like an immense forest fire, the tops of the downs, which the enemy retained, were not of much use to him for observation purposes. In all the dead ground on the northern slopes he had parks of howitzers, mechanically firing at fixed ranges, in answer to the bright rocket signals which his infantry sent up. The original Saxon garrison was reinforced by Brandenburg and Baden divisions, and, after a swaying struggle south of Moronvilliers, the French centre drew back from the Casque and the Téton, and only the attacking left wing around Beine and around Nauroy achieved any important gains.

Yet the fierce operation by General Gouraud was far from being fruitless. It was principally designed as a preliminary measure to draw off forces from the Aisne front by shaking the enemy's left wing and threatening him with a great new offensive all along the Champagne line. On May 1st the German Command **Moronvilliers Battle** resumed the Moronvilliers Battle, and **resumed** after a violent artillery action tried to recover the ground that the French had won around Casque Down. Twice the enemy masses charged forward from the village and the high ground north and south of it. But all the grey waves were broken by the guns and machine-guns of the French.

For some weeks afterwards there were only local hand-bomb actions and raids amid the clump of Champagne Downs, as the high tide of battle turned elsewhere. Yet the German High Command remained very apprehensive of the consequences of the loss of the chief heights in the great buttress system of its central line. Hindenburg came in person to inspect the sector, and earnestly discussed with Ludendorff the prospects of a new counter-offensive. Preparations were energetically made for a grand attack, but they were anticipated by General Gouraud and the Staff of General Pétain. Barely two days before the enemy's arrangements were complete the French commander of the Champagne front again struck heavily in the direction of Moronvilliers village.

On Sunday, May 20th, the French guns opened a terrific bombardment on Casque Hill, Téton Down, and the neighbouring points. The reinforced German artillery replied with equal intensity, endeavouring to overwhelm by counter-battery work the attacking batteries. On each side there were sudden concentrations of numerous batteries against single batteries; most of the guns being howitzers concealed on reverse slopes. Hundreds of dummy guns were employed to produce smoke and flame and to distract and mislead hostile observing officers.

In the end the superb gunners of France won the mastery. Under the cover of their devastating fire their infantry carried the larger part of Casque Hill and Téton Down, and threw the enemy from trench after trench on the northern slopes of Mont Cornillet. A thousand prisoners were taken, and all the most important observation-posts in the Moronvilliers buttress were finally occupied by the victors.

The plight of the local German commander in the Moronvilliers sector of the Crown Prince's Command led him to measures of desperation. He had been thoroughly defeated after Ludendorff had taken the trouble especially to strengthen him and bring up the wooden idol of Berlin to inspire his troops. He lashed all his lost positions and all the French front as far as the old Roman road with hundreds of thousands of shell—shrapnel, high explosive, and gas. He turned the chalk summits of the downs from patched green into dirty white, and fired tempests of death over the saddle of land between Mont Haut and Mont Blond. All the shell accumulated in vain for a great German offensive was expended in this extraordinary counter-bombardment. When, however, the German shock troops, with their **Spade-work** strong ordinary infantry supports, **versus artillery** endeavoured to regain the lost downs they were in turn swept by tempests of French shrapnel, followed by plunging machine-gun fire and short-ranged volleys of hand-grenades.

Again there followed a long pause in the Moronvilliers battlefield. Both armies began to burrow deeply in the chalk, sap up and down to each other, make tunnels to secure their communications, and drive mining galleries under enemy posts. In this kind of mole warfare the industrious and hard-driven Teuton proved somewhat more effective than the easier-going and more talented Gaul.

The Western Allies had always been less inclined to extreme labour on earthworks than was the enemy. At the beginning of the war only the small Regular British Army entrenched with the same skill as the German Army. The French infantryman was disastrously averse at the time to digging himself in and saving his life, and the Russian foot-soldier was rather of the same way of thinking, though led by sergeants and officers who remembered the earthwork battles in Manchuria.

By the spring of 1917 the highly inventive French engineers had succeeded in remedying the defect of their infantry. They had obtained a machine that could excavate vast underground shelters in a surprisingly short time. On the British front, as was seen in the Messines action, the coal-miners of Great Britain were able to surpass the greatest burrowing operations of the Teutons. Nevertheless, the enemy continued to maintain, in a general way, a marked superiority in industrious field fortification. It was, perhaps, by reason of the serf-like condition of mind of all German privates that they stuck to their mole-like work with increasing pertinacity. Alarmed by the superior power of the artillery of the Western Allies, they redoubled their efforts to escape destruction by means of spade-work and electrically-driven excavating tools.

In the chalk downs of the Moronvilliers system the Teutonic moles achieved a fair measure of success in the spring and summer of 1917. They tunnelled completely under some of the **Mont Haut partly** downs and created northern and **won back** southern entrances and defences. Then, up the northern slopes of their lost crests they burrowed, until in places their advanced posts were within twenty yards of the forward French positions. Bit by bit they won back part of the western slope of Mont Haut, which was the supreme observation height, and at this point, within bomb-throw of their opponents, they employed all manner of devices to obtain periscopic glimpses of French activity in the valley.

Far more important was the position the enemy succeeded in maintaining on the saddle between Mont Blond and Mont Haut. He erected thickly armoured observation-posts on this neck of downland, and by means of very long and ingenious periscopes, to the making of which all

[*French official photograph.*
NOT MAN-PROOF.
A good example of German thoroughness in trench construction, proof against high-explosive shells and all save French valour.

star-shells, indicating that the German infantry needed help.

But there was no time for any help to reach them. In a period varying from three to six minutes the French attacking forces won the ground they were set to win. The saddle between Mont Haut and Mont Blond was carried on a front of eight hundred yards for a depth of three hundred yards, and the enemy's position on Téton Down was stormed to a similar depth on a front of six hundred yards. Slight as these gains seemed in comparison with the enormous French bombardment, they decided the long struggle in the Moronvilliers Downs. The Germans were at last completely blinded.

This fact was proved by an

the fine science of the Zeiss works went, he continued to direct his howitzer fire upon part of the French communications.

In the first week of July, 1917, Ludendorff again resolved to make a strong effort to recover the Moronvilliers Downs. The French hold on the hills was regarded by his Staff as a serious danger, in that they gave observation over the Plain of Champagne from Beine to the Argonne Forest. For three weeks the enemy's preparations were observed by the French scouting pilots. They saw the Germans busy making new roads and bringing forward supplies. They caught German tractors at work by night, hauling new heavy guns into position, and they discovered various movements of troops. By the middle of July, 1917, it was known to the French Staff that the enemy had three fresh divisions echeloned on an

Gouraud anticipates enemy offensive

attacking front of five miles, and some of the troops were seen making elaborate rehearsals of the assault.

As before, General Gouraud prepared to anticipate the hostile offensive, being a man who believed that attack was the best form of defence. On July 12th he opened a very heavy bombardment on all the German lines, and continued it day and night on a widely extended front, varying his volume of fire so as to leave it uncertain at what point he intended to attack.

After a preparation lasting for fifty hours the French infantry went forward at eight o'clock in the evening of the National Festival day of July 14th. The German gunners threw out a dense and continuous barrage, while the French artillerymen were intensifying their fire behind the hostile crests. The Champagne Hills disappeared from view in volcanic smoke, and against the dark reek there flared innumerable rockets and

French official photograph.
TYPICAL SECTION OF THE HINDENBURG LINE.
German stronghold at Guennevières, on the Oise, after capture by the French. This massive fortification was occupied for two and a half years by the enemy, who deemed it impregnable.

extraordinary phenomenon. Only twenty minutes after the small and widely-extended French infantry forces won their objectives seven German kite-balloons rose low over the northern hills, taking extreme risk in the hope of catching a glimpse of the French movements. But the balloons were too late. Victory was achieved, and no activity was discernible in the French lines. All night long the beaten forces of Prussianism surged up the northern slopes, only to be shattered by the fire of hundreds of defending guns directed from the newly-won observation-posts. So assured was the French hold upon the Moronvilliers system that the Chief of Staff of the Crown Prince of Prussia gave over the attempt to recover the lost dominating heights and, vainly returning to Verdun, reconcentrated there his artillery forces in the design to effect a diversion.

Long before General Gouraud's operation ended in complete success the larger aim underlying it was achieved. From the beginning the Moronvilliers action had been designed to assist the principal Aisne offensive. The first action on April 17th partly helped to relieve the pressure on the main French armies, but it occurred too late to enable General Nivelle to accomplish his plan. On the other hand, the attack of April 30th, undertaken at the time when General Pétain succeeded to the High Command, was a remarkably effective demonstration.

In all probability the German Staff became aware of the change in the French Command, and, knowing that General Pétain had formerly commanded the Champagne group of armies, expected him to strike from the ground that he best knew. The resumption of the Moronvilliers action was calculated to confirm this anticipation of the enemy.

The new French Commander-in-Chief, however, continued the battle along the heights of the Aisne. At the beginning of May, 1917, the Ladies' Walk remained one of the lines of fiercest conflict in military history. The mutual bombardment never ceased, and infantry fighting went on continuously. After a struggle of more than three hundred hours, in which both French and Germans showed marvellous powers of endurance, the attacking forces began slowly to extend their hold upon the northern Hog's Back of the Aisne.

Along the larger part of the great river valley the Chasseurs, Zouaves, Moroccans, and infantry of the line had climbed three hundred feet above the

Tunnels in the Aisne heights river, fighting through ravines, limestone caverns, quarries, and stone-built villages, and over cliffs through which the enemy had driven tunnels from the reverse slope to the front slope. There were holes seeming like entrances to ordinary dug-outs, into which the first troops of assault merely threw bombs in passing, with the result that their successors had to spend weeks, and sometimes months, in underground fighting; for in a remarkable number of cases the small, commonplace holes led, by many steps and galleries, to caverns in which hundreds of fighting men were undismayed and confidently sheltering.

The crest along which the Ladies' Walk ran was pierced, so that German forces could move from the Ailette Valley to the Aisne Valley, and make surprise attacks upon the French advanced forces. The rock was a kind of hard chalk of limestone quality, and some of it had of old been used in building Rheims Cathedral. But the percolating water had eaten into the lime, dissolving

[French official photograph.

CLEARING A FLOODED TRENCH.
Pumping the water from a trench on the French front. Water was a persistent enemy in trench warfare, and in many places regular pumping was necessary to keep the duck-boards clear of it.

it and washing it away, so that German sappers discovered, during their long mining operations, new caverns of which the French themselves were unaware. The deep underground artificial works in soft chalk, which delayed the British Army on the Ancre in 1916, were small in comparison with the intricate natural subterranean labyrinths which in 1917 delayed the French armies north of the Aisne.

No gun could penetrate such places as the Dragon's Cave near Hurtebise. There was seventy feet of limestone between the surface of the ridge and the roof of the immense German shelter. All that the French artillery could do, by the heaviest bombardment, was to drive the German soldiers to earth, shatter some of their observing periscopes, and give the attacking infantry a brief respite from close-range machine-gun and rifle fire. As the Germans retained the highest parts of the great ridge, they still had some deadly advantages over the forces of attack. They could discern many of the movements of preparation, spot the

[French official photograph.

FRENCH TROOPS PREPARING FOR AN ATTACK.
French soldiers about to fire rifle-grenades as a preliminary to going "over the top" and carrying out an attack with the bayonet. They are standing firm, awaiting the signal to commence.

field-guns firing across the river, and steadily direct their parks of heavy artillery concealed in the woods of the northern hills around Laon.

Aeroplane observation was becoming by this time somewhat restricted in importance. Batteries in action were often surrounded by smoke-producing machines, placed ten yards apart. These machines covered the guns in clouds of fume when a hostile aeroplane was seen, and the guns then fired through the smoke in a mechanical way, as directed by far-distant observing officers. The naval smoke-screen, first employed by destroyers to veil the movements of their **The smoke-screen** battleships, became a general military **factor** instrument. It covered an attack; it screened a defence; it decoyed hostile aircraft into the range of anti-aircraft guns, and in the new age of smokeless powder again made the fog of battle a perplexing and most subtle factor in all main operations.

The Germans employed characteristic energy in developing the smoke tactics which the British Army had first introduced. Seldom in history had the Teuton displayed any surprising inventiveness. He imitated and developed, furiously and fairly successfully. In the present case he built smoke machines in tens of thousands, and complicated his system of mole-warfare with squid devices. Yet when the French armies resumed the grand assault upon the northern rampart of the Aisne, all the increasing

operation. At Vauxaillon, south of Coucy Forest, a salient in the Hindenburg line was destroyed, and around Laffaux Mill, at the western end of the Ladies' Walk, the German positions were carried as far as the road running from Soissons to Laon. Then at Braye, in the centre of the Ladies' Walk, a French army corps broke into a stretch of two and a half miles of the Siegfried line. German columns moving up to reinforce the battle-line on the great ridge got caught by the heavy French artillery and dispersed. Below the cliffs of Craonne the German reserves were diverted from the vital scene of combat by another French thrust between Berry-au-Bac and Rheims. At the same time the action in the Moronvilliers hills was resumed.

The British armies also attacked the enemy from the south of Lens to the north of St. Quentin. The result was that the principal forces of Germany were subjected to immense strain along a front of nearly a hundred and fifty miles. Each local action had its carefully designed place in the combined plan of General Pétain and Sir Douglas Haig. Each stroke was a sledge-hammer blow directed at some critical point in the long hostile line.

At the most critical point the German defence was completely broken. The French Alpine troops rapidly overran the trenches surrounding Craonne village, and then, in wide order, swept over the California Plateau and the Casemates level. After fighting along and across the Ladies' Walk the Alpine Division and their comrades

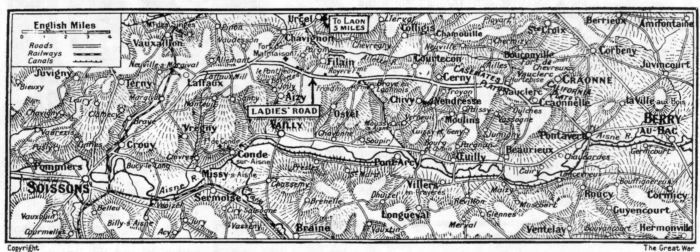

MAP OF THE CHEMIN DES DAMES AND THE CONTIGUOUS COUNTRY.

The Chemin des Dames, constructed in the eighteenth century for the daughters of Louis XV., runs along the crest of the high ridge of ground between the Valleys of the Aisne and the Ailette, from near Craonnelle on the east to Laffaux on the west. From its hard limestone rock was quarried much of the stone of which Rheims Cathedral was built. After intense fighting, the French stormed its positions early in 1917.

machinery of war merely served to reduce the final, decisive stage of combat into more savage hand-to-hand fighting.

The larger machines on both sides tended to balance each other. Gun was arrayed against gun, forts were opposed to batteries, trench-mortars, and "tanks." When the mechanism of attack became equal to or superior to that of the defence, it restored to the human factors in battle their ancient power of decision. The infantryman was the king of the battlefield. With high-explosive bombs in his hand, and light machine-guns and portable mortars immediately behind him, he was a more terrible figure than any foot-soldier of former days.

The famous Alpine Division, formed of mountaineers of France, was given the task of carrying Craonne and the high plateaux above the village. The Alpine Division had fought alongside the British, from Cléry to Bouchavesnes, and had a score of earlier victories to its credit. Many leaders it had lost and many men, but under a young and valiantly gay commander, General Brissaud-Desmaillet, the immortal and invincible hillmen stormed upward to Craonne with winning skill.

A series of fierce thrusts at other points in the enemy's line, on May 4th, 1917, greatly facilitated the main

connected with the French forces already established near the Napoleon monument by the farm of Hurtebise.

The great three-hundred-feet slope, with its ranks of hostile machine-guns above, that had broken General Nivelle's offensive on April 16th, seems to have been climbed and stormed with remarkable speed. The new howitzers of France ranged exactly upon the enemy's topmost redoubts; his tunnel ways were seldom penetrated, yet the entrances were often blocked up by the explosion of huge projectiles. For the rest, the expert manœuvring power of the platoons of **Alpine Division's** French mountaineering troops was such **great victory** as to overcome all the defensive work on which the Germans had laboured since September, 1914.

It was by no means an easy victory. All German commanding officers had orders to hold their positions at any cost in life, and they handled their men with desperate rigour. They still had many first-rate troops, who fought hard and stubbornly, but the French light Alpine infantry, forming the spear-head of the attacking army corps, were not to be denied. Too quickly and too fiercely they moved, under the cover of their superb curtain fire, for the slower-minded Teuton to counter them.

CURTAIN FIRE ON THE CHEMIN DES DAMES.
Enemy curtain fire sent over in anticipation of an attack on the Ladies' Walk, north-west of Rheims. In the right corner French soldiers are seen waiting the moment to go forward and storm the steep slopes.

When they had completely topped the flat and spreading summit, and descended into the wooded Ailette Valley, the local German commander sent a division of the Prussian Guard against them. He reckoned that the victors would be absolutely exhausted by their long, arduous fighting climb, and that ten thousand fresh troops of the best German corps would be able to push the tired Frenchmen back over the great ridge.

The mountaineer races of France were usually of very small stature, with dark hair, dark eyes, and the fine, lively features of the Iberian type. They came from the sleeping volcanoes of Auvergne, from the Maritime Alps, and from the Pyrenees, but had some taller men of the Vosges Mountains among them. **Prussian Guard thrown back** For the most part they represented the Neolithic race which had been driven to the hills in the distant age of bronze by the later and taller races in Western Europe. They were, however, the very best of European hill fighters. Hill fighting, indeed, was an art which they had practised for thousands of years, and in the evening of May 4th they were less fatigued than were the tall, fresh, fair-haired men of the Prussian Guard launched against them.

In the fighting amid crags, woods, and ravines above the Aisne and the Ailette the quick-minded, darting "blue devils of France," as the Germans called them, wore down and threw back the Prussian Guard. In intervals of combat they laboured with peculiar energy amid the broken earthworks of the enemy, turning parapets about, rearranging machine-gun positions, and gathering hand-bombs and other ammunition for the defence of the supreme bastion of the fighting-line in

Western Europe. The gunners of Germany poured an extraordinary number of shells upon them, covered their communications with shrapnel, ploughed up their lines with high explosive, and drenched them with poison gases. But the small, light-blue, masked figures patiently went on with their work, though falling in hundreds. They reorganised, with their comrades, the small California level and the larger Casemates Plateau, and connected their new lines with the downward sloping Forest of Vauclerc.

Across the Ailette Valley, that dipped some three hundred feet between the opposing ridges, the Germans held the more northerly hill line running above St. Croix, Chermizy, and Neuville. Around this northern ridge some thousands of hostile guns were placed in screening woods and hollows. **German hammer and French anvil** By reason of their position the German artillerymen could bring a shorter-ranged and better-directed gun fire to bear in the Ailette Valley than the French gunners could send across the Aisne. Moreover, the German artillery, sited about the lower ground east of the Craonne cliffs, had a large arc of fire against the northern Aisne Plateau. It could enfilade the easternmost French positions, and exactly direct its enfilading fire from the observation-posts on the St. Croix Hills.

For these reasons the victorious French troops were unable to extend very far from Craonne or approach the town of Corbeny, lying on the main road north of Ville aux Bois. In order to achieve an assured success the French commander had to limit his efforts to the conquest of the California and Casemates Plateaux, and thereupon stolidly withstand the stupendous sledge-hammer blows

AN EARNEST OF FURTHER VICTORY.
French infantry raising the Tricolour preparatory to making a ceremonial entry into a town that had been recaptured from the enemy—one of the proud moments for which the men had been heroically fighting.

by artillery and infantry which the Germans directed against him from two sides, eastward and northward.

The victorious forces of France carried out this plan. After breaking the Prussian Guard, the Alpine troops remained upon the highest and easternmost part of the Ladies' Walk, in the position of a menacing spear-head, poised high above the German forces. In co-operation with their fellow-countrymen operating in other sectors, the mountaineers captured in three days 8,200 prisoners, bringing the total of Germans taken since the opening of the Aisne offensive to 29,000.

Ludendorff's fountain-pen success On Tuesday, May 8th, Ludendorff recovered the plateaux above Craonne and Hurtebise by means of his fountain-pen. His communiqué ran: "The French, in fruitless and costly attacks, attempted to wrest from us the high positions between Hurtebise and Craonne, but were not successful anywhere." Then, in order to make good this statement, Ludendorff ordered General Bohm, commanding on the Aisne front and the Chief of Staff to the Crown Prince of Prussia, to retake the lost positions at any cost.

ON THE SUMMIT OF THE LADIES' WALK.
First wave of French infantry surging into the enemy trenches at one section of the great battlefield that extended from Laffaux to Craonnelle along the Chemin des Dames, one of the lines of fiercest conflict in military history.

Large forces of German infantry were continually sent forward under cover of whirlwind bombardments. They attacked, in succession, the ground near Cerny, the Hurtebise position, and the California Plateau. In spite of terrific losses, the grey waves surged up the Ailette Valley, the top of which was flaming with French machine-guns and rifles.

Only for a few minutes did the enemy gain the summit. He tried to hold the north-eastern, horn-like projection of the California level, which he temporarily won by a double flank attack. The Frenchmen, however, returned with the bayonet and pitchforked the enemy back into the valley. Then in the evening of Tuesday, May 8th, the gallant defenders of Craonne in turn attacked the weakened assailers and carried three-quarters of a mile of line north-east of the village of Chevreux, between Corbeny and Craonne.

The local German commander, General Bohm, had then to abandon for a while his attempts to recover the Hog's Back and employ his forces around Chevreux. He sent forward a new division to drive the French back to Craonne, but his fresh troops were caught under artillery fire and shattered by machine-guns. Instead of recovering any ground, they lost two important forts. In the hope of relieving the position around Chevreux the German general once more attacked the French lines on either side of Cerny village, and after fierce hand-to-hand fighting his men were thrown back.

This last counter-attack, delivered on May 10th, marked the close of the second and completely victorious French offensive on the Aisne. Yet, after a short interval of artillery and infantry inaction, the German commander renewed the vain struggle. The earlier pause was merely due to the local shortage in munitions and a lack of further reserves. As soon as more shell and fresh troops arrived, the great ridge again became veiled in flame-shot smoke from Laffaux Mill to Chevreux. For weeks the gigantic wrestle between thousands of guns and hundreds of thousands of men went on, in daylight and darkness, between the Soissons-Laon Road and the Moronvilliers Downs.

Ludendorff's clear intention was to devote all guns and men that he could save from the British front to the extremely costly task of wearing down the spirit of the French people. He tried to turn the Ladies' Walk, with the hill near Berry-au-Bac and the downs above Auberive, into the theatre of a battle of attrition surpassing that of Verdun.

By means of a powerful band of traitors in the world of French politics and journalism the German dictator was, at the time, working strongly upon both military and civilian opinion in France. He supplied his creatures with enormous funds, through banks in neutral countries, and occasionally even succeeded in reaching the French troops in the trenches by means of his agents and their dupes.

The distance between the Ladies' Walk and Paris was so short that the incessant rumble of the tremendous opposing batteries was often borne by favouring winds to the strained ears of the people in the capital. The design of the German Staff was quickly to shake France on the Ladies' Walk into a desire for a negotiated peace, at the expense of Russia, in much the same way as Great Britain was designed to be reduced to a condition of war-weariness by submarine operations and daylight and nocturnal air raids.

General Pétain, one of the master gunners of the world, was, however, well content with the situation that he had obtained. Vast was the increase in his artillery power since he saved Verdun in February, 1916. No longer had he to fight with **German Staff's double design** pieces of inferior range against an overwhelming number of the heaviest kind of German ordnance. He at last possessed guns that enabled him and his lieutenants to display their almost incomparable skill in combination with terrific strength.

Whenever the enemy wearied of counter-attacking, the French commander made some small but intense thrust at the last observation points dominating the Ailette Valley or the Moronvilliers region. The blows were always delivered by gun-power, and often little more than a company of infantry was sent forward to occupy and organise the new position. Thereupon, the Germans

REMARKABLE THREE-MINUTE RAID BY FRENCH TROOPS IN CHAMPAGNE.

This very striking series of photographs, taken by a Frenchman who had already won the Croix de Guerre, shows an actual raid in progress. The first photograph shows the raiding-party leaving their own trenches; in the second they had got beyond their own wire and were crossing No Man's Land; while in the third they had reached the enemy's trenches. To the left a wounded Frenchman is seen returning to his own lines. The raid, in which several Germans were killed and four taken prisoner, occupied from start to finish but three minutes and twenty seconds.

flooded the ground with poison gas, ploughed it up with innumerable shells, and sent out strong storming forces, with ordinary infantry support. Again the French guns created an impassable curtain of fire, causing the enemy to fall back, often before any French machine-guns in the infantry line came into action.

At the beginning of June, 1917, the German High Command launched a grand counter-offensive against the plateaux above Craonne. After a mighty bombardment that continued day and night along the great ridge, two German divisions climbed, in five columns, towards the Vauclerc and California Plateaux. At some points the assailing Germans were packed actually shoulder to shoulder. The heads of the columns were blown away by the massed fire of the heavy French artillery, but one of the main bodies succeeded, by means of a liquid-fire attack, in burning out the garrisons of some of the French forward observation-posts. Part of the main French forces then came into action, and bombed and bayoneted the Germans from the edge of the high level, and pursued them down the northern slope. It was the famous Alpine Division which had taken Craonne on May 4th that broke the two enemy divisions together, and the special German shock troops deployed in front of the routed forces.

Wastage of enemy reserves About this time enemy troops began to arrive in large numbers from the Russian front, and were thrown in violent counter-attacks against the French and British lines. Along the Ladies' Walk the wastage of this large fresh enemy reserve proceeded at a rapid rate, as General Bohm continued to employ forces that often amounted to a whole division in monotonous attempts to drive in some famous French ridge position. Laffaux Mill, Filain, the Pantheon, Royère and Froidmont Farms, the Hurtebise Saddle, and the California Plateau were mentioned almost

daily in official reports of German failures in counter-attack.

The method employed by the Chief of Staff to the Prussian Crown Prince was the same as that he had used at Verdun. He delivered whirlwind bombardments on a large front, and then sent his infantry forward on a comparatively small line of attack. The French forces used their 3 in. quick-firers in the manner of machine-guns, mowing every yard of ground over which the enemy was advancing. Success largely depended upon the condition of communications between French forward observing officers and their light batteries. When a single telephone wire remained uninjured by the German bombardment, the hostile shock troops were generally destroyed. On the other hand, when all telephone wires were broken and other mechanical means of signalling failed the event was an extreme gamble. It depended on the fact whether or no the French runners could get past the enemy's shrapnel curtain and bring their field-batteries swiftly and exactly into play.

Pétain has to take long views

In the cases where the forward light guns were too late to meet the enemy's attempt at a surprise thrust, the battered and shell-islanded French garrison fought as best it could with machine-guns, rifles, and hand-bombs. Continual progress, however, was made in the means of communication between infantry and artillery. Wires were sunk more deeply, and written messages were pitched from the firing-line into the artillery line by means of special mortars. Each improvement of this kind strengthened the French system of defence of the northern Aisne Ridge and the Moronvilliers Downs, and increased the wastage among the German troops that were coming from Russia.

Throughout June, 1917, the French commander remained

[*French official photograph.*

EVERY STREET A HEAP OF RUBBISH: EVERY HOUSE A SHELL.
One of the many villages in the Valley of the Aisne that were razed to the ground by the Germans as they were driven back by the French in the course of the offensive that began in April, 1917.

MUTUAL INSPECTION, CRITICISM, AND ADMIRATION.
Men of a French cycling corps halting on a roadside in Champagne to turn critical inspection on to a passing troop of French cavalry, who returned the gaze of friendly criticism with equal intentness and approval.

largely on the defensive. It served his purpose to allow the strengthening German armies to break against his magnificent system of resistance. General Pétain had to take very long views, by reason of the chaotic weakness of Russia and the unpreparedness of the United States. His position greatly resembled that which had obtained when he was defending Verdun in the spring of 1916 and destroying the Germans there by the hundred thousand, while waiting for the full strength of Great Britain to be thrown against the enemy.

All that General Nivelle accomplished in the offensive of April, 1917, became of local, secondary importance owing to the complete failure of Russia.

Disastrous effect of Russia's collapse In the summer of 1917 the Western Allies were thrown back a year by the unparalleled moral disaster that had fallen upon the Russian people. France, in particular, suffered heavily by the postponement of all hope of obtaining a decisive victory. She had to return to the method she used in the early part of 1916. Steadily and economically she set herself to reduce the power of Germany, while she was gathering sufficient fresh forces to take part, yet again, in a future grand offensive against the common enemy. The French armies above the Aisne and below the Suippe River became, for the time, the anvil of the Entente, of which the northern British armies were the principal hammer. Between anvil and hammer the strength of Germany was to be so broken as to allow General Pétain, by October, 1917, to renew his offensive on the Aisne Ridge.

Meanwhile, nearly all the early line of attack of the Franco-British offensive, from Lens to Auberive, was transformed into a line of resistance. The enemy then had the choice of trying to win back, with the guns and men he was bringing from Russia, either the Vimy Ridge and the Monchy position of the British, or the Craonne Ridge and dominant Moronvilliers Downs of the French. Following the principle of acting against what seemed to

be the lesser force, Ludendorff selected the new French front for persistent and methodical counter-attack. He thought that he could wear France out by means of a war of accelerated attrition more quickly than he could exhaust by submarine operations the resources of the British Empire.

There was another element of importance in the plan of campaign adopted by the German High Command after the failure of Russia. North of the Aisne the Germans had retained a strong and dominating position around Fort Malmaison. From this position they still overlooked part of the Aisne Valley. They also possessed a great upland cavern near Hurtebise Monument, and along most of the high line their advanced forces were within rushing distance of many vital observation points.

The French situation was tantalising to the enemy. At Vauxaillon there was a height known as Monkey Hill, commanding the ravine through which the railway ran to Laon and overlooking the western end of the Ailette Valley. The Germans were entrenched on the reverse slope of Monkey Hill, and had only to climb a few **Stonewall tactics at Monkey Hill** yards in order to snatch all the advantages of the position from the French. The result was that the enemy commander first employed companies, then battalions and brigades, in repeated attempts to regain this critical summit.

Finally he sent an entire Prussian division against Monkey Hill in the last week of June, and reinforced the division with a very large body of shock troops. All his efforts were in vain. After a bitter struggle, lasting a day and night, a much smaller French force counter-attacked and returned to the summit. About the same time the French in turn stormed the enormous grotto that ran below the Hurtebise position. At Hurtebise the Plateau of Vauclerc was joined to a saddle of high land, at which several roads met. The saddle was in many ways the critical position on the ridge, and the French forces could not completely master it because the enemy held the Dragon's Cave.

The French themselves had held this cave in 1915, but had lost it owing to a chance German howitzer shot closing the only southern entrance and imprisoning two of their companies. In turn, two German companies occupied the grottos and apparently enjoyed perfect safety. They had large entrances on the northern and southern sides, and several new vertical exits into the German trenches overhead, around the monument of Napoleon's victory. Their position, moreover, was so close to the French trenches that no heavy artillery preparation was possible.

Story of the Dragon's Cave On June 25th the Dragon's Cave was recovered, in spite of the work that the enemy sappers had spent upon it. The lowest cave was assailed before the action opened, and by certain means made uninhabitable. Then the nests of machine-guns, guarding the main shaft above ground, were overwhelmed by a liquid-fire attack, while the main exit northward was blown in and filled up by heavy howitzer fire based on aerial photographs and directed by pilots. The French infantrymen swept up behind their line of liquid fire and captured all the German machine-guns that were above ground before the enemy gunners were able to fire.

There then followed, however, an amazing scene of confusion. The victors could not find the remaining entrance into the grottos. They were fiercely countered on their left, and compelled to give ground, and swept by a hurricane of barraging shell, for which there was complete shelter beneath their feet, if only they could find it. By a superb rally they recovered the German trenches on their flank. In the meantime their chaplain, Father Py, descending an apparent dug-out in search of wounded, entered the main cavern, in which more than three hundred Germans were collected.

He argued with the enemy officers for a quarter of an hour, and succeeded in inducing them to acknowledge they were prisoners and undertake to lead their men into the French lines. When, therefore, General Bohm launched his main counter-attacks, the men of the 152nd Regiment of France had the caves as cover against the hostile preparatory bombardment, and in almost undiminished strength met and shattered the fresh German forces.

The 152nd Regiment was originally from the Vosges, and was therefore terrible. It was the extreme point of all the spear-head forces of renaissant France. In June, 1917, one officer alone remained of the original cadre. He commanded the machine-guns of the three battalions, and was a very quiet, shy man when he was not actually fighting. He sought no promotion and remained only a captain, but he and his thousands of dead hillmen controlled the spirit of the continual new drafts. He was the complete representative of the idea of the "revanche," a very important French word, which slanderers of the French race in English-speaking countries literally translate as "revenge." The proper modern signi- **Battle motto of the French Ghazis** fication of this word is "return match." The regiment of the French Vosges was personally and intimately acquainted with Prussianism of the school of Zabern. For this reason the men always fought in such a manner that all Germans, Northern and Southern, called them the men of the "devil's regiment."

In the Somme battles it was they who won the chief French successes from Cléry to Sailly-Saillisel. They were the Ghazis of France, and more fearful than any Oriental fanatics. Although their battle motto was: "There are no two ways; there is only one way—Altogether, and as fast as we can!" yet their extraordinary rapidity of attack was enhanced by a solid and cunning science in manœuvre, which made them practically peerless. They were the mad dervishes of France, and at the same time the finest and subtlest of "stunters," to use an expressive military cant term of American origin, introduced by the flying Wright Brothers.

After the capture of the Dragon's Cave and the Napoleonic monument on the Hurtebise level, General Pétain relapsed into a grim state of quiescence, recalling that adopted by Marshal Joffre in his deadliest mood of equanimity. All that the younger Captain of France was for the time concerned about was to kill at least three times the number of Germans for the soldiers that he lost while accumulating a gigantic new park of 15 in. and 16 in. howitzers.

All his local attacks were designed to lure the last reserves of Germany on to the slopes overlooked by his forward observation officers. Unlike the hillmen of the Vosges, General Pétain was no longer obsessed by the idea of a victorious "return match" between the Gaul and the Teuton. Like Joffre, after the disasters of Charleroi and Morhange, General Pétain was essentially a military statesman. His principal aim was to restore that vital balance between the populations of Germany and France which had been lost after 1870. He wanted to save as many as possible of the begetters of the younger generation of Greater France of 1940, and to kill as many as possible of the begetters of the adolescents in Lesser Germany of the same date. So, chiefly he looked to his guns and to his aeroplanes, and stimulated his Staff in the recognition of every inventive mind in his own armies and in the armies of the Allies.

Being himself a tactician, distinguished by inventive ability, and having in the civilian Minister of War, M. Painlevé, one of those political men of science that France alone can produce, the new French Commander-in-Chief had a larger fund of creative imagination at his disposal than any enemy or ally possessed.

Matthew Arnold, the subtlest of modern English anti-Teutons and the most enlightened lover of modern France, would have deeply, **Pétain as military statesman** silently rejoiced over the triumph of the true French spirit in the midsummer of 1917. Every home in France had dead to mourn. They numbered two million. There were many French prisoners in Germany, and the maimed soldiers of France were tragically numerous. Terribly had the country suffered, by reason of the mistaken theories of her former military leaders in regard to the lack of heavy artillery, the want of training in the art of making cover and in the use of machine-guns, and a general imperviousness to the lessons of the South African, Manchurian, and Balkan Wars.

In July, 1914, France was stricken by nearly every malady incident to a middle-class republicanism pillared by international finance. Her political system was based upon the interests of a large class of smallholders in the country and shopkeepers in the towns, who were leagued with large financial houses against all labouring class interests and ambitions. For more than a century France had been the intellectual volcano of Europe, because her governing middle classes were more subtly and more completely tyrannic than had been any similar class in any modern State since the conflicts between governing middle classes and economically oppressed labouring classes in the Italian city republics of the fifteenth century.

France of the twentieth century, however, possessed a more cohesive patriotism than mediæval Italy. The result was that, owing to the sacred union established in August, 1914, the magnificent qualities of the French mind came fully into play, and, in a slowly-organising movement, moulded the main activities of the race into a single, enlightened, branching, saving force that brought such men as Painlevé and Pétain into political and military positions of high command.

The achievement of Carnot, in the early days of the great Revolution, was repeated on a grander scale.

It was repeated with a series of cautious, protective measures against any military despot, which showed that France had learnt much since Waterloo. The French achievement was such as to eclipse all that ancient Greek republics had done in the days of Miltiades and Epaminondas.

It was the finest vindication in history of popular alertness and openness of mind. Voltaire, with all his narrownesses, Rousseau, with all his extravagances, were largely **The immortal** responsible for the salvation of the **spirit of France** French democracy. They had taught Frenchmen for generations to think— to think clearly and keenly, in a way that Darwin and Huxley had largely failed, in a later age, to educate the English intellect.

In reserve strength Great Britain was much superior to the French Republic, but there still obtained more obscurantism of various kinds in Great Britain than in weakened but clear-eyed France. Even the partial success which the treacherous elements in the French political world had obtained after the offensive of April 16th only served to arouse an overwhelming majority of Frenchmen to the internal needs of political and social sanitation.

Love of money is the mother-vice of all middle-class politics. Deeply had France of the Third Republic suffered from it, as Saint-Beuve had foreseen. Yet the Teutons saved her soul while intending to kill her body. Sadly wounded, she emerged from the ambush laid by her assassin; but her temporary physical weakness, by a glorious reaction, indued with fresh power of wing the immortal spirit that animated her. She became the queen of the modern world when, stripped of her light vanities and graces and bleeding from many wounds, she watched the weakening of Russia, upon whose aid she had depended for nearly a generation. Then, having lost much of her wealth and all her early hopes in the Russian catastrophe, she turned with quiet indomitableness to her later Allies, and, in a mood of patient sacrifice, held open the gate to victory until the armies of the English-speaking races could enter.

Gone was her own particular desire for the "revanche." She had proved, in battle after battle, that the Gaul could still prevail against the Teuton. When the opposing populations again tended to become equal, in the healing course of one or two generations, she had little to fear from her secular enemy. For a considerable time married French soldiers had been given special leave at intervals for the frankly-expressed purpose of increasing the number of French babies. The French people intended that their adult members should not only bear the murderous strain of war, but should consciously enter on the task of preventing anything like race suicide.

"Patriotism is not enough," said Edith Cavell, before she was led out to be shot. Many Frenchmen, holding the line of incessant conflict between Coucy Forest and the Champagne Downs in the summer and early autumn of 1917, began to feel somewhat as the murdered English nurse had felt. They became the soldiers of humanity in a larger degree than their ancestors had been during the period between Valmy and Austerlitz; and they fought for the reign of peace upon earth in a manner that foiled all the convulsive efforts of Ludendorff and his lieutenants.

Towards the end of June the Chief of Staff of the German Crown Prince sud- **The soldiers** denly changed the direction of his attack, **of humanity** and, after an intense artillery preparation, endeavoured to break through the western defences of Verdun between Dead Man Hill and Avocourt. After this diversion a great German offensive was launched, along a front of ten and a half miles, upon the Ladies' Walk above the Aisne.

The French troops held remarkably firm, and by July 9th recovered most of the forward positions relinquished under the sudden pressure of overwhelming numbers. This condition of things did not suit Ludendorff. He was in extreme need of a victory on the western front, in order

WAVE OF ASPHYXIATING GAS ADVANCING TOWARDS FRENCH TRENCHES.

Poison gas was first used, at Ypres in April, 1915, by the Germans. The Allies introduced protective gas-masks, and in turn invented forms of gas which were used against the enemy with deadly effect. A German war correspondent, writing of the fighting on the Aisne, in October, 1917, complained that "the Ailette Valley lay for three days under a thick, unbroken cloud of gas, and it was hardly possible to remove gas-masks during that time in order to have a drink of water or eat a bit of food. All the roads at the front lay under poisonous gases."

II

[*French official photograph.*

DESTRUCTION AT ROYE.
Railway bridge at the entrance to Roye as it was demolished by the retreating Germans.

thrusts in the Verdun sector and the Moronvilliers sector, in which Hill 304 was outflanked on the west and Mont Teton carried on the north-east.

For the political reasons already mentioned, the German High Command could not remain contented with the situation thus produced. The grand attempt to push the French forces from the dominating eastern end of the Aisne Plateau was renewed on July 19th. Only two and a half miles of high levels, between Craonne and Hurtebise, were assailed, and a special force of highly-trained veterans, formed into a 5th Division of the Guard, was sent forward, with additional contingents of shock troops.

At seven o'clock in the morning

to strengthen the movement for a negotiated peace, which was being engineered, under his hidden direction, by a majority of the members of the Reichstag. Dr. Michaelis, the new puppet Chancellor, so it was intended, was to be in a position to draw the attention of the world, in the middle of July, to important German successes against France as well as against weakening Russia.

The offensive against the high French positions north of the Aisne was therefore immediately renewed, with an increased number of men and guns. In the evening of Saturday, July 14th, a large German force, including a division of the Prussian Guard, made a magnificent attempt to recover all the ridge positions between Cerny and Craonne. The bearing of the Teutonic soldiers was admirable. Mass after mass of them charged to the death in a way that added to the highest traditions of their Army.

No men under Frederick the Great, Blücher, or Moltke fought with such disregard of their personal fate and such intrepid skill. Yet, brave and highly trained as they were, the Guardsmen met their masters in the comparatively small French garrison clinging to the battered, smoking ground along the eastern part of the ridge. Scores of Germans using flame-projectors were killed, and although their survivors drove the French out of part of their first line and enabled the shock troops to penetrate some supporting trenches, all positions of importance were recovered by the main body of French troops in an intense nocturnal combat that ended only when dawn broke.

Scarcely more than five hundred yards of the forward French line was retained by the Prussian regiments. This small loss was more than balanced by answering French

German Guards meet their masters

A NAME THAT WAS PROPHETIC.
Hotel at Coucy le Château, on the Aisne, as it was when the place was recovered by the French. Nothing but the façade of the "Hotel of the Ruins and of the Terrace" remained standing when the enemy had been driven away from the vicinity.

[*French official photograph.*

the Germans came over their parapets in close formation, and made a frontal attack on the Casemates and California uplands. On the wider parts of the plateaux, where the French artillery had space for barrage work, every assault failed, and a single French company on the west of the Casemates broke every attack there in a conflict lasting for nearly forty-eight hours. Only on the narrow strip of ground between the two main levels was the enemy able to obtain a footing.

But though the French fell back at this point, they held on to the trench running along the southern edge of the ridge. When they were at last reinforced they swept the Germans down the northern slope in a nocturnal battle, and recaptured every observation-post. Still, General Bohm did not abandon hope of recovering the ridge. No doubt he would have lost his command had he done so. He re-formed the new and broken Guards' Division, and added to it the 5th Reserve Prussian Division and the well-known 15th Bavarian Division. He also increased once more the number of his guns; and just before dawn on July 22nd he smote the eastern end of the ridge with such a bombardment as had never before been seen on the French front. Troops who had fought at Verdun declared they had never seen anything like it, and compared it with the Day of Judgment.

There was an element of surprise in the awful bombardment, which was based upon British artillery tactics. The gun fire lasted only an hour. At dawn the three German Divisions climbed up the southern slopes of the Ailette Valley against the Casemates and California Plateaux. There were some thirty thousand Germans, closely arrayed on a front of less than four thousand five hundred yards, with an entire army in immediate support behind them.

Just above the grey masses were a dozen or so surviving French artillery observing officers. But their means of communicating with their batteries had been much improved in the course of three months of unceasing battle. Unfortunately for the Germans, the day broke in an atmosphere of crystal clarity. The German positions could be studied in a minute way as far as telescopes could reach. Any German commander who tried to muster men in the Ailette Valley condemned his troops to death; and in the Champagne Plain, east of the Craonne cliffs, the enemy's camps were shelled with deadly precision at a range of fifteen miles.

A six days' battle

At an utterly disastrous sacrifice the enemy at last reached the first line on the Plateau of California, and, by more reckless daring than had ever been shown before in a bad cause, managed at nightfall to cling to the edge of the level. The whole of the California position measured only four hundred yards by two hundred and fifty yards. The area of the neighbouring Casemates level was sufficient to allow the French artillery to keep the enemy off, and on the smaller plateau the Germans won only the foremost line. The battle continued for six days. In the end not a green thing could be seen on the Ladies' Walk. The ridge was an indescribable dirty-white chaos of tumbled, dusty chalk. Yet, on July 24th, 1917, the men of the 152nd Regiment of France, some of whose former deeds have already been described, were perched upon the extreme northern edges of the California and the Casemates levels, their bayonets red, their faces white with chalk-dust and fatigue, and their eyes blazing with victory. The hillmen of France had conquered. Amid the continuing bombardment they again looked down upon the Ailette Valley, Laon Cathedral, and the Champagne Plain. At least a hundred thousand Germans had died in vain, and General Pétain was at last in so strong a position around Craonne that he could prepare to renew the Aisne offensive eastward against the triangle of fortified hill ground around Fort Malmaison.

100,000 Germans die in vain

[*French official photograph.*

MATTOCK AND SPADE FOLLOWING CLOSE ON THE WHEELS OF THE GUNS.
Permanent repair of the roads followed recovery of invaded districts with a rapidity remarkable even in view of the material and labour available. This photograph shows the station road at Chauny, on the railway line from Noyon to La Fère, approaching completion.

STRANGE CRAFT IN HOME WATERS: A CREWLESS CARGO BOAT PASSING A LIGHTSHIP NEARING PORT.

CHAS. PEARS

With the object of reducing loss of life in the Mercantile Marine, and more probably eluding observation 1917, which carried no crew and were towed by armed tugs. These boats required a smaller margin by German pirates, cargo boats for use in submarine danger zones were constructed, towards the end of of reserve buoyancy than ordinary vessels, and also offered a much less conspicuous above-water target.

CHAPTER CCIII.

WAR-TIME CHANGES IN BRITISH TRADE AND INDUSTRY:
A Record of Remarkable Achievement.
By T. Swinborne Sheldrake.

EDITORIAL NOTE.—This chapter is to be regarded as complementary to others which have appeared already dealing with alterations effected by the war in the national life. While agriculture and commerce and finance are separate activities and, therefore, require separate treatment, their interdependence is so close that no one of them can be discussed without reference to the others. Especially is this seen to be true in the light of the war, which affected all of them by diverting so much of the man-power of the Empire to purely military activity. Mr. Sheldrake's chapter must be read in conjunction with such earlier chapters as that on the Business Side of Armageddon (Vol. 6, p. 337), the Socialisation of Great Britain and Rise of Imperial Democracy (Vol. 8, p. 359), Britain Under the Burden of Bureaucracy (Vol. 9, p. 471), and British Agriculture on a War Footing (Vol. 10, p. 91). Other aspects of the general question will be dealt with in subsequent chapters of THE GREAT WAR, for example, in Mr. Storry Deans' considered summary of the evolution and operation of the Defence of the Realm Act.

THE effect of a great European war upon the industrial and commercial life of the nation was a frequent subject of debate and speculation during the early years of the twentieth century. In order to get into their true perspective the great changes actually resulting from the war it is necessary to consider briefly the position in which Great Britain was previous to its outbreak.

Greater changes had taken place during the preceding sixty years than had occurred previously during almost as many centuries. The era of steam had revolutionised means of transport, and rendered possible the swift and cheap transit of goods from the ends of the earth. The result had been a phenomenal growth in the exchange of commodities between nations. International trade is, and always must be, in the nature of exchange. It is obviously only to the advantage of any country to export its products, while it receives in exchange products of other countries of which it stands in need.

The United Kingdom was the

LORD MOULTON, P.C., K.C.B., F.R.S.
The Right Hon. Lord Moulton, who acted as Director-General of the Department of Explosives Supply in the Ministry of Munitions, received the K.C.B. in June, 1915.

first country to take full advantage of steam-power; it was the pioneer of the modern railway system; the leader in the building of gigantic ships; the first to divert the energies of a large section of its people to industry.

The object of the vast activity of the industrial districts was the acquisition of wealth. By the exchange of the products of the British factories for the raw materials of the world the United Kingdom had not only become a creditor nation—that is to say, other countries were indebted to her for enormous sums over and above the value of the raw materials and other commodities which they sent to her, this balance being, of course, represented by stocks and shares in foreign enterprises and foreign loans which were held in the United Kingdom—but also she had accumulated wealth which was represented in the goodwill and plant of her manufacturing and trading businesses and in the vastly improved homes, furniture, clothing, etc., of her own people.

In order to facilitate this apparently profitable activity, in the middle of the nineteenth century the United Kingdom

245

IN A FACTORY MESS-ROOM.
Dinner-hour in a factory in which women were engaged in making searchlights and signal lamps.

dominions by means of preferential trading arrangements; so that, although the country might not be self-contained, the British Empire—at any rate, so far as its food supplies were concerned—should be so to a considerable extent. The coming of the submarine to imperil the avenues of trade had not been foreseen, and only a comparatively small number of persons had persisted in the demand for more cruisers to protect the commercial highways of the sea.

Meanwhile, a more insidious danger threatened the country, but it was only realised by a very few persons. The German Government, surveying the wide field of industry, realised that

had thrown down the tariff walls which restricted the free importation of foreign goods, and so had enabled the population to buy at the least possible price anything of which they stood in need. This policy of Free Trade was introduced in the interests of manufacturing. Its avowed object was to enable manufacturing operations to be carried on at the least cost in wages, because those wages, when commodities were cheap, would go further. In any country and age, when the cost of living has been low, wages have been low.

It had, however, had other results not foreseen by its originators. It had not been foreseen that the reduction in the cost of the transport of wheat and other articles of food would render it possible to bring agricultural products to this country at so low a price that agriculture in the United Kingdom would become comparatively unprofitable, with the result that the inducements of higher wages and town pleasures would lure a great body of the inhabitants from the countryside to the industrial centres. This rush to the towns, involving shortage of labour in rural districts, combined with the low price of agricultural products, had resulted in a heavy reduction of the arable land of the United Kingdom and a great increase in the proportion of the total acreage given over to grass.

Free Trade and agriculture

It had been foreseen that this system of Free Trade would lead to the United Kingdom becoming more and more dependent upon foreign sources for its food supplies, but it had been urged that it was more important to the country to have cheap supplies than to have those supplies within the realm.

Another school, deploring the great dependence of this country upon foreign nations for food, had urged the encouragement of increased production in British

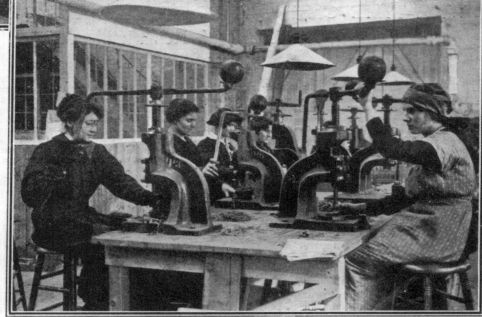

WORKING HAND-DRILLS IN SEARCHLIGHT MANUFACTURE.
Women working hand-drills in a factory where they were largely employed in making searchlights and signal lamps. The way in which women found occupation and proved themselves remarkably efficient in taking up many new industries, was one of the notable changes brought about by the war.

there were certain industries which were absolutely necessary for the prosecution of a number of dependent trades, and it had consequently adopted a settled policy of getting these activities, known as key industries, into the hands of firms in Germany. It would occupy too much space to explain all the methods by which this policy was carried out; suffice it to say that the German Government did not hesitate to give direct and indirect assistance to syndicates, which were enabled to undermine the position of manufacturers in the key industries by selling the products of those industries in the United Kingdom at a price below the cost of their production in the United Kingdom.

Had operations been undertaken in the United Kingdom on the same wide basis as in Germany, it would have been more difficult for the Germans to secure pre-eminence in the key industries; but, since cost of production largely depends on quantity produced, it was of great assistance to the German manufacturer to be assured his home market when making arrangements for attacking markets abroad, and particularly in the United Kingdom, where there was no tariff obstacle. The result was that, on the outbreak of war, it was found that the supply of a great number of articles vitally necessary to the country was almost solely in enemy hands.

The outstanding example was the production of dyes. The invention of modern synthetic dyes was that of an Englishman, but the industry had been patiently developed in Germany, and on the outbreak of war only ten per cent. of the dyes needed in this country were made in the United Kingdom. Approximately, one-third of the value of the total exports of manufactured goods from the United Kingdom was in cotton goods, and not only this trade, but the woollen trade, carpet manufacture, linoleum-making, basket-ware manufacture, commercial printing, and a great many other trades were imperilled by the lack of dyes.

It was found that the manufacture of magnetos had been allowed to fall almost entirely into German hands. The production of spelter—the commercial name for zinc —which was needed for galvanising iron and many other purposes, was largely in German hands, although zinc

Kingdom making optical glass from which telescopic sights, field-glasses, and many other articles needed by the Army and Navy were made. In the pottery trades the making of chemical ware had been almost abandoned to the Germans.

These were some of the difficulties with which British trade and industry were faced on the outbreak of war. We shall see later how they were overcome, to the lasting credit of the British people.

We cannot, however, pass to a review of the achievements of industry without touching for a moment on the question of finance. Commerce, industry, and finance are so inextricably inter- woven that it is impossible to separate them. There had grown up in England during its industrial era a great merchant system. While it was the manufacturer's business to produce goods, it was the merchant's business to sell them, and in this respect the United Kingdom differed very much from other nations. The British merchant system had no counterpart in the world. Its beginning can be traced to the old merchant adventurers who, in the Middle Ages, before commerce and industry were organised on a modern basis, would fill a ship with merchandise and set forth to trade abroad the goods they carried, and to bring back in exchange foreign commodities. So that, when manufacturing developed, there already existed a number of merchants who had connections in foreign fields, and who naturally purchased from the manufacturers the most recent products of their craft to sell to less advanced communities abroad.

The British merchant system

Thus the two activities developed in the United Kingdom hand in hand, and in the early years of the twentieth century there was an enormous army of

WORK FOR THE BLIND.
Learning basket-making at St. Dunstan's Hostel for sailors and soldiers who had lost their sight in the war.

ores were produced to a great extent in Australia. Even in such a comparatively simple article as needles the Germans, by the extent of their operations covering the whole world, had been able to secure so large a part of the trade that, on the outbreak of the war, the supply in the United Kingdom of some kinds of needles was insufficient.

The glass trades were languishing as the result partly of Germany's practical monopoly of the supplies of potash, and partly owing to short-sighted action on the part of the Glass-blowers' Union. In one field—optical glass —the country was terribly handicapped.

On the outbreak of war there was only one firm in the United

IN A WORKSHOP AT ST. DUNSTAN'S.
Men who had become blind in the war engaged in learning boot-repairing at the hostel for blind sailors and soldiers which Sir Arthur Pearson established at St. Dunstan's, in Regent's Park, London. The afflicted men were there taught all kinds of useful occupations in order to minimise their dependence on others.

APPEALING FOR POPULAR SUPPORT OF THE SOLDIERS' CLUBS ASSOCIATION.

Clubs for the use of soldiers in their leisure were recognised as necessary early in the war. The influential men here shown were holding a meeting in Westminster City Hall in the interests of the Soldiers' Clubs Association. Seated and standing at the high table they are from left to right : Mr. Appleton, Labour Adviser to the National Service Department, General Bethune, the Duke of Connaught, the Duke of Portland, the Mayor of Westminster, the Duke of Rutland, Mr. Havelock Wilson, of the National Sailors' and Firemen's Union ; Mr. Reginald Cox, of Cox's Bank.

men engaged not in production, but in merchanting—that is, in handling the products of others and arranging for their disposal abroad. There was no restriction upon anyone who wished to embark upon a merchant's business. The ports of the United Kingdom were filled with foreign merchants, who trafficked sometimes in British goods, and, when it paid them better, in the goods of other countries. Many Germans had settled in the United Kingdom, and having learned the merchant business and secured certain connections, set up in business for themselves, and traded with customers first in British goods; later, if more profits were available, they substituted German-made goods. Nor should it be overlooked that a great number of British merchants saw no reason why they should not handle foreign products if they obtained a better profit on them than they could get by selling British goods.

Introduction of the Black List The illegality of trading with an enemy led to the preparation and publication of the Statutory List (Black List) of firms in foreign countries with whom British subjects were not allowed to trade. This step revealed the extent of Germany's merchanting operations, and led to a most important departure by the Foreign Office, which instructed the British Consuls to supply names of firms who could take the place of those on the Black List. This was a great blow to German foreign trade, and a corresponding advantage to British industry.

One of the principal advantages to the manufacturer of selling his goods through merchants was that he was saved all the trouble of getting payment for them from abroad, and all the worries of shipping and transport. The merchant gave a manufacturer a bill of exchange, in which he promised to pay for the goods in so many days, as might be arranged, after the transaction. The manufacturer promptly discounted the bill—that is to say, he got in cash a little less than its face value, and, unless anything went wrong with the merchant, the transaction from his point of view was closed. The merchant could only give bills if his credit were good. He usually obtained payment from his customers abroad by other bills, and the great machinery of the banking world came into play in clearing these multifarious transactions.

German banks in London

The discounting of foreign bills was profitable, and, as has been shown, so long as a merchant could get bills discounted he could conduct vast operations with comparatively small capital, provided his credit were good. London was the great free market for gold. London was the centre of the world's finance. Naturally, then, German trade desired to take advantage of the financial system of the British Empire, and to do so German banks were established in London to facilitate the discounting of bills, while the great British banks, backed by the Bank of England and the credit of the British nation, assisted their operations by enabling them to discount bills, which in the aggregate amounted to enormous sums, for their customers in all parts of the world.

On the outbreak of war there were hundreds of millions of bills outstanding, and it was only by the prompt action of the Government in shouldering the responsibility that

248

an utter collapse of the financial system was avoided. Had there been an unchecked panic in the first days of the war bills would have been valueless—indeed, not only bills, but every kind of paper-money would have been worthless, since paper-money merely represents a promise to pay in gold, and the total amount of gold in the world is only a fraction of the amount that would be necessary to carry on its commerce in coin, even if such a thing were possible. The whole fabric was based on credit—the belief that when the time came the promise to pay would be fulfilled.

The panic was avoided, and the first great danger to the world was overcome. But one of the first lessons learnt was that the British had been far too generous to the Germans in allowing their merchants to get the benefit of the British system, far too short-sighted and easy-going in allowing the German banks to finance German commerce on British credit. It was also seen that German banks which made a speciality of assisting German international trade were a great advantage to the country, and an agitation for similar facilities in the United Kingdom led to the formation, in 1917, of the British Trade Corporation—in reality, a Trade Bank under Government auspices. Great hopes were centred in this departure.

In the first few days of the war the financial difficulty was the absorbing topic. Business men, until things settled down, did not know how to find ready cash as distinguished from credit to meet such outgoings as wages. The difficulty of meeting many of their other more important obligations was over-

British trade corporation formed come by the declaration of a moratorium, the action of which was to make it legal to postpone immediate payment until the position grew easier, as it speedily did. The moratorium was then declared at an end.

During the next few months of the war there was the greatest difficulty in obtaining raw materials. As we have seen, the Germans controlled the supply of a great number of necessary ingredients, and there was much anxiety on the part of manufacturers in regard to their supplies of raw materials. Extraordinary devices were adopted to meet the difficulty, and great ingenuity shown in finding substitutes.

The third great difficulty was the temporary suspension of purchase by the mass of the public. There was a belief —and the enormous sum contributed to the Prince of Wales's Fund was evidence of it—that war would mean great distress among the population. In order to provide against the evil day, men and women made as few purchases as possible, with the result that for a time there was little business done, except in foodstuffs that could be stored. A comparatively small number of selfish persons rushed to the shops to purchase foodstuffs which they proposed to hoard in case there should be a shortage, and the first real inter- **Decrease in foreign** ference with the liberties of the subject **exchanges** in matters of commerce was the refusal of the stores, backed by the Government, to supply purchasers with more than a reasonable quantity of articles of food needed by the people.

Gold was called in, and new notes of such small denominations as £1 and 10s. were issued in its place. Postal orders became legal tender. Young men in increasing numbers threw up their jobs in order to join the Army as volunteers, and so the commercial community of the United Kingdom entered upon the first stage of the war.

The operations of German commerce raiders were not of long duration. The decline in British commerce with foreign countries was not due to the operations of hostile cruisers, and rates of insurance, which at first were five guineas per cent., very rapidly fell away by the end of the year to one guinea per cent. The decrease in foreign exchanges was due to the shock which the commercial world had received.

In business, nothing is so fatal as uncertainty, and particularly is this the case in regard to transactions with distant countries in which there is time for many things to happen between the despatch of goods and their arrival. It is not remarkable that trade declined during the early days of the war. The extraordinary thing to the student is that the decrease was not much greater.

The shortage of male labour—which, as the war went on, became more and more acute—was met by the introduction of women into occupations for which it had not been hitherto supposed that they were suitable. Every business house concerned itself with the simplification of its methods, and all unnecessary duplication was cut out

MEMBERS ATTENDING THE IMPERIAL CONFERENCE IN LONDON, MARCH, 1917.
Members of the Imperial Conference which met in London in March, 1917. Standing (left to right) : Sir S. P. Sinha, Lieut.-Col. Dally-Jones, Hon. R. Rogers, Sir J. C. Meston, Mr. A. Chamberlain, the Maharaja of Bikanir, Mr. E. J. Harding, Mr. Steel Maitland, and Mr. Henry Lambert. Seated : Sir J. Ward, Sir H. Perley, Lieut.-Gen. Smuts, Sir R. Borden, Mr. Walter Long, Mr. Massey, Sir E. Morris, and Hon. J. D. Hazen.

as far as possible. Even business correspondence became less formal and more direct.

Meanwhile, a remarkable development took place. For years before the war manufacturers had chafed under the inroads of German competition in the home as well as in the foreign markets. A fortnight after war broke out— to be exact, on August 19th, 1914—the " Times " gave a lead which was destined to have important results. On that date its contents bill contained the words, " The War on German Trade." The first of a series of articles was published suggesting that the opportunity should be seized to drive the Germans out of our home and Dominions markets, and hold for the benefit of British industry and British labour the commercial field, where in days of peace Germans had become entrenched.

This lead was followed by the Press throughout the country, and the Board of Trade, acting through its Commercial Intelligence Branch, engaged a special staff, who set to work to disseminate exact **The war on** information concerning German and **German trade** Austrian competition in various lines of trade, and to organise the manufacturers and merchants. This work was very necessary as, owing to the war, merchants who had been obtaining goods from Germany found themselves without sources of supply, and manufacturers who had been selling their products through enemy firms were temporarily unable to market their merchandise.

A number of Exchange Meetings were held under the auspices of the Board of Trade, at which samples of German and Austrian goods which found a ready market in the United Kingdom were displayed. The wholesale prices at which these goods were delivered, and other terms of business, were indicated as far as possible. Manufacturers were invited to inspect these samples, and to meet the merchants who had lent them to the Board of Trade, and others, with the object of making arrangements for British industry in future to supply the goods which heretofore had been obtained from enemy countries.

Excellent results attended these efforts. It was very quickly apparent that British manufacturers were as resourceful and enterprising as ever, and that the British workmen was perfectly competent to do anything that the foreigners had achieved.

What was done in the case of so simple an article as a doll may serve as an illustration of what was accomplished in other directions. In the doll trade it was found that the various parts of an ordinary child's doll were made by a great number of different firms. The china arms and heads were not made in the United Kingdom at all. But the potters took the matter up with vigour. Their first efforts were crude and ugly, but by the end of three years dolls' heads far surpassing anything **Response of British** that had previously been imported from **manufacturers** Germany were being produced in the British potteries. That made the truly British doll possible. Birmingham made the balanced eyes which made the doll appear to sleep ; Yorkshire supplied the wigs for the dolls' heads, and so on.

The glass trade presented greater difficulties, since the skilled hands did not exist. The Government urged British firms to train lads in the art of glass-blowing, and in less than three years even the extremely difficult art of making glass for chemical laboratory work had been mastered in British factories by the aid of British labour.

The problem of obtaining supplies of optical glass, previously referred to, was attacked with vigour. The Government rendered active assistance in establishing this industry, excellent optical glass being produced in large quantities before the country had been at war three years.

Great strides were made in the pottery trades. Porcelain for electrical fittings was, before the war, an enemy product ; its manufacture in the United Kingdom was

soon accomplished. Even the fine chemical ware used in laboratories was available from British sources before the end of the third year of the war.

The dye problem presented, perhaps, the greatest difficulties of all. No one unacquainted with modern science could appreciate the enormous obstacles to be overcome. Germany had been patiently building up this industry with her thousands of trained chemists, while, in every other part of the world, the business was neglected. The making of synthetic dyes from coal-tar products is closely allied to the production of trinitrotoluene and other high explosives used for the first time in the Great War. By monopolising the dye business, Germany had secured an enormous advantage in being in a position to turn out great quantities of high explosives. The German dye-makers had ensured themselves the monopoly by undertaking to supply certain lines, at a rate which left a comfortable profit, to the British firms which formerly made them, and by entering into contracts with the big British gas undertakings to take the whole of their by-products.

The position was so serious that the Government, which had created a special high-explosives branch at the War Office, with Lord Moulton, a judge of the High Court with unrivalled technical and scientific knowledge, at its head, requested the judge to look into the matter. Lord Moulton saw that the weakness of the chemical trade, including the dye trade, in the United Kingdom was the multiplicity of small firms. He saw that it would be necessary to create a corporation with a large capital, if the thousand and one scientific difficulties in the way of making dyes were to be overcome.

At the request of the Government he addressed the great textile firms in Manchester, with a view to inducing them in their own interest to provide capital for the creation of a dye business in the United Kingdom. Money was not the difficulty. The great staple trades of the country were ready to pro- **Formation of** vide any sums that were required, but the **British Dyes, Ltd.** Government would not give any guarantee that the business would be protected from the Germans at the close of the war ; and ultimately, rather than give this assurance, the Government created a company and advanced to it public money on debenture security. The company, British Dyes, Ltd., had other advantages as against its competitors in that firms that subscribed to the capital had the first call on the output, and that was the inducement that led the wealthy textile manufacturers to invest, since, unless they did so, they could not ensure getting from the corporation supplies of dyes that were vital to their business.

But at the end of three years of war, although British Dyes, Ltd., had erected a large number of buildings, the problem had not been overcome. The brightest fast dyes were still not made in the United Kingdom, and in June, 1917, a Dye Commissioner was appointed by the Government. In this particular case Government interference had not, so far, proved strikingly successful, but it is fair to add that the importance of getting supplies of high explosives was to some extent the reason.

The spelter industry affords an illustration of the extraordinary position into which commercial matters had been allowed to drift during years of peace for want of a sound commercial policy and a co-ordinating influence in the Government.

As has been stated, the supplies of zinc ores were in Australia, and these ores were concentrated in Germany, a German firm having a contract with the Australian producers under which they were entitled to take their output. Since zinc was urgently needed in the United Kingdom the question arose whether such a contract could be enforced in time of war, but it was actually upheld in the British courts. That is to say, although the British Empire was fighting for its life, and urgently

Scene at the solemn service held in the metropolitan Cathedral on "the entry of the United States into the Great War for Freedom." The congregation joined in singing Mrs. Julia Ward Howe's famous "Battle Hymn of the Republic," and at the close verses from "The Star-Spangled Banner" and the British National Anthem were sung. The King and Queen, Queen Alexandra, Dr. Page, and Admiral Sims were present.

Singing the American National Anthem in St. Paul's Cathedral, April 20th, 1917.

Parade up Fifth Avenue, New York, of trained drafts for the new American Army.

United States troops marching through London to Buckingham Palace, August 15th, 1917.

The first American troops to land in France marching to camp on arrival, June 25th, 1917.

[French official photograph.

Learning to make trenches: American soldiers at a final training camp somewhere in France.

Arrival of the s.s. Baltic at Liverpool with Lieut.=General Pershing aboard, June 7th, 1917.

Front row (left to right) : Lieut.-Colonel Harbord, Chief of Staff ; General Pershing ; Colonel Alvord, Adjutant-General ; Colonel Brewster, Inspector-General. Standing (left to right) : Lieut.-Colonel Ireland, Medical Officer ; Colonel Taylor, Engineer Officer ; Major Dodd, Aviator ; Colonel McCarthy, Q.M.G. ; Lieut.-Colonel Bethell, Judge Advocate ; Colonel Russell, Signal Officer ; Lieut.-Colonel Williams, Ordnance Officer ; Captain Margetts, A.D.C. General Pershing said : "We are the same kith and kin, and we are now side by side to hammer this thing through."

Lieut.=General Pershing, Commander=in=Chief of the American Army in Europe, and his Staff.

needed spelter for military purposes, the natural resources of part of the British Empire were not available for use because an enemy firm had, in time of peace, entered into a contract to purchase the output. The Australian Prime Minister held up·such legal embarrassments to ridicule, and ultimately the matter was put right; but that it could ever have happened showed that the British Government had not grasped the significance of the war and the principles upon which it was to be waged.

The requirements of the Army naturally led to congestion on the railways, and the shortage of trained men at the docks led to congestion at the ports. It became more and more difficult, as the war went on, for manufacturers to obtain raw materials or to move their manufactured articles. The railways, at the very outbreak of war, were all brought under Government control, and managed by a Board consisting of men drawn from the railway companies themselves. Enormous savings of labour were effected. The railways no longer ran trains in competition one with the other, and everything possible was done to make the railway system equal to the demands upon it. One of the great causes of waste was found to be the system under which the coal trade was conducted. The amount of coal moved every year was something like 260,000,000 tons, and there was little falling-off in total production or demand, but it was no uncommon sight to see coal trains passing each other in opposite directions on the rails. That is to say, coal was being carried to places from which coal was being brought away—an obviously uneconomical method of distribution —and in the third year of the war arrangements were made under which coal was distributed to the places needing it from the nearest collieries. The public was no longer able to purchase the particular kind of coal it fancied. It had to take the kind that was nearest; but even so it was infinitely better off than its Allies in Italy and France, where the shortage of coal **Railway and** was terrible, and householders were **shipping difficulties** obliged to go without coal throughout the winter months.

At the ports the congestion was more serious, as it meant delaying ships, and with the increasing activity of German submarines the need for shipping became of far greater urgency. The unloading and loading of a ship often took longer than its actual journey, and delay in handling cargoes was equivalent to a definite loss of tonnage. As the war proceeded the shortage of shipping became more and more acute, with the result that supplies of raw materials became more and more uncertain, and prices necessarily rose to unwonted heights. In fact, it is not too much to say that the shortage of shipping during the first three years of the war had a greater influence on industry and commerce than any other factor.

The shortage of cotton became extremely serious. Instead of 4d. or 5d. a pound, by June, 1917, there were dealings in cotton for immediate supply at 19½d. a pound. The shortage of the world's cotton crop would probably have been felt had there been no war, since before hostilities there was already evidence of a shortage of supplies owing to increased demand. The cotton spinners of Lancashire, however, were slow to realise the extreme danger of their position, although American spinners were using an ever-increasing amount of the American cotton, and it was evident that without the American supplies there was insufficient cotton in the world to supply Lancashire.

There was a danger, too, that with the increasing shortage of food in the world the cotton planters would be induced to plant more food and less cotton, and so the shortage would become even more marked. In June, 1917, the British Government stepped in, and the Lancashire manufacturers, who had been totally opposed to any kind of Government interference, were glad in their extremity to welcome the assistance of the Government

in allotting fairly among the spinners such supplies of cotton as were available. Still it was evident that the cotton trade would have to be put on short time.

The difficulty in the wool industry was equally serious. The enormous demand for woollen clothing for the Army led to such a shortage of wool that, in the spring of 1917, the Government commandeered all wool and put most of the woollen factories under Government control, so that the amount of wool available for the making of garments for the civilian population was very small.

A similar state of things took place in the leather trade. Enormous quantities of leather used for harness and boots and other requirements led to a shortage of all kinds, and as the war went on boots became increasingly expensive, and various substitutes for leather for making soles were brought out, with varying degrees of success.

In the iron trade energies were bent upon feeding the guns, a subject dealt with at length in Chapter CC. (page 169, Vol. X.). In the spring of 1915 it became known that there was a terrible **Cotton, wool, and** shortage of guns and munitions in the **leather trades** British Army, and that the arrangements made by the War Office were totally inadequate to the needs of the war. A Ministry of Munitions was formed, under the leadership of Mr. Lloyd George, and at once extraordinary developments were seen. The iron and steel trades were set to work to the last ounce of their energy in producing guns and shells. Wherever there was a lathe there was at once established a munition factory, great or small. Shells were turned out night and day. The engineering trades required enormous quantities of iron and steel to supply war requirements. Skilled engineers were forbidden to join the Army. Vulcan's forge was as nothing to the thousand and one forges all over the United Kingdom working to supply the munitions required.

In the shipbuilding yards, at the outbreak of war, attention was diverted from the building of merchantmen, and everything was done to expedite the supply of ships for the Navy. Later on it was seen that, although the Navy was the nation's shield and buckler, the nation could not exist without the Mercantile Marine to bring supplies to its shores, and progress was made in standardising the production of ships—a reform which had been urged before the war, but for which there had been no real demand. Under the pressure of national need the difficulties in the way of standardising shipping were swept aside, a Ministry of Shipping was formed, and ships were laid down on the standard lines, less with a view to their beauty than to their immediate usefulness and cargo-carrying capacity.

Soon after the outbreak of war economists pointed out that with its continuance it would be impossible to allow unrestricted overseas trade. They pointed out that commerce is in the nature of **Standardised ship** exchange, and that although imports into **construction** this country in time of peace greatly exceeded exports in value, the apparent difference was made up by the services rendered by British shipping, by interest on foreign loans, and by investments abroad.

On the outbreak of war there was naturally an immediate decline in our export trade, and great expansion of the imports, due to increased prices and to the purchase by Government of enormous quantities of stores from abroad. Naturally this upset the balance, and soon led to difficulties in regard to the rate of exchange. So long as there is a fairly even exchange between two countries there is no difficulty in financing the transactions of individuals through banks; but when, under abnormal conditions, goods are moving steadily in one direction, it becomes a question how payment is to be made. Clearly, no country at war could allow its gold to be distributed throughout the world, and the rate of exchange, which is the danger signal in foreign trade, began to move against the United Kingdom.

The Government took up foreign bonds which were held in this country, and exported them to the creditor nations, and the creditor nations accepted in payment for their goods many securities and bonds previously held in the United Kingdom. A loan was arranged in the United States. This meant, not that the proceeds of the loan came here, but that they were set off to pay the indebtedness of this country and France to the United States.

Long after the need for such restrictions had been pointed out in the British Press, the Government prohibited the imports of various luxuries into the country. They ought to have been stopped directly war broke out. It may be legitimate to import expensive articles of luxury in peace time, but in time of war their importation not only increases British liabilities abroad, and makes it more difficult to purchase necessaries, but the articles themselves occupy valuable space on ships. There is no excuse whatever for such trades being allowed to continue, and they were abolished without anyone—save, perhaps,

for this country at a lower price than would have been paid had it been left to the unrestricted competition of the market. The tea trade was restricted. Merchants were not allowed to import tea from China because the Indian supply was nearer, and therefore shipping tonnage was saved by bringing necessary supplies from the nearer point. The same reason led to the prohibition of the Soya bean trade. Soya beans are extremely nutritious, but their shipment from Manchuria was held to be wasteful of shipping.

Efforts were made to stimulate the production of food in the United Kingdom, and the Government imported labour-saving machinery of all kinds from the United States, where farming was conducted **The war and the wage-earners** with much less labour than in the United Kingdom. Unfortunately, these efforts were postponed so long that when, in the spring of 1917, American tractors were brought in, the season was too far advanced for any great result to be shown.

All these changes necessarily had a marked influence on the lives of the people. The first fear that there would be destitution soon proved to be quite groundless. There was considerable suffering among the professional middle classes and shopkeepers, but, generally speaking, the working classes of the United Kingdom were much better off than they had ever been before. Work was abundant.

It had been a theory before the war that there was a large class which was unemployable. The war had not been long in progress before that theory was proved to be utterly false. Tramps disappeared from the highways, and the unemployable were found to be employable. People were glad to get anyone to work for them. Wages rose rapidly, but except in certain favourable trades, where supplies were made for the Army and exceptional wages paid, it is doubtful whether the increase in wages during the first three years of the war was greater than the increase in the cost of living.

PREPARING FOR THE POTATO HARVEST.
Arrival of a load of seed potatoes at Epsom for distribution among employees of the L. and S.W. Railway. When, early in 1917, a serious effort was made to increase the home-grown supply of food the railway company made a generous offer of seed potatoes to employees who undertook to cultivate waste land.

a few persons who traded in them—being one penny the worse. This step also had the result of increasing the demand for labour in the United Kingdom, as it became necessary to make substitutes for the goods which were no longer imported from abroad.

But even with these restrictions the pressure on the carrying power of the Mercantile Marine increased, and the Government was obliged to control the supplies of food and raw materials to ensure fair distribution. The problem before the Government was **Government control of supplies** twofold. On one hand, it was imperative to ensure the supply of necessaries reaching this country, and, on the other hand, it was desirable to check the profiteer who made everyday commodities more expensive.

The shortage of foodstuffs led the Government to introduce a lower quality of flour, which was made compulsory. Everything possible was done to decrease the demand for wheat flour, in order to eke out the stocks and the imports from abroad. The price of wheat went up, until, in the first half of 1917, the Government was able to make an arrangement with the United States, under which the crops of North America became available

The greater prosperity of the working classes was due to the fact that everyone was fully occupied; not only the old and infirm, but the cripples were found to have their use and got work. Thus the gross earnings of households were much larger.

The legislation in the United Kingdom which had been framed with a view to improving the lot of the worker was found to hamper the operations of those who desired to increase output. As expeditiously as possible, and under the Defence of the Realm Act, an enormous number of factories sprang up, the building of which would not have been allowed under the conditions of peace times. Most of these factories were erected on good concrete foundations, and built of wood and corrugated iron. Similarly, factories which were capable of turning out munitions were enlarged, and additions were put up in which more people could be employed.

At the end of three years the United Kingdom presented an extraordinary spectacle. The whole country, from one end to the other, was humming with life and activity. The slackness which had characterised its efforts during the prosperous days of peace had disappeared, and young and old, rich and poor, had found occupations, and in many cases happiness, as a result of the needs of the time.

FIRST AMERICAN TROOPS

CHAPTER CCIV.

TRAINING IN FRANCE.

[French official photograph.

AMERICA'S MARVELLOUS MOBILISATION.

By Robert Machray.

State of Feeling in the U.S.A. after War was Declared—Most Citizens Unaware of the Vital Issue for America—Stalwarts' Earlier Campaign for National Preparedness—Comparative Failure—The Nation Not Thoroughly Awakened—The Reasons Why—Defence At Most Contemplated—Increase in Navy—Naval Consulting and Shipping Boards Formed—Small Army Increase—The Council of National Defence and Advisory Commission—Attitude of President Wilson—He Makes Up His Mind Against Germany—First Measures—Special Session of Congress Summoned—Mobilisation of the Politicians—Mass of the American People Not Enthusiastic—Strenuous Action of the President—Endorsed by Congress—Strong Personal Appeal to the Citizens—What the U.S. Must Do to Help the Allies—Seven Billion Dollar War Loan Passed—Three Billions for the Entente—Mobilisation of Finance—Simultaneous Mobilisation of Materials—Intensive Industrial and Commercial Organisation—Splendid Work of the Advisory Commission—Standardising Munitions—Labour Supports the President—The Food Problem—A Million Rifles Arranged For—The Control of Raw Materials—Supplies Dealt With—Large Savings Effected—The Railways Pooled Under the Government—Telegraphs and Telephones Administered—Scientific Research at Work for War—Immense Aircraft Programme Under Way—Mobilisation of the Army and National Guard—Coming of Conscription—The Selective Draft Act—Nearly Ten Million Men Registered—About Seven Hundred Thousand Men Drawn by Lot—Problem of Shortage of Officers—"The First Ten Thousand"—Mobilisation of the Navy—Large Increase in Personnel—U.S. Destroyers Co-operating in European Waters.

CONSIDERED in all its aspects, nothing in the stupendous drama of the world-war was more marvellous in its way than the mobilisation by the United States of America of its vast resources on its entry into the colossal conflict. How the great Republic, thirty-two months after the onset of hostilities in Europe between the Central Powers and the Entente, came to join the Allies was recounted in Chapter CLXXIII. (Vol. IX., page 57). Therein were chronicled in their order the various stages of the prolonged controversy which President Woodrow Wilson had carried on with the German Government respecting the U boats and the dastardly outrages upon humanity—the appalling breaches of international law—that the murderous activities of these pirates involved.

It was shown that the President broke off relations with Germany at the beginning of February, 1917, because of that country's announcement of unrestricted submarine warfare, in spite of specific pledges to the contrary. The narrative concluded with the declaration of war on April 6th, and a brief statement of the steps taken

MR. HENRY D. FLOOD.

As Chairman of the Foreign Affairs Committee, Mr. Flood prepared the resolution declaring that a state of war existed between the United States and Germany, and authorising the President to carry on war.

immediately thereafter by the United States as a belligerent. To the unfeigned joy of the Allies, among whose much-suffering peoples there had been manifested a growing tendency to accuse the Americans of indifference and apathy, the United States, the sole Great Power which had remained apart from the struggle, definitely committed itself to support them in the field. From such a decision there could be no going back, but as a matter of fact there was not the slightest indication of anything of the sort. All the signs pointed in the opposite direction. The nation lined up behind the President and Congress. It was doubtful, however, whether the majority of the citizens of the United States at the outset grasped at all fully the significance of its intervention, which was much more than going to the assistance of the Entente, being nothing less than the making of a new War of Independence on its own account. It would, indeed, have been surprising if they had understood this thoroughly and at once.

Viewed from their side of the wide Atlantic, the war, which they regarded as essentially European, had seemed remote from their life. To most of them it had been something

257

of the nature of a spectacle, which was of absorbing interest in its first developments, but with which they had no intimate concern, and its fascination had palled as month after month rolled by without a "curtain." In some quarters of the United States, as was observed in Chapter CLXXIII., it had ceased for a time to be even a topic of conversation. Particularly was this the case in the West and the South. In the East, on the other hand, it continued to maintain a supreme hold on the bulk of the population, who had a truer appreciation of its vital issues, not only to the Old World but also to the New, and consequently sympathised deeply with the Allies. Not till the publication, on March 1st, 1917, of the letter from Herr von Zimmermann, the German Foreign Secretary, to the German Minister to Mexico, were the West and the South, who saw in that document the suggestion of a menace to themselves from Japan and Mexico respectively, stirred to a consciousness of both the reality and the magnitude of the German threat to their country. Yet so pacific at heart was the United States as a whole, even then, that its participation in the war appeared still to be problematical. It was enormously difficult for the majority of its people to change the standpoint from which they had so long seen the war.

Demand for national preparedness

Nearly two years before its declaration of war on Germany the United States, throughout its vast extent, had been horrified and somewhat alarmed by the torpedoing of the Lusitania. That sinister event, with its revealing light on everything German, caused not a few Americans to understand—what some of them had already perceived—that the real meaning of the world-policy of Germany was no other than the domination of the globe and the destruction of all human liberty. They, therefore, strongly advocated armed intervention on behalf of the Entente. The nation, however, did not respond. It was clear, moreover, that militarily the United States was far from ready for such a course ; even for self-defence it was weak, and hence arose a demand for "national preparedness" from the stalwarts. A powerful organisation, called the National Security League, was formed, which initiated a brisk campaign. Crying out that the country was in danger, the league, by speeches, books, pamphlets, advertisements, film-pictures, and every means open to it, strove to rouse the people to a sense of the dire potentialities of the situation. It pleaded hard for the immediate institution of universal military training. Though the movement was not devoid of some result, the authorities

MR. A. J. BALFOUR IN WASHINGTON.
In April, 1917, Mr. A. J. Balfour, Secretary for Foreign Affairs, visited America as High Commissioner representing the Allies. He was here (centre) leaving the State Department at Washington with Mr. Robert Lansing (right), United States Secretary of State, to call upon President Wilson.

gave it no encouragement, and the reply from the public was not enthusiastic.

The impression made by the torpedoing of the great liner, painful and widespread as that impression had been, quickly passed off from the minds of most Americans as an incentive to action. Nor did the occurrence of subsequent incidents, similar in kind if less notable in degree, quicken American feeling in the mass. The sinking of the Sussex, about a year later, scarcely affected the attitude towards the war that had been taken up generally, although that terrible instance of German methods of inhuman warfare was the main theme of a Note President Wilson addressed to the German Government, threatening a rupture of diplomatic relations if such warfare were maintained. A calculated intermittence of the malign work of the U boats followed, and there were overtures for a negotiated peace, in which the President took a leading part. The view of the majority of American citizens that the war was not a vital matter for the United States appeared to be confirmed, and they "turned down" all proposals for national preparedness in any way whatsoever. They still had no notion that the war was really as much America's as the Entente's, that the self-interest of their country was as genuinely involved in it as was the self-interest of any of the Allies.

One reason for this was the idea derived from authoritative-looking statements that, so far as

BRITISH COMMISSION IN NEW YORK.
Captain Dansen, of the British Army, with Captain John G. Quekemeyer, of the United States Army, on the reception boat crossing the River Hudson when the British Commission headed by Mr. Balfour arrived in New York.

TROOPS PASSING ST. PATRICK'S CATHEDRAL, NEW YORK.
Monsignor Lavelle, Vicar-General of New York and Rector of St. Patrick's Cathedral, reviewing the 69th Regiment before its departure for the State Mobilisation Camp at Beeman, New York.

aims and motives were concerned, there was nothing to choose between the Entente and Germany. Naturally this idea was sedulously fostered by the pro-Germans. The origins, which inspired the aims, of the war were lost in a mist of obscurities. Even President Wilson himself, as late as October, 1916, seemed to be affected by this propaganda. In a speech delivered during his electoral campaign he said: "The singularity of the present war is that its roots and origins and object never have been disclosed." And as for the brutality, bestiality, and general "frightfulness" of German methods of warfare, they were extenuated and glozed over, or excused as being no worse than those employed by their opponents, by those Americans who favoured Germany or wanted peace at any price. A contributory cause, no doubt, of the temporary American obliquity of vision was the prodigious prosperity of the United States, owing to the enormous purchases of munitions, foodstuffs, and other commodities by the agents of the Entente, which flooded the land with money and led very widely to the conviction that it would be the height of absurdity not to take the fullest advantage of such golden—literally golden—opportunities. In addition to these two reasons, there was a third reason which, perhaps, had been prepotent in producing and continuing the detached view of the war that was taken by most Americans.

This reason was the absence for a very long time of any clear guidance of the nation for facing a possible entrance into the struggle, and

the lack of any considerable preparation for such an eventuality on the part of the Government and the political leaders then in control of the destinies of the Republic. Partyism, which was at least as strong in the United States as in any other great community, had a great deal to do with it. Nowhere was the game of the "Ins" and "Outs" played with greater intensity. The people were divided almost equally, as various elections in the past had demonstrated, into Republicans and Democrats. President Wilson and his Ministers, the members of his Cabinet, were Democrats, their party having come into office a couple of years before the war broke out. In the autumn of 1916 another Presidential Election was to take place, and all American politicians were wide awake to that fact. After the despatch of the Sussex Note to Berlin there was a period of quiet, as Germany, for a time at least, complied with its demands respecting submarine action, and the politicians turned their attention from the war to fix it on the approaching electoral contest. Something, however, was done in the way of preparation for eventualities, but it did not amount to much, and certainly gave little sign that there was ground for any apprehension, whether to the pacifists or to the Germans, **Extension of** that the United States would become **naval programme.** a strenuous and aggressive combatant.

Defence was at most what was contemplated. The American "first line of defence" was the Navy, but it had suffered from some years of comparative stagnation. The Secretary of the Navy in the Wilson Government was the Hon. Josephus Daniels, of North Carolina, and under his energetic administration Congress agreed, though with considerable reluctance, to an increase in warship construction shortly after his acceptance of office. In 1916 Mr. Daniels obtained the assent of Congress to a very much larger expansion of the Fleet, the money appropriated to the Navy being upwards of sixty-four millions sterling, or more than double the sum voted for the previous year. Ten first-class battleships of the largest type, six battle-cruisers, ten scout-cruisers, fifty-eight coast submarines, nine Fleet submarines, fifty torpedo-boat destroyers, and other vessels of various types were authorised to be built; but the carrying out of such an extensive programme had to be spread necessarily over a lengthy period. It was provided, however, that four battleships, four battle-cruisers, four scouts, thirty submarines, and twenty destroyers were to be laid down in

BRITISH MILITARY COMMISSIONERS TO THE UNITED STATES.
Major-General G. T. M. Bridges (left) and Captain H. H. Spender Clay on their arrival at New York in April, 1917, as representatives of the British War Office with the British Commission.

the first year. The capital ships were to be super-Dreadnoughts, taking three years or more to build, and they were to be armed with 16 in. guns. In Chapter CLXXIII. it was pointed out that what the United States required in the circumstances of the time were small, fast vessels and quick-firing guns in large numbers ; but the bearing of these circumstances was not realised—when it was, appropriate measures were taken.

Secretary Daniels, who deserved credit for his spirited action so far as it went, did something more than plan and start these great additions to the Fleet. To assist the official Naval Board he organised a Board of civilians, which came to be known as the Naval Consulting Board. It was composed of men of science and of experts, among the first of its members being Thomas Edison, the famous inventor, and it was, therefore, able to give the naval authorities valuable technical and practical help in many ways, both before and after the entry into the war of the United States, and it concentrated on plans for destroying the U boats.

Another of the President's Ministers, the Hon. William Gibbs McAdoo, the Secretary of the Treasury, brought into existence a Shipping Board which dealt with the American Mercantile Marine. When his proposal for its creation first came before the public it was widely ridiculed. In 1914 and 1915 American shipping was not in a flourishing condition ; in the words of a native specialist, Winthrop L. Marvin, "American maritime courage and enterprise were at the very lowest ebb since the Civil War." Hostile legislation had discouraged both shipowners and shipbuilders. More than nine-tenths of the overseas carrying trade of the country was in non-American vessels. But as the war went on and produced a marked shortage of shipping on all the seas, there was a wonderful renaissance of the American marine. After Great Britain and Germany, the United States had the finest ocean shipbuilding plant in the world, and now had come a perfectly magnificent opportunity for its fullest employment. This it was that

MR. THOMAS ALVA EDISON.
The great American inventor who, on the outbreak of war, turned his attention to the devising of new plants for the production of aniline and other chemicals, and on the United States entering the war devoted his entire energies to invention for war purposes.

induced Congress, after two years of opposition, to accept Mr. McAdoo's scheme for the formation of the Shipping Board, which was launched with a vote of ten millions sterling. This Board later stood out as of primary importance for the prosecution of the war by the United States, but in its origin it was designed solely to subserve the American Mercantile Marine.

As with the Navy so with the Army, the United States made no move in 1916 that was in the least indicative of putting itself on a war footing. A new Army Act provided for a small increase in the Regulars, which was to be operative by five annual augmentations of their strength, beginning on July 1st in that year. But the Regulars were still around the 100,000-men mark, as they had been, in fact, for a long time before. So far as size went, the American Army was even more " contemptible " than was the British in 1914. As an American writer phrased it : " Our Army was less than Field-Marshal French's first seven divisions, and the sole powder plant owned by the War Department had a daily capacity of 11,000 lb.—not enough to last the guns of New York Harbour for one minute of firing." The U.S. Army Budget for 1916-17 estimated expenditure at nearly fifty-four million pounds, a figure that showed a rise ; but that considerable sum was discounted, as had been other considerable sums allocated previously for the same purpose, by the well-known expensiveness of the American soldier. But what was perhaps the most remarkable development in the Republic, prior to its declaration of hostilities against Germany, came out of the Army Appropriation Act, which was approved on August 29th, 1916. That Act of Congress definitely organised a Council of National Defence.

By the terms of the Act the Council of National Defence consisted of six members of the Administration—the Secretaries of War, of the Navy, of the Interior, of Agriculture, of Commerce, and of Labour. Its chairman was the Hon. Newton D. Baker, of Ohio, the Secretary of War, who had been appointed to that department by the

DR. HOLLIS GODFREY.
Chairman of the Committee on Science and Research in the United States Council of National Defence.

MR. HERBERT C. HOOVER.
Appointed Food Administrator in the United States immediately after the declaration of war by the U.S.A. against Germany.

MR. JULIUS ROSENWALD.
One of the members of the Advisory Commission appointed to assist the United States Council of National Defence.

PRESIDENT WILSON AND HIS GOVERNMENT.

Front row (from left to right): Mr. William C. Redfield, Secretary of Commerce; Mr. Robert Lansing, Secretary of State; Mr. David F. Houston, Secretary of Agriculture; President Woodrow Wilson; Mr. William G. McAdoo, Secretary of the Treasury; and Mr. Albert S. Burleson, Postmaster-General. Back row: Mr. Josephus Daniels, Secretary of the Navy; Mr. William B. Wilson, Secretary of Labour; Mr. Newton D. Baker, Secretary of War; Mr. Thomas W. Gregory, Attorney-General; and Mr. Franklin K. Lane, Secretary of the Interior.

President on March 7th, 1916. With him were associated Mr. Daniels, the Secretary of the Navy; the Hon. Franklin K. Lane, of California, the Secretary of the Interior; the Hon. David F. Houston, of Missouri, the Secretary of Agriculture; the Hon. William C. Redfield, of New York, the Secretary of Commerce; and the Hon. William B. Wilson, of Pennsylvania, the Secretary of Labour. The organic Act further provided for the appointment of seven public men as an Advisory Commission. The Council, much later, nominated them, and the President ratified the selection, which was of an excellent character and acclaimed by the whole country.

At the head of the Advisory Commission stood Mr. Daniel Willard, the President of the Baltimore and Ohio Railroad, and eminent in the railway world. The other members were Mr. Howard E. Coffin, a famous engineer and Vice-President of the Hudson Motor Company, who had already acted as the chairman of a Committee on Industrial Preparedness; Mr. Julius Rosenwald, one of Chicago's greatest merchants and a man who had built up the largest "mail order" business in the world; Mr. Bernard M. Baruch, a leading financier of New York; Dr. Hollis Godfrey, President of the Drexel Institute of Philadelphia, and a distinguished engineer; Mr. Samuel Gompers, who held the important position of President of the American Federation of Labour; and Dr. Franklin Martin, the Secretary-General of the American College of Surgeons, and himself a surgeon of remarkable talent. Each of these men was an authority in his own line, and, taken together, they covered an extraordinarily wide field. They were in a position, moreover, to enlist the services of civilians of similar calibre. But the Council of Defence, with its splendid Advisory Commission, was not fully organised for business until March 1st, 1917, six months after it had been constituted, and one month after President Wilson had broken off relations with Germany.

By the Act the Council of Defence was charged with the "co-ordination of industries and resources for the national security and welfare," and with the "creation of relations which will render possible in the time of need the immediate concentration and utilisation of the resources of the nation." In performing its functions the Council was directed to supervise investigation, and make recommendations to the President and the heads of executive departments with respect to the railways of the United States, its highways, and waterways, in **Duties of the Council of Defence** so far as they were available for defensive military movements, whether for the concentration of troops at specific points or for the assembling of supplies where required. It was also commissioned to report on the mobilisation of naval as well as military resources, and to say what steps should be taken for increasing the domestic production of articles essential for the support of armies and fleets and of the people during an interruption of foreign commerce. Further, its business was concerned with an inquiry into the possibilities of "sea-going transportation." It was evident that the Council would be of the utmost service in the event of war, offensive as well as defensive, as indeed it was later, but it was not of an offensive that its members were thinking in 1916.

In October and November, 1916, the United States was absorbed, to the exclusion of everything else, by the Presidential Election, as the result of which, after some uncertainty, Mr. Wilson obtained a second term. The Democrats triumphed, and the Republicans were "dished."

A FORTY MILLION LOAN.

United States Secretary to the Treasury signing the Treasury warrant for the first loan of $200,000,000 (nearly £40,000,000) to Great Britain. Left to right: Lord Cunliffe, Governor of the Bank of England; Sir Cecil Spring-Rice, British Ambassador to the United States; Mr. William G. McAdoo; Sir Hardman Lever; Sir Richard Crawford; and Assistant-Secretary Crosby.

AN AMERICAN SUBMARINE AND HER CREW.
The Hon. Josephus Daniels, Secretary for the Navy, induced Congress in 1916 to sanction a large increase of the United States Navy; fifty-eight coast submarines and nine Fleet submarines were included in this programme.

To quote from the "American Review of Reviews" for June, 1917, this came about mainly because Mr. Wilson and his party were regarded as unalterably pacific. "Mr. Wilson was re-elected President because the average peace-loving person of the West and the South believed that in no circumstances could the Wilson Democracy be provoked into assuming the status of belligerency; while, on the contrary, it was feared that if Roosevelt or Hughes (the Republican leaders) should be made President the country would be fighting along with the Allies before the war was ended." It

Mr. Wilson's re-election was as the American protagonist of peace that Mr. Wilson was chosen again as Chief Magistrate. Taken as a whole, the United States, even at the beginning of 1917, did not imagine that it ever would be called on to enter into the war, and this seemed to be the belief of its head, for, as late as January 22nd, Mr. Wilson, in an address to the Senate, and well in line with his speeches during his electoral campaign, still spoke of a negotiated peace, a "peace without victory." But he heard no favourable response from the Allies, and the proposal came to nothing.

Even after February 3rd, when relations with Germany were severed, the country was still far from certain that it was nearing war. Most of its people thought that war could and would be avoided, while others suggested that if war were declared the participation of the United States ought to be strictly limited to the protection of American shipping and the assistance of the Entente with supplies and loans, and not by determined military action, whether on land or sea. The "average peace-loving person" in the great Republic still had no idea that the very life of his country, with all its well-ordered and smooth-running liberties, was involved in the war quite as much as was that of Great Britain or of France. President Wilson appeared still to have hopes of peace, or of limiting war, if it came, to the defensive. On the day after the rupture of relations Mr. Lansing, the Secretary of State, said, in a message to American Ministers to neutral countries, that the President was reluctant to believe Germany actually would carry out her threat against neutral commerce, but that, if she did, he would ask Congress to "authorise the use of national power to protect American citizens engaged in their peaceful and lawful errands on the sea."

The Zimmermann-Eckhardt Note

There was, however, no immediate speeding-up of the preparation of the Army or of the Navy. Probably to the Germanic Powers the threat had an empty sound.

During the next week Americans were called on to submit to the strangest and bitterest national experience of their lives—the humiliation of seeing the St. Louis and other ships of theirs tied up in their harbours though ready to sail, afraid to leave because of the German submarines. As a consequence of this holding-up of shipping, traffic became congested on the railways, and there was a dislocation of business. Prices rose rapidly, and food riots took place in New York and other cities. This was at all events an object-lesson of the meaning of the German submarine blockade, and it did something to educate American opinion. On February 10th it was officially announced, in response to the protests of the shipping people and others, that American vessels might carry guns and ward off an attack, but this permission made matters no better, as neither guns nor gun crews were available except from the Government, which did not supply them. The pacifists, thinking that the President was still bent on peace, redoubled their activities, and under the leadership of Mr. Bryan, Mr. Wilson's former Secretary of State, a strong agitation was set on foot for a referendum on peace or war. But, on the other side of the account, the Democratic Press, notably the "New York Times," the chief organ of the party, supported the Republican papers in urging the President to take action. His next move was, on the 26th of the month, to ask Congress to empower him to institute a policy of "armed neutrality," but the session of Congress came automatically to an end on March 4th without the passing of the necessary legislation, owing to the obstructive tactics of a dozen pacifist and pro-German members of the Senate. The President then summoned an extra session for April 16th for the purpose of legalising the arming of American ships—a process, however, which had been begun already.

President Wilson had in reality long since made up his mind. In his speech to the Senate on February 26th he stated that Germany had not perpetrated against American shipping that overt act that would bring the United States into the conflict, but, though he was not aware of it at the moment, that overt act had been committed by the sinking without warning of the Cunard liner Laconia a few hours before, two American women being among the victims. The incident was followed by similar ones on March 17th-18th, when three American steamers were submarined without warning and with the loss of American lives. His action was prompt and energetic. The Zimmermann Note to Eckhardt had been in his possession—or in that of the Government, which was the same thing—for some time. It was now given to the Press for publication, and on March 1st the President, in answer to a question, told the Senate that the Note was authentic and genuine, and in the hands of the

AMERICAN MIGHT AT SEA: A SUPER-DREADNOUGHT OF THE U.S. NAVY.

Mr. Secretary Daniels' 1916 naval programme included ten first-class battleships of the largest type, four of which were laid down at once. The battleship shown above was 624 feet in length, of 32,600 tons displacement, and her protective armour was of extraordinary thickness. The vessel was equipped with a heavy armament of 16 in. guns, and these were supplemented by secondary batteries.

Government. On March 4th one of the results of this communication was seen in the adoption by both Houses of Congress, after a conference, of a Naval Bill, carrying appropriations of upwards of £107,000,000, authorising a bond issue of £30,000,000 to hasten naval construction, and providing for thirty-eight new submarines. As against that, however, Congress ended on the same day without action by the Senate on the annual Army and Military Academy Bills. The estimate for the Army had been fifty millions sterling, or a good deal less than for the preceding year.

On March 5th the President took the oath of office for his second term, and in his inaugural address declared for armed neutrality, but at the same time he warned the United States that it might be drawn on to a more active assertion of its rights and a more immediate association with the great struggle itself. Four days later he called Congress (the Sixty-fifth Congress, officially) to meet in special session on April 16th, but afterwards, in view of the further hostile acts of the German submarines and the growing pressure of influential American opinion, advanced

AMERICAN DESTROYERS PREPARING FOR SEA.
Destroyers belonging to the American Navy in an English port, getting ready to go to sea. Within a month of the United States entering the war, flotillas of fast American destroyers were energetically assisting in the campaign against the U boats in European waters.

the date by a fortnight. Among the signs of those critical days was a conference on March 12th, at Washington, of Trade Union leaders, who adopted resolutions pledging the support of Labour in the event of war. A second was that next day the Governors of the six New England States met at Boston to discuss measures of national defence. A third was that the Navy Department hastened to award contracts for the construction, by private builders, of four battle-cruisers and six scout-cruisers, involving an expenditure of £22,500,000 for hulls and machinery alone, while the President authorised the Secretary of the Navy to expend on submarine chasers, destroyers, and "mosquito" craft the emergency fund of about thirty millions sterling that had been authorised by Congress. A fourth was that the President directed that the Navy was to be recruited to its maximum of 87,000 men, plus 6,000 apprenticed seamen—an addition to its strength of about 18,000 men—and that he also began calling out the regiments of the National **First steps of the new Cabinet** Guard. He took these steps on March 25th; on the following day he gave orders that the Marine Corps should be increased from 15,000 to 17,400 men. It was during this time also that the Council of National Defence, with its subordinate Advisory Commission, really got down to work, Mr. Willard, of the Baltimore and Ohio Railroad, being elected chairman of the latter early in March.

Meanwhile, Mr. Roosevelt had been strongly advocating the expediting of the meeting of Congress, and that, specifically, in order to declare war on Germany; he demanded that the United States should strike hard for the national interest and honour. Other leaders of the Republican Party spoke in similar fashion, and now were supported by some prominent Democrats. As the third week in March closed, the Press announced that Mr. Wilson's Cabinet was united in support of a strenuous policy. The " New York Times " denounced " apologetic preparedness," and said it must stop. When the date of the meeting of Congress was advanced to April 2nd excitement rose throughout the country. On one hand was the call for war in earnest, on the other the clamour of the pacifists for peace at any price.

GREAT WARSHIP OF THE UNITED STATES NAVY.
Launching of the United States battleship New Mexico on April 23rd, 1917. The vessel was 624 feet long, of 32,000 tons displacement, and was built to burn oil fuel exclusively. It was the first battleship to be equipped with the electric drive, a method of propulsion which had proved most satisfactory in preliminary tests.

The country, as a whole, listening to both call and clamour, was stirred, but it also was bewildered. It hardly yet recognised the inevitability of the war for the independence, even for the existence, of the United States. Goaded on by the Germans, the noisy pacifists brought pressure to bear by getting up demonstrations and by assailing Mr. Wilson, the Government, and the members of Congress in all sorts of ways. The campaign of calumny against Great Britain was actively renewed. Processions of pacifists invaded Washington on the eve of the President's great historic speech to Congress on April 2nd, and were met by processions of patriots red-hot for war. As both pacifists and patriots soon found out, to the confusion of the one and the joy of the other, President Wilson was firm as iron. "We will not choose the path of submission," said the President to Congress. Two months later, in his Note to New Russia, he put the position even more definitively when he stated, "The day has come

Disappearance of Partyism to conquer or submit." These were the alternatives. There was nothing else for America any more than for the Allies.

Most remarkable were the developments which ensued almost at once on the delivery of the President's momentous speech to the joint session of Congress on April 2nd. Partyism disappeared in the United States in the practical unanimity of American politicians for war. The lofty presentment by Mr. Wilson of the American case against the German Government was applauded by Republican leaders like Mr. Roosevelt and Judge Hughes, and by Mr. Root, who had strongly opposed his former policies. What was even more significant was that nearly all the

prominent men among the Democrats swung into line with him. The joint resolution for declaring war, "and making provision for prosecuting the same," was carried in the Senate by 82 votes to 6, and in the House of Representatives by 373 to 50. The dissentients in the Senate were equally divided between Democrats and Republicans, Senator Stone, of Missouri, the chairman of the Senate's Foreign Relations Committee, the man who had been largely responsible for blocking the Armed Neutrality Bill, being among the former. At the head of the minority in the House was Mr. Kitchin, of North Carolina, the Democratic leader on its floor, but when once the resolution was passed he accepted it,

National war loan of £1,400,000,000

as did the others, and he forthwith proceeded to act as manager in the House of the further war measures of the Administration. Complete political unanimity appeared when both the Senate and the House, within less than a fortnight, adopted without one dissenting vote the Government's Bill authorising a national war loan for seven thousand millions (seven "billions," in American parlance), of dollars, or upwards of £1,400,000,000. This swift mobilisation of the politicians of the United States was in itself a wonderful thing.

The concord of Congress was reflected in the newspapers of the United States, which, with very few exceptions and those generally of the irreconcilable Fenian type, ranged themselves solidly in support of President Wilson. The people, taken "by and large," endorsed his action. "A country," wrote an American publicist, "that thoroughly hated war, a country that had obdurately refused to

AMERICAN SUBMARINE "MOTHER-SHIP" IN DOCK WITH HER FLOTILLA OF SUBMARINES.

Until Congress sanctioned Mr. Secretary Daniels' naval programme in 1916, the United States Navy was undoubtedly weak in submarines and in "mosquito" craft generally; even then, however, the existing submarines were of the latest known type, and they were manned by some of the most daring sailors in the world. After the entry of the United States into the war the submarine force was largely increased.
MM

prepare even for its own protection, a country that had re-elected President Wilson because it thought that he was really for peace at any price, a country that cared nothing for the doctrinal rights of American passengers on belligerent ships, a country that longed for the chance to stay at home, mind its own business, and leave Europe to its own strifes and destinies—this country, with amazing unanimity of spirit and purpose, permitted itself to be led to war by its pacifist President within a month after his new term had begun." That the opinion of the politicians, the Press, and the people was mobilised for war in that short time, after nearly three years of insistent national detachment from the struggle, was extraordinary in itself. It was a stupendous triumph for Mr. Wilson, and it made the first phases of the actual mobilisation simply marvellous.

Vital nature of the issue A little later, however, it was noted by a shrewd American observer that the masses of the people were curiously placid and unenthusiastic about the war, as indeed was shown by the disappointing recruiting figures during the next three months, for there was no rush to join the Army. The truth was that they still had to be educated as to the vital nature of the issue for themselves, still had to understand that the war was their war, and that they must fight, and fight with all their might, for the very life of their country and everything that was most dear to them. They were not yet fully awakened—it was a thing that was bound to take time, and that did take time. As late as the fourth week of August, or nearly five months after the entry into the war of the United States, there was published a leading article in the "Tribune" of New York which said : "The mass of the American people have been making up

their minds, and it is plain that the minds of the vast majority are now made up to go forward with the war until there is a solution which shall abolish the perils they now recognise and prevent the repetition of crimes which they now understand. There is not the smallest semblance of enthusiasm of the sort one connects with nations at war, yet it is unmistakable that the people of the United States have gone to this task with an earnestness and determination not at first detected, but no longer to be mistaken."

There was certainly one American who, having made up his mind, went at this task from the start with an earnestness and determination that were absolutely magnificent, and that was the President. As soon as war was declared he threw himself with the utmost energy

"ABOARD-SHIP" IN NEW YORK CITY.
American naval recruits on the U.S.S. Recruit, a land battleship in New York City, used as the headquarters of the Navy recruiting forces, and also as a preliminary training depot.

and devotion into organising the country for war. He took no narrow, restricted, sectional view of the work that had to be done, and he showed that he was resolved that as little time as possible should be lost in overtaking that work. In his address to Congress on April 2nd he had indicated, in a general way, its nature and extent.

First, co-operation in counsel and action with the Allies, and incidentally the extension to them of the most liberal financial credits. Second, the organisation and mobilisation of all the material resources of the Republic. Third, the immediate full equipment of the Navy in all respects, but particularly with the best means of dealing with the German submarines. Fourth, the immediate addition to the armed forces of the United States, already provided for by law in case of war, of 500,000 men, with equal increments later as might be required, who, he suggested, should be selected on the principle of universal liability to service.

On April 15th the President issued a personal appeal to the nation, in which he implored it to rise to the level of the enterprise, and to realise how great was the task before it. He said that the Navy was rapidly being placed on a war footing, and that a great army was about to be created and equipped, but that there were other things besides fighting to which the people of the United States must address themselves. He declared that there must be provided an abundant supply of food, both for Americans and Allies, and he told the farmers that on them in large measure rested the fate of the war. He begged

A GREAT PLANET AND HER SATELLITES.
An American naval observation balloon and a seaplane flying above the cruiser to which they were attached. The rapid development of flying under the stimulus of war necessitated the attachment of aircraft for scouting purposes to battleships.

the farmers in the South to grow foodstuffs as well as cotton. In a striking passage he pointed out :

We must supply ships by hundreds out of our shipyards to carry to the other side of the sea, submarines or no submarines, what will every day be needed there, and abundant materials out of our fields, mines, and factories with which not only to clothe and equip our own forces on land and sea, but also to clothe and support our people for whom the gallant fellows under arms can no longer work, to help clothe and equip the armies with which we are co-operating in Europe, and to keep the looms and manufactories there in raw material ; coal to keep the fires going in ships at sea and the furnaces in hundreds of factories across the sea ; steel out of which to make arms and ammunition both here and there, rails for worn-out railways at the back and at the fighting-fronts, locomotives and rolling-stock to take the place of those every day going to pieces ; mules and horses and cattle for military service — everything with which the people of Great Britain, France, Italy, and Russia have usually supplied themselves, but cannot now afford the men, materials, or machinery to make.

ARRIVAL IN FRANCE OF AMERICA'S VANGUARD.
On June 25th, 1917, an armada of transports escorted by warships reached a French port, bringing the advanced guard of the vast American Army to take an active part in the war in Europe. Along the breakwater gangs of German prisoners gazed in astonishment at the imposing spectacle.

In this most comprehensive appeal the President asked the manufacturer to speed-up and perfect every process, the middleman to forgo unusual profits and expedite the shipment of supplies, the merchant to take as his motto " Small profits and quick service," the railwayman to see that there should be no obstruction in the arteries of the nation's life, the miner, who was as indispensable as the farmer, not to slack or fail — he " also was enlisted in the great service of the Army." To the shipbuilder he commended the inspiration that life and the war depended on him, for no matter how many ships, carrying food and war supplies, were sent to the bottom, more and more ships must be turned out from the

GERMAN SHIPS THAT PASSED INTO AMERICAN OWNERSHIP.
The German auxiliary cruiser Prinz Eitel Friedrich, and (above) the Vaterland, Germany's largest Transatlantic liner, in an American harbour with the Stars and Stripes flying from her stern. Interned at the outbreak of war, these vessels were afterwards pressed into the service of the United States.

yards to replace those lost, and increase the number of vessels on the seas. Lastly, he spoke to the private citizen—by suggesting that everyone who created and cultivated a garden would help greatly in solving the problem of feeding the nations, and that every housewife who practised strict economy put herself in the ranks of those who served the nation. Mr. Wilson concluded by requesting editors, publishers, and advertisers everywhere to give the utmost prominence to his appeal, and by hoping that the clergy of all denominations would give his words widespread repetition, with appropriate comment, from their pulpits. " The supreme test of the nation has come," said the President, " and we must all speak, act, and serve together."

Directed by the President, whom the U.S. Constitution and the war conspired to make almost the greatest autocrat on earth, things had begun to move, even before the declaration of war, in a big way, and in accordance with the plans he outlined to Congress. " Money talks " was a characteristic American saying. The weapon, the instrument of action, that lay most ready to his hand was American money —the vast accumulated and ever-increasing wealth of his country. Never did money talk more impressively. On April 5th estimates were received by the House of Representatives from Mr. McAdoo, the Secretary of the Treasury, calling for the authorisation of a credit of over three and a half billions of dollars, or upwards of £700,000,000, to cover initial war measures, three billions, or £600,000,000, being asked for enlarging and equipping the Army. This was, as it were, a first draft, a preliminary sketch. On the 10th the House Committee on Ways and Means, after a discussion with Mr. McAdoo, whose ideas had grown, agreed to an appropriation that was just double that of five days before. It was for seven billions, or £1,400,000,000. The money was to be raised by an issue of five billions in long-term bonds, and of two billions in certificates of indebtedness to be redeemed at the expiration of one year by revenue derived from increased taxation. It was this enormous war loan that was voted unanimously by Congress, the necessary Bill being passed by the House on April 14th, and by the Senate three days later.

At that time the debt of the United States was only a billion dollars, or £200,000,000, and here were seven times that amount voted almost offhand for war. This was a record in financial history. In August, 1914, Great Britain had entered into the war with a vote of £100,000,000, and that had seemed a large sum then; it appeared almost a small sum, however, as the conflict proceeded. Of the American war loan the sum of £800,000,000 was allocated to the beginnings of the military and naval preparations of the United States, and the sum of £600,000,000 was earmarked for the Allies, who needed cash continually for the purchase of supplies in America. This sum, which had been assigned for their use, was just as good as gold. Investors in the United States had already bought over £400,000,000 of foreign loans since 1915, and had taken back, either by purchase or as

MEMBERS OF THE UNITED STATES AIR BOARD.
Seated (left to right) : Rear-Admiral David W. Taylor, Brigadier-General George O. Squier, and Mr. Howard E. Coffin, Chairman of the Board and Member of the Council of National Defence.　Standing : Messrs. Sidney G. Walden, E. A. Deeds, R. L. Montgomery, and A. G. Cable.

collateral security for loans to the Entente, about an equal sum in American railway and other gilt-edged stocks and bonds. But the holding of the Allies of such stocks and bonds was not unlimited ; it was, in fact, being rapidly used up. In Parliament Mr. Bonar Law, as Chancellor of the Exchequer, stated that when the American war loan was put through, the holding by Great Britain of such securities, not already hypothecated or sold, was reaching the vanishing point. Thus the action of President Wilson was most timely. No doubt he knew the position in which the finances of the Entente stood in the United States, and at the earliest moment, having taken counsel with the Allies about that as about other matters, had determined on its substantial amelioration. For their loans in New York the Entente had been paying

A record in financial operations

5½ per cent. per annum. The American loan was at 3½ per cent., and it was at this much lower rate that the Allies got their share of it, the saving to them thereby being considerable, to say nothing of the gain from the disappearance of commissions to underwriters, brokers, and agents, and of loss from the heavy exchange rates.

On April 24th the President, by signing the seven billion dollar loan Bill, gave it the American equivalent of the "Royal assent," and thus legalised the greatest single financial operation in history. The bonds next had to be marketed, and provision was made for this as it might be required. The Act provided for the issue to the public of U.S. bonds to the value of £400,000,000. Particulars of this loan, which was promptly christened the "Liberty Loan," were not announced till May 9th, and the date of issue was June 15th.

UNITS OF AMERICA'S AERIAL FLEET.
Three aeroplanes rising together from one of the great aviation training camps established in America. The United States' entry into the war synchronised with the general realisation that the air might prove the element in which the final phases of the war would be decided, and America prepared accordingly.

FIXING UP THE ENGINE.
In an American aeroplane factory. Fixing up the engine for one of the new machines which the United States promptly planned to build.

BUILDING AEROPLANE SHEDS.
When the United States entered the war the making of aeroplanes on a colossal scale was decided upon, and extensive camps were immediately erected in various parts of the country, where the men who flocked to the new arm of military service received their training.

But a large sum of money was needed at once. The services of the Federal Reserve Board, a sort of national banking institution which had been created two or three years previously, were brought into play. Then, just as the politicians of the United States had been mobilised, so now were mobilised its financiers in support of the President. The Government was able without difficulty to raise money on short-dated Treasury notes, in advance of the sale of the bonds, and so to meet the current **£500,000,000 loaned to the Allies** requirements of the Allies in America. On the very day after the Loan Act was in force, Mr. McAdoo, who had shown initiative, courage, resource, and other high qualities in his handling of the loan, presented to Sir Cecil Spring-Rice, the British Ambassador, a Treasury warrant for two hundred million dollars, or rather more than forty millions sterling, as a first instalment of America's financial assistance to the Allies. France, Italy, Russia, and Belgium obtained instalments shortly afterwards, and the process went on and on. By the autumn these loans

STAR OF THE WEST.
Painting the "Star" insignia on an American aeroplane—the special distinguishing mark of the aircraft of the great Western Republic.

to the Allies reached five hundred millions sterling. Of course, the money was not lost to the United States even temporarily, for all of it was kept and spent in the country, but the relief to the finance of the Entente could hardly be exaggerated.

To help to pay the war expenditure, Congress agreed to a large increase in taxation. A Bill to raise three hundred and sixty millions sterling in taxes was passed. Later it was discovered that nearly £450,000,000 would be required as the taxable portion of a year's expense estimated

LIKE LARVÆ AWAITING THEIR WINGS.
Aeroplanes nearing completion in an American factory. They were lined up for receiving the finishing touches before being fitted with the planes that would permit of the inert masses soaring like dragon-flies into the air.

at more than twelve thousand millions of pounds. On May 19th the Senate passed, without roll-call, a general War Appropriation Bill, authorising a Treasury expenditure of close upon £670,000,000. New or increased taxes were put on incomes, excess profits, railway earnings, distilleries and breweries, motor-cars, jewellery, perfumes, proprietary medicines, and tobacco, and the price of postage-stamps, telegrams, and telephone-calls was advanced. It was

Mobilisation of money and materials calculated that the new taxation amounted to about four pounds per head of the population.

Simultaneously with this tremendous mobilisation of the money of the United States there proceeded the mobilisation of its materials. With respect to most countries at war their fighting strength, as expressed in terms of Army, Navy, and man-power, is the outstanding feature of their belligerency. While, as narrated later, this ultimately supreme factor was anything but relegated to a secondary place by President Wilson, the special circumstances of the Republic made the emphasis at the outset to be laid on money and materials rather than on men. In this connection "materials" connoted the industrial and commercial resources of America, and everything adjunct thereunto —railways and shipping, as well as farms, mines, shops, and factories. L a b o u r problems necessarily were also involved. From the extent of the United States, its large population, and the multiplicity of its industrial and commercial activities, the mobilisation of materials could not but be a most stupendous undertaking. But there was one key to its complexities, and that was that they all had to be considered with relation to the successful prosecution of the war —that was the main thing, and other interests, while met and

satisfied as far as possible, had to be subordinated to it. More especially was it to these other interests that President Wilson had addressed his moving personal appeal on April 15th, 1917, with its high and resonant patriotic note.

For the intensive mobilisation of materials which he desired President Wilson looked for help to the leading business men of the country, nor did he look in vain. From all quarters they came hot-foot to Washington at his call. Some at once became the efficient assistants of various Government Departments to which they individually were drawn by their special fitness, and others, who formed the majority, joined the forces of the Council of National Defence or of its Advisory Commission, all giving their services gratuitously. Thither also came representatives of Labour—under the leadership of Mr. Gompers, the Labour member of the Advisory Commission—everyone anxious to co-operate. It all was a wonderful demonstration of patriotic feeling. The Council of Defence, with its Advisory Commission, quickly developed into a magnificent war institution, which touched

GUNS FOR THE U.S. NAVY.
Interior of one of the big gun-shops of the Bethlehem Steel Works, Bethlehem, Pennsylvania.

at every point the industrial and commercial life of the community, north, south, east, or west. For administrative purposes Mr. W. S. Gifford, a leading official of the great American Telephone and Telegraph Company, was appointed director of both bodies, and Mr. Grosvenor B. Clarkson their secretary. It was only in the beginning of March that Mr. Daniel Willard became chairman of the Council, but before that month had closed the Council had gone a long way to justify its existence by formally creating the Munitions Standards Board a n d t h e Interdepartmental Advisory Committee, the business of the latter being the co-ordination and expediting of work

HEAVY ARMAMENT FOR AMERICAN SUPER-DREADNOUGHTS.
View of a shop at Bethlehem, Pa., where heavy guns, armoured turrets, and ammunition lifts were in process of manufacture. The Bethlehem works had the largest plant in the world, and it was employed at full pressure directly the United States entered the war as a belligerent.

for national defence, and to prevent overlapping.

The Munitions Standards Board was not in itself a new departure. Some considerable time before March, 1917, it had been organised by Mr. Howard Coffin, later the member of the Advisory Commission in charge of munitions, but the Council took it over and gave it official recognition. This Board consisted of six experts, and the task they set before themselves was the standardising of munitions with a view to increased production. After careful investigations and several meetings with manufacturers of shells, machine-guns, and the like, they were able to introduce such modifications of specifica-

SHELLS, SHELLS, SHELLS!
One of the shops at Bethlehem, Pa., where shells were being made for the American Army in the field.

SHRAPNEL BINS IN AMERICA'S WAR CELLARS.
Tons of metal ready to be placed in shells. Private American manufacturing firms that had been producing vast quantities of munitions for the Allies were tabulated when the United States declared war, and were developed for increased production under the control of the Munitions Standards Board.

tions and design as ensured a vastly larger and speedier output. In this particular field of munitions the United States was far from ill-prepared for war, for, as the Germans knew to their cost, it had been supplying the Allies with enormous quantities since almost the outbreak of hostilities. True, the supplies had come from private manufacturing concerns, but there these concerns were, and the Board made a comprehensive list of them. It did more, for it saw to it that the productive capacity of the country along these lines was developed as well as tabulated. In this way were laid the foundations of something resembling the British Ministry of Munitions.

Among the earliest preoccupations of President Wilson before the declaration of war was the attitude of Labour. Only a few weeks previously strikes on a large scale, which had been fomented by pro-German agencies, had been narrowly averted.

Nothing could be more obvious than that the successful participation of the United States in the conflict demanded the cordial co-operation of its workers, of those who handled its materials. The situation was complicated by the fact that millions of these workers

were aliens, with a not negligible proportion of them of enemy birth. The Census Bureau, in June, 1917, estimated that there were nearly five million persons in the country who had been born in Germany, Austria - Hungary, Turkey, and Bulgaria. The policy of the Government had to be at once broad and strong. The Secretary of Labour, a namesake of the President, was a member of the Council of National Defence, and he was fortunate in having Mr. Gompers—who had thoroughly grasped the meaning of the German menace, and had already done very good work in countering German intrigues in America—as the Labour member of the Advisory Commission.

President of the American Federation of Labour, which had two million men on its roll, Mr. Gompers had the most intimate acquaintance with the workers and their problems, and had the further great advantage of enjoying the confidence and trust of the nation-wide interests he directed. He had realised that the United States must fight Germany, and on the day President Wilson asked Congress to declare war upon her, Mr. Gompers took decisive action.

For the purpose of mobilising Labour for the furtherance of the war, Mr. Gompers called a meeting at Washington, which was held on April 2nd, and attended by both Labour representatives and employers. The officers and executive committee of his own federation were present, as well as leading members of the chief international Labour organisations and of the railway brotherhoods. The employers were represented by delegates of the National Association of Manufacturers. In the report of the work of the Council of National Defence, which was published towards the end of the ensuing June, it was stated that "It was the definite purpose of Mr. Gompers and his

Mr. Gompers and Labour

associates to avoid the unfortunate industrial experiences of Britain in the opening months of the European War." The meeting exhibited the most remarkable agreement, and formed a permanent organisation, with an executive committee of eleven, with a view to Labour's aiding President Wilson and the country in the most effective manner. Subsequently eight sub-committees were created dealing with such matters as mediation and conciliation, wages and hours, women in industry, welfare work, cost of living and domestic economy, and information and statistics. The welfare work was based on the principle that the health and efficiency of the workers in the vital industries, upon which all else depended, were ultimate resources which had to be conserved in the interest of the nation. On the day war was declared the Labour Committee passed a resolution advising workers, as well as employers, not to try to take ad-

British Labour Commission vantage of the country's necessities to alter for their selfish benefit existing standards of wages and hours of work. In a word, American Labour mobilised, and that with a highly intelligent patriotism, under the guidance of Mr. Gompers, supported by the Council of National Defence.

One of the first steps which Mr. Gompers took, with the object of perfecting the mobilisation of American Labour for war, was to cable Mr. Lloyd George, requesting the British Prime Minister to send to the United States a commission of four representatives of British Labour and welfare work. Mr. George gladly complied, and despatched Mr. C. W. Bowerman, M.P., the secretary of the British Trade Union Congress, Mr. J. H. Thomas, M.P., the secretary of the National Union of Railwaymen, Mr. H. W. Garrod, of the Ministry of Munitions, and Mr. J. Davies, one of his own secretaries, to Washington. The British representatives later were joined by two Labour men sent by the Canadian Government. After conferences extending over many days, in which the British and Canadian commissioners placed at the disposal of the Labour Committee the experience of Great Britain and Canada since the beginning of the war in dealing with employment problems, a public session of the full committee was held on May 15th, 1917, when the visiting Labour representatives were heard at **New Boards and Committees** length, and discussions ensued of high practical value. " Let us not repeat the mistakes that were made," said Mr. Gompers wisely. Outside the United States the great war work which was done, and done so admirably, by this able and indefatigable man was perhaps hardly sufficiently appreciated. As an educative force in hardening American public opinion after the declaration of war he constantly rendered splendid service to the common cause.

Another development of the Council of National Defence was seen on April 5th when it created a Commercial Economy Board, with three members, to deal with the problems of war-time distribution. Two days afterwards the council originated a Committee on Food Supply and Prices, and invited Mr. Herbert C. Hoover, chairman of the American Committee for Relief in Belgium, to return to the United States and become the head of this

EARLY RECRUITS FOR THE AMERICAN ARMY.
Soldiers leaving a New York recruiting office. On the United States entering the war, there was no rush to join the Army until the nation realised the greatness and importance to the world and to its own future of the task upon which it had entered.

BRITISH RECRUITING IN NEW YORK.
Scene in a British recruiting office in New York, where many British subjects resident in the United States enlisted for service with the British Army.

new organisation. Mr. Hoover arrived at Washington early in May, but in the meantime the necessary food-supply legislation had not been passed by Congress, and the committee was practically hung up till it was passed, after much opposition, four months later, when the President carried his point, and Mr. Hoover was appointed controller with the title of Food Administrator. Intelligent Americans realised that the food of the United States had to be controlled in the interest of themselves and their compatriots, as well as of the Allies, who were dependent on them for wheat and other of the necessaries of life. The question turned on the nature of the control— how and to what extent it was to be exercised. Mr. Wilson demanded that the control should be absolute, and placed in the hands of a single executive official, Mr. Hoover being the man he had selected.

As it would have been difficult to find in all the world another person who knew as much as Mr. Hoover did with regard to the buying, shipping, and distributing of food, it was evident that he was an excellent choice, and there was no objection taken to him on the ground of want of fitness for the position. What Congress boggled at so long was at putting control of such a vital thing as food under one man, but in the end it accepted the President's scheme, and the Food Act was duly enacted. By that time— August 10th—the American harvest was beginning. Much had been done to make that particular harvest larger than that of the preceding year, which had been unusually small.

In the spring of 1917 the most serious problem of the Allies, and of Great Britain especially, was food. The world's shortage of wheat and the destruction of shipping by enemy submarines had brought about a grave situation, as President Wilson well understood. While legislation for the Committee on Food Supply and Prices was pending, he set in motion, through the Department of

Agriculture, a great food campaign, similar in its general character to that which then was taking place in Great Britain.

All through April and during part of May American official effort was strongly directed towards stimulating increased food production. The Department of Agriculture issued thousands of circulars and bulletins to the farmers, which stated with due emphasis the facts, and urged that while waste should be checked, larger areas of the cultivable soil should be sown or planted with the requisite seeds and roots. In speech after speech Mr. Houston, the Secretary of the Department, and Mr. Vrooman, the Assistant Secretary, sought to rouse the agriculturists of the country. There was no anxiety about feeding the people of the United States; even a comparatively poor harvest was more than sufficient for that. It was the amount of the exportable surplus that was the thing, and the farmers were incited to make it as large as possible.

Stimulating food production

The Government promised them its assistance, even in money, if required. Many employers of labour gave allotments to their operatives. Thousands of gardens were given up to potatoes and other edibles instead of flowers. Many hundreds of Eastern boys went from the cities and towns to work on the Western farms. The food campaign undoubtedly had good results. In New England, New York, New Jersey, and Pennsylvania a decided impetus was given to agriculture and to gardening. Both the West and the South also felt the influence of the movement, the former with respect to wheat, and the latter to maize, or " corn," as it was called in America.

Further important progress in the mobilisation of the materials of the United States was recorded on April 9th, when an organisation, termed the General Munitions Board, began its work under the orders of the Council

RECRUITS FROM THE FAR WEST.
Volunteers presenting themselves for enlistment at a British recruiting office in New York. In oval: Sir Francis Lloyd inspecting men who had returned to London from America that they might join the Army.

of National Defence. The Board was composed of seventeen qualified representatives of the War and Navy Departments, and of eight civilians. Its chairman was one of the latter, Mr. Frank A. Scott, an acknowledged authority on the production of munitions. Before the Board was created the War and Navy Departments could compete with each other in the open market ; it put an end to such a possibility by co-ordinating all the departmental buying. Where manufacturing facilities were inadequate, it developed those in existence or added new ones. As the British Government, because of the enormous growth of its Ministry of Munitions, no longer needed, or could get along without, its small-arms factories in America, it passed them over to the Board on fair purchase terms. In the course of a month from its formation this organisation had arranged with manufacturers for a supply of a million rifles with the requisite ammunition, for artillery in large quantities, for machine-guns at a lower price than had been paid by the War Department, for shells of various sizes, and hosts of other things, including armoured cars and Army vehicles of all kinds. With the most careful attention to economy it supervised all contracts, and, through co-ordination in buying alone, saved many millions of dollars to the Government.

Work of the Munitions Board

To a committee of the Advisory Commission was entrusted the mobilisation of raw materials, and to another that of supplies. At the head of the one was Mr. Baruch, the financier, and the chairman of the other was the merchant prince of Chicago, Mr. Julius Rosenwald. Both "made good," and their efforts resulted in saving the country large sums of money. With the exception of coal, which was dealt with by the Committee on Coal Production of the Council of National Defence, Mr. Baruch and his associates organised the field in minerals and metals, including aluminium, asbestos, brass, copper, lead, mica, nickel, iron, steel, sulphur, and zinc, as well as oil. Within their range also came alcohol, chemicals, and coal-tar by-products, lumber, cement, rubber, and wool. Carefully selected sub-committees concentrated on each of these essentials, and kept in constant touch with the Government Departments, to which they soon proved their value by perfecting early deliveries and in making lower-than-market prices. Among other things the parent committee saved the country two millions sterling in a purchase of 45,000,000 lb. of copper by getting it at half the current rate, while the sub-committee on zinc contracted for 25,000,000 lb. of zinc at a price that was about one-third below that ruling at the time. When ship-plates were selling at £32 a ton the sub-committee on steel got them for the Navy at less than £12 a ton, and the sub-committee on aluminium obtained that metal, the market price of which was nineteen pence per lb., at a cost per lb. of fivepence less. The respective sub-committees on oil and chemicals succeeded in obtaining them for the Government at substantial reductions.

Mobilisation of raw materials

As striking was the success of Mr. Rosenwald and his Committee on Supplies. Their immediate function was to advise and assist the purchasing bureaux of the War and Navy Departments as regards clothing, food, and equipment. They did away with Government advertisement for supplies, as being likely to encourage wasteful competition in war time. The competition of Government Departments with each other was eliminated. Specifications were drafted for providing substitutes for articles difficult or impossible to procure in the quantities required. Middlemen were told that their services were dispensed with. This committee actually bought large supplies for the Government at figures existing at the beginning of the war, and in some cases at prices lower than those which prevailed at that time. It also obtained " options " on extensive supplies of leather and other needed articles at what were practically pre-war quotations. Like the Committee on Raw Materials, and other committees, this committee created sub-committees, and these dealt with the cotton, woollen, shoe and leather, knitted goods, and mattress industries, all of which were mobilised effectively, mills and factories that never before had done work for the Government falling into line. For expediting the delivery of goods " field agents " were appointed to see that no time was lost. As happened with Mr. Baruch and his co-workers, so Mr. Rosenwald and those aiding him were instrumental in effecting large savings in the purchases of the various departments of the Government.

The mining and distributing of coal was mobilised by an organisation set up by the Council of National Defence somewhat later than most of the others. It was called the Committee on Coal Production, and its chairman was Mr. F. S. Peabody, of the Peabody Coal Company of Chicago. Almost at the start it gave much help to the Government in averting strikes among the miners, notably in Pennsylvania. It investigated the problems of haulage, and arranged that coal should be distributed fairly and evenly through the carrying agencies by land and water for the country, while at the same time it saw to the requirements of the Navy and other departments. It conferred with the lake shippers of coal and ore and with the railways, the result being that shippers, railways, and vessels would probably be able to carry to the head of the lakes some additional two and a half million tons of coal, and bring in return the same tonnage of ore, chiefly iron. Prior to this the railways had been completely mobilised, at the instance of Mr. Willard, under the aegis of the Advisory Commission, in co-operation with a special committee, sitting at Washington, of the American Railway Association, comprising the heads of the chief lines of the United States. Over 260,000 miles of railroads were in effect placed in the hands of the Government for war purposes. The railway executives issued orders that coal should be given preference in supply and movement, and that ore should come next.

Government and the railways

Mr. Willard's committee, termed the Committee on Transportation and Communications, took as its slogan railway efficiency for the nation rather than for the individual, and bent all its energies towards that end. It organised co-operative committees and sub-committees on telegraphs and telephones, on military passenger and freight tariffs, on cars and locomotives, on electric railways. It divided up the railway systems of the country into six areas, so as to have local as well as general control. For this purpose it enlisted the services, which were given gratuitously, of all the presidents and high officials of the various lines in each of these areas. A complete scheme was drawn up, in connection with officers of the Army, for facilitating the movement of troops and supplies. The committee, backed by the American Railway Association, made itself responsible for raising nine reserve engineer regiments, composed of skilled railwaymen, to aid in the rehabilitation of the railways in France, as well as in the operation of the French railways behind the British front. Earlier Mr. Willard assisted in the creation of a commission, of which Mr. John Stephens, formerly Chief Engineer of the Panama Canal, was chairman, who with four other prominent railway engineers went to Russia, by way of Vladivostock, to find out what materials or men should be sent to help the Russians. Mr. Willard, through Mr. Theodore N. Vail, president of the American Telephone and Telegraph Company, arranged for the utilisation of the telephone and telegraph systems of the country. This involved the special drilling of some 12,000 telephone long-distance operators, and an increase of wires from 148 to 294 at Washington for long-distance communications. More than 10,000 miles of special systems were taken from commercial use, and devoted exclusively to the Navy and other departments,

Lord Northcliffe, appointed head of the British War Mission in the U.S.A., June, 1917.

The United States Military Academy at West Point was established in 1802 on the site of an old military post on the Hudson, once the headqua of George Washington. A four years' course of training is provided for cadets seeking commissions in the U.S. Army.

Hon. Newton D. Baker, Secretary of War, distributing diplomas to West Point cadets, 19

The U.S. Marine Corps was established in 1793, when war with France was threatened, with a complement of 720 privates, 129 officers, 32 drummers and fife-players. In 1917 the corps comprised over 20,000 officers and men.

Soldiers and sailors too: U.S. Marines from the Atlantic Fleet on parade in Cuba.

rd Kitchener, visiting West Point in 1910, declared that the College stood on the highest level of military instructional institutions, and recommended it to the Australian and New Zealand Governments as the model for the military college they required.

t the graduation exercises at Battle Monument, Trophy Point, 139 lieutenants received commissions.

ressive scene at the unveiling of a memorial to Lafayette in Brooklyn, May 10th, 1917. The ceremony was attended by M. Viviani, Marshal Joffre, and other members of the French Mission to the U.S.A. M. Viviani is speaking after the unveiling.

French commissioners at the unveiling of a Lafayette memorial in Brooklyn, May 10th, 1917.

America mobilises: Fifth Avenue beflagged in honour of the new armies.

while telephone connections were established with all lighthouses and coastguard stations.

Men of science also were mobilised. At the request of the Council of National Defence, the National Research Council maintained at Washington an active committee for co-operation in matters pertaining to scientific research for war objects. The Research Council made a close-knit organisation of the scientific forces of the country, and engaged it in such investigations as the study of devices for detecting completely submerged submarines and mines, of range-finders, military photography, new explosives, and balloon fabrics, besides making improvements in wireless apparatus, and seeing to the utilisation of wastes and by-products. Reports were made on the process to be used for producing nitrates for explosives and fertilisers, and the supplying of optical glass for military purposes was considered. Anti-toxins and serums for diphtheria, tetanus, pneumonia, dysentery, and meningitis were closely studied. Among other matters investigated were the diseases of munition workers, protection of the ear from high explosives, and protection from noxious gases. Some of these labours of the men of science impinged on the work of medical men. Under Dr. Franklin H. Martin, a member of the Advisory Commission, a medical section or committee was created which mobilised the civilian medical resources of the United States, and immediately set about the selection of thoroughly qualified civilian doctors for increasing the medical staff of the Army and Navy. As many as 21,000 competent men were picked out, and the services of 3,500 medical students in their last year were made available. A General Medical Board met at stated intervals at Washington to advise and assist the Surgeons-General of the Army, Navy, Public Health Service, and the Red Cross, and at its instance decisive steps were taken for the hygienic and moral welfare of the soldiers and sailors of the nation.

One of the most interesting, as well as significant, developments of the multitudinous activities of the Council of National Defence was its **Women's work** formation, as early as April 21st, 1917, **in the war** of a Committee on Women's Defence Work, under the chairmanship of Dr. Anna Howard Shaw, by means of which the women of the United States were mobilised. With its centre at Washington, it had head and subordinate organisations of women in every State of the Union, who took charge of the movement locally, and it speedily assumed immense proportions. Among the things that came into its purview were home relief, allied relief, conservation and thrift, the protection of women workers, and the health and welfare of children. It also had courses of instruction concerning women's work in the war and training classes in work for which the Government furnished a demand, such as motor service and wireless telegraphy, a direction in which it found more and more to do as men were called up for the Army.

To the women of America Mr. Hoover, the Food Administrator, issued a special appeal, which the Women's Committee made its own. He asked them to stop throwing any food away if it could be used, to order meals so as not to have too much, to have a proper balance of the most nutritious foods, to stop catering to different appetites, to have no second helpings, no eating between meals, no four o'clock teas, no refreshments at parties and dances, no suppers after the theatre, no young lamb, no veal, no young pigs killed, no young meat of any sort, no butter in cooking. And he also requested them to institute one meatless and one wheatless day a week. He finally invited them all to join in the conservation of food by accepting membership in the Food Administration of the United States, and by signing a pledge to carry out, in conducting their households, the directions of the Food Administrator.

In all the vast mobilisation of the materials of the United States, through the Council of National Defence and its affiliations, there could not help being mistakes, shortcomings, and dislocations. The general unpreparedness of the nation for war, apart from munitions, was such that practically everything else had to be built up from the ground. As was well said, the country was in something of the position of a private manufacturer who was forced, almost over night, to increase the capacity of his work far beyond anything he had ever imagined possible. The truly wonderful thing was that so much was done, and well done. The scale was colossal, the pace prodigious, the results amazing. Hardly anything was omitted. The organisation of an Aircraft Production Board by the Council came somewhat later, but months before the declaration of war Mr. Howard Coffin had an aircraft association in active being, and it eventually received the recognition of the Council. Mr. Coffin had devoted special attention to every phase of aviation, and he consistently urged **Organisation of** that the construction of large fleets of **aircraft production** aircraft, with trained and efficient aviators in proportion, should be made a leading feature of the war programme of the United States. Congress at first, however, did not assign a very large sum for aircraft production, but Mr. Coffin and those who were working with him went ahead, and harmonised, standardised, and unified all branches of the aviation manufacture and service. One of the things they had to do was to find the best type of engine, and they found it. Profiting by expert European assistance and a close study of the machines used at the front, they evolved and perfected an engine of great power.

In the meantime the American public was thinking of aircraft a good deal, as the result of a vigorous aircraft-production "publicity campaign." It was pointed out by Mr. Coffin and others that here was a field that the United States could make peculiarly its own. It was right for this to be done. Was not America the birthplace of the aeroplane? Further, it was contended with much force that if Great Britain and France had possessed overwhelming superiority in the air they would already have won the war. Mr. Coffin and Admiral Peary went before the committees of Congress, stated their case, and asked for an appropriation of over a hundred millions sterling. The country backed them up with enthusiasm. Mr. Baker, the Secretary of War, issued a statement advocating a rapid increase in the number of American machines for the front. In July, Congress voted six hundred and forty million dollars, or nearly £130,000,000, for the development of Mr. Coffin's great aviation plans. No fewer than twenty-four aviation fields were authorised, and some of them were quickly established—notably one at Dayton, Ohio, **Mr. Coffin's** the "home-town" of Orville Wright. **great plans** Nine aviation schools were founded, six being for the Army and three for the Navy. The mark at which the United States aimed was the construction of 22,000 machines in the shortest time.

Thanks also to Mr. Coffin, the Council had on its files more than 27,000 detailed reports from the larger manufacturing plants of the country as to the capacity of those plants to meet the military as well as the industrial needs of the Government in time of war. In the case of only one of the Council's numerous Boards and committees could there be said to be failure, and that later was put right, though not till after a good deal of time had been lost. This was its Committee on Shipping, formed to advise the U.S. Shipping Board, which, as already stated, had been authorised by Congress through Mr. McAdoo's exertions. It was decided in April by the Shipping Board, of which Mr. William Denman, of San Francisco, was chairman, not only to produce all the steel ships possible, but to build one thousand wooden vessels, each of about

GERMAN SAILORS INTERNED IN AMERICA.

Sailors from German ships who were interned at Fort McPherson, Georgia, setting out on their day's task under armed guards. They were set to work constructing new quarters for themselves and other internees.

When the United States entered the war the sailors on the many enemy ships which had sought the security of neutral ports in America were promptly removed to internment camps.

3,000 tons, on a standardised plan, and by utilising small shipbuilding plants and the lumber mills.

This scheme of the wooden ships was approved by the Government, and it was agreed to put the supervision of contracts and the construction of these craft into the hands of a subsidiary organisation, which was designated the Emergency Fleet Corporation. General Goethals, who had been chief of the Board that had completed the building of the Panama Canal, was called in as director of the new corporation; but almost immediately it became involved in controversies with the Shipping Board over technical matters. It became clear presently that he and Mr. Denman could not work together, and serious **Government-built** delays were the result. President Wilson, **merchant marine** who was eager and determined to get as many ships at sea in the shortest time, found it necessary in the national interest to accept the resignation of General Goethals and to request that of Mr. Denman. On July 24th he named as their successors Admiral Capps, Chief Constructor of the Navy, and Mr. Edward N. Hurley, of Illinois, the former chairman of the Federal Trade Commission. Thereafter the gigantic project of a Government-built merchant marine was developed with greater energy and success.

While the United States, under the strong leadership of its President, was mobilising its money and its materials, with their personnel, it was at the same time mobilising its Army, Navy, and man-power under the same energetic driving force. At the beginning of April its Regular Army consisted of about 130,000 troops, but of these nearly 35,000 were stationed in the Philippines, Panama, Hawaii, Porto Rico, and China, and of the rest a considerable proportion were non-combatants. As it could hardly reduce the strength of its forces lying outside its territory proper, it did not dispose in America of more than about 80,000 fighting men. So far as it went, the Army was excellent in quality—well-officered, well-drilled, and well equipped. It was organised in three divisions and a cavalry division; and, besides, there were detachments for coast defence. The infantry consisted of thirty-eight regiments of three battalions, each of four companies, the peace strength of a company being three officers and one hundred men. The cavalry comprised seventeen regiments of three squadrons, each squadron having three officers and seventy troopers. There were nine regiments of field-artillery, each of six batteries with four guns apiece, and three regiments of engineers. In addition there was a coast artillery corps of about 20,000 men. Enlistment was voluntary throughout, but this system worked very imperfectly.

280

As a second line to the Federal Army came the National Guard, an organised militia belonging to the different States of the Union, but controlled by the Central Government, which gave grants in aid to each State's contributions for the maintenance of its own particular militiamen. Though its training and equipment were assimilated to that of the Regulars, it was not intended for service abroad. It comprised over 120 regiments of infantry, besides many separate battalions and companies of foot, three regiments of cavalry with several separate squadrons and troops, nine regiments of field-artillery with separate battalions and batteries, one regiment of engineers with separate auxiliaries, a signal corps, field hospital, and other details, including nearly 150 companies of coast artillery. Of a total strength of about 150,000 men, it could put into the field, according to a fair estimate, upwards of two-thirds of that number. Enlistment in the National Guard, as in the Army, was voluntary, and this system in this regard did not work well. An advocate of "national preparedness" through universal military service wrote: "Simple facts show that volunteering for the Regular Army is a failure, and everyone knows also that the National Guard system is worse than a failure."

Realising how unready for war on the European scale the United States was, the Allies did not expect the immediate or early appearance of American soldiers in the battle-line. It was understood, furthermore, that it was the opinion of the American General Staff that no troops should be sent out of the country to support the Entente Armies until a really large force had been trained and equipped. Not a few Americans maintained, even after war was declared, that it was undesirable as well as unnecessary to despatch troops abroad. On the other hand, Mr. Roosevelt pressed hard for the despatch to France at once of an expeditionary force which he himself was taking steps to raise. **Congress and** His plans went so far that over 200,000 **conscription** officers and men had given him their pledge to join this force as soon as it was authorised. From the very first the President planned to raise very large forces, in addition to vastly increasing the strength of the Regulars and Militia, and among the initial war measures that he submitted to Congress was a Bill to authorise conscription. The Army was to be increased to its full strength of 293,000 men, the National Guard similarly to 440,000 men, by voluntary enlistment; but he called for the formation of a new National Army based on the principle of universal liability to service. Congress did not much like the idea of conscription. Though compulsory service had been introduced in the Civil War, it was as unpalatable to Americans as it had been to the British—and opposition to it was keen, especially in the House of Representatives, where some of the leading Democrats, Mr. Wilson's own political supporters, spoke almost violently against it. The country was divided on the subject, and, generally speaking, looked askance at it. But the President, ably supported by Mr. Roosevelt and other stalwarts, brought both Congress and the country into line—a most notable achievement.

It had taken the British two years to accept conscription ; the United States adopted it in six weeks. After several days' debate, both the Senate and the House, on April 28th, passed Bills for raising an Army of 500,000 men by "selective" conscription, the Senate by 81 to 8, and the House of Representatives by 397 to 24 votes ; but the former put the age-limits at twenty-one to twenty-seven, while the latter fixed them at twenty-one to forty. A storm raged round the limits of age, but the President controlled it. Meanwhile, the Senate adopted a provision authorising him to accept the volunteer expeditionary force which Mr. Roosevelt had offered to raise for immediate service in France, and the House was disposed to agree. While acknowledging the patriotic spirit of Mr. Roosevelt, Mr. Wilson declined the proposal, chiefly on the ground that its plan included the services of officers of the Army who could not be spared —he had already resolved on sending troops to France. The pressure exerted by Mr. Roosevelt was not, however, without a certain effect, as no doubt it prepared the country for the immediate despatch of **The Selective** troops to the front, a request for which **Draft Act** had been made by Marshal Joffre, the military head of the French Mission, who arrived at Washington on April 25th, three days after the British Mission, of which Mr. Balfour was the chief, had reached the American capital.

After various conferences and much discussion, the House finally passed the Selective Conscription Bill in accordance with the views of President Wilson on May 16th, and the Senate followed suit next day. On the 18th the Bill become law on its being signed by him. This Emergency Army Act, generally termed the Selective Draft Act, applied in round figures to ten millions of men between twenty-one and thirty, inclusive, who were to register on June 5th. A noteworthy feature of the Act was its list of exemptions, which was left practically to the judgment of the President ; but it was made clear that there would be no interference with any of the industries essential for the proper conduct of the war or of the national life. As usual with him, President Wilson took pains to impress his views on the people. In explaining and justifying this measure, which was nothing short of revolutionary, he said that it was not so much an army that had to be trained and shaped for war as the nation itself. **The day of enrolment**

The whole nation (he remarked) must be a team in which each man shall play the part for which he is best fitted. To this end Congress has provided that the nation shall be organised for war by selection, that each man shall be classified for service in the place to which it shall best serve the general good to call him.

The preferences of individuals had to give way before the common cause.

Thus, though a sharpshooter pleases to operate a trip-hammer for the forging of great guns, and an expert machinist desires to march with the flag, the nation is being served only when the sharpshooter marches and the machinist remains at his levers.

Local Boards to consider claims to exemptions, and District Boards to revise them, were appointed, but the final adjudication, if such were required, lay with the President. It was alleged by some Americans who were against the war that the registration of the ten million young men would occasion grave disturbances throughout the country ; but when the great day of enrolment arrived, and with it the ten millions, or close on that figure, no serious trouble occurred anywhere, though the noisy pacifists did their utmost to cause it. In some States the number registered was larger than had been expected, in others it was smaller, but the evasions were not important in any part of the land. The final returns registered 9,649,938 names. The draft ultimately yielded 687,000 men for the new army, and, as also had been arranged, for filling vacancies in the ranks of the Regulars and of the National Guard.

What was truly described as the greatest lottery in the history of the world took place at Washington on July 20th

HUTS OF A NEW JERSEY TRAINING CAMP.

Sentry on duty on a raised platform overlooking Camp Dix, in New Jersey. This was one of the extensive training camps established for the conversion of civilians into soldiers on the adoption by the United States of the principle of universal military service, which applied in round figures to ten millions of America's citizens from the age of twenty-one to thirty. The first draft was made on July 20th, 1917.

when the men of the new army were drafted. They had been selected from among the nine million and odd men on a carefully-worked-out system, and the actual drawing was surrounded with every safeguard and with much solemnity, members of Congress and officers of the Army being amongst those present. The Exemption District Boards had previously been told to take all the registration cards in their district, shuffle them, and then number them serially from one to the highest number represented by the total number of the cards. These numbers were published locally, so that each man registered knew his number ; they were also sent to Washington for the information of the War Department. Of the 4,557 districts, the most populous district exceeded 10,200 numbers, and it was determined to draw 10,500 numbers. Slips numbered from 1 to 10,500 were then enclosed in black capsules, which were put in a large glass bowl. Mr. Baker, the War Secretary, was blindfolded and drew the first number, which was 258. This meant that in every district the man whose number was 258 was drafted for the Army. Some of the prominent people present next were blindfolded, and drew from the glass bowl in the same way. Clerks, also blindfolded, drew the rest. The numbers drawn were then telegraphed to the districts and published in the papers, so that everybody knew very soon who had been selected. In the meantime the War Department was preparing sixteen large cantonments for the housing and training of these men, who were to assemble in September. These cantonments, each with a population of about 40,000, were biggish towns, and care was taken to build them well. About the same time sixteen mobilisation camps were established for the National Guard,

Drafting the new army

to the number of 350,000 men, whom the President had called up.

It was evident that there would have to be officers, more and more officers, both for the expanded Army and National Guard, as well as for the new army. Neither the existing Army nor the existing National Guard could supply anything like enough. West Point and the military colleges could do something, and did it ; but hundreds and hundreds more were required. The demand was far in excess of the supply—just as it had been in Great Britain. Then a plan was initiated for an Officers Reserve Corps, from which ten thousand officers were to be provided. To have the honour and glory of being among " The First Ten Thousand " more than forty-five thousand young and able-bodied citizens threw up their jobs or closed their offices to learn soldiering and qualify as officers in sixteen large training camps.

There was, fortunately, already the nucleus of such an

organisation. Years before, General Leonard Wood, a man of the stamp of Earl Roberts, had preached the gospel of national preparedness for war, and, like Roberts, had suffered from officialism for it ; but his words were not altogether without fruit. Thanks to him, there was established a voluntary and self-supporting body called the Officers Training Camps Association, which opened a training camp at Plattsburg, on Lake Champlain. The experiment proved a success, and other training camps modelled on it came into existence and prospered. After war was declared the U.S. Government adopted and developed General Wood's scheme, and these forty-five thousand officers in embryo were the result. The course of training was hard, intensive, relentless, and many could not stand the test ; but the majority persevered, and " won through." As early as August nearly 10 per cent. of them had received their commissions. The aim of each of the sixteen camps was to furnish officers for a division apiece—for infantry, cavalry, artillery, engineers, and the other units— all the officers necessary for sixteen divisions.

In America the military profession had not been a popular one, and the ordinary soldier, or " enlisted man," as he was designated with some contempt by the public generally, was not held in any particular esteem ; he was regarded rather in the light of a special policeman who had certain work assigned to him which the ordinary policeman did not do. War seemed far away, unlikely, almost impossible, and therefore the Army was a very secondary consideration. Compared with the fascinating and absorbing pursuit of the " almighty dollar " it was no-where. But war induced a

REMOVING GAS-MASKS.
[American official photograph.
American troops in training in France undergoing gas-mask drill, in preparation for facing the new horror which Germany had imported into warfare. Inset : Captain Heintz, of the 1st Ohio Regiment, wearing the improved gas-mask that had been adopted by the United States War Department.

different spirit and set up a new standard. Yet such a change in the national outlook could not but take time for its effects to be felt throughout the whole community. In the conditions which still obtained in America in April and May, 1917, the military mobilisation of the .United States, considered apart from its naval mobilisation, presently to be narrated, was not less marvellous than its financial and industrial mobilisation. In the autumn more than a million and a quarter Americans were trained or training for the fighting-line. Within six months the United States had added a million men to its Army, and contemplated with calmness and resolution raising as many more millions as might be thought necessary. A first contingent arrived in France on June 26th.

Mention has been made already of the steps the President took with respect to increasing the strength of the Navy prior to the declaration of war, and of the large additions to the Fleet which Secretary Daniels had induced Congress to authorise. On April 6th the U.S. Navy

Mobilisation of the U.S. Navy had in commission sixteen battleships, three armoured cruisers, one first-class cruiser, two second-class cruisers, eleven third-class cruisers, fifty-eight destroyers, four monitors, thirty-seven submarines, three transports, eighteen gunboats, four supply-ships, twenty fuel-ships, seven converted yachts, forty-eight tugs, and seven tenders to repair vessels. All these ships were fully manned and prepared for war. In commission in reserve there were eighteen battleships, six armoured cruisers, three first-class cruisers, one second-class cruiser, three third-class cruisers, eight destroyers, one torpedo-boat, two monitors, and two gunboats. These vessels had on board from 40 to 50 per cent. of full crews, and enough of officers and men for speedily placing them in commission. In commission in " ordinary " were two destroyers, one monitor, three submarines, and torpedo-boats. These ships had in them only a sufficient number of men to keep them in order and the machinery and equipment from deterioration. As quickly as possible all warships in reserve and in " ordinary " were fully officered and manned, and put into active service.

By an early date in May the mobilisation was complete, and provision besides was made for the officers and men for the additional ships and boats which were being—or were already—taken over by the Navy as scouts, supply-ships, motor-boat scouts, transports, and other auxiliaries. In May, on the President's suggestion through the Secretary of the Navy, Congress voted to increase the enlisted strength of the Navy to 150,000 men. On March 25th the personnel of the Navy stood at 61,000 ; a month later it reached 81,000, and in May it was well beyond 100,000, a gain of over 40,000 men, all voluntarily enlisted, in about two months. In the same time the Marine Corps rose above 20,000 men, an increase of about 6,000. The needed officers for the ships were found to some extent in the regular Navy itself and in the Naval Reserves and Naval Militia. As part of his programme for the enlargement of the Navy, Secretary Daniels had given particular attention to the Naval Academy at Annapolis, and on his recommendation Congress had doubled the number of midshipmen students to provide more officers.

In addition to the existing strength in ships of the Navy, there were under construction, or authorised to be built, fifteen battleships, six battle-cruisers, thirteen scouts, fifty-seven destroyers, one hundred and one submarines, two gunboats, four fuel-ships, two transports, a supply-ship, a hospital-ship, two ammunition-ships, three tenders, and a repair-ship. Three of them were due to be completed in 1917—one of them, the super-Dreadnought New Mexico, was launched that April. All three were super-Dreadnoughts, as were also two other ships which were to be ready in 1918. Of the thirty-two battleships mobilised, fourteen were Dreadnoughts or super-Dreadnoughts, their displacement ranging from 16,000 tons in the older vessels to 31,400 tons in the newer, and their armament from

(Official photograph.

AMERICA'S GREAT LIBERTY LOAN.
The four leading men who took part in the raising of the five billion dollar Liberty Loan in the United States in the autumn of 1917. Left to right they are (standing) : Dr. Nicholas Murray Butler, President of Columbia University, and Mr. J. Pierpont Morgan ; (seated) Lord Reading, of the British Mission, and Mr. Benjamin Strong, jun., Governor of the Federal Reserve Bank.

eight 12 in. to twelve 14 in. guns. The two newest ships, the Pennsylvania and the Arizona, were of the 31,400 tonnage. Besides the twelve 14 in., they had twenty-two 5 in. guns, and their speed was twenty-one knots an hour. They were the largest warships in the world, though Japan could show vessels of nearly equal size and power. The New Mexico and the other four capital ships completing were to have similar batteries and speeds, but had a slightly greater tonnage—32,000 tons. Rapid progress was made with the turning out of new submarine-chasers of a better sort than had been built before. Some were constructed in the New York and New **Allied naval** Orleans Government yards, others in **co-operation** private yards. Within five weeks from the time the first keels were laid down quite a number of these exceptionally speedy craft were on active service. The German and Austrian ships seized in American harbours were, in some cases, turned over to the Navy, the rest being placed at the disposal of the Shipping Board.

During the latter part of March, when war was palpably nearer, the officers and men of the U.S. Navy had been hard at work getting their ships in a thorough state of preparedness, and after war was declared a large part of the Fleet was ready for instant action. The President had resolved on making use of it at once in co-operation with the Fleets of the Allies. In the second week of April a conference of U.S. naval officials took place at Washington, and the British and French naval commanders in the Atlantic participated in it. Rear-Admiral Sims had already left for London to get into closest touch with the British Admiralty, and as early as May 4th flotillas of fast American destroyers were energetically assisting in European waters in the campaign against the U boats.

Unloading the German mine-laying submarine UC5 at 132nd Street, New York, for purposes of exhibition as a specimen of German piracy, and as a stimulus to subscriptions to the Liberty Loan.

Official photographs of a British "tank" from the battlefields of Europe and of the captured submarine UC5 that were sent to participate in the demonstration in New York in aid of the Liberty Loan in October, 1917. A hundred thousand people took part in the display.

SPECTACULAR FEATURES IN THE NEW YORK DEMONSTRATION TO STIMULATE THE SALE OF LIBERTY BONDS.

AMERICAN TROOPS IN FRANCE | CHAPTER CCV. | AT BAYONET DRILL.

FIRST PHASES OF AMERICA'S CO-OPERATION WITH THE ALLIES.

By Robert Machray.

President Wilson's Large Conceptions—Closest Co-operation with the Entente Powers—Offensive, not Defensive, War to be Waged—How Hostilities Began—British Mission under Mr. Balfour Arrives at Washington—Magnificent Welcome—Purpose and Work of the Mission—The French Mission under M. Viviani and Marshal Joffre—American Fast Destroyers Operate in European Waters—Admiral Sims in Command—Coming of the Advance Guard of the U.S. Army—General Pershing, Commander-in-Chief, at Liverpool—Goes to London and Paris—American Troops Land in France—Attacked by German Submarines on the Voyage—The Spy Menace In and To the U.S.—German Intrigue—American Pacifists—Splendid Success of the Liberty Loan—Great Red Cross Rally—The Espionage Act Passed—Embargo on Neutrals Tightens the Blockade of Germany—Lord Northcliffe's Mission—Co-ordination of Mutual Efforts—President's Strenuous Fight for Food Control—Profiteering Denounced—New War Industries Board Created—Allied Purchasing Commission Formed—Germany's Peace Offensive—Effect in America—Hardening of Opinion against Germany—Food Control Act Passed—Herbert Hoover Appointed Food Administrator—Food Problems Firmly Handled—Fresh German Peace Manœuvres—The Vatican Note—President Wilson's Determined Reply—The Gerard Revelations—Growing American War Preparations—" Old Glory " on the March in London—Significant Signs of the Militarising of the U.S.—Sweden and Mexico Involved—America Angry—Vast Expenditures for War Envisaged by the United States—Enormous Sums Again Allocated to the Allies.

 THE American mobilisation, described in our preceding chapter, marvellous in the circumstances as it was, was only the beginning of things. Immediately after the war resolution was passed, President Wilson took such belligerent action as was possible by seizing forthwith the German ships that were lying in American harbours — ninety vessels, with a total of 600,000 tons and a value of £25,000,000. Four days later he did the same with respect to Austrian ships, fourteen in number, and in all of about 70,000 tons, which were in American ports. Most of these vessels, which had been interned since the war began, had been damaged intentionally by their crews, but not to such an extent as to render them beyond repair. Some were handed over to the Navy and the rest to the Shipping Board, the organisation which had been created two years before for furthering the interests of the American Mercantile Marine. Ten days after the seizure of the Austrian ships the President took possession of the fine docks and piers of the Hamburg-Amerika

LORD EUSTACE PERCY.
Lord Eustace Percy, of the British Foreign Office, was a member, as blockade expert, of the British Commission that went to Washington in the spring of 1917.

and the North German Lloyd steamship lines at Hoboken. On April 7th, at the lonely island of Guam in the Pacific, the German auxiliary cruiser Cormoran, which was interned there, was summoned to surrender by the local American forces, but her crew blew her up. Twenty of her officers and upwards of three hundred of her men, however, were captured, and became America's first German prisoners of war. Large numbers of German spies in various parts of the United States were arrested and imprisoned, sixty-five of them being locked up on April 6th alone. All suspected persons were kept under strict surveillance by the clever and vigilant secret service agents of the Government. Troops were detailed to guard docks, depots, public buildings, and bridges, as well as the chief points on the railways and waterways of the country. The Navy put out to sea to protect the coast from attack and to safeguard shipping from the U boats.

From the outset President Wilson was·in close touch with the Allies, and that he might get on still more intimate terms with them he asked them to send special Missions to Washington.

FRENCH OFFICERS REVIEW THE HARVARD REGIMENT.
French Army officers on the steps of the Harvard Club, Boston, Mass., salute the American flag carried past at a review of the men of the Reserve Officers Training Corps of Harvard. The French officers were some of those who had been assigned by their Government to assist the students of Harvard University in their military training.

The Entente Powers gladly accepted the invitation, and selected as members of these Missions the most suitable men — men who were not only distinguished, but who were pre-eminently well fitted for the work that was in view. In the American newspapers it was announced on April 11th that an Allied War Council would be held in the capital very shortly, and that it " would be attended by delegations from Great Britain and France, including British Foreign Secretary Balfour, ex-Premier Viviani of France, and General Joffre," as one New York journal phrased it. But all the Allies had been requested to send special Missions—Russia, for whom since the Revolution the United States showed a particular solicitude, Italy, Japan, Belgium, and the rest. The President wanted to hear everything.

On the day when the news was given to the American public of the coming of the Missions there was a conference at Washington, as the Americans were also permitted to know, of British and French naval officers on the Atlantic stations with high officials of the U.S. Navy, the subject of discussion being the effective participation of American warships in patrolling the Atlantic and destroying the German submarines. The British public in general learned nothing of all the encouraging signs which suggested the fullness of the co-operation of

the United States till some time afterwards. Considerations of prudence sealed for a while the lips of the Governments of the Entente. Some of the Missions had to cross three thousand miles of sea, while others had to make still longer voyages—and there were many U boats about.

The first of the Missions to arrive in America was that of Great Britain. Leaving the shores of England on April 11th, it reached Halifax, Nova Scotia, nine days later, after an uneventful passage. A special train, with steam up, had been waiting for it for some time, and extraordinary precautions were taken to safeguard its journey to Washington, which, however, was made without the occurrence of any misadventure or striking incident. The Mission was in the capital on the afternoon of the 22nd. Its composition was highly significant. At its head was Mr. Balfour, the Secretary for Foreign Affairs, who had been requested by the War Cabinet to occupy that position. With him was Lord Cunliffe of Headley, the Governor of the Bank of England. The other members were Sir Eric Drummond, Mr. Ian Malcolm, M.P., Mr. Dormer, and Mr. G. Butler, representing the Foreign Office ; Rear-Admiral Sir Dudley de Chair and his private secretary, Fleet-Paymaster Lawford, of the Admiralty ; Major-General G. T. M. Bridges and Captain Spender Clay, M.P.

JAPANESE MISSION IN NEW YORK.
Members of the Japanese Mission to the United States, in 1917, with the welcoming committee, on the steps of the New York City Hall. Viscount Ishii, head of the Mission, is in the centre of the front row, with Judge E. H. Gary on his right, and on his left Mr. Mitchel, the Mayor of New York, Mr. Aimaro Sato, Japanese Ambassador to the United States, and Admiral T. Takeshita, of the Imperial Japanese Navy.

with Colonel J. H. T. C. Goodwin, R.A.M.C.; Colonel Heron, C.B., Army Ordnance Department; Major Puckle, Army Service Corps; and Major L. W. B. Rees, V.C., M.C., R.G.A., Flying Corps, representing various branches of the Army; Lord Eustace Percy and Mr. Peterson, of the Foreign Trade Department; Mr. F. P. Robinson, Board of Trade; and Mr. Stephen McKenna, War Trade Intelligence Department, for the Blockade Office; Mr. W. T. Layton, Mr. C. T. Phillips, Mr. M. S. Amos, and Captain J. A. Leeming, R.E., for the Ministry of Munitions; and Mr. A. G. Anderson and Mr. Vigor, representing the Wheat Commission. Some of these and a few other members appeared on the scene soon afterwards, and completed the notable list of experts.

In the personnel of the Mission were included men representing all the manifold activities of Great Britain in the war, and this was precisely what President Wilson had desired. Among the British people there was at first some criticism of Mr. Balfour's appointment as chief of the Mission, but it very quickly disappeared. In his presence misunderstandings disappeared and prejudices melted away.

Combating pro-German misrepresentation

It was well that this was the case, for there was something, despite the enthusiastic reception that was given him on his arrival, that had to be faced and conquered. This was a certain amount—not very large, yet formidable enough—of distinctly anti-British feeling, which arose not so much from out of the old historic background of the two peoples with its antagonisms as from the calculated misrepresentation by German elements in America of British policy in general and of British motives and aims in the war in particular. Mr. Balfour did his best to clear the clouds away, and in a great measure succeeded in doing so by his lucid and logical statements of the actual facts of the case. If he did not make Great Britain universally popular, it was true, at any rate, that, as was said in a semi-official declaration at the time, he placed the relations between his own country and the United States on a better footing than had existed since the secession of the American colonies. That in itself was no small service, whether to the Allies who had already fought so hard for the common cause, or to President Wilson in his persistent effort to educate American opinion in the mass, and concentrate its energies on the most vigorous prosecution of the war.

But Mr. Balfour and his Mission had other ends in view besides charming Americans and creating a clearer and better atmosphere for the British. In reply to a question as to the purpose of the British Mission, Mr. Lansing said that Mr. Balfour and the others had not come to ask for anything, but that a considerable part of their business was to recount the mistakes the Allies had made, and advise opposite courses of action. Naturally, that was not all.

Among the many compliments and attentions showered on Mr. Balfour none was more striking than his being invited to address Congress—an exceptional honour and one that was unique in the case of a British subject. In his speech to the House of Representatives, delivered on May 5th, he said:

> Mr. Speaker, the compliment paid to the Mission from Great Britain by such an assembly, upon such an occasion, is one that not one of us is ever likely to forget. But there is something, after all, of even deeper significance in the circumstances in which I now have the honour to address you than any which arise out of an interchange of courtesies, however sincere, between two great friendly nations. We all, I think, instinctively feel that this is one of the great moments in the history of the world, and that what is now happening on both sides of the Atlantic represents a drawing together of great and free peoples for mutual protection against the aggression of military despotism. . . . It is against that danger that we free peoples of the Western civilisation have found ourselves together. It is in that great cause that we are going to fight, and are fighting at this very moment, side by side.

In these last words was stated the purpose of the Mission—"fighting at this very moment, side by side," America and the Allies. It was on the stern business of war that the Mission had crossed the Atlantic, and on no other. It had come to give and to receive help in the common prosecution of hostilities until the aggression of military despotism was so completely met

MAJOR L. W. B. REES, V.C.
Major Rees, V.C., M.C., R.G.A., Royal Flying Corps, was a member of Mr. Balfour's Mission to the United States in the spring of 1917.

WEST POINT CADETS IN WASHINGTON.
March of West Point Cadets down Pennsylvania Avenue, Washington, at a parade of troops held on the United States declaring that a state of war existed with Germany. They were approaching the Capitol, which is situated at the end of the avenue to the left.

and nullified that never again would the free peoples of the world be called on to undergo a similar experience. Mr. Balfour had brought with him a body of experts in war, and not only in war, but in this particular war, with its individual features. Each of these men got into quick association with the corresponding heads of departments and their experts, discussed matters, and arranged for action with regard to the vital things—naval and military co-operation, tightening the blockade of Germany, munitions, money, food, shipping, and the like. Many of these British experts remained in the United States after Mr. Balfour and the other members of the Mission had returned home. To the British experts with Mr. Balfour were soon added the experts of the French Mission, which arrived at Washington on April 25th, headed by Marshal Joffre and M. Viviani, who not long before had been Prime Minister of France.

GENERAL PERSHING'S ARRIVAL IN LONDON.
The officially formal but sincerely cordial welcome to London of the Commander-in-Chief of the American Expeditionary Force, June 7th, 1917. Left to right : General Pershing, Dr. Page (American Ambassador), Admiral Sims, Lord Derby (Secretary for War), Field-Marshal Viscount French.

Like Mr. Balfour, both Marshal Joffre and M. Viviani met with the most cordial reception. There was no anti-French feeling in the United States ; on the contrary, American sentiment, recalling the assistance given during the War of Independence by Lafayette and Rochambeau, was solid for France. The United States was full of praise of her heroism and of sympathy with her in her sufferings. It was a stroke of genius sending to Washington the victor in the great Battle of the Marne. In any case, the French Mission was sure of the warmest of welcomes from all Americans. Its purpose was identical with that of the British Mission, but hardly had Marshal Joffre reached Washington when he gave a special turn to events by urging with all his might that an American expeditionary force should be despatched to France without delay. He confessed that after nearly three years of the terrible struggle, in which his country had borne, and was bearing, so tremendous a part, France was not so strong in men as she had been, and that help in that direction was most important. He declared that nothing would assist France more, and at the same time more depress Germany, than having American soldiers fighting in the trenches in Europe at the earliest possible moment. He said that while the presence of these troops in France would be most material, it would also have a moral effect that would be incalculable. **Marshal Joffre asks for men** The Marshal's pleadings fell in to some extent with those of Mr. Roosevelt, who, as narrated in the chapter on the mobilisation of the United States, had over 200,000 men pledged to go as volunteers to fight in France, and importuned the President to give his sanction to the project. Mr. Wilson accepted the idea of sending troops to Europe without delay, but feeling that the effort should be made on regular lines, declined Mr. Roosevelt's proposition. The Selective Draft Law, which legalised conscription, had, however, a clause authorising the President, if he saw fit, to raise four divisions of volunteer infantry.

Both the British and French Missions worked hard. On May 1st the Senate received Marshal Joffre and M. Viviani, the latter making a most eloquent speech, in which he thanked the United States for the loan issue and other help to the Allies, and, referring to the measure for conscription, predicted that American troops would soon be fighting side by side with Frenchmen. There were cries of " Joffre, Joffre ! " as soon as M. Viviani had left the rostrum, but, bowing low, the Marshal excused himself, saying, " I don't speak English. Long live America ! "

THE AMERICAN COMMANDER AT LIVERPOOL.
General Pershing (centre) inspecting the Guard of Honour furnished by the Welsh Fusiliers on his arrival at Liverpool as Commander-in-Chief of the American Expeditionary Force.

During the ensuing week the heads of the French Mission made a tour of the Middle West, explaining the situation, and enlisting popular sympathy, and even causing some enthusiasm for the war. There had been an intention that Mr. Balfour should go to Chicago for the same objects, but he remained in Washington, holding a series of conferences with the chiefs of the various Departments of State, and coming to most satisfactory conclusions with them. On May 11th he went to New York, where he was magnificently entertained, and made a great impression. Returning to the capital, he continued to work uninterruptedly till the 25th, when he journeyed into Canada, where another tremendous reception awaited him. On June 9th he was back in London again. In reply to the inquiries of reporters, he said that no man could have been more kindly treated by the Americans, and he added, significantly, that the war spirit in the United States was good. The next day he was received in audience by King George.

Results of Mr. Balfour's embassy

It was scarcely to be expected that Mr. Balfour would make a public statement in detail as to what he and the Mission had accomplished, and none was made; but it was universally understood that very much had been done—and done excellently. All men, moreover, by that second week of June, saw some substantial evidences of that active co-operation of the United States with the Allies, which he had gone to facilitate, for already American fighting ships were in European waters, and American soldiers were in or nearing France in considerable numbers. As the U.S. Navy, or, at least, a large part of it, was not unready for war from the start, the warships came first, but only a few days afterwards the first armed American contingent was in Paris.

Very early in May a powerful fleet of American destroyers and other warships made its appearance off the coasts of Great Britain. These vessels, which were under the command of Rear-Admiral Sims, were actively at work in the war zone, in combination with British ships, on the 4th of that month. Next day Admiral Sims was present at the War Council of the Allies, which was held in Paris, and attended by Mr. Lloyd George and M. Ribot (the British and French Prime Ministers respectively), the Italian and Russian Ambassadors, and the British and French Commanders-in-Chief. Admiral Sims was better known to the officers of the British Navy than any other man in the U.S. Navy, as he had made frequent visits to England in connection with that particular aspect of naval work in which he was most interested. When on one of these trips, a few years before the war broke out, he had created a profound sensation by saying, in a speech at a Lord Mayor's banquet, that when the next war occurred—the implication was with Germany—the Stars and Stripes would fly side by side with the Union Jack. The statement penetrated into Germany, whence an angry protest was sent to the American Government. The Admiral, a Canadian by birth, entered the U.S. Navy in 1876, and was fifty-two years of age when he came to the

"OLD GLORY" BRAVING THE BREEZE ON PLYMOUTH HOE.

An historic event fraught with significance was added to the annals of the famous Hoe at Plymouth on August 4th, 1917, the third anniversary of the outbreak of the Great War, when Dr. Page held a review of British troops upon the heights whence the Armada was first sighted in 1588. These photographs show the American Ambassador taking the salute beneath the Stars and Stripes, and (above) inspecting the troops.

PRESENTATION OF COMMISSIONS TO U.S. OFFICERS.
Mr. Newton D. Baker, Secretary for War, handing his diploma and commission to an officer of the United States Army, in the presence of President Wilson and a distinguished gathering at an American training camp. Behind Mr. Baker stands Colonel Charles W. Fenton, the commandant of the training camp.

British shores with his fleet of fast destroyers. In his younger days he chanced, on the China Station, to meet Sir Percy Scott, then full of those ideas respecting reform in naval gunnery which later brought him fame. Sims was deeply impressed with these ideas, particularly as his own mind had been travelling in the same direction, and presently he tried to get the naval authorities of his country to make such changes as would realise them. But he encountered that stubborn opposition of the conservative old school of thought which also fell to the lot of Scott for a time. Nothing daunted, and sure that he was on the right road, he wrote to the President, who at that time was Mr. Roosevelt, and, over the heads of his superiors, made out such a strong case that Mr. Roosevelt at once ordered him to return to Washington for the further discussion of the subject. When the President heard what young Sims had to say, he was so struck by it that he forthwith gave orders for the departure from use and wont which Sims had advocated. Had the result been otherwise, Sims must have been court-martialled. But thus it came about that, at his instance, gunnery reform on the lines of Sir Percy Scott's ideas was introduced into the U.S. Navy before it was adopted by the British Navy. Afterwards Sims devoted his attention mainly to gunnery, guns, and gun-protection by armour, and was ranked as one of the greatest experts in these and all cognate matters.

Towards the end of May, some time after his arrival in England, Sims was raised to the rank of Vice-Admiral. The public heard little or nothing of the work of his ships ;
American Admiral in the same silence brooded over their
a British Command operations as over those of the British vessels of war, but no one doubted that all were very busy with the U boats. In the fourth week of June an interesting and significant official statement noted that, during the absence on leave of Vice-Admiral Bayly, Admiral Sims had taken over temporarily the Irish Naval Command. For the first time in the history of the British Empire the flag of a friendly and allied Republican nation floated from the flagstaff of the British Naval Headquarters in Ireland, a circumstance in its way as remarkable as the hoisting of the ensigns of Great Britain and the United States over the Palace of Westminster, which gave such memorable announcement of the union of the two countries for war

on Germany ; or as the high, solemn service in St. Paul's, at which the American Bishop of the Philippines preached a noble sermon, King George and Queen Mary and the American Ambassador, Mr. Page, being the chief figures in the congregation. The flag flying over the Irish Station Headquarters spoke eloquently of a real sea-brotherhood in arms —that was its special meaning.

While the naval co-operation of the United States with the Allies was begun and continued under Admiral Sims, its military co-operation—which, in the conditions that existed in America, no one expected to be immediate— was being steadily prepared for and furthered by President Wilson. Both the Regular Army and the National Guard were being recruited up to their full war strength by voluntary enlistment, and on May 18th the great step onward was made by the enactment of conscription. Hardly a day after the passing of the Selective Draft Act the President announced that he had instructed the War Department to send to France approximately one division of Regular troops under the command of Major-General John J. Pershing. A few days earlier it had been reported that General Pershing had been selected to lead the American soldiers in Europe, and the statement had been well received, among the first to express **Despatch of U.S.** hearty approval of the President's **troops to France** choice being Mr. Roosevelt. The various conflicting stories that had been current with respect to the sending of troops, whether Regulars or volunteers, were now definitely set at rest, and Mr. Roosevelt absolved from their pledges all those who had joined his movement.

A complete division was about 24,000 men all told, and it was understood that the expeditionary force would, besides, have a regiment of Marines and include a large number of engineers. With respect to the last, it had been stated on May 17th that nine regiments of at least a thousand men each would be recruited at once from the American railways—as was, in fact, done through the agency of the Railway Committee of the Advisory Commission, the handmaid of the Council of National Defence —and despatched to France with all possible speed to work on the lines of communication. Each of these regiments was headed by engineer officers of the Regular Army, but commissions were given to eminent civil engineers. The creation of these engineer regiments was one of the outcomes of the British and French Missions, it having been suggested that American railroad-men would materially help to solve the problem of transport to and from the front which the Allies found considerable difficulty in coping with adequately. Another direction in which the Missions indicated that America could co-operate at once most beneficially with the Allies was the medical service.

The General Medical Board of the Council of National Defence arranged, after conferences with the medical experts of the British Mission, to have a thousand American surgeons in or near the firing-line in a very short time. The first of the hospital units sailed for France early in May, and Surgeon-General William C. Gorgas claimed that the " first unit of the Army to carry the flag in the Great War would be the Medical Corps.'

But this was not quite the case. For on May 9th a Reuter message from Paris stated that the first armed contingent flying the flag of the United States marched on that day through the streets en route for the front, after being reviewed by Colonel Girard, head of the automobile section of the French Army. The detachment consisted of some fifty university men, thirty of whom were from Cornell University, and it belonged to the new American field service which had been detailed for the transport of ammunition; but at that time it was still officially a part of the French Army. A complete unit of the U.S. Medical Corps, over two hundred in number, including sixty-five nurses, landed in England on May 18th, in charge of Major Henry L. Gilchrist, who only a fortnight before had been summoned from the Mexican border to take command. The unit, accoutred, and dressed in uniforms resembling those of the Australians, presented a very smart appearance when reviewed by the British general **U.S. Medical Corps** who had been sent to greet its arrival. **in France** It was composed of men from Harvard and other American universities and colleges, and of nurses from Lakeside Hospital, the largest institution of the sort in the Middle West. With the unit was Dr. George W. Crile, of Cleveland, a surgeon of world-wide repute, and he acted as director of this medical contingent, which soon proceeded to France.

If it was May that saw these first small beginnings of the co-operation of the Army of the United States with the Allies, it was not a month afterwards when the division,

ordered by the President for service in France was landing in that country. Meanwhile Mr. Wilson had been doing something for Russia, still and for long afterwards in the throes of the Revolution. About the middle of May he despatched to Petrograd a commission, the chief of which was the well-known American statesman, a former Secretary of State, Mr. Elihu Root, whose object was to proclaim the sympathy of **President Wilson** the United States with the Revolution, **and Russia** at the same time offering whatever practical and substantial aid might be desired. About the same date the Treasury Department showed its confidence in Russia by making a loan of a hundred millions of dollars, or twenty millions sterling, to her from the great seven billion dollar war loan. Two or three months earlier President Wilson, knowing that Russia was in bitter need of railway engineers, had sent to Vladivostok Mr. John F. Stevens, formerly Chief Engineer of the Panama Canal, and other railway experts, as was stated in the chapter on the mobilisation of the United States. One of the things that probably was in the President's mind was that America might be called on to double-track the great Trans-Siberian railway.

June, 1917, was a memorable month in the history of the United States from several points of view. To begin with, the 5th of the month saw the registration, as already mentioned, of nearly ten million young men as potential conscripts for the new National Army the President was calling into existence. Then, two days later, General

GREAT RED CROSS DEMONSTRATION IN NEW YORK.

Women nurses marching down Fifth Avenue, New York, during a great Red Cross Demonstration in the autumn of 1917. They met with a most magnificent reception from the crowds that lined the streets.

Women all over America took up Red Cross work with enthusiastic earnestness, and their work was organised on a large and comprehensive scale and carried out in a thoroughly businesslike way.

U.S. MEDICAL CONTINGENT AT BUCKINGHAM PALACE.
King George and Queen Mary inspecting the first American contingent of nurses and surgeons at Buckingham Palace on May 23rd, 1917. They completed their training at Blackpool before proceeding to France.

Pershing and his Staff arrived at Liverpool. On the 8th the " Matin " of Paris announced that the first American warships had reached the shores of France, which indicated the landing of a body of Marines, and on the same day a telegram from Washington stated that a hundred U.S. naval airmen, whose special business it was to aid in detecting submarines, were already in that country. Towards the end of the month the first contingents of the American Regulars were disembarking on French soil— the advance guard of millions to come, if necessary. In the United States itself was witnessed such a " Red Cross Rally " as was never seen in any other land, a fund of twenty millions sterling being raised in a week. Other remarkable features of the month were a Note which

President Wilson addressed to Russia, the passing of the Espionage Act, a clause of which gave him absolute control over exports, the successful close of the great Liberty Loan, the development in the aircraft programme of vast schemes of construction, and the measures taken by Great Britain and France for securing the proper co-ordination of all their activities in America, outside the domain of diplomacy, by appointing High

AMERICAN NURSES IN LONDON.
Some of the American nurses who arrived in London in the spring of 1917, forerunners of the great fighting forces which the United States was rapidly preparing to throw into the struggle.

Commissioners in the persons respectively of Lord Northcliffe and M. André Tardieu.

The appearance on European soil of considerable numbers of American Regulars—in fact, the division, with other details, which the President had directed the War Department to send for service in France—was one of the really great, outstanding events of the war. It was not because of the size of the force, for compared with the armies in the field it was small indeed, but because of all that small force stood for —it implied that the United States was in the war with its whole strength in men and resources till the final victory was attained. The first portion of this combatant force reached Liverpool on the morning of June 7th in the White Star liner Baltic. It was a very important portion, for it included General Pershing and the General Staff of the U.S. Army. The General Staff comprised one hundred and eighty-six officers—a body large enough for a very great army. In addition to a strong guard of Regulars and Marines, there was also with it a considerable number of civilian clerks and other officials. The immediate

WAR COUNCIL OF THE AMERICAN RED CROSS.
Members of the War Council of the American Red Cross. Front row (from left to right) : Mr. W. De Forest (vice-president), President Woodrow Wilson (president), Mr. W. H. Taft (chairman of the Executive Committee), and Mr. E. Wadsworth (executive head of the organisation). Back row : Mr. H. P. Davison (chairman), Mr. G. P. Murphy, Mr. Charles D. Norton, and Mr. E. N. Hurley.

business of General Pershing and his Staff was to prepare the way for the landing in France of the American troops, then about to cross the Atlantic. When the Baltic drew up alongside the landing-stage in the Mersey, the ship was boarded by General Sir Pitcairn Campbell, G.O.C. Western Command, his Staff, and Admiral Stileman, the senior naval officer of the port, who gave a warm welcome to General Pershing and his force.

With the possible exception of General Leonard Wood, who occupied in the United States a position somewhat analogous to that Earl Roberts had held in Great Britain, General Pershing was the foremost soldier of America. When he left West Point in his twenty-sixth year as "Cadet Captain," or head of that famous training school, he was, in the words of Mr. Sydney Brooks, the well-known writer on American subjects, "the most finished, the most all-round, and the most scientific product of the most exacting military curriculum to be found anywhere on earth." Joining the 10th Cavalry as second-lieutenant, he was almost at once called on to take part in a campaign against the Apache Indians of New Mexico and Arizona. In 1897 he was back at West Point as a teacher of tactics, but he threw up that post when the war with Spain broke out, and rejoined his old regiment, participating with it in the fighting around Santiago. After the peace, Pershing organised a bureau of the War Department at Washington to look after the various dependencies of Spain that had fallen to America as the result of the war, and in 1899 he went to the Philippines, where he did some fine work, both as a soldier and as a tactful diplomat, as also was the case later when he was Governor of the province of Moro. Meanwhile, he had been promoted to the rank of brigadier-general by Mr. Roosevelt, who was then President, and had a keen eye for merit, as he had shown in the case of Admiral Sims. Pershing had been a mere captain, and his advancement took place over the heads of eight hundred officers who had been his seniors. He was made military attaché at Tokio soon after the war between Russia and Japan began, and throughout that struggle he was with the Headquarters Staff of General Kuroki, thus gaining knowledge and insight with regard to modern developments of warfare. In 1914 Pershing was placed in command of the U.S. troops patrolling the Mexican frontier, and in 1916 he was selected to lead the expedition into Mexico, the object of which was to catch the brigand Villa, but Villa was not taken, as Pershing and his men were recalled by President Wilson.

Owing to no fault of Pershing, the Villa Expedition was a failure, but the campaign was of considerable value both to him and to the War Department of the United

General Pershing in England

THE AMERICAN FLAG IN ST. PAUL'S CATHEDRAL.
Placing the American flag in position in St. Paul's Cathedral on May 30th, 1917. On that date men of the American Legion serving in the Canadian Army presented the American and Canadian flags to the Cathedral. It was a moving ceremony, at which many distinguished people were present, and as the American Ambassador said, "there was hardly a dry eye in the whole congregation. Because the American flag there symbolised what we all approve, and what moves us to the depth of our being."

States in the way of experience. The National Guard had been called out, and thus an object-lesson in mobilisation was given to the military authorities of America. When General Pershing arrived in England he was in his fifty-sixth year, but looked ten or twelve years younger. In person tall and spare, in character firm and resolute, in military science very thoroughly equipped both from natural bent and by a wide knowledge of actual campaigning, General Pershing was an ideal man for the command with which President Wilson had now entrusted him. Officers who had served with him paid the highest tribute to his courage and resourcefulness, as well as his energy, and none could fail to feel the charm of his frank, friendly, and almost boyish manner. "He is the sort of man who gets on well with everybody," said one who knew him well, and this was also the verdict of those who came into contact with him in London.

Pershing's General Staff comprised Colonel Alvord, Adjutant-General; Colonel McCarthy, Quartermaster-General; Colonel Russell, Signal Officer; Colonel Taylor, Engineer Officer; Lieut.-Colonel Ireland, Medical Officer; Lieut.-Colonel Bethell, Judge-Advocate; Colonel Brewster,

ENGLAND'S KING ON AN AMERICAN SHIP.
During his visit to Liverpool in May, 1917, King George visited two American armed liners, and was interested in a close inspection of them. When he left the crews gave "Three cheers for the King of England!"

Inspector-General ; Lieut.-Colonel Williams, Ordnance Officer ; Major Palmer and Major Nolan ; and Pershing's A.D.C.s, Captain Margetts and Captain Collins. This was a comprehensive list in itself, but other distinguished and capable men were also included in the Staff. Colonel Brewster, the Inspector-General of the force, had but a short time previously been in command of the United States troops in Porto Rico, and on his tunic he wore the only military medal given for gallantry in the Army, having won it during the Boxer affair in China, when he rescued a wounded man from a river under extraordinarily heavy fire. Captain Patten, another member of the Staff, was famous as the crack shot of the Army ; he wore two medals, on one of which was inscribed " Expert Rifleman," and on the other " Pistol Expert."

From Liverpool General Pershing and his men proceeded at once to London, where they were greeted by Lord Derby, the Secretary for War, Field-Marshal Lord

French, General Sir Francis Lloyd, and other British officers, one of whom was Brigadier-General Lord Brooke, who was attached as British officer to the American Staff. Among the company were Mr. Page, the American Ambassador, and Admiral Sims. On June 9th General Pershing paid a visit to Buckingham Palace, accompanied by the chief members of his Staff, and was received in the most cordial manner by King George. Two days later the general lunched with the King and Queen at the palace. General Pershing met Mr. Lloyd George and other members of the Government several times, and held important conferences with them, while socially everything was done to show the Americans honour and esteem. But there was little display of bunting or waving of flags— somehow the thing went much too deep for anything of the sort. In a short speech General Pershing made at Liverpool he said that he and his men were the " standard-bearers " of the United States in the war for civilisation. But there was more than that. The presence of the American Commander-in-Chief and the General Staff of the United States in the capital of the British Empire was the symbol of what **" Standard-bearers** many felt was the most remarkable and **for civilisation "** wonderful movement in the war—the unifying of the English-speaking races against a common enemy. Here was something very great—" deep calling unto deep." The splendid, salient fact was that the Americans and the British had been brought together not so much by their kindred blood—though that, too, was not without its effect—as by kindred ideals, an even stronger force. Never had Germany dreamt that such would be an outcome of the struggle she had so deliberately and wickedly thrust upon the world. As there was very serious and hard work to be done, and done as quickly as might be, there was scant expression of mere sentiment, and the Americans at once set about their special business.

On June 13th General Pershing and the American Staff landed at Boulogne, where they were received by the representatives of France and cordially welcomed, though with hardly any ceremony and with little public demonstration—just as had been the case in England. In the afternoon of the same day Pershing was in Paris. There were many signs of how profoundly France was moved

KING GEORGE'S GREETINGS TO SAILORS AND SOLDIERS FROM THE UNITED STATES.
His Majesty greeting American naval officers on board a United States patrol ship during his visit to Glasgow, and (in centre) examining the equipment of an American soldier during a visit to one of the English camps in which some of the United States troops completed their training before going to France. Right : The King, with Mr. Lloyd George, the Prime Minister, chatting with the officer in command of the American troops, whom he inspected at Buckingham Palace after their march through London on August 15th, 1917.

KING GEORGE SALUTING "OLD GLORY."

American troops marching past King George, Queen Alexandra, and Lord French at Buckingham Palace on August 15th, 1917. As the leading troops reached the Royal party his Majesty saluted the Stars and Stripes carried at the head of the column.

by the arrival of the great American soldier, both on his own account and as typifying the United States in arms with the Allies. One of the most striking was recorded by a British journalist in these words :

Quietly, without any panoply, General Pershing and his Staff were, soon after their arrival in the French capital, taken to see the tomb of Napoleon at the Invalides. Quietly also, as if it were nothing, though it had never been done before, Napoleon's Legion of Honour was taken from its keeping and put on the American Commander-in-Chief. It was the perfect tribute to his captaincy of the sister Republic and to the high call which finds him at the head of an American Army, small as yet, but with millions marching.

It was on June 25th that the first units of the Army, coming direct from the other side of the Atlantic, disembarked at a French port, the name of which was withheld. In command was Major-General William L. Sibert, a veteran of the Cuban, Philippine, and Mexican Campaigns. They came in a veritable armada of huge transports, escorted by at least one large cruiser and flotillas of destroyers under Admiral Gleaves, as well as by some French warships. The inhabitants of the town where the landing was made were told only at the last moment of its imminence, but they quickly turned out to see the wonderful sight, and greeted the Americans with enthusiasm. The force was composed of Regulars, Marines, and recruits, and most noticeable was the look of physical strength and health all of them had. As they formed up on the quays, and then marched on to the places that had been assigned to them, they presented a spectacle that gladdened and uplifted the hearts of the French. It was widely understood that the voyage of the troops had been calm and uneventful, but this was not exactly the case, though no losses of any kind had been incurred. The people of the United States were thrilled with pride when they heard of the arrival of their soldiers " on the other side," but they were thrilled with a very different emotion when, a few days afterwards, they were told that the transports had been attacked by German submarines in circumstances that plainly indicated that spies among themselves had succeeded in conveying to the enemy accurate information of the sailing of the ships.

June 14th was the day on which this expeditionary force had left the shores of the United States, and the authorities had taken every precaution to ensure secrecy. The American Press was silent on the subject. Yet many people knew, and some of them were traitors. On July 3rd it came out that the ships had been attacked twice by

Transports attacked by U boats

U boats. Mr. Daniels, the Secretary of the Navy, stated what had taken place. For convenience the expedition was divided into contingents, each composed of troopships and a naval escort designed to keep off German raiders. An ocean rendezvous had been arranged with the destroyers working under Admiral Sims, in order that the passage through the danger zone might be attended by every possible precaution. The first submarine attack occurred at half-past ten in the night of June 22nd. "What gives it a peculiar and disturbing significance," said Mr. Daniels, " is that our ships were set upon at a point well on this side of the rendezvous, in a part of the Atlantic which might have been presumed free from submarines. The attack was made in force, and although night made it impossible to arrive at an exact count, it was clear that the U boats had gathered for what they deemed would be slaughter." Another attempt at torpedoing was made on a different contingent a few days later at a point beyond the rendezvous, but in each case the submarines were outfought, with a loss of at least one submarine, by the escorting destroyers.

"The whole nation will rejoice," commented Mr. Daniels, " that so great a peril has passed for the vanguard of the men who will fight our battles in France." The nation did rejoice, but both the popular and the official minds were sharply roused to the spy menace in and to the United States. It was even hinted pretty broadly that spies were to be found in the Department of the Navy itself, and there was a loud call for action against them and all other persons in the country who were not free from suspicion. Semi-officially the Government, in reply, stated that if its activities against German spies in the United States could be published, the news would startle the world.

Together with the cry that the country was in danger from spies, an agitation was begun for inciting the

ROYAL VISIT TO AMERICAN OFFICERS' CLUB.

King George and Queen Mary, with Mr. Walter H. Page, the United States Ambassador, and Admiral Sims, at the American Officers' Club, Leconfield House, Mayfair, October 23rd, 1917. Leconfield House was lent by Lord Leconfield for the use of American officers in London.

[French official photograph.

CAMP LIFE OF THE U.S. TROOPS IN FRANCE.
Fatigue-party of American soldiers fetching water. The American Expeditionary Force was completely self-supporting, and imposed a very small strain upon the food supplies of France, from which, in the words of the "Times" military correspondent, they drew nothing "except air, water, fresh vegetables, and eggs."

birthday of the Stars and Stripes that Congress chose as the national emblem on that day nearly a century and a half before.

In his Note to Russia Mr. Wilson alluded to and exposed German intrigue, and denounced the ruling caste in Germany, which, conscious that the war was going against it, was seeking to avoid defeat by any instrumentality whatsoever. Those in authority in Germany, he went on to say, were making use even of the influence of groups and parties among their own people —to whom they had never been just or fair, or even tolerant—to promote a propaganda on both sides of the sea which would preserve for them their power— to the undoing of the very men they were using. The reference here was to the German Socialists and to the suggestion that a conference should be held at Stockholm, where the terms of a democratic (Socialist) peace were to be discussed, drawn up, and settled. The Russian Government of the day was known to regard this proposed Stockholm Conference with favour, and the German Government, which was engineering the whole business, was ready enough to give every facility to such German Socialists to attend the conference as it deemed likely to advance its own interests. In effect, Russia's acceptance of the formula of

Government to deal with the German-language newspapers, as they published disloyal statements. An article in the "Atlantic Monthly" computed that these journals reached and influenced at least a million people. Their editors were careful to keep within the letter of the law, but all the while they were conducting a campaign that was not less dangerous because it was subtle. They sought in every way to diminish enthusiasm for the war, to misrepresent and confuse the aims and objects of the Allies, and to bring about a divorce between America and the Entente Powers.

Their efforts, which were pushed with considerable cleverness, were aided by the pacifists, whether sincere or not, and could not but have some effect on the large numbers of Americans who continued to fail to grasp the deep significance of the struggle for themselves and their country. No direct action against these malevolent papers was taken at the time by the Government, but the President had countered their seditious utterances by his outspoken and clarifying Note to the Russian Provisional Government, which was published in the second week of June, and also by his address at Washington to the employees of the Administration on June 14th—"Flag Day" in the United States, in commemoration of the

AMERICAN ARTILLERYMEN AT GUN PRACTICE.
There was keen rivalry among the U.S. batteries at the front to fire the first shot against the Germans. The privilege fell to a certain Battery C, at the end of October, 1917, and the case of the first shell which they fired was appropriately engraved and sent to President Wilson.

the extreme Socialists, "peace without annexations and without indemnities," meant the return to the *status quo ante bellum.* Mr. Wilson bluntly told Russia this was impossible, for it was out of that very *status quo ante* that "this iniquitous war issued forth—the power of the Imperial German Government within the Empire and its widespread domination and influence outside of that Empire." What had to be done was obvious. "That status," said the President mordantly, "must be altered in such fashion as to prevent any such hideous thing from ever happening again."

In his Flag Day speech Mr. Wilson spoke in scathing terms of the sinister intrigue for peace on German lines that was being "no less actively conducted in this country than in Russia." He knew, he said, that the German Government had many spokesmen in the United States, "in places both high and low." These declared that the war was a foreign war, which held no danger for America. "They set England at the centre of the stage, and talk of her ambition to assert her economic dominion throughout the world. They appeal to our ancient tradition of isolation, and seek to undermine the Government with false professions of loyalty to its principles. But they will make no headway," trenchantly declared the President.

[*British official photograph.*

AN AMERICAN LUMBERMAN AT THE FRONT.
From forest regions of the Far West of the United States lumbermen trooped to the European war zone to co-operate with lumbermen from Canada and foresters from Portugal in the heavy work of felling and shaping the timber required in modern warfare.

Falsehood betrayed them in every accent. The facts of the case were patent to all the world, and nowhere more plainly than in the United States. The great fact that stood out above all the rest was that the war was a peoples' war for freedom, justice, and self-government among all nations. Then Mr. Wilson concluded on a note of warning :

For us there was but one choice. We have made it, and woe be to that man, or that group of men, that seeks to stand in our way in this day of high resolution, when every principle we hold dearest is to be vindicated and made secure for the salvation of the nation. We are ready to plead at the bar of history, and our flag shall wear a new lustre. Once more we shall make good with our lives and fortunes the great faith in which we are born, and a new glory shall shine in the face of our people.

Pessimists were not wanting in Washington and elsewhere in the United States, and their depressing statements all tended to help the disloyal work of the pacifists and pro-Germans. Among other things, they had prophesied that the Liberty Loan would be a rank failure, but this prediction of theirs was splendidly falsified by the American people, who over-subscribed the sum of £400,000,000 required by 50 per cent. Mr. McAdoo, the Secretary of the Treasury, prepared the public for the reception of the loan by a vigorous and ingenious publicity campaign, and he was most generously aided by the

[*British official photograph.*

AMERICAN ENGINEERS WORKING ON LIGHT RAILWAYS IN FRANCE.
In May, 1917, the Railway Committee of the U.S. Advisory Commission recruited nine regiments of 1,000 men each from the American railways and sent them to France to work on lines of communication. Eminent American civil engineers held commissions in these regiments.

RR

American Press in this effort. The Loan closed on June 15th, and in two or three days it was announced that more than four million people had subscribed, the total subscriptions coming to over £600,000,000. Of these persons, three million nine hundred thousand had applied for small allotments, a fact which spoke eloquently of the popularity of the loan.

Another heavy blow at the pessimists, pacifists, and pro-Germans was struck by the wonderful success about the same time of an appeal on behalf of the American Red Cross. A few weeks previously President Wilson had appointed a Red Cross War Council, with Mr. Henry P. Davison, a prominent banker of New York, as chairman; ex-President Taft was chairman of the executive committee. The Council determined to raise a central fund of a hundred million dollars, or twenty millions sterling; and, in spite of the country being tapped at the moment for the Liberty Loan, got the whole amount that had been asked for within about a week—another record for America. A new building in Washington was dedicated to the American Red Cross, President Wilson taking part in the ceremony and delivering an address, in the course of which he maintained that the United States had entered the war because the principles for which the Republic was founded were at stake.

The great Red Cross rally

Besides being the day of the successful close of the Liberty Loan, June 15th saw the enactment of an important, extensive measure to which the title of the Espionage Act was usually given, though it dealt with other matters in addition to espionage, one of its most notable features being a clause authorising President Wilson to employ a power of embargo against neutrals, in order to limit their importation of material likely to reach the enemy.

Introduced early in the session of Congress, the Bill which, changed a good deal, ultimately was this Espionage Law, occasioned much controversy, the discussion turning mainly on a proviso conveying to the President an absolute right of Press censorship, against which every journal in the Union emphatically protested. On May 4th the House of Representatives passed the Bill, after modifying the censorship proviso, and ten days later the Senate cut out the proviso altogether, though it not only adopted nearly all the rest of the Bill, but put in the new clause conferring on the President the power of embargoing exports to neutrals—a striking and significant departure, which doubtless was welcomed by the Government. For some time, however, it looked as if the Bill would be dropped, but towards the end of the month it was revived under pressure from the President, who was anxious that the Bill, including the censorship provision, should go through. But the House of Representatives finally pronounced against the censorship by 184 votes to 144. Several months were to elapse, and certain revelations were to be made before the nation, with its newspapers, realised that the censorship was a necessity of war. But the power of embargo was retained in the Bill when it became an Act.

Espionage and the blockade

The clause empowering an embargo enabled the President to create an Exports Council—or, as it was sometimes called, Embargo Council—the members of which were the Secretary of State, the Secretary of Commerce, the Secretary of Agriculture, and Mr. Hoover.

For this most important and far-reaching effort, which in effect meant a tremendous tightening of the blockade of Germany, the Exports Council received much assistance from Lord Northcliffe, who put before it a mass of convincing statistical information showing how Holland, Denmark, Norway, and Sweden had been fed from outside and largely by America, while " they slipped their dinner " across to the enemy. As head of a permanent British War Mission Lord Northcliffe had arrived at Washington on June 14th, and his exposure of the conduct of these neutrals was one of the first of the many services he rendered to the cause in this capacity, in which he had agreed to act at the request of the War Cabinet. With regard to this appointment, Mr. Bonar Law said in the House of Commons that, in order to co-operate fully with the Government of the United States, Missions representing a number of British Departments had been for some time in America, and as it was necessary that there should be someone at their head to combine and co-ordinate their activities, Lord Northcliffe had undertaken to do this work, which, however, did not interfere with that of the British Ambassador. In a further statement Mr. Law said it was hoped that Lord Northcliffe would be able to carry on the work begun by Mr. Balfour in this respect as head of the British Mission in America, as long as the need for the Mission existed. He quoted the subjoined telegram, which had been sent to the chiefs of the various British Departmental Missions, in explanation of the scope of Lord Northcliffe's functions :

Lord Northcliffe has been appointed by the War Cabinet, with direct responsibility to them, as head of the British War Mission, to co-ordinate and supervise the work of all the Departmental Missions in the United States, to prevent conflict of interests and loss of effort, to determine priority, and to maintain friendly relations both with the Allies' representatives in the United States and with the United States' authorities themselves. Lord Northcliffe will have the right of communicating direct with the Prime Minister, and also with the various Departmental Ministers, either direct or through the Department's representative in the United States. He will have full authority over the various Departmental Missions.

Mr. Law added that Lord Northcliffe had accepted the appointment at the urgent request of the Government, with the full approval of the departments concerned, and that the Government felt that in undertaking this highly important duty, at much personal inconvenience to himself, he was rendering a great public service.

Lord Northcliffe's appointment

In the House of Lords there was some criticism by Lord Buckmaster, who had been Lord Chancellor in the Asquith Government, of Lord Northcliffe's appointment, but it was easily and effectively answered by Earl Curzon, who, in the course of his remarks, indicated that the Departmental Missions in the United States, the work of which would be supervised and co-ordinated by Lord Northcliffe, were those of the Treasury, the War Office, the Admiralty, the Ministry of Munitions, and the Department connected with Food Supplies. He pointed out that Mr. Balfour's Mission, in addition to its diplomatic functions, did initiate departmental work, which it would be the business of Lord Northcliffe to carry on, and that in that sense Lord Northcliffe was Mr. Balfour's successor. No one, he continued, could allege that Lord Northcliffe was not supremely well qualified for his task. He concluded with the observation that, when the appointment was suggested, in no quarter did it receive a more friendly welcome than from Mr. Page, the American Ambassador in London. What the Americans thought of the appointment was shown by an appreciation that appeared in the " New York Tribune," which began with the words: " For the work which Lord Northcliffe is to do in this country the British Government could not possibly have chosen a better man. He fits the situation. He has done more than any other single Englishman perhaps to put England on her feet as a fighting Power." France had sent to America, in a capacity very similar to that filled by Lord Northcliffe, a distinguished member of her Army Commission—M. André Tardieu, who, after remarking that Lord Northcliffe had helped to make Great Britain more efficient, and that his experience and energy would prove of great value to the United States, expressed his extreme gratification that Lord Northcliffe, whom he knew well personally, had been selected for the post.

At Washington Lord Northcliffe had a long interview in private with President Wilson, called on Mr. McAdoo at the Treasury, congratulated him on the success of the

Motor=launch patrol taking in a despatch lowered from an airship.

A seaplane sighted a submarine and dropped a bomb upon it, rending a hole in its hull. Though attacked by two enemy seaplanes and three other submarines, the British seaplane launched another bomb upon its quarry and sent it to the bottom.

A submarine overtook a U boat and fired a torpedo at it. A splash was observed, and immediately afterwards the enemy was seen with stern out of water and conning-tower half submerged. A minute later the pirate disappeared.

Waging war upon enemy submarines by submarine and seaplane.

An auxiliary vessel sighted an attacking submarine and opened fire, causing it to list badly. Some of the crew came on deck making signs of surrender, but, as the submarine attempted to make off when the " Cease fire!" had sounded, it was fired on again and sunk.

A destroyer sighted a submarine disguised with a sail which vanished when approached, disclosing a conning-tower. The U boat dived but presently re-emerged, and the destroyer charged and rammed her midway between the conning-tower and rudder.

Undersea pirates who did not return to their rendezvous.

An alternative to the black smoke screen emitted from warships' funnels. A preparation of carbide contained in a perforated box being put into the water, dense white fumes were instantly generated. These kept to the surface and, travelling with the wind in a straight line, effectively screened vessels from enemy observation.

White smoke screen used by the British Navy.

Liberty Loan, outlined Great Britain's method of raising and expending over four thousand millions of pounds—"twenty billions," as the Americans would have phrased it—in the course of the war, and discussed plans for the further financial co-operation of the United States and the Allies. There also he met M. Tardieu, the French Commissioner, and had several conversations with him about the work on which he was engaged. But Lord Northcliffe had chosen New York as his headquarters, as better adapted for his special business, and his first visit to Washington was short, though he went there frequently afterwards. Great Britain was expending each week from ten to twelve millions of pounds in the country on the purchase of supplies of all kinds, and New York was the money centre of the United States. In a speech delivered in the House of Commons on June 28th, Dr. Addison, then Minister of Munitions, gave the British public some notion of the manifold activities of which Lord Northcliffe was the focus. He stated that Mr. Gordon, who had been Vice-Chairman of the Imperial Munitions Board in Canada, had been moved to the United States, and placed at the head of all the British munitions organisations in that country. "Mr. Gordon," said Dr. Addison, " will report out there to Lord Northcliffe in the same way as the other chief British representatives in charge of shipping, transport, grain purchases, and other services."

Mr. Roosevelt hailed Lord Northcliffe as a " splendid friend of America," and Lord Northcliffe was often asked for his advice and counsel by the Americans. In an informal address to the Players' Club he spoke in favour of the United States permitting its newspaper and magazine writers to be absolutely frank about what was going on. Saying that in his opinion the war was just beginning, he warned his hearers that every ounce of energy and every revolution of America's vast industrial machine would be

Enormous aviation programme needed to bring the struggle to a successful termination, and that it was only by the complete mobilisation of man-power and machine-power that the war could be won. He declared that in the aeroplane lay one great hope of the victory of the Allies. It had so happened that he was in Washington on the day—June 15th—when the Director of the United States Army Aviation Service recommended to Congress an expenditure of six hundred million dollars for a huge fleet of aircraft, " capable of maintaining supremacy for fifty miles back of the German fighting-lines," as an American journalist had it. President Wilson wrote to Mr. Baker, the Secretary of War, warmly approving of this large appropriation. Mr. Orville Wright, one of the fathers of aviation, sent a telegram from Dayton, Ohio, in which he urged the building of aeroplanes in vast numbers, and maintained that ten thousand of them would end the war within ten weeks. The House of Representatives voted the enormous aviation programme on July 14th without a dissenting voice, but there was some obstruction in the Senate, and it was getting on towards the end of that month when the requisite legislation settled the matter, the basis being the construction of 22,000 machines and the training of 100,000 aviators.

Meanwhile President Wilson had put the embargo on neutrals into force. On July 2nd the American Press published a statement of the facts regarding the action of neutrals in supplying Germany with foodstuffs which had been put before the Exports Council by Lord Northcliffe. This statement, which was most impressive, took up in detail the exportation of foodstuffs from Holland, Denmark, Norway, and Sweden into Germany, and it showed that fats sufficient to supply more than seven million men, or virtually the whole of the German effectives, had been, and presumably were still, going to the enemy from these countries. Figures in support were given for 1916. The chief articles on the list included 82,600 metric tons—the metric ton was slightly less than a British ton—of butter, 115,800 metric tons of meat, 68,800 metric tons

of pork products, 70,000 metric tons of condensed milk, 407 metric tons of fish, 80,000 metric tons of cheese, 46,400 metric tons of eggs, 179,500 metric tons of potato meal, 58,500 metric tons of coffee, 74,000 metric tons of fruit, 12,000 metric tons of sugar, and 215,000 metric tons of vegetables—a total of over a million metric tons of food, all of which had gone to feed the Germans.

It was suggested in the statement that all this vast quantity of foodstuffs for the enemy was made possible by the importation from the United States of most of these commodities, or their equivalents—for example, American oil-cakes reached Germany through the sale by the neutrals of their dairy produce to her. The statement went on to point out that obviously a strict enforcement of the blockade through the control of the exports of the United States to Holland and the others would necessarily result in the elimination of **American embargo** these foodstuffs from the German diets. **on exports** It submitted that the blockade had to be strict to be effective, and that the facts presented constituted a definite basis for the embargo on exports on the part of the American Government. It added that the embargo need not in the least endanger supplies of food to Holland and Scandinavia for their own people, but would merely prevent these neutrals from furnishing food to the Germans.

On the evening of July 8th the President issued a proclamation, under the embargo clause of the Espionage Act, prohibiting the export, without licence from the Government, of food, grain, meats, fats, coal, coke, oils, fertilisers, arms, munitions, iron, and steel. The proclamation stated that the embargo would go into effect on the 15th of the month, and that it applied to all the countries of the world and their dependencies, which were named individually from Abyssinia to Venezuela. Mr. Wilson, with his habitual painstaking carefulness, explained in the proclamation the attitude he had taken up. He said that the Government had first and chiefly in view the amelioration of the food conditions which had arisen, or were likely to arise, in the United States itself, and that not only was the conservation of its prime food and fodder supplies a matter which vitally concerned its people, but the retention of an adequate supply of raw materials was essential to its programme of military and naval construction and the continuance of its necessary domestic activities. Next he remarked that it was the obvious duty of the United States, in liberating its surplus products over and above its own domestic needs, to consider first the necessities of all the nations engaged in the war against the Central Empires. Referring to neutrals, he observed that the United States had also a duty with respect to them which it recognised. The Government did not wish to hamper them, and on the contrary intended to co-operate with them in their difficult position as far as possible : but the overriding factor was that no supplies from America would be made **Penalties for** available, directly or indirectly, for **contravention** feeding the enemy. The proclamation imposed a fine of £2,000 on any person found guilty of evading its orders, and directed the seizure of all cargoes shipped in American bottoms in contravention thereof.

As for the neutrals, they were singularly slow in producing the facts and figures which they had promised to furnish to prove that they were not engaged in shipping to Germany the very things they were importing from the United States, or their equivalent. As a matter of course, they could not prove anything of the sort ; and, when the embargo came into force, scores of their ships, which had been ready to sail, were refused the necessary licences, and had to be unloaded. The general working of the embargo was placed in charge of the Department of Commerce, whose head was Secretary Redfield, and the chief of its Bureau for Foreign and Domestic Commerce, Mr. E. E. Pratt, acted as secretary to the Advisory Board of the Exports Council, which had established a Licensing

[French official photograph.

U.S. TROOPS ON A ROUTE MARCH.

Some of the first American troops to reach France setting out on a cross-country route march from their training camp on the Aisne.

RETURNING TO THE TRENCHES.

Company of U.S. soldiers marching to the trenches near their training camp in France, where they finally fitted themselves for taking their places in the fighting-front.

Bureau. Mr. Redfield was determined on the strictest regulation of exports, and finding that Mr. Pratt, who had Scandinavian sympathies, took a lax view, requested him to resign, which he did. The enforcement of the embargo was thorough.

Having struck this heavy blow at Germany and at the rapacity of neutrals, President Wilson was not less determined that the body of the citizens of the country, and the country itself, should not be exploited by " profiteers " among themselves.

In an open address to American business men published on July 11th, he denounced " blood profits," and declared that he would not allow the Government of the United States, the Allied Governments, or the consuming public to be bled by extortionate prices for the benefit of manufacturers, shippers, and others, to whom he gave warning that if they did not reduce prices voluntarily the law would step in. He had already dealt successfully with the price of one great commodity—coal. On June 26th, coal operators, representing both anthracite and bituminous industries, had conferred with officials of the Government at Washington, and agreed to the

establishment of fixed rates much lower than were then current.

He now dealt with steel, perhaps the greatest organised industry in the country. It was much more than a coincidence that the issue of his address to the business men of America synchronised with a meeting of the steelmasters of the United States at Washington in conference with Mr. Baker, Secretary of War, and other members of the Council of National Defence. Mr. Wilson had made it clear that the price of steel must be brought down to a reasonable level.

Next day it was announced that an agreement had been arrived at under which the entire product of the industry was made available at a price to be determined, on the basis of the cost of production, by the Federal Trade Commission.

President Wilson was resolute in laying down as a principle for all trading during the war that there were to be " fair profits " and no others. This, however, raised the question as to what were fair profits, and there was some suggestion that, as a general thing, ten per cent. on the cost of production would meet the case. But the business interests were inclined to grumble, the truth being that the huge profits they had made in supplying the Allies had spoiled them. To end the confusion which was conspicuous in the varying theories and practices as to prices to be paid by the Government, the President appointed on July 28th a War Industries Board, putting at the head of it Mr. Scott, the chairman of the Munitions Board of the Council of National Defence. Its other members were Lieut.-Colonel Pierce, representing the Army ; Rear-Admiral Fletcher, representing the Navy ; Mr. Hugh Frane, a well-known Labour organiser ; Mr. Baruch, chairman of the raw materials committee of the Council ; Mr. Robert S. Brookings, a merchant of St.

Louis; and Mr. Robert S. Lovett, chairman of the executive committee of the Union Pacific Railway.

It was announced that this Board would take measures for increasing the production of war materials, decide on priority of delivery, and furnish a policy and a plan for obtaining reasonable prices for supplies. The last-named work was entrusted to a sub-committee, consisting of Messrs. Baruch, Brookings, and Lovett. Mr. Wilson had said that the Allies were entitled to receive the same treatment as regarded prices as the Government of the United States. Accordingly, early in August, the

Equal treatment for Allies Board declared, in a public statement: "Guns and ammunition employed against our enemy are for our benefit as much when used by our Allies as when used by our own men, and it is obviously unjust to require our Allies, when fighting our battles, to pay our own people more than our own Government pays for the materials necessary to carry on the war." This meant, in practice, a very large saving in money to the Entente Powers. Towards the end of the month, Mr. McAdoo, the Secretary of the Treasury, told of the creation of an Allied Purchasing Commission, to handle British, French, and other Entente purchases in the United States—another step in the realisation of the President's policy of obtaining for the Allies the same price for their war supplies as that paid by the United States Government, and another illustration of his splendid co-operation with the Entente Powers against Germany.

Whatever were her feelings in secret, Germany still professed to regard the intervention of America with derision. During the month of July the attention of the United States, as of the rest of the world, was attracted to the political situation in Germany by the dismissal from the Chancellorship of Herr von Bethmann-Hollweg, after he had held the post for eight years, and the appointment in his place of Dr. George

Michaelis, a comparatively obscure official who had come into some prominence a short time before as Food Controller of Prussia. The change had been brought about by the passing in the Reichstag of the "Peace Resolution," which had been agreed upon by the Catholic Party, the Social Democrats, and the Radicals, the three groups forming a majority of the Chamber, but which ordinarily were completely out of sympathy with each other. The resolution asserted that Germany took up arms in defence of her liberty, independence, and territorial integrity; that the Reichstag laboured for peace and a lasting reconciliation among the nations, and that forced acquisitions of territory and political, economic, and financial violations were incompatible with such a peace. It went on to state, however, that so long as the enemy Governments would not accept such a peace and continued to threaten Germany, the German people would stand together and fight as one man.

There was in all this something of an echo of what had been said in Russia. Pacifists saw in it a deep longing in Germany for peace—what the Kaiser saw in it was that Herr von Bethmann-Hollweg had lost control of the Reichstag and had, therefore, outlived his usefulness.

[*French official photograph.*

"OLD GLORY" AND THE FIRST U.S. REGIMENTAL STANDARD RAISED IN FRANCE.

Part of the first American troops to reach France, with their national flag and their regimental standard. The advance guard of the great United States Army arrived at a French port "in a veritable Armada of huge transports" on June 26th, 1917, and met with a magnificent reception as they landed and marched off to the great camp prepared for them. Inset: A party of American officers at exercise in France.

[*French official photograph.*
GENERAL PERSHING STUDYING A SITUATION.
General Pershing visiting an important observation-post in France with his Staff. The training of the U.S. troops was in general charge of the French, who placed everything unreservedly at American disposal.

So Bethmann-Hollweg had to disappear. Michaelis, his successor, made a temporising speech in the Reichstag, in the course of which he refused to regard America's intervention as worthy of "grave concern," and said he did not believe that the ship tonnage could be supplied to transport American armies to Europe, much less to feed and supply them after they were there. In some quarters there had been a hazy impression that the appointment of Michaelis was a concession to the German Liberals, but events soon showed that German militarism was as rampant as ever, and serious-minded Americans took note of the contemptuous manner in which allusion had been made to their country's participation in the war. They recalled how the Germans long ago had belittled the Kitchener armies, and later had jeered at the British conscripts, and they knew how terribly **German sneering** these sneers had been avenged on the **as a stimulant** battlefield. They vowed that the Germans would be as thoroughly disillusioned with respect to the soldiers of the United States. In a speech to the Officers Reserve Corps, Mr. Lansing, the Secretary of State, said America would fight on until "the military despotism which held the Germans in the hollow of its hand had been rendered impotent and harmless for ever."

In an interview Michaelis tried to influence both Russian and American opinion by saying that Great Britain and France were the only obstacles to peace, the former fighting solely to destroy a hated commercial rival, and the latter only to acquire territory. Why, he asked, should Russia and America support them when such was the case? Mr. Lansing answered him, employing in his speech plainer language in explaining why the United States was at war than had been used by any

previous American speaker. Stating that Germany had promised to refrain from unrestricted submarine warfare merely to gain time to complete her programme of the building of numerous U boats, and that the future of America was at stake, he said to the Officers Reserve Corps, and through them to all the citizens of the Republic:

If any of you have the idea that we are fighting the battles of others and not our own, the sooner he gets away from that idea the better it will be for him, and the better it will be for all of us. Imagine Germany victor in Europe because the United States remained neutral. Who then, think you, would be the next victim of those who are seeking to be the masters of the whole earth?

In the first week of August, it happened that the American Mission, which the President had sent to Russia under Mr. Elihu Root, returned to the United States. Mr. Root spoke hopefully of the Russian situation, and said he was confident that Russia would work out into a great, free, self-governing democracy. But he also warned his countrymen—"As sure as the sun rises to-morrow, if this war ends with the triumph of Germany our people will be a subject nation of the German ruling classes."

Such precise statements of the extreme gravity of the situation for America materially helped the President, and increased his hold on the country, thus enabling him to take a strong hand. The **2,000,000 men for** breakdown of Russia in the field led **France in 1918** him promptly to enlarge his plans for the National Army, and when, about the end of July, it was stated in Administration circles that the sending of two million men in 1918 to France was in contemplation, most of the citizens of the United States heartily concurred, though this was a great increase on what they had supposed would be sufficient.

Nothing touched the masses more nearly than the question of food. Mr. Wilson wished one man to be in control — Mr. Hoover. The Senate voted for a commission of three men, but the President stood firm. After much debate he carried the day, and, under the Food Administration Act of August 10th, Mr. Hoover was given practically unlimited power to regulate the prices, transport, and distribution of food supplies for the United States and for export to the Allies and neutrals.

By this Act Government control was established, for the duration of the war, over foods, feeding-stuffs, fuels, fertilisers, and other kindred things under the designation of necessaries. It gave powers to the Government to ensure adequate supply and equitable distribution, and to prevent monopolies and speculation. It prohibited the manufacture or importation of distilled liquors for beverage purposes, and authorised the suspension of the manufacture of malt, fermented, and vinous liquors, and the limitation of their alcoholic contents. It left to the discretion of the President the commandeering of distilled beverages in bond or in stock, when necessary for military purposes. Accompanying this Act was a cognate measure, known as the Food Survey Act, which provided means for estimating the quantities of foodstuffs available and for stimulating the production of foodstuffs. Congress appropriated £32,000,000 for the working of all this new and well-nigh revolutionary legislation.

Mr. Hoover, with a number of experts, had been studying carefully, for weeks before the Food Administration Act became law, what steps were to be taken, and he lost no time in letting the Americans know his programme for the control of the country's wheat and flour supply in the interests of the United States and the Entente. After stating that the war had destroyed the normal determination of the price of wheat, and that the Allied Governments had placed the whole purchase of their supplies in the hands of one buyer, while the neutral Governments were each buying through a single agent, Mr. Hoover pointed out the dangers of this situation, and announced his plan to meet them. First, in order to eliminate speculation in wheat and flour, all mills and elevators of over a hundred barrels daily capacity had to obtain a Government licence, the conditions of which were that all charges were to be reasonable and customary. Second, no wheat was to be stored for more than thirty days without special permission, and information was to be given regularly of shipments and receipts. Dealings in "futures" were suspended; all transactions were to be for cash only. These regulations came into force on September 1st.

To determine the price of wheat for the 1917 crop a committee was appointed, with President Garfield, of Williams College, as chairman, and it was stated that when this body had arrived at a fair price that price would be fixed for the crop year—which meant that one price, without change or fluctuation, would rule till the coming of the 1918 crop. On the report of the committee President Wilson, at the end of August, fixed the price at eight shillings and tenpence a bushel, which was a compromise between the demand of the farmers for ten shillings and of labour for seven shillings and fourpence a bushel. In the spring of the year speculation had driven wheat up to thirteen shillings and sixpence a bushel. On August 15th Mr. Hoover formed a corporation, with a capital of ten millions sterling, to buy and sell wheat, and opened agencies throughout the country, the usual channels being made use of wherever possible.

All this firm and wise handling of the food supplies of America was conducted during a month when pacifism made special efforts to further the interests of Germany. In Congress a small but persistent group of pacifists kept peace talk alive. On August 11th Mr. La Folette, of Wisconsin, the Republican who had led the opposition to the President's proposal of armed neutrality in March, introduced in the Senate a resolution demanding a "restatement of allied peace terms based on a **U.S. Government** disavowal of advantages either in the **and pacifism** way of indemnities, territorial acquisitions, commercial privileges, or economic prerogatives." The resolution came to nothing. The real attitude of the United States to pacifism was shown next day when Secretary Lansing declined, amid general approval, to issue passports to American Socialists to attend the Stockholm Conference. The great pacifist feature of August, however, was the appeal for peace addressed by Pope Benedict XV. to the belligerents. His pontificate began within a month after the war broke out, and he had more than once previously urged them to take steps towards peace. During Lent, 1916, he had characterised the war as the "suicide of civilised Europe," and in December of the same year he had denounced the "horrible madness of the conflict devastating Europe."

As his appeal, usually termed the *Vatican Note*, virtually suggested a return to the *status quo ante bellum*, it was suspect from the start in the eyes of most of the allied peoples. In the United States the Note brought to light the fact that American opinion was now resolutely and even passionately opposed to any termination of the war except in a complete victory of the Allies. On August 29th the reply of President Wilson to the Pope was issued by the United States Embassy in London. While acknowledging the humane and generous motives which had inspired the Note, Mr. Wilson pointed out that the *status quo* was impossible as a basis for a genuine peace. However much the Allies might wish for peace, they knew they could not find it in the Pontiff's proposal, because they were well aware that the result would be altogether different from that which he desired. Germany was not to be trusted. "We cannot take the word of the present rulers of Germany," said the President, "as a guarantee of anything that is to endure, unless explicitly supported by such conclusive evidence of the will and purpose of the German people themselves as the other peoples of the world would be justified in accepting. Without such guarantees, treaties of settlement, agreements for disarmament, covenants to set up arbitration in the place of force, territorial adjustments, reconstitution of small nations, if made with the German Government, no man, no nation could now depend on." Mr. Wilson's answer to the Pope was endorsed by the vast majority of Americans, gave an immense impetus to the country's measures for hostilities, and utterly nonplussed the pacifists, who were attempting to get up demonstrations in favour of a German peace. Even the German-language papers did not cavil at it.

That hardening of practically all American opinion outside that of pro-Germans and pacifists, with respect to the vital character of the war was ever becoming more and more noticeable. **If Mr. Gerard's exposure** enthusiasm still was lacking, determina- **of Kaiserism** tion was marked. One of the factors that contributed in no small degree to this was the publication in a serial form, beginning about the middle of August, of a book by Mr. Gerard, the American ex-Ambassador to Berlin, containing the most damaging revelations of the lying and duplicity of Germany, as well as the most unflattering views of the United States as expressed by the Kaiser and other German leaders. The personal want of good faith on the part of the Emperor was exposed, and Mr. Gerard stated that in an interview the Kaiser "showed great bitterness against the United States, and repeatedly said 'America had better look out after this war,' and 'I shall stand no nonsense from America after the war.'" These outbursts were occasioned by the fact that the Allies were drawing large supplies from the United States, and were uttered long before the American declaration of war. The words, reproduced all over America, had a prodigious effect. The legend, industriously propagated by far from disinterested people, that the Kaiser was a peace-loving sovereign, was completely shattered. The American Press acclaimed Mr. Gerard's book as the most vitally important contribution that had been made to the true story of the war.

On August 13th the War Department ordered the mobilisation of the new National Army in four instalments, the first being commanded to entrain for the cantonments on September 5th. On August 17th Washington announced

[*French official photograph*.

GENERAL PERSHING VISITING A FRENCH AVIATION CENTRE.

The Commander-in-Chief of the American forces in Europe visiting one of the aviation parks of the French Army. On his arrival in France, in June, 1917, General Pershing paid visits to various centres of activity on the western front, on which his Army was about to take its place.

that two divisions, each of 19,000 men, of the National Guard, which on August 5th had passed into the federal service, were to be organised for an early departure for France, and next day the official figures of the armed forces of the United States were made public: Regulars, 305,700; National Guard, 311,000; Reserve Corps, 93,000—a total of 709,700 men on land; naval forces, 233,117 men. The grand total was nearly 950,000 men. Since April 6th, when war was declared on Germany, America had increased her fighting strength by about 700,000 men, all of whom had enlisted voluntarily. This was the same as saying that, when the conscripted men of the Selective Draft came forward, the armed forces of the United States would number upwards of a million and a half, a truly amazing record for six months.

According to an American authority, a second body of United States troops arrived at a "European port" on July 26th. It was known that American **London's tribute** Army engineers were being trained in **to U.S. soldiers** England. It had been stated in the papers that King George paid a visit to the camp of the United States troops at Aldershot on July 28th. In response to a very general demand, several thousands of these troops marched through some of the principal streets of London on August 15th. These friendly invaders, who bore aloft the Stars and Stripes, affectionately termed "Old Glory," were given a continuous ovation by the enormous masses of people who had turned out to see and welcome them. Such a sight had never been witnessed before in the British capital. It was rightly characterised as one of the great moments of the war, thrilling all with pride and joy; there were those who were touched to tears, but not of sorrow. In four detachments, each headed by a Guards' band playing stirring music, the Americans passed in soldierly fashion through the cheering crowds, saluting on their march Mr. Page and Admiral Sims at their own Embassy, and the King-Emperor at Buckingham Palace, where the popular enthusiasm rose into a great demonstration, at once exultant and sympathetic. In France, American preparations went on apace, among them being the creation of a gigantic aviation camp, where 15,000 flying men were to be "put into shape."

In the United States itself signs multiplied of the militarising of the nation. As August closed, two millions of people stood in the beflagged streets of New York to see and acclaim thirty thousand men of the National Guard, marching through the city from which they were drawn, on their way to cantonments to begin serious training for war. Led by President Wilson, members of Congress, and high Government officials, a thousand soldiers and Marines, and many civic organisations, paraded on September 4th at Washington, as a **New York acclaims** tribute to the men drafted into the new **the National Army** National Army. Congress had adjourned early to take part in the demonstration, which was marked by tremendous enthusiasm. On the same date New York was the scene of another great military display, the second within a week. On this occasion it was the men of the new draft, the conscripts under the Emergency Army Act, as was shown by their wearing a khaki armlet with the letters N.A. (National Army) inscribed on it, who marched through the streets. New York, again in its myriads, turned out to cheer them.

Pacifists and pro-Germans excepted, the war spirit was capturing all America—this was the salient fact of September, 1917. It was somewhat grim, but it was resolute to win. Early in the month the organised labour of the United States mobilised its representatives afresh at Minneapolis with the double purpose of pledging itself anew to support President Wilson's war programme and of sounding a warning to pacifists and pro-German propagandists. The feature of the Labour Day celebrations throughout the country was a practically unanimous declaration of confidence in the Government. Before the Minneapolis Conference was held the President had written to Mr. Gompers, its chairman, a letter in which he said: "While our soldiers and sailors are doing manful work to hold back reaction in its most brutal and aggressive form, we must oppose at home the organised and individual efforts of those dangerous elements who hide their disloyalty behind a screen of specious and evasive phrases." The conference denounced the pacifists and pro-Germans as enemies of the country, the "People's Council of America" being specifically named as disloyal and seditious. At this very time President Wilson struck hard at the "Industrial Workers of the World," a Socialist society financed by Germany money, and at other unpatriotic organisations. In more than fifty cities of the United States agents of the Government raided the headquarters of pacifist and pro-German agitators, and seized their books and correspondence. Some arrests were made, and more were to follow. Simultaneously the Department of Justice conducted a searching inquiry into the utterances of the German-language journals, and the offices of two such papers in Chicago were raided. Towards the end of the month Congress passed an amendment to a measure, called the Trading with the Enemy Act, which gave the Administration control of all foreign language papers published in America. This meant the end of all these organs of Kaiserism.

Not all pacifists were insincere. Many who had been pacifists came to see they had been mistaken and admitted the fact. The most eminent of these was William Jennings Bryan, the ex-Secretary of State, who had left the Administration more than a year before because he disagreed with Mr. Wilson. "I do not know," said Mr. Bryan, "how long this war will last, but I do know that the quickest way out is straight through."

Deeply in earnest in carrying out its plans for war, which were the most colossal in history, the United States during September envisaged a series of enormous financial measures. Legisla- **The U.S. solid** tion was passed to raise new taxation **for war** for the year of £500,000,000, to cover a portion of the war expenditure. A War Credits Bill, authorising the issue of bonds of an aggregate amount of over £2,307,000,000 was ratified by the Senate on the 15th without one dissentient, after only eleven hours' discussion. It had been passed unanimously in the House of Representatives some days previously in an hour less. On the 25th, information submitted to Congress by the various Departments of the Government, for the purpose of drafting a Supply Bill for £1,400,000,000, showed in general terms the military programme to which America was committed, and also indicated that the programme was an everexpanding one. The chief items were concerned with the raising, equipping, and training of an army of *three* million men for foreign service and with the maintenance of a naval force of two hundred thousand men, or fifty thousand more than Congress had voted a month or two before. For artillery ammunition the sum of £400,000,000 was put down, for new destroyers £50,000,000, for the building of merchant ships £400,000,000. Large sums were estimated for the construction of hospitals, and for the making of training camps and cantonments. As the month drew to an end, arrangements were being made for the flotation of a second Liberty Loan, the amount, however, of which was £600,000,000, or three times that of the first. By that time the Allies had received in loans from the United States about five hundred millions sterling, but the War Credits Bill earmarked loans to them for eight hundred millions in addition to the sum which had already been allocated to them in April. As October opened, America presented a picture, vast and impressive beyond description, of nation-wide war-making as gratifying to the Allies as it was confounding to the enemy, though he affected to look on it with contempt.

PIRATES WATCHING A

CHAPTER CCVI.

TORPEDOED SHIP SINK.

THE LAW AND THE DEFENCE OF THE REALM.
By R. Storry Deans.

Disadvantages of Democracy in War Time—Martial Law—Scheme of War Legislation—Skeleton Acts—Their Advantages and Disadvantages—The Moratorium—Averting Financial Panic—Courts Emergency Powers Act—Defence of the Realm Act—Effect on Common Affairs of Life—The New Departments—The First Regulations Under the D.R. Act—Power to Take Possession of Property—Preventive Detention—Espionage—Interference with Trade—Permits—Steel—Leather—Articles of Warlike Use—Shipping Control—National Service—Police Powers—Railway Control—Food Control—Economy of Wheat—" K. J." and His Work—Sugar Control—The Potato Famine of 1916-17—Profiteering—Corn Production—The Allotment Movement—The Liquor Traffic—Less Beer—More Beer—Trial by Court-Martial—The Irish Rebellion—Trading with the Enemy—Enemy Companies —The British Black List—Internment of Aliens—Persons of Enemy Origin or Association.

MEN and munitions were not the only respects in which the declaration of war found Britain unprepared.

It is a well-worn saying, but not the less true, that an autocracy can wage war more easily than a democracy. The reason is not far to seek. An autocracy finds in itself a reservoir of powers. It can by a word, by a stroke of the pen, overturn established conditions. It can, without asking anybody's consent, suspend or abrogate all or any laws or usages that may hamper it in the conduct of war. It can order civilians and soldiers alike to become part of the military machine. It can suppress, without hesitation or delay, all persons and societies that may try to hamper the Government or to endanger the success of the forces. It can confiscate property. It can proclaim martial law.

A democracy has no one in whom such powers reside. And so, while the sudden outbreak of war finds a well-governed and efficient autocracy more efficient than ever, it commonly finds a well-governed and efficient democracy equally inefficient.

Of all democracies, that of Great Britain was the least prepared for war. Its laws were, for many generations, framed entirely in the interests of freedom. Liberty of the subject was a sacred watchword. It had been secured by writs of Habeas Corpus, by Magna Charta, by Declarations of Right, by Trial by Jury. For over a hundred years there had been a Press free to print almost anything it would ; and if there was freedom for the citizen and freedom for the Press, there was no less freedom for property.

A man might do what he would with his own—whether it was land, or factory, or any kind of property such as lawyers call " personal." He could conduct his business, or till his soil, or leave it untilled, as it suited his needs or his caprice.

In most foreign countries there was some indefinite reserve of power in the executive. Even in free France the President of the Republic could proclaim martial law. In most countries the police, representing the executive, could arrest and detain on suspicion of intended harm to the country. In most countries there was power of domiciliary visit and search.

In Great Britain there were no such powers on August 4th, 1914. The law in time of peril was the same as in time of safety. The Executive Government had no power to arrest or detain anyone save by ordinary process of law. It had no power to order a trial except by jury. It had no right to commandeer so much as a mutton chop from a butcher's shop to feed a hungry soldier. If a colonel took his men into the park of Mr. Groggenstein, late of Hamburg, now a naturalised British subject, because the park was the only available ground for drill or camp, he and they were trespassers, and Groggenstein could order them out.

Obviously, in such a perilous moment as the outbreak of the Great War, powers had to be sought. Old and familiar liberties had to be given up for the time. The executive had to be trusted with powers of an autocratic nature. But, such is the way of democracies, and such, in particular, is the way of the British people, that it was only by slow and gradual and

LORD RHONDDA.
Lord Rhondda was appointed Food Controller in succession to Lord Devonport in June, 1917.

BLENDING TEA FOR THE ARMY.
The Port of London Authority blended the tea supplied to the British Army. The varieties of tea were mixed by hand labour, with wooden spades, in one of the Port Authority's warehouses.

even hesitating steps that the Government acquired the powers necessary to govern and direct a nation in a struggle for life.

The result was a body of laws known as Emergency Legislation. The chief of these were the Defence of the Realm Acts; and of hardly less importance were the Aliens Restriction Acts and the Courts Emergency Powers Acts. There were others. In the end, by these Acts, and the regulations made under them, the Executive Government acquired an amount of power such as even the Stuart Kings never dared to grasp at. And, curiously enough, the nation, seeing instinctively that Parliamentary government in a great war was of little more use than a feather-duster in a cyclone, called for more. Some of the consequences of these Acts and regu-
Despotic power of lations have been touched upon in
emergency statutes earlier chapters of this work, notably in "National Psychology and Social Changes" (Vol. 9, p. 395), "The Growth of Officialdom" (Vol. 9, p. 471), and "War-Time Changes in Trade and Industry" (Vol. 10, p. 245).

Not all, however, of the emergency statutes moved in the direction of conferring power on the executive. Some of them were designed to mitigate the financial hardships inseparable from a state of war. Others, again, were intended to curb the greed of Shylock clamouring for his pound of flesh.

Before proceeding to describe in detail the provisions and the working of these statutes, a word as to their general scheme will be useful. Almost all of them were merely skeleton Acts—a form of legislation that had come more and more into favour during the years before the war. Then a great many people objected to it very strongly; for this reason: The skeleton method of law-making consists of procuring Parliament to pass an Act merely enunciating a principle; saying that such-and-such large matters are to be done, and leaving the details and the machinery to be settled by regulations to be made thereafter by some Government department, or some commission or committee. It need hardly be pointed out that this mode of legislation is much easier for the Govern-

ment of the day than it is to pass an Act of Parliament setting out every detail and every item of machinery. It has this merit, at any rate: That if the department-made rules and machinery turn out to be inefficient, they can be scrapped, and new ones made quite easily; but if the machinery and details are part of the statute, the whole stands or falls together. A new statute is required to remedy the least defect.

The drawback of the skeleton law is that it puts into the hands of departments, and Cabinets, and individual Ministers and officials, powers which are, in effect, legislative. A harmless-looking skeleton Act may easily be made anything but innocuous by a set of rules issued under it. They are like the "etceteras"

WEIGHING THE BLENDED TEA BEFORE PACKING
After being blended the tea was weighed and packed in tins holding 15 lb. apiece. More than 50,000 lb. of tea were sent over to France every week.

of Coke on Littleton. The worthy Littleton having written a short sentence winding up with "etc.," Coke proceeds to comment. By this "etc.," he says, "is meant"—and then goes on for three, or perhaps thirty, pages of print. That is why in Coke's commentaries upon Littleton there is much more comment than text. Constitutional purists, therefore, and those to whom the supremacy of Parliament was the main thing to be aimed at in politics, always shook their heads at measures of the kind described.

It can easily be seen, however, of what value such a method might be when it became essential to place in the hands of the Ministry and their servants, the naval and military authorities, powers, not indeed unlimited, but still very loosely defined.

Imagine a case. The Home Secretary and the two fighting departments might have asked Parliament for powers to seize and arrest and detain without public trial all alien enemies. This having been granted, the very first man arrested under the Act might turn out not to be an alien enemy, but a neutral. Parliament is then asked for power to deal with all aliens. A man who speaks broken English is promptly arrested, and quietly produces naturalisation papers. Another Act must be passed to enable the authorities to lay hands on all persons suspected—or on all persons of alien origin. And all these measures would take time, and would occasion discussion ; and the Minister responsible would have had to spend several hours in the House listening to the sarcasm of honourable members who were so much more prescient than he.

Under the skeleton system, having vague, general powers, a regulation is made. If it is not wide enough, another is made the moment the mistake is detected. Time taken—inappreciable.

The first war statute was really passed before Great Britain was at war. It was passed and received the Royal Assent on August 3rd. Its title, the Postponement of Payments Act, 1914, gives some idea of its scope. Power was given to the Government, by proclamation, to authorise the postponement of the payment of any bill of exchange, or any negotiable instrument, or any other payment in pursuance of any contract. The proclamation might impose conditions or limitations to the postponement. Any proclamation

Postponement of Payments Act might be subsequently added to, varied, extended, or revoked by another. It will be observed that this is quite in the skeleton form—merely giving power to act in a certain general direction, and leaving the extent of the action entirely to the executive.

But even before August 3rd the Government had acted, by the issue of a Royal Proclamation on August 2nd proclaiming a moratorium for bills of exchange (other than cheques or bills payable on demand). Moratorium, as the word itself implies—*mora* (Latin) = delay—simply means a period of postponement. And the proclamation allowed anyone who was responsible to pay a bill which had been given (legally called " accepted ") before August 4th, 1914, to refuse to pay it when presented. But, to gain the advantage of delay, the acceptor had to re-accept the bill for a date one month later than its due date, and to pay interest for the month at bank rate.

The Postponement of Payments Act retrospectively confirmed the moratorium proclamation. It is only a curiosity, but perhaps it is some indication of the draughtsman's perturbation of mind, that the Act of Parliament alludes to the proclamation under a wrong date. The

LONDON STREET SCENE DURING THE COAL SHORTAGE.
Coal was another necessary commodity of which there was a shortage in London during the winter of 1916-17, and queues of people, in which children predominated, besieged the retail coal dealers.

A " POTATO QUEUE " IN HOXTON.
During the potato shortage in the winter of 1916-17 the Mayor of Hoxton procured three tons for the poor of the borough. A considerable police force was needed to regulate the crowd of applicants.

hasty drawing of the proclamation itself is evidenced by the minute fact that it speaks of the year as " nineteen hundred " and fourteen. An official document touched by the hand of a permanent official would have said " one thousand nine hundred."

The first moratorium was quickly followed by one on August 6th, extending the postponement to cheques and bills on demand drawn before August 4th, to negotiable instruments and to contracts made before August 4th. The postponement was to be for one calendar month or until September 4th, whichever was the later date. Exception was made for maritime freights, wages and salaries, rates and taxes, bank notes, and a few other matters. It will be seen that this proclamation locked up the money in the banks, and bankers were able to and did refuse to allow their customers to draw on their accounts beyond a certain amount, except by special arrangement. The step was a drastic one, which brought **Protection of the banks** the war home to the business man in the most inconvenient manner. At the same time it effectually stopped runs on banks, and other panicky effects of the declaration of hostilities.

A third proclamation (August 12th) afforded protection to banks of the Dominions, and slightly varied the first moratorium relating to time bills (*i.e.*, not payable on demand and not cheques).

Yet another moratorium (September 1st) was revoked the next day, and by a proclamation of September 2nd the period of postponement was extended for another month—that is, to October 4th instead of September 4th. But before October 4th came round, another period of grace was proclaimed, and the payment of bills and debts was finally postponed until November 4th. But by that time the situation had eased sufficiently to justify the Treasury in ordering that the new period of grace should not apply to rent, nor to any payment to or by a retail trader in respect of his business. The last exception was very necessary, because a whole legion of defaulters had arisen, who could pay their tradesmen perfectly well, but simply declined to do so. Thanks to these measures, people were able to turn round and adjust their affairs to meet the unprecedented conditions.

Of a similar nature was the Courts Emergency Powers Act, passed on August 31st, which provided that where a contract had been made before the war, the creditor could not enforce it by execution (in Scotland, _diligence_) without leave of the court. The creditor's legal rights were not interfered with. But his remedies to enforce those rights were modified.

The Act worked well. Thousands of applications were made under it; and if some debtors thought they were not protected so completely as they wished to be, at any rate thousands were saved from being sold up when they were not to blame for their position.

Some time later it was found necessary to protect two kinds of people interested in land—tenants and mortgagors.

The high hand of authority An enormous number of owners of property have mortgages on it. A man wishes to own his house. It would cost £1,000 to buy it, and he has only £600. So he borrows £400. Before the war he could often borrow at 4 per cent. interest. But after the war, rates of interest began to rise generally. The Government paid 4½ per cent., and afterwards 5 per cent.—even for short loans 6 per cent. There was a great demand, also, for money for trade. So many lenders on house property (mortgagees) began to ask for higher interest, under threat of calling the money in. This was put a stop to by the Increase of Rent and Mortgage Interest (War Restrictions) Act, 1915. So long as the borrower on mortgage of a dwelling-house or houses paid his interest reasonably promptly, the lender could not enforce his security. Nor, in any case, could he, even by agreement, raise the rate of interest from the pre-war rate. A similar provision protected tenants of dwelling-houses (at rents not exceeding £35 in London, £30 in Scotland, and £26 elsewhere) from rent-raising and from eviction.

The Briton of 1917 never had the Defence of the Realm Acts and Regulations long out of his mind. He could not. No man was his own master. His eating and drinking, his house and land, his securities, his labour—all were interfered with, or might be interfered with. He could not go where he pleased; he could not write or speak what he pleased.

Everywhere was the high hand of authority. The State, personified by the police, naval and military authorities, officials of the Ministry of Munitions, the Food Controller, the Liquor Control Board, the Coal Controller, the Press Censor, and other executive departments, new and old, pervaded the land. Britain knew what it was to be ruled. These restrictions and interferences with the old order of things took their rise from the Defence of the Realm Act, 1914, passed four days after war was declared. The purpose of the Act, as its name implies, was to enable the authorities to deal with the new state of things by giving greater powers to the executive. Regulations " for the public safety and the defence of the realm" could be issued by the Crown.

First regulations of D.O.R.A. And as, in Britain, the proclamation of martial law (sometimes called "a state of siege") is unknown, and is, indeed, a meaningless term, the Government was expressly authorised to order that anyone could be tried by court-martial, instead of by the ordinary courts of law, who broke any of the regulations made to prevent communication with the enemy, or obtaining information to assist the enemy, or similar regulations; or who broke regulations referring to the safety of railways, docks, or harbours.

The first regulations were published on August 12th, 1914, and were only thirty-one in number. They were of a strictly naval and military character, though they contained some provisions sufficiently startling—startling, that is, at the time.

A new Act, also passed in August, extended the power of the Government to deal with " reports likely to cause disaffection or alarm." It also added to railways, docks, and harbours such other areas as the naval or military authorities chose to " proclaim." That is to say, such areas came within the jurisdiction of courts-martial.

The regulations under these Acts gave power to take possession of lands, buildings, gas, water, and electricity works; a right to the military to go anywhere, to clear an area near a defended harbour of its inhabitants; a right in similar areas to close public-houses wholly or partially; a right to commandeer vehicles, boats, and warlike stores; a right to demand information; and a right to arrest without warrant. Further, it was not necessary to suspect that the person arrested had broken the regulations. It was enough if the policeman, civil or military, customs officer, etc., suspected that he intended to break them. In other words, preventive detention was established.

The remainder of the regulations were, apparently, intended to deal with espionage. Additional rules, made in September, gave power to stop and seize vehicles on the road and question the owners and drivers; and to take land for military training purposes. They also forbade the keeping of carrier-pigeons without a police licence.

After about three months' trial the two statutes were repealed, and re-enacted, with additions, as the Defence of the Realm Consolidation Act, 1914, passed on November 27th, 1914. The new sections considerably enlarged the powers of the departments. The naval and military authorities acquired power to commandeer any munition factory or workshop, or plant without the factory, or the whole output of the place. Regulations might be made to prevent the spread of false reports likely to prejudice the country's foreign relations; and powers were taken to control the navigation of all ships in British waters, and all British ships wherever sailing.

Extension of State control Even these provisions were not enough. An Act was passed in 1915 (March 16th) giving the naval and military authorities power to requisition any sort of factory or workshop, to convert any factory or workshop into a manufactory of war material; and to regulate a factory so as to assist the production of war material elsewhere.

More stringent still was an amendment contained in the Munitions of War Act, 1915 (S.10), which gave the new Minister of Munitions power over all factories and workshops—the work, the engagement, and the employment of workmen there, and the plant; and also the absolute control of all metals and materials useful for making any article for use in war.

The reader sees how the control of the State, as represented by the naval, military, and now the munitions departments, was mounting up. Starting merely with power to take possession and control of warlike stores, and such land and buildings as might be necessary for immediate warlike use, the Government had gone on to assume control of enormous quantities of raw material, and to exercise an almost despotic power over numerous classes of manufacturers. Nor were merchants and shippers exempt. In time both exports and imports of almost all things were placed under a system of licences.

In June, 1916, the Army Council issued an Order prohibiting all dealings in raw wool grown in Great Britain or Ireland during the season of 1916. This meant that the Government took the whole clip, appropriated for Army clothing as much as was required, and allowed the general trade to have the rest.

As early as March, 1916, the Army Council gave notice to farmers that all their hay and straw was to be held for the Army, and they were forbidden to sell or use any of it except (1) usual quantities to feed their own stock, and (2) under licence to sell or otherwise deal with it. Officers were appointed for every county to grant such licences; and so strict was the order that neither hay nor straw could be removed without such a licence.

Flax was not commandeered wholesale; but as more and more special linen came to be required for aeroplanes, manufacturers were forbidden to use (without the permission of the Director of Aircraft Equipment) flax suitable for aeroplane cloth for any other article. Jute, whether then in the country or to be imported, and not already sold to spinners, was all taken for the Government under an Army Council Order of February, 1917.

Leather of the heavier sort had been similarly commandeered in June, 1916; lighter leather followed in August of the same year; and, finally, in September, almost all leather was taken. There were, in all, seven Orders as to leather, including imported leather, issued in less than two years. This was because the British Government had undertaken to provide what the shopkeeper calls "footwear" for the Russian, Serbian, Italian, and even the French Armies. The result was that leather was hard to come by for civilian boots, and boots and shoes became very dear. To make quite sure of the raw material, dealings in the raw hides were similarly restricted.

A curious list of goods could be compiled **Curious lists of** which were declared to be war material. **war material** Not only were unlicensed dealings prohibited in such main commodities as wool, leather, hay and straw, metals, and the other things already mentioned, but in certain things the warlike uses of which are not so obvious. Who, for instance, would think that goldbeaters' skin was a war material? Yet so it was declared by an Admiralty Order. Binoculars and telescopes were others. Second-hand locomotives and other second-hand railway material were declared in December, 1916, after certain railway engineers had undertaken to improve communications in France. Thus, for the first time, a derelict railway became of value. Photographic lenses were listed in February, 1917, so that the aircraft observers might be amply supplied.

At a fairly early stage of the war the question of shipping became pressing. Many ships, and these of the largest and fastest, were taken by the Navy as auxiliary cruisers. Very many others were necessary to carry supplies to our far-flung Navy. To the Grand Fleet in the North Sea a constant procession of supply-ships ferried backwards and forwards, bearing food, shells, and the thousand and one things **Shipping needs of** necessary for a fleet at sea. Besides, there **the Allies** were ships in the Indian Ocean, ships in the Atlantic, ships in the Pacific. After the overseas expeditions began—first France, then the Dardanelles, Egypt, and German South-West Africa, then Macedonia, Mesopotamia, German East Africa—there were troops to be transported, supplies to be maintained, sick and wounded to be carried. All these things meant ships. Some ships, also, were lost by mines, or sunk by raiders. Again, the British Government undertook to supply many of the shipping needs of the Allies.

As a consequence the mercantile marine was reduced, so far as British trade was concerned, by at least one-half. The first measure taken to cope with the difficulty was the restriction of imports. In 1916 Government forbade the import of many non-essentials except under licence. Towards the end of 1916 legions of dock labourers were formed, who undertook to go to any port where the local supply of men was inadequate. But after the Germans had begun, in 1916, indiscriminate sinking of merchant ships by their submarines, the matter became serious; and in 1917, when the "unrestricted U boat warfare"—a

IN ANTICIPATION OF NEW-LAID EGGS FOR THE SICK-BAY.
Warrant officers building a fowl-run on their allotments. The eggs from the fowls were supplied to hospital-ships. Vegetable-growing and poultry-keeping were encouraged as profitable hobbies for men of the Grand Fleet when ashore.

TRANSHIPPING WHEAT TO A GRAIN BARGE.
Unloading wheat by means of a floating "elevator." Drawn up from
the hold of the ship, and poured through hoppers into sacks, the wheat
was then carried by the men to the barge alongside, for the final stage of
its journey to the flour mills.

polite name for sinking at sight—was applied to all ships,
including neutrals trading to or from the allied countries,
it became acute.

The new Government of Mr. Lloyd George, which
displaced the Coalition Ministry at the end of 1916, for
one of its first measures appointed a Shipping Controller.
This Minister (Sir Joseph Maclay, of Glasgow) had very
drastic powers, and he used them drastically. He entered
at once upon a shipbuilding campaign. For the first time
in these islands it became an offence to buy a ship, or to
charter a ship, or use one for the carriage of goods over
1,000 tons in weight ; or to purchase goods over 1,000
tons abroad on c.i.f. terms.* In effect, this meant that
no one could build, buy, use, or charter a ship without the
Shipping Controller's leave.

Another measure was decided upon which hit many
trades, both employers and men, very hard. In March,
1917, a Director of National Service was
A Director of   appointed. Mr. Neville Chamberlain was
National Service   the first to fill the office. His real
function was to direct labour of all kinds
from non-essential to essential industries. Shipbuilders,
engineers, and farmers were crying out for men. And
there were still able-bodied people working at jobs which
could be done by women, boys, and old men.

Mr. Chamberlain attempted to meet this by two methods.
He appealed for men to volunteer for national service, and
he published a list of non-essential trades. The first of
these methods was not a success. The new department
inspired no confidence. Such things occurred as a piano-
tuner being sent to work as a farm labourer. But the

* C.i.f.=cost, insurance, freight ; meaning that the purchaser buys the
goods to arrive here, at a price which includes the price of the goods, the
freight, and the marine insurance.

second method was successful in driving into the labour
market a considerable bulk of labour. Before the Act
appointing him had been passed—in February, 1917—the
Director of National Service induced the Minister of
Munitions to make the following order : That no occupier
of any factory, workshop, or other premises where certain
trades were carried on should take or transfer into his
employment, whether to fill a vacancy, or otherwise, any
man between eighteen and sixty-one years of age.

The businesses thus declared to be non-essential were
numerous and varied. For instance, they included all
building, house-painting and decorating, the printing trade
(afterwards removed from the schedule), paper-making,
furniture and cabinet-making, many metal industries,
ornamental woodmaking, quarrying, the manufacture of
beer, wine, and aerated-water bottles, bespoke tailoring,
brewing, the confectionery trade, electro-plating, gold and
silversmiths. The whole classes of clerks, domestic
servants, waiters, shop-assistants, and commercial
travellers were comprehended, so that the hotels and
clubs, which had to a great extent voluntarily adopted
female staffs, were now compelled to rely on women
almost exclusively.

Labour, in the great works of the country, had been
placed under control to some extent as early as November,
1914. It had become an offence to attempt to impede, delay,
or restrict the production of war material. This regulation
was made, it should be said, with the
consent of the responsible Trade Union   **The Law and**
leaders. Further, it was made an offence   **the Trade Unions**
to entice away or even to employ a work-
man who had been working at a munition factory. If a
workman turned up late, or went away early, or took a
day off, he was impeding production. If the men in any
shop, in accordance with time-honoured practice, made
up their minds to make only a certain number of shells a
day, they were restricting production. Special tribunals
were appointed to deal with charges of this kind, and
frequently imposed heavy fines. Such a tribunal could,
for just reason, order an employer to grant a leaving
certificate to a workman, but without such a certificate
the man could not leave.

Considering the free and independent character of our
artisans, the long period of complete liberty they had
enjoyed, and the fact that they were being deprived of the
benefit of their cherished Trade Union usages, the amount
of friction was extremely small. This result must be
ascribed to the level-headed good sense of the responsible
union leaders and to the patriotism of the vast majority of
the men.

One of the most remarkable of the changes made in the
extension of executive powers was the very large authority
conferred on the police. An early Defence of the Realm
regulation (November 28th, 1914) gave every police-
constable the right to stop any person and ask him questions.
And if those questions were reasonable and were not
answered, the person refusing or failing to answer might be
penalised in six months' imprisonment with hard labour even
if he was not acting in the enemy's interests. It was for
him to prove that he was not so acting. If the offender
was unable to prove this, he might be sentenced to death.
Vehicles also might be stopped on the road and their
occupants questioned.

A policeman might also arrest without warrant anyone
whose behaviour was such as to give reasonable grounds
for suspecting that he had acted, or was about to act, in a
manner prejudicial to the public safety or the defence of
the realm. Anyone so arrested might be compelled to be
photographed and to have his finger-prints taken.

A superior police officer could go or send to any meeting
or assembly if he thought that an offence against the
regulations might be committed there.

Any policeman might also enter, and even use force to
enter, any premises or vessel at any time of the day or

night, on suspicion that something was being done, or had been done, there prejudicial to the public safety or defence of the realm. And there he might seize anything which was being kept or used in contravention of the regulations, including the type and plant of any newspaper or publication (regulation of April 22nd, 1916).

In June, 1915, after the German airships began those raids which made them infamous for ever, and, it may be said, stiffened the backs of all Britons, the Secretary of State made orders as to extinguishing or darkening lights. To enforce those orders any policeman might enter any premises and extinguish lights or pull down blinds, or stop vehicles and compel the drivers to lower or extinguish their lamps.

All these extra police powers constituted an absolute revolution in the Constitutional government of the country. It says much for the discretion with which they were exercised that they did not cause any appreciable friction.

As has been shown, the Government had acquired the right to take over any land. If the proprietor would not

Land, railways, and mines agree to the price, it was fixed by an arbitrator or referee, or by the commission specially appointed for the purpose. The Government might also take over land without purchasing it outright, and pay such compensation as the Railway and Canal Commission might award. The Government also took powers to control railways and mines. It did, in fact, assume the control of railways in 1914, but this was not under the new legislation. It was by virtue of the Regulation of the Forces Act, 1871, which conferred this power of control in an emergency. The original order was made for a week, and was continued week by week during the war. Traders and merchants found their facilities much restricted as time went on.

Although very unwilling to do so, the Government was at last compelled, in consequence of labour disputes, to take possession of all coal-mines in the same way that it had taken possession of so many factories. That is to say, the Government assumed power to control the management and use of the mines, and could give orders to the owners, agents, and managers. The power to take the mines was

under a regulation made on November 29th, 1916, and it was first applied to the South Wales coal-field. It was in this area that almost the whole of the trouble had arisen. In February, 1917, under the Lloyd George Government, the whole of the coal-mines in the United Kingdom were placed under Government orders.

On the same day the Board of Trade also took possession of the whole of the canals, except those owned by the railway companies, which had already passed into Government possession with the railways.

On March 13th, 1917, a regulation came into force authorising the Minister of Munitions to take possession of metalliferous mines, mines of stratified ironstone, shale, or fire clay.

Thus the State had, by the beginning of 1917, gradually assumed either possession or control of railways and canals, ships and shipping, coal-mines, an enormous number of engineering and other works, the whole output

FOOD ECONOMY OBJECT-LESSON.
Centre of food economy propaganda in Keighley. An enviable fame was gained by this Yorkshire town, the inhabitants of which succeeded in reducing their bread consumption well below that of the "voluntary allowance."

of hay and straw, the whole stock of leather, the whole clip of wool, the whole stock of metals. In fact, it may be said that, having regard to the food regulations, the liquor control, the labour regulations, national military service, and the Government control of all communications and means of transport, as well as fuel and the raw material of manufacture, Great Britain was, for the first time, completely under the thumb of Government departments.

Just before Christmas, 1916, Parliament created a new office of Food Controller. His duties were defined "to regulate the supply and consumption of food in such manner as he thinks best for maintaining a proper supply of food, and to take such

IN A LONDON LOCAL FOOD CONTROL OFFICE.
Preparing for the distribution of sugar cards in the Camberwell Food Control Office. When in the autumn of 1917 the issue of cards to ensure an equal distribution of sugar was decided upon, Food Control Committees were established in all districts throughout the country.

steps as he thinks best for encouraging the production of food."

The first Food Controller was Lord Devonport, a tried business man. For his chief assistant Lord Devonport had Captain Bathurst, M.P., an experienced agriculturist and a man of great public spirit. Prior to this time there had been some attempts to limit the consumption of meat and bread and other food at restaurants, hotels, and clubs. These attempts had been most unlucky. The principal one was an order limiting the number of courses at lunch and dinner, and the result was that unconscientious customers consumed large quantities of meat and bread, as being the most substantial

Powers of the Food Controller

foods. Lord Devonport abrogated these rules and substituted the following: The weight of meat to be supplied to any customer at lunch or dinner was restricted. So was the weight of bread. Tea-shops were not allowed to serve teas at a price exceeding 6d. There were to be two potatoless days a week. At first there were to be two meatless days also, but this was abrogated soon afterwards.

As wheat was the principal concern, on account of the world-wide shortage in the crop and the sinking of so many wheat-ships, millers were prohibited from milling or selling pure white flour. The percentage of flour extracted from wheat was fixed, and it ranged from 78 per cent. for choice Bombay and Australian down to 48 per cent. for No. 6 Northern Manitoba Special Commercial Grade. There was a direction, also, that where the percentage from the mill fell short of the prescribed percentage, flour milled from rice, barley, maize, or oats must be added.

Having thus tried to increase the supply of flour, and having to a slight extent limited the consumption of bread at public meals, the Food Controller tackled the private consumer.

Many people urged the adoption of compulsory rations, like the German bread-ticket system. But Lord Devonport shrank from this for many reasons. One was that hundreds if not thousands of people would have to be taken from other work in order to manage such a system. So an appeal was made to the discipline and honour of the country. Mr. Kennedy Jones, M.P., became the chief apostle of voluntary rations. Aided by a large body of fervent disciples, he preached up and down the country the duty of every individual to diminish his consumption of bread and flour by 25 per cent. He showered leaflets on every householder. He caused mayors and corporations to become his missionaries. Lady lecturers expounded to housewives, cooks, and " generals" the tasty and nutritious properties of ground-rice scones, maize-flour puddings, and oatcakes for breakfast. People were asked to take pledges to go on voluntary rations, and they did it in hundreds of thousands. Thrift and true economy—that is, the absence of waste—became proofs of patriotism.

Sugar was an article of diet which grew very scarce. So much sugar had formerly been imported from Germany, Austria, Belgium, and Northern France, that there was bound to be a shortage. Early during the war the British Government bought up enormous quantities—in fact, there was none left for anybody else—and then sold it in small parcels. Lord Devonport impressed on the public the necessity of economising in the use of sugar. He cut down the amount allowed to confectioners, and forbade several wasteful ways of using sugar. Brewers were given very little for their brewing. As for grocers, they could not obtain half enough for their customers. Long queues of

MR. KENNEDY JONES, M.P.
Director-General of the Food Economy Department of the Ministry of Food, March-July, 1917.

women used to stand at certain shops in London on sugar days. The domestic making of jam was made almost impossible, unless to those who grew their own fruit. Finally, in September, 1917, the new Food Controller (Lord Rhondda) made arrangements, to come into force with the New Year, to issue sugar cards—that is, to put all people on a sugar ration. The local authorities were drawn into the scheme, being ordered to appoint Food Control Committees.

Potatoes were even worse. The crop of 1916 was bad. The Scots, who were generally sellers of potatoes, had become buyers, because their crop was ruined by disease. Twenty pounds a ton was the sort of price that was being paid to the farmer in January, 1917. The public paid 3d. a pound, which is £28 a ton, to the retailers. Very late in the day the Food Controller stepped in. He fixed the price of potatoes, retail, at a maximum of 1½d. a pound. He cut down the maximum price on the wholesale market, with a rising scale from March to June.

" Profiteering" was the next thing to claim attention. It might well have been handled by the Government before, but it had not been the business of anyone to do it. Now, profiteering was nothing more nor less than the dealing on the market by middlemen who were neither growers, nor producers, nor distributors, but merely speculators. Thus, a cargo of 2,000 tons of rice would start from Rangoon, consigned to John Smith, of London, at £2 a ton c.i.f. (See note on page 314.) John Smith would sell the bill of lading of the cargo on the London Produce Market at the rate of £2 10s. to William Robinson the day after the ship sailed—a nice little profit of £1,000 to Mr. Smith. Next day, rice being in demand, Mr. Robinson would sell again to Mr. Septimus Brown for £2 15s.—a nice little profit of £500 for Mr. Robinson. In a few days' time, rice still being in great demand, Mr. Brown would sell out to Mr. Thomas Williams, this time for £3 15s.—a nice little profit of £2,000 for Mr. Brown. And so *ad infinitum*, until, by the time the cargo reached the Port of London, it might have changed hands twenty times, each time at a profit. And the final price to the wholesale distributor, who really took the rice and sold it to the retail trade, might be five, or six, or ten times the price it originally fetched when shipped at Rangoon.

A certain quantity of beans from Burma had been sold and resold by speculators in this fashion until they had gone up from about £15 to £63 a ton. Then the Food Controller stepped in and compelled them to hand over the whole lot at £37 a ton.

Something of the same kind was happening in the meat market, until the Controller forbade intermediate speculations, and said there was to be only one

Restricting the " profiteer "

intermediary between the farmer or grazier and the slaughterer (June, 1917). But the price of meat rose, all the same, until Lord Rhondda fixed maximum wholesale and retail prices (September, 1917). Then the prices became fairly reasonable.

The Food Controller, having power to fix prices, did so in respect of some commodities, more as the war dragged on. Potatoes, beans, oatmeal, tea, all had their fixed maxima. Lord Rhondda, a Welsh commercial magnate, was appointed Food Controller in June, 1917, in place of Lord Devonport, and he at once issued new regulations, giving himself power to commandeer any articles of food on the same basis as the military authorities. In other words, he could buy up stocks of foods at a fair price without regard to any artificial market prices.

But, in 1917, production was even more important than prices, and as soon as a practical man, Mr. Prothero, M.P., was placed at the head of the Board of Agriculture this problem was tackled with a will (1916-17). Corn-growing was encouraged by guaranteeing to the farmer a remunerative price for his corn for five years. If the market price should fall below this, the State was to make up the difference. Thus, at one gulp, Britain swallowed its Free Trade principles. With a hint of compulsion behind the persuasion, landowners and farmers were induced to plough up grass-lands for corn-growing.

Then came also the allotment movement. A Defence of the Realm regulation gave power to local bodies to seize uncultivated lands and let them out as vegetable allotments. All round the great towns and cities tennis-courts, vacant building land, bits of golf-courses, meadows, park-lands, pieces of Hampstead Heath, Highbury Fields, were converted. Local authorities exercised their compulsory powers with a vengeance. They cut up these lands into plots, and let them at trifling rentals to able-bodied citizens. The Archbishop of Canterbury issued a pastoral letter condoning Sunday labour. And so, from March, 1917, onwards, one might see all sorts and conditions of men digging, planting, hoeing, and—sweet moment !—gathering in the crops. Britain had only two passions—to thrash the Germans and to cultivate its soil. A simple idea, a new regulation under the elastic statute, and the country was transformed.

In addition to food, petrol was " controlled " by the Government. All this with intent to save tonnage. No petrol could be purchased without a permit, and permits were so restricted that the private car was practically driven off the road. Even omnibuses had to be cut down in numbers.

Control of the liquor traffic The liquor trade and traffic were thorny subjects. When, late in 1914 and early in 1915, munition workers and other artisans began to earn " big money," a few of them took advantage of the fact to drink more than usually hard. Many temperance reformers began to cry aloud for total prohibition during the war. They cited the Tsar's anti-vodka ukase, which they either misunderstood or misrepresented. For that celebrated decree was not a total prohibition of alcoholic liquors. It was merely a ban on the consumption of certain kinds of highly deleterious beverages of raw alcohol. The " trade," on the other hand, not unnaturally asked to be let alone ; and in this demand it was strongly supported by many working men.

The Government took the usual middle course. The working-class opposition was too strong to allow of total prohibition ; yet it was desirable to stop excessive drinking. Mr. Asquith, therefore, placed the " trade " under the control of a new body called " the Central Control Board," with Lord d'Abernon as chairman.

The Central Control Board had a very wide jurisdiction. It could do practically anything it pleased with regard to the trade in intoxicating liquors and the places where such liquors were sold. It acted not by general decree, but in areas marked out as being areas of military importance, naval importance, or munition-making importance. But the country was so engrossed in arms and armaments that in time the same sort of regulations prevailed almost everywhere. Licensing justices also were given special powers of control, so that Great Britain found itself under regulations which may be thus described : No one could " stand treat " to another in any club or public-house. The interference with clubs was a sign of the importance of the matter. Public-houses and clubs might not be open for the sale of intoxicants except between the hours of 12 and 2.30 in the afternoon, and 6.30 and 9.30 in the evening.

In order to prevent certain classes of workmen from laying in a stock of whisky, bottles of spirits were forbidden to be sold in certain areas between the hours of 2.30 on Friday and 12 noon on Monday. The workmen were paid on Friday night. In the Clyde area some of the men evaded the regulation at first, because they were able to take a tram-ride out of the district where the restriction applied. Eventually the area was extended, so as to entail a long and slow train journey, and thus week-end whisky passed out of the region of practical politics. Besides the curtailment of hours, the price of drink was put up by duties which became progressively heavier. In 1916 the Ministry of Munitions took nearly, if not quite all, the whisky distilleries for the manufacture of alcohol for munitions, and refused to let more than a limited quantity of that already manufactured out of bond.

Beer, too, was cut down in quantity by limiting the barrelage to be brewed—once in 1916, and again, much more stringently, in 1917. The result was, in 1917, a great shortage of beer. Public-houses were rationed. And if a house sold its beer too quickly it might easily find itself without a single pint at the end of the week. To recoup themselves for the limited quantities they

A FOOD MINISTRY SUGAR CARD.
In September, 1917, householders made a return of the number of persons ordinarily resident in their houses, and these received cards authorising them to purchase the per capita allowance of sugar from the retailer with whom they had registered.

had to sell, publicans put up the prices to the public. When the dockers of Liverpool, in the spring of 1917, were asked to pay for their beer about 8d. a pint they wrecked some public-houses and boycotted the others. Stout was 9d. a pint in London.

Notwithstanding short hours of sale, no treating, diminished strength of the beverages, and increased prices, the Government did not manage to make the country teetotal; and in the summer of 1917 was obliged, in order to allay the prevailing discontent, to permit the brewing of 33 per cent. more beer than had been originally intended.

At first all offences under the Defence of the Realm Act could be tried by court-martial. This was the greatest change that had ever been made in the law of the country. But it did not last long. In March, 1915, owing to the attitude adopted by Lord Parmoor, a lawyer, in the House of Lords, the right was given to all

Courts-martial and trial by jury

British subjects to be tried by a civil court and a jury, except for smaller offences which could be tried by magistrates. This right did not extend to persons under naval or military discipline, but it was extended to women who were technically aliens—that is to say, women who had been British subjects but had married aliens. The right given to the British subject was expressed in this way: Within six clear days after he was charged with the offence he could claim trial by judge and jury; and only if he made no claim could he be dealt with by court-martial.

It is a further fundamental portion of British justice that no trial shall take place except in public. In the case of trials under the Defence of the Realm Act, however, if the prosecution applied for it, the court might order all members of the public to be turned out. Even in such a case sentence had to be passed in public.

An extra power was given to the Crown, "in event of invasion or other special military emergency arising out of the present war," to suspend trial by jury. This was the first time that Parliament had conferred upon the Government the right possessed as an inherent power by almost every other Government in the world—namely, to proclaim martial law. And even this fell short of complete martial law, because that phrase on the Continent means the abrogation of all law, and the substitution for it of the will of the military commander. Here it only meant trial by court-martial instead of by the ordinary courts.

The only occasion on which the section was put in force was during the Irish Rebellion of April, 1916. The Government at that time suspended trial by jury and magistrate in Ireland and substituted trial by court-martial.

It was a little odd to the free-born Briton not to be able to go about the country as he pleased. Much too late, indeed, not until May, 1916, was a

The liberty of the Press

regulation under the Act promulgated giving the Admiralty or Army Council power to constitute special military areas, into which nobody might go without a permit, unless he was a member of the forces or police force, a civil servant, or one of a few other limited classes of people. Anyone from outside wishing to enter a military area was obliged to hold a passport very similar to a Foreign Office passport. The first six areas so ruled off from the rest of the island were Dover and a part of its environs, Harwich, Shotley, Felixstowe, the Isle of Sheppey (including Queenborough and Sheerness), Newhaven, Inverness and all Scotland north of it, and the Spurn Head area in the East Riding.

These areas must not be confused with certain others, from which aliens, whether enemies or not, might be excluded.

Quite as radical a change as any of the foregoing was the interference with the liberty of the Press. In English law anyone can publish anything he likes, so long as a jury will find that it is not defamatory, or blasphemous, or seditious. Under the Defence of the Realm regulations the Press was restricted to the publication of such matter as was passed for that purpose through the Official Press Bureau appointed in August, 1914.

By the old common law, when the King was in a state of war, none of his subjects might, without Royal licence, trade or have commercial intercourse with enemy subjects. No contract already made could be carried out, and no new one could be made. Accordingly, on August 5th, 1914, a Royal Proclamation called the attention of the British people to the new state of things.

It is probable that by the old common law of England the term "enemy," for this purpose, included all those who owed allegiance to the hostile sovereign. But by a decision given by the House of Lords at the time of the Boer War, it had been laid down for this purpose that you must look at the place where the trader carries on his business, and not at his nationality. In other words, a German was not an enemy for trade purposes if he lived in British territory or in a neutral or allied country.

As soon as the Law Courts sat after war broke out the full Court of Appeal decided also that a limited liability company, registered in Britain or any British Dominion, was British, and could not be an alien enemy, although every single shareholder might be German, and the directorate consist of Herren Bluchstein, Rosenbaum, and Sauerlein, all of Hamburg. Such a company—trading, it might be, as the British Islands Industries Company, Limited—could carry on as usual; could bring actions; and quite easily remit its profits to Germany via Berne or Milan. Curiously enough, although six learned Lords Justice gave this decision, Lord Justice Buckley took the contrary view, and Lord Justice Buckley was the greatest company lawyer living. After a considerable time the case (Daimler Co., Ltd., v. Continental Tyre and Rubber Co., Ltd.) was carried to the House of Lords, where it was decided that a company which was managed from enemy territory by enemies was

Winding-up enemy businesses

an alien enemy, wherever registered. This interpretation of the law had far-reaching consequences. That it was the common-sense view nobody could doubt, for it was absurd to allow seven Germans possibly to control a whole British industry merely by calling themselves the Something Company, Ltd.

It was not very long before the Government discovered how inadequate the existing law was. It had grown up at a time when trade was a very simple matter, and when there were no banks through whose international operations, and the action of the telegraph and telephone, money paid in one country could be instantaneously transmitted to another and again to a third. International commerce is carried on nowadays by a system of credits at banks. Further, the people of Great Britain began to ask why enemies living in this country should be allowed to carry on business at all, and why German houses should be permitted to keep their British branches open. The two great German banks, the Dresdner Bank and the Disconto Gesellschaft, were shining examples.

To meet this state of affairs an Act was passed in November, 1914, giving power to the Board of Trade to take possession of enemy businesses and enemy property by means of a custodian. A person called a controller might be appointed to carry on and wind up any enemy business. If an enemy held shares in a British company, they might be ordered to be sold, and the money paid to the custodian. When an enemy's business or property had been sold, the money was to be used to pay off any British creditors, and the balance retained by the custodian till the end of the war. In this manner it was hoped to rid the country of the German commercial influence which had become too powerful; and the triumph of the new system was reached when, in June, 1917, the London

TORPEDO PRACTICE FROM A SUBMARINE.

At torpedo practice. Submarine coming to the surface after having fired a torpedo. Its periscope is to be seen in the top right hand corner of the photograph, while the silvery trail of its projectile may be traced across the wavelets. Inset: Another view of a submarine emerging after firing a dummy torpedo—the trail of which is plainly visible—at the cruiser from the deck of which the photograph was taken.

houses of the two German banks were finally wound up and their premises sold by auction in the City.

Yet another step was taken in December, 1915, by way of striking a blow at German commerce. An Act was passed enabling the Government to prohibit British subjects or residents from trading with persons or associations of enemy nationality even though such persons were not residents or carrying on business in enemy territory. For example, the Government could prohibit British subjects from having any dealings with a German carrying on business in the United States, or Holland, or Sweden. In fact, this was actually done, and a considerable number of people who had been endeavouring to help the enemy to elude the consequences of the British blockade found themselves on a black list. The result was that no British ship would carry their **Heavy blows at** goods, no British bank would discount **German trade** their paper, and no British subject would sell them so much as a packet of pins.

The consequences of the enactment were very striking, and few British measures struck German trade harder. There was a time when Englishmen were not fond of foreigners, but nineteenth-century legislation had changed all that. Foreigners, contrary to the old common law, were allowed to be landowners, and had every other privilege of the British citizen, except the vote and the right to own a British ship. If they desired these also, they could easily become naturalised.

On the outbreak of war it became necessary to deal with the enemies within our gates, for every German was an actual or potential spy. In any other country the Government would simply have issued an Order, rounded up all the aliens, detained those who could not clear themselves of all suspicion, tried some by court-martial, and shot a few out of hand. But in this country there was no legal power to do this, and we are incurably addicted to legality. A day after war was declared, however, an Aliens Restriction Act was hurried through, giving the Government power to make Orders-in-Council to deal with aliens. Under this Act regulations were issued giving power of summary deportation, and of prohibiting aliens, even neutral or allied, from landing or embarking except at certain ports. An alien might be ordered to reside or remain in a certain place, and certain areas were prohibited to him altogether. He was obliged to register himself with the police, and his travelling facilities were restricted.

This Act did not, in terms, permit internment—that is, the indefinite detention of a suspect. But such power was taken under the Defence of the Realm Act. By a regulation under that Act the Crown took power to deal with " persons of hostile origin or associations " as well as alien enemies—in other words, with the naturalised German, or the " Swiss," whose name was Heinrich before the war, and had since become Henri.

The regulation was challenged in the courts by one Arthur Zadig, a naturalised subject of German birth. The Home Secretary had caused him to be interned by an Order under the regulation, and he appealed to the courts of law for a habeas corpus to deliver him from confinement. The King's Bench, the Court of Appeal, and the House of Lords successively rejected his contention.

It is interesting to notice that even in such a time the executive power was surrounded by safeguards and hindered by checks. Before the alien or person of alien origin or associations could be interned, these processes had to be gone through : (1) A competent military or naval authority, or an advisory committee had to recommend the internment ; and (2) if the person affected felt aggrieved, he could appeal to the advisory committee, unless he was an alien enemy. Alien enemies could not so appeal.

To make sure of an impartial consideration of such cases, every advisory committee had to be presided over by a judge or an ex-judge. Two of these bodies were constituted—one presided over by Mr. Justice Sankey and the other by Mr. Justice Younger, and they dealt with the cases of thousands of aliens.

It has not been possible to summarise, **Internment of** much less to explain, the whole of **naturalised aliens** the legislative, administrative, and Constitutional changes made in consequence of the war in order to promote the effective carrying on of hostilities. Enough has been written to show the enormous extent of the interference with the ancient currents of life, and the reader is now in a position to appreciate the gentle irony of the first of the Defence of the Realm regulations, which ran thus :

" The ordinary avocations of life and the enjoyment of property will be interfered with as little as may be permitted by the exigencies of the measures required to be taken for securing the public safety and the Defence of the Realm."

HELP FROM THE BRITISH ARMY IN SOLVING THE FOOD SHORTAGE PROBLEM.
Soldier dockers of the Transport Workers Battalion, York and Lancaster Regiment, unloading a food cargo at the Royal Albert Docks, London. These men came chiefly from the North of England, were billeted near their work, and paid at Trade Union rates.

AUSTRALIANS MAKING A

CHAPTER CCVII.

DUCK-BOARD TRACK.

[Australian official photograph.

THE GLORIOUS CONQUEST OF THE WYTSCHAETE-MESSINES RIDGE.

By Edward Wright.

Duel Between German and British Empires—Why Plumer Did Not Attack in 1916—British Geological Advantages—Von Armin Suffers from Over-Confidence—Explosion of One Million Pounds of High Explosive—The Great Gun Rules the Battlefield—Hill 60 and the Miners of Australia—Battling through Battle Wood—Smoking the Enemy Out of White Château—Londoners Checked by Comines Canal—Great Bayonet Charge by the Kents—The Doom of Damstrasse—Terrific Vehemence of the Welshmen—United Ireland at Wytschaete—Orange and Green Compete in Prisoner-Taking—Magnificent Chain of Exploits by the Cheshires—How the New Zealanders Took Messines—One Rifleman and the Institution Royale—Deadly Pause of the Victorious Army—All the Enemy Counter-Attacking Forces are Trapped—Australians as the Pivot of Victory—Their Advance from the Eastern Slope and Long Bombing Conflict in the Plain—Extraordinary Lightness in British Casualties—Sir Douglas Haig Praises Sir Herbert Plumer.

Y the end of May, 1917, the operations of the First, Third, and Fifth British Armies, described in our chapter on "The Epic Battles of Bullecourt" (Vol. IX., Chapter CLXXXVIII., page 409), were completed.

As a matter of fact, the main design of Sir Douglas Haig had been carried out by the middle of April, when the enemy lost Vimy Ridge and the fortressed ground near Arras. The great Battle of the Rivers had then been continued to help the French forces to recover from their partial check in the Aisne offensive. At the time it was advisable, in the common interests of the Western Allies, for the main British armies to continue to press against the main German armies between Lens and St. Quentin, and there wear down the man-power of the enemy by straight, downright, battering-ram blows.

Probably Sir Douglas Haig had a strategic idea underlying his operations from the middle of April to the end of May, though he had no intention of breaking the enemy's front completely, as General Nivelle vainly attempted

to do. The British Commander-in-Chief had long before selected a more delicate part of the enemy's line for an attack that seemed likely to bring about a decision. But, in loyalty to General Nivelle, he first assailed the Hindenburg line in close co-operation with the armies of France.

When, towards the end of April, 1917, General Pétain and General Foch succeeded to the control of the French armies, the British Commander-in-Chief was enabled to prepare energetically for his special plan of campaign. For another month he had to go on with his terrible bludgeon work between Bullecourt and Fresnoy, until General Pétain reorganised and extended the French gain above the Aisne and among the western Downs of Champagne.

As was afterwards revealed in debates in the Chamber of Deputies, a small section of the French troops continued to show signs of weakness at the beginning of June, 1917, and the influence of German agents upon part of the French people went on increasing until Bolo Pasha and other traitors were arrested. In these circumstances General Foch and General Pétain

[British official photograph.

RUINED GERMAN STRONGHOLD ON MESSINES RIDGE.
For two and a half years the Germans on Messines Ridge dominated the Ypres salient. On June 7th, 1917, the British carried the ridge and reduced to dust positions deemed impregnable.

[*Australian official photograph.*
LINKS IN AN ENDLESS CHAIN.
In the British transport service organisation was brought to the point of perfection, and supply trains moved without interruption up to the front and down again, as if upon an endless cable.

arranged to stand largely upon the defensive for a time, and, while holding down strong German forces from St. Quentin to Verdun, to let the British armies fight in their own way a gigantic duel with the main forces of Germany.

There was a complete change in the strategy of the Allies. Instead of Russia, Rumania, Serbia, Italy, France, Belgium, and the British Empire combining in a grand offensive against the Central League, the armies of the British Empire fought a duel with the forces of Germany, and the armies of Italy fought a duel with the forces of Austria-Hungary, while their Allies did little more than retain some of the hostile masses. After the failure of General Brussiloff's gallant attempt at an offensive in Galicia the Russian front became little more than a place of rest cure for enemy divisions exhausted by the Britons and the Italians. In the eastern theatre

Change in Allied strategy

the apprentice pilots of the Central Empires completed their training on Fokker, Halberstadt, and other machines of an old type, and all the later and more powerful battleplanes, together with all the best pilots, were concentrated against the British and Italian fronts and against the persistently indomitable French squadrons and batteries.

Naturally, France was able to second Great Britain in a far more valuable way than disorganised and almost helpless Russia was able to second Italy. The new mighty guns of France, handled by one of the master-gunners of the world, incessantly inflicted considerable losses in men and material upon the Teutons, and cleared the way for brilliant and important infantry movements at Verdun. Nevertheless, there was a profound change in the operations of the Allies in the latter part of the spring of 1917. Great Britain then justified the author of the "Hymn of Hate" by becoming, on land as well as on sea, the supreme foe of his country. Not only was the fiercest

stress of the war removed from the soldiers of France, freeing them for the time being from any further need of making a grand attack, but the dumb, distracted peasantry of Russia was also saved for a while from very grave disaster.

Long had it taken the British governing classes to organise fully for war. The time that had been lost by miscalculations, by half-measures, and by lack of trust in the entire soundness of the British working classes amounted quite to a year. That which Sir Douglas Haig began strongly to achieve in the summer of 1917 might have been successfully commenced in the summer of 1916. When planning the campaign on the Somme, Sir Douglas had intended this great Franco-British operation as a preparatory measure for a thrust against the German lines at Ypres. But after the local reverse between Gommecourt and Thiepval the British commander found that he lacked the men, guns, shells, and railways necessary for the carrying out of his whole design.

When the material and the men he required began to arrive, enabling him to construct an extraordinary system of lateral communications along his front, in the winter of 1916, he was still unable to pursue his own plan of action with all available strength. He had to take into consideration the scheme for a combined offensive which General Nivelle formed. The new French commander reckoned that he would be able to break through the German front, composed of a series of fortified lines six miles in depth. Strangely ambitious as this plan was, the loyal British commander had to do all he could to assist in carrying it out. The result was that another three months was lost before the armies of the British Commonwealth could enter upon their proper campaign, which had been continually postponed since the spring of 1915.

Importance of Ypres sector

Both British and German High Commands had rightly regarded Ypres as the field for decisive effort. After the British victory in the autumn of 1914, Ypres remained the most delicate sector in the German system of defence, for the enemy was at this point too close to the Dutch frontier and too much exposed on his sea flank to avoid at least a local decision if he were forced to retire. As his possession of the Flemish coast increased in importance, with the development of his submarine attacks on shipping, his position around Ypres became more critical. This was the reason why the German High Command exploited the terrifying surprise of poison gas in the Ypres sector in April, 1915, before employing its main strength in new artillery power against the armies of Russia. It was absolutely necessary to close the Ypres gate of attack against the British Army before undertaking the great adventure in the east.

So successful was the enemy's horrible new weapon of poison gas that Sir John French was unable to move onward from Ypres, and had to make the best of his deteriorated general position, by swinging forward south of Lille at Loos alongside the army of General Foch.

Sir Douglas Haig, who as corps commander won the First Battle of Ypres, gave his successor in this sector, Sir Herbert Plumer, the task of liberating and widening the historic British salient by means of an attack upon the enemy's high positions at Wytschaete and Messines. In the spring of 1916 General Plumer prepared for action by driving a series of extraordinary, long mining galleries under the Messines Ridge.

Owing, however, to the first British defeats at the Ancre brook, the Second Army had afterwards to be employed as a reservoir of reinforcements for the Somme actions. Sir Herbert Plumer, therefore, could not undertake the offensive he had prepared. All he could do was patiently to prolong his immense mining galleries, and pile up hundreds of tons of explosive under the enemy's high position.

New Zealand chaplain administering Holy Communion to soldiers before battle.

[Canadian War Records.

Back from the battlefield: Canadian Highlanders, headed by their pipers, returning to rest camp after action

[Australian official photograph.

At the end of a spell: Australians marching to rest billets along a road near Ypres.

[Canadian War Records.

Tired but smiling: Another view of the Canadian Highlanders returning from the front.

[Australian official photograph.

A silhouette of war: Limbers loaded with ammunition "going up" on the western front.

"Faithful unto death": *Wounded British runner dies as he delivers his message.*

The Germans on the Messines Ridge had every advantage except two. They had dominating observation over Ypres northwards, and over Ploegsteert Wood southward, and although the centre of their ridge was in places slightly below the hill positions occupied by the British on Kemmel Hill, west of Wytschaete, they could bring enfilading gun and machine-gun fire to bear upon the low British lines northward and southward. In regard to mining operations, however, the British sappers in the low marshy ground were able' to tunnel deeply under the ridge from comparatively shallow saps in their own lines.

They were at the start a hundred and fifteen feet below the ridge they proposed to blow up. So great was the depth of ground above their galleries that the enemy did not hear the enormous work that was going on. Moreover, there was a stratum of impervious clay in the low ground through which British miners worked, and above the clay there was merely sand, where the Germans were stopped from mining by percolating water.

In regard also to artillery attack, Sir Herbert Plumer and his gunners had, from the beginning of the operations, a certain advantage of ground. They held, near the Spanbroek Inn, west of Wytschaete, part of the summit which was nearly forty-nine feet above the centre of the German ridge. Then when the British artillery became more numerous than the German artillery, the north-western and south-western sides of the hostile ridge were liable to be smashed by downright, overwhelming gun fire, with cannon as well as with howitzers.

In the spring of 1917 Sir Douglas Haig was in the happy position of being able to refrain from withdrawing divisions from the Second Army in order to continue the struggle around Arras. Not only was Sir Herbert Plumer allowed to keep his forces intact, but finally his left flank was gradually strengthened by the trans- **Bombardment of** port of Sir Hubert Gough's army from **Wytschaete** the Bullecourt sector to the northern Ypres sector.

For many centuries Flanders had been the decisive battlefield between the Island race and the War Lords of the Continent of Europe. Philip of Spain had used Flanders as the starting-point for his military invasion of England before the Spaniards failed at sea. Marlborough, Wellington, and other British commanders had entrenched in the Flemish plain in order to decide and direct the future course of civilisation.

By June, 1917, France had partly spent herself in continuing her traditions of making a break-through against her Teutonic invaders, whom she had formerly broken at Rocroi, Valmy, and other places around the Northern Champagne lines. So Great Britain, becoming free to act in her own manner once more, returned to that lowland by the Flemish coast which had been a battle-ground for centuries, and which had been the turning point in the history of the world in October, 1914.

A great bombardment was opened upon Wytschaete on Thursday, May 24th, 1917, after fierce reconnoitring raids had gone on for a week. The bombardment continued to grow more intense and increase in depth and length. Above the flaming parks of artillery British and German pilots fought for the mastery of the air, while the British infantry raided the enemy's lines as far as the support trench around Wytschaete.

By the end of May all the northern British front from Ypres to Armentières flamed and thundered, and the defences of the Flemish coast were assailed by British warships. At first the enemy High Command did not exactly know whether a strong demonstration was intended against Wytschaete and Messines, as a preliminary to the continuance of the Arras battles, or whether a great new offensive was developing.

There were British strokes against the northern defences of Lens, from the direction of Loos, together with movements by the victorious Canadian forces that fought back to their

[British official photograph.

TESTING FIELD TELEPHONE AIR-LINES IN FLANDERS.
Each air-line section attached to Headquarters provided material for erecting twenty miles of air-line, instruments and operators for four second-class offices, and linemen for maintaining forty miles of line.

posts along the Souchez River, south of Lens. The British artillery along the Scarpe River and in the Quéant junction of the Hindenburg line also began to fire heavily and rapidly, while the infantry broke into the enemy's first line.

Sir Herbert Plumer could not conceal his main preparations. There were large new railway junctions just behind his lines, built of tracks removed from the British Isles and Northern America. Hundreds of new locomotives and thousands of trucks had been added to the military rolling-stock by means of the restrictions on British travelling. By obvious multitudes of men the preliminary labour of a grand offensive went on, and, though scores of enemy scouting planes were brought down and a complete local mastery of the **General von Armin's** air obtained, General Sixt von Armin, the **confidence** commander of the German Fourth Army, was well aware that something was intended against him. He and his Chief of Staff, General von Lossberg, had distinguished themselves in the Somme battles by preventing a complete rupture of their line in the autumn of 1916. They were two very capable men, and the choice of them for the Ypres sector showed that Ludendorff was alert to the danger of a Flanders offensive.

Nevertheless, the German High Command, which was hard pressed both around Arras and along the Aisne, did not immediately proceed to shift its main force towards the new front of danger. Either Ludendorff thought that only a strong British demonstration was impending, and feared to move his grand reserve from the old battlefields, or General von Armin was so confident of the strength of his ridge position that he hoped to escape the fate of the commander of the Vimy Ridge, and achieve a result at least equal to that effected by the German commanding officer along the northern Aisne Plateau. He brought up many more large guns and a few fresh divisions, but he had no immense echeloned reserve such as had been arrayed behind the Hindenburg system.

The British attacking forces were comparatively small, but their backing of artillery was tremendous, and the infantry training was remarkable for its minute perfection. General Plumer ordered the construction of a ·model of the ridge, in which the nine miles of German front was

Rehearsing the battle
reproduced on more than an acre of ground. Every detail of contour and natural and artificial feature was studied for hours by the troops.

Bit by bit the battle was rehearsed, until all the soldiers had memorised their parts. They manœuvred over the reproduction of farms, winding roads, trenches, and woods, with drummers and tin-can performers playing before them in imitation of the barrage they were to follow. Many of the men regretted the rest in billets they might have had if they had not been set to play at killing Germans behind a row of tin-cans and drums.

When, however, they at last stood victorious on the ridges overlooking the Plain of the Scheldt, and recognised all the large actual features of their miniature training ground, they had good reasons to be well contented with the time they had reluctantly spent at playing at toy warfare. Their losses were at least one-fifth less than had been expected, and in many cases the number of enemy prisoners exceeded the number of British casualties. There were, in general, about three German prisoners for every Briton, Australian, and New Zealander put permanently out of action. Such was the result of the rehearsals of victory.

Never had any commander been so laboriously and precisely careful in organising a great battle as was Sir Herbert Plumer. He rehearsed his artillery with his infantry. Sometimes the thousands of gunners swept part of the ridge with a devastating whirlwind bombardment. On one occasion, at least, the grand barrage was flung out in full intensity, while hundreds of forward observing officers and aerial scouts studied it in the hope of being able to suggest some improvements in detail.

The plight of the German garrison became desperate, as is shown by the following extracts from the diary of an enemy stretcher-bearer at Messines :

May 27.—The English are firing on us heavily.
May 28 (Whit Sunday).—We have two dead and two wounded. This is a charming Christian festival. One despairs of all mankind. This everlasting murder !
June 1.—The English are bombarding all the trenches and, as far as possible, destroying the dug-outs. They keep sending over shot after shot. To-day we have a whole crowd of casualties. The casualties increase terribly.
June 2.—The English never cease their bombardment. All the trenches are clodded up. Nothing more to be made of them. Casualties follow on casualties.

June 3.—The English are trying to demolish our dug-out, too.
June 4.—The casualties become more numerous all the time. No shelter to bring the men under. They must now sleep in the open ; only a few dug-outs left.
June 5.—Casualty follows casualty. We have slipped out of the dug-out and moved elsewhere. There are many buried by earth. To look on such things is utter misery.
June 6.—The English are all over us. They blow up the earth all around us, and there is shell-hole after shell-hole, some of them being large enough for a house to be built in. We have already sustained many casualties.

In thousands the Germans were driven down into their caverns, and in the early morning of Thursday, June 7th, 1917, as General von Armin sent the Bavarians of the 3rd Division to relieve the shattered Saxon division on the ridge, the grand British barrage struck the enemy in his hour of weakness. The Saxons were partly caught in the disorder of their withdrawal, and the Bavarians, who had to march through a curtain of shell fire, were attacked before they could become acquainted with the position to which they had been sent.

All the dreadful characteristics of the action of Vimy Ridge were reproduced upon the low Flemish slopes, with many technical improvements and a ghastly increase of power. A million pounds of ammonal were exploded at the end of some nineteen mining galleries of extraordinary length and depth. The English, Irish, New Zealand, and Australian troops were impeded by the effects of the great volcanoes that broke through the first German system.

It was death to enter the huge craters filled with the gas from tons of ammonal. Even soldiers who approached to near the lips of the gigantic holes, when trying to skirt round them and help the thrusting movement on the flanks, became dizzy and sick from the drifting fumes. The Germans on the slopes were appalled by the awful nature of the greatest mining operation in the war. The ground around them shook in earthquake tremors,

DEADLY "LIFEBUOY."
An officer inspecting a German "lifebuoy" liquid-fire thrower on a companion's back. It had been captured on the western front.

[Australian official photograph.
GERMAN LIQUID-FIRE THROWER.
Another enemy flammenwerfer of the "lifebuoy" type, which was captured by some of the Australians on the western front, and promptly employed against those who had imported this new horror into warfare.

amid the continual explosion of shells ranging from 15 in.
bolts down to the shrapnel rain of the field-artillery.

Barrels of burning oil tumbled into the enemy trenches
and broke in floods of flame into the dug-outs that
remained uninjured. The concrete caverns and cellars of
the villages, representing the highest developments in the
German arts of defence, were turned into complete death-
traps. The forts of the new model, first known as
M.E.B.U.'s and "Maybushes," and afterwards by the more
scornful term of "pill-boxes," proved to be no more
protection than the Hindenburg tunnel had been. All
definite trench systems, carefully devised by Armin and
Lossberg, in accordance with the lessons they had learnt
on the Somme, went the way of the older works, designed
when the London Scottish were thrust out of Messines
during the First Battle of Ypres and the British cavalry
were driven out of Wytschaete.

The great gun ruled the battlefield as it had not done
even in the days when the old Regular British Army fought
its last battle practically without any cover. For the great
gun had been given "eyes" of far-ranging and precise

CARE OF ARMS AT THE FRONT.
Officer inspecting his men's rifles in a village on the western front. They
were equipped with gas-masks, as it was a point at which the "gas alert"
signal was frequently necessary.

UNDER ORDERS FOR THE FRONT LINE.
Final inspection of the books and identity disks of men of a New Zealand
contingent who were about to leave for the fighting-front in France.

power as well as additional force of destruction. Anything
that could be photographed from the sky could be struck,
and anything that could be seen in movement by aerial
observers could be pursued by the heavy gun and
annihilated.

As the enemy had been at last overtaken in the manufacture of guns and shell, his devices for concealment and
protection were devices of weakness that increased his losses.
Gun alone could properly answer gun. As the Germans
were caught with an inferior amount of artillery, that
suffered under the additional disadvantage of loss of aerial
vision, the battle for the ridge was rather a slaughter than
a conflict.

The attack was made on a front of about nine miles,
from Mont Sorel, south-east of Ypres, to Douve River,
above Ploegsteert Wood. Through Battle Wood, north of
Hollebeke, English troops, with North Country units,
advanced. London men fought along the spoil-banks by
the Ypres-Comines Canal towards the White Château.
From St. Eloi, English County regiments moved south of
the canal into Damstrasse.

Welsh troops stormed into the Grand Bois, north of

Wytschaete, and magnificently battled far across country
into Oosttaverne village. The ridge and village of
Wytschaete were carried by Ulstermen and Catholic
Irishmen. The lowish saddle between the Wytschaete and
Messines heights was gained by more English battalions,
including the Cheshires, who proved they deserved their
name of "the cement of the armies." Messines was
assailed by a New Zealand division, through which
Australian forces passed to extend the victorious advance.

The infantry went over the top of the assembly-trenches
they had recently dug at ten minutes past three in the
morning. There was moonlight dimmed with mist over
all the country, but these natural conditions were smothered
in the great orange and scarlet flames of the mine explosions,
the bursting of barrels of burning oil, rainbow splashes of
signal rockets, white star-shells, and the fire and fume
of millions of projectiles. The British
artillery was reported to have fired four
million shells, and to have made a hole
in every nine square yards of the terrain.

**Rule of the
great gun**

Many of the shells threw their steel splinters over a
radius of two hundred yards, and the mere concussion
effects of their high-explosive charge far overlapped that
of the next shell, only nine yards away.

The German artillery endeavoured to shelter their men
by the usual mechanical barrage over the ground of advance,
but in many places the hostile batteries were unable to
carry out their work. Over each long-studied German
battery site there fell a British standing barrage, and the
unnerved enemy gunners at times displayed extreme
cowardice. Those of the lighter artillery, that fled with
their pieces as the action opened, were not to blame. They
obeyed orders. But there were, in the rear, gunners with
heavy ordnance who remained more or less safe in their
dug-outs, and refused to fight their guns to the death in
order to help their overwhelmed infantry. There were
some similar cases, though fewer, among the well-sheltered
Prussian and Bavarian officers of regiments of the line.
In one case a score of German officers remained in a deep
cavern and let their men struggle on undirected, while they
themselves surrendered as soon as British bombers arrived
at the entrance of their shelter.

The average German has the virtue of prudence. It is
one of the sources of his strength in both business and war.
One of his reasons for first contemning and then ferociously

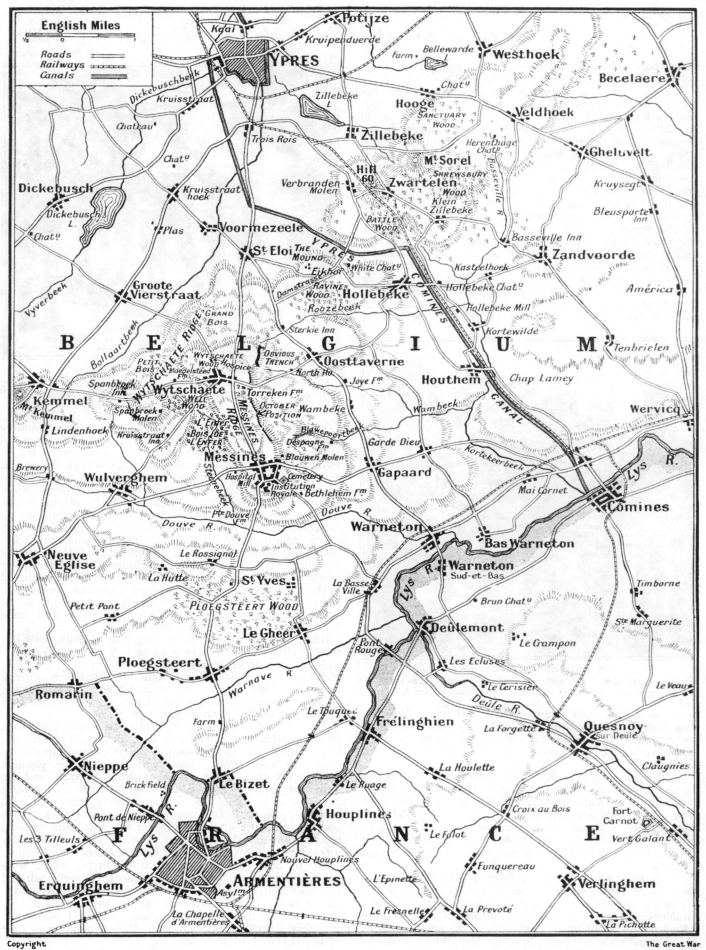

Copyright

MAP SHOWING THE DOMINATING POSITION OF THE WYTSCHAETE AND MESSINES RIDGES.

The high ground between Ypres on the north and Armentières on the south, deemed impregnable by the Germans who occupied it, was long an obstacle to any successful British thrust from Ypres, which both the British and German High Commands recognised as the field for decisive effort. Sir Herbert Plumer was entrusted with the task of liberating and widening the historic British salient by means of an attack upon the Wytschaete-Messines Ridge, and that task was triumphantly achieved by the forces under his command in June, 1917.

hating the " Engländer " was that he naturally disliked the spirit of sport and adventure of which the Anglo-Celt is the modern incarnation. Duty was a thing that the German appreciated, as was seen in many a desperate charge and gallant stand he made. But his feeling of duty was of a gregarious nature, and best expressed itself in massed charges like those that occurred in the First Battle of Ypres.

When the tremendous power of the new British artillery broke the German garrison of the ridge into little distracted groups, seldom amounting to more than **Battle for** two hundred men in the largest tunnels, **Battle Wood** the majority of the officers and men tended to fall back upon the old instinct of prudence which their forefathers had cultivated during the long civil wars in Teutonic countries.

As was often seen, a German machine-gun section that had survived the prolonged bombardment set out with the aim of fighting to the death. The men fired upon the attacking troops to the last moment, but then they became the most currish cowards in Christendom. Instead of dying in desperate bravery, they often tried to save their lives by throwing up their hands in token of surrender. Scores of cases of this kind occurred during the battle, and it need hardly be said that, when the British soldier, with his dead and wounded just behind him, got within bayonet reach of the Germans who wanted to do all the killing possible and yet save their own lives, the death-bed repenters did not always evade the fate they deserved.

At the northern end of the fighting-line the famous Hill 60 was the scene of a long, stealthy struggle months before the action opened. Some Australian and British miners undertook to blow up the mound of raw earth that completely dominated the southern portion of the Ypres salient. Among them were men from Broken Hill and from the great sheep-farms. They bored an elaborate network of galleries and chambers under the ground, where German sappers, working at less depth, succeeded in blowing in their own front line.

Once, without knowing it, the Germans dug so close to one of the Australian chambers that they brought the roofing down upon the tins of ammonal. On another occasion a hundred miners were kept working at an almost unendurable stretch in a gallery, four hundred feet long, pumping out water to save the operation. When at the opening of the battle two great craters were blown in Hill 60, the survivors of a Würtemberg regiment holding the mound were easily conquered by the Australian miners themselves, who had joined with the attacking infantry in order to see at once the effect of their labours.

Apparently, the Australians expected that a mile of Belgium would be blown off the map. After the explosion, however, Hill 60 remained a very strong position. When the German artillery in turn shelled it, their 6 in. shells merely flicked away a bit of roofing concrete the size of a man's hat. The vault of the observing chambers consisted of sixty-pound rails, riveted solidly together, and embedded in six feet of concrete.

From the opening in the outer wall a complete panorama of the British line at Ypres was obtained. When the victors first looked through the slit in the clearing air they saw all their positions minutely exposed. Some of the most important of their places were visible in spite of the camouflage designed to hide them. They could only wonder that the German artillery had not utterly destroyed them. No doubt it would have done so but for the labours of British munition-makers.

Between Hill 60 and the Mound rising near the Comines

Canal there was a large patch of broken trees, wired trenches, and underground and concrete forts known as Battle Wood. It was a most difficult sector to attack, and still more difficult to hold. Being on the flank of the battle-line, it was subject to the cross-fire from German guns on three sides. Moreover, the German commander could pour reinforcements into the blasted woodland from Gheluvelt and Shrewsbury Forest, as well as from the fields and slopes around Zandvoorde.

Some of the English troops who rose to attack Battle Wood were flung down by the force of the explosion on Hill 60. Happily, their comrades met with little resistance, though very heavy fighting had been anticipated. The men of the Würtemberg division that garrisoned the large wooded tract had been terribly hammered in the long bombardment, and were so weak and weary that their central redoubt was speedily silenced. After losing five hundred and forty prisoners the Würtembergers were driven out of the wood in an absolutely shattered condition.

Thereupon, another German division, the 11th, which had been badly punished in the Arras battles and sent to Bruges to rest, was ordered to make forced marches to the southern end of Battle Wood, and there strengthen the

[*Australian official photograph.*

BRITISH SUPPORTS MOVING UP ON THE WESTERN FRONT. A glimpse of that incessant activity behind the lines in France and Flanders which preceded and marked the advances resulting in the capture of the ridges, the principal key position on the western front, and changed the Ypres positions from a defensive salient to a broadened wedge of attack.

men of Würtemberg. The new division had had no draft since its withdrawal from the southern battle, and the wasted regiments had little desire for fight left in them. They were driven back to Shrewsbury Forest, a mile beyond Hill 60, until, with the exception of one corner in the wood, the British line ran without any serious bend from a point about a mile below Hooge to a point about two miles west of Armentières.

On the southern bank of Battle Wood ran the Comines Canal, close to the park and country-house known as the White Château. The position formed the side of the great German ridge salient, and **An impregnable** was itself bastioned by the low hillock **fortress** near St. Eloi known as the Mound, which the Canadian troops had vainly tried to hold earlier in the war. South of the manor-house extended a level drive, built by the owner in the manner of a Roman road. Part of it was banked above a low plain between St. Eloi and Hollebeke, and part of it was cut through the higher wooded ground. This drive was the famous Damstrasse, upon which German engineers had laboured since October, 1914.

Rows of concrete forts were constructed above underground shelters along the Damstrasse and the Comines Canal. Then mounds of excavated earth, called by engineers spoil-banks, were hollowed out by the waterside, roofed with concrete and riveted rails, and armed not only with machine-guns but with artillery. The manor-house was continually strengthened according to the experience obtained in all the battles between Neuve Chapelle and Vimy.

Until the third week in May, 1917, the enemy regarded this northern flank of the Wytschaete Ridge as the most impregnable part of his fortress system. When, however, the heaviest British guns began exactly to register upon concrete armour-plate and the earth cushions above the roofs, there was nothing to withstand the tons of steel and high explosive except the oldest and easiest form of cover. Only where there was an immense cushion of soft earth to act as a pillow to the monster British shells did the garrison beneath escape.

Awful effects of British shell-fire The spoil-banks survived, together with the great Mound and part of the sand-bagged roofed cellars under the broken walls of the country-house. Although six feet of concrete and steel could not generally be broken by 5·9 in. German shells, when enemy gunners were registering upon positions lost by their infantry, the new 15 in. British shell either tore into the forts, or, bursting outside the observing slits, killed or incapacitated the men within by the shock of expanding gases.

A large number of Germans went mad. Some tried to kill themselves or murder their comrades, and especially their officers, or else sat gibbering and clawing at their mouths. Horrible was the stress upon mind and body which the overwhelming British artillery imposed upon the enemy. Thousands of half-broken survivors from shattered redoubts and shelters had at last to lie out in the open ground in shell-holes, and, under a continual rain of death, await the final creeping barrages and the charging British infantry behind the stamping curtains of shell.

The Mound was blown up in the same way as Hill 60. Of the garrison only three stunned Germans remained alive when the huge new crater was explored. It was then discovered that the British infantry had had a narrow escape from the same fate. German miners working from the Mound had driven a shaft a hundred and twenty feet into the British lines on the plain south of Ypres. As it had happened in other battles, there had been a miners' race below the opposing fronts, and it was partly the fact of the British attack occurring at least two or three days before it was expected that saved the assailing troops from a great German mine.

Saved from a German mine

London men, County regiments, including a very fine force of Welshmen and some Irish soldiers, were arrayed between the canal and the ground around the Damstrasse. Some of these troops, who were completely overlooked by enemy observers on high ground, had no assembly-trenches, and gathered for the attack in shell-holes where they were espied by the enemy. Happily, the German officer commanding in the section thought that only a raid was intended. As he did not like unnecessarily to expose all his battery sites, he shelled only a small part of the unprotected men. No German flying machines were available for scouting, as they had either been destroyed in action, or injured in the general bombing attacks upon aerodromes carried out by the Royal Flying Corps.

British observing officers, on the other hand, were able to fly where they liked over the enemy's lines. At times

British official photograph.

ARTILLERY MOVING FORWARD THROUGH A SHATTERED VILLAGE.
Part of an endless procession. It was only by the steady accumulation of artillery and shells that the British attack on the Wytschaete-Messines Ridge became practicable with comparatively small attacking forces.
Even in the preliminary artillery rehearsals of Sir Herbert Plumer's triumphant action thousands of gunners swept parts of the high ground with a devastating whirlwind bombardment.

BRINGING IN BRITISH WOUNDED ALONG A LIGHT RAILWAY. [British official photograph.

Many miles of light railways were laid behind the British front in France and Flanders for facilitating the taking up of munitions and other supplies, and for conveying wounded men back to the bases. This line ran alongside pollarded willows which served to screen it from observation.

they descended within fifty feet of the ground, shooting at gunners, dispersing infantry, blowing up ammunition dumps, and searching for guns amid all the devices of concealment practised by the enemy. A single British squadron marked down some two hundred and ninety German guns, and directed an intense heavy fire upon them until every gun was put out of action. Another British aerial unit of larger size sent three hundred and ninety calls for fire upon enemy gun positions, and directed effective hits upon nearly all the objectives they marked down.

This was the main reason why some of the English County regiments were able to assemble in shell-holes in No Man's Land without being wiped out before the infantry movement opened. The German was so completely mastered in the air that his guns were practically an encumbrance to him, except on the northern and southern wings. He began moving his artillery back a day or two before the assault, and as his retiring batteries had to pass through the persistent barrage maintained by British heavies on the hostile communications, the Germans were far from saving all the guns they hastily withdrew.

British mastery of the air

A large number of the seven thousand prisoners taken in the battle reckoned that they had been betrayed by their commanding general. They were told in an Order of the Day, issued early in June, that the ridge had to be held at all cost by the infantry and machine-gunners, because all positions would be recovered in a great counter-attack for which everything had been made ready. The withdrawal

of many of their guns made the Prussian and Bavarian foot soldiers rather doubt the order given to them.

The increasing intensity of the opposing artillery fire deepened their doubts, and when the great mine explosions occurred, followed by cascades of burning oil, tempests of gas-shells, and tornadoes of high explosive, the spirit of the German soldiers was generally broken. They knew they had been sacrificed in tens of thousands in order that Ludendorff and Armin might be able to save that part of a thousand guns which had escaped the eyes of the squadrons of British airmen.

Men sacrificed to save guns

In spite, however, of the large tendency to demoralisation, there were detachments of Prussians and Bavarians that went on fighting with great courage. The Londoners, who had to clear the spoil-banks along the Comines Canal, met with fierce resistance. By means of skilful rush approaches, trench-mortar fire, and hand-bombs, the men of London managed to work through and around the largest of the works formed out of earth excavated from the bed of the canal. But beyond this triangular system was a smaller oval earthwork, embedded in the water-side, which could not be taken. Neither the ordinary creeping shrapnel barrage that forced enemy garrisons underground nor the heavier roof-smashing line of high-explosive shell was of avail. The loose, deep earth cushioned all the explosions, and the firing slits below could never be reached by shrapnel, and seldom by direct machine-gun or rifle fire. Any attacking-party that came close enough to fire at the slits fell under a lash of bullets from another direction. It

333

POUNDED TO DUST: WYTSCHAETE VILLAGE AFTER THE BATTLES.

[British official photograph.

Wytschaete village as it was when captured by the British after the terrific fighting for the Wytschaete-Messines Ridge on June 7th, 1917. Under the merciless pounding of the British hurricane bombardment, which lasted for seven days, the whole topography of the region was altered; woods were swept out of existence, hill slopes were stripped, and villages, like Wytschaete, were simply obliterated.

took a week of concentrated gun fire and gradual infantry approaches along new saps to break into the oval work.

Checked on the canal, the London men entrenched between the spoil-banks, cleared the Germans out of the dug-outs on either side of the low water, and connected up with other metropolitan battalions who were also fighting under great difficulties around the White Château. As already explained, this country-house, the proper name of which was Château Matthieu, had been transformed into a semi-underground fortress. Near it was a lake—by which were the ruins of what had been fine stables, all surrounded by a wilderness of stumps, broken wire entanglements, blown-in trenches, and sunken redoubts—in what had once been a lovely Flemish park.

The Londoners worked through the blasted woodland with comparative ease, their barrage being far more terrible than it had been in the similar wood fighting on the top of the great ridge along the Somme. They swept through the grounds of the château, and in the first rush entered the ruins. By devious ways, however, some **Capture of the** three hundred Germans climbed up from **White Château** the caverns, and with bomb and machine-gun fire took the men of London at a disadvantage and forced them back. The attacking-party remained within bombing distance and pitched incendiary missiles among the ruins for an hour. During this time a single platoon cleverly worked round the broken walls and completely smoked out sixty Germans remaining from the original garrison of a company and a half.

From the conquered château the troops then worked down to the stables as far as the gate, and into the orangery and other buildings beneath which the Germans were sheltering in their caverns. The new smoke-bombs again proved more effective than the ordinary high-explosive grenade. Every underground retreat was gradually filled

334

with stifling fumes, which compelled the Germans to emerge, breathe, and surrender. The stream running from the lake to the canal had been cleared and occupied, bringing all the Londoners on either side the historic waterway into a new line partly bent around the oval work.

On the right of the London troops were Southern English battalions, who had advanced from the Mound after the great explosion. They pressed forward into the chaos wrought by their artillery and, after a bitter fight with a German detachment, stormed along a ravine where the survivors **An advance with** of a Prussian division were suddenly **fixed bayonets** launched against them in a counter-attack.

The Kents were heading the advance in the ravine and their bayonets were fixed. They rushed upon the Prussians standing behind the stumps of trees. There, crossing bayonets and sometimes firing trickily, they stabbed and shot down every German who showed fight and took prisoner those who dropped their rifles. Eight hundred Germans were taken between the Mound and Ravine Wood, together with a great store of war material.

Several "tanks" climbed over the broken ground in the hope of sharing in the fighting, but they did not find much work to do. The enemy's strongholds were shattered by shell and all his troops broken or dispersed when the landships arrived. German batteries were found knocked out, with the gunners lying dead around them.

The Damstrasse, near by, had been a source of great anxiety to the general commanding the British troops in this sector, and also to the Staff of Sir Herbert Plumer. Aerial photographs had revealed the extraordinary strength of the enemy's defences in the hollow ground along which the drive was made. Special artillery preparation was therefore made in regard to the street of concrete block-houses, and, such was the penetrating power of the storms of heavy British shell that the enemy garrison was practically put out of action before the attacking infantry arrived.

The larger part of the street of fortresses was broken, and the cowed survivors surrendered in hundreds. The unexpected speed with which this victory was gained enabled the English County regiments quickly to bomb their way along the road and reach Ravine Wood in time to break the Prussian counter-attack with the bayonet.

In the afternoon, when the Londoners beyond White Château and their countrymen at the end of Ravine Wood had consolidated on their new line, other English forces went through them in order to drive the enemy farther back to Hollebeke. The men who had been fighting since dawn did not want to be relieved. They wanted to go on and get their fill of fighting, feeling that the enemy and their own artillery had cheated them out of the best part of their job.

Prussian counter-attack broken On the other hand, the fresh troops did not intend to be deprived of their part of the battle, especially as they had rehearsed everything with the men who wanted to do the whole job themselves. Naturally, the first turbulent waves of attack were kept to orders, and the new men went out behind the afternoon barrage and carried out the programme they had practised.

The left wing at first marked time, covered by the wall of smoke and flame in front of them, and the right wing, which had a larger stretch of ground to cover, wheeled onward, fighting all the way. Throughout the Second Army all advances were made with almost mechanical precision by means of thousands of synchronised watches. In the present case the two differently manœuvring wings bore down all the enemy's resistance.

They captured six field-guns and some special trench-mortars, with many machine-guns and three hundred prisoners. Furthermore, the wings joined together on their new line within thirty seconds of each other. The entire casualties, light and **Casualties less than prisoners** serious, were less than the number of German prisoners. One battalion had twenty casualties, mostly light, and a hundred captured Germans. One of the men of this battalion was as disappointed as the Londoners and Kents who were left behind. "The trouble about these easy victories," he said, "is that a man doesn't get any real fighting!"

All the Second Army grumbled. Every battalion either complained that it ought to have been allowed to do something that the afternoon troops did, or, if it belonged to the afternoon forces, it complained that it was not allowed to do all that it could have done. Only the officers were well contented, and they pointed out to their men that, if they went too far, they would get beyond the cover of their own guns and come within easy range of the withdrawn German batteries.

In the matter of fighting, the Welsh troops who broke into the Grand Bois, north-west of Wytschaete, must have

[*British official photograph.*]

BRITISH ARTILLERY DROPPING SHELLS ON MESSINES RIDGE.

Distant view of Messines Ridge under bombardment by the British, preparatory to the "earthquake" mine of June 7th, 1917, when a million pounds of ammonal were exploded at the end of some nineteen mining galleries of extraordinary length and depth. For the victorious attack conducted by Sir Herbert Plumer the British had massed artillery which outnumbered and outclassed that of the enemy.

had all the fierce delight in battle they desired. Some of the Welshmen could not be held back. Their front wave went so fast that it got within fifty yards of one of the largest mines on the whole front at the moment when the explosion occurred. The men were struck with falling fragments and partly gassed by the work of their miners. Yet they went on with the rest, and continued to draw sharp rebukes from their officers because they would not wait sufficiently for the movement of their barrage.

They took the wrecked first trench in a walk, but had some hard fighting in the system of defences just in front of the large wood. **Heroic Welsh machine-gunner** Amid the trees the destruction wrought by the British guns was not complete, missing several machine-gun positions that had to be carried by bomb and bayonet. But one Welsh machine-gunner fought forward in an extraordinary manner. He charged a small redoubt, firing his gun from his hip. So true was his running aim that he killed all eight members of the gun section and, taking the place unaided, released his company for further swift action.

East of the wood was a very formidable obstacle just over the brow of the ridge. It was known as " Obvious Trench," because it was the reverse of obvious, being quite invisible. Happily, it was not invisible from an aeroplane, and the guns had been so exactly directed upon it that all wire entanglements had been cut, and much of the trench and underground work destroyed. There were still many Germans in this high position, but they could not prevent the Welshmen from climbing the slope and killing or capturing them. On the ridge behind the trenches was a hollow in which twelve guns and two heavy trench-mortars were taken.

Then beyond the artillery position was a farm building known as " North House," which was a nest of concrete caverns and gun shelters. There were some well-known football players in the attacking force, and they helped to surround the fortressed farm, and bombed into surrender a regimental commander, " with " his Staff, and a large garrison. In the evening the spirited division, that continually worked in advance of its time-table, made its final drive.

The Welshmen, by savage fighting, pushed through Oosttaverne Wood, and extended their line beyond Oosttaverne village. The German losses in this night attack were uncommonly heavy, by reason of the fact that the Welshmen were engaged in hand-to-hand nocturnal combat with large enemy reinforcements and partly reorganised survivors of the Battle of the Ridge. After overcoming and routing the Germans, the men of Wales proved their qualities as a mining race by digging themselves in deeply and quickly.

Well it was for them they did so. They had reached, at Oosttaverne, the extreme limit of a safe advance, and the long-ranged heavy German artillery shelled them furiously for a night and a day. The victors, however, had few losses, owing to the cover they had made for themselves. When the German infantry at last counter-attacked them on their right and on their left, they did not know there was a movement against them; for their own artillery had been moved up in the interval, **Orange and Green in friendly rivalry** and the hostile waves were broken and dispersed before the Welsh infantry could see and fire on them.

South of the Grand Bois, or Great Wood, was Petit Bois, or Little Wood, with another wood east of it and the village of Wytschaete beyond. There was about three-quarters of a mile of rising wooded ground from the trenches of the attacking force to the northern fortress village on the ridge. Here the left wing of the Irish regiments advanced, while the right wing started from high ground, by Mont Kemmel, over more level ground.

The Ulstermen and the Nationalist men were in a dangerous mood. Their fighting spirit, already proved on the Ancre, in Suvla Bay, and at Ginchy, was edged to harder fineness by emulation. Very friendly were the two forces of Green and Orange. Had they been set together to arrange the solution of the problem of the future government of Ireland, in all probability they would have settled it by mutual magnanimity. Friendly rivalry in games had brought them close together, and not long before the Southern Irishmen had given a silver cup to the Northern.

With inveterate sportsmanship the Protestant and Catholic forces turned the battle into a competition in regard to the capture of prisoners. There was no definite decision on the matter, as when the captives were numbered it was found that North and South had almost even shares of 1,000 prisoners each. But the struggle between the regiments was conducted in a manner disastrous to the enemy.

The earthquake of the exploding mine in the Petit Bois salient killed all the hostile garrison, except two badly wounded men. But, as an Irish sergeant put it, " when the mine went up we went down. The ground rocked under us, and the fumes came back on us and made us dizzy, but we went on to Petit Bois and then to Wytschaete Wood, and other lads passed through us into the village."

Even the timber in the Irish dug-outs was broken by the extraordinary mine in the Petit Bois. The Nationalists formed the left wing that swept into Wytschaete village, while the Ulster right wing of the United Ireland force, keeping in absolute line, drove into the upland fortress of Spanbroek Molen, and, passing by Well Wood, topped the centre of Wytschaete Ridge alongside the conquerors of the village.

At first there was little opposition of importance in Petit Bois, where the Germans were so shaken that many of them met the Irishmen with hands upraised. In Wytschaete Wood, a tract of ploughed earth bristling with branchless and broken trees, sharp fighting occurred. The wood was about **Fighting in Wytschaete Wood** eight hundred yards away, and connecting with it was a ruined hospice and the village on the crest. The Germans had several tunnels, through which they could move quickly and unseen from one threatened point to another. Moreover, the Irish Riflemen on the surface were impeded by broken entanglements, holes, masses of timber, and general wreckage.

There were concrete forts remaining uninjured among other shattered redoubts, from which came streams of machine-gun fire and red and white signals for help from German guns. Upon a neighbouring tree a brave German non-commissioned officer stayed and signalled to his artillery as the Irishmen swept forward from the smoky darkness. He was collected as a prisoner, and the fort was fiercely won by salvos of rifle-grenades that killed almost all the exceptionally resolute garrison. This struggle to the death was costly to the Nationalists, but allowed the attack to sweep on to a further intact block of the enemy's defensive work in the broken circular line around Wytschaete.

A gallant officer, leading a party of men from the South of Ireland, rushed the position, and, as he fell dead, the Riflemen broke into the redoubt, and with the bayonet slew or cowed the Prussians. The swift self-sacrifice of the officer prevented delay, during which the Germans might have begun to reorganise.

As it was, the fresh Irish waves of attack went through the first forces at the newly-won line near the crest, and won the village with remarkable facility. The garrison was demoralised by the devastating bombardment, and there were disgusted companies of Irishmen who had no occasion to fire a shot. They walked up behind their barrage, sat down on their objective, and waited for the fighting to begin, while " tanks " and cavalry patrols went forward to reconnoitre the eastern plain.

After the men had dug themselves in, one of their soldier-poets started a new version of the "Wearing of the Green," while all the batteries rolled forward up the ridge, amid the cheers of the forces of attack resting on the lower slopes. The guns that covered the victorious brigade were dressed in green foliage, as a concealment device. So, as the Irishmen sang:

They love the ould division in the land the boys come from,
And they're proud of what they did at Loos and on the Somme.
If by chance we all advance to Whitesheet and Messine,
They'll know the guns that strafed the Huns were wearing of the green.

Amid the joy of victory there was a feeling of mourning, for Major William Redmond, the brother **Major Redmond** of the Nationalist leader, was killed near **killed** Wytschaete. He was borne away in an Ulster ambulance, thus serving in death to bring North and South into brotherhood of sorrow, as he had striven in life to unite them in a confraternity of heroic adventure.

The Ulstermen set out alongside the Dublins, and began by breaking a brigade of the 4th Grenadiers of Prussians. The German commanding officer did not follow the proper tactics of putting two battalions in line and keeping one in reserve. He placed all his men in action, with the result that all lost heavily and rapidly. One company was destroyed by a gigantic explosion of the mine at the point known at Peckham, and, amid the flaming confusion and smoking obscurity, the Northern Irish charged and broke the Grenadiers. Two other brigades of the 2nd Prussian Division were also routed in the first phase of the advance.

Therefore, about noon, General von **Captives of the** Armin threw into the furnace of the **Red Hand** ridge battle all his 1st Reserve Division; but, as this was thinly extended from the south of Wytschaete to Messines, it could not withstand the combined pressure of Irish, English, and Anzac troops. The Ulstermen also took prisoners from the 40th Saxon Division and from the 3rd Bavarian Division, that had partly relieved the Saxons. There were thus fragments of four enemy divisions in the captives of the Red Hand.

On the right of the Ulstermen was an English force who connected southward with New Zealand troops. Some of the hardest work in the battle was given to the Englishmen. The distance from their starting-place at Kruisstraat Inn to their objective over the ridge was two thousand yards. Fronting them was the Bois de l'Enfer,

[*New Zealand official photograph.*

GERMAN GUN EMPLACEMENT ON MESSINES RIDGE.
Result of the British bombardment on the concrete emplacement of one of the enemy's 77 mm. guns during the attack on the Wytschaete-Messines Ridge in June, 1917. Although the gun had been effectually put out of action, the concrete shelter for the gunners had been only partially destroyed.
Y Y

[*British official photograph.*
GETTING READY FOR ACTION.
Bombers drawing bombs from a well-protected underground supply store during an attack on the western front.

or Hell Wood. North of the wood was a system of concrete blocks, which was hell itself; while southward, behind a labyrinth of fortifications, was Hell Farm. These places formed the central defences of the saddle of the ridge between Wytschaete and Messines, and the enemy fought with especial fierceness in the hope of retaining the means of making a great counter-attack from a position that flanked both hill villages.

On the night before the assault some North Country troops crawled out into No Man's Land, and, clean under the nose of the local German commander, General von Laffert, excavated an assembly-trench four and a half feet deep and two-thirds of a mile long. They had scarcely any casualties while thus reducing the distance between them and the Bavarians and Saxons. When the men leaped out at ten minutes past three, after a most laborious night, there was no symptom of fatigue in their gallant bearing. They broke

Cheshires in Hell Wood

through uncut wire, they stormed fort after fort, and, against the resistance of the best of German troops carried out their time-tabled programme of successes.

Greatly did the Cheshires distinguish themselves in the battle for the saddle. As they advanced they had to fight on the rear as well as on the front. A body of a hundred Germans charged on them from behind, from an ambush in Hell Wood. A young Cheshire officer turned a machine-gun on this enemy detachment and brought many foes down in full career. But he had to stop firing, for his men swept across his sights, met the remaining

Germans with the bayonet, and killed or routed them all.

The Cheshires followed the few fugitives into the wood, and with other English troops rushed the men of the famous 3rd Bavarians in a manner in which that crack German division had never before been treated. Fourteen machine-guns were taken in the lower part of the wood, and more at the top corner. So fast did the Cheshires go through the Bavarians that they ran into the relieved Saxons and also broke them. By the rapid conquest of Hell Wood the battalion closed the gap between them and the troops on their left, and brought all the attacking line forward to the crest without a weak spot in it. They blasted their way into Hell Farm, though they found it deserved its name, and then gained the road connecting Wytschaete and Messines.

Running beyond and parallel

[*Australian official photograph.*
PERILOUS WORK, BUT OF VITAL IMPORTANCE.
Australians going over the top of the trenches to run out new lines of communication during the fighting in the neighbourhood of Zonnebeke, which was an important contributing factor in the capture of Passchendaele on November 6th, 1917.

with the road was an undamaged system of defences known as the October Position. Some Ulstermen had taken part of the trenches, and had orders not to go any farther. They saw the English forces sweep forward on their left, and arrive against a belt of uncut wire near some ruined buildings known as Middle Farm. Enemy gunners and riflemen rose above the parapet and shot down the heroic men who tried by every means to climb over or through the uncut entanglements. With heavy loss some Englishmen got through and began to clear the enemy trenches, but, as the garrison consisted of nearly three hundred Germans, the odds were extremely heavy against the attackers, who had emerged torn and bleeding beyond the wire.

The language of the Ulster spectators, chained down

by Staff orders, became very violent. "To hell to staying here!" said one of the Ulstermen. "To hell with it!" said another. "We could do a power of good up there." They rose, and their comrades followed, and took the German position on the flank, lightened the task of the gallant attackers in front, and saved many of their lives.

Again the English division closed the gaps in its battle-front and carried it unbroken down from the eastern slope of the ridge. On their left they passed another farm, against which their flank and the Ulster flank seemed likely to be checked. But a party went forward with two Lewis guns, stormed into the fortified ruins, chased the fleeing Germans, and made some of them prisoners. This job was not theirs, as they knew from their study of the miniature battlefield; but, like other divisions, they were only too glad for an excuse to expand. On the right flank there was another fortified farm outside the divisional objective, but again a party detached itself, stormed into the wrecked building, bombed the cellars, and apologetically handed over the captured position to the troops it had cheated out of a fight.

It was the Cheshires who again distinguished themselves in the side-shows on the German Warneton line. In the silence that followed the end of this phase of the operations an officer of the Cheshires saw a body

On the German Warneton line of Germans trying to escape from Despagne Farm, well out in that part of the enemy's territory upon which the British barrage was next to play.

Some German machine-gunners were rearguarding the flight of their main body and spraying bullets at three Cheshire men who were reconnoitring. The officer went forward with supports and took the strong point with the bayonet. Then he remembered something and looked at his watch. The dash on the farm had been too late and too premature. It was only a few seconds to the time fixed for the new British barrage. It was too late to try to get back, and the infantry attack itself had been premature.

The Cheshires knew what their barrage was like, and reckoned they were under sentence of death. Each of them dived into a shell-hole, scratched himself as much as possible into the shelving side, and there, like a worm under a plough, endured the storm of flying steel and high explosive. By happy chance the barrage swept over them quickly, and only two men were hurt. Others were somewhat shell-shocked.

Men of weaker fibre would then have been well content with what they had achieved. Not so the Cheshires. They followed their barrage into the next German defences, **A valley of death** and killed part of the garrison and took many prisoners before they dug themselves in on the extreme line of advance in preparation for the enemy's reaction.

They were ready for the foe when he came. Four German battalions debouched from the gully of Blawepoortbeek, that opened in front of Despagne Farm. The Cheshires held back their fire until the German column was at short range. Then with musketry volleys and streams of bullets from machine-guns they shot down the Germans in hundreds, and so turned the little ravine into a valley of death that very few of the enemy were able to escape.

The hostile counter-attack had been so quickly organised and launched that there was no time to warn the British artillery. All the infantry of the Second Army, however, had been strictly maintained by Sir Herbert Plumer in the old and glorious tradition of rapid, deadly musketry fire. The hand-bomb and the bayonet were rightly regarded as secondary weapons, and, like the Australians at Lagnicourt, the Cheshires once more proved that the Lee-Enfield, with a hundred rounds for firing at the fastest speed, was still the master instrument of the British soldier. Many fine acts were performed by the other English troops of the division, and in spite of hard fighting at different points their casualties were not distressing.

Staff work and general organisation were perfect. The men made good their distant final line of victory exactly

HIGHLANDERS STORMING A BRICKWORKS THAT STEMMED AN ADVANCE NEAR YPRES.
During the offensive near Ypres the Highlanders were confronted by a ruined brick factory, heavily armed with machine-guns, which was holding up the advance. A message was got through to the heavy artillery who bombarded the works, sending the bricks flying amid clouds of red dust and silencing some of the machine-guns. The Highlanders then advanced and carried the position with magnificent dash.

THROUGH QUAGMIRE TO VICTORY.

[British official photograph.

Taking up munitions to the guns on the western front after a spell of stormy weather, which had reduced the shell-pounded roads to veritable quagmires. Despite the roughness of the going on certain parts of the front after heavy rains, the men and horses performed their essential task with unflagging perseverance, and the men carried on with a dogged determination which was the best manifestation of the will to victory.

to time. They were all fed on the way. The first waves, that advanced before sunset, breakfasted in comfort one hour after they reached their midway positions. During the hot June day, when the ridge was dry and dusty and steaming with explosion smoke, water went up to them regularly, together with lemons. Carrier-pigeons were employed for some communication purposes, together with other efficient devices.

It was a clockwork battle, for which every individual had been better trained than many Staff officers had been in the first trench conflicts. The general knowledge of the features of all the battleground was of extraordinary value. Owing to the intensive rehearsals, the privates were rather better than many German commissioned officers. In cases where their leaders fell and they took charge of platoons, they continued to develop the long-practised programme without any further guidance.

There was a fine instance of this in a platoon of the Canterbury Regiment during the action in Messines. Officers and non-commissioned officers were shot **New Zealand private** down, and a private went forward with **takes a village** the remnant of men. He conquered the part of the village fixed by the programme, and, digging a splendid trench to safeguard the captured ground, prevented any check to the operations.

The New Zealanders were set to thrust into Messines, through a ring of defences which the enemy had been strengthening since May. On the southern corner-post of the ridge there was an outer defence of an elaborate kind, protected by numerous hedges of wire, both in front of the village and behind it. The inner defence system was based on five concrete works, to which new forts were being added. There were caverns sheltering companies, and smaller dug-outs containing platoons. Tunnels connected the principal underground works, and the Germans continually practised defensive actions, so as to make each machine-gun party capable of acting on its own initiative in critical circumstances.

The left wing of the New Zealand division advanced alongside the Englishmen, and, under their creeping and stationary barrages, took the first position with little loss. Then the second wave passed on to the enemy's second line in front of the town, stormed into an undamaged redoubt, and rushed their objective according to time-table.

Just outside Messines the third wave of attack carried on and, breaking into the northern part of the village, went through the left of the town and joined the Cheshires over the

ridge by Swayne's Farm. On the way German machine-gunners and snipers were found in shell-holes, but so close were the Canterbury, Otago, and Southland men to their barrage that most of the German gunners were captured before they could fire a shot.

One machine-gun position, that was holding up the advance, was carried single-handed by a private. He shot down three of the crew by very rapid fire, and the rest surrendered. In the rush into Messines a sergeant and ten Canterbury men were the first to break into the northern part of the village, where they captured four machine-guns and seventy Germans. Apparently every New Zealander reckoned he was more than a match for half a dozen Germans, and in a general way this was so.

One Southland corporal sprang into a well-garrisoned trench and demanded surrender. As he could see the Germans were not in a mood to yield, he used his bayonet so quickly that he **Splendid dash of** completely cleared the position. Re- **overseas troops** turning to his platoon, he found the officer and sergeant wounded, and in a deadly gay spirit of adventure led the men on to further successes.

The manœuvring skill of the battalions was as remarkable as their flame-like courage. At the opening of the action some of them had to move slantingly to their first objective, at an angle of forty-five degrees. Next, they had to change direction in order to reach their second objective, and finally unite again with the general line. Owing to the darkness, the smoke from the great mine explosions, and the dust and fume from the barrage, the turning-points were completely hidden. Nevertheless, the troops were able to strike exactly at the flanks of their objectives, and take them without delaying for a minute the general movement.

In the cemetery behind the village there was a hostile force which had escaped both bombardment and barrage. The first wave of the New Zealand attack was held up, but, as soon as supports arrived, the graveyard position was taken in a series of springs. In this kind of sprinting race against machine-gun fire the athletic overseas Britons seldom allowed the Germans time to get full on the target.

The forces on the right wing took their first objective in sixteen minutes, and reached the southern outskirts of the village in forty-four minutes. The Rifles, who led the assault, had extraordinarily few casualties in breaking into the hostile points of resistance. "Tanks" that

340

came behind them had nothing to do, every strong post having been stormed or enveloped by the infantry.

During the attack there were more single-handed rushes into enemy machine-gun positions. In one of them a corporal killed five men, wounded another, and took twelve prisoners. The same man next saw a German in a dug-out training a machine-gun on the flank of his platoon. The corporal rushed the gunner down the dug-out, called for surrender, and flung in a bomb. Seven men and an officer came out, but the officer, seeing only one khaki figure, tried to draw his revolver. He was killed. After fishing up four more Germans, the corporal handed his new bag of captives to another party and rejoined his own platoon.

The ruin of the Institution Royale, which was the most striking feature of the Messines Ridge, was expected to give great trouble. A strong party of Germans indeed endeavoured to justify the special training that had been spent on it by making a fierce resistance in the **Rifleman's** cellars. But a corporal and four men **remarkable feat** carried the underground retreat, killing some twenty Germans and driving the rest from the position. As two of his men were wounded during the subterranean fight, only the corporal and one private achieved the victory.

Before this little but important action, the surface position of the battered Institution was the scene of a far more remarkable feat by a rifleman. Through the British barrage he saw the German machine-guns in the ruined buildings firing down the slope. He went through his own shell curtain and attacked the enemy gunners. On finishing this work he was joined by a corporal. With his help the rifleman captured two more machine-guns and killed the fourteen men serving them. Again another German machine-gun fired from an inner wall, and with a grenade the rifleman smashed the gun and killed the gunner. During the whole of this extraordinary series of swoops the rifleman and the corporal darted about, wonderfully uninjured, right inside their own barrage.

This was why the Institution Royale did not hinder the operations of the New Zealand division.

By 7.50 in the morning Messines was not only taken but cleaned up. In the meantime, small columns of Auckland and Wellington men swept by the village to establish a forward line from which the Australians were to jump off. The Wellingtons had some sharp fighting at Blauwen Molen, where a strong party of Germans, with machine-guns, was killed or captured. Then at Fanny's Farm, on the extreme left flank, was another fierce and successful action. By 9.50, when the British barrage had ceased, some of the Aucklanders, like the Cheshires, began to push on towards the afternoon objective, which the Australians in the rear were appointed to take.

Three hours afterwards came the Germans' counter-attack, on which Sir Herbert Plumer had based his final movement. The enemy advanced in ten lines, with the telescopes of British observing officers on the ridge studying the grey waves.

General von Armin thought that the long interval of silence and inactivity of British guns and infantry denoted the end of the attack. So he proceeded to exhaust his reserves in a series of counter-thrusts against the points that promised stra- **Von Armin exhausts** tegical successes. In the case of the **his reserves** New Zealand line there was no hidden valley to screen the enemy's preparations and advance, as there was in the Blawepoortbeek, near the Cheshires.

Consequently, the idea underlying Sir Herbert Plumer's order for the troops to rest awhile on their first line beyond the ridge was fully realised in an abrupt, deadly manner. The field-guns on the newly-won heights and his howitzers on or near the western inclines formed a close barrage that rapidly moved, in flame and smoke and thunder, upon the ten long ranks of enemy infantry. When the air cleared the hostile forces were not visible. The remnants were crouching in shell-holes.

[Australian official photograph.

A MULE TEAM HELD FAST IN THE CLINGING, CLOGGING MUD.

When bad weather set in in the west, mud was the most persistent obstacle to every British movement, straining the strength of mules and horses, imposing the severest task upon the moral of the troops and often taking toll of lives of man and beast. Even on short journeys and quite close to their positions the men had to put shoulder to the wheel and help the animals, while the leader pulled and encouraged them in front.

CARRYING IN THE WOUNDED UNDER HEAVY FIRE.
British stretcher-bearers engaged in their heroic work—" the only living souls to be seen on the vast expanse of the battlefield "—bringing in a comrade during a storm of shell fire on the western front.

There they were attacked at three o'clock in the afternoon by the Victorians and Tasmanians of the Australian force. At the opening of the battle an Australian division formed the flank of the general offensive. The men had to fight over the little valley of the Douve, a stream only three or four yards broad, flowing round Messines Hill. The Douve was the boundary of the Fourth and Sixth German Armies, and the Australians were set the difficult task of cutting off a corner of the ground of the Sixth German Army, and then driving in on the flank of General von Armin's forces.

The attacking division was in turn exposed to a thrust on its flank from the hostile Sixth Army, and a continual enfilading bombardment from the guns ʼ of that army, as well as to direct infantry and artillery attack by the southern wing of the enemy's Fourth Army. Yet the Australian division had to fight forward **Australians at the** and stand firm, because it was the pivot **pivotal point** on which the whole attack of the Second Army was swinging forward over the ridge.

The Douve brook and the ground above it were covered in thick mist, that extended over the lower slope of Messines Hill and hung about densely four hours after the beginning of the attack. The mist served to screen the movements of the first waves of Australians. They threw six wooden bridges over the Douve in ninety seconds, and with equal rapidity overran the German fire and support lines. Even in the shell-holed front beyond few Germans made any attempt to fight. Either they surrendered or they ran.

Only as the rising ground was reached, amid a tangle of battered hedges, rows of branchless forest trees, and the ruins of four farms, was serious machine-gun fire encountered.

Under cover of the mist a Victorian officer, with a small party of men, crept along one of the hedges to a redoubt concealed in foliage. The creepers stormed into the blockhouse, seized a German machine-gun and, turning it upon two groups of Germans, swept them away.

After taking the line of the farms the Victorians and the Queenslanders dug themselves in, two-thirds of the way up the southern slope of Messines Hill, and the lower rise south of the Douve. As the smaller hill was exposed to gun fire on two flanks, the immediate occupation of the crest would have been horribly costly to the storming infantry. By entrenching two-thirds of the way up the reverse slope the attacking troops obtained such shelter from direct gun fire as more than compensated them for other local disadvantages.

In the afternoon other Australians moved through the New Zealanders and the English troops, and carried out, along the southern half of the battle-front, the final advance of the day from the Messines sector. The left of the Australian line met with no heavy opposition. The Germans usually bolted or surrendered, and a couple of "tanks" afforded valuable help against one hostile strong point which threatened to hold up the infantry. When the landships finally became bogged, the crews dismounted some of their machine-guns and fought side by side with the Australians to the victorious close.

There was much stiffer fighting on the right of the line, around the exposed southern shoulder of the ridge. The heavy guns of both the Fourth and Sixth German Armies maintained a violent bombardment, and enemy reinforcements were immediately available from the inactive infantry across the river.

The outworn Bavarian troops, crouching in half broken hedges and behind half ragged trees, were strengthened, and new snipers and machine-gunners poured a continuous fire against the advancing waves of Australian assault, mainly South Australians and Queenslanders. A trench-mortar, intended to deal with the enemy at this place, was destroyed with its team on the way up, and half of a Vickers' gun crew, intended for the same operation, was put out of action. Only an officer and two men remained with the gun. They brought it against the German position, but it was knocked out. The officer repaired the gun only to have it again knocked out.

He then crept forward with his two men and smashed a German machine-gun with two bombs. Other German strong points were either enveloped by Lewis machine-gun parties or rushed with hand-bombs. Scarcely had the new line been established when two German battalions, in dense formation, preceded by a light skirmishing body, charged **German salient** against their lost corner of the ridge. **stubbornly defended** Upon this projected counter-attack the British artillery struck with terrific force, and the assault was not delivered. Thus did the observation value of the ridge quickly tell against the losers of it.

Yet the afternoon action, though generally successful, did not end without some small local checks. In the middle of the British and Anzac new line of attack, near the spot where the Cheshires were pounded by their own barrage, a gap was created in the Australian front by a determined German garrison of a position in a sheltered dip of ground. There was an unbroken wire entanglement at this point, and the enemy commander led up strong reinforcements, and in the night launched a fierce surprise counter-attack without artillery preparations. After a desperate struggle the Germans were thrown back into the hollow. There, screened from direct fire, they held out for three days and nights in a conflict as deadly as that at Bullecourt, though on a smaller scale.

On the fourth night the Australians tried to rush the enemy's salient. They were caught by a heavy German shell curtain, and again held up by barbed-wire, amid which they waged a bomb conflict with the Germans. Only a few men managed to get into the German trench, but on the right flank the South Australians were more fortunate, and, rushing the position in front of them, allowed the other men to move into the captured trench.

On the right some New South Wales men bombed out

the Germans, only to be killed or wounded by a counter-attacking force. Thereupon, some Western Australians attacked the counter-attackers, broke them completely, and, joining with the Tasmanians on the other side, captured all the salient at dawn. So arduous had the fight been that some of the Tasmanians who had borne the main burden of it were found sleeping amid the Germans they had killed.

At the time this prolonged and intense action began the German commander tried to counter-attack along the front with the 1st Guard Reserve Division of some Bavarian forces. On the southern part of the line the counter-attacking brigades were observed as they were getting into position and broken by the British artillery. All that night and all the second day the Germans continued their attempts to form an attacking line. On each occasion, however, they were dispersed by an avalanche of British gun fire.

East of Messines, General von Armin's lieutenants were at first more fortunate in their preparations. They succeeded in forming a line, but the troops that came over the fields were swept away by rifle fire and machine-gun fire. The battle ended a mile beyond Messines, where the enemy was again struck by the Australians as he was about to carry out a peaceful, stealthy retirement to a depth of a thousand yards.

Altogether, the victory south of Ypres was as perfect as superb generalship and magnificent training could make it. The enemy was so stunned that it took him thirty-six hours to collect forces for a counter-attack on a large scale, and this counter-attack completely failed. No doubt General von Armin expected some kind of attack, but he disastrously underestimated the driving power that Sir Herbert Plumer had organised, and he overestimated the strength of resistance in his own men.

All his flying squadrons were struck down, his field-artillery was put to flight, most of his heavy guns were knocked out or smothered, his ammunition dumps were exploded, and his infantry was destroyed. His losses of life were tremendous. The semi-official British estimate of thirty thousand German casualties was well under the mark. It was based on the number of prisoners taken and the dead collected from the conquered trenches.

But for miles beyond the line of victory there were tens of thousands of Germans slain or maimed by the British heavy artillery. For more than a week companies marching towards the ridge, as relief or reinforcements, were sometimes reduced to sixty men before they reached the fighting-front. The permanent British losses in two days of attack and resistance may be calculated at 2,500 officers and men. There were lighter casualties, numbering 7,500, but practically all these only put the men temporarily out of action.

Germans outgeneralled and outfought

The battle, as Sir Douglas Haig pointed out, was a gauge of the ability of German troops to stop the British advance, under conditions as favourable to the enemy as any army could hope for. The British Commander-in-Chief was of a reticent nature. When one of his armies did its duty he did not compliment it. Hard-won victories were the natural meed of the British soldier, he seemed to think, and required no public remarks of importance. But in an Order of the Day he congratulated the Second Army and its chief in a manner very unusual with him. The Order ran :

The complete success of the attack made yesterday by the Second Army, under the command of General Sir Herbert Plumer, is an earnest of the eventual final victory of the allied cause. The position assaulted was one of very great natural strength, on the defence of which the enemy had laboured incessantly for nearly three years. Its possession, overlooking the whole of the Ypres salient, was of the greatest strategical value to the enemy. The excellent observation which he had from this position added enormously to the difficulty of our preparations for the attack, and ensured to him ample warning of our intentions. He was therefore fully prepared for our assault, and had brought up reinforcements of men and guns to meet it. He had the further advantage of the experience gained by him from many previous defeats in battles, such as the Somme, the Ancre, Arras, and the Vimy Ridge. On the lessons to be drawn from these he had issued carefully-thought-out instructions.

Despite all these advantages, the enemy has been completely defeated within the space of a few hours. All our objectives were gained with undoubtedly very severe loss to the Germans. Our own casualties were, for a battle of such magnitude, most gratifyingly light. The full effect of this victory cannot be estimated yet, but that it will be very great is certain. Following on the great successes already gained, it affords final and conclusive proof that neither the strength of a position nor the knowledge of and timely preparation to meet an impending assault can save the enemy from complete defeat, and that, brave and tenacious as the German troops are, it is only a question of how much longer they can endure the repetition of such blows.

Haig's estimate of the battle

Yesterday's victory was due to causes which always have given and always will give success—namely, the utmost skill, valour, and determination in the execution of the attack, following on the greatest forethought and thoroughness in preparation for it. I desire to place on record here my deep appreciation of the splendid work done above and below ground, as well as in the air, by all arms, services, and departments, and by the commanders and Staffs by whom, under Sir Herbert Plumer's orders, all means at our disposal were combined both in preparation and in execution with a skill, devotion, and bravery beyond all praise. The great success gained has brought us a long step nearer to the final victorious end of the war, and the Empire will be justly proud of the troops who have added such fresh lustre to its arms.

The fact was that Sir Herbert Plumer had, abruptly and completely, snatched from the enemy the principal key position on the western front. The German defences were breached between the ridge round Lille and the slopes beyond Ypres. The enemy was thrown back into the plain, there to be killed daily in wholesale manner by British artillery controlled from the ridge. The Ypres positions were no longer a defensive salient, but a broadened wedge of attack, and Sir Douglas Haig at once began immense new preparations for the larger offensive from Ypres, for which Sir Herbert Plumer had decisively cleared the way.

"TANK" SET ON FIRE BY AN ENEMY SHELL.
Occasionally the "tanks" were crippled or destroyed by the Germans by means of a direct hit. In this instance the monster had got bogged on a bad bit of ground, and thus became a stationary target.

WATER FOR MAN AND BEAST: A TYPICAL SCENE IN SALONIKA.

British soldiers watering their horses at a fountain in Salonika, long the headquarters of the Army of the Orient. One of the men is buying a drink of water from a picturesquely attired water-seller; little boys are fetching water from the fountain in kerosene tins, and through the crowd a priest passes, casting haughty glances on the animated scene.

| CHAPTER CCVIII. |

THE SERBIAN OPERATIONS ON THE BALKAN FRONT, JUNE, 1916—JULY, 1917.

By Major Claude Askew, of the Serbian Army.

EDITORIAL NOTE.—In view of the successful reconstruction of the Serbian Army at Corfu, the Editors of the GREAT WAR asked Major Claude Askew—who, with his wife, contributed a personal narrative of the Army's tragic retreat in January, 1916 (Chapter CIV., Vol. VI., page 113)—to write three chapters describing its renewed operations as an effective force when, in his judgment, the time arrived for this to be done with propriety. On August 17th, 1917, the gifted author despatched the chapter here printed, giving an account of the Serbian offensive, June, 1916, to July, 1917, a chapter accurate and complete as it stands and only not longer because of the sequel he then proposed to write. That was one of many projects he was destined to leave unperformed. When Major and Mrs. Askew were returning from Rome to Corfu, after a brief holiday, to continue their devoted work for Serbia, the Italian steamship Bari, in which they were passengers, was torpedoed by the Germans in October, and they were among those who lost their lives. This chapter was the last piece of literary work on which Major Askew employed his pen, and there is a fine fitness that it should have been a record of the splendid work of the heroic Serbians to whose cause he and his wife had consecrated themselves. As having a pathetic interest in the sad circumstances, although not strictly proper to a history, the personal opinions of the writer on the situation and the outlook on the Balkan front of the war at the time of their writing are printed precisely as they reached the Editors. Asterisks indicate where this portion of the chapter begins.

B Y the end of May, 1916, the whole of the reorganised Serbian Army, some 100,000 to 120,000 strong, had been safely landed in the vicinity of Salonika. Their arrival meant the fulfilment of a tremendous task, and one which cannot be overlooked in history's record of great achievements of the war. Barely four months had sufficed to reclothe skeleton frames with warm flesh, to heal open wounds befouled and stubborn through privation and neglect, to put new spirit into tired bodies that had become capable of little else but silent suffering.

To this splendid achievement of French and British endeavour a signal proof of the Allies' effectiveness at sea is to be added. There was no secret about the transport of the Serbian Army from Corfu to Salonika—there could not well be any, owing to the unfriendly attitude of the Greek Government then. Yet not a single transport met with disaster, not a single life was lost.

Only was it to be regretted that one notable figure of the Serbian Campaign was destined to be left behind. The veteran Field-Marshal Voivoda Radomir

Putnik, prostrated by a severe illness which had already in Serbia compelled him to resign his command, and which had been terribly aggravated by the sufferings of the retreat, was compelled to remain behind at Corfu, leading his soldiers in spirit only to the final victory in which he so firmly trusted and believed.

[British official photograph.
A GREAT SERBIAN SOLDIER.
Marshal Misitch, Commander of the First Serbian Army Corps, distinguished himself in the operations which ended in the recapture of Monastir. King George conferred the G.C.M.G. upon him, the decoration being presented by General Milne (right).

Destiny had not willed that he should see victory, though he lived to rejoice at the news of Serbian soil rewon. He died at Nice a year later, leaving behind him a record that will win him a high place among the military leaders and strategic authorities of the world—for he was a writer as well as a soldier.

He took part in the war of 1876 against the Turks, and in that of 1885 against the Bulgars, but it was in the Balkan Campaign in the Great War that he rose to prominence. His name is imperishably attached to the great Serbian victories of Kumanova and Bragalnitza, while the rewinning of Monastir must have particularly rejoiced his heart, for he it was who finally, in 1912, expelled the Turk from that city. To him, too, is due the fine victory of Fser over the Austrians in the present campaign, as a result of which King

ZZ **345**

Peter conferred upon him the title of "Voivoda," or Duke, a title revived for the occasion, and, so far, bestowed upon but three of Serbia's sons.

The Chief of the Serbian General Staff, after the retirement of Field-Marshal Putnik, was General Boyievitch who, born in 1856, had also played a prominent part in the wars of Serbia. He was promoted General after the victories of Kumanova and Monastir. He particularly distinguished himself in the campaign of 1915 by effectively holding up the Bulgar advance through the Gorge of Katchenik, thus delaying the fall of Pristina, and permitting the main body of the Army to effect a safe retreat.

Attached to the person of General Boyievitch—"Adjoint au Chef du l'état Major"—we find an officer, Lieut.-Colonel Pechitch, who won considerable distinction for his qualities, military, diplomatic, and **The new army** literary, and was ranked as one of the **at Salonika** highest authorities in Serbia on strategy and tactics. It is probably superfluous to add that the Chief Command of the Serbian Army remained in the hands of Prince Alexander.

The reorganised Serbian forces were divided, according to the method adopted earlier in the war, into three armies, though now each army contained but two divisions. Later on, owing to losses in the field, and for reasons of convenience, the Third Army was done away with, being merged into the other two.

The First Army, originally under the command of General Vassitch, was now taken over by Voivoda Misitch, a most capable and distinguished officer who had always been closely attached to the person of Voivoda Putnik. Subsequently, for his services on the front, he received from King George V. the 1st Class Order of St. Michael and St. George. The Second Army was commanded by Voivoda Stepanovitch, whose renown as a leader had been vastly increased by his conduct of the recent campaign.

The month of June, 1916, then, saw this notable reinforcement to the troops under General Sarrail's command encamped near Salonika, mainly on the great sun-baked plains to the east of the city. What a change it was from the pleasant olive-groves of Corfu ! Here, no shade was to be found from the torrid heat ; dust lay like a white shroud on the meagre vegetation, and mosquitoes and flies and all manner of insects and other pests abounded. Mikra Bay is not a pleasant place to live in.

Yet among the Serbs there was no complaining ; rather did they rejoice, for they were on Macedonian soil, and Macedonia is closely allied to their own land ; while but a little way off rose the great barrier of mountains that separated them from their country and from all that they held most dear—the old people and the little ones left at the mercy of a cruel foe—and none among them but prayed that the day would quickly dawn when they should be summoned to strike the first blow.

In the meanwhile they were not idle. The work of preparation—of drilling and exercising—effectively initiated by the French at Corfu, was continued unremittingly, and vague intelligence of the arrival of this **A surprise for** new, antagonistic force, springing up like **the Bulgars** ghosts from the shadow of a guilty past, filtered through to the Bulgarian lines beyond. Characteristically, they refused to believe it " There are lying rumours," opined the " Echo de Bulgarie," organ of M. Radoslavoff, " as to the arrival at Salonika of important Serbian reinforcements, which, however, have no existence except in the imagination of Entente journalists."

They were soon to have very practical proof of their error. " What, you are still alive ? " cried the first Bulgar prisoners to be brought in. " We thought you had all been killed off." The mistake was almost excusable, and even when fighting at close quarters might have been persisted in, for the characteristic uniform and kepi of the Serb had largely disappeared to give place to useful metal helmets, and to uniforms of British khaki or French blue. Even

the Balkan sandals had been replaced by stout British boots. Never before, perhaps, had Serbian soldiers been so well equipped and so well fed—which accounted mainly for the large number of Bulgarian deserters who soon came trooping in, and who continued to do so afterwards.

The Serbs did not have long to wait at Mikra. They were soon advanced to their allotted place upon the general front, which had been considerably modified by Bulgar irruptions into neutral Greek territory. The occupation of Rupel and Demirhissar had coincided with the Serbian arrival, while, later on, the invaders had pushed their way on to Seres and Kavalla on the east and on the west to Florina, and well south of the Ostrovo Lake. Here they held the Salonika-Monastir Railway about as far as Vodena, and controlled several important roads, including those to Koritsa and Kastoria, by means of which it was easy for the Germanophil Greeks to communicate with the Central Powers.

The Serbs occupied a long stretch of the front under the great hills which separated them from their own country, extending from Lumnitsa on the east to Sokol on the west, whence it perforce turned south to the neighbourhood of the Bulgar-occupied Ostrovo Lake. The valley is that of the Moglenitza, a river derived from many streams which have their origin among the steep slopes of the frontier mountains, here known by the general term of Moglena. Many of these hills rise to a considerable height, varying from three to eight thousand feet, the latter being represented by Kaymakchalan on the western spur.

On July 28th, 1916, according to English reckoning—July 15th, Old Style—an event occurred which, small though it may appear superficially, will always remain memorable in Serbian annals. It was on that date that the official newspaper issued by Headquarters resumed the publication of bulletins from the front.

The last bulletin to be issued in Serbia appeared on October 20th, 1915, at Krushevatz, the ancient capital of King Lazar. After that date the official publication from Headquarters was sus- **Bulletins from** pended. Serbia was lost for the time **the front** being, and every nerve had to be strained to the saving of the Army. Now and then at towns like Scutari, where prolonged halts were made, it was possible to issue notices of important events, which were posted up in conspicuous places, but of news from the front there was, and could be, no more.

At Corfu, in the fullness of time, the official journal made its reappearance, and continued to be published regularly. By the renewal now of independent war bulletins, Serbia once more stood up proudly by the side of her Allies.

There is a fine and touching, a characteristic, simplicity about the wording of that bulletin of July 28th which makes it worthy to be remembered: " The Serbian troops, trusting in God and in victory, have come into contact with the enemy. For the last three days our troops have been successfully occupied in throwing back the advance of the enemy from Moglena towards the frontier. The engagement still continues."

Simple, straightforward words ! They are like the first manifestations of rude health in a strong man who has been sick unto death and who has aroused himself to the knowledge that his muscles are as firm as ever, his blood as warm, and his brain as keen.

And, what is more, they contained no exaggeration. From the foot of the Moglena Mountains the Serbs had ascended to the slopes, winning every inch of their way by what was practically hand-to-hand fighting, and it was not very long in the history of that year's warfare before heights were gained—and held—which the Bulgars had regarded as natural citadels for their own defence. Thus it was on Vetrenik Kovil, and the tooth-shaped Kukuruz —though the summit of Dobropolye, a point of great strategical importance, was still, up to July, 1917, held by the enemy. Many a time was there premature

British observers escaping by parachute from a kite-balloon fired by a swooping German Albatros.

[Canadian War Records.

Canadian artillerymen in action on the western front loading a 15 in. gun.

[Australian official photograph.

Australians hoisting a shell on to the feeding=tray of a monster piece of ordnance.

Australian official photograph.

Rehearsing for battle: Australians studying a detailed model of the terrain of Messines Ridge.

A little girl, hit by a splinter from a far-flung shell, had the distinction of being the only wounded person in a village. Brought by an orderly to British officers dining in a garden, she was comforted with grapes and much attention.

Resting in the quiet of a château where the war had passed by, a little company of British officers steeped their souls in the singing of a French brother officer, and war-worn soldiers gathered in the hall to enjoy the interlude.

Touches of human kindness in the long=drawn tragedy of " Man's inhumanity to man."

rejoicing over the impending fall of this position, which would have facilitated the eagerly-awaited advance upon Prilep, but Serbia's strength had its limits, and the glorious success of Kaymakchalan had not yet been repeated here. Dobropolye will stand for ever as Nature's monument to many a brave man who laid down his life on the threshold of his heart's desire.

The fighting in the Moglena continued, almost without cessation, from that auspicious day of July, 1916, to July, 1917, practically a year. The Serbs achieved all that was humanly possible of them ; it would have needed stronger reinforcements than General Sarrail was able to afford them to accomplish more. As it was, they gained important points ; they held the Bulgars in effective check, and they gave their enemy no peace by day or night. The guns were never silent on the Moglena, and, in this respect, there is no doubt that in all the Balkan fighting the Allies were eminently stronger than their opponents. In this district the French artillery, assisted later on by heavy British naval guns, subjected the Bulgars to such an unremitting and relentless pounding that their losses, as is known from the statements of prisoners and wounded, were such, from this cause alone, as to compensate in a great measure for the inability to push farther forward the line of advance.

Bulgars heavily punished

There is no doubt that the Bulgars suffered acutely. Constantly harassed by their foes, they were also ill supplied with food, and during the winter months, when snow hung heavy on the mountain tops, they had little to protect them from the extreme cold. The Serbs on the slopes were better off in this respect, and many a time it happened that the Bulgars would steal down, and upon being perceived, cry out : " Brothers, brothers, allow us to come down and cut wood." Sometimes they would actually attempt to do so, but it was at their own risk, and there were few of them who returned. As to the food, thanks to the excellence of the French and British commissariat, the Serbs had all that they needed and more than all. Bulgar deserters came in in regular processions in those days.

Such, very briefly, was a year's history of the Second Serbian Army. Of the doings of the First and Third there is more to say.

They had gone forward, as already mentioned, to the Ostrovo region in order to oppose the continued Bulgar advance into Macedonia, which was assuming threatening proportions. Florina had been seized, and the Bulgarian centre and left attacked, and after fierce fighting thrust back a weak Serbian line from the neighbourhood of Banitsa, and occupied two of the mountain ridges beyond. Their object was clear—if they could penetrate as far as Vodena they would threaten the communications of the Second Serbian Army in the Moglena, while a farther advance on the Vardar would be a menace to Salonika itself.

This was in the month of August, 1916. The Serbs, enormously outnumbered, put up a fierce defence, and it was only after fierce fighting, with heavy losses on both sides, that they were driven back from the first ridge. The Bulgars had the use of the railway direct from Monastir to Banitsa, and could bring up heavy guns and abundant munitions at will ; but the Serbs were less fortunately situated. The railway line, as may be noticed from the map (Vol. VIII., page 420), forms a great curve between Ostrovo and Banitsa, and so they had many miles of mountainous country between them and their nearest rail-head. Nevertheless they performed wonders with their rifles and machine-guns, and with a couple of batteries of " 75's," while here, as on the Moglena front, they showed a special partiality for the use—and the deadly use—of small hand-grenades. But more often than not hand-to-hand fighting was the rule.

Hand-to-hand fighting

This battle endured for the best part of a week. The next critical days were August 21st and 22nd, and it was then that the tide turned in favour of the Serbs, who, established along the summit of the second ridge, had been reinforced by further Serbian detachments and also by the French. The second coveted range of hills did not pass into the hands of the enemy. The Bulgarian advance in this direction had been effectually checked.

Meanwhile, important events were happening in Salonika. On July 30th a strong Russian contingent was landed, and this was followed on August 11th by the arrival of an Italian force of no negligible proportion. Further contingents of both forces followed. The Army of the Orient appeared to be at last in a position to take the offensive.

The offensive was duly taken. The Serbs, upon whom the brunt of the fighting on the west had already fallen, and who were still at grips with the enemy, were reinforced mainly by French and Russians ; but few will deny them the honour that is their due of having taken the main part in subsequent proceedings. The British, occupied on the eastern frontier, had no active share in these events.

It is said that Prince Alexander, as Commander-in-Chief of the Serbian Armies, himself gave the signal for the general attack. He came among his men, and then, baring his head and making the sign of the Cross, he fired the first cannon directed upon the enemy.

Results followed quickly upon the offensive of the Allies. The Bulgars, compelled to abandon the idea of farther advance, and moreover, weakened considerably by the exigencies of the Rumanian intervention, had entrenched themselves heavily in the neighbourhood of Banitsa and along the east side of the Ostrovo Lake. The Serbians were faced by the Malka Nidje Ridge—the same from which they had been beaten back by the Bulgars in their advance. In no way daunted, they began by dislodging the foe from Sorovich and occupying both sides of the lake, after which, by a strong and dauntless assault, they stormed the whole of the fortified ridge, capturing the villages of Gornichevo in the centre and Ekshisu on the left.

Serbians again on Serbian soil

Furthermore, with little delay, they pursued the flying enemy across the River Brod, and occupied the village of the same name, as well as the village of Velyeselo. Brod was found heavily fortified. It is across the frontier, and thus, for the first time, the Serbian soldiers set foot once more upon their own soil.

I felt as if I had crossed the whole width of the world at one step —thus one man described his sensations. Another, who entered Serbia some days later from Krushograd, wrote as follows :

Already the frontier draws near. Only a few steps more. I experienced a most strange and unpleasant sensation. For a moment I stopped, and then suddenly I started and, led by some invisible force, went straight up to the boundary stone. I went by the stone, and it seemed as if it moved on beside me. I cannot explain what it was. I sat down on the ground . . . I don't know why I sat when I really wished to hurry. I cannot tell all I did in those moments of ecstasy, and I do not know how to express all that I felt. I can only say that I kept incredulously asking of myself : " Is that our soil ? Is it possible that this is indeed our soil, our native land ? "

The retreating Bulgars were allowed no rest. Thrown back from Krushograd and Sovich and from the Nidje Mountain, they retreated before the victorious Serbs who, by October 4th, had captured the station of Kenali, crossed the Cherna River in places, and were able to announce that they now held forty kilometres of frontier with two hundred and thirty square kilometres of Serbian soil, including seven villages. Sovich was the first actual Serbian village to be occupied.

The success of these operations followed naturally upon the eventual victory of the Serbs in another and most hotly contested area of the operations. While the Bulgars remained in possession of the great mountain of Kaymakchalan no advance into Serbia and towards Monastir

PRINCE ALEXANDER AND GENERAL LENTIEFF.
As Commander of the Serbian Army, Prince Alexander showed remarkable military skill in the early victories over the Austrians, in the great retreat, and in the campaign which resulted in the recapture of Monastir—a campaign in which he fired the first shot.

was possible; therefore from the very beginning of the Serbian offensive the possession of Kaymakchalan was the first object of their ambition, and on its slopes and around its summit the most violent and most sanguinary battles of the campaign were fought. Kaymakchalan, as already mentioned, is the highest elevation on the frontier. The Bulgars had given it the name of "Fort Crown Prince Boris," and they had been ordered to hold it to the last man.

In spite of this, already by September 18th, the Serbian troops of the Drina Division had occupied the principal summit, and hoisted the Serbian colours upon their native land. The Bulgars, however, reinforced by several battalions from different regiments in the neighbourhood, and, later, by an entire regiment brought over from the Struma, hotly contested the ground and held firmly to the slopes and lesser heights. Again and again determined attacks were launched upon the Serbian position; again and again they were repulsed with heavy and sanguinary loss. The most violent of these, made on September 26th, was falsely announced by the Bulgars as a victory. It was in reality nothing of the sort, for though some of the advanced Serbian trenches were actually occupied, not a single breach was made in the principal line, not a particle of the coveted height was retaken. The battle, which had raged for over five hours, terminated at dawn owing to the sheer exhaustion of the assailants, who, according to very clear evidence, had been well doped with raw spirits before the attack.

The capture of Kaymakchalan

The best evidence of Bulgar failure, however, lies in the fact that a few days later the whole of the coveted mountain fell into the hands of the Serbs, and the Bulgars, utterly routed, were compelled to flee in disorder. This victory it was that enabled the Serbs to effect their advance over the Starkov Grob and into Serbia itself.

The Bulgars were as accomplished as the Germans themselves in claiming victories when things were going amiss. A proclamation issued by Tsar Ferdinand to his "heroic troops" at a somewhat later date caused considerable amusement to the Allies at Salonika. Thus his Majesty:

Heroes of the Eleventh Army, you have just gained a new victory over the common enemy, and you have added a fresh page to the chronicles of your glorious exploits, for you have compelled an adversary attacking with the impetuosity of despair to abandon his efforts after many useless attacks which have cost him enormous sacrifices without the smallest success. Your victory has everywhere aroused the greatest enthusiasm and admiration! Sons of the allied States, you have accomplished your duty with epic self-denial.

There was much more in the same strain, including even the warm congratulations of his Majesty the German Emperor. Yet the publication of this precious eulogy coincided with the allied gains on the hills around Monastir—notably that known as 1,248—and the capture of the villages Kriklena and Snegovo by the French.

Within fifteen days of the fighting around Kaymakchalan the Serbs secured some forty cannon, besides a large amount of war material. The Bulgar losses were very heavy; in the course of the final attack upon Kaymakchalan the 11th Regiment alone lost as many as 73 officers and over 3,000 men. The whole mountain top was converted into a ghastly shambles of the dead. Among all the blood-stained hills of Serbia whose names have been handed down to history, Kaymakchalan must take the foremost place, while the story of its capture and retention against overwhelming odds will constitute one of the most glorious pages in the records of Serbian patriotism and achievement.

The Serbian operations on Kaymakchalan and on the Starkov Grob were happily facilitated by Franco-Russian operations on the left flank in the region of Florina, where important Bulgarian forces were engaged.

Florina taken by the Allies

Florina being now the objective, the allied forces were constituted into three groups, converging towards that town. The Russians, starting from Verria, advanced by forced marches; a French column occupied the centre of the line; while the Serbs, as has been seen, victorious in the Malkan Ridge, throwing back the Bulgars from Ekshisu and Petrsko, pursued their retreating foes westward. Florina could make no long defence. First

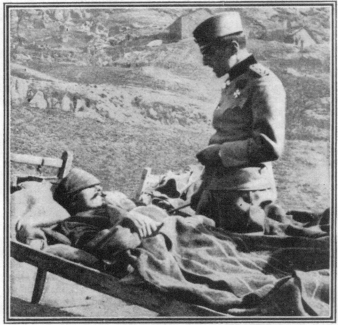

ROYAL SYMPATHY WITH THE WOUNDED.
Prince Alexander talking to one of his soldiers, wounded during the fighting on the Macedonian front which led to the Serbian reoccupation of the ancient town of Monastir.

the station, some six kilometres from the town, fell into the hands of the Allies, and very soon afterwards the town itself.

The three armies had thus come together, and future operations were conducted in unison, Monastir, of course, being the common objective. Its speedy fall was confidently looked for, but there were difficulties in the way which could not be so speedily overcome. It is indeed very much to the credit of General Sarrail and his forces that Monastir fell when it did—on November 19th.

It must be remembered that important as it was to the Allies that Monastir should be taken and this vital centre of Macedonia restored to the Serbs, it was of equal importance to the Bulgars to hold it. Apart from their amour propre, it would be a serious blow to abandon a town the surroundings of which had been transformed into a veritable entrenched camp, and commanded the valley leading to that of the Vardar. Certain it is that for a year, assisted by their German allies, the Bulgars had expended **Victorious advance** much labour upon making Monastir, **on Monastir** as far as possible, impregnable. Moreover, in this they were highly favoured by Nature, which has protected the town by mountain defences by no means easy to surmount.

Another factor at this time rendered difficult the Franco-Russo-Serb advance. Bad weather conditions had set in, and mechanical transport was seriously impeded upon the muddy and broken roads of the plain and among the hills. The railway, although rewon to the Serbian frontier, was of little value, for the Bulgars had naturally destroyed the bridges, notably at Ekshisu. The first and principal line of defence, that of Kenali, was already in the hands of the Allies.

The Serbs, advancing from the east across the Cherna, now found themselves confronted by the powerfully organised positions of Chuké, with the village of Polog for their centre. By a smart attack on November 10th the south part of this village was captured, together with some six hundred prisoners, and a quantity of war material abandoned at Chuké. Several desperate efforts were made by the Bulgars to retake the position, but the only result was the loss of a further thousand prisoners—among whom were many Germans—and much more war material. The fortified Chuké Hill and the whole of the village of Polog fell to the Serbs as well. The corpses of the enemy left on the field of battle were sufficient proof that the Bulgars had suffered here a defeat hardly less disastrous to them than that of Kaymakchalan.

On the 15th the pursuit of the enemy was continued on the left bank of the Cherna River to the fortified line of Ivan Isralok, where further desperate battles ensued, as a result of which the line was broken and several more villages fell into the hands of the Serbs. At the same time the Bulgars on the right of the Cherna were compelled to abandon the rest of their fortified line along the frontier and to withdraw towards Monastir, the villages of Egri, Bukri, and Sredno being vacated.

Heavy snow at this time impeded operations, but the Serbs, supported by the French, pushed on from the west to Tepavtsi, where the enemy was now entrenched. Here the number of Germans brought up to the fighting-line was particularly evident—some five hundred prisoners being made. Tepavtsi offered no long resistance, and the advance was promptly continued—it is not the manner of the Serb to stay his hand when there is an advantage to be pushed.

Within a period of two months to this date the Serbs had captured seventy-one cannon, besides a large number of trench-mortars and other war material. As on the Moglena, their successful advance had been very materially assisted by the efficiency of the French artillery.

From Tepavtsi the Serbs pressed on to Yarashok, taking more German prisoners, while the Franco-Russian forces reached the right bank of the River Viro. This brought

HEIR TO SERBIA'S THRONE.
Prince Alexander of Serbia, Commander-in-Chief of his country's gallant Army, with General Bukovitch, his Chief of Staff, riding through the mountains during the victorious advance on Monastir.

them within six kilometres of Monastir. The capture by the Serbs of the contested Heights 1,212 and 1,718 completed the preliminaries for an attack upon the town itself.

The hill numbered 1,212 saw some severe fighting For the retaking of this eminence from the Serbs in a counter-attack by the "Chasseurs Allemands," the Commander-in-Chief, General Otto von Below, was highly praised and recompensed by the Kaiser himself. It was, however, a short-lived victory, for but two days later this same general, so prematurely honoured, was thrown back upon Monastir, for the fall of which he, too, bore the responsibility.

No resistance was offered to the entrance of the Allies into the town. At eight o'clock on the morning of November 19th the Franco- **Occupation of the** Russian troops took possession, and they **town** were quickly followed by the Serbs. For the latter it was a glorious anniversary, since it was exactly upon the same date in 1912 that they had finally ejected the Turk from Monastir.

To the Bulgars who, a little while earlier, had loudly proclaimed the place impregnable, Monastir now became a town of no importance ; they did not even deign to notice its fall in their early communiqués. The Germans were a little more precise. "After the adversary had succeeded in making progress upon Hill 1,212, on the north-east of Chegen," so they reported, "the Germano-Bulgar troops have occupied a position to the north of Monastir and evacuated that town."

This version, indicating a voluntary retirement is, of course incorrect ; the Germano-Bulgars retreated under the pressure of the Franco-Russian advance from Florina and of the tireless Serbian attacks upon the east. Actually the various attacking armies were by now no longer strictly divided ; there were many French with the Serbs under Voivoda Misitch, while an Italian contingent had joined up with the French and Russians.

News of the impending Bulgar evacuation of the town was received overnight by the Serb and French General Staff. Several violent explosions were heard, and the first impression was that the town had been fired. This, however, was not the case, the explosions proceeding from the blowing up of munition depots which the Bulgars had no time to clear. Heavy artillery fire was opened against the position of the enemy batteries, and since they made no response the conviction was soon acquired that the guns had been removed.

At five o'clock in the morning the Serbs occupied Hill 1,718, while two divisions pushed forward to Hovac in order to threaten the Prilep road. This action virtually completed the capture of the town, though the French batteries at Pozdesh maintained a violent bombardment of the neighbouring heights.

A detachment of the " Chasseurs d'Afrique " was the first to enter the town, and was received with the greatest enthusiasm by the population. Serbian cavalry followed soon after, and several groups of prisoners were made, for the Bulgars were retiring in complete disorder. Curiously enough, a great rainbow hung suspended over the reconquered city, and this very naturally was accepted by the Serbs as an omen of the happiest import.

Flowers were showered upon the incoming troops, the Serbs, with Voivoda Misitch, receiving the welcome that was their due. No time was lost in the re-establishment of order throughout the town, and immediate steps were taken for the distribution of provisions **Welcoming the** —which, indeed, were badly needed, for **victors** a condition not far removed from famine had hitherto prevailed.

General Sarrail was promptly on the scene of conquest, and with the visit of Prince Alexander the town of Monastir passed definitely once more into the hands of the Serbs.

The month of November, 1916, closed thus most auspiciously for the allied cause in the Balkans, and it was confidently hoped both that Monastir would be firmly held and that, after a reasonable delay, the advance into Serbia would be continued. It was assumed that the fall of Monastir would of necessity compel the Germano-Bulgars to evacuate a large tract of Macedonian territory extending westward to Lake Ochrida, and that they would have to retire upon their Prilep defences. "The spring will see us fighting in the Babuna " — such was the Serbian fore- cast.

Unfortunately these aspirations were not destined to be realised. There are many strong places to the north of Monastir, many eleva- tions that are veritable citadels in themselves. Had these places fallen with Monastir, had the Allies pushed their ad- vantage to the full, it is possible t h a t events might have fallen out as foreseen ; but what- ever the cause may have been, certain it is that the enemy was either enabled to retain his hold of these points

of advantage or to regain them after evacuation. The effect upon subsequent proceedings, perhaps upon the whole Balkan Campaign, was enormous. Instead of being securely held, Monastir continued to be subjected to a wanton and profitless bombardment. Hundreds of inoffensive civilians were killed or mutilated ; the town itself—originally largely spared in the hope of reoccupation —was more or less reduced to ruins. Great Britain had to mourn the death of one of her most loyal workers, Mrs. Harley, sister of General French, who was killed by a shell while in the act of distributing food to the needy of Monastir.

* * * * * * *

It is now—July, 1917—over a year since the Serbs came to the threshold of their native land, strong and refreshed, burning with the lust of vengeance. They achieved all that was humanly possible **The situation in** for them to achieve—and it has been with **July, 1917** the loss of more than half of their effec- tives, they who, of all the armies in the Balkans, are the least able to endure the strain. And now they will wait upon the threshold and ask, " How long ? "

For the best part of eight months now the Army of the Orient has remained practically quiescent. We have maintained our positions, but we have not advanced them. It is not for me, here, to question the policy that denies the Balkan front its vital importance ; given that denial, abundant reasons may be found for our inactivity.

For the first and most important, it will be sufficient to quote a few words from the enemy Press. Says the " Balkanska Posta " of August 26th, 1916, after describing the difficulties of the front :

In order successfully to defend such an expanse, 350 kilometres deep (about 220 miles), General Sarrail must have a great force at his disposal. Allowing one division to each ten kilometres, he should have at least thirty-five divisions at his disposal—which means 500,000 men. According to all calculations he has no more than 200,000. It is therefore hardly to be presumed that under present circumstances a great offensive on his part is being contemplated. A defensive, with occasional offensive attack, is far more likely.

The " Balkanska Posta " summed up the situation fairly accurately—and may perhaps have been surprised at the offensive that was actually undertaken. The one certain point is that General Sarrail never had the 500,000 men necessary for an offensive on a large scale at his disposition. It was the policy of the Allies to direct their main energies elsewhere.

We may imagine that with the forces at his command it was no easy task for General Sarrail successfully to maintain his position upon the whole of the extended front. Sick- ness played much havoc in our ranks in 1916, and the reinforcements we received w e r e no more than sufficient to fill the gaps caused there- by. Furthermore, for the whole year, we were covertly threatened by an insidious foe, ready to fall upon us in the rear upon the slightest sign of weakening upon our part, or of material success upon the part of our avowed enemies. This danger has now, very tardily, been re- moved, and it may be possible for General Sarrail to renew his autumn successes of 1916.

[British official photograph.

SEAMEN OF THE SERBIAN NAVY.
Serbian sailors marching through Monastir after its recapture in November, 1916. These men, who did useful work upon the Danube, were trained by British naval officers.

WAR-TIME WORK OF BRITAIN'S SPECIAL CONSTABULARY.
By Basil Clarke.

The Special Constabulary Movement's Welcome—" A Chance to Do Something "—Enrolments from All Classes—The Constable's Oath
—War-Need for More Police—London's 20,000 Constables in Twenty Days—The First Organising Staff—Constables in Bowler
Hats—Anti-German Riots and the Moral Effect of Uniforms—London in the Night Watches—Queer Companions—The Baronet
and His Club Waiter—Extended Duties—Patrol Duty—The " Notebook and Pencil Habit "—" Take Air-Raid Action "—
London Specials at Their Best—The Ambulance Section—The Salvage Section—The Motor Transport Men—Roger Casement
Conveyed by a Special Constable—The 'Busmen Specials and Motor Transport Fleet—The King's Special Constables—
The Man They Arrested at Buckingham Palace—Private Special Constabulary, Clothed and Trained at Employers' Expense—
Constables at Drill—15,000 Proficiency Certificates—A Typical London Division—Observation Posts about London—The City of
London Police—Guarding the Richest Corner of the World—Manchester's Force—Trained as Marksmen—Mounted Specials
for Traffic Duty—The Point Duty Experts—Glasgow's 3,000 Specials—Guarding the Royal Train—Moral Effects Noticed by
Chief Constable—Amateur Firemen Specials at Leeds—Cardiff's Aliens—The Dangers of " Tiger Bay "—In the Country
Districts—Work on the Lone Sea Coasts—Issue of Shrapnel Helmets

NO movement showed the public spirit of the maturer men of Great Britain and their willingness to do service for the nation in its war needs than the Special Constabulary movement, which sprang into being at the outbreak of war and eventually spread throughout the country. It was warmly welcomed by two particular sections of citizens as an opportunity for war service. Men who were above the then military age—which was much lower than in later stages of the war—and men who were not of the high degree of physical fitness then demanded by the Army recruiting authorities found in the Special Constabulary movement a " chance to do something "—the thing for which every good citizen was seeking. The movement appealed also to the great number of citizens who, through business or family responsibilities were not in a posiiton to give up all and join the Army to fight. As the first of many such opportunities for war service that were eventually to offer, the Special Constabulary movement met with an immediate and enthusiastic response. There was hardly a walk of life, from the aristocracy down to the plainest workaday citizen, that did not contribute to the man-power of this new public force. Peers, baronets and knights, doctors, lawyers, journalists, actors, stockbrokers, commercial men, tradesmen, artisans, and even labourers rolled up in their numbers to the police-offices of

FROM THE BENCH TO THE BEAT.
Sir John Knill, Bart., Lord Mayor of London, 1909-10, joined the Blackheath Special Constabulary, and is seen leaving his home in Blackheath to go on duty.

the country to take the King's oath and the constable's warrant and baton, and with them the duties and responsibilities of special police constable, without fee or reward.

I . . . . do solemnly, sincerely and truly affirm and declare that I will well and truly serve our Sovereign Lord and King, in the office of Special Constable for the . . . . District without favour or affection, malice or ill-will: and that I will to the best of my power cause the peace to be kept and preserved, and prevent all offences against the persons and properties of His Majesty's subjects: and that while I continue to hold the said office I will to the best of my skill and knowledge discharge all the duties thereof faithfully according to law.

Such was the declaration they made. Strictly speaking, it was an " affirmation " rather than an " oath," but it was no less solemn and binding. The wording of this affirmation was virtually the same all over the country. It was an old volunteer police oath adapted to modern circumstances.

Here one may pause a moment to note the subtle and unconscious compliment to the regular police forces of Great Britain in this remarkable readiness on the part of the plain citizen to become a " policeman " and to perform ordinary police duties. The fact that, without a moment's hesitancy, without question of any sort, men of the highest standing were willing to join hands with the regular police, and to share their work is proof unequivocal of the very high esteem in which the police forces of this country were held by the

355

Stretcher-bearers of the first-aid section of the New Southgate Special Constabulary at practice. Making the "patients" comfortable.

nation at large. One wonders, in passing, whether there was another country in the whole world wherein an appeal to citizens to become members of the existing police force would have been met with so unanimous and unquestioning a response. It is difficult to imagine German citizens, for instance, joining hands with and assuming the uniform and duties of the hated *Schutzmann*, a policeman disliked even by the people whose interests he is supposed to protect.

The need for special constables to which the war gave rise differed considerably from that of all previous occasions in history upon which they had been used. All previous enrolments of special constables—within memory at all events—had been temporary in character and restricted in area to places wherein some special circumstances, such as strikes or riots, threatened the public peace. Such occasions had been few in number. A big force of these constables was enrolled in some of the Northern cities at the time of the industrial strike riots a few years before the war broke out (1911 and later), but previous to this there had been no occasion for many years when special constables in any great numbers had been required. In the old days, of course, before the appointment of regular police, volunteer police were enrolled from time to time in different localities as and when circumstances required. At a time of disorder public-spirited citizens **Volunteer police of** gathered at the office of their local mayor **former times** and were handed out a small staff (usually bearing a crown) as badge of office, and were turned loose in the streets to keep the peace as best they might. These volunteer police of the old days were no doubt the fore-runners of the special constables of the Great War. One finds no official mention of "special constables" as such before an Act of Parliament of William IV. in the year 1831, which came two years after the passing of the first Metropolitan Police Act. After that year various Acts of Parliament concerned themselves with Special Constabulary, but none of them calls for mention here save the Act of August 28th, 1914, passed to legalise the making of rules and regulations to govern the control and organisation of the great number of special constables which by that time had been enrolled as a war measure. These rules and regulations were forthcoming in an Order-in-Council passed at Buckingham Palace on September 9th, 1914, which formed the "charter" under which the war-time Special

Carrying off the "injured" in a demonstration of efficiency by the men of the first-aid section of the New Southgate Special Constabulary, who prided themselves on being the first fully-equipped section of this kind among the Specials. Inset: Placing a stretcher on its wheeled carriage.

SPECIALS WHO MADE THEMSELVES EFFICIENT IN FIRST-AID WORK.

Constabulary forces of the country gained their authority and official status.

Under this Order-in-Council a special constable was given the same duties, powers, and privileges as a regular police constable, and was made liable to the same penalties in case of failure to perform those duties. Another clause of the Order that is worthy of notice said that, in the event of a special constable being incapacitated or losing his life in the execution of his duty, the authorities "may" grant him or to his widow and children a pension and allowance at the same rates as under the Police Act of 1890. An amended Order passed in May, 1915, provided that a constable contracting illness or injury through the execution of his duties "may" be entitled to certain allowances. All of which, put shortly, meant that any special constable killed, injured, or made ill by doing his duty, "might" get some recompense if the fates and the authorities felt inclined.

Thus the risks attaching to police work fell on the special constables themselves. Nevertheless, citizens did not hesitate to come forward in their numbers to fill this gap in the nation's home ranks which, if unfilled, might have led to serious consequences.

The war created a demand for police that was quite without precedent. In the first place, the existing police forces of the country (which had never been too great for the onerous work they performed) had been suddenly deprived of the services of all their Reservists, both Navy and Army. These local forces had been recruited very largely from men discharged from the fighting Services. Whether this was wise or not is doubtful, but even if unwise it was certainly natural, for in the soldiers and sailors who had left the King's service chief constables and local authorities found policemen almost "ready made"— men who by physical fitness, training, and habits of discipline and responsibility were eminently suitable for the duties of police constable. The recall of these men to the Army and Navy caused great gaps. In the second place, the police forces of the country, thus denuded of many men, were faced with a great accession of duties over and above those they had normally performed. Many of these duties were of a quasi-military nature, such as the guarding of vulnerable points, bridges, waterworks, gasometers, grain warehouses, canals, and the like.

At the outbreak of war it was a vital need that this duty should be done. The country contained an enormous number of alien enemies, German and **Great accession of** Austrian, and other aliens, some of **police duties** whom were undoubtedly active enemy agents. To have left vulnerable points unprotected until such time as proper arrangements had been made for classifying these aliens and ensuring that they were not in a position to do the country harm would have been a fatal neglect. Yet the existing police were far too few to have undertaken these protective duties, and of soldiery there were not enough for active service in the field, let alone for duty at home.

As the war developed, bringing new dangers and needs, and new regulations to meet them, the list of duties falling to the police grew apace. It is not too much to say, in

UNDER A CRITICAL EYE.
Colonel Sir Edward Ward, Bart., Permanent Under-Secretary of State, War Office, 1901-14, inspecting the X Division of the Special Constabulary at Blackheath.

fact, that of the many new orders and regulations for public welfare at home, which were passed from time to time as the war developed, the great bulk could never have been carried out with anything like efficiency but for the conscientious work of the nation's police, working with the loyal support of strong forces of special constables.

As new and increasing duties accrued to the police, the Special Constabulary forces of the country were not left without interference to learn these duties and to perfect themselves. Every change in the re-cruiting regulations and every alteration **The Army and** in the Army age made inroads into the **the police** personnel of the Special Constabulary. Men who had been too old or not physically fit for the Army at the outset of hostilities became so under the altered regulations, and either volunteered or were called up for Army duty. The Special Constabulary, it is pleasing to note, lost more men owing to enlistment of members than from any other cause. In fact, of all the withdrawals and retirements from the police force, nearly half were due to Army calls. As the Inspector-General of the Metropolitan Police Divisions used often to tell special constables when inspecting them : "This is the only way we like to lose our men. Every other retirement from our ranks we regret and grudge, but this mode of retirement, to the fighting forces of the nation, we welcome."

In general terms it may be stated that the duties of the Special Constabulary were virtually the same as the ordinary peace duties of the ordinary police, to which may be added duties essentially of a war character, arising definitely out of regulations passed under the Defence of the Realm Act, either generally or through the medium of local authorities in the form of local Acts.

But to go into these things in more than general terms, and apply them to the Special Constabulary of Great Britain *en masse*, would tend to give rise to error and misunderstanding. For though they were alike in general character, the different forces of special police throughout the country differed very much, both in mode of organisation, equipment, and in the work they did. In London, for instance, one seldom saw a special constable on point duty—*i.e.*, directing traffic at a busy crossing. Manchester, on the other hand, had a little body of picked special constables for this duty, and the writer once watched one of them at work at the busiest crossing in this great city of congested traffic. He was an M.A. of Oxford University, had stroked his college boat, played Rugby football for Lancashire county, and was a man of independent means, but he did his eight hours a day for four days a week in constable's uniform, directing traffic, and directing it with extreme efficiency, too. The city of Cardiff's Special Constabulary—to quote another contrast—helped with the complex machinery of registering aliens, an enormous task in such a cosmopolitan city. Sheffield, on the other hand, with very few moving aliens within its boundaries, has no great need to ask this duty of its special constables, whose chief function was the maintenance of safety and order during alarms of aerial attack. With such difference of police duties and conditions in different places, it will be better for the purpose of this record to deal with some of the country's Special Constabulary organisations in representative cities and areas, to show their different manner of working and to enumerate the facts and achievements of each.

London's Special Constabulary

The order of seniority of the various Special Constabulary forces is a moot point. The Metropolitan district made some claims to have been the first to organise its constabulary on a war footing, but so also did Manchester. The probability is that even before any official hint was given by the Government to the local authorities the more go-ahead among them were already taking steps to "put their house in order" to meet the new needs of war. Certain it is that before Great Britain's declaration of war was many days old, quite a number of cities and districts had begun the enrolment of special constables. Seniority, therefore, is no guide in determining the order of precedence of the various Special Constabulary forces of the kingdom, but as one of them, which was amongst the first in the field, greatly overtops all the others in its size and scope, it may not unfairly, perhaps, be regarded as ranking first. This is the Special Constabulary force of the London Metropolitan district, an area which embraces all the environs of London, and all London itself, except a comparatively small area at the heart of things, which comes under the designation of London City.

It was on the day following the outbreak of war that the Commissioner of Police, Sir Edward Henry, decided to create a Special Constabulary force, and deputed Sir Edward Ward as his chief of staff to organise it. Working with Sir Edward Ward, as helpers, were among others, Major H. F. Wilkinson, who undertook duties concerning general control; Lord Montagu, as director of organisation; Mr. Basil Johnson, as director of transport; Mr. L. L. Ralli, concerned with supply; Mr. R. J. Balfour and Mr. Jeffrey Marks for finance; and Sir H. Cornhill, Captain the Hon. Sir Seymour Fortescue, and others, for special duty in connection with vulnerable points.

Such was the progress made by this go-ahead staff that in the twenty days following the outbreak of war a force of 20,000 special constables had been enrolled and put out on the streets and elsewhere for duty. They were not

GOING ON DUTY.
Detachment of Special Constables marching through Parliament Square on their way to take up duty in lining the streets.

uniformed men, and had no other sign of their office than a blue-and-white armlet, a warrant, a whistle, and a staff. But these things served well for the immediate duties then to be undertaken, the chief of which was the guarding of railway bridges and tunnels, waterworks, gasworks, and canals, and other vital things and places by the destruction of which enemy agents might have tended to incapacitate important public services, thereby rendering the country in a less efficient state for the waging of war.

It was not until some months later that a badge and a blue uniform cap were added to the special constable's equipment, and at the opening of Parliament for the autumn session of 1914 special constables lined Pall Mall

HEADQUARTERS SPECIALS INSPECTED IN THE TEMPLE GARDENS.
The duties of the London Headquarters Central Detachment of Special Constables (which was largely recruited from among members of the West End clubs) included the guarding of Buckingham Palace, Marlborough House, and various public buildings.

and St. James's Park, wearing all sorts of hats—from silk hats and "bowlers" to caps. The issue of uniform caps went a long way towards giving the Special Constabulary of the Metropolis an official appearance, and this at the time seemed as much as was necessary. But the anti-German riots that broke out in the early summer of 1915 showed that there were many people, more especially in the East End and other poor parts of London, who would pay but little respect or obedience to "Authority" so long as its representative was not clothed in full uniform. There was some opposition to the granting of full

BRINGING IN THEIR MAJESTIES' GUESTS.
Early in 1916 the King and Queen entertained a large party of wounded soldiers to tea at Buckingham Palace. Special constables met the guests at various assembly points and escorted them to the palace.

IN THE COURTYARD OF BUCKINGHAM PALACE.
Some of their Majesties' guests were unable to walk, and for these invalid chairs were provided, which were wheeled by special constables into the Riding School, where the reception was held.

uniforms to special constables on the ground of expense, but this was eventually overcome by a compromise that uniforms should be issued to constables, but only after they had completed a certain number of drills and duty "turns."

The uniform was of plain blue with black buttons bearing a crown. Inspectors and other officers wore a similar uniform with silver stars and crowns on the shoulder-straps (after the manner of the Royal Irish Constabulary), corresponding, roughly, to the military rank of lieutenant, captain, major, and colonel. Staff officers wore velvet collar " tabs " of black velvet, broken by a silver line.

The uniform was not only serviceable, but smart in appearance. The difference in the respect accorded by simple people to the wearers was noticeable from the start. The Metropolitan special constable began to inherit some of the respect that had been accorded to his professional predecessor, the regular policeman. Such is the psychological effect on simple minds of a uniform.

It cannot be said that the early duties of the Special Constabulary were pleasant ones. To stand for four hours under a railway arch in some sombre slum through the small hours of a wintry night, or to patrol a monotonous

orbit round the base of some gasometer, was not work that had about it either interest or much of the spice of romance. Yet, throughout the hundreds of square miles of Metropolitan London, hundreds of citizens did this work honourably and well. For duty in all hours of the day and night, for all the districts of London, rich and poor, lovely and unlovely, special constables were forthcoming. They were to be seen together in couples no matter what the hour, no matter how inaccessible or prosaic the point to be watched.

Very often these couples were curiously assorted. Under one bridge in South-East London the director of a bank was often to be seen on duty with a worker at the docks as comrade. At another point a titled actor was seen doing duty with a pawnbroker's clerk. One instance was recorded of a baronet who left his club at midnight to do four hours' constabulary duty with the waiter who only an hour before had served him with supper. It made for a closer sympathy between one rank of life and another. Quiet chats under silent bridges in the night hours made for understandings and friendship which, without that queer duty to be done, could hardly ever have been established.

London in the night watches

Sometimes whole squads of special constables were detailed for duty together. Thus the Newington Road Waterworks every night saw the posting of a troop of thirty special constables to ensure the safety of the water service. That it was saved from pollution and the inhabitants of London from disease may not improbably be due to their zeal in the night watches. More than one instance was recorded of enemy agents attempting to tamper with the water supplies. But for the very thorough precautions taken by the London police, and in fact by the police throughout the country, these attempts at outrage must have been more numerous and more successful than they were.

As time went on the duties of the Special Constabulary in London changed considerably. The internment of alien enemies and the more thorough arrangements that had been made by this time for keeping trace of all aliens lessened very much the risk of outrage at vulnerable points. The police authorities, therefore (with the approval of the military authorities), felt justified in modifying the strictness of the watch kept on these places, and large numbers of Special Constabulary were freed for newer and more pressing police duties. The increase in the number of hostile air raids, and the more complete arrangements made for the warning and protection of the public, threw new duties on the police, with which they could hardly have coped but for the enthusiastic co-operation of the Specials.

Not only in the matter of air raids but in general police duties also the Special Constabulary now became much more part and parcel of the regular police force. In fact, but for the difference in the hours of duty done, which were, of course, less than those of the paid police, the special constable exercised the whole function of ordinary policemen. They patrolled street beats and examined the doors, windows, and locks of shops in the night hours ; they arrested evil-doers, gave evidence in the police courts and coroners' courts, dispersed crowds, directed strangers and leashed homeless dogs, comforted lost children, controlled and reported street accidents, attended to sick and injured people in the streets, and, in fact, performed all the regular and useful duties of the professional constable. They acquired the policeman's habit of notebook and pencil, also something of his calm detachment and impartiality, and even something of his measured walk. They were quite one of the war features of the streets of London.

London "Specials" at their best

But London's Special Constabulary were seen at their best during attacks by enemy aircraft. Before very long they had reduced their measures for coping with these emergencies to routine and method, and the whole procedure went forward as by machine. Sitting in an office of the headquarters in Scotland House on the Embankment was always a staff officer of the force. Day and night alike this central nerve point was always alive. Warning of impending aerial attack was sent to that officer at the earliest moment by the military authorities. He was in touch with every one of the twenty police divisions of Metropolitan London. By the simple act of picking up a telephone receiver and giving the order " Take air-raid action," he could set the whole constabulary of London's 600 square miles—of the most populous district in the world—buzzing into full activity.

The mammoth proportions of this activity may be gauged from the fact that one division alone might cover a district of eighty square miles ; as, for example, the S Division, with its fourteen sub-police stations and more than 2,000 special constables. At the call " Take air-raid action," every constable was summoned to duty. Each division had its own arrangements for summoning its men. These arrangements might vary slightly in different places, but the most common method was to telephone round from divisional headquarters to all stations of the division, each of which in turn telephoned to certain points of its own area, whence started " runners," either by motor-car, cycle, or on foot, to warn individual constables to turn out for air-raid duty. Within very short time of the receipt of the warning at Scotland House special constables in uniform were in the streets and roads of each division carrying their " Take cover " warnings. Others had posted themselves at busy traffic points and in the busier streets, ready to calm any excitement or to cope with any emergency that might arise. Others, again, were on duty at the entrances and on the staircases of the underground railways ready to prevent any block or disorder that might occur through nervous people rushing to take cover. Another special constable was posted by each fire-alarm, ready to give instant warning in the event of bombs causing an outbreak. In this and other ways each constable had a place and a duty in a very carefully-organised scheme of precautions.

" Take air-raid action "

But in addition to these men there were other special constables in almost every division of the Metropolitan area for specialised duties. Great numbers of special constables had voluntarily qualified themselves in ambulance

and first-aid work. A medical officer of each division gave lectures and held classes, and great numbers of the men had gone so thoroughly into this subject as to qualify for the St. John Ambulance certificate and badge. (It was estimated that more than ten per cent. of the Metropolitan special constables were holders of this valuable qualification.) These men of each division, on receipt of air-raid warning, hurried off to their ambulance headquarters, equipped themselves with stretchers and surgical requisites, and stood ready to go off post-haste to any point of the division, or even outside it, to which they might be summoned by telephone. There is no doubt that many lives were saved and many casualties minimised in the course of London air raids by the efficient work of its Special Constabulary ambulances.

Another very useful duty which was learnt voluntarily by many special constables was that of salvage work. It was discovered that for an inexperienced man to enter and search among the ruins of a burnt or bomb-smashed building was merely to do very little useful service, and greatly to jeopardise the life of the searcher. Under tuition, therefore, of experts, such as members of the fire-brigades, members of the London Salvage Corps, engineers, builders, and architects, special constables of a special salvage corps were given instructions to fit them for salvage work.

Among the constables selected for these salvage corps were men who, in ordinary life, were plumbers, gasfitters, watermen, turncock men, and others whose training was likely to prove useful in such work as that of taking control of a wrecked building and making it safe. Waggons and motor-lorries had been provided for the use of these crews by public-spirited citizens, and at a call from any area a " breakdown " gang of the Special Constabulary Salvage Corps could be despatched in their own waggon at the shortest notice. They carried their tools with them, so that they could start work immediately upon arrival at the scene of the damage. These salvage corps were responsible at different times during London air raids for most valuable work. More than one injured person was extricated from the debris of dangerous ruins by members of this enterprising section of the special police. On one occasion a member of the corps saved probably a score of lives by hurriedly shepherding into a neighbouring house a crowd of people who were gazing at a damaged building, quite unconscious of an impending collapse, which occurred only a few moments after they had been got out of harm's way.

Ambulance and salvage work

In addition to ambulance men and salvage men, each Metropolitan police division had a little motor-transport organisation of its own. Motor cyclists and motor-car owners lent their vehicles and their services, and performed duties of a hundred different natures which were invaluable in increasing the efficiency of the police organisation—especially in times of air raids.

It is not generally known that some of the most important prisoners were entrusted for transport to men of the Special Constabulary motor units, and it is worthy of record in history, perhaps, that the traitor Sir Roger Casement was transported across London to Brixton Prison in a Special Constabulary car, in control of a special constable in uniform.

In addition to transport for the purposes of each division, there was a central transport of much bigger dimensions for the work of the Metropolitan force as a whole, by which, in the event of a special emergency in one or more divisions, the constabulary of other divisions might be carried to the spot in maximum numbers in the minimum time. An arrangement had been made with one of the leading omnibus companies by which a fleet of omnibuses was ready for police service at any moment. A force of 350 men, in the service of this company as drivers and guards, had been enrolled also as special constables.

A third of this number was always on duty and available for service. Thus, at a moment's notice, at a call for police into any of the London divisions, a hundred or more motor-omnibuses, if need be, could set off without any delay to bring police from other divisions. On Saturday morning, July 7th, 1917, when a fleet of some thirty German aeroplanes raided London, special police in their hundreds were thus collected from the divisions and despatched to East London, where the damage was greatest. The streets were blocked with traffic and sightseers, but a way was made for the special police omnibuses, and they got through in far less time than would have been possible by other means. Many of the Special Constabulary on that occasion did twelve hours' duty at a stretch without complaint. It was dangerous duty, too.

One London special constable, a lawyer's clerk, was killed by a bomb while on air-raid duty. Many others had very narrow escapes.

Another special feature of the headquarters organisation at Scotland House was a flying motor section which paraded every night and stood ready to do any special transport work that might be necessary between the headquarters and any of the divisions. There was also a central detachment of constables attached to headquarters, among whose duties was the honourable one of providing a special guard of constables for Buckingham Palace. Regularly every night this force, containing not a few eminent citizens of London, marched to the Palace grounds and took their respective stations about the building and the gardens. They patrolled there through the night. To the close of 1917 only one arrest was recorded within the Royal grounds, and the man arrested proved to be the inspector of another division who had gone into the grounds in mufti to see whether the special constables were alert or not. Amid some merriment—when he was examined at the central office as a suspect—he expressed himself quite satisfied that the King's Palace guard of special constables were "watching their job keenly and well."

Many of the big buildings, public institutions, and even private undertakings, of the London district had special

SHRAPNEL HELMETS FOR AIR RAIDS.
In October, 1917, the authorities supplied the special constables with steel helmets to protect them from the hail of steel fragments scattered by the anti-aircraft guns.

constables of their own to guard them. It was felt in many of these cases that some degree of special knowledge was desirable on the part of any special constable having the duty of guarding these buildings, if his services in an emergency were to be of real value. It can be readily believed, for instance, that any layman called upon to do police duty among the retorts of gasworks or the switches of an electricity generating station, would be unlikely to prove of much use ; he could not be expected to know what action to take for the best in an emergency such as, say, the explosion of an enemy bomb. A number of these undertakings, therefore, were allowed to enrol special constables of their own. They were recruited from the men employed in these places, and in some cases were even provided with uniforms and equipment at their employers' expense. Their duties and obligations, moreover, were confined to the particular undertaking to which they were attached.

But they were special constables, duly attested and liable to the same penalties for dereliction of duty as those to which ordinary constables were liable. The General Post Office had its own staff of Special Constabulary ; the Savings Bank at West Kensington had a force of 300 ; a gasworks in the N Division had 200 men. The Government Office of Works and the Marylebone Electric Company had similar bodies, the last-named being uniformed at their employers' expense.

In some cases the firms made private arrangements for teaching the constables drill, ambulance work, and the rest. In other cases they contributed towards the cost of the men attending drill instruction in the divisions to which they were attached, and to the commander of which each of these private forces was responsible.

The drills which these and all special constables of the London divisions attended were a very great and important part of their work. They were attended voluntarily, and were not counted as hours of police duty. They were, in fact, an extra duty undertaken willingly by constables to make themselves more efficient, just as was the ambulance work. Yet with such goodwill and enthusiasm did the members of the force undertake this drill that they

LONG-SERVICE MEN OF THE S DIVISION OF THE METROPOLITAN SPECIAL CONSTABULARY.
March past of the S Division at Golder's Green after the presentation of the medal for long service to members of the Division who had qualified for the honour by continuous service since the inauguration of the force.

BBB

became not only police, efficient in all the little problems of law, tact, common-sense, and ready resource which fall to a man doing police patrol duty, but also trained men. The writer was invited to choose any division he might like to see at work, and choosing at random a station of the Y Division, North London, he saw men, nearly all of mature age, and formerly of sedentary habits (50 per cent. were clerks), drilling with the smartness and " snap " of trained youth.

A few statistics concerning this division will serve as an illustration of the state of things in a typical London division : Area of division, 46 square miles ; nominal strength, 2,000 men ; actual strength, 1,965. Retirements from the force during its existence from August, 1914, to July, 1917, were as follows : Owing to enlistments, Army and Navy, 1,273 ; owing to ill-health, physical unfitness, and business reasons, 1,470 ; transferred to other divisions, 90 ; for reasons of discipline, 15 ; died (2 men drowned while on duty), 14. Total, 2,862. Average age of members at attestation (which in most cases was three years earlier), 42 ; members holding certificates for efficiency in drill, 38 per cent. ; for first-aid and ambulance work, 11 per cent.; highest individual number of turns on duty, 1,736 ; proportion of existing force with three years' service, 35 per

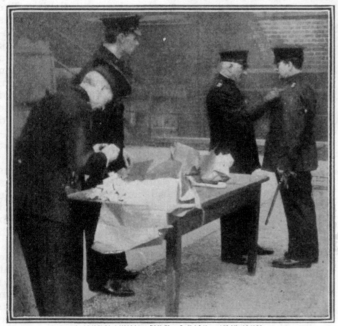

DECORATED FOR LONG SERVICE.
Pinning the Special Constables' Long Service Medal on the tunic of an inspector of the V Division at Lavender Hill Police Station, London.

cent. ; with two years' service, 56 per cent. ; donations made and collected by members of the division for charitable objects, £7,709. Mr. Alfred Collin, the commander, devoted both time and money to improving the force.

With slight variation here and there the statistics of the whole Special Constabulary forces of London showed a similar high degree of efficiency and of enthusiasm on the part of members. The personnel varied, of course, in character in the different divisions, and in place of clerks and business men in one suburb might be found in the next a majority of artisans and shopkeepers. In the East End there were quite a number of dockers and members of the Street Traders' and Hawkers' Union doing conscientious work in their spare hours—and even in business hours during emergencies—as special constables.

Three years of war brought about changes in personnel, and the chief officers in August, 1917, were Major Wilkinson, second in command under Sir Edward Ward ; Mr. Guy Ridley (the chief's former private secretary), Staff Officer ; Mr. W. M. Allen, Director of Supplies ; Mr. Ernest Jacobsen, Chairman of the Discipline Board ; Mr. A. C. Harden, Director of Transport ; Mr. R. F. Balfour, Finance Officer ;

Lieut.-Colonel Reay, Inspector-General of Divisions ; and Colonel Savage, Divisional Drill Inspector.

One interesting and important duty taken over from the military people about this time by London's Special Constabulary was the manning of "observation-posts "— an idea borrowed, perhaps, from the field of war itself. These posts were established at points of high altitude about the city and suburbs, from which a good view was to be had of the surrounding country. They were found to be of great use for observing the approach and movements of enemy aircraft, and for giving warnings and guidance during aerial attack. They were in a favourable position, moreover, for noting outbreaks of fire due to air bombs in their immediate districts, and also for keeping an open eye for over-bright lights and for anything in the nature of signals to the enemy. It was only, in fact, by means of constant observation from vantage points such as these that effectual steps could be taken to lessen the possibility of signals from roofs and other points not open to observation from normal levels. Though many alien enemies had been interned, there is little room for doubt that enemy aircraft did receive signals from the London area in the earlier days of the war. The constant watch maintained by special police, and the vigorous measures taken to suppress anything that might have been of use as a signal, undoubtedly did much to lessen the risks which London ran from the enemy attacks to which it was so often subject. These stations had special instruments for taking the exact bearing of any point of earth or sky, and each was equipped with a special telephone for communicating the results of observations to headquarters.

The small innermost circle of London, previously referred to as outside the jurisdiction of the London Metropolitan Police, had a Special Constabulary force of 2,355 men, and was known as the City of London Police Reserve. The force was divided into four divisions, and the duties were much the same as those of the Metropolitan police—namely, patrol **City of London** duty, the guarding of vulnerable points, **Police Reserve** and special duty during air raids and on the occasion of public ceremonies. In August, 1917, the Special Constabulary Force was commanded by Colonel J. W. Beningfield, who had as Chief Staff Officer, Mr. H. L. Hendricks, and as Staff Officer, Mr. A. H. Veatty. The commanders of the four divisions respectively were Mr. W. G. Lovell, of the A Division ; Mr. A. Hugh Nicholl, of the B Division ; Mr. W. B. Stant, of the C Division ; and Mr. N. Malcolmson, of the D Division. Mr. A. Hugh Nicholl was the Mayor of Lewisham.

As the duties of this force were very much the same as those of the Metropolitan police, and their organisation on very similar lines, there is little need to go very fully here into their work. It may be mentioned, however, that they had the guarding of probably the richest corner of the whole world—the banking and business headquarters of London—and that their duties were made the more onerous by the frequency with which the enemy chose their district for his aerial depredations.

Passing now from the London area to the " provinces," the City of Manchester may be chosen as an example of a city that realised to the full the value in war time of a body of citizens voluntarily undertaking public service to promote the peace and well-being of their city. The big cotton city was one of the best " policed " cities of the kingdom, with a very low proportion of crime and a high level of public morality. In face of this fact the " city fathers " could afford to smile at the little taunts often hurled against their " particular " and " puritanical " police by the thoughtless. The measure of thoroughness expended upon the normal policing of Manchester was extended unstintingly to the establishment of special police, plain citizens sharing with officialdom the work of organising and perfecting this new arm of the law. In less than a month the number of citizens who answered the

Chief Constable's appeal for 5,000 men was 6,300. One hundred and five companies of special police were formed, each with the nominal strength of fifty men, but with an actual strength of considerably more than that number. Each company was placed under the command of its own "leader" and allotted, in the majority of cases, to a special district of its own. Army drill instructors were provided, and each company set out upon a very extensive course of training. It comprised not only the usual squad, company, battalion, and extended order drill, but also physical training, rifle drill, and signalling. Miniature rifle-ranges were opened, four in number, and **Manchester's Special Constabulary** permission was obtained from the War Office to use the full length rifle-range at Diggle, a short railway run from the city. Every member was given the free use of a Service rifle and twenty-five rounds of Service ammunition free of charge. Further ammunition was to be had at a cheap rate. Qualified instructors gave every help to members at the ranges, and before the Manchester Special Constabulary force had been long in existence it comprised not only useful constables but trained men and marksmen—a valuable contribution indeed, at this time to the potential strength of the country for use in any emergency.

At the outset the Manchester special constables, like those of London, confined themselves to quasi-military duties such as the guarding of vulnerable points, but in the early months of 1915 they began to do actual police work, and were soon a common sight, either patrolling the streets or giving evidence in the courts. Meanwhile, one very enterprising new departure, which appeared to be without parallel in the country, was made by the Chief Constable, Mr. Robert Peacock, M.V.O., who from the first had been the prime mover in the organisation of this new police section. He conceived the idea of having a force of mounted special constables for traffic duty. He chose some thirty men, skilled riders—some of whom had hunted regularly in the days of peace with the various hunts of the neighbouring county, Cheshire. After preparatory drill and training they were placed in the streets on traffic duty. Mounted constables had previously been a constant feature of Manchester streets. The day-time traffic in that city was such as to need a readily mobile supervision, for which mounted police had been found essential. The special force of mounted traffic constables was able, after a time, to relieve the regular police of this duty.

Another special force was trained for the direction of traffic, but this force worked on foot and its members were stationed at the busiest crossings. These men were provided with a blue serge suit, peaked cap, black leggings, goloshes, rubber coats, and white gloves. They showed such skill in their work that before long the authorities had no hesitation in handing over even the busiest traffic points to the control of these amateur volunteer constables.

Earlier in the war the Manchester special police carried as signs of their office, like the London police, a uniform hat, official badge, a staff, a whistle, and a warrant card, but later the majority of the men were equipped with uniform, and given an allowance towards boots.

One specially active branch of the force was its ambulance corps, which was one of the largest in the country. The members were trained under Dr. Magian, M.D., who occupied the post of corps surgeon and lecturer. This detachment, in addition to their ordinary police duties, was available for any emergency, and over and above their duties they afforded great help to the Royal Army Medical Corps in removing wounded soldiers from the ambulance-trains and transporting them to different hospitals in and around the city.

Up to August, 1917, no fewer than 700 regular Manchester police had been released for the Army, and 12,000 men had been trained as Special Constabulary. Of this number several thousand passed into the Army, in which they arrived as almost ready-trained men.

The City of Glasgow at the outbreak of war was faced with the need for additional police, owing to the depletion **Glasgow's 3,000 volunteers** of the regular force (of which one-third joined the Army) and other special duties which had to be met. The magistrates of the city accordingly called (on August 19th, 1914) for citizens to act as special constables. The response was large and immediate. Only men over military age were asked for, so that recruiting would not be interfered with, and very soon 3,000 men from all classes were enrolled. They were speedily organised on much the same lines as the regular police, men of experience in discipline and organisation being selected as supervising officers. Under divisional superintendents they became responsible for

A member of the City of London Police Reserve in the uniform issued after two years of service.   Patrol duty in an Essex lane. The man on the right arrested the crew of a Zeppelin.   A stout son of Suburbia. A member of the Hampstead Special Constabulary on duty.

SPECIALS IN LONDON CITY, THE SUBURBS, AND THE COUNTRY.

the protection of vulnerable points specially exposed to risk of attack—waterworks, gasworks, power stations, railway bridges, and the rest. This irksome but necessary duty was undertaken at the request of the military authorities, and for two years it was carried on in an efficient and unostentatious manner.

When the military authorities intimated that they considered it no longer necessary to maintain special protection of railways, bridges, etc., the special constables were withdrawn from this duty, but soon they were called on to undertake fresh ones. The police force was growing smaller and additional duties were being imposed by new Acts of war legislature passed from time to time. The special constables were then employed on patrol duty to

READY TO GO ON DUTY.

Special constables outside a hospital near London preparing to set off on their patrol. Every district had its detachment of Specials, recruited from all ranks of residents in the neighbourhood, who, when their ordinary day's work was done, cheerfully placed their services at the disposal of the authorities.

supplement the regular police. They carried on the ordinary duties of constables, protecting property, dealing with offenders against the ordinary law, and attending courts as witnesses.

In addition to the duties of watching and patrolling, the special constables were from time to time called on for special duties, such as keeping the route on occasions of crowds and processions in the streets, army marches, and parades. A mounted contingent was also turned out on occasion. When the King visited Glasgow in May, 1915, a large number of special constables was employed in keeping the Royal route. His Majesty remarked on their presence, and made inquiry regarding them. The railway-station, where he lived in the Royal train, was guarded almost exclusively by special constables during his Majesty's stay of two days.

In several cases certificates were awarded to special constables of Glasgow for the apprehension of thieves, detection of fires, and other services which successfully protected life and property. There were many instances of the special constables going to the assistance of the regular constables in difficult situations, and the assistance was gratefully acknowledged.

The relations between the regular police and the special constables were uniformly good. There was room for friction where amateurs and professionals had to work together, but no friction arose.

The voluntary response of the special constables to the

call to undertake police duty was noticed to have a good moral effect on the community. On this valuable effect the Chief Constable of Glasgow, Mr. J. V. Stevenson, who from the first had taken the keenest interest in the Special Constabulary movement, said to the writer :

It is really a democratic movement ; it shows that the laws carried out by the police are in full accord with the sentiments of the members of the community, and I have no doubt that it has had a moral effect in other countries than our own. The Continental countries wondered at our voluntary military system. Here they will see great numbers of men over military age coming forward to undertake police duty in order that fit men may be released for military service. It helps to show the spirit in which we entered into this war.

The special constables have also gained by their work. They have gained something by the discipline, which is just self-mastery, enabling a man to follow the rule of duty rather than his own inclination ; they have learned more of their fellow-citizens than they ever knew before ; their knowledge and their sympathies are enlarged, and they have learned to know and appreciate the men of the regular force, who to some extent must stand somewhat aloof from the community in general, and they have the satisfaction of knowing that they have helped in this time of stress.

A fine summary of the benefits that accrued to community and constabulary alike as a result of this great voluntary movement.

The City of Leeds had a Special Constabulary force of a very efficient kind, well adapted to the needs of that busy industrial centre. It was called the Second Police Reserve, and comprised 1,700 constables, 129 sergeants, 45 inspectors, 12 chief inspectors, 7 superintendents, 8 chief superintendents, and a chief administration officer. The force had several very useful branches. A motor section of 127 officers and men, equipped with private cars and transport waggons of various sorts, rendered useful service on many occasions by the rapid transport of men and material to threatened points. There was also an observation section numbering 181 men who, like the similar section of the Metropolitan police, surveyed the town and countryside from convenient points, and were ever ready to report aircraft movements, fires, over-bright lights, and any semblance of enemy signalling. A corps of amateur firemen was also organised by the Leeds **Leeds City** Police Reserve to work in conjunction **Police Reserve** with the fire-brigade. It comprised 93 members who soon became efficient in firemen's duties, and constituted a valuable additional safeguard for the city in the event of fires, whether caused by enemy acts or otherwise. Working in conjunction with this corps was a salvage corps with the strength of 67 men, chiefly skilled artisans and others having special knowledge to qualify them for salvage work.

Among interesting statistics collected as to the work of the Leeds Police Reserve was this table showing in hours the actual duties done by the voluntary police :

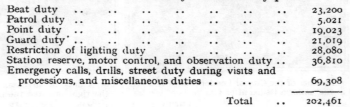

Beat duty	23,200
Patrol duty	5,021
Point duty	19,023
Guard duty	21,019
Restriction of lighting duty	28,080
Station reserve, motor control, and observation duty ..	36,810
Emergency calls, drills, street duty during visits and processions, and miscellaneous duties	69,308
Total ..	202,461

The police problem with which the City of Cardiff was confronted at the outbreak of war was one differing very considerably from that of most British cities, for in proportion to its size Cardiff had probably a bigger alien population than any other. Seafaring men of all the races of the world poured into its docks as the result of Cardiff's world-trade in steam-coal. On shore a resident alien population made a livelihood by catering for the needs of these visiting sailors. On and behind the Bute Road of Cardiff there was an alien population unlike that of any British city. There, mean little shops and rows of cottages contained boarding-houses, restaurants, saloons, and lodgings for almost every race. Some streets were given over to Dutch and Scandinavians, others to negroes and Chinese, and other Asiatics. Police duty along Bute Road and the district—" Tiger Bay " as it was called—was an onerous duty at any time, but when war came and

Onerous duties in Cardiff superimposed the duty of registering and examining individually each member of this floating population, it became more than the ordinary police force of Cardiff could have tackled. An index as to the amount of this work that had to be done is to be found in the fact that in the first three years of the war 300,000 aliens were examined, registered, and " filed for reference " by the Cardiff police. Without substantial help from some outside quarter this work, in addition to all the other police work that arose owing to the war, would not have been possible. This help was forthcoming from the Special Constabulary. A first appeal for volunteer constables brought a response from 557 citizens of all professions and callings. Of these thirty-six elected to act as mounted constables, and they provided their own horses, free of all expense to the city. These men were drilled by a police instructor who was formerly a cavalryman, and on a number of occasions the detachment was used in the streets with valuable effect. The ordinary constables, provided with the usual equipment of armlets, staves, whistles, badges, and warrants, were given an initial period of training, and were then drafted in to fill vacancies caused by the absence of reservists and other constables who had joined his Majesty's forces.

So, with slight fluctuations in strength, the special force continued until the latter part of 1916, when there was a great influx of recruits owing to the action of the tribunals, who called upon many of the men to whom they granted temporary exemption from service to join the Volunteer Special Constabulary Force, and thus perform some additional measure of work of national importance. Owing to these compulsory enrolments the special force rose during the year 1916 from 468 members at the beginning to 1,149 at the close. The scope of the working hours of the Special Constabulary was increased and their duties gradually co-ordinated with those of the regular police. A number of special constables were attached to the fire-brigade as telephone operators; others did work in the Aliens Registration Department. From those who owned motor-cars and motor-cycles a motor reserve was formed for emergency duties. The remaining members did general patrol and traffic duty. A Voluntary Aid Detachment was also organised, and many members

qualified in first-aid. In 1917, when the tribunals were coming to an end of their material, and were refusing to renew temporary exemptions, the strength of the force waned, and by August it had fallen to 863 officers and men. Still, they were a very efficient and enthusiastic force, and the Chief Constable, in giving details of their work, spoke of them in terms of warmest praise. He mentioned that quite a number of them had completed three years' continuous service, and were still working with the same enthusiasm and devotion as when they started.

Bristol's police problem was not unlike that of Cardiff. As a shipping city it had an alien population to deal with, though not perhaps quite so large and varied a one as Cardiff's. At the outbreak of the war a third of the police force went back to service in the Army, and, in the spring of 1915, Mr. J. H. Watson, the Chief Constable, issued an appeal for volunteer constables. On May 6th, 217 citizens, many of them professional men, paraded at the Central Police Station, and were sworn in as special constables by the Lord Mayor. This force gradually increased till, in October, 1917, it numbered 483. The men were allocated to the superintendents of the various divisions, and their turns of duty were four hours a day, Sundays included, every alternate week.

The Bristol Special Police, incidentally, were among the " best dressed " special police of the country. Their equipment comprised cap and badge, button badge, serge tunic and trousers, cloth tunic and trousers, overcoat, cape, leggings, armlet, truncheon, whistle, pocket-book, white cap-cover, waterproof cap-cover, electric torch, cotton gloves, woollen gloves, instruction book, and warrant card. They were also allowed 15s. a year for boots.

AN EMERGENCY CALL.
Assembling of members of the Headquarters Detachment of London's Special Constabulary at Scotland Yard. To members of the Headquarters Detachment was allotted the honourable duty of providing a special guard of constables for Buckingham Palace.

Statistics supplied from official sources concerning the special constables of Liverpool show that at the end of August, 1917, the corps consisted of 1,200 patrol and 520 reserve constables. The former, divided among the city's seven police divisions, performed their duties under the supervision of their own special sergeants, inspectors, and chief inspectors, while the whole force was under the control of the commandant and his assistant, who held the honorary ranks of chief superintendent and superintendent respectively. In the urban areas the special constables did duty from 7 to 11 p.m. one evening weekly, working in pairs, taking charge of beats, or patrolling in company with a member of the regular police. In the suburban districts each special constable paraded for duty twice each week, once from 7 to 11 p.m., and once from 10 p.m. to 2 a.m., taking charge of beats in pairs. In addition, bodies of special constables were made use of on occasions of public ceremony, and on several occasions when disorder was feared, as, for instance, during anti-German riots and demonstrations.

In Cardiff and Liverpool

The administration of the corps was (subject to the direction of the Head Constable) entirely in the hands of the officers of the corps, except in cases of complaint against members, which were dealt with by officers of the

HELP ON A "FLAG DAY."
Members of the Motor Section of London's special constables ready to assist in bringing in the contents of the collectors' boxes on a "Flag Day." Each Metropolitan police division had a motor transport organisation of its own.

regular force. All special constables performing patrol duty were equipped with baton, armlet, whistle, hat badge, coat badge, notebook, and warrant-card, and an allowance of one pound was granted after the completion of twenty-six parades to compensate them for wear and tear of boots and clothing. Mackintoshes and capes were also available at all stations for use in bad weather. In August, 1917, a body of 300 were being fitted with full uniform. These men had undertaken to continue to serve after the conclusion of hostilities.

The Liverpool corps, like the Cardiff force, was recruited in two ways: (1) By enrolling men who volunteered their services, and (2) by the local tribunal making it a condition for those temporarily exempted from military service that they should serve as special constables.

The special constable reserve was composed almost exclusively of these latter men, the majority of whom, for one reason or another, were not suitable for patrol duties. They paraded at a police-station one evening a week at 8.30 p.m., and remained until 1.30 a.m., and were used in an emergency, such as an anti-German outbreak or an expected air raid, for calling up members of the regular and special police who were off duty. They would have proved invaluable in the event of a breakdown of the telephone service, and as it was they reduced the time required for a police mobilisation by about two-thirds.

Speaking on behalf of the Head Constable as to the work

of Liverpool's special police, Mr. L. Everett, the Deputy Head, said to the writer:

I cannot speak too highly of the services rendered by the corps. Without the help it has afforded it would have been impossible for us to have released so large a number of members of the police force for service in H.M. forces and at the same time to give anything approaching adequate police protection in the city. The number of members of the Liverpool police who have joined the forces is now about 800.

Apart from the consistently good services rendered day by day by the special police, probably their usefulness was most apparent during the anti-German riots following the sinking of the R.M.S. Lusitania. I have no hesitation in saying that had it not been for the excellent work done then by the corps the city's heavy bill of about £60,000 for damage done during the riots would have been very much greater.

The war brought new and anxious police duties to the country districts, of course, as well as to the towns. It was in the country, in fact, and especially on lonely coasts, that the acts of enemy agents were especially to be feared. From many of the large and lonely tracts of land about the coast, and its immediate hinterland, enemy agents at the beginning of the war sought to establish signalling stations and depots, and the country police had to be as alive and watchful as the city police. Many country houses and hotels of enemy origin were watched very closely at the beginning of the war, and it was not until after the decision to intern enemy aliens, and definitely to close many establishments of enemy origin, that the countryside of England could be considered incapable of being used for Germanic intrigue.

Almost all the country districts of Great Britain were policed under the authority of the county in which they stood, and it was the County Council and not the local authority who supplied police. In general, these country "beats" were much longer than those allotted to urban policemen, and in place of the two or three hundred yards or less that fell to a city policeman to control, a country constable might have several miles. The county authorities of Great Britain were confronted, therefore, with the need to increase their police force very considerably to cope with their new responsibilities.

No record of the services of the Special Constabulary would be complete without special mention of the highly meritorious work done during the moonlight air raids, which became almost a fashion in the autumn of 1917. Night after night near the days of full moon German aircraft visited the home counties and London, the Yorkshire coast and elsewhere, and though by this time anti-aircraft precautions had become much more efficient, police precautions could not be lessened, and air-raid alarms meant calling out all Specials for duty.

Constables in khaki helmets

The dangers the police incurred in their street duties needed no pointing out to the authorities, and at the beginning of October it was recognised that they should have some better protection. Accordingly, shrapnel helmets were issued to the police of the Metropolitan and City areas for use in air raids. Numbers of helmets, khaki in colour, and of the same pattern as those issued to the troops at the front, were distributed and issued as and when required to constables unable to take cover during air-raid duty.

SOUTH AMERICA AND THE GREAT WAR.

By W. H. Koebel, Author of "Argentina : Past and Present," etc.

Relations of Northern and Southern Halves of American Continent—An Atmosphere of Democracy Observable among South American Indians—Absorption of the Iberian *Conquistadores*—Influence of European Settlements—Great Britain's Links with the Latin Americans—Fresh Influx of Spaniards and Increase in Italian Immigration—German Settlers Who Resisted Absorption—Building Up the Organisation of Teutonic " Peaceful Penetration "—Work of Military Missions from Potsdam in the Various States— German Pre-War Preparations in South America—Sympathies of Latin America Generally with the Allies—Suspicion as to Significance of the Phrase " America for the Americans "—Naval and Military Strength of the Southern Republics—The Naval Battle off Coronel—German Propaganda—Exposure of the Swedish Minister to Argentina—Peru and Uruguay Break off Relations with Germany—Firm Attitude Against the Unrestricted Submarine Warfare—German Minister to Brazil Handed His Passports—Cuba Declares War Against Germany—Brazilian and Argentine Popular Demonstrations Against " German Murderers "—Bolivia Breaks with Germany—Germany Attempts to Conciliate Argentina, and, on Failure, Seeks to Foment Labour Trouble—Count Luxburg's Plots Discovered—Argentina Sends an Ultimatum to Berlin—Brazilian Declaration of War.

IN order to understand the attitude and the actions of the various South American nations with regard to the world-wide war, it is necessary to follow the course of history back along the centuries and to survey the influences that have determined the respective situations of the present-day republics. It will also be necessary to investigate the relations between the Northern and Southern halves of the great American continent—relations which in the past have not been nearly so close as those that have obtained between the Latin republics of the South and the various countries in Europe.

The atmosphere of the Americas would seem to favour the spirit of democracy to a marked extent. This peculiarity has been quite as evident among the Southern Latin communities of the New World as among the Northern people of Anglo-Saxon origin. The circumstance is not a little curious, as the development of the two peoples has been brought about with very little in common save this same atmosphere of democracy and an inherent love for freedom that has manifested itself in the various populations. These characteristics were manifest in the continent even before the advent of the Europeans.

We may begin, therefore, by a very brief study of the aborigines, as they were in the days previous to the Spanish conquests, for the influence of these early native races is marked in many sections of the South Americans, and played a greater part than is generally supposed in determining their attitude with regard to the present war.

The communities of American natives have always shown themselves addicted to a very genuine species of democracy. It is true that in the great Empires, such as those of the Incas and the Aztecs, and the lesser nation of the Chibchas, these characteristics were rather less evident. Nevertheless, a species of Socialism was infused even into these, more especially into the affairs of the Inca kingdom, which, indeed, provides a remarkable example of Indian State Socialism. Nevertheless, the true democracy of the South American Indians was to be met with among the remaining tribes—the Guaranís and the other numerous races of the centre and the north; the Araucanians, the Pehuelches, and the other fierce warrior peoples of the south.

Curiously enough, even among these latter truculent and supremely combative races the power of the chiefs was strictly limited. When war broke out, the man who was considered the best fitted for the task was elected to lead his people into battle, and to act as captain of the warriors. But when hostilities were at an end, he would resume his place as an ordinary tribesman. A similar spirit was observed in the election of the ordinary chiefs. If one of these proved himself incapable or unpopular, he would be deposed with very little ceremony and another would be elected in his place.

The blending of the blood of these liberty-loving spirits with those of the Iberian *conquistadores* undoubtedly worked an important influence on the South American race in general. It was this that helped to cultivate that desire for independence which ultimately led to the War of Liberation and

BRAZIL'S MINISTER OF FOREIGN AFFAIRS.
Dr. Lauro Müller, the energetic Brazilian statesman whose duty it was to conduct the negotiations with Germany which led to Brazil ranging herself with the European Allies.

367

to the separation of the Spanish colonies from the mother country.

We may now deal with the influences which worked upon the South Americans from the outside as well as with the part played by the various foreigners in the development of the continent. In the main it may be said that the actual colonisation of South America was conducted purely by the Iberians. Nevertheless, whether from the point of view of trading and raiding associations, or from the influence of chance settlements, other races—such as the British, French, and Dutch—played their part in the development of the maritime districts, while in the sixteenth century a German community was entrusted with the colonisation of some of the northern districts of the continent, the enterprise being effected through the agency of the powerful Welser Bankers.

Influence of European settlements This, however, proved merely an ephemeral state of affairs, and the same may be said of nearly all the rest. Thus, when the French formed an actual settlement in Rio de Janeiro, before the Portuguese had arrived within the landlocked bay, it appeared for some time as though they had permanently established themselves there. In the end, however, they were driven out by the Portuguese.

The Dutch aggressions in the northern provinces of Brazil were of a larger and more extensive order, and a Dutch chartered company, corresponding in many respects to the British East India Company, was formed in order to administer the great tracts of country of which they had obtained possession. With armies of many thousands of men, and with cities, built on the Dutch model, established on the north-eastern coast of the continent, the Hollanders had every reason to suppose that they had obtained a firm footing—and indeed, their occupation of the Brazilian territory lasted for a

AT THE ATLANTIC END OF THE PANAMA CANAL.
Ships of war at the Atlantic end of the Panama Canal, Colon. A strip of territory ten miles wide, running from Colon to Panama, although within the Republic of Panama, was declared United States territory.

number of years. But in the end they, too, found themselves defeated.

So far as the British attempts on Latin America are concerned, the earlier efforts were aimed chiefly at the Pacific coast and the shores of Central America. An ambitious venture occurred at a later date, when the British expedition to the River Plate at the beginning of the nineteenth century came into possession for a time of the richest portions of the River Plate provinces, including the cities of Buenos Ayres, Montevideo, and other centres along the banks of the great river.

One of the main objects of the British expedition was to bring retaliation to bear on Spain for the part that Power had played in the liberation of the United States of North America, and there is no doubt that the British authorities had anticipated **Achievement of** an important amount of military co- **Independence** operation on the part of the Spanish colonists of the Rio de la Plata, dissatisfied with the methods of the home Government as these were at the time. This was not forthcoming, however, and, after a temporary success, the fate of the expedition was similar to that which befell all similar military forces sent out from Europe with the idea of annexing portions of South America. In this instance the crass foolishness of the British commander, General Whitelocke, completely counteracted the gallantry of his fine troops. Thus in the nineteenth century the sole territories which the European Powers possessed in the South American continent were those of the British, French, and Dutch Guianas.

We may now turn to that important later period, when the various South American peoples emerged from the condition of Spanish dependencies into sovereign nations. With the achievement of independence, the development of the commercial and political relations between the

THE PACIFIC ENTRANCE TO THE PANAMA CANAL.
The gun in the above picturesque scene is trained directly upon the Pacific entrance to the Panama Canal. The islands seen in the photograph have all been fortified for the protection of the canal.

South American States and the countries of Europe and North America proceeded rapidly. Both sentimental and practical motives were concerned in the relations which now sprung into being. Great Britain and the United States had both played a prominent part in the campaign of liberation. France, too, would have undoubtedly assisted with men and munitions to a far greater extent than was actually the case had not the condition of her internal politics and the general state of Europe prevented her participating in the Southern cause of freedom.

Thus the end of the War of Liberation saw the formation of ties of friendship between the recently formed South American republics and the United **Formation of the** States, as well as between the New **" Sacred Alliance "** World and the Old. Of the nations of the Old World, Great Britain, which played the most prominent part, forged the links that were to bind her to the Latin Americans by the effusion of much blood and treasure.

Even so, the future of the new countries was not definitely assured at the conclusion of the War of Liberation itself. The monarchies of Central Europe, alarmed at this great republican success, felt their own thrones shaken beneath them, and, terrified at the prospect, sought a means to delay the spread of the democratic spirit. To this end they formed the " Sacred Alliance," the objects of which were to counteract the republican triumph of the Americas and to restore her one-time colonies to Spain.

Great Britain took up a definite attitude in support of the new republics, and the United States of North America formulated the Monroe Doctrine, which declared that the United States would resist any attempt on the part of the European nations to snatch the newly-won territory from the South Americans

It is a little curious to reflect at the present juncture that the actual birth of the South American States was fostered by Great Britain and the United States of North America, with Prussia and Austria as hostile and opposing agents. The moves of the liberal Powers effectually counteracted the influences of the " Sacred Alliance," and the new Latin countries were thus enabled to begin their early development in comparative peace—that is to say, so far as foreign affairs were concerned, for this peace did not succeed in entering into the domestic affairs of the various Latin American States for a long time.

The Constitutions of these new republics were modelled largely upon those of the United States and of France, although perhaps the majority of the Constitutions made most use of United States' provisions and precedents ; but the spirit in which the actual development occurred was French rather than North American.

As the commercial and political development of the republics proceeded, and the international relations became more complex and extended, it was inevitable that the number of these influences should rapidly increase. With the dying away of the **Spanish and Italian** hostility that the War of Liberation **settlements** had evoked between the former colonies and the mother country, tens of thousands of Spaniards began to accustom themselves to cross the Southern Ocean and to take up their abode in the Latin republics of the South. The Italians, discovering the advantages of settlement in the Southern Latin continent, soon began to arrive in numbers that were at least as great. Up to about the middle of the nineteenth century the influences and ramifications of the continent continued, from the point of view of labour, almost altogether Latin ; while the financial interests and the management of the large industrial enterprises remained largely in the hands of the British.

A MODERN DEMOCRACY WHICH PRESERVES THE STATE SOCIALISM OF THE INCAS.
A scene in the Legislative Assembly of the Republic of Peru, the President delivering his address at the opening of Congress. By the end of October, 1917, Peru had prepared to break off diplomatic relations with Germany, and seized such German ships as were interned in Peruvian harbours.

In 1848 occurred the democratic upheaval which aroused much political turmoil in Europe. The ultimate victory of the old autocratic spirit resulted in the banishment of many of the more liberal-minded Germans from their Fatherland. Many of these political exiles found refuge in Southern Chili, where their communities retained their own speech, schools, and religion. Others settled in Southern Brazil, where a similar state of affairs was inaugurated. The republics to which the refugees went, naturally anxious for immigrants, welcomed the newcomers cordially, and treated them generously so far as grants of land were concerned. The Germans, although rendering passive obedience to the letter of the local State law, did their best to resist the absorbing power of the American atmosphere. In this they succeeded better than the majority of the settlements of other nationalities.

Had they been left to themselves, they would in all probability have become completely absorbed by the units of the South American nations of which they ostensibly formed part ; but, as the ambitions of Prussia spread in Europe, the work of the Prussian agents, passing to and fro, became more active. With the complete militarising of Germany, the attitude of a large proportion of these Germans in South America would seem to have amended itself in proportion as the exhortations from Prussia grew more grandiose and eager ; and ultimately from these communities, which for many decades were regarded merely as collections of patient, hardworking, and non-political peoples, emanated a mass of plottings and intrigue which proved the influence of Prussian world-policy.

Towards the end of the nineteenth century the type of immigrants into South America became altogether cosmopolitan, and Russians, Poles, Scandinavians, Levantines, Turks, and others took to coming out in considerable numbers. They were mainly concerned with labour and with the humbler branches of trade, rather than politics, finance, and more important commercial developments.

German trade and German policy

As the rivalry between Germany and her neighbours in Europe increased and bore fruit in South America, as well as elsewhere, the great Teutonic organisation was built up which had for its aim the so-called " peaceful penetration," as well as elaborate preparation for the ultimate military struggle the Prussian General Staff had continually in view.

The object which the German manufacturer and merchant now set before them was in the first place to make money—not only to enrich their firms, but to place funds at the service of the State which had promised them so vastly extended a field when the ultimate aims of the Pan-Germans had been effected. The policy of the average German merchant, urged by the Prussian bureaucrats and political professors, carried him far beyond that point. It became the aim of the German mercantile community to destroy the commerce of all other nations.

The merchants, in fact, were now part and parcel of the great war-machine of Potsdam, and the result of this policy of flooding South America with German merchants, travellers, goods, and money had the effect of immensely raising the industrial prestige of the German nation throughout the continent. The Teutonic Ministers Plenipotentiary saw to it that this was still further increased by every means in their power.

So close had the alliance between the German State and German commerce become that these diplomatic agents placed themselves unreservedly at the disposal of their mercantile fellow-countrymen in South America. Bribery was resorted to wherever this was thought possible, and in those quarters where this was out of the question, one of the German orders and decorations was nearly always at the service of any local personage who was thought likely to be flattered by the bestowal. Moreover, a telegram from the Kaiser more than once influenced the fate of one of the larger " deals " where international rivalry made the result doubtful.

Perhaps one of the greatest triumphs of the military powers of Potsdam was the organisation of those Military Missions which were sent to various South American republics with the idea of training the armies of the South on the Prussian model. This was followed by the purchase of enormous quantities of war munitions from the Prussian manufacturers.

The countries which accepted the German leadership in the moulding of their armies were Chili, Bolivia, Paraguay, and, to a lesser extent, Argentina. So far as these countries were concerned, not only were numbers of German officers allowed the opportunity of spreading their influence throughout the armies, but many South American officers were sent to Prussia to study the Prussian military system at first hand, and, incidentally, be impressed by its efficiency within in its own limitations.

German Military Missions

The influence of the Germans, of course, varied considerably in these republics. In Argentina it was in many respects the least marked, and many regiments, such as the Horse Grenadiers, originally founded by General San Martin more than a century earlier, retained the style of uniform which more closely resembled the Latin taste. In Chili, on the other hand, the German model was very closely followed, and, so far as uniform and outward appearances were concerned, a Chilian officer might well have been mistaken for a German.

In Brazil the German military spirit did not seem to have penetrated in the least, and it is somewhat curious to reflect that in the south of that great republic, where are situated the very important German settlements, the military training of the armies was undertaken by French officers.

As regards the South American navies, and especially the Chilian Navy, the predominant influence was British.

When the period of war drew near, active preparations were begun by many Germans in various parts of South America to establish points of assistance to the German naval and military forces should the need arise. In those vast and thinly populated stretches of country this was by no means difficult to effect. German wireless stations, secretly erected on South American soil, gave the greatest assistance to the German fleet when cruising off the South American coast.

Despite these facts, the actual sympathies of Latin America in general were undoubtedly strongly extended towards the Allies. The reasons for this were sufficiently deep-seated. In political matters France had stood as a model to the majority of these republics from the date of their foundation. The relations with Great Britain, too, although rather more commercial in some respects, had been always of the friendliest, while the British influence had been evident in the introduction of numerous manners and customs. With Russia, necessarily, the relations had been less intimate, and had been largely confined to the establishment of various Russian colonies.

Relations with Britain and France

The German did not influence the life of the South Americans in any respect beyond that of the barrack-yard, and, although the South Americans entertained a deep sense of his power, they may be said to have regarded him certainly with no affection, probably at the best with indifference, so far as his personality was concerned.

In politics this was not the case. Indeed, for some time previous to the outbreak of the war the two Powers which were regarded with some dread by the South Americans in general were Germany and the United States. It was no secret that Germany coveted large stretches of South America, more especially portions of Southern Brazil. It

A chauffeur of the Women's Army Auxiliary Corps starting the engine of an officer's car.

On this and the three following pages are illustrations of some of the numerous branches of work undertaken by the Women's Army Auxiliary Corps, an organisation formed under the War Office for the performance of all kinds of non-combatant service for the armies in the base camps at home and abroad. By December, 1917, some ten thousand women were employed in different camps. The military authorities pronounced the experiment a complete success, and recommended that outside organisations not controlled by the Army should abandon their separate policies and join the W.A.A.C.

SWEEPING AND SCRUBBING.

REPAIRING AEROPLANE PARTS.

COOKS IN THE KITCHEN OF A MEN'S CAMP ON THE BRITISH FRONT.

ON THE WESTERN FRONT IN THE PRINTING WORKS.

ON THE WESTERN FRONT WOMEN AMBULANCE DRIVERS.

Splendid success of the national organisation of women for military service at home and abroad.

REPAIRING SOLDIERS UNIFORMS.

WOMEN INSPECTING AIRCRAFT FABRIC SEAMS.

WAITRESSES AT AN OFFICERS' CLUB IN FRANCE.

SEARCHING RECORDS OF THE MISSING.

Some occupations in which men were replaced by members of the Women's Army Auxiliary Corps.

Scenes in the daily life of women on active service with the British Army.

was known, too, that the United States had officially taken up the gauntlet, and, basing her stand on the Monroe Doctrine, had declared that no European Power should violate South American territory.

On the other hand, there was a strong suspicion in many quarters—a suspicion keenly fostered and widely spread by German agents—that the United States, although she would permit no one else to intervene, by no means intended to apply the same law to herself. It was frequently said in South America, indeed, that the correct interpretation of the phrase "America for the Americans" was "America for the North Americans." The true aims of those two countries have now been revealed.

From the German point of view, the prospects in the Southern continent had never been more promising than they were at the outbreak of the world-war. For assistance in the South American section of its scheme of world conquest the German Empire, in the first place, relied on the two great German communities of Southern Chili and

WHERE THE INTERNED GERMAN LINERS WERE SEIZED.
Brazilian destroyers and foreign merchantmen in the Bay of Rio de Janeiro, one of the largest and, by general consent, one of the most beautiful harbours in the world.

BRAZIL'S NAVAL BASE.
Harbour and offices of the Naval Base at Rio de Janeiro, one of the three main bases which Brazil possesses.

Southern Brazil. Beyond these were the German Staffs of the various South American armies to which these missions had been accredited, and there was a certain nucleus of well-wishers whom they had succeeded in winning over to their cause, from the sympathetic point of view. Beyond these, again, there were the innumerable agents, secret and otherwise.

That they did not achieve more is due rather to the strong patriotism and common-sense of the South Americans than to the efforts of those who were entrusted with the intrigues. Thus the situation of parts of South America, more especially of Southern Brazil and Southern Chili, resembled that of the United States, where it was confidently predicted by persons of German sympathies that actual hostilities against the Fatherland would be rendered practically impossible by German agents.

In both continents of the Americas a certain number of outrages were committed; but these, through force of circumstances, were limited to isolated criminal acts rather than to the full programme of intimidation and wholesale terrorism which had been intended, and in the course of time the German machinery of sabotage began to fall apart, with the result that many of its grim and savage secrets were exposed **German machinery** to a wondering and angered populace. **of sabotage**

From the point of view of the South American republics themselves, the armaments of the various Southern countries, although admirably adapted for the defence of their frontiers, did not, of course, lend themselves to the transport of troops and to the possibility of sending important expeditions abroad.

We may now survey rapidly the naval and military strength of the various South American republics. Taking the senior Service first, it may be said that the three countries possessing the strongest navies of the Southern

A PEARL OF BEAUTY IN A LOVELY SETTING.
Esplanade and gardens at Botafogo Bay, the pleasure resort of the fashionable society of Rio, and one of the largest indentations and most beautiful recesses in the great main Bay of Rio de Janeiro.

The harbour at Montevideo, the capital of the Republic of Uruguay, showing several of the Uruguayan men-of-war at anchor, and on the left a group of the river steamers which maintain the River Plate traffic between Montevideo and Buenos Ayres.

The Plaza Constitucion, one of the beautiful squares in Montevideo. The edifice on the left is the cathedral; immediately opposite, but not seen in the photograph, stands the old Legislative building.

Montevideo is noted for its fine public buildings; the above, one of the military hospitals, is an indication of the importance which military affairs assume in the life of the energetic little Republic.

Picturesque Bay of Valparaiso, the great port of Chili, on which the Republican Navy is based, and where Von Spee's squadron provisioned before the action with Admiral Cradock off Coronel, farther to the south.

In the various republics are many public tributes from the foreign residents. Above is the arch presented to the city of Valparaiso by the British colony there.

SCENES IN TWO LATIN REPUBLICS OF THE ATLANTIC AND THE PACIFIC.

continent were Argentina, Brazil, and Chili. At the time of the outbreak of war Argentina possessed (or was on the eve of possessing) two Dreadnoughts, each mounting twelve 12 in. guns, some modern destroyers, and a number of armoured and light cruisers of considerably older date. Brazil, too, owned a fairly formidable Fleet, having two fine Dreadnought battleships and a number of fast and modern destroyers as her chief naval assets. The Chilian Navy had from its inception been noted for its efficiency, and was at the time constructing some Dreadnought battleships. It possessed some powerful destroyers, and the majority of its older vessels were in good trim.

The navies of none of the other republics could claim a place of any real importance as regards the part that it was possible to play in modern hostilities.

War forces of the republics These consisted, for the most part, of light cruisers and gunboats, and, indeed, some of the lesser States could boast of no more than one or two tiny vessels for their entire navy.

As regards the land forces, the peace strength of the Brazilian Regular Army was about 30,000, and at war strength its numbers could be raised to some 200,000. The peace strength of the Argentine Army included about 17,000 officers and men, while in war time these forces could be extended to some 120,000 men. Chili, which had bestowed more pains on its Army than the majority of the South American States, numbered about 20,000 men at peace strength, with an efficient scheme to expand to 100,000.

Bolivia's forces were constituted on a somewhat different model, and the total of its active troops and the first reserves slightly exceeded 50,000, there remaining a further reserve that could be called up if necessary. In Peru the standing Army, trained by French officers, was small, and, indeed, did not exceed 5,000 men. In comparison with these, however, there were formidable numbers of reserves on which to draw.

Paraguay's standing Army counted less than 3,000 men. The reserves here,

THE ARGENTINE CONGRESS.
The imposing edifice of the Congress dominates the central scene of Buenos Ayres just as the Capitol does at Washington. It is a magnificent structure, dressed with marble, and in some of its general outlines recalls the proportions of the Capitol.

however, were considerable. The standing Army of Uruguay was about 7,500. This republic, as a matter of fact, formed something of an exception among the South American States, for there military service was voluntary.

In Venezuela, although the standing Army comprised 6,000 officers and men, the reserves consisted of about 100,000 more. In Colombia and Ecuador the Regular forces were small, with a somewhat uncertain number of reserves on which to draw. The combined armies of the continent were fitted much more for defence than for attack.

On the outbreak of war, in Brazil, Bolivia, Peru, and Uruguay, the Governments and the populace moved together towards the side of the Entente. In Argentina and Chili, although the populace was vehemently in favour of the democratic cause (and, indeed, in Argentina, burned various German buildings on receipt of the news of some especial Teutonic atrocity), the Governments maintained a more or less passive attitude, deciding to uphold officially the neutrality that they had declared.

From the very start of the campaign the Southern continent was destined to witness a certain portion of the hostilities at first hand.

History repeated itself. As a base for buccaneers and for the old sailing warships of all nations the archipelago of Southern Chili and the islands of Juan Fernandez had proved of vital strategic value. Admiral von Spee's squadron of German armoured cruisers, accompanied by some lighter vessels, followed much the same tactics as those initiated by the seventeenth and eighteenth century raiders, and the German commander made the most of such sympathies as were afforded to the German sailors by the German settlers ashore in the south of the continent.

The action which ended in the destruction of all but one of Cradock's gallant force was fought

THE NATIONAL HERO OF THE ARGENTINE.
The memory of General José San Martin is perpetuated on every possible occasion throughout the Argentine by monuments and place names, and in a multitude of ways. He was the great liberator of the Republic from the yoke of Spain, and incidentally he helped Chili in her struggle for freedom, so that he is numbered among the heroes of the Pacific Republic as well. The above is a view of the splendid equestrian statue to San Martin in Buenos Ayres, and (inset) a portrait of the hero in later life.

ARGENTINE NAVAL LEADER.
Admiral Howard, although of British origin, proved a thoroughly typical Argentine commander.

GREAT ARGENTINE JURIST.
Dr. L. M. Drago, the originator of the Drago Doctrine, an amplification of the Monroe Doctrine.

off Coronel, which is the centre of the German population in Chili; while on the Atlantic coast German commerce-raiders obtained assistance despite all the efforts of the Government.

The moral effect of these raiding successes on the populations of many parts of South America was very considerable. The destruction of Cradock's squadron lent colour, for some weeks, even to the extravagant boasts which, by wireless and other means, were transmitted abroad. When, however, the last German warship and the last German armoured raider had been sunk in South American waters, the real naval situation was too clearly exposed to be hidden any longer. Although the British liners and merchant vessels in general continued to ply to and fro between South America and Europe as usual, the German mercantile ships—aggregating a tonnage which is estimated at between five and six hundred thousand tons—were all tied to the shelter of the chief ports, there to remain, idle and unemployed, knowing that to venture outside was to court immediate capture.

It was this circumstance which proved, perhaps, the most instrumental of all as a factor in disabusing the public mind of South America of those fallacious notions and sheer inventions in the way of "news" which it had been the object of the German officials to instil into it.

This procedure, indeed, rapidly became part and parcel of the war manœuvres of the Germans in the Southern continent. It took the place of the war of arms in the actual fields of battle, and the endeavour increased in intensity as time went on. Realising

the immense importance of the goodwill of South America to their cause, the Germans threw themselves into the task of propaganda with an energy that had never been approached even by them in this respect until then. Not content with the innumerable attempts to bribe statesmen, editors, and officials in general, they went the length of founding newspapers of their own. Some of them masqueraded under titles which gave them an official air, disseminating the Prussian point of view beneath such headings as "Gaceta Militàr," and similar names.

As affairs went from bad to worse with the military prospects of the Central Empires, the work of their agents in South America took on a more sinister aspect. More ambitious and direct schemes were evolved from the original propaganda, and the scope of these was no longer confined to the South Americans alone. Working in an insidious fashion, the Prussian agents now began to influence some of the neutral Legations which were established in the Latin continent.

As a result of this, in the autumn of 1917 came the amazing exposure of how the Swedish Minister to Argentina had been entrapped, and how the German Minister to Argentina had secretly plotted that Argentine vessels should be "spurlos versenkt"—that is to say, should be sunk without a trace.

The effect of this revelation came as a thunderclap through the length and breadth of South America, and the indignation it aroused was profound. A few days after the publication of the plot Peru and Uruguay broke off relations with the German Empire and ranged themselves, with the other Latin American republics that had already taken this step, on the side of the Allies.

It was at the beginning of the year 1917 that Latin America first began to be directly interested in the war, and we may now follow the chronological order of events from that date.

On January 28th, 1917, the United States forces under General Pershing, which had occupied some parts of Mexico, were withdrawn from that republic, a movement that obviated all chance of unnecessary friction between the two countries, and left the United States general free to occupy

OFFICES OF "LA PRENSA."
One of the sights of Buenos Ayres is the palace of the great daily newspaper "La Prensa" (The Press), in the Avenida. This newspaper has a wide circulation throughout the republic, and during the earlier stages of the war, at least, was inclined to admit a certain sympathy for the Germans.

BEEVES THAT FED THE BRITISH ARMIES.
Picturesque scene in the Argentine "Camp," whence come the exhaustless supplies of cattle for the chilled-meat export trade. A very considerable proportion of the meat supplied to the British Armies in France and elsewhere was drawn from the Argentine.

himself with the study of future events on a larger scale.

From the point of view of the Americas in general, the year 1917 was of particular importance. It was at the beginning of this year that the republics of Latin America were faced by very grave problems consequent on the German declaration of unrestricted submarine warfare.

Throughout the Southern continent it was felt that the menace could not be endured with impunity. On February 4th Dr. Lauro Müller, the Brazilian Minister of Foreign Affairs, had a prolonged conference at Petropolis, the diplomatic centre of Brazil, with the Ministers and representatives of the South American States. Various other conferences succeeded the first, all being concerned with the nature of the protest to be made by Brazil, which had taken the lead in this matter.

The firmness of the Brazilian attitude was strengthened still further by a sinister discovery within her own borders. On February 8th a German wireless station was found to exist at Nictheroy, a town (on the opposite side to the capital) on the Bay of Rio de Janeiro.

As to the other South American countries, the Argentine Government contented itself, on February 7th, with handing to the German Minister at Buenos Ayres a Note of protest against the new submarine campaign. On the same date the Chilian Government, subject to a strong protest against the German marine aggression, decided to maintain an official neutrality. Bolivia entered more warmly into the rights of the neutrals, and on February 6th the Bolivian Minister at Rio de Janeiro visited Dr. Lauro Müller and informed him that the Bolivian Government unreservedly supported the strong policy of Brazil. If anything were needed to spur

HUN-GARBED CHILIANS.
The Chilian Army, which was trained by German officers, adopted uniforms on the Teutonic model, and the above group of Chilian officers, photographed in Santiago, presents the outward features only of a group of modern Huns.

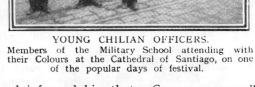

YOUNG CHILIAN OFFICERS.
Members of the Military School attending with their Colours at the Cathedral of Santiago, on one of the popular days of festival.

on the determination of those South American republics who were taking up the matter with energy it was the sinking by a German submarine of the Peruvian sailing-vessel Lorton, which occurred at this juncture.

On February 12th it became known that the Brazilian Government had presented an official declaration to Germany to the effect that it could not accept the blockade as effective, and that, therefore, it protested formally against it.

The great South American republic, moreover, went beyond this point, which, as a matter of fact, had been made by almost every other State in the Southern continent.

It asserted firmly that it would hold Germany responsible in every case where Brazilian interests were damaged, or where Brazilian citizens, cargoes, or ships were harmed.

CHILIAN HOUSES OF PARLIAMENT AND ARTILLERY BARRACKS IN SANTIAGO.
Buildings of the National Congress, the Senate and Chamber of Deputies, in whom the legislative power of the Republic of Chili is vested. Right : A typical artillery barracks. Military affairs enter very largely into the life of Chili, and the Army organisation is the pride of the country.

THE PORT OF TALCAHUANO.
Almost within sight of this busy port in the southern part of Chili, the Battle of Coronel was fought, and it was more than a coincidence that Talcahuano was one of the centres of German influence in the republic.

The Chilian Note to Germany was despatched on February 8th, and took the form of a lively protest against the unrestricted submarine warfare, asserting that profound feeling had been roused by acts which the Chilians considered as restrictions of the rights of neutrality. Uruguay and Paraguay protested in a similar, but still more forcible, fashion.

Germany and Mexico The policy of Germany at this period seems to have been to endeavour to blind the Governments of the Southern continent to the true facts concerning her intentions and actual deeds, while employing every possible means to disorganise the internal affairs of the various republics. Her agents became especially busy, and their work became notably evident in the north of the Latin American world. At the beginning of March it was asserted that Mexico city was in direct communication with Germany by wireless, that large sums of German money were reaching Mexico, while many Germans were leaving the United States for that country.

This somewhat sinister movement, however, had no

effect on the neighbouring republics of Cuba and Panama, which, in April, 1917, associated themselves with the firm attitude adopted by the United States.

In the meantime, affairs had been moving rapidly in Brazil. On the night of April 4th the Brazilian steamer Parana was sunk near Cherbourg. This act aroused a storm of indignation throughout Brazil, and demonstrations occurred in Rio de Janeiro and in the other large cities of the republic which proved plainly that the Brazilians were at the end of their patience.

On April 9th Dr. Lauro Müller refused to receive Herr Pauli, the German

A CHILIAN CRUISER AT TALCAHUANO.
The Chilian Navy was one of considerable strength, as her enormous coast-line involved a greater measure of naval protection than any of the other South American republics, excepting Brazil.

Minister, who, according to the usual German practice, had been endeavouring to justify—or, at all events, to explain—the action of the Teutonic Powers.

Almost immediately after this the full details of the sinking of the Parana were received in Rio de Janeiro, together with the tales of the survivors, who had been picked up by French torpedoboats.

When it became known that shells had been wantonly fired by the submarine at the Brazilian vessel after she had been struck by the torpedo, excitement reached fever-heat, and on April 10th Brazil broke off diplomatic relations with Germany, the German Minister being handed his passports at eleven o'clock in the morning.

When this became known to the sailors on board the German ships interned within Brazilian harbours they endeavoured to render their vessels useless, some by attempts to damage the vessels themselves, and others by making

BRITISH NAVAL OFFICERS AT VALPARAISO.
In the year before the outbreak of war H.M.S. New Zealand visited Valparaiso, and the above photograph shows officers of that warship, together with Chilian officers, at a public function in the Pacific port. The Chilian Navy was trained by British officers.

off for the shore with parts of the machinery.

On April 12th the British, French, and Italian Ministers had a long conference with Dr. Lauro Müller. Brazil now entered enthusiastically into the part which she was determined to play in the world-wide struggle. Feeling confident that the action of their country would be supported by the Governments of Argentina and Chili, crowds of Brazilians gathered to raise cheers outside the Argentine and Chilian Legations. They were somewhat premature, for, although the national spirit of the other two members of the "A.B.C." Alliance was entirely in accord with that of the Brazilians, the official

THE ONLY ACTIVE COLLIERIES IN CHILI.
In the south of Chili there are endless potentialities in the way of coal deposits, but in 1917 the collieries at Lota, near Coronel, on the Pacific. were the only ones worked with energy and success, and the coal produced was somewhat inferior. German influence was predominant.

A CENTRE OF GERMAN INTRIGUE IN CHILI.
The town of Valdivia, in the south of Chili, became for all practical purposes a German colony, the Germans having succeeded in obtaining control of all its public affairs.

very next day the Uruguayan Chamber of Deputies sent a warm telegram of congratulation to the United States Government on its entry into the war.

In the north of the continent the wave of popular sentiment had been flowing with an irresistible force in favour of the Allies. On April 8th Cuba declared war against Germany, and three German ships at the port of Havana were seized without delay, the action being effected just in time to prevent a plot to sink the steamship Bavaria at the entrance to the harbour **Popular feeling in the North** and thus block it. On April 8th, too, the Republic of Panama officially announced its intention of co-operating with the United States, while four days later the Government of Costa Rica proclaimed its determination to adopt a similar attitude to that of Panama.

The influence of all this now became evident in Mexico. On April 12th General Carranza gave satisfactory assurances to the United States that the oil supplies of Tampico, and of the other Mexican oil-fields, would not be refused to the United States or to Great Britain. Thus

attitude was not yet prepared to go to such lengths as were demanded by the citizens at large.

In Argentina strong popular demonstrations occurred, and on April 14th the famous Argentine journal "La Nacion" published a stirring article by the well-known Argentine writer, Leopoldo Lugones, which asserted in a convincing fashion that neutrality was impossible, and that Argentina must break off relations with Germany. Nevertheless, in the face of popular feeling, which now became intense, the attitude of the Argentine Government remained hesitating, and on April 11th the Argentine Ambassador at Washington handed to Mr. Lansing, the United States Secretary of State, a statement to the effect that the Argentine Government would maintain neutrality.

On the same day the Uruguayan Government proclaimed its neutrality; but it was abundantly clear that this proclamation was a mere official form, and that the sentiments of the people were strongly anti-German. Indeed, on the

ANOTHER SEAT OF GERMAN INTRIGUE IN THE REPUBLIC OF CHILI.
The town of Concepcion sheltered a very considerable German colony, and evidences of German taste were to be seen on every hand. The above is a view of the principal plaza, showing the cathedral. In this region there is little doubt that the Germans had secret wireless services at work, which helped to the undoing of Admiral Cradock.

for the time being the German influence here, although by no means destroyed, was, at all events, checked.

In the south, Brazil still maintained the lead. On April 13th Brazilian sailors occupied all the German ships interned in her ports. Three days later the famous Brazilian, Senhor Ruy Barbosa, delivered a speech in Rio de Janeiro which produced a strong impression. In this he urged that the mere abandonment of neutrality was not enough. Nothing short of the definite entry of Brazil into the war would satisfy the nation, he claimed. He explained further that the position of Brazil was identical with that of the United States, and demanded with notable eloquence whether the lives of Brazilians were counted as of less value than those of the North Americans.

In Argentina popular feeling had attained to a pitch which culminated in outbursts of disorder. On April 13th

ROBINSON CRUSOE'S HOME.
View of the coastline of Más-á-Tierra, largest of the Juan Fernandez islands, formerly used as a penal station by the Chilian Government. A wireless station was erected here in 1914.

excited crowds paraded the streets of the capital, shouting, "Down with the German murderers!" and the offices of two German newspapers were obliged to be closed hurriedly owing to the threatening attitude of the crowds. Two days later more serious rioting occurred, when the German Legation and two other German newspaper offices were attacked and the windows of the buildings broken. In this instance several people were injured, including the editor of one of the newspapers. The people, indeed, at this period, showed a disposition to wreck every object that was ostensibly German, and it appeared as if nothing could prevent a rupture of relations between the two countries.

Bolivia breaks with Germany In the meantime the Bolivian Government had adopted a more decided attitude. On April 13th the Bolivian authorities at La Paz handed the German Minister his passports, declaring that diplomatic relations between the two countries were severed. The principal reasons given for this breaking off of relations were the numerous violations by the German Empire of the laws of neutrality and the criminal sinking of vessels by German submarines.

The wave of sympathy now extended over the borders of Bolivia into Paraguay, and on April 14th the only other inland republic in South America declared its full sympathy with the attitude of the United States towards Germany.

In Mexico, on the other hand, German influence would seem to have attained its height. The lives and property of foreigners, with the exception of Germans, were in no little danger ; but no overt acts of hostility were committed, and on April 15th President Carranza announced that Mexico would maintain neutrality.

The situation as regards Central America was considerably improved by the fact that on April 28th Guatemala broke off diplomatic relations with Germany. As Guatemala was the most powerful State in the isthmus, this occurrence was not without its effect on the Republic of Mexico to the north.

In Argentina the popular outbursts had produced a deep impression on the authorities at Potsdam, and Germany now showed a keen desire to conciliate the Southern republic, that held within her frontiers so much German capital as a financial hostage. On May 3rd the Argentine Government received a Note from Germany which, from the point of view of words, gave every satisfaction that could be **Attempt to** desired. It apologised profoundly for the **conciliate Argentina** sinking of the Argentine vessel Monte Protegido, and promised definitely that the Imperial German Fleet should salute the Argentine flag at the first opportunity.

The German Government extended a lesser degree of diplomatic courtesy towards Brazil. On May 3rd it was learned in Rio de Janeiro that the Brazilian Minister in Berlin had been detained. In retaliation, Herr Pauli, the German Minister to Brazil, was in turn prevented from leaving the republic. This produced the desired effect on Germany, and eventually both the Ministers left, on the same day, the respective countries to which they had been accredited.

JUAN FERNANDEZ, RESORT OF THE RAIDERS OF THE SEA.
During the sixteenth and seventeenth centuries the island of Juan Fernandez was the resort of buccaneers, and it was there that the German raider Dresden was rounded up and sunk in March, 1915, by H.M. Ships Glasgow, Kent, and Orama.

The Brazilian steamer Tijuca was sunk by a German submarine off the coast of Brittany on May 26th, and from this date onwards various other Brazilian vessels were sunk by the same agency.

On May 31st the Brazilian Senate finally decided to revoke Brazil's neutrality in the war between Germany and the United States, and to employ for her own purposes the German ships interned in her harbours. The technical result of this was that Brazil allied herself with the great American Republic of the North, but for all practical purposes it amounted to a declaration of war. The number of German ships in Brazilian harbours amounted to forty-two, the tonnage of which comprised nearly a quarter of a million, and these were now prepared for active use.

It may be remarked that the seizure of these ships had a commercial as well as a political significance. For their possession went to serve some way as compensation for six million pounds' worth of Brazilian-owned coffee that the Germans had seized some time previously in Hamburg, and for which they had from the outset definitely refused to pay.

In the middle of June four United States battleships

visited the northern Brazilian port of Bahia, where their crews were welcomed with enthusiasm.

In the countries of the River Plate matters had proceeded more slowly. On June 7th news was received at Buenos Ayres that the Argentine vessel Oriana had been torpedoed by a German submarine. This news, however, did not alter the non-committal attitude of the Government.

In Uruguay, on the other hand, the anti-German feeling was now being given vent to from an official, as well as from a popular, point of view, and the Government officially extended its sympathy towards Brazil and the United States in their joint action.

On June 28th Brazil took a step which regularised her position as regards the belligerents. She revoked her decrees of neutrality in the war between the Allies and Germany, thus making the revocation general. After this, a fresh campaign was instituted against the machinations of Germany in the republic, and one of the results of this was that on July 10th the Brazilian destroyer Matto Grosso discovered at Cambori, near the port of Santos, a hidden prepared base designed to accommodate a submarine. In view of discoveries such as these, further precautions were adopted, and in order to prevent the employment of illicit wireless stations the Brazilian Government issued a decree declaring all the wireless stations in the country to be the property of the Federal Government.

The Brazilian Navy now entered upon its active duties, and undertook the patrolling of the South American coast from the frontiers of Guiana to the south of Brazil.

From the very beginning of the political storm the patriotic unanimity of the Brazilians had been marked. It is true that at one period of the early stages of the final disputes between Brazil and Germany some disturbances had broken out on the borders of the **German intrigue in** States of Parana and Santa Catharina. **Argentina** It was in these southern States that the chief German settlements were established. The outbreak in this case, however, would seem to have been concerned rather with matters of the inter-State frontiers than with the war itself, and order was restored by the late summer.

As in North America, the menace of the German machinations from within was found to be less dangerous than the threats had promised, and such crimes as were undertaken by the agents of the Germans were, for the most part, isolated and intermittent. The work of the agents, however, was by no means confined to the south, for on August 22nd it was discovered that a fire which had destroyed the offices of the newspaper " O Paiz," in Rio de Janeiro, was the work of a German named Hubner.

By the middle of August the peace proposals of the Pope became known throughout America. In remarkably few directions, however, were these received with enthusiasm, or even with approval, and the effect on the people of the South American republics, in general, was not in the least that anticipated by the Vatican.

The Argentine Republic now became again for a time the centre of political interest in South America. Here the work of the German agents had been carried on with an intense degree of energy. The field of its attempts, moreover, had continually grown more ambitious. It was only natural that the weapon of the strike should be one of the chief measures adopted by the " agents provocateurs."

At the close of 1916 a strike of shepherds in the southern town of Punta Arenas, on the borders of Argentina, had been organised in order to prevent wool and frozen mutton from being shipped to England. The movement had been initiated by the Germans, who had provided the necessary financial support, but it was nevertheless settled on January 19th, 1917, when the normal condition of affairs was once again resumed.

Now, far greater and more sinister schemes were set on foot. One of these was to disorganise the entire internal economy of the Argentine Republic by means of the weapon of labour. This was heralded by the strike which occurred on the Central Argentine Railway, and which spread rapidly. Very soon other railways and other enterprises of the kind became involved, and thus was brought about a situation which did, indeed, paralyse for the time being the efforts of the more energetic of the Argentines. The policy of the Argentine Government with regard to this was much criticised, and there would seem no doubt that it lacked firmness and foresight.

We now arrive at that grim and dramatic period of the war when the Washington authorities withdrew the curtain from the vast organisation of crime which had been laboriously brought into being in both the Americas. One of the most striking circumstances revealed was the fact that the German Minister Plenipotentiary accredited to Argentina, Count Luxburg, was plotting to sink

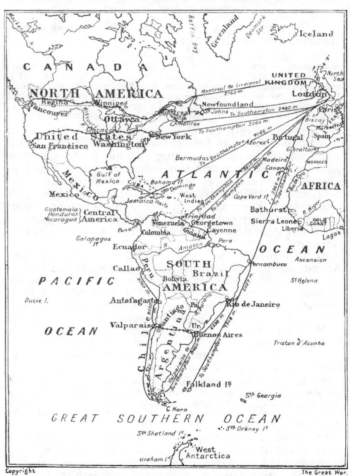

MAP SHOWING THE STEAMSHIP COMMUNICATIONS BETWEEN SOUTH AMERICA AND EUROPE.

Argentine ships, and moreover, to carry out this criminal purpose with a secrecy that should leave no trace of the deed. A strenuous and determined protest arose from all parts of the continent.

On September 12th the Argentine Government delivered passports to Count Luxburg at Buenos Ayres, on the ground that he was no longer a *persona grata*.

It was on that day that the full extent of Luxburg's plot began to dawn on the inhabitants of Argentina, and in Buenos Ayres there promptly assembled great crowds that wrecked German business houses and burned a German club. Count Luxburg himself went in fear of his life, and after various adventures he was interned on the island of Martin Garcia, in the estuary of the Rio de la Plata.

IN THE LEGISLATIVE CAPITAL OF BOLIVIA.
High up in the Andes stands the city of La Paz, one of the two capitals of the Republic of Bolivia, the administrative capital being at the remoter town of Sucre. Bolivia broke off diplomatic relations with Germany on April 13th, 1917.

On September 13th the Argentine Government sent to Germany the following Note :

The Argentine Government recognised and appreciated the magnanimous and high-minded manner in which Germany met the Argentine statement of demands in all its propositions, but it regrets to make known to you that your Minister, Count Luxburg, has ceased to be a *persona grata* on account of the publication of his despatches, and that in consequence the Argentine Government has handed him his passports. (Signed) PUEYRREDON.

On September 17th the German Government determined to cast overboard its too zealous and indiscreet servant, and publicly disavowed Luxburg's actions to the Argentine Minister in Berlin ; but this transparent ruse failed to impress the majority of Argentine statesmen. On September 19th the Argentine Senate, by a majority of twenty-three votes to one, passed a resolution in favour of a severance of relations with Germany, and on September 22nd the Argentine Government sent an ultimatum to Germany.

At this period, the various legislative bodies of the Argentine Republic were no doubt in a somewhat diffuse condition, and it now lay with the Chamber of Deputies to record its vote once again. On September 23rd a dramatic incident occurred in the Chamber of Deputies. Just at the moment when it was about

Mobilisation of Argentine Navy

to vote in favour of a rupture of relations with Germany, a despatch was communicated to the members from the German statesman Kühlmann, which ran as follows :

The Imperial Government keenly regrets what has happened and absolutely disapproves of the ideas expressed by Count Luxburg on the methods of carrying out submarine warfare. These ideas are personal to him. They have not and will not have any influence on the decision or promise of the Empire.

This Note, as a matter of fact, had the effect that had been intended. It exercised a soothing influence, and prevented the proposed vote from being passed at the time. But this passage was only postponed ; for on September 25th the Argentine Chamber of Deputies, by a majority of fifty-three votes to eighteen, adopted a resolution in favour of breaking off relations with Germany.

When it was known on the following day that the mobilisation of the Argentine Navy had been ordered it seemed that the southern republic was on the eve of taking the plunge, and the news was received with much public enthusiasm. On the following day great crowds gathered in the Buenos Ayres streets, and in the demonstration which succeeded a notable part was played by the Uruguayan Parliamentary Delegation which had been especially sent over to take part in it.

In the face of this the underground agents of Germany were now more busily employed than ever with their sinister missions. It is true that the chief of all these, Luxburg, had been prevented from further incitements towards murder and general mischief. Nevertheless,

there remained plenty of lesser agents, and all this time the railway strike, fostered by German money, was continuing and spreading in Argentina. Many acts of sabotage occurred. In the meantime the Luxburg revelations had been followed by the inevitable consequences elsewhere, and the movement of protest against Germany was spreading and growing more determined.

On October 26th Costa Rica broke off diplomatic relations with Germany, and Peru lost no time in seizing German ships interned in her harbours. Although they could not compare in importance with the 235,000 tons that had been taken over by Brazil, these ships confiscated by Peru formed a sufficiently valuable asset.

On October 26th the sinking of the Brazilian steamer Macao became known, and the Brazilian Government officially declared war against Germany—an announcement that was greeted with loud cheers by the Chamber at Rio de Janeiro. It was then declared that Brazil, if necessary, would make all the sacrifices such as were being demanded from the European liberal Powers in order to put an end to the menace of Prussianism. At the same time it was decided to suppress all journals published in Brazil in the German language.

This step was rendered doubly necessary by the discovery, among Count Luxburg's papers, of a definite plan for the invasion of Southern Brazil. At the same time there was strong reason to suspect that there had been a plan to despatch a squadron of German submarines to the waters of Southern Brazil and the Rio de la Plata.

Brazil declares war

On the following day the Brazilian destroyers Piauhy and Matto Crosso proceeded to Bahia with the intention of taking possession of the German gunboat Eber, which had been sheltering there. The German sailors, however, succeeded in setting fire to the gunboat, sinking it before the Brazilian naval forces had time to board the vessel.

The day on which Brazil declared war on Germany was marked by some minor, but none the less sufficiently important, occurrences elsewhere. It was then that a great pro-Ally demonstration took place in Asuncion, the capital of Paraguay, which, notwithstanding the number of German residents in the country who had hitherto done their best to stay the march of events, was enthusiastically attended. On the same day it was decided by the Budget Committee of the Argentine Chamber to do away with the expense of the Argentine Legation in Berlin in 1918.

There was undoubtedly a certain grim humour in this resolution, which, of course, was in accordance with the vote in favour of a rupture of diplomatic relations with Germany. At the same time it became evident that there was a perceptible alteration in the general tenor of the foreign policy of the Argentine Republic, and that it would incline more closely to that of the Allies.

THE PRINCIPAL PORT OF PERU.
The thriving port of Callao, on the Pacific, is only a few miles distant from the capital city of Lima, and is connected therewith by electric tramways. In the roads at Callao there is always a considerable amount of shipping, although the Chilian port of Valparaiso overshadows it in the volume of its trade.

GERMAN ESPIONAGE UNMASKED: A WORLD-WIDE CAMPAIGN OF SECRET SABOTAGE AND MURDER.

By H. W. Wilson.

Gospel of the German " War Book "—Exploitation of Anarchism and Revolutionary Socialism—William II. as Chief Spy—The Case of Colonel Miasoyedoff—Malign Activity of Prince Henry of Prussia—German Crown Prince and Indian Sedition-Mongers—Secret Agents in France, Courland, and Great Britain—Steinhauer, Ernst, Dr. " Graves," Schultz, and Heinrich Grosse—Career of Tribitsch Lincoln—" The Hidden Hand "—Plots in Petrograd and South Africa—German Cipher Codes—Lody and His Work—Kuepferle and Rosenthal—Underground Influences in New York and Washington—Contempt for U.S. Neutrality—Intrigue in Mexico—Offers to Japan—Bolo Pasha and the Pacifists—Almereyda and the " Bonnet Rouge "—German Messages through Neutral Diplomatists—German Agents in Rumania and Italy—Teutonic Triumph in Russia—Guilt of the German Nation.

" BEWARE OF BOLOISM."—*Mr. Lloyd George.*

T HE great struggle between the embattled armies for human freedom was preceded and accompanied by an obscure and noiseless subterranean war. Unseen by the peoples, invisible forces beneath the surface were locked in constant conflict. The colossal Power that had slowly grown up in Central Europe disposed secret emissaries over the whole world to work for it by stealth and to deal blows by treachery and surprise. No form of outrage was too repulsive for the Germans who guided this machine, the working of which has been referred to already in our chapters on " Plot and Counterplot Among the Arming Neutrals " (Vol. 2, Chap. XLI., p. 309; " Germany's World-Wide Campaign of Intrigue " (Vol. 3, Chap. LI., p. 110) ; " The German Conspiracy Against the U.S.A." (Vol. 6, Chap. CIII., p. 83) ; and " The Intrigues and Trials of Neutral Europe " (Vol. 9, Chap. CLXXVII., p. 165).

In no previous age of civilised man had violence and brutality been employed so shamelessly or on so gigantic a scale. For here the source of the wrong was not a single criminal or even an association of criminals, but an immense organised nation with prodigious material resources, which itself formed a vast secret society of immeasurable strength, and also

commanded by its wealth the services of malefactors, desperadoes, traitors and venal newspapers, politicians and writers, in every country on the face of the globe. The stake was the enslavement and exploitation of the world, the slaughter of peoples, the betrayal of whole nations, disaster and agony beyond the imagination of man.

The beings who directed the machine made no secret of their beliefs. They declared publicly in their gospel (the German " War Book," published under official German sanction), " international law is in no way opposed to the exploitation of the crimes of third parties (assassination, incendiarism, robbery, and the like) to the prejudice of the enemy. . . . The ugly and immoral aspect of such methods cannot affect the recognition of their lawfulness." Never was the doctrine, falsely ascribed to the Jesuits, that the end justifies the means, applied with such indifference to every consideration of right and wrong.

In the underground world of Anarchism and revolutionary Socialism this malign influence was specially active. Marx, the creator of International Socialism, was a German who had wished to impose the German type of bureaucracy on all mankind. Stieber, most famous of German spies, who made the arrangements for the subterranean campaign against France in 1867-70, had himself been conspicuous among the revolutionary Socialists. The

THE KAISER'S SPY-IN-CHIEF.
Steinhauer, director of the German spy system, was responsible for the pre-war placing of spies in Great Britain.

connection with them which he established, his successors in the German Secret Service faithfully maintained and tried to extend to the great Labour leaders.

Engaged in this campaign were all classes of Germans. In non-German Royal families the code of honour would have forbidden association with the treachery, crime, and deceit that marked this underground war. The Hohenzollerns and the German princelets entertained no such scruples. William II. was the chief of his own spies, and turned every possible opportunity to advantage. He was a titular Admiral of the Fleet in the British Navy, and proved a most embarrassing visitor to British warships because of the indiscreet curiosity which he showed. He wanted to inspect everything, even the fire-control system and the submerged torpedo fittings, though he always found that his requests were dexterously eluded.

William II. as chief spy At Gibraltar comment was excited by his requests to see the galleries in which the guns were mounted. He examined Malta ; wherever the British flag flew over forts or ships in Europe, there this august person hastened to ply his queries. One of his most characteristic acts was to bring in his train the chief German spy of the Great War, Steinhauer, on his visit to Buckingham Palace in 1911, thereby giving him the run of the palace and an opportunity of convoking other German spies in a great London hotel. The Kaiser assisted this man in every possible way, and allowed it to be known that he expected prominent Germans in London to keep in touch with him.

The Kaiser's direct connection with the work of corrupting officers for the purposes of his Secret Service was signally illustrated in the case of Colonel Miasoyedoff. The colonel was a Russian officer, who before the war commanded the

A SPY CONFESSED.
Dr. Armgaard Karl "Graves," German spy, who wrote a volume of unreliable reminiscences.

military police on the Polish frontier and had his head quarters at Wirballen, the frontier station on the railway from Berlin to Petrograd, only twenty miles from William II.'s shooting-box at Rominten. The German Secret Service desired to get hold of him. Miasoyedoff was therefore invited by the Kaiser to Rominten ; his head was turned by flattery ; and in the company of the extravagant officers in the Kaiser's train he was led to incur expenses which he could not meet. German agents were at hand to lend him money. When they had once involved him he was driven from one betrayal to another. With great influence, urbane, of exquisite manners, knowing all the plans, he was able to supply his paymasters with priceless information.

He was suspected, and accused in 1913 of betraying military secrets when M. Gutchkoff denounced him in the Duma. His reply was to challenge M. Gutchkoff to a duel. It has always been believed that he had a great share in the terrible disaster of Tannenberg, in August, 1914, when a whole Russian army of 200,000 men was destroyed with the loss of almost all its material. A few months later he was on the Staff of the Tenth Russian Army which entered East Prussia in February, 1915, and was defeated. He divulged to the Germans the orders issued, and often delayed their execution so as to give the hostile Staff time to make counter-dispositions. The Russians learnt his guilt from papers found on a German officer captured by the French on the western front. They watched him. At last a letter from him to the Germans, with full details of the Russian plans, was intercepted. The friend of William II. was placed under arrest, tried by court-martial, and hanged as a traitor and a spy in April, 1915. Two of his associates in the upper ranks of the Russian Secret Police, Barons **The hand** Grothus and Freinat, both of German **of Prince Henry** origin, were tried and executed later.

Prince Henry of Prussia was of equal service to the German espionage system. On his visit to the United States he encouraged the foundation everywhere of German societies, which in due time were to act as centres for the Secret Service. He lost no chance of bringing the Irish revolutionaries into sympathy with the Germans. In 1902 the Kaiser told a German-American professor that he regarded the union of Germans in the United States which this visit had produced as its "greatest success and justification." The Germans, thus organised, incessantly stirred up ill-feeling against Great Britain and Japan.

In England, Prince Henry's activity was unremitting. He attempted to bully the Court, felt the pulse of society, conferred with pro-Germans, and, under the pretext of motor-car touring with members of his suite, made a careful road survey of the country. On the eve of war he was in England, nominally to be present at a motor-car

HERR VON KÜHLMANN.
Herr Richard von Kühlmann (left), Councillor German Embassy in London, 1908-14. He was appointed German Secretary of State for Foreign Affairs, on the resignation of Dr. Zimmermann, in August, 1917.

competition; actually, as appeared from the correspondence which has since been published in the two countries, to secure some promise from the King which could be used for purposes of diplomatic blackmail. The King was not caught in this trap, and the prince departed in great discontent.

The two, William II. and Prince Henry, effusively received those British editors, politicians, and literary men who manifested sympathy with Germany and visited Berlin. Lord Haldane, the British Secretary of War, was not only entertained by the Kaiser and provided with advice as to the military measures he should take for the organisation of the British Army; he was also visited in London, on which occasion Mr. Ramsay Macdonald was among the party. From these visits the delighted guests trooped home with busts, statuettes, autographs, and photographs, vaunting the Kaiser's affability and declaiming against the folly and perversity of those who suspected him of mischief. Thus impediments were placed in the way of national defence, for most of these people could never bring themselves to believe that so charming a potentate could entertain hostile purposes. On occasions the Emperor directly entered the battlefield against the British Navy. Thus, in 1908, he wrote to Lord Tweedmouth, then First Lord of the Admiralty, protesting against the suggestion that the growth of the German Navy rendered an increase in the British sea forces essential. The letter became known, and disagreeably affected public feeling. It also appeared that Lord Tweedmouth had communicated to the Kaiser the British Navy Estimates for that year before they were submitted to Parliament. This incident, typical of Hohenzollern intrigue, led to Lord Tweedmouth's early resignation.

The Kaiser's famous interview with the "Daily Telegraph" in October, 1908, was chiefly noteworthy for its audacious assertion that he, who in 1904-5 had planned an alliance of Germany, Russia, and France against her, was Great Britain's only true friend. There were passages in it which suggested that its real object was to create friction between Great Britain and Japan. Another example of Imperial treachery was the despatch of General Emmich to Liège as the Kaiser's envoy, shortly before the war. He was to give the Governor of Liège a reassuring message, and incidentally to reconnoitre the fortress which he was chosen to assault in August, 1914. In 1912, when the situation in Ulster began to grow serious, the Kaiser made advances to Ulster's leading men and attempted to entangle them in an understanding with him. Finding that he had totally misconceived their loyalty, he dropped his overtures. About 1909 he opened relations with seditious Indians, and a bureau was established in Berlin to promote Indian plots.

DR. H. F. ALBERT.
Dr. Albert, Councillor in the German Embassy at Washington, a director of the German secret agency in America.

CAPTAIN KOENIG.
German secret agent in the United States, who was arrested for complicity in an attempt to blow up the Welland Canal.

MR. J. F. J. ARCHIBALD.
American journalist in German pay, who was arrested at Falmouth, in 1915, bearing secret letters from Dr. Dumba, Austrian Ambassador at Washington.

The Crown Prince followed faithfully in the footsteps of his father. During his visit to India persons in his suite were able to meet on the spot Indian sedition-mongers. He himself made certain overtures to native princes, which were received with disdain. He exhibited himself to the Indian peoples as the son of the mightiest ruler on earth, the sovereign destined to wrench the sceptre from feeble British hands. A visit to the British Colonies and Dominions had been planned for him on the eve of war. It would have enabled him to stir up sedition in South Africa and elsewhere. The Reichstag, however, refused the necessary credits. Wherever they went these German travellers and their suites made disparaging remarks upon the incompetence and weakness of the British, contrasting them with the noble, humane, and energetic Germans. This was a subtle form of propaganda which had some effect on simple minds.

Behind the grey cloaks and brilliant uniforms of the German sovereigns and their suites moved those chartered official spies, the German diplomatists, who disregarded all precedents and violated all the rules of honour, and behind them again in the twilight a host of obscure and often sinister figures. The first sign that Germany intended war was given when a multitude of shady, obsequious creatures descended upon the naval ports of Great Britain, the Belgian fortresses, upon France, and upon Poland. The Germans were magnificently equipped for this gigantic campaign of espionage. Their banks in the allied capitals enabled them unsuspected to train agents and to obtain priceless connections. Their vast industries with establishments and branches in allied countries, and the hosts of Germans who gradually wormed their way into the very heart of the commercial world in Great Britain, France, and the United States, gave them unexampled opportunities of procuring the best information. Finance, industry, commerce, intrigue, and espionage were thus interlocked.

The Allies were carelessness embodied, so that it almost appeared as if they wished to render espionage unnecessary. The French Government allowed the firm of Krupp to purchase a site near the all-important fortress of Maubeuge, and to construct on that site concrete platforms which in September, 1914, were used by the German 17 in. howitzers. Near Liège, Namur, and Antwerp the Germans were allowed to make similar siege preparations in the midst of peace. German "insurance" companies and commercial agencies ascertained the exact resources, man-power, and machine-power of every French firm and factory. The British Government permitted Germans to acquire property dominating its naval ports and to obtain employment in local post-offices, so that the Scottish naval bases were infested and watched. Through these offices telegrams and mobilisation notices would pass ; delay in them might decide the fate of the British Empire.

In Courland a German millionaire purchased an estate and built a castellated house with sunk walks, concrete vaults, and concrete artificial ruins. The German armies appeared, and this building became a miniature fortress. Germans acquired property dominating aerodromes and important railway points in France. German pilots were allowed to learn their way in British waters, while German ships took photographs (a series of the British coast hung in the Navy offices in Berlin) and soundings. German airships at night cruised over British soil. German gunboats and torpedo craft constantly anchored in Scapa Flow, the British naval base in the Orkneys. They hovered about the Scottish ports. In the British

German pilots in British waters naval manœuvres of 1913, when invasion schemes were being tested, they redoubled their surveillance. The German cruiser Ziethen and the destroyer D8 put into the Tyne and Sunderland at a critical point in the operations. Germans supplied the Italian Fleet with silver-plate, and so obtained access to Italian dockyards. Germans made electric ventilators for French and Italian forts and installed them. For all this negligence of their Governments the peoples of the Allies had to pay a fearful price in tears and blood.

In Great Britain, where Germany always had many spies available among her clerks, seamen, and business men, she began in 1910 to multiply her agents and to stimulate them to greater efforts. "We have been the subject in the last eight or nine years of careful, deliberate, scientific military reconnaissance," said Mr. Churchill, wise after the event, on September 21st, 1914. Even the British authorities took alarm, and in August, 1911, began a counter-campaign against German espionage by passing the Official Secrets Act of that year. It provided that a person caught with documents or information on him concerning naval or military defences should have to prove his innocence.

At the same time the Post Office began to open letters which were suspected, and gradually a vast spy system was brought to light. The German agents did not seem to know for many months that they were being watched. They were not, as a rule, molested or touched. Only they were followed and their letters were read. The police did not strike unless there was reason to fear that documents and information of importance were being transmitted from the country. As the result of this policy many of the German agents became known to the police. In such trials as took place as little as possible was disclosed.

CAPTAIN VON PAPEN, OFFICIAL MURDER AGENT.
German Military Attaché at Washington, Von Papen was one of the most active and unscrupulous of enemy agents in America. He was recalled to Germany in December, 1915, on representations from the U.S. State Department.

The director of the German spy system, Steinhauer, had been an officer in the German military police, and was a man of some education. His name appeared in many of the British trials. He spoke English well, but with the slight accent which Germans can never disguise. His clothes and his hats were of London make. He gathered about him a large company of Germans who had lost caste at home or served terms of imprisonment abroad. He had two sets of agents, fixed and travelling. The fixed agents were invariably men with a small business of such a kind as to give them some **Steinhauer's agents in Britain** standing and means of obtaining news. The trades patronised were hairdressers, greengrocers, stationers, jewellers, bakers, photographers, tobacconists, and teachers of foreign languages. Publicans abounded in the naval ports, and were strategically distributed through Ireland. Many of these German spies had naturalised themselves under the negligent system of British law and changed their names, so that their identity and nationality were not suspected. They were instructed to be charitable, and were supplied with the necessary funds. Steinhauer, while ready to deal in millions, haggled over small amounts, and gained a hold on his creatures by keeping back a portion of their pay. The German fixed

COUNT JOHN BERNSTORFF: AMBASSADOR AND CONSPIRATOR.
Count Bernstorff, German Ambassador at Washington since 1908, had deeply committed himself to acts of secret war against the country to which he was accredited before being given his passports in February, 1917.

agent Ernst, an Islington hair-dresser, received only the miserable pittance of £1 a month, subsequently increased on his remonstrances to £1 10s. The fact was that the Germans as a people had a bent and liking for espionage, and took to it as a duck takes to water. A spy of higher position, Dr. "Graves," who wrote a book filled with falsehoods, received at the outset £200 a year as retaining fee, 10s. a day as living expenses, and a "bonus" on each piece of work carried out. Correspondence seized by the British authorities showed that he was promised £100 for one errand, which was to obtain details of guns building in Glasgow.

If the spy pitched his demands too high or wasted money without giving value for it he was sharply called to account. Thus the spy Schultz, arrested at Plymouth in 1911, was told by one "R. T.," in a letter from Germany, "unless you obtain something more useful, no more money will be forthcoming from the employer." In another letter he was told to stop " your cursed telegraphing (for money) . . . through your constant telegrams you undoubtedly lay yourself open to suspicion and endanger your safety and our business." He made large promises to people, who at once informed the British police, and they thereupon watched him.

The German agents made many attempts to suborn men in the Navy and Army, but their only success in this **Advances to Naval officers** quarter was the corruption of Gunner Parrott. A most impudent ruse was tried in December, 1913, at a time when, as was subsequently known, Germany and Austria had definitely decided upon war. A document was sent broadcast to torpedo, gunnery, and wireless officers in the British Navy. It stated that a revised edition of a work describing European navies was about to be published by " an important house," and that a collaborator was required to bring the section relating to the British Navy up to date. Officers were invited to communicate with the author of the circular, who promised " extremely high payment " in a " booming business." All communications could, if necessary, be posted by " a very reliable friend." The circular closed with the unidiomatic offer of " a splendid earning of money." In other cases advances were made to officers who had been marked down by the secret agents as in pecuniary difficulties, and here German money-lenders took a hand in the game. To the credit of the British Navy it must be said that in no case except Parrott's was there any hint that an officer had betrayed his duty.

Another device adopted by one of the most important of German spies, Heinrich Grosse, sentenced in 1912, was to publish an advertisement in newspapers circulating in naval ports : " Gentleman wanted to undertake private inquiries ; arrange meeting to suit convenience." A person who answered quite innocently was told, " I am writing a book, and I want to know the amount of coal at Portsmouth. I want to know the number of men stationed in the barracks, and whether it is above or below the normal number at that time of year." Another method was to offer to bet £5 with men who knew as to the number of seamen in the barracks.

In the neighbourhood of Sheerness and Chatham the

HANDIWORK OF GERMAN AGENTS IN PENNSYLVANIA.
In November, 1915, a fire, the origin of which was traced to German agents, broke out in the Bethlehem Steel Works, Bethlehem, Pennsylvania, and was not extinguished before it had effected the destruction of war material of an estimated value of a quarter of a million sterling.

Germans had a stronger organisation than in any other quarter. It has even been suggested that the mysterious explosions in the Chatham ships—Princess Irene, Bulwark, Natal, and Vanguard—were connected with this agency. In Italy no doubt was entertained that the battleships Benedetto Brin and Leonardo da Vinci, in both of which internal explosions took place, were destroyed by treachery. The Gerlach trial early in 1917 showed the existence of a vast German plot in Italy to destroy munitions and warships. In Russia information was obtained in 1917 which indicated that the Russian Dreadnought, Imperatritsa Maria, sunk on October 20th, 1916, was also blown up by treachery.

Once in the German Secret Service, a man or woman could not leave it unless the German authorities saw fit. Those who quitted it without leave were betrayed or mercilessly hunted down. Life was rendered impossible for them. In a few cases they disappeared, and were probably kidnapped or murdered. " If a man left the Secret Service," said Ernst, " he **The case of Tribitsch Lincoln** was suspected of betraying secrets, and was a marked man." So immense was the political and financial power of the German machine that his business could be wrecked and he be ruined if he were not punished in some more terrible fashion. Dr. " Graves " affirmed that he had been deliberately betrayed to the British police because he knew too much.

Spies and German agents were found among the politicians. The famous case of Ignatius Timothy Tribitsch Lincoln illustrated the ubiquity of German influence. He was a plausible, shifty Hungarian, born at Paks, near Budapest, in 1879. In 1896 he was " wanted " by the Hungarian police, and disappeared. He married a German wife at Hamburg, and after a stay in Canada came to England, where he exploited various religions—Presbyterian in 1901, Church of England curate in 1903, Quaker teacher in 1905, spreading pacifist doctrines, till in 1906 he became secretary to a well-known political and philanthropical Quaker, Mr. Seebohm Rowntree. During his many transformations he stole a watch from a friend, who refused to prosecute, and borrowed £10,000 from Mr. Rowntree. In 1909 he descended upon the constituency of Darlington as a Radical Free Trader. He declaimed with special fury against the British Navy, wrote on a blackboard at his meetings demonstrations of the folly of Tariff Reform, spoke with a guttural German accent, and yet was triumphantly returned in January, 1910, receiving the congratulations of the leading Liberal politicians. " When you are M.P.," he remarked, " all doors are open to you."

He disappeared from Parliament after opposing Naval and Military Votes, and thus acting in German interests; but he was employed in the Censor's office on the outbreak of war, and was dismissed for misconduct. On his own confession he became a deliberate traitor in December, 1914. " I hate England," he wrote, and he asserted that he wished first to gain the confidence of the British authorities, and then to betray them and bring about some great British disaster. His scheme, it appeared, was " to lure a part of the British Fleet into a certain quarter of the North Sea on a certain day, and have the German Fleet within easy steaming distance." It is certain that he went to Rotterdam, and there consorted with the head of the German Secret Service in Holland, Colonel Ostersteig, former German Military Attaché in London. He claimed to have obtained from him two spy codes which he revealed to the British. Finding, however, that he was justly suspected, he bolted, and succeeded in reaching the United States, where he published a volume of largely apocryphal memoirs. Thence he was finally extradited for forgery, tried in 1916 in London, and convicted, after a lachrymose defence in which he alternately wept over his own woes and gibed at British incompetence. " You are too slow in England, too slow, in chemistry, in science, in warfare—in everything," he declared.

How much higher in British political life the German organisation extended remained a secret. It was alleged that large German contributions figured in the funds of both parties, and thus swayed their trade policy and attitude to naval and military affairs. It was a curious fact that there were many Germans in Government offices, even in such vital points as the telegraph centres, and that they were allowed to remain there after the war. It was only with great difficulty that their elimination from certain strategically important offices was secured by the naval and military authorities in 1915-16. Whoever attempted to expel them found that he had to encounter the invisible force which came to be known as " The Hidden Hand." It may have been the inertia of bureaucratic scepticism and indolence, or there may have been subtler influences at work, for the Germans had penetrated everywhere, and had on their side social standing and immense financial influence.

Mystery of " The Hidden Hand " London had been gradually overrun by foreigners who manipulated money, dealt in international loans, brought out companies, and could make a man's fortune with a nod or wink. Some of them may doubtless have become loyal British citizens (though as Consul Ahlers said when charged with treason: "Once a German, always a German"). There were others whose German proclivities were barely concealed, and they were the bitterest enemies of British armaments, eager supporters of Free Trade, and, deliberately or incidentally, the auxiliaries of the Kaiser. They claimed to be cosmopolitans, and they provided, secretly or openly, large sums for the pacifists, Socialists, and anti-nationalists of Great Britain, France, Italy, and Russia.

What happened in the United States was full of

ONE OF GERMANY'S MOST NOTORIOUS AGENTS.
Bolo Pasha (second from left) leaving the Palais de Justice, Paris, after interrogation. This industrious German agent was arrested in America in September, 1917, by the American Secret Police, as a result of discoveries made about his world-wide activities.

suggestiveness as to conditions in Great Britain. Germany, said that most restrained and cautious of allied statesmen, President Wilson, filled " even our offices of Government with spies, and set criminal intrigues everywhere on foot, with the support and even under the direction of official agents of the Imperial (German) Government." " When the full secret history of the present war comes to be written," said Lord Robert Cecil on September 9th, 1915, " it will be found that more than one of the civil disturbances that have taken place (in allied countries) have been deliberately fostered with German gold." The Sinn Fein rebels in Ireland were supplied with cash, plans, and arms by **German intrigue** the Kaiser. " The helping hand is **in Ireland** being stretched out again (in Ireland), and the Government know it," said Mr. Duke on October 23rd, 1917. The Ethiopian could not change his colour. German methods were always the same.

On Saturday, August 1st, 1914, one of the most critical in the history of the human race, the tide of peace in the British Cabinet swayed backwards and forwards. France was appealing in bitter agony for help, knowing how terrible an enemy she had to face. It was impossible for British journalists to look their French comrades in the face as the Cabinet sat undecided. From Petrograd came other appeals to the British Ministry not to forsake Russia in her noble effort for a small and weak State. The Russian Ambassador in London told a friend next day that he was quite in the dark as to the British intentions. As Ministers sat in council that stormy afternoon the German armies were already beginning the vast orgy of crime which made shipwreck of all human law, and were concentrating on the Luxemburg frontier, which they had already violated in one place.

When the great battle in the Cabinet ended at last in the only honourable decision, for war, German influence was exerted anew to delay the despatch of British troops to France. Hideous tales of impending bread riots frightened timid Ministers. In the end, after the waste of two precious days in indecision, not the whole

Expeditionary Force of 160,000 men, but only 80,000 were sent. Had two days not been wasted, and had even 80,000 men been promptly sent, according to M. Hanotaux, the British would have been in line on August 20th (instead of on August 22nd), and General Joffre would have outflanked the Germans, and might have routed them in Belgium. Even if this view is rejected as much too hopeful, it is probable that if the whole 160,000 had been sent Germany would never have reached the Marne or conquered the Belgian coast. Such precious results did the Emperor William's friends and agents obtain.

In those dreadful hours German hands were everywhere busy stirring up trouble and suborning rebellion. In Petrograd (where 16,000 Anarchist leaf-

The plot in South Africa lets were seized in a room of the German Embassy, to which Count Pourtalès, the Ambassador, was wont to retire for "amateur photography"), riots mysteriously broke out on the eve of war. In Dublin there was bloodshed. The invisible force, omnipresent, deadly as that of the Mormon "destroying angel," was at work. In Russia thousands of German agents were active as carrion flies. In every neutral country the Germans redoubled their efforts, and in particular in the United States. There a great battle began, which was to continue months and years; thence sedition in India, South Africa, Canada, Australia, Singapore, and a hundred other allied possessions was sedulously fanned. Thence Berlin sent the funds which kept the treasonable Sinn Fein movement burning in Ireland.

A gigantic plot in South Africa was defeated by sheer chance—or what we call chance—the shooting of Delarey on September 15th, 1914. That Boer general, a simple, kindly old farmer of generous disposition, but easy above most men to deceive, was on the point of being hurried off by General Beyers, a South African traitor in British uniform but in the Kaiser's pay. Beyers meant to take him to Potchefstroom, where a large force of South African troops had concentrated. He would lead the troops to imagine that Delarey was a traitor, and lead Delarey to imagine that the troops were disloyal, and thus begin a rebellion. The accident that a gang of motor bandits was active on the Rand led the police to stop Beyers' car. Beyers supposed that he had been challenged because his treason had been discovered, and ordered his driver to go on. The police fired and killed Delarey on the spot. Beyers, imagining all was known, fled, and the Potchefstroom force remained loyal. The whole conspiracy rapidly collapsed before the firmness of Generals Botha and Smuts.

That the German spies proper were able to do comparatively little mischief in Great Britain was due to the prompt arrest of the most important of them on the eve of war, when twenty of the best known were seized and placed in detention, and another two hundred were closely watched and subsequently interned. The British authorities, in their campaign against the spy system, had also discovered the German spy codes. Before the war the Germans generally sent important documents and messages by agents who went to and fro. But when telegraphing, and in some of their letters, ciphers were used.

There were two important kinds of telegraphic cipher. One was known as the "family code," and was in itself not likely to attract suspicion. It gave what was apparently news about some member of the agent's family, and was read in connection with his errand. Thus the spy Lody, shot in November, 1914, after a visit to Rosyth, telegraphed to "Adolf Berkhager, Stockholm," on August 30th, this message: "Must cancel Johnson very ill last four days shall leave shortly." "Johnson" was the British squadron at Rosyth, and the telegram conveyed to the initiated the news that four days later the squadron would proceed to sea. The message seems to have gone through. On September 5th a German submarine was waiting near the Scottish coast, and the British scout Pathfinder was torpedoed and sunk with the loss of nearly two hundred lives. The terrible danger of espionage and the need of iron severity in crushing it were never more clearly illustrated.

The other code involved the use of a dictionary, and was exceedingly complicated. The pattern of dictionary generally employed was one published by Lagenscheidt, which had little vogue in Great Britain. Messages were sent by groups of numbers or values: thus, "I cannot give more than £204 15s.," would mean that the 15th word in page 204 was to be taken. That word might be part of a long message, or might itself be a complete code signal. In that case, however, the spy would have to learn the code

A TRAITOR TRYING TO MAKE TRAITORS.

In October, 1915, it became known in England that Sir Roger Casement had been visiting prison camps in Germany, seeking to induce Irish prisoners of war to join a German-Irish Brigade. At Limburg he was kicked round the camp by the men whom he had sought to make traitors like himself. He also sought to promote sabotage in America. In April, 1916, he was caught trying to land arms in Ireland, and on the following August 3rd was hanged.

COUNT KARL LUXBURG.

Count Luxburg, German Chargé d'Affaires in Argentina, was, in September, 1917, shown to be conspiring against the country to which he was accredited, and cold-bloodedly arranging that Argentine ships should be "sunk without a trace being left." The Argentine Government promptly decreed that Count Luxburg was *persona non grata*.

by heart as, if he carried it about with him, it would have provided damning evidence against him. There was further great risk of mistakes. It was possible to complicate the dictionary code in many ways, by inserting false numbers or adding numbers to the true figures. Thus, by placing arbitrary thousands in front of the figures, the 15th word of the 204th page could be converted into " 3015 1204."

German secret codes The more complicated the code the greater the risk of mistakes. An interesting example of the cipher used by the highest agents of the German Secret Service was this opening of a document seized by the British Government on Captain von Papen :

J. No. 2321/15.

New York, 20 August, 1915.

Über die Zustände 4507 94066 sind folgende Nachrichten 0619 xobakcumf 2289 98022 8443 · · ·

German words were intermingled with code groups of numerals, letters, and phrases. It is an axiom of cryptography that any cipher can be read with sufficient time, patience, and ingenuity, though there have been historic occasions—as twice in the campaign of 1870—when the key of a code was mislaid, and it was impossible till too late to read the messages. The decipherer starts with certain rules, as, for example, that "e" is the commonest letter, and " the " the commonest word in English. But these can be rendered almost useless by such devices as adopting five or six different signs for each letter, or by interposing meaningless letters and numbers in the cipher, so as to hide the length of the words. One of the simplest and easiest ciphers to construct and read is given by taking the

letters of a sentence and numbering them. Thus on the spy Grosse a document was found with this sentence :

"p a c k   m y   b o x   w i t h   f i v e
1 2 3 4   5 6   7 8 9   10 11 12 13   14 15 16 17

d o z e n   o f   l i q u o r   j u g s"
18 19 20 21 22   23 24   25 26 27 28 29 30   31 32 33 34

A message in this code would easily be read by an expert decipherer. But if a few words were added, reading it would become much more difficult, as :

"o f   t h e   s m a l l e s t
35 36   37 38 39   40 41 42 43 44 45 46 47

s i z e."
48 49 50 51

The highest number to which the series runs is 51, and there are several signs for the commonest letters. The number of letters in each word must be hidden, as that would otherwise give a certain clue. Consequently German agents generally divided the signs into **Karl Ernst and Steinhauer** groups of five or six letters, inserting meaningless numbers or letters. Thus in the above code all numbers above 51 would be meaningless. " Sixty battleships " would read:

40.49.09.12.06.   07.02.47.12.44.   25.17.46.13.49.   52.01.94.34.65.
s i x t y   b a t t l   e s h i   p s

Secret inks were also used. But the value of these ancient properties of melodrama is very small in modern times. Simple methods of treatment will bring out the writing, which with good eyesight can generally be detected on the surface of the paper.

On the outbreak of war the police seized the Islington hairdresser, Karl Gustav Ernst, whose correspondence they had long watched with valuable results. He admitted having sent at least two hundred letters to Steinhauer, and he had also re-posted letters to Mrs. Parrott, wife of the spy of that name, to "Graves," to Gould (alias Schroeder, a German spy who kept a public-house at Rochester, and was convicted of espionage), and to a naval stoker who called himself Ireland, but whose real name was Kruger.

Some of the letters which he posted were intercepted, and not allowed to reach their destinations. Among these were circulars addressed to twelve or fourteen naval officers to whom the most tempting offers were made if they would betray their country. Ernst's importance was shown by the fact that Steinhauer visited him at Christmas, 1911, and entrusted many missions to him. As an example, he was requested to go to Sheffield and find out about a person named " P. K. Wohler, care of Mrs. Bartlett." His instructions were precise:

It is possible that a Wohler does not exist at all, and that the name is only fictitious. Great caution is necessary, as one must remember that W. may be only desirous of pumping us. Therefore, go there, perhaps after Whitsuntide, and see whether you are able to ascertain what the fellow is after.

Another letter ordered him to go to

Mr. W. Kronauer, Manor Road, Hampstead, and hand him quietly the enclosed letter without address. K. is a colleague of yours. I do not know whether you know him. If not, then don't make yourself known. Perhaps you can have yourself shaved. Then give him the letter or place it for him in the letter-rack, but he must take it himself without witness.

In this correspondence Steinhauer used the names of " Mrs. Reumers," " Mrs. Reimers," and " Miss M. Reimers." Ernst was sentenced to seven years' penal servitude.

After the destruction of a great part of his system in England, and the arrest of so many of his agents, Steinhauer set to work to establish new connections. The Germans were so widely spread, and had hidden themselves so dexterously and under so many aliases, that it was difficult for the British military and naval authorities to clear them all out. The first German spy to be executed in Great Britain after the outbreak of war was Lody, shot in the Tower in November, 1914. Like most German spies, this man had carefully studied Great Britain before the war. He had constantly visited British ports as a guide attached to the travel bureau of the Hamburg-Amerika Steamship Company, and had twice toured the world and made a study of British coaling-stations. He was a lieutenant in the German Naval Reserve, and had served in the Kaiser's yacht, where the presence of spies would be least of all suspected by the simple British.

He was selected for the work by Captain Boy-Ed, the German Naval Attaché at Washington, an incessant conspirator against the laws of the United States and the organiser of crime in America. Lody was provided with a passport, stolen from Charles Inglis, of Chicago, by the German Foreign Office, which kept the passport when it was sent to be signed and pretended that it had been lost. The description corresponded generally with that of Lody. The man examined London, and noted the steel nets which in 1914 were used to protect certain buildings against bombs. He went to Rosyth and was followed, when he tried "Graves's" trick of complaining to the police. He was allowed to go, and despatched the telegram about "Johnson," which, as has already been stated, resulted in the tragic sinking of the Pathfinder. He was in London on September 15th with a despatch-box, which completely disappeared, and was probably left with some German friend. A few days later he was in Liverpool, then in Killarney. There the blow fell. He was arrested, and on him was found abundant evidence of guilt, a list of names in Berlin, Bergen, and Hamburg, copies of four messages to "Berkhager, Stockholm," £145 in English notes, and £30 in gold and Norwegian notes. A parcel addressed to "Berkhager," known as a German Secret Service agency, was intercepted. It contained reports of great excellence and clarity.

Lody, Kuepferle, and Rosenthal

An important spy, who hanged himself in prison and so escaped execution, was Kuepferle, who reached England in February, 1915, professing to be a traveller in woollens and an American citizen. He posted a letter, which was apparently innocent, but when it was examined by the British censorship was found to contain a message in German, written in invisible ink between the lines. Within forty-eight hours of the letter being posted it had been stopped, opened, tested, and the secret writing exposed. The man was a German soldier, and a letter from a German in Belgium was found on him. The counterfoil of a cheque for £20 paid to him by Captain von Papen, the German Military Attaché at Washington, was afterwards discovered when Papen's cheque-book fell into the hands of the British authorities.

Another spy captured and shot by the British authorities was Rosenthal, executed in July, 1915. He was supplied by Boy-Ed and Papen with a forged American passport. A manufactory of these documents had been installed in the German Embassy in Washington, well supplied with blank forms, stolen or counterfeited, and with forged dies of American seals. Rosenthal paid two visits to Great Britain, posing as an American citizen. He had been in Berlin, but excused this by professing that he had been there to relieve distress among Americans, and gave himself out as a traveller in patent gas-mantles. His career was cut short by a letter which he posted to a German agent,

known to the British Secret Service. It was seemingly of an innocent nature, but its inner meaning was discerned.

The most valuable information obtained in his case was that the Germans were using forged passports wholesale, and were counterfeiting American seals. These facts were brought to the notice of the American Government, while the Allies took precautions of their own. During 1915, 1916, and 1917 various other German spies were caught and shot after trial by court-martial, but the Germans, nevertheless, seem to have obtained much important information, possibly from their highly placed agents using the bags of neutral Ministers, who thus abused British courtesy.

From August, 1914, the headquarters of the German underground war for operations outside Europe—and often inside it—were in New York and Washington. The machine in the earlier period of the war was directed by Dr. H. F. Albert, Councillor in the German Embassy at Washington, and Captains Papen and Boy-Ed, and, when he arrived, Rintelen, the most dangerous of them all, and the only one who in 1917 was still in allied hands. As an American said, they combined the methods of the Mafia (the Sicilian secret society) with the uniforms of diplomacy. The Hamburg-Amerika Steamship Company placed its magnificent offices at their disposal. Koenig, the superintendent of the company's police, was the Steinhauer of the United States, and under the above formidable quartet directed the German spies and criminals.

Conspiracies in the U.S.A.

Abundant and authentic information as to the plots and outrages which these people hatched fell into the hands of the Allies. One batch of papers (a "fat portfolio") they plaintively admitted, was abstracted from "our good friend Dr. Albert" by a clever American journalist. Another set of papers was seized on an American in German pay,

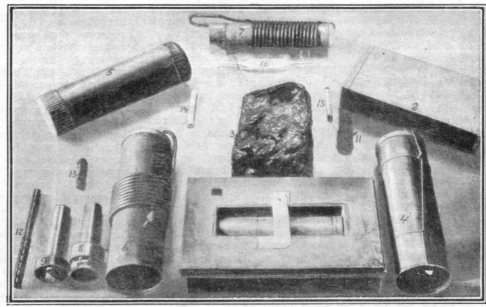

GERMAN INFERNAL MACHINES FOUND IN NORWEGIAN SHIPS.
1 and 2, explosive bombs of tetryl; 3, papier-mâché "piece of coal" filled with tetryl; 4 and 5, incendiary bombs of thermit; 8, clockwork with striker adjustable up to 330 hours; 12, fountain-pen, marked "ideal safety," with electric battery; 13, 14, and 15, chewing tobacco, cigarette, and crayon, marked "Johann Faber," containing powder to be placed in machinery in order to generate heat.

Mr. J. F. J. Archibald, who was stopped by the British Navy at Falmouth, on August 30th, 1915. Yet another series with a number of cheques and counterfoils was captured in Captain Papen's belongings at Falmouth in January, 1916. Others were impounded by the United States Government, which watched the conspiracies vigilantly as a cat watches a mouse through half-closed eyes.

To and fro moved the shadowy figures, American Secret Service men protecting British agents who were openly and honestly carrying on transactions permitted by international law, and German hirelings, criminals, and spies who swarmed into bed-rooms and offices, opened safes, abstracted papers, listened to conversations—so that New York became one enormous whispering gallery—arranged explosions in American munition works, strikes among American munition workers, bomb outrages in munition steamers, and the destruction of important railway junctions and points in Canada, as well as in the United States, as described in Chap. CIII., Vol. 6, p. 83.

Rintelen pressed with furious energy the old plot for embroiling Mexico and the United States. He brought General Huerta from Barcelona, believing him to be personally distasteful to President Wilson, and placed £160,000 in Cuban and Mexican banks for his use. With Papen, Rintelen went down to the Mexican frontier and arranged for the smuggling of arms and ammunition to Huerta's supporters. Finally Huerta **Offers to Mexico** stole off to carry out the plot, but **and Japan** found that the American Government was not so fast asleep as it had seemed to be. He was stopped and sent away.

Rintelen then fell to financing other parties in Mexico. He gave large sums to the bloodthirsty bandit Villa, to Zapata, and others, who are alleged to have absorbed a million sterling without accomplishing what Rintelen wanted. The German Foreign Office was behind these stealthy intrigues. A message from the Berlin Foreign Office was intercepted by the United States on January 19th, 1917. It offered Mexico Japanese support—though the loyalty of Japan to the Alliance was unfailing— promised to hand over three American States to Mexico, and concluded with the assurance that " the submarine war would compel England to make peace in a few months."

The conspirators in the United States were at one and the same time busy making offers to Japan and stirring up American dislike of the Japanese. Their proposals were received by the Japanese Government with cold contempt. If Japan would hold her merchant marine and Fleet aloof, the German agents declared, Germany would make Japanese aims in China her own aims. Viscount Ishii, speaking in New York, referred with indignation and disdain to these intrigues. Viscount Chinda, the Japanese Ambassador in London, in a remarkable speech on October 12th, 1917, recalled how German diplomacy had attempted to aggravate the prejudices against Japan in the United States, and while doing this had sent Germans in Berlin to cheer before the Japanese Embassy on the cool assumption that Japan intended to betray her Allies.

After the disappearance of the original heads of the conspiracy the German machine continued active. In April, 1916, when it was thought that President Wilson intended to enter the war, 100,000 telegrams protesting against this were showered upon him in a single day by German agents. Count Bernstorff directed a political campaign to force Congress into passing an Act **Count Bernstorff's** forbidding American citizens to embark **political campaign** in armed merchant vessels, which was very nearly carried against the President.

Various associates of Sir Roger Casement, the Sinn Fein leader, who had accepted a title from the British Government and had betrayed it for German gold, were in close touch with Bernstorff. Messages intercepted and afterwards published by the United States Government. which passed between Count Bernstorff and Berlin, showed that " the German General Staff desired energetic action in regard to the proposed destruction of the Canadian Pacific Railway at several points," and mentioned certain persons " suitable for carrying on sabotage " who had been " indicated by Sir Roger Casement." " Sabotage," one passage ran, " can be carried out in the United States at every kind of factory for supplying munitions of war. The Embassy must in no circumstance be compromised."

With Rintelen's work interlocked the operations of another gang of German spies and agents led by the famous Bolo Pasha, who himself visited the United States and conferred with the German plotters there. Bolo was the son of a Marseilles notary. Just as Rintelen was connected with persons high in American political life, so was Bolo connected with men high in authority in France. Rintelen was the paymaster of the corrupt German-American Press, Bolo of certain French organs, and it was even suspected that he was the channel by which military information reached the Germans. If that view was correct, he played in France the part of Colonel Miasoyedoff. He had been long at work in Germany's behalf when discoveries made in the United States led to his arrest.

He had a curiously variegated career. In 1888 he tried a lobster business which failed ; he kept a hairdresser's shop ; he was imprisoned for a fraudulent scheme to supply priests with sacramental wine ; he engaged in shady finance ; he ran a champagne agency which collapsed. He then married a rich widow and lived far beyond her means. In 1911 he made himself president of the Wine Growers' Federation, established a newspaper at Lyons, and incited the people of the Champagne district to devastate vineyards and destroy property. Great damage and loss were caused and dangerous riots occurred at the very moment when Germany was preparing to seize Agadir. It was observed that M. Bolo's dupes always avoided injuring German property in their pillaging.

Bolo floated a loan for Turkey in 1913, at a time, as it is alleged, when he knew that Turkey meant to join Germany in the then imminent war, and a little later he went on a secret mission to Mexico. He was also in close touch with the Khedive, who was meditating treachery to Great Britain, and wished to transfer to some serviceable friend his Suez Canal shares and other property which he feared that the British Government might seize. A scheme was prepared, but as it was so drafted that Bolo would have obtained the **The plots of** property for some worthless paper **Bolo Pasha** promises, it was not accepted. At the opening of the war Bolo had contrived to insinuate himself into the French War Office, and was alleged to have had the use of a special telegraph line. Immediately after the Battle of Charleroi, in August, 1914, in which the French suffered a serious defeat, he went to Biarritz, stating to everyone that the defeat was decisive, and declaring that the only course was to make an abject peace.

In March, 1915, he was in Switzerland, intriguing with the ex-Khedive, who had then been deposed, and was acting as a German agent in the vast conspiracy against the Allies. A scheme for Bolo to buy up French newspapers in Germany's interest was submitted to Herr Zimmermann, then German Under-Secretary of Foreign Affairs, who was so enamoured of it that he declared it to be worth a million. The Germans, however, were not ready to place so large a sum in Bolo's hands without some evidence that he could " deliver the goods." Herr von Jagow, the German Foreign Minister, went to see Bolo at Zurich with an offer of £50,000 a month for ten months. In April, £90,000 of German money was handed over to Bolo, less a little perquisite of £4,000 which the ex-Khedive had deducted for himself. The payments were made by the Dresdner Bank through Swiss banks, in order to disguise the source. Bolo was much disgusted with the smallness of the amount, declaring " you cannot buy souls so cheap as that."

He made an offer of £100,000 for " L'Information," a well-known Paris evening paper. He showed such haste to conclude the bargain that the owners became suspicious and broke off negotiations. In April, 1915, he invested £66,000 in shares in the " Rappel," but he was only allowed to do this after careful inquiries had shown him to be a seemingly irreproachable person. He owned the " Aeroplane " and " Motor-Car," two newspapers published in Paris, and described himself as a Chevalier

[Canadian War Records.

On the western front : German shell bursting in a French village captured by the Canadians.

[British official photograph.

Stretcher=bearers carrying wounded into safety during the Battle of the Menin Road.

Portuguese infantry regiment route=marching in field=service uniform and kit.

Cavalry of the Portuguese Expeditionary Force marching afoot to embark for France.

Batteries of Portuguese artillery on a route=march while in training.

Portuguese line battalion marching along a quayside to a transport.

Salute of the sappers: Portuguese General Staff crossing a pontoon bridge over the Tagus.

The girls they left behind them: Portuguese wives and sweethearts speeding their heroes to the war.

of the Legion of Honour, a distinction to which he had no right, and officer of several other orders.

Simultaneously he pressed a scheme for founding a Roman Catholic bank in Switzerland with a couple of millions that the ex-Khedive was to procure for him ; he was to use the money to buy more French newspapers— nominally for religious propaganda. His brother was a Monsignor ; he had himself interested the Pope's brother in the scheme and had obtained a letter of commendation from the Pope. At the end of 1915 Bolo, for £220,000, bought 1,100 shares in the " Journal " from M. Humbert, a well-known Senator, to whom he was recommended by a distinguished French official, M. Monier. M. Humbert at once refunded the money when the truth about Bolo was known.

The investigations of the American police showed that enormous sums were spent in 1916 by Bolo in German interests. He was in the United States in February and March, 1916, professedly to buy paper for his journals. The real object of his visit was to arrange with German agents in the United States a plan for detaching France, so that she would take no part in the Somme campaign, which was preparing. The Battle of Verdun was then in full blast. Bolo spread stories everywhere that France was being " bled white " and was in utter despair. He might have been suspected but for his excellent credentials. He had a letter from M. Humbert, which disarmed distrust.

Many responsible persons were misled. Messrs. J. P. Morgan's Paris branch wrote to New York, " this gentleman is not a Turk, and is in fact the brother of a well-known French archbishop." But he was watched by the vigilant American police, and he was traced to Count Bernstorff. And £320,000 was finally paid over to him by the Deutsche Bank, which remitted the money to France through an irreproachable Canadian bank.

The pacifist pincers in France The German Government did not part with its money without some inquiry. A curious collection of messages exchanged between Count Bernstorff and Herr von Jagow, German Foreign Minister, was deciphered and published by the United States Government. " No. 679," dated February 26th, mentioned the receipt of "direct information from an entirely trustworthy source concerning a political action in one of the enemy countries which would bring peace. The affair seems to me (Bernstorff) of the greatest possible importance."

The Ambassador asked for £340,000. " No. 150 " from Herr von Jagow agreed to the loan, " but only if peace action seems to you a really serious project. If the enemy country is Russia, have nothing to do with the business, as the sum is too small to have any serious effect in that country ; so, too, in the case of Italy, where it would not be worth while to spend so much." " No. 692 " from Count Bernstorff asked " that influence may be brought to bear upon our (German) Press to pass over the change in the inner political situation in France as far as possible in silence, in order that things may not be spoiled by German approval." The last message of the series published, " No. 206," of May 31st, 1916, from Herr von Jagow, showed distinct disquietude. " The person announced has not yet reported himself at the Legation at Berne. Is there any more news on your side of Bolo ? " Throughout 1916 and the first half of 1917 Bolo remained inactive. In September, 1917, he was arrested.

It was the deliberate policy of Germany, as stated by the deputy Herr David at Wurtzburg in October, 1917, " to squeeze her enemies with the military and the pacifist pincers." The Bolo affair showed how the pacifist pincers was set to work in France. There were other strange incidents which revealed the German activity underground against the French nation. In August, 1917, Miguel Almereyda, alias Vigo, editor of the " Bonnet Rouge," and a leader of the pro-Germans and Anarchists in France, was suddenly arrested after M. Clemenceau

had denounced, in the Senate on July 22nd, the negligence of M. Malvy, the French Minister of Home Affairs, in regard to pacifist propaganda.

The " Bonnet Rouge " had been founded in 1913 as the organ of " Apaches " and of sabotage. During the war it had preached the hopelessness of resisting Germany, and incessantly attacked Great Britain. Another journal of a slightly higher class, "Les Nations," to which a number of British pacifists were not ashamed to contribute, was connected with the " Bonnet Rouge," and it and a third paper, " La Tranchée Républicaine," addressed specially to the troops in the trenches, were stopped by the French authorities. Almereyda's past was of a deplorable character. He had been sentenced to two months' imprisonment for theft in 1900, a year's imprisonment for the manufacture of explosives to be used in bomb outrages, in 1901 ; three years' imprisonment for incitement to murder ; three years' imprisonment, in **Affair of the** 1908, for insulting the Army ; and in 1910 **" Bonnet Rouge "** he had been convicted of wanton damage to property. He was an international criminal of the most dangerous type, and therefore a friend of the Germans.

The " Bonnet Rouge " had had 1,400 of its articles obliterated by the censor, but those which remained were poisonous enough. It supported the " embusqués," the French equivalent of the British " Cuthberts," those sheltered in Government offices, and endeavoured in every way to hinder the prosecution of the war.

Almereyda was arrested because his manager, Duval, was found to be in possession of a cheque for £6,300 which appeared to have come from Germany, and because in his belongings a confidential document bearing on French defence was discovered. He was an intimate friend of Bolo, and in touch with that person. As for Duval, sums amounting to £40,000 had been paid to him by Swiss agents. A large part of this was traced to a Mannheim banker named Marx, who, according to Duval, had made enormous payments in order that Duval might prepare reports on the international position in Germany.

Further examination of the case showed that just as Bolo had been set to work in 1916 to dishearten France, so in 1917 Almereyda was employed to preach the futility of continuing the war after the failure of the French offensive in April. It was even alleged that he had communicated the plans of that offensive to the Germans, and had consequently caused a grave disaster. His methods were those usually employed by German agents. The French losses were grossly exaggerated ; bundles of leaflets demanding such a peace as would suit Germany were sent to the French troops. An endeavour was made to destroy the French Army as the Russian Army was being destroyed. Almereyda had some relations with M. Caillaux, the French politician, who was a large shareholder in the " Bonnet Rouge." He was also on good **Almereyda and** terms with M. Malvy, who had given him **a German peace** Secret Service money. On August 14th Almereyda died suddenly in prison, strangled with a bootlace. Though officially he was reported to have committed suicide, it was alleged in Paris that he had been put out of the way. The German murder gang, in fact, had been at work on one of its instruments.

The affair had further consequences. Dr. Michaelis, the German Chancellor, had boasted that he had full information of the secret debate of the French Chamber in June on the war. The military authorities had for a considerable time felt anxiety as to leakages which occurred, and General Lyautey preferred to resign his post of Minister of War rather than divulge certain important information at that debate. The next event was that an usher of the Chamber found a packet of Swiss bank-notes amounting to £1,080 in a locker, together with an eyeglass belonging to a deputy, M. Turmel. This deputy, when questioned about the notes, wrote saying that it was his habit to keep large amounts in the cloak-room, and that the notes had been paid by the Swiss bank for legal services. He had no proof of this, but would go to Switzerland and obtain it ; at the same time he indignantly denied having betrayed the details of the secret session. He was stopped, sent back, and arrested, on October 7th, on the charge that he had carried on relations with subjects of an enemy Power.

The Swiss bank had meanwhile denied having made him payments for the services which he said that he had rendered. It was stated that he had made several visits to Switzerland, and had on each occasion **German use of neutral diplomats** brought back with him a number of thousand-franc (£40) notes, which he had always changed at the same Paris bank. The total he had thus brought from Switzerland was between £8,000 and £12,000.

While these disclosures were coming thick and fast, the American Government revealed the working of the German hand in another direction from its inexhaustible store

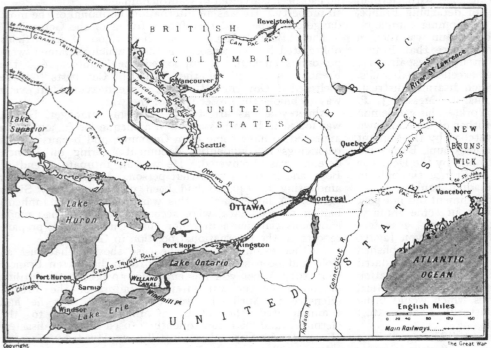

PLACES IN CANADA THREATENED BY GERMAN PLOTTERS.
In September, 1914, Von Papen made payments to many agents with the object of causing trouble in Canada that should prevent the despatch of troops to Europe. The Canadian Pacific Railway was to be destroyed east and west, also the Welland Canal, connecting Lakes Ontario and Erie, and the great grain elevators along the lakes ; while Ottawa, Port Hope, Kingston, and Windmill Point were among other places to be attacked. The scheme was dropped—after 150,000 German Reservists had been reported available, and two million pounds had been subscribed—as Count Bernstorff realised that it would precipitate war with the United States.

of captured and intercepted letters and telegrams. It had long been aware that German messages were being exchanged between Berlin and Washington through neutral diplomatists, who thus disgracefully abused the privileges which they were granted in the belief that they were gentlemen. On September 8th it suddenly published the text of a number of German telegrams, which had been sent for Count Luxburg, German Chargé d'Affaires in Argentina, by Baron Löwen, Swedish Minister at Buenos Ayres.

They covered both the persons concerned with infamy. "No. 3," of May, 1917, asked that certain Argentine steamers then nearing Bordeaux "may be spared, if possible, or else sunk without a trace being left." "No. 64," dated July 9th, repeated this atrocious recommendation to murder neutral Argentine seamen : " I recommend either compelling them to turn back or sinking them without leaving any trace, or letting them through." These messages had to be read in conjunction with the conduct of the German submarines which in 1917, as in the case of

the Belgian Prince, took to murdering deliberately the entire crew of certain submarined ships.

This discovery made the presence of Count Luxburg and Baron Löwen impossible in Argentina. The Swedish Government did not apologise to the Allies, and only ventured to make a timid little protest to Germany. The Kaiser treated it in the usual German fashion. Luxburg was officially censured, while William II. telegraphed to him the " warmest appreciation of the faithful services " he had rendered him. A breach between Argentina and Germany was prevented by another stroke of the German hand. The German agents at Buenos Ayres stirred up a great strike, which was intended completely to paralyse the country. Argentine attention was thus riveted on internal affairs and diverted from Germany. This was fresh evidence, if it were required, that German business men, financiers, and settlers were a constant peril to any country where they were tolerated. Meanwhile the United States had completed the discomfiture of Sweden by publishing another message which showed that a Swedish diplomat in Mexico, Herr Cronholm, had acted as Prussian postman and intermediary.

On the heels of this followed a fresh disclosure of German wickedness. When Rumania entered the war the German Legation in Bukarest was transferred to the custody of the United States, which was then a neutral Power. On October 5th, 1916, before the eyes of the Secretary of the American Legation, quantities of high explosives and virulent bacilli were dug up in the garden of that Legation. The bacilli were in a box bearing certain letters of the name of Colonel Hammerstein, German Military Attaché at Bukarest. Inside the box was a notice in German :

Herewith four tubes for horses and four for horned cattle. For use as directed. Each tube is sufficient for 200 head. If possible, administer direct through the animal's mouth ; if not, in the fodder.

The tubes were tested, and found to contain glanders and anthrax germs of the most terrible violence. The Germans tortured and killed animals with as little compunction as men. Their intention had apparently been to cause a cattle plague in Rumania, and thus prevent her from entering the war.

Allusions to German agents in Italy were found among the German papers by the American police. The chief of these was Monsignor Gerlach, an Austrian cavalry officer, who had entered the **Intrigue in Rumania and Italy** Roman Church and become private chamberlain to the Pope. He fled to Switzerland early in 1917 on learning that his arrest was imminent. Three hundred persons, who were concerned in plots in Italy with him, were seized, and, after a long trial Gerlach, in his absence, was condemned and sentenced to penal servitude for life in June, 1917. His principal accomplice, an Italian named Pomarici, who also made his escape, was sentenced to death, and four other men were sentenced to various terms of imprisonment. The lightness of the punishment caused no little criticism in Italy. Gerlach had behaved quite in the Rintelen fashion. He threw about large sums of money, offered splendid bribes to Italian newspapers which would attack the Allies, and supplied the Germans with information. Agents about him had provided with funds and explosives the gangs which caused great fires at Genoa, and destroyed the battleships Benedetto Brin and Leonardo da Vinci. They steadily undermined the moral of the Italian Army till it gave way in the disasters of October and November, 1917. One of the German masterpieces of deceit was to circulate exact imitations of well-known Italian newspapers containing, besides genuine matter, provocative lies about the British, who were said to have shot down Italian crowds with machine-guns in riots at Turin and Milan. Many persons charged with "Boloism" were arrested in Italy in November and December, 1917.

The greatest triumph of the German underground war was in Russia, where more completely than in any other allied country was the German aim realised of wrecking the State by internal disorder. Under the old régime German influence was strong in Russia ; fifty per cent. of the generals were of German origin ; and Petrograd lay in a district which was largely German. Although German influence was not strong among the wiser men of the Revolutionary parties, it was certainly all-powerful among the extremists.

It can scarcely have been an accident that German names were so common among the Committee of the Soviet, or Council of Workmen's and Soldiers' Delegates, which had so lamentable a share in **Lenin and Russian extremists** destroying the discipline of the Russian Army and the economic power of the Russian nation. Many of these people changed their names, an act which in itself was significant. Lenin, their leader, was given a free passage through German territory by Marshal Hindenburg. Shortly after his arrival at Petrograd the rumour spread that he was receiving German money. Denials were issued, but with him, as with Bolo and Almereyda, the source of these payments was soon discovered. Germany had been remitting funds to him through the Nya Bank at Stockholm and the Copenhagen Loan and Discount Bank.

The events of the Revolution were the culmination of prolonged and careful preparations by the Germans, who had blown up certain of the most important munition works in 1915.

The Russian Woolwich at Ochta, near Petrograd, was thus destroyed.

A Revolutionist named Dolin (believed to have been really of German name and descent) was bought by the German Government, and supplied with large amounts to secure the assassination of M. Sazonoff, the Russian Foreign Minister, to cause fires at Archangel, and to blow up the only Russian Dreadnought complete in the Black Sea, the Imperatritsa Maria, which was sunk on October 20th, 1916. Some parts of these

BARON VON SCHENCK.
Germany's arch-intriguer in Greece during the Constantine régime ; deported from Athens by the Allies, September, 1916.

LIEUT. STEINBRINK.
In November, 1917, First Naval Lieut. Otto Steinbrink announced that his U boat had sunk 198 vessels to date.

plots he revealed to the Russian Secret Police, and received further payment from them. He committed suicide in 1917, apparently because the Germans had discovered his treachery to them and were on his track.

Whether he had any part in the explosions which took place at Archangel was not certain. In November, 1916 314 persons were killed and 642 injured, including a number of British seamen, by an explosion which was believed to have been caused by a bomb placed in an ammunition ship. In January, 1917, a party of four German agents was stopped at the frontier with high explosives (packed as "preserves"), arms, and ammunition. Two of them had but recently come from the United States, where they were connected with the gang of bomb-makers and assassins in the employment of the German Embassy. These arrests did not stop the explosions. A few days later another occurred, in which 30 persons were killed and 344 injured. Under the Revolution, fires and explosions in munition factories became so common as no longer to cause comment.

The German bomb-plotters infested other neutral countries. They were active in Norway, where Baron Rautenfels, a messenger of the Berlin Foreign Office, travelling under the immunities which had been granted in the old days when men recognised a code of honour, was arrested in June, 1917. His luggage contained bombs and explosives, and there was **Baron Rautenfels' explosive luggage** every reason to believe that he had been active in placing the bombs in Norwegian ships, twenty of which had mysteriously vanished at sea. The German Foreign Office declared that "in order to carry out certain warlike operations, it had no scruples in sending explosives over Norwegian territory," and protested against the arrest of its courier, and Norway could get no satisfaction. In the autumn of 1917 German agents deliberately set fire to the stores of food in Norway from sheer malice ; and in October they even proceeded to scatter bombs in Stockholm, the capital of Sweden, which had throughout shown such affection for German methods.

Posterity will know the inner meaning of this tale of crime and murder, the blackest that has disgraced the pages of modern history.

It will be observed that the plots did not succeed where success would have meant the collapse of the allied cause. It will also be observed that the whole German nation shared in the guilt. It knew what was being done ; it had the admissions of its own rulers ; and it never uttered one word in protest. No prophet or patriot arose in that land of tyranny and darkening cruelty to denounce brutality to man and contempt for God.

RUSSIAN BOLSHEVIST LEADERS.
Nikolai Lenin (left) and Leon Trotzky addressing a crowd in Petrograd. Lenin was the man who overthrew Kerensky and plunged Russia into a state of anarchy in the autumn of 1917.

Preparing for their stern work on the western front. Portuguese troops, equipped with their protective masks, engaged in gas-attack drill.

Portuguese soldiers leaving a gas chamber during the period of practical training preparatory to going up to the front-line trenches.

At an infantry training school on the western front. Portuguese soldiers clearing a trench at bayonet practice.

(British official photographs.

Portuguese troops undergoing Lewis-gun drill, and (right) on the march. The soldiers of the Republic of Portugal who went to the western front acquitted themselves well—as was to be expected of the descendants of the fine fighters of the Peninsular War.

SOLDIERS OF PORTUGAL WHO PROVED FINE FIGHTERS ON THE WESTERN FRONT.

CHAPTER CCXII.

PORTUGAL'S PART IN THE WAR.

By W. H. Koebel, author of "Portugal: Its Land and People," etc.

Democratic Tendency of the Portuguese Nation—Alliance with Britain Since 1373—Situation of Portugal on the Outbreak of the Great War—Peace Footing of the Portuguese Army—Popular Feeling with the Allies—Portugal's African Colonies Neighboured by German Ones—Germans Treacherously Attack a Portuguese Frontier Post—Defensive Expeditions Sent from Portugal to Angola and Mozambique—Centre of Political Interest Shifted to Europe : Confusion of Parties in Portugal—Agitation Fomented by German Agents—Attempted Revolution in May, 1915—The Republic Takes Possession of Interned German Vessels—Germany Demands Revocation of the Act, and Declares War—They Had Already Mined the Entrance to the Port of Lisbon—Submarines Indulge in " Shoot and Scoot " Tactics—Important Agreement Between Great Britain and Portugal—Decision to Co-operate Actively on the Western Front—50,000 Portuguese Troops in the Neighbourhood of Ypres—Portugal's Large Expeditionary Force in Africa One of the Largest that Ever Left Europe.

O F the various causes which induced Portugal to enter the war on the side of the Allies, the two most salient were the natural democratic tendency of the nation, which had become very marked during the previous twenty years, and a sense of loyalty to the oldest ally of the western republic, Great Britain. This alliance between the Anglo-Saxon and the Portuguese nations was first established in 1373, and had continued practically unbroken through the centuries.

This alliance, moreover, had been no mere thing of sentiment, theory, and ponderous agreements drawn up on parchment. It had stood the strain of war as well as the tests of peace. From the days of the battles against the Moorish invaders of Portuguese soil, when the Iberian and the Englishman fought side by side, it had held good in the various wars against Spain and France, notably in the Peninsular conflict of rather more than a century before.

The situation of Portugal on the outbreak of the European hostilities in August, 1914, did not

seem to promise any active intervention. Save on the east and west coasts of Equatorial Africa, there was no spot in the world where the frontiers of Portuguese territories ran side by side with those of Germany. But the republic did not hesitate to express the warmth of its sentiments towards Great Britain, and the loyalty with which it was prepared to uphold its treaty obligations.

It was undoubtedly the many hundreds of miles of land that separated the little republic on the Atlantic coast from the Central European States that caused the declaration of war to be postponed until more than eighteen months after the fateful August of 1914.

Indeed, at the first stage of the great conflagration, it seemed quite probable that there would be no necessity for any actual clash of arms between Portugal and Prussia ; but the aggressive policy of the German Empire was not content to leave well—or what might have been considered well for its own interests — alone. The reckless policy which it had carried out in Belgium it was clearly prepared to extend whenever the opportunity offered.

BRITISH CRUISERS VISIT LISBON.
Admiral Yelverton chatting with Sir Lancelot D. Carnegie, K.C.M.G., British Minister to Portugal, during a visit which a British cruiser squadron paid to the Portuguese capital.

From the purely military point of view it was perfectly clear that Portugal had nothing—save the satisfaction of not shirking a grim duty—to gain from her entry into the war. The small western republic had been occupied far more with the arts of peace than with preparation for war. As in the case of Great Britain, the modest scale on which her forces were modelled in itself sufficed to prove this.

At the beginning of 1914 the peace establishment of the regular Portuguese Army did not exceed 32,000, although it was estimated that the war strength could be brought up to about 100,000 men. In any case, the military budget for 1913-1914 had been financially compressed to beneath two millions sterling.

As soon as the first political rupture occurred in Europe the Portuguese Government prepared itself for all eventualities. On August 4th the small Fleet of the republic was mobilised. Three days later full power was given by Congress to the Government to take the necessary measures for the safety of the country. On the same day great public demonstrations took place in Lisbon and Oporto, enthusiastic ovations occurring in front of the Legations and Consulates of Great Britain, France, and Russia.

The feeling in Portugal, indeed, was as unanimous as the somewhat disturbed internal political situation permitted, and the principal organs of the Press, headed by the "Seculo," expressed themselves emphatically in favour of active intervention on behalf of the Allies.

Had any hesitation existed on this point, it would have been rapidly dispelled by the actions of the Germans themselves. True to their policy of launching sudden and unprovoked attacks, the subsequent justification of which it was the business of their professors to assume, the German forces found an almost immediate opportunity of striking in Africa.

Portuguese East Africa bordered German East Africa to the south, while Portuguese West Africa formed the northern frontier of German West Africa. The other

WAR MINISTER IN TWO CABINETS.
Senhor Norton de Mattos, Minister of War in the Portuguese Cabinets of March, 1916, and April, 1917 (left), with Major-General Barnardiston.

neighbours of the German colonies were the British and Belgians, Belgian territory serving as the hinterland of German East Africa, while all the other contiguous frontiers were British.

Thus it fell to Portugal to guard her southern frontier on the Atlantic coast and her northern boundaries on the Indian Ocean. The part that she was to play in this respect was destined to be an important one.

The first of the German "hammer-blows" took effect in the African jungle on August 24th, 1914, when the Portuguese frontier-post of Mazina, north of Mozambique, was treacherously attacked at dawn by a German force, assisted by a number of native auxiliaries. The commandant was in bed when the inrush of assailants surprised him, and he was shot dead as he hastily emerged from his quarters to find out the reason of the uproar. Of the small garrison, those who were not slain on the spot had no option but to flee for their lives, and the place was destroyed. Even after this, curiously enough, no state of war between the two countries was declared in Europe, and the German Minister at Lisbon remained with tranquil effrontery at his post.

The formidable nature of the German forces in East Africa may be gleaned from a report of General Smuts dealing with their numbers during the first three months of 1916, by which time they had already lost very large numbers in killed, wounded, and prisoners. These, according to the estimates made then, amounted to some 16,000 men, with about sixty guns and eighty machine-guns.

The German white forces available in Damaraland have been estimated at nearly 6,000 men, of which 3,500 were European regulars.

Portugal was fully awake to the danger threatening her African colonies, and expeditions were being hastily prepared to protect her possessions in Angola and Mozambique. On September 6th the units of the first African Expeditionary Force assembled in Lisbon. The troops

DR. AUGUSTO SOARES.
Minister of Foreign Affairs in the Portuguese Cabinet of Dr. Affonso Costa, April, 1917.

SENHOR BERNARDINO MACHADO.
Elected President of the Republic of Portugal, August 6th, 1915.

SENHOR AZEVEDO COUTINHO.
Minister of Marine in the Portuguese Cabinet of Senhor d'Almeida, March, 1916.

FIRST SESSION OF THE PORTUGUESE WAR CABINET FORMED MARCH 15TH, 1916.

Left to right : Senhor Pedro Martins, Education ; Senhor Augusto Soares, Foreign Affairs ; Senhor Norton de Mattos, War ; Senhor Mesquita de Carvalho, Justice ; Senhor José d'Almeida, Premier and Minister for the Colonies ; Senhor Bernardino Machado, President ; Senhor Pereira Reis, Interior ; Senhor Affonso Costa, Finance ; Senhor Azevedo Coutinho, Marine ; Senhor Antonio Maria Silva, Public Works.

destined for Angola were commanded by Lieut.-Colonel Alvarez Roçadas, and the expedition to Mozambique was under the orders of Lieut.-Colonel Massano de Amorim. These expeditions left Lisbon on September 11th, the British steamship Durham Castle assisting in the transport.

After this a short lull occurred so far as Portugal itself was concerned, two of the most notable incidents being the official visit of the British cruiser Argonaut to Lisbon on September 28th, and the call of the French cruiser Dupetit Thouars on October 7th with the same object—that of saluting the republic. A circumstance, too, which was of primary importance was the announcement that an expeditionary force was in the course of formation to take part in the hostilities on the western front. Shortly afterwards, however, matters of expediency caused the postponing of this enterprise.

All this time considerable discussion had been going on concerning the extent to which the Portuguese should lend their active support to the Allies, a number of minor politicians being in favour of merely rendering to the Allies such services as were compatible with a benevolent neutrality, although by far the greater proportion of the nation was in favour of active intervention. As leaders of this latter movement, Dr. Alexander Braga and Señhor Leote de Rego were conspicuous in its advocacy.

SENHOR DE CARVALHO.
Portuguese Minister of Justice from March 15th, 1916, to April 23rd, 1917.

SENHOR AFFONSO COSTA.
Prime Minister and Minister of Finance from April 23rd to December 6th, 1917.

On October 20th a revolutionary outbreak occurred at Mafra, the chief incident of which was the attempt to blow up the railway line in the neighbourhood of that town. About seventy prisoners were taken by the Government troops, and the movement failed to spread to any important extent elsewhere. None of these circumstances had any influence on the foreign policy of Portugal, and on November 24th it was officially announced that Portugal intended to range itself side by side with Great Britain in the European conflict. A number of fresh reinforcements in the meantime were being despatched to the threatened colonies.

In Africa the cessation of hostilities had been merely temporary. On October 14th news was received in Lisbon that a Portuguese sergeant and four men had been slain by the Germans in the Nyassa Province of Portuguese East Africa.

The scene of action was then temporarily shifted to West Africa. On October 17th another German force crossed the frontier to Angora, and attacked the military post at Naulila, where they were repulsed. This post of Naulila was of some strategic importance, since it was the nearest to the German frontier of the chain of military stations which ran to Humbe on the left bank of the Cunene River, and included the stations of Otoquero, Daquero, Ancogo, and Rocapalas.

On October 30th the German force, after a night march, surrounded the small fort of Cuangar, situated about two hundred and fifty miles from Naulila. Here they massacred the entire garrison, with the exception of a Portuguese corporal and two native soldiers, who succeeded in making their way from the spot. Two Portuguese officers were murdered in circumstances of extreme brutality; the settlement was entirely destroyed, and from this point the Germans began to march through the Portuguese territory, pillaging and destroying as they went.

The German version of these events, it is almost unnecessary to say, differs entirely from the Portuguese, and affords another of those countless instances of the fixed international policy of the German Empire, since it laid down the reason for these assaults as retaliation for the aggressive policy of the Portuguese, a justification that is difficult to understand when it is considered that it was not German Africa, but Portuguese Africa, in which these unexpected assaults took place.

Shortly after the attack on Cuangar, two hostile columns, comprising about seven hundred men, invaded Portuguese territory. Part of this force had an engagement with a

405

detachment of Portuguese infantry, and were defeated, leaving more than fifty prisoners in the hands of the Portuguese.

The Portuguese statesmen and soldiers now set themselves manfully to the task of military preparation on a large scale and in a manner that did credit to the small western nation.

On December 1st, 1914, there occurred a second engagement at the post of Naulila between an expeditionary force of Portuguese soldiers commanded by Colonel Roçadas and a German force from Damaraland. This attack was effected by about two thousand German troops provided with field and machine-guns, and including a certain number of cavalry. Lieut.-Colonel Roçadas, whose forces amounted to about sixteen hundred men, retreated and took up a defensive position, awaiting reinforcements. The attack was responsible for a spirited engagement, in which the 2nd Squadron of Portuguese Dragoons — v e t e r a n African troops who had long become inured to the climate—rendered signal service, charging the advancing Germans with intrepidity, and saving a situation that looked extremely serious for the main Portuguese force.

Operations in the neighbourhood of Naulila were peculiarly difficult since, it should be explained, away from the neighbourhood of the rivers themselves, there is much arid country, and the lack of water played an important part in the plans of attack and in the general movement of the various forces.

German-inspired native rising

It is possible that a disaster of some magnitude might have befallen the German arms at this juncture, but the germs of rebellion which had been so assiduously spread by the invaders among the Portuguese African natives now bore fruit, and the energies of a considerable portion

GERMANY DECLARES WAR ON PORTUGAL.
Senhor Machado, President of the Republic of Portugal, entering the Parliament House, to be present at the reading of Germany's declaration of war, made on March 9th, 1916.

of the Portuguese forces had to be engaged in suppressing an insurrection of the Cuanhama tribe, which was successfully effected.

At the beginning of 1915 the chief centre of political interest shifted to Europe. The war had caught the Portuguese nation unprepared so far as internal politics were concerned. The nation had enjoyed no real tranquillity since the days of the revolution which turned the country from a monarchy into a republic. Indeed, since a period considerably anterior to that occurrence, any prolonged duration of political peace had been unknown.

In addition to the two main national parties, those of the Republicans and Royalists, many less clear issues were involved, and the rapidity in the changes of government had frequently been amazing. The war had the effect of consolidating the nation to a very large extent, but the political confusion was not to be wiped out at one stroke by even so tremendous a circumstance as this. The beginning of 1915 gave small hope of an improvement in the political evils from which the nation had so long suffered, for on January 24th the Portuguese Ministry resigned, although it had been formed scarcely six weeks before. At the beginning of March, however, a drastic move was made by those in power, and a constitutional innovation was introduced, which it was hoped would have the effect of endowing the country with a spell of tranquillity.

On the 6th of that month the Pimenta Cabinet announced

PORTUGUESE TROOPS FOR THE WESTERN FRONT.
A British general passing along a line of Portuguese troops on the quayside about to embark for France. By the autumn of 1917 about 50,000 Portuguese troops were stationed on the western front.

BRITISH SAILORS ASHORE AT LISBON.
In September, 1914, a British cruiser was sent to Lisbon to pay an official complimentary visit to th
Republic of Portugal. British sailors saluted the Portuguese Headquarters Staff outside the Belem Palace.

enced by the German propaganda, were the Anarchists and the extreme Socialists—the classes whose convictions, it might have been supposed, would have led them to oppose with tooth and nail the aggressive and tyrannical campaign of a brutal autocracy. But the Russian counter-revolution provided further evidence that these are the traitor elements most readily bribed.

A certain number of these, moreover, would seem to have permitted themselves to be completely misled by the German secret agents, and, being disposed to regard the continuation of the war as a crime against humanity, many of them fell easy, possibly innocent, dupes to the specious Teutonic promises.

As elsewhere, one of the chief weapons employed by the Germans in this underhand warfare was the instigation of riots. In almost every riot which occurred in Portugal at this period—and these unfortunately were by no means infrequent — there were agents concerned in the outbreak who were working for German pay.

Nevertheless, the section of the populace actually affected, although turbulent and noisy, remained, as regards its numbers and its influence, comparatively insignificant. This is the more remarkable when the fact is taken into consideration that the **German intrigue in Portugal** enhanced cost of living in the small western republic had increased the difficulties both of existence in general and of the political situation in particular. The contagion, moreover, did not spread to any portion of the Portuguese troops. These remained loyal to their officers and to the republic, even when put to the supreme test of being ordered to open fire on their rebellious fellow-citizens, as on the

the suspension of Parliament, and declared the President to be appointed Dictator. Shortly after this the German submarine campaign occupied the attention of the nation. On April 3rd the Portuguese steamer Douro was sunk by a German mine when on a voyage from Cardiff to Oporto. At the end of the following month another Portuguese merchant steamer, the Cisne, was torpedoed at the entrance of the English Channel.

More subtle, and, indeed, more mischievous, was the internal warfare which the Germans now strained every nerve to carry on in a clandestine fashion in Portugal. German secret agents worked with a feverish zeal, and very large sums of money were covertly sent into the country with the idea of suborning the patriotism of any who could be found to accept heavy bribes. The material return which the German Empire received from this vast expenditure of treasure and intriguing energy was quite insignificant compared with the measures employed, but that the Germans obtained a clandestine foothold here and there among some of the less responsible sections of the community it would be idle to deny.

German gold and German influence were, of course, completely at the disposal of any agitator who could be found prepared to make the attempt to embarrass the Government. The class of people—and they were not numerous—who would seem chiefly to have been influ-

BRITISH ADMIRAL ABOARD A PORTUGUESE CRUISER.
The Admiral in charge of the British Naval Mission went aboard the Portuguese cruiser Vasco da Gama,
lying in the Tagus, and was received with the honours due to his rank and position as representative of an
Allied Power.

occasion of the attempt at revolution on May 15th, 1915, when several hundreds were killed.

It now became evident that the Central Empire was bent on inflicting all the damage it could upon the Portuguese while the latter were reserving their forces for future action. It was not in the power of the small republic to undertake any direct reprisals in Europe, so far as naval action on the high seas was concerned; but in one respect the German statesmen had reckoned without their hosts, for Portugal possessed a German hostage of no small importance. This was represented by the German liners and cargo steamers that, fleeing from the British naval might at the outbreak of the war, had taken refuge in the Portuguese ports.

On February 17th, 1916, the British Minister at Lisbon was instructed by his Government "to urge upon the Government of the Republic, in the name of the Alliance, the requisition of all the enemy vessels lying in the Portuguese ports, which will be made use of for Portuguese trade navigation, and also between Lisbon and such other ports as may be determined by agreement between the two Governments."

On February 23rd the republic took possession of the German vessels in Portuguese harbours, the great majority of these being in the River Tagus.

TORPEDO PRACTICE.
At the moment of discharge. Portuguese war vessel firing a torpedo.

These were thirty-six in number, and among them were many fine vessels accustomed to ply between South America and Europe. The German mercantile officers on board had reason to anticipate such a move, and in consequence they busied themselves, so far as it was possible for them, in the secret destruction of the engines of the steamers. While the hulls were left intact, in almost every case the engines were damaged to an extent which demanded a lengthy period of time for repairs.

On the day the seizure of these vessels took place, the Portuguese Government advised the German Government as to what had occurred. The result was a fierce explosion of Teutonic wrath. A truculent Note from Berlin was received on March 1st, **Germany declares war on Portugal** demanding in no measured terms the instant revocation of the act. On a firm refusal being made by the Portuguese to agree to this, Germany declared war on Portugal on March 9th

On this date, Herr Rosen, the German Ambassador in Lisbon, was instructed to ask for his passports, the same procedure being observed in Berlin by Señor Sidonio Paes, the Portuguese Ambassador at Berlin. So insolent was the wording of the German declaration of war that it had the effect of irritating a proud people profoundly, and made the Portuguese, who were now more than ever the trusted allies of Great Britain, the active and bitter foes of Germany.

On March 14th, as a natural sequel to this, a diplomatic rupture occurred with Austria, and on April 21st there was issued a decree banishing from Portuguese soil and possessions all Germans between the ages of sixteen and forty-five.

WITH THE NAVY OF BRITAIN'S OLDEST ALLY.
Firing practice on board a Portuguese warship. Early in the war the small Portuguese gunboat Ibo beat off the attack of a powerful submarine. In circle: Getting a torpedo ready for firing on board a Portuguese destroyer.

Just as the German sailors on the Tagus had anticipated the seizure of their vessels, so the German Government had made certain that this declaration of war would ensue ; for when war was declared on Portugal by Germany, it was discovered that the Teutonic Powers had once again anticipated matters with that cynical indifference to national honour and human life that had become customary with their officials. They had heavily mined the entrance to the port of Lisbon—which they were the more easily enabled to do, as the sandy bar of the River Tagus rendered the area of navigation somewhat confined and difficult.

The German submarines were now becoming more active, and various encounters at sea took place between these and the vessels of the Portuguese Navy. An attack by a powerful submarine on the small gunboat Ibo failed in its object, the little Portuguese craft successfully beating off its opponent.

In a sense, the most daring feat of the hostile submarines was the rapid bombardment of Funchal, the capital of the island of Madeira, probably with a view to the destruction of the cable station at this place, and the similar attack on the town of St. Vincent in the Cape Verde Islands.

Funchal and St. Vincent bombarded It is true that both of these achievements were of the " shoot and scoot " order, the submarines in each case only appearing above the surface of the sea for a minute or two before submerging and making off at full speed. Nevertheless, the small Portuguese Navy was determined to use its utmost efforts to prevent any repetition of these events, and the keenness with which it carried out its patrol duties was undoubted.

While all these events were occurring, the strain of the financial situation had, as was inevitable, begun to make itself acutely felt in Portugal. Great Britain, when appealed to on this head, lost no time in coming to the assistance of her ally. On August 7th, 1916, the Portuguese Parliament was convoked, when the following Note was read :

The British Government has agreed with the Government of Portugal to grant the latter such loans as may be required for the payment of all expenditure for the purposes directly connected with the war which the two Governments shall agree to incur in Great Britain or, exceptionally, any other allied countries. The British Government will make these loans to the Portuguese Government on the same terms as it may raise money from time to time by means of Treasury Bills. The total sum lent to the Portuguese Government shall be repaid by the latter to the British Government within two years, reckoned from the date of the signature of the Treaty of Peace, out of the product of an external loan to be negotiated by Portugal, and for the remission of which the British Government will give every possible facility.

Shortly after this important agreement had been arrived at, Portugal leased to the British Government a number of the German **Anglo-Portuguese** ships she had confiscated. The direct **agreement** interests of the republic in the war were now increased. In the middle of June, 1916, Portuguese delegates attended the Economic Conference of the Allied Governments in Paris, and on October 8th she announced her definite intention of co-operating actively in the European field of warfare.

From that period Portugal set herself to prepare for operations on European soil. She took measures to improve her Air Service, which, up to that time, had not been extensively organised, although its initiation dated from some years previously.

The Portuguese Air Service was first established in 1912, when three aeroplanes were bought by public subscription. An official Aero Club was opened in 1916, and this included a school of aeronautics. The benefits the Portuguese Flying Corps derived from this initiation were very great, although previously to its opening a number of Portuguese officers had been sent to Great Britain and France in order to be thoroughly grounded in the science of flight. A

PORTUGAL'S MILITARY PREPARATIONS FOR ACTIVE WARFARE.
Cavalry crossing a pontoon bridge over the Tagus. They formed part of a Portuguese division which was on its way to a camp of instruction. The bridge had been thrown across the river for the purpose by the military engineers.

TROOPS FOR WEST
AFRICA.
Men of the Portuguese artillery about to embark at Lisbon for Angola.

Portuguese Aerial Commission, too, was sent to the School of Aeronautics at Lausanne, in Switzerland. The first three pilot certificates were granted to Portuguese officers in March, 1916, and before the close of 1917 the Portuguese military school probably possessed at least a dozen hangars.

Once established in the trenches, the Portuguese lost no time in bringing up their numbers to a formidable basis. By the autumn of 1917, according to a conservative estimate, there were about 50,000 troops stationed on the western front in the neighbourhood of Ypres, some 20,000 more being stationed in readiness in Portugal, while more than 2,000 men of the Portuguese heavy artillery were in training in England.

The Portuguese rank and file have always shown great resolution when ably led, and on the western front these qualities were very freely displayed. This is not to be wondered at by those who have studied the records of the British officers who served in the Peninsular War in the early days of the nineteenth century—

Portuguese troops near Ypres records which frequently bear striking testimony to the qualities of the Iberian troops which these officers had to lead.

The bravery shown by the Portuguese troops on the western front, moreover, was doubly notable, since it frequently shone in somewhat depressing circumstances. Owing to the enthusiasm and the haste with which a number of these troops were despatched to the area of conflict, their equipment had by no means kept pace with their spirit, and, but for the assistance of the Allies, there is no doubt that many of these fine Portuguese soldiers in France and Flanders would have suffered severely in the

PORTUGUESE INFANTRY ON PARADE.
[Portuguese official photograph.
On a peace footing the Portuguese Army consisted of about 32,000 men, but it was estimated that its war strength could be brought up to more than three times that number.

course of the winter, seeing that they were inadequately prepared in the way of clothing for the severities of the climate.

In the neighbourhood of Ypres the Portuguese bore themselves manfully, and did their share of raiding and of resisting attacks. Yet even here they did not seem to be altogether free from the machinations of the Germans, who, realising the very important strategic position of the western republic, would have given much to conciliate its Government.

A remarkable instance of this was testified to by a Portuguese officer in July, 1917, when on the occasion of a Portuguese attack, the 14th Regiment of the Line penetrated as far as the second line of the hostile trenches. The Germans apparently had made no attempt to wait to meet them in the first, and in this a placard had been left, bearing the words, "Long live the 14th Regiment!"

Such amenities, when arising from a Prussian source, were notoriously dangerous. This specious attempt, however, utterly failed, if, as is probable, such results had been hoped for as at an earlier date were tragically achieved on the Russian frontier

The efforts of the Portuguese arms, as we have seen, were not confined to Europe, and we may now turn again to the African theatre of war, where continuous and bitter fighting had been proceeding, although until the summer of 1917 no very definite decisions had been brought about, notwithstanding the fact that the German colonial forces were becoming more and more penned in.

At the beginning of 1916 the East African campaign, after suffering many vicissitudes, was progressing favourably, and the value of the Portuguese assistance to the Allies was increasingly evident. It is certain that, but for the Portuguese garrisons established to the south of German East Africa, the war in this part of the continent would have been far more prolonged, for it was the situation of the Portuguese troops that made it possible for the combined forces to effect the complete surrounding of the German columns and to overcome, little by little, a resistance which was rendered the more effective owing to the very difficult nature of the country. **Progress in East Africa**

As it was, the presence of the Portuguese made a continuous retreat impossible for the Germans, and on the East Coast of Africa these were steadily driven farther south towards the Portuguese border, or else in the direction of the coast. As the area of hostilities lessened, collisions between the hostile forces increased in number, and the excesses of the Germans frequently resulted in a condition of no quarter on either side.

By this time no fewer than 14,000 Portuguese soldiers were fighting in East Africa, while beyond these there were, of course, considerable Portuguese forces in West Africa. These, the Portuguese claimed with some pride, constituted the largest expeditionary force, with the exception of that of the British during the South African War, that had ever been sent from Europe to Africa. These Portuguese troops suffered innumerable hardships in common with their British, French, and Belgian comrades fighting in a tropical country.

In order to secure some idea of the conditions of this tropical warfare, it is essential to realise that the area covered by the East African campaign —including, of course, those operations carried out by Great Britain, Portugal, and Germany — approached 75,000 square miles. Much of this comprised country which, before the war, was practically unexplored. It was necessary to operate in the depths of gloomy and all but impenetrable forests, and among the pestilential, fever-laden swamps of the lowlands.

Hardships of tropical warfare

The heat, of course, was intense, and in the wet seasons the rains fell as only tropical rain can fall. The fate of the wounded was frequently terrible enough, for in many areas lions as well as other wild animals abounded. From time to time, too, swarms of insect pests would attack both men and animals, and on more than one occasion these winged enemies scattered trains of mules and horses.

However, steadily but slowly, the enemy was driven south—from the northern frontier to the Mgeta Valley, thence into the delta of the Rufiji River, and thence into the southernmost areas of the one-time German colony, where the Portuguese forces were waiting to bar further escape, in addition to co-operating actively in Nyassa, where some notable successes were achieved. This brings us down to the middle of 1917, and from that time onwards the position of the German force grew steadily more precarious.

The help of Portugal

In West Africa the operations of the Portuguese were at this period concerned as much with the rebellious natives as with any other enemies, the German intrigues having succeeded in stirring up insurrections in various parts. In the neighbourhood of Amboina the Portuguese troops defeated some rebel forces in July, 1917, while at Gorongosa a strong rebel position was captured on the 17th of that month.

Thus it will be seen that, small though our ancient Peninsular ally may be compared with the great European Powers, she valiantly bore her part, and, in proportion to her resources, Portugal " did her bit."

ARRIVAL OF FIRST DETACHMENT OF PORTUGUESE TROOPS IN FRANCE.
Disembarkation at a French port of the first contingent of troops sent by the Republic of Portugal to fight on the western front, side by side with the Army of the older Republic of France and the troops of Great Britain.

Fine exploit of the Canadians at Passchendaele. On the left of the village, at the cross-roads near Mosselmarkt, Germans in and around a big block-house made a stubborn resistance on November 6th, 1917, but the Canadians, with bomb, revolver, and bayonet, cleared the position.

Seven men who captured a large block-house near Langemarck. Mr. Philip Gibbs, describing this episode of the fighting in September, 1917, told how an officer of the Somerset Light Infantry, with six men, captured forty-two prisoners and eight machine-guns in the block-house.

CANADIANS' AND SOMERSETS' HEROIC ATTACKS ON ENEMY BLOCK-HOUSES.

GERMAN COMMUNICATION TRENCH

[Canadian official photograph.
AFTER BRITISH BOMBARDMENT.

HOW THE PROGRESS OF THE WAR WAS CHRONICLED BY PEN AND CAMERA.

By Basil Clarke.

Threats of War and Newspaper Preparations for Recording It—A Fleet Street Example—How Correspondents were Despatched—Old Correspondents Rush Back to Harness—Changed Conditions of Work—How the Government Made Difficulties—Their Policy of Secrecy—Press Retaliation—Establishment of Press Bureau—How it was Worked—The First Correspondents in the Field—The First War Photographs—Hunting Down and Expulsion of Correspondents Begun—Harsh Treatment of Correspondents—Sir John French's Despatches—Public Demand for More News—Press Correspondents at Last Officially Recognised in the Zone of the Armies—Press Camps Established in the Field—Correspondents Licensed—The Chief Field Censor and his Staff—Correspondents' Obligations and Uniform—Life and Work of Correspondents in France—A Correspondent's Diary, Describing Quarters, Work, and Colleagues—Pen Sketches of War Correspondents—Famous Visitors at the Press Camp—Correspondents on Other British Fronts and with Other Armies—Diplomatic Value of Their Work—Correspondents on the Fringe of the War—Dangers of the Work—The Files of the British Press and Their Place in War History.

AS soon as war became imminent machinery for reporting it was hurriedly prepared, and the moment war was declared that machinery went into motion with a whir. From that day it never ceased. New wheels and cogs and driving-belts were added until it became a mammoth compared with the minnow of August, 1914. Reporting the war became, in fact, a new industry, as distinct and definite in its way as the making of shells, an industry with a story and romance of its own well worthy of a place in any survey of the war which aims at being comprehensive.

War reporting at its birth was an "unofficial" babe. It was not christened and sanctified by the Government until months after its birth. The newspapers fathered it; editors, news editors, and proprietors were its doctors and nurses. Circumstances on almost every big newspaper were much the same. One example from Fleet Street will suffice. Imagine a news editor sitting in his solitary chair, almost without break throughout the Bank Holiday week-end of August, 1914. A tape telegraph machine was spinning its monotonous thread of printed messages in a corner of the room; boys were bringing that thread, length by length, for him to read. The situation grew worse hour by hour. The editor went home at last, but the news editor still sat in his chair passing on to the editor by telephone the more important messages. Some of them found him at dinner, some of them woke him up in the small hours, till finally one message brought him hot-foot to the office. Germany had declared war on Russia.

It was Sunday, but every man of the staff was in the office. The reporters were in their own room awaiting the tinkling of the bell that should summon them to their fate. One by one men were called in to the editor to receive their orders. A grey-haired senior was despatched forthwith to Petrograd; another hot-foot to Marseilles, to be ready there to proceed to any Mediterranean port on instructions by cable; another to Paris, with similar orders; another to Brussels, another to Venice. The trend of war was not yet clearly manifest, but men were being posted at favourable jumping-off points ready to get into the heart of things the moment fighting developed. Half the reporting staff received no marching orders that day. They were the reserves awaiting the development of events.

France joined in. Belgium was ruthlessly violated. That showed the trend of things. One by one reporters were hurried off to Flanders, Holland, Italy, the Balkans—to every country in which war threatened to create events worthy of chronicling.

Stirring newspaper times these were, fraught with suspense and excitement for every journalist. Old journalists and war correspondents who had left the hurly-burly of daily journalism flocked back to besiege editors with requests for war commissions, every one of them as anxious as the youngest reporters to be "in" at the greatest of journalistic ventures that had presented itself since newspapers existed.

And from those early days of the war began ups and downs of fortune for newspaper writers such as none of them could have foretold or even imagined.

[Elliott & Fry.
SIR E. T. COOK.
Sir Edward Tyas Cook, who, with Sir Frank Swettenham, was appointed co-director of the British Press Bureau, on the retirement of Sir Stanley Buckmaster from the directorship, in June, 1915.

MR. RUDYARD KIPLING ON THE ITALIAN FRONT.
Mr. Rudyard Kipling (left) with a friend on a military road near the Italian front, which he visited in 1917. He wrote a graphic series of papers on "The War in the Mountains."

They succeeded in impressing this singular view on the Government, and for a time every attempt was made to keep the war as secret as had been the diplomacy and the treaties and the unpublished agreements that had led to it. To extract from the Government news of the war was, at the outset of things, like drawing teeth. Government departments and officials were besieged with questions by the Press, who received only snubs for their pains. Officialdom raised its eyebrows at merely being asked questions, and gave replies which indicated that it was regarded as a piece of presumption on the part of editors (and the British public for whom they were, of course, acting) to want to know anything about the war at all.

Reporting the Great European War presented problems utterly different from anything in the history of war reporting. Some experienced war correspondents, men with great reputations, failed, in some cases utterly, while men of whom nothing had been heard, some of them quite young in journalism, succeeded. "Form" was no guide, as a racing expert expressed it. Prime favourites were beaten by "outsiders" almost new to the work of journalism.

As the first batches of correspondents sent over to the war zones showed their quality, and failed or succeeded according to their merits—the successful ones going up in the scale, the unsuccessful ones being withdrawn—many new correspondents were sent to try their skill. Among them also were successes and failures, so that by the second year of the war the list of successful war reporters differed utterly from the list of those sent out at the beginning of the war. New names were at the top ; old and in some cases famous names had dropped out.

Before going on to describe war reporting in the field it is necessary for clearness' sake to give some idea of the state of things at home, and of the con-

Government policy of secrecy ditions and official regulations that prevailed to govern and make difficult the collecting and publication of war news.

It is clear that at the beginning the Government regarded the reporting of the war as quite one of the minor considerations, as perhaps it was compared with the many great problems confronting the nation. But though no one claimed that publicity for war happenings should occupy anything but its right and fitting place in the scheme of things, the Government of the day was loath and even unwilling to give it any place at all. Prompted by the myopic view of certain military advisers, the Government began the war with the idea of keeping its details closely to themselves. They failed to recognise that if a war is to be successful it must be waged not by a nation's army and Government alone, but by the whole nation—in spirit, at least, if not in actual participation. The Army leaders quite openly argued that the Army alone was concerned in the subject of war, and that the nation (who supplied the men and muscle and means for that Army, and upon whom future supplies of these things depended) need no more be informed as to how the fortunes of war were going than consulted as to how war should be waged.

[*French official photograph.*]
MR. H. G. WELLS IN THE FRENCH WAR ZONE.
Mr. H. G. Wells (right), the popular English novelist, with three French officers on a temporary bridge at Soissons during a visit which he paid to the French front.

This may seem, perhaps, an exaggerated view of the position, but to anyone who was engaged in the collecting of war news at the outbreak of the war it will be recognised as a fair statement of the position. It was not until the newspapers actually forced the hand of the Government that any attention whatever was paid to the duty of informing the nation of the position of affairs and of seeking to engage their interest, sympathy, and support for the war. Such was the darkness in which affairs were shrouded that a portion of the Press of the country, especially the Radical and Labour Press, was even at the outbreak of war itself hatching an anti-war policy. "Peace" and anti-war advertisements were occupying full pages of newspapers. A group of Radical editors met and were, in fact, deciding to oppose the war, before the Government woke up and in a flutter of concern supplied them with the diplomatic facts of the case. It is probable that never in history had the Government of a democratic nation so failed to realise the importance of reasonable publicity.

By this means were the Government first brought to

some glimmering of its duty to give the nation news. But the lesson was not enough. Under pledge of secrecy they had given the editors of the country certain facts, and had prevented a revolt and the starting of an anti-war campaign in certain political journals. At this they rested on their oars, and carried on the war as secretly as before, in total disregard of a nation that clamoured for war news. Their communications to the Press were of the barest and most meagre kind, and were few and far between.

Again the newspapers forced their hand. For by this time special correspondents and war correspondents were in the field of operations and in prominent centres all about it. They were sending news by telegraph and by couriers from the fountain-head of war, and as yet there was nothing to stop these messages from being printed. Government officials and Army leaders who had formulated the official scheme for keeping the war and **How the Press** all news of it to themselves, saw their **retaliated** plans defeated by correspondents whose messages right from the seat of war were thrilling the nation. Newspaper editions, published at all hours of the day and night alike, began to lend shape to war and its actuality. The policy of secrecy was proving as futile as it deserved to prove.

But even now the Government did not see their mistake. Their first measure that had any bearing on the subject of war publicity was negative rather than positive; it was designed to prevent the dissemination of news rather than to further it; to decide what should not be published rather than that what could be published.

This was undoubtedly the first function of the official Press Bureau which was established, under the Defence of the Realm Act, on August 7th, 1914, under the direction of Mr. F. E. Smith, M.P. Clear indication of its character is to be had in the nickname given to it after it had been at work for a few days **Formation of the** and its methods had been seen, for **Press Bureau** instead of "Press Bureau" it became known among men who had dealings with it as the "Sup-press Bureau."

Outwardly, of course, the duty of the department was made to appear less mediæval in character than this. In official parlance its function was described as the official medium by which all information relating to the war was communicated to the Press. Its secondary function was the censoring before publication of all matters relating to the war which newspapers collected on their own account. The amount of news issued to the Press was of the smallest: its news value of the poorest. Most of the Government departments used the Press Bureau only as a means of getting gratuitous publicity for their needs and requirements for which announcements at ordinary times they would have been charged at advertisement rates. These announcements were solemnly distributed to the Press through

IN A BRITISH PRESS "CAMP" ON THE WESTERN FRONT

British war correspondents and Press officers in the garden of the château which formed their "camp" at the advanced base of General Headquarters in France. From left to right they are (seated): Mr. Percival Phillips, Colonel Hutton Wilson, D.S.O., Press Officer; Mr. Beach Thomas, and Captain Stewart, Assistant Press Officer; (standing) Mr. Basil Clarke, Mr. Perry Robinson, and Mr. Perceval Gibbon.

the Press Bureau as "news. Some of them were denied publication by newspapers of less amenable character. A few outstanding items of news which could not possibly be kept dark were given out at rare intervals. But the Press Bureau's staff of six naval officers, nine military officers, and nine clerks was far more concerned with the mutilation of war news proofs submitted by the newspapers than with providing adequate war news for the nation.

As the first department of its kind in British history, the original Press Bureau is worthy perhaps of a more detailed description. Its home was a battered and mildewed old house, No. 40, Charing Cross, a few doors away from the Admiralty. A policeman guarded its door, and no one but newspaper representatives and the bureau staff was admitted. On the ground floor were two lime-washed rooms containing long tables, made of deal boards, and forms. The walls were mottled with damp, and industrious spiders busied themselves in most of the corners. Small as the rooms were, they held from twenty to thirty Press men, day and night alike.

Filling up half the ground-floor passage outside the first room were telephone boxes, ten or a dozen in number, connected by special wires to the leading newspaper offices and news agencies. Each box was labelled with the name of the newspaper or newspapers jointly to whom it belonged. At the head of a flight of stairs, worn and dirty, were the censors' rooms and the director's room. They were little better than the rooms below, except that the crowding was not so intense. Table telephones in these rooms connected the director and the censors with the various Government departments. As in the Press rooms below,

THE "TIMES" CORRESPONDENT AT A FRENCH COLLEAGUE'S FUNERAL.
Mr. H. Perry Robinson (the grey-haired central figure) by the grave of M. Serge Basset, war correspondent of "Le Petit Parisien," who was killed while on active service, and buried on July 2nd, 1917. Mr. Perry Robinson was first special correspondent of the "Times" and later of the "Daily News."

men were on duty day and night. The censors had no easier time than the journalists below.

The working of the place was curious and complex. At the street door were many newspaper messengers. There was no room for them inside. They raced along the streets with messages to or from the bureau. If a despatch arrived at a newspaper office from a correspondent in the field, it was hurried by messengers to the Press Bureau for censorship, and was in due time returned censored. Statements issued by the Press Bureau, if too long or too unimportant for telephoning, were carried also by messengers, so that the place was generally beset by them and their bicycles and taxi-cabs. A newspaper representative on duty at the bureau had to act as go-between to the censors and his paper, and to act as counsel for his paper. He was allowed in those days to argue with the censors as to whether "copy" should be passed or not, and often by skilful debate and diplomacy he could save a good despatch from destruction. It was his duty, of course, to get as much "copy" passed as possible. One or two of the censors were pompous people who sought to cut down war news by every pretext. Others were quite reasonable men who tried, each according to his lights, to deal fairly with "copy"—so far as the curious and ill-defined rules which had been given to **How the Press** them allowed them to do so. It is actual **Bureau worked** fact that news deleted totally by one censor would often be passed without question by his successor on the censors' rota.

Chaos reigned. The whole of newspaperdom was amazed at the vagaries of the Press Bureau; editors marvelled and wondered what the Press Bureau would do next. Sometimes they visited the bureau to remonstrate in person. Seemingly the explanation of it all was that the Government, instead of considering how much news of the war could fittingly be given to the public, gave the matter no attention at all, and left it to chance and the whims of a few half-pay Army and Navy officers to determine what news collected by the papers should be published. The Press Bureau, its appearance, and its methods, alike reflected the Government's early policy as regards the Press and publicity for the war.

A change for the better came when the bureau was transferred to the Royal United Service Institution, Whitehall, in the middle of September, 1914. The quarters and accommodation were better, and slightly more businesslike methods were adopted for dealing with war news submitted

(*British official photograph.*)

A DISTINGUISHED LONDON EDITOR IN FRANCE.
Mr. J. L. Garvin, editor of the "Observer" (third from the left in the front row), about to start on a visit to Vimy Ridge.

for censorship. But the Government's opinion of the Press was still manifested in queer little ways. Thus, while the censors and officials used the front door of the new bureau, the Press representatives were instructed to use the back door (in Whitehall Gardens).

Some of them objected, and once there was trouble on the subject. It was all very petty, but it is worthy of mention as showing the feeling of the authorities **The Press Bureau** towards the Press at this time, and the **and the " Times "** irritation this feeling caused. Their censoring of despatches and their general attitude towards the newspapers and their representatives were in much the same tenor—an attitude of lofty superiority, which, coupled with an utter disregard of public anxiety for news of the war and an abysmal ignorance of newspapers' needs and methods to supply that want, was no less ludicrous than many of the mistakes made in the handling of affairs in the early days of the war.

Before leaving the subject of the Press Bureau, the centre of censorship and the dissemination of British official news, its later history may be completed in a few lines. Mr. F. E. Smith resigned the directorship immediately after the famous episode of the " Times " despatch. To this message, giving in dark colours details of British defeats in the field in France, Mr. Smith added a few pungent lines of his own in like tone of warning to the British public.

It is possible to see after these years that that " Times " despatch of Black Sunday, 1914, did more to arouse the British public to a sense of the gravity of affairs at the front than any measure the Government had taken. Through their policy people at home were regarding the war more in the light of a picnic than as a matter of life or death. The " Times " despatch woke them up. They turned on the Government, and it was not until a deluge of official " eyewash " had been outpoured and till Mr. F. E. Smith had resigned, that public opinion settled sufficiently to allow the Government to remain alive and continue on their inefficient way.

Mr. F. E. Smith went to the front as a soldier. Sir Stanley Buckmaster went in as director of the Press Bureau. And he went in by the " back door " in Whitehall Gardens !

MR. NEIL MUNRO, LL.D.
This distinguished Scottish novelist, as representative of the "Glasgow News," paid several extended visits to the western front, particularly to chronicle the work of the Scottish regiments.

This mode of entry was regarded as indicating a policy of conciliation. And so it proved. The Government had been wakened to the fact that the Press, much as they disparaged it, might nevertheless upset them yet. They became more amenable, less dictatorial. War despatches were treated more sympathetically, though unfavourable facts were still rigorously deleted from messages from the field of war. Editors still protested, of course. The Press became divided. One **" Tell the truth " v.** half, headed by the Northcliffe Press, **" Hide the truth "** argued that the nation should be told the truth, good or ill, and that by the truth alone could they be roused to war effort and brought to treat the war with the seriousness that it deserved. The other half held that the nation " should not be alarmed "; that the Government must be left to carry on the war as they thought best, without criticism even for their mistakes and failures.

The country at large undoubtedly favoured the " Tell the truth " policy, though the " Hide the truth " party, composed largely of strong party men of the Government side, also made themselves heard. Demands for more news and a less sweeping censorship began to be made on all sides. Hints of bad news that the censors had held back began to leak out ; members of Parliament peppered the Government with questions, and their position became a wobbling one.

Then a " wily " measure was taken. Press Bureau reforms were readily promised and actually carried out. Sir Frank Swettenham and Sir Edward Cook (who six months later, when Sir Stanley Buckmaster was made a peer, became joint directors) were put in as assistant directors, the latter an experienced journalist and editor of repute, who was able to put the management of the place on lines more calculated to meet the needs of newspapers for which it was established. Censorship was speeded up by a great increase of the staff, and a greater uniformity of the treatment of " copy " was brought about, though anomalies of censorship never quite ceased to exist. All this looked most promising to the outside world, and criticism at home was lulled.

But while doing these things at home the Government

MR. J. M. N. JEFFRIES.
Special correspondent of the " Daily Mail " in the Great War on the Belgian, French, and Italian fronts.

MR. MARTIN DONOHOE.
Special correspondent of the " Daily Chronicle " in France, Russia, and the Near East.

MR. PHILIP GIBBS.
Special correspondent of the " Daily Telegraph," and author of many works of fiction, history, and belles-lettres.

took another step less apparent to the country at large. They saw that once the truth about affairs at the front—which were then in a most dangerous position—reached England, it could not be effectually suppressed. The censors might keep it from the public at large, but members of Parliament and others learnt it, and did not hesitate to demand explanations. The Government, therefore, while taking steps to improve the Press Bureau and giving all signs of an eagerness to meet the demand for more news, took steps to cut off the newspapers' news supply at the source— namely, in the field of war.

At the outset of hostilities the newspapers, as mentioned earlier, had sent out correspondents to various war centres to be ready to concentrate upon whatever places should provide scenes of war activity. As soon therefore as the Germans rushed Flanders and France, British newspaper men were ready on the spot. Two days after the outbreak of hostilities Mr. J. M. N. Jeffries, a brilliant young correspondent of the " Daily Mail," was riding about the Belgian front in his own motor-car, and getting long and graphic messages through to London from Brussels, by telephone to Amsterdam or Paris, and thence by cable or telephone. Mr. Philip Gibbs (" Daily Telegraph "), Mr. George Ward Price (" Daily Mail "), the late Alphonse Courlander (" Daily Express "), Mr. Martin Donohoe (" Daily Chronicle ") and others were transmitting messages via Paris from the field itself; Mr. H. R. Wakefield (" Daily Mail "), Lucien Arthur Jones (" Daily Chronicle "), Mr. Raymond Coulson (" Daily Dispatch " and " Sketch "), Mr. Douglas Crawford (" Times "), and others were working via Ostend. Maastricht, in Holland, Dieppe and other points on the fringe of war were being used as bases by correspondents moving in the hinterland of the armies, gathering details of the war's progress. Mr. George C. Curnock (" Daily Mail ") was at Boulogne ready for the arrival of the British Army ; Mr. Beach Thomas (" Daily Mail "), Mr. Percival Phillips (" Daily Express "), Mr. Perry Robinson (" Times "), with roving commissions, were already posted well in the heart of things.

Now, all these men and many others were at first free to move very much as they liked. The French Government and the Belgian Government put no hindrance in their way. In fact, there were many cases in which both these Governments went out of their way to give special passes and privileges to British newspaper men. For weeks this state of things existed, and British correspondents were in the field with the armies themselves, picking up close details of the fighting. Others acted as " long-stops " in the big administrative centres farther back, learning the broader details and policy of the war. Photographers and cinema men alike were in the field. The first photographs of actual fighting were sent to the British newspapers on August 22nd, 1914. They were taken by Mr. Herbert A. Maunder.

First photographs of the war

Then came a sudden change. The hunting down and expelling of correspondents began. It started in the neighbourhood of the British Army. Newspaper correspondents were arrested and sent home on parole, not to come out again. They were not badly treated, except in one or two cases, where younger officers, feeling, no doubt,

MR. HAMILTON FYFE.
As brilliant special correspondent of the " Daily Mail," Mr. Hamilton Fyfe saw service on most of the fronts on which the world war was waged, from Flanders to Italy on the west and from Petrograd to the Danube on the east.

rather big in their new army boots, were perhaps more officious in manner than they need have been. Arrest usually meant being taken before a general, ordered to remain in one's quarters until perhaps the following morning, and then sent to a port of embarkation under escort. Press correspondents and photographers found in the British Army zone were sent home thus in great numbers.

Soon the French Army followed suit in this measure, and here the treatment was not always so gentle as with the British, for the ordinary French soldiers had been led to believe that possibilities of espionage lurked in the correspondents they were ordered to arrest—and, after all, to a simple, uneducated Frenchman an Englishman may look very like a German. Some correspondents were quite harshly treated, and lingered in gaol for periods up to three or four days before they were shipped home or sent to the British Army to be dealt with by their own countrymen. Some of them were stripped stark naked to be searched. Cameras were in some cases smashed or confiscated. In several cases British correspondents on being taken through the streets by guards in were mobbed by French crowds in the belief that they were spies.

The Belgians were the last of the Allies and the most reluctant to trouble correspondents. First they withdrew the privileges and permits they had given them, leaving them to manage as best they could without them. Later, with much politeness and diffidence, they asked such correspondents as came to them for official news to withdraw—but they did not insist on withdrawal, nor did they hunt down correspondents who did not come to them. So long as a correspondent wrote reasonably and guardedly they turned a blind eye to his existence in the zone of the armies, and though no information was given him officially, he was allowed, nevertheless, to roam in the war zone and pick up what information he could. If he obtruded himself, however, or wrote foolishly, he was brought to the notice of the British Staff officer who worked with the Belgian Staff, and through him the correspondent was either arrested or was told in clear terms to leave the war zone.

Harsh treatment of correspondents

As one of the last correspondents to be hunted down and expelled from the Flanders war zone, the writer can supply from personal experience details of how anyone occupying this curious and invidious position of a correspondent " tolerated but not recognised " did his work.

Three bases were used—one in Furnes, which is in Flanders, another in France in a Dunkirk hotel, a third in quiet rooms in Dunkirk. Different " bases " were necessary, because to stay in any one place for more than a day or so at a time brought visits and inquiries from police and others, and once the rank and file, police or soldiers, brought a correspondent officially to the notice of their superiors, these officers, who might themselves have been willing to leave him alone, had to take action. The only official action they could take was to expel him.

To get to the front one could not use a motor-car or a bicycle of one's own. For a motor-car an official pass was required. A pass obtained one month was mysteriously withdrawn next month and never renewed. A bicycle was forbidden to civilians.

[Australian official photograph.

Supports, silhouetted against a sombre sky, going up after a battle to relieve front trenches.

[British official photograph.

Anti-aircraft gun in action near Frezenberg during the battle for Broodseinde Ridge.

[British official photograph.

Shelter for the wounded: A well=screened, sand=bagged dressing=station on the Flanders front.

[British official photograph.

Two=tier bridges over the swamps of Flanders: Cavalry crossing over infantry filing into trenches.

[Canadian War Records.

Canadians looking at the chaos in a village from which the enemy had been expelled.

[Canadian War Records.

Troops from Nova Scotia marching up to the line on the western front.

A hot corner: Sudden attack on motor-omnibuses taking reliefs up to the trenches.

Through sloughs of despond: British artillery advancing through the mud in Flanders.

Journeys to the front, therefore, had to be made either on foot—and the front was fourteen miles from Dunkirk—or by getting a "lift" unofficially on some vehicle bound for the front. The writer travelled at different times in bread-carts, motor-lorries, ammunition-waggons, and even in officers' limousines and armoured cars, for many officers and men were only too glad to give a correspondent whom they knew a "lift" on the quiet.

But to send despatches home to England one had always to return to French territory. There was no means of getting messages away from Flanders. Unable to travel on trains—for to enter a station one needed **The despatches of** an official "laissez passer"—a correspon-**"Eye-Witness"** dent's only method was to engage some Frenchman as courier. A young French-man thus engaged used to make regular journeys carrying the writer's despatches to another courier in Calais, who in turn carried them to London. Occasional short and important messages one might venture to telegraph, but this was risky, because the post-office censors might at any moment have drawn the attention of the authorities to the existence of a Press correspondent in the war zone.

The writer might have gone on indefinitely in this outlaw way so far as the Belgian authorities were concerned, but in January, 1916, on a return to French territory to send home a despatch, he received an official summons to the Prefecture of Police in Dunkirk, where it was given him to understand that the British authorities had sent over special instructions that both he and Mr. Lumby, of the "Times," the last remaining British correspondents in the war zone, were to be hunted out and expelled. There had been previous "round-ups" of correspondents which they had managed to evade, but this one they could not evade.

At the Prefecture and at the Army Permit Office they were told that, however willing the French authorities and the Belgian authorities might have been that they should continue their work, the British authorities were unwilling. The names of the British generals from whom the orders had come were also given.

There is little doubt that the British Government, advised by the then Controller of the Army, Lord Kitchener, who had singular views (views shared by none of his successors) with regard to the Press, was at the bottom of this joint allied arrangement for excluding newspaper representatives from all work in the zone of the armies. The earlier attitude of both France and Belgium showed clearly that no such policy had been contemplated by them at the outset. The persistence of the British Government in putting difficulties in the way of newspaper correspondents, while other allied countries were but luke-warm in the matter, tends to confirm the view that the British were the leaders in this crusade.

For some months after this the British newspapers had virtually no first-hand accounts of affairs in the field save those from little parties of selected correspondents who at rare intervals were taken for motor tours in the war zone under the guidance of officers. These war tours were begun by the French Government, who seemed to regard the newspapers more tolerantly than did the British Government, even though their censorship was closer, stricter, and more intelligent. The British Government, under public pressure at home, followed suit. But, good as were the accounts of doings in the field written by these selected correspondents, they covered too narrow a field of time and place to be anything like a complete and satisfactory service of war news. There was another source of official "war news" at the time—namely, the despatches from the field of "Eye-Witness," but few people took them seriously. They began in the middle of September under the style of "Descriptive accounts of operations in the field compiled by an officer of Sir John French's Staff." Not many weeks later they were issued under the pen-name of "Eye-Witness." Each despatch set out to cover a definite period of operations in the field, and might have been made a most valuable and informative history of the vital events then taking place. Instead of this they were, as one editor expressed it, "charmingly futile descriptions which used to tantalise the British public more than absolute silence would have done — always literary, always elegant, and always—magnificently uninformative."

One exception to the Government's plan of war secrecy stands out clearly in the history of this period — namely, Field-Marshal Sir John French's despatches from the field. Sir John's despatches were models of hard fact and plain state-ments. As such they were splendid. They contained little, however, of the colour and atmosphere and emotion of war. They were also too few in number and too long delayed after the events with which they dealt adequately to fulfil the function of a war news service.

The British newspapers persisted, therefore, in their efforts to obtain greater facilities. They were now backed by politicians and public alike. Members of the Government and even of the Cabinet had begun to rail against the extra-ordinary attitude of repres-sion which had been adopted against the Press in its collection of war news. This pressure at last broke down the resistance—a resistance as stubborn as the military chiefs in whom it centred. Early in May of 1915 the Government at last consented to the sending out of permanent British Press correspondents to the zone of British operations in France to supply a regular service of war news. **Press Camps in** The French Government and other **the field** allied Governments followed suit, and from the beginnings thus made grew a great field organisation for the supply of war news. "Press Camps" were instituted with each army's headquarters in the field. Correspondents, quite representative in the journals and agencies they represented though themselves limited in number, were duly licensed by the War Office and allowed facilities for working with the armies in the field. The British Army established its Press Camps for British journalists and American, for Canadian journalists and Australian, and also for French journalists. Official army

THE AUSTRALIAN OFFICIAL CORRESPONDENT.
Mr. C. E. W. Bean (to the right, wearing sand-glasses) on a light-railway journey with soldiers in the Sinai Desert. As official correspondent with the Australian forces, Mr. Bean wrote admirable despatches from the Gallipoli and Palestine fronts.

photographers were also appointed with commissioned rank ; army cinema operators were also chosen. The French Army established similar camps.

All these new activities, specially designed to meet the loud demands from home for closer and more intimate news of the war than the official communiqués could give or attempt to give, were placed, so far as the British Army was concerned, under the control of an experienced officer, having the title of Chief Field Censor. The officer chosen for this post (General Charteris) had both the necessary military knowledge and the knowledge of Press work to equip him for the post. Under him was an officer holding the rank of Staff Colonel, who acted as " Press officer." Lieut.-

[*French official photograph.*

AT A FRENCH FIELD CENSOR'S HEADQUARTERS.
French correspondents receiving back their " copy " at an Army Field Censor's Headquarters, where, after due revision, it had received the official imprimatur authorising despatch to the journals the correspondents represented.

IN A PRISONERS' CAMP ON THE VERDUN FRONT.
M. Jonas (left), the able cartoonist and war correspondent of the Parisian weekly paper, " L'Illustration," engaged in sketching for his journal. He was making a " note " of a typical Teuton prisoner.

Colonel Hutton Wilson, D.S.O., filled this post for many months, and was succeeded, when he left it to take up other work, by Lieut.-Colonel J. C. Faunthorpe. Under him again were assistant Press officers, some of whom had charge of special departments of Press work, while others acted as conductors in the field to Press representatives. Thus one officer had control of the official photographers and cinema men ; another had charge of the French correspondents posted with the British Army ; others would go day by day with the correspondents themselves to the front lines or elsewhere, helping them to collect information and seeing, incidentally, that they did not exceed the limits of discretion.

The excellent arrangements made by the British Army in France for recording the progress of the war may be taken as typical of those that existed in all the many fields of war in which British armies were engaged, and they may be described in closer detail.

First as to the obligations of the correspondents who were admitted to these facilities. Each had to obtain

from the War Office an " accredited correspondent's " licence, nomination for which was made by one or other of the five papers or groups of papers which alone of all the British Press were privileged to nominate correspondents for the British front. This licence, containing details of the correspondent and a photograph, was issued by the War Office, but had to be countersigned by the Chief Field Censor before it was valid within the " zone of the armies." With it were issued two green brassards, the distinguishing mark of a Press correspondent in the field. These he wore on the sleeves of a khaki uniform of the same cut and kind as a commissioned officer, but without regimental badges or rank badges. A service cap, a Sam Browne belt, field-glasses, and a typewriter completed his equipment, though, on arrival in the fire zone, it was increased by the addition of a shrapnel helmet of green painted iron and a gas-mask in a canvas knapsack. Without these two things no correspondent was allowed in the fire zone.

Life in a French château

The following extracts from notes taken by the writer during time spent as an " accredited correspondent " on the British front in France may help to give some idea of the life and work of correspondents in the field :

Upon arrival at the British base, Boulogne, I had to report to the Acting-Provost Marshal of the port and obtain from him my " field pass," which had been forwarded to him from Headquarters to await my arrival. This pass was in English and French. Guards and sentries would recognise no other. A motor-car had met me at the boat and in this, after my call on the " A.P.M." I was driven straightway to the advanced Headquarters of the British Army. The car was one of five official Press cars provided by the Army and driven by soldier drivers, though paid for, of course, by the Press.

The advanced base at this time was in the city of ——, at which we arrived after a run of about four hours. The Press correspondents' mess, which moved from town to town, whenever advanced Headquarters moved, was at this time in a château off the main street of that city. In the château worked not only the correspondents, but also the Press officer and his assistant officers, a major, captains, and lieutenants, and a staff of typists, orderlies, servants, and others. The correspondents had a room apiece upstairs and shared writing-room, dining-room, and " salon " downstairs. Most of them preferred to do their writing in the quiet of their own room, and at the close of a busy day on the front the polished wooden corridors of the château echoed to the merry patter of industrious typewriters.

My own room was a cheerful little place at the far end of the corridor with a primitive French bath-room attached. My window looked out on the back garden of the château, a roomy square of lawn, shrubs, and path, surrounded, as are most French gardens, by a tall wall. In this room before a fire of sizzling birch logs, lighted after many pains and failures by my soldier servant, Edward, I used to sit at nights writing the events of each day. A paraffin lamp before the mirror on the mantelpiece gave me light. Tall windows, severely clamped and bolted, and equipped with heavy wooden shutters outside, might have dulled for me the never-ceasing rumble of the distant guns had I only **Correspondents' daily programme** been able to keep them shut, French fashion ; but this I could not do, and their solemn "drumble" greeted my waking, droned to my working, and drummed me to sleep at nights. For they never ceased, day or night. Sometimes they rose to a banging tempest—you knew then that a "strafe" was in progress. At other times, especially when the wind was contrary, they sank to a low murmur—constant, regular, and almost soothing, like the rumble of distant trains heard in a quiet countryside on a silent night.

The correspondents' normal daily programme was to meet together after breakfast in a sort of conference, at which the Press officer, their colonel, presided. First, he announced to them in a rough outline any development, changes in position, or actions that had taken place during the night. The correspondents themselves on this information decided their respective programmes for the day. The colonel's information usually made it clear in what districts of the front interesting developments had occurred, and they agreed mutually which of them should visit these districts and obtain full details of what had happened.

Their motor-cars and drivers were by this time waiting at the château gate, and soon they were radiating from the city of —— to different quarters on the front.

MR. DOUGLAS CRAWFORD.

War correspondent of the "Times." Mr. Crawford was in Belgium during the German invasion of that country in 1914, and was later on the western front.

Each car contained, besides one or more correspondents, an assistant Press officer, who served in a curious dual capacity as friend and monitor to the correspondents whom he accompanied. It might fall to this officer to shepherd a correspondent at the risk of his life over a shell-swept waste, or to chaperone him into the august presence of a British general, so that he might glean first-hand details of events that had happened in that general's area of command. Or it might fall to him to pass a quiet veto if the correspondent's innocence or enthusiasm led him to contemplate doing anything that "should not be done."

So far as the writer observed them, they exercised this more unpleasant part of their function sparingly and kindly. In fact, they were excellent fellows. To have gone day after day, as they did, into the most troublous and dangerous places, merely to satisfy the insatiable curiosity and lust for experience which characterise every good journalist, **The assistant Press officers** seemed one of the most thankless of tasks. Yet they performed it not only loyally but good-humouredly. Most of them were officers who through wounds had been invalided and put on "light duty"—a euphemism under which might lurk many onerous and hazardous Army tasks.

If the area to be visited by the correspondent were no great distance from Headquarters he might get home again in time for lunch at the château, but more often his journey and work would occupy the whole day. On these occasions sandwiches and mineral waters and light wine would be taken in the car in a basket—to be eaten on some country roadside, perhaps, or in some trench or shattered village of the front. He might lunch in green, open countryside to the whistling of larks, or in some shell-pitted desert of upturned earth and shattered brick to the whistling of shells.

Often he met kindly people who invited him to a meal with them in their quarters. The writer has lunched, for instance, as the guest of a general in his château, sitting on priceless chairs of two centuries ago, and also by the side of a junior subaltern in a dug-out, with stewed bully beef for a dish and an upturned packing-case for a table, each meal having a subtle charm of its own.

MR. GEORGE C. CURNOCK.

As war correspondent of the "Daily Mail" Mr. Curnock was in France in 1914, and was one of the Pressmen who then suffered arrest.

Everywhere (the notebook records) I found myself received with the warmest hospitality and the keenest wish to help. More than once I dropped across officers who had secretly done me little kindnesses during my "outlaw" days of war reporting in Flanders ; and many a pleasant "crack" (as the Scots say) we had over those early days, and the devices and makeshifts to which one had then to resort to keep out of the military net laid for newspaper correspondents. Meeting these friends again, it was made still

MR. JAMES DUNN.

Having acted as war correspondent of the "Daily Mail" in the early part of the war, Mr. Dunn enlisted in the Artillery in 1916.

MR. EDMUND CANDLER.

A war correspondent of long experience, Mr. Candler was attached to the British Force in Mesopotamia as official Press representative.

LORD BEAVERBROOK.

Sir Max Aitken (Lord Beaverbrook), who was raised to the Peerage in December, 1916, served as "Eye-Witness" to the Canadian Forces, and wrote a spirited account of "Canada in Flanders."

clearer to me how little the Army of that day relished the hunting and baiting of correspondents to which their orders, received from a higher power in England, committed them. Quite naturally, officers, then as now, had been only too pleased that such doings of their units and men as could with discretion be made public should be made public.

With good fortune a correspondent might arrive home in time for a cup of tea at 4.30 with his fellow-correspondents ; and over the tea-cups the news gleanings of the day would be exchanged. One acquired the art of taking notes and munching bread-and-butter simultaneously. After tea each man went to his room to "write up," putting the day's events in such perspective as seemed fitting to him. The news he had himself collected might be the most important of the day, or it might be overshadowed and dwarfed by facts which a colleague had collected.

After a busy day the typewriters upstairs might be tapping till a late hour at night ; and dinner, served about 8.30, might go begging for want of diners. But for the most part despatches were finished by dinner-time, for there was an additional goad to quickness of writing besides that of mere hunger. The despatches were either telegraphed to England —in which case they had to be brief—or they were carried by a King's Messenger who had to leave, of course, in time to catch the boat. The censoring of the despatches was done by the Press officers in the château itself, and they fixed each day a time at which all despatches had to be in their hands so as to leave them an ample margin of time for the censoring before the messenger took them away. Dinner-time was, generally speaking, the time-limit fixed, and by that hour all despatches for transport by boat had to be in the censor's hands. Your despatch, good or bad, complete or incomplete, had to be finished by this time, unless, for some special reason affecting all correspondents alike, an extension of time had first been obtained.

But the time of the boat's departure was apt to vary, and there might be occasions when you arrived

Evening hours in the mess

"home" at night hungry and dog-tired, and with ears still dinning with the sound of shells, only to find that all "copy" had to be handed in in an hour's time. Then for a scrambling rush !

It was after a long day spent at the front, finished up by a lightning literary dash of this sort, that one could with the fullest and most wallowing luxury spread oneself in a big easy-chair with a pipe, in the cosy salon downstairs, tracing the pictures of fancy in the feathery ash of the log fire, or listening to the cheery talk of colleagues whose feet competed with one's own for space on the big square fender.

Looking over his diary for this period the writer finds the following description of those evening hours after work was done and of the colleagues with whom they were spent :

All of them are men of world culture ; men who have seen things and done things. No need to lift one's gaze from the fire to know which of them is speaking. Each voice is distinctive. May be it is Perry Robinson, of the "Times," the oldest man of the little group, though not yet old, who is telling some apposite experience of his varied journalistic days in America. The sentences he uses are short and well-weighed, and, without looking round, you know quite well that the little pauses which punctuate them and make them seem almost halting are taken up in short, quick puffs at his briar pipe, which he nurses tenderly in his fingers as he smokes. Every few minutes there will be a longer pause, and you know that he is "stopping" his pipe with a stopper produced automatically at regular intervals from his right tunic pocket. Turn your head,

[*Annan & Sons.*

LIEUT. MUIRHEAD BONE.
Official artist on the western front ; an etcher and painter of world-wide repute.

and it is to see a face strongly characteristic, a profile finely chiselled, grey hair and moustache of military cut, strikingly contradicted by bushy eyebrows of jet black. When sentries and guards on the road see that face in a passing motor-car they automatically give a "general's salute."

Big Beach Thomas is sitting by him with his long limbs crossed on the fender. He succeeded his colleague, Valentine Williams, who became an officer in the Irish Guards, as representative of the "Daily Mail." Through gold-rimmed spectacles he gazes at the fire, his brown eyes gaining an added twinkle from its light. The ruddy bronze of an outdoor life is on his cheek. It is not many years since he "ran the mile" for his University, Oxford, in which he was president of the Athletic Union. A love of letters and the classics shares almost an equal place with his love of Nature, outdoor life, and pastimes. On a quiet day when there is nothing much to do he is always a "safe" man to look for to go out for a walk. To find him you may look in his room to discover him reading a well-thumbed volume of Virgil or in the château garden to see him kicking a football about. I can see him there now, as I write this in my room—tall, lithe, bareheaded, either kicking his football or bowling imaginary overs at an imaginary wicket by the rose-bush at the bottom of the garden —a boy still, in mind and freshness and jollity of disposition, yet one of the finest and most lovable of men.

Over by the far side of the fire is a short, thick-set figure, with a strong square face, glowing dark eyes, and a shock of shining black hair. You will ransack memory for a moment to think where you have seen a like face, and then the memory comes back in a flash. The head is like **Some representative** Beethoven's. But it is that of Perceval Gibbon. **specials** It is as a short-story writer rather than as a journalist the world knows him best ; it was as a sailor, globe-trotter, and adventurer that he picked up his amazing wealth of experience of men and things. And, to a restless physical energy, Nature has added in him a relentless mental energy. He is in one man two contradictions —roving adventurer and student. His researches in the one capacity touch the remotest corners of the world ; in the other the remotest byways of learning. He has commanded a sailing ship, traded with savages in Central Africa, and yet found time to learn half a dozen languages and to plumb the literature of half Europe. When he talks, it is with all the fire and emphasis of his Celtic blood.

Percival Phillips, of the "Express," from the outer fringe of the circle round the fire, contributes now and again a snappy, dry, and almost pawky comment to the chatter. He has the longest service of all of us in the mess. He came out in May, 1915, when correspondents were first appointed, and is the only survivor of that little band. He speaks but seldom ; a listener rather than a talker, but one of those delightful people whom one can describe as a "merry listener." He was a war correspondent at the age of twenty—when with pack on shoulder, so to speak—he set off on his own account from his home in America to the Greek War, where he wrote war despatches and sent them "on approval" to editors, American and British, who were forced by their very excellence to use them. He soon won for himself a foremost place among English journalists.

MR. HERBERT A. MAUNDER.

Photographer with the Army. He took the first photographs of actual fighting sent to British newspapers, August 22nd, 1914.

A man of fine presence, great unselfishness, courtly manner, and sterling worth, he is a large contributor, in a quiet way, to the happiness and almost family comfortableness (one would have liked to borrow the German word gemüthlichkeit) that characterised our mess.

And, lastly, there is Philip Gibbs, who is next to Percival Phillips in length of service. His broad brow, his pale, finely-chiselled face, thin, sensitive lips, and big clear eyes, show something of the thinker, idealist, and poet that he is by nature. But his spare frame and indolent pose as he reclines—one might almost say, collapses—in an easy-chair belie the fierce unquenchable energy that is his. Few men there are who can idle so unsatisfactorily as he. The cigarette in the fingers of his slim left hand is sending upwards a thin blue line. Through eyes half closed he watches its unwaving course dreamily, apparently the most thorough and most complete of idlers. But it is only for a moment. He moves, I see him turn to catch my eye, and I know full well that it is to challenge me to a game of chess—"à la mort," as we used to say. Over the game he will struggle and wriggle to gain the mastery, finding some outlet in so doing for the restless mental energy that consumes him. But for that game I know he would go to his room and work. It is a kindness to make him play. A man of great sympathy is Gibbs ; a man in whom the soul-wound caused by war and war's horror and war's suffering is ever fresh and raw. Such a war as this weighs heavy on a mind like that.

Later in the evening visitors begin to drift in ; for the correspondents' mess is a popular place of call. Here comes Muirhead Bone, the official artist, a man of world-wide repute, shaped and standardised to Army type by the uniform and one star of a second-lieutenant. He picks up a periodical from the table and would retire shyly to the coldest corner, for he is the most reticent of men. But a gap is made in the circle of chairs round the fire, a new chair inserted, and he is led to it, protesting that he will on no account push anyone from the fire. He begins to tell us some queer happening of his day. He is full of simple, homely anecdote which he retails in a light, flexible voice, in which a trace of his native Scotland still lingers ; though it is the intonation rather than the pronunciation that proclaims it. He talks simply. Even his words, as well as his eyes, seem to have a mischievous twinkle. He sets us all laughing with a little story about the "man who brought coal" that day to the tiny office with which the Army provides him as a studio. He did not want any coal because he had not yet finished his last supply, nor had he room for more coal, but the coalman said he "must

An artist and two photographers
have it ; it was 'Army Orders,' " he was "down on the list" for coal. Out of these and such simple ingredients come his merry stories, told with a shy, dry, kindly humour. A great artist, gentle, diffident ; and, underneath, the sparkling mischief of a boy.

The Press officers have now finished their censoring, and, should no other work present itself, they may stroll into the salon for a chat or a look at the day's papers, which have just arrived by courier and have been spread out on a far table by an orderly. The post has arrived, too, and there is silence while letters from home are read. Then the papers are hunted through and despatches written two days earlier are read through with a microscopic eye for the sins of sub-editors and printers, superadded to one's own ; all stand clearly revealed in that bleak pillory of print.

More visitors arrive, officers for the most part who have come into the city of —— for a few hours' leave from their stations at the front. Brother journalists come in, overseas representatives from the Australian and Canadian Press Camps not many miles away. Among them is Bean, the Australian, whose despatches from Gallipoli earlier in the war will form a great and permanent chapter in Australian history. Tall, with abundant yellow curly hair, his build suggests one of his hardy brother-Australian soldiers, but his head the head of a statesman. In a chance talk that is going on he picks up some item of news about his beloved Australians and hurries out to telegraph it.

Lieutenants Brooke and Brooks, the official Army photographers,

[*British official photograph.*

PRESS COLLEAGUES IN HISTORIC MONASTIR.
M. Albert Londres, French war correspondent, chatting in Monastir with Mr. G. Ward Price, of the "Daily Mail," official correspondent with the British forces in the Balkans.

visit the mess to look at the illustrated papers, which are well filled with examples of their handicraft with the camera. Upon these two men depends the supply of official photographs of the British Army in the field. An orderly enters with drinks and glasses on a tray. Men help themselves.

If the German airmen feel active they may fly over to-night and bomb us. Anti-aircraft guns reply from the streets and gardens about us, and there is a pandemonium of noise. We go through the French windows into the garden and watch the shrapnel bursting against the sky. There is no great concern. One has become by this time almost fatalistic about shell fire and other dangers. Once they bombed us six nights running.

Before midnight, as a rule, all visitors have gone. The "last man up" takes up his oil lamp from the hall-table and creeps off to his room.

This little picture of war reporters and war reporting as it existed at the chief centre of that industry—namely, the British War Correspondents' Camp on the front in France—has only to be altered in details of place and men and extent to illustrate the kind of thing that existed on **Press camps on other fronts** each of the British fronts. The Press camps on other fronts were not so big as the one in France, perhaps, nor were the arrangements for recording the war both in letterpress and in photograph so elaborate. But the mode of life and the fashion of working were much the same everywhere. The British correspondents with the French Army, for instance, worked to almost identical rules ; they lived in almost an identical château. They comprised Mr. G. H. Perris, of the "Chronicle," Mr. Gerald Campbell, of the "Times," Mr. H. Warner Allen and Mr. Lawrence, of Reuter's. The Canadians' Camp was a similar centre of industry and good fellowship, Sir Max Aitken being their "Eye-Witness." The Allied Correspondents' Camp attached to British Headquarters varied

A NARROW ESCAPE FROM THE GERMANS.
Mr. Raymond Coulson, of the "Daily Dispatch" and "Sketch" (in mufti), left Ghent in October, 1914, half an hour before the Germans entered, towing behind his car three British soldiers on commandeered bicycles.

from time to time, but in it were usually three or four leading French journalists, two Italians, a Russian, and a Portuguese. Two American correspondents representing big news agencies worked with the British correspondents.

In the great industry of reporting the war there were also, of course, the outposts—correspondents posted with British armies in the outer fields of the war, and correspondents working with the allied armies. Among the former was Mr. Massey, of the "Daily Telegraph," official correspondent with the British army in Egypt. Mr. Edmund Candler, an old campaigner, was with the British in Mesopotamia. He took part as a war correspondent in General Younghusband's expedition to Tibet years before, and lost an arm in the course of the first battle fought there. Mr. Ward Price was official correspondent with the British forces in the Balkans, where he had previously acted in a similar capacity during the wars of a few years earlier. The allied armies—Russia, Rumania, France, Belgium, Serbia, and Italy—had also representatives of the British Press officially appointed to give the British public full record of what these Allies were doing in the common cause. One need mention only the brilliant work of Mr. Hamilton Fyfe from Russia and Rumania, of Mr. Warner Allen and Mr. Campbell from the French Army Headquarters, of Mr. Crawfurd Price from Serbia and elsewhere, to indicate the calibre of the men engaged with our Allies and the work they did, not only in recording facts of the war, but in winning the sympathy of the British nation for the allied soldiers of whose doings they wrote so well.

All reporting of the war was not official, though all reporting from the actual fields of operations had to be so. Every centre of importance on the fringe of the war had its newspaper representatives eager to collect war news and such news of the enemy countries as came over the frontiers. Holland, Switzerland, Denmark, all had their little groups of British journalists closely watching the trend of things bearing on the war. Amsterdam, Rotterdam, Copenhagen, Basle, and Berne were important centres for war news of the more political and diplomatic kinds. The collecting of news in these and like centres was a very delicate business in view both of the desire of these countries to maintain a strict and impartial neutrality and of the efforts of the Germans and their agents to place difficulties in the way of British correspondents and prevent them from learning the truth about things in Germany. The Germans who found a British correspondent at all successful in getting news of their affairs did not hesitate to denounce him as a spy to the authorities of the country in which he worked; and not a few British correspondents were arrested on charges trumped up by these Germans.

Just as in countries in which fighting actually took place and in countries touching the belligerent countries, the record of war in all its phases, diplomatic, military, and domestic, was faithfully recorded day by day by British journalists, so, too, in countries quite remote from war had a faithful war record to be made and kept. For it is fair to say that there was hardly a country in the whole world in which the war did not bring about great changes and vital events, events that were to leave indelible marks upon the history of these nations. These events were recorded in some cases by correspondents specially sent out from England by British newspapers, in other cases by resident correspondents working for those newspapers or for one or other of the great news agencies. Among the latter none did better or more useful war work than Reuter's.

Thanks mainly to the enterprise of the British newspapers and news agencies, and the sincerity of the men whom they sent out to write records of war's changes and events, the files of the British Press will serve the historians of the time to come as archives of war fact and information, more valuable probably than any other source. The pity of it is that, through official short-sightedness, the making and keeping of this record was given so cramped and inauspicious a start.

LIEUT. J. W. BROOKE.
Official Army photographer with the British Army in the field.

LIEUT. ERNEST BROOKS.
Official Army photographer with the British Army in the field.

CAPT. FRANK HURLEY.
Official photographer to the Australian Imperial Forces in France

CAPT. IVOR CASTLE.
Official photographer to the Canadian Forces on the western front.

MR. HERBERT BALDWIN.
Official photographer to the Australian Forces on the western front.

MR. BERNARD GRANT.
Press photographer, who obtained a commission in the R.N.A.S.

MR. T. E. GRANT,
Press photographer with the British Forces in Salonika.

MR. McDOWELL,
Official cinema photographer on the western front.

ON THE LENS-ARRAS ROAD

CHAPTER CCXIV.

[Canadian War Records.
AS SEEN FROM PETIT VIMY.

THE BRITISH OFFENSIVE AT YPRES AND THE BATTLES OF LENS.

I.—From the Conquest of Hill 65 to the French Victory at Bixschoote.

By Edward Wright.

German Plans Disarranged—Westernism and South-Easternism—Resumption of Lens Operations—Conquest of Hill 65—Battle in a Waterspout—A Memorable Anniversary—Achievements of the New British Armies—Tragic Episode on the Flemish Coast—Heroism of Northamptons and King's Royal Rifles—Eastern Flank Saved by a Sergeant—New Zealanders in La Basse Ville—The Saucer Swamps of Ypres—Ludendorff's " Pill-box " Defence System—Bad Weather and Military Meteorology—General Anthoine's Artillery Success—Frenchmen and Guards Bridge Ypres Canal—Magnificent French Victory at Bixschoote.

AFTER the splendid British victory on the Wytschaete-Messines Ridge in the first week of June, 1917 (described in Vol. 10, Chapter CCVII., page 321), the enemy knew clearly that Sir Douglas Haig intended to strike again, in stronger force, on the Ypres salient.

General von Ludendorff then had an excellent opportunity of renewing his offensive on the western front. The ordinary move for him to make was to attempt to distract the British commander by means of a violent sustained thrust against one of the quiet British sectors. Ludendorff, however, refrained from an attacking defensive. His ruling idea was that attack had become too expensive against such lines, effectives, and armament as the British and French commanders possessed. His strategy largely reposed upon confidence in the success of the intensified submarine campaign against shipping. He reckoned that this naval peril was so deadly as to incite the British Commander-in-Chief to

[British official photograph.
TWO DISTINGUISHED BRITISH GENERALS.
General Sir Henry Horne, K.C.B., commander of the First Army on the western front (on right), enjoying a jest with General Sir Arthur Currie, commander of the Canadian troops in succession to Sir Julian Byng.

hew his way through the German lines at any cost of life. He disbelieved in the official returns of British casualties, and estimated that his own very heavy losses in men and guns were much exceeded by the British losses.

During the interval of preparation on the Ypres battlefield the local German commander, General Sixt von Armin, accelerated the production of armoured concrete forts, known as M.E.B.U.'s or " pill-boxes." These rapidly-made, standardised redoubts were manufactured in such large numbers that the sand-pits of Belgium and the Rhineland were insufficient to supply the material needed. Vast quantities of sand and gravel were obtained from Holland, and mixed at Antwerp with cement to make concrete blocks around the Ypres battleline.

The British Staff knew something of what the German Staff was doing, and trained the infantry in special ways of attacking the new block-houses. Large additions were made to the parks of siege - artillery massed near Ypres, and there

429

British official photograph.]
FAMILIARITY BREEDS
CONTEMPT.
Indifference of two war-seasoned
British soldiers to German shells
bursting within forty yards.

were movements of troops
from the quiet part of the
British line to the critical
northern sector. The enemy
in turn continued to bring
men and guns from the
bankrupt Russian front to
the British front.

So serious did the situa-
tion then seem to the
German High Command
that at the time it allowed
the Austrian Commander-in-
Chief no occasion for profiting by the weakness of
Russia to make another
grand assault upon Italy.
For three months the Italian
armies were enabled to sustain their fierce pressure
upon the Austrian lines.
Even the Russians were left
for a time in possession of
Riga because of the serious situation produced around
Ypres by General Plumer's sudden victory.

The plan which Sir Douglas Haig arranged, with the
approval of Sir William Robertson, consisted in concentrating the main British forces at that point on the
western front where the entire German system might be
endangered, and where the sea passage
Westernism and from England was shortest and the
South-Easternism network of British battle-railways and
motor-roads closest.

This strategy was known as Westernism, and was
approved by the French Commander-in-Chief, General
Pétain. It had the grand merit of conserving the depleted
resources of British transport, as the ships plying across
the Channel were especially protected against submarine
attack, and able to make a large number of voyages in
the time required to carry a small number of troops or a
small cargo of war material, through the zones of enemy
submarine activities, to the south-eastern front.

(British official photograph.
SAFETY BEFORE DIGNITY.
A soldier working on an exposed road crouched low to escape splinters
from a bursting shell, and evinced no little amusement on finding the
photographer had caught him in such a ludicrous pose.

Sir Douglas Haig believed in
the doctrine of striking the enemy
where the enemy was strongest,
because of the peculiar circumstances on the Flemish front.
Naturally, he would have preferred to break through the
German flank, and sweep along
the Flemish coast to the Dutch
frontier by means of a surprise
attack. No surprise attack,
however, was possible, owing to
the long, gigantic, and visible
labour of preparation and the
muddy ground. The enemy had
full opportunity for massing in
utmost strength at the threatened
point.

Thus there was no alternative
to a prolonged pitched battle
between the main forces of the
British and German Empires,
except, perhaps, an adventurous
and weaker attempt at surprise
in a distant theatre of war—the
eastern mountain frontier of Italy.

If General Cadorna had
been strengthened by a large
Franco-British force he
might possibly have been
able to break the Austrian
line. He had apparently
nearly four thousand guns
and a million men between
the Adriatic and the Pre-
deal Pass. If he could have
obtained from France and
Great Britain a considerable
addition of guns and gunners
and ten army corps of
British and French infantry,
there was at least a possibility of his being able to
overwhelm Austria-Hungary
before the Germans and
Austrians moved any im-
portant number of guns
from the Russian front.

But evidently neither
General Pétain nor Sir
Douglas Haig thought that
any important surprise could
be effected in this manner.
They may have held
that any such change of
plan would help the enemy in many ways. All the
successes of the early part of the year would be deprived
of much of their value, and the large new work of
organising offensives at Ypres and along the Aisne would
be wasted. There would also be the difficulty of transporting powerful British and French armies half across
Europe to the Venetian Plain. In a third less time than
this could be done, the Germans, by reason of their
superior railway system, running on interior lines, would
be able to move guns and men down to the new battlefield.
There were also local technical difficulties in regard to
the Isonzo line which confirmed the British commander
in his adherence to the strategy of Westernism. There
was a lack of water on the south-eastern mountain front,
and there was also a lack of immediate cover on the solid
rock, both of which would probably have been factors of
great practical advantage to the enemy. Moreover, the
British troops were neither trained nor especially equipped
for mountain warfare.

Around Ypres, on the other hand, everything was set for battle to the advantage of the British armies. From the newly-won Messines Ridge, and the lower mounds south-east of Ypres, British forward observing officers had a large part of the enemy's lines under view, and could bombard him with masterly effect. The Germans could not afford to refuse a pitched battle in the manner in which they had escaped from a grand trial of strength along the Somme.

They were tied to the Flemish coast by their own submarine campaign, and could not lose their partial hold upon the waters near the mouth of the Thames without the prospect of hampering the plans of their Admiralty and seriously undermining the moral of their people and their allies.

The doctrine of Westernism, therefore, prevailed. An important number of heavy batteries were sent by the British and French commanders to the **Why Westernism prevailed** Isonzo line, together with some of the new British monitors, designed to act against the Austrian sea-flank. But, in a general way, Italy was left for the time to her own resources, while France continued to hold a considerable part of the German strength, and, with weakening Russia, allowed the new armies of the British Empire to attempt to deliver a heavy stroke against the enemy's main forces cornered near the Flemish coast.

The disaster that afterwards happened to the Second Italian Army was at least faintly attributable to the plan adopted on the western front in June, 1917. On the other hand, it must be remembered that, though the suggested Italian grand adventure might have saved an Italian defeat at the cost of British and French successes in Flanders and on the Aisne, it might likewise, through the unaccountable weakness shown by some Italian troops, have ended in a combined Italian, French, and British rout. It must also be borne in mind that the attempt to break the German lines at Loos failed because of insufficient concentration of attacking strength, due to the vain distraction of the Dardanelles affair. The **Italian and** little more effective Salonika Expedi- **Russian problems** tion robbed the allied armies on the western front of the strength needed directly against the principal enemy—the Germans. The chance of breaking the Austro-Hungarian armies before the German armies arrived was extremely problematical. It would have been impossible to rail large numbers of British and French men and guns to the Isonzo line, together with a vast accumulation of shell, general war material, and food, without robbing the movement of all elements of surprise, as well as weakening the western front.

It seems to have been on these grounds, among others, that Sir Douglas Haig and Sir William Robertson, with the approval of General Pétain, decided to resume the Ypres Battle. It was reckoned at the time to be the best of available means for directly helping Italy, because it attracted, for at least several months, practically all German forces released in the east by the chaotic weakness of Russia. Although it was afterwards proved, by terrible evidence in Italy in October, 1917, that the direct,

PRESSING FORWARD ON THE HEELS OF THE ENEMY. *[British official photograph.*
British troops crossing a well-built pontoon bridge during an advance on the western front. The remains of an earlier bridge that had been destroyed by the Germans in their retirement can be seen on the right.

sustained pressure of the great British offensive did not entirely compensate for Russian feebleness, yet the miscalculation was not of a military nature.

It was the new, unexpected, disastrous acceleration of Russian weakness, directly produced by Lenin and his sinister followers, and encouraged by the vacillations of Kerensky and the premature movement of General Korniloff, which, late in the year, introduced a new factor of disorganisation into the general situation of the Allies, and thus, to some extent, checked the complete fulfilment of the Westernism plan of action arranged by the French and British Staffs.

In June, 1917, when the Ypres campaign was being energetically organised, Russia was still of potential strength. The Americans were ready to improve her railway system, and, with Japan and Great Britain, to supply more war material. Discipline could have been restored had the commanders of proved genius been allowed to use stern measures against the elements of corruption and treachery. Indeed, the re-establishment of the death penalty in the disciplinary measures of the Russian Army would alone have upset the plans of Hindenburg and Ludendorff, by **General Currie's appointment** menacing them with another surprise offensive in the eastern theatre. Teutonic guns by the thousand and troops by the hundred thousand would have been held between the Baltic and the Black Sea, and become unavailable for service along the Isonzo, the Aisne, and the Passchendaele Ridge.

Thus little was wanted, in the critical summer of 1917, to turn the balance of victory in favour of the Entente Powers, and the British campaign at Ypres opened under apparently prosperous general conditions.

While selecting Ypres as the scene of the grand duel between the forces of Germany and the British Commonwealth, Sir Douglas Haig also maintained a severe pressure against the enemy around Lens and beyond the Vimy Ridge. The Canadian Army Corps had produced a native commander in General Currie, who had been an estate agent in the days of peace. The former commander of the corps, Sir Julian Byng, had the high honour of being promoted to the control of the Third British Army, in the place of Sir Edmund Allenby, who went to Palestine in succession to General Murray.

The Canadians naturally felt some pride in having produced, by means of their splendid victories, both an army commander and a home-grown army corps general of their own. They remained for many months on the field of their great success, with their infantry crouching

[*British official photograph.*

ON INLAND WATER TRANSPORT SERVICE.
British soldiers navigating a barge on a French canal. The work of the Inland Water Transport Corps was a vital and certainly not the least pleasant part of military service in the Great War

[*British official photograph.*
PILE-DRIVING IN A FRENCH CANAL.
Constructing a new wharf on one of the many fine waterways in France that proved of inestimable value in the war as means of transport for men and munitions.

in shell-holes and rough lines on either side of the Souchez River and in the neighbourhood of Fresnoy. On the northern side of Lens, British troops also pressed the enemy in the blocks of colliers' cottages, and approached the famous rise, Hill 70, against which Sir John French's offensive had failed in 1915.

Lens was an almost hopeless goal. It might have been rushed, at a terrific cost in life to the attackers, immediately after the victory of Vimy Ridge. Probably the German Staff would have attempted such a feat had positions then been reversed. But the British Staff rightly regarded Lens as the most formidable fortress in any theatre of war. Its strength was adventitious, deriving entirely from the **Lens an underground** coal-mining galleries and shafts around **Gibraltar** the town. Only the utterly unforeseen general employment of siege-guns in extraordinary number made the pits and tunnels of the Lens coalfield of magnificent military value.

The enemy won sufficient time to improve and practically perfect the underground system of defence that he found made to his hand. Then, by bringing up large reserves of infantry and many guns liberated from the Russian front, he transformed the mining town into the underground Gibraltar of Europe. Yet Sir Henry Horne, the victor of Vimy, a master gunner of the calibre of General Pétain, possessed in the ridge he had conquered an observation position of supreme importance.

He saw his way to conduct a fierce and deadly conflict of attrition, that promised to reduce the German reserve far more rapidly than the home and overseas British reserve could be diminished by the enemy.

The enemy's scheme of badger defence was not sound, in spite of the extraordinary underground advantages afforded by the coal-mining works; for whenever the Germans lost an important position they had to come out in strength into the open, and counter-attack against one of the ablest artillerists in Europe. If the German commander continually yielded ground in order to save his men he was bound to lose Lens, and, what was of still more importance, he was bound to allow the end of the Hindenburg system at Drocourt to be turned.

In short, it was possible to bring him to battle on fairly equal terms. This General Horne, with the assistance of General Pulteney, continuously did after the conquest of the Vimy Ridge. Bitter fighting went on almost incessantly along the Souchez River, where the Canadians gradually secured a hold upon the electric-power station and the approaches to Avion.

Across the river the enemy held a dominating knoll, known as Hill 65, which rose west of the city, and formed its main direct bastion, linking, across two miles of ruined northern suburbs, with the famous observation height, Hill 70. In the **Midlanders carry Hill 65** middle of June the English troops north of the Souchez River began to work down to a hostile system of fortifications built out of a slag heap and ruined mining works. These were taken completely on June 19th, and though the enemy launched four heavy counter-attacks in twenty-four hours, he failed to recover his lost works.

Then on Sunday, June 24th, a force of Midland men carried Hill 65 with remarkably little difficulty. The hill rose about five hundred yards in front of the English line, and was strongly garrisoned by part of a Prussian division, yet the British barrage of heavy shell was so overwhelming that it entirely broke up the Germans and prevented their machine-gunners from sweeping the approaches. The Midland men carried the western slope in a nocturnal attack, and the Prussians, instead of trying to retain the reverse incline, evacuated the complicated system of **Lens a modern Pompeii** network trenches surrounding the height and fell back into Lens city.

Prisoners reported that the men of the 56th Prussian Division, who had lost the hill, were told that they would be taken out of the line and given a rest if they recaptured the knoll. They preferred not to attempt to do so. As soon as the hill was occupied, the Germans were enfiladed across the river upon all the ground they had been holding against the Canadians. On June 26th they abandoned the wreckage of La Coulotte and the brewery on the Lens-Arras road, together with the approaches to Avion.

As the Germans retired farther into the tunnels and concreted cellars of the mining city, they destroyed streets and blocks of houses to make clear fields of fire for their machine-guns and field-guns, and blew up the roads, leaving enormous mine-craters, and generally transforming Lens into a modern Pompeii. They turned the industrial suburb of the Cité St. Antoine, with its large railway yards, into an artificial lake by flooding the marsh between Lens and Avion. The new lake, a mile long and half a mile broad, prevented Avion from being encircled from the north, and westward and southward the village was

PREPARATIONS FOR THE OFFENSIVE ON THE FLANDERS FRONT.
Busy scene on the road near Pilkem, north of Ypres, where men and munitions were being moved up to the advancing British line. Pilkem was one of the villages recovered from the enemy on the first day of the Franco-British advance along the Flanders front on July 31st, 1917.
I.LL

heavily wired and mined and full of machine-guns. Yet Canadian patrols continued to work forward into the Avion system, and by June 28th they reached the hamlet of Leauvette, by the Souchez River, and penetrated the defences of Avion in two places.

Immediately after this success all the heavy British guns crashed upon Lens in a tumult, increased by a natural thunder-storm. The Midland troops, who had taken Hill 65, again stormed forward and captured a line of the main defences of the city. Then, under cover of high-explosive barrage and smoke curtains, the Canadians stumbled, slipped, and slid into the streets of Avion, where, checked by machine-gunfire at Fosse 4, they swung around this strong-hold and successfully occupied the north-western and south-western sides of the colliery slums.

Complete success was prevented by the torrent of rain that accompanied the thunderstorm. It was like a waterspout. The flooding river poured into the lake, and the lake washed out into new swamps, while the shell-ploughed ground between was turned into a general bog. Soldiers stumbled, often choking their rifles with mud, and falling behind the time-table of the barrages. The delay, due to the unexpected state of the ground, enabled enemy machine-gunners to emerge from their cellars into their forts before the Canadians could get within bombing distance of the principal fosses.

Ludendorff's "official" victory

Yet, though the extraordinary sudden rainfall put an end to the battle by handicapping the Canadians in the latter part of their action, most of the Avion objective was won in the half-hour elapsing between the crash of the British barrage and the bursting of the waterspout. At the same time as the action at Lens opened, a force of English troops attacked the German position at Oppy, beyond the Vimy Ridge, and, on a front of two thousand

BOMBING AN ENEMY CONCRETE "PILL-BOX."
Near Hollebeke and La Basse Ville, during the Third Battle of Ypres, some British troops were held up by a concreted machine-gun fort, which could only be entered from underground. The assailants were equal to the occasion, and secured it by bombing the occupants through the firing slit.

yards, took all their objectives and two hundred and forty prisoners.

The striking feature of this operation was the number of British guns that played upon all the enemy's line from Hulluch to Gavrelle. The batteries were ranged behind each other to the depth of some miles, and their tumult, merging in that of the thunderstorm, was of extraordinary intensity. The enemy's losses from shelling alone must have been very heavy, yet the small number of British infantrymen that went forward merely to seize a few tactical points seemed almost ridiculous after so tremendous a bombardment.

Ludendorff, in his official report, claimed to have won a great victory. This was exactly what Sir Douglas Haig wished him to do. British raids had been made during the bombardment all along the line of gun fire. As the raiding-parties quickly withdrew, after killing the enemy's front-line men, the local German commanders were induced to think that they had repelled a great British offensive movement. They were also disturbed by the unexpected number of guns brought against them, and thereby induced to ask for more artillery in the Lens sector at a time when General Plumer was completing his preparations at Ypres. German infantry reinforcements as well as additional guns were brought to the secondary British theatre of demonstration in order to press the Canadians back. Thereby the lieutenant of the Crown Prince of Bavaria won some advanced posts in the night of July 1st, but he could not shake the Canadian and British troops on the west and south of the town.

July 1st, 1917, the anniversary of the opening of the Battle of the Somme, in which the new British armies were tested, was memorable for the results that had been obtained. In the course of the year the new armies had taken more than 70,000 German prisoners, including 800

DARING ATTACK ON A GERMAN MACHINE-GUNNER.
During the fighting along the Comines Canal, in the Third Battle of Ypres, the British advance was inter-rupted by an enemy machine gunner posted on a railway embankment. A British soldier, who discovered his whereabouts, crept up and, bombing the gunner, captured the gun.

BRITISH TROOPS ENTERING LANGEMARCK.
It was on August 16th, 1917, that the British, continuing the advance north and east of Ypres, which had been begun rather more than a fortnight earlier, carried the village of Langemarck after severe fighting and captured in it 1,800 prisoners.

officers, with 450 German guns and more than 2,000 machine-guns, trench-mortars, and other minor pieces. This represented the capture of a strong German army with all its equipment. Three formidable ridges—the Albert Ridge, the Vimy Ridge, and the Messines Ridge—had been conquered, and every first-rate division in the German armies in turn had been brought against the improvised national forces of the British Empire.

In the line that the British troops had broken, against the strongest military State in the world, there had been at least fifty strong places, each of which was more formidable than Sebastopol or Plevna. During the first six months of the grand British campaign there had occurred a profound change in the character of the war. The offensive, for the first time between opposing modern forces both powerfully armed, became less expensive in life than the defensive. Except on rare occasions, the German losses were heavier than the British losses.

In the last six months of the great campaigning year the German losses continued to increase, owing to Ludendorff's method of strong and continual counter-attack, while the British losses diminished by an average of twenty-five per cent. or thereabouts. The highest casualties in one week, in the first half of 1917, were thirty-seven per cent. less than the lowest casualties in the last part of 1916. The British armies were then undoubtedly winning against the German armies in a measure similar to that in which the Union forces under Grant won against the Confederate forces under Lee.

In July, 1917, when the general situation seemed favourable, in spite of the increasing weakness of Russia, British, French, American, and Italian Chiefs of Staffs met to consider the best means of obtaining unity of action on the western front, by the agency of a permanent Inter-

Allied military organisation. Sir William Robertson, General Pershing, General Cadorna, and General Foch, with some of the commanders in the fields, studied the means of rapid movement of troops and material from one theatre of war to another, and made suggestions towards co-ordination of effort.

As one result, some British and French artillery forces were sent into Italy, and the railway connection between France and Italy was examined in a fashion that afterwards proved very useful. There seems to have been a proposal before the meeting that Laibach should be made an objective for a combined Italian, French, and British Alpine campaign. But the difficulties were very great, and Flanders remained the grand battlefield between the two mightiest concentrations of force in the opposing camps.

In the meantime, the British armies continued their preparations for a conflict surpassing that of the Somme campaign. A British force took over the positions at the edge of the North Sea, by Nieuport and Lombartzyde, to enable the French troops who held this sector to concentrate elsewhere. Among the British forces were the King's Royal Rifles and the Northamptons, who crossed the Yser Canal by the pontoon bridges made by the French, and occupied a narrow belt of sand-dunes along a front of about fourteen hundred yards. The **British force crosses** sector was regarded as fairly safe, in **Yser Canal** spite of the fact that the canal cut the defenders off from their reserves and artillery. For there were British monitors and other warships acting off the coast, and usually ready to help in bombarding the enemy's very powerful coast batteries.

The German Staff, however, had always looked upon this bit of Flemish territory as a thing that could be taken whenever it was worth while to do so. They had only to gather close to it an overwhelming number of howitzers

BRIDGING THE YSER UNDER HEAVY FIRE.
British soldiers engaged in building a bridge under the falling of enemy shells. One of the great features of the advance that began on the Ypres front at the end of July, 1917, was the throwing of bridges across the Yser for the forward-moving troops.

and observation machines, wait until bad weather prevented the British warships from assisting the defence, and then break the pontoon bridges and sweep down to the river. This plan was executed on July 10th, when a heavy gale was blowing on the coast, and the British naval support was temporarily absent. All the formidable armament of coast batteries within range along the dunes was switched on to the mile of trenches held by a British brigade. For an hour the hostile guns swept up and down the British front, smashing breastworks and emplacements, and fouling the Englishmen's machine-guns and rifles with storms of sand.

Tragedy of the sand-dunes The destructive barrage moved on to the support line, broke up all the pontoon bridges, and continued to stamp backward and forward all day long, while German aviators flew down and poured machine-gun fire upon any men who remained visible among the battered sand-hills. The British land batteries were overpowered, in the absence of naval support, and about seven o'clock in the evening the hostile artillery encircled the two British battalions in a cage of fire. A strong force of German Marines then advanced, in crescent formation, between the ebb tide sands on the west and the Lombartzyde position on the east.

The British eastern flank was saved by a sergeant of the Northamptons. Though wounded, he swam the Yser, got round to the troops on the right, and warned them that the Germans were massing against them. Thereupon a bomb-stop was hastily thrown up, about three-quarters of a mile from the shore ; machine-guns were also got into position, with the result that the large force of German Marines were compelled to fall back at this point.

On the Nieuport side of the canal another gallant soldier swam across the water with a rope, and though under heavy fire, succeeded in so fixing it that a few survivors of the two trapped battalions were able to drag themselves across the water. Upon the remnants of the two thousand men, who had lived through the terrific day-long bombardment, disaster fell. Little groups of men fought to the last, without any chance of escape, and without any hope except that of a quick finish, nearly all the machine-guns being filled with or buried in sand.

The fighting lasted from seven o'clock in the evening until half-past eight. The last scene in the struggle, observed by the last wounded man who swam the canal, was that of six officers of the Northamptons, surrounded by bombing-parties of Marines, and fighting to the end with their revolvers. The enemy occupied the British position for the length of fourteen hundred yards, and a depth of six hundred yards. South of Lombartzyde he was driven out of the British lines by means of a counter-attack.

This tragic little episode was acclaimed by Ludendorff as "a great and magnificent success." Happily it was quickly eclipsed by a British aerial victory, in which a practical command of the air was at least temporarily regained by British aviators in the all-important Ypres sector.

A HERO OF THE NORTHAMPTONS.
Sergeant Benjamin Cope, the gallant soldier who swam the Yser in an attempt to save his comrades during the German attack at Lombartzyde on July 10th, 1917.

In spite of the enemy's thorough reorganisation of aircraft production works and flying corps personnel, he was defeated in the air and partly disorganised on land by bombing attacks upon his aerodromes, ammunition dumps, and railway-stations. The British effort in aeroplane and aero-motor production was not then adequate to the occasion, in spite of the urgent public warning given by Sir Douglas Haig in 1916. But British pilots, by their personal qualities, temporarily managed to break up formation after formation of German fighting machines, and thus opened out fields of work and attack for their scouts and bomb-dropppers.

The artillery battle began towards the end of the third week in July, and steadily increased in violence whenever the weather was clear. Strong reconnoitring raids commenced on July 25th, while the British bombardment was at times intensified so as to make the enemy imagine that a great infantry attack was imminent. In one raid, in the night of July 27th, the village of La Basse Ville was stormed by the New Zealanders, but abandoned next morning owing to strong counter-attacks.

All the while the fighting in the air grew fiercer. On July 29th thirty-one German machines were crashed or driven down out of control, at the extraordinarily light cost of only three lost British machines. Day and night the artillery battle went on, and at ten to four in the morning of July 31st, 1917, the great offensive was opened on a front of fifteen miles from La Basse Ville on the River Lys to Steenstraate on the Yser Canal.

A French force, under General Anthoine, operated on the left flank of the British army, and moved forward across the Yser Canal and the Dixmude road towards Bixschoote and the German position south of Houthulst Forest. Just below Dixmude the British army assailed Pilkem and all the swamps and low undulations eastward of Ypres, and some of the ground eastward of the Wytschaete-Messines Ridge.

The main objective consisted of an arc of small hills, rising like the half rim of a saucer, in front of the British valley positions around Ypres. The attack made south of these observation positions was of secondary importance. Sir Douglas Haig's intention was to grind the enemy down between Houthulst Forest and the village of Gheluvelt on the Menin road, between which points there was a crescent of comparatively high ground known as the Passchendaele Ridge. The ridge overlooked on one **British attack on Pilkem** side all the basin of Ypres, and on the other side it gave observation over the Flemish plain as far as Bruges.

In addition to the advantage of possessing the encircling ridge, the Germans had a series of important southernly buttresses at Hooge, Shrewsbury Forest, and Zandvoorde. These heights gave shelter against observation and direct fire from the Wytschaete-Messines Ridge, which was some four miles south-west of Zandvoorde.

Their main forces were on higher and drier ground, and their forward observation officers could observe the movements of British troops in the swamps, and instantly bring to bear upon them a curtain of heavy shell. They made the 5·9 in. howitzer the general weapon of artillery defence. The production of this gun had been enormously multiplied by methods of standardisation, as also had been the production of 5·9 in. shell. Thousands of cannon and howitzers were used against the British Army, and methods of increasing the velocity of shell of all kinds were employed. The 5·9 in. howitzer had become the mainstay of the German defensive system of field fortification.

This system had been altered in accordance with the lessons of the Somme and Scarpe River Battles. The enemy commander relied on a deeper zone of

FRENCH HONOUR FOR BRITISH OFFICERS.
General Anthoine, in command of the French army in Flanders, decorating Major Burkhardt and Captain Napier, of the British forces, with the insignia of Chevaliers of the Legion of Honour.

French official photograph.
FLYING MEN RECEIVE THE LEGION OF HONOUR.
The French commander in Flanders, General Anthoine, decorating Captain Heurteaux (who later shot the German airman who had brought down the great French flyer Guynemer) and Captain Fonck, for their exploits in the air.

garrisoned shell-holes and concrete forts, in order to impede and disarrange attacking infantry formations. There was no definite, well-marked, and connected network of trenches and communicating-ways as in the previous grand battles. Neither the long Hindenburg tunnel system nor the separate great cavern system was used as a backbone for the machine-gun defence. By June, 1917, Ludendorff ordered no new tunnels to be made and all old tunnels to be destroyed at the opening of a battle. His orders were not obeyed, as he afterwards complained.

To a considerable extent the aeroplane had destroyed the value of intricate lines of earthworks. Under the eyes of flying pilots these earthworks merely became easy targets for parks of opposing heavy batteries. The system of defence, therefore, had to be made as inconspicuous as possible, so that hostile guns were not able to register on them night or day for a week. The numberless craters, made by both masses of artillery, afforded the best means

of concealment, and into carefully-selected groups of these craters parties of machine-gunners and snipers were placed, often with a hidden concrete fort behind them as a backing.

Each fort was constructed with a very strong top, and with three very strong sides facing the approaches of assailing troops. But the fourth side, exposed to the fire of German guns, was usually thin, so that it could easily be penetrated by the guns of the defending army if the stronghold were stormed and occupied by British soldiers.

Formidable as these forts were, by reason of their extraordinary number, they did not form the principal obstacle to attack. The low-lying, stream-fed ground of approach was the supreme difficulty. It was swampy by nature in days of peace, when it produced luxuriant pasture and heavy crops. It had been rent and powdered, wildly tossed about and ploughed, deep into the subsoil, by thirty-three months of incessant battering by heavy artillery. All the drainage system was utterly gone. Old shell-holes had silted up and been re-excavated, filled again with mud, and again turned into craters.

Grave British disadvantages

In 1917 unusual torrential summer rains continued to make the great stretch of earthen porridge in the Ypres saucer more watery and deeper.

To this grave disadvantage of ground there was added a rather unaccountable disadvantage in weather lore. British meteorologists had special facilities in forecasting weather disturbances. Nearly all the cyclones arrived from the Northern Atlantic, and could be studied beforehand from Irish weather stations, and from wireless reports from ships at sea passing through zones of bad weather. From Iceland to Spain, with South-West Ireland as a centre of observation, the arrival of bad weather in Flanders could be generally forecasted with a useful degree of certitude.

It was of high importance to Sir Douglas Haig that all his large offensives should be undertaken in as dry summer weather as possible. This was necessary, to save his infantry from an arduous struggle with the mud before the fight around the enemy's positions occurred. Yet in regard to the weather, a succession of extraordinary

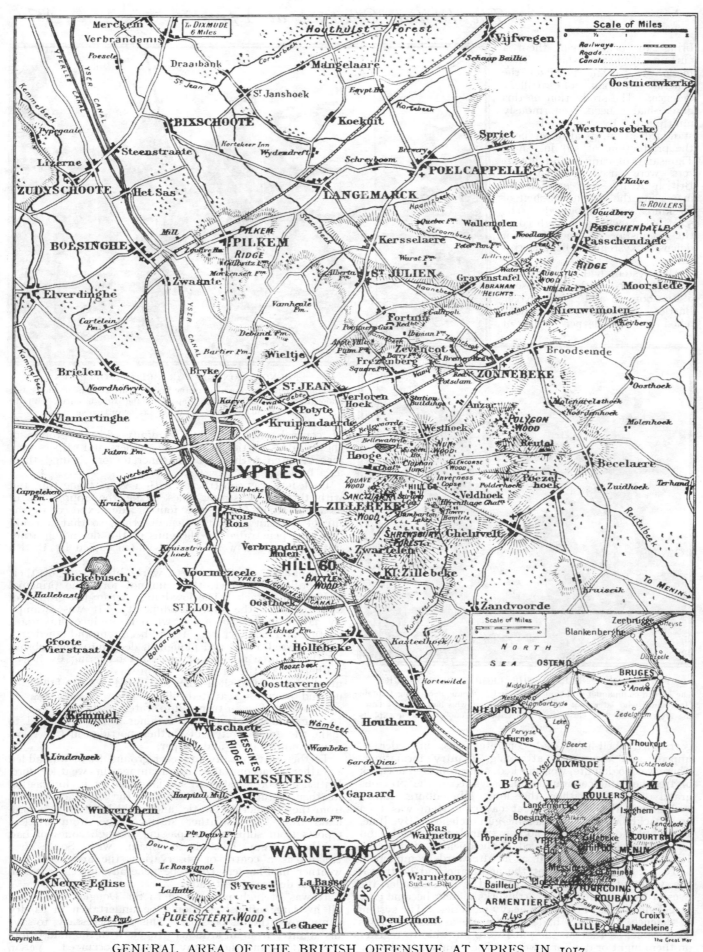

GENERAL AREA OF THE BRITISH OFFENSIVE AT YPRES IN 1917.

On July 31st, 1917, a great British offensive opened on a front of fifteen miles from La Basse Ville to Steenstraate. As a result of bitter fighting the whole of the ridge land in this district was captured by the Allies as far as and including Passchendaele, carried by the Canadians on November 7th.

misfortunes occurred throughout the campaign. It seemed that the British forces in Flanders were very badly served by British meteorologists, or that meteorology was neglected in planning the battles, or less probably that the British commander deliberately selected bad weather in which to attack, because he reckoned that it strained the enemy and hindered his movements of supply and ammunitioning to a greater extent than it impeded the movement of British troops, guns, and supply trains.

Success delayed by weather

It may have been that a very large extension and reorganisation of the British weather forecast system was required, and that the need for this important help to military operations was not foreseen in due time. The fact remains that success was considerably delayed from the end of July to the middle of November.

Sir Douglas Haig originally intended to open his Ypres campaign before bad weather was expected, but circumstances over which he had no control compelled him again to alter his plan. He had had to change his main scheme when General Nivelle was checked along the Aisne, and when he at last was able to break out at the Ypres salient, and prepare his principal campaign for 1917, he ran into the wet season. From July 30th to August 6th there was only one day without rain, and that day was a day of mist. During some of the most important operations, aerial fire control was almost impossible along the entire field of battle. Pilots had to skim over the ground like swallows, beneath clouds hanging two hundred to five hundred feet above the soaking lowland.

The special new arm of British military forces—the "tank"—temporarily lost much of its high value. These mobile forts could not be employed in any considerable number on the fenlike ground; only a few of them managed to escape being bogged and did some service. The British infantry had a terrible time. There were sectors in which the German forces were shattered by gun fire. They offered no resistance of a serious kind, but such was the state of the ground between them and the attacking troops that they escaped capture and had plenty of time to reorganise, receive reinforcements, and make a strong counter-attack.

Many British soldiers found themselves up to the armpits in mud. When comrades tried to pull them out the result was that the would-be helpers were pulled in. In one case two battalions took three-quarters of an hour to get over two lines of undefended trenches. Entire platoons were overwhelmed in bogs like quicksand, into which they slipped back when trying to climb out. When, after the great rainfall, all the hollow between Ypres and the German ridges was mapped out with blue colour, showing the ground covered by water, the battlefield was seen to be a lake, from which emerged islands and promontories of mud all overlooked by the enemy on the hills.

It would not have been worth while engaging in a pitched battle under such tremendous disadvantages, but for the fact that the massing of British artillery around Ypres was on a staggering scale. The British

guns in July, 1917, were many times more numerous than the German guns. In addition to this, British ammunition was also superior in quality to German ammunition. In particular, there was a certain British gas-shell against which the masks worn by the enemy gave only imperfect protection. The Teutonic chemists who began, against international law, the method of poison-gas attack had been overtaken at last by British chemists. It was at Ypres, in April, 1915, that the Germans had first employed chlorine fumes; and in July, 1917, upon the very positions which they had thus won, the British artillery poured a tempest of gas-shells of a novel kind.

The bombardment had opened in the ordinary way on July 18th, 1917, when General Sixt von Armin had deployed some seven divisions of the Fourth German Army around the high circuit of the Ypres salient. After eleven days of incessant British gun fire on all enemy positions and ways of approach, six of the German divisions were in such a state that they had to be relieved. The fresh divisions that relieved them were in turn subjected to a hammering far surpassing any they had experienced along the Somme. Day and night the shells fell; then came the quieter but more destructive explosions of the new British gas projectiles, that cut off reliefs and food supplies, and seriously weakened the holding forces.

On July 30th the bombardment became somewhat less effective. A thunderstorm broke over the battlefield. Rain fell heavily all day long, and continued in a drizzle during the night. Aerial fire-control of the British batteries became impossible, and the gunners could only go on firing at known targets by means of the map. The rain-screen, however, was not entirely to the enemy's advantage. Under cover of it the attacking forces on the northern sectors threw many bridges over the canal, which moated the German positions south of Houthulst Forest, and established bridge-heads on the opposite sides well in enemy territory.

Just as the glimmer of dawn appeared over Menin and Roulers, on July 31st, 1917, French, British, Australian, and New Zealand infantrymen waded forward between the flooded land below Dixmude and the misty river valley of the swollen Lys River. At the northern point a fine French force, containing men from Lille and Roubaix, crossed the Yser Canal, and captured the villages of Steenstraate and Bixschoote, on a front of nearly two and a half miles.

Pilkem carried by the Welsh

Along the canal south of the Frenchmen were the British Guards, who attacked the enemy's intricate system north of Pilkem village. Pilkem itself was carried by a gallant force of Welshmen. English troops in large proportion executed the great central attack, and, with splendid Scottish fighting men, pressed the enemy back towards Passchendaele Ridge and Zandvoorde Ridge. On the south, English troops also fought forward along the spur running from Oosttaverne, on which the Welshmen had got a footing in the Messines Battle. Then, below the British troops, the Australians advanced against a

[Canadian official photograph.
QUEER OBSERVATION-POST.
Observation-post ingeniously arranged by the Germans. It was on ground captured by the Canadians on the western front.

network of fortifications eastward of Messines, while the New Zealanders stormed into the village of La Basse Ville.

The French operation was conducted with uncommon skill and crowned with high success. General Anthoine, though little known to the general public of the allied countries, was one of the great men of the war. He distinguished himself during the most critical period at the end of August, 1914, when, as Chief of Staff to the army of General Castelnau, he took a leading part in snatching victory out of defeat by a flank attack delivered from the heights around Nancy upon the Bavarian army. After winning, with General Castelnau, the first decisive allied success on the western front, General Anthoine remained one of the mainstays of the French Staff, being continually engaged in important actions in the long parallel western battle. In April, 1917, he commanded the army that carried **General Anthoine's** Auberive in Champagne, and worked **success** up and over the highest hills around Moronvillers.

He became as expert in trench warfare as he had proved to be in open field manœuvres, and, as colleague to General Plumer, he displayed in a striking degree the genius of his race. His line originally ran northward from Boesinghe, by the cobbled highway along the Furnes-Ypres Canal. The Germans had erected strong fortifications on the western bank of the waterway, but General Anthoine completely wrecked these works by nine days' gun fire. On July 27th the German garrison abandoned their riverside system of defences, and retired across the canal. French patrols followed, and found the enemy so demoralised that they were able to penetrate into parts of the German second zone of defences around the village of Steenstraate.

On July 28th, without a struggle, the French army occupied the right bank of the canal and formed fifty bridge-heads there, while their pioneers brought up pontoons, and, under a continual storm of hostile shrapnel fire, erected fifty bridges and constructed magazines of bombs in the **The capture of** enemy's territory. Crawling, slipping, **Bixschoote** mud-plastered figures worked into the ruins of Steenstraate, and in three and a half hours attained their principal objectives, between the railway running to Bruges and the river flowing from Houthulst Forest.

French, British, and Belgian batteries from Dixmude to Boesinghe maintained a fierce smothering fire over all known hostile gun sites, and through the torrent of rain the northern French army worked along the road from Lizerne towards Dixmude, capturing the important bastion village of Bixschoote, together with the Kortekaert Inn, which became the connecting point between the British and French forces.

By two o'clock in the afternoon the men from Lille and Roubaix, with their comrades, had broken into the German defences to a depth of nearly two miles. The number of their prisoners was larger than their own total casualties. The conquered positions were of the highest value, as they formed both the rampart and the pivot of the British movement.

[*British official photograph.*

REPAIRING WAR'S BATTERED WAYS ON THE FLANDERS FRONT.

Working-party of British troops making good the ways over captured ground during an advance in Flanders in the summer of 1917, while beyond them their comrades were picking their way over the broken terrain on the way to the fighting-front. The awful state of much of the ground in the successive advances on this part of the line made work of this kind unceasingly necessary.

TAKING UP RATIONS

CHAPTER CCXV.

FOR THE FRONT LINE.

[British official photograph.

THE BRITISH OFFENSIVE AT YPRES AND THE BATTLES OF LENS.

II.—The Storming of Pilkem and Westhoek Ridges and the Struggle on Menin Road.

By Edward Wright.

British Guards' Drive over the Steenbeek—The Cockchafers of Berlin Caught by Gallant Welshmen—Importance of the Pilkem Ridge Conquest—Extraordinary Feat by Herts Territorials at St Julien—A "Tank" Comedy at Pommern Castle—Heroic Achievement of Lancashire Men—Scotsmen and Midlanders Battle Forward Along Roulers Railway—Terrific Enemy Counter-Offensive—How the Gordon and Cameron Highlanders Saved the British Centre—Westhoek Carried by Sherwood Foresters and North-amptons—The Day of the N.C.O.—Check to Advance in Sanctuary Wood—Mud, Blood, and Confusion—Terrible Conflict Along Menin Road Tunnel—Manchesters and Royal Scots Take and Lose Stirling Castle—Conquest of Hollebeke—One Middlesex Man Captures Enemy's Canal Position—Splendid Endurance of Australian Gunners—New Zealanders Take La Basse Ville—General Success of First Offensive.

I N the British preparations for the great offensive at Ypres the place of junction between the army of General Anthoine and the army of General Plumer was a delicate point. As in the Somme campaign, where the French Iron Division was employed to solder the international joint, it was expected that the enemy would make a remarkable effort, in his supreme counter-attacks, to strike between the British and French forces. It will be remembered that he had done this successfully in the Second Battle of Ypres in April, 1915.

He did not, however, even attempt any main thrust at the junction of Franco-British forces in the campaign of 1917. He was not allowed to do so. So violently and continuously was he attacked that, in the northern most critical sector, he could never win time and opportunity for a display of initiative. Moreover, the British force that connected with the French Army was particularly formidable in quality.

The British Guards— Grenadier and Cold-

stream, Scots, Irish, and Welsh—were placed alongside the northern Frenchmen at Boesinghe. The Guards followed the same methods as their French comrades. In the long preliminary bombardment they hammered the enemy from the waterside, between Het Sas and the Ypres-Bruges railway and the western approach to the Pilkem Ridge. Then, three days before the main infantry operation opened, they erected many pontoon bridges over the canal and established bridge-heads. At the dawn of battle they swung alongside the rapid and vehement Frenchmen, and keeping pace with them on the left, fought straight through every trench and fortified copse, capturing six hundred prisoners. Their bridges across the canal were strengthened in a few hours, enabling guns and heavy material to follow quickly.

As in the attack which the British Guards made on the high ridge above the Somme, there were scarcely any distinguishing features in the tract of rising lowland over which they fought. In the report in which he acknowledged partial defeat, Ludendorff afterwards called it the

[Australian official photograph.

OBSERVING OVER THE RUINS OF YPRES.

Observation balloon tethered above the fragmentary walls which were all that remained of the historic and beautiful old city of Ypres—centre of some of the severest fighting on the western front.

shell-hole forefront of the German line; but what he termed a shell-hole position was really the most intricate network of artificial defences that Teuton ingenuity and labour could construct.

In addition to belts of entanglement, earthworks, concrete block-houses, and other ordinary fortifications, the enemy had arranged, wherever ground permitted, a special kind of sniper's and machine-gunner's ambush. Craters left by exploding shells were turned into camouflaged defences by digging out the sides and covering the top with wire netting upon which hay and clay were laid. A high degree of courage was required of the Germans who manned these crater posts. Often they had to stand in water, and they were entirely without protection from shrapnel bullets and high-explosive shells. They remained concealed in the first part of the action and let the waves of attack pass over them. Then they **Ambushed snipers** came head and shoulders out and **in shell-holes** fired in the back of charging troops, raked the flank of passing forces, and tried to stop supports.

These shell-hole snipers and gunners could not have expected to survive, and many of them fought like devils. They killed wounded British soldiers in considerable numbers, but they also fought with extraordinary desperation in an honourable way. Often a single hand-bomb was sufficient to put the crew of a crater out of action. These advanced forlorn hopes of the German line, however, managed in places to do much damage and create spots of local confusion in the British plan of attack.

In the darkness, mist, and rain the covered-in holes were often overlooked during the first movement of advance, and although the British barrage killed or wounded many of the crater forces, sufficient survived to emerge in the rear of the attacking troops. Beyond, yet partly connected with the netted craters, were the blockhouses, which were especially formidable on dry ridges such as Pilkem, where they could be sunk into the ground without fear of drainage water getting into the entrance.

At one important point, by the Steenbeek River, the Guards were held up on the right of their line, so that their destructive barrage went thundering and flaming far in front of them, leaving some German positions untouched. This did not check the advance or cause an interruption in operations at the delicate junction point of the Franco-British armies.

Without the help of their artillery the Guardsmen assailed the enemy works. They stalked the German positions one by one, and rapidly cleared all the ground up to the stream. This they crossed at half a dozen points, and after establishing bridge-heads, went forward, like the Frenchmen, beyond their final objective, and captured several strong places that would have assisted the enemy in his counter-attacks. As in the case of the Frenchmen, their losses were compara-**The "Cockchafers"** tively small, and in spite of the rain **in Pilkem** and oozing water, they ended the day in the best of spirits.

The village of Pilkem, on the right of the British Guards, was held by the Fusiliers of the Prussian Guard, known as the "Cockchafers." The Cockchafer Brigade was in a very strong position. Outside the village the men had a trench, ten feet wide and twelve feet deep, while underneath the wreckage of houses they possessed large concrete-roofed shelters, stored with ammunition, shells, and trench-mortars. Mackensen Farm, Gallwitz Farm, Boche House, and Zouave House were some of the battlefield names of strong points in the Cockchafers' line.

The Welsh went up the ridge in waves, the Royal Welsh Fusiliers climbing up to the village, and the Welsh Regiment moving upward on the right. The Cockchafers had made a song about their own exploits, relating how they had chased the Belgians, broken the French, swept back the British, and destroyed the Russians. When Hindenburg had very difficult work to do—so the song ran—he called for the Cockchafers to carry it through.

They fought well, these three thousand men of the crack Berlin regiment, but some two thousand Welshmen fought better. The Germans stood their ground and engaged in a furious body-to-body fight. The result was that by the afternoon of July 31st Hindenburg had no Cockchafers left for any further difficult work. Most of them were dead or wounded, and six hundred of them were captives of the Welsh. The victors stalked, bombed, or rushed each block-house in their way, getting parties of Prussians as they went up the slopes of the ridge. They captured the headquarters of the hostile brigade, took the great village trench with comparative ease, and had their dinner brought up to them through the enemy's barrage at three o'clock in the afternoon.

Remnants of the 9th Grenadiers of the Prussian Guard and of the 3rd Lehr Regiment were also captured by the Welshmen, showing that the enemy had thrown in very strong forces in order to hold the ridge. The Welsh Fusiliers fought along the south side of the Bruges railway line, and, like their Cymric comrades, were not seriously checked anywhere on their field of operations. In the later stage of the advance the South Wales Borderers, along with some of the tireless Welsh Fusiliers, carried the British line up to the Upper Steenbeek River, alongside the ground won by the British Guards.

The Pilkem Ridge was a position of supreme importance. From it the enemy had dominated Ypres northward since the spring of 1915. Low though the swell of ground was, it was practically as valuable to the enemy as had been the Messines Ridge. It was the upper claw of the German pincers around Ypres. The frontal attack by the Welsh and the flanking thrust by the Guards were carried out in a perfect manner.

Amid weather difficulties that hindered artillery support, aeroplane control work, and the movement of infantry, all parts of the machine of victory acted together in clockwork fashion. The **Difficulties of** result was that the semi-encircling **the ground** movement by Frenchmen, Guardsmen, and Welshmen against the rear and front to the ridge was executed in classic perfection.

Had things gone as well in the centre as they did on the left flank, the battle of July 31st would have ranked among the grand victories of history. But in the central part of the high saucer ridge around Ypres the difficulties of ground were extreme even in dry weather, and appalling when there was a foot of water draining down to the bottom of the saucer.

The commander of the Fourth German Army followed the same defensive tactics that Prince Rupprecht's lieutenant worked out during the second phase of the Arras Battle. He placed very strong advanced forces in his fortified lines, and held still stronger reserve forces under cover of the reverse slopes of the long crescent of the Passchendaele ridge. At Pilkem, where he was assailed both front and rear, he could not bring his main battle divisions into action in a straightforward, sweeping manner. Much of the ground of approach there was held by Frenchmen and Guardsmen in the afternoon and evening of the fatal day.

But along the central line, of which Inverness Copse was the decisive point, and along the southern flank, of which Zandvoorde Hill was the observation pillar, the German commander had abundant room for movement, and only the blind, standing barrages of the British artillery to struggle against. The rain screened the movements of his principal battle forces, preventing them from being traced from the air and swept with exactly-placed hurricanes of shrapnel.

The roads were barred by British heavy guns firing by map, and movement was slow over the sodden fields. Yet, under cover of rain and mist and artificial smoke-screens,

Through desolation to victory: British cavalry passing through a ruined French town.

Pioneers draining the floods and laying duckboard tracks on the way to Passchendaele.

[British official photograph.

British infantry crossing a canal in the eastward push from Ypres to Passchendaele.

[British official photograph.

Highway of a nation's agony: British soldiers working on the Yser Canal.

[British official photograph.

Evening : London troops seeking their billet in a newly recaptured Flanders village.

[British official photograph.

Morning : British soldiers leaving billets in a badly shelled village near Boesinghe.

Reinforcements hurrying to the firing=line cheered by a trophy=laden working=party near Polderhoek Chateau.

Clearing the defeated foe from a formidable machine=gun position.

Victorious troops examining a captured German position in Flanders.

the battle troops of Germany managed to escape from the overpowering British artillery, and gather in force along the ridge, in much the same way as they had gathered along the Sensée and the Scarpe Rivers when the Third Army thrust against the Hindenburg line.

Never, however, did the courage of British troops burn with a steadier flame. The Hertfordshire Territorials won immortal honour, and the Durham Light Infantry, who fought onward when all their officers were out of action, also showed a majestic self-discipline that can never be forgotten. The men of London also finely distinguished themselves.

The Hertfordshire Regiment formed part of a gallant Territorial force that operated below Pilkem, and swept towards the village of St. Julien, over ground made famous by the Canadians in the Second (gas) Battle of Ypres. "Tanks" accompanied the Territorials, but were scarcely needed until Alberta Farm was reached near the village.

Over the rough ground of advance there was some stiff infantry fighting, which, however, went on with fairly regular success. When a wide band of uncut wire was met, a "tank" slid through the edge of the British barrage· and rolled up and down the entanglement, flattening it out, and driving the garrison behind into their dug-outs. Then, in the farm itself, the "tanks" so frightened the Germans that sixty of them surrendered to the travelling fortresses.

This was the most useful "tank" achievement of the day.· It enabled the Territorials swiftly to press into the village of St. Julien and to capture all of it by ten o'clock in the morning. Fifteen 5·9 in. enemy howitzers were taken, together with a large dump of 5·9 in. shell. The German batteries then threw an uncommonly heavy barrage upon the village, and exploded their lost ammunition dump, that went up with the effect of a land-mine.

Hertfordshires' heroism at St. Julien In spite of the enemy barrage, the Hertfordshire men, with some other units, continued their advance beyond the village. They arrived at another German trench, defended by four hundred yards of uncut wire, eighteen feet deep, stretched below a rise occupied by hostile machine-gunners. The Englishmen did not stop. Some went over the wire, some worked around it, and though the men of Herts lost the last of their officers, they won the position, took a considerable number of prisoners, and, with a sergeant as their commanding officer, consolidated, and again went forward to capture another group of Germans who were holding up their hands.

The advance, however, had been too rapid. A sinister rattle of machine-guns in the rear was heard by both Germans and Englishmen. A wide space on one flank was filled only by four Territorials, and the ground behind this flank was occupied by the enemy. On the other side there was a similar situation, with only just a few more Englishmen lining out into hostile ground. The Germans who had been holding up their hands seized their weapons, and even the prisoners in the occupied front trench tried to rise and overcome their captors.

Both prisoners and "hand-uppers" were shot down in scores, in time to allow the Territorials to meet the great counter-attack. The fresh German force came on in waves a hundred and fifty yards apart, and was completely beaten off. Nevertheless, the German machine-gunners in the rear continued to fire, and in the afternoon the men, who had lost all their officers and nearly all their non-commissioned officers, decided to cut a path back, across a tributary of the Steenbeek, to St. Julien village.

With their chaplain in their rear, carrying a wounded man, or dragging him when too tired to carry, the Territorials began to fight their way to the village, while holding off another counter-attack on their flank. The counter-attacking force cut in so deeply that they came within range of a group of German soldiers who, having made

an attack on the other side and failed, were coming forward to surrender.

Then was seen one of the most inhuman sights of the war. The broken German group had dropped its arms, and was covered by the rifles of the retreating Territorials. Yet the German machine-gunners on the other side were moved by so wild a fury that, instead of continuing their attack upon the Englishmen, they turned their guns upon their weaponless countrymen and shot them down. This senseless act of wholesale murder benefited the Hertfordshire men, and enabled them to continue their withdrawal. Thereupon, amid the confusion, the enemy artillerymen intervened in a similar access of disastrous brutality. Upon the entire scene of conflict they threw a heavy barrage of 5·9 and high-velocity shell. **German slaughter of Germans** In a general, blind fashion it swept the counter-attacking German forces on one flank, the broken German force on the other flank, and the small force of Englishmen sandwiched between.

Naturally, the German soldiers were utterly disheartened at being attacked by their own guns. While the murderers were being murdered, the Hertfordshire men remained alert, cool, and determined. With the help of a supporting force they fought their way back to St. Julien, and, when nearly all their ammunition was expended, the remnant of them reached the village.

St. Julien then formed the extreme northern angle of the British advance, and became the most critical point in the new line. It was a weak, improvised salient, subject to attack from both sides, and the enemy possessed, along the road running to Kersselaere and Poelcappelle, a good central line of supplies. Continually and desperately he attacked the diminished garrison, churning up the ruins with shell of all calibre, and delivering infantry storming attacks by day and night.

At British Headquarters it was thought that St. Julien had been lost. The Territorials, however, never gave up the village. They were shelled, gassed, and bombed from the eastern part, and compelled to retire into the western cellars, and there continually hammered and rushed. Yet they held on, though their messengers often could not get through, and no forward observation officer could watch the German assaults and arrange to turn his batteries upon it. It rained for days, causing a flood of water that added to the miseries of the little band of English troops. Still they held on to the storm centre of the entire battle-field, clinging to a ring of posts that afterwards became the jumping-off place for another victorious advance. In addition to the thirteen guns, which was the largest number of German pieces captured in any sector, the Territorials at St. Julien took one thousand prisoners.

On their right, between the Poelcappelle road and the Passchendaele road, there was a splendid force of Lancashire men, who set out from Wieltje towards the Hannebeek stream **Lancashires attack concrete forts** alongside other troops. The advance in this strip of farmland was very arduous, as the fields were closely dotted with concrete forts, ranging in size from the "pill-box," holding a couple of machine-guns, to large labyrinthine defences linked by covered ways and heavily garrisoned.

Every farmhouse was thickly concreted, and usually enclosed in ditches and concealed entanglements. In places the concrete was so thick that the shells of the British "heavies" could not damage it. The enemy's front line gave little trouble, as it had been wrecked, and the remnant of the garrison had retreated to the shell-holes behind it. But the undamaged forts had to be reduced gradually, by bombing-parties and Stokes-gunners, with occasional assistance from a "tank." The ground, however, was very sodden in the streaming hollow below the ridge, and some of the "tanks" stuck in the deep mud.

Plum Farm and Apple Villa were among the places in

EN ROUTE FOR A SPELL IN A REST CAMP.
Men of a Midland regiment entraining in the wet after a turn in the Flanders trenches. They were on their way back to camp for a well-earned period of rest.

German garrison retreated to the redoubt. Upon this stronghold one "tank" worked from the west, and the Germans, more through fright than determination, scurried back into the castle and, in the courage of despair, retook it from the English troops.

When the indefatigable "tank" again lumbered up to the lost castle, the Germans tried to slip back to the Redoubt. As their agility was much superior to that of the steel caterpillar, the remarkable game might have gone on for some time, but was **Pommern position** stopped by the arrival of more English **captured** infantry, who blocked all the bolt-holes and completed the capture of the fortress system in front of the hamlet of Fortuyn.

After the conquest of the Pommern position the Lancashire men again worked forward in successive waves, stubbornly fighting forward against desperate resistance, and swept at times by side gusts of machine-gun fire from the southern flank. Some of the troops on their northern flank were held up by uncut wire, so that the Lancashire men were much exposed on both sides as they went forward. Yet, when they reached their final objective, they,

this sector where "tanks" did useful service. But the great stronghold beyond the Hannebeek, known as Pommern Castle and Pommern Redoubt, was the scene of the greatest "tank" triumph. The fortress system was designed in the manner of Mouquet Farm, though stronger in construction. It was armed with a battery of anti-"tank" guns, and provided with communications between the redoubt and the castle and a southern formidable fortress known as Square Farm.

The English troops worked up to the stream, accompanied by a "tank" that had cleared up the wreckage of another farm. They took Pommern Castle, after a "tank" had worked through it and around to the back, and the

ADOPTING AN INDIAN DEVICE.
Canadian soldiers who made use of the Red Indians' "tump line"—a broad band round the forehead—in carrying heavy materials.

like the Territorials, were not content with their day's work, though their losses were heavy and the German artillery was firing at them in a terrific manner.

They marched out towards the Passchendaele Ridge, far away from all supports, and reached Wurst Farm and the high ground at Gravenstafel. Their situation then resembled that of the Hertfordshires beyond St. Julien. The last remaining officer of the party sent a message to Headquarters saying that his battalion was badly depleted and holding two fortified positions on the high ground by Wurst Farm. Three days passed before this message got through, and, in the meantime, the distant ground so adventurously held had been lost.

COMMUNICATION TRENCH THROUGH A VILLAGE.
British soldiers passing under a barricade built up of barrels and boxes, in a communication trench cut close alongside the houses in a French village. They were on their way to the front line, many of them carrying picks and spades as well as rifles.

The enemy began by making counter-attacks from local reserves. These were swept back. He then pounded the Lancashire position with whirlwinds of heavy shell, and made a continuous series of wave attacks, in which low-flying, armoured German aeroplanes took part. One tide of assault came down from the high ground on the right, while another surged continually upon the exposed left flank. The enemy was in such overwhelming numbers that it seemed impossible to prevent him from breaking through on both sides, and completely surrounding the remnant of the battalion.

Heroic rearguard action

In these tragic circumstances a retirement was effected by means of an heroic achievement ranking with the defence of Rorke's Drift. A hundred and thirty men settled as a forlorn rearguard in the ruins of a farm, which had once been an enemy fortress. There, with Lewis guns, rifles, and bombs, they broke the enemy in front, and enfiladed him on each side, while the main body of Lancashires retreated. One by one the little garrison was reduced, each man selling his life at the price of many Germans. In the end, there were only thirty men able to

[*British official photograph.*

WAYSIDE PITFALLS IN FLANDERS MUD.
Bringing up a water-cart along a track made of fascined tree branches and twigs in Flanders. One of the horses has stepped off the track and taken one of the wheels into the deep, clinging mud.

out against the fresh forces the German commander flung against it. German counter-attacks began, in the mist and rain, at 3 p.m. They were continued at 11 p.m. and again at 1.45 and at 7.15 the following morning. Infernal tempests of shell and shrapnel heralded each grand assault against the wet, tired troops. A few posts were driven in between St. Julien and the Zonnebeke road, but the line held firm.

Alongside the Lancashire men was a magnificent force of Scotsmen, who set out westward of Verlorenhoek, captured this village, and fought into Frezenberg. They continued on each side of the Zonnebeke road, with Square

[*British official photograph.*
WORK OF MERCY IN MUD.
Plucky stretcher-bearers near Boesinghe at times had to pass knee-deep through the terrible mud at their difficult task.

fight in the farm when it was entirely enveloped. They charged upon the enemy on their rear, and fought their way through, twenty of them falling by the way, and ten regaining the line near Pommern Castle.

Another small garrison, which was posted on the right of the line to cover the withdrawal on that side, fought with equal skill and steadiness, suffering themselves, but saving the battalion. In addition to infantry attacks, the little post survived two heavy separate barrages, and only when the Lancashires' line was established did the handful of survivors stab and bomb their way back.

In the afternoon the Germans tried to break into the Pommern Redoubt, but the thin, ragged khaki line held

[*British official photograph.*
"SPOTTING" FOR THE GUNS.
French and British officers engaged as artillery observers watching and directing the fire of their batteries during the forward fighting in Flanders in the summer of 1917. The man behind was in telephonic communication with the batteries.

Farm on their left and the Roulers railway on their right. Around Frezenberg the Germans had constructed one of their large underground fortresses, resembling the Hohenzollern Redoubt, but with improvements. Two of the "tanks" that were assisting the Scotsmen were ditched at that moment when their presence was urgently required by the hard-pressed infantry.

The Germans recovered some of their lost ground, and, seeing the apparently helpless "tanks," came out to capture them. But if the "tanks" were motionless their crews were not. They turned their guns upon the lines of muddy grey figures, while the Scotsmen came forward with their bayonets. Under this combination the counter-attack failed. The Scotsmen fought through the Frezenberg position and captured Square Farm, below Pommern Castle, and went on to two more enemy strongholds, which they broke into and captured. Among the Scottish troops were the Gordon and Cameron Highlanders, who were at last mingled together, alongside English troops, in a stand that saved the British centre.

Connecting with the Frezenberg position was the Ypres-Roulers railway-embankment. This had been transformed by the industrious enemy into a very formidable block-house system. Midland men were sent again to the Roulers railway, and after long and bitter fighting they managed to keep in line with the Scotsmen on the left and swing forward on their right with the **Great German counter-attack** Sherwoods and Northamptons towards the inn on the Westhoek Ridge. In the night the Englishmen and Scotsmen were hammered by shell fire and drenched with rain as they stood almost to the waist in muddy water in the shell-craters.

There they remained until the afternoon of August 1st, when the German commander launched his grand counter-attack. He had taken thirty-four hours to organise it ; but, when it came, the driving-power of it was tremendous. The Germans came down from the Bremen Redoubt, between Frezenberg and Zonnebeke, and from the high ground southward. It was a misty afternoon, and the mist was thickened by a smoke barrage employed by the enemy, with the result that the British barrage did not begin in time.

Behind the smoke, enemy machine-gunners on the spurs of the Passchendaele Ridge maintained a barrage of bullets upon the British line. British machine-gunners answered this fire when the Germans emerged from the mist and smoke, but, in a desperate assault, the line was pierced near the Roulers railway ; while the Scotsmen, in and around the railway-station, and the English troops, between Westhoek and the railway, were held down by the hostile barrage and in extreme danger of being turned around their breaking flanks.

The Gordons were terribly pressed, and about three o'clock in the afternoon of August 1st they were compelled **Young officer saves the line** to swing back and uncover the battalion headquarters, where the adjutant had turned out his staff to fight and defend the position. This officer gathered together all Gordons round about and held on to the station buildings, which then became an outpost to the left wing of the Highlanders, which was moved back to form a defensive flank.

As the Germans came on in great numbers the Gordons in the railway-station swept their rear with streams of fire. Yet, such was the mass of attacking men, that other waves of them regularly continued to surge forward towards the top of the crest, to which the main body of the Highlanders had withdrawn.

For three hours the enemy tried to achieve a decision. At six o'clock in the afternoon he was very near to accomplishing one of the greatest victories in the war by breaking the British line, storming back to Bellewarde Ridge and Frezenberg, and winning, beyond Verlorenhoek, more ground than the British had taken. Ypres itself was, for the third time, in peril. A young officer of the Gordons was inspired by the prospect of a great disaster, and, with the supreme genius of soldiership, he closed the broken line by an action very similar to that with which General FitzClarence had so heroically recovered Gheluvelt during the First Battle of Ypres.

[*British official photograph.*]

BELGIUM'S KING REVIEWING THE BRITISH GUARDS.
"Eyes—right !" King Albert, during a visit which he paid to the British western front in the autumn of 1917, reviewing the Guards Division. In November of that year the Guards fought with their traditional heroism during Sir Julian Byng's surprise attack on the Cambrai front, and in the subsequent counter-attack which somewhat modified the great result at first achieved.

The Englishmen who fought alongside the Scotsmen, and shared with them the honours of the Frezenberg and Westhoek battle, had a very difficult journey to the Westhoek Ridge. They set out in the darkness on July 31st from assembly trenches in front of Bellewarde Park. In the park the Germans had excavated a maze of works, fortified the Manor House and stables, and erected a chain of strongholds around the great lake. The British bombardment destroyed many of the enemy's western works, and drove the larger part of the garrison to the eastern side of the lake. The Sherwood Foresters and Northamptons, with their Midland comrades, met with little resistance at first. They took the rising ground within an hour, and, after some hand-to-hand fighting, formed up in a German support trench.

Beyond this trench the ground sloped into a swamp, in the middle of which rose the ruins of a farm known as Sieben House. Beneath the ruins were six feet of concrete, and below the concrete were cellars containing a large German garrison. **Capture of Sieben House**

These were induced to emerge, by means of bombs, and made prisoners, and the English waves of assault swept forward and up the Westhoek Ridge, where another conflict occurred around the inn at the centre of the village. It took only an officer of the Sherwoods, a sergeant, and a dozen men to capture the inn with the remnant of its garrison, consisting of five enemy officers and about fifty men.

The English line was then finally established on the eastern slopes of the ridge, which gave excellent observa-

[British official photograph.
KING ALBERT IN FRANCE.
The King of the Belgians chatting with General Birdwood during his visit to the British front in France.

He collected the Cameron Highlanders within call, and, with the remnant of his own men, charged down the slopes upon the mass of Germans. Every Highlander fired as he advanced, making gaps in the German line. The enemy stood up to the fire for about two minutes, but by this time the Highlanders were within fifty yards of the grey groups and coming at them with the bayonet. The Germans broke and ran. As they fled, the British gunners in the rear, who had not seen the first S O S signals by reason of the mist and smoke, suddenly intervened in the conflict, and lashed all the enemy's flying forces with a terrific storm of shrapnel.

The barrage surrounded a considerable number of enemy groups, but only one German officer and seven men came safely through the backdoor of the great cage of fire into the British line. Practically all the others were caught in a death-trap. It was, however, entirely a soldiers' battle during the critical period of the fight around the railway-station and the crest. It was the skill, courage, and discipline of a small, half-broken body of troops, lacking artillery support in an artillery battle, that prevented something like a repetition of the disaster which occurred by the Ancre at the opening of the Somme campaign.

[British official photograph.
AN AUSTRALIAN GUARD OF HONOUR.
King Albert inspecting the Guard of Honour formed by men of the Australian Force during a visit which he paid to the British western front in the autumn of 1917.

tion of enemy movements around Polygon Wood, Nun Wood, and Glencorse Wood. Only a little way beyond was the highest part of the crescent-shaped Passchendaele Ridge. From it Bruges could be seen, together with a large part of the plain on which the enemy had concentrated for the great trial of strength between Briton and German.

It was the splendid initial success of the Midlanders on Westhoek Ridge that roused the German commander and the High German Command to extreme determination. When night fell on July 31st it looked as though in its first leap the British Army had almost pushed open the gate to victory, leading to both the Flemish coast and the mining region around Lille.

Westhoek Ridge was one hundred and sixty-four feet above sea-level, and from its southern spur there was a distance of about one thousand yards to the rise known as Clapham Junction, which was about two hundred and ten feet high. An intervening plateau, partly covered eastward by Glencorse Wood, was about sixteen and a half feet higher than Westhoek Ridge, and thus blocked the view of Clapham Junction. Yet the very small distance between the height won by the Midland troops was a matter for high alarm at enemy General Headquarters.

Clapham Junction was the grand buttress of the system of defence based on the Passchendaele Ridge. Together with the lower Inverness Copse it formed the critical southern end of the great arc of observation positions and dry, sheltered gathering places stretching to Houthulst Forest. Had the weather been fine and the air clear, the

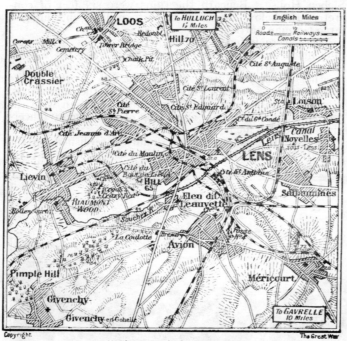

LENS AND ITS SUBURBS.

This plan shows the principal points in the defensive system round Lens, from Avion, captured by Midland troops on June 24th, to Hill 70, carried by the Canadians on August 15th, 1917.

superior power of the British artillery would have quickly broken a path for infantry attack across the intervening thousand yards.

Westhoek would have been a priceless fire-control station for direct work against Nun and Polygon Woods, and for flanking whirlwind bombardments northward and southward. In the prolonged period of rain and mist, however, the air became so thick that British gunners near Ypres could not perceive signal rockets sent up, a mile or so away, at Westhoek. Under these adverse, unexpected conditions the rapid conquest of Westhoek Ridge lost some of its immediately high strategic value. The fruit of victory could be ripened only by fine weather, and was lost for a time in rain and fog.

In the great German counter-attack of August 1st the fighting around Westhoek was a wild soldiers' battle on the British side. The German artillery had everything its own way owing to the mist obscuring the signals of the English and Scottish infantry. Worse than the German shells, however, was the German machine-gun barrage, directed from the dominating ground near Glencorse Wood southward, and from the eastern ridge.

The Midland men had little cover except the enemy's abandoned four-foot wide chambers of concrete, dotted in profusion about the Westhoek and Bellewarde

Ridges. For the most part they fought in the open with rifles, bombs, and grenades, even firing machine-guns from the shoulder. When the officers were killed, the men placed themselves under non-commissioned officers, and an eye-witness who went along the line in rain and darkness during the night of the great counter-attack reported that he found every platoon in its place, responding willingly to sergeants and corporals who were facing greater responsibilities than the commissioned officers had done during the British attacking movement.

Always the British non-commissioned officers had been the backbone of the Army, producing men of the stamp of Sir William Robertson, the Chief of the Imperial General Staff. They had little or none of the book knowledge of the officers, but their large, intimate, practical experience, their very close knowledge of their men, their native strength of character and native mother-wit made them gloriously adequate to the decisive work that fell upon them.

Since the Battle of Arras the troops had been thoroughly trained in the old standard of rapid musketry fire and open field manœuvre. Great as was their peril, they welcomed the opportunity of showing their initiative in open field conflict, and mowed the enemy down in great numbers. For example, there was a gap in the British line occupied only by one man with a Lewis gun. He caught a German company that tried to press through, brought down fifty of the men, and then held the others back until his comrades came up and re-established the line.

Initiative of British N.C.O.'s

All that the enemy, with his broken fresh forces, could manage to do was to climb the eastern slopes and form an emergency line of outposts in the craters and cellars at Westhoek. He took the highest point of the height and part of the village, but could not throw the tired and wasted Midland men off the ridge. The dominating observation points at Westhoek were, however, recovered by the enemy, and held by him for nine days, so that he was able to safeguard the southern end of his main system, on the Menin road in front of Gheluvelt.

Along the Menin road the Germans had pushed into Sir John French's former headquarters at Hooge, where they held a hill as high as Westhoek Ridge, a little more than two miles from the low-lying ruins of Ypres. Immediately south of Hooge was another wooded rise known as Zouave Wood, that connected with Sanctuary Wood, Shrewsbury Forest, and Battle Wood. Battle Wood had been reconquered by General Plumer in the Messines Battle, but the enemy was then very strong in reinforcements at this point, as his entire line was not at the time engaged.

In the Third Battle of Ypres, however, he was pressed severely all along his front, so that none of his deployed forces could come to the help of its neighbouring force. On both sides of the Menin road were wooded tracts, in which the trees survived the bombardment sufficiently to screen some lines of machine-gun redoubts. By Hooge there was a tunnel a mile and a half long, and at its numerous entrances were many undamaged surface

Hooge taken in direct attack

forts. The bombardment had wrecked the enemy's fire trench, which was generally abandoned, and his support trench was also ruined and almost emptied; but the wired and hidden shell-hole posts and "pill-boxes" behind the support trench served to check the advance along the Menin road.

The British attack was made on two sides. One force advanced along the high road direct to Hooge, while other forces battled forward along the south-eastern curve through Zouave Wood, Sanctuary Wood, and Shrewsbury Forest, east of Zillebeke. Had the south-eastern flanking movement proceeded as rapidly as it was designed to do, it would have swept over the enemy's rear at Hooge, just as he was breaking in front, and combined in a strong thrust upon the key position of Clapham Junction and Inverness Copse.

Owing, however, to the previous rainy weather, the ground in front of Zillebeke was soaking in water draining from the German heights above. The ground was littered with coils of rusty wire, and half-filled shell-craters were so numerous that there were only narrow footways between them. Even these passages were composed of such soft mud that the heavily-laden attacking troops sank ankle-deep at each step, as they went forward in the darkness. So many men fell into the shell-holes that some battalions became hopelessly mixed before they engaged the enemy. While floundering forward, they took two hours to cross a narrow strip of ground, and the result was that their time-table barrage thundered away into the distance, leaving the British without the protection it afforded.

[*Canadian War Records.*

STRENGTH THAT AVAILED NOT.
German machine-gun emplacement in the corner of a house shelled and captured by the Canadians. The concrete walls were six feet thick.

LAIR OF A MARKSMAN DISCOVERED AND CLEARED.
German sniper's post made of 3 in. Krupp steel, cunningly concealed in a sunken track and roofed with vegetation-covered earth—one of many similar lairs discovered and cleared by the Canadians in ground from which they drove the enemy.

NO MOVEMENTS ALONG THIS TRACK DURING DAYLIGHT

In the direct attack Hooge was taken with comparative ease, but most of the troops at this point had the Westhoek Ridge as their objective, and swerved away north of the road, with the Sherwood Foresters and Northamptons. The other British forces on the left near Zillebeke, with a line of fortress hills between them and the Menin road, could not make the decisive junction at the appointed time. When the British barrage went too far ahead, the surviving members of the German garrisons emerged from their retreats and fought with resolution and skill. Some of them picked off the British officers with rifle fire; others waited near a "pill-box," and with a machine-gun unexpectedly swept the platoon that was working round the concrete fort. Whenever they were dangerously pressed, the Germans withdrew from one cluster of craters to another, and again made use of their special knowledge of all the defensive possibilities of the ground. Two and a

half hours were spent in reaching the second objective of Sanctuary Wood, and when this was gained, the Germans renewed the conflict from the high ground along the Menin road. Here it was that the hostile machine-gun fire grew very fierce, as the line of forts above the highway tunnel came fully into play against the groups of confused and half-broken British forces.

Nevertheless, the attack was continually pressed. Officers who had lost their men collected other little groups and stragglers and led them upward. Parties of men who had lost their officers were rallied by lance-corporals and privates, and directed against the high tunnelled road; while single-handed Lewis gunners charged the German forts, firing as they ran at the slit in the concrete, which was also at times a target for British hand-bombs. The large mass of ruins on the high ground was the scene of a fight that lasted for hours, and as the Germans had some intact telephone communication, they were able to bring their artillery to bear upon the ground they had lost.

The British troops, on the other hand, lost touch with the headquarters, as their runners could not get through the hostile barrage. When at last there were only one or two officers left in the fighting-line, and they were merely struggling onward with little knowledge of what was happening elsewhere, the brigadier at headquarters, who was also ignorant of the situation sent his brigade major, a young captain, to find out the situation. Going up to the hottest spots, the captain found the mixed units still loosely struggling against enemy machine-gun fire. He reorganised them and, collecting a band of mixed riflemen, took them to the high ground where there was a good field

German counter-attack broken

of fire, moved them over the Menin road, and came across the entrance to the tunnel which ran under the highway. He descended, found only four Germans there, captured them, and so cleared out the tunnel, from which the enemy had already been driven at the eastern end. The tunnel then became an excellent shelter for the British forces. The enemy's counter-attack was broken and the general muddle straightened out.

South of the tunnelled road, and east of Sanctuary Wood, was Stirling Castle, rising on a hill about a hundred and ninety-six feet high. At the northern end of the hill was Clapham Junction, with Inverness Copse behind it. In spite of the confusion and delay in the early part of the attack, the Manchesters and Royal Scots succeeded, with other troops, in reaching Stirling Castle and taking it, after an extremely hard, fierce, and toilsome fight.

Stirling Castle was once a pleasant château surrounded by outbuildings and a park, but British and German guns had completely wrecked the buildings, **Stirling Castle captured** and German engineers had poured concrete upon the cellar roofs and constructed underground strongholds among the trees on the slope. As the Scotsmen and North Countrymen advanced across the valley, machine-gun fire swept them incessantly from neighbouring wooded rises as well as from the slopes they were attacking.

Amid this barrage of bullets, the deadliest of all curtain-fire, the German infantry made small counter-attacks which, though not definitely successful, were strong enough to impede the progress of the thin, slow, wasting waves of assault. The British, however, held on, and after several rushes, the Manchesters and Royal Scots stormed into Stirling Castle, while their comrades captured the trenches around the main fortress.

The victors were spent by their victory. Their labours and their losses during the confused periods of battle left them with insufficient strength when the enemy began to counter-attack under cover of rain and fog that blanketed the scene from the **Germans recover hill position** British artillery. German boys of one of the younger classes were launched upon the circular walls and avenues of Stirling Castle. Unlike many of the recruits of their class, the youngsters fought like tiger-cubs, and with dashing gallantry recovered the critical hill position. They thus made Clapham Junction and Inverness Copse secure against the turning movement that menaced the entire German main line of defence.

Months were to pass before the British Army, so near to success in the afternoon of July 31st, was again in a position from which it was possible to turn the Passchendaele Ridge. The torrents of rain in the first week of August washed out the original plan of attack, and, by preventing a victory in the Messines fashion, resolved the struggle into a close-locked wrestle that swayed for nearly four months over a single mile of ground between Hooge and Gheluvelt.

Below the undulating woodland battlefield south-east of Ypres the enemy held the southern part of the Ypres-

[*Canadian War Records.*]

TRIUMPHANT RETURN FROM THE CREST OF HILL 70.

Canadians who fought at Hill 70 on their way to rest camp after being relieved, headed by their band and attended by an advance guard of French boys. The famous observation height on the northern side of Lens, against which Sir John French's offensive failed in 1915, and which had since been strengthened by every device known to the enemy, was carried by assault by the Canadians in the morning of August 15th, 1917.

[*Australian official photograph.*]

PEACEFUL PATHS ON THE WAYS OF WAR.
Troops being taken up by motor-omnibus to the Ypres salient in readiness for the advance. They were passing one of the long trains of mule-drawn waggons which were ever passing to and from the front.

Comines Canal and high road. The village of Hollebeke formed the base at the end of his line at the Oosttaverne spur, below which the valleys of the Roozebeek, the Wambeek, and the Blaupoortbeek streams broke the land into small ridges. There was a screening by copse of the low rises, and all the broken ground was cleverly organised by the enemy with camouflaged defences.

English troops made the attack upon the Hollebeke sector, conquering the ground to a depth of a thousand yards and taking the village with comparative ease. It was underlaid with cellars and underground shelters, and full of Bavarians, but these were bombed into submission. The trouble occurred in the obscurity of dawn, when the first waves of attack swept over small bunches of Bavarians lying under wire-netted shell-holes.

Hollebeke village taken The snipers attacked the Englishmen from the rear, and not only shot down our fighting men, but slew the wounded lying in the mud. They were men of the 6th and 8th Bavarian Regiments, and but for their merciless barbarity they would have commanded the admiration of the men whom they surprised. They held out nearly all the day behind the English troops, and undoubtedly checked the operation.

Nevertheless, they were at last bombed and bayoneted out of their wire-netted holes, and then the line of concrete caves stretching along the railway that runs by the Comines Canal was taken by a single bomber of the Middlesex Regiment. When all the attacking line was held up, the bomber crept round the railway embankment, killed the men of the machine-gun redoubt, and enabled other bombers to reach the concrete shelters and drop bombs through the ventilating holes. Moreover, in spite of the rear attack by the Bavarians on

the English fighting-line, the casualties of the victors were light.

Had everything gone well in the British centre in the direction of Passchendaele Ridge, it would have been an advantage of importance to obtain more room at the southern flank around Hollebeke, as ground had been obtained on the northern flank around Pilkem. The enemy, however, was very strongly posted in the south, with Zandvoorde and Kruiseik hills as rear observation positions and shelters of concentration. It would have needed another great turning movement along the flats of the River Lys to have shaken the Germans at Zandvoorde.

Against this movement the men and artillery of the Sixth German Army around Lille would have violently reacted, with the result that the British battle-front would have had to be prolonged to the Lille Ridge. Thousands more guns, **German strength at Zandvoorde** fifty million more shells, and perhaps a quarter of a million more men would have been needed, and they could not be obtained without thinning out the forces gathered around Ypres.

The British Commander-in-Chief preferred to maintain at full strength the armament and effectives along his northern fifteen-mile line of attack. The movement he launched from the Wytschaete-Messines Ridge was, therefore, only subsidiary to the main thrust directed immediately from Ypres. Not only was Zandvoorde Ridge neglected, but the English, Australian, and New Zealand troops between Hollebeke and the River Lys were not set the task of gaining all the Ypres-Comines Canal. They moved forward for little more than three-quarters of a mile between La Basse Ville and Hollebeke.

In the circumstances it was well that their objectives were within short range and narrowly limited, for the

[*Australian official photograph.*]

WAR-WROUGHT DESTRUCTION AND DESOLATION.
Views of the ruins of the once-beautiful town of Ypres, as seen from one of its shattered buildings. A British convoy was passing along the devastated street below.

enemy was formidably prepared to meet them in the undulating lowland between the Comines Canal and the Lys River. Although completely dominated by the Messines-Wytschaete Ridge, the German forces had entrenched themselves with amazing industry and magnificent skill. They had been allowed ample time between the Messines and the Ypres Battles to construct new works of defence, artfully concealed from British observers on the western ridge.

Two bodies of English troops assailed the copse-screened ridges between the three little rivers south of Hollebeke. Before the attack they had already pushed into the wood, and, when the grand battle opened, they rapidly overran the enemy's underground concrete works, but were then held up by a machine-gun barrage. The **Difficult task of the** Australians, who attacked between **Australians** Warneton and the approaches to Houthem, had as extremely difficult a task as fell to their lot in the Messines Battle. The artillery of the Sixth German Army enfiladed them on the right by the Lys River, while the guns of the southern wing of the Fourth German Army pounded them in front. The land consisted of small fields, ditched and hedged, and in the hedges the enemy fixed concealed entanglements, so thick that it was very hard to cut them by hand. He had also the usual multitude of crater posts, netted over and camouflaged, with concrete shelters in great abundance. Then, slight as were the swells and knolls he occupied, they were sufficient to shelter, especially on their reverse slopes, some very powerful works that to a considerable extent escaped the destructive fire of the British and Australian artillery.

At quite a short distance from their assembly trenches the widely-spaced platoons of Australians felt the enemy clinch vigorously across the lower part of the road running from St. Eloi to Warneton by Gapaard Farm. There was a terrific conflict around the wreckage of a mill, rising on a knoll near the Lys River. After the Australians had captured it by hard fighting, the Germans returned in the evening, under cover of a smashing barrage, threw out such a succession of waves of counter-attack that they encircled the windmill and compelled the Australians to surrender it. In turn the Australian artillery battered the ruins and ploughed up the ground. Then, towards midnight, their infantry came out again, and with bomb and bayonet recaptured the rise and the rubble of the mill.

In the meantime some of the Australian guns got into difficulty. The guns had been ordered to advance at a stated time, in accordance with the plan of the infantry movement. Along most of the front the batteries went forward smoothly and punctually behind their victorious foot-soldiers, taking less or little more than an hour between ceasing fire in the old positions and coming into action in the new positions. At one point, however, close to the German first-line system the infantry was held up, yet two brigades of artillery, **Bombed by German** apparently not being aware of the **aircraft** situation, proceeded according to the prearranged time-table.

As the leading batteries began to fire over the ridge, the enemy, who was still holding portions of the height beyond, saw them, and concentrated a storm of shell upon them, while the pilot of a low-flying German armoured aeroplane tried to drop bombs upon the guns, missed them, and turned his machine-gun upon the gunners.

Five other German machines, specially designed for infantry and artillery attack, sailed over the ridge and attacked with bomb and machine-guns, while many more spotted for the overwhelming mass of 5 9 German batteries. Machine-gun fire swept the Australian gunners in continual bursts from positions they could not trace. Finding a Lewis gun and a Vickers gun left on the ground, the Australian artillerymen rigged them up so as to beat off the German machines, and collected signallers and batmen with rifles to help against the hostile airmen. Then the gunners went on with their work. The shell fire increased as the day wore on, but the Australian batteries carried out their orders as if they were on a practice ground.

In La Basse Ville the New Zealanders encountered equally strong opposition. The wrecked hamlet by the Lys, on the railway line of Warneton, had been taken by them before the battle, but relinquished under a strong counter-attack. At dawn on July 31st the New Zealanders again drove over the site of the hamlet, and though they found nothing remaining of it above ground, the cellars contained a strong garrison of machine-gunners and bombers, who desperately tried to stem and break the assault. For fifty minutes the conflict swayed over the concrete honeycomb. When the New Zealanders succeeded in mastering the enemy, they could not in turn take to his underground shelters to escape from the storm of German shell. The cellars were so choked with bomb-shattered bodies as to be uninhabitable.

Three times in the course of the day the Germans returned in renewed strength, but only once did they penetrate into the ruins. They were then smashed out once more, and their later attacks were broken by artillery and rifle fire. All the intricately organised region around was cleaned out by the victors of Messines. One New Zealand battalion bayoneted a hundred German snipers in camouflaged shell-holes, the work on this sector being admirably executed, with light casualties to the attacking force.

Regarded as a whole, and in spite of blinding weather and bad ground, the first phase of the Third Battle of Ypres was a very promising opening of a grand campaign It was reported at the time that the German dead found on the conquered field, together with the six thousand prisoners taken, made a total of enemy forces permanently put out of action which was higher than the number of British killed, maimed, and slightly injured soldiers.

Comparatively few enemy guns were taken, for the enemy brought these for- **A cauldron of** ward at night, and withdrew them to his **death** rear before dawn. He still seemed to be more concerned about saving his artillery than economising his man-power. Undoubtedly his fully-developed new system of defence, by means of crater positions and innumerable small block-houses, tended to economise his man-power during the early stage of the battle. There were few large targets for the British siege-guns, and comparatively few men in action against the first waves of British infantry. Everything possible was done by the German Staff to make its machine-gun fire, from protected or concealed positions, a deadly barrier against numerous bodies of British infantry.

On the other hand, the British Staff was not checkmated by the enemy's laborious and skilful development of the old machine-gun defence. On July 31st and August 1st, 1917, the German commander was compelled to bring out on the open field between Bixschoote and La Basse Ville considerably more than a hundred thousand of his infantry forces. They were first swept by rifle fire, by Lewis gun and Vickers gun fire, then bombed at close quarters, and finally overtaken by a prolonged and searching hurricane of shrapnel.

This method of wearing down the enemy was ghastly for both forces. Terrible as had been the blood-bath on the Somme, it was a lighter ordeal for civilised man than the cauldron of death between Passchendaele and Ypres.

The test to which Ludendorff submitted the French race at Verdun scarcely compared in nightmare intensity with the test that Sir Douglas Haig imposed on the German race at Ypres. Heavy was its cost to the flower of manhood in all British Dominions, but the Scots commander sternly went on with his awful work until Passchendaele was won and the enemy so fixed between Gheluvelt and Houthulst Forest that his weakened line southward seemed to lie open to an extraordinary surprise attack.

[British official photograph.

THE LANGEMARCK VICTORY AND THE MENIN ROAD CHECK.

I.—From the Repulse at Glencorse Wood to the Upper Steenbeek Battle

By Edward Wright.

Failure of the Great German Counter-Attacks—In and Out Conflict at Hollebeke—Lancashires Recover All Westhoek Ridge—Unsuccessful Action in Glencorse Wood on August 10th—Gallantry of Bedfords and West Surreys—The Slaughter in Polygon Wood—Battering-Ram Attack and Suction-Pump Defence—Ludendorff Creates a Mass of Manœuvre—Sir Douglas Haig Strives to Wear It Down—Effect on Western Front of Russia's Military Bankruptcy—Racing for Victory Against German Troop Transport System—Splendid Canadian Victory at Hill 70—Resumption of Ypres Offensive on August 16th—Success of Northern French Army at Drei Grachten—Grim Comedy at House of Good Cheer—Reitres Farm Captured by Lewis Gunner—Complete Failure of German Boy Soldiers in the Bog Battle—Somerset and Cornwall Light Infantry Sweep into Langemarck—Strange Adventures of a Somerset Subaltern.

AFTER the opening of the Ypres offensive on July 31st, 1917, there was a pause of a fortnight in the main operations of the Allies. This was not due entirely to the weather. The continual rainstorms and mists were partly an advantage, in that they screened the forward movement of guns and war material, the building of new roads, and the relief of the troops that began the battle. As against this the work of our infantry was hampered. The swampy ground became more watery; the shell-holes filled, and the lowest pastures and woods were covered with a foot of water. The enemy thereby obtained a vast moat in front of the middle part of his fortified ridge.

In his continual counter-attacks, however, he suffered badly. He had in many places to advance over the boggy ground in order to strike. The result was that even when he succeeded in breaking into any new British forward position he was practically at the mercy of the strong British reserves operating from comparatively firm ground. For instance, throughout the morning and afternoon of August 2nd

the German commander launched large forces against the English and Scottish line from St. Julien to the Westhoek Ridge. In every case the waves of counter-attack were broken up and dispersed without any hand-to-hand fighting.

After this repulse the pivoting point of St. Julien village, which the English Territorials were still holding in part, was entirely reconquered, and more ground was won north-west of the village. In the meantime the southern base of the new Ypres salient was subjected to intense bombardment at Hollebeke and along the Comines Canal. On Sunday morning, August 5th, the German infantry swept out and back to Hollebeke, and captured the village, but were in turn pressed and broken by the victorious British counter-attack. On Sunday night another German movement against Hollebeke was crushed before the oncoming Germans were able to reach the English line.

By this time fresh British forces had relieved the divisions that opened the battle. On Westhoek Ridge the Lancashire Fusiliers and North Lancashires, with the Cheshires and other southern battalions, resumed the

[British official photograph.

"TANK" AWAITING THE ORDER TO ADVANCE.
One of H.M. landships at its "jumping-off place" on the western front. The crew, while awaiting the anticipated order to advance, were indulging in a few moments of relief from their somewhat cramped quarters.

(British official photograph.

FIRST CAR ACROSS.
Bridge blown up by the enemy and rapidly reconstructed by British engineers during the advance in Flanders.

July 31st. It was a maze of snipers' nests and machine-gun positions. Between many of the trees were hidden barbed-wire entanglements that could not be seen until they were reached. Where no concealed entanglements were erected, there were death-traps in the form of open pockets, crossed by machine-gun fire, with wire all round them except at the entrances.

A fierce British barrage stamped about the wood, but did not put the garrisoning force out of action. The men from Bedford, from the Surrey-side suburbs of London, and the country around Croydon might have been excused had they failed to climb the wooded hill. Yet they both climbed it and descended the reverse slope,

work of the Sherwoods and Northamptons. The line was continued towards Glencorse Wood by the Bedfords and West Surreys. General Plumer desired to become master of the whole of the Westhoek Ridge in order to launch his second great offensive. The troops had lain out all night in the rain, under a furious bombardment that seemed to show the enemy had observed what was impending. In spite of the furious shelling, the English line went forward at dawn on Friday, August 10th, with irresistible valour.

The Germans fought well. They quickly rallied after every English drive, and when entirely surrounded often fought to the death. Each cellar had to be taken by bombing rushes against machine-gun fire, and, when the concrete forts were broken, the garrison often came out into the open ground and battled hand to hand. For three hours the struggle for the height went on. It ended with the conquest of a stronghold at the southern end of the ridge. The concrete work was battered by Stokes guns and then rushed on either flank. The remnants of the 54th German Reserve Division were pushed off the crest, those who still clung to the lower

Germans driven off Westhoek Ridge ground eastward being practically defenceless against the plunging fire from the victorious Englishmen on the heights. Gunnery observation positions were rapidly established, with appalling consequences to the enemy.

In the meantime the Bedfords and West Surreys and other English battalions attacked the still more difficult forested height of Glencorse Wood. This intervened between the Westhoek position and the enemy's chief base of resistance on the Menin road. The high wood had been refortified since the unsuccessful British attack on

(Canadian War Records.

STRONG POINT DESTROYED BY CANADIAN ARTILLERY.
One of the concrete forts established by the Germans in the vicinity of Lens. The concrete had been reinforced with iron girders, but the position had been effectively smashed by preliminary artillery fire before the Canadians went forward and captured it.

menacing the enemy directly in his key position to the Lille and coast line. The Englishmen broke through the wire entanglements with their rifle-stocks, leaped at snipers and gunners behind the trees, and killed or routed them with the bayonet.

Hard as it had been to gain the Glencorse Hill, it was very much harder to hold it. The German commander could not at any cost allow this dominating point to be lost at this early stage of the campaign. He possessed thousands of guns, with an enormous stock of shell ranged in a short but very deep arc between Zandvoorde and Passchendaele. Hundreds of German artillery observing officers surveyed, from higher positions, the Westhoek and Glencorse Hills, and received signals and messages from their withdrawn infantry line. As soon as the situation was clear to them, they brought the greater part of their gigantic artillery power to bear upon the two miles of new line the Englishmen had gained.

It was a day of clear air, and as such had been selected

for the local British advance. When the main mass of German guns tried to smash up the little victorious English force and cut it off from all supports, the yet more powerful concentration of British artillery worked at extreme speed to save the Lancashire men and their comrades. Large formations of fighting, scouting, fire-controlling, and low-flying machines soared over the thundering and flaming inferno.

The Germans were uncommonly strong in the air, having recovered from their previous defeat. A strong westerly wind and dense clouds made the task of the British pilots very difficult, and the German pilots crossed the British line in many places, and also attacked British bombing and spotting machines. All the best German airmen were concentrated round Ypres in a grand attempt to blind the British artillery.

In this they did not succeed. They lost more than thirty machines and two observation balloons, as against the British air losses of sixteen machines. The vital work of directing the British artillery fire proceeded in a successful manner. In a single day the aeroplane-guided guns silenced seventy-three hostile batteries, and exploded eighteen ammunition stores. Several times in the course of the grand artillery duel the fire of the German guns,

during the turning-points in the general action, was actually perceived to diminish in intensity. The diminution could not have been caused by any pause in the work of the German gunners. Instead of being followed by a sudden resumption in full strength, the slackening of the volume of fire showed a regular regression until nightfall.

The enemy had then to replace some three hundred guns, completely broken or partly damaged. He drew on his artillery reserve both in men and materials, and by labouring strongly all night made a fresh show of full strength the next morning. This was the critical characteristic of the Ypres campaign, until the complete weakness of Russia and

[Australian official photograph.
GERMAN MACHINE-GUN POST.
Looking out through a captured enemy machine-gun emplacement strongly built of concrete and timber in Flanders.

action of the Bolshevists released most of the hostile artillery forces in the eastern theatre of war.

Each forward movement of the British infantry provoked a tremendous conflict between thousands of British and German guns, ranked on either side mile after mile behind each other. On many rainy days and dark nights the opposing artillerists were able to change the sites of batteries that seemed to be known to the enemy, and bring up more guns and more gunners ; then, on the next clear day, they reopened the artillery duel from many new positions. It depended upon the spotting pilots, and the fighting pilots who defended them, to discover the enemy's artillery forces and direct a storm of shell upon them.

When this was done, the infantry was protected against a process of mechanical extermination, and, if other circumstances were favourable, was able to hold on to the line it had gained until relieving forces deployed to continue the ghastly, indescribable grind of conflict between the two principal industrial nations of Europe. Until large quantities of their guns were definitely released from the Russian front, the German gunners, though possessing abundant shell, laboured under a comparative disadvantage in the number of their pieces.

British artillery superiority

The mass of artillery on both sides was, however, so enormous that the comparative superiority of British ordnance did not immediately and continuously afford any marked relief to the advanced British infantry forces. There was also at times a falling-off in British air superiority which affected the artillery work.

When the Bedfords and West Surreys captured the important hill position of Glencorse Wood, the enemy directed upon them an infernal hurricane of shell fire. The troops had not only topped the crest and taken all the wood on the other side, but had pushed the enemy back some two hundred yards towards the main Passchendaele Ridge. The enemy gunners knew to a foot every position in the ground they had lost. They ploughed up the wood with a fire more intense than any known in the Somme Battles.

Then their storming battalions returned from Polygon Wood, Nun Wood, and the upland about Inverness Copse,

[Canadian War Records.
TAKING A PEEP WITHIN A CAPTURED STRONGHOLD.
Part of an enemy fort constructed of concrete and iron girders in the neighbourhood of Lens. The Canadian artillery had been well registered on it, and done considerable damage, before the Canadian infantry advanced and drove out or captured such of the German garrison as remained alive.

thrusting at the front and on both flanks of the English battalions. Two attacks were beaten back, but others followed in rapid succession, until about seven distinct grey waves had surged, ebbed, and returned into the hump of blasted woodland. The fighting was so incessant and so confused that it was almost impossible to separate the enemy commander's efforts into a series of operations. He simply fed his men forward, first in battalions, then in brigades, until by pressure of numbers he bore the Bedfords and West Surreys back to the western edge of the Glencorse Wood.

In this retirement the flank of the Lancashires on and around the southern end of the Westhoek Ridge became exposed to a side attack. But the men of Lancashire did not lose their critical ridge position. They were largely saved by a happy call for artillery support made by the commanding officer of the Lancashire Fusiliers. He saw only some seventy Germans, coming forward on his left, to recover one of their gun emplacements. From this he rightly deduced that a general attack **German infantry** was imminent, and sent through a **waves broken up** message for the guns. A great curtain of shrapnel and high explosive was flung over Polygon Wood just as the German troops were moving out for action. They were brought down in full career.

British guns of every calibre were turned upon Polygon Wood and Nun Wood; 15 in. and 12 in. monsters, miles behind the lines, got on the large target. The 9·2 in. and the 8 in. guns answered the call in large numbers, together with the 6 in. and the 4·2 in., making salvo after salvo of registering shots, followed by the long and overpowering roll of drum fire. Six times in the afternoon and evening of Friday, August 10th, the dense waves of German infantry emerged into the horrible curtain of British shell fire, wavered under it, and broke up into dazed parties.

The remnants wandered about the open fields below the ridge, where they were shot down by the Lancashires and Cheshires on Westhoek Ridge. The English troops also maintained a widespread barrage of machine-gun fire from the high position they occupied. When night fell, with the enemy's artillery blazing away with dreadful

power, all the ridge was still held, except the extreme eastern part at Glencorse Wood.

The strength shown by the enemy along the Menin road positions, on the right of the line of the Bedfords and West Surreys, was prophetic of his main course of action throughout the campaign. He held more determinedly to the end of the Passchendaele Ridge than the French Army at Verdun had held to Dead Man Hill. The early check to the English forces in Shrewsbury Forest had given the German commander time to organise Stirling Castle, Clapham Junction, and Glencorse Wood into most formidable outworks of the main German system of defence around Inverness Copse, Herenthage Château, and the high ground in front of Gheluvelt.

The German commander employed a kind of suction-pump defence against the British battering-ram attack.

[British official photograph.
LIGHT ON THE ROAD TO VICTORY.
British soldier attending to an oil lamp near the fighting area. In its small wooden case the lamp served to give a guiding glimmer of light, in one direction only, to the advancing infantry during the obstinately contested Battle of the Menin Road.

He could not help losing some of his forward positions whenever the British ram struck with full force, but he always endeavoured, by answering whirlwind bombardments and rapid storming actions with fresh forces, to pump out the bodies of British troops from his forward positions around Inverness Copse, and thus resume the struggle on much the same terrain.

The question was whether the wear on the battering-ram was greater or less than the wear on the suction-pump. In actual terms of human life the conflicting processes were horrible. The marvel was that either Briton or Teuton stood the **Battering-ram and** unparalleled, prolonged strain. Both **suction-pump** undoubtedly were fighting men of the highest order, possessing a power of endurance beyond any calculation made in days of peace. They greatly surpassed the quality shown by the Japanese in the Manchurian War.

The German Command sometimes had to employ very harsh methods of discipline and bring up some of its forces under armed guards. Nevertheless, this method of action proved effective. It enabled the defence to be maintained for many months, and, although the cost in man-power was very heavy, the German system endured until the strain on it was relieved by the open, complete bankruptcy of the military power of Russia.

It was on this event that General von Ludendorff

[British official photograph.
KEEPING THE LINES IN COMMUNICATION.
Signalling-post, near the firing-line on the British western front, keeping in communication with a support line. Many forms of visual signalling were employed where telephoning was impracticable or interrupted. The man at the telescope was engaged in reading the answering message.

speculated. Possessing many agents in the new Russian Government, he was able to foretell the dissolution of Russia with a fair degree of certainty. This enabled him to go on sacrificing men in tens of thousands around Ypres, in the confidence that he would have large reinforcements available for removal from the eastern theatre wherewith to open the winter campaign.

Naturally he was well aware of the preparations of the United States. Although in Press communications he ridiculed the American effort, in order to calm public opinion in Germany, yet in his strategy and general military arrangements the capable German dictator fully allowed for the American factor.

This became, indeed, the unseen but dominant feature in his view of the situation. In the spring of the year he had regarded the submarine campaign as the master factor

[*British official photograph.*
SPEAKING BY FLASHES OF SILENCE.
Trench signalling-point on the Flanders front. The two British soldiers were engaged in communicating with a support line by means of a system of flashes from an electric lamp, which was connected with a portable battery placed by them in the trench.

[*British official photograph.*
"WIRE" THAT HELPED INSTEAD OF HINDERING.
British soldier testing the telephone-wires somewhere near the front line in France. Dwarf poles were employed, which just sufficed to carry their complement of wires clear of the ground, and so served to minimise visibility for the enemy artillery observers.

in the last phase of the war. He had then thought that the murderous pressure exerted undersea would compel Sir Douglas Haig to press forward and attempt a complete break-through at the cost of a million men or more. When in July and August, 1917, the total monthly British casualties, serious and light, in all fields of war showed that the actual attrition of British man-power was being very skilfully kept down, Ludendorff had to augment by more furious and longer battles the wastage of his own men in order to inflict heavier losses upon the British troops.

Ludendorff a Westerner

Ludendorff had become a Westerner. He was still hopeful of achieving a decision on the western front and ending the war with the complete triumph of Germany. The suggestions of a negotiated peace made by his puppet politicians in August and September, 1917, were designed merely to undermine the resolution of the British, French, and Italian peoples, the German people being meanwhile saved from revolutionary and pacific influences by the rigorous domestic action of the German war-machine.

In spite of all appearances, Ludendorff was confident of success. He converted Hindenburg, the East Prussian, into a Westerner, and inspired the Kaiser with the hope that the Hohenzollern would yet practically become the

lord of the world. His aim was to wear down the mighty British Army in France and Flanders in a campaign lasting from the summer until the autumn. Then, when the unenlightened peoples of the Grand Alliance thought that the striking power of Germany was exhausted, he meant to open a new German offensive in the west, directed against the French or British lines and conducted by an infantry force likely to amount to nine hundred thousand men. Ludendorff expected that the armies of the British Empire would be defeated before the United States could arm, train, and transport to France her first million recruits.

A strong propaganda was organised throughout the German Army and Navy by the chiefs of the military caste and the coal and steel magnates. Although this propaganda was modified in appealing to the rank and file, in order to make it appear that Germany was still only fighting for a reasonable peace by negotiations, the officers who carried out this extraordinary affair revived among themselves all the old ideas of August, 1914, regarding a practical universal dominion of the Teuton. Gradually a general lust for world-power was excited anew throughout the Army, while the German working men were inspired with a deadly envy of the better-paid British working men by means of a Social Democrat evangel of hate.

Propaganda of Pan-Germanism

Early in the year Sir Douglas Haig had been almost as confident of forcing a decision as Ludendorff was in the late summer. In fact, the British commander had published his opinion in an interview with some French journalists. This, however, occurred before the Russian Revolution, and long before the final disaster to Brussiloff's armies in Galicia. When the Teutons recovered the capital of Bukovina on August 3rd, 1917, the plans of General Pétain, Sir Douglas Haig, and General Cadorna had to be altered in accordance with the catastrophic situation on the eastern front.

Each of the western Commanders-in-Chief endeavoured to snatch some important advantages from the enemy before the German and Austrian forces could swing over in full strength in men, guns, and ammunition against the Entente armies. On August 19th General Cadorna opened

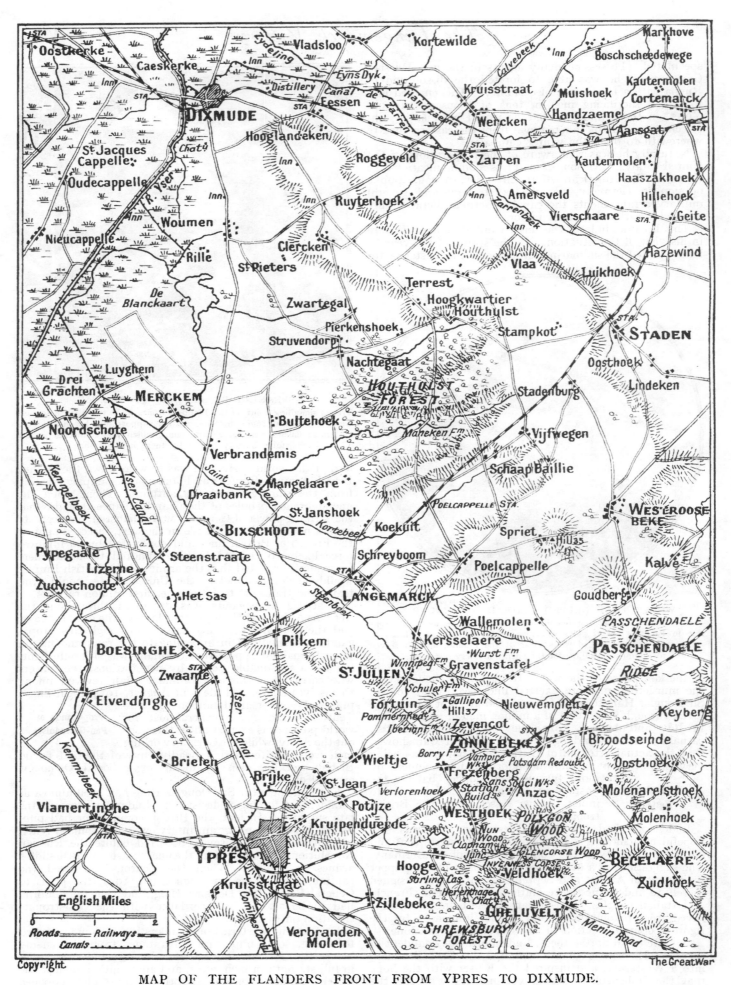

MAP OF THE FLANDERS FRONT FROM YPRES TO DIXMUDE.

Showing the area of the fierce battle, to the east and north-east of Ypres, which preluded the capture of Langemarck on August 16th, 1917. Some of the severest fighting took place along the ridge country immediately to the north of the Menin Road—about Glencorse Wood and Polygon Wood.

an offensive from the Carnic Alps to the Adriatic, and pressed on to the Bainsizza Plateau. The day after the opening of the new Italian campaign the French Army advanced from Verdun and threw the Germans back almost to the line from which they had started in February, 1916.

In co-operation with these strong movements Sir Douglas Haig attacked the Germans vigorously in two sectors—at Lens and at Ypres. The temporary effect of these three thrusts was to deprive the Central Empires of their mass of manœuvre, and prevent

Allies attack on three fronts them from undertaking for the time any fresh offensive, by compelling them to engage a considerable part of their general reserve. It was, perhaps, hoped by the three Allied Commanders-in-Chief that they would be able to wear the enemy reserves down to such a point that his reinforcements from the Russian front would be insufficient to supply him with a fresh mass of manœuvre.

If such a design were entertained, it must be regarded as having eventually failed. In September and November, 1917, Ludendorff succeeded in creating two strong masses of manœuvre, first on the Italian and then on the British front. Thus the almost simultaneous allied efforts at Ypres and Lens, the Aisne, and Verdun, and along the tablelands of the Isonzo did not achieve any immediate decisive results, and the subsequent sudden rupture of the Italian lines tended to have a checking influence upon the main offensive of the British Commander-in-Chief.

Meanwhile, the tremendous struggle for the Passchendaele Ridge went on. On August 15th the Canadian Army Corps attacked, with fine impetuosity, the German defences around Lens. It shifted its main thrusting power from the southern inundations at Avion, it relieved the British forces about Loos, and struck at the famous Hill 70, against which the Londoners and the Scots, the Guards, and the 1st Division had gallantly failed in Sir John French's offensive in September, 1915.

The assault was made under surprise conditions. There was only a brief bombardment of the enemy's positions at four o'clock in the morning. Before the sky was clearly lighted the Canadians went over the top on a front of four thousand three hundred yards, thrusting into Lens on their left, storming over Hill 70 in their centre, and taking Bois Rasé and part of Bois Hugo on their left.

The whole of the two industrial suburbs of Cité St. Émile and Cité St. Laurent was captured. The Canadians, at one point, penetrated nearly a mile into the German defences. The recapture of Hill 70, up the slopes of which the London Irish had dribbled a football in the old offensive, while alongside them the pipers played on Scottish battalions, proved quite unexpectedly to be an easy affair.

The defences were intricately strong. The irregular ground was a lacework of trenches, knotted with many machine-gun redoubts and other concrete works, all thickly wired and swept by crossing fires. The local German commander had been so confident of this hill fortress that he had garrisoned it largely with very young recruits. These lads, however, were not of the same fibre as the tiger-cubs that had recently regained Stirling Castle at Ypres.

The new British missile of barrels of running, flaming oil frightened the German boys more than any Teutonic flame-projector ever dismayed British troops. Comparatively few of the lads were captured, because they fled before the hand-to-hand combats began. Older German troops tried to stand their ground, and the Canadians did not win all along the line without some fierce and stubborn actions. Yet, in a general way, the vehemence of the assault resulted in a rapid victory. One Canadian, who walked back wounded in the thigh, said an extraordinary thing : " I enjoyed the show," he remarked, as he was lying in a miner's cottage awaiting his operation ; " it was a fair treat ! "

A remark like this from a soldier, aching with a serious wound, and awaiting chloroform and the surgeon's probe, spoke more for the moral of the victorious corps than any eloquent speech by an unwounded man. The commander, General Currie, who was an estate agent in August, 1914, and who controlled forty thousand men newly trained in arms, had decisively defeated, on one of the best-known battlefields of the modern world, the Army of that military State whose main business for a hundred and fifty years had been war.

At Vimy Ridge the long-trained professional officers of

[*British official photograph.*

HOME COUNTY HEROES AFTER A FIGHT.
Group of men of a Surrey regiment who were engaged against the Germans in the fighting east of Ypres. They fought amongst the mixed English County battalions in the Battles of the Ridges, over extremely difficult country, and, as it was recorded at the time, " behaved magnificently."

Germany could at least find some unction for their wounded pride in the fact that they had been overthrown by an English professional soldier of long experience, Sir Julian Byng ; but in regard to the loss of Hill 70, they had to admit that a Canadian business man, with a couple of divisions of Canadian farmers and working men, had so rapidly learnt all the arts of war that he was master of the strongest defences German ingenuity could devise.

Immediately after the victory the German artillery turned the lost ridge into a volcano of flame-shot black smoke, and smashed up the lost Cités (or mining villages) with heavy shells that **Canadians occupy** came screaming across the wilderness **Hill Seventy** of bricks and slag-heaps. By this time not a Canadian could be seen on the hill or among the miners' cottages.

The victors were sheltering in the great concreted dugouts from which they had driven the enemy. By their successful frontal attack the men of the Dominion threatened to take the whole of Lens by a turning movement between Loos and Hulluch. Their advance brought them against the front and partly against the flank of the Cité

northern defences of Lens, with the object of stone-walling any farther Canadian advance. But the Canadians did not attempt such a movement. Their real work was accomplished. By aggravating the menace to Lens they had disturbed the plans of Ludendorff and compelled him to detach part of his great central reserve.

Yet the German Commander-in-Chief correctly foresaw that he could not weaken himself around Ypres in order to strengthen himself at Lens. He therefore drew on that part of the reserve likely to be needed on the French front. As soon as this was known, General Pétain thrust forward on either side of the Meuse and gained a very important victory at Verdun. Thus

[Canadian War Records.

WAR-WROUGHT DESOLATION.
Ruined lock on the Ypres Canal, a waterway of peace which became an important barrier in the war.

St. Auguste, which the Scotsmen had just reached in September, 1915, but failed to hold, because a couple of supporting divisions came up too late, too tired, and too hungry to deliver the final stroke of victory.

On August 14th, 1917, the Cité St. Auguste was no longer the last line of the enemy's defence. Eastward of it was a series of equally strong positions, and there was a large German reserve ready for rapid transport to any weakening sector. Part of this reserve was hurried towards the

[French official photograph.

PROVIDING FOR ONE OF THE PRIME NECESSARIES.
British soldiers engaged in pumping and filtering water of the Yser for use of troops on the Flanders front. The water supply of the army in the field was under the supervision of the medical and sanitary services, and no water was permitted to be used for drinking purposes that had not been sterilised.

[British official photograph.

IN PREPARATION FOR A RAPID ADVANCE.
Men in a British trench on the western front making and fixing scaling ladders, in order to facilitate "getting over the top" when preparing for a projected raid on the enemy lines.

in the Verdun advance the Canadians indirectly took a very important part, even as they had played at Courcelette, on the Somme, a very helpful rôle in the defence of Verdun.

Although the Canadian demonstration did not draw enemy forces from the Ypres battlefield, Sir Douglas Haig again tested in a great pitched battle the German army around the Passchendaele Ridge. Early in the morning of August 16th, the day after the Lens Battle, the British and French forces advanced between the Houthulst Forest and the Menin road. On the northern wing the army of General Anthoine was admirably successful.

The Frenchmen moved along the flooded Steenbeek River towards the great inundation below Dixmude. The ground was a morass, islanded by floods, and stretched in a tongue of mud to Drei Grachten, which was a junction of Flemish canals. Owing to the shattering power of the French barrage little resistance was encountered in this naturally difficult peninsula. Only in two isolated masses of fortified ruins, Champaubert Farm and Brienne House, did the German garrisons try to make a determined stand. Their positions seemed to be impregnable. The garrisons were able to bring their machine-guns to bear right over the low-lying swamp that the French infantry had to traverse. But, as they flung out a terrible, plunging, raking barrage of bullets, the Frenchmen splashed into shell-holes and saved themselves. For a few minutes hundreds of French guns, heavy and light, shelled the farm and the house. Even with this terrific barrage to help them, the French soldiers did not move, and the shelling went on until the garrison of Champaubert Farm hoisted the white flag. Then, without further loss, the French infantry collected prisoners in both the farm and the house, and began to repair the broken German works against the enemy's great counter-attack.

General Anthoine, however, did not allow his foes even to attempt to return to the long slice of ground they had lost. Strong German reserves had been gathered in Houthulst Forest in anticipation of the Franco-British

[British official photograph.
EN ROUTE FOR REST.
After a bout of fighting at the front British soldiers were taken by 'bus to camps behind the line for recuperation.

[Canadian War Records.
PLENISHINGS LEFT BY LOOTING GERMANS.
Scene in a village near Lens from which the enemy had been driven. The Germans had carried away with them the best of the furniture they had been able to find in the place. Canadian officers were inspecting the pathetic assemblage of articles that had meant "home" to the exiled villagers.

some strong resistance at the fortified position of Au Bon Gîte, where the concrete works were in places ten feet thick, and the entrance was closed by massive steel doors. The fortress, manned by some fifty Prussians, rose on the eastern side of the Steenbeek, and commanded a considerable stretch of country.

The heaviest shells had been unable to damage it, and it became the refuge of the German outposts, when these were driven back by the attacking troops. After the Englishmen had

resumption of the offensive. Yet there was no answering movement from the large undulating forest. Yard by yard it was swept by British and French guns, and in this process of mechanical slaughter the northern body of fresh German forces was so shattered that it could not be brought up into the fighting-line. The French troops continued to advance to Lilas Farm.

South of the shattered forest was the important village of Langemarck, by which ran the railway line to Staden and Bruges. The Upper Steenbeek River ran below Langemarck, and the Saint Jean Kortebeek stream ran above it. A region of ooze and waterlogged craters extended eastward from the Steenbeek, beyond the line that had been won by the Guards and the Welshmen on July 31st. The ground had been muddy in the opening movement, and the long rains had made the swamp in front of Langemarck a mixture of bog and pond. The roads of a century of peace had disappeared in a chaos of shell-holes, and the village was only a clump of grey or blackened ruins, girt by rusty wire entanglements.

In the morning mist and battle smoke the village was hidden, and the attacking forces of Cornish and Somerset Light Infantry and English County regiments were compelled to advance so slowly that enemy machine-gunners were able to bring their deadly little weapons into play between the barrage and the infantry assault. There was

[British official photograph.
ANTI-TRENCH-RAID GATE.
For success in trench raiding rapidity of movement was always essential. At various parts of the British lines easily-closed gates such as this served to hinder and break up enemy raiding-parties.

PPP

surrounded this strange house of good cheer they could not find any kind of opening through which a bomb might be introduced.

All the morning and the afternoon a party of troops sat around the fort, with bombs poised in their hands, and at last their patience was rewarded. The great steel door was cautiously opened by the Prussians. In came a shower of bombs, and before the door could be closed the Englishmen were inside.

Reitres Farm, rising in front of the lake by the manor-house of Langemarck, was a still more formidable work in concrete of impregnable thickness. Its machine-guns commanded the ground between Langemarck and the Steenbeek, and raked the thin lines of muddied figures during all the first part of the advance.

Thigh-deep in the morass, the Englishmen continued to work close up to the fortress, which was at last taken by

Lewis gunner takes Reitres Farm

a single Lewis gunner. He had carried his gun through the swamp as carefully as if it had been a baby, for fear the mud should foul it. When he was near enough to attack, he crept up to a short rushing distance of one of the enemy's machine-gun loop-holes ; thrusting in the muzzle, he worked his drum round, playing about the interior, until one of the surviving twenty Prussians inside pushed a piece of white cotton out of another slit in token of surrender.

Another line of forts along the railway was then captured, together with the station buildings and some battery pits. The enemy's main trench system formed a rough crescent, sweeping half a mile behind the village and dotted with snipers' nests and machine-gun boxes and redoubts. The ground was held by a Prussian division, behind which was a fine Würtemberg division, which had fought with great determination at Le Transloy, on the Somme. The Würtembergers were beginning to relieve the Prussians when the British offensive was resumed, but most of them were curtained off by the British barrage during the struggle for Langemarck.

The Prussian division was largely diluted with boys, who, like the other German lads of eighteen years of age at Lens, were not good fighters. Days and nights of mud and rain had washed the courage out of them, and, although they possibly would have made a dashing charge if brought fresh into the battle, they were unable to endure the long, slow agony of the swamp campaign. When they broke, the older veteran soldiers were quickly defeated, in spite of the fact that a considerable number of them sold their lives dearly by plastering themselves all over with mud, crouching in shell-holes until the first waves of assault had passed, and then shooting the Englishmen in the back.

Against some serious, isolated efforts of resistance Langemarck was carried with uncommon rapidity in the

British capture Langemarck village

circumstances. The condition of the ground eventually told as much against the enemy as against the English. The Germans were not able to fight and run away. They could have ran away had they started very early and gone through the British standing barrage in their rear, but they could not stand and fight for a time at close quarters and then withdraw. The deep, sticky mud trapped them. During the morning the commander of one German brigade launched a counter-attack with one of his battalions. Only forty of the men, however, came within fighting distance, and they were annihilated.

In addition to the Prussian and Würtemberg divisions, a third force of some eight thousand men was deployed round Langemarck by the enemy commander. It was the 79th Reserve Division, and it suffered more terribly than the young Prussian brigades. Some pieces of German heavy artillery were found embedded in the swamp by the river and around the village, and a remarkably large number of German trench-mortars was taken. The enemy had been using his trench artillery in place of his field artillery, in order to save his main armament from capture.

He did not, however, save it from destruction along the Lower Steenbeek line of French and British victories. The larger proportion of his artillery was temporarily or permanently put out of action, with the result that the barrage with which he attempted to stay the advance of the allied troops around the Houthulst Forest was unexpectedly feeble.

The Somerset Light Infantry and the Duke of Cornwall's Light Infantry, with the Rifles, were the conquerors of Langemarck. The Somersets went well beyond the village, northward towards the hamlet of Schreyboom. Along the road was a line of concrete block-houses, whose machine-guns continued to fire on the British troops in the village. A subaltern in the Somersets promptly collected a squad of twenty men to end this machine-gun barrage.

The party surrounded the first redoubt, broke it open with bombs, and extracted thirty prisoners. Their own casualties numbered fourteen. Nevertheless, the subaltern resumed operations with the remaining six Somersets, and encircled the second redoubt. The young officer flung two bombs through a narrow window, and, as they produced no effect, he bombed the steel door.

Finding it too strong to be burst open by hand-bombs, he madly hammered on the doorway with his fist, shouting to the Germans to surrender. This, most strangely, they did. The great steel plate swung backward, and forty-two grey-clad figures came out with their hands up. Inside the block-house was found a wounded Yorkshireman, who had been captured along the Steenbeek some days previously. There were eight machine-guns in this last German block-house, and some of them were worked by an hydraulic lift.

After the conquest of the block-houses the Somerset subaltern raced other Germans down the Schreyboom road, plugging them with his revolver as they ran. Afterwards he collected

Intrepid young Somerset subaltern

a mixed squad of Somersets, Yorkshire Light Infantry, and Rifle Brigade men, and occupied an exposed advance post all the following night with scarcely any ammunition.

Between Langemarck and St. Julien the advance was less successful. The English troops in this sector of the Steenbeek battle met with determined resistance round Kersselaere and Winnipeg Farm, on the road from Langemarck to Zonnebeke, and around the brook-moated stronghold of Schuler Farm. By bitter fighting in the great streaming swamp they won ground to the depth of a thousand yards, and approached Wurst Farm, which had been reached by the Lancashires in the first offensive.

In the afternoon, however, the advanced troops were compelled to draw back to the thousand-yards limit and establish themselves on good defences. Not only did the enemy begin to counter-attack in remarkable strength, but the right flank of the English troops became unfortunately exposed, owing to a serious disaster on the British centre.

For all along the upper course of the Steenbeek, running by Spree Farm, Iberian Farm, Borry Farm, Vampire Works, Potsdam Redoubt, Sans Souci Works, and Nun Wood, Englishmen and Irishmen suffered a defeat comparable with the tragedy of the Ancre action in July, 1916. By unhappy chance the Ulstermen, who fought so magnificently and yet so vainly along the Ancre, were equally unfortunate in the Upper Steenbeek battle. Alongside of them was a Catholic division, which had shared the honours of the Wytschaete victory. They also were overwhelmed and thrown back.

Finally, in the southern part of the line, by Nun Wood and Inverness Copse, the Londoners were also defeated.

Engineers bridging a Flanders waterway, undismayed by a shower of bombs from the air.

Galloping British guns through the shell=damaged Grande Place of a French town.

[British official photograph.

Ammunition column going up to the front past a heavy battery sited beside the road.

[British official photogr

British cavalry watering their horses in a captured village while ammunition waggons go forward.

[British official photograph.

Opening the fourth year of war: General Horne addressing his troops after a solemn service.

[Australian official photograph

Australian infantry filing along a shell=tortured road to relieve the front=line trenches.

[British official photograph.

Highland Territorials jumping a German trench when attacking on the Cambrai front.

[British official photograph.

East County troops snatching a meal in captured trenches of the German second system.

GERMAN PRISONERS BEFORE

CHAPTER CCXVII.

[Australian official photograph.
A CAMOUFLAGE SCREEN.

THE LANGEMARCK VICTORY AND THE MENIN ROAD CHECK.

II.—From the Advance by St. Julien to the Attack on the Passchendaele Ridge.

By Edward Wright.

Enormous Strength of Enemy's Main Block-house System—Only Direct Hit by 12 in. Shell Able to Break Enemy's Armoured Concrete Works—British Infantry Left Unaided Amid Hostile Forts—Inniskillings Capture Hill 37—Irish Rifles Mowed Down by Bavarian Redoubt—Despairing Message from Dublin Fusiliers by Bremen Redoubt—Heroic Effort of Ulstermen between Winnipeg and Gallipoli Positions—Tragic Victory on Hill 35—Only Two Ulstermen Left to Stand Against German Counter-Attack—Peculiar Artillery Advantages Obtained by Enemy's System of Shell-Proof Defences—German Armoured Aeroplanes Swoop Down on Irishmen—Irish Line Pierced—Temporary Success of London Men in Nun Wood and Polygon Wood—German Counter-Attacking Forces Win Back Lost Ground—General British Defeat in Central Sectors—Failure Partly Due to German Aerial Reorganisation—Rekindling Race Fanaticism in Enemy—Heightened Moral of His Forlorn Hopes—Fresh Canadian Successes at Lens—Clash of Infantry between Walls of High-Explosive—Failure of Grand German Counter-Offensive against Canadian Army Corps.

THE general situation on the western front seemed less favourable to the Allies on the night of August 16th, 1917, than it had been on the night of July 1st, 1916. In the Somme offensive the enemy's defences were penetrated at a highly critical sector, and in spite of the failure at other points, he remained exposed to a slow, outflanking movement between Fricourt and Montauban, which was steadily continued until the entire system of defence was outflanked and rolled up.

In the Ypres offensive, on the other hand, it was only a secondary and comparatively unimportant advanced line of the enemy which had been forced in the north, between the Yser Canal and the outskirts of Houthulst Forest. The forest itself remained at the end of the year a cover to the main German position on the northern part of the Passchendaele Ridge, and as an enfilading fire position from which the British centre could be swept. No really decisive effort was possible by French and British forces in this direction. All they did was to widen the base of the Ypres salient, protect it from a

[Australian official photograph.
"THE GATEWAY TO THE BATTLEFIELD."
Avenue of truncated trees which led to the firing-line on the western front. The soldiers were very prompt in giving special names to points along the front, and many of these took fixed places in the cartography of the war.

northern counter-attack, and win a little more room for artillery positions and the deployment of infantry within the salient.

It was the centre of the saucer-shaped battlefield which was the decisive theatre of conflict. And along this centre the British troops were unable at the time to make any important gain of ground commensurate with the forces employed and the losses incurred. Ludendorff was fairly justified in claiming a defensive victory. The value of his improved block-house system was at last triumphantly, though temporarily, vindicated.

The small "pill-boxes" had been overcome at the opening of the battle, with no very excessive loss of life. The new British form of infantry attack, devised since the M.E.B.U.'s were encountered around Arras, seemed at the time to be fairly effective.

Behind the lighter screen of small concrete forts and netted shell-holes, however, General von Armin had erected a great number of large and amazingly strong forts, arranged in great depth, and so placed that each could enfilade with its machine-gun barrage any hostile force that attacked its neighbour.

The steel and concrete roofs and walls were so strong that ordinary shells burst harmlessly upon them. Only a direct hit by the heaviest siege-guns could put one of these main fortresses out of action. The hostile works were so numerous in and around the swamp that they looked, in an aerial photograph, like pepper thickly sprinkled over the Ypres saucer from a pepper-pot.

From the distance at which the British artillery fired the targets were too small to be struck. They escaped all ordinary barrages. The lighter shells that hit only flicked off small pieces of concrete, while nearly all the heavier shells, deliberately aimed at those works which were not concealed by the art of camouflage, failed to hit.

A fleet of British "tanks," carrying field-guns as well as machine-guns, would probably have helped the infantry to overcome the enemy's new fortress system. But the ground was absolutely unsuitable for the operation of a couple of hundred of the new mobile forts. A few of them did good work along some fairly firm ground, but the large extent of swamp and water prevented anything like a general "tank" offensive.

LEWIS GUNNERS AT BAY IN A SHELL-HOLE.
In a counter-attack east of Ypres the enemy penetrated a gap in the British line, and rushed forward in large numbers. They were stopped, with heavy casualties, by a little party of British holding a shell-hole with two Lewis guns until, reinforcements arriving, the Germans were forced to surrender.

The British infantry had usually to work forward, alone and unaided, against a system of concealed and half-concealed strongholds, which the enemy had some reason for regarding as practically impregnable. The hand-bomb, rifle, bayonet, Lewis gun, and Stokes gun were the weapons of attack. The heavy ammunition for the Stokes gun was a serious drawback in the circumstances. It had to be carried over bogs, often against a hostile machine-gun barrage, and always through a more or less intense shrapnel, high explosive, and gas-shell curtain of fire.

Magnificently effective as the Stokes gun might have been in more favourable circumstances, it was seldom available for service, with a plentiful supply of its enormous bombs, in those advanced parts of the attacking line where the issue of the battle was being decided. The upshot was that the Irish and English infantry found that the task set them was too tragically difficult to be carried out with hand-grenades, rifles, and machine-guns. Some of the troops fell back; some fought till they died; some sought a splendid death, by falling in absolutely hopeless charges against the enemy's counter-attacking masses.

The fighting men of Ireland attacked between the Passchendaele road and the Roulers railway. The Ulstermen were on the right, by Pommern Redoubt, with **Irish check at Gallipoli Redoubt** the Germans on Hill 35 dominating the battlefield. The ground beneath was mostly bogged, with a thin crust over it. Consequently, when the men went forward they stuck in the mud and became targets for German machine-gunners and sharpshooters. Beyond the small hill was a saddlebacked ridge, with double spurs, from which other machine-gun barrages came. At the southern end of the ridge was a machine-gun redoubt known as Gallipoli. It was against this ridge that the British offensive of July 31st had been checked, and the new offensive was not more successful.

At the opening of the action the Inniskillings made rapid and gallant progress over the Zonnebeke brook, south of Gallipoli, and captured a small rise, Hill 37, which was one of the keys of the position. On their left the Irish Rifles were held up by a redoubt containing five machine-guns, manned by a Bavarian garrison as expert as it was resolute. The Rifles could not work around the fort, because of the enemy's enfilading fire, so they heroically endeavoured to carry it by direct assault.

DRAWING WATER FROM A WAYSIDE TANK.
The quality of the local water on the western front was not to be relied upon, and all along the lines carefully sterilised water was stored in tanks at fixed stations which were supplied by water-pipes.

In wave after wave the battalion heroically wasted itself. Every man and officer went on until he dropped; but all dropped. Then the victorious Inniskillings tried, with equal valour, to rush the fortress, and they, too, failed. In the meantime, some Inniskillings and Irish Rifles worked through the enemy's fire to a network of trenches and defences, where they fought a fight to a finish with a Bavarian garrison, and drove a wedge into the enemy's block-house line.

Other Irish Rifles, with the Dublin Fusiliers, went through the German works along the Roulers railway. Their first waves of attack were shattered by enfilading machine-gun fire, which the German gunners poured from slits in their block-houses through the British creeping barrage of shell fire.

The creeping barrage, invented by Sir Henry Horne as the main instrument of victory in the Somme campaign, was on this occasion defeated by General von Armin's new block-house system. Quite small enemy forces, scattered in groups of twenty to sixty men, were able to work their machine-guns coolly through the tempest of shell that broke and flamed upon their roofs of **Block-house system** armoured concrete. They maintained an **v. creeping barrage** unending sleet of bullets, whistling about a yard above the surface of the ground.

They did this while thousands of British guns were playing upon them without hurting them. What was needed was a new creeping barrage, formed by hundreds of guns ranging in calibre from 8 in. upwards. Even 6 in. shell seldom could penetrate six to ten feet of concrete reinforced by steel rails.

In spite of the unparalleled strength of the hostile works, the Dublin Fusiliers worked up the railway line until they were held up by the Bremen Redoubt, on the western bank of the Steenbeek, near Zonnebeke village. From this position a message at last came through from a young Irish subaltern: "All officers and men killed or wounded. I am lying out here in a shell-hole." He appears later to have collected a small force of Irishmen, but he and his second party were afterwards cut off by the enemy's counter-attacking forces.

Nevertheless, the attack along the centre might have been successful had the Ulstermen succeeded in storming the enemy's position between Winnipeg and Gallipoli. The Northern Irishmen, however, could not break through the enemy's chain of block-houses. Fusiliers and Rifles laboured through the swamp to Hill 35. They fought the enemy out of the old gunpits at the foot of the rise, and, against plunging machine- **Only two** gun fire, climbed the slope and won the **Ulstermen left** crest; but their losses had sadly weakened them, and they were finally overborne by a German counter-attack when reduced, on the height, to two men!

At this point, and at other critical points won by the wasted first waves of attack, definite success would have been ensured if only supports had arrived to consolidate the positions. This, however, was the stage in the struggle in which the virtues of the new German defensive organisation told with decisive effect.

The supporting British forces were cut off from the advanced British forces. As they moved forward they were swept by machine-gun barrages from the sides of the redoubts that still held out, and they and the troops they were endeavouring to reach were subjected to a terrific general barrage of German shell fire. The armoured concrete roofs and walls of the block-houses were devised for a double purpose. Not only did they protect the garrison from British shell barrage, but they also sheltered them from light German shell fire. German artillery could employ shrapnel shell of any calibre, with a considerable proportion of light high-explosive shell, and blanket the entire fighting zone with dense storms

VENOMOUS GERMAN ATTEMPT TO KEEP BACK A BRITISH WORKING-PARTY.

Just after leaving their trenches early one morning a British working-party was met by a salvo of German gas-shells accurately ranged across the path by which they had to proceed to work. The diameter of the area covered by the poison gas from each shell averaged thirty yards, and dropped in a line these shells provided an extremely effective barrier, but one not impenetrable by these determined men.

of fire without doing any serious injury to their own advanced troops.

The German sharpshooters usually withdrew to the shelter of the block-houses when the attack was at its fiercest. The German artillery was connected, by means of deeply-buried wires, with the most important redoubts. When, therefore, the officers in these redoubts gave the signal for the general curtain of fire, and for the creeping German counter-barrage, the British infantry alone was exposed to the massed fire of thousands of German guns. Hence the enemy commander obtained a peculiar advantage at a time when his advanced forces and

Germans' great artillery advantage the British advanced forces seemed to be inextricably mingled. He swept friend and foe with shell fire, but as his men were mostly under strong cover, the apparent act of indiscriminate wholesale slaughter was really finely discriminating and deadly only to the unsheltered and weakened forces of attack.

The British artillery could not throw a dense shrapnel curtain over all the zone of close fighting, but the German artillery could do so. When the enemy gunners began to intervene in this telling manner, groups of Dublins and Royal Irish were holding out near Zonnebeke, with both flanks exposed ; the Inniskillings were clinging to Hill 37 ;

Orangemen will never forget. Forwards and backwards he went over the battlefield, kneeling in mud beside the dying and wounded, while bullets played around him from the German forts. The troops watched him with a kind of awe as he walked with death, tending hundreds of Irishmen and giving absolution to those who were dying.

Each time he came back across the battlefield his men wanted him to stay in shelter. He smiled, and worked out again amid the storm. At last a German shell killed the priest who would not desert his men in the hours of their agony. Alongside this saint was a doctor attached to the Leinsters. He worked on the ridge, by Frezenberg Redoubt, and, never sleeping for five days and nights, crawled out after wounded men, bandaged them under heavy fire, and carried some of them back on his own shoulders. Shelled, gassed, and sleepless, he continued to labour on the field and in his dug-out, where by candle-light he tended the wounded.

On the right of the Irish divisions were English County regiments and London battalions, who were also thrown back after a gallant advance. They attacked from the neighbourhood of Westhoek Ridge to the woods and rises along the Menin road. The majority of them had lain out in the mud the night before the battle, but this did not chill their ardour in the least.

LETTER LINKS WITH HOME.
Inside view of an improvised camp post-office on the western front. An Australian soldier was handing in a registered letter to be sent half round the world. The regular postal service to and from the men at the front was one of the triumphs of organisation in the war.

The barrage-fire support of the English troops was lost soon after the opening of the attack, for the infantry movement was continually checked by undamaged hostile block-houses and gins and man-traps in the small and large patches of woodland stretching from Polygon Wood to Shrewsbury Forest. In all this sector the Germans had a cross-fire of immense parks of artillery, as well as sweeping machine-gun fire, from high places and advanced concrete works. The London troops, especially, were swept by German artillery on their right, in the neighbourhood of Zandvoorde, besides being exposed, on their front, to the enemy's masses of guns around Gheluvelt and Becelaere.

Yet all the morning they worked forward in groups, each squad selecting some enemy block-house or concreted earth-

but on the other side of the Zonnebeke brook the Ulstermen had been forced from Hill 35.

A low-flying German aeroplane sailed over the confused battlefield, and instructed the German gunners as to the main positions of the opposing forces. Then, under cover of general curtain fire and moving barrage fire, the main German infantry forces counter-attacked from Zonnebeke. The Irish advanced line was pierced in several places, and many of the groups were surrounded. Some fought their way back in the night or the following morning, but the losses were heavy. It was a tragic day for Ireland— troubled, divided, half-doubting, half-despairing Ireland. Her flower of chivalry she gave ; but, after a glorious tale of heroic defeats and shining victories, her noble fighting men failed in strength, because some of their shirking countrymen continued to act like the playboys of the western world instead of carrying on the work of Thomas Kettle and William Redmond.

The bitter, disastrous conflict brought Catholics and Protestants together in a manner that should have shamed refugees from military service in the Sinn Fein camps. There was one Roman Catholic chaplain whom

work as an immediate objective. It is impossible even to indicate generally the character and volume of all these detached heroic efforts. Thousands of shining deeds were obscurely performed, most of them by men who made the final sacrifice when the tragic summer night fell. Some of the London men penetrated into Polygon Wood, and brought prisoners out of that distant goal. They also got into the triangular patch of Nun Wood, though the larger part of this fortressed ground was under water, and wading through it was difficult, because of hidden stumps and deep craters of water. A small fort at the northern end of the **Grim struggle for** wood was conquered by a bombing **Polygon Wood** party, and another machine-gun position on the Zonnebeke-Gheluvelt road, running along the eastern face of Nun Wood, was also stormed. This success helped to relieve the men—ploughing forward into Polygon Wood—of some of the enemy's enfilading machine-gun fire.

The troops then fought grimly across every barrier until they reached the end of the great racecourse in the centre of Polygon Wood. This was their final objective. Had they been able to hold it on Thursday, August 16th,

German prisoners taken by the Canadians during the attack on Hill 70, which resulted in its capture on August 15th, 1917, and along with it the securing of **Cité St. Emile** and **Cité St. Laurent**, two of the industrial suburbs of Lens.

On the way to captivity. Party of the many prisoners taken by the Canadians being marched to their "cage" camp. The extreme youthfulness of many of the Germans taken was a noticeable feature of the fighting at this point.

Officers of the German prisoners being escorted to internment. They did not for the most part seem ill-pleased at the fortune of war which had removed them from the dangers of the German front to the security of the British rear.

PRISONERS TAKEN BY THE CANADIANS AT THEIR CAPTURE OF HILL SEVENTY.

a great and far-reaching British victory would have been achieved, changing the entire complexion of the war of the world. But the Germans still retained dominating positions southward in Inverness Copse and around Veldhoek Hill.

In part of this sector a small group of five German machine-guns, resolutely directed and skilfully placed, held up an attacking battalion. As this battalion wasted itself in gallant but vain attempts to get through the streams of bullets, another battalion also came under fire from the same hostile work, and was compelled to drop into the cover of shell-holes, and leave the small party of Bavarians masters of the battlefield.

German storm troops launched In the afternoon, about two o'clock, the German storm troops gathered around Veldhoek and around Zonnebeke, and swept down upon the skeletons of London and County battalions who were endeavouring to hold the important critical positions they had won right in the centre of the Ypres salient. There was no means of reinforcing the wasted English advanced forces. From the east and from the south thousands of German guns maintained an impassable curtain of shrapnel bullets, high-explosive shell, and gas-shell between the half-conquered woods and the original British lines.

The British artillery could not beat down by counter-battery work the parks of German guns, partly for the reason that adequate provision had not been made in 1916 for the production of aero-motors and armoured aeroplanes necessary to ensure on a narrow front the British command of the air. The British Empire was directly opposed by only one half of the fighting power and munitioning strength of the German Empire. But Germany was better organised. The total available resources of every kind available throughout the British Empire—in

pianoforte-making and furniture-making establishments, in carpenters' shops, and innumerable petrol-engine manufactories and general engineering works—had not been completely organised in time.

The work that Mr. Lloyd George had begun in the summer of 1915, in regard to the accelerated production of artillery and shell, had not been properly undertaken a year later in regard to the production of fighting aeroplanes of all useful types. The Germans, on the other hand, began in July, 1916, more than a year after the reorganisation of British munition production, to turn out standardised aeroplanes of high power at the rate of thousands a year.

Those who were responsible for co-ordinating and fostering private British aeroplane and aero-motor making works seem to have been lacking in intelligent foresight, in organising talent, and in practically everything necessary for a swift, victorious end to the war. They appear to have worked for the most part by a hand-to-mouth method. When by private enterprise, labouring at first under official lack **Inadequate provision** of encouragement, machines were pro- **of aeroplanes** duced of a type superior to that of the Germans, these machines were not rapidly standardised and produced by the hundred, as secretly as possible, before being used in a large way against the enemy. They were employed almost singly against the enemy, and allowed to be overwhelmed by large mass formations of inferior machines, so that their special design fell into German hands before their standardised production was properly organised in Great Britain.

In the Somme campaign the German infantry was often demoralised by machine-gun attacks from low-flying British machines. In the Ypres campaign the director of the German Flying Corps produced a better

PITIFUL WRECKAGE OF A FRENCH COUNTRY TOWN IN THE WAR AREA. *[British official photograph.*

Systematic destruction of all material property was part of the German policy when compelled to evacuate districts, and scenes like that shown above were common throughout the whole war zone. Official inquiry showed that by June, 1917, 50,756 houses had been completely demolished and 52,043 partly destroyed in the districts of France from which the enemy had up to that date been cleared.

infantry-attacking machine than the Royal Flying Corps possessed. It was protected by armoured plate from rifle and machine-gun fire, and, owing to the general weakness, both in British fighting machines and in British contact machines, these enemy armoured aeroplanes were able to move low over the confused fighting-line, signal the position of Irish and English groups to their artillery, and directly attack the British infantryman with raking machine-gun fire. Thus the direct public warning which Sir Douglas Haig had given in his despatch, published at the end of 1916, failed to elicit that grand effort in the production of tens of thousands of aeroplanes of the first class which were most urgently required for the rapid and economical conquest of the Passchendaele Ridge.

The swift conquest of this ridge would have compelled the enemy to evacuate

[Canadian War Records.
"SLIGHTLY WOUNDED."
Canadians who were wounded in the capture of Hill 70 being checked before their train left a casualty clearing-station.

[British official photograph.
HAPPY MOMENTS IN THE MIDST OF UNHAPPY WAR.
There were joyous scenes at the front when leave was opened and passes issued. The men assembling to board the trains bound for the base and "Blighty" behaved with the exuberance of schoolboys breaking up for the holidays—laughing, cheering, and waving their precious passes.

the sole reason that this effort did not include full provision for the material and personnel for aerial warfare on a scale equal to that of the intensified British artillery action.

At best, Germany was only fighting Great Britain with one hand — sometimes with her left hand and sometimes with her stronger right hand. In August, 1914, Great Britain started with the immense advantage of possessing machines made by private firms, such as Messrs. Roe, Messrs. Vickers, Messrs. Sopwith, and others, which were superior to all German machines then encountered. In this field of warfare it cannot be said that the later German successes were due to years of stealthy preparation before the outbreak of hostilities.

Both nations did not start from a level platform. The Germans had to fight against the Russians and against the French, and also help the Austrians, Bulgarians, and Turks. The Britons were almost entirely free to concentrate practically illimitable sources of aerial strength upon only one hundred miles or less of the hostile front. Yet such was the lack of foresight and organising ability on the part of British political and military authorities that between August, 1917, and December, 1917—nearly three and a half years after the war opened—there were times when large numbers of German aeroplanes were able to cross the British lines in daylight, between Cambrai and Ypres, survey all the movements in the British rear, and at times attack, from very low altitudes, the British infantry. It was a sad reversal of the situation obtaining in the Somme campaign.

Sir Douglas Haig and his Staff officers and army

British lack of foresight

the Flemish coast. This loss, in turn, would have very seriously interfered with the enemy's submarine attack upon the merchant shipping of Allies and neutrals, in addition to producing some far-reaching changes in the military situation on the European continent. Later in the year the work of producing an aerial force commensurate with the resources of the British Empire was belatedly undertaken.

The more powerful political directors of the British organisation for war should have, from May, 1915, overseen, remedied, and enormously developed the production of aerial material, in conjunction with their successful efforts in accelerating and increasing the production of artillery material and transport material.

Magnificent as was the achievement of Mr. Lloyd George, it failed of success, and finally left the western front open to a ferocious counter-attack by the enemy, for practically

commanders were in no way responsible for this disastrous condition of things. The directing minds of their country had failed them badly, after public warning of the vital necessity for greatly increased production of machines of the very best quality. Once more the military virtues of an alert, efficient autocracy were contrasted with the military vices of a sluggish, verbose plutocracy, complacently masquerading **Military value of** as a genuine democratic form of govern-**autocracy** ment. The time lost between July, 1916, and December, 1916, in instituting large measures of aerial reorganisation was no doubt chargeable upon the Asquith-Lansdowne Coalition. Yet the new Lloyd George Government did not immediately do all that was necessary.

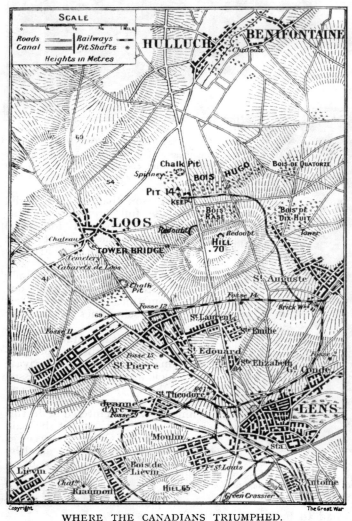

WHERE THE CANADIANS TRIUMPHED.
Map of the area between Hulluch and Lens where Ludendorff's counter-attack on the Canadian victors of Hill 70 was defeated.

British, French, and American politicians unceasingly celebrated all democratic ideals. But at times they seemed to be so carried away themselves by the sounds that came from their mouths that they expected to achieve victory without working with all possible man and woman power, and all resources of intellect and material, to excel the mightiest effort of enlightened despotism known in the annals of mankind. Ten thousand years had passed since something like civilisation, as we understand it, began, and never once in all that period had a genuine democracy been able to withstand the better organised forces of oligarchies and autocracies.

On the whole, the spirit of the enemy soldiery was as strong after three years of incessant warfare as was the spirit of men bred under freer forms of government. Permanent qualities of blood told in either camp. The Briton had the virtues of his island race of born adventurers. The Teuton, with his strong Slav strain, had the virtues of the best disciplined race since the ancient Romans. In the second phase of the Ypres offensive several German regiments, containing many growing and unformed boys, broke and fled between Houthulst Forest and Polygon Wood; but the veteran Bavarians, holding the German centre, sacrificed themselves by the thousand in advanced crater positions and in small and large block-houses. The cool, deadly, imperturbable skill with which the sharpshooters picked off British officers, and the machine-gunners swept and broke company after company of Irish and English troops, were telling tokens that the main German forces retained as high a moral as their opponents.

At times German military authorities in Berlin openly admitted that harsh methods of discipline were required to hold some of their troops and make them fight effectively. As was seen around Langemarck, some of the Prussian garrisons of uninjured forts were liable to be frightened into surrender. This, however, was the exception. The garrisons of the block-house systems between Fortuin and Inverness Copse often held out all day long, even when surrounded. After the new British line was at last broken they maintained their machine-guns in action, and took heavy toll of the retreating fragments of British battalions. There were fortresses fairly close to the British line, such as Schuler Farm and Borry Farm, that proved quite impregnable, owing to the skill and intrepidity of the small parties of Germans that occupied them.

Far from being in any way broken in spirit, the German Army regarded itself as victorious. With determined patience it underwent all the ghastly horrors of the Ypres campaign, **High moral of** in confidence that its terrible sacrifices **German Army** would finally be rewarded by a renewed and overwhelmingly strong offensive in the west.

This offensive was considered by the enemy to be the natural sequel to his great victories in the eastern theatre, which had, in his view, produced not only the military defeat of Russia, but, what was more still important, the entire break-up of the Russian social system.

What war-weariness troubled the German soldiery was adroitly converted into an incentive to fierce action by the brilliant propaganda of Ludendorff. He officially impressed upon his men the fact that " England " was the only formidable obstacle to an early and completely victorious peace. He told them, by means of addresses delivered by their officers and resumed in many newspaper articles, that if the British Army could for a time be held, until overwhelming reinforcements were relieved from the Russian front, the war in the west and south of Europe would be successfully finished some months before any large American army could come into action in Europe.

The German people, as a whole, had never been deluded by the apologies of their General Staff and the political representatives of that Staff. From the beginning they were well aware that their military chiefs had engineered an attack upon the European balance of power, with a view to making the German tribes the practical masters of the world. In dominating numbers the German people tacitly or openly supported this grandiose adventure of their race. Occasionally, when the adventure seemed likely to fail, they pretended to the rest of the civilised world that they had been the helpless helots of the Spartans of Prussia. When, however, Russia was practically knocked out, and France was sadly weakening in man-power, leaving only Great Britain to continue an offensive which should have been conducted by all the Allies, the spirit of the general run of German privates of the veteran

IN READINESS FOR THE BLOW IN FLANDERS. *[British official photograph.*
Heavy British gun being drawn by a steam tractor. It was on the way to the position which it was to occupy when taking part in that fierce and sustained artillery fire which preluded the great fighting in Flanders during the summer of 1917.

ated war more than the British soldiers who endured the extreme horrors of it. Yet these men went on with their terrible work. Seldom or never did they joke and sing as they used to ; they lived in hell, and their strained faces revealed something of what they suffered in mind and body. Defeat scarcely made any difference to them, and neither did victory. In the swamp Battle of Ypres local success and local reverse did not for months change the soldier's lot. Indeed, a victorious advance often resulted in an additional strain upon the men that won the new line and upon the troops that came up to hold it until another forward movement was made.

In the struggle against the despotism of Napoleon Wordsworth had finely sung of that virtue of his countrymen that enabled them to endure unto victory :

> Stern daughter of the voice of God,
> O Duty ! if that name thou love,
> Who art a light to guide, a rod
> To check the erring, and reprove ;
> Thou who art victory and law
> When empty terrors overawe . . .
> Thou dost preserve the stars from wrong,
> And the most ancient heavens, through thee,
> are fresh and strong !

Against the furious fanaticism of the Teuton, whipped afresh to an ecstasy surmounting the fear of death, the Briton opposed just a plain, reticent sense of duty, while grimly battling onward towards the Passchendaele Ridge.

While the battle for the ridge beyond Ypres gathered in an intensity that revealed the enemy's strength, the German and British commanders around Lens likewise increased their pressure against each other, in the common hope of relieving the main armies northward. The rapid Canadian conquest of Hill 70 was a severe blow to the German Headquarters Staff.

The system of army reserves had been abolished by

classes was again wrought up to a high degree of race fanaticism.

In the third year of the war there was seen on the western front something that had not been seen on any front in August, 1914. A very large force of individual Germans, of the peasant and urban working classes, were ready to sacrifice themselves in forlorn hopes along the first zone of defences, in what must be recognised by their

German military fanaticism revived

foes as a magnanimous endeavour to leave to their children the entire earth as a heritage. Not since the Saracens fell at Tours, and the Mongols were broken on the marches of Poland, had Europe seen such an outburst of intense military fanaticism as that which carried the German Army through the campaign of Ypres, and there left it, battered yet still unbroken in spirit.

The Briton had nothing to inspire him but the ordinary strong sense of duty. Victory might bring some of his overseas companions some additional territory detached from German rule. England, Scotland, and Wales, however, whatever might happen in Ireland, would be drowned in debt, crippled for some years in shipping, and sadly weakened of men in the prime of manhood, when victory was won and Europe and the world saved.

There were both shrewd, selfish cynics and flabby pacific cowards in British aristocratic, business, and working classes at home, intriguing openly for a settlement by compromise with the Teutons. The fools among them mistook the character of the German people. The knaves among them inclined to agree with Maximilian Harden that the British and German Empires had so tested each other's strength that the best thing for them to do would be to share together the practical dominion of the earth.

The soul of the British race was tested in all its heights and depths even more thoroughly than the soul of the American race had been winnowed in the American Civil War. There was no sheltered pacifist that abomin-

KEEPING THE FORWARD GUNS WELL FED. *[Canadian War Records.*
Canadian ammunition column passing through a ruined village on the western front. The persistent pressure of the Canadians on the Lens sector meant an incessant supply of munitions passing up from the rear to the front whence the enemy were being hammered back.

Ludendorff. He held a large number of divisions directly under his orders, in the more central districts, and railed part of them to any sector that required to be strengthened. The Chiefs of Staff to the Prussian Crown Prince, Duke Albrecht of Würtemberg, and the Bavarian Crown Prince, together with the army commanders grouped under them, were no longer allowed any important initiative. Their work was to resist to the uttermost with the forces allotted to them. Ludendorff alone decided, on their telephone appeals for reinforcement, whether any and what number of additional men, guns, and shell should be sent to them. He also decided at what point any counter-thrust should be prepared, supplied the necessary forces, and often supervised in person the execution of all considerable efforts.

Ludendorff's method of centralisation

Extreme centralisation on a vast and intricate scale was the characteristic of Ludendorff's method. In regard

WHERE TIME-TABLES WERE CANCELLED. *[Canadian War Records.*
French railway-station near the western front, where trains had for some time ceased to run. Nature was hastening to hide the permanent way with grass and flowering weeds, while soldiers stood fearless in the track despite the signals being " down."

to Lens, he ordered that Hill 70 should be recovered at any cost. He was able to despatch fresh divisions to the battlefield south of Lille as well as to the battlefield north of the city, though he had to weaken his defence against the French armies in order to do this.

The advanced forces of the Canadians, on the low rise between Loos and the Cité St. Auguste, were first attacked by the 4th Prussian Guard Division. The Guards were seen marching in column towards the rows of miners' cottages below the hillock. The Canadian forward observing officers allowed the long, narrow mass to come well within range, then, turning every available gun on them, they mechanically slaughtered the leading brigade. The other brigades changed formation, and worked forward in artillery order towards the Cité St. Auguste and towards the deep chalk cutting lying between the suburb and the lost hill. The Canadian and British gunners, still acting under the advice of their observing officers, made a heavy barrage around the positions which the Guardsmen were trying to reach. Only fragments of the ten thousand Germans got safely through the cataract of high explosive into the shelter of the Cité St. Auguste.

These Prussian Guardsmen, however, nobly upheld their traditions of St. Privat. They reorganised and formed up in the mining suburb, and then came forward in waves. Between them and Hill 70 there was a lower swell of ground, and, as they topped it, their figures stood against the sky-line. Down upon them crashed the withdrawn British barrage. Two waves of attack were completely shattered by artillery fire, leaving the Canadian infantry nothing to do. The third wave moved forward more rapidly, escaped some of the shell fire, and stormed up the hill. The last man fell seventy yards away from the Canadian position. Rifle fire and machine-gun fire completed the terrible work of the guns.

Before the local German commander could get any supporting force through the British barrage, which had again shifted eastward of the Cité St. Auguste, the Canadian infantry went over the top, swept down the eastern slopes of Hill 70, and bayoneted some seven hundred remnants of German regiments in the chalk cutting, and then bombed their way into the cellars of the western part of the Cité.

This second rapid victory, won by the Canadian Army Corps north of Lens, appears to have provoked Ludendorff to fierce efforts that seemed to be out of proportion to the occasion. But the able German dictator had a wide range of knowledge, and acted at times for a political purpose under cover of what appeared to be rather poor military tactics. By every road eastward of Lens and Hulluch and Fresnoy he hurried forward fresh divisions in motor-vehicles and in marching columns the following night and early morning. He also sent more heavy artillery and a larger supply of shell against the Canadian force, and ordered that a bombardment of the utmost intensity should be maintained over the lost positions and over all the area occupied by the troops of General Currie.

For Ludendorff had specialists able to give him fairly exact and minute knowledge of the political situation in Canada. He was well acquainted with the growing division of opinion between the British-Canadians and the French-Canadians in regard to the means of maintaining the strength of the Canadian Army. In his view the Canadians had far too many victories to their credit. He was desperately afraid that, if they crowned their conquest of Vimy Ridge by the capture of Lens and its coal-mines, the movement for complete national service in the Dominion would overwhelm the French-Canadian politicians and priests and the selfish, profiteering French-Canadian farming class, who were opposed to it.

Ludendorff's political strategy

This was most probably the reason why the Canadian divisions were continually exposed to the fiercest blast of war the enemy could concentrate upon them. In a general way all British overseas troops were especially subjected to heavy wastage process, by means of special efforts directed by the political department of the German High Command. The enemy's object was to weaken the links which joined the nations of the British Commonwealth by inflicting uncommon losses on overseas troops.

The hope was that these losses would dishearten the overseas democracies and induce them to slacken in sending more fighting men to Europe.

The German authorities did not always expect to obtain during the war the full fruit of their selective efforts. It was when peace was established, and all nations were mourning their dead and estimating their vital injuries in man-power and breeding-power, that the subtle, far-seeing, yet miscalculating, enemy expected to reap the full benefit of the enormous **German blows** sacrifices he had made in checking the **at Dominion troops** Australians at Mouquet Farm, at Bullecourt, and below Messines, and in breaking into the Canadian line at Ypres, driving the men of the Dominion from Hill 60, and holding them back from Lens.

Wherever it was possible for the German commander to aggravate the task of the men of the daughter nations of Great Britain he sacrificed the human resources of his own Empire with brutal sternness for a far-reaching political aim. He did not know that he was consolidating the British Commonwealth of nations directly by the enormous efforts he continually made to shatter it. He did not know that blood shed in a noble, common cause by nations living by the same traditions and speaking the same language, is the firmest of all cements.

These things he did not know, and therefore he blindly continued his unconscious work of completing the spiritual structure of the British Commonwealth of nations, and bringing this Commonwealth into closer connection with the other great English-speaking federation that sat in power between the Atlantic and Pacific Oceans. In the molten material of the great furnace of war something like a new political structure was shaping, larger than anything yet known in the brief annals of civilisation. Ludendorff, Hindenburg, and Wilhelm II. had the wit to discern what was taking place beneath the battle-smoke, but while trying to shatter the new structure when it was still in the making they only forged it into more tensile strength.

In the afternoon of Thursday, August 16th, when the great German counter-attack was forcing the Irish and English troops back across the swamp at Ypres, a similar counter-offensive was undertaken against the Canadians. At six o'clock in the evening the Germans came out, under cover of a terrific bombardment, and attacked along the entire Canadian front above Lens. All storming forces were broken before they could get to close quarters. Two hours afterwards another grand attack was made, and also shattered completely by artillery, machine-gun, and musketry fire. At eleven o'clock in the night the third attack was made, **Three enemy** and this was also crushed by that **attacks near Lens** famous master-gunner, Sir Henry Horne.

When the broken enemy fled, or crawled back, the Canadians again followed him, and captured some works southward in the Cité St. Theodore, and occupied another portion of the German front line. Another night and day passed, while Ludendorff detached more of his general reserve for the counter-offensive at Lens. Then, in the evening of August 18th, a great gas-shell bombardment poured upon the Canadian Army, and, under the screen of an ordinary stamping high-explosive barrage, a remarkable

[British official photograph.

TAKING PREVENTIVE MEASURES AGAINST ENEMY COUNTER-ATTACKS.
British wiring-party passing a heavy gun when going forward to consolidate a position on the western front. Fixing wire entanglements on which counter-attacks could be held up on spots exactly ranged by the artillery was the first step taken in the consolidation of new positions.

[*Canadian War Records.*

STRONG GERMAN GUN EMPLACEMENT.

Enemy gun emplacement taken by the Canadians in a village near Lens; in which district the Germans had, in the houses and underground, made much use of such masses of concrete as this in their defences.

number of flame-throwers tried to burn the Dominion troops out of the large area of ground they had won.

Behind the men carrying on their backs lifebuoys full of petrol, which they pumped out alight from nozzles they held in their hands, there rushed some ten thousand of the best storm troops that Ludendorff could spare from the Ypres battlefield. The scheme completely failed. The Canadian riflemen and machine-gunners most gallantly stood to battle when the flame fell on them. They shot at the distant end of the flame-jets, brought all the flame-throwers down, and then maintained such a machine-gun and musketry barrage that the German shock troops could not move and live through it.

Later in the night another very violent attempt was made to reach the southern flank of Hill 70 by a flame and shock attack upon Cité St. Emile. At the same time a northern thrust against the hill was attempted at Hugo Wood. While these two flanking operations were proceeding, another general assault along the entire eastern front was undertaken at about half-past one in the morning.

The Canadians had fierce and prolonged fighting on all three sides of Hill 70, and the ground westward in their rear was flooded with poison gas, subtler and deadlier than the chlorine fumes their veterans had first breathed in April, 1915.

When the enemy at last drew back in the flaming, thundering, poisoned darkness of the summer night, another grand victory was added to the list of the men of the Dominion. They still held Hill 70, and all the captured ground in front of it. Four broken German divisions drew away from them, in none of which there could have been left more than three thousand men still fit for action. In all, the Germans appear to have made sixteen powerful counter-attacks. Only a few of them penetrated the Canadian advanced positions at certain points.

Canadians repel counter-attacks

In these affairs the Canadians did not trouble to use their hand-bombs. They went for the enemy with the bayonet, and, according to their own reckoning, killed more Germans with steel in a couple of days than they had done in a year's fighting between the Somme campaign and Vimy Ridge victory and the opening of the Lens campaign. One battalion commander, in an advanced position, did not know that anything was happening to his men until he was called up by telephone from Brigade

Headquarters and informed that the Germans were in his rear.

As he was denying this strange fact in rather emphatic language he suddenly broke off the conversation, saying: "My God, here they are!" For two hours and a half there was no further telephone connection with that colonel. Afterwards he resumed conversation, and informed his chief he had rallied the battalion staff, batmen, signallers, and orderlies, ordered them to fix their bayonets and charge the enemy. The awkward squad did their work so well that they re-established their line, soldered their flanks on to the neighbouring battalions, and enabled their commander to return calmly to the telephone.

[*Canadian War Records.*

REST AND REFRESHMENT FOR THE WOUNDED.

Outside a Canadian Y.M.C.A. hut, where work was carried on within rifle range of the enemy. Wounded men just out of the line welcomed its refreshment before starting for the fuller comforts of a base hospital.

After breaking the last fresh German counter-attacking force—the 220th Division—the Canadians once more attacked the weakened enemy, early in the morning of August 21st, and thereby created a remarkable situation. The Germans had arranged an important storming operation a few minutes before dawn. The Canadian commander had also fixed his attack exactly at that time. Each artillery opened a whirlwind bombardment at the same moment. Simultaneously, the infantry on both sides scrambled over parapets and out of redoubts and followed their barrage. An early autumn mist clung to the damp earth and blurred the faint light of daybreak.

Each storming force was partly smashed by the opposing barrage, and then the equally surprised survivors met in No Man's Land. The Canadians showed more presence of mind. Yelling like madmen, they drove with the bayonet upon the grey forms struggling towards them, and between the two walls of deafening shell explosions the extraordinary conflict was fought to the death. The Germans were desperately brave. They attempted no retreat, but struggled on to the end. Yet it took but a quarter of an hour to overcome them.

The ragged, victorious Canadian line then pressed onward to the German position by the Cité St. Elizabeth, north of Lens. The works were formidably fortified and belted with two zones of wire. In the trenches was a second strong German support force, waiting the signal to follow and support their shock troops. The Germans fought with bombs and revolvers and machine-guns; the Canadians continued to use only their bayonets. They were in very uneven formation, having advanced some hundreds of yards by exceedingly bitter fighting.

In some places they were closely bunched together, in others there was only about one man to a dozen yards. By downright impetuosity and individual enterprise they managed to get through the barbed-wire entanglements, climb the parapet, and clear part of the long trench. The successful men unlocked the position for those that had been checked, and when the artillery on either side ceased for a while to fire, all the line was occupied

[*British official photograph.*
MISHAP, NOT MISADVENTURE.
British tractor that got stuck in bad ground immediately after having delivered a heavy gun at its new position.

by remnants of the first thin Canadian wave of attack.

The action they had won was one of the bloodiest in the war, for both the German forces had, as usual, been used in much denser formation than was employed by British commanders. The Canadians also pressed in towards Lens from the south-western and western sides, taking the defensive works by Fosse St. Louis, which was the last formidable barrier to the old, inner town. During the struggle in this sector Lens itself was penetrated around the point where the main roads met close to the railway-station.

The next day the Germans again counter-attacked persistently but in vain. When they had exhausted themselves General

Currie once more asked his men to resume the assault. They had then been fighting almost continuously for ten days and ten nights, and in one of his official communiqués Ludendorff refused to believe there were only two divisions of Canadians in action, and said there were at least four.

Yet there were only two divisions, wasted in number but amazingly indefatigable. On August 23rd they attacked the Green Crassier, a weed-grown slag-heap rising by the great railway yards of Lens. They hurled themselves against the position and the neighbouring fortresses, smashed their way through hedges of quick-set steel, and stormed over tunnelled machine-gun posts.

They topped the crassier, enveloped its eastern defences, and finally, in the afternoon, fought against the resurgent German forces, and, though losing by mere pressure of numbers the top of the crassier, they were still clinging doggedly when night fell to the western side of the hill of cinders.

By this time it was reckoned they had shattered six German divisions—the 4th, 7th, and 8th Guards Divisions, the 1st Guards Reserve, the 220th Division, and the 11th Reserve. There were also some brigades, at least, of the 185th and **Heroic tenacity** the 36th Reserve Divisions employed **of the Canadians** against the Canadian Army Corps. At times the Canadians themselves were very hard pressed and almost physically exhausted. They came out of the fight with their faces grey and drawn and their eyes heavy, some of them walking like drunken men. "We made 'em pay," was their verdict on their enemies in the prolonged and dreadful southern battle.

While the Canadians were thus pressing the enemy at Lens another British attack was organised, in continual torrents of rain, against the enemy's critical position on the western theatre of war—the Passchendaele Ridge. Undoubtedly the extraordinarily bad summer weather interfered with the execution of the plan of the British Commander-in-Chief. Even when he succeeded in weakening the enemy at Lens, so as to force him constantly to divide his reserves, all the immense work of bringing forward the heavy artillery at Ypres was so delayed that

[*British official photograph.*
ALL HANDS TO THE WHEEL ON THE WESTERN FRONT.
Water-cart which had got stuck in a bad bit of road, having been hastily lightened by the removal of some of the heavy cans of liquid. While the horses tugged, some of the soldiers sought to push and pull the cart level and others to lever the wheel out of the terrible clinging clay.

Ludendorff won sufficient time to make his own full counter-preparations.

The battle became a gigantic slogging match between the two most powerful nations on earth. There was no more strategic play than there had been at Waterloo, the

lists being so set that nothing but battering-ram blows from one side or the other told in any important way upon the result. Each side stated they were losing less than the other side, but the decisive incidence of the mutual process of terrible attrition could not be estimated until the close of the war. It was also hard to decide whether Sir Douglas Haig was merely trying to punish the Germans as severely as possible before all their main forces were released from the Russian front, or whether he was still striving directly to gain the Flemish coast, turn the German flank, and throw into confusion Ludendorff's main armies.

The published list of British casual- **Comparatively light** ties on all theatres of war in August, **British losses** 1917, showed comparatively light losses in the very grave circumstances. In September, 1917, there was a very considerable increase in total British losses on all fronts, yet the figures did not indicate that Sir Douglas Haig was pushing for a decision in such a manner as to cripple his Army by the winter.

He seems rather to have been saving his men as much as was possible under very deadly conditions of continual attack, with the clear prevision of the military bankruptcy of Russia and the resumption of a violent enemy offensive in the west.

[*British and Canadian official photographs.*

DERELICT RAILWAY, LONG IN NO MAN'S LAND.

After having dug-outs made in its embankment, with sand-bag protections, this stretch of railway was found untenable by the enemy on the British western front, and after they had retired it remained for some time a barrier in No Man's Land. When the British went forward and secured it, the rolling-stock had been more or less demolished. Inset: Outside a Canadian dressing-station on the western front.

CHAPTER CCXVIII.

THE ADVANCE ON ZONNEBEKE AND CAPTURE OF POLYGON WOOD AND VELDHOEK.

I.—From the Third Battle for Inverness Copse to the Storming of Bremen Redoubt.

By Edward Wright.

Reorganisation of the British Artillery—Important Action by "Tanks" near St. Julien—Third Attack by English and Scottish Infantry on the Block-house System at Zonnebeke and upon Nun Wood and Glencorse Wood—British Capture Hill 60, Clapham Junction, and Herenthage Chateau—Enemy Storming Counter-Attacks on Clapham Junction Finally Defeated—British Cross the Poelcapelle Road—Results of the First Phase of the British Offensive—German Troops and Munitions Concentrated on the Western Front—Unparalleled Concentration of Artillery Behind the British Lines—British Bombardment Opens September 14th—New British Methods of Barrage Fire and Infantry Tactics—Battle for Passchendaele Ridge Opens September 20th—British Order of Battle—Highlanders at Rose Farm—Londoners at Wurst Farm—Lancashires at Hill 37—South Africans at Bremen Redoubt.

AFTER the check to the British movement against the German Passchendaele Ridge positions on August 16th, 1917, there was a prolonged reorganisation of the heavy artillery of the British Army. In the continual rainy weather the work of moving the big guns forward, digging dry pits for them, connecting them by underground cables, and screening them from enemy aeroplane observers became very arduous and lengthy. The artillery duel went on in darkness as well as in daylight, and squadrons of British and German raiding machines passed over the opposing fronts to work havoc upon the organisations in the rear.

In the interval for these fresh preparations a dozen "tanks" distinguished themselves in an action north-east of St. Julien, which was of strategic as well as of tactical importance. In the dusk of the morning of August 19th the British guns loosened a short, sharp bombardment upon the German salient near St. Julien,

containing the fortified farms of Owl Hill, Cockcroft Farm, and Triangle Farm. The German gunners violently answered the British bombardment, but ceased to fire when no sign of an infantry movement was visible.

Thereupon, the line of "tanks" stole out, and escaped the enemy observing officers. The ground was soft and yielding, but the men inside the armoured forts so manœuvred their machines that none of them was bogged. Helped by a ground mist, the "tanks" reached the German trenches, rushed over them, and swept them with machine-gun fire. Then, encircling the three great strongholds, the "tanks" fired into them at point-blank range until the steel doors were flung back and the garrisons came out with upraised hands. The "tanks" signalled their own infantry to advance, take the hundreds of prisoners to the cages, and occupy a mile of hostile front to a depth of six hundred yards. Although some of the crews of the "tanks" came out with machine-guns and fought in the open, the total casualties for both infantry and

WATER IN STONY WASTES.
British soldiers watering their horses. In many of these pulverised French villages the local water system was destroyed, but the Army brought its own supply forward with it in pipe-lines and fixed water-stations at every convenient point.

[*British official photograph.*]

landship men were under thirty. Small as the affair was, it definitely settled the value of a new arm of the Service, and upon it was afterwards based, when "tanks" were available by the hundred, the great surprise action at Cambrai.

Round Ypres, however, as had been seen in the first two offensives in the new battle, the general swampiness of the ground made "tank" tactics of attack on a large scale quite impossible. On August 22nd a considerable force of "tanks" endeavoured to accompany the English and Scottish infantry in a third attack upon the block-house system in front of Zonnebeke and upon Nun Wood and Glencorse Wood. Although the surface of the shell-broken earth had hardened in a few days of dry weather, there was still only a thin crust over the great swamp. Consequently, most of the new chariots of war sank into the mud not far from their

Midland troops on Hill 35 own lines. Only one of them travelled for about half a mile and arrived close to a German redoubt.

The German artillery threw out a very heavy barrage scarcely a minute later than the opening of the British bombardment. Through the hostile curtain of shell and shrapnel Midland troops passed and met the enfilade fire of machine-guns around Pond Farm, which had shattered the gallant Ulstermen. They pushed on to the slopes of that hill of death—Hill 35—and chased the German block-house garrison along the tunnelled galleries to Schuler Farm, but failed to win this famous fortress.

The Scottish troops were faced by Beck House, Borry Farm, and Vampire Point, all guarding the approaches to Bremen Redoubt. Fierce and strong in spirit were the Scotsmen. Their first waves divided around the enemy's advanced forts, and endeavoured to encircle them and press on to the Bremen position. But the machine-gun fire along the Borry Farm line and the general curtain of shell fire which the German heavy artillery maintained over the entire battleground compelled the attacking forces to desist.

In the southern fighting the Duke **Island height of** of Cornwall's and the Somerset Light **"Clapham Junction"** Infantry—regiments famous for their Langemarck victory—made a splendid effort to achieve a grand decision. They occupied the line to which the London and Middlesex attacking forces had withdrawn after their superb but vain rushes into the enemy's high positions on the Passchendaele Ridge. On their left was Glencorse Wood, in their centre Inverness Copse, on their right Stirling Castle.

All these defence systems ran upon or in front of a long, narrow island of tableland, which we may call Hill 60, as it was generally 60 metres, or about 197 feet, in height. In the centre of this island of dry ground, that rose above the sea of mud in the Ypres swamp, there was a superior knoll, about 13 feet higher than the main hill of which it was the summit. This 210-feet knoll was the memorable and tragic Clapham Junction. It overlooked all the enemy's ridge positions, north-eastern at Polygon Wood, eastward at Gheluvelt, and south-eastern towards Zandvoorde. On the northerly flank of Clapham Junction, Glencorse Wood climbed to the

[British official photograph.

GERMAN PRISONERS TAKEN DURING THE BATTLE OF THE MENIN ROAD.
At a British dressing-station close to the fighting-front. Some of the hundreds of wounded German prisoners who were captured on September 20th, 1917, during the successful combined attack by British, Australian, and South African troops on an eight-mile front between the Ypres-Comines Canal and the Ypres-Staden railway. The enemy wounded were treated with the same care as was given to the British.

THROUGH RUIN ON THE WAY TO THE EXACTING OF REPARATION.

[British official photograph.

British troops marching through a devastated village on the western front on their way to the front-line trenches. In the scenes of destruction through which they had passed the soldiers had object-lessons in what was meant by German lust for power, where towns and villages were wiped out by the methods of modern warfare. Such sights but stiffened the soldiers in their determination to defeat the ruthless enemy.

tableland of Hill 60, and spread over the edge of it. On the southerly flank the park-land of Herenthage Château, part of which was called Inverness Copse, also climbed the slopes of Hill 60, and spread over another edge of it.

Clapham Junction, therefore, could not be securely held and used as a grand observation station, except by the forces that occupied the upper parts of Glencorse Wood and Inverness Copse, and the bare table-**British infantry** land between these high woods. To **capture key positions** the English Light Infantry, on August 22nd, was given the very important task of endeavouring to conquer not only Clapham Junction but all the upland approaches to this supreme key position.

As the Light Infantry went out the German gunners answered the British barrage with a very heavy curtain fire. Through the shells and through the machine-gun barrages from hostile block-houses the Englishmen advanced. They swept around the enemy's works, sometimes blowing in the steel doors by a sapper's high-explosive petard, sometimes reducing the stronghold by hand-bombs dropped through ventilating holes. The Cornishmen were checked by fire from Glencorse Wood, and held up by sixty German machine-gunners near Clapham Junction.

Happily a "tank" managed to survive the German barrage on the Menin road, and, halting near Clapham Junction, fired at the fort and helped to burst it open. The Cornishmen entered with the bayonet and killed all the garrison. This victory brought the large part of the mile-long, narrow tableland of Hill 60 as well as Clapham Junction into British hands.

Meanwhile, the Somerset men fought right through Inverness Copse to Herenthage Château. Below this rubbish-heap was an underground concrete work, in which a hundred and twenty resolute Germans fought to the death. Only their officer was brought out alive when the stronghold was stormed.

In three hours all the key positions on the southern horn of the Passchendaele arc were won. Then, at ten o'clock in the morning, the main battle opened. For miles around, hostile batteries concentrated their tempests of shell upon the Cornishmen and Somerset men. Storming companies assailed the long hill from the east and south of Inverness Copse. Three attacks were broken by the sadly diminished battalion of Somersets, but after each defeat the German commander threw out fresh forces, eastward and southward, until the wasted groups of West Countrymen, being enclosed on both flanks, drew back upon the château and made a new and stronger line through the higher part of Inverness Copse.

There they resisted, from midday to midnight, the incessant assaults of all the German troops that could be collected for action against them. Their line ran east of Stirling Castle and along the crest of Hill 60, with Clapham Junction rising in their **West Countrymen** rear and victoriously held. The enemy **at Inverness Copse** flooded all the long tableland with poison gas, and officers in Brigade Headquarters sat with towels round their heads and eyes, struggling to keep their minds clear amid the poison fumes.

After the gas deluge the German gunners laid a terrific high-explosive fire upon the plateau and the ground in the rear of it. For the first three hours of August 23rd the ground rocked with explosions. Then, at 3 a.m., the

487

IN A SOMEWHAT SINISTER SHELTER.

[Australian official photograph.

Australian soldiers in a dug-out on the western front at a point which had been badly hit—witness the toppled-over remains of transport waggons. The slightly-roofed shelter would have afforded little protection from artillery, had not the fierce storm of war been shifted farther eastward.

balance of opposing forces, each in immense strength, was ultimately so fine that one resolute platoon, or even one gallant individual, made the difference between victory and defeat.

It was the tremendous and long-ranged power of heavy artillery which in the Ypres campaign of 1917 continually narrowed the critical infantry conflict into a tussle between one or two thousand men. The main forces were shut out of the fight by barrage fire. The losses they were likely to incur in moving into the firing-line made their employment in considerable numbers practically impossible. Only by deploying small bodies of troops in very wide order could disastrous preliminary wastage be to some extent avoided. The Germans suffered because their formation continued to be denser than the British waves of reinforcement and attack.

But the enemy's formation was only dense in a comparative way of speaking. British artillerymen

hollows below the high woods were illumined with a red radiance. A line of flame-throwers was advancing, under cover of the intensified bombardment, with special shock troops behind them. Three wide belts of moving barrage fire were employed to prepare the way for this supreme counter-attack.

Historic FitzClarence Farm The Cornishmen were compelled to withdraw from the cascades of flame that fell upon them. But they re-formed near Clapham Junction, and strengthened by Riflemen they charged back on the Germans, and hurled them down the slopes of Hill 60 into the zone of the British barrage. The spirit of the German troops was broken, and when a message came from British Headquarters ordering a retirement from the copse, the West Countrymen and the Riflemen were still holding their line intact. At dawn some of their supporting "tanks" crawled forward to FitzClarence Farm and broke up a German force preparing to renew the attack.

From this historic farm, on October 31st, 1914, Brigadier-General Charles FitzClarence had succeeded in stopping three hundred thousand Germans from reaching Calais, and starving Great Britain into surrender by the development of submarine piracy. General FitzClarence employed barely five hundred men from Worcestershire in inflicting what, up to that time, was the deadliest repulse in the war. On the same ground, on August 23rd, 1917, little more than five hundred men from Cornwall and Somerset decided the issue between two millions of British and German fighting men by breaking all counter-attacks upon Clapham Junction. On each occasion the

made anything like an old-fashioned mass attack impossible, and so imposed open order on the Germans that only small bodies of them could be arrayed on the small front around Hill 60. The German commander exerted mass pressure, by continually launching storming-parties, until he had used in the course of twenty hours thirty thousand men against three thousand men.

The enemy's storming attacks on the Clapham Junction position continued from the afternoon of August 22nd to the night of August 26th. The British line remained intact. Again, on August 27th, the German troops came up the lower slopes of Inverness Copse and made a hopeless

READY FOR THE EMERGENCY.

Highland machine-gunner at his post on the western front, with his weapon at the ready, awaiting an opportunity for action. His position may well have made him think wistfully of the butts on his native moors in days of peace and grouse shooting.

attempt to win back the ground taken by the West Countrymen. There was a very heavy rainfall in the afternoon and a high wind. The enemy forces could not move quickly enough up the hillsides, and as they floundered forward in the mud they were shot down before they could engage. Only a few saved themselves by throwing away their rifles and making a last desperate sprint with uplifted hands to the British line.

In the same tempest of rain a force of Yorkshiremen and other troops set out from the swamp between St. Julien and Langemarck, with orders to strike across the highway to Poelcappelle. They met with the same difficulties in the northern fens as the German shock troops did on the southern slopes. Most of the "tanks" taking part in the northern operation broke the crust over the sea of mud and became bogged. The Germans were numerous in the shell-holes and ready for a fight. Some of them even came out into the open, in the midst of the British barrage, and brought machine-guns into action in the marshes. The fighting was very severe, and oscillated over the crater positions around the shattered farm building of Vieilles Maisons. This seemed to be an utter ruin, but was really a work built of armoured concrete, six feet thick, containing enemy machine-gunners. In spite of the enemy's fierce resistance the Poelcappelle road was crossed, and another jumping-off place secured in the fenland and lakeland of Ypres.

Rain continued to fall heavily until the end of August. By this time the results of the first phase of the British

CLOSE QUARTERS IN A DEEP DUG-OUT.
Australian troops in a dug-out well below the surface of the ground on the British western front. The Australians greatly distinguished themselves in the fighting east of Ypres in September, 1917, notably in the storming of Glencorse Wood and driving through Polygon Wood to the enemy trenches beyond.

offensive included 10,697 prisoners, 38 guns, 73 trench-mortars, and 200 machine-guns. This tale of successes, however, brought little comfort to the British troops. To them the wild, wet weather was a tragic thing, for it served the enemy far better than all his systems and methods of defence could do. At what should have been the height of summer, with parching ground and sinking springs, the little becks, or brooks, running from the long ridge widened into lagoons. Across these broad stretches of water it was impossible for infantry to pass, except at terrible loss, while the enemy held firm ground in front or on the flanks.

Tragedy of the weather

Not until September 3rd was the blue sky seen for the first time in many days. A westerly wind then arose and began to dry the ground, and the resumption of the pitched battle was heralded by intense aerial activity. Under the harvest moon the bombing machines of both armies crossed the lines, and in early morning low-flying aeroplanes came out to attack the infantry. The German airmen at night deliberately attacked hospitals in the British rear, dropping upon them bombs containing some two hundred and fifty pounds of explosive. This was the way in which the Germans showed they felt confident of winning the Flanders battle. The failure of the principal British offensives in August, 1917, made the enemy bestially inhuman.

Actions between patrols and bursts of artillery fire continued for weeks. More than a month was spent by the British commander in making his new preparations. All the best campaigning period had been lost

CANADIAN ARTILLERY IN ACTION.
Artillerymen of the Canadian Army in France loading one of their heavy guns on the western front. The shell had been placed in the tray for pushing up to the already opened breech. An improved system of artillery preparation for infantry attack was one of the features of the fighting east of Ypres in September, 1917.

through the untoward heavy summer rains that occurred at this time.

The original German line of block-houses had ended near Langemarck, Polygon Wood, and Herenthage Park. Had the British forces that penetrated this advanced line on July 31st and August 16th been able to hold their ground the enemy's positions on the long Passchendaele Ridge would have been taken with sufficient rapidity to change the entire complexion of the war in the west. As it was, the enemy was allowed nearly three months' breathing space. He deepened and extended his new system of field fortification and erected hundreds of new concrete forts on each side of the Passchendaele Ridge.

The British Army had to do all its main work over again under heavier disadvantages. For in the long interval General von Ludendorff **Germans from the** practically stripped the Russian front **Russian front** of all good German troops and nearly all heavy and medium guns. Long before any formal armistice was arranged the disorganised Russian forces maintained a practical truce with the enemy, enabling him to reduce his line to a police force of invalid soldiers and Landsturmers. The entire output of German munition factories was employed against the British and French Armies, while the entire output of Austrian factories was concentrated upon the Italian Army.

General von Ludendorff, nevertheless, ordered that a severe economy in the expenditure of shell and wear of guns should be observed. This did not indicate that Germany was running short of munitions at a time when she had knocked Russia completely out. Rather did it indicate that the German Commander-in-Chief was bent upon accumulating so enormous a head of shell as to make the grand counter-offensive he was preparing a thing of overwhelming power.

He knew that the British Army was not even then fully representative of the mobilised strength of the Empire. Sir Douglas Haig was not provided with a sufficient reserve to create an army of manœuvre such as General von Ludendorff had completely organised under General von Below.

Ludendorff, therefore, hoped to exhaust the British Army in the field before it could be strongly reinforced with all the available, yet neglected, numbers of men who remained untrained. Happily, the German dictator was not able to move men and guns from the Russian front very quickly, as his means of transport were wearing out. Both the communications and the munition works of Great Britain were improving in speed and efficiency, so that Sir Douglas Haig was enabled, in September and October, 1917, to strike **Artillery concentra-** the enemy with such terrific force **tion at Ypres** that the principal Passchendaele Ridge positions were conquered just a few days before the strength of the Central Empires was fully consolidated on the western and south-western fronts.

There was an unparalleled concentration of artillery behind the British lines at Ypres in the second week of September, 1917. A great army of labour battalions worked with intense energy, laying cables ten feet below the ground, making new gun positions nearer the enemy's lines, building railways and tracks across the swamps, and accumulating shell by the million within reach of the batteries. The bombardment that opened on September 14th was of an extraordinary nature. It surpassed everything that either belligerent force had before experienced.

It went on increasing in destructiveness for five days. The Germans in the block-houses were apparently safe from anything smaller than a 12 in. shell. Few projectiles of this calibre directly struck the principal concrete works, yet the enemy garrisons had nearly half of their men put out of action by the concussion effects of the bombardment. In intact block-houses were many men bleeding from shell-shock or prostrated by it. When it was possible to relieve them, their successors suffered in the same way.

General von Armin could see and hear what was about to happen. All that he did not know was the hour fixed for the British attack. He came very near to guessing it, however, and about one o'clock in the morning of September 20th he placed a heavy barrage upon the northern part of the British line.

It was a black night, with low-hung clouds and drizzling rain. British and Australian troops were assembled for an attack at dawn, and in one place the Royal Scots were only forty feet from the German position. A grand German barrage might have done great damage, but, owing to Ludendorff's very emphatic order for economy in gun fire, only a partial bombardment was opened, and the packed lines of attacking battalions did not suffer generally.

In overpowering strength the British batteries countered the German guns, putting scores of them out of action and flooding the gunners with poison gas. Through all the remaining hours of darkness the attacking artillery continued to beat down the defending artillery, and at the same time hammer the German infantry. Then, as the British and Australian soldiers were about to advance, at twenty minutes to six in the morning of September 20th, an improved system of barraging the hostile terrain was successfully executed.

There had been continual developments in gun fire since the British invention of the creeping barrage and the French invention of block-system fire. In the present case there were several distinct zones of travelling shell fire in front of the attacking infantry. Each main class of gun was organised into a grand group by means of sunken telephone cables. Then each grand group was connected with the others, so that all enemy forces were subjected to a series of sweeping hurricanes of shell, ranging from the little 3 in. to the great 15 in. projectile. Sometimes the survivors of the first barrages thought that they could emerge **Developing use** with their machine-guns, rifles, and **of gun fire** bombs and make a stand against the usual infantry attack. Instead of any line of khaki figures appearing, another unexpected barrage from a fresh group of guns came roaring over the Ypres swamp.

This improved system of artillery preparation for infantry advances destroyed to a very considerable extent the value of the block-house method of defence perfected by General von Armin and his able Chief of Staff. The garrisons in the concreted works were unable to anticipate the onset of the attacking infantry. They did not know which barrage playing upon them was the last. The result was that the larger part of the enemy advanced forces were still crouching in their shelters, and often suffering from concussion effects, when the first waves of khaki figures began to work around the muddy flanks of the German fortresses.

The British Staff had also worked out an improved method of infantry tactics in regard to the enemy's new fortress system. These tactics, and the improved method of artillery preparation, completely upset the calculations of General von Armin and seriously interfered with the grandiose schemes of General von Ludendorff, compelling him to abandon the idea of economising men, shell, and guns, and forcing him to postpone the offensive in Italy for another month and stand to a terrific, wasting pitched battle along and beyond the Passchendaele Ridge.

The British order of battle, from Langemarck in the north to the Comines Canal in the south, was as follows: The Rifle Brigade, Royal Rifles and other light infantry, Highland Territorials, London Territorials, Lancashire Territorials, all working forward east of Langemarck and St. Julien; South African and Scottish troops operating from the neighbourhood of Frezenberg towards Zonnebeke; Australian forces, based on the Westhoek position, and

Two British airmen taking part in a raid over the German lines on the western front were obliged by the ordered plan to fly low. Presently a shell hit their machine, causing it to sideslip and begin to fall. The pilot used his utmost skill in trying to right the aeroplane, but without effect, and a catastrophe seemed imminent, when the observer unconcernedly walked out along one of the planes, holding on by the stays and struts, until his weight readjusted the balance and brought the machine again under the control of the pilot, who then navigated it back safely to the British lines.

Intrepid British observer's balancing feat in mid=air during heavy attack of "Archies."

Cruiser of the French Aerial Navy approaching a lonely lighthouse while on patrol. These airships, which are larger and faster than the familiar British dirigibles, are used in large numbers near the coasts to guard channels and detect submarines and mines.

French naval airmen manœuvring their dirigible over a vessel with which they desire to communicate. These scouting airships work in liaison with ships' heavily enough armed to prevent enemy submarines from using their guns upon them when detected.

Units of the sea-scouting cruiser patrol of the French Aerial Navy.

View aft of a French dirigible, showing the two motors and members of the crew in their stations at the stern. The motors are strong and light, producing great speed, and the petrol supply is large enough to ensure an extensive range of action.

Mechanic repairing one motor of a dirigible while the airship proceeds upon the other. Even with a single engine the French airships can attain a good speed. A total breakdown can be repaired in the air without having to descend to the surface of the sea.

Aboard a French dirigible in full flight and making repairs in mid-air.

Adjusting the tail vanes of a French large-pattern bomb, whose immense size is shown by the figures beside it.

Fitting the tail vanes into position for sliding the bomb up through the tube into the bomb-chamber of the aeroplane.

Passing the bomb up the tube and testing its smooth running throughout the whole length of the bomb-chamber.

Setting the mechanism of the detonator of the bomb, when lodged in position on board, so as to explode on contact.

Mechanics and pilot arming a French aeroplane for a bomb-dropping raid into German territory.

advancing towards Polygon Wood; Yorkshire and other North Country troops fighting along the Menin road through Inverness Copse to the hamlet of Veldhoek; East Surrey, Kent, and other English County battalions arrayed before Shrewsbury Forest and the woods east of Hollebeke.

The Riflemen in the northern sector of attack were unfortunate. They began to work forward, over the marshes between Langemarck and Schreyboom, and were repulsed by strong hostile forces coming against them from the north and from the east. The check was serious, as the light infantry were the pivot upon which the main attack swung. Desperately the Riflemen and their comrades continued all day long their gallant attempts to win more elbow-room in their critical corner by Langemarck. The enemy commander launched a succession of violent counter-attacks against them, and although they were not able to win much ground, they occupied the Germans while the centre of the hostile line was being conquered.

The Highlanders on the right of the Riflemen had an equally arduous task. They, too, were subjected to tremendous pressure from two sides, northward and eastward, by reason of their awkward situation in the northern corner of the advancing British line. Their operations were at first highly successful. They struck out along the Poelcappelle road, extending out on each side of it, to the Langemarck road and Rose Farm and to the valley of the Stroombeek and Quebec Farm. Their barrage moved before them like a devouring fire, the final smash being delivered by the infantry themselves with Stokes guns. Practically every German in the first crater positions was killed. Only in the block-houses and in the dug-outs along the Lekkerboterbeek did any hostile forces survive. Small parties of Highlanders surrounded the concrete works and **Fine advance of** succeeded in reducing them, and then **the Highlanders** the waves of kilted figures swept on without a check towards the stream running below Poelcappelle.

Here, however, there were German machine-gunners who had survived all the bombardments. They caught one Highland battalion, that was held up by the swamp around the Lekkerboterbeek and by a wire entanglement that had escaped destruction. The Scotsmen fell back and reorganised, and then went forward again, forced a passage over the stream, and advanced against Pheasant Farm and the cemetery, surrounded Rose Farm on the left of the Poelcappelle road, and fought across the swamps to Quebec Farm, in touch with the English forces advancing towards Zonnebeke.

Rose Farm was the decisive point in this splendid Highland advance. The wreckage of the farm, that concealed a strong underground fortress, was only some six hundred yards from the village of Poelcappelle, and commanded the ground about the junction of Langemarck road and Poelcappelle highway. The capture of Poelcappelle was certain to follow the capture of Rose Farm if this were held by the Highlanders. The German commander, therefore, began at ten o'clock in the morning to send brigade after brigade in converging lines upon the small advanced forces of Highlanders stretched between Quebec Farm and Rose Farm.

By this time the sky had cleared, and the air was loud with the hum of hundreds of aeroplanes. The British fighting pilots succeeded in maintaining a practical command of the air, and, though fierce conflict went on, they gave sufficient protection to their comrades at lower altitudes to enable the contact and spotting airmen to accomplish great things.

As the fresh German divisions came up in motor-vehicles to Goudberg and other places by the main ridge, British aerial observers directed whirlwinds of heavy shell upon the lorries and omnibuses. When the German troops descended and began to march towards the firing-line, the British pilots signalled each movement to the British batteries, with the result that the heads of several columns were blasted away and entire divisions often thrown into disorder.

The Germans as a whole showed fine discipline under this nerve-shattering ordeal. The remnants were rallied by their officers, and again sent forward in artillery order towards their goal. At the same time the massed German artillery endeavoured to counter the blow upon their gathering infantry by an intense bombardment of all British forces in sight. Being on high ground in the Poelcappelle sector, enemy forward observation officers had their lost positions directly under view, and could detect any bodies of British supporting troops moving in the lower swamps. They placed a tremendous barrage upon the Highlanders' line. Officers, watching from a little distance, were **Intensity of** horrified by the monstrous belt of **artillery fire** fire that swept over the Scotsmen, and thought that nothing alive could escape so infernal an explosion of power.

Nevertheless, close as were the funnels of the great explosions, and dense as were the showers of shrapnel mingling with the fiery volcanoes and floods of gas, sufficient Highlanders survived to stand to battle. They mowed down the German shock troops for four hours, and their line would have been unbroken when evening fell but for the mischance on their left flank. This was utterly exposed owing to the check to the movement of the Riflemen.

When the Germans discovered the weak side of the Highlanders they made a final thrust at seven o'clock in the evening against the left flank, and the Highlanders fell back from Rose Farm and Delta Farm towards the Pheasant position and the cemetery. There they were rallied by a youthful battalion commander, who supplied them with fresh ammunition and directed them against the temporarily victorious German counter-attackers. With desperate valour the wasted Highland battalions stormed back in the night towards Rose Farm, and recovered sufficient ground to form a jumping-off place for the subsequent advance on Poelcappelle.

The German commander would not submit to defeat at this point. He went on organising counter-attacks on the left and right flanks and on the centre of the Highland line. Some of his fresh forces were broken by British artillery barrages; others that got through the shell curtains were brought down by machine-gun and rifle fire. The Highlanders managed to get thirteen machine-guns into a position from which a barrage of bullets could be maintained upon the upper part of the highway.

The ground was also covered by a male "tank," distinguished from the older, or female, type of "tank" by the power of gun fire, in addition to machine-gun fire. With a cannon in the firing-line and a good number of machine-guns, the expert **In a critical** Highland riflemen worked ghastly havoc **angle** upon the very large number of Germans who vainly tried to break the new British line. The action in this critical angle of the battlefield went on for days and nights until the enemy was exhausted.

On the right of the Highland Territorials were the Londoners. Many of them were rather small in stature, and seemed, indeed, to be troops of the second class. But the city-bred men, on this occasion as on others, proved themselves equal to the best country-bred troops in the world. What they lacked in height and broadness they made up in a peculiar wiriness, and their commander showed something like genius. He had the task of carrying the low ridge rising by Wurst Farm, against which all advances since July 31st had broken. Between him and his ultimate objective there stretched some eighteen hundred yards of swampy ground, dotted with block-houses and the fortressed ruins of farms, beginning with Vancouver Farm, while Tirpitz and other concreted ruins and works rose midway of the ridge.

The ridge ran diagonally across the line of advance. Had the Londoners moved straight forward in a frontal attack they would have been exposed to a withering fire, such as had broken British troops in the previous offensives. General von Armin had placed some of his best troops on and around the ridge. They were the 2nd Reserve Division of the Prussian Guard, and behind the Guardsmen were the men of the 234th Division, ready to make the grand counter-attack when the Londoners were exhausted.

The men of London, however, did not go straight for the Germans and climb the ridge against the impassable machine-gun barrage. While their shell barrages were stamping in succession over all the German line, the Londoners made no movement directly against the ridge. They swerved to the left, and, after surrounding the farms and block-houses northward, they struck sideways at Wurst Farm, and, turning along the summit of the ridge, took the enemy positions on the left flank.

This remarkable manœuvre was conducted in the twilight of early morning, amid the smoke and uproar of one of the greatest battles in history, with enemy machine-gunners playing on the twisting lines and clouds of shrapnel breaking over them.

Yet the Londoners executed their change of direction as steadily and as perfectly as they had practised it beforehand, in clear daylight, on the training-field.

[British official photograph.

LEVIATHAN OF THE MODERN BATTLEFIELD.
British "tank" going forward to destroy German machine-gun positions during the battle along the Menin Road. In the memorable attack on "Clapham Junction," on August 22nd, 1917, a "tank" rendered valuable aid to the Cornishmen who captured that fort.

Their losses were heavy during the manœuvre and rapid action of their left wing. They had to make this sacrifice in order to reach the enemy on the ridge before he became aware of the device that was being employed against him. Everything was done so well that the Prussian Guardsmen were completely surprised, and one of their captured officers had the amazing impudence to complain that the Londoners had not fought fairly. Apparently, from his point of view, the only fair thing for his foes to have done was to make a hopeless frontal attack and allow themselves to be killed in vain by the thousand.

Achievements of the Londoners

When London Ridge was won, the Londoners were fully repaid for the losses incurred by their left wing. The Prussian Guards Division was badly shattered in the rapid turning movement along the high ground, and completely broken by fruitless counter-attacks made by its supporting battalions. Then the German division in reserve poured out for the supreme counter-attack, and met the fate from which the Londoners had escaped.

The new defenders of the ridge had their machine-guns in position, with their riflemen lined out in shell-holes and other defences on the eastern slopes. The German movements were seen from afar, and communicated to the alert British gunners. The three regiments of the fresh German division advanced in turn in the usual way, and either perished in the British barrage or fell under the fire of the London infantry. Some remnants reached the English line by throwing away rifles and coming forward with raised hands as prisoners. Such was the

[French official photograph.

RAPID REPAIR OF THE RAVAGES OF WAR.
Making good the shattered roofs of cottages in a French village, from the neighbourhood of which the enemy had been forced. The homes from which the people had been driven by the invader were repaired as soon as immediate danger of further damage had been removed.

number of living targets that the Londoners used all their cartridges and had to send for small-arms ammunition, which happily arrived in time.

At Wurst Farm, which was a redoubt on high ground between the Hannebeek and Stroombeek, the garrison fought well with bombs and machine-guns, but was overpowered by a young lieutenant and his men, who transformed the fortress into a grand point of resistance against all German counter-attacks. The men found good cover in the broken concrete works, **Counter-attacks on Wurst Farm** and their machine-gunners employed the weapons of the enemy against his counter-attacking forces. In the intervals between the counter-attacks the conquerors of Wurst (or Sausage) Farm strengthened the wrecked works by building more defences eastward, and when in the evening the Germans delivered their final blow, the counter-attacking infantry was smashed up as it deployed in the open ground by the upper course of the Stroombeek.

The Londoners had five machine-guns on the high ground surrounding the valley, and the execution they did was terrible. In one action, against a thousand German shock troops, the five London gunners brought down two hundred of their foes in about a minute, and their riflemen dispersed the other Germans. There was, however, an awkward situation farther along London Ridge, as the enemy was still holding out at Schuler Farm, some seven hundred yards in the rear of the conquered high ground of London Ridge.

Schuler Farm was on the extreme right flank rear of the London advance. It was formed of underground concrete works, covered by the wreckage of the farm, and, lying by the Hannebeek, it had been skilfully moated in the manner of an ancient castle. The water defences made the Schuler galleries impregnable against all attack for months, and many brave men had lost their lives around the water-logged farm since July 31st. When the London brigade won the famous ridge, the brigade-major began to argue with another officer that Schuler Farm must have been captured. As he was speaking a bullet flattened out on the block-house wall behind him, and the brigade-major could then see a German officer in Schuler Farm directing his snipers to pick him off. The Londoners thereupon arranged themselves in a defensive flank, and sent some men down to help the Lancashire Territorials who were attacking the position. All day long the conflict raged around the moated underground fortress in the rear of both the London and Lancashire advanced positions.

The Lancashire Territorials had swerved to the right towards Hill 37, while the Londoners swerved to the left towards London Ridge. The men from Lancashire had very difficult work before them. The ground they were set to attack was covered with block-houses, and commanded by rises against which other Lancashire troops had failed on July 31st, and Irish troops had been tragically checked on August 16th. Nevertheless, the Territorials succeeded, by means of new infantry tactics and stronger artillery preparation, in breaking through the enemy's defences and reaching Hill **Lancashire men's** 37, that rose almost midway between **difficult task** Zonnebeke village and London Ridge.

Schuler Farm, however, could not be definitely conquered, by either the London or Lancashire Territorials. For some time it remained a formidable snag, right in the rear of the two hills captured by the English troops, enabling the enemy to operate along the Hannebeek against the flanks as well as the fronts of London Ridge and Hill 37. It was this remarkable situation that induced the German commander to continue his counter-attacks day and night against the two peninsulas of high

[French official photograph.

FRENCH HONOUR THEIR BRITISH COMRADES IN FLANDERS.

British troops, on their way to the fighting-front in Flanders, passing a French headquarters. The French soldier police-guard stood to attention in honour of their comrades from across the Channel. The joint attack to the north of Ypres was one of the features of the offensive which took French and British troops to the edge of the Houthulst Forest in October, 1917; recalling the dictum that "who holds Houthulst holds Flanders."

Copyright   The Great War

MAP ILLUSTRATING THE ADVANCE EAST OF YPRES FROM LANGEMARCK TO KLEIN ZILLEBEKE.

In the fighting during the autumn of 1917 which led up to the capture of Passchendaele there were many stubborn encounters at places the names of which have been made famous by British troops. These places are dotted along the ridges that lie between Ypres and the higher ground overlooking the Flanders plain to Bruges. The arrows indicate the lines of the advance, and against each is shown the troops engaged.

English ground that extended into the low-lying swamps of the Stroombeek and Hannebeek.

As a matter of fact, there were in all, on September 20th, 1917, four peninsulas of advanced British forces jutting into the German swamp defences between Poelcappelle and Zonnebeke. There was first the wedge of Highland Territorials at Quebec Farm and Rose Farm, commanding the bogs of Lekkerboterbeek and the Lower Stroombeek. Next, partly separated from the Highlanders' positions, was the London salient, overlooking the Upper Stroombeek. Then, about fifteen hundred yards southward, in a direct line across the Hannebeek valley, was the Lancashire wedge on Hill 37. Finally, south of Hill 37 and the Zonnebeke river valley, the South African troops established another wedge in the German defences by the capture of the Bremen Redoubt.

The South Africans, famous for their achievements at Delville Wood and at Arras, worked along the northern side of the Frezenberg and Zonnebeke highway. Facing them were Beck House, Borry Farm, and Vampire Redoubt, each the scene of bitter defeats in the past. Again the new and stupendous barrages greatly facilitated the reduction of the hostile fortresses, and, as the South Africans had very carefully studied the new method of reducing concrete works, their operations were very successful. At Borry Farm they went through their last barrage, and falling on the ruins amid the dust and smoke of the explosions, conquered the Germans before these expected to be attacked. Another fortified farm was rapidly and easily taken in the same way. When, however, the South Africans began to work **Great work of** across the Steenbeek they came under **the South Africans** flanking fire on both sides, from the Potsdam Works on the right and Hill 37 on the left. The enfilading machine-guns on the northern hill were silenced by the victorious Lancashire Territorials. This relieved the left wing of the South Africans, but their right wing continued to be swept by bullets from the Potsdam Works, which a Scottish force was trying to reduce.

The South Africans drew back a little, established a defensive line, and then moved southward to take part in the Potsdam action. The men went out of their own accord, without an officer, and their battalion commander tried to call them back, found he could not get a message through to them, and went out and joined them.

The small party crept up to the cluster of concrete buildings, in which were some sixty Germans, and surrounded the system. Half the Germans then surrendered, but the other half refused to come out, and continued to fire through the loopholes at the sides and backs of the block-houses.

The works were so arranged that they guarded each other by flanking fire, and there seemed no way of breaking into them. A Johannesburg man, however, climbed up the blank front of one building, which was a flanking work with no fire slit westward. On the roof he found a ventilator or periscope hole, and dropped into it an incendiary bomb. The remaining men of the garrison then broke out and ran for it; they were all shot down, and a dozen more of them were found dead inside.

Another fortress, containing seventy Germans, was attacked and conquered by a non-commissioned officer

[*British official photograph.*

VISITORS FROM THE FAR EAST ON THE WEST FRONT.
In the course of 1917 a special Chinese Military Mission visited the western front and are here shown amid the ruins of Bapaume. The group includes Major-General Kouan Hang Chang, K.C.B., Major Tsing Whang, D.S.O., Major Ho Sue, D.S.O., Captain Ting Chia Chur, M.C., Captain Wei Tsang Ki, M.C., and Captain Tegurkia Gen, M.C.

and two men. Before help reached them they captured both the works and the seventy German soldiers. The Bremen position, which was the final objective of the South Africans, was expected to give them very serious trouble, as it had been the enemy's main defence in the previous Zonnebeke battles in the Ypres swamp. The line of works was constructed on high ground above the eastern mud flats of the Upper Steenbeek. The German machine-gunners and riflemen swept the river valley with a plunging fire, and were assisted by flanking posts, some on the Zonnebeke road southward and others in Zevencot hamlet on the northern side.

The South Africans paused for awhile before making their final leap. While they reorganised, the mass of guns supporting them curtained off the enemy's reserve troops, and then hurled barrage after barrage upon the Bremen line. Close behind the last barrage the South African infantry moved forward with remarkable dash, and captured the embattled swell in front of Zonnebeke village at comparatively little cost to themselves.

In the afternoon the Germans attempted the same kind of heavy counter-attack with which they had won striking defensive victories on former occasions. This time, however, no struggle ensued. The British artillery annihilated the counter-attacking forces, and threw a curtain of fire over Zonnebeke, Broodseinde, and the eastern slopes of the Passchendaele Ridge, breaking up the local reserves.

In the evening fresh German forces were brought up against the South Africans. They got through the British barrage, owing to **Triumph for** the obscurity that veiled their move- **South African** ments, but they could not withstand **marksmanship** the rapid fire of the South African rifles. No further counter-attack was made, and the South Africans at the time did not know why they were being neglected.

But on September 24th, after they had extended their line to Zevencot, they found that German searching-parties were still engaged in rescuing troops who had been wounded three and four days before. The rapidity and precision of musketry fire of the marksmen of South Africa staggered the enemy. In spite of the immediate menace to Zonnebeke village, which the South Africans exercised from their Bremen position, the German commander made no further attempt to save his central ridge line.

[Australian official photograph.

German prisoners assisting in bringing in the wounded from the fighting near Passchendaele in the autumn of 1917.

[British and Canadian official photographs.

Loading a light railway with stretcher cases. Inset: A Canadian, severely wounded, arriving on a trolly at a dressing-station. These light railways, laid for the transport of stores and munitions to the front line, were invaluable aids in the transfer of casualties from field to hospital.

TRAINLOADS OF PITY AND PAIN ON THE LINES OF COMMUNICATION.

LINED-UP GERMAN PRISONERS

CHAPTER CCXIX.

[*British official photograph.*
AWAITING THEIR EXAMINATION.

THE ADVANCE ON ZONNEBEKE AND CAPTURE OF POLYGON WOOD AND VELDHOEK.

II.—From Zonnebeke Redoubt to Polygon Wood and Tower Hamlets.

By Edward Wright.

Main Objective the Dominating Ground on the Menin Road—Scotsmen Attack West of Zonnebeke—Australians' Confident Advance on Polygon Wood—Their Flag Flown Over Anzac Redoubt—North Country Troops at Herenthage Château—German Masses at Zandvoorde Vanish Under Whirlwind Artillery Fire—Tower Hamlets Height Taken, Lost, and Retaken—Great Counter-Attack : Heroism of Encircled Scots Companies—British Advance Victoriously Resumed—Capture of Zonnebeke Village and the Remainder of Polygon Wood—Conditions that Prevented the Ypres Campaign from Proving Decisive.

ALL the actions in the northern sectors of the battlefield of September 20th, 1917, as described in the previous chapter, were subsidiary to the operations undertaken south of the Zonnebeke road. The principal aim of the British commander was to conquer in a decisive manner the dominating ground along and on either side of the Menin road between Clapham Junction and Gheluvelt village. He had to engage the enemy between Langemarck and Zonnebeke in order to occupy him all along the Passchendaele Ridge line, and prevent him from concentrating guns and men entirely around the Menin road.

General von Armin could clearly see what was intended. He knew the critical value of the Menin road positions as well as did Sir Douglas Haig and his lieutenants, Sir Herbert Plumer and Sir Hubert Gough. He had to be compelled to deploy a very considerable part of his reserve forces along the subsidiary northern sectors, and thereby weaken his power of resistance on the Menin road. It was the thrust of the South Africans in the direction of

[*French official photograph.*
A "DUD" ON THE MENIN ROAD.
British officers arranging to dispose of an enemy shell that had failed to explode. The "dud" having been wired in for safety, pending its destruction, was then exploded by means of a charge of gun-cotton attached to it.

Zonnebeke, and the support afforded to these gallant oversea troops by the capture of the hills and ridges on their northern flank, that forced the German commander to divert a large number of his reserve divisions from the defence of the southern part of the long ridge.

About seven hundred yards behind Zonnebeke village the Passchendaele Ridge rose to a plateau a hundred and ninety feet high, where the road from Passchendaele to Becelaere crossed the highway from Zonnebeke to Moorslede. The hamlet of Broodseinde rose by the cross-roads on the plateau, and from Broodseinde there was observation over all the heights of the Passchendaele Ridge, with the exception of the southeastern knoll at Clapham Junction. To General von Armin, Broodseinde was more important than Inverness Copse and Glencorse Wood.

For it was under cover of the valleys below the Broodseinde plateau that the German commander collected and manœuvred his principal infantry forces. He had, therefore, to make violent and sustained efforts to defend the approaches to Broodseinde, and, though immediately in front of the plateau he

BRITISH ENCAMPMENT UPON THE RAMPARTS OF AN OLD FRENCH TOWN. [British official photograph.
Picturesque view of an encampment upon the grass-grown, tree-girt ramparts of a town on the western front, with the horses and mules tethered on the road below. Many times throughout the ages had the earthworks of these old places given temporary resting-place to moving troops, but never before the Great War had they themselves been so negligible from any military aspect as modern artillery made them.

was defeated by the South Africans, he continued to assail them indirectly by wasting division after division in counter-attacks upon the northern British flank from Rose Farm to Hill 37.

His disastrous expenditure of large forces above the Zonnebeke road resulted in a classic British victory on the Menin road sector. Immediately south of the South Africans, the Royal Scots and other Scottish regiments drove forward to protect the northern flank of the central Australian troops. The Zonnebeke Redoubt, around **Scotsmen attack the** the Roulers railway, was the final objec-**Zonnebeke Redoubt** tive of the Scotsmen. This work was one of the strongest of all the German defences east of Ypres, being a massive concrete structure at the fork of the Roulers railway and the Zonnebeke road.

The Scotsmen had to fight through fields broken by little copses, with small and large block-houses skilfully placed for cross-firing effects. They rushed from crater to crater along the long railway embankment, where there were dug-outs holding Germans still full of fight. The Scotsmen cleared them out with bomb and bayonet, broke up the 7th Reserve Infantry Regiment that tried to counter-attack in the early phase of the battle, and finally had to be restrained by their officers from trying to take the Passchendaele Ridge.

When they had settled about the Zonnebeke Redoubt and the marshes running down to Anzac Corner, the Scots captured a dog that was carrying a message of high importance to them. It was from a German commanding officer, directing the German artillery to shell the lost positions. The Scotsmen escaped that bombardment, and did all they could to improve their cover. Although they were at last severely hammered by the German

howitzers beyond the ridge, they held on to their new line in a way that excited the admiration of their Australian comrades.

The Australians had a hard time from the beginning. When they came out in the morning twilight the German infantry signalled for artillery support, and a barrage fell upon some of the foremost waves of assault. When the Australians entered the patches of blasted woodland in front of their main objective, Polygon Wood, they found that the enemy had multiplied his devices for slaughter. In addition to stakes, wire entanglements, pits, and machine-gun ambushes, there were in some awkward places trip-mines, such as the veterans of Anzac Cove had first employed against the Turks on the Gallipoli Peninsula.

The Australian line of attack stretched from Anzac Corner to the neighbourhood of Clapham Junction. They fought over the ghastly slopes of Glencorse Wood, meeting there a good many Germans who fought hard in hand-to-hand combats until most of them were killed. There was a long struggle with a block-house on the north-western edge of the wood. The men of the garrison refused to surrender, and kept **Australian line of** their machine-guns going, and were **attack** put out of action by a bombing-party.

Beyond the wood, on the long Hill 60, from which the knoll of Clapham Junction rose, a line of German flame-throwers was surprised and shot down, and connection made with the English troops who were fighting along the southern side of the Menin road.

Meanwhile, the Australian centre, based on Westhoek Ridge, advanced into Nun Wood, which was a difficult region of watery marsh, laced with fallen boles, and bristling with splintered stumps that served the enemy as supports for his wire entanglements. There was stiff fighting in this boggy maze of shattered trees and buried, oozing springs from which the Hannebeek arose. The large German garrison had chosen the driest parts of this drainage patch at the foot of the long ridge, and the succession of British barrages that swept over the men did not destroy all their cover.

They managed to get a shell curtain over the Australians just as the infantry attack opened, and, in the close fighting that followed, the Germans enjoyed considerable advantages. Their weak points had been strengthened since the last English attack; new ambushes had been made, and the ground altered by means of mines and diverted water and new entanglements. Yet the Australians stubbornly fought through this wood of death, and debouched into the eastern open fields for the grand assault upon Polygon Wood as soon as the work between Nun and Glencorse Woods was subdued.

Between them and their goal there was then a stretch of open ground four hundred yards broad. At the end of it Polygon Wood was not visible, for all the tall forest trees, through which Sir Douglas Haig **Attack on** and his 1st Division moved in October, **Polygon Wood** 1914, had disappeared. The timber had remained fairly dense during nearly three years of war, but the last British bombardments had left only stumps sticking out of mud and water around the great oval of the old race-track.

As the Australians lay out in shell-holes they talked about the old race-course, and resolved to commemorate their victory by arranging some sort of race round the oval. They were not troubled at the time by the fact that they had yet to win the victory of Polygon Wood. They were sure of themselves, and sure of the English and Scottish troops on either side of them, and they regarded the Polygon race-course as their possession. The morning papers were brought up to them as they lay out under enemy shell fire, and they leisurely read the news after a good breakfast obtained from the conquered German position. The men lighted the German cigars they had

found, and after a rest of about two hours they followed their new barrage into Polygon Wood, still smoking their spoils of war as they trudged forward.

There was a struggle around a group of concreted craters at the edge of the wood. In this chain of holes were some sixty Germans with six machine-guns and a large store of grenades. By short rushes the Australians got within bombing distance of the crater position and engaged the Germans in a grenade duel, while another party worked around the **West part** Germans, stormed them from the rear, **of the wood won** and took half the garrison prisoners, the other half being dead. The six machine-guns with their ammunition were employed against the enemy, together with the useful stack of hand-bombs.

Like all other attacking troops, the Australians were equipped as light infantry. They carried no packs, but were loaded with hand-bombs, and moved lightly through the mud with bayonets poised. The scantiness of their equipment was compensated by a regular system of supply, which worked with magnificent efficiency, in spite of the enemy's blockading barrages of shrapnel, high explosives, and gas. A constant and unprecedented supply of small-arm ammunition passed to the forward posts throughout the day. Quite a large number of German machine-guns, with ammunition, was added by conquest to the equipment of the attacking forces, so that they were generally very well provided with means of meeting the enemy.

The Australians won the western part of Polygon Wood by eleven o'clock in the morning, little more than five hours after they had entered the battle. They had some fierce combats at the southern end of the wood, by Black Watch Corner and Carlisle Farm. The Germans came out into the open with machine-guns and offered so strong a resistance that the first advance into the wood did not end in a straight line from north to south.

At the bottom was a loop, making a bend westward, and the Germans still held out above the sheltered valley of the Reutelbeek. A fresh Australian force was ordered

LONDON MOTOR-OMNIBUSES BRINGING BACK TROOPS FROM THE TRENCHES TO REST CAMP.

Thousands of motor-omnibuses plied in a regular service between the reserve troops' headquarters and the front lines in France and Flanders. On the outward journey they took up reliefs and reinforcements, bringing back to the rest camps men who had finished their spell in the trenches. These were always a cheerful company, who gaily saluted any despatch-rider or other passer-by encountered on the journey.

forward for the work of straightening the line. When they arrived on the ground they were not needed. The first Australian waves of attack had, in spite of the check, carried on and cleared out all the nests of snipers, bombers, and machine-gunners, and formed a straight line south of Polygon Wood by Hill 55, where the little Reutelbeek rises.

At the northern end of their new line the Australians had another bout of hard fighting around the work named in their honour—Anzac Redoubt. They were determined to achieve an Anzac victory at the Anzac work, and appointed a standard-bearer, in the brave old **Australia's flag over** fashion, to carry the blue and starred flag **Polygon Wood** to the scene of their coming victory. Through patches of shattered timber and fields of ooze the Australians fought forward, alongside the Scottish troops, across the road running from Westhoek to Zonnebeke. The Germans overlooked them from Hill 50, above Polygon Wood, and from Hill 40, by Helles Point, and the garrison of the Anzac Redoubt fought stubbornly and skilfully. But at the end of four hours the flag of Australia rose in the sunlight above the conquered fortress, and an hour later the objectives in Polygon Wood were secured.

At noon the German reserve forces began to counter-attack from the valley of the Polygon brook and the Reutelbeek. They were broken up by artillery fire. At two o'clock in the afternoon another force tried to strike downward from the hills about Zonnebeke village. They also were scattered entirely by artillery fire. The Australians then had a quiet night. But at seven o'clock in the morning of September 21st another concentration of German troops was perceived. Once more the powerful British artillery threw out a great shell curtain, and no Germans came within fighting distance of the Australian lines.

The situation was wonderfully different from that which obtained in the English, Irish, and Scottish attacks in August. The hostile masses of reserve forces were so completely covered by the heavy British guns that along the centre of the Passchendaele Ridge they could not deploy for the routine counter-attacks. They were killed in tens of thousands before they reached the firing-line.

The Royal Flying Corps was still not as strong in machines of superior quality as it should have been. It had no infantry-attacking armoured aeroplane such as the Germans used, but there were more British machines; the pilots fought and manœuvred with superb skill, and the officers in observation planes succeeded in discerning the preliminary movements of many German divisions in the rear, and brought the heavy British batteries upon the enemy with terrifying effect.

In the southern sector of the Ypres battlefield the success of the home troops was as remarkable as that of the overseas soldiers. The North Country troops, who fought on the right of the Australians, advanced along the Menin road upon Inverness Copse. The ground in the blasted park-land of Herenthage Château was like putty, and wherever the attacking **The resourceful** troops plunged into it a shower of **enemy** bullets beat upon them. The Germans had turned a derelict British "tank" into a redoubt in Inverness Copse by running cement around it.

A wrecked mansion north of the road had been changed into a chain of forts by the process of expanding its system of cellars, and this new work, whose machine-guns swept along the Menin road, was linked by firing slits on its northern side with the machine-guns in Fitz-Clarence Farm, rising between Inverness Copse and Glencorse Wood. Then on the south side of the Menin road were the ruins of Herenthage, which was moated by two sheets of water, through which ran two scarcely discernible footways, both covered by German machine-guns.

The artificial lake south-west of Herenthage Château, known to British soldiers as Dumbarton Lakes, had been transformed by inundation into a lagoon, covering the ground for a quarter of a mile. Immediately above the lakes was Hill 55, with Stirling Castle above it, another high hill below it, and Bodmin Copse, Clonmel Copse, and the woods of Pappottje Farm, all connecting in a south-westerly direction with the fifty-metre hill, covered by the deep mud and tree-stumps of Shrewsbury Forest.

The Bassevillebeek, a small brook running from Dumbarton Lakes towards the neighbourhood of Hollebeke, formed a division between the enemy's main positions around Gheluvelt and Zandvoorde, and his advanced positions near Green Jacket Ride and Shrewsbury Forest, Bulgar Wood, and Hessian and Belgian Copses southward. The marshes of the Bassevillebeek valley were defended northward by the inundations of Dumbarton Lakes, and eastward by a great fortress system on the spur of Tower Hamlets Hill. There were many other block-houses, underground works, and organised defences along the Bassevillebeek area.

All the ground from the Menin road to Hollebeke Cemetery had to be forced in order to permit the English divisions to co-operate with the Australian forces in the attack upon the German centre. Veldhoek had to be reached to safeguard Polygon Wood; Tower Hamlets Hill had to be attained to prevent a great flanking counter-attack upon Veldhoek and Inverness Copse; and finally the Bassevillebeek valley had to be secured to permit the attack upon Tower Hamlets.

The southern conflicts may therefore be regarded as a single action. The troops engaged, including Yorkshiremen, Durhams, Northumberland Fusiliers, East Surreys, Kents, Midland, and other regiments, achieved one of the most notable victories in the Ypres cam-paign. Their movement was checked **Our victorious** by the southernmost point, between **troops** Hollebeke Cemetery and Shrewsbury Forest, but this made no difference to the grand result.

The enemy always fought with special strength at the southern basis of the Ypres salient. From the action in Battle Wood in June, 1917, to the end of the Ypres campaign in November, 1917, the Germans made a most determined stand in the Hollebeke sector. They were able to bring up reinforcements from their unengaged wing and launch a flanking counter-attack upon British forces moving forward from the Ypres crescent. On September 20th the English troops waged a series of long and bitter combats between Hollebeke and Shrewsbury Forest, where they were directly overlooked from the Zandvoorde Ridge.

They captured one of the copses, but failed to break through Hessian and Belgian Woods. Nevertheless, their terrible and apparently almost fruitless struggle helped to the main victory. They kept the enemy fiercely engaged around the southern pivot of the moving British battle-line, and thereby formed themselves into an active-defensive flank, behind which their comrades stormed forward to victory.

Just above them the high hill of Shrewsbury Forest, which overtopped the enemy's main positions at Zandvoorde, was conquered in a terrible combat. The high ground was very difficult, and full of new traps as well as strengthened old defences. Owing to a check by one of the uninjured concrete works, one English company on the right of the fortress was swept with a machine-gun barrage. All the officers fell and nine-tenths of the men, leaving only twenty-two privates and one corporal to continue the attack. This undaunted little band continued to fight forward, and after reducing the strong points in front of it, extended in a thin defensive line, under the protection of which the main advance was resumed, and all the desired ground was captured without any further delay.

When the eastern slope of Shrewsbury Forest was reached the difficulties of the advance greatly increased. The enemy could bring machine-guns into action from the Zandvoorde Ridge across the Bassevillebeek valley. He could also watch from his artillery observation positions every English infantry movement and barrage it with strong shell fire. There was no forest screen to serve as cover for the victorious attacking troops, as all the trees had been destroyed by bombardments of unparalleled density and length. Nevertheless, Bulgar Wood was carried to the east of Shrewsbury Forest, and the series of strong redoubts at the southern edge of it were reduced after fierce fighting.

Capture of Shrewsbury Forest

The Shrewsbury Forest victory was a very important element of success in the great advance along the Menin road. It exposed the southern flank of the German centre. The action, however, was also one of great local value. It completely reversed the British and German positions in the Zandvoorde sector, for the enemy commander at once organised a tremendous counter-attack across the Bassevillebeek valley. He collected brigades and massed them on the Zandvoorde heights. Several of his battalions could be seen forming in columns of fours for an old-fashioned mass attack. A line of flame-throwers, distinguished by their white equipment, could clearly be perceived standing in front of the grey ribbons of ordinary infantry and before the more widely-spaced lines of shock troops.

The spectacle resembled more some scene from the Battle of Waterloo than a view of a modern engagement. The local German commander was either incompetent or blindly desperate. At a signal from the English infantry the extraordinary array of enemy forces vanished without striking a blow. At the signal hundreds of British guns of all calibres swept the Zandvoorde heights from end to end and from side to side. The grey columns and lines melted away; no grand counter-attack occurred, and when the German artillery swept Shrewsbury Forest in turn, every flame it made upon the darkening twilight was answered by counter-battery fire from the parks of British guns.

In the meantime, as the infantry action in Shrewsbury Forest was raging, the English troops swept over Green Jacket Ride northward, into Clonmel Copse, Bodmin Copse, and Hill 55, rising between Dumbarton Lakes and Clapham Junction. Everything at first went according to programme. There were scattered actions up and down the line between the Menin road and Shrewsbury Forest, but no serious check occurred until the East Surreys and Kents came upon the uninjured works at Pappotje Farm, between Clonmel Copse and the upper waters of the Bassevillebeek.

Check at Pappotje Farm

The Southern battalions lost their barrage while they were overcoming the garrison of the fortified farm. Yet this did not keep them from their goal. They worked round the woodland fortress, broke into it and took many

LBritish official photograph.

BY QUIET WATERWAYS TO THE WESTERN FRONT.

British soldiers being moved forward towards the battle area in barges along a French canal. A special inland water transport service was organised for the purposes of conveying by canal both men and materials in France and Flanders. This branch of the transport service very materially lessened the demands upon the motor services and the railways in the unceasing task of keeping the armies in the field supplied.

XXX

prisoners, and then fought downward into the brook valley, with Yorkshiremen, the Northumberland Fusiliers, Durhams, and other North Country regiments swinging forward on their right.

The long stretches of fire-swept water at Dumbarton Lakes were a dreadful obstacle to the final movement of the English southern wing. The bogs into which the inundations had oozed added to the complications of the ground. The men who managed to struggle across emerged soaked and plastered with mud and filth. Some of them carried their passion for cleanliness to extreme lengths. They stopped to clean their clothes and puttees with the bayonet, wiped the bayonet on the grass at the foot of the ridge they were set to climb, and then went forward. An eye-witness reported that this extravagance in regard to appearances affected the Bavarians on the ridge in a strange manner. Some two hundred surrendered, others turned and retreated in haste to the redoubts at Gheluvelt. They were appalled by the curious, deliberate calmness with which the Englishmen prepared for the clinch of battle. The legend of the Spartans combing their hair in the Pass of Thermopylæ was matched by the modern tale of English soldiers smartening themselves up for the storming of Tower Hamlets Ridge.

English deliberation scares Bavarians

The larger part of the North Country troops worked around the quarter of a mile of moat at Dumbarton Lakes, while the Southern battalions crossed the stream

[Canadian War Records.

BUILDING DUG-OUTS WITH DESPATCH.
Canadian soldiers unloading trench materials in a village near the line. Standardised sections of iron roofing, on which sand-bags could be superimposed, greatly facilitated the rapid provision of safe cover.

lower down. In front of both of them was the most formidable defensive system in the battle-line. It consisted of a large quadrilateral work, with wing trenches and redoubts on either side, made of steel girders overlaid with concrete. British shells of the largest size had made no impression upon the thick roofs and walls of this great fortress. It rose on a spur of the Tower Hamlets Ridge and commanded the approaches to the high ground.

The English infantry could not capture this great modern stronghold. Every rush they made upon it, with bombs and machine-guns, was broken by a stream of bullets from the loopholes in the castle of armoured concrete. Crawling, darting from shell-hole to shell-hole, the unconquerable Englishmen managed to form a "pocket" around the position, and in reduced strength worked forward on either side of it and occupied the Tower Hamlets Ridge.

The Tower Hamlets position, on the southern side of the Menin road, was about half a mile below the village of Veldhoek. Being a hundred and ninety feet high, it overlooked the Gheluvelt Hill, which was a hundred and eighty feet high, and it still more completely dominated the Zandvoorde Ridge, in direct line with it southward, which was one hundred and forty-four feet high.

British capture Tower Hamlets

On the southern side of the Menin road, Tower Hamlets Hill was the supreme summit on the enemy's remaining portion of the Passchendaele Ridge pillars. Its rapid and definite conquest in the morning of September 20th would have consummated the Anglo-Australian advance along the highest positions of the Menin Gate to Lille and Zeebrugge. Owing, however, to the fire which the enemy kept up from the Bassevillebeek, where the quadrilateral fortress was still unreduced, the attacking troops had to fall back later in the day from the Tower Hamlets height.

The German counter-attacks in this area were, fortunately, ill-prepared, and prisoners captured in them stated that their forces were in considerable confusion, owing to the commanding officers of the fresh forces having no maps of the ground. The Englishmen, on the other hand, were well aware—by experience as well as study of aerial photographs—of the lie of the land and the position of hostile points.

They resumed their attack upon the great quadrilateral system on the spur of the ridge, and by capturing it on the morning of Friday, September 21st, recovered the Tower

[British official photograph.

AT "THE HOLE IN THE WALL."
With a quick eye for opportunity, the soldiers here set up a canteen in a damaged house, where a window enlarged by a shell provided convenient access to the counter.

CEASED RUNNING.

[Canadian War Records.

German locomotive as it was found by the Canadians on their capture of a village on the western front. It had received many hits and been effectually put out of service when a merry party set about examining it.

Hamlets height and completely ensured their hold upon it. Again the enemy counter-attacked with large forces, but after heavy fighting his broken forces were thrown back from the last easterly high position at the end of the Passchendaele Ridge.

While the fight for Tower Hamlets was proceeding amid the lakes, woods, and river marshes south of the Menin road, Yorkshiremen and other Northern English forces drove directly at the centre of the German defences. They worked along the straight highway towards Gheluvelt, that strangely resembled the battle road to Bapaume, being barred by trenches, lined with fortified ruins, and flanked by shell-ploughed pasture-land, thickly sown with pits of sharpshooters and machine-gunners and concrete works.

There was a long series of desperate actions in the Herenthage Park, beginning in Inverness Copse, through which the Menin road ran, and continuing amid the fallen trees and sodden ground southward. Good shooting was the main factor of success. The men of the New Armies moved adroitly between the litter of timber and the shell-craters and poured out a **Fierce actions in** stream of bullets upon each hostile **Herenthage Park** work. Under cover of their rapid and deadly fire their bombers got within pitching distance of German posts and redoubts. When the roofs and walls of concrete afforded no opening for a hand-bomb, charges of high explosive were quickly placed and fired by the steel doors, while the German garrison was being held down by a rain of bullets.

The chain of little forts, built out of the château north of the highway and known as the Towers, was stormed at the same time as the enemy's cross-firing work at FitzClarence Farm was surrounded by English bombers. When all the timbered tract was cleared, the attacking troops advanced across an open field north-eastward against Northampton Farm and against the larger redoubt built out of the ruins of cottages at Veldhoek.

Other English parties continued to work directly along the Menin road towards the hamlet of Kantintje Cabaret. This was a succession of underground shelters connecting with the fortress system of Gheluvelt. Most of these roadside cellars were abandoned by the Germans when they lost Inverness Copse. But, as the enemy forces fled, the victors climbed the northern part of Tower Hamlets on the left, and reached the Veldhoek work on the right. They saw the ground between Polderhoek and Gheluvelt

dotted with fugitives, and covered the open field with a machine-gun barrage northward, while charging with the bayonet below the Menin highway. Very few Germans got through the machine-gun barrage to Polderhoek, while hundreds surrendered near Gheluvelt rather than face the bayonet or run the gauntlet of machine-gun and rifle fire.

As the Yorkshiremen, Durhams, and Northumberland Fusiliers, with their comrades, rested and smoked at the end of their journey, fresh Bavarian battalions endeavoured to mass for a counter-attack in the Polderhoek fields. They were scarcely more than four hundred yards away from the wing of the North Country regiments, and **Sixteenth Bavarian** were shot down as fast as they **Division shattered** made targets of themselves. Three times the Bavarians collected, only to be cut down like corn.

Afterwards, the 16th Bavarian Division was seen coming up the Menin road by a squadron of British aeroplanes. The leading airman flew very low and dropped an enormous bomb on the middle of the highway, blowing the Germans there to pieces. The rest of the British squadron loosed smaller bombs on the foremost Bavarian brigade, and then rose and wirelessed to their guns. Thereupon, a terrifying barrage was flung over the south-eastern approaches to Gheluvelt, and, though the Bavarians gallantly pushed through the thick curtain of fire, they emerged with such heavy losses that this intended counter-attack by nine

[Canadian War Records.

WATER FOR THEIR FEATHERED MESSENGERS.

Canadian soldiers attending to the requirements of their encaged carrier pigeons. They were standing at the entrance to an enemy dug-out in a trench that they had captured on the western front.

MAP OF THE HEIGHTS EAST OF YPRES.
Showing the various parts of the high ground, approached through mud-swamped hollows, over which the British troops fought with combined dash and tenacity during the advance on Zonnebeke.

fruitless counter-attack was the result of the new creeping offensive designed by Sir Herbert Plumer and the Staff of the Second Army. By fixing a series of short-distance objectives for the attacking troops Sir Herbert Plumer won another victory in the classic style of his Messines success, but on a grander scale. He transformed the dispositions of General von Armin into the conditions of a great German defeat.

Had the British troops advanced as far as they would have liked to go, they might not have encountered on the way any immediate serious resistance. But this farther leap over the ridge would have carried them nearer the German main battle masses and taken them farther from their own guns. In particular, the hostile reserve divisions would have had less ground to cover under the British barrage before they closed with the half-spent waves of attack. The limitation of the British offensive, on the other hand, saved the strength of the troops of assault for the main battle, prolonged the distance the hostile counter-attacking forces had to travel into action under heavy British shell fire, made the bombardment of the hostile block-houses more intensive in effect, because concentrated on a slighter depth of ground, and generally enabled the British artillery better to protect its infantry.

For three days the German commander continually tried to win back the most important ground he had lost by means of a stream of reinforcements sent to him by Ludendorff. He attacked from Schreyboom, where the British light infantry had resumed their action in the evening of September 20th and attained all their objectives.

close-packed battalions became merely a weak and futile action. Later, prisoners from other divisions spoke with horror of the sufferings of the 16th Bavarian Division.

General von Armin had been too careful of his large reserve of counter-attacking forces. Being over-confident of the resisting power of the troops he had placed round the Passchendaele Ridge, he had withdrawn his reserve divisions far in his rear, to save them from heavy shelling. When his line broke, the victors had time to settle themselves in defensive positions, because of the temporary feebleness of the enemy infantry. The German commander had to hurry forward his reserves and bring them in motor-vehicles to the edge of the battlefield.

Both when they were being carried forward and when they were marching into the firing-line the fresh German divisions came under whirlwinds of heavy shell that took the strength and heart out of them. Some battalions disappeared so completely that their Divisional Head-quarters had to send out officers to search for the remnants.

The huge wastage of the enemy's principal forces in

He also launched by day and night large new forces against the Durham troops who had regained the Tower Hamlets Ridge.

It was on Saturday, September 22nd, that the Durham troops and their comrades were put to the final test of endurance. Three times in the course of the day the enemy gathered around Gheluvelt and tried to storm up the northern slopes of the famous ridge. On each occasion the Durham men shat-**Gallant Durhams** tered and threw back the picked German **at Gheluvelt** shock forces. Farther south, similar German attacks were repeated, and here the advanced English troops were compelled to fall back slightly from part of the ground they had gained on Friday, September 21st. Nevertheless, all the main positions won in the grand battle on September 20th were retained around the Bassevillebeek valley.

On September 22nd the autumnal mist settled upon the Ypres swamp and on the low heights about it. Both the British and German commanders organised again for battle, under cover of the haze that continued to prevail for the larger part of a week. Aerial observers crossed the lines from both sides and, flying very low, caught glimpses of the new preparations. General von Armin was the first to strike, and he made a series of furious efforts to break up the British order of battle.

At dawn on September 25th, when the mist was very thick, he attacked the Australians in Polygon Wood, and the Scotsmen and Englishmen around Veldhoek and Menin road and Tower Hamlets Ridge. The Australians beat back all assaults, but to the south of their position, at Cameron House, the German shock **Highlanders encircled** troops came up the Reutelbeek valley, **at Cameron House** under the screen of a hill, and broke into the British lines for a short distance.

Two companies of the Argyll and Sutherlands were sent forward to close the gap, but the enemy at this point was in great strength, battalions of some four of his divisions being afterwards identified. The five hundred Highlanders were heavily bombarded for many hours, and were surrounded and regarded as lost.

Lost, however, they were not. They held out when encircled, just as one of their battalions did in the Battle of Arras. Their commanding officer, with another company, tried to reach them and help them, but was curtained off by the British barrage, and held on his flanks by overwhelming numbers of Germans.

The islanded body of Scotsmen piled the German dead around them in a crescent, their only fear being that the British barrage thundering on their rear would stamp over them and destroy them as well as their enemies.

Happily, their barrage

[*Canadian War Records.*
WIDENING THE TRACK.
Ploughing up the earth to be removed prior to laying the ballast on the permanent way.

did not move, and the Australians in Polygon Wood strengthened their right flank and, sweeping out towards Cameron House, helped to break the German cordon and release the Highlanders, amid mutual congratulations. There was another gap in the British line north of the Menin road, and, after the attack he made at dawn and fiercely continued all the morning, the enemy general tried to make a complete rupture in the British line by launching a second grand assault at noon. No further ground, however, was gained by the Germans. As they weakened, the British forces returned, and charging back over their lost ground, re-established their original front.

All this was done without disarranging the array for the new action. On September 26th the British advance was strongly resumed along a six-mile crescent, extending from London Ridge to Tower Hamlets Ridge. Once more a great victory was achieved.

The gallant London troops who had mastered Schuler Farm went on across their ridge to Aviatik Farm and the hamlet of Boetleer, lying due east from Wurst Farm. In and around these **London troops** patches of tumbled ruins, concealing **heavily hammered** concrete fortresses, the London men took prisoners from a Saxon division. But after defeating the German front-line troops with comparative ease, they had to stand a series of terrific counter-attacks.

The German gunners threw out so stupendous a barrage that by shell fire alone they hammered the London men out of the works these had won. Behind this travelling blanket fire the German supporting troops advanced. But as soon as the artillery fire passed, the Londoners reformed, returned to the ground from which they had retired, and reoccupied the block-houses.

[*Canadian War Records.*
RAPID MILITARY LIGHT RAILWAY CONSTRUCTION.
A scraper (shown in circle) followed the plough, and when filled was drawn by the two leading mules along the track and emptied, as shown here, on the embankments or used to level depressions.

BRITISH "TANK" VERSUS TEUTON CONCRETE.
Near St. Julien, on August 20th, 1917, the British infantry was held up by a concrete fort ; a " tank " came along, and in a trial of strength between the landship and the concrete the latter was hopelessly outmatched.

Thereupon, another strong counter-attack was made against them from the north-east. Men could be seen descending the road down the Passchendaele slope—men in omnibuses, men on bicycles, men in marching column. The mist had blown away, and the sun was lighting up the steel hats of the Germans and clearly showing their uniforms, that were supposed to be of an invisible grey-green tint. As the centre of the great column was changing from motor-vehicles into marching order, the British forward observation officers placed their guns exactly upon the hostile force. The London infantry were not attacked.

On the right of the London Territorials, North Midland troops worked across the marshland towards Dochy Farm, on the road running from Zonnebeke to Langemarck. Fortunately, the ground was not very wet, and after some stiff fighting the road was crossed and more ground won close to Gravenstafel and Abraham Heights, above Zonnebeke, and in the direction of Passchendaele village.

Farther south there was an important **Sharp struggle** rise, Windmill Cabaret height, or Hill 40, **for Hill 40** that covered the north of Zonnebeke village and the railway to Roulers. At this point German machine-gunners, firing from the hill-top, gave a good deal of trouble, and the enemy commander skilfully but expensively reinforced them by sending strong counter-attacking forces down the track of the Roulers railway. He succeeded in retaining the eastern slopes of the hill, but the English troops were merely pressed back for two hundred yards.

When night fell they were still clinging to the western side of the rise. Only the enemy's blasting gun fire upon the summit and upon the farther slopes prevented them from occupying all the ground. They could have held the entire hill at some sacrifice of life, but the loss that would have been incurred under the enemy's violent bombardment was not worth the gain of ground.

Zonnebeke village was conquered from the 23rd German Reserve Division. The garrison did not resist in any remarkable way, but the main German battle forces, that made the counter-attack along the railway track, succeeded in winning back a small part of the ruins. They could not, however, shake the British hold upon this very important strategic point by the centre of the ridge. The British troops held the ruins of the manor-house, the church and cemetery, and the houses on both sides of the Ypres highway, while enemy machine-gunners remained in the wreckage of the station and on the high ground around the plateau of Broodseinde.

Below Zonnebeke village the Australian troops completed their occupation of Polygon Wood in the course of three hours. They went forward by means of rifle fire, using few bombs, and by shooting down the enemy at a distance they escaped heavy casualties themselves and inflicted great losses upon the enemy. Only one of their battalions was seriously weakened by some unexpected gusts of machine-gun fire. Firing straight and quick, the men of the Commonwealth crossed the Race-course, and fought the enemy out of the mound that rose by the end of the race-track, somewhat like the bank at Newmarket.

From this mound, so rumour ran at the time, Sir Douglas Haig had conducted the First Battle of Ypres. The enemy had tunnelled under it, and erected machine-gun posts along it ; but his garrison was kept down by rifle fire and then compelled to surrender. The advance to the eastern face of the large wood was made in two leaps. On the northern side flanking fire was encountered from the hamlet of Molenarelsthoek, on the slopes of the Passchendaele Ridge. Here there was a row of posts that maintained a machine-gun barrage, which was supported by rifle fire from many **Australians capture** nests of sharpshooters. With these the **Polygon Wood** Australians engaged in a deadly game of marksmanship and kept them down. Also, on the eastern skirts of the wood, they quelled the enemy by their fine musketry and exhausted his local reserves.

The enemy commander sent forward a fresh division— the 236th—which was brought up in motor-vehicles to Keiberg, and marched to Noordemdhoek, less than a mile from the Australian line east of Polygon Wood. The new German force was followed by the British artillery, and so scattered that its operations had to be postponed for some hours. When at last the counter-attack was made only two of the waves managed to get within range of the rifles and machine-guns of the Australians. In the night some of the remnants of the ten thousand men broken on the Noordemdhoek fields came into the Australian lines and surrendered themselves. In the morning the victors extended their front from the south-eastern corner of Polygon Wood and advanced against little resistance along the Reutelbeek.

In this sector, running from the neighbourhood of Cameron House towards Menin road and Tower Hamlets Ridge, the success of the new British movement of offensive was not so remarkable as in the northern sectors. The thrusts made by the enemy the day before the British attack checked to some extent the forward sweep of the English and Scottish troops around Menin road. The German positions between the Reutelbeek and Polderhoek village, Gheluvelt and Tower Hamlets Ridge, were very strongly held, and the German artillery, arranged in an arc behind Zandvoorde, Kruiseik, and Becelaere, maintained a tremendous concentric fire upon the British troops.

These formed the pivot of the attack, and, as we have seen in our surveys of previous battles, the movement of a pivoting force at the extreme end of an advancing crescent was always conducted with extreme difficulty. In the broken ground on either side of Gheluvelt the enemy had special advantages in the matter of cover, as there were winding hollows, in which his troops could collect with fair security against every form of attack, except direct howitzer fire directed by aeroplane spotters. The British troops were pressed on two sides, and furiously barraged. Nevertheless, they surged forward in a series of violent and sustained hand-to-hand actions, and when the swaying battle ended they were about half-way between their starting-point and their objective at Polderhoek.

In the region of Tower Hamlets the capture of the spur was successfully completed, and the strong German field-work on the eastern slope was taken and held against fierce counter-attacks from Gheluvelt. From four o'clock in the afternoon to seven o'clock in the evening the enemy made seven powerful but fruit-less attempts to recover his lost ground. The next morning he tried again with smaller groups, that worked forward in wide order and slowly on the Australian side of the Menin gate. The Australians waited until the Germans were quite close, picked them off with the rifle, and took three officers and some sixty men prisoners.

The next day fresh battalions of German storm troops emerged from the shell-holes between Polgyon Wood and Menin road, were caught by artillery fire, and scattered. Again, in the moonlight at 1 a.m. on Sunday, September 30th, hostile forces tried to recover some of the ground around Polygon Wood, and were shot down before they could engage. Some six hours afterwards another picked German force advanced against the outworks of the Tower Hamlets Ridge and failed in their design.

Later in the day General von Armin made three more ambitious efforts. He began by directing a large force

NEW ZEALAND HOWITZER BATTERY IN ACTION.
Men of the New Zealand Artillery in a strongly-constructed dug-out on the western front. While the gunlayer looked out to where his weapon was aimed, three of his comrades were engaged in reloading it, while another was getting further shells in readiness for firing.

towards the southern part of Reutelbeek valley. This was overwhelmed by the British artillery before it could come within fighting distance. Then a little stronger force came along the Menin road, preceded by a grand barrage, while, with a travelling line of smoke-shells screening the flame-throwers, the shock troops made the attack. The only result of this costly action was that one advanced British post was occupied until the defending troops returned with **Three German** bomb and bayonet, killed many of the **attacks broken** Germans, took some of the others prisoners, and shot at the rest as they fled. The third attack, which was also made in strength, was completely broken before close fighting became necessary. All that the British artillery spared was swept away by the machine-guns and rifles of the infantry.

The enemy's counter-attacking operations continued on October 1st. Three long waves stormed forward between Polygon Wood and Tower Hamlets Ridge. The first wave was stopped by rifle fire ; the second was completely wiped out by artillery ; and the third wave, after being badly broken by gun fire, was swept by the machine-guns and rifles of the British infantry, who then rose and charged the Germans and occupied the line from which the enemy had started.

Ground to a depth of a hundred yards was won as the result of the heavy German attacks in the morning. This extraordinary revelation of the weakness of his men provoked the German commander to further loss of life. He made two more attempts at counter-attacking, which were so ineffective that on some parts of the British front officers and men did not know that any assault against them had been intended. For very few Germans got through the curtain of shell fire directed

BRITISH ADVANCE AFTER A NIGHT RAID.
In the muddy tracts of France and Flanders night-raiding the enemy trenches was not an easy operation. How effective it frequently was was seen when the British soldiers advancing found German victims of an overnight raid lying dead about the muddy pools.

by British forward observation officers from the dominating ground won all along the southern end of the Passchendaele Ridge. All that the Germans won in five days and nights of continual battle were two isolated posts south-east of Polygon Wood, known as Cameron Covert and Joist Farm.

The September campaign at Ypres was directed by Sir Herbert Plumer and his Staff of the Second Army in a manner that equalled their achievement in the Messines-Wytschaete battle. The British and Australian casualties were light in proportion to the great successes won. Sir Hubert Gough and his Staff of the Fifth Army had not been so successful in the August operations, because they had not completely solved the problem of the strong German block-house system.

In spite of the check to the British advance on the Passchendaele Ridge during the first seven weeks of the campaign, the attacking armies were as generally victorious as they had been in the struggle around Bapaume in 1916.

British continually progressing They fought forward continually, sometimes on the northern flank and sometimes on the southern flank, and their centre was gradually stretched over the highest and most important of the enemy's ridge positions.

In the matter of tactics, after some weeks in which the balance was even, it finally inclined to the British side. What the enemy had first saved by means of his armoured concrete shelters he lost by provoking a reorganisation of the British heavy artillery, which enabled his block-

houses to be conquered at comparatively little expense in life, while exposing his reserve divisions to such dreadful whirlwinds of long-ranged shell as never before had been used on any battle-front.

The Teuton was mastered in material, in personal fighting quality, and in generalship by the forces under Sir Douglas Haig and General Pétain. Had Russia but played an active part in the operations of the late summer and autumn of 1917, the violent **What prevented a** and continual pressure of the British **decision** Army at Ypres would, in all probability, have resulted in a decisive victory. Furthermore, had the Government of the United Kingdom trained and armed more men immediately the weakness of Russia became apparent, Sir Douglas Haig might have been able to force the pace of the grinding conflict along the Passchendaele Ridge, and employ another large army against the thinned and stretched German forces southward, some weeks before General von Ludendorff collected all available guns and men from the eastern front.

In the first week of October, 1917, the prospects of a definite British success, though not certain, were still favourable; the situation resembled that obtaining in front of Bapaume when the enemy was thinking of retiring to the Hindenburg line. He could not retire from the Flemish coast, and he was indeed so confident of his defensive strength that, instead of keeping his reserve army on the western front, he had already detached it for operations in Italy.

[*Belgian official photograph.*

PICTURESQUE IN RUIN: A SHATTERED FARMSTEAD ON THE FLANDERS FRONT.
Soldiers of the Belgian Army Medical Service awaiting the arrival of casualties at an aid-station established in a ruined farmhouse near the battle-front. Peaceful as the spot appears, with its bending willows and reed-fringed pool, it was within range of the guns, and the sand-bags piled high upon the broken outbuildings were necessary precautions by way of protection against splinters from far-flung shells.

CHAPTER CCXX.

[British official photograph.

THE SMASHING VICTORY OF BROODSEINDE.

By Edward Wright.

Advantages of Sir Herbert Plumer's Creeping Offensive on October 4th—General Von Armin Prepares a Knife-like Thrust—Extraordinary Race in Preparations Between Briton and Teuton—One of the Great Surprises of the War—General Von Armin Outplayed and Beaten by Sir Herbert Plumer—How the Australians Rolled Over the Prussian Guard—Rapid and Complete Conquest of Broodseinde Ridge—Brilliant Advance by New Zealanders—Sharp Fighting at Van Meulen and Berlin Farm—Birmingham Men Fight and Endure Grandly—Wading to Victory by the Lekkerboterbeek—Capture of Western Edge of Poelcappelle—Irish Fusiliers Fight Keenly Round the Pilkem-Bruges Railway Line—Dominating Height of Noordemdhoek Rapidly Carried—Arduous Struggle Around the Reutelbeek—Reutel Won, Lost, and Partly Regained—Impetuous Englishmen and Scotsmen at Polderhoek—The Mystery of the Manor House—British Wing Bends Back—Ludendorff Orders a Change in the Defensive Tactics—Results of the British Offensive Already Accomplished Along the Menin Road—Strategic Reasons for Continuance of the Attack Upon the Passchendaele Ridge—Self-Sacrificing Persistence of the British Soldiers.

O NE of the grand advantages of the new method of a creeping offensive employed by Sir Herbert Plumer was that the interval between each leap forward was shortened from weeks to days. The difference between the later movements at Ypres and the movements at Bapaume was evidence of an improvement in general organisation surpassing anything the German Staff had achieved.

The enemy's long pauses at Verdun had been due to factors of labour and transport, which the Western Allies were unable to alter in their offensives of 1916 and the first six months of 1917. But the Staff of the Second British Army, assisted by the General Headquarters Staff, devised in September, 1917, a method for making a surprisingly rapid succession of very violent blows.

After the great victories of September 20th and September 26th, the enemy was again thrown back from an important sector of the Passchendaele Ridge on October 4th. There was an extraordinary race in preparation for attack between the British and German commanders, General von Armin continuing his frenzied efforts to regain the Menin gate and Polygon Wood.

After his long series of local counter-attacks completely failed, he received three fresh divisions from Lüdendorff's general reserve, among them being the 4th Guards Division. He placed two divisions of his own wasted local reserves alongside the fresh forces, and arrayed some fifty thousand bayonets on a front of less than two miles above Zonnebeke village and Polygon Wood. There were thus nearly fourteen Germans to the yard on the short line of the intended counter-offensive, an uncommonly dense formation for a battle in which very heavy guns were used by the thousand on both sides.

In effect, the German commander was still holding to the Prussian tradition of a mass attack, and attempting knife-like thrusts such as he had frequently used against the British right flank in the Somme campaign. In the Ypres operations he again selected the right British flank, by the Menin road, as he was stronger in artillery around Zandvoorde than in the zone within reach of the French and British guns that were still hammering Houthulst Forest.

The German general was a highly capable man, with a first-rate Chief of Staff. Of all the sound, standardised productions of the German General Staff, which was as businesslike as the administration

[New Zealand official photograph.

GERMAN ATTEMPT TO COUNTER THE "TANKS."
Men of the New Zealand Force examining an enemy armoured anti-"tank" gun position captured on the western front. The gunner was enclosed in a small, strong, circular steel fort as shelter from the powerful British landships.

of a great railway, General Sixt von Armin was one of the most remarkable. He had strength of character, in addition to clearness and force of mind, and the fact that he was promoted over General von Below and other army commanders to the position of the defender of the Flemish coast was a sufficient testimony to his proved abilities. For Ludendorff was also a very businesslike man, and, except in the case of his deified figurehead of a chief, Hindenburg, nothing but downright merit weighed with him in choosing men for the most important commands.

Capable, however, as was General von Armin, he was surpassed by the British general who had succeeded Sir Horace Smith-Dorrien in the command of the Ypres sector. After Sir Herbert Plumer's victory at Messines, in which General von Armin's forces had been beaten in geology as well as in artillery tactics, the superiority of the British commander was incontestable.

Von Armin outclassed by General Plumer He had first showed himself slow but sure; he now showed himself sure but quick.

In the race of preparations for attack the British commander won by an apparently narrow margin of ten minutes. In appearance the two offensives clashed, just as the smaller Canadian and German attacks had met in No Man's Land at Lens some weeks before. But in reality the enemy, in the greatest of the Ypres battles, was not just outraced by ten minutes, but anticipated some days beforehand, and then trapped and afterwards slaughtered.

The crisis did not occur at dawn on October 4th, but in the course of previous organisation, when the intentions of the German commander were divined and transformed, by a speeding-up of the larger British preparations, into the means of inflicting upon Germany such rapid, heavy losses as she had not suffered since the slaughter of her recruits in the First Battle of Ypres.

The Germans had an immense concentration of guns southward between Menin and Comines. Consisting mainly of 5·9's and 8·2's, the hostile artillery formed a larger mass than any hitherto brought against the British lines. On October 2nd the preliminary work of smashing up the British right wing was begun by a bombardment of extreme violence.

The Midland troops along the Menin road, and the South of England and West of England forces stationed about Polygon Wood, were savagely hammered. Magnificently did they endure the incessant sledge-hammer strokes, their sufferings being the sacrifice it was necessary to incur in trapping all the forces of the enemy's offensive movement.

In the night of October 3rd the weather again broke, after a fortnight of perfect skies. The troops of the attack stood out in a drizzle, lighted by exploding hurricanes of shell pouring upon them. In their final preparation the German gunners prolonged their

Armies collide at the charge bombardment from the English southern wing to part of the Australian centre.

Then at dawn the German storm troops went "over the top," on a front of some three thousand yards, and met with one of the supreme surprises of the war. Overlapping them on a front of eight miles was the largest Anzac force that ever took the field, with strong bodies of English and Scottish troops alongside it.

Smashing as was the grand barrage which the German gunners threw out to make a path for their infantry, it was clean eclipsed by the stupendous tempest of shell issuing from the parks of British and Australian artillery. When the earthshaking roar of the counter-attacking guns smote the ears of General von Armin, he must have known he was outplayed and beaten. Never before had man produced on earth such a crash of many thunders, such a screaming hurricane of the bolts of war.

Dawn came up in a high wind under dark, sagging clouds, with a mist dragging over Passchendaele Ridge

and veiling the opposing lines. But the gunners on either side went on working with mathematical precision from plans based on the aerial photographs taken in fine weather. When the natural haze cleared away the long, low slant of heights from Gheluvelt to Passchendaele was still veiled in the smoke of explosions. Where, between the drifts, the browning hillsides could be seen, some men were moving upward in an apparently casual way. They were Australians. Here and there bright lights flickered between black bursts of smoke and showers of dull sparks. They were the Australians' signal-lamps, telling the gunners that the infantry was reaching the brow of the hill, and directing them in regard to the attacking barrages.

The Australians and New Zealanders formed a single solid phalanx in the centre of the battle-line, from Gravenstafel spur and Abraham Heights to Broodseinde and Molenarelsthoek. Together they were the greatest overseas force which had ever simultaneously attacked the enemy. The dash which the reunited Anzacs displayed on this historic occasion was largely based on the enthusiasm of Australasian union—a fierce national pride surging in the soldiers from the Pacific. Around Messines the New Zealanders and Australians had not attacked simultaneously, but now they went forward side by side, as the spear-head of the grand Army of the British Federation.

North of them, from the Langemarck sector and the Poelcappelle sector to London Ridge, were Scottish and English regiments. South of them, from Polygon Wood to Tower Hamlets, was an English force—Midlanders, Surreys, West Countrymen, Lincolns, and Londoners— with one Scots battalion.

The central thrust of Anzac was superbly victorious. It penetrated the enemy's lines to a depth of a mile and a quarter. In No Man's Land the Australian right wing, after withstanding the enemy's attacking barrage for half **Australians break the Prussian Guard** an hour, met the Prussian Guard in full career, and struck the leading brigade of another German division just as it was about to storm forward.

The collision occurred between two great walls of gun fire. The German barrage was pounding on the Australian rear; the Australian barrage was more heavily thundering upon the German support and reserve positions. The shells from the contending artilleries rattled in tens of thousands over the neutral zone, where the Australians steadily and grimly worked upward against and through wave after wave of German infantry.

"You are fine troops! Your attack was terribly keen!" So spoke a German battalion commander, streaming with blood from a shell wound and walking to an advanced aid-post. His dug-out had been smashed by a shell, and his men rolled over and overrun with amazing rapidity in No Man's Land. The men of the Commonwealth mounted the ridge as though there were no obstacle to their advance.

Greatly were they helped by their series of barrages. As the German troops tried to work forward they came under line after line of heavy shell. By the time they caught sight of the Australian bayonets the disordered remnants of them were staggered and dazed by their terrifying ordeal.

It must, however, be remembered that a considerable number of the Australians had also come through violent hostile gun fire. The difference was that the Germans had their nerve shaken by the punishment they had received from the guns, while the Australians were maddened by their losses and transformed into stabbing, firing furies. When they reached the high ground and stood against the western sky-line the struggle became harder than it had been against the slaughtered, captured, scattered forces of the enemy's offensive.

German gunnery observation officers saw the ripples of

[Thomson.   [Downey.

HER MAJESTY QUEEN MARY. G.B.E.   HER MAJESTY QUEEN ALEXANDRA. G.B.E.

Dames Grand Cross of the Most Excellent Order of the British Empire.

LADY REID. G.B.E.

THE HON. LADY NORMAN, C.B.E.

MRS. H. O. BARNETT. C.B.E.

DR. A. M. CHALMERS WATSON. C.B.E.

MISS EVA LUCKES. C.B.E.

THE DUCHESS OF MONTROSE. G.B.E.

MRS. LENA SIMSON. O.B.E.

LADY BYRON. D.B.E.

(Portraits by Bassano, Swaine, Lafayette, and Elliott & Fry.

DR. MARY SCHARLIEB. C.B.E.

"For God and the Empire": *Dames Grand Cross, Dames Commanders, Commanders, Officers & Members.*

MISS EDITH PICTON-TURBERVILL, O.B.E.   VISCOUNTESS NORTHCLIFFE, G.B.E.   LADY ARTHUR, O.B.E.

LADY KNOWLES, O.B.E.   LADY HENRY GROSVENOR, C.B.E.   BARONESS AMPTHILL, G.B.E.

[Portraits by Swaine, Hoppé, Lafayette, Barnett, and Speaight.

COUNTESS OF BESSBOROUGH, C.B.E.   MRS. KATHERINE FEDDEN, M.B.E.   LADY ASKWITH, C.B.E.

Of the Most Excellent Order of the British Empire, instituted by King George V., 1917.

THE HON. EMILY KINNAIRD, O.B.E.   MARCHIONESS OF LONDONDERRY, D.B.E   LADY GERTRUDE COCHRANE, M.B.E.

MRS. ADA S. L. HATFIELD, O.B.E.   LADY (RALPH) PAGET, G.B.E.   MISS FRANCES DURHAM, C.B.E.

[Portraits by Swaine, Corbett, Hoppe, and Lafayette.

MISS M. M. STEVENSON, O.B.E   VISCOUNTESS RIDLEY, D.B.E.   DAME MAY WEBSTER, D.B.E

On the Roll of the Order of the British Empire for service during the war.

khaki spreading upward, over the wreckage of their own front-line positions. They brought their line of plunging shells back from the Australian support and rear positions, and concentrated them upon their own lost lines, blanketing all the western hillside.

Also German machine-gunners on the ridge swept the slope with streams of bullets, traversing their guns so that each hose of fire worked like a sickle. In places there were stiff actions around points of resistance in the enemy's ridge positions. But the entire objective was quickly reached, after a struggle by the Broodseinde crossways, and Australians and British stood side by side on the main German position in Flanders, looking down on the country stretching towards Bruges.

There was some difficulty in crossing the marsh in the upper valley of the Hannebeek, above Zonnebeke village. One Australian company there fell behind the barrage and into the mud. Instantly the commander of a reserve company doubled his men around the bog and, catching up with the barrage, carried out the work of the stuck and struggling group.

One Australian lieutenant, single-handed, captured a concrete fortress and all its garrison of thirty-one men. Then there was some sharp fighting along the Roulers railway, where an attacking-party, being annoyed by fire from some German strong points beyond the objective, had a little battle of its own, won more ground to a depth of a hundred and fifty yards, and went on chasing the Germans towards Nieuwemolen.

Here and in other places along the new front the temptation was great to achieve more than the British commander desired, for the Germans were running as fast as they could. The victorious attacking infantry, however, had to be dragged back from the pursuit, as the ground they wished to occupy under the time-table was about to be devastated by British shell fire. More-

Australian triumph completely achieved over, any improvised infantry success beyond the fixed line would have seriously altered the conditions under which the enemy's counter-attacks would be met. The vehement Australians, therefore, had to be pulled back from Keerselaarhoek, at the junction of the Roulers railway and the Passchendaele-Becelaere road.

On the Australian southern wing there was some resistance at Retaliation Farm and Daisy Wood, but in a general way the Broodseinde plateau was won by so perfect an attack that there were no remarkable incidents connected with it. Complete confusion existed in the German lines.

The Guardsmen became jumbled up with other forces. Some regiments overlapped; others were split into helpless fragments. The Staff in charge of the German attack had not expected a resumption of the British offensive for another day or more. With methodical over-confidence they were arranging to surprise their opponents when their own organisation of battle was shattered and scattered.

In the climb from Zonnebeke village no obstacle was met anywhere. The winding, shell-pitted road, the concreted cellars of ruined houses, the fortified cemetery and mill, and the newly-wired line on the tableland were overrun with extraordinary ease. In less than two hours the Australians were lightly thrusting past the Broodseinde cross-roads, round which, three years before, there had been bitter fighting between the little Regular British Army under Sir John French and the immense German army under General von Deimling.

On the heights attacked by the New Zealanders, north of the Roulers railway, the enemy regiments were not caught in the open field. Not only were they purely on the defensive, but they were not aware that the German divisions on their left were about to attempt to recover Zonnebeke and Polygon Wood. All they knew was that the great German barrage was coming at dawn. So that the greater British barrage, with its oil-drums, thermit missiles, and general projectiles, fell upon them with terrifying effect. The New Zealanders worked forward as rapidly and as skilfully as they had done at Messines.

They started under a handicap similar to that at Messines. As their line bulged they could not set out in even waves of assault. Some of them ran backward when their barrage opened, and then rushed forward, carrying out both movements at the double, and coming into line with their comrades on either side. The swamp of the Hannebeek stretched between the New Zealanders and the heights they were set to take.

Continuous British gun fire had lifted the brook out of its bed and turned it into innumerable trickles through the mud. On the level ground men stuck up to their knees; in the shell-holes they went up to their belts. While they were struggling over nearly half a mile of bog in the river valley their **Dashing work of** barrage went ahead of them and was **New Zealanders** almost lost. As the hostile block-houses were strongly manned, the loss of the barrage would have meant practical disaster. But the men from the happy islands struggled against the mud like athletes in the coils of pythons, and by a magnificent combination of strength and agility caught up with their barrage, and under its protection won a complete and rapid victory.

Yet the resistance they met·was very strong. The enemy commander had packed this part of the line with troops, either with a view to developing his expected victory round Polygon Wood, or to breaking a counter-thrust against his assaulting divisions. Otto Farm, close to the jumping-off place of the oversea Britons, was full of hostile machine-guns, as the flames through the loopholes quickly showed. The New Zealanders carried the redoubt, taking fifty prisoners, and went on to the stronger concrete work of Van Meulen, midway between Abraham Heights and Gravenstafel. For half an hour this stronghold held out.

Then there was a lively fight at Berlin Farm, above Gravenstafel, until the New Zealanders brought up Stokes guns and, flinging more than thirty rounds at the fortress in less than two minutes, killed every German in the work. In another fortressed farm the battalion commander and his adjutant were present, yet, far from increasing the resistance of their men for a fight to the death, they surrendered the work.

Above Gravenstafel there was a number of "pill-boxes," from which a party of German gunners under an officer kept up a vigorous fire. When the New Zealanders worked up the road the Germans came out into the open and fought behind tree-trunks until they were nearly surrounded. The officer and his men then put up their hands, but dropped them when the surrender was about to take place. But the New Zealanders were deadlier and quicker. The German **German attempted** officer was shot with his hand on his **treachery prevented** revolver; his gunners were bayoneted.

On the left of the New Zealanders' line one of their battalions could see Germans on the Gravenstafel spur firing at their comrades. Although they had to lose their barrage, they covered the concrete works on the hillside, and under sharp fire worked round the field forts and took numerous prisoners from them. Then arose the question of escorting the captured Germans to the British lines. The victors did not care to miss the next fight, and their brigadier, getting out of his dug-out to see what was happening to his men on the slopes, received the first news of their success from Germans marching westward in company formation under their own officers.

On the left of the Anzac force, between London Ridge and the Stroombeek and the Lekkerboterbeek and Poelcappelle road, South Midland troops and other English forces went forward into the swamps commanded by the central part of the Passchendaele Ridge and the

BATTERY OF BRITISH 18-POUNDERS IN ACTION.

[Australian official photograph.

Artillery played a highly-important part in the Third Battle of Ypres, both in preliminary bombardment and in the varying forms of barrage, behind which infantry went forward to their objectives. In the course of this battle a new system of artillery preparation was employed, which in a large measure destroyed the value of the block-house system of defence extensively utilised by the Germans on the Flanders front.

rises below Houthulst Forest. Against them was a German division, which was so hopelessly smashed up by the British guns as to be generally demoralised.

The only serious delay which the Birmingham men and their comrades encountered was at Wellington Farm, on the eastern side of the Stroombeek swamp. Yet even this stronghold was surrounded and bombed into submission within twenty minutes. The Midland men, like most of the home and overseas forces, were swept by a very heavy German barrage as they were forming for the attack.

Happily, their preliminary casualties were slight, and it was after their victory that their powers of endurance were more severely tested. They were curtained off from their dressing-stations, and shelled steadily and heavily all night as they crouched in beating rain and cold wind on the open field. In spite of the difficulties of communication, touch was never lost with any of the British and overseas outposts along the new line.

On the north of the Midlanders the enemy was stronger and more successful in his defence. He made a stand along the course of the Lekkerboterbeek and upon rising ground between that stream and Poelcappelle. Supported by "tanks," the English troops advanced on both sides of the Poelcappelle road, captured the junction of highways running from Langemarck and St. Julien, and, storming into the village, occupied the ruins of the church and the western half of the wrecked buildings.

Still farther northward, round the railway line running from Pilkem to Bruges, the Irish Fusiliers, who had petitioned for a fighting part in the offensive, made a gallant

"Tanks" assist English infantry

thrust against a series of formidable enemy positions. They had to work over marshes, traversed by two winding streams, towards the railway embankment, from which well-placed enemy machine-gun posts swept all the fenland approaches.

The Irishmen could not, by reason of the difficulties of the ground, move forward in a straight line. They had to turn midway in their operations and swing half-left. So keen were they that many of them went through their own barrage at the start and, in spite of the sea of mud, kept up with the line of shells all the way to the Broenbeek. When they reached their final line they continued to sally out and attack every defensive position which they could espy in front of them.

Gallantry of Irish Fusiliers

When called back, they beat off a counter-attack in the early afternoon, and took many prisoners, whom they treated with especial kindness; for after the fight they found one of their officers in a shell-hole, wounded in the thigh, with a cut artery. Beside him was a German soldier, squatting and pressing both his thumbs on the artery. For two hours the German had sat there with his thumbs strongly pressed on the Irishman's leg— a feat of endurance which undoubtedly saved the officer's life.

Beyond the Bruges railway a force of Scotsmen had the miserable job of pushing over a continuous swamp, about one thousand yards north of Langemarck, to a stronghold known as Japan House. An ordinary advance in line was utterly impossible. The Scottish troops worked forward by whatever channels they could find, and, after reducing some isolated redoubts in the marshes, established a series of posts along the front they desired to reach.

On the north and in the centre the advance was complete. It brought the British troops within two thousand five hundred yards of Passchendaele village and the remaining bit of ridge sheltering Roulers. The belfry of Bruges could be seen clearly from the new British line, and, although the enemy had some cover remaining around the high ground at Moorslede, his general position between Ypres and Roulers was seriously weakened. He remained, however, strong among the low rises of ground southward in front of Menin.

The range of low hills running from Messines to Passchendaele and Staden formed a system shaped like an *S*. Against the lower bend the enemy had ample ground for massing some of the guns of the Sixth Army, as well as part of the artillery of the Fourth Army, and strongly reinforcing this combination of heavy ordnance with artillery brought from the Russian front.

Screened valleys in enemy hands Although General von Armin had lost the highest points by the Menin gate, he yet retained swell after swell of ground eastward. Behind these rises was a fan of screened approaches, along which his troops could reach the firing-line. In particular, he had the valley of the Krommebeek, between Zandvoorde and Kruiseik hills, the Reutelbeek valley, between the Kruiseik rise and the Terhand heights, and the Heulebeek valley, between the Becelaere and

Keiberg slopes and the clumps of Moorslede. British observers on the higher main ridge could not see down into these winding brook-threaded hollows, where the German infantry were safe from practically everything except howitzer fire directed by aeroplane observation.

The gate to Menin was only half open, and Sir Herbert Plumer, instead of again pushing directly against it, tried to wedge it asunder by a turning movement on the northern side. **British try a turning movement** Immediately below the Australian centre a fine force of Surrey, Staffordshire, Devon, Border, and Highland troops advanced from the northern face of Polygon Wood towards the Noordemdhoek height on the Passchendaele Ridge. South of the British force were Yorkshire, Northumberland, Lincoln, and Surrey battalions, who were set to clear the land east of Polygon Wood and seize the village of Reutel.

Farther south, troops from Kent, Devon, and Cornwall, with a battalion of Scottish Borderers, fought forward over Gheluvelt Hill into Polderhoek Château. To protect their flank other English troops moved forward south of the Menin road, from the neighbourhood of Tower Hamlets Ridge towards a short objective among the strong hostile works between Gheluvelt and Zandvoorde.

All the British troops forming the southern wing were severely tried by the enemy's bombardments and barrages. Some battalions had serious losses, and the ordeal of standing under heavy fire for forty-eight hours and getting soaked and chilled, as well as half dazed

[British official photograph.

DRESSING-STATION NEAR THE BROODSEINDE BATTLEFIELD.

Wounded British soldiers at a wayside dressing-station established about some ruined farm buildings on the road to Broodseinde. The men had had their wounds dressed, and were waiting, duly labelled with particulars as to their hurts, for removal to where they could get fuller surgical attention farther behind the line. A welcome drink was served out to such of the men as wished for it while they were waiting.

Cavalry waiting to go forward into action. After the prolonged trench warfare began, cavalry had for the most part they fought dismounted alongside the infantry, and occasionally as mounted infantry. On the few occasions when they could perform few opportunities of exhibiting their prowess. their proper function they showed that they had lost none of their fine horsemanship and gallantry.

Scene at an advanced dressing-station during a battle. Severely wounded men lying on stretchers were to be supplemented by the surgeons in the battered little hut, after which they would be conveyed waiting for the first field-dressing which they had received at the hands of the regimental stretcher-bearers in the waiting ambulances to the hospitals and clearing-stations established behind the line.

ON THE OUTSKIRTS OF THE BATTLEFIELD: BEFORE AND AFTER ACTION ON THE WESTERN FRONT.

by continual shell explosions, would have completely disheartened some of the German forces opposed to them.

Yet when the British were ordered to attack, just ten minutes before the hostile infantry intended to attack them, they went forward with their fine spirit only wrought to harder edge by their sufferings. East of Polygon Wood were three battalions of storm troops of the German 45th Division, assembled for advance in three waves, with an assault battalion to assist them. Behind these shock forces were the 4th Foot Guards waiting to take over the captured line.

Paralysing surprise by British barrages There was also another regiment in reserve ready to make a second assault if the first failed. All these forces were in close formation, and completely veiled in mist and darkness. But the British barrages smashed up all waves and columns in a few minutes. As each German line crumpled under the blaze of shells the swifter British troops were upon them. For there was no answering counter-barrage from the German guns to interfere with the steady surge of the British infantry.

As the front-line German troops were transformed into a defeated mob, the British barrages passed into the reserves and swept through them with terrible effect. "The surprise was paralysing," exclaimed a captured German officer. "No troops in the world could have rallied!"

The men from Surrey, Staffordshire, and Devon, with the Borderers and Scottish Highlanders, worked grimly forward over the crest alongside the Australians. Topping hill after hill, they reached the dominating point of Noordemdhoek, on the road between Broodseinde and Becelaere. Owing to the destructive effect of the British barrages upon the enemy's bunched forces, the attacking troops met with little opposition among the hills just below the crest village.

There was some machine-gun fire from two redoubts upon the cross-roads, but these strong points were reduced without much difficulty. As in the case of the Australian victory, the conquest of the ridge by the Englishmen and Scotsmen was accomplished with a lack of picturesque incidents, which, in the circumstances, was perfect evidence of the condition of the surprised and overwhelmed picked German forces.

In the Reutel sector, immediately below the scene of the Noordemdhoek victory, the Yorkshire, Northumberland, Surrey, and Lincoln troops had a shorter objective, but a more arduous task. They had to advance against the terrific enfilading gun fire from the enemy's southern parks of artillery. The enemy also possessed in the lower Reutelbeck valley a sheltered passage of reinforcement, extending for a mile westward of Reutel village.

He was therefore able in this area to recover from the destruction of his attacking regiments more quickly than he could regain strength on the exposed northern hillsides. The English battalions, sweeping out from the eastern fringe of Polygon Wood, bore down the broken German divisions with the same deadly ease as their home and overseas comrades did.

The Surrey men reported that they killed more Germans than in any previous battle. With their comrades they fought through the belt of wood, six hundred yards deep, which was directly east of Polygon Wood. The stretch of shattered trees was profusely planted with machine-gun posts and diversified into a maze of bogland and dry land by the erratic tributary rills of the Reutelbeck. But for the fact that it was packed with German assaulting troops, who were stricken with moral palsy by the overwhelming fire that surprised them, the terrain would have been as impregnable as Gheluvelt Hill.

When the five waves of enemy attacking forces were caught unexpectedly by the British barrages, shattered, demoralised, and jumbled up in the flame-shot gloom and fog, their machine-gunners in the defensive works were equally taken at a disadvantage. No German had been thinking of defence. Many of the crews in the concrete works had come out to assist, with covering machine-gun fire, in the proposed rushes by the shock troops. Most of them were broken and whirled along in the blind confusion of the general flight, and of those that remained in the concrete works none was able to check the sweeping drive of the English troops.

The whole of Reutel village was taken, and one of the "tanks," crawling onward with attendant infantry, passed the cemetery towards Becelaere. Had all gone well on the extreme flank by the Menin road, Reutel could have been easily held, and the Becelaere Hill

CASUALTIES—BUT INCURABLY CHEERFUL.
[Canadian War Records.
Canadians having their wounds attended to at an advanced dressing-post, one of them—lying on the stretcher and having his head bandaged—being himself a member of the R.A.M.C. Their wounds were unavailing to repress the smile of elation brought to their faces by recent successes.

positions seriously menaced. But the gallant forces who were working through the Upper Reutelbeek valley were impeded by the muddy state of the ground. The Scottish Borderers, Kents, Devons, and Cornishmen had to work forward from Veldhoek and Cameron House, towards Polderhoek Château and the northern flank of Gheluvelt Hill. In their first fine attack they carried the ground beyond the rise on which the manor-house stood, and kept up with the troops advancing on Reutel. They were so eager to catch up with some **Germans overlooked in the advance** fugitive visible Germans that they neglected invisible Germans, concealed in the underground works in Polderhoek Château and in the neighbourhood of Cameron House.

The German machine-gunners emerged from the ruins of the château on the hill above the valley of the Reutelbeek, and began to sweep with fire all the low ground northwards as far as Reutel village. About the same time the hostile guns between Zandvoorde and Comines covered all the southern British lines, new and old, with a tremendous blanket of shell, while strong counter-attacking columns of infantry worked up the river valley and pressed upon the line between Reutel and Gheluvelt Hill.

ON DENTAL PARADE.   [*New Zealand official photograph.*

Soldiers of the New Zealand Force on the western front undergoing inspection by an officer of the N.Z. Dental Corps. This corps undertook everything connected with the preservation and repair of the teeth of the fighting men.

The Englishmen and Scotsmen had to draw back some four hundred yards towards Polderhoek Château. There they discovered the hostile garrisons in their rear, about the mansion and by Cameron covert.

To add to the confusion, a British force in the covert failed to receive the order to retire to the new midway line, and had to be rescued. Once more the British wing went forward, fighting through the enemy positions that had been neglected between the Polygonbeek and the Reutelbeek, and overcoming the Jack-in-the-box garrison of the Polderhoek manor-house.

There then remained a slight dent in the new British front between Reutel and Gheluvelt Hill, and fresh German forces obtained room to make a flanking as well as a frontal attack upon the Englishmen in **German defence** Reutel village. In spite, however, of **methods mastered** continuous attempts to break into the bent British flank, the line between Reutel and Polderhoek held firm against all the enemy's savage thrusts.

Seven counter-attacks were beaten off by exceedingly heavy fighting, and though late in the day an eighth assaulting force succeeded in wresting the eastern part of Reutel village and the Polderhoek spur from the English battalions and Scottish Borderers, the enemy failed to win back the main part of the ground he had lost. South of the Menin road other English troops, about Tower Hamlets, successfully made a short advance, so as to keep in line with the forces on the other side of the Menin gate. In the general operations more than five thousand German prisoners were captured, and the destruction of the German divisions was so complete that General von Armin had not men ready to make any immediate counter-offensive along the critical part of the front after his last reserves had been broken near the Roulers railway.

Documents captured during the course of the battle of October 4th showed that General von Ludendorff and his lieutenants were acutely aware of the fact that their latest novel method of defence was a failure. They had first tried the Hindenburg tunnel system, but found that this only provided burrows for their men who did not want to fight. When the tunnel system was condemned by Ludendorff in person, who gave an order that all tunnels should be partly blown up, the heavy concrete block-house system was developed in an enormous way by frenzied labours.

When, in turn, the concrete forts were mastered by the new armies of the British Empire, they became, like the tunnels, little more than traps for German valour, and ante-chambers to the prisoners' cage for men who only wanted a temporary shelter from shell fire while waiting for a chance to surrender. Ludendorff was therefore obliged to return to the old practice of holding his foremost positions in considerable strength. This meant that he had to expose tens of thousands more infantrymen directly to the whirlwind gusts of British shell fire and all the deadly and terrifying instruments of mechanical assault.

Sir Herbert Plumer and Sir Hubert Gough had thrown the enemy back more than five miles along the Menin road and established a strong ridge-line, with a good defensive flank on the Gravenstafel spur. In these circumstances, Sir Douglas Haig began to doubt whether it was worth while to undertake the conquest of the remaining Passchendaele sector of the ridge before winter set in, for the state of the sodden and shell-ploughed ground was such as to make any further movement through the Ypres swamp seem almost impracticable.

The British commander had to weigh the strength the enemy was receiving from the eastern theatre, and see that his own new lines were not merely jumping-off places for a fresh attack, but well-planned, defensive systems against a possible grand offensive by the enemy. Economy in territorial gains was becoming as important as economy in man-power.

On the other hand, Sir Douglas Haig was desirous of doing all that he possibly could to wear down the enemy's reserves, so that the reinforcements obtainable by the German Command from the Russian front would do little more than serve to replace some of the losses. In this regard, the documents captured from the enemy, showing that he was changing his tactics and putting more men into the firing-line, had a considerable influence on the plans of the British commander. As he was still generally stronger in artillery than the enemy he saw that, by continuing the Ypres offensive for some weeks longer, he could so ravage the more densely-filled hostile lines as to sap the enemy of much of his new strength, as this was being gradually gathered.

Furthermore, General Pétain had arranged an important French operation on the Aisne for the third week of October. It was thus necessary for the British armies to continue to press the German armies severely, so as to keep the German line along the Aisne in its existing weak state. Sir Douglas Haig had found that the Germans were weakening along his southern front in their effort to main- **Why the battle** tain the defence of the Menin gate. **was prolonged** The lines around Cambrai, in particular, were held with inferior forces, and the British commander was preparing to thrust over the Hindenburg line towards Cambrai, as the closing act in the Ypres campaign.

He therefore could not relax his attacks upon the Passchendaele Ridge without giving the enemy time to redistribute his over-concentrated forces and strengthen himself on the Aisne plateau and around Cambrai and elsewhere. So the terrible swamp battle was renewed, in heavy autumnal rain, for certain strategic reasons.

From Messines to Broodseinde Sir Douglas Haig's men were on the hills, while the enemy was spread out on the low ground beneath them, or sheltering under the eastern slopes of lower rises and shell-churned, watery hollows.

But, first to help France and then to assist Italy, the British Army had to plunge again into the most dreadful conditions of battle in military history, and wade in mud and blood to the northern end of the low, insignificant, tragic ridge.

| CHAPTER CCXXI. |

THE CONQUEST OF POELCAPPELLE AND THE REVERSE OF PASSCHENDAELE.

By Edward Wright.

Military Results of False Economy in the Development of the Forecast Division of the British Meteorological Office—Terrible Condition of the Ypres Marshland in the Autumn of 1917—British Attack Opened on October 9th—Superb Performance by the French Sweeping Through Mangelaare to Their Final Objective on the Fringe of Houthulst Forest—British Guards Race the Frenchmen Across the Marshland and Achieve a Dead Heat—Anglo-Newfoundland Battalions Reach Five Roads—Defensive Victories of the Enemy Round Poelcappelle—Agonising Experiences of Lancashire Territorials—Incessant German Machine-Gun Barrages —Wild Soldiers' Battle Round Passchendaele—British Retire Five Hundred Yards During the Night—Second British Assault Opens October 12th, the New Zealand Division Making the Main Attack—Operations Suspended Owing to Weather Conditions —Germans Retire to Keiberg Hill—The Problem of Passchendaele Still Confronting Sir Douglas Haig in View of the Situation on the Italian Front.

IN the science of weather forecasting the meteorological assistants to the British Army seem to have been continuously unfortunate. Immediately after the Battle of Broodseinde, on October 4th, 1917, as Sir Douglas Haig stated in his despatch, he partly based his decision to continue the struggle for the ridge on the anticipation that the weather would not be unusually wet. Very heavy rain, however, went on falling.

By the middle of the month the persistent continuation of wet weather left no further room for hope that the state of the Ypres swamp would enable the whole of the Passchendaele Ridge to be conquered before the arrival of the main German reinforcements of men and guns from Russia. But before this condition of things was admitted, practically all countries lying by the Atlantic were soaking for weeks in rain.

Even in the days of peace the Forecast Division of the British Meteorological Office had not been developed in a way consistent with the agricultural and other interests of the nation that vitally depended on the study of the Atlantic

[*New Zealand official photograph.*
GUIDING THE GUNS.
Telephonist attached to a New Zealand howitzer battery on the western front receiving and recording messages as to the ranges at which the guns of his battery were to fire.

and Continental weather conditions. British politicians had no keen idea of the national value of science, and, like many other branches of intricate research, British meteorology was stunted and starved by the Government. It was also somewhat contemned by farmers and sailors, but this was merely the consequence of inadequate measures of Government support. The vast urban population of the British Isles drew the larger part of its food from foreign countries, and, recking little how the home crops diminished, therefore merely jested at the frequent failures in the official weather forecast, instead of agitating for the expenditure of more money in organising a larger scheme of advanced observations and widely extended research.

Sir William Napier Shaw and his lieutenants were capable men, but they do not seem to have been able, with the small grant of £23,500, properly to extend and reorganise the military branch of their work. Critics might have said that the expenditure of half a million pounds a year, under Major Ernest Gold, of the Military Meteorological Section, might have saved the Empire much treasure and many lives; that apparently,

525

A FIRST-CLASS TRENCH DINING-ROOM.
Dining-room in the officers' quarters in the section of the elaborate underground trench system of the Hindenburg line that was captured by the Allies in the autumn offensive of 1917.

through false economy in one of the most important fields of war, the British Government continued to serve the British soldier far less well than the United States Government had for years served the American farmer.

The control of the Meteorological Office was largely exercised by a committee appointed by the Lords Commissioners of the Treasury. In war time this control should have been in the hands of the British Chief of Staff and a Sea Lord of the Admiralty, and a greatly enlarged Forecast Division should have been placed directly under the Commander-in-Chief of the Grand Fleet and the Commander-in-Chief of the Armies in France and Flanders. They would have spent more than a fraction of £23,500 a year in improving the collection of all available data in the entire areas of cyclone and anti-cyclone movements that conditioned the weather in the North Sea, the Channel, the Flemish coast, and North-Western France. In this case, Sir Douglas Haig might have been provided with definite knowledge on the evening of October 4th that rain was likely to continue for some days, and that there was no reason for supposing that the month would be a fairly dry one.

Appalling mud in the marshland

The swamp of Ypres became terrifying in the autumn of the year of rains. Even in dry weeks in midsummer, shell-holes on high ground round Ypres remained partly full of water. The general surface of the earth was barely above sea-level, and about five feet beneath it was a clay substratum, through which water could not soak. When this clay bottom was dug up by millions of shells the Steenbeek River ceased to flow towards the sea and became an inland lake.

Its many tributaries changed from rills, over which a man could jump, into vague stretches of lagoon and flooded quagmire. The Stroombeek, for instance, completely vanished, losing itself in a wide belt of earthen porridge, under which were the innumerable old shell-craters of suffocating depth. When an advance had to be made without duck-board bridges half a battalion at times would be engaged in wading through the mud above shell-craters, and helping the other half that had slipped into the holes.

Water would have been much easier to pass. Men could have swum through it with a rope and formed a bridge-head under cover of a heavy barrage. But thigh-deep, waist-deep, neck-deep mud proved at last impracticable to the most

athletic, unwearying, and dauntless of men. The Niemen mud, that had hindered Napoleon during his march on Moscow, was not comparable with the Ypres mud that impeded Sir Douglas Haig in his operations against the northern end of Passchendaele Ridge.

The effect of years of heavy artillery fire upon the watery Ypres marshland was to create such an obstacle to all movement as had never been known before in war. The defences, erected with ant-like industry by the German engineers, were utterly insignificant in comparison with the defence that prolonged rainy weather produced. The high Ladies' Walk, with the Aisne in flood below it, was not half so formidable as the low swell of ground by Passchendaele village, moated by the vanished Stroombeek and the vanishing Lekkerboterbeek, the half-obliterated Ravelbeek and Paddebeek.

Happily, the German commander was over-confident of the strength of his position in the morning of October 9th, when the rain ceased for two hours, and left the watery swamp still obscured by a thick, damp mist. Once more German divisions were caught in the disorder of relief, and punished so severely that ground to the depth of twelve hundred yards was conquered without any serious check. The front of attack stretched from St. Janshoek, by Houthulst Forest, to Nieuwemolen, by Broodseinde Hill. In addition to this main assault a subsidiary operation was conducted around Reutel village.

Offensive resumed on October 9th

A fine French corps, forming part of the forces under General Anthoine, advanced along the Corverbeek stream, on the south-western outskirts of Houthulst Forest, to Zevekoten, Mangelaare, and Veldhoek hamlets. The British Guards fought alongside the French troops, and, crossing the Broenbeek water with them, captured Koekuit village and a large number of enemy strongholds on the southern edge of the forest.

On the right of the Guards, English forces worked along the Staden-Bruges railway and won a new line beyond the road running from Poelcappelle to Dixmude. Other English battalions fought forward into Poelcappelle village and through the ruins as far as the brewery. Australian troops, and East Lancashire, Yorkshire, and South Midland Territorials, attacked in the direction of Passchendaele village and the main ridge, reaching the

PAINFUL LABOUR IN DREARIEST CONDITIONS.
British soldiers carrying heavy balks of timber for bridges to be built over the Yser. The labour, heavy enough in itself, was intensified by the mud through which the men had to toil.

[Canadian War Records.

IN LINE OF COLUMN.
A fleet of British landships advancing in single
file towards the front line.

"TANKS" WAITING TO GO INTO ACTION.
[Canadian War Records.
First introduced into warfare at Flers, on the Somme, in 1916, the "tank" caused "indescribable
demoralisation" among the enemy and immediately proved an invaluable aid to infantry advancing
against entrenched positions; and later, before Cambrai, in 1917, was an adequate substitute for
the preliminary bombardment that would have eliminated the element of surprise from an attack.

crest and taking Nieuwemolen. In
the southern action, Reutel village
was wholly regained by the Warwickshire and H.A.C. battalions.

The French attack was conducted
over very bad ground, but handled
with such brilliancy that the swamp
between the Corverbeek and the
Broenbeek was occupied to a depth
of a mile and a quarter on a front of
a mile and a half. For three days
previous to the infantry movement
the French artillery swept each hostile
strong point with whirlwind gusts of
heavy shell. Then at 5.30 a.m. on
October 9th the finely-trained French
soldiers plunged into the almost
continuous marsh of chocolate and
black mud and, shielded by an extremely slow barrage,
toiled forward for two hours towards the vanished village
of Mangelaare.

Though Mangelaare had vanished it was more formidable
than it had been when it existed. Its cellars had been
extended and overlaid with concrete, making it a very
strong submerged fortress amid flood and mud that
might have held up the advance. By the Mangelaare line
the men who got through the mud
rested a while, gathering strength from
men rejoining their lost platoons and
from supports who pushed forward for
cleaning-up work. Only a short stop was made, and the
Frenchmen then swept through Mangelaare with amazing
rapidity and, after another struggle in the slime, reached
their final line on the fringe of Houthulst Forest by 10 a.m.

Their average pace was about four hundred yards an
hour. It was a wonderful speed in the circumstances.
The British Guards had at times to fight desperately in
order to keep up with the vehement Frenchmen. The
worst part of the greatest obstacle race ever devised
would have been easy going in comparison with the

**French sweep
through Mangelaare**

bullet and shrapnel-swept morasses through which the
Frenchmen struggled. Dotting the marsh were many
ruined block-houses and some uninjured strongholds from
which the victors extracted three hundred prisoners.
Lannes Farm, Catinat Farm, London Square, Gambetta
Square, and the organised cellars of Mangelaare were some
of the intact fortresses around and through which the
French had to work, under the fire of enemy machine-
gunners and sharpshooters.

As the attacking troops were often stuck in the mud,
they formed thousands of targets for the enemy forces.
Yet such was their skill, and such was the precision with
which they worked behind their shell curtains, that their
casualties were remarkably light. No hostile block-house
seriously checked the programme of the advance, and at
9 a.m., when messages were received from the Mangelaare
line, the French stretcher-bearers were not working.

The French attack had fallen on two enemy divisions
engaged in a relief. Under the terrific bombardment and
the unexpected infantry assault the enemy forces fell
into complete disorder. They suffered such heavy losses
that they were utterly dispirited, and ran into the French

curtain fire instead of attempting to fight out the awful swamp battle. The French captured two guns as well as many machine-guns.

When a German counter-attacking force struck them on the left flank, and took Victory Farm from them, they not only recovered the farm but pursued the enemy around the crater-pools, chased him into another fortified farm, and occupied it.

It was the way in which the French, British, and Belgian artillery was handled around Houthulst Forest that kept the French casualty list down. All German batteries in and above the forest were hammered with projectiles, and so completely drenched with gas-shells that the enemy gunners could not or would not work. Then the light French field-gun was brought up to the fighting-line and used almost like a machine-gun.

The British Guards had the same kind of ground to traverse as the French corps. In front of them was the little brook, Broenbeek, which had extended from little more than a ditch into an icy mud-flow, some fifty yards broad. Beyond this zone of black liquidity was a waste of pools and ooze, through which ran chaotic fragments of the Ypres-Dixmude road.

British Guards' loyal rivalry

The Broenbeek marsh was cleared by a Stokes-gun bombardment, enabling the Irish Guards to advance some three hundred yards without a single casualty. In this

[*Canadian War Records.*

REPAIRING ROADS BEHIND THE LINES.
At work in a village on the western front in which many of the inhabitants had remained in their homes even during the time that it was under shell fire. The Canadian soldiers were taking a turn at laying down and rolling in fresh road metal on the village street.

sector also the Germans were caught in the process of relief, and the mortar bombardment so dismayed them that many of the survivors, as soon as they saw the Guards coming, ran towards them with their hands uplifted.

Some of the Germans, however, rallied around Strode House. This was a large redoubt, entirely surrounded by wire entanglements, most of which was uncut. Men of the fresh 227th German Division held this work, and by bursts of machine-gun fire and musketry showed they were ready to offer desperate resistance. It appeared to be an occasion for siege work and gradual advances, ending in an attack covered by Stokes guns and machine-guns.

But the Guards could not stop to conduct any slow and economical reduction operations. There was a certain amount of loyal competition between them and their French comrades, and they could not suffer the French advance to be checked by a right flank attack, owing to any delay in their own linking movement. They gathered in the shell-holes about the great stronghold, and then leaped through and over the wire and bombed and bayoneted the garrison into surrender. Farther south another strong fortress was suddenly rushed in similar manner.

The Guards pushed through Koekuit, in line with the racing Frenchmen, and completed their advance at Faidherbe Square, in continual and exact contact with their friendly rivals. "It was perfect," said a French officer. "We were side by side."

[*Canadian War Records.*

LEAVING THE TRENCHES AFTER BEING RELIEVED.
Canadian soldiers whose places in the firing-line had been taken over by their reliefs. They were nearing the end of a communication-trench where weeds had clothed the banks with brief verdure.

His men, as he explained, desired to show the British that they were the finest infantry in the world, and as the Guardsmen were also keen to uphold the particular honour of their corps and the general honour of their nation, the happily competitive combination had a driving power that was terrible to the enemy. The Guards had fought side by side with the French in the opening of the Third Battle of Ypres, and they were sternly resolved that no check which they encountered should interfere with the time-table of General Anthoine. In all, the Guards

Resistance along the railway got some four hundred prisoners, and pushed their line into the wilderness of mud and water by Houthulst Forest.

On the right of the Guards were Newfoundlanders and English troops, who went along the Staden and Bruges railway to the cross-roads of Cinq Chemins, in line with the British Guards and the French corps. The enemy's resistance was stronger along the railway embankment, and some battalions lost many of their officers through having to attack a deep line of German works without the assistance of a close barrage. For while the men were slowly getting through the mud, the British gunners had to keep to the time-table, and sent their squelching, flaming line of shell too far ahead of the bogged infantry. Like the Guards in similar circumstances, the Newfoundlanders and English battalions had quickly to rush block-house after block-house by means of strong bombing-parties in order to attain the pace set by the Frenchmen.

When they arrived at the Cinq Chemins, or Five Roads, some of the Island troops, having reached a point three thousand yards from their starting-place, wanted to pursue the enemy into the maze of the great forest. This, however, would have been a dangerous adventure. The enemy had the advantage of approaches round the Five Roads. Three of the roads ran northwards and eastwards through enemy territory, and were there interconnected by some six or seven straight drives through the southernmost part of the forest.

The Newfoundland and English troops, on the other hand, did not have a single road by which to bring up reinforcements to the crossways. The two southern roads which they occupied ran in lateral directions, towards the top of the French flank on one side and towards the raging conflict in Poelcappelle on the other side.

The enemy commander profited by this situation and delivered his first counter-attack with remarkable rapidity at 8.30 a.m. At this time the French had not reached the fringe of the forest, neither had the Guards, who also were subjected to a counter-thrust. Moreover, the help of the British artillery could not be obtained, yet the spear-head of Newfoundlanders and Englishmen completely broke up the enemy's storm troops with musketry and machine-gun fire. When at 10 a.m. another German force swarmed out of the forest, the victors had settled down, and their Staff in the rear knew the exact line they had won. The result was that the second German counter-attack was wiped out by British field-guns before the infantry could engage it.

Enemy counter-attacks wiped out

Meanwhile the forces on the right, in the neighbourhood

"THE ENEMY'S ARTILLERY HAS BEEN ACTIVE DURING THE DAY."
This photograph of a German shell bursting in the Belgian lines aptly illustrates a phrase that appeared in the communiqués almost daily after the Third Battle of Ypres had ended—showing the enemy's nervousness of further allied offensive action in Flanders.

of Poelcappelle, found themselves unable to make all the progress necessary to cover the right flank of the Anglo-Newfoundland battalions. The enemy began furiously to bombard the salient created by the Five Roads, and in order to save the victors from being assailed on two sides, they were commanded to retire for about a thousand yards towards the Poelcappelle-Staden road. In spite of this strategic surrender of part of the conquered ground, the achievement of the Anglo-Newfoundland force was masterly, and told successfully on the course of all actions in the northern sectors.

Round Poelcappelle village and the brewery on the Westroosebeek road there began a line of German works that stretched south-eastwards to Passchendaele crest and the spurs of the main ridge above Broodseinde. This proved a line of defensive victories for the enemy. For, although he lost the village of Poelcappelle, he stood firm above the ghastly swamps of the Watervlietbeek, the Lekkerboterbeek, Paddebeek, Stroombeek, and the Ravebeek, and broke the thrusting power of the English divisions that vainly endeavoured to reach the central high ground.

Strength of German positions It was not the fighting strength of the Germans that won them, on October 9th, their greatest victory since their repulse of the Fifth British Army on August 16th. Their successful stand was due to the adventitious strength of their positions. Bad weather and bad ground weakened the attacking forces and disastrously delayed their movements. They lost their barrages and became bodily exhausted by the time they arrived within attacking distance of the enemy's main defences.

These defences were certainly held in unusual force. General von Armin brought forward every light and every heavy machine-gun within reach. He removed the gunners from supporting divisions and from his rearmost defences, and posted them alongside the dense garrisons of the main ridge and of the lower spurs and knolls. Thereby he created a machine-gun barrage between Poelcappelle and Passchendaele village such as had never before been employed on any front. While arranging this sheet of incessant fire over the quagmires

of the broken brooks he maintained day and night rolling barrages over the ground where the British troops were assembling for action.

The assembling of the English divisions was as wild and bitter work as the actual advance. In particular, a third-line Territorial division, containing untried men and including Manchesters, East Lancashires, and Lancashire Fusiliers, had an ordeal on the night of October 8th that did not testify to brilliant Staff work. The men set out in the evening on a march to the firing-line by the Gravenstafel spur. It was calculated they would take three hours to get into position, but they were engaged for eleven hours, in a black tempest of rain and heavy hostile gun fire, in winning through the mud to the brimming shell-hole line from which they were to attack. When the men arrived, hungry and exhausted, soaked and chilled to the marrow, they had quickly to go into action. Some of them, indeed, arrived too late for their barrage.

[Australian official photograph.
RISSOLES FOR SUPPER.
Australian cooks busy in their field kitchen preparing rissoles of bully beef for the men's evening meal.

Fighting with the Lancashires were the Warwicks and West Country troops, who were stretched out in the slashing rain and knife-like wind by the slime and foul water that the Lekkerboterbeek and Stroombeek could not carry away. Immediately beside the Lancashires were Yorkshiremen, who kept dreadful vigil near the upper course of the Stroombeek, called the Ravebeek, running through the swamp known as Marsh Bottom. By reason of their terrible march without food or rest the Lancashire Territorials endured the supreme agony, but the lot of their comrades on either side was one of tragic misery.

On this part of the front the Germans were clearly aware that something was impending, and

IN A FIRST-AID DRESSING-STATION NEAR THE FRONT LINE.
Red Cross members of the Australian Imperial Force at work in an advanced dressing-station on the western front. In the cramped quarters casualties received the concentrated attention of highly competent officer doctors and soldier assistants, and bore the dressing of painful wounds with stoic calm.

they gathered in the fragments of the old Staden-Zonnebeke trench system, much of which was still enclosed by wire, and filled all their advanced block-houses and ridge fortresses, besides scattering in innumerable sniping positions on small humps of ground amid the mud.

The Rhinelanders of the 16th Division, good fighting men, after resting for ten weeks by the sea, were the men who held the line against the English. The attacking troops lost their barrage while struggling through water-covered quagmires and wastes of slime. Thereupon the garrisons of intact block-houses and the sharp-

[*New Zealand official photograph.*
A MOMENT IN A MELANCHOLY WASTE.
New Zealand engineers resting in a huge shell-hole on the field where lately conflict had been raging. Toilsome for marching over without opposition, the terrain was described as being only negotiable against opposition by "superhuman exertion."

[*New Zealand official photograph.*
REST BILLETS BEHIND THE LINES.
The commander of the New Zealanders on a tour of inspection of the billets allotted to the men of a Canterbury regiment—havens of peace, indeed, compared with the desolation of the battle area depicted in the upper photograph.

shooters and machine-gunners in crater positions came vigorously into action during the long interval between the last crash of British shell and the slow approach of the haggard, wet, mud-plastered, crawling, stumbling, slipping infantrymen.

The great German machine-gun barrage rattled at long range from the spurs and slopes of the ridge, at middle range from the Staden-Zonnebeke trench system, and practically at point-blank range from the foremost concrete works. The plight of the English wounded was often horrible; lucky were they who rested on some ridge of mud where stretcher-bearers could at last find them. But wounds and death were not the chief source of anxiety to the tragically-heroic Englishmen. Their great trouble was to keep the mud from fouling their rifles and machine-guns, and so disarming them against counter-attacks.

For the confident Rhinelanders came out into the open and amid the sea of mud, and endeavoured to throw back the tired and drenched English troops. This method of active defence completely failed. Whenever the Germans came out they were scattered into cover again. They did their best work sitting behind concrete walls, or sniping from concealed shell-holes, and from the trees

of the little copses between Poelcappelle and Passchendaele. The village of Poelcappelle was taken by a series of rushes from the western part, which had been conquered on October 4th. But about the brewery, some five hundred yards eastward of the ruins, the conflict raged with extreme violence. German sappers had erected great numbers of concrete positions on the north-east and east of Poelcappelle. One of the positions entered by the English troops consisted of nineteen distinct concrete works, all held in strength and bristling with machine-guns. There was another defence near the village, which was a street of massive armoured concrete, under-run by a long tunnel which had chambers opening out into the works of the eastern side. Furthermore, on the western side, the fortress was concealed and cushioned by a bank of earth, so that it should escape the eyes of British gunnery observers. It did so escape; and then, when the Englishmen tried to surround it, they found on the rear side a sheer doorless concrete wall with flaming slits of machine-gun fire.

After clearing out the cellars of the eastern part of Poelcappelle, the Englishmen advanced along the road and bombed their way into the brewery. There, however, they came under enfilading machine-gun fire from the neighbouring works, and the **Violent conflict** enemy commander threw in reserves **at the brewery** from north and east and recovered the brewery fortress. In the end some fine Yorkshire troops made rush after rush upon the brewery, but failed to recover it, owing largely to the check to the English centre.

Had the ground been practicable, the Poelcappelle attack would have been made decisively by means of pincer movements, one force advancing from the north-west across the Dixmude road, while another force worked along the Lekkerboterbeek from the south-west. But the south-western movement was partly lost in the swamp of the spilt and flooded hillside brook. The men could not move quickly enough, and though the enemy counter-attacks were beaten off, the hopelessness of maintaining communications and recovering wounded men from the great swamp brought the troops to a standstill.

The Englishmen in the centre made superhuman endeavours to close around Passchendaele. They battled

THIRTEENTH-CENTURY ART DESTROYED BY TWENTIETH-CENTURY SAVAGERY.

New Zealanders among the ruins at one of the doorways of the once lovely old Cathedral of Ypres, after it had long been the target, deliberately aimed at, of German artillery. Macaulay, when New Zealand was but a new colony, imagined an inhabitant of that distant colony at some distant date contemplating the ruins of London from London Bridge. His fancy could not foretell that well within a century New Zealanders and Londoners would be fighting together through ruins to save civilisation for the world from the recrudescent barbarism of the Teuton.

into the Staden-Zonnebeke system, between Adler Farm and the Ravebeck, and while some of them desperately thrust upon the great hillside fortress of Bellevue, directly in front of Passchendaele, their comrades broke the enemy's line by Wolf Farm and Wallemolen, and mightily endeavoured to work southward by Peter Pan House and thence outflank the Bellevue fortifications.

It is difficult to describe what happened, because the commanding officers did not know at the time what was occurring immediately beyond their view. It was probably the wildest soldiers' battle in British annals. The mud, the snipers, and the machine-gunners hindered lateral as well as rear communications, and the dreadful German machine-gun barrage from the ridge, with the rolling barrages from German artillery around Roulers further bedevilled the connections between all headquarters and the straggling firing-line.

In some places lanes, in other places islands, of enemy forces were situated in the rear of the Midland, West Country, Lancashire, and Yorkshire waves of attack. Battalion and Brigade Staffs were despairingly inadequate in number to maintain touch with and between the attacking groups. Men by the thousand would have been required to connect the scattered, battling groups divided by mud and flood. The messengers took hours to make journeys which on dry land over firm roads would have been accomplished in a few seconds by motor-cycle riders. Most of the runners fell on the way, so that it was only by rare good fortune that occasional directions for team-work reached the infantry officers.

Difficulties of communication

The German commanders were in scarcely better case. They did not know what groups of their men still resisted

in the mad sandwich of conflict amid the copses, block-houses, bogs, and slopes of slime below the ridge around Passchendaele village. Often their machine-gunners, on upland positions, sprayed with bullets friend and foe alike, and the German shell also fell in an indiscriminate way, showing that the enemy had no information regarding his advanced troops.

One party of Territorials was, by error, reported to have entered Passchendaele village, but when night fell some of them were certainly scattered about the high approaches to the main knolls of the ridge. No doubt, had supports arrived in good order, the famous hill village could have been taken by developing the flanking movement towards Bellevue spur and helping the men on the right wing, who were checked about Crest Hill. But the supporting troops were in turn delayed by the state of the ground and by the very difficult work of rounding up the German sharpshooters and machine-gunners who were harassing both the communications and the medical work of the English forces.

Disheartening retirement

When, in the night, the process of cleaning up and organising and connecting the immediate rear of the English attacking divisions was accomplished, it became unfortunately necessary to order a retirement of some five hundred yards from the Passchendaele positions. This was disheartening and arduous work. The scattered groups had to be found before they could be called back, and during the withdrawal the enemy continued to sweep the ground with streams of bullets and fierce bursts of shell fire. He did not launch any counter-attack. Either he was afraid of getting his men bogged in the swamp, or he was staggered by the marvellous driving power displayed by the long-enduring Englishmen and Australians, and was keeping his reserves by the ridge in expectation of having to recover Passchendaele village.

So, without any infantry interruption, the attacking line was drawn back to a point about one thousand yards from the crater positions from which the Territorials had set out. The abandonment of the other five hundred yards' depth of advance was a serious matter, in that it released the enemy forces on the spurs of the ridge from direct and heavy pressure, and enabled the German commander to reorganise and strengthen his already formidable works along the hillsides. It gave his machine-gunners a broader zone of fire during the operations that followed, and greatly increased the distance that other attacking forces had to cover before they could clinch with the main army of the defence.

Yet the withdrawal had to be carried out. Stretcher-bearers were unable to work from the more advanced line. They were tired out and sadly **Heroic** reduced in number when they reached **stretcher-bearers** that line, and when they found the wounded and heroically endeavoured to carry their burdens through shell and bullet barrages, the dark, treacherous reaches of mud and water robbed them completely of their remaining strength. They slipped in the mud, they fell in the mud, they tumbled into the deep ooze and into the shell-hole ponds. Heroes all they were, and the entire Army worshipped them. But, in spite of all their efforts, their physical strength proved

unequal to the intolerable strain imposed on it. They had to cover the miles of ground that had been won, and then carry the wounded over the marshes which some of the attacking troops had taken at eleven hours' traverse with no other burden but their kit.

There was also the problem of supplying food and ammunition to the front-line troops, and providing them with some sort of shelter from rain and wind. The task of getting all this **Problem of** material carried over the Lekkerboter- **supply** beek, Stroombeek, and Ravebeek quagmires was appalling. Only by drawing the front back for nearly a third of a mile was it possible to feed and munition the men in the firing-line.

Adler Farm, Wolf Farm, and Wallemolen Cemetery were among the strong points taken, together with Kronprinz Farm, Peter Pan House, and part of the concrete works behind it. Some of these strongholds, however, were lost during the retirement. Farther south, Keerselaarhoek was captured, and also the cross-road hamlet of Nieuwe-molen, north of Broodseinde and six miles from Roulers.

From Broodseinde the Australians made the most difficult attack they had undertaken since their final advances in the Somme campaign. They plunged eastward into the deluged declines and inclines towards Keiberg, and also fought northward towards the crest position at Passchendaele. Between the Broodseinde fifty-eight metre plateau and Keiberg there were three ridges of forty metres, thirty-five metres, and thirty

[*British official photograph.*

IN MEMORY OF THE HEROIC DEAD OF THE 1st AUSTRALIAN DIVISION.

Australian troops presenting arms and saluting at the solemn unveiling of the memorial to the men of the 1st Australian Division who fell on the western front. This memorial, the tall cross to the right, was a fittingly simple symbol of the brave men who came from the Antipodes to the aid of the Mother Country and her Allies in fighting those who would have imposed upon the world the godless creed that the only right is might.

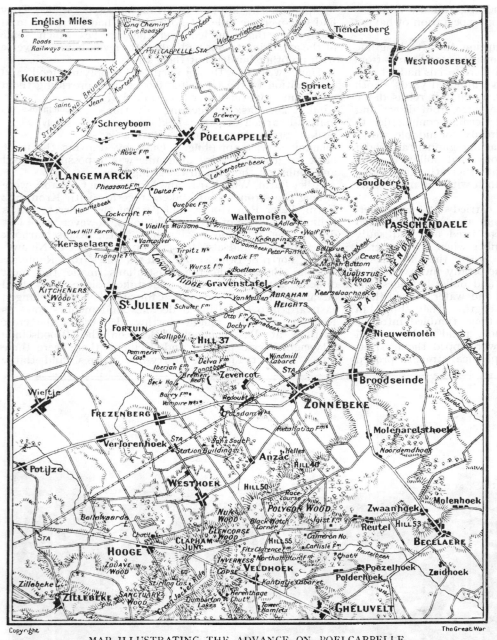

MAP ILLUSTRATING THE ADVANCE ON POELCAPPELLE.
Here is shown in detail the difficult country of small streams that had been converted into broad marsh-lands, and of spurs, across which the British troops fought forward with varying fortunes but unfailing heroism during the first half of October, 1917.

the Australians had to work slowly round the flanks of the copse and leave the enemy gunners still firing in their rear until supports arrived and cleared the batch of broken trees of Germans. The Australians then worked down the slope to the second ridge.

This ridge they took and held after a splendid attack from which their wounded came back strangely smiling. "We got the beggars good on the second ridge," said one lad, limping to the rear, with the blood streaming through the bandages above his knee. By this time, however, the third ridge had been taken and lost. The Australians who topped it were too few in number and too much exhausted to consolidate their line and hold it against the fresh German forces.

Like the Lancashires on their left wing, they had passed over, in the mist and straggling confusion of movements in the mud, nests of hostile sharpshooters and machine-gunners. These emerged in their rear and hindered communications and supporting troops. The advanced force on the third ridge had to fall back, attacked in front and on both flanks and sniped from the rear.

Regaining their supports, they managed to make a consolidation line extending from five to six hundred yards between the Broodseinde Ridge and the Keiberg Hill. On the left of the Australian line the Germans had machine-guns sweeping down the cutting of the Roulers railway through the top of the ridge. In this sector the Lancashire men were more than half an hour late in reaching their starting-point of co-operation with their overseas comrades.

As before explained, the rain-deepened mud had made their march one of heartbreaking difficulty. When the general British barrage began to move forward the Lancashires were quite half a mile behind it. Yet they won the admiration of the Australians by desperately pushing on until they caught up with the travelling line of shell fire and reached a considerable part of their objective.

"Bitterly disappointed we were late," said a mud-caked Lancashireman to some Australians. "It was hard luck on you." But the Australians, when they heard of the conditions of the Lancashires' march, generously recognised that it was only by superb heroism that the English on their right flank had won any ground at all.

Progress to the south

South of the main attacking forces the fine, ubiquitous Warwicks, with London men and South-West Country troops, went through Reutel village in the morning of October 9th, and reached the Wervicq road at a point halfway between Noordemdhoek and Zwaanhoek. The Londoners stormed forward from the western edge of Reutel, bombed the German machine-gunners

metres, with thirty-three metre, forty metre, forty-five metre, and fifty metre heights between Broodseinde and the Roulers railway approaches to Passchendaele. The men were exhausted by their previous efforts, and by the five days and nights of rain and chilling wind they had endured after their Broodseinde victory, while beating back enemy counter-attacks.

The midwinter weather of the night before the battle took the last strength out of the worn Australians. When they went forward in the misty dawn of October 9th the spirit within them, though fierce as ever, could not supply the failing strength of their bodies. Owing to the mud their pace was much slower. Their rifles and Lewis guns were apt to choke, and when Germans were found with some fight in them the combat became most arduous for men who were already worn out with dragging their feet out of heavy mud.

At the opening of the advance a small wood had to be taken in which was a strong group of German machine-gunners. These swept all the direct approaches, and

from the cellars, and, sweeping into the cemetery, silenced a couple of guns there and consolidated on their objective by Hill 53 in front of Becelaere.

Near the Wervicq road there was fierce fighting in Judge Copse and Judge Cottage, while the enemy gunners maintained a steady barrage down the hillsides against the attacking battalions. This long-range heavy machine-gun fire was directed against German as well as against English troops, and wounded German prisoners were maddened by the murderous barrage from their own gunners. Either the men on the hillsides around Becelaere did not mind killing their advanced troops in order to check the progress of the English, or else they were mistaken in respect to the situation, and regarded all the ground as being lost.

British rampart of defence

On the southern flank, however, the British objective was fixed beforehand at a point below Becelaere Hill. Any farther movement forward would only have exposed the attacking troops to larger counter-offensives from the Reutelbeek valley. The enemy retained his hold upon Polderhoek knoll, quite a mile on the rear flank of the conquerors of Reutel Cemetery. Therefore the British line about the Reutelbeek had to be designed mainly as a rampart of defence, behind which all the main movements through the Ypres morasses were conducted.

So it was not safe to make any important movement about the Reutelbeek, and though Polderhoek Château continued to change hands, this little oscillation did not tell upon the balance of great forces at Gheluvelt. The British commander did not want to advance any farther along the Menin road, and the German commander did not care to lose any more men in trying to recover the dominant positions overlooking his centre.

Each side continually swept the opposing lines with enormous tempests of shell, while their infantry extended in two wedges alongside the brook swamp. Polderhoek formed the point of the German wedge, while Reutel Cemetery was the point of the British wedge, with Tower Hamlets spur also jutting into the enemy's southern territory.

After the Battle of Poelcappelle, on October 9th, the unsettled weather continued, and the condition of the ground grew still worse.

Sir Douglas Haig, nevertheless, decided to press onward in spite of all the hardships of his men.

The Italian line had broken, and there was at the time considerable danger that the German and Austrian armies might thrust past Venice and also pierce or turn the Trentino line. Had the German High Command perceived any definite slackening in the British effort in Flanders, Ludendorff would have ceased throwing fresh divisions from the Russian front into the Flemish swamp, and could have detached a part of General von Armin's forces to strengthen the Aisne line, against which General Pétain was just completing his preparations for an attack.

The situation was tragical. The smashing blow against Italy told heavily upon the British Empire. In heroic loyalty to their Allies, the worn and wearied British soldiers had to disregard weather conditions and flooded morasses and resume the struggle for that northern part of the Passchendaele Ridge which their general would have been well content to leave to the enemy.

In mist and twilight, at dawn on October 12th, the Anzac forces again attacked on a front of six miles, between Houthulst Forest and the Staden-Bruges railway. On this occasion the enemy was aware of the coming movement. He began barraging the ground at midnight, and in the darkness pushed his supports forward on the

TENSE MOMENT IN TRENCH MINING OPERATIONS.
British officer on the western front listening, by means of a specially designed apparatus, to the subterranean work of an enemy counter-mining party. The British engineers succeeded in some extraordinary mining operations during the course of the battling on the Ypres sector—the most remarkable being the great earthquake explosion that preceded the capture of the Messines Ridge.

DARING BRITISH AIRMAN'S FINE EXPLOIT.
In the Flanders fighting on October 4th, 1917, a youthful British flying man took his observer close over the enemy lines. Swooping low, he almost skimmed the trenches, and though attacked by rifle fire and heavy guns, fulfilled his work, and with "his aeroplane a rag round an engine" got safely back.

concrete works north of the road, and beat off the storm troops that continually tried in turn to break through them.

It was not a battle. It was a mêlée. The men fought in small parties, with or without officers, clinching with bomb and bayonet, and fighting to the death. Neither side could take prisoners, the fighting was too thick, quick, and merciless. The British were reckless and tigerish. They had suffered considerably in the night, while waiting to attack, and their stretcher-bearers had been deliberately shot by enemy snipers.

When Germans came out with stretchers and ambulances and waved the Red Cross flag, no shot from a British soldier went across the fields where parties numbering as many as two hundred men were visible gathering the wounded. But when a few British stretcher-bearers, with one officer of the Royal Army Medical Corps, came to Poelcappelle to look to the British wounded, German sharpshooters deliberately shot and killed most of the small party.

This was not a single bad case of fiendish barbarism. The same thing occurred in other sectors of fierce conflict. It was a sign that the Teuton was confident that he was winning the battle, and could freely indulge his passion of exterminating hatred which he had to inhibit when he felt himself in peril of death or capture.

Viciously eager was he to deal with the **German attack on** British as the Bulgars had dealt with the **the Red Cross** Serbs, throwing off the last pretence of civilised habit and acting like a human beast of the pagan age. Only when the Teuton thought he was likely to be beaten did he observe any of the conventions of warfare, out of immediate, selfish interest. In the present case he thought he could kill both the British wounded and the Red Cross men and officers tending them without running any personal risk of reprisals. Not until an angry British officer ran towards the German murderers, and pointed

western slopes of the ridge, and brought up reserve divisions into the hollows behind the entrenched heights. Every few seconds flares rose upon the sombre sky, and many other signs of unusual activity in the German lines were perceived.

The German gunners at first tried to break up the coming attack by flooding the swamps with gas-shells and other varieties of projectiles, including British shells sent to the Russian Revolutionary armies and almost given by them to the common enemy. Then, as the British barrage thundered out and the first waves of assault crawled forward, the German batteries intensified and concentrated their fire. They laid a deep curtain right across the British front and held it there to keep back the Anzac main forces. Other groups of German guns tried, in the meantime, to break the infantry that got through the curtain and was working round the outlying redoubts by the centre of the ridge.

In the north, by Houthulst Forest, the indefatigable Guards and some English County regiments advanced on both sides of the Staden-Bruges railway. In spite of all difficulties they attained the positions above Poelcappelle which they had been set to win. There was no need for the French force to struggle farther through the mud, as the line they had won three days before was sufficient protection to the short advance made by the Guards and County battalions. The French gunners, however, brilliantly assisted in barraging the ground in front of the British force and breaking up distant enemy concentrations.

Below the railway there was savage fighting in the streets of fortification just beyond Poelcappelle. Through a dense sleet of machine-gun bullets, Englishmen and Scotsmen rushed from the ruins into the brewery fortress, drove the Germans out of it, and then hacked and blasted their way towards the long range of

MIDLANDERS AIDED BY A TANK TAKE TERRIER FARM.
On October 4th, 1917, some Midland troops, well-nigh exhausted with a long day under fire in terrible mud, but still doggedly attacking, were held up at Terrier Farm. A Tank came to their aid and fired a broadside at the concrete fort, the garrison of which then surrendered.

out that their own Red Cross parties were working in the neighbourhood, did the attack on British stretcher-bearers partially cease.

Meanwhile, the Poelcappelle conflict ended in a check. About five o'clock in the evening, after ground had been gained and lost by the yard and then recovered, another strong German counter-attacking force came down the road from Westroosebeek, drove in the British advanced posts, and compelled the brewery to be abandoned. Between the Lekkerboterbeek and Watervlietbeek and Ravebeek, where the Goudberg and Bellevue spurs rose above the swamps, the attack made by Anzac forces was also a failure.

A storm of wind and rain began at dawn when the British barrage opened, and the ground became a mixture of glue and slush through which the troops could not move with their barrages. The shells thundered with less precision and density than usual along the main road running into Passchendaele village, and swept the flanking ridges where the German commander had massed his men and machine-guns in extraordinary number, according to his new method of defence.

Ineffective British barrage The packed German line on the ridges would have suffered severely from the British barrages in ordinary circumstances. But the circumstances were extraordinary. For the first time since the reorganisation of the campaign the glorious, incomparable British artillery failed its infantry. The attacking troops could see that the travelling line of shell in front of them was thinner and more splattering than ever it had been. This was not the fault of the British gunners. By sustained and most desperate efforts they had done all that men could do, but the rain defeated them. Great difficulty had been encountered in getting the guns up to forward positions, and, when they began shooting, many of the heavier pieces,

CLEARING UP IN A RECAPTURED VILLAGE.
British troops engaged in a systematic examination of a village from which the Germans had been driven. Great care had to be taken in carrying out this work to avoid any remaining enemy machine-gun corners and such "traps" as the Germans frequently left behind them.

as well as some of the machine-guns, shifted upon their foundations. The result was that both the barrages and the counter-battery work were ineffective.

The New Zealand division made the central attack, with the Rifles at the cemetery and Wolf Copse and the Canterbury and Otago troops in the marsh below Bellevue spur. In wave after wave these gallant men went forward, trying to get within bombing distance of the linked concrete works arranged about the slippery slopes, with belts of uncut wire entanglement protecting the approaches. The enemy swept the vile ground with the densest of machine-gun barrages used in battle. He had brought forward more guns since the English Territorial attack.

As before explained, he had taken machine-gunners from reserves and supports, and placed them on the hills, hoping that sufficient would survive the British bombardment to check the attack. As the British bombardment was unexpectedly feeble, the German gunners survived in practically undiminished strength. They poured out such a fire between the Lekkerboterbeek and the Ravebeek as made the situation of the attacking troops impossible.

As the New Zealanders and their comrades were brought almost to a standstill, their officers were shot in tragically large numbers, while they crawled from the brimming shell-holes in order to reconnoitre the field. It was found that no troops could get through the quagmires to the ridge on the left of Passchendaele village, from which two blockhouses were pouring the most destructive fire. For this reason, and for the general reason of the weather and the state of the ground, the operations were suspended, after about a thousand prisoners had been taken.

The check to the New Zealanders on Bellevue spur told on the fortunes of the Australians on Crest Farm spur. These two promontories in the sea of mud were divided by the Ravebeek in regard to attack, but were linked in regard to defence into one

ROUNDING UP ENEMY STRAGGLERS.
Party of British troops engaged in going through a recaptured village on the western front. They had come suddenly upon a group of the enemy hidden in a broken gateway. The small party of cornered Germans at first showed fight, but after a brief skirmish they surrendered.

deadly system by high-placed cross-firing machine-gun positions. The more difficult Bellevue fortifications had first to be taken in order to make the Crest Farm height retainable by troops attacking across the Roulers railway from Broodseinde.

From their drier ridge the Australians went forward more quickly than their comrades in the lowlands after they had traversed a bog by the railway and bayoneted the enemy machine-gunners who tried to hold them up.

Importance of Bellevue Spur

Under a fiercer bullet barrage they entered Augustus Wood and, struggling towards the southern edge of the Rave-beek, came under the Bellevue cross-fire. Above the valley the vehement fighting men of the Commonwealth drove forward for a mile, with close conflicts and with machine-guns rattling viciously all the way to the top of the spur by the outskirts of Passchendaele village.

When they arrived at the rise of Crest Farm, one of the greatest of victories—that would have saved Sir Douglas Haig and his men a month more of battle—seemed about to crown Australian valour. But it was impossible of achievement. So long as the enemy held Bellevue spur

Germans would have been driven from Passchendaele village and from the high ground stretching north-westwards towards Poelcappelle. It was discovered from prisoners that the German forces were also confused by the bad state of the ground, and by the disorder into which reinforcements fell, owing to the interruption of traffic. At least two German groups refused to fight. One was overwhelmed by the Anzac assault while it was suddenly hesitating ; the other made just a feeble feint at a counter-attack between three and four o'clock in the afternoon ; but there was nothing like an organised effort, and few of the men left the watery shelter of their shell-holes. Some Bavarians set out for their homes, a few reaching Nuremberg before they were arrested. The Jaeger battalions of the 195th Division, all young men of fine physique, maintained their moral. Yet even they began to give ground, and the German Staff had to strengthen their battle-front by pressing labour companies and trench-mortar companies into the advanced positions.

Prisoners' tales are not always trustworthy, but in this instance they were confirmed by a remarkable German withdrawal on October 16th. The enemy retired for a distance of a thousand yards between Broodseinde and Keiberg. During the inconclusive battle the Australians drove the enemy down the western slopes of the Heulebeek, where his troops were left in the mud and swept by enfilading fire from the heights south of Broodseinde.

An enforced retreat across the swampy valley would have ended in disaster, so the Germans retired to Keiberg Hill. Some Australian patrols followed them up, and killed or captured some of the rearguard ; but the abandoned ground was not occupied, as the Germans would have been able to enfilade any force that advanced.

After the check on October 12th, Sir Douglas Haig prepared only to make short advances whenever weather permitted, so as to keep the enemy concentrated about the Passchendaele Ridge while larger designs were being quietly carried out.

It was necessary to withdraw considerable British forces for transport to Northern Italy, and Sir Herbert Plumer was appointed commander of the new expedition. A French army had also to be withdrawn, with its guns and train, from the western front and expedited to Italy. These were delicate operations, and any marked enfeeblement of the British pressure around Ypres would have induced General von Armin to release guns and men.

GERMAN OFFICER PRISONERS.
Two German officers who had been taken prisoner by British soldiers on the Flanders front during the Third Battle of Ypres. One of them engaged in talk with one of his captors while they rested awaiting their regular interrogation. [British official photograph.

the Australian flank was too much exposed, and with the rain veiling the gathering of hostile reinforcements a withdrawal was made to the ridge east of Nieuwemolen and the ground by the railway.

The result was in effect as serious as the reverse at Aubers Ridge in May, 1915. The Aubers Ridge action had been undertaken at the time the Russian line was broken ; the Passchendaele Ridge action was fought at a time when the Italian line was breaking. In both cases the urgency of the need for striking at the enemy seems to have prevented adequate preparation. Sir Herbert Plumer had the guns and shell that Sir John French had lacked, but as he was able only to allow his men four days of tempestuous weather in which to drag guns and ammunition forward and build emplacements in the yielding, softening ground, there was again a failure in artillery power which prevented some of the most gallant forces in the world from achieving what they had fiercely determined they would do.

There can be no doubt that but for the bad weather the

He was still receiving fresh divisions from the Russian front. About Houthulst Forest, for example, was the 40th German Division, just arrived from the east. Such troops might have gone to the army of General von Below during the struggle between the Tagliamento and Piave River lines. They had to be hammered until broken, so that as each large fresh body was entraining from Russian territory, its destination might still be fixed for Flanders, in spite of events in Italy. This was the only way in which the general situation of the Allies could be saved from further grave disaster. All that Sir Douglas Haig could do to lighten the terrible burden on his men was to pick a patch of fairly dry weather and, before it completely broke, launch a short attack upon the enemy's weaker positions.

[Swaine.

Lieut.=General the Hon. Sir Herbert Lawrence, appointed Chief of General Staff, Jan., 1918

CCCC 539

The Maple Leaf for ever!   Canadians on the march in France, headed by their band and colours.

In a city of ghosts: Masked ambulance men moving wounded through Ypres.

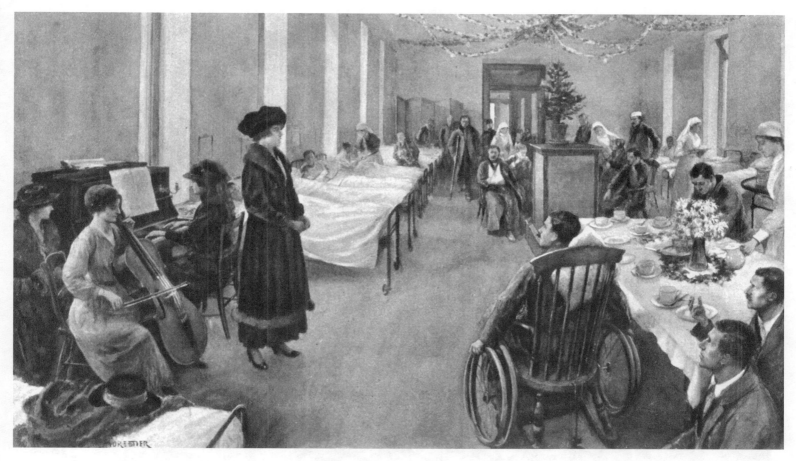

Melody to cheer the soul tired with human strife: A concert in a military hospital.

" Fall in ! "   Unwelcome intrusion of a sergeant into a company off duty behind the lines.

With the enemy driven far enough away to prevent wanton bombardment, the inhabitants of this French village emerge into freedom to feast their eyes upon their own French flag, to chat and fraternise with the friendly British soldiers who rescued them, and to offer what hospitality they can afford to passing despatch-riders speeding upon their business. Proudly wearing the "tammy," of an *Ecossais*, one little chap holds out the Tricolour to be saluted by another still more proudly wearing the captured helmet of a hated Boche. Smiles are on every face, hope in every heart, good wishes on every lip, happiness in the air.

"Sante!" A British despatch=rider enjoying a drink proffered by Frenchwomen in a village he had helped to redeem.

CHAPTER CCXXII.

THE CLOSING VICTORIES ON THE PASSCHENDAELE RIDGE.

By Edward Wright.

Battle of October 22nd—Gallantry of Cheshires and Gloucesters—Canada to the Fore—Great Ridge Victories of October 26th—Heroic Rally on Bellevue Spur—Victorious Ascent of Crest Hill—London Territorials and Naval Divisions in Bog Battles—Magnificent Achievement of French Corps—Swimming to Victory in Luyghem Peninsula—Race between Belgians and Frenchmen—British Check at Gheluvelt—Crowning Success of October 30th—Canadians Storm over Crest Farm—Conquest of Meetchele and Cross-roads Fortress—Unparalleled Artillery Duel over Passchendaele—The Shropshires in Vine Cottages—The Carcanet of Victories on November 6th—Passchendaele, Mosselmarkt, and Goudberg Fall to Canada—When the Shovel is Mightier than the Gun—Westroosebeek Action of November 10th—Masterly Strategy of Sir Douglas Haig—Ludendorff and Armin Completely Deceived—Sir Douglas Haig's Remarks on Ypres Campaign—Failure in British Statesmanship—British Divisions Obliged to Fight Against Doubly Numerous German Divisions—Resemblances and Differences between Verdun and Ypres Offensives—Special Results Attained in the Ridge Battles.

AFTER the severe check to the Anzac force on October 12th, 1917, the weather began slowly to improve, occasional showers being counteracted by drying winds. The swamps were so water-logged by the torrential rains of the previous week that there was no possible chance of their really hardening, but the surface on the high ground would have allowed movement there, had not the ground been continually soaked by columns of water splashing, under intense shell fire, from the network of crater pools and miniature lakes.

From October 14th to October 21st General von Armin fought an amazing artillery duel with Sir Herbert Plumer. In dense parks he crowded guns of every calibre by the northern ridge and the hillocks behind it. Large squadrons of his machines tried to win the command of the air by massed power, and frequently managed to engage with smaller British formations. By personal skill, however, the outnumbered British pilots succeeded in keeping the sky, though they could not prevent enemy aerial observers from crossing the lines and spying out the movements of batteries.

[*Canadian War Records.*
RUINED HOUSE RENDERED TEMPORARILY HABITABLE.
With corrugated iron and tarpaulin sheets some British troops made a shell-destroyed roof weatherproof while they occupied the cottage for a time as their billet behind the lines on the western front.

With his utmost energy the German commander strove to stop the advance of the British artillery. His counter-battery groups used gas-shell by night and gas and high explosive by day, in fierce, prolonged essays to keep down the fire and hinder the forward march of the magnificently toiling and enduring British gunners. Yet nearer crept, by caterpillar traction and other hauling methods, the big, attacking counter-battery guns, closing their range so that each of their strokes should go more powerfully home.

All through the week of fine weather the Germans were nervously expectant of another grand attack. Every minute of the night they sent up flares, and at dawn heavy barrages were laid upon ground where, it was fancied, British troops might have been assembling in the darkness. But it was when the weather once more broke that the offensive was resumed.

On October 22nd, after a rainy night, French, English, and Scottish battalions went out in such a thick mist that the men could not see more than a yard before them. Instead of being able to work forward with little delay, they were impeded by knee-deep mud between wells, ponds and broad zones of ooze.

543

[*British official photograph.*

H.M.L.S. IRON DUKE OUTWARD BOUND TO BATTLE.
A Tank, the Iron Duke, passing down a village street on its way into action, watched with critical interest by British soldiers from the doors of their ruined billets, soldiers making up the broken roadway, and soldiers laden with full packs on their way to or from the front-line trenches.

men with a cross-fire of heavy shell from howitzers above Houthulst and behind Passchendaele; they swept the approaches with long-range machine-gun barrages; they tried to break up the waves of assault by means of sharpshooters distributed in covered craters and machine-gunners in concealed redoubts and isles of concrete amid the swamp and broken jungle.

Slowly and laboriously the British troops fought forward, feeling the weight of the enemy's resistance immediately the attack opened. Some battalions gained ground to the depth of a thousand yards, others won a little more than half that distance confronted by impassable bogs. The hardest fighting fell to the Cheshires and Gloucesters. After driving through to their final objectives with the utmost determination, they were struck by superior counter-attacking forces and compelled to give ground. Back, however, they came, killing or capturing the more numerous Germans and re-establishing themselves upon their objectives.

The Frenchmen had the lighter task, and brilliantly performed it. They advanced a little above Mangelaare and, pivoting on their left, swung their right forward in line with the longer British advance. Going up to their waists in water in places, the Frenchmen bent for a while in their centre, under the lash of enemy machine-gun fire, carried the fortressed points of Jean Bart House and Panama House, took two German guns, and reached some of the outlying spinnies of Houthulst without one serious check.

Alongside the French were Royal Scots, Manchesters, Gloucesters, Cheshires, and Lancashire Fusiliers, moving between the forest and the Staden railway embankment, while Essex and Norfolks, Northumberland Fusiliers, Berkshires, and Suffolks advanced below the railway and beyond Poelcappelle.

By the southern fringes of the forest the Germans were in great strength. They met the Englishmen and Scots-

South of the Staden railway the battle went easier for the Englishmen. This was remarkable in that the Poelcappelle road was the gateway to the Passchendaele positions. For weeks it clearly had been the design of the British commander to widen his wedge about Poelcappelle, in order to get more **English troops win** room to swing down upon the spurs **Poelcappelle** that bastioned the Passchendaele crests.

General von Armin had done his best to prevent this wide flanking movement, but the street of concrete and tunnelled defences extending northward and eastward of Poelcappelle had been especially studied since October 12th by British observing officers. Upon the linked fortresses and the brewery they had directed such a continual tempest of armour-piercing shell that the German garrison had withdrawn, leaving only outposts. Indeed,

[*British and Canadian official photographs.*

TANKS TRAVELLING OVER THE TROUBLED SURFACE OF A BATTLEFIELD.
Barbed-wire lost most of its value in defence when British ingenuity devised the Tanks, whose irresistible mass laid it flat. Only occasional bad luck held one fixed in some exceptionally difficult predicament, as illustrated in the photograph on the right.

the holding force, the 5th Bavarian Reserve Division, had to be relieved, as it began to waver, and was replaced just before the infantry action by the Marines of the 3rd Naval Division.

Yet the fresh Marines did not make any gallant stand. The Essex and Norfolks, with the Berkshires and Suffolks, walked after their barrage, astride the Westroosebeek road, for a distance of nine hundred yards. There was no desperate fighting such as had marked the previous actions round Poelcappelle. Some of the Germans fled from their positions and others surrendered. The enemy machine-gun barrage, maintained from distant uplands, was the source of most casualties; and though the kneaded mire between the Lekkerboterbeek and the Watervlietbeek made going very difficult in the south, in the north the ground was firm enough to permit some English troops to break up an enemy counter-attack with the bayonet.

Staggering ill-luck in regard to weather conditions continued

British official photograph.

TURNING MISFORTUNE TO PROFITABLE USE.
A Tank temporarily disabled on a Western battlefield by the breakdown of its machinery, and the loss of some plates on its endless caterpillar chain, was immediately utilised by adaptable British soldiers as a convenient platform on which to install an observation signalling-post.

to befall the attacking army. As soon as the way of approach was won, from the Lekkerboterbeek line, for a flanking attack on the Passchendaele heights the sky cleared and the sun came out. Again the British commander speeded up his preparations, while a strong gale swept the flats of Flanders, and, under the hard autumn sunshine, stiffened the crust of the battlefield and lightened the work of the gunners and roadmakers.

Canadians closing on Passchendaele

But in the night of October 25th, when a fine Canadian force, with a Naval Brigade, London Territorials, and other English, French, and Belgian troops, assembled for attack at dawn the heavens again opened. A deluge of cold rain washed into the swamps and put a fresh, thick layer of mud upon the slopes of the loamy ridge.

All the operations were designed to assist the Canadians while they closed around Passchendaele village, by Bellevue spur on the north and Crest Farm Hill on the south. At the Menin road the enemy was held and occupied by means of a subsidiary action conducted by English troops who recaptured Polderhoek Château and entered Gheluvelt. Around Houthulst Forest, in another secondary action, the enemy was pressed back farther from the southern outskirts of the undulating wooded marsh, while the French and Belgians drove in on all the western fringes of the forest, and by a northern extension of their victory brought the entire area of the forest screen under direct and complete enfilading gun fire.

The enemy was thus severely hammered on both of his wings around Ypres, and although he preferred to yield a large tract of ground to the French and Belgians, in order to concentrate all his reserves against the Canadians and Englishmen, he was yet unable to resist on his centre, suffering there one of the great defeats of the campaign.

French and British official photographs.

TWO TANKS THAT MET WITH SERIOUS MISHAPS BY THE WAY.
Tanks performed almost incredible feats in moving over shell-torn ground, but their progress was seriously embarrassed when trench systems caved-in under their weight, and they were wedged across the chasm. Right: A derelict tank utilised as armoured cover for a dug-out.

The Canadians followed the same lines of assault along which the Yorkshires and Lancashire Territorials, New Zealanders and Australians had most gallantly but vainly advanced. Like them, they had to conquer the mud before they could attack the enemy. Communications had been improved since the Lancashires took eleven hours to get into position, yet there was still an enormous amount of labour to be performed during the nocturnal deluge that devastated all Staff arrangements. Each duck-board track was so slippery that men with pack and rifle fell at every few steps. Beyond the duck-board ways there was nearly a mile of knee-deep, sticky mud between the left Canadian brigade and their watery assembly line. In darkness, pouring rain, and enemy shell fire the men made their way towards Wolf Farm and Peter Pan House, and then lay out in the mud, hoping that they had not been seen.

But they had been seen, as they came up in omnibuses in the rear, just before the moon went down and the tempest broke. The enemy's guns ravaged the ground, searching for them, trying to poison them and blast them to pieces. The left Canadian brigade rose in the misty, rainy dawn, about a quarter of a mile from the long, bare, brown hummock thrust like a finger from the main ridge. This was the historic Bellevue spur. Beneath it ran the Ravebeek, which was an absolutely im-

Advance over ooze and slime practicable marsh, far too deep for men to get through it, even if the defenders of the spur had only been armed with stone axes instead of being provided with hundreds of machine-guns, trench-mortars, and field-pieces. For on the other side of the Ravebeek marsh was another long finger-like hummock of ground, the Crest spur, whose machine-guns also covered the river marsh.

As the Ravebeek moat had to be avoided as a death-trap, the left Canadian brigade could only try a flanking attack over the northern mud flats below Wallemolen.

They had some six hundred yards of ooze and slime to traverse, and they took an hour to do it. They were little better off than if they had been enclosed by machine-guns, artillery, and riflemen in the Ravebeek marsh. For on the Wallemolen flats they were swept with plunging flank fire from the east, by Goudberg and Mosselmarkt, and also by plunging front fire from the Bellevue slopes and the still higher ground above. There was first a splutter of musketry from thousands of snipers spread about the foot of the uplands eastward and south-ward; then two horribly dense cross-firing machine-gun barrages from the Goudberg, Meetchele, and Bellevue heights, with field-gun and howitzer shells from a deep arc of artillery sited on and behind the main ridge. Some special field-guns were brought down to Bellevue spur, and among the block-houses there they fired at almost a point-blank range upon the Canadians toiling through the morass against the flame-shot rising ground.

Critical moments for the Canadians

The bad weather, however, gave two advantages to the attackers. The mist screened them to some extent, and the mud cushioned the bursting shells, diminishing their concussion effect and their splinters of steel, while the sleet of machine-gun bullets did not ricochet. The left Canadian brigade seemed to have a crippling number of casualties on the mud flats, but many of the men who appeared to have been put out of action were merely bogged. They extricated themselves and, leg-weary but fiercely eager in spirit, caught up with their comrades.

The foremost waves reached the great system on Bellevue spur, and, with slow, grim determination, fought through the tangle of works towards the high main position. But they were too few and too weary to overcome the Bavarians, who brought their guns out into the open by a continuous row of block-houses running by the road on the crest. Under the intense fire the Dominion infantry were compelled to fall back.

MIGHT PUT DOWN FROM ITS SEAT AND MEEKNESS EXALTED.
A column of German prisoners passed through a village in Flanders when the Sunday bells were ringing and Flemish women and girls were on their way to church. The haggard, muddied Huns stared curiously at the scene as they shambled forward between their guards.

LEVELLING THE GROUND FOR SHELL STACKS.
The steady advance of the British Army necessitated the formation of ever fresh ammunition dumps, the sites for which often had to be on the shell-torn terrain of recent fighting. When this happened, horse-drawn scrapers levelled the ground to provide a flat surface for the stacks of shells.

The Naval Brigade, attacking on the left towards Goudberg, was also checked by the Paddebeek swamp and the wire about it, and for a time were unable to maintain contact with the Canadians. Then, however, the astonished enemy, in the hour of his apparent triumph, saw one of the grandest rallies in modern siege warfare. While German gunners were still shelling the vacated crest, the Canadians gathered again below the slopes, and as their barrage returned to them and again ploughed up the spur, they climbed behind it, while the surprised and stricken Bavarians on the top block-houses line were being pounded by both German and British guns.

Grand rally of the Canadians

In small packs the Canadians worked back to the hostile block-houses over their dead and wounded comrades. It was the dread of leaving their wounded on the spur that chiefly urged them upward. They left another trail of fallen men behind them, yet arrived at last on the slopes in strength enough to close round the outer forts and carry the central range of works. They sent down many prisoners, and then broke all counter-attacks, and, under a heavy hostile bombardment, fought still farther forward in the evening to the cross-roads, against another formidable row of concrete and steel-rail redoubts.

By this time the men of the 11th Bavarian Division were completely broken in spirit. They had some eighteen machine-guns on the three hundred feet of block-house line, and plenty of ammunition. But instead of staying in their shelters and trenches, and sweeping back the wearied and wasted Canadian brigade, they fled. In a panic they fled, abandoning their guns and stores, and their weapons were afterwards employed upon their supporting force when these vainly endeavoured to retrieve the situation.

On the southern side of the Ravebeek the right Canadian brigade achieved an equally important success. Having somewhat better ground of approach to the other brown buttress of the Passchendaele main height, the right Dominion force battled forward faster, beyond the defences of Augustus Wood and Heine House, and without attempting to top the second hummock, on Crest Farm line, cleared the Ravebeek edge, and thus assisted their nobly resolute countrymen fighting against extreme difficulties on Bellevue spur.

They drove upwards towards Duck Wood, and with their flank protected at Decline Wood, while machine-guns and artillery searched their front, they arrived within nine hundred yards of Passchendaele village. Between them and their ultimate goal rose the height of Crest Farm. This they neglected for the time in order to give what support they could to the Bellevue attack.

The Britons, Australians, and New Zealanders, who had fallen defeated on the high ground where the Canadians stood victorious, had not died in vain. By their persistent heroism they had explored every possible approach in the maze-like swamps, uncovered the strength of the enemy's defences, shown what improvements were necessary on the attacking side, and pointed the way to eventual success.

Nevertheless, there was historic justice in the achievement by which the Canadians closed upon the central and most famous sector of the Passchendaele Ridge, and brought the Ypres campaign of 1917 to an end by a succession of striking conquests. For it was against the Canadians that the Germans had ferociously turned in the Second Battle of Ypres, when they broke through the French line by means of the fiendish surprise of torture gas.

After their chain of triumphs at Courcelette, Vimy, Lens, and Hill 70, the men of the Dominion were returning,

COURAGE AND ENDURANCE OF THE STRETCHER-BEARERS.
In the hideous water-logged Ypres marshland the work of the regimental stretcher-bearers was incredibly difficult. No troops could have shown more hardihood and endurance. When they could not walk, they crawled forward on all fours, and every man was caked with mud from head to heels.

veterans of a hundred fights, to the battlefield of ghastly memories where their most experienced men had fought as recruits. For certain reasons there was within them a hard, steady flame of passion which, at Ypres, made them the most determined force that Sir Douglas Haig could employ. The Naval Brigade on the left of the Canadians extorted praise from the enemy. Before it was the Paddebeek brook, widened into a flood that seemed unfordable and impassable. Dominating the swamp-framed stretch of water rose on the farther side the northern part of the old Staden-Zonnebeke trench system. The mud before it was wired, and its machine-guns whipped up the flood water as the naval men waded in to the waist.

They were checked, but they returned to their appalling

force of Germans, shaken by the attacking barrage and half-blinded by the mud it splashed in their eyes, held up their hands and waited for the Englishmen to take them prisoners. But the wave of assault could find no way of getting through the deep ooze and water, and the Germans, seeing that their offer of surrender could not be accepted, ran away. Under such prevailing conditions as these, those hostile troops who wished to make something of a stand could easily fire over bog and water, and retire when the Englishmen waded near enough to threaten a close fight. No wrecked hamlet or other object of note in the wilderness of slime and wash gave a name to this northernmost angle of the British wedge. Yet the corner was of high importance, as the continual conflict about it showed.

It was a principal salient of attack, and as it was gradually, grimly extended, heavy counter-attacking forces struck it on three sides—from Houthulst Forest, from Vijfwegen, and from the dominating ground between Stadenberg and Westroosebeek. From the north, from the north-east, and from the east German batteries incessantly swept it, making it the weakest part of the British line.

Fortunately, some of the enemy's pressure against this vital Staden-line salient was relieved by a splendid Franco-Belgian advance opening on October 26th, during the Canadian victory at Bellevue. General Anthoine's troops first made a short advance over the Corverbeek to Draaibank and Owl Farm, swimming the

[*British official photograph.*]

MAKING GOOD NEW-WON WAYS IN FLANDERS.
Men of an English County regiment engaged in roadmaking work during the advance east of Ypres. They were trundling barrow-loads of material across a temporarily constructed bridge.

task, and after heavy losses they broke into the zone of the outer forts, and in a series of desperate attempts took other strong points in the morasses by the inevitable Lekkerboterbeek and its tributary the Paddebeek. Impossible as any definite success then was, their costly, gallant, sustained action was a vital element in the victory of their Canadian comrades. If some force had not strongly pressed upon the Paddebeek line, directly threatening the flank of the Goudberg hump, the central thrust would not have got home.

In the more northerly British subsidiary advances the London Territorials and other English troops also had much dogged holding work in the rather featureless waste between the forest and river swamps. It was a blind country of flood and mud, with camouflaged concrete hutments, old gunpits, and farm ruins, most of which were unmarked on ordinary maps. The chief obstacles, besides the inundations, were the pits and barracks by the Staden railway, once used by enemy gunners for long-range fire on Poperinghe. The long double row of huts had been heavily concreted and transformed into a chain of redoubts, sweeping with their machine-guns all the marshes between Broembeck and the Watervliet-beek. Heavy fighting had already occurred about this four hundred yards' stretch of forts, and the garrison again made a fierce resistance.

In another place, amid the river bogs, an advanced

Fighting in the northern angle

[*Canadian War Records.*]

AN AWKWARD PLACE FOR WALKING.
Canadian soldier returning to his billet through a badly-shelled area. The railway sleepers which formed his open-work bridge were part of a goodly stretch of line left literally in the air.

flood and establishing a bridge-head. Then in the night the sappers and soldiers carried out a surprising engineering feat. Standing up to the shoulders in water, they threw pontoon bridges across the main stream, over which a strong force of infantry passed from the west into the Luyghem peninsula, while another attacking line advanced from the south over the Corverbeek marsh.

Only the night before, the 8th Bavarian Division had come for a rest to the tongue of land between the Dixmude road, the Yser, and the Ypres Canal. Quite unprepared for the sanguinary battle of surprises that opened, the Bavarians were broken with bomb and bayonet and driven from line after line. The Frenchmen had almost to swim to victory. The ground was under mud and water, with islands of machine-gun forts ; and after the amphibians had stormed Aschoop, Kloostermolen, and Bultehoek, the enemy artillerymen tried to keep them off Merckem by a tremendous shell barrage.

But the ranging was bad. The shells hit the water with column-like splashes, but missed the waves of attack, in which the original sky-blue figures were naturally camouflaged by a complete mud covering. Reaching firmer approach by the fortified and strongly-manned village, the Frenchmen took it rapidly with the bayonet. About the same time the hamlet of Kippe, a mile up the Dixmude road, was also carried by close fighting. Then a third force of assault drove upon the enemy's rear from Drei Graachten down the road to Luyghem.

The road was trenched, wired, and blocked by concrete works, and, with the marshes on either side, was commanded by the Germans on the low rise of Luyghem. There were hours of arduous struggle in which the French were repulsed, but on each occasion their own finely-handled field-gun barrage weakened the garrison. By the afternoon the tangle of road defences was cleared, and the victorious troops joined with their comrades pressing northward from Merckem, and in a race with the Belgians forced all the works of Luyghem.

By the Yser the Belgians had been watching their skilful allies, and had a flotilla of flat-bottomed

[Canadian War Records.
IN PREPARATION FOR THE NEXT MOVE.
Canadian soldier cleaning his rifle while standing against a German munition truck from Essen, part of a train that had been secured by him and his comrades on a stretch of captured railway.

boats in hiding, with infantry punters. As the French were wading and swimming towards their closing victory, the Belgians poled across the flood towards the Blanchaart Lake marshes, where the Germans were clinging to the remnant of their broken line. Once more the stricken, reeling enemy was rushed along his rear, while being shattered on his flank and front. Luyghem was first entered from the south by the French, who met the Belgians by a mill on the northern side.

Though thrice outmanœuvred and completely surprised, the Bavarians in many places fought to a finish,

leaving the peninsula littered with their dead. Thousands might have lived, but would not surrender, and fell fighting. Swiftly their choice had to be made when they were in visible groups, for the French gunners, with their mobile 3 in. weapons and their handy 6 in. howitzers, flung their shells out with deadly rapidity and precision.

By this long and deep advance between Bixschoote and Dixmude the French and Belgians extended above the western side of Houthulst Forest to the neighbourhood of Blanchaart Lake, and with their guns brought all the woodland swamp under enfilade bombardment. Ravaged by shell from British positions southward by Langemarck, and swept by French and Belgian batteries westward on the Luyghem peninsula, the enemy's guns and foot on the northern side of the Staden-line salient were

[British official photograph.
MATERIALS FOR TRENCH DEFENCES.
Unloading trucks of sand and cement behind the British lines on the western front. The waiting troops promptly filled bags, and carried them away for the strengthening and building up of trenches.

in an extremely wearing situation. So the British front there was strengthened through the hostile force growing weak.

The southern subsidiary attack on Polderhoek Château was disappointing. The English troops made a magnificent advance over the river bogs and through the marshy park. Screened by the rain, they entered the underground fortress, where a regimental commander and his Staff lived beneath ten feet of concrete and steel with a garrison of four companies. So immense were the defences that even the terrific attacking barrage did not awaken the German fire-control officer from sleep.

It was the bombs of the attacking troops that finally roused all the officers and men. By this time the Englishmen were practically masters of the situation, and they captured the commander and that part of the garrison which was not shot down while trying to bolt. The victorious force then **Disappointment** swept over Hill 55 into Gheluvelt, **at Gheluvelt** from which the enemy ran down the Menin road under the observation of British airmen.

Everything seemed to indicate that another great victory on a sector of historic importance was being achieved. There was, however, a weather defect in the arms of the almost victorious Englishmen. Their rifles were fouled by the deep mud through which they had worked, and some of their machine-guns also became clogged. A tremendous hostile barrage pounded them and curtained off ammunition supplies and supports, the

German commander bringing into action all his gigantic crescent of artillery round the Menin gate. He took a considerable time to rally and reinforce his men, but when the incessant counter-attack increased in strength, the remaining bombs and the bayonets of the English troops were inadequate to the defence of their hasty new positions. Only with rifles in good order could they have held their ground, and they were obliged to fall back and leave both Gheluvelt and Polderhoek Château.

Indeterminate as this action had been, it diverted numerous enemy reinforcements from **Renewed attack** the critical Passchendaele sector, ena- **on Passchendaele** bling the Canadians to tighten their hold upon the spurs of the main ridge and prepare for further advance. On October 30th Sir Douglas Haig ordered another short advance between the Roulers railway and the Westroosebeek road. The Canadians resumed their attack upon the outskirts of Passchendaele village, while their comrades in the former battle—the Royal Naval Division and the London Territorials—endeavoured to press across the Paddebeek and Lekkerboterbeek swamps towards Goudberg.

FAMILIARITY THAT BRED CONTEMPT OF DANGER. *[Canadian War Records.*
Despite the notice posted at the entrance to a captured village warning all whom it might concern that movement in the open there was dangerous, these Canadians preferred walking through its streets, with the risk of being sniped, to taking a safer but more difficult route underground.

In the wild windy night, with an orbing moon peeping through a ravelled curtain of cloud, the opposing guns fought a fierce duel. Then, after working all the night, the muddy, weary, sleepless British gunners put out their grand barrage with marvellous energy at dawn. The masses of German artillery at once answered by a violent curtain fire upon the assembled Canadian and British infantry, striking some of them five minutes before the assaulting movement started.

Happily, the hostile gun fire did very little damage, most of the shells ploughing up the vacant mud. On all the left of the advance, however, the ground was still terribly bad, and although some of the enemy troops actually ran away at daybreak when they saw the khaki figures advancing, the German commander was given time to bring forward fresh forces and re-establish his line among the craters that had melted away around the northern end of the ridge.

Again it was, in places, merely a question of getting through the ooze and water in order to take prisoners with scarcely any fighting. But the journey took so long that, before it was completed, the fugitives vanished, and fresh hostile forces were sufficiently in position to make a stand. In the broadened Paddebeek valley the heavy British shells had blown craters in the soft slime as large as those made in firm earth by ammonal mines.

The block-houses and fortified farms on both sides of the Paddebeek continued to give trouble, even where the German infantry in the open mud line were disposed to run. The work of getting within attacking distance of the dominating machine-gun positions was hopeless. At a few points, where the ground was barely passable, some works were laboriously carried; but, generally speaking, the northern part of the German line held firm because there was no firm ground about it.

While the naval men and Territorials maintained their pressure by heroic and seemingly vain efforts, the Canadian brigades on the drier sandy loam of the Passchendaele heights developed their attack with remarkable speed and success. The brigade on the southern spur, between the Ravebeek and the Broodseinde road, fought up to Crest Farm in less than an hour, and made the eventual capture of the village a practical certainty.

Crest Farm rose on a knoll above the slippery western incline, and formed the outer bastion of Passchendaele itself. On one side its machine-guns swept the spur; on the other side they could be brought against the exposed fortifications of the village. The Australians had reached Crest Farm, but could not hold the ground under the flanking fire from the Bellevue spur. As the Canadians occupied the Bellevue positions across the Ravebeek marsh, their grip upon Crest Farm could not be shaken. They captured the survivors of the garrison and, finding a number of machine-guns still intact in the great concrete superstructure covering the ruins, they turned these upon the village, and there mowed down some of the hostile forces who were trying to throw back other Canadian battalions west of the village.

The left Canadian brigade that worked from the conquered Bellevue position again had the more difficult struggle. As they fought up the road to Meetchele village, on another bastion spur of Passchendaele, they were raked by heavy machine-gun fire from block-houses and redoubts along the broken highway in front of them, taken in the flank northward by bullet barrages from the spur by the Paddebeek, while on their other flank they were harassed by four well-placed machine-guns in Friesland Copse.

Fast and furiously as the Canadians **Struggle on** fought, it took them two hours to **the Canadian left** reach their first objectives. The advance was made in a wriggle around the lips of the craters. The Germans brought into action batteries of their new infantry gun, which was a very mobile piece, running on low wheels and throwing shrapnel at short range. But the British barrage was far more effective and exact. It carried the first waves of attack up both sides of the road, enabling them to take three isolated pairs of " pill-boxes " in the first part of the journey.

A bombing-party encircled and silenced the Bavarian

DEADLY ACCURACY OF BRITISH ARTILLERY.
Rushing a foremost section of the German line, some British troops found that the gun fire which had preceded their attack had smashed an enemy machine-gun and killed its crew.

machine-gunners in the Friesland position, and other men with bomb and bayonet worked into Meetchele, which was nothing like a village, but merely a moonlike craterland, with a few mounds of broken bricks scattered above the reinforced cellar system.

Beyond Meetchele, at the Goudberg cross-roads, was a larger and stronger range of machine-gun fortresses. Here the Germans poured such a barrage of bullets over the bare ground that approach seemed impossible. Shell-holes were numerous, but the Canadians could not use them as cover, for the water in them was so deep that men who ventured in could not get out again. By individual cunning and courage, however, the strong place was stormed. Small parties crawled by the upper lips of the craters, and gradually worked around the sides of the row of block-houses at the cross-roads. As soon as the Bavarians saw that they were likely to be encircled they fled in disorder, floundering wildly in the mud towards Mosselmarkt.

Quickly, however, the local German commander organised a counter-attack with his reserves. About eight o'clock in the morning a mass of grey-cloaked figures could be seen creeping out of Mosselmarkt and forming up for an assault. Then it was that the right Canadian brigade, overlooking the scene from Crest Farm knoll, made use of the machine-guns and abundant ammunition they had taken from the enemy. They poured over the opposite valley a sleet of death, and as the Germans began to give the British artillery also ranged upon them and blanketed them.

German aeroplanes then came out and made daring flights in a strong wind over the new Canadian line. Being unable to see the troops sheltering in the conquered positions, they dived at the supporting columns, raked them with machine-gun fire, and bombed them. Certainly nothing remotely resembling a mastery of the air was held that morning by the fighting pilots of the Royal Flying Corps.

The well-mounted German airmen had become so bold that, in the hour of a Canadian victory, they could swoop low over the British lines and smite the conquering infantry as it was consolidating its ridge conquest. The British aerial position of downright superiority that had obtained in the Somme campaign had not been maintained for want of powerful machines.

Vehemently the German commander worked to save Passchendaele village. At midday the rain and the gathering mist compelled his air squadrons to retire, and he renewed his strong infantry counter-attacks. All of these, however, were beaten off with crippling losses and disorderly flights. **British gunners'** Again he brought all his artillery **superb endurance** to bear upon the British front, hammering it, poisoning it, trying to wreck the rearward organisations, diminish the gun-power, and check the movement of troops.

More heavy British guns came forward for counter-battery work, and the field-guns advanced behind the Canadians, amid the tremendous artillery duel and hurricane bombardment of positions. By night the air was loud with bombing machines and bright with star-shell, rocket, and explosion.

Gunners, squatting on an ammunition-box to eat, fell into a stupor. Officers dropped asleep in the act of giving a command to the guns. What ordinary sleep could be taken had to be snatched on a waterproof spread on the slime. There was no shelter for guns or gunners, either from tempests or enemy fire. Even a brigade commander was lucky if he had a dug-out for Staff headquarters.

Men and guns of the forward batteries stood on the open field, with no cover or concealment, and the lighter shell was brought up on the backs of men, through ground that no mule or pony could traverse. The strain on both guns and foot was such as to test to breaking point the fibre and spirit of the men.

What held the gunners up was loyalty. They would drop from exhaustion where they laboured rather than let

FIRST-AID NEAR THE FRONT LINE.
Australian soldiers coming into a divisional aid-post on the western front—one using his rifle as a crutch, one gripping an injured wrist, and one gallant fellow "borne of four," to whom a comrade, recognising the urgency of the case, signalled and called to make all possible haste.

the infantry down. As was seen in the October 12th battle, where their emplacements gave way through the mud, after heart-breaking slavery in all preparations, the gunners went almost beyond the limit of human endeavour in the hope of breaking a path over the ridge for their quagmired comrades. Finally, they cleared a path for victory. At dawn on November 6th scores of batteries had been dragged through the swamp and fed with ammunition close behind the advanced infantry line, and as the sky began to lighten the Canadians again went forward.

Their front of attack was only about two thousand yards, but it overlapped the Goudberg spur and Mosselmarkt and Passchendaele villages. The attacking troops began by creeping out on their left. By working with two companies of Shropshires through the morass of the Paddebeek, where the Naval Brigade had fought by holding on to exposed outposts, the Canadians won a good position for subsequent operations against Goudberg.

Preparing for the closing battle

The two Shropshire companies were totally barred by a swamp from getting into the wrecked plantation in which was a German concrete work, known as Vine Cottages. Borrowing Canadian guides, they made a wide compass of the morass, and from the territory of the Canadian unit they seized the fortress in the copse, driving a wedge into the enemy's line by Goudberg Hill. A series of other German advanced works, hindering concerted progress through the mud below the ridge, was also won in preliminary little actions conducted during the first five days of November. In one case a small British force clung to an outpost, surrounded by swamp, and there drove the enemy back for four days, until relieved by the Canadian offensive, which it had helped to prepare.

Twice the enemy shelled the Canadian assembly and support positions during the black night, but he was comparatively quiet when, about six o'clock in the morning, a wall of fire began to move over his lines. Only one minute later, however, did he in turn put a wall of fire upon the Canadians, shelling from the north by Houthulst Forest, from the south by Gheluvelt, and from the east along and behind the ridge. The Germans were as ready for the closing battle for the ridge as it was possible to be. They knew what was coming ; they prepared fully against it, and in the clash that followed they were beaten through meeting better men than themselves.

The Canadians went forward quickly, very close after the British barrage, and risking there the shells that chanced to be short. Hindenburg in person had issued an Order of the Day to the 11th Silesian Division that garrisoned Passchendaele, and to the 4th Prussian Division alongside them, stating that the village must be held at all costs, and retaken if lost. It was lost very quickly, but it was not retaken. Some Silesians and Prussians surrendered, more ran away, and none held his ground.

Hindenburg's Order ignored

The Canadians swung forward from the Broodseinde road and the marshes fronting Goudberg in an arc-like formation. They had only three hundred yards to go on the southern side from the Broodseinde road to Passchendaele ruins, but more than double that distance on the northern side. Within twenty minutes they were extracting Silesians from the cellars of Passchendaele. They were raked by machine-gun fire from the skeleton wreck of the parish church and from neighbouring emplacements ; but they went forward so quickly with the bayonet that the defences were surrendered to them before they could close with the enemy. Movement was slow down the High Street. This was merely a jumble of shell-craters, and some entrances to the concrete cellars were difficult to find. As the Canadians were still searching, some of the Silesians bolted from holes that had not yet been reached. But there were Lewis gunners ready for this event, and they killed many of the fugitives on the eastern slope, and took about two hundred and thirty prisoners. By far the larger part of the Silesian force from Breslau had answered Hindenburg's call by running away before the Canadians reached the village.

This, however, did not account for the extraordinarily long time given to the victorious Canadians to rearrange the defences of the most famous of ridge villages. There was no counter-attack of importance. The situation, however, was explained at four o'clock in the afternoon, when two German commanding officers, with a small party, emerged from a " pill-box " which had been neglected by the Canadians when they saw no fire coming from it. One man was commander of the garrison, the other was commander of the supporting force, and with their Staffs they had waited nine hours behind their steel door for sounds of the victorious counter-attack that Hindenburg had ordered. As no counter-attack came, the two commanders decided to surrender. It was no doubt partly because the officer controlling part of the reserve forces was imprisoned in the new Canadian line, while making a call on the front-line commander, that no concerted strong effort was made to recover the most famous of all positions on the long ridge. The British artillery also had a considerable influence upon the fate of the enemy's counter-attacking reserve. From Meetchele to Mosselmarkt and Goudberg the battle was longer and deadlier. The Canadian commanding officer had a difficult problem in tactics, owing to the known nature of the ground by the Paddebeek bogs and the distance of the final objective. Moreover, Brigade Headquarters was intensely shelled during the action, many of its signallers and runners were lost, and the brigadier failed to obtain connection with his soldiers in the swamp. But he managed his main movement with remarkable skill, and for the rest, his fighting men and regimental officers went on from victory to victory.

German fight-and-run method

On their wedge of firm ground, known as Meetchele spur, they were nearly encircled by marshes and, in order to avoid the mud and water, their line had to be wheeled to the left until it stretched almost due east and west across the Westroosebeek road.

As before explained, they fought a preliminary action in the night against Vine Cottages in the corner of the swamp, and then at dawn, with the German barrage beating on them and the country obscured by smoke and haze, they executed their remarkable wheeling manœuvre and became the upper end of the attacking semicircle moving upon the centre of the ridge.

By rare luck the weather was dry, and when the sun came up there was excellent visibility, and the British pilots, though unable to prevent enemy machines raking the Canadian troops, maintained good observation over the enemy lines. The small block-houses were conquered quickly and at light cost. The Prussian infantry gave ground with little or no close fighting, and only at a large redoubt by Mosselmarkt cross-roads was there any prolonged and serious resistance. The Canadians, however, worked round this apparently formidable work, exploded it, and blew the survivors of the garrison into the open.

Scarcely anywhere did the 4th Prussian Division on the left fight harder than the 11th Silesian Division had done on the right. The Prussians used their machine-guns and rifles at long range, and ran when the Canadians worked up for a fight at close quarters. This fight-and-run method angered the soldiers who had come from Lens, hot to end the Ypres campaign in a savage tussle with the men who had first poisoned their comrades from the ground on which they were fighting. The new Prussian method of shooting and running inflicted some losses upon the Canadians, and though these were not very heavy, there was a certain feeling of dissatisfaction in winning ground without a bayonet charge or anything like a hand-to-hand conflict.

Mosselmarkt was taken without any remarkable incident, except the capture of several field-guns—three being immediately taken and two more afterwards found embedded in mud.

When Goudberg, the northern ridge position, was stormed the weather, by rare good fortune, changed in favour of the attack. All that the Canadians then wanted was the opportunity of so consolidating the important stretch of dominating ground they had won as to ensure the holding of it. About half-past eight o'clock in the morning they were rewarded for the remarkable speed of their wheeling manœuvre and double drive by a fall of rain and a gathering of mist consummating the disasters of the enemy.

He could see nothing. The laborious victors and their supporting forces were screened from observation in their period of weakness, when they were improvising means of resisting the expected counter-offensive. Blindly the German artillery smashed upon the ridge, and groped for the new infantry positions and for **Gathering mist** the advancing batteries struggling up **assists Canadians** to take advantage of the dominating ground.

In spite of the rain it was fairly easy for the other stationary British gunners to curtain off the hostile approaches to the new Canadian line, and continue to barrage the well-known communications of the enemy. Before the weather changed, British aerial observers had spied some large bodies of German shock troops and directed swirls of shell upon them. So, from what had been already seen, and from what was known at registered ranges on the map, the enemy's movements could be hampered by almost mechanical bursts of gun fire sent through the rain and fog.

The enemy, on the other hand, could only guess at the places at which he might strike parties of Canadians, changing battery groups, supply columns, and all the tired men and bogged machinery, working with dogged energy for the consolidation of a resounding victory. He slew some of his own troops walking towards the prisoners' cage, he interfered with some of the working units, but he accomplished **Counter-offensive** nothing of importance, while his organi- **disorganised** sation for the counter-offensive that Hindenburg and Ludendorff had clamantly ordered in advance was slackened, mismanaged, and put out of action without any further collision of opposing infantry.

As days passed without any grand counter-attack Sir Douglas Haig went out of his way to provoke the enemy. On November 10th the Battle of the Ridge was resumed by a short, narrow thrust along the crest of the Passchendaele hills towards Westroosebeek. Canadian and English troops took part in the affair. The drive was made in the rain, and upon the firm ground along the Westroosebeek road the Dominion soldiers fought fast and took a series of strong points, while the home battalions, pushing slowly through a morass under machine-gun fire, gained a tract of fortified ground north of Goudberg.

Thereupon General von Armin did what was expected of him. He had been re-grouping his batteries on Roulers Plain and in the little hollows eastward of the ridge. While maintaining a desultory bombardment he had kept an important number of his guns concealed and silent.

[*British official photograph.*

MOUNTED ONCE MORE AND MOVING IN THE OPEN.
British cavalry moving forward upon the western front, crossing trenches still occupied by their comrades of the infantry—alongside of whom they had had a good deal of fighting dismounted during the protracted period of trench warfare when open campaigning was suspended.
DDDD

NORTHERN SECTOR OF THE YPRES BATTLEFIELD.
French and Belgians formed the Allies' left wing, and by fighting around
Houthulst Forest relieved pressure on the forces assailing Passchendaele.

The way to win a battle was to dig until you could not
hold a shovel, and, like the gunners, fell asleep from
extreme exhaustion. The gory romance of bayoneting
Germans, blasting them with bombs, and bringing them
down by the hundred with machine-gun fire served to
cheer the recruit during his training and apprenticeship.
Victories, however, were mainly won by mud-plastered
men with aching limbs, who treated their rifles with more
loving care than a mother treated her first-born baby,
and then dug like moles chased by terriers.

The Canadians were prouder of their rapidly-made
works around Passchendaele than they were of their
ascending victories. Their greatest boast was that, amid
the fiercest hurricane bombardment the enemy had ever
carried out, it was possible to live happily on Passchendaele
Hill. There may have been some exaggeration in this
statement, but in American fashion the exaggeration
merely emphasised a truth.

Sir Douglas Haig succeeded in misleading the enemy
commanders. While maintaining his own ridge positions he
so played his game that the Prussian War Lords continued
to gather fresh divisions and new guns against him in
the wrong place, while he was withdrawing a powerful army
for action in Italy, and out of his small and insufficiently
trained reserves was organising another striking force
for one of the most unexpected blows struck on the western
front since the first weeks of the war.

Ludendorff also possessed an army of manœuvre which
was superior in numbers to the force that Sir Douglas
Haig was building up. But, in the first two weeks of
November, Ludendorff could not seize the initiative and
strike with his large detached forces.

The Canadians and their comrades **Haig misleads the**
around Passchendaele Hill and the **enemy Command**
marshes near Westroosebeek were
apparently so bent upon conquering the last fragment of
the ridge that the enemy Commander-in-Chief decided to
stand to battle, in all available strength on the field
where there was no further intention of attacking him.

About Passchendaele an artillery duel of incomparable
violence opened on November 13th, and on November
16th a most successful imitation of an important attack
upon Westroosebeek was made by some Highland, Lancashire, and Berkshire troops. Nothing like three entire
battalions were engaged, but the men were chosen from
different regiments in order to make the enemy think
that thousands of men were being employed in another
action preliminary to a great offensive.

In a way the attack was a miniature rehearsal of the
Cambrai offensive. The men went forward in the darkness and rain without any clearing bombardment or path-
breaking barrage. They struck the German troops at a
time when the 4th Division was being relieved by the
119th Division. In some positions they killed or captured
double garrisons, and, by the ground that they welded into
their own line, made the enemy commander think that
the gigantic wrestle for the ridge was about to end in
another terrific struggle at Westroosebeek. A few days
afterwards the Hindenburg line covering Cambrai was
abruptly broken, and it certainly was not the fault of Sir
Douglas Haig if the surprise which he and his Staff had
engineered failed of full effect and ended only as a partial
though important victory. The failure of certain forces
who were given a fairly easy task in the Cambrai battle
must not lessen our recognition of the ability with
which the Ypres campaign was concluded, at a time
when the British Army was lacking in well-trained
reinforcements and unexpectedly weakened by the
departure of an army to Italy.

In his despatch on the Ypres campaign Sir Douglas
Haig remarks that the capture of the entire ridge within
the space of a few weeks was well within the power of
his men in ordinary circumstances. To the unexpected
adverse weather conditions in August he attributed his

His design was to throw out, in spite of all preliminary
counter-battery work, an overwhelming barrage so soon
as the extent of the foreseen resumption of British infantry
operations was patent.

When his troops about Westroosebeek sent up S O S
signals, by means of coloured lights, he lashed the lost
part of the road with shell of every calibre and covered
with shell-bursts the country round about. For some
hours the top of the ridge was completely blotted by
battle-smoke from the heaviest bombardment the enemy
had ever organised. The new Canadian-British line had
to be drawn back at some points, reducing the gain to
some hundreds of yards about the crest road.

By this time, however, ground was quite of third-rate
importance. What mattered far more was the complete
revelation of the enemy's new artillery dispositions. This
at once led to a stupendous gunnery conflict. In the
course of it, on November 13th, the
Shovels mightier   Germans at last attempted a serious
than swords   counter-attack, and found that Canada
was secure on the ridge.

The new works, rapidly constructed by the conquerors,
were uncommonly good. The Canadians dug as fiercely
as they fought. In the great swamp battle it was at
times possible for inexperienced men to win ground, but
it took veterans strongly to hold it. Only men who had
lived for months or years under heavy shell fire knew
vividly that the shovel was mightier than the sword.
The Canadians dug as they had never dug before, and
when the battle was won, and every man was weary, he
continued to dig with a conscious frenzy, rivalling the semi-
conscious frenzy with which a drowning man makes his
last struggle for life.

failure to carry quickly the German line and develop the large design for which the operation had been prepared. He points out that from the start he was unable to carry out his original plan as arranged with Marshal Joffre and his first successor in the field command.

His forces were first weakened at the instance of a new French Commander-in-Chief, General Nivelle. He was obliged to take over a further part of the French line and diminish his striking power in order to release French troops for the too ambitious and some-

Adverse effects of Nivelle's offensive what hasty operations which the new French commander undertook along the Aisne plateau and among the Champagne hills in the spring of 1917, before the Italian Army was ready to strike.

As a further consequence of General Nivelle's arrangements, the Third and Fifth British Armies had to continue at heavy cost their successful yet subsidiary operations between Lens and Quéant in order to bring relief to the checked French forces.

As a third result, Sir Douglas Haig began his main operations quite a month late, and instead of having the effectives upon which he and Sir William Robertson had counted, he became so pressed for men that he could not properly train his drafts for offence or defence, and preventable sacrifices were incurred and successes missed owing to troops having to go into battle without special exercise in the tasks they were called upon to perform.

Making all allowance for the disadvantages produced by General Nivelle's masterfulness and over-confidence, the partial failure of the operations which Sir Hubert Gough conducted east of Ypres in August, 1917, seems to have been due to other things in addition to the bad weather. The enemy's improved system of block-house defence, with its thick concrete shelters and elastic cushions of steel rails and air, at first defeated the British artillery. British heavier guns do not seem to have been employed in sufficient number and at

shortened range in forming the barrage under cover of which the infantry could have advanced. They were brought up well for counter-battery work from the beginning, but not close enough to the infantry for block-house destruction.

Regarding the matter in a more general way, it might be held that there was a failure in statesmanship in regard to the British armies on the Flemish and French front. The British Cabinet wasted man-power, war resources, and treasure in attempting to transform the broken, despairing, starving, and disorganised Slav into a free fighting man. The British armies in the field not only lost the powerful new armament provided for the Russians, but had British guns turned upon them firing British shell.

During this great but almost veiled crisis the British nation did not lack courage. The resistance of some British Trade Union leaders was contrary to the main current of character in the people, being indeed considerably influenced by the attitude of young shirkers, who had fled into industrial works of military or national importance in order to escape service in the field. The general character of the race, however, was as firm as it had been in the most desperate periods of the Napoleonic Wars.

Between April 9th, 1917, and November 10th, 1917, 130 German divisions were engaged and defeated, according to the estimate of Sir Douglas Haig, by less than half that number of British divisions ; 57,696 enemy soldiers, including 1,290 officers, were captured, with 393 guns, 561 trench-mortars, and 1,976 **British and German** machine-guns. The new model German **man-power** division contained fewer effectives than an ordinary British division, but the laborious and costly defeat of German divisions numbering more than double the British divisions engaged was not so satisfactory as it might seem. For while the soldiers and their commanders in the field were to be congratulated, not so the higher direction, which could not, in the fourth year of the war, place against the German effectives opposing the British

MAKING THE WAYS PLAIN FOR THE ADVANCE OF THE GUNS.
Upon the artillery most exhausting work fell, but in the " heart-breaking " toil of bringing the guns forward they were helped heroically by the pioneers and labour battalions, who cleared away debris, bridged trenches, and filled in shell-craters, frequently under heavy fire.

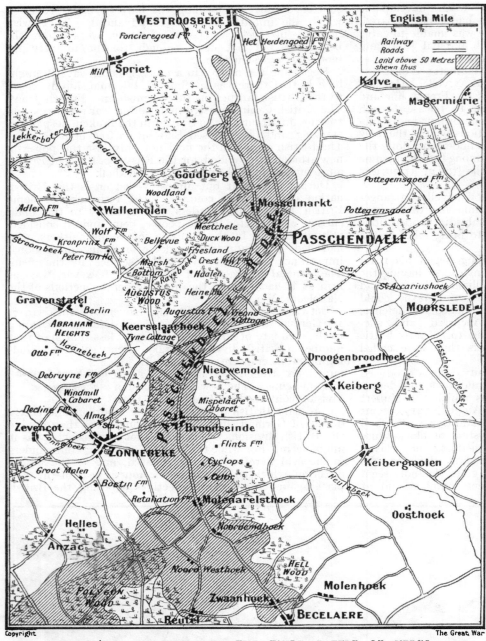

THE FINAL OBJECTIVE IN THE THIRD BATTLE OF YPRES.

Passchendaele, the vital point upon the Ridge dominating the whole Flanders plain towards Ostend and Bruges, was carried by the British on November 6th, 1917, together with the fortified hamlets of Goudberg and Mosselmarkt. Subsequent counter-attacks failed and Passchendaele Ridge was secured.

reasonable design of achieving a decision in Europe before the British Federation was really willing, through its leaders, to make the last sacrifice, and before the United States was ready to fight.

British political strategy was not courageous; British military strategy undoubtedly was. The question rather was whether Sir Douglas Haig was not too stern and stubborn in persisting in attack across the Ypres swamps. The British campaign around the Menin gate has been compared with the German campaign at the Verdun gate. There are points of resemblance. Both operations failed, in the first few weeks, in their original aim, and were then continued as processes of attrition. Snow partly checked the German rapid onset; rain partly impeded the British accelerated attacks.

In both cases an unexpected strength in the hostile methods of defence seems to have been a more important factor than the bad weather. Yet the German casualties of 600,000 men, though terrifying, were not blindly incurred. France was exceedingly hard pressed, and she was eventually saved by what had been the most doubtful factor in the European situation —the untested, hastily-trained, hastily-armed British levies. Germany, in turn, was also very hard pressed, and she was temporarily saved by what had then become the most doubtful factor in the European situation—the re-armed but disorderly Russian private soldiers.

There were, on the other hand, some points of difference between the Ypres and Verdun campaigns. Sir Douglas Haig states : " It is certain that the enemy's losses considerably exceeded ours." This vital superiority in attack over defence did not obtain at Verdun. The French losses there were considerably smaller than the German, and the enemy Staff was only able to maintain a pretence of successful attrition by calculating losses in proportion to French and German populations, and taking no account of British sources of man-power.

Enemy loss of effectives

At Ypres there was absolute attrition of the enemy. He was so worn down that, in the view of the British Headquarters Staff, the addition of strength he obtained from events in Russia and Italy was largely discounted by his tremendous losses in effectives and ordnance amid the hills and hollows of Menin road. So, after all, the Passchendaele Ridge seemed to be, to the men who had gained the dominating heights, the field of a decisive, though arduous, half-veiled success, preliminary to the patent overthrow of the enemy in that or some other theatre of war.

advances a superior or, at least, equal number of well-trained British effectives. By the spring of 1917 the man-power of the German Empire was greatly diminished; the rate of annual recruitment was far below the annual rate of losses by battle and disease. Unlike the British, the Germans had no saving in emigration to help partly to make up for their war wastage. Even their large use of slave labour did not retrieve the situation. Fundamentally, they were gravely weakening in 1917.

On the field of battle, however, they were actually growing stronger, because the United Kingdom and some nations of the British Commonwealth did not yet fully exert in the main, decisive theatre of conflict all their potential might. They were fighting still by instalments, though by larger instalments. Germany and Austria-Hungary were fighting with their entire capital power, borrowing, indeed, as much in advance as possible, in the

THE MAN WHO WILLED THE WAR: WORDS AND WANDERINGS OF THE KAISER WILLIAM.

By Charles Lowe, M.A., author of "Prince Bismarck," "The German Emperor," etc.

Question of the Kaiser's Personal Responsibility for the War—Bishop Boyd Carpenter's Testimony and Criticism—Opinions of Sir George Reid, Lord Morley, Sir Frank Lascelles, Lord Haldane, M. Cambon, and Mr. Wile—War Council at Potsdam; July 29th, 1914—The Kaiser's Rôle of War Lord—The "Willy"-"Nicky" Correspondence—Life in Main Headquarters at Charleville — Imperial Energy Employed in Councils of War — Aspiration to Wrest the Trident of Neptune from Britannia's Hand—Inflammatory Speech at Cuxhaven to Inaugurate the Submarine Blockade—Table-Talk with Max Bewer and Sven Hedin—Ceremonial Degradation from the Garter Knighthood—Eulogy from German Professors, Preachers, and Poets—Pen-Portraits Drawn by Representative Americans—"The Man Who Dined with the Kaiser"—Imperial Visits to Bulgaria and Turkey—Physical and Mental Condition of William II.—Discordant Notes in the German Hymn of Praise of the Emperor—Political Crises Within the Empire—Universal Rejection of the Kaiser's "Peace Proposals" Following Upon the German Defeat in the Battle of the Somme.

THE following narrative will aim at presenting a personal portrait of the German Emperor William II. such as he himself, with histrionic art, was careful to offer to the world throughout the course of the Great War; a picture compounded from his manner of life in the field, his manifold activities as a *soi-disant* soldier, diplomatist, and general showman; his table-talk, telegrams, speeches, and addresses; his shuttlecock flights from one front to another; his meetings with fellow-sovereigns, and other phases of his life.

To what extent was he personally responsible for the world-war?

William II.—who chose to be known as the "modern Attila," from the comparison which he once instituted between himself and that bloody "scourge of God"—never pleaded guilty to the crime of which he was accused by the public opinion of all the civilised world outside the circle of the Central Powers. Far from pleading guilty, he took every opportunity of asseverating his innocence. "A fateful hour has fallen upon Germany," he said in the week before the war: "envious peoples on all sides are compelling us to resort to just defence. The sword is being forced into our hand." That was his invariable phrase, "sword forced into our hand"—a phrase he was to repeat scores of times, especially on the first anniversary of the war, when he said: "Before God and history my conscience is clear. I did not will the war."

WILLIAM II., GERMAN EMPEROR.
Marble bust of the Kaiser, who, while pretending to be a "Prince of Peace," plunged the world into all the unimagined horrors of war.

"I did not want to have this awful war," said the Kaiser to an American interviewer through Herr Ballin, of Hamburg. "I feel that this war was brought on—not by Germany, but by those other nations that are fighting against us." And, again: "God is my witness that this war is no fault of mine, and that it cannot be so. I did not want the war. It has been forced upon us."

William II. always boasted himself to be a "Friedenskaiser," or "Prince of Peace," and undoubtedly there was much to be said in support of his claim to that splendid title. For one thing, in the summer of 1914, he could boast of having kept the peace for over a quarter of a century. But whether he had not gravely meditated a breach of that peace on several occasions during this period is quite another matter. Indeed, it will be shown that on several occasions he did, in fact, seriously imperil peace by his policy of aggression.

Nevertheless, it had been his constant boast that he was a "Prince of Peace," and that this was his conception of his own character may be gathered from the impression which he succeeded in leaving on the minds of many others. Take, for example, Dr. Boyd Carpenter, ex-Bishop of Ripon and Canon of Westminster, than whom no Englishman, perhaps, had better opportunities of studying the character of the Kaiser. A great favourite of his Majesty's English mother, the bishop had been a frequent visitor at Potsdam. It was he who, by the Empress Frederick's special request, conducted

LORD OF THE IRON CROSSES.
The Kaiser in his service uniform, wearing the Iron Crosses of the First and Second Classes.

her funeral service at Kronberg; and there is good reason for believing that he was the anonymous author of a volume, "The Empress Frederick — a Memoir," the work of a most judicious and appreciative mind. It was published in 1913, the year before the war, and in January of that year the Kaiser wrote to the bishop, as appears from his "Further Pages from My Life":

I need not assure you that I am working with the utmost energy to try and secure peace for the world. The task is arduous, and necessitates patience, as the Powers, though in principle all are agreed to preserve peace, yet some of them have their back-thoughts and clandestine ambitions not always in harmony with peaceful issue. However that may be, I don't despair, feeling as I do that I am working at the bidding of a Higher Power, Who said, "Be ye content with My grace; My power is strong in the weak," and as my work is for the good of mankind.

In June of the same year Dr. Boyd Carpenter paid a visit to Berlin, and, as usual, was received by the Kaiser:

He was quite cordial, but he spoke with a note which was new to me; it was no longer the note of hope and joyous anticipation; he seemed to me to be apprehensive; he spoke of the dangerous position in which Germany was placed between two Powers, which understood one another and might prove hostile. When I left him I felt the Emperor was under the influence of a great fear. "He is changed," I said to myself. I was afraid, for I knew that there was no passion so cruel as fear.

Noting that there is a higher and a lower stratum in all personalities, he said of the Kaiser:

In the end the power of the lower vision prevailed; mixed motives and varied influences gave it potency. A mistaken patriotism, mingled with an unworthy jealousy, and driven into action under the pressure of a genuine fear of the growing power of the nations on both flanks, led him to surrender his best principles of action to the unhappy opportunism which was preached, in season and out of season, by a restless military party and by a disloyal and unscrupulous Foreign Office.

Sir George Reid, in his "Reminiscences," thus writes of his visit to Berlin some little time before the war:

I ventured to say to the Kaiser, "What a horrible thing it would be if the German bulldog and the British bulldog got their teeth into one another, allowing some inferior animal to climb over their mutilated remains!" The Emperor's hand flashed from beneath his military cloak, and he exclaimed: "Never! Never!"

My impression then was that the Kaiser looked upon war between Germany and Britain as inconceivable. It has since occurred to me that his Majesty may have scouted the idea that the German bulldog would, in the event suggested, reach the stage of "mutilated remains."

In the late autumn of 1907 the Kaiser during his second State visit to England made this impression on Lord Morley, then Secretary for India, who saw much of him at Windsor and elsewhere:

The general verdict from people well qualified to judge seems to be averse to any claim to a place in the front rank—e.g., with men like Bismarck, or Cavour, or old Metternich, or statesmen of the foxy-breed like Leopold of Belgium. Superficial, hurried, impetuous, badly balanced, these are a few of the descriptive epithets. One impression—and in my eyes it is a golden impression—he appears to have left in the mind of everybody—namely, that he does really desire and intend peace.

The following autumn—1908—completed the thirteenth year of Sir Frank Lascelles' tenure of office as British Ambassador at Berlin, when he retired with this conviction, which he afterwards recorded—not in a despatch, but in a newspaper selection from his "Memories": "I confess that there were as yet no symptoms in the Emperor of other than a pacific turn of mind."

THE HUN IN WINTER'S WEAR.
William II. as he visited the western front during the rigours of a winter campaign.

Such also for long was the opinion of Lord Haldane, who on several occasions went to Berlin as a sort of special or supplementary Ambassador to try and straighten things out, a man who regarded Germany as his "spiritual home," and who claimed to know the Germans and their rulers better than most. To Lord Haldane, therefore, in the first weeks of the war, hurried the London correspondent of the Chicago "Daily News," and said:

"Do you think the Kaiser favoured war?"

"In past years I think the Kaiser undoubtedly opposed war. But I am afraid his opposition to it gradually weakened. He appears to have settled into the war mood about two years ago. You will remember a remarkable communication (published in the French Yellow Book) from M. Jules Cambon, French Ambassador at Berlin, to M. Pichon, French Minister for Foreign Affairs in November, 1913, reporting a conversation between the Kaiser and the King of the Belgians, in the presence of the Chief of the German General Staff, General von Moltke, a fortnight before the despatch was written. 'Hostility against us

WANDERINGS OF A RESTLESS RULER.
The Emperor on one of his incessant journeys to and from the various war fronts, alights from his train to speak with his officers. He was here conversing with General Woyrsch.

is becoming more marked, and the Emperor has ceased to be a partisan of peace.'

"Thus wrote Cambon, and he went on to say that the Emperor appeared to be ' completely changed '; that he had been ' brought to think that war with France must come '; and that he believed in the 'crushing superiority of the German Army.' I think in the end the Kaiser was borne off his feet completely by the military party."

What the French Ambassador had written on November 22nd, 1913, was this:

If I may be allowed to draw a conclusion, I would submit that it would be well to take account of this new factor — namely, that the Emperor is becoming used to an order of ideas which were formerly repugnant to him, and that, to borrow from him a phrase which he likes to use, " we must keep our powder dry."

The same Ambassador had also written:

As William II. advances in years, family traditions, the reactionary tendencies of the Court, and especially the impatience of the soldiers, obtain a greater empire over his mind. Perhaps he feels some slight jealousy of the popularity acquired by his son, who flatters the passions of the Pan-Germans, and who does not regard the position occupied by the Empire in the world as commensurate with its power.

From British Ambassadors at Berlin we got no such personal analysis and enlightenment—in their printed despatches, at any rate—and had consequently to fall back on emissaries of a different kind in the shape of representatives of the Press. Prominent among these was Mr. F. W. Wile, the gifted correspondent of several American journals, as well as of the London "Daily Mail," and many an Ambassador must have envied him the sources of his information and the soundness of his

INVADERS OF ITALY.
William II. at Udine, talking with General von Below, during a visit which he paid to the Italian front after the great Austro-German advance in the autumn of 1917.

judgment. His volume entitled " The Assault " is by far the most interesting account of the incidents at Berlin connected with the outbreak of the war. Though representing a journal which he " could not conscientiously describe as friendly to Germany," Mr. Wile confessed to a belief that William II., " deep down in his heart," did not " crave for war." In other words, he was the instrument of the war party, which " forced the sword into his hand." " I am persuaded," wrote Mr. Wile, " that William II., on July 29th, was confronted with something strangely like an abrupt alternative of mobilisation or abdication."

On the Kaiser's hasty return from his usual summer trip to Norway a nocturnal Council had been held at Potsdam which was to decide the fate—it might almost be said—of the world:

Its precise details have never leaked out. So much, I believe, can be set down with absolute certainty —it was not quite an harmonious Council which finally voted for war. At the outset, at any rate, it was divided into camps, which found themselves in diametrical opposition. The " Peace Party," or what was left of it, was said, loath as the world is to believe it, to have been headed by the Kaiser himself. Bethmann-Hollweg supported his Imperial master's view, that war should only be resorted to as a last desperate emergency. Von Jagow, the innocuous Foreign Secretary, dancing as usual to his superior's whistle, sided with the Emperor and the Chancellor. Falkenhayn and Von Tirpitz favoured war. Germany was ready ; her adversaries were not ; the issue was plain. Moltke was non-committal. . . . Prince Henry of Prussia (just returned from London) did not violently insist on peace. I could never verify whether the Crown Prince was permitted to participate in the War Council or not.

On the western front in France, chatting with Prince Rupprecht of Bavaria.

Talk in France with the general commanding the Prussian Guard.

Discussing the situation with General von Emmich during a trip to Galicia.

THE GERMAN EMPEROR VISITING HIS GENERALS ON VARIOUS FRONTS.

THE KAISER AND HIS HEIR.
The German Emperor and the Crown Prince (in the uniform of the "Death's Head Hussars") inspecting German troops at a parade held during a visit to their front in the Aisne region.

Weeks after the war began it was suddenly discovered and asserted by several Entente journals that this War Council of July 29th, 1914, had been preceded by a still more momentous one on the 5th of the month in the same place, on the eve of the Kaiser's departure for his usual summer trip to Norway, when war was practically decided on. Conclusive proof of this *conciliabulum*—which was said to have been attended, among others, by the Hungarian Premier, Count Tisza, and General von Hötzendorff, Chief of the Austrian Staff—was not forthcoming.

Certain it is, however, that at the Potsdam Council of July 29th the sword was thrust into the Kaiser's willing, or unwilling, hand. William II. has often been called an autocrat, a despot, an irresponsible ruler ; but the public are apt to invest even an autocrat with too much power.

The incarnation of Prussian militarism It might be shown, for example, that Alexander II. was swept into his war with Turkey (in 1877) against his own desire, and that his grandson Nicholas II. was equally powerless to stem the official tide that was setting in for a war with Japan.

Dynastic wars are things of the past, and they have now been succeeded by national wars, in which the soul and will of a great nation are the driving force. The German people—or, at least, their leading and determining portion—had long made up their minds that a war with England for the domination, not only of the sea, but also of the world, was the next great task they had to tackle, and no number of Kaisers could ever have turned them from their purpose.

William II. had thus allowed himself to become the pliable instrument of his people's will, which, however—and now comes the second grand count in the indictment—no one more than he himself had helped to foster and to form. For in spite of all his pretensions to be a " Prince

THE HUN EMPEROR SAFELY SURVEYS THE NEW BARBARISM.
William II. on the western front watching his troops going forward in a poison-gas attack—a barbarism which his Army had the unenviable distinction of introducing into modern warfare.

of Peace," there certainly never was a peace-monarch who looked, and dressed, and talked, and rattled his sabre as did William II., who began his career by solemnly raising himself to the rank of Germany's supreme "War Lord." He was never happier than when posing as a menacing champion in " shining armour." No peace-monarch, which he claimed to be, ever talked or thought of war more than William II. When not blowing his own trumpet he was sounding the war-bugle and seeking to saturate his people with the war spirit. It was ever his aim by his theatrical make-up, his barrack-room harangues, the significant resting of his hand on the hilt of his sword, the harsh, sergeant-major tones of his rasping voice, and his thinly-veiled threats of dire vengeance on the possible foes of the Fatherland—it was ever his aim to pose as the incarnation of the German military spirit, the *furor Teutonicus* of which Bismarck and he were always boasting as something quite terrible and irresistible.

Germany's boastful " Prince of Peace," or " Friedenskaiser," had been the chief creator of the war spirit which, at the crucial moment, he found it impossible to exorcise, and was thus, so to say, devoured by his own offspring. For at the last moment, when shrinking from the results of his own creative handiwork, he allowed the sword to be " thrust into his hand "—which was just as much as if he had drawn it of his own accord—thus proving himself to be a weak-willed, irresolute, and criminal ruler, the most nefarious of his kind who ever sat upon a throne.

He—the self-boasted " Prince of Peace "—had allowed the sword to be " thrust into his hand "

An Imperial Macbeth-Iago

by the war party of his own creating, even as the hesitating Macbeth had equally accepted an assassinating dagger from the hands of his more resolute wife. The comparison is the more apt since the Kaiser himself once referred to daggers as political instruments. This was in his famous " Daily Telegraph " interview, when he protested that " falsehood and prevarication are alien to my nature," and cried out against those British writers " who bade the people of England refuse his proffered hand, insinuating that he held a dagger."

But subsequent events proved this to have been actually true. For while professing the sincerest friendship for England, such as had found expression in his " fraudulent caresses " of his uncle, King Edward, at Kiel in the summer of 1904, he was secretly, and in the most approved Iago fashion, trying to combine Russia and France and Germany in a league against Great Britain, as was conclusively shown by the publication, in 1917, of the " Willy "-" Nicky " correspondence, which also revealed that, in the event of war with Britain on the strength of this alliance, the Kaiser meant to treat Denmark as he was afterwards to deal with Belgium.

" Willy "-" Nicky " correspondence revelations

This contingent occupation of Denmark was even in his mind when an honoured guest at Copenhagen in the summer of 1905. Among other things, he then remarked to M. Isvolsky, the Russian Minister : " In the Morocco affair I threw down the gauntlet to France, who declined to pick it up. Therefore she refused to fight me." Again, in 1909, in connection with Austria's annexation of Bosnia and Herzegovina, the Kaiser, taking his stand in " shining mail," at the side of his aggressive ally, had suddenly threatened to attack Russia and occupy Poland, giving the Tsar only twenty-four hours to make up his mind. In 1911, in the Agadir crisis, he again compelled France to choose between war and giving up a portion of the French Congo.

It was hard to reconcile all these provocative acts with the Kaiser's claims to be a " Prince of Peace "—acts which caused Lord Rosebery to declare that " Germany,

THE TEUTONIC WAR LORD AT A MEMORIAL SERVICE TO HIS HAPLESS ALLY, FRANCIS JOSEPH.

The Kaiser at a service which was held at German Headquarters in memory of the Emperor Francis Joseph of Austria, who, after a reign of sixty-eight years, died on November 21st, 1916. It was the assassination of the Archduke Francis Ferdinand, heir to Francis Joseph, at Sarajevo in the summer of 1914, that was the pretext for the ultimatum from Austria to Serbia which started the Great War.

with genial smiles and Judas kisses, had deliberately and infamously conspired against the liberties of the world."

We have thus seen what sort of a figure was cut by the Kaiser as a pretentious " Prince of Peace " of the prancing kind, at once an autocrat of his people and a weak-willed instrument of their ambitions. Let us now see how this wordy War Lord comported himself in the field when at last compelled by his own acts to exchange the rôle of a statesman for that of a soldier.

His departure from Berlin for the western seat of war was preceded by a torrent of telegrams, addresses, edicts, and speeches. In one of those proclamations to the German people he vowed that " we shall resist to the last breath of man and horse, and shall fight out the struggle even against a world of enemies "; while **The Kaiser draws the sword** in an address to the 1st Foot Guards at Potsdam he drew his sword, brandished it over his head, and cried :

I draw the sword that with God's help I have kept all these years in the scabbard. I have drawn the sword, which without victory and without honour I cannot sheathe again. All of you will see to it that only in honour is it returned to the scabbard. You are my guarantee that I can dictate peace to my enemies. Up and at the foes, and down with the enemies of Brandenburg !

Leaving Berlin on August 16th, with a most elaborate and numerous Headquarters Staff, the Kaiser first of all headed for Mayence, on the Rhine. This was also the place where his grandfather, old King William I.—then in his seventy-third year—assumed command of the united German armies on August 2nd, 1870, exactly seventeen days after issue of the order to mobilise ; and when his grandson similarly left for the front the German Army had been engaged in the same preliminary process for just about as long. Old King William I. had assumed supreme command at Mayence on August 2nd, and in exactly one month from this date all France lay prostrate at his feet—bleeding, disorganised, demoralised, without an Army, without a Government, without an Emperor.

William II. and all his generals had also counted on such a walk-over, but they were to be cruelly disillusioned.

As the war had to be waged on several fronts, and as the Kaiser made a point of trying to present himself at crucial moments on each of them, it followed that his movements were of a very erratic and puzzling kind, like those of the ghost of Hamlet's father, of whom Bernardo, Horatio, and Marcellus successively exclaimed : " 'Tis here ! "—" 'Tis here ! "—" 'Tis gone ! " On the western front the War Lord's Main Headquarters were at Charleville, a charming town on the Meuse, near Sedan.

In the east, on the other hand, his principal residence was at first the Silesian castle of the wealthy Prince of Pless, who had married one of England's fairest daughters in the person of a Cornwallis-West, sister of the Duchess of Westminster. But the fact that the mistress of this lordly mansion was a native of the country against which he was fighting, and on which he had **Main Headquarters at Charleville** poured out all the vials of his venomous hatred, did not deter him from obtruding himself on her presence.

Mr. Gerard, in the account of a short visit he paid the Kaiser at Charleville to discuss the question of submarine warfare, gives this picture of his life :

We were (he wrote) received at the railway-station by several officers, and escorted in one of the Kaiser's automobiles which had been set apart for my use to a villa in the town of Charleville, owned by a French manufacturer named Perin. This pretty little red-brick villa had been christened by the Germans Sachsen Villa, because it had been occupied by the King of Saxony when he visited the Kaiser. A French family servant and an old gardener had been left in the villa, but for the few meals which he took in the villa two of the Emperor's body huntsmen (or " Leibjäger ") had been assigned, and they brought with them some of the Emperor's silver and china.

The Emperor had been occupying a large villa in the town of Charleville until a few days before our arrival. After the engineer of his private train had been killed in the railway-station by a bomb dropped from a French aeroplane, and after another bomb had been dropped within a hundred yards of the villa occupied by the Kaiser, he moved to a red-brick château situated on a hill outside Charleville, known as either the Château Bellevue or Bellaire. The Kaiser's automobile, which he placed at my disposal, had two loaded rifles standing upright in racks at the right and left sides of the car, ready for instant use.

Never did the old Kaiser in 1870 enjoy such comfortable quarters, until at least he got to Versailles. In another respect, too, William II. differed materially from his grandfather, who at Königgrätz, Gravelotte, and Sedan was ever on the battle-front and in the thickest of the fire. But the lot of his grandson had fallen on softer lines, far behind the trenches, amid telephone and telegraph clerks, Staff officers and orderlies, with an easy motor-car for a mount, instead of a restive charger. Yet this, he bitterly complained, was not his favourite way of waging war. What he would have much preferred was to imitate the example of his kinsman, " Brunswick's fated chieftain," who, at Quatre-Bras, " rushed into the field and foremost fighting fell."

Such was the substance of a speech which, in the summer of 1916, on the occasion of a visit to the Somme front, he addressed to a crowd of slightly wounded soldiers waiting to be sent to the rear—officers, ambulance men, drivers, sutlers, and so forth :

It is the most poignant grief of my life that I am unable to take a more active part in this war. It is my earnest desire to take my place in the trenches and to deal such blows at our enemies as my age and strength would permit.

I could take my place with the youngest of you, and I promise that I would leave my mark on the enemy, but the inscrutable Almighty has willed otherwise.

Into my care has been committed by Divine destiny the leadership of our country, of its armies, of its forces on land and at sea.

The burden of thinking, deciding, leading has been laid upon me, and, realising this, I know that my life must not be risked in the foremost line of battle, where my feelings, if unrestrained, would carry me away.

My life must be conserved carefully for the welfare of Germany, to carry out the duties assigned to me by Divine appointment.

It came to this, therefore, that while the dread War Lord held himself to be precluded by Heaven's decree from **Imperial energy in Council** gratifying the dearest wish of his heart by heading a storming column against the British trenches, and showing what he could do by forceful push of pike, his personal combativeness had to restrict itself to the holding of councils of war, now on this front and then upon another.

Solomon, the son of David, King of Israel, laid it down that " in multitude of counsellors there is safety," which, with all due respect for " the wisest man the world e'er saw," was surely a very foolish thing to say, with regard, at least, to the conduct of war, None of the world's great commanders ever acted as Solomon suggested—not Alexander, Cæsar, Turenne, Marlborough, Frederick, and least of all, Napoleon.

As for William I., we have the assurance of Moltke himself, writing to an English correspondent, Professor Spenser Wilkinson, that in 1866, as in 1870-71, a council of war was never called. " If the commander, after speaking with his chosen adviser, feels it necessary to consult others as to what he should do, the arrangements for command are in a sorry plight." That was also what Hindenburg, " with a smile," said to a Viennese journalist in the fourth year of the Great War in allusion to the newly-established War Council of the Entente Allies at Versailles. " Such institutions are always a sign of incapacity and helplessness. When at one's wits' end a war council is established."

Having thus failed to establish a reputation as a soldier, save of the *miles gloriosus* kind, the War Lord began to make a bid for fame as a *miles religiosus*, so to say, claiming more intimate relations with the Almighty and knowledge of His purposes than even his grandfather.

" Soldiers," he shouted to a sort of " Wallenstein's Lager " of his helmeted heroes in Poland—

Soldiers, remember that you are the chosen people ! The spirit

Lieut.=General Travers Clarke, C.B., appointed Quartermaster=General, December. 1917.

Mona's Queen, from the Isle of Man, running down a U boat in French waters.

Hyacinthe-Yvonne, of Sables d'Olonne, sinking a German submarine off the coast of Brittany.

"The Empire's Watchdogs": *Naval patrol on the look=out for enemy submarines in the North Sea.*

Merchantman dropping a screen of black smoke between herself and a pursuing German pirate.

Left to right (seated): Vice-Admiral W. S. Sims, United States of America; Vice-Admiral F. J. J. de Bon, France; the Right Honourable Sir Eric Geddes, First Lord of the Admiralty, Great Britain (who presided); Vice-Admiral Count Thaon di Revel, Italy; Rear-Admiral K. Funakoshi, Japan; Admiral Sir Rosslyn Wemyss, Great Britain. Standing behind the representatives are (left to right): Rear-Admiral S. R. Fremantle, Great Britain; Captain M. C. Twining, U.S.A.; Rear-Admiral Baron de Lostende, France; Captain Thomas E. Crease, R.N., Secretary.

Representatives of the Allied Powers attending the first meeting of the Allied Naval Council, London, January 22nd, 1918.

of the Lord has descended upon me because I am Emperor of the Germans. I am the instrument of the Most High. I am His sword, His viceroy.

Woe and death to all those who resist my will! Woe and death to all those who do not believe in my mission! Woe and death to the cowards!

Let all the enemies of the German people perish. God demands their destruction, God, Who by my mouth commands you to execute His will!

And again, in a proclamation to the Poles at Czenstochowa, he declared:

I had a wondrous dream. To me appeared the Virgin and commanded me to save her holy convent, which danger had threatened. She gazed at me with tears, and I proceeded to fulfil her divine behest.

Know of this, Poles, and meet my troops like brothers and saviours. Know, Poles, that those who are with me will be liberally rewarded, and those against me will perish.

With me are God and the Holy Virgin. She lifted the sword of Germany to succour Poland.

Once, when the British Minister at Berlin—Sir Andrew Mitchell, a shrewd Aberdeenshire Scot, the friend and executor of Thomson, the bard of the "Seasons"—took heart to assure Frederick, in one of his darkest days, that "with the help of God, sire, we shall win through." "With whose help, said you?" replied the sarcastic King. "With God's help, sire, I said," repeated Sir Andrew. "Oh, indeed," returned the mocking atheist on the Prussian throne, who, strangely enough, was known and huzzaed in England as "the Protestant hero," and had country inns dedicated to his name. "Oh, indeed, I was not aware that you had such an ally." "Yes, sire," countered Sir Andrew, with dry Donside humour, "and He doesn't cost us anything like so much in subsidies as does your Majesty." Frederick had been receiving assistance in men and money from England during the Seven Years War.

But there was another Scotsman—John Knox by name—whom William II. must needs impress into his service, **French's "Contemptible little Army"** or, at least, into his sermons. This was when, in the spring of 1915, "in the park of the Castle of Nivbovo," in Russian Poland, he harangued a Sunday conventicle of his soldiers:

We Prussians (he said) are already accustomed to fight against and overcome a superior enemy. We should trust firmly in our Great Allies up above, Who will help our just cause to victory. We know from childhood, and in our study of history when grown up we have learned that God is only on the side of believing armies.

Thus it was under the great Elector and under old Fritz, and in the time of my great-grandfather and grandfather, and so it is now under me. As a great Scotsman, old John Knox, once declared: "A man who walks with God is always in the majority."

The curious thing was that a thorough search by the editors, historians, and divines of Scotland failed to confirm that "old John Knox," whatever he may have thought, had ever said anything of the kind.

One story, or statement, was that, when the Kaiser had his Main Headquarters at Aix-la-Chapelle, he issued the following Army Order early in the war (August 19th, 1914):

It is my Royal and Imperial Command that you concentrate your energies for the immediate present upon one single purpose, and that is that you address all your skill and all the valour of my soldiers to exterminate first the treacherous English, and walk over General French's contemptible little Army.

On behalf of the Kaiser it was officially denied that his Headquarters had ever been at Aix-la-Chapelle (Aachen), or that he had ever issued such an Order. But the coin, counterfeit or otherwise, at once obtained universal currency—all the more readily since, by whomsoever minted or imagined, it was known to crystallise the opinion, if not of the Kaiser himself, at least of the ignorant and arrogant German people and their generals, including Bernhardi, who had practically said the same thing in his book, "Germany and the Next War."

There was, however, the less reason for the Kaiser himself to have fallen into the same error, since he knew the British Army and its history very well indeed, and had frequently sung its praises. With Bernhardi, he may have thought, and even declared, it to be "contemptible" in point of numbers, but certainly not in respect of valour. "Little" he may also have called it, as we all did, but contemptible—never. Germany's War Lord knew perfectly well that the little British Army—like one of its brightest ornaments, on whom even the bestowal of his Black Eagle was powerless to confer additional lustre—was also a "terror for its size," and, if he had failed to realise that truth before the war, was soon to do so.

Well aware—none better—of the truth about the little British Army, the Kaiser was second to none in his admiration of the British Navy. He was not using the language of flattery or hyperbole when he once said that one of the proudest **William's envy of the British Navy** moments of his life was when he had been made an Admiral of the Fleet.

From his very boyhood William II. had always been deeply bitten with mingled admiration and envy of the British Navy, and long even before coming to the throne he had sworn within himself to provide his nation with a Fleet which might one day wrest from his mother's country "the trident of Neptune." His grandfather had taught Germany how to *march*, and he in turn would show her how to *swim*; or, as he once said to his assembled generals, "As my grandfather did for the Army, so I will for the Navy carry out the work of reorganisation."

And when the great Battle of Jutland came to be fought on May 31st, 1916, just missing by a day the glorious First of June, the Kaiser, as "Admiral of the Atlantic," rushed to Wilhelmshaven, where, from the deck of Admiral von Scheer's flagship, he harangued a crowd of delegates from all the vessels which had taken part in the fight, ranked up on the quay—quite in the manner of the Founder of Christianity, Who, from the fishing-cobble of Simon Peter, preached to a press of people standing on the shore of the Lake of Gennesaret.

But the sermons were very different—charity and love to all mankind being the theme of one; while venomous, Lissauer-hymn-like hatred of and exultation over England gave inspiration of the other.

Repeated efforts (he said) had been made, without success, to entice the enemy out into the field of action, but at last "The Day" had come.

The gigantic Fleet of Albion, ruler of the seas, which since Trafalgar for a hundred years had imposed on the whole world the ban of sea-tyranny, and had surrounded itself with a nimbus of invincibility and insuperability, came into the field. . . . And what happened?

The boastful British Fleet was beaten. The first great hammer-blow was struck, and the nimbus of British world-supremacy had disappeared.

Like an electric spark the news rushed through the world and caused unprecedented jubilation everywhere where German hearts beat, and also among our brave allies.

A new chapter in the history of the world has been opened by you. The German Fleet has been able to defeat a superior British Fleet. God Almighty has steeled your arms and kept your eyes clear; but I am standing here to-day **Hysterical exaltation of the German Navy** as your Supreme War Lord, and I thank you from the bottom of my heart.

In these days, when the enemy before Verdun is slowly beginning to collapse, when our allies have driven the Italians form mountain to mountain, and are still driving them back, you have accomplished this grand and beautiful deed. The world was prepared for anything, but never for the victory of the German Fleet over the British. A start has been made. Fear will creep into the bones of the enemy.

This effusion was supplemented by a telegram from the Kaiser to his eldest sister:

Hearty thanks for your dear congratulations. How gloriously God has helped our brave blue lads. To Him praise and thanks for His gracious assistance. I am deeply moved, and I feel proud and joyful that my creation, which has been the work of my life, has proved, with God's help, to be such a good and sharp weapon. The young German Fleet has torn down the nimbus of invincibility of British sea-power. May God help further!

More than a year later, when entertaining at his

The Kaiser with some of his Staff studying the position on a part of his eastern front.

Headquarters a minor poet, Max Bewer, the Kaiser—in spite of his " burning hatred " and " holy wrath " against England — f o u n d a chivalrous word, wrote the bard, for one of his adversaries :

Admiral J e l l i c o e (he said) is a gentleman, an old acquaintance of mine, a nobleman, a seaman from whose lips no lie proceeds. In loyalty to truth he announced the crushing losses England sustained in the Skager Rack battle. Only afterwards, when they observed the full effect on foreign countries, did they exert themselves to falsify defeat into victory over my Fleet. But I know that cab-drivers in Edinburgh publicly hissed the officers returning from that battle.

The Kaiser's victorious High Sea Fleet was in no great hurry to venture out again to complete the annihilation of its opponent.

In recording his conversation with the " Admiral of the Atlantic "—the vicarious victor of Jutland—the minor Poet aforesaid observed that the Kaiser's tone in making these remarks was pained ; as they contained " all the Imperial rancour against England's naval superiority," which thus, after all, seemed to have survived the vicious blow aimed at it in the Skager Rack.

Imperial rancour against England Such was also the Kaiser's vein of thought when, a little later, in a speech to his soldiers on the western front, he drew a comparison—quite in the manner of Plutarch— between the noble-minded French and the sordid, brutal British, " some of his words being drowned by the noise of the engines of aeroplanes keeping special watch overhead in order to frustrate any enemy attack ":

Regarding our French enemies, we can well imagine that the hope of liberating their homeland from the enemy, who had victoriously penetrated it in justified self-defence, spurred them to the highest sacrifices—a motive which a noble-minded enemy will appreciate.

But the English, on the other hand, have no such motive. They

His Majesty in Galicia, where German troops were sent to strengthen the hard-pressed Austrians.

only fight obstinately and tenaciously for the enlargement of their power at our cost.

And so I send you again to the front. It is now our business to hold on, however long it may last.

Thus the time, it will be seen, had now come when the Kaiser no longer talked of " going on " but only of " holding on." It had come to this, in fact, that the Germans, seeing that they had been beaten and baffled by the British on land, now realised that their only hope of salvation lay in their U boats. The Kaiser said so himself in an order to his Navy soon after his resort to " unrestricted submarine warfare."

" In the impending decisive struggle," **The Kaiser's faith** he said, " the task falls on my Navy **in the U boats** of turning the English war method of starvation, with which our most hated and most obstinate enemy intends to overthrow the German people, against them and their Allies by combating their sea traffic with all the means in our power. In this work the submarine will stand in the first rank."

And again : " Our sailors are working to cut piece by piece the vital nerve of the enemy, who devised a base plan to deliver to starvation a whole people, our women and children "—quite in the manner, as he might have added, of the Germans of 1870, who compelled the city of Paris to capitulate by process of famine.

In order to inaugurate his original " blockade " — *à la* Napoleon with his " Berlin Decrees "—the K a i s e r had gone to Cuxhaven to make one of his inflammatory speeches.

He declared himself possessed by a " rock-fast conviction that this weapon will not rest until the enemy is vanquished. To achieve that the help of the

The Emperor in conversation with one of his officers at a point behind the firing-line on one of his flying visits to the Russian front.

THE WAR LORD VISITING HIS EASTERN FRONT.

All-Highest is needed, for it goes without saying that such a task is beyond human strength."

Yet, while boasting of his piracy, the Kaiser was painfully conscious of the fact that the oceans of the world had all been swept completely clear of his mercantile marine, and that those of his subjects who lived by oversea commerce had been utterly ruined. To Max Bewer, the minor poet, his Majesty remarked that " his Hamburg friends had lost millions on millions, some in the Far East, others in Africa and America, but they had not wavered or weakened in their will to

Chats with Bewer and Hedin hold out, especially against England. 'It is envy, envy, and again envy, alone,' exclaimed the Kaiser."

And again, on the Arras front : " In these struggles all the Germans have realised who is the instigator of this war, and who the chief enemy—England. Everybody knows that England is our most spiteful adversary. She spreads her hatred of Germany over the whole world, steadily filling her Allies with hatred and eagerness to fight. Thus everybody at home knows, what you know still better, that England is particularly the enemy to be struck down, however difficult it may be."

Envy and jealousy of Germany as the motives which impelled Britain to enter the war (and without an army) — such was the constant theme of the Kaiser's speeches and table-talk, and his favoured visitors at Headquarters were careful to agree with him completely in this respect. Prominent among those guests was Dr. Sven Hedin, the Swedish explorer, who had always enjoyed the best of British hospitality when travelling in India, but had then

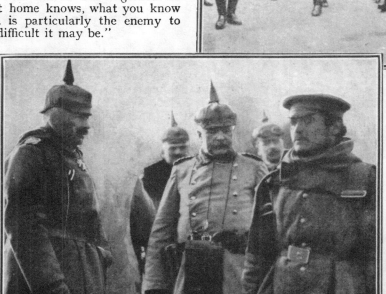

Inspecting his troops at Vilna (Wilna), which they had "captured" after the Russian evacuation.

transferred his sympathies from the Himalayans to the Huns. He spent several months as welcome pervert on the various German fronts, and well repaid his Imperial entertainer by the flattering, not to say fulsome, portrait he drew of his Imperial Majesty in his volume Englished under the title "With the German Armies in the West."

The Kaiser and his Swedish visitor revelled in abuse of England, whom his Majesty was for ever denouncing as the real author and instigator of the war ; and he lost no opportunity of hissing out hatred of his mother's country with a venom unsurpassed even by the " Hate Hymn " of Ernst Lissauer, on whom he hastened to confer the Red Eagle, just as he rewarded the sinker of the Lusitania with the " Ordre pour le Mérite."

The Kaiser, in the field on the eastern front, interrogating a captured Siberian sharpshooter.

In general, it may be said that there had been a marked increase in the acerbity of all the Kaiser's references to England ever since he had been struck off the roll of her Garter Knights. It is **Degraded from the** proper to remember that when his **Garter Knighthood** Majesty, on the first day of the war, divested himself of his British dignities—naval and military—in such a petulant manner, he did not also seek to disembarrass himself of his Garter, and for the simple reason that this was beyond his power. The rules both of the Garter and of the Black Eagle do not provide for the voluntary relinquishment of either, the principle being—once a knight always a knight, except in the case of ceremonial degradation.

This remedy, therefore, had to be resorted to. It used to be accomplished by the hacking of his spurs from a degraded knight, cutting his sword-belt, and breaking his sword over his sconce. But drastic treatment of this

William II. at Riga. Behind him stands General von Hutier, who was in command of the Eighth German Army, which took possession of that city from the demoralised Russians.

REJOICING OVER EASY CAPTURES FROM THE RUSSIANS.

kind evidently required the personal attendance of the knight, and it was impossible in the circumstances for the Garter King to expect the Emperor to respond in person to his summons.

In the Kaiser's case, therefore, as in that of all other German Sovereigns and princes holding the same high English honour, expulsion had to take the place of degradation; and at a Chapter of the Order it was decided that the following should be struck off the Roll of Knights and their insignia removed from the Chapel of St. George, Windsor: The German Emperor, the Emperor of Austria, the King of Würtemberg, the German Crown Prince, the Grand Duke of Hesse and the Rhine, Prince Henry of Prussia, the Duke of Saxe-Coburg and Gotha, and the Duke of Cumberland.

This degradation, in the case of the Kaiser more

if he had known, and that no gentleman would kill so many women and children."

To the interesting narrative of Mr. Gerard, United States Ambassador at Berlin, who paid several visits to Main Headquarters, we have already been indebted for vivid glimpses of the War Lord's life at the front. So now again it is to American writers that we must mainly turn for material to fill in the picture. As for the German journalists, artists, and poets who were admitted, their evidence cannot be accepted, being tainted by flattery of the most servile and shameless kind.

For example. Soon after the outbreak of the war, a Berlin professor of philosophy, Lasson by name, addressed to a friend in Holland a letter in which he described the chief author of this world-war as the "*deliciæ humani generis*," or "darling of the German race," who "has

A ROYAL REVIEW AT NISH.
The German Emperor, accompanied by the King of Bulgaria, inspecting an infantry regiment of the garrison of Nish, on the occasion of the meeting of the two monarchs in that town in January, 1917.

CONFEDERATE CÆSARS.
The Kaiser driving with the King of Bulgaria through the streets of Sofia. Ferdinand vaingloriously assumed the style of Tsar, or Cæsar, and toasted his confederate Kaiser in the Latin of the Roman Emperors.

always protected peace, right, and honour, although it would have been possible for him by his power to annihilate everything."

Akin to this was the effusion of Dr. Vogel, Court preacher at Potsdam, who declared the Kaiser to be "a deeply injured man, a scandalously deceived man, a man with a sore wound in his heart, a man powerful with the sword, victorious against a world of enemies."

After a German professor and a German preacher, let us now take a German poet—a minor one, it is true—in the person of Max Bewer, of Düsseldorf, which happened to be also the birthplace of Heinrich Heine, the most popular of all German singers, and the idolater of the Great Napoleon, on whom he had actually set eyes in his native place. "I saw him," wrote Heine of Napoleon, "and on his brow was written, 'Thou shalt have no other gods but me.'" So now Bewer wrote of William

Adulation from German sycophants

II.: "Hindenburg and Ludendorff, Mackensen and the Bavarian Lion of Arras, the heroes in the air and on the sea, ascended like a wreath of stars about our Kaiser's head. When I saw him at the Great Headquarters he was encircled by Iron Crosses and airmen's crosses, flashing and scintillating on uniforms of field-grey and sea-blue."

Observing that Goethe, Homer, the Northern Scalds, and the Bible describe their heroes by similes from Nature, the minor poet thought that he might as well apply this method to the mighty master of so many million men:

To look upon the Kaiser is like looking upon a wonderful autumn day. Think of fields and woods in all their brown fullness, whilst up above, on the tops of the mountains, there is the first bright, clean, white snow, and above the snow the flashing blue, sunny sky of a wonderful day. There, from the hand of Nature, you have the faithful picture of the Kaiser, as he looks with his great,

particularly, was not in the nature of an act of retaliation for the repudiation of his British naval and military dignities. It was retribution for the crimes, villainies, and barbarities he had been committing, and allowing and ordering others to commit in his name.

Barely a week before his Garter spurs had, metaphorically speaking, been hacked from his heels, humanity had been staggered, as it had perhaps never been before, by the torpedoing and sinking of the huge liner Lusitania, involving an immense loss of innocent life, though the Kaiser was afterwards to say to Mr. Gerard that he "would not have permitted the torpedoing of the liner

blue, flashing, but still good-natured, eyes upon a life that has ripened in fullness of work, and looks blameless into the mists of the war.

A different and a more realistic picture comes from the pen of the representative of the Chicago " Tribune," of the Kaiser's Sunday at the front (November, 1914) :

This morning the Emperor went to church, coming by motor-car from the villa in this town, where he had been in residence for several days. At church I sat fifteen feet from him and watched him as sharply as decency would permit.

This, thought I, as the Emperor seated himself in a drawing-room chair before the improvised altar, is the saddest face I have seen in my life. Not the saddest, either, nor yet the most careworn, but the gravest. In that countenance was no woe, but a solemnity so profound and austere that it moved the heart not to sympathy so much as a kind of awe.

I think that I may say that this man looked his part in the present tremendous drama. He looked not only the warrior-king, but the anxious head of the State, and you said to yourself as you studied the reflective eyes and the motionless lips, " The burden of Empire is upon him." For seconds upon seconds it was like a face of marble — undisturbed by so much as the quiver or the parting of the lips.

This sketch of the Kaiser was drawn by an American Senator, Mr. Berridge, of Indiana, who was received at Headquarters a few months later (March 31st, 1915) :

There is nothing pompous, nothing even pretentious, in the bearing of William II. One's first impression is that of a great man who is also a pleasant, simple-mannered gentleman, with an agreeable personality, charged with that engaging quality called magnetism. One's second impression, following so quickly upon the first that the two are almost one, is that of immense vigour, abounding physical vitality, and searchlight mental alertness. With it all you are instantly put at your ease, although, indeed, the psychological atmosphere is not that of awe or apprehension.

THE KAISER STUDYING THE ITALIAN PROSPECT.
The Emperor William visiting the Italian front. He was engaged in listening to an Austrian officer who was explaining the position of the opposing Austro-German and Italian armies.

The voice is vibrant and strong, without the faintest trace or suggestion of weakness or nervous exhaustion. The step is firm, decided, but not over rapid, and at no time was there the slightest indication of weariness. The carriage is erect, elastic, vigorous. While physically, as well as mentally, the Emperor shows extraordinary animation, there is a calmness, and a steadiness, that surprises you, because of the descriptions to the contrary so universally published.

After the American Senator, let us now take an American Judge (of Cincinnati) in the person of Alfred K. Nippert. As being of German name and descent, he was naturally received with open arms by the War Lord, who greeted him as a quasi-son—perhaps even a lost son—of the Fatherland, and entrusted him with a " message to the American people," through the medium of the " New York Times." With delicate consideration the Kaiser had arranged for his American visitor " to be seated immediately on his right " :

The Kaiser was in splendid spirits when we met at the dinner-table. The menu was simple and short. We sat down at eight o'clock. Including the Emperor's Staff and others, the party was composed of twelve to fifteen persons.

The dinner-party broke up at 8.45 o'clock. We had been served with, first, a plate of clabber—the best clabber I ever tasted in my life. The next thing was pike, then came a plate of roast veal, with peas, beans, and potatoes ; then a side dish of cauliflower, with gravy. There was ice-cream, and the company had its choice of three kinds of wine—claret, Rhine wine, and a strawberry bowl.

After dinner the Kaiser, having lit " one of his favourite Turkish cigarettes," invited Judge Nippert to walk with him, and they spent two hours in " most interesting and many-sided conversation," which impressed the Judge with the opinion that " the Kaiser is one of the few monarchs who are real servants of their people," in

Talking to Baron Conrad von Hötzendorff, Chief of the Austro-Hungarian General Staff, on the Polish front.

Decorating the Austrian Archduke Frederick with the " Ordre pour le Mérite," which is the highest of German Orders.

Meeting of the two Kaisers—the Emperor William and his ally, the Emperor Charles of Austria, at headquarters.

THE "ALL-HIGHEST" KEEPING IN CORDIAL TOUCH WITH WAVERING AND UNCERTAIN AUSTRIA.

accordance with his family motto. The visitor also "became conscious of his absolute optimism and assurance of ultimate and complete victory of the German arms," though this was before the Judge's adopted country had come into the war.

This appreciation may be supplemented by "The Man Who Dined with the Kaiser" and King Ferdinand at Nish, in January, 1916. This daring and deviceful journalist, a young Dutchman, Loopuit by name, acting as special correspondent of the "Daily Mail," actually contrived to be present at the banquet given by the King of Bulgaria to his Imperial visitor, and to furnish his journal with a most vivid and interesting account of the scene.

By the side of the big, clumsy-looking Ferdinand the Kaiser appeared almost insignificant, but it was not his size that so engrossed my attention. All through the meal I could scarcely take my eyes from the haggard face of the author of the world-war who, on this January afternoon, looked so little like a War Lord, as he sat apparently coughing away his life into the Turkish woven handkerchief which he held firmly in his right hand.

His hair was terribly white, darkening a little at the parting where the roots showed. His cheeks were scored with many lines, and when I conjured up the vision of the healthy-looking Kaiser I had seen eight years previously in Amsterdam, I could not help marvelling at the change that those eight years had wrought in him. The only thing about him that was not changed was his upright deportment.

Not content with having conferred on each other high

GERMANY'S CROWN PRINCE AND HIS STAFF.
The Crown Prince (second from the left in the front) surrounded by officers of his Staff at a French château, which he occupied as his temporary headquarters during his command on the western front.

decorations and regiments, the two monarchs now proceeded to exchange speeches of the most adulatory kind, which anyone calling himself a simple soldier of many actions but few words would have blushed to own ; and when at last his native German was no longer equal to the expression of his feelings, the Bulgarian monarch burst out into Latin which would have rather puzzled Cæsar and Cicero : "Ave Imperator, Cæsar et Rex. Victor et gloriosus es. Nissa antiqua omnes Orientis populi te salutant redemptorem ferentem oppressis prosperitatem atque salutem" (*i.e.*, "Hail, dread ruler, Kaiser and King ! Glorious conqueror art thou. Ancient Nish and all the peoples of the East salute thee as their redeemer, the bringer of peace and prosperity to the oppressed !") An Oxford Fellow wrote to the "Times" : "Tsar Ferdinand addresses Kaiser Wilhelm as ' victor et gloriosus.' The meaning of ' victor ' is obvious ; but what does ' gloriosus ' signify ? My Latin dictionary renders it ' vainglorious, boasting, bragging, haughty, conceited, ostentatious.' Was not that the unkindest cut of all at the Nish banquet ? "

Satellites around the planet

After this fulsome flattery, the least thing the Kaiser could do was to return the compliment by presenting the baton of a Prussian field-marshal to his entertainer, of whom General Savoff, a former commander-in-chief of his, had said : "What can you do with a man who always lives in bodily fear, who dares not look at a wounded soldier, who trembles at the sound of the guns, and hides himself in a railway carriage, always keeping as far as possible from the front ? "

Since the very first day of the war, though the fact—which had remained hidden for several months from the British diplomatists on the spot—was only revealed to an astonished world after the deposition of King Constantine and the publication of his private papers, the Kaiser and the Sultan had been treaty allies. No one, therefore could have been more welcome at Constantinople than the chief of the Power that had given the Turks so much material help in men and money, and promised to guarantee the integrity of their moribund Empire ; and one of the first things done by the Kaiser on reaching Stamboul was to go and gloat over the scenes of the fighting at Gallipoli— so disastrous to the Allies.

THE EMPEROR WILLIAM WITH TWO OF HIS SONS.
The Kaiser with his eldest son, the Crown Prince William (centre), and his fifth son, Prince Oscar. This group was taken during one of the visits which the Kaiser paid to the headquarters of the Crown Prince in France.

HEIR OF THE MODERN ATTILA.
The Crown Prince of the German Empire and of Prussia in the garden of the French château which he took as his headquarters on the western front.

At a grand banquet given in his honour at the Dolma Bagtche Palace—where he himself had been welcomed by Abdul the "Damned" just nineteen years previously, he thus referred to his visit to Gallipoli :

Yesterday it was given to me to stand on the ground where Turkish forces by land and sea, in an heroic fight performed immortal glorious deeds, victoriously frustrating the enemy's assault on the heart of the Empire, and thereby rendering immense service to our common cause. Anafarta, Asiburnu, and Seddul Bahr will for ever remain glorious pages in the history of the Turkish Army, which is so crowded with great deeds. To come into personal touch, through my appointment as field-marshal, with such an Army is for me a proud joy and satisfaction.

Before going to Stamboul to embrace and bless his fellow-criminal, the perpetrator of the Armenian massacres, the "modern Attila" had made the tour of the Rumanian battlefields, where victory had been won for him by Generals Falkenhayn and Mackensen. After haranguing in his usual way the troops who had taken part in the campaign of 1916, he indulged in a vitriolic comparison between the noble King Charles, who had ever been true alike to his (Hohenzollern) family and his treaty engagements, and his nephew and successor Ferdinand :

The renegade who, at the time when Germany was engaged in a terrible war, joined the enemies of the Empire as a new opponent. The avenging hand of the Judge above us has sealed the fate of this faithless former friend.

What the Lord of Hosts may still have in store we do not know, but come what may, we are able confidently to look the world in the face.

We did not will this war, and if it be prolonged it is not our fault. Rely upon help from the Lord, but rely also upon your own strength and beat the enemy.

As grim coincidence would have it, at this very time when the War Lord indulged in these assurances, the State Department at Washington was making disclosures proving that the German Legation at Bukarest was a nest of wholesale poisoners.

But, after all, the "perfidy" of Rumania, which had moved the Kaiser to such an outburst, was nothing in his eyes to the "treachery" of another ally and former co-member of the Triplice—Italy. Hastening to the Isonzo front, after the Bolo-bacillus of his devising had done its baneful work on some of Cadorna's troops, the War Lord took his histrionic stand on the Tagliamento and shouted out to his "heroes" : **Physical constitution of the Kaiser**

Acting in concert with the Emperor Charles, we decided to break through the Italian front.
The task appeared to be difficult, but what ensued surpassed all calculations so greatly that a Higher Power than the power of man must have participated in it.
The terrible collapse of the enemy was God's judgment.
Up to the present Heaven has aided us, and it will aid us still further.

A YOUNGER SON.
Prince Eitel Friedrich, second son of the Kaiser, who played a quite inconspicuous part in the war.

The next act of the Kaiser was to congratulate the Emperor Charles on his escape from drowning when trying to cross a swollen mountain torrent in his motor-car. It was natural enough for the War Lord to ascribe this to the special intervention of Divine Providence.

The Kaiser was physically delicate, and no insurance company in the world would have thought him anything but what is called a "bad life." He had always been particularly sensitive to weather changes, and probably no living monarch had spent so much of his time indoors suffering from colds, abscesses, and various other complaints. Once—but this was years before the war—he underwent a somewhat serious operation for a growth in his throat, in precisely the same spot where the fatal illness of his father had first made its appearance, which caused the "Lancet" to remark :

The feeling of every medical man on reading that in a man of forty-five years of age, whose father died from cancer of the larynx,

PRUSSIAN AND SAXON FORGATHER.
The King of Saxony, in the centre, walking with the Crown Prince of the German Empire while visiting the latter's army on the western front. It was to this army that, partly for dynastic reasons, was committed the capture of Verdun—which it failed to accomplish.

THE KAISER AND HIS CONSORT.
Empress Augusta going for a walk with her husband in the grounds of
the Imperial headquarters in Galicia on one of the Emperor's meteoric
visits to the eastern front.

and whose mother succumbed to cancer, a larnygeal polypus had
been discovered and removed was naturally one of uneasiness. . .
The growth, as a matter of fact, turned out to be non-malignant,
but it is a scientific fact all the same that in some cases a development from a benign to a malignant type has been observed.

On such a constitution, however fortified by great physical
and nervous energy, the worries
of the war were bound to produce
a serious effect, so that before it
was six months old the Kaiser's
hair had become white. Frequent were the ailments of which
the outside world was told
nothing, or only at the end of
1915, when the War Lord had to
hurry back from haranguing his
soldiers in Poland—and, probably
enough, on that very account—
to consult the leading throat
specialists of Berlin. Little more
than a year later his health
became so precarious — from
Bright's disease, according to
rumour — that it was thought
advisable for him to take the
waters at Homburg, to which, in
consequence, Main Headquarters
was removed for the duration of
his "cure," with the Kaiserin as
his nurse.

It was at her Kronberg château,
near Homburg, that the
Emperor's mother had succumbed
to the same disease as had

carried off his father thirteen years previously. But the
principle of physical heredity, as referred to by the
"Lancet" in this connection, had a further application to
the case of William II. in respect of the quality of his
mind as well as of the fibre of his body.

For when he behaved in such a way, by word and deed,
as to excite suspicion of his sanity, it was recalled that
some of his relatives had suffered from positive brain
disease, and, above all things, that the mother of the two
mad kings of Bavaria—Ludwig II. and Otto—had been a
Prussian Princess Marie.

Professor Virchow, the famous pathologist, summed up
the mentality of the Prussian reigning house in these
words: "I know a family in which the grandfather
(Frederick William II., nephew of and successor to
Frederick the Great) had softening of the brain; the
father (Frederick William III., our Waterloo ally) hardening of the brain; and the son (Frederick William IV.,
who had to be set aside for his insanity and replaced
by his brother, William I.) no brain at all." William II.,
on the other hand, could not be denied the possession of
a very well-shaped head—the best in
his family since Frederick — and very   **Hereditary tendency**
considerable brain; but it was a question   **to insanity**
of whether this brain was sound or
unsound. Several noted alienists seriously pronounced the
Kaiser to be a lunatic of the criminal kind; while by
Professor Lombroso, founder of criminal anthropology,
William II. was declared to be a "typical mattoid."

Such professional opinions were served up with his coffee
every morning to the Kaiser at Main Headquarters. For,
like his father before him—according to Gustav Freytag,
the intimate friend and biographer of the Emperor
Frederick—William II. had ever made a point of
collecting all the newspaper cuttings about himself, and
of carefully following foreign, especially British, opinion
as reflected in the Press, to several organs of which he was
a private subscriber.

During the war, too, he kept up this practice with the
help of an official whose daily duty it was to paste newspaper cuttings of an essential kind on gilt-edged foolscap
sheets, and from those his Majesty got to know at first
hand what the world was thinking of him.

But it was not alone the elegant extracts from the English

SMILES FOR A SOLDIER BROKEN IN THE WAR.
The German Empress visiting convalescent German soldiers was interested in one man who, having lost
a hand, had elected to be taught gardening as an occupation by which he might maintain his independence
on returning to civil life.

papers which exacerbated the temper of the Kaiser. Cuttings from his own German papers—of the more restrained kind, it is true, in view of the censor's lash—also began to come pouring in to him as counterblasts, so to speak, to the gross adulation of the Ganghofers, the Bewers, the Lissauers, the Sven Hedins, and other flatterers of the Byzantine kind.

Thus, for example, Herr Lebedour, a prominent member of the Minority (or anti-war) Socialists in the Reichstag, rose and roundly declared himself for the abolition of the monarchy. "To-day the Boers were fighting on the side of Britain. Why? Because Britain had at once given the Boers full autonomy. In England, Germans were now called Huns. To whom was that really due?

Rifts in the German lute To the gentleman who, on the despatch of German soldiers to China, exhorted his soldiers to follow the example of Attila and his savage hordes."

Similarly a South German paper characterised one of the War Lord's flaming speeches to his soldiers as "quite incomprehensible and regrettable," while another organ of the same kind plainly told him that he must at once get rid of all his nonsensical notions about Divine right, "in which no one any longer believes. It is absurd to put upon any single man the heavy responsibility of ruling a nation of seventy million souls."

The writer of a pamphlet entitled "The Only Way Out," issued by the "League of South Germans," argued that William II. should be prepared to sacrifice himself for his people as Napoleon I. did after Waterloo. "If the Kaiser abandoned the Imperial throne, and if the whole of the Hohenzollern family voluntarily left Germany, the Allies would willingly negotiate, either with the Imperial Ministers or with the combined Governments of the South German States."

At the same time a prominent journal of Munich made

BLOOD-BROTHERS.
The Kaiser with his brother, Prince Henry of Prussia, leaving the latter's headquarters.

Kaiser, who was assailed for having conducted himself in such a manner as to render inevitable a combination of world Powers against Germany.

Yet another professor, Lezius, of Königsberg, Immanuel Kant's Prussian university, was suspended for reproaching the Kaiser with a lack of courage in hesitating to adopt the complete annexationist programme of the Pan-Germans. The Kaiser was also guilty of a lack of patriotism. "It was a misfortune for Germany to be ruled by a weak Emperor. We must bring pressure to bear on the Emperor to make him adopt a patriotic programme."

That was bad enough for a Prussian professor. But the pillars of the monarchy seemed to be altogether tottering when a Prussian Junker like Count Reventlow positively declared that a German victory and a German monarchy were mutually dependent. Without a German victory a German monarchy would soon cease to exist.

Meanwhile, in March, 1917, the Russian monarchy ceased to exist; and soon after this a member of the Socialist Minority (Herr Kunert) rose in the Reichstag and denounced the Emperor and his Chancellor as the originators of the war. The significance of the Russian Revolution had sunk deep into the Kaiser's soul, and, with the quick intuition which ever distinguished him, he at once decided to throw a preventive sop to his own Prussian subjects in the shape of a promise of a more liberal franchise, while leaving the Imperial Constitution quite untouched.

Several years before this he had dangled electoral reform before the eyes of his Prussian subjects; but it was only this revolutionary pressure, and possible contagion, from Russia which ripened his purpose into promising a sort of reward for the sacrifices made by his people in arms during the war. Yet it really did not matter what sort of a suffrage was enjoyed, either by the German people at large or the Prussians. For as long as the universal right of voting was countervailed by his absolute right of veto the votes of the electors meant nothing.

What was called a political "crisis" now arose. The War Lord himself left the western front and hastened to Berlin, whither he had also summoned his chief generals to take their advice on a purely political question.

Hard upon the heels of this utterly unreal "crisis"

ANIMATION IN THE COURTYARD OF THE PALACE OF POTSDAM.
The Kaiser in conversation with Prince Salm-Horstmar, outside the New Palace at Potsdam. The Crown Princess is on the left, with her eldest son, Prince Wilhelm of Prussia, in sailor dress. This photograph, taken shortly after the declaration of war, was issued in Germany as a war picture postcard.

bold to lecture the Kaiser on his constant forgetfulness of the fact that, after all, he was only President of the United States of Germany, just as Mr. Wilson was President of the United States of America, one being hereditary, the other elective; and that it was quite improper for him to push himself forward and pose as Emperor of the German people when he was only one of the executive kind and not their sovereign head.

In the same way a Heidelberg professor, Max Weber, wrote a series of articles for the "Frankfurter Zeitung," on which, accordingly, the censor's lash was quick to descend, directed against the personal element in the Imperial Government and the usurping character of the

came another rather more serious one in the shape of a change of Chancellor, Bethmann-Hollweg being succeeded by Dr. Michaelis, a man of whom few had ever heard in Germany itself, and fewer still outside its bounds. No definite reason had been assigned for the resignation of the " scrap of paper " Chancellor, but it was felt all over Germany that his position had become impossible after he had written to a Bavarian friend that " the greatest danger came from the Germans who still continued to believe in a German victory. In the best case it could only be a draw."

In writing thus the Chancellor had let the cat out of the bag as completely as when, on August 4th, 1914, he blurted out in the Reichstag that " in invading Belgium, Germany was committing an international crime under compulsion of that necessity which knew no law." He had ceased to serve the purposes of the Hohenzollern.

Kaiser as apostle of peace

Bethmann's fall was a Pan-German victory and a blow to that peace movement which had been initiated by the Kaiser himself—with the approval of his Liberal Chancellor. It was towards the end of the year 1916, after the Battle of the Somme had convinced the Germans that victory in the west was no longer possible for them, that the world was startled by the sudden appearance of the Kaiser—not so much as a mighty War Lord in " shining armour," but as a meek-eyed Apostle of Peace, with a palm-branch in one hand and a gleaming sword in the other. Already, in a bombastic manifesto to his people, this War Lord—after dwelling on the " incomparable," the " unheard of," the " stupendous " achievements of his " invincible," his " unshakable," his " all-conquering " heroes—had hastened to strike a milder note. " The desire for peace," he said, " is stirring in all human hearts, and the blame for further bloodshed rests on our enemies."

This was said on August 1st, 1916, when the iron of the Somme had sunk into the Kaiser's soul, and on December 12th following his Chancellor stood forth in the Reichstag and declared that the time had now come for formally repeating those offers of peace which " had hitherto been evaded by our adversaries."

That this " peace proposal " had emanated from the All-Highest himself he was careful to show by the publication of a letter he had written to " My dear Bethmann " on October 31st, 1916, in which he said :

What is wanted is a moral deed, to free the world, including neutrals, from the pressure which weighs upon all. For such a deed it is necessary to find a ruler who has a conscience, who feels that he is responsible to God, who has a heart for his own people and for those of his enemies, who, indifferent as to any possible wilful misinterpretation of his action, possesses the will to free the world from its sufferings. I have the courage. Trusting in God, I shall dare to take this step. Please draft Notes on these lines, and submit them to me, and make all the necessary arrangements without delay.

The German Note itself, with its " peace offer," was entirely lacking in details. The Allies might as well have been asked to discuss a question of metaphysics. Therefore their reply was as positive as it was prompt, and its general purport was that the Kaiser's " peace proposals " were in the nature of a sham—" less an offer of peace than a war-manœuvre," " a proposal which is empty and insincere," " a calculated attempt to influence the future course of the war, and to end it by imposing a German peace."

A sham offer

Furious at this emphatic and contemptuous rejection of his proffered " palm-branch," he turned to his Army and Navy :

Before God and humanity (he protested) I declare that on the enemy Governments alone falls the heavy responsibility for all the further terrible sacrifices from which I wished to save you. With justified indignation at our enemies' arrogant crime, and with determination to defend our holiest possessions and secure the Fatherland's happy future, you will become as steel. Our enemies

did not want the understanding offered by me. With God's help our arms will enforce it.

Turning then to his people at large the War Lord continued :

Our enemies have dropped the mask. After refusing with scorn and hypocritical words of love for peace and humanity our honest peace offer, they now, in their reply to the United States, have gone beyond that and admitted their lust for conquest, the baseness of which is further enhanced by their calumnious assertions.

Their aim is the crushing of Germany, the dismemberment of the Powers allied to us, and the enslavement of the freedom of Europe and the seas under the same yoke that Greece, with gnashing teeth, is now enduring. But what they in thirty months of the bloodiest fighting and unscrupulous economic war could not achieve they will also in all the future not accomplish . . . . Burning indignation and holy wrath will redouble the strength of every German man and woman, whether it is devoted to fighting, work, or suffering. We are ready for all sacrifices.

Concurrently with its peace overtures to the belligerent Powers the Imperial Government and its allies had addressed to the Pope what was practically an invitation to use his influence in the way of mediation and suggestion, and with this flattering request Benedict XV. decided to comply.

The Pope's reply to the German appeal had at least the merit of being more precise and businesslike than the " peace proposals " of the Kaiser. His Holiness had much to say to the Kaiser about a millennial era of disarmament, arbitration, and other abstract doctrines. But, he went on :

These pacific agreements, with the immense advantages they entail, are impossible without the reciprocal restitution of territories now occupied. Consequently on the part of Germany there must be the complete evacuation of Belgium, with a guarantee of her full political, military, and economic independence towards all Powers whatsoever ; likewise the evacuation of French territory. On the part of the other belligerent parties there must be a similar restitution of the German colonies, etc.

The Pope addressed a copy of his Note to all the belligerents. As in courtesy bound, the Allies—whose ranks had in the meantime been joined by the United States of America — lost no time in replying to the recommendations of his Holiness.

Windy hypocrisy

Their responses may be said to have been summed up in the reply of President Wilson, speaking for a people of a hundred million souls, which took the form of a crushing indictment of the blood-guilty Kaiser, " the ruthless master of the German people," whose " furious and brutal power " had inflicted " intolerable wrongs," and concluded :

We cannot take the word of the present rulers of Germany as a guarantee of anything that is to endure, unless explicitly supported by such conclusive evidence of the will and purpose of the German people themselves as the other peoples of the world would be justified in accepting. Without such guarantees treaties of settlement, agreements for disarmament, covenants to set up arbitration in the place of force, territorial adjustments, reconstitutions of small nations, if made with the German Government, no man, no nation, could now depend on.

As for the German reply, which was practically identical with that of Austria, it made no reference whatever to the evacuation of France and Belgium, which the Pope had specially mentioned as one of the essential preliminaries to a just peace, and simply took the form of another attempt to show that William II. had ever been a pillar and Prince of Peace. " The windiest and most hypocritical document," said a French diplomatist, " ever issued from the Potsdam type-foundry."

Statesmen had said their last word as to the Kaiser's " peace proposals," and now the question was referred back to the soldiers in the words of old Siward in " Macbeth " :

The time approaches,
That will with due decision make us know
What we shall say we have, and what we owe,
Thoughts speculative their unsure hopes relate,
But certain issue strokes must arbitrate ;
Towards which, advance the war.

THE CONQUEST OF GERMAN EAST AFRICA COMPLETED.

By Robert Machray.

Military Situation in East Africa in 1916—General Smuts Reorganises His Army—Recruits More Blacks—Germans from Tabora Break Through—Gallant Defence of Malangali by Rhodesian Native Troops—Large Enemy Force Trapped and Taken—Smuts' New Offensive—Second South African Brigade Cross the Rufiji—Elusive Germans Slip Past in the Centre—Smuts Tries Again—Death of Captain Selous—Smuts Called to London to Represent South Africa in War Cabinet—His Views on Future of German East Africa—General Hoskins in Chief Command—Abnormal Rainy Season—General Northey's Good Work in the West—Belgian Congolese Army Again Co-operates—General Van Deventer Replaces Hoskins—His Fighting Advance in Kilwa and Lindi Areas—Belgians Pressing on to Mahenge—Encircling Move from the Coast—Timely Retreat of the Germans Saves Them—Their Severe Losses—Fall of Mahenge to the Gallant Belgians—Closing Scenes—German Main Body's Flight into Portuguese Territory—Reduced to Two Thousand Men—Force Retreating from Mahenge Enveloped and Compelled to Surrender Unconditionally—A Big "Bag"—Colony Cleared of the Enemy—Summary of Results of Four Months' Operations—Van Deventer's Success Signalised by a Knighthood.

ELEGRAPHING on December 1st, 1917, General Van Deventer reported that reconnaissances had definitely established the fact that German East Africa had been cleared of the enemy. So stated a British War Office communiqué of December 3rd. It added significantly: "Thus the whole of the last of the German overseas possessions has passed into our hands and those of our Belgian allies."

In Chapter CLXXIX. (Vol. IX., p. 207) the story of the East African campaign—under General Smuts in the east and centre, and under General Tombeur in the west — was carried down to October, 1916, when the enemy was hemmed in on all sides, and had lost every healthy or valuable part of the land, with the solitary exception of the Mahenge plateau.

In October, 1916, General Smuts carried out a scheme of general reorganisation, partly because of the evacuation he purposed of his sick men, and partly because the capture of Dar-es-Salaam and the restoration of the Central Railway had given him a new and much better base of operations than Tanga and Mombasa, a thousand miles farther north. At this time his army consisted of three divisions (Chapter CLXXIX., Vol. IX., p. 210).

He now decided to abolish the 3rd Division, which was

MENTIONED IN DESPATCHES.

[Elliott & Fry.

Brigadier-General Sir Charles Crewe, C.B., K.C.M.G., organised the transport and supply service for General Tombeur's force from Lake Victoria and subsequently commanded the advance to Mwanza and Tabora.

commanded by Major-General Brits, including the 2nd South African Mounted Brigade under Brigadier-General Enslin, and to return these officers with their Staffs to South Africa, as well as their men, with the exception of such as were fit, and these were incorporated into the 1st South African Mounted Brigade, of which Brigadier-General Nussey was the head. The 2nd South African Infantry Brigade, under Brigadier-General Beves, which had also formed part of the 3rd Division, was placed in reserve, its immediate control being exercised by Smuts himself. His army consequently consisted of two divisions—one under Major-General Hoskins, and the other under Major-General Van Deventer—in addition to Beves' infantry in his own hands. Further, there was the Nyasaland - Rhodesia force, under Brigadier-General Northey, which was working in combination with Van Deventer. The Lake Detachment, under Sir Charles Crewe, had been abolished as a separate force; some of its units were added to the 2nd Division, and one battalion remained in occupation of a portion of the Central Railway eastwards from Tabora.

Troops had to be found to take the place of the men who had been invalided home, and Smuts obtained them in part by forming and training new battalions of the King's African Rifles. The course of the campaign had demonstrated that some of the native tribes supplied magnificent fighting material, and the Commander-in-Chief sought and obtained the sanction of the War Office for recruiting several thousands of these warlike blacks, or Askaris. Native soldiers were also sent to his assistance from West Africa. Amongst the earliest to arrive was the Gold Coast Regiment. Then followed the Nigerian Brigade, under Brigadier-General F. H. B. Cunliffe, C.B., C.M.G., which reached Dar-es-Salaam in the second and third weeks of December. The Nigerians were thoroughly seasoned, as they had taken a very active part in the conquest of Cameroon, under the leadership of the same distinguished commander (Chapter LXXXVII. (Vol. V., p. 79). Of Smuts' reconstituted army nearly a half consisted of Askaris, about a quarter was white, and the rest was composed of East Indians—Baluchis, Kashmiris, and Punjabis.

In October, 1916, the forces of General Smuts were in three main groups in the south-east of the country. In the east a force of some 2,000 rifles, under General Hannyngton, had been concentrated at Kilwa on the coast. In the centre, opposite the Germans on the Mgeta River, stood the 1st Division, under General Hoskins. In the west the forward troops of the 2nd Division, under General Van Deventer, occupied Iringa and other adjacent points, the remaining men being concentrated north on the Central Railway. Also around Iringa and south of it, in greater strength, on the Ruhudje River, was the force of General Northey. Up till the end of December, when General Smuts began a **Two German forces join** general offensive, interest almost wholly centred in the western area during the last three months of 1916. In this quarter the scene of the fighting was the main road from Lake Nyasa to Kilosa, or on ground in its vicinity. To Van Deventer and Northey had been assigned the difficult task of preventing the Germans, who had retreated from Tabora, from joining up with the considerable body of their troops on the Mahenge plateau. The task, in fact, proved to be an impossible one.

Under General Wahle and Major Wintgens, the Germans from Tabora, mustering about 1,600 rifles, had reached the neighbourhood of Iringa and Malangali in the third week of October. To deal with the enemy, General Van Deventer pushed forward to Iringa the 7th South African Infantry and a cyclist battalion, the latter under Lieut.-Colonel J. M. Fairweather, who for the time being assumed command of the two battalions, as well as of the portion of General Northey's force already there under Lieut.-Colonel T. A. Rodger. The 7th arrived at Iringa on October 23rd, and the cyclist battalion next day.

Before the troops from the 2nd Division had reached Iringa the major part of the Germans from Tabora had broken through southwards between Alt Iringa and Ngominyi. This took place on the night of October 22nd-23rd, and one of its results was to cut all communication with General Northey, who for some time remained without any means of issuing orders to his troops at Iringa. Smuts thereupon placed General Van Deventer in charge of the situation, and gave him **Enemy offensive in the south** control over Colonel Rodger's men. Besides the major German force, many small parties got across the road in the darkness, " which, of course, they were able to do," commented General Smuts, " without any fear of detection over a large front." The passage of the enemy through the British lines occupied some three weeks, and was marked by much fighting on a small scale.

Meanwhile, the Germans from Mahenge, to aid their comrades in the break-through, took the offensive in the south against Northey's troops under Colonels Hawthorn and Murray. The Germans were commanded by Major Kraut, and during the night of October 21st-22nd he crossed the Ruhudje River with about 1,600 men, some of whom were mounted and all well found. His force included the 10th Field Company, two hundred strong,

DUSKY WEARERS OF THE RED CROSS OF SUCCOUR.
British officers in East Africa training natives as stretcher-bearers. In a country where the conditions of campaigning were so difficult, extensive arrangements had to be made for dealing with many sick as well as with wounded, and the natives proved valuable helpers in the stretcher-bearing part of the work. Inset : Trainload of British armoured cars on a German East African railway.

and said to be the best company which the Germans possessed in East Africa. Having despatched a company to block the road to Lupembe, through which Northey obtained his supplies, he proceeded to invest the British at Mkapira, and for three days bombarded them with a 2·4 in. gun. On the fourth day this gun was put out of action by a direct hit from one of the British guns. And all the while the besieged force had managed to keep in touch with a detachment under Captain Galbraith some distance away to the west. On the 30th, Colonel Hawthorn sprang from his trenches, and at dawn attacked the enemy's main position, while a diversion was made by Galbraith. The result was a signal victory. Within an hour the Germans were in full retreat, and hastily crossed the Ruhudje. In this brilliant affair the British captured six European and seventy-five native soldiers, together

Colonel Hawthorn had already been ordered to withdraw. The Germans now made a fresh move by investing Malangali, the supply-depot on the high road lying north-west of that place. From November 8th to 12th, Malangali, which was held by a company of the newly-raised Rhodesian Native Regiment under Captain F. Marriott, suffered serious assaults, three of which were repulsed at close quarters, with heavy loss to the enemy. Led by Marriott, the raw Rhodesian Askaris put up a wonderful defence against considerable odds, in spite of the depressing facts that on the first day of the attack all their stores had been set on fire by a German shell, that food was short, and that the water was bad. On the 12th a relieving force of four hundred rifles under Colonel Murray suddenly arrived on the scene in motor-cars, and taking full advantage of the surprise it effected, routed and

ARTILLERY IN ACTION ON THE VELDT.
British gunners bringing their weapons into action in open country in German East Africa. Phenomenal rains during 1917 considerably delayed the operations, making the movement of guns particularly difficult.

IMPROVISED BRIDGE FOR THE GUNS.
Motor-car drawing a gun over an ingeniously simple bridge for wheeled traffic that had been thrown across a river in German East Africa by the resourceful British engineers.

with the 2·4 in. gun, three machine-guns, and large quantities of ammunition and other war material, including three field telephones.

For a week the Germans remained quiescent. They had left behind considerable numbers of their sick and wounded at different camps, and also had released many of the prisoners they had taken. In the meantime a British column, under Colonel A. J. Taylor, was being concentrated at Dodoma, on the Central Railway, with a view to its being sent to reinforce the troops at Iringa, and the Mounted Brigade of the 2nd Division, which, after the operations in the Uluguru Mountains in August had been resting and refitting at Mrogoro, was despatched to the same point. How striking was the wastage of the campaign was emphasised by Smuts' statement that this brigade had been reduced to 1,000 rifles approximately. These movements were preparatory to a concentration of Northey's men at Lupembe, to which those of them under

drove off the Germans, many of whom, including nine Europeans in one company alone, were captured. For his gallant defence of the post Captain Marriott was awarded the Military Cross. The enemy next attacked Songea, on the 14th-15th, and Lupembe on the 17th, but without success. These rebuffs apparently caused him to abandon further immediate offensive action.

It was discovered that one part of the enemy forces from Tabora was at a point west of Madibira, either having not tried or having failed to break through to the east. On November 21st it was definitely ascertained that this hostile body had occupied Ilembule Mission, which lay north-west of Ubena, on the previous day, and was about to move eastward. Here was an opportunity not to be neglected. Northey arranged to send a force under Colonel Murray by motors to attack the enemy, while Van Deventer was instructed to co-operate from Iringa.

German capitulation at Ilembule

It was anticipated that it might be a costly operation, for the Germans held the mission buildings which they had fortified, but the upshot was as satisfactory for the British as it was unexpected. The enemy was skilfully trapped and captured. By noon on the 24th Murray had drawn a circle round the place, and there was some fighting next day. On the following morning the British lines were moved in closer, and at two o'clock in the afternoon a parlementaire was sent to Colonel Huebener, the German commander, telling him that his water supply was cut off, that he was surrounded without hope of relief, and demanding his surrender. Thereupon Huebener capitulated, with all his stores, guns, and ammunition intact, except for the blowing up of the breech-block of a 4.2 in. Krupp howitzer, dated 1915. The prisoners consisted of seven officers, forty-seven other Europeans, and two hundred and forty-nine native soldiers. The British casualties were only seven men wounded. It was a splendid "bag" at a trifling expense.

In the central area—the Mgeta River front—the conditions were of the nature of trench warfare, and operations were practically at a standstill until Smuts initiated a general offensive at the end of December. The British front line was held by General Sheppard's brigade, while in reserve was the brigade which formerly had been commanded by General Hannyngton, whose place had been taken by Colonel (afterwards Brigadier-General) H. de C. O'Grady. Smuts decided to move O'Grady's brigade to Kilwa. The troops already there were formed into the 3rd East African Brigade, under General Hannyngton, and a new 1st Division was made by the addition of General O'Grady's brigade, the division being commanded by General Hoskins, who, for the purpose, came over from the Mgeta front, arriving at Kilwa on November 15th. By the 29th the whole of O'Grady's force had reached the same base. In this eastern, or Kilwa, area little

Smuts' encircling move

happened at first, but during November and December there was some sharp fighting at Kibata, which Hannyngton had occupied in October.

General Smuts planned a great encircling move south of the Rufiji River, and his intention was, as regarded the eastern end of it, to march towards Liwale, on the road from Kilwa to Songea and Wiedhafen. But information derived from the statements of prisoners and from captured documents, to the effect that the enemy purposed an offensive and an attack on Kabati, induced him temporarily to modify his scheme. In this eastern area the Germans were commanded by Colonel (later General) von Lettow-Vorbeck, their Commander-in-Chief, and it was here that their main strength was now to be found. An assault on Kabati in the second week of November was easily repulsed—it was more of the character of a reconnaissance—but a determined attempt to invest the place was made in December. On the afternoon of December 6th the Germans began an attack, which was intensified on the following day, when they brought several naval as well as field guns into action. Various heavy assaults were delivered on the 7th and 8th by the enemy,

but he was repulsed, although outlying positions changed hands several times. A move of Hannyngton from the west, in co-operation with O'Grady from Kilwa, checked the Germans, and by the 16th the fighting died down, the British holding their positions.

On December 21st General Hoskins reported to General Smuts, then on the eve of launching his offensive, that he believed he would be able to prevent the Germans from retreating to the south by the route from the Matumbi Hills, which lay north-west of Kabati. At this stage Smuts ordered Hoskins to hold some battalions ready to move north-west when the execution of the general plan was undertaken, and advised him of his (Smuts') intention to proceed to the Mgeta front on the following day to direct operations. By December 22nd everything was in readiness on all fronts for the great new movement, and then heavy rains set in which caused delay.

Notwithstanding the weather, Generals Van Deventer and Northey in the western area began their advance on December 24th in a combined offensive to drive the enemy over the Ulanga and Ruhudje Rivers. Between Iringa and the Ulanga, where the former general operated, the

TRAPPINGS OF PRIDE.
An interlude in East African campaigning: Bringing in, as saddle-cloth, the fresh skin of a lion just shot on the veldt.

terrain was very mountainous and covered with dense bush, while all the streams were swollen by the rains. A detachment was held up by the flooded condition of the Lukose River, and was building rafts by which to try to get across it. On Christmas Day the troops of the 2nd Division encountered the Germans, east of the pass known as Magoma, or Lukegeta, Nek. While this frontal attack was proceeding the Mounted Brigade was sent to cut off the enemy's retreat, and a column under Colonel Taylor moved east of Muhenga to join hands with the Mounted Brigade. Fierce fighting continued at the pass on the 26th.

MILITARY USE OF NATURE'S LAW OF MIMICRY.
Painting horses in East Africa with stripes to render them less easily visible to enemy observers. Hunters have declared that the protective colouring of the zebra is the most effective of all, large herds of those animals being quite indistinguishable at quite a short distance.

A SHEER HULK: GERMAN NAVAL POWER IN AFRICA.
The Koenig after destruction by British shell fire. The Germans tried to block the entrance to Dar-es-Salaam Harbour by sinking this vessel in the fairway, but she struck on a reef, where she was subsequently smashed by British gun fire.

When night fell the British pushed up to within three hundred yards of the German position, but when dawn came it was discovered that the enemy had slipped away through the bush. There was still hope, however, that he might be cornered near Muhenga. On the 27th he endeavoured to break through in that district, but was driven back. He had a similar experience next day, yet he "eventually escaped," Smuts recorded, "through the dense bush and forest under cover of darkness and eluded pursuit." The encircling movement had failed, owing to the difficult nature of the country.

Torrential rains descended on January 2nd, 1917, and for a while compelled Van Deventer to confine himself to patrol work. In the meantime Northey had not been idle. On December 26th his forces closed in on all sides of Mfirika and occupied it, after finding out that it had already been evacuated by the enemy, who had retired along the road to Mahenge, having placed a rearguard six miles east of Mfirika. On January 3rd Colonel Murray's column assaulted and captured the southern end of the rearguard's position, and the Germans withdrew to another position eastward. On the 6th the force under Colonel the Hon. J. H. J. Byron, C.M.G., which had advanced north from Songea, dispersed a body of the enemy at Gumbiro. On January 9th

Northey's advanced troops were in touch with the Germans six miles east of Sylvester Falls, and a week later Murray's column secured the bridge over the Ruhudje at Malawis, near Ifinga, which lay to the south-east of Lupembe. Byron had a further and much greater success on January 24th at Likuyu, some sixty miles north-east of Songea, when he forced the surrender of a German southern detachment, consisting of Herr Grawart, its commander, thirty-eight other Europeans, and about 250 Askaris. At this time, everywhere in this area, the enemy, who had been much shaken, was retreating eastward and southward. In recognition of their services, which were very considerable, though they failed of full success, both Van Deventer and Northey were made Companions of the Bath.

Smuts' main offensive was conducted in the central and eastern areas, under his personal direction. On December 22nd he left Mrogoro, and established his General Headquarters at Dutumi, on the Mgeta front, where he had under his immediate command the 1st East African Brigade, later described as the 1st Brigade, led by General Sheppard. The 2nd South African Infantry Brigade, under General Beves, lay on the road between Ruvu and Tulo, and it was ordered to be at Dakawa on the 25th. The Nigerian Brigade, under General Cunliffe, was assembling at Tulo, whence it was to proceed to Dutumi. The 1st Division, under General

GERMANY'S LOST BASE UPON THE INDIAN OCEAN.
General view of Dar-es-Salaam, the capital and principal harbour of the former German colony in East Africa. Above: A German gunboat lying off the town. Dar-es-Salaam was taken by a British combined naval and military attack, September 3rd, 1916.

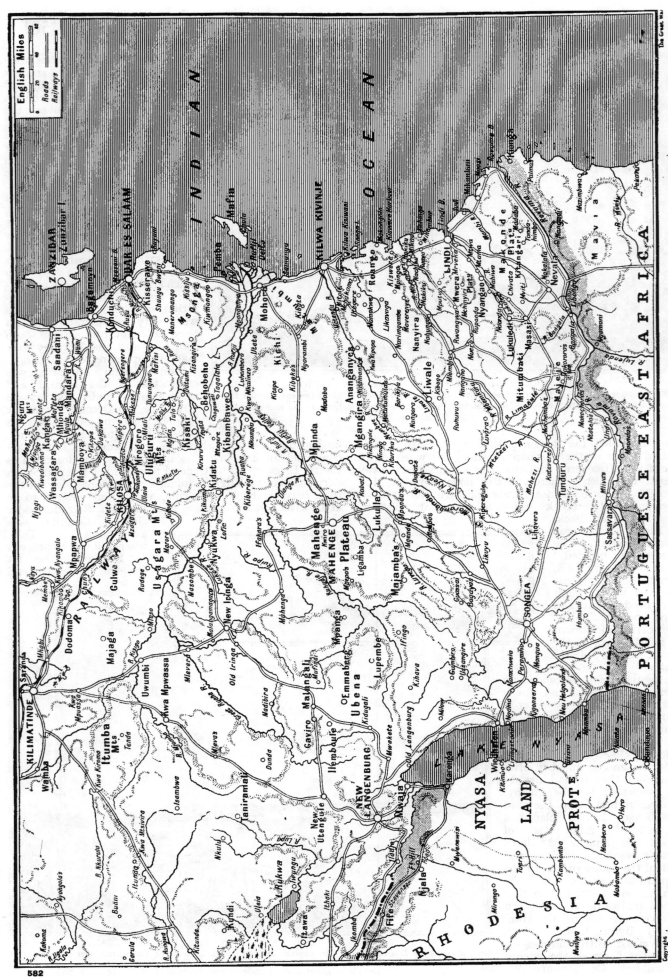

AREA OF THE FINAL MILITARY OPERATIONS WHICH RESULTED IN THE EXPULSION OF THE GERMANS FROM EAST AFRICA.

Hoskins, was in position about Kabati and in the Kilwa district, south of the Rufiji, and its headquarters moved to Mitole on Christmas Day.

Timed to begin on December 26th, the opening movements on the Mgeta front had to be postponed, on account of the rains, to the 31st, when the weather improved ; but this delay was not without a certain advantage, as it permitted the Nigerian Brigade, which was somewhat behind-hand, to complete its equipment and come up. General Smuts said that two main considerations governed the dispositions of his troops. One was the seizure of a crossing

Crossing of the Rufiji

over the Rufiji, and the other was the capture, if possible, of the Germans immediately opposing himself. Attaching the higher importance to the former, the chief problem that he had to solve was the seizure of the crossing over the river without allowing the enemy to become aware of his intention, for he was most anxious that the Germans should not evade a heavy blow by an early retirement from his front. Once he was across the river, his plan was to move to the south-east and join up with Hoskins and the 1st Division, which was to have marched north-west from the Matumbi Mountains. These combined movements, if successfully carried out, would cut all connection between the enemy forces on the Rufiji and at Mahenge respectively. His purpose was either to envelop the Germans on the Rufiji or, at all events, deal them a tremendous blow as they made off to the south.

To secure the crossing over the Rufiji, General Smuts detached the 2nd South African Brigade of Beves to make a wide detour and capture and hold a bridgehead on the river at Kwa Mkalinzo, twenty miles south-west of Kibambawe, and near the junction of the stream with the Ruaha. On January 3rd, a day ahead of the time-schedule, the advanced troops of Beves, after a thirty miles' continuous march, crossed the Rufiji a few miles south of Kwa Mkalinzo and entrenched a bridgehead. Smuts was loud in his praise, declaring that the march of the brigade was a noteworthy achievement, even in a campaign which afforded repeated instances of splendid endurance by every unit of the forces in the most exhausting circumstances. To keep the enemy in his positions while Beves was making this detour, the Commander-in-Chief delivered a holding attack from his forward lines on the Dutumi sector, and at the same time had two columns working their way round the German flanks by the east and west.

At daybreak on January 1st, 1917, Cunliffe's Nigerians, supported by the Army artillery under Brigadier-General Crewe, began the assault in the centre about Dutumi, but did not press home the attack, as their action was contingent on news from the flanks. The left or east flanking column consisted of the 2nd Kashmiris and a battalion of Nigerians, under Lieut.-Colonel R. A. Lyall ; the right, or west, flanking column was Sheppard's brigade. The hope, of course, was that the two columns would surround the force that was engaged by Cunliffe. Lyall's force started from Kiruru, on the Mgeta, while Sheppard's advanced from Kisaki. Lyall came up with and attacked the enemy in the afternoon, taking a 4·1 in. howitzer from him ; but the Germans, now realising that the road of their retreat was blocked on this side, at once commenced to withdraw from before Cunliffe in an endeavour to regain a line of retirement. A heavy attack was made on the Nigerian part of Lyall's column in the evening, but it died down within an hour. Lyall was ordered to keep a sharp look-out for any attempt of the enemy to break through. A column of the 130th Baluchis, under Lieut.-Colonel Dyke, detached from Sheppard's brigade, advanced on the afternoon of December 31st, and early next morning was astride the road by which the left wing of the enemy was retreating before the rest of the brigade, and now unexpectedly found the route barred against it. Trying to force their way through, the Germans made four determined charges on the Baluchis. The fighting, in which the bayonet was used several times at close quarters, was of a severe character, and the casualties on both sides were comparatively heavy. The Baluchis stood their ground, and next captured the enemy camp at Wiransi, but many of the German Askaris made good their escape by breaking formation and taking advantage of the long grass. Elsewhere the encircling movement failed, and, as Smuts put it : " In the course of the morning of the 2nd it became clear that the whole enemy force on the Mgeta front had retired to the south of our forces." It had slipped through the net.

However much Smuts was disappointed with this

COVER FOR GERMANS FROM BRITISH BOMBARDMENT.
A bomb-proof shelter at Dar-es-Salaam provided by the Germans for the use of the civilian population when the town was being shelled by the British. The bombardment from the sea was of short duration, and then seamen were landed in whalers and quickly occupied the capital.

result, he at once determined to try another similar movement. It had long been known that the Germans had a strong position on the Chogowali River, near Beho-beho, and he believed that the retreating force would make for it. He now disposed his troops to surround it. They came into action with the enemy on January 3rd. Next day Sheppard's brigade caught up with and fought a severe engagement with the Germans who were retreating from Beho-beho ; but, though heavily

punished, they once more succeeded in slipping past the British. The brunt of **F. C. Selous killed in action**

this sharp struggle was borne by the 25th Royal Fusiliers, otherwise called the Legion of Frontiersmen, and their casualties included Captain F. C. Selous, the celebrated African big-game hunter, who fell at the head of his company. In June, 1916, Captain Selous, who was sixty-four years of age, had greatly distinguished himself in the battle on the Lukigura River, getting thereby the D.S.O. " for conspicuous gallantry, resource, and endurance."

From Beho-beho the Germans retreated to Kibambawe, where there was a bridge across the Rufiji. The bridge had been damaged by the floods, and had been constantly

FRONTIERSMEN OF EMPIRE: CAPTAIN SELOUS, D.S.O., WITH HIS COMPANY OF ROYAL FUSILIERS.
F. C. Selous, the famous hunter, though sixty-four years of age, joined the Legion of Frontiersmen—the 25th Royal Fusiliers—attained captain's rank, and won the D.S.O. for conspicuous gallantry, resource, and endurance. His regiment took part with Sheppard's brigade in a sharp fight with the Germans on the Chogowali River, near Beho-beho, on January 4th, 1917, and Captain Selous was among those killed.

bombed by British aeroplanes, of which Smuts reported that they did consistently excellent work throughout the operations. When the 1st Brigade, which had been rejoined by the Baluchis and the Kashmiris, arrived at Kibambawe, on January 5th, it found that the enemy had crossed by the bridge, which he had repaired, to the right bank, and had afterwards removed the whole roadway of the bridge. Yet Sheppard got some troops across on the 6th and 7th, among them being the Punjabis, who, on the latter date, had a stiff fight with the Germans and sustained many casualties from accurate gun fire, but kept their position. General Sheppard, however, was not in sufficient strength to proceed further with offensive operations. On the 8th General Smuts arrived at Kwa Mkalinzo, and had a conference with General Beves, who had previously defeated the Germans in that quarter. The men of Beves' brigade had by this time become much exhausted, and Smuts thought it advisable to withdraw them from Kwa Mkalinzo, and concentrate them on the right bank of the river where they originally had crossed it. Some ten days later Cunliffe's Nigerians were despatched to Kwa Mkalinzo, and moved forward to Luhembero, which was occupied on the 18th. At the same time Sheppard and Beves cleared the south side of the river at Kibambawe, and then Cunliffe followed the retreating foe in a south-easterly direction. German forces, as a result of Smuts' advance, withdrew from Kisangire and Mkamba, and crossed the Rufiji at Utete.

Germans withdraw over the Rufiji

While these operations were going on the movement of part of the 1st Division towards the delta of the Rufiji had begun. Marching north from Kabati, the troops were at Mohoro, on the south of the delta, on January 16th. On the way they had come upon a 4·1 in. naval gun which the Germans had abandoned. General Smuts' plan had contemplated a great encircling movement south of the Rufiji, but at this time the gap between the most westerly force of the 1st Division at and north of Ngarambi, south of the Kitshi range, and Cunliffe at Luhembero was far too wide to admit of its realisation, at least by Smuts himself. For on January 20th he handed over the

584

command to General Hoskins, and sailed for Dar-es-Salaam, accompanied by General Van Deventer. Soon after he had started the campaign on the Mgeta front he had been asked by General Botha to go to London to represent the South African Union at the forthcoming sittings of the War Cabinet, and he had consented to do so. The British Government had invited Botha himself to come, but the political situation in South Africa was too anxious and uncertain for him to accept, and he had suggested that Smuts should be released from the East African command so as to be able to attend the conference. This was agreed to, and on January 15th the War Office issued the subjoined statement, which also gave a summary of the general situation:

The military situation in East Africa is fortunately such as to make the change of command and some reorganisation comparatively simple, and, indeed, the steps that are now contemplated, in consequence of the sudden demand for General Smuts' services elsewhere, are those which would have been taken in any case very shortly. In February, 1916, when General Smuts assumed command, the whole of German East Africa and some portion of British territory was in enemy possession. At the present time, eleven months later, nothing of German East Africa remains to the enemy, except a comparatively small and unimportant area in the south and south-east, where his retiring forces are collecting. The enemy does not possess a single railway, town, or seaport. His forces, in consequence of casualties and desertion, are much reduced in strength and moral; his loss in artillery has been considerable; his food supply is dwindling, and he is compelled to remain where he has established magazines. Scanty and shrinking transport resources restrict his power of movement. . . During the last ten days operations on the Mgeta front have caused the enemy to retire across the Rufiji, over which we now hold an important crossing, and can move as occasion requires. On the other fronts the enemy has given way during the same period, evidently in agreement with a plan for a general withdrawal to fresh lines. In these circumstances it has been possible to accede to the request of the Union Government, and arrange for the release of General Smuts from the East African command.

Official summary of the situation

General Smuts proceeded to Cape Town, and saw his fellow-Ministers. In a speech on February 12th, delivered in the City Hall, where he was accorded a most enthusiastic reception, Lord Buxton, the Governor-General, General Botha, and other members of the Union

Cabinet being present, General Smuts took occasion to say that the Union, by sending so many thousands of its sons into the field, had secured a voice in the disposal of Africa, and had a special right to be heard authoritatively in any discussion regarding the fate either of German East or of German West Africa. "Future generations," he remarked, "will never be able to say that we did not peg out our claims." Smuts, who had been made a member of the Imperial Privy Council, arrived in London on March 12th, 1917, and received a hearty welcome. In an interview he said that it was preposterous to suggest that any part of Africa should be returned to Germany, and he prophesied that the struggle in East Africa would be over in a month or two. This, however, was not the case.

That the conquest in all its completeness of German East Africa took a much longer time than had been expected was probably due in large measure to the fact that five days after General Hoskins had succeeded Smuts heavy rains set in, and continued, for an unprecedented number of weeks, with a violence unparalleled for many years. Operations on any considerable scale became so difficult as to be practically impossible until the rainy season was past. In a despatch, dated May 30th, and published on December 25th, 1917, General Hoskins stated that in the Mgeta and Rufiji valley **Abnormal rains suspend operations** roads, which had been constructed with much skill and labour, and over which in January motor transport ran continuously, were traversed with hardship a month later by porters wading for miles in water above their waists. In dry weather the line of communication between Dodoma, on the Central Railway, and Iringa crossed the Great Ruaha by an easy ford. During that abnormally wet period supplies had to be transported not only over a flooded river, but also over a swamp on each side of it six feet deep and as many miles wide. The valley of the Rufiji and its affluents became a vast lake. Patrol work had to be carried out for some time in canoes, and the

men had to make fast to the roofs of the houses which, before the rains, had been their quarters. The conditions of the Kilwa area were not less trying, as roads were impassable for motor transport, and animals died shortly after being landed. And with all this there went, as was inevitable, a most serious increase of sickness among the troops.

It was not possible that in such untoward circumstances General Hoskins could do much against the enemy. Before the rains fell, Utete was occupied by the 2nd East African **Army reconstituted** Brigade, on January 21st, and by **into columns** the beginning of February the north bank of the Rufiji was practically cleared of German troops. During the latter month there was little change in that area. Lieut.-Commander Garbett, of the Navy, made an accurate survey of the delta, and so enabled supplies to be sent regularly by the river to Utete. The enemy showed signs of concentrating near Lindi, on the coast south of Kilwa, and towards the middle of March he was in some strength south of the Matandu River. Meanwhile, Hoskins mainly occupied himself in the work of reorganisation. By this time most of the officers and men of the 3rd Division had gone back to South Africa, and it had been decided to return the 2nd Division there also. This left the command too weak, as it stood, to assume the offensive at the end of the rainy season. But steps were taken largely to increase the King's African Rifles, to reinforce the troops from West Africa, and to bring the Indian regiments up to full strength. The former divisional arrangement of the Expeditionary Force had become unsuitable, and General Hoskins reconstituted his army into columns proportionate to the operations in view once the ground was sufficiently dry. He saw further to a large increase in the medical service, obtained numbers of porters from British East Africa and Uganda, and procured quantities of light motor-lorries from England, South Africa, and

INDIAN GUNNERS AT WORK IN OPEN COUNTRY IN GERMAN EAST AFRICA.
British artillery in action in German East Africa; an English officer observing through glasses the effect of his Indian gunners' fire. The work of the artillery during the campaign was repeatedly referred to in despatches in terms of high praise: "On all occasions when they had an opportunity of preparing the way for and covering the infantry advance their support was most effective."

India. He began building a railway from Dodoma south towards Iringa, and pushed forward a tramway from Kilwa.

Nothing of importance occurred during March in the eastern and central areas. At the end of April several fresh German companies appeared in the Lindi district, and a considerable enemy force under Kraut was concentrated about Tunduru. In February, Kraut had been driven south by Colonel Murray's column of General Northey's command, and he had retreated into Portuguese territory, from which he had returned in March. On April 20th the German hospital at Mpanganya, ten miles north of Utete, was surrendered to the British, who at once evacuated its seventy European and one hundred and forty Askari patients. At the beginning of May the Germans had all moved from the Rufiji valley to that of the Matandu, from fifty to a hundred

Fighting near the coast miles farther south, in the hinterland of Kilwa. Some of them reached the coast, for on May 5th a small gun suddenly opened fire, from the mangrove swamps on the mainland west of Kilwa-Kisiwani, on a British ship at anchor in the harbour of that place. Concerted measures with the Navy were quickly taken, the enemy was compelled to retire, and a British post was established on the mainland. By the close of the month, partly on account of floods and the exhaustion of food supplies, and partly from the pressure of Hoskins, the Germans had given up practically the whole area north of the Matandu. The heavy rain continued in the coastal region well into May.

In the western area the rains had not been quite so heavy as in the central and eastern areas, and consequently there was a fair amount of activity in that part of the country where the various columns of General Northey's command were operating against Kraut and Wintgens. After the German surrender at Likuyu on January 21st, Kraut and Wintgens joined up at Gumbiro, but food was scanty, and they soon separated, Kraut making the raid into Portuguese territory alluded to in the previous paragraph, and Wintgens moving westwards invested Tandala. On the 22nd Colonel Murray relieved that place, and the Germans, not waiting to be attacked, marched northwards, abandoning a 4·1 in. gun. Murray went at once in pursuit, and thus began that long chase which, with Belgian help, ended in the capture of the enemy leader by the Belgians in May, and the surrender of what was left of his force in September. Meanwhile, the British Government had arranged with the Belgian Government that the fine native troops of the latter in East Africa should again co-operate there with the British.

Towards the end of April two German columns, the troops of which had mostly belonged formerly to Kraut's command, got across the Rovuma River, which formed the boundary between German and Portuguese East Africa, and proceeded to occupy the com-

General Van Deventer assumes command paratively fertile districts lying between the Lujenda River and Lake Nyasa. They built fortified camps, sent advance parties to Lake Shirwa, and their patrols even raided into Nyasaland within twenty miles of Fort Mangoche, but these were speedily thrust back over the frontier. Northey now strengthened the garrison of South Nyasaland, and in the latter half of May a Portuguese force left the coast for Mtengula, on Lake Nyasa. The Portuguese were not in strength sufficient to deal with these enemy forces in an effective manner in May, and accordingly British help was sent to them, good results being attained by August. During April, May, and June the Portuguese had been much hampered by having to meet and put down a rebellion among the tribes in their own territory which had been caused by the intrigues of the enemy.

On May 17th the War Office announced that General Van Deventer, who had been given the temporary rank of Lieutenant-General, had been appointed to the East African command in succession to General Hoskins, who retired at the end of the month. Still under fifty years of age, and already proved a most capable commander, Van Deventer was specially well-fitted for the post. A big, broad-shouldered man, typically a Boer in appearance, speaking Dutch more readily than English, he was a favourite with his fellow-countrymen, as Smuts had been, and they had the greatest confidence in his leadership. He knew, moreover, how to handle troops of any sort. Possessed of a wonderful eye for country, he was swift in action and movement, and could be as rapid and judicious in making decisions. When he took over the campaign his forces consisted of Imperial, South African, and Rhodesian white troops to the extent of about forty per cent., and of Indian soldiers about twenty-five per cent., the remainder, or not quite thirty-five per cent., being native East or West Africans, officered like the Indians by whites. The points of concentration were Kilwa and Lindi on the coast, the central Rufiji district, and Iringa and Songea in the west. Kilwa and Lindi were his new sea-bases.

Near Lindi, with the object of clearing the mouth of the Lukuledi River, and thus rendering the port secure, a force was landed on the 10th, under cover of warships, in the neighbourhood of Mrweka on the estuary, and drove out the German detachment which for some time past had occupied the place with a naval gun. A little later an enemy supply depot was destroyed by British patrols at Utegere, some thirty miles south of Kilwa. Towards the close of the month the Germans, under the constant and increasing pressure of Van Deventer, were forced to evacuate the strong positions which they had held south of the Ngaura River in the Kilwa district, and retire for a distance of from seven to nine miles where, astride the tracks from Kilwa leading towards Lindi, Liwale, and Masasi, they took up a new line.

In the district of Iringa a column which Van Deventer had detached from his immediate command was advancing south-eastwards, and was in touch with German companies on and about the **Belgian Congolese** Ruipa River. In the Songea neighbour- **army co-operates** hood a considerable enemy force, after making a half-hearted attack on Likuyu, was falling back along the road to Liwale before General Northey. The Belgian Congolese army under Colonel Huyghe was actively co-operating with a view to surrounding the Germans in the Mahenge area. In the northern part of the colony it was engaged in hunting down some small roving bands, including what was left of Wintgens' troops. From July onward Belgian assistance was of the most material importance in the Mahenge operations. In that month two encircling movements, which were co-ordinated, took definite shape, and might be said to be the beginning of the end of the campaign for the conquest of German East Africa. One was directed against the enemy in the Mahenge area, and the other, which was the larger of the two, aimed at enveloping him in the valley of the Matandu. Kilwa was the main base for the latter movement at that time, and Van Deventer himself was in personal control.

Consisting of broken country covered for the most part with dense bush, the hinterland of Kilwa was extremely difficult. Practically there were no roads, and such poor tracks as existed were impossible for transport. Broad paths had to be cut through the scrub and made available for the advance of troops. On July 12th Van Deventer's right column drove the enemy from Utegere, capturing prisoners and stores, and progressed six miles to Mainokwe. It then moved eastwards towards Chakama, in co-operation with his centre and left columns, and after some fighting reached Roango on the 15th. Here road-cutting caused delay, and two days later it was discovered that General von Lettow-Vorbeck, the German Commander-in-Chief, with the main enemy force under him, had evacuated Chakama, one portion of his troops retreating south-west towards Likavaga, and another, which was

[Russell.

Sir Reginald Y. Tyrwhitt, K.C.B., D.S.O., A.D.C., promoted Rear-Admiral, January, 1918.

General Hannyngton in East Africa interrogating a German native porter guarded by Indian sepoys.

British officers watching the fight for Mombo, on the Tanga-Moshi Railway, in East Africa.

Military motoring by road and railway through the luxuriant forests of tropical East Africa.

Baboons exploring a camp abandoned by the British when driving the Germans out of East Africa.

On patrol over the English Channel: A scouting airship, type S.S., colloquially termed a "blimp."

Homeward bound in the teeth of a winter gale: A British warship steaming to her base.

the more numerous, falling back on Narongombe, lying about seventy-three miles south-west of Kilwa. On July 19th Van Deventer attacked the principal German positions at the last-named place, and severe fighting ensued. The enemy offered the most stubborn resistance, and made repeated counter-attacks, in the course of which he, as well as the British, suffered considerable losses. But by nightfall the Germans were completely defeated and forced to retreat southwards. They then made for the valley of the Mbemkuru. Van Deventer was now held up by heavy rains till July 30th, when his onward march was resumed.

As part of the encircling movement the force which had been assembled at Lindi commenced its advance from that port on August 2nd. Proceeding along the road leading south-west towards Nyangao and Masasi, forty and seventy-five miles respectively from Lindi, it drove the Germans out of their advanced positions on a stream called the Mihambwe, at a point about ten miles distant from the town, and a place known as Schaedel's Farm was occupied. On the following day the main enemy positions on the Mihambwe were attacked frontally and on the flanks. British Askaris gained some ground in the frontal assault, but the flanking attack on the German right was a failure, as the troops encountered strongly-posted defences which were concealed in the thick bush, and so could not make headway, in spite of the utmost gallantry. The British entrenched what ground had been won, and the Germans, who had suffered heavy losses, withdrew farther along the Lindi-Masasi road.

It was not until past the middle of September that the Kilwa-Lindi movement made renewed progress. The country was almost waterless, and transport and supply problems had proved well-nigh insoluble. On September 19th Van Deventer resumed his advance, **Kilwa-Lindi movement renewed** and ousted the enemy from the positions covering the water-holes at Mihambwe. Pressure by his troops at this point resulted in the evacuation by the Germans of Mihambwe, after bitter resistance, and their retreat to Mpingo, a distance of seven or eight miles. Simultaneously other columns of his moved on to attack a larger enemy force strongly established at Ndessa, about fifteen miles south-west of Mihambwe. On the 21st a threat of envelopment forced the Germans out of Ndessa, and on the 23rd the whole body, pursued hotly by the British, was retreating towards the Mbemkuru when it found its line of retreat barred near Maverenye by Nigerian infantry. In the engagement which ensued it lost materially, and broke up into small parties who made a hasty flight to the river. On the 25th the British secured the important crossings over the Mbemkuru at Nakiku, and a strong column marched towards Nahungo, the principal German supply depot in the district, and met with little opposition. Meanwhile mounted troops, making a wide move on the west flank, had effectually destroyed other food depots between the river and the Kilwa-Liwale road, and had advanced close to Nangano, an important enemy supply centre at the place where the main Liwale-Masasi road crossed the Mbemkuru. Farther south the Lindi column, on September 24th, engaged the Germans in strong positions near Mtua, and after severe fighting, which lasted for two days, ejected them, causing a retreat to Mtama, about five miles north-east of Nyangao, the meeting-place of tracks connecting the Mbemkuru valley with that of the Lukuledi. As October opened, heavy fighting was going on midway between Mtwa and Mtama, and higher up on the road to Nangano, about eight miles south of Nahungo, a bitter struggle was taking place.

While these various movements were being conducted by the British forces under Van Deventer in the Kilwa and Lindi areas, with the result that the Germans, who had suffered very substantial losses in men and material, were being swept southward in the direction of the Portuguese frontier, the combined efforts of the Belgians and the British in the Mahenge area had also brought the end measurably nearer. From their base on the Central Railway the Belgians, owing to transport difficulties and the necessity for organising a centre of supply, did not make an appearance in force in this theatre till August. In the meantime the British forces from Iringa, Lupembe, and Songea had harried the enemy in July and driven him towards Mahenge. South-east of Iringa the Germans had been compelled to retreat from their strong lines on the Ruipa River, and the British column marched on towards Ifakara's. Farther south from Lupembe, one part of Northey's command was moving on Mpepo's and Mahenge, a hundred miles away ; while another part, in the Songea district, had driven the entire enemy force north of the Songea-Liwale road, in the direction of Mahenge. East of Mahenge the Germans had fled from **Belgian-British convergent advance** Kitope, and were making for Madaba.

During August a Belgian column under Commandant Hubert, which had come from Dodoma, on the railway, co-operated with the British in the Iringa district, and another Belgian force, commanded by Major Bataille, which had started out from Kilosa, ejected the Germans from their posts north of the Ruaha River, and drove them to its southern bank. A communiqué issued by the War Office on August 31st stated that the convergent advance of these Belgian troops and the British had by that date the effect of clearing the enemy out of the country between the Ruaha and the Ulanga—also called the Kilombero—Rivers, and that all the German detachments in that area were now south of the Ulanga. On the other hand, an enemy force, which had for some time been closely invested at Mpepo's, sixty-five miles south-west of Mahenge, contrived by forming small parties to get out during the night of August 27th and escape towards Mahenge, though not without many casualties. On the 30th the Lupembe column came up with and inflicted still further loss on this German force, three Europeans and ninety-two Askaris being killed or captured.

On the preceding day the Anglo-Belgian troops from Iringa joined up with the Belgians from Kilosa. The latter had effected the crossing of the Ulanga at a point ten miles east of Ifakara's, and within thirty-three miles of Mahenge, and it was at Ifakara's that the allied forces met. The main operations against Mahenge now were left in the hands of the Belgians.

In the second week of September the pressure of the Belgians and British on the Germans in the Mahenge area became very pronounced. The Belgians crossed the Ulanga, and moved on Mahenge from the north. They had successfully negotiated the marshy tracts beside the river, in spite of the keen opposition of the enemy, and now were about thirty miles from their objective. In the south-west the **Allied pressure on Mahenge** Lupembe column, continuing its pursuit of the force from Mpepo's, had occupied Malinje, eighteen miles north-east of the former place. The Germans, however, did not retreat towards Mahenge, but in the direction of Liwale, as doubtless they had heard of the advance of the Belgians towards the plateau. About the same time there was sharp fighting at Mponda's, rather more than fifty miles south of Mahenge. Several of Northey's forces attacked for days, and the enemy counter-attacked with great stubbornness. On September 6th British aircraft successfully co-operated with the infantry, setting fire to the German rampart of trees, and engaging the defenders with machine-gun fire from a height of 700 feet. On the 9th the British were completely victorious. Some days later, after a somewhat severe struggle, the enemy was forced to retire to the north bank of the Luvegu, where, however, he held out till well into October.

Colonel Tafel, who was in general command of the

Germans in the Mahenge country, opposed to the advance of the Belgians from the Ulanga a skilful and obdurate resistance, but all in vain. Taking advantage of naturally good defensive positions in the Kalimoto Hills, he succeeded in holding it up for about seven days, and when compelled to give way retired to strongly prepared lines north and west of Mahenge, where he again stood his ground. According to a Belgian computation, he still had 2,000 men. On October 7th the Belgians attacked him on a wide front on the hills situated to the north-east and north-west of the town, and captured his first line of trenches, after severe fighting in which both had considerable losses. The Belgians next assailed Tafel's second line, and took it, though he struggled desperately to stop them. Then the Germans retreated hastily into the mountainous region to the south, and on the 9th Major Müller, in command of one of the Belgian columns, entered Mahenge, which his troops proceeded to occupy. In its capture the Belgians made prisoner over a hundred European Germans of all ranks and **Belgian column** one hundred and fifty-six Askaris, **occupies Mahenge** besides taking guns and other war material. They also set free a British officer and a number of British and Belgian native soldiers who had been captives. British forces, meanwhile, remained in close touch with German detachments south and south-west of Mahenge, and barred some of the possible lines of retreat from that centre.

In the main theatre—the Kilwa-Lindi areas, including their hinterlands—strong British columns were pressing forward in October through the difficult and waterless country by each of the three principal tracks connecting the lower valleys of the Mbemkuru and Lukuledi Rivers. One from Nakiku was marching by way of Mputva on Nyangao, a second from Nahungo had the same objective but through Rwangwa, while a third from Mlemba, forty odd miles south-east of Liwale, advanced on Lukuledi, which lay west of Nyangao. In the valley of the Lukuledi the Germans still occupied their prepared positions about Mtama, covering the roads leading to this place. Aeroplanes had bombed Masasi and the enemy camps in its neighbourhood. On October 11th the column from Mlemba by a rapid march took and occupied Ruponda, an important meeting-place of tracks on the Mwera plateau,

GERMAN PRISONERS TAKEN IN EAST AFRICA.
Escorting a batch of German prisoners through the East African bush. They had formed part of that remnant of the enemy forces which during 1917 was driven down into the borderland of Portuguese East Africa.

and flanking the line of retreat taken by Lettow-Vorbeck's main body, whose rearguard was being attacked by the column from Nahungo. From Ruponda it established itself at Lukuledi Mission on the 17th, after a march by a waterless track of twenty-four miles and a sharp encounter with the enemy, who withdrew eastwards during the night, abandoning his hospitals. But Lettow-Vorbeck, with his chief forces, succeeded in getting across the Mwera plateau and in reaching Mahiwa, four miles from Nyangao. Van Deventer now began a determined and vigorous assault on the enemy's positions at Mtama and Nyangao, and the fighting which resulted was among the most bitter seen in East Africa.

In conjunction with an enveloping **Mtama and** movement from the north of the **Nyangao captured** Nigerians, who had marched across the difficult Mwera plateau from the Mbemkuru River, a general attack was launched on the German lines at Mtama, which had been strongly fortified, and were held with courage and resolution. The British, however, were well prepared. Supplies now came forward adequately and quickly from Lindi, and the troops were in excellent trim.

The German positions were stormed, and the foe were forced back on Nyangao, to which the main forces of Lettow-Vorbeck were coming up. On the 17th Van Deventer extended his enveloping move from the north and north-east to the north-west, north, and east of the mission, and a severe struggle took place, particularly on the northern flank. Two Nigerian battalions were heavily engaged, and suffered many casualties, but beat off all

NATIVE SCOUTS BRINGING IN REPORTS.
Captain Outram, of the East African Field Forces, receiving reports from some of his native scouts. The German rifle he was holding had been shot through the butt by one of the scouts, who killed its original possessor.

attacks and inflicted heavy losses on the enemy, who fought bravely. On the remainder of the front the British, by dint of sheer hard fighting, in the course of which they repulsed several counter-attacks, captured Nyangao by nightfall. West of that town the battle was renewed next day, and in the meantime the two Nigerian battalions effected a junction with Van Deventer's main forces. Von Lettow-Vorbeck thereupon retreated towards Lukuledi.

Van Deventer did not move on again in strength till November 6th. By the close of the first week of that month the bulk of the Belgian troops, owing to a shortage of food and the approach of the rainy season, had been withdrawn from Mahenge to the Central Railway. But a part of them, led by Commandant Henrien, was conveyed by rail to Dar-es-Salaam, and thence by sea to Kilwa, whence it advanced to Liwale, on the road to Wiedhafen on Lake Nyasa, and occupied that town on October 20th, simultaneously with the British column from Nyasaland which earlier had driven the Germans out of Portuguese territory, and marching on had taken and held, in August, Tunduru, forty-five miles north of the frontier. Before the majority of the Belgians had returned to the Central Railway they had forced Tafel south of Mahenge for over twenty miles of mountain country. Between October 23rd and November 8th the troops of General Northey, operating south of this tract, steadily drove eastwards the German rearguards covering Tafel's retreat towards Mgangira, fifty miles from Mahenge, and captured prisoners and material. On November 6th, at Kabati, on the left bank of the Luvegu, and fifteen miles from Mgangira, three German officers, one hundred and thirty other Europeans, one hundred and forty Askaris, and some carriers surrendered, and on the same day the Belgians received the surrender of eighty-nine Askaris in the district farther north. On that day also Tafel, under Northey's persistent and increasing pressure, broke suddenly southwards from Mgangira, and fled through Kiturika and Dapate. He had escaped from Northey, but had to abandon all his sick and great quantities of war material.

Resuming his advance in the Lukuledi valley, Van Deventer pressed Lettow-Vorbeck and his main body of men out of Mahiwa to the south-west, **Lettow-Vorbeck's disastrous retreat** and his enveloping move through Ruponda and Lukuledi Mission made good progress. The German Commander-in-Chief, in his retreat up the valley, suffered materially in prisoners, killed, and wounded. He also abandoned a 4·1 in. naval gun, and lost substantially in machine-guns, rifles, and ammunition. The process of attrition was now telling very seriously against him, and it was a process that continued. On November 10th the left column of Van Deventer entered Ndanda Mission, and found there a German hospital, with sixty-four European and one hundred and twenty-nine Askari patients. His mounted patrols on reaching Masasi discovered that the town had been evacuated by the enemy, who had left behind him the remains of his last 4·1 in. naval gun, besides over fifty Europeans in the hospital.

As Lettow-Vorbeck retreated to Chivata and Mviti, in the rough hilly country on the west side of the Makonde plateau, he threw away many of his machine-guns and rifles. Van Deventer gave him no rest, for he was ousted from Mviti on the 14th, and from Chivata on the following day, losing in prisoners alone about ninety men, more than half of whom were Europeans. A number of Indian and native African soldiers, who had been taken by the enemy, were released at Chivata. On the 18th Van Deventer's columns occupied what had been a large German camp near Nambindinga,

five miles from the Mission Station at Kitangari, and there received the surrender of twenty German officers, two hundred and forty-two other German combatants, and fourteen civilian Germans, as well as of seven hundred Askaris, while upwards of thirty British, Belgians, and Portuguese were rescued from captivity. Lettow-Vorbeck was driven into the valley of the Kitangari River, about twenty-five miles from the Portuguese boundary.

An effort was made to round up Lettow-Vorbeck in the Kitangari valley, but the wily German was successful in eluding envelopment. **Germans flee into Mozambique** On November 21st the left column of Van Deventer's forces, which had traversed the Makonde plateau, entered Simba's, seven miles northeast of Kitangari Mission, and bagged fifty-two Europeans and seventy-five Askaris. On the same day the right column occupied Nevala, a German Government station, eighteen miles from the Portuguese frontier. There one hundred and twenty-six Germans and seventy-eight Askaris were taken prisoners. Meanwhile, however, the main body of the enemy had escaped. Abandoning what was still left of his artillery and material, the German leader had fled swiftly south and was across the boundary, but his troops were greatly reduced in numbers, and were known to be short of food and ammunition. With only about 2,000 men remaining, he had been driven out of German East Africa and was a fugitive in Mozambique, whither he was pursued by the British, and the result was only a question of time. If General von Lettow-Vorbeck had disappeared from the colony, the force of Colonel Tafel, in retreat from

PRISONERS OF WAR IN THEIR OWN LOST COLONY.
A load of German prisoners in East Africa on their way, by light railway, to a concentration camp. Above: General von Lettow-Vorbeck, German Commander-in-Chief during the fighting in East Africa.

Mahenge and still in some strength, was yet in the country, but its shrift was short.

Breaking across the Songea-Liwale road, Tafel, ignorant or imperfectly informed of what was happening in the south-east to his Commander-in-Chief, planned to join up with him. Harried and attacked in his hurried march by both British and Belgian forces, he stopped to fight at Mandebe, about forty miles south-west of Liwale, on November 15th and 16th, but was defeated, though in **Remaining Germans'** superior numbers, his losses being **unconditional** greater than those of the allied troops. **surrender** Moving down the valley of the Bangala River, he ran into the arms of Van Deventer's leading columns who were pursuing Lettow-Vorbeck, was enveloped, and compelled to surrender at a point south-west of Nevala on November 27th. The surrender, which was unconditional, included twelve German officers, six medical officers, ninety-two other German ranks, and over 1,200 Askaris, as well as upwards of 2,200 native porters and followers. It was the largest single "bag" that had been made by the British in the whole of the campaign for German East Africa, and fitly concluded it.

General Van Deventer's operations, in conjunction with those of the gallant Belgians, had been crowned with success. In addition to depriving the Germans of their last and greatest oversea possession, he had inflicted upon them very heavy losses. Between August 1st and November 30th, said a War Office communiqué, there had been captured 1,410 Germans and other Europeans, 4,149 native soldiers, eleven guns, and fifty-six machine-guns. And of these, 1,212 Europeans, 3,191 Askaris, three guns, and thirty-five machine-guns were taken in November. The War Cabinet sent to him a warm telegram of congratulation, mentioning among other things that in four months he had conquered nearly 50,000 square miles of hostile territory, and felicitating him on the determination and endurance of his forces, which were "beyond praise." Satisfaction was universal throughout the Empire when King George conferred a Knight-Commandership of the Bath on "Temporary Lieutenant-General Jacob Louis Van Deventer, South African Defence Forces, Commanding-in-Chief in East Africa, in recognition of distinguished services in the field." Thus was signalised the passing from the enemy of what had once been German East Africa.

IN TOUCH WITH THE ENEMY MID TROPICAL VEGETATION.
Men of the British force in East Africa who had got in close touch with the Germans whom they were pursuing. They had reached a hot corner, where they were caught by rifle and machine-gun fire, but rapidly dug themselves in, not only securing their position but defeating the enemy.

A WAR-MADE DERELICT

CHAPTER CCXXV.

SOMEWHERE AT SEA.

PRIZES OF WAR: THE ROMANCE OF CONTRABAND AND CAPTURES AS REVEALED IN THE ADMIRALTY COURTS.

By R. Storry Deans, Barrister-at-Law, author of " Notable Trials," etc.

Constitution of Prize Court—Overseas Prize Courts—Enemy Property at Sea—Contraband—The Doctrine of Continuous Transportation Extended —Antiquity of Court of the Lord High Admiral—" The Course of Admiralty and Law of Nations " the Governing Code —Work of Sir Samuel Evans—Practice on Capture of Enemy Vessel—Enemy Cargo in Neutral Ship—Fraudulent Ships' Papers— Declaration of London—Contraband of War: What it Is—Conditional Contraband: What it Is—The Blockade which Was No Blockade—Case of the Kim—Some German Prize Court Cases—The Tomini and Rothersand—Attempted Change of Owner- ship—Property Controlled by German Company—C.I.F. Contracts—Affirmation of Declaration of Paris as to Neutral Cargo in Enemy Ships—Contrasted German Decision—Attempt to Evade Blockade—A Bed of Justice—The Ophelia—Scout Masquerading as Red Cross Boat—The Königsberg—The Airmen's Share of Head-Money.

THE war was not a day old before machinery was established for adjudicating on questions of prizes at sea. A Royal Proclamation of August 5th, 1914, appointed the Lords of the Admiralty as Commissioners to exercise the office of Lord High Admiral, and authorised them to appoint judges of the High Court of Justice to adjudicate on prize questions. To quote the quaint language of the proclamation, the judges were " to take cognisance of, and judicially to proceed upon all and all manner of captures, seizures, prizes, and reprisals of all ships, vessels, and goods already seized and taken, and which hereafter shall be seized and taken, and to hear and determine the same, and according to the course of Admiralty and the Law of Nations, and the Statutes, Rules, Regulations for the time being in that behalf, to ad- judge and condemn all such ships, vessels, and goods as shall belong to the German Empire, or to the citizens or sub- jects thereof."

A similar proclamation with regard to Austria- Hungary followed on August 20th, 1914.

On September 30th the British Supreme Court for Egypt, the British Court for Zanzibar, and the Supreme Court of Cyprus were constituted Prize Courts, with the right to condemn ships and goods " according to the course of Admiralty and the Law of Nations." This was to obviate the necessity of sending ships captured in Eastern waters to England for condemnation.

These phrases, " the Lord High Admiral," " the course of Admiralty," and ". the Law of Nations," carry the mind back to the reign of Prize Courts and their jurisdiction.

Private property belonging to an enemy has always been liable to capture and confiscation if taken at sea ; and seafaring nations have, in addi- tion, always assumed the right of intercepting at sea, and of confis- cating, any goods, to whomsoever belonging, on their way to the enemy country, provided that these goods are in the nature of warlike stores. " Contraband " is the term used in respect of such goods.

Perhaps the most striking feature of the work of British Prize Courts in the war has been the extension of contraband by what is known as the doctrine of " continuous voyage," or " continuous trans- portation." This doctrine was originated by Lord Stowell in the French

" ENEMY IN SIGHT."
Cruisers of the British Navy steaming in single line, and altering their course on receipt of the always eagerly anticipated news that enemy vessels had been sighted.

Wars of the eighteenth and nineteenth centuries ; applied and extended by the American Courts during the American Civil War, and finally consolidated by the British Prize Courts in 1914-17. Its scope and meaning will be explained hereafter. Suffice it here that it is a matter closely and gravely affecting neutrals ; because it necessarily involves an interference with neutral commerce. As such it demands most judicious as well as judicial application.

To turn for a moment to the constitution of the British

Origin of the Prize Court

Prize Court. It is claimed by some that the Lord High Admiral had maritime jurisdiction as far back as Saxon times, and the Privy Council Seal for Admiralty appeals bore the words " Ab Edgare Vindico " (" I give decision on the authority of Edgar ").

At any rate, quite as far back as Henry I. can be traced the Court of the Lord High Admiral, which bore jurisdiction over all matters, civil and criminal, which befell on the high seas. This court dealt with collisions at sea, salvage claims, " droits of Admiralty," piracy, seamen's wages, and a hundred and one other things arising out of or connected with the going down to the sea in ships and doing

[British official photograph.

BROBDINGNAGIAN TELEPHONE APPARATUS.
Sight-setter of a 6 in. gun awaiting orders from the masthead fire-control stations, whence officers communicate the range of the enemy for adjustment of the range used below.

business in great waters. Quite naturally, in time of war this court had jurisdiction over questions of prize. And it is as the successor to the Lord High Admiral that the President of the Admiralty Division of the High Court of Justice sits, with the golden anchor above his chair, to decide questions " according to the course of Admiralty and the Law of Nations."

For, be it observed, sea law has always been of an international character. Seamen have always had, since time immemorial, a code apart from the common law of their respective countries. And although nations did and do make rules, and pass statutes on matters maritime, which only avail in their own courts, it is still true to say that the great body of sea-law is " the course of Admiralty and the Law of Nations." Such British statutes as have been passed to deal with branches of maritime law have been in the nature of codifying Acts rather than the making of new laws.

The office of President of the Admiralty Division was, in 1914, filled by Sir Samuel Evans, and the whole legal profession stood on tiptoe to watch how he would wear the mantle of William Scott, Lord Stowell, the great lawyer who, in the century-old French Wars, made modern Prize Law. The Welshman proved no unworthy successor, and one day his name will be ranked with those of Stowell and of Chief-Justice Marshall, of the United States, who gave the law to the world during the American Civil War.

The classes of cases that came to be dealt with by the Prize Courts may be divided into five. There were German and Austrian ships which had been captured at sea or seized in harbour. There were enemy cargoes arrested in neutral ships. There were goods, the property of neutrals, also arrested in neutral ships, which were alleged to be intended to be transhipped or conveyed to Germany as their ultimate destination. There were neutral ships and cargoes trying to run the blockade. And there were the cases, popularly called the " head-money " cases, where ships of the British Navy made claim to rewards for sinking ships of hostile navies, which have been referred to in Chapter CXCVII. (Volume X., page 105).

The cases of German and Austrian ships captured at sea were very soon dealt with. All that had to be done was this : A merchant ship of German register is found on the high seas by a British cruiser. By the law of nations and the course of Admiralty the cruiser must first summon her to surrender. This is done by firing a shot across her bows. The merchantman can then make her choice. She can elect to fight for it, to run for it, or to give in. If her master resolves to surrender, he hauls down his flag and backs his engines to heave-to, or, if a sailing ship, backs his sails. A boat is then put out from the cruiser, and a prize crew takes possession of the vessel. If the merchantman elects to fight it out—she fights it out.

But in modern times a commercial ship rarely does such a thing. Your old East Indiaman, armed to the teeth, could, and

Capture of enemy ships

did, tackle an enemy frigate at very little disadvantage. If the merchantman chooses to run, again she takes her chance. The warship is at liberty to open fire and stop her that way. And it may again be said that the tremendous range and power of modern guns, not to speak of the high speed of modern ships of war, have much diminished the chances of successful flight on the part of a cargo vessel.

On the capture or surrender of a ship, a prize crew is put on board, whose duty it is to navigate her to the nearest British port, and there to hand her over to an official of the Prize Court, called the Marshal (or his deputy, who is probably the principal Customs officer) for safe custody. When handed over, it is the law that the cargo must be " without bulk broken " (Naval Prize Act, 1864, s. 16, re-enacting the old Admiralty practice). Next, the ship's papers must be secured, if they still exist, and sent on to the Admiralty Registrar. From that moment the matter is in train for the case to come into court, for decision whether the capture is " good prize " or no.

In the cases of enemy cargoes on neutral ships, neutral goods ultimately intended for the enemy, and ships trying to run the blockade, the process is very much the same. A ship flying the Swedish colours, for example, is sighted by a British cruiser. Promptly the warship increases speed, firing a heave-to signal as she flies through the water. The neutral, as in duty bound, will heave-to ; and soon an officer in British uniform is aboard her, with a request to see the papers. The ship's papers are supposed to show at a glance all particulars of cargo carried, and the true names and addresses of the persons to whom such cargo is consigned. Quickly the naval officer scans the record. " Rosenbaum, Hamburg," meets his eye. " I fear, master, I must ask you to accompany us," he says. And the neutral is made to sail his ship to a

British port, where the vessel is searched, and everything suspicious removed from her, handed over to the Marshal of the Prize Court, and a suit begun in the Prize Court.

Before this war a ship's papers were always taken to be correct, but it had not been in progress long before it was discovered that manifests (lists or invoices of a ship's cargo to be exhibited to a Customs House) were false; that valuable munitions were being sent wrapped up in innocent products of commerce; that Germans in America strained every nerve and employed every device to get through to Germany all sorts of contraband under false descriptions. Sometimes the shipowners or charterers were parties to these frauds; sometimes not.

In early days the British Government made an attempt to run their commercial sea-war on the basis of the so-called Declaration of London. We say "so-called,"

CONVEYING AND CONVOYING FUEL FOR CRUISERS.
British tank steamers, guarded by destroyers, taking supplies of oil for cruisers out at sea. The task of transhipping the necessary fuel while at sea was greatly simplified by the extensive use of oil for motive-power in the Navy.

because it never was an effective Declaration, for the simple reason that the British Parliament had refused to ratify it. And this leads us to the subject of contraband of war.

By immemorial usage a belligerent had the right to capture at sea, and confiscate, what is known as contraband of war.

Contraband, absolute and conditional

For some centuries contraband was limited to actual weapons of war, whether manufactured or in parts (e.g., muskets, or musket-barrels), and supplies of food, forage, and equipment consigned to an enemy Government and intended for the Army or Navy. At a later date arose the practice of conditional contraband, which was carried out thus: A belligerent published a list of articles, not necessarily of a military nature, and sent notice to neutral Governments that such articles would be treated as contraband of war if they had an enemy Government destination—that is, they would be captured if possible, and confiscated if captured.

By the abortive Declaration of London (1909) it had been declared that certain goods should never be declared contraband. One was cotton. Another was artificial manures. A third was metallic ores. A fourth was oil-seeds and nuts and copra. Yet others were caustic soda, ammonia, sulphate of ammonia, and sulphate of copper.

A proclamation of August 4th, 1914, published a list of conditional contraband, adhering to the list given in the Declaration of London, and on August 20th another proclamation announced the intention of his Majesty's Government to carry on the sea-war on the basis of the Declaration. Meanwhile the Germans were sowing the North Sea with mines. On September 21st the Foreign Office condescended to include as conditional contraband " copper, lead, glycerine, ferrochrome, hæmatite iron ore, magnetic iron ore, rubber, hides, and skins." Meanwhile the Germans had been laying in a stock of copper, glycerine, and the like, and had been making shells and explosives for shells wherewith to blow to pieces our "contemptible little Army." Likewise, they continued to sow floating mines in the high seas. And, further, to indicate their respect for the finer points of international law, they pursued their well-known frightfulness in Belgium and France.

It is not our purpose in this chapter to follow up all the steps by which the egregious folly of the Declaration of London was whittled away. It is enough to know that on March 11th, 1915, an Order-in-Council was published establishing what was commonly known as a blockade of Germany. It was not really a blockade, because a blockade implies the will and the power to prevent ships going in and out of the ports or coast blockaded. Now the Allies could not blockade Germany's Baltic coast; nor could they prevent ships plying between Holland and Germany. It was, in a legal sense, a declaration of

SELF-DEFENCE AT SEA.
One of the great liners which, in consequence of Germany's piratic method of unprovoked attack on everything that came within torpedo range, were forced to become armed so as to be able to defend themselves in the event of attack by enemy submarines.

reprisals on Germany. The Kaiser's Government had impudently declared the waters surrounding the United Kingdom a "military area" in which all British and allied vessels were to be sunk at sight—by submarine—and neutral shipping would be exposed to the danger of mistakes—German mistakes.

The British Government, therefore, proclaimed, as a measure of reprisals or retaliation, that, so far as the British Navy could prevent it, no commodities of any kind should be allowed to reach or leave Germany. It followed that, after March, 1915, the Prize Court was entitled to condemn as lawful prize any goods, to whomsoever belonging

[British official photograph.

TRANSFORMATION OF ENERGY AT SEA.
Boy wheeling coal from the bunkers along a gangway between two of the huge boilers of a British battleship, into which its latent energy transformed into steam will shortly pass.

and by whatever ships carried, which came directly or indirectly from Germany or which were destined directly or indirectly for Germany. Whether the goods were contraband of war, conditional or absolute, no longer mattered.

The most important case in the Prize Court, both from the amount at stake, the principles involved, and the international consequences, arose out of the capture of four ships in November, 1914. In October and early November, 1914, an American company, the Gans Steamship Line, chartered the Kim, the Alfred Nobel, the Björnstjerne Björnson (all Norwegian), and the Fridland (Swedish) on time charters—that is to say, hired the ships for a certain period. The president of the company, Gans, was a German. The ships carried no less than 73,237,796 lb. weight of cargo, consisting of rubber, hides, lard, hog and meat products, oil, wheat, and other mixed foodstuffs. The lard and meat products were 23,274,584 lb. All the goods were consigned to Copenhagen. One firm, Armour & Co., sent over 9½ million lb. of lard and meat; Morris & Co. sent nearly 7 million lb. Some of the goods were sent by the consigners "to order"—that is, not to any purchaser, but to their own agents, to be sold on arrival. Others were consigned to various firms, chiefly in Denmark; and when the cargoes were seized by British warships and claimed as prize, all these people put in claims.

Gans Steamship Line judgment

These claims were based, to put it shortly, on the ground that the goods were neutral property, consigned in neutral bottoms to neutral persons in a neutral country. The British case was that the goods were, in their nature, conditional contraband; that the neutral country was merely intended as a storehouse for Germany; and that the neutral consignees were merely a blind. For example, one of them was a company with a capital of £120; yet it was importing £280,000 worth of produce. Another was a man with neither warehouse nor office in Copenhagen. His address there was the Bristol Hotel, but he had an office and lived usually in Hamburg. "The real facts are," argued Sir Frederick Smith, "that you dare not try to send contraband to Germany's North Sea ports, so you are trying to send it to her via Copenhagen, either by ship from there or by rail."

The case came before the court for evidence or argument on fourteen days. Six counsel appeared for the Crown, and twenty-two counsel argued on behalf of the fourteen claimants. The judgment of Sir Samuel Evans occupied sixty-seven pages of the Law Reports, and a very masterly judgment it is, dealing with facts, figures, evidence, prize rules, proclamations, and international law without wasting a word. In the end, after allowing one claim for a few thousand pounds of rubber, and eight claims by Danes who were *bona fide* buyers of lard, etc., for home consumption, the President condemned the bulk of the cargoes, over 20 million lb. of food, and practically all the hides and rubber.

It was virtually admitted that the great bulk of the goods would ultimately have found its way into Germany. This was obvious, because the lard consigned by Armour & Co. alone in these ships was twenty times the usual monthly export to all Scandinavia from the whole of the United States. In 1911-13 the average importation of lard into Denmark from all sources was less than 1½ million lb. The quantity in these four ships alone was 19¼ million lb. As a curious coincidence, in August-December, 1913, the United States sent Germany over 68½ million lb. of lard. For the same period, 1914, the quantity was only 23,800 lb.

"Continuous transportation"

The ultimate destination of the goods being thus established by irresistible inference, the President declared that it did not matter that the port to which they were consigned was neutral. The doctrine of "continuous voyage" applied. Now the doctrine of "continuous voyage" had been laid down by Lord Stowell over a century before; and had been applied by American Prize Courts at British expense during the American Civil War, when British shippers used to try to make the British West Indian port of Nassau a jumping-off place for Charlestown. The only new matter added by Sir Samuel Evans was to change "continuous voyage" to "continuous transportation"; and to declare, in advance of the older cases, that it mattered not whether the goods were to be sent on to Germany by rail or by ship. It was thus settled that when contraband of war is ultimately destined to an enemy country, though in the first place consigned to a neutral country, it is to be deemed to be consigned to the enemy country and is liable to capture and condemnation as prize.

This, however, was not enough to conclude the case of the foodstuffs, which were only conditional contraband; that is, only contraband if actually intended for the German Government or to assist German forces in carrying on the war. Sir Samuel Evans held that the probable ultimate destination was the German Army and Navy. He pointed out that some ten million men, between one-sixth and one-seventh of the German people, were under arms; and in that case a large proportion of the food would probably be consumed by these ten million adults. This presumption the claimants were unable to rebut ; and so on this point, too, the court decided against them.

In the case of the Maria the German Prize Court at Hamburg had taken a similar view about corn laden on a Dutch vessel and consigned to Belfast and Dublin. This case was decided in April, 1915. According to The Hague Convention, the Maria's cargo was exempt from capture, because the corn was loaded and despatched before the outbreak of war. And, curiously enough, in a case decided in December, 1914, the same court had decided that " The Hague Convention must be taken into account in a German Prize Court, because it is a State contract ratified by the German Empire." (Case of the Fenix.)

Although the case of the Kim and its three associate vessels was the most important of all those decided by the Prize Court, there were very many other cases of great interest. Very early in the war it was held that a deep-sea fishing vessel did not come within the immunity granted by The Hague Convention and the law of nations to coast fishing vessels. (Case of the Berlin.) At a later period it was held that a fine yacht belonging to the Krupps was not protected from capture after being detained in port (Cowes) at the beginning of the war. Such an immunity only extended to merchant shipping which happened to be in British ports when war broke out—they would be detained, but not captured as prize.

Another curious case was that of the Tomini and the Rothersand. On August 1st, 1914, war having been declared between Russia and Germany, these ships, flying the German flag, were on their way from Danzig to the Thames. That day the Sugar Fodder Company, of Millwall, agreed by telegram with the German owners to purchase the vessels. The Tomini duly arrived at Gravesend on August 5th, the Rothersand at Kirkwall on August 3rd (she did not sail next day). Both ships were seized and detained as enemy vessels. The Sugar Fodder Company claimed them, but the court held that the property in the two ships had not passed to the purchasers, because the formalities of sale had not been completed. Therefore the ships were properly seized and detained. As is well known, on the outbreak of war the German Government seized all British ships in German ports, and all others they could lay their hands on ; and their cruisers sunk British ships which had left port before hostilities commenced. The Hague Convention, 1907, Art. 3, says : " Enemy merchant ships which left their last port of departure before the commencement of the war, and are encountered on the high seas while still ignorant of the outbreak of hostilities, may not be confiscated. They are merely to be detained. . . ." In the case of the Marie Glascer, a German vessel captured at sea on August 5th, it was admitted that she left port before war was declared by Great Britain. It was also admitted that her master knew nothing of war being declared. Sir Samuel Evans, nevertheless, made an order for confiscation of the ship on the ground that Germany had not carried out The Hague Convention towards Britain, and therefore Britain was not bound by it as regards Germany.

The Tomini and Rothersand

In the same case, following a long string of authorities on international law, British and foreign, the President decided that he could not allow the claim of neutrals who had a mortgage on the ship. If a ship was flying the German flag it was German, and there was an end of it.

The case of the Maningtry was one where a British steamship left Australia before war was declared with a cargo of zinc and lead. The firms interested in the cargo were the Australian Metal Company, Ltd., a German-controlled company ; the Metallgesellschaft, of Frankfort-on-Main ; Henry R. Newton & Co., Ltd., of London, another London firm, and a Belgian company. The various firms and companies were all really controlled in German interests by the Metallgesellschaft. The court held that as the metal had really been shipped by a German company, it was their property, and could be seized. Also, that if any of the other persons had advanced money on the cargoes, it made no difference.

But in the case of the Miamichi, where goods had been consigned on a c.i.f. contract (a contract covering cost, insurance, and freight), to Germany, and had been seized at sea, the court held the cargo to be still the property of the consigners. It would not, in law, become the property of the consignees (or buyers) until arrival at the port. In other words, if the goods were captured, the German buyer would not be bound to pay the price, and so he would lose nothing. The loser would be the American consigner.

Declaration of Paris

Once or twice the President took occasion to emphasise that the international law enunciated in the Declaration of Paris (1856) still stood—that neutral cargo (except contraband) carried in enemy ships was not liable to confiscation. This was in striking contrast to the Supreme Prize Court in Berlin, which, in the case of the Glista

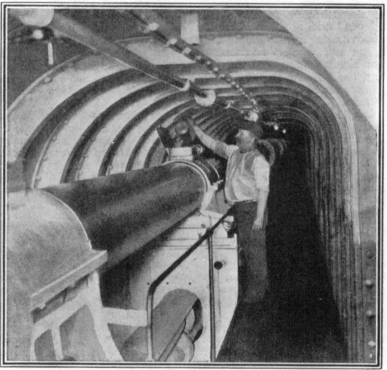

[*British official photograph.*]

ELIMINATING POSSIBILITY OF FRICTION.
One of the lower-deck hands in the starboard shaft tunnel oiling the propeller machinery, on the perfectly smooth working of which the efficiency of every steamship depends.

(September, 1915), decided that neutral goods in enemy vessels are liable to confiscation if the carrying vessel is captured. The " capture " in this case was merely another name for sinking by submarine, and the decision is at once seen to have been very convenient for Germany. If a submarine sunk a British ship laden with, say, American property, the Government relied on this case. It was vain for the neutral to say : " But you never captured it at all. You merely fired a torpedo from under water, and sent ship and cargo to the bottom." The answer was that in German law the ship and cargo had been " captured by H.M. submarine U17." (*German official report of the Glista, September 17th, 1914, in the Imperial Supreme Prize Court, Berlin.*)

Even as late as August 1916, a somewhat impudent attempt to evade the British prohibition of trade with Germany was made in the case of the Axel Johnson and the Drottning Sophia. As a sample of what some neutrals —and probably all Germans—thought was the ease with which the stupid Briton might be hoodwinked, it is hard to beat. It is well known that the chief anxiety of Germany was fat. This substance was a necessity because—quite apart from the food question—without fat there could be no glycerine for explosives and no lubricants for machinery. The direct importation of this important commodity had been put a stop to at a very early stage. Then came indirect importations via the neutral countries. The rationing system curtailed this. Accordingly the German wool-combers arranged the little deal that was explained in the case now under consideration.

Attempts to evade blockade The two ships, the Axel Johnson and the Drottning Sophia, were stopped in the entrance to the North Sea, being bound from Buenos Ayres to a Swedish port. The British found on board one hundred and seventy-nine bales of wool, consigned by one Blombergh, of Buenos Ayres, to the A. B. Skanska Yllefabriken, of Kristianstad, to whose order the bills of lading were made out. The name Blombergh was not one to inspire confidence, and, although it was denied, no doubt the man was not an independent shipper, but a German agent. Moreover, the British Government had found out, somehow, that the bills of lading and invoices had first been sent to Standt & Co. and Hardt & Co., both of Berlin. Confronted with this fact, the Yllefabriken replied that they had purchased the goods from the Berliners, and were the owners at the time of seizure.

It then came out that the plan of campaign was for the Swedes to import the wool and promptly send it on to German and Austrian wool-combers and spinners, who combed or spun the wool, and returned the combed or spun wool to Sweden. This seemed fairly innocent, until it appeared that the Germans and Austrians would retain, as part of their remuneration, all the waste wool and by-products. And amongst the by-products was fat.

The court had no difficulty in deciding that the wool was absolute contraband, and ordered its confiscation. Sir Samuel Evans pointed out that the mere fact of the wool being intended to be sent to Germany and Austria was enough. The contract might be to send the combed and spun wool back to Sweden, but how did anybody know, once the wool was in Germany or Austria, where wool was very scarce, but that the Swedes might be tempted by a high price to allow it to stay there? And, to be quite candid, the President thought that the whole transaction was a "try-on" to evade search and capture.

The foregoing are some of the principal cases in the Prize Court relating to merchant ships, **Abuse of the Red Cross** cargoes, and the "blockade." There were hundreds of these cases, and Sir Samuel Evans spent most of his time in trying them. To minimise delays, and so avoid injustice to neutrals as far as possible, the learned judge sat during the Long Vacation as well as during the ordinary court sittings. And at one time, when he was lying at home with a broken limb, he even heard prize cases in his bed-room.

Besides the contraband and "blockade" cases, there were plenty of others, on more belligerent matters. One, the case of the notorious Ophelia, deserves to be placed on permanent record. The Ophelia was espied by a squadron of British ships openly cruising in the North Sea, neatly painted white, with a red band one and a half metres broad, and flying the Red Cross flag. Before the war she had been a trader, and was, in fact, in the Port of London on August 3rd, 1914. That day the German Consul directed her " to steam to a German port for military duties." Carrying a cargo of three hundred and forty-four German reservists,

she sailed for Hamburg on August 4th, but was diverted *en voyage* to Heligoland, and thence to Hansa Harbour. On August 10th she went to Hamburg and was fitted up as a hospital-ship. A Dr. Pfeiffer took command of her as staff surgeon ; there were sick-bays, orderlies, and all the paraphernalia of a hospital-ship.

Curiously enough, on the morning of October 8th, a British submarine sighted the Ophelia, with no flag, in Dutch waters, and the Ophelia promptly hoisted a large Red Cross flag at the main and ran away. This was very curious behaviour for a hospital-ship, which ought always to be ready to be searched, and had nothing to fear—at any rate from any Navy other than that of his Majesty the German Kaiser. The submarine dived and disappeared, but obtruded its periscope upon the face of the waters a little later, to see the hospital-ship hauling down its Red Cross flag and changing its course.

Nine days afterwards a British patrol boat intercepted two wireless messages in code. One was from Dr. Pfeiffer asking someone at Norddeich for instructions ; and the other from Norddeich to Pfeiffer telling him to "search 3° 55″ East, 52° 51″ North, and neighbourhood." The patrol boat's commander was a little curious. He spoke to another patrol boat, and its commander was curious. So the Ophelia was stopped, boarded, and searched. Lieut. Peters, of H.M.S. Meteor, asked, quite politely, " Why are you to search 3° 55″ East, 52° 51″ North, and neighbourhood ? What are you searching for ? There hasn't been a scrap here." Dr. Pfeiffer blandly answered that he did not know what he was searching for. He had been ordered to search, and he was searching, but what for he knew not. Peters, commanding H.M.S. Meteor, thought this story had better be related to the marines, and so the Ophelia was seized, brought to England, and her history investigated. And, on it appearing that the bland Pfeiffer had thrown certain **The Ophelia** papers overboard when he was boarded ; **condemned** that the Ophelia had a higher speed than she confessed to ; that, although there had been opportunity for it, she had never done any work as a hospital-ship, the court came to the conclusion that the Red Cross was a blind ; that the Ophelia was really a scout, and that the German Navy had one more infamy to its account. The Ophelia was condemned as prize of war.

Another case worth mentioning is that of the Königsberg, a German cruiser, which for a time did damage on the high seas. A day came when she felt it advisable to lie low. So her commander, finding other escape impossible, steered his ship with great skill up the Rufiji River, in German East Africa, and, having reached the farthest limit of navigation, turned his ship into a fort. He constructed land works also, and, " defied " the British " to make good." Eventually two of H.M. monitors, Severn and Mersey, were sent to deal with the business, and this they did pretty thoroughly by lobbing shells over intervening forest and gradually obliterating the Königsberg. The monitors were accompanied by two aeroplanes, forming part of the Royal Naval Air Service ; an aerodrome was made on Mafia Island, and the airmen " spotted " for the monitors and rendered invaluable aid.

Now the question was whether they, having done a lot of the work, could have any share of the spoils. For the Naval Prize Act, 1864, and the King's Proclamation thereunder, entitled " the officers and crews of any of his Majesty's ships of war such as were actually present at the taking or destroying of any armed ship of his Majesty's enemies," to head-money of £5. That is to say, the crews of the ships would be entitled to £5 for every person carried on the books of the Königsberg. In all, it amounted to £1,920. By good luck the airmen had been put on the books of the Severn and Mersey, probably for purposes of messing *en voyage*; and the President of the Court held they were entitled to share in the bounty—which, if it was not technical law, was at any rate substantial justice.

"FOR VALOUR": HEROES OF THE VICTORIA CROSS IN THE THIRD YEAR OF THE WAR.

Statistical Analysis of the Number of V.C.'s Awarded in the Third Year of the War—Ten Awarded to the Navy, Five to the Air Service, Thirty to Men of the Oversea Dominions, Three to the R.A.M.C. and to the Artillery, Two to the Cavalry and to Indian Regiments, One to the Royal Engineers and the Chaplains' Department, Eighty-eight to Regiments of the Line—Boy Cornwell and Commander Loftus Jones at the Battle of Jutland—Lieutenant Leefe Robinson and Captain Albert Ball—Australian Heroes of Gallipoli and Elsewhere—New Zealand and South African V.C.'s—Eight Canadians Win the Cross—Captain Chavasse—Lieutenant-Colonel Campbell, of the Coldstream Guards—Private Jones, of the Cheshires, Single-handed Takes One Hundred and Two Prisoners—The Six V.C.'s Won by the Yorkshire Regiment—Lancashire Fusiliers, Liverpools, and Seaforth Highlanders Each Win Four Crosses—East Yorkshire, South Wales Borderers, South Lancashires, and Durham Light Infantry Each Win Three—Private Readitt, " the Stripling Who Stood Up to a Whole Army "—Fifteen Regiments Win Two Crosses Each—The Regiments that Each Won One Victoria Cross.

IN writing the story of the deeds of exceptional bravery that were rewarded with the Victoria Cross during the third year of the war the chronicler finds himself confronted by a fact that is at once a difficulty and a simplification of his task. This is that—for some reason not readily intelligible to the layman, but which he accepted loyally as being valid on military grounds—the official intimation of the award published in the "Gazette" omitted, in the great majority of instances, the name of the place and the date where and when the conspicuous deed was performed. Although it was possible to make a shrewd and almost certainly accurate guess at the facts suppressed, and although in a few instances the military authorities acquiesced without protest in the early disclosure of them by war correspondents and others, loyalty to authority requires the compiler of the present record to refrain from using knowledge which is not verifiable from the "Gazette" or from other contemporary publications.

As a result, it is not open to him to group the stirring stories in a series of general sketches of particular battles or coherent military operations, which obviously would have given him opportunity for picturesque treatment. Nor is it open to him to deal with them in chronological order, another method which has its peculiar advantages. He is compelled to adopt a plan of arrangement more proper to the auctioneer's catalogue than to a history, and to allocate the space at his disposal first to the three Services—the Navy, the Army, and the Air Service, and then to subdivide that devoted to the second category between the various arms

of that Service and the various regiments of each arm.

These, then, are the broad lines upon which this chapter is planned. A few other prefatory remarks are desirable, relating to the number of Victoria Crosses awarded to different branches of the Empire's huge fighting force, and accounting for the slight variation here made in the main plan. Between August 4th, 1916, and August 3rd, 1917, one hundred and forty-five officers and men of the three Services were awarded the Victoria Cross—in not a few instances, it is to be noted, for deeds performed in the second year of the war. This total of a hundred and forty-five is nearly as great as the combined totals of the first and second years, which were eighty-three and seventy-eight respectively. The fact is worth mentioning, but it has no utility for the doubtfully profitable task of comparative criticism. If, on the one hand, the number of crosses awarded in the third year was nearly double the number awarded in the second, the number of men eligible for the distinction by being on active service was also very much larger. If, on the other hand, the total number awarded during the third year seems small in proportion to the vast Army engaged, it only proves that the high value of the distinction was jealously maintained. The King himself said in a message to his troops, after one of the visits he paid to them in France, that he could not decorate them all, though all deserved it. The heroes to whom he did award the supreme honour of the Victoria Cross were only first among their equals, as they themselves declared on more than one occasion.

Ten crosses were awarded to the Navy, and the stories of the deeds that

REV. W. R. F. ADDISON,
Chaplain to the Forces.

won them are told first in this chapter, precedence being given to the senior Service. Five were won by airmen. Thirty were given to men from the Oversea Dominions —seventeen falling to Australians, eight to Canadians, three to South Africans, and two to New Zealanders. Of the remaining hundred, three were carried off by the R.A.M.C., three by the Artillery, two by the Cavalry, two by Indian regiments, one by the Royal Engineers, and one by the Chaplains' Department. Eighty-eight remain to be accounted for. Of these, two fell to

SEC.-LT. T. E. ADLAM,
Bedfordshire Regt.

awarded to Major Harvey, a member of the Royal Marine Light Infantry, but as it was given for valour exhibited at sea, it is recorded here among those that were credited to the senior Service. Lance-Corporal W. R. Parker, of the same unit, won his when attached to the R.N.D.

There, perhaps, these arid statistics may be left. They have their use in an historical summary, and they serve to introduce the separate stories in a determined order, the only deviation being made in respect of awards allocated in the official "Gazette"

CAPT. W. B. ALLEN,
R.A.M.C.

CAPT. ALBERT BALL,
Notts and Derby and R.F.C.

SEC.-LT. E. F. BAXTER,
Liverpool Regt.

SEC.-LT. D. S. BELL,
Yorkshire Regt.

[Lafayette
CAPT. E. N. F. BELL,
R. Inniskilling Fusiliers.

the Guards, and two to the Honourable Artillery Company. The rest went to regiments of the Line, and, still adhering to the scheme of the analytical catalogue, the names of these regiments are set down now in five classes, distinguished by the number of Victoria Crosses awarded to them.

The Yorkshire Regiment heads the splendid roll with six to its eternal honour. Three regiments carried off four each—the Liverpool Regiment, the Lancashire Fusiliers, and the Seaforth Highlanders. The East Yorkshire Regiment, the South Wales Borderers, the South Lancashire Regiment, and the Durham Light Infantry earned and were given three. Two were awarded to each of the following fifteen regiments: The Royal Irish Rifles, the Royal Lancaster Regiment, the Worcestershire Regiment, the Welsh Regiment, the Royal Welsh Fusiliers, the Rifle Brigade, the Leinster, Bedfordshire, and Middlesex Regiments, the Royal Scots Fusiliers, the Royal Fusiliers, the East Surrey Regiment, the King's Own Yorkshire Light Infantry, the Loyal North Lancashire Regiment, and the Northumberland Fusiliers.

Finally, the following twenty-three regiments were honoured by the award of the cross to one of the heroes on their roll who distinguished himself by almost super-human courage and devotion to duty: The Royal Munster Fusiliers, the Scottish Rifles, the Manchester Regiment, the Royal Irish Fusiliers, the Royal Sussex, West Yorkshire, and Devonshire Regiments, the Royal Inniskilling Fusiliers, the Northamptonshire Regiment, the King's Royal Rifle Corps, the Connaught Rangers, the Cheshire and West Riding Regiments, the Royal Dublin Fusiliers, the Highland Light Infantry, the Royal West Surrey, Border, North Stafford-shire, and Royal Warwickshire Regiments, the Oxford and Buckinghamshire Light Infantry, the Royal Berkshire Regiment, the Argyll and Sutherland Highlanders, and the Essex Regiment. A Victoria Cross was

LT. E. P. BENNETT,
Worcestershire Regt.

[Swaine.
COMDR. HON. E. B. S.
BINGHAM, R.N.

LT. A. S. BLACKBURN,
Australian Infantry.

to specifically mentioned engagements in the Somme and Ancre battles, in Mesopotamia, and upon the Gallipoli Peninsula.

On September 16th, 1916, the "Gazette" contained the notification of the award of three Victoria Crosses for valour displayed in the Battle of Jutland. The recipients were Boy First Class John Travers Cornwell, Commander the Hon. Edward Barry Stewart Bingham, and Major Francis John William Harvey, R.M.L.I. In March, 1917, it was announced that a posthumous award of the cross had been made to Commander Loftus William Jones, R.N., for his extraordinary courage and devotion to duty in fighting his ship, the torpedo-boat destroyer Shark, to the last during the same great naval battle. It is not invidious to assert that two of these four heroes, Boy Cornwell and Commander Loftus Jones, shed new lustre upon the honour that they earned, the one by the quiet devotion to duty and steadfast endurance that he displayed until death at his post, the other by the daring of his fighting and his intuitive response to the call of the blood in the whole performance of an action that rivalled that of Sir Richard Grenville, with his Revenge at Flores, in the Azores, over three hundred years before.

"Jack" Cornwell ranks, indeed, as the boy hero of the war. At one time a Boy Scout in the St. Mary's Mission Troop, East Ham, the lad lived up to the Scout motto, "Be prepared," and the undaunted spirit in which he confronted death immortalised his name and made him the noble exemplar for all boys throughout all time. Mortally wounded early in the battle, the gallant lad, who was under sixteen and a half years of age, remained standing alone at a most exposed post, quietly awaiting orders until the end of the action, with the gun's crew dead and wounded round him. There was nothing spectacular about the deed that won him the cross. It was simply, as Admiral Beatty described it, "a splendid instance of devotion to duty," performed, so far as the young hero knew, without a mortal eye to watch it. The following letter, written to his mother by the captain of H.M.S. Chester, the ship of whose crew he was destined to become the most famous member, gives a few particulars not included in the despatches or in the "Gazette":

I know you would wish to hear of the splendid fortitude and courage shown by your boy during the action of May 31st. His devotion to duty was an example for all of us. The wounds which resulted in his death within a short time were received in the first few minutes of the action.

SERGT. W. E. BOULTER, Northamptonshire Regt.

LT.-COL. R. B. BRADFORD, Durham Light Infantry.

MAJ. C. BROMLEY, 1st Lancashire Fus.

C.-S.-M. E. BROOKS, Oxford and Bucks L.I.

LCE.-CPL. T. BRYAN, Northumberland Fus.

LT.-COL. J. V. CAMPBELL, Coldstream Guards.

He remained steady at his most exposed post at the gun, waiting for orders. His gun would not bear on the enemy; all but two of the crew of ten were killed or wounded, and he was the only one who was in such an exposed position. But he felt he might be needed, as indeed he might have been; so he stayed there, standing and waiting, under heavy fire, with just his own brave heart and God's help to support him. I cannot express to you my admiration of the son you have lost from this world. No other comfort would I attempt to give to the mother of so brave a lad but to assure her of what he was and what he did and what an example he gave. I hope to place in the boys' mess a plate with his name on and the date, and the words 'Faithful unto death.' I hope some day you may be able to come and see it there. I have not failed to bring his name prominently before my Admiral.

This beautiful letter expressed the admiration which was felt throughout the Empire for the heroic conduct of so young a boy. The prompt award of the Victoria Cross only partly satisfied the general desire to pay homage to the dead hero. His body, which had been buried privately, was exhumed and reinterred with full naval honours, a vast crowd attending the funeral, which was at the public charge. As the result of a general subscription a portrait of the boy was presented to and hung in every elementary school in the United Kingdom, while his memory was further perpetuated by the endowment of beds bearing his name in many hospitals and hostels.

Commander the Hon. Edward Barry Stewart Bingham, R.N., H.M.S. Nestor, was awarded the Victoria Cross for the gallant manner in which he led his destroyer division to their attack, first upon enemy destroyers and then upon enemy battle-cruisers. He finally sighted the enemy battle fleet and, followed by the Nicator, the only other remaining destroyer of his division, he closed to within three thousand yards in order to obtain a favourable position for firing his torpedoes. While making this attack the Nestor and Nicator were under heavy, concentrated fire from the secondary

COMDR. G. CAMPBELL, R.N.

C.-S.-M. N. V. CARTER, Royal Sussex Regt.

SERGT. C. C. CASTLETON, Australian M.G.C.

batteries of the German High Sea Fleet. The Nestor was sunk subsequently, and Commander Bingham was taken prisoner by the enemy, being the only winner of the Victoria Cross in the great fight off Jutland who survived the battle.

Major Francis John William Harvey, R.M.L.I., earned the priceless cross when in the very throes of death. Mortally wounded by the explosion of an enemy shell in "Q" gun-house, and almost the only survivor of the explosion, he maintained his presence of mind and ordered the magazine to be flooded, thereby saving the ship. He died shortly afterwards.

On the day that the announcement was made of the King's posthumous award of the Victoria Cross to Commander Loftus William Jones, R.N., for gallantry in the Battle of Jutland, an account of his conduct and that of the crew of his ship, H.M.S. Shark, written by his widow, appeared in the newspapers, furnishing a parallel to the story of Sir Richard Grenville and the Revenge that could not escape observation. In the afternoon of May 31st, 1916, "the captain of the Shark took his division into action against the German battle-cruiser squadron, and there, badly hit, the Shark stayed with her engines and steering-gear out of action, and the pipe which connected up steam blown away." The commanding officer of another destroyer came between the Shark and the enemy, offering assistance, but Commander Jones warned him off, indicating the almost certainty of his being sunk while trying to help. Jones had been wounded in the leg, but went aft to help connect and man the after wheel. All this time the Shark was under very heavy fire. Three cruisers were firing on her at one time, and both the forecastle and the after gun of the Shark were blown away, together with their crews. Commander Jones then proceeded to the midship gun and assisted in keeping it in action. Able-Seaman Hope was at this gun from the beginning till the end of the action, and more than a hundred rounds of ammunition were fired from it. "The captain was so pleased with Hope that he at one time patted him on the back and said, 'Go on, Hope, you are doing splendidly!'" Then ten German destroyers and light cruisers came up out of the mist at close range, about six hundred yards, and all fired on the Shark. A shell took off the commander's leg above the knee, but, undaunted, he continued to give orders to the gun's crew, now reduced to three, while a chief stoker improvised a tourniquet round his thigh.

"As the captain was sitting on the deck he said, 'What's wrong with the ensign?' Hope answered, 'It's shot down, sir.' The captain gave the order, 'Hoist another.' The midshipman cleared the way and Hope hoisted another. There were always spare flags kept for any emergency. The captain then said, 'That's good!' and appeared content. The Shark was sinking quickly now and a German destroyer was coming quite close, so the captain gave the order 'Save yourselves!' And then the German destroyer came near, fired a torpedo into her, there was an explosion, and she sank with her flag flying."

The fight had lasted ninety minutes. The end of the story may be given as told by Mrs. Loftus Jones. Her husband was helped **Commander Jones'** on to a raft by some **glorious end** of his devoted men, and there "presently said, 'Let's have a song, lads!' And the first lieutenant started 'Nearer, my God, to Thee,' and they all sang till they were exhausted. Then some ships came into sight, and the captain asked Filleul if they were British or German. Filleul told him they were British, and he said, 'That's good!' These were his last words. The ships passed on, and shortly afterwards Smith saw him succumb to exhaustion."

So passed as brave a seaman as the British Navy has ever produced. Six of the crew of the Shark survived, and to these the King awarded the Distinguished Service Medal. Of the whole crew it was said that they "left to their Service a tradition, to their country an inspiration, and to their families the legacy of their undying fame."

On January 31st, 1917, the King approved the posthumous grant of the Victoria Cross to Lieutenant Humphry Osbaldeston Brooke Firman, R.N., and Lieutenant-Commander Charles Henry Cowley, R.N.V.R., in recognition of their conspicuous gallantry in an attempt to reprovision the force besieged in Kut-el-Amara on April 24th of the previous year. Starvation was then bringing General Townshend's fine resistance to an inevitable end, and as a last forlorn hope the relief army decided to send a supply ship up the river. Accordingly, at 8 p.m. that day, the Julnar, manned by a crew from the Royal Navy and commanded by the two officers named, left Felahieh with 270 tons of supplies. "Her departure," reported the General Officer Commanding Indian Expeditionary Force "D," "was covered by all artillery and

SEC.-LT. G. E. CATES,
Rifle Brigade.

SERGT. H. CATOR,
East Surrey Regt.

CAPT. N. G. CHAVASSE,
R.A.M.C.

PTE. L. CLARKE,
Canadian Infantry.

MAJ. W. LA TOUCHE
CONGREVE, Rifle Brig.

1ST CLASS BOY J. T.
CORNWELL, R.N.

machine-gun fire that could be brought to bear, in the hope of distracting the enemy's attention. She was, however, discovered and shelled on her passage up the river. At 1 a.m. on the 25th, General Townshend reported that she had not arrived, and that at midnight a burst of heavy firing had been heard at Magasis, some eight and a half miles from Kut by river, which had suddenly ceased." There could be little doubt, the report continued, that the enterprise had failed, and the next day the Air Service reported the Julnar in the hands of the Turks at Magasis. Lieutenant Firman and Lieutenant-Commander Cowley were reported by the Turks to have been killed, the remainder of the crew being taken prisoner.

Official mystery surrounded the details of the "conspicuous gallantry, consummate coolness, and skill in command of one of H.M. ships in action," for which the Victoria Cross was awarded on April 21st, 1917, to Commander Gordon Campbell, D.S.O., R.N. The "Court Circular" announced on March 8th that the King had conferred the cross upon Commander Campbell at Buckingham Palace the previous day, but the official announcement did not appear in the "Gazette" until the following month, and no particulars were supplied then or subsequently. Commander Campbell was gazetted midshipman in 1902, and after serving in the Mediterranean and the Pacific was promoted sub-lieutenant. After varied service he was promoted lieutenant-commander in October, 1915, and in March, 1916, he was made a Companion of the Distinguished Service Order.

Equal obscurity veiled the details of the "conspicuous gallantry, consummate coolness, and skill in command of one of H.M. ships in **A remarkable** action," by which Acting **Service record** Lieutenant (later Lieutenant-Commander) William Edward Sandars, R.N.R., won the Victoria Cross. This gallant man's service record was remarkable. He was commissioned in the R.N.R. as a sub-lieutenant in April, 1916, and although the rule is that an officer shall serve eight years as a lieutenant before obtaining further advancement, he rose to the rank of lieutenant-commander in a little over a year. In August, 1917, it was officially announced that he had been killed.

The two last naval heroes to be mentioned are Lieutenant Ronald Neil Stuart, D.S.O., R.N.R., and Seaman William Williams, R.N.R., of whose crowning deed the official notification of the award of the Victoria Cross in July,

SEC.-LT. G. G. COURY,
South Lancashire Regt.

PTE. C. COX,
Bedfordshire Regt.

SEC.-LT. J. M. CRAIG,
Royal Scots Fusiliers.

1917, merely said that "Lieutenant Stuart and Seaman Williams were selected by the officers and ship's company respectively of one of H.M. ships to receive the Victoria Cross under Rule 13 of the Royal Warrant dated January 29th, 1856."

First in chronological order of the five airmen awarded the Victoria Cross was Captain (Temporary-Major) Lionel Wilmot Brabazon Rees, R.A. and R.F.C. It was his fortune, good or ill, to find himself amongst a squadron of ten hostile aeroplanes, the character of which he had misapprehended. He attacked one of the machines, which, after a short encounter, disappeared, damaged, behind the enemy lines. Five of the others then attacked him at long range, and, coming to close quarters, he dispersed these, seriously damaging two of them. Then he espied two others flying westwards, and gave chase; but, on drawing near, he received a wound in the thigh which caused him to lose control temporarily of his machine. Succeeding in righting

CPL. J. DAVIES,
Royal Welsh Fusiliers.

it, Major Rees closed with the enemy, firing at a close contact range of only a few yards until his ammunition was exhausted, when he returned home, landing safely in the British lines.

Airmen who won the cross

Sergeant Thomas Mottershead, R.F.C., received his cross for most conspicuous bravery, endurance, and skill when, attacked at an altitude of 9,000 feet, he had his petrol tank pierced and his machine set on fire. Enveloped in flames, which his observer, Lieutenant Gower, was unable to subdue, this gallant airman succeeded in bringing his aeroplane back to the British lines. Although suffering extreme torture from burns, Sergeant Mottershead retained his presence of mind, and selected a suitable landing-place on which he brought down his machine. The machine collapsed, however, on touching the ground, pinning the unfortunate pilot beneath the wreckage, from which he was released only to die. His wonderful endurance and fortitude undoubtedly were the means of saving the life of his observer, and he richly deserved the Victoria Cross which was awarded to him.

Whole-hearted popular acclamation greeted the award of the cross to Lieutenant William Leefe Robinson, Worcester Regiment and R.F.C., for his intrepidity and skill in destroying a Zeppelin (type not notified) at Cuffley on September 3rd, 1916. Although not the first airman to destroy a Zeppelin, having been anticipated by Lieutenant Warneford, V.C., Lieutenant Robinson was the first to bring down one of the raiding airships upon English soil, and his achievement was hailed with relief as assurance that the days of the Zeppelin menace were numbered.

PTE. T. DRESSER,
Yorkshire Regt.

The official account of the deed stated that "he attacked an enemy airship under circumstances of great difficulty and danger, and sent it crashing to the ground as a flaming wreck. He had been in the air for more than two hours, and had previously attacked another airship during his flight." The story of the Zeppelin menace and its conquest has been told in Chapter CLVII. (Vol. VIII. p. 219). Lieutenant Robinson's triumph, marking the point when the people at large realised that the defence had overtaken the attack, was rightly regarded as historic. Other airmen of equal intrepidity and skill subsequently destroyed other Zeppelins, and were rewarded with the Distinguished Service Order or the Distinguished Service Cross. As the pioneer who led where others followed, Lieutenant Robinson fairly earned the supreme military honour that was given to him, and his will remain one of the conspicuous names upon the roll of Victoria Cross heroes. Later, he rendered fine service upon the western front, but in April, 1917, he had the misfortune to be shot down by a German airman, and was held a prisoner of war in Germany.

SERGT. R. DOWNIE,
Royal Dublin Fusiliers.

The posthumous award of the Victoria Cross to Captain Albert Ball, D.S.O., M.C., Notts and Derby Regiment and R.F.C., crowned the career of the greatest airman this country produced during the war, some of whose aerial exploits have been referred to in an earlier chapter. He was awarded the Victoria Cross for "most conspicuous and consistent bravery from April 25th to May 6th, 1917, during which period Captain Ball took part in twenty-six combats in the air and destroyed eleven hostile aeroplanes, drove down two out of control, and forced several others to land." In these combats Captain Ball, flying alone, on one occasion fought six hostile machines, twice fought five, and once fought four. When leading two other British aeroplanes he attacked an enemy formation of eight. On each of these occasions he brought down at least one enemy. Several times his aeroplane was badly damaged, once so seriously that but for the most delicate handling it would have collapsed, nearly all the control wires having been shot away. In all, Captain Ball destroyed forty-three German aeroplanes and one balloon, and "always displayed most exceptional courage, determination, and skill." Captain Ball, who was only in his twenty-first year, was officially reported "missing" on May 18th, 1917. In June official information was received by his friends that he had been killed, and was buried at Annoeullin, near Lille. It had been said of him that "beyond doubt his was the most wonderful series of victories yet achieved by a flying man

Captain Albert Ball, V.C., D.S.O., M.C.

SEC.-LT. J. S. DUNVILLE,
Dragoons.
PTE. F. J. EDWARDS,
Middlesex Regt.
SERGT. J. ERSKINE,
Scottish Rifles.
PTE. W. F. FAULDS,
South African Infantry.
LT. H. O. B. FIRMAN,
R.N.

of any nation." Better words could not be found wherewith to conclude this brief record of his inclusion in the most exclusive company of heroes of any nation.

Lieutenant Frank Hubert McNamara, R.F.C., a member of the Australian Forces, the fifth and last airman to win the Victoria Cross in the third year of the war, showed conspicuous bravery and devotion to duty during an aerial bomb attack upon a hostile construction train, when one of the British pilots was forced to land behind the enemy's lines. Lieutenant McNamara, observing the pilot's predicament, and also the fact that enemy cavalry were approaching, descended to his rescue under heavy rifle fire, and despite a severe wound which he himself had received in the thigh. He got the pilot on to his machine and attempted to rise, but the aeroplane overturned. The

WITHIN THE RANGE OF ENEMY ARTILLERY.
[Canadian War Records.
Canadian officers' car passing through the shattered street of a town close to the line held by the Canadians on the western front. The town was one that was daily subjected to enemy shell fire, and its buildings were being gradually reduced to rubble heaps.

two officers extricated themselves, set fire to the aeroplane, and proceeded to the pilot's damaged aeroplane, which they succeeded in starting. Although weak from loss of blood, Lieutenant McNamara flew this damaged machine back to the aerodrome, a distance of seventy miles, and so completed the rescue of his comrade.

In addition to Lieutenant McNamara, seventeen Australian soldiers were awarded the Victoria Cross in the third year of the war, and since the regrettable official silence on the subject of date and locality precludes reference to particular battles, it must be assumed that all were earned in the fighting upon the western front. The story of each of these deeds shall now be told, though with a brevity which it could be wished the exigencies of space did not compel.

Skill, determination, and utter disregard of danger characterised the qualifying performance of Second-Lieutenant Arthur Seaforth Blackburn,

Seventeen Australians win the cross of the Australian Infantry. He was directed, with fifty men, to drive the enemy from a strong point. He personally led four separate parties of bombers, many of whom became casualties, against the enemy trench, and in face of fierce opposition captured 250 yards of it. Then, after crawling forward with a sergeant to reconnoitre, Lieutenant Blackburn returned and attacked and seized another 120 yards of trench, so establishing communication with the battalion on his left—a brave and soldierly act, with a distinct military significance and value which fully merited the high honour with which it was rewarded.

About the same time, judging from the date of the official award, four privates of the Australian Infantry won their crosses. Private Thomas Cooke paid for his determination and devotion to duty with his life. After a Lewis gun had been disabled, he was ordered to take his gun and gun team to a dangerous part of the line. This he did, coming under such heavy fire that at last only he was left alive. He continued to fire his gun and to display all the qualities that have immortalised the Australian fighting man until death overtook him. When the supports at last came up to the point, they found the brave Australian lying dead beside his gun. Equally brave and resolute was Private William Jackson, of whom the "Gazette" declared that "his work has always been marked by the greatest coolness and bravery." Private Jackson had returned from a successful trench raid. Several members of the party were left in No Man's Land seriously wounded by shell fire. After handing over a prisoner whom he had brought in, this gallant soldier went out under very heavy shell fire and helped to bring one of them in. He then went out again, and, with a sergeant, was bringing in another, when a shell blew his arm away and rendered the sergeant unconscious. Private Jackson returned to the British trenches, obtained assistance, and went out once more to look for his two wounded comrades—"a splendid example of pluck and determination."

Several remarkable exploits were performed by Private John Leak. For example, when the enemy's bombs were outranging the British, he jumped out of the trench, ran forward under heavy machine-gun fire at close range, and threw three bombs into the enemy's bombing-post. He also jumped into the post and bayoneted three unwounded German bombers. Later, when the enemy was driving his party back, Private John Leak was always the last to withdraw at each stage, and kept on throwing bombs. Utter contempt of danger was displayed, too, by Private Martin O'Meara while saving many lives. He **Utter fearlessness** repeatedly went out and brought in **and self-sacrifice** wounded officers and men from No Man's Land under intense artillery and machine-gun fire, and carried up ammunition and bombs through a heavy barrage to a portion of trenches which was being heavily shelled.

Sergeant Claude Charles Castleton, of the Machine Gun Company, represented Australia in a list of twelve Victoria Crosses awarded on September 27th, 1916—posthumously, in his case, for he lost his life after saving several of his comrades. By means of intense machine-gun fire the enemy had temporarily driven back the Australian Infantry, who left many wounded behind them in the ghastly strip of ground between the opposing lines. Sergeant Castleton went out twice in face of the raking fire, and each time brought in a wounded man upon his back. He went out a third time, and was carrying in another when he was himself hit in the back and killed instantly.

Captain Henry William Murray, D.S.O., earned the cross by "wonderful work." When commanding the right flank company in an attack he led his men to the assault with great skill and courage, and the position was quickly captured. Fighting of a very severe nature followed, in which three counter-attacks were repulsed. After suffering heavy casualties, the company gave ground for a short way during the night, but the gallant officer rallied his command, and by sheer valour saved the situation. He made his presence felt throughout the line, encouraging his men, heading bombing-parties, leading bayonet charges, and carrying wounded men to places of safety.

A V.C., who had previously gained the Military Cross, was Second-Lieutenant (Temporary Captain) Percy Herbert Cherry. He was awarded the higher decoration for " most conspicuous bravery, determination, and leadership when in command of a company detailed to storm and clear a village,"—a tantalising reference to a gallant exploit at the capture of a world-famous battle place. After all the officers of his company had become casualties, Lieutenant Cherry carried on in face of fierce opposition, and later exhibited qualities of the born leader by taking charge of the situation and beating off the " most resolute counter-attacks " made by the enemy. He was wounded early in the day, but refused to leave his post, where he remained, encouraging his men to hold **Official eulogy of** out at all costs. This most gallant and **Captain Newlands** able officer was killed by a shell late in the afternoon.

In one of the longest lists of awards of the Victoria Cross, containing twenty-nine names, appeared those of six Australians—a most creditable proportion. One of these was Lieutenant F. H. McNamara, R.F.C., the story of whose deed has been told already. Another was Captain James Ernest Newlands, in referring to whom the writer of the official notification seemed to have found difficulty in restraining enthusiasm. " In face of heavy odds " Captain Newlands displayed " most conspicuous bravery and devotion to duty " on three separate occasions. On the first he organised the attack by his company on a most important objective, and under heavy fire personally led a bombing attack. On the following night his company was heavily counter-attacked while holding the captured position. Captain Newlands, by personal exertion, utter disregard of fire, and judicious use of reserves, dispersed the enemy and regained the position. His third example of gallantry was equally fine. The company on his left was overpowered and his own company attacked from the rear. Captain Newlands drove off a combined attack which had developed from these directions. The attacks were renewed three or four times, and it was his tenacity and disregard for his own safety that encouraged the men to hold out. Seldom has the official report been couched in language so glowing as that used in reference to this most brave and skilful company commander, whose gallant stand, it declares, " was of the greatest importance and produced far-reaching results."

His brother-officer, Lieutenant Charles Pope, awarded the Victoria Cross at the same time, showed amazing bravery, and laid down his life for the Empire. He was ordered to hold a certain picket-post at all costs, and was being heavily attacked. Ammunition had run short, and in order to save the position Lieutenant Pope was seen to charge with his picket into a superior force, by which they

were overpowered. By his sacrifice he inflicted heavy loss on the enemy, and obeyed his order to hold the position to the last. His body, with those of most of his men, was found in close proximity to eighty enemy dead.

Sergeant John Woods Whittle received the award at the same time as Captain Newlands and Lieutenant Pope. He distinguished himself on two occasions. On the first he was in command of a platoon when the enemy attacked the small trench he was holding and forced an entry into it by sheer weight of numbers, whereupon Sergeant Whittle collected all **Sergeant Whittle's** the men available, charged the enemy, **two exploits** and recovered the position. On the second occasion the enemy broke through the left of the British line and endeavoured to bring up a machine-gun to enfilade the position. Keeping his men well in hand by his own splendid example, the sergeant rushed alone across the fire-swept ground, attacked the hostile gun crew before the gun could be got into action, and succeeded in killing the entire crew and in bringing the machine-gun into the position.

As picturesque and thrilling an exploit as any that won the Victoria Cross in the first three years of the war was that performed by Private Jorgan Christian Jensen. With five comrades he attacked a barricade behind which more than forty of the enemy were concealed with a machine-gun. One of his party shot the gunner, and Private Jensen, single-handed, rushed the post and threw in a bomb. He still had a bomb in one hand but, taking a second from his pocket with his other hand, he drew the pin with his teeth and, threatening the enemy with the

" NICHT ÄRGERN, NUR WUNDERN ! "

Wrecked buildings in the Grande Place of Péronne as left by the Germans in March, 1917. They deliberately destroyed many towns from which they were forced to retire, and on several occasions vented their humour in such inscriptions—" Do not be annoyed, only wonder ! "

two bombs and telling them that they were surrounded, he induced them to surrender. He then sent one of his prisoners to order a neighbouring party of the enemy to surrender ; this they did, but were fired upon by some other British troops who were unaware of the capitulation. Wholly regardless of personal danger, Jensen immediately stood up in the barricade and, waving his helmet, caused the firing to cease, after which he sent his prisoners into the British lines.

One of Jensen's comrades, Private Thomas James Bede Kenny, performed an act of almost equal super-heroism, very similar to that which won the Victoria Cross for

LT.-COL. **B.** C. FREYBERG,
R.W. Surrey Regt. and R.N.D.

LCE.-CPL. S. FRICKLETON,
New Zealand (Rifle) Brigade.

PTE. J. H. FYNN,
South Wales Borderers.

SERGT. A. GILL,
K.R.R.C.

Sergeant O'Leary at Cuinchy earlier in the war. His platoon was held up by very heavy fire at close range, and Private Kenny dashed forward alone, killed a man in advance of the point who tried to bar his way, bombed the position, captured the gun crew, all of whom he had wounded, killed an officer, and seized the gun. "Magnificent" bravery characterised the behaviour which won the Victoria Cross for Lieutenant Rupert Vance Moon in the course of an attack upon an enemy strong point. His own immediate objective was a position in advance of the hostile trench, and thence he was to proceed against the trench itself, after which it was intended that his men should co-operate in a further assault upon a strong point farther in the rear. Although wounded in the initial advance, Lieutenant Moon reached his first objective. When leading his men against the main trench he received a second severe wound which temporarily incapacitated him. Nevertheless, he inspired his men to capture the trench, and with the utmost valour led his much diminished command in the general attack, which was successfully pressed home. He was wounded for the third time in the course of this attack, and received yet a fourth wound when consolidating the position, this time being seriously injured in the face and compelled to retire from the field.

A very brave Australian, Corporal George Julian Howell, on his own initiative, single-handed, and exposed to heavy bomb and rifle fire, climbed on to the top of the parapet and proceeded to bomb the enemy, pressing them back along the trench. Having exhausted his supply of bombs he attacked the enemy with the bayonet, and shortly afterwards was severely wounded. The gallantry and promptitude of this non-commissioned officer were witnessed by the whole battalion and greatly stimulated it to counter-attack the enemy, who were in a fair way to outflank the position

On the last day of the third year of the war ten Victoria Crosses were awarded, two of them to Australian soldiers. Captain Robert Cuthbert Grieve was the hero of a gallant single-handed deed. **Gallant destruction** During an attack on the enemy he **of machine-guns** located two hostile machine-guns which were holding up the advance. Under continuous fire from these he bombed and killed the two gun teams, reorganised the remnants of his company, and gained his original objective, being wounded during the proceedings. Private John Carroll was also the hero of a single-handed deed. Immediately the barrage lifted in an attack, he rushed the enemy trench and bayoneted four of its occupants. Noticing a comrade in difficulties, he went to his aid and killed another of the foe. With great determination he continued to work ahead, and presently came across a machine-gun with a crew of four men hidden in a shell-hole ; quite unaccompanied, he attacked the crew, killing three of the men and capturing the gun. Later on he extricated two of his comrades who were buried by a shell, being himself exposed all the time to very heavy shelling and machine-gun fire.

SEC.-LT. R. L. HAINE,
H.A.C.

The two New Zealand heroes who were awarded the Victoria Cross were both non-commissioned officers. Sergeant Donald Forrester Brown was one of five soldiers whose distinction was gazetted on June 15th, 1917, but he did not survive to enjoy it, being killed while sniping the retreating enemy at a place and date the particulars of which were not made public. The company to which he belonged had suffered very heavy casualties from machine-gun fire, and, with a comrade, Sergeant Brown succeeded in reaching a point within thirty yards of the enemy, killing four of them and capturing the gun. Then the company advanced, only to be held up a second time. Once more Sergeant Brown and his comrade rushed a gun and killed the crew. He repeated the feat in a subsequent attack, on this occasion killing the crew and capturing the gun single-handed.

Lance-Corporal Samuel Frickleton was the other New Zealander whose bravery and determination, when with troops checked by heavy fire in an attack, were rewarded with the Victoria Cross. Although slightly wounded, he

SERGT. W. GOSLING,
R.F.A.

CAPT. J. L. GREEN,
R.A.M.C.

CAPT. R. C. GRIEVE,
Australian Infantry.

CPL. J. GRIMSHAW,
1st Lancashire Fus.

SAPPER W. HACKETT,
R.E.

dashed forward at the head of his section, pushed into the British barrage, and with bombs destroyed a machine-gun and crew which were causing heavy casualties. He then proceeded to attack a second gun, killing the entire crew of twelve men. It was officially stated that the destruction of these two guns saved his own and other units from very severe casualties, and that Frickleton's "magnificent courage and gallantry" ensured the capture of the objective. During the consolidation of the position he received a second severe wound.

Three South African heroes Private William Frederick Faulds was the first of the three South African heroes to be awarded the cross in the third year of the war, by an exploit characterised by perfect selflessness. A bombing-party under Lieutenant Craig attempted to rush across forty yards of ground that lay between the opposing trenches. The majority of the party were killed or wounded, and Lieutenant Craig lay midway between the two lines, on ground completely exposed. Accompanied by two other men, Private Faulds climbed over the parapet in full daylight, and running out, picked up the officer and carried him back, being severely wounded while so doing. Two days later he again went out and brought in a wounded man, alone on this occasion, carrying him nearly half a mile to a dressing-station. The artillery fire was so intense at the time that stretcher-bearers, themselves the bravest of the brave, were of opinion that any attempt to bring in the wounded must involve certain death. Faulds, however, was not to be deterred, and his unflinching courage was crowned with success.

SEC.-LT. J. HARRISON,
East Yorkshire Regt.

On January 1st, 1917, the official account was published of the deed for which Captain William Anderson Bloomfield, Scouts Corps, South African Mounted Brigade, was awarded the Victoria Cross, as had become customary, without any intimation of the locality where the exploit had been performed. After being heavily attacked in an advanced and isolated position, Captain Bloomfield perceived that the enemy was working round his flanks, whereupon he evacuated his wounded and withdrew his command to a new position, being himself one of the last to retire. Arriving at the new position, Captain Bloomfield found that one of the wounded, Corporal D. M. P. Bowker, had been left behind, and owing to the heavy fire he experienced difficulty in having him brought in. There were some four hundred yards of entirely open, fire-swept ground to be covered in full view of the enemy; but determined to effect the rescue, Captain Bloomfield himself went out, reached the corporal and brought him

back, subjected throughout the double journey to raking fire from machine-guns and rifles.

Sergeant Frederick Charles Booth, of the South African Forces, indubitably earned his Victoria Cross in German East Africa, for he was attached to the Rhodesia Native Regiment, and the wording of the official notification leaves it plainly to be inferred. It was as follows: "For most conspicuous bravery during an attack, in thick bush, on the enemy position. Under very heavy rifle fire, Sergeant Booth went forward alone and brought in a man who was dangerously wounded. Later, he rallied native troops who were badly disorganised, and brought them to the firing-line. This N.C.O. has on many previous occasions displayed the greatest bravery, coolness, and resource in action, and has set a splendid example of pluck, endurance, and determination."

Three Canadian officers and five Canadian private soldiers were awarded the Victoria Cross in the third year of the war. The two who came first in chronological order were Privates Leo Clarke and John Chipman Kerr, both of the infantry, and the date of the award—October 27th, 1916—and the fact that two of the other awards in the same list were made for gallantry at Guillemont and Lesbœufs, suggest with almost certainty that these two Canadians were also heroes of the Battle of the Somme. Private (Acting Corporal) Clarke was detailed with his section of bombers to clear the continuation of a newly captured trench and cover the construction of a "block." After most of his party had become casualties, he was building a "block"

CPL. G. J. HOWELL,
Australian Infantry.

LT. J. V. HOLLAND,
Leinster Regt.

SEC.-LT. D. P. HIRSCH,
Yorkshire Regt.

[Elliott & Fry.
PTE. A. HILL,
Royal Welsh Fusiliers.

MAJ. F. J. W. HARVEY,
R.M.L.I.
[Russell.

LT. F. M. W. HARVEY,
Strathcona's Horse.
[Bassano.

PTE. M. HEAVISIDE,
Durham Light Infantry.

CAPT. A. HENDERSON,
Arg. & Suth'd. Highrs.

LT.-COL. E. E. D. HENDERSON, N. Staffs. Regt.

LLLL

when a counter-attack was made by about twenty of the enemy with two officers. Private Clarke advanced and emptied his revolver into them, and then two enemy rifles which he picked up in the trench. One of the officers attacked him with a bayonet and wounded him in the leg, only to be shot dead for his pains. The enemy then ran away, pursued by Clarke, who shot four more and captured a fifth. Later he was ordered to the dressing-station, but returned to duty next day.

Private Kerr displayed equal bravery and dash. He was acting as bayonet man during a bombing attack and, aware that bombs were running short, he ran along the parados under heavy fire until he was in close contact with the enemy, when he opened fire at point-blank range and inflicted heavy loss upon them. The enemy, thinking they were surrounded, surrendered, and this amazing Canadian thus captured sixty-two **Amazing feats by** prisoners and two hundred and fifty **Canadians** yards of enemy trench. It should be mentioned that before carrying out this most plucky act Private Kerr had one of his fingers blown off by a bomb. With two other men he escorted the prisoners in under fire, and then returned to report himself for duty before having his wound dressed.

Four Canadian soldiers figured in the list of twenty-nine Victoria Crosses awarded on June 9th, 1917, to which reference has been made already. The highest in rank of these, Captain Thain Wendell MacDowell, D.S.O., displayed remarkable bravery and promptitude in rounding up a very strong enemy machine-gun post in the face of great difficulties, actually capturing two machine-guns besides two officers and seventy-five men. Although wounded, he continued for five days to hold the position gained until he was relieved by his battalion.

The second Canadian officer mentioned in this list was Lieutenant Frederick Maurice Watson Harvey. During an attack by his regiment on a village, a party of the enemy ran forward to a wired trench just in front of the village and opened rapid rifle and machine-gun fire at a very close range, causing heavy casualties in the leading troop, of which Lieutenant Harvey was in command. The moment was a critical one, and as the enemy showed no intention whatever of retiring, and the fire was still intense, Lieutenant Harvey ran forward well ahead of his men, dashed at the trench, which was still fully manned, jumped the wire, shot the machine-gunner, and captured the gun. It was a most dashing and courageous act, and had a decisive effect on the success of the operation.

Lance-Sergeant Ellis Welwood Sifton won his cross for locating a machine-gun that was holding up his company, charging it single-handed, and killing all the crew. He also kept off a party of the enemy, who had advanced down the trench, until his comrades had gained the position. The award of the cross was, unhappily, a posthumous one in this instance, the gallant Canadian **Immortality won** being killed while performing his great **in death** deed.

Private William Johnstone Milne also sacrificed his life in winning his Victoria Cross by a deed similar to that of Lance-Sergeant Sifton. He crawled on hands and knees towards a machine-gun that was firing on the advancing troops, reached it, killed the crew with bombs, and captured the gun. Then he stalked a second gun in like manner, and with a like success. Shortly after this second feat he was killed.

Lieutenant Robert Grierson Combe was killed in the action in the course of which he won the Victoria Cross. He steadied his company under intense fire and led them through the enemy barrage, reaching the objective with only five men. With great coolness and courage he proceeded to bomb the enemy, inflicting heavy casualties; and then, collecting small groups of men, he succeeded in capturing the company objective and eighty prisoners. He repeatedly charged the enemy, driving them before

him, and it was while he was personally leading his bombers that he was shot by a sniper.

The last Canadian to be commemorated here was awarded the Victoria Cross on the last day of the third year of the war. This was Private John George Pattison, who also was the hero of a machine-gun exploit. The gun was holding up the advance, and Private Pattison sprang forward and, jumping from shell-hole to shell-hole, reached cover within thirty yards of it. Although under heavy fire, the daring man hurled bombs from this distance, killing and wounding some of the gun team; then he dashed forward again and overcame and bayoneted the surviving five gunners. "His valour and initiative," said the official account, "undoubtedly saved the situation and made possible the further advance to the objective."

No invidious distinction is implied in the suggestion that courage manifested in the saving of life has a higher quality than that displayed in the taking of life. Its utter selflessness makes an irresistible appeal to sympathetic admiration. This quality was the distinguishing one of the deeds that won the Victoria Cross for the three members of the Royal Army Medical Corps now to be mentioned, and for the one member of the Army Chaplains' Department.

Captain John Leslie Green, R.A.M.C., lost his own life while endeavouring to save another's. Himself wounded at the time, he went to the assistance of an officer who was hung up wounded on the enemy's wire entanglements and succeeded in dragging him to a shell-hole, where he dressed his wounds, notwithstanding that bombs and rifle-grenades were being hurled at him the whole time. In endeavouring to bring the wounded officer into safe cover Captain Green was killed.

"Conspicuous bravery and devotion to duty" were exhibited by Captain William Barnsley Allen, M.C., M.B., R.A.M.C., near Mesnil, France, on September 3rd, 1916. Gun detachments **Selflessness of** were unloading high-explosive ammuni- **doctors and chaplain** tion from waggons which had just come up when the Germans suddenly shelled the battery position. The first shell fell in one of the limbers, exploding the ammunition and causing several casualties. Captain Allen at once ran across the open, under heavy shell fire, and by his promptness in dressing their wounds saved many men from bleeding to death. He was himself hit four times during the first hour by pieces of shell, one of which fractured two of his ribs, but he said nothing about this at the time, coolly carrying on until the last man was dressed and safely removed. He then went over to another battery and tended a wounded officer.

Captain Noel Godfrey Chavasse, M.C., M.B., R.A.M.C., was given the Victoria Cross for courage and self-sacrifice "beyond praise." He tended wounded in the open all day, under heavy fire the whole time and frequently in view of the enemy. That same night he searched for wounded on the ground in front of the enemy's lines for four hours. Next day he went with one stretcher-bearer to the advanced trenches, and under intense shell fire carried an urgent case for five hundred yards into safety, being himself wounded on the journey. That night he rescued three more wounded men from a shell-hole near the enemy's trench. Altogether he saved the lives of some twenty badly-wounded men, to say nothing of the ordinary cases which passed through his hands. It was announced in August, 1917, that this gallant officer had died of wounds. He was awarded a bar to his cross in September, 1917.

The one chaplain to whom the Victoria Cross was awarded during the year under review—the second to be so honoured during the first three years of the war—was the Rev. William Robert Fountaine Addison, Temporary Chaplain to the Forces, 4th Class, Army Chaplains' Department, who before joining the forces had been curate of St. Edmund's, Salisbury. He showed

Music and sweet airs after the harsh discords of war : British military band in a square of Arras.

Artillery battle in the snow : New Zealand field-gunners on the western front

Over the top in winter on the western front : British soldiers' camouflage clothing.

Helping hands for the horses: British soldiers as " brake" on a slippery slope in France.

A message to the guns: British soldiers in France firing a rocket to direct their artillery.

614

" For Valour ": King George decorating Private Thomas Hughes, of the Connaught Rangers, with the V.C., in Hyde Park, June 2nd, 1917.

conspicuous bravery in carrying a wounded man to the cover of a trench and assisted several others to the same refuge after binding up their wounds under heavy rifle and machine-gun fire. " In addition to these unaided efforts," it was stated, " by his splendid example and utter disregard of personal danger, he encouraged the stretcher-bearers to go forward under heavy fire and collect the wounded."

It was Sapper William Hackett who placed the one Victoria Cross to the credit of the Royal Engineers in this third year, by marvellous courage displayed when entombed with four other men in a gallery owing to the explosion of an enemy mine. After working for twenty hours a hole was made through fallen earth and broken timber and a meeting was effected with the outside party. Sapper Hackett helped three of the men through the hole and could easily have followed them to safety, but the fourth man had been seriously injured and Hackett refused to leave him. " I am a tunneller," he said. " I must look after the others first." The hole was getting smaller, but Hackett still refused to leave his wounded comrade. Finally the gallery collapsed, and though the rescue-party worked desperately for four days they failed to reach the two men. Sapper Hackett deliberately gave his life for his comrade. He well knew the nature of the sliding earth and the odds against him. His self-sacrifice and devotion were sublime.

Three Victoria Crosses were awarded to the Artillery, a number that seems small in view of the incomparable work done by this arm of the Service. Sergeant William Gosling, R.F.A., won his by an act of courage and promptitude that was supremely great, albeit it had several parallels. He was in charge of a heavy trench-mortar, and, owing to a faulty cartridge, the bomb after discharge fell ten yards from the mortar. The sergeant sprang out, lifted the nose of the bomb from the ground into which it had sunk, unscrewed the fuse, **Conspicuous gallantry** and threw it on the ground, where it **of gunners** immediately exploded. His presence of mind and pluck saved the lives of the whole detachment. Second-Lieutenant Thomas Harold Broadbent Maufe, R.G.A., showed rare initiative as well as great courage. Under intense artillery fire he repaired, unaided, the telephone line between the forward and the rear positions, thereby enabling his battery to open immediate fire upon the enemy. Further, he extinguished a fire in an advanced ammunition dump—in which, it should be mentioned, there were gas-shells—caused by a heavy explosion, thus averting a serious disaster.

Major (later Brigadier-General) Frederick William Lumsden, D.S.O., R.M.A., was the hero of a thrilling exploit, and the first member of his corps to win the cross since the days of the Crimea. Six enemy field-guns had been captured, but it was necessary to leave them in dug-in positions, three hundred yards in advance of the position held by the British troops. The enemy kept the captured guns under heavy fire, and Major Lumsden undertook the duty of bringing them into the British lines. In order to effect this he personally led four artillery teams and a party of infantry through the hostile barrage. As one of the teams sustained casualties, he left the remaining teams in a covered position and, through very heavy rifle, machine-gun, and shrapnel fire, led the infantry to the guns. By force of example and inspiring energy the major succeeded in sending back two teams with guns, and himself went through the barrage with the team of the third gun. He then went back to the position to await further teams, and these he succeeded in attaching to two of the three remaining guns and despatching into safety, despite the rifle fire which had now become intense at short range. By this time the enemy, in considerable strength, had driven through the infantry covering points and blown up the breech of the last gun, but Major Lumsden returned once more, drove

off the enemy, attached the gun to a team and got it away. The two cavalry officers who gained the Victoria Cross might well be included among the infantrymen, for their exploits were performed when dismounted and acting as line officers. Captain (Temporary Lieutenant-Colonel) Adrian Carton de Wiart, D.S.O., Dragoon Guards, won his cross by " most conspicuous bravery, coolness, and determination during severe operations of a prolonged nature." The date of the award, September 11th, 1916, suggests that the Somme battlefield was the scene of the incident. Captain de Wiart displayed utmost energy and courage in forcing an attack home. After three other battalion commanders had become casualties he controlled their commands and ensured that the ground won was maintained. He frequently exposed himself in the organisation of positions and of supplies, passing unflinchingly through barrage fire of the most intense nature.

Second-Lieutenant John Spencer Dunville, of the Dragoons, displayed **Cavalry and Indian** great gallantry and disregard of personal **regiments** danger when in charge of a party of scouts and Royal Engineers engaged in the demolition of the enemy's wire. In order to ensure the complete success of the work, Second-Lieutenant Dunville placed himself between a non-commissioned officer of the engineers and the enemy's fire, and, thus protected, the N.C.O. was enabled to complete a piece of work of great importance. Dunville was severely wounded, but continued to direct his men in the wire-cutting and general operations until the raid was brought to a successful conclusion. The gallant officer succumbed later to his wounds.

One of the two Victoria Crosses awarded to representatives of Indian regiments was won by Naik Shahamad Khan, Punjabis, who, single-handed, beat off counter-attacks with a machine-gun and held a gap in the British line under very heavy fire for three hours. When his gun was knocked out of action he and his two belt-fillers held their ground with rifles until ordered to withdraw. With three men sent to assist him he then brought back his gun, ammunition, and one severely wounded man who was unable to walk. Finally he returned alone and collected and removed all remaining arms and equipment, except only two shovels. But for the great gallantry and determination of this Indian soldier the British line must have been penetrated by the enemy.

In the case of Major George Campbell Wheeler, Gurkha Rifles, Indian Army, it may be assumed from the official account of the exploit that won the cross that it was performed in one of the extra-European battle areas, probably in Mesopotamia. Accompanied by another Gurkha officer and eight men, Major Wheeler crossed a river and rushed the enemy's trench under heavy bombing, rifle, machine-gun, and artillery fire. Having obtained a footing on the river-bank, Major Wheeler was almost immediately afterwards counter-attacked by a strong body of the enemy; with **V.C. heroes of the** his brother-officer and three men he **Guards** charged, and, despite a severe bayonet wound in the head, dispersed the enemy, saved the situation, and consolidated the position.

Fifteen Victoria Crosses were awarded on October 27th, 1916, and two of these went to the Guards. Major and Brevet Lieutenant-Colonel (Temporary Lieutenant-Colonel) John Vaughan Campbell, D.S.O., Coldstream Guards, added a little touch of the picturesque to his gallant deed that was mightily to the liking of the sport-loving British public. A famous sportsman and Master of the Tanat Hunt, he carried into action the horn he was wont to use when out with the Tanat Side harriers in Shropshire, and in the famous charge of the Guards at the Battle of the Somme he rallied his men by blowing this huntsman's horn. On two separate occasions he rallied his men with the utmost gallantry, once leading them against the enemy machine-guns, which he captured, killing their

PTE. J. HUTCHINSON,
Lancashire Fusiliers.

PTE. W. JACKSON,
Australian Infantry.

SERGT. D. JONES,
Liverpool Regt.

teams, and once, at a critical moment, leading them through an intense enemy barrage against the objective, being one of the first to enter the trench. The Coldstreams suffered heavy losses, but when they reached their journey's end Colonel Campbell turned to Major Longueville and said cheerfully : " Never mind ; Tanat Side has it ! "

Lance-Sergeant Fred McNess, Scots Guards, distinguished himself by coolness and resource in some very fierce fighting. When the first line of enemy trenches had been reached it was found that the left flank was exposed, and that the enemy was bombing down the trench. McNess thereupon organised a counter-attack, which he led in person. Although very severely wounded in the neck and jaw he went on, passing through a barrage of enemy bombs, in order to bring up fresh supplies of bombs to his own men. Finally he established a " block," and continued encouraging his men and throwing bombs until he collapsed through exhaustion from loss of blood.

Before proceeding to relate the deeds for which the Victoria Cross was awarded to infantry of the line, it seems expedient to enumerate the few in respect of which it is possible to name the locality where they were performed, and priority is given to four awards made for conspicuous bravery on the Gallipoli Peninsula which, though earned so much earlier, were not notified until the third year of the war.

In March, 1917, it was announced that the Victoria Cross had been conferred upon the following officer and **Crosses won at** non-commissioned officers **Cape Helles** of the 1st Battalion Lancashire Fusiliers in recognition of most conspicuous bravery displayed : Captain (Temporary Major) Cuthbert Bromley, Sergeant Frank Edward Stubbs, and Corporal (later Sergeant) John Grimshaw. They won their honours on April 25th, 1915, during the landing on the Gallipoli Peninsula to the west of Cape Helles, and were selected by their comrades as having performed the most signal acts of bravery and devotion to duty. These three awards are to be read in conjunction with those made for most conspicuous bravery on the same occasion to Captain Richard Raymond Willis, Sergeant Alfred Richards, and Private William Keneally, whose gallant exploits were detailed in Chapter CXLVI. (Vol. VII, page 496), which dealt with the Victoria Cross heroes of the second year of the war. In the case of Major Bromley and Sergeant Stubbs the award was posthumous,

[Lafayette.
COMDR. L. W. JONES,
R.N.

[Vandyk.
LT. R. B. B. JONES,
Loyal North Lancs Regt.

PTE. T. A. JONES,
Cheshire Regt.

the former having been drowned in the Royal Edward on August 14th, 1915, and the latter having died of wounds.

The other Gallipoli hero was Lance-Corporal Walter Richard Parker, R.M.L.I., R.N.D., whose award of the cross was made on June 23rd, 1917, although the deed that earned it was performed so long before as the night of April 30th-May 1st, 1915. During the three previous days Parker had displayed remarkable courage and energy under fire while in charge of the battalion stretcher - bearers, and on this supreme occasion he volunteered, in response to a call for a stretcher-bearer, to join a party to carry water and ammunition to an isolated fire-trench at Gaba Tepe. It was already daylight when the party emerged from shelter, and one of the men was wounded immediately. Parker organised a stretcher-party, and then, going on alone, he reached the **Extreme courage at** fire-trench, where he **Gaba Tepe** rendered assistance to the wounded, displaying extreme courage, coolness, and presence of mind in most trying circumstances. The trench finally had to be evacuated, and Parker helped to remove and attend the wounded, being himself seriously wounded during the operation.

Only seven awards of the Victoria Cross were officially linked with particular battle areas on the western front during the year under review. The first of these in point of date were earned on September 3rd, 1916, by Captain W. B. Allen, R.A.M.C., at Mesnil, as already narrated, and by Private Thomas Hughes, of the Connaught Rangers, at Guillemont. The award in the latter case was announced on October 27th, 1916, as follows : " **Private** Thomas Hughes, Connaught Rangers, for most conspicuous bravery and determination at Guillemont, September 3rd, 1916. He was wounded in an attack, but returned at once to the firing-line after having his wounds dressed. Later, seeing a hostile machine-gun, he dashed out in front of his company, shot the gunner, and, single-handed, captured the gun. Though again wounded, he brought back three or four prisoners."

Private Thomas Alfred Jones, Cheshire Regiment, a native of Runcorn, performed the deed that won him his cross at Lesbœufs on September 25th, and it was one of the most astonishing personal achievements recorded even in the V.C. annals, where the records of heroism are all astonishing. He detected a sniper at two hundred yards

PTE. D. R. LAUDER,
Royal Scots Fusiliers.

PTE. J. LEAK,
Australian Infantry.

PTE. H. W. LEWIS,
Welsh Regt.

distance, returned his fire, a bullet passing through his own coat meanwhile, and killed him. He shot two more Germans who were firing at him, and then, as the firing continued, he said to an officer standing by, "If I'm to be killed, I'll be killed fighting, not digging," and, grasping his rifle, he walked over to the German trenches quite alone. His comrades naturally regarded him as doomed, and about eight minutes later several went out after him. A remarkable sight met their eyes when they reached the enemy trench. "There was Todger Jones," an eye-witness said, "standing by a hundred of the enemy in a bog hollow. He was threatening them with bombs, and they all had their hands up." Officially it was stated that he, single-handed, disarmed one hundred and two of the enemy, including three or four officers, and marched them back

" Todger " Jones' to the British lines through
hundred prisoners a heavy barrage. He had been warned of the misuse of the white flag by the enemy, but insisted on going out after them. The men in the British trench were almost wild with enthusiasm when Jones returned with his captives, and eleven officers joined in recommending him for the Victoria Cross.

Temporary Captain Archie Cecil Thomas White, Yorkshire Regiment, earned his cross at Stuff Redoubt, September 27th-October 6th, 1916, where for four days and nights he held his position when commanding the troops holding the southern and western sides. The Germans, in greatly superior numbers, almost succeeded in ejecting the British from the redoubt, but Captain White led a counter-attack which finally cleared the enemy from the threatened points.

Eaucourt l'Abbaye was the scene of the heroism which won the cross for Lieutenant (Temporary Lieutenant-Colonel) Roland Boys Bradford, M.C., Durham Light Infantry, on October 1st, 1916, when his bravery and leadership saved the situation on the right flank of his brigade and of the division. Colonel Bradford's battalion was in support, and, at a critical moment, he asked permission to command an exposed battalion whose commander was wounded, as well as his own. Permission being given, he proceeded to the foremost lines, where by his fearless energy under fire of every description and by his skilful leadership of the two battalions, he rallied the attack, captured and defended the objective, and so secured the flank.

"Magnificent" was the epithet officially

MAJ. S. W. LOUDOUN-SHAND, Yorkshire Regt. MAJ. F. W. LUMSDEN, R.M.A. [*Russell.*] CAPT. T. W. MacDOWELL, Canadian Infantry.

PTE. W. F. McFADZEAN, Royal Irish Rifles.

LCE.-SERGT. F. McNESS, Scots Guards.

SEC.-LT. T. H. B. MAUFE, R.G.A.

applied to the conduct throughout the day of November 13th, 1916, opposite the Hebuterne sector, of Private John Cunningham, East Yorkshire Regiment, the first Hull man to be awarded the cross. He went with a bombing section up a communication-trench, where such fierce resistance was encountered that all save he became casualties. Collecting all the bombs from his wounded comrades, Cunningham went on alone and, having exploded the entire supply, returned for more. Armed with these, he went again to the trench, where he met and killed a party of ten of the enemy and cleared the trench up to the German line

Lance-Sergeant (later Second-Lieutenant) Frederick William Palmer, Royal Fusiliers, was honoured for "most conspicuous bravery, coolness, and determination" north of Courcelette, February 17th, 1917. He assumed command of his company after all the officers had become casualties, rushed the enemy trench with six of his men, and dislodging the machine-gun which had been hampering the advance, established a " block." Sergeant Palmer held the barricade for three hours against seven counter-attacks; then, during his temporary absence in search of more bombs, an eighth counter-attack was delivered, which drove in his party and menaced the defence of the entire flank. Recognising the critical nature of the situation, Palmer, who had been blown off his feet by a bomb and was terribly exhausted, rallied his men, drove back the enemy, and maintained the position.

Besides these seven men whose heroism was officially announced as having been exhibited in the area of the Battle of the Somme, **Heroes of the** there are two others who **Somme** are known to have been present there, Colonel J. V. Campbell, of the Coldstream Guards, whose story has been told already, and Captain (Temporary Lieutenant-Colonel) Bernard Cyril Freyberg, D.S.O., Royal West Surrey Regiment and Royal Naval Division, who was awarded the Victoria Cross on December 15th, 1916, for his brilliant leadership of the Naval Division, which, with others, captured Beaucourt and Beaumont-Hamel on the previous November 13th. Colonel Freyberg's conduct during the war had already been most distinguished, with the Naval Division at Antwerp, and also in Gallipoli, where he earned the D.S.O. in the Gulf of Xeros, on the eve of the landing, by swimming ashore two miles from a destroyer to light flares on the beach in order to confuse the Turks as to

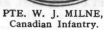

PTE. J. MILLER, K.O. Royal Lanc. Regt. PTE. W. J. MILNE, Canadian Infantry. LT. R. V. MOON, Australian Infantry.

[Australian official photograph.

WHERE A TANK LED THE WAY TO VICTORY.
Flers Church, about four miles south of Bapaume, as it was when the place was taken in the British advance during September, 1916. Flers will always be remembered as the village through which one of the then newly-devised Tanks led the cheering British Army.

the precise spot chosen for the disembarkation. On the occasion when he won the Victoria Cross he carried the initial attack with great personal gallantry straight through the enemy's front system of trenches. His command became somewhat disorganised under the intense fire to which it was subjected, but Colonel Freyberg rallied and re-formed his men, including some from other units who had become intermixed with them. He then led a successful assault upon the second objective, where, unsupported, he held the ground for the remainder of the day and throughout the night. Reinforced in the morning, Colonel Freyberg dashingly led the assault upon Beaumont-Hamel, capturing the village and five hundred prisoners. He was wounded four times during these operations, but refused to leave the line until he had issued his final instructions. The official account of his deed—one of the longest ever issued in the annals of the Victoria Cross—concluded : " The personality, valour, and utter contempt of danger on the part of this single officer enabled the lodgment in the most advanced objective of the corps to be permanently held, and on this point d'appui the line was eventually formed."

As said in the statistical summary at the beginning of this chapter, six Victoria Crosses were awarded to the Yorkshire Regiment during the third year of the war, and

Six Yorkshire Regiment heroes three of these were announced together on September 11th, 1916. The recipients were Major Stewart Walter Loudoun-Shand, Second-Lieutenant Donald Simpson Bell, and Private William Short, not one of whom survived his deed to learn how it had been rewarded. Major Loudoun-Shand leapt on to the parapet when his men were stopped from going " over the top " by savage machine-gun fire, helped his men over it, and encouraged them in every way until he fell mortally wounded. Even then he insisted on being propped up, and continued to encourage and stimulate his men until he died. Second-Lieutenant Bell was killed five days after performing the deed which won him the cross. A very heavy enfilading fire was opened on his attacking company by a machine-gun, and Bell crept up a communication-trench and then, followed by two of his men, rushed across the fire-swept open and attacked the gun, shooting the gunner with his revolver and destroying gun and personnel with bombs. He was in the act of performing a precisely similar deed

when he met his death. Private Short died while performing the act which won him the cross. His leg was shattered by a shell, and being thus unable to stand to throw bombs himself, he lay in the trench adjusting detonators and straightening the pins of bombs for his comrades.

The fourth cross awarded to the Yorkshire Regiment was that given to Captain A. C. T. White for heroism in the Battle of the Somme, as already narrated. The fifth award was made on June 14th, 1917, the recipient being Second-Lieutenant (Acting Captain) David Philip Hirsch, who exhibited remarkable bravery in encouraging his men to dig and hold a hard-won position. Captain Hirsch " continued to encourage his men by standing on the parapet and steadying them in face of machine-gun fire and counter-attack until he was killed." The sixth and last award to the regiment was made in respect of Private Tom Dresser, a Middlesbrough newsagent. He was twice wounded and suffering great pain, but, nevertheless, succeeded in conveying an important message from battalion headquarters to the front-line trenches, where he arrived in an exhausted condition, a feat which " proved of the greatest value to his battalion at a critical period." Private Dresser and Captain White were the only two survivors of the six Yorkshire Regiment heroes.

Three of the four crosses awarded to the Lancashire Fusiliers were for the heroic conduct at the landing on Gallipoli, which has been described already. The fourth recipient was **Lancashire and** Private James Hutchinson, who during **Liverpool V.C.'s** an attack entered the enemy's trench, shot two sentries, and cleared two of the traverses. When a retirement was ordered, Private Hutchinson on his own initiative undertook the dangerous task of covering the retreat, and did this with such gallantry and determination that the wounded were removed to safety.

The first of the four Victoria Crosses awarded to the Liverpool Regiment was gazetted in August, 1916, Private Arthur Herbert Procter being the hero rewarded. In civil life he had been a booking-clerk in a merchant's office and a Sunday-school worker at Stuart Road Mission School, connected with St. Paul's Presbyterian Church, Tranmere, Birkenhead. As secretary of an ambulance class and later as a Red Cross worker, he acquired experience which stood him in good stead when a soldier in France. He won the supreme military honour of the world by crossing open ground under heavy fire to dress the wounds of two comrades, and it is good to be able to record that he was thus instrumental in saving their lives, both of them being brought in at dusk.

Notable selflessness and great gallantry won the Victoria Cross for Second-Lieutenant Felix Baxter, also of the Liverpool Regiment. Before a raid upon the enemy line he was engaged for two nights in cutting wire close to the enemy trenches. He held a bomb in his hand with the pin withdrawn ready to throw. On one occasion the bomb slipped and fell to the ground, but he instantly picked it up, unscrewed the base plug, and took out the detonator, which he smothered in the earth, thus preventing the alarm from being raised, and saving many casualties. Later he led the left storming-party, and was the first man into the trench, shooting the sentry with his revolver. He then assisted to bomb dug-outs, concluding by climbing out of the trench and helping the last man over the parapet. "After this," said the official account, "he was not seen again. There seems no doubt that he lost his life in his great devotion to duty."

Sergeant David Jones, the third hero of the Liverpool Regiment, was rewarded for bravery, devotion to duty, and ability in the handling of his platoon. He led the platoon, occupied the position, and held it for two days and two nights without food or water until relieved, on the second day driving back three counter-attacks with heavy losses.

Captain Oswald Austin Reid, of the Liverpools, was attached to the Loyal North Lancashire Regiment at the time he gained his Victoria Cross " in the face of desperate circumstances." He consolidated a small post with advanced troops on the side of a river opposite to the main body, after his line of communications had been cut by the sinking of pontoons. He maintained this position for thirty hours against constant attacks, and it was due to his tenacity that the passage of the river was effected the following night. The award of this Victoria Cross was announced on June 9th, 1917, and although neither date nor place was mentioned it is permissible to connect the deed with the crossing of the Diala River in the Mesopotamian Campaign in March, 1917, for it was known that the Lancashire men took part in that brilliant episode.

"The highest type of courage and personal initiative " distinguished Drummer Walter Ritchie, of Glasgow, the first of the four Seaforth Highlanders to receive the Victoria Cross during the third year of **Four gallant** the war. He stood on the parapet of **Seaforth Highlanders** an enemy trench and repeatedly sounded the "Charge" under heavy machine-gun fire and bomb attacks, rallying many men belonging to various units ; throughout the day, too, he carried messages over fire-swept ground. This man, a born soldier, had served in the Army for eight years, joining the Colours unknown to his parents and forbidding all attempts to get him back to civil life.

Corporal Sidney William Ware, of the Seaforths, picked up a wounded man and carried him two hundred yards to cover, and then returned for others, moving to and fro under heavy fire for more than two hours, until he had brought in all the wounded and was completely exhausted.

"Beyond all praise " was the official comment on the gallantry and devotion of Lieutenant Donald Mackintosh, Seaforth Highlanders, awarded the cross on June 9th, 1917. During an advance he was shot through the leg, but though crippled he continued to lead his men and captured the trench. Here he collected men of another company who had lost their leader, and drove back a counter-attack. He was wounded again, but, though now unable to stand, he kept control of the situation. When only fifteen men were left, this indomitable man ordered the party to be ready to advance to the final objective, and getting out of the trench with great difficulty he was encouraging them to advance when he was once more wounded, and fell.

Lance-Sergeant Thomas Steele, of the Seaforths, also awarded the cross on June 9th, displayed courage equal to that of Lieutenant Mackintosh. At a critical moment, when the enemy had recovered some captured trenches, Sergeant Steele rushed forward and helped a comrade to carry a machine-gun into position, and then kept the gun in action until relieved, being "mainly instrumental in keeping the remainder of the line intact." Some hours later the enemy again reoccupied a portion of the captured trenches, and Sergeant Steele detected signs of wavering among the troops ; he encouraged them to remain in their trenches, led a number of them forward, and helped greatly to re-establish the line. On this occasion he was severely wounded.

The story of the bombing exploit of Private John Cunningham, V.C., of the East Yorkshire Regiment, in the Battle of the Somme, has been told earlier in this chapter. The other two **Three East York-** members of this regiment to win the **shire V.C.s** cross were Private George William Chafer, the award to whom was notified on August 7th, 1916, and Second-Lieutenant John Harrison, M.C. Private Chafer showed great resourcefulness as well as conspicuous bravery. During a heavy bombardment and attack upon the British trenches, a man carrying an important message to his company commander was rendered unconscious and half buried by a shell. Chafer took the message from the man's pocket and, although severely wounded in three places, ran along the ruined parapet under heavy fire and just succeeded in delivering it before collapsing from the effect of his wounds. Second-Lieutenant Harrison led his company against an enemy trench in a dark wood and, being repulsed, reorganised his command and made a second attack in darkness and under heavy fire—again without success. Turning round, the officer, single-handed, dashed at a machine-gun, helping to knock it out, and so saving the lives of many of his company. At the end of the official report appeared the melancholy words: " He is reported missing, believed killed."

Superb courage of a perfectly selfless type characterised the deeds for which Private James Henry Fynn was awarded the first of the three Victoria Crosses that went to the South Wales Borderers in 1916-17. He was one of a small party which dug in in front of the British advanced line after a night attack and about three hundred yards from the enemy's trenches. Seeing several wounded men lying out in the open, Fynn went forward and bandaged them all under heavy fire, making several

[*British official photograph.*

RUINED BUT REWON FROM THE RUTHLESS INVADER.
British troops entering Péronne, from which the enemy had been forced during the advance of March, 1917. Though the British and French attackers had spared the old place as much as possible, the retreating Germans deliberately burned or blew up all the buildings.

SERGT. E. J. MOTT,   CAPT. H. W. MURRAY,   SEC.-LT. E. K. MYLES,
Border Regt.   Australian Infantry.   Welsh Regt.

journeys for the purpose. He then returned to the advanced trench for a stretcher, and being unable to find one, carried a badly wounded man on his back into safety, and, going back with a comrade, brought in another man. Awarded his cross at the same time as Fynn, Lieutenant (Temporary Captain) Angus Buchanan, of the South Wales Borderers, also assisted to carry a wounded brother-officer into safety, and going back brought in a second wounded man who had gone to the aid of the officer and himself been hit. Sergeant Albert White, of the same regiment, made the supreme sacrifice in an attempt to capture a machine-gun which he realised would probably hold up the whole advance of his company. "He willingly sacrificed his life in order that he might secure the success of the operations and the welfare of his comrades."

The three V.C.'s of the South Lancashire Regiment were Second-Lieutenant Gabriel George Coury, Private John Readitt, and Private William Ratcliffe. Lieutenant Coury was in command of two platoons ordered to dig a communication-trench from the old firing-line **Private Readitt holds** to the position won under intense fire, and **an army** it was mainly due to his inspiring confidence that the task was accomplished. Later he brought in his commanding officer, who was lying wounded in full view of the enemy. He also distinguished himself in rallying and leading forward the attacking troops, who showed signs of being shaken. Private Ratcliffe located a machine-gun which was firing on his comrades from the rear, rushed it, bayoneted the crew, and brought the gun back into action in his own front line.

One of the outstanding Victoria Cross achievements of the war was that performed by Private John Readitt, while fighting against the Turks. The South Lancashires were working down a broad, deep watercourse, and five times Readitt went forward in the face of very heavy machine-gun fire at close range, on each occasion being the sole survivor of the party. These advances drove back the enemy machine-guns, and in an hour about three hundred yards of the watercourse was made good. His officer being killed, Readitt organised and led several more advances, but on reaching the enemy's barricade he was

CAPT. J. E. NEWLANDS,   PTE. M. O'MEARA,   SERGT. J. W. ORMSBY,
Australian Infantry.   Australian Infantry.   K.O.Y.L.I.

forced by a counter-attack to retire, which he did slowly, continuing to throw bombs the while. On supports reaching him he held a forward bend by bombing until the position was consolidated. The Turkish commander, who was captured later in the day, had been a witness of Readitt's heroism, and declared that he had never seen anything finer than the way "that stripling had stood up to a whole army."

Lieutenant-Colonel Bradford, whose work at Eaucourt l'Abbaye has been described already, was the first member of the Durham Light Infantry to win the V.C. during this year. The second was Private Michael Heaviside, a regimental stretcher-bearer. A wounded man was observed in a shell-hole about forty yards from the enemy line making signals of distress and holding up an empty water-bottle. Owing to snipers and machine-gun fire it was impossible during daylight to send out a stretcher-party, but Heaviside volunteered to carry water and food out to the unfortunate man. He succeeded in his task despite the intense fire. The water undoubtedly saved the man's life, for he had been lying out for four days and three nights, and was nearly demented with thirst. The same evening Heaviside went out again with two comrades and rescued the wounded man. The third V.C. hero of the Durham Light Infantry was Second-Lieutenant Frederick Youens. He had just returned to his trenches to have wounds dressed which he had received while on patrol, when warning came that an enemy raid was in preparation. Youens rallied the team of a Lewis gun, and while he was doing so

LCE.-CPL. W. R.   LT. R. E. PHILLIPS,   SEC.-LT. A. O.
PARKER, R.M.L.I.   Roy. Warwicks. Regt.   POLLARD, H.A.C.

an enemy bomb fell on the gun position without exploding. Youens immediately picked it up and hurled it over the parapet. Shortly afterwards another bomb fell near the same spot, and again Youens picked it up. This bomb, however, burst in his hand before he could fling it away, severely wounding him and also some of his men. His prompt gallantry had undoubtedly saved several lives, and his energy repulsed the enemy's raid, but the brave officer succumbed to his wounds.

Self-sacrifice was the distinguishing note of the acts that won the Victoria Cross for Privates William Frederick McFadzean and Robert Quigg, of the Royal Irish Rifles. McFadzean, who was only twenty at the time, threw himself upon a box of bombs which had been dropped accidentally, and was blown to pieces, giving his life without a moment's hesitation to save his comrades. Quigg went out seven times under heavy shell and machine-gun fire to look for his platoon officer, each time bringing back a wounded man, dragging the last one in on a waterproof sheet from within a few yards of the enemy wire. He was engaged for seven hours in this noble work, and only gave up then because of utter exhaustion.

A most dramatic deed that won the cross was that of Private James Miller, of the Royal Lancaster Regiment. He was carrying an important message, and was obliged to cross open ground under intense fire. Immediately he left the trench he was shot in the back, the bullet coming out through the abdomen. With astonishing fortitude he compressed the gaping wound in his abdomen with his hand, delivered the message, staggered back with the answer, and fell at the feet of the officer to whose hand he committed it. Devotion to duty never reached a greater height. The other soldier of the Royal Lancasters to win the cross was Private Jack White, the first member of the Manchester Jewish community to achieve the honour. During an attempt to cross a river, White, who was a signaller, saw the two pontoons ahead of him come under heavy fire from machine-guns, with disastrous effect. When his own pontoon reached mid-stream every man in it except himself was either dead or wounded ; and finding himself unable to control it, White jumped overboard, tied a telephone-wire to the pontoon, and towed it to the shore, thereby saving an officer's life and bringing to land the rifles and equipment of the other men in the boat.

The two V.C.'s of the Worcester Regiment were Lieutenant Eugene Paul Bennett and Private Thomas George Turrall. The former displayed conspicuous bravery in leading the second wave of an attack to its objective. Isolated there with a party of sixty men, he consolidated the position under heavy fire from both flanks, and, though wounded, remained in effective command. Turrall, a Birmingham man, remained with his officer, Lieutenant Jennings, for three hours under continuous heavy fire, and although at one time completely cut off, he held his ground, and at last carried the officer into the British lines. When the King visited the trenches in 1916, Turrall was called out and spoken to by his Majesty. The officer whom Turrall

PTE. A. H. PROCTER,   PTE. W. RATCLIFFE,   PTE. J. READITT,
Liverpool Regt.   South Lancs Regt.   South Lancs Regt.

rescued died upon the operating-table, and a pathetic letter written by his mother to the mother of his rescuer later came to the public knowledge. One passage in this ran : "Will you let me know when your brave son is in England again ? I will go anywhere in England to see him and give him some special thing in memory of Lieutenant Jennings. Your son must be a hero, and so strong, for my son was over six feet."

Second-Lieutenant Edgar Kinghorn Myles and Private Herbert William Lewis brought the two Victoria Crosses that were added to the honour of the Welsh Regiment in 1916-17. The former served in the ranks of a Territorial battalion of the Worcestershire Regiment in France, where his conduct gained him a commission. Subsequently he transferred to the Regular Army and served with the Welsh Regiment in Gallipoli. The official account of his V.C. deed says that he went out on several occasions in front of the advanced trenches and, under heavy fire and at great personal risk, assisted wounded men lying in the open, carrying a wounded officer on one occasion to safety under circumstances of great danger. Private Lewis set " a brilliant example of courage, endurance, and devotion to duty" in a trench raid. Twice wounded and twice refusing attendance, he searched dug-outs and then, again wounded and again refusing attendance, he attacked and captured three of the enemy. During the retirement he rescued a wounded comrade under fire.

The Royal Welsh Fusiliers was represented in the V.C.

MAJ. L. W. B. REES,   LT. W. L. ROBINSON,   PTE. R. RYDER,
R.A. and R.F.C.   Worc. Regt. & R.F.C.   Middlesex Regt.

roll by Corporal Joseph Davies and Private Albert Hill. The former got separated with eight other men from the rest of his company, and was completely surrounded by the enemy. Taking up a position in a shell-hole, the corporal opened rapid fire, and, also throwing bombs, put the foe to flight, whereupon Davies followed them up and ran several through with the bayonet. "Magnificent throughout" was the term applied officially to Private Hill's conduct. His battalion had deployed for an attack upon a wood, and when the order to charge was given he dashed forward and bayoneted two of the enemy. Sent later by his sergeant to get into touch with the company, he was cut off and surrounded by twenty of the enemy, whom he promptly attacked with bombs, killing and wounding many and scattering the rest. He then joined a sergeant of his company and helped him to fight the way back to the lines. Still later he helped in bringing in his wounded company officer, and, in conclusion, himself captured and brought in two prisoners.

Some exploits with bombs

Second-Lieutenant George Edward Cates, Rifle Brigade, was one of the several heroes awarded the Victoria Cross for localising the effect of bombs. He struck a buried bomb while engaged in deepening a captured trench, and it at once started to burn. In order to save the lives of his comrades, Second-Lieutenant Cates placed his foot on the bomb, which immediately exploded, killing the gallant and self-sacrificing man.

The second Victoria Cross to go to the Rifle Brigade during the third year of the war was awarded to Major William La Touche Congreve, who already had earned the Distinguished Service Order and the Military Cross. The supreme honour was conferred as reward for most conspicuous bravery during the period of fourteen days preceding his death at the front in July, 1916. During preliminary preparations for an attack, Major Congreve carried out personal reconnaissances of the enemy lines, taking out parties of officers and non-commissioned officers for over a thousand yards in front of the British line in order to acquaint them with the ground. Later, by night, he conducted a battalion to the position assigned to it, and afterwards returned to it to ascertain the

ACT.-LT. W. E.   CPL. G. SANDERS,   L.-SERGT. T. STEELE,
SANDARS, R.N.R.   West Yorkshire Regt.   Seaforth Highlanders.

PTE. G. STRINGER,
Manchester Regt.

LT. R. N. STUART,
R.N.R.

SERGT. F. E. STUBBS,
Lancashire Fusiliers.

situation after assault. He then established himself in an exposed forward position, whence he successfully observed the enemy and gave orders necessary to drive them from their position. Two days later this gallant officer assisted to remove wounded to places of safety, though he was himself suffering from gas and other shell effects. On a subsequent occasion he "showed supreme courage in tending wounded under heavy shell fire." His end was dramatic. He had returned to the front line to ascertain the situation after an unsuccessful attack, and was in the act of writing his report when he was shot and killed instantly.

The first of the two crosses with which the Leinster Regiment was honoured was won by Lieutenant John Vincent Holland, who led his bombers through the British barrage and cleared a great part of a village in front. He started out with twenty-six bombers and came back with five, after capturing fifty prisoners. His gallantry had the effect of breaking the spirit of the enemy, and thereby saving the British many casualties when the battalion made a further advance. The second cross was awarded to Corporal John Cunningham. While in command of a Lewis-gun section on the most exposed flank of an attack his section came under heavy enfilading fire and suffered severely. Wounded and almost alone, Corporal Cunningham reached the objective with his gun, which he brought into action in face of much opposition. Counter-attacked by a party of twenty of the enemy, he exhausted his ammunition against them, and then, standing in full view, began throwing bombs. He was wounded again and fell; but he picked himself up and single-handed continued to fight the foe until his bombs were exhausted. This most gallant man died in hospital from his wounds.

Two gallant Bedfordshires

Second-Lieutenant Tom Edwin Adlam, Bedfordshire Regiment, displayed courage quite extraordinary in ejecting the enemy from a portion of a village which had defied capture. He led his men in bombing attacks throughout the day, and on the following day exhibited equal bravery, continuing to lead his men after a second wound had incapacitated him from throwing bombs. "His magnificent example and valour, coupled with the skilful handling of the situation, produced far-reaching results." Private Christopher Cox, also of the Bedfordshire Regiment, showed "conspicuous bravery and continuous devotion to duty" while acting as stretcher-bearer. Single-handed he rescued four men, and later he assisted to bring in the wounded of an adjoining battalion.

On November 27th, 1916, two Victoria Crosses were awarded to the Middlesex Regiment, the recipients being Private Frederick Jeremiah Edwards and Private Robert Ryder. The former showed bravery and resource in destroying with bombs an enemy machine-gun which was holding up his part of the line, thus clearing up a dangerous situation. The latter cleared an enemy trench by skilful manipulation of his Lewis gun. "This very gallant act not only made possible but also greatly inspired the subsequent advance of his comrades and turned possible failure into success."

Second-Lieutenant John Manson Craig and Private David Ross Lauder carried off the two Victoria Crosses awarded to the Royal Scots Fusiliers. The officer exhibited courage of the highest order when an advanced post was rushed by a large party of the enemy. He at once organised a rescue-party and was removing the dead and wounded when his men came under heavy fire. He took a wounded non-commissioned officer and the medical officer into shelter, being wounded himself in the process, scooped cover for them, and saved their lives. Private Lauder's qualifying deed of heroism was simpler but not less fine. He threw a bomb which failed to clear the parapet and fell amongst the bombing-party who were retaking a sap. He immediately put his foot upon it, thereby localising the explosion. His foot was blown off, but his comrades escaped unhurt.

Corporal George Jarratt, Royal Fusiliers, won the cross by a similar act of self-sacrifice. Captured by the enemy, he was placed with some wounded men in a dug-out. British troops drove the enemy back, and as they were leaving the position they bombed the dug-outs, including the one in which Jarratt and the others were waiting. Directly the grenade dropped among the

CPL. S. W. WARE,
Seaforth Highlanders.

wounded men, Jarratt placed both feet on it, having both his legs blown off by the explosion. The other wounded were later removed safely to the British lines, but the heroic corporal died before he could be removed. The second Victoria Cross credited to Corporal Jarratt's regiment was that won by Lance-Sergeant F. W. Palmer at the Battle of the Somme, as already narrated.

The East Surrey Regiment's two heroes were Sergeant Harry Cator and Corporal Edward Foster, both of whom won the Victoria Cross by engaging machine-guns which were holding up advances. The sergeant set out with another man, who was killed, and going on alone, he picked up a Lewis gun and some drums and reached the northern end of the enemy trench. Meanwhile, a British bombing-party was seen to be held up by another machine-gun, and taking up a position from which he sighted this,

PTE. E. SYKES,
Northumberland Fusiliers.

SERGT. J. Y. TURNBULL,
Highland Light Infantry.

PTE. T. G. TURRALL,
Worcester Regt.

PTE. T. W. H. VEALE,
Devonshire Regt.

PTE. H. WALLER,
K.O.Y.L.I.

the sergeant killed its entire team and its officer, whose papers he brought in. He continued to hold the end of the trench with the Lewis gun with such effect that the bombing-party was able to work along and capture a hundred prisoners and five machine-guns. Corporal Foster, who had charge of two Lewis guns, engaged two enemy machine-guns which were checking the advance. One of his Lewis guns was lost, but " with reckless courage " the corporal rushed forward, bombed the foe, and recovered the gun. Then, getting both into action, he killed the enemy gun team and captured their gun.

Sergeant John William Ormsby, King's Own Yorkshire Light Infantry, set a fine example of bravery and indifference to enemy fire. After clearing a village and driving out many snipers from forward positions, he took command of the company and led them forward a quarter of a mile to a new position, which he organised and held until relieved. Private Horace Waller, of the same regiment, when with a bombing section forming a " block " in the enemy line, repulsed two counter-attacks, and after all the little garrison had been put out of action and he himself was wounded, he still continued to throw bombs until he was killed.

Lieutenant Richard Basil Brandram Jones, Loyal North Lancashire Regiment, shot fifteen of the enemy as they advanced to recapture a crater, counting them aloud as he did so in order to cheer his men. His ammunition being expended, he took a bomb, but was shot through the head as he rose to throw it.

LCE.-CPL. J. WELCH,
Royal Berkshire Regt.

Lieutenant Thomas Orde Lawder Wilkinson, of the same regiment, with two men, held the enemy up with a machine-gun until relief came, and later, when the advance was checked during a bombing raid, forced his way forward and found four or five men of different units stopped by a solid block of earth, over which the enemy were throwing bombs. Mounting a machine-gun on the top of the parapet he dispersed the enemy bombers. Later still, he made two most gallant attempts to bring in a wounded man, being shot through the heart in the second attempt.

The last regiment of the line to obtain two Victoria Crosses in this third year was the Northumberland Fusiliers, one of them being awarded to Lance-Corporal Thomas Bryan, who did "very far-reaching" work by disabling an enemy machine-gun and killing the team; the other to Private Ernest Sykes, who under intense fire brought in four wounded men.. He made a fifth journey and "remained out under conditions which appeared to be certain death" until he had bandaged all those too badly wounded to be moved.

Second-Lieutenant Reginald Leonard Haine and Second-

SEC.-LT. F. B. WEARNE,   MAJ. G. C. WHEELER,   CAPT. A. C. T.
Essex Regt.   Gurkha Rifles, Ind. Army.   WHITE, Yorks. Rt.

Lieutenant Alfred Oliver Pollard, both of the Honourable Artillery Company, won the Victoria Cross by exploits which deserve somewhat fuller mention. The first-named officer organised and most gallantly led six bombing attacks against a strong point which threatened the British communications, capturing the position, together with fifty prisoners and two machine-guns. The enemy counter-attacked with a battalion of the Guard and recovered the position. Second-Lieutenant Haine formed a "block" in his trench and maintained his position against repeated determined assaults throughout the following night. Next morning he reorganised his men and recaptured the strong point, driving the enemy back for several hundred yards and relieving the situation.

Second-Lieutenant Pollard noticed that troops of various units on the left of his battalion were becoming demoralised owing to their heavy casualties under shell fire, and dashed up to stop a retirement. With only four men he started a counter-attack with bombs and pressed it home until he had broken the enemy's attack, regained all that had been lost, and much ground in addition

Lieutenant Arthur Batten-Pooll, **A West Yorkshire** Royal Munster Fusiliers, displayed conspicuous courage in command of a **hero** raiding-party, directing the operations after receiving a severe wound in the hand, and assisting in the rescue of two wounded men during the retirement, in the course of which he received two further wounds.

Sergeant John Erskine, Scottish Rifles (T.F.), won the cross by rescuing a wounded sergeant and private under continuous fire, and later going out to his wounded officer, bandaging him, and remaining with him for an hour. In assisting to bring him in Erskine shielded him with his own body in order to lessen the chance of his being hit again. Private George Stringer, the V.C. of the Manchester Regiment in the third year, earned the sobriquet of " the one-man army " by the gallantry with which he held his ground when his battalion was forced back from a captured enemy position, keeping the enemy back until all his grenades were expended.

Lieutenant Geoffrey St. George Shillington Catler, Royal Irish Fusiliers, earned the cross by splendid service to wounded men. For five hours at night he searched No Man's Land and brought in three, and next morning he brought in a fourth, and gave water to others, arranging for their rescue later. He took out water to another wounded man, and was going farther when he himself was

SERGT. J. W. WHITTLE,   LT.-COL. A. C. DE WIART,   LT. T. O. L. WILKINSON,   SEAMAN W.   SEC.-LT. F. YOUENS,
Australian Infantry.   Dragoon Guards.   Loyal North Lancs. Regt.   WILLIAMS, R.N.R.   Durham Light Infantry.

killed. Company-Sergeant-Major Nelson Victor Carter, Royal Sussex Regiment, penetrated with a few men into the enemy's second line and inflicted heavy casualties with bombs. Forced to retire to the enemy's first line, he captured a machine-gun and shot the gunner with his revolver. Having carried several wounded men into safety, he was wounded and died in a few minutes.

Corporal George Sanders, West Yorkshire Regiment, was awarded the cross for "the greatest courage, determination, and good leadership during thirty-six hours under very trying conditions." After an advance into the enemy's trenches he was isolated with thirty other men, and, organising his defences and detailing a bombing-party, he resolved to hold the position at all costs. He repulsed three strong attacks, and incidentally rescued some British prisoners, who had fallen into the enemy's hands, before he was relieved. Private Theodore William Henry Veale, Devonshire Regiment, went out to a wounded officer who was lying in growing corn within fifty yards of the enemy, dragged him to a shell-hole, went back for water and returned with it, went back again and returned with assistance, and after several attempts covered an approaching enemy patrol with a Lewis gun and finally achieved the rescue of the officer.

Deed of "great military value"

On September 27th, 1916, the name of Captain Eric Norman Frankland Bell, Royal Inniskilling Fusiliers, appeared among a list of twelve V.C. awards. Captain Bell shot the gunner of a machine-gun which was holding up the front line, and later went forward on three occasions and threw trench-mortar bombs amongst the enemy. When he had no more bombs left he stood on the parapet and used a rifle with great coolness and effect upon the enemy.

Sergeant Boulter, Northamptonshire Regiment, figured in a V.C. list dated October 26th, 1916, for having bombed the team of a machine-gun from the position where they were causing heavy casualties. The official statement explained that the deed was of great military value. On the same date was announced the award of the cross to Sergeant Albert Gill, King's Royal Rifle Corps, for rallying the remnants of his platoon after the enemy had rushed the bombing-post and reorganising his defences, "a most difficult and dangerous task," in which he was killed.

On November 27th, 1916, the award of the Victoria Cross was made to three more single representatives of their regiments. Second-Lieutenant Henry Kelly, West Riding Regiment, twice rallied his company under intense fire, and finally led the only three available men into the enemy's trench, where they remained bombing until two of them became casualties and reinforcements reached the enemy. Kelly then carried his company-sergeant-major back to the British trenches, and subsequently three other soldiers. Sergeant Robert Downie, Royal Dublin Fusiliers, reorganised an attack when most of his officers had become casualties, and at the critical moment he rushed forward alone, shouting, "Come on, the Dubs!" so stirring the men that the line leaped forward after him. He personally accounted for several of the enemy, and in addition captured a machine-gun and killed the team. Sergeant James Young Turnbull, Highland Light Infantry, captured an important post, and was subjected to severe counter-attacks. His party was wiped out and replaced several times during the day, but Turnbull realised that the loss of the post would be very serious, and almost single-handed maintained the position, "displaying the highest degree of valour and skill." He was killed later in the day.

"Come on, the Dubs!"

The Victoria Cross awarded to Sergeant Edward John Mott, Border Regiment, was stated to be "for most conspicuous gallantry and initiative when in an attack the company to which he belonged was held up at a strong point by machine-gun fire." Although wounded in the eye, Mott made a rush for the gun, and after a fierce struggle seized the gunner, took him prisoner, and captured the gun. The cross awarded to Lieutenant and Adjutant Robert Edwin Phillips, Royal Warwickshire Regiment, was earned by "sustained courage in its very highest form." Under intense fire he went out to his commanding officer, who had been mortally wounded, and brought him back to the lines.

Major (Acting Lieutenant-Colonel) Edward Elers Delavel Henderson, North Staffordshire Regiment, awarded the Victoria Cross, brought his battalion up to the two front-line trenches which were under intense fire. The battalion had suffered heavily in a counter-attack when the enemy penetrated the line in several places. Lieutenant-Colonel Henderson, though shot through the arm, jumped on to the parapet and advanced alone some distance in front of his battalion, cheering them on and continuing to lead them, though again wounded, until they finally captured the position by a bayonet charge. This most gallant and fearless officer was wounded yet twice again, and died when he was eventually brought in.

On June 28th, 1917, award of the cross was made to Company-Sergeant-Major Edward Brooks, Oxfordshire and Buckinghamshire Light Infantry, and Lance-Corporal James Welch, Royal Berkshire Regiment. The warrant officer on his own initiative rushed forward from the second wave of a force raiding the enemy's trenches and killed with his revolver one of the gunners of a machine-gun that was checking the advance and bayoneted another. He then turned the gun on the remainder of its team, who made off, after which Brooks carried it back into the British lines. Lance-Corporal Welch entered an enemy trench and killed one man after a hand-to-hand struggle. Armed only with an empty revolver he chased four others across the open and captured them single-handed. He also handled a machine-gun with utmost fearlessness and effect, more than once going into the open under heavy fire to collect ammunition and spare parts in order to keep his gun in action. This he succeeded in doing for more than five hours, until wounded.

"Let us now praise——"

Lieutenant (Acting Captain) Arthur Henderson, M.C., Argyll and Sutherland Highlanders, earned the Victoria Cross during an attack on some trenches when, though wounded, he led his company through the enemy front line to his final objective. He consolidated his position, and by courage and coolness maintained the spirit of his men under most trying conditions. This gallant officer was killed after he had accomplished his task.

The last name to be recorded here is Frank Bernard Wearne, second-lieutenant in the Essex Regiment, to whom the Victoria Cross was posthumously awarded on August 2nd, 1917. He was in command of a small party on the left of a raid on the enemy's trenches when, "by his tenacity in remaining at his post, though severely wounded, and his magnificent fighting spirit, Second-Lieutenant Wearne was enabled to hold on to the flank."

"Let us now praise famous men——" The adjuration inevitably comes to mind on reading the summarised account of the deeds of these hundred and forty-five true heroes. Brief and unadorned as the summary is, owing to the exigencies of space and proportion, it nevertheless stirs that thrill in the heart which responds only to the pure note of the beautiful and the sublime. Completing his task, the chronicler inclines to the view that the style of the seemingly unemotional official award is the proper one for the subject. Statement of the facts is sufficient when the facts are exhibitions of courage, endurance, devotion, self-sacrifice. To apply epithets to these savours of impertinence. It is good to read the story in plain English. It is glorious to know that it is true.

END OF VOLUME 10.